HUMAN–COMPUTER INTERACTION

INTERACT '90

HUMAN–COMPUTER INTERACTION

INTERACT '90

Proceedings of the IFIP TC 13 Third International Conference on
Human–Computer Interaction
Cambridge, U.K., 27–31 August, 1990

Edited by

D. DIAPER
Department of Computer Science
University of Liverpool
Liverpool, U.K.

D. GILMORE
Department of Psychology
University of Nottingham
Nottingham, U.K.

G. COCKTON
Department of Computing Science
University of Glasgow
Glasgow, U.K.

B. SHACKEL
HUSAT Research Institute
and
Department of Human Sciences
Loughborough University of Technology
Loughborough, U.K.

1990

NORTH-HOLLAND
AMSTERDAM · NEW YORK · OXFORD · TOKYO

ELSEVIER SCIENCE PUBLISHERS B.V.
Sara Burgerhartstraat 25
P.O. Box 211, 1000 AE Amsterdam, The Netherlands

Distributors for the United States and Canada:
ELSEVIER SCIENCE PUBLISHING COMPANY INC.
655 Avenue of the Americas
New York, N.Y. 10010, U.S.A.

ISBN: 0 444 88817 9

Printed in The Netherlands.

TABLE OF CONTENTS

Preface xvii

Has done better – the efforts of the '80s in HCI
G. Cockton xix

INVITED PAPERS

SIOIS – Standard interfaces or interface standards
T. Stewart xxix

Empirical studies of the software design process
B. Curtis xxxv

SECTION I: FOUNDATIONS

SI.1 Educational and Social Issues

Why, what and how? Issues in the development of an HCI training course
J. Preece and L.S. Keller . . . 3

University education on human–computer interaction: The Dutch situation
G.C. Van Der Veer and T.N. White . . . 9

Information processing, context and privacy
A. Dix . . . 15

Mac-Thusiasm: Social aspects of microcomputer use
M.R. Jones . . . 21

SI.2 Cognitive Ergonomics

GOMS meets the phone company: Analytic modeling applied to real-world problems
W.D. Gray, B.E. John, R. Stuart, D. Lawrence, and M.E. Atwood . . . 29

The effects of task structure and social support on users' errors and error handling
M. Frese, F.C. Brodbeck, D. Zapf and J. Prümper . . . 35

What kind of errors do Unix users make?
J.H. Bradford, W.D. Murray, and T.T. Carey . . . 43

ECM: A scheme for analysing user-system errors
P.A. Booth . . . 47

How learner characteristics can mediate the effects of giving conceptual details during training
E.J. Lloyd . . . 55

Influencing behaviour via device representation; decreasing performance by increasing instruction
S.C. Duff and P.J. Barnard . . . 61

Pop-up windows and memory for text
H.A. Stark . . . 67

Two ways to fill a bath, with and without knowing it
A. Ankrah, D.M. Frohlich, and G.N. Gilbert . . . 73

The cognitive dimension of viscosity: A sticky problem for HCI
T.R.G. Green . . . 79

The role of games and cognitive models in the understanding of complex dynamic systems
R. Rivers . . . 87

Implications of computer games for system design
L. Neal . . . 93

A study of measures for research in hypertext navigation
D.G. Hendry, T.T. Carey, and S.T. TeWinkel . . . 101

Mental effort and task performance: Towards a psychophysiology of human computer interaction
D. Wastell . . . 107

SI.3 User Modelling

A knowledge analysis of interactivity
R.M. Young, A. Howes, and J. Whittington 115

User's command line reference behaviour: Locality versus recency
A. Lee and F.H. Lochovsky 121

An investigation into quantitative user modelling of user interactions for the purpose of predicting user expertise
R. Spall and R. Steele 129

Constraints in design: Towards a methodology of psychological analysis based on AI formalisms
F. Darses 135

SI.4 Formal Methods

Agents: Communicating interactive processes
G.D. Abowd 143

Pattern recognition and interaction models
J. Finlay and M. Harrison 149

Formal analysis of co-operative problem solving dialogues: Tools and techniques
P. Jeremaes 155

ETAG: Extended task action grammar. A language for the description of the user's task language
M.J. Tauber 163

ETAG: Some applications of a formal representation of the user interface
G.C. Van Der Veer, D. Broos, K. Donau, M.J. Fokke, and F. Yap 169

What is inconsistency?
P. Reisner 175

SECTION II: DESIGN: THEORIES, METHODS AND TOOLS

SII.1 Studies and Analyses of Design

Looking HCI in the I
S.J. Payne 185

Qualitative artifact analysis
W.A. Kellogg 193

Redesign by design
R.K.E. Bellamy and J.M. Carroll 199

What rationale is there in design?
A. MacLean, V.M.E. Bellotti, and R. Young 207

A framework for assessing applicability of HCI techniques
V.M.E. Bellotti 213

Obstacles to user involvement in interface design in large product development organizations
J. Grudin 219

Integrating human factors with structured analysis and design methods: An enhanced conception of the extended Jackson system development method
K.Y. Lim, J.B. Long, and N. Silcock 225

SII.2 Users, Tasks and Organizations: Requirements and Analysis

An investigation of user requirements for broadband communications in the automotive industry
S.E. Powrie and C.E. Siemieniuch 233

Bridging the gap between task design and interface design
W. Dzida, R. Freitag, C. Hoffmann, and W. Valder 239

Supporting a humanly impossible task: The clinical human computer environment
B. Horan, A.L. Rector, E.L. Sneath, C.A. Goble, T.J. Howkins, S. Kay, W.A. Nowlan, and A. Wilson 247

An analysis of the circuit design process for a complex engineering application
L. Colgan and M. Brouwer-Janse 253

Designers-identified requirements for tools to support task analyses
H. Johnson and P. Johnson 259

An application of task analysis to the development of a generic office reference model
J. Hewitt, J. Hobson, and J. Sapsford-Francis 265

Memory–cognition–action tables: A pragmatic approach to analytical modelling
B. Sharratt 271

Analysing focused interview data with task analysis for knowledge descriptions (TAKD)
D. Diaper 277

A plan and goal based method for computer–human system design
D.R. Sewell and N.D. Geddes 283

The use of task allocation charts in system design: A critical appraisal
W.K. Ip, L. Damodaran, C.W. Olphert, and M.C. Maguire 289

The development of tools to assist in organisational requirements definition for information technology systems
S.D.P. Harker, C.W. Olphert, and K.D. Eason 295

SII.3 Prototyping

Hypermedia as communication and prototyping tools in the concurrent design of commercial airplane products
E. Hofer and F. Ruggiero 303

An object-oriented framework for prototyping user interfaces
P. Windsor 309

Paper versus computer implementations as mockup scenarios for heuristic evaluation
J. Nielsen 315

SII.4 Evaluation

Evaluating the usability of user interfaces: Research in practice
A. Vainio-Larsson and R. Orring 323

Evaluating Evaluation: A case study of the use of novel and conventional evaluation techniques in a small company
J. Crellin, T. Horn, and J. Preece 329

Integrated office software benchmarks: A case study
J.R. Lewis, S.C. Henry, and R.L. Mack 337

Comparative study of geometry specification capabilities of geometric modelling systems
K. Case and B.S. Acar 345

Cost-benefit analysis of iterative usability testing
C.-M. Karat 351

Usability statements and standardisation: Work in progress in ISO
J. Brooke, N. Bevan, F. Brigham, S. Harker, and D. Youmans 357

SII.5 Design and Evaluation Tools

Supporting effective and efficient design meetings
J. Karat and J. Bennett 365

The HUFIT planning analysis and specification toolset
B. Taylor 371

The HUFIT functionality matrix
B.J. Catterall 377

Task-based user interface development tools
P. Johnson and E. Nicolosi 383

PROTEUS: An approach to interface evaluation
J. Crellin 389

A knowledge-based tool for user interface evaluation and its integration in a UIMS
J. Löwgren and T. Nordqvist 395

Monitoring and analysis of hypermedia navigation
D. Kornbrot and M. Macleod 401

Towards an evaluation planning aid: A feasibility study in modelling evaluation practice using a blackboard framework
I. Denley and J. Long 407

Providing intrinsic support for user interface monitoring
J. Chen 415

SECTION III: DETAILED DESIGN

SIII.1 Menus

Are all menus the same? An empirical study
Z. Mills and M. Prime 423

Pull-down, HoldDown, or StayDown? A theoretical and empirical comparison of three menu designs
M. Macleod and P. Tillson 429

The use of guidelines in menu interface design: Evaluation of a draft standard
F. de Souza and N. Bevan 435

Decision track: A formalism for menu structure and user's selection behaviour
W. Edmondson 441

SIII.2 Graphical and Iconic Interfaces

A three-state model of graphical input
W.A.S. Buxton 449

Iconic interfacing: The role of icon distinctiveness and fixed or variable screen locations
A.J.K. Green and P.J. Barnard 457

Where to draw the line with text: Some claims by logic designers about graphics in notation
M. Petre and T.R.G. Green 463

The power of parameterizable objects in modern user interfaces
F. Penz, M. Tscheligi, G. Haring, and M. Manhartsberger 469

Alternative bases for comprehensibility and competition for expression in an icon generation tool
S.W. Draper, K.W. Waite, and P.D. Gray 473

Integrating natural language and graphics in dialogue
J. Lee and H. Zeevat 479

Semantics and graphical information
E. Klein and L.A. Pineda 485

Using depictive queries to search pictorial databases
S. Charles and S. Scrivener 493

HyperBliss*: A Blissymbolics communication enhancement interface and teaching aid based on a cognitive-semantographic technique with adaptive–predictive capability
A. Shalit and D.A. Boonzaier 499

A cognitive approach to the definition and evaluation of a standard for naval tactical display symbology
J. Campion, M.A. Brockett, D. Martin, and M. Rate 505

An electronic book: APTBook
M. Miyazawa, K. Kinoshita, M. Kobayashi, T. Yokoyama, and Y. Matsushita 513

"Good" graphic interfaces for "good" idea organizers
K. Sugiyama and K. Misue 521

SIII.3 User Support

Help systems: An information-sharing approach
M. Kurisaki 529

End-user dialogue context management of office automation systems
G. Lu, C. Vanneste, and M. Ader 535

Current approaches and new guidelines for undo support design
Y. Yang 543

Interface usability engineering under practical constraints: A case study in the design of undo support
Y. Yang 549

State versus history in user interfaces
W.B. Cowan and M. Wein 555

The personal touch: A study of users' customization practice
A.H. Jørgensen and A. Sauer 561

Inferring task structures from interaction protocols
F. Schiele and H.U. Hoppe 567

An adaptive system developer's tool-kit
D. Benyon, D. Murray, and F. Jennings 573

SIII.4 **Hypermedia**

Roles for tables of contents as hypertext overviews
T.T. Carey, W.T. Hunt, and A. Lopez-Suarez 581

Navigation in hypertext: A critical review of the concept
A. Dillon, C. McKnight, and J. Richardson 587

Combining hypermedia browsing with formal queries
K.-H. Jerke, P. Szabo, A. Lesch, H. Rößler, T. Schwab, and J. Herczeg 593

SIII.5 **Construction Tools**

An experiment in interactive architectures
E. Edmonds and N. Hagiwara 601

SCENARIOO: A new generation UIMS
B. Roudaud, V. Lavigne, O. Lagneau, and E. Minor 607

MUD: Multiple-view user interface design
D. England 613

PENGUIN: A language for reactive graphical user interface programming
S.-K. Yap and M.L. Scott 619

Petri net objects for the design, validation and prototyping of user-driven interfaces
R. Bastide and P. Palanque 625

An object-oriented UIMS for rapid prototyping
Y.-P. Shan 633

Do-it-yourself iconic displays: Reconfigurable iconic representations of application objects
P.D. Gray, K.W. Waite, and S.W. Draper 639

Localisation of application knowledge in incremental development of user interfaces
P.D. Gray, C.A. Wood, and A.C. Kilgour 645

A UIMS for knowledge based interface template generation and interaction
C. Märtin 651

Incorporating metaphor in automated interface design
B. Blumenthal 659

SECTION IV: INTERACTIVE TECHNOLOGIES AND TECHNIQUES

SIV.1 **Input**

The role of visual and kinesthetic feedback in the prevention of mode errors
A.J. Sellen, G.P. Kurtenbach, and W.A.S. Buxton 667

Windows on tablets as a means of achieving virtual input devices
E. Brown, W.A.S. Buxton, and K. Murtagh 675

Building adaptive interfaces with neural networks: The glove-talk pilot study
S.S. Fels and G.E. Hinton 683

FINGER: A language for gesture recognition
G. Weber 689

A virtual stereographic pointer for a real three dimensional video world
P. Milgram, D. Drascic, and J. Grodski 695

Force-to-motion functions for pointing
J.D. Rutledge and T. Selker 701

Keyboard layout for occasional users
N. Marmaras and K. Lyritzis 707

SIV.2 Output

The simulation of a large image terminal using Heath Robinson techniques
J.R. Harris, M.B. Harris, and D.Th. Henskes 715

Evaluation of flat panel display properties on a high fidelity display simulator
G. Spenkelink, H. Van Spijker, and T.N. White 721

Colour model integration and visualisation
P.A. Rhodes, M.R. Luo, and S.A.R. Scrivener 725

On the visibility of character features on a VDU
D. Bosman and T.N. White 729

Auditory icons in large-scale collaborative environments
W.W. Gaver and R.B. Smith 735

Interactive scientific visualization: An assessment of a virtual reality system
P.J. Mercurio and T.D. Erickson 741

A browser for dynamic multimedia documents
S. Anupindi 747

SIV.3 Speech and Natural Language

An investigation into the use of error recovery dialogues in a user interface management system for speech recognition
M. Zajicek and J. Hewitt 755

Feedback requirements for automatic speech recognition in control room systems
C. Baber, R.B. Stammers, and R.G. Taylor 761

Spoken language interaction in a spreadsheet task
A.I. Rudnicky, M. Sakamoto, and J.H. Polifroni 767

Case study of development of a user interface for a voice activated dialing service
D. Lawrence and R. Stuart 773

A voice recognition interface for a telecommunications basic business group attendant console
I. Sola and D. Shepard 779

Observations on using speech input for window navigation
C. Schmandt, D. Hindus, M.S. Ackerman, and S. Manandhar 787

The design and implementation of a context sensitive natural language interface to management information
A. Burton and A.P. Steward 795

Recent approaches to natural language generation
L. Fedder 801

SECTION V: APPLICATIONS AND CASE STUDIES

SV.1 **Knowledge-Based Systems**

User centered explanations in knowledge based systems
K. Waldhör and H. Anschütz 809

Intelligent user interface for a conventional program
J. Junger, G. Bouma, and Ph. Letanoux 815

Knowledge acquisition and hypertext in manufacturing
S.M. Hajsadr, A.P. Steward, and V. Carroll 821

Knowledge based user interfaces for scientific programs
H.J. Van Zuylen and H. Gerritsen 827

SV.2 **Computer Supported Co-operative Work**

Concurrent editing: the group's interface
J.S. Olson, G.M. Olson, L.A. Mack, and P. Wellner 835

Characteristics of well-designed electronic communications systems
P.A. Holleran and R.W. Haller 841

Process modelling and CSCW: An application of IPSE technology to medical office work
J. Maresh and D. Wastell 849

Tools that support human–human communication in the automated office
I.D. Benest and D. Dukić 853

SV.3 **Applications**

Smartwriter: A tool-based wordprocessor for adult literacy students
D. Ellis, J. Horton, and P. Black 863

The interface to a hypertext journal
A. Simpson 869

A fisheye presentation strategy: Aircraft maintenance data
D.A. Mitta 875

Supporting exploratory learning
A. Howes and S.J. Payne 881

Application of cognitive modeling and knowledge measurement in diagnosis and training of complex skills
Y.M. Yufik 887

SV.4 **Software Development**

Software Reusability: Delivering productivity gains or short cuts
A. Sutcliffe and N. Maiden 895

A project-orientated view of CSCW
N.R. Seel, G.N. Gilbert, and M.E. Morris 903

Satisfying the need to know: Interpersonal information access
R.E. Kraut and L.A. Streeter 909

Conversationbuilder: An open architecture for collaborative work
S.M. Kaplan 917

SV.5 Programming

Learning to program in another language
J. Scholtz and S. Wiedenbeck 925

ϒπADAPTερ: Individualizing hypertext
H.-D. Böcker, H. Hohl, and T. Schwab 931

Minimalist planning tools in an instructional system for smalltalk programming
M.K. Singley and J.M. Carroll 937

Why program comprehension is (or is not) affected by surface features
B.T. Mynatt 945

The generalized unification parser: Modelling the parsing of notations
T.R.G. Green and A. Borning 951

Program comprehension beyond the line
S.P. Robertson, E.F. Davis, K. Okabe, and D. Fitz-Randolf 959

Expert programmers re-establish intentions when debugging another programmer's program
R. Waddington and R. Henry 965

Difficulties in designing with an object-oriented language: An empirical study
F. Détienne 971

The spreadsheet interface: A basis for end user programming
B.A. Nardi and J.R. Miller 977

Action representation for home automation
S. Sebillotte 985

Browsing through program execution
H.-D. Böcker and J. Herczeg 991

Compressing and comparing metric execution spaces
J. Domingue 997

DOCTORAL PROGRAMME

A psychology of programming for design
R.K.E. Bellamy 1005

Cognitive style and intelligent help
L. Coventry 1007

Support for understanding and participation in a distributed problem solving system
C.M. Duursma 1009

The role of analogy in training computer users
J. Elcock 1011

Linguistic models in the design of cooperative help systems
C. Elliot 1013

An environment to support the use of program examples while learning to program in LISP
K.W. Getao 1015

Modelling cognitive aspects of complex control tasks
S. Grant 1017

Using temporal logic to prototype interactive systems
C.W. Johnson 1019

A development environment for the design of multimodal, colourgraphic human–computer interfaces
M. Langen and G. Rau 1021

Advanced user interfaces for distributed group communication
L. Navarro 1025

Logic descriptions in rapid prototyping of applications
L. Oestreicher 1029

Graphical treatment of natural language in HCI
R.A. Singer 1031

Run time interface specification, using direct manipulation
R. Tibbitt-Eggleton 1033

Learning a word processing task: About documentation, help and task complexity
A. Van Laethem 1035

PANEL SESSIONS

HCI seen from the perspective of software developers
Moderator: J.L. Bennett
Panelists: P. Conklin, K. Guevara, W. Mackay, and T. Sancha 1039

User participation in HCI research: Effects on processes and results
Panel Organiser: Y. Waern
Panelists: L. Bannon, T. Timpka, and W. Schneider 1043

Interactively supporting the software process
S.M. Kaplan, A. Finkelstein, G. Kaiser, K. Ryan, and W. Schafer 1047

Task analysis: The oft missing step in the development of computer–human interfaces; its desirable nature, value, and role
Organiser/Moderator: R.I. Anderson
Panelists: J.M. Carroll, J. Grudin, J.F. McGrew, and D.L. Scapin 1051

New approaches to theory in HCI: How should we judge their acceptability?
Organiser: A. Monk
Panelists: J.M. Carroll, M. Harrison, J. Long, and R. Young 1055

Multi-agent interaction
Organiser: N. Seel
Panelists: J. Galliers, G. Kiss, and S. Scrivener 1059

Multi-dimensional interfaces for software design
Organiser: T. Dudley
Panelists: R. Baecker, M. Eisenstadt, E. Glinert, and M.B. Rosson 1063

Usability engineering on a budget
Moderator: J. Nielsen
Panelists: S.M. Dray, J.D. Foley, P. Walsh, and P. Wright 1067

Author index 1071

Subject index 1075

PREFACE

Human-Computer Interaction (HCI) comes of age. This year 1990 can properly be regarded as a significant milestone in the growth of HCI from several starting dates. From various brief histories we know that the first recorded papers in the literature were 30 years ago, including the prospect for 'man-computer symbiosis' heralded by Licklider. It is 21 years since the first conference was held in 1969 (International Symposium on Man-Machine Systems) and the first Journal was established (International Journal of Man-Machine Studies). It is 10 years since four major books were published in the same year 1980, and since the micro-computer came into widespread use.

The last 10 years have seen the growth and diffusion of information technology exceeding most predictions, even those of many optimistic researchers. This decade has also seen a substantial growth in concern for the human aspects of computing and IT systems, even though those working in the field know that much of the work so far has revealed both how little we really know and how much we still have to learn. Nevertheless, this third IFIP Conference on Human-Computer Interaction INTERACT'90, and the continued growth from the previous two Conferences, shows how much more is now being done.

The growth in HCI work is clearly shown by the simple statistics of the INTERACT Conferences. For INTERACT'84, INTERACT'87 and INTERACT'90 respectively, the number of synopses/abstracts offered have increased from 282 to 375 to 500, and the number of papers submitted have increased from 180 to 231 to 312. Each time the increase is of the order of 30% - 35%. For the two previous Conferences, the abstracts were refereed and authors were invited to submit papers which were then also refereed; about 150 papers were accepted finally for each Conference. This year the abstracts were not refereed, and all authors were invited to submit papers except for a limited number which were clearly outside the Conference domain. The refereeing this year has had to be even more selective than in the past, and therefore the 150 papers in these Conference Proceedings are of still higher quality than in the past.

Considerable work has been devoted, by members of the Technical Committee, to arranging the sequence of papers and structuring the Proceedings into related sections. This structure and the contents are discussed fully in the Introduction to the Proceedings by Gilbert Cockton.

A particular new development on this occasion relates to the indexing of the Proceedings' contents. This has been done by the HUSAT Information Service, using the HIS Computer Human Factors Thesaurus and CHF Classification Scheme. This Thesaurus and Classification Scheme have been developed, using professional information retrieval methods, by Kathy Phillips (1990); the extensive work involved in this development was partly funded within the ESPRIT HUFIT project, partly by the Alvey HCI Service and partly by HUSAT funding. The Thesaurus and Classification Scheme are becoming 'de facto' standards for HCI, and copies are available.

Another noteworthy development for the INTERACT series of Conferences is that they are now under the aegis of a full IFIP Technical Committee. At the 1989 IFIP General Assembly two new technical committees were established, the first since 1981, one being IFIP TC13 on Human-Computer Interaction. The scope and aims of TC13 are specified below.

SCOPE - The Technical Committee aims toward the development of a science and a technology of the interaction between humans and computers (under 'computers' we include information technology in general). The main orientation is toward the users, especially the non-computer-professional users, and how to improve the human-computer relationship for them.

Areas for study include:-

* the problems people have with computers
* the impact of computers upon people in both individual and organisational contexts
* the determinants of utility, usability and acceptability
* the appropriate allocation of tasks between computers and people
* modelling the user as an aid to better system design
* harmonising the computer to the characteristics and needs of the user.

While the scope is thus set wide, with a tendency towards general principles rather than particular systems, it is recognised that progress will only be achieved through both general studies to advance theoretical understanding and specific studies on particular practical issues (e.g. interface design standards, software system consistency, documentation, appropriateness of alternative communication media, human factors guidelines for dialogue design, the problems of integrating multi-media systems to match user needs and organisational practices, etc.).

AIMS - To encourage development towards a science and a technology of human-computer interaction, the Technical Committee will pursue the following aims:-

* to promote and provide facilities for the exchange of information
* to encourage empirical research (using valid and reliable methodology, with studies of the methods themselves where necessary)
* to promote the use of knowledge and methods from the human sciences in both design and evaluation of computer systems
* to promote better understanding of the relation between formal design methods and system usability and acceptability
* to develop guidelines, models and methods by which designers may be able to provide better human-oriented computer systems
* to co-operate with other groups, inside and outside IFIP, so as to promote user-orientation and 'humanization' in system design
* to organise specific programmes (e.g. by technical study groups, workshops, etc.) through which to pursue these aims.

The third new development, with this third INTERACT Conference, is that it is the first to be hosted formally by an IFIP Member Society. INTERACT'90 is hosted by the British Computer Society and by the BCS HCI Specialist Group. Therefore it is my great pleasure officially to convey the thanks of IFIP to the BCS and to the BCS HCISG for their invitation and for their extensive and successful work in organising the Conference.

Further, sincere thanks must be recorded to those whose contributions have been essential to create the Conference and this book of Proceedings. We owe a great debt to the Members of the International Programme Committee who laboured long and hard to review the full text of papers and advise on the selections so as to ensure the high standard. Similarly, the Members of the Conference Organising Committee and the Technical Committee, the Chairpersons of all the Subcommittees, and the staff of BISL, deserve much appreciation for their tireless help with all aspects of the planning and managing the many administrative and organisational issues. Finally our thanks go to all the authors who actually did the scientific work.

June 1990

Brian Shackel
HUSAT Research Institute,
Loughborough University, UK

Phillips, K. E. (1990) The Computer Human Factors Database. In: Karwowski, W., Genaidy, A. and Asfour, S. (eds); Computer Aided Ergonomics. London, Taylor and Francis.

Human–Computer Interaction – INTERACT '90
D. Diaper et al. (Editors)
Elsevier Science Publishers B.V. (North-Holland)

Has done better – the efforts of the '80s in HCI

Gilbert Cockton

Department of Computing Science, University of Glasgow, Glasgow G12 8QQ, UK.
gilbert@cs.glasgow.ac.uk

Readers who begin with this introduction and read systematically through all the papers in order will be taken from psychology and mathematics, via design, prototyping, evaluation, interaction techniques and styles, system construction tools and interactive technologies (with real examples all the way) to specific case studies in knowledge-based systems, computer-supported co-operative work, tutoring systems, hypertext journals, aircraft maintainance systems, software engineering and programming. Even though there are uncovered topics and perspectives in these proceedings, the richness of HCI as an area of study and practice should be apparent.

Keywords : Human Computer Interaction, multidisciplinary, interdisciplinary

1. An overview of INTERACT'90

In the 1980s, HCI became recognised as a core topic in computing, taking its place on computing and human science curricula, establishing itself in specialist groups of professional bodies worldwide, and being accepted as a separate area with its own technical committee, TC13, in IFIP. Many papers in this volume report completed work which has reaped the benefits of the expansion of HCI research and development in the 1980s.

This volume contains all the papers accepted for presentation at INTERACT'90, the third IFIP conference on Human-Computer Interaction. All papers were submitted in response to an international call for papers and were each assessed by two to six referees (usually three). All papers in these proceedings had a clear acceptance by the referees (mean rating 6/10 or above). Only 10 accepted papers had conflicting assessments. These were re-assessed, along with the other marginal papers, by different referees on the international programme committee before acceptance.

Some differences are apparent between these proceedings and those of the first two IFIP conferences [Shackel 1985, Bullinger and Shackel 1987]. Higher standards are being set for work in HCI and these standards are being met. But there will always be impatience with progress in HCI: the importance of HCI lies in the importance of interactive systems. Interactive systems are pervasive. Their design is problematic. We are using interactive systems now even though there are many which we would rather not use. Hence the impatience. The problems are not being ignored and the evidence lies in these proceedings.

The evidence is somewhat uneven however. Section SV of the proceedings covers applications and case studies. Over half of these papers are on software engineering and programming. Over half of the remainder are on knowledge-based systems and Computer-Supported Co-operative Work (CSCW). This bias was something of a surprise. The health of these areas is good news for computing personnel, but the apparent under-representation of government, business, medical, industrial and educational applications is a cause for concern. Individual differences too, such as physical and mental disablement, gender, age and culture are not properly represented. There are only a few papers which address the needs of disabled users in the proceedings. The total of two papers on broad social issues is also disappointing, although CSCW papers (especially those in subsection SV.4) do give prominence to social issues. Even so, the bias in the proceedings is towards cognitive mechanisms, with aesthetic, affective, individual and social issues conspicuous by their relative rarity.

The field is consolidating, and if the accepted papers are representative, software design and cognitive ergonomics are the synergistic forces behind the consolidating pull. There are fewer papers on workstation and hardware design, and the papers which have been accepted are encouraging in that user-centred approaches are being taken during the design of new interactive technologies, and not after. Section SIV is dominated by papers on the ergonomic audit of new technologies, and not by those on post-hoc remediations of existing ones. The same pattern is repeated in the software case studies. What was largely academic theory three or six years ago is now part of the best industrial practice. The successful adaptation of knowledge, methods and tools to the practicalities of software production is described in several papers. As a balance to this self-congratulation, there are also papers which reveal the limitations of some proposed approaches. There is still much to be done, and there is no lack of candidates for the outstanding tasks. This volume contains several forward looking papers, with new perspectives on research, design and development. Will they too be conservative practice by InterCHI'93 or INTERACT'96?

A proceedings which is forward looking in part deserved a conference with a similar balance of the old and the new. INTERACT'90 introduced a new approach to visual presentations at conferences. The use of poster presentations for poorer papers was rejected, since for many areas of HCI the interactive and visual potential of "poster" style presentation is more suitable than a verbal presentation in the form of a lecture. Furthermore, material which is presented visually (with several short introductions) is more accessible than a single timed verbal presentation. Two types of paper were thus chosen for visual interactive presentation (VIP) at INTERACT'90:

(i) papers on inherently visual topics (e.g. graphical interfaces, interactive hardware)

(ii) highly-rated papers of interest to all attendees which should be as accessible as possible.

The VIPs did include many of the best papers submitted to INTERACT'90. The majority of the most highly-rated papers were only suitable for verbal presentation, but this was as much due to the nature as to the quality of the content.

There is no distinction between verbally and visually presented papers in the proceedings. The main body of the proceedings is organised into five paper sections, and two further sections for the doctoral programme abstracts and the panelists' position papers. Each paper section is further divided into several subsections. Papers have been placed in subsections without regard to the form of presentation and without regard to the actual conference timetable which, as ever, contained too many logistically driven compromises.

2. Section SI — Foundations

These papers explore the foundations of HCI: educational and social issues, cognitive ergonomics, user modelling and formal methods. Education is fundamental, in the sense that any curriculum commits itself to a model of the discipline of HCI which is passed on to future practitioners (for some possible models see [Long and Dowell 1989]). Such a model is no less fundamental to the success of HCI than its psychological, mathematical or other foundations.

Social issues are poorly covered in these proceedings, and since balance is important, this is disappointing. The two accepted papers are both novel however, and offer new perspectives on the relationship between computers and society. The two papers respectively address particular hopes and fears associated with the widespread use of computing.

Subsection SI.2 on cognitive ergonomics contains several focussed studies which relate the psychology of phenomena such as errors or learning to the process of interacting with a computer. The potential of a cognitive perspective is apparent in the papers on graphical representations and games. However, cognitive ergonomics is still a young area [Carroll 1987] and there are methodological issues which must be resolved before systematic research can deliver unambiguous results. The last two papers in the section address such issues.

Some encouraging results are presented in subsection SI.3. There have long been attempts to formalise what is known about cognition and user performance. User modelling, in its many guises, is a long standing topic in HCI. Four papers introduce the reader to different approaches to the formation and validation of models of users. User modelling is a difficult area which requires the synthesis of psychological and computational models. The papers in this subsection present such syntheses at various stages of their development.

The form and substance of a theory do not come from the body of data which it models. Subsection S1.4 contains fusions of methods of study in the human sciences with computational models from mathematics to provide foundations for design and evaluation. Such methods and models will not emerge from any body of data. They precede it and hence must be of interest (to academics at least) even when their application is unconvincing. Thus the papers in subsection SI.4 examine the application of formal methods to tasks, systems, devices and user interaction. The papers vary in their dependence on established results in psychology. The common theme in this section is the critical analysis of *possible* mathematical models for HCI phenomena.

Some popular views of human knowledge contrast abstraction and reality. The former can never supposedly encapsulate the latter. A blanket rejection of abstraction can only be defended from a position of ignorance which fails to distinguish between invention (where the "abstraction" was never induced from a body of data), flaws (where the induction was wrong) and theory (where the induction stands up). There are sadly too many so-called "abstractions" which are nothing of the sort — the real world has not been studied during the selection and refinement of the non-model. But there are others which are checked against the world and are seen to match it or to miss something. The papers in subsection SI.4 cover abstractions at points beyond that of an interesting idea. Some may be the basis for future established theories. Whatever their status, they are worthy of attention.

There is no doubt that some attempts at generalisation are premature. Those who come looking for ready answers may resent this, but it is discussion of the formation and analysis of hypotheses which is the lifeblood of science, and not the results. The end must not suffocate the means. Thus some papers in section SI challenge the orthodoxy of current "results" as much as they present new ones. Such open, high quality debate can be taken as a sign of young field in the early stages of maturity. This is encouraging, but HCI must continue to resist pressure to grow up too quickly. Real understanding cannot be rushed.

3. Section SII — Design: theories, methods and tools

Section SII brings together papers on current theories, methods and tools for the design of human-computer systems. Subsection SII.1 begins with three symposium papers on the nature of design in HCI and its relation to the science of psychology. These forward looking papers should be contrasted with other papers in subsection SII.1 which address the realities of design, encumbered as it is by the constraints of software engineering practice in current project environments. Two of the cultures of interactive systems construction meet in this subsection. They are not irreconcilable however, and one paper presents an approach to adding HCI concerns to an established structured design method.

An understanding of the tasks which an interactive system will support is central to successful design. Tasks, however, are not abstract, device-dependent entities — they are elements of human work within a social context. Both the workers and their context need to be in understood in conjunction with the tasks which have been identified as the basis of a system. The boundaries between users, tasks and organisations are not clear cut, and many approaches to requirements analyse them together. The eleven papers in subsection SII.2 address requirements from a number of perspectives. Some take tasks and users in isolation, others look at the combinations such as the task and the environment. A number of approaches are contrasted by their juxtaposition in this section. Some papers present detailed case studies in specific application areas. Others present methods and tools which can be employed in such detailed case studies. In all cases, users, organisations and tasks are not studied for their own sake, but with specific design needs in mind [Diaper 1989].

Analytical methods and tools for requirements capture are insufficient — needs may be missed, introduced spuriously, or misrepresented. Subsection SII.3 looks at prototyping which is one means of correcting and extending initial requirements surveys. Prototypes can reveal misunderstandings about requirements as well as problems with the details of interaction and information design which are discussed in section SIII. Given the importance of prototyping, the section is a little thin. There are papers elsewhere in section SII which look at the use of prototypes (e.g. Johnson and Nicolsi, SII.5), but there is little on the ingenious use of existing packages (e.g. [Hewett 1989]). The papers in subsection SII.3 focus on some key issues in prototyping. One key issue is cost. The three papers cover a range of approaches, from low-cost paper based prototypes, via medium-cost package based prototypes, to more expensive re-use of object-oriented software components.

The extent to which requirements have been understood and satisfied by a design is not a matter for casual, "How does it feel now?" analysis. Subsection SII.4 addresses the evaluation of interactive systems, whether they be prototypes or installed final implementations. While evaluation requires discipline, project resources cannot allow for obsessiveness. The practicalities of evaluation demand a balance between coverage, accuracy and cost. Papers explore this balance in the context of real case studies. The final paper in the section describes current work within ISO which is evaluating a draft standard based on menu guidelines (see also subsection SIII.1).

Subsection SII.5 addresses the encapsulation of design methods and knowledge in tools. Tools do need a concrete embodiment, but this need not be a computer program. The cost of the "raw materials" may be low (paper, meetings rooms). This should not be taken as a sign that the thought that has gone into them was limited and that their effectiveness is restricted. On the contrary, far *less* thought can go into a seemingly impressive computer-based tool. The juxtaposition of computer-based, people-based and paper-based tools in this final subsection is a deliberate attempt to encourage reflection on the motivation and knowledge behind design tools, whatever their form. It is this focus which distinguishes interdisciplinary HCI work from narrower technical approaches. In all the papers in this section, the tools are *designed* to meet design needs. They do not come across as solutions seeking a problem.

Like the HCI curricula of colleges and courses, packaged design methods are an important public face of HCI. Methods in widespread use have a narrower focus than the approaches under development in the best HCI R&D laboratories. Both methods and design courses should encourage prospective and practising interactive system constructors to have a broad view of what design entails. The papers in SII indicate the breadth of view which is possible.

4. Section SIII — Detailed Design

Requirements are satisfied by detailed design. The detail required to satisfy an apparently simple requirement can surprise the unwary, even when it is never represented explicitly. Section SIII addresses what we can do to satisfy needs. Evaluation is of little value if we cannot propose solutions to the problems which have been uncovered. The details in this section are part of the design repertoire which can be drawn on during design and the re-designs following evaluations.

Subsection SIII.1 comprises four papers on menu design. Two papers contribute to guidelines with disciplined studies of the details of menu design and the efficacy of these details. Another paper looks at the application of such detailed guidance. The last paper presents a way of specifying menu designs. Such focussed notations should be contrasted with the general purpose formalisms described in subsection SIII.5.

The size of subsection SIII.2 demonstrates the substantial interest in graphical and iconic interfaces. All HCI disciplines have something to contribute. Psychologists, cognitive scientists, ergonomists and computer scientists illustrate the uses of formal modelling, controlled studies, informal interviews, software architectures, design theories, new techniques and novel applications. It is hard to form a synthesis from such a wide range of approaches, but the beginnings of an interdisciplinary fusion are apparent in this subsection. Much still needs to be done, however, before we have a coherent body of detailed design knowledge for usable and useful graphical interfaces.

The initial designs of menus, icons, and graphical controls and displays are more often than not designed with only normal, error-free interaction in mind. For many users, this is not enough, despite the claims for these forms of interaction. Without support, many users will experience very little in the way of error-free, effective and efficient interaction. Close attention to potential errors can result in support being designed into the interaction [Norman 1983]. However, fine tuning of the superficial features of menus and icons is not a remedy for every problem.

The papers in subsection SIII.3 present several approaches to user support. One, the use of people when computers fail, is almost novel now that much research is directed towards placing support in the software. The mainstream of user support is well represented in the papers. Undoing, help, history, user monitoring, semantic modelling, adaptability (tailorability) and self-adaptive systems are all represented in this subsection. Whatever the potential of novel media and interaction techniques, some forms of non-imperative or non-monotonic interaction are going to remain essential in a well-designed system. This subsection shows how varied these supportive forms can be.

Last year's novel interaction technique or medium can be this year's problem (see section SIV for ways to make this less likely). Subsection SIII.4 gathers together three of the several accepted papers on hypermedia. What they have in common is an analysis of user interaction with hypermedia. Hypermedia has substantial potential, as papers elsewhere in the proceedings show. Nevertheless, excessive faith in the interaction style has blinded many to its limitations. The papers in this subsection are both an antidote to this zeal and, in their recommendations for future detailed design, a basis for renewed faith.

The system builders have all the details of their designs: the menus are specified; the icons have been parameterised and endowed with semantic animation; the application structures can be visualised; paths through the application domain have been encapsulated in hypermedia. But what about the construction of the system? The closing subsection, SIII.5, like the closing subsection of SII, concentrates on concrete embodiment, in this case the translation of a design into a working system. The ten papers on construction tools should not be confused with the bare run-time services of cut-down User Interface Management Systems (UIMSs), which neither embrace the whole user interface, provide for its explicit management, or provide any design tools. The papers in SIII.5 differ in one or two ways from toolkit level software support. First, they take the question of interactive architectures seriously. Second, they attempt to support the design specification by providing tools which deliver appropriate formalisms in conjunction with a high-level notation (textual, graphical or hybrid).

Interactive architectures are important because "good" ones provide the basis for re-use of very high level software designs. An initial or lower level of system decomposition is fixed by an interactive architecture. The chosen structure needs to be attractive, and it does this by promising to reduce the possibility of common inflexibilities in system implementation.

There are two views of what a UIMS is. For some, it is like an operating system, a collection of facilities where the only interface provided is one for the application programmer. For others, and this includes the originators of the term [Thomas and Hamlin 1983], it is like a database management system, and includes not only run-time database systems, but management tools for data modelling, database maintainance and performance modelling, as well as query languages for end-user applications. Within the former, more recent (and to some, uninformed) view of a UIMS, the research problems are largely technical and will be solved by computer scientists alone. All the UIMS papers accepted for INTERACT'90 take the wider view. Only a view of a UIMS as a combination of tools and run-time support code will bring the many disciplines of HCI to bear on the problem [Olsen *et al.* 1984].

All of the UIMSs in section SIII.5 include design tools as well as run-time services. The tools try to support good design (as do those in subsection SII.5) rather than just an implementation which will run (but not as fast as the users!) The tools vary in their ambitions. Much of the software in an interactive system is concerned with end-user interaction rather than the underlying functionality. The conservative approach is to support interactive media (presentation) and then simple "reactive" behaviour or dialogue. Half the papers in subsection SIII.5 go beyond this, and address semantic modelling and other sophisticated links between the user interface and the functional core.

Success in tooling further "back" into an interactive system should result in the critical mass required for an Interactive System Design Environment (ISDE, [Cockton 1990]). In the long term, UIMSs may be replaced by ISMSs (Interactive System Management Systems). Advanced design requires the extensive tooling of an ISDE. It is still too early to judge whether the tool designers represented here have succeeded, but the position is certainly improving.

5. Section SIV — Interactive technologies and techniques

In HCI, the knobs and dials of early ergonomics have given way to WIMPs and synthetic speech. Although not every hardware or toolkit producer has an effective human factors team, there is more human factors evaluation of new interactive technologies. A wide range of technologies are covered in this section: foot pedals and their feedback, tablet "windowing", data gloves, gestural input, 3D pointers, force-based pointing, large terminals, flat panel displays, colour, auditory icons and virtual realities, as well as old friends such as text displays, keyboards, speech and natural language.

What is encouraging about the three subsections of section SIV is the pervasiveness of user-centred design. The adoption of a user's viewpoint and usability methods is not even across the papers and more could be done in some areas to increase our confidence in the acceptability of the proposed technologies. Nevertheless, the evidence that more sophisticated approaches to HCI issues are more widespread is encouraging. Even in areas such as speech (subsection SIV.3) where the technical experts have dominated the direction of research, human factors perspectives have now taken their place as an essential component of successful design.

Taken as a whole, the papers in section SIV offer the promise of hardware and software technologies which have been tested on their utility and effectiveness. The need to pay attention to usage issues throughout the design lifecycle for interactive devices seems to be better understood, and furthermore, techniques developed on existing devices are now been transferred successfully to new technologies.

6. Section SV — Applications and case studies

This last paper section gathers together papers which bring together the knowledge, theories, techniques and technologies which were introduced in the first four paper sections. They also introduce perspectives which are not well covered in the rest of the volume. Computer-aided instruction is used in some of the applications. A social perspective is more frequent. Thus the case studies broaden as well as reinforce the material introduced in other sections. Case studies also highlight the need for knowledge and techniques which are still not to hand. Papers in this section not only tell us what can be done if we apply current knowledge and techniques, but also what must still be done without reliable guidance.

The first two subsections address two areas which are still fairly novel and are certainly not yet found in many everyday systems. Subsection SV.1 on knowledge-based systems (KBSs) has examples of the use of knowledge representation techniques from artificial intelligence to improve an interactive system's support for users. We should expect KBSs to be more supportive. They already model the semantics of the application domain. Such a model is an add-on in traditional systems. Some papers in subsection SIII.5 look at how the cost of this additional modelling could be reduced by appropriate design tools. The addition of such a model is the basis of intelligent front-ends. One paper in this section describes the process of adding such a front end to an existing system.

Intelligent front-ends however contain more than an application model. They still require the presentation and interaction components of a traditional user interface. The traditional concerns of information design apply as much, if not more, to fifth generation computing as they do to mainstream computer applications. A difficult design problem involves the explanations common in KBSs. A paper in this section addresses this issue and proposes a new approach.

Subsection SV.2 addresses Computer Supported Cooperative Work (CSCW) and its associated groupware. There are papers on concurrent editing, electronic communication and the application of CSCW approaches to office work. CSCW work is particularly appealing to the HCI community as it is an application area where it is close to impossible to ignore user needs!

The inescapable user demands of CSCW should have important spin-offs for the rest of HCI. From a software stand-point, separable user interfaces are a controversial luxury in single-user applications. In a CSCW application however, there will be considerable separation between the many user interfaces and the shared underlying application. Already, the UIMSs and UIDEs which do exist for CSCW are going beyond minimal support for presentation and dialogue (e.g. LIZA [Ellis *et al.* 1990]). On the other hand, much CSCW work is directed towards sophisticated computer users such as software engineers (e.g. CSCW papers in subsection SV.4). The needs of a wide range of CSCW users will only be met if systems are developed for non-technical as well as technical users (e.g. the office workers of two papers in this subsection).

Subsection SV.3 gathers together the remaining descriptions of applications developed from a user-centred perspective. Three are associated with training, but for very different groups of users (adult literacy students, telephone engineers, complex skills). The other two papers describe the design of an interface to a hypertext journal and the presentation of aircraft maintainance data. In both cases the designs use results from previous research and demonstrate that HCI technology transfer is taking place.

For those interested specifically in the applications of HCI research to real systems, there are several good case studies elsewhere in the proceedings (SII.2, SII.3, SII.4, SIII.2, SIII.3, SIII.4 and SIV.3, as well as section SV). Given the rarity of good applications papers in HCI (e.g. [Gould et al. 1987]), the number of case study papers in these proceedings is encouraging, but we should not be complacent. There is still an apparent imbalance between research and its application. Hopefully, this imbalance will be corrected and the correction will be reported in future international HCI conferences by practitioners who achieve it.

The last two subsections are a case of "physician heal thyself". If HCI cannot improve the production process for software, it is hard to see how it can improve software in general. If computing specialists cannot be helped to understand themselves as users, to understand the tasks associated with their work, and to understand the context in which work, then we cannot expect computing specialists to have full empathy with other users, tasks and organisations. Subsection SV.4 covers the broad topic of software engineering and the large subsection SV.5 concentrates on the specific tasks of programming.

Three of the papers in subsection SV.4 look at the specific application of CSCW to Software Engineering. The pre-eminence of a social perspective in these papers provides some compensation for the dominance of cognition and perception elsewhere. But academic or epistemelogical liberalism is not an end in itself. Rather, a social perspective reveals why the models underlying many project support environments are inadequate. A concern for human issues is thus not just something nice. It is effective. Technically minded designers are too ready to make false claims for tool and application features which the study of real human activities can quickly debunk. Thus one paper combines congratulations for CASE designers (designs are re-used) with a caveat that the resulting re-use is somewhat uncritical (the wrong designs are re-used). The work reported shows the importance of evaluation throughout the design process. What is imagine to be good from an uninformed (and uncritical) technical position may have unforeseen side effects in practice.

Subsection SV.5 covers many aspects of programming: learning, tutoring systems, comprehension, design difficulties and debugging tools. The results are not always restricted to programming. Two papers look at programming in end-user applications such as spreadsheets and home automation. Readers who are not specifically interested in the psychology of programming can still gain much from papers in this subsection.

Programming may appear to involve a well understood group of users and a straightforward set of tasks. As most HCI workers are computer users and have some programming skills, the study of programming should be straightforward. It is not. As user groups go, programmers may have been even more studied than word processor users. The area then is a major corpus of evidence on the pitfalls of various approaches in HCI such as experimental approaches, computational modelling and task analysis.

At the same time, studies of programming are not typical of work in HCI. Programming language designers are not noted for listening to psychologists or taking any notice of the studies that exist. This separation of designers from relevant user studies is somewhat extreme. Papers elsewhere in the proceedings have shown the success which is possible when design is user-centred and when user and task studies can influence design. Where discoveries about users and tasks cannot be directly applied, academic concerns with method and experimental design are more likely to dominate published work than practical success stories. There is an obvious contrast in the final section between studies which have been linked to design from the outset (Böcker *et al.*, Singley and Carroll) and those which are studies where there is no opportunity to apply any new knowledge directly.

7. The doctoral programme

The doctoral programme was a closed session before the main conference. Doctoral students submitted abstracts which were sent for review by the organisers of the doctoral programme. The accepted abstracts are gathered together in the sixth section of this volume.

The range of topics is a subset of those covered in the main proceedings. There is cognitive ergonomics research on training and programming. CSCW research is well represented. There is formal methods research on modelling systems and tasks. There is research into design and design tools, with particular emphasis on user support.

These proceedings face forward to the 1990s as well as backwards to the 1980s. The picture of current doctoral research which this volume confirms that cognitive ergonomics and software design are currently the main forces within HCI, and that application areas such as programming and CSCW are amongst the most popular.

8. The panels

The panel sessions were another forward looking part of INTERACT'90. There were eight panels. Practical issues were well represented. Several panels were concerned with the problem of adapting academic research and R&D work for use in the mainstream of systems development. Two panels looked at ways of improving HCI research, through both user participation and through the proper treatment of new theories. Support for software designers was a popular panel topic as well a popular paper topic. A panel on multi-agent interaction explored the implications of moving away from the typical duo of user and computer.

The emphasis on practical issues in several panel sessions provided a balance to the knowledge generation bias of many paper sessions. With the demonstrations, video show and exhibition, the practical panel sessions provided an important focus on the application of HCI skills and knowledge.

9. More of the different – breadth in HCI research and practice

HCI is multidisciplinary and interdisciplinary. It has been multidisciplinary in its borrowings from psychology, ergonomics, physiology, graphic design, education, management, sociology, anthropology, linguistics, cognitive science, computer science, engineering and even on occasions, drama, film, video, animation and architecture, although these disciplines were not all represented at INTERACT'90. It is interdisciplinary in its practice, applying methods from the human sciences, mathematics and engineering. If either perspective, the multidisciplinary or the interdisciplinary, is denied, user-centred systems will not result. The separation of designers and evaluators in studies of programming (subsection SV.5) is evidence of the benefits associated with fully integrating requirements and evaluation studies within the process of design and construction. This need to unite user studies with artefact construction is elaborated with more eloquence and force in subsection SII.1.

As has been said, these proceedings face forward to the 1990s as well as backwards to the 1980s. In the 1990s, HCI should broaden out and fully accommodate knowledge from disciplines apart from computer science, psychology and ergonomics. The methods of contributory disciplines need to be moulded into an effective process form for user-centred design, just as management, medicine and education have fused several disciplines in the pursuit of organisational effectiveness, health and the dissemination of skills and knowledge. HCI will not be alone; the importance of good design is being recognised in other areas of production, and HCI will share in the general benefits of an increased commitment to quality across all goods and services.

It is the combination of the new research as reported in the doctoral programme and the accepted papers *and* the move towards quality as a key commercial concern which will guarantee some form of progress within HCI. However, there are issues which go beyond individual designs and products which need to be better understood, and there is no strong desire within the majority of national research programmes or industry to expand HCI knowledge in all the contributory disciplines. There is no reason for thinking that there is going to be a trend in future conferences towards more papers on social, individual, aesthetic and affective issues. If this is to be the case, and it is a reflection of slower development in these areas, then our ability to produce interactives systems of quality is going to be affected. Knowledge of cognitive ergonomics and software design is improving and should continue to improve, but progress here will only highlight the lack of progress in other areas of HCI.

It remains to be seen how much progress there will have been by the next IFIP conference on HCI. Let us hope that there will be some real breakthroughs involving a number of contributory disciplines. If we understand where we are now, we will have a better chance of recognising the real breakthroughs when they occur. The papers in this volume are representative of the current state of work in HCI. If we keep up to date and take advantage of the contributions in this volume, we will have more chance of understanding the full implications of the next decade's innovations as they happen.

Acknowledgements

David England let me have his paper (and thus all his setting up for the camera ready format) in electronic form, saving me the frustration of getting things to work in a hurry. The definition of a UIMS as a UIDE plus the run-time support was proposed in a working group at the Eurographics Lisbon workshop on UIMSs in June 1990. Dan Diaper and Nigel Bevan provided many useful comments on this introduction. I am grateful for their suggestions. As programme co-ordinator I have had to familiarise myself with the contributions to this conference. I have based my introduction on my preparations for programme and proceedings structuring. Discussions during paper selection and programme design with David Gilmore, Dan Diaper, Mark Kirby, Brian Shackel and Thomas Green helped to change or widen my view of several of the contributions. Given the nature of these proceedings, this introduction can only be one individual's initial overview — no "official" position is possible.

References

Bullinger, H.-J. and B. Shackel (eds)
Human-Computer Interaction: INTERACT'87, North-Holland, Amsterdam, 1987

Carroll, J.M. (ed)
Interfacing Thought, MIT Press, Cambridge, Ma, U.S.A., 1987

Cockton, G.
"Engineering for Human Computer Interaction: Architecture and abstraction", in *Engineering for Human Computer Interaction*, ed. Gilbert Cockton, North Holland, Amsterdam, 3–8, 1990

Diaper, D.
"Task Analysis for Knowledge Descriptions (TAKD); the method and an example", in *Task Analysis for Human-Computer Interaction,* ed. Dan Diaper, Ellis Horwood, Chichester,UK,108–159, 1989 .

Ellis, C.A., S.J. Gibbs and G.L. Rein
"Design and Use of a Group Editor", in *Engineering for Human Computer Interaction*, ed. Gilbert Cockton, North Holland, Amsterdam, 13-28, 1990

Gould, J.D., S.J. Boies, S. Levey, J.T. Richards and J. Schoonard
"The 1984 Olympic Message System: A Test of Behavioral Principles in System Design", *CACM*, 30(9), 758-769, 1987

Hewett, Thomas T.
"Towards a Rapid Prototyping Environment for Interface Design: Desirable Features Suggested by The Electronic Spreadsheet", in *People and Computers V*, eds. A. Sutcliffe and L. Macaulay, Cambridge University Press, Cambridge, UK, 305–314, 1989

Long, John and John Dowell
"Conceptions of the Discipline of HCI: Craft, Applied Science, and Engineering", in *People and Computers V*, eds. A. Sutcliffe and L. Macaulay, Cambridge University Press, Cambridge, UK, 9–32, 1989

Norman, D.A.
"Design Rules Based on Analyses of Human Error", *CACM*, 26(4), 254-258, 1983

Olsen, D.R., W. Buxton, R. Ehrich, D.J. Kasik, J.R. Rhyne and J. Sibert
"A Context for User Interface Management", *Computer Graphics and Applications,* 4(12), IEEE, 33–43, 1984

Shackel, B. (ed)
Human-Computer Interaction: INTERACT'84, North Holland, Amsterdam, 1985

Thomas, J.J. and G. Hamlin (eds)
"Graphical Input Interaction Technique (GIIT). Workshop Summary" ,*Computer Graphics*, 17(1), ACM, 5–30, 1983

INVITED PAPERS

SIOIS – Standard interfaces or interface standards
T. Stewart xxix

Empirical studies of the software design process
B. Curtis xxxv

Human-Computer Interaction - INTERACT '90
D. Diaper et al. (Editors)
Elsevier Science Publishers B.V. (North-Holland)

SIOIS - STANDARD INTERFACES OR INTERFACE STANDARDS

Tom Stewart

System Concepts Ltd, Museum House, Museum Street, London WC1A 1JT

National Standards have often acted as barriers to trade, requiring manufacturers not only to produce national variants of products but also to undergo costly and time-consuming certification and testing procedures. After 1992, national standards in Europe will be replaced by European Standards, providing manufacturers with a single European market for their products. In the user interface area, and in many other areas also, European standards do not yet exist and so the European Committee for Standardisation (CEN) plans to adopt International Standards, wherever possible. The purpose of this paper is to provide an update on the activities of the committees working at the European and the International levels to create user interface standards.

1. INTRODUCTION

The concern that I wish to address in this paper is that those who are developing user interface standards at a European and at an International level are inhibiting creativity and innovation by insisting that all interfaces look and feel the same ie by creating a standard interface.

If we consider the analogy of the telephone, then to some extent they do all look and feel the same. This is a direct consequence of the required functionality. If the microphone is near the mouth and the earpiece near the ear, then there are limits - human limits - for how far apart they can be. Similarly, if there are buttons to be pressed, then again, unless we redesign the human, there are limits beyond which operation is difficult. There is still scope for creativity and ingenuity in design - telephones are by no means uniform and standardised.

So too with user interfaces. There are some issues where standards will restrict change, both for reasons of good practice or for consistency. There are many other areas where they will not. But it is too simple to talk about user interface standards as if they were a single entity. Even within the International Organisation for Standardisation (ISO) and the European Committee for Standardisation (CEN), there are a multiplicity of committees, nationalities, interest groups, viewpoints and activities. Before going on to review what these bodies are doing and to consider just how much these activities might lead to constrained, uniform or standard interfaces, I believe it is important to consider the historical context.

2. DEUTSCHES INSTITUT FUR NORMUNG

Twenty years ago or more, the German National Standards Organisation (DIN) started to publish a series of standards which shook the computer world. These standards, DIN 66-234, were published in a number of parts and collectively addressed the ergonomics problems of Visual Display Terminals and their workplaces.

At that time, price-performance was the main objective and it came as a major culture shock for the computer industry that ergonomics standards could have such a major impact on whether a product would sell or not.

Note that it was not the DIN standard itself but its integration into workplace regulations (ZH 618 Safety Regulations for Display Workplaces in the Office Sector, published by the Central Association of Trade Cooperative Associations) which gave the ergonomics requirements such 'teeth'. Failure to comply with these regulations leaves an employer uninsured against industrial compensation claims.

DIN 66 234 also contains a number of parts which deal exclusively with software issues. For example, Part 3 deals with the grouping and formatting of data, Part 5 with the coding of information and Part 8 with the principles of dialogue design. Although these are more in the form of recommendations, they have been heavily criticised, particularly for their broad scope and their inhibitory effect on interface design.

Indeed, a major criticism of most early standards in this field is that they were based on product design features such as height of characters on the screen. Such standards were specific to current technology eg cathode ray tubes (CRT) and did not readily apply to other technologies. They may therefore inhibit innovation and force designers to stick to old solutions.

More importantly, the standards specify values for a range of different parameters quite independently and take little account of the complex interactions which take place in real use, for example between display characteristics and the environment. The UK has been a major force in encouraging the international standards work to develop along different lines.

3. THE INTERNATIONAL ORGANISATION FOR STANDARDISATION (ISO)

Two committees in ISO are developing standards directly relevant to the user interface, one from an ergonomics perspective (TC159 SC4) and one from an information technology perspective (JTC 1 SC18).

3.1 ISO TC159 SC4

In our approach, as a Sub-committee (SC4) of the Ergonomics Technical Committee (TC159) of ISO, we have put the emphasis on user performance standards. Thus, rather than simply specify a product feature such as character height which we believe will contribute towards display legibility, we are developing procedures for testing performance such as legibility directly. The standard is then stated in terms of the user performance required from the equipment and not in terms of how that is achieved. The user performance measure includes speed and accuracy and the avoidance of discomfort.

Such user performance standards are relevant to the real problems experienced by users, tolerant of developments in the technology and flexible to cope with interactions between factors.

However, they also suffer a number of disadvantages. They cannot be totally complete and scientifically valid in all cases. They rely on a number of reasonable compromises concerning the performance task, the likely user population, the test conditions and so on. Obtaining the agreement of all the parties in standards setting takes time.

Table 1 lists the parts of the multi-part standard 9241 currently under development. User performance test methods have been developed for two parts. These deal with the legibility of visual displays and the operability of keyboards. In future, a number of other areas of user interface standardisation, especially those concerned with software issues, are likely to be amenable to user performance testing.

Table 1. ISO 9241 Standard

Part 1	General Introduction
Part 2	Task Requirements
Part 3	Visual Requirements
Part 4	Keyboard Requirements
Part 5	Workplace Requirements
Part 6	Environment Requirements
Part 7	VDT Surface Treatments
Part 8	Use of Colour
Part 9	Non-keyboard input devices
Part 10	Dialogue Interface Principles
Part 11	Usability Statement
Part 12	Coding and Formatting
Part 13	Terminology
Part 14	Menu Dialogues

Initially the committee focused on hardware ergonomics issues for office VDU users as these were most pressing and seemed more straightforward. However, as more parts have been added, so the focus of the work has moved and a number of the later parts have far broader applications. The committee is currently reviewing its strategy for dealing with this complex field and recognises that a major restructuring of the parts may be necessary before too long.

The work of the committee is undertaken by Working Groups and WG5 is currently responsible for the five parts concerned with software and man-machine interface issues.

Part 10. Dialogue Design Criteria

This part of the standard presents high level ergonomic principles which apply to the design of dialogues between humans and information systems. These include suitability for the task, controllability and error tolerance amongst others. The principles are supported by a number of scenarios which indicate the relative priorities and importance of the different principles in practical applications. The starting point for this work was the DIN 66234 Part 8 Principles of Ergonomic Dialogue Design for Workplaces with Visual Display Units.

Part 11. Usability Statement

Part 11 provides a framework for an ergonomics requirements specification which includes descriptions of the context of use, the evaluation procedures to be carried out and the criterion measures to be satisfied when the usability of the system is to be evaluated. There are various situations in which usability may be evaluated, for example in product development, in procurement or in product certification. The common framework being developed in this part should be useful in all of these situations.

Part 12. Coding and Formatting

This part deals with the specific ergonomics issues involved in representing and presenting information in a visual or auditory form. It will include guidance on ways of representing complex information, screen layout and design as well as the use of windows. There is already a substantial body of material available in guidelines and recommendations and this part represents a distillation of the most useful and relevant ones. At present, the information is envisaged as guidelines without any need for formal conformance testing.

Part 13. Terminology

There is considerable ambiguity surrounding the terminology of human computer interaction. Although the bulk of the committee work is in English, there is a requirement for the standards to be translated into other languages. There is therefore a need for an agreed terminology to enable those outside the world of standardisation to be certain what is meant and for those inside to be certain that they communicate effectively. This part aims to meet these needs. However, little progress has been made in this area to date.

Part 14. Menu Dialogues

There are a number of recognised dialogue techniques which the multi-part standard is likely to incorporate in time. Rather than create a vast theoretical structure with space for future developments, the strategy adopted has been to develop parts as soon as possible and to review the overall structure of the standard once it has some substantive content. Thus the first dialogue technique for which material is available concerns dialogue menus. This contains a large number of guidelines developed from the published literature and from other relevant research. In view of the range of generality and applicability of the guidelines, a form of conditional conformance is envisaged. Thus, conformance will only be tested on applicable guidelines and these will be identified by satisfying a conditional statement of the form, 'If x is important, then guideline y is applicable'.

Although there has been widespread support for the work from the major manufacturers IBM, HP, DEC, Siemens, Olivetti, ICL and others and from countries East and West, progress is still frustratingly slow. Nonetheless, by the end of 1990, there are likely to be three parts published as full International Standards (Parts 1,2 and 3), one part as a Draft International Standard (part 4) and up to five parts as Committee Drafts (Parts 5, 6, 7, 8, 10 and 14).

3.2 ISO/IEC JTC1/SC18/WG9

After several years of confusion, the ISO and the International Electrotechnical Commission (IEC) formed a Joint Technical Committee (JTC1) to deal with standards in the field of information technology. Sub committee 18 (SC18) is responsible for standards for Text and Office Systems and Working Group 9 is developing standards for user system interfaces.

WG9 is developing standards in keyboard layout, symbols and user interfaces. Some of their activities are described below.

ISO/IEC 9995

This is a new multi-part standard dealing with keyboard layout which replaces 12 existing standards. Twenty parts are envisaged in all and by mid 1990, three are being circulated as Draft International Standards and seventeen as Committee Drafts. It is expected that this multi-part standard will be completed by the end of 1991. It should be noted that WG9 deals with the layout of keyboards, not with the key operation or other ergonomic features which are the responsibility of WG3 of TC159/SC4.

Part 6 of this standard deals with symbols for function keys and for other kinds of equipment.

ISO/IEC 8884

This standard is already published and describes a keyboard layout for multiple Latin alphabet languages. This is particularly important as more and more organisations operate in a multi-lingual environment.

ISO/IEC 6329

This standard deals with graphical symbols on equipment, particularly photocopiers and printers

WG9U

The user interface subgroup of WG9 is working on two main work items.

In collaboration with the symbols group, it is developing a standard for icons and other graphical symbols used on screens.

In the area of Information Processing Standards for Office System User Interfaces, it is working on naming and defining a basic set of objects and actions common in office systems. It is also working on user guidance for and on dialogue interaction.

Committee Drafts on 'Names of basic objects and actions' and on the specification of icons and other graphical symbols used on screens are due towards the end of 1990.

3.3 National Mirror Committees

The members of ISO are the national standards bodies of the member countries. In general, these have their own committee structure which mirrors the international committees. Thus in the US, there is an Human Factors Society - Computer Interaction Committee (HFS-HCI) which mirrors TC159/SC4 and provides major input to WG5 under the auspices of the American National Standards Institute (ANSI). Another ANSI sponsored committee X3V1.9 has the responsibility for user system interfaces and symbols and is the national mirror for JTC1/SC18/WG9.

In the UK, the British Standards Institution (BSI) is the national standards body and it too has mirror committees actively involved in both the ISO committees. PSM39/-/2 mirrors TC159/SC4 and IST18/-/9U mirrors the user interface activity in JTC1/SC18/WG9U.

4. THE EUROPEAN DIMENSION

The European Commission has declared that 1992 represents the end of trade barriers in Europe and that from then there will be a single European market for goods and services. Different national standards are at least potential barriers to trade and so part of this initiative involves the replacement of national standards with European standards. Unfortunately, CEN, the body responsible for producing European Standards, does not have all the standards necessary to replace national standards. There has therefore been a flurry of activity to create CEN standards where none existed before.

The chosen strategy is to adopt International Standards, where appropriate, and thus to short circuit the standards making process. The CEN Ergonomics Committee TC122, through its own Working Group 5, has agreed to facilitate and support the ISO/TC159/SC4 user interface work with a view to adopting the International Standards as European Standards.

The first three parts of the ISO 9241 are already being voted on under the PQ Preliminary Questionnaire procedure as possible European Standards (ENs).

Meanwhile in another part of the EC, the regulation of the user interface is about to receive major impetus.

5. THE EUROPEAN DIRECTIVE ON VDUs

In the Official Journal of the European Communities (C 113,29,4 1988), a Draft Directive was published 'concerning the minimum health and safety requirements for work with visual display units'. It was one of a series of Directives covering the health and safety of workers in Europe.

This Draft Directive has caused considerable concern in the computer industry. It has also caused concern to organisations who have large numbers of staff using VDUs. Part of this concern is that the Directive itself seems to have been created in haste and bears all the hallmarks of its precipitative birth. It is also difficult for all but the most dedicated EEC watchers to anticipate just what its chances are and how it might evolve. Given the potential impact of Directives on member states, (it is mandatory for them to pass appropriate legislation) concern is clearly justified.

Although the bulk of the Directive is concerned with hardware design, there are explicit references to software and dialogue issues. It is therefore important to understand the extent and the implications of this potentially highly significant piece of European legislation.

The Directive applies to the entire work station including 'display screen, keyboard, peripherals, including diskette drive, printer, document holder, work chair, work desk, the immediate work environment' and for some issues the software also (see the discussion of the Technical Annex).

Member States will take different steps to demonstrate that they are providing adequate supervision. In the UK, the responsibility will lie with the Health and Safety Executive and it is likely that it will issue specific guidance based on the final Directive.

'Work stations put into service for the first time' after 31 December 1992 must meet the minimum requirements laid down in the technical annex.

Article 7 stipulates that workers receive training in all aspects of VDU health and safety. Article 7a places a responsibility on the employer to 'ensure that the daily working time on a VDU is appropriately divided up'. VDU work may be interrupted by breaks or by changes of activity.

Article 11 requires member states to 'bring into force the laws, regulations and administrative provisions necessary to comply with this Directive' by 31 December 1992.

The Annex contains a number of very general requirements for display screen, keyboard, work desk, work chair, lighting, reflections and glare, noise, heat, radiation and obscurely but potentially significantly, the operator/computer interface.

> 'Operator/computer interface
>
> The psycho-social factors applicable to the writing of programs (software) and to the tasks resulting from such programs shall be taken into account; no clandestine individual checks (tell-tale devices) may be built into the programs.
>
> The principles of software ergonomics shall be applied in particular to human data processing'

These requirements 'shall apply as and where appropriate, depending on the presence of the components in the work station and on the demands of the task in question'. In other words, there is considerable scope for debate and argument over whether the requirements will apply in a given situation or not - a perfect situation for lawyers!

6. OTHER BODIES

Of course, complex though the above may seem, it is a considerable simplification of the current scene. I describe below some of the other players whose activities are important.

6.1 The European Telecommunications Standards Institute (ETSI)

The European Telecommunications Standards Institute largely replaces CEPT in the field of telecommunications standards. Its members are the national telecommunications administrations, network operators, manufacturers and users in Europe. It has twelve technical committees of which one deals with Human Factors (TC HF). Four working groups are active, dealing with such issues as the usability of telecommunications services and the human factors of telecommunications for people with special needs including the handicapped. The output of the human factors work is likely to take the form of technical reports rather than standards, although that option exists in the future. There is some overlap with the international body, the CCITT SG1 WG2C which is also developing methods for the evaluation of telecommunications usability.

6.2 Information Technology Steering Committee (ITSC)

The Information Technology Steering Committee is a high level European body set up to coordinate the IT work programmes of CEN, CENELEC and CEPT (through ETSI). It has a number of IT Ad hoc Expert Groups (ITAEGs) to advise it and one of these (ITAEGM) deals with Advanced Manufacturing Technologies. This group has a strong interest in user interface standards for advanced manufacturing. At the moment it is reviewing current user interface standards and developments in CEN and ISO to identify what is relevant to advanced manufacturing technology and what gaps exist.

6.3 European Computer Manufacturers Association (ECMA)

The European Computer Manufacturers Association has recently set up a Technical Committee (TC35) on User System Interface. Its objective is to develop an architectural reference model for the user system interface on the basis of which required standards can be identified. Initially at least, its main activities will involve reviewing current work especially in CEN and ISO and acting as a act as a channel for communication between the standards makers and the European computer industry.

6.4 Institution of Electrical and Electronic Engineers (IEEE)

The Institution of Electrical and Electronic Engineers has a standards committee (P1201.2) which has recently started work on Graphical User Interface Drivability. Their objectives are to define a recommended practice that embodies a consistent set of user interface elements to allow users to transfer between environments and applications in order to minimise interference, errors, confusion and retraining. It also aims to form a liaison with other standards groups working in related areas.

7. CONCLUSION

From this brief overview of the international scene, I hope it is clear that the majority of current standards activity does not aim to reduce creativity and innovation, except where this is necessary to protect users from badly designed products. However, although the intention is honourable, the reality is not always quite as intended. I have been informed by some display manufacturers that they have to de-tune their displays to ensure that they conform with certain standards which were originally introduced to improve display quality.

The rapid pace at which technology develops not only outstrips our ability to use it properly but renders conventional standards development timescales inappropriate.

That is why I believe in what we have called the user performance approach. It is possible to create standards which reflect enduring human characteristics and requirements. The technology of keyboards has changed dramatically but it is still possible to construct a valid performance test to compare speed, accuracy and discomfort on an early manual typewriter and the latest PC based word processing package. Thus the user performance approach actively encourages innovation and creativity in user interface design by allowing better design to flourish in appropriate performance comparisons.

Not surprisingly, I am optimistic about the positive benefits to be achieved through well-designed standards. However, it is not just because I believe in standards as end products. Much of the benefit of standards comes through the process of standards creation. It is a slow process involving international collaboration and consensus with all its frustrations and benefits. Over the years, the reaction of the manufacturers has changed from one of suspicion and reluctance even to consider user interface standards to one of active participation in the development process. They have recognised that user interface design, in all its forms, is firmly on the agenda. The slow nature of the standards development process means that by the time the final standard is published most manufacturers are ready with products which comply. This does not mean that the standard is unnecessary, more that its publication may be closer to the end of its period of major influence rather than the beginning.

Improving user interface design through standards is as much about changing attitudes as it is about changing products.

Human–Computer Interaction – INTERACT '90
D. Diaper et al. (Editors)
Elsevier Science Publishers B.V. (North-Holland)

Empirical Studies of the Software Design Process

Bill Curtis
MCC
3500 West Balcones Center Dr.
Austin, TEXAS 78759

Empirical research on software development has shown that the design phase exercises extreme leverage over project outcomes. This paper reviews research performed at MCC on the design process and proposes several research questions whose answers are crucial to improving productivity and quality. One implication of these results is that project outcomes are largely determined before a project begins. *(As is the author's habit, the talk at INTERACT'90 may differ substantially from this paper)*

MCC'S Design Research

Until recently the dominant paradigm for designing software has been top–down, balanced decomposition. Not only is this the dominant paradigm used to structure most software engineering textbooks, but it has been chiseled into the hard stone of many software development standards, most notably the US Department of Defense's MIL–STD–2167A, the process bible of the aerospace industry. Deviations from this model were treated as special cases of behavior to overcome weaknesses of various sorts. Although variations of prototyping models are usually mentioned in texts and standards their value is retarded by either being, 1) merely paid lip service in opening sections while the remainder of the tome is presented in a top–down life cycle organization, or 2) presented as a process that can be executed entirely within the bounds of one phase of the life cycle process.

Realizing that MCC's Software Technology Program could not base its research on advanced software design tools on process models we did not believe, my colleagues and I performed an assortment of empirical studies of the software design process. The guiding philosophy in this program of research was that the design process must be understood at many levels of analysis – cognitive, social, and organizational providing a minimal set. At the level of individual design problem–solving we studied software engineers creating designs for the controls of an elevator system. At the social / team level we observed one of our own teams designing a object–oriented database. At the organizational level we interviewed teams on 17 large software development projects about the problems they experienced.

Design as Cognitive Activity

Early studies of the cognitive aspects of designing software usually presented results without explicitly challenging the traditional model of top–down software design (Jeffries, Turner, Polson, & Atwood, 1983; Kant & Newell, 1985). Although Adelson and Soloway (1985) reported design behaviors that supported other models, they did not go so far as to propose an alternate to the standard top–down model. In fact, their balanced development of the *sketchy model* is similar to earlier models.

Early studies used small problems and did not look at expert design behavior on realistically large tasks. In order to study design on harder problems, Herb Krasner presented the *Lift Problem*, a standard problem used in studying specification techniques, to eight professional designers. In analyzing the thinking aloud protocols from these sessions, Raymonde Guindon (Guindon, 1990a,b; Guindon & Curtis, 1988; Guindon, Krasner, & Curtis, 1987) discovered that an opportunistic model is more characteristic of cognitive behavior in software design. Further, she surmised that top–down, balanced development is a special case that occurs when a designer fully understands the problem, or has solved a similar problem before. This opportunistic model is similar to those developed in the empirical literature on planning (Hayes–Roth & Hayes–Roth, 1979).

A 60 minute slice of the design activities of a designer who holds a Masters Degree in Software Engineering and has 5 years experience in designing real–time systems is presented in Figure 1. This designer is analyzing the problem using the techniques of Jackson System Development (Jackson, 1983), his preferred approach to software design. Notice how this designer bounces back and forth across levels of abstraction in developing his design. This is the hallmark of an opportunistic process, wherein concepts at one level of abstraction trigger thoughts at other levels of abstraction. These opportunistic thoughts at widely different levels of abstraction are often attended to before concepts at intervening levels of abstraction are elaborated. Thus, we have seen that even when a trained software engineer attempts to perform a top–down, balanced development (as represented by the shaded line descending by steps in Figure 1), the process becomes opportunistic as the designer searches for insights or tries to verify design hypotheses through the early exploration of details at much lower levels of abstraction. Recently John Sumiga has been developing a similar model in Great Britain.

The hallmark of Guindon's opportunistic model being the constant iteration between levels of abstraction in the design is not surprising in light of earlier results. Kant and Newell (1984) provided an excellent description of how insight develops in the design process. Insight requires establishing a relation between act of recognition in the problem domain space with structures in the solution space. This act of recognition in the problem domain usually involves abstracting higher order relationships from known relationships among the existing components. However, the importance of this insight is lost if it is not related to the emerging solution structure. Thus, the identification of a key insight requires that the problem domain space and the solution space be developed (decomposed, elaborated, etc.) simultaneously. If the problem domain is underdeveloped it cannot serve as basis for simulating test cases (Adelson & Soloway, 1985). If the solution space is underdeveloped an insight in the problem domain will be lost to the design process. In actual software development there is a severe problem in that the models of the problem domain and the solution space are developed 1) at different times, 2) by different people, 3) to different levels of elaboration. Thus, the process of developing insight that we observe in single designer experiments is thwarted by the context of design in actual software development environments. A crucial question that must be answered

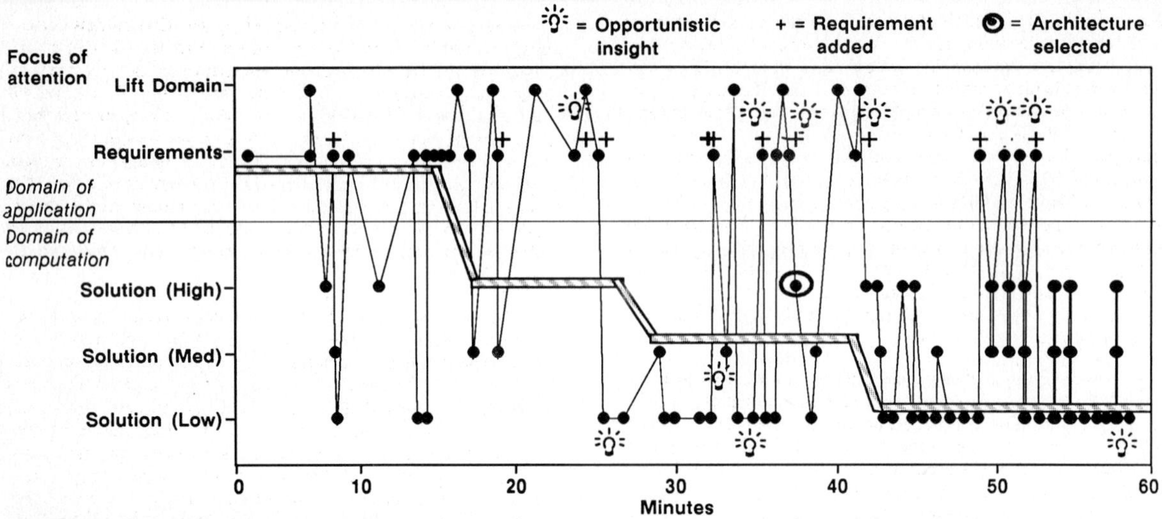

Figure 1. The process map of a Lift design session (Guindon, 1990a,b)

for software productivity and quality is how to integrate these disparate design functions into a conceptual whole that looks as if one designer had developed the insight from comparing problem domain and solution space information.

Most researchers stress the importance of mental simulations in supporting design activity. Yet there has been little systematic study of this simulation process. Adelson and Soloway (1985) observed that mental simulation was difficult when the designer lacked problem domain knowledge. Guindon (1990a) observed that the structure of a given simulation was driven by the structure of the design problem to be addressed, and that the depth of a simulation was driven by the depth of the questions being asked. Often new or inferred requirements are discovered through this process. A crucial question for future research involves how designers acquire the scenarios from which these problem domain simulations are developed.

The amount of research on mental simulations in design problem-solving has not been commensurate with their importance in this process. I am going to speculate a bit on what future research may find. These speculations are influenced by the research on qualitative physics (Weld & de Kleer, 1990). Mental simulations do not appear to be like the mathematical simulations that characterize performance modeling or operations research. Rather the objects within the scenario simulated are chosen because they are the ones recognized as relevant to the designer's understanding of the behavior being simulated, and may not form a complete model of relevant parts of the system. Further, designers generally do not mentally reconstruct a replica of the actual continuous behavior that a system will exhibit. Rather they jump through discrete states that represent significant points in the process they are considering. These points emerge from memory as being significant to the behavior under analysis.

The designer is forced to use cues in a static representation as an index into information about the dynamics implied by these structures. Thus, a designer will sense that a throughput problem may exist because it has occurred in previous systems that share some structural characteristics and/or a similar operational context. An interesting research question that emerges here is whether exceptional designers differ from competent designers in how they organize their knowledge of previous designs they have worked on, and how they use structural cues in the current design as a means of accessing this knowledge for mental simulations.

The nuggets of design knowledge extracted from previous experience are crucial to aiding designers in future projects. They represent the designer's understanding of the states a system may enter, and as such, provide a measure of the completeness of the designer's understanding of the problem domain. These nuggets may be triggers recognizing problematic configurations in the solution space or they may be different events, data loadings, exception conditions, constraints, etc. in the problem domain. If design performance is related to the quality of simulations of information in the problem space, then the depth of a designer's understanding of the application (problem) domain is crucial. Software design tools will not solve this problem, since designers cannot enter information they do not know. That is, the tools cannot simulate the effects of exception conditions and data throughput factors that the designer has not entered into the simulation model. An important problem for an applied research project is to test vendors' claims about whether representing a design in any of the CASE tools currently available assists designers in identifying flaws or gaps in the design of which they were otherwise unaware. Further, do these tools help or hinder the designer in developing and analyzing a design at multiple levels of abstraction simultaneously, as suggested by Guindon.

Application domain knowledge is not trained in computer science departments, it is gained through experience on a job. Another description for on the job training is disorganized education. Future research on the cognitive aspects of design should investigate how application knowledge is acquired over a career and how it is used at increasing levels of sophistication in the design process. This research needs to move beyond the traditional expert–novice paradigm, and investigate the historical development and use of deep knowledge. One reason the traditional expert–novice paradigm is not adequate, is that software designers are forced to integrate knowledge from many different knowledge domains, and we need to study how this integration process occurs and how knowledge is reorganized across domains with continued experience. Are there characteristic phases that could be identified? If phases can be identified, how can career paths be designed to accelerate this intellectual growth. For cognitive scientists these are exciting new research challenges. Industry should be interested in funding this research, because companies bet millions on design decisions made by senior system engineers, and they have no idea how exceptional designers are developed. Perhaps they are just born and in any random personnel selection process you will hire a few of them. I doubt it.

Design as Group Activity

In the 1990s we will begin to see software development environments that embed models of the software process in the control of their tools (cf. Dowson, 1987). These process models will too often be based on traditional life cycle models, models of individual activity, or idealized models of team process. If these environments are to be successfully employed in software development, they must operate in a way that supports team activity rather than hindering it. Of the few studies of multiple agents performing complex design activities (cf., Basili & Reiter, 1981; Boehm, Gray, & Seewaldt, 1984), none have investigated the integration of knowledge across experts in different domains or the communication processes required to develop a common model of the application and the system design across the entire design team. As a result, design in team situations is typically treated as an outgrowth of individual design activities, avoiding the multi-agent problem-solving and communication issues.

In order to study software design team behavior, Herb Krasner and Jeff Conklin videotaped every design meeting of an MCC team designing an object-oriented database. They held 37 team meetings over five months, some of which involved interactions with customers. In a dissertation using these data directed by Joyce Elam, Diane Walz (1988) devised a method for scoring the verbal protocols of design teams into categories tailored to the semantics of the design process. The analysis emphasized the team's information requirements and their effect on the group process, especially information sharing. She began by assuming that the conflicts within a software design team were not solely the result of incompatible goals and/or opinions, but also represented the natural dialectic through which knowledge was exchanged and terminology was clarified (Walz, Elam, Krasner, & Curtis, 1988). Analyses of the protocols and follow-up questions to team members indicated that design meetings were generally dominated by a few individuals to whom fellow participants attributed the greatest breadth of expertise. These individuals appeared to form a coalition that controlled the direction of the team.

In reading the transcripts of these team meetings you are struck with the amount of time designers spend trying to develop a shared model of the design. There are many aspects to this effort. First, many design meetings can be devoted to filling knowledge gaps, such as learning about the application (e.g., lectures from outside experts about object-oriented programming and the requirements for object repositories). Next, the team must come to a common understanding of the semantics of the symbol or diagrammatic system they are using to represent design information. The longer they go without establishing this consensus, the more communication breakdowns will occur. Next they must try to comprehend the differences in their initial model of the application and the design solution. Without understanding these individualized starting points, the team is unable to detect when a breakdown in establishing consensus is likely to have occurred. Finally, they must come to negotiate a common understanding of the architecture. This common model allows them to work on different components of the system without violating interfaces or architectural constraints. Problems of this nature usually do not show up until integration test, and are much more expensive to remove than they would have been in the design phase.

There is an interesting trade-off that a manager must make in staffing a design team. The more similar the design knowledge of team members, the faster they can reach consensus and the more productive they are during design. However, if it is important to challenge design assumptions (as would be true when undertaking design in a new application area are with new technology), then such a team would be sub-optimal. The greater the diversity of mental models of designs brought together in a design team, the greater the challenging of assumptions that will occur. This challenge is important if design flaws and gaps are to be detected early. Thus, the tradeoff a project manager faces in staffing is between speed of reaching consensus versus the breadth of exploring alternatives. The context surrounding a project and the nature of the design challenges faced will influence the appropriate choice.

Divergence among the application or solution models held by designers must be related to a multi-agent problem-solving model in two ways. Divergence among designers has the advantage of surfacing alternative designs. On the other hand, divergence has the disadvantages of reducing an individual's ability to contribute to the current state of the design, and requiring greater team overhead in coordinating an understanding of the design among team members. Much of the communication in design meetings is in the service of building and maintaining common models of the emerging design. One measure of communication effectiveness is in the problems experienced in integrating components produced by various designers.

The existing research on team problem-solving led us to expect monotonically increasing consensus among design team members on design issues. A simplistic model assuming that cooperative design activity requires agreement among team members would lead us to hypothesize this monotonic increase. However, an interesting pattern in the verbal acts representing agreement within the team was observed across the 17 meetings that constituted the design phase of this project. As the data in Figure 2 demonstrate, Walz observed a surprising inverted U-shaped curve (verified through logistic regression) that characterized verbal acts of agreement. The level of agreement increased until meetings 7-10, when the design team released a document presenting its functional specification in response to customer requirements. In subsequent meetings the level of agreement began to decrease. There are several possible explanations for the observed pattern.

First, there may be an inflection point in the middle of a group process where the team is forced to come together and agree on their technical plan and operating procedures. Gersick (1988) observed such a point in a study of project teams. Rather than the standard group process of form-storm-norm-perform, Gersick suggested there came a point halfway through a group project where the team faced its lack of progress during its early stage, and came to a consensus about how it would attack the objective. Often this critical point involved an insight into the problem's structure. Group process was relatively stable and productive until the delivery of the final product. Although this model suggests that significant changes occur in a group's process midway through its history, it does not explain the downturn (the drop in consensus) of the inverted U-shaped curve.

A second hypothesis is that this curve results from the integration of two processes in these data. There is a intellectual process of integrating technical ideas and resolving inconsistencies. Overlayed on this process is a project process of meeting scheduled milestones. Meeting the milestone forced a contrived consensus (a "cut-the-bull" phenomena) that did not resolve underlying technical disagreements, but allowed production of a document. However, the existence of this document disguised the lack of intellectual integration that remained in the design. These disagreements began to dominate design meetings immediately after document delivery. Having completed their obligations the team was free to reopen the conflicts that were temporarily suspended to meet the milestone. Thus, we would expect that we would see this inverted-U phenomenon of agreement repeat at any point where the team must achieve some shared milestone (as opposed to individual milestones). Since we only looked at the design phase, we were only subject to observing one such curve. Looked at over the course of a project we would expect to see the level of agreement represented as an oscillating curve with the upper inflections occurring at deadlines for milestones. However, the magnitude of these oscillations should decrease over time as the team resolved more of their underlying technical disagreements.

A third explanation is not unlike the second, but emerges more from modeling the stepwise refinement (decomposition) of the artifact. In this model the team struggles to resolve technical conflicts at the initial level of refinement required of them (eg., functional specification, system architecture, detailed design,

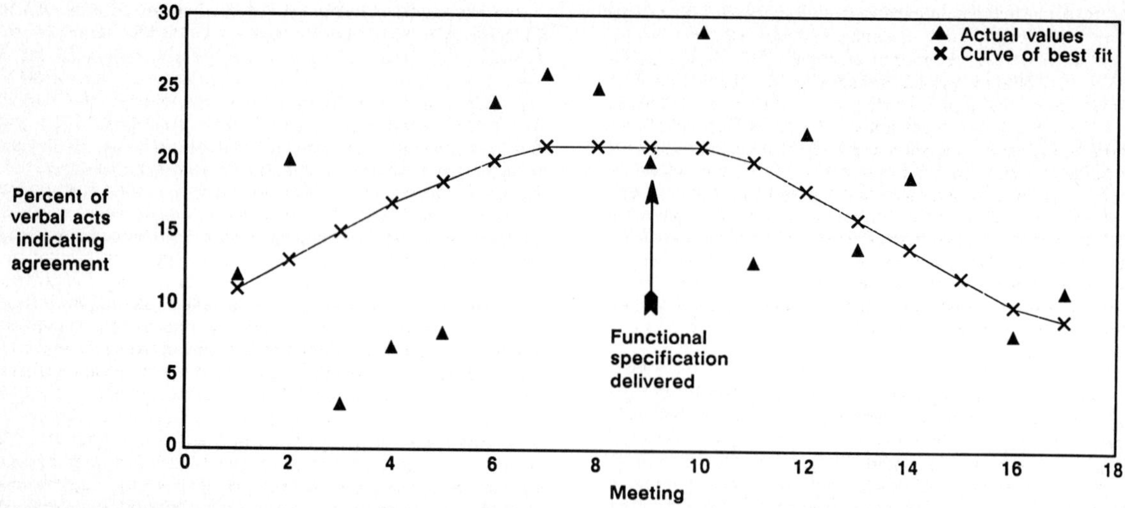

Figure 2. Level of agreement among designers working together on subtasks (Walz, 1988).

etc.). After the artifact or this level is produced, the next level of refinement presents a host of new technical issues for the team to begin struggling to achieve consensus over. Thus, we would again expect to see an oscillating curve of agreement as succeeding stages of refinement present new sets of problems for the team to resolve. This model might differ from the second by not requiring a decreasing magnitude for the oscillations, since each oscillation represents a new wave of problems, rather than the continuing struggle to resolve disagreements that have existed from the project's start.

Of these three explanations I prefer the second because I believe that on many, perhaps most, real projects there are people present who recognize early some of the fundamental problems that must be resolved. Their understanding of these problems cuts across several levels of abstraction or refinement as we saw in Guindon's analysis, and they are able to articulate the implications of these issues for several levels of refinement early in the design process. The levels of refinement notion may enter the picture in that the problems that are attended to early are those that must be resolved to get the impending artifact produced. Thus, levels of refinement provides a model for selecting among problems in order to achieve progress toward a milestone. There is much research ahead before we can feel comfortable selecting among these speculations or other explanations of our observations.

We believe we are investigating questions about team cognitive phenomena for which we cannot obtain adequate explanation from the existing literature on group behavior (Shaw, 1981). From our observations of design teams, we concluded that the team design process should be modeled as a multi–agent cognitive process, on which the social processes of role development, coalition formation, communication, etc. are superimposed. The evidence in our protocols suggested that on intellectually complex tasks like system design, traditional group processes are played out on a foundation provided by the cognitive aspects of team problem–solving (Curtis & Walz, 1990). Thus, we believe we must model multi–agent cognitive processes as the fundamental element of team behavior in design, rather than beginning with the more traditional group process elements of role formation, leadership style, etc. In order to explain the team design process, we model group dynamics by their effect on team cognitive processes. Social psychologists have studied social cognition, but this applies primarily to group attitudinal processes rather than to problem solving processes usually studied by cognitive psychologists. Thus, we have an opportunity to contribute theoretically to the cross–fertilization of social and cognitive psychology.

Since we analyzed data from only a single team, it is difficult to draw conclusions that we would generalize to other software design episodes. However, there are some intriguing possibilities that lead to new models of how design teams operate. We will not be able to make a definitive assessment of conflict resolution in design teams until we have studied other teams and compared our data to those produced by other researchers who study design teams longitudinally. We are hoping to gain further insights from analyses being conducted by Judy and Gary Olson and their colleagues at the University of Michigan in a joint research project with MCC and Andersen Consulting on coordination technology being funded by the National Science Foundation.

Design as Organizational Activity

The paradigm of organizational behavior provides multiple levels for analyzing external impacts on programming teams. These levels include the parent organization, the local division, the customers, the business marketplace, the management structure, the administrative procedures, the physical environment, the psychological environment, the professional environment, etc. Although there is a large body of empirical research on organizational behavior, little of it has been performed in programming organizations. Most current thinking on organizational processes in software development comes from anecdotes in books like those by Weinberg (1971), Brooks (1975), and DeMarco and Lister (1987). This area badly needs new research, especially with the growing size and complexity of software products, and their effect on the size and complexity of the organizations that build them.

In order to obtain insight into large system development problems, we conducted a field study of large software development projects (Curtis, Krasner, & Iscoe, 1988). The field study was designed to provide detailed descriptions of development problems in such processes as problem formulation, requirements definition and analysis, and software architectural design. We sought to study projects that involved at least 10 people, were past the design phase, and involved real–time, distributed, or embedded applications. We interviewed 17 projects from nine companies in such businesses as computer manufacturing, telecommunications, consumer electronics, and aerospace. Our objective was to get software development personnel to describe the organizational conditions that affected their work.

Three crucial problems were identified in the Field Study. First, knowledge about the specific application (avionics, sensors data processing, telecommunications, etc.) was thinly spread across software design teams. Second, the requirements to be satisfied by the system were constantly changing. Third, large multi-team projects suffered serious breakdowns in coordination and communication. We expanded the model of the systems design process developed in our team study to include processes related to organizational communication and coordination, but we found no evidence to challenge our fundamental assumption about superimposing group and organizational processes on top of cognitive problem-solving models. Rather we found additional evidence that team design processes are often dominated by one or two team members and that viable coalitions posing alternate designs were infrequent. Dominant designers were characterized by an unusually deep understanding of the application domain coupled with the ability to translate application behavior into computational structures.

The importance of application domain knowledge was highlighted earlier in describing the results of our cognitive research, because of its importance in developing design insights and mental simulations. Given the thin spread of application domain knowledge on most projects, breakdowns in communication seriously hindered integrating the knowledge required to develop a successful design and transfer it to the many independent thinkers constituting a project. A coordinated project requires tens, perhaps hundreds, of engineers who share the same mental model of the system architecture. Otherwise, a manager is faced with tens to hundreds of different projects loosely confederated under one funding source.

Organizational boundaries to communication among development groups often inhibited the integration of knowledge about the system. These communication barriers were often ignored, since the artifacts produced by one group (e.g., marketing) were assumed to convey all the information needed by the next group (e.g., system design). However, designers complained that constant verbal communication was needed between customer, requirements, and engineering groups. For instance, organizational structures that separated engineering groups (e.g., when software and systems engineering report to different vice presidents) often inhibited timely communication about application functionality in one direction, and feedback about implementation problems that resulted from the system design in the other direction.

Most project members had several networks of people they talked with to gather information on issues affecting their work. Similar to communication structures observed by Allen (1970) in R&D laboratories, each network might involve different sets of people and cross organizational boundaries. Each network supported a different flow of information; for example, information about the application domain, the system architecture, and so forth. When used effectively, these sources helped coordinate dependencies among project members and supplemented their knowledge, thus reducing learning time. Integrating information from these different sources was crucial to the performance of individual project members

Imagine for a moment that an organization is a cognitive system with a sensible architecture for design problem solving. How would this architecture be organized for combining inputs from different knowledge domains for integration into an architecture from which pieces can then be redistributed for development? It is tempting to over-generalize results from research on distributed artificial intelligence (Bond & Gasser, 1988), but nevertheless there are some initial models of distributed cognition that could act as a starting place for modeling the system building ability of an organization. The purely cognitive paradigm must be overlaid with social and organizational processes in order to understand the real behavior in a large system project. But the problem remains, how do we design the team and communication structures for best integrating the intellectual talents of the engineers involved? We will have to be clever in designing this research, since I doubt many corporations will volunteer a sufficient number of multi-million dollar projects to populate both the experimental and control conditions.

The fundamental research themes emerging from our research on the design process are the need to integrate the opportunistic model of design problem-solving with the multi-agent problem-solving dynamics of design teams and organizations. Although there is some research on problem-solving systems with distributed intelligence in the artificial intelligence world, the nodes in these systems only have access to limited knowledge bases and do not resemble the richness of human interaction and problem-solving. There is little theoretical research on distributed problem-solving among humans on complex tasks requiring longitudinal interactions. There is little research on how to integrate sources of expertise in a design process and at the same time manage the overhead of multiple interacting agents in a social situation.

What is the design space of a project? Is it what is in the documents? Is it what is on the blackboards? Is it what information most designers currently agree on? Is it what a prototype currently does? Is it what is in the head of the brightest designer? Is it all of the above? Is it any of the above? The answer, of course, depends on who you talk to – the manager, the customer, the designer, etc. However, from the point of view of determining whether a system's design is coalescing, it is crucial to determine what representation you will accept. Studying design as an organizational activity opens a Pandora's box of where and how things are represented and how information in these different locations and sources are brought together to create an architecture for a system that displays a unity of concept. The 1990s will see the growth of a new field of research that I will call organizational cognition (until it is supplanted by a better buzzword).

Implications for Software Productivity and Quality

Most current proposals for improving software productivity and quality start too late in the development process to have the impact advertised for them. That is, techniques such as software design methods, formal representation languages, and Computer-Aided Software Engineering (CASE) tools can only have impact within the constraints of the cognitive, social, and organizational factors that form the context for a software project. Improving the outcomes of software development requires improvement in the context that is set for a project before it begins.

The most important components of the context for software development are the human and organizational capabilities available for application on a project. The design process is designed by an organization's level of preparedness for undertaking the design of a new system. An organization controls this preparedness not at design time, but in its ability to design a business process that prepares it's staff for increasingly difficult tasks.

The crucial issue from the perspective of organizational performance is how to grow the amount of knowledge available in a firm for application to future projects. Knowledge growth allows similar projects to be undertaken with increasing productivity and quality over time. On the other hand it allows projects of increasing complexity to be undertaken without a dramatic loss in productivity and quality. In particular, increasing the spread of application domain knowledge across the staff is a crucial component of increasing their proficiency in tackling new design problems. Four methods of increasing the growth of application knowledge are formal training, planned job placements, libraries of reusable design templates, and an apprenticeship or mentor program. The level by which the organizational knowledge pool is increasing may be measured by the decrease in design iterations observed on succeeding projects. In particular, the capture of reusable knowledge (design templates, domain models, etc.) is a valuable area for behavioral researchers to contribute to work in computer science.

Space limitations will not allow continued elaboration of the implications of our observations on the software design process, but from the descriptions provided herein, I encourage you to speculate about how empirical and behavioral scientists can lend their efforts to solving practical problems. In return we are offered a nice reward in problems that force us to stretch our theoretical horizons in the next decade.

References

Adelson, B. & Soloway, E. (1985). The role of domain experience in software design. *IEEE Transactions on Software Engineering*, 11(11), 1351–1360.

Allen, T.J. (1970). *Communication networks in R&D laboratories* (Tech. Rep. RM–1195). Cambridge, MA: MIT Sloan School of Management.

Basili, V.R. & Reiter, R.W. (1981). A controlled experiment quantitatively comparing software development approaches. *IEEE Transactions on Software Engineering*, 7(3), 299–320.

Boehm, B.W., Gray, T.E., & Seewaldt, T. (1984). Prototyping versus specifying: A multiproject experiment. *IEEE Transactions on Software Engineering*, 10(3), 290–302.

Bond, A.H. & Gasser, L. (1988). *Readings in Distributed Artificial Intelligence*. Los Altos, CA: Morgan Kaufmann.

Brooks, F.P. (1975). *The Mythical Man–Month*. Reading, MA: Addison–Wesley.

Curtis, B., Krasner, H., & Iscoe, N. (1988). A field study of the software design process for large systems. *Communications of the ACM*, 31 (11), 1268–1287.

Curtis, B. & Walz, D. (1990). The psychology of programming in the large: Team and organizational behavior. In D. Gilmore, T.R.G. Green, J.M. Hoc, & R. Samurcay (Eds.), *Readings in the Psychology of Programming*. Chichester, UK: Wiley.

DeMarco, T. & Lister, T.A. (1987). *Peopleware*. New York: Dorset.

Dowson, M. (1987). ISTAR: An integrated project support environment. *ACM SIGPLAN Notices*, 22 (1), 27–34.

Gersick, C.J.G. (1988). Time and transition in work teams: Toward a new model of work development. *Academy of Management Journal*, 31 (1), 9–41.

Guindon, R. (1990a). The knowledge exploited by experts during software system design. *International Journal of Man–Machine Studies*, in press.

Guindon, R. (1990b). Designing the design process: Exploiting opportunistic thoughts. *Human–Computer Interaction*, in press.

Guindon, R. & Curtis, B. (1988). Control of cognitive processes during design: What tools are needed? In *Proceedings of CHI'88*. New York: ACM, 263–268.

Guindon, R., Krasner, H., & Curtis, B. (1987). Breakdowns and processes during the early activities of software design. In Olsen, G., Soloway, E., & Sheppard, S.B. (Eds.), *Empirical Studies of Programmers: Second Workshop*. Norwood, NJ: Ablex, 65–82.

Hayes–Roth, B. & Hayes–Roth, F. (1979). A cognitive model of planning. *Cognitive Science*, 3(4), 275–310.

Jackson, M.A. (1983). *System Development*. London: Prentice–Hall.

Jeffries, R., Turner, A.A., Polson, P.G., & Atwood, M.E. (1981). The processes involved in designing software. In J.R. Anderson (Ed.), *Cognitive Skills and Their Acquisition*. Hillsdale, NJ: Erlbaum, 255–283.

Kant, E. & Newell, A. (1984). Problem solving techniques for the design of algorithms. *Information Processing and Management*, 28(1), 97–118.

Shaw, M.E. (1981). *Group Dynamics: The Psychology of Small Group Behavior*. New York: McGraw–Hill.

Walz, D. (1988). *A Longitudinal Study of Group Design of Computer Systems*. Unpublished Doctoral Dissertation. Austin: Department of Management Science and Information Systems, The University of Texas.

Walz, D., Elam, D., Krasner, H., & Curtis, B. (1987). A methodology for studying software design teams: An investigation of conflict behaviors in the requirements definition phase. In Olsen, G., Soloway, E., & Sheppard, S.B. (Eds.), *Empirical Studies of Programmers: Second Workshop*. Norwood, NJ: Ablex, 83–99.

Weinberg, G.M. (1971). *The Psychology of Computer Programming*. New York: Van Nostrand Reinhold.

Weld, D.S. & de Kleer, J. (1990). *Readings in Qualitative Reasoning About Physical Systems*. Los Altos, CA: Morgan Kaufmann.

SECTION I: FOUNDATIONS

SI.1 Educational and Social Issues

Why, what and how? Issues in the development of an HCI training course
J. Preece and L.S. Keller 3

University education on human–computer interaction: The Dutch situation
G.C. Van Der Veer and T.N. White 9

Information processing, context and privacy
A. Dix 15

Mac-Thusiasm: Social aspects of microcomputer use
M.R. Jones 21

Human–Computer Interaction – INTERACT '90
D. Diaper et al. (Editors)
Elsevier Science Publishers B.V. (North-Holland)

WHY, WHAT AND HOW? ISSUES IN THE DEVELOPMENT OF AN HCI TRAINING COURSE

JENNY PREECE AND LAURIE S. KELLER

PACIS Research Group, Computing Dept, Open University, Milton Keynes MK7 6AA UK

Lack of tradition in teaching HCI and the multi-disciplinary nature of the subject creates challenging problems for those developing a curriculum to teach it.

In this paper we discuss the development of a postgraduate course for practicing professionals in industry and commerce. The course is taught by distance teaching, which means that students study texts integrated with other media on their own.

Three questions are considered: why we teach HCI, what we teach and how we teach. In additon, we discuss how problems arising from the multi-disciplinary nature of HCI pervaded course development and how the development process itself resembled user-centred HCI design practices.

1 INTRODUCTION: WHY TEACH HCI?

Awareness of HCI continues to grow as product developers realise that sales depend on usability as well as on functionality. But what makes one computer system enjoyable to use and another a nightmare? As researchers and developers strive to find the answers, the need for training which facilitates putting this rapidly growing body of knowledge into practice also grows. What is more, as systems get more complex and multi-media and multi-tasking environments become the norm, the need to understand human needs and to design and tailor systems to meet those needs will be even greater.

Demand for knowledge is an obvious reason for developing training materials; small companies and many large companies cannot afford to have their own HCI specialists yet they need HCI knowledge. Another reason is to make sense of HCI knowledge and skills so that they can be more easily understood by those who need to apply them. This is particularly the case in HCI where the multi-disciplinary nature of the subject, its newness, its poorly developed and incomplete knowledge base, lack of established theory and methodology and ambigous terminology means that it is not easy for an outsider to make sense of and apply it.

A pragmatic reason for developing a course is that there is nothing else suitable around. This is not to say that the subject is not being taught, but rather that there is a lack of a traditition which gives rise to standard texts, styles of teaching, syllabuses and formal accreditation and recognition by bodies such as the British Computer Society and the American ACM. All of these things are now happening. (Both the BCS and the ACM are currently preparing syllabuses.) Given this state of affairs, developing training materials to teach HCI is not straightforward. Many of the problems arise from the nature of HCI itself and, in particular, its multi-disciplinarity and newness.

For the remainder of this paper we discuss the multi-disciplinary nature of HCI and other issues about what to teach and how to teach in the development of an HCI course for industrial and software practitioners. We then provide a brief case study of the development of the course and discuss how the process had many aspects in common with 'user-centred' system design.

2 WHAT AND HOW?

'What should we teach and how should we teach it?' These basic questions are asked when designing a syllabus for any kind of course. The issues to be considered are fairly obvious too - see Figure 1. It depends on who will study the course, what they need to know, the nature of the subject to be taught, who does the teaching, what facilities are available and how the course will be delivered.

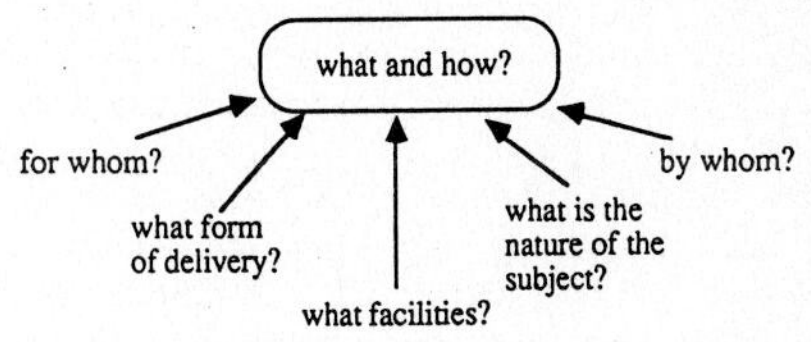

Figure 1 Key questions to ask

For each question there are a number of different factors to consider and some of these are summarised in Figure 2. Understanding the influence of these factors,and particularly the far-reaching nature of some of them is easiest done through an example. We shall, therefore, briefly describe the course on HCI that has recently been developed at the Open University.

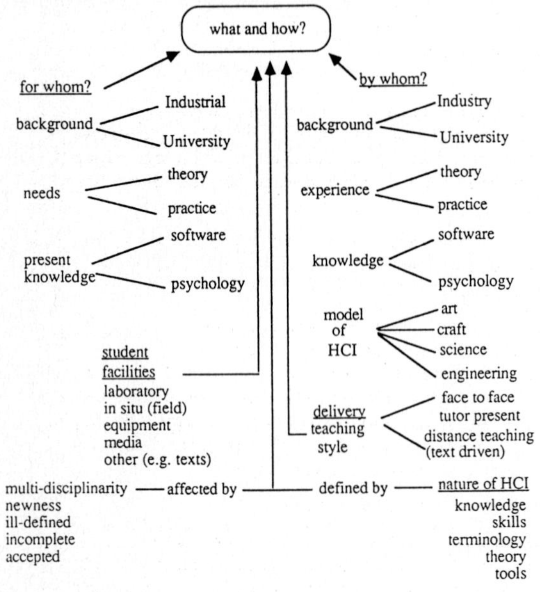

Figure 2 A range of factors to consider

For whom: the course is designed for industrial and software practitioners and is aimed particularly at those involved in the design and management of computer systems. The needs of these people (whom we shall refer to as students) is for *relevant* knowledge and skills which they can put into practice rather than for esoteric theory. The majority of our students have software experience (for example, many are programmers and many have some from of computing or software engineering qualification). Very few have much psychological knowledge and many are sceptical about the value of psychology unless they can see how it relates to and helps to answer practical problems.

Delivery: like the majority of Open University courses, the course on HCI is a distance learning course. This means that students study on their own, at work or at home, from specially prepared correspondence texts (known as units). Television, video, audio, practical computing and computer assisted learning may also be used for delivery of the material. A tutor is also available for telephone tuition, to give a few tutorials and to mark assignments. The materials are carefully structured and integrated to make the learning experience as interactive as possible. The text drives the course; tutors are not readily available as in conventional universities.

Facilities: although practical computing forms a part of many Open University courses, it was not possible in this case to provide computer-based practical work for a specific configuration of machine or to bring the students into the laboratory. Consequently, we have had to design practical activities which take advantage of the students own working environments. However, this has turned out to be an advantage since it encourages us and the students to relate what is taught to their own work experience and environment.

By whom: the course was developed by a team from the British and Dutch Open Universities who prepared the texts with a number of consultants from other universities. Academic and industrial assessors and critical readers drawn from industry and academia commented on the content, appropriateness and style of draft materials. This meant that a wide range of ideas and experience could be capitalised upon as shown in Figure 3, which summarises the logistical influences on the course. The predominant influences (shown in bold on Figure 3 with less important but still significant influences in italic) however, came from the core team.

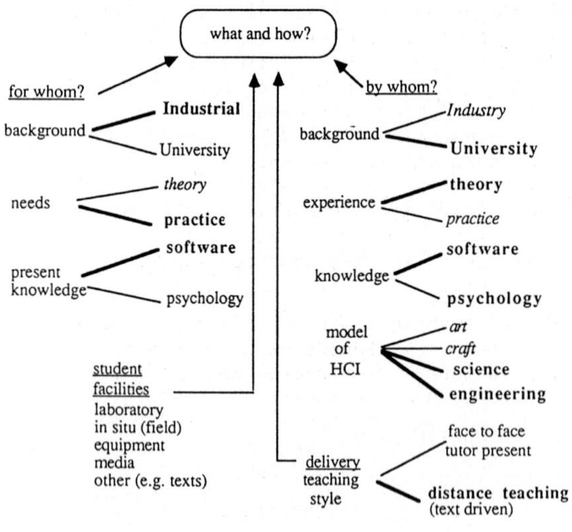

Figure 3 Logistical influences on the Open University HCI course

Many of these issues needed very careful consideration, such as the issue of how to teach HCI by distance methods so that it could be applied and used to practical advantage by people in industry without being able to rely on students having access to a specific configuration of computer. However, these issues paled to insignificance by comparison with some of those relating to the nature and content of HCI, which are shown in Figure 2, especially as they interacted or impacted upon each other. Space precludes a detailed discussion of these issues here, and in any case this is available elsewhere (Preece and Keller, 1990a). We shall, therefore, only list them below and proceed to consider how the multi-disciplinary nature of HCI impacted upon so many other aspects of the course.Consequently, multi-disciplinarity can be thought of as a 'meta-issue'.

Meta-issue

The interdisciplinary nature of HCI

Major issues

The balance between teaching theory and following practice.
The balance between providing knowledge and tools

Other issues

Capitalising on 'in situ' and coping without the laboratory
Making psychology palatable and relevant for sceptics
Design - what is it?
Lack of good, applicable case examples
Terminolgy - lack of it and inconsistency

Long and Dowell (1989) have identified and analysed three different perspectives of HCI which they describe as frameworks; these are craft (e.g. the heuristic approach), applied science (a hypothesize-and-test approach) and engineering (the use of prescriptive knowledge applied to design). Explicitly defined frameworks like these can be useful for explaining and identifying the nature of different perspectives both when examining research issues and when developing a curriculum.

The relationship between the other issues is not always straightforward; many are closely interrelated. (see Preece and Keller, 1990a) for further discussion.

3 WHAT WE DID

3.1 The course components

Our course consists of eight booklets (units), each with a different area of content. These are:

Unit 1: Introduction to Human-Computer Interaction (scene setting)
Unit 2: Input, Output and Communication Style (devices and dialogue)
Unit 3: Applied Cognitive Psychology
Unit 4: Knowledge and Action: Mental Models in HCI
Unit 5: Fundamentals of Design (user-centered approaches and techniques)
Unit 6: Design: Analysis and Representation (analysis of formal design and notations)
Unit 7: Evaluation
Unit 8: Design Support (guidelines, tools, prototyping and UIMSs)

The basic contents of the course (Open University, 1990) can be inferred from these titles.

A published collection of specially selected readings (Preece and Keller, 1990b) provides extension material and alternative views on subjects.

A seventy-five minute video entitled 'Industrial applications of HCI' provides case studies that illustrate the concepts taught in the units and show how they have been applied in industrial examples.

The course assessment is in two parts; an end of course examination and continuous assessment.

The course is designed to take about one hundred hours of study time and it is normally studied over a period of four to six months. The students' progress through the course is scheduled by a work plan and also by 'cut-off dates' which are the dates by which assignments have to reach tutors.

3.2 Interaction style

Material in the units and the reader is broken down into assimilable 'chunks' of sections (bands in the video). The student moves from reading a unit to reading a chapter or section in the reader, back to the unit, and thence to a band of the video as directed. The size of such sections and bands has to take into account attentional constraints; the movement from one medium to another helps to keep the student alert and reinforces teaching by restating topics in a variety of ways and introducing variations. However, this movement between different items could be a potential problem and clear 'signposts' are needed.

Learning is not merely a passive activity. The texts contain two types of activity for the student. One is the self-assessment question, which is a question that directs the student to *rephrase or integrate* knowledge taught within a unit section or a reader chapter. This helps to reinforce the material. The student who gets a 'wrong' answer (answers are given at the back of the unit booklet) can re-read the material again. The second type of activity, an exercise, asks the student to *apply* the knowledge taught in a practical way (for example asking the student to read a scenario and then select suitable evaluation method(s) for the situation described in the scenario, giving reasons for her choice). Some exercises call upon the student to relate her own experience to concepts through demonstration (for example, demonstrating running a mental model by asking the student to recall the number and placement of windows in her home or place of work). Others provide genuine scope for developing concepts. Feedback is provided in a 'comment' immediately following each exercise. The comment may be a firm answer where this is appropriate, an example answer, or consist of a discussion of the issues raised by an exercise.

At three points in the course the student undertakes much more extended exercises in the form of three assignments, which are marked and commented on extensively by a tutor. In these, the student selects an existing computer interface with which she is familiar, analyses it for its strengths and shortcomings, selects one aspect of it which is particularly 'poor' for redesign, and then evaluates her new design. This virtually constitutes a project, but it is carried out during the learning process. Feedback from the tutor thus provides more than correction of error - it also provides suggestions for altering the project as it is in progress. This form of project enables the students to relate what they learn about HCI with the practical design work that forms part of their jobs.

Self-contained support is of major importance in distance learning (Neil, 1981). This is ensured by the development process described below, which has some interesting similarities with user-centred design.

4 HOW WE DEVELOPED IT: 'USER-CENTRED' COURSE DEVELOPMENT

4.1 The team

The development team reflected the multi-disciplinary nature of HCI: one of us is a 'straight' computer scientist, one a cognitive psychologist and one of us a computer scientist coming from an educational background with a strong interest in science teaching and psychology. This team was assisted by academics from the Dutch Open Universiteit, consultants, assessors (who assess the academic and industrial suitability of the material), critical readers (subject experts) in cognitive science, human factors, educational technology, computer science and industrial research and development and student testers.

4.2 The process - iterative development with evaluation and redesign

The course team developed the materials through sessions of discussion and intra-team negotiation by working iteratively, criticizing, assessing and testing material as it is developed. This is analogous to user-centered iterative design process advocated by many HCI specialists (e.g. Gould, *et al.* 1987). The material passes through five draft stages. Stage one is commented on by the team alone, with stages two and three commented on additionally by the critical readers and assessors. The fourth draft is tested by student testers, and the final draft again assessed by the assessors. This accords well with Jones' (1981) description of the design process: 'Simulating what we want to make (or do) before we make (or do) it as many times as may be necessary to feel confident in the final result.'

At those draft stages where material is commented on by team members, critical readers and assessors, suggested changes are negotiated and incorporated. Students who test the material are selected on the basis of how typically they represent the target audience. These students 'do' the course, including assessment material, reporting on how long it took them, any parts of the material they experienced difficulty with, and any suggestions they have. All this is taken into account in the preparation of the final draft, which then passes to an editor, an illustrator and a graphic designer and is published, much as a book is. Figure 4 summarises this course development cycle.

Just as in the design of an interface the team has to work within a tight schedule, financial and practical constraints such as lack of control over the students' access to computing facilities. Similarly, there are also trade-offs to be made, decisions made at one stage in the development process affect what is done later. For example we adopted various stragies for teaching psychology to sceptics which determined what, how and when the material was presented, which in turn had a number of knock-on effects.

5 SUMMARY AND CONCLUSIONS

In the development of a course on HCI the developers are bound to spend time attempting to resolve basic questions such as whether or not even to teach HCI, what to teach and how to teach it. A certain amount of this type of questioning is inherent in the development of any course, but in the case of HCI, the newness of the subject and lack of tradition exacerbate the need for such questions and also creates a very large initial design space in which to take initial decisions about course content and stucture. In addition, its multi-disciplinary nature has far-reaching implications. In this respect multi-disciplinarity can be regarded as a meta-issue.

The development process that we followed had much in common with user-centred system design and by adopting the language used to describe the latter, the similarities become even more apparent. For example, the success of our course relies on good interaction style, and just as in the design of an interface, there is no prescribed formula to

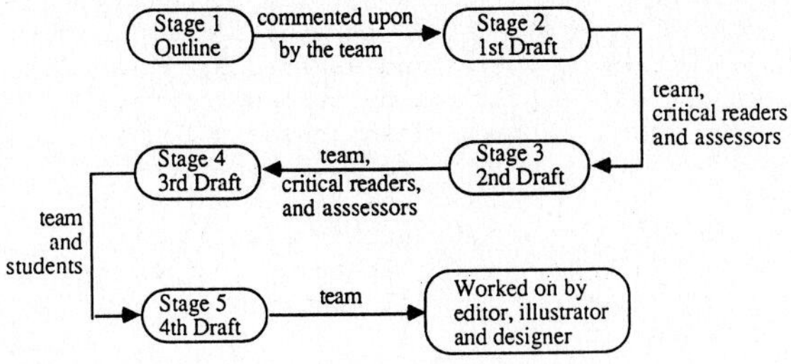

Figure 4 The course development cycle

guarantee success. Experience has resulted in a body of design knowledge, and for new authors there is even the equivalent of a set of guidelines. However, in the end, the quality of the material is largely dependent on attention to detail; in this there is no substitute for expert and user testing and several iterations through the 'design - evaluate - redesign' cycle are essential.

ACKNOWLEDGEMENTS

The authors would like to acknowledge the other members of the course team, particularly Dr. Yvonne Rogers. We also wish to thank the student testers, consultants, contributors and assessors and those who provided administrative and secretarial support. We are grateful to them all.

REFERENCES

GOULD, J. D., BOIES, S. J., LEVY, S. RICHARDS, J. T. and SCHOONARD, J (1987) The 1984 Olympic Message System: a test of behavioural principles of system design, *Communications of the ACM,* Vol. 30, No. 9 (Sept.) pp. 758 - 769. Reprinted in PREECE, J. and KELLER, L. (1990b).

JONES, C. C. (1981) *Design Methods: Seeds of Human Futures, 2nd Edition,* John Wiley and Son, London.

LONG, J. and DOWELL, J. (1989) Conceptions of the discipline of HCI: craft, applied science, and engineering, in SUTCLIFFE, A. and MACAULAY, L. (1989) *People and Computers V - HCI '89,* The Cambridge University Press, Cambridge, pp.9 - 32.

NEIL, M. W. (ed.) (1981) *Education of Adults at a Distance, A Report of the Open University's Tenth Anniversary International Conference,* Kogan Page Ltd., London. p. 98

OPEN UNIVERSITY (1990) *Human-Computer 1*

Interaction (Code: PMT607) ISBN 0 7492 4230 2. Open University Press, Milton Keynes, England.

PREECE, J.J. and KELLER, L.S. (1990a) Empowering the practice of HCI through curriculum design: some key issues. (To appear in *Interacting with Computers*)

PREECE, J. and KELLER, L. (eds) (1990b) *Human-Computer Interaction: Selected Readings,* Prentice-Hall, Englewood Cliffs, New Jersey.

Human–Computer Interaction – INTERACT '90
D. Diaper et al. (Editors)
Elsevier Science Publishers B.V. (North-Holland)

UNIVERSITY EDUCATION ON HUMAN-COMPUTER INTERACTION - THE DUTCH SITUATION

Gerrit C. van der Veer[*], *Ted N. White*[#]

[*]Department of Cognitive Psychology,
Department of Computer Science, Free University, Amsterdam

[#]Ergonomics Group,
Twente University of Technology, Enschede,

1. Introduction

It is generally accepted that scientific theory and research are indispensible as a basis for the design and development of interfaces between a computersystem and the end-user (e.g. Norman & Draper, 1986). For the design of user interfaces, both ease of use and efficiency are strong requirements. Moreover, end-users need education and information regarding the system they are going to use. In the current situation there is a general trend towards increasing use of computers by "professionals", people who apply a computer system as a tool in their professional environment, without being a computer scientist. There is therefore an increasing demand for designers of user interfaces and for qualified instructors. We address the question whether there is one specific faculty in which education and training on this topic is or should be concentrated, and how in general the education regarding human-computer interaction (HCI) is structured. In the international literature, few sources on this subject can be found. As far as we know, the current study is the first of its kind in the Dutch situation.

The designer of an system for end-users has to think about the user having abilities as well as limitations. He has to keep in mind for which circumstances the system is applied, by whom and even why the system is used. The central question is what does the system add to what has allready been obtained? In the short history of automation systems the examples are numerous about projects lasting longer than planned, products which had less impact than expected, or systems promising to solve all problems but finally lacking quality. One may ask why is the case. The computer is a fast machine which looks very intelligent but can behave rather stupid in comparison with human beings, and in fact stupid with the high speed promised by the manifacturer. What is wrong is that the information technologist has, in general, not been educated to weight the value of the meaning of the information. He has been tought only to manipulate information to search structures and to generate models about related data. In fact the information technology student is thought to search for hard facts and structured information.

If a system engineer, novice in the field with clientele, happens to built a system for a customer, there is a fair chance that the customer complains about the fact that he has not got what he wanted, and that the technologist reasons that the specifications where too fague. If the architecture is built as a truly open system, to adapt for wishes from the customer, the chance is substantial that system development is unacceptably slow. Besides, the longer the construction of the complete system takes, the larger will be the chance that changes have to be accepted in the specifications, required from developments in the outside world. Besides, the more complicated the system becomes, the more time it takes to add all issues in a logical and coherent way.

So next to teaching the students Information Technology from the technological side, one should also teach design and software engineering with reference to the human part in HCI.

In the United States of America the ACM (Association for Computing Machinery) is the forum for recommandations on educational curricula. In 1978 the program recommended for Undergraduates in Computer Science hardly included HCI (Austing et al., 1979). The course on Software Engineering contained only technical design methods and a unit on organisation and management in relation to project teams. The course "Computers and Society" contained a section on "the Computer and the Individual" of which the content, however, was not elaborated. In 1985 this was the base for the recommendations of the Chines Computer Federation (Wilson et al., 1988). Here we find a section on user interfaces, regarding mainly graphics and character set translation. Human factors do not seem to be involved. Recently SIGCHI (the Special Interest Group on Computer and Human Interaction of ACM) is actively involved in a discussion on curriculum development (Carey, 1988, 1989, Baecker, 1989, Mantei, 1989, Strong, 1989). In Carey's proposal the three main parts of an undergraduate program (with the tentative name "Information Systems and Human Behavior") are Computer Science, Psychology, and Sociology. Human-Computer Interaction is a separate unit from Software Engineering, and both are parts of the course on Computing and Information Science. Besides there is an important course on Psychology, containing among other subjects cognitive processes and perception. These recommendations are a topic of discussion at this moment.

2. Objectives

In this study we present an overview of the current situation in HCI education at the Dutch university (undergraduate) level. In order to elaborate on our investigations we need a description of the concept "HCI education". We developed a structured list of possible topics. This list is not complete, reflecting the content of existing courses, and the available literature on HCI curricula.

2.1. A tentative description of HCI education

In our framework a destinction is made between (a) design and evaluation (of application systems, of user interfaces, and of documentation), (b) input and output, (c) communication between user and system, and (d) motivational aspects. The complete structure of topics envisaged, is as follows:

DESIGN AND EVALUATION
- *design of application systems*
  . *tasks analysis (what can be done with the system, what not)*
  . *functionality (quality of task delegation, time constraints)*
- *evaluation of applications (requirements, checklists)*
- *design of user interfaces (user friendliness, ease of use, adaptation)*
- *evaluation of user interfaces*
- *design of end-user documentation*
- *evaluation of end-user documentation*
- *standards and guidelines*
  . *for user interfaces*
  . *for end-user documentation*
  . *for end-user languages*
  . *for human computer interaction*

INPUT AND OUTPUT
- *input*
  . *keyboard ergonomics (posture, movement, skill)*
  . *ergonomics of the working place (spatial arangement, adaptation to individual differences)*
  . *speech recognition*
  . *other media (mouse, drawing tablet or writing pad, etc.)*
- *output*
  . *VDT ergonomics (visual aspects, health)*
  . *speech generation*

COMMUNICATION
- *dialogue styles (menu, command language, object manipulation)*
- *languages for end-users*
- *natural language processing*

MOTIVATIONAL ASPECTS
- *computer literacy*
- *mental load*
- *work satisfaction*

This list was used to structure the inventory sent to the relevant educational institutes. We indicated clearly that the list was not complete, but merely functioned as a guide. In fact the list aimed at helping the respondents to identify which parts of a course or curriculum could be considered to be part of the field of HCI.

2.2. The target population

In the Netherlands higher education is provided in different types of institutes. There are a relatively small number of Universities and comparable institutes, which provide scientific education in a variety of faculties. On the other hand there is a larger number of institutes for "Higher Professional Education", of which some aim at a relatively small set of professions, although there is a strong tendency for these institutions to fuse, resulting in large schools with a diversity of curricula.

In this study we concentrate on the university situation. Educational institutes in this field traditionally are of two types: (a) the classical Universities and (b) the Universities of Technology. The latter originally concentrated on technical education of the university level, but currently there is a tendency to broaden the scope of education and of establishing departments that traditionally would only be found in the classical Universities.

In the Netherlands there are 7 universities of the former type, and 3 universities of technology. In table 1 we list their names and the code we will use to indicate them in this publication. Apart from these institutes, we investigated the situation on HCI education at the Dutch Institute for Post Academic Education in Computer Science), the Dutch Open University, and some commercial institutes at the level of post-higher professional education (this last category is fragmentarily represented, only to provide some comparison to university education in this field).

type of institute	name/location	code
University	U of Amsterdam	UA
	Free University	UF
	Groningen	UG
	Leiden	UL
	Nijmegen	UN
	Tilburg	UT
	Utrecht	UU
U of Technology	Delft	UoTD
	Eindhoven	UoTE
	Twente	UoTT
Post Acad. Educ.	PAO comp. sc.	PA
Open University		OU

Table 1. The Dutch population of institutes for university level education

3. Method

An inventory was sent to all teachers of relevant courses. In order to locate these, course descriptions, department guides and comparable documents were collected. Some non-university institutes did not react even on repeated requests for documentation, so they were left out of the report.

A thorough reading of all material collected provided us with a nearly complete list of all courses that (according to title, to description of contents, or by referring to relevant literature) might contain even a small amount of HCI knowledge. We tried to be very carefull, and included e.g. a course of which the title did not show any relation to the subject, but for which one of the books listed as compulsary reading contained a single chapter on user-interface design.

As completeness was not guaranteed, all teachers approached were asked to mention any comparable course knewn, or formally related to their course (in the way of being prelimimnary to it or a possible continuation to it). In this way some additional courses were added to the list.

The second phase of the search consisted of the actual data collection by sending a questionnaire to teachers responsible for all known courses. In case more than one teacher was mentioned, we usually chose the first one. A letter was sentexplaining the goal of our project, the list of HCI topics (see section 2.1) and a 2-page questionnaire. Filling these two pages took between 15 and 30 minutes. Teachers responsible for more than one course, were sent a list for each course.

The questionnaire covered the following information:

a. identification of respondent, office address, name of the course;

b. content of the course, to be indicated by a short description of objectives and a list of units that were related to HCI;

c. prior knowledge required, supplementary courses, target students (department, curriculum), and year;

d. estimate of total time spent, classified in lecture hours, practical sessions, and self-study. Moreover we asked to estimate which part of this time was spend on topics directly relevant for HCI;

e. compulsory and recommended literature, including, if applicable, a table of content of the reader composed by the teacher;

f. final assesment if any (written exam, oral exam, piece of work, thesis);

g. "age" of the course, i.e. calendar year in which the course was given for the first time.

All university departments and institutes approached, responded, as did three of the five commercial institutes addressed (one respondent made use of the same external educational institute as one of the non-respondents). Some university institutes returned an incomplete reaction, and three teachers failed to meet the deadlines, but in these cases we tried to complete the information frome the department guides and other sources available.

4. Results

4.1. HCI as part of a curriculum

In most universities Education on HCI is part of a curriculum in Social Sciences. This education is provided by institutes in the Departments of Social Sciences known as "Social Science and Information Technology" (UA, UG, UL, UN), or in sections for "Educational Technology" or "Psychonomic Science" (UF, UU, UoTT).

HCI education is part of a curriculum in Computer Science in three universities (UF, UL, UoTD). Mainly in Universities of Technology there are courses in the Departments of Ergonomics (UoTD, UoTT, UT), and in curricula on "Technology, Labour and Organisation" (UoTD, UoTE).

Both the Open University, and the Dutch Institute for Post Academic Education in Computer Science, present a course on HCI, and a course on "Designing Modern Software / User Interfaces" is provided by two commercial institutes. Courses in this last group are not part of an official curriculum, but there are clear descriptions of prior knowledge required, that indicate at least University level.

The majority of these courses have originated within the last five years, some were given this year (1988-1989) for the first time. Only two curricula originated between 1970 and 1980 (UoTD - product-ergonomics, UoTE - Technology and Organisation). PA and commercial courses started in 1987, and the Open University plans to present the course on MCI in 1990 (in cooperation with the British Open University).

4.2. Target students

Parts of the curriculum that cover HCI aspects are normally not a part of introductory courses. With a single exception the topics are treated from the 3th year in university.

Courses that are part of a curriculum in Social Science and Information Technology and related institutes, are offered as a free choice for all students in the Department of Social Sciences, or, alternatively, are a compulsory course for students specialising in Social Science and Information Technology. Educational Technology institutes provide their education in HCI mainly for students graduating in this field.

Ergonomics Departments and Departments for Technology, Labour and Organisation provide education for a broad range of students, in fact these courses are open for students of all kinds of technical curricula.

Departments of Computer Science present their courses on HCI partly as an option for various departments, but at the same time they provide specialised courses as a compulsory part of curricula in Software Engineering.

4.3. Content of HCI courses

From the description of content and objectives differences in curriculum in the different disciplines involved have become clear. The name of the course, in the first place, shows a clear difference between departments. Departments of Ergonomy list courses like "Ergonomy of Office Automation, of Telecommunication, or of VDU", "Ergonomics and Information Technology", of "Methods of Systematic Analysis of Labour Situations".

Courses in institutes for Social Science and Information Technology contain "Human-Computer Interaction", "Human Factors", but we also found "Dialogue Design". Educational Technology courses often refer to "Computer Aided Education" or "Educational Programming".

Titles of relevant courses in Departments of Computer Science are "Software Engineering" or "Very Interactive Software", but also plain titles like "Human-Computer Interaction".

Looking at the actual content of the courses, design and evaluation of user interfaces is almost always addressed, but there is a differential attention to applications. Educational Technology focusses on Computer Aided Education (as does one curriculum in Ergonomics), on Intelligent Tutoring Systems, and on Artificial Intelligence. Ergonomics and the non-university institutes in our sample pay a lot of attention to general problems of design and evaluation of applications. Standards and guidelines are among the topics treated in some Departments of Computer Science, and in institutes for Technology, Labour and Organisation. Documentation is only mentioned in courses in the Departments of Computer Science, and in Social Science and Information Technology (and in one single course in Technology, Labour and Organisation). These same Departments stress the importance of models of human information processing, and pay attention to modes of representation, knowledge, and mental models, as developed by users of computer systems.

Input and output technology in relation to human users is mentioned in Departments of Social Science and Information Technology, and in Ergonomics, Educational Technology, and sometimes in Computer Science or in Technology, Labour and Organisation. The non-university institutes show a clear specialist character in this respect (interactive video or VDU ergonomics).

Communication and dialogue styles are mentioned in curricula in Social Science and Information Technology, Psychonomics, and Educational Technology (these latter stressing natural language interfaces), and in a more general sense also in the other curricula. Motivational aspects are solely mentioned in some courses in Social Science and Educational Technology.

4.4. Time aspects of the courses

Of the courses described, the part that is devoted to HCI varies considerably, from about 10 per cent in "Software Engineering", 20 to 40 per cent for courses in "Knowledge systems" and "Tutor Systems", to 100 per cent in courses named "Human-Computer Interaction" or "Human Factors". These data, however, are not always very clearly reported, so it is dangerous to draw conclusions.

Stand-alone courses spend from 1 to 60 hours to HCI teaching. Departments that offer an integrated curriculum containing HCI components (Ergonomics, Social Science and Information Technology, Educational Technology) claim to devote 40 to 200 lecture hours to HCI education, including practical sessions. If these are part of the course, they require normally more than half of all teaching hours and of all hours students spend.

Final assessment for lectures normally is of the written examination type, sometimes requiring students to produce an essay. Practical sessions are concluded by the presentation of piece of work or a written report on the session.

4.5. Literature

Many teachers produce their own syllabus or lecture notes, the contents of which reflect the content of their course. Readers are often mentioned, but, alas, the content is hardly ever mentioned in the questionnaires returned (we recorded a striking number of reprints from the International Journal of Man-Machine Studies, and from the book "Man-Computer Interaction MACINTER I, eds. Klix and Wandke). Apart from these a multitude of books are mentioned. Some titles clearly show the intention to introduce a programming language (like "Turbo PASCAL", or "PROLOG programming for Artificial Intelligence").

Specialised courses refer to titles like "Educational application of computers", "The role of HCI in intelligent tutoring systems", "Computer simulation as a teaching aid", "Knowledge systems in services", "Management information systems", "Ergonomics at work", or "VDU ergonomics" (a publication of the Dutch Ergonomic Society, referred to several times), or "Computer graphics".

General literature stressing the design of user interfaces is mentioned with titles like "User centered system design" (Norman & Draper, referred to by four different departments), "Designing the user interface" (Shneiderman, mentioned three times), "Applying cognitive psychology to user-interface design" (Gardiner & Christie), "Human factors in engineering and design" (McCormick & Sanders), "Software engineering concepts" (Fairley), "Software engineering" (van Vliet).

A general theoretical approach is supported by works like "The psychology of HCI" (Card, Moran & Newell) or "HCI - a multidisciplinary approach" (Baecker & Buxton), both mentioned twice.

5. Summary and conclusions

The general picture of Dutch curricula that include HCI aspects is very unsystematic. Both the duration and the content vary considerably, partly in connection with the discipline that provides the course. The literature recommended is also strongly dependent on the department, but here there is some systematic relation: some sources are mentioned in several comparable situations.

We would like to stress the interdisciplinary character of the field, in which mainly software engineering, ergonomics, and applied cognitive psychology participate. Each of these disciplines contributes specific theories and specialised methods. The integration of these contributions will lead to new models and methods that are unique for the new discipline of HCI. This requires a dedicated curriculum at the level of scientific education.

5.1. HCI as part of a curriculum

It seems to be possible to incorporate courses on HCI in several departments and curricula. The content of these courses has to be tuned to the anticipated careers and jobs of the students. In some curricula HCI is compulsory, in other situations it is recommended as a useful possibility for specialisation.

a. Social Sciences (and Information Technology)
   Application of cognitive psychology, possibly complemented with organisational psychology, in situations of HCI seems to fit well in a specialisation. Students may draw a link to other courses in the field of "cognitive science" (artificial intelligence issues), or to educational technology. Post graduates may apply for jobs related to the design of application systems, user interfaces, documentation or training. In these situations they will need some knowledge of software engineering theory and methods.

b. Ergonomics
   The ergonomy of HCI may be seen as a relatively independent domain separate from "hardware ergonomics". This makes sense if we interpret ergonomics as a professional discipline that provides knowledge on behalf of experts in a different field. In this sense ergonomics may support a technical designer. The ergonomist should be able to communicate in the language of the discipline concerned (e.g. software engineering). At the same time he may be considered to supply guidelines and methods on behalf of the designer.

c. Computer Science
   Education on HCI can be an integral part of a curriculum on software engineering. In this way a direct link is provided to methods of user-interface design, and to the development and use of UIMSs (user-interface management systems). In this case a selection of cognitive psychological theories and methods have to be included in the curriculum.

5.2. Cognitive ergonomics as a separate curriculum

As an alternative structure, education in HCI may develop into a separate specialised curriculum Cognitive Ergonomics (the label Software Ergonomics refers to a somewhat too narrow concept: spatial and physical aspects of HCI need to be included, mainly in relation to perception and motor skill). The scientific research community preceeded education in this respect. A number of specialised international journals of high standard allready exist (International Journal of Man-Machine Studies, Behaviour and Information Theory, Interacting with Computers, and Human-Computer Interaction). Organisations such as IFIP, IEEE, and ACM have their own journals, bulletins, and conferences in this field. One can hardly keep up with the number of international conferences and workshops, and with the stream of literature.

5.3. Some examples of instruction

For the benefit of stimulating discussions about the necessity and possibility of HCI-education in university curricula two examples of instruction will be worked out.

a. Example on the visual display of trends
   Suppose a designer / software engineer acts in team of control engineers. These have described the control loops, the control settings ect. The software engineer is requested to design all software including the user interface. In bulletins the software engineer read about userfriendliness of interfaces and he has even seen a checklist during college education. It sayd things like "present as few information on one screen as possible",

and "don't use too much colours". The problem now encountered is that there is a technical systems with hundreds of loops, all supplying a multitude of information. In this situation the checklist does not give any help. Straight forward questions on what kind of information the operator requires at what time, and what kind of additional information does support the operator during the supervision of the multidimensional and complex system are not answered by ordinary checklists. Scientific research could answer some of the questions by laboratory experiments. However, the information should be available within a short time frame. Therefore knowledge about HCI on the level of defining the problem and posing the right questions is the first step in such a case. Thereafter the level of expertise of the operators and supervisors has to be known and with their help and participation the interface can be designed. Quick experiments and well specified literature scans belong to the design of the interface, but still seldom tought on a level to be of any practical use in itself.

If we focus on only one topic of layout design it becomes clear what kind of problems may be encountered. Suppose the software engineer concludes that graphical trend representation is needed in order to see the present values of system outputs as well as their recent history. He designs representations by defining time and amplitude axis and determines whether trends share the same baseline or, alternatively, are displayed separately. Then he counts how many trends will fitt on one screen and concludes that colour will help to distinguish the different trends. If then several alternative representations are written in software and showed to the operators to give their opinion, trend representations which show the output signal rather smoothly may well be selected as best representation by the operators.

Students of the second author have performed trend scaling experiments, and they have seen that subjective preference and face validity are not valid determinants for the design of trend lay-out. In contrast, these factors contradict objective performance on trend prediction. These experiments, including preparation, data analysis and writing a scientific report, take about 50 hours of student time.

b. Example on colourblindness
Suppose a software designer is working for a Workstation/PC manufacturer. One of the advantages of this manufacturer's hardware is that a hudge amount of different colours can be displayed. Unfortunately some of the future users are diagnosed as colour deficient and have difficulties in colour selection. In fact 8% of the male European population has defects in colour perception. Although not digging to deeply into this matter, still it can be said that ergonomic guidelines can be misleading in this sence especially in the hands of naive users. The checklist that our designer may remember from college might have guidelines like "don't use too much colours on your screen (prevent a christmas tree effect)", but also "use preferably green as the colour to indicate a safe condition and red as an indication of a nonsafe or danger condition. If no indication is needed don't use any. Select grey for the background colour (no attention attractor)".

But a "deuteranopian" (5% of the male population) confuses red and green and perceives them both as some sort of grey, which indicates the hazard of some of the ergonomic guidelines. As a matter of fact, the increase of distance to the screen will increase the effect of confusion. Moreover, colour deficiency is not only a matter of congenital defect but that it can also happen temporally, Temporal deficiency may occur when people are ill or use drugs, when they have consumed much alcohol or when they are suffering a (not necessarily noticed) brain tumor. Regarding the use of colours in the user interface, designers have a responsability.

Once again students may be explained these aspects of colour vision. As the second author showed in his classes, some experimentation, based on the concepts and theories of colour perception, may reduce the 8% of colour deficients to less then 0.01% having trouble with the misperception or confusion of colours on well designed user interfaces.

We propose to incorporate in the education of Information Technologists some practical instruction based on experimental psychology, cognitive ergonomics, technology assessment and impact studies, and industrial engineering. Both authors have experience in the field of social sciences and technology and feel that the necessary practical knowledge can be supplied.

5.4. Concluding remarks

The main problem, as it turned out from our review, is that much of the available knowledge on HCI education is unevenly spread over the universities. Many faculties are not yet aware of the existence of practical knowledge, or they do not appreciate the benefits of sharing this knowledge with others. Our primary aim is to make the inventarisation available for all who might be interested in HCI-education in the field of information and technology.

6. References

Austing R.H., Barnes B.H., Bonnette D.T., Engel D.T., and Stokes G. (1979) Curriculum '78 - Recommandations for the Undergraduate Program in Computer Science. *Communications of the ACM*, 22 (3), 147-166.

Baecker R. (1989) A vision of education in user-centered system and interface design. *SIGCHI Bulletin*, 20 (3), 10-13.

Carey T. (1988) Education. *SIGCHI Bulletin*, 20 (2), 16-17.

Carey T. (1989) Position paper: the basic HCI course for software engineers. *SIGCHI Bulletin*, 20 (3), 14-15.

Mantei M.M. (1989) An HCI continuing education curriculum for industry. *SIGCHI Bulletin*, 20 (3), 16-18.

Norman D.A. & Draper S.W. (1986) *User centered system design*. Lawrence Erlbaum Associates, Hillsdale, NJ.

Strong G.W. (1989) Introductory course in human computer interaction. *SIGCHI Bulletin*, 20 (3), 19-21.

Wilson J.D., Adams E.S., Baouendi H.P., Marion W.A., and Yaverbaum G.J. (1988) Computer education in the People's Republic of China in the late 1980's. *Communications of the ACM*, 31 (8), 956-964.

Human–Computer Interaction – INTERACT '90
D. Diaper et al. (Editors)
Elsevier Science Publishers B.V. (North-Holland)

INFORMATION PROCESSING, CONTEXT and PRIVACY

Alan Dix†

Human-Computer Interaction Group and Department of Computer Science,
University of York, YORK, YO1 5DD
0904 432778, alan@uk.ac.york.minster

This paper is about an old concept, data processing, but one that has taken on new meaning with the increasing complexity and interconnection of systems and the burgeoning of expert systems and connectionism. Classical information theory has been found to be inadequate even in the relatively formal context of security, but this inadequacy is intensified when we consider more human issues like privacy. Further, writers like Suchman and Winograd & Flores emphasise context in understanding communication and information. Relating these issues to a simple information life-cycle, this paper questions how we can retain an understanding of human issues when interacting with such complex systems.

Keywords: Information theory, information processing, privacy, formal analysis

1. Interacting with computers

As I write this I am sitting at my desk at home using a personal computer. Later, I shall take the disk into the University and read it into a compatible computer. On my desk there I have a workstation which I will use to format and print this paper. I am also networked to various other computers in the department, which I occasionally use more or less transparently. These are simple face-to-screen interactions, and are obvious examples of personal interaction with computers, but the majority of our interactions with computers are less direct.

There are, of course, the large range of embedded microprocessors in day to day equipment such as washing-machines, electric drills, hi-fi, and cars, but as these are not information systems, they are not relevant to this paper. Moving outside our homes, we might use automatic bank teller machines, pay for goods using electronic funds transfer at a supermarket, or stand behind counters in various institutions while those we talk to enter information about us and consult terminals to national networks. However, there are many more systems that we never even see at all, with which our interactions are totally indirect. Electricity, gas and telephone companies all hold records and have largely automatic billing. Both the university which employs me, and SERC which pays my grant, use a mixture of manual and automatic mechanisms, as do insurers, credit card companies, and mail order firms. Some systems are so diffuse that it is hard even to be aware of their importance: corporate decision support systems, simulations for local government road planning, party political and media planning. All of these are supported to some extent by automated information systems, all clearly affect us by their decisions but, less clearly, all take input from us: market research and sales figures, monitoring of traffic flows, opinion polls and audience viewing figures. Finally, there are those systems which are most discussed and of which (perhaps) least is known, that is, governmental, police and security service files, including social security, tax and census information.

We are also, of course, the recipients and users of many information systems. In addition to direct services such as bank teller machines, we have television, radio, newspapers, tele-text services and direct mailings. Further, we are affected by the diffuse decision-making processes mentioned above.

Privacy and bugs

When considering large corporate computer systems, both governmental and private, the emphasis is frequently on the deliberate misuse of personal data. It is to counter such misuse that privacy legislation such as the Data Protection Act in the UK is aimed. To make an assessment of the acceptability of various uses of personal data and of the adequacy of such legislation, we need to understand the nature of information and the ways it is transformed and used.

A further problem is bugs. In private or embedded computer systems these are relatively well understood, and we can notice and deal with them at a local level. Large numbers of breakdowns can of course have very damaging results, just as large numbers of engine breakdowns would clog up the rail system, or misbehaving telephones damage communications. However, from just such analogies we have some idea of how to deal with local breakdowns. Even though it can be very distressing to lose a file or deal with a bad interface, it is comparable to a typewriter with sticking keys and probably less damaging than a leaking gas appliance. Thimbleby [1] has noted that the attitude to bugs in the software industry is far from professional, and this bodes ill for the correspondingly more obscure errors of design

† The author is funded by a SERC Advanced Fellowship in Information Technology

and interpretation possible in more complex systems.

When we look at large scale information systems, in addition to the familiar bugs in the access mechanisms and their interfaces, there are a whole new set of problems connected with the access to and interpretation of the large information bases involved. In the early days of data processing such bugs usually involved multi-million pound electricity bills or alternatively sudden massive bank balances. The current equivalent would be credit blacklists, where people find themselves mistakenly refused credit because someone with a similar name or a previous occupier of the same address once defaulted. Less clearly mistaken is the use of neighbourhood as a basis for assessing creditworthiness, or to demand additional deposits. For example, I was recently told by one of my banks that they could not post cheque books to my home address as I had a "high risk postal code". One wonders seriously about the quality of information used for such decisions, especially as the frequent response to queries is that the "system says so". Bugs in information systems may also be just as life threatening as bugs in aircraft control systems; Vallee [2] quotes an example where French police shot a motorist due to mistaken information in the computerised record system.

From a management perspective, poor, mistaken or misunderstood information could easily lead to corporate ruin. For instance, credit companies do not really want to refuse credit to a good potential customer (or allow it to a bad one) any more than the electricity companies wanted to send out silly bills. In the same way as we had to understand the nature of information to assess the deliberate misuse of information, we need a similar understanding to detect and prevent its accidental misuse.

In some ways, it makes little difference to the above examples whether the relevant systems are computerised or not. Large corporate information systems are by their nature complex and can easily use, or misuse, poor quality information. Similarly, they are often hidebound by arbitrary rules which differ little from those executed in a computer system. In fact, the rules may be inferior if they deliberately ignore information to make the human processing task simpler. It is the massive quantitative increase in the complexity of information *processing* that gives a different qualitative nature to computer centred information systems.

2. Formal models of information

As we have noted, in order to assess issues of privacy and misuse of information we need some understanding of the nature of information. One simple requirement is to measure how much information we have, and where the information is going. The simplest measure of information is length. For instance, this paper is aiming to be about six pages long, and at various stages I will do a word count to see how I am getting along. However, when thinking of formal treatment and measures of information, one turns to classical Shannon and Weaver information theory [3]. Its concepts colour the understanding of information even among those who have little grasp of its mathematics and range of application. Indeed, one would surmise that the popular idea of information lies somewhere between classical information theory and word counts! In fact, such a model turns out to be inappropriate when considering human issues like privacy.

Classical information theory

The origins of classical information theory lie in the analysis and design of data channels and optimal data transmission strategies. The information content of a message is given a precise value in the context of the ensemble of possible messages and their likelihoods. Information is measured using entropy:

$$I(\textit{message channel}) = -\sum p_i \log_2 p_i$$
$$I(\textit{particular message}) = -\log_2 p_i$$

where the p_i are the probabilities of the various alternative messages. The information conveyed by a message of fixed length is maximised when all alternatives are equally possible.

Of course, this is a more subtle measure of information content than the simple expedient of measuring the length of a message. However it has no idea of the content of the message except in so far as this is captured by relative probabilities. This means, for instance, that in a nuclear reactor control room a light indicating that the kettle has boiled for tea carries more information content than an indicator of potential meltdown! It also takes no account of the context of interpretation so that translating a message into Swahili would leave its information content unchanged (reasonably) but of course would not be equally acceptable in a British power station. (In fact the opposite is far more likely to occur in practice.)

The vital importance of context in understanding language, and, by extension, computer data, has been emphasised by authors such as Winograd and Flores [4]. To be fair, however, the Shannon and Weaver definition was not intended for such purposes. The problem is that its conceptual impact is pervasive and is likely to be translated to inappropriate areas.

One of the nice things about an entropy-based definition is its pleasant mathematical properties; for instance if A and B are two independent messages then

$$I(A+B) = I(A) + I(B)$$

In general there is correlation between messages (for instance after reading the letter "q" the successive letter "u" has little additional information). In this case we have the inequality:

$$max(I(A), I(B)) \leq I(A+B) \leq I(A) + I(B)$$

the left hand side equality being obtained when the correlation is complete, and the right when the messages are independent as above. We can summarise these properties as "linear" behaviour.

Security

Interest in security comes from two main groups, commercial and military. The desire here is to minimise the "information" obtained by an adversary, either the enemy or the competitor. Some work in these fields has concentrated on classical concepts of information, reducing the bandwidth of information loss, ideally to zero, but more practically merely to insignificant levels (eg. a bit a day) [5].

Even in this relatively formal field, however, the classical approach has been found inappropriate [6]. One reason is the relative importance of different messages, alluded to above. For instance, if an enemy spy opening and shutting a blind means "D-day tomorrow", then it is clearly a more important "bit" of information than "fish and chips in the mess again".

In addition, measures of security which include importance (related to military or commercial damage) do not follow the simple linear patterns of composition. For instance, enemy knowledge of *either* a ship's latitude *or* longitude may not be important, whereas the combined information is highly secret. That is, security measures exhibit "super-linear" behaviour:

$$\exists\, X, Y \quad s.t. \quad S(X+Y) > S(X) + S(Y)$$

It is crucial to be aware of this behaviour as it denies the intuition obtained from classical information theory. The fallacy of linearity (albeit essential when appropriate) is as dangerous when applied to information as it is to environmental damage or straws on camels backs.

Privacy

Privacy, whether personal or corporate, is subtly different from secrecy. Things are private because the very fact of another person *knowing* them is as important as what they might do with that knowledge. Private things may be secret (because we do not want others to know) but not necessarily vice versa. For instance, the formula for a paint would be secret, because one would not want other manufacturers to copy it. The dumping of residues from its manufacture in the North Sea would be private as it would damage the corporate image. Similarly troop strengths would be secret from an enemy, to prevent them using the information in planning their attacks, but private from ones own population to guard morale.

The properties of privacy are more complex again than those of secrecy. It is usually the case that the more pieces of secret information someone has the less happy we are. This is not true of privacy. It is frequently the case that you do not want someone to know something, but, if they do find it out, you want them to know something else as well. For instance, a business man may not want his wife to know that when he said he was working late he was actually with another woman. However, if this fact comes to light he may reveal to his wife that the other woman was a silver-smith with whom he was agreeing the details of a bracelet for their wedding anniversary.

We could call this behaviour "sub-linear", that is, given a measure of privacy P:

$$\exists\, X, Y \quad s.t. \quad P(X+Y) < P(Y) < P(X)$$

There are parallels with this behaviour in the security world, like flooding an adversary with useless information to hide the important bits. However, these trade on the inability of the adversary to access the relevant information; in the case of privacy we may not mind other parties *knowing* something so long as they know the context as well.

This sub-linear property of privacy is related to the need for context that Winograd and Flores [4] demonstrate in the understanding of language. One could characterise problems of privacy like the example above in terms of context/understanding. Essentially, there is some information that has some meaning in its true context with which we are happy. However, if someone attempts to understand it without that contextual background their understanding will inevitably be based on some assumed context yielding a damaging interpretation.

Sub-linear behaviour reminds us that we must be as worried about too little information being stored as too much. Automated systems are particularly worrying as, if there is one thing that computers do better than remembering, it is irrevocably forgetting. This concern about loss of context is important both for individual and official information. Most government and corporate misinformation is true.

Resumé - formal properties of information and privacy

It is obvious that, on the one hand, bringing together seemingly innocuous pieces of data can produce something valuable, and, on the other hand, ignorance of relevant data or context can significantly alter the interpretation of other data. However, these obvious facts violate the two inequalities in the linearity equation implied by classical information theory, the very measures that colour our perception of modern information systems.

3. Information life cycle

The foregoing discussion concentrates on "information" as a passive item. However, any understanding must look at the *process* by which data is gleaned, analysed and used rather than just the stored entities. A simple model would be to divide the information life cycle into three parts:

- Collection
- Processing
- Use

This is clearly an over-simplification. For instance, there will be various phases of analysis before data is collected, the use of one piece of data will affect subsequent data collection, and there are likely to be feedback loops. However, since the purpose is to show the complexity of the process, considering such a simplification will be sufficient.

To each phase in this life cycle we can add various attributes:

Collection

Who (or what) is the subject of the information and in which of its attributes are we interested? Who is collecting the information, for what purpose and in what context? When the information is gathered in, who owns it? This last question probably has different answers depending on whether one looks at it from an ethical, legal or de facto point of view.

Processing

Once data has been codified it will be processed in some way. It is important to know the intentions and purpose behind the algorithms used for processing the data. There is no reason to assume that this purpose is related to the purpose for which the data is collected or for which it is eventually used. By whom is this processing done? There is a wealth of difference between an application for postponement of tax payments being considered by the district inspector of taxes and an application for housing benefit being considered by a programmer in Bletchley.

Use

Finally, how is the processed information to be used? Someone (or something) will use it for some purpose (not necessarily related to the reason for collection). The actions that arise are likely to affect the original subject, amongst others. Of course, even if these actions are acceptable and "correct", there are many issues to consider in the way this process interfaces to the user, and whether the manner of collection and use are consistent with the dignity and privacy of the subject. Automation may help in this respect: it is far less humiliating to be refused money by a bank telling machine than to be refused cash over the counter.

One could expand upon each of these phases but it is the processing which I consider central. It is interesting that over the years the phrase "data processing" has become rather out-dated, even "information processing" sounds a little too technical and we are all now engaged in "information technology" (note my funding!). The processing aspect is played down, and yet it is precisely this processing that gives computer based information systems their power and danger.

Examples of the information life cycle

In the simplest human information systems, the collection, processing, and use would all be carried out by the same individual, perhaps at the same time. The context is taken into account when analysing and acting on the data and the purpose for which the data is to be used is apparent when it is collected. There is, of course, plenty of room for misinterpretation and misunderstanding but it is *relatively* easy to focus on these and correct them. An example of this would be if the businessman in §" 2 met his wife while with the silver-smith.

An example of a more complicated human information system would be a small building society. A borrower is behind with her payments partly because of a delay in receiving her salary after a job change and partly because of delays due to a postal strike. She phones up the building society to apologise and explain and a note is made in the margin of the *paper* records. Later, she goes to request an extension of her mortgage to cover some new central heating. The manager looks up her payment record and notices the period of arrears. At first he is reticent but then, perhaps after discussion with the borrower, he sees the marginal notes and agrees the loan.

Imagine now that the building society computerises its records. There is no room for the marginal note and the information is lost. This time, if the borrower submits her (streamlined and efficient) postal application she is refused. Perhaps she follows it up and the matter is cleared up, perhaps she gets finance elsewhere, or perhaps she sticks with her coal fire.

Finally, let us consider a totally automated system. The effects of the need for automatic processing are felt even at the collection stage. Usually only predefined information can be entered, so that additional marginal notes would never have existed in the first place. Also the information collected will have to fit into categories that may not be appropriate for the actual data subject. For instance, I was once computerising the personnel records system for an education authority. The teachers' titles were given code digits, and I was specifically requested *only* to allocate codes for Mr, Mrs and Miss. Clearly the teaching profession contains no Doctors, no Nobility and no Feminists!

In this last example the failure of the information system is apparent even before processing begins. What hope is there that sensible decisions can be made by the eventual user of the information after it has been changed in form by the processing stage?

4. The nature of processing - alienation

From the increasingly automated examples above, we see that the role of automatic processing in the middle of the information life cycle separates the user of the information from its source. This means that valuable contextual and hard to codify information is not available. Furthermore, the processing itself may make it hard to trace back to the original data, such as it is. We shall now look at the way that different types of processing relate to the properties of information discussed in section 2.

Again, we will grossly simplify and consider processing under three headings:

Selection

This is direct access to data stored in the system, by some sort of query. Information is of itself useless without an effective access mechanism and it is the ability of modem data base systems to access data quickly and by various mechanisms which has revolutionised this aspect of information systems. This is probably the type of processing envisaged when people consider privacy issues: can someone get at information about me? The Data Protection Act recognises this and makes allowance for personal information that can be accessed by keys not actually held upon computer. A better use of computer facilities is perhaps the indexing of data stored manually, the prime example being library indices. As far as I am aware the UK legislation makes no special provision for computer indices to manual data. However, in terms of accidental misuse this form of processing is probably the most benign, because it at least presents the user with the data as originally collected. (One could even make provision for free format fields on all records and thus approximate the paper form.)

Collation

This is the gathering together of related information and is a crucial requirement of any data base query facility. This bringing together of disparate data brings into play the super-linear behaviour discussed under security. From the point of view of privacy, items of personal information gathered separately which individually I am willing to divulge may be brought together, and thus compromise my privacy. On the other hand it is exactly this super-linear behaviour that gives collation its power. The query yields information of greater quality than the sum of the data brought together. On the whole the major problem here is from malicious misuse of information. However, the fallacy of linearly additive information might lead someone to use collated information in a way which infringes one's privacy without considering that there are any human or ethical questions involved.

Filtering

This is where we deliberately throw away unwanted information. It is similar to selection, but there we were considering selecting entire data records, whereas here we consider the extraction of parts of a single record for some purpose. Formally, the two are pretty much equivalent, but if we consider a record to be the total of the information collected about a single subject we see that filtering has a quite different effect. If we recall the sub-linear behaviour of information with respect to privacy, we see that filtering of data can invade privacy by losing relevant information. In fact, we have already seen that all data collection involves some loss of context and this is especially so when the data is intended to be entered into a computer system. Thus filtering really begins at the collection stage. The collector may well be aware of the paucity of the information gathered, whereas the eventual user may be blissfully ignorant. It is well known that the choice of indicators to be taken into account when describing people can be used as a subtle means of discrimination against specific groups. Thus deliberate misuse under this category is possible. However, it is probably one of the most frequent ways in which information is unintentionally misused and it is important principally for this reason. In fact, most of the modern "bugs" in information systems seem to stem from the ignoring of pertinent information.

Statistical analysis

Statistical measures of large data bases may be seen as protectors of privacy, by hiding the particular in the whole. For instance, UK census data is deliberately only supplied in aggregate form. Clever use of multiple statistical queries may in fact compromise individual information [7], but this problem is well understood and techniques are available to protect against it. It is unlikely that such a circumstance would arise unintentionally. There is however again the problem of loss of context. A parent may drive his child 100 metres down the road to school because the road is unsafe to cross. On the way, he passes an observer measuring road usage. Because the road is used such a lot it is widened, attracting more traffic and thus making it more dangerous.

Mathematical and symbolic analysis

We are thinking here about applying complex algorithms to derive information about a specific subject. This relates to statistical analysis in the same way that selection relates to filtering. It comprises aspects of both collation and filtering, for instance, $a+b$ brings together two pieces of information while at the same time losing their individuality. Further, the very complexity of the operations may make it almost impossible to relate the derived information to the originally collected data.

We notice that once we take into account the super-linear and sub-linear nature of human information, each of the modes of processing has the possibility of violating privacy or misusing information due to loss of context. If the information system has been designed as a whole, these effects may be taken into account, but it is more likely that users of information will come to an existing information system. The data with which they work may have been collected for a totally different purpose. Important facts may be missing, and even where data is complete the way in which the real world has been disambiguated in order to codify it may not be pertinent for the new purpose. Further, the user may not have the raw data available, but will instead access it in an already processed form. Again, the purposes of this processing will affect the way information is collected together or ignored. With the best of intentions the user is forced to take action on the basis of this incomplete and possibly irrelevant data. Any statistician knows the problem of being asked to produce some sort of analysis from derived statistics, where perhaps the wrong type of data was gathered and the original data lost. One could compare this situation with the industrial revolution. At that time, workers became alienated from the source and purpose of the material artifacts they produced. Today, information workers are similarly alienated from the subject and context of the data which they process and use.

Connectionism and expert systems

Until quite recently, the majority of processing has been of a fairly simple algorithmic nature. In *principle*, one could analyse the method of collection and processing to decide whether the derived information was suitable for the purposes required. For some time now, expert systems have been used as part of the processing element in information systems. The complex nature of their decision-making can increase the distance between the user and the original data. To some extent, the problems of alienation have been recognised; users are unwilling to trust the conclusions of such systems without access to the decision-making process, and explanation facilities are often included.

The advent of connectionism into commercial systems poses more severe problems again. Amongst others, credit companies are considering the use of neural networks in assessing creditworthiness. The problem with such systems is that the processing they perform is so diffuse and unstructured (and deliberately so) that it may be theoretically impossible to obtain a similar explanation. That is, the processing may contain elements of collation and filtering, but it will be impossible to know what information is being ignored and what brought together. Information users may violate the personal rights of a subject without being aware of it, and without the ability to detect that they are so misusing the data. Although research is being done to address the "explanation" of neural net decisions it is likely that the use of such systems will fast outstrip the ability to understand them.

5. Addressing the problem

The picture painted is a trifle gloomy. One reaction might be to eschew all complex processing because of the inherent dangers. For instance, I used to have a book dating from the late 1960s [8] that suggested, amongst other anti-computer measures, magnetically "wiping" your cheques to force them to be processed by hand. Luddism has a bad name, but faced with technologies that benefit the powerful at the expense of the ordinary man and woman such a response may well be defensible [9]. A second reaction is exemplified by the Data Protection Act in the UK, which, continuing the analogy to the industrial revolution, we may see as following in the tradition of reformers by statute such as Wilberforce and Shaftesbury. Finally, and most relevant to the reader, there are the awareness and professional standards of information technologists. But what measures, if any, can we take to make effective use of information systems and to protect the integrity of their subjects?

The value of processing

No one would bother with the costly business of processing information unless it yielded some value. In this the super- and sub-linear behaviour of information is specifically used. We collate disparate data or discard unnecessary data because that enhances the value of the derived data. If the derived data is of more value to the data user it is not surprising that it may also be of more value to the subject.

This leaves us in somewhat of a dilemma. It appears that it is fundamentally impossible to process data effectively without necessarily also causing problems of ownership and privacy. Of course, some types of processing may maximise the commercial value of derived information whilst causing few personal problems, and vice versa. However, the connection between power and privacy does imply that we cannot simply bar classes of processing as unacceptably violating civil liberties and allow others wholesale; any type of processing, if it is useful, is a potential privacy problem.

On the one hand, the value of correctly processed information can be a strong argument for avoiding misuse, as this misuse is just as harmful to the data user as to the data subject. On the other hand, data collection, storage and processing is costly in itself. One reason why bugs in information systems (such as the problems of credit blacklisting) persist is that the costs of proper processing and use outweigh the losses due to misuse. Unfortunately, as in many spheres, the costs to the individual are not included in this formula.

People-friendly processing

Is there such a thing? As with all areas the solutions to the problems cited will be as varied as the systems designed. One can however give a few suggestions.

To begin with, knowing that the problem exists is the key to solving it. In particular, the most potent and most easily overlooked cause of information misuse is due to the sub-linear nature of information, ignoring pertinent knowledge which could lead to better systems both for users and subjects. A "people-friendly" company would include these factors in their assessment of appropriate information processing strategies.

Processing as the source of alienation is the key problem. We can therefore design systems that attempt to bridge the gap between collection (and subject, context etc.) and use. Traditional data files mirrored the constrained fields of punch cards and the fixed field approach has been uncritically extended into more advanced data base architectures. One could imagine data base designs that include space for free format comments or perhaps have several different answers to the same question related to some (coded?) indication of the context of use. Even more unconventionally, we might imagine doubtful or special items of information being active so that if they are used in any calculation they could signal to the user their specialness. On a more traditional level, we could just choose that wherever we can, we present as much of the original data as possible even when this is done in conjunction with derived data.

Auditing may well be at the heart of a people-friendly company's information policies. At a per transaction level this would imply that as far as possible the user was made aware of the source of information used, perhaps in the ways described above. More importantly, this should be a professional activity in its own right. In the same way as we might assess the energy efficiency of a factory or check for financial irregularities in a company's accounts, the professional information auditor would examine the information systems for the way they use or misuse personal information. They might well be able to tell the company how better to use their information as well as giving it a "people clean" bill of health.

Even more radically, one could attempt where possible to replace 'information up, decisions down' processing with one where strategic information was passed down for local, contextual, decision making. This has its technical problems, as the local structure of use may differ from the structure of the data it depends on. However, the main problem with such an information structure is not technical, but that it would conflict with the corporate power structures.

6. Conclusions

We have seen how classical information theory, the basis of much of our intuition about information flows, fails to provide appropriate measures of privacy and personal importance. Processing, at the heart of the information life cycle, may thus violate personal rights subtly and perhaps unintentionally. Moreover it causes a separation between the user of information and the subject of that information which makes effective and proper use impossible. Some strategies have been suggested for tackling this alienation, but whether complex systems can be tamed in this way is debatable. Of particular concern is the prospect of connectionist approaches to the processing of personal information, which make it impossible to tell whether or not privacy is threatened.

References

1. H. Thimbleby, *Bugs : The Issue Facing H.C.I.*, Department Of Computer Science, Stirling University, Scotland (May 1989).
2. J. Vallee, *The Network Revolution*, Penguin Books (1982).
3. C.E. Shannon and W. Weaver, *A Mathematical Theory of Communication*, Univ. of Illinois Press (1949).
4. T. Winograd and F. Flores, *Understanding Computers And Cognition*, Addison-Wesley (1987).
5. DoD, "Trusted Computer System Evaluation Criteria", (CSC-STD-001-83), US Department of Defence (15 Aug 1983).
6. J E Dobson and J A McDermid, "Security Models and Enterprise Models or Information Flow Models considered a Denial of Service Attack on Computer Security", *Proceedings of The 1988 Workshop on Database Security*, Kinsgton, Ontario,Canada (Oct 5-7, 1988).
7. Wiebren do Jonge, "Compromising statistical databases responding to queries about means", *ACM Trans. on Database Systems* **8**(1), pp. 60-80, ACM (March 1983).
8. *The Beast of Business*, author and publisher unknown.
9. E.P. Thompson, *The Making of the English Working Class*, Pelican Books (1968).

Human–Computer Interaction – INTERACT '90
D. Diaper et al. (Editors)
Elsevier Science Publishers B.V. (North-Holland)

MAC-THUSIASM: SOCIAL ASPECTS OF MICROCOMPUTER USE

Matthew R JONES

University of Cambridge, Management Studies Group, Department of Engineering, Mill Lane, Cambridge, CB2 1RX

The success of the Apple Macintosh computer is normally ascribed to the quality of its user interface. This paper presents evidence from interviews with Macintosh users of the importance of social and organisational factors in influencing their choice of microcomputer and their pattern of, and attitude to, computer use. Many of the users held strongly positive views about the Macintosh computer and some possible reasons for this enthusiasm are discussed.

1. INTRODUCTION

"Macintosh users love their computer".
"The Macintosh is fun to use".
"Macintosh users are different".
"The Macintosh puts the user in control".

Comments such as these will be familiar to most people who have come across users of the Apple Macintosh microcomputer. Similar comments are difficult to imagine from users of other types of microcomputer, except perhaps from members of the select band of devotees for whom particular computer systems become the centre of their social existence [1]. They suggest that the Macintosh is seen differently from other computers.

Most research on the Macintosh, however, has concentrated, usually in generic terms, on the qualities of its direct-manipulation interface. Yet, as the comments above suggest, user attitudes toward the Macintosh are not simply a product of its technical functionality. Other factors, notably those concerning the social and organisational context of computer use would also appear to play an important role. For example, the comments given above would seem to suggest that there is a distinct sense of identity among Macintosh users which positively influences their attitudes.

Our understanding of this phenomenon, however, needs to move beyond the simply anecdotal level of these introductory comments and to locate these attitudes within an appropriate theoretical framework. This paper reports the results of a series of interviews with Macintosh users which has sought to address this issue.

Although the analysis presented here relates to the views of a small number of users of a particular computer system, the results have a broader relevance in relation to human computer interaction. Firstly, in emphasising the social and organisational aspects of computer use and their interrelationship with technical factors, the paper seeks to redress an imbalance in much of the HCI literature. Secondly, in drawing on insights from from social and organisational theory, the paper seeks to introduce a number of analytical approaches which may enhance our understanding of the way that humans interact with computers in practice.

2. RESEARCH METHOD

2.1 The Interviews

Semi-structured interviews were held with ten academic Macintosh users from a variety of disciplines. The interviews lasted approximately one hour and covered a number of topics as shown in Table 1.

Table 1 Topics covered in Macintosh user interviews

Primary and other uses of the microcomputer;
History of Macintosh use;
Experience of other computer systems;
Comparison (where appropriate) between Macintosh and other computer systems;
Interaction with users of Macintosh and other computer systems;
Views on Macintosh functionality;
Perceptions of Macintosh use;
Commitment to Macintosh use;
Knowledge of, and views on the Apple computer company.

Users were encouraged in all interviews to expand on any points they wished to make, and to discuss any other issues relating to their use of the Macintosh which they considered important. The interviews were tape-recorded, and the recordings were used in conjunction with written notes to provide the basis for the discussion below.

3. TECHNICAL FACTORS

In drawing attention to the importance of social factors in influencing user attitudes toward the Macintosh, it is not intended to deny the importance of technical factors. Indeed, one of the striking aspects of user perceptions was the complex relationship between social and technical factors. For example users' positive views on the quality of the user interface were associated with perceptions of a Macintosh culture committed to design quality. This issue will be discussed again in more detail in a later section of this paper, but the reason for raising it at this point is to emphasise that to consider technical factors in isolation may be to miss out on potentially important social factors which may be associated with them. The discussion in this section, therefore, should be viewed in the context of the discussion of social factors which follows.

3.1. The quality of the interface

All of the interviewees specifically commented on the quality of the Macintosh user interface. In terms of principles of interface design [2], it would appear that the Macintosh is highly successful. Interviewees particularly emphasised the transparency of the interface. This was generally related to the close correspondence between the user's actions and the task to be completed. The consequent elimination of a layer of complexity enables the user to concentrate on the task at hand rather than on how to achieve it.

Closely related to the transparency of the interface was its simplicity. Several interviewees commented on the ability of their children to use the Macintosh often at what was considered to be a remarkably early age. The ability of novice users, especially those with no prior experience of computers to grasp quickly the basic principles of Macintosh use was also noted. The key factor in the simplicity of the user interface was held to be the small repertoire of basic techniques which could be applied across nearly all functions and applications, thus obviating the requirement to remember complex or obscure command sequences.

This last point identifies another important feature of the interface in the view of the interviewees: its consistency. Knowing that all applications have the same visual appearance and can be used with the same basic techniques was widely felt to be highly advantageous. Other features of the interface which were considered beneficial were the visibility of objects of interest (all tasks ultimately being accessible via continuously displayed menu options) and reversibility of actions (permitting exploration of a program without fear of permanent damage).

The only area in which there were reservations expressed about the interface was in the ease of use for experienced users. The extent of this problem was considered to vary between different programs, but those that did not provide keyboard-based shortcuts as alternatives to mouse and menu-based commands were felt to unduly restrict the speed of work of experienced users and could evoke frustration. More generally, it was felt that experienced users who had overcome the initial difficulties of command-based interfaces could achieve a degree of facility with such systems which would exceed that possible with equivalent packages on the Macintosh. For those experienced with command-based systems, the Macintosh interface, particularly in its use of the mouse and menus, could pose difficulties, it was felt, largely due to lack of familiarity.

3.2. Physical qualities

For some interviewees, the physical appearance of the Macintosh was considered important. The single box design with small desktop footprint and high resolution screen were commented on favourably by a number of interviewees. Others, however, found the screen size in particular to be constraining, especially when seeking to work with multiple windows.

The quality of design of the Macintosh and the recognition of a unified design concept was also felt to be a distinctive feature. This was described by interviewees in the following terms: "the whole ensemble is rather nicely put together"; "the original designers obviously paid a lot of attention to detail and seem to have got it right on the whole .... a good choice of hardware and software".

The main drawback of the Macintosh, in terms of hardware, was felt to be the closed design, although some interviewees actually liked the idea of the computer being a black box. The cost of moving to an open design was seen as an expansion of the size of the machine, as illustrated by the Macintosh II. For at least one interviewee this was seen as a mistake.

4. SOCIAL ASPECTS OF COMPUTER USE

The use of a computer is not simply a matter of physical and cognitive tasks, but is shaped by, and itself shapes, a variety of attitudes and perceptions. These attitudes and perceptions are not the unique product of isolated individuals, but are influenced by the users social environment. In seeking to understand the origins of these views as they relate to the Macintosh, therefore, we need to consider the social context within which computer use occurs.

4.1. Changing Attitudes to Computer Use

In discussing their adoption of the Macintosh, most interviewees affirmed that their use of the Macintosh had changed their attitudes to computing, although not always very substantially. For some, who had prior experience of computing on other systems, the primary change was related to the simplicity of the interface. The more direct engagement with the task at hand facilitated by the Macintosh was seen as eliminating or reducing a 'psychological barrier' to effective use. Even tasks which had previously been carried out on a computer, such as word-processing, were felt to have become qualitatively closer to hand. As one interviewee expressed it, the Macintosh was a "jolly good pencil" for which the relationship "from [the user] to the paper is absolutely straight". This was contrasted with other systems which introduced "mechanical things ... between you and whatever you want to do".

For interviewees for whom the Macintosh was their first computer the change in attitude corresponded mainly to a loss of fear of computing. This was also observed to be the case with other computer-phobic novice users, particularly in the arts and humanities, where it was stated " [the Macintosh] had a very easy interface to use and this was important in the minds of [arts academics] who had a particular fear of the computer". Similarly, arts students who might say "oh I couldn't [use a computer] or I wouldn't know how", within "probably, literally five minutes", would be happily using the Macintosh. Experienced users also perceived a benefit from loss of fear when using new programs where "the fact that it looks familiar means that you are not scared of it".

Another related feature of changed attitudes is attested to in the last of the introductory quotes. Several interviewees referred to feelings of greater control over the technology. There were two aspects to this control. Firstly, a feeling that the computer was docile - without any specialised knowledge you would generally be able to "get the computer to do the things you want to do", even to the extent of damaging it (whether accidentally or on purpose) one interviewee suggested; and secondly that the computer was pliable - it could be easily customised to suit your requirements.

The first aspect of control was the source of some disagreement among interviewees. Most considered that the simplicity of the interface obviated the need for manuals. Indeed, two of the interviewees specifically identified this as a central feature of their appreciation of the Macintosh. Another, however, argued that this was an illusion. Although it may be possible to achieve desired functionality solely through searching the menus, this was considered likely to lead to users missing out on important features or adopting inefficient methods. In addition, the apparent saving in time from not needing to consult the manuals may be a false economy, as more time may actually be spent in searching, or trial and error tests, or inefficient task performance. This difference in viewpoint was not accounted for by differences in computing experience or type and range of applications used. Some of the interviewees who argued that manuals were not required recognised this problem, but persisted in their views, arguing that learning by doing was central to the whole Macintosh philosophy. It would appear that the feeling of being able to do things oneself is an important aspect of Macintosh use, notwithstanding its potential limitations.

Autonomy and engagement with the work task are characteristics of the 'craft' mode of production and are identified as an important source of employee motivation, exemplified in the 'Quality of Working Life' and sociotechnical approaches to job design. Historically, they have been associated with a mythology of the independent craft worker, who it is argued has been largely eliminated in the modern industrial organisation in favour of Taylorite management control [3,4]. More recently, the concept of post-Fordism, has sought to identify in recent trends in organisational practice and developments in Information Technology, a re-emergence of the autonomous unalienated worker (at least within the organisational core)[5].

The Macintosh with its emphasis on user control may thus appear to act as a post-Fordist technology, permitting a return to craft-based work practices. To what extent it actually re-skills users is debatable, but it would appear that it is perceived as substantially less alienating than equivalent computer systems. The motivational benefits of enhanced user control may also be a factor in positive user attitudes.

4.2. The Macintosh as a Non-computer

Several interviewees specifically stated that before using a Macintosh they viewed computers with antipathy. For some, this attitude has persisted, despite their use of a Macintosh, and it was also observed that "Macs are at their best for people who don't like computers at all". In some way, therefore, the Macintosh was seen as a non-computer. This raises the question of what the intrinsic qualities of a computer are seen as and what the Macintosh is seen as, if not as a computer.

4.3. What Makes a Computer?

The evidence gathered from the interviews can provide us with no more than a few preliminary ideas of what qualities users associate with computers, but some initial criteria suggest themselves. For a number of interviewees, computers were associated with programming, particularly in a high-level language such as Fortran and with scientific, or at least primarily mathematical tasks. Programming was combined (confused?) with a view of interaction with a computer as being characterised by complex, arcane and possibly arbitrary command languages. The effectiveness of interaction with a computer was also seen as being heavily dependent on keyboard proficiency.

The physical appearance of a computer was also considered important. A typical computer was seen as consisting of several large boxes of severely functional design, which, combined with great weight, identified it firmly as a desk-bound, primarily office-based, machine. The Macintosh being a small, 'luggable', single-unit machine of distinctive design was therefore seen as not fitting this stereotype.

In addition to these practical aspects of computers and computing another important factor may be perceptions of values associated with computers. Franz & Robey [6] have argued that computers are seen as "icons of rationality in cultures commited to the idea of intelligent choice". Computing in organisations is also generally seen as a serious business, directed at functional ends [7].

4.4. The Macintosh as a Consumer Device

One interviewee, well-versed in Apple's original design philosophy for the Macintosh (or the myth thereof, as will be discussed later), viewed it as being a consumer device, like a telephone. Such devices are used as black boxes without questioning how they work, and provide the rationale for the closed design of the Macintosh. The transparency of the Macintosh interface was considered to enable this perception (largely) to be sustained.

Other interviewees, usually those who used the Macintosh almost exclusively as a word-processor, also talked of the Macintosh as a high-powered typewriter. Although this description may seem extremely prosaic, it does suggest that the computer-like qualities of the Macintosh are not perceived as dominant, as interviewees suggested they were for other systems.

4.5. The Macintosh as a Toy

A number of interviewees referred to the Macintosh as a toy. Often this was cited as the (negative) perception of the Macintosh by 'real' computer users. In some cases this aroused a defensive reaction from the interviewee who sought to discredit the view arguing that this was a, possibly understandable, misconception based on the 'user-friendly' interface. In fact, in their view, the Macintosh was just as capable of 'real' computing as any other comparable machine.

Other interviewees, however, saw this as a positive feature of the Macintosh. There appeared to be two reasons for this response. The first, was that the toy-like appearance acted as a means of encouraging novice users with a negative view of computers to try using the Macintosh in a game-like way. The second was because of the perceived benefits from play in terms of creativity, interest and motivation as will be discussed later.

4.6. The Macintosh as a Cult Object

One notable feature of several of the interviews was the identification of the Macintosh as a cult object. One interviewee compared the Macintosh and the Volkswagen

'Beetle' car as functional machines which have become accepted as design classics. Another identified the Macintosh with the childrens' toy *lego*. Such comparisons imply not merely a perception of the Macintosh as well-designed, but also the additional mystique of the cult object which enables it to transcend its original function and to acquire almost iconic qualities [8]. Concepts of 'design', 'style' and 'chic' associated with such objects also have an important role as marks of social distinction [9], transforming them into symbols of subcultural identity [10]. The Macintosh may therefore be seen as an emblem of a particular social group, and ownership/use of one as a statement of group identity. We will return to this issue later in this paper in considering the existence of a Macintosh community.

'Style' and 'design', however, need not operate solely as sources of social exclusivity. Commercially, the importance of design in product marketing has become widely recognised [11]. In the last decade in particular, the concept of 'design' has been adopted as a mass marketing device, particularly in the retail sector, as the spread of the epithet 'designer-' illustrates, being applied to everything from clothes (designer-label) to facial hair (designer-stubble)[12]. The Macintosh as a 'designer- computer' may therefore acquire a mass market cachet.

5. THE EXPERIENCE OF MACINTOSH USE

Apart from the practical aspects of direct manipulation, for a number of interviewees there was also a number of characteristics of the experience of Macintosh use which distinguished it from use of other computer systems.

5.1. Spatial Thinking

For some interviewees, especially those with artistic or architectural training, the Macintosh was liked for the spatial quality of its interface. Used to expressing themselves through drawing, the interface had a "visual logic" that suited them.

Even where the Macintosh was not being used for drawing, the spatial quality of the interface was felt to be beneficial. For example with 'outlining' software, where the relationships between the topics was felt to be much clearer when visualised within more than one dimension. The nature of the interface would thus appear to enable users to employ types of visual thinking [13] which may be inaccessible in command-based systems.

Other users also conceived of the interface in spatial terms, talking of the Macintosh opening up space or expanding horizons for productive work by cutting back on the space required for learning how to use the system. Spatial metaphors were also evident in talking about the experience of using multiple windows with several different applications open at once. The various applications, it was suggested, "don't feel very far from one another", and the easy way in which they are integrated creates a "larger task space".

5.2. Aesthetics

Another factor identified by some users as being important in their appreciation of the Macintosh was aesthetics. The high resolution screen, the graphic quality of the display, and also in some cases the design of the computer itself were identified as important. This was particularly notable in the case of one interviewee who used the Macintosh for writing arabic script, where the aesthetic appearance of a text is essential, and was one of the main reasons for his choice of the Macintosh.

Aesthetics were also frequently mentioned with respect to the quality of the output. Quality of presentation was mentioned by all interviewees as being a significant factor in their preference for the Macintosh, and as an important factor in persuading other people of its benefits. The ability to control the appearance of the output was considered valuable, although it was suggested by a number of interviewees that this also had its drawbacks in raising one's expectations of what should be achieved. This could lead to a lot more time being spent on 'perfecting' the appearance of a document than was the case with alternative systems.

It may be argued that the 'look and feel' of the Macintosh was also an aesthetic criterion. All interviewees recognised a distinctive Macintosh style, based at least in part on the appearance of programs. It was suggested that some programs, particularly those 'translated' from other types of microcomputer, were unsatisfactory in this respect because they "don't feel right". While it was difficult for interviewees to define precisely what the 'right feeling' was, they could easily identify programs that didn't have it. Factors mentioned included the similarity of appearance and operations, the shape of icons and fonts used in menu text. Interviewees generally had positive views about the look of Macintosh programs, and felt that their design exhibited a distinctive "elegance" and "clarity". Admiration was also expressed for the designers of the Macintosh in having achieved this aesthetic quality.

5.3. Fun

A feature of Macintosh use commented on by several interviewees was that it was generally fun to use. As one interviewee put it "after an afternoon's hard work, one can nevertheless come away with not just a feeling of having accomplished a task, but also a feeling of somehow having had fun". In addition, use of the Macintosh was frequently referred to by interviewees as "playing". This did not appear to be simply a matter of the humour evident in some of the icons, although this was mentioned by a number of interviewees, but relates to a more general quality of Macintosh use.

This perception may underlie the concept of the Macintosh as a toy, but also has other potentially important influences on creativity and motivation. It is argued [14] that play creates conditions under which individuals are enabled and encouraged to re-combine behaviour or ideas in novel ways, and may thus be an important source of creativity. The importance of play in organisations has been identified [15, 16]. The potential contribution of play as a source of intrinsic motivation for computer users has also been described [17].

6 THE ORGANISATIONAL CONTEXT OF MACINTOSH USE

To consider the use of the Macintosh simply in terms of the individual's personal experience, however, is to neglect the potentially important influence of the organisational context within which the individual is located. The organisational context may be considered in terms of three elements politics, culture and communication (here identified in the interacting community of Macintosh users) [18]. Each of these may have an influence on the way in which the individual uses a computer.

6.1. The Politics of Macintosh Use

The use of a computer in an organisation involves a network of power relationships which may shape the nature of the interaction. In the context of the use of the Macintosh, organisational politics may intrude in a number of ways. Several interviewees commented on the initial hostility of computer support staff toward the Macintosh, and the way in which control over access to resources of finance, technical support and infrastructure was used to restrict its adoption. A crucial factor in the acceptance of the Macintosh was also seen to be the emergence of a powerful 'champion' able to overcome organisational resistance to its use.

The perception of the Macintosh as not a 'real' computer may be a source of political difficulties in organisations, or groups within organisations, heavily committed to the scientific/rationalist perspective. Status within such groups and organisations is likely to be associated with support for this perspective, thus the 'irrational' aspects of the Macintosh (non-computer, toy) may mean that senior members of the organisation will be unwilling to use one [19]. Conversely, within an arts or humanities department, for example, the Macintosh may be supported precisely because it is seen as in opposition to conventional scientific notions of computing.

Power is not unidirectional, but is the product of a relationship between groups and individuals whose enforcement depends upon the acceptance of its legitimacy by the subordinate partner [18]. Thus subordinates have power through their potential for resistance. Where the use of the Macintosh in an organisation is prevented or actively discouraged, therefore, it may become a symbol of resistance. For a number of interviewees, this "subversive" quality was considered to contribute to their positive attitude toward the Macintosh. That is to the say they liked to see their use of the Macintosh as striking a blow for individuality in a conformist computer world ("an enlightened minority in a faceless business world" as one interviewee put it).

Another interesting issue concerning the politics of Macintosh use is the fact that a number of the main advocates of the Macintosh are women. It is also reported that the proportion of female Macintosh users is higher than that for other microcomputers (although still only 10%) [20]. It is argued that the image of computers is predominantly male [21]. In this context, the Macintosh, as a non-computer, may seem more neutral in its identity. Part of the attitude toward the Macintosh in technically-dominated organisations may also be a result of this identification of the Macintosh with the 'negative' pole of the constructs rational/irrational, power/weakness, technical/social, machine-centred/human-centred, male/female.

6.2. Macintosh Culture

The perception of the Macintosh as a non-computer was one element of a distinctive Macintosh culture. Characteristics of this culture were identified by interviewees as being an individualistic and rather anti-establishment outlook, a genuine commitment to the individual user and a reciprocal commitment by users to the machine. Macintosh users were considered to be different from the general run of computer users. They do feel that the computer has been designed with the a genuine understanding of the needs of the user in mind. Macintosh users do talk about loving their machines.

It could be argued that this Macintosh culture is simply an extreme form of brand loyalty which has been created by the Apple Computer company. That is to say Macintosh users want to feel that their computer is special, to justify their investment in such an idiosyncratic system and Apple encourage this. Certainly, Apple has been assiduous in cultivating elements of this culture, notably in its (in)famous Superbowl adverts which presented Macintosh users as standing out from the crowd. Yet is this very different from other advertisements, often for alcoholic beverages which seek to emphasise the individuality of their consumers? Is there something that makes the Macintosh special? The interviews clearly do not provide sufficient evidence to give a definitive answer to this question, but a number of factors considered relevant by the interviewees, such as the design, the view of it as a non-computer, the cult status, have already been identified.

An additional factor, which was explored in the interviews was the influence of perceptions of the Apple Computer Company itself. The mythology surrounding its origins in a Californian garage, the sense of vision upon which the company is felt to be based, perceptions of the company structure as being very youthful, dynamic and informal were all mentioned by interviewees. These perceptions, while not determining user attitudes (several interviewees had no knowledge of the Apple Company), appeared to reinforce, by confirming the cultural values, user commitment to the Macintosh.

6.3. The Macintosh Community

Most interviewees also talked of, and identified with a Macintosh "community" (compared by one interviewee to a car owners club), based largely upon the shared culture discussed above . This feeling was particularly strong in the early days of the Macintosh (a number of interviewees talked of themselves as pioneers of Macintosh use) when its minority, cult status, the hostility of other computer users and the then distinctive qualities of its appearance and interface served to encourage a sense of solidarity. Interviewees talked of the enthusiasm among early Macintosh users meeting to swap tips, ideas and programs and of the feeling of identity with other Macintosh users facilitated, perhaps fortuitously, by the distinctive typeface of the Imagewriter printer. Apple's encouragement of new software and its enforcement of a unified interface were also seen to have reinforced this community feeling.

Interestingly, the community was identified by most interviewees as being outside their own immediate group of colleagues. There did not appear to be a clustering of enthusiasts, rather, there was an identification with other Macintosh users in the wider academic community. This may be explained by the individualistic nature of the Macintosh culture. Interviewees often referred with pleasure to the spread of the Macintosh amongst colleagues, but this was seen as resulting from a process of osmosis rather than through an act of evangelism on their part.

It was generally felt that the sense of community had diminished in recent years. This was attributed to a number of factors. The growing acceptance of the Macintosh in even previously hostile environments had reduced the exclusiveness of the 'following' and had taken away the feeling of being members of an oppressed minority. Changes in the Apple Computer Company and its increasing emphasis on the corporate sector in its marketing were also felt to have changed the nature of the relationship between the individual user and the company. New models which were much more evidently real computers also evoked negative reactions from some interviewees. What had previously seemed something special, was now becoming just like any other computer, and the company just like any other large multinational corporation. This view was not universally shared, though, and some interviewees welcomed the arrival of 'proper' computing facilities in the Macintosh world. These changes to Apple and the Macintosh were generally seen as inevitable as the company and the technology developed, but, ironically, also seem likely to lead to a loss of its distinctive identity.

7. CONCLUSION

This paper has sought to identify the distinctive characteristics of the Apple Macintosh microcomputer which encourage the loyalty and enthusiasm of its users. Although technical factors were found to be important in users' attitudes, the influence of social and organisational factors was also found to be strong. In particular, a greater sense of control over the technology, the social image of the Macintosh, and the visual, aesthetic and "fun" qualities of the interface, appeared to be important. In the organisational context political factors and the existence of a Macintosh culture and community were identified as influential.

While the results of this small number of interviews can only provide us with an initial outline of user attitudes and perceptions, the recurrence of a number of themes does seem to suggest several factors which merit further investigation. This paper has sought to locate these factors within the framework of a number of social theories and thus to illustrate their relevance to the study of human computer interaction.

REFERENCES

[1] Kiesler, S. and Sproull, L. The Social Process of Technological Change in Organisations, in: Kiesler, S and Sproull, L (eds) Computing and Change on Campus (Cambridge University Press, Cambridge, 1987).

[2] Shneiderman, B. Designing the User Interface, (Addison Wesley,Wokingham, 1986).

[3] Mullins, L.J. Management and Organisational Behaviour, (Pitman, London, 1985).

[4] Zuboff, S. In the Age of the Smart Machine, (Heinemann Professional, Oxford, 1988).

[5] Mulgen, G. The Power of the Weak. Marxism Today, December 1988, 24-31.

[6] Franz, C.R. and Robey, D. An Investigation of User-led System Design: Rational and Political Perspectives, Communications of the ACM (1984) 27.

[7] Carroll, J. The Adventure of Getting to Know a Computer, IEEE Computer 15 (1982), 49.

[8] Baudrillard, J., Selected Writings (ed Poster, M.), (Polity Press, Cambridge, 1988).

[9] Bourdieu, P. , Distinction: A Social Critique of the Judgement of Taste, (Routledge and Kegan Paul, London, 1984).

[10] Hebdige, D. , Hiding in the Light, (Comedia, London, 1988).

[11] Lorenz, C., The Design Dimension, (Basil Blackwell, Oxford, 1986).

[12] Polan, B. Defunct, The Guardian, December 16, 1989, 18-19.

[13] Arnheim, R. Visual Thinking, (Faber and Faber, London, 1970).

[14] Miller, S., Ends, Means and Galumphing: Some Leitmotifs of Play, American Anthropologist, 75, (1973) 87-98.

[15] Weick, K., The Social Psychology of Organizing, (Random House, New York, 1979).

[16] Kallinikos, J. Play in Organisations in: Jackson, M.C., Keys, P. and Cropper, S.A. (eds) Operational Research and the Social Sciences (Plenum Press, London, 1989).

[17] Carroll, J.M. & Rosson, M. B. Paradox of the Active User in: Carroll, J.M. (ed.), Interfacing Thought, (MIT Press, London, 1987).

[18] Giddens, A., New Rules of Sociological Method, (Hutchinson, London, 1976).

[19] Owen, W. Computers: toy or tool. Management Today, December 1988.

[20] Dvorak, J.C. The Last Men's Club. MacUser, August 1987.

[21] Lloyd, A & Newell, L. Women and Computers. in: Faulkner, W. & Arnold. Smothered by Invention: Technology in Women's Lives, (Pluto Press, London, 1985).

SECTION I: FOUNDATIONS

SI.2 Cognitive Ergonomics

GOMS meets the phone company: Analytic modeling applied to real-world problems
W.D. Gray, B.E. John, R. Stuart, D. Lawrence, and M.E. Atwood 29

The effects of task structure and social support on users' errors and error handling
M. Frese, F.C. Brodbeck, D. Zapf and J. Prümper 35

What kind of errors do Unix users make?
J.H. Bradford, W.D. Murray, and T.T. Carey 43

ECM: A scheme for analysing user-system errors
P.A. Booth 47

How learner characteristics can mediate the effects of giving conceptual details during training
E.J. Lloyd 55

Influencing behaviour via device representation; decreasing performance by increasing instruction
S.C. Duff and P.J. Barnard 61

Pop-up windows and memory for text
H.A. Stark 67

Two ways to fill a bath, with and without knowing it
A. Ankrah, D.M. Frohlich, and G.N. Gilbert 73

The cognitive dimension of viscosity: A sticky problem for HCI
T.R.G. Green 79

The role of games and cognitive models in the understanding of complex dynamic systems
R. Rivers 87

Implications of computer games for system design
L. Neal 93

A study of measures for research in hypertext navigation
D.G. Hendry, T.T. Carey, and S.T. TeWinkel 101

Mental effort and task performance: Towards a psychophysiology of human computer interaction
D. Wastell 107

Human–Computer Interaction – INTERACT '90
D. Diaper et al. (Editors)
Elsevier Science Publishers B.V. (North-Holland)

GOMS Meets the Phone Company: Analytic Modeling Applied to Real-World Problems

Wayne D. Gray[1], Bonnie E. John[2], Rory Stuart[1], Deborah Lawrence[1], & Michael E. Atwood[1]

[1]NYNEX Science & Technology Center, 500 Westchester Avenue, White Plains, NY 10604, USA.
[2]School of Computer Science, Carnegie Mellon University, Pittsburgh, PA 15113, USA.

GOMS analyses were used to interpret some perplexing data from a field evaluation of two telephone operator workstations. The new workstation is ergonomically superior to the old and is preferred by all who have used it. Despite these advantages telephone operators who use the new workstation are not faster than those who use the old but are, in fact, significantly slower. This bewildering result makes sense when seen with the aid of GOMS. With GOMS we can see that very few of the eliminated keystrokes or ergonomic advantages affect tasks that determine the operator's work time. Indeed, GOMS shows that some presumed procedural improvements have the contrary effect of increasing the time an operator spends handling a phone call. We conclude that if GOMS had been done early on, then the task, not the workstation, would have been redesigned.

1. INTRODUCTION

In the world of the phone companies, small differences in time per call can result in large savings of dollars. For example, NYNEX estimates that each second reduction per call in work time for its Toll & Assistance Operators (TAO) saves three million US dollars per year. With such an economy of scale, a newly introduced workstation that promised up to 2.5 seconds reduction in average operator work time (AWT) (or $7.5 million US per year) appeared very attractive[1]. However, the potential savings in yearly operating costs must be balanced against a capital cost of $10 to $15 thousand (US) per workstation. Since NYNEX has approximately 1,000 TAO workstations the initial investment in new technology is large and the cost of making a bad buying decision is great.

To evaluate the actual AWT saved by the new workstation with realistic call traffic, our group at the NYNEX Science & Technology Center helped to conduct a six-month field trial. Unfortunately, empirical trials are often long, expensive, and hard to control under real-world conditions. Analytic models, such as GOMS (Card, Moran, & Newell, 1983), have the potential to replace empirical trials but have not been validated with large-scale, complex systems. Therefore, in addition to the empirical component of this project, we have built GOMS models and are testing their predictions against the empirical results.

With its ergonomic enhancements, the new workstation was expected to improve (decrease) AWT. The new workstation had a 1200-baud, graphic display while the old workstation was a line and character-oriented 300-baud display. The new workstation eliminated many keystrokes and those that remained took place on a keyboard specifically designed for the TAO task. In contrast, the old keyboard had evolved through years of functional changes, adding new keys wherever space allowed.

As we framed it, the job was clear cut. We would collect data showing how much better the new workstation was than the old. Of special interest to the phone companies would be data showing for which call-types the new workstation had the greatest advantage and for which it had the least advantage. For the GOMS part we would compare the empirical data with GOMS models for accuracy, reliability, and cost (Gray, et al, 1989).

The empirical data surprised us. No matter how we looked at it, it showed that operators who used the old workstation to be faster than those who used the new workstation. To understand this unexpected result we turned to the GOMS analyses. These analyses show why the old workstation is faster than the new, and, most importantly, they indicate that it would be very difficult for any new workstation to be faster than the current one.

In this paper we provide an overview of the methodology of the study, the ***WHAT*** of the empirical data, and the ***WHY*** provided by GOMS. This is our first published report, more detailed reports will follow.

2. METHODOLOGY

2.1. Design

2.1.1. Task

The task of the TAO is to assist the customer in completing calls and recording the correct billing. Among others, TAOs handle person-to-person calls, collect calls, credit-card calls, and calls billed to a third number.

2.1.2. Office

The phone company office used in the study employs over 100 TAOs and handles traffic in the Boston, Massachusetts area. For purposes of the study, 12 existing workstations were removed and 12 new workstations installed.

2.1.3. Participants

All participants were NET employees who had worked as TAOs for a minimum of two years. Twenty-four participants were selected for the new workstations (the ***NEW*** condition) from a list of approximately 60 volunteers. Each new participant was paired with an ***OLD***, control participant matching for shift worked (that is, time of day), and AWT on the old workstation. The NEW condition was assigned a full-time manager from the management staff of the office.

2.1.4. Training

All NEW participants went through three days of training on the new workstation. The course was conducted on-site, by regular NET trainers. The course taught the techniques and procedures advocated by the manufacturer. The course itself was for ***conversion*** training, not new training; that is, it was intended for TAOs familiar with call handling and billing, who were simply being taught a new workstation. As such, it was very similar to other commonly taught conversion training courses .

2.1.5. Duration

The trial began in April 1989 and was originally scheduled to continue for six months. It was interrupted during the fifth month by a work stoppage (AKA strike) that affected all 60,000 NYNEX employees who belonged to a union. NEW and OLD participants worked their normal shifts during the trial. From the perspective of the NEW participants their tasks and duties as a TAO was identical to their pretrial job in all respects but one; namely, a new workstation was used. For the OLD participants nothing had changed.

2.2. Empirical Data Collection

In GOMS terminology, TAO performance is tracked at the level of the ***unit-task***, where a unit-task is one completed phone call (one completed customer request). For billing purposes, a database is maintained of every completed customer request handled by every operator in each office. Reports generated for each office randomly sample one out of every ten calls that pass through that office. We used this office database to extract data on the calls handled by our 24 NEW and 24 OLD participants.

In the database each completed call is classified as one out of over 250 call-types. Pretrial analysis showed that 19 call-types accounted for over 90% of all completed calls. Both the empirical and GOMS parts of this study included just these 19 most frequent call-types.

2.3. Data for GOMS

The GOMS analyses are based on previous human performance research and task specific information (John, 1990). The task specific information includes commonly used TAO training materials, observations of TAOs handling actual calls with the old workstation, pretrial AWT statistics, and videotapes of TAO handling staged calls with the old workstation. Staged calls, placed by a TAO supervisor and identified for the TAO, are a standard phone company practice used to debug new equipment or software; for this study, they were videotaped. Using these sources we can estimate the knowledge and procedures used by experienced TAOs, and produce estimates of system response times and customer conversation time. GOMS analyses for the new workstation are based only on manufacturer-supplied training materials and performance estimates from the old workstation. No observations or AWT data for the new workstations were used because our goal in using GOMS was to predict performance on the new workstation without empirical evidence.

3. WHAT: EMPIRICAL DATA

3.1. Pretrial

Pretrial matching of participants was based upon data collected by TAO managers at the phone company office. After the trial began we were able to use database information to check whether our two groups showed pretrial equivalence on this measure. The average difference between groups was small, 0.06 seconds, and insignificant, $F(1, 46) < 1$[2,3]. From this we conclude that our two groups, NEW and OLD, were equivalent on pretrial performance on the old workstation.

3.2. Trial

3.2.1. By Month

For the analysis by month we collapsed over call-type and chose the median time for each participant for each month. The data show that median work time (MWT) for the NEW group is 104% that of the OLD[4]; that is, the new workstation requires 4% more time on an average call than does the old workstation. This difference is significant. A two (group) by four (months) ANOVA (with months as a within subject variable) yields $F\ (1, 44) = 4.17$. The main effect of month is also significant, $F\ (3, 132) = 12.11$. This main effect reflects seasonal fluctuations in call-mix that affect MWT for both groups of TAOs.

More interesting, as shown by a non-significant interaction ($F\ (3, 132) = 1.39, p > 0.10$), between group differences in work time do not converge over the four month period. (From April through July work times for the NEW group are, respectively, 6%, 3%, 5%, and 4% higher than for the OLD.) This lack of an interaction suggests that the NEW participants master the new workstations very fast and reach asymptotic performance during the first month of the trial.

3.2.2. By Call-Type

For the analysis by call-type we collapsed over months and chose the median time for each participant on each of 18 call-types[5]. The two (group) by 18 (call-type) ANOVA (with call-type as a within subject variable) yielded a significant effect of group, $F\ (1, 46) = 5.92$, again indicating that the new workstation was slower than the old.

The main effect of call-type was also significant, $F\ (17, 782) = 101.27$, indicating that different call-types required different amounts of time to process. To our surprise, call-type did not interact with group, $F\ (17, 782) < 1$.

3.3. Summary of Empirical Results

Not only was the new workstation NOT faster than the old, but it was significantly slower. The approximate 4% difference translates to about a one second loss in MWT. Using the heuristic of $3 million (US) dollars per second per year, the 1 second difference would cost NYNEX $3 million per year.

Clearly something is wrong. How could an ergonomically engineered, modern workstation be slower than ergonomically indifferent, 5 year old technology?

The obvious answers seem to be wrong. First, the NEW participants were very motivated and very interested in "beating" their old work times. Managers reported that the NEW participants enjoyed the new workstations and actively tried to lower their work times. Second, although the study lasted for four rather than six months, all the data we have examined indicates that the NEW group had already reached asymptote and would not have improved their MWT with more practice. Indeed, preliminary analyses suggests that asymptotic performance was reached in the first week of the study.

4. WHY: GOMS

TAO's do several things in parallel when processing a customer's request: they listen to the customer, they perceive information on the CRT screen, they move their hands to appropriate keys and strike them. We represented this parallelism in a PERT chart, displaying all perceptual, cognitive, and motor operators (as boxes) and the dependencies between them (as lines connecting the boxes) according to goal decomposition and operator-placement heuristics (Card, et. al, 1983; John, 1990).

Figures 1 and 2 show the first and last segments of a GOMS analysis for one 15 second phone call. For each figure, the top chart represents the call using the new workstation while the bottom shows the GOMS analysis for the same call using the old workstation. For this report we make a virtue of necessity. A readable version of the full GOMS analysis would require more pages than this proceedings permits; also, a readable form would tend to draw the reader's attention to details which, while interesting in their own right, are tangential to this paper. The reduced version allows us to avoid such details while drawing attention to the overall pattern.

An important concept in analyzing the total task time for complex parallel tasks is "critical path". In project management, the critical path is "the sequence of tasks that determines the soonest the project can finish" (p. 6, CLARIS Corp, 1987); in GOMS analyses, it is the perceptual, cognitive, and motor operators that determine the total time for the task. For example, consider three partially overlapping activities: the TAO saying "New England Telephone, may I help you?", the TAO moving his/her right hand towards specific function keys, and the customer's saying "Operator, bill this to . . ." The TAO must perceive the customer's request before s/he can either press the appropriate key or make the appropriate verbal response, however, experienced TAOs can prepare for the most likely request in advance. In this case, the TAO moves towards likely function keys while still saying the greeting. Since saying the greeting takes longer than moving to the function keys, and customers typically wait for the operator to finish the greeting before they state their request, the movement toward the function keys is said to have "slack time" and is not on the critical path. This slack time is observed in the videotapes as the TAO hovering over some function keys waiting for the customer to give information that will dictate which key is to be pressed. In Figures 1 and 2, the critical path is shown as bold lines and boxes.

Figure 1 has two striking features. First, the analysis for the new (top) workstation has 10 fewer boxes than the analysis for the old (bottom) workstation, representing two fewer keystrokes. Second, none of the deleted boxes were on the critical path so the total task time for this portion of

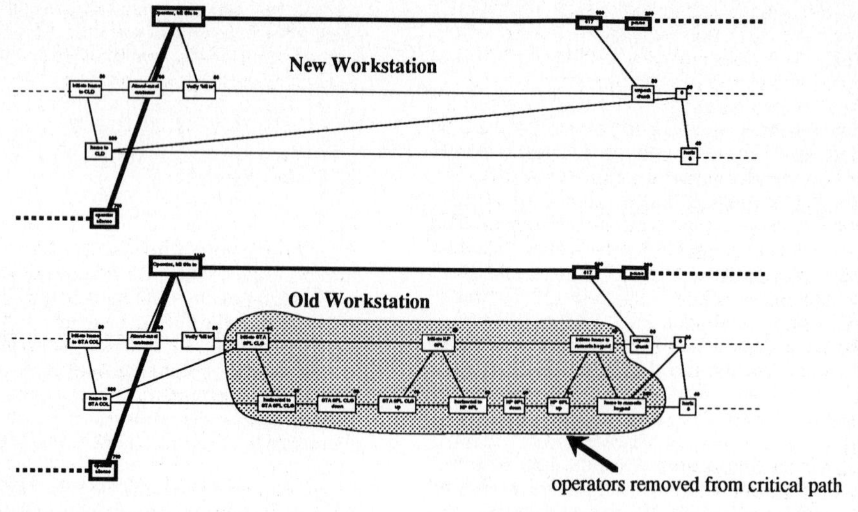

Figure 1. Section of GOMS analysis from near the beginning of the call. Notice that the new workstation (top) has removed two keystrokes (which had required 7 motor and 3 cognitive operators) from this part of the call. However, none of the ten operators removed were along the critical path (shown in bold). (Note: the print in the boxes is intentionally illegible.)

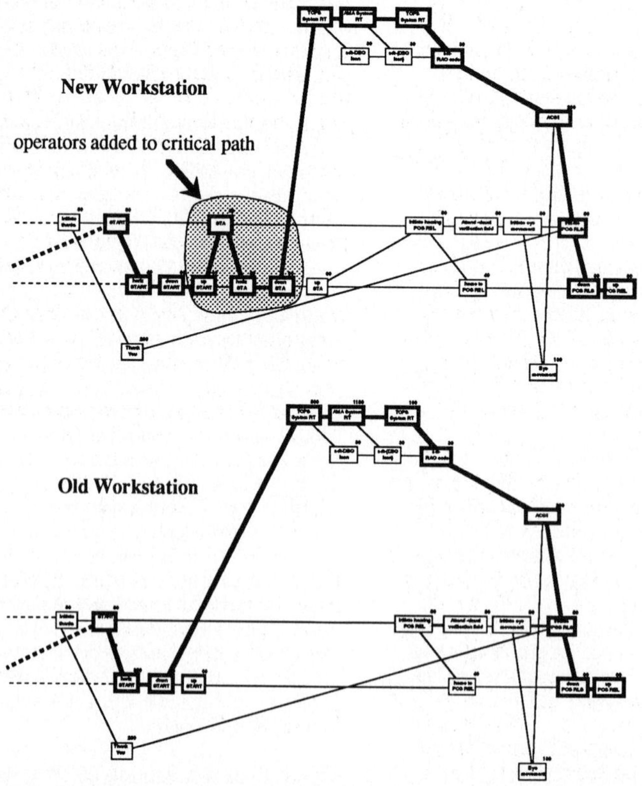

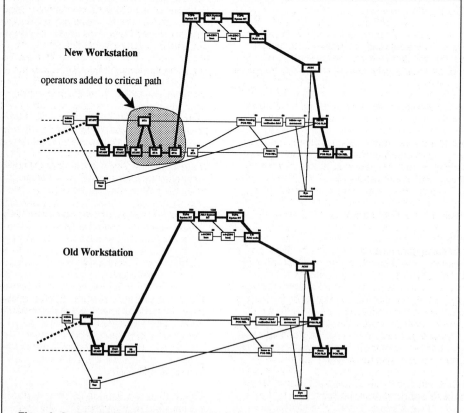

Figure 2. Section of GOMS analysis from the end of the call. Notice that the new workstation (top) has added one keystroke to this part of the call which results in four operators (three motor and one cognitive) being added to the critical path (shown in bold). (Note: the print in the boxes is intentionally illegible.)

the task would not change between workstations. At this point in the task the critical path is determined by the TAO greeting and getting information from the customer. Removing keystrokes here does nothing to affect the TAO's work time; that is, work time is controlled by the conversation, not by the keystrokes and not by the ergonomics of the keyboard.

The missing middle of the analysis (the activities between those shown in Figures 1 and 2) is identical for both workstations and essentially shows the critical path being driven by how fast the customer says the ten-digit number to which the call should be billed. TAOs are taught to "key along" with the customer. While a rapidly speaking customer could force the critical path to be determined by the TAO's keying speed, given that both workstations use the standard numeric keypad, the critical path (and resulting speed of keying in numbers) would be the same for both workstations.

If the new workstation simply eliminated the two keystrokes required by the old workstation in the beginning of the call, then GOMS would predict equivalent performance. However, for the new workstation, the procedure has been changed so that one of the keystrokes eliminated at the beginning of the call (Figure 1) now occurs later in the call (Figure 2). In this analysis, the keystroke moves from a position off of the critical path to one that is on the critical path. Hence, the cognitive and motor time required for this keystroke now adds to the time required to process this call. Thus, GOMS predicts that the AWT for this call would be slower for the new workstation than it would be for the old workstation. Indeed, the empirical data show that this call is 5% slower on the NEW than OLD workstation (a marginally significant difference, $F_{(1,46)} = 3.14$, $p < 0.10$).

This analysis also speaks to the unexpectedly fast learning curve found in the empirical data. On the old workstation, the critical paths for many call-types are dominated by TAO and customer conversation time, and system response time, with individual keystrokes having as much as several seconds of slack time. Previous research with expert typists suggests that at most, the duration of keystrokes would increase from approximately 100 msec to approximately 1000 msec for the least experienced, hunt-and-peck keying on an unfamiliar keyboard (John & Newell, 1989, Card, et. al., 1983). Thus, it is unlikely that initial difficulty with the new workstation would change the critical path to being dominated by keystrokes. Therefore, most of the learning would be off the critical path and thus unobservable in the MWT.

To date, we have performed GOMS analyses for five call-types. The above example is representative of what we are finding. Generally the new workstation removes keystrokes that are off the critical path. Most of these are eliminated while some are placed onto the critical path. Current analyses are very specific to protocols obtained from individual TAOs. It is our intention to generalize the analysis for each call-type to all TAOs and to then assess the goodness of fit against the empirical data.

5. CONCLUSION & SUMMARY

The new workstation is ergonomically superior to the old and is preferred by all who have used it. Despite these advantages TAOs who use the new workstation are not faster than those who use the old. Indeed, statistical analyses show that the NEW TAOs are significantly slower than the OLD.

This bewildering result makes sense when seen with the aid of GOMS. With GOMS we can see that very few of the eliminated keystrokes or ergonomic advantages affect tasks that are on the critical path of the example call. Indeed, GOMS shows that some of the procedural changes moved previously non-critical keystrokes onto the critical path. Such changes add to the predicted work time even when the net result is fewer keystrokes.

Although the GOMS analyses is ongoing, the emerging conclusion is that there is very little that could be done to a workstation itself that would decrease work time for TAOs. The factors most limiting performance are neither the display nor entry of information, but system response time (other than workstation time) and customer conversation time. Clearly, if GOMS had been done early on, then the task, not the workstation, would have been redesigned.

For the TAO job, GOMS can be used in one of two ways. First, based upon GOMS, we can redesign TAO procedures to reduce the number of bottlenecks along the critical path. Second, and longer term, we can use GOMS to redesign the task itself. With GOMS we can ask whether it is worth while to speed up a component of the system. For example, when calling cards are used, a database is accessed to verify the number. What affect would a 50% decrease in time for database access have on operator work time? (If waiting for verification is not on the critical path then a faster access time would not reduce work time.) As another example, we can ask whether some parts of the customer interaction might best be automated.

Our main conclusion concerns GOMS itself. GOMS is an important and valuable tool that can be applied to tasks other than text-editing or spreadsheets. While it will continue to be useful to academic researchers, the time is ripe to apply GOMS to complex, real-world tasks.

ACKNOWLEDGEMENTS

Thanks are due to Karen O'Brien for her sponsorship, support, and assistance throughout all stages of the trial. Thanks also to Sandy Esch.

FOOTNOTES

[1] Reductions in AWT is just one of the many features of the new workstation. Its other features are such as to make it attractive to NYNEX even if AWT remained constant.

[2]Note that all all comparisons, ANOVAs, and figures are based upon median work time (MWT).

[3]The level of significance chosen for this report is $p < .05$.

[4]Note that the absolute magnitude of work time of NYNEX TAOs is considered proprietary information. Therefore, here and in several other places in this report, we have made an attempt to accurately depict the relative results without compromising corporate information

[5]One of our call-types was chosen not because of its frequency but because of interest in the procedure required to process it. Because many of our participants had such low numbers of recorded calls of this type (< 16) we excluded it from the current analysis.

REFERENCES

Card, S. K., Moran, T. P., & Newell, A. (1983). ***The psychology of human-computer interaction.*** Hillsdale, NJ: Erlbaum.

CLARIS Corporation (1987). ***MacProject II Manual.*** Mountain View, CA: CLARIS Corporation.

Gray, W. D., John, B. E., Lawrence, D., Stuart, R., & Atwood, M. E. (1989). ***GOMS meets the phone company, or, can 8,400,000 unit-tasks be wrong?*** Poster presented at CHI '89 (Austin, Texas, April 30-May 4).

John, B. E. (1990). Extensions of GOMS analyses to expert performance requiring perception of dynamic visual and auditory information. In the ***Proceedings of CHI, 1990*** (Seattle, WA, April 1-5). New York, ACM.

John, B. E., & Newell, A. (1989). Cumulating the science of HCI: From S-R compatibility to transcription typing. In ***Proceedings of CHI, 1989*** (Austin, Texas, April 30-May 4 1989). New York: ACM, pp. 109-114.

Human–Computer Interaction – INTERACT '90
D. Diaper et al. (Editors)
Elsevier Science Publishers B.V. (North-Holland)

THE EFFECTS OF TASK STRUCTURE AND SOCIAL SUPPORT ON USERS' ERRORS AND ERROR HANDLING

Michael Frese, Felix C. Brodbeck, Dieter Zapf & Jochen Prümper

Dept. of Psychology, University of Munich, Leopoldstr. 13,
D- 8000 München 40, Federal Republic of Germany
Electronic mail address of Michael Frese:ub121ai at dm0lrz01.Bitnet
Tel.: 89/33 19 82

Abstract:The relationship of four organizational variables - job complexity, job discretion, social climate, and the organization of the computer advisory service - with number and type of errors and use of support facilities was studied in a field observational study. 198 subjects from 12 different public and private companies in the southern part of the Federal Republic of Germany (secretaries, typists, specialists, low level managers) were observed for 2 hours while they used computers during their work. They also filled out a questionnaire (N=232). There were a number of small but significant and practically important relationships, e.g. errors pertaining to conscious strategies happened more often in more complex jobs. Perceived support by supervisors and co-workers was related to whether these people were asked in case of an error. Decentralized advisory services were preferred and used more often by users than centralized services.

1.Introduction

User errors play a prominent role in the literature on human-computer interaction (e.g., Card, Moran & Newell, 1983; Lewis & Norman, 1986; Shneiderman, 1987). This is not surprising. Errors have been used to establish bench-mark tests for systems (Roberts & Moran, 1983). Errors are stressful and because of errors people sometimes give up using computers. Moreover, errors are economically costly; errors usually take more time to correct than it does to work slowly.

Although errors have a prominent place in the field of human-computer interaction, errors are usually not observed at the work place but in the laboratory. While laboratory studies are very useful, larger impact factors like organizational variables cannot be observed. Therefore, the results are often taken to mean that only the human factors area is important without reference to the larger organizational setting. In our study, we have observed users in their usual work situation with office software. Organizations have an impact on particular work settings by determining the concrete task structure and the social climate. Therefore, these two sets of variables and their relationship with how users deal with errors were studied.

The influence of task structure variables and social support is interesting for theoretical and practical reasons (cf. Frese, Ulich & Dzida, 1987 for an overview on this issue). Theoretically, it is interesting to know whether or not high level organizational variables can have an impact on low level errors and error handling. Practically, show-ing some kind of correlation means that an exclusive concern with the human factors side is not sufficient to reduce errors or error handling time but that the role of organizational variables has to be taken seriously as well.

Traditionally, the two most important task structure variables have been (1) job complexity and (2) job discretion (or control at work). The two social climate factors studied here were (3) social support by supervisors and co-workers. An additional organizational factor important for our field is (4) the organization of the computer advisory service because it influences error handling.

1) *Job complexity*: The organization of work determines which tasks have to be done by each individual worker. The complexity of each particular work task influences which errors appear and how they are dealt with. For example, jobs with highly complex tasks may show more errors (at least errors involving the more complex tasks).

2) *Job discretion*: A high level of job discretion implies that the workers can decide many issues at work, e.g. the timing, sequencing and the content of plans and goals at work (Frese, 1987). Does the discretion level at the work place have an impact on errors and error handling? The discretion level has been shown to reduce stress at work (Karasek, 1979; Semmer & Frese, 1989) and to increase the transfer of computer skills from training to work (v. Papstein & Frese, 1988). Similarly, it might also increase certain errors and decrease the emotional impact of errors. While there are similarities between job complexity and job discretion - and usually high correlations - there are important conceptual and empirical differences (cf. Frese, 1987).

3) *Social climate*: The social climate at work may have an impact on error handling. Aspects of the social climate are social support by supervisors and by co-workers. Social support implies that the supervisor or the co-worker will listen to problems appearing at work, will

give emotional support as well as actual help in dealing with these problems. This may also affect a person's behavior in an error situation. Users who feel that their supervisors support them, will be more likely to ask them for help once they are in an error situation. Similarly, users who feel that their co-workers support them, are also hypothesized to ask co-workers more often in case of an error.

4) *Organization of the computer advisory service*: Most larger organization provide some direct support for error handling. Many organizations have a centrally localized computer advisory service. Other organizations have developed a more local decentralized service with local experts (Dutke & Schönpflug, 1987; Scharer, 1983). We hypothesize that the computer advisory service is more often used when it is decentralized because local experts know more about the users' tasks and are more quickly available (less psychological distance).

Error handling is actually quite a complicated concept embracing many variables. There is no error handling without error detection. After error detection, the error has to be localized. Localization may sometimes result from being able to explain the error. The explanation of the error may facilitate error recovery. Error recovery may take different forms, direct corrections like backward operations (e.g. using the backspace key) or repetition of an action (e.g. rewriting a lost letter) or compensatory actions like using a set of procedures to resurrect a file that was erased.

Actually, all of these different parts of the error handling process are intermingled and it is not necessary that each step has to be done. Sometimes an error is recovered without explanation, sometimes localization is not necessary (e.g. when the system has an UNDO key), sometimes explanation is achieved while the error is localized or recovered, etc.

Additionally, users may react with emotional upset for having made an error, (actually, the emotional upset may develop at any point of the error handling process, e.g. when it turns out to be difficult to diagnose the error).

Not all of these concepts can be differentially observed in a field study of work behavior. Therefore, we shall concentrate on the following aspects of error handling:
- How many errors does a user make (number of errors)?
- How long does it take to handle the error (error handling time)? This is the time after an error is discovered up to the time the user finishes error recovery.
- How much outside support is needed for error handling, e.g. by co-workers, by supervisor, calling up the help system, asking the computer advisory service, etc.? How useful are the support functions judged to be?
- How many negative emotional reactions does the user show, once he or she gets into an error situation?

Organizational variables do not affect all kinds of errors in the same way. We have developed an error taxonomy based on some theories of errors and inefficiencies (Norman, 1981; Semmer & Frese, 1985; Rasmussen, 1987; Reason, 1987) and have shown its usefulness and its construct validation (Zapf, Brodbeck, Frese, Peters & Prümper, 1990). For reasons of space, the whole error taxonomy cannot be presented here. It may suffice to say that organizational issues should have a higher impact on those errors that arise in the conscious and problem oriented approach to a task in which controlled processes and conscious attention dominate, than in more routinized and automatized actions. The most important errors that pertain to the conscious approach are: knowledge errors that appear if the user does not know how to deal with a certain task; thought errors that happen, when the steps for dealing with a task are not planned out well; memory errors, when some part of a conscious plan is forgotten; and judgment errors when the feedback of a system could not be interpreted correctly. The last three - thought, memory, and judgment errors are part of the intellectual level of regulation of action (the concept of different levels of regulation is described in Hacker, 1986 and in Semmer & Frese, 1985, a similar concept is used by Rasmussen, 1987). This means that the problem is consciously and deliberatively tackled. In contrast to the intellectual level of regulation, the lower levels of regulation imply that the actions are routine and need only minimal conscious attention.
Up to this point, only usability problems were described which are a result of a mismatch between the user and the system (Zapf, Brodbeck & Prümper, 1989). There is also a second class - functionality problems - which appear when there is a mismatch between the task and the computer system. The mismatch concept is important in that it suggests that errors can never be blamed on either the system or the human but that errors arise when a mismatch occurs (Rasmussen, 1987). This mismatch may occur between the user and the system (usability problems) or between the system and the task requirements (functionality).

In general, we do not expect the hypothesized relationships between organizational variables and error handling to be very large. This is so because a task structure variable such as complexity does not directly translate into more errors or longer handling time. Rather, there are many intermediate steps: Complexity of the work task implies that one does not only deal with one particular problem area alone but with a wide range of tasks. Each task implies that a different set of commands has to be used. None of these tasks (and commands) will be completely routine because many different tasks have to be done. Therefore, there are more errors on the intellectual level of regulation. These errors are more complex to deal with and therefore demand a longer handling time. Similarly, social support by co-workers should not directly translate into asking co-workers for help in an error situation. First, the co-workers may not know enough about the user's problem. Second, the user may appreciate the emotional support of his or her co-workers but does not necessarily want to ask them for help in a problem with the computer. Third, the co-workers who the user relies on for support may not be readily available for questions when he or she works with the computer. Thus, all the correlations will be low. This does not mean that they will be unimportant. In different areas it was shown that even small correlations translate into important practical effects (Frese, 1985; Funder & Ozer, 1983; Ozer, 1985).

2. METHODS

2.1 Subjects

We observed and gave questionnaires to 259 office workers using computers from 12 different public and private companies in the southern part of the Federal Republic of Germany. The mean age was 31.1 years, 73% were women. They worked as secretaries, typists, specialists and in lower level management. Not all subjects could be observed (N=198). In all, 174 subjects were both observed and responded to the questionnaire. (Details on the sample are given in Zapf et al., 1990). There is an additional reduction of the N in the analyses since a few subjects did not make certain kinds of errors (e.g. no intellectual level errors) and were, therefore, not included.

2.2 Methods

Before observing the subjects, a short job analysis was done to describe the tasks which were performed at the observed work place. This was also necessary for the observers to receive an overview of the tasks they were to observe. Since errors are always defined by the goal, the knowledge of the task structure helped the observers to determine what goals the subjects were trying to achieve. In a second step the subjects were observed doing their normal work with the computer. In some cases, people also did a lot of non-computer tasks. Here it was necessary to ask them to do their computer tasks during the observation period. Since we did not want to make the work situation unrealistic for them, they were also asked to perform their non-computer tasks if this was part of their usual working procedure. The observation period lasted for two hours. The observers had two different protocol sheets. One protocol kept a record on the type of computer task on which the subjects worked on and the amount of time required. This protocol was also used to record all interruptions, either by another person or a telephone. A second protocol was kept for all errors, and the subsequent recovery actions. Here, the observers gave a written prose description of each error. They also responded to a standardized questionnaire on how the subjects handled each error, whether they worked systematically or not; whether they used a manual, help system or asked a colleague; and, what amount of time was needed for error handling.

Observations of number of errors, error handling time, outside support, and negative emotional reactions: The errors were immediately classified in a taxonomy (more on its reliability and validity in Zapf et al., 1990). To increase the validity, only those errors were included in this analysis which could be re-rated consistently by two raters (N=1306). In this article, we are concerned mainly with errors on the intellectual level of regulation. The observers also noted how long it took to handle the error. Due to some regulations in the German industry, we could not use stopwatches to record error handling time; instead the observers made rough time estimates (these estimates were reliable, with a Spearman correlation of .68 for two observers, observing the same subjects). For expository purposes, these estimates were then transformed into a real time scale (the chi^2 tables are difficult to interpret - there are no differences between the correlational treatment used in this article and chi^2). Additionally, it was observed whether or not the subjects required the use of some outside support (using help texts, asking coworkers or supervisors, looking into manuals, asking the computer advisory service and asking others outside the company). The nature of the observation had some impact on the use of supports, e.g. the users tended not to ask the supervisor any questions while we observed, they probably called up the advisory service less often or did not leave their work place to ask a coworkers as often as they might have done otherwise. We, therefore, had the subjects rate the frequency of their use of external support. Additionally, working through an error without external help was included in this list. These external supports were also ranked on two dimensions, preference ("Whenever you encounter a problem or an error which have difficulties to deal with it, which of the following possibilities do you employ first, second, third etc.") and usefulness of information ("Whenever you encounter a problem or an error which you have difficulties to deal with it, which of the following possibilities do you expect to be the best, second best, third best etc. support").

The observers also gave a rough estimate, whether the subjects reacted with anxiety, frustration and anger to errors.

Complexity at work and job discretion were also observed. In another study, the validity and reliability of these variables was shown (Semmer, 1984; Zapf, 1989).

Social support by supervisors and by co-workers is very difficult to observe and they were, therefore, ascertained by a questionnaire. The social support variables have been shown to have good reliability and validity (Frese, 1989).

3. RESULTS AND DISCUSSION

Observed complexity of work was significantly related to the number of errors on the intellectual level of regulation ($r=.22$, $N=176$, $p<.01$), to error handling time for all errors ($r=.17$, $N=168$, $p<.05$) and to a lack of emotional reaction ($r=-.20$, $N=177$, $p<.01$). This is in line with our hypothesis that more complex tasks will lead to more complex errors. Since there are fewer routine actions in a complex job, each error takes longer to correct. On the other hand, errors are less upsetting, probably because jobs of higher complexity usually allow a more leisurely work style than highly supervised non-complex jobs.

Observed job discretion showed similar correlations: $r=.14$ ($N=178$, $p<.05$) with the number of errors on the intellectual level of regulation, $r=.28$ ($N=169$, $p<.01$) with the error handling time, and $r=-.16$ ($N=177$, $p<.05$) with negative emotionality with regard to making errors.

Job discretion and complexity of work tasks are highly correlated as well ($r=.72$, $N=203$, $p<.01$) because more complex jobs usually also allow more leeway in how the job is done.

The social climate at work - social support by supervisors and co-workers - was weakly but significantly related to whether or not supervisors or co-workers were asked for help in an error situation. Social support by co-workers correlated r=.15 (N=222, p<.05) with the frequency of asking co-workers (questionnaire version) and social support by supervisor r=.17 (N=219, p<.01) with the frequency of asking supervisors. Thus, organizational variables can translate into asking for help in a very specific error situation.

The general data on the use of supports are presented in Tables 1 and 2. Table 1 presents the observed and the reported frequencies of supports (reliance on self was always included in addition). Both frequencies showed quite a similar picture. In both cases, co-workers were relied on most often. Co-workers were asked in 60 of 118 cases in which the subjects required any kind of help (sometimes more than one support was used for handling one error; therefore there were 139 uses of support for handling 118 errors). The second most frequently used support was observed to be calls on help texts and exploration of menus. The subjects did not think that they were doing this as often as it was observed. However, the observers also included explorations of menus in this category; thus differences between subjects and observers were to be expected.

Table 1:

Frequency of Use of Supports (Questionnaire and Observations)

	Means (Questionnaire)	Absolute Frequency (Observations)
Without external help	3.68 **	--
Asking a co-worker	3.09 **	60
Looking up in user manual	2.05 ns	15
Use of help/menu facilities	1.93 *	45
Asking user advisory services	1.75 ns	19
Asking superordinates	1.70 **	--
Asking other outside the company	1.11	--

Friedmans
Chi^2 511.833,n=214
$p < 0.01$, df = 6

Chi-Square test
Chi^2 = 25,68,n=198
$p < 0.01$, df = 3

Paired t-test for dependent samples
** $p < 0.01$
* $p < 0.05$

Table 2:

Mean Rank Orders for Supports with Regard to Preference and Usability (Questionnaire)

Preference	Usability
1.Asking a co-worker ns	1.Asking a co-worker ns
1.Without external help ns	2.Use of help/menu facilities ns
1.Use of help/menu facilities ***	2.Asking computer advisory service **
4.Looking up in user manual ***	4.Looking up in user manual **
5.Asking computer advisory service ***	4.Without external help ***
6.Asking superordinate ***	6.Asking superordinate ***
7.Asking others outside the company	7.Asking others outside the company

Friedmans
Chi^2 386.358, n = 133
$p < 0.01$, df = 6

Friedmans
Chi^2 425.252, n = 198
$p < 0.01$, df = 6

Wilcoxons test for single differences
*** $p < 0.01$
** $p < 0.05$

Surprisingly, users thought that they used the manual more often than we observed them doing it. One possible interpretation is that users have great difficulties with manuals and hence still vividly remember how they used the manual. Thus, recall is better and the number of manual use is overrated. Another possible interpretation is that during observation subjects did not want to use the handbooks because they knew that they would have difficulties using them (correspondingly, preference for them is not very high). We did not observe asking supervisors or people outside work.
Table 2 gives an overview on two questions in the questionnaire: How much do you prefer a certain support to solve an error situation and how good is the quality of the information that you receive from these sources of support. All patterns are significant ($p < 0.01$). This Table corroborates the findings reported in Table 1. Asking a

co-worker is preferred most often (even preferred to just solving the problem on one's own). Co-workers usually know the task best (e.g. in contrast to a centralized computer advisory center) and they are readily available. As one would suppose, getting along without any external help is most often done and it is also highly preferred. But it is considered not to be the most appropriate possibility to gather information for error coping (ranking on 4th place, Table 2).

Whether or not a supervisor is asked may also depend on how much a user feels to be supported by the supervisor. The Spearman correlations showed that the more social support was given by the superordinate the higher was the ranking of preference of asking the supervisor (r=.25, N=199, p<0.01) and the usefulness (r=.28, N=217, p<0.01). A similar tendency appeared for social supportiveness of co-workers with preference for using co-workers (r=.16, N=222, p<0.01). However, there was no significant relation with respect to usefulness.

The final point of our discussion was a comparison of *centralized versus decentralized computer advisory services*. The computer advisory services were not used very often (Table 1). However, the computer advisory service was actually considered to be an informative support facility (ranking 2 on usefulness), but it was considered significantly less helpful than consulting a co-worker. Why is this so? Qualitative analysis of the interview data showed that the computer advisory service was often centrally organized, technically oriented, not task oriented and it was highly overloaded.

In an additional analysis the subjects were grouped according to whether the advisory service of their department was decentrally or centrally organized. The hypothesis was that those people with a decentralized advisory system would use them more frequently and find them more useful. The average ranking of advisory services differed significantly (Kruskal-Wallis one-way ANOVA). Decentralized advisory services were used more frequently (chi^2=12.5, p<0.01, n=129) and they were ranked higher in preference (chi^2=9.3, p<0.01, n=116) and in the quality of information (chi^2=15.1, p<0.01, n=130) than centralized advisory services.

These data speak for the usefulness of the local experts (Dutke & Schönpflug, 1987; Lang, Auld & Lang, 1982; Scharer, 1983). Local experts combine the advantage of being co-workers with high expertise; they know the tasks and the computer program and can integrate task knowledge with computer knowledge; additionally, they are readily available.

4. OVERALL DISCUSSION

In summary, task structure variables showed significant correlations with number of errors and error handling time. The most important findings concern organizational issues and the use of supports once an error appeared. Social support by co-workers and supervisors influenced who was asked in an error situation. This influence showed up for preferences and the usefulness of the support as well. Finally, it made a difference whether the advisory services of a company were organized centrally or in a decentralized manner. The decentralized computer service was strongly preferred. The results speak for the concept of local experts rather than for a more central advisory system. Although the centralized systems often employ the more knowledgeable experts, they do not know the users' tasks and they are not available enough.

Figure 1: Complexity at work and errors on the intellectual level of regulation

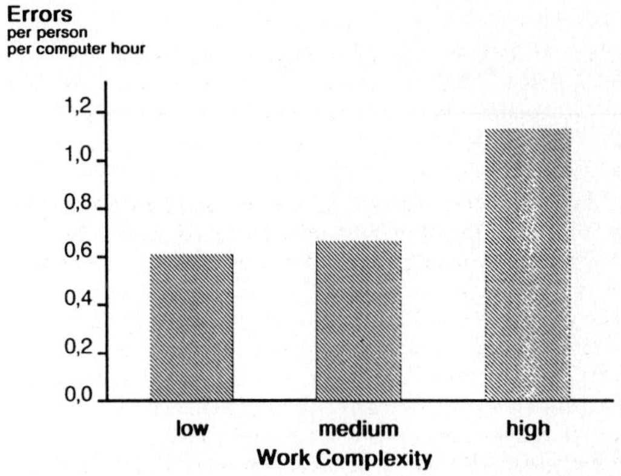

The correlations are by and large small. In so far, this study is suggestive only. However, even small correlations are of practical importance. Figure 1 translates the correlation of .22 between job complexity and number of errors into a different picture; the mean number of errors was calculated for three levels of complexity. It shows that for high complexity mean number of errors is nearly double as high as for low and medium complexity (Scheffé p<0.05) - this is clearly an effect size that is important for practical purposes. Furthermore, the data are largely based on observations in an ecologically valid work setting, using computers in normal day to day work.

The data cannot be interpreted causally. While it is unlikely that number of errors and error handling influenced job complexity, job discretion, and social support, it is possible that third variables may have brought forth job complexity and longer error handling times, etc. Nevertheless, the correlational evidence should be taken to mean that there is a relationship between organizational variables and errors.

Although, they were all ascertained by the observers, we are quite confident that the measures on the number of and handling time for errors were not confounded with the measures of job complexity and job discretion. The observers were not aware of this particular hypothesis and a confounding would presuppose that the observers made a count of the errors depending upon the intellectual level of regulation or not (the observers rated each error individually and after the observation answered a set of questions with regard complexity and job discretion).

Note that the errors reported in this study did not directly refer to organizational issues. Actually, we also observed a few additional organizational errors, which we called interaction problems. 2.1% of all errors (n=28) were interaction problems. They included, for example, errors using a computer tool that had been changed by another person without indication that this was done. A second example: a user could not start working because the commonly used password of the shared work-station was changed by his co-worker without leaving any message.

Finally, the system manager changed an array of system defaults but the users were not informed properly. Thus, interaction problems directly imply that an implicit or explicit organizational rule was violated or an organizational rule had not be drawn to fit the case.

The data suggest that it is useful to enlarge the picture of software ergonomics to include organizational variables. The human-computer dialogue is clearly also a determinant of the errors and error handling (Peters, Frese & Zapf, 1989) but it may not be the only important factor. The influence of organizational variables on the daily activities with the computers has been underresearched and is usually only paid lip service to. It is necessary to develop a comprehensive concept of how organizational variables enter into each action dealing with the computer and which mechanisms are responsible.

REFERENCES

Card, S. K., Moran, T. P., & Newell, A. (1983). The Psychology of human-computer interaction. Hillsdale, N.J.: Erlbaum.

Dutke, S., & Schönpflug, W. (1987). When the introductory period is over: learning while doing one's job. In M. Frese, E. Ulich, & W. Dzida (Eds.), Psychological issues of human- computer interaction at the work place (pp. 295 - 310). Amsterdam: North-Holland.

Frese, M. (1985). Stress at work and psychosomatic complaints: A causal interpretation. Journal of Applied Psychology,70, 314 - 328.

Frese, M. (1987). A theory of control and complexity: Implications for software design and integration of computer system into the work place. In M. Frese, E. Ulich, & W. Dzida (Eds.), Psychological issues of human-computer interaction at the work place (pp. 313 - 337). Amsterdam: North-Holland.

Frese, M. (1989). Soziale Unterstützung: Gütekriterien der Operationalisierung. Zeitschrift für Arbeitswissenschaft,43, 112 - 121.

Frese, M., Ulich, E., & Dzida, W. (Eds.) (1987). Psychological issues of human computer interaction at the work place. Amsterdam: North-Holland.

Funder, D. C., & Ozer, D. J. (1983). Behavior as a function of the situation. Journal of Personality and Social Psychology,44, 107 - 112.

Hacker, W. (1986). Arbeitspsychologie. Bern: Huber.

Karasek, R. A. (1979). Job demands, job decision latitude, and mental strain: Implications for job redesign. Administrative Science Quarterly,24, 285 - 311.

Lang, K., Auld, R., & Lang, T. (1982). The goals and methods of computer users. International Journal Man - Machine Studies,17, 375 - 399.

Lewis, C., & Norman, D. A. (1986). Designing for error. In D. A. Norman & S. W. Draper (Eds.), User centered system design (pp. 411 - 432). Hillsdale: Erlbaum.

Norman, D. A. (1981). Categorization of action slips. Psychological Review,88, 1 - 15.

Ozer, D. J. (1985). Correlation and the coefficient of determination. Psychological Bulletin,97, 307 - 315.

Papstein, P. v., & Frese, M. (1988). Transferring skills from training to the actual work situation:The role of task application knowledge, action styles and job decision latitude. In E. Soloway, D. Frye, & S. B. Sheppard (Eds.), CHI'88 Conference Proceedings. Human Factors in Computing Systems. Special Ussue of SIGHI Bulletin (pp. 55 - 60). Washington: Association for Computing Machinery.

Peters, H, Frese, M. & Zapf, D. (1989). Funktions- und Nutzungsprobleme bei unterschiedlichen Dialogformen. University of Munich: Manuscript.

Rasmussen, J. (1987). Cognitive control and human error mechanisms. In K. Rasmussen, J. Duncan, & J. Leplat (Eds.), New technology and human error (pp. 59 - 61). London: Wiley.

Reason, J. (1987). A framework of classifying errors. In J. Rasmussen, K. Duncan, & J. Leplat (Eds.), New technology and human errors (pp. 9 - 14) London: Wiley.

Roberts, T. L., & Moran, T. P. (1983). The evaluation of text editors: Methodology and empirical results. Communications of the ACM,26, 265-283.

Scharer, L. L. (1983). User training: Less is more. Datamation,29, 175-182.

Semmer, N. (1984). Streßbezogene Tätigkeitsanalyse: Psychologische Untersuchungen zur Analyse von Streß am Arbeitsplatz. Weinheim: Beltz.

Semmer, N., & Frese, M. (1985). Action theory in clinical psychology. In M. Frese & J. Sabini (Eds.), Goal directed behavior: The concept of action in psychology (pp. 296 - 310). Hillsdale, N.J.: Erlbaum.

Semmer, N., & Frese, M. (1989). Control at work as a moderator of the effect of stress at work on psychosomatic complaints: A longitudinal study with objective measurements. Bern and München: Manuscript.

Shneiderman, B. (1987). Designing the user interface: Strategies for effective human-computer interaction. Reading, Mass.: Addison-Wesley.

Zapf, D. (1989). Selbst- und Fremdbeobachtung in der psychologischen Arbeitsanalyse. Göttingen: Hogrefe.

Zapf, D., Brodbeck, F.C., Frese, M., Peters, H., & Prümper, J. (1990). Errors in working with office computers. A first validation of a taxonomy for observed errors in a field setting.University of Munich:Manuscript.

Zapf, D., Brodbeck, F.C., & Prümper, J. (1989). Handlungsorientierte Fehlertaxonomie in der Mensch-Computer Interaktion:Theoretische Überlegungen und eine erste Überprüfung im Rahmen einer Expertenbefragung. Zeitschrift für Arbeits- und Organisationspsychologie,33, 178 - 187.

Human–Computer Interaction – INTERACT '90
D. Diaper et al. (Editors)
Elsevier Science Publishers B.V. (North-Holland)

What Kind of Errors Do Unix Users Make?*

James H. Bradford, William D. Murray, and T.T. Carey+

Department of Computer Science
Brock University,
St. Catharines, Ontario, L2S 3A1
Canada

ABSTRACT. This paper describes a large scale analysis of user error in the Unix environment. Over 300,000 commands were logged containing approximately 16,000 errors. The errors detected included various kinds of token entry problems, mode errors, keyboard errors and grammatical mistakes. The relative frequency of each type is presented. The paper concludes with a discussion of a number of improvements that could be made to the Unix csh command interface.

1. BACKGROUND

This study grew out of our research into user error correction. In particular we are in the process of developing an integrated strategy for handling both syntax and spelling errors in user input [Murray (1990)]. An analysis of an extensive log of user interactions with a Berkeley 4.2 Unix csh command language interpreter was done. The data was collected by Saul Greenberg [Greenberg (1988)] while working at the University of Calgary. The interactions were logged over a four month period and involved 168 users of various levels of computer experience. The result was an 21 Megabyte file containing a record of 303,628 individual commands.

1.1. Sources of Error

There is an extensive literature on spelling correction [Damerau (1964), Peterson (1980)] that shows the most common spelling errors are: insertion of an extra character, deletion of a character, substitution of one character for another and transposition of pairs of characters. Based on the spelling of the word, "table" examples of the four most common errors are shown below:

Insertion: taable	Deletion: tabe
Substitution: tible	Transposition: talbe

Most spelling mistakes involve single errors although multiple errors do account for a noticeable fraction of all mistakes. If an error is made in two different tokens in the same command, we record this as two single errors rather than as a multiple error. The decision to use tokens rather than commands as the unit of context for counting errors is based in part on tradition (most other research on user error also treats errors this way) and in part on our desire to formulate a correction strategy that integrates spelling correction with grammar correction. In this case, tokens represent the natural working level for both grammar and spelling.

A special class of error is the separator error. This occurs when the blank that normally separates two tokens of a command is omitted. The new token formed by the merging of two legitimate tokens is usually unrecognizable and therefore classed as an error. Separator errors can, of course, be combined with other forms of error to produce combination errors.

From the point of view of error correction, it is easier to handle errors in command keywords than it is to handle errors in command arguments (such as file names). This is because the keywords are known in advance, whereas arguments are essentially free form. As a consequence, our study also measures the relative frequency of errors in command keywords and in command arguments.

At the grammatical level the errors of token insertion, deletion, substitution, and transposition were measured. At the grammatical level, additional sources of error were noted that could not easily be captured by our automated data collection routines. For example, a significant amount of error seemed to arise because the user was in the wrong context for the given command. We call these "mode errors," and they will be discussed more fully in section three.

1.2. Our Data Gathering Approach

The data contained thousands of commands that produced error messages. In some cases the user made multiple attempts to correct the error and in others the attempt to correct the error was abandoned and the user proceeded with other commands. Since the amount of the data to be analysed was very large, we needed to develop software that would extract the command lines containing errors and somehow identify the intended command. Our approach was to collect commands containing errors that were followed immediately by a correct command. This process yielded the almost 16,000 command lines containing errors that formed the basis of our study.

---

* This research was supported by the Natural Sciences and Engineering Research Council of Canada grant OGPIN007.

+ Department of Computing and Information Science, University of Guelph, Guelph, Ontario, Canada N1G 2W1

The csh command processor provides a number of special features which allow users to customize their interaction. Thus, part of the data contained special character sequences that caused the command processor to perform aliasing, string substitution, command expansion, file name substitution, and a number of other pre-processing operations. In addition, users could enter and modify commands through the use of a history mechanism. Since we were interested in the frequency of spelling and grammatical errors, we needed to study commands for which the spelling and grammar was known. Thus, to proceed with our data analysis we filtered out these non-standard interactions. This left a total of 6,112 standard UNIX commands that contained one or more errors, and it was these commands that formed the basis of our study.

2. RESULTS

Of the total of 6,112 command lines containing errors, 1,831 of these were typographical errors committed during the entry of one or more tokens, 528 of these were errors in the syntax of the command and 3,753 were errors due to other causes. It is clear that a significant portion of the errors were neither typographical nor syntactic. Rather, these represented problems such as "mode errors" in which the user entered a technically correct command in the wrong context. This will be discussed in more detail in section 3.

The 1,831 errors in token entry were analysed in three categories: commands containing a single token entry error, commands containing multiple errors in a single token and commands containing errors in several tokens. It is important to remark that the ease with which these kinds error can be corrected depends heavily on what kind of token contains the error. Errors in command keywords are relatively easy to correct because the correct word is known. Errors in file names are difficult to correct because they are essentially free form (the possibility of computing lists of file names to be used as candidates for correction will be discussed in section 3). Errors in tokens expressing command options (e.g. the "-c" in "cc -c chrec.c") were somewhat more difficult to evaluate since the composition of such option strings is quite variable.

The single token errors could be any one of the four kinds mentioned in section 1 (insertion, deletion, substitution or transposition). Of the 1,494 single token errors, 601 (40 %) involved the insertion of an extra character, 392 (26 %) involved the deletion of a required character, 340 (23 %) involved substituting an invalid character for a valid one, and 161 (11 %) involved the transposition of two characters. The following table shows the relative frequency of each kind of error.

Error Type	Frequency	% of Total
Insertion	601	40 %
Deletion	392	26 %
Substitution	340	23 %
Transposition	161	11 %
Total	1,494	100 %

Table 1 - Single Token Error Distribution

The instance of multiple errors in tokens represented only 307 of the 1,831 token errors (17 %). Like single token errors, multiple token errors can be recovered through the use of standard string similarity measures [Wagner (1974), Bradford (1987a)]. However, in command languages such as UNIX, commands and keywords tend to be short. Multiple errors may transform keywords to an extent where they are unrecognizable. This has been studied in more detail in some of our earlier work [Bradford (1987b)].

In a few cases, users made errors in more than one token in a given command. Such errors were present in only 30 commands (2 % of the sample). Concurrent errors in more than one token do not present any particular problem from the point of view of correction.

To detect and correct UNIX command language errors it is particularly important to identify the intended command. Once this identification has been achieved, knowledge of the command's syntax can be used to identify the expected arguments, secondary keywords and options. This greatly simplifies the search for the valid tokens against which the tokens in the user's command line are compared. Our analysis has shown that errors in command names occurred 1,538 times (this represents 84 % of the total number of token errors we detected).

We identified 528 commands which contained grammatical errors. It must be emphasized that the UNIX command language has a relatively weak grammar (i.e. many commands may be entered in a nearly free-form manner). Thus we would expect there to be fewer grammatical errors than there would be in a more structured command language.

Grammar errors were analysed in terms of token insertion, deletion, substitution, and transposition. We also collected data on errors in command arguments since the correction problem for arguments is a special case (i.e. such things as file names were not a predefined part of the command language). In addition we recorded data for errors resulting from the misuse of command delimiters (see the discussion on separator errors below). The following table shows the distribution of these error types.

Error Type	Frequency	% of Total
Insertion	0	0 %
Deletion	249	47 %
Substitution	85	16 %
Transposition	0	0 %
Argument	12	2 %
Separator	182	35 %
Total	528	100 %

Table 2 - Syntax Error Distribution

A special problem concerns typographical errors involving blanks (we call these "separator errors"). The omission of a blank merges two adjacent tokens. In this case, the search for a correction must follow a different strategy than in cases where any other character has been omitted from a given (single) token. Similarly the substitution of a non-blank character for a blank merges tokens, the insertion of a blank splits a token and the transposition of a blank with an adjacent character splits a token in the wrong place (this would normally be detected as two errors: the omission of a character in one token and the insertion of a character in the adjacent token). Separator errors were detected 182 times in our analysis (35 % of the total sample).

The knowledge of how user errors are distributed in a large sample of UNIX commands can be used to devise strategies for handling these errors. The error distribution also suggests ways that the design of the UNIX command language might be changed to enhance error recovery. These issues are addressed in the following section.

3. DISSCUSSION

In our sample of 6,112 distinct user interactions, we found a total of 2,359 command lines containing either typographical or syntax errors. Thus these kinds of errors occurred in 39 % of the sample. It must be noted that users often experience errors as a "cognitive discontinuity." To correct an error, a user must: (a) recognize that an error has occurred, (b) divert attention from the task at hand, (c) diagnose the error, (d) develop a strategy for dealing with the error, (e) implement the strategy, (f) monitor the results, and (g) revert attention to the interrupted task (assuming the error correction strategy was effective). These 7 logical states tend to interrupt a user's flow of thought directed towards achieving a sequence of job related tasks. Thus the 39 % of the interactions containing grammar and syntax errors may strongly influence user satisfaction and productivity.

3.1. Discussion of Error Classes

In this particular command line interface, typographical errors predominate over grammar errors. However, this may be a peculiarity of UNIX. UNIX has a relatively unstructured format for commands and as a consequence it is relatively unlikely that users will make grammatical errors. This may not be true of other command languages. When a grammar is present, its very structure provide clues for correction. It becomes possible to deduce that missing or mistyped tokens are in specific grammatical categories. This reduces the search space for the correction algorithms as well as the number of candidates for correction that result from the search. For these reasons, we would expect other command languages to be at least as correctable as UNIX.

A surprisingly large portion of the errors (59 %) were neither typographical nor grammatical. Some of these seemed to be the result of serendipitous events. For example, in a number of cases, users entered long sequences of repeated characters. This might have been caused by leaning a book on the keyboard or some similar event. Another class of errors seemed to arise through a misunderstanding of the text editing keys. For example, there were a number of cases where the backspace key was used when the delete key was intended. Both keyboard errors and serendipity accounted for a comparatively small fraction of the errors (11 %). The major class of user error other than the typographical and grammatical classes consisted of "mode errors" (48 % of our 6,112 command sample).

Mode, or state errors occur when the user issues a technically correct command that is inappropriate for the current state of the system. For example, attempting to access a file with insufficient privilege. We believe that such errors not only represent a significant source of error in this study, but are almost certainly an important source of error for many other interfaces as well.

3.2. Discussion of Possible Improvements

Our analysis has suggested a number of things that might be done to improve the correctability of UNIX-like interfaces. One of the most important issues has to do with the number of possible candidates that could serve as the correction for an unrecognized token. If the tokens of the language were sufficiently dissimilar from each other, then a single error in the entry of a target token would produce an unmatched token that is more similar to the intended token than to any of the others. The use of token dissimilarity to design correctable command interfaces is explored more fully in our earlier work [Bradford (1987b)]. In the system we studied, such single errors represented 30 % of the recorded errors, and thus the capacity to find unique corrections for this class of error would be of major benefit to the user.

The problem of mode or state errors is a special case. Such commands are often technically correct but are rejected because the user does not have an accurate understanding of the state of the system. Although this is beyond the scope of our study on command entry errors, a few remarks may be appropriate. It is clear from a review of the state errors included in our data, that in the majority of cases, the cause of the error (insufficient permission, files not found, etc.,) could be mechanically deduced. At the very least, an accurate diagnosis of mode errors would represent a significant improvement to the interface.

Errors in command arguments (such as file or directory names) ought to have been more correctable than they were. Part of the problem is that in UNIX, the currently active paths through the directory structure can be quite complex. Nevertheless, the operating system already contains code to search the active directory paths to find valid files and directories. Something similar could be used by the interface to generate a list of names which would serve as the search space for an argument corrector. This would significantly improve the correctability of the interface since a number of the detected errors were due to errors in command arguments.

We conclude with the observation that UNIX is rapidly becoming the interface of choice for many microcomputer systems. As its popularity increases it is likely that many more of its users will be novices and non-technical personnel than has been traditional for UNIX. Because of the cryptic nature of the UNIX command language, user error is likely to become even more of a problem in the future. A knowledge of how these errors are distributed may help to inspire future versions of the interface that make user interaction friendlier and more robust.

REFERENCES

Bradford, James H. (1987a). A Symbolic Representation of Human/Computer Interaction, Proceedings of the 1987 IEEE International Conference on Systems, Man and Cybernetics, pp 339-343.

Bradford, James H. (1987b). A Symbolic Representation of Human/Computer Interaction, Computer Science Technical Report CS-87-01, March 1987.

Damerau, F.J. (1964). "A Technique for Computer Detection and Correction of Spelling Errors," Communications of the Association for Computing Machinery, Vol 7 #3, March 1964, pp 171-176.

Greenberg, S. (1988). "Using Unix: Collected Traces of 168 Users," Research Report 88/333/45, Department of Computer Science, University of Calgary, Calgary Alberta, Canada.

Murray, W.D. (1990). An algorithm for Integrating Token and Grammar Level Correction (M.Sc. Thesis). Department of Computing and Information Science, University of Guelph, Guelph Ontario Canada.

Peterson, J.L. (1980). "Computer Programs for Detecting and Correcting Spelling Errors," Communications of the Association for Computing Machinery, Vol 23 #12, December 1980, pp 676-687.

Wagner, R.A. & Fischer, M.J. (1974). "The String-to-String Correction Problem," Journal of the Association for Computing Machinery, Vol 21 #1, January 1974, pp 168-173.

Human–Computer Interaction – INTERACT '90
D. Diaper et al. (Editors)
Elsevier Science Publishers B.V. (North-Holland)

ECM: A Scheme for Analysing User-System Errors

Paul A. Booth

Department of Computing, Manchester Polytechnic, UK.

This paper addresses the question of how best to consider and eliminate the errors that occur during human-computer interaction. Firstly, a distinction is drawn between human errors and user-system errors. A further distinction is then made between different types of user-system error; mapping mismatches and incongruity mismatches. Following this, a classification scheme (an Evaluative Classification of Mismatch, ECM), for analysing user-system errors, is defined, and a study into its usefulness reported. A system that had been refined using ECM was shown to be significantly better, in terms of time, errors and user attitude ratings, than both the original system and a system that had been refined without using ECM. The results of this study suggest that schemes for analysing user-system errors can play a significant role in improving the performance of human-computer systems.

It is suggested that an effective means of optimizing user-system performance is to concentrate upon the errors that occur during interaction. A consideration of errors is already the major focus of concern during many usability tests (Booth, 1989), and such phenomena might be viewed as the most useful source of information about interaction. The advantages of considering errors are fourfold: Firstly, concentrating upon errors can reveal mismatches that actually occur, rather than mismatches that might or should be present, as is the case when employing some predictive human factors tools. Secondly, such an approach might also allow us to model just those aspects of a task that require analysis; those parts where the user experiences difficulty with the system. Thirdly, a consideration of errors can help to highlight those parts of a design that require attention, and can help to direct resources to these areas. Fourthly, in most large IT companies systems are iteratively developed, and many are presently tested with users in usability laboratories.

Error terminology

Although we might be clear as to why we are considering errors, the terminology surrounding human errors and the errors that occur at the interface is sometimes a little confusing. Consequently, it may be useful to suggest some loose definitions of one or two terms. These terms and distinctions have been explained in greater detail elsewhere (Booth, 1990). However, it may be useful to briefly reiterate this framework.

During interaction it appears as though we rarely, if ever, directly observe these errors. What we see are *dialogue failures*. A dialogue failure is *a breakdown in communication between the system and the user; it is where either the computer or the user do not understand one another, or some information about the nature and structure of the task is not properly communicated.* Such a failure is considered to be evidence that some sort of error has occurred.

It is suggested here that there are two basic types of error that occur during interaction:

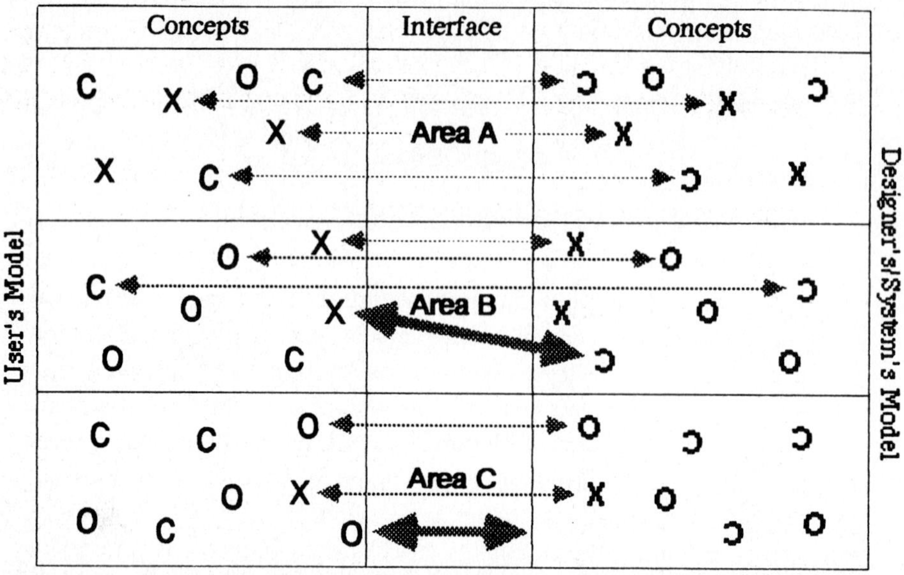

Figure 1. An abstract representation of a user's and a designer's/system's model of a task. Area A shows where the models are identical and the mappings between the models are correct. Area B shows where the models are identical, but the mapping between the models is incorrect (the incorrect mapping is shown with a thick arrow). Area C shows where the models are incongrous, and cannot be mapped onto one another (a thick arrow shows the mapping that cannot be achieved).

human errors and user-system errors. A human error is an error within one cognitive system (this definition is narrower and more precise than that previously employed, where the term *human error* has been used to mean almost any error that could be related to human action of some sort.) On the other hand, a user-system error is an error between two cognitive systems, it is not an error within one. In essence, user-system errors are mismatches between the user's and the designer's or system's model of the task in hand. These mismatches can be of two sorts; either mapping mismatches or incongruity mismatches. An abstract representation of a user's model and a system's/ designer's model, illustrating these different types of user-system error, can be seen in figure 1. Here, parts of the two models are identical, and correctly map onto one another (see area A in figure 1). Other parts are identical, but have been incorrectly mapped onto one another (see area B in figure 1). These are mapping mismatches; where the problem is with the mapping between the two models. Finally, some parts are not identical, but are incongruous to one another (see area C). These are incongruity mismatches, where the models *cannot* be mapped onto each other because the model elements are not the same, or are in different positions in relation to other elements.

Analysing user-system errors

Given that we are clear about the terminology used in this paper, it may be useful to consider the question of how we might analyse the errors that occur during interaction. The approach that is favoured here is to classify such errors. Classification need not be viewed as a totally restrictive process, where the central aim is to slot events neatly into categories. But, rather, may be considered as an exercise where the quality of information regarding an error is increased, as it is classified according to its central underlying causes. Such benefits, however, assume that any classification addresses fundamental concepts.

Such an approach has been adopted within the study of human error. However, directly applying human error classifications may not be appropriate. This is because human error classifications are generally intended to classify errors that occur within one cognitive system (that of the human) not errors that occur between two or more cognitive systems, as is the case with user-system errors.

A number of classification schemes have been suggested for dealing with the errors that occur during interaction (e.g. Davis, 1983a & b, Welty, 1985). Possibly the best known, however, is Norman's (1983) scheme. This classification scheme deals with both human and user-system errors. The human error side of the classification is covered by the *mistakes* and *slips* distinction (Norman, 1981; Reason & Mycielska, 1982). The user-system error aspect of the scheme is the distinction between *description* and *mode* errors. A *mode error* is where a person believes a system is in one mode when it is in another, and, consequently, performs an action that is inappropriate for that particular mode. A *description error* is where there is insufficient specification of an act, resulting in an erroneous action. An example Norman (1983) provides is where a row of identical switches have been provided, and distinguishing these switches is difficult. Interestingly, although Norman's scheme is undoubtedly a useful way of thinking about some errors, not all errors can be classified under the scheme. For instance, the scheme cannot account for situations where the operation the system performs is not exactly what the user wanted (an incongruity mismatch). An example is to be found on the Memomaker system (a small word-processing package produced some years ago by Hewlett Packard) where the operation to re-justify paragraphs, also joins these paragraphs into one continuous piece of text. It is not clear how might this be usefully classified as either a mode or a description error.

The general approach adopted by Norman (1983) and others, however, does appear to offer an adequate means by which we might analyse user-system errors. Consequently, a scheme aimed at just such an analysis has been developed. Essentially, the scheme represents an attempt to use some of the concepts and definitions developed for early evaluation of systems (i.e. using cognitive grammars) and apply them in the context of late evaluation. The development of this scheme has been described in more detail elsewhere (Booth, in preparation). Nevertheless, it might be useful to briefly define the scheme.

An Evaluative Classification of Mismatch

The approach adopted here is one where classification is based upon the user's perspective. What is *right* and *wrong* in the system relies entirely on the user's view of the system and task. In the context of usability testing; the purpose of the scheme is to provide a uniform and helpful way of thinking and talking about the different causes or elements of user-system errors.

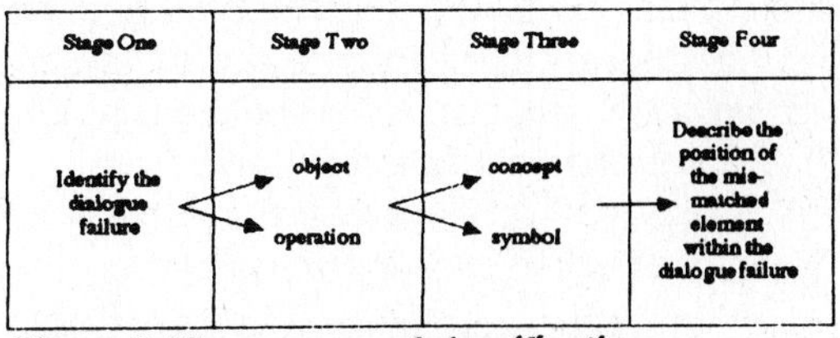

Figure 2: The process of classification.

Stages of Classification

The classificatory scheme has four stages. However, these stages are not hierarchical representations of the user interface or of human-computer interaction generally; the four stages only illustrate the steps through which the proposed classification process should proceed (see figure 2). The four possible classes of mismatch following the identification of a dialogue failure can be seen in figure 3. In the following sections the classes of mismatch will be defined and discussed. Examples will be provided to illustrate the definitions and a practical *rule of thumb* will be suggested for distinguishing the different categories of mismatch.

	Object	Operation
Concept	object-concept mismatch	operation-concept mismatch
Symbol	object-symbol mismatch	operation-symbol mismatch

Figure 3: ***The four classes into which a mismatched element should fit.***

Stage 1: Identifying a Dialogue Failure

The first stage of the classification process involves the identification of a user-system error. In practical terms, this means the detection of a failure in the dialogue between the system and the user. A definition of a dialogue failure was given earlier. However, it might be useful to consider an operational definition:

- the user reports any degree of misunderstanding during the interaction (i.e. the system does not do what he or she wanted it to do),
- the user asks for help in any form,
- the user enters an illegal command that is not purely the result of a keystroke error.

Stage 2: Identifying an Object or Operation

Having identified a user-system error then the next stage is to identify the object or operation associated with the failure.

Objects
A data file in a system, an applications package, a figure, character or window on a screen might all be considered to be objects. An object is, in essence *a thing to which something is done or about which something acts or operates,* (Oxford Universal Dictionary, 1944, third edition). An object mismatch can take the form of one of two possible types; an object-concept mismatch or an object-symbol mismatch. These terms will be defined and explained in greater detail in the next section.

Operations
An operation *is an action which is performed upon an object or objects within the system.* Saving a file, deleting a character, changing a shape in a graphics package, creating text in a word processing package are all operations. As before, there are two types of operation mismatch; operation-concept and operation-symbol mismatches. The notions of concept and symbol will be explained in greater detail in the next section.

A rule of thumb
A general rule of thumb for distinguishing objects from operations is that an operation is something that is done to an object whereas an object has operations performed upon it. Therefore an applications package is an object while the act of loading the package is an operation. A data file is an object which when examined will be seen to contain further objects. This view necessarily implies that users never see an operation, they only observe its effects upon the objects within the system.

Stage 3: Identifying the Mismatch Type

Once the user-system error and the associate (an object or operation) of the dialogue failure has been identified then the next stage is to classify it regarding its cause.

Concepts
For the purpose of this classification it is suggested that *a concept may be either an object or operation whether represented*

mentally (the user) or computationally (the computer). A concept mismatch is *a fundamental difference in the understanding and representation of system or task objects or operations.* In essence, under the ECM scheme an incongruity mismatch is described as a concept mismatch. One example of an operation-conceptmismatch can be found on the Hewlett Packard *Memomaker* word processing package. Most users expect the *backspace* key to delete as well as move the cursor backwards. The key will not delete and is, in effect, only a further cursor control key.

An object-concept mismatch is where the object is not in a form that the user would expect. If the object were a data file then it might contain information which is unnecessary as far as the user is concerned. Alternatively, it may lack information which the user feels is important. An example of an object-concept mismatch can be found on the ICL Perq running PNX. In order to print a file to a quality standard the user must issue a command not only to print but to create a print file (a configured file). Many first-time users have no idea as to why this object is needed.

Symbols

The term *symbol* is taken to mean *a word, character, sign, figure, shape or icon employed by either the user or the system to represent an object or operation within the system.* A symbol mismatch is not one of fundamentalunderstanding, *but occurs where the computer and the user adopt different terms or visual images to represent the same concept.* Again, under the ECM scheme, a mapping mismatch is described as a symbol mismatch.

An example of an operation-symbol mismatch can be found on the Prime 750 system. To print a document the user must type *spool* while the command to save a document is *file.* Most inexperienced users appear to believe this to be an illogical choice of terms. An object-symbol mismatch is where an object which is part of the task or system is what the user would expect if it had not been misnamed; that is to say that the object is correct but the symbol used to represent it is inappropriate as far as the user is concerned. An example of an object-symbol mismatch can be found in some library systems. Some naive users may search for a *catalogue* number for a publication only to discoverlater that the system they were using refers to these as *accession* numbers.

A rule of thumb

A rule of thumb for distinguishing symbol from concept mismatches might be whether the users' symbols for the systems objects and operations easily map onto the designer's version of the task or system. For example; if it can be seen that the *spool* and *file* operations on the Prime 750 system mentioned earlier, are in essence, the same concepts as the user terms 'print' and 'save' then the mismatch might be considered to be of the operation-symbol variety. That is to say, that the user and the system have the same model with the same concepts, but that these concepts have not been correctly mapped onto one another. If terms cannot be easily substituted then the problem may be of a more fundamental kind, where the designer's and user's conceptualizations of the concepts or structure of either the system or the task (their models of each) are inharmonious.

Stage 4: Positioning a Mismatched Element

Once a dialogue failure has been identified, and its causes classified, these causes (or mismatched elements) need to be described with respect to their position within (or contribution towards) the dialogue failure. In the example given earlier, the symbol *spool* appears to be almost totally responsible for the dialogue failures that relate to it. However, in more complex dialogue failures a number of mismatched elements may have contributed towards the misunderstanding. If this is the case then the description of the position and role of the mismatched element is more important. The crucial question that is addressed at this stage in the classification process is; *what role did the element play in the dialogue failure?*

The important point about distinguishing mismatches is that to properly classify a dialogue failure the observer must not only discover what happened (i.e. which operations were applied to which objects) but must also elicit the user's view of the task and system. For example; if a user intended an action that the system can perform then this is an operation-symbol mismatch, but if the user desired an operation which is not possible then the mismatch is more fundamental (a concept mismatch). In short; *the physical actions and consequences may remain constant, but the classification depends upon the user's view of the task and system.*

The Usefulness of ECM

The purpose of this experiment was to discover whether a small system could be improved using ECM. To this end, a system was developed, and then refined by two pairs of "designers." The first pair did not use ECM, whilst the second pair did. This resulted in three systems; the original, an iteration produced without using ECM (the non-ECM system), and an iteration produced using ECM (the ECM system).

Hypotheses

1 The version of the system produced using ECM will enable users to perform the tasks faster that users of the system modified without the use of ECM.
2 Users of the system produced using ECM will make fewer errors than users of the system where ECM was not used.
3 User attitude ratings be more positive towards the system produced using ECM rather than the system produced without using ECM.

Method

In the first stage the system was designed and built by the author. For convenience the system was briefly titled Train Timetable and Prices System (TTPS). It was considered important that the system be kept as small as practically possible (both in terms of functionality and code). The small size of the system enabled a simple experimental comparison, without the added complexity of changing a large system.

In the second stage the system was tried by just two users. These users were given a set of instructions and tasks to perform. This use of the system was supervised by an independent judge. This judge constructed problem descriptions from the difficulties the two users reported, and these were put into a list.

In the third stage four "designers" familiarized themselves with the system, and with the instructions given to the users. Following this, they were given the problem descriptions and asked to use these descriptions to produce a list of recommended changes to the system. Two of the designers were asked to use ECM to analyse the problems before they produced their recommendations, while the other two designers did not use ECM.

In the fourth stage the recommendations of the designers were compiled by an independent judge to produce two lists: one list of changes recommended by the two designers who used ECM and another list of changes recommended by the designers who used only the problem descriptions. These two lists of recommendations were then implemented by the author to produce two further systems: one system that was produced from the recommendations of the designers who used ECM, and one system produced from the recommendations of the designers who did not use ECM. At the time of programming these systems, in order to avoid a possible source of bias, the author was not aware of which recommendations were produced by which set of designers. This was known only by the independent judge.

In the fifth and final stage of the study the three systems (the original and the two iterations) were subject to an experimental comparison. Twenty four subjects (eight for each system) were run, and the major measures were the number of errors subjects made, the time subjects took to complete the tasks and attitude scores of the subjects towards the system they had just used.

Design

The independent variable in the experimental comparison was the system the users were asked to use; either the original, the iteration produced without using ECM, or the iteration produced using ECM. The dependent variables were the errors subjects made, the time subjects took to complete the tasks, and the subjects' attitude scores on a questionnaire. This questionnaire was administered immediately after the subjects completed the experimental tasks on the system. In more detail:

1 Errors; these were defined in terms of *any incorrect entry into the system.* This applied whether the entry was a keystroke error or not. It was assumed that a source of bias would be introduced if the experimenter had to judge which were keystroke errors and which were not.
2 Time; this was the time from the subjects beginning the tasks to them finishing these tasks.
3 Attitude scores; these were the attitudes of the subjects to the system they had just used, measured using a questionnaire.

Results

Hypothesis 1

Will the version of the system produced using ECM enable users to perform the tasks faster than users of the system modified without the use of ECM? The times that the subjects from each group took can be seen in figure 4. This result supports the idea that ECM *accurately* classifies user-system mismatches, as the system produced using ECM enabled users to perform their tasks in a shorter space of time than users of either the original system, or the non-ECM iteration of the original system. An analysis of variance demonstrates that this difference is highly significant ($F = 43.41$, $df = 2,21$, $p < 0.0001$).

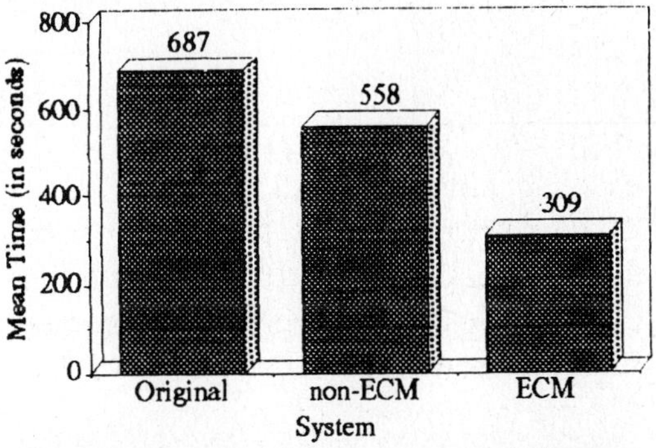

Figure 4. The mean time for task completion for each system.

Hypothesis 2

Will users of the system produced using ECM make fewer errors than users of the system where ECM was not used? The number of errors that each subject made can be seen in figure 5. This result further supports the idea that ECM *accurately* classifies user-system mismatches, as the system produced using ECM enabled users to perform their tasks with fewer errors than users of either the original system, or the non-ECM iteration of the original system. An analysis of variance demonstrates that this difference is highly significant ($F = 105.35$, $df = 2,21$, $p < 0.0001$).

Hypothesis 3

Will user attitude ratings be more positive towards the system produced using ECM rather than the system produced without using ECM? If ECM accurately classifies user-system errors then we might expect user attitudes towards the system produced using ECM to be more positive than those towards both the original system and the non-ECM iteration of the system (see figure 6). Again, this result supports the idea that ECM *accurately* classifies user-system mismatches, as the system produced using ECM provoked better attitude ratings than either the original system, or the non-ECM iteration of the original system. An analysis of variance demonstrates that this difference is highly significant (F = 232.02, df = 2,21, p < 0.0001).

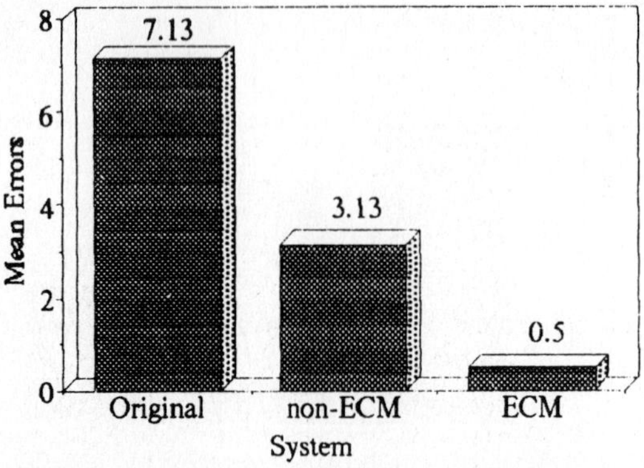

Figure 5. The mean number of errors for each system.

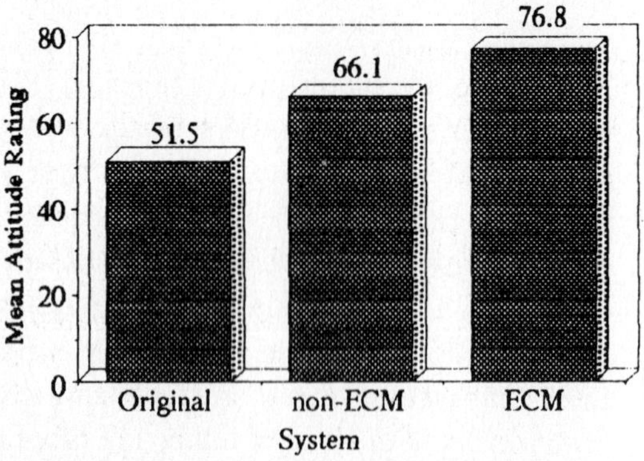

Figure 6. The mean attitude score for each system.

Conclusion

Within the HCI field relatively little attention has been paid to the issue of how user-system errors might be analysed, despite a general recognition that errors offer us some of the most revealing insights into the interaction between a computer and a user (Lewis & Norman, 1986; Norman, 1983). It has been arguedthat present classification schemes do not deal adequately with user-system errors. A classification scheme (ECM) has been suggested in an attempt to overcome some of these drawbacks, and to take into account the theoreticaldistinctionbetweenincongruity and mapping mismatches. In essence, ECM represents an attempt to use some of the concepts present in a number of early evaluation techniques, and apply them in the context of late evaluation.

The study reported here provides indications that ECM could be employed to improve the quality of a system. Overall these results, togetherwith others regarding the usability of the scheme (Booth, in preparation) suggest that evaluative classification schemes may have a useful role to play within the design and development process, and that using evaluative classification schemes might be one route towards a better understanding of the user within the context of the design process.

Acknowledgements

I would like to thank Gill Brown, Adrian Castell, Simon Davis, Ken Eason, Chris Fowler, Mark Kirby, Linda Macaulay, Phil Marsden and Deborah Twigger for their help with this research.

References

Booth, P. A. (1990) Modelling the user: User-system errors and predictive grammars. In: G. A. Weir (Ed) *HCI and Complex Systems.* London, UK: Academic Press.

Booth, P. A. (1989) *An introduction to human-computer interaction.* Hove, UK: Lawrence Erlbaum Associates.

Booth, P. A. (in preparation) Analysing User-System Errors: An Approach to Improving System Design. *Submitted to Human-Computer Interaction.*

Davis, R. (1983a) User error or computer error? Observations on a statistics package. *International Journal of Man-Machine Studies, 19,* 359-376.

Davis, R. (1983b) Task analysis and user errors: a methodology for assessing interactions. *International Journal of Man-Machine Studies, 19,* 561-574.

Lewis, C. & Norman, D. A. (1986) Designing for error. In: D. A. Norman & S. W. Draper (Eds.), *User centred system design: New perspectives on human-computer interaction.* Hillsdale, New Jersey, USA: Lawrence Erlbaum Associates.

Norman, D. A. (1983) Design rules based on analyses of human error. *Communications of the ACM, 26 (4),* 254-258.

Norman, D. A. (1981) A psychologist views human processing: human errors and other phenomena suggest processing mechanisms. In: *Proceedings of the International Joint Conference on Artificial Intelligence, Vancouver.*

Reason, J. & Mycielska, K. (1982) *Absent-minded? The psychology of mental lapses and everyday errors.* Englewood Cliffs, New Jersey, USA: Prentice-Hall.

Welty, C. (1985) Correcting user errors in SQL. *International Journal, of Man-Machine Studies, 22,* 463-477.

Human–Computer Interaction – INTERACT '90
D. Diaper et al. (Editors)
Elsevier Science Publishers B.V. (North-Holland)
IFIP, 1990

HOW LEARNER CHARACTERISTICS CAN MEDIATE THE EFFECTS OF GIVING CONCEPTUAL DETAILS DURING TRAINING

Elizabeth J. Lloyd*

Department Of Engineering Production,
University Of Birmingham, P.O. Box 363, Edgbaston,
Birmingham B15 2TT

Giving a conceptual model has often been hypothesized to aid learning and subsequent use of computerized devices, but scant attention has been paid to the role of learner characteristics in mediating this training outcome. An experiment was conducted to investigate such aspects further. Two groups of computer-naive subjects were taught to use a text editing system. One group was taught by procedures alone; the other group also received procedures, but in addition was given concurrent conceptual information. The results demonstrated that giving conceptual details during training may not be universally beneficial; overall, there were no great performance differences between the two groups. However, when learner characteristics were examined, it was found that certain individual characteristics interacted with training type to determine the learning outcome. The results imply that conceptual training is only efficacious for certain people, and that it may be possible to predict who those people will be.

1. INTRODUCTION

1.1. The Mental Model

A mental model is a cognitive mechanism used for representing the structure, rules, and internal relationships of a system. It can be run to give a "qualitative simulation" of a device, and hence guide user interactions by helping explain and predict device behaviour.

The user can develop a mental model of the device he is interacting with either by training or via the device's own design. Because systems are rarely designed to give a clear conceptual model to their users, it is consequently usually in training and documentation that the conceptual model must be given, and much of the published work is in this domain e.g. Borgman [1], [2]; Halasz [3]; Mayer [4], [5]; Sein et al. [6].

The general paradigm adopted to discover the utility of giving conceptual model information is to compare training where both conceptual and procedural details are given with training where only procedures are provided. The conceptual details are either given concurrently or in the form of an advance organiser. Where procedures alone are taught the target, device is treated as something that cannot be understood, and whose control manipulations must be memorized. When giving conceptual information too, the user is taught how the control manipulations in question are related to changes in the internal state of the device. This is learning by understanding. Several researchers have demonstrated the relative efficacy of the conceptual model approach to training; this has led to the prevailing viewpoint that only this mode of instruction can lead to the adaptive learning of complex computerized devices. For example, Halasz [3] showed that conceptually trained subjects performed better on certain problem types. He found that only complex (far transfer) tasks showed beneficial conceptual model effects. Where simple tasks (involving near transfer) were performed, giving a conceptual model was of little benefit. He hypothesized this was because it was only in far transfer tasks that the mental model was needed; it was unnecessary in more routine tasks. Kieras & Bovair [7] demonstrated strong beneficial learning effects where conceptual details were given for

* Now at IBM (U.K.) Laboratories Ltd., Hursley Park, Hursley, Winchester, Hampshire SO21 2JN.

+ This work was funded by the U.K. Government, through the Science & Engineering Research Council.

learning a simple control panel device. Similar beneficial effects were demonstrated in the text editing domain by both Jamar [8] and Sebrechts et al. [9]. Unfortunately few studies apart from Halasz's [3] have incorporated any analysis of task type when looking at performance effects.

1.2. Individual Differences

Several researchers have noted individual differences in the way people learn about and interact with computerized equipment. For example Egan and his associates (Egan & Gomez [10]; Gomez et al. [11]) have shown certain characteristics can distinguish learners in their facility and ability to learn (for example reading skill, spatial memory, age). Others, for example Van Muylwijk et al. [12], have examined how personality affects computer learning and use. Field Dependence/Independence has also been applied to the HCI situation. Van Der Veer et al. [13] broadened previous analyses of this factor by including it in an analysis of mental model use, positing that Field Dependents would be less likely to use any mental model for task completion than Field Independents.

The most thorough analysis of differences in learning style in HCI has been provided by Pask [14] (see Coombs et al. [15]) - The Conversation Theory. These are exeplified by *Comprehension Learners,* who take a holistic approach and attend to global aspects and relations in a system, and *Operation Learners,* who take a more local approach, concentrating more on procedural details and rules. Several researchers have given support for this theory e.g. Van Der Veer & Beshuizen [16]. Extrapolating from such findings, we could expect that learners would respond differentially well to training based on either general concepts or local procedures. Unfortunately, there is little hard experimental research to support this supposition, as most researchers comparing procedural with conceptual approaches have ignored individual factors in their analyses.

1.3. Mental Models And Individual Differences

As mentioned in the previous section, people differ in the ways they can learn about and use computerized devices, and there are indications that these differences are governed by innate predispositions. Frequently the impact of such factors are omitted when assessing the impact of a certain training type. For example, most researchers who have given learners conceptual models have ignored individual factors. They have assumed all recipients will respond in the same manner to these conceptual details; that they will all build a mental model and use it in future device interactions. Thus, the approach has usually been to look at average effects over all tasks and ignore individual factors e.g. Kieras & Bovair [7]. This may have excluded an important factor that could have served to mediate their results. When results have shown that subjects who were given a conceptual model performed better than those who were not given such a model, they have concluded that conceptual model provision aids performance for <u>all</u> people on <u>all</u> tasks. Only Mayer [4], [5] has explored in any great depth the possibility that conceptual model information may be helpful on some tasks for some people but impair the performance of others (that is, produce an Aptitude Treatment Interaction - ATI). He looked at people learning to program, and found high ability subjects fared worse when presented with a conceptual model. He posited this result was obtained because such subjects already possessed models with which the new conceptual information interfered.

1.4. Research Issues

It is clear from past research that there are situations where conceptual details can help learners assimilate and build a mental model, but what is not so clear is how this process is affected by characteristics of the learners themselves. To look at this in greater depth it was decided to compare procedural versus conceptual training. A further aim was to look at the interaction between individual characteristics and the type of training given, and thus see whether conceptual details were universally beneficial.

Previous work in the HCI domain suggests that personality may be an important determinant of computer learning and use. There are indications from Mayer's [4], [5] work that not all recipients of conceptual information respond advantageously; intellectual ability was an important predeterminant in his studies. In an effort to combine these factors, measures of personal learning strategy and ability were investigated.

As far transfer problems involve extensive use of the mental model, it was on these problems that the individual factors investigated were expected to have the strongest effects.

2. METHOD

2.1. Experimental Design And Materials

Training groups were matched for I.Q. via the Wechsler Adult Intelligence Scale (WAIS) (Wechsler [17]). There were two experimental groups, based on the type of training subjects were to receive. One group received only procedural details on how to use WordStar (MicroPro International Corp.). The other group received, in addition, further details that were designed to give information from which a mental model could be assembled. The dependent variable throughout the experiment was the performance on various editing tasks given during tests following each training session. The five training/test sessions, each lasting approximately two hours, took place every other day.

Measures of Achievement Potential and Intellectual Efficiency from the California Psychological Inventory (CPI) (Gough [18]) were used to give scores on the individual measures of interest. In particular, three scales were used - Achievement through Independence (Ai), Achievement Through Conformity (Ac), and Intellectual Functioning (Ie). Those who Achieve through Independence do better where initiative is necessary and need less direction and guidance. Those who Achieve through Conformity like clear-cut rules and regulations to follow. Intellectual Efficiency score indicates the degree of personal and intellectual efficiency gained, and those scoring high here are intelligent, resourceful, and efficient.

Thus the independent variables were:-
1. Provision or absence of conceptual details
2. Achievement Through Independence score
3. Achievement Through Conformity score
4. Intellectual Efficiency score

2.2. Subjects

Twenty unpaid volunteers acted as subjects. All were totally computer-naive; none were trained typists. They were of varying academic backgrounds and qualifications; none were students.

2.3. Procedure

Initially the WAIS was administered to determine training group allocation. On subsequent visits subjects learnt about WordStar using the appropriate manual, which they read through at their own speed. As they read the manual they practised the exercises in it. On completion of each manual an editing test was administered. This test contained both near and far transfer problems. Performance was monitored online, giving a time-stamped performance protocol after each test session. At all times subjects were urged to complete the tasks using the knowledge they had gained during training, but if they were unable to complete an edit after several attempts they left it and carried on with the next one. Following session two, subjects were given the CPI to complete. More details of procedure and training/ test materials can be found in Lloyd [19].

3. RESULTS

3.1. Performance Metrics Used In Results Analysis

The major performance metrics, listed below, were derived for the editing tasks both over all tasks and for those involving far transfer alone. Error data include behaviour devoted both to the making and correcting of errors.
1. Total length of time spent
2. Total number of keys taken
3. Time spent on all errors made
4. Keys taken on all errors made

(3) and (4) can also each be divided into error relating to "Slips" and that relating to "Mistakes" (see Norman [20]), to give the following:-
5. Time spent on Slips
6. Keys taken onSlips
7. Time spent on Mistakes
8. Keys taken on Mistakes

3.2. Data Analysis

Data were analysed using SPSS-X. Separate two way (2X2) ANOVAS were performed for each dependent variable for each task type. To enable the three CPI scale scores to be examined, median splits were performed for each scale on the scores of each training group. This gave groups of high and low scorers on each scale for each training group.

3.3. Major Findings

No significant Main Effects for training type were found, so no evidence was gained to show that overall conceptual details produce markedly superior learning outcomes. There were wide variations in performance within the training groups. There were several significant Interaction Effects between training type and the individual differences studied. Only some of the more major of these will be covered; more detailed results are available in Lloyd [19]. These interactions all showed that giving conceptual details produced either very good or very poor scores where it interacted with individual factors; procedurally based training gave far less diverse effects.

Intellectual Efficiency (Ie). Several significant interactions were obtained between this variable and the keystroke metrics. For example, the interaction between level of Ie (high, low) and training type (procedural, conceptual) on the number of keys spent on Mistake-type errors for all task types gave significant results $F (1, 16) = 6.351$, $p < 0.05$. When looking at this same data subset for far transfer tasks alone, the following significant result was obtained - $F (1, 16) = 7.401$, $p < 0.05$. The significant interaction between Ie and training type for the total number of keys spent on errors for far transfer tasks ($F (1, 16) = 4.811$, $p < 0.05$) is shown in Figure 1. Keystroke metrics can be used as a way of looking at editing efficiency and planning. As edits came to rely more on mental model use (far transfer edits), the importance of Ie increased. Those subjects who were more Intellectually Efficient performed best when given conceptual details, but if such subjects were given procedural details their performance was substantially degraded. On the other hand, subjects scoring low on this scale fared better when given procedural training; if they were given conceptual training it had extremely detrimental performance effects.

Achievement Through Conformity (Ac). Analyses here also gave numerous significant interactions. For example, the interaction between level of Ac (high, low) and training type (procedural, conceptual) on the number of keys spent on Mistakes for all task types was significant $F (1, 16) = 11.967$, $p < 0.01$. A similar analysis for far transfer tasks alone gave the following significant result - $F (1, 16) = 10.584$, $p < 0.01$. Figure 2 shows the significant interaction ($F (1, 16) = 16.595$, $p = 0.001$) between Ac and training type for the total number of keys spent on errors for far transfer tasks. All results showed those scoring high on this variable to perform better when given conceptual training; when they were given procedurally based instructions their performance was degraded. Those scoring low on this scale produced the opposite interaction effects. Once again, these findings were particularly strong on the keystroke metrics, especially on far transfer tasks. This suggests Achievement Through Conformity score influenced the selection and derivation of methods, particularly where the conceptual model needed first to be operationalized and then used. On the whole,

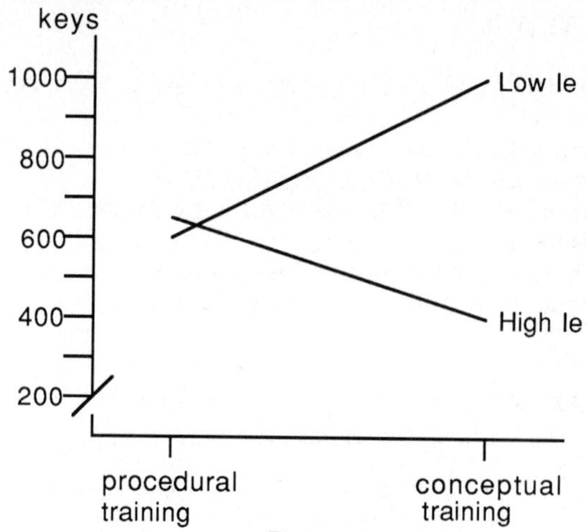

Figure 1

results suggest conceptual details will or will not be developed into a usable mental model depending on learner characteristics.

Achievement Through Independence (Ai). Results here were very similar to those for Ac. The interaction between level of Ai (high, low) and training type (procedural, conceptual) on the number of keys spent on Mistakes for all task types was significant $F (1, 16) = 11.050$, $p < 0.01$. A similar analysis for far transfer tasks alone also gave significant results $F (1, 16) = 6.130$, $p < 0.05$. The significant interaction between Ai and training type for the total number of keys spent on errors for far transfer tasks was $F (1, 16) = 13.317$, $p < 0.01$. Subjects who showed high levels of Ai were better able to text edit if they were given conceptual information; when they were given procedural details alone their performance suffered. A person scoring low on this scale fared better with procedural details, performing worse if conceptual details were also provided. Once again, these effects were particularly strong for the keystroke metrics, although time metrics also gave some significant findings.

Individual Characteristic Correlations. These findings suffer from the fact that all three CPI scales used were positively correlated. (Ai/Ac $r = 0.7035$, $p = 0.001$; Ai/Ie $r = 0.3939$, $p = 0.043$; Ie/Ac $r = 0.5025$ $p = 0.012$.) Those scoring high on Ai also scored high in Ac and Ie. This limits the number of available conclusions that may be drawn. However, this is in common with population norms from the CPI manual (Gough [18]) and suggests the three measures together show those who have a tendency to achieve will do so in any circumstances since they are able to learn and act in a conforming or independent manner according to situational requirements.

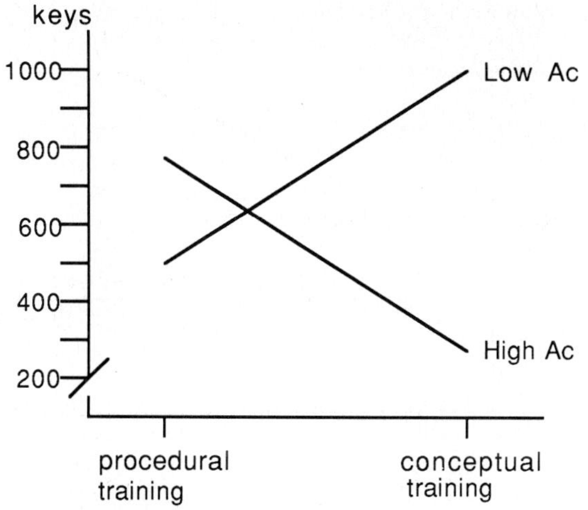

Figure 2

4. DISCUSSION

The results provide little evidence to support the contention that giving conceptual details is universally beneficial to learners. The conceptually trained group did not perform substantially better than those who had been trained with procedures alone, even on far transfer tasks. Instead, there were wide variations within groups in the ability to use WordStar to perform the editing tasks. These results thus contrast strongly with those of, for example, Kieras & Bovair [7].

However, when the individual characteristics of the learners themselves were included in the analysis, an interesting picture emerged. Many of the performance metrics showed strong interactions between these characteristics and training type. Individual characteristics mediated learning outcome. More able learners, who were able to adapt their strategy to meet situational requirements, performed far better if they were given conceptual details. If subjects of lower ability were given these details their performance suffered. These effects were particularly numerous where subjects needed to derive methods from their model (far transfer tasks). As such, there is some support for Jamar [8], who suggested students were better able to deal with conceptual details than secretaries (with the implication that students would be of a higher ability than secretaries). There is also experimental support for the more general proposal of Bayman & Mayer [21] - there are differences in the ability to use model information. The findings in this study do not convey whether such differences are due to variations in the ability to assimilate and build a mental model or due to differential abilities to use that model once built. Perhaps those who scored low on the three CPI scales built models from the conceptual details, but were unable to run them.

The results do contrast somewhat with those of Mayer [4] where high ability subjects performed *worse* when given conceptual details. He felt this was because those details interfered with previous models his subjects had of the domain. Such an interference effect was unlikely to occur here, as subjects were computer and typewriter naive.

In terms of previous research that has not looked at ATI effects, the results here suggest they have ignored an important aspect of their findings. Many studies finding strongly beneficial model effects have used students (who presumably are of high ability), and this may have inadvertently biased their results and produced findings in favour of providing conceptual details. Furthermore, the underlying rationale (as noted by Young [23], Norman [24]) of all similar didactic comparisons has been that to present a conceptual model is enough to instill a usable mental model in the recipient's head; this supposition is not supported here. Those, for example, Foss et al. [22] who found non significant model effects have also attributed this solely to training factors. This study shows type of training alone does not determine learning outcome.

One point which is underlined by this work is that there is no good substitute for a clear conceptual design. It is unsuitable for system designers to develop an opaque application and then assume the system documentation and training will solve all their problems. A complex design means the conceptual model (both given by the design and given by documentaion and training) will be complex.

As regards system documentation and training development, the results imply the decision of what type of information to provide is not a clear cut one. Conceptually based training produces very diverse effects; people either learn very well or very badly. Procedural details alone produce a much less diverse response from learners. High ability trainees are hampered with procedural details, but not as much as those of low ability if they are given conceptual details. Thus, only giving procedural details minimizes the possibility of very poor performance. The best solution would be to provide both types of information in a mutually exclusive way. Thus, learners who want and can use conceptual details can have them as well as learning the procedural aspects of system use. Similarly, those who neither want nor can deal with conceptual details can devote their attention wholly to the procedural details. It is as Deck & Sebrechts [25] say; some people like procedures and some people like concepts; system information should be designed to suit the needs of both.

REFERENCES

[1] Borgman, C. L. (1984). The user's mental model of an information retrieval system. *Ph.D. Thesis*, Dept. of Communications, Stanford University.

[2] Borgman, C. L. (1986). The user's mental model of an information retrieval system: an experiment on a prototype online catalog. *International Journal Of Man-Machine Studies*, 24, 47-64.

[3] Halasz, F. G. (1984). Mental models and problem solving using a calculator. *Ph.D. Thesis,* Department of Psychology, Stanford University.

[4] Mayer, R. E. (1975). Different problem-solving competencies established in learning computer programming with and without meaningful models. *Journal Of Educational Psychology*, 67, 725-734.

[5] Mayer, R. E. (1981). The psychology of how novices learn computer programming. *Computing Surveys*, 13, 121-140.

[6] Sein, M. K., Bostrom, R. P. & Olfman, L. (1987). Conceptual models in training novice users. In Bullinger, H.-J. & Shackel, B (Eds.), *Interact '87.* Amsterdam: Elsevier Science Publishers.

[7] Kieras, D. E. & Bovair, S. (1984). The role of a mental model in learning to operate a device. *Cognitive Science,* 8, 255-274.

[8] Jamar, P. G. (1986). Lost in Computerland: functional model-enhanced training and interface designs. *Proceedings Of The Human Factors Society 30th. Annual Meeting,*

[9] Sebrechts, M. M., Deck, J. E. & Black, J. B. (1983). A diagrammatic approach to computer instruction of the naive user. *Behaviour, Research Methods, Instruments, And Computers*, 16, 234-237.

[10] Egan, D. E. & Gomez, L. M. (1985). Assaying, isolating, and accomodating individual differences in learning a cognitive skill. In Dillon, R. F. (Ed.), *Individual Differences In Cognition.* New York: Academic Press.

[11] Gomez, L. M., Egan, D. E. & Bowers, C. (1986). Learning to use a text editor: some learner characteristics that predict success. *Human-Computer Interaction*, 2, 1-23.

[12] Van Muylwijk, B., Van Der Veer, G. C. & Waern, Y. (1983). On the implications of user variability in open systems. An overview of the little we know and the lot we have to find out. *Behaviour And Information Technology*, 2, 313-326.

[13] Van Der Veer, G. C., Tauber, M. J., Waern, Y. & Van Muylwijk, B. (1985). On the interaction between system and user characteristics. *Behaviour And Information Technology,* 4, 289-308.

[14] Pask, G. (1977). *Learning Styles, Educational Strategies, And Representation Of Knowledge: Methods And Application.* Richmond: System Research Ltd.

[15] Coombs, M. J., Gibson, R. & Alty, J. L. (1981). Acquiring a first computer language: a study of individual differences. In Coombs, M. J. & Alty, J. L. (Eds.), *Computing Skills And The User Interface.* London: Academic Press.

[16] Van Der Veer, G. C. & Beshuizen, J. J. (1986). Learning styles in conversation - a practical application of Pask's Learning Theory to human-computer interaction. In Klix, F. & Wandke, H. (Eds.), *Proceedings Of The 1st. MACINTER Seminar.* Amsterdam: North Holland Publishing Company.

[17] Wechsler, D. (1955). *The Wechsler Adult Intelligence Scale Manual.* New York: The Psychological Corporation.

[18] Gough, H. G. (1975). *California Psychological Inventory Manual.* California

[19] Lloyd, E. J. (1989). Training with a conceptual model: short and long term effects and the mediating influences of learner characteristics. *Ph.D. Thesis,* Department of Engineering Production, University Of Birmingham.

[20] Norman, D. A. (1981). Categorization of action slips. *Psychological Review,* 88, 1-15.

[21] Bayman, P. & Mayer, R. E. (1984). Instructional manipulation of user's mental models for electronic calculators. *International Journal Of Man-Machine Studies,* 20, 189-199.

[22] Foss, D. J., Smith-Kerker, P. L. & Rosson, M. B. (1987). On comprehending a computer manual: analysis of variables affecting performance. *International Journal Of Man-Machine Studies,* 26, 277-300.

[23] Young, R. M. (1983). Surrogates and mappings: two kinds of conceptual models for interactive devices. In Gentner, D. & Stevens, A. L. (Eds.), *Mental Models.* Hillsdale, New Jersey: Lawrence Erlbaum Associates.

[24] Norman, D. A. (1983). Design rules based on analyses of human error. *Communications Of The ACM,* 26, 254-258.

[25] Deck, J. G. & Sebrechts, M. M. (1984). Variations on active learning. *Behaviour, Research Methods, Instruments And Computers,* 16, 238-241.

Human–Computer Interaction - INTERACT '90
D. Diaper et al. (Editors)
Elsevier Science Publishers B.V. (North-Holland)

INFLUENCING BEHAVIOUR VIA DEVICE REPRESENTATION; DECREASING PERFORMANCE BY INCREASING INSTRUCTION

Simon C. DUFF and Philip J. BARNARD

MRC Applied Psychology Unit, Cambridge, England.

Several studies including those of Duff (1989) suggest that prior knowledge plays a crucial role in learning operating procedures and problem solving with computer based systems. This paper tests a counter-intuitive prediction derived from Barnard's (1987) Cognitive Task Analysis. The analysis predicts that the advantageous effects of device knowledge can be offset by providing users with additional procedural instructions during the learning phase. Experimental evidence in support of this prediction comes from users learning to control a simple laboratory application.

1. INTRODUCTION

Research in Human-Computer Interaction, (HCI), suggests that there are internal mental structures which contain knowledge and descriptions concerning devices or interaction media, most often referred to as "mental models". With a history of troubled usage of computer technology, one of the aims of HCI has been to investigate the role of knowledge content and structure, and thus mental representation, in interaction. A number of studies, from various perspectives, have looked at this, e.g. Hammond et al. [1], Kieras & Bovair [2], Berry & Broadbent [3], Frese et al. [4] and Duff [5]. Although effects have not always been easy to establish, most suggest that mental representation, and the knowledge which it supports, plays a crucial role during interaction. They also suggest that the mental models which users develop are almost unitary and 'static', descriptions of some aspect of a system or device.

A number of recent studies carried out by Duff [5,6] suggest that this view of mental representation is not flexible enough to explain user behaviour controlled by complex cognitive processes. The studies involved subjects learning to control computer implementations of various kinds of system under differing constraints and given different forms of knowledge, and then controlling these under novel conditions. The overall effects can be summarised as follows. Knowledge form plays a role in accuracy and speed of action execution both during learning and problem solving. Knowledge which describes relationships between system components, "how-it-works" or Figurative knowledge, leads to mediocre accuracy whilst learning, but improves accuracy under novel conditions, at the cost of speed. Knowledge which provides lists of actions, "how-to-do-it" or Operative knowledge, leads to faster and more accurate performance during learning, but poor accuracy under novel conditions. Learning via Exploration, where no device information is provided, leads to fast execution, accuracy dependent on the extent to which general principles and heuristics are available for abstraction from the device. Supporting knowledge, either supplied, as in the case of figurative knowledge, or inherent, as when controlling a familiar device, will improve accuracy with a loss of speed during problem solving. However, this is only if that supporting knowledge leads to the development of a coherent and integrated representation which is easily accessible.

To explore the theoretical basis of these findings, the Interacting Cognitive Subsystems framework (ICS - Barnard [7]) was used for analysis. This framework distinguishes between different levels or types of cognitive representation, proposing that 'mental models' are not unitary bodies of knowledge. Rather, they should be considered as being based on a range of representations containing different forms of knowledge. Most important for this paper are three types of representation, each dealt with by a different cognitive subsystem. One deals with the surface structure form and content of verbal material (Barnard's Morphonolexical subsystem), another its underlying meaning (Propositional subsystem) and another the relevant inferential connections within broader, schematic knowledge structures (Implicational subsystem). What a user knows about a system will be reflected at each of these levels. The different types of representations can be called upon strategically to help a user decide what to do. The precise properties of performance will depend upon the particular mix of mental representations used and their inherent properties (see Barnard [7]).

Figurative knowledge describes a system in terms of propositional and semantic relationships, requiring the drawing of inferences for utility. The consequences of the relationships for action selection must be processed. Operative knowledge describes a device through surface information, relying on the reuse of recent memory records. As action sequences are described, little inferential processing is required, so relationships, heuristics etc. are unlikely to develop. Knowledge derived from exploration describes a device via surface and inferential representations dependent on the extent to which general principles about the device can be abstracted. To reduce cognitive load, Exploratory learning acts to identify heuristics to constrain behaviour. Earlier studies show that these differences in representation strongly influence the strategies which subjects invoke in order to carry out the tasks under learning and problem solving conditions. In addition, the levels of representation develop over time, both in the quantity of knowledge which is represented, and the extent to which this knowledge becomes integrated with other relevant knowledge.

Within Barnard's approach, an important feature of the subjects' knowledge is represented through the concept of a Common Task Record (CTR). These records detail "what must be done" to achieve a certain goal. This mental representation of information typically describes the device at the propositional level as a series of structures which are related. It indicates the complexity and flexibility of the information, and thus how it may be able to constrain the use of knowledge whilst carrying out a task. It is the content and structure of the CTR which influences user behaviour.

Barnard [7] argues that users will, if possible, rely on the propositional CTR for the execution of tasks. However, where a propositional structure is insufficient to resolve uncertainty concerning a specific sequence of actions, surface structure representations and schematic knowledge may be called into play. In many settings, users provided with only Operative knowledge of the steps in a procedure will be able to determine what to do largely on the basis of very simple propositional and surface structure representations. Inferential representations will only be required to tackle novel tasks. Users given only figurative knowledge will have to actively construct propositional and surface representations of what to do, via inference. Likewise, users left to explore a device will have to determine the relevant propositional and surface structure representations, but without the benefit of the constraints embodied in figurative knowledge.

The general framework suggests that users will tend to rely on the type of mental representation that most readily enables them to determine "what to do". So, for example, if the users only have figurative knowledge, but no operative knowledge, they must use inference to determine the relevant propositional and surface structure for task execution. If the instructional material is operative and specifies the action sequence, inferential processing would not be a necessary requirement.

On the face of it, providing users with both operative knowledge of task procedures and figurative knowledge about how the device works would seem to give them the best of both worlds. However, if it is assumed that users typically rely on the specific form of mental representation that can be used most readily to execute a sequence of actions, then a counter-intuitive prediction can be arrived at. If users are provided with sufficient figurative knowledge of device constraints for them to infer action sequences and add to this some operative information about the sequence itself, then they will make less use of inferential processing. As the amount of operative knowledge added to figurative knowledge is increased, so the need for inferential processing will effectively decrease. The direct consequence of this should be three-fold. First, users will increasingly rely on surface structure and simple propositional representations, the consequence of this being reduced ability to solve novel problems. Second, the CTR that develops at the propositional level will not in itself reflect the structure implied by the figurative knowledge, and hence the specific pattern of performance errors should change. This is because the CTR representation constrains interaction through the structure of device knowledge. For example in Figurative cases where information is given about pairs of controls, the CTR will not describe relationships between individual pairs, thus errors would be expected to occur more often on commands used first in a pair, than on subsequent commands. When the use of Operative information supersedes this, the structure of knowledge describing pairs of controls will break down, so errors will begin to occur in later positions also. Third, since inferential processing of a similar but less constrained nature is involved in exploratory learning, we should expect an analogous pattern of overall performance to that for figurative knowledge but at a lower level of accuracy. Further, in the absence of figurative knowledge, the pattern of errors should resemble those from operative knowledge.

2. METHOD

These basic predictions were tested by users learning sequences of actions for a minimal office system. The individual actions were presented in an icon array (with verbal labels) using a MacIntosh. The user's task was to select the appropriate sequence of commands in their correct serial order using the mouse.

There were three independent groups of eight subjects and each of which had to learn six different sequences of actions, three of length six, and three of length eight. One group were given operative instructions detailing the sequence of command operations. e.g. "...3. Check, 4. Start, 5. Close, 6. Filter, ...". A second group of subjects were provided with figurative knowledge, which in principle would enable them to infer the actual operative sequence. e.g. "Files must be checked before the filing operation is started to ensure that there are files for this process to operate on." The third group were instructed to explore the device to establish the sequences of actions. For the two experimental groups (figurative & exploratory) the amount of operative information given was varied over the task sequences. For one task sequence of each length, users were given 0% operative information, and for subsequent pairs, the amount of operative information varied. This allows the performance of these groups to be assessed in relation to the performance of the operative group on identical task material, and thus provide a clear view of the effects of additional operative knowledge.

Within each pair of command sequences, there were a series of positional and semantic regularities to determine the extent that such information would be abstracted under various conditions. That is, command names or command meanings were shared between paired lists,which might be used to predict command positions in the sequences. This was important in the case of the EK group, whose main strategy has been proposed as the abstraction of generalities.

The experiment took place in two phases, learning and problem solving. During learning, subjects practised each of the command lists three times in succession. The order in which lists were presented, and the list/knowledge pairings were balanced to reduce effects of any possible interactions between specific lists. Pairs of lists were practised consecutively in order that the generalisations which applied, and the knowledge conditions, were not separated. To overcome positional practice effects, on each of the three trials the positions of commands within the icon array varied randomly. During the problem phase there were three trials in which each command list was carried out once. Pairs of lists were not presented together, presentation counterbalanced by list, knowledge type and number of commands required. In these problem trials, the set of commands which were available was reduced.

Condition 1 was essentially a replication of earlier comparisons between operative, figurative and exploratory learning. In Condition 2, the exploratory group received additional operative knowledge describing the half of the command sequence positions (those which could not be predicted from the system generalities). The figurative group received additional operative knowledge for 50% of the figuratively described controls. In Condition 3, the exploratory group received additional operative information about sequence positions of commands which could be predicted from system generalities. The figurative group received approximately 75% of additional operative information.

3. RESULTS

User responses were logged as was the time taken to select each command. Graphs 1 and 2 (Figure 1) show the learning data as commands per required action and time per command respectively. During initial learning, the provision of additional amounts of operative knowledge for the figurative and exploratory groups clearly facilitates performance. In Condition 1, these groups behave at the same levels as during previous studies, performance reliably less accurate than for the other tasks ($F_{2,42}$=38.05 $p<.0001$). For the time data there is also evidence of an increase in speed associated with presence of additional operative knowledge. Speeds of command selection for figurative and exploratory groups in Condition 1 are slowest ($F_{2,42}$=80.5 $p<.0001$).

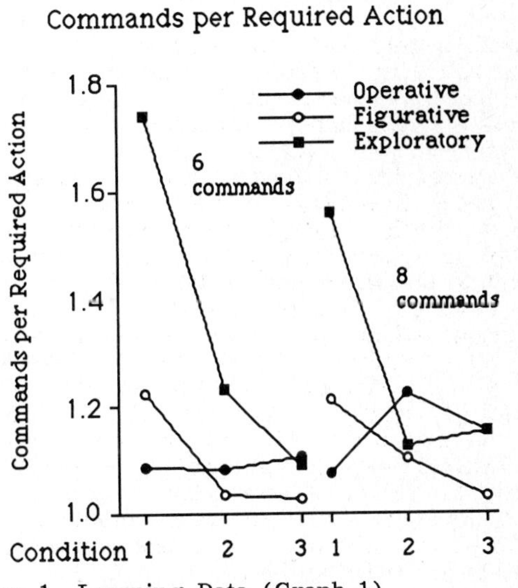

Figure 1 Learning Data (Graph 1)

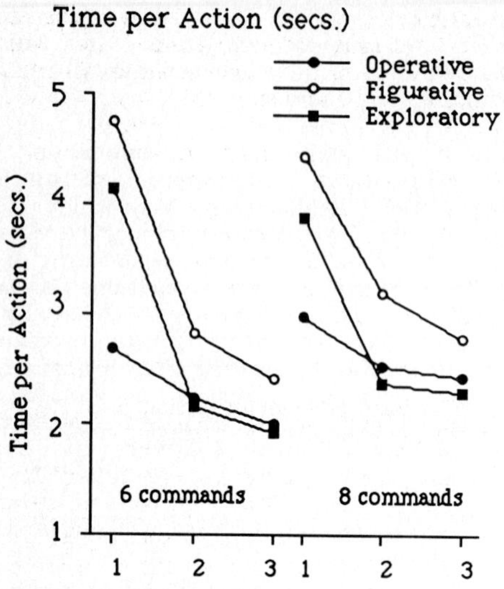

Figure 1 Learning Data (Graph 2)

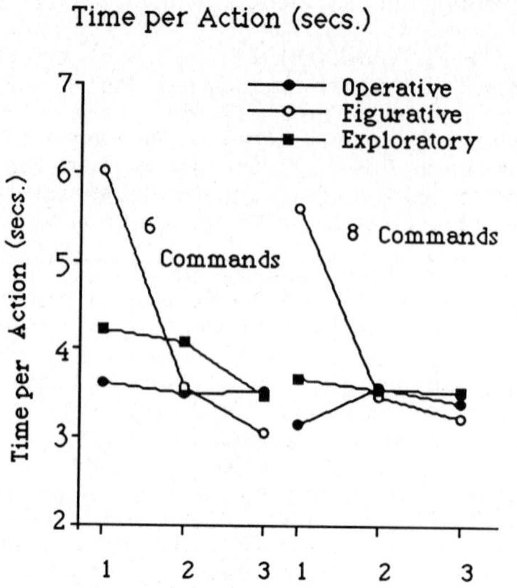

Figure 2 Problem Data (Graph 4)

During the problem solving phase, the overall pattern changes markedly in line with the predictions. The data (Graphs 3 & 4 - Figure 2) show how the provision of operative knowledge to exploratory and figurative groups influence their behaviour. Increasing operative knowledge reduces figurative group problem accuracy for both sequence lengths, and operative knowledge which describes generalities results in less accurate exploratory group behaviour, Conditions 1 and 2 differing ($F_{2,42}$=19.87 p<.0001)). Time data shows an associated decrease in command selection time, indicating that the amount of inferential processing is probably reduced.

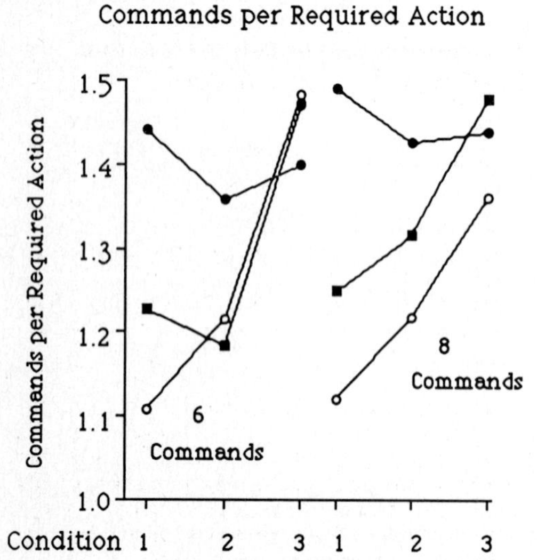

Figure 2 Problem Data (Graph 3)

Graph 5 (Figure 3) shows the error pattern, by serial position, for the command sequences involving six operations. The patterns for the sequence of eight operations is the same. The data shows how figurative knowledge constrains behaviour when it is used to develop a CTR (Condition 1). More errors are made on controls that are described first in a pair, suggesting that the mental representation has developed to reflect the relational knowledge given in figurative instructions. Where additional operative knowledge is provided, (commands so described are marked "*") it is clear that the neatly structured pattern of errors does not occur, suggesting that surface information was being used preferentially during learning. Relational information present in the initial figurative information is not reflected in the representation used to support performance. However, those controls which are described as pairs still show the error pattern of more errors on the first member of the pair.

Space precludes the inclusion of more graphical data, but the pattern of data for the operative group does not match that of the figurative group. More errors are made on later commands in the sequence, indicating that this representation supports a primacy effect. In line with the predictions, the error data for the exploratory group shows a similar pattern as the operative group in the six sequence case in Condition 1. With eight actions, and the benefit of the use of generalities between pairs of command lists, this pattern breaks down, greater accuracy attributed to where the generalities exist. In Condition 2, a similar pattern emerges, though the differences between commands is reduced by the presence of operative knowledge describing non-inferential command positions. In Condition 3 this pattern no longer exists, and generalities are no longer of any more benefit.

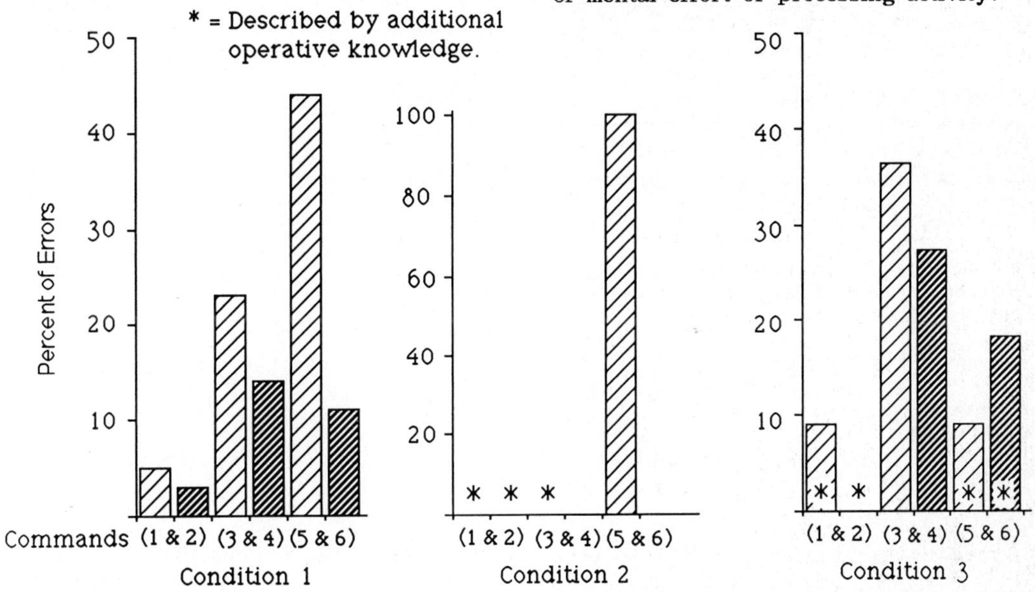

Figure 3 Graph 5. Learning Phase Error Data for Figurative Group

4. DISCUSSION

This experiment replicates a core phenomenon often observed when comparing figurative, operative and exploratory learning. Figurative knowledge requires high numbers of command transactions and relatively slow performance during learning, but the knowledge structures which develop facilitate performance when users need to infer novel sequences of actions. By contrast, providing operative knowledge leads to accurate and fast performance during initial learning, the accuracy dropping in novel contexts. Exploratory learning is initially fast, but obviously highly error prone. Such a pattern of findings is generally consistent with the earlier findings of Duff [5,6] and those of e.g. Kieras and Bovair [2]. However, it should be remembered that there are studies which have failed to demonstrate such effects e.g. Foss, Smith and Rosson [8].

However, the experiment also shows how fragile the potential advantages of providing figurative knowledge can be. Users only appear to benefit from such knowledge if they are forced to use it. Only then will the mental representation develop with the kind of form and content that can support inferences in novel task settings. These benefits are relative. The additional operative knowledge does reduce errors and increases speed of performance during learning. Nonetheless, the overall pattern of the data is generally consistent with the conjecture that users will mentally resolve what-to-do on the basis of the representation that reduces the overall amount of mental effort or processing activity.

The precise patterns of the error data suggest that it is not only the structure, but also the form of mental representation which is important for behaviour. The figurative group demonstrate that the relations they receive are able to constrain behaviour, presumably because these are internally represented at the propositional level. The exploratory group data suggest that with no external learning aids, system generalities can be abstracted to aid accuracy of performance. Operative knowledge appears to provide users with a representation of lists of actions to perform, which is well suited to initial learning. However, such knowledge does not support the development of mental representations that are flexible under novel conditions.

5. CONCLUSIONS

The potential benefits of figurative knowledge for learning human-computer dialogues started with a chequered history, empirical paradigms eventually emerging which could demonstrate clear findings. By further investigating the causes of these effects, it appears that the key aspects of such knowledge are its form and structure and the necessity for it to be inferentially processed. In addition, this determines the level at which the mental representation is instantiated, contributing towards the flexibility and, as suggested by earlier work, the memorability of the information. Analysing such data using ICS strongly suggests that the idea of a mental representation of a device is incompatible with the range of performance which can be found. It is more the case that there are internal representations at different cognitive levels, which are responsible for describing the device in different ways, and which are constantly evolving. The particular effects presented here, and the reasoning about their causes go some way towards developing and understanding the precise relationships that hold between performance, mental processing and the structure and content of knowledge relevant to system use.

REFERENCES

[1] Hammond, N., Morton, J., MacLean, A., Barnard, P. and Long, J. IBM Hursley Research Report HF071, December 1982.

[2] Kieras, D. and Bovair, S. Cognitive Science 1984 8 255-273.

[3] Berry, D. and Broadbent, D. Quarterly Journal of Experimental Psychology 1987 39a 585-609.

[4] Frese, M., and Albrecht, K. Behaviour and Information Technology 1988 7 pp. 295-304.

[5] Duff, S.C. Reduction of Action Uncertainty in Process Control Systems: The Role of Device Knowledge, in: Megaw, E. (ed.), Contemporary Ergonomics (Taylor & Francis 1989) pp. 213-219.

[6] Duff, S.C. Device Knowledge and the Reduction of Action Uncertainty. Paper presented at ECCE 4, Cambridge 1988.

[7] Barnard, P.J. Cognitive Resources and the Learning of Human-Computer Dialogs, in: Carroll, J.M. (ed.), Interfacing Thought (MIT Press, 1987) pp. 112-158.

[8] Foss, D. Smith, P. and Rosson, M. The Novice at the Terminal: Variables affecting understanding and performance. Paper presented at the Psychonomic Society meeting, Minneapolis (1982).

Human–Computer Interaction – INTERACT '90
D. Diaper et al. (Editors)
Elsevier Science Publishers B.V. (North-Holland)

POP-UP WINDOWS AND MEMORY FOR TEXT

Heather A. STARK

MRC Applied Psychology Unit, 15 Chaucer Road, Cambridge CB2 2EF, United Kingdom

This study investigates the effect of pop-up windows in hypertext on readers' memory. One group of readers read "plain" descriptions of properties for sale in conventional linear format. Another group read descriptions with the same content, but with some sentences ("new details" about the property) in pop-up windows. Readers judged the suitability of these properties for clients, and then were tested on their memory for property features. For the pop-up group, pop-up property features were recognized more quickly than main text features, and the description they came from was identified more quickly. These sets of features did not differ significantly for the plain group. Pop-ups may be useful ways to emphasize information.

1. INTRODUCTION

1.1. Pop-ups and memory for text

Electronic documents such as hypertexts support many ways of organizing, presenting and accessing information. Effective use of these options by authors requires knowledge about what effects these choices have on the cognitive representations and processes of users.

This empirical study looks at how the use of pop-up windows in a hypertext affects readers' memory for what is read. The study compares a hypertext containing pop-up windows with a "plain" one that has the same information content, but no pop-ups. The plain version of the hypertext contains conventional textual descriptions of properties for sale. In the pop-up version, the descriptions contain pop-up windows that show "new details" about the property. (See Figure 1, below.) The pop-up version of the hypertext was generated from the plain version by selecting sentences from the plain descriptions to serve as new details.

1.2 Function and form of the pop-ups in the study

The semantic and rhetorical link between main text and pop-up window in this study is relatively neutral: almost any sentence in the plain version that is not the sole antecedent for an anaphor can be described as "new". This is not always the case: a pop-up may, for instance, always display a definition of a selected word from the main text.

However, the present arrangement has two advantages. First of all, it permits naturalistic comparison of linear and pop-up display of the same information. Secondly, it allows the effect of the pop-up display to be evaluated without the confounding influences of a highly specific textual relation.

In this study, the pop-up windows displaying new details appeared centred over their navigation cue within the text, partially occluding it. This style is frequently used in hypertext, and may make pop-ups less of a bother to look at by minimizing the visual excursion from the source window to the pop-up and thus minimizing any consequent disruption of the reader's focus of attention. However, this occluding style may have interesting adverse consequences for certain aspects of readers' memory for the text.

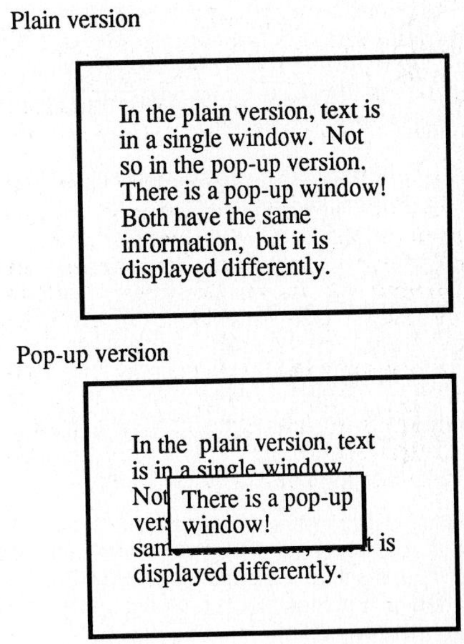

Figure 1
Plain and pop-up versions of the same text

1.3. Predicted effects of pop-up windows on memory

Putting information in a pop-up may make that information more memorable. A pop-up window separates the "popped" information from the mass of content in the main text both visually, by setting the information in a new frame, and behaviorally, by making a break in the reading process a prerequisite to displaying and hiding the pop-up. This separation may make the "popped" information more salient to readers during reading, and more memorable afterwards.

However, this same separation may result in poor *linkage* between readers' representations of popped information and their representation of information from the source window. Pop-ups may make readers less effective at integrating popped information with their knowledge of the property as a whole (global linkage), and with their knowledge of the information presented immediately before and after (local linkage). Occluding pop-ups, especially, may interfere with the reader's local links between the main text occluded by the pop-up, and the content of the pop-up. The present experiment was designed to explore whether using pop-up displays has global and local effects on memory.

2. THE STUDY

2.1 Overview

Two groups of adult volunteers were paid for their participation in the study. Both groups read hypertext descriptions of properties, and decided how strongly to recommend them to clients. One group read property descriptions with "new details" presented in a pop-up window. For the other group, all descriptive information was presented in conventional linear format within each window of text.

Subsequently, the groups were tested on their memory for features the properties had. This memory test assessed both the salience of property features, and how strongly these features were linked to their local text environment and to the global representation of the property.

All activities in the study were self-paced, but their time of occurence was monitored unobtrusively.

2.2. The reading task

Each property description consisted of a introductory page describing the property's address, age, and exterior, followed by three pages of prose description. Each screen page was 512 pixels wide by 340 pixels high. Readers advanced through a description by clicking an arrow a corner of the window. On the last page they had a choice between clicking a "Read again" button, or a "Recommend" button.

The pop-up version of the property descriptions had one new detail per page of property description, which was indicated by an asterisk within the text. Clicking the asterisk displayed the new detail and hid the region of text around the asterisk. Clicking again hid the new detail.

On the client recommendation page, readers saw a short description of a client (e.g. "Company seeks prestigious address to be used as venue for expensive business seminars"). Subjects used a clickable rating scale below the client description to judge how strongly they would recommend the property to that client. The rating scale was a continuous seven point Likert scale verbally labelled "Absolutely do not recommend" at one end, and "Recommend very strongly" at the other. After deciding on their rating, subjects clicked a "Done" button to see the description of the second client. The rating task had two purposes: to consolidate readers' memory for what they had read by encouraging them to think about it immediately afterwards, and to provide readers with a meaningful but not too difficult task to perform with what they had learned.

Subjects read and rated the suitability of a set of three properties before performing the memory task for that set of descriptions. There were four sets of properties in all: the first and third sets were descriptions of terraced houses, and the second and fourth sets were descriptions of stately homes. The purpose of this alternation was to reduce interference between sets. All descriptions were "factional", and described properties that might be found in the neighborhoods in which they were located.

2.3. The memory task

After reading each of the four sets of three property descriptions, subjects performed an online memory probe task in which they had to answer ten sequences of multiple choice questions. Each question sequence was based on a pair of property features. These features were either unique noun phrases from one of the three descriptions, or novel noun phrases that had not been seen in any of the descriptions.

For the pop-up group, the previously seen noun phrases had either been displayed in a pop-up window, or in the main text of a description. For the plain group, all these phrases had been displayed in the main text.

The canonical question sequence was:

1. Memorability:
   Was there a property with a *feature-1*?
2. Local link:
   Did that property also have a *feature-2*?
3. Global link:
   Which property had the *feature-1*?

If neither *feature-1* nor *feature-2* were recognized, the global link question was not asked. If a subject failed to recognize *feature-1*, they were asked about *feature-2* using the wording of the recognition question. If they correctly rejected a novel feature, no further questions in the sequence were asked, but if they incorrectly recognized it , an novel *feature-2* local link question was shown, followed by an global link question for the novel *feature-1*.

The memorability questions were designed to see whether putting information in a pop-up made it more memorable. Table 1, below, shows the text locations (for the pop-up group) of the memorability question features.

Table 1
Text location of features in memorability questions

Text location	Number
Pop-up	12
Before pop-up	6
Main text	6
Not in any text	16

The local link questions were designed to see whether putting information in a pop-up interfered with the local link between the popped information and occluded adjacent information from the source text. Table 2, below, shows (for the pop-up group) the text locations of the features asked about in local link questions, and the text location of the features in the memorability questions that occurred immediately before.

Table 2
Text location of features in local link questions

Memorability text location	Local link text location	Number
Pop-up	After pop-up	6
Pop-up	Other description	4
Pop-up	Not in any text	2
Before pop-up	Pop-up	6
Main	Other description	4
Main	Not in any text	2

If the pop-up display interferes with the local links in readers' representations of the description, subjects in the pop-up group should be slower or less accurate in answering two types of local link questions: those which follow memorability questions about a pop-up and ask about information after the pop-up, and those which follow memorability questions about information before a pop-up and ask about information in the pop-up.

The global link questions were designed to assess whether pop-ups interfered with reader's global links between individual features and the properties they belonged to. If pop-ups interfere with global links, responses to the features seen in pop-ups should be slower or less accurate.

Accross the four property sets, the location of all features in feature pairs was counterbalanced for position on page (top or bottom), page in description (1, 2, or 3), and order of property in set (first, second or third). The order of feature pairs in the question sequences was also counterbalanced as to the match between serial order in the property set and serial order in the memory task, the recency of a question in the memory task relevant to the same property, and the previous two correct answers (Yes or No) in the memory task.

The question sequence was controlled by "hot buttons", which the subject had only to touch with the mouse pointer to register a response or request the next question. This was done to give faster RT's by eliminating the click movement. The layout of the question page is shown in Figure 2, opposite. Subjects touched the black up-arrow with the mouse pointer when they were ready to see the next question. For the memorability and local link questions, responses were made by touching a "Yes" button or a "No" button with the mouse pointer. For the global link question, response buttons were labelled with the information on the introductory page of the description.

2.4. Subjects

All subjects in the study were drawn from the APU subject panel, and were paid for their participation. All had some form of tertiary education, and either lived or worked in the Cambridge area. Fuller details are given in Table 3, opposite.

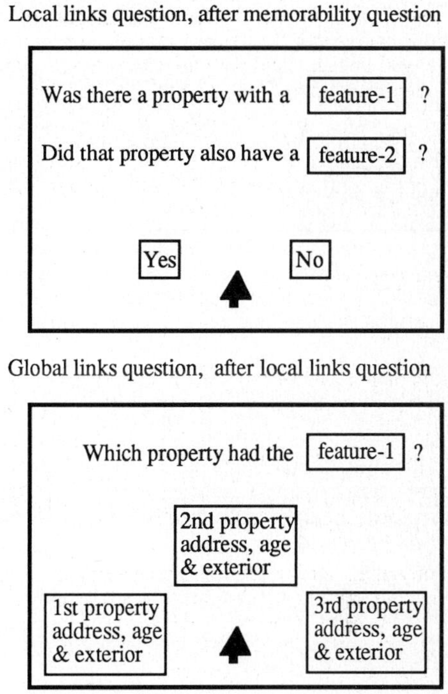

Figure 2
The interface for the memory task

Table 3
Composition of the pop-up and plain text groups

	Pop-up	Plain
N	12	12
Age		
Range	20-38	19-37
Median	23.5	27.5
Gender		
Female	43%	50%
Male	58%	50%
Handedness		
Right	100%	83%
Left	0%	17%
Time of testing		
morning	25%	25%
afternoon	50%	25%
evening	25%	50%
Previous mouse experience		
<= once	42%	42%
> once	58%	58%

2.5. Procedure

All subjects had self-paced practice (approx. 7 minutes) at moving and clicking the mouse.

Next, a sentence verification task was given which introduced the "hot buttons" interface used later for the memory task following a property set. In this task, subjects moved the mouse pointer to an up-arrow to display a sentence, and touched a "Yes" button or a "No" button to indicate whether the sentence was true. There were no trick questions. After initial explanation and practice, all subjects judged twenty sentences as quickly as possible. This task provides an independent check on the comparability of the two groups of subjects, as at this point in the procedure the groups have received identical practice, materials, and instructions.

After the sentence verification task, there was an on-line tutorial on the use of the hypertext. The instructions received by the pop-up group were identical to those received by the plain group, except for an additional screen giving explanation and practice at viewing new details. During the two practice properties, pop-up subjects were reminded to look at new details if they forgot, but afterwards looking at the new detail was left up to them.

Materials were presented using HyperCard running on a RAM disk, on a Mac II with 2 megabytes of RAM. A HyperCard script kept a timed record of all actions resulting from mouse presses and clicks.

3. RESULTS AND DISCUSSION

3.1. Analysis of "good" subjects only

In both the pop-up group and the plain group, some subjects were unable to cope effectively with the memory task. One subject in each group behaved at chance level or worse in rejecting novel information; one subject in the plain group always gave false positive responses to Feature 2 questions concerning features from other properties; two subjects in the pop-up group, and one subject in the plain group had more than 40% (mean 48%) missing or wrong replies to questions features in the descriptions.

The three subjects in each group who did not deal with the memory task effectively were excluded from subsequent analyses.

3.2. Sentence verification task

Surprisingly, the sentence verification task given as a part of subjects' "mouse training" was performed more quickly by the Pop-up group (Pop-up group: 1.65 sec, Plain group: 1.93 sec, $t(17)= 2.079$, $p<.10$, two-tailed). The Pop-up group was also slightly more accurate, although not significantly so (Pop-up group: 2% wrong, Plain group: 4% wrong, $t(17)= 0.83$, *n.s.*). This verification time difference is worth taking seriously because it of the cloud it casts on between group comparisons for the two groups. If the Pop-up subjects are faster in the introductory practice, where they have had *exactly* the same tasks and materials as the Plain group, the speed of their recognition judgments cannot be compared directly with the Plain group.

The best solution this problem is to collect more data, assigning subjects to conditions on the basis of their sentence verification task performance, in order to ensure that the two groups' performance on the sentence verification task are equivalent. Such data collection is currently underway. The interim solution, which is presented here, is to analyze the memory task results in terms of within group comparisons for each of the groups. (There are not enough data points for matched pairs analyses of the memory task, where matching is based on sentence verification performance.)

3.3. Memorability Questions

The purpose of the memorability questions is to assess whether information is more memorable when displayed in a pop-up window. Figure 3, below, shows the time each group takes to correctly recognize pop-up and main text features. (For the Plain text groups, of course, all features were mentioned in the main text.) Figure 4, following, shows the error rates for the recognition judgements.

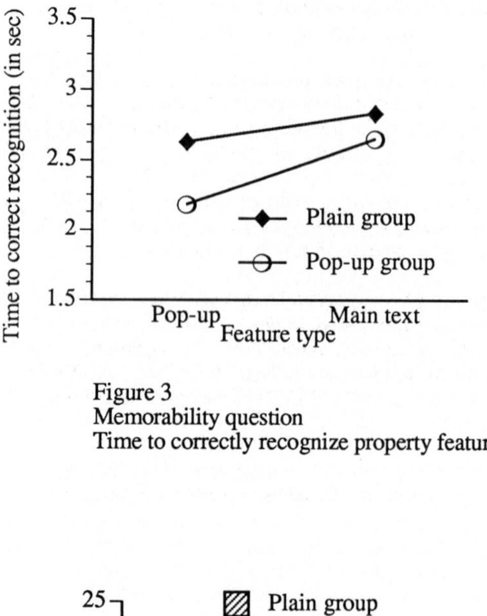

Figure 3
Memorability question
Time to correctly recognize property features

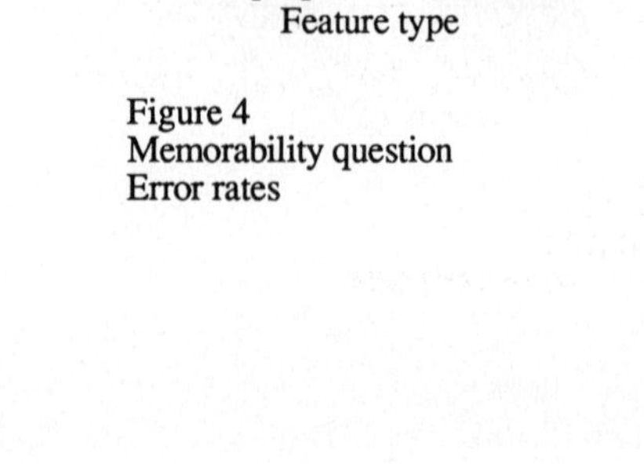

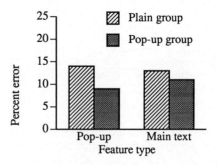

Figure 4
Memorability question
Error rates

For the Pop-up group, the pop-up features were recognized faster than the source features (Pop-up features: 2.18 sec, Source features: 2.65 sec, $t(8)= -2.79$, $p<.05$, two-tailed). This effect is not likely to be due to pop-up subjects learning the contingency that pop-up information was likely to be asked about, because the same pattern of results obtains when only the questions after the first set of properties are considered.

For the Plain group, who saw both sets of features in the source window, pop-up features were not recognized significantly faster (Pop-up features: 2.63 sec, Source features: 2.83 sec, $t(8)= -1.24$, *n.s.*). The differences in error rates for the two types of features were not significant for either group.

3.4. Local link Questions

The initial purpose of the local link questions was to assess the strength of local links between pop-up features and main text features before and after the pop-up which were hidden when the pop-up was displayed. However, since assessment of this effect relies entirely on a between groups comparison, it is inappropriate for the current sample.

Instead, the local link questions were analyzed to provide another assessment of the memorability of pop-up information. Within each group of subjects, responses to local link Questions in which *feature-2* was a pop-up feature were compared with responses to the memorability questions in which *feature-1* had been a main text feature. Times for correct responses for the two groups are shown in Figure 5, below, and error rates in Figure 6, opposite.

For the pop-up group, pop-up *feature-2*s were recognized more accurately than source *feature-1*, although this difference was only marginally significant (Pop-up *feature-2*s: 2% wrong, Source *feature-1*'s: 11% wrong, $t(8)=1.89$, $p<.10$). For the plain group, there was no difference in error rate (Pop-up *feature-2*s: 12% wrong, Source *feature-1*s: 13% wrong, $t(8)=0.14$, *n.s.*). For neither group was there a significant difference in the time it took to answer the pop-up *feature-1* questions and the source *feature-2* questions.

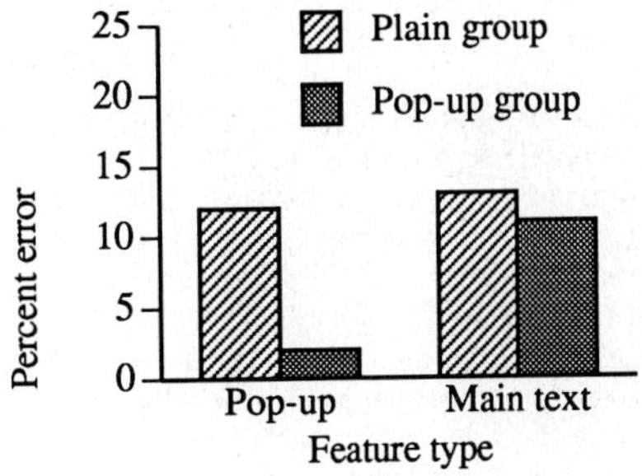

Figure 6
Local links question
Error rates

3.5. Global link Questions

The purpose of the global link questions is to assess whether pop-up windows disrupt reader's global links between the information in a pop-up and knowledge of where the information came from. Figure 7, below, shows how quickly the two groups can correctly identify which property a feature came from, and Figure 8 on the next page shows the error rate.

For the pop-up group, pop-up features were verified much more quickly than source features (Pop-up features: 2.76 sec, Source features: 3.95, $t(8)=3.49$, $p<.02$). This was not the case for the plain group (Pop-up features: 3.45 sec, Source features: 4.06 sec, $t(8)=1.33$, *n.s.*). Differences in accuracy were not significant for either group.

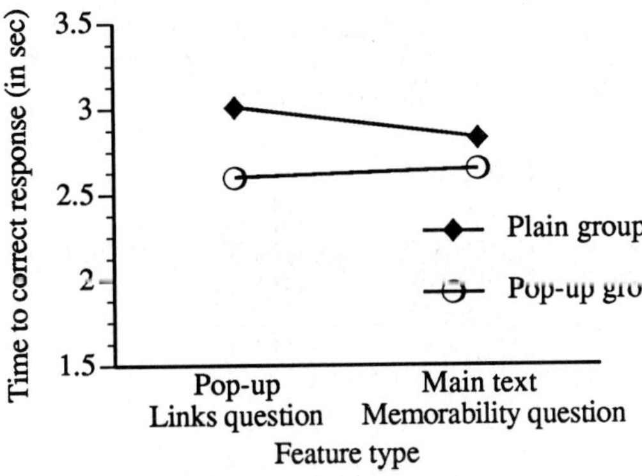

Figure 5
Local links
Time to correct response

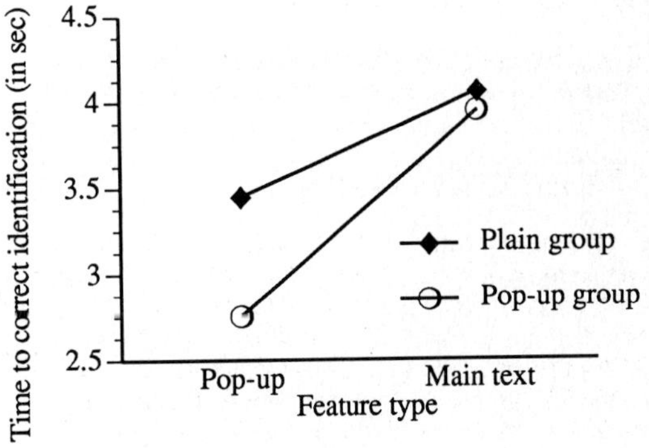

Figure 7
Global links question
Time to correctly identify property

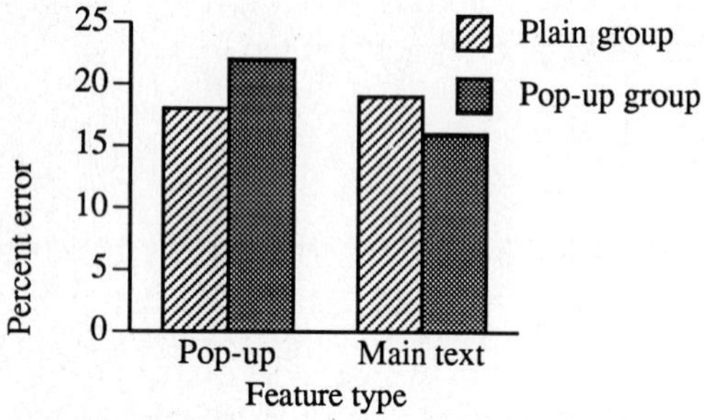

Figure 8
Global links question
Error rates

3.6. Reading and rating

The two groups did not differ significantly in how long, on average, they took to complete a set of three properties (Pop-up group: 10 min 6 sec, Plain group: 11 min 35 sec, $t(17)= -0.74$, *n.s.*).

On average, subjects in the Pop-up group re-read property descriptions more often than subjects in the Plain group, but this difference was not statistically significant (Pop-up group: 80% of properties re-read, Plain group: 57% re-read, $t(17)= 0.95$, *n.s.).* Partitioning results in the memory task by subjects' re-reading strategies results in subgroups that are, at the present moment, too small to be meaningful, but this analysis will be undertaken when more data is collected.

Perhaps because the Pop-up subjects were reminded to look at pop-ups during initial practice, subjects in the Pop-up group almost never forgot to look at the new details in pop-up windows. The pop-up features queried in memorability questions had been read by subjects 99.1% of the time.

There was substantial agreement between the groups in average ratings given for the 24 clients (Spearman $r = .92$, $p<.001$). While the pop-up group performed these ratings somewhat more quickly than the plain group, this difference was not statistically significant (Pop-up group: 13.4 sec, Plain group: 16.2 sec, $t(17)= -1.58$, *n.s.).*

3.7. Discussion

Because the Pop-up group was faster than the Plain group prior to any divergence in their experimental treatments, futher data collection is being undertaken to enable between groups comparisons to be made. However, using within groups comparisons it was possible to assess some of the questions asked by the study.

Pop-up features were recognized more quickly than main text features in the Pop-up group, but not in the Plain group. This shows that pop-up windows can make their contents more memorable for readers. This conclusion is also supported by the better accuracy for pop-up features in the Pop-up group, but not the Plain group, in the local link questions.

Investigation of whether pop-ups disrupt local text links must wait until between groups comparisons can be made. However, pop-up windows did not adversely affect reader's global links between the pop-up information and the property it came from. Instead, readers seeing pop-up windows were *faster* to identify which property a pop-up feature had come from. It could be that the visual and behavioral framing of material in pop-up windows results in an overall improvement in how well the information is encoded.

The two groups of subjects did not appear to differ on gross measures of performance, total reading time and agreement and time to client rating. The effect of pop-up windows on readers' appears to be one of stylistic emphasis, which is more appropriately evaluated with techiques that probe the organization of readers' representation of the text.

With the present sample size, it was not possible to tell whether readers with pop-up windows developed a different reading strategy, and were more likely to re-read the property descriptions. This is one of the questions which will be answered by the collection of further data.

4. CONCLUSIONS

In this study, text presented in a pop-up window was better remembered than material in the main text, both in terms of speed of recognition and speed of identifying the text from which the material came. This result suggests that, rather than being just a vehicle for "footnotey" asides, pop-up windows could be a useful way to display information an the author wishes to emphasize.

It would be interesting to see whether pop-up information is more memorable when other types of semantic and rhetorical links are implied by the use of a pop-up.

It would also be useful to extend the investigation to evaluate whether the superior memorability of pop-up information persists when a main text window has several pop-up windows leading from it. In this study, each screen of main text had only one pop-up window in it. Remembering where information comes from may be more difficult when there are more places it could have been.

ACKNOWLEDGEMENTS

Pat Wright and other members of the APU have been very helpful in discussing all stages of this work.

Human–Computer Interaction – INTERACT '90
D. Diaper et al. (Editors)
Elsevier Science Publishers B.V. (North-Holland)

TWO WAYS TO FILL A BATH, WITH AND WITHOUT KNOWING IT†

Anne Ankrah, David M. Frohlich* and G. Nigel Gilbert

Social and Computer Sciences Research Group, University of Surrey, Guildford GU2 5XH, UK

It is generally thought that direct manipulation interfaces are those based on some clear metaphor for interaction which encourages the user to draw an analogy between the machine and some familiar situation. In this paper we challenge this view by showing how it is possible to vary metaphor and directness of manipulation independently in interface design, and that the influence of these factors on usability is not simple. We report findings from an experiment in which 40 users were presented with the same process control task through four different interfaces incorporating different combinations of the two factors. The task was based on the familiar situation of filling a bath.

1. INTRODUCTION

The development of interactive computer systems appears to have entered a period of theoretical consolidation in which explanations are sought for the quality of interaction enjoyed by different groups of users on different kinds of system. The goal of this activity is to establish a theory (or theories) of *usability* which will allow systems to be designed in a principled way and will provide starting points or 'survival forms' (Dreyfus 1955) for system prototypes.

A particularly high quality of interaction has been enjoyed by the users of the Xerox Star information system (Johnson et al 1989) and its style of interaction has been widely adopted or adapted by companies such as Apple,Microsoft, the Open Systems Foundation and many more. Success stories like the Star's have prompted the formulation of two candidate theories of usability.

Firstly, there is what may be called the theory of *direct manipulation*. This proposes that usability is related to the directness with which psychological variables of interest to the user (goals) can be mapped onto physical variables (actions) at the interface. According to this theory, a system will be easier to use, the more direct the mapping is. The term direct manipulation was coined by Shneiderman (1982, 1983) to describe the properties of certain kinds of graphical interfaces which allow the user to perform physical actions on objects displayed continuously on the screen. Subsequent work by Norman and colleagues on the psychological basis of using such interfaces has lead to the formulation above (Hutchins et al 1986).

The second theory of usability may be called a theory of *metaphorical interaction.* This proposes that usability is related to the extent to which an interface encourages its users to reason analogically about the operation of the system (i.e. from previous experience of the world). A system embodying appropriate or stimulating metaphors for interaction will be easier to use than a system without such metaphors (eg.Carroll & Mack 1985,Wozny 1989).

The Xerox Star serves as a exemplar of how these theories may be related to usability. The Star was targeted at users who were skilled office workers and

> casual, occasional users rather than people who spent most of their time at the machine. This assumption led to the goal of having the Star be *easy to learn* and *remember* (Johnson et al 1989: p 11).

In order to meet this requirement the Star interface was based on the 'desktop metaphor'. Familiar office objects were displayed on the screen as icons (Smith et al 1982). Users were able to manipulate the icons on the screen by a mouse driven cursor and thus control the system. The design emphasized two features:

1. The transfer of prior knowledge from the office environment to the computer environment.
2. Control of the system through recognition rather than recall.

The latter is facilitated by the fact that the

> Star's Desktop metaphor is based on a more general principle of direct manipulation (Johnson et al 1989: p 14).

This strong association between metaphorical interaction and direct manipulation is frequently made, often to the extent that the two properties are discussed as if they are

† The authors acknowledge the support of the Economic and Social Research Council, grant GR/ ROOO231480
* Now at Hewlett-Packard Laboratories, Filton Road, Stoke Gifford, Bristol, BS12 6Q2

synonymous.

Metaphorical interaction and direct manipulation are, however, quite separate as illustrated by the fact that they can be defined without reference to one another and could in principle be found in isolation . It is impossible to assess the validity of the theory of direct manipulation based on trials of a system incorporating metaphor which may equally account for its high degree of usability. The same may be said for a theory of metaphorical interaction. To suggest that systems with both characteristics are easiest of all to use is to assume ,without warrant ,that their effects are additive and precludes the possibility of interactions between them. What appears to be required is the direct testing of each of these theories in a context where both their separate and combined effects can be measured.

This paper describes such an empirical investigation. Four independent groups of subjects were presented with the same computer-based task through one of the following interfaces:

1. Indirect without metaphor
2. Direct without metaphor
3. Indirect with metaphor
4. Direct with metaphor

The task was based on an example used by Norman (1986) to explain the concept of direct manipulation: filling a bath. The psychological difficulty of the task differs according to the type of taps used. The goal is always to fill the bath to a desired level and water temperature. However this can be done more easily with American style taps which control the rate of flow and water temperature directly. The separation of hot and cold water supplies with British style taps leads to a less direct relationship between goals and actions.

By simulating the task of filling a bath with either British or American style controls, it was possible to experimentally vary the degree of *directness* of manipulation in Norman's (1986) terms. Furthermore, by varying the visual presentation of the task, it was possible to offer or withold the bath-filling metaphor. It remained only to define the outcome, the degree of usability of the four interfaces.

Following Bennett (1984), we have characterized usability along four different dimensions: throughput, learnability, flexibility and attitude. In this paper we focus principally on traditional throughput measures of usability based on the speed and accuracy of task performance. Although some indication is also given of interface usability along the other dimensions, later reports will consider these in greater detail.

In short, this study aims to demonstrate that direct manipulation and metaphorical interaction may,in practice, be viewed independently, and that when they are combined they may not produce a simple additive effect on system usability as characterized by throughput, evidence of learning and retention. The results of this study should show exactly what the individual and combined effects of each factor are for the task described.

2. METHOD

2.1 Design

The experiment had a two factor independent groups design. The two independent variables were:

(i) the directness of manipulation of the subject's goals (direct or indirect)
(ii) the presence or absence of an explicit metaphor.

All combinations of these two factors were presented through four different interfaces to the same computer-based process control task.

2.2 Subjects

Forty paid volunteers were randomly assigned to one of four experimental groups in equal numbers of males and females. Subjects varied in age from 20 to 37, and most were undergraduates from the University of Surrey.

2.3 Apparatus and Materials

The four versions of the task were implemented using HyperCard on an Apple Macintosh llcx. Subjects interacted with the Macintosh via a mouse. The process control task underlying all of the interfaces was a computer simulation of filling a bath. The physical dynamics of mixing water at varying temperatures were maintained for all interfaces, but the control dynamics and the visual presentation were varied as follows:

1. Indirect manipulation without metaphor.

The visual presentation of the task (Figure 1) suggests no explicit metaphor. However, in terms of the physical dynamics underlying this version's behaviour, the larger box represents a tank filling with water and the smaller box, a gauge monitoring the temperature of water in the tank . The horizontal lines within these boxes correspond to water level and temperature level. The level in the larger box may only move upwards (there is no way to 'empty the tank'), but the line in the smaller box moves up and down (corresponding to varying temperature). There are two sliding scales, the top one having the same effect on the water as a hot tap (90 F) and the bottom one having the same effect as a cold tap (10 F).

The subjects were thus provided with indirect control over the goal: to get both horizontal lines to their target positions as quickly and accurately as possible. When either slider is moved to the right, the horizontal line in the larger box will rise. The line in the smaller box rises and falls according to the ratio of the integral of the sliding scale positions.

2. Direct manipulation without metaphor.

This version shares the same visual presentation as version (1). However, the top sliding scale corresponds to a single tap controlling water *rate* and the bottom sliding scale corresponds to a temperature control for the water flowing from this tap. The subject is thus provided with more direct control over the goal, but no access to the bath-tub metaphor. The further to the right the upper slider is moved the faster the 'flow' and the further right the lower slider is moved, the hotter the 'water'.

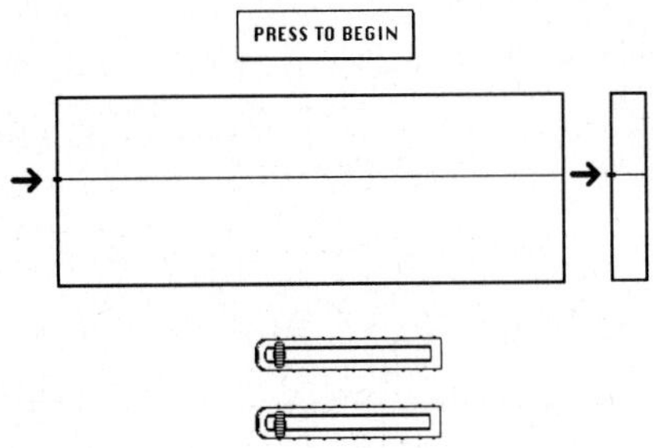

Figure 1 Visual presentation of the task for versions without the metaphor.

3. Indirect manipulation with metaphor.

The visual presentation of the task (Figure 2) explicitly suggests a bath-tub. The top sliding scale has the effect of a hot tap and the bottom one a cold tap, once again providing the subject with indirect control over the goal.

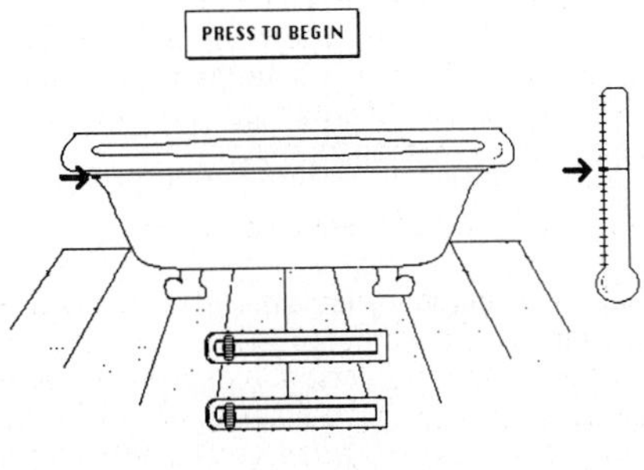

Figure 2 Visual presentation of the task for versions using the bath-tub metaphor.

4. Direct manipulation with metaphor

This version shares the same visual presentation as version (3), but in contrast to that version the top sliding scale simulates a tap controlling water rate and the bottom scale simulates a temperature control for the water flowing from this tap. Subjects are therefore provided with relatively more direct control over the goal.

A simple automated monitoring technique allowed each subject's interaction to be recorded. The interaction monitoring device was also implemented in HyperCard, inspired by an idea from Macleod (1989). Each subject had their own experimental stack through which they were presented with the appropriate interface. Interaction data was collected in this stack and task performance was recorded so that it could be played back for post-experiment investigation.

A questionnaire was used to structure a post-experiment interview. It consisted of 18 statements relating to the learnability, throughput, flexibility and attitude towards the system. Subjects' retrospective protocols and evaluations were audio recorded.

2.4 Procedure

There were four experimental groups each made up of five male and five female subjects. Subjects were individually instructed in one of two ways depending on the group they were assigned to.

All subjects were informed that the experimenter was investigating how people interact with the computer while performing a task. They were shown a summary of what they would be doing, displayed on the first card in their HyperCard experimental stack. They were then presented with the appropriate version of the task on a practice card in which the lines did not change when the sliding scales were operated. This allowed them to practice using the mouse and sliders without affecting the lines.

Groups 1and 2 were told that the goal was to get both the horizontal line in the large box and the line in the smaller box to their target positions as quickly as possible. Groups 3 and 4 were told that the goal was to fill the bath to its target level at its target temperature as quickly as possible.

Subjects were then presented with a working card, the target water level was 80% full and the target temperature was equivalent to 60 F. The trial began when the subjects pressed the 'PRESS TO BEGIN' button, it ended either when the water level was halted at or above the target level, or when the water passed an overflow level near the top of the bath. After 10 trials the subjects were moved to another card on which the target temperature level was lowed to 30 F.. After trial 11 subjects were asked to complete the questionnaire. A post- experimental interview followed in which subjects were asked to describe what they had been doing and what they thought the dynamics of their particular version of the task were. All subjects returned after a two week interval and performed one trial, trial 12, on the same version of the task they had experienced on trials 1-10 .

2.5 Measures

Throughput was measured by a standardized composite performance score based on
(i) time taken to complete the task for each trial
(ii) error: the absolute number of pixels between the achieved level and the target level (water and temperature)

These scores were then converted to z scores reflecting the deviation of each score from its sample mean. In order to qualify this metric the following were also considered:

Learning was measured by the change in performance scores between trial 1 and 11. *Retention of learning* was measured by the change in performance scores between trial 11 and 12. *Subjective impressions* of the task were collected during post-experimental interviews.

3. RESULTS

3.1 Learning and Retention

Task performance for the four experimental groups is illustrated in Figure 3. Group 1 (Indirect manipulation without metaphor) does not appear to improve across trials. Their performance deteriorates dramatically on trial 6 and continues to fall until trial 11. There is a slight improvement after two weeks on trial 12. Group 2 (Direct manipulation without metaphor) does appear to improve as the trials progress. They seem to have learned the task to the highest level of performance by trial 11 and retain this over the two week interval. Group 3 (Indirect with metaphor) appear to have mastered the task from the beginning. Their level of performance deteriorates over trials and has fallen considerably by trial 11. However a high level of performance is displayed again after the two week interval. Group 4 (Direct with metaphor) show evidence of learning during the first session and this is retained relatively well after two weeks.

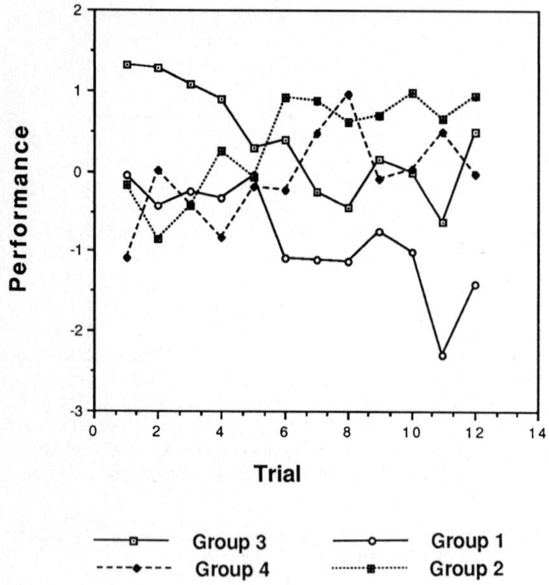

Figure 3. Task performance by group over twelve trials.

Paired score t tests were administered to each of the experimental groups' task performance scores to test the differences in task performance between trial 1 and trial 11(learning), and trial 11 and trial 12 (retention), (Table 1).

Table 1. Evidence of learning within groups during trials 1-11 and for retention of learning after two weeks

<u>LEARNING</u>			
Group 1	Deterioration	(t = -3.24,	df = 9,**)
Group 2	Improvement	(t = 2.50,	df = 9,*)
Group 3	Deterioration	(t = -3.62,	df = 9,**)
Group 4	Improvement	(t = 2.05,	df = 9,*)
<u>RETENTION</u>			
Group 1	No change	(t = 1.69,	df = 9,ns)
Group 2	No change	(t = 1.50,	df = 9,ns)
Group 3	Improvement	(t = 2.75,	df = 9,**)
Group 4	No change	(t = 1.72,	df = 9,ns)

* p<0.05 **p<0.01 ns = not significant at 5% level

These results support the summary of trends observed from the mean performance scores. Group 2 and Group 4 learn the task and retain their ability after two weeks. Group 1 and Group 3 deteriorate over trials, but Group 3 significantly improves after two weeks.

3.2 Throughput.

In order to quantify the effects of directness and metaphor on throughput, a two-factor analysis of variance test was applied to the composite performance scores for trial 11. There was a highly significant main effect for directness on usability, such that subjects presented with the direct manipulation interfaces performed consistently better than those using the indirect interfaces. (Directness: F = 17.44, df 1 36, p<0.001). This can be seen from Figure 4. The absence or presence of a task metaphor did not, in itself, significantly affect usability Metaphor: F = 0.16,df 1 36, ns). However, the presence of a metaphor appeared to reduce the difficulty of using the indirect interface, as shown by the interaction which fell just short of conventional significance (F = 4.16, df 1 36, p<0.1).

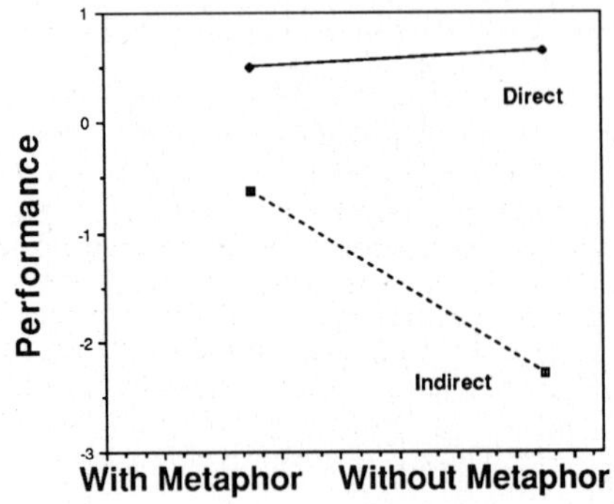

Figure 4 Interaction diagram for task performance (Groups 1-4) Trial 11

A two-factor analysis of variance was also applied to the combined performance scores for trial 12. There were no significant main effects (Directness: F = 2.34,df 1,36, ns. Metaphor: F = 0.63, df 1 36, ns). There was, however, a significant interaction between the two factors (F = 5,87,df 1,36; p<0.05). As may be seen from Figure 5, subjects presented with an *indirect* manipulation interface achieve a higher level of performance when the metaphor is *present*, while subjects presented with a *direct* manipulation interface achieve a higher level of performance when the metaphor is *absent*.

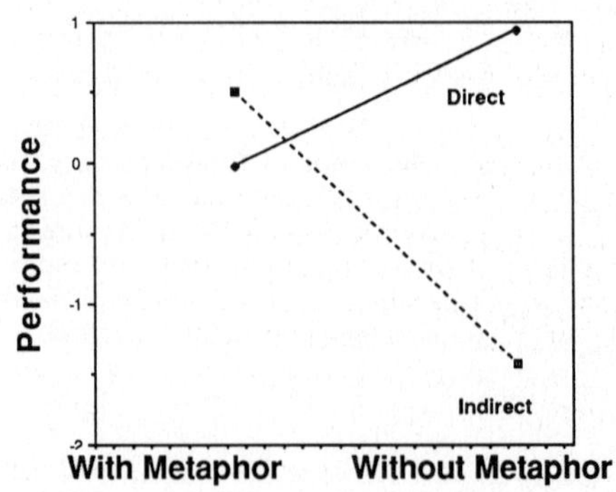

Figure 5 Interaction diagram for task performance (Groups 1-4) Trial 12

The occurrence of a significant interaction in trial 12 as opposed to trial 11 is related to the significant improvement of Group 3 after the interval of two weeks,there was no other significant improvement or deterioration in performance for the other groups during this period.

3.3 Subjective Impressions

The subjects' own evaluations and retrospective protocols shed some light on these statistical results:

Group 1 (Indirect manipulation with no metaphor): Most subjects were unable to describe the relationship between the two sliding scales and the horizontal lines. They were aware of the interdependence of the two scales and described the task in terms of "balancing" and setting the distance between the sliders relative to one another. Even after trial 12, they felt that they had more to learn about the task and that what understanding they had acquired had been achieved towards the end of the trials. They did not find the interface easy to learn to use.

Group 2 (Direct manipulation with no metaphor): Most subjects achieved an understanding of what the two sliding scales were controlling. They described the upper scale as a speed control over the horizontal line in the large box and the lower scale as controlling the line in the small box. Many described the specific strategies they used to achieve their goals in terms of "speed" and "fine tuning". They felt that they had learned all they needed to know by the end of the trials, and that this understanding had occurred toward the beginning. They found the interface easy to learn.

Group 3 (Indirect with metaphor): There was a clear split in this group, most subjects achieving a high level of understanding while some remained completely confused to the end of the trials. The majority of subjects described the top sliding scale as a hot water control and the bottom one as a cold water control. They described their strategies in terms of adding more hot and cold water. They felt they had learned all they needed to know and that the task was very easy. The minority could not understand what the two scales were controlling. They reported that the task had been extremely difficult to learn although they had expected it to be easy.

Group 4 (Direct with metaphor): Most subjects in this group understood what the two sliding scales were controlling. They described the top scale as the water rate control and the bottom scale as the temperature control. They felt they had learned all they needed to know towards the beginning of the trials. They thought the task had been easy to learn.

Subjects in Groups 1 and 2 ,and to a lesser extent, those in Group 4, felt a strong sense of achievement on completing the task. However, competent subjects in Group 3 appeared bored and dispirited by the end of the trials, those who had not succeeded in understanding the interface were frustrated and angry with the experimenter and the system.

4. DISCUSSION

The theories of direct manipulation and metaphorical interaction propose that directness of manipulation and the presence of a metaphor respectively increase the usability of an interface. If the directness and metaphorical nature of an interface independently increase its usability, one would expect that the interface design which incorporates both of these features would facilitate the highest level of performance. Figure 6 illustrates the effect which would be obtained if the two effects were simply additive. The results, summarized in Figures 4 and 5, show that the situation is in fact considerably more complicated.

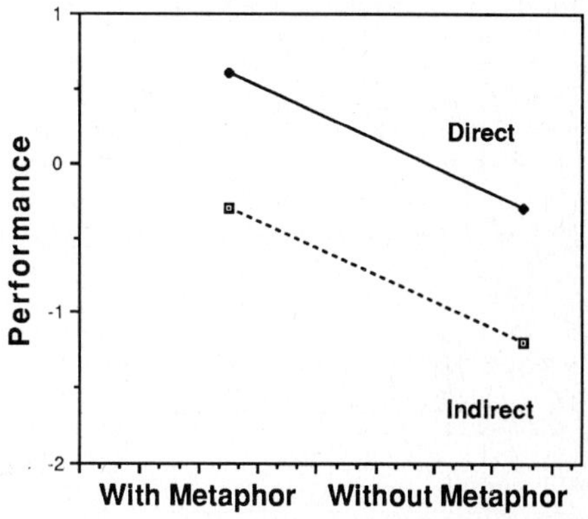

Figure 6 Interaction diagram for performance showing an additive effect of the 2 factors

The clearest finding was in the form of support for the theory of *direct manipulation.* The direct manipulation interfaces were significantly more usable than the indirect interfaces after 10 practice trials. Thus, subjects in Groups 2 and 4 who used the direct interfaces showed significant improvement in task performance over 11 trials, were able to sustain the same level of performance after a two week break, and for the most part, reported finding the task easy to learn. Conversley, subjects in Groups 1 and 3 , who used the indirect interfaces exhibited signifcant deterioration in task performance with practice. However this distinction between direct and indirect interfaces is by no means clear cut. While subjects in Group 1 performed comparitively poorly after the two week break and reported finding the task difficult to learn, most subjects in Group 3 reported that the task had been easy to learn and actually performed significantly better after the break. In contrast to the other groups, these subjects appeared bored and lacking enthusiasm by trial 11. The deteriorating performance displayed by Group 1 appears to reflect the counter intuitive nature of the relation between the controls and the visual representation, in which a single slider could influence the level of both horizontal lines. Many subjects began with the view that a single slider would affect a single line, became gradually more anxious, confused and ultimately demoralized as they realized this was not the case, letting their performance scores slip so as to understand the true relationship. The deteriorating performance displayed by Group 3 may reflect their boredom and lack of attention.

There was no direct support for the theory of *metaphorical interaction.* Providing subjects with an understanding of the task which the system simulated did not, in itslelf, enhance their performance on trial 11. This is not to say that the presence of a metaphor did not affect usability at all. On the contrary, it appeared to have different effects on the usability of the direct and indirect interfaces. This was shown by the significant or near significant interactions between directness and metaphor on trials 12 and 11 respectively. The results show a consistent effect of metaphor on use of the indirect interfaces, such that these were easier to use with the metaphor (Group 3) than without it (Group1) . In contrast, the direct interfaces were easier to use without the metaphor (Group 2) than with it (Group 4).

This interaction is understandable in terms of the interplay of task and device knowledge encouraged by the design of each interface. For British subjects familiar with hot and cold running water, the presence of the bath-tub metaphor is likely to call into play device knowledge consistent with the design of the indirect but not the direct manipulation interface. This would tend to enhance the performance of subjects in Group 3 and degrade the performance of subjects in Group 4. Furthermore the absence of the metaphor is likely to call into play more intuitive knowledge about control display relations, part of which seems to be the assumption that there will be a one-to-one mapping between a control device and a display indicator (Poulton 1974). This knowledge is consistent with the design of the direct but not the indirect manipulation interface, and would tend to enhance the performance of subjects in Group 2 and degrade the performance of subjects in Group 1.

5. CONCLUSION

This study has shown that *direct manipulation* interfaces need not be those based on a 'desktop' or other real world metaphor. It is possible to design both direct manipulation interfaces which lack metaphorical images and to to design indirect manipulation interfaces based on some clear task metaphor. For this reason we reiterate Norman's (1987, p 333) observation that the term itself has been over-generalized and misused, and suggest that the interfaces originally characterized by Schniederman (1982, 1983) be referred to as 'WIMP -style' interfaces.

The psychological definition of 'directness' of manipulation provided by Hutchins et al (1986) serves as a foundation for the empirical investigation of its effect on the usability of interactive systems, and the data reported in this study provide preliminary support for the claim that control systems based on close action-goal mappings are easier to use than those based on distant mappings. However, the results have also shown that the extent to which directness will enhance usability is affected by the model of the task projected to users by its visual presentation at the interface.

In conclusion, the observed interaction between the effects of directness and metaphor implies that more sophisticated theories of usability are required, which acknowledge the interplay of control system design, task presentation and prior learning in computer use. Further empirical studies of their relationship would help in this endeavour.

ACKNOWLEDGEMENTS

The authors acknowledge the encouragement and assistance of the other members of the Social and Computer Sciences Research Group.

REFERENCES

Bennett, J.L. (1984) Managing to meet usability requirements: Establishing and meeting software development goals. In: J. Bennett, D.Case, J.Sandelin, and M,Smith, (Eds), *Visual Display Terminals*, (Prentice-Hall, Englewood Cliffs,NJ), 161-18

Carroll, J. M. and Mack, R. L. (1985) Metaphor, computing systems and active learning. *International Journal Of Man-Machine Studies 22:* 39-57

Dreyfus, H. (1955) *Designing for people*, (New York : Simon and Shuster).

Hutchins, E.L., Holland J.D and Norman D.A. (1986) Direct Manipulation Interfaces. In D.A. Norman and Draper (Eds.) *User Centred System Design.* Hillsdale, NJ: Lawrence Erlbaum Associates.

Johnson, J., Roberts,T.L., Verplank, W., Smith, D.C., Irby, C.H., Beard, M., and Mackey, K. (1989) The Xerox Star: A Retrospective *IEEE Computer*, September.

Macleod, M. (1989) Direct Manipulation Prototype User Interface Monitoring. In *People and Computers: Designing for Usability*, (Eds. A. Sutcliffe and L. Macauly). Cambridge University Press: Cambridge .

Norman, D.A. (1986) Cognitive engineering. In D.A. Norman and S. Draper (Eds.) *User Centred System Design.* Hillsdale, NJ: Lawrence Erlbaum Associates.

Norman, D.A. (1987) Cognitive engineering or cognitive science. In J.M. Carroll (Ed.) *Interfacing thought: Cognitive aspects of human- computer interaction.* MIT Press

Poulton, E.L. (1974) *Tracking skills and manual control.* (New York: Academic Press)

Smith, D., Harlsem, E., Irby,C., and Kimball, R. (1982) The Star user interface: an overview. *Proceedings of the 1982 National Computer Conference* .

Shneiderman, B. (1982) The future of interactive systems and the emergence of direct manipulation. *Behaviour and Information 1:* 237-256.

Shneiderman, B. (1983) Direct Manipulation : A step beyond programming languages. *IEEE Computer 16* : 57-69.

Wozny, L, A. (1989) The application of metaphor, analogy, and conceptual models in computer systems. *Interacting with computers* Vol 1 no 3, 273- 283.

Human–Computer Interaction – INTERACT '90
D. Diaper et al. (Editors)
Elsevier Science Publishers B.V. (North-Holland)

The Cognitive Dimension of Viscosity: a sticky problem for HCI

T R G Green

MRC Applied Psychology Unit, 15 Chaucer Road, Cambridge, UK

'Cognitive dimensions' are features of interactive systems considered as information structures, capturing significant commonalities across many types of system. Examples include the presence of asymmetric dependencies; consistency in the command language; and viscosity, or resistance to local change, the subject of this paper. In viscous systems users need many 'internal tasks' to accomplish one 'external task' of adding, removing, or altering a plan-level component. Opportunistic planning can be thwarted by undue viscosity. Two types are distinguished: Knock-On viscosity, where a goal-related action violates a notational constraint, and requires additional, non-goal-related actions to rectify the problem; and Repetitiousness viscosity, where to achieve a singe goal many individual actions are required. Examples of viscosity from many areas are given and some solutions are noted.

Introduction: the 'cognitive dimensions' framework and its aims

The motivation for this paper is that HCI needs a more universal language to describe features that are common across many different areas. The discipline is fragmented into database-talk, hypertext-talk, graphics-talk, etc., with poor communication across the boundaries. Yet there are important commonalities to be observed, one of which is the subject of this paper. Briefly it may be expressed as "how much work you have to do if you change your mind".

The framework of 'cognitive dimensions' of notations and their environments was coined by Green (1989). These 'dimensions' are intended to be applicable to many different kinds of HCI activity, to be related to existing cognition-based theory, and to lead to useful statements about cognitive demands and users' behaviour. They are necessarily rather general, but by analysing briefly the Smalltalk-80 environment it was shown that they can be effective at revealing problems in existing designs.

The framework is intended for situations where someone ('the user', or author, designer, or programmer, as appropriate) is building something, such as a program, a musical score, or a database model. These can all be considered as 'information structures' represented in some *notation.* Well-structured text, with headings and subheadings, figures and captions, would also qualify. The framework distinguishes between the notation and the *support environment.* The support environment is the medium of interaction: it may provide 'power tools', such as global search-and-replace, and it controls such aspects as how much the user can see at one time. The combination of notation and environment is the system that the user interacts with, and it is this total system to which the dimensions apply.

Example systems include any combination of a programming language and a text editor, or a programming language and pen-and-paper (considered here as an editor system), or a programming language and a telephone (also an editor system, but with very different properties!). Other examples will appear below.

It should be clear that the aim of this exercise is to present a set of well-analysed terms which can be used as part of the language of discussion of HCI. If we are to use results from one domain (say, studies of word processors or programming languages) to predict any aspects of usability in other domains (say, data base query languages, CAD-E systems, or hypertext systems), then we need terms to express relevant commonalities. These commonalities will largely exist at the structural level rather than at the level of detailed specification of individual devices or systems; hence, the focus of this research is on properties of information structures that are relevant to users' behaviour and understanding.

Interaction Layers

In the simplest case the cognitive dimensions framework is applied to uninterpreted information structures, such as musical scores or database models, which are built using some type of interactive editor. In these cases, the notation is the 'interaction language' (Reisner, 1981) in which the user works the editor. (A good analysis of this, in terms of 'device space' and 'goal space', is given by Payne, 1987.)

'Executable' structures, such as programs and documents marked up for formatters, go one step farther. Consider a document formatting language, such as Generalised Markup Language. In preparing a document using GML we have two layers: we apply a text editor to the GML commands, and in due course we execute the GML commands to format the body of the text. So we use a notation of text editor commands to build an information structure of GML commands, and that information structure is itself a notation which affects the information structure comprising the final document.

Examples of cognitive dimensions

A few examples of dimensions that were identified in Green (1989) will be given, although there is no space to discuss either the complete set or their relationship with underlying theory. (1) Asymmetric or 'hidden' pointers: two components of the information structure are related, but the relationship is only visible in one direction. Example: spreadsheet cells, where cell A refers to cell B, but it is not easily determined that changing cell B will affect cell A. (2) Role-expressiveness: the functional role of a component may be highlighted by distinctive lexemes or syntactic constructions (called 'beacons' in the psychology of programming) or in various other ways. Without distinctive cues, determining the functional role of a component may be very difficult. Example of poor role-expressiveness: identifying functional roles in low-level notations (assembly code, flowcharts). (3) Consistency: the alignment between task semantics and syntactic constructions. Example of poor consistency: in the early text editor TECO every semantic task was expressed by a unique single letter. In contrast, in MacWrite, related tasks are performed by similar actions, leading to savings in learning. This dimension has been explored via Task-Action Grammar (Payne and Green, 1986; Schiele and Green, 1990). (4) Viscosity: resistance to local changes. Read on!

Incidentally, these cognitive dimensions, like the physical dimensions, are not easily manipulated independently. The *concepts* are independent, just as the concepts of mass, length, and time are independent: but to change the viscosity of a notation it is usually necessary to change other dimensions as well, just as to change the volume of a mass of gas it is necessary to change its temperature or its pressure or both. Thus, evaluating a notation and environment requires consideration of trade-offs.

Dimensions are task-related. Behaviour is conjointly determined.

The relevance of each dimension can only be determined in relation to what users are trying to achieve and their mode of working. In Green (1989) I considered *opportunistic design*, which has been identified as a typical preferred mode of working in many situations (Flower and Hayes, 1980; Guindon et al., 1988; Visser, 1988; Hartson and Hix, in press). In this mode of working, users explore possible solution paths, and frequently change their minds. The externally-expressed design is being used both as an aide-memoire and as a vehicle to allow consequences of design options to be explored. Requirements include easy conversion of goals into actions and easy modification of the design as it progresses. Users will also need to be able to 'unbuild' the design and to recreate the steps that led to an option: its functional role and the associated reasoning. Otherwise they will not be able to make safe modifications.

A second mode of working is *one-way transcription,* in which a structure expressed in one notation is translated into a second notation (eg. a functional specification in a program design language is translated into code). The requirements here will be somewhat different. Notably, the need for easy modification is much less. Changes will be required only when the user mistranslates.

The dimension analysed in this paper, viscosity, is particularly relevant to the first mode. It need hardly be demonstrated that opportunistic design will be easier when the frequent modifications, characterising this mode of working, require fewer actions, impose less cognitive load, and break up the context of working less often. But it must be emphasised that users respond to the entire set of cognitive dimensions, not just to one, and that they are able to adapt their working style in many ways, including by changing the mode of working. In an excessively viscous system which makes opportunistic design difficult because modifications need too much work, users can adopt a different environment (eg. pen-and-paper) to create the design opportunistically, then translate the completed design into the target notation. Thus they have adopted a *two-stage process*, first using the opportunistic mode, then switching to the transcription mode.

Illustrative example

Viscosity in hydrodynamics means resistance to local change – deforming a viscous substance, e.g. syrup, is harder than deforming a fluid one, e.g. water. It means the same in this context. As a working definition, a viscous system is one where a single goal-related operation on the information structure requires an undue number of individual actions, possibly not goal-related. The 'goal-related operation' is, of course, at the level that is appropriate for the notation we are considering. Viscosity becomes a problem in opportunistic planning when the user/planner changes the plan; so it is changes at the plan level that we must consider. This is important, since changes at a lower level can sometimes be purely syntactic, giving a misleading impression of low viscosity. So, in general, *viscosity is a function of the work required to add, to remove, or to replace a plan-level component of an information structure.*

To illustrate cases of high and low viscosity I shall use a programming example, partly because it is compact and partly because it is familiar in the literature on novice programming (Soloway et al., 1983) and on program comprehension (Pennington, 1987). Suppose we wish to write a program to compute the average of a series of numbers, representing orders from clients over some time period. First we produce a program that finds the average of the list, then we modify it so that it also computes a filtered average in which zero entries, representing clients who have placed no order during the time period, are excluded. In terms of the 'programming plans' literature, we wish to insert a Filter plan and a Count plan. Figure 1 displays a solution in Microsoft Basic; underlinings show portions that must be added to the code in order to insert these plans. Figure 2 shows Prolog solutions for the two versions. (Note: to simplify the problem the solutions do not include a guard for the case when no orders are placed and the average becomes undefined.)

To change the Basic only needs three short insertions. But the second version of the Prolog is more than twice as long as the first – and moreover, even the lines that were present before have all been changed.

We have not necessarily shown that Prolog is more viscous. That depends on the environment as well as the notation. If the the user has a support tool that allows programs to built and modified at the plan level (eg. Bundy, 1988), the system may turn out to be pleasantly fluid. If, like the rest of us, the user is stuck with an ordinary text editor, then the Prolog system certainly is viscous, and there will be exclamations of "Bother. I wish I'd thought of that earlier!"

This toy example is only meant as an illustration. Real-life problem cases usually concern deleting or altering components, rather than inserting them; moreover, comparisons should be made using realistic-sized examples; and finally, the viscosity of the information structure will depend partly on the skill and care of the creator. So no conclusions about Prolog and Basic should rest simply on this example. The viscosity of a large, badly-written Basic program may well be much greater than that of a large Prolog program.

Viscosity types

In principle we can distinguish two types of viscosity, although most real systems have elements of both. Type 1 is Knock-on Viscosity: performing action A, which is goal-related, requires us also to perform a train of further actions, B, C, D, ... which are not directly goal-related. This is caused by a high *constraint density* in the notation: action A causes the new structure to violate some constraint, which must be rectified by action B, which in turn leads to a different violation, etc. Paradigm example: inserting a sentence near the start of a document, using an editor with no widow control, leads the author to have to page through and possibly adjust headings so that they all lie on the same pages as the bodies. That in turn will require the contents list to be updated, and if other documents cross-reference this one, then they in turn will need to be updated. All for one sentence!

```
NClients = 0
NActive = 0
Sum = 0
READ Order
WHILE Order <> 9999
   Sum = Sum + Order
   IF Order > 0 THEN NActive = NActive + 1
   NClients = NClients + 1
   READ Order
WEND
PRINT Sum/NActive, Sum/NClients
```

FIGURE 1: Basic program for versions 1 (plain text) and 2 (underlined) of the averaging problem.

```
average1( L, A ) :-
    sumAndCount( L, Sum, N ), A is Sum/N.

sumAndCount( [], 0, 0 ).
sumAndCount( [A|B], S, N ) :-
    sumAndCount( B, S1, N1 ),
    S is S1 + A, N is N1 + 1.
```

Figure 2a Prolog program for version 1.

```
average2( L, A1, A2 ) :-
    sumAndCount2( L, Sum, NClients, Nactive ),
    A1 is Sum/Nactive, A2 is Sum/NClients.

sumAndCount2( [ ], 0, 0, 0 ).
sumAndCount2( [ 0|B], S, Nt, Na ) :-
    sumAndCount2( B, S, Nt1, Na ), Nt is Nt1 + 1.
sumAndCount2( [ A|B], S, Nt, Na ) :-
    A>0,
    sumAndCount2( B, S1, Nt1, Na1 ),
    S is S1 + A, Nt is Nt1 + 1 , Na is Na1 + 1.
```

Figure 2b: Prolog program for version 2. Note the extensive changes from version 1.

Type 2 is Repetitiousness Viscosity: to achieve the desired goal, instead of a single action A we have to perform a string of virtually identical actions a1, a2, a3, ... Here, the problem is that the support tools are *missing an abstraction.* Paradigm example: changing all occurrences of a string in a document, where the editor has no search-and-replace mechanism (i.e. has no abstraction mechanism for "all strings of this pattern").

Viscosity is a wide-spread problem

In this section several examples are given to support the claim that viscosity is a concept relevant to all areas of HCI. Because the aim of this paper is to demonstrate the universality of the concept, no one system is analysed in depth. In practice, any system has some areas of high viscosity and some areas of fluidity – i.e. some operations are hard work, some are not. Generalised assessments of systems should not be made from the examples, which are only designed to illustrate some patches of viscosity in particular cases.

1. *Music notations used with pen-and-paper.* Among the many systems in use, most, including the 'standard' staff notation, assign a unique and absolute symbol to each combination of a note name and a note-length. Changing the key of a piece requires every single note to be altered. In contrast, 'tonic sol-fa' expresses each note as a combination of an absolute note-length and a *relative* note-name. The note names are conventionally given as do, re, mi, .. but they can be read as 0, 1, 2, .. steps from the key-note. A single component of the structure defines the key-note. ("Tonic = G" for instance). Thus, to change the key, only that one component need be altered. For any moderately long piece of music, the saving may amount to something like four orders of magnitude (say, one second to 3 hours). This is Repetitiousness Viscosity: same action many times.

2. *Word processors and document formatting languages* are staple diet for HCI concepts, so the framework must be shown to apply. We saw above that adding material, in some systems, can run into Knock-On viscosity. Adding a new section to a document with numbered sections creates different problems. In a simple-minded word-processor, like MacWrite, the section numbers are assigned by the author, and to insert a new one requires all following ones to be incremented. This is another case of Repetitiousness Viscosity.

The document formatters (Generalised Markup Language, Scribe, TeX, etc) solve that problem by offering a changed *notation:* instead of writing, as with a typewriter, "Section 2.5: Viscosity and the Meaning of Life" the author writes something like "@subheading{Viscosity and the Meaning of Life}". Section numbers are 'soft' and are assigned by the formatter. The Repetitiousness Viscosity goes away, but notice that to use this method authors must understand a vocabulary of heading, subheading, caption, and so on.

We can also consider a second example in this domain, also a case of Repetitiousness Viscosity, where the solution is to change the *environment.* This is the allocation of typographical styles to particular components. Certain word processors maintain a library of styles, such as "Heading: left-flush, bold, space before and after". By choosing a style from the library, authors can easily maintain a consistent layout in their document. What happens when the author decides to change the style of headings, perhaps by putting them in the centre of the page? In some systems, all previously-set headings must be altered individually. But in some other systems (e.g. Microsoft Word), redefining the style definition changes all previous uses of it, so only a single action is required. In this pair of examples, then, the notation is unchanged, but the environment offered by Word is different.

In both these cases, fluidity has been bought at the expense of increasing the number of abstractions. When you need a special term to denote 'an inset paragraph, close-spaced, with the first line indented and the tab settings just *so*', it is clear that the ontology (the set of things-in-the-world) has been uncomfortably expanded, and the problem of finding an appropriate name for each new style is going to become irksome.

3. *Painting and drawing on screen.* Little needs to be said here. Typical painting programs, such as MacPaint, work at the pixel level; typical drawing programs work at the object level. They can be considered as picture editors for our purposes. Drawing a rectangle requires very similar actions in the two systems, but subsequent manipulations are very different. In a pixel based system, all the pixels must be erased and a new rectangle drawn; in a object-level system, the original rectangle can simply be re-sized. Thus, pixel-based systems are viscous with respect to object-level tasks.

There are converse cases, where the object-level system is viscous: one example is the application of graded shading. Unless the shading can be defined algorithmically it will be easier to apply it at the pixel level.

The importance of this example is that attempts to provide both levels in a single system have been hard to bring off. Initial efforts were too complex to understand readily. It was too difficult to discover which component of the drawing had been created at which level, and what operations could be performed upon it in consequence. As a design solution, low viscosity had been achieved at too high an expense. A recent and more successful Macintosh system, Superpaint 2, provides operations to move components from one level to the other, thereby simplifying the notational problems.

4. *Hypertext structures*, although easy to create, can become extremely viscous. Fischer (1988), describing what appears to be the process of opportunistic design that takes place while creating a hypertext structure, writes " ... For many interesting areas, a structure is not given a priori but evolves dynamically. Because little is known at the beginning, there is almost a constant need for *restructuring*. [But] despite the fact that in many cases users could think of better structures, they stick to inadequate structures, because the effort to change existing structures is too large."

This quotation demonstrates equally clearly the need to improve hypertext systems and the need to improve the HCI vocabulary, so that we can express ourselves more succinctly: "hypertext systems are too viscous".

5. *Programs and programming languages* provide numerous examples of viscosity of both types (at least when used with conventional text editors), one of which was shown above. Where possible, experienced programmers define a frequently-used constant (e.g. 'number of records') in a single place, rather than using a number in many places throughout the program. This design avoids Repetitiousness Viscosity. Experienced programmers are also recommended to maintain low interconnectivity between modules – in fact, there are rule-of-thumb scoring systems to evaluate a connection between modules: where the calling modules can both access and reset values in the called module, the interconnectivity is high, and so on. Alterations to such programs are likely to be difficult because of high Knock-on Viscosity.

Languages which maintain an identifier hierarchy, such as Pascal, possess high constraint density which can therefore create substantial Knock-on Viscosity. For instance, no procedure definition may invoke another identifier unless that identifier has already been defined, either higher in the identifier hierarchy or else earlier in same level. Under these conditions, if it proves necessary to relocate a procedure (e.g. to move an error-reporting procedure to a higher level in the hierarchy, to provide for errors of a new sort taking place before lower levels can be invoked), substantial revision may be necessary. Pascal is one possible solution to the varied problems of designing a language for computer efficiency, avoidance of ambiguity, and compile-time detection of many kinds of user mistake. The high viscosity of certain operations is a by-product that many find acceptable – especially as the viscosity is quite low for many other operations.

6. *Data base systems* also offer plenty of examples of viscosity. Few amateur users are likely to design their data model perfectly first time: but to evaluate their model, and thereby discover the imperfections, they have to to try it. (In terms of the dimension framework, the system is enforcing 'premature commitment' – see Green, 1989, for further examples.) When they discover their problems, it may be too late to modify the design. Some data base systems allow fields to be altered or deleted and new fields to be defined, and adjust the existing data to fit; others refuse to allow such modifications, so that users are faced with an impenetrable wall, the ultimate viscosity, between what they would like and what they have. Another design implication here: the premature commitment problem is hard to avoid, but is acceptable so long as the system is relatively fluid so that second thoughts are always possible.

7. *Tailorable systems* seem to create opportunities for viscosity at the *organizational* level. Examples of these systems include customizable settings and macros for spreadsheets and word-processors, and other systems allowing users to tailor their office environment. The problem here is that users lose the ability to exchange tools and working environments; moreover, the arrival of a new release of the software may mean that it has to be tailored all over again, possibly with few records of what had been done before.

Indeed, many organizations are repositories of information among many people ('distributed cognition') and the organizations themselves can be therefore be considered as information structures. Changing a component of the information held collectively by the organisation may be a matter of telling every single person separately (Repetitiousness Viscosity), or it may, in a hierarchical or bureaucratic organization, only need one person to be told. The levels of the hierarchy have the same role as the abstractions in other systems.

8. Finally, *diachronic aspects of viscosity*. In many design systems, the viscosity of any one structure or design tends to increase as it grows. In the context of CAD-E design, one workplace has reported that their practice is to explicitly declare a point after which a design can no longer be changed in any substantial way. At that point the design is said to have 'congealed', in their terminology, and opportunistic design must be restricted to details.

There is at present no reported data, to my knowledge, describing in detail the time course of viscosity in different systems. The impression is that certain programming languages, such as Basic, have low initial viscosity, but as programs grow their viscosity increase steeply. Pascal starts higher but increases more slowly, because more is done in the initial abstractions. Object-oriented systems are intended to preserve fluidity even better, by using late binding and the inheritance mechanism to minimise the effort needed to modify a program. Some of the investigations made under the banner of software lifecycle studies may prove to be revealing.

Remedies for viscosity

One of the claims of the cognitive dimensions framework is that remedies for problems found in one domain may be applicable to similar problems in other domains. Thus, a collection of remedies and treatments would be desirable. We can pick out a few from the foregoing examples.

1. *Notational redesign.* Repetitiousness Viscosity can be mended by changing the abstraction level. The 'knowledgeable environment' offered by GML and other formatters is only available if the author is prepared to learn a new ontology, in which headings, subheadings, lists, captions, etc., are distinguished, in place of the undifferentiated world of marks on paper that characterised old-fashioned typescript.

In some cases, ridding the notation of absolute references is effective – eg. in the music example.

2. *Organisational and methodological solutions.* The author can be exhorted to use a design discipline that minimises viscosity within the structure: avoiding interconnecting modules, for instance. Structured programming made much of this. In some worlds, this will impose organisational requirements for various layers of expertise: some changes to tailorable systems would be made by local experts, say.

3. *Two-pass design.* It has been mentioned above that users faced with too much viscosity can change their mode, by sketching out a design in some more relaxed system, such as pen-and-paper with an informal notation. Expert programmers habitually do this (Petre, 1988). This has been formalised in the notion of stepwise refinement, where no code is written until the design is complete. However, the implication is that during the final phase, where the design is transcribed ('coded') into the target notation on the target system, no modifications are likely to be required. A study by Hoc (1983) on learning to use Warnier-Orr design methodology indicates that this is a difficult condition to meet.

4. *Environmental support.* Powerful environments can provide help. Repetitiousness Viscosity can be handled by providing more powerful abstractions. Sometimes these can be created on the fly, as in the case of search-and-replace. Hypertext systems need such 'virtual structures'; graphics systems are now beginning to acquire them, although until recently they were a prerogative of text-based systems.

Design Choices

It should not be assumed that viscosity is an unnecessary evil to be stamped out. It probably provides error protection, through interlinking redundancy, and it can aid comprehensibility by providing better cues to indicate the functional roles of components. The designer of a design system (either a notation, or an environment to support it) must therefore make many difficult choices. Some of the trade-offs are as follows.

1. Abstractions vs. fluidity. Lowering viscosity by creating new abstractions will tend to increase the system complexity: more commands, more learning, more possible surprises, as Algol 68 and typical OOPS languages illustrate. Mastering the range of abstractions in a mature OOPS takes a very long time (the difficulty of understanding certain Smalltalk-80 abstractions, such as the metaclass and the Model-View-Controller system, has become legendary). Once achieved, the user has a profound understanding, and can make profound changes to the system very easily. On the other hand, slight mistakes may well also be 'profound' (i.e. based on a deep misunderstanding) and therefore be hard to discover. It is widely believed in OOPS circles that using many abstractions helps to slow the rate at which viscosity increases with program size, but this may be unsupported.

2. Security vs. fluidity. In safety-critical systems, for example, the ideal design mode would probably *not* be exploratory. The one-way transcription mode would be desirable because it increased the level of processing and made it more likely that mistakes would be spotted. In such a context it might pay to deliberately increase viscosity to force users to think ahead.

3. Launch speed vs fluidity: Some contexts require a small quick patch, others require a massive edifice. You cannot get a fast launch if you have to start by defining a large object hierarchy, nor if you need to make many redundant declarations about your identifiers and their machine-level representation. Systems that achieve fluidity by asking for many abstractions, and others that achieve security by imposing many checks, are poor for quick patches. Thus, Basic is good for a quick-and-dirty job, Algol 68 is not; ditto with various types of word processor, etc. This seems to imply a dilemma: one can get the program (or whatever) set up fast, *or* one can be able to change it quickly, but getting the best of both worlds requires really clever design.

4. Permanence and transience: By the same token, contexts where structures are transient (e.g. quick-and-dirty patches) will not be likely to acquire a growth of modifications. Contexts where structures survive for many years will have higher demands for modifiability, and users should be prepared to trade initial effort in defining abstractions against subsequent fluidity.

Relation to other frameworks

Moran (1983) distinguishes between internal and external tasks. In these terms, a highly viscous system is one where a single external task demands many internal tasks for its completion.

Previous analyses of effort or number of actions, such as the Keystroke Level Model and the GOMS model, have concentrated on the effort required to achieve single internal tasks. Most of our examples of Repetitiousness Viscosity and Knock-on Viscosity therefore lie outside the scope of those models, at least as normally construed (eg. Olson and Olson, in press). Essentially, those models concentrate on the *interface,* while the cognitive dimensions framework concentrates on the *logical structure* behind the interface. As a distant prospect one can envisage a unified account dealing with both aspects: complex, but immensely rewarding.

Changing our implicit model of design

The design of many of the systems mentioned suggests that their designers had overlooked the need to support opportunistic planning, and therefore the need to assist users make frequent small changes to information structures as they were built. Elsewhere (Green, in press) I have argued this point in detail for many types of programming language and environment. The systems support one-way transcription well enough – it's easy enough to add a new section or to start a data base or construct a first version of a program – but the exploratory mode is something else again. Too often, Fischer's description of the hypertext user accepting a poor design because changing it is too hard would depict the user of many another system.

We researchers have been equally limited. HCI evaluations of interactive systems have often given excellent assessments of the difficulty of internal tasks, typically tasks of adding material or making very localised changes to a structure (e.g. Olson and Nilsen, 1987-8; Polson, 1988; Young and MacLean, 1988), but there has been little said about the difficulty of alterations at the 'plan' or external task level, and how this might affect users' choice of strategies. We need studies of the same quality addressing the problem of modifying structures as they are built and analysing the relationships between the notation, the support environment, and the user's strategies.

Conclusions

The relevance of the viscosity concept to a wide range of HCI domains has been demonstrated, together with the existence of standard solutions. At present, experimental studies of the effects of viscosity on strategies for design and authoring have not been reported, but it is easy to anticipate that the effects will include an avoidance of early exploration and a reluctance to change designs once started: initial mistakes will lead to attempts to wriggle out, possibly to massive kludges. Both as designers and researchers, we should amend our implicit theory, and provide as much support for modifying structures as we do for creating them.

Acknowledgements Rachel Bellamy, David Gilmore, Steve Payne, Marian Petre, Darrell Raymond, and Simon Shum have listened patiently, offered examples and re-interpretations, and criticised some bits. Thank you to them and apologies to anyone I've missed out.

References

Bundy, A. (1988). Proposal for a recursive techniques editor for Prolog. Research Paper 394, Department of Artificial Intelligence, University of Edinburgh. To appear in *Instructional Science*, special issue on Learning Prolog: Tools and Related Issues.

Fischer, G. (1988) Panel on Critical assessment of hypertext systems. *Proc. CHI 88 ACM Conf. on Human Factors in Computing Systems,* p 224. New York: ACM.

Flower, L. and Hayes, J.R. (1980) The dynamics of composing: making plans and juggling constraints. In L.W. Gregg and E.R. Steinberg (Eds.) *Cognitive Processes in Writing*. Erlbaum.

Green T. R. G. (in press) Programming languages as information structures. In J-M. Hoc, T.R.G. Green, D.J. Gilmore and R. Samurçay (Eds.) *Psychology of Programming*. Academic Press (forthcoming).

Green, T. R. G. (1989) Cognitive dimensions of notations. In A. Sutcliffe and L. Macaulay (Eds.) *People and Computers V*. Cambridge University Press.

Guindon, R., Krasner, H. and Curtis, B. (1988) Breakdowns and processes during the early activities of software design by professionals. In G. Olson, E. Soloway and S. Sheppard (Eds.) *Empirical Studies of Programmers: Second Workshop*. Ablex.

Hartson, H. R. and Hix, D. (in press) Toward empirically derived methodologies and tools for human-computer interface development. To appear in *Int. J. Man-Machine Studies.*

Hoc, J.-M. (1983) Analysis of beginners' problem-solving strategies in programming. In T.R.G. Green, S.J.Payne and G.C. van der Veer (Eds.) *The Psychology of Computer Use*. Academic Press.

Moran, T. P. (1983) Getting into a system: external-internal task mapping analysis. *Proc. CHI 83 ACM Conf. on Human Factors in Computing Systems,* pp 45-49. New York: ACM.

Olson, J. R. and Nilsen, E. (1987-88) Analysis of the cognition involved in spreadsheet software interaction. *Human-Computer Interaction*, **3**, 309-349.

Olson, J. R. and Olson, G. (in press) The growth of cognitive modelling in human-computer interaction since GOMS. To appear in *Human-Computer Interaction.*

Payne, S. J. (1987) Complex problem spaces: modelling the knowledge needed to use interactive devices. In H.-J. Bullinger and B. Shackel (Eds.) *Human-Computer Interaction – INTERACT '87*. Elsevier (North-Holland).

Payne, S. J. and Green, T. R. G. (1986) Task-Action Grammars: a model of the mental representation of task languages. *Human-Computer Interaction*, **2**, 93-133.

Pennington, N. (1987) Stimulus structure and mental representations in expert comprehension of computer programmers. *Cognitive Psychology*, **19**, 295-341

Petre, M. and Winder, R. (1988) Issues governing the suitability of programming languages for programming tasks. In D. M. Jones and R. Winder (Eds.) *People and Computers IV*. Cambridge University Press.

Polson, P. (1988) A quantitative theory of human-computer interaction. In J.M. Carroll (Ed.) *Interfacing Thought.* MIT Press.

Reisner, P. (1981) Formal grammar and human factors design of an interactive graphics system. *IEEE Trans. Software Engineering*, SE-7, 229-240.

Schiele, F. and Green, T. R. G. (1990) HCI formalisms and cognitive psychology: the case of Task-Action Grammar. In M. Harrison and H. Thimbleby (Eds.) *Formal Methods in Human-Computer Interaction.* Cambridge University Press.

Soloway, E., Ehrlich, K. and Black, J.B. (1983) Beyond numbers: Don't ask "how many" – ask "why". *Proc. Conf. Human Factors in Computer Systems*, Gaithersburg, MD.

Visser, W. (1988) Towards modelling the activity of design: an observational study on a specification stage. Technical Report, INRIA, Rocquencourt, France.

Young, R.M. and MacLean, A. (1988) Choosing between methods: analysing the user's decision space in terms of schemas and linear models. *Proc. CHI 88 ACM Conf. on Human Factors in Computing Systems,* pp 139-143. New York: ACM.

Human–Computer Interaction – INTERACT '90
D. Diaper et al. (Editors)
Elsevier Science Publishers B.V. (North-Holland)

The Role of Games and Cognitive Models in the Understanding of Complex Dynamic Systems

Rod Rivers

Logica Cambridge Ltd., Betjeman House, 104 Hills Road, Cambridge CB2 1LQ

Computers are being applied to increasingly complex real time monitoring and control tasks. What is the best way to develop this type of computer application? This paper argues that the development of games can reveal a great deal about the complexity of the application, its users and the circumstances in which it will be operated. The development of a game plays a similar role to the development of a prototype or simulation in identifying the most critical factors pertinent to a design. However, developing a game often focuses more attention on the user, his tasks, strategies and learning. Cognitive modelling techniques are especially relevant to understanding the user and contribute to the development of games and to understanding the very nature of complexity.

1. INTRODUCTION

With generally increasing levels of technological sophistication, the world contains more and more real time monitoring and control tasks. Examples include the control of power stations, chemical and manufacturing processes, traffic control (air, ship, train and road) , dealing in financial markets, defence systems, resource management, crowd control, communications, and organisational management. These tasks are highly interactive requiring the human operative to make many small interventions to keep their systems in efficient, predictable and safe states. Inevitably, computers are now used in a wide variety of these applications to provide the human operator with information and to allow him/her to make interventions within tight constraints of time, economy and safety.

What are the appropriate methods for building computer systems for these challenging applications ? Clearly the range of techniques applicable to the development of traditional batch data processing applications are quite inadequate. For example, moving from requirements specification, to design specification and building, in a linear sequence of activities with little planned feedback, cannot hope to deal with the complexity of predicting how the design of a system may predispose the operator to making particular (perhaps inaccurate or unsafe) interpretations of what is going on in a highly complex and changing system. New techniques are required for developing appropriate systems for these applications.

This paper considers the role of games and cognitive modelling techniques as a contribution to new development methods for designing computer-based real time monitoring and control system. It is argued that games provide a useful way of understanding complex dynamic systems. The developer of the game, the player of the game and the analyst of game playing behaviour can all benefit.

In order to be useful a technique must also be cost effective. The paper argues that games are a cost effective method because they allow a high fidelity modelling of critical aspects of the real situation they are mimicking. This leads to games providing a higher quality end product than alternative methods. By carefully selecting which aspects of a situation to include in a game, and the degree of fidelity required, the costs can be minimised for a given level of quality of results.

Cognitive modelling techniques have a significant role to play in determining which factors are critical and what degree of fidelity is required. There are a wide range of techniques for modelling users of complex systems. These range from models of human sensory/motor performance, through cognitive to social and environmental models. Within this range different models focus on different aspects of human performance. Some provide general explanatory frameworks, some describe human processes while others focus on human error. The paper gives examples of some of these techniques.

Complexity itself can only be understood as a function of the mechanism of human cognition. Complexity is as much a function of the person perceiving it, as it is of the situation or system itself. The development of computer systems in relation to real time monitoring and control tasks must, therefore, include techniques which focus on the user in the entire human-computer system.

2. DEFINITIONS

A game is understood to be some more or less formally defined system with which a person interacts but where the consequences of their actions do not impact on the real world. Games can be abstract (e.g. Chess) or they can attempt to simulate some aspect of the real world. In the second case, the game plays the role of the real world while the player plays the role that he/she would normally play in relation to the real world situation that the game depicts. However, a game is more than a domain model. It includes a specification of the way in which players may interact with it and a specification of the state that the player is trying to achieve or maintain.

It is not the intention to distinguish in detail between the terms 'game', 'simulation' and 'prototype'. With prototypes the emphasis is on the design of the artifact with which a person will interact. With games the emphasis shifts to include the human element ; the player, his performance and skill development . The term 'simulation' seems relatively neutral in this respect. Much of what is said about games applies equally to simulations and prototypes so the definition can be taken quite broadly.

Complex dynamic systems are systems which comprise a number of inter-relating variables that change over time. They are complex if it is difficult for a person to understand the relationships between the variables or keep track of their progress over time. Complexity is a property of the interaction between the person, the task and the view that the system presents of itself, not just a property of the system.

Cognitive modelling techniques are more or less formal theories about how people learn and make decisions. They are usually descriptive or predictive techniques rather than normative techniques designed to guide how people should learn or decide.

3. DEVELOPING GAMES

Several requirement must be met in order to model a complex dynamic system. The method used must be sufficiently precise that the model is not open to interpretation. It must be able to deal with change over time. It must be testable and it must model those characteristics of the system that are essential in being able to predict its behaviour. The last of these implies that, where appropriate, it must take into account the whole system including the human element. Games provide the driving force for the development of models that meet these requirements in a way that other methods do not.

A narrative description of a complex system (such as a written specification), for example, will often fail because it lacks sufficient formality. The meanings of the terms used in the descriptions are not tightly defined and can shift in response to challenges about the accuracy of the model. Although narrative descriptions can provide coverage of a wide range of potentially important variables their lack of precise semantics means that they are essentially untestable. Also, much of the complexity of systems arises from the way in which variables interact over time. Once again, the informality of narrative descriptions leaves the precise nature of these interactions largely undefined.

Given these deficiencies it is tempting to jump to the other extreme of using very rigourous and precise mathematical or logical descriptions. However, many formal approaches to modelling cannot be used for all aspects of the description because they lack expressive power. For example, they may not be able to cope adequately with the description of change over time. Systems with very few variables often display dynamic behaviour of such complexity that they defy description using currently available formalisms. The effects of variables feeding back on each other may results in sudden changes to the global state of a system which look chaotic from the perspective of many formal techniques. Also, although formal models may be useful in describing deterministic aspects of the behaviour of complex systems, they provide little help in the description of the relatively unpredictable components, such as the human element.

The requirement is for some half way house between free form narrative descriptions which provide breadth but little precision, and rigourous formal approaches which provide precision but lack expressive power. Developing a game may provide that half-way house.

Even a simple game can involve variables which interact over time in a combinatorially explosive fashion such that it is not possible to describe all possible legal paths through it. While the dynamic behaviour of the game may defy complete formal description the rules by which the complexity unfolds can be described sufficiently formally to provide a model which is both executable and testable. When more formal techniques fail, a games approach encourages the development of an executable model which can be studied in a more empirical manner in order to reveal its behavioural characteristics.

Games are just one type of executable model offering the benefits of formality and testability. Any executable simulation of a complex dynamic system has these features. However, in contrast with other approaches the notion of developing a game also encourages the modelling of the interaction between players and the essential domain variables. It is necessary to distinguish between these essential domain variables and the view that a player has of them at any particular time. The rules of a game normally include a reasonably precise and explicit statement of the ways in which players may interact with and influence the essential variables.

Developing a game requires modelling the complexity of real world systems such that a player of the game believes it to be an accurate depiction of the essential features of the world. For this to happen the game must respond to the players interactions with it in a way that is either expected or can be justified as the way in which the world would actually behave. The player acts as a test of the fidelity of the model. If the player cannot be convinced the fidelity of the model is in question.

Stammers [1] lists several dimensions of fidelity. These include display / control relationships and feedback, task complexity, temporal aspects, environmental factors, and situational payoffs. In the main these dimensions are not concerned with the underlying complexity of the systems that are being modelled. Rather they are to do with the way in which the systems are represented to the player, and social / environmental factors.

The domain model represents the complex interactions of variables in the real world but does not pre-suppose a particular view. There may be many possible and partial views that a person may have of the domain model. Building one deep model of the domain facilitates the development of several partial views which are consistent even though they may not immediately appear to be when comparing then. The game developer must not only achieve fidelity in the domain model but must also achieve it in the view of the model that a player sees. He must consider exactly how the player will interact with the domain. In the real world information may arrive through a variety of communication channels (electronically, on paper, over the phone, from conversation with someone in the same room etc.) and over different sensory channels (e.g. visual and auditory). Similarly, actions resulting from decision making may be executed over a variety of channels. The player's conceptual model of the overall state of the system may be critically dependent on his partial view of particular system states. Designing systems to ensure fidelity in this area is difficult. Work on the integration of formal techniques for system modelling and techniques for cognitive modelling in the design of interactive systems is working towards improved methods (Barnard and Harrison [2]).

There are many complex dynamic systems that evolve in ways that people do not anticipate, and this is more likely if the player has only a partial view of the domain model. It is possible that a player will question the underlying model rather than question his/her own ability to make sensible decisions and anticipate their outcomes. The evaluation of a game by players is not, therefore, a sufficient basis on which to make changes to the underlying domain model. In addition it may be necessary to test the game against reality. A game depicting a historical incident can be tested to see whether it is possible, within the rules, to reconstruct the way in which the real situation did unfold over time.

The use of the most effective development techniques involves borrowing from the experience of other game developers and avoiding the pitfalls they have already encountered. Huxham et al [3], for example, emphasize the need to base game development on an understanding of the processes of human decision making and being sure to include subjective accounts of decision making when collecting data for analysis. However, there are dangers in placing too much emphasis of verbal accounts (Berry and Broadbent [4]). Bainbridge [5] warns against the dangers of extrapolating about performance from one task to another and proposes a set of dimensions for the definition of complex dynamic tasks. Klein [6] examines the dimensions along which reality can be abstracted in a game and notes that anything more than trivial abstraction in the dimension concerned with the player's subjective model will alter the meaning of the model to the extent that it will not be understood.

In summary, games constitute testable theories about complex situations. Developing a game helps the understanding of a complex dynamic system because it encourages the design of a formal and testable model of the essential characteristics of the system including its human elements. The model is formal because it is necessary to specify precisely how the game will operate under the envisaged circumstances that may arise. It is testable because playing the game or comparing its operation against real situations will reveal ways in which the model is incorrect or needs refinement. Testing will tend to weed out the non-essential aspects in favour of only those important variables and relationships that give the game appropriate fidelity.

4. PLAYING GAMES

While developing games enables the developer to understand complex dynamic systems, playing games enables the player in a similar way. Through contact with the game the player is expected to become aware of the variables involves, their interactions and the way in which their own behaviour effects how the games develops.

Another possible method of instruction would be to present the variables, their interactions and the underlying essential model in the manner of a textbook or lecture. There are two broad arguments as to why actually interacting with the model in a game is better that simply studying it in abstract form. These are :

1. Textbooks and lectures miss out many of the essential aspects of the model

2. Transfer of learning / training is poorer from textbook / lecture material to the real situation than it is from game playing to the real situation.

Both these arguments concern the relationship between the learning / training situation and execution of the real task. The elements missing from the abstract model presented in a textbook or lecture include a failure to represent the dynamic aspects of the essential model in detail, a failure to represent the way in which the user of the model (the trainee) can influence the state of the variables, a failure to provide an environment in which the model can be explored by the trainee experimentally (for example, to test the sensitivity of variable values to other model parameters), a failure to convey information about frequency (of events and situations), and a failure to involve the trainee in the learning process adequately. These arguments also apply to much of the learning material presented in traditional computer based training and hypertext systems.

Whether or not transfer of learning / training is better as a result of interacting with a game than being presented with an abstract textbook account is a question open to empirical investigation. However, there are also a priori theoretical arguments which suggest that game playing may be more effective. The 'Encoding Specificity Principle' (Tulving [7]), for example, predicts that a memory is more likely to be retrieved the closer the match between the context of retrieval and the context of learning.

In summary, it is argued that playing games is a training method that leads more readily to improved performance in the real situation than other training methods. This is because games have closer fidelity to the real task than do other methods, and there are a priori theoretical grounds in the form of psychological models of learning and memory, to suggest that increased fidelity should lead to better transfer.

5. ANALYSING GAME PLAYING BEHAVIOUR

The analysis of game playing behaviour can help in understanding both aspects to do with modelling the real world and aspects to do with the player or human operative engaged in the real world task.

The first of these concerns how analysis can lead to greater insights about the essential domain model that underlies the game and the way in which the player is given a view of the model. Simply logging information about the way in which particular runs of the game progress can give an indication about the validity of the domain model. This can lead to changes in the game's design at the level of the domain model or at the level of the way information about states of the domain model are presented to the player(s). Many analytic techniques can be used including formal mathematical or logical analysis of information logged during runs of the game and semi-formal / informal gathering and analysis of data about the users subjective reactions to the game. All such data can contribute to improving the fidelity with which the game represents the real world situation.

Better understanding of the domain model is not only relevant to improving the game. It may actually lead to better performance in the real world. The analysis of the game may reveal misconceptions about the operation of the domain model which lead to a revised understanding about how the world operates. For example, it may be revealed that in an apparently complex situation there are, in fact, only two variables that matter at all. Analysis of games data allows these types of hypotheses to emerge so that they can be investigated in greater depth.

The player or human operative adds to the complexity of dynamic situations and needs to be studied both as part of the whole system and separately from any particular system so that the results can be generalized. Much of the benefit of analysis concerns gaining a better understanding of the human element and it is expected that understanding the player of the game will help in understanding the human operator in the real situation. There are several questions that need to be addressed. These include :

1. How do people generally make decisions and cope with complexity ?

2. How does the surface representation of the underlying dynamics of a situation effect peoples understanding of it ?

3. How do people generally learn to behave in relation to complex dynamic systems ?

4. What is the variability between individuals on these dimensions ?

5. To what extent are outcomes (in a game or in a real situation) influenced by the properties of the situation itself and to what extent can it be influenced by the human participant ?

6. To what extent is it possible to predict performance in the real situation from performance in a game (what is the validity and reliability of games as an approach to understanding real complex dynamic systems) ?

These are some of the research questions which the analysis of games playing data should aim to address. They are also some of the most important questions because the human element can have a large impact in the way a complex dynamic system develops and other techniques of analysis do not touch on them.

For the detailed analysis of the player of a game there are more sophisticated techniques than arbitrary data logging. For example, it is possible to incorporate within a game an Embedded User Model (EUM - Rivers [8]). An EUM is a description of a user of a computer application. The description takes the form of computer code and can be maintained by a computer program during the course of a users interaction with a computer based application. The EUM is the computer's model of the user. This model may be generic (of users in general), stereotypical (relating to particular classes of users) or individual (relating to one particular user). An individualized user model can be updated in real time during the course of a game playing session. It can be inspected at various points in time in order to monitor changes in the user's behaviour or the system's beliefs about the user's changing state of knowledge. The method by which the computer updates its model of the user is crucial because it is not neutral (as exhaustive data logging might be). It constitutes a theory about how the user is changing and needs to be developed and guided by an advanced understanding of cognitive modelling techniques. EUMs are not restricted to monitoring. A computer program may change its output depending upon the state of the user model and thereby adapt to changes in the user. In a game playing situation, for example, an EUM could keep track of an individuals skill development and adapt the difficulty of the game accordingly.

6. COGNITIVE MODELLING TECHNIQUES

The human element in a complex dynamic system can have a great effect on the way in which it develops over time. People differ in their ability to interpret and control complex dynamic systems and within an individual this ability changes over time. The same underlying system is easy or difficult to interpret and control largely as a function of the way it is represented, and the same underlying system represented in the same way may be interpreted and controlled differently as a result of various social and environmental circumstances.

Dixon [9] presents anecdotal evidence about how errors due to factors like boredom and stress have lead to a whole catalogue of train, plane and other transport disasters. He has also looked at the way these same factors have lead to a series of military disasters through-out history (Dixon [10]). In addition, there is experimental evidence. It has been known for some time that the way in which information is presented can be critical to task performance. A task presented as an abstract problem cannot be solved but becomes tractable when presented in a concrete situation (Wason and Johnson-Laird [11]).

There are a large number of models of human error. Kahneman et al. [12] identify many different biases that creep into human judgement and decision making. One specific example is the anchoring bias which may lead two decision makers who have been presented with exactly the same information but in different orders, to assess the same situation completely differently. There are also some process models of human error that have been implemented as computer programs. Sleeman [13] describes a computational model of error in terms of 'perturbations' to decision making rules which result in 'mal-rules'.

There are theories concerned with describing human understanding and decision making, with respect to complex systems, in terms of mental models (Johnson-

Laird [14], Gentner and Stevens [15]). These are important because they view the individual decision maker as an active agent who is trying to make sense of the environment or some system in terms of his own mental representation. Norman [16] gives a useful common sense accounts of how psychological theory can be applied to design and describes how many very ordinary designs are totally unusable because human factors issues are neglected.

How can cognitive models and theories be of use in building better games? The requirement is that they should give the game designer an orientation to the type of factors to consider and the type of systems that will meet the requirement. Specific theories should help in the detailed design of features in the system. Cognitive models should help answer questions such as : what is appropriate fidelity?, how do people learn to deal with complex dynamic situations?, and what should be studied in order to understand more about the complex dynamic systems and the people using them?

However, there are problems with the application of science to design. Scientific accounts are often too restricted to apply to the real issues. Theories often only account for some small aspect of human behaviour and, at worst, this behaviour may only exhibit itself within some restricted laboratory setting. Theories may not, therefore, have scope or relevance. Even when they do, it may be difficult to trace how a good theory should or can be translated into a specific design. An account of some of the problems of applying cognitive theories to the design of systems and artifacts is given by Barnard [17].

General theories of cognition not only help to understand design but also implicitly influence design (Carroll and Campbell [18]) and an inadequate cognitive theory may influence design for the worse. For example, early theories of human decision making were based on the theory of subjective utility. This theory assumed that a decision maker knew all his options in advance and could accurately evaluate the implications of selecting each one. Several decision support systems have been built based on this normative model. However, it is inappropriate for many decision making tasks and totally inadequate for real time monitoring and control tasks where decisions have to be made with limited information and under time and cognitive resource constraints (what Simon [19] calls 'bounded rationality').

There are now more sophisticated general models of human cognition which imply quite different designs for learning and decision support systems, and computer interfaces to real time monitoring and control tasks. Two leading candidates which have resulted in implemented computer models are SOAR (Laird et al [20]) and ACT (Anderson [21]). SOAR gives insight into how decisions are made with limited cognitive constraints and also provides a theory for explaining how many small learned tasks are chunked into higher level units. ACT attempts to account for how appropriate information is available to a decision maker within limited working memory, in terms of a theory of spreading activation around a network of related concepts. Both SOAR and ACT can be considered as both process and architectural theories. Their computer implementations aid the formulation of precise predications about what is going on in cognition and the resulting performance on some task. At the same time they both propose quite general mechanisms for cognitive processes that might operate across a wide range of cognitive tasks.

What is a complex system and how can complexity be measured? The world would be a much more straightforward place if it were possible to assess the complexity of a system independently of the way in which people perceive and understand it. A naive view is that it is possible to measure complexity by performing objective counts of such matters as the number of variables involved in a system and the extent of interactions between variables. However, it is clear from the large amount of psychological evidence available that such a method will not work. Quite independently of whether a game is being developed, played or analysed cognitive modelling has a fundamental role to play in the understanding of complexity. Some theories of cognitive complexity are now sufficiently well developed that they have resulted in computational approaches to the measurement of complexity (e.g. Kieras and Polson [22]).

These examples illustrate how theories of cognition tend to shape the way artifacts, including games, are designed. Different theories have different implications for design and using the best and most appropriate theories can make significant differences to the design and the way in which studies of human learning and behaviour should be analysed and interpreted. These theories provide some support along the spectrum from cold analytic decision making through to 'hot cognition' in complex dynamic real time tasks. Without these theories of cognition to guide design at an early stage the developer risks making many expensive mistakes.

REFERENCES

[1] Stammers R.B., 'Simulators for Training', In : T. O. Kvalseth (ed), 'Ergonomics of Workstation Design', Butterworths, 1983, 229-242

[2] Barnard P. and Harrison M., 'Integrating Cognitive and System Models in Human-Computer Interaction', Discussion paper for ESPRIT Basic Research Actions Project 3066, 1989, (In preparation)

[3] Huxham C.S., Bennett P.G., Lozowski M.V. and Dandos M.R., 'The Study of Human Decision-Making : A Cautionary Tale from the World of Experimental Gaming', Journal of the Operational Research Society, 1981, 32, 173-185

[4] Berry D.C. and Broadbent D.E., 'On the Relationship between Task Performance and Associated Verbalizable Knowledge', Quarterly Journal of Experimental Psychology, 1984, 36A, 209-231

[5] Bainbridge L., 'Extrapolating from one task to another', Proceedings of BCS HCI Special Interest Group Conference 'Simulation in the Development of the User Interface', Brighton, 1989

[6] Klein J.H., 'The Abstraction of Reality for Games and Simulations', Journal of the Operational Research Society, 1985, 36, 8, 671-678

[7] Tulving E., 'Recall and Recognition of Semantically Encoded Words', Journal of Experimental Psychology, 1974, 102, 778-787

[8] Rivers R.E., 'Embedded User Models - Where Next ? ', Interacting with Computers, 1989, 1,1

[9] Dixon N, 'Our Own Worst Enemy', Futura, 1987

[10] Dixon N, 'The Psychology of Military Incompetence', Futura, 1979

[11] Wason P.C. and Johnson-Laird P.N., 'A Conflict between Selecting and Evaluating Information in a Cognitive Task', British Journal of Psychology, 1970, 61, 509-515

[12] Kahneman D., Slovic P., and Tversky A. (Eds), 'Judgment under Uncertainty : Heuristics and Biases', Cambridge University Press, 1982

[13] Sleeman D.H., 'Inferring Student Models for Intelligent Computer-Aided Instruction', In Machine Learning, Michalski R.S., Carbonell J.G., and Mitchell T.M., Morgan Kaufmann, California, 1983

[14] Johnson-Laird P.N., 'Mental Models', Cambridge University Press, UK, 1983

[15] Gentner D. and Stevens A.L., 'Mental Models', Lawrence Erlbaum, Hillsdale, NJ, 1983

[16] Norman D., 'The Psychology of Everyday Things', Basic Books, NY, 1988

[17] Barnard P., 'Bridging between basic theories and the artifacts of human-computer interaction', (Seminar paper), 1989

[18] Carroll J.M. and Campbell R.L., 'Artifacts as Psychological Theories : The case of Human Computer Interaction', Technical Report RC13454, IBM Yorktown Heights, 1988

[19] Simon H.A., 'Alternative Visions of Rationality', In : Arkes H.R., and Hammond K.R. (eds), 'Judgment and Decision Making', Cambridge University Press, 1986

[20] Laird, J.E., Rosenbloom P., and Newell A, 'Universal Sub-Goaling and Chunking', Kluwer Academic Publishers, 1986

[21] Anderson J.R., 'The Architecture of Cognition', Harvard University Press, 1983

[22] Kieras D.E. and Polson P.G., 'An approach to formal analysis of user complexity', International Journal of Man-Machine Studies, 1985, 22, 365-394

Human–Computer Interaction – INTERACT '90
D. Diaper et al. (Editors)
Elsevier Science Publishers B.V. (North-Holland)

IMPLICATIONS OF COMPUTER GAMES FOR SYSTEM DESIGN

Lisa Neal†

Aiken Computation Laboratory, Harvard University, Cambridge, MA 02138 USA

Abstract

Computer games "hold an inexplicable fascination for many people" [Rich 83] and they often provide striking examples of highly motivating activities [Malone 80]. We present a empirical study of game use, focusing on features of games, such as feedback, help, and levels of difficulty, which significantly influence the interaction with a user. We discuss the implications of this research for improving the design of systems, showing that systems not designed for entertainment can benefit from the features incorporated into computer games.

1. Introduction

Traditionally, system design decisions have been made on an ad hoc basis,[1] based on the experience or instincts of the designer [Good 81], which does not necessarily produce systems that match the needs and abilities of users. An alternate approach to design is to systematically examine systems in order to determine the ways in which they are successful or unsuccessful and to use this information to influence future designs. Computer games can be be viewed as providing a testbed for design, demonstrating elements of an interface that are effectively or poorly designed, implemented, and integrated into an environment. Also, "games provide an extremely compelling interface whose advantages should be considered for more standard applications" [Krueger *et al.* 85].

An empirical study of four computer games was performed [Neal 89b]. Descriptions of the games, methodology and the features of the games which influenced the interactions of users are presented. In particular, we discuss goals, competition, help, levels of difficulty, control, strategy, the discovery and understanding of information, and feedback. We found that many of the ways in which games are successful can be attributed to specific aspects of their design. The implications of these features for improving more general system design are presented. While the effect of incorporating randomness, for example, into a tool could be detrimental rather than beneficial, the use of other features described here could lead to systems which are easier and more fun to use [Carroll and Thomas 88] and aid in the "design [of] a system that has the right functions in it so people can do their work better and like it" [Gould 87].

2. Selection of Games

A number of games on the Macintosh computer were considered for this study; role-playing games, which tend to be very time-consuming to play, games involving specialized knowledge, and multi-player games, in which an additional human player was needed, were ruled out. The final decision about which games to use was based on a preliminary study, which served to eliminate games for which there were significant problems with the interaction, such as difficulty with control. We present a description of the games we selected.

2.1. Mystery Box

In Mystery Box, the computer "hides" between two and eight balls, where the number of balls is selected by the player, in an 8×8 grid and the player tries to find the balls by firing rays into the grid. The behavior of the ray depends on the locations of the hidden balls; the rays can be absorbed, deflected, or returned. The player places balls on the squares in which a ball is thought to be hidden, and gets points for correctly placed balls while losing points for incorrectly placed ones. The score is lowered by each ray that is fired, and the maximum possible score, given the number of balls and the number of rays that have been fired, is always displayed. After all the balls have been placed, the player finds out if the placement of the balls is correct when the solution is displayed, and gets points for correctly placed balls while losing points for incorrectly placed ones. Scores are not saved. The difficulty increases with the number of balls, which is explicitly stated in the introductory help window.

Help is invoked from a poorly-labeled pull-down menu, making its presence less noticeable, especially to a novice Macintosh user who is not aware that options are typically available through pull-down menus. There are eight help windows and in addition to the help system, there was a small window which displayed messages describing the ray behavior; for instance, stating "Ray Deflected."

2.2. ThinkAhead

ThinkAhead is a number game in which a player competes against the computer to obtain the highest score. It is played on an 8×8 board, of which the initial configuration contains a starting marker and 63 numbers. The first player, who is chosen randomly, makes a vertical move in the same column as the starting marker, and the second player makes a horizontal move in the same row as the number previously selected, and so on. Most players perceived that the game got easier as it progressed because there were fewer numbers to consider; this is in contrast to many games in which the level of difficulty can be selected or increases based on the player's achievements. Sounds mark each move, with the pitch of the sound varying dependent on the value of the selected number. The score is the sum of the numbers in the boxes selected by a player, and it is always displayed. Neither scores nor the number of games won is recorded.

An extensive help system is provided, which is automatically invoked when the game started. The eight window help system is far more extensive than was warranted by the simplicity of the game, especially in terms of the information that was necessary to start playing. Instructions, such as "Make vertical move," are given to the player in a window on the playing screen.

† This research was supported, in part, by U.S. Army Research Office Grant #DAAG29-83-G0008 and, in part, by the Defense Advanced Projects Research Agency under contract N00014-85-C-0710.

2.3. Crystal Quest

In Crystal Quest, the user moves a "ship" through space, accumulating points by gathering crystals and by firing at a wide variety of "nasties," all of whom have different appearances, sounds, and behaviors. "Smart bombs" can be used to remove all the "nasties" on the screen The graphics are sophisticated and the sounds and behaviors of the "nasties" often quite humorous. There are multiple levels, which increase in difficulty due to the larger number of increasing more complex "nasties" and the resulting increase in difficulty of avoiding or shooting at them. The fifteen high scores of the day are saved, in addition to the thirty best scores.

Crystal Quest provides a help system and demonstration games. The help system explains how to play the game and how the score is calculated, and displays all of the "nasties," describing their attributes. Help and the demo are selected from the initial screen.

2.4. Tetris

Tetris is a game involving eye-hand coordination and spatial reasoning, in which different arrangements of four blocks fall from the top of the screen and can be moved left or right, rotated, or dropped. Filled-in rows disappear, and the game continues until there is no space left. There are multiple levels at which a player can start, and each time a player fills in ten rows the level increases automatically, increasing the speed at which shapes fall. The score is based on the number of shapes that are placed, the height from which they are dropped, and the speed at which they are falling. The ten best scores are saved. In addition to selecting the initial level of difficulty, a player can select the height to which rows will be filled with random blocks.

No help is provided other than a window displaying the key bindings for the keys used to manipulate the blocks. As a result, players had trouble determining what the point of the game was, in addition to having trouble determining how to play the game.

3. Method

Twenty-five subjects participated in the experiment; the subjects were undergraduate and graduate students at Harvard University, and computer and non-computer professionals. An effort was made to have as wide a variety of subjects as possible; subjects ranged from infrequent users of word processors to heavy computer users with over ten years of computer experience and from infrequent players of computer games to people who play games for hours daily.

Subjects were given the following task: to play four Macintosh games, Mystery Box, ThinkAhead, Crystal Quest, and Tetris. Subjects were told that they could play each game for as long as they wished, for up to one hour, playing each game at least once. Sessions lasted from one to four hours. Subjects were videotaped while they performed the task, resulting in fifty-four hours of videotape. Transcripts were produced from the tapes containing the verbal data and the visual data necessary to support the verbal data.

Subjects were observed while engaged in the task, and were asked to think aloud [Ericsson and Simon 84], which allows a more in-depth analysis of system use. In particular, subjects were asked to talk about what they were doing and why they were doing it, what were their goals, what they were learning or understanding about the game, what made them feel they were progressing and/or made them feel successful, why they stopped playing and what they thought what would happen if they continued to play, and what they liked and disliked about each game.

4. Game Characterization

Even seemingly simple computer games are complex when examined in terms of their features and skill requirements. The games we used involved fundamentally different skills and a diverse set of non-trivial tasks. A characterization follows, which is based on the elements that a game can include and the skills or abilities that are needed to play a game, specifically: goals; competition; help; levels of difficulty; control; strategy; the discovery and understanding of information; and feedback.

Additional features will not be discussed here that have less impact on general system design. For example, games vary in the extent to which timing and speed of response are factors, which primarily impacts the scoring and the development of control. Games vary in their complexity, differing in the number of actions valid at a given time and in the size and complexity of their rule set. The availability of options contributed to complexity, where some affected the playing of a game and others altered the playing environment. The perceived complexity of a game depended on the individual player and was influenced by factors such as experience.[2]

Among the game features we will discuss, some are more important than others for a player to achieve objective success.[3] In addition, many of the features listed are among those that have been shown to contribute to making a computer game successful[4] and suggest what to be aware of in analyzing what makes a game fun and motivating [Malone 80]. A discussion of the features which characterize games, and their impact on users, follows.

4.1. Goals

Computer games are typically designed with clearly-defined, built-in goals, the achievement of which is generally synonymous with objective success. The goals built into a game include beating the computer, obtaining a high score, and solving a puzzle. The existence of an obvious built-in goal has been shown to be of importance for a game to be popular and successful among elementary school children [Malone 80]. However, we found that game players frequently generate their own goals, which can upstage the built-in goal. Turkle [84] looked at how children use microprocessor-based toys and similarly found that children often use them in other than the ways they were intended, generating their own goals for the use of the toy. The goals that players try to achieve can be quite different from the game's built-in goal; they include reaching a certain level within a game which the player feels is achievable, developing the eye-hand coordination necessary to play a game, understanding an aspect of a game, such as the computer's playing strategy, or generating pleasing sounds or visual displays.

Games differ from other types of software in that they "are used for their own sake with no external goal [while tools are] objects that are used as the means to achieve some external goal" [Malone 80]. While the goal of producing a program or document can be viewed as a fixed, predetermined goal, additional goals often arise during system use. An understanding of a user's goals can be useful to detect mismatches between a user's intentions and actions [Whitefield 87] and to provide effective system feedback, which should be at the level at which the user is forming intentions [Norman 84].

4.2. Competition

The computer's role ranged between active and passive for the different games. We define an active role as one in which the computer provides competition and we define a passive role as one in which the computer responds to a player's actions or commands. We additionally define a semi-active role as one in which the computer performs actions of its own initiative, yet is not competing.

Paranoia was the primary consequence of the computer's role in terms of player's perceptions of the games. Players of all four games occasionally attributed the computer's actions to an attempt to "trick" or "second-guess" them or thought that the computer's actions could not be attributed to randomness.[5] In ThinkAhead, in which the computer plays an active role, many players thought that the computer was unbeatable. The computer was sometimes anthropomorphized by players when it played an active or a semi-active role. Such reactions occurred less often when the computer played a passive role.

4.3. Help

The help systems included in games vary in how they are accessed and in the amount and content of the information they provide. Help was typically invoked through a pull-down menu or labeled button. In ThinkAhead, the help system was automatically invoked when the game started. Access in Mystery Box was through a pull-down menu which was not well-labeled, creating difficulties in locating help.[6]

The size of the help systems ranged from a small window displaying key bindings in Tetris to extensive systems in Mystery Box and ThinkAhead. When help is too short there can be too little information, while when it is too long, the user often became overwhelmed or overloaded. The type of information varied in content and representation. Mystery Box's help explicitly states the object of the game and how to play. ThinkAhead, more typically, never specifies the mechanics of making moves.

The representations of information include text, drawings, and examples. The graphic representations included in the text of Crystal Quest's help system depicted the objects that appear in the game. Many subjects found the graphic representations in Crystal Quest especially useful. Mystery Box and ThinkAhead both include examples which present snapshots of games. The windows displaying examples were the most heavily used of the help windows. Many players expressed that they were more useful than the text. The examples aided in understanding the instructions, possibly because it facilitated the building of a mental model of the game. Examples have been shown to play a large role in expert performance [Gorry 74] and to be useful as part of the programming process [Neal 89a]. Another form of example was the demo in Crystal Quest. In addition to the help systems, some games provided a window containing context-sensitive information which described a move's outcome or prompting the user's next action.

4.4. Levels of Difficulty

Games typically provide explicit levels of difficulty. Other types of software, like games, allow user-selection of the command set size, but, unlike games, do not guide a user's selection of an appropriate difficulty level. Levels of difficulty in games can be controlled by the user or the system. When the user has control, selection criteria include what the user deems appropriate, the default, or a recommendation from the help system.

ThinkAhead was the only game we examined which did not provide explicit levels; in fact many players perceived that each game became easier, rather than more difficult, because there were fewer choices to consider as a game progressed.[7] In Mystery Box, the difficulty increases with the number of balls that the user selects. In Crystal Quest, the system increases the level of difficulty when the user completes a level. Successive levels include more and increasingly complex objects. The levels of difficulty in Tetris are user-controlled and system-controlled. A player selects the initial level, and, once a player has filled in ten rows, the level increases automatically.

4.5. Control

Minimally, in a game, some amount of motor control is needed as part of the interaction, but many games require extensive control. Control is often simple to develop in games in which the mouse or keys are used to select, rather than move or manipulate, elements. Control can be difficult to develop in a real-time system where speed is a factor. The former case includes Mystery Box and ThinkAhead; the latter includes Crystal Quest and Tetris. In both cases, control is a necessary but not sufficient condition for "successful" play; a player needs an understanding of the game and a strategy as well, even in games involving extensive eye-hand coordination.

An explanation for why games are captivating is that they give players a sense of control [Malone 80], where perception of control is more important than actual control. A perception of control depends on the extent to which a player controls the likelihood of an outcome occurring and can be produced through responsiveness and "the provision of explicit choices;" however, providing too many choices can cause one "to devalue the importance of choice and to experience frustration instead of satisfaction" [Malone and Lepper 87].

4.6. Strategy

Strategies used to play games are typically to determine the optimal next move or the optimal manipulation of an object. Strategies are often based on inference from available information or prior experience or knowledge. This is especially the case when randomness occurs in the game, and the use of a playing strategy is primarily to predict random events or placements of objects. An additional type of strategy that might be employed in playing a game is a search strategy for determining the next move to make.

McKinsey [52] found that "after optimal strategies for a game are known it ceases to offer any intellectual challenge and people stop playing it." The straightforwardness and variety of strategies contributes to the difficulty and interest of a problem. For instance, in a game such as chess, the cognitive limitations of players prevent them from knowing the optimal strategies, while in a game such as tic-tac-toe, the optimal strategy can be determined, making the outcome certain and the game uninteresting [Malone 80].

4.7. The Discovery and Understanding of Information

An understanding of a game, along with control, is necessary for "success" in playing the game. However, information in games is often incomplete or partially-specified. This includes a comprehension of the rules for a game, the elements of a game and their behavior, and playing strategies, i.e. how to use the knowledge about the rules and elements of the game. The discovery and understanding of this information is an integral part of playing a game. A discussion of the different types of information and their impact on the player follows.

Games and other forms of software provide incremental learning situations, in which learning certain rules or elements is necessary for successful use. Learning a game is accomplished through the use of prior knowledge and analogies and through exploration, and is facilitated through the use of help. However, some people do not use help, either by choice or because they can not find it, and some games provide inadequate help, for instance, by not providing information on the mechanics of playing.

Learning also occurs through the use of prior knowledge and the use of analogies. New knowledge is comprehended in terms of existing knowledge and metaphors and analogies can aid a learner in applying old knowledge to understand new things [Malone 80].[8] For instance, when a computer game is an on-line version of a card or board game, control must still be learned, while knowledge and skills are transferable.[9] Many players used analogies when learning a game, which was helpful when the analogy was accurate, but detrimental to their progress when faulty. In addition, learning can occur through exploration,[10] which is often motivated by curiousity. In general, curiosity is "a desire to bring better 'form' to one's knowledge structures," which is stimulated when the amount of information presented makes a learner's existing knowledge seem incomplete, inconsistency, or unparsimonious [Malone 80].

Games differ in what information is unspecified and why. A player often needs to be able to predict hidden information, for instance, by having a sense of which events are likely to occur. This, in addition to maximum utilization of and inferencing from available information, and determining what is of importance,[11] increases a player's likelihood of success.

4.8. Feedback

Feedback is used to provide players with measures of progress and success. A score is the typical feedback mechanism used in games; other types of feedback include a solution and visual and auditory effects. The amount and variety of feedback which is provided by games contributes to making games successful and fun and is a significant way in which games differ from other types of software.[12]

4.8.1. Scoring Mechanisms

The score measures the player's success at achieving the game's built-in goal. Scores vary in how they are calculated and presented. Scores are usually additive; this can be straightforward and obvious, as in ThinkAhead, where the number that a player selects is added to the player's score, or can be complex, as in Tetris, where the greater the distance from which a piece falls and the greater the speed, the larger the amount that is added to the score. Scores can be calculated in other ways; for example, Mystery Box has a maximum possible score which depends on the number of balls selected, and the score is decremented as each ray is fired. Mystery Box presents the maximum possible score that players can get if their final solution is correct.

Some games record scores in high score lists; players of a game where a score is kept often had the goal of beating their own or someone else's previous record. When there is no high score list, players have less feedback on what constitutes a good, bad, or typical score. Information about a game and how to play it can be inferred from recorded scores; for instance, users can determine that greater mastery is obtainable by seeing that scores are higher than their highest score. This can provide a source of motivation to continue playing if high scores seem achievable. A large difference between scores or clusterings of scores can indicate that use of an option, knowledge about an element of the game, or a different strategy may account for the range of scores.

Players often infer that they have improved on achieving a score higher than their previous best; however it is often difficult to accurately determine improvement in playing since there is a high standard deviation between plays of a game due to randomness in the game and variability in performance. Games typically record only high scores, not a mean or an average, so that a player's perception of progress may be inaccurate.

4.8.2. Additional Measures of Progress and Success

A game can have multiple built-in measures of success and players sometimes generate their own or devise their own use of the game's measure, which were often more compelling or of greater importance than the score. Players frequently employ measures which reflect the achievement of their own goal, rather than the game's goal. This can be seemingly irrelevant to the game because the the scoring mechanism does not support such a goal. There are additional measures, many of which are blatantly subjective. Measures other than the score are often more meaningful to a player.[13] Visual and audio effects provide feedback and are often used as a reward for good performance.[14]

Measures of progress and success can not only provide a sense of accomplishment, but also influence further play. Some games provide more constructive feedback than others, giving information about the closeness of an answer. In particular, a solution indicates that a player's guess is close or far from being correct, instead of only that it is right or wrong. Regardless of the outcome, most players examined the solution to understand their errors. A. Collins, in [Malone and Levin 84], defines the hindsight principle as when you can see at the conclusion of an activity how you could have done just a little better.[15]

4.8.3. Problems with Feedback

Although games are designed for appeal, they are often poorly designed from a usability viewpoint. Game playing, in general, is not an intrinsically difficult task, even though games may be quite complex. Unlike other software, which may require specialized knowledge or abilities, games should be usable by anybody, including non-computer-literate people. In a critical evaluations of games, it becomes apparent that design flaws make tasks which are not intrinsically difficult beyond the capability of many players. In general, poorly-designed features were more apparent than well-designed features because frustration was more strongly expressed than satisfaction.

There were many problems with feedback and control in games. A common problem with the games we examined was that not every area of the playing screen was either reactive or clearly not usable. As a consequence, there were frequent problems with players selecting areas of the screen with the mouse and receiving no feedback.[16] While the feedback that a system could provide in such instances is not detrimental to experienced players, it is helpful to novices. Mystery Box provides a good example of this, when a player made a guess prematurely, by giving a message that all of the balls must be placed before making a guess. Since players who made a premature guess were typically engaged in figuring out how to play the game, they inferred from the message that they needed to place the balls on the playing screen.

Design flaws and control problems can overwhelm a user and narrow a user's focus and the resulting preoccupation can prevent the accomplishment of a task. For instance, the importance of designing an interface to allow an appropriate margin of error was demonstrated by some of the games which we used in our preliminary study. In many instances, what appeared to the user to be correct placement of an object was not sufficiently accurate; this often resulted in an assumption that the action was incorrect, rather than imprecise.

5. Implications for System Design

We will mention some of the implications of our work for system design. Command design, measures of progress and success, help and system response, and challenge are examined.

5.1. Command Design

An area of system design for which our research has direct implications is the design of commands, such as the reversibility and consistency of commands. We found evidence that inconsistency and irreversibility of commands caused problems even in the case of games, which generally have a small command set. Such problems are likely to be more extensive in a system which has a large command set. Consistency is important for learning and for allowing a user to predict that if an operation has a certain effect, it is likely that a similar operation will have a similar effect, given the same context. Reversibility is important for a user to be able to undo an action and it can facilitate freer exploration of a system.

Command overloading and underloading are also problems that become apparent during observation of system use. Placing and replacing the ball, in Mystery Box, was an example of command underloading. There was a separate command to replace a ball, but most players assumed that it was dragged with the mouse in the same way that it had been placed. While it is not a design flaw to have a separate command, it adds to the complexity of learning and causes frustration. In this case, as in other instances, there was no advantage to the separate command since the commitment to a choice was made when "Make Guess" was used, not when a ball was initially placed.

5.2. Feedback and Measures of Progress and Success

One of the ways in which games are more successful than other types of software is the extent to which they provide measures of progress and success to users. We discuss the means by which mechanisms can be incorporated into the design of systems in order to likewise provide measures to users. Since the mechanisms by which progress and success were measured often differed from a game's measures and were often of greater importance to the user than the score, we also explore the means by which a system can support individual measures.

While users of software can develop internal measures of progress or success at accomplishing a task or achieving a goal, this is not explicitly supported by tools. As a result, users frequently have little sense of whether they are making progress, whether their goal has been achieved, or how well a task was done [Carroll 82]. For instance, a programmer might have the goal of compiling a program with no compile-time or run-time errors or to write terse or efficient code. The scores which a system could provide to a user include how many language features were used in a program or how well documented the program is. Likewise, measures can be used to indicate efficiency of command use or how quickly or efficiently a task was accomplished. A number of scoring mechanisms could be made available for a system, allowing users the choice of which reflect their concerns about the use of the system or the resulting product from the system use. In addition, users could automatically or upon request find out how they are doing with respect to previous users, typical users at the same level of expertise, or past performances through recorded scores. In addition to the provision of a number of predefined measures which are likely to be relevant to users, a system could allow the specification of user-defined measures.

5.3. Help and System Response

The role of feedback and help in a system are to aid a user in accomplishing a task and to prevent problems with the use of a system. A help facility should be easy to locate in order to avoid initial usage problems and the accompanying frustration. The frustration experienced by game players who were unable to locate help often influenced their feelings about their later success. A system can make help available through a clearly-labeled button or pull-down menu, and first time users can be placed directly in the help facility.

A closely related area of system design is the system's feedback or response characteristics. System response is important, especially for risk-averse users [Neal 87]. For such users, system commands which have no associated system response can induce anxiety that an unnoticed action occurred. If an invalid command is used, a risk-averse user is more dependent on explicit and clear system feedback. Visual feedback can be used to highlight information and to direct a user's attention, also reducing anxiety.[17] For such users, it will be worthwhile to expend additional effort to produce system responses which, besides indicating the problem, suggest which command to use instead. The latter is quite feasible since there usually is only a limited number of valid commands at any cursor location, and in many cases it is possible to infer the user's intention.

5.4. Graduated Challenge

The major way present computer games already exploit challenge is by providing multiple levels of difficulty for the player. In other games, notably in computer chess, the player can choose the level of difficulty at which to play or at which the computer, as the opponent, will compete. This "graduated challenge" principle of game design is not shared by the design of other software artifacts, or if used at all, is used in a very rudimentary way. For instance, while users of a system can select a command subset and choose to eventually expand it, explicit levels of difficulty are rarely provided. Designing in multiple levels of difficulty is a device which will aid in keeping users challenged.[18]

Tools which provide explicit levels typically present only a novice mode and an expert mode. While a novice mode can be effective at providing entry into a system, tools provide no assistance to the user in going between modes. The increments in modes are generally much greater than the difference between subsequent levels of difficulty in a game.

A further way a sophisticated system design could aid a user is by determining when to change modes and by providing a greater number of levels so that it is easier to make incremental steps. Thus the system adapts more to a user's increasing expertise and abilities. Subsequent modes could be based on classes of commands which are of the same difficulty level and are likely to be needed by someone who has mastered the previous level. For example, a user would be likely, after initial use, to want to know simple options to commands, and eventually may want to know more complex options. Tracking the commands that a user has mastered can provide an indication that a user is ready for an increment. A system could use such information either by automatically and transparently switching modes or by providing guidance that the user is ready for a more advanced mode or level of difficulty.

6. Conclusions

We performed an empirical study of computer games, and describe the salient features which impact the interaction between the user and the systems. Implications are drawn from the results of the study, and we show that there are significant ways in which system design can be improved through the incorporation of techniques and features borrowed from games, in particular, command design, measures of progress and success, help and system response, and graduated challenge. Some of these principles arise from a detailed examination of the problems with the use of computer games, while others arise from a careful consideration of the ways in which successful features from games can be incorporated into more general system design.

Acknowledgements

I would like to thank Ugo Gagliardi for his support of this work.

Notes

1. In a plenary address to CHI'87, T. Landauer noted that "the egocentric intuition fallacy of designers" was the basis of the typical design process.

2. For instance, a subject who was playing her second game of ThinkAhead said, "I feel like the game has all of a sudden become much more complex than it was last time... in that I know I can recognize more of the ramifications of each move."

3. Objective success for each game is generally well-defined, since games tend to have clear goals and to provide a scoring mechanism. Subjective success, however, varies for each player for each game, depending on factors such as their goals and level of expertise, and it can vary significantly over time since the factors on which it depends, such as expertise, change with time and continued system use.

4. The features that make computer games successful include that skilled performance is instrumental to attaining an objective posed by the rules of the game, that a game increases in its ability to challenge the player, that audio or visual effects are used to reward success, that the possibility of competition exists, that random elements are part of a game, that a game incorporates fantasy elements, that a game allows opportunities for cooperation, and that the computer times a player's responses and factors speed into scores [Banet 79].

5. Randomness affected players' perceptions of their performance and of the computer's actions, for instance, often creating an erroneous perception that a player has improved. In games in which the computer's role was active or semi-active, players often erroneously attributed randomness to being intentional actions on the part of the computer. For example, a Tetris player said, "The computer knows how I'm playing this, because it won't give me a straight one any more." A reaction by a player of ThinkAhead was, "It seems that all the rows have bad numbers and the columns have good numbers. But that's impossible."

6. A subject compared Mystery Box and ThinkAhead, saying, "[ThinkAhead] explained itself to me from the start, which was good. I guess [Mystery Box] I had a negative feel towards it when I had to figure out how to get the help. It didn't have something that said 'help'."

7. While "competition is often an effective and natural way of providing an appropriate difficulty level for the individual motivation of challenge [Malone and Lepper 87]," this was not the case in ThinkAhead, where many players perceived that the computer was or should be unbeatable. This perception might not have existed had there been user control of the level at which the computer competed.

8. The use of metaphors and analogies is becoming more common in other types of systems. For example, the icons used by the Macintosh, such as the trash can and file folders, provide pictorial, easy-to-understand representations. In addition, most users perceive the task of dragging a file to a trash can as being more fun than typing a command which has the same result.

9. In general, the design of systems for optimal transfer is too restrictive [Norman 84], but it can be a factor in the design process.

10. Rasmussen [87] found that "to be successful, a new system has to motivate its users to explore its capabilities." Carroll [82] found that Adventure has an environment that motivates people to explore, which is accomplished through features such as responsiveness and benchmarks to indicate progress.

11. Some facts or rules might be necessary to know or understand, while others are less important or ones for which a faulty understanding does not impact success. When erroneous rules are developed, in some cases successful play is still possible, while in other cases misconceptions become repaired, aided by feedback [Suchman 85].

12. Carroll [82] found that the level of motivation shown by game players is often higher than that of users of other types of software, and that complex games are mastered more easily than computer tools, primarily because of the increased feedback provided by games. There are few liabilities to the inclusion of better feedback; for instance, the inclusion of error messages impacts new users who are experiencing problems without adversely impacting experienced users. Not only can feedback potentially increase the motivation to use and master tools, but it can also help in the prevention of problems during use. For instance, while there are few consequences to failing with a game, there are major consequences to problems with tool use, such as lost information [Carroll 82].

13. In ThinkAhead, a measure of success was when a player had the goal of understanding the computer's strategy and measured success by the accuracy of a prediction of the computer's next move. Another subject described her measure of success at playing Crystal Quest as being "any time the bridge opens up I think I am doing well, but I still can't get through it..." A Tetris player described her measure as "when I was able to position something from the top and then hit the space bar to drop it down really quickly instead of letting it sort of fall where it may...that was one of my measurement things to see that I was getting better."

14. Users can more quickly and easily assimilate a graphical display than a textual one [Myers 83], and games currently utilize more visual and audio information than do other types of applications.

15. A subject said the following about Tetris, but could as easily have been describing any of the four games: "Each time you play you figure out a different strategy, a different way that all the blocks could possibly fit and you could possibly get the line completed. Maybe each time you make different mistakes, but at least you feel as though you're getting closer to understanding how these are going to fit."

16. Dragging a ball was an instance in which players had problems. When the mouse was moved on top of a ball, the cursor changed to a hand, which to most players indicated that the ball could be moved. However, the ball disappeared between its original location and the playing screen. Most players stopped trying to drag it once they could no longer see the ball, and were very confused over how to move it. The hand icon was informative enough so that many continued to try, until they were successful.

17. For instance, "percent-done progress indicators" are a technique which graphically depict how much of a task has been completed [Myers 85]. They have been shown to be effective at reducing anxiety and allowing users to better utilize the time that they are waiting.

18. While games become boring after too much mastery has been achieved, tools become usable almost instinctively once mastery has been achieved. Malone [80] found that "tools should be made as efficient and reliable as possible [because] unnecessary difficulty or complexity may prove frustrating rather than rewarding." One of the consequences of achieving mastery of a tool is that a user has less incentive to switch to a new tool unless their are enormous benefits associated with its use.

References

Banet, B. Computers and early learning: A new direction for High/Scope Foundation. *Calculators/Computers* (1979) 3, 17.

Carroll, J. M. The Adventure of Getting to Know a Computer. *Computer Magazine*. (1982).

Carroll, J. M. and Thomas, J. C. Fun. *SIGCHI Bulletin*. V. 19, N. 3, January 1988.

Ericsson, K. A. and Simon, H. A. *Protocol Analysis Verbal Reports as Data*. Cambridge, MA: MIT Press, 1984.

Good, M. Etude and the folklore of user interface design. In *Proceedings of the ACM SIGPLAN SIGOA Symposium on Text Manipulation* (Portland, Oregon, June 1981).

Gorry, G. A. *Research on Expert Systems*. MIT Laboratory for Computer Science, Technical Memoranda 56, 1974.

Gould, J. D. How to Design Usable Systems. In Bullinger, H.-J. and Shackel, B. (editors), *Human-Computer Interaction - INTERACT'87*. Amsterdam: North-Holland, 1987.

Krueger, M. W., Gionfriddo, T., and Hinrichsen, K. VIDEO-PLACE -- An artificial reality. In *Proceedings of CHI'85 Conference on Human Factors in Computing Systems* (San Francisco, April 14-18, 1985), ACM, New York.

Malone, T. W. *What Makes Things Fun to Learn? A Study of Intrinsically Motivating Computer Games*. Technical Report CIS-7, XEROX PARC, 1980.

Malone, T. W. and Lepper, M. R. Making Learning Fun: A Taxonomy of Intrinsic Motivations for Learning, In Snow, R. E. and Farr, M. J. (editors), *Aptitude, learning and instruction: III. Conative and affective process analysis*. Hillsdale, N.J.: Erlbaum, 1987.

Malone, T. W. and Levin, J. Microcomputers in Education: Cognitive and Social Design Principles. in Walker, D. F. and Hess, R. D., Instructional Software, Wadsworth Publishing Company, Belmont, California, 1984.

McKinsey, J. C. C. *Introduction to the Theory of Games*. New York: McGraw-Hill, 1952.

Myers, B. A. The Importance of Percent-Done Progress Indicators for Human Computer Interfaces. In *Proceedings of CHI'85 Conference on Human Factors in Computing Systems* (San Francisco, April 14-18, 1985), ACM, New York.

Myers, B. A. Incense: A System for Displaying Data Structures. In *Computer Graphics: Proceedings of SIGGRAPH '83* 17(3), July 1983.

Neal, L. R. Cognition-Sensitive Design and User Modeling for Syntax-Directed Editors. In *Proceedings of CHI+GI'87 Conference on Human Factors in Computing Systems and Graphics Interface* (Toronto, April 5-9). ACM, New York, 1987.

Neal, L. R. A System for Example-Based Programming. In *Proceedings of CHI'89 Conference on Human Factors in Computing Systems* (Austin, April 30 - May 4). ACM, New York, 1989a.

Neal, L. R. *The Role of User Models in System Design*. TR-18-89 (Ph.D. Dissertation), Harvard University, October 1989b.

Norman, D. Stages and levels in human-machine interaction. *International Journal of Man-Machine Studies* (1984), 21.

Rasmussen, J. Cognitive Engineering. In Bullinger, H.-J. and Shackel, B. (editors), *Human-Computer Interaction - INTERACT'87*. Amsterdam: North-Holland, 1987.

Rich, E. *Artificial Intelligence*. New York: McGraw-Hill, 1983.

Suchman, L. *Plans and Situated Actions*. Palo Alto: XEROX Corporation, 1985.

Turkle, S. *The Second Self: Computers and the Human Spirit*. New York: Simon and Schuster, 1984.

Whitefield, A. Models in Human Computer Interaction: A Classification with Special Reference to their Uses in Design. In Bullinger, H.-J. and Shackel, B. (editors), *Human-Computer Interaction - INTERACT'87*. Amsterdam: North-Holland, 1987.

Human–Computer Interaction – INTERACT '90
D. Diaper et al. (Editors)
Elsevier Science Publishers B.V. (North-Holland)

A Study of Measures for Research in Hypertext Navigation

D.G. Hendry, T.T. Carey and S.T. TeWinkel

Dept. of Computing and Information Science
University of Guelph, Guelph Ontario Canada N1G 2W1

Abstract : The research described here investigated the strategies people use to navigate a hypertext document in reading comprehension tasks. We present the results from experiments where people were initially instructed to browse and later to study a document containing expository information on 35 mm. cameras. The users interacted with the document through one of two presentation methods : traditional page sequences or access by hypertext links. A variety of measures were used to illuminate users' navigation strategies : Each of these measures contributes in a different way to our overall understanding of users' navigation (and raises additional questions).

1.0 Introduction

Documents presented with hypertext systems offer the potential of much more flexible access to information than traditional linear, paper-based documents. But flexible access requires choice—the reader must make decisions about what to read next. The process of choosing an access sequence is often described as analogous to navigating around a physical space.

Navigating in spatial environments can be both frustrating and rewarding—frustrating when you get disoriented, rewarding when it leads to increased understanding. Consider, for example, the experience of driving yourself somewhere to which you have previously been driven by others. You can be suddenly aware of how little you have absorbed as a passenger about the structure of the neighbourhood. Navigation can be an important learning process in its own right.

There are numerous reports of hypertext navigation being disorienting [e.g. Edwards and Hardman 88]. But our knowledge of navigation is limited, particularly in terms of its potential to be a learning experience in itself rather than just a means to get to document content.

Understanding navigation is an important research goal for understanding hypertext : how do people navigate through hypertext documents, how does that differ from their navigation through traditional documents, how the navigational strategy is formed, and what impacts—positive and negative—it has.

This paper reports on a research study of hypertext navigation. A variety of research measures are necessary to gather information about this process : we report here on the role of different data gathering techniques in filling in our picture of hypertext navigation. Section 2 describes the experiment, Section 3 presents the results from the various measures used. Section 4 compares the roles of the various research measures and discusses further ongoing work.

2.0 The Navigation Experiment

2.1 Choice of task

Research has been done on how people retrieve information from hypertext systems (e.g., [Campagnoni Erhlich 89]) and how well people use systems to answer open-book essay questions [Egan et al 89]. However, despite obvious implications [Charney 87], little research has been done on how hypertext systems affect our *comprehension* for the content of a text. Since many hypertext systems are used for more that just information retrieval, we decided to investigate how a hypertext system affects comprehension outcomes, resulting from various reading tasks. Further, it was decided that we would initially investigate the essence of hypertext—making decisions about where next to read—without the influence of navigation aids such as maps [Monk et al 89] or more elaborate methods for signaling document structure [Conklin Begeman 88].

In the experiment, subjects were given two reading tasks: browsing and studying. Subjects always browsed first, then studied. For browsing, subjects were instructed to "quickly browse through the document, trying to determine its organization and the nature of its contents". For studying, subjects were instructed to "learn as much as possible" and to expect a test. The instructions did not specify the nature of the test, but did describe a scenario in which students might use the information.

2.2 Choice of document

We decided to use expository text passages, which had been used in previous experiments [Bromage Mayer 81]. These passages explained the operation of a 35mm camera and the experiments examined what good problem solvers learn from them. Two reasons led us to this decision. First, the text passages were designed for subjects from a subject-population similar to the one available to us, namely undergraduate students. While the passages contain complex expository information, (as do many commercial hypertext documents) no specialized background knowledge was needed of the topic. Second, cued-recall questions for measuring subjects' comprehension had already been prepared; thus, using these text passages gave us a method for measuring comprehension. Using existing expository text passages and cued-recall questions gave us time to concentrate our efforts elsewhere, as well as the potential to compare results and methods.

2.3 Converting to hypertext

To develop the hypertext document, we first decided upon a strategy for transforming the expository passages into standard topologies of nodes and links. These logical structures (i.e., the topologies) together with the physical structure (i.e., the manner in which titles, passages, and links are shown) constitute a rhetorical convention for organizing the hypertext. This rhetorical convention can be summarized by describing the topologies, the methods for connecting the topologies, and the physical structure.

Three topologies are used in the document: simple-, sequenced-, and complete-collection. Each topology consists of a *topic* node and several *descriptive* nodes. A topic node introduces the subject matter for its topology. How the descriptive nodes are linked together (i.e., how they are related) is what distinguishes the three types of topologies. In the simple-collection, each descriptive node has a link to-and-from the topic node. In the sequenced-collection, the descriptive nodes are sequenced in some order, and the topic node has a link to the first descriptive node and the last descriptive node has a link back to the topic node. In the complete-collection each descriptive node has a link to-and-from the topic node and all descriptive nodes have links to each other. An illustration of these topologies appears in Figure 1 : the vertical line on the left side links together a simple collection, the box clusters together a complete collection, and the loop on the right side links a sequenced collection. These topologies were chosen because: (a) they reflect common methods for structuring text [Meyer Freedle 84] and (b) similar topologies have been used to create topologically complex but purposeful hypertext documents [Bernstein 87].

Two methods can be used to connect topologies together. First, collections can be embedded in each other, by making the topic node for one collection a descriptive node in another. This method is used to create hierarchies. Second, topologies can be connected together by what are called *associative* links. These links provide efficient access to nodes that are otherwise far away (i.e., several links have to be followed up and down a document) and they allow an author to show important relationships between nodes that, for expository reasons, are most effectively placed in different topologies.

Figure 1 shows the nodes titles and topology which make up the document hierarchy for the experiment. All links are two-way unless explicitly marked with an arrow. Figure 2 shows the 26 associative links. The document consists of 30 nodes, 92 links, and 2088 words.

Figure 3 shows the physical appearance of a node. All nodes contain a thematic title that is elaborated by a text passage. Links (i.e., titles of other nodes) are shown beneath text passages. The positions of the links are random, because a systematic method for placing links (e.g., all links going down the hierarchy are shown on the left) might induce a navigation bias, a complication we did not want to face in our initial work.

Experience in creating hypertext documents is showing that strategies for linking nodes (i.e., structuring text) are often subjective, taking the form of authors' personal (nonstandard) tastes [Alschuler 89]. The rhetorical convention, described above, was intended to provide a general approach for creating a class of documents, all with the same style. Criticism about the idiosyncrasies of the hypertext document can thereby be deflected, to some extent at least, to the the rhetorical convention. But, the convention only reduces the possibility of ad hoc document structures, it does not eliminate it. On the one hand, decisions about choice of topology can usually be based on the nature of the ideas in the text. These decisions are relatively straight-forward. For example, passages on the steps of taking a picture naturally fit into a sequenced-collection, whereas the parts of a camera, having no inherent sequence and being relatively independent, fit best into a simple-collection. On the other hand, decisions about when to use associative links are not straight-forward. (An informal exercise showed that when given the hierarchical structure of the document as a basis, and asked to add about 30 associative links, two people experienced with hypertext had about 50% of their proposed links in common.)

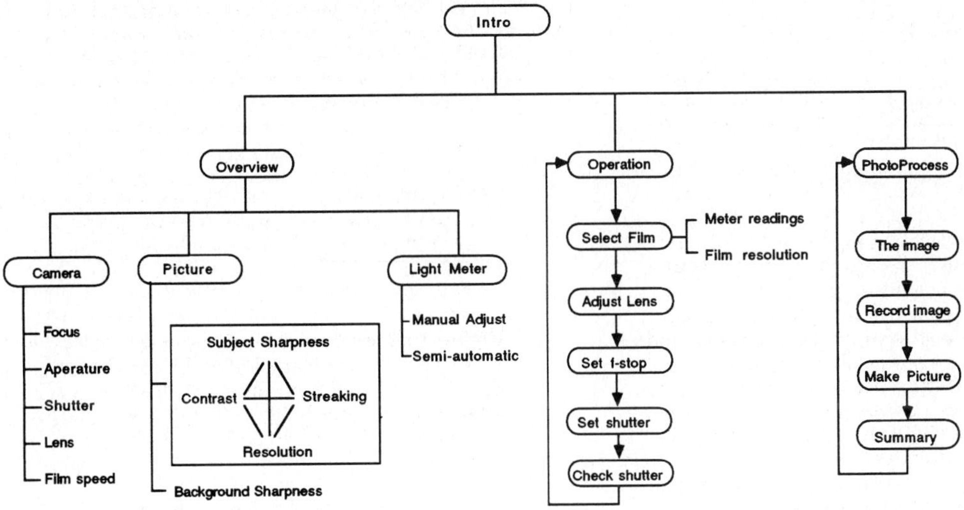

Figure 1: Node Titles and Topology for Document

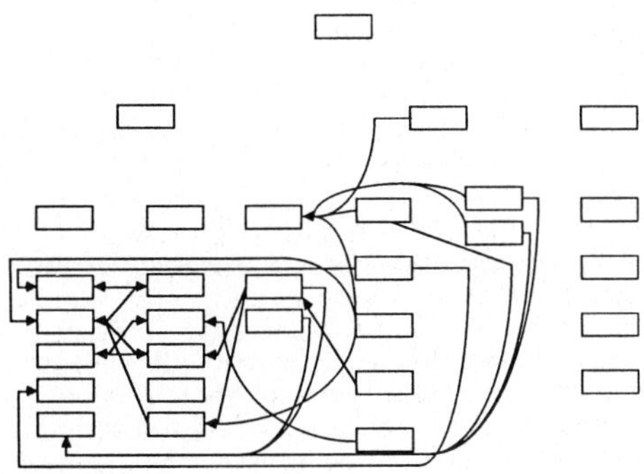

Figure 2: Associational Links in Document

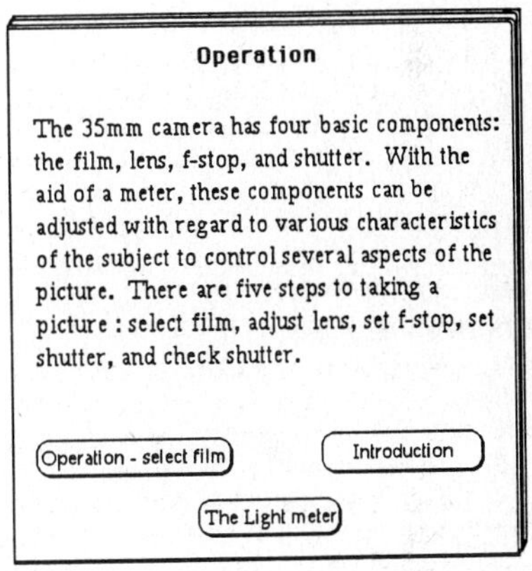

Figure 3: Example Information Node

2.3 Procedure

The measures and results discussed in the next section are part of a larger experiment, reported elsewhere [Hendry 89]. This section summarizes the procedure for that experiment.

Forty-four undergraduate students, who reported no familiarity with operating 35mm cameras, were randomly assigned to experimental or control groups. The experimental group subjects read the hypertext document by navigating through links, whereas control subjects read a linearized version of it by paging. (The control and experimental groups were in fact subdivided further, but we do not discuss those results here.)

After subjects completed a tutorial, they were instructed to browse the document (6 min). Then, they were asked to recall as many nodes titles as possible. Next, they were asked to study the document (15 min). Finally, they were again asked to recall as many node titles as possible, and to then answer several cued-recall questions, which appraised their comprehension of the material. The experiment was thus a mixed design: task instructions were an incomplete within-subject variable, and user-interface for reading was a between-subject variable.

3.0 Measures and Results

In this section the details of the experiment are summarized; in the next section we discuss how the various measures of performance contribute to our understanding of users' navigation.

3.1 Measures of comprehension

The results show that reading by navigating neither enhanced nor hindered comprehension for the material, as measured by the cued-recall questions. However, subjects who read by navigating recalled more node titles than subjects who read by paging (33% vs. 20%, $F(1,40)=19.1$, $p<.001$). Similar results were found in an experiment where subjects were instructed to find information using either SuperBook or a page-bound manual: users of SuperBook recalled more section titles than users of the page-bound manual [Egan et al 89]. Taken together, the results from this experiment suggest that navigation enhances the learning of incidental information but does not affect learning for content.

3.2 Measures of node access and coverage

Subjects who read by paging covered more of the nodes than subjects who read by navigating (92% vs. 82%, $F(1,30)=29.1$, $p<.001$), apparently because it is harder to assess one's coverage and strive for complete coverage when reading a hypertext document. This result reminds us of the importance of providing navigation aids that help people obtain a sense of closure. As expected, there was a positive correlation between scores on comprehension questions and coverage of the document (Pearson $r=.57$, $F(1,31) = 15.0$, $p<.001$).

When subjects browsed the hypertext document they generally had shorter node visiting times than when studying (19 vs. 23 sec, $F(1,30)=7.2$, $p<.025$) and the standard deviations of node visiting times were shorter when they browsed than when they studied (10 vs. 16 sec, $F(1,30)=26.7$, $p<.001$). This data suggests that the task instructions did affect the way subjects read. Browsing might be characterized by relatively short visit times, with low variance, whereas studying might be characterized by relatively longer visit times, with high variance.

3.3 Comparisons with original study (paper-based text)

We did not duplicate the experimental conditions of Bromage and Mayer, so that comparisons between our results and the original study were not straightforward. For one thing, while we reproduced their comprehension questions, their marking scheme was not recorded so we had to estimate how the scoring was done. For factual questions this was simple, but for more complex questions we adopted a conservative scoring which may have varied considerably from the original. On the factual questions, the scores were very similar (mean of 7.1 in our study vs. 7.3, out of a possible score of 17 in each case). On more difficult questions, our subjects were considerably lower. We did not attempt statistical comparisons—it is not clear whether these differences were due to differences in experimental conditions, subject populations or scoring methods.

A second difference in experimental methods occurred in the instructions to subjects. The browse/study distinction was not presented in the original experiments. Subjects were instructed there to "read the document through once", in preparation for answering questions. This does not translate easily into the hypertext condition, in which a number of nodes may be revisited before the entire document has been read. We attempted to achieve the same effect by asking subjects in the browse condition to try to cover the whole document and restricting the time allowed based on pilot studies. In the actual experiments the subjects did not always achieve complete coverage of the document. This illustrates the way in which media considerations complicate comparisons between conditions.

3.4 Measures of navigation patterns

The sequences of nodes that users create as they navigate is an important source of data about the the usability of hypertext systems. Analyzing these sequences seems to have been first proposed and explored, in an experimental setting, by Canter and his colleagues ([Canter et al 85 & 86]), but has been used informally in practical settings to evaluate the usability of both help systems ([Campagnoni Ehrlich 89] [Campbell 88] and walk-up-and-use information systems [Mountford 89].

For this research we adapted some indices for characterizing navigation [Canter et al 85] so they could be used to characterize subjects' navigation through the hypertext document. We computed the extent that subjects covered all nodes in a topology before moving on to another one; the extent that subjects moved through the document by going up and down, instead of following associative links; and the extent that subjects made loops back to a topology in the cases where an associative link was followed. We anticipated, as have others (e.g., [Canter et al 85] [Bernstein et al 88]), that indices such as these could be used to discriminate paths through hypertext documents under varying task conditions.

Contrary to our expectations, the indices failed to show any systematic differences in the way subjects sequenced nodes during browsing and studying. Furthermore, when subjects were divided into two groups, subjects scoring low in comprehension and those scoring high (16 vs. 28 points, $F(1,20)=57.4$, $p<.001$), there were no significant differences in the navigation indices across the two groups. It appears that a particular sequence for visiting nodes is as likely to occur during browsing as it is during studying, and that good-comprehenders do not sequence their access to nodes (as characterized by the indices) any differently than poor-comprehenders.

3.5 Verbal protocols and debriefing

To supplement the controlled experiment, several additional subjects were presented with the hypertext condition. They were encouraged to verbalize while they read, and questioned afterwards about aspects of their strategies. We were particularly interested in their perceptions of their strategies during the browse and study stages. We also wanted to assess whether the recall of node titles was an aid to searching in the document, so subjects were asked to search through the document to find answers to several of the original comprehension questions.

During the browse condition, subjects focussed on the goal of covering the document, skimming the text of nodes and concentrating to some extent on titles. This was particularly evident towards the end of the time period allotted for browsing. During the study condition, subjects' goal was to remember the document contents that they considered "testable". The instructions, which indicated they would be tested, seemed to have biased them away from information suited for their own use, such as photo processing.

While subjects did indicate these different strategies for the browse and study conditions, they did not differ in directedness. This is in line with the navigation path data described above. Our experimental conditions did not induce the kind of undirected browsing we were seeking, which may explain in part why the navigation indices did not differ. To create an undirected browsing condition, we would have to remove the goal statement. The best way to do this appears to create a "waiting" condition, in which subjects are ostensibly waiting to participate in an experiment and are given the opportunity to use the hypertext system to fill in their time. All the people we debriefed indicated that they found using the medium enjoyable, so that the hypertext environment would probably be attractive enough to engage subjects outside an explicit experimental instruction to use it.

When asked to search for the answers to questions, navigation became the primary task rather than studying for recall. People experienced more frustration using the document for this purpose, because they wanted to home in on the desired information but were often unable to quickly find it. They did frequently verbalize node titles as search objects. The rhetoric conventions adopted to guide reading in the document were counter-productive for searching, e.g. the sequenced-collection topology. The presence of associative links was noticed more during search, where it tended to diminish subjects' initial perceptions of the document as solely hierarchical.

Subjects also differed considerably in their search strategies. One subject deliberately returned to the initial node to start each search, but tended to use associative links during traversal more than other subjects. Another person, who had focussed in the browse and study stages on learning where information rather than details of content, performed very efficient searches on general questions but had difficulties on specific questions (where the answer was in a single node).

4. Conclusions and further work

Each of the measures employed supplied complementary information about the experiment. The comprehension measures demonstrated that hypertext users were not at a significant disadvantage over readers of the paged text, despite the need to navigate explicitly through the document. The recall of node titles suggested that hypertext users might be able to use titles to navigate in search tasks, which was confirmed by the verbal protocol sessions. The node coverage statistics showed that coverage of the document was uneven, and that people who scored higher on the comprehension measures had been more successful at exploring the whole document.

The verbal protocol sessions showed that different strategies were used in the browse and study stages, but the navigation data showed that these strategies did not differ overall in terms of node access patterns. The verbal protocol data also demonstrated how the task instructions influenced the navigation. This suggests aspects of the experiment not considered in the original Bromage and Mayer study. For example, the original study noted that subjects scoring higher on comprehension questions also scored higher on general problem-solving ability. They did not consider whether the differences in recall were due to more accurate guesses about the "testables" which the experimenters would ask about. The verbal protocols make it clear that subjects' perceptions of the probable questions influenced their navigation strategy.

A number of extensions to our study are now underway. The most obvious addition is a map of the hypertext document. Other studies have demonstrated the positive effects of a visual overview to guide navigation [Monk et al 88, Hammond & Allison 87 & 88], and the verbal protocols of subjects searching for information indicate frustration at the absence of such an aid. During browse and study stages the same comments are not frequent, although there are other indications that subjects would have appreciated a map.

For example, some subjects were distracted by a node title "Overview" which occurred at the second level of the document hierarchy (below "Introduction", see figure 1). In the browse stage, they failed to return up the hierarchy past this point, thinking that "Overview" was the main topic node rather than a subnode of "Introduction". As a result, they failed to cover the several parts of the document until the study stage—when they were returned to the top node automatically and remarked on what they had missed.

We are particularly interested on the effect of a map on navigational patterns, compared with the data on use without a map. Does a map change the navigational strategy or just facilitate it? We currently have map prototypes with different appearances (topological network vs. table of contents) and different features (static map, map which records current position, map which allows direct access). Our concern at present is not to choose an optimal map format, but to first understand the effects of various map structures in different conditions.

A second area of further work is the rhetorical conventions used to organize reading for comprehension. Our subjects received no introduction to these conventions, and the verbal protocols indicate discovery about the role of hierarchical vs. associative links occurring after considerable navigation. We want to compare the impact of instruction in the conventions against the impact of a map (and against both a map and instruction). We also need to study how the rhetorical conventions affect navigation during search, and to what extent people are disoriented by an associative access which bypasses the organizational structure. We also want to observe the search process on parts of a document which have not previously been browsed, to determine the role which browsing plays in formation of a navigational strategy.

Acknowledgements

This research was supported by Cognos Inc., the Ontario Technology Fund and the Natural Sciences and Engineering Research Council of Canada.

References

Alschuler, L. (1989). Hand-crafted hypertext—Lessons from the ACM experiment, in E. Barrett ed., *The Society of Text*, MIT Press, 1989. pp. 343-361.

Bernstein, M. (1987). *Hypertext '87 - A Digest* [hypertext document for *Hypergate*, a hypertext system]. Cambridge, MA: Eastgate Systems Inc.

Bernstein, M., Feiner, S., & Drexler, K. E. (Organizing Committee). (1988, August). *AAAI-88 Workshop on AI and Hypertext: Issues and Directions.*

Bromage, B. K., & Mayer, R. E. (1981). Relationship between what is remembered and creative problem-solving performance in science learning. *Journal of Educational Psychology, 78*, pp. 451-461.

Campagnoni, F. R., & Ehrlich, K. (1989). Information retrieval using a hypertext-based help system. *ACM Transactions on Office Information Systems, 7*, pp. 271-291.

Campbell, R. L. (1988). *Evaluating online assistance empirically* (Report No. 13410-60030). Yorktown Heights, NY: IBM Research Division, T. J. Watson Research Center.

Canter, D., Rivers, R., & Storrs, G. (1985). Characterizing user navigation through complex data structures. *Behaviour & Information Technology, 4*, pp. 93-102.

Canter, D., Powell, J., Wishart, J., & Roderick C. (1986). User navigation in complex database systems. *Behaviour & Information Technology, 5*, pp. 249-257.

Charney, D. (1987). Comprehending non-linear text: The role of discourse cues and reading strategies. *Hypertext'87 Position Papers* (pp. 109-120). Conference held at the University of North Carolina, Chapel Hill, November 1987.

Conklin, J., & Begeman, M. L. (1988). gIBIS: A hypertext tool for exploratory policy discussion. *Proceedings of the ACM SigOIS Conference on Computer-Supported Cooperative Work*, pp. 140-152.

Edwards, D. M., & Hardman, L. (1989). a hypertext environment. In McAleese, R. (Ed.), *Hypertext: Theory into practice*, Norwood, NJ: Ablex, pp. 103-125.

Egan, D. E., Remde, J. R., Landauer, T. K., Lochbaum, C. C., & Gomez, L. M. (1989). Behaviour evaluation and analysis of a hypertext browser. In K. Bice & C. Lewis (Eds.), *Proceedings CHI'89 Human Factors in Computing Systems* New York: ACM, pp. 205-210.

Hammond, N., & Allinson, L. (1987). The travel metaphor as design principle and training aid for navigating around complex systems. In D. Diaper & R. Winder (Eds.), *People and Computers III* Cambridge University Press: Cambridge, pp. 75-90.

Hammond, N., & Allinson, L. (1988). Travels around a learning support environment: Rambling, orienteering, or touring? In E.Soloway, D. Frye, & S. B. Sheppard (Eds.), *Proceedings CHI'88 Human Factors in Computing Systems* New York: ACM, pp. 269-273.

Hendry, D. (1989). *The relationship between navigation and comprehension in a hypertext environment.* M.Sc. Thesis. Department of Computing and Information Science, University of Guelph, Ontario, Cananda.

Marchionini, G., & Shneiderman, B. (1988). Finding facts vs. browsing knowledge in hypertext systems. *IEEE Computer, 21*(1), pp. 70-80.

Meyer, B. J. F., & Freedle, R. O. (1984). Effects of discourse type on recall. *American Journal of Educational Research, 21*, pp. 121-143.

Monk, A. F., Walsh, P., Dix, A. J. (1988). A comparison of hypertext, scrolling and folding. In D. M. Jones and R. Winder (eds.), *People and Computers IV*, Cambridge: Cambridge University Press, pp. 421-435.

Mountford, J. (1989). Comments during presentation at User Interface Strategies '90, Satellite course December 9, 1989.

Human–Computer Interaction – INTERACT '90
D. Diaper et al. (Editors)
Elsevier Science Publishers B.V. (North-Holland)

MENTAL EFFORT AND TASK PERFORMANCE: TOWARDS A PSYCHOPHYSIOLOGY OF HUMAN COMPUTER INTERACTION

David WASTELL

Department of Computer Science, University of Manchester, Oxford Road, Manchester, M13 9PL, U.K.

Empirical methods play an important role in the science of HCI. The limitations of introspective and behavioural techniques are discussed, using mental workload as an example. The case is argued for a psychophysiological approach to the study of HCI (i.e. the interlocking study of behaviour, experience and bodily processes), adducing as evidence two field studies in which physiological measures played a decisive role. A laboratory study is described in which a physiological measure of mental effort is used to resolve the confounding of effort and cognitive demands inherent in performance measures of workload. The psychophysiological perspective broadens the scope of HCI to include such issues as stress and job design. The paper concludes with a discussion of the possible influence of psychophysiological thinking upon the design of systems for supporting co-operative work.

1. The empirical-analytic paradigm in HCI

The study of human-computer interaction is a diverse and eclectic enterprise. One scientific tradition has a pre-eminent place, the *empirical-analytic* paradigm inherited from positivist experimental psychology, particularly the practice of quantitative behavioural testing in a well-controlled laboratory situation. A wide variety of empirical methods are in use, including detailed behavioural observation using video recording, collection of verbal protocols etc. Performance testing, in particular, has been widely employed in design, evaluation and theory-development. Bewley et al (1983), for instance, in a classic report describe the role of "human factors testing" to resolve well-defined design questions in the design of the Xerox Star Workstation (eg to determine the best method for selecting text). Performance studies have also played a significant part in developing and testing information processing theories of human-computer interaction and in evaluating the psychological validity of various task analytic formalisms (eg Card *et al*, 1980). Performance metrics also figure prominently in system evaluation (eg Brooke, 1986; Roberts and Moran, 1983). Outside the laboratory, the empirical inheritance is reflected in the pursuit of nomothetic field studies (using survey methods) to evaluate aspects of technical quality, to study user attitudes etc.

The application of empirical techniques is not without methodological controversy, although these debates typically do not bring into fundamental question the validity of the scientific method as they have in the neighbouring field of Information System research (Wastell, 1988). Some issues are particularly intriguing, such as the contentious status of verbal protocols (Bewley and Buxton, 1983). This issue, of course, reflects a wider controversy in cognitive psychology (Claxton, 1980) which recalls those formative debates that characterised the early years of scientific psychology, leading to Watson's rejection of introspection and the ascendancy of behaviourism. The external validity of laboratory studies is a serious issue (Monk, 1986) although the problem is perhaps "more honoured in the breach than the observance". The question of external validity is not just a question of recruiting representative subjects. The laboratory situation itself is an artificial one, which exerts a characteristic influence over behaviour (cf the Hawthorne studies), which Orne (1962) famously dubbed the *demand characteristics* of the experimental situation. Experimenter effects also exercise a powerful but covert influence over the results of experiments as Rosenthal's classic studies (Rosenthal, 1966) demonstrate.

Interpretation of the humble performance measure itself is not uncontentious. Measures of task performance are used widely thoughout HCI, in much the same way as they are used throughout applied psychology where they operationalise the related constructs of task difficulty and mental workload. Like many ostensibly simple concepts, the innocent ideas of difficulty and workload have provoked enormous "sound and fury" and a burgeoning of techniques, dogmata and factions (Gopher and Donchin, 1986). Primary task performance, of course, suffers from a fundamental ambiguity; that it is inextricably confounded with effort. The problem is easy to state. Gopher and Donchin comment: "Neither can it be assumed that quality of performance is a good measure of the difficulty of a task. People often cope with an increase in task difficulty by increasing mental effort so that performance may remain stable despite a great increase in difficulty".

We clearly face a vicious circle here involving performance and effort. The need to break out of this circle, coupled with distrust of introspective techniques, has led researchers such as Gopher and Donchin to champion physiological measures of workload.

2. The psychophysiological perspective

The methodological problems of empirical HCI are, of course, no more and no less than those besetting its parent discipline, experimental psychology, and HCI has been no more and no less negligent in the face of what are very difficult and inconvenient issues. This paper concentrates on one main topic, that of mental workload, as a bridgehead for developing the case for a psychophysiological approach to the study of HCI. The issue has been chosen for three reasons: because workload is an important issue in HCI (the cognitive demands of computer-based work are frequently cited as being of major concern to the field (Briner and Hockey, 1988)); secondly, the workload issue brings into foveal view the inherent ambiguity of the ubiquitous performance metric, i.e. the problem of interpreting performance without an independent measure of effort; thirdly, physiology affords a number of indices of mental effort which have achieved varying degrees of respectability and which thus allow the psychophysiological approach to be shown off in a rather favourable light.

The argument of this paper is that the study of HCI requires a greater depth than can be provided by any single domain of description, be it behavioural, subjective or physiological. Introspection is unreliable and limited in scope. Much of information processing is non-conscious; moreover, an inverse relationship between awareness and behaviour often prevails (eg skilled performance) which severely limits subjective techniques. Behaviour, as we have seen, is intrinsically ambiguous. Specifically, the case is put forward that a psychophysiolgical approach, in which physiology, subjective experience and outward behaviour are simultaneously examined, provides a richer and firmer base for the scientific study of HCI. Gale and Christie (1987) have recently called for a psychophysiological approach to research into the office of the future, the *electronic workplace*, basing their argument on similar grounds: "it is possible for subjects to dissemble, to give responses they believe to be desirable, to construct feasible *post hoc* accounts of the reasons for their actions...physiological response systems can provide us with objective information that is unlikely to be open to access by other means".

I will begin with a field study by Rissler and Jacobsen (1987) from the last INTERACT meeting, which cogently illustrates the stereoscopic depth-of-view provided by psychophysiology. Then a further field study will be described, executed by one of the authors, in which physiological indices played a decisive role. Then I describe a preliminary example of the use of physiological recording within the HCI laboratory before concluding with a speculative discussion of the possible influence that psychophysiological thinking might work on the evolution of the field. First though, we will examine Rissler and Jacobsen's elegant psychophysiological field study.

The study in question concerned performance and workload amongst software engineers working to tight deadlines. The authors' prime interest was in the cognitive efficiency of the engineers, and especially the possibility that under the pressure of high workloads and oppressive schedules, the critical faculties of working memory and reasoning power might be subject to serious impairment. Two tests of cognitive prowess (grammatical reasoning, letter substitutiuon) were administered over a four week period at the end of a six month work period. Contrary to expectations, no decline was observed. On the surface then, the cognitive efficiency of the engineers appeared unimpaired. But as well as measures of cognitive performance, Rissler and Jacobsen also measured catecholamine excretion. These physiological indices told a much more interesting story; they revealed that for a significant number of the engineers, keeping up a high level of performance exacted a conspicuous biological cost: "cognitive efficiency [was maintained] at the price of a very substantial increase of effort", reflected by "mobilising a high level of adrenaline". Thus monitoring physiology (effort) as well as behaviour turned what would otherwise have been a highly misleading null result into a rather important insight.

3. Case Study One: The Psychophysiological Field Study

In Rissler and Jacobson's study, the results at the behavioural level were transformed by sweeping in physiological measures. Other Scandanavian field studies have also shown the great value of the psychophysiological perspective, particularly the insights revealed by measuring levels of stress hormones. The distinguished research of Johansson and Aronsson (1984) on computer-based work needs must be mentioned. A further field study involving the present author will now be described in which physiological measures played a significant role in augmenting a purely behavioural evaluation of man-machine interaction.

The background to the study was the modernisation by British Telecomm (BT) of their national network of telephone exhanges in the 1970s. The modernisation programme involved the replacement of the old style of *cord* switchboard (calls connected by the physical insertion of jackplugs; operators sitting facing tall cabinets of sockets and signal lights in generally austere and uncomfortable surroundings) by the *CSS1* switchboard (operators sitting conformatably at ergonomically well-designed consoles in carpeted, quiet surroundings) Despite the superior design of the new system (which was reflected in laboratory testing which showed that less work was required per call), performance and job satisfaction amongst staff suffered deleteriously with the introduction of the new switchboard designs, to the extent that BT had been forced to increase staffing levels in their switchrooms to maintain the same level of service. A psychophysiological field study was put in place to determine why (Brown *et al*, 1982).

The study was conducted at the Bristol telephone exchange where operators routinely used both styles of switchboard. 17 experienced operators were monitored over the course of one days interaction with each system, in their normal milieu. The study was a thorough-going psychophysiological exercise: subjective experience (mood questionnaires), task performance (key press times, call-handling rate) and physiology (EEG, evoked potentials, heart rate) were simultaneously recorded. In particular, physiological measurement was necessitated in order to winkle out whether the anticipated differences in performance were accompanied by differences in effort/stress for the two switchboard designs. As expected, feelings of greater well-being and higher performance levels (workload, keyboard performance, responsitivity to fluctuating call traffic demands) were observed for cord board interaction. Physiological parameters for the cord board showed a consistent pattern of increased activation and mental effort: heart rate was 5% higher, heart-rate variance 7% lower, alpha abundance attenuated by 4%, and EP (N1-P2 amplitude) augmented by 10% for cord board interaction.

Integrating the subjective, behavioural and physiological findings the authors were able to conclude decisively that the superior performance for the cord board interaction was associated with "greater alertness and higher levels of mental effort, without apparent signs of stress". The authors went on to develop an interpretation of the paradoxical impact of the "improved" system design in terms of Job Design theory. The adverse impact of the CSS1 switchboard was attributed to its degrading effect on the operator's work (skill variety, task identity and other job indices were attenuated) resulting in lower *motivating potential* for CSS1 interaction, reflected in lower levels of effort and hence performance. As well as showing the deeper causal insights afforded by the psychophysiological approach, the study also highlights the Taylorism implicit in much human factors engineering and the questionable validity of generalising from laboratory situations to real settings.

4. Psychophysiology in the HCI laboratory: mental workload

It is striking that our two illustrative case studies are both field studies. Other examples might have been described in which physiological recording played a decisive role: eg. Gomer et al's (1987) EMG study of man-machine interaction in postal sorting rooms. The psychophysiological approach has also been applied in laboratory settings. A wide variety of such studies may be found, such as Kuhman's (1989) study of the stressful effects of system-response times; Sundelin and Hagberg's (1989) EMG study of the therapeutic value of different pause types during VDU work; Tanaka *et al*'s (1988) study of catecholamine excretion in simulated VDT work. The issue of mental workload has attracted concerted interest and a small corpus of studies has grown up concerned with the physiological measurement of mental workload during HCI. Much of this work involves cardiac indices, but there is also interest in the use of EEG measures and evoked potentials (Wastell, 1989).

The most systematically explored physiological candidate for assaying mental workload has been heart rate variance (HV), where the work of Mulder and colleagues at Groningen has been pre-eminent (eg Aasman *et al*, 1987). Concern with mental effort is closely associated with the information processing paradigm of cognitive psychology which has been centrally influential in HCI. As well as questions relating to the architecture of the cognitive machine (the articulation of the sensorium into a number of discrete processing mechanisms), there is also deep concern amongst cognitive psychologists regarding the energetics of the machine, and in particular with the limits on human performance imposed by its finite resources. Kahneman's original notion of undifferentiated mental energy has been superceded over recent years by a more sophisticated multiple-resouces theory in which each component in the cognitive mechanism (encoding, central processing etc) is now believed to be powered by its own (limited) supply of mental energy. This material is excellently reviewed by Gopher and Donchin (1986).

Mulder defines mental effort as the amount of *controlled processing* required by a task. In a typical experiment, Aasman et al (1987) demonstrate that HV closely reflects variations in working memory load by varying memory set size in a counting task in which the subject is required to maintain a number of counters for different types of event. Typically, HV (and especially the 0.10 Hz component of the cardiac spectrum) steadily decreases (reflecting increasing mental exertion) until, and this observation is rather compelling, the cognitive demands apparently overwhelm the subject, whereupon HV increases again as the subject gives up. Encouraged by these demonstrations, several investigators have enthusiasticaly looked to HV as a method for measuring mental effort/workload during human-computer interaction.

Of the growing number of studies reported thus far in the HCI literature, the overwhelming majority can fairly be described as preparatory studies. Characteristically, HV is correlated with objective task conditions and subjective experience with a view to 'validating' the physiological index as a workload metric. The study of Itoh *et al* (1989) is typical. The cardiac activity of a group of skilled pilots was studied in a flight simulator.

HV was found to co-vary in the expected manner with the objective difficulty of different flight phases (landing, cruising etc) and with subjective reports of workload (using the tried and tested Cooper-Harper scale). Despite such promise, the potential of physiological metrics in the laboratory study of HCI is as yet largely unfulfilled. The studies conducted by Sauter's group at NIOSH are markworthy for their use of HV but are disappointing in the sense that interpretation of HV does not decisively influence the conclusions drawn. Henning et al (1989) for instance, report a study of microbreak length, performance and stress during a simulated data entry task, but inexplicably fail to appeal to HV when making claims for the presence of compensatory effort as a factor offsetting fatigue.

5. Case Study 2: Physiological measurement of workload during HCI

In this section, I describe some preliminary results from an embryonic programme of experiments aimed at appraising the value of physiological recording by re-addressing some of the classic problems of HCI. One of the studies simply demonstrates the use of heart rate parameters (especially HV) to assess variations in mental load as a function of text editor design, using the comparison of a screen-based editor with a line-based editor in celebration of Card et al's landmark experiments with GOMS and the keystroke-level model. The detailed task-analytic approach characteristic of GOMS continues to represent an important theme in contemporary HCI and finds expression, for instance, in the development of formal methods such as Cognitive Complexity Theory (Kieras and Polson, 1985) which have been advocated for appraising usability (and cognitive demands) without the expense of running experiments (Sutcliffe, 1988)

The results for a pilot experiment involving three subjects are described. Heart rate and HV were measured while subjects carried out various manuscript editing tasks. Marked scripts were drawn up in the manner of Card et al (1980). Each script was approximately 60 lines long and contained around 50 simple corrections involving line positioning and text replacement. The experiment was carried out on an IBM PC using two MS-DOS editors, the public domain PC-WRITE (screen based word processor) and MS-DOS's EDLIN (line-oriented). Subjects were observed under four conditions: a) resting, b) screen editing with instructions to "take your time", c) screen editing under orders to carry out the task with the maximum celerity and with as few errors as possible, d) line editing under the same time and accuracy requirements. Three scripts were used. Subjects edited each script under all three conditions in a latin square design that balanced order effects. Recordings were also made while subjects were typing, also under different regimes of effort.

Let us begin by considering the behavioural data on its own. First it was noted that the average time on task for screen editing was significantly shorter (12 mins) in the *full-speed* condition than in the *relaxed condition* (17 mins). Turning now to the use of the line editor, time on task (26 mins) was manifestly much longer than either screen-based condition. Here now we confront the central dilemma of a purely behavioural analysis: time on task may reflect either presumed differences in the efficiency of the two editors (a keystroke-level analysis predicts unit operations to take roughly twice as long for EDLIN), or perhaps subjects were simply not trying as hard with EDLIN, possibly responding to the tacit expectations of the experimenter that line editors are less effective tools.

Activity	Heart Rate bpm	HR Variance msec
Rest	75	49
PCWRITE full effort	88	28
PCWRITE relaxed	81	36
EDLIN full effort	90	27
Copy typing	81	36
Typing,time pressure	92	24

Table 1: Heart rate and HV shown as a function of type of task activity. HV was measured using the successive difference mean square statistic (Wastell, 1981).

Happily, the physiological data shown in table 1 allow the inherent ambiguity of primary task performance to be resolved. The sensitivity of HV to mental effort is trenchantly revealed in several comparisons. HV is at its zenith in the rest condition. It is over 40% lower in the full-effort PCWRITE condition, where the figure is also conspicuously lower than the corresponding relaxed condition. The comparison of typing under pressure with unpressed performance reveals the same phenomenon. Thus, the fact that the HV value for the EDLIN condition corresponds with the full-speed PCWRITE condition strongly suggests that subjects were indeed applying a comparable effort, and hence that there are genuine differences in the efficiency of the two editors.

The present results powerfully suggest that HV usefully reflects mental effort and that it can be of great value in disambiguating situations where behavioural measures are equivocal. In the interests of due scientific propriety, it must, however, be cautioned that the relationships between cardiac dynamics and human information processing are in general complex and imperfectly understood. Broadly speaking, there is consensus that cardiac deceleration reflects attention to the input of information, that cognitive operations (eg mental arithmetic) are marked by cardiac acceleration and that HV covaries inversely in many circumstances with mental workload (Gale and Christie, 1987), although one should note that Mulder's studies typically involve a well-controlled memory component. Computer-based work, such as text editing, involves a largely undefined and uncontrolled blend of sensory input, internal manipulation and motor activity; some circumspection is therefore due in interpreting results.

These provisos notwithstanding, the promise of HV as a workload metric appears to be confirmed by the present study. As well as quantifying average effort, there exists the more intriguing possibility that dynamic moment-by-moment changes in physiological reactions can help pin-point areas of specific difficulty (eg high cognitive demands) in the real-time use of systems. In the course of informal observations during the text editing experiment, for instance, there was some evidence that lowered HV was associated with periods of smooth productive work (*throwness*, Ehn 1988) and contrasting evidence that when disruptive problems arise (*breakdown*), HV tends to rise. These early studies thus suggest that HV represents a practical method for quantifying mental workload during HCI, for ascertaining effortful task engagement and for complementing verbal and behavioural techniques in diagnosing user problems.

6. Towards a radical psychophysiology of H.C.I.

Despite considerable promise, it is disappointing that psychophysiological methods have had so little influence within cognitive psychology, perhaps because psychophysiology is perceived, indeed often championed, as a reductionist enterprise, aiming to explain cognitive processes in terms of physiological concepts. In many ways, however, it is the potential for *disagreement* (rather than regularities) between the physiological, phenomenological and behavioural domains that gives psychophysiology its unique importance. Under many circumstances (eg danger), a dissociation between behaviour, experience and bodily processes (Gale and Christie, 1987) is observed and in general the relationship between conscious experience and cognitive processes is problematic. Since Jung's early advocacy of GSR recording to explore "the secrets of mental life" (Stern, 1982) there has been a long history of the use of psychophysiological techniques in psychology to complement behavioural and experiential data: lie detection is perhaps the most celebrated example but there are also applications in areas such as personality assessment (eg Nelson and Epstein, 1962) where physiological techniques give priviledged access to areas of unconscious anxiety and conflict which are putatively obscured by the ego's defense mechanisms.

The psychophysiological approach thus provides, as it were, a method of triangulation that brings depth to our description and understanding of psychological phenomena. The present paper may be seen as an initial response to Gale and Christie's rallying call for a psychophysiological approach to research into the *electronic workplace*. The paper is a credo reflecting my conviction that psychophysiology has an immensely valuable role to play in deepening our understanding of HCI, especially in real-world settings, and helping us to design better systems. I have identified one area where physiological recording is especially helpful, namely the real-time unobstrusive monitoring of mental effort, which should augment our understanding of the energetics of information processing during HCI. Currently we know how effectively a device is used (output); psychophysiology makes available the biological cost (the resources mobilised) underlying a given level of performance, allowing efficiency (i.e. output/input) to be properly determined. Both controlled laboratory studies and field research must be carried out in an integrated programme of psychophysiological research. The need for ecological validity of laboratory studies is critical and calls for the careful construction of simulated environments; Gale and Christie's (1987) description of the "Cafe of Eve" is inspirational.

We have hinted that the psychophysiological perspective should have a strong normative flavour, that it should help us design better systems. An important aspect of psychophysiological thinking is that it naturally opens up a stress and health perspective on the interrelationship between people, work and technology. Pollock (1988) has commented on the ideological colouring of the stress concept, and it is indubitably true that much of stress research has a strong normative impetus: that work systems *should* be designed with worker health and well-being as design goals of equal importance with technical efficiency. (In this respect psychophysiological thinking is in close sympathy with the philosophy of sociotechnical systems design, Wastell (1988)). One area of HCI in which such a *radical psychophysiology* could exert a decisive and benign influence is the recently fashionable area of Computer Support for Cooperative Work (CSCW). We may see how the infiltration of a psychophysiological concept of stress could contribute to the design of CSCW systems by considering the Scandanavian field studies of stress and its modulation by personal and collective control.

The classic sawmill studies of Johansson et al (1978) demonstrate that "more autonomous work" is associated with better health. Such studies provide powerful arguments for developing forms of work organisation that emphasise group autonomy. In designing systems for CSCW, we confront head-on the question of work organisation, i.e. the division of labour and the social structures of co-operation and managerial control. Technology in itself does not determine how work should be organised; technology makes available many options and the designer has the responsibility of choice. The influence of a radical psychophysiological attitude would, I propose, orient the designer to champion personal and group autonomy as design ethics, predispose the CSCW design process in favour of technological options that support such concepts, emphasise the importance of well-being and health as design goals, help in the proselytizing of sociotechnical design ideals, and stimulate the selective use of physiological recording in design and evaluation to operationalise the essentially psychophysiological concepts of stress and well-being.

7. References

Aasman, J. Mulder, G. and Mulder, L. (1987). Operator effort and the measurement of heart rate variability. *Human Factors*, 29, 131-144.

Bewley, W.L., Roberts, T.L. *et al.* (1983). Human factors testing in the design of the Xerox Star workstation. In *Proceedings of CHI 83* 72-77.

Bewley, W.L. and Buxton, W. (1983) *Readings in HCI: a multidisciplinary approach.* Kaufman: Los Altos.

Briner, R. and Hockey, G. (1988). Operator Stress and Computer-Based work. In *Causes, Coping and Consequences of Stress at Work* (Eds. Cooper and Payne). Wiley: New York.

Brooke, J.B. (1986). Usability engineering in office product development. In *People and computers: designing for usability* (Eds. Harrison and Monk). British Informatics Society: London.

Brown, I.D., Wastell, D.G. and Copeman, A. (1982). A psychophysiological investigation of system efficiency in public telephone switchrooms. *Ergonomics*, 25, 1013-1040.

Card, S.K., Moran, T.P. and Newell, A. (1980). Computer text editing: an information processing analysis of a routine cognitive skill. *Cognitive Psychology*, 12, 32-74.

Claxton, G. (1980) *Cognitive psychology: new directions.* RKP: London.

Ehn, P., (1988) *Work-oriented design of computer artifacts* Arbetlivcentrum: Stockholm.

Gale A. and Christie B. (1987). *Psychophysiology and the Electronic workplace.* Wiley: New York.

Gomer, F.E., Silverstein, L.D. *et al.* (1987). Changes in EMG activity associated with occupational stress in the workplace. *Human Factors*, 29, 131-143.

Gopher, D. and Donchin, E. (1986). Workload- an assessment of the concept. In *Handbook of perception and human performance, vol 2* (Eds. Boff, Kaufman and Thomas). Wiley: New York.

Henning, R., Sauter, S *et al* (1989). Microbreak length, performance and stress in a data entry task. *Ergonomics*, 32, 855-864.

Itoh Y., Hayashi Y., Tskui H. and Saito S. (1989). Heart rate variability and subjective mental workload in flight tasks. In *Work with Computers: organisational, management and stress and health aspects* (Eds. Smith and Salvendy). Elsevier: Amsterdam.

Johansson, G. and Aronsson, G. (1984). Stress reactions in computerised administrative work. *J. Occup. Beh*, 5, 159-181.

Johansson, G, Aronsson, G. and Lindstrom, B.O. (1978).Social psychological and neuroendocrine stress reactions in highly mechanised work. *Ergonomics*, 21, 583-599.

Kieras, D. and Polson, P.G. (1985). An approach to the formal analysis of user complexity. *Int. J. Man-Machine Studies*, 22, 366-394.

Kuhmann, W. (1989). Experimental investigation of stress-inducing properties of system response times. *Ergonomics*, 32, 271-280.

Monk, A. (1986). *Fundamentals of H.C.I.*. Academic Press: London.

Nelson, J. and Epstein, S. (1962). Relationships between three measures of conflict over hostility. *J. Consult. Psychol.*, 26, 345-350.

Orne, MT (1962). On the social psychology of the psychological experiment with particular reference to the demand characteristics *American Psychologist*, 17, 776-783.

Pollock, K. (1988). On the nature of stress: production of a modern mythology. *Soc. Sci. Med.*, 26, 381-392.

Rissler A. and Jacobsson L. (1987). Cognitive efficiency during high workload in final system testing of a large computer system. In *INTERACT87* (Eds. Bullinger and Shackel). Elsevier: Amsterdam.

Roberts, T.L. and Moran, T.P. (1980). The evaluation of text editors: methodology and empirical results. *Comm. ACM*, 26, 265-285.

Rosenthal, R. (1966). Experimenter effects in behavioural research. Appleton: New York.

Stern R. M. (1982). *Psychophysiological recording.* Oxford University Press: Oxford.

Sundelin, G and Hagberg, M. (1989). The effects of different pause types on neck and shoulder EMG activity during VDU work. *Ergonomics*, 32, 527-537.

Sutcliffe, A. (1988). Some experiences of integrating specification of HCI within a structured development method. In *People and Computers* (Eds. Jones and Windsor). Br. Informatics Soc.: London.

Tanaka, T, Fukumoto, T *et al* (1988). The effects of VDT work on excretion of catecholamines. *Ergonomics*, 31, 1753-1763.

Wastell, D.G. (1981). Measuring heart rate variability: comments on the successive difference mean square statistic. *Psychophysiology*, 18, 88-90.

Wastell, D.G. (1988). Phenomenology and participation: alternative principles for information systems development. *Lecture Notes in Medical Informatics* 717-721.

Wastell, D.G. (1989). Psychophysiology and system usability: the evoked potential as a metric of cognitive complexity. In *Proceedings of HCI 89, Boston (poster supplement)*, 1989.

SECTION I: FOUNDATIONS

SI.3 User Modelling

A knowledge analysis of interactivity
R.M. Young, A. Howes, and J. Whittington 115

User's command line reference behaviour: Locality versus recency
A. Lee and F.H. Lochovsky 121

An investigation into quantitative user modelling of user interactions for the purpose of predicting user expertise
R. Spall and R. Steele 129

Constraints in design: Towards a methodology of psychological analysis based on AI formalisms
F. Darses 135

Human–Computer Interaction – INTERACT '90
D. Diaper et al. (Editors)
Elsevier Science Publishers B.V. (North-Holland)

A KNOWLEDGE ANALYSIS OF INTERACTIVITY

Richard M. YOUNG, Andrew HOWES and Joyce WHITTINGTON

MRC Applied Psychology Unit, 15 Chaucer Road,
Cambridge CB2 2EF, U.K.

Most existing techniques for predicting users' behaviour do not cope well with highly interactive computer usage, such as is typically found with workstations or personal computers. This paper explores the interactivity inherent in a simple task on an Apple Macintosh computer. An analysis of the knowledge required for performing the task provides the basis for understanding how internal knowledge and information present in the display are combined to guide the behaviour of users spanning the spectrum of expertise from novice to expert .

1. INTRODUCTION: MODELLING INTERACTIVITY

Within the field of Human-Computer Interaction, several kinds of models now exist for predicting aspects of users' behaviour, and have been developed to the point where they can be applied by HCI researchers, even if not yet routinely by the interface designers who are their intended clientele. (For surveys of the current state of user modelling in HCI, see e.g. Olson & Olson, 1990; Butler, Bennett, Polson & Karat, 1989.)

However, although these models deal with users' behaviour with interactive computer systems (typically based on VDUs, personal computers, or workstations), they are all relatively poor at reflecting the interactivity of such behaviour. In this context, we use the term *interactivity* to refer to the way in which information available in the external situation — in this case on a computer display — combines with the user's internal knowledge in order to determine behaviour. In the well-known GOMS family of models, for example (GOMS itself, the Model Human Processor, and the Keystroke Level Model: Card, Moran & Newell, 1983; and the closely associated Cognitive Complexity Theory of Kieras & Polson, 1985), although of course the models include actions of reading from an external display (e.g. GOMS: **get-next-task**; CCT: **screen**), the role of such actions is merely to retrieve specific items of information. The use to which this information will be put has been decided beforehand. Thus it plays a severely restricted part in guiding behaviour.

This neglect of the role of interactivity within HCI mirrors the neglect within Cognitive Science generally of the importance of the external situation in guiding behaviour (Suchman, 1987). Only in the last few years has attention turned to this point within mainstream cognitive psychology. Larkin (1988), for example, lists six characteristics of what she terms "display-based problem solving", including the ideas that the task behaviour is largely error free, that the component steps can be taken in a variety of orders, and that fluent task performance requires learning.

An experiment by Mayes, Draper, McGregor & Oatley (1988) provides a starting point for our examination of interactivity. The experiment demonstrates that even highly experienced users of the Apple Macintosh cannot necessarily recall the names for the headers of the menus used to perform a routine task. One possible explanation is that when such users invoke a particular pull-down menu, they choose that menu on some basis other than by knowing the name of its header. Howes & Payne (1990) show how such behaviour by expert users might be modelled. According to their analysis (the spirit of which is followed in the present paper), expert users have a *semantic* specification, but possibly not a *lexical* specification, of the menu to be used. In other words, they know something precise about the meaning of the menu header, but not necessarily the actual word. They can therefore invoke a simple procedure to scan the headers presented on the screen and find the one which best fits the semantic specification. This account illustrates in a simple way how information from the screen can combine with knowledge held by the user in order to guide behaviour. But it can explain only limited aspects of interactivity, since the model applies only to the behaviour of *expert* users.

Our own approach to the predictive modelling of user behaviour, which makes use of "Programmable User Models" (PUMs: Young, Green & Simon, 1989), has a more flexible control structure than the GOMS models, and can therefore predict the user's sequence of actions rather than requiring it to be pre-specified (Young & Whittington, 1990). In the present paper we explore how to extend the PUMs technique to deal with behaviour exhibiting higher interactivity than we have been able to model so far. We do this by considering in some detail the cases of three hypothetical users of different degrees of expertise, all attempting to carry out a simple task on the Macintosh similar to that examined by Mayes *et al.* That task is treated as the basis for a scenario (Young & Barnard, 1987) for driving the theoretical technique, which here takes the form of an analysis of the knowledge needed by the different users to carry out the task.

2. THE TASK AND THE USERS

The task we choose to analyse is that of arranging for a text file to have its contents manipulated by a text-editing program, which we assume to be already running. We suppose that users wish to update the draft of a party invitation which they had prepared previously, to finalise it for printing and circulation. For concreteness, we will use the MacWrite editor as our illustration, although the procedure is closely similar for most programs on the Macintosh. In Macintosh jargon, this task is described as "opening a document within a running application", from which it can be seen that the terms *open, document,* and *application* have a specialised meaning in the Macintosh domain, not exactly coincident with their meanings in general computing parlance. These specialised meanings, of course, may or may not be known to a particular user.

In order to perform the task, the user needs to carry out four mouse-and-button actions in succession. On the actual Macintosh these four actions are all subtly, physically different: one is a 'press', one is a 'drag-release', one is an 'item selection', and one is a 'button click'. For present purposes we will ignore these fine distinctions, since they carry no extra communicative information, and simply refer to all four actions as *clicks*. Initially, the user is faced with an almost blank screen, showing just a horizontal bar at the top of the screen bearing the names of seven menu headers:

 File **Edit** Search Format Font Style

(where the headers shown here in outline are displayed on the screen as being "greyed out"). The user clicks on **File**, and the Macintosh displays a vertical pull-down menu, containing entries such as

New **Open** Close Save ... Print **Quit**.

The user clicks on **Open**, and the Macintosh replaces the menu by a dialogue box, which in its left half has a scrollable vertical menu of file names. The user searches through this list, scrolling it if necessary, looking for the name which plausibly indicates that it holds the desired party invitation, and clicks it once it is found. The Macintosh puts the selected item into inverse video, but otherwise leaves the display unchanged. In the right half of the dialogue box are four buttons, labelled **Eject**, **Drive**, **Open**, and **Cancel**. The user clicks on **Open**, waits while the disc drive clunks and whirrs, and then a few seconds later the party invitation appears on the screen.

We note in passing that, from an informal standpoint, this dialogue seems to be fairly well designed and conceptually straightforward for the user, since the required actions correspond clearly to different aspect of the information needed to specify the task: that it is an operation concerning a *file*, that the file should be *opened*, and which *particular* file is intended. Equally, though, the fourth and final action presents something of a hiccup since it appears to require the user to repeat some information already communicated earlier in the dialogue, and we would not be surprised to find users who baulk at the idea of having to specify **Open** twice.

To pursue our analysis of interactivity in this task, it will be sufficient to focus discussion on just the first action to be taken, the click on the **File** header. Our three hypothetical users are considered to possess differing amounts of expertise:

- The *expert* has plenty of experience with using the Macintosh, and is familiar with the details of how to get tasks accomplished with it. This user is able to perform the steps of the task fluently and rapidly.

- The *intermediate* might be an occasional user who also has plenty of experience with the Macintosh, but with long intervening periods of disuse during which details are forgotten. This user makes the same choices as the expert, but more slowly, and has to consider the alternative header items rather than going straight to the right one.

- The *novice* is assumed to have used the Macintosh before, but not this particular text-editor. The novice is again slower than the intermediate and has to ponder each header item. This user often has to make repeated passes through the set of headers, sometimes has difficulty in deciding between two or more candidates, and picks the wrong one more often than the intermediate or expert.

It is characteristic of the Macintosh, and a significant feature of the scenario, that users at three widely separated points on the spectrum of expertise all produce the same sequence of actions, even though they have to undertake varying amounts of problem-solving and decision-making.

3. KNOWLEDGE ANALYSIS

3.1 Classes of Knowledge

Our modelling of interactivity in this task centres on a *knowledge analysis*, i.e. a classification of the kinds and contents of what the different users know about the Macintosh and the task. We distinguish several different classes of knowledge that users may or may not have:

- *Screen interpretation and affordances:* knowledge about how to parse the visual layout of the display into separate items, and about what actions are possible on them. For example, Macintosh users need to be able to recognise the bar of menu headers, and to know that clicking on any of its items invokes the corresponding pull-down menu. Similarly, users may or may not be able to parse the dialogue box into its constituent parts, and to recognise the buttons and know what can be done with them.

- *Conceptual model:* a simple story about how the Macintosh (and other similar computers) work, able to support reasoning and explanation (Young, 1983). This might take the form of a description of the computer as consisting of notional objects at notional locations, with many operations interpreted as the movement or copying of an object from one location to another (*cf.* Mayer, 1979). For example, opening a document inside a running editor might be conceptualised as moving the document from "permanent storage" on the disc into the "active data storage" area of the computer's memory.

- *Specialised Macintosh meanings:* knowledge of the meanings of the specialised jargon words used in menus and headers. For example, the word *Open* has a rather generalised meaning of making available to the user, on the display, the contents of some object which previously were hidden. An expert Macintosh user might know that the word *Edit* has a specific, but widely applicable, meaning centered on the notions of copying and deleting objects, and does *not* have the sense common in computing of applying an editing program to a file of data.

- *Everyday semantics:* Users' knowledge of the ordinary meaning of common words can be relevant to the analysis. Thus both task-related terms, such as *invitation*, and Macintosh-related terms such as *file*, *open*, and *edit*, have everyday senses which are known to users and may be involved in thinking about the task.

- *Specific item* knowledge: what actual word is used in a particular context. For example, an expert might know that the appropriate target item for the first action in the task is the word *File*.

- *Locational* knowledge concerns the position on the display of relevant items. For example, an expert might know that the header to be chosen for the first action of the task is located near the extreme left of the header bar.

- *Decomposition:* knowledge of how to break a given task apart into several subtasks which can be performed separately. For example, it is common on the Macintosh to perform tasks in two steps, first to select a relevant object and second to invoke an appropriate action on it. Applied to our present task, this knowledge suggests that it be done in two steps, first selecting the desired file and then specifying that it be opened. This suggestion is not totally correct — as we have seen, the task actually requires the specification of three aspects, and takes four actions — but can still be helpful. The expert may know the full four-step decomposition of this specific task. In any case, decomposition knowledge may or may not include partial or complete information about the ordering of the subtasks.

- *Translation:* knowledge of how to take a specification or meaning expressed in one domain, and formulate its equivalent in another. For example, an experienced computer user knows how to translate a problem given in terms of *kinds of documents* (e.g. reports, invitations, memoranda, etc.) into the language of *computer file systems* (e.g. files, directories, etc.). In the case of the Macintosh, the famous "desktop metaphor" is intended to minimise the amount of such translation knowledge needed in order to accomplish tasks. Hence the use of the non-standard term *documents* to designate what would usually be referred to as "data files".

3.2 Knowledge Configurations for the Three Users

Our analysis of interactivity assumes the existence of a single mechanism common to all users. It consists of laying out what knowledge in the various categories the users have, and then showing how that knowledge, in interaction with information from the display, leads them to exhibit their individual behaviours. Although we discuss explicitly just three users located at particular points on the spectrum of expertise, the analysis is clearly intended to extend to other cases too. Other patterns of knowledge would correspond to users lying at other points along the continuum from novice to expert.

We now consider the three hypothetical users one by one, and show how assumptions about the knowledge plausibly held by each of the them yield an account of their characteristically different performances on the task.

3.2.1 *Expert*

The expert knows the four actions required, and the order they need to be done in. In line with the results of Mayes *et al* (1988), we assume that the expert is not aware of the actual target words (**File, Open**). On the other hand, since the expert knows the actions and their order, at each step he or she can be assumed to have a precise semantic specification of the next action. So for this user, the task involves four repetitions of the procedure described by Howes & Payne (1990) of scanning the current options to find the one that satisfies the current specification, and then clicking it.

So the expert begins with a specification of the task expressed in domain-oriented terms, along the lines of *"Get the draft of the party invitation ready for updating"*. The expert then applies translation knowledge to map this specification into an equivalent one expressed in terms related to the conceptual model of the Macintosh, something like *"Bring the file holding the party invitation into the working area of the text editor"*. Decomposition knowledge then breaks this specification of the overall task into four sub-tasks. The expert may well know that the first sub-task involves telling the Macintosh that the kind of object to be operated on is a file (where of course 'file' is to be understood in this analysis as a conceptual term, not a reference to the word *file*). At this stage the user has a tight semantic specification for the first target item to be clicked, and so scans the menu header for a term that fits the specification, choosing as the only plausible candidate the word **File**. The rest of the task behaviour proceeds in a similar manner.

Individual experts might additionally have specific item knowledge telling them explicitly that **File** is the word to use. This would allow them to employ a faster kind of scan, one looking for a particular target word rather than one for a word meeting a given semantic specification (Neisser, 1964). Similarly, expert users might have locational knowledge informing them of the approximate position of the target within the header bar. This too would enable them to find the target item more quickly, by biassing or restricting the scan to the appropriate region.

3.2.2 *Intermediate*

There are many plausible *intermediate* users. The one we will follow through is someone who has most of the knowledge the expert does, but is not aware of the order of the steps. Before looking at the screen, then, this intermediate user knows that various aspects of the task need to be specified (i.e. that the operation is on a *file*, and which *particular* file, and that it is to be *opened*) but does not know which of them will be relevant for the first action.

This intermediate user therefore, unlike the expert, is unable to form a unique semantic description of the target action and simply scan for it. Instead the user has a number of possible semantic descriptions. This slows down the scanning of the header bar, with each candidate header having to be considered against each of the descriptions. Alternatively, the user might guess at which semantic description will be needed first, but on average this will also slow down the processing since it increases the risk of being distracted by spurious partial matches and of requiring multiple scans. In any case, once the match between semantic description and target item is found, this tells the user not only which header to choose but also which sub-task is being performed — another aspect of interactivity.

3.2.3 *Novice*

The *novice* is assumed to be familiar with the basic mechanics of using the Macintosh, such as how to use the mouse and how to invoke and select from pull-down menus, but knows little about how to carry out our particular task. In particular, the novice does not know how to translate the requirements of the task as originally formulated into the specialised language of the Macintosh, nor how to decompose the task into a number of separate aspects. The novice may also not know the specialised meaning of some of the header terms. Thus the novice user has to proceed by seeking inspiration, as it were, from the information present on the display. The user will have to ponder the candidate items in turn, and ask of each "Given what I know about the task, can I see any plausible connection with this word, strong enough to make me want to consider selecting it?"

So the novice begins the task by reading the words in the header bar. Knowledge of screen interpretation informs the user that these *are* headers and can be used to invoke actions by pull-down menus. The user has to attempt to assess each header word by a process of internal problem solving and semantic search. With the header **File**, for example, the novice might have enough computing knowledge to connect it to the general sense of *document* which is relevant to the task. If not, depending on the idiosyncratic everyday connotations the user has for the word, he or she might still make the connection. (And if not, the novice is likely to fail on this first choice of menu header.) Without the specialised Macintosh knowledge, the item **Edit** is likely to seem plausible, since both the everyday meaning and the general computer meaning suggest that indeed the user wants to *edit* the party invitation. Similarly, the greyed-out items **Format** and **Style** may appear to be plausible candidates, since they characterise the kinds of changes that need to be made to the invitation.

Thus the novice user faces more uncertainty of choice than the intermediate or expert, and has to expend more effort in assessing each candidate header. The result is that novices take longer to find their target item, and make more mistakes on the way.

3.3 Simulating the Model

We are in the process of building a simulation of our model in SOAR, a problem-solving architecture built round a nested series of problem spaces (Laird, Newell & Rosenbloom, 1987) and offered by Newell as a candidate "Unified Theory of Cognition" (Newell, 1990; Waldrop, 1988). In the SOAR model, most of the classes of knowledge described earlier are realised as specialised knowledge sources residing within their own problem spaces. SOAR has been used in a similar way as a vehicle for previous PUMs work (e.g. Young & Whittington, 1990), in part because it "can be regarded as an engine for applying knowledge to situations to yield behaviour" (Young, Green & Simon, 1989). SOAR is particularly appropriate for supporting the present kind of knowledge analysis, because the architecture provides a mechanism which automatically tries to compensate for any lack of immediately applicable knowledge by initiating a subgoal to search for a way to derive the needed knowledge from what is available in the different problem spaces. Such searches can be expensive in time and effort, offering an explanation for the differences in speed, fluency and accuracy between novice, intermediate, and expert. SOAR also offers a framework for integrating different kinds of knowledge in order to guide behaviour (Steier, 1989).

One of the primary mechanisms in SOAR is to set up a subgoal whenever it is unable to proceed with its current goal without further problem-solving, i.e. whenever it encounters an *impasse*. In the model of the expert, almost all the knowledge is represented in a form in which SOAR can apply it to the task without running into impasses and invoking subgoals. Thus the task is performed without problem-solving and without internal search. For the intermediate user, the model lacks knowledge about which sub-task is to be done first, and SOAR therefore sets up a subgoal which is resolved only when that decision is made. The model of the novice has none of the immediately applicable knowledge, and so SOAR sets up subgoals to access whatever knowledge is available (such as everyday semantics) in order to help resolve the problem.

In this way, SOAR provides a single set of mechanisms to model the behaviour of the expert, the intermediate, and the novice, by making use of whatever knowledge it is given and indulging in problem-solving as needed to bridge the gaps. The interactivity emerges because in doing so, it combines internal knowledge with information from the display.

4. DISCUSSION

This paper has put forward an account of a certain aspect of interactivity that arises in the use of the Apple Macintosh. The account is based on an analysis of the different kinds of knowledge that users may or may not possess about the Macintosh and the task. The central theme of the story is that there exists a kind of trade-off between, on the one hand, specific knowledge about the procedure to be followed to achieve a given task, and on the other , what can be inferred about the necessary steps from information present on the display. In this way, instead of viewing interactive behaviour as the unfolding of a sequence of actions determined by prior procedural knowledge or internal problem solving, we see it as being guided by an interplay between internal knowledge on the one hand, and information provided by the external device on the other.

A simple and clear illustration of this situationally determined behaviour emerges from the case of the intermediate user. We saw that the match between an item on the display and the specification of a particular action informs the user not only which menu header to click on, but also which of the several aspects of the task known to be relevant is the one to be specified first. This same example indicates that our analysis goes beyond the scope of models such as the GOMS family. Such models are unable to handle this degree of flexible ordering because they require the procedure followed by the user to be specified beforehand — a point emphasised by Young & Whittington (1990).

The analysis has also provided some incidental insights into the strengths and weaknesses of this corner of the Macintosh design. The main result of course is a confirmation of the quality of the interactivity for which the machine is famous. We have examined in detail the means by which it is possible for the single design both to allow experts who know exactly what to do to perform the task as a sequence of four pre-specified actions, and also to provide novices, who know little about the Macintosh or how to perform this task on it, with enough information to let them figure it out. Secondly, we have uncovered some ways in which certain aspects of the design provide a kind of robustness against minor ambiguities in the user's knowledge. Thus the menu header **File** can be chosen both (a) by users who are following the general Macintosh principle of specifying objects before the operations on them and therefore think that they are about to specify the actual file, and who interpret the header as meaning something like *File-identification*; as well as (b) by users who believe they are about to specify the operation first, for whom it should be glossed as something more like *File-related operations*. This means that users will correctly click on **File** as their first action, whether they believe the first step is to specify the file itself (wrong) or the operation (right).

The analysis of interactivity we have presented in this paper is a prerequisite for the construction of a computational model implemented in the SOAR architecture. One of the lessons to be drawn from the recent interest in "situated action" (e.g. Suchman, 1987) is a reminder that anyone engaged in interactive problem solving or behaviour has two kinds of resources available to them: those arising from their own internal knowledge and those arising from the external situation. The account offered here can be regarded as a rough sketch of a cognitive, information processing account of how those two kinds of resources interact in order to guide behaviour.

Acknowledgements. This work was supported in part by a grant from the UK Joint Research Councils Initiative in Cognitive Science and HCI, and in part by AMODEUS, European ESPRIT Basic Research Action 3066.

REFERENCES

Butler, K., Bennett, J., Polson, P. & Karat, J. (1989) Report on the workshop on analytical models: Predicting the complexity of human-computer interaction. *SIGCHI Bulletin, 20 (4)*, 63-79.

Card, S. K., Moran, T. P. & Newell, A. (1983) *The Psychology of Human Computer Interaction*. Hillsdale, NJ: Erlbaum.

Howes A. & Payne, S.J. (1990) Display-based competence: Towards user models for menu-driven interfaces. *International Journal of Man-machine Studies* (in press).

Kieras, D.E. & Polson, P.G. (1985) An approach to the formal analysis of user complexity. *International Journal of Man-machine Studies*, 22, 365-394.

Laird, J. E., Newell, A. & Rosenbloom, P. S. (1987) SOAR: An architecture for general intelligence. *Artificial Intelligence, 33*, 1-64.

Larkin, J.H. (1988) Display-based problem solving. In D. Klahr & K. Kotovsky (Eds) *Complex Information Processing: The Impact of Herbert A. Simon..* Hillsdale, NJ: Erlbaum.

Mayer, R. E. (1979) A psychology of learning BASIC. *Communications of the ACM* , 22, 589-593.

Mayes, J.T., Draper, S.W., McGregor, M.A. & Oatley, K. (1988) Information flow in a user interface: the effect of experience and context on the recall of MacWrite screens. In D.M. Jones & R.Winder (Eds) *People and Computers IV*. Cambridge University Press.

Neisser, U. (1964) Visual search. *Scientific American, 210*, 94-102.

Newell, A. (1990) *Unified Theories of Cognition: The 1987 William James Lectures*. Harvard University Press (in press).

Olson, J. R. & Olson, G. M. (1990) The growth of cognitive modelling in human-computer interaction since GOMS. *Human Computer Interaction* (in press).

Steier, D. (1989) *Automating Algorithm Design within a General Architecure for Intelligence*. PhD thesis, Computer Science Department, Carnegie-Mellon University. Report CMU-CS-89-128.

Suchman, L. (1987) *Plans and Situation Actions: The Problem of Human Machine Communication*. Cambridge University Press.

Waldrop, M. M. (1988) Toward a unified theory of cognition. *Science, 241*, 27-29; Soar: A unified theory of cognition? *Science, 241*, 296-298.

Young, R. M. (1983) Surrogates and mappings: Two kinds of conceptual models for interactive devices. In D. Gentner & A. Stevens (Eds) *Mental Models*, 35-52. Hillsdale, NJ: Erlbaum.

Young, R. M. & Barnard, P. J. (1987) The use of scenarios in human-computer interaction research: Turbocharging the tortoise of cumulative science. In J. M. Carroll & P. P. Tanner (Eds) *CHI + GI Conference Proceedings: Human Factors in Computing Systems and Graphics Interface*, 291-296. New York: ACM.

Young, R.M., Green, T. R. G. & Simon, T. (1989) Programmable user models for predictive evaluation of interface designs. In K. Bice & C. Lewis (Eds) *Proceedings CHI'89 Human Factors in Computing Systems*, 15-19. New York: ACM Press.

Young, R. M. & Whittington, J. E. (1990) Using a knowledge analysis to predict conceptual errors in text-editor usage. In *Proceedings CHI'90 Human Factors in Computing Systems*. New York: ACM Press.

Human–Computer Interaction – INTERACT '90
D. Diaper et al. (Editors)
Elsevier Science Publishers B.V. (North-Holland)

USER'S COMMAND LINE REFERENCE BEHAVIOUR:† LOCALITY VERSUS RECENCY

Alison Lee and Frederick H. Lochovsky

Department of Computer Science
University of Toronto
Toronto, Ontario CANADA

The techniques of *working set* calculation and *locality set* determination from computer memory management research are applicable to HCI research. Working sets can be used to analyze the *recency* characteristic (favouring recent interactions) and locality sets can be used to analyze the *locality* characteristic (clustering of interactions) in user behaviour. We present two computer simulation studies and their results. The first study found that locality exists in users' command line references. The second study found evidence to suggest that the locality characteristic is better at predicting candidates for recurrence than the recency characteristic. Both of these results have positive implications for the design of tools that allow users to reuse their past interactions.

1. WORKING SET & LOCALITY SET

In the course of a computer program's execution, it makes references to portions of the computer's memory in units known as *segments* or *pages*. This sequence of memory reference is known as the *memory reference string*. It is neither feasible to allocate all of the computer's memory to a program nor efficient to overcommit at the penalty of other simultaneously executing programs. The strategy is to assign memory to those portions of a program's memory space that will be needed immediately. This strategy is possible because of the fact that memory references repeat. Denning 1980 and others have found that a candidate set of segments can be determined by sampling the past references and characterizing their behaviour.

A *working set* is the collection of unique segments that are referenced within the last *T* references (commonly referred to as the window of the working set) [Denning 1980]. In the example in Figure 1, the working set consists of 6 segments { A, C, D, E, G, H } for T=10. Studies of program reference behaviour have found that at certain extended reference intervals (called *phases*) a program's references are limited to a subset of its segments (called a *locality set*). In Figure 2, a number of locality sets of various sizes and composition for the same reference string used in Figure 1 are shown.

† This research was supported by the Natural Sciences and Engineering Research Council of Canada under grant OGP0003356.

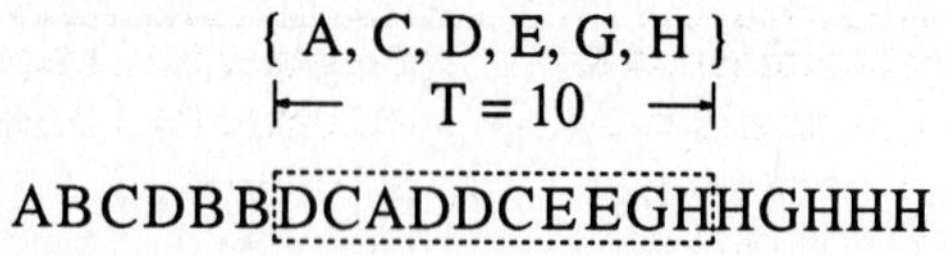

Figure 1: Working set of size 6 (T = 10)

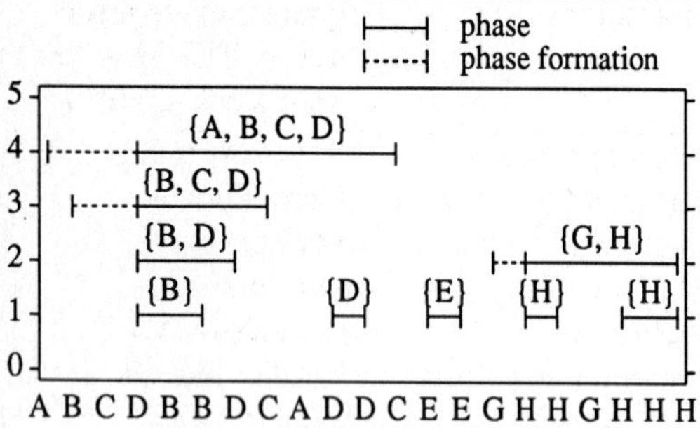

Figure 2: Locality Sets of Various Sizes

A *locality set* is not a *working set* or vice versa (compare Figures 1 with 2). The latter is an intrinsic measure of a program's memory demands while the former characterizes a program's reference behaviour in a way that permits the detection of boundaries between phases. The working set metric is ineffective for identifying locality of reference or boundaries between shifts in the locality sets. Locality sets can be an approximate measure of a program's memory demands (within phases) which is not dependent on an arbitrary parameter as in the case of the working set [Henderson and Card 1986, Denning 1980].

However, the working set is an indirect indicator of when references are being made to segments that are not part of the current working set by the *inter-reference distribution*. This distribution represents the number of times segments are referenced as function of the interval between two consecutive references (i.e., inter-reference interval, the *T* in working sets) to the same segment. The nature of the distribution may suggest interesting behavioural characteristics. For instance, when the distribution is skewed towards low inter-reference intervals, it illustrates a strong *recency* characteristic (i.e., preference for near adjacent segments) and possibly *locality* (i.e., clustering of segments into groups).

1.1. Application to HCI

Both recency and locality arise because of recurrence in the reference string. Recurrence is a critical property in user's interaction behaviour [Card et al. 1984]. As such, there has been previous HCI efforts to employ these concepts in a) the analysis of a user's interaction behaviour and b) the design of user interfaces involving the use of a scarce resource. Card et al. 1984 and Henderson and Card 1986 used the working set and locality set notions to analyze the effects that limited screen space has on the use of windows in a multiple window environment. They found evidence to suggest that users exhibit recency and locality of window references. These patterns can be attributable to activity switching behaviour [Bannon et al. 1983, Cypher 1986, Henderson and Card 1986].

The working set notion was used in an analysis of the relationships and dependencies of the command line sequences of UNIX™ C Shell users [Greenberg and Witten 1988a, Greenberg 1988a]. They found that, on average, 74% of the command lines issued were recurrences. Furthermore, the inter-reference distribution was skewed towards the lower distances (i.e., recency of recurrences). The previous 7 or so inputs contribute to the majority of the recurrences with the second last dominating the distribution. These findings were corroborated by a similar analysis of session traces of a functional programming language [Greenberg 1988a].

1.2. Limitations of the Two Studies

Like Greenberg, we are interested in the design of the *interaction history tool*. An *interaction history* tool permits the user to have access to past interactions kept in a history and to incorporate them into the context of the current situation. Analogous to the computer memory management problem, we have the problem of

are most relevant to the user currently [Lee in preparation]. However, the findings of the two studies cited above have two limitations with respect to the analysis of a user's command line reference behaviour and the design of an interaction history tool for reuse.

First, Greenberg's study found recurrences of individual command lines, but is inconclusive about whether locality set sizes larger than 1 are possible. While there is evidence to suggest locality in window references, this does not imply locality in command line references. Window reference behaviour is at a grosser and conceptually higher level than command line reference behaviour. Our own informal examination of session traces in 3 different UNIX™ command interpreters have found that users repeated and/or cycled over groups of command lines (see Table 1) [Lee and Lochovsky 1990a]. That is, larger locality set sizes are apparent.

Second, one of Greenberg and Witten's design guidelines, based on the observed recency behaviour, says "*simple reselection of the previous five to ten submissions provides a reasonable working set of possibilities*" (i.e., window size) [Greenberg and Witten 1988a, Greenberg 1988a]. However, their analysis shows that a significant number of recurrences are not covered by these window sizes. Only 45% of the maximum 74% recurrences are covered by a window size of 10. Doubling this window size would increase the 45% to 55%. Further improvements can be obtained by suitable conditioning techniques like context sensitivity, pruning duplicates, and partial matches. However, we speculate that before applying these conditioning techniques, the coverage can be improved by exploiting the locality behaviour, if it indeed exists. In Greenberg's study, the assumption has been made that each point in the user's session is likely to exhibit recurrence and this is incorrect as only about 74% of the command lines are recurrences. We speculate that recurrences would be likely only in situations when the user is within a phase (i.e., in a locality set) or a phase formation period and not so outside of phases (i.e., in a *transition*).

Repetitions	Example
repeat commands & parameters literally	spell paper.tex | page spell paper.tex | page
repeat commands diff. parameters	rlogin utworm rlogin utbugs
repeat parameters diff. commands	page draw vi draw
cycle a number of commands with same or diff. parameters	setenv TERM xterm gnuemacs –e mh-r setenv TERM xt100+ gnuemacs –e mh-r setenv TERM vt100 gnuemacs –e mh-r
repeat commands in a group	S < draw > draw.out page draw.out vi draw vi draw page draw.out S < draw > draw.out page draw.out vi draw

Table 1: Examples of observed repetitions.

1.3. Outline

In sections 3 and 4, we describe two computer simulation studies we conducted and the respective findings. The first study investigates the question "do the user's command line references exhibit localization patterns?" The second study examines the question "is the locality characteristic better at predicting candidates for recurrence than the recency characteristic?" Before beginning, we describe the session traces that were used in our studies.

2. USERS' SESSION TRACES

We used the session traces from Greenberg's study in our two simulation studies [Greenberg 1988b]. A total of 168 users made up Greenberg's subject population and they came from four groups:

a) *novice programmers* — 55 students from an introductory Pascal course with little or no previous exposure to programming, operating systems or UNIX-like command-based interfaces.

b) *experienced programmers* — 36 senior computer science undergraduates with a fair knowledge of programming languages and the UNIX environment.

c) *computer scientists* — 52 faculty, graduates and researchers from computer science department at U of Calgary having varying experience with UNIX™ but all being experts with computers in general.

d) *non-programmers* — 25 office staff and members of the Faculty of Environment Design at U of Calgary who were primarily application users (e.g., word-processing) and required minimal knowledge of UNIX in order to do their job.

For each user, we treated the trace as one long session. Every command line in the trace was used. A command line was treated as a recurrence if the command line matched exactly with a previous command line.

3. STUDY 1: LOCALITY?

Using the algorithm developed by Madison and Batson 1976, locality sets were detected and observed for all users. The observed set sizes were 1-11 and 13. Figure 3 illustrates where the locality sets of size 1-6 were found for one user's session.

While the data shows that users generate locality sets, the question "is this is due to chance"? Can *pseudo users* generate locality sets in the proportions that were observed for real users?

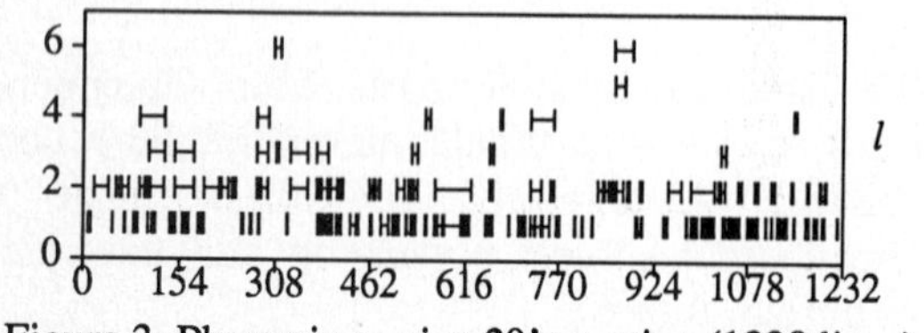

Figure 3: Phases in novice-29's session (1230 lines)

Pseudo users are capable of generating legitimate command lines but the ordering of their command lines are totally random.

We hypothesize that it is possible for locality set sizes of 1 to occur (i.e., recurrence of individual command lines) because of the 74% average recurrence rate. However, locality set sizes greater than 1 are less likely to occur compared to real users. We investigated this question in the following study.

3.1. Analysis Method

We generated 100 pseudo sessions by computer simulations for each user's session and ran each through the locality set detection algorithm. Each pseudo session was generated by randomly permuting the command lines of a user's real session using a different random number seed. In total, 16,800 pseudo user sessions were generated and analyzed.

We collected the number of locality sets that occur for the sizes we observed in the real user's traces (i.e., 12 sizes). Each of the 12 x 16,800 results were normalized by computing the percentage ($L_{p,l}$) of the total observed locality sets in the session that were of the particular locality set size l.

For each l, a histogram (percentage frequency) plot was produced using the 16,800 normalized results. The histograms are a good representation of what would occur by chance for the respective locality set size because of the large numbers of sessions generated. Furthermore, the population frequency distribution for each locality set size is well approximated by the relative frequency histogram. Two of the histogram plots (for locality set size 1 & 2) are shown in Figures 4.1 and 4.2. The other 10 plots are extremely skewed to the low values of $L_{p,l}$ [Lee in preparation]. The 168 results for the real user's session were also collected and normalized in a similar fashion (i.e., $L_{r,l}$).

3.2. Test and Results

A one-tailed statistical test was performed as the histograms were skewed distributions (see Figures 4.1 & 4.2). For each locality set size l, the null hypothesis is H_0: $\bar{L}_{p,l} = \bar{L}_{r,l}$. The alternate hypothesis is H_1: $\bar{L}_{p,l} > \bar{L}_{r,l}$ or $\bar{L}_p < \bar{L}_{r,l}$.

For each locality set size l, the null hypothesis is rejected if the cumulative probability of the observed average lies at the extremes of the pseudo-user's population. Simply, we determine whether the probability that the statistic (the real users' average $\bar{L}_{r,l}$) falls below α percent of the pseudo-users' population (i.e., compute either the $P(L_{p,l} > \bar{L}_{r,l})$ or $P(L_{p,l} < \bar{L}_{r,l})$, whichever is the one that represents the extreme condition). The P values represent the α value (level of significance) in a test of a statistical hypothesis.

From Table 2, we can see that for all but locality set size 4, the P values are less than 1% (i.e., test is significant at 1%). In the case of locality set size 4, the P value is less than 5% and the test is significant at 5%. Thus, we reject the null hypothesis and accept the alternate hypothesis at $\alpha = 5\%$. Namely, real users exhibit locality sets and not by pure chance. Figure 5 graphically illustrates the difference between $\bar{L}_{p,l}$ and $\bar{L}_{r,l}$ $(\bar{L}_{p,l}, \bar{L}_{r,l})$ at each of the locality set sizes l.

Size l	Test	P
1	$P(L_{p,1} < 62.5962)$	.00095
2	$P(L_{p,2} > 27.2488)$	.00149
3	$P(L_{p,3} > 6.8558)$	.00565
4	$P(L_{p,4} > 2.0594)$	.01244
5	$P(L_{p,5} > 0.8514)$	.00804
6	$P(L_{p,6} > 0.2369)$	.00720
7	$P(L_{p,7} > 0.0766)$	.00393
8	$P(L_{p,8} > 0.0560)$	.00161
9	$P(L_{p,9} > 0.0061)$	.00089
10	$P(L_{p,10} > 0.0064)$	.00036
11	$P(L_{p,11} > 0.0056)$	.00024
13	$P(L_{p,13} > 0.0009)$	.00012

Table 2: P's for observed locality set sizes l.

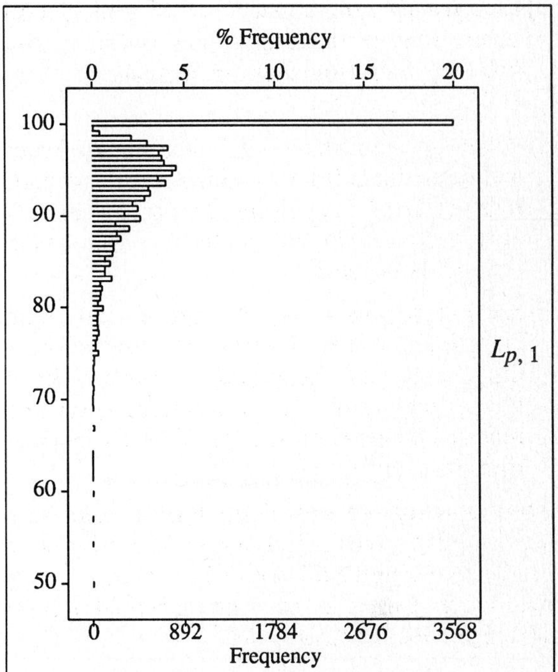

Figure 4.1: $L_{p,1}$ histogram (l=1)

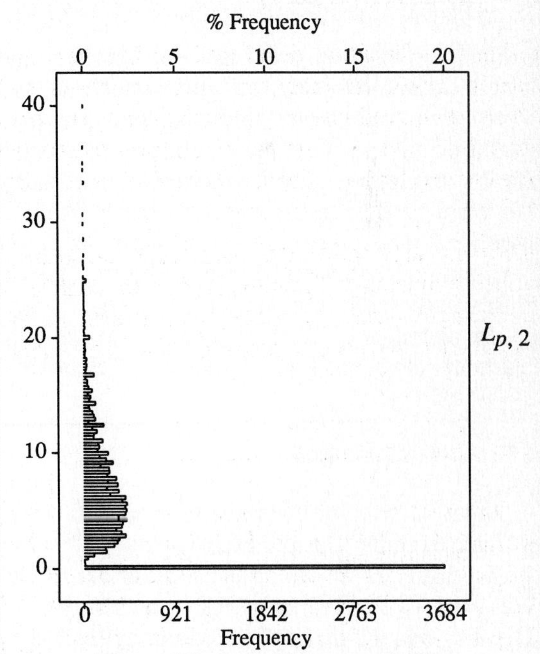

Figure 4.2: $L_{p,2}$ histogram (l=2)

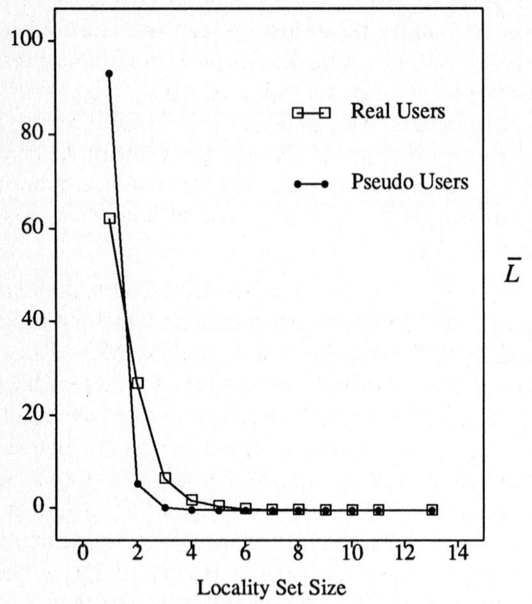

Figure 5: $\bar{L}_{p,l}$, $\bar{L}_{r,l}$ versus locality set size

4. STUDY 2: PREDICTOR'S QUALITY

In this simulation study, we were concerned with whether we could better predict when recurrences would occur and what the candidate recurrences are by exploiting locality rather than recency. The view is that recurrences are more likely in situations when users are in a phase or at the beginning of a phase than throughout the session. If this is the case, the candidate elements would be the elements of the locality set, otherwise the candidate elements would be the last T elements.

4.1. Analysis Method

A common basis for comparison is needed before we can examine the predictive quality of either the working set model or the locality set model. We used two versions of each user's session. The first was the original session trace (called S). The second was a transformation of S (called S'). The transformation removes all command lines in S that were part of a transition leaving only the command lines that were in the phase formation interval or in the phase (see Figure 2).

We took both the session traces (S and S') and performed computer simulations for each using the working set algorithm. The hit percentages for T (window parameter of the working set) ranging from 1 to 50 were determined for both session traces of each of the 168 users. Also, the average hit percentage of each of the traces was determined.

4.2. Results

The results are tabulated in Table 3 and shown graphically in Figure 6. The average recurrence rates for the S and S' are 72.18% and 74.55% respectively. Note that our observed recurrence rate for S (72%) is lower than the value Greenberg reported (74%). This may be attributed to the fact that we used every command line whereas he may have screened the non-shell command lines. Furthermore, the session traces we used were modified to ensure confidentiality of the data (i.e., user names were replaced by x's). The resultant S' had a slightly higher recurrence rate due to the fact that the transformation removed command lines that were not part of in phase formations or in phases. This would have the effect of reducing the number of unique command lines for each user.

As the data indicates, the hit percentages for the locality set model are higher than the hit percentages for the working set model at the same recurrence distance (T) for ($1 \leq T \leq 50$). For T=10 we get a 6% increase in the locality set model compared to that of the working set model. Doubling T (i.e., 20) results in a lesser increase (4.6%) of the locality set model's hit percentage over the working set model compared to that obtained for T=10. In general, the incremental gain for T>3 of the locality set model versus the working set model diminishes. From the data in Table 3, T=3 appears to be the threshold point.

T	S	S'	$S'-S$
1	11.08	17.73	6.65
2	33.05	41.12	8.07
3	43.45	51.68	8.23
4	49.71	57.59	7.88
5	54.42	61.90	7.48
6	57.75	64.80	7.05
7	60.48	67.22	6.74
8	62.71	69.18	6.47
9	64.54	70.78	6.34
10	66.16	72.20	6.04
20	75.69	80.27	4.58
30	80.40	84.25	3.85
40	83.39	86.67	3.28
50	85.55	88.38	2.83

Table 3: Hit % for various *T*s for S, S', $S'-S$.

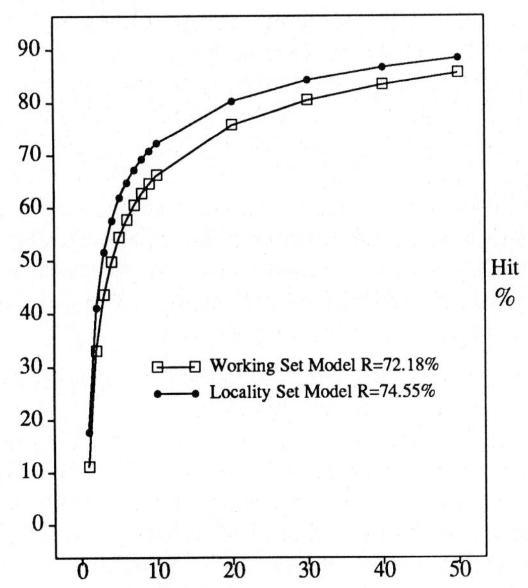

Figure 6: Hit % versus recurrence distance

5. DISCUSSION

The findings of the earlier studies and our studies are applicable to our investigation into the prospects for using the interaction history tool for user support [Lee in preparation]. A survey of the functionality provided by current systems suggests a number of different ways (e.g., reuse) that the interaction history can be used [Lee 1990]. A large majority of the efforts have been directed at various shades of reuse (e.g., commands, interaction objects, individual directives as well as groups of directives). However, there are no studies to suggest that reuse would indeed be the primary or preferred use of interaction history as a user support tool.

Similarly, very few studies have examined the question "do users use interaction history tools and how"? Greenberg and Witten 1988a found that despite the high recurrence rate, actual uses of the UNIX™ C Shell history were minimal. 54% of the users (largely computer sophisticates) recalled at least one previous action. Of those, on average, 3.9% (*std dev* = 3.8) of the command lines referred to an item through the interaction history. There are many reasons why actual usage is low. The two main reasons are design considerations and physical and cognitive overhead with using the tool [Greenberg 1988a, Lee 1989b, Lee in preparation]. Both of these considerations are important and need to be addressed.

The findings of locality and the preliminary results of the predictive quality of the locality set model are steps being made towards addressing the issue of better designs of interaction history tools. One of the basic questions addressed by our research is "*when is the interaction history suitable for reuse of a user's command lines*"? By exploiting the locality phenomenon, an interaction history tool can present a set of candidate items for reuse to users during periods when they are in a phase.

This leads to another interesting observation. While the analysis and the results of the analysis are important, the method used to obtain the results can be in and of itself important in tools that we design that exploit the results of our analysis. At least in the design of an interaction history tool for reuse, the algorithm used to detect locality set is also be useful in the operation of an interaction history tool for identifying phases and locality sets.

ACKNOWLEDGEMENTS

We would like to thank Marilyn Mantei and Mark Tapia for their comments and suggestions during the development of the simulation studies; Ruth Croxford and Prof. Tibshirani of the statistics department for their guidance in the statistical analysis; and Blaine Price for comments on the paper.

REFERENCES

L. Bannon, A. Cypher, S. Greenspan, and M.L. Monty (Dec. 12-15, 1983). Evaluation and analysis of users' activity organization. In *Proceedings of the CHI'83 Human Factors in Computer Systems*, pages 54-57, Boston, Massachusetts.

S.K. Card, M. Pavel, and J.E. Farrell (September 4-7, 1984). Window-based computer dialogues. In *Proceedings of Interact'84 First IFIP Conference on Human-Computer Interaction*, Volume 1 , pages 355-359.

A. Cypher (1986). The structure of users' activities. In D.A. Norman and S.W. Draper (editors), *User-Centered System Design: New Perspectives on Human-Computer Interaction*, pages 243-263. Lawrence Erlbaum Associates.

P.J. Denning (January 1980). Working sets past and present. *IEEE Transactions on Software Engineering*, **SE-6(1)**, pages 64-84.

S. Greenberg (1988a). Tool use, reuse, and organization in command-driven interfaces. Research Report 88/336/48, 187 pages. PhD Dissertation, Department of Computer Science, University of Calgary, Calgary, Alberta, Canada

S. Greenberg (1988b). Using UNIX: Collected traces of 168 users. Technical Research Report No. 88/333/45, 13 pages. Department of Computer Science, University of Calgary.

S. Greenberg and I.H. Witten (May 15-19, 1988a). How users repeat their actions on computers: Principles for design of history mechanisms. In *Proceedings of the CHI'88 Human Factors in Computer Systems*, pages 171-178, Washington, D.C. Also appears as DCS, University of Calgary Technical Report No. 87/279/27 (February, 1987).

D.A. Henderson Jr. and S.K. Card (July 1986). The use of multiple virtual workspaces to reduce space contention in a window-based graphical user interface. *ACM Transactions on Graphics - Special Issue on User Interface Software Part II*, **5(3)**, pages 211-243.

A. Lee (August 21-25, 1989b). Issues in design of history tool for user support. In *Proceedings of the Working Conference on User Interfaces (Engineering for Human-Computer Interaction)*, Napa Valley, CA.

A. Lee (May 14-18, 1990). Taxonomy of uses of interaction history. In *Proceedings of Graphics Interface'90*, Halifax, Nova Scotia.

A. Lee and F.H. Lochovsky (1990a). Study of command usage in three UNIX command interpreters. In *Proceedings of the Second Conference on Work with Display Units*, (September 11-14, 1989), Montreal, Quebec. Also appears in F.H. Lochovsky (editor), CSRI-238 Technical Report, University of Toronto, pages 6-11.

A. Lee (in preparation). Use of interaction history for user support. PhD dissertation. Department of Computer Science, University of Toronto.

A.W. Madison and A.P. Batson (May 1976). Characteristics of program localities. *Communications of the ACM*, **19(5)**, pages 285-294.

Human–Computer Interaction – INTERACT '90
D. Diaper et al. (Editors)
Elsevier Science Publishers B.V. (North-Holland)

AN INVESTIGATION INTO QUANTITATIVE USER MODELLING OF USER INTERACTIONS FOR THE PURPOSE OF PREDICTING USER EXPERTISE

R. Spall and R. Steele

Department of Computer Studies, Sheffield City Polytechnic, Pond Street, Sheffield S1 1WB

This paper examines the topic of Quantitative User Modelling. After initial definitions and background work, the potential of computable Quantitative User Models is explored, with particular emphasis given to their application to Intelligent Interfaces. Finally, an example Quantitative User Model is presented in order to highlight the pertinent issues which need to be addressed within this field. This work forms part of an SERC sponsored Research Project being pursued at Sheffield City Polytechnic, which is concerned with the implementation of a complete Object Oriented UIMS.

1. BACKGROUND AND DEFINITIONS

This paper is concerned with the application of User Modelling to the field of Human Computer Interaction, and how user models may be built into a human computer interface. User models attempt to describe those properties and characteristics of humans which affect their interaction with computer systems. It is a description of how users interact with software interfaces [1]. Within this field, models serve main two purposes. Firstly, models may be used as a design tool to assist the interface designer in generating usable interfaces. Knowledge of how a particular person interacts with and uses a computer system should improve the design of computer systems which that person may use. This knowledge does not need to be available as an Expert System, and may take the form of written user interface guidelines [2]. These types of models have arisen out of considerable empirical cognitive psychology research involving the analysis of users using real computer systems. This typically identifies which human qualities and characteristics affect human computer interaction, and explains these affects and their interrelationships. Appropriate guidelines and recommendations concerning interface software design improvements can then be compiled. Due to the individuality of users, it is very difficult to define the 'best interface' for all users. Cognitive psychology research can only suggest which interface techniques or styles are best suited to which user characteristics or traits. It is the job of the interface designer, or an adaptable intelligent interface to select the 'best interface' for a particular user, or user group.

Alternatively, a user model may be used by an actual software interface in order to infer certain values, or characteristics, about a user. An expert system is therefore needed to implement this type of user model. An intelligent interface is required to make full use of computable user models, and this is comprised of many different interrelated components. These components attempt to improve an interface's usability by applying the results of work in the field of Artificial Intelligence [3].

A computerised user model is necessary if an intelligent interface is to adapt itself to the requirements of individual users. This adaption may be performed by the user, or by the interface itself, and requires that knowledge be stored concerning individual users. For example, a user model may describe user style preferences, or a user's expertise with particular tasks.

Two broad types of User Model can be identified, namely: conceptual and quantitative models [4]. Conceptual models are chiefly concerned with representing human cognitive processes. They serve to identify the cognitive processes, structure, and strategies involved in human computer interaction. For example, work by Norman [5] classifies the user's cognitive strategy using 7 stages:-

1. - Establishing Goal,
2. - Forming an Intention,
3. - Specifying the Action Sequence,
4. - Executing the Action,
5. - Perceiving the System State,
6. - Interpreting the State,
7. - Evaluating the system state with respect to goals and intentions.

Quantitative user modelling deals with the numerical representation of user performance at the interface. That is, performance as it relates to human information processing capabilities and limitations. For example, the keystroke model developed as part of GOMS [6].

Various user characteristics may be modelled in order to provide useful knowledge for an intelligent interface. User preferences could be modelled as a means of describing a user's personal tastes, for example prefering menu style interaction to command language, or certain text styles and colours. The modelling of user motivations and objectives could provide knowledge concerning the tasks which a user is trying to achieve. This should enable intelligent planning techniques to be applied to assist the user in accomplishing these tasks. The modelling of user expertise should provide knowledge concerning a user's understanding of the computer system being used. This can then be used to control the amount of user assistance given by an intelligent interface. Similarly, modelling of user interaction skills such as mouse movement, keyboard recognition, etc should also prove beneficial, especially where disabled users are concerned. Psychological, or behavioural modelling should provide helpful knowledge concerning a user's overall character and profile [7]. This can be used to match specific interface and human computer interaction styles to individual users. Finally, the modelling of a user's background with other computer systems should enable an intelligent interface to make analogies with other computer systems, and possibly adapt itself to mimic them.

A computable user model may use several techniques in order to determine the knowledge it contains. Stereotyping can provide an initial user model based upon pre-described user groups. A particular stereotype is chosen from a set of general user stereotypes, according to information supplied by user in reply to an initial question and answer session. Alternatively, the appropriate stereotype may be directly specified by the user / interface designer, or automatically selected based upon initial user interactions. This approach limits the flexibility of a user model, and assumes that it is possible to classify users into groups according to psychological or behavioural frameworks. Instead, a user model may determine its knowledge using an extensive question and answer session with the user. This approach makes use of well proven psychological / behavioural written questionnaires and analysis techniques. A finer granularity is achieved however, this technique is obtrusive and requires that the user answers questions accurately. It also assumes that users can correctly describe themselves, and that the appropriate analysis technique works. Finally a user model may derive its knowledge from actual user interactions which take place. This requires that the model monitors human computer interaction and infers knowledge about a user's characteristics. The user model must be capable of inferring a user's intentions and recognising any difficulties. This technique is relatively unobtrusive, but problems may arise due to incorrect inferencing. Some models may in fact combine these techniques. For example, using stereotyping to determine the initial user model knowledge, while employing interaction inferencing techniques to later refine the model.

Several types of information concerning user interactions are available to a user model for inferencing purposes. These include correct application usage, incorrect usage or errors, requests for help and tutorial support, and time lapses between usage. These interactions can each be used to infer different type of knowledge concerning the user. They can also be used to infer different things at different times, depending upon the context of their occurrence. For example, correct application usage can be used to infer user development, that is progression towards an expert user. However, application errors can be used to infer user regression at certain times, while at other times they may be used to infer user progression. This may occur when an expert user is exploring a new application, or is using negative error responses to interrogate an information system. Inferencing based upon user interaction is also dependent upon a user's learning abilities which therefore must also be represented within a user model.

This work tests the hypothesis that a user's interactions with an application can provide the basis for a predictive quantitative user model. This model can then be used to predict a user's expertise with an application, and therefore provide useful knowledge which can be used within an intelligent interface; for example, by an intelligent help system for the purpose of tailoring its response to a user's request for assistance. The proposed model was developed as a 'test vehicle', and uses a mathematical approach to describing knowledge concerning a user. It embodies knowledge concerning correct and incorrect application usage, and takes full advantage of the principles and benefits of object oriented design. Please note that the model does not attempt to suggest the 'best approach', instead it is intended to focus attention upon the issues which need to be addressed within the user modelling field.

2. QUANTITATIVE USER MODELLING OF USER INTERACTIONS FOR THE PURPOSE OF PREDICTING USER EXPERTISE

A user's expertise with a computer application must be divided into different conceptual levels. For example, overall interface expertise, overall application expertise, and both individual interface and application component expertise. The proposed model only considers a user's expertise with an application, and organises this according to three conceptual levels. These are overall application expertise, expertise with component objects, and expertise with object functions.

Individual user expertise classification is required for the various objects and functions at different conceptual levels. This classification may be stored directly as a value, or inferred from other knowledge contained within the model. This model uses a broad classification of either Expert, Intermediate or Novice user. This classification is maintained for individual components at each conceptual level, rather than as a general level classification. For example, users are classified accordingly for each individual object, application and function rather than being given a single classification which generally applies to all applications, objects or functions.

Usage of functions and objects at different conceptual levels will indirectly affects the user's expertise with other functions and objects. For example, individual function usage may well affect a user's overall expertise with an application. Similarly, use of one function may affect a user's expertise with other related functions. This shows the need for an explicit application model which describes the relationship between various application functions, and the objects on which they act.

Traditional procedural languages do not provide this self describing function, and the application architecture is often hidden within the program structure. Because of this, separate application models are required which must be specified in computable formats [8]. These can then be extended to incorporate knowledge which describes the relationships between individual functions and conceptual objects. Fortunately, object oriented languages support a self describing explicit application architecture based upon an application, its component objects, and their behaviour (which is determined by their explicit message protocol). This is utilised by the proposed model.

The proposed model, examines the hypothesis that correct application usage can be used to infer user development. Although incorrect application usage, and time lapse between usage is represented in the model, this is not considered when inferences are made. Finally it uses a learning curve to describe a user's ability to learn and forget new knowledge.

3. STRUCTURE OF THE PROPOSED QUANTITATIVE USER MODEL

Figure 1 illustrates the basic model architecture, and information flows between the model and any application. An object oriented application is used by sending messages between different self contained objects. The architecture uses this feature to determine what objects and functions have been correctly or incorrectly used. The model is implemented separate from the Smalltalk message handling mechanism. It therefore expects to be independently informed of the correct and incorrect messages issued by the user, and those arising from communication between various application objects.

The model is clearly divided into knowledge and heuristics. The knowledge describes a user's usage of an application, while the separate heuristics access and modify this knowledge. The knowledge concerning a user's application usage is structured according to the applications architecture. Knowledge concerning the application architecture is therefore included.

The application architecture is represented at three conceptual levels. These are based upon the object oriented concept of an application comprised of objects which provide a specific function, or method protocol. The three levels are :-

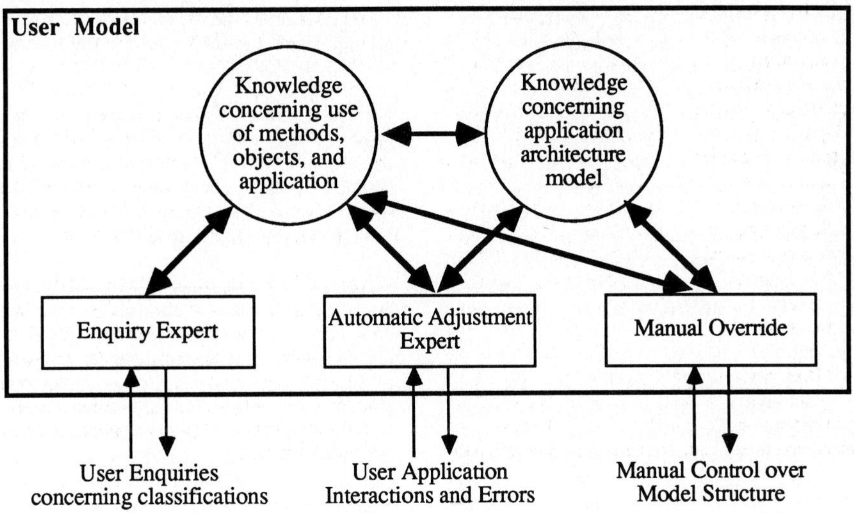

Figure 1 - Quantitative User Model Structure

- Application,
- Application objects,
- Object methods or functions.

The application effectively represents the highest conceptual level, while object methods denote the lowest. There may also be many objects and methods at the respective object and method conceptual levels. Each of these must therefore be individually represented within the internal application model. Grouped with the application, these are collectively referred to as application components. As described below, the relationship between individual application components is also contained within the internal application architecture model.

The following information is stored within each user model, for each application component :-

- Number of uses,
- Date of last use,
- Number of errors (for each error type),
- Number of uses since last error (regardless of error type),
- Intermediate Classification Trigger (controls move from Novice to Intermediate),
- Expert Classification Trigger (controls move from Intermediate to Expert),
- Current Experience Classification (when set to nil, user classification is inferred from knowledge contained within the model. When set to a numeric value between 1 and 3, it is assumed that the automatic inferencing is to be overridden with a classification specified by the user. A value of 1 implies Novice experience, while 2 and 3 imply Intermediary and Expert experience classifications),
- Usage Transfer factor, i.e. the effect of usage on higher conceptual level (not maintained at application conceptual level).

- A single mathematical formula is also maintained for each user model to represent a user's learning curve.

This knowledge is constantly updated according to a user's interactions, and is maintained between different sessions. The purpose of this knowledge is described in section 4 below.

The complete model is implemented as a single Smalltalk Class, with the internal knowledge encapsulated within instances of the Class. The necessary heuristics are implemented as instance methods using Smalltalk code. A user requires a separate quantative user model for each application, and this is achieved by creating new instances of the quantitative user model Class. Each instance effectively contains separate model knowledge, but shares the same instance methods or heuristics defined by the Class.

Individual application objects are described using the object oriented Class mechanism [9]. Application objects which share the same Class definition behave identically, and knowledge concerning their usage need only be modelled at the Class level. Multiple instances of the same Class are therefore represented as a single Class within the quantitative model, and usage of individual instances only affects the one quantitative model Class representation.

Objects sharing the same Class definition may also be used within different applications. The objects used within a specific application are not explicitly described, and the model needs to be told which Class definitions relate to which application. As shown in figure 1, this knowledge is incorporated into an internal application model. The first step in using a model must therefore be to define the Classes used by an application, and also the messages which any Class instance, or object can understand. This is achieved by sending the appropriate messages to the user model.

4. FUNCTIONING OF THE PROPOSED QUANTITATIVE USER MODEL

Three function or method subsets are provided by the model. The first 'Automatic Adjustment Expert' subset enables the model to be informed of application usage. It contains the necessary heuristics to modify the model according to specific user interactions. The second 'Enquiry Expert' subset provides inferencing heuristics for classifying a users expertise. Finally, a third 'Manual Override' subset allows the model's internal knowledge to be manually modified, thus providing an override facility.

The Automatic Adjustment Expert provides a set of messages which must be used to inform the model of specific application user interactions. Interactions may occur at the application, object or method levels and must be identified using appropriate names. When object usage is reported, the application in which it is being used must also be identified. Similarly, when method usage is reported, both the object to which the method applies or belongs, and the application in which the object is being used must be specified. This enables both correct and incorrect application usage to be monitored.

If the model is informed of an interaction using an object or method which is not described within its application architecture model, the new object or method is automatically added. In doing so, default values are automatically set for the usage transfer factor, and classification triggers.

When the model is informed of correct application usage, the appropriate internal usage count is incremented. Similarly, when incorrect usage occurs, the relevant error count is increased. The date since last usage and number of uses since last error are also updated accordingly.

Using a particular method not only affects a user's expertise with that method, but also with the object to which it belongs. Similarly, use of an object also affects a user's expertise with the application of which it is a part. The model tries to capture this effect by providing a transfer factor for each application component. This determines the effect of a component's usage upon another component at a higher conceptual level. For example, the effect of a method's usage upon the object to which it belongs. As illustrated in figure 2, this transfer factor is a simple decimal number which is passed on to the component at the next conceptual level (to the object conceptual level in the case of a method usage, and to the application conceptual level in the case of object usage). This number can be set for individual application components and should be in the range of 0 to 1. As an example consider an object which understands the *age* message. Use of the *age* method increases the models usage count for *age* by one. If this method has a transfer factor of 0.2, then using it causes the model's usage count for the Person Class to increase by 0.2, i.e. 1 * 0.2. Assuming that the object's Class has a transfer factor of 0.1, the appropriate application usage count is finally increased by 0.02, i.e. 0.2 * 0.1.

An application may comprise of many objects, each of which has a separate transfer factor. Similarly, each object may have many methods each of which has also has a separate transfer factor. A components usage count may therefore be directly affected by a specific use by a user, or indirectly by the use of a component at a lower level which is related to it.

Although the model does not provide any error recognition or classification facilities, it does support more than one error count for each component in order to represent different types of error. It is up to the implementor of the quantitative model to interpret the meaning of different error types, and to inform the model when errors of a particular type arise. When the model is notified of an error made while using an application component, the appropriate component's error count is incremented by one. Knowledge is also maintained concerning the application component use since the last error was made, and this is reset to one whenever an error of any type occurs.

Unlike correct interactions, the effect of an error is passed onto the next conceptual level on a one to one basis. This is analogous to setting the transfer factor to 1. For example, consider the effect of a user who makes an error of type One with a particular method. This would cause an increase of one in a model's type One error count field for that method, the Class to which it belongs, and the application in which it is being used.

In order to represent a user's learning ability, a Learning Curve is maintained within each model. This depicts a user's ability to learn new knowledge, and is stored as a mathematical formula. This curve is used to define the rate at which a user learns knowledge, and assumes that the user learns all knowledge at the same rate across different conceptual levels. As figure 3 illustrates, this formula is used to plot a graph showing usage count against user knowledge. The user knowledge is shown along the vertical axis, and ranges from 0

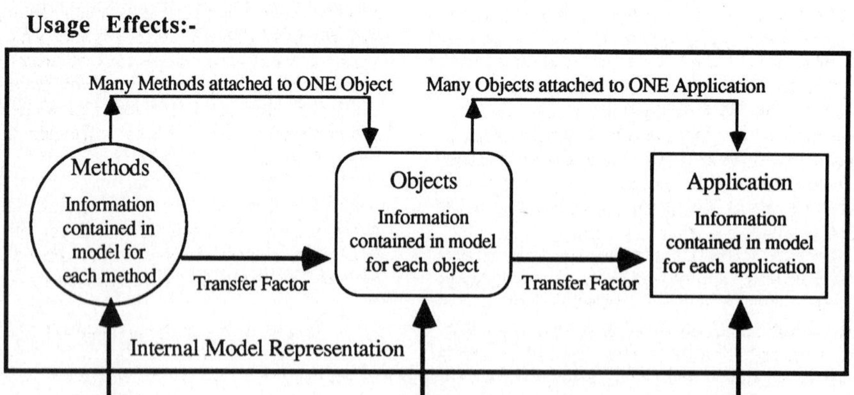

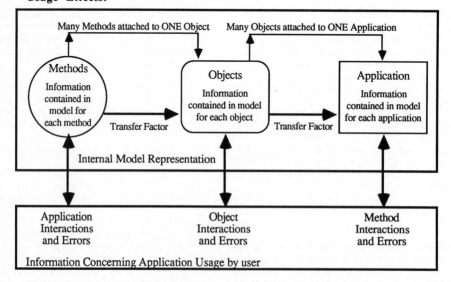

Figure 2 - Usage Relationship Between Different Conceptual Levels

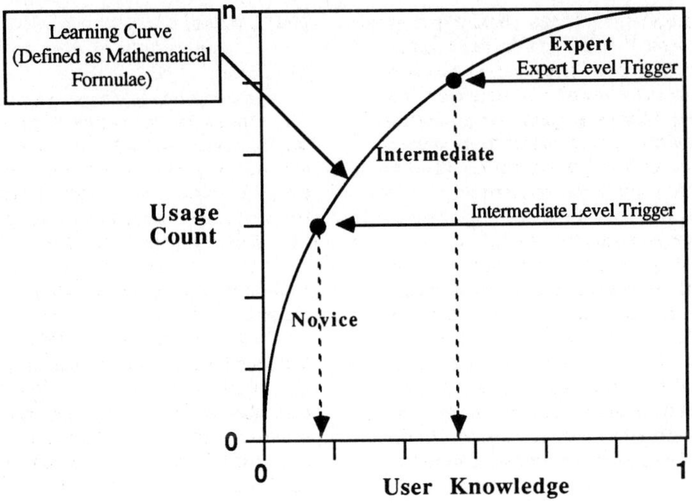

Figure 3 - User Learning Curve

(Novice) to 1 (Expert). The usage count is shown along the horizontal axis, and its range may differ between models. The learning curve formula is stored in the form X = f (Y), where usage count can be substituted for Y, and X represents actual user knowledge.

Two triggers, Intermediate Classification Trigger and Expert Classification trigger, are used to calculate a user's classification for a particular application component. These triggers represent the user knowledge required for a user to move from novice to intermediate classification, and intermediate to expert classification respectively. Their values should range from 0 to 1, and the Expert Trigger should always be greater than, or equal to the Intermediate Trigger.These triggers break the learning curve into three regions, namely: novice, intermediate, and expert. Using these triggers, the learning curve formula and the current usage count, a user's classification at a particular conceptual level may be computed. Although a single learning curve formula is used for the entire model, the two triggers may be set for individual application components.

The model's internal knowledge is automatically updated according to user application interactions. However, this knowledge may also be directly modified using the Manual Override methods provided. These enable the internal application architecture model structure to be changed, as well as the information stored for each application component - as listed in section 3 above. The model learning curve may also be modified. Finally, the automated expertise classification mechanism may be overridden, and an explicit experience value set for each application component. This may be set to either 1, 2, or 3 implying Novice, Intermediary, or Expert knowledge with the appropriate component. Automatic classification may be resumed at any time by setting this value back to nil. Again, appropriate model methods are provided to simplify switching between manual and automated classification.

5. CONCLUSIONS

After initial testing, it was realised that the proposed model could not accurately predict a user's expertise based upon correct usage only. In response, attempts were made to modify the model's heuristics to take into account both errors and time lapses. Again, the model failed to accurately predict a user's expertise. The reasons for this inaccuracy appear to lie in the complexity of structuring, acquiring, and inferencing from quantitative knowledge concerning a user.

Determining the initial model knowledge was very difficult. In particular, it was hard to fix the component classification level triggers, learning curve formula, and transfer factors. Assuming that these values could be accurately calculated, further extensive empirical work would be required to investigate the mathematical relationship between the different values and the real knowledge that they are modelling. This definition stage would also take a very long time as there are numerous inter related components at the different conceptual levels.

User interaction is very complex, and the relationship between correct usage and user expertise is difficult, and may be impossible to mathematically express completely. Similarly, the effect of errors and time lapse is also difficult to mathematically represent. User interactions can not be considered independently of other factors which also affect human computer interaction. These include work environment, personal motivations, work pressures, stress, 'off days', etc. Again, assuming that this extra knowledge can be acquired, the complex relationships that result will require tremendous computing power to solve.

While using the model, it was realised that certain types of knowledge concerning the application bore no direct relationship to the actual application architecture. For example, knowledge describing a user's general understanding of information systems, or of an object oriented system. Similarly, knowledge concerning a user's understanding of the application domain and terminology was not described. Without this knowledge it would not be possible to accurately determine user expertise with different application components. The user model's knowledge would therefore have to be expanded to include information concerning these and other general concepts.

In effect a large amount of extra knowledge is required to improve the accuracy of this model. This raises the issue of organising, capturing, and using this extra knowledge within a user model. Reflecting upon the complexities of these issues, the implementation and use of accurate user models will undoubtedly require both tremendous computer resources and intelligence.

Another problem identified by this work was that of inconsistency between the model and the real user. If small inconsistencies are not immediately corrected, the user model very quickly becomes inconsistent with the real user, and therefore useless. Ultimately, this implies that a user model has to exactly represent the user at all times or not at all. This could be achieved by periodic question and answer sessions with the user. However, this overhead may defeat the very purpose of user models. Alternatively, the heuristics for updating and inferencing from the model must take account of every factor which can possibly affect the user's real interaction processes.

A final problem is that of heuristics which may themselves change. The heuristics for updating the user model and for inferring knowledge about it, were themselves subject to change. For example the effects of errors and correct usage upon user expertise changes, as a user moves from a Novice to Expert. Similarly, these effects are probably different during each cycle of the repetitive move from Novice to Expert, and Expert back to Novice over a period of time. Adding to the problem, it is probable that the mechanisms for changing the heuristics are themselves subject to change and so on.

The very least that this work shows is that an object oriented design facilitates the definition and updating of a quantitative user model to represent a user's interactions with a software applications.The mechanism for monitoring and describing user interactions are relatively straight forward, and can be implemented within the interface software. The body of knowledge required to define the parameters influencing the 'shape' of a user's learning curve is less clear, and needs to be extracted from the fields of educational psychology, cognitive psychology, artificial intelligence. Given the success of these fields in solving the problems identified, predictive quantitative user models should serve a useful function within an intelligent interface.

REFERENCES

[1] Clowes, I. 1985.
User Modeling Techniques for Interactive Systems. HCI 1985 Proceedings, Cambridge Press.

[2] Thimbleby, H. 1983.
Dialogue Design: Principle or Prejudice? 'Generative User-Engineering Principles'. The User Interface: Human Factors in Computer Based Systems.

[3] Carroll, J.M. 1987.
Interface Design Issues for Advice Giving Expert Systems. Communications of the ACM, Jan 1987, Volume 30, Number 1.

[4] Williges, R.C: 1987
The Use of Models in Human Computer Interface Design. Ergonomics Society Lecture, Swansea, Wales, 6-10 April 1987.

[5] Norman, D.A.
Cognitive Engineering, User Centred System Design (edited by D.A. Norman and S.W. Draper). Erlbaum: New Jersey, pp 31-61.

[6] Fountain, A.J. 1985.
Modelling User Behaviour with Formal Grammar. People and Computers:Designing the Interface. Johnson, P. and Cook, S. (editors). Cambridge Press 1985.

[7] Benyon, D. 1988.
Experience with Adaptive Interfaces. The Computer Journal, Vol. 31 No. 5, 1988.

[8] Carberry, S. 1988.
Modelling the User's Plans and Goals. Computational Linguistics, Volume 14, Number 3, Sept 1988. [9]Goldberg, A. 1981. Introducing the Smalltalk 80 System. Byte, August 1981.

Human–Computer Interaction – INTERACT '90
D. Diaper et al. (Editors)
Elsevier Science Publishers B.V. (North-Holland)

CONSTRAINTS IN DESIGN: TOWARDS A METHODOLOGY OF PSYCHOLOGICAL ANALYSIS BASED ON AI FORMALISMS

Françoise DARSES

C.N.R.S, Paris 8, U.R.A 1297, Equipe de Psychologie Cognitive Ergonomique, 2 rue de la Liberté, 93526 Saint-Denis, France
INRIA, Domaine de Voluceau, Rocquencourt BP 105, 78153 Le Chesnay Cedex, France

More and more CAD systems are founded on a constraint posting approach. In order to know whether such an approach is compatible with the cognitive activity of the designers, this paper focuses on the crucial role of constraint in the cognitive processes of design. We first highlight how the notion of constraint is referred to in the psychological models of design. A constraint posting approach for design is used to set up a specific methodology of analysis. Based on AI formalisms, this methodology has to be enlarged to give an account of some psychological charateristics of the designers activity. An empirical assessment of the method has been conducted in the domain of computer network design. The results highlight that half of the activity of the experts can be understood in terms of constraint posting. Moreover, we show that the ability to handle the constraints differs, depending on the level of expertise of the designers and according to the nature of the constraints. But above all, this assessment lays down the limits and the benefits of the methodology. It sketches the directions in which the method will have to be enlarged.

INTRODUCTION

The concept of constraint is inherent to the design activity. It is often referred to by the designers when they report their solving process. They readily describe the problems they have to cope with in terms of constraints: the technological properties of the equipment, the priority to be given to particular characteristics of the problem, the order in which the actions have to be achieved, the specifications expressed by the customer, all these are viewed as constraints to be satisfied.

From that point of view, an increasing number of CAD systems have been developed from the constraint satisfaction paradigm. Those are for instance scheduling problems [1, 2], resource allocation [3, 4, 5] or spatial arrangements problems [6, 7]. For this class of problem, the process of solving is viewed as a progressive reduction of an initially very broad search space: a good means of achieving this limitation is to satisfy the constraints linked to the object. However, these CAD systems have not been psychologically and ergonomically evaluated yet.

The question is to know whether designers effectively represent to themselves the problem they have to cope with as a set of constraints to be satisfied. Up to now, cognitive processes involved in design have been described in the psychological models essentially as the result of planning activities, where the development of the solution is viewed as the outcome of top-down and bottom-up strategies [8]. Although the crucial role of constraint is often referred to in these models, the way the designers deal with the various constraints bounded to the problem has not been stressed yet and this concept remains vague or incomplete. In a first section, we show that the notion of constraint is at the core of the cognitive processes in the activity of design . In a second section, we outline a methodology to be applied to a psychological analysis in terms of constraints. Then, an empirical assessment of the method is presented.

1. CONSTRAINT AND COGNITIVE ACTIVITY IN DESIGN

Whatever features the psychological models emphasize, the notion of constraint is underlying. It is in some cases explicitly integrated as a whole component, but most of the time, it is implicit.

Constraint and least commitment strategy

The hierarchical models of planning consider that the design process is developed from the definition of a general goal to be decomposed into sub-goals which are themselves decomposed, until elementary actions are achieved. This strictly top-down point of view of the design process has been reinforced with an influential artificial intelligence trend, the best known contribution of which being the Hierarchical Planners [9, 10]. A top-down modelling of design permits to express two characteristics of the psychological behaviour of the designers which are tightly tied to the notion of constraint.

The first one is known as a least committment strategy [9]. The idea is that the designers try to keep open as late as possible the choices to be made. By deferring as long as possible the decisions, they avoid prematurate and inappropriate decisions which would narrow the possibilities and create unsolvable conflicts between sub-problems. This behaviour has been observed by Lebahar [11] in a psychological study of the architectural design. Therefore, one can consider that the interactions between the sub-problems, the management of which appears crucial in design, can be seen like the expression of constraints bounded to the problem [12]. As a matter of fact, the conflicts which emerge in the course of design are

themselves. For instance, a conflict can arise between the hierarchical network architecture which is achieved and the budgetary limits which are overpassed.

Constraint and evaluation activity

A second characteristic of the psychological behaviour which is highlighted in hierarchical models of design is the evaluation activity developed all along the solving process. Each time an intermediate state of solution is built, evaluation knowledge intervenes. Thus, the relevant points to be modified are pointed out. In Sacerdoti's program [9], the evaluation knowledge is formalized with the introduction of criticalities. These are a set of procedures the role of which is to control the effects of any action which could jeopardize the plan. Criticalities are very similar to the notion of constraint, since they are the formulation of the specifications of the problem domain, their weight being the expression of their importance and priority in the solving process.

Constraint as initial data

The notion of constraint as a set of initial data, or as the specifications of the solution has been emphasized in the opportunistic models of design. The idea of these models is that it is necessary to articulate both top-down and bottom-up processes to give an account of the process of design [13, 14, 15]. Thus, the steps of the solving process are triggered by information that the designers notice about the current state of the problem. This suggest to them possible decisions to be implemented at any level of the plan. Various psychological observations [16, 17, 18] have highlighted and confirmed that planning is developed either through top-down or bottom-up processes. In the Hayes-Roth model [13], constraints act, but they are formulated as initial data and they are simply mixed together with other records on the blackboard. They are for instance time constraints such as groceries perish, people get hungry at lunch time, and so on. In computer network design, initial data and specifications of the final solution are also expressed as constraints: "the building is six floor high", "the thin cable cannot overpass 185 meters", "the professional units located on the second floor must be isolated from the other units".

Type of constraints

Eastman [19], analyzing the activity of architectural designers, suggests distinguishing more accurately the type of constraints handled in the course of the design process. Some constraints are identified before trial sketches were made ("designing a more luxurious bathroom"); this set of constraints is itself divided into constraints given ("cost = existing + 100 $") and constraints retrieved ("set the plumbing on one wall"). Some constraints are identified while making the trial sketches ("no exposed bathtub corners"). Moreover, the author notices that the competence of the designers depends much on the type of constraint they deal with and on the way they have organized and structured these constraints in memory.

Empirical observations

The prominent part of constraint in design is also pointed out by some empirical observations. When talking with the designers, it appears that they are always looking for the solution which will represent the best compromise. They know that it is not possible to achieve a solution where the constraints would be all equally satisfied. Thus, priorities have to be made, according to the features of the problem and according to the individual choices. The greatest difficulty the designers have to cope with arises from this hierarchy to be built.

The previous remarks highlight that the notion of constraint is at the core of the design processes. Therefore, one might justifiably assume that the cognitive activity involved in design can be interpreted in terms of constraint posting. Such an approach implies to set up a specific methodology for describing and analyzing the psychological behaviour of the designers. The next section outlines this methodology.

2. A METHODOLOGY OF ANALYSIS OF DESIGN IN TERMS OF CONSTRAINT POSTING

For a psychological description of the process of design in terms of constraint, we found that it would be fruitful to set up a methodology based on one hand upon the formalisms developed in AI, but enlarged on another hand by an analysis of verbal protocols collected from design sessions. We outline the rationale of the constraint posting approach, as it has been developed in some computational programs. We explain how we made use of it to build a methodology of analysis and how it had to be complemented with additional descriptors in order to give an account of the psychological activity involved in design.

2.1. Constraint: a relation between variables

Constraint

From the Constraint Satisfaction Problem paradigm, the concept of constraint can be understood as a relation between variables. The rationale is that it exists a set of variables, each to be instanciated in an associated domain, and it exists a set of constraints, limiting the set of allowed values for specified sub-sets of the variables [20, 21]. Consequently, a constraint is viewed as the set of possible combinations between the values of its associated variables [12]. In the domain of network design, the constraint "length-compatible" bounds the variable "type of cables, regarding their maximum length {thin -> up to 185 m; thick -> up to 500 m; optic fiber -> up to 3000 m}" and the variable "segment to be cabled { 0 to n meters}". This example refers to a binary constraint, but a lot of unary constraints are used in design situations, such as "the building is six floor high". As the instanciations of the constraints can differ according to the individual choices of the designers, many different solutions can be drawn. This corresponds very well to the psychological observations which have pointed out that a remarkable characteristic of design situations is the elaboration of numerous solutions from a same initial problem.

Actually, a constraint can be either formalized as a relation among variables, or as rules (productions) or objects (schemas or frames) [22]. For instance, the system GARI [3, 4] implemented for generating the machining plans of mechanical parts uses a rule-based approach. Here, a constraint is for instance: "if a hole H1 opens into another hole H2, then one is recommended machining H2 before H1 in order to avoid the risk of damaging the drill". In the verbal protocols, a constraint item is isolated eachtime a relation among variables is highlighted. For instance, a constraint is "as there are many separated buildings, I will put optic fiber for the security".

Deduced and Prescribed constraints

From a psychological point of view, it seemed necessary to add a distinction between two kinds of constraints. The first have been named Deduced Constraints, because their instanciation is submitted to the decision of the designers. For example, it is up to the designer to choose the type of cable according to the length of the segment to be cabled. On another hand, the Constraints are Prescribed when the values of their variables have been previously set, as for instance "the building is six floor high" or "we want optic fiber to be used".

Validity constraint and Preference constraint

The necessity to account for the fact that the designers range the constraints involved in the problem according to their importance or their priority has been introduced in the computational systems in several ways. Descotte et Latombe [4] confer weights to the constraints. Since these are expressed as production rules, each right-hand side of the rule is weighted according to the importance of its satisfaction in the human expert's view. Janssen et al [23] have distinguished Validity constraint from Preference constraint. A Validity Constraint must be verified in the solution for it to be admitted. Most of the validity are about the technological prescriptions, topological prescriptions or customer specifications. For instance, the compatibility between the type of the cable and the length of the segment to be cabled is a Validity Constraint.

But the designers choose a solution rather than another in the set of all the allowable solutions upon Preference Constraints. Whether their terms have been applied or not, the object to be designed remains an allowable object. In networking design, a preference constraint is for instance to provide the possibility of a further extension of the configuration. But the limits between preference and validity constraints are sometimes fuzzy. As a matter of fact, some constraints can be considered either upon validity or preference criteria, regarding to the problem. For instance, the final cost of the network is a validity constraint when the customer has initially specified that it must not overpass such an amount. But this can be viewed as a preference constraint if the designers impose to themselves a "reasonable price" criterion, although it was not specified by the customer.

2.2 Constraint posting

Beyond the difficulty of expressing the constraints, a greater complexity arises from their management during the planning process. It is unavoidable that conflicts occur because of uncompatible constraints. The designers have to post the constraints in order to minimize these conflicts, avoiding prematurate choices to be made, taking into account their importance and their priority. The constraint posting approach distinguishes three operations on the constraints. All of these operations could be broadly characterized as inferences in problem solving. These operations [12, 24], considered in terms of the different roles they play in the problem solving process, provide an interesting frame for a psychological analysis and outline the treatments which are applied in the design activity.Constraint formulation is the adding of new constraints in the design process. The traditional constraint satisfaction approach works with a fixed number of constraints that are all known at the beginning. But the designers' behaviour is much different. When starting to solve the problem, the set of constraints is not entirely delimited. Moreover, the constraints are usually not tightly specified at the beginning but progressively expressed during the solving process. For this reason, some authors suggest allowing a progressive refinement of the constraints [12] and their progressive introduction in the solving process [23].

Constraint propagation is the creation of new constraints from old constraints. When constraints are propagated, they bring together new requirements from separate parts of the problem. These modifications can be adding or suppressing some values; they trigger new modifications, or they trigger the formulation of new constraints. This operation makes possible the least-commitment strategy. It also accounts for an implicit propagation of the constraints, observed in the design process.

Constraint satisfaction is the operation of finding values for variables so that a set of constraints on the variables is satisfied. When a constraint is satisfied, a part of the solution is described more accurately and the set of possible solutions is then restricted.

When analyzing the protocols, the formulation and the satisfaction of the constraints have been indicated, depending on their occurrence in the process: constraint formulated only, constraint formulated and satisfied simultaneously, constraint formulated and satisfied later on in the process (the satisfaction is differed). The nature of the constraint (validity or preference) has also been distinguished.

2.3 Other units

But some steps of the solving process are unlikely to be interpreted in terms of constraint, as for instance when the designers execute a procedure. Some utterances of the protocols have to be assigned to additional categories in order to report the cognitive activity occurring during design. Additional descriptors were defined by a preliminary analysis of verbal protocols:

- *meta plan* contains all the utterances which give an account of the decisions about the planning process ("a project must be carried out through different steps; here a basic solution has to be settled, and the general feature of it has to be exposed") or general strategies of resolution ("minimize the prices as much as possible and propose something substantial without care of the traffic optimization");

- *abstract plans* qualify any solution described at its abstract level. It refers to the intention of elaborating a solution; here, this is more an idea of solution rather than an accurate description which is given;

- *executed plan* qualify any solution which is described at a low level of abstraction; in this case, the designers do implement mentally the solution they thought about.

3. AN EMPIRICAL ASSESSMENT OF THE METHOD

The methodology has been applied to the analysis of computer network design. This assessment provides some clues about the cognitive processes involved in the activity of design. But above all, the purpose of this empirical assessment is to lay down the lacks of the method and the features to be improved in thought of a psychological model in terms of constraint posting.

In network design, the experts have at their disposal initial data, such as the type of the machines to be connected, their location, the plan of the building and some specific requirements listed by the customer. From these data, choices must be done: topological (location of the cables in the building), technological (specific properties of the network equipment), functional (architecture of the network according to the foreseen applications, depending on the distribution of the professional units,...) [25]. An experiment has been conducted, which consisted in asking six designers (3 experts and 3 novices) to deal with the same problem of network configuration. As a matter of fact, we found that precious information about the management of constraints would be brought through the comparison of the solving process from various levels of expertise. The data collected are verbal protocols obtained through simultaneous verbalization. Applied to the analysis of these protocols, the methodology highlights some interesting findings [26].

A first point is that the level of expertise is correlated to the ability of handling Prescribed and Deduced Constraints: the experts make use of prescribed constraints for about 30% of the total of items, when novices use them for 20% only and rely their process more on deduced constraints.

The distinction between Validity Constraints and Preference Constraints is pointed out, in that the way they are posted differs much: Preference Constraints are expressed at the beginning of the solving process and are satisfied late in the solving process, when Validity Constraints are formulated and satisfied simultaneously in the process.

Moreover, a remarkable difference between experts and novices is outlined in their competence of managing Preference Constraints: the novices are unable to handle these constraints by postponing their satisfaction, when this way of doing is readily used by the experts.

4. CONCLUSION

Beyond these first results, this study highlights a few spots to be investigated. A first point concerns the meta activity which is developed in the design process. Should the meta knowledge be considered as a set of meta-constraint, as Stefik does [27], or should it be understood as a set of strategies, strictly distinguished from the set of constraints? A second major point is the question of level of constraints. As a matter of fact, it seems that the constraints cannot be seen as an homogeneous set of items, regarding the level of abstraction they belong to and regarding the system of representation they refer to. The question is to know whether specific sets of constraints might be drawn, depending on how they are embedded, or according to the way they are linked [28]. Actually, this point is very dependant on the characteristics of the mechanism of constraint propagation.

These points, which have not been tackled with yet, reveal some lacks in our method. The methodological frame will have to be enlarged in these directions so as to allow a description of the processes of design in terms of constraint. This will make possible to sketch the limits and the benefits of a psychological model based on a constraint posting approach and to provide some ergonomic specifications for the implementation of CAD systems.

REFERENCES

[1] Fox, M.S., Allen, B., Strohm, G. (1982) Job-shop scheduling: an investigation in constraint directed reasoning. Proceedings of AAAI-82, Pittsburgh.

[2] Chandra, N., Marks, D. (1986) Intelligent use of constraints for activity scheduling. Applications of IA in engineering problems.

[3] Descotte, Y., Delesalle, H. (1986) Une architecture de système expert pour la planification d'activité. Proceedings of Sixth International Workshop Expert Systems and their Applications, Avignon, 1986 May.

[4] Descotte, Y., Latombe, J.C. (1985) Making compromises among antagonist constraints in a planner. Artificial Intelligence 27, 183-217.

[5] Oplobedu, A., Marcovitch, J.,Tourbier, Y. (1989) CHARME: un langage industriel de programmation par contraintes, illustré par une application chez Renault. Proceedings of Ninth International Workshop Expert Systems and their Applications, May 29-June 2 1989, 1, 55 -70.

[6] Manago, C. (1985) Lego: un système qui traite des contraintes. Proceedings of Cognitiva 85, Application à la CAO dans le bâtiment. Paris, June, 4-7.

[7] Brinkley, J., Buchanan, B., Altman, R., Duncan, B., Cornelius, C.(1987) A heuristic refinement method for constraint satisfaction problems. Knowledge systems laboratory (Report n° 87-05). Computer science department, Standford University, 1987, January.

[8] Hoc, J.M. (1988) Cognitive psychology of planning. London, Academic Press.

[9] Sacerdoti, E.D. (1974) Planning in a hierarchy of abstraction spaces. Artificial Intelligence, 5, 115-135.

[10] Sacerdoti, E.D. (1977) A structure for plans and behavior. New-York: Elsevier.

[11] Lebahar, J.C. (1983) Le dessin d'architecte. Roquevaire: Parenthèses.

[12] Stefik, M. (1981) Planning with constraints (MOLGEN: Part 1). Artificial Intelligence, 16, 111-140.

[13] Hayes-Roth, B., Hayes-Roth, F. (1979) A cognitive model of planning. Cognitive Science, 3, 275-310.

[14] Nii, H.P. (1986a) Blackboard Systems: Part One: The blackboard model of problem solving and the evolution of blackboard architectures. AI Magazine,

July 1986, 38-53.
[15] Nii, H.P. (1986b) Blackboard Systems: Part Two: Blackboard application systems, blackboard systems from a knowledge engineering perspective. AI Magazine, August 1986, 82-106.
[16] Hoc, J.M. (1983) Analysis of beginners' problem-solving strtategies in programming. In T.R.G. Green, S.J. Payne, G.C. van der Veer (Eds). The psychology of computer use. London: Academic Press, 143-158.
[17] Bisseret A., Figeac-Letang C., Falzon P. (1988) Modeling opportunistic reasonings: The cognitive activity of traffic signal setting technicians (Report #898). Rocquencourt, France: INRIA.
[18] Visser, W. (1987) Giving up a hierarchical plan in a design activity.(Report #814). Rocquencourt, France: INRIA.
[19] Eastman, C. (1970) On the analysis of intuitive design processes. Emerging methods in environmental design and planning. Gary Moore (Ed.) Proceedings of the design methods group. First International Conference, Cambridge, Mass.: MIT Press, june.
[20] Mackworth, A.K. (1987) Constraint satisfaction. In S.Shapiro (Ed), Encyclopedia of Artificial Intelligence. New-York: Wiley, 205-211.
[21] Nadel,B.A.(1986) The general consistent labeling (or constraint satisfaction) problem (Technical Report). Department of Computer Science, University of Michigan.
[22] Sriram, D., Maher, M.L. (1986). The representation and use of constraints in structural design. Applications of AI in engineering, April 1986.
[23] Janssen, P., Jégou, P., Nouguier, B., Vilarem, M.C. (1989) Problèmes de conception: une approche basée sur la satisfaction de contraintes. Proceedings of Ninth International Workshop Expert Systems and their Applications, May 29-June 2, 1989, 1, 71-84.
[24] Meseguer, P. (1989) Constraint satisfaction problems: an overview. AICOM, 2 (1), March 1989.
[25] Darses, F., Falzon, P. (1989) The design activity in networking. General remarks and first observations (Technical report). Rocquencourt, INRIA, 1989, March.
[26] Darses, F. (1989) Gestion de contraintes au cours de la résolution d'un problème de conception de réseaux informatiques (Report in print). Rocquencourt, France: INRIA
[27] Stefik, M. (1981) Planning with constraints (MOLGEN: Part 2). Artificial Intelligence, 16, 141-170.
[28] Berlandier, P. (1988) Intégration d'outils pour l'expression et la satisfaction de contraines dans un générateur de systèmes experts (Report #924). Sophia-Antipolis, France: INRIA.

SECTION I: FOUNDATIONS

SI.4 Formal Methods

Agents: Communicating interactive processes
G.D. Abowd . . . 143

Pattern recognition and interaction models
J. Finlay and M. Harrison . . . 149

Formal analysis of co-operative problem solving dialogues: Tools and techniques
P. Jeremaes . . . 155

ETAG: Extended task action grammar. A language for the description of the user's task language
M.J. Tauber . . . 163

ETAG: Some applications of a formal representation of the user interface
G.C. Van Der Veer, D. Broos, K. Donau, M.J. Fokke and F. Yap . . . 169

What is inconsistency?
P. Reisner . . . 175

Human–Computer Interaction – INTERACT '90
D. Diaper et al. (Editors)
Elsevier Science Publishers B.V. (North-Holland)

Agents: Communicating Interactive Processes

Gregory D. Abowd
Human-Computer Interaction Group
Department of Computer Science, University of York
Heslington, York YO1 5DD, UK*

Abstract

In this paper we extend the theory of communicating interactive processes based on the formalisms of CSP and Z first presented by Sufrin and He. We then use this theory to show how specifications of complex interactive systems are composed from smaller and simpler components. The theory provides a formal foundation for the investigation of multiagent models and allows the precise formulation of design principles for the development of interactive systems. We view an interactive system as a closed collection of communicating interactive processes, or agents. An agent can represent both an application and its users. We develop an example of a mouse and keyboard input to a simple display manager. This will serve as a small but realistic example to explain the features of the model.

Keywords: *interaction model, formal methods, software architecture*

1 Introduction

A theory of interactive processes was first presented by Sufrin and He [6]. This theory applies the more general work on state-based CSP to the design of interactive systems. We extend the ideas of Sufrin and He through a more constructive model. We consider an interactive system to be a collection of *communicating* interactive processes representing both a computer system and its users. The entire system is built up from the smaller components by describing how the components interact with each other.

We call these communicating interactive processes *agents* in deference to the multiagent models described in the literature. A multiagent model is similar to a stimulus-response system in which individual agents are transformed by external events or stimuli. The agents respond by producing new events that will in turn affect other agents. A formal definition of an agent will in the future allow comparison of the different multiagent architectures in order to lay bare their advantages and disadvantages as real tools for the design of complex interactive systems.

Another motivation for our agent model is the need for a scientific approach to the incorporation of psychological principles of interaction in the design of real systems. This has been the theme of much research at York with work on the PIE model [4]. The formal definition of an agent and explicit rules governing their interaction in a given system enable us to precisely translate the psychological principles into concrete design principles.

The paper proceeds by presenting the definition of the agent as a communicating interactive process. This definition is split into two parts—one part for the description of the explicit state and operations to be performed on the state and one part for the description of the ordering of events which are linked to the operations performed on the state. We next discuss the observational properties of an agent within a system and how to combine simple agents in various ways to specify complex system architectures.

To make the presentation more understandable we have chosen to describe a simple interactive system consisting of a mouse and keyboard serving as concurent input devices for a display manager. This example is realistic and adequate for explaining how to put the theory into practice. It demonstrates the power of describing simple agents and then combining them in various ways to achieve more complex concurrent systems. The use of formal methods to investigate these various constructions of concurrent systems is far less expensive than actual implementations and so we will be able to more fully explore all design possibilities. A fuller explanation of this example is contained in an ESPRIT AMODEUS working paper [1].

*This work is funded by the ESPRIT Basic Researh Action 3066, the AMODEUS project.

2 Agent Definition

As we described earlier, an agent accepts stimuli from other agents, undergoes some transformation because of those stimuli and then responds by sending out stimuli to other agents. The stimuli are *events* and we describe them as messages passed between agents along channels. We choose two sets to represent all possible channels and all possible messages. An event is an ordered pair consisting of the channel name and the message communicated along that channel. For any event e, the channel along which e occurs is given by $chan(e)$ and the message content of e is given by $mess(e)$. An event (c, m) can also be written $c.m$ to correspond to the convention used in CSP.

$$E == CHAN \times MESS$$

2.1 State description

The agent has an underlying state description. Given a particular description of the possible states S of an agent, transitions in the state space reflect the agent's response to certain stimuli. We can describe the transitions using Z schemas that contain the declaration ΔS, which represents the state before and after the transition. Any input and output for the transition are also included in the Z schema and decorated with a ? and a !, respectively. These input and output are events and correspond to the stimuli that cause the state transitions and responses that will cause transformations in other agents.

As an example, we will describe the possible states and transitions relevant to a single button mouse. It has an underlying state which contains its current position and the status of its one button. The position values are just ordered pairs of natural numbers constrained to be within some finite coordinate plane. The status of the button is either up or down. The set of states is described by the schema *MS*.

$$xmax, ymax : \mathbb{N}$$
$$Pos == 0..xmax \times 0..ymax$$
$$STATUS ::= up \mid down$$

```
_MS______________________
| position : Pos
| button : STATUS
|________________________
```

The mouse position may be changed by a move operation. The event that causes the move operation is called *delta?*, where *mess(delta?)* contains the distance by which the mouse position will change. The mouse position after the move is the output event *new_pos!* with message content equal to the new mouse location *position'*. The status of the mouse button after the move operation is the same as it was before. The channels along which the input and output events occur is as yet undetermined.

```
_MOVE____________________
| ΔMS
| delta?, new_pos! : E
|________________________
| mess(delta?) ∈ Pos
| position' = position + mess(delta?)
| mess(new_pos!) = position'
| button' = button
|________________________
```

The status of the one button on the mouse is changed by one of two operations, depending on whether the button is depressed or released. The *DEPRESS* operation is given below. The *RELEASE* operation is described similarly.

```
_DEPRESS_________________
| ΔMS
| press?, status! : E
|________________________
| mess(press?) = button_down
| position' = position
| button' = down
| mess(status!) = button'
|________________________
```

One part of the definition of an agent concentrates on the definition of the state transitions and the events linked with particular transitions. The link between sets of events and state transitions is called the *behaviour* of the agent. A behaviour function is, therefore, a mapping from sets of events to state transitions. Both the inputs *and* the outputs are linked to the state transitions. For example, the *delta?* event and the *new_pos* event are linked to the transition from original mouse state (denoted ΘMS) to the new mouse state (denoted $\Theta MS'$). We introduce the generic type $Behaviour[S]$ as a synonym for all behaviour functions definable on the state S.

$$Behaviour[S] == \mathbb{P}\, E \twoheadrightarrow (S \leftrightarrow S)$$

The notation $\mathbb{P}\, E$ describes the powerset of set E and represents all possible subsets derivable from the set E.

All of the events in which an agent may participate are given by its alphabet. The final piece of information needed to define the state-based description of an agent is its set of initial states. For any given state space S, the specification of the state-based description of an agent is as follows.

$\_\_STATE\_BASED[S]\_\_\_$

$alphabet : \mathbb{P}\, E$

$beh : Behaviour[S]$

$init : \mathbb{P}\, S$

$\mathrm{dom}\; beh \subseteq \mathbb{P}\; alphabet$

We can complete the state-based description of the mouse by noting that all of its possible states can be initial states, i.e., the mouse can be in any position in the finite coordinate plane with its button up or down. The channel along which the mouse receives events is cryptically referred to as *tom* (for "to mouse") and the channel used for output is called *mtod* (for "mouse to display").

$\_\_MOUSE\_ST\_\_\_$

$STATE\_BASED[MS]$

$$\begin{aligned} alphabet = &\\ &\{p : Pos \bullet (tom, p)\}\\ \cup\; &\{p : Pos \bullet (mtod, p)\}\\ \cup\; &\{(tom, button\_up), (tom, button\_down)\}\\ \cup\; &\{s : STATUS \bullet (mtod, s)\} \end{aligned}$$

$$\begin{aligned} beh = &\\ &\lambda\, delta?, new\_pos! : E \bullet \{MOVE \bullet \theta MS \mapsto \theta MS'\}\\ &\quad \cup \ldots \end{aligned}$$

$init = MS$

2.2 Event description

Another part of the definition of an agent describes the possible sequences of events, or *traces*, in which the process can participate. This method of description mentions no explicit state. Instead, we focus on the exact sequence of events in which the agent can be observed to participate. The method for describing the event-based description of a process is based on the traces model of CSP [5]. Because of this, we refer to the event description as being of type *CSP*. The formal definition of elements in *CSP* is given elsewhere [6, 1]. The construction of CSP-like processes is familiar to some HCI practitioners and has been used by Alexander in a rapid prototyping system [2]. For example, if P is an element of *CSP* and b is in the alphabet of P, then $b \rightarrow P$ is another element of *CSP* which participates in the event b first and then behaves as P. With the mouse, we would expect its event description to allow movement events (input along channel *tom* of how far to move the mouse and output along channel *mtod* of the mouse's new position) to be arbitrarily interleaved amongst successive depress and release events. This can be described by

$$MOUSE\_EV = CLICK \;|||\; GESTURE$$

where

$$\begin{aligned} CLICK = \;& tom.button\_down \rightarrow mtod.down \rightarrow\\ & tom.button\_up \rightarrow mtod.up \rightarrow\\ & CLICK \end{aligned}$$

$$\begin{aligned} GESTURE = \;& in : \{p : Pos \bullet tom.p\} \rightarrow\\ & out : \{p' : Pos \bullet mtod.p'\} \rightarrow\\ & GESTURE. \end{aligned}$$

The astute reader may have noticed that there are discrepancies between the state-based and event-based descriptions of the mouse. The state-based description will allow two successive depresses or releases of the button (not very realistic!), whereas the event description will only allow (quite reasonably) a depress followed by a release, and so on. On the other hand, the event description will allow the output of new mouse positions that will not be allowed by the state description. This is not a problem, since the union of the state-based and event-based descriptions will only allow the agent to engage in events that are allowed by both descriptions, as we shall see in Section 3.1.

2.3 Tying it all together

An agent has both a state-based and an event-based description. We next make explicit the input and output channels and stipulate that no channel can be both an input and output channel for the same agent.

$\_\_AGENT[S]\_\_\_$

$STATE\_BASED[S]$

CSP

$inputs, outputs : \mathbb{P}\; CHAN$

$inputs \cap outputs = \varnothing$

The agent description of the mouse is completed by noting that the input channel is *tom* and the output channel is *mtod*.

$\_\_MOUSE\_\_\_$

$AGENT[MS]$

$MOUSE\_ST$

$MOUSE\_EV$

$inputs = \{tom\}$

$outputs = \{mtod\}$

---

3 The Agent in the System

3.1 Observing an agent

The environment observes the sequence of inputs and outputs in which an agent engages. We call these sequences of events the *traces* of the agent. The traces of the agent are only those sequences of events allowed by *both* the event-based description and state-based description of that agent.

A trace of an agent, therefore, contains a history of all communicated events. Assume we have an agent A. We are interested in the relationship between the inputs to and the outputs from A because these inputs and outputs represent the interface between A and its environment. If A were an interactive system minus the user agents, these inputs and outputs would represent the user interface. By making precise the relationship between these inputs and outputs we can make restrictions on them that are in accord with psychological claims about the usability of the user interface.

Sufrin and He give sufficient motivation for using the process model as the vehicle for precise formulation of usability constraints. Our model is equally expressive and has the added advantage of being more constructive. The restrictions that are based on psychological knowledge of user interfaces become design principles for someone familiar with our agent model. Hence, it may be possible to bridge the gap between cognitive psychology and computer science in an attempt to build usable interactive systems. We will now concentrate in the rest of this paper on explaining how our agent model can be used to build specifications of interactive systems.

3.2 Combining agents

Given two agents A and B, we can form a third agent which behaves like A or B. If the choice is made by another agent—possibly a user agent—then we call the choice external. The external choice between A and B will be denoted

$A \Box B.$

If the choice is not made by another agent, then we call the choice internal. The internal choice between A and B will be denoted

$A \sqcap B.$

The observable behaviour of the new agent will correspond to that of exactly one of the components.

We can use external choice to provide another description of the mouse that may better point out the choice a user has between moving the mouse and pressing or releasing one of its buttons. One agent will govern the movement of the mouse and the other agent will govern the status of the button. The whole mouse will then be given as the external choice between moving—the *SWEEP* agent—and clicking the one button—the *BUTTON* agent.

There are two advantages to describing the mouse this way. One advantage, which we mentioned already is that it makes more obvious the actual functionality of the mouse as an input device. Every input event in which the mouse engages is actually chosen by the agent that interacts with the mouse, typically the user. The other advantage is that the individual agents which make up the mouse will be even simpler to describe than the description we gave in Section 2. We will use the external choice combinator to construct the mouse from its simple parts.

As an example, the SWEEP agent has as its state simply a location in the finite coordinate plane.

```
┌─ LOCATION ─────────────────
│ position : Pos
└────────────────────────────
```

The mouse position may be changed by a move operation identical to the one given in Section 2 except without mention of the button status. Any state is a possible initial state and the input and output channels are again *tom* and *mtod*. The event-based description is given by the CSP description *SWEEP_EV* and stipulates that the agent can participate in one moving operation and then it terminates successfully. That is the purpose of *SKIP* in the definition; it signals successful termination by participating in the special event $\surd$.

```
┌─ SWEEP ──────────────────────────────────
│ AGENT[S]
│ SWEEP_EV : CSP
├──────────────────────────────────────────
│ alphabet =     {p : Pos • (tom, p)}
│              ∪ {p : Pos • (mtod, p)}
│              ∪ {√}
│ beh = Link(MOVE)
│ init = LOCATION
│ SWEEP_EV = p, p' : Pos • tom?p → mtod!p'→
│       SKIP_alphabet
│ inputs = {tom}
│ oututs = {mtod}
└──────────────────────────────────────────
```

The *BUTTON* agent is similarly described. The agent which represents one action of a mouse, either a movement or a button click, is described as

$ACTION = SWEEP \Box BUTTON.$

Sometimes it will be easiest to define an agent by specifying that it behaves as one agent followed sequentially by another. If A and B are agents, we write the sequential composition of A followed by B as

$A \mathbin{;} B.$

A full description of the mouse now involves the successive sequential composition of single mouse actions. We use * to represent the repetition of composition.

$MOUSE = ACTION^*$

As an aside, we point out that many mouse-based systems rely on the coordination of clicks and moves to carry out a rich set of operations in the application domain. It may appear that we are not allowing this kind of flexibility in our description of the mouse by separating the movements and clicks. What we are actually doing is separating the operations performed on a mouse by a user from the operations that those combined mouse events cause in the application.

When agents are intended to perform concurrently it matters whether or not they operate independently. If they are intended to operate simultaneously and independently, then we write their *interleaved* combination as

$A \mid\mid\mid B.$

Interleaved agents in our model correspond to PAC agents on the same level of a hierarchy, (see [3]). Instead of using external choice to model the separability of mouse movements with button clicks, we could have chosen to model the mouse as the interleaving between an agent which governs the continual motion of the mouse and an agent which governs the continual clicking of the button.

$MOUSE2 = SWEEP^* \mid\mid\mid BUTTON^*$

This may be a more intuitive way to model the mouse. The external choice variant emphasizes a continual choice of either a move or a click. The point we would like to make in presenting alternative ways to model the same mouse is that there are advantages in investigating all of the options. We are able to investigate many options and analyze their consequences on the user interface without having to do any expensive implementation.

If the concurrent behaviour of two agents requires some synchronization, then we need another combinator to reflect this interaction. In the PAC model, this kind of cooperating behaviour is seen between a PAC agent and one of its direct descendants in the hierarchy. The synchronization we now discuss is when the two processes participate in the same event. This occurs when the output from one agent must become input for the other, if the communicated event occurs along a common channel. We represent this synchronized interaction as

$A \mid\mid B.$

When building complex agents from smaller interactive processes, it may be desirable to hide the events that occur on internal channels. Then the traces of the complex agent will only reveal the communication events that happen on channels into or out from the environment. Given a set of channel names CS, we denote the hiding of events along that channel as

$A/CS.$

We will discuss an example of this interaction and hiding when we present the display manager in Section 4.

4 The display manager

The other common input device in most interactive systems is the keyboard. In our model, each key is an agent which participates in only one *PRESS* operation. The input events, which occur along the input channel ***tokb***, will be name of the key pressed and the output events, which occur along the output channel ***kbtod***, will be the character value associated to the key. The translation from key name to character value is contained in the state of the key agent. If the agent for the **a** key is called $KEYA$ and a similar convention is used for the naming of the other key agents, we can represent a keystroke agent as the external choice between all of the key agents.

$KEYSTROKE = (KEYA \,\square\, KEYB \,\square \cdots)$

The input stream to a display manager is then the repeated iteration of an external choice between a keystroke action and a mouse action.

$INPUT = (KEYSTROKE \,\square\, ACTION)^*$

Next we define a simple display manager that accepts input from the mouse and keyboard along channels ***mtod*** and ***kbtod***. The display manager's state consists of the current insertion point, the mouse location and a mapping from the finite coordinate plane (the model of the screen) to visual images. The visual images are either the characters or the mouse cursor or the insertion point cursor. These visual images are described by the type V. The display manager's state is given below.

DST
$cursor : Pos$
$mouse\_loc : Pos$
$display : Pos \rightarrow V$

Input from the keyboard is echoed by altering the *display* mapping at the insertion point to be equal to the character value received in the message on channel ***kbtod***. The insertion point is incremented by one (with due consideration of boundary conditions) and the new *display* mapping marks the insertion point's new location. The output event from this operation is the *display* mapping. When the mouse button is depressed, the insertion point is changed to the current mouse location and the *display* mapping reflects this change. Releasing the mouse button has no effect on the underlying state.

The formal definitions of the insert, move cursor, and move mouse operations are omitted. The event-based description of the display manager adds no further stipulations to the sequences of events, and so is given the weakest definition, which simply means that any sequence of events in the alphabet A is allowed. Any state of the display manager is a possible initial state. The input channels are *mtod* and *kbtod*, while the output channel is *dout*. All of this information is sufficient to define the display manager as an agent, $DISPLAY1$.

It is not necessary to model the display manager state with the mapping from coordinate positions to visual objects. Instead, we could view the display manager as a driver for yet another agent, which is the actual display. In this case, we would want the agent defined by synchronous interaction of the new display manager with the visual agent,

$DISPLAY2 \parallel VISUAL,$

to be the same as the original display manager. Then, since it would not matter to the environment which display manager was involved, we could model the display manager as the internal choice between the two display managers described above.

$DISP\_MAN = DISPLAY1 \sqcap DISPLAY2$

Together, the mouse, keyboard, and display manager make up a simple system whereby the user can echo character messages to a visual display. This system is a complex agent formed from the agents already described. The output from the input devices becomes the input for the display manager, so we must combine the agent $INPUT$ with the agent $DISPLAY$ using the interaction combinator of Section 3.2.

$ECHO\_1 = INPUTS \parallel DISP\_MAN$

In addition, we want to hide the communication that occurs along the channels *mtod* and *kbtod*, because those are internal to the agent $SIMPLE$.

$ECHO = ECHO\_1 \ / \ \{kbtod, mtod\}$

5 Conclusions

The agent model we have presented very briefly above provides a general tool for describing and analysing interactive systems. We have demonstrated how this model allows the description of a simple interactive system based on the construction of smaller subsystems. A formal approach has also allowed investigation of alternative design decisions without expensive implementation costs. A concise presentation of design options can then be offered to psychologists for analysis of the user interface at its most primitive level. We have extended the work on abstract models of interaction, elevating the results of prior work done at York and other places to a more constructive level that can positively affect the designers of interactive systems.

Acknowledgements

Many thanks go to my colleagues in York for their careful consideration of the ideas behind this paper and for their many welcome comments and corrections of previous drafts. I would especially like to single out Michael Harrison and Roger Took. A special thanks also goes to Bernard Sufrin from the Programming Research Group at Oxford for his initial inspiration of this work.

References

[1] ABOWD, G. D. Communicating interactive processes. Esprit BRA project AMODEUS working paper RP2/WP2, February 1990.

[2] ALEXANDER, H. *Formally-Based Tools and Techniques for Human-Computer Dialogues.* Ellis Horwood Ltd., Chicester, 1987.

[3] COUTAZ, J. PAC, an object oriented model for dialog design. In *Human-Computer Interaction — INTERACT'87*, H. J. Bullinger and B. Shackel, Eds. North-Holland, Amsterdam, 1987, pp. 431–436.

[4] DIX, A. J. *Formal Methods and Interactive Systems: Principles and Practice.* PhD thesis, University of York, 1987.

[5] HOARE, C. A. R. *Communicating Sequential Processes.* Prentice Hall International, UK, Ltd., London, 1985.

[6] SUFRIN, B., AND HE, J. Specification, refinement and analysis of interactive processes. In *Formal methods in Human Computer Interaction*, M. D. Harrison and H. W. Thimbleby, Eds. Cambridge University Press, Cambridge, 1990, pp. 153–200.

Human–Computer Interaction – INTERACT '90
D. Diaper et al. (Editors)
Elsevier Science Publishers B.V. (North-Holland)

Pattern Recognition and Interaction Models

Janet Finlay and Michael Harrison
Human-Computer Interaction Group
Department of Computer Science, University of York
Heslington, York YO1 5DD, UK*

Abstract

Human Computer Interaction can usefully be described in terms of a sequence of user and system events. *A priori* traces of such event sequences, as specified by a mathematical model, can be used in the evaluation of interactive systems by contrasting them to *a posteriori* traces of actual user behaviour. We use pattern recognition techniques to automate this comparison, identifying points in the interaction where a user's behaviour is sub-optimal. We describe work in this area relating to a bibliographic database system.

1 Introduction

Human Computer Interaction can usefully be viewed as a sequence of events. The confluence of actions taken by users, and states within an interactive system, form a "trace". This view underlies models of interactive behaviour developed at York by Dix et al.[3]. A trace produced from such a model can be considered as an *a priori* trace and can be contrasted with the *a posteriori* traces recorded with the purpose of analysing user behaviour. (We will for clarity refer to these as "trace" and "log" respectively). However at an appropriate level of abstraction there is a morphism between these two. We aim to use this morphism to strengthen the use of both, and show an example of an initial study to illustrate how this might be achieved.

Neural-based pattern recognition techniques, which learn by example, may be used to analyse the traces. Our aim is twofold: we can detect points in a log where a user has deviated from the predicted trace, allowing us to easily identify "critical incidents" (Wright and Monk[6]) in the interaction; and we can suggest possible traces on the basis of a generalization across a number of logs. In this paper we concentrate on the former. In the next section we discuss the nature of traces in general before going on to consider an example trace from the system under consideration.

2 Traces

We can distinguish three models of an interactive system: the system model (S); the interaction model (M); and the implementation (I). The system model is an abstraction of interactive behaviour that may be used as a basis for the implementation (I). S describes features of interactive behaviour in terms of the computer system, in a way that aids understanding of the structure of the implementation. The interaction model embodies claims about usage as a superstructure on S incorporating knowledge of the user, application and environment. Superfluous mappings and structures, such as the display templates and cycle structures described elsewhere by Harrison et al.[4], are added to the system model. Thus M is a filtered view of the system which captures claims about how the system will be used. It then becomes possible to consider mismatches between the interaction model's predictions about use and actual use, making it possible to analyse usability problems.

Associated with M and S are sets of traces, *traces*(M) and *traces*(S). These sets, which are analogous to those of Hoare's CSP[5], contain admissible dialogue sequences of M and S. The set *traces*(M) takes into account claims about the usability of S.

Complimentary to the set of Hoare-like rules, we are also interested in the set of logs that is generated by means of an experiment with the system (*exp*(I)). This set of logs is generated by observing actual behaviour of the user by experiment.

2.1 An example: REF

We will illustrate these concepts by means of a concrete example, a bibliographic database system, REF. REF supports conventional database operations including *search*, *delete*, *insert*, and *alter* as well as providing

*This work was funded by ESPRIT Basic Research Action 3066, the AMODEUS project.

facilities for creating and maintaining libraries of references. It has a menu-based interface, where items are selected by typing the initial letter at the keyboard.

An interaction model of REF has been derived based upon the notion of cycles (Harrison et al.[4]). REF usage is characterized by a cycle structure, where the appearance of the Main menu indicates the start (and end) of a cycle, and where the result is not modified until the end of the cycle. The cycle structure is a required property of the model M, but is not necessarily a property of the model S. This clarifies the distinction between the two models: the structures in M are intended to elucidate the interaction and may not be reflected in the implementation.

The cyclic pattern can be seen when we describe REF in terms of event sequences, in a notation such as CSP. Space does not permit us to provide a full description so we shall concentrate on a single example, the select operation. The process MAIN describes the presentation of the main menu, the available choices, and subsequent events. It is shown in part. The process SELECT describes the events involved in executing a select operation. In both cases events may be either user or system events. We have in view a collection of events in this description, some of which are internal system events (for example "search!y" denoting the system event of searching the database on the value "y"); these are unseen by the user, although their effects are important. Again we can illustrate this more clearly by considering the models S and M. The event "search!y" is in S, since it is an important part of the implementation of the database system. However it is not in M as it is unseen by the user and does not therefore form part of the interaction *per se*.

```
MAIN=(main_menu ->
       ( choice_s -> SELECT
       | choice_d -> DISPLAY
       | .......))

SELECT=(select_menu -> choice?x
        -> panel!x -> in_data?y
        -> search!y
        -> show_selection_box
        -> MAIN)
```

The cycle pattern can be clearly seen. Using a description such as this, we can produce a CSP trace to describe the behaviour of the system under certain conditions, for example where the user selects references by the author Smith:

```
< main_menu, choice_s,
  select_menu, choice.n,
  panel.name, in_data.Smith,
  selection.Smith,
  show_selection_box, main_menu
>
```

This is a member of the set *traces*(M), rather than *traces*(S), since we are only concerned with interaction events (note that the internal system event "search!y" is not included in the trace). A complete set of valid traces can be produced in this way. These are *traces*(M).

In addition to formal analysis of this type, use of REF is logged for evaluation purposes, resulting in the set of logs *exp*(I). These also contain user and system events, but no internal system events. Although different in form and notation, both *traces*(M) and *exp*(I) deal with the interaction in terms of events. Assuming the level of description is compatible we can therefore compare the traces of expected behaviour (*traces*(M)) with the logs of actual behaviour (*exp*(I)). This enables us to identify problematic areas in actual use. Two types of problem may arise: incidents where the user's behaviour is sub-optimal but correct; and those where the user's action is erroneous and requires recovery. Both can be considered as clashes between *traces*(M) and *exp*(I), that is, between the designer's model of the interaction and the user's. In the next section we propose a method by which such comparison can be automated in order to facilitate evaluation, and we demonstrate how this method might be exploited.

3 Pattern Recognition

A way of viewing traces (and logs) is as patterns of interaction, where each trace event is an element in a pattern string. So for example a trace such as the one cited in the previous section can be abstracted or "coded" into a simple character string:

```
MsSn?1M
```

In this code each character represents a particular event, M is the appearance of the Main menu, for example. Certain information is abstracted out, such as the value of data entered, since this is variable and cannot be predicted. However the event of data entry is retained (represented in the abstraction by "?").

This is an encoding of an instance of *traces*(M), representing a cycle. The return to the display template of the Main menu (represented by "M") can be seen, as can the update of the result at the end of the cycle (represented by "1", indicating that a single reference has been extracted as the current selection).

The comparison between traces and logs can now be framed as a pattern recognition problem, in which automatic pattern recognizers such as neural networks can be used. The set of traces forms the training set and the logs represent potentially noisy patterns to be classified.

There are a number of advantages in using neural techniques in this area. They learn by example and are therefore trained by the presentation of known patterns rather than by, for example, explicit rule formulation. This is useful since we have a set of known patterns in *traces*(M) and we may not easily be able to characterize these in rule form. In addition neural pattern recognizers have generalization properties which enable them to interpolate from the known examples to classify unseen and untrained patterns. This allows us to present patterns from *exp*(I) which are not in the set *traces*(M), and still expect recognition to the closest match.

In this work we use a neural system developed at York, ADAM (Advanced Distributed Associative Memory). This system has the advantage over more conventional back-propagation techniques that it is relatively efficient and learns without iterative training. Its operation is explained in detail elsewhere by Austin[1] but is summarized in the next section.

3.1 ADAM

The ADAM system is an associative memory, and as might be expected, operates by "associating" a response to a particular known input, so that when that input (or a significant part of it) is presented to the memory the associated response is given. Each input pattern is translated into a bit pattern, by a process known as "n-tupling", where the complete pattern is sampled by a number of tuples, each of which will set a unique bit in an input vector, according to its input. The mapping of elements onto the tuples may be random, or specific, for example, mapping each element of the original pattern onto a tuple which will set a unique bit in the input vector, as a function of the element's ASCII code. The advantages of tupling are twofold. Firstly, each element of the pattern is treated separately (rather than taking the pattern in its entirety) so that any pattern containing that element in that position will get a response from that tuple. This allows the system to recognize patterns that it has not seen before. Secondly, a sparse input is provided, avoiding saturation which would prevent the memory from being able to distinguish patterns accurately.

The memory can be visualized as a matrix of initially unlinked wires, a horizontal wire for each bit position in the input vector, and a number of vertical wires. In training, each of the input vector bit patterns is presented to the memory along with a unique, randomly generated, sparse bit pattern representing the class to which the example belongs. The class pattern has a known number of bits set. The input appears on the horizontal wires, while the class pattern is presented on the vertical wires. A link is made in the memory wherever an active vertical wire crosses an active horizontal wire. On recall, a pattern is presented as before, and the class pattern is calculated by summing the number of links in each column which are on an active horizontal wire. This is "n-point thresholded", by retrieving the n highest values (where n is the number of bits set in the class pattern) to return the class pattern which matches the input most closely. It should be noted that the class pattern can be recovered even if not all the elements of the originally taught input pattern are present in the target pattern, since the thresholding provides us with the best match.

This process is illustrated in the following diagram which shows an example of training and recall in the memory. The first matrix shows the links set in the memory for the input pattern 1011001, following the training of that pattern. The second matrix shows the same memory, after training with many more patterns (hence many more links are set). The first pattern is presented again and the correct class pattern recalled by n-point thresholding.

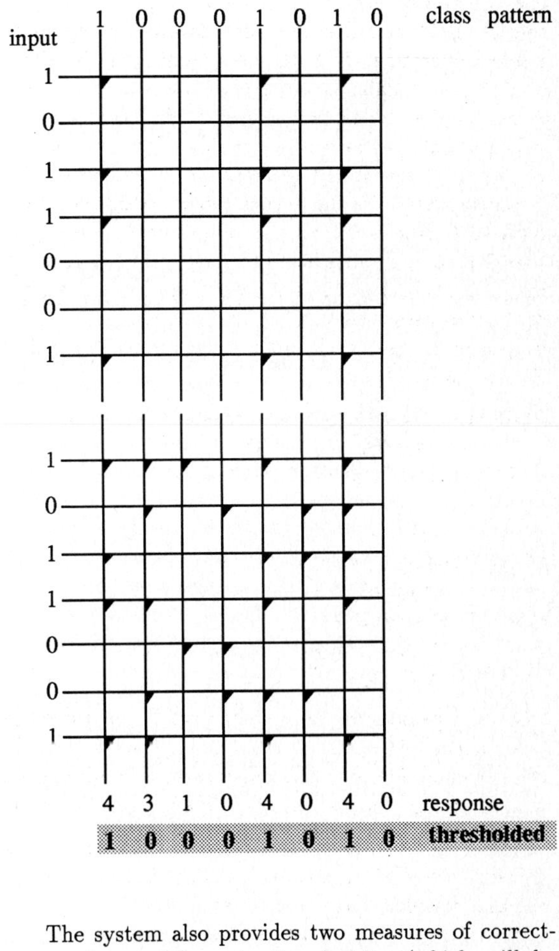

The system also provides two measures of correctness: the confidence in the decision (which will be 100% only if all input lines are identical to the pattern trained), and a distance measure, which indicates how far the pattern is from the next nearest class.

4 Testing the theory

Previous work at York, by Beale et al.[2], has exploited this view of traces as patterns of interaction in the area of automatic user modelling, using ADAM experimentally to classify users on the basis of expertise and task. Following on from this work, we carried out a small experiment using traces and logs from REF, to illustrate how the technique can be used to detect deviations from valid use in actual usage logs. Evaluative work has identified many "critical incidents" in REF usage where the user follows a sub-optimal or erroneous solution path (Wright and Monk[6]). We took four such known critical incidents and attempt to detect them in logs using ADAM trained on valid trace patterns.

The training set comprised 529 examples of valid traces, representing eleven cycles or "classes". Some examples are shown below.

Class/Cycle	An example pattern
Alter	MaCaV?d9%%
Select	MsSn?234%%
Selwhere	MsWaSk14%%
Display	MdDf34%%%%
Library	MwLa00%%%%

These were mapped onto an input pattern of 10 characters (the average trace length) since the current implementation requires a fixed length input vector. Traces longer than this were curtailed; those shorter were "padded" with a neutral character (in the examples above %). The specific meanings of the particular abstractions shown here is not important; however in general a capital letter represents a menu display, a lower case character input to a menu, "?" represents data entry, and a numeric character a display of selected references. In terms of our previous discussion of S, M, and I, these patterns can be viewed as an alternative representation of *traces*(M). The input pattern was "tupled" to produced a sparse bit pattern, the tuples sampling each element in the pattern and setting 1 bit in 96 using a function of the element's ASCII code. This vector formed the input to the memory, together with a unique bit pattern, with 4 bits set in 40, representing the class to which the pattern belongs. When trained as described previously, the memory achieves 100% recognition of the training set, with 100% confidence and high distance measures, indicating that the patterns can be easily distinguished, as would be expected.

In addition, the memory was presented with 94 logs containing one of four known critical incidents, produced by actual users under experimental conditions; these are examples of *exp*(I) patterns. The four critical incidents are as follows:

1. failure to save alterations to a reference;
2. typing an ineffectual command;
3. typing data input without first selecting the field name;
4. accidentally escaping from the main menu resulting in a costly reload of the library.

The first occurs when the user performs alterations to a reference but fails to save these by entering a "done" command. Instead they type "escape", as this is a means of moving up a menu level. This is an error caused by the user's failure to notice the "done" command, and can be costly as the alteration must be redone. The second incident happens when the user selects a command which is currently disabled because a prerequisite to valid use of that command, usually that there be a selected reference, has not been met. Examples of such commands are display, alter, and remove. These commands make no sense if there are no selected references. This is not an error which requires recovery; the usual effect is that nothing happens. However it does represent sub-optimal behaviour. The third incident is another example of sub-optimal behaviour, which may, as a side effect, cause an error from which the user will have to recover. The user types a data string (such as an author's name) without first selecting a field (such as "author"). The effect of this will depend on what characters are typed: if they are not valid menu options nothing will happen and the input will be treated as ineffectual; if one character is a valid input the system will treat it as a command and the resulting action may require error recovery. The final example of a critical incident occurs because the user does not notice a change in the display which indicates a return to the main menu, and so "escapes" to reach this menu. Since the user is already there the effect is to take her to the next menu level, which is the menu for choosing a new library. The result is that the user must reload the library, a time-consuming operation. Again this is an example of an error which requires the user to take action to recover. Each of these critical incidents is an instance of a clash between *traces*(M) and *exp*(I). Examples of logs containing these critical incidents are shown below (the abstractions used are the same as previously; in addition > signifies "escape").

Incident	An example pattern
1	MaCn9?9C>%
2	MdMsSy?2%%
3	MsSSmith?>
4	M>La00%%%%

It should be noted that in attempting to classify examples of these critical incidents, we do not expect the system to identify them as critical incidents, since it has not been trained to do so. Rather, we are looking for deviations from perfect patterns which may indicate the presence of a critical incident, and for consistency in these deviations which will enable us to cluster similar incidents. For example we would hope that incidents of the first type would be classified as imperfect Alter cycles.

4.1 Results

The examples of the first critical incident (17 logs) were all classified as Alter cycles, but with between 80-90% confidence, indicating that they vary by between 1 and 2 characters from the valid trace.

The second set of critical incidents (24 logs) are more variable since several commands can be ineffective if there are no selected references (for example display, alter, remove etc.). However these logs generally have a similar form: a command is issued at the main menu, the main menu reappears immediately, and a select cycle follows. Most of the logs (79%) are classified as Selwhere cycles (i.e. select where there is already a current selection), with lower confidences than previously (between 50 and 80%) and with low distances, indicating that the patterns contain elements of several classes. This is due to position dependence: because the logs typically have two characters before the select cycle they are generally more similar to the Selwhere cycle (which also has this pattern) than the Select cycle itself. The other logs are classified as Select or Display, where these represent the main elements of the trace. All the logs match the class representing the ineffectual command on at least one point, indicating that a small part of the pattern is recognized as that cycle. "Fine tuning" of the thresholding technique could identify this if necessary.

The third set of critical incidents (36 logs) is perhaps the most variable as what the user types as a data string is recorded fully. However most of these incidents occur in select cycles of some type. All are classified as Select or Selwhere cycles with varying confidence (47-90%), but generally high distance measures, indicating that they are not close to any other class.

The final set of incidents (17 logs) are all classified as Library (selecting a new library) or Initial (selecting the first library). Confidences are relatively high (but below 100%) suggesting that there is only one element difference between the incident and a valid cycle (corresponding to hitting the "escape" key rather than the key to select the "change library" option). Distances are fairly low, due to the fact that these are short cycles which contain several padding characters, a common factor with other cycles.

The results are encouraging and indicate that it is possible to automatically recognize these types of deviation from valid traces. Interpreting the results of the net must currently be done manually but in the next section we suggest ways in which parts of this too could be automated.

5 Future Work

The current ADAM system has demonstrated several limitations which must be overcome. Firstly the length of the input trace is currently fixed so that inputs shorter than this length are "padded out" and inputs which are longer are curtailed, diluting the information content and losing perhaps vital information. A version of ADAM which is currently under development will resolve this problem by providing the facility to feed output back into the memory, so allowing varying length patterns to be built up.

Secondly, the current system can identify occurrences of deviations but cannot diagnose them. The extended version provides an occlusion function which will give the difference between the new pattern and the original, which can then either be identified manually or recognized by a second memory trained on critical incidents.

Other limitations are associated with the nature of abstraction itself. In treating the trace as a pattern we dispose of information which is variable, such as the values of data entered. However it is at this level that several critical incidents occur. A possible approach is to take a finer grain of abstraction, perhaps considering the traces at a keystroke level. This is problematic in that there is a potentially infinite set of valid traces at this level. However it may be possible to achieve satisfactory results using variables for training purposes.

Finally, several critical incidents can only be recognized in the larger context, since they may be valid in themselves, but are actually sub-optimal to the user's current task. This problem may be helped by providing a series of memories each identifying logs at different levels. In this way a particular incident can be placed within a wider context.

In summary, the work described here is in its early stages, but the results to date (and in related work) suggest that it has potential in aiding the identification of mismatches between traces and logs. The limitations can be reduced or resolved by using more complex memory configurations. It should be noted that some critical incidents are very difficult to identify from logs manually, and require re-enactment of the user's behaviour, since they demand knowledge of the user's intention which may not be available. These are unlikely to be identified by an automatic pattern recognizer. This work should therefore be seen in the context of other research, particularly that of Wright and Monk[6], which handles more complex incidents. However if even the simpler incidents can be handled automatically we have a useful tool to aid evaluation.

Acknowledgements

The authors would like to thank Russell Beale for his work in developing the implementation of ADAM used here, and his comments on earlier drafts of this paper; and our colleagues in the HCI group at York for much useful discussion.

References

[1] J. Austin. Adam: A distributed associative memory fo scene analysis. In M. Caudill and C. Butler, editors, *Proceedings of the First International Conference on Neural Networks*, pages IV–285. IEEE, San Diego, 1987.

[2] R. Beale, J. Finlay, J. Austin, and M Harrison. User modelling by classification: A neural-based approach. In J. G. Taylor and C. L. T. Mannion, editors, *New Developments in Neural Computing.* Adam Hilger IOP, 1989.

[3] A. J. Dix, M. D. Harrison, C. Runciman, and H. W. Thimbleby. Interaction models and the principled design of interactive systems. In H. Nichols and D. S. Simpson, editors, *European Software Engineering Conference*, pages 127–135. Springer Lecture Notes, 1987.

[4] M. D. Harrison, C. R. Roast, and P. C. Wright. Complementary methods for the iterative design of interactive systems. In G. Salvendy and M.J. Smith, editors, *Designing and Using Human-Computer Interfaces and Knowledge Based Systems*, pages 651–658. Elsevier Scientific, 1989.

[5] C. A. R. Hoare. *Communicating Sequential Processes.* Prentice Hall International, 1985.

[6] P. C. Wright and A. F. Monk. Evaluation for design. In *People and Computers V.* Cambridge University Press, 1989.

FORMAL ANALYSIS OF CO-OPERATIVE PROBLEM SOLVING DIALOGUES: TOOLS AND TECHNIQUES

P Jeremaes

Hewlett-Packard Laboratories, Filton Road, Bristol BS12 6QZ, England

We are developing task specific theories of co-operative problem solving and using these theories to derive methods for engineering knowledge-based systems which support co-operative human-computer interaction. Research to date has concentrated on the collection of empirical data to support the hypothesis that co-operativity in this context is warranted and to develop our initial theories of co-operative interaction. This paper presents an overview of the role that formal tools and techniques have played in helping to analyse that data and in formulating tentative theories of co-operation.

1. INTRODUCTION

The primary focus of our research is on developing task specific theories of co-operative problem solving. These theories are being used to derive methods for engineering knowledge-based systems which support co-operative human-computer interaction. It has been established that only limited notions of co-operativity are currently supported by interactive knowledge-based systems and it is believed that additional features characteristic of human-human co-operation play an important role in making these systems more useful to the user (Stenton (1987)). Research to date has concentrated on the collection of empirical data to support the hypothesis that co-operativity in this context is in fact warranted and to develop our initial theories of co-operative interaction. This paper presents an overview of the role that formal tools and techniques have played in helping to analyse that data and in formulating tentative theories of co-operation.

The formal tools that we speak of are formal logics, of various flavours, and specification techniques which are based upon these logics have been employed to characterize principles of co-operation and components of domain knowledge upon which these principles are applied. From a software engineering perspective the need for specification techniques requires no special introduction; specification is considered to be an integral component of all principled approaches to software development. However, the major benefit of these techniques has been as a conceptual aid in helping to extract from the empirical data dialogue control strategies that capture specific properties of co-operativity whilst ensuring that such strategies are computationally tractable.

It has been found that much of the related research on dialogue theory establishes high-level descriptive principles that participants engaged in dialogue of a particular kind (eg. co-operative, competitive, argumentative, etc.) adhere to. These principles, although sometimes accepted intuitively, are often difficult to translate into meaningful statements that may be used to design implementations of knowledge-based dialogue participants. The pragmatic conventions established by Grice provide examples of this high-level analysis of dialogue (Grice (1975)). A conceptual leap has to be made to convert high-level descriptive principles into prescriptive dialogue rules and strategies (the role of dialogue rules and strategies is explained in Sections 2.2 and 2.3, respectively). This is necessary to prescribe the behaviour of a knowledge-based dialogue participant. Use of formal tools and techniques is intended to aid the process of defining dialogue rules that characterize co-operative interaction and dialogue strategies for specific problem solving tasks. The formal rigour helps to establish an appropriate level of analysis that avoids unnecessary conceptual gymnastics.

The progress that has been made so far has shown that a number of elementary properties of interest can be characterized with well established formal machinery (ie. a sorted first-order logic). Insight has also been gained in understanding some of the logical extensions that are required in order to continue with our approach to constructing theories of co-operation dealing with more complex interactions. More specifically, a dynamic logic of actions was introduced to characterize the dynamic constraints of a configuration task. This particular task domain identifies the need to be able to characterize behavioural information about dialogue participants interactively performing a configuration task and about the planning activities that underlie co-operative response strategies. Formally this is achieved by extending the dynamic logic with deontic operators that express the rights (permissions) and commitments (obligations) of co-operating dialogue participants. These logical extensions are described informally in this paper in the context of the empirical results that motivated the need for them. A formal account of the logical issues involved is given in Jeremaes et al. (1986).

The empirical data consists primarily of query response pairs, ie. a problem solver (or user) formulates a query and an expert supplies a co-operative response. Clearly the use of the term dialogue in the title of this paper is being used rather loosely inasmuch as sequences of such pairs or other forms of user-expert interaction containing, for example, assertions, retractions, denials, etc., are not being considered. However, the framework for dialogue analysis that is being developed and used in our investigations is of more general applicability and will at a later stage facilitate the analysis of contextual information, user intentions, and other features of more complex dialogues.

In what follows an outline of the framework used for dialogue analysis is introduced in Section 2. In Section 3 the results of an experiment will be discussed with respect to the standard and non-standard logical tools used in the analysis of the empirical data generated. The experiment deals with the configuration of HP computer hardware products. A résumé of our research results with respect to the formal tools and techniques that have been employed is given in Section 4.

2. A FRAMEWORK FOR DIALOGUE ANALYSIS

2.1. The Expert Knowledge Base

Before taking a look at some of the results from our analysis of empirical data, it is first necessary to identify the basic components of co-operative interaction and to construct a framework for dialogue analysis. Figure 1 shows the two participants involved in the interaction, ie. the User and the Expert, and the Knowledge Base (KB). The Expert generates the responses ($R_1, \ldots R_n$) to the User queries

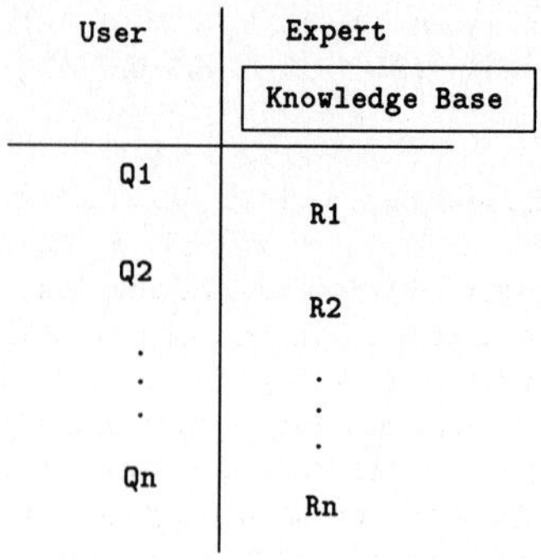

Figure 1: Components of Dialogue Analysis

($Q_1, \ldots Q_n$) based upon the knowledge in the KB. The Expert KB is looked upon as being a theory of the task domain. In simplistic terms it contains the axioms that define how that domain works. Something more will be said about the required structure of the KB in Section 2.4.

To infer that our analysis framework is based only upon query/response pairs is, of course, not strictly true. The User makes other forms of input (akin to a speech act) in the dialogues considered, ie. assertions, denials, etc., and the Expert responds in a variety of ways. Further to this, all forms of user-system interaction are being considered when talking about User input and Expert output, ie. direct manipulation, menu selection, command assertions, iconic prompts etc. Co-operativity is something that we believe will be realized through many different interface media. Our current interest in human-human natural language dialogue merely provides a starting point from which an understanding of co-operative dialogue in general can be developed.

2.2. Dialogue Rules

The next important component to consider in the framework for dialogue analysis is the set of rules which characterize what is allowed to happen at any stage of a dialogue with respect to the User input and Expert output. These are called the Dialogue Rules. It is important to distinguish the role of a Dialogue Rule from that of a Dialogue Strategy to be introduced below. In every day conversation Dialogue Rules are (nearly always) implicitly understood by the participants involved. Protocols of turn taking, question-answering, etc., are considered to be fundamental to the definition of rational behaviour itself (Cohen & Levesque (1987)).

If on the other hand more formal interactions are considered, such as court room proceedings or debate in Parliament, then immediately explicit rules of interaction are revealed. To define what constitutes a legal (ie. valid) dialogue requires the explicit definition of DIALOGUE RULES in our analytical framework. DIALOGUE RULES deal with the rights and commitments that participants have at any particular stage in a dialogue. Indirectly DIALOGUE RULES characterize the style of interaction that is desirable, they describe the step-by-step development of dialogues. It is hoped that attention to naturally occurring dialogues will enable us to define *descriptive* DIALOGUE RULES from which potentially useful *prescriptive* rules for user-system interaction can be designed. They do not say how particular responses are generated but stipulate the effects that those responses have on the rights and commitments of participants (Barth & Krabbe (1982)). Our current interest is in simple query/response pairs, accepting implicitly the rule that responses follow queries, consequently nothing further will be said about DIALOGUE RULES in this paper.

2.3. Dialogue Strategy

When the EXPERT is placed under a commitment to respond to the USER there has to exist a method for generating an appropriate response. This method is referred to as a DIALOGUE STRATEGY. This paper only considers the types of strategy required for generating responses to USER queries. In addition to these the EXPERT requires strategies to deal with other forms of USER input. Whether or not a formulation of USER problem solving strategies will also be required in our analysis remains an open question. If any notion of USER modelling becomes important in our treatment of co-operativity then such strategies are an integral part of understanding and predicting USER behaviour. This has not been the case so far. An example of a DIALOGUE STRATEGY derived from the empirical data is given in Sections 3. Tentative theories of co-operativity will be realized in the prescriptive strategies used by the EXPERT participant.

2.4. Formal Query Evaluation

The components of the framework presented so far serve to provide a conceptual picture of the USER/EXPERT interactions. The pictorial presentation of these components (in Figure 1) is also theoretically motivated. Proof methods for formal logics can be presented in a variety of ways ranging from axiomatic systems through sequent systems to tableaux techniques. These modes of presentation have been developed to explore alternative ways to construct formal proofs and to understand the properties of different logics. The intended connection between the presentation of human-computer dialogues and dialogue tableaux proofs has been made previously in Jeremaes (1987). In this paper it is sufficient to note that a logical query addressed to a KB is represented formally as:

$$\Delta \vdash_L \alpha$$

where α is a well-formed formula (wff) of the logic L, Δ is the set of KB axioms, and $\vdash$ is the consequence relation such that α is a logical consequence of the theory Δ, in the logic L. Logical deduction is the foundation of our formal analysis and abstract characterization of USER/EXPERT interaction. We claim to avoid the criticism of formal languages being used to analyse natural language interactions simply because our interest is in the inter*actions* (of a co-operative nature) across a restricted communication medium (ie. the USER interface) and not in the subtleties of naturally occurring dialogue in the large. Our approach, however, does presuppose that it is possible to characterize the logical content of a USER query and the EXPERT KB theory in a formal system.

In this paper consider the EXPERT KB as a single theory encompassing both the domain theory and the domain model. For example if we assert in the domain model the tuple $< Peter, John >$ in a relation $son\_of()$, then this is regarded as a ground atomic formula $son\_of(Peter, John)$. In this way the domain theory and domain model constitute the proper axioms of the EXPERT KB theory. This is generally the approach to KB implementations when the logic programming language PROLOG is used. Of course it is well known that there are restrictions with this approach particularly with respect to the expression of negative facts as proper axioms in PROLOG, which means that the notion of integrity constraint, for example, is not supported at all. In future refinements of our dialogue analysis framework, therefore, it is likely that we shall adopt a different approach to the structure of the EXPERT KB. Further research is required to uncover the limitations of various KB structuring proposals (Frost (1986)).

2.5. Dialogue Analysis

Although a relationship exists between a formal query and the KB (ie. as a logical deduction), this is not all that is required to analyse the empirical data. It has been made quite clear that our interest is not in natural language, but the data collected and analysed is of natural language interaction. Therefore, to provide a clear separation between the original form of the data and its logical content, a two part analysis of queries has been developed, based upon the principle of using a locution modifier to account for the 'force' of a query. Locution modifiers are typically used to distinguish between different types of statement. In J. Mackenzie's work on argumentation, for example, he extends a propositional language of statements to include locution modifiers. In addition to the assertion of propositional statements and their denials, this enables him to define questions, withdrawals, challenges, and a number of other locutions to enable dialogue participants to make objections on the grounds of inconsistency (Mackenzie (1985)). The use of locution modifiers in this instance is an extension to the basic idea and enables distinction between query types and to classify responses in relation to those types. The LOCUTION MODIFIER identifies the type of information requested in the query whereas the FORMAL QUERY represents the logical content, represented simply as a wff as shown in Section 2.4. For example, consider the following two queries:

Q1 ''Does John have a son ?''
Q2 ''How many sons does John have ?''

One interpretation of the logical content of these queries identifies the following FORMAL QUERY:

FQ1 $\exists x\ son\_of(x, John)$

Although the FORMAL QUERY for both Q1 and Q2 is the same with this interpretation the response required to Q1 is clearly different to that required for Q2. In the first case the USER wants to know if John has a son, whereas in the second case the USER effectively presupposes that John has at least one son, but wants to know how many sons he has. The difference is accounted for by the use of two LOCUTION MODIFIERS. However, the same LOCUTION MODIFIER and FORMAL QUERY used for Q2 would be used for the query:

Q3 ''What number of sons does John have ?''

This simple two part analysis of USER queries is course grained as far as natural language is concerned. The key point is that the information in the query referring to how the response should be presented to the USER is separated from the logical content of the query itself. Our main interest is in the nature of co-operative responses to USER queries. The analysis of experimental data now under consideration concentrates on the formulation of dialogue response strategies and on formal query analysis. The description of these components in our analysis framework is being used to guide the development of prototype co-operative problem solving systems that exhibit the experimentally generated response behaviour.

3. AN EXPERIMENTAL CONFIGURATION TASK

3.1. HP3000 Computer Equipment

The first reasoning task being studied is configuration, ie. the arrangement of objects of a certain kind (eg. equipment) to satisfy constraints on their connectivity. The intended task domain involves a sales person configuring a computer system which has to satisfy the customer's requirements and the system constraints. This configuration task is performed whenever a sales order is created for a new system. Having chosen configuration as a reasoning task it was necessary to gain experience with configuration problems in general and to develop our research method. Consequently a small experiment was conducted which involved a configuration task with HP 3000 computer equipment. Details of this experiment are given in Kidd (1989). An approximation to *real* configuration data was sought but with a restricted range of USER queries. By controlling the USER input the experiment set out to show if it was possible to: (1) generate ''apparently useful'' co-operative responses as a function of the query category and the state of the current configuration search space alone, (2) consistently obtain these co-operative responses across a number of EXPERTS.

3.2. Specification of Constraint Information

In dealing with the configuration task domain for HP 3000 equipment a great deal of attention has been paid to the constraint information. Although only a subset of this information was used for the experiment itself, prototype configuration systems are being built that use these constraints, consequently a clear understanding of the role of each constraint was necessary. The configuration domain knowledge of interest is contained in a configuration manual and from the analysis of this knowledge a number of important characteristics have been identified.

1. The activity of constructing a configuration involves performing a sequence of ordering and configuring actions.
2. A class of legal configurations is characterized by the constraints that restrict and permit actions being performed.
3. Performing certain actions can force or permit the performance of other actions.

There are many explicit as well as implicit features of the configuration knowledge that can be deemed to be important from different viewpoints. The role of heuristic information, for example, has not been mentioned here as being characteristic of this domain, although in reality it has a very important role to play. However, the current conceptual level of interest is one characterized by actions, the constraints on performing actions and the consequences of performing actions. Appropriate formal machinery to help disambiguate the manual information and to specify the domain knowledge of interest has been introduced.

Our approach is based upon the idea of using a dynamic logic. This is a well understood logical tool that has a wide range of applications, especially in computer science (Harel (1979)). Basically, a dynamic logic is seen as a modal logic that facilitates reasoning about state relations. Think of the modal logic framework as introducing the notions of necessity and possibility such that $[]\alpha$ represents that the condition α is necessarily the case (ie. true) in all possible worlds or states accessible from the current world, and likewise $<> \alpha$ represents that α is the case in some possible world accessible from the current world. What dynamic logic gives us is the ability to specify, for example, $[a]\alpha$. This can be read as saying that after the action a is performed then the condition α is necessarily the case. Thus a statement is being made not only about state information but also about the relationship between states. This is ideal for our present purposes as our primary interest is in understanding the state transitions that take place when actions are performed to extend a configuration. More specifically, the dynamic constraints in the domain theory are represented by expressions of the form $\alpha \rightarrow [a]\beta$ which is intuitively read as follows: If the condition α is true of the current configuration state, then if the action a is performed, and the action terminates, then the condition β will be true of the resulting configuration state. The formulae α and β are well-formed formula of the extended first-order sorted language and may themselves contain modalities.

Although this machinery allows us to reason about a configuration state and the effect of actions performed on that state, in its primitive form it does not allow us to say anything about the behaviour of the USER, ie. the person performing the configuration actions. Recall that the third characteristic of interest in this domain is that some of the constraints force or permit actions to be performed. To accommodate these prescriptions the dynamic logic can be extended to include first the notion of an agent being responsible for performing actions and then the deontic operators $obl(A,a)$ and $per(A,a)$. These are read as agent A is obliged to perform action a, and agent A is permitted to perform action a, respectively. This enables us to express constraints of the form

$$\alpha \rightarrow [A,a]\beta$$

where α and β are wff that may contain deontic prescriptions for agents to perform actions. These extensions were originally carried out in the Alvey sponsored FOREST project to enable the formal requirements of real time embedded systems to be specified (Jeremaes et al.(1986)).

3.3. Query Response Strategies

If the configuration constraints are viewed as dynamic constraints of the form $\alpha \rightarrow [a]\beta$ then the analysis of the empirical data generated from the experiment can proceed as follows. Three query types were used in the experiment:

1. Can I $< a,n >$?
   Example : Can I add 2 HP-IB cards?
2. If $< a,n >$ do I have to $< b >$?
   Example : If I add 5 HP-FL cards do I have to add another CIB adaptor?
3. How many $< a >$?
   Example : How many HP-IB cards can I add?

A statistical analysis of the experimental data identifies important responses for each query type. For example, in query category 1 three forms of response were identified:

''Yes''
''Yes, as long as b''
''No, the maximum is n' ''

A descriptive strategy can then be formulated to account for these responses in terms of the appropriate formal query. In the case of query category 1 this strategy relies on being able to search for a sequence of actions that the USER is permitted to perform (from the current state of the configuration) such that it includes n action a's. Note that we are dealing with atomic actions in our analysis at present, ie. add HP-FL and add HP-IB are distinct atomic actions. An informal description of the response strategy for this query category can be structured as follows:

```
If there is a sequence of actions that includes
   n action a's and the USER is permitted
   to perform each action in the sequence
then
   if no action in the sequence is obligated
   then RESPOND ''Yes ''
   else RESPOND ''Yes, as long as you perform
                  the obliged action(s) ··· ''
else
   if there is a sequence of actions that
      includes n' action a's, with n' < n, and
      the USER is permitted to perform
      each action in the sequence
   then RESPOND ''No, the maximum number is n'''
```

We introduce appropriate notational conventions to characterize sequences of actions, eg. allow the variable S range over sequences of action, then

$$\Delta \vdash \exists S : seq\, InSeq(a, S, n)$$

represents the formal query to search for a sequence of actions such that the action a occurs in the sequence S, n times. This is not all that is required, however, to characterize the response strategy above. The process of creating a configuration is one that is characterized by the performance of actions. Each action that is performed transforms the state of the configuration into a new state. These transformations, as well as building up the configuration itself, also alter the permission structure for potential USER actions. Consequently, in searching for a sequence of actions to satisfy the USER query it is necessary to check that all actions in the sequence are permitted. For example,

$$\forall n_{(0 \leq n < len(S))} [S_{a_1 \cdots a_n}] per(a_{n+1})$$

In a similar way it is quite straightforward to express the restriction on obliged actions in generated sequences.

Results from the experiment show that the dynamic action logic with deontic extensions is well equipped to characterize the response strategies. It should however be pointed out that some technical issues have yet to be resolved with respect to establishing an appropriate semantics for our notion of obligation. Currently the existence of an obliged action for a dialogue participant implies that the obliged action must be the next action performed by that participant, if any action at all is to take place. We believe that a weaker notion of obligation is required. It should be possible for a participant to have a number of outstanding obligations whilst being committed to ensure that all obligations are met, or discharged, over some period of time. In the USER/EXPERT interaction such a commitment should be met before the end of the dialogue. Interestingly recent work on a commitment logic for legal reasoning explores the relationship between obligation and commitment, casting new light on possible ways of making further progress (Fuks et al.(1989)).

4. RÉSUMÉ OF RESEARCH RESULTS

We are primarily concerned with developing task specific theories of co-operative problem solving and on using these theories to derive methods for engineering knowledge-based systems which support co-operative interaction. Formal tools and techniques are being employed to help analyse the empirical data collected and to express our developing theories of co-operation. This paper has presented an overview of that work to-date.

An outline framework for dialogue analysis has been established that clearly identifies the components of interest in co-operative interaction. So far the project has concentrated on query/response pairs generated from two experiments dealing with the task domain of configuration, consequently the full potential of our framework has yet to be explored. However, within this framework EXPERT dialogue strategies are responsible for generating appropriate responses to USER queries. It is here that the use of formal logic has been most beneficial as a conceptual aid in helping to formulate dialogue strategies to account for our experimental results. Ultimately components of these descriptive strategies will become control strategies for knowledge-based implementations of co-operative dialogue participants. Attention to formal rigour helps to establish an appropriate level of analysis for the empirical data and provides guidance relevant to the computational tractability of formulated dialogue strategies.

In selecting appropriate formal tools for dialogue analysis a balance has to be struck between the temptation to design from scratch the appropriate logical apparatus and the potential vice of forcing the analysis problem to fit a ready made tool. A similar tension exists when considering the choice of programming language and delivery environment for system implementation. Strategically we have allowed the empirical data to guide and help establish the requirements of the analytical tools and then conservatively customized established formal machinery to meet those requirements.

The task domain of interest is currently system configuration. To date two experiments have been conducted in this task domain. Analysing the results of these experiments has enabled us to develop techniques for categorizing co-operative responses in relation to user query types. Dialogue response strategies have been formulated for a number of query types. A two part analysis of USER queries into a locution modifier and a formal query enables us to write response strategies in terms of formal deductions from the domain KB theory. Using logical deduction as the corner-stone of our analysis provides a clear picture of the computational mechanisms that will be required to support knowledge-based implementations of dialogue strategies. However, in no way does it provide all of the answers as to how these mechanisms will in practice be realized.

A key development has been the use of a dynamic logic of actions to characterize USER/EXPERT interaction. This logic includes a deontic component that enables us to specify behavioural information about dialogue participants performing configuration actions and structural information about the consequences of performing actions. The notational elegance of the action logic has enabled us to clearly specify the dynamic constraints of a configuration KB and to express the formal component of a number of query response strategies. Although further research is called for to rigorously define this logical apparatus, significant insight has been gained into the nature of co-operativity and the way in which it can be supported.

REFERENCES

Barth, E. M. & Krabbe, E. C. W. (1982) From Axiom to Dialogue. Walter de Gruyter.

Cohen, P. R. & Levesque, H. J. (1987). Rational Interaction as the Basis for Communication. In Formal Theories of Communication. (Eds. P. Cohen & C. Perrault). Linguistic Institute, Stanford University, 1987.

Frost, R. A. (1986). Introduction to Knowledge Base Systems. Collins.

Fuks, H., Ryan, M. & Sadler, M. (1989). Outline of a Commitment Logic for Legal Reasoning. In Proceedings of 3rd International Conference on Logica Informatica Diritto. Florence.

Grice, H. P. (1975). Logic and Conversation. In Syntax and Semantics. (Eds. P. Cole & J. Morgan). Academic Press. 41-58.

Harel, D. (1979). First Order Dynamic Logic. LNCS, Vol. 68. Springer Verlag.

Jeremaes, P. (1987). Specifying the Interface Logic. In Proceedings of Interact '87. (Eds. H. -J. Bullinger and B. Shackel). Elsevier Science Publishers B.V. (North Holland).

Jeremaes, P.,Khosla, S. & Maibaum, T. S. E. (1986). A Modal [Action] Logic for Requirements Specification. In Software Engineering '86. (Eds. D. Barnes & P. Brown), pp 278-294, Peter Peregrinus.

Kidd, A. L. (1989).Deriving Principles for Generating Co-operative Responses, Hewlett Packard Technical Memo HPL-ISC-TM-89-137.

Mackenzie, J. (1985). No Logic Before Friday, The Logic of Dialogue, (Ed. D. Walton). Synthese, Vol. 63, No. 3, June, 1985.

Stenton, S. P. (1987). Dialogue Management for Co-operative Knowledge-Based Systems. Knowledge Engineering Review. Vol. 2, No. 2, 99-121.

Human–Computer Interaction – INTERACT '90
D. Diaper et al. (Editors)
Elsevier Science Publishers B.V. (North-Holland)

ETAG: EXTENDED TASK ACTION GRAMMAR - A LANGUAGE FOR THE DESCRIPTION OF THE USER'S TASK LANGUAGE

Michael J. Tauber

University of Paderborn, FR Germany

1. Introduction

In the paper, we present the fundamentals of ETAG (Extended Task Action Grammar) a language for the representation of a user's task language.

One central aspect of a human-machine interface is the language to be used by a user in order to specify task related actions to the system. This language can be seen from two different views, a *cognitive view* and an *implementation view*. In the cognitive view, we will call the language *task language*. Otherwise we will speak of the *dialog language*.

Let us explain the conceptual difference by a sample system we use as an example through the whole paper: PMAIL, a UNIX like electronic mail system which is consistently designed around a user's mailing tasks. PMAIL was designed in the course of the COST11ter research project "Human Factors in Teleinformatics". In the project, the design of PMAIL serves as a prototypical example for user- and task-oriented design. PMAIL was designed with several different interfaces (based on common dialog styles like command language driven dialog or direct manipulation) to the same functionality. In the command language version, the following phrases are regular in a user's interaction with the PMAIL system:

TABLE 1: Simple phrases of the PMAIL dialog (task) language

(phrase-1):	copy 3 5 7 folders/interact
(phrase-2):	copy read letters
(phrase-3):	mark 2 3
(phrase-4):	tidy

From an implementation point of view, such phrases keyed in by the user run the dialog. The dialog language can be represented by a context free grammar, regular phrases of that language can be sucessfully parsed by this grammar and after parsing, a protocol links the parsed input phrase with both internal processes and a phrase of the output language producing perceptible output to the screen or other physical devices in the user interface.

From a user's point of view, such phrases are (intermediate) results within a complex and structured task solving acitivity. They are preceeded by mental activities like "forming an intention", "specification of an action", and "executing an action", stages of a user's mental activities as introduced by Norman (Norman, 1986). If a user wants to save all messages already read in a folder with the name "letters", his task solving process starting with the intention will end-up in issuing phrase-2 of the above sample phrases. The task language is a means to have tasks done.

We introduce the concept of *the competent user* being competent in using a particular system (like PMAIL) for particular tasks (like administration of messages). Since even experts have misconceptions about systems the competent user is not reality. It is a model of complete knowledge of the tasks which can be accomplished with a system, the task related semantics of the system and the way the tasks are to be specified in terms of a language. Given certain tasks, the competent user knows how to decompose them into tasks which can be accomplished by the system. An ETAG description focuses on the "smallest tasks the system offers" (*basic tasks*) and the way how a regular phrase is formed to a given basic task.

In PMAIL, for example, basic tasks which can be accomplished with the system are "marking messages for deletion", or "deleting all messages marked for deletion". There is no chance to "delete messages" directly. Competence with respect to PMAIL means now to decompose a unit task like "deleting the messages 2 and 3" into "marking the messages 2 and 3 for deletion" followed by "deleting all the messages marked for deletion". The two basic tasks are issued then by the phrases 3 and 4 of table 1.

The examples demonstrate the concept of a task language. For the user, the dialog language which runs the dialog with the system is the only means to accomplish tasks with the system. For this scope, it is not of interest how the system analyses regular phrases but how the user produces correct specifications (regular phrases) for particular tasks. An ETAG description aims at the structural analysis of a task language in terms of the competent user.

The specification of the task language is an important part of designing a system. By determining a model of a competent user as knowing the basic tasks which are feasible with the system and the language to specify them, the system's requirements to its users are identified.

The two different views to the user's language are strongly related to the two different views of the human-computer interface: the *cognitive interface* as "all those part of the system a user comes in contact with conceptually, perceptually, and physically" (Moran, 1981) and the *observable interface* as "input language and output language linked by a protocol" (Chi, 1985). Like the task language, the cognitive interface is the scope in the design process. The observable interface and the dialog language as input language, however, are the focus in the implementation of a user interface.

The design of ETAG was influenced by several representational languages like C(ommand)L(anguage)G(rammar) (Moran, 1981), Action Grammar (Reisner, 1981), and T(ask)A(ction)G(rammar) (Payne and Green, 1986).

ETAG was first presented in 1988 (Tauber, 1988). Since that time it has changed and improved in many respects. In the paper, we give a sketch of the main features of an ETAG representation by examples. The whole concept of this representational language and its formal definition will be published elsewhere.

2. Components of an ETAG Representation

After a task analysis which identifies the space of tasks feasible with the system (including their decomposition into unit tasks) decisions about the *basic* (no more decomposable) *tasks* the system allows can be made. Basic tasks are determined by the simple phrases of the task language. Since the phrase is no more decomposable the basic task is no more decomposable too even if it has a complex meaning. Hence, we speak of basic tasks instead of simple tasks (Payne and Green, 1986).

Task delegation to a system can be characterized as mapping the task to conceptual objects and conceptual operations represented on the system's side for this task. (Tauber, 1985, 1986). The description of the task related semantics of a system (**user's virtual machine**) is the first part of an ETAG description. It is the conceptual analysis of the knowledge needed to understand the task related work of the machine. A **canonical basis** of concepts and conceptual relations used for this conceptual analysis must be determined before.

Once the task related semantics is determined the meaning of the basic tasks can be identified in terms of conceptual events in the user's virtual machine. The **dictionary of basic tasks** lists all the basic tasks with their meaning. The dictionary of basic tasks also links conceptual meaning of the basic tasks to the related regular phrases of the task language: regular phrases give the user explicit control to some or all conceptual aspects of the related basic task; for each basic task, the conceptual aspects which are under explicit control of the user and also the implicit conceptual effects (defaults, side effects) are listed in the dictionary of basic tasks.

The **production rules** describe the production of a regular phrase in terms of the keystroke level (keystrokes, mouse actions) starting at the conceptual description of a basic task. These production rules go down through four levels: specification level, reference level, lexical level, keystroke level.

In the following, we give examples for each component of an ETAG description. Most of the examples are related to the regular phrases of table 1.

2.1. Canonical Basis of Basic Concepts

In ETAG, knowledge of tasks and the task-related "machine's work" (often called "how it works knowledge") is described in a declarative way.

The formal structure of such a knowledge representation is influenced by Sowa's conceptual graphs (Sowa, 1984). In fact, the definition of the user's virtual machine (see 2.2) in terms of conceptual objects, attributes, and events can be easily translated into a conceptual graph. This is the formal aspect of the knowledge representation.

The content, however, depends on a canonical basis of basic concepts from which other concepts can be introduced incrementally. We will not argue for or against the idea of a general ontology of basic concepts from which all the concepts represented by a human can be derived. However, for representing an application domain by conceptual structure we need a canonical basis constraining the type of concepts and conceptual relations as well as providing a basic conceptual view to the domain.

Elsewhere, we already pointed out that understanding systems and their work in terms of concepts like [OBJECT], [PLACE], [STATE], and [EVENT] and conceptual relations like <ATTRIBUTE> might be a useful canonical basis for the representation of knowledge of many system's work (Tauber, 1985, 1986, 1988). Table 2 shows a part of the canonical basis we introduced for the conceptual analysis of PMAIL and many other tools. In this basis, concepts are denoted by [], conceptual relations by < >.

Structural relations between these basic types of concepts are denoted by a functional description (Jackendoff, 1983). Concept-functions like *place-functions, state-functions,* or *event-functions* denote concepts defined in terms of other ones. The functions (like *event.MOVE-TO* or *place.IN*) denote a simple concept in which other concepts (the function's parameter) are involved.

The conceptual structure as introduced by table 2 is more or less self explaining. It can be understood in the following way: "In representations based on this canonical basis, objects exist which may have attributes and values with respect to the attributes. These objects stay on places provided by other objects. The state of a collection of objects can be described by their locations (places) and their values with respect to certain attributes. States can be changed by changing the locations of objects and / or their attribute-values."

2.2. The User's Virtual Machine

When solving tasks in cooperation with a machine people delegate parts of the tasks to the machine. Task delegation is specified in terms of the task language. Phrases of the task language (like the ones in table 1) have meaning. They denote task related conceptual actions a user wants to run at the machine. The competent user knows the conceptual structure (objects, attributes, events) of the machine with respect to his tasks.

TABLE 2: Canonical basis

```
[CONCEPT] ::=
        [OBJECT]  |
        [VALUE]  |
        [PLACE]  |
        [STATE]  |
        [EVENT]

<RELATION> ::=
        <ATTRIBUTE>

[PLACE] ::=
        [place.IN ([OBJECT])]            |
        [place.ON ([OBJECT])]            |
        [place.ON-POS.(i) ([OBJECT])]    |
        [place.ON-TOP ([OBJECT])]        |
        [place.ON-TAIL ([OBJECT])]

[STATE] ::=
        [state.IS-AT ([OBJECT], [PLACE])]  |
        [state.HAS-VAL ([OBJECT], <ATTRIBUTE>, [VALUE])]

[EVENT] ::=
        [event.KILL-ON ([OBJECT], [PLACE])]   |
        [event.MOVE-TO ([OBJECT], [PLACE])]   |
        [event.COPY-TO ([OBJECT], [PLACE])]   |
        [event.SET-VAL ([OBJECT], <ATTRIBUTE>, [VALUE])]

type [EVENT > event.MOVE-TO ([OBJECT: *o], [PLACE: *p])]

    precondition: [state.IS-AT ([OBJECT: *o], [PLACE: *p0])];
    clears:       [state.IS-AT ([OBJECT: *o], [PLACE: *p0])];
    postcondition: [state.IS-AT ([OBJECT: *o], [PLACE: *p])],

end [EVENT].
```

The user's virtual machine (UVM) (Tauber, 1985, 1986, 1988) is the description of a machine's work (in terms of competence) with respect to a certain task domain. For the task language, the UVM defines the task related semantics of the machine and serves as the semantic basis for the task language.

A description of the UVM consists of two parts: the description of the conceptual objects, and the description of the conceptual places.

2.2.1. Conceptual Objects and Attributes

Table 3 shows a few examples for the description of conceptual objects.

The second definition, for example, says that "in the system" are some individual objects which can be classified as being a [MESSAGE_FILE] (head of the type definition) which is a [TEXT_FILE] (supertype slot). Type hierarchy is an important part of a description of the UVM. Informations on it are provided by the head of a type definition ([OBJECT > MESSAGE_FILE] saying that [MESSAGE_FILE] has [OBJECT] as supertype) and by the supertype slot. Type hieararchy is the precondition for reasoning by inheritance.

The themes slot defines the type of objects which can be "placed spatially on the object under definition". For the [MESSAGE_FILE], objects of type [MESSAGE] can be placed there. *x stands for an arbitrary individual and {*x} means many (a set) of them. After the "@" informations on how many themes may exist might be provided (0 to indefinite many messages in the case of a message file).

The relations slot defines the possible relations between the object under definition and its themes. For a [MESSAGE_FILE], these are spatial relations ([PLACE]) saying that a theme object [MESSAGE] can be placed on places like "on the top", "on the tail", or "on a position i". Those places are generic to the object under definition and are provided for certain themes.

The style how attributes are defined can be seen in the definition of a [MESSAGE] (attribute slot). One of its attributes (<STATUS>) is defined at the end of table 3.

TABLE 3: Conceptual objects of the PMAIL-UVM

```
type [OBJECT > DIRECTORY]

  themes:     [ONE-OF {FILE, DIRECTORY} : {*x}@0-inf];
  relations:  [place.IN ([DIRECTORY])];
  attributes: <PATH_NAME>, <NAME>;

end [DIRECTORY].

type [OBJECT > MESSAGE_FILE]

  supertype: [TEXT_FILE];
  themes:    [MESSAGE : {*x}@0-inf];
  relations: [place.ON-POS.(i) ([MESSAGE_FILE])],
             [place.ON-TOP ([MESSAGE_FILE])],
             [place.ON-TAIL ([MESSAGE_FILE])];

end [MESSAGE_FILE].

type [OBJECT > MESSAGE]

  supertype:  [TEXT];
  themes:     [HEADER], [BODY];
  relations:  [place.ON-POS.(1) ([MESSAGE])] for [HEADER],
              [place.ON-POS.(2) ([MESSAGE])] for [BODY],
              [place.POSS-AT ([MESSAGE])] for [HEADER], [BODY];
  attributes: <SENDER>, <SENDING_DATE>, <RECEIVING_DATE>,
              <STATUS>, <DELETION_MARK>;

end [MESSAGE].

type <ATTRIBUTE  > STATUS>

  object type: [MESSAGE];
  value set:   {"composed", "unread", "read"};

end <STATUS>.
```

2.2.2. Conceptual Events

An individual state is determined by the location of individual themes on individual objects and individual values of an individual object's attribute. "Message *x with the status "read" is in the message_file *y at position 8" is a typical statement about a current state of the UVM. There are different types of [STATE], two of them are listed in the canonical basis (table 2). [STATES] are expressed in terms of [OBJECT], [PLACE], <ATTRIBUTE> and [VALUE].

Conceptual [EVENT]s change a conceptual [STATE]. Some basic [EVENT]s are already listed in the canonical basis (table 2). [EVENT]s specific to the UVM (and therefore specific to the scope of tasks considered) has to be defined in terms of the [EVENT]s of the canonical base. Conceptual events are the focus of a user's tasks. The events specified by the simple phrases of the dialog language (basic events) are the focus of the basic tasks (see 2.3). All the phrases of table 1 are simple phrases and therefore refer to basic events. So, it is evident that a UVM definition of PMAIL must contain basic events like "copying messages from a message file into a message file", "marking messages within a message file for deletion", or "cleaning up a message file by deleting all messages marked for deletion".

Table 4 shows the definition of the basic events of PMAIL which are addressed by the phrases of table 1. The definitions are more or less self explaining.

TABLE 4: Conceptual events in the PMAIL-UVM

a) conceptual event denoted by the phrases 1 and 2 of table 1:

```
type [EVENT > COPY_MESSAGES]

  description:
      for {[MESSAGE: *x]}
        [event.COPY-TO ([MESSAGE : *x],
              [place.ON-TAIL ([MESSAGE_FILE : *y]) : *p2])];
  precondition:
      [state.IS-AT ([MESSAGE : *x],
        [place.ON-POS.(i) ([MESSAGE_FILE : *z]) : *p1])];
  comments:
      "copying messages x from a message file z onto the end of a message file y";

end [COPY_MESSAGES].
```

b) conceptual event denoted by phrase 3 of table 1:

```
type [EVENT > MARK_FOR_DELETION]

  description:
      for {[MESSAGE: *x]}
        [event.SET-VAL ([MESSAGE : *x], <DELETION_MARK>, "marked")];
  precondition:
      [state.IS-AT ([MESSAGE: *x],
        [place.ON-POS.(i) ([MESSAGE_FILE: *y])])];
  comments: "marks messages for deletion";

end [MARK_FOR_DELETION].
```

c) conceptual event denoted by phrase 4 of table 1:

```
type [EVENT > TIDY_MESSAGE_FILE]

  description:
      for {[MESSAGE: *x]}
        [event.KILL-ON ([MESSAGE: *x], [PLACE : *p])];
  precondition:
      [state.HAS-VAL ([MESSAGE: *x], <DELETION_MARK>, marked])],
      [state.IS-AT ([MESSAGE: *x],
        [place.ON-POS.(i) ([MESSAGE_FILE: *y]) : *p];
  comments: "discards within a message file all messages marked for deletion";

end [TIDY_MESSAGE_FILE].
```

2.3. Dictionary of Basic Tasks

Basic tasks of the competent user are related to basic events of the UVM. All basic tasks and the related basic events are listed in the dictionary of basic tasks.

There is another important information listed in the dictionary of basic tasks which links a basic task conceptually to the regular phrase denoting it. This information is about the control on the conceptual components of the related basic event. Some of the conceptual components might be explicitly determined through the task language other might be determined by the system. In PMAIL, for example, the specification of a basic event MARK_FOR_DELETION (like "mark 2 3") in the course of the related basic task T9 refers to the type of the event ("mark") and the messages involved ("2 3"). According to table 4, also the message file to which these messages belong must be determined. Since this task language was designed for the context of a (default) current message file, this paramater in the conceptual description of the basic event is not to be specified in the task language and is therefore determined by default.

Each entry into the dictionary of basic tasks characterizes a basic task and is of the following form:

> **ENTRY** *id:*
> *basic task,*
> *related basic event,*
> *system controlled concepts,*
> *task symbol with associated user controlled concepts,*
> *comment.*

The *related basic event* links the *basic task* to the UVM, the *task symbol with associated user controlled concepts* links the *basic task* to the regular phrase denoting the *basic event*. The *task symbol with associated user controlled concepts* is also the starting form for the production of the related regular phrase (see 2.4).

For the production of a regular phrase to a basic task of type MARK_FOR_DELETION, the form

> **T9** [EVENT > MARK_FOR_DELETION] [OBJECT > MESSAGE: {*x}]

is the starting form (see table 5). Here, the concepts [EVENT > MARK_FOR_DELETION] and [OBJECT > MESSAGE: {*x}] are associated to the unique task symbol (T9). This concepts are therefore to be specified through the task language in the course of the basic task T9.

Table 5 gives examples of entries into the dictionary of basic tasks. Again, the examples were chosen in the light of the regular phrases of table 1.

TABLE 5: Dictionary of basic tasks for the PMAIL task language

ENTRY 6:
[TASK > COPY_MESSAGES],
[EVENT > COPY_MESSAGES],
[MESSAGE_FILE: *z],
T6 [EVENT > COPY_MESSAGES] [OBJECT > MESSAGE: {*x}]
[OBJECT > MESSAGE_FILE: *y],
"copy messages from the current message file into a message file".

ENTRY 9:
[TASK > MARK_FOR_DELETION],
[EVENT > MARK_FOR_DELETION],
[MESSAGE_FILE: *y],
T9 [EVENT > MARK_FOR_DELETION] [OBJECT > MESSAGE: {*x}],
"mark messages of the current message file for deletion".

ENTRY 5:
[TASK > TIDY_CURRENT_MESSAGE_FILE],
[EVENT > TIDY_MESSAGE_FILE],
[MESSAGE_FILE],
T5 [EVENT > TIDY_MESSAGE_FILE],
"removes all messages marked for deletion from the current message file".

2.4. Production Rules

The production rules of an ETAG description determine the grammar of the task language. For each basic task, the regular phrase for the specification of the related basic event can be produced by applying the production rules (generative grammar). The productions run over 4 levels which are described below.

So far, we considered as task language a language in the style of a classical command language. Now we will consider two alternative task languages for the same functionality (same UVM, same basic tasks). One is the already sketched language in the style of a command language (version C) the other is a language in the style of direct manipulation (version D). With these two alternative languages, we want to demonstrate several aspects. First, also direct manipulation can be regarded as a language and that even from the user's point of view. Second, direct manipulation is mainly another style of reference to the objects of interests. Third, several types of task languages can be easily designed for the same tasks and the same functionality.

2.4.1. Specification Level

The production rules start from a form which identifies the basic task and the conceptual components associated with the task and controlled by the task language (see 2.3). The first level of productions mainly determines in which sequence these conceptual components are to be specified. These productions model semantics-syntax alignments.

There is a well known discussion on the sequence of commands and arguments. Classical command languages have a structure "command first, argument then" or in the terminology of ETAG "specification of the event first, specification of the object involved then". Direct manipulation interfaces prefer for several reasons another sequence: "specification of the object first, specification of the event then".

The examples of table 6 are production rules on the specification level. For the two versions (C, D), the different sequences of specifying semantic components can be easily seen. The examples for Version C are chosen in the light of the regular phrases of table 1. We leave it to the reader to sketch examples for regular direct manipulative actions in Version D.

The rules of the specification level do not contain any dialog style dependent information except informations on sequencing of semantic components which might be dialog style dependent. How each of the semantic components is to be specified is determined by the rules of the next level.

TABLE 6: Specification level production rules

a) Version C:

T6 [EVENT > COPY_MESSAGES] [OBJECT > MESSAGE: {*x}]
[OBJECT > MESSAGE_FILE: *y] ::=
specify [EVENT] + **specify** [OBJECT > MESSAGE] +
specify [OBJECT > MESSAGE_FILE] + **end-input**.

T9 [EVENT > MARK_FOR_DELETION] [OBJECT > MESSAGE: {*x}] ::=
specify [EVENT] + **specify** [OBJECT] + **end-input**.

T5 [EVENT > TIDY_MESSAGE_FILE] ::=
specify [EVENT] + **end-input**.

b) Version D:

T6 [EVENT > COPY_MESSAGES] [OBJECT > MESSAGE: {*x}]
[OBJECT > MESSAGE_FILE: *y] ::=
specify [OBJECT > MESSAGE] + **specify** [EVENT] +
specify [OBJECT > MESSAGE_FILE].

T9 [EVENT > MARK_FOR_DELETION] [OBJECT > MESSAGE: {*x}] ::=
    specify [OBJECT] + **specify** [EVENT].

T5 [EVENT > TIDY_MESSAGE_FILE] ::=
    specify [EVENT].

c) Both Versions:

specify [OBJECT > FILE: {*x}] ::=
    specify [OBJECT > FILE: *x] |
    specify [OBJECT > FILE: *x] + **specify** [OBJECT > FILE: {*x}].

specify [OBJECT > MESSAGE {*x}] ::=
    specify <ATTRIBUTE> [VALUE: {*v}] |
    specify [PLACE: {*p}].

specify <ATTRIBUTE> [VALUE: {*v}] ::=
    specify <ATTRIBUTE> [VALUE: *v] |
    specify <ATTRIBUTE> [VALUE: *v] +
        specify <ATTRIBUTE> [VALUE: {*v}].

specify [PLACE: {*p}] ::=
    specify [PLACE: *p] |
    specify [PLACE: *p] + **specify** [PLACE: {*p}].

2.4.2. Reference Level

Production rules at this level determine on the left hand side the conceptual component to be specified and on the right side the style of reference to this component. Version C like all command languages gives reference by names, version D mostly handles the reference problem by selection (pointing) of a visible symbol denoting the referred conceptual component.

The right hand side of reference level production rules contains forms enclosed in ' '. This forms are left hand sides of production rules on the next level, the lexical level. The ' ' indicate replacement in the following sense: identify the production starting with the form enclosed in ' 'at the lexical level and replace the form at the reference level by the right side of the production found at the lexical level. This replacement fills into the phrase under production the lexical items denoting the considered conceptual components. Since the semantic expressiveness of lexical items is an important aspect in the design of a task language we decided to put this information in an extra level (lexical level; see 2.4.3) and to isolate it from the reference level productions.

When you follow the productions

specify [EVENT > MARK_FOR_DELETION] ::=
    name 'symbol [EVENT > MARK_FOR_DELETION]'

symbol [EVENT > MARK_FOR_DELETION] ::=
    [%COMMAND% : "mark"] **(see table 8)**

the replacement will change the first production to

specify [EVENT > MARK_FOR_DELETION] ::=
    name [%COMMAND% : "mark"]

Note that ETAG production rules chunk rules to classes of rules. The first rule in table 7, for example, says that the specification of each [EVENT] is to be done in the same way. Above we instantiated the rule for the [EVENT > MARK_FOR_DELETION].

Additionally, the rules at the reference level contain informations for the production of new rules as shown by the above example. These new rules model a conceptual break: from semantic concepts to syntactic concepts. The above produced rule says: the specification of an event of type MARK_FOR_DELETION (semantic concept) is done by using the command (syntactic concept) "mark" as a name for the event.

The following table 7 shows a few examples of rules at the reference level.

TABLE 7: Reference level production rules

C: **specify** [EVENT] ::= **name 'symbol** [EVENT]'
D: **specify** [EVENT] ::= **select 'symbol** [EVENT]'

C: **specify** <ATTRIBUTE> [VALUE] ::=
    name 'symbol <ATTRIBUTE> [VALUE]'
D: **specify** <ATTRIBUTE> [VALUE] ::=
    select 'symbol <ATTRIBUTE> [VALUE]'

C: **specify** [PLACE: *p] ::= **name 'symbol** [PLACE]'
D: **specify** [PLACE: *p] ::= **select** 'icon [PLACE]'

2.4.3. Lexical Level

The lexical items of the task language are verbal and / or visual symbols. The relation between the semantic concept denoted by the lexical item and the syntactic concept to which it belongs is expressed by the production rules at the lexical level. In order to distinguish them from semantic concepts names for syntactic concepts are enclosed in % %. Table 8 shows some examples for productions at the lexical level.

TABLE 8: Lexical level production rules

a) Version C:

symbol [EVENT > COPY_MESSAGES] ::= [%COMMAND% : "copy"]
symbol [EVENT > MARK_FOR_DELETION] ::= [%COMMAND% : "mark"]
symbol [EVENT > TIDY_MESSAGE_FILE] ::= [%COMMAND% : "tidy"]

symbol <DELETION_MARK> [VALUE] ::= [%MARK% : {"m", "u"}].

symbol <STATUS> [VALUE] ::= [%STATUS% : {"read", "unread", "composed"}]

symbol [PLACE > *place.ON-POS.(i)* ([MESSAGE_FILE])] ::= [%POSITION% : i]

b) Version D:

symbol [EVENT > COPY_MESSAGES] ::=
    [%MENU% : "message"] [%MENU_ITEM% : "copy"]

symbol <DELETION_MARK> [VALUE] ::=
    [%DIALOG_BOX% : "deletion"] [%BUTTON% : {"marked", "unmarked"}]

icon [PLACE > *place.ON-POS.(i)* ([MESSAGE_FILE])] ::= [%IMAGE% : "X"]

2.4.4. Keystroke Level

As shown, lexical level production are used to produce new production rules at the reference level. In the above example, we arrived at the production rule

specify [EVENT > MARK_FOR_DELETION] ::=
    name [%COMMAND% : "mark"]

Production rules at the keystroke level extend the right hand side of those derived rules to the keystroke level. For our example, we would instantiate the following rule from the first rule of table 9:

name [%COMMAND% : "mark"] ::= **KEYS** [%COMMAND% : "mark"]

which says that the string "mark" has to be typed in.

Table 9 contains some examples of keystroke level productions and we leave it to the reader to explore the different versions and the different basic tasks by "running" the productions from the specification level down to the keystroke level.

TABLE 9: Keystroke level production rules

a) Version C:

name [%IDENTIFIER% > ONE-OF {%COMMAND%, %MSG_ATTRIBUTE%}] ::=
KEYS [%IDENTIFIER%]

end-input ::= **KEY** ("RETURN")

b) Version D:

select [%MENU%] [%MENU_ITEM%] ::=
MOUSE-POSITION (POP-UP-AREA [%MENU%]) +
PRESS_RIGHT_BUTTON +
DRAG-TO [%MENU_ITEM%] +
RELEASE_RIGHT_BUTTON

select [%IMAGE%] ::=
MOUSE-POSITION [%IMAGE%] +
KLICK-LEFT-BUTTON

---

3. Outlook

Although ETAG is based on the idea of Action Grammars (Reisner, 1981) and TAG (Payne and Green, 1986) it was not developed as an analytical tool for predictions about the learnability of systems. The main motivation for developing ETAG was to provide more "descriptive power". As such we understand a description of the task language as complete as possible with respect to a competent user's knowledge. Descriptive power is a relevant aspect for using ETAG in the design of a task language. A good design is properly represented and makes relevant design decisions explicit (Webster, 1988). There is a remarkable lack of techniques for the representation of user oriented views of a system in the design process. Computer science is not really concerned with those problems of "early design". With presenting ETAG, we want to open the discussion on more strong approaches to the design of user-oriented systems.

However, ETAG description may also be of interest in other respects. Since chunking of concepts and rules to supertypes and "superrules" is a basic aspect in an ETAG description there is possibility to consider the value of ETAG descriptions also for predictions on learnability based on user perceived consistency. We are currently working on this aspect. There are two other activities which might be worth to be mentioned: currently we expolore the potentials of ETAG descriptions as a knowledge base of the task language for use in an expert system answering user questions on "how to work with the system"; already developed (but based on an earlier version of the ETAG language) is the prototype of a translator which accepts an ETAG description and produces natural-language answers to typical user questions (see the related paper of Veer et al. in this volume).

Acknowledgements: I would like to thank Diederick Broos, Felix Yap and Mark Fokke for their contributions to the improvement of the ETAG language.

References

Chi H.U. (1985). Formal Specification of User Interfaces: A Comparison and Evaluation of Four Axiomatic Approaches. IEEE Transactions on Software Engineering, Vol. SE-11, No. 8, 671- 685.

Jackendoff R. (1983). Semantics and Cognition. Cambridge, MA: MIT-Press.

Moran, T.P. (1981). The Command Language Grammar: A Representation for the User Interface of Interactive Computer Systems. Int. J. Man-Machine Studies, 15, 3 - 50.

Norman D.A. (1986). Cognitive Engineering. In D.A. Norman and S.W. Draper (Eds.), User Centered System Design. Hillsdale, NJ: Lawrence Erlbaum.

Payne S.J. and Green T.R.G. (1986). Task Action Grammars: A Model of the Mental Representation of Task Languages. Human-Computer Interaction, 1986, Volume 2, 93 - 133.

Reisner, Ph. (1981). Formal Grammar and Human Factors Design of an Interactive Graphic System. IEEE Transactions on Software Engineering, Vol. SE-7, No.2, 229 - 240.

Sowa J.F. (1984). Conceptual Structures. Reading, MA: Addision-Wesley Publ.

Tauber M.J. (1985). Top Down Design of Human-Computer Systems from the Demands of Human Cognition to the Virtual Machine - An Interdisciplinary Approach to Model Interfaces in Human-Computer Interaction. In Proceedings of the IEEE Workshop on Languages for Automation, Palma de Mallorca, Spain, June 28-29, 1985, IEEE Computer Society Press, Silverspring.

Tauber M.J. (1986). Top-Down Design of Human-Computer Interfaces. In Chang, Ichikawa, Ligomenides (Eds.), Visual Languages. New York: Plenum Press.

Tauber M.J. (1988). On Mental Models and the User Interface. In Veer, Green, Hoc and Murray (Eds), Working with Computers. Computer and People Series. London: Academic Press.

Webster E.A. (1988). Mapping the Design Information Representation Terrain. IEEE Computer, December 1988, 8 - 23.

Human–Computer Interaction – INTERACT '90
D. Diaper et al. (Editors)
Elsevier Science Publishers B.V. (North-Holland)

ETAG - SOME APPLICATIONS OF A FORMAL REPRESENTATION OF THE USER INTERFACE

Gerrit C. van der Veer, Diederik Broos, Kenneth Donau, Mark J.Fokke, Felix Yap

Free University, Dept. Mathematics and Computer Science,
Amsterdam, The Netherlands

Based on the theoretical work described in the contribution by M.J. Tauber (this Volume), we conducted several studies aiming at the application of the ETAG formalism. We concentrated on 3 aspects of user interface design and analysis:

- The application of ETAG based evaluation methods for the analysis of existing systems from the point of view of learnability and usability;
- Formal representation methods like ETAG based formalisms, for the analysis and formal description of user's tasks;
- The use of ETAG and related formalisms for the design of user interface modules (automatic generation of on-line manual and help text, and modules for answering users' questions about the system).

1. Introduction

There are many different approaches to design specifications for user interfaces (see for instance van der Veer et al, 1988). In our project we used a formal representation method of the user interface called Extended Task Action Grammar, Tauber (this volume). This representation is developed with the explicit aim to represent the user interface or "user virtual machine" in such a way as to describe all aspects of the system that are relevant from the point of view of interaction with the end-users (actually, at the physical level of interaction - hardware of the terminal and peripherals that the user is in direct contact with - the method is not complete, but we leave this level out of our analysis for the moment). ETAG was developed originally as a tool for the design and analysis of user interfaces (in the broad sense, including the functionality provided for the user). Tauber (1988) shows an example of such an analysis, regarding some elements of MacWrite. Innocent and Tauber (1988) present an ETAG description of UNIX binmail. In Tauber (in preparation) the method is applied in the course of designing a new (electronic mail) system. These are the only applications of ETAG available at the moment.

In this contribution we will first of all show some further applications of ETAG to the analysis and comparison of existing systems (section 2). To this end we choose two different systems for the same task domain (page tools for a UNIX environment). In section 3 we will show how ETAG may be extended in order to describe not only systems' basic tasks, but also users' tasks, that normally are at a higher level in task-decomposition hierarchies, and, moreover, sometimes have to be described without complete knowledge of the user interface (e.g. in the case of novice users, and in the case a system is still to be designed). The last two sections show ETAG applications towards a goal that was not envisaged in the first place in Tauber's work. If ETAG provides a description of a system that is complete and sufficient from the point of view of the knowledge of the intended user, this description should in principle be an adequate source for teaching, documentation, and on-line help for users. Section 4 presents a software engineering solution for translating ETAG descriptions into quasi natural English. Section 5 shows a method to use ETAG as a knowledge base for answering end-user questions on the system.

2. An example of ETAG applications

The formal interface description method ETAG by Tauber still lacks empirical validation. We describe the project which entails deriving two ETAG descriptions from the interfaces of the page tools *less* and *pg*.

Tauber (in preparation) derived ETAG descriptions of the UNIX bin/mail interface and Write (a subset of MacWrite) for analysis. The very same ETAG descriptions were used by Boeijink (1987) and Broos (1989). Boeijink developed an instrument to measure the functionality of user interfaces. He tested this instrument on an ETAG description of UNIX bin/mail. Broos built part of an ETAG-based help system, making use of the ETAG descriptions of bin/mail and Write.

Apart from Tauber, nobody has ever tried to derive formal descriptions of user interfaces using ETAG. As a matter of fact, the UNIX bin/mail and Write ETAG descriptions Tauber derived were sometimes rather informal, with a number of ad hoc constructions. In addition, there is no methodology for deriving such descriptions.

ETAG is a promising formal interface description method, but up until now it has only been used to describe some rather trivial user interfaces. Besides that, nobody knows how to make an ETAG description of an arbitrary user interface.

2.1. Project goals and objectives

The first objective of this project was to validate ETAG. To establish its general applicability we used it on a different type of user interface than the UNIX bin/mail program, which has already been extensively analysed.

Moreover, we wanted to see if ETAG is able to compare two user interfaces which offer more or less the same functionality. In other words, we wanted to know that if the user interfaces of the two page tools can be compared, their ETAG descriptions can be compared as well.

The second objective of this project was to provide a methodology which can be used as a manual for using ETAG, i.e. making ETAG descriptions of an arbitrary user interface.

2.2. Page tools

In UNIX environments files can be one of two kinds: binary files or text files. Text files can be created and edited by screen editors like *vi*. To read the text file people can make use of so-called *page tools*, although more often than not they just *vi* them.

A few of the more well-known page tools are UNIX *more*, UNIX *less* and AIX *pg*.

These page tools allow the user to *page* through a text file (hence the name *page tool*). Text files too large to fit into one screen, are neatly chunked so that the user can read the next screenful of text at the press of a key. Page tools differ in functionality. The more advanced ones allow the user to jump to arbitrary pages or even to do some string searching ("find the string: ETAG").

Another difference between the page tools is the mapping of system objects to the user objects. For example, *more* has no concept of "the previous page" whereas *less* and *pg* do.

We chose the page tools AIX *pg* and UNIX *less*, which both run on an IBM PC/RT under the AIX operating system as examples to validate ETAG. The reason for this choice is that we believe that with data increasingly being stored in computer files, the functionality of page tools will become a focus of interest in the near future.

2.3. Development of ETAG descriptions

To start with, the then current version of ETAG did not provide sufficient expressional power. For one thing, ETAG's Dictionary of Basic Tasks was unable to cope with arguments interspersed in the command (like *+numl*). For another, it was impossible to describe different views on objects in ETAG. How to describe text searching was another problem altogether.

The improved ETAG version by Tauber, though, was able to solve all these problems.

2.4. Some results

For the empirical validation of ETAG we admit that ETAG should be tried on a wider variety of user interfaces. The two ETAG descriptions of the page tools *pg* and *less* are far from sufficient to validate ETAG. Nevertheless, we showed that ETAG is truly a formal method capable of describing arbitrary user interfaces. In addition, ETAG has proven to be a valuable tool to analyse and compare user interfaces. The ETAG descriptions of the page tools *pg* and *less* showed significant differences in functionality, and in the system objects offered. The complexity of the UVM descriptions provide an index of the learnability and usability of the user interfaces (Boeijink, 1987).

Another result of this project was a methodology which can be used to make ETAG descriptions of user interfaces.

3. ETAG and the description of users' unit tasks

User tasks can be decomposed into unit tasks. We define unit tasks, following Card, Moran, and Newell (1983) as the smallest subtask that a user is intrinsically interested in. Decomposing this unit task does ask from the user to bother about details of the system for the system's sake, not for the sake of interest in task details. Unit tasks are user defined control constructs. When unit tasks are executed on a system they have to be decomposed into basic tasks. Basic tasks in the sense of ETAG are designed and implemented by the system designer and are equivalent to executable commands offered by the system. Basic tasks can be described using the ETAG formalism. Both the context in which the tasks are executed and their effect are both represented within this formalism. Unit tasks however are represented by simple phrases like:

"Delete the first sentence"

"Assign a value to some identifier"

A representation for unit tasks can be useful for several purposes. It would be possible to give a formal characterization of unit tasks before a system is even built, to determine what set of basic tasks should be implemented. It would also be possible to describe part of a user's knowledge about the system to determine the usability and learnability of the system. Knowledge of users can be organized differently. The more familiar a user is with a system the more he is inclined to describe his unit tasks in terms of basic tasks.

3.1. An event representation of unit tasks

In order to avoid the use of basic tasks in the description of unit tasks, unit tasks may be represented by their initial situation and their final situation. Additional knowledge about the execution of the unit task on the system may be represented by describing in what order some specific states or actions should occur.

We extended the ETAG manner of describing basic tasks in order to describe unit tasks. I.e. using the event functions as introduced in the basic task descriptions to describe effects of actions. Both the situations before and after the unit task are denoted by event functions.
The subparts of this unit task description are:

Virtual Machine:
The virtual machine denotes the content and structure of the object space.

Pre-condition:
The event funtions in the pre-condition denote the events that are required to have occurred prior to the unit task (these events however do not have to be caused by the user executing the task).

Restriction-pre:
This restriction part is present to give an unambiguous interpretation of the pre-condition. Details can be specified on the initial state. Some history information about actions prior to the unit task can be specified, as well as information about the order of the events that led to the initial state.

Post-condition:
The post-condition denotes the effect of the unit tasks and consists of an enumeration of all the event functions that are supposed to have happened when the unit task is completed.

Restriction-post:
This restriction part denotes the allowed and necessary sequences of event functions.

In this representation method it is still necessary to have knowledge about the event functions. The event functions from the basic task description also occur in the unit task description. This link has the drawback that a lot of knowledge of basic tasks and their event functions is required to give a valid description of a unit task. A representation free of events information needs constructs to describe the effects of the unit tasks.

3.2. Representation of unit tasks by state primitives

To denote system states the following properties are important:

active — denotes if an existing object is directly available for use.

current — denotes if an instance is the last used instance of its type and still active.

place — denotes the place of an instance within the User Virtual Machine

exist — denotes the existence of an instance

display — denotes if an instance is displayed through the available hardware

attribute — denotes the attributes of an instance

These properties of instances may be described by introducing state-primitives. For every distinct property two different state-primitives have to be introduced. One state-primitive to denote that the property holds and one state-primitive to denote the opposite.

The following state-primitives will thus be introduced:

[active(<instance>)]
[not active(<instance>)]
[current(<instance>)]
[not current(<instance>)]
[place(<instance> , <place function>)]

[not place(<instance> , <place function>)]
[exist(<instance>)]
[not exist(<instance>)]
[display(<instance>)]
[not display(<instance>)]
[attribute(<instance> , <type> , <value>)]
[not attribute(<instance> , <type> , <value>)]

A set of state-primitives describes a state by explicitly denoting which properties hold in that state.

The unit task description method using explicit state descriptions consists of:

- A description of the state before the task has been performed
- A description of the intended effect of the unit task
- A optional description of necessary information during unit task execution

The description of the state of the instances before the task has been performed, the pre-state, consists of that set of state-primitives which defines the context which is necessary before the unit task can occur. There has to be some restrictions on the environment before any unit task can take place and these restrictions are given in the pre-state. If the pre-state of a unit task is not met, the unit task cannot be performed. There is not a basic task sequence that will deliver the desired result in that case.

The description of the intended effect of the unit task gives a description of all the necessary effects at unit task completion time. Sometimes the intended effect cannot be described by a single state. The effect of the unit task "look at all messages" cannot be described by a single state. The intended situation is not that all messages *are* displayed, but that all messages *have been* displayed. This situation cannot be described by a single state, but needs multiple states to be described. Note that in these cases of using multiple states for describing the intended effect of a unit task no order is needed on the states. If the multiple states of the intended situation need an explicit order, this would imply that the task can be decomposed into subtasks. Therefore this task would be no unit task.

These descriptions are still independent of the set of basic tasks, therefore the necessary effects do not include all the effects which have to occur because of the side-effects of the necessary basic tasks, but they only include the effects that are explicitely controlled by the phrase denoting the unit task.

The last part in the description of a unit task, the path constraints, is an optional part and requires knowledge of the possibilities and effects of the basic tasks. It takes care of the necessary intermediate states implied by the set of basic tasks. Necessary in this context means that for every basic task sequence that could complete that unit task, this intermediate state would occur. If a unit task cannot be completed without the occurence of a particular state, it seems useful to allow a possibility to denote this state in the unit task description. Furthermore there might exist some intermediate states that would make it impossible to complete the unit task

3.3. Comparison of the two methods

Information about actions can be better handled with event functions than with state-primitives. On the other hand, solely a description of the intended effect, with no strings attached (i.e. free of any action information) is better expressible with state-primitives. Expert users will have knowledge of basic tasks. This knowledge will influence their representation of unit tasks. Novices, but also all future users of systems yet to be designed, will only be able to represent knowledge of task states, derived from their ideas of the unit tasks they want to delegate to the system. In the latter case state primitives seem to be a usefull medium for the representation of unit tasks, whereas in the former case the event representation may be more valid.

4. ETAG based help text

Although ETAG is a complete description method, it is in no way understandable for any reader who is not an expert in computer science or formal languages. We needed a translation of this formal representation into a description in a "natural language". The way to arrive from the ETAG formalism to English texts is the subject of this section.

4.1. A few considerations

Because an ETAG-description is a static description of the *Users' Virtual Machine* (UVM), questions about the state of the system the user is working with (like "Have I sent the letter?", "Am I still inside the system", etc.) cannot be answered on the basis of an ETAG-description. What we *can* do, is to present the user help on various aspects of the UVM. For this purpose we decided to base the kind of help the system should give on the four levels of Moran (Moran, 1981).

a. *Task level.* At this level the user views the computer system as a tool to perform a certain task (unit task). The user needs to know what tasks the system can perform and how these tasks can be delegated as part of a unit task. It's difficult to give good help on the task level. Especially on the basis of an ETAG-description, for here only the *basic* tasks (identified with one command) are described. Therefore we did not incorporate this level in the help system. Teaching and documentation will have to supply this, outside the system.

b. *Semantic level.* The task level maps onto conceptual operations and entities within the user's virtual machine. On the semantic level these operations and entities (objects and their attributes) are described.

c. *Syntax level.* On this level the lexicographic structure of the commands for accomplishing the conceptual operations defined on the semantic level is given.

d. *Keystroke level.* On this level the physical actions a user has to perform for issuing a particular command are described (e.g. use of keyboard or mouse).

Following the last three levels, our help system provides help text for the following kinds of questions:

- "What is a ...?": i.e. a *semantic* description of the objects in the UVM.
- "What is the effect of a particular operation (basic task)?": a *semantic* description of the basic task in question.
- "How do I perform a certain basic task?": a description of how to perform the basic task in *syntax* terms ('actions'). For example: 'select the WORD and select the ITEM "copy" from the MENU "edit"'.
- "How do I perform an 'action'?": *keystroke* level. E.g. "select a WORD: point the mouse to the WORD and click the mouse button twice".

We implemented a system that translates relevant parts of an (arbitrary) ETAG-description into natural(-like) language (English). In this paper many semantical, grammatical, notational, implementational and other problems are not discussed. For an elaborate discussion of these, see Broos (1989).

4.2. Translation of ETAG-constructions

For our purposes we view an ETAG-description as consisting of three parts: the UVM, the dictionary of basic tasks and the replacement rules. The elements of these three parts impose different requirements on the translation method. We'll give a few examples of the three types of elements and their translation(-method) in section 4.1 to 4.3.

Our system takes the following approach.
We start with the original ETAG-description of an ideal user's mental model, as written for the original purposes (mainly describing and analysing user interfaces). This is given as input to a *preprocessor*. This system performs some transformations on its input, in order to make the parsing by the real translator easier/possible. Its output is a description in an extended or semi ETAG-notation, and is the input to the *translator*. This system translates its input into English and outputs the help messages in their raw form. These translations do not have a good lay-out, and also some overhead is output. That is why its output is fed into a *postprocessor*, which makes "nice" help messages out of its input. The eventual help messages are output. This is where this project stops. A possible continuation could be that the help texts are used by a "real" help system, in order to consequently provide the user with state-independent help.

The main part of our translating system, the translator, is written in the SYNICS-language, a system for writing general purpose translators (Guest, 1982; Edmonds & Guest, 1978). In SYNICS one can define a BNF of the input, along with statements that make transformations on the input and output the result. This is a very useful feature for our translation purposes. In short, we defined a BNF of the ETAG-formalism and rewrote this in the SYNICS language, along with the output statements. In essence this constitutes the whole of the translator program.

4.2.1. The UVM

This is a description of the concepts and objects that are relevant to the user. The descriptions are mainly based on mutual (spatial) relationships, like supertype, subtype, etc. The elements of the UVM are translated in a rather straightforward manner. An example is:

```
type [OBJECT = SPACE = SYSTEM_MAILBOX]
    supertype: [UNIX_MESSAGE_FILE];
    instancies: [SYSTEM_MAILBOX: #mailbox]
    where
      val ([SYSTEM_MAILBOX], [NAME]) = "$USER"
      val ([SYSTEM_MAILBOX], [PATH_NAME]) = "/usr/spool/mail/$USER";
end [SYSTEM_MAILBOX].
```

Translation:

> SYSTEM MAILBOX
> Here is some information on the type SYSTEM MAILBOX: It is a special kind of UNIX MESSAGE FILE. There is a SYSTEM MAILBOX, indicated with "mailbox", which NAME is "$USER" and which PATH NAME is "/usr/spool/mail/$USER".

This example shows that for the UVM the spatial structure implied by the ETAG-description is maintained. If the user wants to know what the function of a SYSTEM MAILBOX is, he is referred to the type UNIX MESSAGE FILE. Types are translated as they occur in the ETAG-description, that is, in capitals. We made this decision, because it clearly indicates that it is a type, on which the user can get further help/explanation.

4.2.2. The dictionary of basic tasks

This is a description of the basic tasks the user can perform and their operation on the objects in the UVM (a basic task is the smallest unit of functionality offered by the system to the user, always connected to one command or one basic action). Consider the following basic task in ETAG-notation:

```
ENTRY 8:
[EVENT = QUIT_WITH_CHANGES],
[event.KILL-ON( [MESSAGE: {*x}] , [place.IN( [MESSAGE_FILE: *y] )])];
[event.LEAVE( [UNIX_MAIL_ENVIRONMENT] )],
*y = get-current( [MESSAGE_FILE] )
AND
[state.ATTRIBUTE( [MESSAGE: {*x}], [TO_BE_DELETED], "true")],
T8,
"remove messages marked for deletion and quit".
```

Because of readability we want to remove the references 'x' and 'y'. This is done by syntactic transformations on the original basic task, performed by the preprocessor (we cannot consider *semantic* matters, because this is in conflict with our goal to develop a general system, usable for an arbitrary ETAG-description). After these transformations the resulting basic task can be translated as:

> QUIT WITH CHANGES
> (remove messages marked for deletion and quit) Description: the MESSAGEs, of which the attribute TO BE DELETED is "true", are removed from the current MESSAGE FILE and discarded. Then the UNIX MAIL ENVIRONMENT is left.

4.2.3. The replacement rules

There are two kinds of replacement rules. One kind describes how to perform a certain basic task in syntax-terms (we call these *actions*). The other kind describes how to perform a (syntax-) action in keystroke terms. We will give a simple example of one of each. The translations are rather straightforward after letting the preprocessor remove all variables (references, like 'x' below) that are the only one of their type and that have only one type (this doesn't necessarily have to be the case in ETAG).
syntax-rule:

```
T4 [OBJECT: *x] ::=
  select [OBJECT:*x] + use-key [LABEL = "backspace"]
  where: [OBJECT: *x] = ONE-OF {[STRING], [WORD], [RULER], [PICTURE]}.
```

The translation is:

> DELETE OBJECT IN DOCUMENT *(name of corresponding basic task)*
> Select the OBJECT and use the "backspace"-key. The OBJECT can be a STRING, a WORD, a RULER or a PICTURE.

Keystroke-rule:

```
select [OBJECT = STRING: *x] ::=
    MOUSE-POINT (first (image [STRING: *x])) + MOUSE-BUTTON-PRESS +
    MOUSE-DRAG-TO (last (image [STRING: *x])) + MOUSE-BUTTON-RELEASE |
    MOUSE-POINT (image [STRING: *x]) + MOUSE-BUTTON-CLICK.
```

The translation of this rule should speak for itself:

> Select a STRING, Point the mouse to the first place on the STRING, press the mouse button, drag the mouse to the last place on the STRING and release the mouse button. Or: point the mouse to the STRING and click the mouse button.

4.3. Conclusions

A useful feature of the messages is their generality. We focussed on generating them and not on how they are to be used. They can be used in on-line manuals, form the basis for the writing of the user-manual, be a help in reading and understanding the sometimes rather cumbersome ETAG-notation, etc. But of course they have to be supplemented by other types of help (task-level help, state-dependent help).

It seems that the main purpose of the help messages would be for reference documentation, which a user who has been sufficiently trained and educated (in the use of the system) can consult in order to refresh his memory and/or learn more about the specific workings of the system.

Our method poses restrictions on the form and structure of the help messages. The matter of improving the help on objects in the UVM is the subject of the next section.

5. An interactive question/answering system based on ETAG

We wrote part of a Help Machine that can answer users' questions about the information that is contained in an ETAG description only. Although ETAG was not designed for this purpose, it would be very useful if a Help System could be automatically generated from an ETAG desciption. In general, a Help Machine can be decomposed into three smaller machines (programs):

1. A machine that can answer questions stated in a formal language. The answer to those questions is also formal.
2. A machine that can translate a natural language query into a formal query that is suitable for the first machine to answer.
3. A machine that can translate formal answers from the first machine into natural language.

We wrote the first program, to which we will from now on refer to as the **interpreter.** The programming language in which this program was written is the Prolog programming language. There were two reasons for this choice:

For one thing, Prolog has always been one of the most heavily used programming languages in the field of natural language processing. It was in fact designed for this purpose. So it would be wise to write the interpreter, on top of which the natural language processing system is to be built, in Prolog as well.

The second reason is that Prolog already provides me with an interactive Question/Answering system. All we have to do is to provide the desired predicates in which the questions and answers can be expressed, and a suitable framework to use these predicates.

To make the information in an ETAG description, which is just a text file, accessible to the interpreter, we wrote a second program that converts the description into an equivalent Prolog database. We will refer to the program that performs this function as the **translator.** The translator is little more than a parser of ETAG that produces the same information in a different notation. However, since the grammar of ETAG is rather rich, it is not a small program. The translator was written in the C programming language, with code from the Lex and Yacc programs. Figure 1 shows the relations between the two programs (in boxes) and the data (in circles) they act upon.

The Prolog database is sufficiently general to be useful to other applications written in Prolog. An application other than the interpreter could be a program that performs semantic consistency checks on an ETAG description. It is the general intention that all ETAG related programs are 'building bricks' that can be used by other people to build their own particular applications.

5.1. Some examples

In this section we will illustrate how the translator and the interpreter perform their function by supplying an example from both programs. Due to space limitations we will not explain everything in full detail here, but the example should make the general intention clear. The example in this section is taken from an ETAG description of PMAIL. PMAIL stands for Prototype Mail, and it is the description of a mail system, that is yet to be.

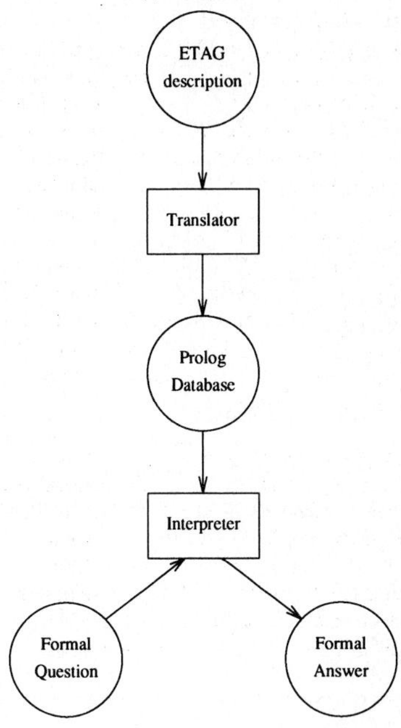

Figure 1.

5.1.1. The translator

The following is a type definition of a DIRECTORY as found in the ETAG description:

```
type [OBJECT = DIRECTORY]
  themes: [ONE-OF{ FILE, DIRECTORY }: {*x}];
  relations: [place.IN( [DIRECTORY] )] for all;
  attributes: <NAME>, <PATH_NAME>;
  comment: "Whatever..."
end [DIRECTORY].
```

In words, it says that a DIRECTORY can be related to OBJECTS, which are either of type FILE, or of type DIRECTORY. The number of OBJECTS that can form a relationship with an instance of DIRECTORY is specified by the referent; zero or more. The possible kinds of relations are mentioned in the *relations* slot. In this example, the themes can be in the relationship *place.IN* with an instance of DIRECTORY, meaning that a theme can be located in a DIRECTORY. A DIRECTORY has attributes NAME and PATH_NAME. The translator produces the following Prolog structure for this example:

```
object( directory,
        [],
        [],
        [ concept( one of( [file, directory] ), set( x, [] ) ) ],
        [ for( all, place( in, directory ) ) ],
        [ name, path_name ],
        "Whatever..."
).
```

The slots in the *object()* predicate correspond to the slots from the ETAG notation. The order of the slots in the predicate are: supertypes, subtypes, themes, relations, attributes and comment. Note that this is just a different notation to represent the same information.

5.1.2. The interpreter

This is the program that answers the users' questions through a Prolog-like interface. The following Prolog rule shows the role of the interpreter in the Help Machine as described at the beginning of this chapter.

```
help :- display_prompt,
        input( NL_Question ),
        nl_to_formal( NL_Question, Formal_Query ),
        query_answer( Formal_Query, Formal_Answer ),
        formal_to_nl( Formal_Answer, NL_Answer ),
        output( NL_Answer ),
        help.
```

The work of the interpreter is done by the predicate *query_answer()*. The task of machines 2 and 3 are performed by the predicates *nl_to_formal()* and *formal_to_nl()* respectively.

From the example of the previous section we can already answer a lot of questions. The question that involves all information encoded above is "What is a directory?". This question can be posed to the interpreter by asking all you want to know about the object. A question about what the attributes of a DIRECTORY are, is given to the interpreter as:

```
query_answer( [attributes( directory, A0 )], Formal_Answer )
```

After which the variable Formal_Answer will be instantiated to:

```
Formal_Answer = [attributes( directory, [ name, path_name ] )]
```

Which could be translated into english as "The attributes of a directory are name and path_name." Questions on the other slots are similar. If these are combined into a single question, then the answer will give the information that is necessary. For the case of the directory, the question "What is a directory?" is written as:

```
query_answer( [ supertypes( directory, Sp ),
                subtypes( directory, Sb ),
                themes( directory, Th ),
                relations( directory, Re ),
                attributes( directory, At )
              ],
              Formal_Answer
)
```

Note that the amount of information that is given depends entirely on what you want to know. For example, the instances are not mentioned in the above example. Also, it would be possible to leave out the themes, since these are also mentioned in the relations. The themes are a bit of a problem because it is not clear how to translate them into english. Broos (1989) uses the verb 'contains', which is suitable for most cases, but the meaning of theme is more general. Another possible translation is 'consists of'. The example given in this section is very simple. A more complete treatment with some less trivial examples is given in my thesis. The most important things that are handled by the interpreter are the following:

- Providing predicates for expressing questions and answers. These are predicates as mentioned above, but there are more like *cause(), keystroke()* etc.
- Inheritance of attributes, themes and relations from supertypes to subtypes. Attributes are always inherited, themes and corresponding relations are only inherited if ETAG says so.
- Collecting all possible answers in a list in the Formal_Answer. We decided that every answer should give as much information as possible. Queries like "Give a single theme of type ...", "Give an example of an instance of type ..." are not supported.
- duplicating the predicates from the question into the answer to make the work of *formal_to_nl()* easier, especially if the query consists of more than one predicate. The translation of the answer into English can be done in a way that is similar to what Broos did in his thesis.
- Providing only two out of the four layers used in the Replacement Rules section of an ETAG description. These two layers correspond to the syntax and keystroke levels from Moran. Roughly stated, the syntax layer describes **what** to do, the keystroke layer describes **how** to do it.
- Just as in real Prolog queries, it allows more than one question to be asked at the same time, where two questions can have 'sharing variables'. This allows queries like "What are the attributes of the subtypes of directory?". If it does not know the answer to some question, the interpreter still continues to answer the remaining questions.

References

[1] Boeijink P. (1987). *On Predictive Validity of HIDM with respect to Functionality*. Masters thesis, Free University, Amsterdam.

[2] Broos D. (1989). *ETAG-based Help - Generating Human-readable Explanation from a Formal Description of the User Interface*. M. Sc. thesis, Free University, Amsterdam.

[3] Card S.K., Moran T.P., and Newell A. (1983). *The Psychology of Human-Computer Interaction*. Hillsdale, NJ., Lawrence Erlbaum Associates.

[4] Edmonds E. & Guest S. (1978). SYNICS, a Fortran subroutine package for translation. *Man-Computer Interface Research Group report* no. 6. Leicester Polytechnic.

[5] Guest S. (1982). Software Tools for Dialogue Design. *IJMMS*, 14, 263-285.

[6] Innocent P., and Tauber M.J. (1988). Representation of the User Interface. In: van der Veer G.C. (ed.) *An Interdisciplinary Approach to Cognitive based User-Interface Design: Theory, Methodologies, Methods, and Tools*. Amsterdam, Free University, Department of Psychology.

[7] Moran T.P. (1981). The Command Language Grammar: a representation for the user interface of interactive computer systems. *International Journal of Man-Machine Studies*, 15, pp. 3-50.

[8] Tauber M.J. (1988). *On Mental Models and the User Interface*. In: van der Veer et al., 1988.

[9] Tauber M. J. (in preparation). *Course: Human-Computer Interaction*, Unit 7. Open Universiteit, Heerlen (The Netherlands), Open University, Milton Keynes (England), PMT607.

[10] van der Veer G.C., Green T.R.G., Hoc J. & Murray D.M. (Eds) (1988). *Working with computers: Theory versus Outcome*. London, Academic Press.

Human–Computer Interaction – INTERACT '90
D. Diaper et al. (Editors)
Elsevier Science Publishers B.V. (North-Holland)

WHAT IS INCONSISTENCY?

Phyllis Reisner

IBM Almaden Research Center, 650 Harry Road, San Jose, California 95120

One of the basic tenets of interface design is that an interface should be consistent. However, the meaning of the term remains elusive. Recently, there have been several attempts to represent inconsistency formally. A goal of such representation is to identify the inconsistency automatically. This paper (1) shows how each new formalism has increased our understanding of the nature of inconsistency, by expressing assumptions that had been hidden in earlier ones, (2) argues that none of the current formalisms will be able to identify consistency reliably because of an assumption that is still missing, and (3) presents a formal framework, APT, which includes the missing assumption. APT (Agent Partitioning Theory) is used to explain why user errors - a result of inconsistency - occur.

1. INTRODUCTION

One of the basic tenets of interface design is that an interface should be "consistent." (Rubinstein and Hersh, 1984; Shneiderman, 1987). However, precisely what is meant by this term remains elusive. For example, Payne and Green (1986) state:

> Consistency is difficult to define and therefore difficult to measure, but it is informally recognized to be a major determinant of learnability.

Similar comments can be found in Kellogg (1987), and Reisner (1981). According to Grudin (1989), in 1988 a two-day workshop of 15 experts was not able to produce a definition.

Several attempts have been made to represent consistency (and inconsistency) formally (Green and Payne, 1984; Payne, 1985; Payne, 1987; Payne and Green, 1983; Payne and Green, 1986; Payne and Green, 1989; Reisner, 1981). These attempts all describe inconsistency by variations on a theme: inconsistency is represented by "extra" rules in a grammar. Some of these attempts imply, state (or hope) that such formalization can be used, in a mechanical fashion, to identify inconsistencies in an interface. They would thus form an addition to the growing arsenal of design tools aimed at finding flaws in an interface design prior to time-consuming behavioral testing. These formalisms embody an increasing understanding of what inconsistency is. Hidden assumptions in the earlier formalisms become increasingly explicit with later ones. However, although the assumptions are becoming more explicit, there is still something crucial missing. Consequently, none of the formalisms are likely to succeed in the goal of automatically identifying inconsistency. In this paper we introduce a formal framework, called APT, which attempts to synthesize the previous work and to add the missing component. We are not concerned with the "form" of the formalisms, but with their meaning. To show the development, we use the same simple, easy-to-understand example throughout. This same example has been used by various authors. The paper focusses only on one kind of inconsistency - that of the syntax of a command language. However, the APT framework is probably quite general.

Loosely, consistency has been described as "doing similar things in similar ways." Grudin (1989) gives the following example of inconsistency. This example was the impetus for writing this paper. We consider later whether this example completely represents inconsistency.

> Consider the household interface design problem of deciding where to shelve imple-

ments, specifically knives. Butter knives, table knives, steak knives -- all may be kept in the same drawer. Consistent, easy to learn, easy to remember: there is one place to go for knives.

Grudin considers the above system *consistent.* But if the silverware knives are placed with the crystal and china, the putty knive is in a workbench drawer in the garage, or the Swiss army knive is with the camping gear, Grudin considers this *inconsistent.* The error, of course, would be to look in the wrong place for the knife.

In the example to be used throughout this paper, an early version of a simple graphics program, ROBART 1 (Reisner, 1981), was inconsistent; the methods for selecting lines, circles or squares were all similar, setting a switch for line, for circle, or for square. However, the method for selecting text differed. There was no "text" switch. Users were expected to just start typing. This action was inconsistent with the others. Users consequently made mistakes, and looked for a text switch which did not exist. In a redesigned version, ROBART 2, the methods for selecting line, circle, square and text were all the same; put a cursor in the appropriate icon. This system was consistent. There were no comparable errors in ROBART 2.

2. FOUNDATIONS

2.1. Rules and "Extra Rules"

In the ROBART system described above, a BNF-like notation was used to describe the "action language" of the system (the series of user actions needed to use the system, such as moving a cursor or setting a switch). The rules were then just the production rules in that notation. In the ROBART 1 example the rules were, e.g.:

```
to select line   -> SET LINE SWITCH   + GO
to select circle -> SET CIRCLE SWITCH + GO
```

Since these rules were of essentially the same form they were combined into one, more general rule which was called a "necessary" rule, for creating shapes. A second "necessary" rule described the manner of creating text, viz:

```
to select shape -> set shape switch + GO
to select text -> NULL
```

Other rules defined the shapes that applied to these rules, e.g.:

```
shape -> LINE | CIRCLE | SQUARE
```

Since there were two "necessary" rules for selecting items, the system was "structurally inconsistent," and, as mentioned above, during behavioral tests, users erroneously looked for a "text" switch. Since, however, in the redesigned, consistent ROBART 2, all forms, including text, were selected in the same way, the selection actions could be described by one necessary rule and the defining rule, viz:

```
to select shape -> PUT CURSOR IN SHAPE ICON
shape -> LINE | CIRCLE | SQUARE | TEXT
```

This work demonstrated that a user action language could be described formally. It also made explicit a criterion for inconsistency: the "extra" rule needed to describe ROBART 1. Notice that the formalism was intended to describe the action language of the *system.* This is the language *as the designer intended it to be used.* If we look at the informal definition of consistency, "doing similar things in similar ways," the rules describe the "similar ways." The "similar things," however, are not handled explicitly.

2.2. Set Grammar

Next, Payne and Green (1983) introduced the notion of *Set Grammar* to represent "perceived organization of a grammar." According to the authors, consistency involves *family resemblances between rules.* This is the notion that was hinted at in the "necessary rules" of ROBART. In Set Grammars, furthermore, these rules apply to *sets of objects.* Both family resemblances and sets of objects can be represented in the BNF-like notation used for ROBART, although not as explicitly. However, Set Grammars introduce a very important new notion - that elements within sets are *semantically* similar; they have some element of meaning in common. Payne and Green rewrite the ROBART 1 rules as follows:

```
SETS
SHAPES :: {circle, line, square}
RULES
select SHAPE -> select SHAPE switch + "GO"
select TEXT -> NULL
SELECTION RULE
Uniform replacement, use same selection
rule throughout
```

This very neat and easy to read notation explicitly labels both the sets and the rules which have a family resemblance. The notion of "selection rule," which solves a notational problem, is included for completeness but is not necessary to our discussion. The two notions introduced by Set Grammar make the correspondence of the notation to the early informal definition of consistency clearer. The "similar things" are members of the set, and the "similar ways" are the rules. The criterion for identifying inconsistency is still an "extra" rule. There is, however, an apparent difference. Instead of seeing the grammar that is being described as the action language of the *system,* as in the ROBART example, the grammar is seen as the *Grammar in the Head (GIH),* the knowledge of this action language that an ideal, experienced user of the system would have. Furthermore, according to the authors, Set Grammars represent user "competence" - what an experienced user *can* say or do, rather than what he/she actually *does* say or do. This distinction between competence and performance is well-known in linguistics (Chomsky, 1965).

Something very strange is happening. We see two very similar approaches, differing largely in notation, both describing inconsistency as an extra rule - but one sees the extra rule as being in the system language while the other sees it in the head of an ideal, experienced user. We will return to this difference later. The apparent difference is not a real one, but the different points of view do hide a real difference!

2.3. Task Action Grammars

In Set Grammars, similar things are in the same set. But what makes them similar? Task Action Grammars, or TAGs (Payne, 1985; Payne and Green, 1986; Green, Schiele, and Payne, 1988; and Payne and Green, 1989) introduce the notion of "semantic features" to label this similarity.[1] In TAGs, the authors make explicit the notion found in the earlier Set Grammar, by specifically identifying the "semantic features that underlie the grouping of rules sharing family resemblances into single rules." TAG now makes explicit in its notation the *criteria* (features and their values) that are used to treat rules that show family resemblances as similar. Also in TAGs, there are higher level rules to show the family resemblances, now explicitly called *rule schemata.* A TAG notation for the ROBART 1 example is shown in Figure 2. Inconsistency, in TAGs, as in Set Grammars, is represented by extra rules. ("... a highly consistent system will be representable by fewer rules than an arbitrary system" (Green et al., 1988, p.21)). However, the reason that the rule is extra is now explicit. Both rules contain the same semantic feature, "unit," which I prefer to call "things to be selected." Also in a similar vein to its predecessor, TAG is seen as modelling the "competence" of the user - what the ideal, experienced user *can* do, not what s/he actually does.

Returning to the informal definition, the "similar things" are similar because they have some element of meaning in common. This similarity is explicitly labelled by the semantic feature in the formal notation. We are getting closer to an understanding of what inconsistency is, but there is still something crucial missing.

```
select(Unit = ONE-OF:{circle, square, line}) ::= select-switch (Unit) + PRESS_GO
select (Unit = text) :: NULL
```

Figure 2. TAG notation for ROBART 1. In this example, "unit" is a *feature*, with *values* circle, square and line in the first *rule schema*, and *value* text in the second. The example is drawn from Hoppe et al., p. 17.

Task	select circle
Task Set	TASKSET = {circle, line, square, text}
Rule Instance	to select circle -> set circle switch up + go
Rule Schema	to select SHAPE-> set SHAPE switch up + go
Schema Set	SHAPE = {line, circle, square}
Semantic Feature	SHAPE (or UNIT, or whatever one labels a set).

Figure 1. Examples of terminology used to discuss inconsistency.

3. ELEMENTS OF APT

3.1. Terminology and Notation

Some concepts have not been clearly differentiated. We will use the following terminology and notation for the subsequent discussion.

We will assume that the meaning of task is self-evident. We will need to be able to talk about a task set - the set of tasks that could, according to some criterion, be treated as similar. We need to distinguish rule instances from rule schemata. Rule instances relate a single task (on the left hand side) to the syntax for that rule (on the right hand side). Rule schemata are meta-rules. They apply to a set of tasks. I like to think of rule schemata as statements or rules with variables. They can be expressed, in BNF notation, by rules with non-terminal symbols. A schema set is a set of tasks that can be used in a rule schema. If we think of rule schemata as rules with variables, then the elements of the schema set are the values (constants) for those variables. A schema set is a subset of a task set. A semantic feature is a name for a schema set. It is a name for the set of items that has "something in common" that resulted in their being grouped together. A semantic feature is *not* a semantic "attribute" - the reason things are in the same set. (For example, circle and square have the attributes of being two- dimensional, enclosing space in a certain way, etc.). The notation is illustrated in Figure 1.

3.2. An Important Detour : Semantic Relativity

To see what is missing from the above attempts to describe inconsistency, we detour to discuss an important philosophical point which has serious pragmatic consequences. *Semantic features do not exist in the real world.* This is not an academic position. Rather, it is at the very heart of what is involved in inconsistency. If "semantic features" were inherent in the world, all we would have to do is look for them, and hope to eventually come up with a definitive set, analyze tasks into semantic features, and automatically identify inconsistency. *Semantic features are LABELS.* In order to make sense of the world, we classify things into sets of "similar" things and assign labels to those things. That piece of vegetation ("vegetation" itself is a label) with light and airy things (branches) drooping over a riverbank is a "willow"; the thing in my back yard is an "ash." We decide that they have enough in common to call them trees. *Semantic features are (probably) context dependent.* But what about "text"? Why does it "belong" with the geometric shapes, line, circle and square? In the classic kinds of classification experiments ("here are a number of items; put those that are similar together") would text be identified as belonging to the same class as line, circle and square? Not necessarily. Suppose, for example, there were a system with (1) many kinds of fonts (2) font selection physically separate from shape selection (3) different modes of selection (buttons for text, switches for shapes) and (4) text selection at least as frequent as shape selection. My guess is that such a system would not be perceived as inconsistent by users. *There is more than one way to partition the universe.* Let us look at another simple thought experiment. The task is to classify, into sets of similar things: red balls, green balls, red cubes and green cubes. They could be classified by shape (all balls together) or by color (all red things together). A water-dweller of the planet Venus (known as watery to science fiction fans) might well classify on the basis of "floatability."

3.3. The Missing Pieces

Given this "semantic relativity," our notions of consistency and of inconsistency require more than we

Tasks
TASKSET = {circle, square, line, text}

Schema Sets
SHAPE = {circle, square, line ...}
TEXT = {...}

Partitioning rules
ROBART 1, Inconsistent
text ∊ TEXT for agent (designer)
text ∊ SHAPE for agent (user)
ROBART 2, Consistent
text ∊ SHAPE for agent (designer)
text ∊ SHAPE for agent (user)

Figure 3. Some possible partitioning of tasks in ROBART systems

have so far: rule schemata, schema sets and semantic features. We need to know:

1. Which things belong to which set, and
2. Who says so.

To describe the first, we need an *assignment rule*, e.g. circle ∊ {SHAPE}. To describe the second, we need an *assigning agent.* The combination of assignment rule and assignment agent we will call a *partitioning rule*, e.g. circle ∊{SHAPE} for agent (designer). For our purposes, there are (at least) two possible assigning agents, the designer and the competent user. We prefer to describe inconsistency in terms of a "competent user" rather than the "ideal" user of Payne and Green. An ideal user knows how to use a system, hence will not make mistakes. But in an inconsistent system, users do make mistakes caused by that inconsistency. By a "competent" user we mean one who makes mistakes common to many users, and probably ascribable to some system design feature. The competent user, however, does not make spurious errors.

Our central claim is that, when a system is inconsistent, ***DIFFERENT ASSIGNING AGENTS USE DIFFERENT ASSIGNMENT RULES.*** Specifically, in the case of interface inconsistency ***THE DESIGNER AND THE COMPETENT USER EMPLOY DIFFERENT ASSIGNMENT RULES.*** Hence they partition the set of tasks to be performed differently. Different possible partitionings are illustrated in Figure 3. The examples shown have been discussed earlier in this paper. Two others are possible. The notation and interpretations would follow the same format.

What then is consistency? When a system is consistent, a given task set is partitioned in the same way by both designer and user into sets of "similar tasks." The "schema sets" resulting from this partitioning are thus the same for both designer and user. These schema sets of similar items are used in the generalized "rule schemata" - the "similar ways" of handling the similar things. So consistency involves not only rules and sets of similar tasks, but also agreement between people about what things are similar.

5. DISCUSSION

5.1. Finding the Knives

Returning to Grudin's knife example, we can ask whether putting the knives in different places is truly inconsistent. From the information about knife placement alone, we can not tell. Let us formalize the discussion, as show in Figure 4. If the putter-away-of-knives and the seeker-of-knives both classify knives by function, the system will be con-

```
Tasks TASKSET = {knives of all kinds}

Agents
  Agent 1 =   putter-away-of-knives
  Agent 2 =   seeker-of-knives.

Sem. Feature 1 = function (things which cut)
  SCHEMA SET 1  =  {things which cut}
  Rule schema 1  =  put t-wh. cut in drawer

Semantic feature 2 = intended use
  SCHEMA SETS 2A, 2B, 2C =

• 2A = {things to be used in the garage}
• 2B = {things to be used in the kitchen}
• 2C = {things to be used on holidays}...
  Rule schemata, e.g.
       put things to be used in garage together

Partitioning Rules

Consistent System
  silverware ∊ SCHEMA SET 2C for agent 1
  silverware ∊ SCHEMA SET 2C for agent 2

Inconsistent System
  silverware ∊ SCHEMA SET 2C for agent 1
  silverware ∊ SCHEMA SET 1 for agent 2
```

Figure 4. APT description of knife placement consistency.

sistent. Likewise, if they both classify by intended use, the system will also be consistent. Only when one classifies by function, and the other by intended use, will the system be inconsistent - and the knives not found.[2]

5.2. Related work

The notion of two agents is conceptually related to the "mappings" described in various contexts. ETIT analysis (Moran, 1983) describes a mapping from external to internal tasks. The mapping rules can be used to indicate the complexity of a system. Green et al. (1985) discuss "expert slips" in terms of a mapping between the "task structure" and the language. However, they discuss inconsistency in terms of more than one way of organizing rule-schemas, rather than the multiple agents suggested here. Payne (1987) talks of two state spaces, the goal space and the device space, and a semantic mapping between them. He uses these concepts to distinguish between rote and meaningful learning. The notion of "semantic relativity" draws its inspiration from the considerable work in the field of linguistics to explore the "whorfian hypothesis." Whorf (1965) assumed that people in different cultures perceive the world differently, and that this is correlated with differences in their language.

5.3. Theoretical and Practical Implications

What is consistency? If we look at the informal definition of consistency as "doing similar things in similar ways" then we have to add to the definition - "agreement between agents about what things are similar." Likewise, inconsistency would be disagreement on such similarity judgements. *Where is consistency?* Contrary to popular belief, consistency is not a *property* of a system language. Likewise, consistency does not reside in the head of the user, alone. If consistency is not a property of either the system or the user, what then is it? By now, the answer should be obvious. It is a relation between two languages, that of the system, as the designer intended it, and of the competent user. We now understand the apparent anomaly noted earlier: in one case the grammar described the system, and in the other, it described the user. Both views are correct, and both are incomplete. *Where is the extra rule?* There is clearly an extra rule, but where is it? The answer depends on what is meant by a "rule" and on the point of view. In our example, from the point of view of the user, the system has an extra "rule schema." But from the point of view of the system, the user has created an extra (incorrect) "rule instance." *Where do errors come from?* Errors arise when the user substitutes an incorrect variable (drawn from his/her own classification) into a rule schema to produce an incorrect rule instance. *What are the practical implications?* Since consistency is not a property of a system interface, it is unlikely that ANY formal description of that interface alone will be able to identify inconsistency mechanically. Likewise, since inconsistency is not a property of the GIH (grammar in the head), NO formal description of the GIH alone will be able to identify it. None of the current efforts will suffice. *What is needed?* We need a discovery procedure that describes and compares *both* interface and user languages and looks for mismatches. We also need to study classification criteria - why do people treat certain tasks as similar?

Caveats. This paper discusses only one kind of inconsistency. The rules relate a task to the syntax for that task. The reasoning behind this discussion is probably quite general. But other dimensions have not been examined. Furthermore, APT is a representation framework, not a causal analysis. It is not clear how much inconsistency is due to carelessness, to different people designing different parts of a system or to different world views. Likewise, APT is not a discovery procedure. It does not show how to identify inconsistency, only what its components are.

6. SUMMARY

Consistency of an interface, "doing similar things in similar ways," is important but not well-defined. The ROBART work described inconsistency as an "extra rule" in a grammar. This described the "similar ways" but said nothing about the "similar things." Set Grammar grouped the "similar things" into sets, but said nothing about what made them similar. TAG said that the similarity was "semantic" and labelled the "semantic feature" that named the set and the "values," the members of the set, but said nothing about who did the labelling. The current work, APT, adds the notion of agents assigning a value to a particular set, or class. When agents (e.g. designer and user) agree in this classification, a system is consistent, otherwise it is inconsistent. Because all previous attempts at formalizing inconsistency are missing the notion of multiple agents, none of these attempts, in spite of their claims, are likely to provide a reliable method of automatically identifying inconsistency. It will probably be necessary to look at two languages, not one, and find a method for discovering mismatches between them.

ACKNOWLEDGEMENTS

I would like to acknowledge Ron Fagin, Jonathan Grudin, Ben Shneiderman and Irv Traiger for their provocative and thoughtful comments, and Mark Harwood and Sharon Lee for invaluable help in formatting the paper.

FOOTNOTES

1. I want to emphasize that the interpretation of both Set Grammars and of TAGs is mine and may or may not correspond to the intention of the authors. If not, I claim their indulgence. Just as they acknowledged that the starting point of their work was mine (Payne and Green, 1983), I in turn acknowledge that the starting point of my current work is theirs.

2. Many fine points are made in the Grudin paper. We pick this example only to illustrate the missing assumption.

REFERENCES

1. Chomsky, N. (1965). *Aspects of the theory of syntax*. Cambridge, Mass: MIT Press.
2. Green, T. R. G. and Payne, S. J. (1984). Organization and learnability in computer languages. *Intl. J. Man-Machine Studies, 21*, 7-18.
3. Green, T. R. G., Payne, S. J., Gilmore, D. J. and Mepham, M. (1985). Predicting expert slips. In B. Shackel (Ed.), *Human-Computer Interaction - INTERACT '84* (pp. 519-525). Amsterdam: Elsevier.
4. Green, T. R. G., Schiele, F. and Payne, S. J. (1988). Formalisable models of user knowledge in human-computer interaction. In G. C. van der Veer, T. R. G. Green, J-M. Hoc and D. M. Murray (Eds.), *Working with computers: theory versus outcome* (pp. 3-41). London: Academic Press.
5. Grudin, J. (1989). The case against user interface consistency. *CACM, 32* (10), 1164-1173.
6. Hoppe, H. U., Tauber M. and Ziegler, J. E. (1986). A survey of models and formal description methods in HCI with example applications. *ESPRIT PROJECT 385 HUFIT, Report B.3.2a.* Fraunhofer-Institute.
7. Kellogg, W. A. (1987). Conceptual consistency in the user interface: effects on user performance. In H.-J. Bulinger and B. Shackel (Eds.), *Human-Computer Interaction - INTERACT '87* (pp. 389-394). Amsterdam: Elsevier.
8. Moran, T. P. (1983). Getting into a system: external-internal task mapping analysis. *CHI '83 Proceedings* (pp. 45-49). New York: ACM Press.
9. Payne, S. J. (1985). Task action grammars. In B. Shackel (Ed.), *Human-Computer Interaction - INTERACT '84* (pp. 527-532). Amsterdam: Elsevier.
10. Payne, S. J. (1987). Complex problem spaces: modelling the knowledge needed to use interactive devices. In H.-J. Bulinger and B. Shackel (Eds.), *Human-Computer Interaction - INTERACT '87* (pp. 203-208). Amsterdam: Elsevier.
11. Payne, S. J. and Green, T. R. G. (1983). The user's perception of the interaction language: a two level model. *CHI '83 Proceedings* (pp. 202-206). New York: ACM Press.
12. Payne, S. J. and Green, T. R. G. (1986). Task-action grammars: a model of the mental representation of task languages. *Human-Computer Interaction, 2*, 93-133.
13. Payne, S. J. and Green, T. R. G. (1989). The structure of command languages: an experiment on task-action grammar. *Intl. J. of Man-Machine Studies, 30,* 213-234.
14. Reisner, P. (1981). Formal grammar and human factors design of an interactive graphics system. *IEEE Trans. on Software Engineering, SE-7* (2), 229-240.
15. Rubinstein, R. and Hersh, H. (1984). *The human factor, designing computer systems for people.* Burlington, Mass: Digital Press.
16. Shneiderman, B. (1987). *Designing the user interface: strategies for effective human-computer interaction.* Reading, Mass: Addison-Wesley.
17. Whorf, B. L. (1971). *Language, thought and reality, selected writings of Benjamin Lee Whorf.* (J. B. Carroll, Ed.). Cambridge, Mass: MIT Press.

SECTION II: DESIGN: THEORIES, METHODS AND TOOLS

SII.1 Studies and Analyses of Design

Looking HCI in the I
S.J. Payne 185

Qualitative artifact analysis
W.A. Kellogg 193

Redesign by design
R.K.E. Bellamy and J.M. Carroll 199

What rationale is there in design?
A. MacLean, V.M.E. Bellotti, and R. Young 207

A framework for assessing applicability of HCI techniques
V.M.E. Bellotti 213

Obstacles to user involvement in interface design in large product development organizations
J. Grudin 219

Integrating human factors with structured analysis and design methods: An enhanced conception of the extended Jackson system development method
K.Y. Lim, J.B. Long, and N. Silcock 225

Human–Computer Interaction - INTERACT '90
D. Diaper et al. (Editors)
Elsevier Science Publishers B.V. (North-Holland)

Looking HCI in the I

Stephen J. Payne

User Interface Institute
IBM T.J. Watson Research Center
P.O. Box 704
Yorktown Heights, NY 10598

Despite its name, the field of human-computer interaction has not devoted much research attention to the nature of interaction. This paper begins such an effort by focussing on the role of the user interface as a resource for action. A simple notation for describing human-computer interactions, based on Clark and Schaefer's (1987, 1989) theory of conversational contributions is motivated and described. Interaction trees allow descriptions that expose the role of the device's detailed output dynamics in user activity.

1.0 USER INTERFACE: GULF OR RESOURCE?

Almost all psychological research in Human-Computer Interaction has framed the issue of usability as a problem of complexity: why are computer systems so difficult to learn and use? This perspective has led to a dominant characterization of the user interface as a gulf that the user must cross. The term "gulf" is due to Norman (1986), but similar perspectives underlie the work of Moran (1981, 1983) and Young (1981), as well as work that draws on traditions outside the cognitive literature, such as Bodker (1989). In this vernacular, good design helps bridge the gulf by bringing the machine "closer" to the user's real task. The style and name of "direct manipulation" interfaces exemplify and encourage this characterization.

At the last Interact conference, I expressed the nature of the interface gulf by contrasting HCI with the puzzle solving tasks from which cognitive models of goal-directed behaviour are derived (Payne, 1987). It seemed to me that there are at least two critical differences between HCI and puzzles like the Tower of Hanoi: 1) The user can only act on objects in the goal space indirectly, via the device's representation of the goal space. 2) Operations cannot be applied directly, a mapping from operations onto actions is defined by an artificial interface language.

Both these aspects of the interface gulf create special learning problems for the user, on which cognitive analyses may be brought to bear. For example, Task-action Grammar (Payne and Green, 1986) seeks to analyse the perceived structure of the mapping from operations onto actions, and the Yoked State Space hypothesis (Payne, Squibb and Howes, in press) seeks to analyse device-centered problem spaces.

However, one might take a different view of these two distinctive features of HCI, illustrating a different conception of the user interface. Instead of viewing them as a learning problem one can view them as providing the potential for a new kind of action: 1') The user is able to apply operations without immediately affecting the external world, enabling experimentation and simulation. 2') The user is able to specify operations in a language, with all the potential for vagueness, indirectness, negotiation that languages allow.

Viewed in this way, the user interface is not a gulf, but a resource for action. Unfortunately, current cognitive models of how action is generated do not throw much light on the way such a resource might be exploited.

2.0 DISPLAY-BASED ACTION AT THE USER INTERFACE

Most current models of action, in HCI and in cognitive psychology, assume that skilled actors know what they are doing. Users form goals, decompose these into subgoals, and further into sequences of operations, which can be expressed directly as actions. In routine skill, this decomposition can take place without problem solving: sequences of actions are remembered as pre-packaged methods for the direct accomplishment of goals (Newell and Simon, 1972; Card, Moran and Newell, 1983). Information from the world plays a limited role, that of feedback, allowing an evaluation of the effects of actions against goals (Miller, Galanter and Pribram, 1960; Norman, 1986).

This account is very succesful at modelling many aspects of skilled and unskilled human behaviour, including time to perform tasks at the user interface, but it underplays the role of perception in cognitive skill, and thus underestimates the extent to which a user interface can act as a resource. Several researchers have noted that the external "display" on which a skill is enacted serves as a repository for much search control knowledge, thus relieving working memory from the onerous jobs (such as maintaining long stacks of subgoals) assigned it by the classical account. For example, Green, Bellamy and Parker (1987) and Young and Simon (1987) have argued that actions are often enacted before plans are complete, allowing intermediate states to be picked up from the world, rather than remembered. Larkin's (1989) analysis of "display based problem solving" similarly stresses that the current problem state is often directly available from the display.

Larkin's work and that of Young and Simon suggest that many of the senses in which action is "situated" may be amenable to accounts within the goal-planning account of action (for the opposite conclusion from similar observations, see Suchman, 1987). However, Payne (in press) notes a further two phenomena of display-based action, that are particularly relevant to HCI, and particularly hard to address within the confines of the plans framework. First, users may rely on recognizing the actions required to effect operations, rather than having to recall them. Second, users may be uncertain as to the precise effects of operations until they have enacted them. Payne (in press) illustrates both these phenomena through simple experiments in which experienced users of computer systems fail to recall the names of menu-items (see also Morton, 1967, Mayes et al 1988) and exhibit inaccurate recall of the effects of commonly used actions such as find commands or cursor movements. Users need not know what they are doing in as strong a sense as that implied by deterministic plans.

3.0 TOWARDS A MODEL OF INTERACTION AS CONVERSATION

How can we develop a model of performance that respects these phenomena of display-based action? A model in which users may recognize the operation they need from the current display, rather than generate it from their memory, and in which they may be uncertain of an operation's precise effects until after it is issued, instead of choosing between operations on the basis of their known effects? A model in which an important aspect of becoming skilled is to learn to gather and use information from the interface during action sequences?

These properties are reminiscent of human conversation, and may underly the popularity of a conversation metaphor for HCI. Much previous use of the metaphor has been limited to generation of wishlists of features to support convivial computing (eg Nickerson, 1977). Here the metaphor will be used for a different purpose, as the platform from which a cognitive model of interaction can be developed. I start with a specific model of human conversation due to Clark and Schaefer (1987,1989).

3.1 Conversational contributions

Clark and Schaefer (1987, 1989) suggest that conversation is structured not just at the level of turns but also at a level of contributions. A contribution is a collaborative achievement in two phases. In the first phase, presentation, one of the participants makes an utterance that is intended to specify the content of a contribution. This is followed by acceptance, in which participants collaborate to establish the mutual assumption that they have all understood the contribution satisfactorily for current purposes (the "grounding criterion"). Acceptance may take several turns, or it may be established by default, if the conversation is simply continued at the same level. Both the presentation and the acceptance phase of a contribution may have other contributions nested within them, so that a conversation is a sequence and a hierarchy of contributions.

Clark and Schaefer describe the machinery of presentation and acceptance in some detail, paying particular attention to the conversational structures which allow the grounding criterion to be achieved. Much of their analysis need not concern us; the important aspects of contribution theory for our rather separate purposes can be illustrated using a single example.

Consider the extract of a conversation described in Figure 1. This fragment of conversation comprises two contributions, the first complex, the second simple. Both presentation and acceptances can be simple or complex. All utterances are presentations at some level and so initiate a new contribution at that level. Contributions may be accepted by one participant simply continuing the conversation at the same level, marked in the tree by diagonal acceptance arcs. All acceptances must ultimately be completed in this way.

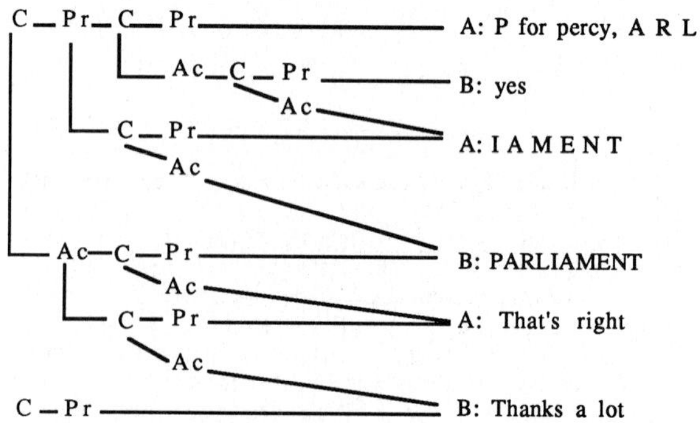

Figure 1. A contribution tree for a conversation in which A spells "parliament" to B.

The heart of Clark and Schaefer's proposal, then, is that participants in a conversation are doing two things at once: they are communicating, and they are attempting to ground the communication in a mutual belief that it is being successfully achieved.

3.2 A model of interaction

At first glance, contributions may appear to be an unsuitable basis for a model of action, even "interaction" with a machine. Contribution structures emerge because of the requirement to ground conversations in mutual understanding, but it is surely fanciful to apply this criterion to current technology?

Nevertheless, I suggest that users of a computer system, like conversationalists, are doing two things at once: they are acting, and they are attempting to account for their actions in terms of their purposes. This dual thread structures interactions, like conversations, into the two phases of presentation and acceptance. However, the nature of the phases, especially the nature of acceptance, is radically different. In recognition of the shift, HCI-Contributions are renamed unit interactions. A unit interaction is an interchange between the user and device, which begins with a presentation by the user or the device, and ends when the "accounting criterion" is satisfied - when the user has accounted for the presentation's role relative to her purposes. Much action at the interface plays the role of accepting some earlier presentation, as later actions give meaning to earlier actions.

Replacing the grounding criterion with a user-task oriented accounting criterion leads to different structures for HCI than for conversation. All default acceptances, those that are signalled by moving on to a new presentation at the same level, are done by the user. This marks the asymmetry of HCI, and a radical breakdown in the conversation metaphor for HCI. In most conversations each partner is autonomous to a degree; in HCI the user is in global control, although locally the device may lead the interaction.

Some basic properties of this model of action at the user interface are illustrated in Figure 2, which shows an interaction tree for deletion of a file in DOS. (In all interaction tree figures, I stands for a unit interaction, U and D mark actions by user and device respectively).

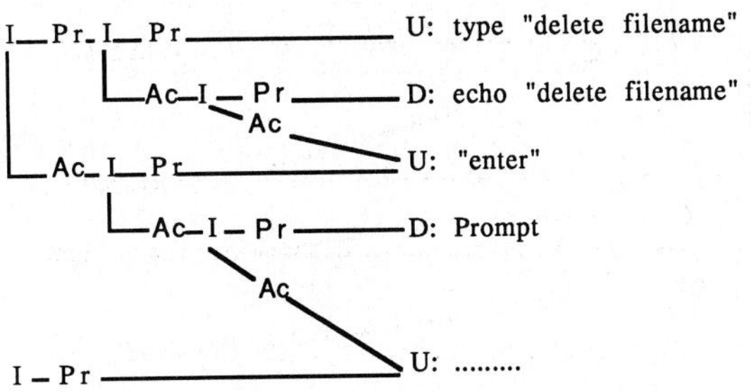

Figure 2. An interaction tree for file deletion in DOS.

The interaction divides into two main phases. In the first presentation phase, the user specifies the intended interaction, and the device echoes the specification. At this stage the user is free to edit the specification, which would show in an interaction tree as part of the "acceptance" phase, although in this instance, the function would, of course, be non-acceptance of the intial presentation. The user (eventually) initiates acceptance of the presentation by hitting Enter, to which the device, rather uninformatively, responds with a new prompt, which the user accepts by moving on to the next unit interaction. In an alternative scenario, if the user makes a typing error, for example, the device may respond "Bad command or file name". At this point, the user, rather than merely moving on, may repair the initial command, by reentry, or by using the command-line editor. In this case the unit interaction is extended, with the repair working to accept the device's error message (see Figure 3).

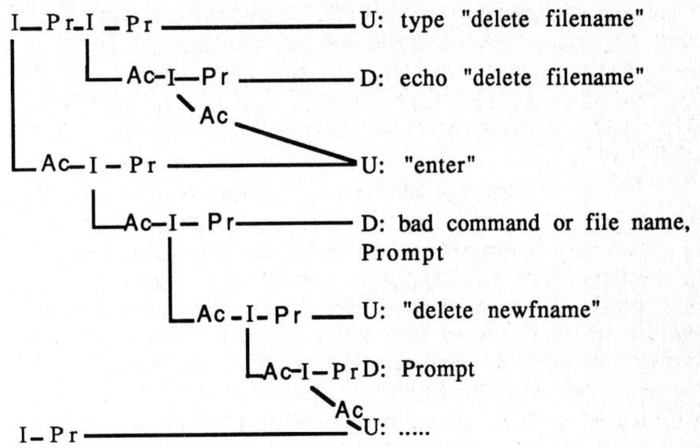

Figure 3. Interaction tree for repairing file deletion in DOS.

4.0 ANALYSING ARTIFACTS WITH INTERACTION TREES

4.1 Supporting exploration and repair

Our first example shows how an adaptation of Clark and Schaefer's distinction between presentation and acceptance might underly the structure of interactions in which the user is initially uncertain about the effects of operations. The example also shows that one of the roles of acceptance phases, in HCI as in conversation, is to allow repair. Repair is a routine aspect of conversation, described in detail by Schegloff, Jefferson and Sacks (1977). I claim that repair is also a routine part of interaction with a machine, but its facility depends on good design. In the basic DOS deletion interaction, the opportunities for repair are quite limited, for there is but a single acceptance unit.

By way of contrast, consider file deletion on a mouse-driven system, like the Apple Macintosh. During such a transaction there is a great deal more detailed interaction between user and device. The sequence of actions for (one method of) file deletion on the Macintosh is as follows:

User: Move mouse to file icon; Device: Pointer moves to file icon; User: Depress mouse button; Device: File icon highlights; User: Drag mouse to bin; Device: Outline of icon moves to bin...Bin highlights; User: Release mouse button; Device: File icon and outline disappear, bin reverts to normal

A contention of this article is that these details of the device behaviour and the way they interact with user actions - the interactivity of the system - is a critical feature of interface design. And, to reiterate another of our main points, standard models of action cannot throw any light on these features. This is well illustrated by the work of Karat and Bennet (1989) who attempted to analyse the difference between a DOS-like interface and the Macintosh interface, using the Cognitive Complexity model of Kieras and Polson (1985). They found that, through the filters of GOMS, transactions like file deletion appeared identical under each design.

How can interaction trees help us to understand interactivity? Figure 4 shows an interaction tree for Macintosh file deletion.

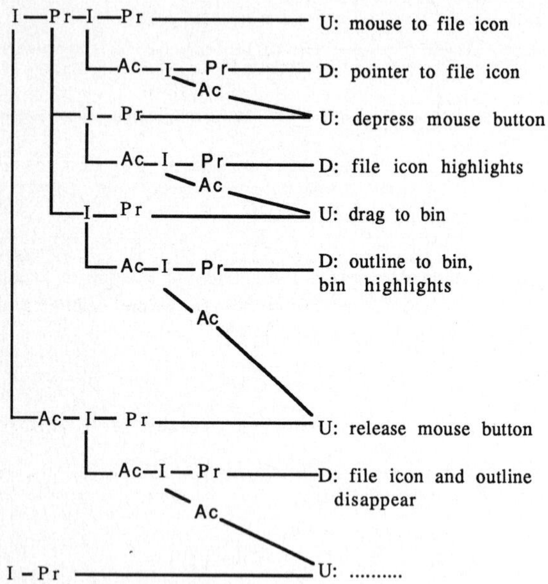

Figure 4. Interaction tree for file deletion using an Apple Macintosh.

According to the model, the interaction is structured into a presentation phase and an acceptance phase. The main presentation is itself a sequence of three unit interactions, led by the user moving the mouse, depressing the mouse button and dragging to the bin. At each stage the device responds, and the user implicitly accepts the device's response by moving on. But note that at each step the user could repair the interaction, by moving the mouse elsewhere, or deselecting the icon. This smooth, versatile repair, is a feature of the interaction. The main acceptance is led by the user releasing the mouse button.

One interesting point to emerge from the analysis is the role of the "bin highlights" device-response. According to the interaction tree, this response is accepted by the user proceeding to accept all the previous interactions, by releasing the mouse button. Yet its content appears matched only the "drag to bin" presentation. One is led to wonder whether the interaction design would not be improved if the feedback here matched its true role - perhaps the icons should disappear when the bin is reached, not only after release? Such a design would maximize the potential for exploratory action, as the effects of the interaction could be reviewed before the interaction is finally accepted (by releasing the mouse button).

Conversations with Macintosh users offer some confirmation for this speculation that the bin-highlight response is inadequate. Several users that I have spoken with recall difficulty as novices with this operation, inadvertently "missing the bin" and leaving the file icon nearby on the desktop. Some users even report a strategy of opening the bin to ease deletion, though this is surely unneccessary for users who have realized that moving the pointer over the bin, indicated by the bin highlighting, is always enough to achieve successful deletion. The problem these users face is that they have not induced the necessary condition for completion of the presentation phase of the deletion operation. Yet for many actions the highlighting of the pointed-to icon is seemingly perfectly adequate. If this line of reasoning is correct, it shows the importance of interaction structures for the design of detailed device responses, and it suggests that interaction trees might provide a useful tool for the analysis of such structures.

4.2 A parsing error

Our next example is also taken from the Macintosh interface. Consider the selection of drawing tools in MacDraw. Each tool is selected by pointing to and clicking on the appropriate icon (square, circle, line etc). Figure 5 shows an interaction tree for this sequence.

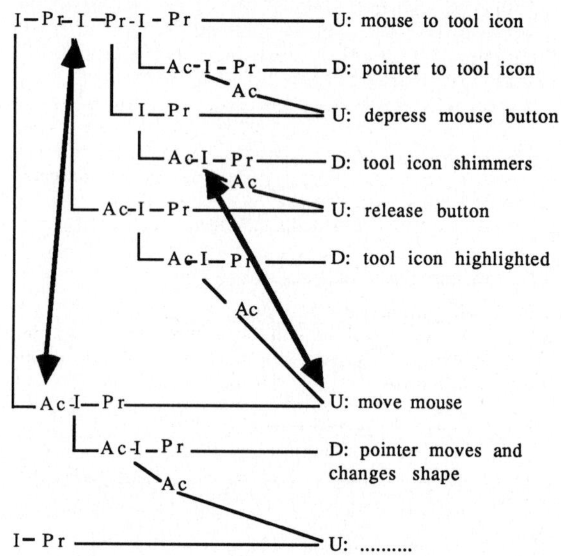

Figure 5. Interaction tree for tool selection in MacDraw. Bold acceptance arcs show a misparsing error.

In this case, we can see that the interaction has been specifically designed to address the issue raised in our discussion of file deletion. When the user depresses the mouse button, the pointed-to tool icon shimmers, indicating that this icon will be selected when the user accepts by releasing. This feedback plays an important role, especially when user selections are made near the boundary of two tools (the tools are lined up in a vertical array). If the wrong tool is selected at this stage, the user can repair by simply dragging the mouse to the correct tool.

However, in this case, the informative design leads to problems of its own, for some novices. In observational studies of MacDraw, I have recorded several novices drag off a tool icon to the workspace, only to be surprised that the tool icon then becomes de-selected (the distinction between depressing the button and clicking it is often a problem for novices). In one case, this cycle of selection to inadvertent deselection was repeated over ten times by a hapless subject. Interaction trees can offer an account of the nature of this error. It seems that the novice is misparsing the structure of the interaction. As shown by the error arcs in Figure 5, the novice is assuming that the shimmering icon marks the end of entire tool-selection interaction, and that moving off the icon constitutes a valid acceptance of the shimmering by continuing to the next interaction.

One test of theories of action is that they should be readily perturbed to model errors, and interaction trees clearly score in this case. However, with regards to recommendations for design, we seem to have unearthed something of a paradox: errors in file deletion arise because intermediate device-responses do *not* properly signal completion of a presentation phase; errors in tool selection arise because intermediate device-responses *do* attempt to signal presentation completion. If bin-highlighting was redesigned along the lines we suggested, conveying the pending file-deletion, would not novices make a parallel to the tool error, dragging off the bin and inadvertently failing to accept the deletion?

We suspect that this may well be the case, but still prefer the more informative feedback. What we have discovered is not a paradox, but a tradeoff, that most pevasive of interface decisions. Interaction trees do not resolve the tradeoff, in this case, but they do expose it's dimensions to support a more informed decision.

4.3 Reusing device outputs

The above examples have focussed on one of the ways in which the user interface can be a resource for action, allowing exploratory action and repair. What of the other resource listed in the introduction, the recognition of operations? To see some of the issues here, consider yet another example of file deletion, this time imaginary (though it might well correspond to the design of some real system). Imagine deletion is achieved by first selecting the file icon, then popping up a menu, and selecting "Delete" from the menu. The interaction tree would be as shown in Figure 6.

The point to make about this tree is that the selection of delete from the pop-up menu is treated as an acceptance of the popping up. It is through the action of selection that the user gives an account of popping-up the menu for the current purpose. This example introduces another kind of acceptance that is at the heart of many current interactive systems, where the user accepts a device-action by actually using it in the specification of the next presentation (Draper, 1986, observed the importance of this feature, which he dubbed inter-referential I/O).

Our treatment of inter-referential I/O as interactive acceptance may provoke criticisms of inconsistency. In our earlier examples from the Macintosh interface, we should surely have regarded pointing to icons as reusing a device's output, and thus accepting some tacit presentation? Indeed, file icon selection could have been treated this way, but was glossed for simplicity. The resulting interaction tree would contain that which appears in figure 3, unchanged but at a lower level, as the acceptance phase of a larger interaction, in which the presentation displayed the file icon.

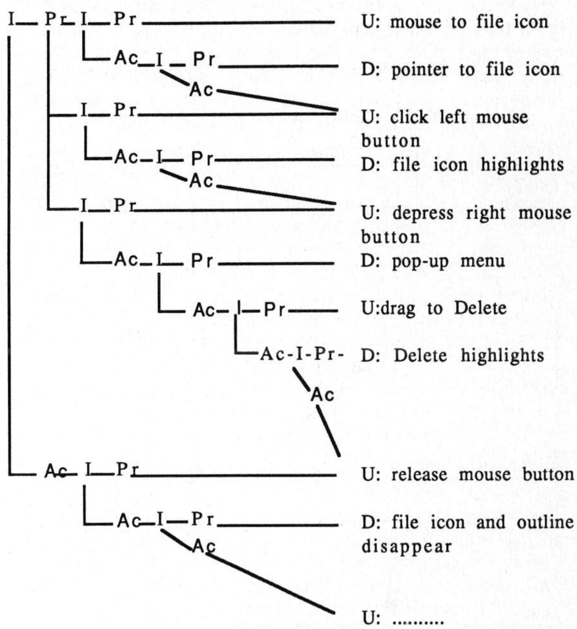

Figure 6. Interaction tree for deletion using a pop-up menu.

However, there are two types of reuse for which the issue is more complex, which can be exemplified within the described interactions. First, for icons which are a permanent part of the application's appearance such as the waste bin, or the MacDraw tool icon, it seems unnatural to regard use of the icon as acceptance of a device presentation, yet interactions with such icons must surely have a different status to, say, the typing of names. Second, the reuse of device-responses may be interleaved with intervening interactions. Imagine a user displaying the contents of three disks before selecting a file from the first. This kind of interleaving of reference happens on occasion in human conversation ("let's go back to what you said about..."), but it is rife in HCI where the persistence of many device outputs means that the history of an interaction is often avaliable to the user without any dependence on memory. In summary: interaction trees appear to provide the basic vocabulary for analysing the inter-reference of device and user actions, but we have yet to develop a full, satisfactory treatment.

5.0 FUTURE PROSPECTS

The three file deletion interaction trees show the radically different structures that can be needed to describe superficially similar interactions. It must be noted that there is no simple metric that can be applied to these trees to gauge the quality of the interaction, but it is tempting to speculate that the depth of the tree gives some indication of the "feeling of engagement" with the interface - the deeper the tree, the richer the interaction. This speculative account of perceived interactivity differs from that of Hutchins, Hollan and Norman (1986), who regard the directness of manipulation as the major determinant of the affective quality of an interface. Any resolution of this nascent dispute must await empirical and theoretical developments.

One key to such a development within the current framework is a better understanding of the nature of acceptance. In the course of analysing the examples of this paper, several distinct types of acceptance have been proposed - acceptance by reuse, acceptance by continuation, acceptance by reiteration, acceptance by completion (as in Entering a command, or releasing the mouse button). To this list we might add acceptance by undoing and acceptance by confirmation. This list is a start towards a classification of acceptances, a classification of the ways of interacting to satisfy the accounting criterion. Such a classification may be a useful step towards a taxonomy of user interface techniques, which currently exist as a large unsystematic collection of widgets.

This paper reports work at an early stage, and there is no pretence that interaction trees provide a fully polished lens through which we can look HCI in the I. Even in the simple examples we have chosen, some interesting issues lie outside the scope of the model. Indeed, some of these issues can be addressed by existing interface-as-gulf models; it is not suggested that the complexity perspective be replaced by this paper's stress on the interface as a resource, but rather that both perspectives are necessary for a full analysis of interactive artifacts. The goals of this paper are to promote the need to examine the close detail of interaction sequences as a vital part of such analyses, and to advance the potential for bringing cognitive models to bear on that problem.

ACKNOWLEDGEMENTS

I am grateful to Tom Moran for prompting the inital development of these ideas. This project began on a working visit to Rank Xerox EuroPARC, while I was employed at Lancaster University.

REFERENCES

Bodker, S. (1989). A human activity approach to interfaces. *Human-Computer Interaction, 4*, 171-195.

Card, S.K., Moran, T. P. and Newell, A. (1983). *The Psychology of Human-Computer Interaction.* Hillsdale, NJ: Erlbaum.

Clark, H.H. and Schaefer, E.F. (1987). Collaborating on contributions to conversations. *Language and Cognitive Processes, 2,* 19-41.

Clark, H.H. and Schaefer, E.F. (1989). Contributing to discourse. *Cognitive Science, 13,* 259-294.

Draper, S.W. (1986). Display managers as the basis for human-computer interaction. In D.A. Norman and S.W. Draper (Eds.) *User-Centered System Design.* Hillsdale, NJ: Erlbaum.

Green, T.R.G., Bellamy, R.K.E., and Parker, J.M. (1987). Parsing and gnisrap: a model of device use. In G.M. Olson and E. Soloway (Eds.). *Empirical Studies of Programmers: Second Workshop.* Norwood, NJ: Ablex.

Hutchins, E. L., Hollan, J.D. and Norman, D.A. (1986). Direct manipulation interfaces. In D.A. Norman and S.W. Draper (Eds.) *User-Centered System Design.* Hillsdale, NJ: Erlbaum.

Karat, J. and Bennet, J. (1989). Modelling the user interaction methods imposed by design. IBM Recarch Department Report, RC 14649, IBM T.J. Watson Research Center.

Kieras, D.E. and Polson, P.G. (1985). An approach to the formal analysis of user complexity. *International Journal of Man-Machine Studies, 22,* 365-394.

Larkin, J. (1989). Display-based problem solving. In D. Klahr and K. Kotovsky (Eds.) *Complex Information Processing: A Tribute to Herbert A. Simon.* Hillsdale, NJ: Erlbaum.

Mayes, J.T., Draper, S.W., McGregor, A.M. and Oatley, K. (1988). Information flow in a user interface: the effect of experience and context on the recall of MacWrite screens. In D.M.Jones and R.Winder (Eds.) *People and Computers IV.* Cambridge University Press.

Miller, G.A., Galanter, E. and Pribram, K. (1960). *Plans and the structure of behaviour.* New York: Holt Rinehart and Wilson.

Moran, T.P. (1981). The command language grammar. *International Journal of Man-Machine Studies, 15,*3-50.

Moran, T.P. (1983). Getting into a system: external-internal task mapping analysis. In Proc. CHI 83 Human Factors in Computing Systems. New York: ACM.

Morton, J. (1967). A singular lack of incidental learning. *Nature,* 215, 203-204.

Nickerson, R.S. (1977). On conversational interaction with computers. *User-Oriented Design of Interactive Graphics Systems.* New York: ACM.

Newell, A. and Simon,H.A. (1972). *Human Problem Solving.* Englewood Cliffs, NJ: Prentice Hall.

Norman, D.A. (1986) Cognitive engineering. In D.A. Norman and S.W. Draper (Eds.) *User-Centered System Design.* Hillsdale, NJ: Erlbaum.

Payne, S.J. (1987). Complex problem spaces: Understanding the knowledge needed to use interactive systems. In H. Bullinger and B.Shackel (Eds.) *Human-Computer Interaction - Interact 87.* Amsterdam: North Holland.

Payne, S.J. (in press). Display-based action at the user interface. *International Journal of Man-Machine Studies.*

Payne, S.J. and Green, T.R.G. (1986). Task-action grammar: A model of the mental representation of task languages. *Human-Computer Interaction, 2,* 93-133.

Payne, S.J., Squibb, H. and Howes, A. (in press). The nature of device models: the yoked state space hypothesis and some experiments with text editors. *Human-Computer Interaction.*

Schegloff, E.A., Jefferson, G. and Sacks, H. (1977). The preference for self-correction in the organization of repair in conversation. *Language, 53*, 361-382.

Suchman, L.A. (1987). *Plans and Situated Actions*. Cambridge University Press.

Young, R.M. (1981). The machine inside the machine: Users' models of pocket calculators. *International Journal of Man-Machine Studies, 15*, 51-85.

Young, R.M and Simon, T. (1987). Planning in the context of human-computer interaction. In D.Diaper and R. Winder (Eds.) *People and Computers III*. Cambridge University Press.

Human–Computer Interaction – INTERACT '90
D. Diaper et al. (Editors)
Elsevier Science Publishers B.V. (North-Holland)

Qualitative Artifact Analysis

Wendy A. Kellogg

IBM T.J. Watson Research Center, P.O. Box 704, Yorktown Heights, NY 10598, USA

The psychology of HCI in the 1990s will be concerned with *embodied* cognition and action: helping us understand real people acting in real situations, and doing so in a way that enhances existing design practice. One proposal for meeting these objectives is qualitative artifact analysis: specifically, creating psychological design rationales by extracting claims from scenarios of use. I describe our method for doing this and its key requirements, and suggest how artifact analyses of this kind can serve to cumulate knowledge about usability in a form useful for design. A critical requirement for deriving benefit from analyses of human-machine interaction is expressing understandings and usability outcomes in terms of the artifact's design. In support of this, I reconsider an example of the analysis of situated action from the point of view of artifact analysis.

1.0 SHIFTING PERSPECTIVE

Every representation of a problem constrains the possibilities for its solution. Some aspects of a problem are brought into relief, others are recessed. More than this, the very framing of the problem determines what it is critical to represent, the aspects most relevant to creating a solution. And, of course, sometimes the only way to make progress on solving a problem is to change the way it is being framed.

A prominent framing of the "problem" of human-computer interaction has been applying models of human cognition to the design of computer artifacts. This perspective has led to an emphasis on representations that illuminate the cognitive processing or knowledge requirements imposed by an artifact's design. Thus, models of task performance (e.g., Card, Moran & Newell, 1983; Kieras & Polson, 1985), cognitive grammars (e.g., Reisner, 1981; Payne & Green, 1986), or sometimes cognitive processing models or architectures (e.g., Barnard, 1987; Young, Green, & Simon, 1989) have been employed in an effort to bring the constraints on interaction introduced by human users to bear on design.

These models represent an intentional strategy for building a psychology of HCI through comprehensive analysis of specific design issues. The final verdict on this approach to HCI is not yet in, but examples of how the approach could work are now sufficiently developed to assess its impact. The critiques are by now familiar: models of information processing or cognitive structure as sole representations of users are too impoverished for many design purposes; perhaps as a result, they have failed to have any pervasive or fundamental impact on design practice.

In recent HCI a new perspective is emerging. Within this perspective is a fundamental commitment to understanding what we might call embodied cognition and action: to build an analysis that embraces *real people in real situations whose activities involve computer artifacts.* This perspective differs from the conventional perspective at least in setting very difficult requirements for representing the HCI problem: representations must be capable of adequately expressing the rich detail of real-world situations and of realistically describing the characteristics of people acting in these situations.

Specific proposals for how this perspective can be realized in HCI are now being developed. Suchman (1987) argues for an analysis of human-machine interaction that focuses on the differential resources for situated action that humans and machines can recruit, and calls for "building generalizations inductively from records of particular, naturally occurring activities" (Suchman, 1987, p. 179). Whiteside, Bennett, and Holtzblatt (1988) describe contextual inquiry, a research method for discovering and articulating requirements and usability issues of users in their real work environments. Thomas and Kellogg (1989) describe ways to address discrepancies between the development or research laboratory and real usage environments. Norman (1990) calls for a psychology of cognitive artifacts, an analysis which focuses on the properties of artifacts and how their design affects people and tasks. Our own work develops the proposal that the task-artifact cycle can serve as a framework for HCI research and design through the analysis of psychological design rationales for artifacts and the use of scenario-based design (Carroll, 1990b; Carroll & Campbell, 1989; Carroll & Kellogg, 1989; Carroll, Kellogg, & Rosson, 1990).

The aim of this paper is to further explicate our approach to artifact analysis: producing psychological design rationales via claims extraction. The kind of qualitative analysis we seek to develop will fulfill the requirements of representing realistic users in situations of use, and being applicable to existing design practice. We believe there is leverage to be gained from artifact analyses both "locally" for redesign within a given domain of artifact-tasks, and "remotely" for design in unrelated domains. A critical requirement for obtaining leverage, however, is codifying our understandings and observations of usability outcomes in terms of an artifact's design.

2.0 CLAIMS ANALYSIS

The objectives of having realistic scope and being applicable to design practice impose constraints on the utility of possible artifact analyses. These constraints might be phrased as the following concerns: 1) *how well does the analysis illuminate and cover important issues for real users in real contexts of use?* 2) *to what extent does the analysis enable something getting done to improve the artifact's usability?* While undoubtedly there are many possible appropriate responses to these concerns, here I outline the approach of developing psychological design rationales via claims extraction.

The basic organizing structure of our analyses is key scenarios of use: the core productive tasks the artifact is intended to support, and problematic (error) scenarios that the artifact is intended to manage. The scenarios chosen for analysis might come from cumulated knowledge of core tasks for the application domain (e.g., typing and printing documents for word processors), from an analysis of an artifact supporting similar tasks to support comparison, or from empirical observations of users, for example, to support understanding aspects of use that are giving users trouble.

For each scenario, a detailed analysis of embodied psychological claims is made. The key requirement for a claim is that it must relate some aspect of the artifact's design to an important consequence for the user. A claim attempts to specify how the artifact positively supports the user; in this sense, each claim is a piece of design rationale for the artifact. A claim can analyze, for example, aspects of displays (e.g., visual characteristics, prompts), effects of interface techniques on interaction (e.g., *blocking selection* in menu dimming), or things a user might experience or do in the course of the scenario (e.g., redisplay of a menu, work opportunistically, accomplish the task). Psychological consequences can refer to the user's cognition, actions, motivation, work or social context, etc. The range of issues that can be addressed by claims is thus broad; the object of the analysis is to articulate the *leading* or most powerful claims for the scenario.

A second important aspect of claims is that they detail any downside of the way the user is supported, by being stated as tradeoffs. Recognizing the tradeoffs associated with claims can make explicit the limits of the claim's applicability; for example, a particular kind of feedback might be prone to misinterpretation by users under certain circumstances. Tradeoffs reveal the usability gambles taken by a design. In this way, they are also part of the artifact's design rationale: they represent the artifact's wager that the circumstances leading to realization of the positive consequences of the design are more prevalent than the conditions leading to the negative consequences detailed by the tradeoff.

Claims analyses are intended to support a variety of levels of detail. For example, the analysis of a single artifact might contain scenarios at different levels of abstraction. Thus, the analysis might consider the interface broadly and ask how user learning is supported by the design (e.g., the analysis of HyperCard in Carroll & Kellogg, 1989). Alternatively, the analysis might address a particular error that arises in the course of a specific task (e.g., the background error in HyperCard stack creation; Kellogg, 1989). At the highest levels of abstraction, claims the artifact as a whole makes for the user's work context might be assessed.

Claims analyses support different levels of detail in another way as well. The core scenarios of the claims analysis represent abstractions from particular instances of the scenarios; for example, observations of users engaged in those tasks. Further abstraction from these core scenarios can reveal common user concerns and differentiate design strategies employed by different artifacts to address these concerns (Carroll, Kellogg, & Rosson, 1990).

Finally, a critical requirement for claims analyses is that they be in the language of design (Carroll, 1990b). Individual claims refer to tradeoffs associated with particular aspects of a design. Collectively, claims represent a special kind of description of an artifact: a view of the psychological dynamics of its real usage situations, expressed in terms of its design and the tasks it supports.

From these primary characteristics -- being organized by scenarios of use, associating aspects of design with important consequences for users, being stated as tradeoffs, comprising and supporting a variety of levels of detail, and being in the language of design -- psychological design rationale via claims analysis derives its ability to meet the objectives of realistic scope and relevance to design. Realistic scope is possible through the basic organization of scenarios of use ranging from narrowly-defined system tasks to real work activities, and through the broad range of issues claims can address.

One way claims analysis can apply in design is to guide an artifact's redesign within the ongoing task-artifact cycle. By providing an account of usability successes and failures, claims analysis naturally gives rise to objectives for the redesign. Carroll, Kellogg, and Rosson (1990) provide an example of how the design of a successful training system for a word processor could have arisen from an analysis of the claims made by the word processor.

Claims analysis may also be applied to design in new domains through analogy or abstraction. For example, the analysis of the Training Wheels error blocking technique (Carroll & Kellogg, 1989; Carroll, Kellogg, & Rosson, 1990) and related techniques that manipulate the availability of function (menu dimming, function hiding), can be the basis of a more comprehensive and abstract view of design strategies for error management (Carroll, Kellogg, & Rosson, 1990). The *idea* of designing to exploit errors by helping users to manage the experience can arise from analyses of artifacts that do this (e.g., from Training Wheels). Abstractions from claims analyses also demonstrate possible techniques for doing this. Conversely, given the abstraction, specific claims analyses provide contextual examples of how and why the design supports the constructive use of errors. Of course, abstractions will not guarantee applicability to new domains just in virtue of being abstract. But if similar abstractions arise in many design domains, confidence in their usefulness in other domains is increased.

For example, the error management abstraction, described above in work on office systems, is also found in the domain intelligent tutoring systems (Burton & Brown, 1982; Brown & Newman, 1985). Under the guise of "the constructive use of trouble" or "managing for trouble," similar abstractions and design strategies have been articulated for students interacting with intelligent tutors. This is just what would be expected if the abstraction is useful.

An important consideration from the point of view of artifact analysis, however, is to be able to ground abstractions in specific analyses of artifacts that instantiate them. In the case of managing for trouble, understanding how specific cases work in different domains like office systems and intelligent tutors can provide a broader view of what design strategies are possible. A claims analysis can help illuminate how these strategies succeed and fail in particular situations.

Another example is the "system for experts" described in "Computers in Context" (1987), a videotape presenting design projects using the Scandinavian approach. Two versions of an artifact designed to assist in diagnosis and prioritization of aircraft maintenance jobs were described. The first, an expert system, was found to have an overall negative impact on user's work activity and the quality of work. The explanation of this usability outcome was that the expert system did too much of the wrong sort of thing for the workers; for example, it deskilled their work by making the judgments of what needed to be done for them, and it controlled their work activity by recommending the order in which work should proceed. The redesigned system was described as a "system for experts" rather than an "expert system" which did not give rise to these difficulties.

A design experience such as this may illustrate an important usability issue: the artifact's role in the wider context of the user's work activities. But to be able to develop a general analysis of the way work activity is affected by artifacts, and to preserve this particular experience as a rich, contextualized example to assist in applying it to other design situations, more is needed. What was it about the design of the expert system that made it fit the way it did into the workers' activities? What, specifically, about the design of the system for experts changed that relationship? Taking an artifact-centered view and attributing consequences for users to the details of the artifact's design is critical for getting the most from previous design experience.

3.0 AN ARTIFACT-CENTERED VIEW OF SITUATED ACTION

A similar critique can be made of analyses of situated action. One of Suchman's (1987, pp. 166) examples, from her corpus of interactions of new users with document copiers, can serve to demonstrate how taking an artifact-centered view of situated action provides design leverage. In this scenario, the user is in the midst of a fairly complex (though routine) copying task involving multiple copies of a multiple-page document that is bound. The user has succeeded in making a "master" from the bound document -- a single copy of the complete document. She is ready to perform the last part of the task, in this case, generating 4 copies of the complete document from the master. Unfortunately, however, at this juncture the user and the copier part company. The user, for whatever reason, has the idea of an iterative, one-page-at-a-time procedure for producing the final copies. The copier is all set to handle the whole document at once in its "Recirculating Document Handler (RDH)."

Suchman's analysis shows how and why the interaction goes awry. When the machine instructs the user "Place all of your originals in the RDH," the user puts in only the first page instead. The machine, sensing that *something* has been placed in the RDH, accordingly tells the user to press the Start button. The user does, and the machine produces the copies of the "document." From the machine's point of view, the task is complete except for removing the document from the handler. The user waits in vain for the machine to request the next page. She removes the first page and places the second in the handler. The machine, still detecting a document in the handler, continues to request its removal. The interaction is at an impasse.

In this analysis, the impoverished resources of the copier and its consequent insensitivity to the user's circumstances and actions is responsible for the impasse and the bleak prospects for its repair. In support of the analysis, Suchman notes that the user's utterances ("So it made four of the first?" and "Does it say to put it in yet?"), which are inaccessible to the machine, could be readily interpreted by any human observer as indicative of the misunderstanding. Another example is the machine's having to rely on detection of *any* document in the document handler to indicate that the instruction to "place all originals" has been satisfied. Finally, Suchman argues that the impasse is not a case of failing to anticipate the problem. On the contrary, the "place all originals" instruction was there specifically in anticipation of the problem. However, she reports that in her observations there was "no evidence ... that the instruction [was] consulted" (p. 166).

The asymmetrical resources analysis of situated action in this scenario, and others described by Suchman, lead her to propose three general design strategies for improving human-machine interaction: 1) extend the machine's sensitivity to user circumstances; 2) make users more cognizant of the machine's limited sensitivity; and 3) employ computationally feasible alternatives (e.g., advice based on a user model) to substitute for actual increased sensitivity.

An underlying assumption of these strategies, indeed the entire analysis, is that the chances of felicitous human-machine interaction *within* the constraints imposed by the asymmetry are vanishingly small. At the very least, there is no account of when interaction under these circumstances *is* successful, and why it is successful.

In contrast, artifact analysis seeks to understand the potential for both successful and unsuccessful situated action in this situation, and to do so in terms of the copier's design. From this point of view, attributing usability problems to impoverished machine resources is premature. An artifact analysis details how an artifact's design contributes to and detracts from productive interaction. The design strategy it recommends is not to fundamentally change or compensate for machine limitations, but to design *for* productive situated action given those limitations. Unless this option is fully exploited, what is actually entailed by the machine's limited resources cannot be accurately assessed.

An analysis of claims associated with the design of the copier for the "iterative copy procedure" scenario is shown below.

Iterative Copy Procedure Claims

1. A familiar task suggests that prior knowledge of the task can be applied in the current situation (*but inappropriate parts of this knowledge may also be applied*)
2. Task instructions will be used prescriptively by users (*but may not be if the user already has an idea about what to do next*).
3. The "place all originals" task instruction conveys that the whole document is to be placed at once in the handler (*but may also confirm the iterative procedure to a user with this idea*).
4. The key function of the RDH as whole document handler is evident to users (*but may not be to users unfamiliar with this technology*).
5. Displaying the "Press Start button" instruction upon detection of a document in the handler is adequate feedback that the "place all originals" instruction has been satisfied (*but is misleading if the user has not satisfied the instruction*).

The design goal for the iterative copy procedure scenario is to make the iterative interpretation of the task unlikely, or at least to support detection and repair of the error. Ideally, this can be done relying only on the user's spontaneous efforts after meaning in this situation. The claims made by the artifact identify aspects of the design that are responsible or partially responsible for the emergence and perpetuation of the problematic scenario. Many of the claims in Figure 1 reflect Suchman's perceptive analysis of what transpires in the scenario. But there is a subtle, yet important, difference in restating the analysis in terms of *claims* the design makes: the effectiveness of the design in supporting situated action is implicitly questioned.

Claim 1, for example, raises an issue not considered in Suchman's analysis, namely why the user might have the idea of an iterative copy procedure to begin with. There are several possibilities: the user might be familiar with older technology that requires originals to be handled one page at a time; the task the user has just completed (producing a master copy from a bound document) on the *current* copier requires one page at a time copying; or the iterative procedure might simply have been the first idea that occurred to the user about how the task should be done. For any particular user on a particular occasion, any or all of these factors might contribute to the misconception. We do not have to know how the misconception arises on a particular occasion to make productive use of its possible occurrence. We can both attempt to keep the factors giving rise to the misconception from exerting an influence on the user, and attempt to counteract their implications if they nevertheless do arise. In the case of a user adopting the iterative copy model based on prior knowledge, for example, nothing in the design can *prevent* that factor from operating; but the design *can* try to make it harder for the user to maintain the misconception, perhaps by making the multiple-page capability of the document handler unmistakable. Recognizing the copier's claim that knowledge of "older" copiers will provide an appropriate model suggests an explicit design objective of making any discrepancies salient to users.

Indeed, the point of analyzing the iterative copy procedure scenario at all might be taken to answer the question of how the copier's design might prevent users from acting on the basis of this misconception. A general answer is represented by Claim 2, that (step-by-step) task instructions will be heeded by users. But in fact, it is already known that this is often a false claim (e.g., Carroll, 1990a; Wright, Creighton, & Threlfall, 1982). A more specific remedy, represented by Claim 3, is that a specific instruction countering the "one page at a time" model is adequate for conveying the "all at once" model. The downside of this claim is that if the user already has the wrong idea in mind, the wording of this instruction allows it to be misinterpreted as congruent with the iterative procedure (i.e., completing the task will involve placing all of the originals in the document handler, one by one).

Claim 4 asserts that the ability of the RDH to handle whole documents is self-evident. The design challenge for the copier here is to make every aspect of the RDH bespeak its (new) technological capability. The claim implicitly asks what affordances for handling multiple pages might have been created through the physical design of the RDH, or through judicious labelling (e.g., perhaps "Whole Document Handler" or "Multiple Page Document Handler"). The name *Recirculating* Document Handler seems to demonstrate a familiar design flaw of naming things from the system's or designer's rather than the user's viewpoint. At the very least, it emphasizes an aspect of the document handler that is irrelevant to any user concern (i.e., that pages to be copied are passed in a circle).

Finally, Claim 5 captures the copier's gamble that any document detected in the handler is the "right" document. Suchman correctly identifies the nature of this gamble: that the user will "anchor" the relative quantifier "all" in the "place all originals" instruction to the particular (whole) document the user is concerned with on a particular occasion. But as discussed above, the gamble also relies on the user attending to the instruction, an event made *unlikely* rather than likely by the very circumstances the instruction is attempting to address.

Once again, the claim implicitly raises the question of how well the design succeeds in creating the desired consequence (here, confirming that the last user action was appropriate). But the copier's reliance on detection of any document in the handler means that the feedback of moving to the next instruction will be misleading whenever the user has failed to place the whole document in the handler. Interestingly, in this case the copier apparently *did* have access to relevant information about the user's circumstances that it failed to apply at the propitious moment. Users were required to describe their job to the machine at the beginning of the interaction, including the approximate number of pages in the original to be copied. Thus there was a possibility for the machine to compare the number of pages placed in the document handler with the number of pages declared by the user, leading to repair of the error. A less technically demanding possibility might be performing the comparison after the user has initiated the task on a single page; since the copier can count the number of pages in the handler as it copies, it has the resources available to repair the misconception after its occurrence.

4.0 CLAIMS ANALYSIS: A SUMMARY

Articulating claims and their tradeoffs for scenarios of use can be a way to understand real episodes of user-machine interaction and a way to probe designed interactions before empirical observations are available. A claims analysis of an artifact in use can raise pertinent questions for the redesign of the artifact. And abstracting from analyses of real interactions can identify broader user concerns and design strategies which may be applied in new design.

The psychology of human-computer interaction is taking the notion of embodied cognition and action seriously. Expressing understandings of embodied cognition in terms of the design of artifacts is the key to reaping benefits from earlier design experience. The design of artifacts is under our control, and through design, we influence human-artifact interaction. We want to improve the usability and usefulness of existing cognitive artifacts. We need to be able to anticipate interaction with new technology. An understanding of how artifacts enable and constrain human cognition and action is critical for creating more usable systems.

Making our analyses "artifact-centered" does not mean replacing our primary concern with users, their experience, or contexts of use. It does not mean failing to recognize that action is situated. It does mean trying to understand how human-machine interaction in particular situations succeeds and fails, and learning to express our understanding in ways that support cumulation of knowledge and its broadest application to design.

The case for artifact analysis follows a simple logic for framing the problem of how to intentionally design more usable cognitive artifacts. It claims that what is needed is a representation that can bring together the worlds of real users, designers, and researchers. And it claims that the artifact, as the common ground, is the appropriate source from which to construct sharable understandings of the relationship of user experience and design.

5.0 ACKNOWLEDGEMENTS

Thanks to the members of the User Interface Theory and Design group, Jack Carroll, Rachel Bellamy, Steve Payne, and Kevin Singley, for ongoing discussion and collaboration, and to John Thomas for comments.

6.0 REFERENCES

Barnard, P.J. (1987). Cognitive resources and the learning of human-computer dialogs. In J.M. Carroll (Ed.), *Interfacing thought: Cognitive aspects of human-computer interaction.* Cambridge, MA: MIT Press.

Brown, J.S. and Newman, S. (1985). Issues in cognitive and social ergonomics: From our house to Bauhaus. *Human-Computer Interaction*, **1**(4), pp. 359-91.

Burton, R. and Brown, J.S. (1982). An investigation of computer coaching for informal learning activities. In D. Sleeman and J.S. Brown (Eds.), *Intelligent tutoring systems.* London: Academic Press.

Card, S.K., Moran, T.P., and Newell, A. (1983). *The psychology of human-computer interaction.* Hillsdale, NJ: Erlbaum.

Carroll, J.M. (1990a). *The Nurnberg funnel: Designing Minimalist instruction for practical computer skill.* Cambridge, MA: MIT Press.

Carroll, J.M. (1990b). Infinite detail and emulation in an ontologically minimized HCI. In J.C. Chew and J. Whiteside (Eds.), *Proceedings of CHI'90: Conference on Human Factors in Computing Systems.* New York: ACM.

Carroll, J.M. and Campbell, R.L. (1989). Artifacts as psychological theories: The case of human-computer interaction. *Behavior and Information Technology*, **8**, 247-256.

Carroll, J.M. and Kellogg, W.A. (1989). Artifact as theory-nexus: Hermeneutics meets theory-based design. In K. Bice and C.H. Lewis (Eds.), *Proceedings of CHI'89: Conference on Human Factors in Computing Systems.* New York: ACM, 7-14.

Carroll, J.M., Kellogg, W.A., and Rosson, M.B. (1990). The task-artifact cycle. In J.M. Carroll (Ed.), *Designing Interaction: Psychology at the human-computer interface.* Cambridge, MA: Cambridge University Press.

Computers in Context (1987). Videotape published by California Newsreel, 149 9th Street, Suite 420, San Francisco, California, 94103, U.S.A.

Kellogg, W.A. (1989). Extracting psychological claims from artifacts in use. *Research Report RC 15511*, IBM Thomas J. Watson Research Center, Yorktown Heights, NY 10598.

Kieras, D. and Polson, P. (1985). An approach to the formal analysis of user complexity. *International Journal of Man-Machine Studies*, **22**, 365-394.

Norman, D.A. (1990). Cognitive artifacts. In J.M. Carroll (Ed.), *Designing Interaction: Psychology at the human-computer interface.* Cambridge, MA: Cambridge University Press.

Payne, S. and Green, T.R.G. (1986). Task-action grammars: A model of the mental representation of task languages. *Human-Computer Interaction*, **2**, 93-133.

Reisner, P. (1981). Formal grammar and human factors design of an interactive graphics system. *IEEE Transactions on Software Engineering*, **SE-7**(2), 229-240.

Suchman, L.A. (1987). *Plans and situated actions: The problem of human-machine communication.* New York: Cambridge University Press.

Thomas, J.C. and Kellogg, W.A. (1989). Minimizing ecological gaps in interface design. *IEEE Software*, January, 1989, 78-86.

Whiteside, J., Bennett, J., and Holtzblatt, K. (1988). Usability engineering: Our experience and evolution. In M. Helander (Ed.), *Handbook of human-computer interaction.* Amsterdam: North-Holland.

Wright, P., Creighton, P., and Threlfall, S.M. (1982). Some factors determining when instructions will be read. *Ergonomics*, **25**(3), 225-237.

Young, R.M., Green, T.R.G., and Simon, T. (1989). Programmable user models for predictive evaluation of interface designs. In K. Bice and C.H. Lewis (Eds.), *Proceedings of CHI'89: Conference on Human Factors in Computing Systems.* New York: ACM, 15-19.

Human–Computer Interaction – INTERACT '90
D. Diaper et al. (Editors)
Elsevier Science Publishers B.V. (North-Holland)

Redesign by Design

Rachel K. E. Bellamy and John M. Carroll

User Interface Institute, IBM T.J. Watson Research Center
P.O.Box 704,
Yorktown Heights, NY 10598 USA

The evolution of HCI technology has been characterized by the task-artifact cycle, raising the question how do artifacts change tasks? In answer we have started to analyze personal redesigns of Smalltalk/V tools, to understand how and why the programming environment and the tasks it supports evolve. We interviewed designers working with Smalltalk/V, and asked them to describe their personal redesigns of the system tools (browsers, inspectors etc.), motivations for redesign, and typical scenarios of use before and after redesign. We found that designers do consider usability issues, but sometimes not *all* the usability strengths and weaknesses of existing interface techniques and of their redesigns. We show how psychological claims analysis can support and guide such redesign work.

1.0 INTRODUCTION

Technological development can be characterized by a task-artifact cycle; an artifact is built to support a task, but then the very existence of the artifact changes the task it was built to support introducing further requirements for redesign (Carroll and Campbell, 1989). Consider the task of writing. First came the quill and ink; then the typewriter, and eventually the word processor. Each new artifact brought significant changes to the activities it was designed to support. It de-skilled the original task, but at the same time introduced new tasks, requiring new skills. So although the word processor added considerable power and flexibility to authors, it also added complexity to the task: now authors need to understand rules of formatting, constraints of the publishing industry, etc.

At the IBM research center, we are developing a methodology for incorporating psychological theory into design based on the analysis of design as a task-artifact cycle (Carroll, 1990). We think that for psychology to impact design, we need representations that support understanding the psychology within existing designs, and applying psychological theories to design. Psychological claims analysis (Carroll and Kellogg, 1989) is such a representation. It can be used both for understanding the usability of an existing artifact, and to drive its redesign. A claims analysis describes the psychological consequences of features of the interface. The claims are not independent, but interrelated, coherent chiefly because they inhere in a coherent artifact. Scenarios provide a specification of the task-oriented functionality for redesign (Carroll and Rosson, 1990).

In this paper we use claims analysis to re-express redesigns of Smalltalk/V, an object-oriented programming system particularly well-suited to the rapid development of interactive applications. Our goal is to exercise claims analysis and to explore its application in software design.

2.0 THE STUDY

We interviewed 4 designers all of whom had made enhancements to the generic Smalltalk/V programming system. All of the designers had considerable experience in programming in Smalltalk/V, each spending the majority of their time prototyping interactive applications. A list of specific issues was used to structure each interview. Each designer was told that we were interested in how they had changed the Smalltalk/V programming language and environment; either how they had redesigned the system, or how they had made enhancements to the system. We asked them to describe the changes they had made, their motivation for making these changes, and how the changes had affected the task of programming in Smalltalk/V. To get detailed information on the latter point, we asked them to generate scenarios describing how the task would be done before and after making the changes.

We were interested in changes designers had made that they considered to be fundamental to the Smalltalk/V system. Any programming done in Smalltalk/V can be considered to be changing the system. All programming, whether it be changing the programming environment, or building an application, consists of adding classes and methods to the basic class hierarchy. These classes and methods are then available for reuse by other programmers; they also provide additional functionality. For instance, writing a hypertext application in Smalltalk/V might mean adding a class for a hypertext pane, and methods to display information in this pane. A programmer coming to this enhanced system not only has access to the functionality provided by the hypertext

Goal: Knowing the class of an object which is receiving a message, find where that message is implemented.	
Generic Environment	Redesigned Environment
Scenario: In the class hierarchy browser select each super-class in turn and browse the method list	**Scenario:** Get an inheritance browser for the class
1) Navigating over a complex information structure like the class hierarchy supports serependitious search and incidental learning of the hierarchical organisation, *but it distracts from the original task and can lead to dissorientation.*	6) Displaying inherited information in a separate user-controlled window results in less nested action sequences which is less stressful for planning and working memory, *but it increases window management and is distracting.*
2) A large library of code provides a rich source for software reuse, *but the number of classes and methods in the hierarchy makes locating the inheritance path difficult for novices.*	7) Reducing the amount of information to be browsed makes it easier to keep track of context, *but reduces the opportunity for incidental learning of the whole hierarchy.*
3) Supporting all information look-up tasks from within the same screen context focuses user activity, *but changing the screen context during information look-up increases memory load because users have to remember intermediate results.*	8) Seeing all the methods a class responds to supports incidental learning of inheritance relationships.
4) Highly sensitive navigation tools increase precision, *but demand skilled motor coordination.*	9) Maintaining two tools on the screen separates the information used for different tasks and helps users with screen management, *but increasing the amount of duplicated information on the screen is visually confusing.*
5) Indentation is a good cue to hierarchical decomposition, *but additional cues are needed to facilitate judging the exact size of an indentation.*	

Figure 1. Some claims inherent to the inheritance method browser

application, but can also use the newly defined pane to create new applications. Given the problem with defining what is fundamental to the system, we elicited this information by asking the designers whether they thought the changes they had made should be shipped with the generic Smalltalk/V image.

Using the scenarios generated by the designers, and our own usability analysis of Smalltalk/V (Bellamy and Carroll, in preparation), we developed a psychological claims analysis describing usability for the generic Smalltalk/V and for the personalized versions of Smalltalk/V described in the study. Some examples are shown in Figures 1 - 3. In developing the analyses we tried to be aware not only of those scenarios generated by the designers, but of possible programming scenarios for the generic Smalltalk/V and the redesign. We tried to understand how the scenarios supported by the generic system had been affected by redesign. We were also concerned to indicate not only how a design can lead to usability problems, but also how it supports a task. These are reflected in the analysis as trade-offs, i.e. Figure 1, claim 5, shows that highly sensitive navigation tools entrain the positive psychological consequence that they increase precision, but they also entrain the negative psychological consequence that they demand skilled motor coordination. For each redesign, we indicated the claims pertaining to each scenario for both the generic system and the redesign. We used the claims analyses to understand how designers dealt with usability issues.

We conducted a follow-up interview with the designers after analyzing the designs described in the primary interview. We used this second interview both to verify our own claims analysis against the designers' experiences, and to see if the analysis would provoke them to reconsider any of their original design decisions.

3.0 REDESIGNING SMALLTALK/V

We collected descriptions of redesigns of both Smalltalk/V286 and Smalltalk/VPM. For reasons of space we have chosen to discuss only redesigns of Smalltalk/V286 in this paper (for the rest of this paper we use Smalltalk/V to mean Smalltalk/V286). Here we describe three redesigns; the inheritance method browser, the instance variable pop-up and the change manager.

Goal: Find the instance variables of a class during methods development		
Generic Environment	Generic Environment	Redesigned Environment
Scenario: Use two class hierarchy browsers, one for developing code and one to look at class definition	**Scenario**: Save method and select the class to get class definition in method text pane	**Scenario**: Get pop-up window for the selected class showing the list of instance variables
1) Simultaniously displaying information sources in separate windows is less stressful for planning and working memory, *but it increases window management.*	3) Supporting all information look-up tasks within the same screen context focuses user activity, *but changing the screen context during information look-up makes recovery of the original task difficult.*	5) Displaying information in pop-up windows reduces window management, *but limits the amount of time the information is displayed on the screen.*
2) Using two class hierarchy browsers allows simultaneous access to multiple places in the hierarchy, *but it increases the amount of duplicated information leading to discrimination problems.*	4) Hiding the class definition when method code is being written constrains the information to be considered, *but increases planning during code development.*	6) Specialized tools supporting specific tasks such as instance variable look-up reduce actions necessary for a single goal, *but increase the amount to be learnt.*
		7) Information should appear at the focus of user activity, *but overlaying information increases memory load for overlaid info while looking at the pop-up window*

Figure 2. Some claims inherent to the instance variable pop-up.

3.1 The inheritance method browser (IMB)

Code in Smalltalk/V is arranged as a functional hierarchy of classes. Methods encode behaviors, and are associated with a class. Classes lower in the hierarchy inherit methods from their superclasses. Programming in Smalltalk involves adding classes to the hierarchy, or enhancing the behavior of existing classes by adding methods. The main programming tool is the class hierarchy browser. The browser consists of three panes: one contains a list of classes, the second contains a list of methods for the class selected in the class list, and the third the text for the method selected in the method list. The class list is organized hierarchically and indentation is used to indicate inheritance.

In Smalltalk, methods inherited from superclasses are not displayed in the method list for the currently selected class. The designer described a before-redesign scenario for the task of finding the implementation for an inherited method. *"...I could see that message X was being sent to some object, and I could look at that object's class and then see, oh well, X wasn't in that class. Let me check the superclass. Well, it's not in the superclass; let me check the superclass of that..."* The programmer felt that this task was *"sometimes confusing or taxing"* because it required excessive amounts of navigation. To overcome this problem, the designer built the IMB, a hypertext window that shows all the methods of a class in the same window. The methods can be ordered alphabetically or in inheritance order. Users can access the IMB via the class pane menu of the class hierarchy browser. The IMB consists of two panes, an upper pane containing the complete list of methods to which the class responds indicating in which class they are implemented, and a lower pane showing code corresponding to the method selected in the upper pane.

3.2 The instance variable pop-up (IVP)

Another task identified by one of the programmers was looking for the instance variables of a class. Instance variables are specified in the class definition and define the state of an object. Selecting a class in the class pane of the class hierarchy browser when no methods are selected, causes the class description to be displayed in the method text pane. Thus it is not possible to see both a method text and the class definition using the same class hierarchy browser.

The programmer identified two before redesign scenarios for accessing a class definition whilst developing code. In one the method currently being edited in the method text pane is saved and the class in the class list pane is reselected, which gives the class description in the method text pane. In the other, a second browser is opened in which to view the class definition. The designer had learnt Smalltalk with Smalltalk 80, and liked its use of pop-up windows to display information about the class and instance variables. Pop-up windows differ from the hypertext window used in the inheritance browser, in that they only display the information until the next user input. The programmer used this design to alleviate the problems he found with Smalltalk/V. In the redesigned Smalltalk/V, the user can pop-up a list of instance

Goal: share application code with other programmers	
Generic Environment	Redesigned Environment
Scenario: Edit the change log	**Scenario:** Use change manager
1) People are skilled at editing text files and can use this knowledge when editing the change log, *but editing the change log is tedious and overwhelms the user.*	2) Indicating which methods and classes have been added to the system and which changed facilitates sharing code, *but increases the amount of information to be managed.* 3) Multiple organizations of code increase the ease of finding methods, *but increases the number of representations to be learnt* 4) Automatically adding changes to a selected change group keeps users actions to a minimum, *but indicating the change group in a peripheral tool increases possibility of adding changes to wrong group*

Figure 3. Some claims inherent to the change manager

variables for the selected class by selecting instances from the class pane menu.

3.3 The change manager (CM)

One of the aims of Smalltalk is to support code sharing. One designer in our study pointed out that the original designers of Smalltalk/V had intended code to be shared by exchanging a copy of a complete system. This has proven cumbersome: in practice, programmers maintain their own system image and share code by adding classes and methods representing applications. This necessitates editing text files containing all the changes made to the system. The text file or change log contains not only the changes made to the system for the application currently being developed, but also any changes made to the system previously. There are ways of reducing the size of this file so that only the final changes to a method or class are recorded and not all the intermediate versions; nonetheless editing this file by hand is, as the designer put it, *"a process somewhat painful of going through on a line by line basis and throwing out that which was not the part that you wanted to remember"*.

The CM was designed to facilitate sharing code by allowing programmers to group all the changes to their system into different change groups. Thus sharing an application consists of giving a fellow programmer a change group. The CM provides a browser for viewing change groups and manipulating the contents of the groups, joining groups, taking the intersection of two groups, etc. It is tied to the class hierarchy browser in that any changes made in the class hierarchy browser are added to the currently selected group in the CM. There is also a menu facility in the class hierarchy browser for adding methods selected in the class hierarchy browser to a selected change group in the CM.

4.0 THE ANALYSIS

Design problems like any complex problems are hard to solve without supporting representations (Newell and Simon, 1972). This means that even when designers do consider usability issues (Hammond *et al.*, 1983), they may fail to be sensitive to all the important issues. Here we look at the kinds of information that designers can miss due to the inherent complexity of the design process. We discuss how psychological claims analysis can support design by enabling designers to externalize information pertinent to design and to focus their attention on specific aspects of this information.

4.1 Designers may focus on a few salient usability claims

When talking about their motivations for redesign, the designers tended to concentrate on one or two salient claims Smalltalk/V makes with respect to a task, and not on the whole set of claims pertinent to a task. This is also the case for their redesigns: they focused on a few features of their redesign and how these affect the task rather than on the whole set of claims determining the task they seek to support. For instance the generic system supports users in learning the hierarchy and in serendipitous search for classes and methods (see Figure 1, claim 1). These positive features of the generic system were not noted by the designer of IMB and were not incorporated in its design.

Designers not only miss usability claims made by the generic Smalltalk environment, but also claims made by their redesigns. In CM, new or changed methods in the class hierarchy browser are added to the change group currently selected in the CM. As programmers are working in the class hierarchy browsers they often forget that their changes are being added to a change group, and add or change a method which does not belong to the currently selected group (see Figure 3, claim 4). This can increase the programmer's work and lead to frustration.

Usability depends on the whole set of psychological claims pertaining to a task. Emulation of designs without a full understanding of their usability in both the original and new context can result in less than optimal design solutions. In both the redesigned Smalltalk/V and Smalltalk'80, the IVP appears on the screen so that the cursor appears in the middle of the pop-up. In Smalltalk/V the IVP typically obscures the method text which can be annoying as the method text contains the instance variable you want to check in the pop-up (see Figure 2, claim 7). This is not the case for the same design in Smalltalk'80. In the Smalltalk'80 used by the programmer, the screen was much bigger, the font relatively small, and most importantly, the class hierarchy browser in Smalltalk'80 organizes classes into categories. Thus in Smalltalk'80 only those classes of a selected category appear in the class list pane, making a considerably shorter list. When selecting the class from which to pop-up the instance variable list in this system, programmers are relatively high in the class pane and thus the IVP rarely obscures the method text. This is an example where the very fine detailed context of a technique has considerable impact on usability.

In this study, designers behave like problem solvers in other domains in that they tend to fixate on a single view of the initial problem (e.g. Maier, 1931). People do this because it constrains the problem solving, and so reduces the complexity and amount of information to be considered in finding a solution. However, it can also reduce the success of a solution. Representations such as claims analysis can reduce the complexity of problem solving by allowing designers to externalize some of the information and by introducing a limited number of dimensions around which to analyze the problem and structure a solution. This allows designers to take a more complete view of the initial problem.

4.2 Designers may focus on a single task

Only for one redesign, the IMB, was more than one scenario of use generated, and in this case, like the others, the same before-design scenario was used to illustrate usability problems of the generic system. This is another example of where taking an overly focused view of the design problem affects the usability of the final solution.

The IMB supports both the task of accessing inherited methods, and finding method name clashes (not shown in Figure 1). In the interview, the designer explained that the IMB had been initially designed just to support the former task. Thus, the methods were only displayed in inheritance order. After building and using the IMB, the designer realized that it also supported finding method name clashes and ordering the methods alphabetically would better support this task. We questioned the usefulness of the inheritance ordering for either task. The designer agreed and even pointed out that because the default order was inheritance, he was making programmers constantly have to bring up the menu and change the ordering to alphabetic. Having alphabetic as the default would make the system more usable, but he said that he was not interested in redesigning it now. Describing the initial redesign in terms of functional scenarios and their claims might have suggested the task of finding name clashes, and led to using alphabetic ordering as the default in the initial redesign.

Focusing on a single task not only affects the ease of use of the redesign, but can also mean that designers don't exploit the full potential of a redesign. We thought the IMB not only supported information finding, but also learning (see Figure 1, claim 8). Novice programmers find the class hierarchy overwhelming (Rosson, Carroll and Bellamy, 1990). Using the IMB novices can learn about inheritance relationships whilst browsing just a single branch of the hierarchy. When we suggested that it was a tool for learning, the designer said he had not thought of it in this way, but accepted our analysis and added that personally he found the tool less useful now that he was familiar with the hierarchy.

It is not that designers are unable to generate scenarios; rather, focusing on a single task is another example of functional fixity. Designers did generate other scenarios in their second interview. Mostly they had to be prompted with a certain task goal before they could generate other scenarios, but the designer of the IVP spontaneously generated a second scenario (not shown in Figure 2). The IVP has additional functionality in that when one of the instance variables displayed in the pop-up is selected, a hypertext browser appears which displays all the methods that touch this instance variable. This supports understanding the role of an instance variable.

The claims analysis had already helped us realize that the IVP supported comprehension even without knowing about this additional functionality. In Smalltalk code, instance variables and method names can only be distinguished by their syntactic position (Green, 1989). Being able to access a class' instance variables whilst reading method code provides an additional cue to help programmers distinguish instance variables from method names.

Designers sometimes realize their designs could support additional tasks, but make a conscious decision not to. This was the case with CM, which can be used not only to share code, but also to organize classes and methods into application groups (not shown in Figure 3). Grouping code into applications is important. In fact, programmers tend to misuse the functional hierarchy so that they can locate applications code in one place, rather than it being distributed throughout the hierarchy. The designer of CM said that programmers sometimes tended to view the CM as an application browser, but he did not want to develop it in that manner. This is understandable, but we think that in this case the system should be redesigned so people cannot use it in this way. If the tool suggests it can be used for a certain task, then programmers will try to use it in that way and get frustrated when it does not fully support this task.

Although all the designs discussed in the study were used by people other than the designer, the designers tended to be the *primary users*. In fact the designer of the CM was disappointed that others were so timid in their use of the full functionality of the CM. We suggest that this is because the tasks the designers focus on are those they want to accomplish. This is not surprising as in general people tend to rate commonly experienced events as the most important (Tversky and Kahneman, 1973). However, these event might not be as important or obvious to other programmers. Perhaps programmers do not realize the full functionality of the CM; the designer himself suggested that some of the menu items may be obscure. Obviously this cannot be a problem for the designer who built the system.

Claims analysis supports the design of more generally useful tools because by structuring the information to be considered when designing it encourages designers to think about the set of tasks a system supports, and to identify those which there redesign is affecting.

4.3 Designers may under-evaluate trade-offs

Critical analysis of the generic system and positive analysis of their redesigns was common. That designers focus on the positive aspects of their designs is supported by a number of studies showing that people tend to ignore negative evidence that might contradict their conclusion (e.g. Adams and Adams, 1961; Lichtenstein, Fischoff and Phillips, 1982). Perhaps, it is also easier to be critical than positive about a situation.

In this study, it was not that designers were unaware of trade-offs, rather they did not explicitly state them. For instance, when shown the claims analysis (see Figure 2), the designer of the IVP said he was not concerned that programmers were not always able to see the referent in the method text pane because you only had to remember it for a short time and anyway it was easy to go back and look and then get another IVP if you did forget. Although the designer thought obscuring the referent trivial, articulating these trade-offs may have led to a more usable design. The IVP could have been designed so that it appeared next to the class hierarchy browser rather than over it. In fact, this is what the programmer himself suggested when we gave him the claims analysis.

4.4 Designers may miss interface features

It is not a single interface feature that supports a task, but multiple interacting features. Identifying the specific interface feature that leads to a usability problem can be hard. The designers in this study occasionally missed some of the interface features we felt were important contributors to usability problems. The IMB is an example where the designer identified navigation as a difficult task, but attributed this solely to the fact that the information to be browsed is distributed throughout the hierarchy. The IMB groups all the information to be browsed into one pane. We think that the navigation tools and size of the hierarchy may be significant contributors to this usability problem (see Figure 1, claims 2 and 4). Perhaps redesigning the tools for navigation would have supported not only the task of browsing inherited methods without having to build a specialized tool, but also supported other tasks in which browsing the hierarchy plays a significant part.

Claims analysis encourages designers to think specifically about which interface features lead to psychological consequences. Existing examples of claims analysis can also help designers in analyzing other systems. Although this does not guarantee a complete or correct analysis, we found it useful when thinking about the designs in this study.

5.0 CONCLUSIONS

Design is complex problem solving and designers are unable to take into account all factors pertaining to a particular redesign because humans have a limited processing capacity (Guindon, Krasner and Curtis, 1987). The design process reflects this problem, for instance designers focus on a current subproblem (Guindon and Curtis, 1988; Simon, 1971), or single task in this case, and over-rate its importance (Thomas, 1989). They then try to integrate other parts of the problem into this existing solution structure. This usually results in a sub-optimal solution to the original problem. Cognitive dissonance makes them unwilling to start over and construct a solution that addresses all the constraints.

Claims analysis offers a structured problem solving representation that can be used by designers to alleviate the inherent complexity of the process. It offers support consistent with the existing design trajectory and so can be incorporated into current design practice without disruption.

This study suggests that claims analysis of an artifact can support redesign and perhaps speed-up the task-artifact cycle. The designers in this study were able to use the claims analysis of the generic system, or their redesign, to produce alternative redesigns of the system. We hope that by giving designers examples of both positive and negative claims we will encourage them to think more critically of their own redesigns, and not miss positive claims embodied by the generic system.

In this study we produced the claims analyses and designers were able to use these to better understand and drive their designs. Whether designers can and will develop and use claims analysis remains an open question. However, we were encouraged by designers' reactions to the claims analysis. In one case, the designer actually started talking about redesigning his redesign based on claims the system was making. In addition, we think that existing claims analyses may help designers develop and use their own.

6.0 NOTES

Rachel Bellamy is a graduate intern from Cambridge University and the MRC Applied Psychology Unit, Cambridge, UK.

7.0 REFERENCES

Adams, J.K. and Adams, P.A. (1961). Realism of Confidence Judgements. *Psychological Review*, 68, pp. 33-45.

Bellamy, R.K.E. and Carroll, J.M. (in preparation) Smalltalk/V as a Theory of Programming.

Carroll, J.M. (1990) Infinite Detail and Emulation in an Ontologically Minimized HCI. In *Proceedings of CHI'90*, Conference on Human Factors in Computing, Seattle, USA. ACM, NY.

Carroll, J.M. and Campbell, R.L. (1989). Artifacts and Psychological Theories: The case of Human-Computer Interaction. *Behaviour and Information Technology*, 8.

Carroll, J.M. and Kellogg, W.A. (1989). Artifacts as Theory Nexus: Hermeneutics Meets Theory-Based Design. In K. Bice and C. Lewis (Eds.), *Proceedings of CHI'89*, Conference on Human Factors in Computing Systems, Austin, USA. ACM, NY.

Carroll, J.M. and Rosson, M.B. (1990). Human-Computer Interaction Scenarios as a Design Representation. In B.D. Shriver (Ed) *Proceedings of the Twenty-Third Annual Hawaii International Conference on Systems Sciences*, Hawaii. IEEE Computer Society Press, CA.

Guindon, R., Krasner, H. and Curtis, B. (1987). Breakdowns and Processes during the Early Activities of Software Design by Professionals. In G. Olson, S. Sheppard and E. Soloway (Eds.), *Empirical Studies of Programmers: Second Workshop*. Ablex, NJ.

Guindon, R. and Curtis, B. (1988). Control of Cognitve Processes during Software Design: What Tools Would Support Software Designers. *Proceedings of CHI'88*,Conference on Human Factors in Computing, Washington, D.C., USA. ACM, NY.

Green, T.R.G. (1989). Cognitive Dimmensions of Notations. In A. Sutcliffe and L. Macauley (Eds.), *People and Computers V*. Cambridge University Press, Cambridge.

Hamond, N., Jorgenson, A., MacLean, A., and Barnard, P. (1983) Design in Practice. In *Proceedings of CHI'83*, Conference on Human Factors in Computing, Boston, USA. ACM, NY.

Lichtenstein, S., Fischoff, B. and Phillips, L.D. (1982). Calibration of Probabilities: the State of the Art to 1980. In D. Kahneman, P. Slovic and A. Tversky (Eds.) *Judgement under Uncertainity: Heuristics and Biases*. Cambridge University Press,.

Maier, N.R.F. (1931). Reasoning in Humans II: the Solution of a Problem and its Appearance in Consciousness. *Journal of Comparative Psychology*, 12, pp. 181-94.

Norman, D.A. (1986). Cognitive Engineering. In D.A. Norman and S. Draper (Eds.), *User Centered System Design: New Perspectives on Human-Computer Interaction*. Lawrence Erlbaum Associates, Hillsdale, NJ.

Rosson, M.B., Carroll, J.M. and Bellamy, R.K.E. (1990). Smalltalk Scaffolding:. In *Proceedings of CHI'90*, Conference on Human Factors in Computing, Seattle, USA. ACM, NY.

Simon, H.A. (1971). *Models of Bounded Rationality*. MIT Press, Cambridge, MA.

Thomas, J.C. (1989). Problem Solving by Human-Machine Interaction. In K.J. Gilhooly (Ed.), *Human and Machine Problem Solving*. Plenum Press, London.

Tversky, A. and Kahneman, D. (1971). Availability: a Heuristic for Judging Frequency and Probability. *Cognitive Psychology* , 5, pp. 207-32.

Human–Computer Interaction – INTERACT '90
D. Diaper et al. (Editors)
Elsevier Science Publishers B.V. (North-Holland)

WHAT RATIONALE IS THERE IN DESIGN?

Allan MacLean, Victoria Bellotti and Richard Young[1]

Rank Xerox EuroPARC, 61 Regent Street, Cambridge CB2 1AB, England
[1] Also MRC Applied Psychology Unit, 15 Chaucer Road, Cambridge CB2 2EF.

Design Rationale is a framework for locating a proposed design within a design space. It incorporates an explicit representation of design *Options*, and an explicit representation of *Criteria* for choosing among the *Options*. This paper explores the relationship between Design Rationale and design practice. It uses Design Rationale as a way of analysing the content of a design session to help us understand requirements for future ways of improving the design process.

1. DESIGN RATIONALE

The Design Rationale framework (MacLean, Young and Moran, 1989) is a central part of a long term project in which we are interested in helping software designers reason about design and produce an output which can help others to understand why the design is the way it is. This paper explores the relationship between Design Rationale and design practice with the aim of developing the framework and understanding how it might be supported with computer based tools, so that ultimately it can improve the design process. The framework generalises to a wide variety of design domains, but our current interest focusses on user interface design.

The approach contrasts with the traditional conception of design which assumes that the eventual output is a specific artifact (which ultimately only reflects a small fraction of the thinking and problem solving which went into its creation). Instead, we suggest that a more appropriate output from design activity would be what we refer to as a Design Rationale. (See MacLean et al., 1989, for a more comprehensive discussion). A Design Rationale is not simply a record of a design process – it is a co-product of design along with the artifact and itself has to be designed. Briefly, Design Rationale is a semi-formal notation which is used to represent the design space around an artifact being produced. This space is an explicit representation of alternative design options, and an explicit representation of reasons for choosing among those options. We characterise the main concepts we are currently using for the representation as *Questions* which highlight key issues in the design, *Options* which are effectively answers to the questions and *Criteria* which are the reasons that argue for or against the possible options.

Our goal with Design Rationale is to develop a representation which can help designers reason about design and produce an output which can help others to understand why the design is the way it is. Such a representation should be able to support communication between people with different backgrounds and goals, for example between members of a design team working on an initial design, between the original designers and designers of a later generation system who want to re-use parts of the original design, and even between the designers and users of a computer system. It provides a theoretical framework for design which we have already found useful for helping us better understand design issues (see MacLean et al., 1989; MacLean, 1990). This theoretical approach drives such activities as understanding the design process and how it can be improved; requirements for tools to support the creation of a Design Rationale (and thus the design process); and the integration of other approaches to HCI, such as modelling techniques, into design.

The development of Design Rationale so far has relied on analysing existing designs (effectively reverse engineering the Design Rationale), and on limited use in our own in-house design projects. It is clearly important that Design Rationale is found to be of value when we use it to guide our own thinking, however it is also important for longer term development that it can provide benefits to others as well. The main aim of the study reported in this paper is to help us understand how compatible the main concepts we use are with the kinds of concepts designers "naturally" rely on for problem solving in design. There are a number of potential outcomes to such a study. We might want to modify our views of Design Rationale to make it more compatible with design practice; we would hope to begin to understand what support might be necessary for a design methodology which aimed at producing a Design Rationale; we would hope to be in a better position to understand requirements for tools to support the creation and use of a Design Rationale. A complementary aim is to produce a Design Rationale from the activity of designers other than ourselves.

2. THE ATM DESIGN STUDY

This paper looks at two professional software designers (who have worked together in the past) carrying out a design problem "in the zoo", by which we mean that they worked on a realistic design problem of our choosing in our laboratory. Such a setting is halfway between an artificial laboratory task and uncontrolled free behaviour "in the wild".

Standard ATM

The National Barklands Bank (NB) Automated Teller Machine (ATM) is a fairly typical ATM. If you want to get cash from it, you would go through the following steps:

- Push card into slot
- Type PIN number when prompted
- Select *Cash Withdrawal.* (from the several Services offered).
- Select *Another Amount.* (You could have selected one of five preset amounts)
- Type in amount required and press *Enter* key.
- Select *No* (when asked if you would like to request another service).
- Remove card from slot
- Take cash from drawer, and receipt from slot.

But...

The NB bank noticed that long queues sometimes built up at these standard ATMs. They asked their design staff to see if they could speed the process up. Their proposed design (FATM) presents the customer with the following procedure:

The Fast ATM (FATM)

- Select cash amount (Must be one of six preset amounts)
- Insert card.
- Remove card.
- Type in PIN number.
- Take cash and receipt from drawer

Your task...

You are brought in as design consultants by NB, who would like to know whether you think they have produced a successful design for the FATM. We would like you to analyse the new design and

(1) summarise for us what you feel are the main advantages and disadvantages of the FATM;
(2) suggest any further improvements to the design, or better design alternatives.

Figure 1. The problem presented to the designers.

The designers (Jaimie and Donald) were given an outline of a proposed new design for a bank Automated Teller Machine (ATM) to criticise and improve relative to an earlier version. The problem presented to them is shown in Figure 1. We chose the ATM as an example domain as it is sufficiently simple to make it possible to carry out a "complete" design task in a relatively short time. We gave a problem which contrasts two designs in order to encourage a discussion of design alternatives and criteria. This is the first stage of a strategy to put us in a position to look for similar discussions in more open ended design.

The two designers sat in a room on their own, on either side of an electronic whiteboard which they used heavily. We watched them working over a video link and video recorded the session. The designers spent about forty five minutes on the problem on their own, then about ten minutes summarising their conclusions to us, and then about fifteen minutes on a debriefing during which they told us their backgrounds and experience both as software designers and as users of bank ATMs.

The video record was transcribed and annotated so that the protocol produced could be understood without referring back to the video tape. Our focus was on analysing the content of the meeting, so we were prepared to lose information about the detailed dynamics of the session in exchange for moving towards building a coherent representation of the main concepts discussed. Asides and redundant remarks were filtered out and the protocol was segmented into about 360 assertions, each of which captured a substantive point in the discussion. This gave a convenient index into the session. These assertions were then linked into clusters identified by the first occurrence of each of 80 key concepts, which were then structured into a Design Rationale. We found areas where our Design Rationale framework appears to be compatible with the design behaviour observed and areas where we think Design Rationale could potentially improve the quality of design. We also identified some difficult challenges which Design Rationale based support tools will have to face. In this paper, we will illustrate these findings with excerpts from the protocol.

3. THE DESIGN SESSION

The designers' task was to analyse the proposed new design for the Fast ATM (FATM) which had been proposed in response to queues building up at standard ATMs, critique it relative to the standard ATM and suggest further alternative designs if appropriate. They jumped straight into the task and started off by trying to understand the differences between the two ATMs described. They did not see a good reason for the FATM to use a different order of steps. They moved towards a design solution which simply reduced the number of services available on the standard machine but preserved the order of the remaining steps. Their final proposal was a switchable ATM which the bank staff could set into a "fast cash mode" offering restricted services during busy periods.

3.1 *Options* and *Criteria* Observed

When we look at the protocol of the design session to see to what extent Design Rationale concepts can be directly observed, many examples of *Options* and

Criteria are easily discernable. Many of the options which were discussed are in fact variations on those suggested in the original problem statement. Figure 2a shows an example of a novel option being discussed. This is where they first came up with the solution of a combined ATM which could be switched between a "Fast Cash" mode and a "Full Services" mode. Here they are discussing using a light above the machine to indicate the current mode to the customers.

00:21:30

185. Jaimie: So **we could use** um *(waves his hands around in the air, and they both laugh)* **a "Fast light"**

186. *(he writes* ***"'fast' light - operated...")*** **presumably by the bank staff**.

Donald: Yes.

Jaimie writes "... by the bank staff to restrict machine to just fast cash withdrawals -delete other operations".

187. Donald: Yes, and **you could say like five items only in supermarkets** or whatever. And you could say that this would make...

188. **there'd be a light above it** *(pointing at the "Other operations" item in the screen diagram)*, and also

189. **other options wouldn't appear on the screen**.

Figure 2a. Discussion of "fast light" option.

00:39:55

311. Jaimie: [if the problem is] **too many people** [the solution is] to

312. **provide more machines,**

313. **with a potential for a "fast light" machine.**

Donald: Yes.

314. Jaimie: [if the problem is] **Lots of transactions per person** [the solution] is

315. **again this fast light thing,**

Figure 2b. Revisiting "fast light" option and justifying it against different reasons for queues building up.

The figures show time into the session, assertion number and key attributes of the assertion in bold.

Options are not discussed once and then decided upon. An option often comes up several times, temporally distributed over the design session. Figure 2b shows the "fast light" option being raised again later in the session, in the context of possible reasons for queues building up. Two different reasons for queues are suggested, and in each case the "fast light" machine is confirmed as a suitable design solution. This example not only illustrates the discussion of details being distributed throughout the session, it also shows the common tendency for seeking evidence to confirm one's own views. This is basically the same phenomenon noted in faulty reasoning where people tend to look for positive instances in support of their argument rather than examples which contradict their argument (e.g. Wason, 1968). Counterexamples are of course one powerful way of detecting flaws in arguments. We claim that exploring alternative and conflicting design options is a fruitful way of detecting flaws in the argument behind a given design (MacLean et al, 1989). Searching for counterexamples is a form of reasoning we would expect a Design Rationale based approach to promote, thus improving the quality of design reasoning.

Criteria are also fairly well represented in the design protocol. For example, Figure 3 shows a discussion of error recovery from pressing the wrong button. Jaimie rather unequivocally claims that if a mistake is made the customer should try again from the beginning. Donald justifies this by appealing to a trade off between speed and security, and effectively makes the claim that security is more important.

00:41:07

331. Donald: Yes, now **if you press the wrong one**...

332. Jaimie: **That's tough.**

333. Donald: It is basically, because **otherwise you trade off speed against security**.

Figure 3. Discussion of error recover calling on speed and security as criteria to be traded off against each other.

3.2 Impoverished *Questions*

The appearance of explicit *Questions* (in the Design Rationale sense) are rather more impoverished than *Options* and *Criteria*. It is rare in this protocol for alternative options to be directly compared. Rather, individual options are discussed. The option is often expressed as a binary choice - i.e. the *question* is to have that *option* or not. For example, one discussion revolved around whether or not to give the customer a receipt for the transaction. This was discussed in terms of a trade off between a safeguard against an error in the machine and the avoidance of litter or saving paper. One of the claims we have made is that appropriate *Questions* serve an important role in helping to generate new *options*. In this case, if a question such as "Should the customer be given a record of the transaction?" had been asked first, followed by a question such as "What form should the record take?" a wider range of possible options such as marking the ATM card, giving a reference number etc. may have emerged as being alternatives to a receipt.

3.3 Assertions with Multiple Roles

The previous sections illustrate that it is generally not too difficult to identify *options* and *criteria* when they explicitly appear in the protocol. *Questions* are more difficult to identify, in part because relatively few are explicitly stated and when they *are* stated they tend to be fairly impoverished in their potential scope. Another reason is that the questions are effectively implied by the options being discussed. For example, when moving on to talk about how to have the card read, the topic is changed by Jaimie saying "You've got to insert and remove the cards...". So this statement serves the dual role of bringing up a new question, and doing it by making a statement about the likely options which will be appropriate. Another multiple role we occasionally observe is *options* and *criteria* more closely intertwined in an assertion than we have so far seen. For example, when talking about how to give the customer a receipt, Donald says "...no one's going to remember to take it out of a drawer." He is effectively saying that a drawer is an inappropriate option for handing over the receipt because it will rely on fallible human memory to open the drawer.

3.4 Concrete *Options*

When *options* are discussed, it would appear that in some cases, the option is not meant precisely as stated. Rather, a concrete option is proposed as an example – in fact, perhaps more of a caricature as only some of its attributes are seriously being evaluated. For example, Figure 4 shows an extract from the session in which the designers are discussing what preset amounts of cash the machine should offer. They discuss the options by proposing alternative combinations which could be offered. Note first that there are two criteria implied in this segment. In assertion 198, they want to provide the most common amounts, and in assertion 202 they are talking in terms of "covering the spectrum" - i.e. providing an adequate range of options. In both of these cases they are also working to a criterion to minimise the number of choices (implied by assertion 193). However, they discuss the possibilities by proposing a series of very specific options - e.g. twenty and fifty; ten, twenty, fifty a hundred, and in fact settle for ten, twenty, thirty and fifty in their final written design. The point is that they clearly do not mean these as specific proposals, rather they exemplify relevant *attributes* of the solution, *viz*: to look for what they think are the most common sums required; to minimise the number of different ones; and to cover the range of values required. The easy acceptance of different alternative proposals, and especially the abstraction of the minimal set of two sums to "a big red button and a big blue button" serve to support this argument. If this form of reasoning is recorded, there is a danger that unintended attributes will migrate into the design description.

00:22:50

193. **I'm not sure whether you need that many.**
194. It would depend, **you could just do a survey** though. Couldn't you just sort of
195. **attach something from the inside which just looked at what most people mostly chose.**
196. **In fact that's probably what they've already done.**

Jaimie: Yes.

197. Donald: Trying to decide **which were the most common ones.**
198. They probably are **twenty and fifty are the most common ones.**
199. In fact **that would probably do**, almost.
200. **Just a big red button and a big blue button.**

Jaimie writes "4, Survey most common cash withdrawals.

201. Donald: **Especially since people tend to fit in.**

202. Jaimie: That's right, I mean **if you've got ten, twenty, fifty and a hundred this covers the spectrum** doesn't it ?

Donald: That's it.

Figure 4. Discussion of what preset amounts of cash to offer.

3.5 Implicit Rationale

We have so far focussed primarily on what Rationale can be observed explicitly in the protocol. However, trying to understand what is not mentioned explicitly is perhaps even more important for some of the Rationale which drives the design. One clear tendency was for few options to be discussed which differed significantly from the overall style of ATM machine with which the designers were presented. Indeed one might go so far as to say that there was a strong tendency for them not to deviate far from the standard ATM design, with which they were both more or less familiar as users. Indeed, in the debriefing after the session when asked how much they felt they had assumed from their own knowledge of ATMs, Donald said "A hell of a lot." and Jaimie expanded to say he felt they had "...made assumptions, but not consciously." Their own shared experience of bank ATMs clearly shaped the way they approached the problem, and they seemed to effectively accept the assumptions behind the designs with which they were familiar.

Another example of implicit rationale can be seen when the designers are comparing the two ATM designs from the problem statement. Donald says "Ah, I'll tell you what I do like though is this *cash and receipt from drawer*. Taking both from the same place is quite a good idea." In this case it seems unnecessary to produce a more explicit rationale. Jaimie does not question the assertion that it is "a good idea", because it is "obvious" to both of them from the context of the discussion that the effect is to collapse two steps into one. In these cases, if the Rationale were made explicit it would help others revisiting the design at a later time to understand it better.

3.6 Missing Rationale

So some information which might be helpful in forming a Rationale for the design is clearly implicit, but nonetheless influential in shaping the way the design goes. Other potentially relevant information however may not be thought of at all. For example, early in the design session when the designers are comparing the standard ATM and the Fast ATM, they explicitly ask if there are any advantages in the different order of steps (Figure 5). The immediate reaction is that there is no advantage – in fact that there is a disadvantage – but although they both seem to agree they obviously feel uncomfortable as they pause and think and eventually Donald rather unconvincingly suggests that people are not going to like to learn two different ways of doing things. This is another illustration of the phenomenon noted earlier where the tendency is to confirm their own views rather than look for evidence which opposes them. In this case, for example, they fail to note that for a very simple machine like the Fast ATM, users probably do not "learn" how to use it - rather the machine guides them through the steps. A possible advantage for the ordering might be that by insisting on a sum of money being selected first, the machine makes it immediately clear that all it can do is provide cash. Had the designers followed this kind of reasoning, their later conclusions may have been very different.

The above example suggests a line of reasoning which may have influenced the course of the design session had it been discussed. A related example shows a line of reasoning which was eventually discussed, but only late in the session. It was thirty minutes into the session before the designers started to ask why queues were building up. Understanding the possible reasons would presumably have influenced how the designers interpreted the differences between the two ATM designs earlier. As it turned out, they asked the question late in the session and their strategy was simply to look for confirmation of the design they had already come up with rather than to question it (see Figure 2b).

00:04:51

34. Jaimie: Right. **Any more advantages,**

35. **is there any advantage to the ordering ?**

36. **Seems like a disadvantage to me.**

Pause

Donald: Yes.

Pause

38. Donald: No **I don't think there's any advantage in the ordering**. In fact

39. **I think there's a disadvantage**. In fact you could write that down.

40. **If you have a different order on different machines**, this is going to, er, you know, **people are going to have to learn two different ways of doing things;**

40a. **they're not going to like that.**

Figure 5. Discussing order of steps on the two ATMs.

---

4. IMPLICATIONS FOR DESIGN RATIONALE

This study provides us with three distinct types of information to help towards our goal of producing computer based Design Rationale tools to assist with software design. First, the relatively close correspondence between much of what is explicitly discussed and the key concepts we want to represent with Design Rationale suggests that, with suitable tools, it should be possible to record much of what would happen "naturally" in an appropriate form for a Design Rationale representation, and therefore make it more accessible for other people who need to understand the design.

Secondly, the kinds of things which do not appear explicitly in the protocol point towards areas where a Design Rationale based approach to design might improve the final design. If designers conducted their problem solving in terms of Design Rationale we would expect the conceptual structure that it provides to assist them with structuring their problem solving. Burgess et al (1989) describe design meetings where a paper based method for structuring discussions based on the IBIS representational scheme (Kunz and Rittal, 1970) was perceived to help in structuring design problem solving. In particular, "problem finding" is known to be an important part of problem solving (e.g. see Hayes, 1981). The emphasis on structuring design Options around Questions in the Design Rationale framework is geared towards helping focus on the questions and thus assisting with understanding the real problem. We would expect a Design Rationale based approach to help highlight important questions sufficiently early to allow them to be properly addressed.

It was noted that much of the design progressed by continually revisiting points which had been discussed earlier. Even in a small problem such as this one it appeared that the designers are likely to lose track of issues they discussed earlier. As Olson and Olson (in press) point out, in more complex design meetings many issues and ideas are raised and lost. Laying out considerations in an appropriate structure should therefore help to remind participants about points they have already visited. Also, it is clear from the debriefing that it is possible to access information which implicitly shapes design (such as experience with other ATMs in this case). We would expect that working to an explicit structure such as Design Rationale would make it more likely that such information would be represented, thus communicating its relevance to other people who need to understand the Rationale for the design at a later time.

Finally, the data from the design session presented here also highlights challenges for design support tools. Since some assertions in the protocol have multiple roles, it would clearly require extra work to mould them into a form (or forms) appropriate for mapping onto a structured representation such as Design Rationale. Explicitly working to a structure may of course reduce the number of such situations, and encouraging decomposition may help clarity of thought, but it is likely that enforcing (rather than encouraging) structure will impede the flow of design. Similarly, if ideas are discussed in relatively concrete terms as observed in this study and then have to be effectively abstracted for "appropriate" representation in a structure, the overheads for the user of the design tool may be excessive. One potential solution is to encourage regular periods of reflection on the more intense creative periods of design. Current tools, such as hypertext based tools, typically enforce either premature commitment to represent the content of ideas in a structure, or require excessive duplication of effort to restructure them (see Halasz, 1988 for further discussion of such issues).

If we are successfully to introduce new design tools into design practice, it is essential that we understand how people naturally carry out the tasks we are trying to support. Only by seeing where current practice can be improved and where its characteristics set particular challenges for support can we hope to understand whether our proposed solutions are likely to be acceptable and useful. The study reported here helps us along the road to evolving requirements for design tools based on Design Rationale.

ACKNOWLEDGEMENTS

The work reported here was partially funded by the European Commission Esprit Basic Research Action 3066. We would like to thank Judy Olson and Bill Gaver for insightful comments on an earlier version of this paper.

REFERENCES

Burgess, K.C., Yakemovic and Conklin, J. (1989) *The Capture of Design Rationale on an Industrial Development Project.* Preliminary Report, MCC TR STP-279-89, (July, 1989).

Halasz, F. (1988) Reflections on NoteCards: Seven Issues for the Next Generation of Hypermedia Systems. *Communications of the ACM*, 31, 836-852.

Hayes, J.R. (1981) *The Complete Problem Solver.* Franklin Institute Press, Philadelphia.

Kunz, W. and Rittal, H. (1970) *Issues as Elements of Information Systems.* Technical Report S-78-2, University of Stuttgart.

MacLean, A. Young, R. and Moran, T. Design Rationale: The Argument behind the Artifact. In *Proceedings of CHI'89: Human Factors in Computing Systems.* Austin, Texas. ACM, New York, 247-252.

MacLean, A. (1990) Design Rationale: Developing a Usable Representation for Design Knowledge. In *Proceedings of AAAI Spring Symposium on Knowledge Based Human-Computer Communication.* March 27-29, 1990, Stanford University.

Olson G. and Olson J. (in press). User Centered Design of Collaboration Technology. To appear in *Organizational Computing.*

Wason, P.C. (1968) Reasoning about a Rule. *Quarterly Journal of Experimental Psychology.* 20, 273-281.

Human–Computer Interaction – INTERACT '90
D. Diaper et al. (Editors)
Elsevier Science Publishers B.V. (North-Holland)
IFIP, 1990

A FRAMEWORK FOR ASSESSING APPLICABILITY OF HCI TECHNIQUES

Victoria M.E. Bellotti

Queen Mary and Westfield College, London University.
(Now at Rank Xerox EuroPARC, 61 Regent Street, Cambridge CB2 1AB, England)

The findings from three studies of applied and commercial design practice provide the basis for a framework for assessing the applicability of HCI analytic techniques. This framework embodies an explicit view of the design process, HCI oriented design roles, and a scoping matrix designed to represent breadth of a design or evaluative approach. These components assist in the identification of a list of desirable features for more applicable techniques, derived from interviews with practising HCI specialists in commercial software houses.

1. INTRODUCTION

1.1 Background and Motivation

The assessment of usability of a design specification or existing computer system becomes more complex as computing technology and functionality advances. Approaches to modelling knowledge representation or performance of system users, such as GOMS (Card et al, 1983) and TAG (Payne & Green, 1986) aim to enable the prediction of usability in the absence of user evaluations of prototypes. Such techniques are usually developed and tested by HCI specialists in research and laboratory environments, rather than in practical design situations. A question asked here is; what impact have these techniques had on practice ?

We can posit two alternative, roles for HCI modelling techniques:

Role I; as scientific explorations which enhance our understanding of usability and the essence of which "percolates" through to design practice in some form.

Role II; as design and evaluative techniques which can be directly applied to support practitioners of user-oriented systems design.

On the basis of explicit claims made by the authors of some techniques it appears that they are, at least in part, addressing the more ambitious Role II. Examples of the claims made are as follows:

"Task-action grammars ... provide *designers* with an analytic tool for exposing the configural properties of task languages." (Payne & Green [1986] p 93)

"Our implicit advice to the *system designer* has been to use these [GOMS] models in design."
"We have expressed some of the results in this book as a set of design principles to *aid in the design of systems* for human-computer interaction." (Card et al [1983] pps 417 & 424)

"...the formal representations that have been represented in this paper [on CCT] provide the tools necessary to explore the psychological aspects of the complexity of a device, and provide the quantitative metrics for user complexity that are necessary for applications of these theoretical ideas for the *design of actual products*." (Kieras & Polson [1985] p 393)

"CLG *guides the designer* by ordering the decisions he must make."
"Several...evaluation measures could be derived from CLG descriptions to guide the designer..." (Moran [1981] pps 45 & 47)

Many other modelling techniques do not make such explicit claims, but still focus on analysing and predicting system usability. I assume that all such approaches represent a serious attempt by HCI researchers to help designers to design and evaluate for more usable systems. This paper asks why HCI design and evaluative techniques (DETs) are not being used and addresses features which would make them more appropriate for practice. To that end an empirically based framework is described which is designed to structure the assessment of the practical applicability of HCI techniques from a number of design perspectives.

1.2 HCI Modelling Techniques and Design Practice

Some HCI DETs have no clear view of the practicalities of design and how they would fit into systems development lifecycles. The Action Language (Reisner, 1981), TAG (ibid), and ICS (Barnard, 1986), for example, make little attempt to account for the nature of design practice and how they might integrate with the other necessary activities which have to take place in order to produce a complete system. In some cases it may be argued that the technique aims only to fulfil Role I. TAG however comes with more serious claims about its utility to design practice.

GOMS (ibid), CCT (Kieras & Polson, 1985) and CLG (Moran, 1981) do have explicit views of the design process. For example, the authors of GOMS present ten principles which should guide the UI designer. The design process itself is viewed as being made up of design functions belonging to the categories of *Structural Design*, where the system, or system part, is actually configured or restructured to satisfy requirements specifications; *Evaluation* where the system (or part) has been built or specified and requires an analysis of its performance and *Parametric Design* where the structure of the system (or part) has been fixed and quantitative performance parameters, or ranges of parameters, need to be defined (Card et al, 1983).

Despite explicit statements about the expected design process, there is little evidence of use of HCI DETs in practice. Concern about this fact has been expressed by various researchers in the field. Hammond et al (1983) note that much HCI literature runs the risk of being inapplicable for systems design, with overgeneralisation of recommendations based on artificial experimentation. Smith & Mosier (1984) suggest that blame for poor UI design approaches may lie at the door of HCI specialists who lack the knowledge and tools, and consequently the influence, to deal effectively with design. Rosson et al (1987) report an interview study based upon the idea that, if specialists are ever to provide useful design tools, they must look at design practice. They found that user testing was mostly informal, ranging from active user involvement, to belated user testing. They did not report use of HCI techniques. It appears that, if any user-oriented evaluation takes place, designers prefer to prototype and test their designs on real users rather than use modelling techniques.

Hannigan & Herring (1987) describe a study of the experience of designers from five major manufacturers. They compared practice with generic design cycle models both from research and from the companies themselves and found that extreme deviation from these models was the rule rather than the exception. This suggests that ideal views of what occurs in design practice are unlikely to be representative, and that design or evaluative techniques which rely upon them may not prove to be applicable.

This paper describes work which aims to relate the scope and methods of HCI DETs to design practice, in order to assess how applicability of such approaches can be improved. Three studies contributed to the assessment:
1. A questionnaire based analysis of features of user-oriented design practice, information sources, and design constraints. This study was aimed at revealing some basic characteristics of typical design projects.
2. An interview based analysis of more general characteristics of user-oriented design. This study aimed to provide more contextual information about design projects and the relationships between constraints and problems which emerge.
3. An interview based analysis of the activities and particular techniques used by HCI practitioners in commercial environments. This study provided contrasting information to that obtained in the first two studies about methods applied by those who specialize in addressing user-oriented design aspects.

Eight modelling techniques were reviewed and characterised according to their analytic scope. The techniques were BIMs (Morton et al, 1979), Reisner's Action Language, TAG, GOMS, CCT, (including analysis of the ACT* model of human information processing; Anderson, 1985), ICS and CLG. A comparison between the practical implications of applying these techniques to system design and evaluation, and evidence from studies of actual design practice drove the development of the application assessment framework which is outlined below.

2. ASSESSING APPLICABILITY OF HCI TECHNIQUES: A FRAMEWORK

2.1 A List of Desirable Features for HCI Techniques

The main component of the for Application assessment Framework (AF) is a list of ten "desirable features" for applicable techniques which are derived from the interviews with HCI practitioners in commercial environments. These interviews focused around the good and bad features of the user-oriented design and evaluation techniques which these specialists had experience of applying in real design projects, as opposed to in laboratory studies. Four features are examined in the rest of this paper;

1. **Breadth of Scope** across different contextual views of the system and usability principles
2. **Richness of User Characterization;** both Cognitive and Behavioural
3. **Realism of the design view**
4. **Coherence of Support** for the role based activities of intended users of the technique

For completeness the other desirable features, which are not discussed here are simplicity, explicitness, expressiveness, low visual complexity, high generality and preservation of information. The rest of this paper focuses on the characterization of the first four features which are the best articulated by the AF in its current form. At present the framework is comprised of four components:
1. Desirable Features List for Applicable HCI Techniques
2. Usability Matrix
3. Activities Support Matrix
4. Design Schema

The *Desirable Features List* highlights areas of weakness in existing HCI techniques as far as application is concerned. The *Usability Matrix* lays out an analytic space for HCI techniques and designs. It is used to represent feature 1; *Breadth of scope* across views of the system and usability principles and feature 2; *Richness of the User Characterization* in terms of cognitive and behavioural properties. The *Design Schema*, which is empirically derived, is intended to represent common design attributes relevant to HCI techniques. In so doing it facilitates the identification of feature 3; *Realism of the Design View* of a technique. The *Activities Support Matrix* is used to represent feature 4; the *Coherence of*

Support provided by a technique. It characterizes user-oriented design roles in terms of the types of activity they involve which are likely to require support from a technique. The following discussion outlines the nature of the Usability Matrix, the Activity Support Matrix and the Design Schema.

2.2 A "Usability Matrix" for Scoping HCI DETs

In order to assess appropriateness of HCI modelling techniques to the analytic requirements of design projects they can be characterized explicitly in terms of what they describe or predict. A Usability Matrix has been developed (Bellotti, 1990) as an expansible, visually appealing means of characterizing the scope of HCI DETs and the user-oriented analytic requirements of design projects. Figure 1 shows a simplified example of a matrix characterization of the breadth of the CCT approach.

The *context* of the systems design is represented by five "evaluation factors." These are perspectives on a design product which temper whether it will be judged usable or not. A single system would vary in usability with changes in these factors. The *breadth* of user-oriented design issues is represented by a number of "usability principles. The Usability Matrix maps usability principles, or ideal properties of a system, against factors of the context within which they may be evaluated in order to lay out a broad space within which to scope possible approaches to assessing usability.

Evaluation Factors	**Usability Principles**		
	Simplicity	Compat-ibility	UCTDs
Users	Yes		Yes
System Application			
User Interface	Yes		Yes
Target Tasks	Yes	Yes	Yes
Acceptable Performance	Yes		Yes

Figure 1.
Simplified Usability Scoping Matrix Characterising CCT (Kieras & Polson 1985)

The principle of *simplicity* is based upon extensive research (e.g. Thimbleby, 1984 and Dix et al, 1986) that examines aspects of UI design which can be formally specified and which, when embodied in a system, yield better usability. The principles of *compatibility* and *user-centred task dynamics (UCTDs)* are based on research into human representation and processing (e.g. Wilson et al, 1988) which suggests that users are better able to learn to use systems that exploit existing knowledge structures which they have acquired from previous experience.

The matrix represents an expandable, two dimensional view of a design space within which the scopes of different HCI techniques can be characterized and quickly distinguished from one another in terms of their appropriateness for certain kinds of analysis. Additional usability principles may be included such as *observability, consistency* and *reachability* (Thimbleby, 1984).

An additional advantage of using this characterization is that it is capable of representing analytic issues which are important to a particular design project. If, for example, the application happens to be in a high risk domain such as power generation process-control, designers may want evaluation techniques which can predict human performance and the probability of error, and which are sensitive to the semantics of the application and its behaviour. Such an application might require an HCI DET to be sensitive to underlying system state behaviour and its observability and that the UI be as simple as possible in order to avoid human error. These analytic requirements would be represented by marking or describing the nature of the intersection of observability with the system application factor, and the intersection of simplicity with the users factor in the Usability Matrix.

The desirable feature; Richness of the User Characterization can also be captured within the Usability Matrix by expanding the user-factor row into rows of sub-factors such as visual processing, memory characteristics, social aspects and so on. Each sub-factor can then be mapped to usability principles where appropriate (some principles may not relate well to certain user sub-factors) and HCI modelling techniques can be characterized within the resulting space in terms of the Richness of their User Characterization.

2.3 An Activities Support Matrix.

The Usability Matrix relates the breadth of issues addressed by any HCI descriptive or predictive technique to the intended product of the design process in terms of its properties and context. It does not, however illuminate the activities which must be undertaken in order to carry out the required analyses. In other words it cannot show whether a technique provides Coherent Support for its intended users, which is one of the desirable features of applicable approaches. It is possible to assess the types of activities necessary to carry out a complete analysis using an HCI DET (Bellotti 1990). These might include information collection activities such as interviewing and observation for task analysis. Such an assessment produces an informal activity profile. It is then possible to determine whether a given technique provides support in terms of guidance and tools for the activities necessary to its implementation.

Study of design projects revealed that systems engineers and HCI practitioners carry out various activities which applicable HCI techniques may usefully support (Bellotti, 1990). From the study focused on HCI practitioners in commercial environments it was possible to derive a characterization of five user-oriented design roles in terms of types of activity which are important to them. If a technique were to be applied by an analyst in a design project, it would be helpful if it supported the activities of the practitioner in a particular role, rather than some arbitrary subset of activities reflecting interests of researchers. In other words an applicable technique should ideally provide Coherent Support for at least one of the characterized roles in the Activities Support Matrix in terms of the activities the role requires.

Roles	**Activity types**		
	Invention	Analysis	Communication
Designer	S	S	S
Technology Transfer Agent			S
Supported			
by CCT	No	Yes	No
S = an important activity to be supported			

Figure 2.
An Example Activities Matrix Representing Coherent Support Requirements for Roles in Design Projects

Figure 2 presents a simplified Activities Support Matrix showing two of the roles which HCI specialists were observed to undertake in commercial environments (presumably systems designers could also carry out these roles). The roles are characterized in terms of types of activity which they may or may not involve to a significant extent. CCT is represented as being unable to support either of the roles in figure 2. It provides little guidance on how to collect the appropriate information to generate realistic task descriptions and write psychologically plausible production system simulations of users. It does not support invention (e.g. novel ways to improve the UI), but concentrates on identification of the source of problems with the design and the performance effects these can be expected to have on users. CCT does not support communication as it relies on complex and esoteric specifications of task structures and user knowledge representations.

Like the Usability Matrix, this Activities Support Matrix can be expanded in terms of the roles and activity types it contains, according to assessment requirements. If particular roles are expected to be involved in a design, these can be characterized in as much detail as necessary and compared, in terms of the activities they involve, with those supported by a selected technique. Furthermore it can be used to characterize the precise activities required to apply an HCI technique and to contrast these with the activities which that technique effectively supports (with guidance, explicit methods, or tools perhaps).

2.4 A User-Oriented Design Practice Schema

As stated earlier, many HCI DETs have no view of the design process into which they expect to be assimilated. Those which do possess views of the design process may be misrepresenting what actually happens in practice. For this reason an empirically based Design Schema is presented which captures common, goal-oriented design activities, information sources exploited, and design constraints, which are drawn from two studies of systems designers' practice (see figure 3).

The intention of this representation is to provide a basis for determining whether an HCI DET possesses the feature of a Realistic Design View, or implicit assumptions about its application which are consistent with such a view.

The design activities are minimally structured with the middle three, main activities being potentially parallel and iterated. They are classed according to their goal rather than their actual nature with formal, informal, top-down, middle-out, object-oriented, bottom-up, data-driven, and functional specification, design or evaluation approaches all having to be included as possibilities, but which have some basic, common goals.

The information sources and design constraints represent the limitations of what is possible within most design projects, in terms of user-oriented investigations, analysis and evaluations. The constraints succinctly capture a wide variety of forces which have a negative impact on the effort to ensure usability.

With this schema the explicit and implicit requirements an HCI DET has for activities, information sources and other resources can be represented in a suitable form and compared with the Design Schema which which is derived from common attributes of *real* practice, rather than an idealized structured design methodology. It should then be possible to assess how likely it is that the technique has few unusual overheads for a design project. If the technique is too demanding it risks being rejected as inappropriate or too time consuming and expensive (Bellotti, 1988).

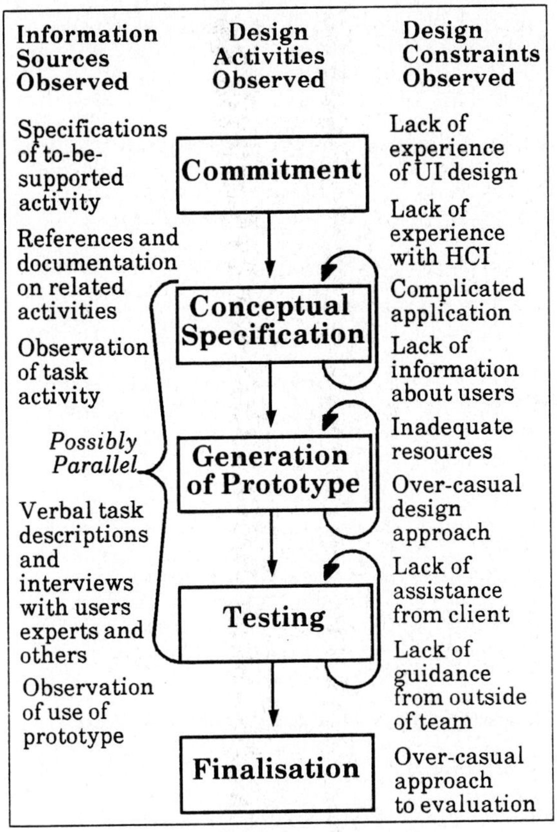

Figure 3
Schema for User-Oriented Design Practice: Based On Findings from Two Empirical Design Studies

Within the AF the existing "default" Design Schema can be modified if the framework is to be applied to a particular project, or set of projects, about which more is known. Known activity types, information sources and constraints can be inserted. However, by adhering to the existing outline, over-complexity can be avoided, in terms of representations of the system life-cycle which cannot be related to the requirements of HCI DETs.

2.5 Four Roles for the Application Framework

The framework outlined above is intended to fulfil a number of possible roles. These are:

1. A way of viewing common characteristics of applied and commercial design practice.
2. A concise basis for critiquing HCI approaches to design and evaluation.
3. An HCI technique development guide.
4. A potential HCI technique selection tool for systems designers.

The first role is the most straightforward. The AF summarizes research based on three empirical studies of design practice in a way which makes it possible to relate the findings to the application of HCI in general.

The second and third roles require that an analysis of one or more HCI DETs be carried out to the extent that characterizations within the terms of the framework are possible. Some adaptations of the Usability Matrix and the Activities Support Matrix may be necessary to suit stated aims of the technique in question. The technique might focus on particular principles in the Usability Matrix, or it might be intended to support an unusual design role involving special activities.

With further development the framework may help to make HCI modelling techniques more accessible to HCI practitioners in commercial environments and even systems designers who have so far been reasonably justified in their complaint that HCI modelling techniques are impractical (Bellotti, 1988).

3. SUMMARY

Four components of the Application Framework for assessing HCI techniques have been outlined briefly. The main component; the Desirable Features List provides the context for the other three which are aimed at assisting in the identification of presence or absence of such features in HCI techniques which would make them more applicable to practice. The Usability Matrix, Activities Support Matrix and the Design Schema are all intended to be flexible, emphasizing the form, rather than the precise content of the representations. The reason for this is the diversity of existing techniques and their aims, together with the extreme variation in approaches to design practice.

Each component serves as a basis for keeping a broad view on diverse, practical aspects of HCI approaches and their implications for real design situations. The simplicity of the representations is aimed at allowing techniques to be succinctly summarized and quickly compared with one another, and with the requirements of individual design projects, if necessary, in terms of their utility to design practitioners.

REFERENCES

Anderson, J.R. (1985) *The Architecture of Cognition*, Harvard University Press.

Barnard, P.J., (1985) "Interacting Cognitive Subsystems: A Psycholinguistic Approach to Short-Term Memory," in *Progress in the Psychology of Language, Vol 2*, A. Ellis, ed., London, Lawrence Earlbaum, pp 197 - 258.

Barnard, P.J. (1987) "Cognitive Resources and the Learning of Human-Computer Dialogues," in *Interfacing Thought: Cognitive Aspects of*

Human-Computer Interaction, J.M. Carroll, ed., MIT Press, Cambridge, Massachusetts.

Bellotti, V. (1988) "Implications of Current Design Practice for the Use of HCI Techniques," In *People and Computers IV; Proceedings of the Fourth Conference of the BCS HCI Specialist Group*, D.M. Jones & R. Winder, eds., C.U.P., pp 13 - 34.

Bellotti, V. (1990) "Applicability of HCI Techniques to System Interface Design" *PhD Thesis Submitted to the University of London.*

Card, S.K., Moran, T.P., & Newell, A. (1983) *The Psychology of Human Computer Interaction*, Lawrence Earlbaum Associates, Hillsdale, New Jersey.

Dix, A.J., Harrison, M.D., & Miranda, E.E. (1986) "Using Principles to Design Features of a Small Programming Environment," in *Proceedings of the Software Engineering Environments Conference, Lancaster*, I. Sommerville, ed., Peter Peregrinus, pp 135 - 150.

Hammond, N.V., Jorgensen, A., MacLean, A., Barnard P.J, & Long, J.B. (1983) "Design Practice and Usability: Evidence from Interviews with Designers," in *Human Factors in Computing Systems, Proceedings of CHI'83, Special Issue of the SIGCHI Bulletin*, A. Janda, ed, ACM, Boston, pp 40 - 44.

Hannigan, S., & Herring, V. (1987) "Human Factors in Office Product Design - European Practice," in *Cognitive Science in the Design of Human-Computer Interaction and Expert Systems*, G. Salvendy, ed., Elsevier Science Publishers B.V., Amsterdam, pp 225 - 274.

Kieras, D.E., & Polson, P.G. (1985) "An Approach to the Formal Analysis of User Complexity," *IJMMS, 22*, pp 365 - 394.

Moran, T.P. (1981) "The Command Language Grammar: A Representation for the User Interface of Interactive Computer Systems," *IJMMS, 15*, pp 3 - 50.

Morton, J., Barnard P.J., Hammond, N.V., & Long, J.B. (1979) "Interacting with the Computer: A Framework," in *Teleinformatics'79*, E.J. Boutmy & A. Danthine, eds., Holland: North-Holland.

Payne, S.J., & Green , T.R.G. (1986) "Task Action Grammars: A Model of the Mental Representation of Task Languages," *Human Computer Interaction, Vol 2*, Lawrence Earlbaum Associates, pp 93 - 133.

Reisner, P., (1981) "Formal Grammar and Human Factors Design of an Interactive Graphics System," *IEEE Trans. Software Engineering, Vol SE-7, No. 2*, pp 229 - 240.

Rosson, M.B., Maas, S., & Kellogg, W.A., (1987) "Designing for Designers: An Analysis of Design Practice in the Real World," in *Human Factors in Computing Systems and Graphics Interface, Proceedings of CHI + GI Conference'87, Special Issue of the SIGCHI Bulletin*, J.M. Carroll & P.P. Tanner, eds., ACM, Toronto, Canada, pp 137 - 142.

Smith S.L., & Mosier, J.N. (1984) "Design Guidelines for User-System Interface Software," *The Mitre Corporation, Report No. ESD-TR-84-190*, Bedford M.A.

Thimbleby, H. (1984), "Generative User Engineering Principles for User Interface Design," in *Human-Computer Interaction, Proceedings of INTERACT'84*, B. Shackel, ed., Elsevier Science, B.V., Amsterdam, pp 661 - 666.

Wilson, M.D., Barnard, P.J., Green, T.R.G., & MacLean, A. (1988) "Knowledge-Based Task Analysis for Human-Computer Systems," In *People and Computers: Theory Versus Outcome*, G.C.Van Der Veer, T.R.G. Green, J.-M. Hoc, & D.M. Murray, eds., Academic Press, London.

Human–Computer Interaction – INTERACT '90
D. Diaper et al. (Editors)
Elsevier Science Publishers B.V. (North-Holland)

OBSTACLES TO USER INVOLVEMENT IN INTERFACE DESIGN IN LARGE PRODUCT DEVELOPMENT ORGANIZATIONS

Jonathan Grudin

Computer Science Department, Aarhus University, Ny Munkegade, 8000 Aarhus C, Denmark

Development of an "off-the-shelf" product typically starts with a product idea and limited knowledge of the eventual users. Since the functionality is partially predefined, the most natural focus for user involvement in design is the human-computer interface. However, large product development organizations contain inherent obstacles to involving existing or potential users even in interface design. Formed before the human-computer interface attained its present prominence, their organizational structures and development processes have evolved with minimal consideration of the particular needs of interface development. This paper outlines the problems in achieving and benefiting from user involvement in design that stem from typical divisions of responsibility and development processes. While overcoming such organizational constraints may ultimately require organizational change, those working within such an organization must be aware of the problems and constantly seek constructive paths around them.

PRODUCT DEVELOPMENT ORGANIZATIONS

This paper focuses on large companies that develop software systems and applications for wide distribution. A direct sales force, independent sales organizations, or value-added resellers may stand between development and the customer. This paper does not address internal development groups within a large organization, whose software is not developed as a product to be marketed externally. Also not considered are development groups formed to work on specific contracts. These other types of development groups have different advantages and disadvantages in obtaining user participation in design. Of course, a company may straddle categories: a product development company may bid on government contracts, an internal development group may decide to market a system built initially for internal use, and so forth. In addition, small product development companies may not find the problems associated with division of labor and management practices described here, while companies of moderate size may experience some of them but not others.

Thus, the obstacles to user involvement described below affect a fraction of systems developers -- perhaps only a small fraction. However, it is a significant fraction, especially in the United States. These product development companies have hired and trained large numbers of user interface specialists, recruiting heavily from leading research universities. They have recently been prominent in promoting the importance of usability and "look and feel." Their user interface specialists have dominated the conferences and journals in the field of human-computer interaction, especially in the United States.

These companies grew up primarily in the 1960s and 1970s. At that time, profits came from selling or leasing hardware; software functionality was secondary, and the human-computer interface received little attention. Since then, software has come to rival hardware in importance -- many of the successful new product development companies of the 1980's were primarily software companies. The focus has been on functionality and price, not the interface, but the success of the Macintosh in the late 1980s is changing that. The interface has become important, and its importance will grow (Friedman, 1989; Grudin, 1990).

Unfortunately for those whose concern lies with the interface, these companies organized their business operations and development procedures when hardware and software functionality were the only important considerations. It is therefore not surprising that existing organizational structures and processes do not facilitate interface development. In fact, they often systematically *obstruct* the design and development of good interfaces (Grudin, 1986). One way they do so is by blocking user involvement in the process.

INTERFACE DEVELOPMENT IN PRODUCT DEVELOPMENT ORGANIZATIONS

Drawing a line between software functionality and its "user interface" is notoriously difficult. Nor is it necessarily a significant distinction -- since both interface and functionality determine how computer systems support work, user involvement could span them. In practice, however, a project to develop or upgrade a system begins with general preconceptions about the functionality to be provided. In a product development company in particular, a project typically begins with a product idea, defined in terms of hardware and software function. Product ideas do not arise in a vacuum; some market research may take place, and individuals within a company develop varying degrees of intuition and domain expertise, in part through direct or indirect contact with users of existing products. One might suppose that better product ideas would emerge from involving users without preconceptions, but one has to start somewhere, and product development companies often find themselves with existing products in clear need of improvement as well as a wealth of new product proposals to select among.

Thus, user participation in product development environments typically occurs, if it occurs at all, in defining the human-computer interface (assumed here to include low-level functionality). Interface builders are thus natural advocates within product development companies for greater user involvement. This paper outlines the obstacles to user participation that they encounter. A market research group focusing on deeper aspects of product direction might experience quite different obstacles and opportunities in involving users.

APPROACHES TO UNDERSTANDING COMPUTER USERS

There are many possible approaches to understanding computer users, not all of which require direct user involvement. The problem is clear: As computer users become less technical and more diverse, there is greater need for developers to obtain information about them and their work environments. The most direct solution to this problem may be participatory or collaborative design, engaging potential users as full members of the design team (e.g. Bjerknes, Ehn and Kyng, 1987). Where its drawbacks are not serious, it may be the most effective. A limited form of this may be obtained by hiring people from user organizations to work as "domain experts." A more common but also more circumscribed form of direct user involvement is limited-duration study by developers of existing or potential users, or individuals presumed to be much like them. Indirect approaches to obtaining a better understanding of users and their environments include hiring knowledgeable consultants, who serve as "surrogate user representatives"; organizing "focus groups" of user representatives, who often end up being information system specialists rather than end-users; and obtaining information about customers and users through sales, marketing, field service, management and other contacts.

ORGANIZATIONAL STRUCTURE AND DEVELOPMENT PROCESSES

The division of responsibility within product development companies separates software developers from the users (or their "representatives") of the companies' products. Points of contact are typically in other organizational divisions: sales, marketing, training, field service, customer support, and perhaps upper management. But the people assigned these tasks are not primarily concerned with the interface, their relevant knowledge is not systematically organized, and they are often located far from the development groups. In sum, they probably have a limited sense of what information would be useful or to whom it might be forwarded.

Many standard software development procedures and techniques used in large projects were developed in the context of government contracts. On such projects, which are often sought by primarily product development companies, product definition precedes the designation of the development group. User contact following the earliest design phase is usually difficult and may be explicitly forbidden. In any case, standard approaches to development were developed with minimal consideration of interface requirements. Also working against interface optimization is the pressure for a product development company to respond quickly to competition by releasing frequent enhancements, which inhibits scheduling adequate time for user participation.

The next several sections detail specific obstacles to user involvement that result from these structural and procedural characteristics of organizations, as well as pointing to positive contributions of these organizational characteristics -- that is, their reasons for existing. The remainder of the paper describes approaches to removing or working around these obstacles.

CHALLENGES TO IDENTIFYING APPROPRIATE USERS[1]

Obstacles to identifying appropriate users stem from the nature of developing products intended to appeal to a broad range of people, many of whom are not identified in advance. To understand how serious this problem is, consider the experience of some of the Scandinavian researchers and developers who have pioneered user involvement through "participatory" or collaborative design. These projects, where potential users of a system become full-fledged members of the design team, have started by defining relatively constrained user populations, within one industry or even one organization. Even then, selecting "representative" users can be a challenge (e.g., Ehn, 1988, pp. 327-358). Clearly, these problems will be greater for developers of generic products.

Further obstacles are found in the division of responsibilities within organizations that are set up to develop and market such products. User interface specialists rarely have "the big picture." They typically work with a development team assigned to a single application or even to part of an application. Not even the project manager has a perspective that encompasses the application mix that customers are expected to use, the practices and preferences of the installed customer base, and strategic information about the intended market for a product (e.g., banking or insurance industry; private doctors or those in an HMO or group practice). This broad perspective may be found in Marketing or Sales divisions, which are often geographically and organizationally distant from the development groups. The projected market -- the identity of the future users --may be closely guarded by high-level management due to its competitive importance.

In large companies, marketing and sales representatives are almost themselves "users" of products emerging from development. They typically consider themselves internal advocates for the customers, who may not actually be "end-users." One or more marketing representative may track a project through written communication or by attending meetings. People in an International Marketing group may review designs to insure that they can be easily translated. But mutual respect between marketing and development is often low (e.g. Kapor, 1987; Poltrock, 1989a), so even this indirect connection to product users is not a strong one.

Another complication in identifying appropriate users is that a system is often modified substantially after the development company ships it but before the users see it. This may be done by a software group within the customer's organization, by a "value-added reseller," or by another third party that tailors the product for specific markets. These developers not only are in a real sense "users" of the product, but may be the most important potential users. It may be *their* job to involve actual end-users. In any case, the initial development team is well-advised to discover which aspects of their design are likely

---

[1] ***A note on terminology.*** The term "users" focuses on a limited and increasingly unexceptional part of people's lives: their use of computers. The full term "computer users" is rarely used, although it has the virtue of avoiding a perspective in which the centrality of the computer is silently assumed. In this paper, "users" unavoidably appears, designating existing or potential users of computer systems who might play some role in the product development process.

to be "passed on" to users. Third-party intermediaries can represent an opportunity, but their role also makes the selection of "representative end-users" more difficult.

CHALLENGES TO OBTAINING ACCESS TO USERS

Once candidates have been identified, the next challenge is to make contact with them. Obstacles here may be found within either the users' organization or the development organization, or both.

Perhaps the potential user is *within* the development company. This is convenient, but it is a dangerous special case to rely on. The company is not in business to build products for itself. Involving internal users brings with it a host of unique advantages and disadvantages. If, as it is better to assume, the prospective user works for a potential customer, that company may see little benefit in giving the employee much time to work with an outside design group. What's more, contacts with customers are often with managers or information system specialists, rather than with the computer users themselves. Getting past these people may not be easy, as their job is precisely to represent the users.

Within the product development company, *protecting (or isolating) developers from customers is traditionally an important priority*. The company cannot afford to let well-intentioned developers spend all of their time customizing products for individual users -- the priority is on developing generic improvements to benefit scores or hundreds of users. Savvy customers are well aware of the value of having the phone number of a genial developer. Of course, barriers erected to keep users from contacting developers also prevent developers from easily connecting with users. The relationships and channels aren't there.

Another problem is that the development company's sales representative may be reluctant to let developers meet with customers. The developer, coming from a different culture, might offend or alarm the customer, or create dissatisfaction with currently available products by describing developments in progress. Similarly, Marketing may consider itself to be the knowledgeable conduit into the development organization for information about customer needs, and may fear the results of random contacts between developers and users. In at least one company, developers, including Human Factors Engineers, were strongly discouraged from attending the company's annual User's Group meeting. The meeting was organized by the Marketing Department, who saw it as a show staged strictly for the customers.

CHALLENGES TO BENEFITING FROM USER CONTACT

Given the typically uncertain identity of future users, and the wide range of possibilities that may exist, assessing one's experiences with a small number of possible users can be difficult. The Scylla of over-generalizing from a limited number of contacts is accompanied by the Charybdis of bogging down when users disagree, which is more likely to happen with a diverse set of user-participants. Finally, if user involvement succeeds in producing design recommendations, the work has just begun. Design recommendations, whatever their source, must be steered through a software development process that is typically fraught with obstacles to interface optimization. One outcome of user involvement may be to increase the odds of successfully navigating this course, but the journey is rarely easy, for reasons described below.

CHALLENGES TO OBTAINING FEEDBACK FROM USERS

Feedback from users may be collected, often quite haphazardly, either informally or from bug reports and design change requests. These typically focus on hardware and high-level software functionality, rather than on interface features, because the former are still of primary importance in the marketplace. Unfortunately, even the little information that *is* collected rarely gets back to developers. As mentioned above, the organization may consciously shield developers from external contacts. In addition, field service or software support groups typically maintain products and work with customers on specific problems, while the original product developers move on to develop new releases or product replacements, are reassigned to altogether different projects, or even leave the company, in this industry marked by rapid turn-over.

The extent of feedback may vary with the pattern of marketing and product use. A company such as Apple, historically relying on purchase decisions initiated by the actual users rather than by management or information systems specialists, may benefit from having a particularly vocal user population. In general, though, the lack of user feedback may be the greatest hindrance to good interface design in product development organizations and among the least recognized problems with standard software development processes. It is true that system developers cannot spend all of their time fielding requests from customers, but their overall lack of experience with feedback is an obstacle both to improving specific products and to building developer sensitivity to the potential value of user participation in design. Developers rarely become aware of the users' pain.

The neglect of on-line help systems is a good example of how division of labor impedes interface design. Developers are not notoriously sympathetic to less experienced users to begin with, so encouragement to provide on-line help may be necessary. A good help system might save the company a substantial amount of money in customer "hand-holding," service calls, printed documentation, and so forth. But the principal beneficiaries would be in Customer Service. The savings would be in their budget, while the effort and expense would come from Development. As a result, help systems typically have very low development priority.

This point deserves emphasis. Engineers are engaged in a continuous process of compromise, of trading off among desirable alternatives. They would give more weight to interface improvements if they were more aware of the far-reaching, lasting consequences of accepting an inferior design. Consider some typical tradeoffs: "This implementation will save 10K bytes but be a little less modular." "This design will run a little faster but take a month longer to complete." "This chip provides two more slots but adds $500 to the sales price." Each requires a decision. Once the decision is made, the price in development time, memory size, or chip expense is paid and the matter is left behind. In this environment of tradeoffs, the interface is just one additional consideration. "This interface would be nicer, but take two months longer to design." The developer does not get feedback from users, so once this decision is made, it too can be forgotten. The decision may adversely affect thousands of users daily for the life of the product, but the developer remains unaware of it. The interface *really is* special, but developers don't recognize that -- once it is built and shipped, they are on to the next job, and other people (including users) must do the sweeping up.

TRYING TO FIND THE DESIGN TEAM

User involvement would be easier and make more sense if there were a single group with interface responsibilities. But the "user interface," broadly defined, is not often the province of one easily-identified team. The hardware is designed by one group, the software by another, the documentation by a third, and the training by a fourth. Representatives from other groups may have continual or periodic involvement -- reviewing design specifications, for example. A product manager with little direct authority over developers may coordinate scheduling. Individuals from several different marketing groups, such as competitive or strategic analysis[2] and international marketing, may occasionally contribute. Members of support groups such as human factors or performance analysis may participate. Several levels of management may monitor the process and comment at different stages. In concert, these people contribute to defining a computer user's experience with the system or application, yet communication among them may be surprisingly sparse. With whom is a user to participate? In addition, turnover in personnel at the core of a development project is common, a further obstacle to sustained user involvement.

THE SOFTWARE DEVELOPMENT PROCESS

When today's software methodologies were being developed in the 1960s and 1970s, interface requirements were not important. Input and output channels were limited and computing resources were too expensive to devote much to the interface. Furthermore, most computer users were engineers with an understanding of the system. The interface that emerged during development and debugging was often adequate or even appropriate for the very similar "user environment." In general, the interface was ignored or received minor adjustments at the end of development.

Over the past ten to fifteen years, pressure has mounted to abandon "engineering interfaces" and develop interfaces for an increasingly diverse user population. This follows a pattern seen in other maturing technologies (Gentner and Grudin, 1990). Not surprisingly, software development methodologies did not anticipate this change. New approaches to development are emerging in response to the challenge (e.g., Boehm, 1988; Perlman, 1989), but have yet to be proven or widely adopted. Natural inertia is perhaps abetted by youth; software developers emerging from comparatively homogeneous academic environments may lack the experience with other workplaces and the people in them that would help them appreciate the diversity among computer users.

One aspect of this inertia is the persistence of the belief that the interface can be handled by tidying up at the end of development. Late involvement in the software development process is a chronic complaint of members of support groups such as human factors and technical writing (Grudin and Poltrock, 1989). They are the project members most likely to advocate user involvement -- if management is unaware of the need for *their* early and continual involvement, how much support will early and continual *user* involvement receive?

Yet early and continual user involvement is one of Gould and Lewis's (1985) widely accepted principles for designing usable systems. Late involvement is particularly problematic for the software interface developer. Once the underlying software code is frozen, a fully functioning system is finally available on which users might be tested. Unfortunately, at that very moment documentation moves into the critical path to product release. Because it is the software interface that is being documented, the interface is also frozen -- before a user has the chance to try it out!

Gould and Lewis's other principles for designing usable systems are prototyping and iterative design. These go hand in hand -- there is little point to prototyping if the design cannot be changed. Unfortunately, the high visibility of the interface works against iterative design in three ways: a) the interface is naturally grouped with aspects of the product that must be "signed off" on early in development; b) support groups, such as those producing documentation, training, and marketing, cannot avoid strong dependencies on the interface; c) iteration that takes place is evident, which can create uneasiness in an environment where early design is stressed.

The emphasis on careful early design and review makes sense for software, where a development course is relatively predictable. But it works less well for the interface, where it is uncertainty that motivates prototyping and iterative design in the first place. As the interface grows in importance, the desire to see it alongside the proposed functionality in the preliminary design will only grow. And once management has "signed off" on a design, changes require approval. Poltrock (1989b) observed the unique problems that high visibility and dependencies create for the interface development process. One developer summed it up: "I think one of the biggest problems with user interface design is that if you do start iterating, it's obvious to people that you're iterating. Then people say, 'How is this going to end up.' They start to get worried as to whether you're actually going to deliver anything, and they get worried about the amount of work it's creating for them. And people like (those doing) documentation are screwed up by iterations. They can't write the books. Whereas software, you can iterate like mad underneath, and nobody will know the difference."

The key here is the distinction between interface development and other software development. Solutions to these problems can be found -- *will* be found -- but because the problems are new and unique to interface development, the solutions will require procedural change. And an innovative process proposal is unlikely to leave management as comfortable as a detailed product design specification.

---

[2] Competitive analysis may seem to be a logical ally of a development organization. However, in practice their efforts may be directed far more toward the effective marketing of existing products against competition than toward the planning of future products.

THE ROUTINIZATION OF DEVELOPMENT[3]

As competition and the pace of change increase in the electronics industry, product development companies feel growing pressure to turn out new products or enhancements in a reliable, predictable fashion. This may be a legitimate concern, as reflected in this analysis: "Ashton-Tate's decline began with what is becoming a well-worn story in the industry: failure to upgrade a market-leading product. Dbase III Plus went for almost three years before being upgraded, while competitor's products were upgraded as often as twice in that time," (Mace, 1990). A similar pattern is found in other maturing markets, from automobiles to stereo systems. The result is pressure for a predictable and controllable software development process: for routinization of development. Parker (1990) describes a perceived solution to the problem described in the previous quotation: "Lyons (an Ashton-Tate executive) responds that he can keep customers by providing predictable if not always exciting upgrades. 'Customers don't want to be embarrassed; they want their investment to be protected. If you are coming out with regular releases, even if they skip a release because a particular feature is missing, they will stay (with the product) because the cost of change is large.'"

This perceived need for controlled development creates difficulties for design elements or approaches that have uncertain duration or outcome. Interface design in general has a relatively high level of uncertainty, and user involvement may increase the development time while also introducing the possibility of changing the direction of development. This is the intent, of course -- to produce a better design -- but it nevertheless works against these powerful pressures within the organization.

ASSISTANCE FOR USER INVOLVEMENT IN LARGE PRODUCT DEVELOPMENT COMPANIES

The picture is a little grim, but some support for involving users in interface design can be found. These companies are motivated to distinguish their products and to increase their acceptance in a competitive marketplace, some of which is characterized by increasingly discretionary application use. In addition, large product development organizations often have considerable resources to devote to usability -- the cost of development is highly amortized. As noted before, these companies are major employers of human factors engineers and are heavily represented in conferences focused on interface issues. There is also a positive potential in these companies' relatively frequent upgrades to or replacements of existing products: developers can more easily break out of "single-cycle" development. Evaluation of the use of existing products can feed into the design of a later version, and good ideas that arrive too late for use on a specific development project can be retained for use later. Another advantage is the large supply of potential users for most products. Also, the successful completion and evaluation of the system doesn't ride so precariously on the wide range of tangential factors that operate in any one given site.

OVERCOMING THE OBSTACLES

To someone working within a large product development organization these obstacles sometimes seem insurmountable. But as just noted, the company has a powerful incentive to improve its product interfaces. As software products mature, ease of learning and use becomes a more important marketing edge. Adding a new bell or whistle may not help much if the already available functionality is underutilized. In addition, declining hardware and software costs permit more resources to be directed to the interface. These forces have already pushed large product development companies into the forefront of human factors research and development in the United States. In the long term, organizational structures and development processes may evolve, institutionalizing solutions to the problems described here. This is likely because the forces in development companies that work systematically *against* user involvement stand in the way of product optimization and success. In fact, the directions that these companies will take are not obvious. As the focus of development shifts from generic products to systems and applications that meet the needs of different specific markets, companies may have to choose between working closely with independent developers, working with value-added resellers who in turn work with "end-users," or working with the diverse computer users themselves. Each alternative will benefit from "user involvement" -- but the identity of the "users" will vary.

In the meantime, practitioners may find a growing climate for limited experimentation. But even to *begin* working effectively requires a clear awareness of the obstacles, an understanding of why they are there, and a tolerant recognition that their source is in institutional constructs, not in unsympathetic individuals.

ACKNOWLEDGMENT

I thank Don Gentner for suggestions and Morten Kyng for useful comments on an earlier draft.

REFERENCES

Bjerknes, G., Ehn, P. and Kyng, M. (Eds.) (1987). *Computers and democracy: A Scandinavian challenge.* Brookfield, VT: Gower Press.

Boehm, B. (1988). A spiral model of software development and enhancement. *IEEE Computer, 21,* 5, 61-72.

Ehn, P. (1988). *Work oriented design of computer artifacts.* Stockholm: Arbetslivcentrum.

Friedman, A.L. (1989). *Computer systems development: History, organization and implementation.* Chichester, UK: Wiley.

Gentner, D.R. and Grudin, J. (1990). Why good engineers (sometimes) create bad interfaces. In *Proceedings CHI'90 Human Factors in Computing Systems,* (Seattle, April 1-4).

Gould, J.D. and Lewis, C. (1985). Designing for usability: Key principles and what designers think. *Communications of the ACM, 28,* 3, 300-311.

Grudin, J. (1986). Designing in the dark: Logics that compete with the user. In *Proceedings CHI'86 Human Factors in Computing Systems,* (Boston, April 13-17).

[3] Friedman (1989) suggests that claims for a trend toward routinization and deskilling of programming have been exaggerated. This may be true, but his focus is on the internal software development centers of large corporations engaged in the support of business operations, not product development. Some of the competitive and marketing pressures described here as promoting direct control of development are less evident in such environments.

Grudin, J. (1990). The computer reaches out: The historical continuity of interface design. In *Proceedings CHI'90 Human Factors in Computing Systems*, (Seattle, April 1-4).

Grudin, J. and Poltrock, S. (1989). User interface design in large corporations: Communication and coordination across disciplines. In *Proceedings CHI'89 Human Factors in Computing Systems*, (Austin, April 30-May 4).

Kapor M. (1987). Interview, *INC. Magazine*, January, 1987.

Mace, S. (1990). Defending the Dbase turf. *InfoWorld*, *12*, 2 (January 8), 43-46.

Parker, R. (1990). Bill Lyons' task: Incremental moves to consistency. *InfoWorld*, *12*, 2 (January 8), 44.

Perlman, G., 1989. Design/evaluation methods for hypertext technology development. In *Proceedings Hypertext'89*, (Pittsburgh, Nov. 5-8), 61-81.

Poltrock, S.E. (1989a). Participant-observer studies of user interface design and development. MCC Technical Report ACT-HI-125-89.

Poltrock, S.E. (1989b). Innovation in user interface development: Obstacles and opportunities. In *Proceedings CHI'89 Human Factors in Computing Systems*, (Austin, April 30-May 4).

Human–Computer Interaction – INTERACT '90
D. Diaper et al. (Editors)
Elsevier Science Publishers B.V. (North-Holland)

Integrating Human Factors with Structured Analysis and Design Methods: An Enhanced Conception of the Extended Jackson System Development Method

Lim, K. Y., Long, J. B. and Silcock, N.

Ergonomics Unit, University College London, 26 Bedford Way, London WC1H 0AP, U. K.

The potential benefits of integrating Human Factors (HF) with structured analysis and design methods have been described previously, along with an initial conception for integration instantiated using the Jackson System Development (JSD) method (termed JSD*). Based on a case-study test, the initial conception has been enhanced by further extensions and developments of its HF design stream (termed JSD*(HF)) and these are reported in this paper. The case-study which involves the re-design of a recreational facility booking system (RFBS) is used to illustrate the enhanced conception. It is concluded that the conception shows promise. Future developments of JSD*(HF) are also proposed.

1. INTRODUCTION

Previous papers on this research (Walsh et al. [1] and [2]) have proposed an initial conception of JSD* which comprises an explicit HF design stream within JSD. It was suggested that integration be achieved by inter-weaving the stage-wise design scope, processes and products (including notations) of HF with those of JSD. In other words, stage-wise inter-linking occurs between parallel HF and Software Engineering (SE) streams within an integrated design process. In this way, the communicability (format), timeliness, scope and granularity of HF inputs are sensitized to the needs of SE designers at each stage of design development. Such a conception thus not only facilitates early consideration of HF, but also supports its participation throughout the design process. This participation is intended to enable the generation of systems with better usability and more appropriate functionality.

Two research constraints are relevant to enhancing the conception of JSD*:

(a) the JSD method should, as far as possible, be left unchanged. Familiar reference points within JSD* should encourage positive transfer of SE designers' knowledge of JSD. Thus, existing JSD design notation and process structure are maximally exploited. Familiar aspects of JSD* will be expected to facilitate communication of intermediate design products and so encourage uptake of JSD*.

(b) JSD* should accommodate the incompleteness of current human-computer interaction (HCI) and particularly HF knowledge, by including prototyping as a supporting technique for analytic design; e.g. for early evaluations of models generated during the detailed design phase (see later). For further information concerning the research requirements and strategies, see Lim et al [3].

In the following section, the enhanced conception of JSD* will be described.

2. AN ENHANCED CONCEPTION OF JSD*

JSD* comprises two design streams: namely an SE (JSD*(SE) which closely resembles JSD) and an HF design stream (JSD*(HF)). Figure 1 is a schematic representation of this conception. As the SE stream is essentially unchanged except for points of contact between the streams, it will not be discussed further (see texts on JSD for further information; e.g. Jackson [4] and Cameron [5]). Instead, the paper will focus on JSD*(HF) and identify inter-linkages with the SE stream as appropriate.

The JSD*(HF) design stream comprises four phases, each of which is composed of proceduralised stages. These design phases represent a refinement of the phases of JSD, and derive from a set of wide perspectives on the system design process (e.g. Newman [6], Aze et al [7], etc.). The concerns of each of the design phases of JSD*(HF) are summarised as follows:

(a) Design Conceptualisation Phase: this phase addresses concerns relating to overall task or system level definition. Associated design stages are: Statement of Requirements (SoRe); Task Description (TD); Generalised Task Model (GTM); Statement of User Needs (SUN) and Composite Task Model (CTM).

(b) Detailed Design Phase: this phase addresses design concerns relating to interaction task definition; e.g. specification of feedback and error messages, physical layout, etc. Associated design stages are: User Task Model (UTM); User Interface Constraints and Environment (UIC/E); Interface Model (IM); Interaction Task Model (ITM) and User Interface Specification (UIS).

(c) Implementation Phase: the function of this phase may be regarded as the conditioning of specifications (of the preceding two phases) to hardware characteristics (e.g. technological limitations and economic concerns which have not emerged during the SoRe stage).

(d) Evaluation Phase: this phase may be regarded as late evaluation. (Early evaluation would have occurred during the first two phases as part of iterative design. Iteration would be expected to be supported by the stage-wise documentation required by JSD*.) During this phase, the designed system would be assessed against criteria provided by both intermediate design documentation (e.g. SoRe and SUN, and stage-wise models developed and documented during design, e.g. IM, ITM, etc.), as well as final design specifications of the user interface (UI).

Following this overview of JSD*(HF), each of its design stages will be described and illustrated by reference to a simple case-study involving the re-design of a recreational facility booking system (due to space constraints the illustration can only be selective). Since this paper is primarily concerned with design specification (rather than implementation or evaluation), the description will be confined to the first two design phases which are particular to JSD*(HF). This description comprises the stage-wise scope, process and notation associated with intermediate design products. Obligatory linkages with JSD*(SE) will also be indicated as appropriate. The design stages of JSD*(HF) will be presented in the order in which the design is progressed. Thus, products of any design stage constitute the input of the stage immediately succeeding it. Indirect relationships between design stages will be indicated as they arise.

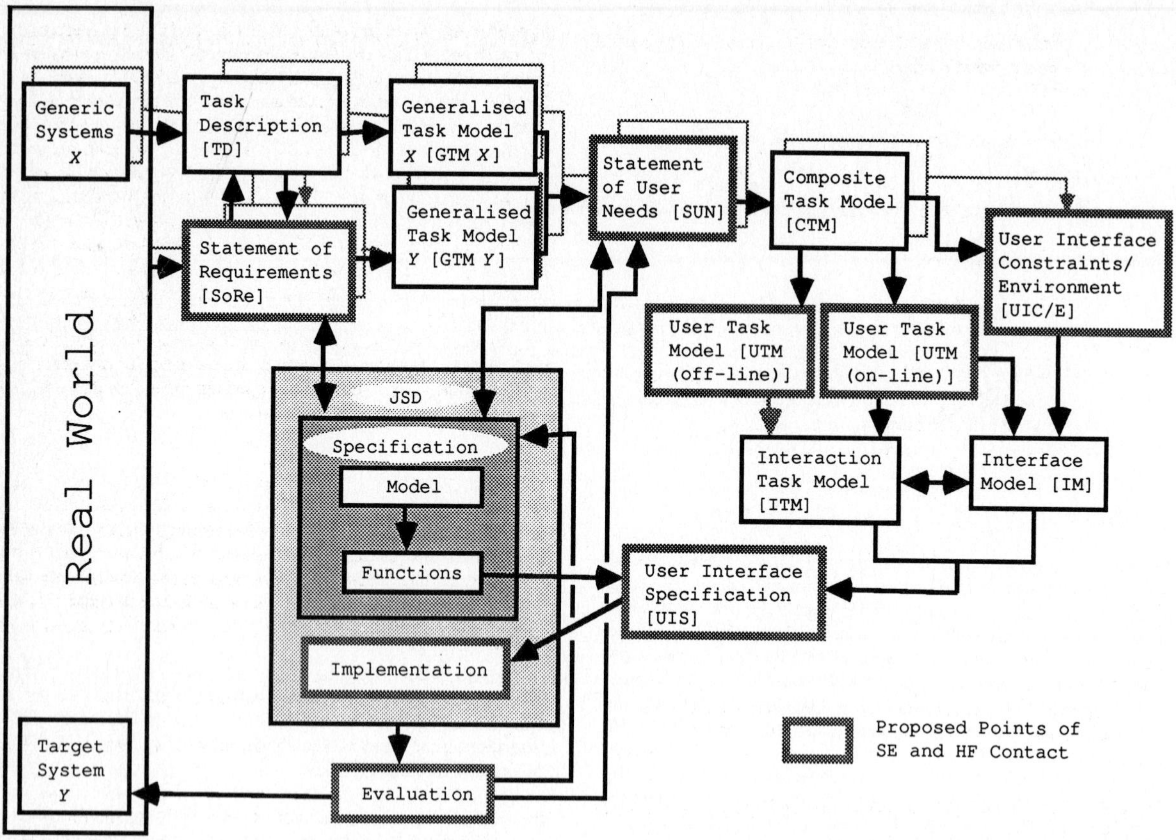

Figure 1 : A Graphical Representation of the Enhanced Conception of JSD*

Before describing the stages of JSD*(HF), a brief account of the RFBS case-study illustration is appropriate. The RFBS supports two major task activities:

(a) it allows authorised users to effect advance bookings (one week) of recreational facilities on a first-come-first-served basis.

(b) it permits the checking of bookings made during the current day and a week in advance.

The design scenario adopted by the research is one of re-design or variant design. The motivation for the re-design of the RFBS is the provision of more effective support to users. This scenario provides the background against which the stages of JSD*(HF) will now be described. (Note that in the following sub-sections: the *target* system (*Y*) refers to the system to be designed; the *current* system (*CS*) is its predecessor, currently in use; *related* systems (*RS*) are similar systems in use elsewhere; and *generic* system (*X*) is a general term referring to the class to which both the current and related systems belong.)

2.1 STATEMENT OF REQUIREMENTS (SoRe) STAGE

The SoRe prescribes characteristics desired of *Y* (in this instance the target RFBS), i.e. the work to be accomplished by the RFBS (the assignment of temporal rights over the recreational facility); technological or hardware constraints, etc. These statements, which may be general, usually comprise a mix of task and hardware requirements which have been collated from informal and contractual documents and verbal exchanges. They may also include concerns relating to perceived future needs and desirable characteristics of the *CS*. This set of characteristics required for *Y*, should be available to both HF and SE designers. These expressed requirements then form the basis on which the search for possible design solutions is conducted by both design streams, i.e. it defines the scope of concerns for design development. For example, designers may then plan detailed observations of specific aspects of the *CS* on this basis. In addition, a preliminary definition of work domain semantics may also be undertaken to help identify *RS* for analysis (to increase the information available to form the basis of the design). The product is represented as a semantic network termed the 'Domain of Design Discourse'. A simple illustration for the RFBS is shown in Figure 2.

It is important to emphasize that the analysis of *RS* may be carried out explicitly or implicitly; i.e. the designer might explicitly select an *RS* for study or implicitly apply past experience acquired in the design of other systems. These analyses are carried out in the next stage.

2.2 TASK DESCRIPTION (TD) STAGE

Having identified *CS* and *RS* for analysis, more information may be needed by designers. This information can be obtained from manuals,

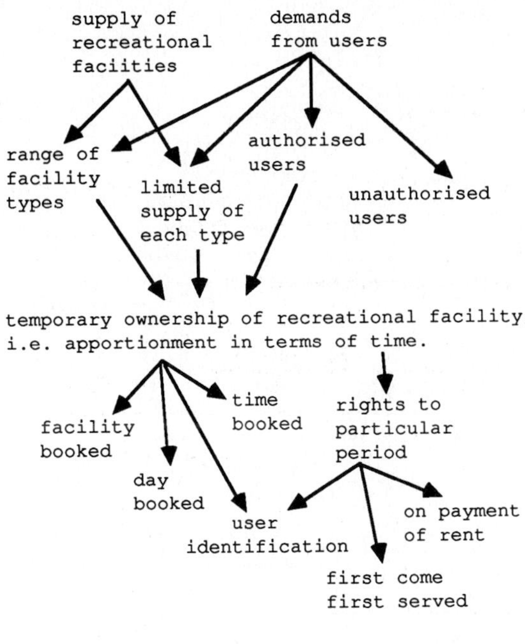

Figure 2 : The Domain of Design Discourse Associated with the RFBS Case-Study

verbal protocols, observational studies, etc. The objective is to capture details of X (the generic class of systems to which both the CS and RS belong), such as the current allocation of function between user and device, the rationale underlying generic designs, current user tasks, needs and problems, etc. This information may include roles; tasks; sub-tasks; goals; plans; system information requirements, and the utilisation and exchanges of information within the system. Appropriate collation and assessment of this information would subsequently support design decisions concerning what design features of X might be beneficially ported across to the design of Y. It would also highlight shortcomings and required extensions of existing designs. Thus, to facilitate later uptake of the products of the TD stage, the generated information is processed into descriptions corresponding to products of the stages of JSD*(HF); i.e. GTM, UTM, UIC/E, IM and ITM. Prominent UI design characteristics are also noted. In other words, the products of the TD stage feed into several stages of JSD*(HF). (For a description of the processes involved in the derivation of these products, see Silcock et al [8]). In accordance with the requirements of JSD*, these products are then expressed using JSD modelling notation and supported by text (this use of the JSD modelling notation has also been suggested by others (Sutcliffe [9]; Carver [10]; Carver and Cameron [11]). The utilisation of a class of products from the TD stage will now be illustrated by the GTM stage.

2.3 GENERALISED TASK MODEL (GTM) STAGE

There are two products from this stage; namely an overall GTM(x) description which derives from the compilation of GTM(cs) and GTM(rs) descriptions; and GTM(y) which is abstracted from the SoRe. Since GTM(y) is a precursor of CTM(y), it may be regarded as a preliminary expression of the conceptual model of the user's task(s). Although both GTMs are expressed using JSD modelling notation and are essentially device independent*, they serve different functions. While GTM(x) facilitates the evaluation and subsequent recruitment of design characteristics of X towards CTM(y), GTM(y) exposes new and/or salient characteristics required for Y. Thus, in addition to being a precursor description for CTM(y), GTM(y) sets the scope and structure for expressing GTM(x); i.e. it supports, in addition to the SoRe, the identification of X for analysis at the TD stage. For instance, in the case of the RFBS, GTM(y) may indicate that user authorisation is to be controlled by access to the system. Access then becomes one of the features included in the scope of the survey of generic systems; e.g. authorised users may be identified by: their identification cards (CS); passwords (RS); and the magnetic strip-cum-personal identification number system used for automatic cash teller machines (RS). The GTMs are then brought forward to the next two stages which determine the CTM.

2.4 STATEMENT OF USER NEEDS (SUN) STAGE

This stage draws together the conclusions from the analysis of the design of X and summarises them with respect to the user. The purpose of the SUN stage is thus to augment the initial SoRe for Y and so sensitise it further towards user needs and requirements. The products of the SUN stage are expressed primarily in text, and would include the following:

(a) the identification of user problems with X.

(b) a summary of the rationale, requirements and constraints underlying the design features of X.

(c) the expression of design criteria (e.g. for performance) for obviating the problems in (a), and upgrading/extending existing design solutions identified in (b). These criteria should take the SoRe into account.

The SUN products are made available to SE designers. The design is taken further by HF designers, and progresses to the CTM stage where the GTMs are synthesized on the basis of the SUN.

2.5 COMPOSITE TASK MODEL (CTM) STAGE

The design concerns of this stage are two-fold:

(a) the synthesis/generation of CTM(y) by combining GTM(y) with desirable and appropriate features (with respect to the SoRe and SUN) of GTM(x) which have been identified during the TD and GTM stages.

(b) the documentation of design concepts destined for Y; e.g. insights associated with the design features selected from GTM(x), and the rationale underlying particular design characteristics originating from GTM(y). This documentation of GTM features would support subsequent evaluation and iterative design, as well as post-implementation modifications and maintenance.

JSD modelling notation supported by tabular form-fill schemes suggested by others (specifically Owen [12]; Frohlich and Luff [13]) may be used for documenting this information. The resulting product of the CTM stage, thus provides the conceptual foundation/design model of Y; i.e. it provides the basis on which decisions on the allocation of function may be made. Figure 3(A) shows a small part of the CTM(y)

*The extent of abstraction of these analytic descriptions to device independence, is determined by how dissimilar the requirements and characteristics of the GTM(x) are with respect to the intended target system; i.e. GTM(y).

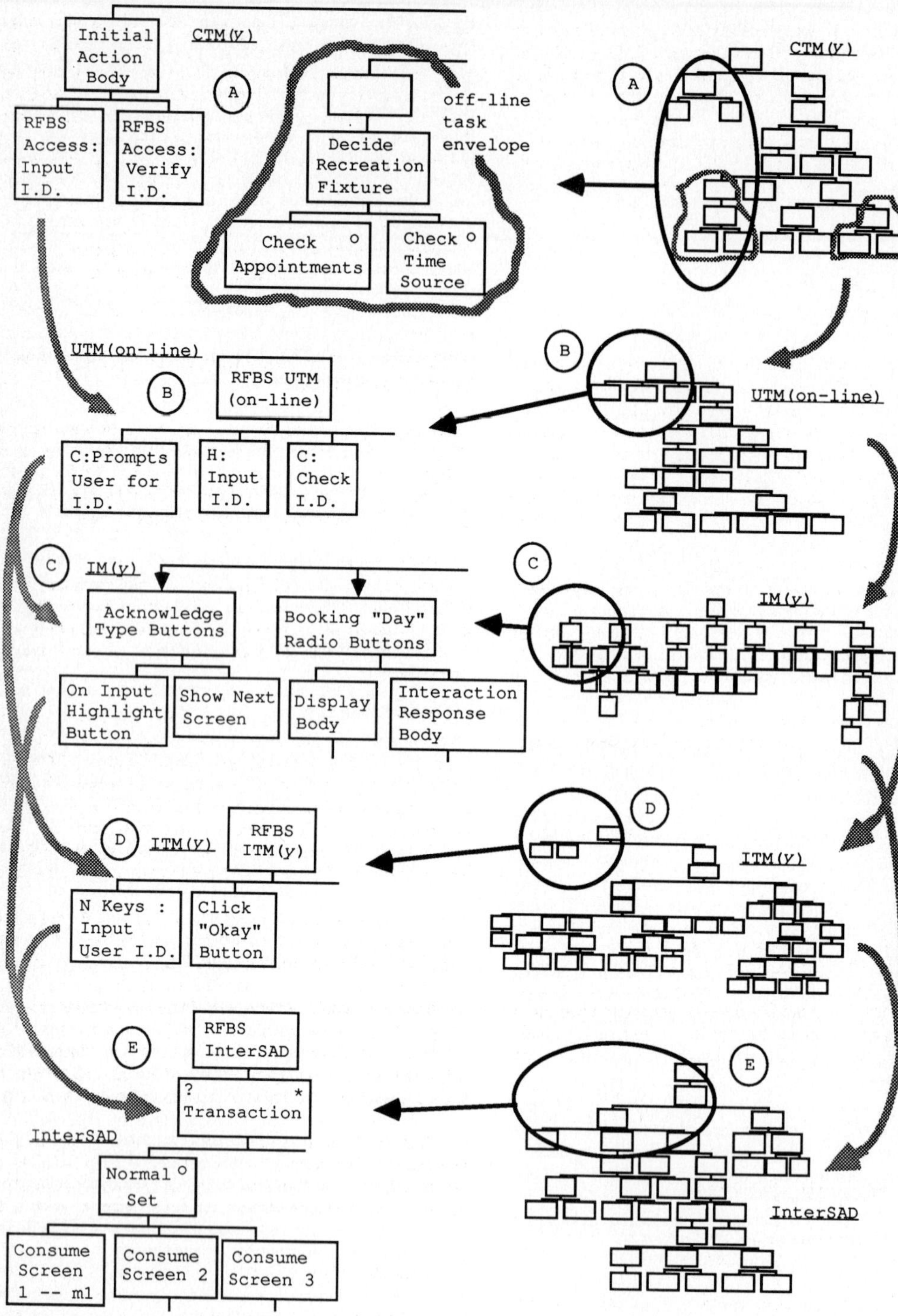

Note: "*": "iteration"; "0": "selection"; " ": "sequence"; "?": "posit" (for an explanation of these constructs, see Jackson [4] or Cameron [5].
" ↓ ": "consists of"

Figure 3 : Samples (Post-CTM Design Stages) of JSD*(HF) Intermediate Design Product Descriptions and Transformations for the RFBS Case-Study which describes initial actions of the RFBS. They involve checking whether the user is authorised to make recreational facility bookings. On positive verification, the user can then proceed to match recreational facility/day/time preferences with available booking slots. This facility booking process is expressed by CTM(*y*) for both successful and unsuccessful booking outcomes. Decisions on function allocation are then made, by marking out envelopes of off-line tasks (Figure 3(A)); e.g. selection decisions and conditions for booking preferences are too varied among users and are thus designated as off-line tasks. These tasks (both on-line and off-line) are then re-described at lower levels in the succeeding UTM stage.

2.6 USER TASK MODEL (UTM) STAGE

This stage is concerned with extending the CTM(*y*) further on the basis of the SoRe and SUN, and the incorporation of UTM(*x*) corresponding to features of GTM(*x*) that have been recruited to CTM(*y*). The objective here is to re-describe the allocated functions of CTM(*y*) with respect to inputs and outputs. In this regard, two descriptions result; namely UTM(on-line) and UTM(off-line). These correspond to user tasks which are supported and unsupported by the computer system respectively. Task characteristics of and information flows between on- and off-line tasks should also be noted explicitly as both UTMs influence the design; e.g. UTM(off-line) may affect the content and format of information displayed to the user. This information concerning UTM(off-line) should be borne in mind, when interaction design for *Y* is pursued via the UTM(on-line). Thus, the primary product of this stage, the UTM(on-line), represents a preliminary model of the human-computer (H-C) dialogue that is required for the achievement of the overall task goals of the user; i.e. it is a conceptual precursor of ITM(*y*). In other words, it describes both the task of interacting with the device and the computer-supported part of the overall task. The UTM(on-line) is expected to further the design in two ways:

(a) it may be decomposed to lower levels of description to generate ITM(*y*).

(b) it provides early identification of suitable UI environments and objects for recruitment to the development of *Y* via IM(*y*).

The products of the UTM stage are described using JSD modelling notation. Figure 3(B) shows how the flow of inputs and outputs between the human and computer is expressed using this notation. It describes an interaction loop on the RFBS corresponding to the verification of user status. Such descriptions are to be shared between HF and SE designers.

So far, no indication has been given of the following UI design concerns:

(a) the manner by which input is to be effected.

(b) the behaviour of UI objects in response to user input and/or changes in state attributes to either the system or the real world.

(c) the appearance of communication tokens and the content of H-C messages.

These are addressed in the remaining design stages which will now be described.

2.7 USER INTERFACE CONSTRAINTS OR ENVIRONMENT (UIC/E) STAGE

At this stage, applicable generic UI features of the adopted UIC/E or house-style (if any) are assessed and selected on the basis of the SoRe, SUN, CTM(*y*) and UTMs(*y*). This preliminary conception of the UI style for *Y* is documented with respect to the representation, behaviour and interaction rules which govern this initial set of UI objects. Required modifications and further extensions of the UI description are then undertaken in subsequent ITM and IM stages, e.g. generic UI objects may be renamed/modified to conform to the context set by the Domain of Design Discourse of *Y*. In the case of the RFBS, the chosen implementation environment was HyperCard on the Macintosh. In this regard, characteristics of UI primitives are noted, e.g. the function, presentation and interaction rules associated with buttons, fields, etc. This information is carried forward to the ITM and IM stages.

2.8 INTERFACE MODEL (IM) AND INTERACTION TASK MODEL (ITM) STAGES

These two stages will be discussed together as they are undertaken at about the same time, i.e. they overlap each other. At this point in the design process, information set down in the UTMs(*y*) and UIC/E is brought forward for collation in the ITM and IM stages respectively. The resultant products may be characterised as follows:

(a) IM(*y*) which exhaustively describes the characteristics and behaviour of UI objects of *Y*, incorporating and extending information captured in the UIC/E stage. Figure 3(C) shows part of the description of the classes of generic UI objects. Instances of each of these classes (e.g. 'booking day' button for the RFBS) are then summarised using a tabular format.

(b) ITM(*y*) which is a keystroke level description of *Y* derived predominantly on the basis of the UTM(on-line). This is either expressed in terms of object/action primitives of the UIC/E and basic keystrokes of the designated hardware; or described at a level that is easily understood among design team members. For instance, the description for the RFBS was taken down to the level of mouse clicks (see Figure 3(D)), instead of further defining mouse clicks to be an action sequence comprising a mouse-down followed by a mouse-up.

These two products are inter-dependent, i.e. they are derived interactively and in tandem with each other. For instance, from the ITM stage, bespoke UI commands and objects may be determined by decomposing the 'leaves and sub-nodes' of the UTM(on-line); e.g. 'User Identification', 'Book', 'Search', etc. These designations should also be compatible with the properties of UI objects that comprise IM(*y*); e.g. if integer keys (N keys) are used to input the 'User Identification' then IM(*y*) (attributable to HyperCard) would suggest that an input field is needed. In addition, a suitable conceptual structure may be imposed on these objects, on the basis of their inter-relationships as described by the Domain of Design Discourse; e.g. using concepts of analogical reasoning to identify a suitable metaphor for incorporation into the UI design. The users are then provided with a familiar conceptual structure that would support their interpretation of the design of the UI.

2.9 USER INTERFACE SPECIFICATION (UIS) STAGE

Having derived UTM, IM and ITM descriptions for *Y*, the HF designer can then set about: designing the computer display (i.e. the layout and presentation of UI objects and actions); composing system dialogue and error messages; and demarcating within and between screen actuations (termed inter-screen actuation descriptions (interSADs). These describe the dynamics of the computer screen display, and map out the locations and conditions for triggering system dialogue and error messages with respect to the interaction cycle. Figure 3(E) shows a sample of an InterSAD for the RFBS.) These specifications of the UI are described using JSD modelling notation and are supported by text, index tables and scaled drawings (for screen layouts). These facilitate subsequent design team discussions, during which HF specifications of the UI may be checked against functional specifications generated by SE designers. (Further illustration of these specifications is obviated for reasons of space).

3. CONCLUSIONS

This paper proposes an enhancement of the conception of JSD* reported in previous papers. It presents an overview of an attempt at integrating an HF design process into an existing structured analysis and design method. Case-study tests indicate the present JSD* conception to be promising. The research is still on-going, and further tests on the conception are needed. These have been planned using more complex case-studies (more specifically, using a network management system). Future papers will report the results of these tests, and provide a more detailed account of the procedures of JSD*(HF). It should be clear from this and earlier reports that the scope set for the current research, is confined to the verification of the method by case-study demonstrations. As a result, follow-up work to this research needs to be undertaken in the field so that the efficacy of JSD* for facilitating the generation of more effective systems may be validated.

ACKNOWLEDGEMENTS

The research associated with this paper is being carried out for the Ministry of Defence (Royal Armament Research and Development Establishment) under Contract No. 2047/130 (RARDE). Views expressed in the paper are those of the authors and should not necessarily be attributed to the Ministry of Defence. Particular acknowledgement is made to M. Carver, D. Clenshaw, and D. Myles who originally initiated the work and who have supported and contributed significantly to its progress.

REFERENCES

[1] Walsh, P. A., Lim, K. Y., Long, J. B. and Carver, M. K., Integrating Human Factors With System Development, in: Heaton, N. and Sinclair, M. (eds.), Designing End-User Interfaces (Oxford: Pergamon Infotech, 1988), pp. 111-120.

[2] Walsh, P. A., Lim K. Y. and Long, J. B., JSD and the Design of User Interface Software, in: Barber, P. and Laws, J. (eds.), Ergonomics (Special Issue): Methodological Issues in Cognitive Ergonomics, in print.

[3] Lim, K. Y., Long, J. B. and Silcock, N., Requirements, Research and Strategy for Integrating Human Factors with Structured Analysis and Design Methods: The Case of the Jackson System Development Method, in: Lovesey, E. (ed.), Proceedings of the Ergonomics Society's Annual Conference (London: Taylor Francis), in print.

[4] Jackson, M. A., System Development (New Jersey: Prentice-Hall International, 1983).

[5] Cameron, J.R., An overview of JSD, IEEE Transactions on Software Engineering (1986), SE-12, 2, pp. 222-240.

[6] Newman, W., User Interface Design Practice, (Tutorial Notes of HCI'88 Conference, Manchester, 1988).

[7] Aze, P., Bazargan, M., Burton, P., Dillon, A., Fallon, E., Fehrenbach, P., Finkelstein L., Herring, V., Sweeney, M., Warren, C. and Whitefield, A., A User Modelling Tool for MMI Design Final Report -- Alvey Project MMI/142, (1988), pp. 32-44.

[8] Silcock, N., Lim, K. Y. and Long, J. B., Requirements and Suggestions for a Structured Analysis and Design (Human Factors) Method to Support the Integration of Human Factors with System Development, in: Lovesey, E. (ed.), Proceedings of the Ergonomics Society's Annual Conference (London: Taylor Francis), in print

[9] Sutcliffe, A., Some Experiences in Integrating Specification of Human Computer Interaction within a Structured System Development Method, in: Jones, D. and Winder, R. (eds.), Proceedings of the Fourth Conference of the BCS HCI SIG (Cambridge University Press, 1988), pp. 145-160.

[10] Carver, M. K., Practical Experience of Specifying the Human-Computer Interface Using JSD, in: Megaw, E. (ed.), Proceedings of the Ergonomics Society's 1988 Annual Conference, (London: Taylor Francis), pp. 177-182.

[11] Carver, M. K. and Cameron, J., The Jackson System Development Method: A Framework for the Specification of the Human-Computer Interface, Unpublished Internal Report of Michael Jackson Systems Limited, 1987.

[12] Owen, C. L., Structured Planning: A Concept Development Process, Internal Paper of the Institute of Design, Illinois Institute of Technology, Chicago, 1986.

[13] Frohlich, D. M. and Luff, P., Some Lessons From an Exercise in Specification, in: Moran, T. P. (ed.), Human-Computer Interaction (Lawrence Erlbaum Associates Inc., 1989), Vol. 4, pp. 121-147.

SECTION II: DESIGN: THEORIES, METHODS AND TOOLS

SII.2 Users, Tasks and Organizations: Requirements and Analysis

An investigation of user requirements for broadband communications in the automotive industry
S.E. Powrie and C.E. Siemieniuch 233

Bridging the gap between task design and interface design
W. Dzida, R. Freitag, C. Hoffmann, and W. Valder 239

Supporting a humanly impossible task: The clinical human computer environment
B. Horan, A.L. Rector, E.L. Sneath, C.A. Goble, T.J. Howkins, S. Kay, W.A. Nowlan, and A. Wilson 247

An analysis of the circuit design process for a complex engineering application
L. Colgan and M. Brouwer-Janse 253

Designers-identified requirements for tools to support task analyses
H. Johnson and P. Johnson 259

An application of task analysis to the development of a generic office reference model
J. Hewitt, J. Hobson, and J. Sapsford-Francis 265

Memory–cognition–action tables: A pragmatic approach to analytical modelling
B. Sharratt 271

Analysing focused interview data with task analysis for knowledge descriptions (TAKD)
D. Diaper 277

A plan and goal based method for computer–human system design
D.R. Sewell and N.D. Geddes 283

The use of task allocation charts in system design: A critical appraisal
W.K. Ip, L. Damodaran, C.W. Olphert, and M.C. Maguire 289

The development of tools to assist in organisational requirements definition for information technology systems
S.D.P. Harker, C.W. Olphert, and K.D. Eason 295

Human–Computer Interaction – INTERACT '90
D. Diaper et al. (Editors)
Elsevier Science Publishers B.V. (North-Holland)

AN INVESTIGATION OF USER REQUIREMENTS FOR BROADBAND COMMUNICATIONS IN THE AUTOMOTIVE INDUSTRY

S E Powrie and C E Siemieniuch

HUSAT Research Institute, The Elms, Elms Grove, Loughborough, Leics LE11 1RG, England.

This paper discusses a user-centred research methodology for the investigation of the role for multimedia integrated broadband communications (IBC) in the automobile industry. The derivation of a comprehensive user requirements set is described, key requirements outlined and the usefulness of the methodology itself considered.

1. INTRODUCTION

1.1. The CAR project

The CAR project (CAD/CAM in the Automotive Industry in RACE) focuses on the identification of new opportunities made possible by the use of IBC in the domain of CAD/CAM applications for the European automotive industry. The four year project is part of the European RACE programme which is concerned with establishing the requirements for multimedia integrated broadband communications networks. This paper details work carried out in the first year of the project.

The aim of the project is to improve the effectiveness of the European automotive industry by accelerating design-to-production timescales through the concept of 'simultaneous engineering' or co-operative working. By doing this, it is intended to improve the quality and reduce the costs of the design process. In addition to high speed data communications, the project will also investigate the use of multimedia communications as a means of strengthening human-to-human interactions in a high tech environment.

Collaborators in the project include three internationally prominent user companies, together with well-known organisations providing expertise in computing, video- and telecommunications technologies and leading academic institutions.

1.2. Need for 'simultaneous engineering'

Current technology available to the automotive industry allows sequential integration of design and manufacturing activities, but simultaneous engineering is carried out only at the risk of prejudicing work elsewhere. Hence the overall integrity of the design is endangered, and design mismatches can occur, leading to costly and time consuming remedial work. There is also an increasing emphasis on a requirement for much closer working with suppliers and sub-contractors, but little technological support exists for such activity.

Today the automotive industry uses highly sophisticated CAD/CAM tools and there is also a strong demand for integrated communication facilities. Due to the fact that the industry has a wide distribution of its various activities, there is an important requirement for distributed computing enabling interaction between all the parties involved (often in different locations), from the initial design to the manufacture of the component concerned ie sales, finance, maintenance and in particular between design, engineering and production personnel. The CAR project focuses particularly on the communication of multimedia objects between these last three, possibly between remote sites, demonstrating the use of both public IBC networks and their local interfaces (workstations, LANS etc).

1.3. Potential applications of IBC

From the user organisations' perspective several potential applications had been identified: multi-user interaction with CAD systems and the substitution of point-to point multimedia electronic conferencing for costly face-to-face meetings being two examples. Technology already exists to support most tools of this type in stand-alone mode: it is their simultaneous use in parallel with other applications by widely distributed users that gives rise to the application for an IBC system. The research aimed both to investigate and validate these initial perceived requirements and to generate a detailed user requirements specification.

1.4. Focus on user requirements

Since one of the main principles underlying the CAR project was that of *user centred* design, the user requirements specification has been the driving force within the project. Accordingly the project's first emphasis was to provide an in-depth initial user requirements specification to be iteratively translated into an Initial Functional Specification. Running alongside this was an investigation of the user companies' current technical base and any emerging technology which might influence or assist in the design of the application pilot. Therefore investigation and analysis of both the organisational/end-user and the technical components of the proposed system were studied in parallel. As the project progresses the user requirements and functional specification will be further refined and developed as prototype systems are built and evaluation work carried out.

It should be emphasised that only by carrying out these initial investigations was it possible to show how end-users could make effective use of IBC systems. Novel applications have been identified, problem areas highlighted and potential blind alleys avoided. It is firmly believed that only by matching user requirements with available and emerging technology can the true potential of IBC in this context be demonstrated in the application pilot(s) to be built at the end of the project.

2. METHODOLOGICAL APPROACH

It has been the intention in this work to strike an effective balance between technocentric and humanistic approaches to design. While the substantial contribution of classical socio-technical design theory to the design of properly integrated systems is acknowledged, it is considered that in its application this approach has sometimes demonstrated a failure fully to apprehend the technological basis of the organisation; the result being implementation mismatches.

There were also the more specific problems of finding a methodology capable of deriving requirements for multimedia applications some of which were as yet undeveloped even in stand-alone form, and very few of which had been integrated into coherent systems. Associated with this issue was the need to capture implications for organisational change inevitably arising from the implementation of new technology.

For these reasons it was felt necessary to develop a purpose built strategy for organisational and end-user requirements capture, which ensured equal emphasis was given to both human and technical issues. The primary aim of the methodology was to establish a set of organisational and end user requirements for an application pilot demonstrating the use of an IBC system in the automotive industry; a secondary aim being to establish a preliminary set of evaluation criteria to be applied and developed throughout the rest of the project as prototype systems were designed and implemented.

3. THE METHODOLOGY

The methodology adopted is based on established techniques used within HUSAT, documented in Gardner and McKenzie [1]. The main elements of the methodology are presented below:

3.1. Site Identification

A list of criteria was presented to the user companies to help in the selection of appropriate sites to be studied, eg there must be frequent interactive communication between the separate sites, the sites should be linked by a common element such as a body shell or an engine component etc. For the sake of relative simplicity and the maintenance of consistency between user companies, it was agreed to focus on sites concerned with the design and production of mechanical components as opposed to body styling. It was also decided to limit consideration to design and manufacturing planning before the start of final production. Eight sites across the three user companies were identified as primary sources for user data.

3.2. Stakeholder Analysis

Stakeholder analysis identifies and describes the people who have a legitimate 'stake' in the new system and identifies the scenarios (eg circumstances of use) with which the new system is to cope. Key stakeholders within the various user sites were identified by the user companies, again based on criteria provided by HUSAT. These included probable primary end users of the IBC system eg designers, process engineers, material specialists, production engineers; managers of end users; experts in computing and communication systems and strategic planning; possible secondary users. These people were then interviewed both to confirm their own role as key stakeholders and to identify other potential stakeholders.

3.3. Data Acquisition

Three main techniques were identified:

Interviews. The purpose of the interviews was to establish detailed descriptions of the roles currently undertaken and the tasks performed by end users, with particular reference to those areas likely to be affected by the introduction of an IBC system. These details included data sources, information flows and applications of knowledge and expertise. The interviews were semi-structured in that a number of identified topics were covered for each interviewee, although not necessarily in a fixed format. This ensured that sufficient uniformity existed between different interviewers and different interviews to ensure comparability of data. The interviews varied in duration from one to two hours: some were held on a one to one basis, others in a group format. Three sets of interviews were held in order to gain progressively more focussed and detailed data on user companies and their needs.

Topics covered in this first set of interviews included:

- general company organisation structure
- organisation of design and manufacturing planning
- roles of different actors in design and manufacturing planning and their location
- mechanisms for project control and management
- relationships with outside organisations such as suppliers, sub-contractors and clients
- role of applications software in design and manufacture
- existing means of communication (person-to-person, paper-based and system based)

A good account was obtained of how design and manufacture was organised in each of the user companies, each company's structures, activities and communication patterns, their current preoccupations and problems and of general areas where an IBC system might be of use. While some of this information was not directly relevant to CAR in itself, it helped to flesh out knowledge of organisational climate and culture.

The second round of interviews were more sharply focussed and based on the scenarios described in section 3.4 below. In the main these concentrated on working practice in specified areas, the use of particular sorts of information and specific communication links. Interviewees at this stage were for the most part middle management, end-users and specialists. It was now possible to draw up a list of specific user requirements based on user actions as described in the scenarios. The list was augmented on an on-going basis as further data was obtained.

The main purpose of the third round of interviews was to check points raised by the second stage analysis and therefore, the type of personnel interviewed and data obtained varied between user companies. The interviews were structured and conducted as as described above. At this stage, as expected, no major revision of the scenarios etc was necessary, but minor modifications and additions were made as appropriate. The list of user requirements could now be considerably expanded and detailed with confidence, and this provided the basis for the final stage of data analysis and review described in section 3.4 below.

In total fifty-three people in the user companies were interviewed, either singly or in groups, the interviews lasting from one to three hours. Some individuals were interviewed more than once, so the total number of interviews conducted is rather larger. The breakdown is as follows:

- senior management (6)
- project management (4)
- communications experts (4)
- computer systems experts (3)
- CAD/CAM system development and support (10)
- CAD/CAM end-users in design and manufacturing planning (17)
- Specialists from QA, finance, security, legislation, plant engineering, structural engineering and purchasing. (9)

Tracer Studies. Whereas the interviews provided personalised views of an organisation and its procedures, user roles and tasks, tracer studies are intended to take a different view. In this type of study, a packet of information is usually followed from its source to its destination(s), identifying how it is transferred, used and for what purposes. A tracer study will highlight the knowledge and expertise brought to bear on the information tracked. It also serves to extend and substantiate the data obtained from the interviews. These studies will be carried out in the second year of the project.

Observational Studies. These studies have two purposes: firstly to provide detailed information about real time usage of information and application of knowledge and secondly to corroborate what was found in the previous two exercises. Again these studies will be carried out in the second year of the project.

3.4 Data Analysis

The following techniques were adopted:

Modelling the design process. This was done for three main reasons: firstly to understand the interactions between individuals and/or departments within a given design 'project' in relation to the design process as a whole; secondly to define a simple 'staged' model for the design to build process for the CAR project to facilitate analysis of the data collected; thirdly to highlight major areas of discrepancy and commonality across the three user companies.

A stage-based model of design as practised within the user community was constructed as shown in Figure 1.

The model was then expanded to include both the types of people/roles involved and some examples of knowledge and/or data used at each stage. The model was not intended to be seen as 'complete' - it was a device used to order and rationalise the data obtained. Considering the apparent diversity of user company practice, a surprising degree of commonality was found once terminological differences had been stripped away.

Market Requirement → Formal Statement of Intent → Live Project

Establish project team
Fix project plan eg milestones, budget constraints etc.
Conceptual design/alternative solutions
Test and evaluate
Select and detail design
Test and evaluate
Review and release design
Define manufacturing processes
Select suppliers
Manufacture

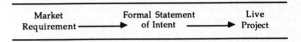

Figure 1: Design Viewed as a Series of Stages

Scenario development. In order to focus down on a more manageable set of 'design stages', three text-based scenarios or hypothetical problem situations were devised for each user company. Each scenario described in detail a sequence of events in cooperative design problem solving. At each stage actors concerned, their locations, the nature of data transferred, the type of interactive working and the means of communication were specified. The scenarios were developed iteratively with end-user companies and then three generic versions produced, which again reflected the large degree of commonality between the three companies and helped to establish those areas of important conflict between them. This last point is important: in order to design applications of genuine usefulness it is vital that provision is made to accommodate company specific modes of working.

The scenarios helped to link users' knowledge of their current circumstances with the future possibilities offered by an IBC system and thus stimulated informed comment and debate. For this reason the scenarios were very much set in the future and therefore pre-supposed the existence of high-speed communication links.

Rich Pictures. 'Rich pictures' were used to complement the text form of the scenarios in order to provide a graphical snapshot of the whole scenario. The rich pictures did not seek to capture every detail of the scenarios, but rather to provide an overall view of the main 'players', the data to be communicated, the main communications routes between the players, and the form or medium used for the various types of communication in the scenarios. This representation of the scenarios was extremely useful as a means of communicating user requirements to the developers of the Initial Functional Specification.

Action Diagrams. As the 'rich pictures' did not provide a representation of the events in the scenarios in time, a simple action diagraming technique was also applied to each of the generic scenarios to give a time-based view.

User models of system diagrams. Users' views of a system and its actual configuration are often at variance: these diagrams were used to illustrate the system as it would appear to a user.

Workshop/Delphi analysis. This technique involved circulating an initial draft set of user requirements to individual experts and end users within the consortium for comment prior to a workshop which was attended by a range of experts and end-users. At the workshop different working groups were set up to consider core topics such as security, interactive graphics, workstation design and the control of user conferencing, but most importantly to derive a minimum set of user requirements for implementation in the application pilot. The individual topic-related working groups verified existing material and provided some new elements, while the minimum set of user requirements were drawn up and a set of priorities for their implementation established. In this way the set of end user requirements was reviewed and a consensus view achieved.

Information Maps and Knowledge Maps. These representations will be distilled out of the Action Diagrams in order to view the data contained within them at a higher level. This will serve to highlight any mismatches between these maps and organisational structures, tasks and procedures. This technique will be applied later in the project.

4. METHODOLOGICAL DIFFICULTIES

4.1 Linguistic ambiguities.

All interviews in one user company were conducted in French. It was considered that this was important in order to allow interviewees to express themselves as fully and naturally as possible. Where appropriate, supporting documentation for the interviews was also provided in French. This inevitably resulted in a double translation problem, in that not only was a great deal of technical and company specific vocabulary used but translation errors occasionally compounded the problem.

4.2 End user representation

Potential end-users are possibly under-represented in the sample, because users supplied by the end companies tended to be management and system support staff who do not always reflect the view of this community accurately. In addition to this users were frequently interviewed in the presence of more senior members of staff. This may have constrained, for example, discussion of current communications problems and hence limited the range of potential applications for IBC systems considered.

5. RESULTS

5.1 Categories of user requirements

A set of over seven hundred user requirements was derived as described above using the three scenarios. Each scenario was broken down into a series of user actions and for each user action, four categories of user requirements were identified:

- User requirements for sending/receiving a message
- User requirements for interaction using graphics
- User requirements for database access and control, including high speed file transfer
- User requirements for user conferencing

These categories were also used for the Initial Functional Specification. A further four groupings of requirements were also identified which detailed issues more generally applicable. These included:

- Security
- Workstation design
- Organisational/Job design
- Implementation

5.2 Minimum Set of user requirements

Due to resource constraints within the project it was decided to define a minimum set of user requirements for the application pilot that would be acceptable to the user companies involved. After careful discussion of all three scenarios, it was decided to concentrate on those areas and applications that offered something new to users. The minimum set of user requirements was agreed with users and can be encapsulated in three main statements:

- The application pilot should demonstrate communication between three workstations across Europe. This presupposes a user requirement for low cost high bandwidth readily available.

- The application pilot should demonstrate both synchronous interworking and asynchronous interworking. This type of interaction should occur between like with like workstations, like with unlike workstations and like/unlike with a low cost workstation. An additional point here was that a suppliers catalogue of standard components should be included.

- The application pilot should demonstrate communication of each (and any combination) of the following objects:

  - text
  - audio
  - video, both 'full motion' and 'snapshot'
  - CAD/CAM files
  - graphics pictures
  - images (scanned)

It should be emphasised that the minimum set of user requirements in no way negates the value of the complete set of user requirements. It should be seen as the minimal set acceptable to users. The other requirements have been validated and agreed by users and other experts and will be incorporated into the application pilot if resources permit.

5.3 Example user requirements

Below is a extract from the user requirements specification relating to 'interaction using graphics' for the user action shown in italics.

The supplier process engineer reviews the data received from the design company

- Non-specialist users should have access to a sub-set of facilities to enable them to view CAD data. Note that this form of interaction should not permit any changes to be made to the CAD data itself.

- A user, receiving a CAD document should not have to own the same CAD package or system as the originator of that document in order to have access to the sub-set of facilities mentioned above.

- Users should have access to facilities that allow them to express and explore their ideas formally and informally using graphics.

- Graphics facilities should allow for a range of use from free-hand sketching to more formal use of graphical applications eg manipulation of solid models. *(Detailed user requirements for personal use of the sketchpad not included in this extract...)*

- User interaction with different graphical applications should be consistent as far as possible.

  (The above user requirements imply a need for facilities to manage interaction with a formal graphics application whether one or more users are involved.)

6. FUTURE WORK

6.1. Amplification and continued refinements of the user requirements

It has been stressed throughout this paper that the initial set of user requirements must be further developed throughout the lifetime of the project. It is also important to note that they were generated without reference to cost or current software limitations. This approach was adopted as technical constraints can change rapidly over time and something considered impossible at the start of the project might become readily available by its conclusion. Likewise, limiting the user requirements by cost could result in failure to include certain leading edge technologies. It is considered far better to explore the alternatives before rejecting certain components based on an informed cost-benefit decision, rather than to select on this basis at an early stage.

It has been emphasised in this paper that the introduction of broadband systems will entail a considerable amount of organisational change both at corporate and individual user level. This subject has only been touched upon to date and will be approached in more depth, at a generic rather than specific company level, as the project continues.

6.2. Evaluation criteria

Similarly, evaluation criteria and methods have only received brief consideration and will be developed as prototypes are designed and built. In the context of the CAR project the term 'evaluation' refers to the eventual formal evaluation of all the elements of the prototype(s) and the application pilot itself. Therefore appropriate evaluation criteria and metrics must be developed to validate the user requirements, the functional specification and the technical components (both individually and as an integrated whole) which make up the system. In addition, to ensure successful implementation of the application pilot in a user company, the degree of task and organisational match must also be assessed. Evaluation in the wider sense of the word is a continuing exercise which will begin as soon as possible.

Some work has been done in this area, particularly with regard to the prioritisation of the minimum set of user requirements, as it was recognised that some requirements in the minimum set varied in criticality in terms of providing immediate and visible benefits to user companies, while others varied in their degree of current technical feasibility.

The following criteria were identified for the prioritisation exercise on the minimum set:

- Feasibility of implementation
- Timescale of implementation
- Upgradeability (hardware and software)
- Conviviality (ease of use)
- Plausibility (face validity)
- Degree of innovation
- Perceived impact on efficiency

It will also be necessary to monitor that the Initial Functional Specification is accurately, successfully and completely reflected in the design and build of the prototype and the application pilot itself. This work will inevitably involve expansion and clarification of the user requirements as translated into the Initial Functional Specification and also the development of a set of targets and metrics designed to provide answers to the following types of questions:

- Does the system function and does the functionality provided accurately reflect the user requirements?
- Can the system be used 'easily'?
- Does use of the system result in a better end-product and/or shorten the design to manufacture cycle?

Not all the targets and metrics derived will be capable of application in the early stages of prototype and pilot building: at one extreme some elements such as screen design can benefit from a useful amount of early evaluation when the system exists in paper form only, while at the other many more important aspects of the system can only be evaluated once a near-complete pilot is in place at a user site. Evaluation, like design, will thus be an iterative process.

6.3 Design notations for user requirements

It is an on-going problem that, although user requirements can clearly be specified in great depth, it is difficult to express them in a form that is truly communicable to system designers. Because of this, user requirements are often misrepresented in system design and build, not because designers disagree with them, but more often because they have difficulty in correctly interpreting a text based specification, particularly when development takes place in isolation, prior to full system integration. Therefore within the CAR project, some effort will be devoted to deriving a more structured means of communicating the organisational and end user requirements to those responsible for designing and implementing the application pilot.

7. CONCLUSIONS

7.1. Derivation of a well-founded user requirements set

The user requirements were seen as the starting point for the specification, design and construction of an application pilot demonstrating the use of IBC based systems in the automotive industry. By applying the methodology as described, large quantities of user generated information on a variety of issues were obtained. These included the companies current design practices, potential advantages of installing high speed communications systems, software and hardware requirements for such systems.

Analysis of the data then revealed a range of issues common to all three user companies. These include: cost, security, change control, requirement for true interactive working, potential for voice/video conferencing on a one to one or one to many basis, client/supplier communications problems, quality assurance of design, the range and disparate locations of individuals involved in the design and manufacture of products, the need for improved communications. Additionally a host of potential implementation problems emerged, amongst these are software and hardware issues, and organisational, task and usability considerations.

7.2. Lessons learnt

In all important respects the user requirements specification went according to plan and should help to ensure that the application pilot will not only meet genuine end-user needs but also be designed in such a way as to meet real-life organisational constraints. With hindsight one or two minor aspects might have been conducted differently:

- More attention should have been given to ensuring that interview subjects were fully briefed about the project, prior to the interviews being held, this would have released valuable interview time.
- Analysis time might have been shortened by the development of methods to limit the collection of extraneous data.
- More stress should have been placed on persuading senior representatives of companies to realise that although they represent one level of user, it is always necessary to cover the whole range of primary and secondary end users in a company - there is occasionally a suggestion of 'I was a user once, therefore I know' or 'J' étais, donc je sais!'. This policy is not intended to imply that the management are unaware or negligent of the circumstances and needs of their staff, but as a means of viewing the problem from all perspectives.

7.3. Biases and omissions in the data

It should be noted that some user requirements are specified at a greater depth than others. This is illustrated by the considerable detail found in the specification for the sketchpad facility, which was considered to be a key component, compared with the higher level requirements specified for the proposed sub-conferencing facility, an item not selected as a minimum requirement.

It is also acknowledged that the research so far has concentrated more on the 'in front of the screen' user requirements and less on technical demands on the communication systems. That is, the user requirements concern to a great extent those facilities that the user can see and manipulate at the user interface and specifies in only general terms the 'behind the screen' database and file transfer requirements, eg how many messages are likely to be passed at a given time.

Whilst acknowledging these omissions and biases it must be stressed that work on the user requirements will continue throughout the project using feedback from and feeding into other Work Packages in the project. Any missing details eg the speed, frequency and size of files to be transferred, will therefore be amongst the subjects of further investigation, and communicated to the rest of the project in an appropriate form.

Finally the authors feel it is worth emphasising that the methodology outlined in this paper, used within the framework of a user centred approach to design, offers a greater probability of successful systems design and implementation in a wide variety of application areas.

ACKNOWLEDGEMENTS

The authors wish to acknowledge the substantial contributions of our colleagues in the CAR team at HUSAT to the work described in this paper and the co-operation and support of our partners in the CAR project.

REFERENCES

[1] Gardner, A. and McKenzie, J., Human factors guidelines for the design of computer-based systems. Parts 1-6, Issue 1, 1988. Ministry of Defence (PE) and the Department of Trade and Industry. (Distributed by the HUSAT Research Centre.)

Human–Computer Interaction – INTERACT '90
D. Diaper et al. (Editors)
Elsevier Science Publishers B.V. (North-Holland)

Bridging the Gap
Between Task Design and Interface Design

Dzida, W., Freitag, R., Hoffmann, C, and Valder, W.

German National Research Center for Computer Science
P.O. Box 12 40, 5205 St. Augustin, West Germany

"Work context" is an ergonomic and technical concept for user interface development. Essentially, interface development is taken to mean more than screen layout, explanatory dialogue or something like that; it is the user's way of performing a task which is developed. Software developers are the particular user target group. For the technical and ergonomic ideas to become illustrated, the prototype of a user interface - called ERGO-Shell - has been constructed. The shell assists the user to apply a plan-oriented style of dialogue in that the system provides facilities for work preparations in complex task settings. Thus, ERGO-Shell enables the user to interact with the system on a demanding level.

1. Introduction

The concept of "work context" has been introduced for user interface design of complex application systems (Dzida et al., 1987). A work context displays a combination of tools, objects as well as associated knowledge about their application in a certain problem domain. A work context is intended to assist the user in exploiting the functional spectrum of a complex application system more effectively. A work context provides a sufficient transfer of knowledge about the application of that system. Thus, the notion of work context contributes to human-computer interface design.

Essentially, "work context" is taken to mean more than interface design; it is the user's way of performing a task which is developed, particularly the way of preparing work steps. Given a specific problem, the preparation of work is an essential prerequisite to achieve an efficient solution. This particularly holds in complex problem domains, such as the development of software. Due to the complexity it is necessary to care for an adequate preparation of solution approaches and to ensure that they are well set up for later reuse. A work context provides a means for making up work preparations as part of a problem solution. Thus, the notion of work context also contributes to the design of human task performance.

A work context is suitable for human-computer interaction, if the application system as well as the problem to be solved are complex. Complex areas of work may be characterized by a lack of generally accepted methods and techniques to be used for problem solving and task performance.

In order to illustrate that a work context is a suitable approach for bridging the gap between task design and human interface design both the task and the interface aspect are outlined here.

The target group of our investigation are software developers; the target system of our own implementation activities is UNIX.

2. The design of task performance

An approach to problem-oriented preparation of work, called "work conception", is introduced, especially for the field of engineering tasks. A work conception is a collection of elaborated proposals for the application of a software engineering method, including the instrumentation of the method application. A unique characteristic of engineering tasks is that their performance is aided by certain professional methods. An engineering method including its "instrumentation" is called an "engineering work conception". The notion of instrumentation refers to available tools as well as rules of expertise which represent experience about the application of tools or heuristics which apply, if tools are not available to tackle a problem.

We distinguish work conception and work context, with the first being the task design part (chapter 2) and the second being the interface part (chapter 3) of our approach. Work conceptions are introduced as results of problem-oriented work preparations. A prerequisite, however, is an investigation into the work tasks and work styles of our target user group.

2.1 Analysis of work styles of software engineers

From published literature, we know two work styles which can be considered as opposite incarnations on a scale of work styles: the "hacker" (also described as "compulsive programmer" by Weizenbaum, 1976) and the "cooperative programmer" (Yourdon 1977).

"Compulsive" programmer

- s/he likes to work away
- s/he hardly produces documents giving information about the state of a development
- s/he is hardly interested in other tasks

"Coopérarative" programmer

- s/he does extensive preparatory work
- s/he works prudently, i.e. considers the products of his/her colleagues
- s/he does administrative work in parallel

The extreme incarnation of the "cooperative" programmer is presumably as rare as that of the "hacker"; both types are overdrawn.

Nevertheless, these work styles were also observed in work situations in which no programming was done (e.g. Triebe, 1977) so that, in more general terms, we distinguish between a "momentary strategy" and a "planning strategy" (cf. Hacker, 1986, p. 332 ff.). In the extreme case, "momentary" means that work steps and their results are hardly anticipated mentally while "planning" points to a prudent approach which pervades the essential relationships of the construction process mentally. Empirical findings show (Hacker, 1986) that this style of working yields higher efficiency though requiring less stress. For our target user group efficiency can be improved, if the UNIX interface is designed such that users are enabled to adopt a planning strategy.

2.2 Analysis of work preparation

Some computer systems provide support for work preparation which is, however, restricted to the administrative parts of task performance. A typical example is the UNIX program "make" which assists the user in maintaining computer programs so that he/she needs not bother with the administration of dependencies between files during an actual problem solving process. In contrast to administrative work preparation our approach is aimed at the design of problem-oriented preparation. Since our target user group are software engineers, we always suppose a user acting problem-oriented when he/she is applying an engineering method. Hence, we regard engineering problem solving as an application of a method.

Additionally, problem solving implies the provision of an instrumentation enabling the user to apply a method. Problems are regarded as complex, if there is no generally accepted way to pursue the application of a method. For this reason it is impossible to construct software tools which cover the solution of such a problem completely and in a generalizable manner. Due to this difficulties the solution of a problem depends on expertise, the knowledge and skill of an expert who spent considerable time to incrementally develop one or more solutions approaches. It is the evolutionary process which finally evolves mature solutions. Even if a solution approach on an engineering method is only a fragment, it should be kept to become available later as a provisionally developed component of a more mature and complex solution.

We observed UNIX users who applied this system as a basis for software development. UNIX does not provide special tools for, let us say, the application of an engineering test method, such as "black-box test". The UNIX tool repertoire is incomplete; it only serves as a basis for a further development of an instrumentation. We observed that an engineer's solution approach mostly comprises a collection of UNIX tools and highly specialized tools developed by the engineer for a limited area of the problem. Such solution approaches often include good ideas which are worth to be stored, advanced and then made generally accessible. The result of such an evolutionary approach is what we call a work conception. It is regarded as a work preparation representing the technical "know how" for the application of an engineering method.

2.3 Design of work conceptions

A work conception is the result of an evolutionary process. The development of work conceptions proceeds as follows:

I. Preparation of work performance:

Establish an individual working environment:

- Select from the set of available tools and objects a subset needed for work performance.
- Arrange the selected tools and objects in such a way that they are easily accessible during work performance.

II. Analysis of solution approaches:

Collect re-usable solution approaches:

- Select the steps or sequences which are re-usable from the set of performed dialogue steps.
- Edit proved dialogue steps or sequences for re-use and integrate them into the working environment.

III. Installation of work conception:

Present proved and generalizable solution approaches:

- Present the collection of well-elaborated proposals for a problem solution clearly in the "work context".
- Provide the experiences with the proved solution approaches in a special "context info" so that they can easily be accessed.

In professional software development a work conception is to be generally accepted for a class of tasks to be performed when applying an engineering method. In contrast to traditional work conceptions such as "CASE" which guides the user to act in a schematic way, our approach allows a flexible handling of the solution fragments. Users of work conceptions are encouraged to utilize them as proposals for individual solution approaches. They find it feasible to amend these proposals according to their actual problem situation. To achieve this flexibility a close cooperation with the users during the development of work conceptions is necessary.

Encourageing users to participate requires that precautions have to be made at the user interface to prevent them from regarding such kind of anticipatory work preparations as an additional burden. Hence, our design approach to work preparation is closely associated with an ergonomic interface design approach (see chapter 3).

2.4 Requirements for interface design

The analysis of work steps which are to be assigned to the planning strategy distinguishes the categories "preparatory control" and "preparatory activity" (Dzida, 1986). Work preparations in the sense of "preparatory control" are analyzed in order to provide a better overview of task and system contexts at the user interface. For example, the user should check preventively whether essential parts of a compound command input are available. In addition, "preparatory activities" are investigated for providing technical components that facilitate a reuse of work steps already performed. Reusable solutions (even fragments) should also be easily adaptable to the actual execution context of a user's task.

Work preparations leave "traces" which can be re-used later during work performance. Individual preparation and execution should be integratable at the workstation. This can be achieved technically by window systems. Various display areas enable the user to set up overviews on elaborated solution fragments (for instance, structured files, stored sequences of dialogue steps, commented command sequences). The analysis of work preparation is aimed at a user interface which assures that the already structured or preselected input objects are considered such that superfluous (error-prone) input effort is avoided.

Additionally, the investigation is aimed at a user's execution of a task which is not dictated by the momentary system status, but rather by the state or extent of his/her preparatory activities. Work preparation relieves the user of a high degree of intensity of attention at the moment of task execution; i.e. the submission of a compound command. A command need not be split atomistically only to enter it step by step; rather, the user can plan large sequences of dialogue steps. Consequently, input errors which are based on an insufficient logical penetration of a complex command are avoided more easily.

Work preparations can be utilized much more efficiently upon a later execution, if these work traces are stored in an appropriate form. If structured or already well-considered solution approaches are to be made reusable for other users, such intermediate products have to be "dressed" in a special manner. In the most simple case, it can be useful to complete a proven sequence of commands (a macro) by explaining comments. This will facilitate the reuse or possible advancement of the solution approach by a colleague.

Doubts about the benefit of this kind of individual and collective work preparations can be removed easily at least by theory. Schönpflug (1986) regard the external storage of knowledge not only as an extension of individual cognitive capacities, but also a progress for collectively usable knowledge. There are however many questions to be answered: "Which knowledge is relevant?" "Is storage useful without refining or "dressing" the knowledge especially for reuse?" "Who is reponsible for updating and maintenance of such knowledge?"

With the development of the ERGO-Shell, we attempt to find practical answers to these questions. This can be done by implementing components of a user interface which supports storage and reuse of individual work preparations.

3. The design of an interface

According to the task and work requirements of software engineers a user interface has been implemented. It is called ERGO-Shell. Components of the shell are introduced here, particularly with regard to the requirements outlined in chapter 2. The ERGO-Shell as a whole serves as a support for problem-oriented work preparation for an engineering environment on the basis of UNIX.

The prototype ERGO-Shell is implemented on BSD-UNIX and is based on the X-window system. The ERGO-Shell is developed in an Shell in the development process.

3.1 Components of the ERGO-Shell

The classical UNIX-shells (Bourne-shell, C-shell) provide the user only with a rudimentary support for the formulation of commands. There is only a command line for the user to enter a command; as system reaction an output appears on the display. The C-shell also supports the re-execution of commands and provides a directory-stack to store and regain locations in the file system. But due to lack of missing visual support, searching through the file system and accessing files, for example, is very time-consuming, selecting a command for re-execution is complicated and structuring the tool inventory is difficult. The user has to concentrate on activities which divert his/her attention from the virtual task.

The ERGO-Shell consists of a set of components which facilitate the software developer's input and support him/her in work preparation (Fig. 1). The "command listener", the central component, is the main working area of the user. Here, s/he formulates his/her commands to the UNIX system as usual. As the components are technically integrated, the work preparation accomplished in other components of the ERGO-Shell can be included into the "command listener" with minor effort. The components of the ERGO-Shell enable the user to create an individual working environment to adapt the task planning and accomplishment to his/her own work style.

To arrange his/her individual working environment, the user is provided with components as follows:

- "command listener"
- "history tracer",
- "file-system browser",
- "work context".

"History tracer", "file-system browser" and "work context" are implemented as independent components which the user may add to the "command listener" if required. All components support collecting, editing and presenting proved commands, subcommands and command strings.

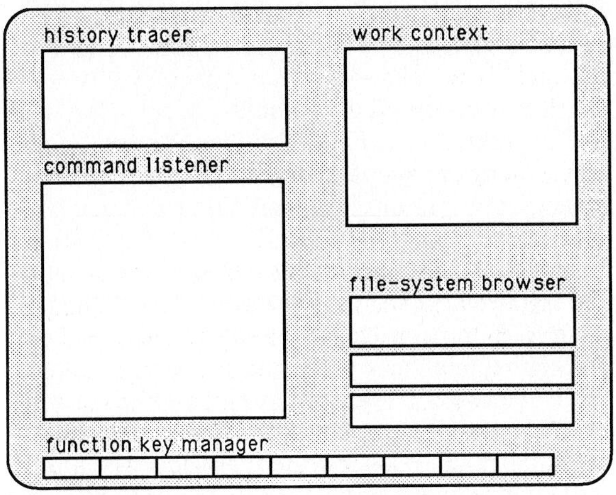

Fig. 1: Components of the ERGO-Shell.

3.2 The command listener

The "command listener" consists of a command editor, a separate output area for system output and a menu bar.

In the command editor, commands are edited and/or composed of already prepared parts. The user facilitates his/her work by re-using prepared subcommands, commands or command sequences. Using already existing command parts relieves the user of reconsidering e.g. the parameters a command requires for a specific purpose, the command sequence which accomplishes a special subtask or the complete path name of a file s/he needs in this context.

After a command has been entered, the command and the relevant system output are displayed in a separate window. By means of "Cut&Paste" operations, parts of the system output are re-usable in the formulation of a new command.

In the menu bar, the user keeps self-defined menus and macros s/he requires for performing his/her task.

3.2.1 Adaptable menus

An important work preparation consists of identifying and providing necessary tools. ERGO-Shell supports the providing of tools by adaptable menus.

Menus are used to combine tools (with suitable parameter assignments) or files to groups belonging to a specific task area. In self-defined menus, the user can assign names to tools s/he considers appropriate in the task context, thus performing a problem-specific structuring of the tool set and the object set. Menus can therefore be used to support orientation and recognition for a subset of tools in the intransparent tool set of UNIX.

Menus are generated with the aid of a special purpose editor. The menu descriptions are stored in files and can therefore be easily transferred to other users.

If the user prepares the handling of a complex task, s/he provides the menus generated for this purpose or adopted from other users in the menu bar of the "command listener". The execution of a menu item makes the relevant command (or subcommand) to be automatically inserted into the command editor of the "command listener". Here, it is available to the user for execution or further editing if required.

3.2.2 Adaptable macros

Complex sequences of work steps can be stored in the form of conventional command procedures or in macros. Unlike command procedures which instrument mostly a specific solution and which are of a final character, macros are more suitable for storing preliminary solution approaches.

Macros are produced by means of the macro editor and can be provided for execution in the same way as menus are provided in the menu bar. In contrast to the execution of a command procedure, the macro body is displayed before it's execution. The call of a macro makes the sequence of commands to be copied into the command editor where adaptations to the current task are still feasible. Macros are therefore open to further development. This characteristic is an important requirement for the incremental development of work conceptions. It is not the schematic execution of a command string which is decisive, but rather the presentation of the sequence so that it can be re-used in an adapted or unchanged form.

The dialogue history can be used to generate macros. The recording of the dialogue history is performed in the "history tracer".

3.3 The history tracer

To support the recognition of re-usable command sequences in the course of work and the access to them, the executed commands can be recorded in a "history component" of the user interface.

The dialogue history stored in the "history tracer" of the ERGO-shell is available for editing. The user can remove erroneous commands from the dialogue history, e.g. if s/he wants to store only proved dialogue steps. By commenting, experiences or special conditions for command applications are recorded. Entire sessions can also be stored in a file and reloaded from there to resume an interrupted work or to reconstruct a past working situation.

From the "command listener", the user has direct access to the commands in the "history tracer". The re-execution of commands or command sequences requires only little input effort. If a re-execution is done repeatedly or if command sequences are recognized as re-usable, a macro can be defined in addition and made available in the "command listener".

Macros which result from editing the dialogue history are often ad hoc solutions for a special case. Many of such solutions contain approaches which can be generalized so that they are usable for a whole class of tasks. Elaborated solution approaches of this type with suitable comments can also be made available to other software developers (see chapter 3.5 "work context").

3.4 The file-system browser

The hierarchically organized file system of UNIX provides facilities for structuring objects and tools. Searching through the file system and accessing files is, however, difficult for the user, because there is hardly any possibility of visualizing the tree-like structure of the file system.

A special component of the ERGO-shell, the "file-system browser", supports the orientation in the file system. The user can make several levels of the file hierarchy to be displayed simultaneously or can get an overview of larger subtrees. The search for files is thus facilitated.

Work preparation with the aid of this component means to ascertain whether and where the files to be modified for a current task are available. The necessary files can be marked as a preparatory task. If needed, the user accesses the files thus provided without any additional search effort.

Furthermore, the "file-system browser" offers via menus a direct access to functions the user needs for important preparatory work such as file management, file attribute manipulation etc.

The "file-system browser" is designed for tasks of file management and manipulation. The assignment of UNIX tools to these tasks is unambigious. Another typical task area in which a defined tool set is accessed is system administration. At the user interface, components supporting the user selectively in such defined routine tasks are therefore developed.

3.5 The work context

In contrast to routine tasks, an assignment of tools to tasks is a priori not possible in a complex problem area such as software development. However, individual work preparation can gradually lead to the result that a set of useful commands, command sequences and objects is evolving for a class of tasks. The collection of such elaborated results of work preparation is a work conception (see chapter 2). Its presentation on the display is called a "work context".

Both the selection and the combination of the tools reflect user experiences gained in problem solving. It can be useful to store such experiences over the momentary work performance. This enables other users to obtain individual results of preparation and thus to participate in the evolutionary development of "work conceptions".

The re-use and transfer of results of preparations presupposes that they can be accessed selectively. A problem-oriented combination of the available solution fragments at the user interface is required.

Within the ERGO-Shell, the component "work context" is supplied to this end. It displays a combination of tools and objects which are usable for a task area. Information concerning application purpose and user experiences is furthermore provided in a "context info". Users need help to trace and classify work preparations done by other developers. Therefore, it has to be possible to document both the used solution fragments and the knowledge about the approach to a problem solution. The documentations are filed in the explanation component of the "work context", the "context info".

If certain solutions of a problem are equally instrumented by several users, a new UNIX tool of the corresponding functionality could be developed. Thus, fragmentary work preparations lead to tools which are characterized by the fact that they are derived from generalizable concrete problem situations. Such a tool can then be included in the corresponding "work context".

The situation is however different if generalizable solutions are not obtained, since the work preparations have to be modified repeatedly to make them usable in the concrete work situation. In this instance, information concerning selection and adaptation of tools is provided to the user at the user interface. It is essential for the usability of work preparations that they can be adapted to the features of special problem situations with relatively minimal effort.

The "work context" provides the user with a collection of well-elaborated solution approaches and problem-solving proposals s/he can use for his/her individual problem solving. The flexible handling of solution fragments should replace the schematic application of ready solutions and encourage the user to add problem-oriented extensions instead.

4. Perspectives

ERGO-Shell components are designed such that the user can adhere to the tradition and "philosophy" of the UNIX system. Each component can be taken as a generalized solution. The user can configurate an individual ERGO-Shell according to his/her special purpose of application. A single component can also be used for another environment than the originally intended one. Nevertheless, the ERGO-Shell as a whole is designed for the assistance of users in developing a "work conception".

The ERGO-Shell provides a technical basis for the re-use and transfer of work preparations. The development of work preparations should contribute to a gradual improvement of the instrumentation of software engineering methods as a result of gained experiences. This requires not only a technical support as provided by the ERGO-Shell, but also the willingness to organize a transfer of experiences. Managers and staff members in the software development departments should discuss the extent to which the transfer of expertise will lead to the advancement of method instrumentation.

The developers of the ERGO-Shell expect that an incremental realization of "work conceptions" will also lead to an increased qualification of software developers. Since almost all staff members can participate in the development of "work conceptions", the methodological and technical know-how of a development department is getting more transparent to all participants.

5. References

Dzida, W. (1986). Computer assisted know-ledge acquisition. Towards a laboratory for protocol analysis of user dialogues. In: Man-Computer Interaction Research: MACINTER-I. (Eds.: F. Klix and H. Wandke). North Holland, Amsterdam, 139-150.

Dzida, W., Hoffmann, C., Valder, W. (1987). Mastering the Complexity of Dialogue Systems by the Aid of Work Contexts. In: Human-Computer Interaction-INTERACT '87. (Eds.: H.-J. Bullinger, B. Shackel). Elsevier: North Holland, Amsterdam, 29-33.

Hacker, W. (1986). Arbeitsspychologie. Huber, Bern.

Schönpflug, W. (1986). The trade-off between internal and external information storage. Journal of Memory and Language, 25, 657-675.

Triebe, J.K. (1977). Entwicklung von Handlungsstrategien in der Arbeit. Zeitschrift für Arbeitswissenschaft, 31, 221-228.

Weizenbaum, J. (1976). Computer Power and Human Reason. From Judgement to Calculation. W.H. Freeman and Company, New Jersey.

Yourdon, E. (1977). Structured Walkthroughs. Prentice-Hall.

Human–Computer Interaction - INTERACT '90
D. Diaper et al. (Editors)
Elsevier Science Publishers B.V. (North-Holland)

SUPPORTING A HUMANLY IMPOSSIBLE TASK: THE CLINICAL HUMAN COMPUTER ENVIRONMENT

B. Horan, A.L. Rector, E.L. Sneath, C.A. Goble, T.J. Howkins, S. Kay, W.A. Nowlan and A. Wilson

Medical Informatics Group, Department of Computer Science, University of Manchester, Manchester M13 9PL, United Kingdom.

Medicine has proved a fruitful field for developing knowledge based systems. Paradoxically, the General Practice medical environment has a number of characteristics which make the introduction of such systems difficult. Attempts to produce systems for other professional users — e.g. architects, lawyers, and executives — have had somewhat similar experiences. However, doctors work under severe time pressure in a complex social environment. The neatly confined problems most tractable to expert systems have limited relevance to doctors' decision making in practical situations. Furthermore, doctors already have a well developed system of sharing expertise.

Extensive user centred design studies have led us to propose an alternative model for *augmenting* doctors' performance. Rather than an expert system, we propose an intelligent human–computer environment for maintaining medical records and 'throwing light' on the complex data of patient histories.

1. INTRODUCTION

Medicine has proved a fruitful field for developing knowledge based systems. The existing knowledge sources are relatively systematic with well–defined subproblems of a tractable size. It has also been possible to recruit interested experts (Shortliffe, 1987). Paradoxically, the medical environment has a number of characteristics beyond those previously identified, which make it difficult to introduce expert systems into routine use (e.g. Lucas, 1976). Doctors work in a complex social environment under severe time pressure. A large number of people must agree to use a system before it can be successful. The neatly confined problems most tractable to expert systems often have limited relevance to doctors' decision making in practical situations. Furthermore, doctors already have a well developed system of referrals and sharing of expertise, so that there is no glaring gap waiting to be filled by an expert system. Consequently, much of the effort invested in developing medical applications of artificial intelligence has failed to have a major impact on routine clinical care.

Traditional expert systems focus on the core of doctors' skills — *diagnosis.* We put forward the hypothesis that it is much more difficult to introduce systems which impinge on users' primary expertise than those systems which assist with peripheral, probably irksome, tasks. For example, our experience of introducing computers in hospitals is that word processors were taken up first by academic consultants and by staff in departments which were short of secretaries. Most secretaries accepted them only reluctantly, at least at first. Similarly, we found that spread sheets were taken up instantly by departments such as catering, estates management, and the various laboratories, but that it took much longer before the finance department made extensive use of them.

Is there then a role for knowledge based systems in medicine? In the PEN&PAD[1] project we are taking a step back to re–examine the major requirements of general practitioners by involving them intimately in the design process. The design which is emerging from our work emphasizes cooperative, mixed–initiative problem solving. It embodies a view of 'Artificial Intelligence' as 'Building artifacts compatible with intelligent users'. While based specifically on the problems faced by British general practitioners, we believe many of the features are more generally applicable. The paper that follows traces our motivations and some of the basic principles that are emerging.

2. COMPUTER SUPPORT FOR PROFESSIONAL ACTIVITY

2.1. Common Issues

A distinction can be drawn between systems which *augment* skilled performance and systems which *substitute* for some skill or knowledge. Whereas augmentation systems are *used*, substitution systems are *consulted*. Classic expert system paradigms such as MYCIN (Shortliffe, 1976) or INTERNIST–I (R.A. Miller et al, 1982) substitute for an expert. Perry Miller's critiquing systems ATTENDING (P.L. Miller, 1984), ONCOCIN (Shortliffe, 1986), the recent adaptation of INTERNIST to become QMR (R.A. Miller et al, 1986) and the Oxford System of Medicine (J. Fox et al, 1987) are steps towards systems which aim to augment experts' abilities rather than replace them.

While this distinction is not absolute, the goal of most augmentation systems is to become one of the regular tools of the trade, 'readily to hand' in the users' environment. Consequently, we consider our work to be the design of a 'human computer *environment*' rather than a 'human computer *interface*'. We believe that it is not just a matter of making systems *usable* but of making them *useful* to their users, and consequently *effective* in patient care. Furthermore, we take as our starting point the premise that only users can judge whether or not a system is *useful*. This is in contrast to the '*benefits*' of the system which may accrue to users, clients, the organization, or society at large.

2.2. Special Problems of Doctors

The term 'knowledge workers' was coined by Engelbart (Engelbart, 1963, 1984) to cover a wide variety of professionals. However, along with many others in the same tradition, he considered 'knowledge workers' primarily within the context of business management. Medicine, particularly general practice and other forms of 'primary care', presents its own special problems for the design of a human computer environment. For example:

- Doctors' primary attention should be on the patient rather than the system. An engineer using a CAD/CAM system, or perhaps even an executive using an executive information system, will intensively use the system for a period ranging from a few minutes to a few hours. During that time their attention will be primarily on the system. For doctors, the system can only be 'to hand' if it is present during the consultation, but the patient must always remain the focus of attention.

- Doctors work in brief consultations under severe time pressure. In most medical fields the average consultation with a patient lasts only five to fifteen minutes; in British general practice, it lasts only seven minutes (Wilkin et al, 1987). The consultation involves little long term planning, instead the focus of each problem–solving episode is to find an immediate solution to the current problem and 'get the patient out the door'.

- The variety of problems with which any general practitioner is presented in the course of a week is enormous and no one condition occurs sufficiently frequently to justify a specific system to deal with it.

- Doctors already work under an information overload. There is every danger that any information system will simply aggravate the overload.

- General practitioners work in comparative isolation from their colleagues. Much of the 'training' in how to use systems in other fields occurs through informal contacts between users. The structure of medical practice makes such informal contacts less frequent.

- Although most encounters with patients occur in the consulting room or at the bedside, there are many variations. Home visits, 'bed borrowing' in hospitals, casualty wards, and specialist laboratories all have special needs. Experience with conventional information technology in medicine gives many warnings that failure to satisfy critical variations can make otherwise desirable systems unworkable in practice.

- Psychological and social issues are an integral part of medical practice, and much of the information needed to deal with them is 'soft', poorly characterized, and therefore difficult to evaluate.

- Many 'Executive Information Systems' exist as a means of manipulating and re–assessing previously entered information. However, users of consulting room systems are required to enter significant amounts of new information.

3. PRINCIPLES OF DESIGN FOR A MEDICAL DECISION SUPPORT SYSTEM

3.1. Basic Principles

How can the problems outlined above be overcome? Our approach is based on:

- A broad vision of a 'clinical information environment' based around the medical record, which we hope will become doctors' primary means of gathering and retrieving information and of communicating with other parts of the health service.

- A fresh examination of the functions of the medical record and the full context in which it is used.

- The determination that a sufficient number of doctors will be involved in the design of the system tha it will reflect the real needs of a significant segment of the medical profession.

Within this framework, we have been conducting a series of workshops with general practitioners and observing them during simulated consultations, as well as examining a range of systems aimed at doctors in various specialities. The involvement of doctors in the design process is critical. It dictates an 'evolutionary' approach through rapid prototyping and experimentation, since neither doctors nor designers can predict with any accuracy how new ideas will work in practice, and doctors can only explain their needs in response to examples of the possibilities. Furthermore, the use of task analysis techniques has assisted us in gathering user requirements and identifying user variability. Finally, by presenting 'mockups' of proposed screen displays (for example), and by demonstrating small–scale prototypes we have produced sets of recommendations for features to be subsequently included in larger prototypes.

3.2. An Intelligent Medical Record — Information Readily to Hand.

Where should we start? What does having information readily to hand mean to the practising doctor? The basic information used by doctors is about the patient, therefore our design starts with the fundamental source of patient information — the medical record. A patient with a complex history may have a paper record several inches thick containing over 10,000 'observations'. Typically, it is minimally indexed, mainly handwritten, with no reliable summary. Not surprisingly, errors which occur because doctors fail to find important information are common (Fernow et al, 1978).

Most existing computer–based medical records do little more than create an electronic equivalent of the paper record, a simple chronological record of what has occurred with little or no indexing. The task we have set ourselves is to provide a self–organizing and well summarized record that can be viewed in a variety of ways. Much of the 'intelligence' is devoted to making data entry as easy and as quick as possible. The goal is to completely replace the paper record so that the system truly becomes a part of routine practice. We expect most of the 'decision support' in the system to come from the effective presentation of information and from implicit prompting by data entry formats — for example by the use of forms (Figure 1). Our metaphor is one of 'throwing light' on the medical record so that doctors can see the information more clearly and thus perform more effectively.

3.3. Summarization and Chunking: An Expert System to Answer the Question "What Next?"

Fundamental to the design is the need to provide answers to the following questions:

1) What information is the doctor likely to want to record about the current situation?

2) What one 'pageful' of information does the doctor currently need — and how can it be presented so as to be easily assimilated ?

3) Is the doctor proposing or omitting anything that is sufficiently worrying to merit a warning?

Successful answers to the first two questions involve establishing the appropriate 'chunks' for medical dialogue. One of the chronic complaints about many existing systems is that they demand too much detail. Doctors usually communicate using a shorthand of syndromes or 'super syndromes', for example 'pneumonia and heart failures' or 'disabling migraine'. For most situations this is all the information that is needed; it may even be all that it is appropriate to record. The third question requires a clear distinction to be made between what can be taken to be true by default and what is actually recorded.

To reduce keyboard use, the prototype utilises a method of constrained selection for data–entry — pointing, menus, and direct manipulation. For this to be successful, the user should only be presented with those options that are most likely to be needed. This requires a visual language and something approaching semantic and pragmatic grammars of clinical practice. Fortunately, much of medical knowledge is inherently visual, and the association of a physiological system with an anatomical region appears to present a surprisingly powerful basis for such a language.

The distinction between the semantic and pragmatic components of the underlying 'grammar' is critical to the system. The semantic component answers the question "*What can be said?*", whereas the pragmatic component answers the questions "*What is likely to be said?*" and "*What needs to be said?*". Data entry is organized in layers, such that the doctor can always request to enter more detail than is currently provided. The top layers follow the pragmatic component of the knowledge base. If the pragmatic component were totally successful (and if the world were completely predictable), this would be all that was needed. However, inevitably from time to time the doctor will need to get beneath the level of what is *expected* to the level of what is *possible*. It remains to be seen how often this will occur in practice.

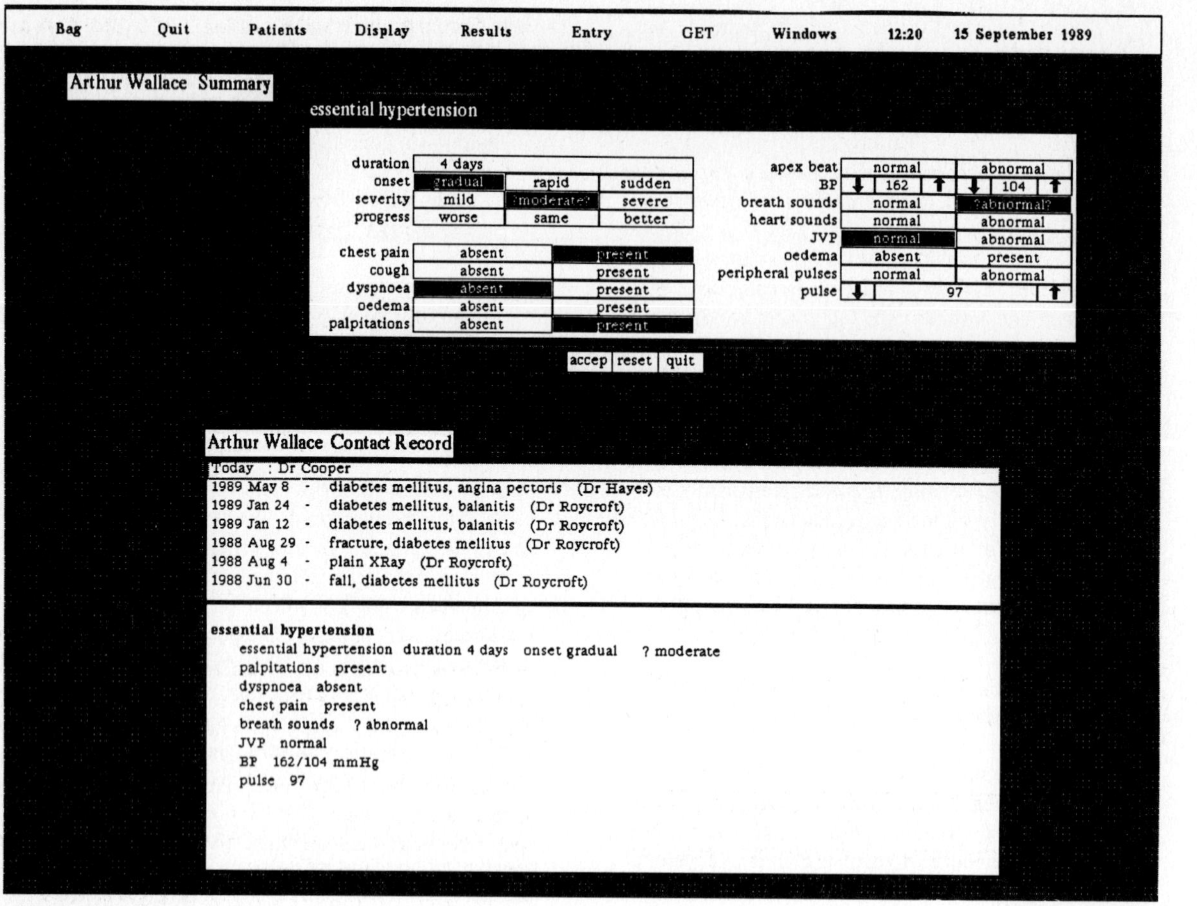

Figure 1: A form–filling dialogue is used to constrain data entry

4. ARCHITECTURE OF THE SYSTEM

The overall structure of the system is summarised in figure 2. The relations within the knowledge base form one axis of the system, time and space form the second axis. The basic data of the system or '*things*' are the '*occurrences*' which occupy the the plane formed by the knowledge base axis and the time/space axis. The third axis of the system is formed by the layers of the application and user interface and represents progressive degrees of cognitive and perceptual organisation, '*things*', '*perspectives*', '*presentations*' and '*displays*'.

The bottom layer, the *things*, are the objects in the semantic network itself. The *thing* layer is responsible for maintaining basic integrity constraints and has a straightforward translation into standard data base structures.

The *perspective* layer provides (i) filters and transformations so that the *things* can be viewed in different ways; and (ii) interpretation of the commands from the *presentation* layer into operations on the *thing* layer. Most of the 'intelligence' of the system lies in the *perspective* layer. Different *perspectives* perform summarizations, decide on appropriate chunking and levels of abstraction, and restructure the information into database–like views.

The *presentation* layer manages (i) the 'topological' information concerning presentations — i.e. information which is relatively independent of the details of the screen itself such as the tabbing and indentation structure of a piece of formatted text; and b) the conversion of the 'tokens' from the display layer into 'commands' to the *perspective* layer.

The *display* layer manages the actual mechanics of the screen display and the conversion of 'lexical' input from the user into 'tokens' to be dealt with by the *presentation* layer. In our current Smalltalk–80 implementation, the *display* layer is a view—controller pair.

This multi–layered model has many features in common with other layered models widely discussed in the HCI

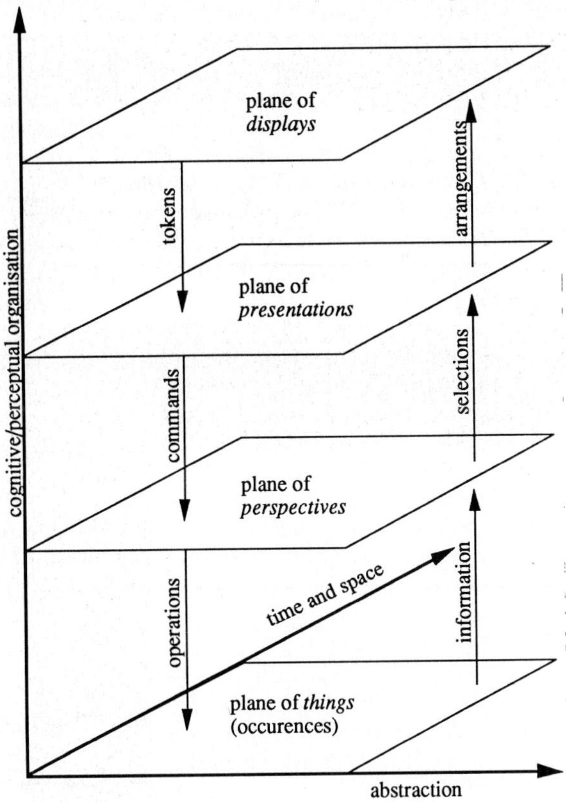

Figure 2: Layered Model of User Interface management

community (e.g. Cockton, 1986; Pfaff, 1985). It also serves two functions: it allows a complex interface to be factored into pieces which are practical to implement and maintain; and it also allows multiple views of the same information to be maintained simultaneously and consistently. There can be any number of *perspectives* on the same *thing* and any number of *presentations* of the same *perspective*. (In theory there can also be more than one *display* of a *presentation*, but we have not been able to find any use for such an arrangement.) All changes are ultimately made in the *thing* layer and the effects are propagated back to the multiple *presentations* via a dependency maintenance system. The display of any individual patient's record consists of a number of windows each of which *displays* a *presentation* of an alternative *perspective* on that patient.

5. CONCLUSION

Professionals have a wide range of skills only some of which are easily captured by the formal descriptions of their disciplines. They carry out a wide range of tasks, only some of which fit formal or academic stereotypes. While not sufficient, the formally described tasks are a necessary part of performing effectively, and limitations on human cognitive processes make errors inevitable. However, professionals are not novices; they are broad experts, and systems which treat them as novices are likely to be rejected.

From our current work, we can see at least three different ways of augmenting the abilities of one group of professionals — doctors in general practice — to carry out their tasks:

- Performing tasks such as retrieving, sorting, transforming and displaying information which 'throw light' onto the problem in question and provide cues that would otherwise be missing.
- Monitoring and anticipating the situation according to formalized rules of the discipline to anticipate or correct errors.
- Performing those tedious subtasks which are outside the doctors' primary expertise.

To achieve any of the above, systems are required that are *useful* in doctors' daily tasks and which are matched to their usual practices and concepts. We conclude that the development of such systems requires a user–centred approach in which a sample of the intended audience participate in the design process. In the PEN&PAD project we believe this is leading to a productive relationship where users and designers create a common language. That language inevitably requires the use of prototypes without which it is almost impossible to discuss user interface issues.

As a result of user involvement and the more general considerations outlined earlier, a set of key maxims have emerged to guide the design:

- Make the system useful to doctors in day–to–day patient care.
- Do not overload the doctor. One of our central efforts is to find a means of summarizing and 'chunking' information so that it can be quickly assimilated within the limits of human short term memory. The top level of information should cover only the detail normally needed. Further information can be sought by expanding individual items.
- Minimise the number of interactions with the system. Doctors' attention should be on their patients; having to manipulate the system is a distraction. Within the medical consultation little clinical effort is spent diagnosing patients *de novo*. In addition, consultations usually follow a stereotyped script. The system should take advantage of these facets to ensure that, as far as possible, the 'next step' should

always be natural and immediately to hand, thus making the system quick and efficient for those common situations which constitute the vast bulk of clinical care. However, the course of an individual consultation cannot always be predicted in advance and the system must therefore allow the user to pursue as many parallel threads as necessary at any point in the consultation. Finding the right balance between the amount of information on the screen at one time and the number of interactions required to access or enter a particular piece of information is one of the functions of the experimental prototypes.

- Minimise the extra memory load necessary to operate the system. Use direct manipulation metaphors and make the navigation through the system visually obvious.

- Make the system flexible and tailor it to individual doctor's requirements. Medicine is not a precise science, and individual variations range from substantive issues — such as differing opinions on alternative drug regimens or the use of diagnostic tests — to superficial issues such as preferences for icons or text in a given context and whether or not the user is willing to use the keyboard. No one interface will fit everyone all of the time.

- Never *require* that the doctor do anything. All data fields and all actions should be optional.

- Always look for the *disadvantages* of using the system and the potential harm it might do as well as the potential good.

Ultimately we hope that clinical information systems will become 'intelligent assistants' which provide a wide range of services ready to hand, some of which will resemble knowledge based systems, others of which will be more mundane.

ACKNOWLEDGEMENTS

This paper is based on the collaborative effort of the Manchester Medical Informatics Group. We are particularly grateful to the doctors collaborating with us on the PEN&PAD project. The research is funded in part by the Medical Research Council (grant #SPG8800091) and the Department of Health.

FOOTNOTES

1. Practitioners Entering Notes, Practitioners Accessing Data.

REFERENCES

Cockton, G. (1986). Where do we draw the line? Derivation and evaluation of user interface software separation rules. In People and Computers: Designing for Usability (Eds. M.D. Harrison and A.F. Monk). Cambridge University Press, England.

Engelbart, D.C. (1963). A conceptual framework for the augmentation of man's intellect. In Vistas in Information Handling, vol.1 (Ed. P. Howton). Spartan Books, Washington DC.

Engelbart, D.C. (1984). Towards high performance knowledge workers. In Proceedings of Office Automation Conference, 1982. AFIPS Press.

Fernow, L.C., Macki, C., McColl, I. and Rendall, M. (1978). The effect of problem–oriented medical records on clinical management controlled for patient risks. Medical Care, 21, 143-148.

Fox J., Glowinski, A. and O'Neil, M. (1987). The Oxford System of Medicine: a Prototype information system for primary care. In AIME–87, Proceedings of the Second European Conference on Artificial Intelligence in Medicine (Eds. J. Fox, M. Fieschi and R. Engelbrecht). Springer Verlag, Berlin.

Lucas, H. (1976). Why Information Systems Fail. Columbia University Press, New York.

Miller R.A., Pople, H.E. and Myers, J.D. (1982). INTERNIST-1, an experimental computer–based diagnostic consultant for general internal medicine. New England Journal of Medicine, 397, 468-476.

Miller, P.L. (1984). ATTENDING: Critiquing a physician's management plan. IEEE Transactions on Pattern Analysis and Machine Intelligence, vol. PAMI-5, 449-461.

Miller, R.A., McNeil, M.A. and Cahllinoor, S.M. (1986). The Internist–1 Quick Medical Reference Project: Status Report. Western Journal of Medicine, 145, 816-822.

Pfaff, G.E. (1985). User Interface management Systems. Springer Verlag, Berlin.

Shortliffe, E.H. (1976). MYCIN: Computer Based Medical Consultations. Elsevier, New York.

Shortliffe, E.H. (1986). Medical Expert Systems: Knowledge Tools for Physicians. Western Journal of Medicine, 145, 830-839

Shortliffe, E.H. (1987). Computer programs to support clinical decision making. Journal of the American Medical Association, 258, 63-68.

Wilkin, D., Hallam, L., Leavey, R. and Metcalfe, D.H.H. (1987). Anatomy of Urban General Practice. Tavistock, London.

Human–Computer Interaction – INTERACT '90
D. Diaper et al. (Editors)
Elsevier Science Publishers B.V. (North-Holland)

AN ANALYSIS OF THE CIRCUIT DESIGN PROCESS FOR A COMPLEX ENGINEERING APPLICATION

Lynne Colgan
Imperial College
Department of Electrical Engineering
London, UK

Maddy Brouwer-Janse
CFT-Automation
Philips
The Netherlands

An approach for improving human-computer interaction in a complex engineering domain is presented. A multi-disciplinary team addresses the issue of finding an appropriate environment for analogue circuit optimisation. This environment has to bridge the gap between users in the electrical engineering field and numerical techniques. Our solution is to adopt a long term system-design approach integrating cycles of prototyping with user evaluations. This approach highlights the conflict between designing a controlled psychological experiment from which conclusions can be drawn with statistical confidence, and a practical, incremental system development. The general philosophy of the approach is to enlist users tackling realistic problems in everyday settings.

1. INTRODUCTION

The task of analogue circuit design has long been recognised as a skilled, creative process utilising many sources of knowledge built up through experience. Circuit design is also a complex, iterative process in which, after a creative beginning - the development of the circuit topology - the circuit designer has to pass through several cycles of adjusting circuit parameters to achieve the acceptable circuit performance, or, if this is not possible, return to the circuit to adjust the topology.

Circuit design and optimisation can be seen as multi-criteria decision-making processes. On many occasions the circuit designer is confronted with a decision in the face of competing objectives. To meet design objectives, design variables have to be chosen and adjusted in the presence of several performance trade-offs. In addition, the designer will also have a number of constraints which must be satisfied. The overall aim is to achieve the optimum circuit when confronted with competing criteria, keeping design variables within bounds and performances within constraints.

This process can and often does take several months to complete. The majority of this time (often as much as 80%) is spent understanding the circuit behaviour: recognising trade-offs and identifying design variables. A smaller fraction of time is spent developing topologies and making topological adjustments. Once the circuit designer has created a circuit and explored its behaviour, the tasks humans perform well are concluded. The process of achieving the optimum performance from the circuit can be considered a purely mechanical task. Adjusting components, finding inter-dependencies and finding the optimum combinations of parameter values in high-dimensional space are tasks humans are not usually good at.

There is a definite role for some kind of automated *tool* in order to capitalise on the diverse abilities of humans and machines. Adopting a support approach will ensure that humans continue to gain satisfaction from the creative side but can oversee and control the optimisation of parameter values. High-level marketing decisions such as the choice between a high performance, high cost tool and a low performance, low cost tool are difficult to model mathematically and lie firmly in the human domain. Brooks [1] noted the importance of providing people with tools for the interactive watching and steering of searches through parameter space. Providing the appropriate graphical displays to make this possible is an essential ingredient.

2. CONTROL AND OBSERVATION OF CIRCUIT OPTIMISATION (COCO)

The aim of the project is to provide circuit designers with a new circuit optimisation tool which will address long-standing problems encountered by recent attempts to introduce numerical techniques into the circuit design field. In particular, it attempts to provide intelligent support in the mathematical and electrical domains using an expert system approach, and to make optimisation algorithms accessible to circuit designers via a novel user interface. The designer interacts with the system via a graphical user interface. The electrical subsystem sets up monitors to ensure electrical realisability and helps in the formulation of the optimisation problem. The mathematical subsystem defines the problem, selects an algorithm, and invokes the optimiser. The power of these mathematical methods in improving productivity and circuit performance has already been demonstrated.

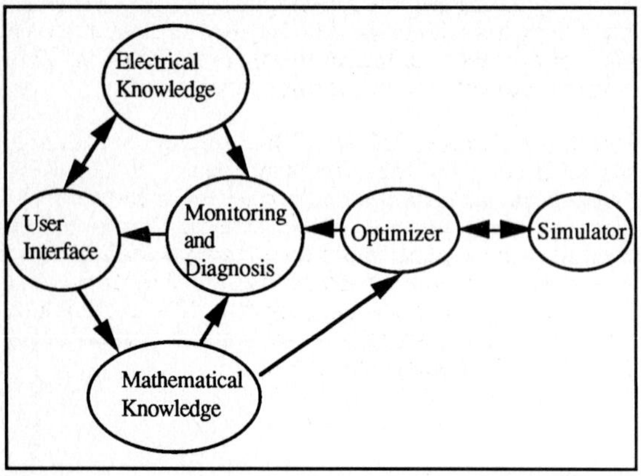

Figure 1: Structure of COCO

3. USER MODELS

Boyle [2] has pointed out that in designing an engineering support system, the roles that human and machine are going to play should be established. He notes that machines are good at executing complex procedures, searching through data and presenting information to the user, whereas humans are good at high-level decisions, setting and refining objectives.

It is also essential to have a clear model of the task the human will be carrying out. Mostow [3] maintains that developing better models of the design process is a key research problem in AI-based design. Having constructed this model, we can ensure that circuit design stages are supported in the system. We can establish those areas of the design process in which human cognitive limitations impede progress and those areas in which a machine would excel.

The system must take account of the cognitive processes involved in circuit design and attempt to compensate for any working memory limitations and information processing weaknesses. As Baker et al [4] note "To be a useful adjoint to human performance, the tools must closely match the cognitive processes associated with the various design activities."

Allowing system designers to speculate about users' needs, and impose their own unjustified models of the task on the system can lead to unusable systems. The COCO project team is multi-disciplinary and includes members who have had personal experience of circuit design. The team advocates a philosophy of incremental refinement for system development. A first prototype of the system based on concepts developed by experienced team members is developed. This prototype, although far from the optimum, acts as a medium for talking to circuit designers.

Incrementally building up the user model can be seen as part of a more general system design philosophy of ensuring user involvement in all stages. As a first step, the method the user currently employs to tackle design tasks needs to be studied. Then as prototypes of the system evolve, each needs to be conveyed to the user for evaluation. This may involve intermediate user models of how the prototypes are affecting the manual design process.

4. A FIRST PROTOTYPE

The user studies were carried out at one of the intermediate stages of system development. A prototype of the whole system (MOUSE [5]) provided us, for the first time, with a vehicle to approach users and watch how they utilised the tool to design circuits, and indeed observe the process of circuit design. As the development of this system took a considerable amount of effort (four person-years) the importance of the results from user evaluation are apparent.

This system offers major enhancements to the facilities to which subjects were accustomed. A circuit simulator encased in a front end graphics environment was usually employed. Embodied in the prototype is an optimisation package which can link a numerical optimisation algorithm with a circuit simulator.

The user communicates with the optimiser via a graphical user interface (MOUSE). The user can enter a circuit via a schematic editor, access a circuit simulator for analysis, view results graphically, enter specifications for circuit optimisation, and identify design variables and design priorities for the optimisation package. It provides a starting point for communication with circuit designers. This is extremely important when no other product exists as a control or a basis for comparison. MOUSE does not support electrical and mathematical aspects at this stage: the experimenters have to substitute this knowledge either by training or assistance.

5. AIMS FOR USER STUDIES

The user studies had numerous and ambivalent aims. We needed to evaluate MOUSE in its role as an automated optimisation system. Inevitably, this involves collecting low level data such as unforeseen system and interaction bugs. These hide the deeper issues we are interested in. As circuit designers have never had the opportunity to use mathematical methods to optimise their circuits in the past, they can be considered as naive users and their use of the system is critical. We also need to know how to improve the system for the next prototype. CoCo proposes the addition of mathematical and electrical subsystems, and the creation of a new user interface: we need to know if this is the correct approach. It is notoriously difficult to get users to say exactly what they want, it is far easier to attempt to use a prototyped system and note user criticisms.

As we are introducing experts in circuit design to numerical techniques, we need to know to what degree they are prepared to be involved in these issues. Should mathematical aspects be completely hidden from the users, or with adequate documentation and training, could these aspects become interesting and useful to them. This has important implications for the user interface.

There are situations in which circuit designers consider specifications to be too obvious to state, for example, minimising power and chip area are always desirable specifications. We need to know what should be automated and what should be left to the designers to specify. Situations exist in which the algorithm may act in a non-sensible way, for instance, it may suggest negative values for physical components in the circuit. We need to equip the system with electrical "common-sense" to eliminate these situations.

We need to examine the stages of circuit design and investigate whether these stages can be contained in a model which accurately reflects the design process. We must find out if the system we are producing will hinder the established design process or if it will allow designers to work through their usual design stages in a more efficient way.

6. EXPERIMENTAL DESIGN: USER STUDIES VS CONTROLLED EXPERIMENTS

There are formidable problems associated with attempting to carry out user studies in a complex engineering field. Not least is the problem that the circuit design process usually takes place over a period of several months. The difficulties are evident when we consider trying to conduct a one week study of a process that normally occurs over a much longer time span. The proposed solution was to have a short study in which subjects are trained on the system and then continue with a longitudinal study in which subjects keep diaries of their progress.

Psychologists in the field of HCI often advocate consistent, controlled experiments as a reliable method from which to draw inferences. When studying complex circuit design problems carried out on a non-trivial system, this is not possible. For instance, it was impossible to provide a standard, realistic problem that all circuit designers could tackle on the system. To ask a subject to attempt a problem from an unfamiliar electrical sphere would lead to low motivation levels. More significantly, the system needed to be tested on as many different types of circuit design problems as possible to ensure generality.

The usual controlled approach of finding an independent variable to vary and a dependent variable to measure is not appropriate in this field. Each circuit design problem is a problem-solving exercise that involves long periods of thought and investigation. It is difficult to compare time taken to solve problems manually with time taken when using the system. We cannot ask the subject to design the same circuit twice, and the variation in circuit design problems and circuit designers mean that it would not be applicable to use two different designers or two different designs.

Psychologists also advocate keeping conditions static during the experiment to maintain consistency. In contrast, from the system development viewpoint, an incremental approach is the best policy. The pilot study alone supplied a comprehensive list of user problems with clear solutions, for example, incorrect terminology, unforeseen bugs and system crashes which could be improved before the next trial. This incremental improvement ensured that low-level problems did not obscure more important issues.

Carroll and Campbell [6] state "Methodology should fit the subject matter, not the other way round." With this in mind, we are left with a compromise: an unrealistic "toy" problem to be used as a benchmark during which conditions are kept as consistent as possible, followed by free sessions in which subjects use the system to solve their current, topical design problems. The prototype is incrementally improved between sessions but no major redesign of the system takes place.

7. SUBJECTS

One subject from an industrial research department took part in the pilot study. Three subjects took part in the main experiment. One from a university research department and two from a commercial environment. Four more subjects from industrial sites are planned for the near future.

8. METHOD

Before the experiment was carried out, MOUSE was subjected to testing by a hostile user. A pilot study also uncovered unforeseen system errors and protocol oversights. The approach of incremental refinement was applied to the experiment format as well as the system throughout the study. The first experimental sites were protected environments with sympathetic users. As MOUSE and the protocol become more stable more hostile users are planned. The experiment has the following format:

Tutorial: The experimenter administers a standard tutorial, giving the subjects enough information to complete the benchmark problem.The subjects are deliberately undertrained in order to gauge the level of training needed and also to retain an element of the naive user.

Benchmark Problem: Subjects are given an electrical design problem. This problem is directed to test low-level aspects of MOUSE such as menu handling and accessing different modes when the subject is not engaged in complex problem-solving. Subjects are encouraged to attempt as much of the problem as possible without asking for help. The point at which they start to ask questions is noted. They are asked to think-aloud while they attempting the problem and the session is recorded on audiotape, and accompanied with time-stamped screen dumps. Hesitations, mispicks and losses of orientation are noted.

Questionnaire A: The questionnaire consists of a mixture of rating scales, yes/no and open-ended questions. It attempts to test understanding of system and other subsystem-specific aspects.

Advanced Tutorial: The experimenter administers a tutorial on the more advanced features of the system. Difficulties are noted.

Free sessions: The experimenter and an adviser on mathematical and electrical aspects of the system sit with subjects while they solve their own circuit design problems. The adviser plays the roles the mathematical and electrical subsystems will play in the final system. Screen dumps are made and the sessions are audiotaped.

Questionnaire B: Again a mixture of question types this time testing the use of MOUSE for subjects' specific circuit design problems.

Debriefing: A structured session based on questionnaire answers, followed by open questions and discussion. This gives the subjects a chance to qualify their comments and discuss further issues. These sessions are audiotaped.

The experiment was punctuated with discussion encouraged by the electrical and mathematical adviser. This discussion covered the aim of the circuit designer at this state in the design; the design strategy; alternative strategies; and rational for design decisions. This discussion was not tightly structured, but was deliberately intended to create an atmosphere of trust and mutual sympathy for the aims of all participants.

9. DATA LOGGING

Notes were taken throughout the study, but in addition audiotaped material is available from the benchmark problem-solving exercise, the free sessions, and the debriefing. This experiment generated a large amount of audiotaped material (15 hours per subject). As transcription and editing takes approximately two days for an hour of tape, only selected segments were transcribed. The screen dumps provided snapshots of the design process and were in a form which was easier to handle than videotape. Any notes, sketches and formulae used by the subjects were also collected.

10. ANALYSIS AND INFORMATION EXTRACTED FROM THE DESIGN PROCESS

10.1. Design Trace

As a first analysis of the data, a design trace was created. This was a complete review of all stages the designer had gone through. It was produced by pasting together annotated screen dumps to result in a series of design stages. This provided a detailed case history for the circuit design being considered. It looked very much like a flow chart: a set of static screens with arrows between them. Each screen contained the current state of the circuit and what the design options were at this stage. At each node in the chart, several issues were made explicit. The plan the designer was following, the strategies being considered, and the design variables being investigated made up some of screen annotations. A picture of the designers' exploration of the circuit was being built up (a section is shown in Figure 2). When completed this series was taken back to the designer for confirmation of the data produced.

This stage functioned as a mode of verification of the design with the circuit designers. Being couched in circuit design terms, designers were comfortable with it. It was a useful way to record and condense detailed information about the circuit design problem. Another diagram was produced: one at a slightly higher level of abstraction.

The intention was to remove much of the detail obscuring more general issues and to reveal any stages the designer had iterated through. A much shorter, condensed version of the design was created. This moved away from domain-specific terminology and towards the goal structure of the circuit design problem. This diagram was colour-coded to emphasise several categories which had been observed: strategies; goals; subgoals; and verification of circuit hypotheses. This pattern emerged in a cyclic fashion throughout the condensed history (shown in Figure 3).

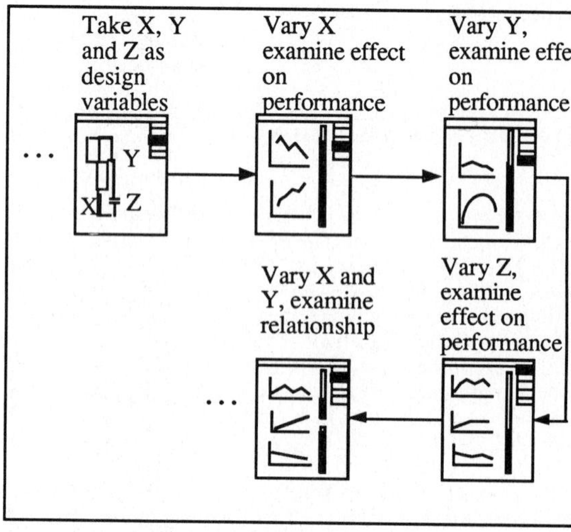

Figure 2: A Section of a User's Design History

These stages are accommodated in the main modes of MOUSE. From questionnaires, the users stated that the main system modes were adequate, although it became evident that there is a need for an "Explore" mode. This will provide the designer with facilities for the investigation of circuit behaviour. This should allow for multiple, approximate simulations of the circuit to gauge the response. These simulations should be rapid as subjects' design priorities were influenced by the speed of the system. Faster simulations which give the designer some idea of how the circuit behaves, even if inaccurate, can avoid much of the frustration caused by long simulation times.

10.2. Procedural knowledge

At regular points throughout the circuit development each subject was observed to be utilising sources of procedural knowledge. This knowledge was partly based on electrical engineering first principles and partly on experience of other circuits. This knowledge was also being appended

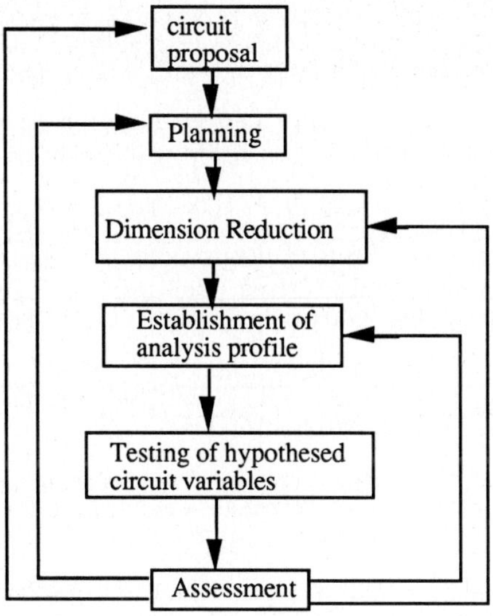

Figure 3: Circuit Designers' Stage Diagram

with specific information being built up through exploration. This knowledge was in the form of a set of circuit-specific rules. They took the following form:

"If the loading factor is approximated to a value of X pF per micron
then the settling time will be closer to specifications"

These rules were often hypotheses which the designer attempted to verify by simulation. The designer could often be seen to take extrapolative leaps to bypass the time consuming justification stage. Using their own set of rules, users could be seen to jump from the half finished testing of one topology to a new topology.

10.3. Chunking of Circuit Diagram

A strategy of "chunking" the circuit into smaller blocks about which knowledge existed already was observed. This could be seen as an assignment of functional roles to groups of components. The circuit behaviour associated with these smaller blocks was adapted as a result of their present location in the circuit. Subjects were observed adjusting the component roles as their knowledge of the circuit grew.

10.4. Working memory limitations

Subjects often looked back at aspects of the circuit design problem that were not available in the present mode. The user cannot keep all current values of circuit components, or values of design variables in his mind at once. This had important implications for screen design of the new system.

It was detected that users had difficulties with thinking in more than two dimensions at once. This made it difficult identifying interdependencies amongst design variables especially when these variables interacted in a complex fashion.

The process of finding strong design variables and investigating how they interact or affect circuit performance is a task humans find difficult. As the number of design variables increases and as combinations of variables start to have an effect, the more difficult the task becomes. Using mathematical techniques eliminates the need to think in several dimensions at once as, given a set of design variables, the algorithm should arrive at optimum values, but the user still has to choose these design variables at the outset. The length of time the algorithms take and the inability to view progress interactively mean users still spend much time on manual investigation and do not use the full potential of the system, possibly due to mistrust of results simulating reality. This suggests a new user interface should be provided which allows the user to view progress interactively through the use of graphical displays and interrupt whenever the optimiser takes a step in the wrong direction or the time factor becomes unreasonable. This interface should specify the most sensitive and the redundant design variables for achieving the desired results.

10.5 Interface Findings

The subjects often had the "where am I" feeling, and usually stated so during the sessions. MOUSE makes use of a complex hierarchy to formulate the optimisation problem. The user's path through this hierarchy is invisible, and inconsistencies in the method of opening and closing menus initially left users slightly confused.

Deficiencies were discovered in the way the user could view optimisation results. Screen dumps often had to be enlisted to compensate for missing screen views. The users needed to view circuit performance results together with some aspects of mathematical results. This was not available on the current system but will be accommodated in the new system user interface [7].

It was evident that users were unable to make the most of available mathematical facilities. Naturally, circuit designers unskilled in the numerical methods found it difficult to specify their electrical problem in mathematical terms. The mathematical terminology utilised in the system was unfamiliar to them and they avoided these facilities whenever possible relying on default values not necessarily the best for their circuit problem. Mathematical help which is planned for the CoCo system in the form of a mathematical knowledge base may alleviate some of these problems.

11. CONCLUSIONS

We have received confirmation of our initial ideas, and reassurance for the design of CoCo subsystems and future full prototypes. If the final system is successful, the benefits delivered to circuit designers by the use of numerical techniques could include increased productivity, heightened job satisfaction and better circuit designs. More user studies are planned at strategic points in the system development and our knowledge of circuit design will evolve in parallel with the evolution of the system.

The user studies have meant we have been out into the field studying real users solving real problems in real settings. Previously sceptical team members are now convinced that there is no substitute for sitting at the designers elbow and observing the design process. Our approach will have important implications for other complex engineering applications in which previous studies on simpler systems do not hold much relevance.

ACKNOWLEDGEMENTS

The project is supported by Philips Research Laboratories (PRL), Redhill, UK. The authors would like to thank Paul Rankin of PRL for his help in the user trials. They would also like to thank him and Robert Spence of Imperial College for ideas and useful comments.

REFERENCES

[1] Brooks, Jr, F.P., Grasping Reality Through Illusion - Interactive Graphics Serving Science CHI'88, Washington (1988) pp 1-11.

[2] Boyle, J-M., Interactive engineering systems design: a study for artificial intelligence applications Artificial Intelligence in Engineering (1989) Vol. 4, No. 2.

[3] Mostow, J., Toward Better Models of the Design Process The AI Magazine. Spring (1985) pp 44-56.

[4] Baker, K.D., Ball, L.J., Culverhouse, P.F., Dennis, I., Evans, J.St.B.T., Jagodzinski, A.P., Pearce, P.D., Scothern, D.G.C. and Venner, G.M., A Psychologically Based Intelligent Design Aid, Eurographic Workshop in Intelligent CAD (1989).

[5] Rankin, P.J. & Siemensma, J.M., Analogue Circuit Optimization in a Graphical Environment, IEEE ICCAD-89 (1989) pp. 372-375.

[6] Carroll, J.M. and Campbell, R.L., Softening up Hard Science: Reply to Newell and Card, Human-Computer Interaction, (1986) Vol. 2, pp. 227-249.

[7] Colgan, L., Spence, R., Rankin, P. & Apperley, M.D. Designing the 'Cockpit': the application of a human-centred design philosophy to make optimization systems accessible, SIGCHI Bulletin, July (1989) pp. 92-95.

Human–Computer Interaction – INTERACT '90
D. Diaper et al. (Editors)
Elsevier Science Publishers B.V. (North-Holland)

Designers-identified requirements for tools to support task analyses

Hilary Johnson & Peter Johnson

Department of Computer Science.
Queen Mary and Westfield College.
University of London.
Mile End Road.
London, E1 4NS.

Abstract.
The authors are presently developing tools to enable software designers to carry out task analyses (TA). The tools will support a methodology comprising techniques for carrying out task analyses and will also take account of integrating the resulting TA information into system design. To support integration and to identify the requirements for TA tools, a group of designers were surveyed. The survey identified whether designers believe TA would be of use to them and also how, why and where TA might contribute to design. The designers' views of the desired characteristics of TA tools, was also sought. This paper outlines the results of this small, detailed survey of what designers want, need and expect from TA tools.

1. Introduction.

A major goal of HCI is to assist software designers to construct useful and usable computer systems. Rosson, Maass and Kellogg [1] have identified that designers consider obtaining information about users and tasks as a major contributor to the generation of design ideas. Information about how users plan and carry out goal-directed behaviour is one aspect of users and tasks that can be identified and analysed. In recent papers we (Johnson, Johnson, Waddington & Shouls, [2]; Johnson, Johnson & Russell, [3]; Johnson & Johnson, [4] have outlined an approach to task analysis (TA) which comprises techniques for gathering and analysing information about users and their tasks, and then subsequently building task models in the form of "task knowledge structures", (TKS). Frame-based representations have been used to represent appropriate aspects of system design in terms of those task knowledge structures. However, more recently we have been identifying the requirements for, and constructing task analysis tools which will enable software designers to carry out task analyses within their chosen design process in the hope that more useful and usable computer systems will result. Rosson et al [1] distinguish between design idea generation and design development. The results of their survey suggest that design idea generation is facilitated by task/user analysis tools and techniques, while design development is facilitated through the use of specification and prototyping tools. User Interface Management Systems (UIMS) and prototyping tools ease the process of creating user interfaces resulting in the speeding up of the design process thereby allowing for a greater amount of iteration. We argue that the design process can be made more efficient or optimised by the use of tools to aid interface design, and the quality of the design can be improved by the designer knowing, or having reliable and detailed information about users and their tasks. By carrying out task analyses, users and tasks will be taken into account in the formation of the design idea. If this is the case then interface and system design will take place from an informed position on the part of the designer, resulting in the need for *less* iterations. Rapid prototyping without an awareness of users and tasks leads to post-hoc usability design. However, using task analysis *in conjunction with* rapid prototyping is tackling the usability issues from a more informed and hopefully principled position of design generation followed by design development through prototyping and specification with appropriate testing and re-design.

At present the authors are constructing tools (see Johnson & Johnson [5]) which will enable designers to carry out task analyses. In this paper the term design "tool" is something quite specific such as a piece of software that can be used by a person to assist their design activities. A method or methodology is a procedure or approach to be followed. Techniques are subsets of a methodology. The three terms are related in this paper in that techniques of data collection have been combined to form a method of TA. Tools are being developed to make it easier and more efficient for members of a design team to use and apply the method in design. These tools can be divided roughly into two sets; the first set will provide on-line techniques and help to aid the designer in collecting, analysing and modelling user/task data which might aid design idea generation. The second toolset is intended to support the incorporation of the data contained in task models (TKSs) into design development. In order to build the TA toolset it became imperative to identify what the designers wanted in the way of tools to support task analysis and also to integrate TA into system design. Consequently, a small, but detailed study was carried out to provide information about whether designers believe that task analysis would be of use to them and if so for what reason(s), and how and where might task analysis contribute to design? We wanted to identify the desired characteristics of the TA tools and what criteria they must satisfy.

None of the designers had undertaken a task analysis. Consequently, it would have been meaningless to have asked them directly to provide user requirements for TA tools. Instead, designers were first asked if they needed further information about users and tasks. This lead us to ask what kind of information about users and tasks they felt would be useful and also to identify where they presently made guesses or weakly-supported assumptions about users' tasks. Finally, we asked designers how they would use this information, in what form of expression would user/task information be relevant and if they would require any software support in order to use this information. From the replies we obtained to these questions we were able to derive a set of requirements for TA tools in design.

Because only three designers participated in this survey we are reluctant to make a statement about how representative these designers were of system designers in general, and how representative their views of design are of design processes generally. However, all three designers were in a position to argue that they as designers carrying out system design were representative of their respective companies.

In this study the authors used a structured interview to obtain details about design processes and designers' needs. Of course this is not the only method of collecting information, (see Johnson & Johnson, [6] for an extensive report on data collection techniques). Ideally, the interview would have provided an initial view of how designers design systems and what they might expect to be the characteristics of any tools. This would then have been supplemented by observing designers undertaking system design, followed by a series of experiments to test the validity of our findings. However, in this case it was not possible to observe designers actually designing systems due to time constraints on the part of the researcher and the designer. Constructing computer systems can take several months from the initial stages to completion. Also not all design activities are immediately observable. Another factor was that projects are confidential and therefore details cannot be shared with a third party.

<u>The study</u>.
Three system designers participated in the study, each were interviewed at length, from a minimum of one and three quarter hours to a maximum of two and three quarter hours. The basis of the interviews was a structured questionnaire which was to guide the interviewer and was not to be completed by the designers. The interviews were audio-taped and later transcribed. The designers all of whom worked on product development projects, each had a number of years experience of system design (from three to ten years), although only one of the three was experienced in interface design.

Each of the following sections relate to questions relevant to our aim to produce TA tools that can be used by designers.

2. Do designers believe TA can be of use to them, and if so why?
For all three designers there was very little, if any, end-user involvement in system design. Neither were TA or HCI methods and principles used. The reasons why TA and HCI principles and methods generally, are not more widely used are many, (see for example, Bellotti [7]). Hammond et al [8] argued that designers rely more on their own common sense when making interface design decisions rather than on human factors advice. Hannigan and Herring [9] also state that there is little evidence of the use of human factors advice in system design. They believe this low take-up to be due to the perceived high cost of access to, and familiarization with human factors material outstripping the perceived benefit. However, with regard to the argument about the high cost of incorporating human factors into system design, Mantei and Teorey [10] argue that including human factors stages in the design process is cost-effective.

Rosson, Maass and Kellogg [1] argue that the reason why HCI is not more extensively used in system design is due to the system designers belief about the usefulness of user input in design. Other reasons relate to the fact that designed systems have to be successful, usually cost-effective and often meet strict deadlines and HCI integration is seen as an activity which will prolong the design process and increase the cost.

Anderson [11], himself a designer, states that human factors is not widely applied to system design because it is not in a form suitable for systematic application as part of current design practices. According to Anderson, what is needed is a step by step approach which incorporates HCI as an integral part of the structured analysis and design methods (SADM) already in use. Clearly, this is one solution, however it assumes that a particular design process is itself likely to be widely used.

Given that end-user involvement, HCI methods and principles were rarely considered, did the designers believe that TA would be of use to them in system design, and if so why? All three designers thought that information about how end-users carried out tasks would be useful to them. Each designer was able to say in what way they might benefit from knowing about how people carry out tasks. Two of the designers had general comments such as any further information leading to more precisely documented requirements would be greatly appreciated by the designers, if this resulted in less end-user problems after the system had been built and released to the customer. A commercial argument for the importance of HCI issues was that if there was not much choice between the functionality of competing systems in the market place then user friendliness was one of the factors affecting ultimate choice of the system.

One designer argued that user/task information could be useful because the bulk of the development effort and lines of code were devoted to the user interface. If the interface could be developed initially by taking into account what the user needed, wanted and expected to see represented at the interface, then this could be an improvement on the designer having to rely on his own past experience. Lack of information about how users carry out tasks had he felt resulted in end-users having problems with the dialogue sequence and screen layout of systems where he himself thought that these were compatible with end-user tasks.

3. How and where might TA contribute to usability issues in system design?

Although many researchers (Moran, [12]; Card, Moran and Newell, [13]; Kieras and Poulson, [14]) ourselves included (Johnson, [15]; Johnson and Johnson, [6]; [16]), have made claims about what TA, HCI principles and methods might contribute to system design, the views of the designers who participated in this survey were of particular interest to the authors.

The designers who participated in the survey thought that the contibution of TA might be:

At the feasibility/initial planning stage:
*Identifying and documenting any new functions/new tasks the computer may support.
*Identify potential functionality of the system from user perspective.
*Identify user population and characteristics of that population.
*Identify characteristics of interface to be developed.
*Allocation of function between user and system.
*Assess scope/degree of larger-scale TA to be undertaken later in development lifecycle.

At the requirement/analysis stage:
*Identify and document user/UI requirements comprising details about;
*hierarchical structure of tasks (goals and subgoals)
*how users achieve goals and subgoals
*listing and ordering of undertaking task procedures
*frequency with which particular procedures were carried out by users
*reasons why and circumstances under which one procedure was used in preference to another
*inputs and outputs from each procedure
*events, data used, actions, objects
*standard set of properties relating to objects and actions, e.g. frequency, time taken, etc
*expectations the user entertains about the system after user has carried out an operation
*division between user and system.

At the Design stage/ User interface Development/ Dialogue design.
*Provide initial input to guide dialogue and screen design, comprising;
*details of what users expect to have available to them at any one time;
*the structure and sequence of their usage of system facilities;
*the names and form of representation to be given to screen-presented objects and events;
*information that should be available in given contexts,(i.e. design of screens);
*structure between contexts, (i.e. mapping between screens)
*how much to put on the screen at once with reference to number of commands
* what information to go on screens and the grouping of that information
*what commands are needed to support user operations and what those commands will be
*User testing.

At the prototyping stage:
*Guide initial format and presentation of prototype by indicating what the screens should look like
*Identify data that has to be displayed.
*Identify operations and sequencing of procedures
*Ensure dialogue specification is represented in a format that can be understood and verified with end users and to carry this out.

At the validation stage :
*User testing

At the update and maintenance stage:
*Identifying, documenting and cataloguing user problems.

In addition to the information contained above, other issues arose in carrying out the survey, concerning the integration of TA into system design. For instance, all of the designers argued that a small-scale TA at the feasibility stage would aid in firming up requirements in the analysis stage. Furthermore, the format of the TA information should enable the requirements to be checked and verified with end-users and managers, and also between designers and design teams. The same TA information at the requirements/analysis stage should be i) integrated with the functional requirements specification to provide more complete end-user requirements, and ii) re-formatted to support a mapping onto functionality design.

Two of the designers argued that the TA would have to be cross-referred to the data and functional models in order that a coherent view might result of what was required by the end-user of the system. This mapping could be carried out by matching all end-user task "operations" against the functional and data models; for instance in data flow diagrams end-user task operations should correspond to some input in a process box. At this point omissions could be identified and rectified. A data dictionary of objects and actions, common across the task, data and functional models was considered to be appropriate, and there was the suggestion by two of the designers that each of the models should use the same object or entity names and descriptions.

All of the designers considered that TA data should not be provided in data flow diagram format. Rather, it was recommended that task modelling should be simultaneous with, but separate from data flow modelling. It was envisaged that the TA at this stage could help to "flesh out" user/task operations and also identify boundaries between system aspects to be captured in data flow diagrams versus those that might not. The reason for the designers reluctance to have task modelling in the form of data flows stemmed mainly from the fact that end-users task behaviour and interactions with the computer are spread across a number of data flow diagrams representing the system functions. More specifically, one role of TA is to support end-users at the interface and the end-users responsibilities are spread across a number of data flow diagrams. The designers argued that a number of end-user tasks will map onto several elementary functions. However, these functions will not all be represented on the same data flow diagram.

The comment by two of the designers that TA would provide an initial input at the interface prototyping stage, and thus influence what was presented by the prototype was particularly pertinent in view of what we have said earlier in this paper about the use of TA in conjunction with design generation and development by the use of principled and informed prototyping.

The designers thought that the results of TA would be most useful and allow maximum flexibility to designers at various stages of design if they were provided in alternative format. A report giving a full narrative account of all aspects of users tasks (see Johnson and Johnson, [16]) appears to be appropriate to most stages in a design process, supplemented by Structured English and diagrammatic or graphically represented task models. The reports should contain as little technical jargon as possible in order that they might provide a medium of communication between end-users and designers, thus allowing the verification of statements within the report and also a vehicle for the designers' and end-users' common interpretation of those statements. Such reports would also serve the purpose of passing information from designer to designer within a non-technical environment.

4. What are the desired characteristics of the task analysis tools, and what criteria must they satisfy?

Currently a number of task analysis and HCI tools and techniques are available for use by designers, for example Moran's [12] Command Language Grammar (CLG) and Barnard's [17] Cognitive Task Analysis (CTA). A review of task analysis techniques, some of which are supported by tools is provided by Wilson [18]. However, it is unlikely in the case of the majority of these developed techniques or tools that the software designers requirements of TA tools were identified beforehand. In this survey we have attempted to identify what designers would like, need and expect in the way of TA tools in order that we would have a clearer view of the criteria to be satisfied by TA tools and by which they might be judged.

The designers were asked about the desired characteristics and criteria they thought that the proposed TA tools must satisfy; the results are summarised below:

*easy to use
*on-line
*can be used on a small-scale at first then used more later
*must have a facility for registering objects and actions and defining what they are
*facility to list characteristics and attributes of objects
*facility to help in constructing procedures and task hierarchy
*facility to show task hierarchy and procedures graphically - and allow procedures to be expanded into detailed operations by some diagrammatic convention
*assist in process of transforming task model into representations used by designers.

Two of the designers said that first and foremost, the tools must be easy to use. The irony of this statement coming from software designers to an HCI researcher was not lost, but from the opposite point of view we also appreciated a designer's dilemma when confronted with such a vague request. All three designers argued that the tools must be on-line and that it was important for the tools to be potentially integrated into a project on a small scale initially, and for the use of the tool to not delay project development. By this the designers meant that it must be possible to use the tools partially, thereby building up such use until the whole tool could be employed. In this way the designers could learn to use the tools over a length of time and this would lessen the likelihood of putting project development in jeopardy assuming that learning to use the tools would take time. The facility of allowing designers to use sections or parts of the tools would also increase the likelihood of their adoption by the designers.

Two of the designers also argued that the tools must incorporate a number of facilities for registering and defining actions and objects, listing the characteristics and attributes of objects, constructing procedures and task hierarchies or goal structures. Additionally, it should also be possible for the tools to show the task hierarchy and procedures graphically and allow the procedures to be expanded into detailed operations using some diagrammatic convention. The final requirement identified by all of the designers was that the tool should assist the designer in the process of using the task model as an input to the creation of design models.

The first two requirements; that the tools be easy to use and also on-line were more general requirements than the more specific facilities that the designers would like to be made available to them. At present we do not know of any TA tools already constructed which satisfy all of these requirements, although there might be some in existence.

Having identified the TA tool requirements, how could a TA toolset meet those requirements? Taking the designer-identified requirements first, we intend that the tools shall be on-line and that the interface to those tools will be designed from an informed and principled position and tested extensively on designers in the hope that this will result in the tools being easy to use. This will be supplemented by help facilities and introductions to TA itself. The tools will support the construction of a task model but this can be undertaken to a lesser or greater extent thereby making the tool appropriate for small scale use at first and more extensive use later.

An object/action database or dictionary will allow TA tool users to register, define and characterise attributes of objects and actions and their interrelationships to each other and amongst themselves. A goal-oriented structure (see Johnson and Johnson; [16]) to be completed by designers should aid in the construction and graphical representation of task hierarchies and procedures, along with appropriate help facilities. We are still considering the best way to support task models and their use in design modelling.

A non-uniform view of design practices and minimal end-user involvement (see Johnson & Johnson [19]), leads us to conclude that the tools must be versatile and flexible, capable of integration with different approaches to, and stages in design, should not impede design stages and should be capable of integration into both structured design methods and other design lifecycles.

The content and function of the task analysis tools should provide end-user/task information and users' interface requirements, relate identified requirements back to end- users in a non-technical fashion, and lessen the need for designers to have to rely only on their experience of the market place. The TA tools should also provide the basis for getting user feedback, decrease the number of end-user problems associated with using the system in undertaking tasks and provide a basis for including end-users in quality assurance procedures.

In addition to the TA tools being general purpose we decided that an independent subset of these tools should be specifically tailored to one of several potential structured design methods.

Adapting TA and the tools to support the integration of TA into design can be enhanced by the integration of TA processes into particular structured design methods. One opportunity of integrating TA into design practices is when structured design methods are introduced into the design environment. It might be easier to introduce TA at such a time, especially if the TA is appropriate to, and an integral part of the system design methodology. SSADM has been chosen, for a number of reasons, largely beyond our control, as the structured design method for our tool subset.

5. Summary and conclusion.

We began this paper by suggesting that one way of assisting designers to build usable and useful computer systems was to provide them with information about how users plan and carry out goal directed behaviour. To this end we are currently constructing task analysis tools which designers themselves can use. The paper has outlined the results of a survey which was concerned with identifying what designers wanted, needed and expected in the way of tools to support task analyses and their integration into system design. Earlier we identified that one contribution of task analysis to system design in the present climate is to guide the input to rapid prototyping. The cost/benefit relationship, must be considered, between building the interface following an informed and principled approach versus building an interface in an unprincipled manner and then constantly updating and modifying it to achieve user satisfaction.

Acknowledgements. We are grateful to ICL URC for funding the project "The development of task analysis as a design tool". Our thanks go to the ICL designers who participated in this study, and also to Phil Stradling, then of Data Logic.

References.

[1] Rosson, M.B., Maass, S., and Kellogg, W.A. The designer as user: Building requirements for design tools from design practice. Communications of the ACM, 31, (1988), 1288-1298.

[2] Johnson, P., Johnson, H., Waddington, R., and Shouls, A. Task-related Knowledge Structures: Analysis, modelling and application, in: Jones D.M. & Winder, R. (Eds,). People and computers IV. (Cambridge University Press, 1988).

[3] Johnson, P., Johnson, H and Russell, F. Collecting and generalising knowledge descriptions from task analysis data. ICL Technical Journal, 6, (1988), 137-155.

[4] Johnson, P and Johnson, H. Knowledge Analysis of Tasks: Task analysis and specification for human-computer systems, in: Downton, A (ed) Engineering the human-computer interface. (London: McGraw Hill 1989).

[5] Johnson, H and Johnson, P. The development of task analysis as a design tool. Design specifications for tools to support task analyses. Report to ICL, October, 1989.

[6] Johnson, H and Johnson P. The development of task analysis as a design tool. A methodology for carrying out task analyses. Report to ICL, March 1987.

[7] Bellotti, V. Implications of current design practice for the use of HCI techniques, in: Jones, D.M and Winder, R. (eds.), People and computers IV. (Cambridge University Press, 1988).

[8] Hammond,N., Jorgenson, A., Maclean, A., Barnard, P. and Long, J. Design practice and interface usability: Evidence from interviews with designers. IBM UK Laboratories Report HF 082 August 1983.

[9] Hannigan, S. and Herring, V. , Human factors in office product design - European Practice. 2nd International Conference on Human-Computer Interaction, Hawaii, 1987.

[10] Mantei, M.M. and Teorey, T.J. Cost/benefit analysis for incorporating human factors in the software lifecycle. Communications of the ACM, 31, (1988), 428-43.

[11] Anderson, J. M. The integration of HCI principles in structured system design methods. In Proceedings of Milcomp, September 1988.

[12] Moran, T.P. The command language grammar: A representation for the user interface of interactive computer systems. Journal of Man-Machine Studies, 15, (1981) 3-50.

[13] Card, S.K., Moran, T.P., and Newell, A. The psychology of human computer interaction. Hillsdale, N.J: LEA (1983).

[14] Kieras, D. and Poulson, P. An approach to the formal analysis of user complexity. International Journal of Man Machine Studies, 22, (1985), 365-394.

[15] Johnson, P. Towards a task model of messaging, in: Johnson, P and Cook, S (eds.), People and Computers: Designing the user interface. (Cambridge, Cambridge University Press 1985).

[16] Johnson, P and Johnson, H. Practical and theoretical aspects of human computer interaction. Journal of Information Technology, 3, (1988), 147-161.

[17] Barnard, P. Cognitive resources and the learning of human-computer dialogues, in: Carroll J.M. (ed.) Interfacing thought: Cognitive aspects of human computer interaction. (Cambridge, Mass: MIT Press 1987).

[18] WILSON, M. D., BARNARD, P. and MACLEAN, A. 1986, Task analysis in human computer interaction. IBM Hursley Research Centre Report No HF122.

[19] Johnson, H and Johnson, P. The development of task analysis as a design tool. Designer-identified requirements for task analysis tools. Report to ICL, May, 1989.

Human–Computer Interaction – INTERACT '90
D. Diaper et al. (Editors)
Elsevier Science Publishers B.V. (North-Holland)

AN APPLICATION OF TASK ANALYSIS TO THE DEVELOPMENT OF A GENERIC OFFICE REFERENCE MODEL

Jill HEWITT, John HOBSON, John SAPSFORD-FRANCIS

Hatfield Polytechnic, College Lane, HATFIELD, Herts. AL10 9AB
Tel: 0707 279327 e-mail: comqjah@hatfield.uk.ac

The roles of task analysis in the software engineering life cycle are considered, and a method is described which is suitable for capturing the high level communication tasks in offices. The contribution of this method to the building of a generic office model and its role in the generation of scenarios for future early requirements analysis are discussed.

1. THE GENERIC OFFICE REFERENCE MODEL

Work carried out with the Human Factors Division, British Telecom*, over the past year has led us to the design of a multi-perspective office reference model. It incorporates four views: the high level organisational (goal) view, the task view, the linguistic view and the operational requirements (support services) view. The task analysis described in this paper contributes to this model at the organisational and task levels. The model itself and the interfaces between the views have been described elsewhere (Watkinson 1990). The role of the model is to provide a benchmark for the evaluation of the potential effects of new systems and products in a very early requirements analysis. Scenarios of office activities may be generated from the model, they are used either as the basis for further investigations or to formulate hypotheses about possible future activities in selected areas.

1.1 The Role of Task Analysis

Task Analysis techniques have been shown to be useful in various stages of the Software Engineering Life Cycle. TAKD (Johnson & Diaper 1989) and TKS (Johnson et al. 1988) aim to capture some of the different types of knowledge that are recruited in task behaviour and to provide a generic task model which can be used as the basis for subsequent system design. TKS considers the broader concept of roles, made up of collections of tasks; this concept also plays a major part in the early stages of CORE (SD-Scicon), a more traditional requirements analysis technique, where viewpoints are considered as a starting point of the analysis. Although Sutcliffe (1988 (a)) describes task analysis as synonymous with requirements analysis, there do appear to be major differences between the approaches of (say) TKS and JSD (Sutcliffe 1988 (b)) in that TKS allows for consideration of cognitive tasks, whereas JSD is more concerned with modelling communicating processes and their data.

Other task analysis methods concentrate more on the cognitive limitations of tasks and are employed in the process of interface design; methods such as GOMS (Card et al. 1983) and TAG (Payne & Green 1989) allow for a specification of user-system interaction and provide the designer with a way of evaluating alternatives.

In the context of the generic office model, a method was required that allowed capture of high level task descriptions so that they could be viewed in the context of a company's organisational structure. The more detailed descriptions of user-system actions and the design of any particular new system were not to be considered.

2. THE METHOD

The analysis in this section is based on data collected from a variety of offices, mainly in the form of recorded interviews and conversations with key company personnel.

2.1 The High Level View

The high level view which has been developed seeks to elicit and describe the structure of relationships between task performers (Checkland 1981), and provide a referential framework for further analysis. The basis of the method is the same semi-structured interview used for the more detailed task analysis, enhanced with formal organisation charts, job descriptions and plans of office layout.

The method seeks to create an overall picture of an office environment showing the inter-relationships between the office personnel and the flow of information between them, it thus provides a frame of reference for any subsequent task analysis or systems analysis and gives the essential organisational overview when considering a change to some part of the system.

It is important to be able to relate the analysis back to the original transcript of the semi-structured interview, subsequent analyses can then be more easily cross-related. Figure 1 gives an example of a structure chart developed from a paragraph of transcription which is an interview with an accountant's secretary (Liz) talking about her boss, Alec. This has been used as an example throughout the text.

*Research Project A114929/P (IOD) Hatfield Polytechnic and British Telecom.
Sponsored by: Human Factors Division, British Telecom Research Laboratories, Martlesham Heath, Ipswich IP5 7RE.

Interview 1.
Para 4.
E: *I suppose right he gets the post opens it delegates to whoever his next assistant in line em like he's got someone working for him - em he deals with his own clients. em he'll dish out the post to him and anything general to me that's not worth bothering with ......*

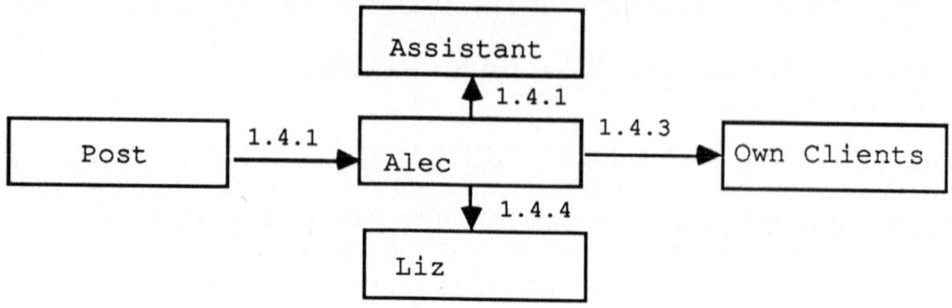

Figure 1. The Structure Chart derived from part of an interview

Cross referencing is provided by the numbering, thus 1.4.3 refers to interview 1, paragraph 4, line 3.

These structure charts give a useful visual overview of the roles of individuals, they can be overlaid to show all the activities relating to an individual, derived perhaps from several interviews. A complete analysis of the office revealed a large number of structures in which Liz was involved, highlighting her pivotal role in the day to day running of the office. They provide a useful mechanism for cross-checking information in any subsequent interviews and can highlight areas of interest where formal and informal structures differ.

These discrepancies between formal and informal structures were found to fall into two categories; the first is a set of tasks which are natural extensions of the job description and are part of a job expansion, for example a secretary using a word processor to create letters where previously a typewriter was used. The second category are tasks which bear no obvious relationship to the job description. This second set of tasks may be further sub-divided into those which would generally be expected to be done by someone less qualified, and those tasks which have developed through some change in the system.

An example of a less-skilled task is that of Alec opening the post; this was seen to be a hang-over from the early days of the office when the first person in opened all the mail, but a closer investigation may discover a covert role in that it provides him with knowledge of the performance of other partners. The role of computer expert undertaken by one of the other partners provides a set of tasks which would not have been included in his job description, but which provide him with a certain amount of control over the administration of the partnership.

Any proposed changes to the office would need to acknowledge such covert control mechanisms if they were to be successfully implemented and it is important that subsequent task analysis takes such possible covert goals into account.

2.2 The Task View

Following the high level structural analysis, a more detailed task analysis is carried out with the aims of: gaining a better insight into the tasks as viewed by individuals, identifying roles as collections of tasks fulfilled by individuals, providing a basis for comparing activities between roles and between companies and providing a generic model against which future requirements models may be compared.

The method used draws on those developed by Diaper and Johnson, but with important differences. In particular, we recommend the incremental building of a generic task model and the maintaining of close references back to the source material; this allows actual data to be used by subsequent scenarios rather than the more sanitised generic items, thus giving them a more 'real' flavour.

The first step is to translate the task performance descriptions into standard 'sentences' of the form:

Performer: Action, On Object (With Object) ,
From/initial state --> To/final state

This standard format allows the controlled inclusion of contextual information, which is critical if one is to make meaningful generifications. The sentences are then grouped by task. From the paragraph given in Figure 1 we can identify the 'sentences' shown in Figure 2.

In the case of this example, the 'with' object is not required, although it does occur in other sentences such as:

liz: send,letter (fax), alec --> client
liz: send,letter (post), alec --> client

The next stage is to build the Generic Task Representations (GTR's), as shown in Figure 3. This may involve the analyst in the inference of some of the sub-tasks, actions and objects, although these should be checked where possible with the task performer. Inferred items are shown in italics in the figure. Some generic terms may be introduced, and new terms added to cope with the inferred structures. Figure 4 shows extracts from a thesaurus which is developed to keep track of generic names their pseudonyms and origins;

```
1.4.1   alec: get, post (_), _ --> alec
        alec: open, post (_), _ --> _
        alec: delegate, post (_), alec --> next-assistant-in-line

1.4.3   alec: deal-with,own-clients (_), _ --> _
        alec: dish-out-to,post (_), alec --> him
        alec: dish-out-to, post-general-not-worth-bothering(_), alec --> me
```

Figure 2.

GTR: Handle incoming post

Plan: Handle Incoming Post (only 1 plan in this case)
Goal: Overt: Sort Incoming Post
Covert: Check progress on cases
Overt Subgoals:
get new post
identify post owner
distribute post
Covert Subgoals:
get new post
identify post owner
scan letter
note progress
distribute post

Subtask: get new post
manager:get, post(_),*post-box* --> self
Subtask: identify post owner
manager:open, post(_),_-->_
manager: read, subject (_),opened_letter --> self
Subtask: scan letter
Subtask: note progress
Subtask: distribute post
Condition: subject is manager's _client
manager: *allocate*, post(_),self-->self
Condition: subject is general_post
manager:*allocate*, post(_),self--> secretary
Condition: default
manager:*allocate*, post(_),self--> *assistant*

Figure 3 A Generic Task Representation

Figure 5 gives an example of the context information that would need to be recorded for each generic task.

Generification is carried out by associating terms that are used in similar ways then finding a generic term that can be substituted for each (Diaper 1989). Because we are dealing with sparse information it may be necessary to infer some generic terms. Thus the generic term 'manager' is substituted for 'Alec' etc. As new analyses are undertaken, the analyst should refer back to generic terms already introduced, adding new ones only where necessary, thus gradually building up the generic model.

Some tasks may be cognitively complex, in these cases the tasks are not analysed further. Such is the case with 'scan letter' and 'note progress'. It is not clear what Alec is looking for nor how he notes progress.

A role consists of a group of Generic Task Representations, so that for an individual we can identify a number of roles. The decision as to which role a task 'belongs' to may be somewhat arbitrary, but roles provide a useful mechanism for comparison across individuals and across companies and allow the construction of a generic role model.

In our analysis of five companies we were able to identify generic roles such as *Typist* (Transcribe Dictation, Copy Typing, Photocopying, Filing and Distributing Documents), and *Personal Assistant* (Arrange Meetings, Answer Phone, Deal with Callers, Reply to General Mail). These roles formed part of the work of each senior secretary interviewed, but they each also played other roles which were not generally applicable, e.g. *Trainer* (of other secretarial staff) or *Database Manager* (of staff cv's). It was thus easier to

Generic Terms	Class Members and Origins
get	(1.4.1)
post	(1.4.1, 1.4.3)
open	(1.4.1)
manager	alec (1.1.1) implied (1.4.1, 1.4.3)
manager's clients	own clients (1.4.3)
post-box	implied (1.4.1)
read	implied (1.4.1)
opened-letter	implied (1.4.1)
subject	implied (1.4.1)
allocate	dish out to (1.4.3), delegate (1.4.1), deal with (1.4.3)
default	implied (1.4.1-2)
assistant	next assistant in line (1.4.2)
general-post	general not worth bothering (1.4.4)
secretary	me (throughout)

Figure 4 Thesaurus

Generic Name	Subtasks
get	get new post
post	get new post, identify post owner, distribute post
open	identify post owner
manager	get new post, identify post owner, distribute post
manager's clients	distribute post
post-box	get new post
read	identify post owner
opened-letter	identify post owner
subject	identify post owner, distribute post
allocate	distribute post
default	distribute post
assistant	disribute post
general-post	distribute post

Figure 5 Context table for the GTR 'Handle Incoming Post'

genericise at the role level than at the job level, although identification of generic jobs is not ruled out.

As the analyses proceed, a generic task model is built up which can be related at the role level to a higher level organisational view and at the task level to the operational requirements (e.g. communication services) needed to support the tasks. A linguistic analysis at the task level can give further information about dialogues which adds to the richness of the generic office model. This model should be used as the starting point for new analyses, thus providing a framework for the first structured interviews and a benchmark for the new analysis. Ideally, the iterations should be repeated until the information gained from a new analysis does not make substantial changes to the generic office model; a stable state thus being reached.

3. SCENARIO BUILDING

As identified in the introduction, the generic office model is to be used in establishing requirements for new systems where actual customers have not yet been identified. We may want to answer such general questions as "What will be the effect of this innovation on an office organisation?" or "What can be built in order to improve this aspect of an office organisation?" In both cases, the generation of a scenario can help to clarify ideas by providing a "snapshot" of activities in the area under review. For example if we were developing an electronic diary management system that could be accessed over the telephone we could extract from the generic office model all those roles containing tasks that were related to scheduling and recording appointments. These could be used to generate a "typical office" scenario involving the use of diaries, which could be enriched by the inclusion of actual dialogues and task information. A hypothesis about the proposed new system could then be made and a new scenario developed to show how the electronic system could be used. This would form the basis of early discussions about the functionality of the proposed system, and would provide valuable metaphors to be used in the design of the first user interface prototype.

4. COMPUTERISATION OF THE ANALYSIS

Carrying out this kind of task analysis for a group of organisations requires continual cross referencing throughout a large body of data. The computerisation of parts of the task analysis process has been considered. The use of a database is favoured for maintaining 'sentences' of actions and objects drawn from the interview material as well as the thesaurus and context table. This should allow sophisticated questions that can extract, for example, all instances of the use of a particular object or a particular action. This should help considerably in the generification process.

The use of a Hypermedia environment would allow data to be stored in its original form giving easy access for researchers to browse through it, perhaps listening to recorded material or viewing photographs of office layout.

We are also investigating the possibility of setting up a simulation of parts of the model. This would provide an important check on the completeness and consistency of the model and greatly facilitate the process of scenario building and testing.

5. CONCLUSIONS

We have developed a method of task analysis that contributes to the multi-perspective office reference model whilst maintaining useful links back to the source data to enable realistic scenarios to be evoked. This approach has required the development of new procedures and notations. The use of a standard 'sentence' as a contextual structure for actions and their objects makes it possible to generify actions and objects using limited context. The brevity and consistency of the 'sentence' improves its comprehensibility. Our approach provides support for searching and cross referencing in the generification process.

6. REFERENCES

Card S, Moran T, Newell A, (1983). The Psychology of Human Computer Interaction, Lawrence Erlbaum Associates, Hillsdale, New Jersey.

Checkland P, (1981). Systems thinking, Systems Practice, Wiley.

CORE - SD-Scicon, Pembroke House, Pembroke Broadway, Camberley, Surrey, GU15 3XD.

Diaper D. (1989) Task Analysis for Human-Computer Interaction Chapter 4. Ellis Horwood.

Johnson P, Diaper D, (1989). Task Analysis for Knowledge Descriptions: Theory and Application in Training. in Cognitive Ergonomics.Long & Whitefield (eds.)

Johnson P., Johnson H, Waddington R, & Shouls A, (1988) Task Related Knowledge Structures : Analysis, Modelling and Application, in People & Computers IV, Jones D, & Winder R (eds) Cambridge University Press.

Payne S.J. & Green T.R.G. (1989) ,Task Action Grammar: the model and its developments in Task Analysis for Human-Computer Interaction Diaper D (ed), Ellis Horwood.

Sutcliffe A, (1988) Human-Computer Interaction. MacMillan

Sutcliffe A, (1988) Jackson System Development. Prentice Hall.

Watkinson N, (1990) A Multi-Perspective Office Reference Model, Human Factors Division, British Telecom - Internal Report.

Human–Computer Interaction – INTERACT '90
D. Diaper et al. (Editors)
Elsevier Science Publishers B.V. (North-Holland)

MEMORY-COGNITION-ACTION TABLES: A PRAGMATIC APPROACH TO ANALYTICAL MODELLING.

Brian Sharratt

Logica Cambridge Ltd, Betjeman House, 104 Hills Road, Cambridge, CB2 1LQ, England.
(Phone: +44-223-66343 E-mail: brian@logcam.co.uk)

Current analytical models have a number of practical problems - they use complex notations, produce very detailed task descriptions and tend to be difficult to use for anything other than small examples. This paper describes a simple analytical model based on multi-columed tables, called Memory-Cognition-Action (MCA) tables which is used to address these problems. The paper concentrates on the production of MCA tables and the analytic metrics derived from these tables. The metrics cover task complexity, cognitive processing and task consistency and can be used to locate potential user problems in the task structure. Features of the MCA tables such as their extendability, reusability and handling of task closure are discussed.

1. INTRODUCTION

Key elements in the design, development and evaluation of computer interfaces are the range of tasks supported by the interface and the user actions associated with these tasks. Usually the tasks identified during the initial requirements analysis become woven into the interface design process and often form the basis for subsequent evaluations of the prototyped interface. The HCI research concerned with user tasks has addressed two issues:

- Task Analysis - where then user's real-world tasks are decomposed into ordered sets of sub-tasks [9,10];
- Cognitive Task Modelling - where a representation of the tasks from the user's perspective is constructed which reflects the task/interface knowledge required and the sequencing of physical and cognitive actions to perform the tasks [4,5].

A wide variety of cognitive task models have been developed (see [14]) and the potential and actual rôles of these models in interface design is attracting some interest [1].

The term "analytical model" has been introduced by Butler et al [1] and refers to a model (typically a cognitive task model) which can be used by a designer to examine the potential usability of a particular interface design and assist in making design decisions. According to them an idealised analytical model would "take some form of representation of the design as input, and then provide the designer with output in the form of estimates of user response to that design " ([1], pp.65). Current practice falls a long way short of this situation and various problems have been encountered when trying to use current cognitive task models as basic analytical models. This paper addresses some of these problems, in particular those associated with the description of user tasks in a cognitive task models and what estimates of task operation can be made using those models.

When using a cognitive task model as an analytical model there are production and feedback problems. On the production side, using a cognitive task model can be a complex and demanding exercise. Kieras [7] has noted the difficulties in constructing cognitive task models based on production rule formalisms and has likened it to programming in assembler language. Sharratt [12] analysed a design exercise involving a multi-layered cognitive task model and noted the high complexity and error-proneness of the task models produced. The cognitive task models which are relatively easy to use are restricted to short component tasks that may have a timeframe of about 5-20 seconds and contain a very simplistic representation of cognitive activity, e.g the unit tasks and single mental operator used in the Keystroke-Level Model [3]. On the feedback side, a variety of analytic metrics have been derived from different cognitive task models, however, these metrics tend to summarise potential user performance (usually in terms of task execution or learning time, e.g. [7]) and are of limited use for locating specific problems in the design or comparing design alternatives (see [11], p.350).At present the benefits and cost-effectiveness of analytical models are open to debate (see [1]).

This paper presents a cognitive task model that is relatively simple to construct and which contains details of the cognitive activity occurring within specified tasks. The model is represented as a series of multi-columed tables, where each task is placed in a separate table and the columns deal with different types of task activity. These columns cover the user's memory operations, cognitive operations and physical actions and the tables are referred to Memory-Cognition-Action (MCA) tables. The following sections describe how MCA tables were derived from research on cognitive task models, provide examples of MCA tables, indicate important aspects of the tables and discuss the various analytic metrics which can be calculated.

2. ORIGINS OF MCA TABLES

The present model was based on two sources. Specific

features contained in the Natural GOMS Language (NGOMSL - [7]) were used in conjunction with some general features taken from Moran's Command Language Grammar (CLG - [8]). The two features extracted from the NGOMSL approach were: (i) a standard set of physical and cognitive operators, which form the building blocks for tasks descriptions; and (ii) the use of decision points embedded in the task sequence. The more general features taken from CLG were the layering of the model, with task descriptions at different levels of abstraction, and the emphasis on procedural task descriptions.

When using these features care was taken to avoid some of the practical problems associated with CLG and NGOMSL. In the case of CLG, the person using it is faced with a complex syntax and has to construct a multi-level structure where the task descriptions at each level are preceded by lengthy declarations of all the objects and actions used at that level. NGOMSL provides a much simpler structure and syntax, however, its main drawback is that it leads to a very fragmented description of cognitive and physical actions (NGOMSL produces a decomposition of task goals into a hierarchy of sub-goals with short sequences of user actions attached to these sub-goals).

The general approach taken in the development of MCA tables was to make them easier to construct: (i) by focussing on task procedures; (ii) by altering the balance between declaration and description; and (iii) by adopting a tabular format. In MCA tables the need for a long declaration process is avoided as they use a standard set of cognitive and physical operators (to which new operators can be added if necessary) and a separate list for the objects used in the task descriptions is produced as the task description develops. The tabular format has a number of advantages in terms of:

- Flexible Construction - the starting point for task descriptions can be either physical, cognitive or memory components;
- Linkage of Task Components - the tables illustrate how different types of components are linked together to create task descriptions;
- Indication of Task Complexity - the tables provide a direct indication where task complexity occurs and what it is producing it.

3. PRODUCTION OF MCA TABLES

The production of a cognitive task model relies on an initial task analysis of the user's activity at the interface. In many cases the task analysis is hierarchical nature and consists of an iterative process where tasks are identified, placed in an operational sequence and decomposed into more detailed sub-tasks (see [13]). The production of MCA tables fits in well with hierarchical task analysis (HTA). One useful feature of MCA tables is that they are suitable for three levels of task in a HTA, and can be used to represent:

- Decomposition Tasks - the breakdown the overall task into tasks executed at the interface (the top one or two levels of the task hierarchy);
- Main Tasks - the series of task performed at the interface (the middle of the task hierarchy);
- Sub-tasks - the basic repetitive tasks associated with interface use, such as menu selection and window scrolling (the bottom level of the task hierarchy).

To illustrate these three task levels Figure 1 shows part of a task hierarchy for the creation of a one-page flyer containing boxed text and lines using MacDraw™.

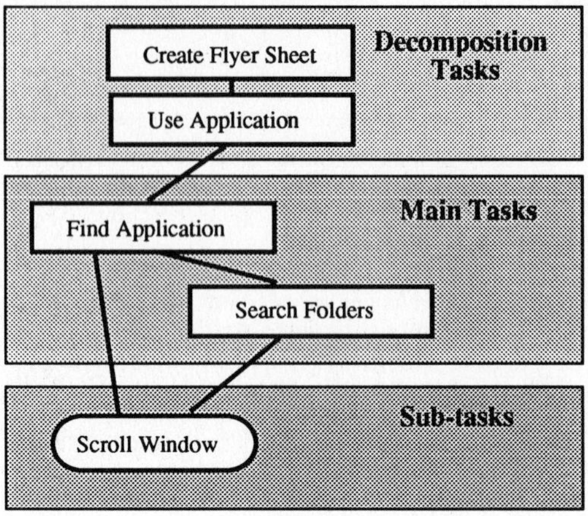

Figure 1

These three types of task use two types of MCA table. The decomposition tasks are simply represented by simplified MCA tables that have a title bar (containing the task name and a statement of the task goal) followed by an ordered list of tasks (either further decomposition tasks or main tasks). The main tasks and sub-tasks are represented by full MCA tables which have a title bar followed by separate columns for memory, cognitive and physical actions. The set of operators used in these columns are derived from Kieras [7], with the addition of physical operators taken from the Keystroke-Level Model [3] and cognitive operators taken from CLG (i.e. *Look* and *Read*).

Following NGOMSL a very simple memory model is used for the actions in the memory column - items are stored in either Long Term Memory (LTM), which is a permanent memory store, or Working Memory (WM), which is a temporary store used for items for the current task and related sub-tasks. The use of WM requires explicit operations, i.e. items are placed in WM (Retain operator), taken from WM for use (Recall operator) or removed when no longer needed (Forget operator). Another noticeable feature of the MCA tables are the use of optional operator sequences. These sequences are incorporated into the MCA tables via decision points placed in the cognitive actions column and, to aid identification, these optional sequences are boxed in. Figure 2 presents the MCA table for the Find Application task shown in Figure 1.

The actual construction of an MCA table is relatively straightforward process. Usually the process starts with the physical actions needed for the task and these are prefaced by their immediate cognitive actions. These cognitive actions can be viewed as the instructions given to the user before they perform the physical actions, e.g. looking at the screen for a particular icon before moving the cursor to select that icon. The memory operators are then added to "glue" the task sequence together by recalling and storing the items needed by the cognitive and physical operations.

Task: Find Application Goal: Find chosen application in file structure on Macintosh		
MEMORY	COGNITION	ACTION
Recall LTM (AN; HDI)		
Retain WM (AN; HDI)		
Recall WM (HDI)		
	Look at (desktop) for (HDI)	
		Home to mouse
		Move cursor to (result of look)
		Double click mouse
Forget WM (HDI)		[closure point]
Recall WM (AN)		
	Look at (window) for (AN)	
	Decide:	
	IF (AN present) THEN	
	(end task) END	[closure point]
Recall LTM (scroll bar & elevator)		
	Look at (window) for (scroll bar & elevator)	
	Decide:	
	IF (elevator present and not at bottom of scroll bar) THEN	
Retain WM (elevator posn)		
		Sub-task Scroll Window
	(goto Recall WM (AN)	
	ELSE	
		Main Task Search Folders
	END	
	END TASK	[closure point]

Key AN - Application Name HDI - Hard Disc Icon
WM - Working Memory LTM - Long Term Memory

Figure 2

To ensure consistency in the location of memory operators a set of five rules are used. These rules determine where memory operators are sited and they place limits on the use of items recalled from WM (see Table 1). These memory location rules guide the process of recalling items from LTM when they are needed for certain tasks and using them to support particular cognitive and physical actions. In practice rule 5 is the most difficult to apply as the task sequence has to be 'chunked' into sequences that require related memory items and task closure points placed between these chunks. How this task chunking is done depends very much on the nature of the tasks represented in the MCA tables.

A secondary process accompanies the production of the MCA tables in which the task objects are listed. This list contains the object's name, its properties (i.e the effects physical operations on that object) and other objects with a functional connection to that object (e.g. pull-down menus are connected to the object "menu-bar"). The task object list is then used for the task consistency calculations briefly described in section 5.

4. FEATURES OF MCA TABLES

Three interesting features of the MCA tables are:

4.1. Task Closure

Task closure refers to the points in a task where it can be easily suspended before completion and the point (or points) where the task is eventually completed. These task closure points provide some flexibility for users so that they can deal with interruptions (such as phone calls or visitors), have rest breaks during the task or switch to another concurrent task (see [2], for an interface which supports task switching). Whilst the need for task closure has been stressed in the guidelines literature (e.g. [16]) there have been few attempts to locate closure points within task descriptions. Some cognitive task models, such as NGOMSL, contain implicit closure points when each of the task's sub-goals are satisfied.

The MCA tables contain explicit closure points linked to either task completion or the Forget operator. These closure points provide the main sites for task interruption or switching and show the potential fragmentation of the task. Furthermore, the cost of task interruption or switching can be assessed in terms of the items requiring retention in WM or repeated operator sequences needed to re-establish the task state and WM contents.

4.2. Extendability

The present format can be extended by adding further columns to the MCA tables or connecting with other multi-columned notations. Two columns can be added to reflect the occurrence of task dependent and design dependent components in the task tables. Task dependent components deal with how the tasks are structured make best use of the functionality of the interface, e.g. the use of keyboard shortcuts to avoid dialogue boxes or menus. Design dependent

Rule 1	Use Recall LTM at start of task or when sub-task is about to be used to recall all items needed in task (usually 2-4 items).
Rule 2	Recall LTM is usually followed by Retain WM so that items are stored prior to use in task or sub-task.
Rule 3	Recall LTM can be used directly as a single item recall (i.e. item recalled and used in next operation), but groups of task related items are put into WM and then recalled as required. Single item recall is used for main operational features of interface, e.g. window scroll bars.
Rule 4	When Recall WM is used the items recalled are only available for 2 subsequent cognitive or physical operations. (In practice Recall WM often preceeds physical actions or Look operator).
Rule 5	Forget WM is used to clear items from WM on point of closure in task (closure occurs when WM items are no longer required due to unrelated set of actions being started or end of task being reached).

Table 1

components deal with assumptions occurring in the task sequence concerning the presence and operation of specific interface features, e.g. in a direct manipulation interface a "hand" tool to move screen contents would be assumed to operate using smooth scroll and not jump scroll action [2].

In terms of other notations, MCA tables have a clear connection with the multi-columned User Action Notation (UAN - [15]). MCA tables are concerned with the memory and cognitive operations driving physical actions and UAN starts with physical actions and covers the interface feedback and system state. An interesting feature of MCA and UAN are the differences in notation for physical actions. UAN uses a heavily abbreviated action notation and parameterisies the physical actions to show the system dependent features of the input [6]. In contrast, MCA tables provide textual descriptions of physical actions without parameterisation as the other columns provide direct indication of input needed for the current task. Despite notational differences, linking MCA and UAN is relatively straightforward.

4.3. Reusability

With current analytic models it is often difficult to assess the effort required to generate a new task description for a different task or interface application, i.e. their reusability is unclear. The MCA tables have a high degree of reusability owing to their tabular format and the separation of main and sub-tasks. Dividing the task structure into a series of tables means that the task sections which can be reused are more easily identified - sometimes whole tables can be reused and other may require only minor modifications. As for sub-tasks, they describe the basic features of the interface style being used and can be adopted by other tasks/applications sharing that style. For example, in Figure 2 the sub-task Scroll Window can be used by other Macintosh™ tasks or applications.

5. METRICS FROM MCA TABLES

Using the MCA tables analytic metrics for task structure/performance, cognitive processing and interface comparison can be derived. The important feature of these metrics is the use of the decision points embedded in the tables to calculate the minimum and maximum paths through the task tables. To calculate the maximum path various assumptions have to be made concerning task components (e.g. the maximum number of folders searched when finding a particular application) and cognitive components (e.g. whether the location of a menu item is forgotten and how many menus have to be searched to find it). The metrics used are:

Task Complexity	the number of operators in the minimum and maximum paths;
Performance Time	the performance time for both paths (the time values for the different operators are derived from Card et al ,[4]);
Cognitive Load	the percentage of task time spent in memory and cognitive operations for both paths;
Memory Load	the number of items in working memory for both paths (taking into account the use of Forget operators in task sequences);
Task Consistency	indicates the percentage change in operator sequence and task objects when the MCA tables are applied to the same tasks on another interface or a different version of the same interface (this metric is based on the consistency measure used by Kieras, [7]).

To get a more detailed picture, a task-metric table is constructed which contains the metric values for each MCA table in the task hierarchy. From the task-metric table the "blackspots" in the task structure can be identified, the efficiency of sub tasks can be considered and special features (such as default values and consistency) can be examined. The blackspots are places where the performance time and memory loads are high for minimum paths and there is a large difference between the maximum and minimum task complexity values. Once identified, the contribution of task and cognitive components to these blackspots can be assessed. The sub-tasks are an important interface element as the efficient use of the interface depends on them having short, fast-executing task sequences (see [7]). Default values are usually indicated by high cognitive loads for minimum task paths (i.e. the task sequence contains little physical action) and the effects of changing these values are shown in the maximum path metrics. Finally, the potential ease-of-transfer between different applications and interfaces are covered by the task consistency metrics.

In the present approach, the two path lengths form limiting values for the MCA tables, the assumptions indicate how the task reaches its maximum complexity and the metrics measure various aspects of task use. Using the task-metric table specific problem areas can be identified and their underlying roots in either task structure, interface operation or cognitive features can be identified.

6. CONCLUSIONS

The majority of current analytical models use complex notations, produce very detailed task descriptions and tend to be difficult to use for anything other than small examples. The aim of the present approach was to provide a notation that has expressive power, can be applied to real tasks and is easy to use. In MCA tables the multi-columned format captures the procedural detail of tasks and forms a basis for various analytic metrics and further consideration of task dependent and interface dependent components. The metric-task tables not only summarise potential user performance at different levels in the task hierarchy but also enable the location of potential problems in the task structure. Current work with MCA tables has addressed task transfer between Macintosh™ drawing applications, such as MacDraw™ and Illustrator™, and future research includes: the refinement of metrics, especially consistency metrics; the application of MCA tables to concurrent user tasks and task switching; and study of the connection between task structures and interface design features.

ACKNOWLEDGEMENTS

The research reported in this paper was supported by Alvey

Grant GR/D 42412 and undertaken at Scottish HCI Centre. My thanks go to Rex Hartson and colleagues at the Scottish HCI Centre for their helpful comments during the refinement of the MCA tables.

FOOTNOTES

MacDraw™ is a trademark of Apple Computer Inc.
[2] It may be noted that the hand tool in MacDraw™ uses smooth scroll whereas the same tool in Adobe Illustrator™ uses a jump scroll action.

REFERENCES

[1] Butler, K., Bennett, J., Polson, P. and Karat, J. Report on the workshop on analytic models: predicting the complexity of human-computer interaction, SIGCHI Bull., 1989, 20(4), pp.63-79.

[2] Card, S.K. and Henderson, A. A multiple, virtual-workspace interface to support user task switching. In Carroll, J.M. and Tanner, P.P. Proc. CHI+GI 1987 (ACM Pubs., 1987) pp.53-60.

[3] Card, S.K., Moran, T.P. and Newell, A. The keystroke-level model for user performance with interactive systems, Comm ACM, 1980, 23, pp396-410.

[4] Card, S.K., Moran, T.P. and Newell, A. The Psychology of Human-Computer Interaction (Erlbaum, Hillsdale) 1983.

[5] Carroll, J.M. and Olsen, J.R. Mental models in HCI, In Helander, M. (ed) Handbook of Human-Computer Interaction (North-Holland, Amsterdam, 1988) 1988, pp.45-65.

[6] Hartson, R.H. Personal communication, April 1989.

[7] Kieras, D.E. Towards a practical GOMS model methodology for user interface design. In Helander, M. (ed) Handbook of Human-Computer Interaction (North-Holland, Amsterdam, 1988) pp.135-173.

[8] Moran, T.P. The Command Language Grammar: a representation for the user interface of interactive computer systems. Int. J. Man-Machine Studies, 1981, 15, pp.3-50.

[9] Olsen, J.R. Cognitive analysis of people's use of software. In Carroll, J.M. (ed) Interfacing Thought (MIT Press, London, 1988) pp.260-293.

[10] Phillips, M.D., Bashinski, H.S., Ammerman, H.L. and Fligg, C.M. A task analytic approach to Dialogue Design. In Helander, M. (ed) Handbook of Human-Computer Interaction (North-Holland, Amsterdam, 1988) pp.835-857.

[11] Reisner, P. Discussion: HCI, what is it and what research is needed? In Carroll, J.M. (ed) Interfacing Thought (MIT Press, London, 1988) pp.337-352.

[12] Sharratt, B.D. Top-down interactive systems design: some lessons learnt from using Command Language Grammar, In Bullinger, H.J. and Shackel, B. (eds) Proceedings INTERACT'87 (North-Holland, Amsterdam, 1987) pp.395-399.

[13] Shepherd, A. Hierarchical task analysis and training decisions, Programmed Learning and Education, 1985, 22, pp.162-176.

[14] Simon, T. Analysing the scope of cognitive models in HCI: a trade-off approach. In Jones, D.M. and Winder, R. People and Computers IV (Cambridge University Press, Cambridge, 1988) pp.79-93.

[15] Siochi, A.C. and Hartson, H.R. Task-orientated representation of asynchronous user interfaces. In Proc. CHI'89, ACM Pubs, 1989.

[16] Smith, S.L. and Mosier, J.N. Guidelines for designing user interface software, Technical Report ESD-TR-86-278, Mitre Corp., Massachusetts, 1986.

Human–Computer Interaction - INTERACT '90
D. Diaper et al. (Editors)
Elsevier Science Publishers B.V. (North-Holland)

Analysing Focused Interview Data with Task Analysis for Knowledge Descriptions (TAKD)

Dr. Dan Diaper

Department of Computer Science, University of Liverpool, P.O. Box 147, Liverpool L69 3BX, United Kingdom.

While Task Analysis for Knowledge Descriptions (TAKD) is now a reasonably well established task analysis method, its use to date, in the published literature, has been principally concerned with the analysis of observational data from task performance exercises. The paper describes the use, in an industrial context, of TAKD to organise data from interviews, albeit where there was a focus on the interviewees' tasks and subtasks.

Keywords: Task Analysis, Interview Data, Automatic Test Equipment.

1. Introduction

In the early 1980s, Task Analysis for Knowledge Descriptions (**TAKD**) was first developed to provide a specification of the knowledge that 16 year old trainees needed to acquire about Information Technology (**IT**) on the United Kingdom's one year Youth Training Scheme (Johnson, Diaper and Long, 1984; 1985; Diaper and Johnson, 1989). The knowledge specified in the developed syllabus was based on the observation of relevant IT tasks that such trainees might be expected to be competent to perform after training. TAKD has subsequently been developed and used for system design (Johnson, Diaper and Long, 1985), electronic mail interface design (Johnson, 1985), message system requirements (Diaper, 1988), hypertext document annotation system requirements (Diaper, 1989a), and collaborative authoring system requirements (Rogers, 1989). While TAKD is quite a complex method, its basic analytical stages have been described with some completeness (Diaper, 1988; 1989a), as have the methods of acquiring observational data for analysis (Diaper, 1989b).

All of the above applications of TAKD have involved data from the observation of people carrying out tasks. While many of these studies have also recorded verbal data in either concurrent protocols, or from post-task walkthroughs of video recorded task sessions, none have used only verbal data as a source for analysis. Given that interview data is the other main source of data in Human-Computer Interaction (**HCI**) research, and is nearly always available even when the main data capture method is observational, then it would be highly desirable for both interview and observational data to be representable, following analysis, in a single format. This paper describes how TAKD is able to represent interview data in the same manner as it represents data from task observation. However, the current work used interviews that were focused on task performance, although a considerable amount of non-task information was also collected. The paper includes a demonstration of how at least one class of such non-task data can be accommodated in the output from TAKD.

2. Introduction to TAKD

A reasonably complete description of the TAKD method can be found in Diaper (1989a). TAKD starts with a written input, an activity list, that contains a prose description of the activities carried out by an observed task performer. Data is extracted from this description in the form of *specific objects* and *specific actions*. Specific actions are behaviours carried out by the task performer using the specific objects. Specific objects may be physical objects such as a screwdriver, a mouse, a QWERTY keyboard or specific keys on a keyboard, screen contents (text, graphics, etc.) or informational objects such as files, programs, etc. The output from this initial stage of TAKD is thus two lists: (i) *The Specific Action List* (**SAL**); and (ii) *The Specific Object List* (**SOL**). Experience indicates that the SOL is generally much larger than the SAL.

The primary analytical phase consists of building a *Task Descriptive Hierarchy* (**TDH**) and is the major step in TAKD that relies on the subjective expertise of the task analyst. The main effort has previously been with the SOL and the TDH. A TDH possesses levels of generality: at the lowest level are the SOL members (usually shown on the right of the TDH); at the highest level, are a few, easily identified, *generic objects*. These highest level generic objects are easy to identify, given that the purpose of the analysis is known (i.e. the type of system and its functionality have been approximately decided) as they are few in number and at far too high a level of description to be useful. The TDH is constructed by the task analyst working in both a bottom–up and a top–down manner. The TDH provides a description that allows a single path to be plotted through the TDH from every low level specific object to a single high level object.

There are three types of logical relationship that are possible at a level in a TDH: (i) XOR; (ii) AND; and (iii) OR. The XOR relationship is the most frequently used and denotes that an object is either one thing or another. AND relationships tend to be used most frequently at the higher levels of the TDH to denote several properties possessed by all objects, whereas the OR relationship tends to be used at the lower levels to mark that an object may possess a subset of several properties. The TDH representation, while developed independently, thus resembles that of Systemic Grammar Networks (Johnson, 1989; Halliday, 1978; Bliss et al., 1983), but with additional descriptive power provided by the three logical relationship types. The final stage in constructing a TDH, once it has been tested to ensure that every specific object does possess a single route through the hierarchy from lowest to highest level, is to align the levels so that similar levels of generality are matched. Thus in some paths levels may be skipped (e.g. See Figure 1 `INSPECT` and `REPAIR`). Furthermore, while called a hierarchy, a TDH is not a true one as nodes may be repeated at a level, typically where OR relationships are used.

While it is usual to use the SOL when building a TDH, it is possible to use the SAL instead. Rogers (1989), for example, used TAKD to examine individual and collaborative authoring where the only objects were pen and paper and a TDH was successfully constructed using the SAL alone. Usually, however, the SAL is sufficiently brief that higher level generic actions can be readily identified and these are usually appended directly to the highest levels of the TDH. Diaper (1989a) used only a single generic action (mark text) when analysing annotation behaviour on paper documents and in the syllabus design work (e.g. Diaper and Johnson, 1989) only 11 generic actions were required across a range of tasks from microelectronics to programming and automated office applications of IT.

While not relevant to the interview analysis reported later in this paper, one of the strengths of TAKD is that an analytical method is available that allows the graphical representation of the TDH to be converted in to a more useful notation for statistical analysis. Each route from specific object to highest level generic entity can be represented by a sentence in a Knowledge Representation Grammar (**KRG**). Once complete, the representation of a TDH as a set of KRG sentences is automatic and requires no intelligence. A tool is currently being designed to fully automate this process and the subsequent statistical tests that may be applied either to full KRG sentences or generic KRG sentences, (produced by truncating the lower levels of the TDH).

3. TAKD with Interview Data

While this paper describes only a quarter of the results collected, this is sufficient to illustrate how TAKD can be used on interview data and doesn't compromise commercial confidentiality.

3.1 Background to the Study

Racal Automation Ltd. (**RAL**) manufacture a range of Automatic Test Equipment (**ATE**) for both military and civil use. Each ATE may cost up to £1M, typically there may be up to 50 ATE units of a particular type produced and the life expectancy of each unit may be in the order of 20 years. However, RAL's current family of ATE are based, for a number of goods reasons, on conventional technology and RAL have plans to launch a new generation of ATE, using state-of-the-art technology, in the near future. The author was commissioned to carry out a pilot study using RAL employees to uncover and systematise the believed nature of this new generation of ATE. RAL were interested in ATE interface specification, although it was agreed that it would be necessary to identify both current ATE problems and issues and also the desired functionality of the next generation ATE prior to providing an interface specification.

There were also several secondary motivations to the pilot project. First, RAL were interested in task analysis and particularly in TAKD. Second, the study provided an opportunity for the author to acquire a knowledge of ATE prior to embarking on a larger study. Third, the author was interested in extending the scope of TAKD.

In the negotiations involved in setting up the study it was decided that four classes of personnel would be interviewed with respect to their ATE related work: (i) operators; (ii) maintenance and service engineers; (iii) programmers; and (iv) marketing staff. The latter were included as the first ATE product of the next generation is to be a demonstrator ATE to be used by the marketing staff to obtain orders for the new style ATE. The demonstrator would also allow RAL to test new interface and ATE functionality options quickly and cheaply without the considerable expense associated with developing a full ATE.

The only source of data for this pilot study was to be interviews conducted by the author with RAL personnel, or personnel attached to RAL (e.g. military personnel on the Test Package Evaluation and Advisory Team).

3.2 Data Collection

Twelve interviews were conducted over a three day period, with each interview lasting between 1 and 2 hours. Interviewer and interviewee sat at the same side of a large desk in a quiet room. The interviews were recorded on a high quality stereo cassette recorder and the interviewer made extensive notes during the interview. The notes, which the interviewee could see, and which were often immediately read back by the interviewer to check their correctness, were the major data source; the audio recording was only used to disambiguate notes during the subsequent data extraction and analysis phases.

The style of interview used was unstructured but focused (Cordingley, 1989). The interviewer had thirteen prepared questions. The first four were about the interviewee and were in part intended to allow the interviewee to get settled into the interview. Questions 5 and 6, 7 and 8, and 9 and 10 were identical in form and were targeted at ATE operator's, maintenance engineers, and ATE programmers respectively. Normally, only one set of these paired questions were used per interviewee and answering them formed the bulk of the interview session. The question pairs, particularly the latter, focused on the relevant ATE personnel's tasks and the interviewer was provided with a set of prompts about the sort of content that should be covered by the interviewee in answering the question.

The two questions for the ATE operator, for example, were:

5. *"What sort of person is an ATE operator?"* (General background, qualifications and training, personality, intelligence, life goals, sex).

6. *"A UUT (Unit Under Test) has been mounted on an ATE - describe what are the critical steps performed by the ATE operator. Start at the beginning of the task. Don't get bogged down with the fine details of current ATE. If you like we can work on a diagram/flow chart together."* (What does the operator do?, What decisions does he make?, What does he have to know?, What ATE output does he want?, What are his options?, What happens if the ATE is faulty?).

Question 11, used with marketing staff interviewees, concerned what functionality was needed for a next generation ATE demonstrator and how such demonstrators should be used.

Question 12, which was put to all interviewees, as was question 13, asked "Describe what your future, ideal ATE would be like" and interviewees here were encouraged to provided a *"wish list"* for ATE.

Question 13 asked "Is there anything else that you would like to say that you feel has not been covered in this interview?". Here, interviewees were encouraged to fill in gaps they felt they had left in answering the paired questions and to allow them to expose any other ATE issues that they were particularly concerned about.

The interviews went very smoothly and the interviewer's main problem was restraining the responses from interviewees, so as to maintain focus and relevance in the time available. The interviewees were generally willing to take part in the exercise because they saw the research as an opportunity to influence their future working life and many of them appreciated the chance to talk about their work unencumbered by considerations of company policy or practices. The interviewees were not identified with particular points in the final report to RAL.

3.3. Data Extraction

The interviewer's notes, with occasional help from the audio recordings, were used to cumulatively (i.e. combining data across interviewees) construct four data sets, one for each of the four types of ATE personnel. Three main classes of important data were extracted: (i) a list of tasks; (ii) descriptions of the steps in particular tasks (an activity list); and (iii) a task improvement suggestions list, or wish list.

The following typical, but briefer than usual, task description of the ATE operator's task was provided by one interviewee:

connect UUT
select jig (test interface adaptor)
login in to ATE
select ATP (program) for UUT
run ATP (Automatic Test Program)
select output option
read screen instructions
probe at UUT test points
read/check probe output
select/confirm output options
IF fault run diagnostic ATP and repeat to locate fault
repair
retest UUT to pass
disconnect UUT
logout ATE

Each of these steps, of course, was further expanded in detail during the interviews, although this level of detail is sufficient for many purposes for those who have an understanding of ATE operations.

The same interviewee provided the following task improvement suggestions for the ATE operator:
UUT easy to connect – use non-compatible connectors
User profile at login (3 levels – novice, intermediate and expert) selected automatically – can be changed by the operator later in software
Hierarchy of diagnostic ATPs selected by operator or from login profile

3.4 Data Analysis

There were two stages to the analysis of the data extracted from the interviews. The first stage used TAKD and involved the construction of a TDH which could then be used to redescribe in a common format the task steps represented in the activity lists. The second stage involved the task improvement suggestions, which were mapped on to the TDH, so as to provide an organising principle for what was otherwise a set of four unstructured lists.

3.4.1 TDH Construction

A generic TDH, missing the lowest level nodes, was constructed in parallel with constructing each of the four TDHs; one for each class of ATE personnel. Figure 1 shows the TDH constructed for the ATE operators. The generic TDH, which is common to all four specific TDHs is represented by nodes in upper case. In the case of this research project, the upper 5 levels of the TDH consist of actions which become more specific as the hierarchy is descended. The only logical operator required to connect nodes was the XOR function, which is usually the one most commonly used in TDHs. As is usual with TDH construction, it was ensured that every element in the activity list was redescribed by a single route through the TDH. Each of these routes can be expressed as a KRG sentence and thus the activity lists can themselves be redescribed in the common format of KRG sentences.

Figure 1. TDH for ATE Operators.

```
ACT
|__PHYSICAL ACTIONS
|  |__TO ATE
|  |  |__MANUAL
|  |  |  |__CONNECT/DISCONNECT
|  |  |  |  |__jig  (1 9 20)
|  |  |  |  |__probes
|  |  |  |  |__uut
|  |  |  |
|  |  |  |__TURN ON/OFF
|  |  |  |  |__ate
|  |  |  |
|  |  |  |__LOAD
|  |  |     |__floppy discs
|  |  |
|  |  |__KEYBOARD
|  |     |__COMMANDS
|  |     |  |__login/out  (2)
|  |     |  |__run stp  (8)
|  |     |  |__run atp
|  |     |
|  |     |__SINGLE KEY/MOUSE
|  |        |__menu option
|  |        |__probe located
|  |        |__confirm
|  |
|  |__ELECTRICAL
|     |__TEST
|     |  |__LOCATE PROBES
|     |  |  |__ate probes  (21)
|     |  |
|     |  |__ADJUST
|     |
|     |__REPAIR (REMOVE/REPLACE)
|        |_____boards
|        |_____board components
|        |_____wires
|        |_____connectors
|
|__COGNITIVE ACTIONS
   |__PERCEPTUAL
   |  |__READ
   |  |  |__SCREEN  (13)
   |  |  |  |__instructions  (12 14 15
   |  |  |  |__option menus          16 22)
   |  |  |  |__help
   |  |  |  |__diagnostics  (18 19)
   |  |  |  |__stp error reports
   |  |  |  |__probe readings  (4 11)
   |  |  |
   |  |  |__OTHER
   |  |  |__PAPER
   |  |     |__repair request
   |  |     |__uut label
   |  |     |__inspection chart
   |  |     |__probe point diagram
   |  |     |__pin numbers  (23)
   |  |     |__repair instructions
   |  |     |__help
   |  |     |__circuit diagrams  (10)
   |  |     |__special procedures
```

```
|  |
|  |__INSPECT
|      |_____uut
|      |_____wires
|      |_____connectors
|      |_____boards
|      |_____components
|
|__CONGNITIVE
   |__INTELLECTUAL
   |  |__IDENTIFY
   |  |  |__uut
   |  |  |__uut requirements
   |  |  |__are requirements
   |  |
   |  |__SELECT
   |  |  |__floppy discs
   |  |  |__programs
   |  |  |__program modules  (3 5)
   |  |  |__menu options
   |  |
   |  |__DIAGNOSE
   |  |__UNDERSTAND/SOLVE
   |
   |__SOCIAL
      |__WRITE/PRINT
      |  |__uut inspection certificate
      |  |__fault log
      |  @__logs  (6 7)
      |
      |__DISCUSS
```

3.4.2 Suggestions Analysis Organisation

The complete list of suggestions for each of the four ATE personnel types were, wherever possible, appended to the appropriate TDH's lower nodes. These are represented by numbers on the left for the ATE operator's TDH in Figure 1. Thus the TDH provided a method of organising the unstructured improvement suggestions lists and demonstrates how the task focused TAKD analysis, represented by the TDHs, can be used for the analysis of non-task orientated data gathered from interviews.

In a few cases the suggestions list items could not be appended to the appropriate TDH. There were two classes for such suggestions. First, were suggestions related to ATE facilities that are not available on current RAL ATE, or were never mentioned by interviewees. The "logs" node at the bottom of Figure 1 represents just such a case in that current RAL ATE does not maintain a permanent log of either each UUT subjected to test, or the running of each test program. In such cases a new node was constructed, representing a desirable future ATE facility and is represented on the TDH by an @. Second, were suggestions that could not be accommodated by the TDH because they did not represent specific ATE operations. Suggestion 17 from the operator's suggestion list is of this type and stated that it was important that future generations of ATE should have "improved reliability". However, the latter type of suggestions were comparatively rare and for the total data set constituted only 13%, and 69% of these were from the ATE demonstrator's data, which was less task orientated than that of the operators, maintenance engineers, and programmers data.

3.5 Interpretation and Design

There were two, related uses made of the analyses described in the previous sections. Of considerable interest was the similarity and differences between the tasks carried out by the four types of ATE personnel. Such comparisons can be made because the tasks of the different personnel are all represented by TAKD in a common format as either TDHs or as KRG sentences (N.B. the content of these different representational forms is identical). It turns out that there is considerable overlap between the contents of the operators, maintenance engineers, and programmers TDHs such that the operators' tasks are generally a subset of the maintenance engineers, and the latter a sub-set of the programmers. However, and this is not contained in the interview data, the frequency of task components will be different for these classes of user. The most important exceptions to this result are in the social skills associated with the different jobs of these personnel. This finding supports the claims made by several of the maintenance engineers that RAL underestimated the importance of their interactions with the users and managers when visiting an ATE site to carry out maintenance, repair or calibration jobs.

This task similarity result then led to a proposed interface design for the next generation of ATE which could take advantage of this finding by providing a single, modeless type of interface to such ATE. Different classes of user would then be restricted to only a subset of the interface, depending on their needs and level of expertise. There are immediate commercial advantages to having only to design one interface, rather than several. Furthermore, reliability and consistency is likely to be enhanced as an ATE programmer, for example, can test, during design, the consequences of a section of code on the same interface as will be provided to the end users, because it is the same interface as that being used by the programmer. The details of this interface design proposal are commercially sensitive and are deliberately not reported here.

The main use of the ATE demonstrator analyses

was to identify the important functions of a full ATE that need to be built into an ATE demonstrator which can then be used as a marketing tool to attract customer interest from ATE clients for the next generation of RAL ATE.

4. In Conclusion

Until this study, TAKD had been used exclusively for the analysis of data obtained from the observation of tasks. That it can be used on interview data provides an important extension to TAKD. In particular, on future projects, TAKD can be used in the early stages to elicit an approximate or general TDH which can then be extended in detail by the observation of tasks. It is likely to be of considerable interest to analysts when situations arise where a major mismatch is found between how people report they carry out tasks and how they are observed to carry them out. There is a considerable literature on the difference between the verbal description of tasks and their actual performance (e.g. Bainbridge, 1979; 1986; Diaper, 1987; 1989b; 1989c). The use of TAKD on data from both sources will allow such differences to be easily detected and they can be characterised in a systematic fashion using TAKD's representational formalisms.

A further advantage of first using TAKD on interview data is that this is likely to lead to a better selection of the tasks that need to be observed and perhaps to a reduction in the total number of tasks that have to be observed. This in itself is likely to reduce analysis costs as, whereas interview data is quick and cheap to collect, task observation, if done at all well, is both costly and time consuming.

Aknowledgement

The work reported in this paper was wholly funded by Racal Automation Ltd. The views expressed, however, are entirely the responsibility of the author. The author expresses his thanks to Racal's managers and to the personnel who took part in the interviews. In particular, thanks are directed to Mr. Paul Tyson who organised the project at Racal.

References

Bainbridge, L. (1979) *Verbal Reports as Evidence of the Process Operators Knowledge*, International Journal of Man-Machine Studies, 11, 411-436.

Bainbridge, L. (1986), *Asking Questions and Accessing Knowledge*, Future Computing Systems, 1, 143-150.

Bliss, J., Monk, M. and Ogborn, J. (1983) *Qualitative Data Analysis: A Guide to the use of Systemic Networks.* Croom Helm.

Cordingley, E. (1989) *Knowledge Elicitation Techniques for Knowledge Based Systems*, in (Ed. Diaper, D.) Knowledge Elicitation: Principles, Techniques and Applications, 89-172. Ellis Horwood.

Diaper, D. (1987) *Designing Systems for People: Beyond User Centred Design*, in Software Engineering, Proceedings of the SHARE European Associated Aniversary Meeting, 1, 283-302.

Diaper, D. (1988) *Task Analysis for Knowledge Descriptions: Building a Task Descriptive Hierarchy* in (Ed. Megaw, E.D.) Contemporary Ergonomics 1988, 118-124. Taylor and Francis.

Diaper, D. (1989a) *Task Analysis for Knowledge Descriptions (TAKD): The Method and an Example*, in (Ed. Diaper, D.) Task Analysis for Human-Computer Interaction, 108-159. Ellis Horwood.

Diaper, D. (1989b) *Task Observation for Human-Computer Interaction*, in (Ed. Diaper, D.) Task Analysis for Human-Computer Interaction, 210-237. Ellis Horwood.

Diaper, D. (1989c) *Designing Expert Systems: From Dan to Beersheba*, in (Ed. Diaper, D.) Knowledge Elicitation: Principles, Techniques and Applications, 1-46. Ellis Horwood.

Diaper, D. and Johnson, P. (1989) *Task Analysis for Knowledge Descriptions: Theory and Application in Training*, in (Eds. Long, J. and Whitefield, A.) Cognitive Ergonomics for Human-Computer Interaction, 191-224. Cambridge University Press: Cambridge, UK.

Halliday, M. (1978) *Language as a Social Semiotic.* Edward Arnold.

Johnson, N. (1989) *Mediating Representations in Knowledge Elicitation*, in (Ed. Diaper, D.) Knowledge Elicitation: Principles, Techniques and Applications, 177-194. Ellis Horwood.

Johnson, P. (1985) *Towards a Task Model of Messaging: An Example of the application of TAKD to User Interface Design*, in (Eds. Johnson, P. and Cook, S.) People and Computers: Designing the Interface, 46-62. CUP.

Johnson, P. Diaper, D. and Long, J. (1984) *Tasks, Skills and Knowledge: Task Analysis for Knowledge Based Descriptions* in Interact'84: First IFIP Conference on Human-Computer Interaction, 1, 23-27. Elsevier.

Johnson, P., Diaper, D. and Long, J. (1985) *Task Analysis in Interactive Systems Design and Evaluation*, in (Eds. Johansen, G., Mancini, G. and Martensson, L.) Analysis, Design and Evaluation in Man-Machine Systems. OUP.

Human–Computer Interaction – INTERACT '90
D. Diaper et al. (Editors)
Elsevier Science Publishers B.V. (North-Holland)

A PLAN & GOAL BASED METHOD FOR COMPUTER-HUMAN SYSTEM DESIGN

Daniel R. SEWELL

Search Technology
4725 Peachtree Corners Circle #200
Norcross, GA 30092 USA

Norman D. GEDDES

Applied Systems Intelligence
3453 Point View Circle
Gainesville, GA 30506 USA

A methodology for designing computer-human systems based on explicitly representing the user's hierarchical plan and goal structure is presented. The methodology provides an advance over traditional task-analytic methods by providing representational structure that captures both causal relationships of the operational domain and cognitive states of the system user. The plan-goal graph representation maps directly to system functions and actions, aiding both design and implementation of the system. This methodology is illustrated with a review of a recent application to designing an information retrieval and analysis system for system designers attempting to access and apply human performance information to design problems.

1. INTRODUCTION

The purpose of this paper is threefold: to describe a Plan & Goal Graph (PGG) based method for computer-human system design based on the goals, plans, and actions of the human operating the system; to describe how such a design methodology would be used; and, to briefly review the use of this methodology in the development of a particular product. Each of these is briefly characterized here and discussed in detail in later sections.

Current system design methods describe the tasks a user performs and the knowledge a user needs as the basis for system design. This task-analytic approach is taught and practiced in various forms throughout the software and engineering design communities [4,12] and even appears, in principle, in other forms such as the language/action design perspective of Winograd [20]. There are weaknesses to this traditional approach and its offshoots, which has resulted in a plethora of task analytic methods, none of which have been broadly accepted [3,18] and all of which have significant weaknesses [19].

Most task-analytic methods do not distinguish between the goal component and the process component of a task. As a result, both the existence of alternative processes and the commonality of processes across the system can be overlooked. This obscures the mapping from task element to system function in the design, often leading to a proliferation of functions whose purposes are unclear. To improve design methods requires going beyond the surface features of the user's actions to examine their intentions and the processes governing those intentions.

A PGG-based design method is based on the concept of a PGG as a description of both the cognitive states and physical actions of an operator of the system under design. The PGG requires developing a complete description of the actions of the user in and knowledge about a particular domain so it can be used to infer goals or predict plans and actions [11]. To the extent a PGG can be developed for building a system, it should be possible to develop functionality that directly supports the plans and goals; and, to develop system actions that correspond to the user's intended actions. After constructing a PGG, one must develop functionality reflecting the plans and goals of the user and develop a detailed description of system actions that complement the primitive user actions in the PGG.

The PGG methodology shares common ideas with the goal-oriented GOMS model of human performance [2]. It has been developed in parallel with the GOMS-based design approach reported by Kieras [14]. That work develops general goals and specific methods for achieving them. However, recent work by Elkerton & Palmiter [5] from their study of a GOMS-based user interface design provides evidence that users do not always associate specific methods with higher-level goals. An advance in the PGG approach is the use of both abstract plans and scripted procedures as the means of pursuing goals rather than only specific methods. This advance alleviates much of the need to make specific judgment calls on exactly how a goal might be pursued in terms of specific primitive operator actions. The PGG abstract plans approach has been used for system development [13] and has been empirically tested [6].

Current work with this methodology has contributed to a design for an information retrieval system and simulation environment that is currently in rapid prototype development. The added value of the PGG design method for this particular implementation is to point out new functionality such as user-understanding and information mapping; ***and***, since the PGG is based in the user psychology, to provide indications of where in the psychological research literature to look for possible solutions to design and implementation problems.

2. PLAN & GOAL BASED METHOD FOR DESIGN

The PGG design method consists of the following five elements problem and domain definition, plan, goal, and action definition and decomposition, function composition, interface development, and implementation

2.1 Design Problem and Domain Definition

The *design problem definition* consists of specifying the purpose of the PGG, as distinct from the purpose of the user that the PGG represents. The purpose of the PGG provides a statement of what the designer wants to accomplish by creating the PGG representation itself. This step is an explicit recognition that the content of a specific instantiation of a PGG is not a general representation of the user's task domain, but rather is tailored to provide a semantically strong characterization of the user's task domain from the viewpoint of a specific design problem (e.g., information management solutions may not be error monitoring solutions).

The *design domain definition* deals with the world in which the user operates and his purposes in that world. This step in the design identifies those attributes of the world and the activities of the user that are relevant to the purpose of the system under design. The design problem definition acts to bound the design domain definition by determining what is relevant. Unlike traditional scenario-based approaches to characterizing the operational setting of the user and system, the design domain definition is an explicit causal "theory of operations" for the user and his system, specific to the actual target domain. The definition establishes the attributes of the user, the system, and the world that are causally connected, either as intentional inputs, intentional outputs, side-effects or disturbances.

The domain definition is documented as a set of attributes each characterized by how it is measured or determined, and by its relevance to the purpose of both the system and the design problem. The attributes provide a description of the system, the user, and the environment that is used in the plan and goal decomposition to determine the context for user interaction with the system.

2.2 Plan, Goal, and Action Definition and Decomposition

Once the domain has been characterized, the effects of user interaction with the system is formulated by defining primitive actions. A primitive action is a user interaction with the system under design that results in changes to values of some of the attributes that were identified in the domain definition. While a primitive action must affect at least one value from the domain attributes, interactions with broader effect may also be defined as primitive. Again, the design problem definition mediates the selection of primitive actions. Primitive actions represent the lowest level of description of user activity that will be reached in the PGG decomposition.

The primitive actions themselves however are like an "assembly language" for the user--a higher-order organization of the primitives is vital to successful user interaction. This higher level organization is provided by the PGG.

The construction of the PGG is accomplished by a decomposition of the top-level purposes of the system into plans and goals at successively increasing levels of resolution or preciseness until plans are reached that can be decomposed completely into primitive actions. The formalism of the relationships between plans and goals guides the decomposition process. The definitions of and relationships among plans, goals, and actions in the PGG are shown in Figure 1.

As the decomposition of plans and goals proceeds, some plans may be defined to achieve more than a single goal, and goals defined which may be sub-steps of more than one plan. The PGG allows multiple parents for a plan, goal, or action. This structure results in a directed acyclic graph, rather than a more traditional tree structure typical of task analysis. The decomposition continues until either plans are decomposed into strictly primitive actions, or until additional decomposition of the plans into subgoals would not increase the value of the PGG for the purpose of addressing the chosen design problem. At this point, each plan not yet decomposed into primitive actions is linked to the primitive actions implied by the content of the plan.

The process of decomposing the plans, goals, and actions of the intended system user is typically a complex process requiring communication and cooperation among several people or organizations. It is necessary to build the PGG from both top and bottom; and, to develop and maintain definitions of all elements and relationships in the PGG as it is developed.

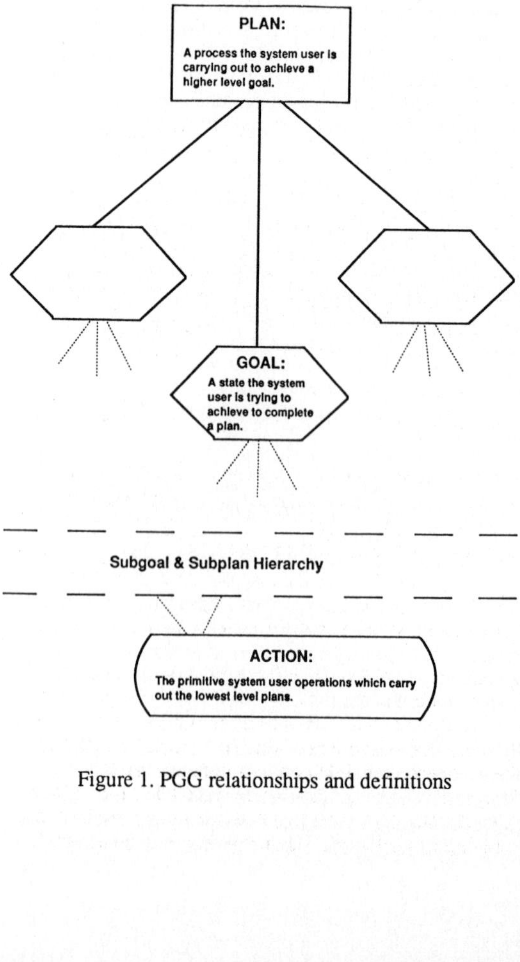

Figure 1. PGG relationships and definitions

2.3 Function Composition

The means for achieving the required functional capability definition is a recursive process of taking plans at all levels of the PGG and developing functions that match them. Eventually, the system designer should produce functionality that reflects every plan in the PGG. This functionality takes on the same hierarchical nature as the PGG and, in fact, could be the basis of a complete menu driven system. Ultimately, the system designer can take the PGG and develop a table of mappings between every plan and every system function (see Table 4 for a partial example).

Defining system actions requires the system designer redefine the primitive user actions from the PGG in terms of system actions that produce data for the functionality of the system. This means the system designer must define both the activity involved and the effects that activity is expected to have. As primitive user actions are mapped into system actions, it is possible that constraints will force changes in the system actions that cause the PGG developer to reconsider the possible primitive user actions in the PGG.

2.4 Interface Development

For this design method, developing the interface consists of defining the means by which system actions will be carried out, the nature of interactions among the primitive actions, and the higher level functions the system user will see during the system operation. This is the point at which a GOMS based design methodology becomes complementary to the PGG methodology.

2.5 Implementation

At the level of user actions in the intended system, the definition of primitive actions are directly programmable as system actions that the user can carry out. The lowest level plans are programmed as routines or sub-routines which receive inputs directly from the system user (in the form of actions) as well as from other functions. Higher level functions are calling routines or control structure which pass data and initiate implied functionality. These design-to-implementation characteristics readily lend themselves to a structured or object-oriented programming approach.

3. A PLAN & GOAL BASED DESIGN EXAMPLE

This section presents a partial description of a PGG based design that has been implemented in prototype. We will cover each aspect of the design in some detail but will not discuss the prototype implementation.

3.1 Design Problem and Domain Definition

The requirement for this example design is to provide an information search and retrieval system for a user-designer who is attempting to develop a computer-human interface to a complex system. Examples of the interface being designed by the user-designer might be a new computer system interface, an aircraft cockpit, or a point-of-sale cash register. In general terms, the user-designer needs human performance information to solve some design problem and the design goal of this new system is to make information accessible and useable.

What the user does. The most general activity of interest the engineering designer as user performs is to *apply human performance information to design problem X*. Of course, this activity is subordinate to many other activities this individual performs but it is the top-level focus for the following analysis. This happens during problem formulation, tradeoff analysis, detailed design, and so forth.

How the user does it. The four general activities that the user-designer engages in when trying to apply information to a particular problem are *scope/select information sources, access information from/within sources, understand information,* and *map/extrapolate information to current context.* These activities are a general distillation from the results of descriptive studies of users and information seekers [1,4,6,7,9,12] and are defined and described below.

Scope/Select information sources. This is the activity during which user-designers consider or seek the possible information sources from which they might obtain the information necessary to solve the current design problem (e.g., handbooks, guidelines, journals, etc.). Some of the important domain attributes needed to characterize the causal relationships underlying the selection process are attributes that define the contents, nature, and treatment of these various sources as they are relevant to the problem being addressed by the user-designer.

Access information from/within sources. This is the activity during which user-designers identify possibly relevant information through a more considered examination of selected sources. The processes related to accessing information are mediated by attributes such as the presentation medium, access time duration, depth and breadth of coverage, and the extent to which the desired information is intermixed with other data (signal to noise). These attributes can depend on the source that is accessed, the user himself, and the problem under consideration.

Have information/concepts. This is the activity during which designers try to assimilate the information they have found into their own framework for understanding. For example, the designer finding information about proceduralized performance may or may not find information that is described in a vocabulary, set of examples, or theoretical framework the designer understands. Attributes which characterize the specific background, experience of the user, and depth of understanding sought are relevant to the process. Consequently, the depth and scope of the accessed information are important considerations.

Extrapolate information to current context. This is the activity during which designers try to apply the understanding they have gained to the current problem on which they are working. Extrapolation of the information to the specific problem is affected by attributes of the problem, the information, and the user. The degree of generality of the problem and that of the information accessed are strong factors in extrapolation of the information.

3.2 Plan, Goal, Action Definition and Decomposition

Intended system users can be viewed as planners who operate in a plan-goal space similar to the multiple spaces of design rationale [15], the goal structures of Mostow [16,17], and design as constraint exploration [10,11]. In this particular case, the PGG will describe how the designer does the activity of applying information to a design problem. As an activity with particular actions that could carry it out, *applying human performance information to design problem x* will be viewed as the top level plan from which the rest of the following plan-goal graph will be developed.

The initial description of the user illustrated four general activities that the designer performs when *applying human performance information to design problem x.* These four activities can be converted into goals the designer must achieve in order to complete that activity as a plan. In essence, these become the four states the designer must achieve to carry out the plan. They are described in Table 1.

Table 1. Descriptions of top level goals.

1. Have Selection (Info Sources) - Achievement means the designer will have selected among or within varied sources such as colleagues, experts, system users, design handbooks, engineering handbooks, archival information sources, empirical tools, analytical tools, and so forth.
2. Have Access - Achievement means the designer will have browsed through sources to select and obtain specific pieces of information; or, will have searched explicitly through sources to identify, retrieve, and obtain specific pieces of information.
3. Have Information - Achievement means the designer will have gained definitions of the relevant concepts in the information, will have seen or developed an interpretation of concepts in terms the designer already understands; or, will have seen or experienced the effect that concepts are intended to characterize.
4. Have Extrapolation - Achievement means the designer will have applied the information gathered to the design problem in some way; and, at the most will have solved the design problem or made the design decision at hand. The designer must search for the relevant case or model, develop appropriate representations for the case/model and the problem, match between the case/model and the problem, project values from the case/model to the problem, and evaluate the projection.

For the purposes of this paper, only part of the PGG decomposition will be shown to provide more discussion of the design and implementation; a general overview of the PGG is provided in Figure 2.

At the same time that the plans and goals are being developed, it is necessary to develop the primitive actions that are expected from the system user. Since the actions are the means for carrying out plans, as new plans are developed it may turn out that existing actions are unnecessary or that new actions are necessary to adequately describe the PGG for the user. Table 2 provides partial descriptions of the actions for the example design.

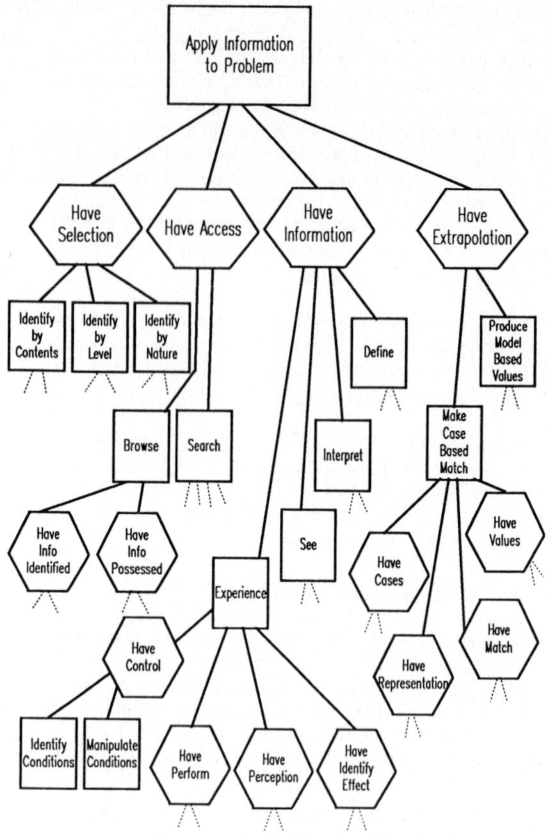

Figure 2. Top level plan & goal graph

Table 2. Partial description of primitive actions

1. select - Characterized by the indicated choice of one item from the possibilities in the interface.
2. open - ...
3. view - Characterized by the fact that a viewable item has been opened for some amount of time that is a function of its content. May also be characterized by selection of functions such as scrolling or pagination.
4. enter - ...
5. match - ...
6. execute - Characterized by the initiation of a process that takes input and/or produces output.
7. terminate - ...
8. close - Characterized by the fact of a previously opened item no longer being opened.

Table 3. Partial listing of PGG to function mapping

PLAN & GOAL GRAPH	DESIGN FUNCTIONALITY
Have Access	
Browse material	**Browser** - a function providing a means for examining series of text items
Have info identified	
View entries	**Viewer** - a subfunction providing a port through which examination is carried out
.	.
.	.
Select	**Mouse-select** - a subfunction providing a means for carrying out action select
.	
.	
Have Understanding	
Experience effect	**Simulation** - a function providing a means for simulating processes
Have control of conditions	
Identify conditions	**Simulation exploration** - a subfunction providing means to develop simulation conditions
.	.
.	.
Manipulate conditions	**Control panel** - a subfunction providing means to manipulate simulation conditions
.	
.	
Interpret effect	**Interpretation** - a function providing means for developing explanation in the form of a model, case, or conditions
Have mapping	
Depict relationship	**Analogize** - a subfunction providing means to compare base and target stimuli for match
Have formal representations	
Develop F-B rep	**Model-builder** - a subfunction providing means to develop models
.	.
.	

3.3 Function Composition

Table 3 partially illustrates the mapping between the PGG and the functions composed for the example system design. The process of composing functions from the PGG required explicit mapping from plan to function. These are denoted by boldface in the table. For example, the plan to browse material mapped directly to a function for browsing, its subplan for viewing material mapped directly to a function for viewing, and so forth down to the primitive user action of select which mapped directly to a system action for mouse-select. During the process of composing this function mapping, it became apparent that the goals serve the function of guiding the nature of the outputs of the functions. The goals indicate the state the system user should have attained by performing the function associated with the goal's subplan. Therefore the output of the function should match or directly correlate with the attributes necessary to the goal.

There are two important points to remember about the composition process. One is that straightforward composition of functions and the development of actions from the PGG is dependent on clear definition of of the goals, plans, and actions in the PGG. The other is that recursive definition of goals, plans, and actions appears to be a requisite part of the design process. These and other implications of this application of the PGG design methodology are discussed in the following section.

4. DISCUSSION

About the use of this method. Application of the PGG design method has illuminated several important issues. One is the importance of "nailing down" the top-level goals and the primitive actions as early as possible. Changes in the PGG have to be propagated throughout the PGG; and, there are changes as the design process continues. However, to the extent that the endpoints of the process are fixed by having defined both the top and the bottom of the PGG then the possibilities are much reduced in number and the degree of change to be propagated at any time is much reduced.

It is important to reconsider all related elements when any one element is changed. These changes lead to a more complete PGG and they enhance the possibility of uncovering previously unrecognized functionality for the intended system.

A final issue in the use of the method is the importance the method has in promoting concrete definitions of possible system functions, states, and data from a very early stage. In traditional task-analytic approaches, the analysis process is divorced from the design and implementation process so there is very little chance for the needs of one process to affect the other. In this approach, the early development of actions and the existence of goals as achievable states both drive the direction that the system takes and are affected by the capabilities of the intended system environment.

On the good side, this need promotes early definition that can be examined from an implementation perspective. Such definition feeds current concepts for rapid prototyping and concurrent engineering. On the bad side, this early definition can lead to an early rigidness in the concepts that might be incorporated in the design to the exclusion of other potential concepts. This kind of functional fixedness is well documented in other problem solving areas.

About the form of this method. In the course of developing the first design with this method we learned that the PGG provides strong drivers toward particular system design. For example, at the interface level, it would be possible to convert a PGG directly into a menu hierarchy that could even take all options away from a user. At the system level, it would be possible to convert a PGG into a calling sequence of literal functionality that could make most or all of a system invisible to the user. Neither inflexibility nor invisibility are particularly desirable in most system functionality.

About the conceptual basis of this method. The central issue with respect to the conceptual basis of this methodology is related to the use of cognitive states as indicators of goal achievement in the intended system user. Our intuition was that defining goals in terms of cognitive states (as opposed to our earlier work with physical states) might be more difficult but not impossible. This intuition was well founded, though aided by our willingness to firmly define those states. For example, the goal of *have-information* had to be defined as occurring even if we did not know what particular information the user had. Also, it turns out that defining cognitive states required more time and more interaction with domain experts than did defining physical states. This was not completely unexpected; however, the degree of analysis and reiteration that was necessary to reach a deep yet coherent PGG is worth noting for future development.

Conclusion. As illustrated, PGGs are capable of describing the possible states and processes of an intended user of a system under design. Consequently, the PGG can be used to derive the functions such a system ought to have to support that user's intended goals, plans, and actions. In this respect, the PGG design method holds much promise for the future of designing systems toward the psychology of intended users. Future work will further develop this promise by exploring the issues raised above and by applying the method to many designs, computer-human and otherwise.

ACKNOWLEDGMENTS

We wish to acknowledge projects funded by AF-F33615-86-C-0542, the Designer's Associate and AF-F33615-85-C-3804, the Pilot's Associate. They did not support this work but have provided excellent technical domains and work environments in which to develop and pursue the ideas.

REFERENCES

[1] Bruns, G.R. & Gerhart, S.L. (1986). *Theories of design: An introduction to the literature.* MCC Technical Report Number STP-068-86, Austin, TX: Microelectronics and Computer Technology Corporation.

[2] Card, S.K., Moran, T.P., & Newell, A. (1983). *The psychology of human-computer interaction.* Hillsdale, NJ: Lawrence Erlbaum Associates.

[3] Companion, M.A. & Corso, G.M. (1982). Task taxonomies: A general review and evaluation. *International Journal of Man-Machine Studies, 17*, 459-472.

[4] Curtis, B., Krasner, H., & Iscoe, N. (1988). A field study of the software design process for large systems. *Communications of the ACM, 31*, 1268-1287.

[5] Elkerton, J. & Palmiter, S. (1989). *Designing help systems using a GOMS model: Part 1 - An information retrieval evaluation.* Report CHE-ONR-3, Center for Ergonomics, University of Michigan.

[6] Dagwell, R. & Weber, R. (1983). System designers' user models: A comparative study and methodological critique. *Communications of the ACM, 26*, 987-997.

[7] Fischer, G. & Nieper-Lemke, H. (1989). HELGON: Extending the retrieval by reformulation paradigm. *CHI'89 Proceedings*, 357-362.

[8] Geddes, N.D. (1989). *Understanding human operators' intentions in complex systems.* Ph.D. Dissertation, Georgia Institute of Technology.

[9] Goel, V. & Pirolli, P. (1989). Motivating the notion of generic design within information processing theory: The design problem space. *AI Magazine, Spring Vol.*, 18-36.

[10] Gross, M.D. (1987). Design and use of a constraint-based laboratory in learning design. In Lawler, R.W. & Yazdani, M. (Eds.), *Artificial intelligence and education, Volume one.* Norwood, NJ: Ablex Publishing (p. 167-182).

[11] Gross, M.D., Ervin, S.M., Anderson, J.A., & Fleisher, A. (1988). Constraints: Knowledge representation in design. *Design Studies, 9*, 133-143.

[12] Hales, C. & Wallace, K.M. (1988). Detailed analysis of an engineering design project. *International Journal of Applied Engineering Education, 4*, 289-294.

[13] Hoshstrasser, B.D. & Geddes, N.D. (1989). OPAL: Operator intent inferencing for intelligent operator support systems. In V.L. Shalin & G.A. Boy (Eds.), *Proceedings of the IJCAI-89 Workshop on Integrated Human-Machine Intelligence in Aerospace Systems*, 53-70.

[14] Kieras, D.E. (1988). Towards a practical GOMS model methodology for user interface design. In M. Helander (Ed.) *Handbook of human computer interaction*, pp. 135-157.

[15] MacLean, A., Young, R.M., & Moran, T.P. (1989). Design rationale: The argument behind the artifact. *CHI'89 Proceedings*, 247-252.

[16] Mostow, J. (1985). Toward better models of the design process. *AI Magazine, Spring Vol.*, 44-57.

[17] Mostow, J. (1989). Design by derivational analogy: Issues in the automated replay of design plans. *Artificial Intelligence, 40*, 119-184.

[18] Price, (1985). The allocation of functions in systems. *Human Factors, 27*, 33-45.

[19] Webb, B.W., Geddes, N.D., & Neste, L.O. (1989). Information management with a hierarchical display generator. In *Proceedings of the '89 NCGA Conference, 1*, 52-62.

[20] Winograd, T. (1988). A language/action perspective on the design of cooperative work. *Human-Computer Interaction, 3*, 3-30.

Human–Computer Interaction – INTERACT '90
D. Diaper et al. (Editors)
Elsevier Science Publishers B.V. (North-Holland)

THE USE OF TASK ALLOCATION CHARTS IN SYSTEM DESIGN : A CRITICAL APPRAISAL

W K Ip
Now at BT Research Laboratories,
Martlesham Heath, Ipswich.

L Damodaran, C W Olphert and M C Maguire
HUSAT Research Institute,
Loughborough, Leics.

The design of IT systems has traditionally failed to take account of the job design requirements of end users, resulting in negative and unplanned effects on user acceptability and system efficiency. A technique based on the idea of Task Allocation Charts was developed to enable job design issues to be represented and considered in the early stages of IT system design. This attempts to address the problems of Requirements Capture and the limitations of traditional Systems Analysis in identifying job requirements in system specification. A description of the notation and usage of the charts is followed by a critical appraisal of their application in a real design situation. The paper concludes with proposals of future research and the development of a CASE tool to support the technique.

1. INTRODUCTION

The design of IT systems has traditionally failed to take account of the task allocation and job design requirements of its end users. This has often resulted in negative, unplanned effects on the final system implementation. Consequently, these systems are often under utilized and incur high running costs in the form of work re-organization and the human costs involved in poor job design.

Many design methodologies, particularly structured methodologies, now address the requirements of 'end users'. But on closer examination they are still heavily data-driven and technology centred. This results in a lop-sided view of the organisational system into which the computer system under design is to be integrated.

Gould and Lewis [1] state that while there should be an early focus on users and tasks, this is rarely applied in practice. According to Buckle et al [2] requirements capture and analysis is "the first step in a series of transformations from a vaguely expressed need for an information system to an actual working manifestation". As such, it is the basis of all further work and also the means by which the quality and applicability of the final system can be measured (Ceri [3]). Miller [4], in considering the failures of Management Information Systems, believes that this can be traced to a lack of organisational understanding amongst analysts. He says "it is almost impossible to separate the content of managerial information systems from the field of organisation theory", because "you cannot determine the information that a manager needs without considering his responsibility and organisational skills during the analysis".

The technique of Task Allocation Charting (TAC) has been developed to meet these limitations in conventional systems analysis. The TAC notation allows task allocation decisions and job design options to be addressed during the early stages of IT system design. The technique has been tailored to be integrated into a structured system design methodology based on SSADM used by a large Government Department.

2. PROBLEMS IN TRADITIONAL SYSTEMS ANALYSIS

2.1. Narrow Focus

Traditional system analysis focuses on those aspects of a work system which are to be computerised or given updated IT support. Yet in reality a work organisation is an 'open system' and a complex socio-technical system. Many activities and decisions associated with, for example, relationships, communication and informal working practices will not be computerised. These will therefore be disregarded in any narrowly defined analysis process however significant they are for the functioning of the work organisation. Thus in many IT applications, vital aspects of work such as contact with customers, adaptation to novel situations, problem-solving and negotiation are likely to continue to be uniquely human activities. Nevertheless these activities will have impact upon, and be affected by, the IT system. The effective functioning of the total socio-technical system requires compatibility of the IT-based activities with other activities. Such compatibility can only be achieved through a design specification which is the product of a broad based analysis process.

2.2 Lack of tools and techniques

Techniques to support such requirements capture and analysis processes have not been readily available although some are now emerging (e.g. Sutcliffe [5], Fowler et al [6], Galer [7] Gardner and McKenzie [8]). The narrow focus of conventional system analysis generally yields an inadequate and highly constrained representation of what the user requires. Thus the users' flexibility in performing tasks become closely circumscribed by the IT facilities. The serious outcome is that a smaller repertoire of problem-solving skills is available and thus a measure of flexibility and adaptability is lost to the organisation.

Currently, none of the commonly used structured system design methodologies explicitly address the job design requirements of end users. The fact that the design of the computer system and the tasks and jobs that people do are inextricably linked has still not made its way into the thinking of those responsible for upgrading these commercial methodologies. This is a major weakness in them.

Those that mention 'job design' only really pay lip service to the concept as the claims are not supported by parallel tools and techniques, training and skill requirements, nor built into the project management structure - the hallmarks of true integration into a methodology.

2.3 Limited role and training

There are many factors which serve to perpetuate this unsatisfactory state of affairs. The limited role of the analyst and the narrowness of his training are especially pertinent factors. For example the analyst's responsibilities, particularly where structured design methodologies are in place, are often defined in terms of 'deliverables' such as an 'Outline User Requirement Specification'. There is generally no incentive for the analyst to show awareness of the likely future impact of the proposed IT changes. Nor will the analyst generally have to live with the resultant system and thus experience its strengths and weaknesses first hand.

2.4 Poor communication between users and designers

There is often a breakdown in communication between the end users and the designers which can be attributed to various factors:

- They often have very different backgrounds in terms of training and expertise.
- Their concerns regarding the computer system are different i.e. the designers are more concerned about the processing and data-flows whilst the users are more concerned about the functionality of the system as it is presented at the user interface.
- There is no appropriate communication 'tool' which system designers use that end users can easily relate to. Diagramming tools such as Entity Life Histories (ELH's) and Data-flow Diagrams (DFD's) do not support the users in visualising the system and tend to obscure job design issues - of particular concern to them.

In conclusion, the fundamental problem posed by these limitations is that a mismatch between user need and the developed IT system is established early in the analysis phase. To reduce or eliminate this mismatch requires improved techniques to analyse the rich and complex world of the user organisation in a way which requires designers to develop IT which will support the reality of the user situation, not an over-simplified, impoverished representation of it. Only when the design of IT recognises and reflects the entire socio-technical system (of which it is part) can it really achieve its full potential. This paper reports the first steps towards this goal.

3. THE TOOL AND THE TECHNIQUE

3.1. Notation and Structure of TAC's

Task Allocation Charts (TACs) shows how particular work processes may be organised between people and computers. Each chart consists of two or more labelled columns, one containing the tasks to be performed by the computer, the others containing the tasks performed by people.

Each task is shown as a rectangle with the particular task named inside it. Tasks are connected to each other by arrows indicating task sequences.

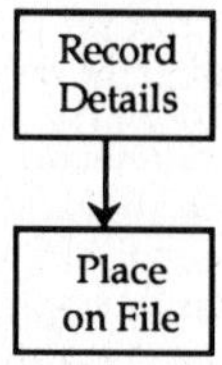

When tasks pass from person to person, or from person to computer, a shaded interface box is used to indicate that consideration needs to be given to what form the flow of information will take.

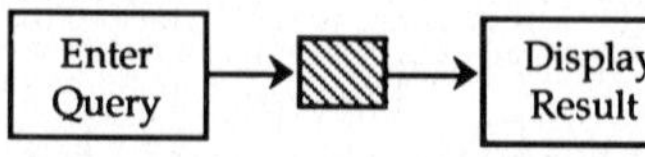

Conditional tasks are represented by a small open circle in the top right corner of each conditional task box. The condition is described on the flow line.

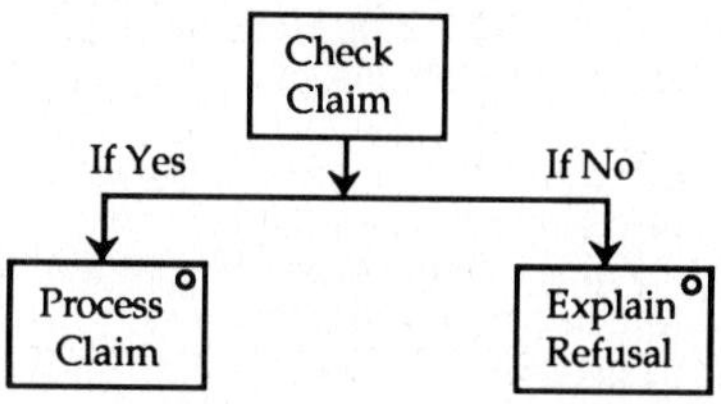

Where a task flow splits into two or more parallel tasks, all of which must be performed, these are shown with a small solid circle in the top right corner of the first box in each flow.

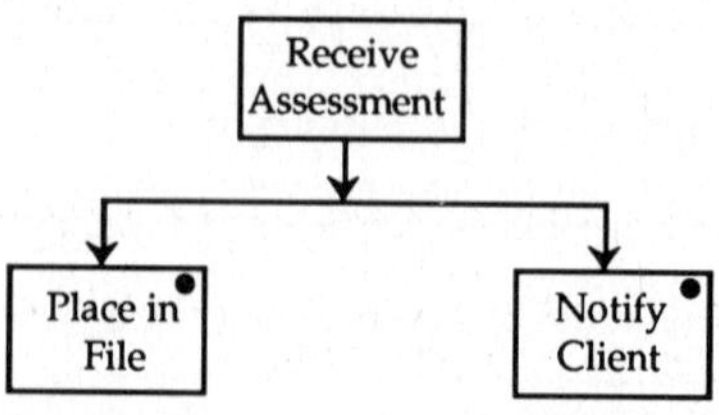

Iterative tasks are shown with an asterisk in the top right corner of the box.

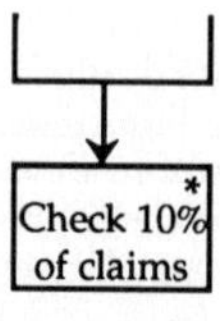

Entities (e.g. people and organisations) which are external to the system are shown as ellipses. They are also given a separate column on the TAC.

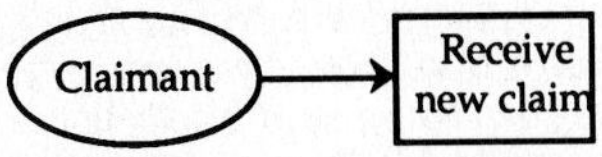

It is important to note that TACs need only be sketched, rather than drawn as 'works of art', thus encouraging the development of a range of task allocation options for each work process.

There follows 3 simple TACs showing the different options for organising the work process: 'Receiving insurance claims by post and Locating the corresponding records'.

In option 1, the Junior Clerk opens the post, delivers the claims to the Claims Clerk who enters each the client's identification number into the computer. The computer then displays the locations of the client records (i.e. filing cabinet numbers) which the Junior Clerk then fetches for the Claims Clerk to process. Note that a section is reserved at the bottom of the TAC for user/staff representatives to record their comments. These will help to choose the best task allocation option.

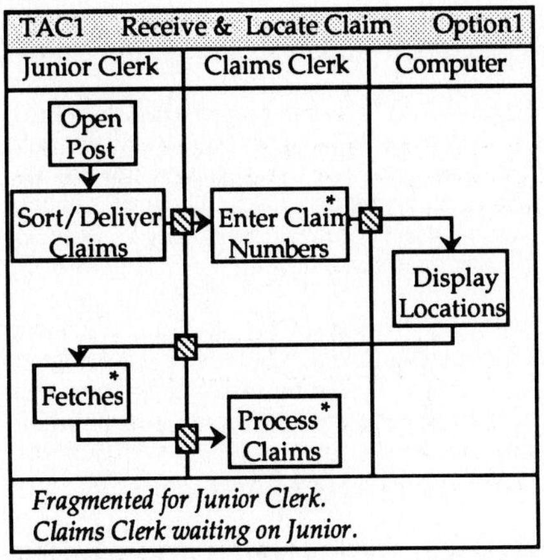

Fig 3.1 Task Allocation Chart - Option 1

In option 2, the Junior Clerk opens the post, sorts out the benefit claims and uses the computer him/herself to locate the records in the filing cabinets. He or she then fetches the records for the Claims Clerk to process.

In option 3, the computer holds the records on file. The Junior Clerk sorts out the claims, delivers them to the Claims Clerk who then calls them up on the computer as and when he or she wishes to process them.

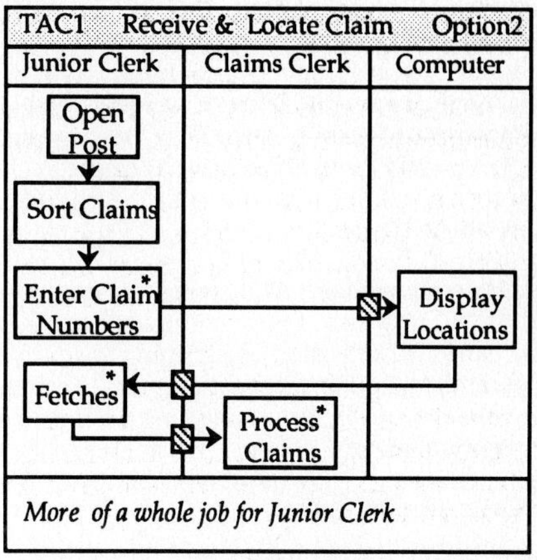

Fig 3.2 Task Allocation Chart - Option 2

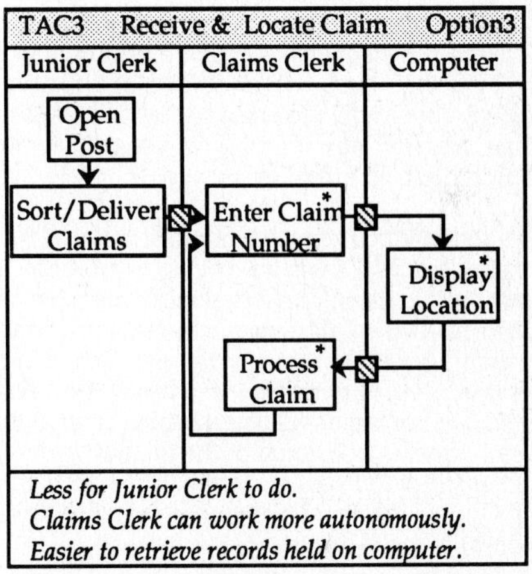

Fig 3.3 Task Allocation Chart - Option 3

3.2. What to use TAC's for.

Task Allocation Charts can be used in the system design process to achieve several ends. These are:

1. *Determining the boundary of the computer system.*
2. *Exploring job design options.*
3. *Communicating design options to users.*

Determination of the system boundary (the allocation of tasks between users and the computer) should take place at an early stage of design. From the end users' point of view, the acceptability of each task allocation option will very much be judged on its impact on their jobs. TACs help the users to visualise what that impact might be and contribute to the decision making process. For example, in Figure 3.1, the users can respond to the appropriateness of the allocation between the manual and the automated system. Of course a TAC may elicit different reactions from different user roles. A supervisor may be able to identify potential problems at a higher level whilst the claims clerk may be able to highlight the problems to do with the actual execution of the tasks.

TACs can also be used to explore different job design options by allocating the tasks in different ways (see Figures 3.2 and 3.3). It can be seen that each option have different job design implications for different user roles as highlighted in the comments under each chart. Analysing the charts in this way will enable the users and management to choose the most appropriate option or options while taking into account the impact on job design.

The above two uses of the TACs facilitates communication with end users. However, this communication need not be limited to the above activities. By keeping an up-to-date record of the allocation decisions, designers can always use them as a reference when discussing later design decisions with user representatives.

3.3. When to use TACs

The TACs can be used at various points in the development lifecycle, particularly during the early stages of system development (see Figure 3.4).

As shown, TACs can be drawn to explore the system boundary with reference its potential impact on the "users' system". Typically, there will be several options for where the boundary should lie. On analysis, some of these options will be discarded because they are not congruent with either the organisational, technical or user goals.

In parallel with the activity of defining functional requirements, the TACs will be used to explore the job design options i.e. the allocation of tasks between the user roles involved. These will impact upon the functional requirements, hence the two activities are carried out simultaneously and with reference to each other. As before, some job design options will be discarded as inappropriate. The overall effect is to firm up of the boundary and the requirements prior to Logical Design. The added value of using TACs is to incorporate the users' view more fully into this process.

4. APPLICATION OF THE TOOL

4.1. The application context

TACs have been built into the structured design methodology used by a large Government Department. They were not intended to stand alone, but to be supported by training. In the first large computerisation project to use the methodology, the User Team had the benefit of some initial (albeit necessarily superficial) Human Factors training and subsequently HF consultants providing on-going advice and support. The system to be designed was a large payments administration system, to be implemented in a network of more than 800 offices nationwide (Olphert & Damodaran [9]).

Although some of the functions of the Department were already computerised, the new system was intended to automate a much greater percentage of the work in order to improve the efficiency of the service and to reduce costs. In addition to these aims, however, there was also an explicit commitment to the creation of satisfactory jobs for staff.

By the time the technique was released to the project, the current systems analysis stage had been completed and outline functional requirements for the new system had been identified. The User Team and end users had been extensively involved in these two activities, but had not used TACs as part of the process.

The first use of TACs on the project was, therefore, at the point of defining the detailed functional requirements on the system and specifying the users' job design and work organisation requirements. These two activities took place in parallel, with different teams (consisting of both users and designers) assigned to each task.

The users found it relatively easy to draw TACs and to evaluate them using an extended list of job design evaluation criteria which they themselves had drawn up after their training. Having generated and compared a number of options for each of the functions, they were able to identify their preferred options in each case.

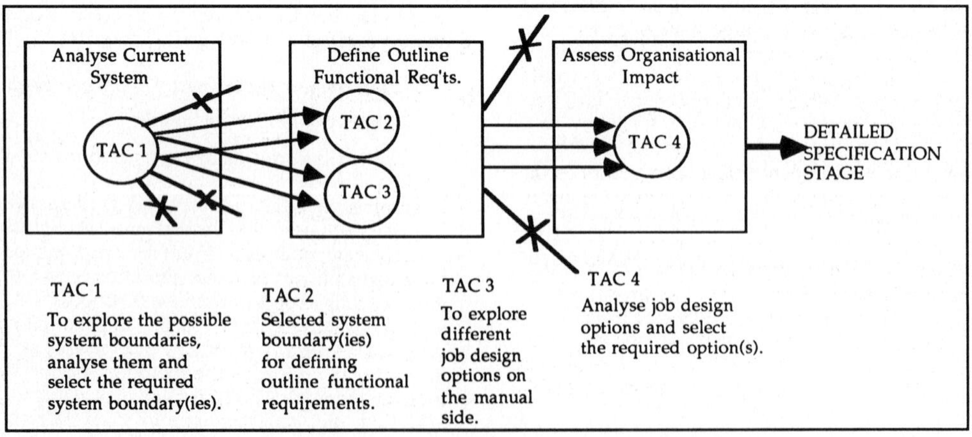

Fig. 3.4 Where to use TAC's in the System Development Lifecycle

At the end of the design stage, the TACs showing the preferred option for each function were included in the User Specification, which was then reviewed by a group of end users drawn from Branch Offices as part of the QA process. The TACs provided a unique means of visually representing the procedures associated with the functions and linking the text descriptions of the functions with the proposed screen formats.

4.2. Achievements and strengths of TAC's

Although this was the first project to use TACs, they proved to be a useful and usable tool. TACs enabled the teams to explicitly and systematically explore the feasibility of various task allocation options in relation to the design of the computer system prior to its final specification. This seemed to be a radical enhancement to existing practice.

Users found that the process of drawing TACs actually elucidated potential problems which they had not thought of. The charts modelled a different view of the same (total) system to that of DFD's and provided a different perspective on the problems. Indeed questions were asked of the whole organisational set-up.

Users found that highlighting the interface between the manual and automated sides of the system at the task level focussed their attention on the user-computer interfaces in terms of screen design and information requirements. It also powerfully illustrated the direct impact that dialogue and screen design has on the jobs that people do.

4.3. Weaknesses of TAC's

A number of problems emerged through use of TACs. Some were context-specific in that the late release of the methodology containing TACs to the project, limited the complete range of activities which they could inform. Other problems were more general but point the way in developing TACs as a systems design tool. These can be considered under three headings:

4.3.1. Volume/quality
Several TACs were drawn for each function to explore job design options. The exercise was both time consuming and labour intensive, and resulted in a large stack of paper! If TACs had been drawn in the earlier stages of the project (i.e. TAC 1 and TAC 2 in Figure 3.4 above), the problem would have been compounded. Whilst it is intended that TACs be used as an exploratory technique in the early stages of system design, and therefore need not be perfect in every detail, there was also a significant amount of variation in the quality and accuracy in spite of the training which had been given.

4.3.2. Using the TACs to specify job design requirements
A second problem (related to the first) is that the level of detail to which TACs can be drawn, makes it difficult to decide on the preferred allocation of functions for the overall design of jobs or work organisation. This points to the need for 'higher level' TACs representing more global units of the organisation.

4.3.3. Integrating TAC's into the system design process
As it stood, it was difficult to integrate this technique with the products from other techniques used in SSADM. It was difficult to make direct links in terms of inputs (to the drawing of TAC's) and outputs (in terms of feeding into the development of the system specification). Typical questions asked by the users was whether each chart should be based on a single 'Function', 'DFD', 'Entity' or 'Process' (SSADM terms), or any other 'chunk' of data. Clearly there was a need to clarify the relationship between TACs and the other SSADM entities. It was later found that the charts can be develop ed from the SSADM 'Event Catalogue'. A TAC will typically cover several events which tend to form a 'task' (from an end user's point of view).

5. THE WAY FORWARD

5.1. The case for CASE

To be effective, TACs need to be drawn for all aspects of the job that is defined as 'critical' both to the organisation and the design of the computer system. To reduce the effort involved, the process of drawing them can be automated. To realise its full potential however, it is not sufficient to just develop a graphical drawing tool. Some form of analysis needs to built into the tool encapsulating a certain amount of job design and evaluation expertise to support the human evaluator.

5.2. Translating job design requirements into system specifications

Job design is not solely about maximising the effectiveness of technology, nor even about ensuring that the human components of the socio-technical system have a meaningful, and satisfactory role to play. It is also about achieving overall organisational effectiveness. All of these factors must be taken into account when designing a system to meet an organisation's job design requirements. TACs appear to provide a useful technique for projecting a proposed computer system in terms of its job design implications and user interface requirements, at least at the micro level of functions. The technique requires further development if it is to be used to explore work organisation options at a global level before any systems design decisions are taken (ie before the boundary is established). Work is now progressing to achieve this goal.

REFERENCES

[1] Gould J D & Lewis C , "Designing for Usability - Key Principles and What Designers Think", Communications of the ACM, 1985, 28, 300-311.

[2] Buckle J K, Langefors B, Mayr H C, Solvberg A, 1979. Position papers: "What is a formal requirement?" In 'Formal Models and Practical Tools for Information Systems Design', H J Schneider (ed.), North Holland (IFIP TC-8).

[3] Ceri S, "Requirements Collection and Analysis in Information Systems Design" In Information Processing 86, H J Kygler (ed). Elsevier Science Publishers BV (North Holland), 1986.

[4] Miller J C, "Conceptual models for determining information requirements". Proc. of the Joint Computer Conference, 1964, 609-620.

[5] Sutcliffe A, "Some Experiences in integrating specification of HCI within a structured system development method". In People and Computers IV, DM Jones & R Winder (eds.), HCI Conference, Manchester, 1988.

[6] Fowler C, Macaulay L, Hutt A, and Kirby M, "User Skills and Task Match (USTM), A Human Factors based methodology for determining product requirements". Proc. of the Alvey Conferences, Swansea, July 1988.

[7] Galer M D, "The HUFIT Toolset: Human Factors Tools for Designers" (in publication). HUSAT Research Institute, The Elms, Elms Grove, Loughborough, Leics.

[8] Gardner A and McKenzie J, "Human Factors Guidelines for the design of computer-based systems". Parts 1-6, Issue 1, 1988. Ministry of Defence (PE) and the Dept. of Trade and Industry. Distributed by the HUSAT Research Institute.

[9] Olphert C W and Damodaran L, "Job Design, Work Organisation and System Design: Payfund" in 'Case Studies in Information Technology' (eds.) Legge K, Clegg C, and Kemp K, Blackwell 1990.

Human–Computer Interaction – INTERACT '90
D. Diaper et al. (Editors)
Elsevier Science Publishers B.V. (North-Holland)

THE DEVELOPMENT OF TOOLS TO ASSIST IN ORGANISATIONAL REQUIREMENTS DEFINITION FOR INFORMATION TECHNOLOGY SYSTEMS

S D P Harker, C W Olphert & K D Eason

HUSAT Research Institute
Loughborough University of Technology, Loughborough, Leics. , U.K.

The 5-year CEC ESPRIT II Project 2301, begun in January 1989, aims to create a methodology called ORDIT (Organisational Requirements Definition for Information Technology systems) which will enable those engaged in systems analysis and design to identify and address organisational requirements. The methodology will use concepts at the organisational and work role levels of description to represent these requirements, and will also provide a variety of tools (including software tools) for using this representation as a simulator to explore the implications of systems at various stages in their development. This paper discusses the concepts which underpin the Project, the emerging methodology, and prototype tools.

1. RATIONALE FOR THE ORDIT PROJECT

It is widely recognised that the design of a product can only be as good as the statement of requirements for that product. This means making the requirements specification unambiguous, as complete as possible and consistent, so that progress towards the goals specified can be verified in the course of design. When errors are detected only at the application stage, they are 30 to 100 times more costly to correct that those detected earlier, and most of those errors can be attributed to failures during the stages of requirements capture and design (Groh and Lutz [1]).

The elimination of such errors in the early stages of design is therefore a high economic priority for systems designers. This task is however made increasingly complicated by the growing significance of user and market forces which must be fully represented in the process of requirements capture and representation. One of the major and continuing problems for the information technology community is the tendency to create technically excellent and advanced products which do not meet the needs of user communities.

Considerable progress has been made in recent years with the development of methods to analyse requirements and represent them within the systems development process (e.g. CORE diagrams [2]). Whilst these are important advances, they nevertheless focus on the functionality of systems, and do not treat as significant a range of requirements which might be described as 'non-functional' or organisational. Such requirements are outside the scope of most structured design methodologies, and therefore when they are dealt with, it is often in an informal way.

There is ample evidence that the failure to treat such requirements as central topics in the systems design process leads to problems when systems are implemented. The slow rate of IT uptake is often attributed to the failure to deal with these issues (see, for example, the analysis presented by Hirschheim [3]). Some of the requirements can be managed at the time of implementation, but others (e.g. ease of use, privacy, security and reliability) demand appropriate provisions within the technical system.

It is widely accepted that future generations of

The authors gratefully acknowledge the contributions made by our colleagues in the HUSAT Research Institute and in our partner organisations - MARI Applied Technologies Ltd, Computing Laboratory, University of Newcastle-upon-Tyne, The Work Research Centre plc and Algotech srl - to the formulation of the ideas contained in this paper and to the ORDIT Project.

information systems will be integrated, multi-media, multi-user systems rather than stand-alone products. These systems will have to be carefully matched to organisational requirements if they are to be successful, which suggests that such issues will become progressively more central to systems design. Since many of the analytic and design methods already exist, the most important need, it is argued, is to find a method of formalising non-functional requirements which will act as a focus for analytic and design efforts. It is to this end that the ORDIT project is directed.

2. ORGANISATIONAL (NON-FUNCTIONAL) REQUIREMENTS

The first requirement that an organisation will have of a technical system is that it has the functionality necessary to serve the organisation's purposes. These are the functional requirements of the system. Of equal importance, however, is the need for the system to support these functions in a way which matches the structure, objectives and characteristics of the organisation - i.e. the organisational requirements. Whilst the term 'non-functional' has sometimes been used to describe these requirements, it is the aim of the ORDIT Methodology to allow such requirements to be expressed in a precise form which will enable them to be directly dealt with in the specification of a system; thus, it is hoped that most organisational requirements will eventually be operationalised as functional requirements.

A number of lists or classifications of organisational requirements have been produced. The following is taken from Herbert and Monk [4]:

1. Power
2. Financial Security
3. Responsibility
4. Mistrust
5. Ownership
6. Value
7. Privacy
8. Secrecy
9. Fear of Failure
10. Fear of Injury and Damage
11. Fear of Alienation
12. Fear of Loss
13. Ethics
14. Reasoning, creativity and decision-making capability
15. Arrangements of objects
16. Aesthetics and Presentation
17. Avoidance of Tedious Work
18. Frustration

This list conveys the range and nature of the requirements. Others have concentrated upon grouping the factors and seeking ways of treating them. Dobson and Martin [5], for example, have identified a group of requirements that extend the concept of 'dependability' to subsume reliability, availability, safety and security. Their analysis recognises that these requirements are of overall concern to an organisation, but also that individual users may have specific and important requirements of their own.

ORGANISATIONAL STRUCTURE	ORGANISATIONAL ISSUES	TECHNICAL REQUIREMENTS
Organisational Structures	Power Structures, Control, Monitoring, Accountability, Values	Monitoring, Authorisation, General Access
Multi-User Co-operation	Shared Access, Role Definition, Co-operation and Control	'Read Access', 'Write Access', Change Control
Individual Work Role	Responsibility, Ownership, Autonomy, Information, Reward, Tools	Privacy, Reliability, Flexibility, Personalisation

Figure 1
Organisational Reality and Technical Requirements

3. IMPLICATIONS FOR TECHNICAL SYSTEMS DESIGN

Many of the items which appear in the above list of organisational requirements (e.g. privacy, security, dependability) have different forms of expression and different implications for systems design depending on the level at which they are expressed. This is reflected in Figure 1.

4. ORGANISATIONAL REQUIREMENTS CAPTURE

The need to capture and deal with organisational requirements in the systems design process has long been recognised, and there are a number of methods now in existence to support the handling of such issues in IT systems design. These include forms of analysis which can detect and classify the range of 'non-functional' or organisational requirements within an organisational setting. One example is Checkland's Soft Systems methodology [6] which provides methods for developing a 'rich picture' of organisational needs, incorporation 'soft' and 'hard' requirements and showing their interdependencies.

Other authors, notably Pava [7] and Mumford [8] with the ETHICS methodology, have developed socio-technical systems theory into analysis processes which show the requirements which the social system will lay upon any new technical system. The forms of task and user analysis developed, for example, within the ESPRIT HUFIT programme [9], are also capable of revealing the detailed requirements of users on usability and acceptability criteria.

In addition to analysis methods, there are many sources of design guidance to help design teams meet this kind of requirement. These are at their most developed with respect to the design of usable human-computer interfaces - see, for example, Shneiderman [10]. Methods also exist to support broader issues acceptability and organisational match. Models or profiles have been developed, for example, the model of the occasional, discretionary user presented by Eason [11].

However in spite of the development of techniques to identify and incorporate organisational issues in the systems design process, there is very little evidence that they are widely used. A survey of design process in use, undertaken by Harker et al [12] as part of the Alvey programme, identified the following problems.

- The methods of analysing requirements did not formally collect information about organisational requirements, and even when these needs were recognised by designers, their methodologies did not provide ways of formalising the requirements.

- In the design of technical solutions, there tended to be 'design drift' on organisational issues, as each designer made their own decisions as to what was important and how to treat it. The absence of a formal means of stating the requirement and offering support took this set of issues into the realm of opinion and guesswork.

- Finally, the methods of evaluation rarely incorporated any test against these criteria until the acid test of implementation, when it was usually too late for major redesign.

The conclusion to be drawn from this review is that it is imperative to bring organisational requirements into the mainstream of systems analysis and design. Since many of the analytical and design methods already exist, the most important need is to find a method of formalising organisational requirements which will act as a focus for analytic and design efforts.

5. THE REPRESENTATION OF ORGANISATIONAL REQUIREMENTS

There are many prescriptive theories of organisations that could provide the basis for representation of organisations, for example Beer's cybernetic model of the firm [13]. However, it is not the aim of the ORDIT project to specify ideal organisational forms, but to enable systems designers to build IT systems which match the critical features of a given organisation. In order to achieve this, it is essential to be able to represent organisations as they actually exist or as the policy makers propose that they exist, rather than as they should exist according to theory. The approach adopted is therefore to look for the most common denominator in organisations; the basic objects and the relationships between them.

Organisational theory emphasises one feature of all enterprises; they operate by division of labour. The large tasks that are the 'primary tasks' (Rice [14]) of enterprises, e.g. manufacturing cars, are divided into smaller manageable tasks, that are co-ordinated by control systems. These sub-tasks and their relationships give rise to information needs and information flows, and it is these which define the functionality requirements on an IT system to serve the organisation. Consequently, traditional systems analysis techniques concentrate on capturing these aspects of organisational life.

However, division of labour is not only concerned with the division of tasks. In any organisation consisting of more than one person, there will be a division of labour between members of staff, and normally this differentiation produces different responsibilities. It is useful to describe this division as producing work roles which staff occupy. Each work role defines the responsibilities laid upon the role holder, the relationships with related roles (the 'role set') and the expectations placed on the role by the role set.

The work role defines the task responsibilities of the role holder and therefore the functionality required in an information system to support the role holder. It also defines the rights and obligations of the role holders and therefore many features of expected role holder behaviour which define non-functional requirements; for example, we have expectations that a doctor will treat patient information as confidential and we have other expectations about the behaviour of priests, school teachers, nurses, salesmen, journalists and many others. A work role analysis can therefore reveal many attributes that specify non-functional requirements.

There are two other powerful features of work roles. First a work role can be defined separately from the individual; it is the receptacle the human being fills. We can therefore separate that which is common across a given work role from that which is attributable to the personal characteristics of a particular holder. The latter characteristics have to be mapped by local customisation whereas the former can inform the design of a system to serve many users.

The second attribute of a work role is that it does not require a comprehensive or logical structure. Many of the concepts in role theory exist in order to describe the uncertainties of organisational life; role ambiguity describes the difficulties a role holder may feel in understanding what is required and role conflict describes, for example, the situation where other roles expect incompatible things from the role holder. A role analysis of an organisation would therefore permit the expression of tensions and uncertainties in the social structure and permit an expression of reality rather than the formalised unreality of the published organisational structure.

It is proposed that the concept of describing an organisation as a set of related work roles is used as a basis for representation of organisational requirements because:

1. The work role makes it possible to move between organisational requirements and the requirements of individual users .

2. The work role defines task responsibilities and thereby functionality requirements.

3. The work role defines the relationships between role holders and the behaviour they expect of one another, which defines many 'non-functional' requirements.

4. The work role is a descriptive concept which can be used to represent many different organisational realities from the formal and structured to the fluid and unconstructed.

The project aims to provide formal definitions and languages based on a suitable logic to support these representations.

As well as the key concepts of activity and actor, our approach stresses the logic of information structures and relations between the formalisation of the a) activities and information, and b) actors and information. The former set of relations leads to issues of access modes (eg read, write) and the relation between role and access mode(s); the latter set of relations leads to issues of rights of access and the relation between role and access rights (e.g. to create or to destroy). Again these are important aspects of a role which can be formalised and analysed.

Formalisation of a role is not, of course, an end in itself. The importance of the proposed formalisation is that for the first time it enables roles to be related to requirements in a rigourous manner. In the past, work on formal requirements analysis has proceeded on the assumption that there is a unique set of requirements to be captured, which can then be taken to define the system to be engineered or improved. Our experience of analysis in many systems shows that in many cases this is simply not so. A system is seen from many viewpoints, each of which places its own set of requirements on it. Clearly, these various sets may mutually reinforce each other, or be independent, or conflict. What is needed is some method for detecting conflicts and identifying the means or authority for conflict resolution. Our claim is that our formalisation of roles permits the formal analysis of conflict detection and resolution.

6. THE ORDIT METHODOLOGY

The development of ORDIT as a means of suporting the capture and representation of organisational requirements for IT systems will involve the creation of a methodology (to be known as the ORDIT Methodology) which will describe the way in which these goals may be achieved. The Methodology will set out what should be done, and how the necessary activities will be carried out. It will also specify the relationships between the parts and, where necessary, the timing and order in which activities are to be pursued. It is not the intention to create a complete systems design methodology, but rather to identify a series of complementary activities to existing requirements capture and systems design techniques. The main activities which will form the basis of the ORDIT Methodology are summarised in Figure 2 below.

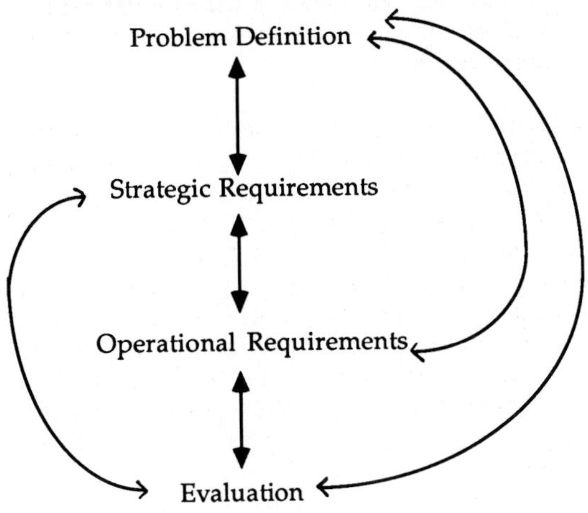

Figure 2
Architecture of the ORDIT Methodology

The central part of the Methodology will be a representational medium in which the organisational world which is to be served by a planned technical system will be described as a network of inter-related work roles. The medium will be capable of distinguishing boundaries between and within organisations. The Project is currently developing a representation medium based on enterprise modelling concepts (see [5]) which will enable work roles in an organisation to be depicted in a set of role relation diagrams (ORDIT Diagrams).

Each work role should be describable by a set of attributes which include task responsibilities (and therefore functionality requirements), work role rights and obligations (and therefore user acceptability requirements), and the required attributes of the role holder (and therefore usability requirements).

It should be noted that whilst the main function of the Methodology is to represent organisational requirements in a way which will facilitate their inclusion in the technical specification for a system, the approach also represents functional requirements. This is necessary because of the tight interdependence of the two types of requirements. There is no need for security or reliability if no information of functional value is supplied, and if the human-machine interface gives access to useless information, the usability of the interface is academic. The type of functionality specified is, however, important to define. It is a macro, or organisational task view of functionality, i.e. facility needed to edit text. The identification of the major areas of functionality related to specific work roles is vital to the acceptability of the technical system.

The process by which the ORDIT methodology will be developed forms an additional and important objective, i.e. that it should be developed in a manner compatible with the philosophy underlying its purpose. That is, it should be a process paying full attention to the functional and organisational requirements of its potential users in design teams. To this end, the proposed development process is user-centred, and will involve a number of iterations over the duration of the Project (5 years from January 1989) in which the proposed product is tested against the requirements of design teams. The intention is that at the end of the Project, the delivered Methodology and supporting Tools are not only demonstrably functional but are also usable and acceptable.

7. THE ORDIT TOOLS

The ORDIT Methodology will be supported by a set of ORDIT Tools, at least some of which will be automated. In the first instance, the Project is creating a software vehicle for the creation and manipulation of ORDIT Diagrams. In line with the principle of iterative development stated above, this and other Tools will be developed through a series of prototype stages and tested against increasingly real design problems. The first prototypes will be demonstrated in mid-1990.

8. APPLICATION DOMAINS AND USERS OF THE ORDIT METHODOLOGY

It is anticipated that the use of the ORDIT Methodology will be concentrated, initially at least, on larger, bespoke systems design projects. These are the systems where organisational requirements provide the greatest explicit challenge, and where there is potentially the greatest cost-benefit to be derived from the use of such a methodology. The Methodology is intended to be applicable in a wide variety of application domains, but this will be subject to field testing throughout the course of the Project.

REFERENCES

[1] Groh, H and Lutz, K, 1984
Outside-in Instead of Top-down: Industrial Scale Software Production with CADOS
Data Report XII, No 4, 19-25

[2] Mullery, G P, 1985.
Acquisition-Environment
In Paul, M and Siegart, H J (Eds)
'Distributed Systems'
Lecture notes in Computer Science, No 190, Springer-Verlag

[3] Hirscheim, R A, 1985
Office Automation: A Social and Organisational Perspective
Chichester, Wiley

[4] Herbert, A J and Monk, J (Eds), 1987
The ANSA Reference Manual
Cambridge, Advanced Networked Systems Architecture

[5] Dobson, J E and Martin, M J, 1986
Modelling Real-World Issues in Dependable Communications Systems
Technical Report No 1,
Computing Laboratory, University of Newcastle-upon-Tyne

[6] Checkland, P, 1981
Systems Thinking, Systems Practice
Chichester, Wiley

[7] Pava, C, 1983
Managing New Office Technology: An Organisational Strategy
New York Free Press

[8] Mumford, E, 1983
Designing Human Systems
Manchester Business School Publications

[9] Galer, M. D. and Taylor, B.C. 1989
Human Factors in Information Technology: ESPRIT Project 385 HUFIT . In:
Contemporary Ergonomics 1989,
Ed. Megaw, E. Taylor & Francis

[10] Schneiderman, B, 1986
Designing the User Interface
Wokingham, Addison-Wesley

[11] Eason, K D, 1988
Information Technology and Organisational Change
London, Taylor and Francis

[12] Harker, S D P et al, 1987
Classifying the Target for Human Factors Output.
Proc. of Alvey Annual Conference, UMIST, Manchester, July 14-16

[13] Beer, S, 1981
The Brain of the Firm
Chichester, Wiley

[14] Rice, A K, 1985
Productivity and Social Organisation: The Ahmedabad Experiment
London, Tavistock

SECTION II: DESIGN: THEORIES, METHODS AND TOOLS

SII.3 Prototyping

Hypermedia as communication and prototyping tools in the concurrent design of commercial airplane products
E. Hofer and F. Ruggiero 303

An object-oriented framework for prototyping user interfaces
P. Windsor 309

Paper versus computer implementations as mockup scenarios for heuristic evaluation
J. Nielsen 315

Human–Computer Interaction – INTERACT '90
D. Diaper et al. (Editors)
Elsevier Science Publishers B.V. (North-Holland)

Hypermedia as Communication and Prototyping Tools in the Concurrent Design of Commercial Airplane Products

Elfriede Hofer and Frank Ruggiero
Training and Computing Technology
Boeing Commercial Airplanes
P.O. Box 3707, M/S 2T-62
Seattle, Washington 98124-2207, USA

This paper discusses the utility of hypermedia technology as a communications and proto-typing tool for a "concurrent" or "integrated" product design approach. This design approach uses multifunction teams, called Design-Build-Support Teams (DBST's), with members from the design, manufacturing, and customer service disciplines working together from the outset to communicate effectively and produce a robust design--one which requires a minimum of change throughout the product's full life cycle. Examples of hypermedia-based simulation applications from the commercial airplane domain are discussed. These applications in-clude a B747-400 full-flight simulator instructor control station, an animated simulation of the B737-300 airplane pneumatic system and a user-interface prototype of an avionic module.

INTRODUCTION

As in most traditional product design environments, commercial airplane design and development takes place over a number of self-contained, sequential steps or phases starting with: preliminary design or requirements specification, and moving on to product design, analysis and testing, to production and finally, to operator training, system operation and maintenance. Using this serial process, it is very expensive to maintain the high level of product quality demanded by the commercial aviation industry.

One way to improve the process is by providing for a cooperative exchange of information, from the outset of the design sequence, by members of all groups involved in the full life cycle of the product. This concurrent design approach [1] allows designers to anticipate downstream shortcomings or problems, early in the process and make modifications before critical design decisions have been "frozen". Thus optimal product quality and defraying unnecessary development costs can result, as illustrated in Figure 1 below [2] :

This design optimization, however, requires an "egalitarian" communication medium, one which allows all the stakeholders to truly see and understand the design on equal footing with the most sophisticated engineer or human factors specialist. Fundamental to this approach is an increased awareness of the socio-technical context [3] in which new technologies and design methodologies will be used.

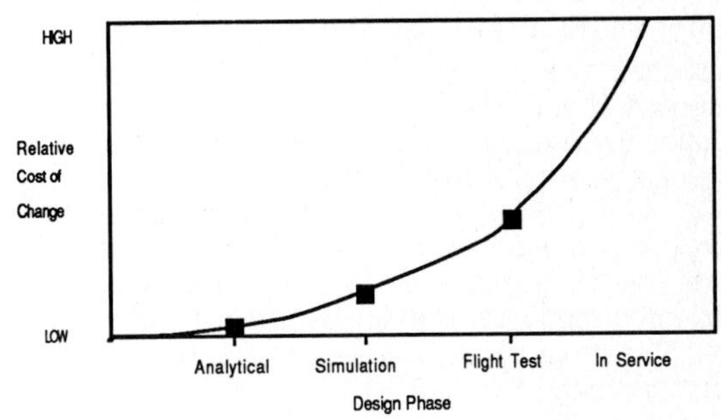

Figure 1. Cost of design change per design phase.

The remainder of this paper will discuss the use of hypermedia-based tools to produce animated simulations, which are being evaluated as possible collaborative computing aids for concurrent design teams that are developing new airplane components and systems.

CONCURRENT DESIGN

A design methodology in which integrated activities are conducted between parallel teams, that communicate and coordinate from the early design stages on through the full life cycle of the product, is labelled by Winner et al. [1] a *concurrent design* methodology:

> *Concurrent design is a systematic approach to the integrated, concurrent design of products and their*

related processes, including manufacture and support. This approach is intended to cause developers, from the outset, to consider all elements of the product life cycle from conception through disposal, including quality, cost, schedule, and user requirements (p. 659).

In a similar vein, Gould [4] advocates *integrated design,* which focuses early and continually on the end user and product usability. Both methodologies yield tremendous payback, because they allow the development of a robust design--one which requires a minimum of change over the course of the product's full life cycle.

A specific implementation of concurrent design methods under evaluation at Boeing Commercial Airplanes are Design-Build-Support Teams (DBST's). DBST's have representatives from each of the major product disciplines, Design, Manufacturing, Customer Service, and Materiel work together to define requirements and jointly evaluate the downstream consequences of the design as early as possible in the product development cycle.

The potential for improved productivity is enormous. For example, using conventional design and development methods, the "learning curve" for hands-on labor tasks, can represent an 80-90% reduction over the first 100 units. If DBST's using concurrent and integrated design practices could reduce the amount of change required so that this learning curve plateaus, at say, 30 units or 10 units, then these methods represent a marvelous opportunity to improve factory productivity. In another area, the B747-400 airplane design, we have used this integrated approach to develop the flight deck [5]. The structure and make-up of that DBST is represented in Figure 2.

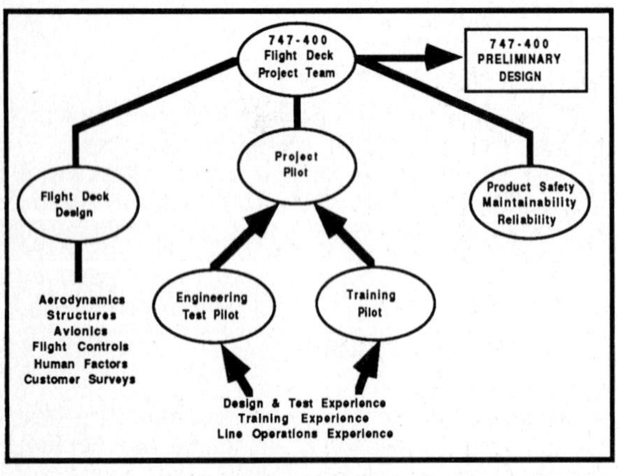

Figure 2. DBST approach to preliminary flight deck design.

Although there seems to be good agreement on the utility of such a concurrent or integrated approach in the design communities, its practical implementation is still not a reality. As pointed out earlier [6], computers and selected computer architectures may constitute enabling technologies in support of concurrent or integrated design. Providing consistent sets of graphical images and sharing engineering databases from the beginning will improve standard, sequential methods of communication and ultimately the product and its quality.

Although later design stages intend to refine proposals made in earlier stages, there still exist communication problems between the technical subject matter experts from various disciplines. (A detailed account on this can be found in [6]). Hopes of remediating the problem with the use of state of the art technologies such as artificial intelligence (AI) or computer aided design (CAD) have fallen short.

The shortcomings of AI occur because it is based on a "linguistic model of reasoning [6] and cannot capture, for example, the intelligence provided by an animated presentation--visual models, which simplify relationships and focus on essential elements, and are still the most powerful method of communicating to others the intended operational aspects of the design.

While AI has proven less than satisfactory in the spatial problem domain, simple CAD systems turn out to be little more than picture generators, unable to communicate the designer's intent or to reason about lifecycle problems. More sophisticated 3-dimensional CAD systems, which can model a large number of system operational attributes, are in development and show great promise. The downside of these newer systems is high cost and a complex user-interface, which requires considerable training and fulltime use to realize the full potential.

According to Williams et al. [6], design knowledge cannot be communicated and practical experience seems to be the only way to gain proficiency in the "black art" of design. They argue that an enabling tool is needed which keeps the people who are involved in the various stages of product design, production and operation in the loop by allowing them to communicate ideas and issues among each other from the early stages onward. Our experience today suggests that hypermedia may constitute such an enabling tool.

HYPERMEDIA FOR PRODUCT LIFECYCLE SUPPORT

Software applications like HyperCard™ and

Supercard™ are new graphics oriented programming environments. They provide powerful visualization and simulation technologies, which have the potential to greatly enhance interdisciplinary communication throughout the lifecycle of a product such as a commercial airliner.

Hypermedia Simulation Capabilities

Both HyperCard™ and Supercard™ are object-oriented programming environments that use a "program generator" and high order scripting language to produce sophisticated *animated simulations* of airplane structures, systems and their interfaces, down to the component level. In addition, complex sounds can easily be added for enhanced realism.

Hypermedia not only enable designers to build systems simulations of high physical fidelity, but also allow for the design of high functional fidelity simulations. Norman [7] advocates that human interfaces should correspond to conceptual models that are easily understood by its users. This can be accomplished through simulations that not only look but also function like the real system that is being simulated. Earlier instructional research [8] also underscores the importance of the functional fidelity of simulations to improve learning outcomes.

Technical Hypermedia Properties

The hypermedia interface has been described as the "universal interface" [9]. A designer can construct just about any type of interface inside HyperCard™/SuperCard™, or modify existing programs created externally or inside the application. The result is an appealing, easy to work with end user-interface.

Hypermedia environments provide a virtual world in which the designer can construct and manipulate objects ("buttons", "fields", graphics, etc.) which may be manipulated by means of scripts (HyperTalk™ / SuperTalk™ programming statements) associated with individual objects. Hypermedia objects can be linked in any desirable combination to create dynamic simulations of airplane systems. The basics of HyperTalk™/ SuperTalk™ scripting can easily be learned by non-programmers such as subject-matter experts who want to build their own systems simulations.

Hypermedia have been employed to produce a number of pilot projects at Boeing's Customer Training organization, and several examples will be discussed. HyperCard™ and SuperCard™ were selected for the featured prototype applications, primarily for their widespread availability, ease of use, and high fidelity graphics and animation capabilities.

Ease of use of HyperCard™ and SuperCard™ by non-programmers was a key factor in its selection for the featured simulations. Since both applications conform to the standard Macintosh user interface, they are easy to learn. The ease of integrating graphics, sound and animation was also an important consideration.

SuperCard™ projects can be saved as stand alone modules making them very portable. When saved this way, a run-time module (necessary to make a project work without the SuperCard™ application) is built in. Each of the application prototypes discussed, fits on a single 800K floppy disk which will run on any of the Macintosh II family of computers, with 5MB of RAM and 256 colors.

For a more complete discussion of hypermedia see [10] - [13].

Hypermedia Prototype Applications

Three prototype simulations will be discussed. They include the following:

- A B747-400 full flight simulator instructor control station.
- An avionic "BITE" control module interface prototype.
- An animated simulation of the B737-300 airplane pneumatic system.

<u>Simulator instructor station prototype.</u>
The 747-400 full flight simulator instructor control station prototype development illustrates, on a small scale, many of the benefits of concurrent design. This workstation, located in the rear of the full flight simulator, allows the flight instructor to program the simulator lesson plan for a crew, including inflight faults and other unusual situations. The instructor station interface makes use of two 19 inch touch sensitive monitors. Simulator flight profiles and option menus appear on the screen and the instructor touches the areas representing his choices.

Initially, the engineering team defined requirements by using a series of drawings representing the screens for the system. The team then built storyboards with McDraw™ screen drawings. To explain to the simulator manufacturer how the touch sensitive screen of the instructor interface would operate. As the design progressed, the number of branching possibilities from each screen also increased and it became cumbersome to explain how the system would work.

Midway through the requirements definition phase, HyperCard™ became available and the design team was able to quickly develop (within nine days) a working simulation by incorporating the prototype screen drawings into an operational HyperCard™ stack. The DBST, which included engineers, instructors, and suppliers, used the prototype stack to communicate design requirements, evaluate the design's usability and prototype the "functional specification".

With each design change the prototype stack was updated and passed between the airframe manufacturer and flight simulator supplier. As the simulator was brought into service the prototype stack was "frozen" and it became the chief means of verifying the correct operation of the instructor station. At the simulator manufacturer's facility, the stack became the only device capable of training the simulator engineers on how the simulator should operate, since no real equipment was available.

Following full acceptance of the flight simulator, the stack was modified into a computer-based training lesson and used for new or refresher training of simulator instructors. About 90% of the instruction could be accomplished using the stack, eliminating the need to schedule the full flight simulator just to train instructors. The most recent application of this stack has been as a demonstrator for the simulator manufacturer. Prospective customers are shown how the basic 747-400 instructor station operates and new features or functionality requested by the customer are prototyped using the stack.

To summarize, this HyperCard™ stack has served very well during: requirements definition, design evaluation, procurement verification, acceptance testing, instructor training, and sales/marketing for the supplier.

Avionic control module prototype.
The BITE (Built-in Test Equipment) module simulation was developed to reflect design proposals and modifications for a new, standardized user-interface to maintenance electronics equipment used to troubleshoot faults on airplanes. The simulation was done in HyperCard™ and represents the proposed requirements and specifications.

The new BITE prototype was the direct result of a redesign effort aimed at standardizing the control panels for some 29 different BITE modules by proposing one common user-interface for all future BITE modules.

The BITE system is an avionic control and monitoring system designed to collect electronic signals from specific airplane systems sources (e.g., power, hydraulics, electrical, etc.) that it monitors. It records and reports in-flight and on-ground faults, does automatic tests and can be used for troubleshooting faults by means of interactive testing.

During the course of the design requirements specification phase, the standardized BITE prototype simulation was employed in usability tests with airline maintenance technicians. For the usability tests a tutorial on how to operate the module was added to the simulation and troubleshooting scenarios. Subjects were first asked to troubleshoot without any instructions. Then they were stepped through the interactive tutorial and asked to do additional troubleshooting. The results of the usability studies were used to make modifications to this preliminary design.

Airplane pneumatic system simulation.
This simulation of the B737-300 pneumatic system is one of several such simulations developed at Boeing's Customer Training organization. The intent of these systems simulations is to serve as exploratory instructor led training aids, supplementing more traditional, computer-based airplane systems and operations training. This animated simulation concept is also being tried by design-build-support teams (DBST's), as a communication and design medium for new airplane systems.

The pneumatics system simulation was developed with SuperCard™ in conjunction with several other software applications, including an animation program and a color paint program.

By clicking on airplane components, this animated simulation takes the user on a structured walk-through starting from the airplane exterior, on to the flight compartment, electronics bay, or any other desired location, down to the component level. Graphical images, originally scanned from photographs or digitized video images, can be manipulated via zooming and spatial rotation functions. Valves can be opened and closed to simulate the dynamics of propagating hydraulic fluid flow, for example. Most importantly, the pneumatics system not only has structural similarity with the real system, but it also simulates its operational characteristics with a high degree of fidelity.

COMPUTER-SUPPORTED COLLABORATIVE WORK

Judging from our experience with the applications discussed in the previous section, hypermedia appear to have great potential for supporting concurrent and integrated design activities. However, the implementation of hypermedia into the existing design process requires careful consideration of the organizational and social context in which the new technology is to be embedded.

The proliferation of computer networks and software applications supporting group work activities has resulted in a recent surge of interest in computer-supported cooperative work (CSCW) or *groupware* which is defined as follows [14]:

> *GROUPWARE = intentional GROUP processes and procedures to achieve specific purposes + softWARE tools designed to support and facilitate the group's work*

Geirland [15] points out that the potential benefits of computer-supported cooperative work in organizations is profound, but that the potential for user resistance is also great. Similarly, the potential usefulness of hypermedia for DBST's in the airplane design domain is great, given their implementation into the existing design environment is carefully planned.

To avoid the pitfalls associated with the implementation of new technologies targeted for use by work groups, Geirland [15] recommends a *macro-ergonomic approach.* This approach advocates a careful consideration of not only the task at hand and the selected work methodology, but also of the social structure and organizational culture of the environment in which a system or new enabling technology is used. He maintains that:

> *inadequate attention to social and environmental aspects of the sociotechnical system may result in development of a sophisticated technology that does not meet the need of users, does not fit into the social and cultural milieus in which users operate, and does not support the larger mission of the group or organization in which it is introduced* (p.2)

If CSCW approaches are to realize their full potential, then empirically based models of cooperative work must be developed to prototype and test potential applications. User groups must be targeted, a taxonomy of cooperative workstyles developed, and the interdependencies, functions, and socio-cultural forces must be assessed in a naturalistic setting or everyday work groups.

FUTURE OUTLOOK FOR CONCURRENT, COLLABORATIVE DESIGN

In order to increase product effectiveness and efficiency throughout its lifecycle, concurrent engineering will be a necessity in future design efforts. *Design-Build-Support Teams (DBST's)* will play a major role in the realization of concurrent engineering practices, given they are provided with carefully implemented, powerful enabling technologies supporting their collaborative work efforts.

Hypermedia represent an enabling technology capable of bridging the communication gap that still exists between the various stakeholders in the design process. By means of animated simulations, which can be rapidly created and modified, design ideas may be communicated without ambiguity and issues documented and resolved, sometimes even during the course of group meetings.

Finally, to realize the potential of hypermedia and current design, greater emphasis must be placed on the socio-technical context in which these new media and methods will be used. A careful study of the social and organizational changes, likely to result from increased interactions between people sharing new technologies, will facilitate the implementation of concurrent design.

REFERENCES

[1] Winner, R., Pennel, J., Bertrand, H., and Slusarczuk, M. *The role of concurrent engineering in weapons system acquisition.* Institute of Defense Analysis Report R-338.

[2] Sandry-Garza, D.L., Boucek, G.P.Jr., Logan, A.L., Biferno, M.A., and Corwin, W.H. *Transport Aircraft Crew Workload Assessment-Where Have We Been and Where are We Going?* (Warrendale, PA: SAE Technical Paper No. 871769).

[3] Smith, A. W. *Management systems: Analyses and applications.* (Hinsdale, IL:Dryden Press, 1982).

[4] Gould, J. D., How to design usable systems, in: Bullinger, H.-J. and Shackel, B. (eds.), *Human-Computer Interaction - INTERACT'87* (North-Holland, Amsterdam: Elsevier, 1987).

[5] Higgins, J. K. and Braune, R. J., The Manufacturer's role in training program development. Paper presented at the *Fifth International Symposium on Aviation Psychology,* (The Ohio State University, Columbus, Ohio, April 17-20, 1989).

[6] Williams, J., Pentland, A., and Connor, J., Interactive integrated design - visualization of form and process, in: Salvendy, G. and Smith, M. J.(eds.), *Designing and Using Human-Computer Interfaces and Knowledge Based Systems.* (North -Holland, Amsterdam: Elsevier, 1989).

[7] Norman, D. A. Interface critic considers visual cues. *MacWeek* 3(12), (1989), 19-20.

[8] Alessi, S. Fidelity in the design of instructional simulations. Paper presented at the Annual Meeting of the American Educational Research Association, Washington, D. C. (April, 1987).

[9] Swaine, M. Bullish on the stack market. *MacUser,* 5(5), (1989), 211-212.

[10] Mourant, R. R. Designing human inferfaces with Hypercard, in: Salvendy G. and Smith M. J. (eds.), *Designing and Using Human-Computer Interfaces and Knowledge Based Systems.* (North-Holland, Amsterdam: Elsevier,1989).

[11] Conklin, J. Hypertext: An Introduction and Survey, *IEEE Computer* 20(9), (1987), 17-41.

[12] Goodman, D. *The complete HyperCard Handbook.* (New York: Bantam Books, 1988).

[13] Nicol, A. Interface design for hypermedia: models, maps, and cues, in: *Proceedings of the Human Factors Society--32nd Annual Meeting.* (Santa Monica, CA: The Human Factors Society, 1988), pp. 308-312.

[14] Johnson-Lenz, P. and Johnson-Lenz, T. Groupware: The process and impacts of design choices, in: Kerr, E. B. and Hiltz, S. R. (eds.), *Computer-mediated communication systems.* (New York: Academic Press, 1982), pp. 45-55.

[15] Geirland, J. Developing design guidelines for computer-supported cooperative work: A macroergonomic approach. *Human Factors Society Bulletin,* 32(9), (Sep. 1989), pp.1-4.

Human–Computer Interaction – INTERACT '90
D. Diaper et al. (Editors)
Elsevier Science Publishers B.V. (North-Holland)

AN OBJECT-ORIENTED FRAMEWORK FOR PROTOTYPING USER INTERFACES

Peter Windsor

Logica Cambridge Ltd, Betjeman House, 104 Hills Road Cambridge, CB2 1LQ, UK
email: petew@logcam.co.uk

We have developed a software framework for prototyping user interfaces combining the technology of user interface management systems and window system toolkits. The architecture provides: support for the overall structure of the interface, the means to define and control the dialogue at high and low levels and control over the fine details of presentation and interaction style. The design is object-oriented and achieves great flexibility through inheritance and polymorphism. The framework has been used to produce operational prototypes as part of the requirements analysis for a new workstation for the Oceanic Air Traffic Control Centre

1. Introduction

We have recently completed a project for the UK's Civil Aviation Authority to determine the user interface requirements for upgrading their Flight Data Processing System (FDPS) for the Oceanic Air Traffic Control Centre (the MMI PARC project). The principal means used to elicit these requirements was to build a series of prototype user interfaces and run trials with the Air Traffic Controllers and Assistants. In this paper, we describe the SIRIUS software that formed the basis for these prototypes.

The need to prototype user interfaces is now an "almost universally accepted principle" (Baecker & Buxton 1987, preface to Part III). However, there is wide variety of prototyping approaches differing in sophistication and complexity from "slide shows" through to full simulations (Hekmatpour & Ince 1986). In the MMI PARC project we were tackling a complex system and we expected that many of the requirements would derive from the detailed aspects of the task and from timing and sequencing considerations. Our initial analysis confirmed this; we found three major areas that our prototypes would have to address:

- Air Traffic Controllers need to build and maintain a mental picture of the traffic under their control. To explore this requirement we would have to display realistic volumes of data that changed over time.
- There is potential for break down of communications both between members of a watch and with external control centres, especially for uncommon events. To analyse this requirement needs either a multi-user system or the ability to simulate the operational environment.
- Air Traffic Control Assistants are required to enter and correct flight plans and other complex data, sometimes under considerable time pressure.

This made it clear that we would ultimately need full-scale, operational prototypes, although we also wanted to use partial prototypes as a means to check the validity of our ideas before proceeding to the full, integrated system. Therefore, we decided to build a user interface prototyping framework – SIRIUS – as a platform that would allow the later work to concentrate on the requirements analysis.

2. Requirements for a User Interface Prototyping Tool

We saw three fundamental requirements for SIRIUS:

- It should be flexible. It should allow a wide range of possible user interface designs.
- It should allow designs to be changed. In particular, it should be possible to change the overall structure of the interface yet still retain and re-use those portions that were still appropriate to the design.
- It should include an incremental development environment which would allow prototypes to be run and modified concurrently.

A possible fourth requirement was for high level tools to allow prototype user interfaces to be designed directly with minimum recourse to programming. We decided against this for several reasons. Firstly, we recognised that the design of such tools is a research topic in its own right; while we had well developed ideas for the architecture of a prototyping framework we did not believe we could develop design tools within the constraints of the project. Secondly, the commercially available tools were predominantly 'facade builders' and could not easily be used to develop fully functioning prototypes. Where such tools did include a code generator, they did not provide an appropriate development environment.

The changeability requirement had the biggest impact on our software architecture. To achieve this goal, it was clear that that we needed a structure that separated the application from the user interface software. Moreover, within the latter we had to establish a model that distinguished those aspects of the interface that could be independently changed and ensured that the software design kept them apart.

3. Separating the User Interface from the Application

In an idealised and abstracted view, the user interface and (non-interactive) application software are quite separate and communicate through a well-defined protocol. In the extreme case, they may even be separate processes. Hence, the idea of a UIMS (Pfaff 85)– a general purpose software tool which can implement a user interface from a high level, declarative description. In practice, the appearance and behaviour of the user interface are heavily application dependent, and its description needs the power of a programming language. This motivates the idea of a User Interface Framework (UIF) – a software tool within which application specific user interface software resides.

Separation of user interface and the application remains a crucial design goal for such a framework. For the SIRIUS software, we used two techniques to achieve this objective. Firstly, we developed a model that allowed us to describe the combined system at several levels. Secondly we used the object-oriented approach to software design which gave us the means to integrate application specific semantics into a general purpose design.

3.1. The User Interface Model

The user interface model describes aspects of the interactive system as a series of layers, starting with the highly abstract 'non- interactive core' and moving towards a concrete view of the user interface. Within the layers, there are both application and user interface elements, but the emphasis shifts from the former to the latter as the description becomes more concrete. Figure 1 shows the user interface model.

The Stateless, Non-Interactive Core of the system is the application database and its associated functions. It is stateless in the sense that notions such as 'current selection' are removed and that there are no 'modes'. It can be described as a semantic data model (Hull & King 1987).

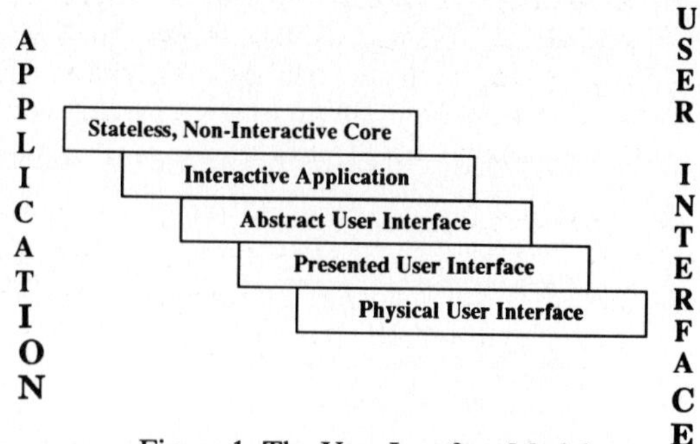

Figure 1: The User Interface Model

The Interactive Application augments the semantic data model by describing the overall state of the system and the high level dialogue through which the user interacts with it. It introduces a number 'state variables' typically to contain references to the database objects with which the user is working. The combination of the Stateless and Interactive descriptions of the application form the designer's conceptual model or system image. (Foley 1988, Norman 1986, 1989)

The Abstract User Interface describes the structure of the user interface. It specifies the different displays presented to the user and the information they are intended to convey, the commands that the user may give to the system and the behaviour of the user interface as the application responds.

The Presented User Interface describes the concrete appearance of the system to the user and its behaviour in response to the user's actions. This is the level which is most commonly used to describe a user interface.

The Physical User Interface describes the details of the presentation and behaviour of the system at the device level.

A particular benefit of this model for prototyping user interfaces is that it allowed us to understand what we were changing between two series of prototypes. The significant changes were all in the Interactive Application layer, the Stateless Application did not change at all. The Abstract and Presented User Interface aspects of the design changed in response to the higher level changes and the individual parts were then refined at those levels.

3.2. The Object-Oriented Approach

Object-oriented programming languages are characterised by four features: information hiding, data abstraction, dynamic binding and inheritance (Pascoe 1986). They all contribute to making object-oriented paradigm appropriate to the implementation of a User Interface Framework:

- Information hiding and data-abstraction are key elements of all modern programming languages. They give the means to control the complexities of a software system by allowing parts of its state to be localised in a module and then accessed through a well-defined abstract interface. Graphical user interfaces inevitably have a complex state which demands careful encapsulation.

- Dynamic binding or polymorphism allows different types of data to respond to the same instructions (messages). In a UIF, polymorphism lets the framework software function with a variety of different application supplied software.

- Inheritance allows application software to use standard mechanisms where they are appropriate and replace them with specialised versions where they are not. Inheritance in a UIF means that the user interface is not constrained by the pre-defined facilities of the framework. The framework becomes an open system which can be extended and modified by an application.

In addition, the Smalltalk-80 system which was used to implement the framework provides an extremely productive development environment (Goldberg & Robson 1983, Goldberg 1984).

4. The SIRIUS Interactive Architecture

The architecture of the SIRIUS software is a synthesis of ideas from UIMS, user interface toolkits and computer graphics. The overall structure follows the Seeheim architecture for a UIMS (Pfaff 1985) with presentation and dialogue manager components implementing the user interface between the application and a device interface. However, an additional mechanism is introduced at the interface of these two components to provide the Abstract User Interface layer of the SIRIUS model. It also differs from UIMS approach in that there is no explicit specification language to configure the UIMS; the user interface is implemented in the high level language as sub-classes of the framework classes.

The architecture supports the user interface model as follows:

- the non-interactive core of the application maintains a database; this is shared with the user interface software, but only updated by the core application

- the dialogue manager maintains the overall state of the user interface and coordinates the various elements

- the abstract user interface is represented as a collection of components or 'models' each of which has a number of views (corresponding to the windows and panes seen by the user); this is based on the Smalltalk Model-View-Controller paradigm (Goldberg 1984)

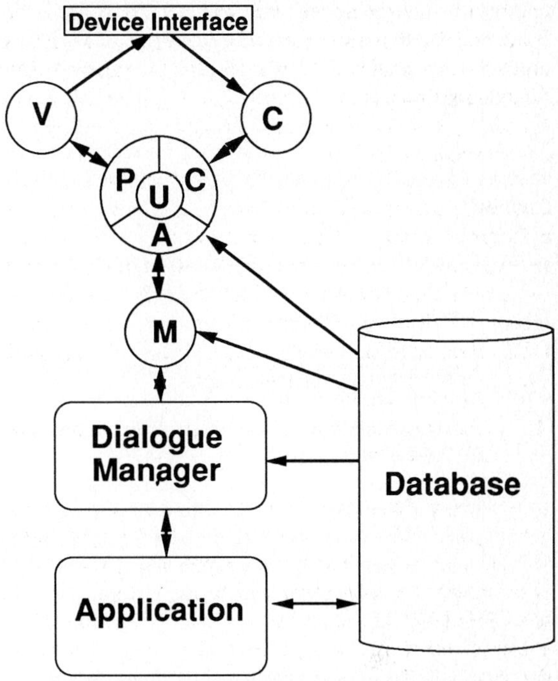

Figure 2: The SIRIUS Interactive Architecture

- the detailed appearance and behaviour of the interface is implemented as hierarchies of Presentation-Abstraction-Control objects (Coutaz 1987, 1989)

- the device interface provides an object-oriented interface to a window server plus device independent graphics output

This layered organisation gives a powerful means to break up the interface software and is efficient because the deeper layers are only invoked when they are needed.

Figure 2 shows the Sirius architecture.

4.1. The Application Interface

The interface between the application and user interface software is in three parts. Firstly, instances in the user interface hold references to the relevant application data. By strict convention, they do not change application data, but generate copies when needed and ask the application to make updates. This is efficient and provides support for one form of undo, but does increase the coupling between the interface and the application.

Secondly, when application data is changed, the application software tells the dialogue manager which data is affected and the aspects of it that have changed. The dialogue manager uses a broadcast mechanism to propagate this information to the components. The dialogue manager also broadcasts changes in the global state of the interface using the same mechanism.

Finally, the mechanism for the user interface to issue commands is based on 'Action Packages' with the following features:

- there is a class of action package for each application function, appropriate instances are generated as the user enters commands
- action packages can be treated as models and hence have views; this allows the options and parameters for the command to be entered (cf dialogue boxes on the Macintosh)
- when a command is issued, the dialogue manager passes it to the application to be executed. In the object-oriented style, the processing is controlled from the action package, the application provides 'atomic' operations.
- a list of action packages provides a logging mechanism; it could also be the basis for an undo mechanism such as that found in Apple's MacApp framework. (Schmucker 1986)

For the Oceanic prototypes, the application is a simulation of the existing FDPS driven by a scenario script. This scenario processing runs as a separate, low priority process using Smalltalk's cooperative scheduling mechanism. As a consequence, the user interface needs to respond to changes in application data that were not initiated by the user. The same broadcast mechanism was used for both scenario and user initiated updates.

4.2. The Dialogue Manager

The dialogue manager is the core of the SIRIUS architecture, but, capriciously, there is relatively little generic software. Instead, the dialogue manager is a framework into which the parts of the application that can directly impact the user interface are placed. The dialogue manager performs the following tasks:

- it maintains a set of variables defining the global state of the system
- it instantiates the components of the abstract user interface according to that state
- it modifies the state as requested by the components (or possibly in response to application events) and informs the components of the changes
- it allows the components to pass instructions to the application in the form of action packages
- it informs the components of changes to application data

The framework software supports these functions, but additional application software is needed to implement them. An important aspect of the generic software is that the mechanism for broadcasting changes to application and global state data executes as separate process that is blocked while the user interface is active. This ensures that changes are batched together and that the user interface does not change unexpectedly during drag interactions.

An additional point to note is that the SIRIUS architecture is an external control system with the application constrained to respond to user requests and not able to request input directly. However, application specific specialisation of the dialogue manager can impose a sequence on the interaction if required. This follows the user interface model in separating out the state dependent parts of the application.

4.3. The Abstract User Interface

Between the dialogue and presentation managers, the SIRIUS architecture introduces an additional mechanism to implement the Abstract User Interface layer of the user interface model. The functions it provides could potentially be seen as part of either dialogue or presentation management. This part of the software is based on the Smalltalk Model-View-Controller approach and describes the user interface as a collection of 'models' each of which has a number of views through which it is presented to the user and a set of abstract functions to which it responds.

The architecture recognises two categories of model. 'Component' models correspond to the windows presented to the user. The views of a component model are the panes of the window and may have scroll bars and other border decoration. The framework software provides the means to define components and their views plus a mechanism for updating the user interface in a wholesale manner, replacing the contents of a view with a significantly changed presentation. Component models are instantiated by the dialogue manager and typically persist for long periods, often throughout a session with the system.

The second form of model are the action packages used to enter commands. These are instantiated by the component models as required and viewed 'within' a component model view, that is the component model obtains the contents of the view from the action package. The action package approach allows the component models and the dialogue manager to be significantly insulated from details of application commands.

Further, the user interface software for a particular command is localised in a single class. It has proved very simple to implement additional commands within this structure.

Pop-up menus are supported as part of the abstract user interface; the framework allows a model to provide a menu for each view and for the whole window. This can be overridden to provide context sensitive menus associated with the individual elements displayed within a view.

4.4. The Presentation Manager

The contents of a view of a model is defined as a 'control panel', a hierarchy of Presentation-Abstraction-Control objects (Coutaz 1987) called controls. Each control provides an abstract interface to the model, knows how to display itself and how to respond to input events. Internally, controls have an update mechanism that is used by the control and abstraction software to initiate updating of the presentation.

The root object of the hierarchy, the control panel itself is typically an application specialisation of the general control panel class. It implements any interaction between the controls and provides an abstract interface with the model. This ensures that the model is unaware of the details of the view apart from instantiating a particular class of control panel. The controls themselves were selected from a library of generic controls – buttons, selection controls etc – plus application specific controls for particular displays and interactions.

The framework includes a configuration mechanism that allows one of a number of equivalent classes to be selected when creating specific instances. Although this could be used to select different models, or even different dialogue managers, it was most useful for selecting different controls. In this way, it is straightforward to switch between different presented user interfaces with a common abstract structure.

In the prototyping environment, we found it to be useful to use deeper nesting of controls than was strictly necessary. For example, our flight plan display control has offspring for organisational sub-divisions – route, overall description, status – and grandchildren for the individual displayed items – positions, times, aircraft type. This was motivated by the desire to make it simple to re-arrange the layout of the display and select alternative presentations using the configuration mechanism. It also proved advantageous for two further reasons. Firstly, the individual items contain the software to present their data, so presentation of each type of data is located in a single class. Secondly, the individual items decide if their data has changed when a general change message is broadcast; this allows incremental updating of the displays.

4.5. The Device Interface

The device interface comprises an object-oriented interface to the workstation window server, a graphics substrate for generating images and an input manager which receives and distributes input events. The window server interface supports multiple, overlapping windows each of which is sub-divided in non-overlapping panes. It did not allow full use of the hierarchy of sub-windows allowed by current window servers.

The graphics substrate provides a rich set of facilities for generating images:

- An object graphics system allows pictures to be built from graphics primitives (lines, arcs, text etc); the pictures can then be updated or otherwise manipulated conveniently and rapidly; this is similar to the structure store of PHIGS (ISO 1988)

- Each view has an 'abstract drawing surface' (known colloquially as 'paper') which has an application specified co-ordinate system and a suite of drawing functions

- Arbitrary transformations can be imposed to create a 'model' coordinate system relative to the 'world' system of the drawing surface; this allows components of a display to be built using convenient coordinates and then scaled, rotated and translated to their required position.

- Named 'styles' are used to select graphics attributes: colours, fonts etc; by using a separate style for each distinct display the interface is made very flexible in this aspect of its appearance. The use of names for styles makes it possible to refer to them directly in the user interface software. Styles are similar to the primitive representation numbers of GKS (ISO 1985).

Conclusions

Our experience in using the SIRIUS software to develop prototypes is that it met our design goals of changeability and productivity and proved sufficiently flexible for our purposes. As a general tool, it is limited in the range of user interfaces that it can implement. The most apparent weakness is that the device interface restricts the user interface to put all output into panes of windows. This does not allow a system to make full use of hierarchical sub-windows supported by window servers such as X11 and NeWS.

The productivity derives primarily from the incremental development capabilities of Smalltalk 80. This is supplemented by the framework's use of object-oriented techniques as relatively little software is needed to specialise the general purpose classes. While it was specifically not an objective, the framework would benefit from the addition of design tools particularly for the layout of elements of the interface. In general, Smalltalk was found to work both as a high level, declarative language for specifying the structure of the system and as a procedural language for implementing its behaviour.

The software certainly met the primary objective of allowing us to experiment with different prototype designs. We believe that this derives from our model of gradual separation between the user interface and application software combined with the innate flexibility of the object-oriented approach.

Acknowledgements

The MMI PARC project team all contributed to the design and implementation of SIRIUS either directly or as designers of prototype user interfaces it had to support. Graham Storrs was the project manager, Kate Blackman, David Brazier, Colin Grant and the author formed the project software team and Simon Dickens and Ged Morrisroe designed prototype user interfaces. The project was funded by the UK Civil Aviation Authority and we would like to thank both the project management from CAA House and the staff at the Scottish and Oceanic Air Traffic Control Centre, especially Roger Wannop who provided our main contact with the ATC operation.

References

Baecker, R. M. and Buxton, W.A.S. (1987). Readings in Human-Computer Interaction: A Multidisciplinary Approach. Morgan Kaufman Publishers: Los Altos, California

Coutaz, J. (1987) PAC, an Implementation Model for Dialog Design. Interact '87, pp 431-436

Coutaz, J. (1989) Architecture Models for Interactive Software. ECOOP '89, pp 383-399

Goldberg, A. and Robson, D. (1983) Smalltalk-80 The Language and its Implementation. Addison-Wesley Publishing Company: Reading, Mass.

Goldberg, A. (1984) Smalltalk-80 The Interactive Programming Environment. Addison-Wesley Publishing Company: Reading, Mass.

Foley, J., Gibbs, C., Kim, W.C. and Kovacevic, S. (1988). A Knowledge-Base User Interface Management System. CHI '88, pp 67-72.

Hekmatpour, S. and Ince, D. C. (1986). Rapid Software Prototyping. Open University Computing Department Technical Report 1986/4.

Hull R. and King R. (1987). Semantic Database Modeling: Survey, Applications and Research Issues. ACM Computing Surveys, Vol 19, No. 3 pp 201-260.

ISO 1985 International Organisation for Standardisation: Information Processing Systems - Computer graphics - Graphical Kernel System (GKS) functional description; ISO IS 7942, July 1985.

ISO 1988 International Organisation for Standardisation: Information Processing Systems - Computer graphics - Programmer's Hierarchical Interactive Graphics System (PHIGS) Part 1 - functional description; ISO IS 9592, 1988.

Norman, D.A. (1986). Cognitive Engineering. In User Centered System Design (Eds D.A. Norman and S.W. Draper. Lawrence Erlbaum Associates, Publishers: Hillsdale, New Jersey.

Norman, D.A. (1988). The Psychology of Everyday Things Basic Books Inc: New York.

Pascoe, G.A. (1986). Elements of Object-Oriented Programming. Byte Magazine, August 1986.

Pfaff, G.E. (ed) (1985). User Interface Management Systems. Eurographics Seminars, Springer-Verlag: Berlin

Schmucker, K.J. (1986). "Object-Oriented Programming for the Macintosh". Hayden Book Company: Hillsdale, New Jersey.

Human–Computer Interaction – INTERACT '90
D. Diaper et al. (Editors)
Elsevier Science Publishers B.V. (North-Holland)

Paper versus Computer Implementations as Mockup Scenarios for Heuristic Evaluation

Jakob Nielsen
Technical University of Denmark *)

A taxonomy of the various forms of scenarios in the user interface field is given, including a discussion of different forms of mockups. A single interface design for a videotex system was implemented as a mockup in two different mediums: As a paper mockup and as a running prototype using HyperCard. These two versions of the same design were then subjected to heuristic evaluation by two similar groups of evaluators. Both versions contained the same fifty usability problems, but there were great differences in the types of problems found by the two groups of evaluators. This indicates that the medium in which a design is presented will have a major impact on what kind of usability problems can be discovered using heuristic evaluation.

Introduction

Heuristic evaluation [Nielsen and Molich 1990] is an informal method of usability analysis where a number of evaluators are presented with an interface design and asked to comment on it. This method forms a significant part of the "discount usability engineering" approach [Nielsen 1989b] of improving user interface under severe resource constraints. See Molich and Nielsen [1990] for a completely documented example of a heuristic evaluation of a user interface.

One advantage of heuristic evaluation is that it can be performed at a very early stage in the usability lifecycle since it does not require the existence of a complete implementation. Specifically, one can perform heuristic evaluation on user interface scenarios as discussed here.

Scenarios in HCI

Just as it has long been the case with terms like "model," "user model," etc. [Nielsen 1990a], the term "scenario" has recently seen widespread use in the user interface community with slightly different meanings. Carroll and Rosson [1990] give examples of the term in at least seven different meanings. Therefore it seems reasonable to try to clarify the terminology by giving the following more precise definitions:

The main characteristic of a scenario is that it is an *encapsulated* description of

- a single *user*
- using a specific set of computer *facilities*
- to achieve a specific *outcome*
- under specified *circumstances.*

This is in contrast to e.g. statistical averages of measurements of many users' interaction with a system or a complete specification of a user interface which typically needs to support many different activities under many different circumstances.

The main types of scenarios are:

Archetypical interactions: These scenarios are descriptions of typical previous observations of user behavior which can be used to assess theories of human–computer interaction by analyzing how each observed phenomenon would be described in the terminology of the

*) Author's current address: Bellcore, 445 South Street, Morristown, NJ 07960-1910, USA. This paper was written while the author was at the Technical University of Denmark and does not represent views or policies of Bellcore. Email: nielsen@bellcore.com

theory and whether the theory can account for it [Young and Barnard 1987].

Illustrative scenarios: Striking observations of usability problems which can be used to argue for the change of a specific design or for the relevance of some user interface issue. For example, [Nielsen 1990b] illustrates the problems with navigating large information spaces in a traditional hierarchical file system with a scenario of a user having to move between subdirectories a total of nine times to get an address for a letter.

Design scenarios: Design scenarios are used to develop specifications for a system by providing examples of possible goals users may have when using the system [Carroll and Rosson 1990]. A design scenario can gradually develop into a presentation scenario as it gets more detailed and approximates a full design of a given set of system features by including not just descriptions of user goals but also descriptions of the actions users may take to reach these goals.

Presentation scenarios (storyboards or videotaped): Presentation scenarios are intended to be shown to an audience to communicate the nature of a proposed interface better than can be done with a textual description. They are frequently videotaped [Vertelney 1989] but can also be presented to the audience by a speaker showing a series of slides with the relevant screens. Presentation scenarios that are only implemented as a series of screen shots on paper are often called storyboards. In a similar analogy with filmmaking terminology [Chell 1987], the videotaped presentation scenarios could be seen as a kind of "pencil test" of the final interface. The audience can be managers or programmers who need to know what the proposed system will be like, or it can consist of user representatives who are asked to comment on the design as early feedback to check whether the design matches their requirements. The difference between an illustrative scenario and a presentation scenario is that the presentation scenario is intended to give the audience as good an understanding of the proposed design as possible while the illustrative scenario is aimed at giving an example of a usability issue and is intended to help the audience understand that issue. This means that the presentation scenario should have fairly comprehensive coverage of the design while the illustrative scenario can be more focused.

Mockups (paper or computer-based): A mockup is an especially cheap kind of interface prototype since it only implements a single scenario of an interaction with the computer [Nielsen 1987]. The difference between mockups and the other scenarios considered in this list is that mockups can actually be used interactively by users and therefore form a generic fame for a set of interactions which are instantiated by the individual user as he or she uses the mockup. A paper mockup consists of a series of screen designs only, and needs a human to "play computer" and present the screens to the user in the right order according to the user's (simulated) actions. A computer mockup does run, but only allows the user extremely limited freedom of action in each system state since it only supports actions within the scenario it implements.

Experimental setting: Used to provide the subjects in a usability test with an artificial background for the tasks they are asked to perform. For a test of a word processor a user might be asked to imagine that he or she works as a secretary for a manager writing a proposal which needs to be changed before a certain deadline. This experimental setting scenario can also be used by the experimenter to come up with a reasonable and coherent set of tasks for the subject to perform.

Generic test suite: Generic test suites describe a set of tasks that is reasonable to use for the testing of a given class of computer applications. For example, a generic test suite for hypertext authoring could present a scenario of a university course catalog where the user was asked to add a node describing a new course and the links to other courses related to the new course with prerequisites relations as well as links to navigation screens presenting classifications of courses. Roberts and Moran [1983] present a classic example of a generic test suite for text editing. A person wanting to test a new system can construct test tasks for the subjects from the generic test suite and would have the advantage of being able to compare the results from the new system with similar results from previous tests of old systems.

Documentation scenarios: Used to provide users with task oriented instruction by giving them specific examples of what their new system is good for. These documentation scenarios are most frequently in the form of text in a manual but many recent software packages have been released with a video tape showing examples of their use or even with a hypermedia-based documentation scenario [Eisenhart 1989]. Finally, many systems include tutorials which allow the user to work through a specific scenario with the actual software using files supplied with the tutorial.

A Taxonomy of Scenarios

The types of scenarios presented above can be classified according to the following three dimensions:

Purpose:
- Communicate user interface issues to an audience
  - —managers, colleagues
  - —users
- Structure thinking and provide background for refinements
- Testing
  - —interfaces
  - —HCI theories

Medium of expression and implementation:
- Textual description
- Storyboards (screen designs on paper, video, etc.)
- Running system on an actual computer

Source of inspiration:
- Empirical observations
- Designer's ideas and analysis

The types of scenarios listed above were distinguished by their purpose. The medium of the scenario seems to be an orthogonal dimension since each type of scenario could conceivably be implemented in each of the three media, even though not all media are equally suited for all purposes. Finally, the source of inspiration for the content of the scenario is a more fluent dimension where a given scenario can shift its classification as it is further developed and gets inspiration from additional sources. Table 1 presents a classification of the scenario types listed above according to these three dimensions. Even though only design scenarios are listed as having the explicit purpose of structuring thinking, there is obviously also an implicit side effect on the designer's thinking from the development of other scenarios like presentation scenarios, mockups, and documentation scenarios (if the latter are developed *before* implementation and not after as it is usually done).

An Evaluation of Two Mockups

Heuristic evaluation can be performed on all forms of scenarios but is probably best suited for mockup scenarios. To compare the use of the method for evaluating paper and computer mockups, we constructed both kinds of mockup of a single interface. The interface was an approximation of the Danish videotex system, Teledata. There were minor differences such as the use of a monochrome screen in the scenario compared to a

	Inspired by empirical observations			**Inspired by designer's ideas**		
	Text	*Storyboards*	*Running system*	*Text*	*Storyboards*	*Running system*
Communication	Illustrative scenarios	Extended illustrative scenarios		Documentation (manual)	Presentation scenarios, Documentation (video)	Documentation (tutorial)
Structure thinking	Refined design scenarios			Design scenarios		
Testing	Archetypical interactions	Iterative test of mockups (paper)	Iterative test of mockups (running)	Experimental setting, Generic test suites	Mockups (paper)	Mockups (computer)

Table 1. *Scenario types classified according to the three dimensions: Source of inspiration, medium, and purpose.*

color screen in the real system. The scenario consisted of ten screens showing the finding of certain information about Scandinavian Airlines flights. The HyperCard implementation of the computer mockup is discussed further in [Nielsen 1989a]. It is important to stress that both versions had exactly the same screen designs and dialogues. The paper version contained the dialogue behavior as written specifications and the computer version implemented those specifications.

Both versions of the user interface were evaluated using heuristic evaluation. Two different (but similar) groups of evaluators were used to eliminate the transfer-effect. The number of evaluators was 37 for the paper version and 29 for the computer version. The original study evaluating the paper mockup is described as the "Teledata" study in [Nielsen and Molich 1990].

Virzi [1989] discusses the differences between "low-fidelity" and "high-fidelity" prototypes, defining fidelity as the extent to which a person cannot distinguish a prototype from the final system. According to this definition, our paper mockup was a very low-fidelity prototype, while the computer mockup had somewhat higher fidelity. It is therefore of interest to compare the

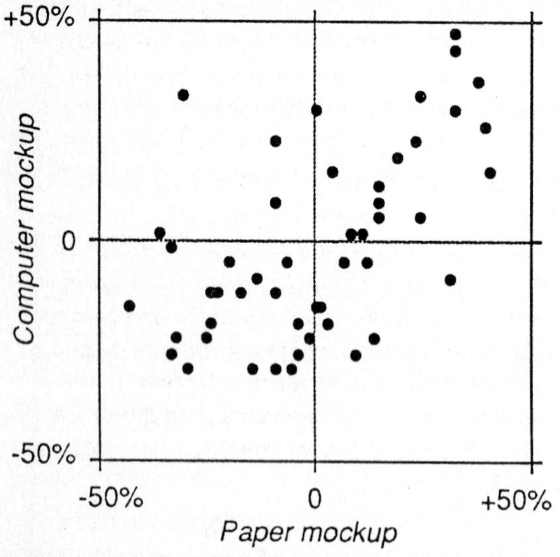

Figure 1. *Comparing the relative difficulty of finding the same usability problems in two versions of a user interface. Each dot represents one usability problem, and its position indicates whether the probability for finding that problem was larger (positive numbers) or smaller (negative numbers) than the average.*

ease with which the usability problems were found by the evaluators in the two cases.

Both versions of the user interface contained the same 50 usability problems. Actually, the paper mockup contained a further two usability problems which had to be eliminated in the computer mockup simply because of the instantiation of the paper specification in a running implementation. This is in itself an indication that a higher-fidelity prototype will give a different evaluation result than a low-fidelity prototype.

Results: Finding Usability Problems on Paper vs. the Computer

From Figure 1 we observe that most usability problems were either easy to find in both versions (dots in the upper right hand corner) or difficult to find in both versions (dots in the lower left hand corner). There are some differences, however, and a regression analysis comparing the two evaluations only gives $R^2 = 0.37$ which is rather minimal, considering that we are talking about two studies of the same interface.

Table 2 provides some insight into the differences between the two evaluations by listing those usability problems that were much easier to find in one version than the other.

Of the 50 usability problems, 15 can be classified as major, while the 35 are minor or cosmetic problems. On the average, the major problems were found 6% *less* than the minor problems in the paper mockup while they were found 25% *more* in the computer mockup. This indicates that the computer mockup tended to focus the evaluators more on the major usability problems while the paper mockup tended to focus evaluators somewhat more on minor problems. A similar conclusion can be drawn from Table 2 which lists only two major problems in the group of problems scoring much better in the paper mockup than in the computer mockup, while it has five major problems among the group of problems scoring much better in the computer mockup than in the paper mockup.

Let us analyze these seven major errors in slightly more detail to see why they differed so much between the paper and the computer mockup.

Problem (short description)	Paper Rank	Computer Rank	Difference
The term "INTERCONT" is not Danish	19	45	–26
"ExDB" is not user-oriented language	16	41	–25
Menu choices should have consecutive numbers	8	29	–21
Same error message is used for more than one error	30	47	–17
Need consistent rules for the concept "index"	***28***	***44***	***–16***
Inconsistent listing of actors for inflight films	33	49	–16
UNKNOWN IP error message should confirm user's input	***23***	***38***	***–15***
UNKNOWN IP error message needs constructive addition	***50***	***34***	***+16***
Last two lines in Screen 2 are strange	***34***	***17***	***+17***
Long strings of digits (page #) are hard to remember	***25***	***7***	***+18***
Menu choices should not start with zero	32	10	+22
Columns are too far apart in list of cities (hard to read)	47	23	+24
No exit from SAS-subsystem back to main system	***49***	***21***	***+28***
No heading in Screen 2 to tell user what to do	***45***	***6***	***+39***

Table 2. *List of problems with a difference in rank ordering of 15 or more. Ranks are from 1 to 50 such that problems having small rank numbers would have been easy to find in the interface, while problems with large ranks numbers were among the most difficult to find. This means that the top half of the table lists those problems which were easier to find in the paper mockup while the bottom half lists the problems that were easier to find in the computer mockup. The problems in* ***bold italics*** *belong to the category of major usability problems while the rest are minor or cosmetic problems.*

The problem of *needing consistent rules for the concept "index"* relates to the hierarchical navigation principle in the videotex system. The term "index" referred to some kind of higher-level node in the hierarchy than the current screen but in an inconsistent manner. Evaluators of the paper version were able to understand this problem better because they could get an overview of the hierarchy and the different uses of the concept from looking at several screens at the same time.

The *UNKNOWN IP error message should confirm the user's input* by restating the name of the information provider that could not be found. This problem was found less by the evaluators of the computer version because the prototype implementation did not include a real search facility. Instead of actually allowing users to type in a name, it just referred to a specification of the search procedure. This specification was identical to the part of the paper version having to do with the search facility, but apparently the computer version evaluators focused on the running parts of the interface when writing their evaluations.

The *UNKNOWN IP error message needs a constructive addition* in the form of a reference to the system's list of known information providers. This is the one case where it is hard to find an explanation for the difference between the two groups of evaluators. Maybe the evaluators of the computer version had spent more effort on understanding the screens listing information providers (because they did not have access to the specification of what these screens would do) and were therefore more explicitly aware of their potential use for user assistance.

The *last two lines in Screen 2 are strange* and not related to the rest of the screen. The difference in this case was probably due to the same effect as the one discussed below for the other major problem on Screen 2. In the paper version, evaluators were implicitly told how to interpret this screen by having the specification state the result of each menu selection. In the computer version, evaluators had to guess the meaning if the dialogue elements when they first arrived at the screen.

The system provided an option to jump directly to a screen by *typing in a long string of digits that was hard to remember*. These page numbers could be up to eight digits in length for the screens used in the mockup. In the paper version, the evaluators could simply note the existence of the facility in the specification and might have felt that it was a nice feature to be able to jump directly to a screen. The evaluators in the computer version were better able to understand this problem because they actively got to type in the long numbers rather than simply glancing at them on a piece of paper.

The *lack of an exit from the SAS-subsystem back to the main system* would entrap users in a part of the videotex database without any explicit menu options to return to the rest of the system. In the paper version, evaluators did not feel this problem themselves as they could move between screens simply by turning the pages of the printed specification, and they were therefore less able to find the problem.

The problem that there was *no heading in Screen 2 to tell user what to do* relates to a menu showing all the letters of the alphabet where the user is expected to choose a single letter to look up in the index of information providers. In the paper version, this use of the screen was evident from the next screen showing a list of information providers for the letter "S" and the specification's statement that that screen would be displayed if the user made the menu selection corresponding to "S." In the computer version, however, the evaluator would at first be presented simply with the screen containing the alphabet without knowing what might come out of it. Because they had faced the problem themselves, the evaluators in the computer case were better able to understand the problem of showing such a screen to users without any instructions.

Conclusions

The same user interface can be prototyped as either a paper mockup in the form of a series of screen dumps or a computer mockup in the form of a running implementation. Both can be used for heuristic evaluation but there are differences in what usability problems are easy to find in the two cases.

The computer mockups seem to focus the evaluation on the major usability problems and offer the evaluator an experience closer to that of a real user. Paper mockups are better with respect to showing certain inconsistencies in a design. Since paper mockups are also significantly cheaper to produce, we would recommend using a mixture of the two types of mockup.

References

Carroll, J.M. and Rosson, M.B. (1990). Human–computer interaction scenarios as a design representation, *Proc. IEEE HICSS-23, 23rd Hawaii International Conference on System Sciences* (Hawaii, 2–6 January), **Vol II,** pp. 555–561.

Chell, D. (1987). *Moviemakers at Work,* Microsoft Press.

Eisenhart, D.M. (1989). 1-2-3 goes TV: Interactive multimedia at Lotus, *Boston Computer Society BCS Update* (September), 14–17.

Molich, R. and Nielsen, J. (1990). Improving a human–computer dialogue, *Communications of the ACM* **33**, 3 (March), 338–348.

Nielsen, J. (1987). Using scenarios to develop user friendly videotex systems, *Proc. NordDATA'87 Joint Scandinavian Computer Conference* (Trondheim, Norway, 15–18 June), 133–138.

Nielsen, J. (1989a). Prototyping user interfaces using an object-oriented hypertext programming system, *Proc. NordDATA'89 Joint Scandinavian Computer Conference* (Copenhagen, Denmark, 19–22 June), 485–490.

Nielsen, J. (1989b). Usability engineering at a discount. In Salvendy, G. and Smith, M.J. (eds.): *Designing and Using Human–Computer Interfaces and Knowledge Based Systems,* Elsevier Science Publishers, Amsterdam, 394–401.

Nielsen, J. (1990a). A meta-model for interacting with computers, *Interacting with Computers* **2**, 2 (August).

Nielsen, J. (1990b). Applying traditional principles of dialogue design to modern user interfaces, manuscript submitted for publication.

Nielsen, J. and Molich, R. (1990). Heuristic evaluation of user interfaces. *Proc ACM CHI'90 Conf. Human Factors in Computing Systems* (Seattle, WA, 1–5 April), 249–256.

Vertelney, L. (1989). Using video to prototype user interfaces, *ACM SIGCHI Bulletin* **21**, 2 (October), 57–61.

Virzi, R.A. (1989). What can you learn from a low-fidelity prototype?, *Proc. Human Factors Society 33rd Annual Meeting* (Denver, CO, 16–20 October), 224–228.

Young, R.M. and Barnard, P.B. (1987). The use of scenarios in human–computer interaction research: Turbocharging the tortoise of cumulative science, *Proc. ACM CHI+GI'87 Conf. Human Factors in Computing Systems and Graphics Interface* (Toronto, Canada, 5–9 April), 291–296.

SECTION II: DESIGN: THEORIES, METHODS AND TOOLS

SII.4 Evaluation

Evaluating the usability of user interfaces: Research in practice
A. Vainio-Larsson and R. Orring 323

Evaluating Evaluation: A case study of the use of novel and conventional evaluation techniques in a small company
J. Crellin, T. Horn, and J. Preece 329

Integrated office software benchmarks: A case study
J.R. Lewis, S.C. Henry, and R.L. Mack 337

Comparative study of geometry specification capabilities of geometric modelling systems
K. Case and B.S. Acar 345

Cost-benefit analysis of iterative usability testing
C.-M. Karat 351

Usability statements and standardisation: Work in progress in ISO
J. Brooke, N. Bevan, F. Brigham, S. Harker, and D. Youmans 357

Human–Computer Interaction – INTERACT '90
D. Diaper et al. (Editors)
Elsevier Science Publishers B.V. (North-Holland)

EVALUATING THE USABILITY OF USER INTERFACES: RESEARCH IN PRACTICE

Arja Vainio-Larsson

Department of Computer and Information Science
Linköping University, S-581 83 Linköping, Sweden

Rebecca Orring

Network Department, Systems Division
Swedish Telecom, S-123 86 Farsta, Sweden

A prototype for a network operation and control system has been evaluated as part of a study on methods for evaluating usability. Interviews, direct observations, video recordings and thinking aloud techniques has been employed to collect information from users. Additionally a checklist was used as a guide for an expert assessment of the prototype. The methods were chosen on the basis of suitability for data collection in a field study. The approach generated considerable amounts of data, and several usability problems were identified. However, analysis and compilation of the data was time consuming, difficulties were also encountered in feeding back the results of the evaluation into the design process. Since evaluation is more than merely an exercise in data collection these issues must also be considered in selection of evaluation methods.

1. INTRODUCTION

Swedish Telecom and the Department of Computer and Information Science in Linköping have recently carried out a joint project to study methods for the evaluation of user interfaces.

The project was divided into two phases:

1. An extensive literature study with the aim of investigating reported uses of HCI evaluation methods.

2. An evaluation of a prototype for a system to support the operation and control of telecommunication networks.

This paper describes phase two, in which some of the methods reported in the first phase were tested in evaluation studies at five operation and maintenance centres.

Since the studies were carried out in an industrial context while the system was in use, the choice of methods was limited to those specifically suited for easy application in natural work settings.

In section two the concepts of usability and evaluation are introduced and defined. Section three describes an evaluation study of a prototype system for network operation and control. Finally, a summary is presented in section four.

2. USABILITY - A DEFINITION

Usability defined from a human factors perspective "... is the extent to which a user can exploit the potential utility of a system" [1]. Bennet [2] emphasizes the importance of realizing the distinction between the *functionality* (or utility) and the *usability* of a system. The functionality of a system describes how well a system fits a set of particular task needs; the usability relates to the extent to which the system matches users' characteristics and skills for the task concerned. A third factor related to these is *user acceptability*, which describes how willing users are to use a system in their own organizational context [3].

2.1 The Role of Evaluations

Evaluations vary in terms of *when* they are performed (e.g. during development or after end-user installation), *what* they attempt to measure (e.g. user acceptance or productivity increase), *how* they are performed (i.e. the methods and techniques used), and whether they are *comparative* (i.e. a comparison of two or more similar systems) or *focussed* (i.e. focussed on one system).

Formally, an evaluation of the usability of a system (or part of a system) consists of comparing the characteristics of the system with some set of preestablished criteria and determining the degree of correspondence to these criteria [4]. Evaluations are often performed as part of the development process of a system in order to catch any potential problems at an early stage. Other reasons for evaluating a system include to identify problems encountered by end-users and to determine what proportion of a system's functionality is utilized. In such cases the evaluation results may be applied to the development of future products or upgraded versions of the current system [5]. Finally, evaluations may be of use to system purchasers as a decision aid [6].

3. A PROTOTYPE SYSTEM FOR NETWORK OPERATION AND CONTROL

In 1985 Swedish Telecom initiated a development project for the design and implementation of a computerized system referred to as NOAC, (Network Operation and Control). The NOAC system will be used to monitor telecommunication, radio and data networks. It will also support related activities such as operational planning and follow-up and provide a single and consistent user interface for the underlying systems and applications.

A working prototype was constructed as a temporary solution to acute problems, thus alleviating the necessity to rush the main development project. The prototype was also used to test the feasibility of a number of issues, for example the use of a general database management system for an alarm presentation system. The prototype was developed in a short time and on a small budget. It was installed at five operation and maintenance centres in central Sweden.

In the original plans for development of NOAC, the design team made no provision for evaluation of the user interface of either the prototype, or any of the early versions of NOAC. However, the importance of making use of previous experience was recognized and this study was initiated, but was separate from, instead of being included within, the development project. In the autumn of 1988 evaluations were made of the prototype with the aim of feeding back into the NOAC system development process information on user opinions and usage of the system.

3.1 The System and Its Users

The system is based on a VAX computer with the VMS operating system and the majority of terminals are connected to the computer by modem. At the four smaller centres, the terminal consists of an alphanumeric display screen and a keyboard. At the main operation and maintenance centre there is in addition a graphic colour display, which is controlled from the same keyboard as the alphanumeric screen. Other equipment includes printers, wall displays and various alarm units.

The number of people working with the system on a daily basis varies from 1 - 4 at the smaller centres to approximately 30 at the main centre. The user group is relatively homogeneous. Most users are male between the ages of 25 and 45 and have considerable experience both of operating and maintaining the network as well as of various computer-based support systems. Many of the users have a technical education equivalent to senior high school level, supplemented by job-oriented training provided by the company.

3.2 Evaluation Methods

Usability engineering becomes more and more important when developing systems that are both easy to use and hard to misuse. Ideally usability criteria must be specified in a way that make them not only measurable but verifiable as well. Since the aim (the output) of this study was not to provide a formal usability specification the results only define areas where such criteria can be sought when designing and developing the full system.

In order to evaluate the usability of a system it is often necessary to use several methods in combination. This is partly due to the fact that, as previously discussed, there are many aspects to usability, and also that most modern user interfaces employ a combination of graphic and alphanumeric techniques.

The prototype system was already in use, and thus in addition to the usual criteria of ease, effectiveness and comprehensiveness, it was necessary to select methods that caused as little disturbance as possible to the running of the centres.

Since a primary aim was to access the richest possible data on the actual use of the system this evaluation was carried out with real users working with real problems in real work settings. All five operation centres where the prototype is installed were included in the study. In all 20 users participated in the evaluation, only one of whom withdrew during the course of the evaluation. One of in total seven evaluation sessions was terminated because users' workload made it impossible for them to participate in evaluation activities.

3.2.1 An Evaluation Checklist

Initially the system was evaluated using a modified version of a checklist for analyzing direct manipulation interfaces presented in Ziegler et al. [7].. The aim was partly to test an aid for expert based evaluation and partly to obtain a concise and coherent description of the system in terms of objects, attributes, functions, relations between objects as well as between objects and functions, dialogue states, selections and estimated usability. However, the graphics for the prototype evaluated in this study were primitive, and the interface was primarily text-based, whereas the checklist tested was developed for graphic, direct manipulation user interfaces. Thus only a small part of the checklist was relevant.

3.2.2 Think-Aloud, Walk Throughs and Interviews

The users were encouraged to "think-aloud" while interacting with the system and to demonstrate as much of the system's functionality as they normally made use of, as well as to comment on the system in general. A checklist had been prepared in advance, and users were questioned about any points on the checklist they did not mention spontaneously, in order to obtain as a complete description of the system as possible. In some cases, opinions were collected from users in small groups.

When necessary, for example if a user felt uneasy or for other reasons was reluctant to think aloud, this method was combined with "walk throughs" where each function of the system was checked systematically.

Requiring the users to think aloud while interacting with the system is hence not always an effective method when used in a real work context. However, the objective in this particular study was not to obtain precise measures of, for example, time and error performances, but to collect information on users' own reasons for their behaviour. The ability of users to observe their cognitive processes has been discussed elsewhere [8]. Sometimes users accurately describe what they are doing, i.e what users say they are doing seems also to be the things they actually do, but sometimes there is a discrepancy between what they do and what they say they do. The latter can lead to paradoxical effects such as *users get things right but for the wrong reasons, and users get things wrong for the right reasons* .

Thinking aloud techniques and walk throughs are not to be recommended in stressful situations. The thinking aloud method presupposes that users are able to describe their actions. This may be true for users trained to be verbally explicit about their behaviour, but many users have difficulty in acting and reflecting simultaneously. When the thinking aloud technique is supplemented with guided and supportive informal interviews the evaluation becomes more relaxed and can more easily be adapted to stressful situations.

3.2.3 Logging

A log was made of users' interaction with the system. Normally this method is an effective way of recording breakdowns in interaction and to record how often different commands are issued. The log function used in this particular evaluation study could only record syntactically correct commands, and there was no way of recording other kinds of input and output, for example form input or system output. In order to make up for these shortcomings video recordings of the interaction were also made. In all the study resulted in 15 hours of film.

3.2.4 Video Recording

Video recordings were made of the user interaction, primarily by filming the display screen. This produced a great mass of data, but a considerable amount of work was required to extract the interesting material. The process of analysis consisted of viewing the tapes several times to find interesting segments and then reviewing these segments to capture details. Various methods exist for simplifying this work [9].

Some usability criteria cannot easily be formulated in technical, quantitative terms and this may create communication problems within the design team between members with different backgrounds. The video material can act as a visible link, illustrating phenomena that cannot easily be formulated or understood. Often the design team as a whole can benefit from such a process in that the different aspects of usability are clarified, and even though difficulties caused by differences between "soft" and "hard" data are not eliminated, they can at least be overcome.

3.3 Results

User representatives from the main operations centre were actively involved in the design and installation of the prototype, building up the database and introduction and training of users at the local centres. They were also available to deal with problems as they arose at any of the centres, and collected information from other users about necessary changes. However, representatives from the local centres were not involved in the design of the prototype, with the result that it more effectively supported tasks carried out at the main operations centre than tasks specific for the local centres.

Users make use of only a minor part of a system's total functionality. This subset of course varies between different user groups. Hence, it is important to identify potential groups of users and their needs early in the design process. The users' own experience of the prototype is an important source of information for determining its usability. The methods and tools for evaluating the usability of a system are only valuable to the extent that these actually tell us something about the users' own experience of the system. This experience should, as is also pointed out by Whiteside [10] , always be the real justification for all usability criteria. The most important results obtained are discussed below.

3.3.1 Design Problems and Their Effects on Evaluations

The users experienced both the system and the interaction as far too slow, especially the search mechanisms provided. Once a search had been initiated, the user could neither obtain any information about the retrieval process, nor interrupt the search. Certain operations on the database, such as search and updating, effectively blocked alarm presentation.This not only reveals the shortcomings of this particular prototype and its underlying database, but also illustrates a potential hazard in evaluating prototype systems. One of the benefits of using a working prototype in a real application setting is that a part of the full system can be installed and tested during a lengthy design and implementation phase. However, this also raises problems concerning the correspondence between the prototype and the full system. Users often know that it is necessary to make a distinction between them, but at the same time the prototype often functions as a partial model of the full system. In our study this ambiguity is reflected as an uncertainty as to how to refer to these systems, i.e. the need to relate and to separate these two systems becomes a dilemma in itself. There is also a potential risk that shortcomings (such as failures in performance, lack of features etc.) attributed to the fact that the system is a prototype may conceal other real usability problems in the full system. In some cases, such problems can be identified by carefully planned and executed evaluation studies.

3.3.2 User Expectations

The fact that different command based interaction styles use graphic or alphanumeric techniques does not guarantee the success or failure of the user interface, although text based command languages are often particularly difficult for non-native users. The command language used in this prototype system was highly appreciated by the users. It was experienced as natural and consistent with the underlying tasks.

Users were also required to enter data in the form of function codes and abbreviations. The code systems had evolved and expanded and users found it increasingly difficult to learn and to recall these changes. Nonetheless, users often want the computers to do the right things although they themselves make mistakes. This particular system allows mis-spellings (commands can be undone, mis-spelled commands can be corrected). The problem is that it does not handle this kind of failure in what users perceive to be an intelligent manner.

This phenomenon of seeing the computer not as a basically mechanical thing, a machine among others, but as something that has, or ought to have, human qualities such as intelligence, understanding, fault tolerance etc. has become more common. What exactly is meant by this kind of attributes is not always clear, and an important task is hence to clarify these, although often strongly formulated, infinite demands. It can be argued that usability studies are in many cases already too expensive and time consuming, and extending them will only exacerbate this. However, this kind of expectation must be taken into account in order to be able to decide whether or not it may be ignored.

3.3.3 User Interface Design Trade Offs

When designing the human - computer interaction component of a system a decision must be made as to whether efforts should be concentrated on the command language itself, or on the design of a sophisticated support system. The former is a *"design for success"* approach, based on the assumption that users will not make mistakes with a command language that is easy to remember and simple to use. The latter is a *"design for failure"* approach,where users are expected to make mistakes and as far as possible the system should support their correction. The nature of the application determines the appropriate balance between these two extremes. Applications with a rich command structure, and hence many opportunities for making mistakes, are the most difficult to handle, since users cannot be expected to interact with the system without errors, and the support system cannot effectively cope with all possible mistakes. For applications with a simple command structure and limited arguments, users can be expected to be exact in their communication with the system and the system is able, if necessary, to provide effective support.

Function keys and shortcuts were used in the prototype to make interaction more direct and effective. Although users appreciated the various possibilities for interacting with the system they also pointed out that the use of function keys had the negative effect of turning them into simple "button pressers", dependent on the function keys provided and never really learning the command language. While it was possible for them to change these and define their own function keys, many users were either unaware of this possibility, or doubtful of their own ability to accomplish the task.

3.3.4 Considerations When Integrating Several Systems

Today several different systems, each with its own user interface, are employed in the monitoring and control of communications networks. The NOAC system will collect information from some of these systems, and provide the user with an integrated presentation. The benefits are several: users need learn fewer command languages, the integration of information will give users a better overview of the situation in the network and the exchange of information between different users and groups will be facilitated. However, some users pointed out the risk that an integrated system will lead to a more sedentary work situation. This risk is more marked at the operation and maintenance centres where monitoring the network is the operators' primary function.

3.3.5 Factors Influencing System Usability

While theoretically it may be possible to separate the concepts of functionality, usability and acceptability, this separation is more difficult in practice, especially since users often motivate their preferences and points of view with aspects of all three factors. Similarly, it is difficult to restrict an evaluation as in the case reported here to include only human computer dialogue, and to exclude other aspects of the interface. This may be a weakness of the methods and the manner in which they were employed, but it may also reflect users' greater concern with social, organizational and functional aspects of the system than with details of interaction.

Although the user group was highly homogeneous with regard to variables such as sex, age, education and work tasks, there were surprisingly large variations in how the users carried out their tasks and in their demands and expectations concerning interaction with the future system. The user's need to adapt system function to his own personal work style may conflict with requirements of in-house work routines. A system has the twofold function of guiding (and thus also controlling) the user's actions according to common requirements, and also of assisting the user in carrying out his tasks with as little hindrance as possible. Factors which are basically independent of the system may thus affect users' experience of system qualities such as usability and interactivity. These findings not only illustrate the breadth of these terms, but also indicate the need to distinguish between usability in flexible or adaptive systems (*interactive systems*) and in systems that guide user interaction in order to establish effective working habits (*reactive systems*).

4. SUMMARY

This paper has reported on the evaluation of a prototype for a network operation and control system, as part of a study on methods for evaluating usability. Interviews, direct observations, video recordings and think-aloud techniques have been employed to collect information from users. Additionally a checklist was used as a guide for an expert assessment of the prototype. The methods were chosen on the basis of suitability for data collection in a field study. The approach generated considerable amounts of data, and several usability problems were identified such as deficiencies in system performance as well as in the interactivity of the system. However, the results also reflect users' often greater concern with social, organizational and functional aspects of the system than details of interaction.

The potential hazards of evaluating prototypes, and the need to take into consideration diffuse expectations formulated by the users have also been discussed in this paper. Two different design approaches, design for success and design for failure, have been formulated. The evaluation was carried out in the real work setting, and while this is recommended for future studies, it would be an advantage to complement workplace studies with controlled laboratory studies in order to achieve an appropriate combination of qualitative and quantitative data.

LIST OF REFERENCES

[1] Eason, K. D., Behaviour and Information Technology, vol 3, nr 2 (1984).
[2] Bennet, J. L., Managing to Meet Usability Requirements. Establishing and Meeting Software Development Goals, in: Bennett, J. and Case, D. et. al (eds), Visual Display Terminals (1984) pp. 161-183.
[3] Richardson, S., Operationalising Usability and Acceptability: a Methodological review, in Wilson, J. R. and Corlett, E. N. (eds.), New Methods in Applied Ergonomics (1987) pp. 125-134.
[4] Howard, S. and Murray, M. D., A Taxonomy of Evaluation Techniques for HCI, in Bullinger, H.-J. and Shackel, B. (eds.), Human-Computer Interaction -INTERACT '87 (Elsevier Science Publishers B V, North-Holland, 1987) pp. 453-459.
[5] Novara, F., Bertaggia, N., Allamanno, N. et. al., Usability Evaluation and Feedback to Designers - an Experimental Study, in Bullinger, H.-J. and Shackel, B. (eds.), Human-Computer Interaction -INTERACT '87 (Elsevier Science Publishers B V, North-Holland, 1987) pp. 337-340.
[6] Brooke, J., Background, Objectives and Scope of Usability Engineering Standards for Software Systems, Digital Equipment Corporation, pp. 1-15.
[7a] Ziegler, J. E., Vossen, P. H., Hoppe, H. U. et. al., Analysis of Direct Manipulation Interfaces, ESPRIT Project HUFIT Report B3.1a (1985).
[7b] Ziegler, J. E., Eichhorn, H. U. et. al., Analysis of Direct Manipulation Interfaces.Part 3: Direct Manipulation in a General Framework of Human-Computer Interaction, ESPRIT Project 385 HUFIT, Wp. B3.1b (1986).
[8] Nisbett, R. E. and Wilson T. DeCamp, Psychological Review (1977), volume 84, number 3, pp. 231-259.
[9] Neal, A. S. and Simons, R. M., Playback: a Method for Evaluating the Usability of Software and its Documentation, in Proc. CHI '83 , pp. 78-82.

[10] Whiteside, J. and Wixon, D., The Dialectic of Usability Engineering, in Bullinger H.-J., Shackel B. (eds), Human-Computer Interaction -INTERACT '87 (Elsevier Science Publishers B V, North-Holland, 1987) pp. 17-20.

Human–Computer Interaction – INTERACT '90
D. Diaper et al. (Editors)
Elsevier Science Publishers B.V. (North-Holland)

EVALUATING EVALUATION: A CASE STUDY OF THE USE OF NOVEL AND CONVENTIONAL EVALUATION TECHNIQUES IN A SMALL COMPANY

Jonathan Crellin, Thomas Horn* and Jenny Preece

People And Computer Interaction Systems Research Group (PACIS), Computing Department, Faculty of Mathematics, The Open University, Walton Hall, MILTON KEYNES, MK7 6AA.

*BRAMEUR, 237 High Street, ALDERSHOT, Hants, GU11 1TJ.

During recent co-operative working with an industrial partner, a number of usability evaluation techniques were compared in an evaluation of seven interface prototypes. A detailed real-time software log of the interaction was recorded and video and audio records of the interactions were kept. Additionally, a novel experience elicitation technique, based on knowledge elicitation techniques was used. Keystroke and BNF analyses were also prepared. This material has allowed a comparison of the different methods to be made, and recommendations as to their use to be drawn up.

1 INTRODUCTION

1.1. Designers and Users

Software designers and software users have different views of software. Designers see all the parts that make up a system, including those parts which are usually hidden from the user. Users on the other hand only ever experience the interface. Conventional usability evaluation methods strive for objectivity in their measurement of user/system interaction, yet it is often the subjective experience of using a system which is important. Currently, a range of different approaches to evaluation are practiced. These approaches differ greatly in their under-lying philosophies; consequently they also vary along a number of dimensions related to data collection and analysis. In our case study we selected some well established and some novel techniques from four different evaluation approaches and we compared them in terms of their ease of use and how well the information derived from the data revealed usability problems and represented users' attitudes towards the prototype interfaces. The four evaluation approaches are:

- formal analysis, which Grudin (1989) defines as analysis of the form of the interface in isolation from users
- empirical approaches, which test the interface in an experimental (or, more often, semi-experimental) setting such as a usabililty laboratory;
- contextual research, in which users and researchers attempt to understand users' naturally occuring experiences in their normal work environment; and
- another ethnographic method which is based on construct elicitation (Crellin, 1989, 1990).

1.2. Formal Analysis

Focusing on the interface in isolation from users can be an attractive proposition (especially to many system designers) as the interface is always readily available and, unlike users, it never complains. In addition, formal analysis holds the possibility of automation of some aspects of evaluation and it is also possible to assess an interface from a specification without an existing prototypes. Unfortunately, however, focussing only on the structure of the interface often leads to interfaces which are difficult or unpleasant to use.

1.3 Empirical Approaches.

Generally in empirical approaches, formal benchmark tasks are set and user performances on different versions of the prototype are compared. This involves identifying important usability criteria and setting measurable behavioural goals . These operationalised goals are based on ergonomic and cognitive science knowledge and they form the yardsticks by which progress towards a final interface design is measured.

In the empirical approach the criteria for design are no longer focus purely on the formal aspects of an interface, but also include observation of people using the interface. However, the 'agenda' of interface evaluation issues remains clearly in the hands of the evaluators. Gould et al (1987) provide a clear account of such a procedure for developing a complex interface.

1.4 Contextual Research

Empirical evaluation has contributed to the successful design of usable interfaces, but as awareness increases of the generally large gap between the evaluator's knowledge and experience and that of the user, there is a growing concern that evaluators may not always be addressing the right issues. This suggests that the important data that needs to be collected during evaluation is that relating to the actual experience of using the interface. One way of obtaining this type of data is by contextual research as proposed by Whiteside et al (1988).

Contextual research is an attempt to understand the use of the software in ecologically valid situations. It involves replacing the empirical positivist approach, in which the user is viewed as another object in the human-computer system, with a user as subject focus. A number of methods are associated with this approach. Whiteside et al., for example, concentrates on recording experience as it happens in order to avoid post-hoc rationalisation; this, therefore suggests the pre-eminence of direct observation techniques in contextual research.

Unfortunately, however, there are a number of problems associated with observing users in this way. For example, it is difficult to observe users in context without intruding and altering the nature of the interaction, especially as much of the interesting parts of an interaction are internal to the user, and not available for direct observation. Methods such as think aloud (TA) verbal protocols (which may make such phenomena explicit) are both intrusive, and usually alter the phenomena being observed.

1.5. Another Approach: The Construct Elicitation System (CES).

If the process of using an interface provides information about the usability of the interface, then it appears that techniques derived from knowledge elicitation may be appropriate, Briggs (1987). Although the user is not an expert in interface design, he is certainly an expert on his own experience. Several knowledge elicitation techniques, including Crellin's construct elicitation system, involve questioning the user after the event. This form of data collection does not interfere with the processes as they take place. However, it has the potential disadvantage that post-hoc rationalisation may occur and conceal evidence of the actual processes that took place.

In traditional non-computerised versions of this approach an interviewer asks open ended, none-leading questions of the user. This may introduce other problems; bias, inexperience or fatigue on the part of the interviewer may also distort the data. Computer presentation of questions, however eliminates the possibility of these problems. In addition the anonymity which results is preferred by many interviewees. Particularly, as there is the added advantage that the interviewee can do the elicitation task anywhere, providing that a suitable computer is available; enhancing ecological validity. Since the technique used in this study was also designed to be ethnographic the questions are in part supplied by the interviewee (i.e. the user) in his own terms. (See Crellin, 1988, 1990 for details). In essence, this technique involves repeatedly asking the interviewee variations on the same question, collecting the replies, and then feeding these back to the interviewee for clarification and elaboration. Like most techniques of this type, it is based on Kelly's repertory grid (Kelly, 1955) and follows an approach similar to Boose's Expertise Transfer System (Boose, 1985). Similar approaches have also been used in marketing (Stewart et al., 1981), and in architectural evaluation (Honikman, 1976).

Key aspects of the four evaluation approaches are summarised in Table 1. Notice that both contextual research and construct elicitation are described as ethnographic; the main difference concerns when data is collected.

	Empirical	Ethnographic		Formal Analysis
		Contextual	CES	
Philosophy	Traditional engineering/scientific perspective. Measurements are allocated to assessed named attributes of the system.	Ethnographic. Context and naturalness of the interpretation are important. No preconceived ideas about what to look for.	Ethnographic Post-event elicitation of users' opinion. No preconceived ideas about what users will say.	Theoretical models are used to measure a hypothetical expert users' performance.
Location of Study	Laboratory or field.	Always field. Users' normal environment .	Field- wherever user chooses to work.	Paper and pencil exercise.
Methods and Techniques.	Quasi-experimental;. Specific Tasks. Observation leads to measurement of user performance. Attitudes quantified by questionnaire ranking. Often supported by field observation and interview.	User and researcher observe user doing what s/he wants to do when and how she wants to do. (Data in the trad. sense is often said, not to exist e.g. Whiteside et al., 1988).	Post-event elicitation of users' opinions which are collected by a special computerised tool. (Crellin, 1988).	Various techniques available such as Keystroke Level Analysis (Card et al) and BNF Grammar analysis (Reisner, 1984).
Test system required.	Prototype or final.	Prototype or final.	Several prototypes for comparison.	System specification.

Table 1: A comparison of usability evaluation approaches

1.6 Two Important Conclusions about Evaluation

The same techniques can be used with different approaches. Evaluation approaches can be distinguished partly by the data collection and analysis techniques employed. However, there are often occasions when the same technique is used in different ways in two approaches. For example, TA protocols are collected in both the empirical approach and the contextual approach. In the empirical approach the data is usually analysed according to a pre-defined categorisation, which may be based on a cognitive psychological abstraction. In the contextual approach, however, there would be greater openness to the natural form of the data and an over-riding desire to interpret it within its natural context. In addition, users would often be invited to participate in the interpretation. Consequently, the use of a particular data collection technique *does not alone* indicate that a certain evaluation approach is being adopted; other factors must also be taken into account.

Pure approaches are rarely used . Although, an evaluation is generally biased strongly towards a particular approach, in practice the boundaries are much less distinct and a mixture of approaches usually results. This can be brought about by logistical constraints. For example, it is not always possible to follow Whiteside et al.'s (1988) contextual philosophy as time constraints dictate users' and researchers' schedules. Similarly, a video camera in an office is often far from unobtrusive and may threaten the ecological validity of a study. It is also well recognised that empirical findings are often enriched by ethnographic data and vice versa, so many researchers adopt both approaches.

What is more, it is quite feasible to collect data within an ethnographic paradigm and to analyse it by developing categories more akin to those used in empirical approaches. In some respects, for example, the Construct Elicitation System behaves in this way in that the data is presented semi-quantitively in the form of graphs and percentages. We, therefore, assert that life is not as simple as it might at first appear; although one paradigm may dominate, few studies operate within a single paradigm except in formal analysis.

1.7 Background to this Study

This case study involves the collection of data by two formal analysis techniques and a variety of other techniques normally associated with empirical and ethnographic approaches.

The laboratory-like feature was that the task was not a real world task, due to the underlying functionality of the prototypes being so restrictive. However, formal benchmark tasks were not set and although subjects did not work at their own desks, they did whatever they liked with the prototypes. They also worked in Brameur's offices and asked for help and frequently broke off to do other things. Consequently, there were aspects in common with contextual research. The aim of the study was to observe how well a range of evaluation methods captured the real usability issues concerned with the prototypes and to determine how usable the techniques themselves are for use in small companies like Brameur.

2. METHODOLOGY

2.1. The Participants' Task

Each participant calculates the cost of telephone calls, using different versions of a prototype application. Most people are familiar with telephone usage so that the task domain should not be unfamiliar to any user. However, the method of call charging employed by BT is not particularly obvious, so many people will not be familiar with exactly how telephone charges are calculated. Some calls are more expensive than others, due to the distance called, or the amount of equipment used. BT cope with this by allotting different amounts of time per unit to each distance band, additionally BT vary the amount of time per unit according to the time of day. (British Telecom, 1987).

In this study the functional part of each of the seven prototypes is identical; it is simply a timer which increments the cost of a call by the cost of a unit, as each unit is completed. The functional system is also clearly separated from the interface. Each interface is radically different from the other interfaces, there is plenty of opportunity for variation in the way a user enters call parameters (distance and time of day). Also the way a user calls the different application functions provides considerable scope for interface variation. The different interface versions were implemented on a Mac Plus computer using a rapid prototyping environment . Where relevant the final interfaces conform to Macintosh interface guidelines. Each of the stimulus interfaces was given a short meaningful name to assist users recall during the CES task.

The interface issues explored included:

* Depth versus breadth in menu structure.
* Command language versus graphic user interfaces.
* Different graphic user interfaces formats.
* The use of icons.
* Mouse versus keyboard input.
* User event based versus system directed.
* The amount of information displayed at any one time.

2.2 The Participants

The six subjects came from industry, having a broad range of backgrounds and experience. Clerical, technical and managerial users were represented, with experience of computers ranging from novice to very experienced.

2.3. Data Collection

Formal Measures: A BNF description of each interface of the system was developed along the lines of Reisner (1981). The BNF description was used to derive two metrics measuring 'string simplicity' (how many actions in a task) and 'structural consistency' (are semantics reflected in syntax). A Keystroke Level Analysis was also performed to enable comparisons of predicted and observed expert behaviour to be made (Card et al., 1988)

Observational Data.: Users were asked to verbalise their thoughts: to explain what and how they were going to tackle the tasks. Video was also used to record evidence of users' intentions and emotions; this can be compared to actual user behaviour on the system, which was collected by interaction logging. This recording was done using a Macro writer application which collects a real time record of system usage (i.e. key presses and mouse movements). The recording can be replayed in synch with the video and audio data, and it also provides a text description of the actions performed.

Construct Elicitation: The PROTEUS shell was used to elicit participants' opinions; this is an integrated environment in which interfaces, evaluation and help systems can be easily accessed. A system usage log is also collected by the shell. The shell controls presentation of an on-line questionnaire and rating scales when programmed to do so but in this study only the rating scales were used (Crellin 1988, 1990).

3 RESULTS

For usability evaluations to be viable within the working environment of a small company such as Brameur it must be relatively cheap; that is, be quick to carry out and not require expensive specialist equipment or expertise. It should also not disrupt employees normal working patterns unreasonably. In addition the information derived from the assessment must provide a good overall picture of the usability of the prototypes.

The suitability of the methods described in the previous section can, therefore be examined with three questions in mind:

1) What equipment, time and expertise was required to collect the data and how much disruption did employees incur?

2) What kind of data was collected, how was it analysed and what equipment, time, and expertise was required for the analysis?

3) What were the main findings from the data?

Tables 2 to 6 summarise the results and observations relating to each of the questions.

	Setting Up			Running		Comment
	Equipment	Time	Expertise	Reliability	Disruption	
Video	Good definition portable camera which will operate in normal room lighting.	1 hour.	Positioning and co-ordinating with interaction log.	Good.	More than desirable.	Initial expense or hire fees.
Audio	Directional microphone, recording onto audio track of video.	20 minutes	Checking sound quality.	Good.	More than desirable also TA protocol is disruptive to colleagues.	Initial expense or hire fee.
Interaction Log	Appropriate software. System requires additional RAM.	5 minutes	Needs co-ordination with video.	Poor, kept running out of memory without warning and recording was lost.	Much more than desirable, but not when working properly.	Could be made automatic with no effect on users, very low cost.
System Usage Log	Software on users system.	None.	Automatic.	Excellent.	None.	Low cost.
Construct Elicitation System	Program called in normal way by user.	None.	None.	Excellent.	A separate activity which must be carried out by user. No disruption during evaluation task itself.	Low cost.
Keystroke/BNF	None.	None.	N/A	N/A	N/A	Time and expertise required to decompose task.

Table 2: Analysis of data collection techniques

Table 2 shows that, in our opinion, video recording was far from unobtrusive. In fact, we remain to be convinced that contextual research, in which video is used, is as ecologically sound as the overall philosophy suggests it should be. Table 3 examines analysis techniques.

Table 3: Analysis of data analysis techniques

	Data Type	Analysis	Equipment	Time	Expertise	Comment
Video Observation	Record of users body language. (Qualitative).	Differences noted in relation to events in interaction (Plus log and verbal protocol).	Good playback, pause and search facilities.	Approx 1 hour per user.	Previous experience helpful.	Sparse source of data, but valuable in conjunction with verbal protocol of interaction.
Audio (verbal protocol).	Protocol of users thoughts and actions. (Qualitative).	User perceived difficulties, and user intentions noted.	Playback facilities	Approx 1 hour per user.	Previous experience helpful.	TA protocol is difficult for users. Video and Int. Log provides context.
Interaction Log	Record of all keystrokes, mouse actions. (Qualitative but can be interpreted quantitatively).	Problems noted. Timings can be taken and metrics applied. Number of types of errors recorded.	System prototype. Appropriate monitoring. Ideally real-time playback, and text description of events should be available.	Depends on nature of analysis. Can be qualitative or quantitative.	Intimate knowledge of prototypes being tested.	Rich and detailed data about user behaviour. Less useful without intentional context provided by audio and video.

Construct Elicitation System	Numerical ratings data, textual construct labels.	Computer aided cluster analysis. Graphical display of analysis.	Several prototypes of system. Appropriate elicitation software.	Varies.	Experience of technique.	A standalone analysis, which provides a user interpretation of other data.
System Usage Log	Quantitative record of time used on each interface.	Supplements other data.	Several prototypes of system. Appropriate software shell.	Short amount of time.	Little required.	
Keystroke and BNF	Quantitative Helps determine possible expert performance.	Formal, using prescribed model	None		Previous experience useful.	

An important conclusion that we drew from our data analysis experience was that video recording, audio recording and interaction logging are individually impoverished forms of data collection. However, when analysed in conjunction 'the sum is far greater than the individual parts'. The data becomes very rich and this justifies the time, expense and disruption to work that occurs during its collection.

Full records for all six participants cannot be included but table 4 gives an overall summary of the findings for one (AA). Notice particularly, the information about body language obtained from the video; these findings were also supported by audio data. From the interaction log we can see that the subject did not know the syntax of the command language nor how to get the 'help screen'. Three distinct problems can be detected: incorrect use of the delimiter; lack of understanding of parameters and the syntax for setting them; confusion between the use of the underscore to set parameters and hyphens in parameter names. A number of typing errors are also apparent.

From the rest of the participants' data we gain a clear picture of how her confidence grew along with her knowledge of the task until she understood it completely and became bored. This data, like that of most of the subjects, showed that the command language interface had poor usability and that there was little to choose between the others; possibly because the underlying functionality of the system was very limited. The usage logs also supported these findings, with most subjects spending longer on the command language interface or not completing the task.

The CES data, however, indicated distinct differences in the way that users themselves viewed the interfaces even though they appeared to perform on all but the command interface with similar competence. The analysis of this data is done using the FOCUS algorithm, Shaw (1980), Jankowicz and Thomas (1982). Results from the analysis are displayed as two binary trees per subject; these graphs show the similarity matchings for the constructs elicited from subjects, and for the interfaces as the subject saw them. In this study, for example, the data suggests that subjects view the two menu interfaces as being very similar even though their appearance on the screen is quite different, and so is the depth of the menus. However, in this study, one of the keyboard menu interfaces is, in fact, very similar in appearance on screen to the checkbox interface (where selection of the menu items is by ticking checkboxes), These interfaces are also similar in inter-menu structure. Few subjects seem to notice this. The former has keyboard input and the latter, mouse input and these features appear to dominate users impressions.

The construct trees help to make apparent the ways that individuals distinguish between different interfaces. Unfortunately, lack of space precludes the inclusions of the trees but a summary of the findings for participant AA are shown in table 4. (C3, C6 etc.are construct numbers; the subjective usability is the participants' own rating on a given ten point semantic differential scale, with poles 'Pleasant to Use' and 'Unpleasant to Use'.)

	Observation (Video, Audio, Interaction log).	Usage Log	Subjective Usability 1=low, 10=high.	Construct Elicitation System (C=construct number).
Checkbox	Body language stiff. User doesn't understand task requests help.	Used twice: 186 and 108 secs.Total 294 secs.	8.5	Highly differentiated on C3: simple to use and C6: presenting information on the screen.
Command Language	Syntax causes problems, omits delimitter, reads error message, adds delimiter. Doesn't set parameters, comment "I havn't got a clue what I am doing". Eventually finds the HELP screen. Works out how to set parameters. Confuses underscore with hyphen. Does not complete the task.	Used twice: 654 and 199 seconds. Total 853 seconds.	1	Highly differentiated on C1: Keyboard based, C2: Requires help, C3: Difficult to use, C6: Implying rather than displaying information.
Icon	Now understands the task well. Puzzled when clicking on the desk icon returns him to the shell program.	Used twice: 110 and 75 seconds. Total 185 seconds.	5.5	Highly differentiated on C4: Drawing based rather than reading based and C6: Implying rather than displaying information.

Menu-A	Complete quickly. Now understands task and how to use menus so no challenge.	Used twice: 176 and 99 seconds. Total 275 seconds.	5	Highly differentiated on C4: Reading based.
MenuB	Decides to experiment with changing the order in which the parameters are set.	Used twice: 153 and 77 seconds. Total 230 seconds.	5.5	Highly differentiated on C4: Reading based and C6: Displaying information on screen.
Dialogue	Didn't complete the task.	Used twice: 184 and 52 seconds. Total 236 seconds.	8	Highly differentiated on C1: Keyboard based and C3: Simple to use.
Macintosh	Likes this one "When you go to rate you can see which ones are available".	Used twice: 158 and 72 seconds. Total 230 seconds.	7	Highly differentiated on C1: Mouse based, C2: Does not require help, C3: Easy to use, C4: Reading based, C5: Uses pull-down menus, and C6: Implying rather than displaying information.

Table 4: The main findings from the data for user AA

An interesting point to notice in the CES data is how the participants' apparent understanding of the way that this data collection technique works seems to affect the quality, though not necessarily the content, of the data.

Tables 5 and 6 contain the data from the formal analyses. Applying the Keystroke Level Analysis (Card et al., 1988) yielded the following predictions for expert performance:

ChBx	Cm.L	Icon	Mn.A	Mn.B	D.log	Mac
21.4	30.8	42.7	32.8	30.6	23.7	43.4

Table 5: Predicted times (s) for interfaces

These results suggest that the checkbox interface would be the expert's choice and not the command language as might be expected. (Interestingly, the checkbox faired well on other measures.) The BNF metric (table 6) also gave high rating for the checkbox but only the command language interface differed markedly from the others on this measure.

ChBx	Cm.L	Icon	Mn.A	Mn.B	D.log	Mac
5	13	6	5	5	7	6

Table 6: Reisner's metric for string simplicity

4 DISCUSSION AND CONCLUSIONS

The aim of this case study was to evaluate a number of data collection and analysis techniques, using mainly ethnographic but also empirical and formal approaches, within the context of a small company. As a focus for this evaluation we have examined the usability of seven different prototype interfaces.

Although it is not possible to draw any but conclusions from a single case study with out further investigations, there is sufficient evidence for speculation. Our results suggest that, although the command language interface has very poor usability, there is little evidence to discriminate between the others at the level of analysis that we have performed on the observational and usage data so far. This leads us to suggest that, providing users understand the task that is to be performed and know how to map this onto the design of the system, then carefully designed interfaces of any type are likely to have similar usability. This result concurs with a report by Whiteside et al. (1988a) of a similar study. Although predictions from the the formal analyses suggest that the checkbox interface is good for both experts and novices, they provide somewhat conflicting indications about the other interfaces.

Given the lack of discrimination using these techniques, the deciding factor (for any designer) surely ought to be the participants' own opinions of the systems, which can be obtained from construct elicitation. In the next part of our study we shall replay our data (video, audio and interaction log) and invite the participants to discuss it. This ought to reveal how well the CES data represents their opinions.

On the logistical side both we and the Brameur employees consider that it perfecting the combined observational data collection method is worth doing. The intrusiveness of the video recording could be reduced by using smaller lower quality equipment and accepting a loss of recording quality. Since the video is only really useful for providing context, giving information about body language and making data analysis more palatable, this reduction in quality would be acceptable. The TA technique is unsuitable for use in work situations since it disturbs colleagues and is embarrassing. Audio is, however, valuable for collecting details of users requests for help, comments and discussions with other colleagues. It is probably worth investing in a lapel, or remote directional microphone. In addition, the video, sound recording and interaction logging must be easy to synchronise.

The CES system is easy and cheap to run as a researcher is not required to collect the data and the first part of the analysis is done by the computer. The main disadvantage of the technique remains the need for multiple prototypes.

In the introduction we argued for mixed approaches to evaluation; the evidence from this case study suggests that this is sound. Table 6 provides a summary of the strengths and weaknesses of the techniques used in this evaluation.

	Data Collection		Data Analysis	
	Strengths	Weaknesses	Strengths	Weaknesses
Video	None	Intrusive. Recording equipment required	Provides context, can be used to stimulate post-hoc user comments.	Playback equipment required
Audio	None	TA is very intrusive	Provides context.	Equipment. required
Keystroke logging	No additional equipment needed. Very unobtrusive.	Present software not very reliable.	Good real time record of user behaviour. Adds to video and audio recordings. Text description a useful resource.	Can be time consuming to analyse.
Usage Logging	Unobtrusive	None	Useful extra information	None, but rather impoverished data on its own.
Construct Elicitation System	Can be used by users on their own.	Users need to understand construing if high quality data is to be collected.	Initial quantitative analysis carried out by computer. Graphic representation of data provides basis for qualitative analysis.	Sometimes difficult to work out what users really mean. Some experience is needed to interpret data.

Table 6: Summary of the strengths and weaknesses of the techniques used in the case study.

ACKNOWLEDGEMENTS

The evaluation of usability evaluation techniques was sponsored by Brameur as part of ESPRIT Project 1257, Muse. The authors wish to thank the Brameur participants and members of Muse for their support and, in particular, Dr. J. Hemesley, Director of Brameur and Mr. M. Kelley organiser of the Muse Project at Brameur.

PROTEUS and CES are part of Mr. J. Crellin's Ph. D. work which is supported by The Open University and supervised by Mr. D. Benyon and Dr. J. Preece.

We should also like to thank the employees of Brameur who participated in the study.

REFERENCES

Boose, J. H., (1985) A Knowledge Acquisition Program based on Personal Construct Theory, Int. J. Man-Machine Studies, 23, 495-525.

Briggs, P., (1987) Usability Assessment for the Office: Methodological Choices and their Implications, in, Psychological Issues of Human-Computer Interaction in the Workplace, (Frese, M., Ulich, E., and Dzida, W), North-Holland, Amsterdam .

British Telecommunications PLC, (1987) International Telephone Guide, ITG6 RES November, Collier and Searle Ltd..

Card, S. K., Moran, T. P. and Newall, A., (1980) The Keystroke-Level Model for User Performance Time with Interactive Systems, Communications of the ACM, 23, 7.

Crellin, J. M., (1988) Personal Construct Psychology and the Development of a Tool for Formative Evaluation of Software Prototypes, in: Proceedings of the Fourth European Conference on Cognitive Ergonomics, (Green, T. R. G. et al. ed.), Cambridge.

Crellin, J.M., PROTEUS: an approach to interface evaluation, this volume.

Gould, J. D., Boies, S., Levy, S., Richards, J. T., and Schoonard, J., (1987) The 1984 Olympic Messaging System: A test of behavioural principles of system design, Communications of the ACM, 30, 9.

Grudin, J., (1989) The Case Against User Interface Consistency, Communications of the ACM, 32, 10.

Honikman, B., (1976) Construct Theory as an Approach to Architectural and Environmental Design, in The Measurement of Interpersonal Space Vol 1, (P. Slater ed.) Wiley, London.

Jankowicz, D. and Thomas, L., (1982) An algorithm for the cluster analysis of repertory grids in human resource development, Personnel Review, 11, 4, pp.15-22.

Kelly, G., (1955) The Psychology of Personal Constructs, Norton, New York.Stewart, V., Stewart , A., and Fonda, N. (1981) Business Applications of Repertory Grid, Mcgraw Hill (UK) Ltd.

Reisner, P., (1981) Formal Grammar and Human Factors Design of an Interactive Graphics System, IEEE Transactions in Software Engineering, 7.

Shaw,M., (1980) On Becoming a Personal Scientist Academic Press.

Stewart, V., Stewart , A., and Fonda, N. (1981) Business Applications of Repertory Grid, Mcgraw Hill (UK) Ltd.

Whiteside J., Bennett J., Holtzblatt K., (1988) Usability Engineering: Our experience and evolution, in: Handbook of Human Computer Interaction, (M.Helander ed.), Elsevier Sciences Publishers, Amsterdam.

Whiteside, J., Wixon, D. and Jones, S. (1988a) User Performance with Command, Menu and Iconic Interfaces, in Advances in Human-Computer Interaction, Vol. 2. (H.R. Hartson and D. Hix eds.), Ablex.

Human–Computer Interaction – INTERACT '90
D. Diaper et al. (Editors)
Elsevier Science Publishers B.V. (North-Holland)

Integrated Office Software Benchmarks: A Case Study

James R. Lewis
Suzanne C. Henry
Robert L. Mack

User Interface Institute IBM T. J. Watson Research Center, Hawthorne P.O. Box 704, Yorktown Heights, NY 10598

In this paper we present a case study of a benchmark evaluation of integrated office systems. The case study includes developing scenarios, benchmark measures, and quantitative and qualitative analysis of user performance and user problems. We studied two systems, one loosely integrated windowing environment and one more tightly integrated (with respect to consistent graphical interface style). Multivariate analyses showed that significant differences were attributable to performance/analytical variables and to patterns of error impact classifications, but not to subjective ratings. Somewhat surprisingly, users experienced serious problems with the seemingly more integrated (consistent) system largely because of a handful of serious problems. This was taken as evidence that improvement of the poorer performing system should be based primarily on an analysis of errors. Some examples are presented to indicate the potential diagnostic value of analyzing problems and the development of testable behavioral objectives from benchmark measures.

1.0 INTRODUCTION

Evaluating computer systems using realistic scenarios is a common practice in the software industry. Formal quantitative benchmark evaluations, in particular, are useful in a usability engineering context to help set measurable usability targets to guide iterative design of developing systems (see Gould, 1988; Whiteside, Bennett & Holtzblatt, 1988). The key characteristics of benchmarking are measuring user performance across a set of systems or techniques of interest, using common scenarios, measures and test procedures so that meaningful comparisons can be made of these measured objects (Williges, Williges & Elkerton, 1987). Surprisingly few such benchmark studies have been published however, particularly for software applications reflecting the current generation of integrated applications and graphical direct manipulation interface styles. Roberts and Moran (1983) published an early benchmarking case study involving text editing systems and tasks, and relatively expert users. Roberts and Moran conclude that as a whole, the evaluation methodology provided an objective, multidimensional picture of the functional and usability characteristics of text editors. In a more recent case study, Whiteside, Jones, Levy and Wixon (1985) compared seven systems contrasting command-, menu- and direct manipulation interface styles for relatively novice users performing a complex file manipulation task. Their main conclusion was that graphical direct manipulation interfaces had numerous problems of their own, different from, but comparable in impact to problems commonly associated with command and menu-based interface styles.

In this paper we present a case study of comparative benchmark evaluation in the domain of integrated office software, and non-expert users for whom problems may be a more salient experience than through-put. Our method is similar to that described by Roberts and Moran (1983), but we focus on on the rationale for the specific scenarios we selected and the results of a benchmark evaluation aimed at answering three questions:

- What are the obtained values of our usability measurements?
- How good (reliable and valid) are these measurements?
- How can this information be used to improve a system?

In order to set reasonable behavioral objectives, a limited number of human-system usability characteristics should be measured. The reliability and validity of these measurements necessarily influence the degree of confidence placed in the objectives derived from the benchmark data. We are especially interested in the possible diagnostic value of user feedback obtained in the benchmark evaluation. Such diagnostic information is often associated with more informal qualitative evaluation methods (Gould, 1988; Whiteside, Bennett & Holtzblatt, 1988; Lewis, 1982), in contrast to formal quantitative benchmarking. Both methods are needed in a development context, but we believe there is considerably more diagnostic information in benchmark evaluations than is often appreciated.

2.0 THE OFFICE SCENARIOS: CONTENT AND RATIONALE

Table 1 summarizes ten scenarios we developed to evaluate different implementations of integrated office software packages, along with key subtasks comprising the scenarios, and the total steps in each subtask and scenario. As we write, we know of no single software package for the office which offers integrated text editing, mail, calendar, and decision support (e.g., database, spreadsheet, chart applications) for the PC hardware and system environments we are interested in. It is possible, however, to integrate individual applications to some extent using windowing platforms that enable data transfer between applications, using cut, copy and paste functions.

These scenarios are motivated by several sources, including internal marketing expertise, and published field studies and analyses of integrated software (Nielsen, Mack, Bergendorff, and Grischkowsky, 1986; see also Mack & Nielsen, 1987). Based on this work content analysis and discussions with relevant development personnel involved in office systems we initially developed a large number of tasks. Potential tasks were defined by crossing all possible objects with all possible actions, similar to the procedure described by Roberts and Moran (1983), but at a somewhat higher level. A subset of these tasks was then organized into ten scenarios. These scenarios were designed to fulfill the following goals:

- Broad coverage of the types of applications used in an office setting, such as text editing, mail, calendar, and decision support. Since office work consists of a complex set of tasks, scenarios intended to sample this task set are necessarily broad in scope.
- Some scenarios which would be accomplished most efficiently by using techniques for data transfer between applications or presenting multiple applications in windows.
- A set of scenarios which could be performed in one day by most users. This reduces the likelihood of participants dropping out of the study and allows the study to be completed in a reasonably short time.
- Scenarios which required a minimum of typing to reduce performance variability attributable to typing skill.
- Scenario tasks which are written at a high enough level for use across systems. The tasks are specific with respect to text and objects such as files, but step-by-step procedures are not specified.

Table 1. Scenario Descriptions.

- Mail 1 (M1): Open, reply to, and delete a note.
- Mail 2 (M2): Open a note, forward with reply, save and print the note.
- Calendar 1 (C1): Create a calendar entry and print today's appointments.
- Calendar 2 (C2): Open a note, open specified calendar entries, compare the note and calendar entry information, delete a calendar entry. (*)
- Address 1 (A1): Create, change, and delete address entries.
- File Management 1 (F1): Rename a file, copy a file, and delete a file.
- Editor 1 (E1): Create and save a short document.
- Editor 2 (E2): Locate and edit a document, open a note, copy text from the note into the document, save, mail and print the final version of the document. (*)
- Decision Support 1 (D1): Create a small spreadsheet, open a document, copy the spreadsheet into the document, save and print the document, save the spreadsheet. (*)
- Decision Support 2 (D2): Locate information in a calendar entry, revise a spreadsheet title using the calendar information, create a pie chart from the spreadsheet, print and save the chart, save the spreadsheet. (*)

* indicates a scenario which tests integration by requiring data transfer between applications or window manipulation.

3.0 APPROACH TO THE BENCHMARK EVALUATION

3.1 Participants

Thirty employees of temporary help agencies participated in the study, with two groups of 15 hired for evaluations in two locations. Each group of 15 consisted of three groups (five participants per group), with the following characteristics:

- Clerical/secretarial with no experience using a mouse.
- Business professional with no experience using a mouse.
- Business professional with at least three months experience using a mouse with a computer system.

All participants had at least three months experience using some type of computer system. They had no programming training or experience, and had no (or very limited) knowledge of the DOS operating system.

3.2 Measures

The measures collected for each scenario are described below.

- Performance
  - Time on Task: The time to complete a scenario successfully.
  - Completion Rate: The percentage of participants completing a scenario successfully. The participant may have experienced problems (as defined below), but must have completed the scenario without assistance and with correct outputs in order for the completion to be considered successful.
  - Error Free Rate: The percentage of participants completing a scenario without any problems.
- Analytical
  - Step Counts: A step is really a subtask, and not individual physical actions. For example, *opening the file pull-down menu* is a step, but not *moving the pointer to the action bar option "file"*, followed by *pressing mouse button down.* Steps generally were chunks of relatively routinized and generic actions (select, open, drag) applied to diverse objects. Steps also tended to be subtasks for which substantive mistakes were possible, i.e., a mismatch between what the user might want to do, and how the user tried to it with the system (see Norman, 1982; Carroll & Mack, 1984).
- Opinion:
  - Satisfaction with (1) the ease of scenario completion, (2) the amount of time required, and (3) the support information (help, messages, and documentation).
  - The frequency with which these types of tasks were done in the real work environment.

  For these opinion measures, participants were asked to complete a short questionnaire at the end of each scenario. The satisfaction items used 7-point scales. The frequency item had four points corresponding to Daily, Weekly, Monthly, and Never.
- Problem Analysis: Specific user problems were also recorded. Any deviation from the optimum sequence of actions required to complete the scenario was considered to be indicative of a problem. These problems were classified in terms of impact on scenario completion and frequency (number of users experiencing the problem). Four impact levels were defined:
  1. Scenario failure or irretrievable data loss. A scenario could be failed if the participant required assistance to complete the scenario, or if the participant believed the scenario to be properly completed, but the output of the scenario was incorrect (excepting minor typographical errors).
  2. Considerable recovery effort. The recovery effort was defined as considerable if a participant worked on recovery for more than one minute or repeated the error within a scenario.
  3. Minor recovery effort. The recovery effort was defined as minor if the error only occurred once within a scenario and required less than a minute for recovery.
  4. Inefficiency. A problem was considered to be an inefficiency if it did not fall within any of the impact classifications above.

3.3 Systems and Environment

Two office systems were put together by installing a word processor, a mail application, a calendar application, and a spreadsheet on two different platforms which allowed a certain amount of integration among the applications. Both platforms allowed participants to cut, copy, and paste data between applications and to present data from several applications simultaneously in windows. System I was more tightly integrated than System II (see Mack & Nielsen, 1987) with respect to consistency of graphical interface style across applications. In System II e.g., the address and calendar applications were host-based menu- and text-based applications quite different from other component applications in the software environment.

3.4 Procedure

Introduction Participants began with a brief tour of the lab, a description of the study's purpose and events of the day, and completed a background questionnaire. Participants who used System I began by working with the interactive tutorial which was provided. Those who used System II were given a brief demo about how to move, point and select with a mouse, how to open the icons for each product, and how to minimize and maximize windows.

Task Scenario Activity Following the system familiarization, participants worked on Scenario M1. Following this, the ten scenarios (including a different version of Scenario M1) were presented in mixed orders. The instructions emphasized that we were especially interested in what happened when people first began to use a new system and assured the participants that we did not expect perfect performance. The instructions also focused on working "at your own pace" and using supporting documentation "whenever you like". If it became clear that a participant had failed to complete a scenario successfully, he or she was helped to finish, and then began the next. At the end of the day, participants were debriefed.

4.0 RESULTS AND DISCUSSION

4.1 What are the obtained values of our usability measurements?

Table 2 shows a subset of the usability measurements gathered in this study. The table is organized by scenario and dependent measure.

Table 2. Subset of Scenario Data (System I/System II).

Scenario	Comp. Rate (%)	Med. TOT (min)	Step Count	Impact 1 Errors	Impact 2 Errors
M1A	33/80	*/10	15/13	21/4	36/10
C1	57/80	10/15	14/13	12/2	19/16
A1	64/93	7/15	28/32	8/1	10/17
D1	36/47	*/*	43/62	20/13	15/30

* If the Completion Rate is less than 50%, then the Median Time-on-Task cannot be calculated.

Statistical analyses can be used at various levels for various reasons. Univariate analyses such as t-tests may be used to determine for which variables and scenarios a behavioral objective has been exceeded beyond a statistical criterion such as alpha $< .05$. Analyses can be conducted at the participant or scenario level. It is reasonable to consider the scenario as a unit of analysis because scenarios, like participants, are sampled from a larger population and are expected to exhibit individual differences. At this level of analysis, it is possible to include analytical information such as step counts as well as measures calculated from the participant sample (e.g., completion rates, median subjective ratings).

We experimented with multivariate statistical techniques at the scenario level. Multivariate techniques are of value when dependent variables are expected to be correlated, or when one is concerned with patterns of dependent variables. For example, we conducted three discriminant analyses (Cliff, 1987; SAS, 1979) to help discover if some variable sets of a priori interest were useful in discriminating the systems. The first set included the performance/analytical variables of completion rate, error-free rate, and step count, and was significant ($F(3,18)=4.98$, $p=.01$). The next analysis used the error counts by impact level, and was significant ($F(4,17)=9.87$, $p=.0003$). The discriminant analysis using the three subjective ratings was not significant ($F(3,18)=.27$, $p=.84$).

The three discriminant analyses indicated how one might begin an exploration of the data. The most significant discriminant function was obtained by examining the error counts by impact rating. System I had significantly more high impact problems than System II, that is, problems which could not be resolved without help, and which may have led to loss of data. The analysis using completion rates, error-free rates, and step counts was also significant. Participants using this system completed significantly fewer tasks without assistance for System I compared System II (about 50 % vs 69%, respectively). The systems did not differ in frequency of tasks users were able to complete with no help and no problems, a low frequency outcome for both systems in any case (about 20% and 17 % for System I and II respectively). The subjective ratings, however, provided a poor discrimination between systems. These patterns of results indicated that, in this case, we should focus on user problems when providing design guidance.

4.2 How good (reliable and valid) are these data?

One of the goals of quantitative benchmarking is to develop a cumulative and reliable database of benchmark assessments for systems over time and investigators, in the face of known sources of variation in human performance (e.g., individual differences, see Egan, 1988). To establish this goal requires (1) reliable data measurements, (2) standard data collection and analysis methods (applicable across time and development groups), and (3) valid measurements with respect to providing representative and diagnostic information about user's experience in the real workplace. We discuss each issue in turn.

4.2.1 Reliable benchmark measures

The reliabilities of the benchmark measures were estimated by creating subsamples of the data for each system. Subsamples consisted of two representatives from each participant group for a total of six participants per subsample. Dependent measures were calculated for each subsample by scenario, and correlations were calculated by system for each measure of interest (median time-on-task and satisfaction ratings, completion and error-free rates). Of the eleven correlations computed, only one was clearly nonsignificant (System II Time Rating, $r=.29$). The others ranged from .5 to .8. This is encouraging since there were only six participants in each subsample, consistent with many industrial benchmark evaluations. Although some reliabilities fell slightly below the recommended values of .7 to .8 (see Landauer, 1988) most of the coefficients were fairly high considering the small number and heterogeneous quality of the participants in the subsamples. These measurements should be adequate for most system evaluative purposes, since they are more experimental and exploratory in nature than they are psychometric and normative (see Nunnally, 1978).

4.2.2 Reliable Data Collection and Analysis Methods

In each study, the data were collected by a different set of observers in a different location. We do not have any quantitative assessment of the inter-rater and inter-location reliability. It may be that the values we have reported represent the upper limit for reliabilities since they are based on measures collected in the same location by the same set of observers. The lead observers for each study were in constant communication to ensure that consistent methods were followed, both for procedure and judgements. At the conclusion of the study, all recorded errors were reviewed by the lead observers to ensure that all disagreements were resolved before the summary measures were derived.

4.2.3 Validity of Scenarios and Measurements

The ultimate validity of our laboratory benchmarks is in predicting the success of our product in the marketplace. We know of no actual statistical interpretation of validity assessed from the laboratory (or even field) and the marketplace. Rather, we relied on the content validity of our scenarios, the usability attributes we develop, the way we measure those attributes, and the design guidance these measurements provide. It is possible in some cases to obtain converging evidence for these conclusions. For example, our confidence in the validity of the scenarios is based not only on earlier field work and collective judgment of office system experts, but also on judgments we elicited from participants in this study about the frequency with which they performed tasks corresponding to the scenarios. For this judgement, averaged across participants by scenario, the correlation between the systems was .92 ($p<.001$), indicating that the estimates were very reliable. This result is consistent with our belief that these scenarios are representative of real office work.

4.3 How can this information be used to improve a system?

4.3.1 Testable Behavioral Objectives

Although it is not presented in the form usually associated with behavioral objectives, the data presented in Table 2 can be considered a matrix of testable behavioral objectives. The data in the upper left cell imply that the objective for a system under development should be that, under the same measurement conditions described in our Methods section, the successful completion rate for Scenario M1A should exceed 80%. In the same way, the median Time-on-Task should be no greater than 7.0 minutes for Scenario A1. It may not be realistic to expect the system under development to exceed the better competitive system for every measure and every scenario, but these targets enable the developer to understand those tasks and measures for which the system under development is failing to be competitive. With this knowledge, the developer can make more appropriate engineering decisions and tradeoffs than would otherwise be possible.

4.3.2 Qualitative Diagnostic Information

On the quantitative side, our classification of user problems by severity was similar to alternative methods of characterizing the impact of problems (see Good, Spine, Whiteside and Peter, 1986), but did not involve estimating time spent recovering from errors based on video data. Error impact turned out to be an important factor discriminating the systems we evaluated. In particular, high impact errors are precisely those which a developer is likely to want to solve to achieve usability objectives.

On the qualitative side, we are interested in diagnosing the possible causes of user problems and possible design solutions. Diagnostic information can be obtained from other kinds of evaluation, often qualitative, informal and exploratory such as thinking aloud, methods which may preclude obtaining reliable quantitative performance assessments (see, e.g., Nielsen, 1989; Landauer, 1988; Lewis, 1982). However, we believe that substantial qualitative, and diagnostic information is available from benchmarking studies if the investigator records participants' errors and comments.

Several psychologically grounded frameworks are useful for interpreting problems users experience in various human-machine and human-computer domains (examples include Arnold and Roe, 1987; Norman, 1982; Rasmussen, 1988; Reason, 1988; Lewis & Norman, 1986; Carroll & Mack, 1984). We have found that design-relevant interpretations of problems often do not involve deep psychological analysis but seem to point to violation of basic, commonplace guidelines associated with usable interfaces. Many of the high severity problems in Table 2 resulted from problems with lack of feedback, lack of consistency in operation, unintuitive modes and lack of visibility in system states. These observations apply to both systems, and in the case of System I were somewhat surprising because of the seeming surface consistency and intuitiveness of the interface style. We illustrate these general observations by discussing some serious problems users experienced.

Lack of feedback: Many problems observed simply involved lack of feedback about outcomes or states of the system relevant to successfully accomplishing a task. Copying and pasting between applications was a problem for both systems and was relatively severe in impact and frequency (47% of the participants had trouble using the functions on both systems). Users did not always specify a to-be-cut object first, or did not recognize when selection has somehow failed. The result in both cases is that either nothing was pasted or some prior material was incorrectly pasted. There was no feedback when "cut" or "copy" was executed without specifying an object. These problems suggest providing more feedback about what has been copied (prior to pasting) and/or to somehow reinforce the need to select to-be-copied material before selecting the copy action. Note that solving these problems would improve the System I completion rate for the spreadsheet scenario D1 from 36 % to 50 % (assuming the solutions created no new problems).

Consistency of operation: Another basic guideline is to implement functions consistent with users' tasks and expectations. The cut/copy/paste problem may also be an example of inconsistency with users' expectations. Users who selected copy or paste actions before selecting relevant to-be-copied information seemed to expect an action-object style of interaction, at least in this instance. Another example involved calendar use (Scenario C1) for System I compared to System II. The quantitative data in Table 3 shows that for Scenario C1, users' completion rate was 57% for System I and 73% for System II. The most serious error for System I was that 40% of the participants had great difficulty simply printing daily appointments. The proximate cause of the difficulty was that users misinterpreted an instruction in the user manual. The deeper cause, however, may be that the calendar application for System I did not implement that function in a way consistent with its other print options. Instead, users had to print the screen for that subwindow, a procedure that is actually part of the operating system, not the application, and covered in documentation, but not referred to within the application. Given development resources one would obviously recommend implementing this print option consistent with other available print options. The correction of this problem would improve the completion rate for this scenario to 80% (assuming the solution did not create additional problems).

These analyses are highly interpretative and based on user actions rather than immediate comments (e.g., thinking aloud). Two aspects of this analysis should be clear. Interpreting user problems in a design-relevant way is highly contextual in that it often depends on the details of the application, interface implementation and user task. Also, more than one interpretation is possible, and even useful: e.g., more than one guideline or psychological generality may provide a useful interpretation.

4.4 Conclusions

The benchmarking methodology described here provides a reliable and standard framework. In this paper we described a set of integrated office scenarios, their rationale, and their use. The scenarios were useful in developing both quantitative and qualitative descriptions of two integrated office systems. Users experienced many serious problems with both systems. We were somewhat surprised to find that the system that was seemingly more tightly integrated (with respect to data transfer and consistency of interface implementation) did not provide clear usability advantage for users in terms of our benchmark measures and our broader set of integrated office tasks. Equally surprising, these problems seem to involve failure to observe basic user interface design guidelines as well as a deeper failure in some cases to match user's expectations or intuitions about how tasks can be accomplished using computers. These problems could be analyzed both quantitatively and qualitatively to help diagnose system differences and provide clues to possible system improvements.

5.0 REFERENCES

Arnold, B. and Roe, R. (1987). User errors in human-computer interaction. In M. Frese, E. Ulich, and W. Dzida (Eds.), Psychological Issues of Human Computer Interaction in the Work Place. Amsterdam: North-Holland.

Carroll, J. and Mack, R. (1984). Learning to use word processors: By doing, by thinking and by knowing. In J. Thomas and M. Schneider (Eds.) Human factors in computer systems. (13-52), Norwood, N.J.: Ablex Publishing.

Cliff, N. (1987). Analyzing multivariate data. San Diego: Harcourt-Brace-Jovanovich.

Egan, D. (1988). Individual differences in human-computer interaction. In M. Helander (Ed.) Handbook of human-computer interaction. North-Holland: Elsevier Science Publishers.

Good, M., Spine, T., Whiteside, J., and Peter, G. (1986). User-derived impact analysis as a tool for usability engineering. In Proc. CHI'86 Human Factors in Computer Systems. (Boston, April 13-17), 265-283.

Gould, J.D. (1988). How to design usable systems. In M. Helander (Ed.), Handbook of Human-Computer Interaction. New York: North-Holland Press.

Landauer, T.K. (1988). Research methods in human-computer interaction. In M. Helander (Ed.), Handbook of Human-Computer Interaction. New York: North-Holland Press.

Lewis, C. (1982). Using the "thinking aloud" method in cognitive interface design. Research Report RC 9265, IBM Thomas J. Watson Research Center, P.O. Box 704, Yorktown Heights, N.Y..

Lewis, C. and Norman, D. (1986). Designing for error. In D. Norman and S. Draper (Eds.) User-centered system design: New perspectives on human-computer interaction. Hillsdale, N.J.: Lawrence Erlbaum Associates.

Nielsen, J. (1989). Usability engineering at a discount. In Proc. Third International Conference on Human-Computer Interaction, (18-22). Boston, MA.

Nielsen, J., Mack, R.L., Bergendorff, K.H., and Grischkowsky, N.L. (1986). Integrated software usage in the professional work environment: Evidence from questionnaires and interviews. In CHI'86 Proceedings, (162-167). New York, NY: ACM.

Mack, R. and Nielsen, J. (1987). Software integration in the professional work environment: Observations on requirements, usage and interface issues. Research Report RC 12677, IBM T.J. Waston Research Center, P.O.Box 704 Yorktown Heights, NY.

Norman, D.A. (1982). Steps toward a cognitive engineering: design rules based on analyses of human error. In Human Factors in Computer Systems, (378-382). Gaithersburg, MD: ACM.

Nunnally, J.C. (1978). Psychometric theory. New York: McGraw-Hill.

Rasmussen, J. (1988). Human error mechanisms in complex work environments. Reliability Engineering and System Safety, 22, 155-167.

Reason, J. (1988). Modelling the basic error tendencies of human operators. Reliability Engineering and System Safety, 22, 137-153.

Roberts, T.L. and Moran, T.P. (1983). The evaluation of text editors: Methodology and empirical results. Communications of the ACM, 26, 265-283.

SAS Institute. (1979). SAS User's Guide. Cary, NC: SAS Institute, Inc.

Whiteside, J., Jones, S., Levy, P. and Wixon, D. (1985). User performance with command, menu and iconic interfaces. In Proc. CHI '85 Human Factors in Computing Systems (185-191). San Francisco, CA: ACM.

Whiteside, J., Bennett, J., and Holtzblatt, K. (1988). Usability engineering: our experience and evolution. In M. Helander (Ed.), Handbook of Human-Computer Interaction. New York: North-Holland Press.

Williges, R., Williges, B., Elkerton, J. (1987). Software interface design. Handbook of human factors. G. Salvendy (Ed.), New York: J. Wiley & Sons.

Human–Computer Interaction - INTERACT '90
D. Diaper et al. (Editors)
Elsevier Science Publishers B.V. (North-Holland)

COMPARATIVE STUDY OF GEOMETRY SPECIFICATION CAPABILITIES OF GEOMETRIC MODELLING SYSTEMS

K Case, Department of Manufacturing Engineering
B S Acar, Engineering Design Institute

Loughborough University of Technology, Loughborough, Leicestershire, LE11 3TU, UK.
email kcase@mansun.lut.ac.uk

This paper describes experimentation carried out with a novel computer aided design system which uses 'manufacturing features' as the principal method by which the designer specifies the geometric part of design. The approach has been experimentally compared with the more traditional methods of two dimensional computer aided draughting and solids modelling. With skilled industrially-based design engineers such a features approach compares well with the other methods in terms of the user time and the accuracy and completeness of the final models.

Learning studies in the new technique and a large scale attitude survey are also briefly described.

1. INTRODUCTION

The integration of the design and manufacturing functions is important not only for greater efficiency, but also to improve quality in both respects. In some industries, such as electronics, highly integrated Computer Aided Design, Manufacture, Assembly and Test (CADMAT) systems are already heavily used. However similar success has not been achieved in that part of manufacturing industry devoted to mechanical components where more complex design geometry is often present.

The 'traditional' approach to the problem involves the design office encoding information into a standard format such as an engineering drawing. The drawing contains dimensional details of the final geometric condition of a component plus manufacturing information. Process planning is, in part, the task of recording this into a (textual) form representing the creation of the shape by a sequence of operations carried out on stock material. Data from design and process planning may then be transmitted onward for further decoding/encoding into a program to drive a numerically controlled machine tool and programmable inspection devices such as Co-ordinate Measuring Machines (CMM). This frequent recoding of information may not be too onerous in some circumstances, but it remains an objective to integrate more closely and automate the various activities.

As the central consideration is the geometry of the component, much research effort has been put into determining a representation which is at the same time compatible with the internal representations of the commonly used varieties of geometric modelling, is easy and natural in use, and a suitable basis for automatic determination of manufacturing method.

One promising line of research lies in the use of features (Gindy,1989). Thus a component could be described as a set of recognisable and describable groups of geometric entities. It may be useful to describe the collection of geometric entities according to their function in the finished component. These would then be described as 'design features'. As an alternative the geometry might be described according to the method of producing the shape, in which case they would be described as 'manufacturing features'. These manufacturing features might be used in the planning of the manufacturing method by feature recognition or feature specification techniques.

With feature recognition the designer works geometrically and computer techniques (Herbert et al, 1990) are used to 'recognise' features. Thus two circles, one on each of two parallel planes might be recognised as a hole. Such techniques are computationally intense, and in their purest forms appear to enhance the divisions between design and manufacture by assuming that the single state end condition of the design geometry is the only information available. (Whereas the designer has based this on some functionality and hopefully with a knowledge of likely methods of manufacture).

As an alternative, feature specification enables parametrically defined shapes to be used by the designer and with retention of the feature description subsequent processes do not need to 'recognise' the implications. Attempts are now being made to structure and formalise this technique whilst, at the same time, associating manufacturing methods with the geometric feature definition. This can be seen for example in the work of the Geometric Modelling Project (Eckersley, 1988) and CAM-I (Brimson and Downey, 1986).

Although the use of features in one way or another is a very widely accepted approach to problems of integrating Computer Aided Design (CAD) and Computer Aided Manufacture (CAM), we wished to formally and experimentally confirm their suitability from the user's point of view. To this end a prototype system embodying some of these ideas has been built and used as an experimental vehicle. It is known for convenience as CAPE-LUT (Computer Aided Production Engineering - Loughborough University of Technology).

The objectives of the research were then to discover:-

(a) the efficiency with which a manufacturing features interface might be used in comparison with a geometric interface. (In the hands of experienced CAD users).

(b) the relative ease with which a manufacturing features approach might be learned.

(c) what additional benefits might be obtained in the true integration of CAD and CAM systems.

2. THE CAPE-LUT SYSTEM

The CAPE-LUT approach is a variety of the feature specification technique with the following salient characteristics:

(a) a single representation for geometry definition (component design) and specification of manufacturing method (outline process planning).

(b) a natural, easily understood method of defining the representation.

(c) methods of presenting the information for design and process planning purposes.

The CAPE-LUT System

Starting from stock material or a pre-formed shape, the designer/planner explicitly states the method and sequence by which the material is progressively transformed into a finished part. This initial state and the transformations are the internal representation of the CAPE-LUT method.

The representation is defined using a familiar engineering language of which two forms are possible - a syntactical textual language for turning operation (Hart, 1986), or a set of interactive techniques for milling and similar operations based on metal removal terminology (Acar et al, 1986). The model is transformed by the sweeping of a tool through a path representing the cutting motion.

The information is presented for design purposes by the graphical display of a solid geometric model derived directly from the internal representation and generated by a subroutine driven version of a commercially available solid modeller (Boxer, Pafec, 1986a). The internal representation is a set of transformations plus the initial geometric condition, so that the effects of changing parameters or the order of transformations can be investigated. Process planning information can be presented by the output of descriptive text based on the current state of the transformations and is typically output in the same form as the familiar engineering language used for input. (Figure 1).

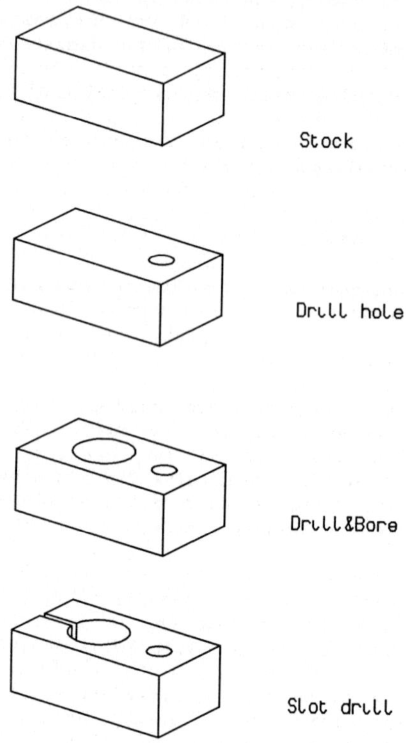

Figure 1. Fragment of a Graphical Outline Process Plan.

3. GEOMETRY EXPERIMENT

Any proposed new method of geometry specification must be efficient and accurate when in the hands of knowledgeable and experienced users. Hence, the first set of experiments was designed to compare the performance of CAPE-LUT in this respect with a solid geometry modelling system and a two dimensional draughting system.

The experiments were designed to enable the investigation of performance variation within groups of industrially based design engineers when using three different methods of specifying geometry. Performance measures used included time taken, accuracy and completeness. Time taken can be considered as the main variable cost in the use of CAD systems, whilst accuracy and completeness are important measures of the quality of design information. Clearly the quality of design information has major implications on 'downstream' costs associated with manufacture, assembly, in service use, etc.

3.1. The Experiment

Three methods of specifying geometry were used by the subjects to generate geometric models of two real components. These were the use of a two dimensional draughting system for the production of engineering drawing (Dogs Drawing Office Graphics System, Pafec 1986b), a Constructive Solid Geometry System (Boxer, Pafec 1986a), and the CAPE-LUT system. The two methods chosen for comparison with CAPE-LUT were selected as being representative of current CAD methods and as they both came from the same supplier it eased the task of locating subject which had experience in both approaches. Furthermore, CAPE-LUT is based upon the solid modeller selected and thus a direct comparison of interface characteristics is possible without interference from underlying system differences in functionality or performance.

3.2. Subjects

Experimental subjects were selected from the engineering staff of eight companies. The CAPE-LUT system is restricted to a class of component that can be described as 'a single part machined from stock material or blank'. Therefore we were mainly interested in subjects whose work was predominantly or substantially involved in this area. We choose to call such people 'designers', whilst fully realising that in other contexts a wider meaning should be ascribed to this description. Hence eighteen designers experienced in the use of Boxer and Dogs were chosen from eight collaborating engineering companies. All subjects were totally without experience of CAPE-LUT. The subjects were formed into three groups according to age, engineering experience and CAD experience. Group one was formed by young subjects with relatively little engineering and CAD experience, whereas the second and third groups were formed by relatively older subjects with group II having more engineering and group III more CAD experience. Later in the procedure, three persons were replaced by members of the University's full-time technical staff with similar qualities, due to the unavailability of some industrial subjects.

3.3. Methods of Presenting Test Pieces

The objectives of the experiment required the tests to be carried out on real parts, displaying a range of geometric characteristics. Thus test piece 1 is a simple part containing a small number of non-interacting features, whilst test part 2 contains more complex geometry due to the interaction of features (Figure 2). The method of presentation was considered to be very important as it could seriously influence the results. For example, if the parts were presented to the subjects in the form of engineering drawings, then this might favour the draughting approach, whereas isometric sketches might favour the three dimensional solid modelling approach. The method finally selected was to use physical 'models' by producing the components (in metal) to full scale. The subjects were then required to extract geometric information from these models by use of a rule. This inevitably compromised accuracy to an extent, but the application of a plus or minus 1 mm tolerance criterion on dimensional accuracy when analysing the results totally removed any such effect.

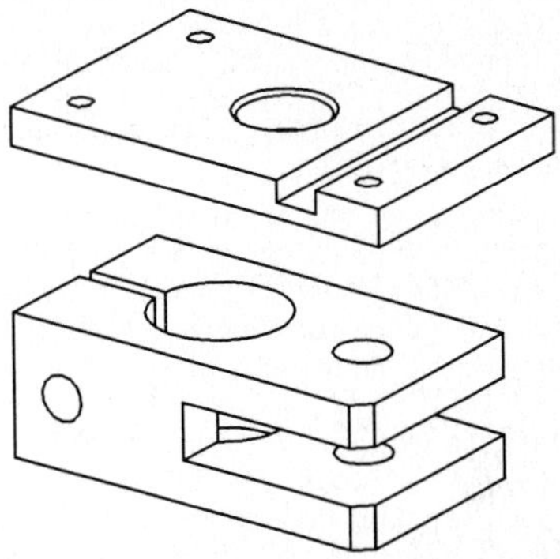

Figure 2. The Test Pieces

3.4. Trials

A pilot study was carried out prior to the main study with the purpose of establishing and validating a detailed experimental procedure (see Case & Acar, 1988 for details). After selection the subjects' age and experience in engineering and CAD were recorded to form the experimental groups. The methods were allocated to experimental cells on the basis that six permutations of ordering were possible and these should be allocated with equal probability. This was done to remove any effects such as nervousness on the first method or false confidence on the last. Table 1 shows the ordering within a particular group of six subjects

Table 1. Experiment Sequence

	Sequence of Methods		
Subject	First	Second	Third
1	DOGS	BOXER	CAPE-LUT
2	DOGS	CAPE-LUT	BOXER
3	BOXER	DOGS	CAPE-LUT
4	BOXER	CAPE-LUT	DOGS
5	CAPE-LUT	DOGS	BOXER
6	CAPE-LUT	BOXER	DOGS

Each subject was required to generate the geometry of the test pieces on each of the systems. Six hours were spent with each subject, allowing two hours for generation of the geometry of both test pieces on each system. The general objectives of the trials were described to the subjects and they were familiarised with the computer equipment (they were not permitted to use their own in case this influenced the results). A brief demonstration of the CAPE-LUT system was given, but not for Boxer and Dogs with which the subjects were already experienced. The subjects were presented with the physical models and instructed to generate a complete and accurate geometric specification as quickly as possible on the appropriate computer modelling system. In the case of Dogs it was made clear that a 'geometric specification' excluded the dimensioning and annotation normally to be found on an engineering drawing, but other than this the subjects placed their own interpretation on the requirement. Manuals for the systems were available and the experimenter would respond to specific questions on the operation of the various systems. The subjects made their own decisions as to when the trial was finished (ie the geometry specification completed) and all finished within the allotted time.

User time and the number of system errors were recorded. Generated models were saved for the post assessment of the model in respect of accuracy and completeness. User time was defined as the amount of time taken by the user to isssue commands, and excluded the time taken by the system to execute the command. System errors were defined as incorrect actions taken by the computer system outside the control of the user, and were recorded to shed light on future studies, but were not analysed as part of this experiment.

Accuracy was defined as the extent to which the completed part of the geometry specification matched the correct information. This was measured by comparing the geometry specification prepared by the subject against a template. The template consisted of a physical drawing in the case of Dogs, and a solid model specification for CAPE-LUT and Boxer. The accuracy of representation was scored on the basis of the ratio of the number of correct statements to the number of incorrect statements. Missing features were scored under 'completeness' and not considered as inaccuracies.

Completeness is a measure of the extent to which the geometry specification is complete. Failure to complete the geometry specification is useful as a measure of the subjects' abilities with the system and of the ambiguity of the techniques used. Completeness was scored on the basis of missing features when compared with the geometry template.

3.5. Results and Analysis

To test whether there is significant difference between the time taken to specify geometry by using different systems, we have to allow another source of variation - the difference between groups - since the various levels of experience of the users was summarized by arranging them into three groups. Thus statistical analysis of the data obtained from experiments to compare the performance of CAPE-LUT with the solid geometry modelling system (Boxer) and two-dimensional draughting system (Dogs) was made by employing a two factor experiment with a replication model (details to be found in Case and Acar, 1988). Tables 2 and 3 show the data relating to time taken for both of the test pieces.

Table 2. User times for both test pieces (decimal minutes)

Subject	Test Piece 1			Test Piece 2		
No	DOGS	BOXER	CAPE	DOGS	BOXER	CAPE
1	25.67	5.37	7.13	21.53	15.08	11.82
2	17.63	20.97	6.60	24.73	15.47	16.67
3	13.93	58.00	15.27	32.72	25.90	34.20
4	36.58	29.75	20.65	66.40	29.15	27.37
5	11.88	15.27	13.20	31.27	31.20	28.55
6	16.12	16.48	8.57	15.10	15.38	22.80
7	5.02	31.53	6.40	21.08	20.80	13.65
8	10.77	68.37	12.65	13.02	22.03	27.93
9	20.20	31.82	12.13	27.52	39.90	23.58
10	17.57	14.57	11.47	18.57	22.22	21.03
11	17.42	12.18	8.05	16.53	37.73	17.20
12	14.20	18.45	8.42	25.43	15.67	20.23
13	6.28	11.90	5.75	13.07	16.78	17.17
14	15.37	14.20	7.45	11.38	13.25	16.12
15	14.70	10.40	13.73	25.42	14.13	14.75
16	17.27	8.90	7.07	15.48	14.50	29.92
17	31.60	34.02	7.28	23.68	34.52	21.72

The statistical analysis leads to the conclusion that the implementation of CAPE-LUT on test piece 1 produced a significant decrease in the time taken to specify geometry compared with Dogs and Boxer; Dogs being second best. There is no statistical evidence of the existence of a significant difference between the performance characteristics of the three groups.

Analysis of the results for test piece 2 were less conclusive in that although the largest source of variation is in fact between the goups this is not statistically significant. It is even more difficult to discern any performance difference between the three alternative systems.

As has been mentioned, accuracy was determined by comparison with a template using a tolerance of plus or minus one millimetre as an accuracy criterion against certain 'key' dimensions. The ratio of correct statements to the number of key statements, when the groupings of the subjects are considered, is almost identical for each model. The scores clearly indicate that there is no significant difference between the systems. On the other hand, when we observe the data closely, we see that CAPE-LUT users, unlike Boxer users, never make positioning mistakes. However due to unfamiliarity with the system, they sometimes give wrong parameters, eg radius instead of diameter, which makes overall performance comparable to the other systems.

The Boxer and CAPE-LUT models were all complete (with one exception). However, almost half of the Dogs models were incomplete, mostly because of the lack of hidden detail, which reveals the vagueness of the completeness concept in two-dimensional engineering drawings.

4. LEARNING STUDIES

The 'manufacturing features' approach is often proposed as a method of geometry specification which is easier to learn as well as more efficient in the hands of fully experienced users. A second part of our study sought to formally establish this by a series of experiments using subjects who had some engineering experience but little or no CAD experience, the hypothesis being that subjects could attain a target performance level more quickly with the proposed system. This experimentation is described more fully in Case and Acar (1989) and only a brief description is given here.

Learning involves a complex combination of habits and responses which cannot be measured in absolute terms. However, established techniques (Restle and Greeno, 1970), suitably modified (Acar and Case, 1989), provide a method with which to compare the time taken to learn the use of alternative methods of specifying geometry within a solids modeller. Production of learning curves for a range of geometric features for CAPE-LUT and the alternative solid modeller together with statistical analysis formed the basis of the method of comparison.

The objectives of this experiment required the subjects to be inexperienced in the solid modelling aspects of CAD, but to have a basic understanding of geometry and the elementary concepts of manufacturing engineering. Hence ten undergraduate manufacturing engineering students were used as subjects, selected from a larger group on the basis of evidence of ability in engineering drawing. Six hours were spent individually with each subject in ninety minute sessions. During this time each subject used CAPE-LUT and Boxer to generate solid models of basic manufacturing features (hole, step, slot, fillet, keyway, chamfer, copy hole, counterbore and countersink).

The test parts were presented as a series of annotated isometric sketches and represent a variety of complexity within a simple stock material (the block). The subjects were required to repeatedly produce solid models of geometric features in the same order using a different set of parameters each time. No time limit was imposed, but the trials were terminated when the time taken to produce a particular feature converged within a 10% band after at least eleven attempts. Each subject carried out this procedure for each of the ten different features using both CAPE-LUT and Boxer (200 sets of experiments and at least 2200 trials across the entire experiment).

The primary measure of performance was response time which was defined as the time taken (seconds) to complete one feature with given dimensional parameters. Calibration was provided from earlier experiments to determine an expert user unit time per feature, and thus any inherent performance differences between the systems was eliminated. A typical pair of learning curves is shown as figure 3.

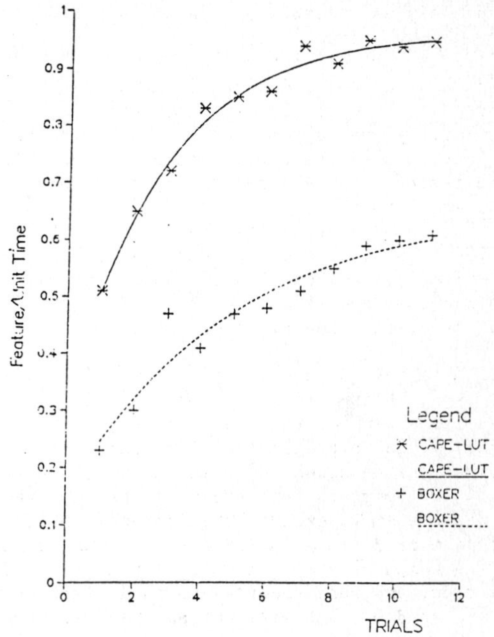

Figure 3. A Learning Curve

The learning time for a feature was determined by taking the cumulative time of the inverse of the learning curves and accepting 60% of the expert's performance as a measure of having 'learned' a system. Table 3 shows these cumulative learning times.

Table 3. Cumulative Learning Times at 60% level

Feature	CAPE-LUT	Boxer
Block	6.77	18.89
Hole	7.47	14.80
Step	2.94	25.59
Chamfer	2.79	7.66
Fillot	2.53	5.52
Keyway	2.07	22.58
Slot	2.73	20.15
Copyhole	4.57	21.62
Countersink	2.62	10.84
Counterbore	1.42	15.47
Mean	3.59	16.32

The clear difference in the data is supported by a one-tailed test at the 0.0005 level of significance that makes us 99.95% confident in claiming that the learning time for CAPE-LUT with its features interface is shorter than that for

Boxer with its mainly geometric interface.

5. ATTITUDES TO INTEGRATED DESIGN AND PROCESS PLANNING

The experimental work relating to learning and efficiency in use by experienced users demonstrates that the manufacturing features approach can be beneficial in both respects. This is encouraging for these reasons alone, but assumes increased significance when the deeper reasons for considering manufacturing features are considered. The hope is that this approach will provide a means of integrating the design and manufacture planning activities. Clearly the evidence so far is that there will be no detrimental effect on performance, but we are also concerned that such an approach be acceptable to practising engineers. This is by no means a certain proposition as it cuts across very clearly demarked areas of responsibility in existing organisations.

It was not possible to experimentally evaluate the proposition, partly because of the extended nature of any such experiments, and partly because features-based systems were not commercially available (CAPE-LUT was an experimental vehicle which would not be sufficiently developed for this purpose, and features systems which are now beginning to emerge were not available at the time).

Consequently a large scale questionaire survey was undertaken instead. This had the objective of determining attitudes to the close integration of design and manufacturing planning, particularly through the mechanism of features and the graphical outline process plan provided by CAPE-LUT.

Twenty-one percent of the 1200 companies contacted replied, and although the results are discussed more fully elsewhere (Case and Acar, 1988), a generally favourable response was received. It is perhaps wise to treat questionaire results with some caution but there seemed to be a genuine willingness to consider new methods in a part of industry which is often accused of adhering rigidly to traditional methods.

6. CONCLUSIONS

This experimental work has provided formal evidence to support the widespread adoption of manufacturing features as the interface to three-dimensional CAD systems. It has been shown to have no detrimental effect on performance, and to be a considerable aid in the learning of systems. Initial subjective evidence suggests that the approach is acceptable to practising engineers.

7. ACKNOWLEDGEMENTS

This research work was funded by the Application of Computers in Manufacturing Engineering (ACME) Directorate of the Science and Engineering Research Council (SERC) under grant number GR/C/89007.

REFERENCES

Acar, B S and Case, K, 1989, CAD systems ... easy to learn? Interaction with Computers.

Acar, B S, Case, K and Bennaton, J A, 1986, Evaluation of a new approach to design and process planning. Proceedings of the 4th Conference on UK Research in Automated Manufacture (London: Institute of Mechanical Engineers).

Brimson, J A and Downey, P J, 1986, Feature Technology: a key to manufacturing integration. Spring CIM Review (Arlington, Texas: CAM-I).

Case, K and Acar, B S, 1988, Computer Aided Production Engineering Linking CAD, Process Planning and Tool Design - Experimentation. Final report to Science and Engineering Research Council GR/C/89007, Loughborough University of Technology.

Case, K and Acar, B S, 1989, Learning Studies in the use of Computer Aided Design Systems for Discrete-Parts Manufacture. Behaviour and Information Technology, Vol 8, No 5, 353-368.

Eckersley, J S, 1988, Features as an Interface between CAD and CAM. Manufacturing Systems Group Survey paper. Geometric Modelling Project, Loughborough University of Technology.

Pafec, 1986a, Boxer User Manual 3.2, Pafec Limited, Nottingham.

Pafec, 1986b, DOGS User Manual 3.2, Pafec Limited Nottingham.

Gindy, N N Z, 1989, A Hierarchical Structure for Form Features. International Journal of Production Research, Vol 27, No 12, 2089-2103.

Hart, N M, 1986, A CAD Engineering Language to Aid Manufacture. Ph.D Thesis, Loughborough University of Technology.

Herbert, P J, Hinde, C, Bray, A, Launders, V, Round D and Temple D, 1990, Feature Recognition within a Truth-Maintained Process Planning System. International Journal of Computer Integrated Manufacture. In print.

Restle, F and Greeno, J G, 1970, Introduction to Mathematical Psychology (Reading, MA: Addison-Wesley).

Human–Computer Interaction – INTERACT '90
D. Diaper et al. (Editors)
Elsevier Science Publishers B.V. (North-Holland)

COST-BENEFIT ANALYSIS OF ITERATIVE USABILITY TESTING

Clare-Marie Karat, Ph.D

IBM T. J. Watson Research Center, P. O. Box 704, Yorktown Heights, NY 10598, USA

A methodology for computing the value of iterative usability work is presented using data from a series of three usability tests of a software application. The cost-benefit analysis methodology provides software development managers a basis for making pragmatic decisions about human factors work. The projected dollar value of the reduction in end user time on an application task based on data from the first to the third test is compared to the costs of the usability work. The analysis of initial end user application use shows a two dollar return on every dollar invested in usability project activities and highlights sources of additional savings. Two methodological techniques employed during the iterative usability testing are highlighted and the decision process concerning use of these techniques for human factors, software development schedule, and economic reasons is discussed.

1. INTRODUCTION

Software development managers have to make pragmatic decisions regarding the inclusion of human factors work in their projects. Towards this end, it is important for human factors professionals to address project management concerns regarding time schedules and resources required for human factors work and the benefits that will be derived from its inclusion in the project cycle. The inclusion of human factors work in software development can result in both short-term and long-term benefits. During the development stages of a project lifecycle, human factors work can result in development cost reduction through the identification and resolution of design problems prior to coding and integration testing (Mantei and Teorey, 1988). These design problems can be identified through human factors work early in the project cycle in the form of end user requirements definition, benchmarking, design reviews (Karat and Bennett, 1989) iterative prototyping and testing of designs (Gould, 1988), and through studying the context of the users work environment (Whiteside, Bennett, and Holtzblatt, 1988). After a system has been coded and delivered, prior human factors work on the system can result in lower training and help support costs, and savings due to reduced user errors, increased user productivity, and increased user acceptance of the system (Karat, 1989; Mantei and Teorey, 1988; Norman and Draper, 1986). Finally, human factors work completed during system development can result in lowered expenses for system maintenance as the need for costly system fixes is greatly reduced (Rubenstein and Hersh, 1984). This final benefit of human factors work is of growing importance as information systems organizations in both the public and private sectors are by necessity spending increasing proportions of their resources on maintenance and costly fixes to existing systems rather than on the development of new systems.

Human factors professionals have an opportunity to make a significant contribution to the financial outlook of software development organizations. In order to effect these changes, objective financial data on the value of human factors work needs to be available to software development managers to justify its inclusion in project plans.

The purpose of this paper is to present a methodology for computing the value of iterative usability work using data from a series of three usability tests of a software application. This methodology illustrates a successful attempt to provide software development managers a basis for deciding to include human factors work in their projects. Moreover, the different methodological techniques used in this study provide an indication of the appropriateness of different techniques in various situations. Human factors techniques can be tailored to fit the particular size of a project, its schedule, and resource constraints. Sometimes a low-technology human factors technique is the technique of choice for a software project (Nielsen, 1989). For example, in smaller development projects and in situations were a project schedule is extremely constrained, use of low-technology alternatives such as foil prototypes (described later in the document) rather than online prototypes (high-technology alternative) may provide a low cost and timely solution for completion of human factors activities.

The software application that will be used to illustrate two innovative human factors techniques and the cost-benefit methodology is a security application recently developed to improve the dialog of 23,000 end users (IBM employees in branch offices across the US) with a large data entry and inquiry mainframe application. Prior to this application, end users had to reidentify themselves when they wanted to perform each of a series of related transactions that composed a business process and they had to remember the separate code or mnemonic for each transaction and sign-on with the mnemonic to use it. From the user's perspective, working with the mainframe application was like a series of disconnected conversations. The new security application simplifies the sign-on process by providing a seamless environment for end users across transactions within an application. This was accomplished through an architectural change that grouped mnemonics for related business application tasks under one master mnemonic. End users need to remember only one master mnemonic rather than the many each had to recall previously. The main usability goal for this project was to ensure that the transition from the old to the new sign-on process for business transactions was completed smoothly, without disrupting end users or business, and without requiring formal user training. The end users sign-on to the target mainframe application which resides on a target business system an average of a dozen times a day. The specific project usability objective was for 95% of the end users to sign-on error free after three attempts.

2. METHOD

2.1. Participants

The participants for all three usability tests were IBM administrative staff from the New York metropolitan area. The first test employed 5 participants, the second test employed 10 participants, and the third test employed 12 participants. Summary background data for participants across the three tests was highly comparable. Participants in each test had an average of 2 years experience in their current jobs and had worked for IBM an average of 5 years. They have college degrees and work with computer terminals on a daily basis in the performance of their jobs. Their self-assessed experience level with the target business system was above average and their experience level with the target business application resident on the target business system was average.

2.2. Design

The first usability test (Test 1) was a field prototype test conducted in a branch office, the second test (Test 2) was a laboratory prototype test, and the third test (Test 3) was a laboratory integration test of the live code on a test system. Since the usability performance objective for this application concerned how quickly the end users would learn to use the system error free, all three tests were designed to measure learning that occurred across several repetitions of the same task. Each participant in each test performed a set of four typical sign-on tasks to a variety of business transactions three times. Each time the set of tasks was performed (called a trial), the tasks were presented to the participant in random order.

Both field and laboratory tests were conducted for several reasons. The initial field test provided usability data in the context in which end users complete their work. The need to test systems in real work environments is receiving increased attention (Whiteside et al, 1988). The end user's social and physical environment is not replicated in the laboratory, and these factors influence the way an end user works with an application. Some physical environment factors are the layout of an office space in the work environment, crowding, and noise level. Some social environment factors are the office atmosphere and pace that in this case resulted in the typical end user's "rote" attention to the terminal screen while juggling a variety of tasks simultaneously, and communication among the staff (telephone calls, people stopping by and requesting information).

During the field test, usability staff were alerted to end user issues related to the work context that were not observed in the laboratory tests. Another advantage of the field test was that it was less obtrusive on participants. Participants in the field test were in their normal work environment whereas in the laboratory tests they were isolated in an unfamiliar setting (the test studio) with its configuration of office furniture, terminal, and phone as well as cameras, microphones, and one-way mirrors. Finally, because the experimenter did not have to spend time orienting participants to the testing environment and moved quickly from participant to participant within the branch office, the field test was completed in 25% of the time and at approximately 25% of the cost required to complete a comparable laboratory test. Usability field tests that collect performance and opinion data are an innovative human factors technique that may provide critical data at nominal cost as compared to usability laboratory tests.

The laboratory tests provided the ability to collect videotape data for later review, a more controlled environment, and facilitated the observation of end users by, and education of, development and application owner staff. There are possible problems in comparing the results of the different tests; however, the benefits of having both types of test data outweigh the negative factors. Iterative testing was crucial to the success of this project as it provided an opportunity to test the impact of design changes made to the interface (Gould, 1988). It also provided a reliability check on previous results. By combining use of field and laboratory tests and testing prototype and integrated code, usability staff were able to collect complementary information that together provided a more complete understanding of the end user, work context, and panel issues and resulted in a better final interface design than would have been possible without iterative testing using different methodologies. The three tests were completed across a period of seven months and were scheduled to fit within the existing project time table without adding additional days to the schedule.

2.3. Test Materials and Procedure

Four sign-on tasks that covered different aspects of changes to the sign-on process were used in the three tests. These tasks were developed in consultation with end users and other support personnel. An example of a sign-on task is as follows: "Please sign-on to the XXX system to perform an authorized inquiry function (e.g. CMINQ) on the XXX application."

The first two tests were completed using foil prototypes of the panels, while Test 3 was completed using the integrated code on a test system. For the foil prototype, one overhead projection color foil was developed for each panel using a PC graphics application. Usability prototypes are usually online prototypes written using one of a variety of tools available. Because of the extremely tight project development schedule, there was insufficient time to develop and test an online prototype. Instead, a reusable color foil prototype of the sign-on panels was developed in 20% of the time it would have taken to develop the online prototype based on estimates of development time from programming staff and actual time developing the foil prototype. Since a lower level of skill and less time was necessary in developing the foil prototype than the online prototype would have required, the reduction in development cost for this task was approximately 90%. The reusable foil prototype provided a realistic approximation of the interface panels and navigation. One limitation of this methodology is the number of panels an experimenter can work with and test at once; twenty-five panels is probably a reasonable maximum.

To perform the sign-on tasks on the foil prototype, usability staff placed a large sheet of white paper in front of participants to serve as a backdrop and then provided participants with the foil version of the sign-on panel. The participants used an audiovisual pen to write the information they would normally type on the panel, and then usability staff removed the first foil and provided participants with the panel foil they would encounter next based on their previous input. This pattern continued until the task was completed or participants said they did not know how to continue. An audiovisual pen was used so that entries made on the foils could be wiped off and the foils could be repeatedly used in the sign-on tasks.

The same performance and opinion measures were used in all tests. The performance measures included time on task , the time from the first to the last keystroke (or character written on the foil prototype) in completing the task; cumulative error free rate, the number of sign-on attempts required until 95% of the participants sign-on error free without backsliding; and completion rate, the percentage of participants completing each task (regardless of the number of errors made along the way). The debriefing questionnaire concerned the changes participants thought had occurred to the sign-on process, how they figured out the changes that had occurred, whether they read information and error messages, what was confusing about the sign-on process, and what changes needed to be made to the sign-on panels. Finally, participants were asked a key forced-choice question called the End User Sign Off rating at the end of the debriefing sessions. They were asked to respond yes or no as to whether the product they had worked with was good enough to deliver without any changes.

The same procedure was used in all tests with two exceptions. In the field test participants sat at their desks and the experimenter, research assistant, and one application developer sat nearby. In the laboratory tests participants were brought into the test studio and oriented to the office configuration as well as the microphones, cameras, and one-way mirror. In the field test a research assistant unobtrusively collected timing data with a stopwatch while the experimenter worked with the participant and in the laboratory tests the research assistant used a PC logging program to collect timing data and also ran the videotape and cameras. In each test the experimenter worked with one participant at a time. After introducing them to the usability session, each participant performed three trials of a set of four sign-on tasks that were presented in random order. At the end of the third trial, each participant was debriefed and asked to make recommendations about needed changes to the panels and completed an opinion measure.

3. USABILITY TEST RESULTS

The correct sign-on procedure for each of the four sign-on tasks in the tests was the same. Therefore data for completion rates and error free performance were each collapsed across tasks. The majority of participants were able to complete the sign-on process (although committing numerous errors in Tests 1 and 2). The completion rate for sign-on tasks was 92% for Test 1, 98% for Test 2, and 96% for Test 3.

Data on error free performance of the sign-on process were collapsed across the tasks and the cumulative percentage of participants performing error free from the first to the twelfth sign-on attempt was calculated for each test. In Test 1 80% of the participants never understood the sign-on process changes and completed all twelve attempts incorrectly (see Figure 1). During the debriefing participants talked about the office environment and the way they juggled several assignments at once. They remarked about the rote manner in which they worked at the terminals and how information needed to be presented to them given this context. Usability staff developed four recommendations to resolve the end user issues identified and three were implemented by development staff. These end user problems involved the content of error and informational messages and their position on panels.

Error free performance improved markedly in Test 2 in that 90% of the participants signed on correctly after 7 attempts; however, the number of learning attempts required remained unacceptable. The end user problem identified in Test 2 was a reoccurrence of one left unaddressed after Test 1. This end user issue involved a problematic navigational flow where users navigated down two different paths depending on the mnemonic chosen at sign-on. One path was clear to the end users, the second presented problems which because of technical limitations, were difficult to address. This time a new technical solution to the problem was determined and implemented; the navigational flow was simplified and standardized for end users. The navigational fork, the two separate paths mentioned above, was replaced by a bridge that all end users employed regardless of the mnemonic chosen at sign-on. In Test 3 100% of the participants signed on error free after the third attempt, thus meeting the usability objective set at the beginning of the project. The solution to the problem identified in Test 2 created one minor end user problem in Test 3. This issue was resolved prior to delivery of the code.

Additional performance data that illustrated end user issues with the application were the time on task data (see Figure 2). The ideal time to complete the task was 6 seconds and was determined by timing an expert at the task. Across the three tests, participant median time on task for Trial 1 ranged from 195 seconds on Test 1 to 24 seconds on Test 3. Median time on task for Trial 2 ranged from 76 seconds for Test 1 to 8 seconds on Test 3. Trial 3 data for median time

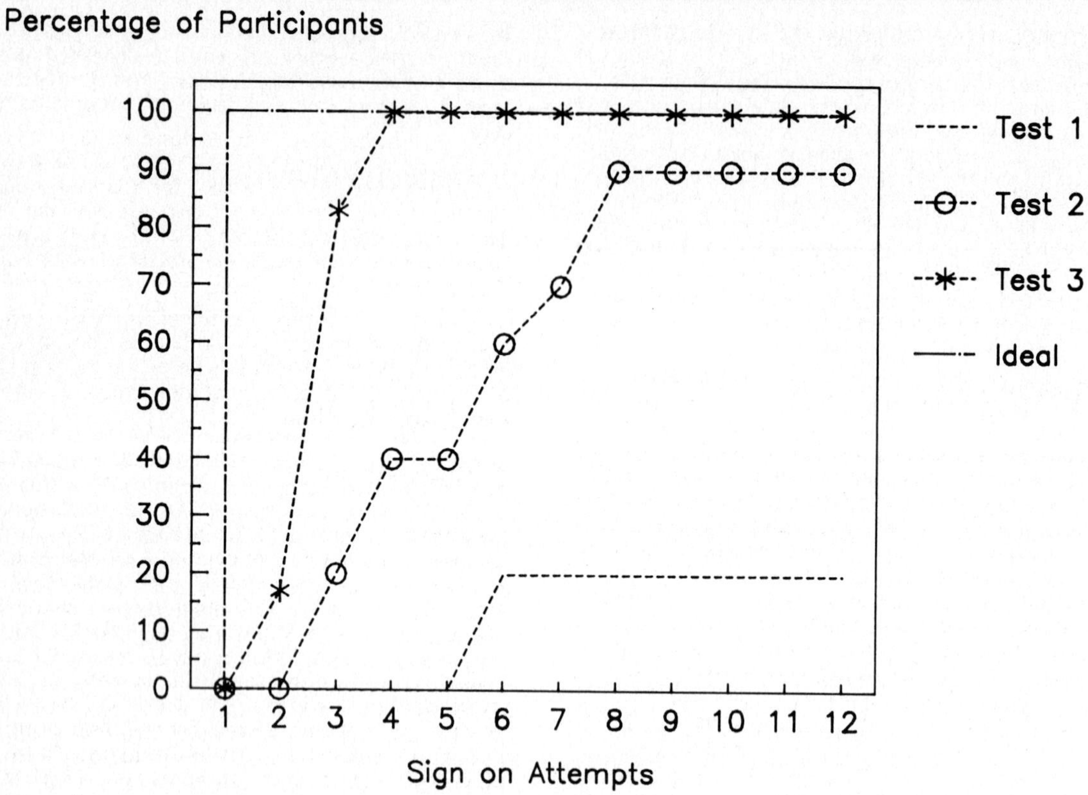

Figure 1. Cumulative percentage of participants performing error free.

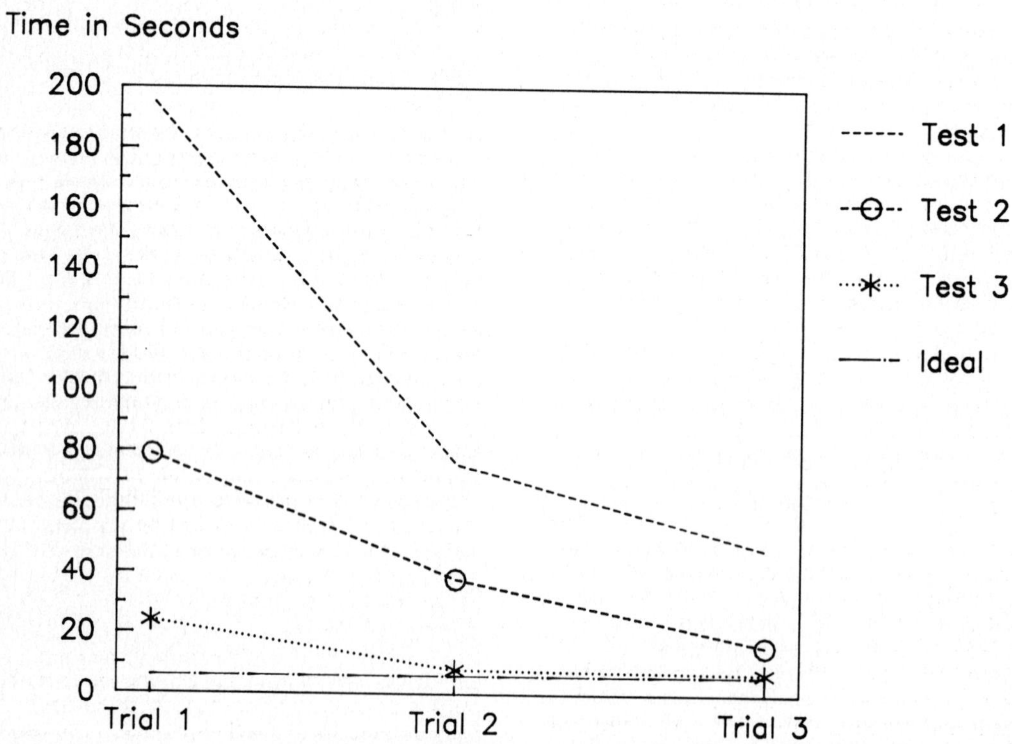

Figure 2. Median time on inquiry task.

on task ranged from 48 seconds on Test 1 to 7 seconds on Test 3. By Trial 2 of Test 3, the participant time on task was nearly equivalent to the ideal time on task.

The End User Sign Off data reinforced the performance data. No participants in Test 1 thought the new sign-on process was satisfactory as it was whereas 60% of the participants in Test 2 and 100% in Test 3 thought the new sign-on process was good enough to deliver without any changes. The low participant opinion score after Test 2 helped provide the impetus to correct the remaining end user problem identified.

4. COST-BENEFIT ANALYSIS

The methodology for the cost-benefit analysis is based on the assumption that had the human factors work on this project not taken place, the design established in Test 1 would have been coded and delivered. The value of the human factors work on this project was calculated by determining a dollar value for the reduction in time to complete the first three attempts at a task across iterations of the design (see Figure 2). The benefit of the human factors work was defined as the area between the lines for Test 1 and Test 3 on Figure 2. The projected dollar value of these savings was calculated for the end user population who would use the application. Most end users completed their first three sign-on attempts in the first few hours they worked with the new system following its installation.

The calculation of the dollar value of this usability work is conservative as it does not include:

- Cost savings related to further sign-on attempts - an average of twelve sign-ons per user per day,
- Cost avoidance due to fewer user errors,
- Savings related to the greatly reduced disruption of end users,
- Cost avoidance due to the reduced burden on Help support staff and the elimination of training for users, and
- Cost avoidance in system maintenance activities - Mantei and Teorey (1988) estimate that the cost of changes to a released system is four times the cost of these changes at the prototype stage.

The first step in the cost benefit analysis was to calculate the savings produced by the human factors activities. The time on task on Test 3 was subtracted from Test 1 for each of the three trials. The values were as follows:

- Trial 1: 3.25 - .40 = 2.85 minutes
- Trial 2: 1.27 - .13 = 1.14 minutes
- Trial 3: .80 - .12 = .68 minutes

The differences in time on task across the three trials sum to 4.67 minutes. This sum was multiplied by the end user population (22,876), and then converted to hours (1,781). The hours were multiplied by a productivity ratio and then by the personnel costs for the administrative staff for a total of $41,700 in savings.

The costs of usability work included time spent by development and usability staff and travel money for test participants. The costs were as follows:

- Usability resource $18,000
- Participant travel $ 700
- Test related development work $ 1,200
- Total cost $20,700

The costs of the three usability tests are combined in the cost data provided above. The cost of the field test was approximately 25% of that for a laboratory test. The laboratory prototype test cost less than the laboratory integration test since the latter required programmer time to facilitate the usability staff's use of the live code on a test system.

The analysis of the value added of usability work produced a conservative estimate of the net savings as $21,000 on the first three sign-on attempts which is a two dollar return on every dollar invested in usability project activities.

5. DISCUSSION

This analysis shows that the inclusion of human factors work in this software development project was a sound financial decision for the project manager to make. It is compelling that the analysis resulted in a one-to-two cost-to-savings ratio given the limited scope of the analysis and the small size of the project. If the analysis had covered savings across twelve sign-on attempts and included values for the cost avoidance of system maintenance and user support activities, the cost-benefit ratio would have been significantly larger. To give an indication of the difference that the size of a project can make, the cost-benefit ratio for a larger project at the same site using this methodology was 100 to 1 and was determined to be $6.8 million worth of end user time. The human factors work on that project included development of a large online prototype and three iterations of testing.

The cost-benefit analysis for the study reported here underscores the need to carefully consider the human factors techniques employed on a particular project. The size of the project and the time schedule constraints led to the choice of a low-technology tool to complete the human factors work. Using the reusable foil prototype of the interface panels, it was possible to efficiently and effectively identify end user problems, make design changes, and retest the panels. The use of a field test was a timely and low-cost alternative to a laboratory test and provided contextual data that was unique, necessary to understanding end user issues, and that complemented the later laboratory tests. Iterative testing of the interface provided the opportunity to assess the impact of changes made to the interface and provided a reliability check on previous results. The iterative testing was conducted within a short span of time and was cost-effective even for this small project. The system was delivered on schedule and users made a smooth transition to it. The human factors work resulted in a positive and cost-effective addition to the project.

It is important to note that the human factors work on this project might not have been cost-effective if other human factors techniques had been employed. If an online prototype had been developed by programmers, and all three tests had been conducted in a laboratory setting, it is unlikely that a cost-benefit analysis would have resulted in a favorable outcome. Since the methodology described here provides a conservative estimate of savings, it is possible that a more comprehensive analysis that included other areas of savings (e.g. further sign-ons and system maintenance) would show a favorable cost-to-savings ratio for this project even if high-technology human factors techniques had been used. The larger issue, though, is that it may be incumbent on human factors professionals to weigh the financial factor associated with a human factors technique along with the myriad of other relevant factors in making methodological decisions. The two project examples provided above illustrate that it may be cost-effective to include human factors work in small to large sized projects depending on the techniques employed. Human factors techniques can be tailored to fit the financial aspects and time schedules of projects and thus remain cost-effective.

Finally, in order to provide cost-benefit data to software development managers, an organization might chose one project as its test case, and then provide the resulting cost-benefit information to other software development managers before their upcoming project plans are finalized. Cost-benefit estimates for human factors work on individual projects could be made and then checked against usability test results. This growing body of data could provide the basis for decisions regarding human factors work. The cost-benefit data could also be used in project business cases to justify human factors work. At a minimum, cost-benefit data may help human factors professionals communicate with software project managers about their areas of concern and may facilitate their understanding of the value of incorporating human factors work in software development. Human factors work is an added value in software development and the challenge is to determine a more accurate and complete methodology to illustrate that contribution to a software project's success.

6. REFERENCES

Gould, J. (1988). How to design usable systems. In M. Helander (Ed.), *Handbook of Human Computer Interaction.* Amsterdam: Elsevier.

Karat, C. (1989). Iterative usability testing of a security application. In *Proceedings of the Human Factors Society.* Denver, Co. 273-277.

Karat, J., and Bennett, J. (1989). Modelling the user interaction methods imposed by designs. *IBM Research Report RC 14649,* Yorktown Heights, NY.

Mantei, M.M. and Teorey, T.J. (1988). Cost/benefit analysis for incorporating human factors in the software lifecycle. *Communications of the ACM, 31,* 428-439.

Nielsen, J., (1989). Usability engineering at a discount. In *Proceedings of HCI International,* Boston, MA.

Norman, D.A., and Draper, S.W. (1986). *User centered system design: New perspectives on human-computer interaction.* New Jersey: Erlbaum Associates.

Rubenstein, R., and Hersh, H. (1984). *The human factor: Designing computer systems for people.* Mass.: Digital Press.

Whiteside, J., Bennett, J. and Holtzblatt, K. (1988). Usability engineering: Our experience and evolution. In M. Helander (Ed.), *Handbook of Human Computer Interaction.* Amsterdam: Elsevier.

Human–Computer Interaction - INTERACT '90
D. Diaper et al. (Editors)
Elsevier Science Publishers B.V. (North-Holland)

Usability Statements and Standardisation - work in progress in ISO

John Brooke[1], Nigel Bevan[2], Fred Brigham[3], Susan Harker[4], and David Youmans[5]

[1]Digital Equipment Corporation, [2]National Physical Laboratory, [3]Nederlandse Philips Bedrijven B.V, [4]Loughborough University, [5]IBM United Kingdom Laboratories

Address for correspondence: John Brooke, Digital Equipment Co Ltd., REO2-F/B8, PO Box 121, Worton Grange, READING RG2 0TU, United Kingdom

This paper describes work in progress in Working Group 5 of the International Organisation for Standardisation Technical committee 159 subcommittee 4 (ISO TC159/SC4/WG5). While many standards are concentrating on what guidelines can be given regarding the design of user interfaces and dialogues, subgroup 2 of TC159/SC4/WG5 is taking a holistic approach to the issue of the usability of products. A standard is being developed which will specify how producers and consumers of products may communicate with each other about the usability of products.

1. Introduction

There is currently a great deal of activity in a number of standards organisations towards the development of standards for user interfaces and software ergonomics. Committees of international bodies such as ISO (International Organisation for Standardization), CEN / CENELEC (European Community), and national standards bodies such as ANSI (USA), BSI (United Kingdom), and DIN (Germany) are working on this topic. In addition, there are a number of activities within industry organisations such as OSF and X/Open to apply some standardisation to dialogues between users and machines. Some of these activities are reviewed by Holdaway and Bevan[1] and by Abernethy [2].

2. What is being standardised?

The questions that inevitably arise when considering work in this area are "*what is the purpose of producing standards for designing dialogues between users and systems?*", and "*what sort of standard best serves that purpose?*". There are a number of motives for producing standards.

One reason for standardising user interfaces and dialogues relates to the maintainability of software. If a number of software products use a common user interface, it is easier to maintain changes across the set of products, especially if all use a common tool kit. Interfaces built with a common tool kit also have other advantages - they may be reusable, they may give a common identity to a number of products, and they may lead to greater consistency both within and between user interfaces.

Another reason is that software engineers are increasingly concerned with a need for practical guidance to incorporate ergonomics into their software and dialogue design because specific markets demand that they do so. As Taylor and Harker[3] point out, the problem is not one of absence of information - Smith and Mosier[4] cite the existence of at least 580 guidelines for human factors of dialogue design. Taylor and Harker suggest that the problem is rather to relate this mass of information to the actual task that the designer has in hand. Eason and Harker[5] suggest that the chief reason why difficulties arise is that there is a high degree of task dependency in the design of usable software which means that decisions can only be made on the basis of an understanding of specific task and user needs.

A further objective of standardisation may be to make products *more usable*. However, it is appropriate to be cautious in this area. For example, consistency can increase the predictability of system behaviour, but it can also be a two-edged sword as Grudin [6] has pointed out. (Grudin argues that even where some kind of consistency is desirable, the hard part is to discover which dimensions to be consistent along and that many interface problems arise because, for instance, the interface is consistent with the underlying implementation but inconsistent with how the user sees things).

In general, it can be questioned whether prescriptive user interface standards will lead to greater usability, or whether it will simply lead to interfaces which represent the lowest common denominator. Some of these arguments are considered by Holdaway and Bevan[1]; they point out that a full understanding of usability requires an understanding of the cognitive processes which enable users to achieve their goals in a satisfactory manner. Since nobody can know absolutely what these processes are, standardising the detail of the interface may not address those elements fundamental to the cognitive processes. Thus, Holdaway and Bevan argue that it is better not to attempt to standardise the detail of interfaces, but to standardise the principles to be followed when designing an interface.

2.1 What is usability?

When considering the issue of whether standards will improve the usability of products, one must step back and understand what is meant by the term usability. It is the belief of the authors of this paper that usability cannot be defined except in operational terms, and that to define usability one must consider :-

- the users who will use the product
- the tasks for which the product will be employed
- the conditions under which those users will perform those tasks

There is no absolute quality of usability; any given product may be usable for one combination of users, tasks and circumstances, but unusable for another.

Furthermore, there are many different aspects to usability; in some circumstances usability may be reflected in the fact that the system assists the user to achieve error-free performance, whilst in others as long as the error rate is kept to tolerable proportions,it may be more important to achieve fast throughput. Usability may be measured in terms of the completeness with which a product allows users to achieve their task goals. There would be little point in producing, say, a word processing product which allowed typists fast and error-free production of text but then failed dismally to allow them to print out the finished document. Even allowing that a product permits users to achieve their goals efficiently and without error, usability of that product depends to a very large extent on subjective factors; if users do not like a product, they will not continue to use it, in which case it can be regarded as "unusable".

The definitions of measures of usability and usability attributes of systems currently used by ISO TC159/SC4/WG5 subgroup 2 are:

"Usability measures: the effectiveness, efficiency and satisfaction with which specified users can achieve specified goals in a particular environment

Usability attributes: the features and characteristics of a product which influence the effectiveness, efficiency and satisfaction with which particular users can achieve specified goals in a particular environment".

It should be noted that although the work of ISO TC159/SC4/WG5 is concerned primarily with the usability of systems for office work with visual display terminals, this definition of usability and the usability assurance standard can be applied in principle to all products and systems.

2.2 How do standards and usability relate to each other?

Given the discussion above, it might be argued that since usability is situationally determined and there are innumerable combinations of users, tasks and conditions of use there is little standards can do to improve the usability of products since any standards would have to describe either a very limited set of conditions or would have to be so general as to be difficult to apply to any particular situation.

The authors believe that there are two major issues relating to usability which can be addressed by standardisation.

- products which are used in conditions for which they were not designed are likely to be unusable. The issue that needs to be addressed here is that those who use a product should understand the intentions of the designers of the product so that appropriate people use the product for appropriate tasks. This points to a need for **better communication of information about usability** between the producer and the consumer.
- In a similar vein, designers of products must be able to understand the criteria by which the user will judge usability, and the user must therefore be able to communicate usability requirements to the designer of a product in terms of conditions of use and criteria by which the usability of the product will be judged.

Taking both of these issues into account, it seems clear that standards can provide a valuable service by attempting to ensure that both producers and consumers communicate information about usability in a way that is as comprehensive and as precise as possible.

2.3 The Usability Statement

To address this need, subgroup 2 of ISO TC159/SC4/WG5 has produced a draft proposal for part 11 of ISO standard 9241 ("Ergonomics Requirements for Office work with Visual Display Terminals (VDTs)"). Part 11 as currently envisaged will specify the form of a **Usability Statement** (US) which is the proposed mechanism that should be used to communicate information about product usability.

The Usability Statement as specified in the draft proposal consists of a series of headings that should be included, and notes guiding the user of the standard as to how to provide information under each of the headings.

The Usability Statement performs the following functions:

- it draws attention to usability variables that should be addressed. If product producers are completing a Usability Statement, they will have to specify the intended users, uses and conditions of use of the product, and the aspects of usability (effectiveness, efficiency and satisfaction) that were addressed during development of the product. Similarly, if potential product users are specifying usability requirements, by following the form specified by the standard they should give a reasonably complete description of the meaning they attach to usability so that developers of the product can understand it.
- The Usability Statement not only communicates information about the **intended** usability characteristics of the product but it also communicates what **action has been taken (or should be taken) to achieve** those usability characteristics. The proposed standard recognises that although it is important to understand the usability characteristics, understanding alone will not guarantee usability and the producer of the product should undertake some activity to assure that the product conforms to those characteristics.

The Usability Statement is intended to contribute to greater precision in specification and assessment of usability. Although it does not directly provide a basis for quantitative evaluation, the identification and definition of context (users, tasks and environment) and the aspects of usability to be assessed (effectiveness, efficiency, and satisfaction) provide a basis for definition of usability metrics which are appropriate to a particular set of circumstances. Other groups within ISO are investigating the possibility of defining usability metrics; for instance, ISO JTC1/SC7/WG3, who have identified usability as one of six software quality characteristics.

The approach being taken in developing this standard is intended to be complementary to the work being carried out in other committees which are working on standards based on design guidelines; rather than specifying guidelines to be followed in designing interfaces, the Usability Statement outlines issues that should be addressed and draws the attention of the user of the standard to processes that should be carried out, without actually specifying what those processes are. This process orientation has something in common with standards relating to quality such as ISO 9000.

2.4 Defining usability characteristics of a product

The proposed standard outlines the way in which information about the various usability characteristics of a product should be described. An important aspect of this part of the standard is that it lays emphasis on using precise and verifiable descriptions of these characteristics. For instance, in specifying the intended users of a product, the information conveyed by saying that "*this product is intended for use by office workers*" is neither precise nor verifiable. What is an "office worker"? A secretary? A chief executive? A programmer who happens to work in an office? If it is not possible to define which of these is meant by office worker, it is not possible to verify whether any particular user of the product falls into the categories of intended user.

On the other hand, a statement such as "*intended for use by workers who produce documents to be read by others*" conveys a good deal more precise information. It is verifiable in the sense that it is possible to observe whether any particular users undertake such activities in the course of their duties.

There are obviously other areas where the description could be tightened up as well. For instance, usability may be affected by whether the product is designed for frequent use by an expert, or whether it is intended for the document producer to use it occasionally. This also has further consequences in terms of the types of expectation of training and experience that the designer might expect the user to have, and these are all important characteristics which potential users of a product may wish to know about in order to understand whether it fits their requirements or not. A reasonably precise definition of the characteristics of the user might be "*intended for use by workers who produce documents to be read by others, whose job entails production of such documents for at least 20% of their working hours,and who have taken the training course provided with the product*".

This precision needs to be applied not only to the description of intended users of the product, but also to the tasks the product is intended to be used for, and the conditions under which it will be used.

2.5 Usability assurance activities

The Usability Statement also provides for the description of activities which have been undertaken to assure usability of the product for the users, tasks and conditions of use. It is recognised that there is no one correct way of assuring usability. There would be little point in insisting on particular sets of guidelines being applied, or conformance to a particular standard, if the user population at which a product was aimed had a background of using products built according to a different set of guidelines or standards. Even allowing for the general desirability of empirical validation of usability, there is no one correct technique for this, and it would be excessively restrictive to prescribe such activities. However, it is important that some activity should be undertaken to assure activity, and that the user of the product should be aware and understand this activity.

Anyone completing a Usability Statement is therefore expected to detail the nature of these activities, without being required to disclose the details of what has been found since it is recognised that such information may be proprietary. The producer and the consumer may, of course, agree to share such information if disclosure is mutually acceptable.

2.6 Assuring the usability of the standard

Since the standards relates to usability, the members of the committee were particularly concerned that the standard should itself be usable. A usability test plan has been put into place and is being followed as the draft proposal progresses. Part of the usability test plan, is, indeed, to produce a Usability Statement *for the standard itself.* It is hoped that following good usability assurance procedures will result in a standard which is not only usable, but which provides positive benefits through its use, since the purpose of the standard and the users of the standard will have been addressed in detail.

3. Conclusion

Subgroup 2 of ISO TC159/SC4/WG5 has produced a draft proposal for a usability statements standard which is intended to improve communication between producers and consumers of software and other products. The draft proposal (ISO 9241 part 11) has been circulated as a draft proposal to the member countries of ISO in early 1990. It is expected that it will progress to draft international standard status later on in 1990. It is hoped that the concept of the Usability Statement will provide a strong impetus for both producers and users of products to pay attention to the issue of usability and to think about what it means in the context of the use of products.

References

[1]Holdaway, K, and Bevan, N (1989) *User product interaction standards.* Computer Communications, 12, April 1989, 97-101

[2]Abernethy, C (1988) *Human computer interface standards: origins, organizations and comment.* International Review of Ergonomics, 2, 31-54

[3]Taylor, B.C and Harker, S.D.P (1985) *Developing human factors standards for dialogue design: a case study.* In: Brown, I.D., Goldsmith R. Coombes, K. and Sinclair, M.A. (eds) Ergonomics International. London: Taylor and Francis.

[4]Smith, S and Mosier, J (1984) *The user interface to computer-based information products: a survey of current software design practice.* Proc. INTERACT 84, First IFIP Conference on 'Human-Computer Interaction', London.

[5]Eason, K, and Harker, S.D.P (1984) *The production of usable dialogue design guidelines.* In: Proc NATO Advanced Research Workshop on Research Needs in User-Computer Interaction.

[6]Grudin, J (1989) *The case against user interface consistency.* MCC Tech Report ACA-HI-002-89.

Acknowledgments

A number of our colleagues have participated in this committee and have contributed to the development of the proposed standard. In particular, we would like to acknowledge Chris Marshall, Marion Wittstock, Eva Brenner-Wallius, Nadia Bertaggia, and Donald Anderson, all of whom have spent long days sitting wrangling in subgroup meetings.

SECTION II: DESIGN: THEORIES, METHODS AND TOOLS

SII.5 Design and Evaluation Tools

Supporting effective and efficient design meetings
J. Karat and J. Bennett 365

The HUFIT planning analysis and specification toolset
B. Taylor 371

The HUFIT functionality matrix
B.J. Catterall 377

Task-based user interface development tools
P. Johnson and E. Nicolosi 383

PROTEUS: An approach to interface evaluation
J. Crellin 389

A knowledge-based tool for user interface evaluation and its integration in a UIMS
J. Löwgren and T. Nordqvist 395

Monitoring and analysis of hypermedia navigation
D. Kornbrot and M. Macleod 401

Towards an evaluation planning aid: A feasibility study in modelling evaluation practice using a blackboard framework
I. Denley and J. Long 407

Providing intrinsic support for user interface monitoring
J. Chen 415

Human–Computer Interaction – INTERACT '90
D. Diaper et al. (Editors)
Elsevier Science Publishers B.V. (North-Holland)

SUPPORTING EFFECTIVE AND EFFICIENT DESIGN MEETINGS

John Karat and John Bennett

IBM T. J. Watson Research Center, P. O. Box 704, Yorktown Heights, NY 10598, USA

We present a description of the methodology employed in our evolving user-centered design framework. Our experience suggests that the quality of human-computer interaction (HCI) supported by a system design will be strongly influenced by the insight generated in design work at early stages of development. Our methodology focuses on creating a shared vision and working environment within the design team for productive action on system objectives, constraints, resources, and proposed designs. Two aspects of the methodology which we focus on are use of the walls of a "design room" to hold representations of the design-in-progress, and fostering collaboration through discussions by team members with different skills and perspectives. Our experience indicates that the framework and techniques used within it are generally applicable, but that successful use requires attention to characteristics of each particular design project and group.

1. INTRODUCTION

We are articulating a user-centered design framework for supporting the development of systems which meet user requirements. We start with an assumption that maintaining a user-centered perspective during design is both challenging and necessary, and then we examine the role of various techniques within the system design environment. In a broad sense, we are attempting to synthesize a model of the design process in-the-large (i.e., to distinguish components of successful HCI design processes). Our purpose is to understand how we might improve the quality of human-computer interaction (HCI) made possible in the systems resulting from the design process.

In our study of the design process, we have observed a variety of activities which occur in system design meetings. Generally speaking such meetings are held between individuals with different roles in the design of the system, and they occur throughout the life of a design and development process. We will refer to such meetings as design meetings, suggest that they are a pervasive activity, and limit our consideration to events in which a number of individuals meet to discuss some aspect of the system being designed.

While some design tasks may be carried out by individuals or small teams in close contact, most commercial system development involves a fairly large group of people. Even those design breakthroughs created by individuals are explained and worked out in groups. In these cases, and in the case of work in large teams, it is particularly important to achieve a ***shared understanding of the objectives and of the the suggested design.*** Through group discussion the participants in meetings can develop a common vision of how to meet requirements. But, such meetings can also be viewed as a waste of time by participants for a variety of reasons (e.g., lack of focus, failure to produce follow-up results, poor leadership). The center of our activity is identification of techniques that will raise the probability of producing productive results in meetings.

In this paper we describe briefly some aspects of our user-centered design framework and present a summary of our experiences with design meetings. Our purpose has been to gain a better understanding of where support might be useful in the design of systems and where it might help bring focus to, and help resolve, the user-centered design issues that arise. We use experiential exploration in developing our ideas rather than formal experiments. This is motivated by a belief that such exploration will serve our goals much more effectively. Our work has aspects of theory, modelling, science, and engineering.

2. BRINGING USER-CENTERED VIEWS INTO DESIGN

An essential aspect of the HCI design process is a search for workable answers (in contrast with searching for THE single "right" answer). Such design is a complex synthesis involving trade-offs among multiple perspectives. Managing design in such an environment is so difficult that issues which are not clearly represented as a part of the design activity simply become lost in the sea of those issues which are in focus.

We have detected an unspoken, perhaps unconscious, general background perception on the part of many working within the software development process -- usability topics have "very little technical content". That is, the evaluation of HCI quality is considered to be an ultimately "arbitrary, idiosyncratic, subjective opinion". As a result, while designers genuinely believe that they are addressing usability issues, in practice these issues do not remain in focus. A contributing factor seems to be our inability to provide engaging representations for user-centered concerns. The problem is one of when and how to get user considerations reliably inserted into the search for workable designs.

We have found that the process of responding to user needs involves consideration of the user's perspective throughout the design process. Though user requirements may be explicitly considered at some points (e.g., in developing objectives or in behavioral testing), the continued focus needed for quality systems is difficult to maintain. In fact, we observe that it is best to consider design as an iterative spiral or wheel rather than a set of linear steps (see Figure 1). As an example, the initial motivation for choosing objectives from a universe of perceived user requirements often results in a loosely stated goal for the system (e.g., build a system to facilitate software development). As design proceeds, focus turns to considerations of constraints (e.g., cost and schedule), the techniques to be used by the designers (e.g., prototyping tools, problem analysis techniques), and then the specifics of the design-in-progress. Through this series of activities the nature of the objective is often lost or translated into function-centered rather than user-centered goals.

The next question is how to bring topics of system use into focus so that they are more concrete. We see a variety of candidate techniques which can contribute to developing and maintaining an effective perspective on the user. Examples we have found useful in design settings are:

1. Tabular formats for representing system objectives, including those relating to usability (Whiteside et al., 1988),
2. Abstract statements of guiding visions for design including the qualities to be observed by users as they carry out tasks (e.g., interface style guidelines such as IBM (1989)),
3. Early design prototypes to serve as a basis for iteration (Gould et al., 1987),
4. A focus on the objects important to users and the actions that users take on those objects (Wegner, 1987), and
5. Scenarios of use (from a user perspective) concentrating on what the user will see, what the user must know in order to interpret what the design presents, and what the user can (or in some cases must) do to achieve the needed task results (Karat & Bennett, 1989).

It is important from the outset to consider how any suggested innovation will fit into existing design activities and how it will be recognized by designers to demonstrate "obvious value" during the design and development process. Our focus has been on how each innovation might be constructively used in design meetings rather than on an abstract test of "which is best". Our experience suggests that each has a place in providing a focus on user-centered issues in design (though using techniques to guide design is far from a cookbook exercise).

2.1. 4-Walls Design Room

Team design can take place in many ways. An individual can develop and maintain a "vision" of what is to be designed and can distribute sub-problems to members of the team. To the extent that the leader understands the system to be developed (i.e., has a vision for the system that matches user needs) and is successful in decomposing design problems, such a design approach can succeed without all members of

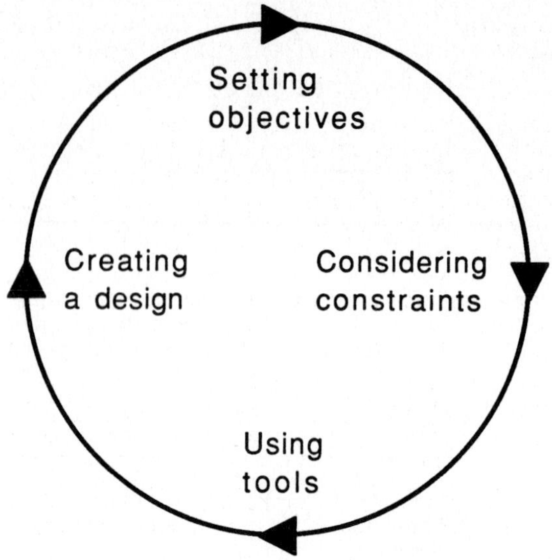

Figure 1. Generic system design iterative activities

the team understanding the "vision". Small teams working in close partnership can often develop shared understanding of the design vision without public documentation. However, we have observed that developing this type of shared understanding can be problematic in larger design groups.

The common practice for systems developed in an industry environment is to describe the design in a product specification document. This enables opening the design vision for inspection and modification by diverse members of a design team and for review by marketing and management personnel outside the team. While such documents are intended to capture the product vision, they often concentrate on details of the implementation technology and fail to present user-centered content effectively (a comment which has been echoed by colleagues in other software development companies). Participants in current design reviews must study the specification, deduce implications for the user interface from clues distributed over a (typically) 300 page document, and synthesize the results into an effective analysis of the evolving system.

In addition, Conklin (1989) points out that what is often missing in current design process documents (such as product specifications) is the rationale (the "why") of a given design. Because the rationale for design decisions is frequently unavailable when system maintainers alter a design, we are also interested in how representation might be used to "capture" the reasoning for later access. We believe that an important part of supporting design meetings is enabling better capture of, and access to, such rationale.

Advocates of usability engineering (Gould and Lewis, 1985; Gould et al., 1987; Whiteside et al., 1988) strongly recommend iterative design and testing as an important factor in successful user interfaces. Quite aside from user interface considerations, the cognitive capacities of designers are already taxed by the design challenges faced when using computer-based technology to meet demands for software performance and integration (Guindon, Krasner, and Curtis, 1987). Trying to maintain a cumulative user perspective (i.e., design a system that meets user needs) simultaneously with a technology perspective (i.e., design a system that can be built within resource constraints) is very difficult. Thus, shifts in focus and repeated iteration are essential to keep user and computer aspects evolving in parallel. Techniques which support a group "memory" for important discussions leading to prototype development and iteration seem not to be in common use.

We have attempted to address some of these issues. In our evolving user-centered design framework we have focused on ways to bring a user perspective to design reviews and to maintain it throughout the design process. To facilitate a user-oriented overview, we have brought together on the walls of a room (large enough for 2-8 people, small enough so that the walls are nearby) an organized and high-level view of the entire context within which the development process takes place (see Figure 2). The use of walls provides a large space with distinct regions (different walls) to help with the separation of complex issues within the problems often encountered in design. As a general guideline, each of our walls contains representations for an aspect of the design environment.

Using walls to post various design representations is not entirely new to design. We have heard reports that "war rooms" containing various diagrams arrayed on walls have been used during development. Individual experience and guidelines for use seem quite varied, but typically these rooms are used to help interpret a large quantity of information. Walls seem particularly useful as providing a surface for easy manipulation of content readily visible to the group.

We organize content through the use the four walls to present descriptions of the emerging system objectives, constraints, resources, and design-in-progress. The material on some of the walls (e.g., constraints and resources) might be seen as remote from being user-centered. By bringing these concerns within the broader context of objectives and design-in-progress, we find that discussions which balance such concerns are facilitated.

On one wall we outline the product objectives in a tabular format, identifying the factors and features thought to be critical to success (Whiteside et al., 1988). Such objectives, typically developed by the team using input from people familiar with marketplace requirements, can serve as a basis for making design trade-offs in the allocation of development resources (design skill, development optimization, manpower, scheduled attention). For example, in reviewing the design for one system we collected text describing the high level goals (in this case, to "meet the information needs of business professionals"). Below this we placed information describing what some of those needs were perceived to be (e.g., provide a tool for easy data access, provide tools for data analysis and presentation). Placing these objectives on the wall led to a variety of discussions (What are the information needs of business professionals?

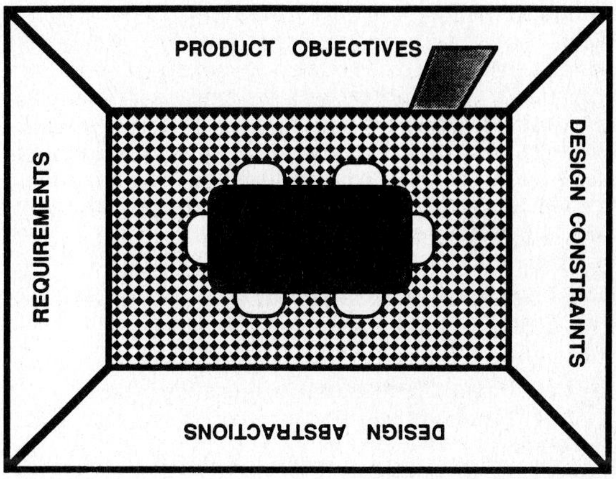

Figure 2. Room layout for 4-walls design environment.

What would constitute "easy access" to data?) which helped us form an understanding of the objectives for the group. We do not claim that placing the descriptions on the wall "caused" the questions to be asked nor answered clearly or correctly, but we do claim that such representation can help trigger the exchange.

On another wall (spatial separation emphasizes the different dimensions under consideration) we outline constraints such as evolution from previous systems, guideline compliance, and likely user and management expectations (e.g., must code in C++) not covered under objectives. In continuing our analysis of the system mentioned above, we gathered information concerning guidelines that were intended to influence the design. These guidelines (in the form of user interface design principles), were placed on the wall and discussed. The wall included items such as "make rigorous use of a small set of common commands", and "use see and point rather than remember and type". Discussion of such constraints can lead to a better understanding of the range of possibilities for the design of the system.

On a third wall we outline resources and tools available for constructing the system (e.g., data base support, data interchange architectures, libraries of existing programs). For example, these might include tools for software engineering (CASE tools), rapid prototyping, or user interface screen design, which are used within the organization. While the general objective of providing such tools is to facilitate system design and development (compatible with project schedule and resource demands on the project), invariably they will also place constraints on what can be designed. By explicitly including the tool capabilities in this environment, discussion of possible impact on user-centered objectives represented on other walls is encouraged.

On a fourth wall we extract from the functional specifications and from any available prototypes some representative images of the interface that will be seen by users. Rather than show these on a display screen, we provide an overview of the entire system on a wall with screen images arrayed horizontally and in a menu-accessed hierarchy, if that faithfully reflects the design approach. In this way observers can see at a glance how the entire system fits together (from a user perspective). In addition, this array facilitates walk-throughs of typical scenarios reflecting user learning and productive user work to bring out the dynamics of system operation. The size of the area required can itself give some sense of how much the user will have to learn.

This fourth wall is an arena for analysis and action at a variety of design levels and perspectives.

- Questions can be asked about the infrastructure in the organizations that will use the system -- how much resource will be required for training and who will provide it, how the data needed by users will be supplied, and how the system will fit with existing systems.
- Questions can be asked about the system design itself -- aspects of intra-system consistency and on what dimensions consistency is to be measured, a static description of system objects (such as files and directories), actions that the user can take on those objects, how the parts of the system fit together, and conceptual and path-length distance between parts traversed in typical scenarios.
- Those providing the underlying utility services (communications, the database) can debate the likely response time and data access requirements of users.

We consider the room with the information arranged on the various walls to be our model-in-the-large of the system. Each wall serves as a focus for particular design questions, and the whole room provides an arena for holding questions open while the team searches for solutions. Rather than looking for a single form to represent the various views, we recognize the benefits of using various forms (such as object/action tables or scenario descriptions) at different points in the design discussion. These and other techniques serve to provide a group working on a problem with a basis 1) for forming a shared understanding of system technology and user-centered opportunities and 2) for probing issues which may not seem clear. Through this approach we hope to to describe and develop additional specific techniques effective in supporting the ***highly interpretive*** process of design.

2.2. Supporting group processes in design

The social context in which the design activity takes place is very important for the quality of the resulting design (Bennett, 1986; Bennett, 1987). This is a large and challenging area, and we have space here only to recognize it as an issue.

One obvious aspect of group processes in design is the composition of the group. It has been clear from our experience that many groups succeed or fail because of personality and skill factors of individuals within the groups. First, teams composed of individuals with a range of skills seem to facilitate good discussion (though it is difficult to specify the dimensions on which to establish this range). Second, many have commented on the need for user representation on design teams. This might be accomplished through a team member whose goal it is to provide a user focus, or through inclusion of representatives of the user community in the design group. Our own experience has been to work as user-centered representatives, often providing user focus by asking questions which bear on user interactions with the system. We hold that input from a user's perspective is necessary for much of the design activity (e.g., it may be difficult to develop appropriate scenarios of use for a system without this background).

In this regard, we do not seek to provide an environment in which we can guarantee that the "right" thing happens. Design of complex systems is not a domain in which such a goal is realistic. We do feel, however, that the four-wall environment is one in which constructive group activities can occur. For example, the process of laying out the representations on any of the walls has invariably led to questions and discussions which probe the reasons for the content of that wall. Any explicit representation will include a background of assumptions which may not initially be shared by all in the design group. Some of the discussion may simply lead to clarification (e.g., "Yes, I think we all understand that to be the case"), but often we find that it points to areas in which something overlooked is recognized or disagreement surfaces. While no technique can guarantee catching all oversights or resolving all disagreements, we feel that a variety of representations can support design by encouraging comprehensive discussion.

3. OBSERVATIONS

While it is difficult to offer a case study which "proves" the value of our evolving framework - we consider it very much work in progress - we have had some productive experiences which lead us to believe the direction is useful. We have taken part in a number of design reviews for products under development, and we have been able to assist the design teams in "discovering" issues. In some cases, the discoveries have related to items such as "holes" in the design (e.g., differences in the actions available to users with respect to similar objects with no known motivation for the differences). In other cases the discoveries have been in the nature of clarifications of what different members of the team thought was contained in the existing design specification (e.g., typically characterized by a "Oh, so that's what you meant" response). The environment has been useful in helping design teams focus on "real" objectives (such as making a system easy to use), in contrast with translation of such objectives (e.g., "use menus for all interactions" because that will -- is assumed to -- make a system easy to use). We can not directly attribute such insights to any particular aspect of our process, but we do note that such discoveries are important and that they had not occurred previously in these particular design groups.

3.1 Analytic models

Within the four-walls environment there are many techniques which can be used to derive representations of different design aspects. In looking at ways to represent the design-in-progress, we have borrowed from analytic techniques developed for modelling the complexity of user actions required when people interact with computers. Examples of analytic approaches are the goals, operators, methods, and selection rules of Card, Moran, and Newell (1983), the extensions of Kieras and Polson (1985), the formal grammar of Reisner (1983), and the task-action grammar of Payne and Green (1986). Central to all of these techniques is a rather loosely defined task analysis (which includes hypothesized user mental operations as well as physical actions) and some level of language for modelling the distinctions presented by the theory.

For several years we have been exploring whether approximate models of human-computer interaction could become useful in the design of computer systems (Karat et al., 1987; Bennett et al., 1987). This theory-based methodology might help designers to "understand the users" and to "analyze the users' tasks". We found the prospects for quantitative predictions (which would be quite valuable if available to designers) of particular interest in the NGOMSL modelling framework of Kieras and Polson (Kieras and Polson, 1985; Kieras, 1988). We viewed this as one possible process in the user-centered design framework, applied when considering what users see, what they must know, and what they must do to carry out typical tasks. The value could be realized through considering the impact of alternative designs on the amount, content, and transfer of user knowledge (Polson, 1987).

We investigated the role of GOMS-like models in design by selecting a "design scenario" focused on commands needed for managing files. We began by modelling user actions on files in two existing systems, and we established "use scenarios" for important tasks. The details of this design analysis exercise are presented elsewhere (Karat and Bennett, 1989); we offer here a brief summary of our experience.

In initial modelling work we looked at user actions required to carry out the low-level operations for elements of file maintenance ("move", "copy", and "delete" files), and we derived quantitative estimates for comparative "ease of use". This led to much discussion about the relative merits of the two systems. We then repeated the modelling at a different level of granularity, (e.g., backup files), and now the command default structure of each system came into play. The quantitative results comparing "ease of use" ***reversed*** for the two systems. Rather than being a straight-forward exercise with a single output (a stable quantitative prediction), we observed the sensitivity of the quantitative modelling results to the analysis perspective taken.
However, we found that the discussions (which led to the different view of what a user might want from a file management system) were quite valuable, though less quantifiable than the model predictions. The modelling activity provided us with a focus for reviewing low-level alternatives available in design. However, the power resided in qualitative questions which arose opportunistically rather than in quantitative answers (of doubtful accuracy). We strongly suspect that the quality of the questions formed has important implications for revealing discussion, and this is an aspect of design that HCI research might well address directly.

3.2 Scenario Analysis

Rather than developing quantitative measures of usability to aid in user-centered discussions, we have turned to a more general use of scenarios in design meetings. By scenarios we refer to descriptions of user work to be carried out with the system. In recent projects we have found it quite useful to articulate the design-in-progress by iterating through descriptions of tasks which the system is to support at increasing levels of detail.

We currently describe scenarios using the following elements. First, a ***situation description*** provides a high-level account of the task to be carried out. Next we expand the description to include ***logical essentials*** required for completing the task. For example, if two items are to be linked, it is logically necessary to identify the objects to the system and to specify the kind of connection to be made -- note that there are many possible designs for accomplishing this. The description of the scenario continues by adding ***generic steps*** (which are relatively implementation independent), and finally ***specific steps*** (to complete the task given the design-in-progress).

Again, this is not a cookbook process. All of the description is captured on the walls of the design room, and it is subject to discussion as it develops. Once a design-in-progress begins to unfold, focus can be developed through questions related to the specific steps. Questions which we have found useful in this process concern how the user might know what to do next in a sequence of steps, what happens if an error is made, what is the recovery path from errors, and where does the sequence fit in the expected use of the system (frequency of use).

3.3 Capturing Process

More goes on in design room discussions than can easily be captured in a paper document. Design team members seem to be able to recreate a good deal of the discussion process on returning to the room over the course of several meetings which may be separated by days or weeks. Physical locations along the walls of the room become "tied" to particular issues and to other locations in the room (we have had one design team report using color-coded ribbons to connect various areas).

One way to preserve some of the context is to videotape a member of the team walking through the information captured on the walls at the end of a meeting. The process of creating this review can itself be revealing (which aspects are featured as results; the comments added by other team members as they hear the summary). Those team members who can not be present for a particular meeting can get some sense of the status, but we have found that much of the value to the team lies in the process that preceeds the "snapshot" captured on the video summary.

4. CONCLUSIONS

We characterize design as creative synthesis and complex problem-solving situation in which multiple views of the problem (e.g., users' need for function and effective access to that function, development time constraints, cost of development resources, hardware capabilities) must be considered. A primary problem in existing design is that it is difficult to construct a total design environment in a way that promotes effective discussion of user-related issues within the design team.

Our experiences in developing our user-centered design framework have led us to the following conclusions in considering future work.

- A variety of representations (or models) can be used to describe system objectives, static features of a system (tables of system objects and actions), dynamic uses of a system (descriptions of scenarios), and other important system constraints (such as hardware capabilities). Central to this work are representations that enable participants in the design process to understand an important aspect of the design context and that serve as a basis for insightful discussion and fruitful revision.
- Some of our experience suggests that a number of techniques for representing parts of a large design problem might be useful in user-centered design even though they are not well established as accepted cognitive theory. MacLean has suggested (Butler et al, 1989) that though the science base lags far behind the needs of designers, cognitive science can contribute to design by making the concepts behind developing theories known to the HCI design community.

We believe that work to support group design activities is a critical and overlooked area in HCI research. Further, we believe that providing support for group meetings does not require technology solutions so much as it requires attention to communication within a team committed to a common objective. HCI design research needs to consider the social context. Additionally, while we emphasize a framework for early design meetings, we believe that the results of the activities should be viewed as useful throughout the design process. We view the impact of our work as extending into iterative design stages by providing a framework for capturing and communicating the rationale used in decision making at such stages. We expect that our continued experience working within the design context will shed light on effective support for design group meetings.

5. REFERENCES

Bennett, J.L. (1986) Observations on Meeting Usability Goals for Software Products. *Behaviour and Information Technology*, 5, 183-193.

Bennett, J.L. (1987) Collaboration of UIMS Designers and Human Factors Specialists, *Computer Graphics*, 21, 102-105.

Bennett, J.L., Lorch, D.J., Kieras, D.E., and Polson, P.G. (1987). Developing a user interface technology for industry. *Proceedings of the INTERACT'87 Conference.*, H. Bullinger, B. Shackel, eds., Participants Edition, North-Holland, 1987, 21-26.

Butler, K., Bennett, J.L., Polson, P., and Karat, J. (1989). Predicting the complexity of human-computer interaction. *SIGCHI Bulletin* New York: ACM.

Card, S.K., Moran, T.P., and Newell, A. (1983). The Psychology of Human Computer Interaction. Hillsdale, NJ: Erlbaum.

Conklin, J. (1989). Design rationale and maintainability. *Proceedings of the 22nd HICCS. IEEE Computer Society Press.*

Gould, J. D. and Lewis, C. (1985). Designing for usability: Key principles and what designers think. *Communications of the ACM, 28,* 300-311.

Gould, J.D., Boies, S.J., Levy, S., and Richards, J.T. (1987). The Olympic Message System: A case study in system design. *Communications of the Association for Computing Machinery, 30,* 758-769.

Guindon, R., Krasner, H., & Curtis, B. (1987). Breakdown and processes during early activities of software design by professionals. *Proceedings of the INTERACT'87 Conference.*, H. Bullinger, B. Shackel, eds., Participants Edition, North-Holland, 1987, 383-388.

IBM Corporation (1989). Common User Access, Advanced Interface Design Guide. Systems Application Architecture, SC26-4582.

Karat, J., Fowler, R. and Gravelle, M. (1987). Evaluating user interface complexity. *Proceedings of the INTERACT'87 Conference.*, H. Bullinger, B. Shackel, eds., Participants Edition, North-Holland, 1987, 489-495.

Karat, J., and Bennett, J. (1989). Modelling the user interaction methods imposed by designs. *IBM Research Report RC 14649,* Yorktown Heights, NY.

Kieras, D.E. (1988). Towards a practical GOMS model methodology for user interface design. *in: M. Helander (Ed.): Handbook of Human-Computer Interaction.* Amsterdam: Elsevier.

Kieras, D.E. and Polson, P.G. (1985). An approach to the formal analysis of user complexity. *International Journal of Man-Machine Studies, 22,* 365-394.

Payne, S.J. and Green, T.G.R. (1986). Task-action grammars: a model of the mental representation of task languages. *Human Computer Interaction, 2,* 93-133.

Polson, P.G. (1987). A quantitative model of human-computer interaction. *in: J.M. Carroll (Ed.): Interfacing Thought: Cognitive aspects of Human-Computer Interaction.* Cambridge, MA: Bradford, MIT Press.

Reisner, P. (1984). Formal grammar as a tool for analyzing ease of use. *in: Thomas, J. C., and Schneider, M. L. (eds.): Human Factors in Computing Systems.* Norwood, NJ: Ablex.

Wegner, P. (1987). Dimensions of object-based language in design. *in: N Meyrowitz (ed.), Object-oriented Programming Systems, Languages, and Applications (OOPSLA) Conference Proceedings (pp. 168-182).* NY: ACM.

Whiteside, J., Bennett, J., and Holtzblatt, K. (1988). Usability Engineering: Our experience and evolution. *in: M. Helander (Ed.): Handbook of Human-Computer Interaction.* Amsterdam: Elsevier.

Human–Computer Interaction - INTERACT '90
D. Diaper et al. (Editors)
Elsevier Science Publishers B.V. (North-Holland)

The HUFIT Planning Analysis and Specification Toolset

Bronwen Taylor

HUSAT Research Centre
The Elms, Elms Grove, Loughborough, Leicestershire, LE11 1RG, U.K.

The Planning Analysis and Specification (PAS) Toolset has been developed to improve the requirements capture and specification of IT products. The tools are structured techniques which help to develop User and Task information into appropriate product requirements specifications. They have been developed iteratively, in collaboration with product Planners, Marketeers, Developers and Testers in large European IT manufacturers for use by these groups in the planning of generic IT products. The tools present a user-centred approach to design with a number of beneficial features: they improve communication in design teams, structure and support design decisions about user needs and record information for reference by other participants in the design process. Experience in training designers and human factors practitioners in the use of the tools has confirmed the usefulness of this approach.

1. Introduction

The aim of the HUFIT project was to promote the use of human factors methods within IT manufacturing companies [1]. Work by HUSAT over many years research and consultancy with a wide range of client organisations had shown the importance of a good understanding of the target user population and their tasks as a basis for human factors and other work later in the design process, ie a user-centred approach to design. It is also known that many problems in the use of IT systems stem from difficulties in the planning and analysis stages of the design process, where methods are often lacking or poorly understood and implemented [2,3]. Concentrating effort into the early stages of the design process can save costly errors later in development or worse still the problems of recalling or maintaining poor products [4]. The goal of this part of the HUFIT work was therefore to develop the user-centred methods used by HUSAT in consultancy into tools which could be used by designers themselves to help them consider user-task needs and translate them into product requirements specifications. In this way the resulting IT products would be better suited to the needs of the users, which would in turn contribute to their commercial success.

2. Key Features of the PAS Tools

Human factors expertise is in short supply so that to promote widespread use of human factors methods and principles it is necessary to develop techniques which can be handed over to the designers of IT products. The Planning Analysis and Specification Tools were developed to meet this need with the intention that they would be used by Planners, Marketeers, Developers and Testers, who have no particular training or experience in human factors, to use by themselves with a short period of training. The tools are therefore procedures to be followed at various points in the planning and analysis phases of the design process. The procedures have a number of beneficial features which address problems commonly encountered in product design:

The Workshop Forum
A workshop forum is recommended for the use of the tools. One major benefit arises out of bringing together representatives from Marketing, Planning, Development and Testing as appropriate in a workshop where they are able to share their knowledge and discuss the needs of the product user in order to develop appropriate product plans. This discussion process also benefits the company in the long term by raising the general level of awareness of user and task issues and improving communication between different sections of the company. The workshop method also facilitates the progressive

introduction of the tools by training teams as they work on products. A small amount of human factors knowledge in a company can be spread to other team members during the work processes required to use the tools.

Structured Methods

During the development of the tools they became more structured, evolving into a set of form-based procedures. This makes the tools easier to pick up and use. The structure of the tools is also appreciated by people with previous knowledge of human factors as it provides a framework which helps to formulate solutions to meeting user needs. Human factors practitioners are also attracted to the tools because the structure helps them to communicate ideas and methods to their non-human-factors colleagues.

Recording Information

A function of the tools which is expected to have great benefit for the success of the design process is the capture of information from the discussions, recording this on paper or on-line. In this way the tools build up a dossier of information about the users and tasks for which a product is planned and the design decisions or suggestions which are based on this information. This is available for other participants later in the design process, for instance the software designers in development or technical authors producing documentation. The different groups are then better informed about the target users of the product and have a basis for informed decisions. In this way change control is facilitated and design drift reduced.

3. Development of the PAS Tools

A user-centred design approach was followed in the production of the Planning, Analysis and Specification Tools, involving their intended users and also human factors experts. The process began with studies of the design process in the project partner companies [5]. Further discussions were carried out with Planners and Designers in these companies focusing on user and task information issues. These led to the aims given above of creating tools which would be straightforward and quick to use. Draft tools were then developed, based on methods used by HUSAT over a number of years and on ideas developed in work with other organisations, notably the collaboration of Professor Ken Eason and Susan Harker of HUSAT with Andrew Hutt of ICL and Linda Macaulay, then at Huddersfield Polytechnic, in the development of an extensive methodology called User Skills Task Match [6].

The drafts of the tools were first tried out in-house with human factors experts. Improved versions were then taken to designers in the partner companies and tried out in workshops. These steps were repeated so that the tools evolved into a linked set of structured procedures with accompanying examples. Once satisfactory draft tools had been developed on paper, on-line demonstrators were begun. Some people, especially system designers and programmers, are known to prefer to work with a keyboard rather than using paper and pencil. It is envisaged the on-line version will have more appeal for them.

There are certain benefits to be gained by putting the tools on-line, in that information input in the early stages of the process can automatically be carried over into the later stages. In addition the explanation and notes can be made more easily accessible on-line. There are disadvantages to the on-line version which will have to be overcome in use. For example, the recommended use of the tools in a workshop forum could be inhibited, as it is difficult for more than two people to work together around a small screen. To overcome this problem it is envisaged that a workshop using the paper tools would gather information and develop ideas while an on-line tool would be used as a convenient way of capturing the results of the discussion for storage and use later in the design process.

The on-line versions are demonstrations for adaptation to the software environments in use in individual companies. Further information about the on-line development of the tools is in the publication in Computer Aided Ergonomics [7].

In this way the tools were developed by a process which incorporated continous user evaluation. At a later stage the tools were considered to be sufficiently well formed for use in training seminars offered to the European IT community as a whole. The courses have also provided useful feedback on the usefulness and usability of the tools to designers from a wide range of design contexts, both supplier companies and bespoke design in-house. The development workshops and subsequent training seminars have shown that the tools are usable by designers with a short period of training followed by support in the early stages of the use of the tools.

4. The Six Tools in the PAS Toolset

Considering user and task requirements throughout the design process in an integrated

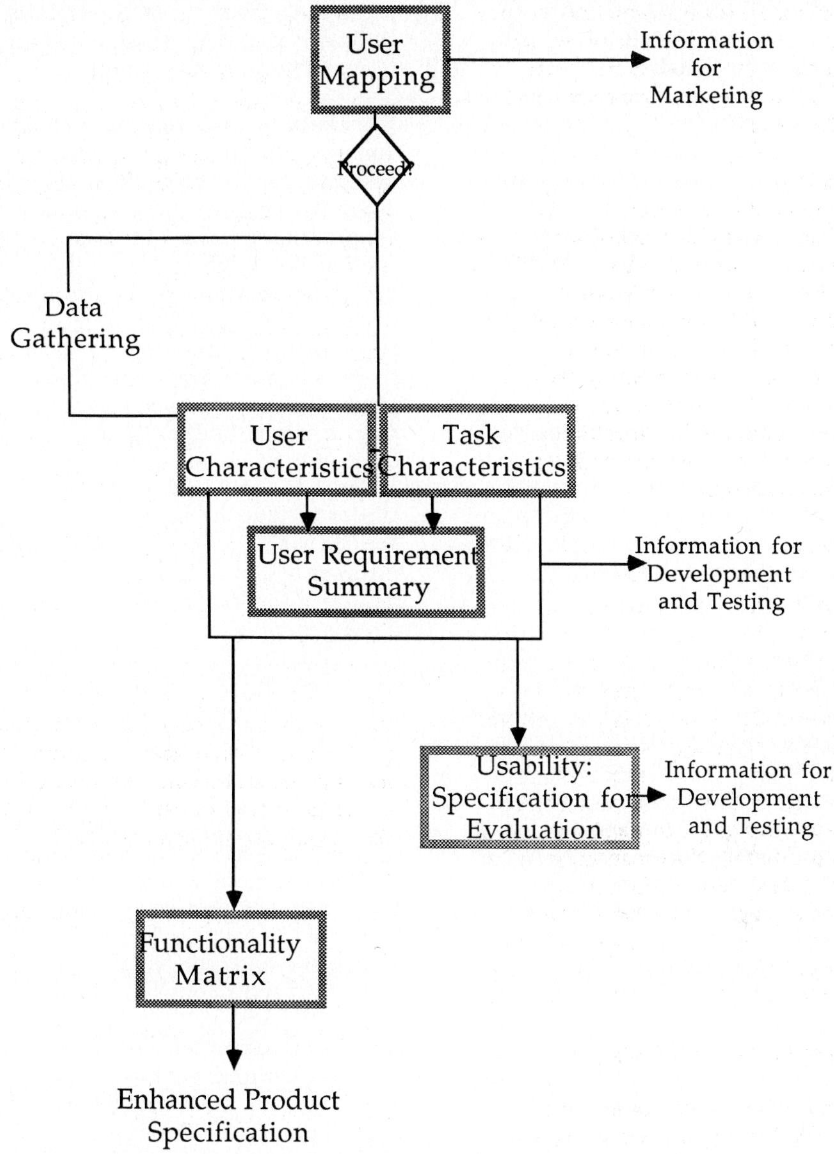

Figure 1
The PAS Toolset

information further. Each one however produces outputs which are of use to various participants in the development stages of the product life cycle. The tools are also capable of modular use and may be tailored to fit existing design methods.

User Mapping
This tool is intended for use very early in the product life cycle when a product idea is being considered.

The tool has four steps. The first is to identify users and stakeholders, i.e. all those who will use the product and other people who have a stake in it. The job goals for these groups are then identified in order to examine the benefits and costs to them of using the proposed product.

The information gathered in the User Mapping Tool is important for the later planning activities since it identifies the users whose tasks will have to be supported by the product, and who therefore form the basis of further data gathering and analysis activities. In drafting the PAS tools it was recognised that during the manufacture of generic office products it is not always possible or necessary to mount a full scale study of users in the field. There may be data already available in the company from previous studies or information may be obtainable from training, sales and maintenance personnel about the use of existing products. This information is used in the following tools to generate product requirements.

User Characteristics and Task Characteristics Tools
Experience in bespoke product design at HUSAT has shown that various attributes of the users, their tasks and the context in which the tasks are carried out are important for the design of successful IT products. Traditional systems analysis methods do not usually consider these attributes. The User and Task Characteristics tools have been developed to provide a structured method by which planners and developers of IT products can include these issues in product plans. These tools complement the usual analysis of task content, using one of the many charting techniques available.

The tools elicit a general description of the direct user groups and their task environment and conditions which is intended to highlight unusual or important factors which will affect the use of the product. They then concentrate on the user and task characteristics which are known to be important in the design of office technology. At each step product requirements are derived to meet the user and tasks characteristics under consideration. The examples provided in the notes which support the process set out in the tool show what kind of product requirements may be indicated by each user and task characteristic.

The information generated by these tools is useful in many stages in the design process. The product requirements feed into the specification of the product. The descriptions of the user groups and their task conditions are in testing for developing appropriate user tests. The information is also of use to all groups in development, including documentation and training developers, to focus their activities on the correct users and tasks.

The User Requirements Summary
The product requirements, generated in the User and Task Characteristics tools are collated into a summary which may be inserted into the product functional specification. The process highlights conflicts arising from the requirements of different user groups or different task characteristics. These conflicts may in part be resolved now, or flagged for special attention during development and testing. The requirements are also redistributed in this tool to suit the structure of the development process, eg. information for Training and Documentation will be separated for use by the relevant development groups.

The Usability Specification for Evaluation Tool
The research carried out in the partner company design teams [5] showed that designers often encounter problems because of lack of clarity in the product specification. In some cases a formal specification might not be written before development begins or the specification might be unclear. Decisions taken to meet problems encountered during design also change the specification but this is not always recorded. If the product is then evaluated according to an out of date or incomplete specification it is clearly difficult to reach any satisfactory conclusions either as to the quality of the product or what should be done to improve it. For these reasons a method which clarifies product goals in the planning stages of a product is useful to both designers and evaluators. This led to the development of the USE - Usability Specification for Evaluation Tool. This tool is linked to the other Planning, Analysis and Specification tools drawing particularly on the information developed in the User and Task Characteristic Tools.

The USE tool comprises tables which provide a structure to lead the Planner, Designer and Evaluator through a series of steps until the specification of product goals and criteria is complete. These steps are supported by notes which give suggestions for the sort of goals which may be set and examples of the tests and measures.

A set of preparatory tables are included in the tool which gather together the necessary data about the users and their tasks and the environment in which they work. The core of the tool is the Usability Specification for Evaluation table itself, which helps to identify the separate elements of usability for testing purposes. It is based on the work of many authors, particularly [8, 9, 10, 11]. The table leads the designer through four steps:

These steps are:

1. Defining usability goals for the product. The designer is encouraged to set high level human factors goals which are specific to the product and capable of being measured.

2. Setting tests to find out if the goal is met. Keeping the test specification closely linked with the goals ensures that realistic goals are set.

3. Identifying measures to use in the test. With the help of examples and notes it is possible for designers to find tests and measures for all purposes, which may include subjective assessment as well as the more frequently discussed metrics involving timings and error rates.

4. Setting criteria by which to judge success or failure. Two levels of criteria are set, a desired and a minimum level.

When completed this table provides a high level plan for all user evaluations of the product. The goals and tests are very product specific and practical. Goals specified here may also indicate issues for performance and technical testing. Indeed the same format could be used to specify technical and business goals for inclusion in product evaluations.

A further table shows how this information is expanded to form a test plan. It divides the test procedures into the different kinds of testing to be carried out ie. performance tests, user trials in the laboratory and field testing. At this stage it is necessary to specify which user groups will be required, the kinds of tasks to be carried out, etc. In this way a high level test plan is developed.

The Functionality Matrix
Having completed the User Requirements specification phase, the design team must then amalgamate these requirements with the proposed technical specification in order to begin the process of functional decomposition and subsequent implementation. The Functionality Matrix provides a procedure to check items of proposed functionality against user and task characteristics. This tool is describe in detail in a separate paper [2]

5. The HUFIT Training Seminars

The HUFIT PAS Tools are designed for use by designers, who have little or no previous experience of human factors. The main delivery mechanism for the tools is a training seminar which shows the designers how to use the tools, introducing the human factors concepts, while showing how the procedures contribute to the design process.

The course is very practical, based on a series of exercises which allow designers to work through the tools using data from a real-life interface design exercise from HUSAT's recent consultancy experience.

The seminar was developed for designers without a human factors background, but we have consistently had requests from human factors practitioners, who want access to the tools for use in their companies and for training purposes.

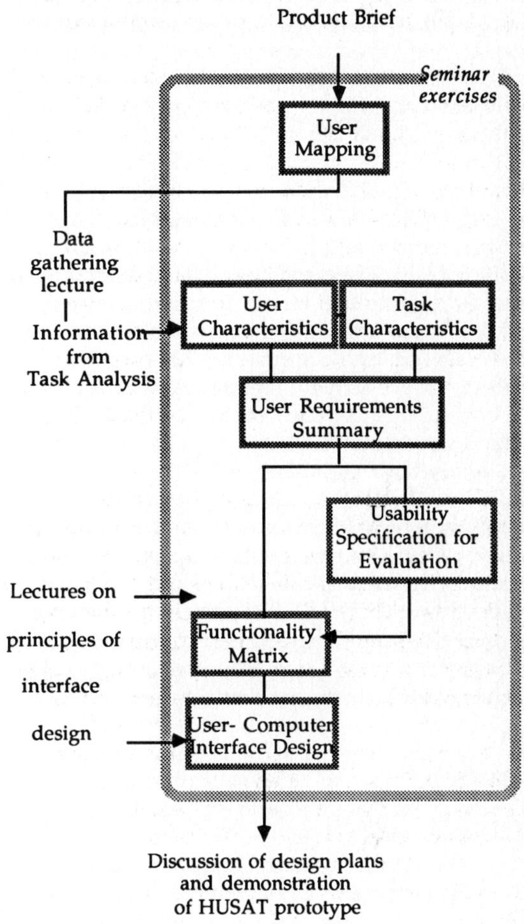

Figure 2
The Seminar for Designers

A separate seminar for Human Factors practitioners has been developed to meet this demand. The exercises have been suitably shortened and additional sessions have been included. Firstly, an outline of the training strategy required for the introduction of the tools and secondly, a discussion of possible implementation and tailoring strategies.

The seminars have been running successfully since 1988 and are continuing beyond the end of the HUFIT project into the early 1990s to support the uptake of the Toolset by both Designers and Human Factors Practitioners.

6. Conclusion

The tools have been well received by designers coming from a far wider range of design contexts that the generic, office products manufacturing setting, for which they were developed. It is clear that the structured procedures are appreciated by designers involved in many areas for instance in-house systems design, where they can be tailored to fit into and complement the existing systems analysis methods.

This approach of developing of techniques to aid the communication and incorporation of human factors methods and principles in the design process is considered to be the key to gaining wider acceptance of human factors in systems design and thereby improving the quality of systems delivered and their acceptability to users. At HUSAT we are actively seeking ways to further the development of basic tools, like the HUFIT toolset, which can be handed over to designers to use themselves. A further ESPRIT project - ORDIT - is looking into the difficult area of organisational requirements to develop methods for capturing and communicating these in order to improve system specifications [13]. Further developments of the HUFIT toolset are planned including the development of a distance learning package for the tools and the integration of these methods into existing methodologies.

REFERENCES

[1] Galer, M. D., 1990
The HUFIT Toolset: Human Factors Tools for Designers of IT Products
In this volume

[2] Harker, S. D. P., Eason, K. D. E. & Poulson, D. F. 1987
Classifying the Targets for Human Factors Output
Proc. of Alvey Annual Conference, UMIST, Manchester, July 1987

[3] Antill, 1986
The Information Systems Design Process: Many Views of One Situation
Design Studies, Vol 7 (2)

[4] Boehm, 1981
Software Engineering Economics
Englewood Cliffs, N-J Prentic Hall

[5] Hannigan, S., & Herring, V., 1986
The Role of Human Factors in the Design of IT Products
HUFIT Deliverable A1.2b, HUFIT/3-HUS-11/86

[6] Hutt ,A., Donnelly, N., Macauley L., Fowler, C. & Twigger, D. 1987
Describing a Product Opportunity: A Methodology for Understanding the User's Environment
In People and Computers III, Diaper & Winder (Eds), Cambridge

[7] Galer, M.D., Taylor B.C., Dowd, M., Catterall, B.J., Maguire, M., Allison, G.
An Integrated Human Factors Input to the Design of Information Technology Products
Chapter for Computer-Aided Ergonomics, Taylor & Francis, London. In press.

[8] Macaulay, L.A., 1988
A Process for Deriving Product Dependent Usability Metrics
DTG Report 88/AN, Design Technologies Group, UMIST (internal report)

[9] Bennett, J., 1984
Managing to Meet Usability Requirements: Establishing and Meeting Software Development Goals
In Visual Display Terminal, Bennett et al (Eds), Prentice Hall International, London

[10] Shackel, B., 1986
Usability - Context, Framework, Definition, Design and Evaluation
SERC CREST Advanced Course, HUSAT, Loughborough.

[11] Gilb, T., 1977
Software Metrics
Winthrop, Cambridge Mass., USA

[12] Catterall, B. J., 1990
The Functionality Matrix
In this volume

[13] Olphert, C. W., Poulson, D.F., Powrie, S.E., 1990
Teh Development of Tools to Assist in Organisational Requirements Definition for Information Technology Systems
Proceedings of "Computer, Man and Organisation", Nivelles, Belgium, May 1990

Human–Computer Interaction – INTERACT '90
D. Diaper et al. (Editors)
Elsevier Science Publishers B.V. (North-Holland)

The HUFIT Functionality Matrix

Bernard J. Catterall.

HUSAT Research Institute, The Elms, Elms Grove, Loughborough, Leics, UK.

The Functionality Matrix, part of the HUFIT Planning Analysis and Specification Toolset for IT Product Designers, cross references user requirements information with the technical proposal in a first-pass assessment procedure which seeks to arrive at an enhanced functional specification. In business terms, the Matrix provides an explicit mechanism for assessing user and task-related issues within the context of the other business trade-offs which are made during real product development.

1. INTRODUCTION

The rationale behind all user requirements capture, analysis and specification techniques is that it is both possible and desirable to derive functional product requirements from user and task-related data. However, the skills required to perform such a detailed human factors analysis and specification procedure are seldom combined with skills to translate identified requirements into functional terms which are of meaning to product designers. Too often, the outputs of user requirements exercises are criticised for being high-level and non-specific. In the worst case, the purpose of user requirements capture may be misunderstood as synonymous with *purchaser* requirements. So-called *user* requirements are then expressed in marketing terms such as the need for 'modularity', 'flexibility' or 'adaptability'. Equally problematic for the human factors practitioner is gaining acceptance of the need for the inclusion of human factors information in the technical specification at all, where either designers or management are sceptical of the worth of such information in a business setting. They may feel that human factors has little part to play in product definition in the real world environment of production and marketing and the pursuit of increased sales volumes. These problems may appear to be insoluble, since the parties involved express their understanding of the actual product or system features required to meet identified needs in entirely different terms.

A further problem is that in proposing a set of functional requirements for an application the human factors expert is still making a creative leap in translating identified user needs into detailed functional solutions. Any tool which purported to be able to provide prescriptive, context-specific, *and definitive* human factors answers in functional terms would assume that there is 'one correct solution' to all problems. In reality, a variety of possible implementation solutions can be offered for any given product development. Whilst there may be very specific experimental data, or 'best-practice' design guidelines to draw on, the fact remains that at the holistic level of whole-product design, a bewildering set of mix-and-match possibilities exists. Trade-offs are inevitably made.

The Functionality Matrix has been developed to assist in alleviating these problems. The designer, with little or no human factors knowledge, and the user requirements analyst with only limited technical knowledge, are provided with a means for cross-referencing their separate views of the functional specification. They work together to agree an enhanced specification which demonstrably addresses the full range of technical factors, managerial factors, and human factors trade-offs which inevitably occur in real-time cost-effective product development. Completion of the matrix *by a development team including designers themselves* assists in the process of refining product proposals. Equally, the need for user and task-related functionality is demonstrated through a simple rating and assessment procedure. The value of an early input of user and task data for documentation, training, maintenance, system-testing and marketing is also made clear through the evolution of directed outputs to relevant departments. Information is provided for each of the subsequent stages in the product life-cycle with outputs rooted firmly in a practical human factors and commercial context.

2. THE HUFIT CONTEXT

The Functionality Matrix evolved as a part of the HUFIT Toolset which was developed by members of the HUSAT Research Centre, Loughborough, UK (Galer &Taylor[2]). The aim of this work was to develop tools and methods which would enable the wide variety of personnel involved in the design of IT products to take account of ergonomics/human factors *for themselves* as a normal part of the product design process (Taylor[5]). The individual items of the Toolset (Catterall,Allison & Maguire[1], Taylor[4], Taylor & Bonner[6]) are intended to encourage the establishment of more explicit information pathways between design team members who too often fail to pass on their implicit views of the product in any tangible form. The Functionality Matrix is the final tool in the HUFIT Planning Analysis and Specification (PAS) Toolset. In the HUFIT context, the Functionality Matrix receives its user- and task-related input from the earlier components of the PAS Toolset and outputs its interface data directly to the User Computer Interface Design Tool.

3. THE FUNCTIONALITY MATRIX (FM)

Figure 1 shows a highly schematic representation of the functionality matrix.

3.1. When the tool is employed

The matrix is completed during a workshop in the later stages of product planning, prior to the outline functionality specification being approved for prototyping or first build. The workshop involves representatives from all business -related departments - i.e., planning, design, system test/QA, management, finance, and marketing.

3.2. Expected benefits

The completion of the matrix demands a cooperative effort from all participants in product development and each benefits from its outputs:

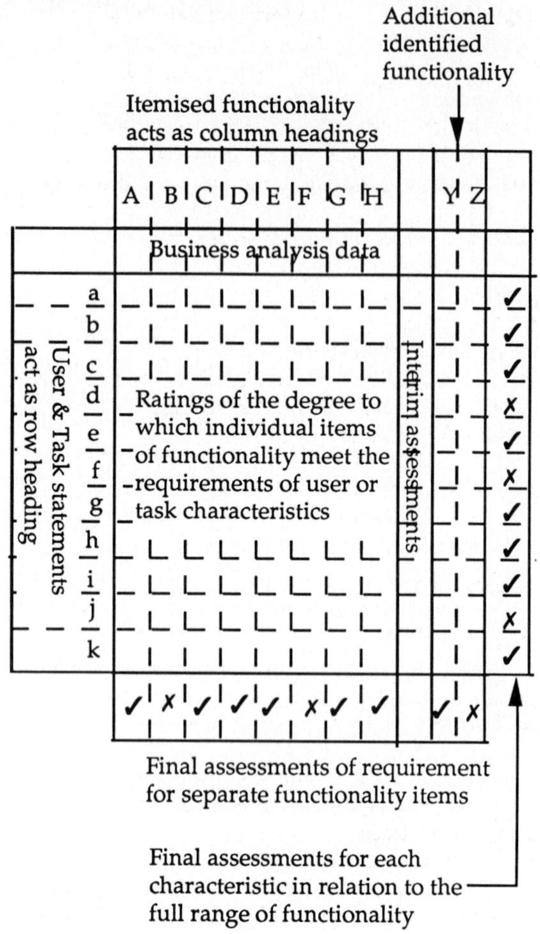

Figure 1. A schematic representation of the Functionality Matrix

- The matrix ensures a realistic and demonstrable consideration of early user and task issues in product functional specification.
- The matrix is highly tailorable to suit varying design processes and in-house styles. Output, therefore, can be made both corporately recognisable and understandable. It is, therefore, likely to be highly usable by its target audience.
- The matrix presents complex data in an easily recognisable and usable form. This allows product planners to address the complex inter-relationships of the various business, human factors and technical constraints represented in real-world trade-offs.
- Additional functional items required to meet user and task requirements are identified.
- Functional items identified as superfluous to user and/or task requirements are identified.
- The proposed functional specification may not adequately meet important user or task

characteristics. The matrix will identify these gaps, which will have important marketing, documentation or training implications.

- Functional items rated as either vital to a sufficiently wide range of user and task requirements or which alone meet a given important user/task requirement are flagged for possible prototyping and/or quality assurance (QA) testing. Again, there will be marketing, documentation or training implications.
- Detailed design implementation proposals/solutions begin to emerge as consideration is given to the various issues involved in completing the matrix.
- Functional alternatives can be discussed and rated in order to narrow down the number of possible options for later prototyping.
- Once completed, the matrix is available for reference in all subsequent stages of the PLC and may be updated in the light of prototyping, testing or marketing feedback. Subsequent releases can be assessed and developed more easily on the basis of referral to well-documented and fully-recorded design decisions.

3.3. Inputs

The functionality matrix uses information from a variety of sources:

- The proposed technical specification. These specifications exist in a wide variety of forms. In practice, the FM can yield useful data at whatever the level of description - either helping to increasingly refine generalised statements or through promoting design teams to understand the grouping of highly-detailed technical descriptions in terms of their practical representation to users. By promoting the process of increasingly detailed redescription of functional items the matrix also assists the human factors practitioner in his or her common difficulty of translating ideas to an adequate level of design detail.
- The functional requirements derived from earlier user and task analysis are combined with the elements of the technical specification to provide a comprehensive outline specification for use in the FM. The set of detailed statements describing the full range of defined, agreed user and task characteristics (from which the initial user requirements were derived) are also required.
- Marketing information feedback
  i) competition analysis - the presence or otherwise and perceived competitive advantages or disadvantages of particular functional items in relevant competitive products
  ii) purchaser ratings - the perceived importance of particular functional items to prospective system/product purchasers - who will often have very different requirements from end-users.
- Likely development costings in terms of time, manpower/resource commitments, and capital expenditure - which may over-ride any other factors in later trade-offs.

3.4. Form of the Tool

The FM can be used in both paper-based and spread-sheet formats. Gill ([3]) has shown that the most effective and practical technique for employing the Matrix is that the rating procedures be performed on-line using a suitable spreadsheet package, with the assessment procedures being completed off-line using an enlarged print-out from the spreadsheet to avoid on-line 'window' restrictions. Assessment results are then transferred to the spreadsheet upon completion for recording purposes.

4. HOW THE FUNCTIONALITY MATRIX IS USED

4.1. Preparing the Matrix

Step 1. The technical specification is concatenated with the product requirements derived from the earlier user and task requirements specification exercise to generate a complete initial functionality listing. These items act as the individual column headings. Logical or technical subsets are used to divide the whole into more manageable groupings.

Step 2. Assessments are made for each of the functionality items (or sub groups) in terms of:-
a) estimated development time
b) estimated development effort - i.e., man allocation, level of technical difficulty, resource allocation, etc.
c) estimated development cost - a function of items a) & b) expressed in financial terms

Step 3. Assessments are then made for each functionality item (or grouping) based on marketing feedback in two main areas:-
a) purchaser ratings
b) competition assessment

Step 4. The user and task characteristics statements derived from earlier analysis are entered separately in the left hand column to act as the individual row headings.

4.2. Completing the matrix

Step 5. Ratings are completed which individually cross-reference proposed functionality items against each identified user and task characteristic.

The design teams, using a simple 5-point rating scale, make individual assessments of the degree to which the separate (or logically grouped) functionality items meet the underlying requirements of the separate user and task characteristics. A view can then be established of the degree to which the *overall* proposed functionality is seen as adequately meeting user and task-related requirements.

All background design proposals, refinements or revisions which inevitably emerge in performing the rating procedure are also separately recorded for later reference. Additionally, where alternative functional proposals exist, these can be assessed by opening the required number of spreadsheet columns, performing interim ratings and assessments (as below), and consequently discarding the least desirable item columns - continuing as before. This is a particularly cost-effective exercise in choosing between possible prototyping options.

Step 6. An assessment can now be made (across each horizontal row) of the degree to which the underlying requirements of each user or task characteristic are, or are not, being met by the totality of the proposed functionality. Again, further clarification of design proposals often results as a by-product of this procedure and is recorded for future reference.

Step 7. Where overall product functionality has been assessed as failing to adequately meet the requirements of a given individual characteristic, additional functionality is, where possible, now identified to meet that need. User trials have demonstrated that the clarification of design implementation proposals which occurs as a result of the earlier procedures will also tend to suggest a number of additional functionality requirements (or redefinition of existing items) which are then added here.

Steps 8, 9 &10. Any additional functionality items proposed in step 7 may or may not adequately address the problem of meeting the requirement of a given characteristic and may, in any case, have considerable knock-on (or, more correctly, knock-*back*) effects for the earlier assessments made. It is important, therefore, that additional functionality is itself assessed and rated as in steps 2, 3 and 5. Further additional required functionality may again be identified during this process and an iterative procedure is followed until no further effective proposals can be made.

At the end of this process final assessments can be made (in the horizontal dimension) of the degree to which the underlying user and task requirements are being met (using the same procedure as in step 6).

Step 11. An assessment is now made in each vertical column. The actual requirement for each item of functionality is demonstrated in the context of the separate user and task characteristics. No reference is made, at this stage, to the compounding business factors contained in the cells at the top of the Matrix since the purpose of this interim stage is to isolate the user- and task-related judgements ready for the trade-off procedure in step 12.

Steps 12. Final assessments can now be made of the *overall* requirement for each separate (or suitably grouped) item(s) of functionality. This is the trade-off process between the often conflicting business interests now represented in the vertical dimension of the matrix.

The output of each assessment, and the impact on the product development process as a whole, will carry with it detailed implications for future stages in the product life-cycle and for specified members of the multi-disciplinary design team.

In addition, it cannot be stressed strongly enough that there is further major output of the Matrix *procedure*. All relevant ideas and implementation proposals, together with the hitherto implicit decisions made throughout the rating and assessment procedures are suitably recorded for forwarding to appropriate parties involved in the later stages of the design process. The completed Matrix and its accompanying notes act as an explicit record which can be used for referral throughout the design process and can, if required be used as part of an attributable 'sign-off' procedure.

5. THE FUNCTIONALITY MATRIX IN ACTION

Whilst results from early user trials in the HUFIT partner companies and in a number of industrial field sites have been noted in describing the operation of the Matrix, a number of additional points are of interest. Development and initial validation of the Matrix followed an iterative procedure which began with in-house trials employing the wide range of human factors expertise within the HUSAT Research Institute. Later versions were then trialed with designers from the HUFIT industrial partner companies in a series of workshops and assessed in follow-up interviews. Other additional field-sites were obtained as a result of requests to participate resulting from general HUFIT promotional activities. As a result of these contacts, field testing of the Matrix in real-time product developments has been conducted (and continues) in a wide variety of locations throughout Europe.

Industrial users of the matrix have commented on its effectiveness as a positive step in ensuring a human factors representation in the earliest stages of IT product development. Designers are said to be 'at ease' with the matrix format and, even where they have been previously hostile, become quickly involved in making qualitative 'human factors' judgements. Whilst a 'first-run' of the matrix is necessarily a lengthy process, Gill ([3]), along with our own experience, has demonstrated an approximate 50% saving in completion time for second and subsequent runs.

An industrial advantage of the Matrix has been that, in common with the other components of the HUFIT PAS Tools, its uptake is demonstrably costable (both in terms of predicted training times, and in predictions for first and subsequent run-times). In addition, as a precursor to any prototyping exercise, the Matrix assists in choosing between possible prototyping options - thus reducing development costs. Prototyping, vital in the still continuing process of user requirements capture and testing, can begin from a more directed base.

In conclusion, two particular benefits of the Matrix have been most highly valued in industrial settings. Firstly, that it provides an explicit mechanism for human factors issues to be equally represented in the business trade-offs which inevitably occur in any cost-pressured product development. Secondly, and perhaps most significantly, that in completing the Matrix, designers find themselves actively involved in detailed technical discussions about user issues which they themselves have generated and see the necessity to resolve. The need to have to fight for the inclusion of human factors issues in the early planning stages of the product life-cycle is superseded by the adoption of such issues as one of the full range of business factors impinging on early product development.

REFERENCES

[1] Catterall, B. J.; Allison, G.; Maguire, M., HUFIT: specification and design tools. Proc. of the Ergonomics Society Annual Conf. "Contemporary Ergonomics 1989" (97-102). Megaw, E. D. (ed), Taylor and Francis (1989).

[2] Galer, M.D.; Taylor, B., Human factors in Information Technology - ESPRIT Project 385, Proc. of the Ergonomics Society Annual Conf. "Contemporary Ergonomics 1989" (82-86), Megaw, E. D. (ed), Taylor and Francis (1989).

[3] Gill S., Towards an on-line version of the Functionality Matrix, M.Sc IT Diss'n, LUT,(1989).

[4] Taylor, B., HUFIT: user requirements toolset. Proc. of the Ergonomics Society Annual Conf. "Contemporary Ergonomics 1989" (87-91) , Megaw, E. D. (ed), Taylor and Francis (1989).

[5] Taylor B.. The HUFIT PAS Tools, this volume

[6] Taylor, B.; Bonner, J. HUFIT: usability specification for evaluation. Proc. of the Ergonomics Society 1989 Annual Conf. "Contemporary Ergonomics 1989" (92-96), Megaw, E. D. (ed), Taylor and Francis (1989).

Human–Computer Interaction – INTERACT '90
D. Diaper et al. (Editors)
Elsevier Science Publishers B.V. (North-Holland)

Task-based user interface development tools

Peter Johnson & Emma Nicolosi*

Department of Computer Science,
Queen Mary and Westfield College,
University of London.
Mile End Road,
London E1 4NS.

ABSTRACT

The generation of design ideas can be facilitated by user/task analysis. Task analysis can influence the design of functionality, dialogue and presentation characteristics of user interfaces. A case history of designing a user interface to a CAD system using Knowledge Analysis of Tasks (KAT) is reported. Methods and tools to assist designers in carrying out user/task analysis have been developed and are described. These include a hypercard task simulation tool (DETAIL) and a task based prototyping tool which allows user interfaces to be developed from task analysis data.

Keywords: Task analysis; prototyping and simulation tools; Computer Aided Design.

Introduction

In a recent attempt to identify the design characteristics for effective tools for user interface designers Rosson et al [1] and Johnson & Johnson [2] have carried out studies of the target users and their tasks, namely, software developers and their design practices. Both studies came to similar conclusions about the use of task analysis in design and the requirements for tools to support design. The majority of problems identified by designers in [2] were concerned with the information and contact they had with end-users. In many cases they had little or no information about the end-users' tasks. Often the user requirements were derived from a log of problems with the current system together with added information about what they thought the system could or should do. At best the designers had implicit and indirect information about the end-users and their tasks.

The designers studied in [2] all reported that they required more detailed information about users and tasks. They also stated that usability and efficiency evaluation requires clear design requirements based on users and tasks. Finally they felt that evaluations would be easier to perform if prototyping could be done in terms of user tasks (eg, if the prototype could be used to simulate how an identified end user task would be performed).

Rosson et al examined how designers generated and developed their ideas. Figure 1. gives a diagrammatic summary of the most frequently identified design activities reported by Rosson et al. Several techniques were found to be used by designers for 'idea generation'. 53% of the interviewed designers used task analysis; 23% used external sources such as available literature; 16% used meta-strategies such as concentration; 13% used interaction with others; 12% used design activities like charts and diagrams; and 6% used trial and error.

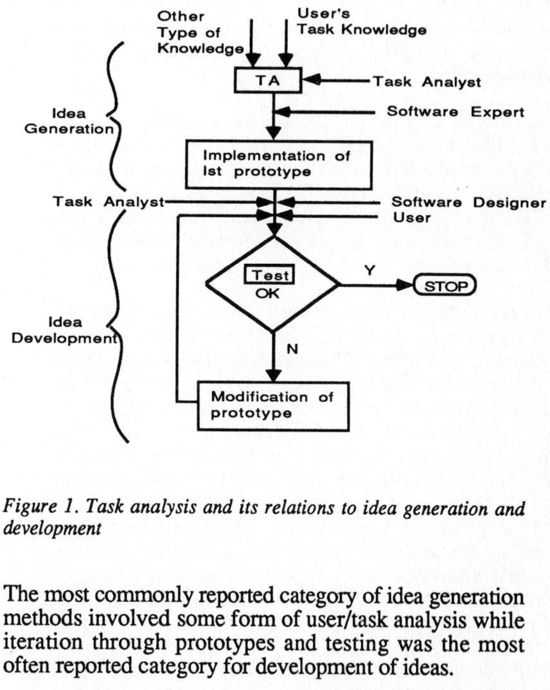

Figure 1. Task analysis and its relations to idea generation and development

The most commonly reported category of idea generation methods involved some form of user/task analysis while iteration through prototypes and testing was the most often reported category for development of ideas.

From the results of surveys [1] & [2] we conclude that designers would welcome some form of task-based design tool to assist with the design and evaluation of interactive software.

Task Analysis and Design.

Three aspects of design have been identified in [2] where TA might usefully contribute to design idea generation. These were; first, to identify the functionality of the system; second, to identify stylistic and presentation characteristics of the UI requirements; and third, the design of the dialogue.

* Emma Nicolosi is now at CISE, Segrate, Italy

Let us consider what task analysis involves. There are two aspects to task analysis, first gathering information and analysis of the users' tasks; second the development of task based design specification models. Some form of transition between task analysis and design specification and modelling is required. The reality of providing tools which could support these activities requires the development of methods of task analysis and an understanding of the relations between the output from task analysis and design development. Aspects of task analysis and design will be considered in subsequent sections of this paper.

Knowledge Analysis of Tasks; a case study.

In constructing a method for analysing users and tasks, Johnson et al. [3] have identified aspects of user knowledge that relate to task behaviours and task performance. This is covered by a theory of Task Knowledge Structures (TKS) [3]. Also, they have identified a number of techniques that can be used to gather this information.These are detailed in a method of TA known as Knowledge Analysis of Tasks (KAT) [4].

KAT has been used in real design projects in which the design has had to be carried out in tight time constraints and within limited resources. A case history of a commercial design project in which KAT was used is presented below.

A commercial design project was undertaken using KAT. The project produced a prototype user interface and recommendations for the design of a direct manipulation interface to a CAD system to be used in the jewellery industry. The purpose of the system was to allow jewellery designers to undertake some aspects of the design of jewellery products such as rings.

A systems analysis had already been carried out by the client and this had produced a functional specification for a database. However, it did not describe in any detail the nature of the jewellery design tasks. A task analysis was performed using KAT, to gain some understanding of how jewellery design tasks were carried out by an experienced and practicing jewellery designer. One expert jewellery designer was contacted (due to time constraints only 15 person days were available to complete the design and prototyping). The results of the task analysis cannot be considered to be generally applicable to all aspects of jewellery design. Accessing many experts to validate and augment the analysis obtained from any one expert is recommended. However, the client required an early prototype system to demonstrate the potential capabilities of applying interactive computers to jewellery design. It was felt that the results of the TA would serve the purposes of providing a suitable input to the design of an early prototype and provide a basis for making some user interface design recommendations. It also proved to be an ideal opportunity to show that TA does not necessarily increase the overall timescale of a project, can be usefully carried out in short timescales and can provide useful information with minimum additional overheads to the project.

The method used for data collection was a structured interview supported by a written questionnaire. This technique of data collection was used in preference to others such as collecting detailed protocols because of the short time constraints of the contract. Two visits to the jewellery designer's premises were organised. During the first visit the expert was interviewed. The interview was recorded and the expert provided drawings and gave demonstrations of parts of tasks. From these data an initial analysis of the task was undertaken. The second visit gave us the opportunity to show the initial results of our task analysis to the expert and to consolidate issues which had not been fully covered during the first visit. In addition a third meeting with the client and the expert was also held to check the results of the task analysis and to agree on the format of the TA report. Each meeting lasted approximately four to six hours.

The use of KAT in this project is summarised in figure 2. The data collection techniques were as described in the preceding paragraph. The analysis identified and described in detail Task Knowledge Structure (TKS) elements in the form of goals, procedures, objects and actions [3]. In addition generic, specific, typical and central elements were identified. An object is one task element and is used here to exemplify the above terms. A generic object represents a class of specific objects (i.e. instances). A specific object represents an instance of a generic object. A typical object is the "best example" instance of a generic object. A central object is an object which is essential for carrying out a task.

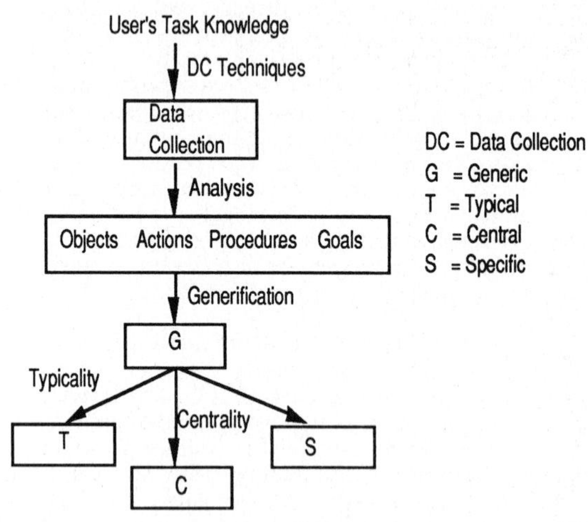

Figure 2 Decomposition of Task Analysis

Developing Designs from Task Analysis

The TA contributed to the design of the system in a number of ways. For example, the results of KAT helped us to identify how much information should be provided on the screen at any one time; to give recommendations and suggestions on how to present information on the screen and, to design the dialogue. Moreover, typical objects were used to define default values; central objects were treated as essential to the functionality of the design; generic objects were used as menu or window titles; and specific objects were used as the items of particular menus or windows. An example of the user interface design is shown below in figure 3.

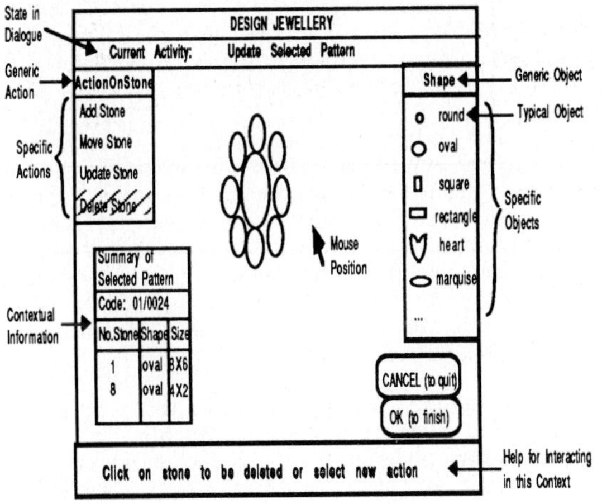

Figure 3. Example of User Interface Design with Generic, Typical and Specific Objects and Actions in a System for Jewellery Design.

The task analysis enabled us to identify all the information necessary to be represented at any one time for a particular task. As can be seen from figure 3 the amount of information is large, and would be complex if not well structured. The structure of this information was also developed from KAT by identifying classes of actions that are carried out on classes of objects, the procedures used for particular activities and the context in which those procedures occurred.

"Lookalike" screen dumps or storyboard interaction scenarios were developed by using the information derived from KAT together with our experiences in designing user-interfaces. These designs were then passed to the prototype implementors who constructed a prototype user interface on the basis of these designs. KAT provided an invaluable source of information for generating the initial user interface design to a significant level of detail.

In summary the KAT contributed to design idea generation in this case study in three ways; first, to identify the functionality of the system; second, to identify stylistic and presentation characteristics of the UI requirements; and third, the design of the dialogue. KAT helped to identify what users expected to have available to them at any time, their likely usage of system functions, the names and form of representation to be given to screen presented objects and events, and the information that should be available in a given context (eg screens) and the structure between contexts (eg moving between different screens).

Tools to support task-based design.

KAT provides a method of TA that can complement UI design. Two categories of tools have been developed in initial versions, a notation for specifying UI designs in terms of user tasks, and two software tools, one for simulating tasks and a second for prototyping UI designs. The notation and DETAIL, a HyperCard tool have been described in full elsewhere [5, 6 & 7]. An early version of this prototyping tool is described in the remaining sections of this paper.

A Task-Based Prototyping Tool

One aim of our research activities is to provide an integrated task-based approach for system design and evaluation in the context of prototyping. Task analysis is an integral part of such an approach in order to better inform the initial prototyping phase and to incorporate users' requirements more fully into the system design.

We have identified at least three different aspects of the design of software systems to which KAT can contribute namely, the design of **functionality**, **dialogue** and **presentation**. There is quite a clear distinction between presentation and functionality since presentation is concerned primarily with the visual appearance and screen layout of the user interface, whereas functionality has to do with the performance and capability of the system. The dialogue is concerned with accessing the functionality through the presentation 'layer' of the user interface design. The dialogue must support users in achieving their goals and to do this it makes use of both the functionality and presentation aspects of the design.

An illustration of the differences between functionality, dialogue and presentation aspects of design can be given using the jewellery design system, described earlier.

The system functionality for a jewellery CAD system might include create, edit, select, display and delete bejewelled products.

The dialogue is concerned with the structure of the permissible links between different states of the system. Dialogues include the interaction necessary to access a particular function of the application, and the interactions that occur in applying the available functions in the context of particular tasks.

The presentation includes the design of pop-up menus, windows, icons, buttons, text-fields, command names etc. The presentation aspects of the design are the media through which the state of the application, accessible functions and feedback are presented to the user.

Initial implementation of a task-based prototyping tool

Some initial ideas of how the tool should look have been implemented in KEE, a knowledge engineering tool developed by IntelliCorp and running on a SUN 3/160 with 16mgb of memory and 280 mgb discs. KEE provides a powerful and flexible environment which supports objects (called units), object oriented programming, rules, backward and forward reasoning, active values and active images. Moreover KEE supports worlds or states of a background world. Worlds consistency is given by an Assumption Truth Maintenance System (ATMS) which provides justifications every time an inconsistency occurs. KEE handles multiple windows and the creation of new classes of objects. It provides an integrated knowledge engineering environment. KEE is being used, by us, to investigate the advantages and disadvantages of alternative representations of TKS elements and to develop an architecture for relating the different representations of TKS elements and design outputs (ie functionality, dialogue and presentation characteristics of a system design).

As shown in figure 4 a background window called 'Create a new TKS' is the area where creation, editing and deleting of TKS elements happen. The buttons on the left hand side of the background window refer to the TKS elements represented by the tool. Clicking on a button makes a pop-up menu appear with several options available (e.g. Create, Delete, Edit).

Objects, actions, procedures and goals can be created, etc. Every time a new object, for example, is created its name is entered and its properties are recorded. The user is be able to begin the task-based design by defining any of the TKS elements. Appropriate links between TKS elements can be either automatically or user generated. For example, if the definition of a new procedure, action or goal refers to an existing object then the tool will automatically add the name of the newly created procedure, action or goal to the list of procedures etc associated with that object (the properties of an object include 'used in procedure: action: goal:'). If the definition of a new procedure refers to a non-existent object, action or goal then the tool will ask the user to define the missing element.

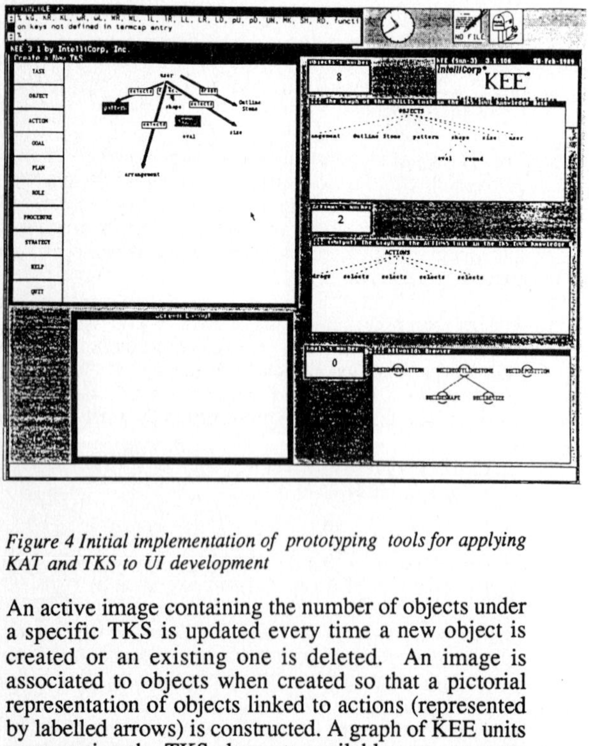

Figure 4 Initial implementation of prototyping tools for applying KAT and TKS to UI development

An active image containing the number of objects under a specific TKS is updated every time a new object is created or an existing one is deleted. An image is associated to objects when created so that a pictorial representation of objects linked to actions (represented by labelled arrows) is constructed. A graph of KEE units representing the TKS elements available appears every time a change is made in the current TKS. Objects and actions are shown as members (dashed lines) of the classes OBJECTS and ACTIONS respectively. All these different pictorial summaries of existing TKS elements allow the user (designer) to have an exact picture of the state of the model at any one time.

Every time the user has to enter textual or numerical information then the interaction is transferred to a window which appears for the time it is needed.

Goals are represented as 'worlds'. Worlds and background world are KEE concepts which can represent state, time or hypothetical situations. Goals are, by definition, different states of the world under examination. A set of conditions may allow you to move from one goal to another. This can be well represented by KEE-worlds and -rules respectively. Rules in KEE are expressed in the form 'IF <premises> THEN <conclusions>'.

An initial attempt to represent goals and subgoals as worlds of the background world which is the current task is shown in figure 4. Rules can be associated to each world so that the current task, 'TASK' is successfully completed if 'GOAL1' and 'GOAL2' are both completed. However, 'GOAL2' is completed only if 'GOAL3' has been satisfied. Note, goals can have sequential, concurrent, unordered, or independent relations to other goals.

The tool can be used to design user interface components (functionality, dialogue, presentation) and express these in terms of task scenarios. The tool should provide further support for KAT to be used in design and to allow prototype interfaces to be designed. User interface components are designed by relating them to a TKS element which then has appropriate links to other existing TKS elements.

The tool allows the designer to define a task object action, procedure or goal and then choose the form of presentation and/or dialogue of the user interface. The design and the TKS model can be viewed in different but proximal windows. Thus the tool has both a UI design window and a TKS window. The designer can edit either window and the reciprocal window is updated.

The main use of the tool is to allow the designer to move between representations of user tasks and representations of user interfaces in a single environment. To support design the tool offers a mechanism for rapidly modifying either the user task or the user interface. The tool could also be used to provide an insight to and test of the user's understanding of the design.

The task-based prototyping tool is designed to support the design of the functionality, dialogue and presentation of a computer system alongside a KAT derived model of the user tasks or conversely to produce a user interface design, another to identify the tasks associated with that design. Thus, task-based design can be directly supported. The design of the user interface or the task is quite open to changes by the tool user as far as design decisions are concerned. Since designers want to be able to experiment with new ideas all the time, the tool should not be seen as an obstruction to their activity by delivering rigid designs. One possible extension to the tool would be to provide usability guidelines that would help the designer in making sensible decisions about the choice of functions, dialogues and presentation characteristics. A further development would be to implement the tool outside KEE.

Summary and Conclusion

HCI research aims to develop high quality, usable systems. HCI researchers have developed methods and approaches to meet this aim and are working on the development of tools and more formal support for the approaches to design that are emerging. Tools and methods have been developed to support TA and design development.

We have discussed some aspects of interactive system design to which we believe TA can contribute. Some initial ideas of a task-based design tool have been developed which will support the task-based design of interactive systems.

ACKNOWLEDGEMENTS

The work referred to in this paper has been supported by SERC/Alvey grants, PRJ/MMI/122. We thank Hilary Johnson, Ray Waddington, and Christine Knowles for help through discussions and comments on this paper.

REFERENCES

[1] Rosson, M.B., Maass, S. & Kellog, W.A. (1988) The designer as user: building requirements for design tools from design practice. Communications of the ACM, 31, 11 pp. 1288-1298.

[2] Johnson, H. & Johnson, P. [In press) Integrating task analysis into system design; surveying designers needs. Ergonomics.

[3] Johnson, P. Johnson H. Waddington R. & Shouls A. (1988) Task Knowledge Structures. In Jones D. & Winder R. (eds.) People and computers IV, Cambridge University Press.

[4] Johnson P. & Johnson, H. (1990) Knowledge analysis of tasks: task analysis and specification for human-computer systems: in Downton A. (ed.). Engineering the human-computer interface. McGraw Hill, England.

[5] Waddington, R. & Johnson, P. (1989) Designing and evaluating interfaces using task models. In proceedings of IFIP 11th World Computer Congress, San Francisco. North Holland.

[6] Waddington, R. & Johnson, P. (1989) A family of task models for interface design. In A. Sutcliffe (ed.) People and Computers V : HCI'89 Cambridge University Press.

[7] Edmondson, D. & Johnson P. (1989) DETAIL: An approach to task analysis. Proceedings of Simulation in the Development of User Interfaces, Brighton, UK.

Human–Computer Interaction – INTERACT '90
D. Diaper et al. (Editors)
Elsevier Science Publishers B.V. (North-Holland)

PROTEUS: AN APPROACH TO INTERFACE EVALUATION

Jonathan Crellin.

People and Computer Interaction Systems Research Group (PACIS), The Computing Department, Faculty of Mathematics, The Open University, Walton Hall, MILTON KEYNES, MK7 6AA. United Kingdom.

PROTEUS is a number of software tools which allow the implementation of an iterative, user centred approach to software (particularly interface) design, using rapid prototyping. The tools allow automated collection of questionnaire data, logging of system usage, and the central technique which is the collection of a qualitative representation of users perception of an interface design space, using the Construct Elicitation System. This data is fed back to the designer, and increases understanding user needs in relation to an interface. The paper describes the development of PROTEUS as an integrated evaluation tool, and reports on some of the empirical work underlying the approach embodied by PROTEUS, including its integration into the design of a small but real system.

1: INTRODUCTION

1.1. The failure of analytic approaches

It is possible to distinguish between interface evaluation methods, and interface evaluation approaches. Approaches is used here to describe the underlying philosophy of the evaluation. Methods are the techniques of data collection employed. Different approaches may use the same methods of data collection, but analyse the data in different ways. Formal approaches focus on the structure of the interface, within the context of human cognition models. They evaluate features of interface such as complexity and consistency, Grudin (1989). Such methods frequently fail to predict the future success of interfaces.

1.2. Problems with Empirical Approaches

Empirical approaches use an experimental or controlled observational paradigm. They involve evaluating performance of users with the interface on bench mark tasks aiming to predict how effective the interface will prove to be in real use. External variables (such as interruption) are controlled, and clear behavioural performance measures for performance on the interface are stated before evaluation takes place. However such evaluation approaches still fail to predict performance in real situations.

1.3. Contextual Approach

Whiteside et al (1988) suggests a contextual approach to interface evaluation. Such an approach collects experience as it happens, in the context where it usually occurs. This approach seeks to understand the experience of using an interface, as it is used in a real situation.

1.4. The problems of contextual methodology

The methods employed by contextual approaches are usually video observation, verbal protocols, and software logging. Unfortunately the first two methods for collecting experience are usually highly intrusive, and likely to alter the very phenomena which one wishes to observe.

1.5. Knowledge elicitation techniques as a basis for evaluation.

Techniques used for knowledge elicitation for expert systems may offer some useful methods for use within software evaluation, Briggs (1987). If such techniques are used it remains necessary to distinguishing between an objective description of an interface, and the subjective experience of using the interface. The knowledge elicitation approach can be used to identify users mistaken assumptions about an interface. However what does mistaken actually mean in this context? It could be argued that user mistakes are actually due to designers poor conception of a users viewpoint. Such users mistakes highlight a difference in designer and user perspectives.

1.6. Designer and Users

Designers and users have distinct differences. Designers see systems as a whole, they see the source code which makes up the system, and by the nature of their profession they spend a lot of time considering the link between the underlying system and the interface. Users are only directly aware of a systems interface, and knowledge of the underlying system is inferred from their experience with the interface. There are also differences which stem from a different knowledge of what is possible within the technology. The lack of knowledge of what is possible can make users ask for things that are difficult to achieve (for example a natural language interface), but at the same time, that lack of knowledge can mean users do not think of possible alternative ways of doing things (for example considering using pull-down menus rather than buttons).

Involvement of users in the design process is usually considered a 'good' thing, as it helps avoid the most obvious design trap, of ending up with a design that is considered at best uncomfortable or unpleasant to use, or at worst simply unusable. The term 'user-centred design' has been used to describe a range of design methodologies. At one end of the range of user centredness this can be a fairly small amount of evaluation of the software as it is used by a number of typical users. The evaluation can often involve looking at a feature of the interaction which the designer has decided (in the light of psychological/ergonomic guidelines) to be relevant to the performance of the system. At the other end of the spectrum, the user can design the majority of the system himself, by using some type of application-builder. The dimension here is one of emphasis on a designers design skills. At one extreme the responsibility for identifying the important features of the design lie with the designer, at the other end the responsibility is entirely placed on the user. One can see advantages with both approaches. Designers are expected to have knowledge which transcends a particular domain, and thus can see things about a design which may not be apparent to users-as-designers. If designers have any value this is what their value must be. Marcus(1983) refers to three perspectives on design.First the outerface, which are the final products of computation, text, tables, graphics. All of these can be printed, projected, or can appear on a VDU. People who use this information need have very little real understanding of how computers work. Second the interface which is the frames for command/control and documentation, that the computer system user encounters. This human computer connection allows the human to manipulate and control the machine, without which the computer is a useless tool. Thirdly the innerface which is the frames of command/control and documentation that are avaialble to the designer and only he sees. They depict programming languages, software tools and operating systems. This special perspective that only a designer has can lead to enhanced control over the design space but also misunderstanding of user perspectives.

System designers are used to dealing with computer system concepts, and use language to express those concepts. Users language is usually specialised to cope with their own task domain. These specialised languages form a signifigant barrier to communication between users and designers.

1.7. An ideal method for evaluation

An ideal method for interface evaluation will have the following characteristics:-

* Scope for automation
* User centred
* Not intrusive into the experience of using an interface
* Supports communication between users and designers.
* Quantitative and qualitative data.
* Ecological validity supported

The repertory grid, which is used as a knowledge elicitation tool, is an obvious candidate for software evaluation. The method has been used for the collection of evaluative data in a number of different domains, architecture, Honikman (1976), marketing Stewart et al (1981). The Construct Elicitation System (CES) has been developed at the Open University for collection of repertory grid information in evaluation tasks, Crellin (1988). The system has also been used in an investigation of the meaning of a researchers abstraction, Robson and Crellin (1988).

2. DESCRIPTION OF PROTEUS

PROTEUS is not designed to replace existing methods of evaluating usability and performance, but to provide a parallel analysis of user centred issues, and an input into the design decision making. It is a tool designed to aid the social process of designing a piece of software. The social process is one of extending the mutual understanding between the designer and the user. As such the tool is best suited to circumstances where a designer is not very experienced, and lacks the ability to gain a users perspective, or where the perspectives of designer and user might be expected to be radically different.

The components of PROTEUS are a shell, the different software prototypes, a help system, and the Construct Elicitation System. The methodology of PROTEUS is to allow users to use the prototype systems in as near as possible an ecologically valid environment. The system is therefore robust, and portable, and can be used in a normal workplace. PROTEUS can be used on a minimal Macintosh system (Mac Plus with single internal drive), and is consistent with the Macintosh interface guidelines. It therefore requires no special equipement, and can be used in a normal working environment by any Macintosh user. Usage data is recorded unobtrusively by the system during use, additional system logging (for example keystroke level recording) can be recorded by code embedded in the prototype systems. Data elicited by the Construct Elicitation System is available for user editing, during the session. The aim of the approach is to collect the maximum of information about user behaviour and experience, without intruding on the experience of using the prototype systems. The user should feel comfortable in the use of the system, and not feel themselves to be the object of unwanted scrutiny.

The PROTEUS shell presents an on-line questionnaire to collect demographic data. Access to the Construct Elicitation System is controlled via the shell. A user can only start using CES when she has used all the prototypes.

The Construct Elicitation System is an open ended description and rating system, based on the Personal Construct Psychology repertory grid Kelly (1955). Users are asked to provide textual labels for the ways in which they discriminate between the different prototypes. These verbal labels form the basis of semantic differential grids, which provide information both about the similarities between different ways of rating, and between the different prototypes.

3. PROTEUS AND THE RAS HELP SYSTEM

3.1. Introduction: The RAS System

RAS is a demonstration relational database program to be used as a teaching resource in the Open University's undergraduate program for 1990. Its primary role is to demonstrate the structure of a relational database, and to introduce the interrogation of relational databases using Standard Query Language (SQL).

Although most of the system was specified by teaching requirements, the HELP system had not been finalised. The role of a HELP system in a teaching package is to assist the student in completing their exercises, but not to provide a substitute to the course material, through which primary teaching takes place, or to distract learners from the course material.

3.2. Subjects

Subjects were of varying backgrounds. Some were post-graduate students working in the Faculty of Mathematics (n=4), others were Open University technical and research staff (n=2), and tutors from the Database course (n=4). All subjects had prior experience of micro computers. Only the tutors on the database course had more than a slight knowledge of SQL and relational databases. Additionally the system's designer completed the task.

3.3. Materials

The experimental materials consisted of two floppy discs. A 3.5 inch Macintosh boot-up disc, which contained the PROTEUS shell, including the CES program, and a number of prototype help systems for the RAS teaching material. Each of the prototype help systems were implemented on the Mac, running in a command language environment which was very similar to the MSDos RAS environment. Only the help commands were implemented on the Mac versions of RAS, other functional aspects of the RAS system were not implemented, and returned a short message to that effect if the user attempted to type them on the Mac version of the RAS system. Three distinct HELP systems were devised, and one more system was added by combing elements of the others. The HELP systems provided were:-

Declarative Textual Help, describing the purpose and effects of the commands in detail, but not providing information about how to implement the command.

Exemplar Help, which consisted of a valid example of the command (executable on the RAS system), and an example of the reply RAS would deliver if such a command was executed.

Syntax Help, which provided a BNF syntax diagram of the command.

Finally, *Declarative and Syntax*, which combined the contents of Declarative and Syntax above.

Each of the Help systems is syntactically identical, having a simple structure of the HELP command and a single argument. The screen display of each system is also very similar, resembling a message output from an IBM PC.

Subjects were also given a 5.25 inch MSDos floppy disc which contained the RAS program, and MSDos system files. In addition to the floppy discs subjects were given copies of the relevant OU teaching material. This consisted of an audio tape containing a guided tour of the RAS program, and a draft copy of the written OU course material. The course material introduces the RAS system and teaches interrogation of the database using SQL.

Subjects who completed the study in the computing laboratory had available a twin drive Amstrad 1512 PC, a Mac Plus computer, and a tape cassette player equipped with headphones. This equipment was located in a section of a computing laboratory partitioned off from the 'public' area, and was available for use anytime during the test period.

3.3. Procedure

Two procedures were adopted. The first was closer to a laboratory procedure, with subjects working in a variable number of sessions on the laboratory Macintosh and Amstrad PC away from their normal workplace. The audio material was available to these subjects and was listened to through headphones. A draft copy of the database teaching material was also available. The sessions took place in a screened off section of a computing laboratory.

The second procedure was more ecologically valid, and involved giving the subjects discs of the materials, and allowing them to work on them in their normal place of work, using familiar equipped. The return rate from this procedure, was however much lower. Data from this group is still being analysed and is not reported in this paper.

Both groups were given the experimental materials and were asked to listen to the audio tape (introducing the RAS system). They then had to read the extract of OU teaching material, and try the exercises in using SQL. When they needed help on the RAS system they were instructed to use the help systems running on the Macintosh, although the exercises themselves were completed on the Amstrad PC version of the RAS system.

On booting the Macintosh, demographic data was collected from subjects by a computer delivered questionnaire. After this each of the prototype HELP systems were available to subjects, accessed by clicking the appropriate button on the Mac screen. A graphic indication of the time spent on each prototype HELP system was given by the gradual filling in a pie chart next to the appropriate button. Additional help on the experimental procedure was given to subjects on screen, accessed from a pull down menu. Finally one more button was available on the screen, allowing access to the Construct Elicitation System. This button could not be selected until all the prototype HELP systems had been tried.

After completing the RAS exercises (which took up to one hour to complete) subjects went on to the Construct Elicitation task. Before they started generating constructs they were asked to rate the prototype HELP systems on a ten point semantic differential scale, with poles Unpleasant to Use, and Pleasant to Use. The Construct Elicitation System was loaded and the process of triadic elicitation started. The CES uses both an open ended way of asking questions about what characteristics of individual interfaces make them distinct from the other interfaces (triadic elicitation) and an ethnographic method (implication laddering) for gathering correlates of the elicited constructs. The elicited constructs form the poles of bi-polar semantic rating scales, on which all the interfaces are evaluated. Feedback of the data is given to subjects as an aid to further construing. Finally the subject is asked to give an extended text description of each construct.

When subjects have finished generating constructs they can leave CES and then quit from the PROTEUS shell. If at any stage a subject wants to refresh her mind about the prototype HELP systems, she can leave CES and view the particular prototype HELP system, then return to CES. When subjects leave CES for the last time they are again asked to rate the prototype HELP systems on the ten point semantic differential scale. These ratings are currently used to estimate if the process of construing alters how the interfaces are perceived, but also provides a mean subjective usability rating for each interface by each subject.

The users actions inside PROTEUS are monitored. When a stimulus interface is called logging is suspended unless supported by code inside the prototype. It is possible for subjects to leave the RAS shell, and continue the evaluation task at another time. Such breaks are also logged

3.5. Data

Subjects spent between two hours seven minutes and four hours forty seven minutes on the task, and completed the task in between one and three sessions. Between five and ten constructs were elicited from each subject.

3.6. Analysis of Data

A review of the data is presented in table 1. This shows the quantitative data from the experiment.

Table 1: Review of Quantitative Data collected by PROTEUS.

	INTERFACES			
	Syntax Help	Textual Help	Exemplar Help	Syntax and Text Help
Ratings Data (1=unpleasant, 10=pleasant) (ranking).	1=7(2) 2=4(2.5) 3=4.5(2.5) 4=1(4) 5=7.5(3) 6=3.5(4) 7=2.5(3) average=4.3(3)	1=8(1) 2=4(2.5) 3=3(4) 4=2(3) 5=6(4) 6=5(2) 7=1(4) average=4.2(2.9)	1=3.5(3.5) 2=4(2.5) 3=7(1) 4=8(2) 5=9(1.5) 6=4.5(3) 7=6.5(1) average=6(2)	1=3.5(3.5) 2=4(2.5) 3=4.5(2.5) 4=9(1) 5=9(1.5) 6=7(1) 7=6(2) average=6.2(2)
Number of Uses	1=1 2=2 3=3 4=3 5=6 6=6 7=3 average=3.4	1=3 2=5 3=3 4=4 5=6 6=5 7=3 average=4.14	1=2 2=3 3=2 4=3 5=9 6=2 7=2 average=3.28	1=2 2=4 3=2 4=3 5=2 6=6 7=2 average=3
Total Usage (seconds)	1=2651 2=1261 3=2014 4=321 5=327 6=404 7=305 average=1041	1=294 2=183 3=309 4=173 5=393 6=532 7=176 average=294	1=819 2=816 3=1532 4=142 5=852 6=653 7=244 average=723	1=315 2=223 3=109 4=154 5=386 6=4626 7=191 average=858

The quantitative data shows that subjects used the different help systems between three and four times during the study. Total usage times are probably less informative in this study than number of uses, since users spent time doing the RAS learning task whilst a particular help was running. Number of uses does not vary significantly between the different interfaces. The ratings data does give a clear indication of user preferences regarding the different systems. The Syntax and Text help and the Exemplar Help systems are rated higher than the Syntax on its own or the Text on its own. This observation is reflected in the CES data of most subjects, with the exemplar and text and syntax help systems matching closely on six of the seven element trees.

The data from the Construct Elicitation System has been analysed using the FOCUS algorithm, Shaw (1980), Jankowicz and Thomas (1982). Results from the analysis are displayed as two binary trees per subject. The binary trees show the similarity matchings for the constructs elicited from subjects, and for the interfaces as the subject saw them. This method of displaying the construct data makes certain features more apparent. It is possible to see which interfaces are seen as very similar, and which interfaces are seen as quite different. It is also possible to compare individuals and see if those similarities are common to most people or unique to individuals.

In this study the element trees of most subjects showed a high level of correlation between the Exemplar and Text&Syntax help. This supports the view that the CES data is reflecting perceived usability, as intuitively the Text and Syntax help system would be correlated more closely with the either of the other two systems, which are identical in part. The CES data appears to reflect perception of the system as a whole, rather than simply the physical characteristics of the systems.

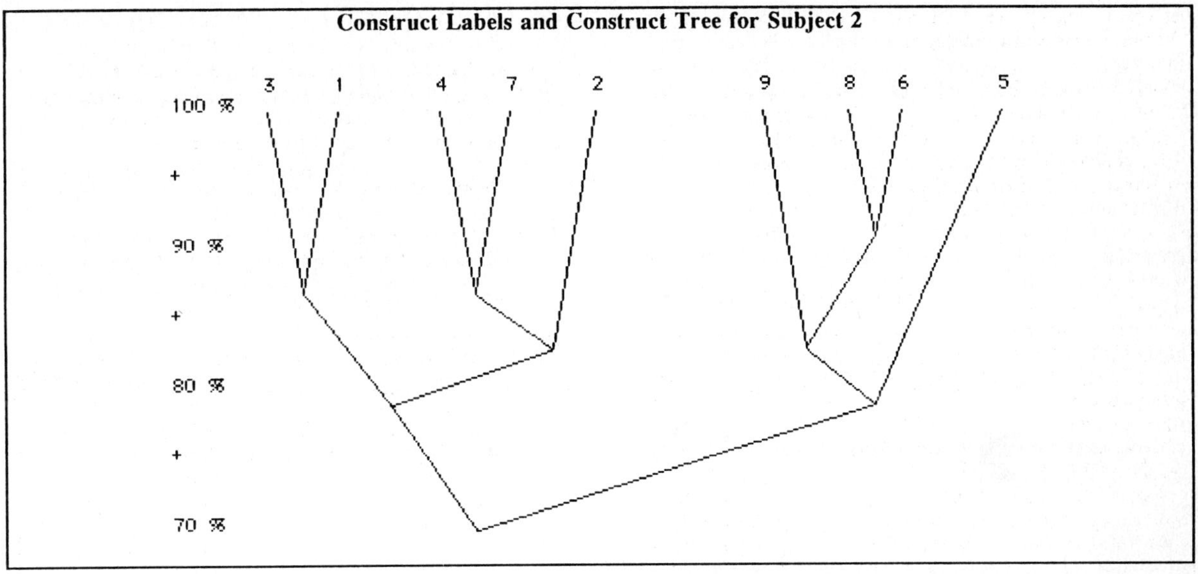

CONSTRUCTS:-

1: EXPLANATION STRATEGY
A: DESCRIPTIVE
B: EXEMPLARY
"Descriptive attempts to explain the relevant process, whereas exemplary shows it."

2: FORM
A: STRUCTURAL
B: NON-STRUCTURAL
"Structural uses a formal notation, the other a natural language description"

3: CONTENT
A: FORMAL
B: SUBSTANTIVE
"This distinction is between showing the form or grammar of a command, and giving the substantive application of it"

4: STYLE
A: EXPLANATORY
B: DEMONSTRATIVE

5: APPROACHES TO EXPLANATION
A: SINGLE
B: MULTIPLE

6: SCOPE
A: MINIMAL
B: FULL

7: UTILITY
A: USEFUL
B: LESSUSEFUL
"I avoided the phrase useless, as I found all of the systems had some utility, depending on the nature of my problem eg. wanting to know the correct grammar, or reminding myself of the meaning of a particular term"

8: ELEGANCE
A: ELEGANT
B: INELEGANT
"An aesthetic response."

9: EASE
A: INTUITIVE
B: OBSCURE
"Whilst the syntactic form has elegance, it is not immediately intuitive to me"

The construct tree for subject 2 is fairly typical of the structure of data generated by CES. The construct trees make more apparent the number of distinct ways an individual is using to distinguish between the different interfaces. For example it may be that constructs with very different verbal labels attached to them are used in approximately the same way by an individual. This is true in the Subject 2's construct tree, where 'Style' is seen as similar to 'Utility'. Looking at the raw rating data from subject 2 it is possible to see that this construct is used in a similar way to describe all the help systems, although the poles are reversed, so that 'Useful' systems are aligned with 'Demonstrative' systems, and 'Less Useful' systems with 'Explanatory' ones. This helps illuminate one aspect of the task presented in this study, where subjects were asked to complete simple operations in SQL. In this task understanding of syntax is much more useful than understanding why a particular command should be use. From the point of view of a learning package, this type of help can distract attention from the underlying principles that are being taught.

3.6. Giving the Data back to the Designer...

PROTEUS allows the identification of user significant issues, within an overall context of designer significant issues. It does this by identifying both a verbal description of the issue, and its relationships to other issues, and to particular designs, and their features. It also allows a designer to identify the extent to which he is cognizant of particular issues, even though they may be expressed in different linguistic terms. Constructs are not represented only by verbal labels, which are open to misinterpretation and misunderstanding especially where designers meet users of a fairly different background (for example system designers and OU students). The ratings data provides a framework in which the verbal labels take on an extra dimension.

Currently the system designer is evaluating the data from this study, and will consider what form of improvements should be made to the RAS help system.

4. SUMMARY

Although the study was not taken in an optimally ecologically valid setting, in practice the laboratory environment used was probably not distinctly different from an ideal students learning setting. Equally the subjects used were not directly concerned with studying an Open University course. Fortunately all the subjects were interested in finding out about the learning material, and after the study all the subjects stated that they had learned a little more about relational databases.

Although the systems evaluated were very similar to each other, the PROTEUS methodology has produced distinguishing data between the prototype systems. The process of producing recommendations for the system designer is still to be completed, and further work is being undertaken to develop methods for giving the data back to the designer. These include improved interactive graphical representations of the data.

5. FURTHER WORK

The issue of giving back of data to the designer has not been fully addressed in this paper. Current work involves exploring ways of making the significant aspects of the CES data more explicit to designers. Data from the CES is currently essentially individual data, however because the data is generated by experience of the same set of interfaces, it becomes possible to look for similarities in construing between individuals. Further work is currently being undertaken in the representation of group data generated from clustering algorithms.

ACKNOWLEDGEMENTS

The work described in this paper was supported by an Open University research grant.

REFERENCES

Briggs, P., (1987) Usability Assessment for the Office: Methodological Choices and their Implications, in, Psychological Issues of Human-Computer Interaction in the Workplace, (Frese, M., Ulich, E., and Dzida, W), North-Holland, Amsterdam .

Crellin, J. M., (1988) Personal Construct Psychology and the Development of a Tool for Formative Evaluation of Software Prototypes, in: Proceedings of the Fourth European Conference on Cognitive Ergonomics, (Green, T. R. G. et al. ed.), Cambridge.

Grudin, J., (1989) The Case Against User Interface Consistency, Communications of the ACM, 32, 10.

Honikman, B., (1976) Construct Theory as an Approach to Architectural and Environmental Design, in The Measurement of Interpersonal Space Vol 1, (P. Slater ed.) Wiley, London.

Jankowicz, D. and Thomas, L., (1982) An algorithm for the cluster analysis of repertory grids in human resource development, Personnel Review, 11, 4, pp.15-22.

Kelly, G., (1955) The Psychology of Personal Constructs, Norton, New York.

Marcus, A., (1983) Graphic Design for Computer Graphics, in: Readings in HCI:A multidisciplinary approach, (Buxton, W., and Baecker, R.), Morgan Kaufmann, Los Altos, California.

Robson, J. I., and Crellin, J. M., (1989) The Control Implications Program, in: Contemporary Ergonomics 1989: Proceedings of the Ergonomic Society's 1989 Annual Conference, (Megaw, E. D. ed.), Taylor and Francis, London, pp.172-177.

Stewart, V., Stewart , A., and Fonda, N. (1981) Business Applications of Repertory Grid, Mcgraw Hill (UK) Ltd.

Whiteside J., Bennett J., Holtzblatt K., (1988) Usability Engineering: Our experience and evolution, in: Handbook of Human Computer Interaction, (M.Helander ed.), Elsevier Sciences Publishers, Amsterdam.

Human–Computer Interaction - INTERACT '90
D. Diaper et al. (Editors)
Elsevier Science Publishers B.V. (North-Holland)

A Knowledge-Based Tool for User Interface Evaluation and its Integration in a UIMS

Jonas Löwgren
Dept. of Computer and Information Science, Linköping University
S-581 83 Linköping, SWEDEN

Tommy Nordqvist
National Defense Research Establishment (FOA52), P.O. Box 1165
S-581 11 Linköping, SWEDEN

Abstract

This paper describes and discusses a knowledge-based user interface evaluation tool, based on the *critiquing* paradigm. The tool uses knowledge acquired from experts and from collections of guidelines to evaluate a formal description of a user interface design, generating comments as well as suggesting improvements.

After describing the system architecture and reporting some experiences, the paper focuses on the possibility of incorporating a knowledge-based design tool in a *User Interface Management System* (UIMS), making it possible to give constructive advice to the designer as well as comments. We report some preliminary results from a project aimed at this integration.

1 Introduction

User Interface Management Systems (UIMSs) were originally conceived as tools for facilitating user interface development within the existing software development process. Issues such as rapid prototyping and reusability are well understood and often put forward as advantages gained from using a UIMS. Recently, however, there has been a notable interest in additional support and functionality, not earlier considered part of normal user interface development software. For instance, Myers writes:

> [UIMSs] do not support evaluation. Very few user-interface tools provide any support for evaluating the user interface. More research into how the computer could do such evaluation is needed before such support is practical. (Myers 1989, p. 23)

Similar observations have been made by several authors, including Olsen *et al* (1987) and others. This paper presents a contribution to the research called for by Myers in that we present a knowledge-based system that illustrates the feasibility of computer-supported user interface evaluation. Furthermore, we show how a tool of this kind can be incorporated into a UIMS, providing support for user interface designers in designing and evaluating user interfaces.

Other researchers have contributed work in the same area, notable contributions including the Framer system (Fischer and Lemke 1988, 1989) and a tool called Designer (Weitzman 1988). However, whereas the Framer project focussed on an argumentative environment for design, and Designer only represents low-level graphic design knowledge, our aim is to support *evaluation* of user interfaces on several levels, as we shall see presently.

2 The KRI system

The KRI system (Knowledge-based Review of user Interfaces) was developed as a pilot project in order to assess potential advantages and disadvantages with a knowledge-based critiquing approach to the problem of supporting evaluation of user interfaces. To be precise, we are dealing with what is known as *expert-based* evaluation (Howard and Murray 1987) which comprises evaluation based on an expert's subjective knowledge. The project addressed evaluation of form-filling user interfaces with menu-driven navigation by means of function keys. This section describes the prototype system and discusses some results and conclusions that arose.

2.1 System architecture

The KRI system, being a fairly traditional stand-alone knowledge-based system, comprises the following principal components:

- a knowledge base containing evaluation knowledge;
- a database with user interface design guidelines;

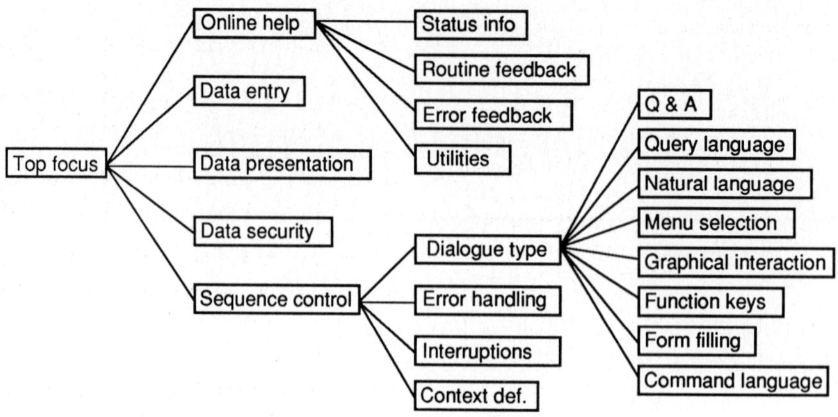

Figure 1: A part of the user interface aspect taxonomy.

- a user interface aspect taxonomy.

The *evaluation knowledge base* is represented in rule form and contains evaluation knowledge from two main sources: (i) transcripts of several expert evaluations of a user interface under development, and (ii) the expert's interpretations of the general user interface design knowledge compiled in guideline documents (Smith and Mosier (1986) and others). In the KRI system only knowledge pertaining to the user interface levels of layout and syntax was implemented. The reason for this, as we shall see in the subsequent section, was that the user interface representation used in the system only supported reasoning about these levels.

The inference mechanism of the system is forward chaining, with the rules designed to detect and report mistakes in the design. This is the most straightforward way of building a critiquing system, but as we discuss in section 4, it is not the only way.

The *guidelines*, which were taken from Smith and Mosier (1986), are not in themselves actively used in the reasoning process of the system. Since the rule base contains interpretations of some of the guidelines, the contents are still there, but the reason for storing the guidelines also in a textual form is different. They are used as justifications for some of the comments generated by the system. We found this to be reassuring to the users of the KRI system.

The *aspect taxonomy*, part of which is illustrated in Figure 1, is used in two ways. First, it is presented to the user of the KRI system as a graph, in which the user can mark the topics of interest for the current session. Secondly, it is used internally as a means of structuring the knowledge base.

2.2 User interface representation

In order for the KRI system to be able to reason about properties of the user interface that is being evaluated, the user interface has to be represented in the system in some way. Given the type of user interfaces that we chose to focus on, viz. systems where the user employs function keys to navigate in a number of menus and a tree of forms to be filled out, we selected a simple version of a transition network where the nodes contain information about which objects (menus and forms) that are currently visible and active, and the tokens labeling the arcs correspond to keystroke commands. The systems are supposed to run on a character graphics terminal with a keyboard featuring arrow and function keys. The objects of the interface are also represented separately with information about their appearance. Thus this representation gives us both lexical and syntactical properties of the user interface.

2.3 System operation

In this section, we describe the work sequence of an evaluation session using the KRI system.

When the designer has developed a design suggestion or a part of a design, it is possible to have this evaluated by the system in the following sequence. First, the user interface representation is loaded into the system.

Next, the evaluation session is initiated. The first thing that the user has to do is to select relevant aspects of the evaluation taxonomy for this session. This selection phase is performed in an interactive way, where the system decomposes the current selections into more detailed topics, at each stage giving the user the opportunity to select the ones that are of interest. To let the user compose his own evaluation plan is a convenient way of addressing the generally very difficult problem of planning evaluation sessions in a supportive way. When the user is satisfied with the foci of interest for the review, the system starts evaluating the user interface design.

In this phase, the system walks through the evaluation plan that the user has just specified and executes the rules that are associated with each evaluation domain. The forward chaining reasoning process generates conclusions and comments about the aspects of the evaluated interface that the knowledge in the rulebase covers. The system also processes the messages somewhat; for instance, when the same flaw is detected in several components of the evaluated user interface, the messages are aggregated to one single comment.

When the system has completed the evaluation, it is possible for the user to browse through the results and examine the comments generated in the evaluation phase. The user can select evaluation domains to analyze further. He can also select specific messages and have the system present the reasons for generating the messages along with suggested improvements. It is also possible to have the system search the guidelines database and present directly quoted guidelines as a source of reference. The following example, where the KRI tool was applied to evaluate an independently developed application, illustrates the kind of comments that the system generates.

2.3.1 Example of evaluation comments

The user interface under evaluation consisted of three separate tables where the user could enter data. Six pull-down menus were available in the top area of the screen. Each table had to be activated before data entry, i.e., the cursor had to be moved to that table. This could be accomplished either by menu selection or by using dedicated function keys. When the evaluation reached the "Function keys" evaluation domain, the following comment was generated (translated to English by the present authors):

> There is a mismatch between the presentation order of the tables and the implicit (ASCII code) order of the function keys used to access the tables.

The reason why the system generated this comment is that the tables (counting from the top of the screen) were activated with function keys 3, 1, and 2, respectively. The most interesting thing about this comment, however, is that it came as a surprise to the designer of the user interface in question. He had used the function keys to reflect the order that he intended to be the most suitable for carrying out the task, not considering the more simple-minded, lexical interpretation of the ordering. His conclusion was that it might be worth considering changing the screen layout.

3 Epistemological issues

In this section we discuss the evaluation knowledge represented in the system and how it can be acquired. Since the level of knowledge is inherently related to what it is intended to reason about, i.e., the user interface representation, we also discuss briefly the issue of user interface representation levels.

User interface design knowledge is compiled and publicly available in collections known as *guideline documents.* Consider and compare the following two guidelines:

1. [For a menu,] related options should be grouped from general to specific.

2. [For a button,] the selectable area should be at least 0.25 in (0.6 cm) square.

They are both taken from a collection of computer graphics guidelines compiled by Davis and Swezey (1983, p. 122), and illustrate well the span of such guideline collections. Ranging from presentation aspects through syntactic and semantic (related to meaning) to pragmatic (task-related) considerations, these guidelines are written for humans to use and interpret. When we want to implement this knowledge in specific design rules, we have to interpret and tailor the guidelines in order to arrive at something usable. As Smith (1988) points out, this tailoring is also related to the specificity of the guidelines: the more general they are, the more they have to be qualified before they can actually be applied.

3.1 Knowledge acquisition issues

As pointed out above, the available collections of guidelines provide an immense source of knowledge about user interface design. This knowledge has to be classified and sometimes specialized before it can be used in a reasoning system, and a highly relevant question is to what extent the guidelines are applicable at all for this purpose. Let us dwell for a moment upon how the guidelines relate to the actual knowledge acquisition that was carried out within the KRI project.

Our main method of knowledge acquisition was collecting transcripts of a human factors expert evaluating several user interfaces. The transcripts were then "played back" to the expert and the resulting discussion generated the major part of the knowledge implemented in the system. However, we found that many of the expert's comments pertained to higher levels such as task- and user-related issues (pragmatics) that we were unable to handle due to the fact that our user interface representation concerned only presentation and syntax. The issue of user interface representation level is further discussed below.

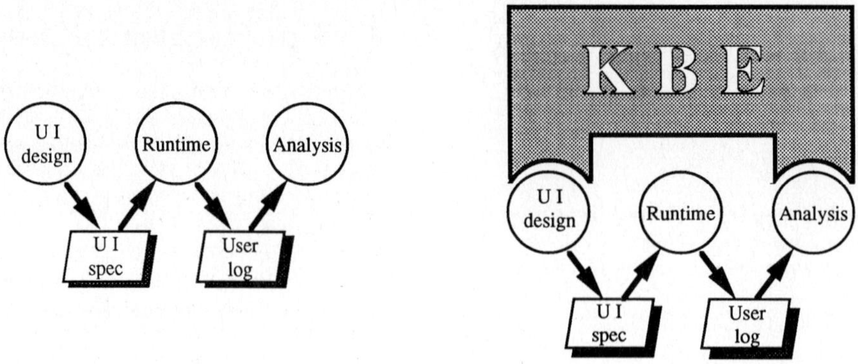

Figure 2: The Seeheim UIMS runtime model (adapted from Tanner and Buxton (1985)), left, and our proposed enhancement, right.

The generality of the guidelines was demonstrated by the observations that (i) it was almost always possible to find a guideline that catered for a remark made by the expert, but (ii) there were almost no guidelines that were specific enough to be implemented directly in the system. Those that were, tended to generate comments that the expert perceived as trivial. In conclusion, guidelines do not seem to replace human experts for knowledge engineering purposes.

3.2 User interface representation

When experts examined the comments generated by the KRI system, a number of these comments were judged either trivial or failing to take semantic aspects or user- and task characteristics into account. The reason for the system's inability to evaluate user interfaces on these levels is of course that the user interface representation used is not concerned with them. This turns out to be a difficult tradeoff situation: high-level representation techniques such as, for instance, the semantic-level representation used in the UIDE system (Foley *et al* 1987) are not commercially feasible when considering compatibility and methodology issues. They are also sometimes very demanding to use. On the other hand, they open up possibilities for user interface evaluation on a level that can not be attained in the more conventional presentation and syntax representations.

4 Enhancing a UIMS

In the previous section, we saw that the KRI system indeed demonstrated the feasibility of a knowledge-based critiquing approach to user interface evaluation support. However, for a system of this kind to support design-time evaluation and hence the user interface designers, it has to be integrated in the design environment (the UIMS). Furthermore, as pointed out by Fischer and Lemke (1988), the integration of working and learning that would be obtained by integrating an evaluation package in the design environment has many potential educational benefits. The rest of this section is devoted to describing a current project that is being carried out with the aim of augmenting an existing UIMS with a knowledge-based evaluation module, designed along the lines of the KRI system. In this context, we also discuss how some of the problems of attaining an adequate user interface representation can be addressed using the UIMS runtime structure. For reasons of space, we can not go into detailed discussions. The interested reader is referred to Löwgren *et al* (1989) for a more thorough treatment of this integration project.

4.1 An architecture

Already in 1983, Tanner and Buxton formulated a model of the runtime structure of a UIMS (Figure 2, left). This model, which has gained widespread acceptance, covers the activities involved in designing a user interface using a UIMS, and the resulting specifications and data. The design process results in a user interface specification (in some representation format) that is executed together with the application at runtime. The UIMS is responsible for collecting a log of all interactions occurring between user and application across the interface. This log may then be evaluated in some way, not further detailed by Tanner and Buxton.

Our proposed enhancement is shown to the right in Figure 2. We can see that the knowledge-based evaluation module (KBE) is intended to support user interface generation as well as evaluation of the interaction log. The current project that we describe below mainly addresses the issue of design-time support. However, we submit that using the interaction log can contribute to the quality of the evaluation in several ways. For example, it is possible to use information from the log to compensate for a less expressive user interface representation. These two aspects of evaluation are discussed in the two following subsections.

4.2 Design-time support

During the phase of user interface design, the KBE module is used for evaluating the user interface specification being constructed. This is accomplished by integrating the evaluation functionality into a design tool, a UIMS. We are currently in the process of integrating evaluation support into TeleUSE, a commercially available UIMS developed by TeleSoft (TeleSoft 1989). It is a general UIMS for graphical interfaces based on the Seeheim model, dividing the user interface into presentation, syntax, and semantic components. The presentation level is expressed in terms of X Windows widgets, while the syntactic aspects of a user interface is implemented in an event handling language based on the D language developed by Hill (1986) in his Sassafras UIMS. This language supports multithreaded dialogue and is responsible for synchronizing the presentation with the application functionality.

The current objective of the project is to support evaluation on the presentation level, i.e., we are augmenting the TeleUSE graphical editor with a knowledge-based module that is capable of evaluating a textual representation of a collection of X widgets. We have decided to implement evaluation on demand as opposed to continuous monitoring. In other terms, there is an evaluation command available for the user of the graphical user interface editor. When this command is invoked, the selected interface objects or the whole interface constructed so far is sent to the evaluation module which generates comments and possibly suggestions for changes.

4.2.1 Functionality of the KBE at design-time

There are a number of interesting design decisions to be made when integrating a KBE into a user interface design tool, including:

- TYPE OF ADVICE. Should the system only point out flaws in the design (like the Framer system), or should it have (at least limited) capabilities of generating design solutions?

- SPECIFICITY. A system based on general design knowledge of the type found in guidelines collections can of course only generate comments on a general, domain-independent level. We feel, however, that one of the most important benefits of an evaluation system integrated into the design environment is its potential to support and enforce organization- and end user-specific design rules.

- LOCUS OF CONTROL. Should the system automatically comment upon every mistake it detects, or should we leave to the designer to call upon the evaluation functionality?

4.3 Post-runtime evaluation

As was demonstrated earlier, the level of user interface representation determines the level of reasoning in the evaluation system. X widgets only determine appearance, and hence that is all that we can evaluate at design-time. But by using the interaction log, it is possible to compensate to some extent for this deficiency. This log, which is essentially a time-stamped protocol of all events pertaining to the user interface, contains a lot of information that can be potentially useful for evaluation purposes. Even though the information is on a lexical level, it allows us to reason about several aspects of the user interface design, including *selection frequencies* (for menu items and the like); *user proficiency*, quantified analogously to the keystroke model (Card *et al* 1983); *common subsequences* that could possibly be factored out; the *empirical syntax* implicitly formed at runtime; *errors* and *help requests*, indicating the dialogue states that are particularly difficult for the user to handle.

In conclusion, we believe that using the runtime log for evaluation purposes is a way of addressing the difficult tradeoff between powerful user interface representations and designer acceptance.

5 Conclusions

The KRI project has indicated a certain potential for success in using knowledge-based techniques for UI design support and evaluation. We have illustrated how this kind of support tool may be used to enhance a traditional UIMS. In addition to supporting the designer in his construction of user interfaces, the tool we propose would also make use of the interaction log collected at runtime. This would to some extent address the problem of needing a very rich user interface representation for the purposes of adequate evaluation, a representation that may be too demanding to use to gain general acceptance. The interaction log to some extent compensates for deficiencies in the user interface representation of the UIMS. Work is under way to implement this architecture, which we feel would be a most valuable tool in the hands of a user interface designer.

Smith (1988) acknowledges that a design tool such as the one outlined in the present paper would shorten the design time and ensure design consistency. However, as he correctly points out, a tool that enforces design guidelines may not be capable of accommodating desirable exceptions and innovative concepts. This is precisely why a critiquing approach to design support is so attractive, combining compliance and non-intrusiveness with the design power equivalent to that of an enforcing tool.

Acknowledgments

The authors are grateful to Sture Hägglund for his valuable comments which helped improve this paper. Göran Forslund and Björn Peters did a nice job of implementing the KRI system. The current project group includes Per Asplund at FOA, Kent Lundberg, Karl-Erik Hedin and Leif Larsson at TeleSoft, Staffan Löf and Göran Forslund at Epitec, and Sture Hägglund at Linköping University, all of whom contributed to the work described in the latter parts of this paper.

References

S. Card, T. Moran, and A. Newell (1983). *The Psychology of Human-Computer Interaction.* Lawrence Erlbaum Associates, Hillsdale, NJ.

E. Davis and R. Swezey (1983). Human factors guidelines in computer graphics: a case study. *Int. Journal of Man-Machine Studies*, 18:113–133.

G. Fischer and A. Lemke (1988). Framer: integrating working and learning. Manuscript submitted to IJCAI 89.

G. Fischer and A. Lemke (1989). Design environments: from human-computer communication to human problem-domain communication and beyond. In *IJCAI'89 Workshop: A new generation of intelligent interfaces*, pages 53–58. Position paper.

J. Foley, C. Gibbs, W. C. Kim, and S. Kovacevic (1987). *A Knowledge Base for User-Computer Interface Design.* Technical Report GWU-IIST-87-11, The George Washington University, Washington DC, August.

R. Hill (1986). Supporting concurrency, communication, and synchronization in human-computer interaction—the Sassafras UIMS. *ACM Trans. on Graphics*, 5(3):179–210.

S. Howard and M. D. Murray (1987). A taxonomy of evaluation techniques for HCI. In *Proc. Interact'87*, pages 453–459.

J. Löwgren, T. Nordqvist, and S. Löf (1989). *Knowledge-Based Support for User Interface Evaluation in User Interface Management Systems.* Research report LiTH-IDA-R-89-32, Linköping University.

B. Myers (1989). User-interface tools: introduction and survey. *IEEE Software*, January.

D. Olsen, M. Green, K. Lantz, A. Schulert, and J. Sibert (1987). Whither (or wither) UIMS? In *Proceedings of CHI+GI'87*, pages 311–314.

S. L. Smith and J. N. Mosier (1986). *Guidelines for Designing User Interface Software.* Report ESD-TR-86-278, Mitre Corp., Bedford, MA.

S. L. Smith (1988). Standards versus guidelines for designing user interface software. In M. Helander, editor, *Handbook of Human-Computer Interaction*, pages 877–889, Elsevier Science Publishers (North-Holland).

P. Tanner and W. Buxton (1985). Some issues in future user interface management system (UIMS) development. In G. Pfaff, editor, *User Interface Management Systems*, Springer Verlag, Berlin.

TeleUSE Reference Manual (1989). 1.0 edition, TeleSoft AB, Linköping, Sweden.

L. Weitzman (1988). *Designer: A Knowledge-Based Graphic Design Assistant.* Technical Report ACA-HI-017-88, MCC, Texas.

Human–Computer Interaction – INTERACT '90
D. Diaper et al. (Editors)
Elsevier Science Publishers B.V. (North-Holland)

MONITORING AND ANALYSIS OF HYPERMEDIA NAVIGATION

Diana KORNBROT and Miles MACLEOD

Hatfield Polytechnic, College Lane, Hatfield, Hertfordshire, AL10 9AB, UK

The use of an interaction monitoring tool in conjunction with commercial spreadsheet and statistical packages is described. The tool was used to monitor and analyse M.Sc. students' use of a hypermedia system with multiple navigation structures to study course content. The final product of the analysis is a description of the navigation routes and methods used by individual students to acquire information from the courseware. Post hoc, students were clearly separable into those who performed relatively more, and those who perfomed relatively less, actions per minute. These two groups were also different in terms of their use of the available navigation structures and the content they chose to visit. The role of high level monitoring tools and associated analysis packages in evaluating hypermedia material, and in answering questions about human learning, is discussed.

1. INTRODUCTION

This paper describes the use of a specialist monitoring tool, in conjunction with commercial general purpose analysis packages, to investigate students' behaviour using Hypermedia learning materials composed of multiple navigation structures. There are two major aims of the research. The first is to answer substantive questions about how students use the courseware in terms of routes and methods of navigation, and topics explored. The second is to illustrate the systematic use of the monitoring and analysis tools, from collection of the raw data in the form of time-stamped protocols, through to the production of results in a form which can shed light on substantive theoretical and pragmatic issues.

Hypermedia systems have the potential of allowing users to follow their own paths through a body of information; but all too easily they can create confusion, if navigation proves too difficult.

Of particular importance for ease of navigation may be the designer's conceptual model of the system structure, of the organization of its nodes and links, and the cues which help a user to form a coherent model. Wright and Lickorish (1989) categorize navigation structures as linear sequences; modules; matrices; hierarchies; & networks. Some structures can be portrayed via a map (Nicol, 1988). Hammond and Allinson (1989) view maps and indexes as access and guidance tools, and show that learners' use of a system is substantially influenced by the tools provided. Monk, Walsh and Dix (1988) describe the use of a hierarchical map, and conclude "It would seem that providing a map ... is of crucial importance".

Monitoring learners' interaction with hypermedia has the potential to provide information of importance to teacher-authors about the content explored in terms of the cards visited, text fields activated and simulations performed. Monitoring can also provide information on the modes of navigation used by learners to control their pathway through an information structure. Such information is important for hypermedia designers because it can give a systematic account of the navigation methods students actually use. It is important for authors because it can provide a principled way for guiding decisions about the presentation and linking of topics. It is important for cognitive scientists because it highlights the processes involved in student initiated learning.

1.1. An Example of Hypermedia Courseware

'HyperCard Basic Concepts' (Macleod, 1989b), is an example of hypermedia courseware presenting the concepts underlying HyperCard™. It employs what may be termed *'conducive redundancy'*: the co-existence of multiple navigation structures, presented to the user in a manner which seeks to enable the formation of complementary conceptual models. The structures are designed to allow the user to explore the system in different ways at different stages of learning, to have multiple means of recovering from getting lost, and to have information available about unvisited nodes.

Some of these structures are represented in the map shown in Figure 1. In total, they comprise the following.

A. *A linear sequence,* intended to allow the student to step gently through the major concepts, using standard arrow screen-buttons, or keyboard arrows. The order of topics in the sequence is given in the topic codes listed in Fig. 1. Cards which exemplify or make subordinate points are only accessible via other links and are deliberately excluded from the linear sequence, they comprise the advance field material and some advanced button material.

B. A *network* of hypermedia links for exploring individual concepts and their connections. The network is designed to provide easy access to related ideas at all points. Network "jump" opportunities are signalled by enclosing the destination name in a box. It has been found necessary to *qualify some of the jump links* with a dialog box outlining the knowledge needed to understand what lies at the end of the link.

C. A graphical *'active MAP'* (or browser) is accessible from any location. This provides a spatial representation of the nodes and their links, a current position indicator, and an immediate means of going to any card (point and click). The map emphasizes a *hierarchical structure* within the network, by highlighting the relevant links.

D. Sub-sequences or topic *modules.* Strongly related adjacent cards are indicated on the MAP by overlapping their icons, and on the cards themselves by signal arrows pointing forward and/or back, within the topic module.

E. Notes and simulation *loops.* Certain words are marked *, signalling that a field with additional text will appear when the user clicks on them. A user may re-hide the note field by clicking it, or by re-clicking the * word (toggle). All still visible notes are hidden by the system when a user leaves a card. Simulations which loop back to their starting point can also be activated by clicking within a card.

1.2. Investigation of Navigation and Content

Hypermedia encourages active learning, but as yet relatively little is known about the global characteristics of its use. The first goal of this study was to obtain a descriptive overview of interaction.

A more detailed analysis of navigation explored the different paths learners took, by comparing the number of actions in each of the navigation structure categories listed above. The means used for navigation were determined by comparing counts of the different kinds of user action in terms of mouse clicks, hypercard menus and hypercard command keypresses. Content was investigated by examining the number of cards visited and time spent per card in each of the major courseware topic areas shown in Fig. 1. Monitoring and analysis was at the level of individual students. This enabled identification of generalizations across students and of individual peculiarities.

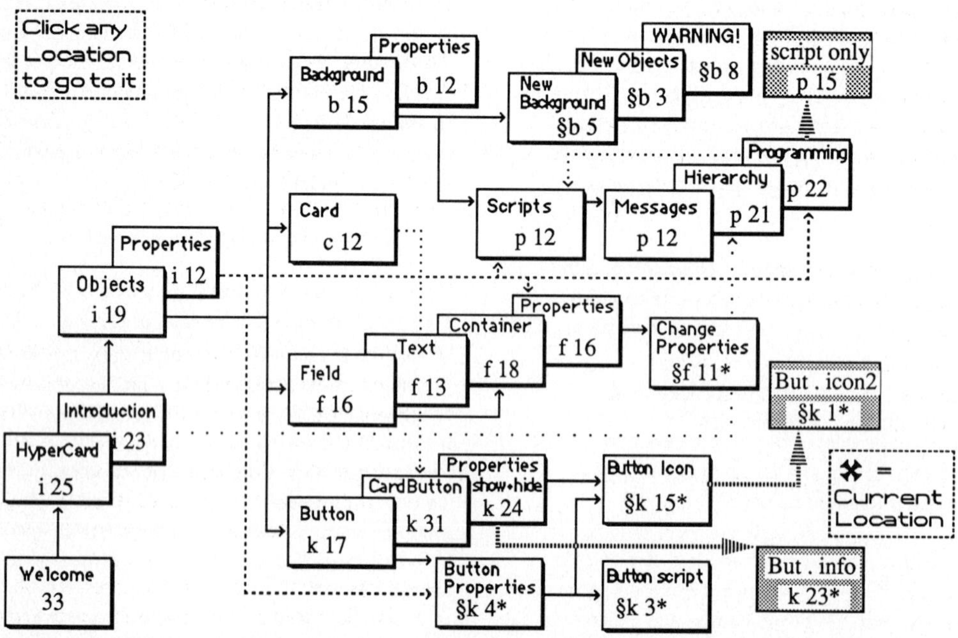

Figure 1. Cards in 'HyperCard Basic Concepts. White background objects and names on them comprise the MAP, as seen by students. In addition, the following items are superimposed and were not seen by students:
(a) grey background cards, reachable as shown by striped arrows; (b) topic area code and total number of visists from all students combined, shown in bold beneath the card name. Topic code in linear sequence order: i=intro; c=card; f=field1, intro; b= background1, intro; k=button1 (key), intro; p=script; §b=background2, adv; §k=buttpon2, adv; §6f=field2, adv.

2. THE MONITOR & ANALYSIS TOOLS

To be useful in answering substantive questions, a monitoring tool has to produce output in a form which is easy to analyse. This is often not the case. The output may require new software to be written for each investigation, (Bull & Kornbrot, 1985; Kornbrot, 1990), or may be very low level (Maguire & Sweeney, 1989). Automonitor output can be easily entered into standard spreadsheets for coding and simple statistical analyses, and thence transferred to statistical packages for more complex analyses.

2.1. The Monitoring Tool: AutoMonitor

AutoMonitor (Macleod, 1989a) is a software device which can capture a time-stamped record of interaction between a user and a HyperCard stack. It is unobtrusive, both in its physical presence, and its effects upon interaction, and is simple to use. AutoMonitor records interaction at the level of user actions upon discrete interface objects, such as buttons, fields and menu items. This avoids the common problem of being overwhelmed by information at the lower pixel and mouse co-ordinate level. The output of the interaction record is in text format. All objects are described by their object type and their name as given by the courseware author. Macleod (1990) describes substantial refinements made to AutoMonitor since Macleod (1989a).

An auxiliary tool, StackMonitor, provides a facility for listing the names of every background, card, field and button in a stack. This can facilitate both the tailoring of object names within a stack, and the subsequent interpretation of actions upon those objects. The object list may be used for inspecting existing object names; checking for missing or duplicated names; and for the creation of an index of stack objects

The AutoMonitor record enables identification of several classes of event which are important for the evaluation of hypermedia systems.
• *Navigation or browsing* through the system.
AutoMonitor records a trace of cards and backgrounds opened and closed, timed to 1/60th second.
• *Display* of pop-up text material ("loops").
The timing of presentation and hiding of fields can be derived from the record.
• *Actions chosen* by users in order to navigate and browse. In HyperCard, these actions may be mouse clicks on buttons and fields, command / keypress combinations, menu choices, or keypresses on the arrow keys, so AutoMonitor records all these individual user actions timed to 1/60th sec.

2.2. Analysis of Automonitor Output

The text form of the output identifies objects by their author-given name. Hence, even non-automated visual inspection enables identification of which navigation structures have been used at which times. In 'Basic Concepts', for example, linear navigation employs the 'Next' and 'Prev' buttons (or arrow keys); use of the map employs the 'MAP' button; and exploration of the network of links employs embedded text buttons.

The spreadsheet EXCEL™ was used for more detailed analyses. Raw data from each student together with the complete objects list from 'StackMonitor' was read into EXCEL. Encoding schemes for grouping together like objects were devised, and implemented using EXCEL's powerful logical functions. For example all buttons with names starting 'go_' were given the navigation action code 8 which corresponds to "jump" in Figure 2. Buttons which initiated jumps but had other names were also given this code. Similarly, each card name was assigned a topic area code. Two versions of the coded data were made for each student: one sorted by card and then by time; the other by user action and then time. Two group sheets containing data from all 8 students were created: one for actions and one for cards and topics. These group coded sheets were transferred to the statistical analysis package STATVIEW 512™ to obtain the statistics which are reported in the results section.

Once the templates have been created, the mechanics of the process of getting the results of a single student/session into the file for STATVIEW analysis takes about 20 minutes. The EXCEL coding frames are available from the authors in a form which could be used as a template for similar investigations of other HyperCard stacks.

3. METHOD

The data for the analysis were captured by monitoring the use of hypermedia courseware in a normal educational environment. Subjects were 4 male, and 4 female students, aged between 25 and 49, in the second year HCI option of a part-time Computer Science MSc 'conversion course'. All had been introduced to HyperCard, and had some experience of beginning to create stacks (programs).

The students were informed that the purpose of the study was to find out about how people use the courseware, 'HyperCard Basic Concepts', when trying seriously to understand and learn about the concepts it presents. They were asked to study the information available in the courseware, for a period of 20 minutes, after which they would have 5 minutes in which to write down what they understood of the concepts presented, for subsequent assessment.

The courseware was used on Macintosh™ IIs, in a relatively uncrowded teaching laboratory. External circumstances were in keeping with the students' experience of studying at a computer.

The verbal instructions were backed up by an instruction sheet introducing the study, and explaining how to use the monitor system, AutoMonitor. This simply required entry of a user name before starting, and the filing of the results at the end. Otherwise, AutoMonitor did not intrude upon their use of the courseware. The monitor data and the students' written analyses were collected for assessment.

4. RESULTS

Table 1 summarizes overall navigation activity and behaviour on card visits for all 8 students.

Overall activity rates ranged from 2/minute to 7/minute and appeared to separate the students into two groups. The "less" active group had activity rates lower than 4/min. while the "more" active group had activity rates higher than 5/min. More detailed analyses shows that there are also differences between the two groups, both in how they navigate and in the topics they explore.

The groups did not differ in the total time spent on the task, or in the number of visits per card. For both groups about a third of the cards are visited only once. The "more" group also use generic hypercard menu and command-key actions more often than the "less" group. Students' median perusal time per card ranges from 13 sec to 50 sec. All time distributions are highly skewed with several visits under 5 sec. and at least some visits over 2 minutes.

Table 1

student	activity				card visits		
	rate[a]	time[b]	mse[c]	mnu+[d]	all[e]	#/card[f]	time[g]
cl	2.0	11.7	57	7	33	1.9	50.3
jo	3.2	5.2	63	4	51	2.6	31.7
ji	3.8	8.5	75	22	46	2.2	23.1
pe	3.9	8.4	90	22	62	2.6	21.5
ha	7.0	5.6	121	29	58	2.8	14.4
je	5.9	5.7	115	33	72	2.4	13.6
br	6.8	5.8	128	36	69	2.8	18.7
bl	5.4	4.1	159	51	71	2.7	23.9

a. overall activity rate, user actions per minute
b. median time between mouse-up actions, seconds
c. mouse up user actions, count
d. HyperCard menu and command/key actions, count
e. card visits, total count
f. number of visits per card, count
g. mean of median card visit time, seconds

4.1. Navigation

Figure 2 show the frequency of different types of navigation action for the "less" and "more" groups. For the "less" group the preferred method of transferring to a new card is via the *linear sequence* using the "next" forward

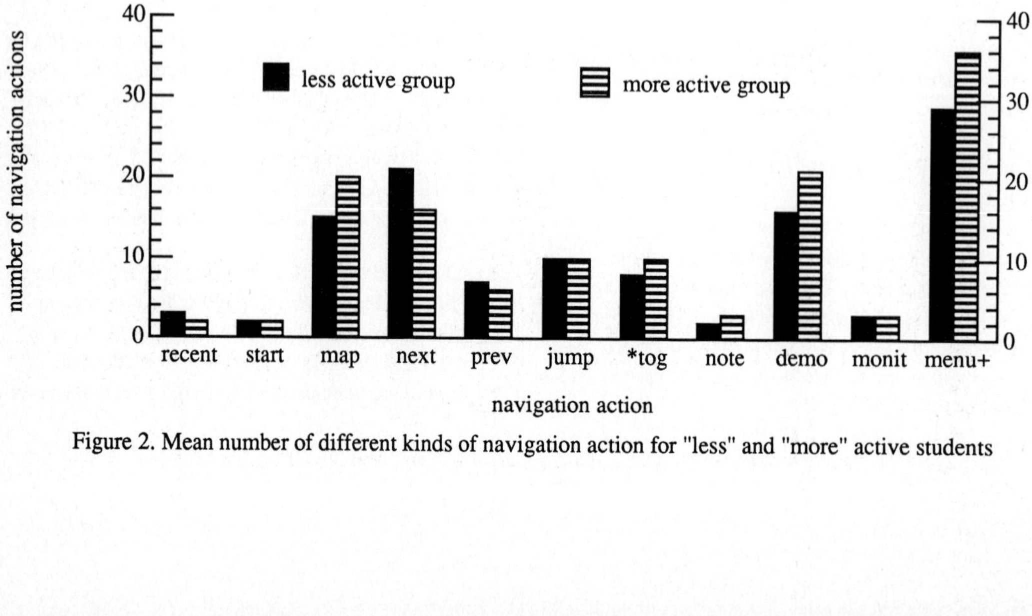

Figure 2. Mean number of different kinds of navigation action for "less" and "more" active students

arrow button. The use of the *network* "jump" method which takes them via one of a small number of author-prescribed routes indicated by an outline box frame is next in order of frequency of use. There is also substantial backtracking using the "recent" and "previous" arrow buttons. Navigation using the "MAP" is relatively rare. By contrast, the "more" group uses "next", "previous" and "jump" with similar frequency to the "less" group, but makes far greater use of the "MAP" route.

In terms of *loops* which occur during a card visit, "more" and "less" students make about equal use of the toggle switch to examine additional note material indicated by the symbol *. The "less" students do *not* click on the notes to make them go away. They either use the toggle by re-clicking on the starred item or leave the item to be closed automatically by the system when they leave the card. The "more" students also spend more time "playing" with the demonstration simulations.

Finally, the "more" students perform more actions on general hypercard objects, as is also shown by their use of the hypercard menu and command key presses in addition to mouse clicking (shown as menu+ in Figure 2).

4.2. Topics

The total number of visits to each card summed across all students, together with the associated topic code, is shown in Figure 1, superimposed on the relevant cards. Cards which accessed simulations have number of visits marked with a *. Only three students visited all the topics and all advanced material was omitted by at least 2 students.

Figure 3 shows the mean time students spent on each major topic content area. The "less" group averaged 18.9 out of 22.6 minutes on content cards while the "more" group averaged 18.7 out of 21.2 minutes on content cards. What is salient is that the "less" group spent more time on the introductory material, while the "more" group spent

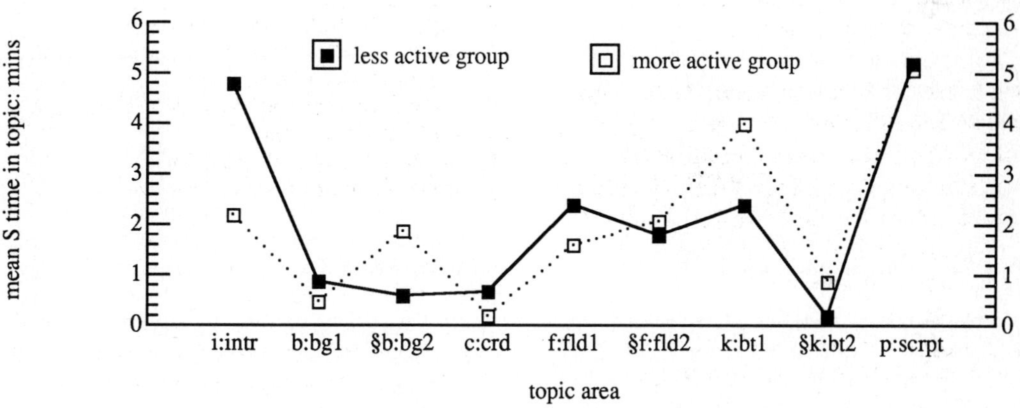

Figure 3. Mean total time in minutes spent in topic area by "less" and "more" active students

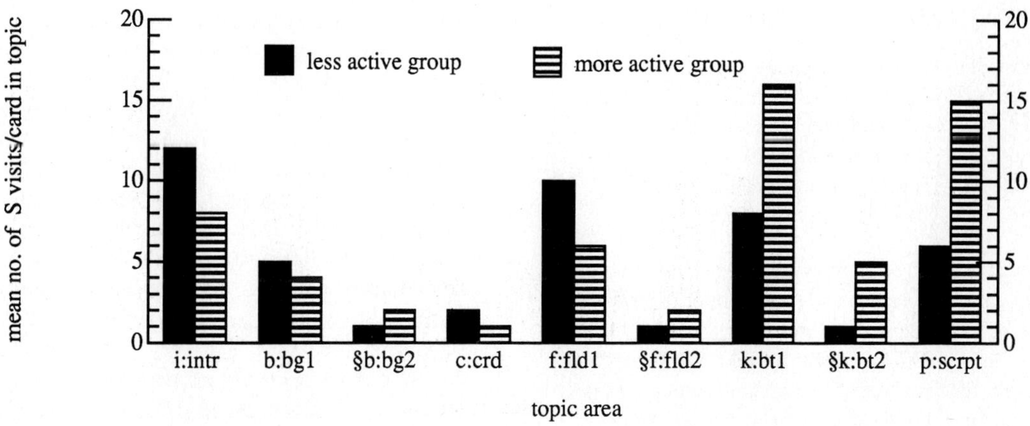

Figure 4. Mean number of card visits in a topic area by "less" and "more" active students

more time on the buttons and the more advanced material. Neither group spent much time on cards and backgrounds.

Figure 4 shows the average number of visits to cards in each topic area. The pattern is obviously similar to that in Figure 3 for time, but there are some important differences. In particular the "less" students make *more* visits to the more elementary topics: introduction , background1 and field1. The "more" students pay more visits as well as spending more time on buttons and background2. However they make more visits to the script topic than "less" students, although total time on this topic is identical.

5. DISCUSSION

The use of AutoMonitor in conjunction with EXCEL and STATVIEW enabled us to produce a clear picture of how students used the 'Basic Concepts' courseware in a real learning task, where they might be motivated to acquire the knowledge for their own purposes, as well as to satisfy course requirements.

Interesting features emerge from the analyses of students' interactions. In terms of navigation, all students used all the available navigation structures. However, "more" and "less" active students had discernibly different patterns of behaviour. In particular, the "more" active students did more navigating via the MAP; spent more time on the interactive simulations; and were more likely to use the generic HyperCard menus and command keys.

In terms of topics visited, all students explored at least some of the less advanced material. There was little difference between students in number of card visits or number of visits per card. Interestingly, all students made multiple visits to more than half the cards, seeming to prefer 'little and often' to a single extended visit. This may may be a general feature of the way people study complex information which merits further investigation.

These substantive findings would have been difficult, if not impossible, to acquire without the use of an object level monitor. Co-ordinate based automatic records do not produce results in interpretable cognitive units. On the other hand, video-recordings do not provide detailed counts and timing of precisely specified events.

The present study serves to illustrate the potential of object based monitoring in general, and AutoMonitor in particular. The logical capabilities of spreadsheets such as EXCEL make it possible to specify any event for analysis, even after the data has been collected, not just those investigated here. For example, one might wish to examine particular sequences of card visits where a student looks successively at all cards which mention 'properties'.

Using AutoMonitor to analyse a considerable body of data with particular substantive questions in mind has led to several changes which materially improved the power, functionality and usability of AutoMonitor. Progress, both in understanding the use of hypermedia for learning, and in the development of better monitoring tools, is likely to result from close collaboration between workers in the role of tool developer, author and HCI psychologist.

In summary, this work serves to show how an object-level monitoring tool can be used to discover psychologically important features of how people use hypermedia for learning. It also relates the use of hypermedia to the available navigation structures.

REFERENCES

Bull, G. and Kornbrot, D. E. (1985). The design of user interfaces to interactive computer systems. Final Report of SERC grant GR/B/70896.

Hammond, N. and Allinson, L. (1989). Extending Hypertext for Learning: An investigation of access and guidance tools; in People and Computers V (Proc. of HCI'89 Conf, Nottingham, U.K. 5-8th September) (Eds. A. Sutcliffe and L. Macaulay), CUP, 293-304.

Kornbrot, D. E.(1990). Situated action and mental models: effect of query language form and function on the formulation of queries to a relational database. Submitted.

Macleod, M. (1989a). Direct manipulation prototype user interface monitoring. In People and Computers V (Eds. A. Sutcliffe and L. Macaulay), CUP, 395-408.

Macleod, M. (1989b). HyperCard Basic Concepts (Macintosh HyperCard software).

Macleod, M. (1990). Tools for monitoring and analysing the use of hypermedia courseware. (Invited paper, NATO Advance Research Workshop, Espinho, Portugal, April 19-24 1990).

Maguire, M. and Sweeney, M. (1989). System monitoring: garbage generator or basis for a comprehensive evaluation system? In People and Computers V. (Eds. A. Sutcliffe & L. Macaulay), CUP, 375-394.

Monk, A.F., Walsh, P. and Dix, A.J. (1988). A Comparison of hypertext, scrolling and folding. In People and Computers IV (Proceedings of HCI'88 Conference, Manchester) (Eds. D.M. Jones and R. Winder), CUP.

Nicol, A. (1988). Interface design for hyperdata: models, maps and cues. In Proceedings of The Human Factors Society - 32nd Annual Meeting), pp 308-312.

Wright, P. and Lickorish, A. (1989) The influence of discourse structure on display and navigation in hypertexts. In Computers and Writing, (Eds. P. Holt and N. Williamson). Ablex.

Human–Computer Interaction – INTERACT '90
D. Diaper et al. (Editors)
Elsevier Science Publishers B.V. (North-Holland)

TOWARDS AN EVALUATION PLANNING AID: A FEASIBILITY STUDY IN MODELLING EVALUATION PRACTICE USING A BLACKBOARD FRAMEWORK

Ian Denley and John Long

London HCI Centre and Ergonomics Unit, University College London, 26 Bedford Way, London, WC1H OAP

This paper assesses the feasibility of the blackboard architecture as an organisational schema with which to model evaluation practice, and to provide an initial input to the development of an evaluation planning aid for practitioners. The paper illustrates the potential of a blackboard framework as a structure for making explicit the classes of knowledge used by human factors practitioners in the evaluation of interactive human-computer systems. A number of case histories of evaluation practice are modelled in terms of the framework, and provide examples of its applicability. It is concluded that the blackboard architecture has potential as a structure with which to model evaluation practice.

1.0 INTRODUCTION

The intention of this paper is to assess the feasibility of the blackboard architecture as a structure within which to model current evaluation practice employed in the development of human-computer interactive work systems. Current evaluation practice is based largely on expert problem solving, by use of implicit knowledge and experience in particular commercial contexts. It is intended here to appraise whether these characteristics of evaluation practice are amenable to analysis using the blackboard architecture as a means both to represent the outcomes of the evaluation activity and to make explicit the classes of knowledge involved. This modelling activity is intended to form the basis for the construction of a planning aid that will contribute to the London HCI Centre's evaluation activities.

The notion of 'blackboard systems' originated in the field of Artificial Intelligence as a means of constructing knowledge based systems to solve complex problems which are dependent on different kinds of knowledge and expertise, (for example, the Hearsay II speech understanding system, Erman et al 1980). The architecture of a blackboard system is based on a metaphor of group problem solving whereby a number of 'experts' are assembled to solve a given problem using blackboard and chalk.

2.0 REQUIREMENTS ON THE BLACKBOARD ARCHITECTURE FOR MODELLING EVALUATION PRACTICE.

The activity of modelling evaluation practice is intended to provide an organisational schema within which to systematise the collection of data and knowledge concerning current evaluation practice. The aim of this activity is not only to create an opportunity to improve understanding of the structure and limitations of such practice, but also to provide an initial input to the development of an evaluation planning aid.

These goals place a number of requirements on the blackboard framework for the modelling activity. First, the framework must be capable of supporting the modelling of different types of evaluation behaviours and knowledge (for example, that of human factors practitioners and that of software engineers). Second, although the blackboard framework must be capable of modelling an individual evaluator's behaviour, there is no necessary requirement here for such models to represent explicitly the mental processes of that evaluator. Rather, the blackboard framework should support the understanding of evaluation practice more generally, such that the strengths and weaknesses of evaluation practice can be made sufficiently explicit to support the development of an evaluation planning aid. In addition, some technical shortcomings of the blackboard framework (such as its difficulties in modelling control or meta-knowledge) may be of no consequence, since there is no intention to implement the planning aid in software as a blackboard system. Indeed, the first version of the planning aid is likely to be a paper-based version.

Taken together, these considerations suggest that the blackboard architecture may be a suitable structure with which to model evaluation behaviour. The purpose of this paper is to assess this suitability on the basis of a rapid 'first pass' at modelling a number of examples of evaluation practice.

3.0 A FRAMEWORK FOR EVALUATION PRACTICE

An earlier paper proposed a framework for evaluation practice that attempts to provide a structure within which to identify common components of the practice of human factors evaluation regardless of the wide variation that exists in that practice. Two key concepts were identified, namely: *performance setting* and *performance evaluation.* (Denley and Long, 1990)

The framework is represented schematically in Figure 1, and briefly described in the following section.

Figure 1 - Schematic of the Framework for Evaluation Practice as Components of System Development Practice

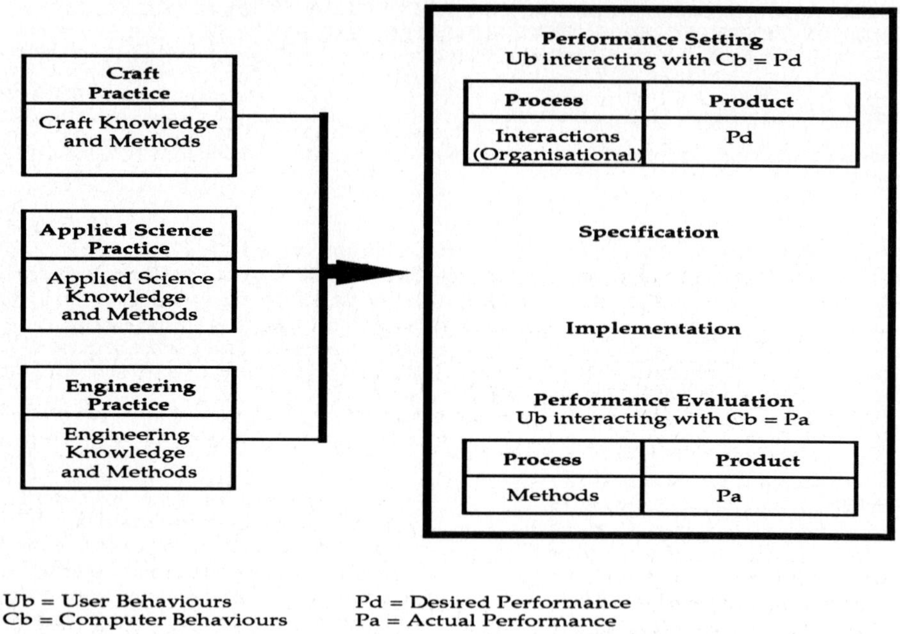

3.1 Performance Setting

For the purposes of evaluation practice, performance setting has both a *process* and a *product*. The *process* of performance setting focuses on the (organisational) interactions between the human factors evaluation practitioner, the system developer, the system sponsor and the user in agreeing the purpose, tasks and effectiveness of the interactive work system, the system development role of the evaluation to be performed and its goals. This agreed position should define the task performance which is desired and which is to be evaluated. The *product* of performance setting is the specification of criteria and metrics for the agreed desired performance. Desired performance will be expressed according to the type of system development practice in question. i.e. craft, applied science or engineering (see Long and Dowell, 1989).

3.2 Performance Evaluation

Performance evaluation assesses the actual performance (P_a) of the implemented interactive system against the criteria for desired performance specified during performance setting. As with performance setting, performance evaluation has both a *process* and a *product*. The *process* of performance evaluation is essentially the use by the human factors practitioner of suitable evaluation methods. The *product* of performance evaluation is a value for the actual performance (P_a) of the interactive work system expressed in the same terms as the criteria and metrics for desired performance (P_d) agreed during performance setting.

4.0 THE BLACKBOARD FRAMEWORK

It must be emphasised that the blackboard framework that supports the modelling activities presumes the general framework for evaluation practice proposed here and which is intended to support a common and coherent perspective for all types of evaluation practice.

The blackboard architecture is generally agreed as comprising three defining features, (see for example, Craig 1988). These are:

1) The *blackboard*, which is a structured database which organises the information leading to solution of the problem of concern, and whose state expresses that solution (or some intermediate form thereof).

2) The *knowledge sources*, which represent the knowledge necessary to solve the problem, and which communicate information to the blackboard one at a time.

3) A *control mechanism*, which decides between knowledge sources competing to communicate information to the blackboard at the same time.

Each of these architectural features, and their relevance to modelling evaluation practice is described next.

4.1 The Blackboard

The blackboard is a structured database that mediates the interactions between different knowledge sources and contains the current state of the problem solution. The blackboard supports two functions: it records in turn entries communicated by knowledge sources (activated by the preceding entry), and so represents in aggregate at any one time the intermediate states of problem solving activity.

The blackboard can have a number of dimensions. The vertical dimension distinguishes different *levels of abstraction*, and the horizontal level may reflect other dimensions of the solution, (for example temporal, spatial or conceptual). The process by which blackboard systems construct solutions is incremental and is based on the progressive application of knowledge solution elements at various levels of abstraction. This process allows the problem under consideration to be addressed at different levels of description. The partial results generated during problem solving by the knowledge sources are stored on the blackboard as *entries*.

4.2 The Knowledge Sources

A knowledge source is an independent collection of knowledge(s) appropriate to the problem space, in this case the planning and implementation of human factors evaluations of interactive worksystems. The knowledge source can be conceived as as a set of production rules, such that if a rule's conditions are satisfied (by an entry on the blackboard) then its actions are implemented and a new entry is communicated to the blackboard. Such a rule might be: *if* time is short, *then* use a human factors expert walkthrough evaluation method. The knowledge sources can either propose solution hypotheses or can test solution hypotheses currently on the blackboard, that is they can be *generative* or *evaluative*. (Whitefield and Warren, 1989). They also contain different *classes* of knowledge.

4.3 Control

The final component demanded by the architecture is a control mechanism, or scheduler. The control mechanism determines the system's problem solving activity when alternative activities are possible. During the problem solving process, many different knowledge sources may be triggered either by data entered onto the blackboard or by previously generated partial solutions. At each point in the solution process, several new blackboard entries would be possible, since a number of knowledge sources may be simultaneously activated by the same entry to communicate information to the blackboard, and it is the responsibility of the control mechanism to decide which knowledge source should be allowed to communicate its entry to the blackboard.

5.0 MODELLING EVALUATION PRACTICE USING THE BLACKBOARD FRAMEWORK

The blackboard framework described earlier was applied to a number of examples of commercial evaluation practice carried out by the London HCI Centre. These case studies are described below, and are then examined using the framework. The results of the modelling activities have been pooled to identify a set of knowledge sources that are applicable **only** to *performance setting*, (this set, however, is not claimed to be exhaustive at this time). The modelling reported here is limited to performance setting to reflect the current state of the research, and to accommodate the limitations on space. However, since performance setting and performance evaluation have much in common (see below), if the framework is shown to be feasible for modelling setting, it would also be expected to be feasible for modelling evaluation.

On the basis of this pooled set of knowledge sources, an hypothetical example of performance setting is examined to suggest how the modelling activities may contribute to the development of a planning aid. The contribution results from identifying the classes of knowledge necessary at particular levels of abstraction in the human factors evaluation activity of performance setting.

5.1 Three Case Studies of Evaluation Practice

The three examples of evaluation practice modelled later were carried out by consultants from the London HCI Centre:

5.1.1 Integrated Project Support Environment - IPSE 2.5

The work described here was conducted by the London HCI Centre as part of a project entitled *Developing a Service for the Evaluation of Advanced Interactive Software Engineering Systems*. (Funded by the DTI).

The IPSE 2.5 project is developing a generic IPSE tool based on integrating the *processes* of information systems development, rather than (as in most IPSE projects) on integrating the *entities* of information systems development (i.e. data and tools). Thus, the project seeks a generic tool to support the whole development process rather than a collection of tools which assist particular activities within that process.

IPSE 2.5 has been planned to support an extensive range of development processes, both because no two development processes will be identical and because each development process will necessarily evolve throughout its life-cycle. The approach relies upon explicit process descriptions written in a Process Modelling Language (PML) that allows different development processes to be described.

The evaluation in this instance was not one of investigating the performance of the IPSE 2.5 system concerning its effective use, but of introducing the system into a new organisational environment.

5.1.2 Integrated Project Support Environment - Analyst Assist

The work described here was conducted by the London HCI Centre as part of a project entitled *Developing a Service for the Evaluation of Advanced Interactive Software Engineering Systems*. (Funded by the DTI).

Two integrated tools have been developed by the Analyst Assist project to support the tasks of the systems analyst. These are a fact finding tool to assist requirements analysis; and a specification builder for translating these requirements into a Jackson System Development (JSD) specification.

The Fact Gathering Tool requires that analysts enter information in the form of Conceptual Graphs which are formalisms for representing concepts. The evaluation in this instance focused on the ease of learning and use of conceptual graphs in general, and their use within the context of the integrated toolset.

5.1.3 RACE Project 1054 - Application Pilot for People with Special Needs

The work described here was performed as part of a European collaborative project (funded under the RACE program - Research and Development in Advanced Communications Technologies in Europe).

This case study focuses on the specification of an evaluation plan, designed for use by European service organisations which are being established to provide viodeotelephony-based support services for the elderly. These organisations provide information and counselling to elderly people in their own homes via a videotelephony system.

5.2 Data collection

Two techniques were used to obtain information from the case studies mentioned above. The first procedure is based on observing human factors practitioners interacting with clients during commercial consultancy, this is called *Observing Interactions*. Case study notes were taken by the observer which were supported where possible by tape recordings and verbal protocols. Following the observations, semi-structured interviews were also conducted with the consultants to identify important classes of knowledge and clarify areas of uncertainty. These interviews included *expert walk/talk-throughs* during which the consultant was asked to talk the observer through aspects of the case in order to identify the consultants' solutions to specific problems.

5.3 Identification of the Levels of Description for Performance Setting and Performance Evaluation

The data collected from the case studies were analysed and classified. Analysis of the problem solving behaviours of the human factors consultants resulted in the identification of three levels of problem description for the activities of performance setting and performance evaluation. Whitefield (1989) suggests that such an hierarchic view of design problem setting and solution is corroborated by much of the psychological literature on design. These levels of problem description are reflected in the models. The models have two blackboards - one representing "*performance setting*" and the other representing "*performance evaluation*"- both of which contain three levels of abstraction. These levels are shown in Table 1.

Each of these levels constitutes a complete (but re-expressed) description of the information appearing at any other level, and this transformation between levels is mediated by the appropriate knowledge sources. The levels on the performance setting blackboard represent the outcomes of the dialogue between the client and the evaluator as expressed in agreement and specification of their goals and requirements, and in the conceptualisation, specification and implementation of the desired

Performance Setting Blackboard	Performance Evaluation Blackboard
Performance Conceptualisation	Method Conceptualisation
Performance Specification	Method Specification
Performance Implementation	Method Implementation

Table 1 - Levels of Abstraction of the Blackboards

performance (P_d) of the system. (Note that, implementation on the performance setting blackboard refers to the re-expression of the higher level descriptions of performance setting, and not to the instantiation of desired performance). On the performance evaluation blackboard, the levels of abstraction represent the outcomes of the evaluator's behaviour as expressed in the conceptualisation, specification and implementation of the evaluation methods necessary to meet the requirements agreed in performance setting and to obtain a value for actual performance. (P_a)

On the horizontal dimension, each blackboard has a *time line* that reflects the outcomes of the activities of the client and the evaluator. Both the problem setting and the evaluation solution spaces can be developed incrementally, temporally and at different levels of abstraction. The two blackboards are not able to write to each other, but communicate via the entries of *communication knowledge sources*, and so share partial results, and refine both the problem and the solution. This 'communication' between the blackboards may be especially important in complex, novel problems where little *a priori* knowledge is able to specify an optimal sequence of necessary decisions.

5.4 Identification and Classification of the Knowledge Sources for Performance Setting

The data were also analysed to classify the knowledge sources used by the evaluation practitioners. The classification comprises a number of dimensions. First, in common with evidence from the design literature (see Whitefield, 1989), it became apparent that knowledge sources can be *generative* or *evaluative*. Generative knowledge sources create new solution entries either within or between blackboard levels, and evaluative knowledge sources assess, and so may modify, existing entries on the blackboards, but can only act at a particular level. It should be stressed that evaluative knowledge sources are not simply those pertaining to the evaluator, but also include those of the system developer. Second, analysis of the content of the knowledge sources used by the practitioners allowed the identification of two dimensions of concern; these were knowledge sources associated with *performance knowledge,* and the knowledge sources associated with the *process of organisational interaction.*

The above, then, provides a classificatory system for identifying and examining the knowledge sources used in evaluation practice. Such a classification applies to each level of abstraction of both blackboards.
Tables 2, 3 and 4 present the results of the modelling activities with respect to the performance setting blackboard (the results are not claimed at this time to be exhaustive).

	Generative	Evaluative
Performance Knowledge	Problem statement concerning system and its use (1) Client product development objectives Client's evaluation goals (5)	Current HF state Project status and history (2) System state
Process Interactions (Organisational)	Client's view of HF Client's view of evaluation Roles and outcomes	Management strategy Competence level of client Evaluation end-user status External influences

Table 2 - Example Knowledge Sources for Performance Setting at the Level of Performance Conceptualisation

	Generative	Evaluative
Performance Knowledge	Software/hardware Technology state Users (3) Tasks (4) Usage environments (6) Sub-problem statement (9)	Domain access System development cycle Problem tractability
Process Interactions (Organisational)	Budgets Deadlines	Project deliverables Project timescale HF evaluator's experience

Table 3 - Example Knowledge Sources for Performance Setting at the Level of Performance Specification

	Generative	Evaluative
Performance Knowledge	System availability Subject availability	Consultant's training needs System familiarisation
Process Interactions (Organisational)	Workgroup roles Personnel (7) Payment	Information exchange mechanisms Detailed expected outputs Client support (8)

Table 4 - Example Knowledge Sources for Performance Setting at the Level of Performance Implementation

The tables represent the knowledge sources of both the evaluator and the system developer. Those knowledge sources that are numbered in brackets are examined in more detail in Section 5.5, and also relate to Figure 2. The identification of knowledge sources is an on-going activity, and a more complete set (including a consideration of the activity of performance evaluation) will be reported at a later date.

5.5 An Example of Modelling Performance Setting.

This section illustrates how the modelling activity could be applied to a simplified example of performance setting based on the knowledge sources identified in the above case studies. The purpose of this description is to show how the outcomes of a dynamic problem solving activity for a particular performance setting cycle is capable of being modelled by the blackboard framework. The example also shows the iterative nature of the relations between knowledge sources and between blackboard levels. This description offers some insight into the nature of the proposed planning aid, insofar as it suggests the scenario of its use, i.e. the aid is likely to have a structured format offering appropriate knowledge and advice at different levels of description.

Performance setting can be conceived as a problem solving dialogue between the evaluation practitioner and the system developer. The blackboard framework, by modelling the outcomes of the client's behaviour (the system developer) and the consultant (the evaluation practitioner), provides a means of making explicit the knowledge sources relevant to this dialogue cycle, and important for the setting of the desired performance of the interactive computer system in question.

In this section, the knowledge sources that have been identified as important for performance setting (Tables 2, 3 and 4), are used to exemplify an hypothetical cycle of a performance setting dialogue between the client and the consultant. Knowledge sources associated with the evaluator and the system developer are not distinguished, since the likely use of the planning aid has no requirement at present for them to be distinguished.

Figure 2 illustrates the modelling of an hypothetical individual cycle of performance setting. The figure should be interpreted in conjunction with Tables 2, 3 and 4.

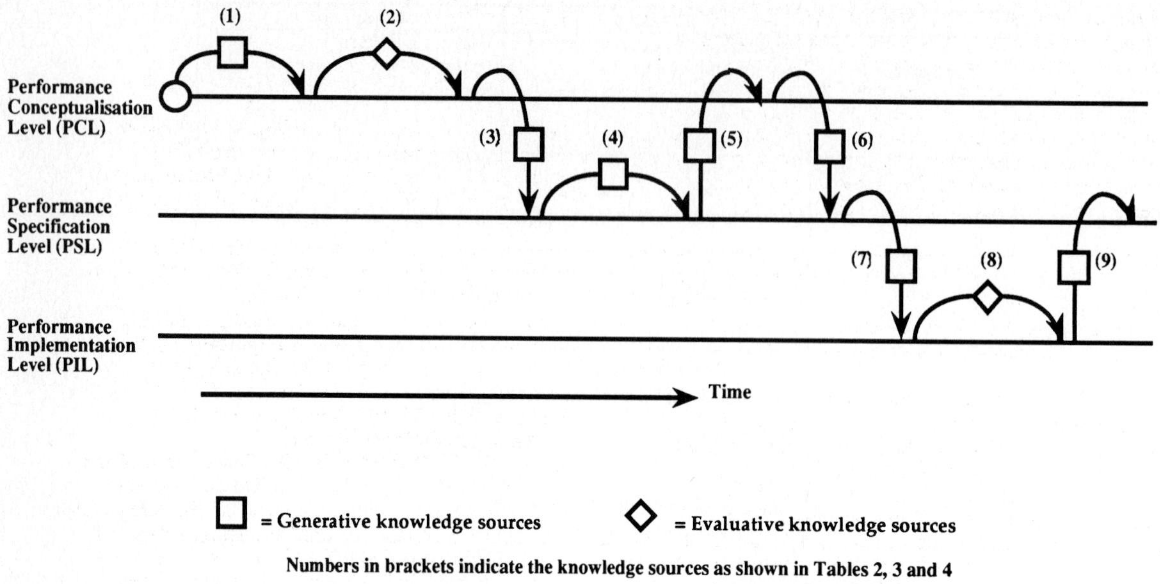

Figure 2 - Modelling a Performance Setting Cycle

Figure 2 shows that the dialogue begins with a problem statement by the client concerning the system (under consideration for evaluation) and its use, modelled by an entry from generative knowledge source 1 (GKS 1) at the Performance Conceptualisation level (PCL) of the blackboard. (Note, initial entry to the blackboard can be at any level i.e. the model can support both top-down decomposition and bottom-up abstraction of the problem.) The consultant responds by evaluating the statement in terms of the status of the system development project and its past history, modelled by an entry from evaluative knowledge source 2 (EKS 2) at the same level (PCL). Details concerning the users (GKS 3, PSL) and the tasks (GKS 4, PSL) envisaged for the system under development are exposed. The details result in a general description of the client's evaluation goals (GKS 5, PCL), which in turn leads to the provision of details concerning the target usage environments for the system (GKS 6, PSL). Concern with the target environments results in the disclosure of information concerning the personnel of the client, for example, whether any of their usage environments approximate to that of the target system (GKS 7, PIL). Reference to the client's personnel leads to an assessment of their willingness to take part in user evaluation trials of the system (EKS 8, PIL). The result of the assessment is a sub-problem statement concerning the specification of problem setting (GKS 9, PSL). This interplay between generation and evaluation of entries continues until performance setting is completed. The completion reflects the achievement of the dialogue in conceptualising, specifying and implementing the performance setting for the system.

6.0 CONCLUSIONS

The main purpose of constructing models of current evaluation practice is to make explicit the classes of knowledge used by human factors evaluation practitioners, and to improve understanding of the relations between these different classes of knowledge. This paper has attempted to show how the blackboard framework is a suitable structure for this purpose. Additionally, a number of case histories were modelled in terms of the framework, and have provided some simple examples of the applicability of the framework.

Given the current analysis, there are a number of problem attributes to which a blackboard architecture can be applied (Englemore and Morgan, 1988), and which make it particularly suitable for examining current evaluation practice. These problem attributes are examined below, and their relationship to evaluation practice, as evidenced in the examples (and more widely), is suggested:

1) *The need for distinct and specialised knowledge in problem solving*. It is clear that evaluation practice is dependent on a wide range of classes of knowledge, and the blackboard architecture allows this diversity to be identified and modularised as distinct and independent knowledge sources.

2) *The need to integrate a variety of sources of information.* The blackboard architecture allows different kinds of information to be organised at different levels of abstraction. This structure is important for evaluation practice, where the evaluator may be drawing on many different kinds of information and knowledge exposed at different levels of detail.

3) *A requirement for hierarchical concepts*. The more obvious is the need for concept hierarchies, the more attractive the blackboard framework. Evaluation practice is a component of system development practice which is itself essentially hierarchical in nature, in that its general process abstractions, such as specification, can be decomposed, for example, into detailed procedures. Likewise, knowledge of the domains of application of the interactive computer systems to be evaluated can also be decomposed.

4) *The need for incremental problem solving*. Blackboard systems build solutions incrementally, such that there is always a partial solution at any given time. This approach has similarities with the design behaviour of system developers. (Lawson 1980; Whitefield 1989).

Additionally, as mentioned earlier, control is a problem for the implementation of blackboard systems, and so constitutes a shortcoming of the blackboard framework. However, the current purpose is not to implement a system, but to use the blackboard framework as an organisational schema within which to systematise the collection of data and knowledge concerning current evaluation practice in order to provide an input to the development of a planning aid. Control knowledge to support the use of the planning aid could be provided by the planning aid itself, in terms of advice, for example, about evaluation *per se*, and by the user of the aid in terms of their own control knowledge of system development and problem solving more generally. The shortcoming of the blackboard framework concerning control, then, does not constitute a problem for the construction of the planning aid.

In sum, it is proposed here that the blackboard framework is a useful means to represent and analyse evaluation practice, and that results are sufficient to warrant the use of the blackboard framework in a more extensive and complete modelling of that practice. It is intended that this extended modelling will provide an important contribution to the development of a planning aid to support evaluation practitioners. In this respect, identifying the class and status of knowledge used in evaluation practice allows reasoning about how this knowledge may best be applied and supported, and improves the focus of the planning aid currently under development.

ACKNOWLEDGEMENTS

Thanks are extended to colleagues at the London HCI Centre who contributed to the case studies reported in this paper. I am particularly grateful to Andy Whitefield and Carolyn Selby for the IPSE evaluations, and to Mick Ussher and Margaret Welbank for the RACE videotelephony study. This research is carried out with funding from the Science and Engineering Research Council (SERC) as part of an ALVEY project (MMI 151).

REFERENCES

Craig, I. (1988). Blackboard Systems. *Artificial Intelligence Review,* 2, 103-118

Denley, I., and Long, J.B. (1990). A Framework for Evaluation Practice. In: E.J. Lovesey (Ed). *Contemporary Ergonomics 1990*. Proceedings of the Ergonomics Society's 1990 Annual Conference, Leeds. Taylor and Francis. London.

Englemore, R., and Morgan,T. (1988). (Eds). *Blackboard Systems.* P 561-563. Addison-Wesley Publishing Company. Wokingham, England.

Erman,L.D., Hayes-Roth, F., Lesser, V.R., and Reddy, D.R. (1980): The Hearsay-II Speech-Understanding System: Integrating Knowledge to Resolve Uncertainty. *Computing Surveys, 12, (2).*

Lawson, B.R. (1980). *How Designers Think.* Architectural Press. London.

Long,J.B. and Dowell,J. (1989). Conceptions of the Discipline of HCI: Craft, Applied Science, and Engineering. In A. Sutcliffe and L. Macaulay (Eds): *People and Computers V. Proceedings of the Fifth Conference of the BCS HCI SIG*, Nottingham 5-8 September 1989. Cambridge University Press.

Whitefield,A.D. (1989). Constructing Appropriate Models of Computer Users: the Case of Engineering Designers. In: J.Long and A.Whitefield. (Eds) *Cognitive Ergonomics and Human-Computer Interaction.* Cambridge University Press

Whitefield,A.D., and Warren,C. (1989) A Blackboard Framework for Modelling Designers Behaviour. *Design Studies,* Vol 10, No 3, July

Human–Computer Interaction – INTERACT '90
D. Diaper et al. (Editors)
Elsevier Science Publishers B.V. (North-Holland)

Providing Intrinsic Support for User Interface Monitoring

Jolly Chen

Laboratory for Computer Science
Massachusetts Institute of Technology
Cambridge, MA 02139, U.S.A.

Effective user interface evaluation requires unobtrusive recording of dialogue data. This paper examines how dialogue information can be acquired from monitoring the communication channels between different linguistic levels in the user interface model. Adding built-in monitoring mechanisms to the architecture permits recording of dialogue information not otherwise accessible from low level input recording techniques. Intrinsic support also allows an application program to be monitored without modifying the application source code. Enhancements have been made to the Xt Intrinsics architecture as a sample implementation of this approach.

1 Introduction

Interactive programs today are expected to provide sophisticated graphical user interfaces. These user interfaces are generally time-consuming to create and traditional approaches to software design have proven inadequate in addressing the difficulties specific to the development of interactive programs. Only recently have methods, techniques, and tools been developed to support construction of complex user interfaces. It is now generally accepted that quality user interfaces can only be constructed by using an iterative design strategy[4]. Iterative design involves constructing prototypes, evaluating those prototypes, and then modifying the design based on the evaluation. Evaluation of an user interface involves recording dialogue information and using that information to make design changes. The process is repeated until an acceptable user interface is reached. More tools are becoming available that enable the interface designer to rapidly construct prototypes; however, few automated tools exist to help the designer evaluate those user interface prototypes. The tools that do exist predominantly monitor dialogue at a low level. As a result, the burden of adding instrumentation to monitor human-computer dialogue is usually left to the application programmer.

This paper introduces the strategy of recording dialogue information at the boundaries of the linguistic layers of the user interface model. Such recording can be supported directly by the intrinsic architecture itself and requires no modifications to the application program. A sample implementation of this approach is discussed in relation to the Xt Intrinsics[7, 8] architecture.

1.1 Terminology

Dialogue is the observable exchange of information between two parties. In this document, the term dialogue refers to communication between the user and the computer unless otherwise specified. The *user interface* is the software and hardware that supports this dialogue. The user interface includes the windowing system and the window manager as well as hardware such as graphical displays, keyboards, and pointer devices. The *application* is the computational component of an interactive program. The application performs the algorithmic transformation of inputs into outputs. *Evaluation* refers to the process of assessing the system according to some set of objectives or criteria. In this document, evaluation refers to empirical evaluation rather than analytical evaluation, i.e. the aim is to evaluate the interface based on data from actual usage sessions rather than to evaluate the design of the interface apart from a working prototype. Furthermore, only the software portion of the user interface is considered. *Monitoring* means observing in an unobtrusive and non-invasive manner. Monitoring also includes some means of *recording* the dialogue information.

2 Linguistic Model

The linguistic model views the interaction between the user and the computer as a dialogue. The dialogue can be partitioned into four layers: lexical, syntactic, semantic and conceptual[5]. The lexical layer translates raw user inputs such as keystrokes and pointer movements into tokens. Sequences of tokens are formed into commands in the syntactic layer. The semantic layer gives meaning to those commands. Tasks that users wish to accomplish and objects that the users are familiar with make up the conceptual layer. Though not universally applicable, the linguistic model provides a good framework for reasoning about user interfaces.

3 Higher level dialogue information

Most dialogue recording is currently done at a very low level. In the X Window System[1] environment, some work has been done to provide means of recording input and output events[6, 9]. Events are the information units by which the X servers and the X clients communicate. While capturing raw events is useful for reproducing a user session, that level of detail is not as helpful in reasoning about the user interface as a whole. The interface designer is more likely to be interested in knowing that the third item of a particular menu has been selected than in knowing that the mouse pointer has moved to coordinate (103,320). The former kind of dialogue information is that which is communicated between the syntactic and semantic levels, i.e. commands. The interface designer is often more interested in the sequence of coarse grain commands formed by the user than in the sequence of fine grain raw input events.

In addition to knowing which commands were formed, the interface designer may also be interested in knowing how the command was formed. For instance, the designer may want to know whether a certain command was invoked by a button press in a window, by highlighting an item in a list, or by a keyboard accelerator sequence. This type of information is that which is passed between the lexical and the syntactic layer, i.e. tokens. It is useful to know which tokens formed the command because the token usage pattern may show how the user is adapting to the dialogue model presented him by the user interface. For example, a novice user and an expert user may use very different sets of tokens to form the same command.

Dialogue information at the semantic level is also important. Such information, however, can usually be recorded only by explicit mechanisms in the application program itself. Since modifying the application source is undesirable, that type of monitoring will not be discussed here. Higher level dialogue information will be broadly referred to as *incidents.*

3.1 Incidents

An *incident* is defined as a user-initiated occurrence which generates a reaction from the program. The reaction may not necessarily be a visible response. The program may make some logical response that does not affect input or output directly. An incident can be considered, in some sense, an event in which the program is interested. Incidents, however, are not necessarily raw user events. Incidents are at a higher level of abstraction that may represent a sequence of user events.

An incident requires that the program react in some way. The reaction must come from the program, not other parts of the environment like the windowing system. The reaction must also entail more than simply recognizing the occurrence. For example, if the program completely ignores button presses on inactivated menu items, then those button presses are not incidents. On the other hand, if the program performs error handling when inactivated items are chosen, then those button presses are incidents. Another example is pointer movement. Moving the pointer generates a visual response of updating the cursor. This response, however, usually comes from the windowing system and does not involve the application. In that case, pointer motion itself is not an incident. On the other hand, an application may perform recalculations based on the change in coordinates of the pointer. In such a case, pointer motions would be incidents.

The definition of an incident may seem rather arbitrary. Since the granularity of an incident varies and can be as fine as a raw user event, why must

[1]X Window System is a trademark of M.I.T

there be a distinction between the two? Because an event is too general in nature, there needs to be a way to distinguish between all events and those events that are interesting to the particular program. The reason that the granularity of incidents is not specified is that different applications will require different granularities to suit their evaluation needs. For example, in most text applications, keystrokes would not be incidents. The application probably does not react directly to each letter entered because it is more interested in the entire text string. It would be more important for the dialogue designer to know that a certain string has been entered than to know that a certain key was pressed multiple times in the formation of a word. In other words, the application may not be interested in knowing that the user had to backspace several times to correct typographical errors. On the other hand, in an application like a typewriter simulator, it may well be important to know exactly which key were pressed. In that case, key presses would be incidents.

An important aspect of incidents and events is that they are information units that can be communicated. Events are already handled via explicit channels between the server and the client. Similarly, it is much easier to deal with incidents if they are communicated through explicit channels in the user interface architecture.

3.2 Incidents in the Xt Intrinsics model

The Xt Intrinsics model provides a measure of separation between the application and the user interface. It provides a policy-free substrate on top of which toolkits and application environments can be built. The Intrinsics layer supports abstract user interface components called widgets as well as inter-component and intra-component communication. Thus, the concepts of incidents and communication channels can be mapped fairly well unto the Xt Intrinsics model. The Xt Intrinsics supports objects and class hierarchy. Methods can be added to existing object classes via extensions.

This document will focus on two kinds of incidents: tokens emitted from the lexical layer, and commands emitted from the syntactic layer. In the Xt model, the latter corresponds roughly to *callbacks* and the former corresponds roughly to *actions.* A callback is an incident that generates a reaction from the application component of the program. For example, by clicking on a command widget, the user invokes a callback procedure. A particular widget class may service various kinds of callbacks but only those callbacks for which the application registers procedures are considered incidents. This is consistent with the definition that incidents must generate a response from the program. Empty callback procedures are not incidents. Actions correspond roughly to tokens in that a sequence of events is translated into a sequence of actions. An action can be considered an incident that generates a response from the user interface component of the program. For example, clicking on a scroll button in a viewport widget generates an action that is serviced by the widget and not the application. Another example of an action is the highlighting of a command button. The command widget does not require application intervention to highlight itself when the pointer enters the window. In the Xt model, actions can also encapsulate application semantics because the application programmer is not restricted to the actions provided him by his toolkit. Thus, actions do not always correspond exactly to tokens emitted from the lexical layer; however, actions are always incidents because they elicit response from the program.

4 Recording Incidents

An incident recording tool should meet several criteria. First, the tool must be able to access incidents and allow the user of the tool to specify incidents of interest. Second, the tool must be unobtrusive. The less the application program needs to be modified in order to interface with the monitoring tool, the more immediately useful the tool will be. Third, the tool must be efficient. The monitoring mechanism must not incur a costly performance overhead. The more the speed or feel of the original interface is compromised because of recording requirements, the less accurate the evaluation will be.

4.1 Instrumenting the intrinsic architecture

The requirements outlined above can be met quite satisfactorily by instrumenting the intrinsic user interface architecture. Given an object-oriented architecture and a logical division between the application component and the user interface component, it is possible to make modifications to monitor the communication channels. The modifications are straightforward if the communication mechanism is well isolated. In the Xt Intrinsics, the code controlling the invocation of callback and action procedures is relatively easy to isolate and modify. In other object-oriented architectures, changes may need to be made to message passing channels.

The modifications involve adding an observer at the appropriate location in the communication channels. The automated observer examines the communication traffic and notes those incidents which have been specified by the user interface designer. The user interface designer specifies in advance those incidents that are *interesting.* If an interesting incident passes, then the observer queries the sender of that incident for a more detailed description of the incident. Identification and querying of source and targets in the communication channel is made possible because source and targets are objects. Each object class that can send incidents is required to provide a query method. The detailed description returned by the query procedure is logged by the observer.

In the Xt model, interesting incidents can be easily specified because callbacks and actions can be identified by name. In addition, widgets are partitioned into classes so they may be specified by class or instance. For example, the evaluator may specify a menu widget named "Folders" or the entire class of pulldown menu widgets. Naming is a powerful feature of the Xt intrinsics that may not be available in other user interface architectures.

The communication channels provide good access for monitoring incidents. In comparison, if monitoring support was added on the application end, it would be difficult to locate the source of the incident as the application may be sent a similar incident from different user interface objects. For example, in a mailer interface, the application program may be sent the incident **OpenFolder** by a number of different user interface objects, corresponding to the different ways that that command may be invoked. By the time the incident reaches the application, it is difficult to tell from which widget it came. If, on the other hand, the monitoring support was added only on the toolkit end, it would be more difficult to selectively log incidents of interest. Each widget class would need some way of checking whether or not it should be logging dialogue detail. The incident recording would be tied to the toolkit so that if a different toolkit were used, the entire incident recording mechanism would need to be moved. In either case, code would be repeated and scattered in either the application components or the widgets.

Placing the monitoring support at the architectural level is both unobtrusive and efficient. The application component does not need to be modified at all. The user interface toolkit does need to provide some query procedures that supply information about widget state. As long as the toolkit provides such query procedures, any toolkit built on the same intrinsic layer can be monitored. Aside from adding query procedures to existing toolkits, incident monitoring can be achieved with a simple relinking of code. The proposed monitoring mechanism is also quite efficient. The incident detail is sent by the observer to another logging process to be saved and processed. The performance of the application component remains largely unaffected because no code changes were required there. The performance of the user interface toolkit may be slightly affected due to the need to respond to queries and report incident detail. The overall performance of the program is slightly affected due to the presence of the additional logging process in the system. Because incidents are not as fine grain as raw events, efficiency hits are taken much less frequently than a similar event recording mechanism.

5 Sample implementation

The changes proposed above have been made to the R4 version of the X11 Intrinsics. The modifications required only a small number of code changes. To take advantage of the monitoring, an application program needs to be relinked with the new Xt library. The monitoring mechanism makes use of the resources mechanism in X to specify incidents. Below are some sample specifications for monitoring the mail handler xmh.

`XtMonitor*Xmh*Action: On`
- monitor all actions in Xmh-class programs

`XtMonitor*Xmh.comp*Callback: On`
- monitor all callbacks in the comp widget in Xmh-class programs

`XtMonitor*Xmh*XmhIncorporateNewMail: Off`
- do not monitor the action XmhIncorporateNewMail in Xmh

`XtMonitor*xmh-jc*toc.ScrollBar*Action: On`
- monitor all actions of Scrollbar widgets inside the widget toc in the xmh-jc program.

`XtMonitor.xmh.xmh.tocMenu.inc.callback: On`
- monitor the callback in the inc button on the tocMenu menu

The monitoring mechanisms assume that the widget classes provide well known query procedures. A simple query procedure has been written for the core widget class so that those widget classes that do not have more specific dialogue detail to return can simply inherit the default query procedure. By using the extension mechanisms in Xt, an easy way of adding query procedures to existing widget classes has been provided for toolkit writers. The query procedure is allowed to return arbitrary text information concerning the state of the widget. The default query procedure returns information about the widget name, the widget class, and the time used by the application response to the incident. The duration is a conservative estimate of the amount of "wait time" the user faces. It takes as least this long before the user can do something again with the user interface. This time is easily measured in single-threaded systems because the user interface blocks while the application procedure is executing. The user interface is able to continue only after the application returns.

Currently, the format of the incident description is simple ASCII text. This makes processing of the data somewhat unwieldy because of the volume of the dialogue information logged. As an interim solution, the output of the logging mechanism is piped to an awk[3] script that compresses and stores the information to file. A better solution is to store compressed, binary information.

A sample post-processing analyzer has been written to manipulate this data. The user interface analyzer is essentially a small database management system tailored to handle dialogue data. The analyzer is able to sort the data by fields as well as provide summaries by field. For example, the analyzer is able to tell the interface designer such things as how often a certain incident occurred, which incidents had the longest wait time, and what the breakdown was between the different kinds of gestures that caused an incident. The analyzer is also able to perform some simple pattern matching. For instance, the interface designer may query the analyzer for all incidents patterns that begin with the **Help** action and end with the **Cancel** action. That kind of information would give the designer a sense of how and when Help is being requested and canceled. The analyzer is able to handle wildcards so that if the incident names were indicative of their functions, multiple incidents can be searched via wildcards. An example of a valid query is a request for all sequences of four incidents or fewer where the first incident matched **Xmh***. The analyzer itself provides a graphical user interface so its user interface can also be monitored and analyzed.

Some data has been gathered from recording usage of the Xmh mailer interface. Analysis of that data is in progress. Unfortunately, there are currently few other applications written with the R4 Xt Intrinsics. Motif[2][2] and OPEN LOOK[3][1], are examples of widget sets built on top of Xt. More applications built on top of those toolkits are expected in the near future.

The intrinsic recording mechanism proved to be efficient. There were no noticeable delays in use of an instrumented version of Xmh. More careful timing measurements showed the overhead per incident was in the range of a few milliseconds. The most frequent incident in Xmh proved to be character entry. Even the fastest typist can not notice per character delays of less than 10 milliseconds. Other types of direct manipulation interfaces, however, may require a lower overhead. Further improvements and speedups are both possible and anticipated.

6 Future work

Much improvement can be made on this initial implementation. More work needs to be done in determining exactly what kind of dialogue detail should be logged. The sheer volume of data to be logged remains a problem. Although incidents may be selectively recorded via the resources specification, it is often useful to see the whole transcript of incidents throughout the entire session. One possible improvement would be to allow different levels of detail to be specified. Instead of a simple on/off in the resource specifications, different values could signify different levels of detail. In this way, detailed descriptions of special target incidents would be recorded while much less detailed

[2] Motif is a registered trademark of Open Software Foundation

[3] OPEN LOOK is a registered trademark of AT&T

descriptions of other incidents would be recorded to show context.

The current approach also does not take into account output incidents originating from the application end, namely. Much more consideration needs to be given to that area. The prospect of playing back incidents seems possible but exceedingly difficult. It would be useful to be able to replay the incidents at some level even if the use session cannot be reproduced in its entirety. Complete reproduction does not seem possible without additional lower level event information and output incidents.

7 Conclusion

In summary, recording incidents seem to be a good way to complement existing methods of recording dialogue information. Incident recording can be supported by adding recording mechanisms to the user interface architecture itself. The conditions are that the architecture must be object-oriented and that the communications channels must be somewhat accessible. A sample implementation of the proposed approach has been made to the Xt Intrinsics architecture. The modifications were easy to make and the same approach can be applied to other user interface architecture. The benefits of adding monitoring support in the intrinsic layer are ease of specifying target incidents, unobtrusiveness, efficiency, and the ability to monitor the dialogue without changing the application source code.

More work needs be done with the incident monitoring approach proposed here. The sample implementation should give way to more efficient and more robust implementation. This monitoring mechanism should be integrated with other monitoring mechanism to provide a more complete user interface evaluation tool. Good evaluation tools will enhance the productivity of user interface designers and enable them to create better user interfaces for the future.

References

[1] An OPEN LOOK Toolkit for the X Window System.

[2] Open Software Foundation. *Application Environment Specification (AES) User Environment Volume.* Prentice Hall, 1990.

[3] A.V. Aho, B.W. Kernighan, and P.J. Weinberger. *The Awk Programming Language.* Addison-Wesley, 1988.

[4] W.A. Buxton and R. Sniderman, *Iteration in the Design of the Human-Computer Interface*, Proceedings of the 13th Annual Meeting of the Human Factors Association of Canada, pp 72–81.

[5] J. Foley and A. van Dam, Fundamentals of Interactive Computer Graphics, Reading, Massachusetts, Addison-Wesley. 1982.

[6] A.G. Jamison, *Experiences Developing X Server Support for the Programmed Control of a X Window Workstation*, 4th Annual X Technical Conference, Boston, MA, January 1990.

[7] J. McCormack, P. Asente and R.R. Swick, *X Toolkit Intrinsics – C Language Interface, X Window System, X Version 11, Release 3*, X11R3 distribution, 1988.

[8] R. Rao and S. Wallace, *The X Toolkit: The Standard Toolkit for X Version 11*, USENIX Summer '87 Conference, pp 117–130.

[9] L. Woestman, *X11 Input Synthesis Extension Proposal*, X11R3 distribution.

SECTION III: DETAILED DESIGN

SIII.1 Menus

Are all menus the same? An empirical study
Z. Mills and M. Prime 423

Pull-down, HoldDown, or StayDown? A theoretical and empirical comparison of three menu designs
M. Macleod and P. Tillson 429

The use of guidelines in menu interface design: Evaluation of a draft standard
F. de Souza and N. Bevan 435

Decision track: A formalism for menu structure and user's selection behaviour
W. Edmondson 441

Human–Computer Interaction – INTERACT '90
D. Diaper et al. (Editors)
Elsevier Science Publishers B.V. (North-Holland)

ARE ALL MENUS THE SAME ? - AN EMPIRICAL STUDY

Zsuzsanna Mills and Martin Prime

Rutherford Appleton Laboratory, Chilton, Didcot,
Oxfordshire, OX11 OQX, England.
martin@uk.ac.rl.inf

In the "direct manipulation" style of interacting with computers pop-up menus are becoming increasingly popular. The present study looks at the speed and accuracy of six different menu styles falling into two main groups, "moving" and "static" menus. After an initial "ballistic response task", subjects carried out a block of 15 selections with each menu style. The order of the menu styles was randomly varied for each subject to counter-balance possible "fatigue" and practice effects over subjects. The order of the items on the menus was also randomised to force subjects to use visual search at each trial rather than relying on their memory of the item's position from previous trials. The analysis of the response latencies for menu item selection indicates a clear performance advantage with static menus. There was no interaction between "skill level", determined by the ballistic response task, and performance on the menu selection task. The fastest and least error prone amongst the menu styles proved to be the circular menu.

1. INTRODUCTION

Pop-up menus are an important interactive technique used increasingly in direct manipulation environments. A popular misconception is that expert users view menus as a cumbersome method of interacting with the computer. Antin found, that "although command entry produced performance superior to the other two modes [menu selection and a combination of command and menu selection mode], there was a strong user preference for the combined mode. These results dispel the notion that menus are necessarily viewed as a hindrance by experienced users of a computer system." [1]

Poorly designed menus may affect the usefulness of a program; may require a long time to get used to and may even become a constant source of irritation to the user.

Research has been carried out into many aspects of menu design. A good survey of them can be found in Shneiderman's book [7] about user interface design. Issues such as command language versus menu selection; names versus numbers versus icons as menu constituents [2]; the semantic organisation of menu items [7]; trade-offs between height, breadth and width in tree-structured menus [5]; alphabetical versus probability of selection versus random versus positionally constant menu arrangements [8]; colour-coding categories in menus [6]; and pie versus linear menus [3] have all been studied. This latter study found, that target seek times were faster and error rates were lower with pie menus, than with linear ones. However, it would seem that there was a potential confounding of target area with menu type which could have given rise to the advantage of pie menus.

The present study is an empirical comparison of 6 different menu styles falling into two main groups, "moving" and "static" menus. Moving menus are classified as such because items on them move as the mouse is moved. The scrolling menu, used by many application programs, is a good example of this category. On the other hand, items remain stationary on static menus and users select a required item by either moving a highlight bar or a pointer to it.

2. METHOD

2.1 Subjects

30 subjects of both sexes, aged from 21 to 50, took part in the experiment. All were members of Informatics Department at the Rutherford Appleton Laboratory. 15 subjects were experienced Sun users, 9 used Suns occasionally and 7 were inexperienced.

2.2 Apparatus

All subjects used the same Sun 3/75 workstation, Sun Workstations® is a registered trademark of Sun Microsystems, Inc. The Suns had a monochrome (black and white) display (1152 by 900 resolution) and a three-button optical mouse on a movable mousepad coated with a specially formatted reflective material. The mouse speed used was that of SunView's default setting. (SunView™ is a trademark of Sun Microsystems, Inc.) Mouse speed is the ratio of physical movement on the optical pad to on screen cursor movement. SunView's default setting is scale factor of 2. The experiment was controlled entirely by software. 6 pop-up menu styles were used, 3 moving and 3 static. All menus displayed the same 8 items resembling typical wordprocessor selections, like "delete", "replace", "search". The menu items were displayed as black characters on white background using "screen.r.14" font. The precise sizes of the font in pixels was width: 8; max. height: 11; capital letters: 11, height of lower case x: 7; baseline: 11 Highlighting or inverse video (white characters on black background) indicated selection.

The 3 stationary menus were:
1. Regular Menu: was similar to SunView's default menu. On pop-up all 8 items were visible with a horizontal pointer pointing to the first item, but items were not separated by lines. Subjects selected an item by moving the pointer to it, thus highlighting it and releasing the left mouse button.

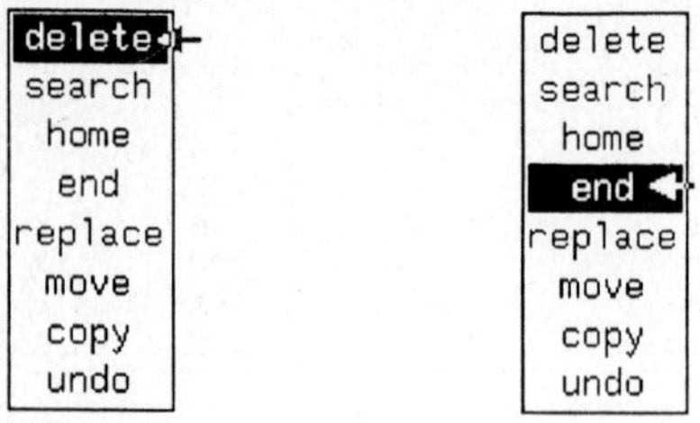

Pop-up Selection

2. No Pointer Menu: was similar to the regular menu, but had no pointer. Subjects moved the highlighted bar up or down by moving the mouse up or down.

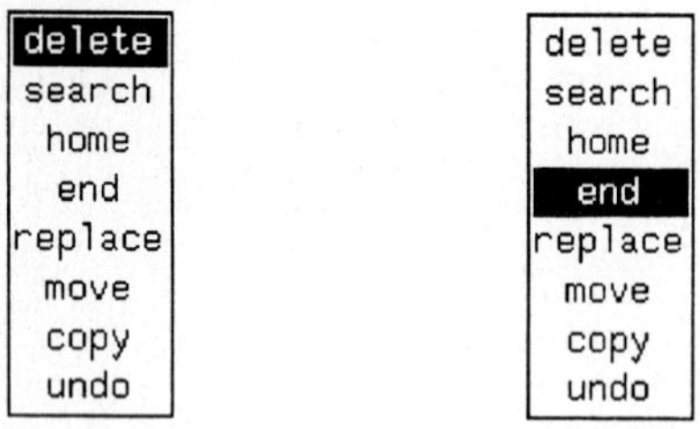

Pop-up Selection

3. Circular Menu: was circular as its name suggests with the 8 items distributed evenly in an equi-angular fashion. On pop-up the menu was centred at the cursor position so the pointer had to be moved an equal distance to highlight the required item. The area of activation was the same as for other menus and the same kind of highlight bar indicated selection.

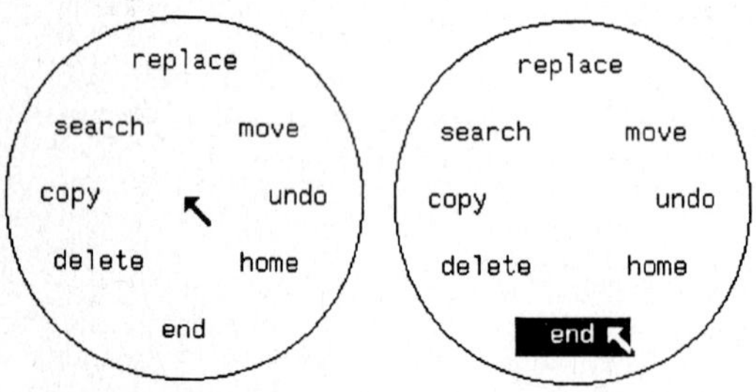

Pop-up Selection

The 3 moving menus were:

1. Rotating Menu: on popping up the menu all items were displayed and the first highlighted. To select the required item, subjects had to rotate it under the highlighted bar, which never moved. Items could be rotated in either direction by moving the mouse up or down.

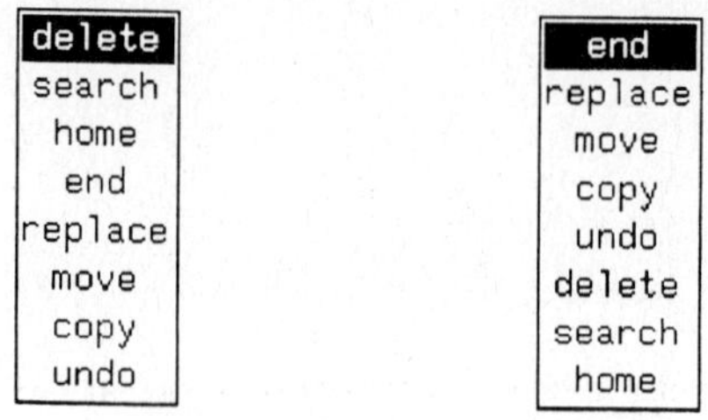

Pop-up Selection

2. Shifting Menu: on menu pop-up all items were displayed and the first item highlighted. The highlighted bar stayed in the same position and the whole menu shifted up or down as the mouse was moved. To select an item subjects had to shift it underneath the bar.

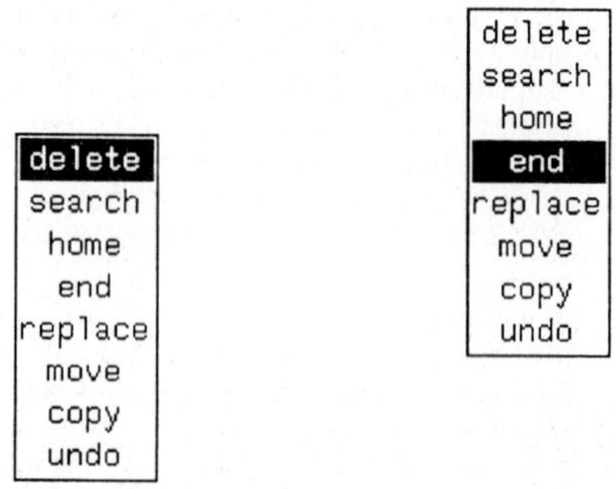

Pop-up Selection

3. Scrolling Menu: only 5 items were displayed on pop-up together with a scroll bar on the side of the menu. The pointer was already in the top portion of the scroll bar. Subjects could either scroll by dragging the scroll bar up or down, or they could select an item on the visible portion of the menu by pointing at it and thus highlighting it.

Pop-up Scroll Selection

2.3 Procedure

The experiment was carried out in the same room and all subjects read the same instructions on the screen. During the experiment subjects' reactions to the different menu styles were observed by the experimenter who sat behind the subjects.

To start with subjects were asked to perform a simple "ballistic response task"to determine their skill level in controlling the mouse and to familiarise themselves with the experimental setting. A circle appeared on the screen and as soon as subjects clicked inside it a square area appeared somewhere nearby. Subjects had to move the cursor into the square as fast as possible and click the left mouse button. They were timed from clicking in the circle to clicking in the square. The task was repeated 15 times. The position of the circle as well as the position and the size of the square was randomly varied by the program.

Having completed the first part, subjects were given the chance of trying out each menu style twice.

In the main part of the experiment subjects were asked to select a particular item from the menu. Each subject went through all menu styles, selecting 15 items from each. Subjects were first informed which menu style was next, they then had to click on a CONTINUE "button" to start each block of trials.

Thereafter the menu style they were using stayed visible through the block of 15 trials. The item subjects were required to select was displayed below the name of the menu style. Subjects could pop the menu up anywhere in a rectangular target area. There was no visible or audible feedback of errors, the program merely noted them in the data files.

Having made a selection, the required item disappeared and subjects had to click on a NEXT button to proceed with the next trial.

This way, each subject could carry out the experiment at their own pace. Time was measured from menu pop up to selection or the release of the left mouse button without selection. The order of the menu styles was randomly varied from subject to subject to control for possible "fatigue" effects being confounded with the "menu" effects. The order of items on the menus between each trial was also randomised to force subjects to do a visual scan rather than relying on their memory of the item's position. The required item was randomly generated by the program.

At the end subjects were asked which menu they liked and disliked most. Some responded by giving a particular menu style as the one most liked and disliked; some just said "I didn't like any of the moving ones, the rest I didn't mind", and quantified their preferences only when asked specifically.

3. RESULTS

3.1 Analysis of selection time differences between menu styles (with subjects divided according to the ballistic response task)
Subjects' responses in the menu task were analysed using a mixed design analysis of variance, where speed (fast/slow) on the ballistic task was the between subject variable, menu style and trial number were the within subject variables. On dividing subjects up into two groups at the mean ballistic response time (0.969 seconds), no significant differences could be found on performance of the menu task between groups. This is interpreted as indicating that "fast" and "slow" subjects had no measurable preferences for a particular menu style.

3.2 Analysis of selection time differences between menu styles (with subjects treated as one group)
As no significant differences were found between subjects, the analysis was carried out on the 30 subjects as one group.
A two factor repeated measures analysis of variance was carried out on the raw selection time scores with menu style and trial number as the independent variables. The results show a significant difference between menu styles ($F(5,145) = 24.33$, $P < 0.001$).
Summarised in the table below.

MENU STYLE	MEAN (sec)	SD	SE
Circular Menu	1.862	0.665	0.031
Regular Menu	1.894	0.704	0.033
No pointer Menu	2.048	0.890	0.042
Shifting Menu	2.444	1.291	0.060
Scrolling Menu	2.647	2.060	0.097
Rotating Menu	3.114	2.414	0.113

Table 1

There seemed to be a significant learning effect over 15 trials as well ($F(14,406) = 6.90$, $P < 0.001$). Figure 1. shows it graphically.

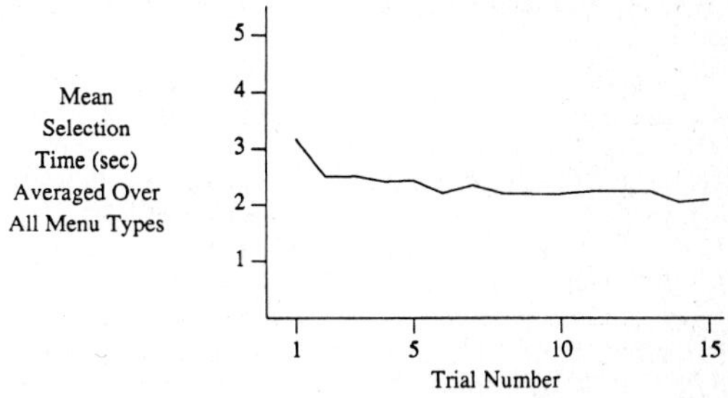

Figure 1

The interaction between menu styles and trials also proved to be significant ($F(70, 2030) = 1.452$, $P < 0.01$).
Figures 2. and 3. show the means for each menu style over the trials.

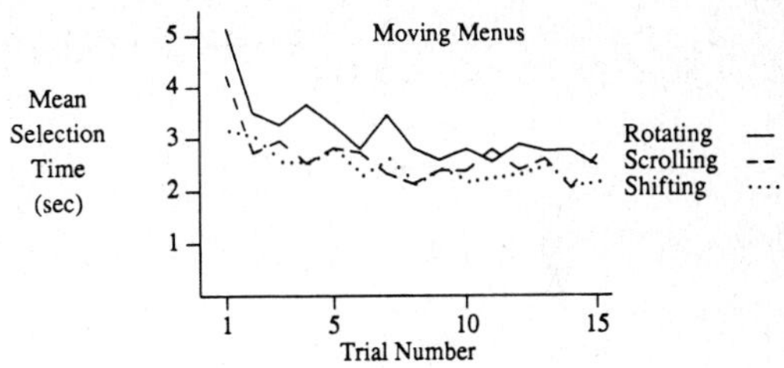

Figure 2

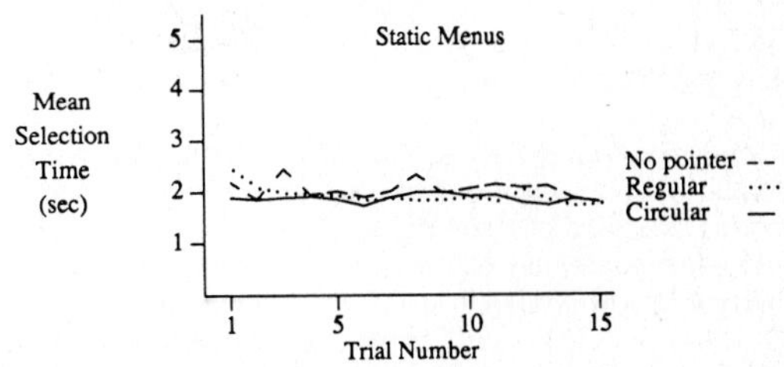

Figure 3

3.3 Errors

The two factor repeated measures analysis of variance on the raw scores with menu style and error as the independent variables, also showed a significant difference between menu styles ($F(5,145) = 4.782$, $P < 0.001$). However the effect of learning over trials, i.e. making less errors on successive trials, was not significant ($F(14, 406) = 1.360$, $P < 0.05$). The table below shows the actual number of errors made over 450 trials and the mean error rates across menu styles.

MENU STYLE	ERRORS	MEAN	SD	SE
Circular Menu	2	0.004	0.066	0.003
Shifting Menu	29	0.064	0.245	0.011
No pointer Menu	30	0.066	0.249	0.011
Rotating Menu	36	0.080	0.271	0.012
Scrolling Menu	46	0.102	0.303	0.014
Regular Menu	50	0.111	0.314	0.014

Table 2

4. DISCUSSION

There was an agreement between performance measured and subjects' expressed preferences.

17 subjects (57%) preferred the regular menu, mainly because they were used to it. It is perhaps worth mentioning that having watched subjects do the experiment, it seemed they did not pay as much attention to this menu style, because of their familiarity with it, as to novel styles. This is reflected in the high mean error rate for the regular menu (See Table 2. above).

The remaining subject (3%) preferred the menu without the pointer giving the reason that the pointer did not obscure the item chosen.

This result is broadly in agreement with the findings of the pie versus linear menu study [3], despite the differences in experimental and pie menu design of the present study. Callahan's study used three task groupings as one of the independent variables and menu styles as the other. The three groupings were defined as pie task, such as choosing points of a compass; linear task, such as selecting numbers, and unclassified tasks, such as choosing from a list of unrelated items. According to these definitions the present study used only the unclassified task. It was not clear from this report though, whether the order of the items on the menu were varied from trial to trial on the unclassified task.

Callahan's selection mechanism for the pie menu was also different. The menu centered on cursor position; the cursor changed shape into a circle with a cross in it; and the activation regions were "pie" shaped sectors of the circular menu. Subjects had to move the mouse only a small distance towards the target to highlight it. It can be argued that the target area of the circular and linear menus were more comparable in the present study.

Subjects reported difficulty in finding items in the lower half of the circular menu, the top half was scanned first every time. They also remarked that moving the cursor into the top half was easier as the mouse only had to be pushed away from the resting position of the hand, whereas pulling the mouse down to an item in the lower half required lifting one's hand first and then pulling it down. It might be worthwhile investigating the difference between semi-circular menus, sometimes called rainbow menus, i.e. just the top half of a circular menu, and circular menus.

The worst menu proved to be the rotating one. 19 subjects (63%) disliked it most. The scrolling menu, was disliked most by seven subjects (24%) and four (13%) thought that the shifting menu was the worst.

What seemed to emerge from the study and from subjects' remarks was that anything "moving" was confusing and was therefore disliked. "Static" menus were preferred by all. I did not find a single subject who chose a moving menu as favourite.

Taking this into consideration, the selection time data was reanalysed. Rotating, scrolling and shifting menus were classified as moving; circular, regular and the menu without a pointer as static.
The two factor repeated measures analysis of variance on the raw selection time scores with moving versus static menus as one independent variable, trial numbers as the other clearly show that static menus are easier to use ($F(1,29) = 96.95$, $P < 0.001$).
The table below shows the means.

MENU STYLE	MEAN (sec)	SD	SE
Static Menus	1.935	0.266	0.048
Moving Menus	2.735	0.614	0.112

Table 3

The learning effect was obviously the same as in Figure 1. and the interaction between menu styles and trials was found to be more significant then when analysing the menu styles individually ($F(14, 406) = 3.85$, $P < 0.001$).
Figure 4. below shows this.

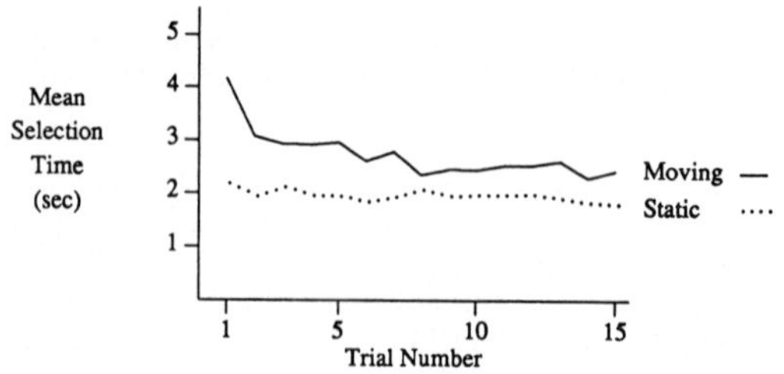

Figure 4

It appears that performance is more consistent with static menus than with moving ones and less time is required to get used to these menu styles.

There did not seem to be a significant difference between static and moving menus from the point of view of errors ($F(1, 29) = 2.45$, $P < 0.05$), which may be due to the fact that so many mistakes were made with the regular menu.

One of the limitations of this study was, that the scrolling menu, used widely by application programs, did not seem very appropriate. A better comparison of moving versus static menus might be if 20 or 30 items were used rather than eight.

5. CONCLUSIONS

This study indicates that for small number of items the circular menu has a distinct advantage. Item seek times are marginally better than with the regular menu and error rates are the lowest. However, if more than eight or ten items have to be displayed, circular menus would be impractical, they would cover too large an area on pop-up. But even with only eight or ten items displayed, should functions be difficult to express in a short word, the size of a circular menu may have to be increased to an unreasonable size. One way to get over this limitation might be to use icons instead of words.

Scrolling menus are a popular way of displaying large number of items, however this study suggests that any "moving" menu is slow in use and confusing. Static menus show a clear advantage over moving ones, so hierarchically structured menus may be a better option in displaying large number of items. Kiger's study

[5] investigated the depth/breadth trade-off in hierarchical menus and recommends minimising the depth by providing eight or nine selections on each menu. Somberg's paper [8] looked into the different organisations of menu items and concluded that during the initial stages of practice, rule-based approaches produced faster search times, but after a moderate amount of practice a positionally constant arrangement appeared to be more efficient.

This study was focusing on the visual search aspect, which is probably the way novice or casual users would use menus. Experienced users may be aided by their memory of the items' position as Somberg's study indicates [8]. It would be interesting to see whether positional constancy over a larger number of trials would yield a different result.

ACKNOWLEDGEMENTS

The authors would like to thank 'T. Conway of the Rutherford Appleton Laboratory for his help and support.

REFERENCES

[1] Antin, J.F. (1988) An Empirical Comparison of Menu Selection, Command Entry and Combined Modes of Computer Control. Behaviour and Information Technology Vol. 7. No. 2, 173-182

[2] Baecker, R.M. and Buxton, W.S., Readings in Human-Computer Interaction: A Multidisciplinary Approach (Morgan Kaufmann Publishers Inc, 1987).

[3] Callahan, J;., Hopkins, D., Weiser, M., and Shneiderman, B., An Empirical Comparison of Pie vs. Linear Menus (Conference Proceedings of CHI' 88, 95-100, 1988).

[4] Foley, J.D. and Van Dam, A., Fundamentals of Interactive Computer Graphics (Addison - Wesley Publishing Company, 1982).

[5] Kiger, J.I., The Depth/Breadth Trade-off in the Design of Menu-driven User Interfaces (International Journal of Man-Machine Studies. Vol. 20. No. 2., 201-214, 1984).

[6] MacDonald, J.E., Molander, M.E., Noel, R.W., Colour - Coding Categories in Menus (Conference Proceedings of CHI' 88, 101-106, 1988).

[7] Shneiderman, B., Designing the User Interface: Strategies for Effective Human-Computer Interaction (Addison - Wesley Publishing Company, 83-130, 1986).

[8] Somberg, B.L., A Comparison of Rule-based and Positionally Constant Arrangement of Computer Menu Items (Conference Proceedings of CHI' 87, 255-260, 1987).

Human–Computer Interaction – INTERACT '90
D. Diaper et al. (Editors)
Elsevier Science Publishers B.V. (North-Holland)

PULL-DOWN, HOLDDOWN, OR STAYDOWN? A THEORETICAL AND EMPIRICAL COMPARISON OF THREE MENU DESIGNS

Miles MACLEOD and Penelope TILLSON

School of Information Sciences, Hatfield Polytechnic, College Lane, Hatfield, Herts, AL10 9AB, UK.
Email: comrmm@hatfield.ac.uk

Pull-down menus can be cumbersome to use when making multiple choices, as they become hidden after each choice. They may also be criticized for paucity of feedback about choices made. This paper considers two alternative designs, which help overcome these shortcomings: a menu which can be set to stay visible until closed by the user; and a menu which can be held in view while required, by pressing a 'hold' key. The user actions required by these design alternatives are evaluated theoretically, with the help of user action notations, and predictions generated about some aspects of usability. The implementation in HyperCard™ of working, self-monitoring prototypes is described. An empirical comparison for usability of the implemented designs is reported, where the StayDown and HoldDown menus were found to be significantly faster than a pull-down menu for making multiple choices, and to be subjectively preferred, especially for their enhanced feedback about currently chosen attributes.

1. INTRODUCTION

In the current generation of direct manipulation user interfaces to computer systems, pull-down menus are often employed by designers as a convenient means of enabling the user to *choose* which *operations* are to be performed on selected system objects. They are also employed for a different purpose: allowing the user to choose and *set* certain *attributes* of system objects, such as the style and size of text.

When setting attributes which are not mutually exclusive, the user may wish to choose more than one from a given menu. Pull-down menus in this usage are effectively a terse and transient form of property sheet: terse because they lack detailed information about the choice relationships between menu items; transient because they disappear from view once the first choice has been made.

While users seem not to be unduly handicapped by the lack of information about the logical relationships between choices, the need to pull down the menu repeatedly to make successive choices is a time-consuming source of irritation. In addition, with Macintosh™ pull-down menus, the feedback about currently chosen attributes – in the form of checkmarks against the menu items – is not displayed until the next time the menu is pulled down. Users may be observed pulling down a menu simply for reassurance that the intended choice has indeed been registered.

1.1. Alternative Menu Designs

The problem of inappropriately disappearing menus can be solved in several ways. Recent versions of Macintosh system software have enabled the implementation of 'tear-off' menus, which, if detached from the menu bar by dragging, then remain displayed until closed by the user. Such menus are commonly used for tool palettes. The HoldDown and StayDown menu designs, introduced in this paper, possess different control features:

• A HoldDown menu can behave exactly as a standard pull-down menu, if the user makes no choice or a single choice, disappearing from view on mouseUp. When the user wishes, *it can be held in view by pressing a hold key* while choices are made. In the implementation described here, the option key was used. Feedback, in terms of changing check marks indicating the currently chosen attributes, is then immediately visible. When display of the menu is no longer required, the hold key is released; an action which can easily be carried out in parallel with other user actions.

• A StayDown menu *stays in view* after a menu item is chosen. It can be made to stay in view even if no choice is made, by dragging the cursor beyond the menu boundary and releasing the mouse button (the location of the menu does not change). Any number of choices may be made, without having to pull the menu down again. Feedback is constantly visible, indicating the currently chosen attributes. The menu can be re-hidden by clicking on its title.

2. THEORETICAL ANALYSIS

Theoretical approaches to the analysis of user actions and tasks have the potential of providing predictions about aspects of a system's usability, before implementation. However, they often fail to represent many of the factors which may influence usability, and they can be complex to apply.

The long established Keystroke-Level Model (Card, Moran and Newell, 1980) provides a simple method for generating predictions of the time for error-free performance of tasks by an expert user. Such an analysis fails to take account of the feedback given to the user, and provides only a limited treatment of the cognitive aspects of the tasks. A Mental operator, M, averaged at 1.35 seconds, is used to represent thinking / preparation time for actions. The set of heuristic rules for the assignment of the M operator, provided by Card et al, is aimed at the analysis of command-entry tasks. The assignment of M in the analysis of direct manipulation tasks is more problematic. Experience with HCI students using the model suggests that most variance in estimating task performance time arises from different decisions about where to assign this operator.

An example keystroke-level analysis of the task of choosing two menu items from a single menu is shown (Figure 1) for each of the three menu designs. Such analyses clearly express the differences, between menu designs, in the clicking and pointing actions necessary for task performance. Totals P1, H1 and S1 show the predicted performance time where the user makes no explicit action to hide the menu after making both choices. Note that times for subsequent double-choices via the *pull-down* design would be *the same* as P1, but times with the other designs would be *faster* than H1 and S1, since the menu would already be displayed. Totals P2, H2 and S2 show predicted times *including* explicit closing of the menu.

Siochi and Hartson (1989) introduce a User Action Notation which, as well as expressing user actions, makes explicit the feedback presented to the user in response to each action. [Macleod (1989a) describes a less concise notation which serves a similar purpose]. Such notations can be used to describe aspects of alternative designs for a user interface, with the aim of providing a means for considering and communicating their precise differences in action and feedback, before implementation.

An example of the use of the notation for describing the behaviour of Macintosh pull-down menus, offered by Siochi and Hartson (1989), is shown in Figure 2.

METHODS FOR A TWIN-CHOICE TASK

Pull-Down Menu

Point to menu title	**MP**[mTitle]	1.35 + 1.1
Press mouse button	**K**[mouse]	.2
(System response time)	**R**[display menu]	.2
Drag to menu item 1	**MP**[mItem1]	1.35 + 1.1
Release mouse button	**K**[mouse]	.2
(System response time)	**R**[change text + hide menu]	.5
Point to menu title	**MP**[mTitle]	.85 + 1.1
Press mouse button	**K**[mouse]	.2
(System response time)	**R**[display menu]	.2
Drag to menu item 2	**MP**[mItem2]	1.35 + 1.1
Release mouse button	**K**[mouse]	.2
(System response time)	**R**[change text + hide menu]	.5
	TOTAL TIME (P1=P2):	*11.5 secs*

HoldDown Menu

Point to menu title	**MP**[mTitle]	1.35 + 1.1
Press mouse button	**K**[mouse]	.2
(System response time)	**R**[display menu]	.2
Press hold key	**MK**[hold]	1.35 + .2
Drag(or Point) to menu item 1	**MP**[mItem1]	1.35 + 1.1
Release(Click) mouse button	**K**[mouse]	.2
(System response time)	**R**[change text + check menu]	.5
Point to menu item 2	**MP**[mItem2]	.85 + 1.1
Click mouse button	**K**[mouse]	.2
(System response time)	**R**[change text + check menu]	.5
	TOTAL TIME (H1):	*10.2 secs*
Release hold button	**K**[hold]	.2
(System response time)	**R**[hide menu]	.1
	TOTAL TIME (H2):	*10.5 secs*

StayDown Menu

Point to menu title	**MP**[mTitle]	1.35 + 1.1
Press mouse button	**K**[mouse]	.2
(System response time)	**R**[display menu]	.2
Drag to menu item 1	**MP**[mItem1]	1.35 + 1.1
Release mouse button	**K**[mouse]	.2
(System response time)	**R**[change text + check menu]	.5
Point to menu item 2	**MP**[mItem2]	.85 + 1.1
Click mouse button	**K**[mouse]	.2
(System response time)	**R**[change text + check menu]	.5
	TOTAL TIME (S1):	*8.65 secs*
Point to menu title	**MP**[mTitle]	.85 + 1.1
Click mouse button	**K**[mouse]	.2
(System response time)	**R**[hide menu]	.1
	TOTAL TIME (S2):	*10.9 secs*

Figure 1

TASK: select-menu(x, choice') RETURNS: choice'		
USER ACTIONS	FEEDBACK	SYSTEM STATE
~[x-menu-bar-choice] Mv	x-menu-bar-choice ! , show x-menu	
select-pull-down-choice(x-choice')	hide x-menu	return choice'

Key: ~[object] move cursor into context of object
[object]~ move cursor out of context of object
! highlight an object
-! dehighlight an object
Mv press mouse button down (mouseDown)

Figure 2. UAN Task Description for selecting a Macintosh pull-down Menu (Siochi and Hartson, 1989).

Siochi and Hartson's example describes moving the cursor to the menu title, then depressing the mouse button. In fact, this is *only one of the ways* of pulling down a Macintosh menu. Once the mouse is pressed down while the cursor is within a menu-title, then dragging the cursor (i.e. with mouse button held down) from one menu title to the next *will cause each menu to pop into and out of view as the cursor enters and leaves its menu-title.* Figure 3 seeks to express this, by means of an extension to Siochi and Hartson's description.

This feature of menu display enables the rapid, low cost exploratory behaviour which is characteristic of Macintosh users when seeking to locate a menu item.

TASK: select-menu(x, choice') RETURNS: choice'		
USER ACTIONS	FEEDBACK	SYSTEM STATE
~[x-menu-bar-choice] Mv	x-menu-bar-choice ! , show x-menu	
([x-menu-bar-choice]~	x-menu-bar-choice -! , hide x-menu	
~[x'-menu-bar-choice]	x'-menu-bar-choice ! , show x'-menu	
x := x')*		
select-pull-down-choice(x-choice')	hide x-menu	return choice'

Key: ( ) grouping of actions
* 0 or more repetitions

Figure 3. UAN Task Description for selecting a Macintosh pull-down menu (extended to include the menu-bar tracking-highlighting / menu-display behaviour).

The task descriptions in Figures 2 and 3 do not identify the effects of releasing the mouse button without making a menu choice. These effects are different between the StayDown design and the standard pull-down. Even with a notation as clear and concise as UAN, more comprehensive descriptions of actions and feedback soon become very complex, especially when expressing alternative available actions.

3. DESIGN OF PROTOTYPE MENUS

The menu selected for use in the study (Figure 4) is a simplified version of the standard Macintosh 'Style' menu (Apple Computer, 1987) which is used, for example, in MacWrite. The contents of this menu are familiar to Macintosh users, and provide ample opportunity for multiple choices of attributes. On careful inspection, the logic of the choice relationships between the component items of the style menu is revealed to be of surprising complexity. It has been analysed in detail by Apperley and Spence (1989), who provide a neat, comprehensible notation for its expression.

Choices of text *size* are mutually exclusive; hence no more than one size choice will be required in any single text attribute-changing task. Choosing an already chosen size results in that size remaining chosen (i.e. size choices do not toggle).

A task may require that a size choice be made in combination with *any legal combination* of choices from the text *style* part of the menu. **Bold** and *Italic* may be chosen independently of each other. Choosing one of these, when it has already been chosen, causes it to be unchosen (i.e. these style choices toggle). Choosing Plain causes all other style items to be unchosen, whatever their previous state. Plain does not toggle.

As a consequence of these relationships, more than one combination of choices can be used to change a chunk of text from, say, bold to italic. For example:

[unchoose(bold) + choose(italic)]
OR [choose(plain) + choose(italic)].

3.1. Implementation of Prototypes

Fully working prototypes of all three designs were implemented using HyperCard, a task of some complexity. HyperCard's limited set of object classes does not include menus. Several menu XFCNs and XCMDs (compiled resources which extend HyperCard's capabilities) are available, but none of these is sufficiently flexible to allow the easy implementation of a menu exhibiting the required non-standard behaviour. The HoldDown and StayDown menus were constructed using a combination of a pop-up menu XFCN (Drazga, 1988), a large number of low-level MENU resources, and button and field objects.

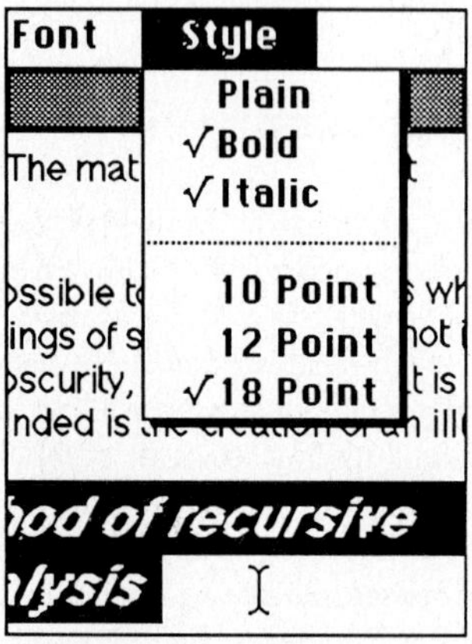

An example of a HoldDown menu implemented in HyperCard

Figure 4

The requirements were that the menus should:

- change the text style and size of currently selected text
- possess the correct logical choice relationships between menu items
- change their menu item check-marks to give the correct feedback both when new choices are made, and when different text is selected
- display reverse-video tracking highlighting (as found in standard Macintosh menus) up to the first user menu-choice, then display their own individual characteristic behaviour.

A major shortcoming of HyperCard for these purposes is its inability to display more than one text style and size at any one time in any given text field. Using a single text field, the implemented style menus would change the style and size of all visible text; and hence give the same attribute feedback information, whichever word the user selects. This was circumvented by employing two adjacent text fields, both under the control of the same style menu.

Interpreted systems – particularly one such as HyperCard, which makes frequent disk accesses – may be conspicuously slow in executing complex procedures. A satisfactorily fast response time was achieved by running the prototype on a RAM disk, on a Macintosh II.

4. EMPIRICAL STUDY

A complete experimental environment was designed, and created in HyperCard, for the presentation of conditions and the recording of data. This incorporates the implemented versions of the three designs of menu, and employs a tailored version of AutoMonitor (Macleod, 1989b) to capture a detailed, time-stamped record of their use, at the level of subjects' actions on the component interface objects: menu titles, menu items, fields and buttons. It records subject and session details, and exports the data from each session to an external text file, for analysis.

After a small pilot study, the experimental tasks for the main experiment were specified in detail. These were designed to be representative of the kind of *multiple* menu choice tasks encountered in text editing. They involved selecting chunks of text in the fields, and using the style menu to choose two or more new attributes for each chunk. A set body of text was used, in which style and character size could be changed, but character order was fixed. This was to some extent enforced by implementation constraints, but enabled identical tasks to be presented to each subject, and under each menu condition. It also made it possible to ensure that tasks were presented which tested possible weaknesses of the designs, for example where the menu staying displayed obscures the chosen chunk of text.

4.1. Method

Subjects were 20 Computer Science MSc 'conversion course' students (with first degrees in other disciplines), 14M and 6F, aged between 22 and 42. All were well-practised at using the standard Macintosh user interface and pull-down menus, with at least nine months' experience.

Subjects were given a standard introduction and demonstration of the menus and the experimental system. Written instructions were displayed alongside the computer screen, detailing the set of training tasks. Each subject performed the set of tasks three times, once with each menu type. Order of presentation was chosen randomly from the possible orders. Subjects paused between menu types to complete a questionnaire eliciting their subjective views. They were asked to rate each design for ease of use, on a scale of 1 to 4, and to express their opinions.

At the completion of all menu tasks, subjects were asked to rank the three designs according to preference. While sitting at the computer, they were then asked to visualize – and if possible, to act out – the use of each of the menus in an everyday, real-world, word processing situation; and to express their resulting opinions.

4.2. Results

Task performance times for each subject were extracted from the monitor output. Each task was deemed to start at the point of successful selection of the chunk of text, and finish when the menu choice was made which completed operations on that chunk. Total task times for each menu design, within subject, were ranked. Task performance with the standard pull-down menu was significantly slower than with the novel designs. A Friedman two-way analysis of variance by ranks of pull-down vs. HoldDown vs. StayDown showed a highly significant difference ($p < 0.001$). There was no significant difference between HoldDown and StayDown.

Choice error rates showed no significant difference between the three designs. Re-display of a menu by a subject, immediately after making a choice, was found to occur highly significantly more often with the pull-down menu than with the other designs. This is an action often performed in order to confirm that the correct choice has been made, by inspecting which items have become checked in the menu. HoldDown menus give the user an opportunity to hold the menu in view to inspect these. StayDown menus remain in view displaying the new information, without the need for any user action.

The significant incidence of longer total performance time with the pull-down menu, for a set of tasks each involving multiple menu choices, is consistent with predictions derived from the keystroke-level analysis of one representative multiple choice task.

Subjective evaluation showed an overwhelming preference for the StayDown design for performing the experimental tasks. A Friedman test on the overall preference ranking (P v H v S) was significant at $p < 0.001$, and a comparison of HoldDown vs. StayDown was also significant at $p < 0.001$.

Comments volunteered by subjects indicated that the increased feedback about currently selected style – presented through the menus remaining visible – was helpful; the pull-down menu seemed impoverished in comparison. This must be traded off against the area of screen text hidden by the menus.

5. CONCLUSIONS

That the novel menu designs can offer clear performance advantages over a standard pull-down menu for some tasks is supported both by the theoretical analysis and by the empirical study. However, these two approaches to *evaluation* each have weaknesses when it comes to generating predictions about the performance of real-world tasks in the work environment.

The Keystroke-Level Model analysis successfully predicts the faster performance times possible with the novel menu designs, in error-free expert performance of the experimental tasks. It is less successful in expressing the element of parallel user actions made possible by the HoldDown design. Further, by not expressing feedback, it has no mechanism for considering some important factors, such as a user's need to check that subtasks have been successfully performed. Siochi and Hartson's UAN enabled the designs to be described both in terms of user actions and feedback, and allows consideration of the detailed differences between the designs. It offers no explicit guidance in predicting the implications of those differences.

Empirically, it was found that StayDown and HoldDown menus were each significantly faster for making multiple choices than pull-down menus, as predicted for the given tasks. An experimental study can also achieve what no theoretical analysis yet approaches: assessment of people's relative preferences for the different menu types. A significant subjective preference was found for the ease of use of the StayDown design. These findings, of course, relate to the performance of a specific set of experimental tasks, in which many menu choices were telescoped into a short period; and to the performance of tasks in synthetic circumstances. In the subjective evaluation, subjects placed a high level of importance on the *increased feedback about current attributes,* provided by the StayDown and HoldDown designs.

The HoldDown design has some conceptually appealing features: it behaves *precisely* as a standard pull-down menu when the hold key is not pressed, thus is unlikely to induce errors from negative transfer of pull-down menu knowledge; and it can be held in view just as long as required for multiple menu choices, by an action of the user's non-mouse hand. The learning time required for use of a hold key has not been established. It is possible that insufficient training time was allowed in the empirical study.

This study has demonstrated that StayDown and HoldDown menus can offer significant performance advantages over a pull-down menu, when making multiple choices. Further work is required to evaluate the use of these designs for making single and multiple choices embedded in real-world computing tasks.

REFERENCES

Apperley, M.D. and Spence, R. (1989). Lean Cuisine: A Low Fat Notation for Menus, Interacting with Computers, 1 (1), 43-68.

Apple Computer (1987). Human Interface Guidelines: The Apple Desktop Interface, Wokingham, England , Addison-Wesley.

Card, S.K., Moran, T.P. and Newell, A. (1980). The Keystroke-Level Model for User Performance Time with Interactive Systems, Communications of the ACM, 23 (7), 396-410.

Drazga, S. (1988). PopUp menu XFCN; AnalytX, Box 388, Southampton, PA 18966.

Macleod, M. (1989a). Integrating Task Analyses in the Design of Direct Manipulation User Interfaces; Unpublished Technical Report, Hatfield Polytechnic, Hatfield, UK.

Macleod, M. (1989b). Direct Manipulation Prototype User Interface Monitoring; in Sutcliffe, A. and Macaulay, L. (Eds) People and Computers V, Proceedings of BCS HCI'89 Conf., (Nottingham, 5-8th September), CUP, pp 395-408.

Siochi, A.C. and Hartson, H.R. (1989). Task-Oriented Representations of Asynchronous User Interfaces; in Proceedings of CHI '89 Conference on Human Factors in Computer Systems (Austin, TX, May).

Human–Computer Interaction – INTERACT '90
D. Diaper et al. (Editors)
Elsevier Science Publishers B.V. (North-Holland)

THE USE OF GUIDELINES IN MENU INTERFACE DESIGN: Evaluation of a draft standard

Flavio de Souza*
University College London
Ergonomics Unit, 26 Bedford Way
London, WC1H 0AP, England

Nigel Bevan
National Physical Laboratory
DITC, Teddington, Middlesex
TW11 0LW, England

This paper reports a case study of the evaluation of the effectiveness of a draft standard containing human factors guidelines for menu interface design. Three designers were given a week to study the guidelines, before spending a day using the guidelines to redesign a menu interface. They were asked to justify their design in terms of the guidelines. The designers made errors or had difficulties with 91% of the guidelines. The cause of the errors and difficulties was analysed, which enabled recommendations for improvements to be made. Despite the difficulties with interpretation of the guidelines, the resulting interfaces only violated an average of 11% of the guidelines which could be assessed. It is concluded that it was difficult for the designers to integrate detailed design guidelines with their existing experience.

INTRODUCTION

In the 1980's the point was reached where the downward spiral in cost of computer technology made it more cost-effective for computers to serve the needs of people, than for people to serve the needs of computers as had previously been the case (Bevan and Murray, 1985). To create systems which are subservient to human needs requires a change of priorities in the design process. Ideally this means that systems designers should also be experts in human factors. However, not only are such multi-disciplinary individuals very rare, but there are not even enough trained experts in HCI to participate in every design team.

There is thus a great demand for mechanisms to transfer human factors knowledge to existing designers (Hannigan and Herring, 1987). One widely-used means is collections of design guidelines. These vary in their degree of specificity, ranging from those which state a small number of general principles (eg DIN, 1987), through those giving detailed guidance derived from cognitive psychology (eg Marshall, Nelson and Gardiner, 1987), to specific advice based on empirical evidence (eg Smith and Mosier, 1984b).

Guidelines can be used in a number of different ways. They are a useful compilation of HCI knowledge, and can provide the human factors professional with an authoritative source of advice for designers. They can also be used as a means of transferring knowledge to designers as part of educational or training courses. But the most valuable role they could play would be as a direct source of reference and guidance for designers to use during the design process. However, surveys have shown that in practice only a minority of designers consult such guidelines (Smith and Mosier, 1984a, Hammond et al, 1983).

* now at Birkbeck College, Psychology Department, Malet Street, London, WC1E 7HX, England.

The ISO Software Ergonomics group (Holdaway and Bevan, 1989) in conjunction with the American National Standards Institute has been developing a set of guidelines for menu interface design (Williams, 1989), incorporating material from the MITRE Corporation guidelines (Smith and Mosier, 1984b). It is shortly intended to publish these guidelines as the first draft of an ISO standard. The objectives of the study reported here were to evaluate the extent to which designers are able to use such guidelines to design menu interfaces, and to suggest how the guidelines could be improved.

METHOD

A task such as using guidelines to design a menu interface can be analysed in terms of the reduction of the 'designer costs' (cognitive and affective) when using guidelines, and the improvement of the 'quality of the product' (in this case the designed interface) (Dowell and Long, 1989). For the purpose of this study 'cognitive costs' are expressed in terms of errors (recognized and unrecognized) and difficulties in using the guidelines, and 'affective costs' refer to the feelings of distress (irritation, annoyance, anger) experienced by the designers using the guidelines. The 'product quality' can be assessed by comparing the the initial and redesigned interfaces.

It should be emphasised that what is being tested here is the extent to which the guidelines successfully transfer human factors knowledge, and not the correctness of the scientific findings or principles that constitute their basis.

Analytic Structure

The evaluation is based on an extension of the formal-empirical approach to analysis of user behaviour proposed by

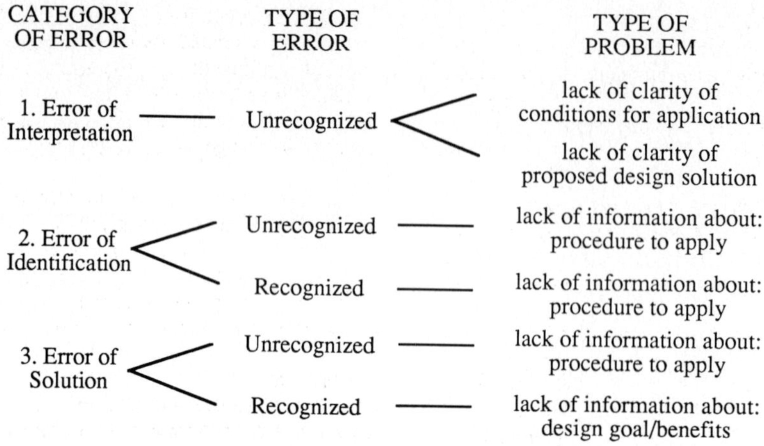

Figure 1. Sources of errors and difficulties

Long and Buckley (1987). The analytic models concerned have been described and illustrated in de Souza, Long and Bevan (1990). The source of errors or difficulties can be divided into four categories.

1. Interpretation of the guidelines.
2. Identification of the design problem.
3. Solutions to the design problem.
4. Implementation of the solutions.

In order to interpret the designers' behaviour, an initial 'Model of the Sources of Errors and Difficulties' was constructed (see Figure 1) which identified problems which could be due to lack of information, either about the procedure to follow to apply a guideline, or about the design goals and benefits; or lack of clarity of information, either about the conditions under which the guideline should be applied, or about the precise nature of the proposed solution.

In this analysis, *errors* are design decisions which contravene a guideline. The errors may be *recognized* or *unrecognized* by the designers. *Difficulties* are design decisions which are consistent with the guidelines, but which have a high cognitive or affective cost for the designer (eg in terms of work load, effort or frustration).

The Experimental Design

Three interface designers used the guidelines to improve the design of the structure and presentation of the menu options of a badly designed traditional menu-style interface for an electronic mail system. The technique employed for the assessment of designers' cognitive and affective costs was an interventional observational study. The experimental sessions were video-recorded, and the errors and difficulties in using the guidelines were identified by means of protocol analysis and observations made by the experimenter.

The Subjects

The three subjects employed in the experiment were designers with a minimum of 1 year of experience in designing interactive programs.

The Guidelines

The guidelines used were those drafted for the International Standards Organisation (Williams, 1989) and consist of 87 guidelines. However, because of time constraints, the present experiment addressed only those guidelines concerned with 'design requirements for menu structure' and 'design requirement for menu presentation', which constituted a total of 45 guidelines.

Preparation of the Subjects

Seven days before the experiment the designers received the set of guidelines, and general instructions for the experiment, which informed them about the objective, methodology and scheduling of the experiment. They were asked to read the guidelines very carefully and to mark the parts that they found unclear, and to make notes about any difficulties (particularly about the interpretation of the guidelines and their applicability to real interface problems).

The Task

The designers were instructed to improve the design of the structure and presentation of the menu options of the initial interface. In order to do this they were required to use and apply the menu interface guidelines.

The initial version of the interface design was presented to the designers on paper and they were asked to redesign it by drawing on a white board. In order to make the task more realistic the designers were given the objective of designing for a real-world problem, which included relevant information about the characteristics and objectives of the organization which would use the system, including the characteristics of the users and their tasks.

Procedure

1 Study of the set of guidelines

During the preparatory part of the experiment the designers were asked to study the guidelines for 45 minutes. This was to ensure that they had sufficient knowledge of the guidelines and to serve as a warm up period for the actual experiment.

2 Familiarisation with the initial interface
The second phase of the experimental session consisted of presenting the initial version of the interface to the designers. The designers were asked to read the contents of the menu panels, the description of the functionality and the instructions about how the system worked.

3 Use of the guidelines in the experimental session
It was observed during a pilot study that designers tended to identify and solve the design problems by an iterative and random procedure. Even a designer who was emphatically asked to use the guidelines tended to put them to one side and rely on his existing experience and prior reading of the guidelines. When asked from time to time to justify his implemented design solutions by referring to the relevant guidelines, the designer appeared to become confused, unable to find where most of the supposed justifications were in the guidelines. It was therefore decided to divide the design process into two distinct parts.

Part I
The experimenter clarified the nature of the task, and explained how the initial menu interface worked. During this session the designers were oriented towards changing every feature of the interface design that they thought should be immediately changed, based both on their previous study of the guidelines and on their own experience. They were not obliged to follow the guidelines but they were asked to think aloud and justify every design decision that they made without necessarily showing the specific guideline that they were applying. The designers had one hour to check and design the main features of the new version of the interface.

Part II
During this phase (lasting three hours) the designers were asked to change the new interface to make it consistent with the guidelines by using and applying all the guidelines systematically one by one. The designers were asked to apply each guideline to 'identify' and 'solve' design problems in the new version of the interface (the product of the design process part I). During this part of the design process (the most relevant to the experiment) the experimenter asked the designers to clarify what they were trying to do (intended design solution), why they were trying to do it (identified design problem) and indicate which guideline they were using throughout the design process. It was made clear to the designers that the intervention was not intended to change the designers' behaviour.

Application of the guideline either led to confirmation of an already identified problem and implemented design solution (in either version of the interface), or to the identification of a design problem and the implementation of a design solution proposed by the guidelines, changing the feature of the current interface under consideration.

The interview
After the design task the designers were interviewed by the experimenter for 45 minutes. The objectives of the semi-structured interview were: (a) to collect complementary information to support the assessment of the affective and cognitive costs to the designer, (b) to discuss the doubts, comments, criticisms and suggestions made by the designers before and during the experimental session, to help the experimenter to identify and understand any sort of difficulties and errors that may not have been observed during the experiment and (c) to discuss and clarify, if necessary, any difficulties and errors observed by the experimenter during the experimental session.

RESULTS

Evaluation of Effectiveness

Cognitive Costs
On average each designer had errors or difficulties with 66% of the guidelines, and 91% of the guidelines produced errors or difficulties for at least one designer. The percentage of guidelines which showed at least one error or difficulty in each category was:

1. interpretation: 44% (none were recognized);
2. identification: 47% (including 2% which were recognized);
3. solution: 31% (including 18% which were recognized).

designer	percentage of guidelines causing errors or difficulties				percentage of guidelines violated
	interpretation	identification	solution	% of guidelines affected	
1	27	33	16	62	6
2	27	18	22	65	19
3	36	31	7	71	9
mean	30	27	14	66	11
% of guide-lines affected	44	47	31	91	19

Table 1. Errors, difficulties and violations

No errors or difficulties of implementation were observed. This is probably the result of the simplified simulation of the menu design task without on-line implementation.

Examples of the errors and difficulties are given below. In some cases a designer made more than one category of error on a guideline.

Affective Costs
The observed affective costs of the guidelines were low: no evidence was detected in the protocol analysis or interviews made by the experimenter.

Quality of the Product
The degree of inconsistency of each designed interface with the guidelines was expressed as the percentage of guidelines violated in relation to the total number of guidelines which could be assessed (32). (The remaining 13 guidelines were either not applicable to the interface design process or to the quality evaluation process.) The assessment of product quality was made by expert analysis of the extent to which the final interface conformed with the guidelines (irrespective of the encountered errors or difficulties).

As can be seen in Table 1, on average only 11% of the guidelines were violated in the final design. In many cases it was possible to produce a satisfactory design despite the difficulties experienced in applying the guidelines. (However, there are other aspects of the quality of the design not represented by this particular assessment which may also be related to the number of errors and difficulties.)

Types of Problem and Design Recommendations

This section illustrates with examples the different types of problem observed for each category or error, explaining the cause and making appropriate design recommendations. The same types of problem could also cause difficulties, where the correct solution of a design problem was preceded by difficulty of interpretation of a guideline.

1. Interpretation of the Menu Guidelines

Example 1.1. Lack of clarity of the conditions under which the guideline should be applied, causing an unrecognized error of interpretation of the guidelines

Guideline 5: 'Natural grouping: group options by function or into logical categories which are meaningful to users'

Comment by Designer: "To some extent it is repeating what has already been referred by the guideline 1."

Cause: the textual structure. This guideline is about groups within a menu panel while Guideline 1 is about the design of menu panels (group the options into menu panels).

Recommendation: structure the text of the guideline so as to prevent the designer from misinterpreting the condition under which the guideline should be applied. For example, reword using italics, as follows: '*In designing groups within a menu panel*, group options by function or into logical categories which are meaningful to users.'

When the designers went through the guidelines they tended to forget that guidelines were listed under headings (in this case: 9.2.4.1.B Groups within a menu panel). Another reason why this designer interpreted guidelines 1 and 5 as the same may have been because both of them are based on the same principle and have similar headings: 'Natural groups' and 'Natural grouping'.

Example 1.2. Lack of clarity of the conditions under which the guideline should be applied, causing a difficulty in interpretation of the guideline.

Guideline 12: 'Distinctive designators: if designators are used (a) the user should be able to clearly distinguish the designator for each option, and (b) do not mix upper and lower case codes for menu option designators.'

Comment by Designer: "I ignored that because I did not know what 'designators' meant"

Cause: the word 'designator' was not understood..

Recommendation: replace 'designators' with another word better known to designers, eg 'labels'.

Example 1.3: Lack of clarity of the nature of the proposed design solution, causing an unrecognized error of interpretation of the guidelines.

Guideline 25: 'Horizontal space columns: columns of options should be separated, horizontally, by at least three character spaces.'

Comment by Designer: "I have applied it in all the menu panels by putting a gap of three spaces between the labels and the option names."

Cause: lack of clarity of the term 'columns of options' which is intended to include option names and associated labels.

Recommendations: provide clarification of the term 'columns of options', eg by a note such as: '*column of options* refers to the option names and respective labels'. It may also reduce the cognitive costs of the designers if the implicit conditions to apply this guideline are made explicit, eg: '*If a menu panel has more than one column of options* the columns of options should be separated, horizontally, by at least three character spaces.'

2. Identification of Menu Design Problems

Example 2.1. Lack of information about the procedure to apply a guideline, causing an unrecognized error of design problem identification.

Guideline 10: 'Frequency ordering: If the frequency of options use is known and option groups are small (eight or less), place the most frequently used options first.'

Comment by Designer: "Frequently used will be 'redisplay' and 'logout'. On the basis of the available information this is the best that can be done, no information is available about it. Based on the lack of information I have to use what I call an intuitive order."

Asked about the specific information that was not available he said: "I need information like, for example: if you have only one list you would be more likely to use this list more frequently. 'Display list' option in the 'Mail list menu' could be *there*, but I do not know, it is a bit vague. I need to know what is exactly in there in order to infer the most frequently used options. Not having the exact information about what is on the list I cannot think about a better ordering."

Cause: lack of information about the procedure to apply and assess frequency of options use. When the designer referred to the need for exact information he does not mean empirical information about frequency of use by the users. He refers to the need to have a well-structured and explicit system in order to make a logical inference about frequency of options use.

Recommendation: provide a procedure for how to assess 'frequency of options use'. The designer inferred that 'logout' will be frequently used because the users will have to use it every time that they logon to the system. However this does not necessarily mean that it is going to be frequently used. This incorrect inference reinforces the need for a very clear guideline.

Example 2.2. Lack of information about the procedure to apply a guideline, causing a recognized error (a design decision inconsistent with the guidelines).

Guideline 1: 'Natural groups: If options can be arranged into natural or conventional groups known to users, organize the options in levels and groups consistent with the natural hierarchy.'

Comment by Designer: "This guideline would be applicable for partition of options into menus. I am confused: does it apply to options within the menus? It would be more applicable to group the options into menu panels." He went on to apply the 'natural grouping' prescriptions to organise menus within panels, a design problem not addressed by the guideline.

Recommendation: The scope of the guideline should be clarified.

3. Solution of Menu Design Problems

Example 3.1. Lack of information about the procedure to apply a guideline, causing an unrecognized error of design problem solution.

Guideline 39: 'Familiar terminology: use terminology familiar to users.'

Comment by Designer: "There is no standard person, so what is familiar to me is not necessarily familiar to the users. Some of the users might have some knowledge of computers as a hobby and others not. That is why I have tried to use simple words."

Cause: Lack of information about the procedure to apply the guideline and assess familiar terminology. Even though this guideline explicitly demands consideration of the knowledge of the end user, the designer relied on his own intuition or common sense on which to base the design decision.

Recommendation: provide information about the procedure to apply the guideline and assess familiar terminology. For example: 'Note: make sure that the terminology used is familiar to users by carrying out an empirical test using a sample of the target population.'

Example 3.2. Lack of information about the design goals and benefits, causing a recognized error of design problem solution.

Guideline 45: 'Branching to submenus: if an option leads to another menu rather than to executing an action, then provide appropriate cues to the user. Example: options leading to a submenu could be followed by a right-pointing arrow at the end of the option label or "menu" might be included in the option name.'

Comment by Designer: "I would not implement this guideline in this interface because it does not add anything. It is of no utility at all to this interface, because so long as you select an option you change the thing that you were displaying. I think that it would be useful for menus that use a mouse because you would be able to move the cursor to the 'arrow', click on it and another menu would appear on that point in particular."

Cause: lack of information about the design goals and benefits. It seems that this designer has misinterpreted the guidelines based on previous experience with pop-up menus. He may not have experienced this guideline implemented on a traditional menu interface, and so did not envisage the utility (design goal) of implementing it.

Recommendations: provide information to the designers making explicit that the design goal is to improve perceptual distinctiveness among the option names.

CONCLUSIONS

It can be seen from the detailed analysis of the errors and difficulties that if guidelines are to be correctly interpreted, it is essential that they contain clear information about:

- the design goals and benefits
- the conditions under which the guideline should be applied
- the precise nature of the proposed solution
- any procedure which must be followed to apply the guideline

To produce effective guidelines requires careful attention to these design principles for guidelines, complemented by an empirical evaluation such as the one described in this paper. The finding that only 4 guidelines out of 45 did not produce any problems for the three designers illustrates the importance of designing a set of guidelines which are not only accurate, but also usable. This is potentially a problem when publishing guidelines as a standard, as existing rules for producing standards (eg ISO, 1989) which are concerned with technical accuracy, make it difficult to present the information in a manner which optimizes usability.

With iterative development of the guidelines it should be possible to rectify the errors and difficulties of interpretation, identification and solution. The recognized errors are the most difficult to deal with, as they suggest that designers may apply what they understand to be the principles underlying the guidelines, to design problems for which they were not intended. In other words, designers are not passive consumers of guidelines advice, but actively seek to interpret them in the light of their own experience. This makes it particularly important to clarify the design goals and objectives, and the procedures which may be used to achieve these objectives. This will reduce the cognitive costs to the designers and decrease the likelihood of the guidelines being misinterpreted.

Iterative refinement will maximise the potential usefulness of the guidelines, but it cannot itself guarantee that designers will actually use them. The experience in this study was that designers were very reluctant to make explicit reference to individual guidelines, except when directly asked to do so. The attitude is summarised by one designer:

"I see these guidelines as an explicit statement of my intuitive knowledge. I had already got this information but I had not perceived it. So, I would know what is wrong and I would have an idea about what is right on the interface but I would not be able to explain these perceived ideas. ... I do not need these guidelines because I know how to do it [design interfaces] already. I think that it is important to read it one or two times and once you have got this information from the back of your mind to the front of your mind, you do not need it anymore, so you put it away. I think that you will forget about it. Possibly, if you have a problem you might have a quick look at it."

The results from these designers support the view (Taylor and Galer, 1989) that the most effective way to ensure that human factors are addressed is to integrate the human factors issues into the normal design process. Guidelines alone do not appear to be a very effective way of achieving this.

The guidelines are likely to have more impact when they are published as a standard. The ISO group has yet to decide whether it is possible to measure conformance with a guidelines standard. If a solution is found it will provide a powerful incentive for designers to carefully evaluate the design for a menu interface against the individual guidelines. More generally, it may be useful to establish instructional workshops to give designers the opportunity to integrate the principle in the guidelines with their existing expertise.

ACKNOWLEDGEMENTS

This paper is based on research carried out by the first author in conjunction with the National Physical Laboratory in part fulfillment of the degree of MSc. (Ergonomics), University of London and was funded by Coordenadoria de Aperfeiçoamento de Pessoal de Nível Superior and Universidade Federal Fluminense (Brazil).

The authors would like to acknowledge the contributions made by Prof. John Long.

REFERENCES

Bevan N. and Murray D. (1985). *Man-Machine Integration. Infotech State of the Art Report,* **13**, 1, (Maidenhead: Pergamon Infotech Ltd).

DIN (1987) *DIN 66234 Part 8: Principles of dialogue design.*

Dowell J. and Long J.B. (1989). Towards an engineering conception for the human factors discipline. *Ergonomics,* (in press).

Hammond, N.V., Jørgensten, A.H., MacLean, A., Barnard, P.J. and Long, J.B. (1983). Design practice and interface usability: evidence from interviews with designers. In *Proceedings of CHI'83*, Boston. (New York: ACM.)

Hannigan S. and Herring V. (1987). Human factors in office product design: European practice. In: *Cognitive engineering in the design of HCI and expert systems,* ed. G. Salvendy (Amsterdam: Elsevier).

Holdaway K. and Bevan N. (1989). User system interaction standards. *Computer Communications,* **12**, 2, 97-102.

ISO (1989). *Directives Part 3: Drafting and presentation of international standards.* (Geneva: International Standards Organisation).

Long J.B. and Buckley P. (1987). Cognitive optimization of videotex dialogues: a formal-empirical approach. In *Psychological Issues of Human Computer Interaction in the Work Place.* eds. M. Frese, E.Ulich, W. Dzida (Amsterdam: Elsevier).

Marshall C., Nelson C. and Gardiner M.M. (1987). Design guidelines. In *Applying Cognitive Psychology to User-Interface Design*, eds. M. M. Gardiner and B. Christie (Chichester: Wiley & Sons Ltd).

Smith S.L. and Mosier J.N. (1984a). The user interface to computer-based information systems: a survey of current software design practice. *Behaviour and Information Technology,* **3**, 195-203.

Smith S.L. and Mosier J.N. (1984b). *Design guidelines for user-system interface software.* Technical Report NTIS No. AD A154 907.

de Souza, F.L. (1989). Ergonomic evaluation of menu interface guidelines. (National Physical Laboratory Technical Memo).

de Souza F.L., Long J.B. and Bevan N. (1990). Types of error and difficulty in using human-factors guidelines. In *Contemporary Ergonomics, 1990.* (London: Taylor & Francis).

Taylor B. and Galer M. (1989). User-centred design practice in office automation. In: *Proc. HCI International 89.*

Williams J.R. (1989) *Menu Design Guidelines.* ISO TC159/SC4/WG5 WD 9241-14 (17 March 1989).

Human–Computer Interaction – INTERACT '90
D. Diaper et al. (Editors)
Elsevier Science Publishers B.V. (North-Holland)

Decision Track: A Formalism for Menu Structure and User's Selection Behaviour

William Edmondson, CSRC, School of Computer Science, Birmingahm University, England

The paper presents a new notational formalism designed to permit the recording of sequences of selections, and also to express the space of possible selections, in menu-based interfaces. The fundamental insight is that when people make selections from a menu they do so as part of a process of decision making; selections are organized into sequences, and it is these which characterize the expression of decisions. It is intended that the notation will be used as the output of task analysis and as the input to both the formalism of Lean Cuisine (Apperley & Spence, 1989), and the formalism of User Action Notation (Siochi & Hartson, 1989). Decision Track is one of the formalisms in the proposed framework for Systematic Menu Design (Edmondson and Spence, 1990).

Introduction

0.1 The structure of this paper is as follows. The central idea of a Selection Track is introduced first, in the context of a task analysis scenario based on a user's selection of various values which determine the characteristics of a 'font' in a typical Macintosh™ application.* The second section develops the notion of a track diagram, a depiction of all possible selection sequences in the 'font' scenario. In the third section the basic idea of Decision Track is explained. The short concluding section relates the formalism to other formalisms - Lean Cuisine and User Action Notation.

Selection Track

1.0 When a person uses a menu-based interface the observable behaviour is that of sequences of selections, or choices. Physical constraints on behaviour ensure that actual choices are expressed one at a time, and this aspect of behaviour is the basis for the formalism presented here.

1.1 Assume, for the purposes of exposition, that a person is using a typical word processing application in an environment such as the Macintosh™ computer. Assume also that the user is specifying the characteristics of the font which s/he wishes to see on the printout. If questioned, the user might indicate that they began by choosing 'font' on the menu-bar at the top of the screen, and that when the list of font-names appeared they moved up and down the list until happy with the particular font-name highlighted, whereupon they selected that font, and then went away and did something else. If asked whether that is all they expected to be able to do under the heading 'font' in the menu-bar, they might reply - "yes, in this package", or "no - but I can do things in 'style' as well", or some such comment.

1.1.1 The basic element in the formalism developed here is the Selection Track; it provides a precise means whereby the user's behaviour can be recorded and used. A Selection Track has an *entry*, and an *exit*, and it expresses the presence of selectable entities. A selectable entity may be a selection value, as in the font-name example (it may be other things too - see 2.2). The notation for this font-name example (where the user can choose between 'Athens', 'Boston', 'Cairo', or 'Chicago') is shown in Figure 1. The notation expresses a general temporal flow from entry (top left) to exit (lower right). Having entered a track the user can assess the values on offer before making a choice (this can include acceptance of a default, i.e. 'do nothing'). Having chosen, the user can evaluate the choice before exiting. Clearly, one cannot choose before entering, and one cannot exit until one has assessed, chosen, and evaluated.

1.1.2 The user can only choose one thing at a time. If, therefore, one is attempting a task analysis for the purpose of constructing an application, or for evaluating an application, the track would record the individual selections and thus each section of the track would show just one selection value (i.e. between an entry and an exit). However, the set of values available to the user (i.e. those actually offered) can be assembled, by the analyst, or observer, or designer, and expressed as a single Selection Track Diagram with all the relevant selection options. The Selection Track Diagram is constructed by combining individual paths, or tracks, which proceed from an entry node to an exit node.

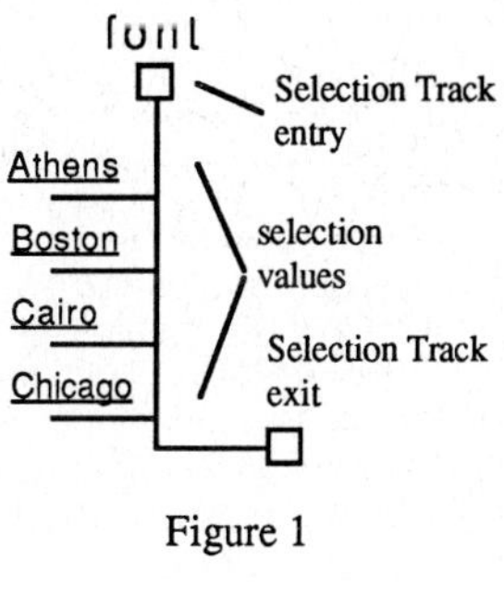

Figure 1

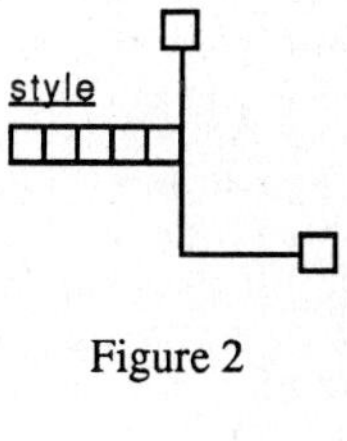

Figure 2

* Macintosh™ is the trademark of Apple Computer, Inc.

Mutual Compatibility

2.0 An important concept in the construction of menus is mutual compatibility (as identified by Apperley and Spence). The discussion in the preceding section dealt with selections (shown in a vertical arrangement) where the values available to the user are mutually exclusive - a font can be 'Athens', or 'Cairo', but not both. Mutually compatible values are depicted in a horizontal fashion in Lean Cuisine, and this idea is also carried over into the Selection Track notation. However, there are some differences in detail.

2.1 The selection of mutually compatible values, to provide values for a 'style' variable in an application (for instance) results in several component arguments being determined as a group (assuming for expository purposes that 'style' is defined as taking several arguments). However, the order of selection of arguments is irrelevant - provided the grouping of argument component values is an acceptable version of the initially desired configuration.

2.1.1 The notation depicts mutual compatibility in two ways - a short form and a full form. The short form for a set of 5 style values (bold, italic, underline, outline, shadow) is shown in Figure 2. In order to see how the full form is derived one has to consider the selection process over time. One can make any selection, followed by another selection, and so forth, until the required arrangement is achieved (deselection is addressed below, in section 2.1.2). The formalism must reflect this repeated selection activity; the notation is augmented by placing within the entry and exit node symbols a dot, and by arranging the set of selection values horizontally, as shown in Figure 3. This augmentation is to be read as 'repeat node'; movement along the Selection Track through an exit repeat node can recommence at any entry repeat node. Having entered 'style' one is free to proceed through any of the the sections of track until one selects the track which does not exit via a repeat node.

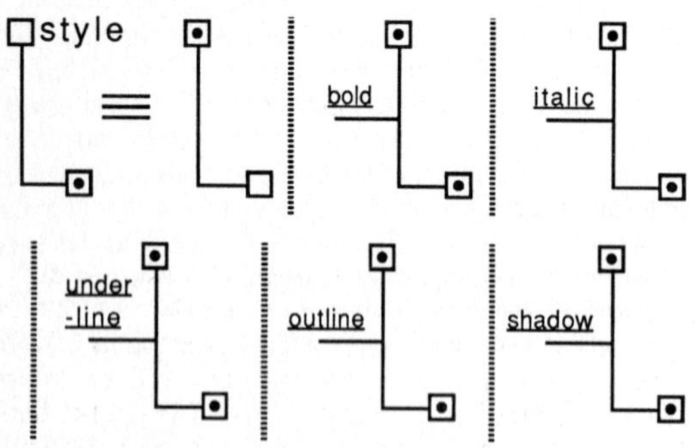

Figure 3

2.1.2 Augmentation of the formalism to show deselection is straightforward. Figure 4 shows the addition of appropriate de-selection 'selection values': the notation for de-selection is the 'bar' above the value, which is shown without the underline. The labelling system is quite straightforward: labels to the left of the track are values - underlined or 'overlined'; labels for the entry nodes are in plain text (cf. Figure 1), and are only inserted where necessary (the entry node in Figure 2 could be labelled, but is not).

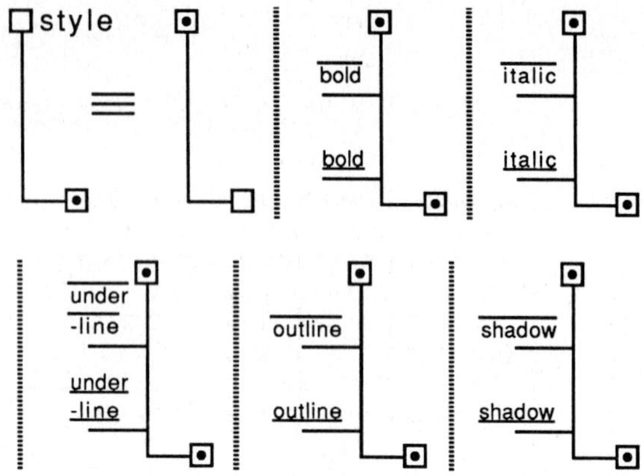

Figure 4

2.1.3 Consider now a representation of a more recognizable 'style' Selection Track. This is offered in a short form - Figure 5a - and in two full forms - Figures 5b & 5c. The expansions of 'b' and 'c' are shown in abbreviated form for convenience, an addition to the formalism which is readily appreciated (another addition, the depiction of 'fancy' as an option node is discussed below, in 2.2.1). Note that the short form, as depicted in Figure 5a, is ambiguous because two full form diagrams are possible, one with the repeat entry node positioned in the main Selection Track. This addition to the formalism is designed to show how re-entry to the main track is notated - an important distinction which is required in the detailed diagram because the selections offered the user under 5b are not equivalent to those under 5c. The 'style' track shown in Figure 5, complete with either expansion to the full version, also illustrates an important point about deselection which is not immediately obvious from the earlier diagrams. The explicit incorporation of deselection is only required in the mutually compatible selection values. To see this reflect on the vertical arrangement of the values plain text and fancy. These are mutually exclusive, which means that selecting one deselects the other; in the mutually compatible arrangement deselection has to be provided explicitly.

2.2 The discussion above presumed that all selections are of values, shown to the left of the vertical track. However, it was noted earlier (1.1.1) that selectable entitites are not just values. In fact, the full definition of a selectable entity is that it is either a value or an option. An option is defined as a Selection Track, and an option is selected by passing through a node where one leaves one track and enters another.

2.2.1 By way of illustration of the concept, consider Figure 5 again. One of the notational additions shown there depicts fancy as an option - a labelled node to the right of the track - instead of five mutually compatible values (the row of five 'node symbols' to the left of the track, labelled fancy) . The two full versions - 5b & 5c - are correctly, and completely, represented. The difference between them is quite subtle.

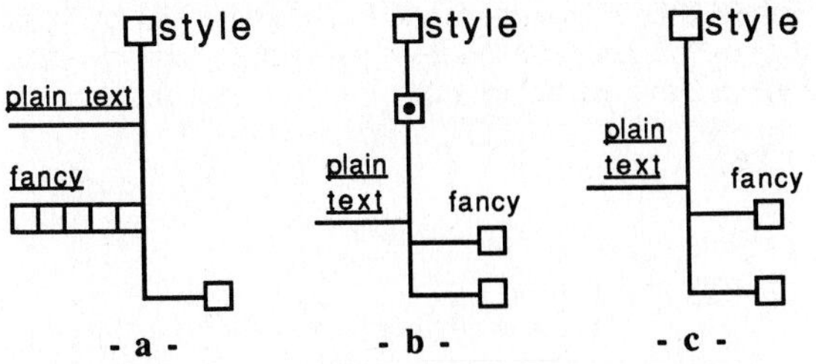

Short form **a** expands to full form **b** or full form **c**

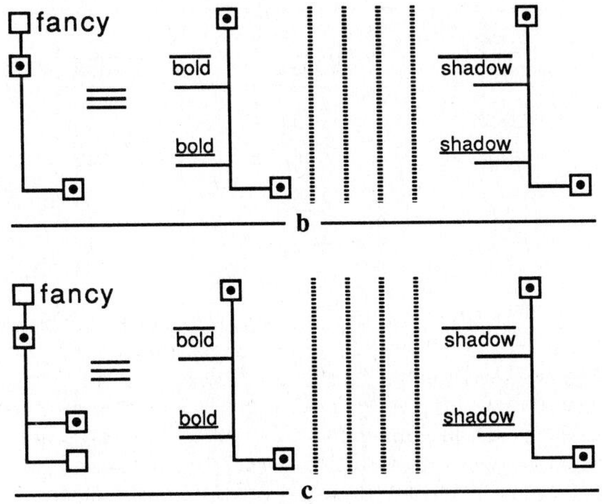

Figure 5

Figure 5b shows 'fancy' as an option which provides for the selection of the mutually compatible values (endlessly, if desired), and also provides for selection of plain text, from the main Selection Track, without leaving the 'style' Selection Track and re-entering it (this is possible because the repeat nodes are not paired off; entering the main track through the repeat node is permitted). By contrast, Figure 5c provides for appropriately free selection of mutually compatible values in 'fancy' but does not permit selection of plain text without using the exit node in the 'fancy' track and re-entering the main Selection Track through the 'style' entry node. This may seem a cumbersome way of going about the business of making selections, but in fact some applications force this on users.

2.3 The introduction of selection options - shown on the right of the vertical track - introduces another selection possibility with diagrammatic implications. It is possible to have mutually compatible options (as distinct from values) and these require a notational convention. Unsurprisingly, the device used for selection values can be reused.

2.3.1 In Figure 6 we see a selection track, with the label 'format', comprising two mutually exclusive options - 'layout' and 'font' - where 'font' is shown as three mutually compatible options ('layout' is not further elaborated here). The arrangement of repeat nodes in Figure 6 permits re-entry to the track at any appropriate point for revising a selection, for making a selection regarding name, size, and style without re-entering at the top (menu-bar) level, and so forth. This should be contrasted with the arrangements frequently encountered in commercial software, where, for example, the font name, size and style may be grouped arbitrarily, and re-entry is usually forced at the top level.

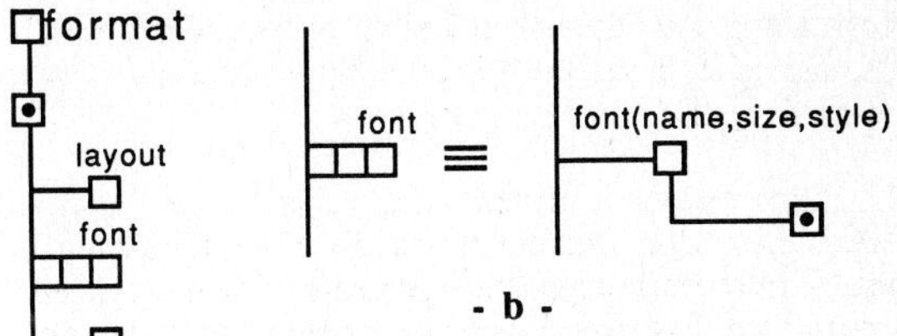

- a -

where the font option is detailed in **b,c,d,e**

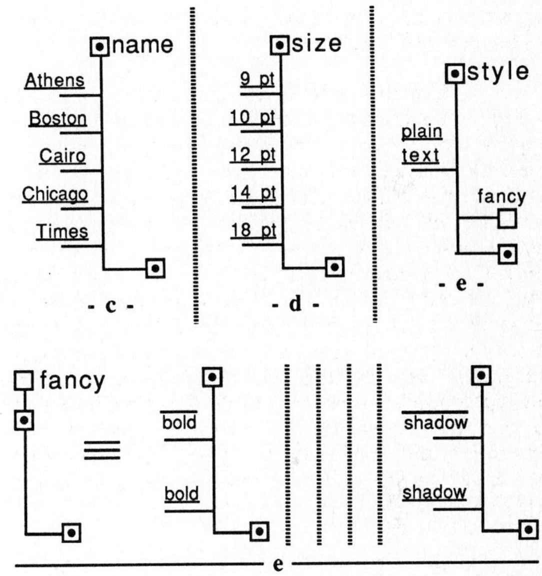

Figure 6

Decision Track

3.0 Thus far the following notational details have been introduced. Selection Tracks comprise at least an entry node, an exit node, and a selectable entity. Selectable entities can be values (shown on the left, underlined or overlined) or options (shown as a labelled node, to the right). Mutual exclusivity is shown by vertical arrangement, mutual compatibility by horizontal arrangement. Mutually compatible selectable entities can be shown in short-form and in full form, and the full form requires the use of a special node (the repeat node) and explicit expression of de-selection as a value. A sequence of single selections can be described as a sequence of Selection Tracks, or sections, and these may or may not have a single value between a pair of entry and exit nodes. Each exit node from one section serves as the entry node for the next, and Selection Tracks comprise these sections joined 'end to end'.

The set of all possible Selection Tracks (for a given portion of selection space) is a Selection Track Diagram (e.g. Figure 6 is the Selection Track Diagram for 'font' under 'format').

3.1 The formalism developed thus far lacks an essential layer of structure - something which has been hinted at in the foregoing, but which needs explicit introduction and discussion. This structural detail is the organization of Selection Tracks, or sections, into larger units. These larger units are called Decision Tracks. A Decision Track (DT) and a Decision Track Diagram (DTD) can be described in various ways: it (DT) is a 'meta Selection Track'; it (DT) is a Selection Track which is entered at the 'top level' - e.g. at the menu-bar at the top of the screen; it (DT) is the set of Selection Tracks which lie between "deciding to do 'X'", and "knowing that 'X' is done"; it (DT & DTD) is a 'natural unit' or 'natural domain' of decision making; it (DT & DTD) is a 'natural grouping' of Selection Tracks.

3.1.1 The notion of Decision Track is best clarified through discussion of examples. A diagram such as Figure 6 shows 'font' as comprising 'name', 'size', and 'style'. There is a naturalness to the grouping of these three components as definitional of 'font'; a naturalness which is lost if other 'irrelevant' components (e.g. tabulation settings) are added, or if one of the three components is separated from the others - but which is retained if a relevant detail is added (e.g. super- and sub- script under 'style'), and which is reinforced if a new, but appropriate, component is added (e.g. dealing with letter spacing, or with some sort of geometric adjustment of the type in a uniform manner different from point sizes).

3.1.2 In circumstances where users only, habitually, or mainly adjust font 'size' (say) one might suppose that 'size' is the natural domain for decision making. The user would, in this case, "decide to alter size" rather than "decide to alter the size component of font". The 'size' Decision Track would be entered, values selected, and the DT exited. This account is not unattractive - and indeed the formalism is developed further to account for this - but ultimately one is left with the recognition that 'font', as described above, is indeed plausible as the natural unit, or domain, regardless of the use of one particular component.

3.1.3 The notation used for Decision Track is a simple modification of that used for Selection Track. The entry and exit nodes are shown filled, instead of hollow (see Figure 7). As noted earlier, a track diagram may contain repeat nodes other than those required in relation to the full forms of mutually compatible selections (see Figure 6). The effect of this use of repeat nodes is to constrain the diagram to contain only one exit node. Without repeat nodes many exit nodes are required, and changing one's mind requires exit and re-entry - circumstances which can be considered 'bad practice' (see 3.2.2).

3.1.4 Where it is apparent that a component of a Decision Track is itself a natural domain, or cognitive unit (cf. 3.1.2) which could well, in principle, be available at the top level menu-bar (for instance), then such a component is indicated by a modified Selection Track node - a half-filled symbol as illustrated in Figure 7. Put simply, this node indicates that a

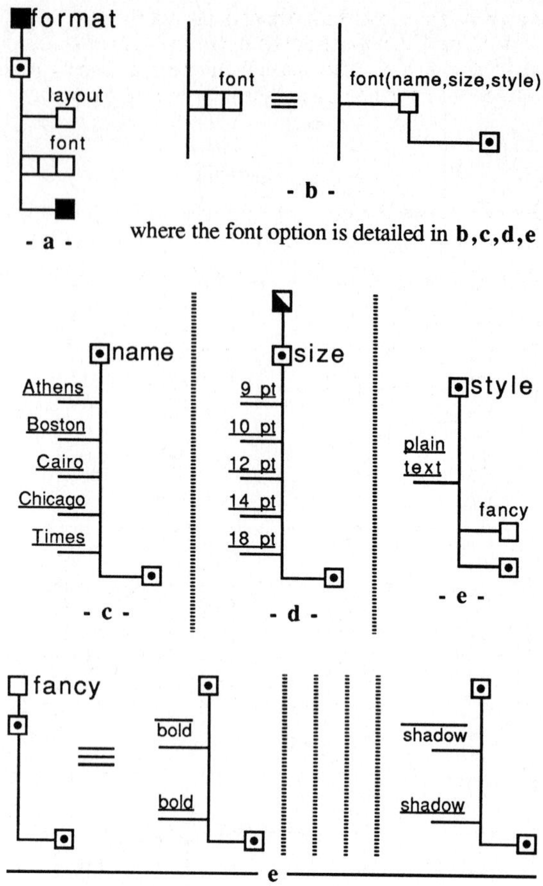

Figure 7

Decision Track is functioning as a Selection Track (see also Edmondson 1990). Figure 7 shows that 'size' has been recognized as a Decision Track in its own right, incorporated as a Selection Track in the 'font' Selection Track in the 'format' Decision Track. The reader should beware the temptation to think of these diagrams as Lean Cuisine diagrams - they are not; the selectable entities are not necessarily menemes (e.g. 'font' could be a virtual non-terminal meneme, just like 'fancy' often is). The diagrams represent the structure of decision space, as derived from introspection or task analysis, rather than the menu structures which are presented to users (see below, and Edmondson and Spence, 1990).

3.2 Decision Track Diagrams incorporate, and express, a cognitive coherence not apparent from individual tracks as observed in users' behaviour. To be sure, fragments of observed behaviour are expressed in Selection Tracks and ultimately in Decision Tracks, where a user confirms that the behaviour under discussion does indeed have the characteristics derived from the diagram. However, the diagrams are representative of more than just a single person's behaviour, even though individuals, and individual Selection Tracks, provide the input for the designer to use when deriving the diagram.

The process of constructing, or assembling, the Decision Track Diagram from all the components is not automatic, or inevitable, and it is at this stage, therefore, that mistakes can be made. The use of the formalism is described below.

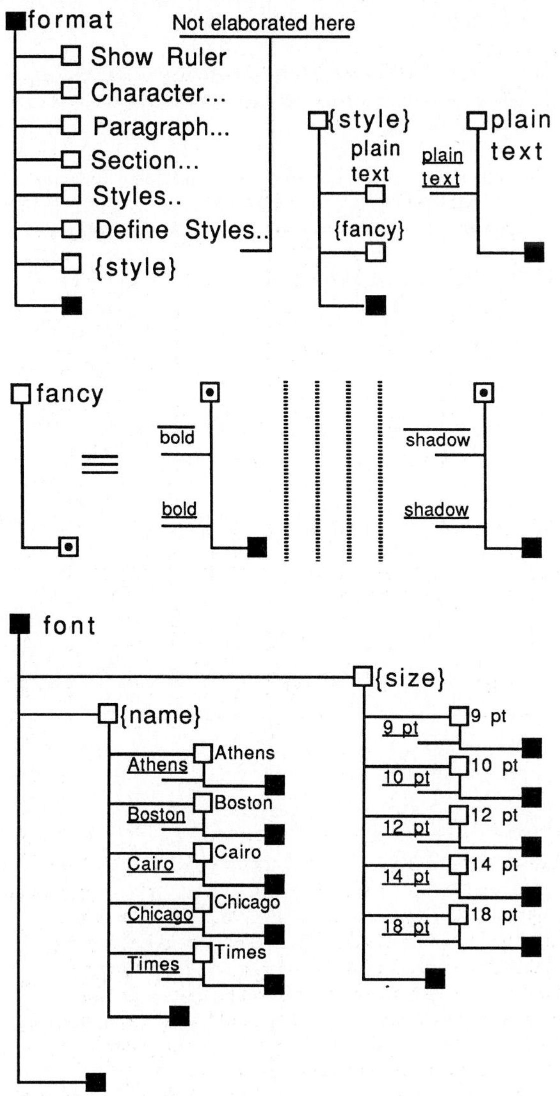

Note 1 Many more fonts are selectable by name than those shown.

Note 2 When an entry node ■ leads to only one □ option and thence to an exit node ■ we have in effect ⧄ (entry) and ⧄ (exit).

Figure 8

3.2.1 Consider first a success story. Referring again to the example in Figure 7, we should note that if the basic structure shown was a) derived from the behaviour of users, b) reflected in the operation of the relevant item in a typical menu, and c) confirmed as 'natural' by users, then we could feel secure with the identified Selection Tracks and Decision Track. And if we had relied upon intuitions, then provided that b) and c) held we could still feel secure. If in addition, and by virtue of comments from experts, we recognized that 'font size' had a status closer to that of Decision Track than Selection Track we could, firstly, record this fact in the notation and secondly attempt to modify the top level menu-bar accordingly. This latter design alteration might result in a (user controllable) enhancement whereby 'font' is replaced by 'font:size' in the menu-bar, both words being independently selectable and resulting in different drop-down menus. The above scenario is an attempt to show how real behaviour (even intuitions) can lead to good design when the intermediary description of behaviour is a comprehensive formalism like Decision Track.

3.2.2 Consider next the use of Decision Track notation to describe the use of (part of) an existing interface, rather than to record users' aims, desires, etc., in relation to the same acitivity. The diagrams in Figure 8 show how, using a widely known commercial word processing package, one effects changes in the style, size and name of the font used in a document. Several points should be noted - the separation of components within the different Decision Tracks, the number of exit nodes (i.e. lack of facilities for changing one's mind), the need to exit from one component and re-enter at the top level in order to adjust another component. This last point is interesting because it has the effect of making each Selection Track feel like a Decision Track, something which can be read off the notation, as noted. In short, the interface should be considered an example of poor design - something which is evident from the diagram.

3.2.3 Space limitations prevent a full discussion here one further augmentation to the notation (shown in Figure 8). One encounters, in assessment of menu-based interfaces, instances of bad practice which can be summarized as inappropriate elevation of a Selection Track to a Decision Track. This too can be expressed in the Decision Track formalism and the node symbols for this are open squares with a diagonal line (see Edmondson, 1990). Figure 8 shows clearly how excessive use of DT exits changes the menu into a collection of falsely elevated Selection Tracks.

Conclusion

4.0 In this last section we consider briefly the implications of the DT formalism in relation to other formalisms (see also Edmondson and Spence, 1990). DT expresses both structure and sequence, and thus provides a link to more specialized formalisms in these two separate domains.

4.1 The structural patterning of DT is intentionally close to Lean Cuisine and this permits straightforward derivation of LC structures. However, some modifications to the detailed formalism of LC appear to be required in order to utilise DT fully (see Edmondson and Spence, 1990). In particular, the

DT records the decision space with little regard to the specifics of menu presentation - menemes are not identified, for example. One would expect that a normative reading of the DTD's would lead to some insights into, and specifications for, the structures required in both applications and menus - but there is no inevitability about this.

4.2 With regard to sequences of selections, and to users' actions therein, the notation usefully captures all the important points. Users can 'browse' up and down a track (between nodes) considering options, and after making a choice they should be free to consider this (cf. Norman, 1986). There are subtleties here which should not be overlooked. The trajectory, or path, from selection to exit node is depicted as being under the user's control. However, in many menu driven interfaces a fixed and short time is allowed for evaluation with exit proceeding automatically thereafter (i.e. selecting a value automatically takes the path through the exit node after a brief pause for 'notification' of the user). Users report having to go back and re-enter the top level Decision Track just to check that the value required was indeed selected - a habit reinforced by the need to re-enter the track to change something else which is mutually compatible with the first. This concern for the actions which users make is appropriate as regards DT (because the whole process is sequential), and provides the motivation for use of a different formalism for just this component of behaviour. There is a formalism available which, with some modifications relating to menu appearance, is well suited to the requirements. User Action Notation, developed by Siochi and Hartson (1989), can take DT as partial input and yield suitable details of user behaviour with menu selections (for further details see Edmondson and Spence, 1990).

4.3 In conclusion it is worth reiterating that the aim of a good formalism is that it should be precise and perspicuous to the extent that it triggers insights and offers concise accounts with a readily appreciated sense of obviousness to them, and it should do all these things usefully in relation to other relevant formalisms. DT, it is suggested, meets these aims.

Acknowledgements

This work has been developed out of many valuable and enjoyable discussions with Robert Spence, especially, but not exclusively, on Systematic Menu Design. However, he is not responsible for any errors.

References

Apperley, M.D., and Spence, R. 1989. Lean Cuisine: a low-fat notation for menus. *Interacting with Computers,* **1**(1):45-68.

Edmondson, W.H. 1989. Asynchronous parallelism in human behaviour: A cognitive science perspective on human-computer interaction. *Behaviour & Information Technology*, **8**(1):3-12.

Edmondson, W.H. 1990. Decision Track. CSR-90-1. Computer Science Department, Birmingham University.

Edmondson, W.H., and Spence, R. 1990. A Framework for Systematic Menu Design. CSR-90-2. Computer Science Department, Birmingham University. Also submitted to INTERACT'90.

Hill, R.D. 1987. Event-response systems - a technique for specifying multi-threaded dialogues. *CHI + GI'87 Conf. Proc.*:241-248.

Norman, D.A. 1986. Cognitive engineering. In D. A. Norman and S. W. Draper (eds.), *User Centered System Design.* New Jersey: Lawrence Erlbaum Associates.

Siochi, A.C., and Hartson, H.R. 1989. Task-oriented representation of asynchronous user interfaces. *CHI'89 Conf. Proc.*:183-188.

SECTION III: DETAILED DESIGN

SIII.2 Graphical and Iconic Interfaces

A three-state model of graphical input
W.A.S. Buxton 449

Iconic interfacing: The role of icon distinctiveness and fixed or variable screen locations
A.J.K. Green and P.J. Barnard 457

Where to draw the line with text: Some claims by logic designers about graphics in notation
M. Petre and T.R.G. Green 463

The power of parameterizable objects in modern user interfaces
F. Penz, M. Tscheligi, G. Haring, and M. Manhartsberger 469

Alternative bases for comprehensibility and competition for expression in an icon generation tool
S.W. Draper, K.W. Waite, and P.D. Gray 473

Integrating natural language and graphics in dialogue
J. Lee and H. Zeevat 479

Semantics and graphical information
E. Klein and L.A. Pineda 485

Using depictive queries to search pictorial databases
S. Charles and S. Scrivener 493

HyperBliss*: A Blissymbolics communication enhancement interface and teaching aid based on a cognitive-semantographic technique with adaptive–predictive capability
A. Shalit and D.A. Boonzaier 499

A cognitive approach to the definition and evaluation of a standard for naval tactical display symbology
J. Campion, M.A. Brockett, D. Martin, and M. Rate 505

An electronic book: APTBook
M. Miyazawa, K. Kinoshita, M. Kobayashi, T. Yokoyama, and Y. Matsushita 513

"Good" graphic interfaces for "good" idea organizers
K. Sugiyama and K. Misue 521

Human–Computer Interaction – INTERACT '90
D. Diaper et al. (Editors)
Elsevier Science Publishers B.V. (North-Holland)

A THREE-STATE MODEL OF GRAPHICAL INPUT*

William A.S. BUXTON

Computer Systems Research Institute, University of Toronto, Toronto, Ontario, Canada M5S 1A4

A model to help characterize graphical input is presented. It is a refinement of a model first introduced by Buxton, Hill and Rowley (1985). The importance of the model is that it can characterize both many of the demands of interactive transactions, and many of the capabilities of input transducers. Hence, it provides a simple and usable means to aid finding a match between the two.

After an introduction, an overview of approaches to categorizing input is presented. The model is then described and discussed in terms of a number of different input technologies and techniques.

1. INTRODUCTION

All input devices are not created equal in their capabilities, nor input techniques (such as pointing, dragging, and rubber-banding) in their demands. The variation in each is both qualitative (types of signals) and quantitative (amount of signal, or bandwidth). Because of this variation, it is important that designers be able to answer questions like, "What particular demands does dragging make of a transducer, compared to selection?" or "How well are these task requirements met by a touch screen or a trackball?" Unfortunately, there is little available in the way of help from either theory or guidelines.

If language is a tool of thought, then a start to addressing this shortcoming is to develop a vocabulary common to both devices and techniques, and which augments our ability to recognize and explore relationships between the two.

In the remainder of this paper, a model which contributes to such a vocabulary is presented. It is a simple state-transition model which elucidates a number of properties of both devices and techniques.

2. TAXONOMIES OF INPUT

Traditionally, input devices have been discussed in terms of their mechanical and electrical properties (Foley & Van Dam, 1982; Sherr, 1988). Discussions centre around "joysticks," "trackballs," and "mice," for example.

Several studies have attempted to evaluate the technologies from the perspective of human performance. Many of these are summarized in Greenstein and Arnaut (1988) and Milner (1988). A common problem with such studies, however, is that they are often overly device-specific. While they may say something about a particular device in a particular task, many do not contribute significantly to the development of a general model of human performance. (There are exceptions, of course, such as Card, English and Burr, 1978.)

With the objective of isolating more fundamental issues, some researchers have attempted to categorize input technologies and/or techniques along dimensions more meaningful than simply "joystick" or "trackball." The underlying assumption in such efforts is that better abstractions can lead us from phenomenological descriptions to more general models, and hence better analogies.

An early development in this regard was the concept of *logical devices* (GSPC, 1977, 1979). This occurred in the effort to evolve device-independent graphics. The object was to provide standardized subroutines that sat between physical input devices and applications. By imposing this intermediate layer, applications could be written independent of the id-

---

* The research reported has been sponsored by the Natural Sciences and Engineering Research Council of Canada and Xerox PARC.

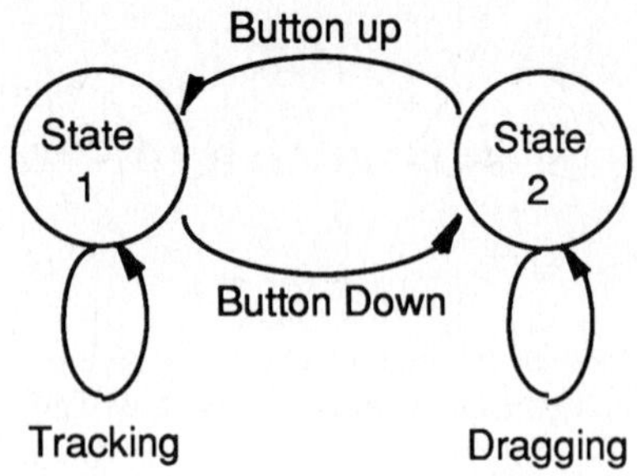

Figure 1. Simple 2-State Transaction
In State 1, moving the mouse causes the tracking symbol to move. Depressing the mouse button over an icon permits it to be dragged when the mouse is moved. This is State 2. Releasing the mouse button returns to the tracking state, State 1.

iosyncrasies of specific devices. The result was more standardized, general, maintainable, and portable code.

As seen by the application, logical devices were defined in terms of the type of data that they provided. There was one logical device for what the designers felt was each generic class of input. Consequently, we had the beginnings of a taxonomy based on use. The devices included a *pick* (for selecting objects), a *locator,* and *text.*

Foley, Wallace, and Chan (1984) took the notion of logical devices, and cast them more in the human perspective than that of the application software. They identified six generic transactions (which were more-or-less the counterparts of the GSPC logical devices) that reflected the user's intentions:

- *select* an object
- *position* an object in 1, 2, 3 or more dimensions;
- *orient* an object in 1, 2, 3 or more dimensions;
- *ink,* i.e., draw a line;
- *text,* i.e., enter text;
- *value*, i.e., specify a scalar value.

They then proceeded to enumerate a relatively comprehensive set of techniques and technologies capable of articulating each of these basic primitives.

Buxton (1983) introduced a taxonomy of input devices that was more rooted in the human motor/sensory system. The concern in this case was the ability of various transducers to capture the human gesture appropriate for articulating particular intentions. Consequently, input devices were categorized by things such as the property sensed (position, motion, or pressure), the number of dimensions sensed, and the muscle groups required to use them.

Recent research at Xerox PARC has built on this work (Card, Mackinlay and Robertson,1990; Mackinlay, Card and Robertson, 1990). Their taxonomy captures a broad part of the design space of input devices. The model captures both the discrete and continuous properties of devices, (unlike that of Buxton, which could only deal with the latter).

Together, this collected research begins to lay a foundation to support design. However, none of the models are complete in themselves, and there are still significant gaps. One is the lack of a vocabulary that is capable of capturing salient features of interactive techniques and technologies in such a way as to afford finding better matches between the two.

In what follows, a model (first suggested in Buxton, Hill and Rowley, 1985) is developed which provides the start to such a vocabulary. It takes the form of a simple state-transition model and builds on the work mentioned above. In particular, it refines the notion of device state introduced in the PARC model of Card, Mackinlay and Robertson (1990) and Mackinlay, Card and Robertson (1990).

3. A THREE-STATE MODEL

The model can be introduced within the context of a direct manipulation interface, such as that of the Apple Macintosh. Consider moving the mouse without the button pushed. One way to characterize the state of the system at this point is as *tracking.* If, however, we point at an icon, depress the mouse button and move the mouse while holding the button down, we have entered a new state, *dragging.* These simple states are represented in Fig. 1.

Consider now the situation if a touch tablet rather than a mouse was connected to the system. For the

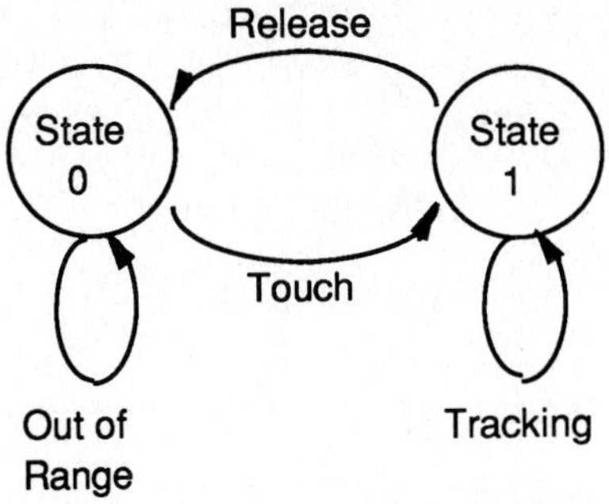

Figure 2. State 0-1 Transaction
Assume a touch tablet. In State 0, moving the finger is out of range (OOR), so has no effect. When the finger is in contact with the tablet, the tracking symbol follows the finger's motion (State 1: tracking). The system returns to State 0 when the finger releases contact from the tablet surface.

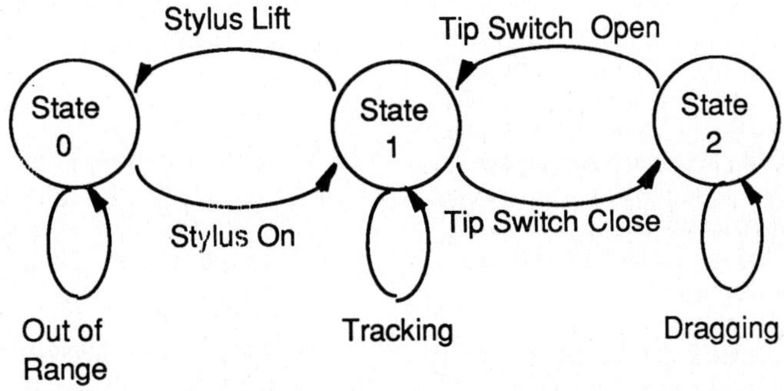

Figure 3. State 0-1-2 Transaction
Assume a graphics tablet with stylus. In State 0, the stylus is off of the tablet and the tip switch in its open state. Moving the stylus has no effect since it is out of range (OOR). When the stylus is in range, the tracking symbol follows the stylus' motion (State 1: tracking). Extra pressure on the stylus closes the tip switch, thereby moving the system into State 2.

purpose of the example, let us assume that the touch tablet is capable of sensing only one bit of pressure, namely touch or no-touch.

In this case we also get two states, but only one is common to the previous example. This is illustrated in Fig. 2. The first state, (State 0), is what we will call *out of range*, (OOR). In this state, any movement of the finger has no effect on the system. It is only when the finger comes in contact with the tablet that we enter the State 1, the tracking state seen in the previous example.

Each example has one state that the other cannot reach. Lifting a mouse off of one's desk is not sensed, and has no effect. No interactive technique can be built that depends on this action. Consequently, State 0 (the OOR condition) is undefined. Conversely, without some additional signal, the touch tablet is incapable of moving into the dragging state (State 2). To do so would require a signal from a supplementary key press or from a threshold crossing on a pressure-sensitive tablet (Buxton, Hill and Rowley, 1985).

There are, however, transducers that are capable of sensing all three states. A graphics tablet with a stylus would be one example.[1] This is illustrated in Fig. 3.

The three states introduced in the above examples are the basic elements of the model. There can be some variations. For example, with a multi-button mouse (or the use of multiple clicks), State 2 becomes a set of states, indexed by button number, as illustrated in Fig. 4.

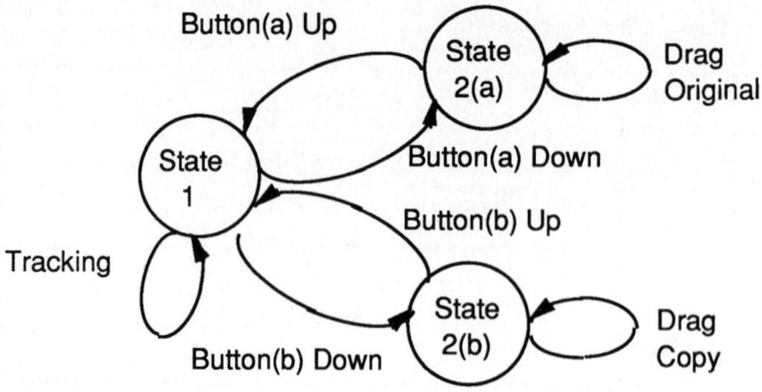

Figure 4. State 2 Set
With a multi-button mouse, for example, multiple State 2's are available. For example, selecting an object with button$_a$ may cause the selected object to be dragged, whereas selecting the object with button$_b$ may mean that a copy is dragged. Multiple State 2s can also be realized by multiple clicks on the mouse, as with the Apple Macintosh, where single clicks are used to select and double clicks to "open."

While the model is simple, it will be shown how important properties of devices and interactive techniques can be characterized in terms of these three states, and how this representation can be used in design. Weaknesses of the the model and areas for future research will also be discussed.

Note that in what follows, states will be referred to by number (State 1, for example) rather than by description. The consequences of the action performed in a particular state can vary. For example, State 2 could just as easily been "inking" or "rubber banding" as "dragging." The ordinal nomenclature is more neutral, and will be used.

4. DEVICES AND TRANSACTIONS: TABULATING ATTRIBUTES

Two tables are presented. The first summarizes the demands of a number of transaction types expressed in terms of the states and state transitions that they require from a supporting transducer. The second summarizes the capabilities of a number of input devices, expressed in terms of this same type of state information. By comparing the two tables, a simple means is provided to evaluate the match between transducers and transactions.

4.1 State 1-0 Transitions and Gestures

Transitions from State 1 to State 0 are not significant in most direct manipulation systems. As stylus-driven interfaces using character and gesture recognition become more important, so will this class of state transition. The reason is that this signal is a prime cue to delimit characters. You can think of it as the need for both the system and the user to be able to sense and agree when the pen has left the "paper."

If this cue is to be used in this or other types of transitions, it is important to note that input devices vary in how well they signal the transition. In particular, the majority of tablets (touch and otherwise) give no explicit signal at all. Rather, the onus is on the application to sense the absence of State 1 tracking information, rather than on the transducer to send an explicit signal that the pointing device has gone out of range.

Not only does this put an additional burden on the software implementation and execution, it imposes an inherent and unacceptable delay in responding to the user's action. Consequently, designers relying heavily on this signal should carefully evaluate the technologies under consideration if optimal performance and efficiency are desired.

4.2 Point/Select and State Transitions

Point and select is an integral component of most direct manipulation interfaces. The transaction is compound: pointing, which is a continuous task, and selection, which is binary. In our vocabulary, the binary selection signal is represented as a state change.

As commonly implemented, the pointing task is undertaken in State 1, and the selection is articulated by

Transaction	State 0	State 1	State 2	Notes
Point		√		
Point/Select		√	√	
Drag		√	√	State 2 motion
Rubber Banding		√	√	State 2 motion
Sweep Region		√	√	State 2 motion
Pop/Pull Menu		√	√	State 2 motion
Ink		√	√	State 2 motion
Char Recognition	√	√	√	State 2 motion

Table 1: State Characteristics of Several Classes of Transaction
A number of representative types of transactions are listed showing their state and state transition requirements. This table is of use as a means to help verify if a particular transducer is well suited to that class of transaction.

Device	State 0	State 1	State 2	Notes
Joystick		√	4	
Joystick & Button		√	√3	
Trackball		√	4	
Mouse		√	√	
Tablet & Stylus	√	√	√	
Tablet & Puck	√1	√	√	
Touch Tablet	√	√	4, 5	
Touch Screen	√	2	√2	6
Light Pen	√	√	√	6

1. The puck can be lifted, but shape and weight discourages this.
2. If State 1 used, then State 2 not available.
3. Button may require second hand, or (on stick) inhibit motion while held.
4. Has no built in button. May require second hand. If same hand, result may be interference with motion while in State 2.
5. State 1-0 transition can be used for selection. See below.
6. Direct device. Interaction is directly on display screen. Special behaviour. See below.

Table 2: State Characteristics of Several Input Devices
A number of representative input devices are listed showing their state and state transition properties. This table is of use as a means to check if a transducer meets the state characteristics required by a particular type of transaction.

a State 1-2-1 transition, with no motion in State 2. This can be easily supported with any of the devices in Table 2 that have plain check marks (√) in the State 1 and State 2 columns.

Some transducers, including trackballs, many joysticks, and touch tablets do not generally support State 2. For the most part this is due to their not having buttons tightly integrated into their design. Therefore, they warrant special mention.

One approach to dealing with this is to use a supplementary button. With joysticks and trackballs, these are often added to the base. With trackballs, such buttons can often be operated with the same hand as the trackball. With joysticks this is not the case, and another limb (hand, foot, etc.) must be employed[2]. As two-handed input becomes increasingly important, using two hands to do the work of one may be a waste. The second hand being used to push the joystick or touch tablet button could be used more profitably elsewhere.

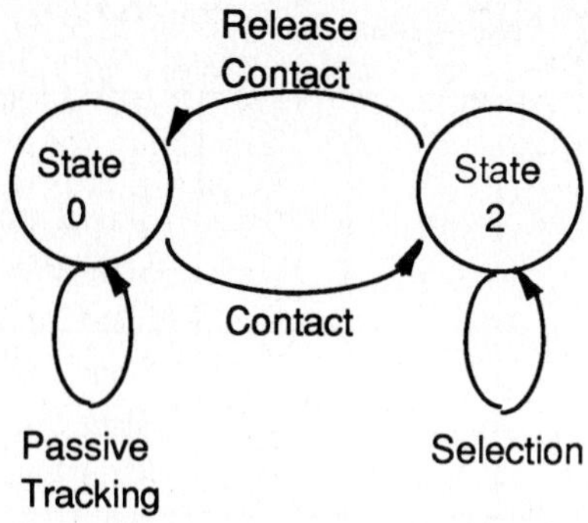

Figure 5. State 0-2 Transitions
With direct devices such as a light pen and touch screen, the pointing device (pen and finger, respectively, is the tracking mechanism. Hence, State 1 is bypassed. Since the tracking is passive (the system does not know what is being pointed at until contact), this tracking state should not be considered as State 1.

An alternative method for generating the selection signal is by a State 1-0 transition (assuming a device that supports both of these states). An example would be a binary touch tablet, where lifting your finger off the tablet while pointing at an object could imply that the object is selected. Note, however, that this technique does not extend to support transactions that require motion in State 2 (see below). An alternative approach, suitable for the touch tablet, is to use a pressure threshold crossing to signal the state change (Buxton, Hill, Rowley, 1985). This, however, requires a pressure sensing transducer.

The selection signal can also be generated via a time-out cue. That is, if I point at something and remain in that position for some interval Δt, then that object is deemed selected. The problem with this technique, however, is that the speed of interaction is limited by the requisite Δt interval.

4.3 Continuous Motion in State 2

Unlike *point and select,* most of the transactions employing State 2 require continuous motion in that state. These include:

- *dragging:* as with icons;
- *rubber-banding:* as with lines, windows, or sweeping out regions on the screen;
- *pull-down menus;*
- *inking:* as with painting or drawing;
- *character recognition:* which may or may not leave an ink trail.

Consequently, two prerequisites of any supporting technology are:

- State 1 to/from State-2 transitions
- Ease of motion while maintaining State 2.

The first is more obvious than the second, and has been discussed in the previous section.

It is this more obscure second point which presents the biggest potential impediment to performance. For example, this paper is being written on a Macintosh Portable which uses a trackball. While pointing and selecting work reasonably well, this class of transaction does not. Even though both requisite states are accessible, maintaining continuous motion in State 2 requires holding down a space-bar like button with the thumb, while operating the trackball with the fingers of the same hand. Consequently the hand is under tension, and the acuity of motion is seriously affected, compared to State 1, where the hand is in a relaxed state.

4.4 Direct Input Devices are Special

Direct input devices are devices where input takes place directly on the display surface. The two primary examples of this class of device are *light pens* and *touch screens.*

In terms of the model under discussion, these devices have an important property: in some cases (especially with touch screens), *the pointing device itself (stylus or finger) is the tracking "symbol."* What this means is that they "track" when out of range. In this usage, we would describe these devices as making transitions directly between State 0 and State 2, as illustrated in Fig. 5.

Another way that one might think of characterizing this would be as a simple State 1-2 transition, as shown in Fig. 1. There are at least two reasons that this is not done, however. First, in this case the tracking is passive. The system has no sense of what the finger is pointing at until it comes into contact. This is a significant difference.

Second, there are examples where these same direct devices are used with an explicit State 1. For example, light pens generally employ an explicit tracking symbol. Touch screens can also be used in this way, as been shown by Potter, Shneiderman, and Weldon (1988), and Sears and Shneiderman (1989), among others. In these touch screen examples, the purpose was to improve pointing accuracy. Without going into the effectiveness of the technique, what is important is that this type of usage *converts the direct technology into a State 0-1 device.*

Consider the case of the touch screen for a moment. Choosing this approach means that the price paid for the increased accuracy is direct access to State-2 dependent transactions (such as selection and dragging). Anything beyond pointing (however accurately) requires special new procedures (as discussed above in Sections 4.1 and 4.2).

5. SUMMARY AND CONCLUSIONS

A state-transition model has been presented that captures many important aspects of input devices and techniques. As such, it provides a means of aiding the designer in evaluating the match between the two. While discussed in the context of well-known devices, the model can be applied to newer classes of transducers such as the VPL dataglove (Zimmerman, Lanier, Blanchard,Bryson & Harvill, 1987).

The model goes beyond that previously introduced by Buxton (1983) in that it deals with the continuous and discrete components of transducers in an integrated manner. However, it has some weaknesses. In particular, in its current form it does not cope well with representing transducers capable of pressure sensing on their surface or their buttons (for example, a stylus with a pressure sensitive tip switch used to control line thickness in a drawing program).

Despite these limitations, the model provides a useful conceptualization of some of the basic properties of input devices and interactive techniques. Further research is required to expand and refine it.

ACKNOWLEDGEMENTS

I would like to acknowledge the contribution of the members of the Input Research Group at the University of Toronto and colleagues at Xerox PARC who provided the forum to discuss and refine the ideas contained in this paper. In particular, I would like to acknowledge Abigail Sellen and Gordon Kurtenbach who made many helpful comments on the manuscript. This work has been supported by the Natural Science and Engineering Research Council of Canada and Xerox PARC.

NOTES

1. For the example, we are assuming that stylus position is only sensed when in contact with the tablet. This is done for purposes of simplicity and does not detract from the model.

2. I distinguish between joysticks with buttons integrated on the stick, and those that do not. With the former, the stick and button can be operated with one hand. With the latter, two handed operation is required. Note, however, that in the former case operation of the button may affect performance of operation of the stick.

REFERENCES

Buxton, W. (1983). Lexical and Pragmatic Considerations of Input Structures. *Computer Graphics*, 17 (1), 31-37.

Buxton, W. Hill, R. & Rowley, P. (1985). Issues and Techniques in Touch-Sensitive Tablet Input, *Computer Graphics*, 19(3), Proceedings of SIGGRAPH '85, 215-224.

Card, S., English & Burr. (1978), Evaluation of Mouse, Rate-Controlled Isometric Joystick, Step Keys and Text Keys for Text Selection on a CRT, *Ergonomics*, 21(8), 601-613.

Card, S., Mackinlay, J. D. & Robertson, G. G. (1990). The design space of input devices. *Proceedings of CHI '90*, ACM Conference on Human Factors in Software, in press.

Foley, J. & Van Dam, A. (1982). *Fundamentals of Interactive Computer Graphics*, Reading, MA: Addison-Wesley.

Foley, J.D., Wallace, V.L. & Chan, P. (1984). The Human Factors of Computer Graphics Interaction Techniques. *IEEE Computer Graphics and Applications*, 4 (11), 13-48.

Greenstein, Joel S. & Arnaut, Lynn Y. (1988). Input Devices. In Helander, M. (Ed.). *Handbook of HCI*. Amsterdam: North-Holland, 495-519.

GSPC (1977). Status Report of the Graphics Standards Planning Committee, *Computer Graphics*, 11(3).

GSPC (1979). Status Report of the Graphics Standards Planning Committee, *Computer Graphics*, 13(3).

Mackinlay, J. D., Card, S. & Robertson, G. G. (1990). A semantic analysis of the design space of input devices. *Human-Computer Interaction*, in press.

Milner, N. (1988). A review of human performance and preferences with different input devices to computer systems., in D. Jones & R. Winder (Eds.). *People and Computers IV, Proceedings of the Fourth Conference of the British Computer Society Human-Computer Interaction Specialist Group*. Cambridge: Cambridge University Press, 341-362.

Potter, R., Shneiderman, B. & Weldon, L. (1988). Improving the accuracy of touch screens: an experimental evaluation of three strategies. *Proceedings of CHI'88*, 27-32.

Sears, A. & Shneiderman, B. (1989). High precision touchscreens: design strategies and comparisons with a mouse, *CAR-TR-450*. College Park, Maryland: Center for Automation Research, University of Maryland.

Sherr, S. (Ed.)(1988). *Input Devices*. Boston: Academic Press.

Zimmerman, T.G., Lanier, J., Blanchard, C., Bryson, S. & Harvill, Y. (1987). A Hand Gesture Interface Device, *Proceedings of CHI+GI '87*, 189-192.

Human–Computer Interaction – INTERACT '90
D. Diaper et al. (Editors)
Elsevier Science Publishers B.V. (North-Holland)

ICONIC INTERFACING: THE ROLE OF ICON DISTINCTIVENESS AND FIXED OR VARIABLE SCREEN LOCATIONS

Alison J. K. GREEN AND Philip J. BARNARD

MRC Applied Psychology Unit, 15 Chaucer Road, Cambridge, UK, CB2 2EF.

This study examined the ease with which icons differing in visual distinctiveness are learned and searched in either fixed or variable screen locations. Previous research by Arend, Muthig and Wandmacher [4] found that with random arrays, abstract icons were searched faster than representational icons. The present experiment manipulated the degree of locational ambiguity within arrays of abstract and representational icons in order to identify general principles governing the learning and searching of icon arrays. Results clearly show that differences between search times for abstract and representational icons are substantially reduced with arrays in which the position of all icons remained fixed. These and more detailed findings are used to frame constraints which may be governing cognitive activity in search and select tasks.

1. INTRODUCTION

Despite the popularity of iconic interfaces there is a surprisingly small quantity of systematic experimental evidence which directly examines user learning and performance with different types of icon. We know remarkably little about the kinds of tasks where icons may or may not prove to be effective, or even what aspects of icon arrays enhance the ease with which they are learned and searched.

In spite of this, there has been considerable general discussion about why icons might be effective and what type of icon will be most effective. Rogers [1] argues that the effectiveness of an icon will depend upon the nature of the mapping between the physical form of the icon and its referent, the suggestion being that the more direct the mapping, say with a "concrete" as opposed to an "abstract" form, the easier the icon will be to comprehend. A similar point is made by Hutchins, Hollan and Norman [2] through their notion of "articulatory distance". This refers to the relationship between the meaning of an expression and its physical realisation. Icon sets comprising concrete, or representational, icons minimise articulatory distance and so should be more readily learned than more abstract icons.

However, the effectiveness of an icon set is unlikely to be established through such gross distinctions. Within earlier work on non-computerised symbolic and pictographic forms of communication, numerous more detailed issues are raised concerning meaning and its visual realisation in non-verbal form (e.g. see Barnard & Marcel, [3]). These concern not only properties of the meaning expressed, such as whether it primarily depicts reference, relational (e.g. actions), or purely semantic information (e.g. negation), but also set effects, communicative issues, and those dealing with the history of use and the likely task context. Obviously, an icon constructed visually in a way that might help a user to infer its meaning may nevertheless be hard to locate in a structured array of visually similar icons.

Indeed, in one study by Arend, Muthig and Wandmacher [4] icons that were constructed with informative elements superimposed upon a representation of a document were found to be searched more slowly than abstract icons. One of the main points of this particular study was to test an hypothesis derived from basic psychological research in visual perception [5]. The hypothesis suggested that figures differing from each other in terms of their "global" features (e.g. size, shape, colour) would be searched and identified more rapidly than figures differing from each other in terms of "local" features (e.g. lines and structures within figures). Using highly practised subjects, Arend et al. also demonstrated that increasing the number of icons in an array slowed search times for the "representational" icons to a much greater extent than the corresponding abstract icons. From this they argued that the abstract icon arrays were more likely to be searched in parallel.

The present paper is also concerned with extending our empirical knowledge of learning and search performance with structured arrays of icons. It takes the Arend et al. experiment as its point of departure.

However, the study to be reported here is part of a broader project in which we are attempting to create theoretical apparatus that will enable us to predict key attributes of user performance. The overall approach is based upon a particular architecture for human information processing, *Interacting Cognitive Subsystems*. This is used as a basis for describing the cognitive activity underlying user performance [6]. The longer term objective is to further develop an expert system that will automatically construct predictive models of cognitive activity [7].

A major strategic aspect of this approach is the use of experimental evidence to motivate the general principles that govern the construction of such predictive models. Without going into the details of the underlying theory, it is assumed that the various subsystems of cognition handle representations in different mental codes (e.g. in visuo-spatial or auditory-verbal domains). Each type of representation has a structural description and specific content. The general principles

1(a)

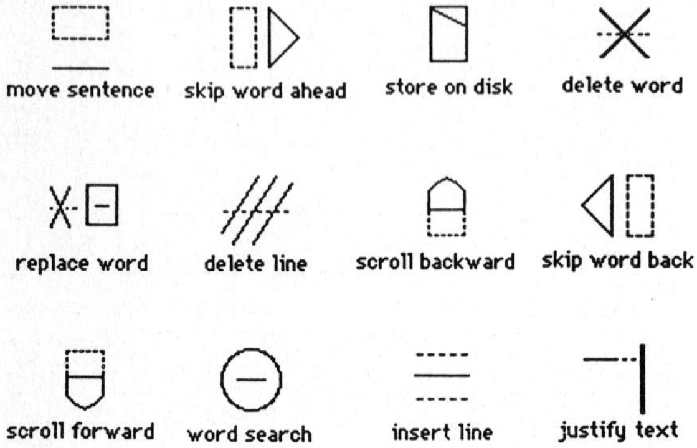

1(b)

Figures 1 (a) & (b) The "abstract" and "representational" sets used in the Arend et al study

that are sought include a subset specifically designed to inter-relate key aspects of structural description and content with human information processing activity. Principles explored so far [6] have largely concentrated on lexical reference to command operations. Icons obviously have visuo-spatial form and content.

Figures 1 (a) and (b) show the actual sets of icons from the Arend et al. study. In terms of their form and content, the two sets clearly differ in a number of respects. The representational icons share a document-oriented shape and have a *larger* number of *smaller* constituents than their abstract counterparts. As basic visual objects the representational icons clearly have more complex structural descriptions with similar gross characteristics, factors which may themselves be important candidate general principles governing the information processing activity underlying the search and verification of a particular target operation.

Clearly, search performance is going to be governed not only by the internal form and content of the target icons but also by the properties of the broader structure in which they are embedded, in this case, an array. Locational cues and knowledge of positioning are known to exert a major influence on search performance. A well-known graphical structure, like a map, can substantially enhance speed of locating targets on a menu display of target words or numbers [8]. There is also evidence specifically concerning icons that locational knowledge can act as an important retrieval cue [9].

In the search for broader principles, the Arend et al. study has a key restriction. On each search trial, the position of individual icons was randomised. In most real applications, users are likely to be able to capitalise on at least some locational stability from one occasion to the next, or upon other positional cues in an icon array. Over the course of extended learning the effect of locational cues could conceivably come to over-ride simple effects of icon-internal form and content.

Accordingly, the study reported below was designed to examine the effects of icon type on initial learning and locational stability on search performance. The point at stake in the experiment is not so much whether locational stability will enhance performance, almost any useful theoretical apparatus would predict this. Rather, we are concerned to identify more detailed properties and constraints that would need to be reflected in specific principles for modelling the cognitive activities involved in icon use. Using the Arend et al. materials and paradigm, we set out to establish whether the basic phenomena with icons located at random held firm for less highly trained subjects. At the other extreme, we examined performance when icons always appeared in exactly the same position from trial to trial. However, by their very nature, most iconic interfaces are designed to permit users, at will, to add icons or to tailor the positioning of a given set. From both practical and theoretical points of view, it is therefore perhaps most important to establish what happens in intermediate ranges - where some icons appear in a fixed location, but the position of others varies from trial to trial.

2. METHOD

2.1. Design

The experiment occurred in three phases: an initial period in which users studied the icons and their meaning; a training phase in which they carried out the basic search task to a criterion of three successive correct responses to each and every icon in the full set; and the main search-and-respond phase.

The two sets of 12 abstract or representational icons shown in Figure 1 (but obviously without the verbal labels) were used and three independent groups of subjects were tested on both sets. The number of icons in a fixed screen location was varied across groups (0, 6, or 12 fixed). Each group of subjects was trained and tested on one type of icon and then trained and tested on the other. Order of icon set was counterbalanced over subjects. The group with all twelve icons in a fixed location were divided into 3 subgroups each receiving a different spatial arrangement of the items. The group with six icons in a fixed position were divided into two subgroups. The particular items that were fixed for one subgroup were varied for the other and vice-versa.

2.2. Procedure

Study phase.
At the beginning of each session, the task was explained to subjects and they were practised on a variety of mouse move and click tasks. For ten minutes, they then studied a sheet describing one set of 12 icons and their functions. They were asked to learn the text editing functions of each of the icons because the sheet would not be available for inspection during either the training or experimental trials. The training and experimental trials were implemented in Hypercard on a Mac 2.

Training phase.
During this phase, subjects carried out the search task interactively, with performance feedback. As in Figure 1, the 12 icons were presented in a 3 X 4 matrix with the columns spacing at 4 cm and the line spacing at 3 cm. At the top left corner of the screen was a function statement. This function statement remained on the screen whilst subjects searched the array and selected the intended target with the mouse. The function statement corresponding to the selected item then appeared below it. This process was repeated until subjects had correctly selected each icon from the set three times (i.e., 36 correct responses). During this initial training the actual screen locations of all 12 icons remained constant for all experimental groups.

Search and respond phase.
For the main experimental phase subjects were assigned at random to a condition and subgroup and they received no further feedback on the accuracy of their responses. The target statement (e.g. You want to scroll forward) appeared as a button located in the upper half of the screen. Subjects were asked to read the statement and then to click on it when they were ready to proceed. The statement disappeared and the 3x4 icon array appeared. They responded as before and the speed and accuracy of their selection was assessed. Subjects each had 84 trials - 7 blocks of trials on each of the 12 target operations. For each block, the order of target statements was randomised, with the constraint that the last target statement within a block differed from the first target in the following block.

Once subjects completed the testing procedure for one set of icons (abstract or representational), the three phase procedure was repeated for the other set (except for mouse practise). For the groups with 6 and 12 icons in a fixed position, icons were fixed to screen locations during experimental trials which differed from those they were fixed to during the initial training trials.

2.3. Subjects

36 female subjects aged between 18 and 50 (mean age 38.1 years) were randomly assigned to the 3 experimental groups (n = 12). The full experimental procedure took around one hour.

3. RESULTS

3.1. Learning trials

Training data from 4 subjects were lost due to an equipment problem. The number of trials to criterion for abstract icons was 38.37 (min. 36, max. 62, SD 4.71), and for representational icons, it was 40.19 (min. 36, max. 58, SD 4.80). Although users took more trials to learn the representational icons, the overall difference was not reliable ($F_{1,30}$ = 3.48, p = 0.074). There was, however, an interaction between icon type and order of learning,

$F_{1,30}$ = 5.11, p = 0.032. For the first set of icons learned the means were: abstract 38.83 trials; representational 41.94. For the second set, they were abstract 37.91 trials; representational 38.44. While it should be remembered that these training trials were preceded by a study phase, the initial training data would not seem to indicate a substantial or enduring influence in overall learnability of the two forms of icon set examined here.

During training the mean response times for abstract icon set (5587 ms) were substantially faster than for representational set (7791 ms), $F_{1,30}$ = 123.51, p < 0.001. Again, the interaction between icon type and order of presentation was significant, $F_{1,30}$ = 4.63, p < 0.04. Response times for abstract icons were similar regardless of whether subjects learned abstract or representational icons first. However, response times for representational icons were faster when subjects had had prior experience of the abstract set.

3.2. Experimental trials

Response times are from the offset of the target statement to the mouse click that selected the response. The times therefore include a component of system response time, search time, the physical movement of the mouse and the actual act of clicking over the target itself. In general subjects did not appear to move the mouse until they had decided where they were going to move it to. Response times were discarded for trials in which an error was made (3.74% of all responses). The remaining time data were subjected to analysis of variance with any missing observations filled.

The overall pattern of results clearly replicates the basic phenomenon observed by Arend et al. [4], but for considerably longer basic response times. Mean response times to targets in the abstract icon set were substantially faster overall (4496 ms) than those for representational set (6013 ms), $F_{1,33}$ = 179.86, p < 0.001. For individual items in the abstract icon set, means ranged from 3933 ms (word search) to 5350 ms (replace word). For the representational icon set, means ranged from 4535 ms (store on disk) to 7602 ms (move sentence). There was little overlap in performance. Performance with ten of the representational icons being slower than responses to the slowest abstract exemplar. Furthermore, the relative rankings of performance with individual icons obtained here correlated highly with the individual item data published by Arend for highly practised subjects with considerable faster overall response times (for abstract icons r_s = 0.804, p < 0.01, and for representational icons, r_s = 0.853, p < 0.01).

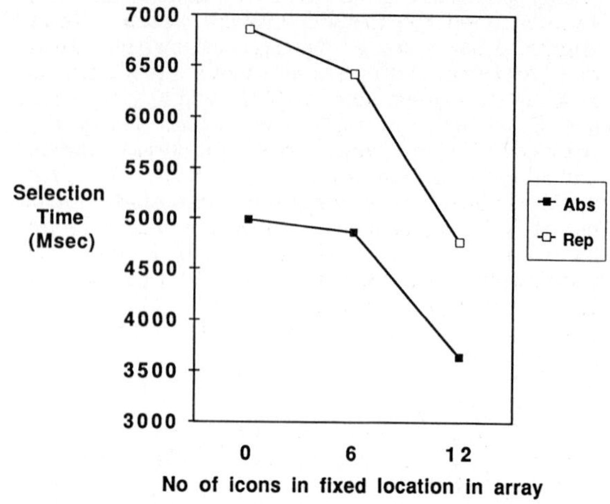

Figure 2 The interaction between icon type and number of icons in a fixed location.

The number of icons allocated to a fixed screen location had a substantial influence on performance ($F_{2,33}$ = 11.64, p < 0.01). There was also a significant interaction with the icon type ($F_{2,33}$ = 3.53, p < 0.041). These data are shown in Figure 2. Two things should be clear from this figure. First, the relative difference between the two types of icon is smaller when all icons occupy fixed positions. Second, by far the larger difference is between arrays in which the locations of all twelve icons are fixed, and the other two groups in which the position of half or all the icons varied. The average increase in search time from 12 fixed to 6 fixed was 1438 ms, but only 278 ms from 6 fixed to 0 fixed. Multiple comparisons showed that the arrays with 12 fixed icons were searched reliably faster than those with only 6 or 0 fixed for both types of icon (abstract, q = 9.378 and 8.84 respectively; representational q = 15.03 and 11.911; in all cases p < 0.001). The step from 6 fixed to 0 fixed was reliable for representational icons (q = 3.119, p = 0.035) but not reliable for the abstract ones (q = 0.895 p = 0.531).

The data for the group with half fixed and half randomly positioned icons were decomposed into the search times for positionally fixed icons and those for the randomly positioned ones. In the case of abstract icons, those items that are positioned at random in this kind of array are found slightly more slowly (5187 ms) than the average for a wholly random array (4991 ms). In the case of representational icons located at random among other fixed position icons, targets are located at the same speed (6757 ms) as they are in a wholly random array (6850 ms). However, for both the abstract and representational sets, items occupying a fixed spatial position in the mixed array are located very much slower than their counterparts in an array with all items occupying fixed positions (abstract 4478 ms vs 3631 ms; concrete icons: 6002 ms vs 4746 ms).

Unsurprisingly, there was a large overall effect of experience, $F_{6,198} = 62.15$, $p < 0.001$, the average latency on the first block of trials being 6638 ms, decreasing to 4665 ms by the seventh block. There was an interaction between trial and the number of icons occupying fixed positions ($F_{12,198} = 2.45$, $p < 0.005$). Arrays of 12 fixed icons

3(a)

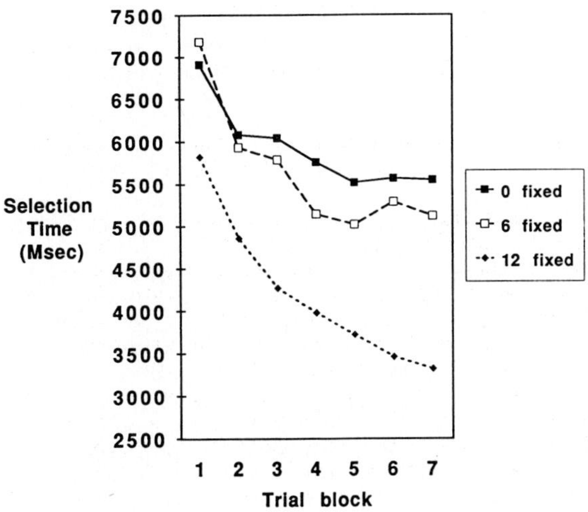

3(b)

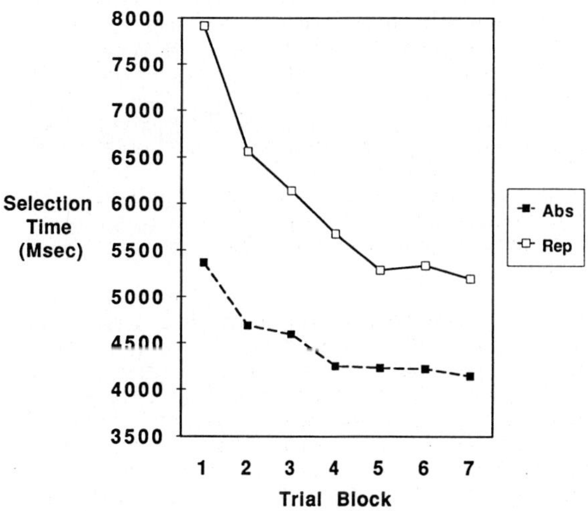

Figure 3 The upper panel (a) shows the interaction between the number of icons in an array occupying a fixed position and trial. The lower panel (b) shows the interaction between icon type and trial.

showed the greatest increase in search and respond times. The interaction between icon type and trial, $F_{6,198} = 12.37$, $p < 0.001$, showed that response times for representational icons decreased more rapidly than those for abstract icons. These two interactions are shown in Figures 3 (a) and (b). The interaction between icon type, trial and extent to which icons were given fixed, mixed or random locations was not statistically reliable ($F_{12,198} = 1.32$, $p = 0.209$).

4. DISCUSSION

Our initial concern in framing this study was to identify properties and constraints that would need to be reflected in general principles for modelling the kinds of cognitive activities involved in icon use. The data reported here confirm certain aspects of earlier results reported by Arend et al [4] and extend them considerably.

For relatively inexperienced subjects trained to criterion performance, the kind of abstract icons examined here are generally located much faster than their representational counterparts, irrespective of the array context. Performance with the representational icons also developed more rapidly relative to the abstract set. Both these effects would be consistent with a constraint on the formulation of a general principle which held that, for a given size of icon, a more complex internal structural description of the iconic form will initially require additional mental processing in controlling search and evaluating the appropriateness of scanned items in relation to the specified goal. Naturally, since the two sets of icons differed on more than one feature of their internal structural descriptions, the data presented here do not permit further elaboration of this constraint.

Both the present and the previous data indicate further constraints that arise not from the iconic form, but from the array context. Whereas Arend et al. showed that decreasing the number of items in the array speeded up search for the representational set relative to abstract set, the present data shows that for a constant array size, fixing the positions of all the icons has an analogous effect in differentially enhancing search for the icons in the representational set. Subjects can capitalise upon learning item-location mappings rather than relying wholly upon generalised search procedures. Since the precise locational knowledge of any given array must develop through experience, the interaction of trial block with the number of items was to be anticipated.

The fact that fixing the positions of only half of the icons gives rise to levels of performance not too far short of those for wholly random arrays is rather more surprising. It also has strong implications for the formulation of general principles for modelling cognitive activity. Although the positionally fixed items are located faster than those whose position varies from trial to trial, subjects gained nothing like the benefits they did from wholly fixed positioning. This suggests that, in mixed arrays, the development of search performance for the positionally fixed items is impeded by uncertainty as to exactly which of the items in the set occupies a fixed position. This would naturally tend to increase reliance on generalised search strategies as opposed to the learning of specific item-location mappings.

Although the three-way interaction between trial block, icon type and number of icons with a fixed spatial position failed to reach significance over the course of learning studied here, a number of more absolute points are nevertheless worth noting. By the final block of trials the difference between search and respond times for abstract and representational items in wholly positionally fixed arrays was reduced to a mere 389 ms (abstract - 3124; ms representational - 3513 ms), whereas the comparable final difference for wholly random arrays remained at 1665 ms (abstract - 4719 ms; representational 6384 ms). These compare with overall differences in the Arend et al. array size twelve of approx.1200 ms (abstract - approx. 1200 ms; representational - approx. 2400 ms) based upon vastly greater experience. The absolute numbers here are at least indicative that the learning of item-location mappings in spatial fixed arrays would, with greater experience, come to minimise performance differences between the abstract and representational sets.

5. CONCLUSION

The present empirical study has helped us to move towards the formulation of a number of empirically motivated principles concerning the properties of cognitive activity in the use of icon arrays. Here, we have not attempted to present these in their ultimate form, which depends upon the particular "theoretical language" of *Interacting Cognitive Subsystems* e.g. see Barnard et al. 1988 [7]. However, such findings should not be viewed as of theoretical interest alone. From a more practical viewpoint, they underline the interdependence of icon form and array structuring. In the specific context of arrays that are spatially tailorable by users, they should at least be made aware of the potentially negative consequences of certain forms of positional strategies. In this, users may not always naturally exhibit the best judgement (cf. Grudin & Barnard [10]).

REFERENCES

[1] Rogers, Y., Icon design for the user interface, International Review of Ergonomics 2 (1989) 129-154.

[2] Hutchins, E.L., Hollan, J.D. and Norman, D.A., Direct Manipulation Interfaces, in: Norman, D.A. and Draper, S.W. (eds.), User Centred System Design (Erlbaum, Hillsdale, NJ , 1986), pp. 87-124.

[3] Barnard, P.J. and Marcel, A.J. Representation and Understanding in the Use of Symbols and Pictograms, in: Easterby, R. and Zwaga, H. (eds.), Information Design (Wiley, Chichester, 1984), pp. 37-76.

[4] Arend, U., Muthig, K-P., and Wandmacher, J., Evidence for global feature superiority in menu selection by icons, Behaviour and Information Technology 6 (1987) 411-426.

[5] Pomerantz, J.R., Global and local precedence: selective attention in form and motion perception, Journal of Experimental Psychology: General 112 (1983) 516-540.

[6] Barnard, P.J., Cognitive Resources and the Learning of Human-computer Dialogues, in: Carroll, J.M. (ed.), Interfacing Thought: Cognitive Aspects of Human Computer Interaction (MIT Press, Cambridge, MA, 1987), pp. 112-158.

[7] Barnard, P.J., Wilson, M. and MacLean, A., Approximate modelling of cognitive activity with an expert system: A theory-based strategy for developing an interactive design tool, The Computer Journal 31 (1988) 445-456.

[8] Barnard, P.J., Morton, J., Long, J.B., and Ottley, E.A., Planning Menus for Display: Some Effects of their Structure and Content on User Performance, in Displays for Man-Machine Systems, IEE Conference Publication No. 150, (IEE, London 1977), pp. 130-133.

[9] Lansdale, M.W., On the memorability of icons in an information retrieval task, Behaviour and Information Technology 7 (1988) 131-151.

[10] Grudin, J. and Barnard, P.J., When does an abbreviation become a word? And related questions, Proceedings of CHI '85 Human Factors in Computing Systems (ACM, New York, 1985), pp. 121-125.

Human–Computer Interaction – INTERACT '90
D. Diaper et al. (Editors)
Elsevier Science Publishers B.V. (North-Holland)

WHERE TO DRAW THE LINE WITH TEXT: SOME CLAIMS BY LOGIC DESIGNERS ABOUT GRAPHICS IN NOTATION

M. PETRE

Institute for Perception Research/IPO, Postbus 513, 5600 MB Eindhoven, Netherlands

T.R.G. GREEN

MRC Applied Psychology Unit, 15 Chaucer Road, Cambridge CB2 2EF, England

Is graphical notation really superior to text, or just different? This paper reports observations of professional hardware designers and considers claims they make about graphics and text on a variety of issues: overviews, zooming, adjacency, detail, viscosity, searching, and space consumption. This paper concludes that the key factor in choosing between graphics and text is the accessibility of information demanded by the user's task.

1. INTRODUCTION

Some writers on visual programming assume that graphical representations are self-evidently superior to text in all conditions and for all purposes (Shu, 1988, is one instance). We doubt that. This paper asserts that graphics and text each have their places, and that the determining factor is the user's task (cf. Bouwhuis' goal-directed analysis of reading, 1989, and Pennington's suggestion that a programmer's task goals influence mental representations, 1987).

Electronics designers have been using a graphical notation for years. This paper considers in detail some of the claims about graphical notation made by expert hardware designers and CAD-E (Computer Assisted Design systems for Electronics) users. Where possible, relevant psychological considerations are brought to bear on those claims.

1.1. Introduction to CAD-E

Schematic drawings for electronics are largely, but not exclusively, graphical. (See Figure 1.) The notation is multi-layered, although not strictly hierarchical. Text is incorporated as annotation or addenda to diagrams, and sometimes as the lowest level in the design (e.g., parameters of a component). Often the schematic is only a partial representation of the final object, dependent on information held elsewhere for the complete implementation. What began as a paper- and-pencil notation has adapted well to computer technology, and some of the most advanced graphical interfaces have been developed for CAD-E. Although systems are available for PCs, those used by engineers in this study ran on workstations, with large, high- definition screens.

1.2. The nature of the experts and interviews

Five expert digital electronics engineers and CAD-E users, all with ten or more years of experience and all members of hardware design teams in industry, were interviewed and observed *in situ*. All use CAD systems (mainly commercially-available systems, but some 'home-grown') running on workstations, and all are familiar with more than one system.

The interviews were informal, set (confidentially) in the context of the engineers' current work-in-progress, so that the engineers provided their own examples. Having been asked to discuss and demonstrate the CAD-E systems they use and what they use them for, the engineers needed little further prompting, so that the interviews were led by the experts, supported by a fixed agenda of questions from the interviewer.

2. THEMES FROM THE INTERVIEWS

We report seven major themes, each mentioned in some form by every designer. All quotations are from these interviews.

2.1. Overviews

Claim:
Graphics is better for overviews.

> *"In a case where you've got things like the flow of a signal, the graphics makes it a hell of a sight easier to understand what's going on."*

> *"The shape of the diagram gives information about the content of the diagram, at least for the initiated."*

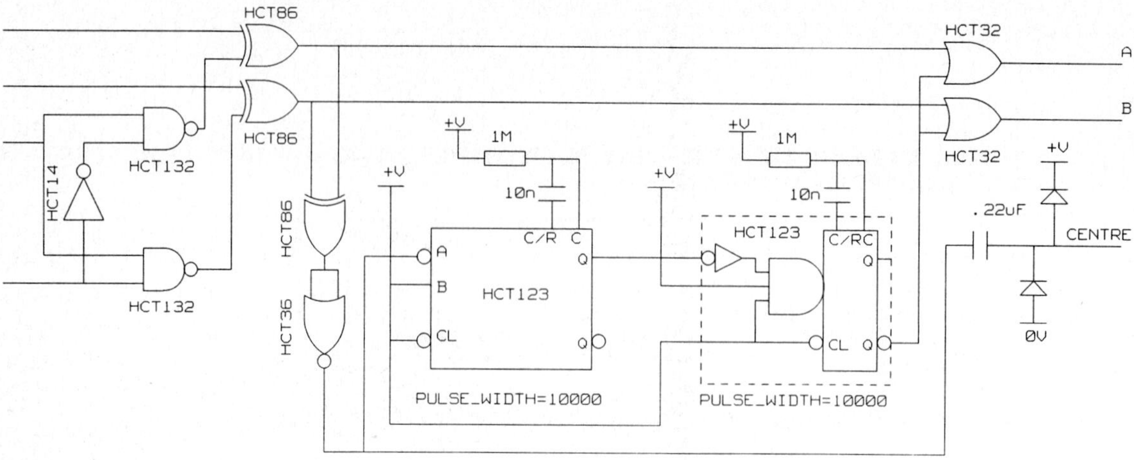

Figure 1: This fragment of a schematic illustrates a simple *stepped zoom:* the components enclosed in the dashed box are an expanded version of the rectangular component (also labelled HCT123) to their left.

Comment:
There appear to be three explanations.

First, discussions about graphical notations frequently incorporate some notion of a 'gestalt', an informative impression of the whole diagram which provides insights to structure or flow and is useful as a reference for navigation. It is argued that this distinguishes graphical representations from text. Results in visual perception (e.g., Humphreys and Bruce, 1989, or Treisman, 1986) suggest that, for plain, unformatted text at least, this is true.

The effective visual field is determined largely by visual grain, by the number of visual elements in the objects under scrutiny. Because of the complexity and density of the characters, text is more affected by actual distance than pictographic information in terms of overall perception. Hence, 'stepping back' from a slab of text may well put it out of effective visual range. Moreover, because letters are not simple, and because the density of plain text minimizes the distinctions between global and local features, the very nature of plain text counteracts the simple perceptual interactions of visual elements (e.g., perception of texture, clustering, 'pop-out' of shapes and boundaries) that might produce 'gestalt' effects. Further, the learned associations with text disrupt automatic perceptual processing.

Second, Kosslyn (1978) and Rohr (1986) suggest that relations among objects are visually/spatially grasped, and so it is easier to derive a mental model of a system structure from a graphical representation than from a textual one. In mental simulation, people often use visual/spatial models which they place themselves inside and move through mentally. In general, if mental representations are visual, there will be be less translation between external graphical and internal representation, at least in the early stages of comprehension and acquisition. It is worth noting that most electronics diagrams are fairly flat, usually with no more than two or three layers (although there may be more for more complex problems treated in more detail), so that the structures discussed are broad rather than deep--just the sort of map-like, mainly two-dimensional abstractions that people handle well (see, e.g., Gilhooly et al., 1988).

Of course, not everything is grasped visually/spatially, just as not every entity has spatial components. Rohr (1986) concluded that highly abstract and more exclusively event-related functions (''existential functions'') are ill-served by visual concepts; these may be grasped verbally. Hence, this study observed the transition to text for component properties that are not spatial.

Third, an entirely different type of explanation relies not on matches between external representation and supposed internal representation, but on accessibility: with a graphical overview we can more readily scan elements within their structure of relations, because the search path to each of those relations is shorter and less difficult.

The three explanations offer different (and complementary) ways to improve systems and notations. There are two mechanisms provided in CAD-E that are relevant to providing information to help form overviews: zooming devices and the use of neighborhood. These will be considered in the next two sections.

2.2. Zooming

Claim:
Designers emphasize the need for the improved detail or

the overall gestalt-like views obtained by changing scale, i.e., *zooming.*

> *"...Zooming for instance. There's something you can't do with text. You can get information standing back from a diagram, seeing the whole thing at once, but it doesn't tell you anything with text."*

Comment:
The term 'zooming' is applied to two sorts of facilities: *uniform zooming,* in which the content is uniform but the view varies, usually continuously, as though moved closer or farther away; and *stepped zooming,* in which 'pushing' on an object causes a move to a lower-level representation of that object in the same physical position, as though the object were opened up or expanded in place.

Uniform zooming is often used as an aid to navigation, with a 'far' view acting as a map and a position reference. This is often used in combination with windowing, so that different windows are opened on near and far views of the same diagram. Few, if any, text editors support uniform zooming.

Stepped zooming (illustrated in Figure 1) is something like macro expansion in programming, or, if the technique were available, like seeing a function expanded at the place where it is called. By unfolding objects in place, and allowing the engineer to trace from the outside of the object to the inside continuously, stepped zooming permits bridging among levels of abstraction by making it possible to interleave several different levels in a single view. Interleaving levels helps designers to perceive the functionality of lower-level components by showing them set in a higher level or, if necessary, in the level above that. Importantly, the stepped zoom exposes calls to still lower levels. The nearest text equivalent is probably hypertext. However, in early hypertext systems users easily lost context, which was not mentioned as a problem in these graphic CAD-E environments, where the context is maintained in the same view.

2.3. Neighbourhood: adjacency and locality

Claim:
The nature of graphics allows *connectedness* to be represented by a line, and thus kept separate from *relatedness* (represented by adjacency). Hence, adjacency or position is always, even locally, a secondary cue, a manipulable variable, available for reinforcing associations, for suggesting structure, or for giving hints to the reader. Text, however, must either use adjacency to indicate *both* relationships, or introduce symbolic links (e.g., cross-references or variables).

> *"You get less clutter in graphics. There aren't arbitrary extra variables running around; you just link one thing explicitly to the next."*

> *"Adjacency is what you use to make things clear, it's not automatic. Think about the mess they got into with automatic generation of flow charts from code. There's implicit information in grouping and adjacency: long lines, short lines, which way round things go."*

> *"The difference in the design between mechanically identical designs done by a novice and an expert, is the novice engineer's will be more difficult to comprehend because of the layout.".*

Comment:
It appears that the *extra dimension* of adjacency is used to express something akin to the notion of *programming plan:* a description in a functional domain (e.g., Gilmore and Green, 1988, Pennington, 1987). Unenhanced text displays plan structures badly, precisely because no extra dimension is available.

Electronics design conventions attempt to reinforce meaningful use of adjacency and to avoid awkward distances between related things. Hence, signals tend to be local, appearing on a few pages of the many that specify a large system. But, as a manipulable quality, adjacency in graphics is subject to personal style and skill, and is not used well automatically. *"Engineers will discourse for hours on the disgustingness of badly done circuit diagrams."* It is not unusual for engineers to re-draw a circuit from a document in order to put it into a form meaningful to them. Similarly, programmers often fail to take advantage of what local organization *is* available in text (cf. Waller's argument that text designers can make better use of the perceptual cues, 1980).

2.4. Shifts from graphics to text, or, what *text* is good for

Claim:
Text has its uses; even after reasonable evolution, electronics schematics remain a multi-level system with alternative representations in text.

> *"The purpose of the schematic is to show connectivity--what's used where and how it's used. What it's very bad at giving you is a description of the components therein."*

> *"[Schematic representation has] stood everybody in great stead and still does, apart from special cases where the implementation constraints start becoming important and you have to mention them on the same piece of paper as the schematic, by text...where the physical constraint is of the properties of the things you're indicating by objects on a schematic."*

Comment:
Three important shifts from graphical notation to text were noted, in addition to annotations to the diagrams (e.g., labels or component values):

1. the lowest level of description, usually library information concerning properties of components (this may or may not be available from the CAD system);
2. appendices, often parts lists or textual descriptions (usually not handled within the CAD system);
3. the net list, a list of all connections among elements (produced automatically by the system from the schematics).

In each case, the text offered the most precise and detailed view of the aspects of the diagram covered. The net list, primarily an interchange mechanism between the graphic editor and all the other programs in the CAD suite, is still used by engineers in checking designs, as a sort of 'representation of last resort'.

Often the schematic is only a partial representation of the final object, dependent on physical details expressed in text. The graphic representation abstracts from physical details (e.g., physical packaging and implementation constraints), just as any formal notation is a deliberate abstraction. The persistence of text in CAD-E highlights the need in any formal notation for some underlying--and preferably accessible--universal form that can capture the details outside the formalism. Text is also used for compiling parts inventories and net lists, because there is no graphical equivalent for ordered look-up.

The engineers associated shifts from graphics to text with shifts from functional reasoning to implementation reasoning and with shifts from general functional and structural information to details and constraints. They refer to text more often with more difficult designs, ones that use the components closer to their specified limits.

2.5. Viscosity

Claim:
Massive changes to graphic representations are hard work: if a group of components is moved, connections have to be re-established. Similarly, the cases where moving a piece of text is difficult are where connectivity has been established explicitly; in other cases, blocks of text may be moved freely without difficulty.

> *"Small changes are small and large changes are large, but the definition of small is more strict than it is in text, by which I mean that a small change is a change to a few things connected to each other at one level in the hierarchy, whereas a large change would be a change at many levels of the hierarchy, or a similar change at lots of different places...That's where it's very different to text...which relies on symbolic similarity, not the semantic similarity."*

Comment:
Replacement in CAD-E is nearly always manual, and global replacement is available only in the form of object re-definition: *"Change all somethings is usually done by changing the library entry, i.e., change not what is being called but the substance of the thing which is being called...There's a difference of opinion about whether it [global search-and-replace] should be doable: it's like changing a system call on a multi-user operating system."*

Green (1989) points out the universal HCI problem of *viscosity:* resistance to change of a design. The apparent high viscosity of graphics systems provokes changes in the designers' strategies; because the absence of 'power tools' discourages the types of change that require global thought or global manipulation, designers cope by applying a more local method or a more hierarchical structure. For example, electronics, like software, has used modularity to control signal complexity. A hierarchy is applied to signals, so that the signals in a sub-component are local to the diagrams concerning that sub-component.

2.6. Search trails

Claim:
Searching is well supported in CAD-E in the domain of connectivity, but not in the domain of functionality.

> *"Schematics show connectivity, but they're bad at showing any other things, like the precise actions applied to the signals. Sure, the symbol suggests the function, like a* **print** *statement suggests what it does, but the parameters may vary, and those may be fiendish to get at."*

> *"...It's possible to make assumptions about what a symbol means that turn out not to be true in practice. That's the sort of thing that results in masses of text appended or long amounts of time spent debugging or things going wrong in the field."*

Comment:
Following a signal in a schematic is a matter of following a line or of following a signal name from one page to the next. The CAD system can help by highlighting the whole signal path or by stepping along it. The search may be more complex than following a single line; some signals have many sources and many 'sinks'. Notable is the symmetry of the signal trail: a signal can be traced to its source or followed to its destination. This is in contrast, for example, to a spreadsheet program, which provides pointers only in one direction, and to many other information designs (Green, 1989).

Although the signal path is explicit (as wires), the action that a component has on a signal may be affected by a parameter buried in a lower level. Such side-effects may be difficult to unearth. Symbol shape is associated with component function. Implicit in this evolved use of perceptual cues (embodied in the symbol) is a notion of what information is of primary importance to designers, i.e., function over value. But the engineers also mentioned ambiguity resulting from this sort of abstraction, because parameters constraining the function are less accessible.

2.7. Vocabulary and space consumption

Claim:
Although it is commonly believed that graphics is more compact than text, the comparison is not straightforward, particularly because most graphical notations rely to some extent on text to keep their vocabularies manageable. *Complete* system descriptions tend to be massive in either graphics or text.

> *"You can get more on a page [with graphics]..."*

> *"The early pictorial version of the schematic had the advantage of telling you what type of a component you were dealing with; the schematic now gives you no hint as to its physical representation...In the beginning, there were two or three types of resistor [and a symbol for each]. You're now dealing with several hundred, so the schematic representation has gone from three to one...what will help is the text normally appended to a schematic, a parts list or whatever."*

Comment:
A survey of the contents of the components libraries used by the engineers in this study suggested that CAD-E libraries used for designing large digital systems in a given technology are likely to contain in the range of 50 to 65 basic component symbols, which are used with textual labels to represent 100 to 500 actual part types. Symbols for given functions are similar across technologies. Symbols for similar functions share some resemblance. A variety of attributes distinguishes the symbols: shape (with smaller units, like gates, having varied shapes, and composite units, like memories, typically being variations of rectangles), aspect ratio, size, numbers of inputs and outputs.

The resistor example that appears in the quote above illustrates an important trade-off in graphical notation: between graphical purity and vocabulary size. Should each sort of resistor have its own symbol, or, given that all resistors serve the same basic function, should they be represented by a single symbol annotated with text indicating their individual values? Conciseness and discriminability among symbols argue for the annotation.

The numbers of components employed in a single design varies tremendously, depending on the problem, but for medium to large digital designs the number of different component types (and hence different symbols) seems to range around 50 to 70. Although plotter size can be a variable in how the engineer lays out a design because of transitions from one page to the next, density apparently increases approximately linearly above the minimum useful page size, usually A3 in Britain. The engineers studied usually produce A3 drawings, on which they expect to place 20 to 60 components. Although symbol size varies somewhat with enlargement and reduction, and symbol size is affected by the numbers of input and output wires that must be accommodated, symbols tend to be roughly the same size (say, within a factor of 2), fitting in an area around 3 to 5 centimeters square.

Whether or not "you can get more on a page" using graphics (at least annotated graphics) rather than text, is uncertain. Arguments about relative usable density of graphics and text are inconclusive because of the difficulty in identifying comparable units in each style of notation. Certainly, in schematics, reduction is limited by the textual annotations, whose smallest elements (the characters) are smaller than the graphical symbols, and which in the scale typically used are close to their minimum usable size. (Imagine trying to read a diagram with graphical symbols the size of text characters.)

3. CONCLUSION

> *"Forget* 'all the information'; *what you want is the* **salient** *information and let the rest go hang."*

A decade ago, Fitter and Green (1979) argued that the critical factor determining comprehensibility of notations was accessibility of information. They listed five criteria: "A good notation [1] should present *relevant* information in a perceptual form, or [2] should use *redundant recoding* to present important parts of the symbolic information in a perceptual code as well; [3] it should *restrict* users to objects that can readily be understood; [4] it should *reveal* the underlying mechanisms and be *responsive* to manipulation; and [5] it should allow easy and accurate *revision.*" [Emphasis and numbers added.]

Seven themes emerged from the interviews. They can be related easily to these criteria. First, the designers favoured graphics for its better presentation of *overviews.* This is a standard claim. It indicates not only the undisputed importance of perceptual organization [1], but also the sometimes-overlooked importance of having all requisite information simultaneously available, as indicated by the next two themes: the increased *zooming* capabilities of graphics, and the 'extra dimension' of *adjacency,* used heavily by the designers as a perceptual cue to implicit organization [2]. Text was not just favoured but required for the next theme: the presentation and *manipulation of detail* (e.g., ordered sets, physical packaging, implementation constraints), elements excluded from the graphical formalism [4]. Theme five was the problem of changing designs, the *viscosity* problem that afflicts any notation, which is severe enough in these systems to make it difficult to rework poor designs [5]. Theme six was *search trails:* signal flow is well revealed and responsive to exploration [4], but constraints on functionality are not; text is required for these. Lastly, text annotation is used to restrict the *vocabulary* of graphical symbols [3], but no clear statement could be made about *space consumption.*

Fitter and Green's criteria do not cover two other aspects of the results. One is individual skill differences. Even a well-evolved notation is vulnerable to weaknesses in individual expressive skill. On the other hand, skill may help compensate for weakness in a notation (e.g., the engineers described how they use modularisation to help combat viscosity). The second aspect is the need to escape from formalism. Every notation, graphical or symbolic, is a formalism, designed to present a simplified view of the world. In laboratory study, formalisms may be adequate, but in real-life professional-level design there must be a mechanism to express arbitrary constraints outside the formalism.

Bouwhuis (1989), in his analysis of reading as goal-driven behaviour, characterizes the tradeoffs among criteria: "Reading is a fight for percentages." So it is with electronics schematics. Bouwhuis observes that text is well-evolved: "...there is an almost perfect correlation between the temporal organization of the reading process and the spatial organization of text." Similarly, electronics schematics have evidently evolved well in their own terms.

We argue that the observations presented indicate *not* that graphical systems are universally superior to text, but that the two systems, text and graphics, each have preferred uses; and, moreover, that the uses of each are exactly in line with the argument that accessibility of information is a key factor.

4. ACKNOWLEDGEMENTS

We thank the engineers for their cooperation and enthusiasm, Peter Eastty for invaluable comment, and Jackie Harper for facilitating our communications. Part of this research was performed while TG was seconded to Rank Xerox EuroPARC; we thank Tom Moran and Rank Xerox EuroPARC for providing facilities for MP.

5. REFERENCES

Bouwhuis, D.G. (1988) Reading as a goal-driven behaviour. In: B.A.G. Elsendoorn and H. Bouma (eds.), *Working Models of Human Perception*. Academic Press. 341-362.

Fitter, M., and Green, T.R.G. (1979) When do diagrams make good computer languages? *IJMMS,* **11** , 235-261.

Gilhooly, K.J., Wood, M., Kinnear, P.R., and Green, C. (1988) Skill in map reading and memory for maps. *Quarterly Journal of Experimental Psychology* **40A** , 87-107.

Gilmore, D.J., and Green, T.R.G., (1988) Programming plans and programming expertise. *Quarterly Journal of Experimental Psychology,* **40A** , 423-442.

Green, T.R.G. (1989) Cognitive dimensions of notation. In: A. Sutcliffe and L. Macaulay (eds.), *People and Computers V*. Cambridge University Press.

Humphreys, G.W., and Bruce, V. (1989) Visual processes in reading. In: *Visual Cognition: Computational, Experimental, and Neuropsychological Perspectives*. Lawrence Erlbaum. 227-286.

Kosslyn, S.M. (1978) Imagery and internal representation. In: E. Rosch and B.B. Lloyd (eds.), *Cognition and Categorization*. Lawrence Erlbaum. 217-257.

Pennington, N. (1987) Stimulus structures and mental representations in expert comprehension of computer programs. *Cognitive Psychology,* **19** , 295-341.

Rohr, G. (1986) Using visual concepts. In: S.-K. Chang, T. Ichikawa, and P.A. Ligomenides (eds.), *Visual Languages*. Plenum Press.

Shu, N. C. (1988) *Visual Programming*. Van Nostrand Reinhold.

Treisman, A. (1986) Features and objects in visual processing. *Scientific American,* November 1986, 106-115.

Waller, R.H.W. (1980) Graphic aspects of complex texts: typography as macro-punctuation. In: P.A. Kolers, M.E. Wrolstad, and H. Bouma (eds.), *Processing of Visible Language 2*. Plenum Press. 241-253.

Human–Computer Interaction – INTERACT '90
D. Diaper et al. (Editors)
Elsevier Science Publishers B.V. (North-Holland)

THE POWER OF PARAMETERIZABLE OBJECTS IN MODERN USER INTERFACES

Franz PENZ, Manfred TSCHELIGI, Günter HARING

Abteilung für Angewandte Informatik
Universität Wien, Lenaugasse 2/8, A-1080 Wien
EARN/BITNET: A4424DAF@AWIUNI11

Martina MANHARTSBERGER

Vienna Software Publishing GmbH
Darnautgasse 13, A-1120 Wien

Design alternatives for modern object based user interfaces are presented trying to reach a second generation of enjoyable graphical user interfaces. The objects are designed following the real life paradigm, yielding to intuitive human computer associations. Objects are parameterized to give the user some possibilities to adjust his operating environment, according to his special needs. Menus, highly used in traditional user interfaces, are superfluous in our introduced system.

1. INTRODUCTION

Initiated by Xerox`s Star System [1,2] graphical user interfaces are gaining widespread use in the computer community [3]. Modern, graphical user interfaces are now available for different operating system platforms, reaching from single processing systems to the long neglected UNIX-systems.

Modern user interfaces are associated with the terms WYSIWYG (What You See Is What You Get) and DM (Direct Manipulation). The characteristics of these approaches are well known. A valuable treatment of these topics is given by Shneiderman and Hutchins et. al. [4,5]. The functional features of such systems are presented to the user through objects and their attributes. The objects are presented visually and the user is able to operate directly on the objects, trying to reach his goal.

However this spatial approach to effective human computer communication is not restricted to operating systems. In the meantime application programs of different kinds are available, which utilize the graphical features of display screens and pointing devices. Windows, menus and icons are widely used to compose a graphical user interface. User interface realizations for different functional problems exist and are used. These have to be evaluated and refined to remove existing usage problems, yielding a next step in the direction of enjoyable user oriented user interfaces.

In systems which are developed according to the object oriented paradigm, an extensive pursuance of the WYSIWYG and DM naturally results in Real-Life-Look-User-Interfaces (RLL-UI) [6]. In RLL-UIs the system functionality is presented to the user by elements he is familiar with from his daily (real) life. The appearance of the system elements imitates the real life model, forming the real life metaphor. In the course of the development of an integrated office automation system using an object oriented environment we use the real life metaphor to design the coexistence of word-processing-, graphics-, database- and spreadsheet capabilities.

In our system some new design approaches are introduced. Due to the space limitations we concentrate on one particular property of the system in question.The user interface is based on various types of real-life-objects representing a wide range of functionality. With extensive use of objects we minimize the usage of menus, used in conventional systems to give the user the possibility to execute commands or to select attributes. This and some related concepts (necessary for understanding) of our system are first introduced in general and then two special example objects are presented in detail. Additional features of these two objects are also emphasized.

2. BASIC CONCEPTS

The whole user interface is built out of objects. These objects present the data and the functions, mirroring the underlying semantics. A document object is dedicated to user data, and a trash can represents the delete function. The objects can be manipulated in and between different workspaces, represented by rooms. Various rooms are possible, giving the user some help in a multiuser situation. The rooms are connected by doors. Other structuring mechanisms are also available in the rooms, e.g. filing cabinets and drawers. The objects are manipulated directly, reflecting a real life situation. Some impression of our simulated office environment is given in Figure 1.

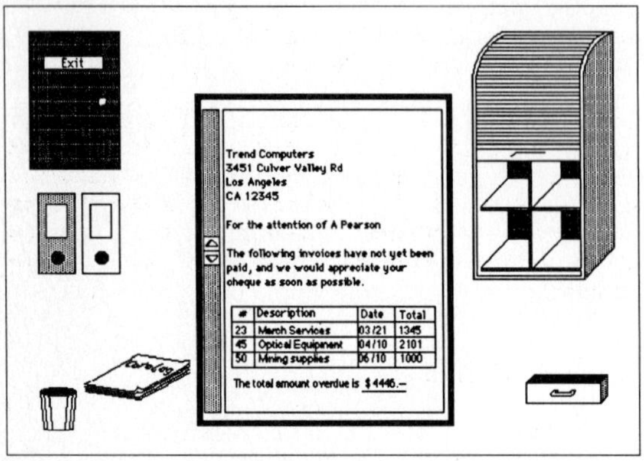

Figure 1

The user defines the available objects as operands or operators by different input actions (normally done with a mouse). The system then uses this information to simply present a different object state (a previously closed folder is opened) or to initiate more complex semantic actions. The action associated with the operator object is executed on one or more operand objects. It is this interaction relation between operator and operand which determines the semantics of the system. If no interaction relationship between two objects is defined a special parameterized error object is presented.

Two distinct strategies for the definition of operand-operator-relationships are available to the user. The first one is to mark one or more operand-objects (e.g. a single click with a mouse button) and then to activate the intended operator-object (e.g. a single click with the other mouse button). Activation means the execution of the semantic action defined by the operand-operator-relationship. The other possibility is to drag one or more operand-objects to the intended operator-object. The activation is carried out after the mouse button is released.

The user employs as many instances of the same object type as desired. A catalogue contains all possible objects in any number for the user to choose from. New object instances are dragged out of the catalogue. The object instances can be parameterized through special value settings (the selection is presented to the user by a dialogue box), and are thereby adjusted to the user´s needs. Different object instances of the same type hold different value settings, and therefore are available in parallel. These objects are used as operators to initiate some semantic action. The user does not need to activate one special menu and alter the adjustments for every slightly different usage. Also the catalogue with all possible objects can be adjusted to different user classes.

3. THE PENCIL OBJECT

3.1. Function

Todays word processors offer their users the possibility to write text with variable appearance. Therefore the system must supply a function to set the character attributes for the next character entered (the current text attributes). We use pencil objects to present this function to the user.

We identified three frequent user intentions for the selection of the current text attributes:

a) The user might want to continue with the attributes of a character close to the text insertion location (to select the character to the left is a suitable but not perfect algorithm, see Figure 2).

b) The user might want to continue with the attributes he has used last.

c) The user might want to continue with completely different attributes.

> The character to the left is suitable to define the current text attributes in the middle of a word. The character to the right is a better choice at the start of a new line or a new word. We indicate the choice by an L or reverse L shaped cursor **respectively.**

Figure 2

If a user changes the text insertion location only the first and third intention is supported by most of todays word processors. Using the real life metaphor of pencils we found a presentation which supports the second intention and can easily be extended to the other. The real life metaphor of selecting a pencil to select text attributes naturally leads to the understanding of writing with the same attributes as long as the user holds the same pencil in his hand.

3.2. Usage

Every pencil defines a special set of attributes. You change the current text attributes by taking a different pencil into your hand. You do so by activating one of the pencils lying on your desk. The activated pencil is slant to show its working situation (Figure 3). The previous active pencil returns into its horizontal position. You click with the right mouse button into your text to write with the active pencil at a certain location.

Most word processors allow to continue with attributes of a character to the left of the insertion location. This possibility is included by a "pick up pencil" function.

If the user defines the text insertion position by double clicking with the left mouse button, the pencil used for writing a close character becomes the active pencil. If this pencil does not exist in the users environment a temporary pencil holding the same attributes appears as the active pencil. This temporary pencil becomes permanent if it is manipulated, e.g. moved on the desk.

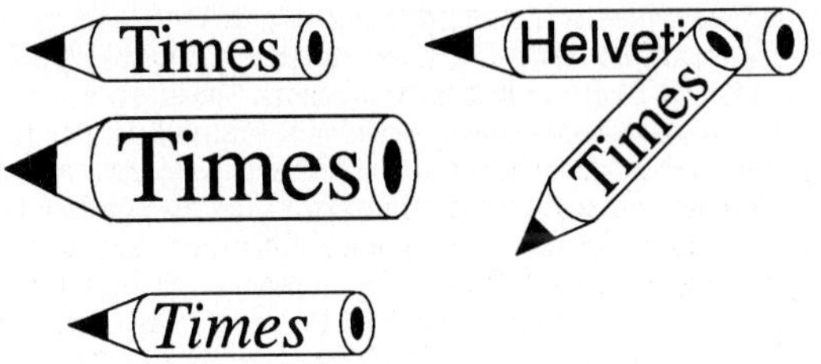

Figure 3

Pencils are parameterizable objects. You adjust its settings to alter its associated text attributes.

3.3. Interaction with other Objects

Pencils are "tool objects". At any time there is exactly one pencil active. The active pencil is valid to determine text attributes at all places where text is entered into the system.

3.4. Parameters

The parameter dialogue box lets you edit the text attributes associated with a pencil (Figure 4). In this dialogue box the usual choices are supported. The user selects the font, size and style of the text which will be written with this pencil. The attributes attached to a pencil are easily identified by its appearance. The form and size of the pencil icon corresponds to the selected attributes. Each pencil is labeled adequately to provide an example text and additional textual information.

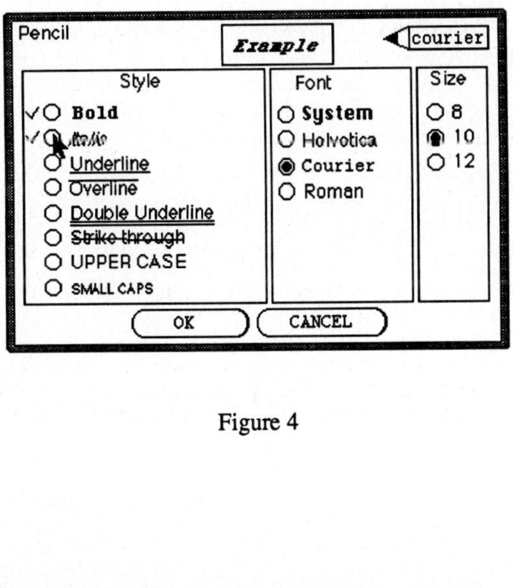

Figure 4

3.5. Comparison to other Representations

Menus are a usual interaction technique for the selection of the current text attributes. Every time you want to use attributes different to the attributes of a character close to the text insertion location you have to select separately the new font, size and style. The pencil metaphor allows you to prepare all the attribute sets you will use. Thereafter you have an easy access to these pencils while you need not remember their settings.

Like in real life a typical user will have about four pencils lying on his desk defining his favorite text attributes. The easy access to the prepared pencils leads to uniformity in the documents produced. In an institutional environment uniformity can also be achieved by supplying the same set of pencils to all members.

4. THE DOG OBJECT

4.1. Function

The dog represents the search and replace function. The function may be applied to a variety of objects. A string is searched and/or replaced in a document, folder, drawer, filing cabinet or room. Multiple search conditions are adjustable for this parameterizable dog object instance.

4.2. Usage

To search for a string you first open the dog-related dialogue box to enter the string to search for. The search-string is a permanent parameter of the dog and can only be changed by entering a different string into the dialogue box. Then you mark (right mouse click) the object in which to search for and activate (left mouse click) the dog. The dog moves its head to the floor as if sniffing on the ground to present that the search function is in progress. When it has found the string in the object, the part of the object containing the string is shown (e.g. a document is opened and/or scrolled) and the string is marked. The dog lifts its paw to show that the string was found. If no such string has been found the dog has its normal presentation (Figure 5). If the user wants to search on the dog is activated again.

Figure 5

4.3. Interaction with other Objects

The interaction-relationship determines the objects, where the dog searches in. The marked objects are the operands and the activated dog is the operator of the search function. The search proceeds in all objects the user marked before activating the dog. Searches for strings can take place in sheets, documents, folders, filing cabinets etc. There is also a search for objects which may be in different rooms and are not visible.

4.4. Parameters

The parameters of the dog can be edited in the related dialogue box which is shown in Figure 6. Some selections are supported at the moment (e.g. search mode, case sensitivity, attribute sensitivity).

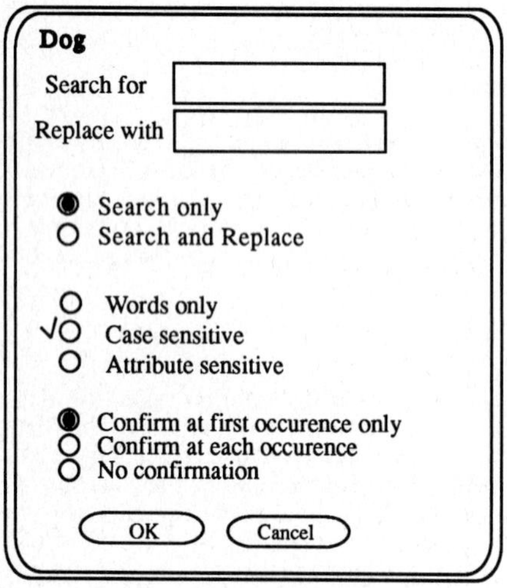

Figure 6

4.5. Comparison to other representations of the search function

Many graphical user interfaces let the user activate the search function via an always present menu bar and a pull-down menu which opens a dialogue box where the string to search for is entered. When opening the dialogue box again some systems use the last string as a default. The search proceeds in the active window.

In our system the search string remains permanent with the dog unless it is changed by the user. That means that the user can always keep one dog to search for a special string. If someone changes the name of his company, he can use a dog to search for the old company name replacing it with the new name. He uses a different dog to search for different strings. To differentiate the dog with the company name from other dogs he gives it a special colour by using a presentation object. Parameterizable presentation objects are used to set forms and colours. If the dog is not used any more its string is changed or it is thrown away by activating the trash can.

5. CONCLUSIONS

This paper presents an ongoing work. The emphasis lies on the study of several drawbacks in existing user interfaces for different application systems. Wordprocessing-, graphics-, database- and spreadsheet features of existing systems are taken into account. Novel design approaches are introduced to improve the access to the application system functionality for the user. Our user interface is highly based on the real life metaphor. Special parameterizable objects are available to the user offering him a lot of functionality. Different value settings are possible in parallel with instances of the same object type. So confusing menu paths are prevented. The major part of our objects (including the two example objects presented) are now in a prototyping state, where some tests are carried out with different user classes. In addition the visual appearance of the objects has to be controlled by an aesthete as in artistic rather than a rational endeavor.

REFERENCES

[1] Smith, D.C., Irby, C., Kimball, R., Verplank, B., and Harslem, E. Designing the Star user interface, in: Degano, P. and Sandewall, E. (eds.), Integrated Interactive Computing Systems (North-Holland, Amsterdam, 1983).

[2] Smith, D.C., Harslem, E., Irby, C. and Kimball, R. The Star user interface: an overview, Proceedings of the AFIPS 1982 National Computer Conference, June 1982, pp. 515-528.

[3] Apple Computer Inc. Inside Macintosh. Vol I-III (Addison-Wesley, Reading, Mass., 1985).

[4] Shneiderman, B. Direct Manipulation: A Step Beyond Programming Languages, IEEE Computer 16,8 (August 1983), pp. 57-69.

[5] Norman, D.A., Hutchins, E.L. and Hollan D.J. Direct Manipulation Interfaces, in: Norman, D.A. and Draper, S.W. (eds.), User Centered System Design: New Perspectives in Human Machine- Interaction, (Lawrence Erlbaum, Hillsdale-London, 1986) pp. 87-124.

[6] Haring G., Penz F., Tscheligi M. Real Life Look: A Paradigm for Intutitive User Interfaces (Technical Report, Department of Statistics and Computer Science, University of Vienna, TR-ISI/ANGINF-57, March 1989).

Human–Computer Interaction – INTERACT '90
D. Diaper et al. (Editors)
Elsevier Science Publishers B.V. (North-Holland)

Alternative Bases for Comprehensibility and Competition for Expression in an Icon Generation Tool[§]

by Stephen W. Draper[‡], Kevin W. Waite[†] and Philip D. Gray[†]

[‡]Department of Psychology
[†]Department of Computing Science
University of Glasgow, Glasgow, United Kingdom, G12 8QQ

Abstract
We have constructed an icon generation tool (called "Iconographer"), as reported in a companion paper [1]. It can be regarded as possessing multiple inheritance of research areas: either as a user interface management system (UIMS) narrowly specialised on iconic presentation, or as a data visualisation package specialised to apply to user interfaces. There are similarly contrasts in whether the icons are hand drawn or generated, and in the sources of knowledge which users bring to bear in interpreting graphics: resemblance to known objects (e.g. little drawings of printers), or comparison with the other icons in view and with axes and keys drawn on the background. The work of Gaver and J.J. Gibson suggests the possibility of a closer synthesis of these approaches.

The information competing for expression comes from several distinct general sources. We distinguish three: the central arena of system objects offering system properties such as file size, the semantic arena of concepts coded by the user such as "all files to do with my current project", and the articulatory arena concerned with interactive properties such as "this object may be clicked on".

1. Introduction

We have constructed an icon generation tool (called "Iconographer"), as reported in a companion paper [1]. Its central feature is a switchboard with a left hand menu of object properties (e.g. file size, access permissions), and a right hand menu of pictorial properties (e.g. icon size, border colour). Our users link items on the left hand menu to items on the right hand menu, and Iconographer immediately redraws the display pane to show the current set of objects using the set of mappings just specified by the switchboard settings. Figure 1 shows a schematic diagram of the Iconographer.

This system can be seen from either of two perspectives, corresponding to the two research areas from which it derives in a kind of multiple inheritance. In one, Iconographer can be seen as a UIMS specialised narrowly but intensively for the rapid prototyping of alternative iconic representations of application program objects. Its users would be designers of user interfaces, or possibly other applications of iconic design. This is the perspective emphasised in the companion paper [1]. The alternative perspective sees it as a kind of data visualisation program, specialised for "data" that are objects in application programs (e.g. UNIX[1] files, the machines of a local network, Smalltalk classes). Its users would be individuals interested in those data, developing and changing the representation interactively to suit their personal needs at a given moment. Thus users are expected to have moment to moment control over the representation, rather than for it to be optimised and fixed by a designer. This is the perspective emphasised here.

§ This research has been funded by SERC grant number GR/F 67129.

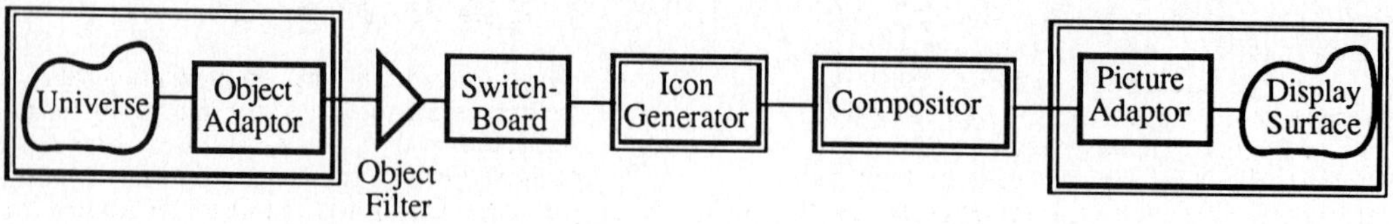

Figure 1: The Structure of the Iconographer

1.1. Data Visualisation

We were influenced here by MacKinlay's work [2] on the automatic generation of a visualisation for data retrieved from a database. This work shares with our main examples to date the feature that what is represented is a set of objects of the same type, but differing in the values of their attributes; and that the choice is basically one of how to use the available expressive dimensions of a picture to represent those values. The idea that pictures have dimensions of expressiveness which the designer may exploit is most fully explored in Tufte [3].

On this view, the heart of the program is a parameterised function which generates a drawing (one instance for each application object). In principle any drawing function could be used (some examples are described in [1]), and its parameters form the switchboard's right hand menu. For instance one such function might draw spirals of varying diameter, number of turns, and "pitch" (turns per centimetre). An elaborate function might be taken from the realm of 3-D graphics and produce detailed rendered drawings with many parameters. At the other extreme, a degenerate "function" of no parameters could produce the fixed icons that are common today.

2. Set versus Object Presentation

We call this function the "icon generator", and its role is to present a single object. This can be usefully distinguished from another module whose role is that of set presenter: the "compositor" whose job is to coordinate the presentation of the set of objects in a single picture. The need for such a function first appeared in the need to scale the mapping of an object property such as file size to fit the available range of a picture property such as X position. But equally some of the drawing actually appearing in the final composite picture may not correspond to any object e.g. the axes of a graph, or a key explaining what the different shadings or colours represent. Thus there are concerns on the "right hand" side about the picture as a whole, and concerns on the "left hand" side about properties not of a single object but of the set e.g. the number of members, the maximum value of some attribute. Furthermore some compositors may present the set or some aspect of it without calling on an object presenter (icon generator) at all. For example if the set is very large and the display space small, a summary statement "There are 300 files in this directory, with sizes from 1k to 543k" might be appropriate. Again, if we consider a histogram or bar chart presentation (figure 2), then the bars might be built up of unit squares corresponding to individual objects but their position depends not just on individual object attributes but partly on their position in the set. More generally, any presentation that orders the objects by some attribute (e.g. sorts them alphabetically by name, or positions them at equal spacing ordered by size) is showing a set property rather than a strictly individual one. Finally if a histogram is represented by a series of lines whose height represents the number of objects in that category, then there is scarcely any sense in which individuals are represented at all. Thus the distinction between object and set presenters (icon generator and compositor), allows us to generalise the representations offered by Iconographer far beyond the simple case of one fixed size icon per object.

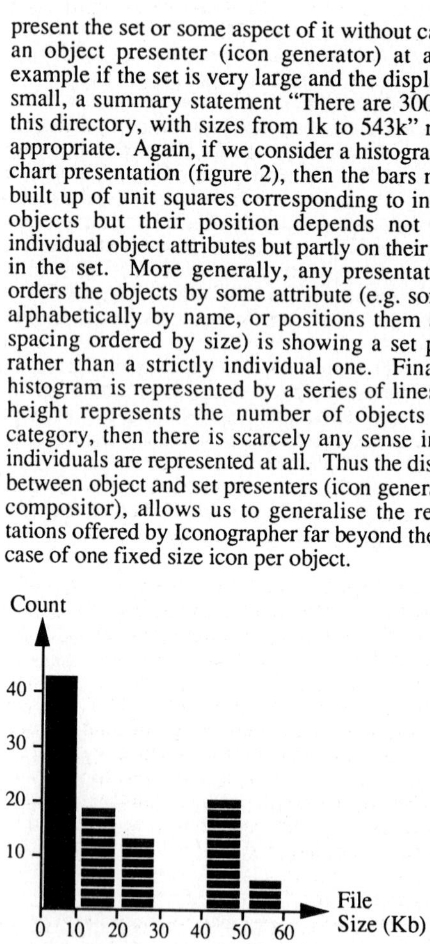

Figure 2: Histogram Plot of File Sizes

Another aspect of this distinction between presenting sets of objects and individuals, is that the viewer's understanding of a display is often heavily dependent on visual comparisons between the objects. You can see at a glance that a file is large, if file size is represented by X position say, not because its icon is positioned at coordinates (900, 900) but because most of the other icons are far to its left. Much of visual perception is implicitly relative in this way. The usefulness of graphs, and more generally of the wider class of representations offered by Iconographer, apparently depends on this advantage of presenting sets rather than isolated individuals. It seems to allow a quick grasp of a representation that the viewer may not have seen before.

3. Set Presentations versus Universal Icons

This aspect of our work, although a natural consequence of the data visualisation perspective, is in contrast to much previous work on iconic representation e.g. [4, 5]. Work has often concentrated on how to represent concepts iconically, so as to replace words and language by picture symbols. In that approach, the question is how can a picture remind a viewer of a previously known idea, by means either of a previously acquired knowledge of natural or conventional appearance or failing that by making it mnemonic and memorable after a single explanation. In other words, the icons are supposed to be informative in isolation; and the criterion of successful design tends to be guess-ability on first exposure or learn-ability (i.e. being highly mnemonic). In contrast in data visualisation users already know what the icons represent (e.g. files) because they themselves set the domain and the choice of representation. Instead, the question is how usable the representation is: not whether the user can decode it at all, but whether the information can be easily read off, grasped as a whole, and implicit relationships perceived (e.g. picking out the largest file, or a group of files that were worked on together grouped by having a similar last-access date).

Thus in studying representations of sets, as in a data visualisation approach, the emphasis is on expert usability rather than on guess-ability or learn-ability; end users understand the representation through local, temporary knowledge from comparisons, keys, and having set it up themselves, rather than through more general and permanent knowledge of conventions, symbol systems, or analogies with appearances in the real world; the information conveyed tends to be quantitative and comparative rather than the identity of unique objects; and the icons tend to be generated by algorithms rather than designed and drawn by hand. Similarly it seems appropriate to consider an analysis of the encoding and flow of information along the lines of Dretske [6], rather than to concentrate on an analysis of users' prior knowledge, mental models, use of analogies etc. which is more useful when explaining how fixed pictures remind users of knowledge from other situations.

4. A Unified Framework

Despite our initial focus on presenting sets of objects, we have attempted to design Iconographer to support fixed, individually designed icons as well. One kind of icon generator opens a file of stored pictures (icons) and allows the user to attach an object property (e.g. file type) to the picture property "stored picture". An editor may be opened to tailor this mapping, so that the user can further specify which picture is to be used to represent which value of the represented object property. This allows us for instance to use fixed icons to represent document type.

A development of this is to have more structure in the files of stored pictures. In a generalisation of SAPPHIRE [7], which divided an object's icon into 8 subareas, each independently varying to represent different attributes, one of our icon generators produces faces with mouth, eyes, and hair style independently variable by selecting different stored versions to represent different values of object attributes. Figure 3 shows examples of generated faces.

Figure 3: Examples of Generated Faces

In this way, pre-drawn icons or parts of icons may be added to Iconographer and offered to the user as an alternative representation of objects. They may be drawn with some other tool and are easily imported and converted to the format required. Such icons may of course be designed to resemble familiar things, and to trade on a user's prior knowledge of the world, as in work on universal icons (although our program will of course not understand that aspect of them).

5. The Three Arenas

In the above we have mentioned a contrast in the kind of knowledge which users may bring to bear in order to interpret graphics: resemblance to known objects (e.g. little drawings of printers) and knowledge of general cultural conventions, versus local and temporary comparison with other icons in view and with axes and keys drawn on the background.

Another contrast is the several distinct general sources of the information competing for pictorial expression. Almost always our users must decide which information will, and which will not, be expressed in any given switchboard setting: in effect there is competition for expression. Yet the object properties which we have up to now exclusively discussed are not the only properties competing in general. We distinguish three such general sources.

The properties of application objects may be said to come from "the central arena". (The term "arena" is taken from Young [8].) Arenas are a conceptual space of objects and operations within which an agent such as a user plans and acts. The central arena is the highest level within a system or program to which system operations generally apply. For instance, UNIX files and the common operations on them form such an arena. In Iconographer, the object adaptor (see [1]) is primarily a connector to such an arena.

Users however are often thinking at a higher level that represents their own tasks in terms external to the system: this is "the semantic arena". For instance, a user may think of one set of files as the chapter of a book in progress, and another set as "general odds and ends". These are the user's own terms, and we are using "semantic" here in the sense of [9]: as denoting the user's side of a gulf which good system design must help to bridge in order to reduce the cognitive load of translating from system terms to user or task terms. This is relevant to Iconographer, because most systems, while not supporting such user level concepts in system operations, still allow users to record private references to such concepts. For instance file names mean nothing to most systems except as arbitrary identifiers, but they are important and often systematic descriptors to users. The Macintosh[2] Finder further allows users to record arbitrary text in "info boxes", and to associate an arbitrary X,Y position with each icon — arbitrary that is to the system, but usually important and meaningful to the user.

We are extending Iconographer to allow such properties recorded by the system, but actually from the semantic arena, to appear on the left hand side of the switchboard and to be represented iconically. For instance a user could choose to have all files with the word "project" in their file name appear a special colour, or files with "magic" in their info box text to have a thicker border. Similarly in systems which allow users to choose and store icon positions manually, Iconographer will extract this and present it on the left hand switchboard menu e.g. as "stored X position", and the user may then choose (or not) to connect it to the "X position" picture property on the right hand menu. Thus properties from the semantic arena, manually encoded by the user and stored by the system without understanding, should appear and compete for representation. In this way, icons may present properties of importance to the user (such as "to do with the book in progress") even though they are not object attributes in the sense of being used by the system.

The third arena is the articulatory arena. It concerns the interactive properties of objects, which may be classified as to do with feedback, affordance, or articulatory state. Thus buttons may highlight or change shape or beep when clicked (feedback). Areas of the picture which may be clicked on should suggest this to the user, items which be dragged should suggest this etc. (visual cues to the operations afforded by the object). In many systems icons highlight when selected to represent a sub-state which is persistent over the short term and important to executing larger operations, but is not in itself significant in the sense of changing objects or properties in the central arena (articulatory state). We have not yet addressed this problem, because we shall deal with user input only in the next phase of the project. When we do, articulatory properties should appear at the switchboard so that the user can experiment with alternative pictorial expressions of them.

Thus all three arenas compete for expression in terms of the same limited set of picture attributes.

6. Conclusion: from Proximal to Distal Dimensions

We have discussed how in principle it is desirable to represent many features in an interface, and that these features come from three general sources — the central, semantic, and articulatory arenas — which must compete for expression in terms of limited pictorial dimensions. This expressive potential too may be organised in different ways. One obvious source of variation is the extent to which the icons are generated as opposed to hand-coded and pre-stored. Generally there is a corresponding variation in the type of knowledge a user will deploy to interpret these alternative types of icon. Generated icons will often depend on local particular knowledge of the representation used, relying on the fact that the user set up the mapping or on axes and keys drawn on the background to explain the mapping used. In contrast, hand drawn icons usually aim at being guessable by relying on more general prior knowledge of the world or of conventions.

Gaver, in his work on auditory icons [10], draws on J.J. Gibson's theories of perception to make an interesting distinction between analysis of the proximal stimulus (the wave energies as they arrive at the sense organ) and the distal stimulus — the remote object whose properties (according to J.J. Gibson) we perceive directly e.g. its size and surface colour. Proximal stimulus dimensions for auditory icons are pitch, rhythm etc., and for pictorial icons are colour, size on the screen, X and Y position etc. — the dimensions which most of the icon generators we have written so far use. Hand drawn icons which attempt to remind users of real world objects do so by capturing distal dimensions: similarities which artists, but usually not algorithms, can capture. Gaver's contribution is to suggest that we should be attending not just to isolated one-off examples (like drawings of printers, pens, etc.) but to varying dimensions of object properties. Thus he has auditory icons which sound like objects falling and vary in the apparent weight of the object.

An important future challenge for Iconographer is to present distal perceptual properties such as depth, apparent weight, age, and age. It will be fairly easy to present depth by an icon generator that offers three not two position parameters (X,Y,Z) and generates a perspective drawing. Adopting computer graphics techniques offers many possibilities here. Furthermore work in human perception has shown that it is possible to find mathematical transformations which appear to encode "age": for instance a "neonate" distortion of a drawing of a face (or even a car) that enlarges the eyes (headlamps) and forehead (radiator grille) increases apparent youth. Thus the work of Gaver and J.J. Gibson suggests the possibility of a closer synthesis between our original focus on continuously variable properties expressed in automatically generated icons (inherited from the field of data visualisation) with the essence of earlier work on icons that tries to use visual similarity to achieve instant comprehensibility (guess-ability) by reminding viewers of familiar objects (and shares with the field of UIMS the idea of hand tuning appearances). Iconographer's existing structure is sufficient for this, but great innovation will be needed in methods for designing icon generators.

Acknowledgements

The authors would like to thank their colleagues in the Graphics and HCI group at Glasgow University for providing a stimulating environment for this research. In particular, Catherine Wood, Tunde Cockshott, Alistair Kilgour and Stephen Todd have all helped hone our ideas and early implementations.

References

[1] Gray, P.D., Waite, K.W., Draper, S.W. "Do-It-Yourself Iconic Displays: Reconfigurable Iconic Representations of Application Objects", this volume.

[2] MacKinlay, J. "Automating the Design of Graphical Presentations of Relational Information", *ACM Transactions on Graphics*, **5**(2), April 1986, pp.110–141.

[3] Tufte, E.R., *The Visual Display of Quantitative Information*, Graphics Press, 1983.

[4] Rogers, Y., and Oborne, D.J., "Pictorial Communication of Abstract Verbs in Relation to Human-Computer Interaction", *British Journal of Psychology*, **78**, 1987, pp.99–112.

[5] Rogers, Y., "Icons at the Interface: their usefulness", *Interacting with Computers*, 1989.

[6] Dretske, F., *Knowledge and the Flow of Information,* Basil Blackwell, 1981.

[7] Myers, B.A., "The User Interface for SAPPHIRE", *IEEE Computer Graphics and Applications*, **4**(12), December 1984, pp. 13–23.

[8] Young, R.M., "The Machine Inside the Machine: Users' Models of Pocket Calculators", *International Journal of Man-machine Studies*, **15**, 1981, pp.51–85.

[9] Hutchins, E.L., Hollan, J.D., and Norman, D.A., "Direct Manipulation Interfaces" in Norman, D.A. and Draper, S.W. *User Centered System Design* Erlbaum, 1986.

[10] Gaver, W.W., "The Sonic Finder: an Interface That Uses Auditory Icons" *Human Computer Interaction*, **4**(1), 1989.

---

[1] UNIX is a trademark of AT&T Bell Laboratories.
[2] Macintosh is a trademark of Apple Computers Inc.

Human–Computer Interaction - INTERACT '90
D. Diaper et al. (Editors)
Elsevier Science Publishers B.V. (North-Holland)

INTEGRATING NATURAL LANGUAGE AND GRAPHICS IN DIALOGUE

John Lee & Henk Zeevat

EdCAAD & Human Communication Research Centre/Centre for Cognitive Science
University of Edinburgh, 20 Chambers Street, Edinburgh EH1 1JZ

Abstract

Natural interfaces to "intelligent" systems have much to gain from the integration of natural language and graphics. Neither medium is sufficient alone. Experience in the development of an integrated interface (the ACORD demonstrator system) indicates that graphical visualisation must include syntactic specifications of interactions and their semantic interpretations. These issues are discussed in the context of moves towards unifying the specifications of graphical interactions and natural language sentences in a single formalism.

1 Introduction

If interfaces to "intelligent" systems are to become as effective and natural as possible, especially for naïve users, they will have to make use of natural means of communication. This has long been thought to mean natural language (NL). However, NL is often not the most natural means to convey a certain intention of the user. In describing the shape of a house, or indicating the position of the on/off button on a PC, a graphical medium is much more natural. Often, combinations of graphical input with labels in NL form the most natural form of expression. Similarly, there are situations where a formal language is the most natural solution (e.g. calculation).

This observation relates to problems in the development of NL as a form of HCI. The most obvious is the inefficiency of having to type NL sentences describing complicated states of affairs or properties such as shape or structure for which there seem to be no appropriate words. Another is the difficulty of accommodating to the inevitably restricted coverage and robustness of the system's grammar. These problems have not been solved, and have often been added to, by proposals involving speech I/O and the use of "semantic parsers" more tolerant of the user's grammatical waywardness. A pure NL interface is therefore currently only possible for systems that involve a very limited functionality; a functionality that precludes the necessity of expressing complex states of affairs and of searching for means of expression to replace more natural ways of conveying the intention.

We believe that important progress can be made by linking NL to another communication medium which is of great importance in human communication, namely graphics.

We envisage an interface to a knowledge-based system which presents the user with information either in graphical or, if more appropriate, in linguistic form, and allows the possibility of interaction in either medium. Thus the user may ask questions or make statements using NL, but he may alternatively create, delete or change pictures or parts of pictures. Most importantly, he may do both at the same time, using NL to explain and supplement his graphical editing activities and the graphics to replace complex definitions. Another important aim is to allow for reconfiguration of the interpretation of the graphical depictions in the dialogue, allowing a reinterpretation of drawing components and of their attributes.

Graphics can then typically take over from NL in areas where NL descriptions become unwieldy and inefficient as in e.g. defining shapes or relative dimensions or when describing complex relations. Combinations of graphics and NL add an extra group of natural means of expressions, e.g. flow diagrams, labelled assembly instructions, spreadsheets etc.

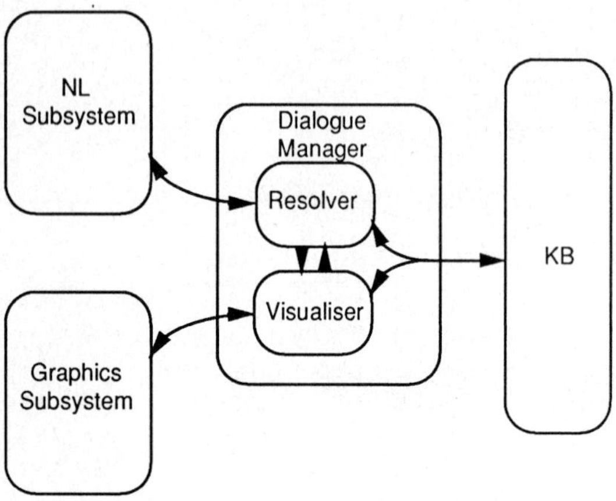

Figure 1: Architecture of the ACORD Demonstrator

The embedding of graphics in NL dialogue creates an interaction which promises to be far more congenial and efficient than can be achieved in either purely NL or purely graphical interfaces.

2 ACORD: Towards an Integrated System

In this paper, some of these issues are discussed in the context of research done as part of the ESPRIT project P393 (ACORD), of which a major purpose was to investigate text/graphics integration. The project has recently been concluded, but we will also introduce some current research which follows it up. Although this paper is not primarily about implementational matters, it will be useful to describe the general outline of the ACORD demonstrator system. There are four major components, crudely represented in Figure 1. A central Dialogue Manager (DM) connects a knowledge-base complex (KB) to subsystems dealing with communication through NL and graphics. The NL component is rather sophisticated and contains both parsers and text-generators for three languages (English, French and German). Two crucial elements of the DM are the *resolver* and the *visualiser*. The link between these is the meeting-point of the NL and graphics processing streams.

The ACORD project has moved towards the goals suggested above by examining text/graphics links involving deictic expressions, by building graphical feedback into text-generation strategies, and by allowing the user free use of graphical direct manipulation. This leaves many issues almost untouched, especially the potential role of the user in establishing visualisation strategies.

3 Graphical Semantics and Visualisation

The most obvious way in which NL and graphics are linked is by *deictic* expressions, by which we mean specifically demonstrative or ostensive referring expressions, such as *this, that, here,* and so on, naturally referring to objects that are indicated by pointing by the user of the expression. Selecting an object in the graphic representation is a direct analogue. Suppose the display features a truck and some cities; the user might say, e.g. ***This truck moves to here*** while pointing at the truck and then a city (say Paris) with a graphical pointing device. Several things are already presupposed in this case. One is that the graphical depiction is "understood" in terms of the information that it represents. What the user means, of course, is that the truck moves to Paris, not merely that its screen position is to be changed. So there must be some connection between the KB and the display, which allows the former to be updated consistently with changes specified via the latter. There must also be some connection between the NL processing and the processing of the graphical interaction, so that a coherent semantics can be given to the sentence.

The first of these requirements, the connection between KB and display, is conditioned by a specification of how KB objects and relations are to be graphically realised. We call this the "visualisation" of the KB information. A truck, for instance, is visualised by a small icon which happens to be recognisable as a picture of a truck; a city is visualised as a labelled circle, but if the city contains a truck-depot it becomes a triangle. Similarly, the presence of a truck in a city is visualised by the graphical relation of spatial proximity between the truck-icon and the city-shape. More problematically, the position of a truck may become unknown (eg. it may be known to have left a certain city, but not to have arrived anywhere else). There is at present no clearly general solution to such problems; one has to adopt more or less *ad hoc* conventions on a case-by-case basis. In ACORD, we visualise such a moving truck by animating the icon, so that it is clearly moving (the wheels rotate!) although it does not change its position. In an extension to the system, one might have a library of options for expressing such situations and allow the user to select one that suits him best.

It is important to recognise that there is always this element of relatively arbitrary convention in graphical depiction. The location of an icon by a circle seems "naturally" to indicate the location of a truck in a city, but the vagueness allowable in the proximity relationship is not obvious and may differ for different users. Indeed, it is easy to think of many different possible "meanings" for any spatial relationship between depictions of objects. This is how graphics — especially simple, diagrammatic graphics — acquires its power and flexibility. It would be intuitively strange to use an icon clearly resembling a truck to depict something with completely different spatial properties, but this case reflects a mismatch between the analytical capabilities of a human user and those of the graphical system. For the former, the icon is a complex object with many graphical properties; for the latter it is a simple primitive, like a circular blob. There is a good argument here for insisting that the graphical object should have no more properties than are represented within the graphical system, as might be the case with a blob, so that the user's perception of it should approximate the system's. However, it appears that people are reluctant to accept the visually impoverished displays this policy results in. So we may agree to use icons as if they were labelled blobs, recognising that most of their graphical properties are irrelevant to their use by the system, which is specified by an arbitrary convention meaningful only to the user.

The extra properties, of course, are set up by a system designer who anticipates that the user will find them natural: they should make the convention easy to remember and to recognize. But in any other than very simple cases, he might well be mistaken about this. Accordingly, we would like to see the development of a means whereby the user himself could specify some of these conventions, or constraints upon them. The use of NL is a natural course here, as one thinks of people, among themselves, drawing sketches and saying "*This* is Edinburgh, and *this* is London, and *this line* is the A1 ..." — but note the difference in this case from the above. Here, the objects referred to by the deictic expressions are *not* objects in the domain of depicted knowledge (ie. cities), but rather are graphical objects, components of the drawing for which interpretations are being specified. The deictic references are, as it were, in quotation marks. With respect to the combined text-graphics system as an extended language, this is a metalinguistic activity concerning the meanings of terms, rather as if in ordinary English one were to say "'Dunedin' is Edinburgh".

In the ACORD project, a deliberate decision was taken to leave aside these cases, and hence remove the nature of the visualisation relation entirely from the user's control. However, related research, primarily by Luis Pineda (Pineda et al. 1988, Pineda 1989) has begun to address the issues in this area, in particular to elaborate a formal theory of semantics and reference for graphical constructions which allows the distinctions between these kinds of activities to be examined in detail.

Support for interaction implies that there must be a continually accessible internal representation of the visualisation relation. The system must treat graphical objects immediately in terms of their "semantics". But additionally, interaction implies a dynamics. Graphical objects may move and change in meaningful ways. Hence we maintain in the graphics system itself a local knowledge-base which holds not only referential information but also details of domain-dependent constraints that may govern changes to the depicted objects, and interpretations for allowed changes. Trucks, for instance, may be allowed to move only along roads; cities may not be allowed to move at all: these are facts constituting as vital a part of the visualisation as static appearance.

Changes to the depiction ("graphical edits") could in principle be handled by noting simply that a change has occurred and then reinterpreting the resulting picture. We reject this approach for a number of reasons. Problems can arise, for instance, when there is no visible difference as the result of a change: an edit exchanging the positions of two identical trucks cannot be distinguished from one leaving them both where they were. Of central importance is that we are interacting with *pictures*, images that have a very strong semantic basis in some application domain. The semantics of a transition from one state to the next is commonly a domain event that happens smoothly and continuously.

If, as in the example in Figure 2, a truck is moved from one location (a) to another (c), our understand-

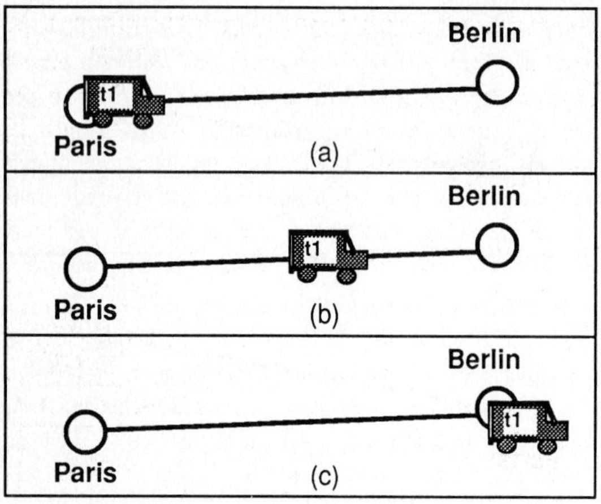

Figure 2: An interaction event

ing of the event is that the vehicle has passed through intermediate positions, e.g. (b). Ideally, the user will want actually to see it pass through these positions in some form of graphical feedback during the editing action. We can achieve this, while also avoiding the above problem, by deriving interpretations for interactions as they happen. (Which also seems more efficient.)

It is evident that typical interactions concern events that are otherwise in principle describable in natural language. *Truck1 goes from Paris to Berlin*, for instance, seems to describe the event in Figure 2. Interactions can thus be treated as having an essentially linguistic semantic structure. Moreover, at the syntactic level they consist of temporal sequences of tokens (derived from mouse events). This has lead to the evolution of a "grammar" for interactions, which treats a series of interaction tokens as analogous to a textual string, parsing it in context to produce a semantic representation for the whole action. The obvious advantage for integration is that graphical interactions can share essentially the same semantic representation formalism as NL sentences.

The handling of this idea in ACORD is described in more detail in Lee et al. (1989), but we shall return to it below.

4 Discourse and Deixis

In the ACORD project, semantic representation output by the parsers uses a formalism called InL (for "indexed language") (Zeevat at al. 1987) based on a linearised version of Kamp's (1981) "discourse representation structures". This amounts to a form of first-order predicate logic, but augmented with some syntactic information about the references in the original NL sentence. Where a sentence has an incomplete semantics, due to the presence of pronouns such as *it, him* or of deictic referring expressions, InL contains information useful to the system in *resolving* the reference and arriving at a complete interpretation. The DM's resolving component collects this information along with other information it may need to find in the knowledge base itself or, in the case of deictic references, in the graphical representation.

Deictic references appear in InL essentially as uninstantiated variables, flagged as deictic and numbered in sequence (since, as in the above example, there may be more than one in a sentence). The job of the resolver is to find a value for the variable, which must be an object selected from the graphics display. The graphics system provides a queue of selections the user has made since the previous interaction was completed. A problem — graphical input is often highly ambiguous — is that there may be more than one object mentioned in each selection. If a truck on top of a city were selected, for instance, there would be two. The resolver is able to cope with cases like this by using syntactic and other information in the InL expression so that, obviously, if the reference is *this truck*, a city can be ruled out as a referent, whereas if it is *here* it must be a location (which a truck is not). Another way in which the right element can be determined is by invoking the conceptual frames in the knowledge base. In the following example,

This goes to Munich

the verb *go* must take a subject that can move, such that the alternative *Paris* is ruled out. The fully-resolved InL can then be used by the DM to update or query the KB.

Use of deixis is not confined to the user. The system itself may wish to draw the user's attention to particular graphically-displayed objects, which it can achieve by highlighting them. This is done as routine useful feedback whenever such an object is referred to, but can be used more constructively when the system has no determinate name by which to refer to an object. The planning component in the text-generation subsystem follows a general strategy in referring to objects, using the highest possibility from the following list for which the preconditions are fulfilled.

(i) personal pronoun
he, she, it
(ii) deictic expression
this, that, this truck, there
(iii) anaphoric definite description
the truck, the depot, the city
(iv) defining definite description
the truck from Paris, the depot in Frankfurt
(v) indefinite referring expression
a truck in Paris, a truck with peripherals

So a deictic expression is chosen if the object is not in the dialogue focus (this would result in a pronoun) but visible on the screen, as in the following simple dialogue:

A truck is in Munich.
It carries 50 PCs.
Which vehicle carries 50 PCs?

to which the system replies ...

This vehicle transports the PCs

...highlighting the truck, which was drawn on the screen in response to the first sentence. A future use of this facility may be in selecting objects for graphical manipulation, e.g. when one cannot identify the object on the screen, or when manual selection would be inadvisable given the overcrowding of that particular region of the screen.

Very often, of course, NL with deixis is better replaced with purely graphical interaction. Our original example (*This truck moves to here*) is a case in point, since it is possible and much simpler just to move the truck directly on the face of the screen. We do not wish to suggest that text/graphics interaction should be indulged in for its own sake, but there are many instances where it allows a more comfortable interaction than either medium alone.

5 Improving Integration

It has been mentioned that the graphical direct-manipulation system uses an approach based on parsing a stream of interaction events. This idea was introduced comparatively late in the project and stands in need of further investigation. A followup project currently under way is looking at (among

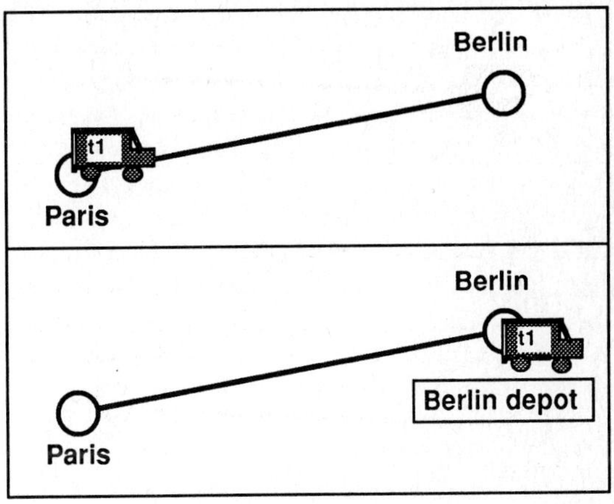

Figure 3: Changing focus

other things) the relationship between this technique and the parsing of NL.

NL in the ACORD project (at least for English and French) has depended on the use of Unification Categorial Grammar (UCG) (Zeevat et al. 1987), a technique which represents grammatical information as part of the lexicon. The lexicon itself is built as a set of "feature-structures", or more generally directed acyclic graphs (DAGs). Parsing proceeds by successive applications of graph unification to these structures. The experimental graphical parser implementation (described in Lee et al. 1989) uses a set of rules based on an approach resembling direct clause grammars. This is likely to prove too restrictive in a more complex system, and we intend to investigate the potential of applying similar graph- unification based techniques both for enriching the representation of graphical interaction and for improving the integration of NL and graphical processing.

We want to move to a tighter integration: a single component parsing a stream of events that can be either graphical action tokens or natural language words, sharing information with a visualisation component on the one hand and a knowledge base on the other. The crucial point is the harmonising of the different events, as illustrated in the example in Figure 3.

button down on truck
movecursor
button up in Berlin
It goes to the depot.

The first three events are recognised as the movement of the truck from Paris to Berlin. Because the truck and Berlin were selected, these become the focus of the interaction. The NL event is bequeathed the focussed elements of the graphical event and hence these can be used to identify the referent of *it* (the truck) and of *the depot* (the depot at Berlin not depicted before). The NL event changes the focus of the interaction: it becomes the truck and the depot. The depot is now visualised in the picture, and both objects are selected for possible graphical manipulation in a new event, and equally may play a role as pronoun referents in a new NL event.

The integration of this system is further shown by the definition of "combined medium" events, such as drawing a box with some text in it. The depot in Figure 3 might be drawn in this way: we assume a "button" called *labelled box*, click on it and move the cursor to the point in the drawing where we want the box to be. On a button-up we are prompted for the content of the text box, and the following NL event (terminated, say, by a double click) is interpreted as associating the description in the box with the object depicted by the box: in this case that it is a depot and that it is located in Berlin. Much more elaborate text could be used in such cases, defining quite complex relationships.

Our emphasis has been all along on *dialogue*. There are many difficult problems in the treatment of this topic in the domain of NL (cf. Grosz and Sidner 1986), and it might be thought that integrating graphics will effectively compound these. This should not be so quickly assumed, however. One thing that is crucial in all accounts of dialogue processing is some sort of representation of the current state of the dialogue. Such a representation has to keep track of what objects have recently been mentioned (the dialogue focus), and it has to be able to accommodate interruptions that unexpectedly switch to a different topic, or a whole different subdialogue. We propose that these functionalities will actually be aided by an NL dialogue being linked to a continually present representation of much of the subject matter, which is made visible in graphical form and constantly involved in the user's activity. Just as pencils and paper help people to focus their dialogue on a topic, so the externalisation of a dialogue context in a graphical representation available for deictic reference will facilitate a shared response to a developing dialogue in HCI.

6 Acknowledgements

Our current work is part of the project "Foundations for Intelligent Graphical Interfaces", funded by the U.K. Joint Research Councils' Initiative in Cognitive Science and HCI. The ACORD project was funded by the CEC ESPRIT programme (project 393). The results described here are of course due to the whole consortium as well as EdCAAD and the Centre for Cognitive Science, including: the Fraunhofer Gesellschaft IAO/452, Stuttgart; the University of Stuttgart IMS; the University of Clermont-Ferrand II (Section de Linguistique); the Laboratoires de Marcoussis (prime contractor); TA Research, Nürnberg; BULL SA, Louveciennes. In particular we thank Traude Manz (FhG/IAO) for her work on the visualisation component.

7 References

Grosz, B and Sidner, C [1986] "Attention, Intentions and the Structure of Discourse", *Computational Linguistics*, 12, 3.

Kamp, JAW [1981] "A Theory of Truth and Semantic Representation", in *Formal Methods in the Study of Language*, ed. JAG Groenendijk et al., Mathematical Centre, Amsterdam.

Lee, JR, Kemp, B and Manz, T [1989] "Knowledge-Based Graphical Dialogue: A Strategy and Architecture", in *ESPRIT '89*, ed. CEC-DGXIII, 321-333, Kluwer Academic Publishers.

Pineda, LA, Klein, E and Lee, JR [1988] "GRAFLOG: Understanding Drawings through Natural Language", *Computer Graphics Forum* 7, 97-103.

Pineda, LA [1989] *GRAFLOG: A Theory of Semantics for Graphics with Applications to Human-Computer Interaction and CAD Systems*, PhD Thesis, University of Edinburgh.

Zeevat, H, Klein, E and Calder, J [1987] "An introduction to Unification Categorial Grammar" in *Categorial Grammar, Unification and Parsing*, ed. NJ Haddock et al., Working Papers in Cognitive Science, vol. 1, Centre for Cognitive Science, University of Edinburgh.

Human–Computer Interaction – INTERACT '90
D. Diaper et al. (Editors)
Elsevier Science Publishers B.V. (North-Holland)

SEMANTICS AND GRAPHICAL INFORMATION*

Ewan Klein & Luis A. Pineda

EdCAAD and Centre for Cognitive Science, University of Edinburgh

1 Introduction

Standard computer graphics systems for drafting and CAD support the creation and manipulation of a predefined set of graphical symbols in the production of drawings. In design activity, drawings are taken to be *representational* with respect to some intended domain, and what they represent can radically affect the way in which their components should be manipulated. However, the ability of current computer graphics technology to deal with issues of interpretation is seriously limited. The major problem, we believe, is lack of *explicitness*: that is, the intended interpretation of synthetic drawings is not an explicit parameter of the program, but is either encoded in the algorithmic knowledge embedded in so-called application models, or else is left to the intuitions of end-users.

From this follows an important practical problem. Since the interpretation of drawings is not made explicit in the system, users have no opportunity to inspect or modify the interpretive conventions. Yet computer graphics programs are used for the production of many different drawings in the system's life time, and what varies from application to application is the interpretation that is assigned to graphical symbols and relations.

Making the interpretation of drawings an explicit parameter of the graphics programming environment can lead to a more efficient definition, use, and understanding of computer graphics technology. In our approach, the intended interpretation is explicitly stated in the course of the graphics interactive session by means of natural language input from the user. This allows the system to check whether particular design decisions made by the user conform to conceptual constraints holding in the domain-specific knowledge base. When such constraints are violated, the system should initiate a dialogue with the goal of eliciting new design moves which will converge on a point of equilibrium relative to the constraint set.

Natural language has been used before in computer graphics for providing and querying information expressed in an alternative communication channel [1,10]. However, we believe that the use of a linguistic channel to interactively impose meanings on drawings in computer graphics is a novel step. Our starting point is the GRAFLOG system [4,5,6,7], which has been implemented in Prolog and takes important steps towards the desired functionality. In this paper, we outline some existing results achieved by GRAFLOG, together with some extensions which are currently under investigation.

In § 2, we give a simple example of interaction in GRAFLOG, illustrating the basic environment and the kind of dialogue that might be natural in both the expert and the naive mode of interaction. We point out that graphical symbols and relations have different meanings under different interpretation contexts, and that the meaning that is relevant in particular applications can be expressed through natural language. We suggest that *deixis* [1] is central for establishing the basic layer of spatial interpretation, and show how the relation between linguistic and graphical knowledge is established. In § 3, we illustrate a way in which conceptual constraints can be entered into the system's knowledge base, and in § 4, we show how these constraints can be invoked in an intelligent dialogue to guide the end-user in a design task.

2 The Semantic Interpretation of Drawings

Suppose that you have at your disposal a graphics interactive enviroment in which drawings can be made out of three kinds of graphical symbols, namely lines, rectangles, and polygons. You can add, move, scale, and delete instances of these symbols on the computer screen by means of standard interactive techniques. Suppose that you have edited a line. How would you answer the

*This paper has been written under the auspices of the project *Foundations for Intelligent Graphical Interfaces* (FIG), supported by Special Project Grant 8826213 from the Joint Councils Initiative in Cognitive Science/HCI. We are grateful to John Lee and Henk Zeevat for their substantive and substantial contributions to this research, and to David Beaver, Lex Holt, Neil Leslie and Henry Thompson for conversations and suggestions.

question, *What does this line mean?* Out of context, there is no sensible answer to the question. Yet this is not because graphical symbols are incapable of bearing interpretations, but rather because they are capable of bearing *arbitrary* interpretations. [2] For example, if you are engaged in the production of, say, an architectural drawing, the line might be intended to represent a wall, or perhaps the roof of a house. In practice, we normally have no difficulty in interpreting computer drawings, so long as there is a sufficient context of discourse.

Of course, the semantics of drawings depends on very specific conventions which are established on a largely *ad hoc* basis, and is highly dependent on which graphical symbols are taken to be basic. It is often unclear how such conventions evolve, and whether they are only present in the user's mind, or are also represented in the computer program. Within the limited class of applications that we are considering, these difficulties can be overcome by formally stating the interpretation of a graphical symbol in a second symbolic system, such as a logical calculus, or a logic programming language like Prolog.

Imagine, therefore, that a user *U* is interacting with GRAFLOG, and has just added a line on the screen, as shown in Figure 1.

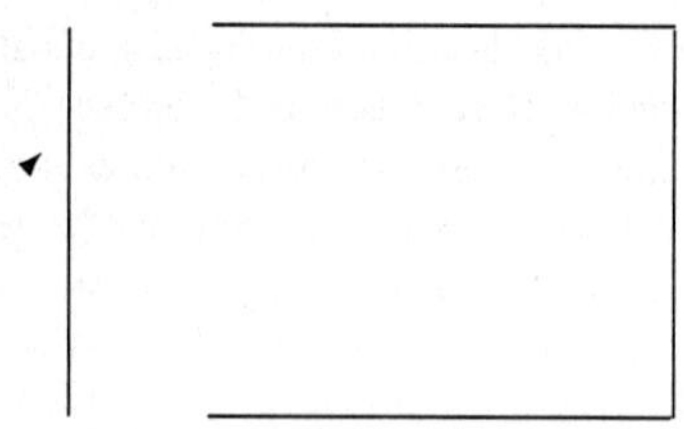

Figure 1: Classifying a line

U then asserts (1) (e.g. by typing into an input window, and by pointing with a mouse; the pointer is displayed as ◂).

(1) `This is a wall`

This statement has a metalinguistic role, in that it serves to make explicit the intended interpretation of the graphical symbol, relative to a particular application domain. If accompanied by an appropriate pointing action, the pronoun `this` can be used *deictically*, in the sense that it identifies a referent in the spatio-temporal context; in fact, in the context consisting of the configuration of graphical objects displayed in Figure 1, it identifies the line which has just been introduced.

There are two components of GRAFLOG which have to be updated by such assertions:

- The domain-specific knowledge base, KB_D
- The graphical knowledge base, KB_G

KB_D contains information about the intended representation of particular graphical symbols in the given domain, together with general conceptual relations which hold in the domain. KB_G encodes information about geometrical properties of symbols in the current configuration, allows inferences to be carried out using geometrical reasoning, and acts as a bridge between the symbols and their intended interpretation.

In order to add the proposition expressed by (1) to GRAFLOG's two knowledge bases, we first have to find some way of referring to the graphical object which *U* picked out with the use of `this`. Conveniently enough, when the line is drawn on the screen, GRAFLOG automatically generates an arbitary identifier for it, say the constant $\mathtt{l}_1$. Within KB_G, therefore, we will be able to state that $\mathtt{l}_1$ is a line, at a certain coordinate position. However, we also want to be able to say what $\mathtt{l}_1$ represents in the intended domain, i.e. that it represents a wall. We therefore postulate a translation function * which will map any graphics identifier α into a domain-specific constant α^*. Consequently, we add to KB_D the assertion that $\mathtt{l}_1^*$ is a wall. The mapping of the graphical object into these two internal representations is depicted in Figure 2.[3] Thus, KB_D will contain the Prolog fact:

(2) $\mathtt{wall(l_1^*)}$

In KB_G, the relation entry for graphical symbols is of the following form:

(3) `graphics(Id, Type, Parameters)`

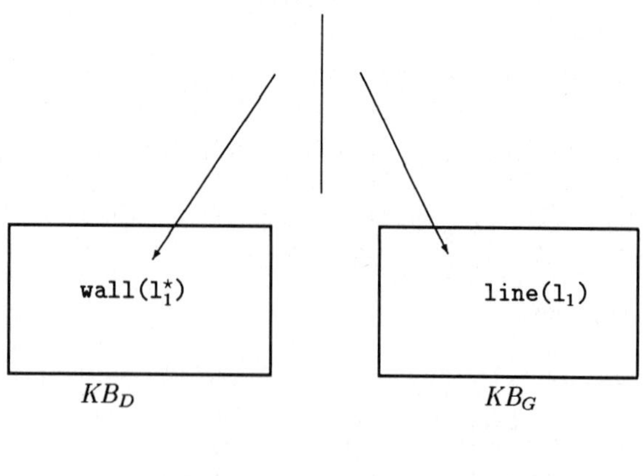

Figure 2: Relation between KB_D and KB_G

As just indicated, `Id` will be an identifier generated by GRAFLOG. The metavariable `Type` ranges over sorts of graphical objects; for example, we will have the sorts `line, point, polygon`. [4] Of course, GRAFLOG has to be able to construct and manipulate such objects. Consequently, each sort of graphical object is associated with an algorithm which constructs the appropriate spatial features. The parameters for the algorithm are listed in the slot **Parameters**. This can be illustrated by the graphical database entry for our current example, where [p_{origin}, p_{end}] is a list of points determining the origin and end of the vector:

(4) graphics(l_1, line, [p_{origin}, p_{end}])

Notice that if *U* were to address the system with the question **What is this?**, while pointing to the line in Figure 1, there are potentially two valid answers:

(5) It's a wall.

(6) It's a line.

However, GRAFLOG will only respond with (5), since we assumed that the graphical medium is being employed to model a particular application domain, rather than being an object of interest in itself.

Let us continue to develop the interactive scenario. Suppose that *U* types the assertion (7) while defining the configuration of lines shown in Figure 3.

(7) These are walls

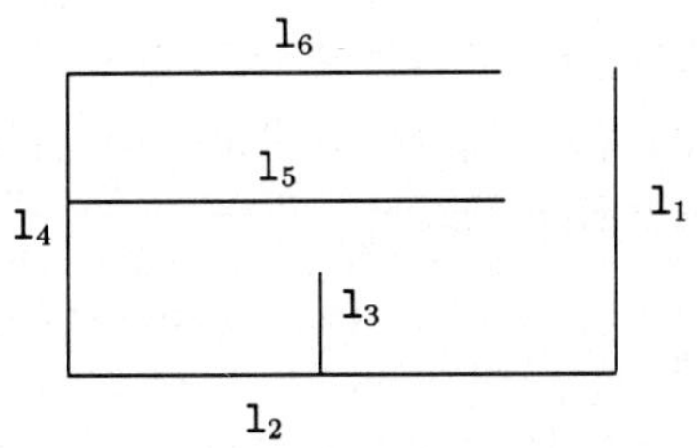

Figure 3: Building a house

The numerical ordering of identifiers for the six lines in the drawing are intended to reflect to the order in which the lines were added. The basic facts asserted in the linguistic domain are shown in (8)–(13):

(8) wall(l_1^*)

(9) wall(l_2^*)

(10) wall(l_3^*)

(11) wall(l_4^*)

(12) wall(l_5^*)

(13) wall(l_6^*)

In (14)–(19), we show the corresponding entries in the graphical data-base, where an identifier of the form $p_{o(i)}$ names the *origin* of line l_i and similarly $p_{e(i)}$ names the *endpoint* of line l_i:

(14) graphics(l_1, line, [$p_{o(1)}$, $p_{e(1)}$])

(15) graphics(l_2, line, [$p_{o(2)}$, $p_{e(2)}$])

(16) graphics(l_3, line, [$p_{o(3)}$, $p_{e(3)}$])

(17) graphics(l_4, line, [$p_{o(4)}$, $p_{e(4)}$])

(18) graphics(l_5, line, [$p_{o(5)}$, $p_{e(5)}$])

(19) graphics(l_6, line, [$p_{o(6)}$, $p_{e(6)}$])

It can be observed that plural definitions like (7), used in conjunction with a set of pointing acts, express a large amount of conceptual information in a very economical fashion.

Continuing with our example, suppose that we want to impose a further conceptual layer of interpretation on our basic symbols. Note that in an architectural drawing it is not only overt symbols (e.g. the lines standing for the walls) which can carry an interpretation. Space partitions that 'emerge' from configurations of overt symbols can also be given a domain-specific interpretation. In Figure 4, the walls determine a set of rooms and a house, but the interpretation of these latter, *emergent* objects cannot be inferred by the representational environment; instead, it must be explicitly stated.

We use symbols of type **polygon** to indicating space regions. However, rather than postulating polygons as primitive graphical objects, we define spatial regions as functions from lists of points to polygons. In order to characterise the geometrical and topological structure of the spatial region that denotes the house, *U* can input expressions like (20), at the same time as pointing to a sequence of vertices. These in turn form a list of reference points that parameterise the polygon. This is illustrated in Figure 4.

(20) This is a house

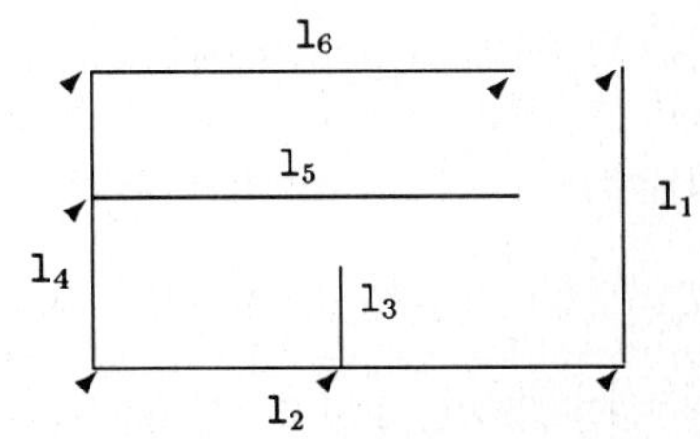

Figure 4: Defining the house

As with our earlier examples, this emergent object has both a linguistic and a graphical representation. The corresponding entries in the KB_D and in the KB_G are shown in (21) and (22), respectively.

(21) house($poly_1^*$)

```
(22) graphics(poly1,polygon,[origin_of(l1),
                    e_joint_at(l1, l2),
                    t_joint_at(l3, l2),
                    e_joint_at(l2, l4),
                    t_joint_at(l5, l4),
                    e_joint_at(l4, l6),
                    end_of(l6)]
```

Note that in the linguistic domain, the representation of the house is similar to the other linguistic objects. However, the entry in the geometrical data-base is more complex. The polygon's `Parameter` attribute depends on a sequence of points. However, these points are given by *description* rather than as explicit values in the current graphical configuration; i.e. they are expressed as terms, constructed from functors of type $line \times line \mapsto point$. For example, `t_joint_at(l3, l2)` is a term which denotes, in any particular configuration, the *point* at which two lines `l3` and `l2` form a t-junction. The denotation of these terms thus gives the actual polygon vertex. There are good reasons for adopting this intensional characterisation of emergent objects. Suppose, for example, that the graphical configuration Γ_1 in which the polygon `poly1` was defined changes to a new configuration, Γ_2; as a result, the lines `l3, l2` were modified, and their t-junction is moved to a new position. In typical interactive situations, we would want the new configuration of lines to still constitute a house. However, if we had given a purely extensional definition of the polygon `poly1`, by using the values at Γ_1 of the point-descriptions, rather than the point-descriptions themselves, then `poly1` would no longer correspond to the pattern of lines occurring in Γ_2. Thus, our intensional definition of emergent objects provides us with a means of giving them a stable identity across the different graphical states which develop in the course of an interaction.[5]

3 Conceptual Knowledge

The knowledge that has been expressed by means of the linguistic and graphical dialogue illustrated above involves specific individuals, and corresponds fairly accurately to the functionality of GRAFLOG as currently implemented. We assume that this kind of definition would occur when an end-user, say an architect, is engaged in developing the layout of a house in a particular project. As was mentioned, the use of deixis made it possible, at least in our simplified model, to partially determine the design object without relying in a predefined layer of conceptual knowledge. However, in a more realistic design task, we would rely on a great deal of conceptual knowledge of the current discourse domain. We know, for instance, that a house is related to other kinds of objects, such as rooms, kitchens, sinks, and waste-pipes, among other things. These considerations suggest a number of ways in which a system like GRAFLOG might be extended, and it is to these that we turn now.

Suppose that an expert user is customising our general drafting environment for use in architectural applications. The expert must be able to define a large amount of knowledge of the application domain. Some of this knowledge is abstract in nature, and might be expressed through natural language; other facts can be expressed through a combined dialogue. For example, the expert might input the following statements:

(23) `A house has rooms`

(24) `A house has a front door`

(25) `A room is a kitchen`
`or a bedroom or a sitting room`

(26) `A kitchen has a sink`

(27) `A sink is connected to a waste-pipe`

(28) `Every waste-pipe is connected to a gulley`

In similar fashion, other properties and relations of individuals that are relevant to the subject domain might be defined. We take it that these definitions amount to a (partial) specification of the design object. Moreover, to simplify our discussion, we assume that their content can be represented in Prolog, and that the standard back-chaining proof procedure of Prolog provides a good first approximation to the way in which specifications can be refined.

Thus, let us assume that the preceding natural language input has been parsed and regimented into the following clauses:

```
(29) house(X) :- room(Y), has(X, Y),
         front_door(W), has(X,W)

(30) room(X) :-
         kitchen(X) | bedroom(X) | sitting_room(X)

(31) kitchen(X) :-
         sink(Y), has(X, Y)

(32) sink(X) :-
         waste_pipe(Y), connected(X, Y)

(33) waste_pipe(X) :-
         gulley(Y), connected(X, Y)
```

When the user engages in the task of designing a house, relative to this conceptual knowledge, she is initially trying to satisfy the top-level goal expressed by (29). The latter provides a specification of a house: for some object `X` to be a house, `X` must have a room and a front door.

Now when U starts to draw a house, the system should check whether the intended object satisfies the specification. When the assertion `This is a house` is made of some polygon $\mathtt{poly}_1$, the system should try to prove the goal $\mathtt{house(poly}_1^\star)$. This will trigger the following new (pairs of) sub-goals:

(34) $\mathtt{room(Y),\ has(poly}_1^\star\mathtt{,\ Y)}$

(35) $\mathtt{front\_door(W),\ has(poly}_1^\star\mathtt{,\ W)}$

Since neither of these sub-goals can be satisfied in the current state of KB_D, a certain kind of 'instability' results in the system as a whole. At this point, there are a number of ways in which equilibrium could be achieved. The main possibilities appear to be the following:

1. The system adds new objects to KB_D which satisfy these sub-goals, presumably updating the graphical display where necessary. In many cases, there will have to be an arbitrary choice about where new graphical symbols are located.
2. The system flags the existence of these sub-goals, and U instructs the system to put them 'on hold', while continuing to elaborate other parts of the drawing.
3. As before, the system flags the the new sub-goals, and U elects to input more information which will lead to their satisfaction.

For our current purposes, it is most interesting to explore the ramifications of taking the third option. We will explore this further in the next section.

4 Interactive Refinement

It should be apparent from our earlier example that there are potentially a very large number of unsatisfied sub-goals thrown up by a specification such as (29). It seems essentially arbitrary which of them is resolved first, and an adequate interface should enable U to choose. However, let us simplify matters by assuming that the system follows usual Prolog conventions, and starts by trying to prove the leftmost sub-goal(s) in (29), namely (34). Since the attempt fails, the system presents U with the corresponding natural language statement:

(36) `A house has rooms`

U could now define some sub-polygon within the house as being a room. However, we know from (25) that a room also has to meet a specification, of being a kitchen, a bedroom or a sitting room. In view of this, U can shorten the interactive cycle by asserting something stronger, namely (37), while selecting the polygon in Figure 5.

(37) `This is the kitchen.`

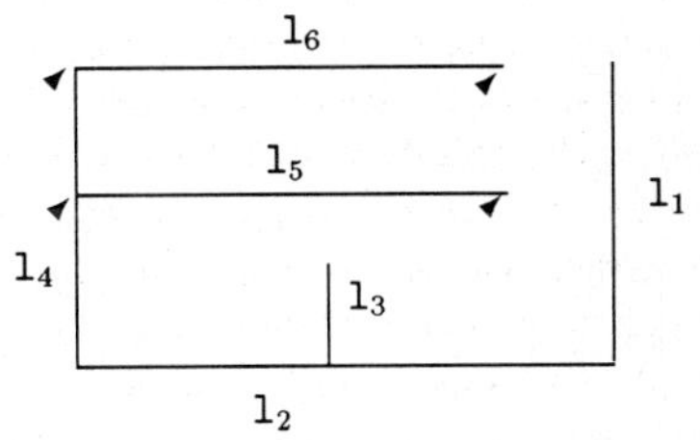

Figure 5: Defining the kitchen

As with our earlier deictic definitions, this new individual is represented in both the graphical and the domain-specific domains:

(38) $\mathtt{graphics(poly_8,polygon,[end\_of(l_5),}$
$\mathtt{t\_joint\_at(l_5,\ l_4),}$
$\mathtt{e\_joint\_at(l_4,\ l_6),}$
$\mathtt{end\_of(l_6)]}$

(39) $\mathtt{kitchen(poly}_8^\star\mathtt{).}$

The addition of (39) to KB_D allows us to prove the first part of the current goal (34). However, the system still needs to satisfy the condition $\mathtt{has(poly}_1^\star\mathtt{,\ poly}_8^\star\mathtt{)}$, and this relation is not deducible from the current information in KB_D. Intuitively, it seems that the house does have a kitchen because the space region which was labelled as a kitchen in Figure 5 is included in the region which as defined as the house. That is, the relevant information appears to be recoverable from the graphical domain. In order to implement this, we flag certain relation symbols in KB_D as being 'graphically verifiable'. When such a relation occurs as the main functor of a goal, the interpreter does not attempt to prove the goal within KB_D; instead, the goal is redirected to the graphical knowledge base, KB_G.

Let us assume, therefore, that there is an inverse $^{\star-1}$ of the translation function such that for any graphifically verifiable n-ary relation symbol ϕ,

$$\phi(x_1,\ldots,x_n)^{\star-1} = \phi^{\star-1}({x_1}^{\star-1},\ldots,{x_n}^{\star-1}).$$

Moreover, we stipulate that $\texttt{has}^{*-1}$ is the KB_G relation in of geometric inclusion. Then the goal $\texttt{has(poly}_1^*\texttt{,}$ $\texttt{poly}_8^*\texttt{)}$ will be satisfied just in case the condition

(40) $\texttt{in(poly}_1\texttt{, poly}_8\texttt{)}$

is verifiable in KB_G. At this point, we have to depart from logical deduction. Conditions like (40) can be checked by means of *geometrical reasoning*; that is, by algorithms which are computed over the coordinate space occupied by the current graphical configuration. In the example we are considering, this verification succeeds, and hence the current sub-goal, of showing the house has a room, also succeeds.

At this point, the interpreter again enters the consistency checking phase of its cycle. The specification of a kitchen, namely (31), throws up a new sub-goal, as indicated by (41), whose satisfaction will recursively give rise to the further goals in (42)–(43):

(41) `A kitchen has a sink`

(42) `A sink is connected to a waste-pipe`

(43) `A waste-pipe is connected to a gulley`

The strategy for satisfying these new sub-goals can proceed much as before, by adding new objects to the drawing in the appropriate manner. However, it is worth observing that the user might wish to adopt a different response to (43). Suppose, in particular, that the current house is one of several sharing a common gulley. Rather than explicitly drawing the gulley, *U* should have the choice of responding to the system with

(44) `Assume there's a gulley.`

At this point, there will be a discrepancy between the domain-specific and graphical knowledge bases. For example, KB_G might be displayed as in Figure 6, where the arrow-head on the line indicates that the waste pipe extends beyond the boundaries of the current drawing. However, KB_D will contain the assumption that there is

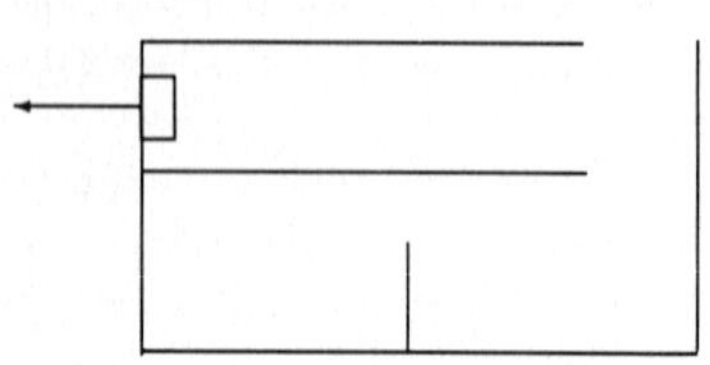

Figure 6: Defining the waste-pipe

such a gulley:

(45) $\texttt{gulley(x}_{100}\texttt{), connected(l}_9^*\texttt{, x}_{100}\texttt{)}$

The identifier $\texttt{x}_{100}$ is an internal name for an arbitrary object which satisfies the condition (45). It is distinct from a constant such as $\texttt{l}_9^*$ in not corresponding to a graphical object in the current state of KB_G, and will have to be flagged as an 'undischarged assumption'. A record of such objects will have to be maintained so that the user can ensure that in the final design, some provision, graphical or otherwise, is made for this part of the specification.

5 Pointing to the Future

Let us attempt to summarise our main points. First of all, we want to emphasise that natural language can do more than just act as an alternative input and output command language. As we have shown, it can also be used to impose an interpretation on graphical symbols and relations. We have briefly indicated the architecture of a system which allows graphical knowledge to be set in correspondence with an intended domain of interpretation by means of a translation function which maps between two knowledge bases.

Second, natural language can be used by the interpreter to taking a active role in an interactive refinement of a design specification. Concepts are expressed by the user through natural language and represented within the system. The interaction should be guided not only by the desires and intentions expressed by users, but also by the conceptual world of the system and the logic of the specification task. It should be obvious that we have said nothing about the precise way in which natural language design specifications are in fact translated into appropriate representations in the system. The problem here is not so much to find a method that works, but rather one that is theoretically well motivated. We leave this as a topic of future research.

Finally, we would like to briefly comment on the general utility of graphics-NL integration. As Negroponte [3] has recently pointed out, communication is greatly enhanced by redundancy, when users can access information from a variety of concurrent channels. It should be obvious that computer systems which can 'talk about' what they are displaying visually give the user information which is redundant in this valuable sense. At the same time, there is also another kind of redundancy, in that the computer 'knows about' (*via* its internal representation of graphical symbols) what the user is pointing to when she says `This is a wall.` A theory of shared graphics-NL semantics will be vital, we believe, in developing future generations of intelligent machines.

Notes

[1]The term *deixis*—derived from the Greek word for pointing—is used to cover linguistic expressions whose interpretation depends on the time and place of utterance (cf. Lyons [2]).

[2]Recall Saussure's [9] fundamental insight that within a sign, the relation between *signifiant* and *signifié* is essentially arbitrary.

[3]Incidentally, Figure 2 provides further illustration of the communicative lability of drawings—here, rectangles represent 'modules' in a program, rather than plans of houses.

[4]In a more formal treatment, Pineda [6,7] develops a multi-sorted algebra for modelling graphical configurations.

[5]It should be noted that our use the 'intensional/extensional' distinction is drawn from modal logic; this differs from the usage which is common in the CAD literature (cf. [8]), which seems to correspond more closely to our distinction between the graphical knowledge base KB_G and the domain-specific conceptual interpretation in KB_D.

References

[1] Bolt, A., "Put-That-There": Voice and Gesture at the Graphics Interface, in: J.J. Thomas (ed.), ACM Siggraph'80 Conference Proceedings, Computer Graphics, 14 (1980).

[2] Lyons, J., Introduction to Theoretical Linguistics (Cambridge University Press, Cambridge, 1968).

[3] Negroponte, N., An Iconoclastic View Beyond the Desktop Metaphor, International Journal of Human-Computer Interaction 1 (1989) 109–113.

[4] Pineda, L.A., Klein, E.H. and Lee, J., GRAFLOG: Understanding Graphics Through Natural Language, Computer Graphics Forum 7 (1988) 97–103.

[5] Pineda, L.A., A Compositional Semantics for Graphics, in: D. Duce and P. Jancene (eds.), Eurographics'88 Conference Proceedings (Elsevier Science Publishers B.V., North-Holland, 1988).

[6] Pineda, L.A. and Klein, E.H., A Graphical and Logical Language for a Simple Design Domain, in: P. ten Hagen and P. Veerkamp (eds.) Intelligent CAD Systems III (Springer-Verlag, Berlin, to appear).

[7] Pineda, L.A., GRAFLOG: A Theory of Semantics for Graphics with applications to Human-Computer Interaction and CAD Systems (PhD thesis, University of Edinburgh, 1989).

[8] Rossignac, J., Borrel, P. and Nackman, L., Interactive Design with Sequences of Parameterized Transformations in: V. Akman, P.J.W. ten Hagen and P.J. Veerkamp (eds.) Intelligent CAD Systems II: Implementational Issues (Springer-Verlag, Berlin, 1989) pp.93–125.

[9] de Saussure, F., Course In General Linguistics (Peter Owen Ltd, London, 1974).

[10] Tabata, K. and Sugimoto, S., A Knowledge-based System with Audio-Visuals Aids, Interacting with Computers, 1 (1989) 245–258.

Human–Computer Interaction – INTERACT '90
D. Diaper et al. (Editors)
Elsevier Science Publishers B.V. (North-Holland)

Using depictive queries to search pictorial databases

Stephen Charles and Stephen Scrivener
LUTCHI Research Centre, University of Technology, Loughborough, Leicestershire, UK.

This paper argues that pictorial databases are becoming, and will continue to be, important in information systems because pictures can be used to depict information which is difficult to describe or perhaps incomprehensible in non-pictorial form. It follows that when searching for a picture the user might find it easier to depict the query by means of a picture. This paper describes a method for searching pictorial databases where the user essentially constructs a sketch (which combines depiction and description) of the target picture.

1. INTRODUCTION

In the past databases have consisted purely of text. However in recent years techniques for the storage, retrieval and manipulation of pictorial information within computers have become possible, due largely to the increase in resolution and processing power of the latest range of image display hardware. As a consequence it has become practical to construct databases that store large quantities of pictures. Chang [1] defines a pictorial database as an integrated collection of shareable pictorial data encoded in various formats to provide easy access by a large number of users. However, given technical feasibility, why should people wish to construct and use pictorial databases?

In some instances the answer to this question seems obvious: because the pictures exist. For example in remote sensing applications large quantities of digital image data are being constantly generated by sensing devices and surely these must be stored, ready for the user who wishes to analyse them. Another example of this kind that we can envisage is an art gallery, such as the Tate, that might wish to keep visual records of its collection. In this case a pictorial database is a necessity, is it not? Well in the case of remote sensing, if we were able to extract and describe all the relevant information in the remotely sensed image surely we could discard the picture. We may not be sure that we could do this, and if we could it might prove impossibly expensive; but at least in principle the proposition is logically reasonable. Perhaps we could treat the Tate's Picassos in the same fashion. To some this might seem to be the best thing to do with them; others, whilst perhaps being prepared to contemplate the idea of describing remotely sensed images will now balk at the suggestion. For them, at least, there is some fundamental difference between words and pictures; between description and depiction.

The difference between description and depiction has been the subject of considerable debate in discussions about representations Paivio, [2]; Palmer, [3] &[4]. Fish and Scrivener [5] summarise some of the suggested differences between descriptive and depictive representations. Descriptive representations involve signs systems , such as language, which have arbitrary learned rules of interpretation linking the sign system to the represented objects or concepts. Descriptions are useful for representing classes and properties of things. In addition, descriptive representations allow us to separate important from unimportant information. For example, specifying the relationship "on" without specifying position, or specifying the type of object without specifying its size or colour, say. The information in a description is extrinsic, meaning that it only exists by being associated with externally defined rules of interpretation.

In contrast, a depictive representation, sometimes termed analog, is not dependent on externally defined rules of interpretation because it causes visual experience which is similar to that associated with the object, or scene, or event represented. The colour of a cat may be described by the word "black" or depicted by spatially extended paint generating a similar colour sensation to the represented cat. Depictions represent spatial structure in a two or three dimensional spatial medium in which there are correspondences between spatial position in the medium and spatial position in the thing represented. Much of the information in a depiction is intrinsic, meaning it is not represented explicitly but can be extracted by inspection. Depictions are commonly associated with specific modes of perception. Apart from being necessary to represent detailed concrete spatial information, visual depictions facilitate the search for information not easily represented descriptively, or not easy to find because it is not represented explicitly. Perhaps, then, it is the depictive power of Picasso's painting that causes us to feel there is no descriptive substitute for his work.

It seems reasonable to suggest that often a picture is as much a thing of depiction as description. It is the potential of the picture as a medium of depictive representation which, in our view, provides the most compelling reason for their inclusion in information systems. Descriptive representations are amodal, they are not specific to, and as such do not benefit from the specific processing capabilities of a mode of perception. On the other hand visual depictions rely for their effectiveness on the processing power of visual perception and must be seen, hence pictures containing a depictive component must be available to the user. We shall argue here that "easy access" to pictorial databases implies an ability to search the database, when necessary, in terms of the depicted properties of the represented "world".

2. PICTORIAL DATABASE SYSTEMS

Early pictorial databases consisted of both textual information and images. However, they were constructed by storing textual information separately from pictorial data, linked only by textual registrations of the images. Examples include medical databases storing X-ray images linked by textual registrations of patient name and patient number Assman, Venema and Hohne [5]. In such systems the user can only get to the picture by providing queries that match simple descriptions of the contents of the picture. Furthermore, it was not possible to search on depicted properties of the patient, such as the spatial arrangement of the heart and lungs, say.

Gradually systems using computerised digital analysis techniques were introduced in an attempt to automatically analyse the actual images within pictorial databases thereby converting from depiction to description. These systems have been further developed by the inclusion of textual picture query languages such as GRAIN Chang Reuss and McCormick [6] and IMAID Chang and Fu [7] which enable users to construct their own queries about the information depicted within the images. IMAID for example is an integrated relational database system interfaced with an image analysis system. By using pattern recognition and image processing manipulation functions, symbolic descriptions of depicted structures can be extracted from images and stored in relational form. User queries about pictures can be manipulated through the relational database and pictures matching these queries displayed. In this way the need to process vast amounts of imagery data at query time is eliminated. If a user's requirements can be expressed in terms of the extracted descriptions, then there is no need to retrieve and process the actual pictures. If on the other hand the stored information is not sufficient, all pictures satisfying selection criteria can be retrieved and processed until the required precision is obtained. Such systems, which integrate conventional and picture query languages Chang and Fu [7], are flexible tools for analysing the contents of a pictorial database. However, such systems suffer from a number of limitations. The processes for extracting descriptions are highly application specific. For example, we would not expect the process that extracts the descriptor "highway" from a satellite picture to be very successful when presented with a picture of a highway taken from a land vehicle. Also, there is difficulty in extracting information about spatial arrangement depicted in the picture

The relational model used within such systems has been amongst the most popular techniques by which to analyse information within images. However, the use of relational calculus for manipulating locational data has been shown to have severe limitations Peuquet [8]. The basic set of operations of union, intersection and containment hold in a spatial sense, but this approach is derived purely from traditional mathematical concepts, and there is no ability to handle inexact, context-dependent relationships, set-oriented or otherwise, or of defining higher-order relationships on the basis of simpler in-built operators. Hence, even given that spatially depicted information could be translated into descriptions, the method of query provided to the user is unsuited to searching on these descriptions.

Meier and Ilg [9] have demonstrated that an extended relational database management system approach in which spatial relationships within a picture are directly encoded within a textual database is also severely limited. Such systems use a set of primitive textual relationships when storing spatial data Peuquet [8]. Here the designer views the spatial description of an entity as another attribute within the database. Various lists of "primitive" spatial relationships have been derived. These include spatial relationships such as "below", "left-of", "right-of", "above" etc. However, the difficulty of describing spatial relationships between entities in this way makes the use of such systems problematic. Here again, as for conventional text based relational systems, textual descriptions of relationships depicted in a picture are inadequate.

In current approaches to pictorial databases, then, there is a failure to handle effectively the problem of searching for a picture, or pictures, on the basis of depiction. The user has to describe the things of interest, and these descriptions are matched to descriptions derived from the pictures. However this is not fundamentally a machine problem. It may be that in the end, when all arguments are resolved, it will be demonstrated that everything that can be represented depictively can be represented descriptively. In such a case, it may prove possible to implement representational systems in the machine capable of fully describing what a picture depicts. The problem is that humans' find it difficult to use natural descriptive systems (such as language) to adequately describe certain properties of the visual world or information depicted in pictorial representations. It is the nature of human perception and cognition that limits the usefulness of description and explains the potential of depiction. Consequently it is the nature of the pictorial query language that the user employs in searching the pictorial database that is at the heart of the problem.

3. PICTORIAL QUERY AND THE SKETCH

As we have seen, previous pictorial query languages have been text based; queries are entered by constructing sentence like statements. Of course, it was not the development of pictorial databases that first necessitated descriptions of the visual world. The very pictures stored in pictorial databases are often themselves examples of such representations (eg ordinance survey maps). More importantly, such representations are usually both descriptive and depictive. For example, on an ordinance survey map three towns will be identified by their names (description) and their relative distances from each other by the the relative distance between their locations on the map (depiction).

Typically visual design starts with a number of vague ideas which are clarified and developed with the aid of sketches. Fish and Scrivener [10] have argued that sketches are two-dimensional sign systems used, in general, to represent three dimensional visual experience. They do this in two ways. For example, lines used in drawing have a variety of meanings which are (partly at least) culturally acquired. These descriptive sign systems are frequently supplemented with written notes. However, unlike purely descriptive sign systems such as writing, sketches are also depictive in the sense that they promote visual experience resembling that associated with the objects or scene represented. Sketching is a method by which a person can, with little material and some skill, produce representations of mental constructs. At any time the sketcher is free to use description and depiction as appropriate.

The sketch, then, provides an insight into how we might go about providing interfaces to pictorial database systems that allow a user to search for pictures (which are partly at least depictions) using a query method which is both depictive and descriptive. That is to say, the depictive component of the query might be provided graphically and descriptive component textually, or by the selection of other descriptive symbols, such as icons. In the following sections we describe a prototype pictorial database system that uses such a query method.

4. PICTURE PROPERTIES

Before proceeding to describe our system it is important to consider exactly what spatial and visual properties of the target picture we are expecting the user to depict. Frequently a picture represents properties of a three-dimensional medium on a two-dimensional medium. One approach then is to allow the user to depict properties of a three-dimensional "world". Answering a query of this form would require machine processes capable of inferring properties of the three-dimensional "world" from two-dimensional depictions.

Although recognising the potential of such an approach we have not chosen to go in this direction. In the first place not all pictures are representations of a three-dimensional world, or the world "as seen". Many of the representational systems that humans have developed to communicate with other humans (eg circuit diagrams, flowcharts, data flow diagrams, architectural plans and elevations) represent non-visual systems, concepts and conceptual structures, or views of the world in which the third dimension is not relevant (eg architectural plans). In such instances extracting three-dimensional information from pictures is either meaningless or serves no useful purpose. In the second place, and with practicality in mind, we wished to provide some facility for querying by depiction quickly in order to investigate its value in practice, and mapping from two-dimensions to three-dimensions is by no means straightforward.

Instead we have chosen to provide methods that allow the user to enter two-dimensional properties depictively. The nineteenth century artist and critic Maurice Denis, in a statement that has often been used to justify the movement towards abstraction in painting, wrote that before being a horse or a battle a picture is a collection of shapes and colours arranged on a surface. Similarly a picture can be described in terms of surface shapes, colours and arrangement. We have chosen to explore methods that allow a user to query by the depiction of pictorial properties.

5. QUERY FEATURES OF THE SYSTEM

We can identify two extremes of query. At one extreme a query in terms of objects, attributes, and visual and spatial properties of a picture can be constructed purely descriptively. At the other extreme they can be constructed using depiction only. Between these two extremes lie queries that combine both description and depiction. In the following sections we provide examples of how the above query types are supported by our system.

5.1 Query by description

Descriptive tables are provided that allow a user to describe target pictures textually. This is achieved by selecting objects and attributes (including visual and spatial) by moving through a textual menu hierarchy. Words describing an object or its attributes can be typed directly into the appropriate field or, alternatively, the user can enter information into a field by selecting words from a mouse controlled pop-up menu. Thus, for example, clicking on the OBJECT name field would show all objects within the database, and clicking on the word LOOM puts the object name into the object field.

Selecting one of these values moves the user to a different menu until at the lowest level the actual images are located. Therefore the textual menus reflect the logical linking of data allowing a user to navigate through the database.

In practice a user has two initial choices when searching for a picture descriptively :

1) items can be selected directly from the relational database, or
2) objects can be selected by moving through the database structure via direct manipulation.

Using 1), on selecting an appropriate object name and choosing SELECT from the database management system, all records in the relational database which match the query will be displayed. Thus selecting 'fisherman' from the object name field will display all pictures within the database that contain fisherman. Other attributes can be entered if a more

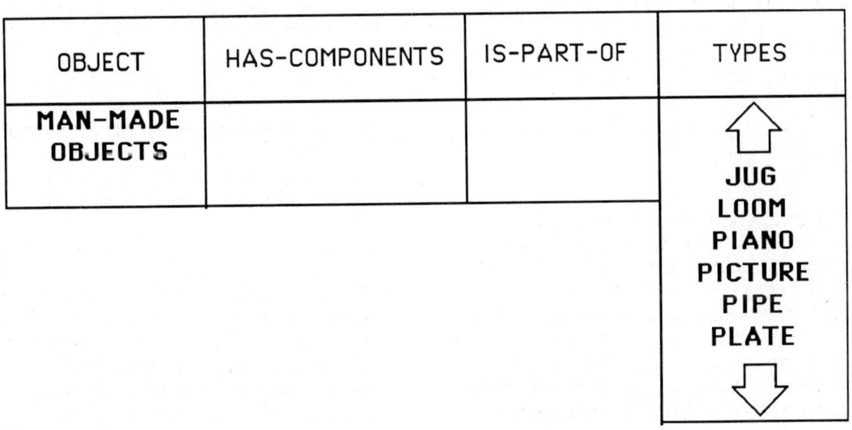

OBJECT
HAS-COMPONENTS
IS-PART-OF
TYPES
MAN-MADE
OBJECTS
JUG
LOOM
PIANO
PICTURE
PIPE
PLATE

Figure 1: Example of interface for constructing textual queries

specific query is desired.

Using 2) the user moves through the textual database by directly manipulating the menus in order to locate a specific object after which attributes of that object can be selected. Thus for example moving through the hierarchical menu might involve selecting the following:

PEOPLE------>MAN--------->FISHERMAN

Having identified the object (in this case a fisherman), visual and spatial attributes (currently relative size, orientation, colour, length, width, and position) can be entered into the appropriate relational database query field. Thus at present the text menu structure is designed to assist the selection of an object name, and it is only after this is done that object attributes are entered by typing in values.

5.2 Query by depiction

Pure depictive techniques of picture query allow a user to construct a graphic depiction of the target picture. Shapes on a picture surface can be depicted by manipulating a depictor , Figure 2a. The rectangular part of the symbol depicts size, the bars depict length and width and their intersection the position of a shape. The thicker bar depicts the orientation of a shape and by default its length. Size can be specified by varying the rectangle; width and length by varying the bars; and orientation by rotating the entire symbol, Figure 2b. In this way visual and spatial attributes of shapes in a picture can be specified depictively. Currently, no facility exist for specifying colour depictively but we can see ways of achieving this in the future.

manipulated. In this way combinational descriptive and depictive queries can be used to identify pictures from a pictorial database, since the icons have names attached to them and hence placing a wine glass icon in the picture surface area is equivalent to writing the words "wine glass". Figure 3a, which is a query for figure 3b, illustrates this idea. Here some objects have been identified by manipulation of the shape symbol. Also a representation has been selected from an iconic menu and placed in an appropriate position in the picture field. This type of query corresponds closely to a sketch in the sense that it combines both descriptive and depictive components.

6. REFINING CHOICES

One of the major advantages of such a system is that choices can be refined. When a query is satisfied the first picture in the set of "matching" images is displayed. The user can compare the picture to the specification in the table, and as a consequence refine the query.

This facility is probably more applicable in the descriptive case rather than the depictive, since in the depictive case the pattern that the user constructs should match closely the patterning in the pictures retrieved from the database. However, where a description of a picture is used the user will not know how these descriptions will appear (in the sense of predicting matching pictures). On seeing a "matching" picture displayed the user can enter more accurate quantities based on a comparison between the displayed picture and the mental image of the target shape.

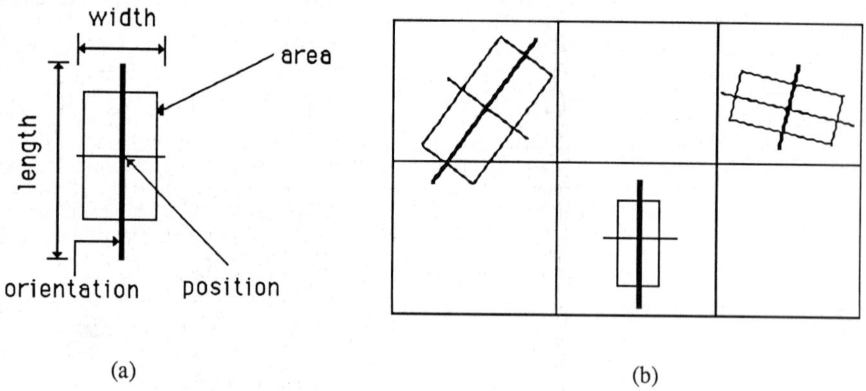

Figure 2: Depictive symbol and example of its use in pure depictive query

The method by which a query is constructed using purely depicted techniques is shown in figure 2b. First the user selects the entity depiction symbol and locates it in an area of the screen representing the picture surface (which can be user defined). Currently this field is divided into a number of sectors and when a symbol is placed its location is defined by the label of the section in which it falls. Many such symbols can be placed into the picture field and manipulated, thus allowing the user to depict visually complex queries.

In addition, icons depicting objects can be selected from menus and located in the picture field and subsequently

For example, on selecting an object name LOOM" descriptively (either textually or iconically) the system retrieves twenty pictures containing a loom. Seeing that the picture of the loom on the screen is of size six (say) the user may conclude "well I want a loom much smaller than that" and consequently enter two as the new loom size. Other attributes can be altered in this way, so refining the query on the basis of what is seen on the screen.

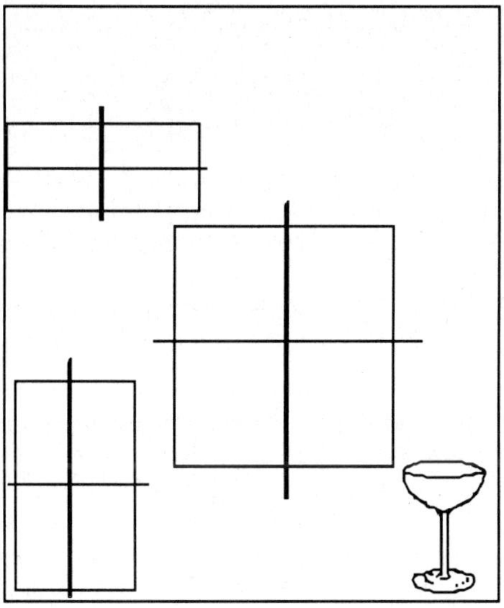

a) b)

Figure 3: Querying by depiction and description

7. SYSTEM CONFIGURATION

The system is implemented on an Apple Mackintosh IIx connected to a Philips VP835 laserdisk. Information from the laserdisk is displayed on a 14 inch colour television. The application runs on Hypercard version 1.2 and the relational database (built using ORACLE, version 1.1 for Mackintosh) stores descriptions of paintings by the nineteenth century post-impressionist artist Van Gogh, recorded on the laser disk titled "Vincent Van Gogh (a portrait in two parts)", published by North American Philips Corporation.

8. ENTERING PICTURE DESCRIPTIONS INTO THE DATABASE

So far we have described how the user can query by depiction but we have not explained how the descriptions of the pictures against which queries are matched are entered into the database. For the Van Gogh database this was done manually. All pictures were inspected in order to identify objects, and quantify, by visual judgement, the location and attributes of shapes. Clearly, this was a time consuming process but was adequate for our purposes. In the future we will explore a number of ways of simplifying this activity. As we have already mentioned, a sketch provides a way of representing a picture. It can be used to represent a picture in mind (for search) or a visible picture. Initially, we propose to modify the system so that a picture can be entered into the database by constructing a sketch. In this later case the sketch will be constructed over a displayed image of the picture that is to be aquired.

We will also investigate the use of image analysis techniques Scrivener and Schappo [11]. This will allow greater drawing freedom using a painting system. Here a sketch will be painted and the sketch processed automatically to derive shapes and attributes of shapes. Methods for doing this have already been developed Woodcock et. al [12], what remains to be done is to implement them for the pictorial database application. It is possible to get the descriptions directly from the picture using these techniques, but we foresee difficulties with this and prefer to follow the more practical path described above.

9. CONCLUSIONS

We have argued that information technology systems are capable, in general, of storing at a low cost large volumes of pictorial data. We have suggested that because of the depictive power of pictures we should anticipate a growth in the use of pictures and hence an increased reliance on pictorial databases. However, pictorial databases will only be useful to the extent to which that allow the flexible and rapid search.

We have drawn a distinction between depictive and descriptive representations and have argued that pictures are important because they, in part at least, depict and hence allow the viewer to take up information more efficiently because of the way in which they address visual perception and cognition. It follows from this that when searching for a target picture a user might find it easier to depict the picture (since a picture is itself a visual and spatial thing and pictures are useful for representing such things) rather than, or as well as, describing it. Earlier methods for accessing pictorial databases make no provision for depictive search. In this paper, we have described a system that provides methods that include search by depiction. Essentially the user creates a "sketch" of the target picture from which the system extracts descriptions that are matched to descriptions of the pictures in the database.

Currently a shape and its gross attributes, including position, can be specified depictively. As a consequence the system is application independent. In the future we will attempt to maintain this application independence whilst investigating how other properties of a picture might be communicated depictively, including for example shape, and relationships between shapes (eg adjacency), and how to improve the ease with which descriptive-depictive queries can be constructed and manipulated.

REFERENCES

[1] Chang,S.K., Pictorial Information Systems. Computer. November 1981. pp.10-11.

[2] Pavio, A., Imagery and Verbal Processes (Holt, New York,1971).

[3] Palmer,S.E., Visual Perception and World Knowledge. Notes on a Model of a Sensory-Cognitive Interaction , in: Norman,D.A. and Rumelhart,D.E. et al (eds.), Explorations in Cognition (Freeman, San Francisco, 1975).

[4] Palmer, S.E., Hierarchical Studies in Perceptual Representation, Cognitive Psychology, No 9, (1977) pp.441-474.

[5] Fish,J. and Scrivener,S.A.R.S., Amplifying The Mind's Eye; Sketching And Cognition. LEONARDO. (to appear) (1990).

[6] Assman,K. Venema,R. and Hohne, K.H., The ISQL Language: A Software Tool for the Development of Pictorial Information Systems in Medicine, in: Chang,S.K. Ichikawa,T. and Ligomenides,P.A.(eds.), Visual Languages (Plenum Press 1986). pp.261-284.

[7] Chang,S.K. Reuss, J. and McCormick,B.H., Design Considerations Of A Pictorial Database System. Policy Analysis and Information Systems. vol 1, No 2, (1978) pp.49-70.

[8] Chang,N.S. and Fu,K.S., Picture Query Languages for Pictorial Data-Base Systems. Computer. November 1981. pp.23-33.

[9] Peuquet ,D.J., Towards The Definition And Use Of Complex Spatial Relationships. Proceedings of the Third International Symposium on Spatial data Handling. August 17-19. (1988) pp. 211-223.

[10] Meier,A. and Ilg, M., Consistent Operation on a Spatial Data Structure. IEEE Transactions on Pattern Analysis and Machine Intelligence. Vol 8. no 4 (1986) pp.532-538.

[11] Scrivener,S.A.R. and Schappo, A., Perceptual Approach to Picture Interpretation'. Knowledge Based Systems. Vol 1. No 2 (March 1988) pp 105-113.

[12] Woodcock,A. Plant,T. Schappo,A. and Scrivener,S.A.R., A Psychological Oriented Approach to Picture Interpretation. Poster Paper. HCI 88, Manchester. (1988) pp. 1-12

Human–Computer Interaction – INTERACT '90
D. Diaper et al. (Editors)
Elsevier Science Publishers B.V. (North-Holland)

HyperBliss*: A Blissymbolics Communication Enhancement Interface and Teaching Aid Based on a Cognitive-Semantographic Technique with Adaptive-Predictive Capability

Ami Shalit and David A. Boonzaier

Department of Biomedical Engineering
University of Cape Town Medical School and Groote Schuur Hospital
Observatory 7925 RSA. Fax:+27-21- 47.8955 Tel: +27-21- 47.1250 x 235

Blissymbolics is a semantically-based graphic language. It is internationally accepted as a comprehensive and effective alternative communication system for severely disabled people. A new approach to the selection of Blissymbols has been implemented as a HyperCard™ application for the Apple® Macintosh™ computer. The result is a user interface designed to enhance communication through Blissymbolics and facilitate the learning thereof. Following an introduction to the context within which **HyperBliss** has been developed, some of the features which are unique to this programme are illustrated and discussed.

Keywords: Blissymbolics, User Interface Design, Augmentative and Alternative Communication, Semantics, Graphic Language, Special Education

Introduction

Augmentative and Alternative Communication

Internationally, Augmentative and Alternative Communication (AAC) has become a core science in the field of Rehabilitation Technology. It is now accepted that comprehensive treatment of multiple handicaps which include speaking disability should offer an appropriate solution to the prime need of the individual: Communication. This need is arguably the most serious and often the most neglected. The ability to respond, converse, and convey coherent messages can ease the frustration of severely disabled people and help them achieve a more rounded physical and emotional existence. With AAC, conventional physical therapy becomes more efficient because a "communicative" patient can offer the therapist valuable feedback. Furthermore, AAC technology enables non-speaking pupils to explore new linguistic horizons which are otherwise out of their reach. Being "communicatively independent" gives disabled people better prospects of integration with the community at large. Job placement, for instance, is no longer an impossible task. Complementary AAC technology can help those who under different circumstances impose an unnecessary burden on the ever shrinking welfare budgets to become self supporting and even tax payers.

Blissymbolics

Blissymbolics is a semantically-based graphic language. C.K. Bliss developed this logical and unambiguous symbol system in the hope that it would become a universal channel of communication to promote world peace (Bliss, 1965). Instead, In 1971, Blissymbolics was introduced as a communication-enhancement system for pre-reading non-speaking children (McNaughton 1985).

Blissymbolics has a core vocabulary of more then 2000 symbols (Blissymbols). They derive from a fixed set of "key" graphic forms made of standard geometric shapes and international marks:

♡□○△ − + ? 1 2 3 etc...

Every "key" symbol is assigned a root meaning. Most Blissymbols are, therefore, ideographs. They represent the summed semantic value generated from their meaning-based symbol composition. Others are pictographs (or icons). They graphically depict the outline shape of the object which they represent:

♡↑ -ideograph: (feeling + up) = "happy".

 -pictograph = "grapes".

Users who need to expand the system can modify existing symbols or generate new ones by applying a variety of logical strategies and simple syntactic rules.

Communication Boards

Typically, individuals who communicate through Blissymbolics do so by pointing at symbols laid out on communication boards. Their communication partners can read the verbal meaning which accompanies each symbol. As an alternative communication system, Blissymbolics is advantageous to people with multiple disabilities because it enables them to communicate and converse effectively with minimal 'actuations'. Moreover, Blissymbolics transcends traditional orthographic literacy. The semantic basis of the system makes it possible for pre-reading users to transmit meaningful and comprehensive messages without the need to be familiar with the writing system relevant to their audience.

Communication Boards are an inexpensive and easily accessible entry-level solution to very basic communication requirements. However, they are quite inadequate for the more elaborate social interaction and academic needs of most users. Microcomputers with Bliss-based software on the other hand offer the flexibility and versatility users may need for enhanced communication and effective education.

Computerized Applications

Over the last 10 years a number of multifunctional programmes which manipulate a stored set of Blissymbols have been developed. **None** of these programmes, however, allows a cognitive approach by which the user can interface the stored "lexicon" through a logically consistent symbol retrieving procedure. For example, the most popular programme to date, "Talking BlissApple™" (Kelso & Vanderheiden 1980), has been translated into several languages, and has faithfully served Blissymbolics users around the world. However, the programme is not a good mechanism for users to access large vocabularies. It is so because each symbol stored in BlissApple™ must be retrieved by calling the arbitrary numerical code assigned to it. Users must therefore rely on auxiliary boards or otherwise memorize long lists of cognitively non-related numbers associated with the symbols.

HyperBliss

A Cognitive "Semantographic" Technique

A study entitled "Multidimensional Scaling of Blissymbolics Data" (Shalit et al, 1988) provided statistical evidence in support of the hypothesis that ***the semantic comprehension of Blissymbols is elicited through conscious or subconscious reference to their component composition.***
A direct consequence of this study was the development** of a microcomputer-based semantographic technique by which users access stored Blissymbols by cognitively referring to their semantic content and retrieve them by logically relating to their component parts.

Retrieval

HyperBliss users must apply their acquired knowledge of Blissymbolics to synthesize, consciously or subconsciously, the precise or an approximate (even partial) graphic representation of the concept or object they wish to "talk" about. The users then retrieve the symbol by selecting one of its component parts from the keyboard. If the desired symbol does not appear in the visible portion of the "Options Field" then the user may either scroll the display to look for it, or select another component from the keyboard. [see Figure 1].

Adaptive-Predictive Algorithm

This retrieval mechanism is augmented by an adaptive-predictive capability. The algorithm "learns" the Bliss communication patterns of the user. It constantly updates frequency, recency and pairing tables which reflect the user's symbol selection history. By manipulating these records the system is able to predict the most likely selection trajectory to be taken by the user. Therefore, a frequently used system can offer its user (from the beginning of almost every selection process) an "intelligently" prioritized list of potential Blissymbols to choose from.

Output

There are a message display, text-editing facilities and a syntactically-based option generator . Symbols are automatically presented with the orthographic representation of their meaning. However, once a symbol is selected the user can reassign to it any chosen syntactic and morphological form which is also presented as audio output by the text-to-speech generator.

Figure 1. Hyperbliss "Communication Board"

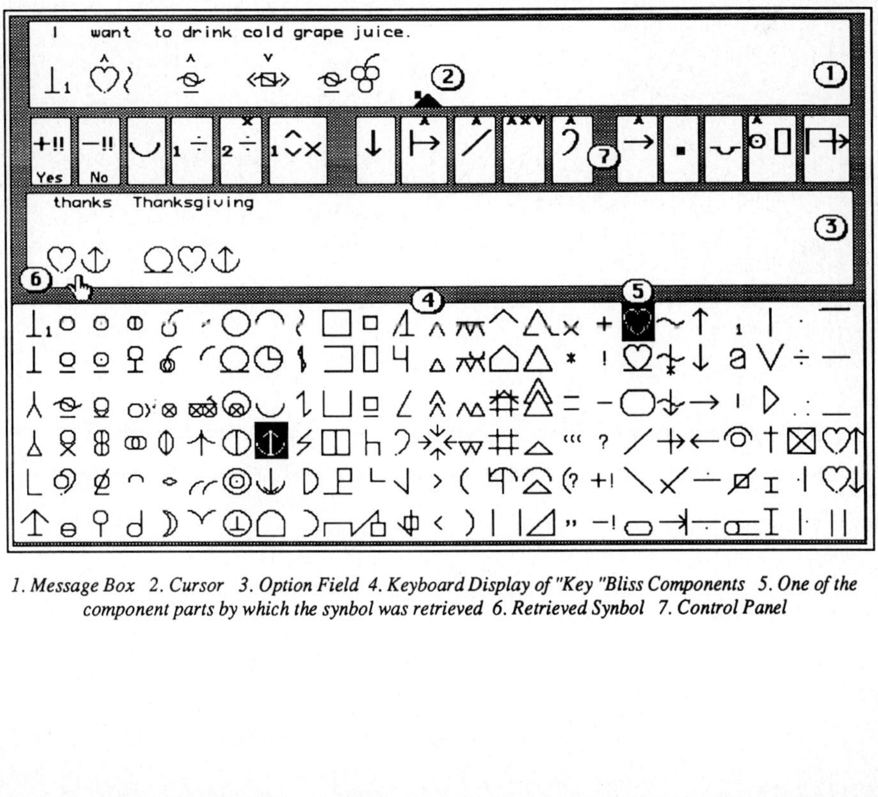

1. Message Box 2. Cursor 3. Option Field 4. Keyboard Display of "Key "Bliss Components 5. One of the component parts by which the synbol was retrieved 6. Retrieved Synbol 7. Control Panel

Teaching Aid

This powerful and personalized communication interface is integrated with a versatile teaching aid [Figure 2] designed to prepare the user for proficient utilization of this communication device. It features semi-automatic teaching and testing routines based on the present cognitive semantographic method. The tutorial "teaches" the symbols to the user in a manner which is believed to facilitate a more effective learning of the system. The two test routines allow the teacher or the therapist to monitor the user's progress. These are briefly discussed below:

(i) The tutorial demonstrates to the user how symbols are analyzed into their component parts. Each symbol is shown with its meaning while a voice output repeats the word twice. The "key" components which form the symbol are then "highlighted" one by one on the "Keyboard".

(ii) The first test routine checks if the user is able to analyze symbols that had already been taught to him/her. The user is asked to indicate which "key" components on the Keyboard match the ones that form the particular symbol that appears on the screen. There is instant vocal and visual feedback. If a selection is correct then the respective "key" component is highlighted and the machine responds with "Very Good". Otherwise, the response is "Sorry". However, before the user is tested on the next symbol, the components of the present one are highlighted. This way the user can see how successful he/she was. At the end of each test the teacher can obtain a full report on the user's performance.

(iii) The second test is a simulation of the actual retrieving routine which the user must perform while communicating through HyperBliss. The test checks if the user can synthesize (partially or fully) a given set of familiar symbols. The test is almost identical to the previous one, except here the user does not see the symbol. In other words, the user is asked to recall Blissymbols by semantographically structuring these symbols in his/her mind and to refer, in no particular order, to some or all of their component parts which may appear on the "keyboard" display.

Figure 2. Hyperbliss Tutor and Tester for Bilssynbolics

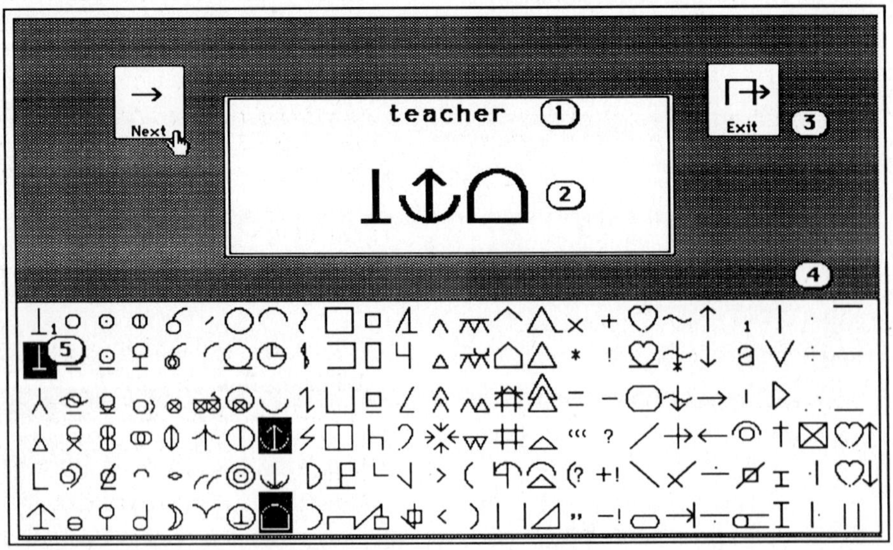

1. Gloss 2. Symbol 3. Fubction buttons 4. Keyboard display of "Key" Bliss components 5. Correct component selection

Additional Features

An automatic scanning mechanism is installed in relevant parts of the package to facilitate a 'one switch' selection preference. Other useful features include: a sophisticated lexicon (i.e. symbol-library) maintenance; statistical analysis of the user's communication performance; a print-shop for easy "drawing", storing and printing of existing and new Blissymbols; and desktop facilities to print Symbol-Charts and 'Bliss' dictionaries. Segments of HyperBliss have already been translated into several languages (e.g. Afrikaans, Xhosa, Hebrew and Hungarian) and were used to produce the respective 'Bliss' dictionaries.

Conclusions

Preliminary clinical tests of HyperBliss (currently under way) suggest that the present programme supports effective teaching of Blissymbolics and facilitates learning thereof. This could be attributed to the more stimulating interaction environment which HyperBliss helps create for the users. However, further research is being planned to establish the relative contributions of various components within this software package in order to optimize it as a broad multi-functional blissymbolics interface.

Acknowledgements

The authors would like to thank The Chairman and the board of the Mauerberger Foundation, Cape Town, RSA for their Support.

Footnotes

* HyperBliss was conceptualized, designed, specified and coordinated by the first author and supervised by the second. Low level programming was done by Michael Brand, Tony Stein and Marion Baxter (Department of Computer Science, University of Cape Town.

**Three factors facilitated the completion of the HyperBliss project in a rather short time: The graphic capabilities of the Apple Macintosh™ Computer; HyperCard™ which proved to be an ideal environment for the development and implementation of the programme; and BlissTemplate™, a special Macintosh-based non-spacing font, used in the programme to "draw" Blissymbols. [BlissTemplate was developed in 1988 by Dr Peter Reich, Department of Linguistics, University of Toronto, Toronto, Canada. It is now available from 'Blissymbolics Communication International': 250 Ferrand Drive, Don Mills, Ontario, M3C Canada].

References

Bliss, C.K., (1965). Semantography (Blissymbolics): A logical Writing System for an illogical World. Semantography Publications, Sydney, Australia.

Kelso, D.P. & Vanderheiden, G.C., (1980). Talking BlissApple: Multifunctional Blissymbol Display and Printing Program for the Apple II. Madison, Wisconsin: Trace Research and Development Center.

McNaughton, S., (Ed.) (1985). Communicating with Blissymbolics. The Blissymbolics Communication Institute, Toronto, Canada.

Shalit, A., Boonzaier, D.A., & Underhill, L.G., Williams-Short, R., (1988). 'Multidimensional Scaling of Blissymbolics Data'. An Interim Research Report. Submitted to the Department of Biomedical Engineering. University of Cape Town, RSA.

Human–Computer Interaction – INTERACT '90
D. Diaper et al. (Editors)
Elsevier Science Publishers B.V. (North-Holland)

A COGNITIVE APPROACH TO THE DEFINITION AND EVALUATION OF A STANDARD FOR NAVAL TACTICAL DISPLAY SYMBOLOGY

John Campion[1], Martin A. Brockett, Dan Martin and Michele Rate

Admiralty Research Establishment, Procurement Executive, Ministry of Defence,
Portsdown, Portsmouth, Hants, PO6 4AA

A cognitive approach to systematically and objectively defining and evaluating options for a standardised coding scheme for naval tactical displays was described and illustrated through the partial development of a method. The method comprises three parts; a consideration of the process of defining the standard, an evaluation framework for the coding schemes which considers system effectiveness and the general nature of command level tasks associated with tactical displays, and a task model derived from analysis of a typical display user's task. The model was used to interpret data from an experimental study, also based on this task.

1. INTRODUCTION

1.1 Aim of the paper

The work described in this paper forms part of a wider project - to develop experimentally based methods for the evaluation of parts of prototype naval command systems. The problem presented to the authors, and described in this paper (to evaluate three candidate symbology coding schemes for the development of a NATO standard), is an "instance" of the sort of problems to be addressed. It is used to illustrate the approach adopted in developing these methods. The aim of the paper is not to develop substantive design recommendations, nor to develop a method itself, but rather to justify and illustrate the approach through the development of part of a method.

1.2 Aims of the approach

Many decisions associated with the design of naval command systems are made by committees of experts. Decision makers may be users (naval personnel), system designers, ergonomists etc. Decisions are made on the basis of individual subjective judgement and discussion. Disagreements are resolved by rational argument, arbitrary compromise and the exercise of authority.

Such a decision making process is unsatisfactory because the status of its product (some design recommendation) is uncertain. This uncertainty is of two sorts. First, it is uncertain if the design recommendation is a "good one". Second, even if it turns out to be a "good one", the reasons for its being so are likely to be unknown, thus rendering uncertain the scope of its validity (e.g DefStan 00-25 [1])

The approach adopted here attempts to remedy this situation by providing decision makers with design advice which is demonstrably true (i.e. objective) and which is supported by explanation (i.e. principled). In doing so it embraces the concept, as adopted by Dowell and Long [2], that human factors should aim to develop into a more serious engineering discipline.

1.3 The domain problem

A naval command system is the system within a ship which draws together all the information from the ship's sensors and other sources, interprets it and uses it to support the generation and implementation of tactical plans. The focus of this study is the command system tactical display. This display presents to the command a synthetic real-time "picture" of the tactical situation in the form of a plan position indicator. An example of such a display is shown in Figure 1 in order to indicate the typical range and type of symbols used and their configuration on the display.

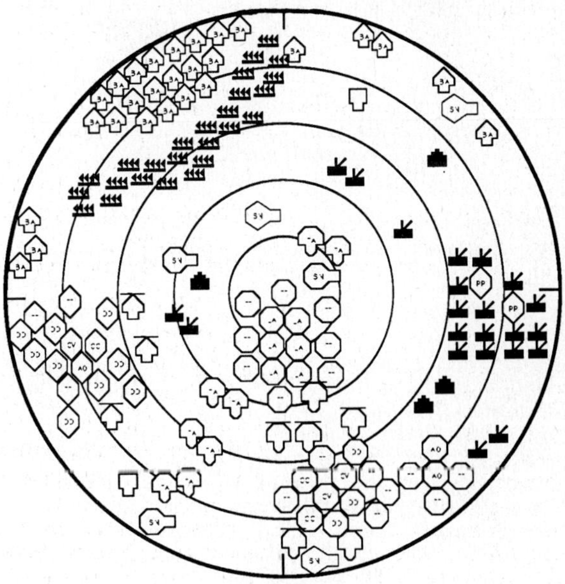

Figure 1
A Tactical Display

Currently, different nations within NATO use a variety of symbols on their tactical displays. Geometric shapes,

[1] All correspondence should be addressed to Dr. T.J. Campion, now at Electronic Facilities Design Ltd, Unit 8, Grove Park 2, Waltham Road, White Waltham, Maidenhead, Berkshire, SL6 3LW, England.

pictograms, alphanumerics, and various combinations of these are used at present. Operational requirements (e.g. the increasing scope and integration of naval operations) and enabling technologies (e.g. the advent of high speed data links) have led to a large increase in the amount and type of data to be handled by naval command systems and encouraged a proliferation of new or modified coding schemes for representing it. Many schemes could not be adapted to handle the extra information without degradation. This led to a move to establish a NATO standard - a STANAG.

Discussion between nations established a short-list of newly developed candidate coding schemes. Examples of each scheme are shown in Figure 2. The aim of the study reported here was to evaluate the alternative schemes with a view to developing an optimal one. This could be a single scheme, a modified single scheme or an amalgam of more than one scheme.

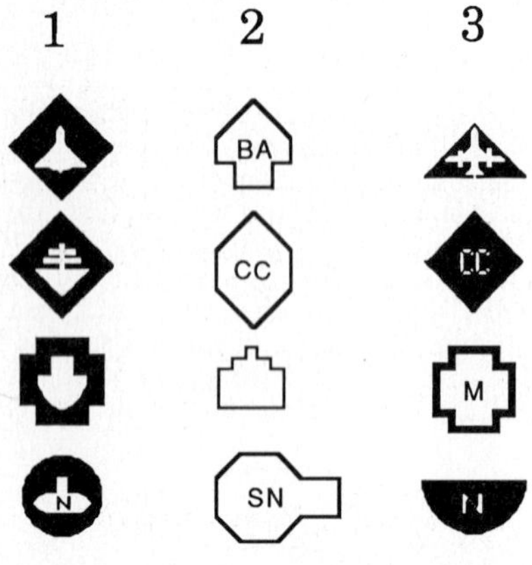

Figure 2 Coding Scheme Options
1st row: hostile bomber, 2nd row: hostile cruiser,
3rd row: neutral merchant ship,
4th row: friend nuclear submarine

A critique of the previous symbol set evaluation work by the authors was used to determine the form of the method.

2. THE METHOD

The method (which is only partially described in this paper) comprises three parts. The first is a definition of the form a standard such as the STANAG should take. The second is a framework for the evaluation of coding schemes designed for the standard. The third part is a task model, designed to support the analysis of such an evaluation. The first two parts are briefly introduced here, followed by the rationale for and procedures used in the development of the task model. The main substantive contribution of this paper is the task model itself. (See Section 3).

2.1 Definition of the standard

A major weakness of the approach adopted by the group developing the STANAG was to assume that all types of similar information, wherever situated, had to be coded in precisely the same way. However, this was unnecessarily constraining, and would probably have led to a sub-optimal display design if it was adhered to. Our attitude has been that the form of the STANAG should follow from the purpose for which it is created.

The purpose has been declared informally as being to expedite the movement of senior naval officers between ships of different navies so that they may easily and rapidly appreciate the tactical situation. Firstly, the aim of the STANAG is primarily one of *coherence of form*, and only secondarily one of *quality assurance*. Secondly, this coherence could take many forms. For example, it may be important for the standard coding scheme to be coherent between nations for certain ship roles (e.g. anti-submarine warfare, area air defence etc.), but that the scheme be allowed to vary between these different roles. Also, the coherence may be only loosely specified e.g. use pictograms rather than letters to represent objects, or it may be precisely specified e.g. use pictograms of a particular form (such as those shown in Fig 2. column 1.) It is an important aspect of our approach that we see the form of the STANAG as free to vary.

2.2 An Evaluation Framework

One coding scheme may be preferred over another for a number of reasons. We can divide these into two types of criteria; *functional* and *non-functional*. The former implies that one scheme may be preferred because it is easier or more powerful in its use than another, whereas the latter implies that one scheme may be preferred because of pragmatic considerations such as being more readily familiar (as with the "qwerty" keyboard) or perhaps more adaptable to technological change. We address functional criteria only in this paper.

Functional criteria imply that the scheme to be preferred is the one best supporting the tasks associated with it. The method to be defined is therefore *Task Oriented*. The first part of the general framework we work within is shown below. Thus the *effectiveness* of a system is given by:

$$\mathrm{Att}_c \times \mathrm{Att}_u \text{------>} \mathrm{DP}_S \;\; W \;\; \mathrm{Costs}_c + \mathrm{Costs}_u$$

This means that attributes of the computer (Att_c) interacting with attributes of the user (Att_u) meet to some degree the demanded performance (DP_S) of the system whilst incurring costs to the computer and costs to the user.

The rest of the framework considers the general nature of command level tasks. The user is concerned with inferring states of real world objects, for example the likelihood, time and type of attack by them. He does this by using representations of these states (in the form of symbols) on his tactical display. These states are computed from classes of *information primitives* contained on the tactical display and other information sources. These information primitives are of three classes; location of object, type of object and status of object (radiating, releasing missile etc). These will vary over time. Information primitives have a number of *quality attributes,* which combine to specify the quality of this information. These are; appropriateness - the extent to which the information supplied meets the needs of the user for a particular purpose, accuracy - the correlation of the information with the actual state of the real world, timeliness - the availability of the relevant information as and when it is needed, and truth value - the confidence the user has that the information is of the type and quality declared.

The tactical requirements may be regarded as setting up a *profile of required information primitives together with their quality attributes*. The inferred state of the world is not a simple function of this profile, but a function of the tactical requirements which establish the appropriate accuracy / timeliness / truth value trade-offs. These ideas are set out in Figure 3.

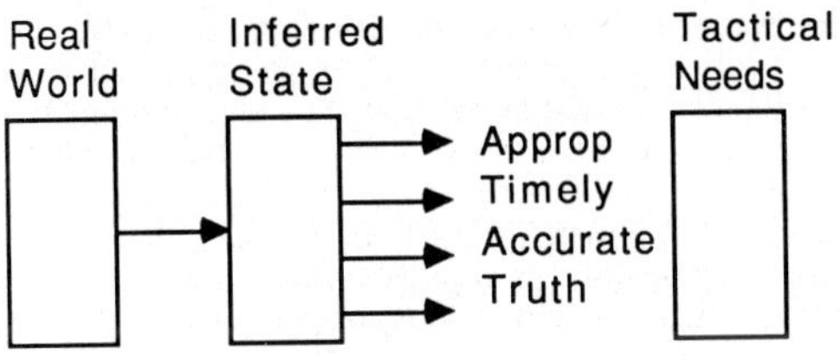

Figure 3 Formation of information primitives
Appropriateness, timeliness, accuracy and truth are the quality attributes of the information primitives.

Finally, we need to consider the role of symbology in this system and, in particular, how we should view it in relation to the system's performance. We start with the assumption that the type of symbology scheme "matters" i.e. there is some rational basis for preferring one scheme over another on usability grounds. This is intuitively plausible because some displays (e.g. those with colour and shape) feel easier to use than others (e.g. those without colour and alphanumerics only). Also, as guidelines indicate, there are clearly some design options to avoid.

However, performance of a system is unlikely to be some simple function of symbology type. Firstly, symbology is likely to be a relatively unimportant determinant of overall system performance. Secondly, there may be many schemes which are of equal value and therefore no usability grounds for choosing between them. Thirdly, even when there are usability differences, there are likely to be complex cost and benefit relations. Fourthly, because of the properties of human minds interacting with task demands, the benefits of one scheme over another are likely to show in the amount of *effort* required to use the display effectively rather than in the effectiveness itself. Lastly, all of the above are likely to be a function of the number, size and distribution of objects on the screen and the type of tasks associated with it. It is this task dependency which is the focus of the remainder of this paper.

2.3 Justification for the task model

Conventional methods of evaluating coding schemes (and in a wider context - prototype system designs) are unhelpful for three reasons. Knowledge gathering activities are typically *atheoretical* in style. Implicit performance measurement frameworks are typically unsuited to human systems and the purpose addressed here. Knowledge obtained, whether in the form of system specific recommendations or general guidelines, is thus uncertain with respect to its truth or scope.

Dowell and Long [2] point to one of the problems of traditional human factors - the lack of coherence in the definition of some of its basic concepts. Here, we see a similar problem. It is well known that the influence of colour is heavily task-dependent (see for example the work of Christ & Corso[3]). The conventional wisdom is that generally colour aids symbol grouping tasks. However, the extent to which colour aids grouping more or less than some other coding parameter is strongly dependent on (a) what is meant by "grouping" and (b) what it is that is being grouped. A similar problem arises with the use of standard guidelines (e.g. Def Stan 00-25 [1])

Consider information used in committee for the STANAG development. One guideline used was that shape codes should employ no more than six items in the set (from Smith & Mosier [4]). In fact naval officers can readily identify and use many hundreds of different shapes, both on displays and in ship recognition, because the task is necessary and much overlearned. A traditional laboratory-based experimental paradigm (albeit using a relatively authentic looking tactical display and naval officers as subjects) was used to evaluate three candidate schemes. Coding scheme was employed as an independent variable, performance on a simple grouping task was measured and statistically significant improvement of one scheme over the other was taken to indicate a superior scheme.

The data from the above experiment were unsatisfactory for three reasons. First the *causes* of any superiority were unknown, and this could have been some chance configuration of features of the particular display and/or task employed rather than the intrinsic superiority of the general approach. Second, the task employed was unlikely to have been similar to the tasks carried out by naval command level officers, and even if it were, it would represent only a single task rather than a representative range of tasks. Third, the magnitude of any alleged superiority in terms of operational significance was unknown.

2.4 Procedure of task model development

The problems associated with this unsatisfactory data may be overcome by developing a model of a task associated with the tactical display. However, because of the complexity of such a task, and the novelty of the approach used here, the first step was to develop a task model based on the experimental task used in an earlier evaluation for the NATO group. This task was labelled "grouping". The procedure for the development of this task model is set out here.

Seven subjects took part in this study, six novices and one experienced naval officer. Subjects sat in front of a computer-generated display using a 19 inch colour monitor of resolution 1024 x 768 pixels. They were first trained to perfect knowledge of the symbols in one of the schemes whilst the experimenter explained the principles underlying the scheme design. They were then asked a sequence of 20 questions relating to a simulated tactical display shown in Figure 1.

The questions asked were of the form "click with the mouse on all X" where X was either general (e.g. surface tracks) or specific (e.g. hostile submarine). They were instructed to work as quickly as possible without making errors. Of the novice subjects, two performed on each of the three schemes with one subject's question sequence of increasing specificity and the other's of decreasing specificity. Timing and movement of the mouse and clicks of the mouse were recorded by the computer along with video-recording of the screen and recording of verbal protocols at the end of each trial and a de-brief session at the end of the experiment.

The authors also acted informally as subjects. Combining all the data, a preliminary model of the task was constructed which was used to interpret the data. This model, when developed and applied to naval users would form part of the overall method being developed.

3 GENERATION OF THE MODEL

3.1 General description of the task

The experimental task was originally classified as a "grouping" task . On the basis of our understanding of this task and the task performance data, a task model was generated. This incorporated the hypotheses that the subject uses three stages of cognitive operations to perform the task. These operations are GROUPING, SEARCHING and IDENTIFYING. The particular form of these is determined by a PLAN which is GENERATED, IMPLEMENTED and EVALUATED. These operations are intended to represent cognitive processes. Although yet to be fully defined technically, the definitions given below serve to introduce the model.

The term "grouping" is given to the process of selecting a spatially contiguous set of objects by virtue of some common physical attribute. Attributes may be colour, texture (common shape) and spatial separation from some other group. "Searching" is the process of sequential focussing on a set of selected objects from a group (the search set). "Identify" is the process of trying to match some physical feature or set of features of a selected object from the search set to some mental template. For example, consider the task "click on the hostile aircraft carrier" with reference to the display shown in Figure 1 in which the designated symbol is arrowed. We hypothesized that, to complete this task, the subject performs the following operations using informational cues from the long term knowledge base, and symbol / screen cues from experimental knowledge and the display:

OPERATION	INFORMATION	SYMBOL AND SCREEN CUES
Group	Standard Identity (hostile)	Colour (red objects) Position (left of screen)
The subject considers only the hostile force, all the red symbols, most of which are on the left of the screen.		
Group	Environment (hostile surface)	Texture (similar lozenge shapes) Position (lower left of screen)
The subject then considers only the hostile surface ships, all of similar shape and spacially contiguous (giving a texture), which are situated in the lower part of the hostile force.		
Group	Task Group (hostile surface ship formation)	Configuration (group of organized similarly shaped objects)
The subject uses knowledge of expected naval formations to isolate the group of hostile surface ships most likely to contain an aircraft carrier.		
Search	Capital Ships (hostile surface capital ship)	Configuration (central symbols of task force)
The subject, knowing that the aircraft carrier is the most important ship looks toward the centre of the task group for it..		
Identify	Aircraft Carrier	Letters (carrier denoted by CV on symbol)
The subject identifies the target symbol finally using remembered letter designator and looking at each individual capital ship symbol, finding CV = aircraft carrier.		

In order to generate such a plan, the subject needs (a) general tactical knowledge e.g. the expected configurations of groups of ships in operational situations, (b) knowledge of the symbol set, e.g.that red symbols represent hostile objects, (c) knowledge of the particular tactical display, e.g. that all the hostile forces are on the left of the screen, and (d) a general plan. The general plan consists of the three operation stages group, search and identify and is motivated by the principle that the search space should be minimised.

Minimisation of the search space follows the principle of cognitive economy. According to this general principle grouping is the most efficient initial operation for reducing the search space, *providing* there is some code available which enables easy grouping. So, in generating the plan, hierarchies (in the sense of spatial embeddedness) of groups are formed until no further grouping is possible. A search group is then identified and a search plan devised, consisting of a target feature and search sequence, which maximises the chance of locating the target feature quickly and with acceptable degree of confidence. Each of the objects within this set is then identified using this plan and target feature. If it is known that there is only a single target object, the search is terminated when the target is found.

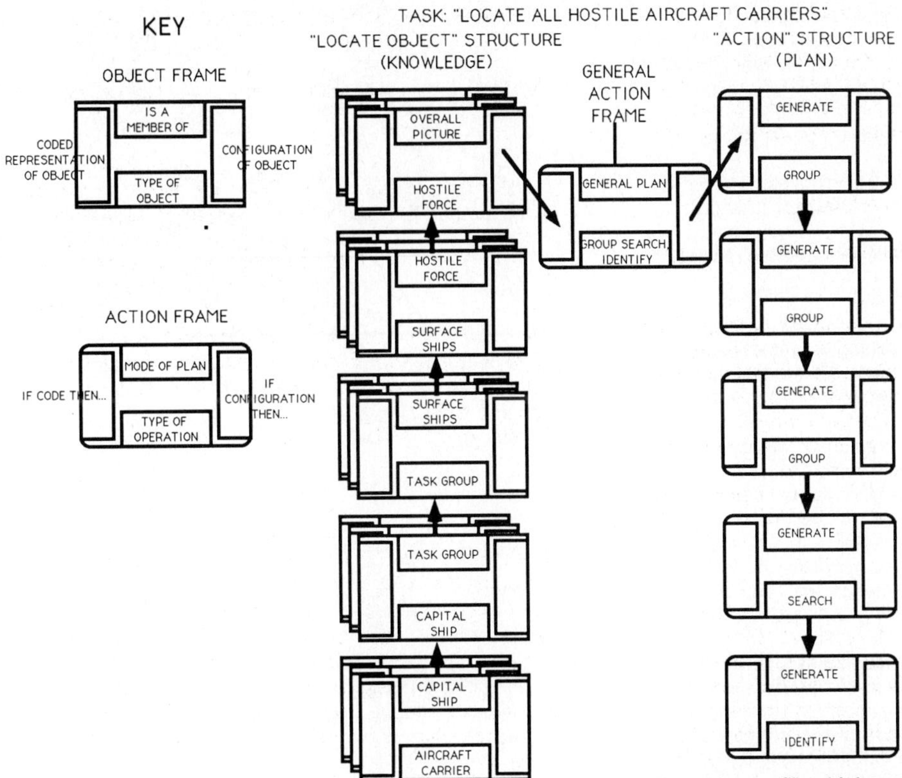

Figure 4
The structure of the model

The structure of the model is explained and its use demonstrated with reference to the sources of redundancy within the task environment, and those which have an important influence on the functionality of display codes. For example, two sources of redundancy in tactical displays are the non-random distribution of objects on the screen (by virtue of their tactical coherence) and the knowledge that the naval user has of the tactical situation.

A tactical display conveys three types of information; types of object, their status and their location. The key attributes of a tactical display are its *tactical structure* in terms of the types of object that go together in groups, the structure within a group and their relationship to other groups. We posit that the subject brings to the experiment a permanent store of knowledge relating to tactical displays in general which is recruited to form a temporary store relating to the particular experimental display. This temporary store is used to generate plans necessary to execute the experimental task.

Research in cognitive psychology and AI by Minsky [5], combined with the apperent use of recognitional strategies in command decision making (Klein [6]) led us to employ a frame-based notation for modelling the task. This is not yet completely worked out and what we present is merely illustrative of the value of the general approach. We posit a knowledge structure composed of two types of frame - *object* frames and *action* frames.

Object frames form a hierarchy as shown in Figure 4 and describe the objects on the tactical display. Object frames have three classes of slot; *relation slots* ("is a member of" or "is made up of") which establish the object's place within the hierarchy; *identity slots* ("type") which establish the name of the object e.g. aircraft carrier; and *method* slots ("code" and "configuration") which define the means by which it can be located and recognised. Before the structure is activated and brought into working memory, the code slot is empty.

Action frames are used to generate the plan in conjunction with the knowledge structure described. They also have three classes of slot; *mode slots* ("generate", "implement", "evaluate") indicate the mode of planning activity that is taking place, *type slots* ("group", "search", "identify") show the task process in operation, and *conditional slots* ("if code" and "if configuration") which are used to test the conditions within the object structure necessary to carry out the action indicated by the value of the *type* slot. Both object and action frames exist in three memory states; long term (existing before the experiment), short term (existing only during the experiment) and working (existing only for a single trial).

The model works in the following general way. We consider the *generate* phase only:

1. General knowledge structures of objects and actions exist in the subject's long term memory when he comes to the experiment. Also general knowledge of code types (in a form not specified here) exist.

2. Exposure to the experimental situation causes a general knowledge structure of objects and actions (of the form shown in Figure 4) to be constructed in short term memory. A locate question causes the form of the object structure recruited to include "is a member of" for the relationship slots.

3. Exposure to the experimental question completes the object structure by filling in the code slots and activates the action structure This, through acting on the object structure, generates a plan.

The last stage, in more detail, consists of the following:

4. The verb contained in the experimenter's question causes activation of "locate" form of object structure.

5. The object name causes the activation of the code (colour, shape etc).

6. The object name causes the construction of an hierarchical knowledge structure using values contained in all "is a member of" slots , which attach to all identical values in "type" slots in other frames.

7. Code is entered as value into empty activated "code" slots. The code is suitably transformed for the level of the object frame. For example"shape" at the force level would be coded as "texture".

8. The general action frame is applied to the activated object structure. It starts at the highest level activated slot and works down.

9. The general action frame contains the general plan:
   • Generate actions in the order - *group, search, identify*.
   • Starting at the highest level activated frame, and working down, apply test conditions to the activated frame *code* and *configuration* slots.
   • If there is a match, then generate a plan frame of the appropriate type.
   • Continue down the hierarchy until a mismatch is found.
   • Goto next frame type (e.g. *search*) and continue.
   • Continue to until *identify* frame completed then STOP.

10. Working memory now contains a frame based knowledge structure consisting of a set of grouping, searching and identifying actions. These are performed on the appropriate features of the display.

3.3 Data Interpretation Using the Model

Mouse tracks, including timings and clicks, for two sets of experimental trial data are shown in Figure 5. The data are for two subjects, each performing with a different coding scheme. Two question types are discussed for each subject: "locate all neutral tracks" and "locate all hostile destroyers" but only the data from the latter appears in figure 4. The tactical display used is shown in figure 1. The interesting feature of these data is that Scheme 1 appears best for Task 1 and Scheme 2 appears best for Task 2. The aim is to use the model to interpret in what manner the schemes are strong and weak.

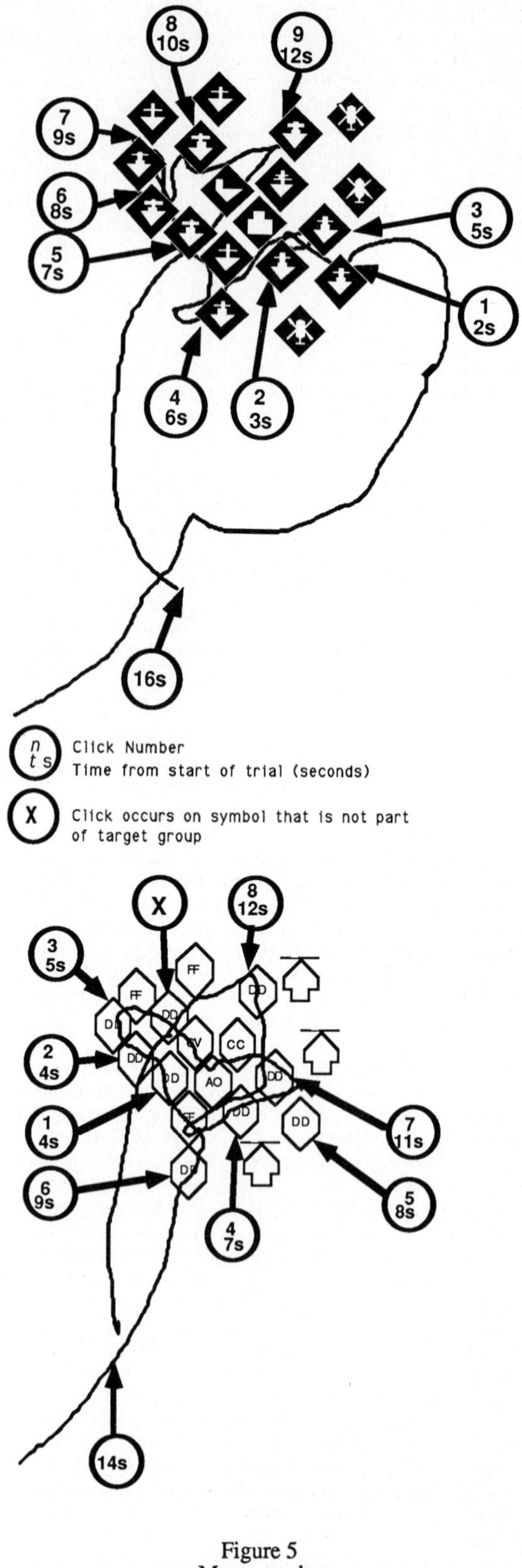

Figure 5
Mouse tracks

From the data we can infer the following. First, the time spent pausing at the beginning of the trial before moving the mouse onto the display (pre-move pause) is related to the amount of time spent planning. Second, the time spent after completing the task (post-move pause) is related to the amount of time the subject spends evaluating the effectiveness of his implemented plan. These two times are typically inversely related, presumably because a hastily generated poor plan leads to low confidence that the task has been sucessfully completed. This was supported by the protocol data.

Other data we can extract are, the symbols clicked on (and hence accuracy), the path taken to click on all the symbols (the search plan), and the time between symbol clicks. It is important to emphasise that we are not claiming that the interpretation we give of the data is well supported or true. Rather, we are supposing it to be true in order to illustrate the function of the model.

The overall times are not very different between the trials. What is more interesting from our point of view are the different behaviour patterns within the trial. In the case of the "neutrals" question, Scheme 1 seems to support good planning and a fast time whereas Scheme 2 seems to support poor planning and a relatively slow time. The fact that this tendency is reversed for the "hostile destroyers" question suggests that there might be a true coding scheme effect. Other possible interpretations are chance inter-subject variability or differential learning.

The distribution of the neutral tracks may be seen in Figure 1. Scheme 1 only is shown, in which the neutrals are filled black symbols. In both schemes they would be coloured green. According to the model, this would activate the "force" level frame only and generate a "search" frame only indicating a search set consisting of "all green tracks" together with some search strategy based on spatial distribution. We would not, in fact, expect much difference between the two schemes since the green objects appear equally distinct from all other objects in both schemes. Colour alone is used in the task and the use of colour does not differ between schemes.

Of greater interest are the performances on the "hostile destroyers" question. Here there seems to be some clear evidence that Scheme 1 is poorer than Scheme 2 in some important respects. The subject appears to spend little time planning, and the long post-move pause, together with observation of his behaviour, suggest that he had little confidence due to poor stopping criteria. In Scheme 2, there appears to be a longer period devoted to planning with a consequent rapid and certain finish (although the subject missed one destroyer in the upper part of the group). There is evidence that at least some parts of the searching and identifying are better carried out in Scheme 2. However, there appear to be complex effects of pattern of distribution and adjacency. For example the average inter-click time is shorter in Scheme 1 than in Scheme 2.

With a small number of naive subjects, these objective data are weak in supporting substantive claims, but they serve to illustrate how they may be interpreted with the model. Together with observational and protocol data we could conclude the following about the coding schemes in our evaluation.

Colours, spatial contiguity and bold, simple, easily discriminable shapes; all are good codes for rapid grouping (where "grouping" is defined technically in terms of our model - in contrast to the original NATO evaluation). Colour, relative spatial distribution (as in the "High Value Units" and "Defence Screens" of the task groups), together with shapes related to the spatial distributions, are good codes for defining search sets (as defined technically). Pictograms (if well designed and well-learned) are probably as good as letters for identification (as defined technically). Letters need to be self-evidently related to their designated objects and can probably cope with a large object set. Pictograms can have the benefit of rapid grouping properties (because of the potential for forming common shape features) as well as rapid identification properties. However, there is some conflict between the two requirements. They can suffer poor discrimination if, in trying to keep to the "spirit" of pictographic representation, they contain many minute physical differences (as in Scheme 1). On the other hand, the requirement to preserve common general shape tends to drive design towards this attribute.

4. SUMMARY AND CONCLUSIONS

This paper has described and illustrated part of a method being developed to evaluate standard display coding schemes. This is an instance of a general approach being evolved which aims to bring objectivity and generality to human factors evaluation within a cognitive framework.

The parts of the method described and illustrated are the definition of the NATO standard, an evaluation framework and the construction of a cognitive model of the display user's task. Emphasis is placed on the rationale for and the structure of the model. This is used to demonstrate the functionality of the various coding attributes in terms of users' tasks. The model has been partially developed and validated with novice users in order to illustrate the value of the method and approach. This was motivated by the nature of tactical displays and tasks and the requirement to expose the functionality of the display codes. The framework posits long term, short term and working knowledge structures used to generate, implement and evaluate plans for obtaining tactical information from the display.

The task illustrated for model construction was chosen because it was the one used in the original NATO evaluation and also could be viewed as a likely component of tactical planning using a dynamic tactical display. The next stage of the research will involve refining the model, validating it further on novice subjects and then using it to model real naval user tasks. The appropriate form of design advice that would evolve from this approach still needs to be addressed.

REFERENCES

[1] Ministry of Defence, Defence Standard 00-25 Human Factors for Designers, Section 7:Visual Displays (1986)

[2] Dowell J. & Long J.B. Conceptions of the Discipline of HCI: Craft, Applied Science and Engineering - *in* (ed) Sutcliffe A. & Macaulay L. People and Computers 5. Cambridge University Press (1989)

[3] Christ R.E.& Corso G.M., The Effects of extended Practice on the Evaluation of Visual Display Codes. Human Factors (1983) 25(1), 71-84.

[4] Smith S. L., Guidelines for Designing User Interface Software. Mitre, Bedford, Massachusetts, (1986).

[5] Minsky M., A Framework for representing Knowledge - *in* (ed) Haugeland J., Mind Design. MIT Press (1981)

[6] Klein G.A., Strategies of decision making. Military Review, May 1989, 56-64.

Human–Computer Interaction – INTERACT '90
D. Diaper et al. (Editors)
Elsevier Science Publishers B.V. (North-Holland)

An Electronic Book: APTBook

Mitsumasa Miyazawa, Kaoru Kinoshita, Minoru Kobayashi,
Teruo Yokoyama, Yutaka Matsushita

Department Of Instrumentation Engineering,
Keio University
3-14-1 Hiyoshi, Kohoku-ku, Yokohama, 223, Japan
Tel: +81-44-63-1141 Fax: +81-44-62-7625 Email: on@inst.keio.ac.jp

Abstract

This paper describes an electronic book named APTBook in which we can leaf through the pages of it, furthermore we can either paste it with a memopad, or make a dog-ear, underlines. Since this APTBook is realized by the hierarchical data structure in which the more upper layer has the more rough information, the system can show many pages in a short time by using the animation of leafing through the pages. Furthermore, we can access a page in which a photograph is located in the upper-right corner by an access method similar to the memory structure of human being based on spatial location, nevertheless existing electronic media cannot manage it.

Thus, by using APTBook, we can access the data without using database access based on keywords.

1. Introduction

Recently computers for office-automation are getting lower in price and higher in performance so that they are much closer to many people and can be individualized for many users. But there are many people having the feeling such that it is not easy to use them. For example, when we want to write a report by using a word-processor, only a part of the report is shown on the screen area, since the most part of it are stored in the memory of it.(eg. H.Rex(1989))

Human beings are good at managing and memorizing many objects spatially.(eg. Andrea(1986),Richard(1984) ,Richard(1987)) For example, in the case that we go shopping at a supermarket for the first time, it often take a long time to find out something we want to buy. It is because we don't know the location where the goods are placed (that is called goods-location map). At the favorite supermarket, we can find out them easily by using such a map. Thus, information can be managed spatially in the brain of human beings. At present, since most computers can show the data on the screen area by scrolling or poping up the next frame, such schemes cannot manage information spatially.

In order to improve the man-machine interface, many kinds of metaphors are often introduced.(eg. D.Austin(1986)) Since there are many existing media in which human beings can manage the memorization based on spatial location, it is very important to realize such media electronically. However now, most of information is stored on paper media and transmitted through paper media. Furthermore, even the information on electronic media is often employed by printing it on paper. Thus, since paper media is recognized as one of the oldest and the most familiar interface for users, paper media, especially the form of books, should be paid attention. In spite of the appearance of a radio and a television, paper media have been still used by many people. Moreover, they will be expected to use much in future. A book assign the contents spatially, in which the two dimensional page space and the three dimensional thickness of piling the pages are used. It is worth while to realize electrically the advantage which book media have. In this paper, we describe an implemented electronic book to be realized, named APTBook (Animated Book by Paging Through).

In APTBook, the data of it are provided by using the animation of leafing through the pages. We can underline to emphasize the part of the page so that we can catch the part easily and quickly. Furthermore, we can paste a memopad on a particular page in order to add supplemental information, or make a dog-ear to emphasize the page itself. So we can access the data without using database access based on keywords and can obtain required pages by using the operations of APTBook, which is designed to realize the concept similar to the memory structure of human beings based on spatial location.

Section 2 describes the overview of book media and electronic media. Section 3 mentions the overview of APTBook, and section 4 the detail of APTBook. Current status is described in Section 5. Future directions and Conclusions are discussed in Section 6 and Section 7.

2. Overview of book media and electronic media

2.1 Book media

The following two style of reading a book are studied; reading the book for the first time, and reading the book read before.

1) Reading the book for the first time.

At a library or a book store, according to books-location map we go to the bookshelf on which the books of our interesting field are. Thus, if an interested book is beforehand, we run our eye over titles of some books on the bookshelf in order to find out it. Otherwise we look for some books with an appropriate title. When the interested book is found, we take it in our hand, and open it. Some may see the table of contents, others the index with keywords. It is usual that we leaf through the pages to find out something interested. At that time, all data are not paid attention, and only impressive data, such as chapter titles, figures, tables, etc catch our eye.(eg. Carmen(1988)) When you leaf through the pages of Bible in which the unrelated sentence of " Mt.Fuji in Japan burst into eruption last night!" is inserted, do you have a confidence with which you can find out the sentence? If the objects of something interested are found out, leafing through pages will be stopped, and we begin to read near the object.

After we finished to read the interested objects of the book, we may buy it. If we have enough money to buy it, we should restore it to its proper place and usually memorize the location where the bookshelf are.

2) Reading the book read before.

We often read the book read before, we want to confirm the contents again, quote from it or show it to other people. It is usual to find out an object of the book by means of our spatial ambiguous memorization, such as the page in which a photograph is located in the upper-right corner, as illustrated in figure 1. A page which is similar to our memorization can be found out by leafing through the pages. Furthermore we often underline and make notes to emphasize an important part of the page so that the part emphasized will be the objects for retrieving.(eg. John.D(1987))

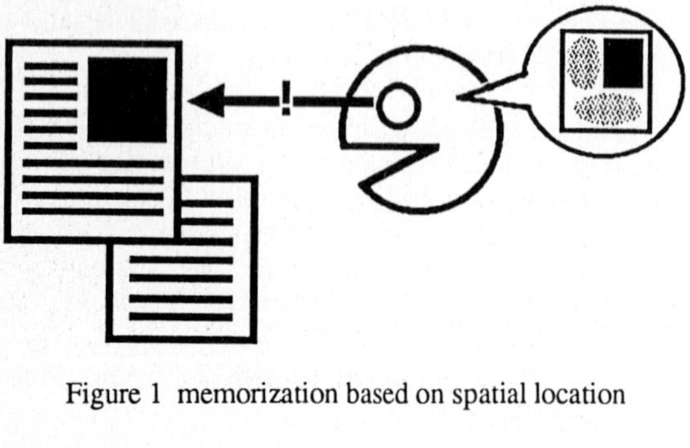

Figure 1 memorization based on spatial location

While searching the objects in above two ways, we usually catch some words, figures and tables unexpectedly. If we are interested in one of them, we stop leafing through pages and read its contents in detail. In some case, we continue to leaf through pages in order to memorize the outline of book. In other case, we read a book by leafing through the more pages of it, the more the impressive objects increase. Such seemingly futile access to a book may be very effective in some case.

In electronic media, the access to the data by using database access based on keywords is easier and quickly than that based on the index of a book. But, if we cannot remind an appropriate keyword, we cannot catch the expected data based on the keyword. Book media makes it possible to access an object by means of such vague information so that we can catch the correct keyword and expected data based on keywords, nevertheless existing electronic media cannot manage it.

As described above, a book fits the memory structure of human beings based on spatial location. So we itemize the features of book media as follows.

- A book is easy to operate.
- A book is portable.
- It is possible to read in comfortable position.
- It is possible to emphasize an important part of the page.
- It is possible to add supplemental information on paper.
- It is possible to refer multiple books at the same time.
- It is possible to predict time needed to read a book by thickness of it.
- It is possible to buy in a low price.

Some of them are difficult to be realize on the electronic media, but in APTBook we realized most of them.

2.2 Electronic media

Some features of the electronic media is mentioned in section 2.1. In this section, we itemize the features of electronic media as follows.

- It is possible to handle the realtime information such as animation and sound.
- It is possible to access the contents asynchronously.
- It is possible to store the information in small size media like a floppy disk.
- It is possible to copy and modify the data easily.

3. Overview of APTBook

In order to design APTBook, the following points are considered.

In an APTBook, we can leaf through pages of it with animation. As mentioned in Section 2, when leafing through the pages of a book, we pay attention to only the impressive data, such as chapter titles, figures, tables, etc. So in an APTBook, only the impressive data are shown in detail, and the rest are shown in rough style keeping the spatial location of the page. APTBook has the hierarchical data structure in which the more upper layer has the more rough data. This system can show many pages in a short time by means of leafing through many pages. In APTBook, we can view simultaneously much information like fisheye without distortion.(eg. George(1986))

Many other features of book media are also realized in APTBook, in which we can underline to emphasize the part of a page, we can paste a memopad on a particular page in order to add supplemental information, and further, we can make a mark in a page with a dog-ear. When an user is leafing through the pages, emphasized parts can be shown in detail. In the background environment, we can access the data by using the database access based on keywords, and furthermore, the asynchronous link such as hypermedia can be used.

4. APTBook

4.1 Data display levels and high speed leafing through

In APTBook, the data of each page such as text, figure, and table are shown by using the animation of leafing through pages. In a CRT display, we can see many page by scrolling or popping up the next frame, but the both schemes have such drawbacks that it is far from the feeling of leafing through pages and also it is difficult to comprehend the position of a book where the displayed screen is located. By displaying users the animation of leafing through pages, we can easily understand the direction for leafing through (forward or backward) and also understand the amount leafed through from the thickness of the rest pages.

This system has the layered structure of data display levels. In the layered structure, the more upper layer has the more rough(compressed) information, and the lower layer has the more detailed information. For instance, in the lowest level, APTBook shows characters in detail, and in the upper layers, it displays only impressive characters like chapter and section titles and the rest is displayed in the compressed form by converting from characters to halftone dots. Furthermore, the figure data are also displayed in the compressed form by converting it to a mosaic figure. A user can select the data display level according to his request. The more compressed level is used, the more fast we can leaf through pages. If we want to run our eye verbatim, we have to use the lowest data display level. When this high speed leafing trough is stopped by the user who detects his interested object (title, figure etc), the roughly displayed data shown in figure 2 are changed to the detailed display as shown in figure 3.

4.2 Notes written on APTBook

As we can write notes (underline, memo, etc) on a real book, a user also can do them on APTBook. We call these kind of notes on APTBook "Memo", and it has four kinds of "Memo" as follows:

Underline. It is used to emphasize the important words, phrases, figures, and tables. We can select its thickness freely. By moving the mouse from a point to another point keeping it clicked, an underline can be drawn.

Memopad. We sometimes make a note on a piece of paper and paste it on the book. Similarly, we can paste a note (called memopad) on the page of APTBook. If a user clicks on the MemoPad button, drags by keeping it clicked,

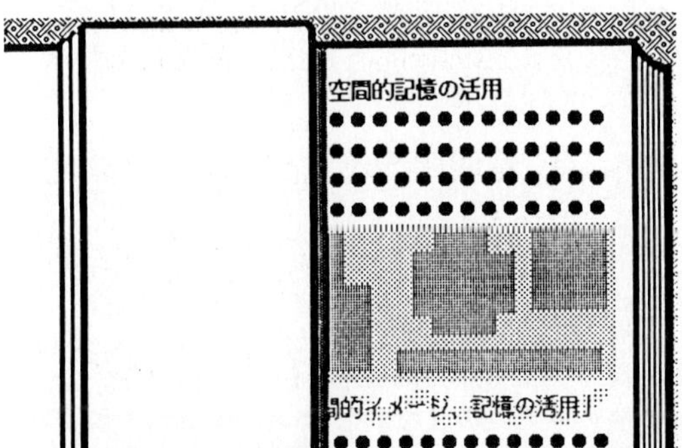

Figure 2 Leafing through pages by rough display

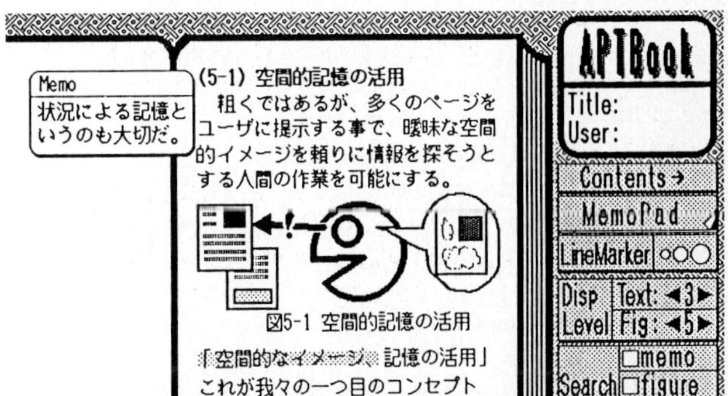

Figure 3 Detailed display

and releases it at any position on the page, "Memo Editor" as shown in figure 4 will be opened. After we write supplement information on the memopad, "Memo Editor" will be closed, and an icon which shows the existence of the memopad is put at the place "Memo Editor" is opened on the behalf of it.

Link. This is the function which only electronic media have, and makes possible to connect from the particular word to another related information. We have two kinds of links, organizational link and referential link. The former is provided before hand in APTBook, and a user cannot freely modify it, for example, by clicking a part of contents, a user can open the expected page. The latter is freely made and canceled by a user whenever he wants.

Dog-ear. We use it as shown in figure 5 to put a mark on a leaf. By clicking the corner of a leaf, it is folded down, and also it can return.

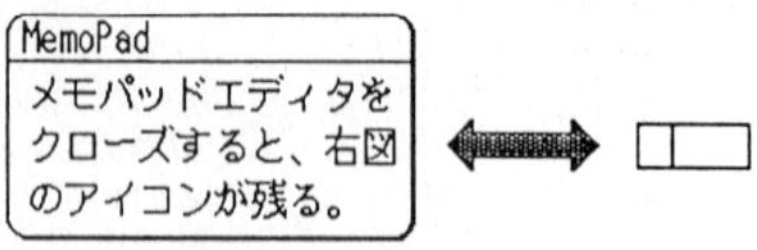

Figure 4 Memopad and its icon

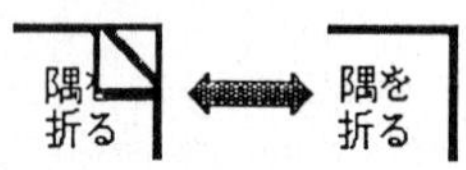

Figure 5 Dog-ear

We can handle these "Memos" as personal data apart from the data of a book itself (called book data) which is provided in APTBook. In the case that multiple persons each have same books, they are quite same books when memos are not added. On the other hand, in proportion as memos are added to each book, we each have our book. Similar function are realized in APTBook by creating a user's own personal data file when he reads it for the first time.

When a user leaf through pages at high speed, the location in which "Memos" are placed can be shown in detail. Thus "Memos" are used to match the grade in which the information is provided with the user's needs.

4.3 Hierarchical tree structure

In our APTBook, hierarchical tree data structures are used to realize the features described in previous sections. The hierarchical tree structures are organized so that the more rough information can be obtained from the more upper layer.

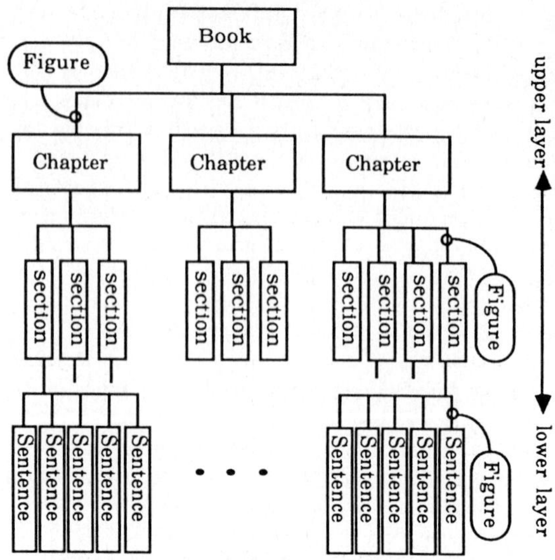

Figure 6 Hierarchical tree structure of a book

Figure 6 illustrates the hierarchical tree data structure of a real book. A book is composed of multiple chapters which consist of multiple sections including several sentences.

APTBook has such a hierarchical tree data structure similar to that of a real book. Each node of APTBook's hierarchical tree structure, as shown in figure 7, has the rough information of its descendants and has the pointer to the next lower node in the tree. If a user does not require the detailed information, APTBook can display rough page images using the data of the upper layers. On the other hand, if he requires the detailed information, it can display the more detailed page images using the data of the more lower layer. For example, by using the data of node A level of figure 7, we can get a rough page image shown in figure 8. If the data of node B level is used, we can get more detailed image as shown in figure 9. Since APTBook has the hierarchical tree structure mentioned above, it is possible to display either rough page images or detailed page images according to the user's interest.

Each figure image appeared in the tree structure also has a hierarchical tree structure as its internal structure which is similar to 'quadtree', a computer graphic technique appeared in [(eg. Donald)]. The trees are generated by successively dividing a two-dimensional region into quadrants. The algorithm for generating a tree divides the original space into quadrants. And for each regions, the successive subdivision into quadrants continues until the size of the regions is 4*4 dots. Each node in the tree has four elements, one for each of the quadrants in the region(Figure 10). And each data element in the node stores the density of dots in corresponding quadrant. If there is no dot in quadrant 3 of figure 10, Zero (which means that there is no dot in the region) is then placed in

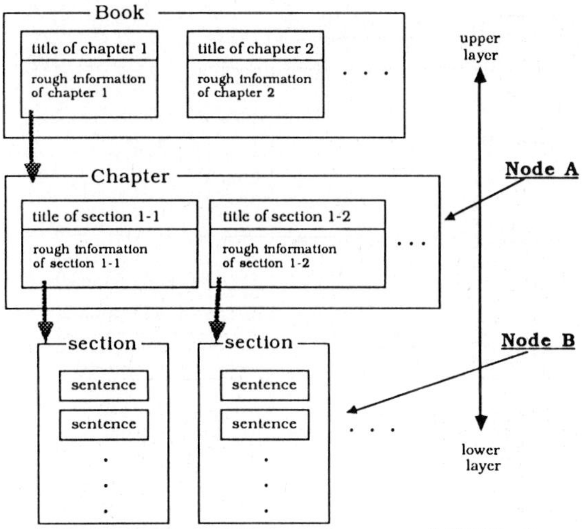

Figure 7 Hierarchical tree structure of APTBook

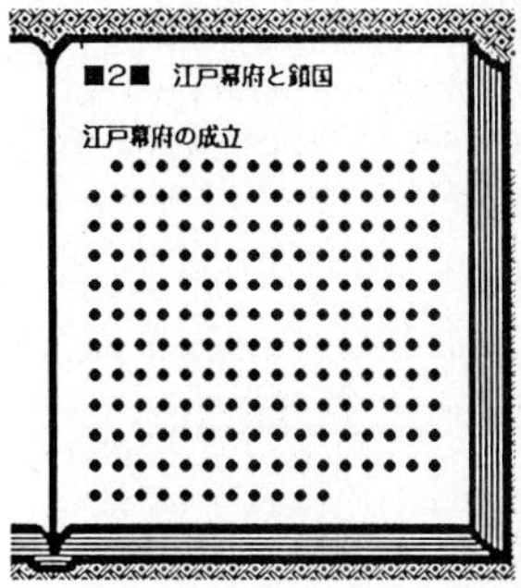

Figure 8 Rough display image

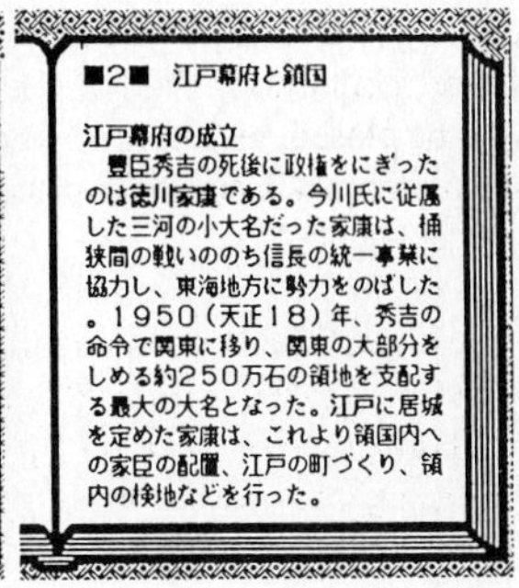

Figure 9 Detailed display image

data element 3 of the node. Otherwise, the element stores another value. It is possible to display figure images either roughly or in detail, in the same way as the text hierarchical tree structure, namely the more upper layer can display the more rough image. Figure 11 shows the relation between the layer and the displayed image.

Furthermore, it can be realized in APTBook that only the part in which a user is interested in a page is shown in detail, and the rest of it is shown roughly, because the system has a hierarchical tree data structure. If underlines or memopads are found in a node while an APTBook's display manager is displaying a page image at a certain level, the part underlined and the position in which the memopads are located are displayed in detail, and the rest of the page is displayed roughly, as shown in figure 12. We call such a display scheme "partial detail representation".

This display scheme is also available for figures, the outline of which is shown in figure 13. APTBook displays a figure image more clearly in the neiborhood of the "Memo" which the user drew before than around. How to realize this is shown in figure 14. To display figures at a certain level which the user set, the figure display manager traces the tree to the level. If the corresponding node of the personal tree which represents the user's "Memo" on the figure has descendants, it traces more deeply. This tracing continues while both nodes of the tree of the figure and those of the personal "Memo" have descendants. The information of each node is displayed at the time when the tracing stops. Doing the procedure mentioned above repeatedly, the display manager draws clearly near the "Memo" in a figure, the rest of which is displayed roughly.

APTBook can display a page image by changing the detail degree according to the user's interest. This comes to be possible by means of the hierarchical tree structure mentioned above.

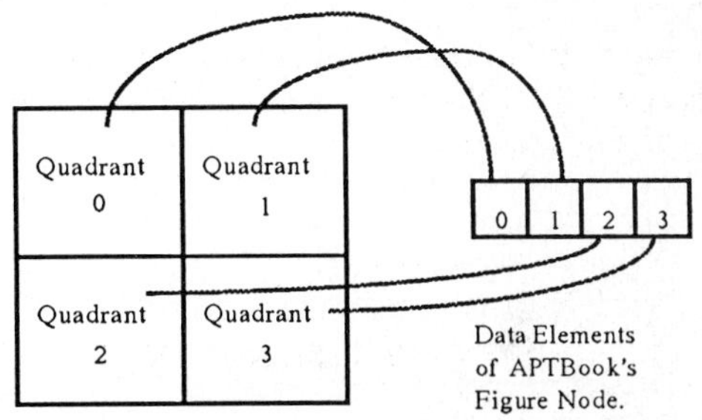

Figure 10 A region and the data elements of a node

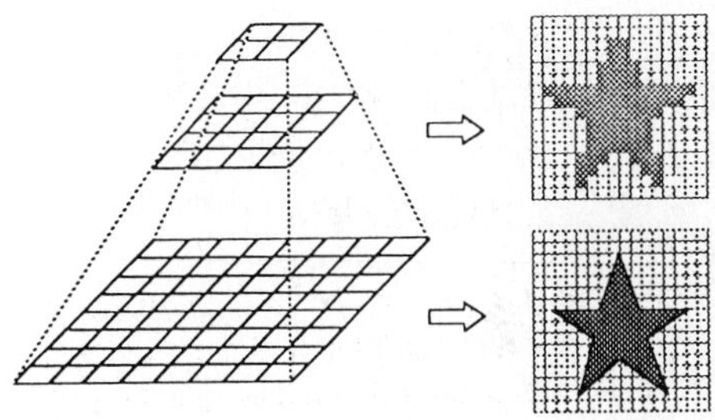

Figure 11 Relations between the layer and the image

5. Current status

APTBook is currently implemented on a personal computer. The program in the system consist of roughly 10000 lines of source language, of which about 2000 lines are written in the assembly language and about 8000 lines are written in C language.

We point out our subjective evaluation to APTBook as follows:

Text representation. We can quickly find out an expected word by leafing through at high speed, but there is such a problem that the more the number of impressive words increases in a page, the more the number of words we overlook increases.

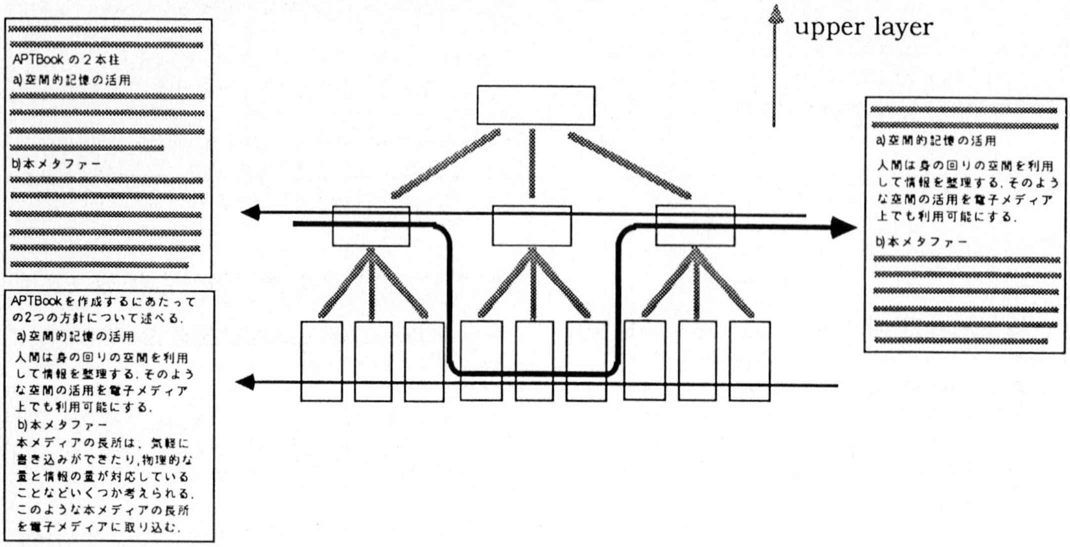

Figure 12 Partial detail representation

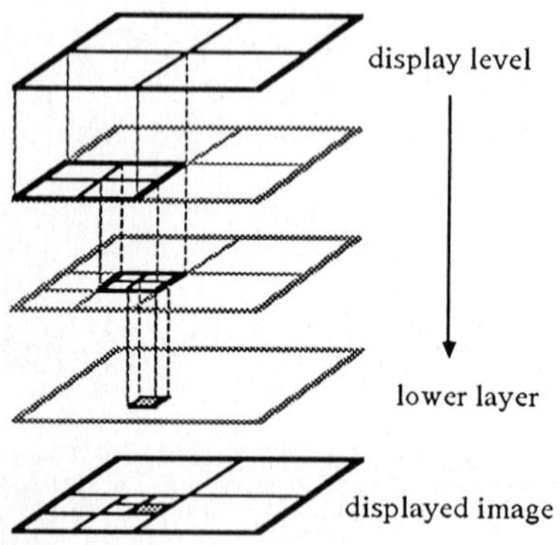

Figure 13 Partial detail representation for a figure

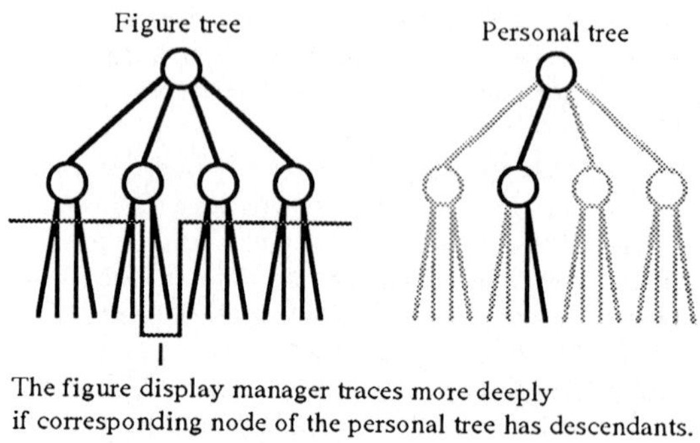

Figure 14 Figure tree and Personal tree

Figure image representation. When a user leafs through pages, APTBook displays figure images in compressed style. But, under the high speed leafing through, further discussions are needed whether or not it is preferable to display figure images in this style. It is because an image itself has much information.

"Memo". Since APTBook currently provides only one book as a prototype, we cannot make links among different books. In future, if APTBook can supports the field of very wide range, the employment of links will be much effective. Memopads, underlines, and dog-ears can be used independently according to each user's interest. Regarding the memopad, although we have to write on it through keyboard, if handwriting input is supported, it will be more and more useful.

Animation of leafing through the pages. When we want to refer to a document, the animation of leafing through pages is one of the effective referencing scheme, since we can easily understand the direction for leafing through and also understand the amount leafed through from the thickness of the rest pages.

6. Future directions

Recently, the portable computers such as lap-top computer are large in number on the market. Although our current system can only access the data on a floppy disk, if the APTBook which are installed in those portable computers can access the electronized library in future, we will be able to browse our favorite information light-heartedly at anywhere and any time. Using this APTBook, we could read books, magazines, and newspapers in a train, if a radio data communication network were realized.

From now on, in order to make our system practical, we must increase the volume of information in each page and enhance the quality of representation.

7. Conclusion

We have discussed a newly developed information providing system based on book metaphor, named APTBook. Since APTBook can show the parts in detail in which a user interested, the form in which we read the only eyecatching part in a magazine, we buy something after running our eye through a catalogue, or we buy a book after stand-up reading will be able to be realized on electronic media. Although the research is not completed yet, the current implementation suggests the success of our system, APTBook.

Acknowledgements

Many people have assisted this project with information and ideas. We would particularly like to thank Dr. Ken-ichi Okada and Mr. Hiromi Mizuno for their encouragement and suggestions.

References

ANDREA A. diSESSA, HAROLD ABELSON(1986): BOXER: A RECONSTRUCTIBLE COMPUTATIONAL MEDIUM,Communication of the ACM September 1986 Volume 29 Number 9

BARTLETT W. MEL, STEPHEN M. OMOHUNDRO, ARCH D. ROBINSON, STEVEN S. SKIENA, KURT H. THEARLING, LUKE T. YOUNG, and STEPHEN WOLFRAM(1988): TABLET: Personal Computer in the Year 2000,Communications of the ACM June 1988 Volume 31 Number 6

Brad A. Myers(1989): User-Interface Tools: Introduction and Survey,IEEE Software January 1989

Carmen Egido, John Patterson(1988): Pictures and Category Labels as Navigational Aids for Catalog Browsing,ACM SIGCHI CHI'88 Proceedings

D.Austin Henderson, Jr., and Stuart K. Card(1986): Rooms: The Use of Multiple Virtual Workspaces to Reduce Space Contention in a Window-Based Graphical User Interface,ACM Transactions on Graphics, Vol.5, No.3, July 1986

Donald Hearn, M. Pauline Baker: COMPUTER GRAPHICS,PRENTICE-HALL,INC.

George W. Furnas(1986): Generalized Fisheye Views,ACM SIGCHI CHI'86 Proceedings

H. Rex Hartson and Deborah Hix(1989): Human-Computer Interface Development: Concepts and Systems,ACM Computing Surveys vol.21, No.1, March 1989

JEFFREY MITCHELL, BEN SHNEIDERMAN(1989): DYNAMIC VERSUS STATIC MENUS: AN EXPLORATORY COMPARISON,ACM CHI BULLETIN APRIL 1989

John D. Gould(1987): WHY READING WAS SLOWER FROM CRT DISPLAYS THAN FROM PAPER,ACM SIGCHI CHI+GI'87 Proceedings

John D. Gould(1987): BEHAVIORAL EXPERIMENTS ON HANDMARKINGS,ACM SIGCHI CHI+GI'87 Proceedings

Mark A Linton, John M. Vlissides, and Paul R. Calder(1989): Composing User Interfaces with Interviews,IEEE Computer February 1989

Richard A. Bolt(1987): The Integrated Multi-Modal Interface, Trans. IEIC Japan, Part D November 1987

Richard A. Bolt(1984): The human interface, Van Nostrand Reinhold, New York(1984)

William Buxton and Brad A Myers(1986): A STUDY IN TWO-HANDED INPUT,ACM SIGCHI CHI'86 Proceedings

Human–Computer Interaction – INTERACT '90
D. Diaper et al. (Editors)
Elsevier Science Publishers B.V. (North-Holland)

"GOOD" GRAPHIC INTERFACES FOR "GOOD" IDEA ORGANIZERS

Kozo SUGIYAMA and Kazuo MISUE

International Institute for Advanced Study of Social Information Science
FUJITSU LIMITED, 140 Miyamoto, Numazu, Shizuoka, 410-03 Japan

"Good" graphic interfaces are indispensable for "good" idea organizers to arrange and organize lots of segments of information. We analyse the KJ Method, an idea organizing method famous in Japan, and consider graphic interface aspects of human-computer interactions. Some novel techniques such as automatic graph drawing, incremental editing, fisheye, diagram-document conversion etc. are presented. These techniques are useful also for browsers of hypertexts, collaborative work and so on.

1. INTRODUCTION

In developing "good" *idea organizers*, "good" graphic interfaces are indispensable to arrange and organize lots of segments of information. Such interfaces are required to provide facilities for editing diagrams of relational networks and showing them in a readable way to stimulate human's abductive thinking abilities.

The *KJ Method* (KJM) was developed by Jiro Kawakita[1,2]. It is famous in Japan as an effective *card-based* method for organizing ideas and solving problems. Developing a *computer-supported KJ Method* (CSKJM) is not only interesting itself but also useful for investigating "good" graphic interfaces for idea organizers.

In this paper we analyse idea organizing processes in KJM and consider graphic interface aspects of human-computer interactions. Some novel techniques for the graphic interface such as automatic graph drawing, incremental editing, fisheye, diagram-document conversion etc. are discussed. These techniques are useful also for *browsers of hypertexts*[3], *collaborative work* such as Colab[4] and so on.

2. GRAPHIC INTERFACE ASPECTS OF CSKJM

2.1. Process of KJM

KJM contains four basic steps as follows[1].

(1) *Label Making* : We start with a supply of *labels* or *note cards* on which *ideas* or *information* (text or image etc.) relevant to our problem are written. We collect and record ideas until we feel we have exhausted all information necessary to solve the problem.

(2) *Label Grouping and Title Making* : The labels are shaffled well and spreaded on a large *sheet*. Then all the labels are read several times. If there exist such lables seemed to belong together, we make a *team* of the lables. This process is repeated. After about two-thirds of all the lables are arranged in teams, making *titles* for the teams is started. The titles should clearly describe the essence of all labels in the team. Once a title is made for a team, we put all the labels together in a *pile* with the title clipped on its top. Next, we arrange the teams in *larger teams* in the same manner. This iterative process of grouping labels may be repeated as many times as necessary. Usually it is terminated when the number of the teams is reduced to less than ten.

(3) *Spacial Arrangement and Chart Making* : We find carefully the *arrangement* of the final groups in which a consistent understanding of all the groups can be obtained. Then we proceed to arrange all *sub-teams* or *elements* in the same manner. After completing this *spatial arrangement*, we draw a *chart* in own handwriting by showing the relationships using various *symbols* and *signs*.

(4) *Verbal or Written Explanation* : To explain the chart clearly, we try to describe the chart *verbally* or *in writing*. As a general rule our explanation should proceed to a team adjacent to where it started. The cumulative effect of idea generation will continue to increase as our explanation advances.

The process of KJM can be represented well schematically using *KJM diagram-matrix* shown in Figure 1, where the process starts at the left-bottom corner(*Label Making*), goes up from diagram 1 to 9(*Label Grouping*), goes down from 10 to 15(*Spacial Arrangement and Chart Making*) and ends at the right-bottom corner (*documentation*). Diagrams 10' to 13' mean images which its user might have in his mind when he is arranging diagrams 10 to 13.

2.2. Features of KJM and Subjects for Developing CSKJM Interfaces[5]

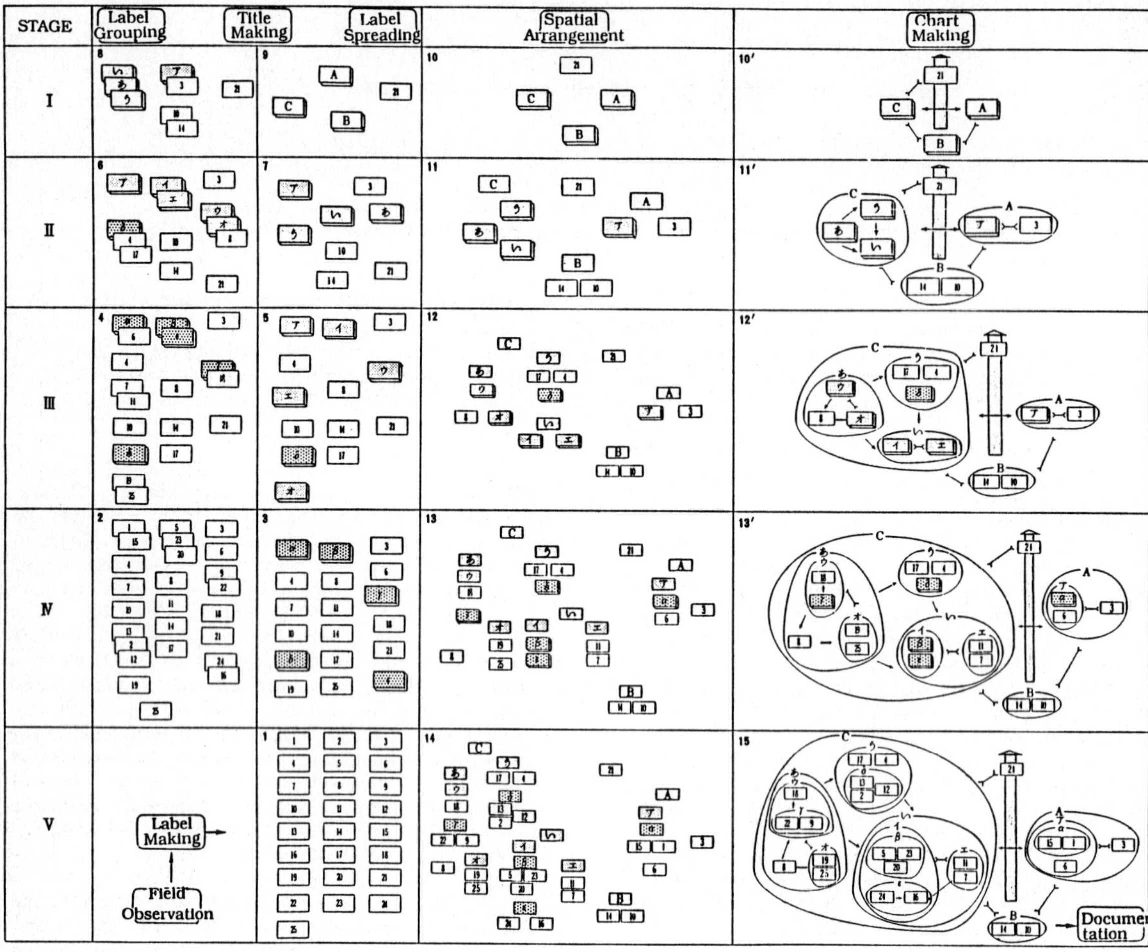

Figure 1 KJM Diagram-Matrix.

In KJM, diagrams are utilized as a map of user's image. We need to develop an *advanced graphic editor* which can progressively organize labels according to the image *without non-intrinsic operations* for generating and editing diagrams.

KJM emphasizes that organizing labels should be conducted through viewing the whole structure. We should develop a method to display *the whole and detail* effectively on a small bit-mapped screen of a workstation.

Kinds of diagrams, *drawing convensions*, *operations* etc. are restricted in each KJM step and *guides* for the process to organize labels are given as shown in Table 1. These restrictions and guides, however, might be mainly due to "manual" processes of KJM. It is important to make *experiments* of making and organizing labels under *different* restrictions and guides.

Information written on lables is most important in the KJM process though it is omitted in the diagrams shown in Figure 1. *Automatic spatial arrangement* and *title making* based upon semantic analyses of the information on labels are challenging subjects.

Final results are written in documents. We need to support the step for *coversing diagrams to documents*.

2.3. Desirable Graphic Facilities for CSKJM

Based upon the analyses of KJM, graphic facilities desirable for CSKJM are summarized as follows[5]:

(1) aesthetic printing of diagrams*
(2) incremental editing of diagrams*
(3) chaging drawing styles*
(4) swiching outline/detail diagrams*
(5) viewing the whole and detail of diagrams effectively*
(6) conversing a diagram to a different kind one*
(7) supporting diagram-document conversions*
(8) memorizing history, backtracking and retrying*

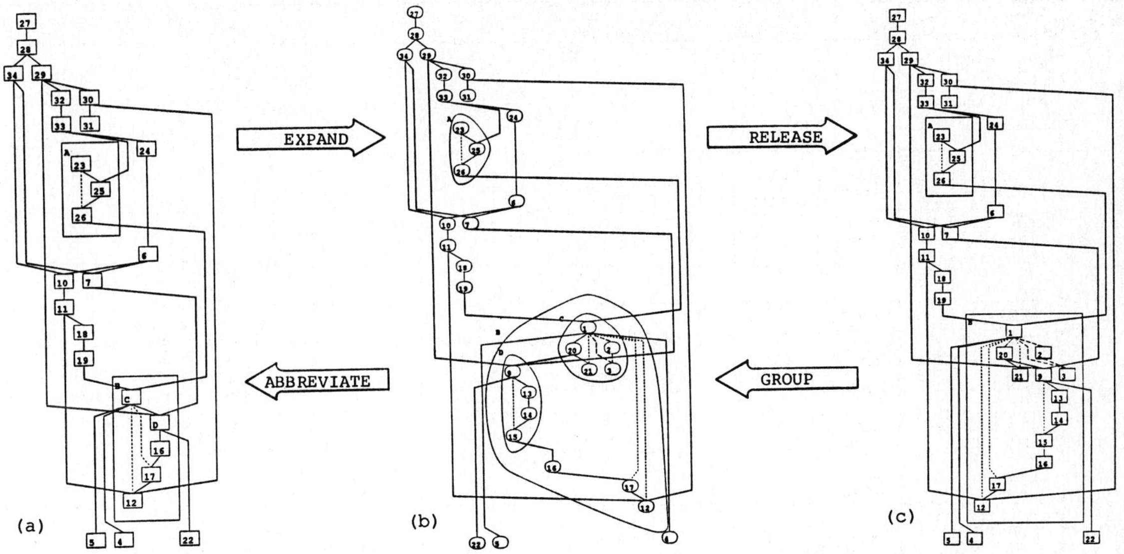

Figure 2 Area-Net Diagrams Drawn Automatically and Command Primitives.

(9) selecting an adequate guide among several prepared guides

In the above, items marked with * mean that they relate to *automatic drawing of diagrams* (or *graphs*).

3.DEVELOPING ELEMENTARY GRAPHIC TECHNIQUES

3.1. Automatic diagram Drawing

Diagrams provide the user with a *friendly interface* where an important quality required to the diagrams is *readability*. Diagrams so far have been drawn manually or with the aid of a graphic editor, where placement of nodes and routing of links have been under responsibility of the user. This means that drawing "readable" diagrams has often been a time-consuming and neglected activity. This can be overcome by providing an automatic drawing capability.

Diagrams treated in algorithms developed so far have been *net diagrams* which represent adjacent relations among nodes[6]. The framework and algorithms for drawing net diagrams are summarized in APPENDIX. Diagrams we utilize in KJM, however, are *area-net diagrams* (diagrams with both inclusive and adjacent relations among nodes) where nodes are drawn as *closed curves*, inclusive rela- tions as *geometric inclusion* among the closed curves and adjacent relations as *links*.

We have developed an algorithm for drawing net diagrams[7,8] and some improvements of the algorithm have been carried out[9,10,11]. An *algorithm for area-net diagrams* is developed as an extension of the algorithm for net diagrams[12,13]. We first identify readability elements for area-net diagrams, i.e. *drawing conventions* and *drawing rules* such as *minimization of line crossings, close placement of linked nodes, minimization of line bends, balanced layout of lines* and so on. Then we specify *priority* among the rules empirically and develop a heuristic method to generate "readable" diagrams in a *hierarchical form*. Figure 2 shows hierarchical drawings of three area-net diagrams where nodes are drawn as boxes in (a) and (c) *while as closed curves in (b) to improve the readablity* [12].

It has been implemented in SKETCH-II, written in C, on a workstation. The computational time for applications shows that the algorithm achieves satisfactory performance. Large diagrams can be drawn with fast heuristics although exact optimizations are characterized as NP-complete problems[12].

3.2 Swiching Outline/Detail Diagrams and Incremental Editing of Diagrams

The automatic drawing of area-net diagrams can provide us prominent and powerful facilities for representing and manipulating structural information. One of the most remarkable facilities, for example, is a "grouping" of vertices or "labeling" of a subdiagram which ordinarily means *generalization, abstraction, aggregation or integration of concepts* assigned to the nodes or elements of the subdiagram. Another is the facility for the *refinement of concepts* assigned to nodes, which can be realized by "expanding" the nodes into more

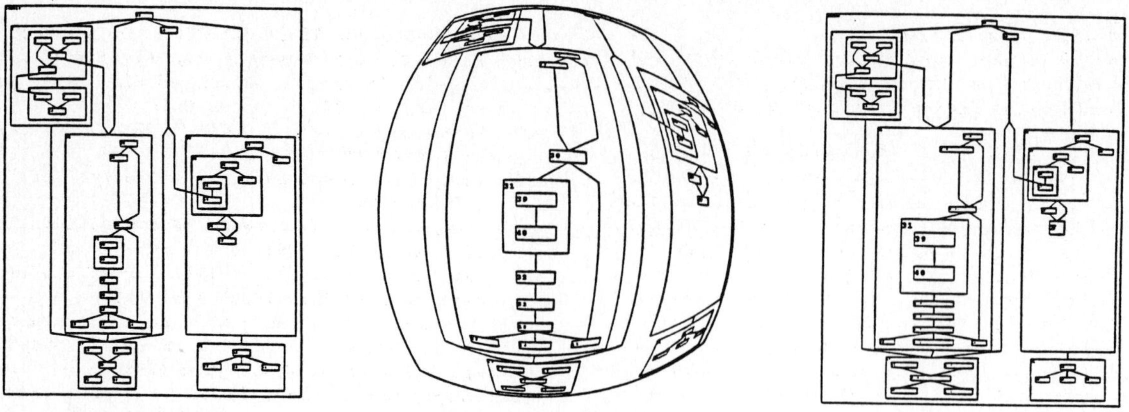

(a) original (b) natural fisheye (c) biforcal fisheye

Figure 3 Fisheyes for Area-Net Diagrams.

refined structures. Figure 2 explain the possibility of a set of command primitives for reorganizing structures within the extent of our diagram formalism[12]. Meanings of primitives in Figure 2 are as follows:

(1) EXPAND: construct a more refined structure within a node
(2) ABBREVIATE: eliminate all the structures which a node includes
(3) RELEASE: eliminate a node and release the structure which the node includes
(4) GROUP: create a node including the structure which is constituted by some other nodes

It is desired to investigate how to use the automatic drawing capabilities in *dynamic thinking processes* under *more general* visual formalisms.

3.3 Viewing the Whole and Detail of Diagrams

Furnas[14] proposed the concept of *fisheye* and its formalization. We have developed fisheyes adecuate for our area-net diagrams.

To display a large diagram on a small bit-mapped screen of a workstation, multi-window techniques are often employed; the whole of the diagram is outlined on a window and a focussed part of the diagram is detailed on another window. We have proposed methods to map a large diagram on *one window* where we can see both details of focussed parts and an outline of the rest.

In Figure 3, (b) and (c) show two types of mappings of the diagram presented in (a); (b)*natural fisheye* and (c)*biforcal fisheye*. The latter has good characteristics such as:

(1) Focussed boxes are magnified with *geometrical similarity* and *orthogonality*, and other part is de-magnified with orthogonality.
(2) *Nevertheless, form and space of the whole drawing area are preserved* [15].

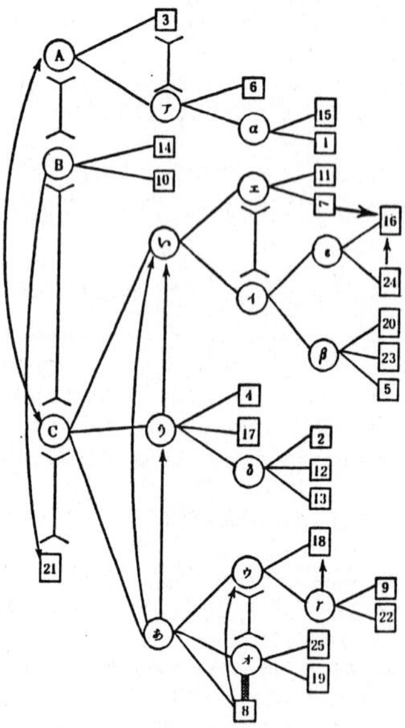

Figure 4 A Net Diagram Convenient for Diagram-Document Conversion.

3.4 Supporting Diagram-Document Conversions

A diagram has a network structure while a document has a linear structure. Therefore, in order to convert a diagram to a document, we should determine a *description order* among nodes in the diagram. KJM suggests some principles in determining the order as follows:

(1)First, determine a *starting node*.
(2)Determine the description order among nodes of each depth according to (i) ordinarily, moving to adjacent nodes, (ii) moving to any node, however, if it seems to be more adecuate, and (iii) connecting nodes logically inserting con-

junctions, reasons and so on.
(3) Determine the description order among sub-nodes according to (i) moving from top to bottom, or (ii) moving from bottom to top.

In considering a description order, net diagrams are more convenient than area-net diagrams since linear orders among nodes of each depth are expressed explicitly in the former. Figure 4 shows a net diagram converted from area-net diagram 15 of Figure 1 where the order of top nodes, A, B, C and 21, for example, means the description order[5]. If we want to describe B preceeding to A, we can easily modify the diagram using the automatic drawing capability.

REFERENCES

[1] Kawakita, J., The KJ Method - A Scientific Approch to Problem Solving (Kawakita Res. Inst., Tokyo, 1975).
[2] Kawakita, J., The KJ Method (Chuo-Koron-Sha, Tokyo, 1986). (in Japanese)
[3] Conklin,J.,IEEE Comput.,20(9) (1987)17-41.
[4] Stefik,M.et al., CACM, 30(1) (1987) 32-47.
[5] Sugiyama,K.,Proc.5th Symp. on Human Interface (Kyoto,Oct 1989) 325-330. (in Japanese)
[6] Eades,P. and Tamassia,R., Algorisms for Drawing Graphs: An Annotated Bibliography, Tech. Rep. CS-89-09, Brown Univ. (1989).
[7] Sugiyama,K. et al., IEEE T.SMC, SMC-11(2) (1981) 109-125.
[8] Sugiyama,K.,Cybernetics and Systems, 18(6) (1987) 447-488.
[9] Rowe,L.A.et al.,Software :Practice and Experience, 17(1) (1987) 6-76.
[10] Gansner,E.R.et al., Software:Practice and Experience, 18(11) (1988) 1047-1062.
[11] Messinger,E.B., Automatic Layout of Large Directed Graphs, Tech. Rep. 87-07-08, Dept. Comp. Sci., Univ. Washington (1988).
[12] Sugiyama, K. and Misue, K., Visualizing Structural Information: Hierarchical Drawing of a Compound Digraph, Res.Rep. No.86, IIAS-SIS, FUJITSU LTD (1989).
[13] Misue,K. and Sugiyama,K., T. IPSJ, 30(10) (1989) 1324-1334. (in Japanese)
[14] Furnas,G. W., Proc. CHI'86 (Boston, 1986) 16-23.
[15] Misue,K. and Sugiyama,K.,Proc. 5th Symposium on Human Interface (Kyoto, Oct 1989) 463-468. (in Japanese)
[16] Sugiyama, K., Systems, Control and Information, 33(11) (1989) 559-567. (in japanese)

APPENDIX: FRAMEWORK AND ALGORITHMS FOR AUTOMATIC DRAWING OF NET DIAGRAMS

The extensive survey of automatic drawing algorithms for net diagrams is conducted and *the framework for the automatic drawing* is developed, which is summalized in Table A.1, where:

(1) Variations of *standard coordinates* are shown in Figure A.1;

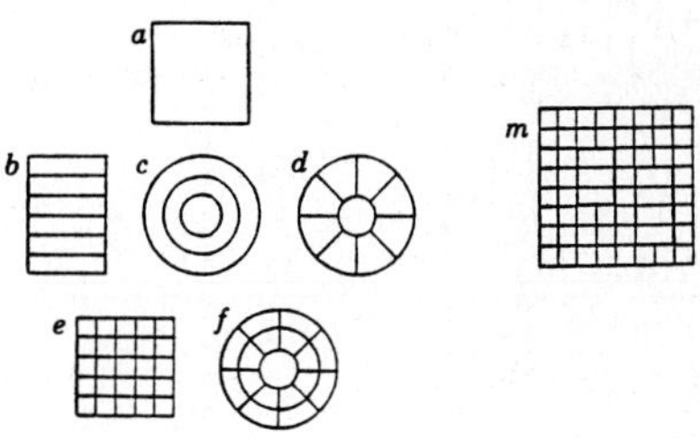

Figure A.1 Variations of Standard Coordinates.

(2) *Drawing conventions* are as follows:
- (i) conventions for *placement of nodes*
  - C1p:no restriction
  - C2p:positioning on pararell lines
  - C3p:p. on grid points
  - C4p:No overlapping among nodes
- (ii) conventions for *routing of arcs*
  - C1r:routing by straight lines
  - C2r:r. by polygonal lines
  - C3r:r. by curves
  - C4r:r. on grid lines
  - C5r:no restriction
  - C6r:no overlapping among arcs
  - C7r:no overlapping among nodes and arcs;

(3) *Drawing rules* are as follows:
- (i) *semantic rules*
  - R1a:p. of specific nodes on a line
  - R2a:p. of specific nodes on a curve
  - R3a:specifying sizes of nodes
  - R4a:p. of specific nodes on a boundary
  - R5a:close p. of specific nodes
  - R6a:central p. of specific nodes
  - R7a:limit of crossings of specific arcs
  - R8a:limit of bends of specific arcs
  - R9a:limit of lengths of specific arcs
- (ii) *structural rules*
  - R1b:central p. of highest degree nodes
  - R2b:unique drawing of isomorphic graphs
  - R3b:un. p. of nodes of isomorphic graphs
  - R4b:hierarchical layout
  - R5b:minimizing line crossings
  - R6b:balance of vertical/horizontal ratio
  - R7b:presentation of symmetries
  - R8b:minimizing bends
  - R9b:maxinizing convex surfaces
  - R10b:symmetrical layout of sons
  - R11b:no crossing among subgraphs
  - R12b:uniform positioning
  - R13b:minimizing drawing area
  - R14b:minimiing total length of arcs
  - R15b:minimizing differences of node sizes
  - R16b:minimizing average length
  - R17b:min. dif. of n. outline and a. leng.
  - R18b:min. differences of arc lengths
  - R19b:minimizing maximum arc length
  - R20b:uniform positioning on a boundary;

(4) *Taxonomy of drawing rules* is as follows:
- (i) for axis I(solution), U:unique; N:not unique

Table A.1 Summary Table of Drawing Algorithms for Net Diagrams.

CONVENTIONS & RULES		TAXONOMY	TREES				DIRECTED GRAPHS								PLANAR GRAPHS						UNDIRECTED GRAPHS					REMARKS
		I II III IV	①	②	③	④	⑤	⑥	⑦	⑧	⑨	⑩	⑪	⑫	⑬	⑭	⑮	⑯	⑰	⑱	⑲	⑳	㉑	㉒	㉓	
ST. COORDINATES			b	b	b	b	b	c	b	d	b	c	b	c	a	a	e	b	b	e	a	a	a	e	m	○: fall on
DRAWING CONVENTIONS	C1p														○	○					○	○	○			△: fall on partially
	C2p		○	○	○	○	○	○	○	○	○	○	○	○				○								
	C3p																○		○	○		○		○	○	
	C4p		○	○	○	○	○	○	○	○	○	○	○	○	○	○	○	○	○	○	○			○	○	
	C1r		○	○	○	○	○	○					○	○	○	○		○		△	○	○	○			□: given as constraints
	C2r								○	○	○						○	○	○	△				○	○	
	C3r											○	○													
	C4r								△								○	○	○					○	○	■: optimized
	C5r		○	○	○	○	○	○	△	○	○	○	○	○						○	○	○	○			
	C6r		○	○	○	○			○	○	○	○	○	○	○	○	○	○	○		○			○	○	
	C7r		○	○	○	○			○	○	○	○	○	○	○	○	○	○	○		○			○	○	
SEMANTIC RULES	R1a	USLB							□1																□2	▪: optimized easily
	R2a	USLB												□1												
	R3a	UMLB					□1		□1				□1											□1	□1	
	R4a	NTLB																			□1			□2	□2	
	R5a	NTLB																							□2	●: heuristic method with some guarantees
	R6a	NTLB																							□2	
	R7a	NTLF																							□2	
	R8a	NSLF															□1								□3	
	R9a	NMLF																							□4	
STRUCTURAL RULES	R1b	UTLB																								◎: heuristic method without guarantees
	R2b	USGB				■3			■1				▪1													
	R3b	USGB										■2														
	R4b	NTLH	▪1	▪1	▪1	▪1	▪1		■2		■1	▪1	▪2												(●)2	
	R5b	NTGB	▪1	▪1	▪1	▪1	◎3		◎3		◎2	◎3	◎3	◎1	■1	■1	■1	■1	■1	■1	◎1			◎1	◎1	
	R6b	NSGB																								
	R7b	NSGB				■3																◎2	◎1			
	R8b	NSGB							◎4		◎3						■2	■2	●2	◎3				■2	■2	
	R9b	NSGF													■2	■2					■2					
	R10b	NSLH	●3	■2	■2	■2	◎3		◎5		◎4		◎4												(●)2	( ): Only when hierarchical structures exist
	R11b	NMGH											■5													
	R12b	NMGB							◎6		◎5												◎2			
	R13b	NMGB	■2	●3	■3	●4							■6				●3		●3	●2				●3	●3	■1: Numbers represent priorities
	R14b	NMGB					◎2		◎2		◎1														●3	
	R15b	NMGB																								
	R16b	NMGF																								
	R17b	NMGF																								
	R18b	NMGF																				◎1				
	R19b	NMLF																								
	R20b	NMLF																								
COMPLEXITY	n		○	○	○	○										○			○							n : # of nodes
	$n^{1.5}$														○											s : # of simulation steps
	n^2								○		○						○			○						k : k-gonal graph representation
	sn^2																					○				
	$(n+c)^2$																							○		
	$n \sim (k(n+c))^2$																								○	c : # of crossings
	n^3																						○			
	?						○					○	○	○				○			○					

(ii) for axis II (phase), T: topology; S: shape; M: metrics

(iii) for axis III, G: global; L: local

(iv) for axis IV, H: hierarchical; F: flat; B: both common.

We adopted empirically *general priorities among conventions and rules* such as:

(1) placement conventions > routing conventions
(2) conventions > rules
(3) semantic rules > structural rules
(4) U > N (5) T > S > M (6) G > L
(7) H > B > F.

In Table A.1, conventions and rules are ordered from top to bottom according to the *general priorities*. In Table A.1, numbers attached to symbols mean priorities of rules adopted in the respective algorithm. It should be noted that *the practical priorities conform well to the general priorities*.

Numbers in circles mean algorithms: i.e., 1,2: Wetherell & Shannon (1979); 3: Vaucher (1980); 4: Reingold & Tilford (1981); 5,6: Carpano (1980); 7,8: Sugiyama et al. (1981), Sugiyama (1987); 9: Rowe et al. (1987); 10: Reggiani & Marchetti (1988); 11: Itsumi & Kogure (1988); 12: Nakamori & Murasaki (1989); 13: Tutte (1963); 14: Chiba et al. (1985); 15: Tamassia (1987); 16: Otten & Wijk (1978); 17: Tamassia & Tolis (1986,87); 18: Woods (1982); 19: Hara & Kaya (1984); 20: Eades (1984); 21: Kamada & Kawai (1988); 22: Batini et al. (1986); 23: Tamassia et al. (1987). (See [6] and [16].)

SECTION III: DETAILED DESIGN

SIII.3 User Support

Help systems: An information-sharing approach
M. Kurisaki 529

End-user dialogue context management of office automation systems
G. Lu, C. Vanneste, and M. Ader 535

Current approaches and new guidelines for undo support design
Y. Yang 543

Interface usability engineering under practical constraints: A case study in the design of undo support
Y. Yang 549

State versus history in user interfaces
W.B. Cowan and M. Wein 555

The personal touch: A study of users' customization practice
A.H. Jørgensen and A. Sauer 561

Inferring task structures from interaction protocols
F. Schiele and H.U. Hoppe 567

An adaptive system developer's tool-kit
D. Benyon, D. Murray, and F. Jennings 573

Human–Computer Interaction – INTERACT '90
D. Diaper et al. (Editors)
Elsevier Science Publishers B.V. (North-Holland)

Help Systems: An Information-Sharing Approach

Masayuki Kurisaki

Information & Communication Research Laboratory
Matsushita Electric Industrial Co., Ltd.
1006 Kadoma, Kadoma, Osaka 571, Japan

Although the knowledge-based approach has allowed the development of extensive help systems, it seems impossible to build a complete knowledge base for a large complex system such as an operating system, in advance. This paper describes the need for and the basic design of a help system which asks other users for help when it encounters an unknown situation. Only frequently asked questions and their solutions are stored in the initial state. However, a user can ask any question and is almost guaranteed to receive an answer even if it comes later by electronic mail. The collected solutions are kept in the knowledge base for future use. The system is intended to help non-expert programmers find a UNIX command or get advice from other users who belong to the same working group. The knowledge base of the system is regarded as an extension of the human memory shared by a group of users.

1 Introduction

Help capabilities are often considered to be essential components of well-designed computer systems. Most existing help systems, however, have failed to be helpful because they don't have enough knowledge about the users and the help domain (Kearsley, 1988). In response, intelligent online aiding became an active research area and many such systems have been developed (e.g., Fischer et al. 1985; Hegner, 1988; Jackson et al. 1984; Kemke 1988; Wilensky et al. 1984, 1988). Although many demonstration systems have shown their "intelligence", most of the knowledge-based help systems cannot produce answers when they encounter a situation where they lack the knowledge necessary to answer the user's questions. Little is known about the usability of intelligent help systems (e.g., Carroll and McKendree, 1987; Carroll and Aaronson, 1988).

One of the other reasons why users prefer to consult other persons rather than use help systems is that they can get "something" even if the user cannot formulate the "right" questions. It is also observed that many users tend to adopt a trial-and-error approach, exploring the situation (e.g., Carroll and Rosson, 1987; Coventry, 1989), and they quickly stop using a help system which cannot give them a beneficial response or even any answer at all. Therefore, it is necessary for help systems to always give users a response which leads to the solution, even if it is not an exact solution for an immediate problem.

Artificial intelligence techniques are indispensable for intelligent help systems. We should not forget, however, to consider other people as an integral part of computer support environments. As Bannon (1986) pointed out, more effort should be put into better exploiting the natural intelligence of the other users available in the user community.

2 Help Domain

2.1 Expertise in UNIX

The UNIX operating system is widely used around the world. However, because it was developed for programmers, it is difficult to learn to use, especially for people unfamiliar with computer systems. It is a common view that a user gradually becomes an expert from a novice as he gains experience, and experts know everything that novices know. User levels are often classified as novice, beginner, intermediate, and expert (Chin, 1989). These levels differ in more than just their command vocabulary. In the programming domain, the differences in semantic and strategic knowledge are also important (Mayer, 1988). Empirical investigations show that only a small number of commands are known to most users, including well-experienced users (e.g., Draper, 1984; Greenberg and Witten, 1988). It seems people don't learn commands which aren't related to their immediate tasks. Draper (1984) argues that all users will be experts in relation to some parts of the system, novices in relation to other areas they have never used, and intermediate elsewhere.

The UNIX system includes several hundred utility programs, and by using the shell facility, a user can easily combine these programs to build entire applications. It is highly probable that the functions a user wants have already been created as a shell command by other users. There is also much lore about system usage that cannot be found in manuals or textbooks. This information is usually spread only within a small group at their workplace, mostly orally.

2.2 How People Get Help

UNIX provides a keyword help and an online manual (e.g., "man", "apropos", "whatis" command) as a help facility. Although potentially useful for skilled users, they are inadequate for most users. One of the reason is that it contains too much information and the user must search through irrelevant material to get to the information actually needed. In other words, the cost of searching for the particular information is potentially quite large. Things get worse if a user has difficulty understanding the material because of the language used. Today, a great deal of information is available in English but may not be also available in a language familiar to the user.

It is widely observed that learners at every level of experience try to avoid reading, preferring to consult their colleagues or a local expert. (e.g., Lang et al. 1982; Hiltz, 1984). When users cannot find any person who knows the solution in their local community, they can send a message to other people on the network and receive an answer by electronic mail or on a bulletin board. Some people tend to ask even basic questions to which the answers can be easily found in any textbook or reference, while other people hesitate to ask questions at all.

2.3 The Problem

Ideally, human consultants are available anytime anywhere; however this is not always the case. Then it becomes very important to know whom to ask. Although there often is a local expert among a group of users, he will not want to spend too much of his time as a consultant unless consulting is his job. A help environment based on an electronic message database can be useful, but it doesn't usually have the comprehensive and systematic structure of built-in help systems and people often overlook or neglect the topics that aren't relevant to their immediate tasks. There are questions which are frequently asked by different users, and the human consultant, whether they are expert or other users, should not be disturbed by such questions.

Intelligent interfaces (e.g., Tyler and Treu, 1989; Jerrams-Smith, 1989) are one approach to make a system easier to use, especially for novice users. However, they require a great deal of knowledge or system description in advance. In order to provide sophisticated help, a sophisticated knowledge representation and inference system is necessary. Usually, the more detailed the knowlege representation, the more effort is required to acquire such knowledge. It is almost impossible to build a complete knowledge base for all UNIX aspects.

While formulating a question is itself a difficult problem (e.g., O'Malley, 1986), even if a user does know what he wants to know about, current standard help systems seem hard to use. This is not an uncommon situation in the real world. People often remember that some command or a method exists, but they don't remember the exact name or how to apply it. Although there have been many studies on novice users and many systems have been developed to help such users, there are few practical systems that support beginner or intermediate programmers, who already have a conceptual model of the system. For those users, a more easy and efficient way of accessing relevant information is necessary.

3 Help Systems as Information-Sharing Systems

One of the strongest needs of users for command-based system is a help facility which helps them to find the existence of a command or a utility program that performs required functions. (Utility programs include shell programs written by other users.) It is important because if a user can find the function, he doesn't have to spend his time writing a program by himself. In order to enhance the productivity of a working group, it should be possible for any information that would benefit other users to be archived and retrieved whenever needed.

In our view, the knowledge base or data base of the help system is an extension of the human memory shared by a group of users, and the help system is meant to be the user's assistant rather than a expert advisory system. The function of the system is not to produce the solution by itself, but to provide information collected from other users. The system doesn't have to have a perfect knowledge base from the beginning; instead it must increase its knowledge through use. The user who asks for help must be given the needed information even if it comes later.

The system works as follows:

1. A user ask for some information. For example, he might be looking for a command or wants to check the availability of some utility programs.
2. If the system has an answer, it will give it to the user. Alternatively, the user may search for the information by browsing the knowledge base by himself.
3. If the system lacks the information and the user approves, the system sends a message which describes the question to some or all other users.
4. Users who know the answer or have suggestions respond to the system. The responses are sent to the original questioner by electronic mail, and also kept in the system's knowledge base.
5. If more than one different answer is collected, everyone who contributed will be informed of the other solutions.

4 System Overview

This section proposes an architecture that addresses the issues raised above.

4.1 Natural Language Query

Although natural language is too verbose for routine use through a keyboard, many users would prefer it when they have goal-directed questions (e.g., "I want to...", "How can I...?") because it allows them to directly specify their problem relatively easily. There are many categories of user utterances in advice-seeking dialogues (e.g., Ringle and Halstead-Nussloch, 1989); however, it is not always necessary to handle all of them in natural language dialogue even if possible. Help systems should provide an appropriate access method to each type. In this paper, we describe only the case of How-type questions.

The Natural Language Query Analyser of the system takes as input a sentence typed by a user, and builds a meaning representation using KODIAK-like knowledge representation. KODIAK (Wilensky 1986) is a relation-oriented system, where objects are thought of as atomic elements, and knowledge is captured by the relationship in which these objects participate. Although the analyser must produce the meaning representation as specifically as possible, it must not expect that all the inputs are well-formed in a real situation. The analyser is able to handle undefined words in certain cases. Even if the system cannot understand the whole meaning of the user's query, it must extract critical concepts because the user's interest or topic area can be often guessed from them and used to access the relevant information in later processing. There are many methods for doing this, including even simple techniques such as keyword-based approaches (e.g., Whalen and Patrick, 1988; Roberts, 1970).

The most important feature is that the users in a group can share their knowledge through the system. This is not specific to UNIX help systems; it can be seen, more generally, as a tool for computer-supported cooperative work.

4.2 Operation Hierarchy

The core knowledge about UNIX operations is represented by a network called the Operation Hierarchy. Basic nodes represent a user's specific goal (e.g., deleting a file, changing a password) and each has a solution for its goal, while the other nodes have abstract meanings (e.g., file manipulation) and are used to group basic nodes. Each node has a brief description and hierarchical relations to other nodes, and also the following information.

- Associated Key Concepts

  This information will be used by the search process (described in 4.3) to constrain the number of nodes selected as candidates. Key concepts that trigger the node are described using AND and OR relations. For example, if the abstract node "File-Manipulation" is linked to the concept "File", and the concept "File" appears in the user's query, then the node "File-Manipulation" is activated as one of the candidates.

- Condition Test

  This information is used to select nodes from the candidate set returned by the search process. The test, which checks whether the node is appropriate or not, can be performed by pattern matching and/or querying the user. It is usually done by pattern matching on the meaning representation of a user's question, but, if there was an unknown object and the match was partial, the user is asked predefined questions. For example, if the user asks "How can I copy a file from renoir to magrit?" and the system doesn't know "renoir" and "magrit" are machine names, it will ask the user "Do you mean that you want to copy a file between machines?" assuming this question was prepared as a alternative to the pattern matching. Any other additional data can be collected in such a way.

Basic nodes have solution parts, which describe the corresponding solutions or advices, ie. how to achieve the user's goal. A solution part contains the following information.

- Solution Type

  Solutions are classified by their types. The types include Command, Shell scripts, and other advice. At present, the distinction is only made between Commands and others.

- Solution

  When an exact command is available, only the command name and, if necessary, its option are described. The actual command description, which contains a minimum of information, is kept in another file. Other solutions, including advice, are kept here as text.

- Possible Failures and Their Solutions

  These are kept as a pair list, where each pair consists of a description to check against the context and another solution to be tried.

4.3 Information Search Process

Although users must be able to obtain specific information they requested, it is not always easy for users to express exactly what they want. Even if a user enters only a fragment or a phrase, the system must guide him to specific information or provide related information.

In practical systems, menu-driven interfaces are often introduced to compensate for the shortcomings of a natural language interface (e.g., Uehara et al. 1988). More importantly, using menus seems to have the effect of helping the user to develop a mental map of the structure of the system and its knowledge base. One of the advantages of menus is that users can see what information is available by scanning them, and this is a good opportunity for them to find a new function which they might never have thought of otherwise.

When the system cannot find exactly appropriate information for the user's initial question, the rest of the help session becomes a information-finding process, similar to that of menu-based information retrieval systems.

Step 1
A user's query is now represented as a kind of semantic network, and some nodes of the network have links to the nodes in the Operation Hierarchy. When there is a concept which has such links, the associated operations are activated as a candidate set of the user's goals. For example, the phrase "to delete a file" activates at least three operation nodes: Deleting Operations, File Operations, and File Deletion. The first two are abstract nodes which don't have specific solutions.

At this point, usually, too many operation concepts are activated, as in a keyword-based information retrieval.

Step 2
After a candidate set is chosen, the system checks each condition test to find an operation which corresponds to the meaning of the user's question. If the selected node has a solution, it is displayed. If no particular operation (node) was found and there remains an activated abstract operation, the system makes a menu consisting of more specific operations and lets the user choose. When the user needs help in order to select from the menu and there are un-asked questions, the system asks those questions to decrease the number of candidates. After the solution is shown, the system ask whether it worked or not. If the answer is "No" and the solution has a possible failure list, each possibility is checked.

Step 3
If no solution is found, or all candidates are found to be useless, the user is asked if he wants the system to post the question on the net and find the answer from other users. In this case, the question is kept along with relevant information such as its meaning representation and the network position where the new node would be added.

4.4 Asking Other Users for Help

When a user searches for a command by describing his goal, his interest is usually in finding a method to achieve his goal. The user should be given advice or other relevant information if such a command doesn't exist. This can be done by asking other users for help, because there is a high possibility that many people had similar goals before, especially in the domain of computer programming.

When the system fails to answer the user's question, it requests help from other users by sending a message describing the problem. If someone knows the solution or he can give advice, he should respond to the system as a knowledge provider. He can add the knowledge in two ways. One is by invoking the system and the other way is by replying to the mail. The system uses the template shown in Fig. 1 to acquire knowledge from other users.

```
1. Problem and Explanation: (given)
2. Assumption:
3. Solution
     If a command exists,
        Command Name:
        Option to Use (if necessary):
     Other advice or comment:
4. Alternative Solutions
     Further Assumption (if any):
     Solution
     ......
```

Fig. 1 Template for Knowledge Acquisition

When a user who wants to add knowledge invokes the system, the recent question list appears and he is prompted to select a question. Since there may be many solutions, the questions are kept for a while even after the first answer is given. If he is the first user who responds, the blank template is given, otherwise, he will be shown the solutions which other people made. In the latter case, he can compare them with his own solution, and modify them only if he has an alternative solution or wants to add a comment.

When the system sends a message to ask for help, the template can be included at the end of the message. Users can respond by replying to the mail with the filled-in form. In this case, there is a possibility that the same answers are collected from different users. The system checks only command-type solutions to remove the duplicates. In order to check other types of solutions, text and program understanding ability is required for the system, which is not realized in the current version. For practical reasons, all the other replies are appended without any processing and left to be modified by human advisors.

4.5 Tracking Other Solutions

In general, there exists more than one solution to any problem. Furthermore there is a possibility that the given solution has a bug, or there exists a better solution. When a user gives the system a solution, he is asked whether he wants to follow that problem. That is, if he wants, he can receive other solutions posted by other people and check their solutions.

As new problems are posted, all participants have the chance to learn new knowledge. If they are interested in the problem, they can also be kept informed of newly added information. They can, of course, retrieve the solution at any time they want.

5 Discussion

One of the advantages of this system is that a user is guaranteed to get a response even if he cannot get it during the help session. Responding with some useful information at every interaction is critical for help systems, because many users don't attempt to use a help system with which they have unsuccessful experience. Although this is an obvious need, many systems fail to meet this expectation. Most knowledge-based help systems try to avoid this by preparing a complete knowledge base; however even if possible this requires a great effort. Moreover, it is not always necessary to prepare a complete knowledge base, if the system can handle the cases when it lacks the knowledge. Building a help facility which exploits system code as part of the its knowledge base (Rich, 1982) is one solution. In the Unix help domain, although it is possible for a system to exploit an online manual by itself, this is currently impractical and more research is needed. Although our approach, asking other users for help in one-shot dialogue, would not be suited for complex problems where more user-advisor interaction is needed, it is observed that users use face-to-face interaction for more serious, or urgent problems (e.g., Aaronson and Carroll, 1987). Our system is intended to be used mostly for checking for commands or utility programs that are available in his working environment. In practical situations, it is important for a help system to show its limitation so that users don't expect too much from the system and get frustrated as a result.

By incrementally adding only the knowledge which is actually required, the knowledge base can be kept as small as possible. The traditional way to maintain a knowledge base is similar to this, but it is usually done by a knowledge engineer or by a learning component of a system at regular time intervals. In these cases, the original user who brought the question is usually left unanswered. The incremental knowledge acquisition for help systems should be done whenever a problem is found.

The most significant difference between this approach and other help systems is that we regard other users as an important component of the system. Although it causes extra work for the other users, they also benefit from contributing because they have an opportunity to check their solution when other solutions are collected. The main goal is to create an environment where the users in an organization can share their knowledge through the system to enhance their productivity. If people have easy access to useful information shared by a user group, they can spend more of their time working on the unique aspects of their project.

We didn't describe the system structure in detail, because each component can be built in different ways by using different techniques. For example, the use of hypertext seems suited for information search by browsing, if a user is given an appropriate starting point. Also, Yoder et al. (1989) describes a shared hypermedia system which supports collaborative work. Many intelligent help systems have been based on client-consultant dialogues in natural language dialogues. However, more empirical studies of human-computer dialogues are needed to design *truly* useful interfaces.

6 Conclusion

We have described the need for and the basic design of a help system which relies on other users in the group. A prototype which handles questions in Japanese is currently under development.

The knowledge base of the help system is regarded as the shared extended memory of the user group, and every user will be able to benefit from using the help system. Actual data on system usage over time must be collected to determine the usability of this approach.

Acknowledgements

The author would like to thank Robert Wilensky and the members of UC Berkeley BAIR group, especially Michael Braverman, Dan Jurafsky, Eric Karlson, Peter Norvig, Nigel Ward, and Dekai Wu.

Note

UNIX is a trademark of AT&T Bell Laboratories.

References

Aaronson, A. and Carroll, J. (1987). Intelligent Help in a One-Shot Dialog: A Protocol Study. *Proc. of Human Factors in Computing Systems and Graphics Interface, CHI+GI '87,* 163-168.

Bannon, L. (1986). Helping Users Help Each Other. In *User Centered System Design: New Perspectives on Human-Computer Interaction* (Eds. D. Norman and S. Draper). Hillsdale, NJ: Lawrence Erlbaum Associates.

Carroll, J. and Aaronson, A. (1988). Learning By Doing With Simulated Intelligent Help. *Communications of the ACM*, 31(9), 1064-1079.

Carroll, J. and McKendree, J. (1987). Interface design issues for advice-giving expert systems. *Communications of the ACM*, 30(1), 14-31.

Carroll, J. and Rosson, M. (1987). Paradox of the Active User. In *Interfacing Thought: Cognitive Aspects of Human-Computer Interaction* (Ed. J. Carroll), Cambridge, MA: MIT Press.

Chin, D. (1989). KNOME: Modeling What the User Knows in UC. In *User Models in Dialog Systems* (Eds. A.Kobsa and W.Wahlster). Springer-Verlag.

Coventry, L. (1989). Some effects of cognitive style on learning UNIX. *International Journal of Man-Machine Studies*, 31, 349-365.

Draper, S. (1984). The nature of expertise in Unix. *Proc. of IFIP Conf. on Human-Computer Interaction, Interact '84*, 182-186.

Fischer, G., Lemke, A., and Schwab, T. (1985). Knowledge-based Help Systems. *Proc. of Human Factors in Computing Systems, CHI '85*, 161-167.

Greenberg, S. and Witten, I. (1988). Directing The User Interface: How People Use Command-Based Computer Systems. *Proc. of 3rd IFAC/IFIP/IEA/IFORS Conference on Analysis, Design and Evaluation of Man-Machine Systems*. 349-355.

Hegner, S. (1988). Representation of Command Language Behavior for an operationg System Consultation Facility. *Proc. of the forth Conf. on Artificial Intelligence Applications*, 50-55.

Hiltz, S. (1984). *Online Communities: A Case Study of the Office of the Future*. Norwood, NJ: Ablex Publishing.

Jackson, P and Lefrere, P. (1984). On the Application of rule-based techniques to the design of advice-giving systems. *International Journal of Man-Machine Studies*, 20, 63-86.

Jerrams-Smith, J. (1989). An attempt to incorporate expertise about users into an intelligent interface for Unix. *International Journal of Man-Machine Studies*, 31, 269-292.

Kearsley, G. (1988). *Online Help Systems: Design and Implementation*. Norwood, NJ: Ablex Publishing.

Kemke, C. (1983). The SINIX Consultant: Requirements, Design and Implementation of an Intelligent Help System for a UNIX Derivative. In *User Interfaces* (Ed. T. Bernold) Elsevier Science Publishers, North Holland.

Lang, K., Auld, R., and Lang, T. (1982). The goals and methods of computer users.*International Journal of Man-Machine Studies*, 17, 375-399.

Mayer, R. (1988). From Novice to Expert. In*Handbook of Human-Computer Interaction* (Ed. M.Helander) Elsevier Science Publishers.

McKevitt, P. and Wilks, Y. (1987). Transfer Semantics in an Operating System Consultant: The formalization of actions involving object transfer. *Proc. of IJCAI-87*, 569-575.

O'Malley, C. (1986). Helping Users Help Themselves. In *User Centered System Design: New Perspectives on Human-Computer Interaction* (Eds. D. Norman and S. Draper). Hillsdale, NJ: Lawrence Erlbaum Associates.

Rich, E. (1982). Programs as data for their help systems *Proc. of AFIPS National Computer Conference*, 481-485.

Ringle, M. and Halstead-Nussloch, R. (1989). Shaping user input: a strategy for natural language dialogue design. *Interacting with Computers*, 1(3), 227-244.

Roberts, R. (1970). HELP: A question answering system. *Proc. of AFIPS Fall Joint Computer Conference*, 547-554.

Tyler, S. and Treu, S. (1989). An Interface architecture to provide adaptive task-specific context for the user. *International Journal of Man-Machine Studies*, 30, 303-327.

Uehara, S., Yamomoto, R., and Ogawa, T. (1989). LISP-PAL: An Approach to Natural Language Consultation in a Programming Environment. *Proc. of 8th Phoenix Conference on Computers and Communications*, 601-605.

Whalen, T. and Patrick, A. (1989). Conversational Hypertext: Information Access Through Natural Language Dialogues With Computers. *Proc. of Human Factors In Computing Systems, CHI '89*. 289-292.

Wilensky, R. (1986). *Some Problems and Proposals for Knowledge Representation*. Report No. UCB/CSD 87/351 University of California, Berkeley.

Wilensky, R., Arens, Y., and Chin, D. (1984). Talking to UNIX in English: an overview of UC. *Communications of the ACM*, 27(6), 574-593.

Wilensky, R., Chin, D., Luria, M, Martin, Mayfield, J., and Wu, D. (1988). The Berkeley UNIX Consultant Project. *Computational Linguistics*, 14(4), 35-84.

Yoder, E., Akscyn, R., and McCracken, D. (1989). Collaboration in KMS: A Shared Hypermedia System. *Proc. of Human Factors In Computing Systems, CHI '89*. 37-42.

Human–Computer Interaction – INTERACT '90
D. Diaper et al. (Editors)
Elsevier Science Publishers B.V. (North-Holland)

End-User Dialogue Context Management of Office Automation Systems*

Gang Lu, Claude Vanneste and Martin Ader

Bull. S.A.
7 rue Ampere, 91343 Massy Cedex, France

Abstract: Office work is characterized by concurrency and exception handling. While switching frequently back and forth between many concurrent activities, the office worker finds it difficult to manage dialogue context, (i.e., to restore quickly dialogue context regarding his(1) current activity, manipulate numerous objects belonging to different activities on the limited size screen, coordinate the execution of all concurrent activities, and so on). Based on field observation we analyze the multiple activity characteristics of office work concerning dialogue context management. We postulate the requirements for an office automation system to assist end users in overcoming the difficulty of dialogue context management. Finally, we describe how a prototype office automation system IWS can partially meet these requirements, and propose future research directions.

Key Words: user interface, dialogue management, office automation, end-user assistance, multiple activity environment, object-oriented systems

1. Dialogue Context and Multiple Activities

A system reacts to an incoming event according to the circumstances in which it occurs (i.e., its context). When two persons are engaged in a dialogue, each interprets the other according to his own context. The dialogue context should be well understood by both persons. Just as important is context understanding in man-machine interactions. This context understanding becomes difficult when the user interacts with the system in performing many concurrent activities. The memory capacity of the user is limited, and restoring dialogue context becomes problematic.

Office work is characterized by concurrency and exception handling because office work depends heavily on external environment. It is, therefore, important for an office automation system to help end users manage dialogue context, such as restoring the dialogue context of their current activity quickly, manipulating numerous objects belonging to different activities on the limited size screen, and coordinating the execution of numerous concurrent activities.

This paper represents an attempt to synthesize some research results in software ergonomics and computer sciences. Data were gathered via field observation (Section 2) and they were analyzed to formulate the requirements (Section 3) of an office automation system (Section 4) to assist the end user in managing dialogue context. These requirements provided us with some pointers regarding the type and nature of tools needed to satisfy there requirements, at least partially. We constructed a prototype system to demonstrate how these tools could be used (Section 5 - 7).

* The research was funded by the Commission of the European Economic Communities through the Esprit projects IWS and Ithaca.

2. Office Work Observation

2.1. Methodology of Field Observation

Different models have been proposed to model office work (e.g., [Bracchi 84] and [Conrath 89]). Instead of relying on these models and formalisms, our methodology focuses on field observations of office work. Two fundamental components of office activities concerning the dialogue context management are: action unit sets which are meaningful to the user, and their distribution over time. The basic objective is to avoid separating the activity description from the user's actions. Our approach, based on [Pinsky 89]'s "course of action", is:

- to observe office work
The observation is carried out by a video recorder. This improves the objectivity and preciseness of collected data for subsequent analysis.

- to discuss the observation results with the office worker
The objective is to explain the observed results and identify those action unit sets which are meaningful to the observed worker vis-a-vis his work.

- to present the observation results in form of action graphs
The objective is to see how action unit sets are interleaved in chronological order and ascertain their interrelations.

2.2. Action Graph

The action graph (refer to Fig.1) consists of:

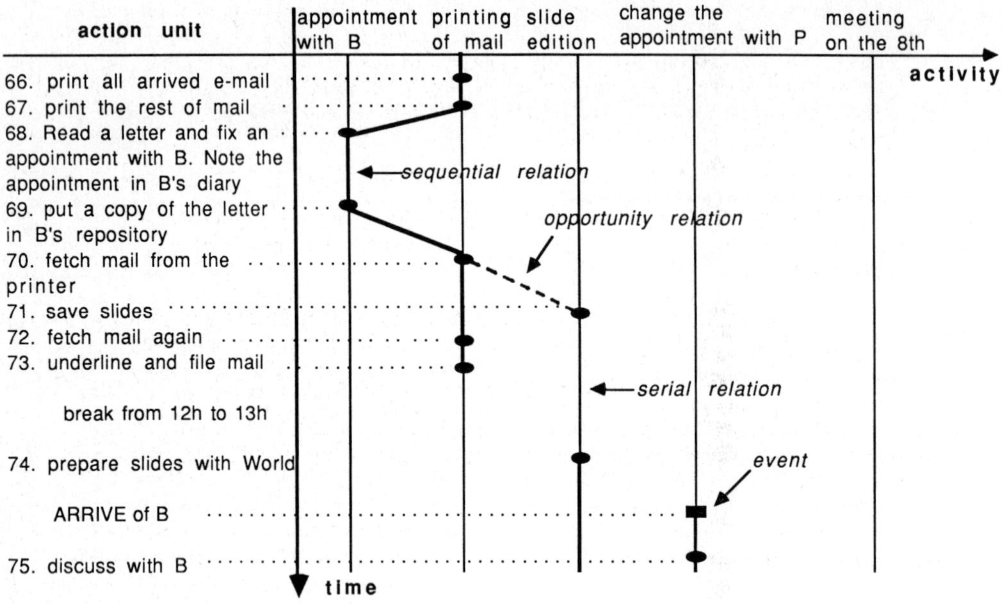

Fig. 1 Action graph of a secretary's activities

- action units
A circle node represents a significant unit of a user's action. Every action unit is numbered according to its operation order. A square node stands for an event.

- time axis and activity axis
Action unit interrelations with respect to time sequence and different activities are clearly presented.

- sequential relations
Action units concerned with causal relations and not subject to long interruption are connected by sequential relations (boldface lines).

- serial relations
Action units belonging to the same activity but subject to interruption by action units of other activities are connected by serial relations (normal lines).

- opportunity relations
Action units connected by sequential or serial relations have a semantic relationship. Action units connected by opportunity relations (dashed lines) do not have this kind of relationships. Such action units are interrelated through vicinity considerations or digression actions.

In summary, the action graph presents the end user the basic points regarding dialogue context management (e.g., the context of activities, the overlap of the action units concerning different activities, and the causes of activity switching) in a concise and meaningful way.

3. Requirements of Dialogue Context Management

Using the methodology described in Section 2, we observed the work of a manager's secretary [Vanneste 89]. After analyzing the action graph, we think that the requirements of dialogue context management can be considered along the three facets: (1) activities and applications, (2) supporting routine work, and (3) metaphor of user interface.

3.1. Activities and Applications

It is necessary to distinguish between activities and applications. In this paper, an "activity" means a series of operations that have to be executed to reach a goal from the view of the end user. An "application" refers to a series of sequential operations whose successful execution is necessary to reach a goal from the view of the system. An activity is defined dynamically by the end user when he uses the system, while an application is defined by system developers when the system is built.

3.1.1. Observation Summary

The action graph of the observation presents clearly the activities involved, the time and duration of the activities, the tools used, and the synchronization between these activities. The secretary handled about 20 activities during the observation period. Five activities concerned document preparations, four related with communications, and eight diary keeping (such as conference room reservations and appointment arrangements). The secretary spent most her time on editing documents and slides.

It would be ideal if the end user can always find a matching application for each of his activities. However, this is very difficult since office work varies considerably, and office environment evolves constantly. Observational data showed that on the one hand, an activity could involve several applications. From the viewpoint of the user, there were dependencies between some applications. For instance, the secretary often used the editor, the electronic mail and the diary in conjunction to carry out a specific activity. On the other hand, an application could serve several activities (either with same or different type) simultaneously.

The secretary had to deal with a lot of coexisting activities (often more than four) and rarely carried out an activity without interruption. The main causes of activity switching are:

- interruptions by external events
The secretary was continually interrupted by telephone calls or persons passing through her office (e.g., the arrival of B after action unit 74 in Fig.1). These interruptions lasted over different durations. Some of the durations were quite long.

- association and vicinity
The secretary initiated the change of her current activity according to the semantic interrelations between different activities, or simply "by the way" or "while waiting for". For instance, in Fig.1, before the secretary fetched the mail again (action unit 72), she thought of saving the slides to forestall cases of accident.

- synchronization
The need to synchronize activities with related persons often made the secretary suspend an activity for a quite while before resumption.

- deadlines, priority, and periodic activities
The secretary had to change her current activity because of scheduling and planning. The secretary often looked at her notes or diary to avoid missing deadlines or urgent activities.

- maintenance of coherence
Since different activities were interrelated through constraints and shared resources (e.g., the printer, the common diary of a group, and manager's working hours), the operations of one activity could not, sometimes, be carried out straightaway. The secretary took some measures to avoid the conflicts. For instance, she allocated alternative time slots or doubled the reservation period for important interviews.

3.1.2. Recommendations

The system needs to help the user to associate his activity with available applications. A kind of "generic application" can be envisaged. Through the specialization (such as parameters or functions) of the generic application, the user can define various applications corresponding to his activities. The generic application should be manageable by the end user.

The system should guarantee the continuity of an activity's progress and, at the same time, allow the user to resume easily other existing activities. When the user wants to initiate another activity, the system should not enforce him to abort the first one. This allows the user to resume the first one at the point where he left. The system should provide various mechanisms to deal with interruptions. For instance, a special module to deal with telephone interruptions is needed. In general, more research is needed for the presentation of interruptions and the precondition of the presentation.

In situations where many activities coexist, with numerous interruptions and micro-decisions, the user needs assistance to remind him of the existence of unfinished activities and help him schedule. The system should help recognize and recall some elements which are not presented on the screen, but are related with the current activity. The problems are: What kinds of reminders are needed? How and when are the reminders specified? How are the reminders presented?

3.2. Supporting Routine Work

3.2.1. Observation Summary

We derived some points about the automation of office activities:

- The secretary spent a lot of time on the telephone trying to contact a person or some person related to that person. There was a similar problem concerning document circulation. The secretary had to ensure that the various portions of a document were collected from their respective sources on time.

- Some activities were highly repetitive, such as sending a document to different persons, telephoning persons to ensure their presence at a meeting, distributing periodic reports, and updating information.

- There exists obviously some periods of time, such as the beginning of morning or afternoon, when the secretary dealt with miscellaneous matters.

- The secretary spent a lot of time to maintain the data consistency.

3.2.2. Recommendations

The system needs to provide some user-friendly tools with which office workers can delegate some responsibilities to the system and reduce the interruption frequency. When a secretary telephones somebody who is absent, the system should be able to suggest whom the secretary can speak to. The system can also generate acknowledgements for received mail, and notify incoming events and changes of information.

Parallel processing can increase the efficiency for the user to launch and deal with highly repetitive routine activities. Parallel processing capability enables the user to deal with miscellaneous matters while waiting for execution results. For instance, the user can deal with something else while a file is being printed or a complicated retrieval in a database is being carried out. While dealing with such long duration operations, parallel processing can improve not only working efficiency of the user, but also the quality of the interface. The system can display a living image to show that the user's request is being executed. The user can also suspend his request which is being executed.

The system should maintain information consistency and propagation between different activities and applications so that the user does not have to make a lot of notes and duplicate documents. Providing triggers with respect to specified activities is also helpful. Scheduling tools should be provided so that various activities can be activated, resumed, or sorted according to timing requirements.

3.3. Metaphor

The system tries to model the real world. The user views the model world through the metaphor of the system. The metaphor is, therefore, concerned with two aspects: the presentation of system functionality and dialogue context, and the facilities of manipulations.

3.3.1. Observation Summary

The action graph revealed some interesting points about how the secretary organized her work. The secretary had her own way to recall events and activities. She placed various documents on the desk in such a manner as to remind herself what to do with the documents. For instance, she placed Mr. B's document in a prominent place so that she could pass the document to him when he happened to walk past her office. The secretary needed a proper perspective about all existing activities. The secretary often asked herself, "Where am I? What have I done? What am I doing now?"

What the secretary was required to do is often quite independent of what she was doing. In such cases, the secretary, instead of interrupting her current activity immediately, often used desk pads to remind herself of the requests to be processed. The secretary also used desk pads to communicate with her manager.

3.3.2. Recommendations

All the above recommendations can benefit only through an informative and manageable metaphor. The accessibility of system functionalities and the information about dialogue context should be well studied.

The explanation of dialogue context is necessarily both time-oriented and activity-oriented. It is important to have a historical view (time sequence) about the operations of different applications. Just as important is an understanding of the interrelations between different applications concerning a given activity. The system should allow office workers to retrieve existing activities using relevant parameters (e.g., activities within a given time period, activities related to document preparation). The system can construct the trace using activities as organizing cores so that the user can easily recall what he had done about a specific activity. The level of detail of the trace (such as only the last step or several last steps) can be controlled by the end user in order to facilitate the identification or the reconstruction of previous steps.

The user needs assistance in managing and coordinating numerous coexisting activities through a well designed user interface. He needs help to remind himself of what to do. The user needs operational tools, such as redo, undo, dairy, desk pads and screen layout management.

4. Architecture of IWS

In order to validate the above analysis, we implemented some of the recommendations on top of a prototype intelligent office workstation IWS (Esprit project number 82 [Ader 87]). IWS aims at providing office workers a complete and integrated office automation environment in a knowledge-based solution for: (1) representing office activities (e.g., documents, organizations and procedures); (2) advising user's actions; (3) automating routine office procedures; and (4) monitoring the sequences of the office procedures until their goals are achieved. The last three points are the initiatives of IWS.

The dialogue context concerns both application nature and dialogue scenarios so that both their architectures are important for dialogue context management. On top of KRS (Knowledge Representation System [Von Marcke 87]), we have simulated an object-oriented database to manage organizations, documents, facilities, time and procedures. Basic operations are concatenated using AMS (Activity Management System [Tueni 88]) networks so that various administration routines can be automated. High declarativity, powerful and simple retrieval capability, and dynamic consistency maintenance of KRS and AMS provide a good basis for dialogue context management.

In the UIMS (user interface management system) of IWS, there is a separate dialogue layer which controls all interactions between one end user and multiple concurrent activities. The layer carries out implicit operations to help the user manage dialogue context. For example, each active application has a standard window on the screen (refer to Fig.2). The data-exchange area corresponds to a request from the application. The user views the man-machine interaction as answering a series of such data-exchange areas. For the application, the interaction with the end user

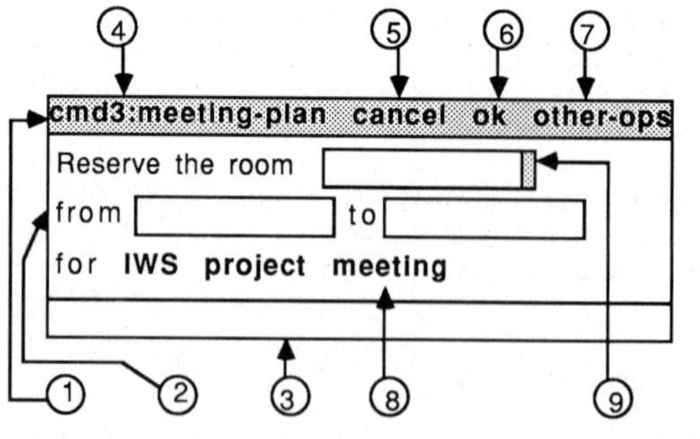

NB: (1) title (2) data exchange area (3) explanation message area (4) Clicking "cmd3:meeting-plan" will display the functionality of the application in the explanation message area. The unique window number 3 is given by the UIMS. (5) Cancel the application and related ones (6) The user's inputs are sent to the application. Then the application is resumed. (7) explanations and related operations concernig the application. (8) Clicking a boldface item will give its explanation. (9) input help

Fig.2 A standard application window with a data-exchange area of an explainable natural language-like sentense

is considered as exchanging a series of high-level declarative messages with an interface object (standard window). As such, the UIMS provides both the application and the end user with an activity-oriented view about the man-machine interaction.

From the implementation viewpoint, the recommendations in Section 3 can be summarized as follows:

- to provide explanations about dialogue context in both activity-oriented and time-oriented ways, and to retrieve and navigate among concurrent activities;
- to provide an integrated view of information and applications, ensure the consistency of applications, propagate information and associate interrelated information;
- to enable the user to deal with interruptions with minimum efforts and resume interrupted activities easily;
- to provide an informative and manageable metaphor, and to assist in manipulating numerous objects (windows) on a limited size screen.
- to provide parallel processing capability for repetitive or time-consuming applications; and
- to automate some routine activities so as to reduce the interruption frequency of office workers, and to remind, retry or resume automatically suspended activities based on time schedule or semantic conditions.

In the rest of the paper, we will briefly describe how IWS can support the recommendations about context explanations, the integrated view of information and operation, and informative and manageable metaphor.

5. Context Explanations

The dialogue layer has a global view about all man-machine interactions. The application layer specifies the requirements to the end user with the declaration of the necessary context. Based on the global view and the declared context information, IWS can provide various explanations in both activity-oriented and time-oriented ways.

From the top-level metaphor, the user can list all existing activities according to creation order, execution priority or the catalogue of activities. From the window of a given application, various explanations adapted to the demanding context are available by simply clicking. Some of the available explanations are as follows:

- functionality of the application;
- interaction trace concerning the application;
- application state (Why is the application suspended? Why is such a request being asked? etc);
- interrelations with other existing applications (creation order and related windows concerning the same activity); and
- terminology (the meanings and contents of displayed objects).

Two of the principles to present and explain dialogue context are activity-oriented explanation and explainable natural language-like sentence.

5.1. Activity-Oriented Explanation

In IWS, when one application is activated, a standard window is created (refer to Fig.2). The window remains on the screen until the application completes its run, and the execution of the sequential operations of the application is presented as the evolution of the data-exchange area of the same window. As such, the explanation concerning the given application can be obtained directly from the window.

One activity can involve several applications so that the end user hopes to know all existing applications concerning a given activity. As the interrelations between existing applications concerning different activities depend on the operation sequences, these interrelations have to be built dynamically. Because every active application corresponds to a unique window, the dynamic association of related applications vis-a-vis a given activity becomes the dynamic association of related windows vis-a-vis the activity.

The reference network derived from the dynamic associations is used to explain the interrelations between existing windows. For instance, Fig.3 tells us there are currently 4 active applications related to "cmd3:show". Both "cmd2:revise" (e.g., revise a database instance) and "cmd5:reply" (e.g., reply to a letter) invoke "cmd3:show" to retrieve a database instance. "cmd3:show" invokes "cmd4:show" and "cmd6:show" to find out complement information. The reference network of a given window consists only of the windows which are currently associated to the given window, instead of all available links in the underlying model. By clicking the window's name in the reference network, the user can directly access the explanations about each window, such as the functionality, the interaction trace and the interrelation with other windows. Such a concise global view of the interrelations between existing windows is very helpful for the user to understand the role of each window in the whole situation.

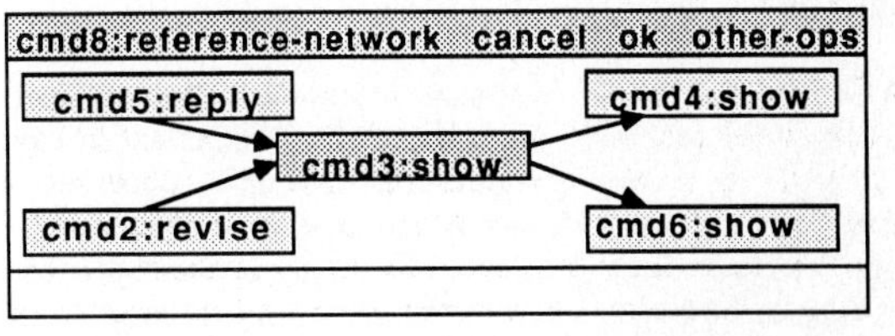

Fig.3 Reference-network of "cmd3:show"

5.2. Explainable Natural Language-Like Sentence

The request from an application to the end user is usually presented in explainable natural language-like sentences (refer to Fig.2). The main reasons to introduce the explainable natural language-like sentences as the basic form of man-machine interaction are as follows:

- Since the end user cannot fully devote his attention to one activity without interruption, brief questions, such as "how many year?" or "unit?", will only render it more difficult for him to provide inputs when he resumes the activity. The semantic completeness of natural language-like sentences can help the user restore dialogue context quickly.

- The sentence is called explainable because further explanations will be shown by clicking related boldface items in the sentence (i.e., "IWS project meeting" in Fig.2). In this way, the original sentence can be concise (for occupying minimum screen space and highlight important information) without sacrificing details (allowing the user to retrieve the context further in a hypertext way).

- The input help (see Section 7) will reduce the requirement of the preciseness of the context restoration.

- The trace in natural language-like sentences concerning an application provides a good historical explanation of the application evolution.

6. Integrated View of Information and Applications

All IWS applications are implemented on top of an object-oriented office model which guarantees a consistent way to present organizations, documents, facilities, time and procedures. Once an object has been created, it can be used in several different activities and can migrate from one activity to another. Thanks to KRS, different objects can be interrelated by a consistent and powerful reference formalism so that the consistency and propagation of information can be guaranteed.

From the viewpoint of the end user, the integrated view is due to the consistency of man-machine interaction convention. This consistency is guaranteed by the UIMS because the applications only specify the requirements of man-machine interaction. It is the dialogue layer which decides the request presentation and the interaction sequence.

When several activities use the same application for a same problem (e.g., using the text editor to modify the same file), the UIMS guarantees there is no double activation of the application. Windows, where the displayed information is no longer valid, are also deleted automatically.

The integrated view can be further improved if the different applications can exchange information. The user can use clipboard to exchange information between different windows (applications). The uniform message-exchange convention between the dialogue layer and the application layer is also an important means to facilitate such exchange.

7. Informative and Manageable Metaphor

The graphical presentation and the operation sequences are controlled by the UIMS so that the metaphor can easily adapt to the habits of different users. A graphical explanation of the functionalities of all top-level options can be generated automatically by the UIMS in order to assist the user in finding available operations (applications).

When the user deals with an application, he needs to consult related information or to activate a needed operation. For instance, when the user receives the reply to a letter, he may need to retrieve the original letter. In the example shown in Fig.2, the user may need to create "G301<Meeting Room" when the system indicates that the instance has not been created. Thanks to the architectures of both applications and the UIMS, a supporting environment can be dynamically constructed for the user to deal with application requests. That is, when the user deals with an application, he can usually activate related operations directly from the window of the application, instead of having to find them from the top-level metaphor. In other words, related applications can be activated directly from the current one.

Two advantages accrue from this modus operandi. First, it renders the user's operation easy and manageable. Second, it allows the system to gather the semantic relations among active applications so that all windows regarding a given activity can be manipulated as a whole. For example, when an activity is completed, all exclusively related applications will disappear automatically.

The application requests are displayed on the screen. The user is notified, but is not forced to deal with the requests in order to enable the user to access different existing activities. The user is totally free to decide whether he replies to the requests, and if so, when. When there are several input fields, the user can give inputs in any order.

According to dialogue context, the system always tries to verify, complete and normalize user inputs, and allows the user to give inputs by selecting, instead of only by typing. When the user clicks the black vertical rectangle in Fig.2, the pop-up menu will list all existing meeting rooms. The input assistance will reduce the user's memory load and render the input process easy and flexible.

When there are only a few windows on the screen, all of them can be kept on the screen so that the user can easily resume an interrupted activity. When there are too many windows on the screen, the user can hide the visibility of some activity. When the visibility of an activity is hidden, all windows belonging to the activity will disappear together. When the activity is resumed, all its windows will be restored to their original positions.

IWS has a diary for the end user to schedule and plan his work. The user can easily define an activity to be activated at a given time. As such, the user can use the diary to remind a periodic or deadline activity, or retry an unsuccessful activity.

8. Conclusions

Office workers usually have to deal with a lot of concurrent activities. In doing so, they have to switch frequently back and forth between these activities. Window-based interfaces alleviate the cognitive load of end users in dealing with concurrent activities. Different activities are placed in different windows. This, however, is not enough since the end user needs assistance to restore the dialogue context vis-a-vis his current activity, manipulate numerous objects belonging to different activities on the limited size screen, coordinate correctly the execution of all concurrent activities, etc.

In order to resolve this problem. we think that it is necessary to study how office workers work in a real office environment and articulate their difficulties regarding the dialogue context management. We used a video recorder to capture the activities of office workers. Data collected were discussed with the observed worker so as to understand the raison d'etre behind their actions. Action graphs were plotted using these data. These graphs make sure that we understand the context of the worker's actions in a precise and unambiguous way. Such a mode of collecting and analyzing data should produce valid results.

We implemented some of the recommendations on top of IWS in a way simple enough for office workers. The thrust of the solution lies with the architecture of both applications and interactions. Many existing solutions are inadequate because they concern only either the application aspect or the interaction aspect. In IWS, an object-oriented database system (simulated in KRS), a set of coordination tools (AMS) to concatenate the basic applications, and an activity-oriented UIMS are the three pillars for our solutions.

The examples of remaining problems vis-a-vis the requirements of dialogue context management are:

- In IWS, the associations between different applications for a given activity are limited by the predetermined links at the application level. Simple and flexible ways for the end user to define the associations dynamically are needed; and

- The management of dialogue context and the schedule of activities are inherently interrelated, and they have many points in common. This should, therefore, provide the end user with an integrated view of dialogue context management, internal activity coordination tools and user's diary.

We will try to resolve these problems in the Esprit Project of Ithaca [Proefrock 89].

9. Acknowledgement

We gratefully acknowledge Mr. Najah Naffah for his support of this research and Mr. Bernard Mazoyer for his valuable recommendations for both the research and the paper. Observational data were gathered by Mrs. Isabelle Lambert and Mr. Francois Jeffroy. We would like to thank Dr. James Ang for his comments on an early draft of this paper.

References

Ader,M. and Tueni,M. (87). An Office Assistant Prototype Using a Knowledge-Based Office Model on a Personal Workstation, *ESPRIT Results and Achievements,* North-Holland (Amsterdam), 1205-1225.

Bracchi,G. and Pernici,B. (84). Design Requirements of Office Systems. *ACM Trans on Office Information Systems, vol.2, no.2,* 151-170.

Conrath,D. and Dumas,P.(Eds) (89). *Office Support Systems Analysis and Design,* T.O.T., Munich.

Pinsky,L. (89). User's Activity Centered System Design, *Proc. of Work with Display Units,* Montreal, Canada, Nov. 1989.

Proefrock,A, Tsichritzis,D, Muller,G, and Ader,M. (89), Ithaca: An Integrated Toolkit for Highly Advanced Computer Applications, *Object-Oriented Development,* Univ. of Geneva, July 1989, 321-344.

Tueni,M., Li,J. and Fares,P. (88). AMS: A Knowledge-Based Approach to Tasks Representation, Organization and Coordination, *Forth Conference on Office Information Systems,* Palo-Alto, U.S.A., March 1988, 22-45.

Vanneste,C. (89). Analysis of Office Requirements, *Technical Report of the Software Ergonomics Unit of Bull,* July 1989.

Von Marcke,K., Jonckers,V. and Daelemans,W. (87). Representation Aspects of Knowledge-Based Office Systems, *Esprit Results and Achievements,* North-Holland (Amsterdam), 1226-1238.

Note: (1) Through this thesis, the pronoun "he" is used in the nature sense.

Human–Computer Interaction – INTERACT '90
D. Diaper et al. (Editors)
Elsevier Science Publishers B.V. (North-Holland)

CURRENT APPROACHES & NEW GUIDELINES FOR UNDO SUPPORT DESIGN

Yiya YANG

Informatics Department, Rutherford Appleton Laboratory, UK

Task-oriented commands cause essential steps in performing tasks within a system's scope whereas support-oriented commands inform a user about appropriate task-oriented commands, facilitate user-computer interactions or assure the integrity of a user's work. An undo capability is a support-oriented command facility which allows a user to reverse the effects of commands. It supports the fallible and fickle nature of users. In this paper major current undo support facilities are reviewed and critically compared. Design guidelines for undo support derived from a research project which prototyped sophisticated undo support in a widely used editing environment are then formulated.

1. INTRODUCTION

Current conceptions of undo support reflect received HCI wisdom as to the reasons for having it and these ideas shape current undo support facilities. Received wisdom in the literature on undo support suggests that undo support is a recovery and usability feature which permits ready recovery from many simple errors. It avoids creating frustration where a user discovers that an unexpected result of a command cannot be reversed and encourages exploration of unfamiliar options. It can be used to deal with mode errors, interactive deadlocks, and changing one's mind [5, 6, 17].

2. CURRENT UNDO SUPPORT FACILITIES

Undo support facilities have been provided within several contexts including programming languages, editors and formatting systems, and program development environments. These systems' undo support provision varies considerably. By distinguishing undo support into its various aspects their undo support provision can be compared and contrasted.

Granularity affects how many commands an undo command can reverse at one go. An undo command with one command granularity can only reverse the effects of one command whereas an undo command with multiple command granularity can reverse the effects of many commands at once. Undo commands with one command granularity can be restrictive or non-restrictive. The former can only reverse the system to its immediately previous state. A second successive such undo command will reverse what the first one has done. The latter issued n times can reverse the system n steps back. Under multiple command granularity, three types of provision can be distinguished, local, global and restrictive. An undo command with local multiple command granularity can reverse commands only from the present command. One with global multiple command granularity can reverse multiple commands anywhere within the range of undo support. One with restrictive multiple command granularity can return a system to a state which is set by a user in advance or return the system a fixed number of steps back. An undo command with global multiple command granularity subsumes the power of an undo command with local or restrictive multiple command granularity, but not vice versa.

The range of undo support indicates how far the undo capability can reverse a system state. Undo support with one-step range only has the ability to reverse the system state one step back. Two types of undo support with whole current session range can be distinguished by whether the range can be limited or not. If the range can be made more limited than the whole current session, it is limitable. Otherwise, it is fixed. Table 1 summarises the characteristics of current undo support facilities.

2.1. Programming Language and Development Environments

Representative examples of programming languages and program development environments with undo support are Cope, Gandalf, Interlisp, PE, Pecan and Smalltalk. Cope is an integrated program development environment [2]. Gandalf is an incremental programming environment generator working for several algebraic languages [10]. Its editor, Aloe, is interactive, structure-editor based [16]. Both Aloe and Cope provide an undo command with non-restrictive one command granularity. The undo command cancels the effects of the last task-oriented command and

Table 1. Characteristics of Current Undo Support Facilities

Type of environment	System Name	granularity of undo command					maximum range of undo support			
		one command		multiple command			part of session		whole session	
		restrictive	non restrictive	restrictive	local	global	one step	multiple step	fixed	limitable
programming languages & development environments	Cope		*						*	
	Gandalf		*						*	
	Interlisp	*		*		*	*			*
	PE		*		*				*	
	Pecan		*		*				*	
	Smalltalk	*					*			
editors and formatting systems	Aldus FreeHand				*			*		
	Emacs		*		*			*		
	Etude	*			*				*	
	Interleaf	*		*				*		
	Lisa	*					*			
	Macintosh	*					*			
	Poe		*					*		
	Poiite		*	*					*	
	Sam		*		*				*	
	VED		*		*				*	
	Vi	*		*				*		
other interactive systems	CSS				*				*	
	Designbase				*				*	
	Higgens		*	*				*		
	MMS			*					*	
	US&R		*						*	
	X-AiD				*				*	

it can be used consecutively. Their undo support facilities have the fixed range of a whole session.

Interlisp, a dialect of LISP, is a programming environment [14]. Among its many utilities, the Editor and History Package provide undo support. An Editor command's effects can be undone using the UNDO command. An alternative form, !UNDO, undoes all structural changes made during the current editing session. The undo support provided by the Editor has only one-step range. The History Package provides an undo command with global multiple command granularity. The undo support provided by the History Package has the limitable range of a whole session. Undoing from the current state in the reverse order of execution will restore the system to its correct previous state. If a user undoes events in any other order, the state of the system is unpredictable because the evaluation of expressions may have been dependent upon the sequence of execution.

PE is an integrated, interactive and incremental programming environment. Its evaluator can have many dynamic modes. One of them is the inverse mode which corresponds to an undo support facility. Two possibilities exist: either a user undoes in a step by step manner or a user undoes until the occurrence of a special event [29].

PECAN is a family of program development systems. Its data management facility, PLUM, allows changes to data structures to be undone and redone. Its command facility, CMD, provides a global undo/redo support facility which allows a user to undo the last command. A user can also point with the locator device at a particular command, to cause the system to undo or redo to the chosen point [23].

Smalltalk consists of an object-oriented programming

language and environment. It has an undo command in a pop up menu which will reverse the effects of all the users' typing and backspacing since the selection made last with the pointing device. Issuing two undo commands in sequence leaves a user in the state the user was in prior to the first undo [8].

2.2. Editors and Formatting Systems

Representative examples of text/graphics editors and formatting systems with undo support are Aldus FreeHand, Emacs, Etude, Interleaf, Lisa, Macintosh, Poe, Polite, Sam, VED and Vi. Aldus FreeHand is a comprehensive drawing program for producing high-quality graphics on the Apple Macintosh. Its first advertised editing function is undo and redo options which allow up to 100 actions to be undone and redone [1].

Emacs is a real-time display editor. It has a powerful undo command. The first time the user issues an undo command, it undoes the last change. Consecutive repetitions of the undo command undo changes further and further back. Any command other than an undo command breaks the sequence of undo commands. Starting at this moment, the previous undo commands are considered ordinary changes which can themselves be undone [24].

Etude is an interactive editor and formatter. It provides an undo command which can reverse the result of the immediately proceeding operation or sequence of operations. The user interface presents a list of the preceding operations as a menu and asks the user to specify how far back the undo should go [9].

Interleaf is a publishing software package. One of its commands for modifying diagrams is an undo command which allows a user to reverse certain changes to an object. Besides undoing the most recent operation, a user can undo more than one operation so long as the user has not de-selected the object(s) in between commands [12].

Lisa is a word processor. The "Undo last change" command is available in every program which allows a user to undo the effects of the last command he issued [18]. Macintosh is a mouse-window-desktop word-processor which provides an undo menu item to undo the last text-editing action [13].

Editor POE (Pascal Oriented Editor) is a full-screen display editor which knows the structure and rules of Pascal. At any time, the most recent POE command can be undone by an undo command. Entering this undo command n times causes the most recent n commands to be undone. The number of commands which can be undone is limited by the depth of an internal history stack. At present the maximum depth of this stack is 10 [7].

POLITE is a real-time editor-formatter for compound documents containing images, data, graphics and handwriting as well as text. Every operation may be undone by a command UNDO. UNDO can be issued until the state at the beginning of the session is reached. A user can UNDO up to a specified checkpoint. A user can also UNDO to a specific time. A facility for UNDOing across multiple sessions has also been designed [21].

Sam is an interactive multi-file text editor. It has an undo command which allow a user to undo the last n changes, no matter how many files are affected. Multiple undo commands move the editing state further back in time [20].

VED is a specialized editor for network representations. It provides state-oriented and function-oriented undoing. State-oriented undo is defined as returning to a previous checkpoint without extending the corresponding dialogue protocol. Function-oriented undo is defined as evaluating an inverse function and thereby producing a new checkpoint [22].

Vi is a screen editor of the Unix system. It has undo commands to undo the last change including itself and all changes made to the current line [3].

2.3. Other Interactive Environments

Representative examples of other interactive environments with undo support are CSS, Designbase, Higgens, MMS, US&R and X-AiD. CSS is a computer Cricket Scoring System designed to control an electronic scoreboard. Its recovery facility allows a user to change what has previously been specified. The user may choose to undo some events specified (in effect delete them) or backtrack over events (but save them so that they can be redone later) in order to return to a point in the past at which a deletion or insertion of an event can take place [4].

Designbase is a solid modeling system all of whose high-level operations are implemented using primitive operations. All primitive operations used in a design are stored in a tree representing the history of the solid design process. A user simply specifies a path moving up the tree to UNDO a sequence of operations [26].

Higgens is a user interface generation system. A user

command is decomposed into internal primitive commands. Each internal primitive command has an internal primitive command as its inverse. Undoing a user command is achieved by executing inverses of all the internal primitive commands corresponding to the user command [11].

MMS is a Message Management System. A small set of universal commands, applicable to any MMS object, is defined in MMS. One is a MARK command which allows a user to set checkpoints before a set of operations. Another is an UNDO command which allows a user to undo the effects of a set of operations just completed back to the last checkpoint [15].

US&R is a component of an interactive graphics system. It has UNDO, REDO and SKIP commands. UNDO reverses the last action of the current state of the system and it can be used consecutively. SKIP causes some primitive command which was previously undone to be skipped. REDO causes some action which was previously undone to be re-executed [27].

X-AiD is an adaptive knowledge-based interface management system. It has a sophisticated UNDO support facility allowing the user to operate on the dialogue history and transform the state of the object instances under development by undoing or redoing sequences of dialogue steps already performed [25].

2.4. Comparison of Current Undo Support Facilities

According to our previous definitions, an undo command with global multiple command granularity is most powerful because its functionality subsumes any undo command with other kinds of granularity. An undo command with local multiple command granularity is as powerful as an undo command with non-restrictive one command granularity. However, the former is more convenient to use because issuing an undo command with non-restrictive one command granularity many times does the same thing as issuing an undo command with local multiple command granularity only once. After these, an undo command with restrictive multiple command granularity is more powerful than an undo command with restrictive one command granularity because it can reverse the effects of more than one command.

Besides the granularity of undo commands, the range of undo support is also important because it determines how far back a previous system state can be restored. A multiple step range is better than a one step range because the latter can only sustain undo commands with restrictive one command granularity which are the least powerful. An undo support facility with the range of a whole session is obviously more powerful than one with the range of part of a session. Undo support with limitable range is as powerful as that with fixed range although it provides for better control of computer resources. However, such flexibility has pitfalls for an unwary user who may find he has removed the safety net of recovery from himself by overly limiting how far back he can undo.

Thus, if only functionality is considered, Interlisp is the most powerful. Aldus FreeHand, Cope, Gandalf, PE, Pecan, Emacs, Etude, Poe, Polite, Sam, VED, CSS, Designbase, Higgens, MMS, US&R and X-AiD are the next most powerful although their degrees of convenience vary, depending on how aptly they provide their functionality to the user. Interleaf and Vi are the third most powerful and the rest are the least powerful. However, practical situations are not as simple as one would like. Functionality is not the only consideration because convenience is also important for support features like undo. There is always a trade-off between powerful functionality and the number and form of commands which provide such functionality.

Table 1 does not include information about whether undo support provides recovery across multiple sessions. Among all the undo support facilities described above, only Polite provides undoing across multiple sessions. Certainly, undoing across multiple sessions is more powerful than undoing only within the current session. The question remains as to whether it is worthwhile to provide undoing across multiple sessions with the extra resources it consumes. Since the main purpose of providing undo support is to help a user to use software better to do his job, the user's task structure is important to consider. Generally speaking, a session is the period between entering and exiting a system. The moment of exiting a system is normally the closure point for the user's tasks. If confirmation of the command to exit a session is required, a user is unlikely to want to undo something once a task or task phase is finished. Of course, there are cases where a user mistakenly types the wrong command or clicks the wrong button for confirmation. There is also the possibility that the habit of unthinkingly confirming such a request may result in the user doing what he did not really mean to do. However, having a clearly defined point of no-return at the closure point of a user's task crystallizes the moment of commitment for a user in a natural way. It helps foster a forward looking approach to the next job while discouraging the temptation to tamper and meddle with work that has already been completed in a previous session. For this reason, the capability to undo across several sessions may actually work against the natural grain of user's tasks and hinder rather than promote productivity.

Besides the above common granularities, some of the systems mentioned above have some other unusual and system-dependent granularities. They are

1) undo all changes to current line --- Vi
2) undo to a time --- Polite
3) undo to the last selection --- Interleaf
4) undo all changes in a session --- Polite

All these granularities are system-dependent because they depend upon whether relevant grain concepts are supported in a system. The concept of granularity was only introduced to compare different forms of undo support and to guide a designer in considering the granularity of undo commands. Interface requirements and interaction styles are so diverse that there are probably no mandatory guidelines as to what forms of grain a particular undo command must have and what specialised forms of granularities of undo commands must be provided by a system. It is up to the designer to balance all tradeoffs and to decide on whether specialised command grains are appropriate.

However, undoing all changes in a session is a general grain capability that is important for designers to consider also having in a system if they only opt for undo support with a limited range. Most editors like Vi already support this capability indirectly. They allow a user to undo all changes within one session by letting the user exit the editor without saving his changes. Other systems like Polite and Emacs provide a command to restore the file being edited to its original form. Based upon this basic capability, many other variations can be provided. For example, an editor can reduce the grain of undoing from a whole interactive session to the interval between two saving commands by writing the current state of the file back to its stored form on disc.

3. DESIGN RECOMMENDATIONS

Table 1 shows that there is simply too much diversity in what functionality is offered to be able to distil a common wisdom for undo support provision. This prompted a user-oriented research project into the design of undo support. The methodology adopted by this research and its results are reported on in [28]. The following lists the general recommendations and conclusions drawn from the analysis and empirical evaluations conducted during this research.

1) Early design of undo support:
It is recommended that undo support should be considered when the analysis of functional requirements for a system is conducted. It is more difficult to realize an undo support facility after a system is built.

2) Minimal undo support.
In order to enhance the usability of an interactive system, it should at least provide minimal undo support in terms of being able to reverse the last command including itself.

3) Undo support as a safeguard.
Minimal undo support only safeguards a user against his last action being a mistake and not against any earlier errors. An interactive computer system that aims to provide a safeguard against errors has to provide undo support in terms of being able to reverse multiple task-oriented and undo commands.

4) Direct advertisement of undo support.
A direct method to advertise undo support is recommended. It can employ visible buttons on the screen, keys on the keyboard or menu items in a pop-up menu. Its use should be consistent with the style of invoking the interface.

5) Different commands for redo and undo functions.
It is possible to combine a redo function and an undo function into one command in non-minimal undo support as is done by Emacs. However, this combination is confusing for a user. Separate commands for undoing and redoing should be provided.

6) Granularities of undo support commands.
An undo command should at the very least be able to reverse the effects of a basic command. The combination of n-step undo support and aggregate undoing functions can compensate for the absence of task-oriented granularities.

7) History oriented undo support.
It is recommended that undo support for sophisticated environments should provide a command history recording executed and undone commands.

8) Structure of history information.
If an interactive computer system is designed for a cooperative environment, it is desirable to provide user-oriented or task-oriented history information for users with respect to undo support. Otherwise, it is easier to design and implement shell/window-oriented histories.

4. CONCLUSIONS

This paper compares critically major current undo support facilities. This survey was the starting point for a user-oriented research project into the design of undo support. Although the methodology and the results of this research are not reported here, the main recommendations for designing undo support are presented. These recommendations can be used to guide the practice of designing an undo support facility for an interactive system.

ACKNOWLEDGEMENTS

This work was supported by an Alvey grant GR/D 424125 and carried out at the Scottish HCI Centre of Hriot-Watt University. Thanks are due to my husband and my colleagues.

REFERENCES

[1] Aldus Europe Limited, Aldus FreeHand Facts and Features (UK, 1988)

[2] Archer, J. E. & Conway, R., COPE: a Cooperative Programming Environment, TR81-459 (Department of Computer Science, Cornell University, 1981)

[3] Bourne, S. R., The Unix System (Addison-Wesley Publishing Company, 1983)

[4] Briggs, J. S., Generating Reversible Programs, Software-Practice and Experience (1987) pp. 439-453

[5] Carroll, J. M. & Mazur, S., Lisa Learning, Computer (1986) pp. 35-49

[6] Darlington, J.; Dzida, W. & Herda, S., The Role of Excursions in Interactive Systems, International Journal of Man-Machine Studies (1983) pp. 101-112

[7] Fischer, C. N.; Johnson, G.; Pal, A. & Stock, D., An Introduction to Editor Allan POE, Proceedings of the First Conference on Software Development Tools, Techniques, and Alternatives (1983) pp. 245-250

[8] Goldberg, A., Smalltalk80: The Interactive Programming Environment (Addison-Wesley Publishing Company 1984)

[9] Good, M., An Ease of Use Evaluation of an Integrated Editor and Formatter, MIT/LCS TR 266 (MIT, 1981)

[10] Habermann, A. N., The Gandalf Research Project (Department of Computer Science, Carnegie-Mellon University, 1979)

[11] Hudson, S. E. & King, R., Efficient Recovery and Ueversal in Graphical User Interfaces Generated by the Higgens System, Proceedings of the 11th Canadian Conference (1985) pp. 151-158

[12] Interleaf, Inc., Reference Manual of the Technical Publishing Software (Cambridge, Massachusetts, 1986)

[13] Kaehler, C., Macintosh Plus (Apple Computer, Inc. 1986)

[14] Kaisler, S. H., Interlisp: the Language and its Usage (John Wiley & Sons, Inc. 1986)

[15] Lee, A. & Lochovsky, F. H., Enhancing the Usability of an Office Information System through Direct Manipulation, Proceedings of Human Factors in Computing Systems (ACM 1983) pp. 130-134

[16] Linxi, C., Habermann, A. N., A History Mechanism and Undo/Redo/Reuse Support in ALOE (Department of Computer Science, Carnegie-Mellon University, 1986)

[17] Monk, A, Mode Errors: a User-Centred Analysis and Some Preventative Measures Using Keying-Contingent Sound, International Journal of Man-Machine Studies (1986) pp. 313-327

[18] Morgan, C.; Williams, G. & Lemmons, P., An Interview with Wayne Rosing, Bruce Daniels, and Larry Tesler, Byte (1983) pp. 90-114

[19] Norman, D. A., Design Rules Based on Analyses of Human Error, Communications of the ACM (1983) pp. 254-258

[20] Pike, R., The Text Editor Sam, Software -- Practice and Experience (1987) pp. 813-845

[21] Prager, J. M. & Borkin, S. A., POLITE Project Progress Report (G320-2140, International Business Machines Corporation, 1982)

[22] Rathke, M., Application Independent Undo/Redo --- a Programmer's Guide (WISDOM-forschungs-bericht FB-INF-88-14, Universitat Stuttgart, 1988)

[23] Reiss, S. P., PECAN: Program Development Systems That Support Multiple Views, IEEE Transactions on Software Engineering (1985) pp. 276-285

[24] Stallman, R., GNU Emacs Manual, Version 17 (Free Software Foundation, Inc. 1987)

[25] Thomas, C. G., Kellermann, G. M., & Hein, H., X-AiD: an Adaptive and Knowledge-Based Human Computer Interface, Proceedings of INTERACT'87 (1987) pp. 1075-1080

[26] Toriya, H.; Satoh, T.; Ueda, K. & Chiyokura, H., UNDO and REDO Operations for Solid Modeling, IEEE Computer Graphics and Applications (1986) pp. 35-42

[27] Vitter, J.S., US&R: a New Framework for Redoing, IEEE Software (1984) pp. 39-52

[28] Yang, Y, User-Oriented Design of Undo Support, PhD Thesis (Heriot-Watt University, 1989)

[29] Wertz, H., The Design of an Integrated, Interactive and Incremental Programming Environment, Proceedings of the Sixth International Conference on Software Engineering, Japan, September 13-16, (1982) pp. 157-165

Human–Computer Interaction – INTERACT '90
D. Diaper et al. (Editors)
Elsevier Science Publishers B.V. (North-Holland)

INTERFACE USABILITY ENGINEERING UNDER PRACTICAL CONSTRAINTS: A CASE STUDY IN THE DESIGN OF UNDO SUPPORT

Yiya YANG

Informatics Department, Rutherford Appleton Laboratory, UK

Employing usability engineering methods during interface design contributes to making the final product more usable. However, although classical evaluation methods are scientifically sound and can be effectively used for usability engineering, they are not practical, because system developers see them as too time consuming, expertise intensive and expensive to apply. Finding usability engineering methods, which can be applied under the practical constraints of time, cost and available expertise that normally shape interface development, is an important challenge for HCI. This paper discusses a project which shows how inexpensive and practical usability engineering methods can be employed during interface development to enhance its usability using the design of undo support as a case study.

1. INTRODUCTION

The usability of a computer interface determines how successfully and efficiently a user is able to employ the system to carry out required tasks. During interface development many design techniques can assist in enhancing its usability. However they are not widely used in the real world because developers of interfaces are put off by the complexity of these techniques and perceive them as expensive and time-consuming to apply [1, 4, 5]. In order to make HCI knowledge serviceable to the real world, Nielsen has advocated the compromise of using 'discount' methods which stand a better chance of actually being used in practical design situations [7].

User commands can be classified into two kinds: task-oriented and support-oriented. Task-oriented commands cause essential steps in the performance of any task within the scope of the system. They are directly involved with the manipulation of application objects and provide an incremental progression toward the user's task solution. Support-oriented commands enable the user to acquire knowledge of appropriate task-oriented commands, facilitate user-computer interaction or assure the integrity of a user's work. An undo facility is a support-oriented interface feature which allows users to reverse the effects of executed commands. It does not change the functionality of a system but enhances its usability and learnability.

Current conceptions of undo support reflect received wisdom as to the reasons for having it. The HCI literature views undo support as a recovery and usability feature which permits ready recovery from many simple errors. It avoids creating frustration where a user discovers that an unexpected result of a command cannot be reversed and encourages safe exploration of unfamiliar options. It can be used to deal with mode errors, interactive deadlocks, and changing one's mind [2, 3, 6, 8].

Recent HCI research has brought the importance of user-centred and user-oriented design to the fore [9, 10]. Using this approach enables designers to consider users' abilities, limitations, and preferences prior to detailed design. In this way design becomes objective-driven rather than technology-driven. This paper brings out how inexpensive discount methods can be used in each stage of a user-oriented design process of undo support. Although they may lack the scientific rigour of more advanced empirical methods they can bring many usability problems to light. As the case study in developing undo support will illustrate, they are surprisingly effective as well as cheap.

2. USERS' REQUIREMENTS

Basic requirements guidelines for undo support state that [11]

. any user action should be reversible
. an undo action should be able to reverse more than the most recent command
. an undo action itself should be reversible

Whether these requirements are general enough and how

a user uses existing undo support are not explained in the guidelines. Since a primary purpose of providing undo support is to improve the usability of software, knowing whether users use undo support is important for deciding whether software should provide undo support. In order to find out about users' requirements for and attitudes to undo support, some evaluation methods need to be employed. Electronic mail systems over wide area networks provide a cheap, timely and available method for conducting an informal survey of users' views. In order to elicit user requirements five questions were asked of subscribers to JANET's news network (British Academic Network):

1) Are there any undo/redo commands in the system you use?
2) What forms do they have?
3) How often do you use undo/redo commands and in what circumstances?
4) Is it easy to use the existing undo/redo commands and how do they meet your needs?
5) What are your ideal undo/redo commands?

The questions were brief and the sample size was small but that did not diminish its usefulness. The survey aimed at bringing to the fore issues about undo support which users thought significant or problematic. 8 responses from experienced computer users were received to the inquiry. Their salient points can be summarised as follows:

1) *Popular undo support facilities and their usage circumstances*

   Five systems with undo support, Vi text editor, Macintosh tools, SunView text editor, Smalltalk-80 and Emacs were popular with respondents. The reported circumstances in which they are used are:
   . correcting wrong commands
   . rectifying typing mistakes
   . coping with unwanted outcomes
   . changing one's mind

For these respondents undo support is useful for text writing and programming. They recognised that undo support has at least three advantages: saving keystrokes, correcting errors and allowing a user to change his mind.

2) *Preferred undo/redo commands*

   Respondents described their preferred undo and redo commands in the following terms.

   a) An undo support facility should provide n-step undo commands which can be reversed themselves.
   b) An undo support facility should be context-based and able to undo almost all aspects of the system state as perceived by the user, not just the file contents, but also the cursor position (or focus), meta-information like the printer setup (for a Mac) and actions among files. It should be able to undo any command. If it is impossible, the user should be told that a command cannot be undone and confirmation should be received before its execution.
   c) An undo support facility should be multiple-level and provide undo commands with variable granularity which either undo a single command at once or multiple commands at once. It should provide a query-undo by which a user can have more control over undoing.

From the respondents' preferences it would seem that experienced users want an interactive system to provide different options which can be used in different situations. They prefer an environment where they have significant undo functionality and usable control over that functionality.

Based on the information obtained from the network survey and a literature review, general functional requirements for undo support were elicited and a user's model of undo support was constructed [13]. The general requirements can be expressed as properties: reversibility, inversibility, self-applicability, unstacking and thoroughness. The property of reversibility concerns whether the state of a system can be reversed to a previously existing state after a sequence of task-oriented commands have operated on it. The property of inversibility concerns whether effects of an undo command can be reversed by one or more undo commands. The property of self-applicability concerns whether an undo command can reversed its own effects. The property of unstacking for an undo command states that this undo command is not self-applicable. The property of thoroughness concerns whether the situation where the effects of a command are reversed is equivalent to the situation whether that command was not executed from a user's point of view. The user's model supports cancelling, sequential undoing/redoing, partial undoing/redoing, pattern undoing/redoing and conditional undoing/redoing functions.

3. FUNCTIONAL DESIGN

Once a user's model of undo support was constructed,

three functional models of undo support, primitive, meta and triadic models were specified [14]. The primitive undo support model sustains history undo/undo [12] in which only one self-applicable undo command is provided. The meta undo support model sustains linear undo/redo [12] in which an unstacking undo command and a redo command are provided. The triadic undo support model sustains the specified user's model in which an undo, a redo and a rotate command are provided. Comparing these three functional models using the general requirements shows that the triadic model is the most powerful and subsumes the functionality of the primitive and meta models.

When the project reached this stage, some evaluation was needed to assess received HCI wisdom on undo support and to derive information upon which to base detailed design decisions. A mail questionnaire evaluation with a sample population of 534 was conducted. It got a 65.7% response rate and a 53.6% useful response rate. The details were analysed [15]. The main conclusions and recommendations based upon the information yielded by the questionnaire for the design of undo support can be summarised as follows:

1) Most users agree that the capability to undo the last command are important and that undo support is useful for saving typing, correcting mistakes and safely exploring new functions.
2) Users learn by reading manuals and trying things out more than by any other general method. Since undo support allows users to explore safely new functions, it encourages the dominant learning practice.
3) On the one hand users consider the capacity to undo the last command to be rather more important than the capacity to undo any previous command. On the other hand the forms of undo support users prefer most among a choice of four undo/redo models are history undo/undo and reference undo/redo [16] in which a rotate command is provided so that a user can specify which command is to be redone. Therefore to square users' perceptions of the utility of undo support ranges with their preferences for types of undo support, simple undo support should provide history undo/undo with a single command grain and range and sophisticated undo support should provide reference undo/redo with a multi-command grain and range.
4) There is no single best grain for a recovery command. The number of commands a recovery command should reverse is application- and user-dependent. Undo support should provide at least a recovery command which can reverse the effects of a basic command and can reverse the effects of n basic commands by being issued n times successively where more than the last command can be undone.

4. DETAILED DESIGN

After balancing different trade-offs, GNU Emacs was chosen to be the prototype environment . GNU Emacs combines undo function and redo function into one command called undo. The first time this undo command is issued, the last change is undone. Consecutive repetitions of the undo command undo earlier and earlier changes. Any command other than an undo command breaks the sequence of undo commands. Starting at this moment, the previous undo commands are considered ordinary changes that can themselves be undone.

Since GNU Emacs has its own undo support, an informal network survey was carried out to solicit Emacs users' opinions as to whether GNU Emacs's current undo support capability was adequate and as to which aspects of undo support in Emacs might be improved. The following questions were broadcast in the news group Comp.emacs through the JANET network.

1) How often do you use GNU Emacs undo commands? In which circumstances?
2) In which aspects do the undo/redo facilities of Emacs need to be improved?
3) In the Emacs environment, what kind of undo/redo commands are ideal?

Seventeen replies were received. Their recommendations for improvements to GNU Emacs can be summarised as follows.

1) GNU Emacs should provide an easy way to tell what commands have been issued, what commands have been executed and what commands have been undone. For example, a window might be brought to the screen which contains numbered lines of keystrokes or command names and details the execution status of each line.
2) The command to undo task-oriented commands should be different from that to undo undo support commands. It should provide a sort of undo checkpoint (or implicit one) at the last undo that was not preceded by an undo so that a whole sequence of undos could be undone at once.
3) Undo support should have an option to specify what

range it is possible to undo over. It should also have some coarser granularity optionally available to mark and undo commands. It should be able to wipe out a sequence of commands followed by a sequence of undos so that a user can skip over the whole undone sequence when using undo again later.

4) Undo support should have clearly defined boundaries for commands which have sub-dialogues. The current undo support facility does not have the right boundaries for query-replace. For example, a whole query-replace should be able to be undone as a unit as well as a lot of individual replacements.

5) If there are other ways than through using undo support to undo a command, undo support should be at least as powerful as these other ways. Currently, a yank command can deal with some situations which undo support cannot handle.

The survey shows that Emacs users want Emacs to provide undo support more transparently, more thoroughly and more consistently. They want a better presentation of the execution and undo history. They want different granularities of undo support commands and a flexible range of undo support. They also want more consistency and coherence in undo support's provision. So the survey shows that although Emacs provides quite powerful undo support, it does not meet all users' requirements and can be improved in a number of ways. Based on the information obtained, a new undo support facility within the Emacs environment was designed and a document was written to describe the new undo support facility.

5. DESIGN REVIEW

Before a prototype was developed, the design proposal was used for an expert walkthrough and design review. It described the current undo support capability in Emacs, summarized suggestions extracted from the previous informal network enquiry, and described the proposal for an improved undo support facility with abstract task examples to illustrate how this facility might work. This document also expressed different FOR and AGAINST arguments for some issues and explicitly asked for opinions. The document was given to two HCI experts who were told the purpose of the document and asked to evaluate what the document described. Their feedback was used to draft a second version of the document [16] which was individually sent to 137 representative Emacs users who were chosen from the network group called Comp.emacs.

32 of the 137 Emacs users replied to the survey by electronically mailing responses. From the 32 responses and the comments of two HCI experts, it was clear that three kinds of people responded to the survey. HCI experts were largely concerned with issues about interface consistency and interface presentation. Emacs users were largely concerned with what functions they liked or disliked. Emacs programmers were largely concerned with how difficult it was to implement the proposal and which techniques should be used for the implementation. Among the 32 electronic mail replies, most of them broadly agreed with most ideas presented in the document. Some rejected or raised doubts about some issues and others proposed new methods to deal with undo support. The detailed analysis was reported in [16]. The following summarizes the points which differed from, opposed or amplified some of the ideas of the original document.

1) There should be separate commands for undoing changes to the current buffer and undoing changes to the state of the system. It would be undesirable for the same commands that undo text changes to undo cursor motions or window switches as well.

2) Currently undo is done on a per-buffer basis: each undo affects just one buffer. This is simple to understand and to use. It would not be possible to keep undo on a per buffer basis if undo is on a command basis rather than on a buffer change basis, because a command in general affects more than one buffer. Nor would it be possible to do this if you keep undo information for other Lisp data structures since they may not be clearly associated with any buffer.

3) It is not feasible to undo absolutely everything Emacs does. Emacs commands are Lisp programs. To make Lisp programs generally undoable, you would need to make setq, fset and many other Lisp functions undoable.

4) If you are going to deal with different granularities, you may want to have the commands "undo-bigger" and "undo-smaller" that adjust the granularity. "Undo-bigger" would redo the previous undo, increase the size of the undone chunks, and undo one of them. "Undo-smaller" would redo the previous undo, decrease the size of the undone chunks, and undo one of them. The idea is that when you notice that the granularity is wrong, you do an "undo-bigger" or "undo-smaller" as appropriate.

5) Sub-dialogue-initiating commands need an internal undo or redo. Sub-dialogue-initiating commands should start the compilation of a list of the whole sub-dialogue in reverse order. One kind of undo command

should undo the whole sub-dialogue and a different kind of undo command should work through all steps in the sub-dialogue in reverse order.
6) In an editor where there are often many different ways of achieving the same end, a user may regard several of his commands as being part of a higher-level operation to perform some desired task. Therefore, undo support may need to be high level.
7) Regional undo and redo commands should be provided. This would allow a user to undo or redo only commands which modified the region between the current cursor position and the latest marked position. This is useful if the user has made lots of modifications to a Lisp buffer and only wants to undo the changes to one region.
8) Regarding the suggestion for Query Undo Support, one way to present it is to follow the method of M-x list-buffers. A user can move around in the *Undo history* buffer to undo/redo individual commands by pressing **r** and **u** or to undo/redo a sequence of commands by marking that region and pressing **r** or **u**.
9) The idea of marking checkpoints called undo barriers is attractive. It may be useful if a user could indicate them explicitly.

It can be seen that the points raised were both pertinent and helpful. After careful analysis significant changes were made to the original proposal and a prototype was implemented [16].

6. OBSERVATIONAL EVALUATION

Once the initial prototype of the undo support sub-system was considered to be usable, an inexpensive post-mortem evaluation was carried out. The whole evaluation procedure consisted of several sessions across a couple of days. Two end users were asked to assess the system informally. One of them went through three evaluation sessions (about one hour each) in three days and the other went through only one evaluation session. Their comments were used as feedback for improvements. The evaluation was incremental in the sense that some changes were made on the system after each evaluation session.

The evaluation method used was the paired-user protocol. Each evaluation session was carried out in the following way. Before the interaction between the end user and the system, the end user was provided with a written manual on how the system works and what functions the system has. After reading the manual, the end user was asked to use the system and to provide verbal comments while an experienced Emacs user was observing and taking notes. During interactions with the system, there was also interaction between the end user and the observer. If the end user had any question, the end user could ask the observer for an answer. After each evaluation session the end user was asked to give his views on the undo support sub-system and to suggest improvements. The findings elucidate some of the successes as well as the shortcomings of the system. Six issues raised during the evaluation are summarised as follow.

1)The undo history does not need to show minor cursor movement commands. Cursor movement commands for short distances are not significant and their appearance in the undo history window clutters it and crowds out significant commands.
2) The keystroke for the self inserted space should be a space rather than SPC
3)When the keystrokes for a command are too long to be displayed on one line, they should be shown in an abbreviated form by the first few keystrokes followed by three dots.
4)The display of the history list for redoing commands could be made more compact for a common case of redoing. If the commands to be redone are successively undone commands that include the last one in the undo history, it would be better, when these undone commands are redone, that the mark * opposite each of these commands be removed rather than adding new entries for each redone command to the history list.
5)The way of listing commands in the undo history does not support the normal order of writing later commands below earlier commands. It would be more natural to support this ordering than a bottom to top ordering.
6)The system should provide a convenient way to re-organise undoing by user-defined task-oriented units rather than by commands. For example, chunk-based self-insert-command should be word-based or phrase-based rather than letter-number-based.

After the evaluation, the first five suggestions have been implemented. The sixth suggestion is very attractive. But it cannot be implemented easily with current techniques. Defining the granularity of commands in a user and task-oriented fashion is a research topic itself.

When finishing the evaluation procedure, the end user was asked to give his or her overall impressions of the undo support facility. They can be summered as follows:

1) This new undo support facility was rather better than the existing Emacs undo support facility because

   a) it is more powerful and flexible
   b) it can show the undo history making it easy to select which commands to undo
   c) it has a separate redo command

2) An undo support facility is a nice feature for editors, but it may be more important for a programming environment because text is written in natural language and programs have to be written in an exact form of a programming language. A large proportion of debugging time is spent on correcting syntactical errors. If a programmer changes a program wrongly, the programmer can return it to its earlier form easily by undoing.

7. CONCLUSIONS

This paper illustrates how different inexpensive usability engineering methods can be incorporated into the HCI design process and provide detailed, pertinent and helpful knowledge for improving the design of an interface. The detailed analysis can be found in [16]. This paper only describes the methods and the information obtained. From this discussion, it is clear that informal evaluation methods can be used to collect information on which design decisions are made in the early design stages and to assess the impact of design decisions at later design stages. It proves the point that informal and inexpensive evaluation methods are already available for making real improvements to the usability of software.

ACKNOWLEDGEMENTS

This research was supported by an Alvey grant GR/D 424125 and carried out at Scottish HCI Centre of Heriot-Watt University. The author would like to thank her husband and her colleagues for their valuable comments and support.

REFERENCES

[1] Bellotti, V., Implications of Current Design Practice for the Use of HCI Techniques, in: Jones, D. M. & Winder, R., (Eds.), People and Computer IV (Cambridge University Press, 1988) pp.13-34

[2] Carroll, J. M. & Mack, R., Learning to Use a Word Processor: by Doing, by Thinking and by Knowing,. in: Thomas, J. & Schneider, M., (Eds.), Human Factors in Computing Systems (Ablex Publishing Corp., 1984) pp.13-15

[3] Darlington, J.; Dzida, W. & Herda, S., The Role of Excursions in Interactive Systems, International Journal of Man-Machine Studies (1983) pp.101-112

[4] Gould, J. D. & Lewis, C., Designing for Usability: Key Principles and What Designers Think, Communications of the ACM (1985) pp.300-311

[5] Harker, S., The Implications of Current Practice and Future Trends in the Design and Use of Prototyping Systems (Department of Human Sciences, Loughborough University of Technology, UK, 1989)

[6] Monk, A., Mode Errors: a User-Centred Analysis and Some Preventative Measures Using Keying-Contingent Sound, International Journal of Man-Machine Studies (1986) pp.313-327

[7] Nielsen, J. (1989). Usability Engineering at a Discount, In: Salvendy, G. & Smith, M. J., (Eds.), Designing and Using Human-Computer Interfaces and Knowledge Based Systems (Elsevier Science publishers B.V., 1989) pp.394-401

[8] Norman, D. A., Design Rules Based on Analyses of Human Error, Communications of the ACM (1983) pp.254-258

[9] Norman, D. A. & Draper, S. W., User Centred System Design (Lawrence Erlbaum Association, Hillsdale, 1986)

[10] Rouse, W. B. & Cody, W. J., On the Design of Man-Machine Systems: Principles, Practices and Prospects, Proceedings of the 10th World Conference on Automatic Control, (1987) pp.295-302

[11] Smith, S. L. & Mosier, J. N., Guidelines for Designing User Interface Software (ESD-TR-86-278, MITRE, Bedford, Massachusetts, 1986)

[12] Vitter, J. S., US&R: a New Framework for Redo, IEEE software (1984) pp. 39-52

[13] Yang, Y., A New Conceptual Model for Interactive User Recovery and Command Reuse Facilities, CHI'88 Conference Proceedings: Human Factors in Computing Systems, Washington, D.C., (1988a) pp.165-170

[14] Yang, Y., Undo Support Models, International Journal of Man-Machine Studies (1988b) pp.457-481

[15] Yang, Y., Survey Steered Design: Evaluating User Recovery and Command Reuse Support by Questionnaire, Behavior and Information Technology (1989a) pp.437-460

[16] Yang, Y., User-Oriented Design of Undo Support, PhD Thesis (Heriot-Watt University, UK, 1989b)

Human–Computer Interaction – INTERACT '90
D. Diaper et al. (Editors)
Elsevier Science Publishers B.V. (North-Holland)
IFIP, 1990

STATE VERSUS HISTORY IN USER INTERFACES

W.B. Cowan, Computer Graphics Laboratory, University of Waterloo, Waterloo, Ont., Canada

M. Wein, Laboratory for Intelligent Systems, National Research Council of Canada, Ottawa, Ont.

ABSTRACT

Recent growth in window-oriented user interfaces with the implied evolution of interaction styles has led to two distinct approaches to user interfaces. The older style is terminal oriented and can be characterized as history-based: the current state of the system is inferred by the user from his or her knowledge of the sequence of previous commands. The newer window-oriented style is state-based in that the current state of the system is displayed in the window or the dialog box. Many interfaces attempt to combine elements from the two styles. This paper discusses the distinctive characteristics of each interface style, considering particularly user requirements that are inconsistent with the conceptual organization of the interface. We conclude that the two styles provide an almost non-overlapping set of capabilities, and that the choice of interface should be determined by the user's task requirements. The inevitable desire to encompass all capabilities in one interface demands significant generalization of the interface metaphor.

1. INTRODUCTION

The emergence and rapid growth of window-oriented user interfaces has popularized an entirely new style of interaction. This paper identifies significant qualitative differences between the style of interaction in a window oriented system and that in the older, terminal-based system.

The earlier command-line oriented interfaces, of which the Unix* shell (Bourne, 1978) is a classical example, can be thought of as being history-oriented because previously executed commands scroll upwards and remain as a (partial) visual record of the changes of the state that have occurred to the system, caused by the execution of user commands. There is a clear concept of time inherent in this interface. Present time is associated with the line containing the cursor. A time-line goes back from that point, being represented by the sequence of commands. As will be discussed later, the term *history* is used in this paper to convey a different concept from that of reuse of previously issued commands (Greenberg and Witten, 1988 and also Yang, 1988).

In a window oriented system the essential perceptual quality is a visual representation of state. The window system in its pure form presents on the screen an instantaneous snapshot of the system as seen by the user. A Macintosh Finder (Apple Computer, 1987) presents a snapshot of (a portion of) the file system. The only state that is being presented is the *present* state.

This paper analyses the interfaces from the point of view of state vs. history and demonstrates how the two approaches can coexist and how they had been combined in the past with highly unsatisfactory results.

* Trademarks are acknowledged in the context by a reference to the product documentation.

2. PROPERTIES OF INTERFACES

2.1 Command-line Interface

The classical command-line interface was originally based on the hard-copy terminal. In response to a system-generated prompt the user issues a command as a string of text, terminated by the new-line character. The paradigm assumes that the user is at a character-oriented terminal, more recently a *glass teletype*, but currently a more likely device is a virtual terminal program or terminal emulator running on a personal computer either under a window system, or not. In all cases the two-way dialogue is based on the concept of a temporally ordered byte-stream. Virtual terminal programs typically have a scroll buffer that retains a much larger number of user commands than the typical 24 lines on a screen. The local scroll buffer retains both the user-generated commands and system-generated responses.

The visual record of past commands and system responses seen on the screen (or scrolled back from the scroll buffer) represents the history of transactions: the system response following each command indicates the incremental change in the system.

Output in the history-based system is static: it is never updated retroactively. When a sequence of commands *ls* and *rm* is executed, the result of the *ls* command, being the list of files appearing on the screen above the current line, is not updated following the *rm* command, as shown in Figure 1.

The user infers the current state based on the history of commands and responses. He needs to know the current

```
%cd fig
%ls
part1  part2  part3
%rm part1
%ls
part2  part3
%
```

Figure 1.

Results of a series of commands ls, rm, ls in cshell.

state in order to predict the operation of his commands. The most difficult problem encountered by a new user is confusion over the current state: He may not know what commands to type or even where to look in the manual to find a command that would get him to a known state.

In the history oriented system the user maintains a mental image of the state and updates the mental image based on specific events. Thus an *rm* command updates the mental image that the file is no longer there, even though it is plainly visible in the output record following the earlier *ls*. The sequence of commands *ls, rm, ls,* is a useful tool for teaching the effect of the *rm* command.

Occasionally, even the most experienced user performs a sequence of actions from which he or she cannot infer the state of the system, usually as the result of a command that produces unexpected results. In such a case it is essential that the user know a set of actions that is guaranteed to bring him or her into a known state. Otherwise he or she will remain lost forever! This essential feature is often not present in systems, and even when it does exist it is rarely taught explicitly. For example, vi, the Unix screen editor, has such a sequence where repeated ESC brings the editor back into the command state, with the bell rung to indicate to the user that ESC has been typed in the command state. New users, however, are forced to learn this sequence by trial and error, even though it is one of the first things that should be taught.

2.2 State-Oriented Interface

The window system provides the user with the visual cue of the context. How the mental image of the context is maintained represents the most profound difference between the history and state oriented systems. One associates the state-oriented interface with a window oriented one, but that is true only in those systems in which a full graphical user interface is implemented and includes a static representation of the relevant part of the file system.

The state-oriented interface emerged largely from the work at Xerox Palo Alto Research Center on the SmallTalk System (Goldberg and Robson, 1983), the Cedar system (Teitelman, 1984) and other related systems. The dialogue is via dialogue boxes and graphical representations of the state of the system. This style of interaction is at the root of the pure window system. The window, representing the current state of the system, is being updated continuously and usually irrevocably. The Macintosh Finder or its equivalent on a Unix (e.g.. Finder-like interface on the Silicon Graphics Personal Iris or on Sun 386i) always represent the current state of the file system. Any event in the shell causes an update of the 2D surface representing the state of the file system.

In a state-oriented interface history exists but it is neither recorded nor explicitly shown. Since history is evanescent in state-oriented systems the display surface must contain enough information for the user to infer the state information needed to predict the result of any command he or she may wish to use. Note that executing commands to discover more about the state of the system, such as opening a folder in the Macintosh, changes the state, an example of the probe effect, which is analogous to the Heisenberg uncertainty principle. In this example the working directory changes as a result of the operation, with far reaching implications: the display configuration, the set of available commands, the file selection dialogue, and many other things, all change.

Consequently, there is a far greater requirement for the *Undo* function. Single-level *Undo* is inadequate. The editor QUED/M (Lewak and Robbins, 1988) available on the Macintosh, for example, has up to 32K levels of undo, although a practical limit of 64 is reasonable. The multi-level undo is, in fact, a mechanism for recreating history in a state-oriented system. An interesting model to support user's perception of the complex state of the system is discussed in Card and Henderson (1987).

2.3 Page System vs. Text System

First, no interface is really pure history. Buffering a line on input, for example, makes line editing possible. A small subset of history, the current line, can be revoked. The user learns a model of the interaction that is centered on commands, from which the name "command line" interface is taken. Thus one line, the current one, stays in the present and is entered into history when RETURN is typed. This capability is generalized in two ways: page-oriented interfaces and history for re-use (discussed elsewhere).

In a true history system the line representing the present is always at the bottom of the scrolled text. If a previous command is invoked again, it is copied to the bottom line, i.e. the present line and executed. In a hybrid, modified history system the previous command is executed at its original location in the scroll buffer and that point becomes the present. An example of a modified history is the Macintosh Programmer's Workshop (MPW). There, it is impossible to reconstruct history by examining the record of the scrolled text. Present time is established wherever the mouse is clicked. Other hybrid systems are the X Window System (Jones, 1988), and in some ways the VAX/VMS system (Digital Equipment, 1988). Managing of commands in a multi-window system is discusses in Barnes and Bovey (1986).

There is actually a second and distinct hybrid system: the page- or block-oriented display found on terminals communicating with mainframes in a half-duplex block-oriented mode. The goal in those interfaces is to minimize network communication and especially the reversal of direction of transmission.

Page-oriented interfaces expand the input buffer to a whole page, which can be used as a form by the user. Output is continuous, as in pure history systems, though accessible only one page at a time, with moving back and forth, as in a book, possible. Page breaks are put between the output from different commands in some systems, keeping the metaphor more consistent and playing the role of the prompt. Input shows the problem with such a system. Some applications, such as reservation systems, deal naturally with page-sized and -formatted chunks of data. In such applications form-filling followed by a command that effectively means TRANSMIT is logical, and may be followed by re-transmission of the form with errors marked, re-transmission of the form with an okay message, and so on. Other applications naturally have smaller commands. Three choices are possible: a COMMAND request which produces a new blank window to contain the command and associated output, the ability to type a command followed by an ENTER request at the bottom of the currently displayed output, and the creation of a special area on the screen into which commands are typed, followed by an ENTER request. Each choice has problems. The first causes useful history to vanish from the user, often just when it is most needed. The second creates a pseudo-glass-teletype inside the page oriented system with scrolling inconsistencies to be resolved by the user. The third creates a confusion between two different types of commands: form-filling ones that require no input to the command buffer and other commands that do. Many ad hoc solutions have been considered to handle one problem or another, none of which comes to grips with the underlying problem: two distinct types of command, one creating history and the other obliterating it. Accommodating both within the same user interface cannot be done without inconsistency.

2.4 History for Command Reuse

In order to clarify the difference between the two uses of the term *history,* its other use, that of the concept of reuse of previously issued commands will be reviewed here. The operating system shell includes a history capability and retains a separate copy of user-generated commands, but does not retain system responses. In the cshell in Unix bsd 4.3 it is implemented as *.history* file and there is an equivalent facility in DEC VAX/VMS. More modern shells go even further by maintaining history across login sessions.

The preserved sequence of commands in the shell history file serves only one purpose: it provides the user with the ability to reuse a command without having to retype. Here the burden of remembering past commands is placed on the user. Not surprisingly, an experienced programmer tends to reach further into the past to retrieve a command, than an inexperienced one (Greenberg and Witten, 1988). This ability to remember past commands is somewhat analogous to the uncanny ability of an experienced bridge player to remember all cards that have been played.

There are subtle differences how this input history is used: in VMS Command Line Interface lines are copied from history buffer to current position and then executed as current. In cshell in bsd 4.3 command lines are numbered and can be invoked by reference, subject to a simple editor for minor fixes or modifications. In this sense, the interface approaches that in Commodore C64, where the command line interface is accessed always through a simple full-screen editor.

History for re-use must decide where to put its output. History-oriented systems recopy the command in the present then put output directly after it, just as though the command had been typed by the user. There is a page-oriented re-use which is not possible in this way. Suppose I want to build up a sequence of commands that do a single job for me. A typical operation might be incremental creation of a script. I type the command for the first action; verify that it does what I want; add the second command; run the two together and verify the result; and so on. This is a page-oriented, form-filling interaction and, like page-oriented applications, benefits from a separation of input from output since incrementing requires a representation of the script uncontaminated by output. History-oriented systems put that representation into some kind of command file. (E.g. Unix with job control: edit, write, ^Z, run and observe output, fg, edit, write, ^Z, run and observe output...). The more state-oriented a system the more suitable it is for keeping that representation on the display surface. Page-oriented systems with separate input and output streams allow building the script in the input area while output is separately observed in the output area.

The MPW program development environment on the Macintosh attempts a more complicated solution. The command is not repeated: when it is rerun output is inserted into history directly below the position of the first instance of the command. Since history is completely editable the script can be built up by inserting the second command immediately before the output from the first. Then the two are selected together and run, creating a composite output directly below the second command. A third command is then added below the second and so on.

The effect is history that branches, making time tree-structured and creating and awkward artifact in the user interface.

3. PSYCHOLOGY OF INTERFACES

The record in a history based interface preserves a linear time-line into the past. The interface is intrinsically linguistic, textual and inherently linear. The interface is essentially an analytic one, in that the current state is perceived by the user, based on a mental image of the state changes that have occurred. Context switch is mainly mental and implied. This style of interface appeals to an analytic minded person who is proficient at visualizing large hierarchical structures and who is aware of his or her current place in the hierarchy. The user never needs to execute *pwd* as a reminder.

One experienced Unix user, observed anecdotally, was seen usually to change directories using the sequence

% cd
% cd <path name relative to the home directory>

Clearly this user could easily maintain a mental image of his elaborate directory structure from the viewpoint of the home directory but not from the viewpoint of his current directory and that the extra typing was less costly than manipulation of the complicated mental image. In similar ways it should be possible to infer quite a lot about how users maintain their mental models of the system state by looking at how they use the commands that are available on their systems.

A state oriented interface appeals to the visually oriented mind. The context of each activity is captured in the state of each window. Context knowledge for the user is achieved by visual inspection to select the desired context. The state is always valid and there is no need to extrapolate from an older state. In a history oriented system the context can be remembered, because the number of default states is severely limited. Then changes in context are followed incrementally as the session proceeds. In a state oriented system the context can be discovered by inspection of the display surface. Of course context is so rich that only part of it is available at any time and state-oriented interfaces have problems with the probe effect as noted above.

Consequently state-oriented interfaces try to show not the complete context but those parts of the context that are needed to allow the user to determine the results of any command. Because context in history interfaces is known from a state sequence that starts from a known state applications cannot maintain rich context across invocations, but should always start in a default state: suppose for example that you forget the defaults you have set in a program. State interfaces, on the other hand can maintain context across invocations, because they don't require incremental inference. The history tradition has been very deep rooted: Macintosh applications took a long time to discover such simple things as the benefits of leaving the cursor in the file at the point where it was when the file was last edited.

Communication with a typical shell has evolved from the raw essentially unbuffered and unforgiving style, to one permitting command line editing with arrow keys (VMS CLI), and finally to an interface that permits full editing through a basic editor (X Window System, Commodore C64, Macintosh MPW Shell). Every action performed since the last ENTER is the present and is revokable. But as the amount of stuff taken into the present gets bigger and bigger the problem of maintaining sequence gets harder and harder.

4.0 INFLUENCES OF INTERFACE STYLES ON APPLICATIONS

The difference between the two types of user interfaces and the underlying psychology, can be illustrated in the context of two popular classes of programs: electronic mail and editors.

4.1 Mail

The two mail systems that characterize the two extremes are the mail system in Unix on the one hand and QuickMail on the Macintosh on the other. The latter is being used as an example because it is relatively popular, but it is based in concept on Cedar, which is the originator of many concepts of the state-oriented interface. A compromise between the two styles is the VMS mail system

The Unix mail system presents a view of a terminal, or multiple terminals through instantiation. The system preserves the model of a linear record of history. The interface is sparse with minimal messages to the user. The current context of the mail system is established entirely by the sequence of preceding commands and its view is maintained by the user, who must remember that sequence. Of course, there is the associated problem of state overload in mail because of the many available commands. The Unix mail system is history oriented but it is not sequential: At any time it is possible to add Subject: and Cc: items. If desired the mail system can be used such that it has no interface at all, it is intended to be called from shell scripts. E.g. Create the message using vi, including such things as Subject: and Cc: lines if you want them, then use

% mail user < message

to send it.

The context of QuickMail (CE Software, 1988) is established entirely visually, as shown in Figure 2. All of the components, such as: "To:" and "Subject:" fields appear in dialog boxes. If the user wishes to prepare the message using a separate and free-standing editor, the mail system window remains on the screen, available to re-establish the context visually.

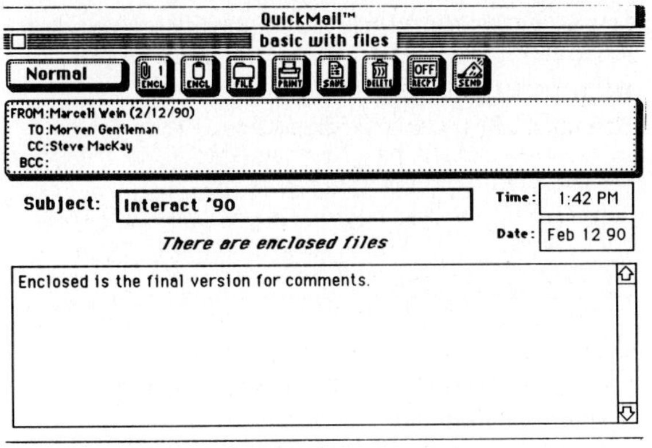

Figure 2.

State-oriented interface in QuickMail (CE Software, 1988)

A compromise between the two styles tends to produce a very unsatisfactory interface. One of the more obnoxious mail systems is the VAX/VMS mail system. It is verbose making automated procedures, designed by the user, difficult to write. The system uses structured encoded files, so that only system programmers are able to write programs that manipulate mail messages. Worst of all, the system modifies the history by using the terminal in the paged mode, which clears all top-of-screen text. This quirk prevents one from seeing the text being replied to, or the recipients path, etc. In short, this modified history interface proves to be an extremely poor compromise. Even though it is hybrid the mail system is highly sequential: it is possible to add Cc: recipients only at the beginning of the process.

4.2 Text editors and Word Processors

Almost all interaction a user has with a system occurs via a text editor. (Obvious exceptions are the power switch and the reset button.) The editor, several of which normally comprise the interface, must be well integrated with the style of interaction for which it is used. For example, history-oriented interfaces generally use a simple editor that provides line editing on the command line, for which little more than delete and kill operations are provided. History for re-use requires a somewhat more complicated editor, containing substitution for correcting spelling and for generalization. The creation of general text files in a history-oriented interface is more conveniently done using a full screen editor like vi or emacs (Stallman, 1980).

Notice that some editors are implicit, like command line and history substitution editors, while others, like vi, are run explicitly as separate programs. State-oriented systems, which allow any displayed element to change, typically use display editors for all editing, and many attempts have been made to have a single editor that works on any item. Two examples are the Commdore 64 Basic editor and the Tioga editor in Cedar (Teitelman, 1984). Not surprisingly there are always a few items that cannot be edited, such as the title bars in the Macintosh interface, or incoming text in a mail system, and the fewer they are the more they confuse the user when he or she tries to edit them.

History and state oriented systems diverge most strongly in how they define a file in the middle of an editing operation. History systems are procedural, and change state as the result of an ENTER command. Write corresponds to ENTER for display editors in history-oriented systems, so the current value of any file is its value when write was last performed. Thus, in Unix if a file is edited with vi, during which an escape is made to the shell using job control, a compilation does reflect changes made since the last write. In state-oriented systems the user always sees the current state of the system, so that when the screen representation of a file changes the change should be reflected in any operation concerning the file. Thus, a compilation should affect the editor's copy of the file. Since compilation should not imply an implicit write of the file it requires close cooperation between the editor and the compiler. This basic property of state-oriented interfaces greatly complicates interworking, with two consequences. First, most programs include an integral editor, which is needed to make the state-oriented file transfer possible, and so that the need for interworking is minimized. (This restriction is an infringement on programmer's right to choose an editor.) Strong interface discipline is needed to keep the editors similar enough to minimize learning transfer problems. Second, most data files are so strongly identified with the application that created them that interworking using them is not possible. Transfer of data files between applications is only possible via standardized formats and temporary files such as the Macintosh clipboard and scrapbook.

Word processing significantly complicates problems of editor functionality. History-oriented system characteristically do word processing in batch mode: a formatter, like TeX or troff, processes a source file into a set of commands that can be used to drive a printer or previewer. The source document and its formatted counterpart both exist as different points in the history of the document. State-oriented system, on the other hand, immediately convert input into formatted form. The benefits of the latter are evident, but it does have drawbacks. First, in complicated documents there is a many to one mapping between source and formatted documents. The extra information in the source document is sometimes discarded and sometimes held as a part of the document's state that is invisible to the user. Microsoft Word for the Macintosh, which has a large amount of hidden structure, adds a few small windows to its display, each containing a more or less cryptic comment pointing to hidden information. In batch-oriented systems this information is visible in the source file, where the user's interaction occurs. Second, since state-oriented word processors attempt to reformat after every key-stroke, they are at present unable to perform the global format optimization that formatters like TeX do. Without this capability they are unlikely to attain the standards of human formatting, which takes into account global features ignored even by programs like TeX.

5. SCRIPTING

History-based interfaces with sparse textual dialog offer one advantage in ease of preparation of command scripts. In particular, there is a growing trend to replace terminals with personal computers, running a terminal emulator program. If the command shell keeps replying with additional state information, those replies can get seriously in the way of the emulator running a script in the virtual terminal. The extra verbiage has to be parsed by the script, acted upon and usually thrown away. An example of a verbose system is the VAX/VMS command interface which, combined with awkward syntax makes it difficult for end users to compose command procedures.

Also, the history-based interfaces are entirely text stream oriented, so that complex editing scripts can be run under the Unix shell. One example illustrates the process. There was a real, though uncommon, requirement to take a large file, separate it into tens of little files and to send each to a different receiver. This task proved to be easy because the underlying file in the Unix mail are text files that can be edited by the user.

Scripts or macros in state-oriented interfaces are still evolving. There are those macro tools that accumulate mouse clicks and other interface events and which are programmed interactively through gestures. Examples are Tempo (Affinity Microsystems, 1986) and MacroMaker (Apple Computer, 1988). More satisfactory ones for the more serious user are those that revert to textual specification. Examples of this type are scripting tools in the Macintosh Programmer's Workshop (Apple Computer, 1989) and in the programmer's editor QUED/M (Lewak and Robbins, 1988). The latter ones represent an excellent combination of advantages of shell scripts (as in cshell) and the ability to execute scripts line at a time with immediately visible results in the state-oriented presentation. Another approach is discussed in Siochi and Hartson (1989).

6. CONCLUSION

The detailed analysis of the user interface considering state versus history orientation of various features leads to a better understanding of a user's perception of the inter- face. We are currently witnessing the merger of interface styles found in "popular computers" like the Apple Macintosh with those on Unix workstations. The issues discussed in this paper are a contribution towards creating hybrid systems that take advantage of both cultures.

These issues become particularly important in the context of distributed computing. The greater use of agent/server models for distributed computing has triggered a renewed interest in investigation of partitioning applications across the network. It has become evident that the transport of mouse clicks and window updates across the network results in unresponsive and unsatisfactory interfaces. An understanding of the underlying perceptual issues with respect of state, history and context is a good starting point for the development of models for more satisfactory interfaces.

REFERENCES

Affinity Microsystems, Product Manual, Tempo, Intelligent Macros for the Macintosh, Affinity Microsystems, Boulder CO, 1986.

Apple Computer Corp (1987) *Human Interface Guidelines, The Apple Desktop Interface*, Addison Wesley.

Apple Computer Corp (1988), *Product Documentation, MacroMaker, System 6.0,* Apple Computer Corporation: Cupertino CA.

Apple Computer Corp (1989), *Product documentation, Macintosh Programmer's Workshop 3.0*, Apple Computer Corporation: Cupertino CA.

Barnes, J.D, and J.D. Bovey (1986), Managing Command submission in a Multiple Window environment, *Software Engineering Journal*, (1) 5, Sept, 177-183.

Bannon, L. , A. Cypher, S. Greenspan and M. Monty (1983), Evaluation and Analysis of Users' Activity Organization, *Proc CHI (SIG ACM)*, 54-57.

Bourne (1978), An Introduction to the Unix Shell, *Technical Report,* Bell Laboratories, Murray Hill, NJ.

Card, S.K. and D. Austin Henderson (1987), A Multiple Virtual Workspace Interface to Support User Task Switching, *Proceedings. CHI '87*, 53-59.

CE Software (1988), *QuickMail 2.0 User Manual*, CE Software: West De Moines IA.

Digital Equipment Corporation (1988), *VAX/VMS 5.0 Document Set*, Digital Equipment Corporation: Maynard, MA, April.

Goldberg, A. and Robson (1983), *Smalltalk 80, The Language and its Implementation*, Addison Wesley.

Greenberg, S. and I.H. Witten (1988), How Users Repeat their Actions on Computers: Principles for Design of History Mechanisms, *Proceedings CHI '88*, Washington, DC, 171-178.

Jones, Oliver (1988), *Introduction to the X Window System*, Prentice Hall: New York .

Joy, W.N. , (1986), Introduction to cshell, in *UNIX User's Supplementary Doocuments, 4.3*, 4:1-46, Berkeley Software Distribution, UNIX Association: Berkeley CA.

Lee, A. (1990), A Taxonomy of Uses of Interaction History, *Proceedings GI '90*, Graphics Interface Conference, Halifax, May 14-18. Canadian Information Processing Society.

Lewak, J. and G. Robbins (1988), *QUED/M - The quality Editor for the Macintosh*, (User Manual), Paragon Concepts: Solana Beach CA,.

Siochi, A.C. and H.R. Hartson, Task Oriented Representation of Asynchronous User Interfaces (1988), *Proceedings CHI '89*, Austin TX, 183-188.

Stallman, R.M. (1980), EMACS: The Extensible Customizable Self-documenting Display Editor, *Proceedings ACM SIPLAN/SIGOA Conference on Text Manipulation,* Portland OR June 8-10, 147-156.

Teitelman, W. (1984), A Tour Through Cedar, *IEEE Software* (1) 2, 44-73.

Yang, Y. (1988), A New Conceptual Model for Interactive User Recovery and Command Reuse Facilities, *Proceedings CHI '88*, Washington, DC, 165-170.

Human–Computer Interaction – INTERACT '90
D. Diaper et al. (Editors)
Elsevier Science Publishers B.V. (North-Holland)

The Personal Touch: A Study of Users' Customization Practice

Anker Helms Jørgensen
Dept. of Psychology
Copenhagen University
Njalsgade 88
DK-2300 Copenhagen S
Denmark
anker @ vax.psl.ku.dk

Allan Sauer
Denmark Credit Association
Dp-department
Jarmers Plads 2
DK-1551 Copenhagen V
Denmark

Modern computer systems provide a rich variety of customization features that allow individual users to tailor the systems to their own needs. Although these features have existed for many years, very little is known about their actual use. This paper reports three studies of users' customization practice. The users ranged from fairly dp-naive professionals using pc's to experienced systems programmers using mainframe systems. About half of the experienced users applied the customization features and the other half had tried them, whereas the novice users had not used them at all. The changes made in the systems were mainly related to appearance, such as screen colour changed due to personal preferences or visual handicaps, and to task tailoring, such as redefinition of function keys and start-up functions. The satisficing principle explains the cases where the features are not used. The results indicate that user experience play an important role in customization practice.

1. Introduction

Modern computer systems provide customization features that allow individual users to tailor the systems to suit their personal needs. Typical examples are menu set-up, adjustment of cursor speed, and screen colour.

Indeed there are many reasons for customizing computer systems. Firstly, there are large individual differences between users, e.g. in terms of visual and verbal abilities, cognitive style, learning mode, and motor skills. Thus a user might want to change the background colour in a word processor due to impaired eye sight.

Secondly, users develop from novices to experienced users over time. Novices are often overloaded with information and they may prefer to customize the system to a simple set-up - or keep away from customization features altogether as the features require extra work. Experienced users often develop particular routines and they may wish to customize the system in order to facilitate the application of these routines.

Thirdly, users perform different tasks. Therefore one user may wish a particular system to start in the e-mail program while another prefers the same system to start in the word processor.

Finally, environmental factors may create a need for customization. The background noise in a workshop may for example cause a user to increase the "beep" level.

These customization features have been available in computer systems for many years. They are, in fact, often used as a selling point. Many researchers have also called upon the need for customization features, for example Newmann (1978):

> *"Each user ... has an internal 'model' ... and it is very unusual to find two users with the same model ... Thus every user will potentially need his own private interface to the system."*

This can be done in two ways: by having the users adapt the system to their needs (adaptable system) or by having the system adapt to the users' needs (adaptive system). This paper focusses only on adaptable system. Firstly we find adaptable systems more relevant as the users themselves take the initiative to change their tools; secondly, we do not know of any adaptive systems accessible to us; thirdly, the literature abounds with papers addressing adaptive systems, e.g. Greenberg and Whitten (1985), Mason (1986), and Innocent (1982).

What characterizes an adaptable system? Which features does it include? To provide answers to these questions seems deceptively simple - but not so. Rather than going into lengthy discussions of the issue we will rely on the readers' intuitive understanding supplemented by the examples given in the paper.

Although adaptable system have been in use for a long time, little is known about the actual use of the features in practice. Only a few studies exist - focussing on related topics. As an example, Rosson (1984) investigated the effect of experience on learning and using a text editor. She found that most users had used customization features and it was strongly dependant on experience. Brooks and Thorburn (1988) report a comparison between a system with a regular help system and a system where the users could choose between three dialogue modes - i.e., customize the system. The help system group requested help more often than the other group, otherwise no differences were found.

The present paper addresses the following issues regarding users' application of customization features:

- Which parts of the systems are changed?
- Why are they changed?
- Which factors influence the changes?

We conducted three studies of users' customization practice in a building society in order to answer the questions above:

1. An interview study of 10 computer-naive valuers working locally with an integrated pc package.
2. An analysis of the system user profiles of 720 professionals and computer programmers working centrally with mainframe-based systems. This study included only choice of colour, location of prompt line, and start-up command.
3. An interview study of 20 of the professionals and 7 of the programmers from study 2 eliciting their reasons for customization.

2. The three studies

We planned for inclusion of a broader range of users in the investigations. We were, however, seriously constrained in our access to users and information about their customization practices. For example, in Study 2 we couldn't get access to the information about the users' redefinition of function keys for technical reasons, although the information existed in the user profiles. In the three studies we employed both qualititative and quantitative methods in order to obtain a broad coverage of the issues.

Study 1: Ten evaluators using pc's locally

The 10 evaluators worked individually in branches of the building society in Denmark. They had little contact with other users and with the dp-department. They had been trained in IBM Assistant, an integrated pc package, 8 months ago. The package included word processing, graphics, spreadsheet, and data base. They used the package daily for document processing and calculations. The 10 evaluators were interviewed on the phone.

The customization features were accessible via two function keys:

F2 "Make ready"
- format of currency
- format of date
- format of numbers
- format of time
- screen colours
- active library
- working drive

F3 "Menu maintenance"
- change format of date
- change screen colour
- change menu selection
- sort menu selections
- add a program to the menu
- delete a program from the menu

The two function keys F2 and F3 and the associated labels were listed in the bottom of the main menu.

It turned out that none of the evaluators were using any of the customization features, nor had they been using them previously. Only one of them knew about the features but

> *"I didn't dare touch them in case something went wrong."*

One evaluator exclaimed

> *"I'm not curious as long at it works!"*

The evaluators stated that they hadn't had the time to look at the features due to workload, personal factors, etc.

Next the interviewer asked them about the possible sources of information on the customization features. None of the evaluators had discussed the features with collegues, nor had any read about them in the manual, neither did anyone recall anything from the training courses.

Finally the interviewer explained the customization features and asked the evaluators if they could think of any use for the screen colours. The answers were as follows:

6 were satisfied with the screen colours
5 suggested colour for marketing materials
3 related colours to familiar systems
1 suggested a change of screen colours: from blue/white to green/yellow
2 had no suggestions

Study 2: 720 mainframe users

This study comprised 720 users of a business application package running on a mainframe computer. The package supports basically the same functions as the IBM Assistant package in Study 1. The system is menu-driven but supports also execution of commands from the surrounding operating system (TSO). The users worked in the head office of the building society.

The users comprised 552 professionals dealing with mortgages, investments, etc. who had little or no training in computing. They were, however, generally experienced as end-users. The remaining 168 users were systems programmers and application programmers from the dp-department.

We had a systems programmer code a program that searched the 720 user profiles in the mainframe computer. For technical reasons we could only get access to the following three customization features: Use of colour, location of prompt line, and start-up command.

Use of colour

The system at hand accomodated 7 colours: white, blue, turqoise, green, yellow, red, and pink. These colours could be used for the following items on the screens: headings, normal text, highlighted text, field labels, input fields, messages, and options. The colour customization screen was accessible from the main menu by a single selection.

It turned out that only 203 of the 720 users were using colour terminals. 96 of the 203 users (48%) had changed the colour of at least one item (programmers 59%, professionals 43%). Below is listed the number of users having changed the colours.

Number of items changed	Number of users
1	7
2	15
3	13
4	16
5	13
6	20
7	12

The figures show that users do not just change one or two colours. Six is the most frequent number of changes and the median is 4 changes.

We also looked at the type of screen items where the users had changed the colour.

Screen item	Percentage of changes
Highlighted text	18%
Input fields	16%
Headings	15%
Normal text	14%
Field labels	14%
Options	12%
Messages	11%

It appears that the distribution is quite even. Not surprisingly, the most popular item is highlighted text. But the difference between the items is rather small with a factor of less than two 2 between the extremes.

In terms of colour, the customization resulted in the following selections (absolute numbers in decreasing order)

Colour	Number of selections
Yellow	76
Red	68
Pink	67
White	66
Turqoise	60
Blue	51
Green	40

The bright colours are favoured at the expense of the darker and less obtrusive colours.

Prompt line position

The system accomodated two positions for the command prompt line: in the top of the screen (default) and in the bottom. This customization feature was also accessible from the main menu.

This feature turned out to be used extremely rarely. Only 2 of the 720 users had changed the position from the default top position to the bottom position.

Start-up command

The user can specify a sequence of commands to be executed when the system starts up, e.g. to start in the editor with split screen. This customization feature was also accessible from the main menu. The commands used are TSO commands that require some dp-experience to, although some of them are also used regularly in the menu-driven business system, e.g., "end".

Of the 720 users, 59 had used this customization feature (8%); 15% of the programmers and only 6% of the professionals.

As to the number of commands in the start-up commands, the programmers used on average 4 commands, while the professionals only used 1.

Study 3: Interview with 27 users

This study was a follow-up to Study 2. We interviewed 20 of the professionals and 7 of the programmers in their workplace in order to get the rationales behind their customization practice. The professionals worked in the planning department bridging between end-users and the dp-department. The users were typically bank professionals with about 3 years of experience as end-users. The programmers were employees of the dp-department. As the responses from the two groups were very similar, we collapsed the data.

As none of the programmers were using colour terminals, the data here only comprise the 20 professionals.

Nine of the professionals had changed the colour (45%). The reasons why the colours had been used are listed below:

Fun, exciting	4
Taste	3
Eye problems	2
Nice change	2
Different	1

Ten of the users who had not changed the colours were satisfied and one did not care about colours. However, half of them had tried to "play around" with the colours.

Prompt line position

None of the users had changed the position of the prompt line (cfr. only 2 of 720 had changed in Study 2).

The reasons why they had not used it are listed below.

Habit	13
Not considered	10
Satisfied	9
Didn't know	4

Start-up command

Three of the professionals (15%) and one of the programmers (14%) had used this feature.

The four users had used the feature because they for the time being were working with a particular type of task and could therefore benefit from starting with a certain program in the system. Another seven users had used the feature previously.

The reasons why the remaining 23 users did not use the feature are listed below:

Task variation	16
Not considered	5
Didn't know	5

Function keys

In this study, contrasting study 2, we also asked them about their customization of the function keys. These keys are also customized on a display accessible from the main menu.

Twelve of the professionals had used function key customization (60%) and four of the programmers (55%). The work routine was the overall reason for using this feature.

The reasons why the remaining 11 users did not use the feature are listed below:

Satisfied	5
Habit	3
Task variation	3

Sources of information

Finally, we asked them about the sources of information regarding the use of customization features. Hardly no one had looked in the manual, a few had discussed them with collegues. None of the users recalled anything about customization features from the training courses.

We also asked them if they found the features easy to use. In general the answer was yes. This applied also to the features they were not using.

3. Conclusions

This study is based on users from only one business organisation employing software and hardware from only one computer manufacturer. The results should therefore be interpreted with caution.

The study shows that almost all experienced users apply customization features; half of them applied one or more customization feature at the time of the investigation, while the other half had tried used them before. Contrasting this, none of the novices had used the features and only one knew about them.

Satisficing seems to be the overall reason for not changing the systems. Another reasons is lack of knowledge about the features.

Overall two types of changes in the systems are made. Firstly the appearance of the system such as screen colour, where changes are made due to visual handicaps, personal preferences or even fun. Secondly changes are made that are directly related to the users' tasks and the working routine, such as function keys and start-up command. Programmers seem to make a few more changes than professionals.

4. References

Brooks A. and C. Thorburn: User-driven adaptive behaviour, a comparative analysis and an inductive analysis. In: D M Jones & R Winder (eds): People and Computers IV. Cambridge Univ. Press, pp. 237-255, 1988.

Greenberg, S. and I.H. Witten: Adaptive interfaces - a question of viability. Behaviour and Information Technology, vol. 4, pp. 31-45, 1985.

Innocent, P.R.: Towards self-adaptive interface systems. International Journal of Man-Machine Studies, vol. 16, pp. 287-299, 1982.

Mason, M.V.: Adaptive command prompting in an on-line documentation system. International Journal of Man-Machine Studies, vol. 25, pp. 33-51, 1986.

Newman, I.A.: Personalized interfaces to computer systems. Proc. Eurocomp 78, Wembley, London, 1978.

Rosson, M.B.: Effects of Experience on Learning, Using, and Evaluating a Text Editor. Human Factors, vol. 26, pp. 463-475, 1984.

Human–Computer Interaction – INTERACT '90
D. Diaper et al. (Editors)
Elsevier Science Publishers B.V. (North-Holland)

INFERRING TASK STRUCTURES FROM INTERACTION PROTOCOLS

Franz SCHIELE & H. Ulrich HOPPE

GMD - Integrated Information and Publication Systems Institute (IPSI)
Dolivostr. 15, D–6100 Darmstadt, FRG
Email: schiele@darmstadt.gmd.dbp.de

Powerful multi-purpose software may be used for an unforeseeable variety of tasks. To redesign, or to dynamically adapt such systems to the users' specific task requirements, new task structures must be inferred from the users' actual use of the system. An inductive method for inferring task schemata from protocols of user input has been explored, using different heuristics to filter out implausible task structures. An empirical study in the domain of file-handling tasks provides evidence for its ability to acquire meaningful task schemata.

1. INTRODUCTION

Task analyses are an essential prerequisite for designing user interfaces which meet the users' needs. However, users differ as to how they go about performing tasks; their expertise differs and changes over time, and so does the range of tasks for which they use a system, particularly in the case of powerful, multi-purpose software. Ideally, this situation would require repeated task analyses and re-design of systems, and it has motivated much of the research on adaptivity and individualized tailoring of user interfaces. For intelligent user interfaces based on user and task models, the same basic problem has to be solved: to respond adequately to different individual needs and to changing task requirements of users. User-specific task models must be updated dynamically, and it is most desirable that this knowledge acquisition process be performed to a large extent by the system itself.

Hoppe & Plötzner [1] developed a method for inferring task structures from protocols of user actions. The method works inductively by searching protocols of low-level tasks for sequences (compositions) which are likely to correspond to meaningful procedures, and then generalizing them to operational task schemata in the form of grammar rules. While this method grew out of research on task-oriented user support in intelligent user interfaces, it may potentially be used for the intelligent analysis of task performance for a variety of purposes, including e.g. usability evaluations.

In the work presented here, an empirical study was carried out with two aims: a) to evaluate more systematically the performance of the inductive learning mechanism, which had previously only been tested informally, and b) to explore the usefulness of additional heuristics for increasing its precision in learning relevant task schemata.

2. LEARNING OPERATIONAL SCHEMATA

Different methods for automatically acquiring operational schemata, or macros, have been developed as extensions of problem solving or planning architectures. Macro learning in the robot planner STRIPS [2] is an early example of such an approach. More recent suggestions for macro learning in a problem solving framework have been made e.g. by Korf [3], Minton [4], or Iba [5]. From a more general perspective, macro learning can be seen as a special case of *knowledge compilation*. In a production system architecture, this coincides with the chunking of action patterns and the discrimination of applicability conditions [6,7].

The different approaches to macro learning can be further subdivided into those based on an analysis of general characteristics of a given problem space and those relying on given problem solving episodes. Korf's method [3], which uses the concept of operator decomposability for an a priori analysis of the problem space, is an example of the first category, whereas the other methods mentioned are *inductive* in that the selection of examples is based on experience in the form of problem solving protocols. Such protocols may be generated automatically or by humans.

A fundamental problem of inductive macro learning is the selection of operator sequences which are promising candidates for being transformed into macros. Although the transformation step usually involves generalization over parameters, resulting macros may still be too specific to shorten the solution path under sufficiently general conditions. This, however, is required to outweigh the increase in the branching factor of the search tree which ensues from introducing macros. Several heuristics for the extraction of promising subsequences from problem solving protocols have been proposed to overcome this problem: In Minton's approach [4], the selection of macros is based either on the empirical criterion of *frequency*, or on a comparison of estimated and actual progress which favours "non-obvious" solutions. Progress towards the final goal is measured by an evaluation function. Iba [5] introduces a "peak-to-peak" heuristic which is also based on an evaluation function.

Inductive approaches to macro learning would appear to be well-suited for the acquisition of *individualized* task knowledge in intelligent user interfaces, since they rely on empirical observations. But human-computer interaction has specific characteristics which differ from those of automatic problem solving. In the typical puzzle solving applications, we can assume that there is *one* final goal and potentially a number of derived subgoals. This allows to define an evaluation function which measures the distance between any given state and the goal state. But with multi-purpose software tools, users may pursue many different goals. Often, we do not even have practical means to enumerate all potential goals nor could we control them in the task environment. This precludes the use of heuristics for the selection of macro candidates which are based on an evaluation function that measures progress towards a final goal. Applicable criteria include e.g. the frequency of subsequences in action protocols and parameter constraints between the component actions. The next section will describe such an approach in more detail.

Our aim is to develop methods for assessing task structures and reasoning about them on a *symbolic level*. In order to explore the characteristics and viability of such an approach, we have concentrated on purely symbolic processing mechanisms. This does not mean that we deny the usefulness of numerical performance measures, particularly time measurements, for task analysis in general (cf. [8]). Within the paradigm of symbolic information processing, we have drawn on a core of syntactic processing mechanisms in the sense of "general weak methods".

In our approach to learning task schemata from action protocols, we have been influenced by Lewis' EXPL system [9]. EXPL learns "causal" links between input actions and system responses from demonstration sequences. The learning material is provided in an abstract representation and is only treated syntactically. Several heuristics are used in order to detect causal links between different component patterns. A central one is the *identity heuristic* which establishes links between components sharing identical elements, e.g. if an argument of a command also appears in a system response or in another argument. EXPL simulates the construction of explanations by a human learner. In the situation we have to deal with, the machine is the learner, and the learning material is provided as a list of the user's input actions. We look for regularities in this material in order to induce meaningful operational schemata. It turns out that heuristics similar to those in EXPL can be used in this situation.

3. TASK INDUCTION

A method for the inductive acquisition of operational task schemata from protocols of user actions has been developed by Hoppe & Plötzner [1]. The method is based on frequency analysis as the primary criterion for the extraction of macro candidates from a session protocol. It also comprises a generalization mechanism as well as a component for restructuring the set of acquired task schemata in order to account for subsumption and hierarchical dependencies.

We have to distinguish between two different representations in the knowledge acquisition process: the source representation of the learning material and the target representation of the newly acquired knowledge. In our case, both are consistent with the representations used in *Task-Oriented Parsing* (TOP), a method which performs plan recognition and automatic plan completion and can be used as an "intelligent" component of interactive user interfaces [1,10]. The task instances in the learning material (task protocol) are represented as lists of attribute/value pairs. The operational task schemata, or plans, to be acquired in the task induction process are represented as attribute grammar rules, i.e. in the format used by the Task-Oriented Parser.

Given a certain subsequence of the transcript, the *generalization mechanism* transforms the example into a grammar rule by establishing constraints between attributes with identical values. Identity constraints between attributes are expressed by equal names and imply a unification of the respective attribute values. Sometimes new attribute names have to be introduced in order to avoid constraints between identical attribute names of the component tasks which do not share identical values in the source pattern. Figure 1 gives an example of such a generalization step.

```
Command Sequence:

10> cp mbox mbox.old                 copy
11> cat mbox letter > temp  ┐
12> rm mbox                 ├        append
13> mv temp mbox            ┘
14> rm letter                        delete

        TOP ↓

Task Protocol (source representation):

[ [type, copy], [source, mbox], [target, mbox.old] ]
[ [type, append], [source, letter], [target, mbox] ]
[ [type, delete], [file, letter] ]

        Generalization ↓

Generated Rule (target representation):

copy&append&delete [source, target, source2]
::=
sequence-of(  copy    [source -> source,
                       target -> target ],
              append  [source -> source2 ,
                       target -> source],
              delete  [file -> source2 ] )
```

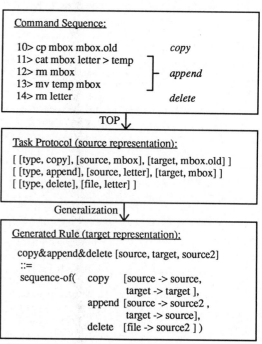

Figure 1: An example of the generalization mechanism

The example is taken from the domain of file handling with the UNIX operating system. The initial command sequence is interpreted as a sequential composition of the tasks *copy*, *append*, and *delete*. (Here, the task-oriented parser has interpreted commands 11-13 as an *append* task, based on a known composition rule.) A new rule describing the composition of these three tasks with attributes *source, target,* and the newly introduced attribute *source2* is generated. The *internal attributes* of the component tasks are mapped onto these *external attributes*. Thus, identity constraints are established, here e.g. between the *source* of the *copy* and the *target* of the *append* and between the *source* of *append* and the *file* which is *deleted.*

In order to be selected, a sequence has to appear with a certain frequency in the task protocol. The required frequency can be specified either as an absolute value or relative to the length of the protocol. The selection algorithm is parsimonious in that it only extracts *maximal sequences* which comply with the frequency criterion. Maximal sequences are those which cannot be enlarged without violating the frequency criterion. Subsequences are only considered as candidates for the introduction of hierarchically nested task structures if they also appear independently of the maximal pattern they are embedded in.

The initial frequency analysis is performed on the level of task types, irrespective of the instantiation of the other task attributes. After the generalization step, different instances of sequences of identical task types may produce rules with different attribute constraints. The *restructuring mechanism* first orders each class of rules with identical type sequences according to their generality. In terms of constraints, a rule A is more general than a rule A' (or: A *subsumes* A') if the constraints of A form a subset of the constraints of A'. This relation '*subsumes*' induces a *partial ordering* within each class. Only the maxima with respect to this ordering are further considered (principle of *most general representatives*). A similar subsumption analysis on substructures of tasks is performed when hierarchically nested task-subtask structures are introduced (cf. [1]). The restructuring component serves as a filter which reduces the number of new rules. For each of the rules which passes this filter, the frequency criterion is again checked through a comparison with the entire set of initially constructed rules. Here, attribute constraints are taken into account.

The method as described so far is generally applicable to any protocol comprising task descriptions in the required format of lists of attribute/value pairs. It is implemented in IF/Prolog and runs on SUN 3 or 4 workstations. The implementation is efficient enough to analyze protocols of a hundred commands in less than one minute. This makes online applications possible.The costliest step is the selection of maximal sequences from the task protocol according to the frequency criterion. It involves comparisons of single task instances with respect to the identity of the *type* attribute. Since we can assume the maximum length of potential sequences to be independent of the length of the protocol, the number of comparisons required is at most quadratic in the length of the protocol.

The method was initially tested with UNIX protocols. Another application was macro detection for an eight puzzle problem solver. In both cases, informal analyses suggested that the frequency criterion was not selective enough. Therefore other filters have been added in the form of different *selection heuristics*. The basic concept employed in the formulation of these heuristics is the notion of constraints between attributes, which is an explicit feature of the target representation. As constraints in the rules reflect identity links in the source representation, this principle is comparable to Lewis' *identity heuristic* (see previous section).

Motivated by the observation that not all attribute constraints seem to be equally relevant, we have introduced the notion of *essential attributes*. An attribute is defined to be essential if it denotes a parameter which is necessary to specify the effect of the task in a given environment. For instance, in our task representation of the UNIX '*rm*' (delete-file) command we would declare the filename *(file)* to be essential, but not the directory *(dir)*. However, if this task appears in combination with other operations which involve changes of the directory as essential parameters, the directory attribute has to be considered as essential as well. Therefore, attributes are defined to be essential for a composite task if they are essential for at least one of the components.

The basic notions of attribute constraints and essential attributes, which are operationalized as specific predicates, are the building blocks for the definition of a variety of heuristics. A minimal amount of semantic modeling is required for the definition of the essential attributes of elementary tasks. A selection heuristic is specified as a separate module and simply added to the previously described components of the inductive mechanism without further modification.

4. EVALUATION

4.1 Data Collection

In order to assess the performance of the learning mechanism and the contribution of different heuristics to the selection of plausible candidates for new task compositions, comprehensive interaction protocols were collected from subjects who performed a variety of file-handling tasks.

This was done in a simulated UNIX environment (implemented in Prolog) which comprised 13 basic commands for performing operations on files and directories. Using this simulation enabled us to have immediate access to environment parameters which do not appear in the user input but which are part of the representation of commands as elementary tasks (e.g. the current directory).

Twelve subjects, ranging from regular to sporadic users of UNIX, took part in the study. They had to transform a file-system from a given initial state into a specified goal state. This involved a number of independent tasks, each of which required the execution of several commands. Seven such self-contained task concepts occured at least twice in the overall task, although in different contexts and with different parameters (filenames, etc.), and thus represented possible candidates for operational task schemata. Figure 2 gives an example of such a task, using a STRIPS-like notation where the goal is given in terms of add- and delete-lists.

Initial State:		file(F1), file(F2), cont(F1,C1), cont(F2,C2).
Goal State:	ADD:	file(F3), cont(F3,C1), cont(F1,C1+C2).
	DEL:	file(F2), cont(F1,C1).

Figure 2: The task concept of *backup-append-delete*

This task requires a backup file F3 to be created with the same content as an existing file F1, while the content of another existing file F2 is to be appended to F1, whereupon F2 is to be deleted. At least three UNIX commands (*cp, cat, rm*) are necessary and different operationalizations are possible. Another example is the transposition of file contents, which also requires at least three commands and allows for different operationalizations.

Subjects were given general instructions describing the overall task and the commands available in the simulation. After establishing that they were familiar with these commands, they received a detailed description of a first set of tasks which, when completed, was followed by a second and third set. Since we were interested in heterogeneous interaction protocols reflecting variation in goal decomposition and methods, the task descriptions were devised in such a way as to avoid direct procedural instructions on how to perform the tasks. They consisted of:

a) a description of the goal state in terms of directory contents as well as file contents, and
b) a description of the differences in the goal state as compared to the initial state.

The latter was given to focus the subjects' attention on the state changes they had to bring about. To compensate for possible order effects that might occur due to subjects proceeding through the list of state changes in a top-down fashion, half the subjects received an alternative version of this list with a different order of items.

All data collection was done within the UNIX simulation. The data recorded included: the initial and final state of the file system; a protocol of the executed commands; and a transcript of the user input which served as a documentation of the session. The command protocols were parsed by the TOP interpreter to convert them into protocols of elementary tasks, which were the input to the learning mechanism.

4.2 Analysis and Results

Several heuristics had been devised for incorporation into the learning mechanism. All of them search for identical attribute values among the tasks contained in the sequences found according to the basic criteria described above. The set of heuristics explored in this study was the following:

- Heuristic 1 requires each component task in a candidate sequence to have at least one identity constraint with some other task in the sequence, and thus checks what could be called the *connectedness* of a task composition.
- Heuristic 2 reflects the observation that in self-contained task compositions, the last task is often to a high degree determined by the immediately preceding tasks, i.e. many of its attributes show identity constraints with attributes of these. This heuristic requires that half of the attributes of the last task must have identity constraints with preceding ones.
- Heuristic 3 is a more restrictive version of Heuristic 1: in addition to the identity constraint required for each task in the sequence, the respective attributes showing these constraints must be in the total set of *essential attributes* (see above) of all the tasks in the sequence.
- Likewise, Heuristic 4 is derived from Heuristic 2: half of the *essential attributes* of the last task in the sequence must have identity constraints with preceding tasks.
- Finally, Heuristic 5 is a combination of Heuristics 3 and 4, and thus represents the most restrictive one in this set.

Since the emphasis in constructing the overall task was on including a variety of different tasks, only few repetitions of variants of these tasks could be included if the sessions were not to become too tedious. (Even so, completion time ranged from 30 to 60 minutes among our subjects). Consequently, the minimal frequency criterion of 2 was chosen for the learning mechanism, i.e. task sequences had to occur at least twice in the protocol for them to be considered as candidates for composition rules. Otherwise, learning of more complex task composition rules which cover operationalizations for such task concepts as described above would have been impossible.

The status of output-oriented commands (e.g. *'ls'*, *'pwd'*) for the learning of composition rules is ambivalent. Since they occur quite irregularly (being rather more determined by imponderable factors such as the users' attention, familiarity with the system, etc. than by the semantics of task procedures), it seems not desirable to incorporate them into composition rules which ought to have some degree of generality. Moreover, they may have an undesirable impact on the learning of task composition rules in the first place: when segmenting a task protocol interspersed with output-oriented elementary tasks according to the frequency criterion, many sequences which include only small parts of task procedures are likely to be found. On the other hand, these commands often represent 'natural' delimiters between (sub-)tasks, and ignoring them in the segmentation of a task protocol may also lead to adverse results in some cases. Their undesirable effects seem to prevail particularly when the data available is limited and the efficacy of empirical filters therefore low. In our case they were rather reinforced by additional factors due to the task setting. Therefore output-oriented commands/elementary tasks were ignored when the protocols were processed by the learning mechanism.

To assess the performance of the learning mechanism in finding useful generalizations of task compositions, we used the following criteria for judging the relevance of the composition rules learnt: A composition rule is considered relevant with respect to a self-contained task concept T, if

a) it achieves all goal conditions of T, i.e. if it operationalizes T as a whole, or
b) it achieves a subset of the goal conditions of T with more than one effective command (*'cd'* is non-effective, since it does not affect the file-system).

In the first case, an additional condition was that rules were not to cover more than one task. In both cases it was required that rules achieve the respective goal conditions by necessity, i.e. that they are not over-general, but have the appropriate constraints.

subject	coms	coms (- output)	rules	relevant rules	coverage (indiv. r.)	coverage (other r.)
1	90	52	4	4	46%	31%
2	130	82	8	4	22%	32%
3	79	57	3	2	21%	46%
4	107	65	5	3	37%	35%
5	120	75	8	6	51%	39%
6	131	74	5	2	16%	54%
7	59	44	5	2	23%	50%
8	124	75	5	2	16%	55%
9	91	47	3	2	17%	43%
10	100	65	4	3	46%	28%
11	118	70	4	0	0%	51%
12	144	72	6	2	24%	42%
mean:	108	65	5	2.7	27%	42%

Table 1

Table 1 shows various measures which characterize the general performance of the basic learning mechanism (no additional heuristics employed) with respect to the twelve protocols obtained.

The second and third column show the number of commands per session, including vs. excluding output-oriented commands. Due to the demands of the task (subjects had to manipulate files and directories they were unfamiliar with and had to acquire their goals from compact declarative task descriptions), the proportion of output-oriented commands which served the subjects' orientation and the verification of the effect of operations is presumably higher than would normally be the case.

The fourth and fifth column of Table 1 show the number of task composition rules learnt from each protocol (without output-oriented commands) and the respective number of rules which were judged to be relevant. There is one extreme case (subject 11), where none of the rules acquired satisfied our relevance criteria; but one of the rules was in fact a composition of two task sequences, each of which corresponded to a complete operationalization of a self-contained task concept. Thus, it is very likely that a larger empirical basis with more varied task sequencing would have led to the acquisition of at least two complex task schemata in this case.

From a total number of 60 composition rules, 32 were relevant. The majority of rejected rules failed on the relevance criterion which required rules to contain more than one effective elementary task/command. Of the relevant rules, 23 were unique. Of these, 15 rules (which included 2 hierarchical ones), represented complete operationalizations of task concepts, including at least one for each of the seven concepts mentioned above. 8 rules represented partial operationalizations of task concepts, 5 of which corresponded to repetitive procedures (e.g. *delete, delete, delete*). The average number of component tasks (either elementary or composite) comprised in the 23 composition rules was 2.8.

To see how much of a protocol can be accounted for by the relevant composition rules learnt from that same protocol, each was parsed by the TOP interpreter using exactly these rules. Column 6 (coverage by individual rules) shows the percentage of elementary tasks which are covered by these rules, i.e. which are interpreted as elements of composite tasks. As one would expect, there is a positive correlation between the coverage of the protocol and the respective number of relevant rules; but, of course, other factors such as the length of the respective rules (number of components), their "universality" (range of applicability), and also the total length of the protocol (see e.g. subject 2) co-determine this measure.

In addition to the coverage of protocols by the individual rules, each protocol was parsed using the complement of the set of individual rules in the total set of 23 unique composition rules, i.e. each protocol was parsed with those rules only which were <u>not</u> acquired from that same protocol. The resulting coverage (by "other" rules) is given in the rightmost column of Table 1. An inverse relation can be observed between coverage by individual rules and coverage by "other" rules. There are several reasons for this: Individual coverage is mainly determined by the number of relevant rules acquired, and these in turn are largely due to the subjects' consistent or inconsistent use of methods for similar (sub-) tasks. Thus, since subjects with low individual coverage of their protocol are likely to have been inconsistent in their use of methods, the chance for various "other" rules to match with procedures used by these subjects was high, especially considering that the number of these "other" rules used for parsing the protocols was between 17 and 23, depending on the respective number of individual rules. This phenomenon also reflects the fact that rules are related to tasks and not just representations of idiosyncratic command sequences. Conversely, subjects/protocols with high individual coverage show low coverage by 'other' rules. Since these subjects must have been rather consistent in their use of methods, chances for "other" rules to cover sizeable parts of their protocols were low. This expresses another aspect of rules: they capture individualized methods or procedures.

The preceding results refer to the performance of the basic learning mechanism, which defines the baseline as to the number of task schemata acquired. The heuristics we explored were devised to filter out composition rules which are not relevant according to the criteria we used, while preserving the relevant ones. Table 2 describes their effectiveness in achieving this. The top row shows the percentage of relevant rules among all composition rules accepted by the respective heuristic (*precision*). The bottom row (*loss*) gives the percentage of relevant rules filtered out by Heuristics 1 to 5, i.e. the price that is paid for being more precise.

Heuristic	none	1	2	3	4	5
precision	53%	55%	58%	56%	60%	66%
loss		0%	6%	13%	16%	16%

Table 2

The loss is mainly caused by employing the notion of *essential attributes* in Heuristics 3, 4, and 5. However, all the rules lost by applying any of the heuristics represent repetitive partial operationalizations of task concepts (e.g. *delete, delete, delete*). Also, a closer look at these rules shows that half of them are difficult to interpret as meaningful self-contained macro operations. This qualifies the significance of the observed loss and rather indicates that the second condition of our a priori relevance criterion may not be specific enough.

Heuristic 1, which checks the *connectedness* of task schemata in terms of identity constraints between attributes of component tasks, achieves only a slight improvement in precision as compared to the baseline. Roughly the same holds if these identity constraints occur with *essential attributes*, as is the case with Heuristic 3. More successful are Heuristics 2 and 4, both of which check the proportion of attributes/essential attributes in the last component task which have identity constraints with preceding ones. Thus, the principle of considering the *degrees of freedom* for the attribute values of the last component task appears to be a valuable heuristic. As can be seen from the result for Heuristic 5 (i.e. 4 combined with 3), its power can be increased by combining it with a check for connectedness: This heuristic achieved the highest precision – at no further cost in terms of loss. (A similar, though less strong effect could be observed for the analogous combination of Heuristics 2 and 1 which yielded a precison of 60% while keeping the loss at 6%.)

5. CONCLUSIONS

The results of this study indicate that the inductive learning mechanism, despite its basically syntactic nature, does acquire meaningful task schemata which represent procedures users actually apply in their task performance, and which can capture user-specific methods. Also, some of the additional heuristics explored proved to be useful for filtering out schemata which are unlikely to correspond to (sub-) tasks in the users' decomposition of higher-level tasks. With respect to the acquisition of user-specific task schemata we can expect that a larger empirical basis than was available here would lead to an increased coverage of user actions. On the plausible assumption that users do exhibit routine methods in their performance of tasks, the cost/benefit relation of the method (in terms of the analytical effort required and the resulting task schemata as well as the size of the ensuing knowledge base) appears to be particularly favourable for individualized approaches to user support.

REFERENCES

[1] Hoppe, H.U. & Plötzner, R. (1989). Inductive Methods for Acquiring Task Knowledge in Adaptive Systems. GMD-Arbeitspapier No 392 (GMD: Birlinghoven).

[2] Fikes, R.; Hart, P. & Nilsson, N. (1972). Learning and executing generalized robot plans. Artificial Intelligence, 3, 251-288.

[3] Korf, R.E. (1985). Learning to Solve Problems by Searching for Macro Operators. Pitman: Boston.

[4] Minton, S. (1985). Selectively generalizing plans for problem solving. In Proc. of 9th IJCAI, 596-599. Morgan-Kaufmann: St. Paul.

[5] Iba, G.A. (1989). A heuristic approach to the discovery of macro operators. Machine Learning, 3, 285-317.

[6] Laird, J.E.; Rosenbloom, P.S. & Newell, A. (1986). Chunking in SOAR: The anatomy of a general learning mechanism. Machine Learning, 1, 11-46.

[7] Langley, P. (1985). Learning to search: From weak methods to domain-specific heuristics. Cognitive Science, 9, 217-260.

[8] Ackermann, D. (1987). Handlungsspielraum, Mentale Repräsentation und Handlungsregulation am Beispiel der Mensch-Computer-Interaktion. PhD Thesis (Univ. of Bern)

[9] Lewis, C. (1988). Why and how to learn why: Analysis-based generalization of procedures. Cognitive Science, 12, 211-256.

[10] Hoppe, H.U. (1988). Task-oriented parsing - a diagnostic method to be used by adaptive systems. In Proc. of CHI' 88, 241-247. ACM: Washington.

Human–Computer Interaction – INTERACT '90
D. Diaper et al. (Editors)
Elsevier Science Publishers B.V. (North-Holland)

AN ADAPTIVE SYSTEM DEVELOPER'S TOOL-KIT

David Benyon*, Dianne Murray$ and Frances Jennings*

* PACIS research group, Computing Department, Open University, Milton Keynes MK7 6AA, U.K.
$Department Business Computing, The City University, Northampton Square, London EC1V 0HB, U.K.

Adaptive systems share some characteristics with other knowledge-based systems, but differ in other important respects. In particular, adaptive systems require a comprehensive model of the system users and have to make inferences not just about the domain, but also about the users' knowledge of the domain. This paper describes the design of a User Modelling Shell - a system designed to meet the needs of adaptive system developers. The paper outlines the architecture of the system and the reasons for the chosen design and illustrates these principles with examples from an application of the system.

1. INTRODUCTION

An Adaptive System may be defined as a knowledge-based system which automatically alters aspects of the system functionality and interface in order to accommodate the differing preferences and requirements of individual system users. In order to do this, an adaptive system must possess models of each individual or class of system user and must relate the contents of this model to some theory of interaction.

Adaptive systems share many characteristics with all knowledge-based systems, but they also possess their own, particular features. Firstly, an adaptive system must possess an explicit and comprehensive model of the system's users. Such a model has been termed an Embedded User Model (EUM) by Murray [1]. This is a model of the classes, or stereotypes of users and/or of each individual user of the system which is embedded in the system in a form suitable for the adaptive system to access. The explicit nature of the user model is vital. Systems which adapt but do not explicitly model the characteristics of the users are not considered adaptive systems in this context.

Secondly, adaptive systems must not only make inferences about the domain, they must also make inferences about the users' knowledge of the domain. Hence adaptive systems must be capable of representing knowledge of the domain and of acquiring and representing the user's knowledge of the domain. Such inferences can only be made by monitoring and evaluating aspects of the interaction between users and the target system.

These two features of adaptive systems have lead us to believe that a general-purpose knowledge engineering environment is insufficient for developing adaptive systems [2]. A software tool-kit aimed specifically at developers of adaptive systems is required. This tool-kit is known as a User Modelling Shell (UMS).

This paper describes the implementation of a UMS and its use in the development of an exemplar and test-bed adaptive system. The exemplar system is in information retrieval, using a mail-order shopping catalogue as the domain. This system has a single task - select items from the catalogue which some criteria - and five representative interfaces; a command interface, a menu interface, a question and answer interface, a mouse and button interface, and an iconic interface. Like the UMS, the exemplar system has been implemented in KEE on a SUN workstation.

This work represents the first year of a two year project called Adaptive Systems and User Modelling Tools. We are currently using the adaptive system in a number of experiments which are aimed at identifying and isolating cognitive characteristics of users which are real predictors of user performance on the various interfaces. The data from these experiments feed into the enhancement of both the adaptive system and the UMS. Further details of the project, the UMS and the exemplar system can be obtained directly from the authors and documentation is currently being prepared.

2. OVERVIEW

As part of a general trend in the development of computer aided software engineering (CASE) tools, attention has been focussed on the needs of interface designers and the development of design environments. There has also been considerable interest in the development of User Interface Management Systems (UIMS). In common with other authors we separate the primarily run-time concerns of UIMS from the development orientation of the design environment. The User Modelling Shell described here is a designer's tool-kit which tailors the general-purpose nature of KEE to the specific needs of an adaptive system developer and which exploits the facilities of KEE at run-time.

The UMS is similar to the concept of an expert system shell. During the development phase of building an adaptive system, the UMS has to play two separate but related roles. In the first instance the developer employs the UMS to specify the characteristics of the target adaptive system and its users, their interaction and the rules which will guide the inferencing and adaptations which are to take place. These features are represented in the adaptive system's knowledge-base. Once the structure of a particular adaptive system has been established, the developer uses the UMS to specify the values of relevant attributes of individual or classes of user and the inferences which are to be made from these values. The user interacts directly with the target system which exploits its knowledge of users and the domain in order to adapt aspects of the interaction in accordance with the specified rules. At present, the designer implements the I/O format and dialogue directly in the target system. In the future we see these aspects as being specified through the UMS. The interaction of the UMS with an adaptive system is illustrated schematically in Figure 1.

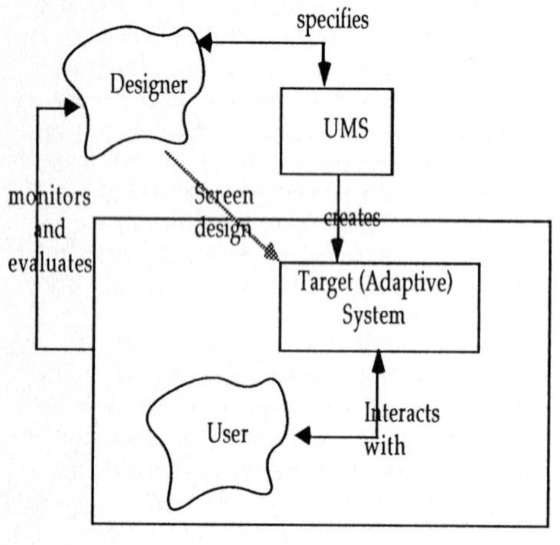

Figure 1 Relationship between the UMS and an adaptive system

The focus of this paper is to elaborate the architecture of a UMS and to show why this architecture is necessary by illustrating the principles in the context of the exemplar system. The rationale for adaptive systems has been well rehearsed previously [3], [4]. However, an analysis of these experiences led us ([2], [5]) to produce an outline architecture for an adaptive system and hence for the UMS itself. An adaptive system has three main components; the application, task or *Domain* model, the *Embedded User Model* and the *Rule-base*. These are considered individually below.

There are other components of adaptive systems which do not concern us and hence are not considered in detail here. For example, some systems require a representation of the teaching strategy to be employed and for a model of an expert's goal-seeking strategy. Other systems require the provision of a learning environment. Our interest is with intermediate rather than novice computer users and we do not attempt to model and infer user goals. These are two aspects which we expect to be added to the UMS in the future.

3 DOMAIN MODEL

The Domain model describes the structure and functioning of the domain of the target (adaptive) system. The domain model has to fulfil three related purposes. Firstly, the system designer uses the model to specify the structure and functionality of the domain. Secondly, this specification has to be instantiated in the target system as a knowledge-base. Thirdly, the domain model provides the basis of an 'overlay' model which is used as a the representation of the user's knowledge of the domain. This is stored in the user model (see Section 4). The domain model, therefore, has to be simple enough to be easily specifiable and implementable, yet detailed enough to provide the basis for the adaptations which we are seeking.

We examined a number of domain modelling techniques (see [3] for a discussion of this) before settling on a three-level model which appears to provide an appropriate degree of detail for our purposes. We represent the domain in terms of the task(s) which it supports, the logical functions and related concepts which it embodies and the physical functions and concepts which are required in order to carry out the logical functions. The logical/physical distinction is one which is used in many areas of computer science; for example, in database design [6] structured systems design [7] and UIMS design (the presentation and abstraction components of Coutaz's PAC system [8]) Similarities can also be seen with Rasmussen's means-end analysis [9] and the original four levels of Moran's Command Language Grammar[10].

External to the system is the Task level which corresponds to the external level of Moran's ETIT technique [11] and to the task space, or goal space described by Payne [12]. The task level details the task(s) and concept(s) which the system is capable of achieving and is described in terms that the user can understand. For example, the exemplar system has the single task of displaying all the items from an on-line shopping catalogue which meet some specified criteria of cost, size and colour.

In order to complete the task, the system has to perform a number of logical functions which in turn require the use of a number of logical concepts. This logical level of the domain model describes the system functions and concepts which are strictly necessary to complete the task(s). Some of these are user functions and concepts - e.g. the user must enter the name of an item from the catalogue and its attributes expressed in terms of cost, size and colour - and some are system functions and concepts - e.g. the system has to open the 'catalogue'. Thus, in this case, the user has to understand the concepts of 'item', 'size', 'cost', and 'colour' and the user function of 'entering' these to the system in order to make any use of it at all. The user must also understand, to some extent, what the necessary system functions and concepts are. (In this case the concept of a catalogue, or file and the function of opening)

In order to enact these logical functions, the system needs to describe physical interactions - the physical level of the domain model. The system needs to describe the logical functions in terms of physical functions (keystrokes, mouse actions, command syntax etc.) and these may reference physical concepts (e.g. the concepts embodied by the mouse buttons). A coherent set of physical functions and concepts in known as an *interface*. For example, using a command interface, the user has to physically type in the name of an item which is in the catalogue followed by the three parameters cost, size and colour. This input must be enclosed in parentheses and be terminated by pressing the <enter> key. The user has to understand this physical function and the physical concept of an <enter> key. This physical model of the domain clearly has a mapping to the logical model and the complexity of this mapping may be a good metric of the complexity of the system. There is no guarantee that the physical-logical mapping is one-to-one, and indeed frequently it is not.

The three levels of description of the domain model are shown in Figure 2. Notice how the user interacts only at the physical level, but has to try and understand the logical functions and concepts through this physical manifestation. This is similar to the view of Norman [13] who describes the 'gulfs' of execution and evaluation in his seven stage model of interaction. The user has to understand the (physical) output and interpret that in logical terms in order to understand the logical functions and concepts which underlie the system.

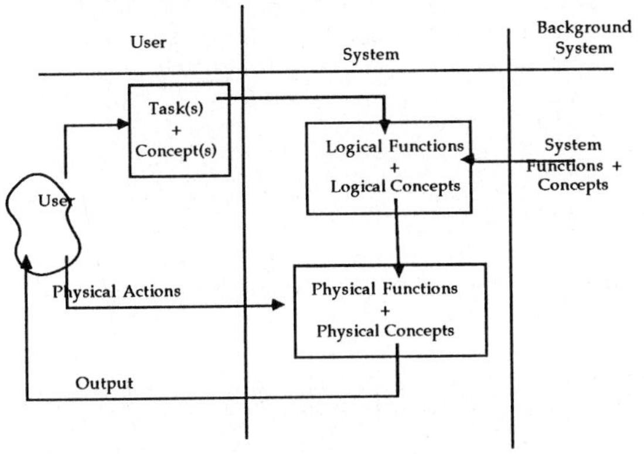

Figure 2 The three descriptions of the domain model - task, logical and physical

Each concept and function at the logical and physical levels of the domain model is represented as a KEE object. The intra- and inter-level mappings between the concepts and functions are represented as relationships between the objects. As with all aspects of the UMS, the domain model is constantly under review and results from the experiments feed back into its design.

4 EMBEDDED USER MODEL

The embedded user model is a KEE knowledge-base which contains information about users which will have a bearing on the most suitable combinations of functions and concepts (logical and/or physical) to present to a user in order to perform a task. The user model may also determine which subset of the full range of tasks the user will have access to. The embedded user model is in fact a family of user models. There is one instance of the user model for each user of the system. In any particular adaptive system there may be anything from a single model for all users of the system to a model for each individual user. Following Murray [5], we can identify three components in the user model - a personal profile, a cognitive model and a student model.

The personal profile contains information such as the job, needs and interests of the users, their experience with other systems, their age, sex and other general, domain-independent characteristics. The cognitive model contains information about users' personality, learning strategy and cognitive style. The student model contains information about a user's level of understanding of the concepts and functions in the adaptive system they are using.

Each user (individual or class) is represented in the adaptive system as a KEE object. The attributes are represented as slots in the objects and hence all members of that class of user automatically inherit all the attributes of the class. The facilities of KEE and the concept of inheritance which it offers is particularly appropriate for the user model. Initially, the designer specifies the characteristics of classes, or stereotypes [14] of user using the UMS. For example in the exemplar system there is a class of user characterised by having a high spatial ability. Standard interactions are established for stereotypes of user. When individuals use the target system, they are allocated to one or more stereotypes on the basis of the knowledge which the system has acquired about the user (either by questioning the user, or by inferring characteristics from the interaction). The individual then becomes a member of that class and inherits the characteristics of the class. Conflicting classifications can be handled through the conflict resolution mechanisms provided by KEE. As the system learns more about the user, so the user model becomes increasingly individual.

One of the most important aspects here is that the model of each user is explicit and can be displayed and edited if necessary. This facility is vital both in respect of the privacy of individuals and their rights under data protection legislation, and in order to maintain the accuracy of the model. However, as yet the user models are still very simple, consisting of only five cognitive and three personal profile attributes.

The relationship between the user profile and the cognitive user model is complex and is still under experimental investigation. We recognise that considerable work needs to be done in this area in order to determine the relationship between cognitive characteristics and interaction and indeed much of our experimental work is orientated to this end. However, we believe that adaptations to individual differences in cognitive characteristics are vital to the effectiveness of user-system interactions and that an explicit and separable cognitive model of users is required. In the first series of experiments we are testing for correlations between spatial ability (following Vicente and Williges [15]), verbal ability, short-term memory, logical- intuitiveness and field-dependence and individual performance on the five interfaces to the exemplar system. Early results suggest that the level of spatial ability does correlate significantly with the time taken to complete a task using a command interface. We are currently seeking to confirm these results.

In order to understand the system, a user must understand the tasks the system supports, the logical functions and concepts underlying the tasks, and the physical functions and concepts which they are using to complete the tasks. The student model part of the embedded user model is an 'overlay model' and consists simply of a list of all the tasks, concepts and functions, at a physical and logical level, with an indication of a user's inferred level of knowledge of each of these. The student model inherits all the domain concepts and functions automatically when the domain model is specified through the UMS. When the adaptive system is being used, the student model indicates a user's level of understanding and experience with the system's functions and concepts which can be used by the rules to suggest changes to the functions the user should be using.

5 THE RULE BASE

The Rule-base consists of three types of rules; *adaptation* rules which control the system adaptations, *inference* rules which exploit the data collected in order to infer user characteristics and update the user model and *evaluation* rules which feed the inference rules with data concerning the effectiveness of the interaction.

The Rule-base lies at the heart of the system and is open to considerable development and change as the system evolves. An initial specification of rules is required, but subsequent modification and enhancement is needed during the prototyping of the adaptive system as the effectiveness of the rules are monitored. In our experience, a serious bottleneck in the development of adaptive systems has been the difficulty in extracting and modifying rules. Making the model explicit and separable from the other components of the adaptive system facilitates changing the rules as details of the interaction are understood.

The designer enters the rules through the UMS. The facility used for this at present allows a reasonably natural language method of entering rules. The next stage of the implementation of the UMS is to restrict the allowable attributes of the premises and conclusions of the rules to be attributes which have been previously defined in either the domain or user models. The advantages which such a facility provides are significant - allowing the rapid specification and tuning of the rule-base.

We are concentrating at present on the adaptation rules. These take the general form of:

IF <attribute1> has <value1> AND <attribute2> has <value2> AND...etc.

THEN present a particular interface, present a particular function, etc.

Adaptations may be quite subtle. For example, some early evidence suggests that the amount of information on a help screen which accompanies the command interface should be adapted according to an individual's level of short-term memory. Alternatively, adaptations may be larger as when, for example the whole interface is changed. In the latter case, the user is consulted before the adaptation is made.

The next stage of the adaptive system development is to implement the inference rules. The Vicente and Williges work (e.g.[15]) reports that users with a high spatial ability performed a task of locating a specific record in a database system twice as quickly as those with low spatial ability. Moreover, they suggest that there is a correlation between users' use of particular commands and their level of spatial ability. This suggests that inference rules can be formulated which monitor the interaction and allow spatial ability to be automatically and unobtrusively inferred from command usage. In a similar vein, work by Mason and Thomas ([16], [17]) indicates that users' propensity to explore a command set can be quickly inferred from monitoring their use of commands.

The final aspect of the rule-base - the evaluation rules - will evaluate the effectiveness of the suggested or actual adaptations provided. As with the adaptation rules, inference and evaluation rules are specified through the UMS.

6. DISCUSSION

In this paper we have outlined some important features of a User Modelling Shell. A UMS is an adaptive system developers tool-kit. A broad architecture of such a system has been outlined, consisting of a domain model, a user model and a rule-base. A system based on this architecture has been implemented in KEE and is currently being used and evaluated. In our research in this area, we have come across few other attempts to develop a UMS. One is a front-end to a standard knowledge engineering environment to assist the developer in specifying the basics of a student model for a tutoring system [19]. Finin [20] describes GUMS which appears strong on the implementation of user stereotypes. These stereotypes include inference rules. However, GUMS does not place so much emphasis on the domain modelling or adaptation and evaluation rules, preferring to see these as parts of the user model. Two other systems were described at a recent user modelling workshop ([23], both concentrating on the domain model). Kay's system ([21]) used concept mappings and Kobsa's ([22]) employed a graphical function/concept tool similar in structure to the domain model described here.

The UMS described in this paper is a more comprehensive adaptive system development tool than these because it integrates the three main components. We see the UMS as a first generation system which will evolve and develop within the architecture outlined during the remainder of this project. Ultimately, the UMS should play a much more active role in the development of adaptive systems, advising the designer on aspects of the system which may be suitable for automatic adaptation. However, before it can do this, there must be much more research in order to develop a knowledge-base of individual differences and their importance for human-computer interaction. Our experimental work should contribute to this debate.

ACKNOWLEDGEMENT

This work is funded by the National Physical Laboratory, Teddington, UK under extra-mural research agreement 82- 0486.

REFERENCES

[1] Murray, D.M (1987) Embedded User Models, In [18]

[2] Murray, D.M. and Benyon, D. R. (1988) Models and Designers' Tools for Adaptive Systems, presented at ECCE-4, Cambridge, UK, September 1988.

[3] Benyon D. R., Innocent P. R., Murray, D. M.(1987) System Adaptivity and the Modelling of Stereotypes. In [18]

[4] Benyon, D.R. and Murray, D.M. (1988) Experience with Adaptive Interfaces, The Computer Journal, Vol. 31(5).

[5] Murray, D.M. (1988) Building a User Modelling Shell, Proceedings of of 6th EFISS Conference, Atlanta, Ga, October 1988, Plenum Press.

[6] Date, C.J. (1986) An Introduction to Database Systems, 4th edition, Addison-Wesley.

[7] Skidmore, S.R. and Wroe, B. (1990) Introducing Systems Design, NCC/Blackwell .

[8] Coutaz, J. (1987) PAC: An object orientated model for implementing user interfaces, SIGCHI Bulletin, Vol. 19(2), October.

[9] Rasmussen, J. (1987) Information Processing and Human-Machine Interaction, North-Holland.

[10] Moran, T.P. (1981) The command language grammar, International Journal of Man-Machine Studies, Vol. 15.

[11] Moran, T.P. (1983) External-internal mapping analysis, Proceedings of of CHI '83 Conference on Human Factors in Computing Systems, ACM Press.

[12] Payne, S.J. (1987) Complex problem spaces: Modelling the knowledge needed to use interactive devices, In: [18]

[13] Norman, D. (1986). In: Norman D.and Draper S.(Eds.) User Centred System Design, Addison-Wesley.

[14] Rich, E. (1979) User Modelling via Stereotypes, Cognitive Science, Vol. 3.

[15] Vicente, K. and Williges, R.C. (1987) Visual momentum as a means of accommodating individual differences between users of a hierarchical file system, In: Rasmussen, J. and Zunde, P.(Eds.) Proceedings 5th EFISS, Plenum Press.

[16] Mason, M.V. & Thomas, R.C. (1984) Experimental adaptive interface. Information Technology Research & Development, Vol. 3.

[17] Mason, M.V. (1986) Adaptive command prompting in an on-line documentation system, International Journal of Man-Machine Studies, Vol. 25.

[18] Bullinger, H-J and Shackel, B. (Eds.) Proceedings of Interact '87 - Human-Computer Interaction, North Holland,.

[19] Tang, H., Major, N., and Rivers, R. (1989) From Users to Dialogues, In: Proceedings of People and Computers V, CUP.

[20] Finin, T. W. (1989) GUMS - A General User Modelling Shell, In: Kobsa, A. and Wahlster W. (Eds.) User Modelling in Dialog Systems, Springer-Verlag.

[21] Kay, J. um. A tool-kit for user modelling. In [23].

[22] Kobsa, A. Modelling the user's conceptual knowledge in BGP-MS, a user modelling shell system. In [23].

[23] Proceedings of 2nd International Workshop on User Modelling, Hawaii Mar 30 - Apr 1 1990.

SECTION III: DETAILED DESIGN

SIII.4 Hypermedia

Roles for tables of contents as hypertext overviews
T.T. Carey, W.T. Hunt, and A. Lopez-Suarez 581

Navigation in hypertext: A critical review of the concept
A. Dillon, C. McKnight, and J. Richardson 587

Combining hypermedia browsing with formal queries
K.-H. Jerke, P. Szabo, A. Lesch, H. Rößler, T. Schwab, and J. Herczeg 593

Human–Computer Interaction – INTERACT '90
D. Diaper et al. (Editors)
Elsevier Science Publishers B.V. (North-Holland)

Roles for Tables of Contents as Hypertext Overviews

T.T. Carey, W.T. Hunt and A. Lopez-Suarez

Dept. of Computing and Information Science
University of Guelph, Guelph Ontario Canada, N1G 2W1.

Abstract : Hypertext documents can provide increased access to information. However, users can experience disorientation as they jump between units in a document. This "lost in hypertext" phenomena is often thought of as a way-finding problem, to be solved by overviews of navigational structure. But we argue that it is often a problem of making sense of the document when the access sequence does not reflect its organizational structure, so that overviews must preserve and extend the user's organizational view.

The paper describes a prototype overview aid, TableView, for users of hypertext systems. Extensions to traditional tables of contents allow TableView to integrate several roles for hypertext navigation aids. We discuss application of TableView for an online help system, and future extensions to incorporate additional overview roles.

1. Introduction: Way-Finding versus Sense-Making in Hypertext

Hypertext technology is a method to organize information for electronic retrieval. Using this approach, an information base is fragmented into a collection blocks (nodes) which are then interconnected through a variety of links. Thus, the essential idea of hypertext is the organization of information as a network of nodes and links which is meant to facilitate its retrieval using a variety of strategies [Conklin 87].

Documents prepared using hypertext technology encourage users to find information by following a likely path amongst a set of alternatives until they reach their objective. However, in the absence of contextual information and other visual cues, this method of search can easily lead users to become disoriented.

Disorientation has been characterized in two ways:
- a navigational view of getting lost, losing one's way [Mantei 82; Edwards & Hardman 89] or
- a conceptual view of confusion about the logical structure, losing one's sense of the document [Akscyn et al. 88].

Which perspective we take on disorientation will affect how we propose to alleviate it:
- a navigational overview which shows where to go or
- an organizational overview which shows the logical structure.

Whether we see the use of hypertext documents as way-finding or sense-making will depend on the document content and the users' tasks. In the applications which we are addressing, such as online help, users often need to make sense of their current situation in order to find the information they need. The hypertext document has to help in this task, since otherwise they may not recognize the information they need even if they do navigate to it.

In the research described in this paper, we attempt to diminish way-finding behaviour by increasing users' ability to make sense of logical document structures. Section 2 discusses the organizational differences between paper-based and hypertext documents. Section 3 examines the roles of hypertext links and overviews in making sense of organizational structures. Section 4 shows how a familiar organizational aid for paper-based documents, tables of contents, can be extended to create organizational overviews for certain links of hypertext documents. This is done by a usage scenario from our TableView prototype system, with information from an online help manual. Section 5 describes our ongoing work with the TableView design, including future enhancements to provide additional aids to assist in making sense of a particular session of use.

2. How does Hypertext improve Documents: Access or Organization ?

2.1 Document organization

The author of a document attempts to arrange the contents in order to meet the specific needs of the 'typical' reader. The achievement of this goal is complicated by the existence of different categories of readers, the nature of the subject, and the purpose of the document. Due to this range of requirements there is not a single best method of organization. Weisman [85] identifies several schemas for structuring a document: chronological, functional, spatial, general to particular, simple to complex, or cause and effect. These schemes do not need to be mutually exclusive, but in paper-based documents usually only one of these determines the overall structure.

A table of contents is usually inserted at the beginning to provide a compact systematic list of headings identifying the items discussed in detail in the document. It helps readers find desired information and also lets readers see how the author has organized the contents of the document; it is an aid to both way-finding and sense-making.

Selecting a particular scheme for organizing a document is often a challenging task. The author needs to balance both the readers needs and the nature of the subject (for example, describing the process to operate a tool). This task must also be achieved within the linear layout of paper-based documents. In order to reduce the limitations imposed by these constraints a single organization scheme can be complemented in three ways:

a) Within the document, by interrupting the linear sequence: footnotes, appendixes, and the use of pointers like 'See also ..' or 'To find out more about .. refer to section ..'.

b) At the document level, by providing other search tools like indices, cross-references, or virtual tables of contents

c) External to the document, by producing additional documents, each with a different organization and often with considerable redundancy: a scope-oriented primer, a task-oriented user's guide, or a reference-oriented manual.

Each of these organizational supplements presents different problems in use.

2.2 Organization of hypertext documents

The design of an information base using hypertext technology offers several opportunities for overcoming these limitations, but it also introduces a new set of problems. Information designers have the possibility of establishing a rich set of interconnections (links) among blocks of information (nodes), thus eliminating some of the constraints of having a single organizational schema and a single linear sequence. Readers of hypertext documents can easily follow links that depart from a linear organizational path and follow other connections, as well as backup from link trails followed. However, the incorrect design of hypertext documents, the lack of contextual information, or the provision of cumbersome navigation facilities can actually make it more difficult to find the desired information.

Hypertext systems explicitly implement accelerated versions of the techniques listed above for complementing the single linear sequence of a paper-based document. References between nodes allow users to move around quickly, notes and expansions allow additional material to be accessed easily when desired, and indices or hierarchical overviews permit immediate access to desired nodes. The SuperBook text browser [Egan et al. 89] uses a weighted table of contents based on the frequency of occurrence of words being searched, to provide access superior to printed documents.

On the other hand, very few hypertext systems attempt to relax the constraint Of a single organizational structure. (The notable exception is Intermedia [Yankelovich et al. 88], which allows "webs": subspaces of the overall information topology.) This is the deficiency which our work is intended to address.

We believe that the *lost-in-hypertext* phenomena is at least partly due to this mismatch in the improvements hypertext offers over linear text. By accelerating access without enhancing structural cues, we can make it more difficult for users to make sense of where they are. Indeed, the access path they have followed may explicitly make no sense, in terms of the document's apparent organization. One example of this organizational deficiency is presented by users' experience with hypertext documents implemented in the Guide system [Brown 86]. Users show a marked preference for replacement and annotation links, which preserve their logical place in the document, over reference links which alter their organizational location [Hardman 89]. This need to maintain a sensible view of the information space is supported by experiments disrupting that view [Edwards & Hardman 89].

To overcome some of the disorientation problems, several systems provide the display of graphical network diagrams as a navigational interface. Examples of systems using this approach are NoteCards [Halasz 87], Intermedia [Yankelovich et al. 88], and gIBIS [Begeman & Conklin 88]. This technique works for way-finding in relatively small networks. However, in large information bases with an extensive set of interconnections, graphical displays often lead to user information overload [Conklin 87]. In the next section, we examine some of the reasons these overviews may not be effective for making sense of a document - small or large.

3. Roles for Links and Overviews

The previous section concluded with examples of hypertext overviews, and a further example is presented in section 4. An overview of hypertext links is a representation mechanism which visually reveals the interconnections amongst information nodes [Halasz & Conklin 89]. Given the essential character of hypertext, this also means that the overview reveals the possible node accesses, and in many cases elements in the overview can be selected to accomplish the access.

The nature of the links determines the nature of the overview. The relationships represented by some links exhibit global properties like transitivity: if A and B are linked, and B and C are linked, then some relationship also exists between A and C. This is true of hierarchical relationships like part/whole - A is a component in object B - and of thematic relationships - A and B both contain information about printing. We call such relationships, and their corresponding links, *organizational*, because they can be used to organize the contents of a document. The part/whole relationships lead to an hierarchical organization; other relationships lead to document organizations based on commands, events, etc., which may not be hierarchical (Winston et al.[87] provide an analysis of part/whole relationships and transitivity).

Other links in hypertext may not exhibit global properties, representing associations between nodes which have only local meaning. For example, an information unit about the history of a city might have links to two political leaders who had visited there at different times. There is no implied relationship between the two individuals. The event of visiting may be very important for understanding the city and thus well worth hypertext links, but it is not a relationship around which a logical structure for several cities or individuals could be built. We call these links *associational*.

An overview of organizational links should help readers both in making sense of a document and in finding their way in it. But an overview of associational links can serve readers only for way-finding: the visual representation will not make sense as a global structure, because it reveals relationships with only local meaning. Note that we refer here only to readers. If the user is an author or organizer of the information, then an associational overview is often a prerequisite aid to seeing the potential organizational links. Notecards [Halasz 87] is an example of a system designed for this purpose. But for people who are seeking information, rather than generating it, an overview without structure is unlikely to aid in sense-making unless it has very limited scope (there is a celebrated example of a "nonsense-making" overview in [Conklin 87]).

We come to two conclusions:

i) an organizational overview will only be effective for one organizational paradigm. For documents with sets of orthogonal organizational links, a *set* of organizational overviews will be required to make sense of their link structure.

ii) in some hypertext systems, many of the links that seem to be associational are really organizational links "struggling to be get out" . That is, some hypertext documents make it easy to get lost, by providing long chains of (transitive) links which are not reflected in the document's organization. When the user stops to ask "where am I", there is no good answer in terms of the document's structure. An overview of the document's organization is at that point of little use. It's like having a map of a city's rapid transit system when you are trying to get around on foot: you may recognize an occasional landmark, but generally your view will be too distorted to be helpful.

One strategy for reducing the disorientation problem is to reduce the number of such disorienting associational links by presenting them in their natural organizational form. The next section describes some of our experimentation with this strategy.

4. Extending Tables of Contents for Organizational Overviews: TableView

Many online information retrieval systems also use an implicit table of contents scheme by the provision of several layers of menus. An example of this approach is found in typical videotext systems developed in the 1970's. Some recent experimental studies on the use of hypertext systems [Campagnoni & Ehrlich 89; Marchionini 87] have shown that browsing through a table of contents is often a preferred approach over analytical methods (e.g., query formulation).

TableView allows the representation of several tables of contents on a hypertext network; this enables the selection and display a more relevant contextual structure in different situations. In order to reduce information overload, TableView also uses the concept of adapting a table of contents based on user needs and semantic rather than syntactic cues. For example, Figure 1 shows a contextual structure, given by a semantically adapted table of contents (on the left), of a selected (page) block of information being displayed (on the right). Thus, TableView may be seen as an representation mechanism for the provision of overviews.

The online help facility provides user-requested help for the Data Modeller prototype of Cognos Inc. This experimental tool is a knowledge-based aid for the conceptual data modelling process performed during a database design. The knowledge base consists of rules for properties like consistency and heuristics for design quality. The users are experienced database designers and database administrators. The Modeller prototype uses a mix of dialogue styles, including direct manipulation, form filling, and a command language.

The TableView design relates to the Modeller as follows: initial context-sensitive information is provided to give a 1-3 line message when users request help or the system cannot process the input. If additional help is requested, an appropriate TableView window is opened. Access to the TableView help system is provided through a separate process. Therefore users can resume work with the Modeller or close the TableView window at any time.

Figure 1 shows the format of a TableView window. The panel on the right contains the help system information; the panel on the left contains the table of contents overview. (Information panel text has been shortened for this paper.) The current information is the introduction node of the Assert Level section in the table. The table adjusts automatically to always show the subsections of the current node. The user may have been placed here by the basic help system, or may have selected this node as explained below.

The table entry in reverse video show the current cursor position in the table. If the user moves the mouse, the cursor position will change, but the current information panel only changes with a deliberate selection. Moving the mouse over the table initiates browsing. When the user is browsing through the table to see what other topics are available, we need two pieces of context to make sense of the current situation: the context of the browsing, and the context of the current information

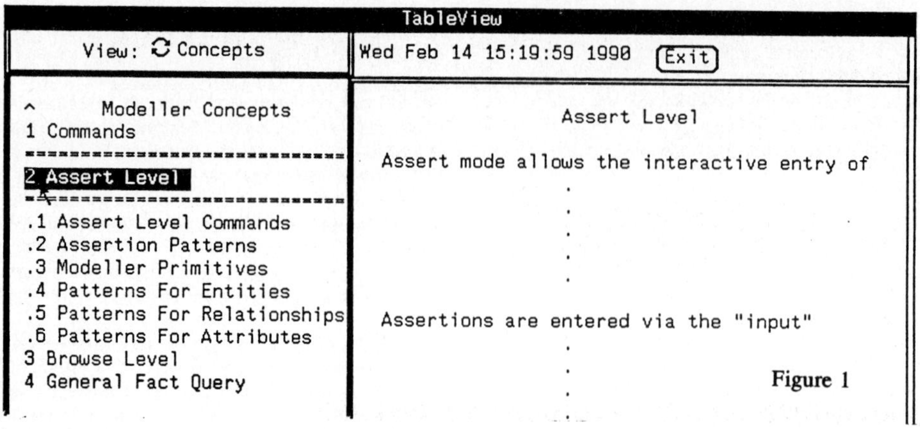

Figure 1

panel. Figure 2 shows the TableView window during browsing. The user moved the cursor away from the position in Figure 1. This opened up a Preview panel to the left of the Figure 1 display (the display is actually updated whenever mouse movement stops, although TableView has been processing the mouse movements so that the update is almost instantaneous. Continuous display update is both distracting and unnecessary.)

In the Preview table, the cursor has become an arrow. The user can browse through the entries in this panel. The entry with the double line highlighting around it represents the point at which the user entered this preview table, and links back to the original table. The original table panel continues to show the context of the information panel actually displayed.

If the user wants to access one of the topics in the Preview panel, selecting that entry with the mouse will change the current information panel: in the navigational metaphor, the user has moved to that location. If selection had occurred from Figure 2, the result would produce the window of Figure 3.

The displays so far have relied on a single organizational structure: the tables have all taken a 'Concepts' view of the information. The information in the Rename Entity node can be viewed from other perspectives: it is information about the Entity object, about a class of Commands that relabel objects, about actions used in certain task steps, about actions available to certain classes of users, etc. Each of these views will contain a different set of connections to other nodes. The nodes most similar to Rename Entity under a given view will be closer in the appropriate table of contents. A useful strategy in searching for relevant information is therefore to change views and scan the neighbourhood of the current information in the new view.

Figure 4 shows the result of changing the view from Figure 3. The View rotator at the top of the overview panel. By changing the view, the user can scan quickly through several information neighbourhoods. Note that displaying all these connections in a single overview diagram or network would produce an overwhelmingly dense picture of inter-connections. The TableView overviews separate out the connections as organizational paradigms, as an aid to making sense of the inter-connections.

For the user of a help system, this represents a rethinking of the problem, e.g., as a difficulty related to objects rather than commands. Error recovery often requires just such a reconception of the situation [Bagnara & Rizzo 89].

In any complex set of information, some of the interconnections will not fit an overall organizational paradigm. So any hypertext information space will contain some associational links. Figure 5 shows how TableView provides access to these links. The user has encountered a problem with the Enter command. In the overview panel, this command appears logically with other window commands: other views might show other rational organizations. But the problem in this case does not have a rational explanation - at least from the user's perspective. The link shown at the bottom of the information panel has been placed there after-the-fact, when the difficulty was first discovered: the transcript of entered commands can sometimes overflow with bizarre consequences. Users can preview the link, as shown in Figure 5, and select it as they would with any other table entry. These associational links also provide a mechanism for site-specific link to be added within the help system.

5. Current Status and further Work

The TableView prototype is currently implemented as a research pilot system, undergoing testing to address various design issues. We are converting the documentation for two software systems into the TableView hypertext structure. One is the Modeller tool for database experts used above for the examples; the second system is a visual database query product for non-expert users. For the latter, TableView will be compared with the existing (non hypertext) online help panels. Considerable experimentation will be required before we understand the implications of the various design tradeoffs. For example, we have another version of the TableView prototype in which the information panels are tied to the preview table and change contents with it - this rapid change appears to be favoured by experienced users.

We have development work underway to add additional types of information and additional mechanisms for access. For example, the table of contents overview can easily incorporate additional aids for making sense of the current interactive session, such as bookmarks or a

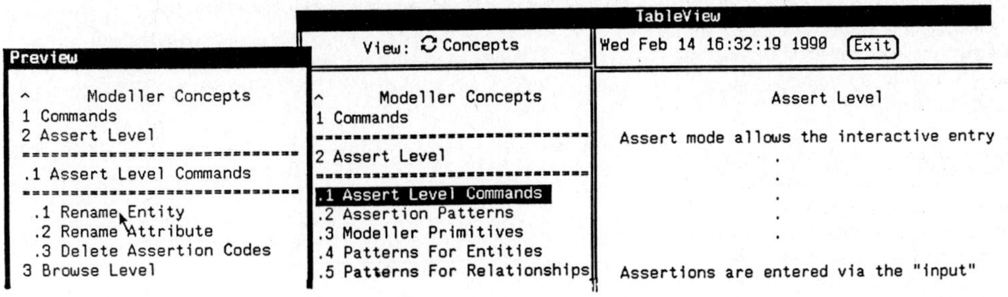

Figure 2

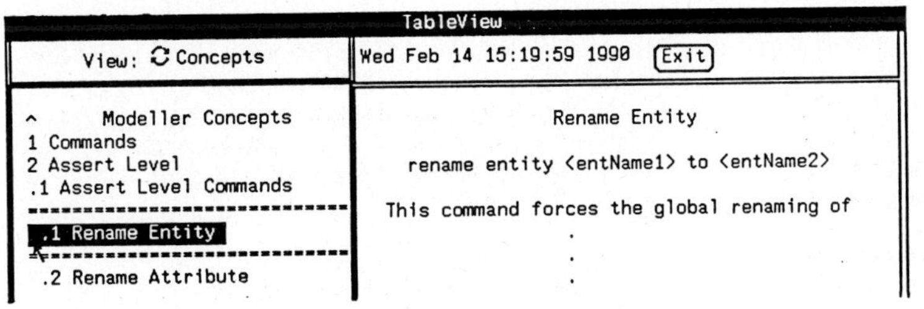

Figure 3

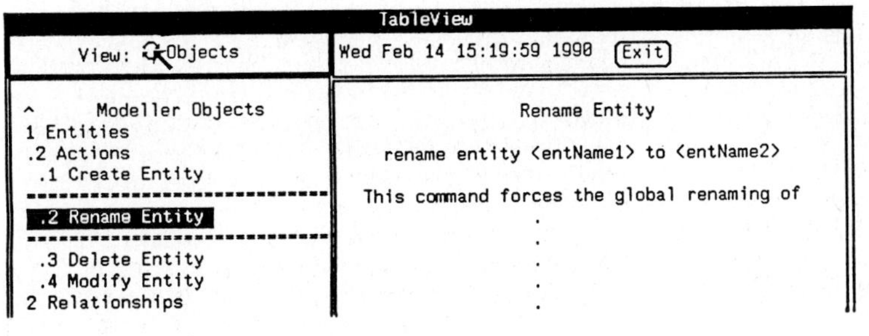

Figure 4

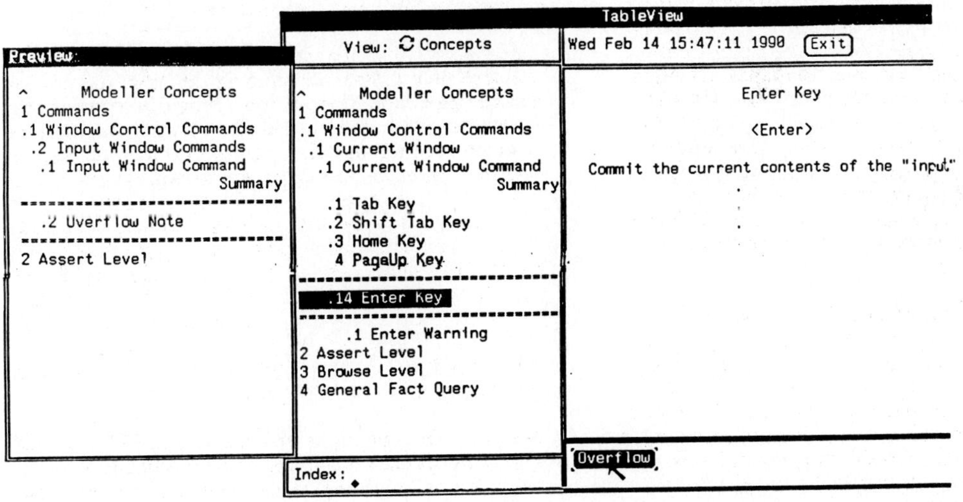

Figure 5

history record. The other access mechanism which has been designed but not yet implemented is an index facility. In the future we would like to address the content creation process, through computer-aided semantic analysis of existing documentation.

One common mechanism we do not currently have is a link facility within the information panels, which would move users to a new panel. This leaves us on the periphery of hypertext as some people define it, although with a more extensive link structure than some other hypertext help systems [Campagnoni & Ehrlich 89]. While TableView appears at any given moment to be relying on an hierarchical structure, the presence of multiple views supplements the limited associational links to provide a rich structural perspective on the information space.

Acknowledgements

This work was sponsored by Cognos Inc., the Ontario Technology Fund, and the Natural Sciences and Engineering Research Council of Canada.

References

Akscyn, R., E. Yoder and D. McCracken 1988. The Data Model is the Heart of Interface Design, in E. Soloway, D. Frye and S.B. Sheppard (eds.), *Proceedings CHI'88 Human Factors in Computing Systems*, ACM: New York NY. pp. 115-120.

Bagnara, S. and A. Rizzo 1989. A Methodology for the Analysis of Error Processes in Human-Computer Interaction, in M.J. Smith and G. Salvendy (eds.), *Work with Computers: Organizational, Management, Stress and Health Aspects*, Elsevier: Amsterdam, pp. 605-612.

Begeman, M. and J. Conklin 1988. The Right Tool for the Job, *Byte*, October 1988, pp. 255-266.

Brown, P.J. 1986. Interactive Documentation, *Software - Practice and Experience,* 16, pp. 291-299.

Campagnoni, F.R. and K. Ehrlich, 1989. Information Retrieval Using a Hypertext-Based Help System, *ACM Tran. on Information Systems*, vol. 7, pp. 93-102.

Conklin, Jeff 1987. Hypertext: a Survey Introduction, *IEEE Computer*, vol. 20, September 1987., pp. 17-41.

Dumais, S.T. and T.K. Landauer 1982. Describing Categories of Objects for Menu Retrieval Systems, *Behaviour Retrieval Methods, Instruments and Computers*, 16(2), pp. 242-248.

Edwards, D.N. and L. Hardman 1989. 'Lost in Hyperspace': Cognitive Mapping and Navigation in a Hypertext Environment, in R. McAleese (ed.), *Hypertext: theory into practice*, Ablex Publ., 1989. pp. 105-125.

Egan, D.E., J.R. Remde, T.K. Landauer, C.C. Lochbaum and L.M. Gomez 1989. Behaviour Evaluation and Analysis of a Hypertext Browser, in K. Bice and C. Lewis (ed.), *Proceedings CHI'89 Human Factors in Computing Systems Conference*, ACM: New York, NY. pp. 205-210.

Frisse, M.E. 1987. Searching for Information in a Hypertext Medical Handbook, in *Hypertext '87 Position Papers*, University of North Carolina, Chapel Hill, NC, pp. 57-66.

Furnas, G. 1986. Generalized Fisheye Views, *CHI'86 Conf. Proc.* (Boston, 1986), pp. 16-23.

Halasz, F.G. 1987. Reflections on NoteCards, in *Hypertext '87 Position Papers,* University of North Carolina, Chapel Hill, NC, 1987, pp. 253-258.

Halasz, F.G. and J. Conklin 1989. Issues in the Design and Application of Hypermedia Systems, CHI'89 Tutorial, May 1989.

Hardman, L. 1989. Personal communication.

Landauer, T.K., S.T. Dumais, L.M. Gomez, and G.W. Furnas 1982. Human Factors in Data Access, *Bell System Technical Journal*, 61 (9), 1982, pp. 2487-2509.

Mantei, M. 1982. A Study of Disorientation Behaviour in ZOG, Ph.D. dissertation, University of Southern California, Los Angeles, CA.

Marchionini, G. 1987. An Invitation to Browse: Designing Full-Text Systems for Novice Users, *The Canadian Journal of Information Science,* 12 (1987), pp. 69-79.

Remde, J.R., L.M. Gomez, and T.K. Landauer 1987. SuperBook: An Automatic Tool for Information Exploration - Hypertext ?, *Proceedings Hypertext'87*, University of North Carolina, Chapel Hill, NC, 1987, pp. 175-188.

Weisman, H.M. 1985. *Basic Technical Writing*, Charles E. Merril Pub.

Winston, Morton E., Roger Chaffin, and Douglas Herrmann 1987. A Taxonomy of Part-Whole Relations, *Cognitive Science*, vol 11 pp. 417-444.

Yankelovich, N.B, J. Haan, N.K. Meyrowitz, and S.M. Drucker 1988. Intermedia: The Concept and the Construction of a Seamless Information Environment, *IEEE Computer*, Jan. 1988, pp. 81-96.

Human–Computer Interaction – INTERACT '90
D. Diaper et al. (Editors)
Elsevier Science Publishers B.V. (North-Holland)

NAVIGATION IN HYPERTEXT: A CRITICAL REVIEW OF THE CONCEPT

Andrew DILLON, Cliff McKNIGHT and John RICHARDSON

HUSAT Research Institute, Elms Grove, Loughborough, Leics. LE11 1RG

With the advent of hypertext it has become widely accepted that the departure from the so-called "linear" structure of paper increases the likelihood of readers or users becoming lost. In this paper we will discuss this aspect of hypertext in terms of its validity, the lessons to be learned from the psychology of navigation and the applicability of the navigation metaphor to the hypertext domain.

1. IS NAVIGATION A PROBLEM?

There is a striking consensus among many of the "experts" in the field that navigation is the single greatest difficulty for users of hypertext. Frequent reference is made to "getting lost in hyperspace" (e.g. Conklin 1987, McAleese 1989), and Hammond and Allinson (1989) speak for many when they say:

> "Experience with using hypertext systems has revealed a number of problems for users..... First, users get lost... Second, users may find it difficult to gain an overview of the material... Third, even if users know specific information is present they may have difficulty finding it" (p294).

In the following section we will discuss what is known about the psychology of navigation in physical environments and show how this might have relevance to the 'virtual' worlds of information space.

2. THE PSYCHOLOGY OF NAVIGATION

2.1. Schemata and Models of Generic Environments

Individuals possess schemata or models of the physical environment in which they find themselves. This is acquired from experience and affords a basic orienting frame of reference for navigatory purposes. Thus, we soon acquire schemata of towns and cities so that we know what to expect when we find ourselves in one: busy roads, numerous buildings, shopping, residential and industrial areas, many people, churches, pubs, etc. According to Downs and Stea (1977) such frames of reference exist at all levels of scale from looking at the world in terms of east and west or First and Third Worlds, to national distinctions between north and south, urban and rural and so on down to local entities like buildings and neighbourhoods.

Such frames of reference also guide our responses to the environment in terms of how we should behave. Therefore we soon realise that to interact effectively with an urban environment (e.g., to get from A to B) there are probably a variety of information sources available to us such as maps, street-signs, landmarks, tourist information facilities and so forth. In this sense the frame of reference is identical to the concept of script (Schank and Abelson 1977).

While schemata are effective orienting guides, in themselves they are limited. They do not reflect specific instances of any one environment and provide no knowledge of what exists outside of our field of vision. Yet humans have such knowledge of places with which they are familiar. So what is this detailed knowledge that we acquire of our environment and how does it emerge?

2.2. The Acquisition of Cognitive Maps

Current theories of navigation vary and it is no longer the province of psychologists alone. Geographers, anthropologists and urban planners all show an interest (see for example Downs and Stea, 1974). However, Tolman's (1948) paper on cognitive maps is frequently cited as seminal. Tolman postulated the existence of a cognitive map, internalised in the human mind which is the analog to the physical lay-out of the environment. In dismissing much of the then popular behaviouristic school of psychology, Tolman argues that information impinging on the brain is:

> "worked over and elaborated....into a tentative cognitive-like map of the environment indicating routes and paths and environmental relationships..."

Recent experimental work takes the notion of some form of mental representation of the environment for granted, concerning itself more with how such maps are formed and manipulated. Many theorists agree that the acquisition of navigational knowledge proceeds through several developmental stages from the initial identification of landmarks in the environment to a fully formed mental map. One such developmental model has been discussed by Anderson (1980) and Wickens (1984) and is briefly described here.

According to this model, in the first instance we represent

knowledge in terms of highly salient visual *landmarks* in the environment such as buildings, statues, etc. Thus we recognise our position in terms relative to these landmarks, e.g., our destination is near building X or if we see statue Y then we must be near the railway station and so forth. This knowledge provides us with the skeletal framework on which we build our cognitive map.

The next stage of development is the acquisition of *route* knowledge which is characterised by the ability to navigate from point A to point B, using whatever landmark knowledge we have acquired to make decisions about when to turn left or right. With such knowledge we can provide others with effective route guidance, e.g., "Turn left at the traffic lights and continue on that road until you see the Bull's Head public house on your left and take the next right there..." and so forth. Though possessing route knowledge, a person may still not really know much about his environment. A route might be non-optimal or even totally wasteful.

The third stage involves the acquisition of *survey* knowledge. This is the fully developed cognitive map that Tolman (1948) described. It allows us to give directions or plan journeys along routes we have not directly travelled as well as describe relative locations of landmarks within an environment. It allows us to know the general direction of places, e.g., "westward" or "over there" rather than "left of the main road" or "to the right of the church". In other words it is based on a world frame of reference rather than an ego-centred one.

It is not clear if each individual develops through all stages in such a logical sequence. Obviously landmark knowledge on its own is of little use for complex navigation, and both route and survey knowledge emerge from it as a means of coping with the complexity of the environment. However, it does not necessarily follow that once enough route knowledge is acquired it is replaced by survey knowledge. Experimental investigations have demonstrated that each is optimally suited for different kinds of tasks. For example, route knowledge is better for orientation tasks than survey knowledge, the latter being better for estimating distance or object localisation on a map (Thorndyke and Hayes-Roth 1982, Wetherell 1979). Route knowledge is cognitively simpler than survey knowledge but suffers the drawback of being virtually useless once a wrong step is taken (Wickens 1984). Route knowledge, because of its predominantly verbal form, might suit individuals with higher verbal than spatial abilities, while the opposite would be the case for survey knowledge.

While such theoretical work on navigation is primarily concerned with travels through physical space such as cities and buildings it does offer a perspective that might prove insightful to the design of hypertext systems, where navigation is conceptualised as occurring through an information space. Variations in navigational knowledge might account for many of the opposing views expressed on the validity of navigation problems.

3. NAVIGATION APPLIED TO ELECTRONIC DOCUMENTS

3.1. Schemata and Models

The concept of a schema for an electronic information space is less clear-cut than those for physical environments or paper documents. Electronic documents have a far shorter history than paper and the level of awareness of technology among the general public is relatively primitive compared to that of paper. Exposure to information technology will almost certainly change this state of affairs but even among the contemporary computer literate it is unlikely that the type of generic schematic structures that exist for paper documents have electronic equivalents of sufficient generality.[1]

Obviously computing technology's short history is one of the reasons but it is also the case that the media's underlying structures do not have equivalent transparency. With paper, once the basic *modus operandi* of reading are acquired (e.g., page-turning, footnote identification, index usage and so forth) they retain utility for other texts produced by other publishers, other authors and for other domains. With computers, manipulation of information can differ from application to application within the same computer, from computer to computer and from this year to last year's model. Thus using electronic information is often likely to involve the employment of schemata for systems in general (i.e., how to operate them) in a way that is not essential for paper-based information.

The qualitative differences between the schemata for paper and electronic documents can easily be appreciated by considering what you can tell about either at first glance. A paper text is extremely informative. When we open a hypertext document however we do not have the same amount of information available to us. We are likely to be faced with a welcoming screen which might give us a rough idea of the contents (i.e., subject matter) and information about the authors/developers of the document but little else.

Performing the hypertext equivalent of opening up the text or turning the page offers no assurance that expectations will be met. Many hypertext documents offer unique structures (intentionally or otherwise) and their overall sizes are often impossible to assess in a meaningful manner (McKnight *et al.* 1989). At their current stage of development it is likely that users/readers familiar with hypertext will have a schema that includes such attributes as linked nodes of information, non-serial structures, and perhaps, potential navigational difficulties! The manipulation facilities and access mechanisms available in hypertext will probably occupy a more prominent role in their schema for hypertext documents than they will for readers' schemata of paper texts. As yet, empirical evidence for such schemata is lacking.

The fact that hypertext offers authors the chance to create numerous structures out of the same information is a further source of difficulty for users or readers. Since schemata are generic abstractions representing typicality in entities or events, the increased variance of hypertext implies that any similarities that are perceived must be at a higher level or must be more numerous than the schemata that exist for paper texts.

3.2. Acquiring a Cognitive Map of the Electronic Space

The roots of this issue can be traced back to the literature on users interacting with non-hypertext databases and documents as well as with menu-driven interfaces, where it has been repeatedly shown that users can lose their way in the maze of information (Canter *et al.* 1985). Hagelbarger and Thompson (1983) claim that when users make an incorrect selection at a deep level they tend to return to the start rather than the menu at which they erred. Research by Tombaugh and McEwen (1982) and Lee *et al.* (1984) indicates that the actual to minimum ratio for screens of information accessed in a successful search is 2:1, i.e., users will often access twice as many menu pages as necessary. All of this leads such researchers to conclude that navigation through electronic (but non-hypertext) databases can pose severe navigational problems for users.

In terms of the model of navigational knowledge described above we should not be surprised by such findings. They seem to be classic manifestations of behaviour based on limited knowledge. For example, returning to the start upon making an error at a deep level in the menu suggests the absence of survey type knowledge and a strong reliance on landmarks (e.g., the start screen) to guide navigation. It also lends support to the argument about route knowledge that it becomes useless once a wrong turn is made. Making "journeys" twice as long as necessary is a further example of the type of behaviour expected from people lacking a mental map of an environment and relying on landmark and route knowledge only to find their way.

3.3. Acquiring a Cognitive Map of a Hypertext Document

McKnight *et al.* (1989) looked at navigation in terms of the amount of time spent in the contents and/or index sections of the documents employed using two hypertexts and two linear documents. They found that subjects in both hypertext conditions spent significantly greater proportions of time in the index/contents sections of the documents. They noted that this indicated a style of interaction based on jumping into parts of the text and returning to base for further guidance (a style assumed not particularly optimal for hypertext) and concluded from this that effective navigation was difficult for non-experienced users of a hypertext document.

Once more this is a classic example of using landmarks in the information space as guidance. Subjects in the linear conditions (paper and word processor versions) seemed much happier to browse through the document to find information, highlighting their confidence and familiarity with the structure presented to them. Similar support for the notion of landmarks as a first level of navigational knowledge development are provided by several of the studies which have required subjects to draw or form maps of the information space after exposure to it (e.g., Simpson and McKnight 1989). Typically, subjects can group certain sections together but often have no idea where other parts go or what they are connected to.

Unfortunately it is difficult to chart the development of navigational knowledge beyond this point. Detailed studies of users interacting with hypertext systems beyond single experimental tasks and gaining mastery over a hypertext document are thin on the ground. Edwards and Hardman (1989) claim that they found evidence for the development of survey type navigational knowledge in users exposed to a strictly hierarchical database of 50 screens for a single experimental session lasting, on average, less than 20 minutes. Unfortunately the data is not reported in sufficient detail to critically assess such a claim but it is possible that given the document's highly organised structure, comparatively small size and the familiarity of the subject area (leisure facilities in Edinburgh) such knowledge might have been observed. Obviously this is an area that needs further empirical work.

4. PROVIDING NAVIGATIONAL INFORMATION: BROWSERS, MAPS AND STRUCTURAL CUES

4.1. Graphical Browsers

A graphical browser is a schematic representation of the structure of the database aimed at providing the user with an easy to understand map of what information is located where. According to Conklin (1987) graphical browsers are a feature of a "somewhat idealized hypertext system", recognising that not all existing systems utilise browsers but suggesting that they are desirable. The idea behind a browser is that the document can be represented graphically in terms of the nodes of information and the links between them, and in some instances, that selecting a node in the browser would cause its information to be displayed.

It is not difficult to see why this might be useful. Like a map of a physical environment it shows the user what the overall information space is like, how it is linked together and consequently offers a means of moving from one information node to another. Indeed, Monk *et al.* (1988) have shown that even a static, non-interactive graphical representation is useful. However, for richly interconnected material or documents of a reasonable size and complexity, it is not possible to include everything in a single browser without the problem of presenting 'visual spaghetti' to the user. In such cases it is necessary to represent the structure in terms of levels of browsers, and at this point there is a danger that the user gets lost in the navigational support system!

Some simple variations in the form of maps or browsers have been investigated empirically. Studies by Simpson (1989) requiring users to locate information in hypertexts have experimentally manipulated several variables relating to structural cues and position indicators. In one experiment she found that a hierarchical contents list was superior to an alphabetic index and concluded that users are able to use cues from the structural representation to form maps of the document. In a second study she reported that users provided with a graphical contents list showing the relationship between various parts of the text performed better than users who only had access to a textual list. Making the contents lists interactive (i.e., selectable by pointing) also increased navigational efficiency. In general, Simpson found that as accuracy of performance increased so did subjects' ability to construct accurate post-task maps of the information space.

4.2. The Provision of Metaphors

A second area of research in the domain of navigational support concerns that of metaphor provision. A metaphor provides a way of conceptualising an object or environment and in the information technology domain is frequently discussed as a means for aiding novices' comprehension of a system or application. The most common metaphor in use is the desk-top metaphor familiar to users of the Apple Macintosh amongst others. Prior to this metaphor, the word processor was often conceptualised by first-time users as a typewriter.[2]

The logic behind metaphors is that they enable users to draw on existing world knowledge to act on the electronic domain As Carroll and Thomas (1982) point out:

> "If people employ metaphors in learning about computing systems, the designers of those systems should anticipate and support likely metaphorical constructions to increase the ease of learning and using the system."

However, rather than anticipate likely metaphorical constructions, the general approach in the domain of hypertext has been to provide a metaphor and hope (or examine the extent to which) the user can employ it. As the term 'navigation' suggests, the most commonly provided metaphor is that of travel.

Hammond and Allinson (1987) report on a study in which two different forms of the travel metaphor were employed: "go-it-alone" travel, and the "guided tour". These two forms were intended to represent different loci of control over movement through the document, the first being largely user-controlled and the second being largely system-controlled. Additionally a map of the local part of the information structure was available from every screen. Hammond and Allinson stress the importance of integrating the metaphor in the design of the system, which they did, and not surprisingly they found that users were able to employ it with little difficulty.

Of course, one could simply make the electronic book look as similar to the paper book as possible. This is the approach offered by people such as Benest (1989) with his book emulator and as such seems to offer a simple conceptual aid to novice users. Two pages are displayed at a time and relative position within the text can be assessed by the thickness of pages either side which are splayed out rather like a paper document would be. Page turning can be done with a single mouse press which results in two new pages appearing or by holding the mouse button down and simulating "flicking" through the text. The layout of typical books can also be supported by such a system, thereby exploiting the schematic representations possessed by experienced readers.

If that was all such a system offered it would be unlikely to succeed. It would just be a second-rate book. However, according to Benest, his book emulator provides added-value that exploits the technology underlying it. For example, although references in the text are listed fully at the back of the book, they can be individually accessed by pointing at them when they occur on screen. Page numbers in contents and index sections are also selectable, thereby offering immediate access to particular portions of the text. Such advantages are typical of most hypertext applications. In his own words:

> "the book presentation, with all the engrained (*sic*) expectations that it arouses and the simplicity with which it may be navigated, is both visually appealing and less disruptive during information acquisition, than the older 'new medium demands a new approach' techniques that have so far been adopted."

This may be true but at the time of writing no supporting evidence has been presented and in the absence of empirical data one should view all claims about hypertext with caution.

It is interesting for two reasons that Benest dismisses the 'new medium demands a new approach' philosophy of most hypertext theorists. Firstly, there is a good case to be made for book-type emulations according to the arguments put forward above about schematic representations. As outlined earlier, such representations facilitate usage by providing orientation or frames of reference for naïve users. Secondly, the new approach which rejects such emulations has largely been responsible for the adoption of the concept of navigation through hypertext.

In response to the first issue it is worth noting that Benest's approach is, to our way of thinking, correct up to a point. We ourselves have been developing a hypertext journal database and have decided that, on the basis of some of our studies on usage styles and models of academic articles (see McKnight *et al.* 1990), emulating the structure of the journal as it exists in paper is good design. However, we are less concerned with emulation as much as retention of useful structures. This does not extend as far as mimicking page-turning or providing splayed images of the pages underlying either opened leaf. Furthermore, while we advocate the approach of identifying relevant schematic structures for texts we would not expect all types to retain such detailed aspects of their paper versions in hypertext. There seems little need, for example, to emulate the book form to this degree for a hypertext telephone directory. Benest does not seem to draw the line however between texts that might usefully exploit such emulations and those that would not, or state what he would expect unique hypertext documents to emulate.

In response to the second point, it is worth asking whether there is an alternative to navigation as a metaphor. Hammond and Allinson (1987) argue that there are two relevant dimensions for understanding the information which metaphors convey: *scope* and *level* of description. A metaphor's scope refers to the number of concepts that the metaphor relates to. A metaphor of broad scope in the domain of HCI is the desk-top metaphor. Here, many of the concepts a user deals with when working on the system can be easily dealt with cognitively in terms of physical desk-top manipulations. The typewriter metaphor frequently invoked for explaining word processors is far more limited in scope. It offers a basic orientation to using word processors (i.e., you can use them to create print quality documents) but is severely limited beyond that since word processors do not behave like typewriters in many instances.

The metaphor's level of description refers to the type of knowledge it is intended to convey. This may be very high level information such as how to think about the task and its completion, or very low, such as how to think about particular command syntax in order to best remember it. Few, if any, metaphors convey information at all levels but this does not prevent them being useful to users. In fact, few users ever expect metaphors to offer full scope and levels of description.

According to Hammond and Allinson, the navigation metaphor is useful in the hypertext domain and when users are offered "guided tours" through an information space they do not expect physical manifestations of the metaphor to apply literally but might rely primarily on semantic mappings between metaphor and system much more heavily. There are numerous rich mappings that can be made between the navigation metaphor and hypertext and thus it seems sensible to use it.

Benest's book emulation is also a metaphor for using the system and in some instances would offer a broad scope and many levels of description between the paper text and the hypertext. The fact that we can talk about navigation and book metaphors in the one system shows that mixed metaphors are even possible and (though awaiting confirmatory evidence) probably workable in some instances.

It is hard to see any other metaphors being employed in this domain. Navigation is firmly entrenched as a metaphor for discussing hypertext use and book comparisons are unavoidable in a technology aimed at supporting many of the tasks performed with paper documents. Whether there are other metaphors that can be usefully employed is debatable. Limited metaphors for explaining computer use to the novice user are bound to exist and where such users find themselves working with hypertext new metaphors might find their way into the domain. But for now at least it seems that navigation and book emulation are here to stay.

5. CONCLUSION

The concept of navigation is a meaningful one in the hypertext domain in the sense that we can view user actions as movement through electronic space. Research in the psychology of navigation in physical environments has some relevance but needs further empirical investigation to identify the extent to which it may map directly onto users of electronic documents. Limitations in scope and level of application need to be made explicit. The expression of navigation difficulties is rarely supported with clear evidence, however, and the need for sound empirical work here should not be underestimated. The psychological model of navigation knowledge could prove a useful research tool in these circumstances.

FOOTNOTES

1. It is worth noting that, in part, this might be because the electronic document is usually only a stage in the production of a paper one. Few pure electronic texts exist, thus any unique forms have yet to emerge.

2. The history of technological progress is littered with such metaphors e.g., the car as the "horseless carriage", the first typefaces were imitations of script and so forth.

REFERENCES

Anderson, J. (1980) *Cognitive Psychology and its Implications*. San Francisco: W.H. Freeman.

Benest, I. D. (1989) A hypertext system with controlled hype. Paper presented at *HYPERTEXT II*, the Second Annual UK conference on Hypertext, York, July.

Billingsley, P. (1982) Navigation through hierarchical menu structures: does it help to have a map? *Proceedings of the Human Factors Society 26th Annual Meeting*.

Canter, D., Rivers, R. and Storrs, G. (1985) Characterising user navigation through complex data structures. *Behaviour and Information Technology*, 4(2), 93-102.

Carroll, J. and Thomas, J. (1982) Metaphor and cognitive representation of computing systems *IEEE Transactions on Systems, Man and Cybernetics*, SMC-12(2), 107-116.

Conklin,J. (1987) Hypertext: an introduction and survey. *Computer*, September, 17-41.

Downs, R. and Stea, D. (1977) *Maps in Minds: Reflections on Cognitive Mapping*, New York: Harper and Row.

Downs, R. and Stea, D. (eds.) (1973) *Image and Environment: Cognitive Mapping and Spatial Behaviour*. London: Edward Arnold.

Edwards, D. and Hardman, L. (1989) "Lost in Hyperspace": Cognitive Mapping and Navigation in a Hypertext Environment. In R. McAleese (ed.) *Hypertext: Theory into Practice*, Oxford: Intellect.

Hagelbarger, D. and Thompson, R. (1983) Experiments in teleterminal design, *IEEE Spectrum*, 20, 40-45.

Hammond, N. and Allinson L. (1989) Extending hypertext for learning: an investigation of access and guidance tools. In: A. Sutcliffe and L. Macaulay (eds.) *People and Computers V*. Cambridge: Cambridge University Press.

Hammond, N. and Allinson, L. (1987) The travel metaphor as design principle and training aid for navigating around complex systems. In D. Diaper and R. Winder (eds.) *People and Computers III*, Cambridge: Cambridge University Press.

Lee, E., Whalen, T., McEwen, S. and Latrémouille, S. (1984) Optimizing the design of menu pages for information retrieval. *Ergonomics*, 27(10), 1051-1069.

McAleese, R. (1989) Navigation and browsing in Hypertext. In R. McAleese (ed.) *Hypertext:Theory into Practice*. Oxford: Intellect.

McKnight, C., Dillon, A. and Richardson, J. (1989) A comparison of linear and hypertext formats in information retrieval. Paper presented at *HYPERTEXT II*, the Second Annual UK conference on Hypertext, York, July.

Monk, A., Walsh, P. and Dix, A. (1988) A comparison of hypertext, scrolling and folding as mechanisms for program browsing. In D. Jones and R. Winder (eds.) *People and Computers IV*. Cambridge:

Cambridge University Press.

Schank, R. and Abelson, R. (1977) *Scripts, Plans, Goals, and Understanding*. Hillsdale, NJ: Lawrence Erlbaum Associates.

Simpson, A. (1989) Navigation in hypertext: design issues. Paper presented at International OnLine Conference '89, London, December.

Simpson, A. and McKnight, C. (1989) Navigation in hypertext: structural cues and mental maps. Paper presented at *HYPERTEXT II*, the Second Annual UK conference on Hypertext, York, July.

Thorndyke, P. and Hayes-Roth, B. (1982) Differences in spatial knowledge acquired from maps and navigation. *Cognitive Psychology*, 14, 560-589.

Tolman, E.C. (1948) Cognitive maps in rats and men. *Psychological Review*, 55, 189-208.

Tombaugh, J. and McEwen, S. (1982) Comparison of two information retrieval methods on Videotex: tree structure versus alphabetical directory. *Proceedings of the Conference on Human Factors in Computer Systems*. Gaithersburg, MD: ACM. 106-110.

Wetherell, A. (1979) Short-term memory for verbal and graphic route information. *Proceedings of the Human Factors Society 23rd Annual Meeting*.

Wickens, C. (1984) *Engineering Psychology and Human Performance*. Columbus: Charles Merrill.

Human–Computer Interaction – INTERACT '90
D. Diaper et al. (Editors)
Elsevier Science Publishers B.V. (North-Holland)

Combining Hypermedia Browsing with Formal Queries

K.-H. Jerke, P. Szabo, A. Lesch, H. Rößler
SEL Alcatel, Postfach 1760, D 7530 Pforzheim

T. Schwab, J. Herczeg
Universität Stuttgart, Herdweg 51, D 7000 Stuttgart 1

This paper describes a system for retrieving and presenting multimedia objects (e.g. text, picture, graphic, video and audio) that are organized in an information network. The system combines the approaches of hypertext and formal query: at any time the user can express his intentions both by a formal query or navigate through the information space according to the hypertext paradigm.

1. Introduction

The aim of the ongoing research project MCPR (Multimedia Communication, Processing and Representation, RACE 1038 – Research and Development in Advanced Communications technologies in Europe) is to integrate broadband communication with current workstation and video technology in order to develop an architecture (hardware and software) for hypermedia applications with particular emphasis on the user's needs. Multimedia information is already used in application areas such as libraries, education and travel agencies. These are locally available as brochures, reports, slides and videos and can be retrieved from various communication services (telephone, fax, videophone, digital data communication, videoconferencing and video library facilities).

To integrate and process this highly interconnected multimedia information hypermedia has been taken as the underlying concept for supporting multimedia applications in the domains mentioned above (Halasz (1988), Yankelovich et.al. (1988)). Moreover, hypermedia provides the user with mechanisms for the organization of distributed multimedia information and enables navigation therein. Broadband Communication Networks introduced by the RACE program will provide appropriate means for the interchange of large amounts of hypermedia information. These networks will operate with a bandwidth of up to 600 Mbit/s.

A travel agency scenario has been chosen as a typical multimedia application to demonstrate the final model at different locations (project partners*) connected via IBCN – Integrated Broadband Communication Network.

The approach of combining formal queries with hypermedia browsing is an attempt towards a user friendly human computer interface for the multimedia system outlined above.

2. Querying and Browsing in a Hypertext Environment

Today, there are two contrary approaches to represent and retrieve data from complex information spaces. In the more traditional way, the information base is represented as a (relational) database, and retrieval is done by formulating queries in a formal language. On the other hand, there are *Hypertext* systems, in which the data is represented as a network of information nodes. The user may navigate in these systems by following links connecting the nodes.

Each of the two approaches has inherent drawbacks that may be overcome by the other. To get information from a database system, for example, the user has to be familiar with the structure of the underlying database and the syntax of a formal language. On the other hand, users of Hypertext systems often find it difficult where to start searching for information and after a few browsing steps they get "lost in space" (Conklin (1987)). Therefore, a combination of both techniques is a promising solution to benefit from their respective advantages: the user may specify his overall intentions by a formal query which results in appropriate starting points for navigation through an information network according to the Hypertext paradigm.

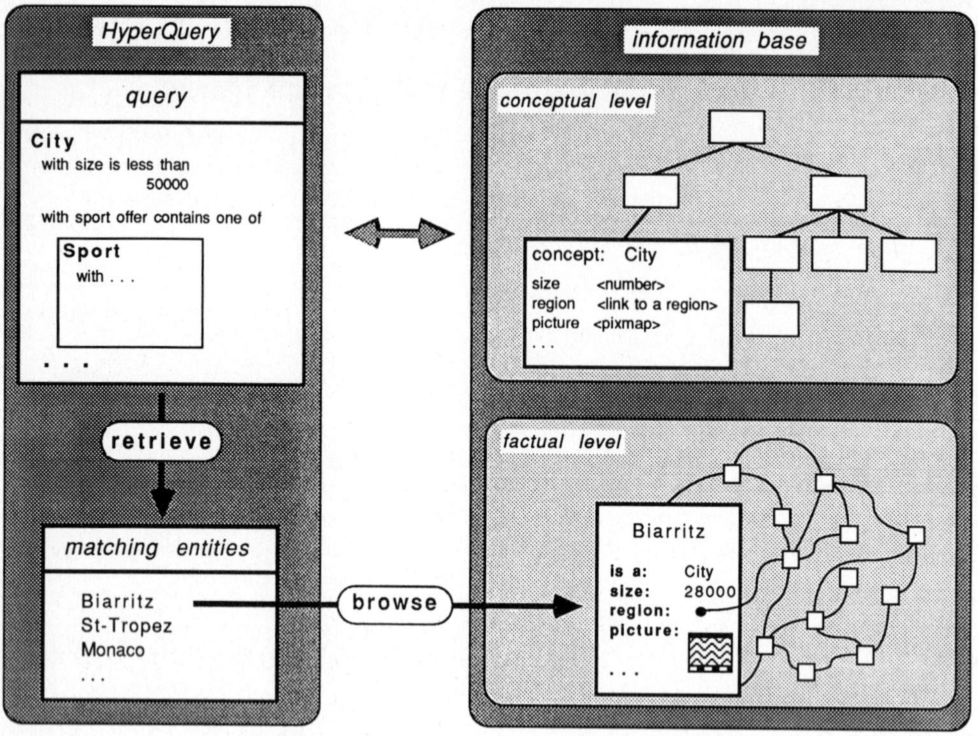

Figure 1: The Architecture of the hypermedia system

Following this idea, in MCPR, a hypermedia system will be developed that consists of two main parts (Figure 1):

– A *query component* to specify a formal query. To this end, a conceptual description of the entities in the information network is required. The formulation of the query is strongly guided by the system so that the user does not need to be familiar with these concepts in advance, preventing incorrect or incomplete queries. The dialogue starts with a simple query which may be incrementally modified by gradual refinement. The entities retrieved from the information base form the starting points for the hypermedia browser.

– A *hypermedia browser* to allow navigation through a network consisting of discrete information units presented in the form of multimedia documents. These documents extend the notion of printed (static) documents by integrating audio and video information into them. The browser enables free, associative exploration of the information space in contrast to the analytical methods. The combination of these two 'orthogonal' approaches is likely to support a wide range of user's needs in information retrieval (Campagnoni et. al. (1989)).

3. The information base

The information base that is used by both components contains travel information which has been extracted from the Baedekers travel guide. The travel information is represented as a network of information nodes with additional links to multimedia information like picture, video, and speech annotations. These interconnected information nodes form the *factual level* of the information database. In addition to this level there are descriptions that define the *conceptual level* of the information nodes.

The Conceptual Level

The conceptual level is represented in form of *concepts*. The information nodes on the factual level of the database are instances of these concepts. Each concept defines a set of *attributes* for its instances. The concepts resemble classes in object oriented languages: they are organized in a specialization hierarchy; each concept inherits the attributes of its superconcepts.

Two different types of attributes may be defined by concepts: *primitive attributes* that may have single Lisp objects or a set of Lisp objects as values and *link attributes* that may contain one or more links to instances of a specific concept. Links to multimedia information are implemented via primitive attributes. The values of these attributes are pointers to multimedia objects.

The top node of the concept hierarchy is the concept THING which defines the most general entity in the database. The only attributes that are defined by THING are the primitive attributes *external–name* (an external name for the information node), *description* (a textual description), *picture* (an associated picture), *video* (a videoclip), and *voice* (a voice annotation). Each information node on the factual level has at least these attributes.

The Factual Level

Each concept may have *instances* with individual attribute values (e.g. *Baden–Baden* is an instance of the concept CITY). An attribute may be a property of the instance (e.g. the attribute *size* contains the number of inhabitants of a city), a link to one or more other instances (e.g. the attribute *region* is a link to an instance of the concept REGION), or a multimedia object (e.g. the attribute *picture* contains the pixmap obtained from a photograph of the city). The set of all instances forms the *factual level* of the information base. The architecture of multimedia objects is outlined in chapter 5.

4. The Formal Query

The formulation and modification of queries in the retrieval system is performed with the query component. It provides general mechanisms that are independent from the contents of the information base and therefore portable to different domains.

During the retrieval process the user interacts with the system via a direct manipulation interface. He starts with a simple initial query which may be incrementally modified by stepwise refinement or by reformulation. This approach is strongly influenced by the systems: Rabbit (Tou et.al. (1982)) and Argon (Patel–Schneider (1984)).

Corresponding to the query built up by the user there is an internal representation which may be evaluated to find the entities of the information database matching the formal query. These entities may serve as entry points for the browser component.

The formal query is internally represented as a hierarchical structure. Each query is a description on the conceptual level of the information base and represents a set of instances that match this description. The possible modifications of the internal query description are driven by the conceptual structure of the database (concept hierarchy and attribute definitions) and will always lead to a correct query that may be evaluated at any time to recompute the set of matching instances. The simplest complete query from which all other queries may be derived is the 'initial query'. It represents the set of all instances of the information base. Attribute descriptions within a query may again contain subqueries that may be evaluated for their own. To enable the user formulating the query solely by means of direct manipulation the query component starts with the initial query, which refers to the concept THING and has no further restrictions. This query may be incrementally modified.

Figure 2 shows a query which may be formulated as follows:

"Find a spa which offers casinos and restaurants."

The evaluation of this query leads to the set of cities presented in a map. The names of the retrieved cities are selectable. In this case Baden–Baden has been chosen. The next navigation step leads to the city map as shown in Figure 2.

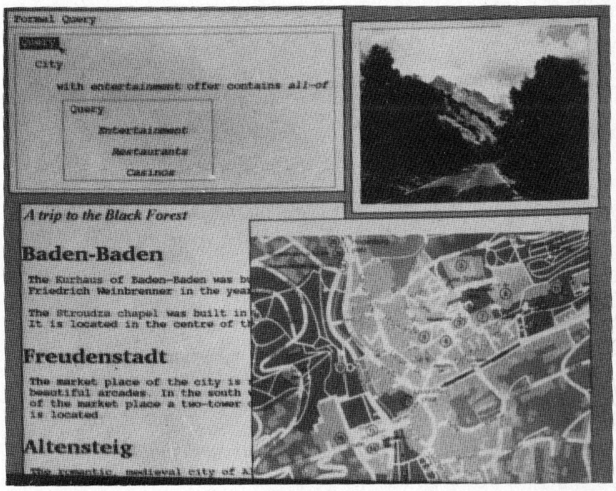

Figure 2. A query with multimedia browsing

Each query description may be evaluated to compute the set of instances that is represented by the description. This is done recursively by computing the sets of instances for concept descriptions and query descriptions from the bottom to the top of the tree. For efficiency reasons the results are stored at the nodes of the tree and kept as long as this subtree is not modified so that a later re–evaluation minimizes the access to the database.

5. Hypermedia Architecture

For the purposes of this project both techniques, formal queries and browsing, will be provided. In terms of the data model the hypermedia system manages information in a network which is organized as independent, small and discrete units, called nodes. Furthermore, these nodes are interconnected by links. The nodes correspond to multimedia data which belongs to one of the following information types: text, picture, graphic, audio and video. This means that each node has associated content of only one of the above types. In terms of the implementation model, the term 'particle' will be used for these nodes. For collections of particles which are presented together the term 'page' will be used. This can be considered as a generalization of a printed document page which can speak, play music or show a movie in addition to the traditional static information. A particle consists of content of a specific type and some linking information. Currently, linking information has a source, destination and presentation description. The presentation description deals with visualization of the location in the source particle, from which the link starts. The perception of a link will be a multimedia object (often a graphic object), which is called a 'marker'.

The implementation model is realized as object-oriented architecture. The fundamental objects of this architecture are classes, instances, generic functions and methods. The following terminology expresses the most important relations in this architecture:

- *is–a* denotes the class–instance relationship;
- *depends–on* denotes the inheritance relationship, which is the sharing of characteristics and behaviour among a set of classes;
- *part–of* denotes the ability to create composite objects.

At the current design stage the classes belong to the categories: *media objects* (e.g. text, picture, video and audio), *presentation objects* (e.g. windows, icons, etc.), *manipulation objects* (e.g. menus, control–sheets, etc.).

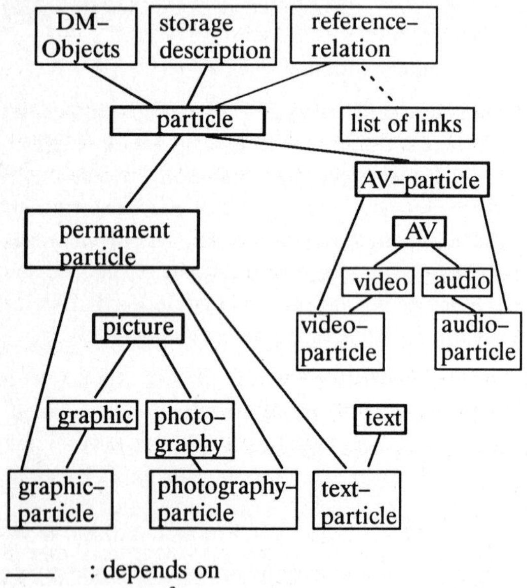

Figure 3. illustrates an example of some fundamental objects related to these categories.

The following taxonomy of classes has been developed so far. Classes TEXT and PICTURE represent the data structures and operations for text and still images. PICTURE is specialized to GRAPHIC and PHOTOGRAPHIC types to distinguish computer generated images and real world images. Class AUDIO-VIDEO (AV) represents common properties of sound and video information. AUDIO and VIDEO are subclasses of AV. To describe storage representation of multimedia objects the class STORAGE-DESCRIPTION is introduced. Objects of this class contain in addition to retrieval also administrational information such as author, creation date, version, etc. Layout information will be mixed with the internal structures of the media objects. Class BASIC-LAYOUT describes common properties of spatial information for visual presentation. Therefore TEXT, PICTURE and VIDEO inherit this information. The abstract class PRESENTATION-SUPPORT describes the ability to maintain the audio–visual appearance of objects and supports the identification of objects. Another abstract class MANIPULATION-SUPPORT provides the necessary mechanisms for applying operations on objects and their attributes. Finally the composition of the above two classes is specialized to the class DM-OBJECTS (i.e. Direct Manipulation Objects). Class LINK models the concept of linking and class REFERENCE-RELATION summarizes common properties of linking behaviour.

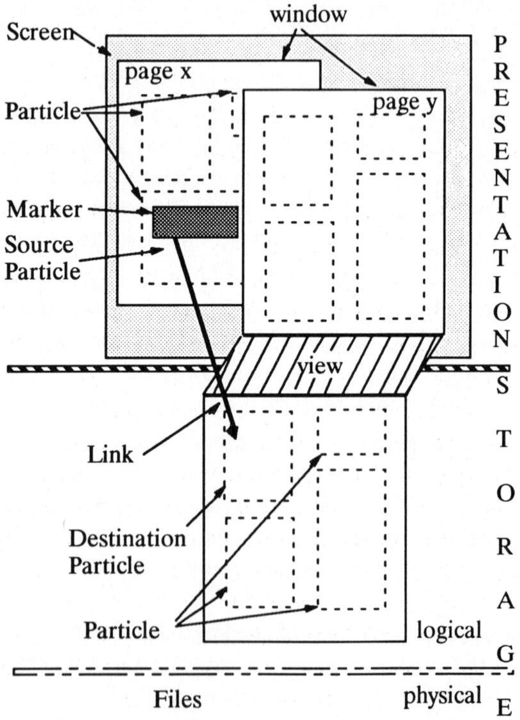

Figure 4. Relationships of some classes.

Class PARTICLE is a specialization of the classes DM-OBJECTS, REFERENCE-RELATION and STORAGE-DESCRIPTION which represents the information units (nodes) as mentioned above. A meaningful collection of particles is represented by an instance of the class PAGE. Figure 4. illustrates the relationships amongst some of the above classes.

Current findings indicate that a simple data model based on labelled directed graphs is not sufficient for modelling the hypermedia applications addressed in this project. At the current stage a data model based on hypergraphs (Tompa (1989)) is under consideration. For example one of the major requirements is to separate the linking structure from the content so that different network structures can be superimposed over the same media objects. That is there should be a strong distinction between archived material (such as picture documents, text documents, video clips, etc.) and navigational structures. Another major requirement is to have an appropriate concept which is able to express the notion of the class PAGE in terms of the data model. The hypergraph model provides appropriate descriptive means for coping with problem, resulting from the requirements mentioned above.

6. User Interface

On the physical level the system is a workstation with a high resolution color display and a pointing device. The workstation is enhanced by HiFi sound equipment and a facility for inserting real time video into the display. Design principles such as metaphors from the real world, desktop concept, see–and–point and direct manipulation, which are familiar from the WYSIWYG based publishing systems, guide the prototyping of the user interface (Lesniewski et.al. (1987)). The user interface itself is viewed logically as an event based model, i.e. the user generates events by interacting with input/output devices. Event–based mechanisms are currently the most–used control and communication techniques upon which asynchronous dialogue is constructed. Physical actions are discovered by media devices and passed to the interface software as events. The events will then be received and processed by appropriate objects (Hartson et.al. (1989)). Most of the objects the user deals with are direct manipulative objects (DM–OBJECTS). They also receive events and are responsible for appropriate reactions and feedback. In this way the user works with a direct manipulative system, in which objects are identifiable and tangible with the pointing device.

To give an impression of the systems surface at the current stage of the project a photographic image of the screen is shown in Figure 5. On the left of the screen a text particle with markers designating the links is visible. In the top right hand corner a video clip is running and beneath it a color picture is shown. But the true impression of colors, motion and audio can only be demonstrated with the system running.

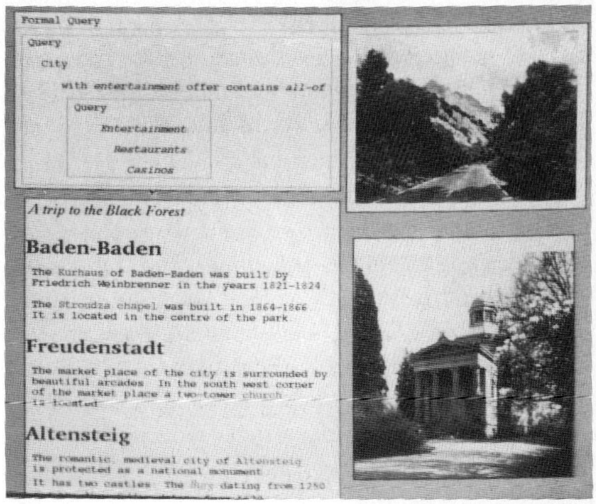

Figure 5. Photo of the screen

The interaction methods used to set up a formal query mainly depend on the selection of DM–OBJECTS. This has several advantages:

- There is no need for the user to learn the syntax of a formal language. The syntax is incorporated into the query–manipulating operations, which are selected from menus.
- Semantic values to be specified in the query are also selected from menus which provide all possible values. So, the user does not have to know the contents of the database.
- No incorrect query may be formulated since the whole process of formulating a query is guided by the query component and the database.

The interaction makes extensive use of pointing device and dynamic menus. Each part of the external query representation is directly manipulable.

7. Implementation Aspects and Future Work

The prototyping started with the implementation of a tool for readers where the user can query and navigate through the hypernet by following predefined links. In this case the user is not allowed to modify or to extend the information base. But the design and the implementation of the software structure already incorporates the concepts needed for an authoring tool where the user has the freedom to extend the system both on the content level (multimedia documents) and on the structural level (query and navigation).

The development environment consists of SUN and SYMBOLICS workstations and a system–independent video mixer which inserts realtime video on the high resolution color display. Several video sources such as video disc, video tape and video camera are controlled by the system. An integrated FDDI interface allows the experimentation with broadband communication facilities. The final demonstrator will be running on a SUN Sparcstation.

Communication and system related software has been implemented using the programming languages C and C++. Querying and browsing facilities as well as the user interface were written in Common Lisp (Steele (1984)) and PCL/CLOS (Keene (1989)) and the Common Lisp X–Window Interface (CLX) (Scheifler et.al. (1988)). Interaction objects are implemented using the user interface toolkit **Xit** which is based on the principles of general user interface management systems and toolkits (Herczeg (1989)).

One of the major implementation goals is a high degree of portability. Therefore system components such as UNIX, C, Common Lisp, X–Window and s.o. which are already available on many systems where chosen. Objectoriented programming techniques have been used to reduce dependence on these standard interfaces.

In the near future an object–oriented data base will be used to deal with the problem of persistency of hypermedia objects.

Starting the navigation from one of the results of the formal query is rather straightforward and has been outlined in this paper (see Figure 1). Working in the other direction is more complicated and requires additional elaboration. The problem is to construct the intentional description of a subset containing the node reached by the navigation. To achieve this the observation of the attributes of objects inspected during the navigation may be helpful. Furthermore, some dialog will be necessary during the construction or relaxation of constraints for the new query.

The communication part of the project will enhance the system by providing a video conferencing facility. This facility will allow the user to establish a video phone connection with one or two other parties on the workstation's screen. In this way they will be able to discuss the content of a multimedia document presented on the screen. This provides the basic features of a system which supports cooperative distributed working.

---

* SEL ALCATEL – Standard Elektrik Lorenz AG (D), Alcatel Standard Electrica SA (E), TELENORMA – Telefonbau und Normalzeit GmbH (D), CSATA – Tecnopolis (I), Industrie FACE Standard SpA (I), ALCATEL STK – Standard Telefon og Kabelfabrik A/S (N), University of Stuttgart, Institute of Computer Science

References

Halasz F.: Reflections on Notecards: Seven issues for the next generation of hypermedia systems, CACM 31, 7 (1988) pp. 836–851.

Yankielovich N., Haan B., Meyerowitz N., Drucker S.: Intermedia: The concept and the construction of a seamless information environment IEEE Computer 21, 1, (1988) pp. 81–96.

Conklin J.. Hypertext: An Introduction and Survey. Computer, 20, 9 (1987) pp.17––41.

Campagnoni F.R., Ehrlich K.: Information Retrieval Using a Hypertext–Based Help System. ACM Trans. on Inf. Syst. Vol 7, No 3, (1989) pp. 271–291.

Tou F.N.,. Williams M.D, Fikes R.E. Henderson A., Malone T.W.: RABBIT: An Intelligent Database Assistant. In Proceedings of AAAI–82, Second National Conference on Artificial Intelligence (Pittsburgh, PA), (1982) pp 314––318.

Patel–Schneider P.F., Brachman R.J., Levesque H.J.; ARGON: Knowledge Representation meets Information Retrieval. Fairchild technical report no. 654, Schlumberger Palo Alto Research, (1984).

Tompa F., A Data Model for Flexible Hypertext Database Systems, ACM Transactions on Information Systems Vol 7 Nr 1 (1989) pp. 85–100.

Lesniewski A., H. Roessler, P. Szabo, K.–H. Jerke, Designing an User–Oriented Interface to a Document Management System, HCI–Interact'87 (1987) pp. 541–546.

Hartson H. R., Hix D., Human–Computer Interface Development: Concept and Systems, ACM Computing Surveys, Vol. 21 Nr. 1 (1989) pp. 5–92.

Steele Jr. G. L.: Common LISP: The Language. Digital Press, Digital Equipment Corporation (1984).

Keene S.E.: Object–Oriented Programming in Common Lisp, Addison–Wesley (1989).

Sheifler R.W., LaMott O.: CLX – Common LISP Language X Interface. Texas Instruments Incorporated, PO Box 655474, MS 238, Dallas, TX 75265, (1988).

Herczeg M.: USIT: A Toolkit For User Interface Toolkits. In Proceedings of Third International Conference on Human–Computer Interaction, Boston, Massachusetts, (1989).

SECTION III: DETAILED DESIGN

SIII.5 Construction Tools

An experiment in interactive architectures
E. Edmonds and N. Hagiwara 601

SCENARIOO: A new generation UIMS
B. Roudaud, V. Lavigne, O. Lagneau, and E. Minor 607

MUD: Multiple-view user interface design
D. England 613

PENGUIN: A language for reactive graphical user interface programming
S.-K. Yap and M.L. Scott 619

Petri net objects for the design, validation and prototyping of user-driven interfaces
R. Bastide and P. Palanque 625

An object-oriented UIMS for rapid prototyping
Y.-P. Shan 633

Do-it-yourself iconic displays: Reconfigurable iconic representations of application objects
P.D. Gray, K.W. Waite, and S.W. Draper 639

Localisation of application knowledge in incremental development of user interfaces
P.D. Gray, C.A. Wood, and A.C. Kilgour 645

A UIMS for knowledge based interface template generation and interaction
C. Märtin 651

Incorporating metaphor in automated interface design
B. Blumenthal 659

Human–Computer Interaction – INTERACT '90
D. Diaper et al. (Editors)
Elsevier Science Publishers B.V. (North-Holland)

AN EXPERIMENT IN INTERACTIVE ARCHITECTURES

Ernest Edmonds, LUTCHI Research Centre, Loughborough University of Technology, Loughborough, UK
and
Noriko Hagiwara, Software Product Engineering Laboratory, NEC Corporation, Tokyo, Japan

The paper considers the interactive architecture known as the "Seeheim Model". A problem which emerged with that model as direct manipulation became more important is identified. A solution to the problem was proposed which involved the introduction of active objects in place of the application interface model. This proposal was evaluated by constructing a direct manipulation graphical interface using that architecture. Certain problems were encountered which were solved by modifying the architecture again. The paper describes the experiment and its results. A new interactive architecture is presented and its relationship to the source models demonstrated.

1. INTRODUCTION

Since William Newman's early work on his system for interactive graphical programming (Newman, 1968), considerable attention has been given to architectures for interaction and related systems. Much of this work has evolved around the specific issue of user interface separability, as described in an historical survey by Edmonds (1990). The degree to which separability can be achieved, and the architectural requirements for it, have been the questions most frequently discussed in reports on research into interactive architectures. Early thinking, such as that of Moran (1981) and Edmonds (1982), was brought together at a 1983 workshop in Seeheim and the result is now widely known as 'The Seeheim Model' (Green, 1985). As shown in Figure 1, the separation, in that model, was intended to be achieved through the 'Application Interface Model'. Thus, for example, an object in the Presentation layer would only have a link to the Application through Dialogue Control and, afterwards, the Application Interface Model or, in special cases, directly to the Application Interface Model. In those cases where a high band-width communication was needed, it was proposed that Dialogue Control directed the communication, by controlling the Switch, even though the data was never seen by the Dialogue Control module itself.

At Seeheim, the interest was in the separation of concerns between different software modules, in a way that provided the designer of an interactive system with a means of effecting modularisation and, with it, greater clarity. A number of authors have, since, tried to extend this basic concept. For example, Cockton (1987) suggests that in the ideal case, the application and the user interface might be such that changes to one component cause no change to the other. As has been argued elsewhere (Edmonds, 1990), this ideal goal is probably not achievable and, as the work reported here suggests, even a more specific objective, that of partitioning an interactive system in a way which does not result in performance disadvantages, leads to interesting architectural developments. It is expected that each component in such an architecture will need modification in order to build any particular interactive system.

2. SUPPORTING DIRECT MANIPULATION

Direct manipulation interfaces (Shneiderman, 1983) have become very important in recent years and many authors have noted that they pose particular problems for interactive architectures. Hudson, for example, (1987), points out that the problem of organising the software so as to provide appropriate feedback can be quite difficult:

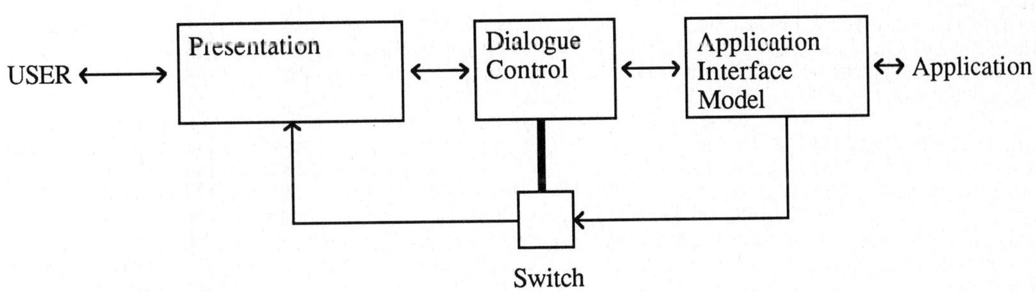

Figure 1

"... in the Macintosh desktop interface in some cases, such as putting a file in a folder, one may drag objects *into* other objects. In other cases dragging one object on top of another has no special semantic consequence. The semantic difference between these lexically identical operations is clarified by highlighting..." (Hudson, 1987).

Dealing with these problems led Hudson to propose a modified architecture, see Figure 2. Here, the Application Interface Model is replaced by an Application Data Model that is shared by the user interface and the application code. At the same time, the Dialogue Control module is removed. In this approach, the Application Interface Model becomes a collection of active application objects that are available to both the user interface and the application which might, alternatively, take the name Application Object Models. Semantic information, therefore, should be much more accessible to the Presentation layer because, for example, semantic changes can be directly reflected in the information available for presentation.

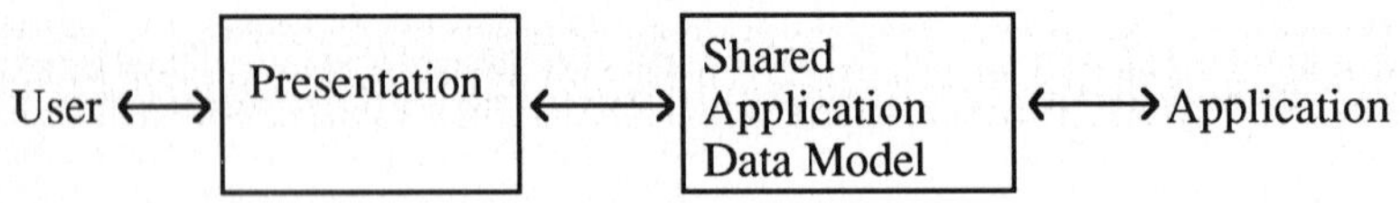

Figure 2

The goal of the experiment described here was to evaluate this architecture in practice. It was not necessary to construct a complete User Interface Management System (Pfaff, 1985), or even implement a significant application, in order to study the architecture. In fact, a restricted and well-defined problem was found that enabled a careful study of the significant issues to be made. The problem was to construct a particular interactive system tool for the definition of icons and to carefully consider its architectural requirements. This tool is described in the next section.

3. PIT: A GRAPHICAL ICON TOOL

The problem selected for the experiment was that of devising a tool for the construction of new icons, each of which could to be associated with some particular semantics. The role of the Programmable Icon Tool (PIT) was to deliver the icon and its semantics into the interactive system in a usable form. Thus, the tool can be seen as an essential element of a User Interface Management System and, hence, one which must generate a result that can operate successfully within the interactive architecture employed.

In practice, the tool adds facilities to MacProlog using the 'Graphic Editor' Program provided by LPA MacProlog (LPA, 1988). The new tool provides a graphics editor to draw an icon and gives the designer an ability to define the semantics that underlie it. An example semantic definition is provided as a guide to the designer. It can be used as a semantic definition template.

To help the designer to define icons, the system provides the following facilities:-

1) a display of icons from which a selection may be made.
2) a graphics editor with which to design new icons.
3) an editing facility for the association of semantics with an icon.

In the first instance, for the purpose of the experiment, the system provides icons that represent the following graphical facilities: rubberband line, arc drawing, scaling, copying. In addition, of course, designers can add their own icons and there own semantics to the set of templates provided.

PIT generates graphical descriptions of programs from the designer's own definition of an icon and its associated skeleton semantics. The semantics provide a description of the actions that the system should perform when a particular icon is selected. For the purposes of our experiment, when the designer specifies an icon, the system generates associated semantics that, as a default, draws a picture of the icon on the drawing area. The designer can then choose, as an alternative, a semantic description from the templates provided by the system and modify it to adapt it to his or her requirements.

The key point to notice is that the activation of an icon does not necessarily lead to an application action. Indeed, it can generate a change that exists purely in presentation or can cause actions that change presentation and more than one application action, if the designer so desires.

4. AN EXAMPLE OF PIT IN USE

In this section, an example showing how to make a graphics editor for dialogue box design is presented.

The following description covers the instructions that should be followed in order to complete the procedure that is needed in order to build the example graphics editor.

1) Select 'new item' from the 'tool pane' menu and then give the name of the intended graphics editor for building dialogue boxes, say 'test'.

2) Set the chosen tool provided by the system onto the tool pane of the new graphics editor; select the 'set default' tool item, and the list of default tools appears (Figure 3); choose the tools which are needed to build the required editor. The tools for selecting, information, eraser, scaling, rubberband-line, rectangle and copying are selected. The selected items then appear in the 'tool pane' of 'test' (Figure 4). In Figure 4, the window 'scaling:desc' shows the associated semantics expressed in Prolog.

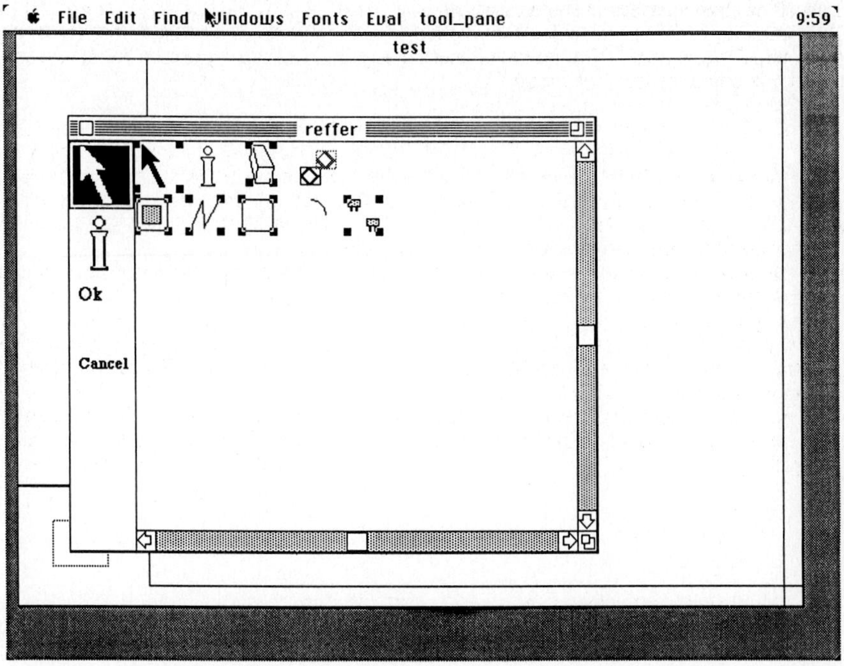

Figure 3

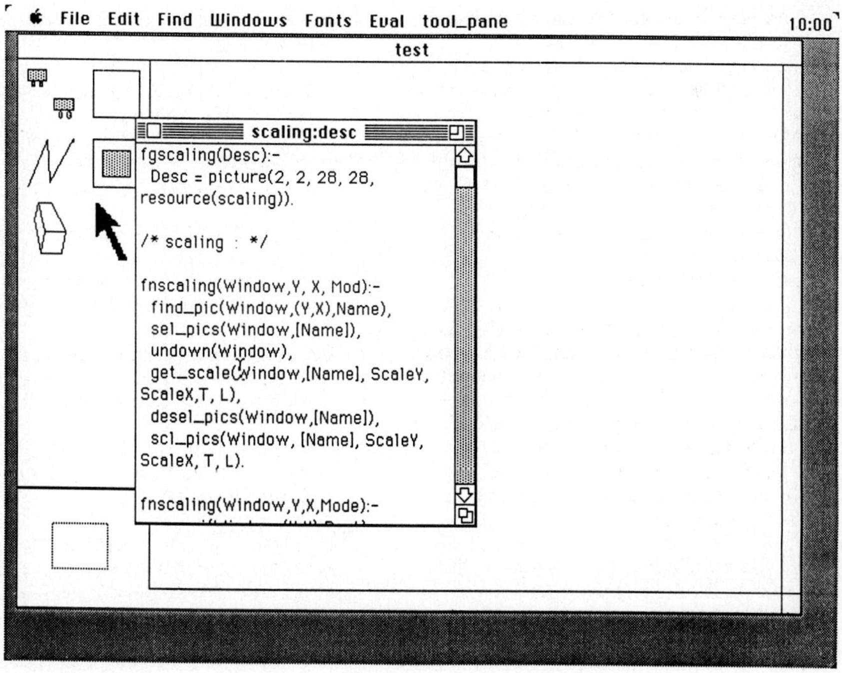

Figure 4

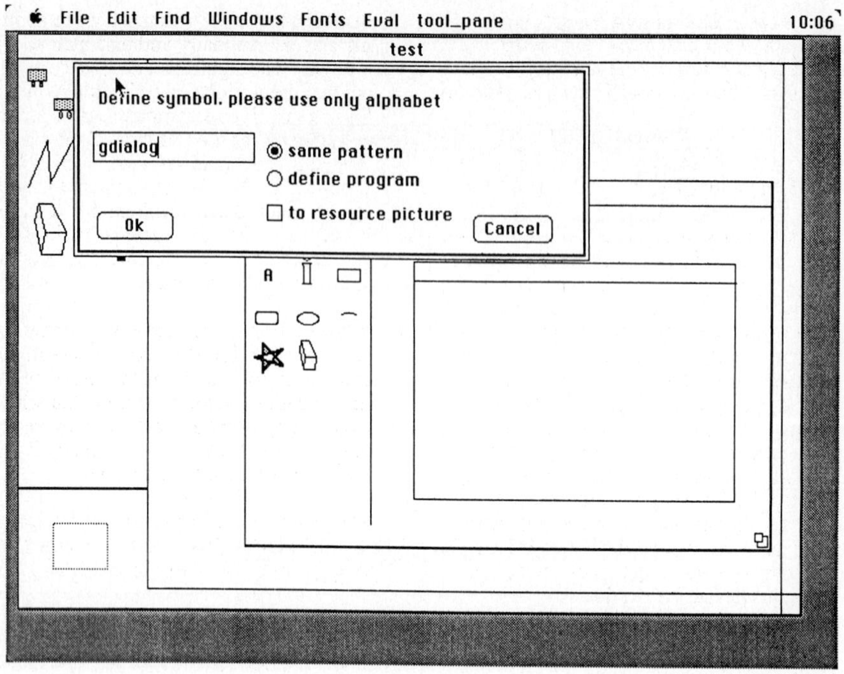

Figure 5

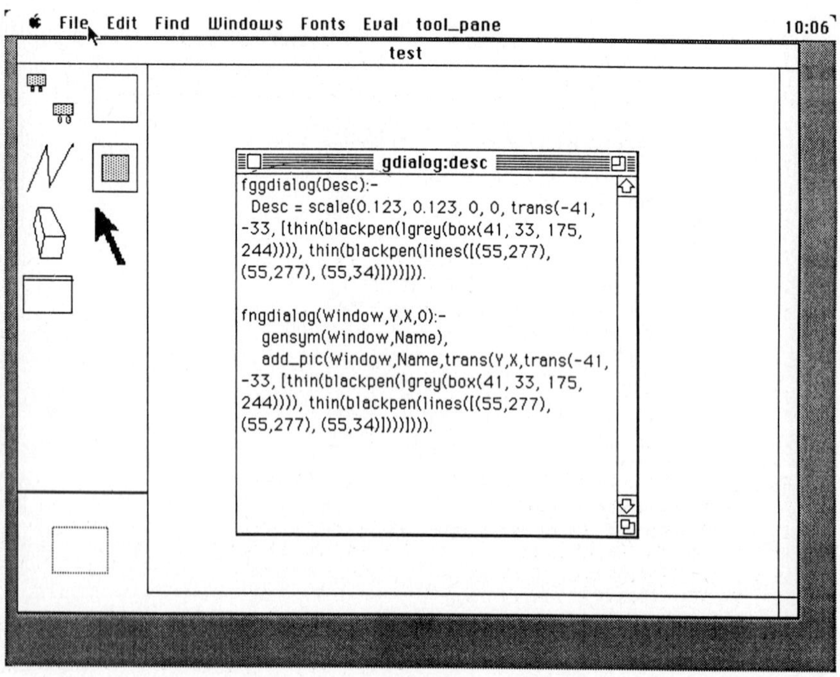

Figure 6

3) An extra icon can then be drawn using the graphics editor. In Figure 5, the dialogue box boundary is defined and the default semantics of the tool (drawing the same figure) is selected. Finally, the semantics are modified to deal with text input (Figure 6).

5. THE REVISED ARCHITECTURE

In constructing PIT, an attempt was made to apply Hudson's model. However, in the event, it did not prove practical to follow it fully. The particular problem which arose was that an icon did not necessarily map directly onto a single application object, i.e. a single entry in the Shared Application Data Model. In fact, the system designer is able, for example, to associate a complex set of inter-related application actions with a single icon or, at the other extreme, to decide that an action associated with an icon only affects the Presentation layer. It was not practical to view the control of the icon-related actions and their consequences as part of the application and, thus, it was necessary to introduce an Action Control module to handle them, as shown in Figure 7. This module contains the description of the actions resulting from a designer action on an icon in terms of presentation changes and operations on the application objects, as represented in the Shared Application Data Model. Communications are required between each of the three user interface components. Thus, all of the communications proposed by Hudson are supported, together with the extra ones required by the introduction of the Action Control module.

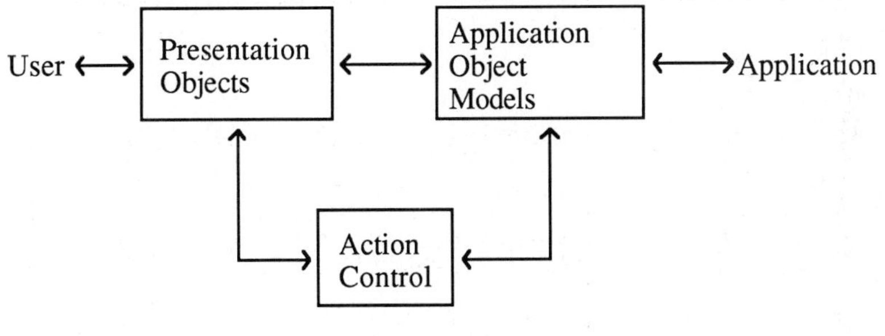

Figure 7

Comparing Figure 1 with Figure 7, we can see that a similar set of three components exists in both. An important consideration for both is that they contain links which must be high bandwidth; the link through the Switch in Figure 1 and the link between Presentation Objects and Application Object Models in Figure 7. The distinction between the two figures is that the link between Presentation and Application objects is central to Figure 7 but an exception route in Figure 1.

6. CONCLUSIONS

It is interesting to compare the interactive architecture described above and the early Seeheim model. It turns out that the early view was much more appropriate for modern interfaces than many authors, such as Hudson, have thought. The significant difference between the two views are that the Action Control module does not have access to a Switch that directs communication between the other two components, as the Dialogue Control module did in the Seeheim view and that 'switch' route is not seen as exceptional. We would not wish to assert that an arrangement like the Seeheim Switch is not required at all; it is only clear that it is not required in the handling of the particular User Interface Management task that formed the subject of our experiment.

In the early work on interactive architectures, the issue of whether each different module should exist in a different process or not was not identified. Considerations of direct manipulation, however, dictate that with the currently available technology, it is probably necessary for the complete user interface to reside within a single process, as was was done in our experiment.

The experiment has concluded with a new Architecture which has much in common with the Seeheim Model but that is appropriate for direct manipulation interfaces.

ACKNOWLEDGEMENTS

The work described in this paper was partly conducted with the generous support of the NEC Corporation. André Schappo provided helpful advice during the development of the experiment described and Linda Candy provided valuable comments on an earlier draft of the paper.

REFERENCES

Cockton, G. (1987). A new model for separable interactive systems. In Human-Computer Interaction - INTERACT '87. Bullinger, H-J and Shackel, B. (eds). North-Holland. pp 1033-1038.

Edmonds, E.A. (1982). The man-computer interface: a note on concepts and design. Int. J. Man-Machine Studies, 16. pp 315-326.

Edmonds, E.A. (1990). The emergence of the separable user interface. ICL Technical Journal. (To appear).

Green, M. (1985). Report on dialogue specification tools. In Pfaff. pp 9-20.

Hudson, S.E. (1987). UIMS support for direct manipulation interfaces. Computer Graphics, 21, 2. pp 120-124.

LPA (1988). LPA Mac PROLOG reference manual, LPA Ltd., London.

Moran, T. (1981). The command language grammar, a representation for the user interface of interactive computer systems. Int. J. Man-Machine Studies, 15. pp 3-50.

Newman, W. (1968). A system for interactive graphical programming. Proc. of Spring Joint Computer Conference. pp 473-86.

Pfaff, G.E.(ed.). (1985). User Interface Management Systems. Springer Verlag.

Sheiderman, B. (1983). Direct manipulation: a step beyond programming languages. IEEE Computer, 16, 8. pp 57-69.

Human–Computer Interaction – INTERACT '90
D. Diaper et al. (Editors)
Elsevier Science Publishers B.V. (North-Holland)

SCENARIOO: A New Generation UIMS

Brigitte ROUDAUD, Valérie LAVIGNE, Olivier LAGNEAU, Earl MINOR

CAP SESA Innovation, 7 chemin du Vieux Chêne, 38240 Meylan, France

UIMS technology and tools are still an evolving research area in the domain of human computer interaction. Although some techniques are today well defined, the user interface designer still has few tools to prototype, develop, debug, and assess a user interface. SCENARIOO [1] is a rich UIMS which provides many of these tools. SCENARIOO allows the user interface designer to prototype, develop, test and debug a user interface, either in a simulated or true application environment, with one or multiple running applications. It provides interactive graphical editors for development of each part of the user interface (presentation, dialogue control), and automatically generates the code of the final program. Thus, the interface designer can concentrate on good interface design, not programming details. Here we describe SCENARIOO.

1. Introduction

In modern workstation applications the portion of code devoted to implementing the user interface is often a significant proportion of the overall code. This code has become highly specialized, requiring mastery of accepted user interface design principles and knowledge of standard graphics libraries. In fact, the design of user interface code now demands as great a knowledge of workstation interface techniques as of the application functionality. At the same time, networks are opening up new possibilities for distributing applications and interfaces on multiple processors to increase performance and throughput.

The development of User Interface Management Systems (UIMS) has occurred in an effort to find better and easier ways to implement the user interface portion of applications software. A UIMS is based on the idea of the interactive application model [2], which subdivides an interactive application into three parts (figure 1).

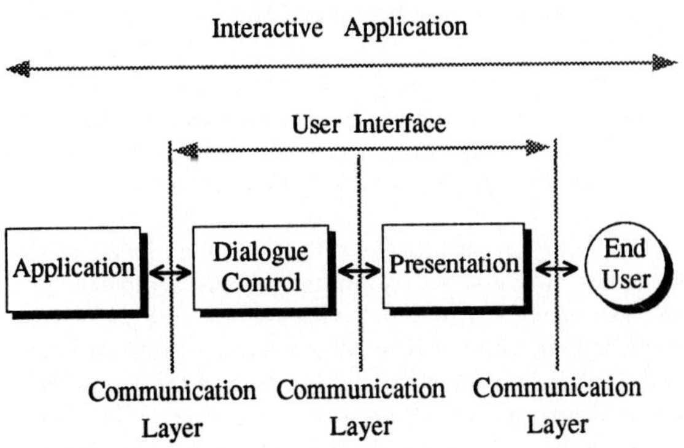

figure 1: The Interactive Application Model

In this model the application functionality is separated from the functionality of the user interface, thus lending several advantages. Most important, the interface and the application can be developed independently, and by different people. Such an approach fits well into a team effort and permits faster development by allowing specialists to work in parallel. Also, several previously independent applications can be integrated into a single larger application by creating an interface which coordinates and communicates with them all. Since the interface and the application are independent, they can be run on separate nodes, making the migration to distributed environments easier. Finally, existing applications with poor interfaces can be upgraded by connecting them to new and better interfaces.

In the application model the user interface is subdivided into two layers; the presentation layer and the dialogue control layer. A UIMS provides tools to aid in the development of both layers, and then to integrate the user interface into the interactive application. In this paper we describe such a UIMS, called SCENARIOO. SCENARIOO is a complete UIMS, containing tools for each phase of the user interface development process. In addition, SCENARIOO aims to extend the current functionality of UIMSs in the areas of dialogue representation and interactive test environments for debugging.

Dialogue in SCENARIOO is represented visually by event graphs. This approach is based on the idea that a well chosen visual representation conveys a better understanding of a system than an abstract (language, or programming) representation. The SCENARIOO test environment is directed towards the very practical consideration of using a UIMS in a production setting, where a major portion of the effort is devoted to making modifications and debugging. In the remainder of this paper we will look at SCENARIOO in detail, concentrating particularly on the dialogue representation and the test environment.

2. SCENARIOO Overview

The global functional architecture for SCENARIOO is presented in figure 2. The grey arrows correspond to interface creation time, and the solid black arrows correspond to interface run time. The two arrows marked with asterisks are mutually exclusive; i.e. at run time only one of these links really exists. This means that at run time you can run either the real application or the simulation, but not both together.

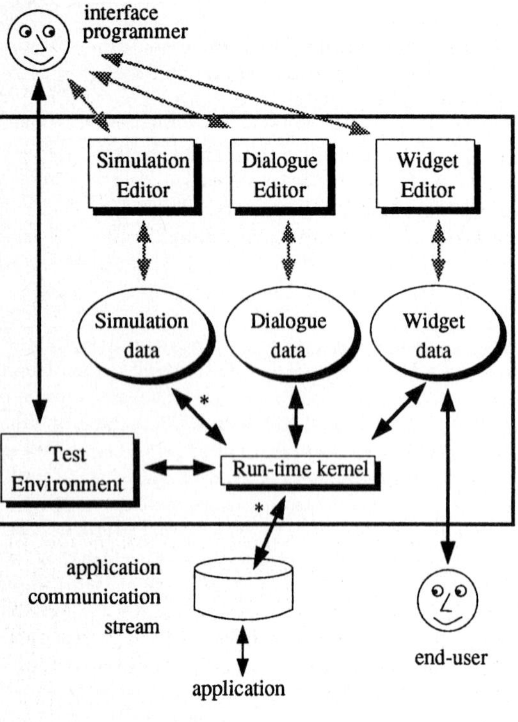

figure 2: Global Architecture for SCENARIOO

The process of building an interface using SCENARIOO essentially consists of generating and modifying three internal data bases; the Widget data, the Dialogue data, and the Simulation data. The Widget data contains *widgets*, which are the visual objects that compose displays. Examples of simple widgets are menus, push buttons, and text boxes. Widgets can contain other widgets, so that an entire display can consist of a single *composite widget*, constructed from simpler widgets. The Dialogue data contains a set of event graphs. Each graph provides a visual representation of the dynamic behavior for a part of the interface. All of the graphs taken together specify the complete interface dialogue. The Simulation data contains one or more sets of application simulation data. Each data set simulates values for all of the functions in the application. The different sets simulate different application behavior.

Each data base has its own interactive editor. These editors permit the user interface designer to build the interface using direct manipulation of graphical objects, rather than by programming. The Widget Editor allows widgets to be created, modified, and assembled into composite widgets using simple interactive graphical manipulations. The Dialogue Editor allows event graphs to be constructed from basic graphical elements. The conditions and actions associated with event graph transitions are entered using forms, menus, and icons. The Simulation Editor is used to generate sets of application simulation data. It provides features to aid in reproducing and modifying multiple sets of data.

The heart of SCENARIOO is the run-time kernel. The run-time kernel accesses the internal data bases to implement the user interface. It reads the Widget data to obtain the specification for the visual aspect of the displays. It continuously interprets the graph set in the Dialogue data to carry out display changes and application communications. To perform the application communications, the run-time kernel is connected either to the simulation data base or to the actual application. Typically, the simulation data base is used during prototyping and early debugging, and the connection to the actual application is made for final debugging and tests. The simulation data base allows the interface development to be carried out in parallel with the application development, and permits a significant amount of testing and debugging to be done independently of the application.

Prototyping and debugging are supported by the SCENARIOO test environment. The test environment allows the user interface developer to invoke the run-time kernel with a list of parameters which control the execution of the interface. For example, the test environment can direct the run-time kernel to single step, or to execute the number of steps needed to reach the next breakpoint. The test environment also contains a facility for generating a history file of all interactions which occur during the current session of the interface interpretation. The history file can then be used instead of user input to drive the run-time kernel through a standard sequence of operations. The test environment provides a convenient step by step debugging facility.

3. Communication with the Application

The user interface can be thought of as a separate, self contained system which communicates with the application according to a well defined protocol. This is the model of the interactive application presented in figure 1.

Since the application and the interface are independent, a mechanism must be established for the communication between them. SCENARIOO requires that each application communicate with the interface via a single input stream, a single output stream, and a single error stream. On a UNIX system, these streams could correspond directly to the well known standard input, standard output, and standard error files for applications. This requirement insures a very robust and portable communication link between the application and the interface, at the expense of limiting the flexibility of the communications permitted to the application. The application does not need a flexible communication link, however; the basic input, output, and error streams are sufficient to support the interface.

Most communications between the interface and the application are synchronized according to a simple query response model. Messages originate in the interface, often as a result of user actions, and are sent to the application in its input stream. It is assumed that the application sends reply messages in the same order as the received inputs. There is also a mechanism for handling unsolicited messages originating in the application. All incoming messages to SCENARIOO are first examined by a low level process. If the message format does not match the format for the pending reply message it is treated as an unsolicited message. Such messages can be routed to special graphs in the dialogue. Messages coming into SCENARIOO via the error stream are always handled as unsolicited massages. All such messages can be routed to graphs in the dialogue which are concerned with handling errors.

It is possible to connect more than one independent application to a single interface. Each application must communicate via its own input, output, and error streams as described previously. SCENARIOO manages the multiple applications in parallel, maintaining separate communications queues for each one. The coordination of events between applications is controlled by the dialogue, which can specify sets of conditions and actions dependent on more than one application. In this way a single integrated application can be created from several smaller independent applications. In a distributed environment it is possible that the independent applications, and the interface itself, could all be run on different nodes.

4. The Dialogue Management

This section describes why Event Graphs can be useful in the development of User Interfaces and especially how they are used to specify the dialogue in SCENARIOO.

4.1 What is the dialogue?

Recall that a user interface has two parts :

- the presentation : consists of all the windows, forms, messages and images that can be displayed on the screen;
- the dialogue : describes the way the user interface is animated, that is to say when such window is displayed or removed, when such button is available or not, when such message is displayed or removed, and so on. The dialogue also represents how End User's actions and interventions from the application are taken into account. In other words, the dialogue specifies what to do on End-User's actions (click on a button, selection of an item in a menu), or on application requests (display of an information or of an error message).

The specification of the presentation of the user interface is not really a complex problem, but it can be tedious and time consuming to specify each form or window, and to write each message to be displayed. Today there exist a number of tools allowing this specification to be done graphically and interactively saving a lot of time. These tools or editors generate from the graphical specification an associated textual specification or code implementation.

The specification of the dialogue, however, is more difficult. As the dialogue becomes sophisticated and complex, so does its specification. Very quickly the specification can become a mess and the developer is easily lost. Up to now there is no tool that can aid in this specification by hiding the complexity. Some progress has been made in giving the dialogue a formalism such as *grammar based systems* [3][4], or *rules based systems* [5], but although these systems provide a way to specify the dialogue, they do not help in controlling and managing its complexity. SCENARIOO attempts to provide such a tool by allowing a complex dialogue to be broken into a set of simpler ones, and by providing a visual representation of dialogue.

4.2 The Event Graphs system

What is missing from the dialogue representations of today is: 1) a way to structure the dialogue; 2) a way to visualize the dialogue. Event Graphs as they are used in SCENARIOO can provide solutions to these two problems first because graphs can be used to decompose a complex dialogue into simpler ones (a graph can be divided into several graphs), and second because they can contribute a very powerful visual aspect of the dialogue. Before going into more details, we will present a short overview of the kind of Event Graphs we are talking about.

4.2.1 The Event Graphs overview

In this paper we use a definition for Event Graphs which was developed for the ESPRIT-1 QUIC project [6]. The definition consists of two parts:

- a model that represents graphs,
- a principle for evaluating them.

The three main components in the Event Graphs model are places, transitions and tokens. A place does not contain any information, but it can be marked with a token or not. All the places marked in a graph represent its current state. A transition has a condition and a set of actions. A transition can be seen as a *rule* just like in rules based systems. The transition supports the actions that are performed under its condition. A transition can be fired if all its input places are marked and its condition is true. When a transition is fired, its actions are executed and the tokens are removed from the input places and each output place of the transition is marked with a token.

Figure 3 shows the different basic schemas that can be used to build a graph :

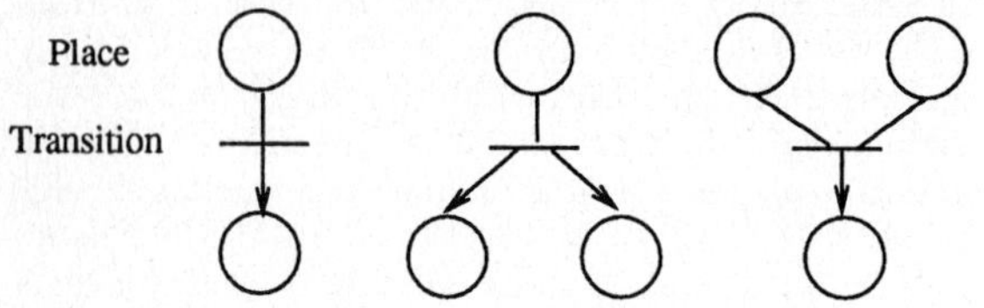

figure 3: Event Graphs basic schemas

A graph must have at least one initial place, but there can be several. An initial place is a place that is initially marked with a token. This is used during the "evaluation phase" and the set of initial places in a graph represents its initial state.

Once one or more graphs have been specified, they can be evaluated according to the following principle.
Repeat for ever :
For each graph:

- make a list of the firable transitions (all the input places marked);
- fire the first transition with its condition to true.

This means that all the graphs evolve concurrently. But for each graph, no more than one transition is fired during an evaluation cycle. The evaluation of the graphs is ended when no more firable transition can be found.

4.2.2 Formalization of the dialogue using Event Graphs

One of the main purposes of our system has been to use Event Graphs to specify the dialogue of the user interface. The specification of a dialogue consists of the specification of series of actions and the conditions of their activation. Conditions mainly consist of testing for the occurrence of a particular event or testing the state of some object in the presentation; actions mainly consist of modifying the presentation or calling a function in the application.

For example, consider an interactive application which requires the entry of a password. The user interface can be the following :

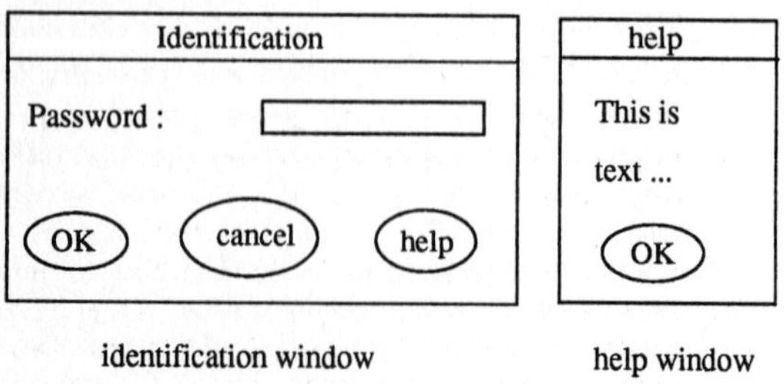

figure 4: Windows of the user interface

The user enters his password in the password field, then activates the OK button to validate his action. Activating the CANCEL button forgets the text entered and destroys the window. Activating the HELP button disables the identification window until the user activates the OK button of the help window.

The specification of the dialogue using rules can be :

- *if* the OK button of the identification window is activated *then* verify the password
- *if* the CANCEL button of the identification window is activated *then* destroy the window
- *if* the HELP button of the identification window is activated *then* disable the identification window, open the help window
- *if* the OK button of the help window is activated *then* destroy the help window, enable the identification window.

The same example can be represented using Event Graphs like this :

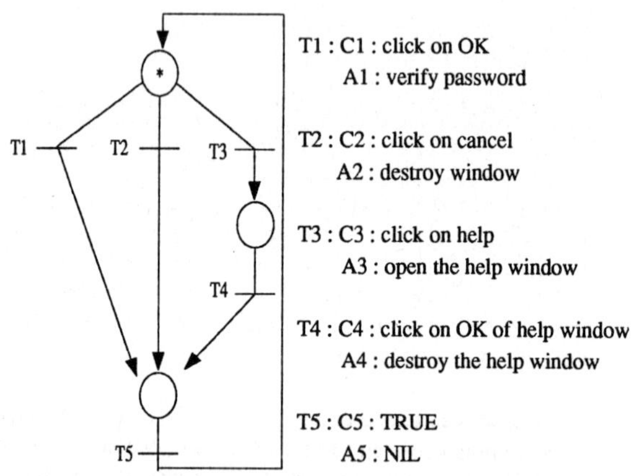

figure 5: Event Graphs specification

It is important to note that this graph represents only part of a more complex dialogue, but it is easier to specify it as an independent entity. Thus, the Event Graphs let one specify the dialogue using a set of graphs, instead of a single graph, allowing a complex dialogue to be broken down into a collection of simpler ones.

The visual aspect of the Event Graphs is also very important because it can help in hiding or at least in managing the complexity of a dialogue. A dialogue is more understandable if it is seen as a set of graphs instead of a set of textual rules! Indeed, a graph and the widget which it references have almost the same structure. As the widget offers three possible actions (three buttons), the graph has three transitions. In addition, because of its structure a graph implicitly defines a sequencing of actions. This sequencing must be made explicit when using rules. Also, using rules one has to specify on which window the event occurs (click on the OK button of such window), while it is implicit in a graph if the graph is dedicated to a particular window. Of course, this example is a very simple and short one; Event Graphs become really useful when one has a complex dialogue to specify.

Finally, the descriptive power of the Event Graphs is equivalent to event based systems, and there exist results showing that such systems are the most powerful [7]. This means that using Event Graphs will not impose any important restrictions on the kind of dialogue that can be developed. As we have already seen, Event Graphs allow multiple graphs to work concurrently, allowing multi-thread dialogues to be specified.

4.2.3 The Dialogue Management in SCENARIOO

Our goal is that the dialogue be as easy to build as is the presentation of the user interface. A widget editor provides an easy way to interactively specify a presentation, the same thing should be possible with a dialogue editor. The dialogue should be specified interactively by building the associated graphs.

SCENARIOO provides a dialogue editor based on Event Graphs. First, it provides facilities to interactively and graphically specify the dialogue by helping one input the "places" of a graph, and interconnect the places with "transitions". Then it provides a set of predefined skeletons for possible conditions (such as to test for a particular event or a particular widget attribute value), and for possible actions to perform (such as open a window, or modify a widget attribute).

Now we will explain more precisely how the specification of the dialogue is connected to the presentation. The graphs of a dialogue are not explicitly linked together in a hierarchy to form the whole dialogue. Instead, each graph is independent and describes just a part of the dialogue. However, each graph can be associated to one widget (at least the graphs that describe the reactions to End User's actions!). This association can be a solution to the problem of the decomposition of the dialogue into several graphs.

Indeed, how can one find a decomposition that is efficient at run time and that still keeps the dialogue understandable by the developer ? What SCENARIOO proposes is to decompose the dialogue into subdialogues corresponding to the subdialogues that occur in each widget. SCENARIOO recommends to attach a graph (ie a subdialogue) to each widget that has a significant dialogue. For instance, one will attach a graph to a form or to a dialogue box with different possible choices in it; on the contrary there will be no graph attached to a single button. SCENARIOO does not pretend to provide a methodology nor to impose constraints for decomposing the dialogue. It just gives the following advice: attach a graph to each composite widget. Of course, this is just advice and the developer can decide to describe the dialogue as a single graph attached to the main window !

The graphs attached to composite widgets represent only that part of the dialogue which is a reaction to End User actions. As mentioned earlier, another part of the dialogue is concerned with reactions to application requests. This part can be specified in SCENARIOO by defining "daemon graphs". These graphs describe what to do when an unexpected application request occurs. These graphs, as they have nothing to do with widget and End User actions, are not attached to a widget but to a special graph called the *InitGraph*. This graph is started when the interface starts. It is in charge of displaying the initial windows of the user interface, of activating the attached graphs, and also of activating the "daemon graphs". These "daemon graphs" are always active, and function just like background processes which run throughout the time the interface runs.

Our system is dedicated to interactive applications where it is the user interface that has the control of the dialogue. But with the "daemon graphs" the application can also take the control of the dialogue. So, our system supports user interface control, application control or mixed control of the dialogue.

5 Test and Debug

As seen before, Event Graphs provide a powerful visual aspect to specify the dialogue. This aspect can also be used efficiently in the Test Environment to show visually what happens when the interactive application is running.
We are going to show how Event Graphs are used to help in debugging a user interface, but first here are the main functionalities of this tool :

1. the user interface can be tested in "simulation mode" (simulating the I/O of the application) or in "real mode" (the application being really connected).
2. in "simulation mode" one can define several test sets and test with one particular one.
3. the test can be done step by step. One step corresponding to one evaluation cycle in the Event Graphs interpreter (see section 4.2.1).
4. the step by step test can be started only after an event has occurred (this provides a way to identify a particular point in the user interface).
5. an history of the session is maintained, providing a simple way to start a test from a particular point of a previous session history. Indeed the system will run automatically the user interface using the history file until the point which has been defined. At that point the user interface will go on as usual.

Finally, within this environment one can specify which graphs one wants to visualize. This is the most important aspect of this tool. Indeed, this allows one to test the user interface by seeing where one is currently in the dialogue. The graphs one chose to visualize are displayed on the screen all the time the user interface is tested. By this way one, can see the tokens moving from one place to another as the dialogue evolves.
In fact, it is a debugger of the Event Graphs. With it, one can see if the dialogue is well specified (that is to say if the dialogue evolves the right way), and also if an error occurs in the user interface where it occurs (when the error occurs one can have the global state of the dialogue with the Event Graphs : the global state can be represented by the position of all the tokens in all graphs).
Here again, the Event Graphs are used for the powerful visual aspect they provide. On the one side one can see its user interface running, and on the other side the associated graphs evolve !
The principle of the Event Graphs interpretation is also very helpful to implement the step by step test.

6. Conclusion

In this paper we have described the SCENARIOO User Interface Management System. We have concentrated on the aspects of the system which we consider the most innovative and useful: representation of dialogue by a visual formalism based on event graphs, and usage of a test environment to provide a high-level tool for user interface development.

Up to now, a prototype of SCENARIOO has been developed using Intellicorp's KEE environment. The purpose of the prototype has been to explore the use of event graphs for specifying and implementing user interface dialogue. Apart from the fact that the current prototype works only in simulation mode, that is without any real application, the runtime kernel and test environment have been fully implemented. The Widget and Simulation editors are simplified versions, and the dialogue editor is derived from the QUICs [6] graph editor. Our largest application so far for event graph based dialogue has been the prototype itself; the top level interface displays for managing files and invoking the editors and test environment have been implemented using event graphs.

To validate our ideas concerning the communication with the application we have developed a 'demonstrator' which communicates with multiple independent applications. This demonstrator provides an integrated high-level graphics interface for a collection of bibliography generation utilities (the 'bib' commands under UNIX). It can be run in a distributed environment, with the interface on a either a PC or a SUN, and the applications on a SUN. The interface and each application communicate via input, output, and error streams, with an intervening mailbox mechanism.

The prototype and the demonstrator have served as important 'proof of principle' tests for many of the ideas on which SCENARIOO is based. We have now begun the next step in our project, which is a full implementation of the SCENARIOO system using C++ and OSF/Motif. This version of SCENARIOO is to be a true 'interface builder', which can be used in a production setting to build user interfaces for large applications. It will be running by the end of 1990.

REFERENCES

[1] This work is supported in part by the Commission of the European Community under the ESPRIT-2 project TROPICS.

[2] Gunther E. Pfaff, editor. User Interface Management Systems. Springer Verlag, 1985.

[3] D.R. Olsen Jr. Syngraph : A Graphical User-Interface Generator. Computer Graphics, 43-50, July 1983.

[4] Michael L. Scott and Sue-Ken Yap. A grammar-based approach to automatic generation of user-interface dialogue. CHI'88 Conference Proceedings, 73-78.

[5] Ralph D. Hill. Supporting concurrency, communication and synchronization in human computer interaction - the Sassafras UIMS. ACM Transactions on Graphics, 283-317, October 1986.

[6] Reference Manual of the QUIC ESPRIT-1 Project, 820.

[7] M. Green. A Survey of Three Dialog Models. ACM Transactions on Graphics, 244-275, July 1986.

Human–Computer Interaction – INTERACT '90
D. Diaper et al. (Editors)
Elsevier Science Publishers B.V. (North-Holland)

MUD: Multiple-view User interface Design

David England

Department of Computing Science, University of Glasgow, Glasgow G12 8QQ, UK.
de@cs.glasgow,.ac.uk

The communication and visibility of information in a software engineering project is essential. In the user interface component of a project these needs are even more acute. This arises from the increasing underlying complexity of user interfaces and the multi-disciplinary nature of the teams required for their construction.This paper describes MUD, a Multiple-view User interface Design tool. This tool follows the hypertext paradigm by providing integrated, multiple instances of tools and browsers with which to view the attributes and relationships of a user interface. The base views include: end-user views, geometric views, structure views and object behaviour views.

Keywords : User interface design, rapid prototyping, hypertext

1. Introduction

In the pursuit of finding better means of constructing human-computer interfaces many solutions have been proposed in the areas of programming toolkits, User Interface Management Systems (UIMS) and graphical tools. Each proposed solution category has its own attendant problems. [Myers 89] outlines some of the limitations of current approaches, mainly in terms of tool functionality (or lack of it) and the restrictions that tools may impose on individual designers.

From a wider perspective many current approaches can also be criticized for their lack of support in terms of the software engineering aspects of user interface construction, i.e. lack of support for

- communication between project team members,
- change control during prototyping
- configuration management of user interface components.

A further broad inadequacy in current approaches is their hindrance to a User Centred Systems Design (UCSD) [Norman 86] approach. For example conventional programming toolkits do not support rapid prototyping hence it is difficult for the designer to quickly create and modify a system. It then follows that end-users cannot be directly involved in the early design stages, resulting in ambiguous, or under-specified, user requirements.

Programming tools in themselves do not provide methods. However, tools can dictate how much or how little support is provided to a designer within a given design method. In this paper we look at the area of graphical support for user interface design. In particular we look at the problems associated with a specific graphical tool set and see how some of these problems can be overcome by applying hypertext mechanisms.

2. Approaches to Interface Construction

Current techniques for user interface construction can be split into three broad groups

- Programming Toolkits
- UIMS
- Visual Tools

2.1. Programming Toolkits

Programming toolkits are the most widely used and available construction method. Many such toolkits are available, including several for the X window system [Scheifler 86], e.g. Athena Widgets, Motif [Young 89] and OpenLook [Sun 90]. Others include, SunView [Sun 86] and the Macintosh Toolbox [Apple 85]. All these toolkits share the same advantages of providing a conventional and familiar programming interface and some familiar set of user interface components. They also share the same deficiencies, namely; a restricted (or at least difficult to extend) range of components, lack of support for ease of prototyping, difficulties in ease of use at least as great as the base language, no abstraction mechanisms and they offer no path of communication between the user interface designer and the end-user.

2.2. UIMS

UIMS (User Interface Management Systems) attempt to provide solutions to some of the problems of conventional programming toolkits. For example; they provide abstract user-system dialogue specification mechanisms, usually in the form of transition nets (e.g. [Jacob 83]) or production systems (e.g. [Hill 87]). Their descriptions are generally interpreted thus aiding prototyping to some degree. They still, however, require programming. Also they offer limited support for graphical interaction with semantic feedback.

2.3. Graphical tools

Visual programming tools offer advantages over toolkits and UIMS inherent in their direct manipulation approach, i.e. no programming language has to be learnt, immediate feedback is provided to the designer. Visual user interface tools fall into two categories, those built on existing programming toolkits and those aimed at more general user interface construction. The former category - including ExperInterfaceBuilder for the Macintosh [EXPER 87] and TAE+ [Nasa 88] - are restricted to the manipulation of the components of their foundation system. The later category includes, Trilium [Henderson 86], Peridot [Myers 87] and DoubleView [Holmes 87]. With these tools user interfaces are built from a set of user interface primitives. They are thus more flexible. Peridot is perhaps the best example of this class of tools, offering programming by demonstration for component construction and component behaviour specification. The same mechanisms that support programming by demonstration are also the weak point of Peridot, i.e. the information used to construct an interface is implicit and therefore hidden in the system. Also the interventions of the inference mechanisms can become tedious for an experienced user. From a software engineering point of view a system which offers an explicit notation for user interface appearance and (dialogue) behaviour would aid communication about the system between user interface designers.

3. A Graphical Toolkit

One example of an explicit description system, supported by visual interaction is described in [England 88]. This tool set provides the interface designer with three interactive, direct manipulation, tools;

- A graphical layout tool for component composition. Components are built from graphical primitives,
- A graphical net editor for the construction of transition nets to describe an object's interaction behaviour,
- An interface executive to run the constructed interface following a Video Recorder metaphor.

3.1. Aims of the toolkit

The toolkit aims to fulfil some of the deficiencies outlined in other tools above. It succeeds to some extent in that it enables the designer to quickly and easily build small, graphical components by direct manipulation. The behaviour of each component is explicitly defined by a transition net [Jacob 86] which is constructed graphically. Thus the designer has a document of the specification of the components and can easily demonstrate the interface to the end user. In addition the executive tool is able to record and play-back a user's interaction session for evaluation purposes.

3.2. Limitation of this toolkit

This toolkit, however, suffers from some serious limitations. These limitation stem mainly from a lack of integration between the individual tools. This leaves the designer to manage changes in the interface description between tools, e.g. when attaching a net description to an object within an existing group. Also the designer must keep track of the senders and receivers of messages between user interface objects when placing labels on the nodes and arcs of a transition network. As the size of the interface grows so these problems become a greater burden for the designer and interfere with the main task of prototyping the user interface.

4. Hypertext as a design aid

Hypertext systems [Conklin 87] provide a non-linear view of textual information. Hypertext readers are able to follow links between related text items. Systems such as Apple's Hypercard present just one view of the information at any one time. Others such as Notecards [Halasz 87] provide many views so that the user is able, for example, to simultaneously view related items. One solution, explored here, to the limitations, described in section 3.2 above, is the exploitation of hypertext mechanisms as a basis for a user interface design environment. Work on the Designer's Notepad (DNP) [Sommerville 89] has demonstrated that a hypertext architecture can form the basis of an integrated tool set for the informal description of software systems. The DNP follows a similar model to Notecards in that it provides a set of graphical tools and browsers with which to create and browse the relationships and attributes amongst a network of entities. In the DNP the entities represent software components. The central tool in the DNP is the entity browser which allows the designer to create and link entities. The designer can also spawn sub-entity browsers on any entity. Overview mechanisms for the whole network are provided by maps and outline browsers. In addition attributes can be added to entities in the form of text notes, sketches and options.

By treating the components of a user interface system as entities in a hypertext network we have the basis for an integrated design system on which various user interface "authoring" tools and browsers can be built. The hypertext mechanisms are used in their conventional role in supporting a non-linear document and, more importantly for this work, the same mechanisms are also used to support an enhanced construction environment for user interfaces. Thus we are able to have multiple, integrated instances of our existing tools described in section 3. above. We are also able to support new representations of the user interface and relate these interactively to the existing tools.

4.1. Examples

In this section we show how the addition of hypertext mechanisms extends the existing tool kit. We describe the composition of a simple pull-down menu and represent it in terms of its layout, the underlying structure of that layout and its interaction behaviour.

4.1.1 Composing/Decomposing a pull-down menu

Figure 1

Figure 1 shows the layout of a typical pull-down menu consisting of a permanently visible label and an intermittently visible menu-part. The menu part itself consists of a hierarchy of graphical regions. This is shown in figure 2 and is the *structure* view of the menu.

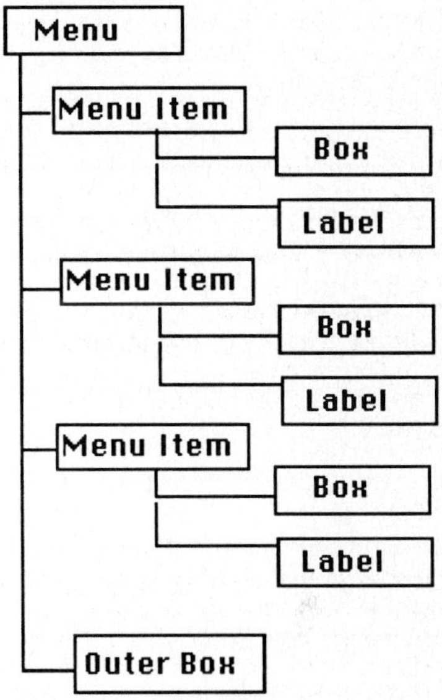

Figure 2.

This is the internal view of the menu as constructed by the layout tool. When constructing the menu the designer would group together the individual items of the menu with the layout tool. However to make changes to the individual items the designer would have had to ungroup the menu to make the individual parts selectable. The structure view gives an alternative access path to the individual items without decomposing the graphical view. This is similar to the two views of DoubleView. However, in this case the designer is able to simultaneously view as many structure views of composite objects as he/she requires.

4.1.2. Message names as Hypertext links

The dialogue or interactive behaviour of user interfaces objects is often specified via augmented transition nets (ATN) or condition-action rules. The traditional problem of ATN's is that they become unmanageable as the size of interface grows. Jacob's alternative model of placing a transition net on each interaction object (an object oriented rather than functional model) helps the designer by providing a data abstraction on top of ATN's. However as far as the designer is concerned the problem now shifts to one of interfacing between objects and their associated transition nets. Each transition net can respond to tokens generated by user input. It can also respond to tokens generated by other objects. Tokens on transition nets thus specify a link between one object and another. Using the pull-down menu again, we can represent a partial specification of the interactive behaviour of a single menu item. For reasons of space this is presented here as a table of conditions and actions which is logically equivalent to the transition diagram.

Condition		Action
mouseDown, containsEvent	=>	selectItem
selectItem	=>	highlight
mouseUp, containsEvent	=>	action, * popdown*

Figure 3.

For each token received by an object the appropriate condition flag is set. When a condition is completely satisfied the associated action(s) on the right are executed. The actions may act locally by setting other condition flags (e.g. selectItem) or executing local methods (e.g. highlight). Alternatively the token may be sent to another object (marked here with an asterisk). So in the above example when the user releases the mouse pointer over a selected menu item two messages are generated, *action* and *popdown*. The designer is able to select these two messages as links and trace them to the corresponding object [Figure 4] and invoke the network editor. In this case *action* maybe a method in the underlying (and perhaps as yet undefined) application, whilst *popdown* is set to the geometric parent of the menu item - the menu itself - removing it from view. Thus what were implicit relations in the existing toolkit are now explicit hypertext links.

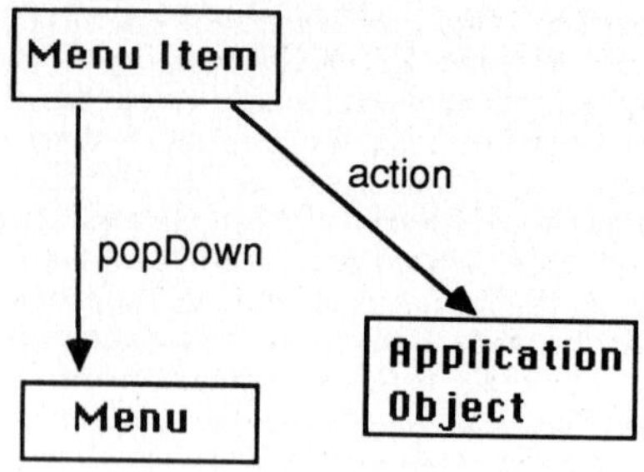

Figure 4.

5. Current Status

The prototype system is currently implemented using X windows + Athena Widgets as the input/output environment with the underlying hypertext and user interface structure written in Objective C. The system provides two classes of tools

User Interface Construction tools

- Layout editor
- Transition network editor
- End-user view

Hypertext tools

- Entity/Structure browser
- Map and outline overview tools
- Text note annotation
- Sketch annotation

The two classes of tools are fully integrated and can be called from each other at any point in the designer's prototyping session. The designer is able to construct standard user interface components such as, buttons, menus and scrollbars. In addition novel devices, more appropriate to a particular application, can be built.

6. Conclusions

In this paper we have presented a multiple view approach to user interface design and documentation. This approach assists the designer in the wider aspects of user interface design and construction. By integrating a toolset via a hypertext mechanism user interface component configuration problems are eased and hence change control during prototyping is assisted. This integration is achieved by forming implicit relations in an existing toolkit as explicit hypertext links. Conventional hypertext components (for annotating and browsing) integrate documentation with the design process. The same mechanisms also permit the inclusion of multiple views of the structures of the user interface thus providing more access paths to those components.

Several improvements could be made to this work. For example, the area of application interfacing is weak. Similar work at Glasgow is being undertaken by the Druid project [Gray 88]. The Chimera UIMS of the Druid project has a graphical toolset, Chime, which allows the graphical manipulation of *dialogue units* . Chimera also provides a separable linkage unit, the Applications Interface [Wood 90]. This aids the separate development of the application and user interface components and could be integrated into the hypertext network.

This work does not address the problems of hypertext in the navigation of large networks. However, as we are using hypertext in a specific application, navigation techniques could be tailored to aid the designer. For example [Parunak 89] suggests the examination of the topology of a hypertext system in order to design navigation aids.

A more serious and specific limitation is the transition net notation. Though this may be adquate for the description of many current interface technologies it cannot handle multi-user or multi-device interactions. As these more complex styles of interaction become more common so new interaction notations and models will be required. The Actor model [Agha 86] of concurrent object-oriented computation is one possible candidate. Future work with this toolkit will involve the enbeddding of an actor-like model into the hypertext mechanism. Thus the toolkit will in future support the user interface designer in the exploration of new styles of interaction.

Acknowledgements

The hypertext foundation of this work stems from the Designer's Notepad, which was designed and constructed by Ian Sommerville and Neil Hadley as part of the Esprit Dragon Project. The author is supported by an SERC IT Fellowship. Thanks to Cathy Wood for her comments on this paper.

References

Agha 86
G Agha, "Actors: a model of concurrent computation in distributed systems", MIT Press, Cambridge, MA, 1986.

Apple 85
"Inside the Macintosh Vols. I-V", Addison-Wesley, 1985.

Conklin 87
J Conklin, "Hypertext: an introduction and survey", IEEE Computer, 20 (9), pp 17-41, 1987.

England 88
D England, "Graphical Prototyping of Graphical Tools", in People and Computers IV Proceedings of BCS HCI '88, Cambridge University Press, 1988.

EXPER 87
"The ExperTelligence Guide to ExperInterface Builder", ExperTelligence Inc. 1987

Gray 88
P D Gray, A Kilgour, C A Wood, "Dynamic reconfigurability for fast prototyping of user interfaces", Software Engineering Journal, pp. 257-262, November, 1988.

Halasz 87
F G Halasz, T P Moran, R H Trigg, "Notecards in a Nutshell", Proceedings of the ACM GI+CHI conference, pp.44-52, ACM, 1987.

Henderson 86
A Henderson, "The Trillium User Interface Design Environment", in Proceedings of CHI '86 , ACM, 1986.

Hill 87
R D Hill, "Event-Response Systems - A Technique for Specifying Multi-Threaded Dialogues", in Proceedings of CHI+GI '87, ACM, 1987.

Holmes 87
S Holmes, "DOUBLEVIEW - A Prototoype User Interface Design Tool for the Presenter Environment", Alvey MMI Workshop, University of York, 1987.

Jacob 86
R J K Jacob, "A Specification Language for Direct Manipulation User Interfaces". ACM Trans. on Graphics 5, 1986.

Myers 87
B A Myers, "Creating Dynamic Interaction Techniques by Demonstration", in Proceedings of CHI+GI '87, ACM, 1987.

Myers 89
B A Myers, "User-interface tools: Introduction and survey", IEEE Software, Vol. 6, No. 1, January, 1989.

Nasa 88
"TAE Plus Workbench user guide", NASA Goddard Space Center, Document No. 88-TAE-WBU1, 1988.

Norman 86
D A Norman, S Draper, "User Centered Systems Design, LEA, 1986.

Parunak 89
H Van Dyke Parunak, "Hypermedia Topolgies and User Navigation", Hypertext '89 proceedings, pp. 43-50, SIGCHI Bulletin special issue, ACM, 1989.

Scheifler 86
R W Sheifler, J Gettys, "The X Window System", ACM Trans. on Graphics No 63, ACM, 1986.

Sommerville 89
I Sommerville, N Haddley, J Mariani, R Thomson, "Designer's Notepad - a hypertext system tailored to design", Hypertext II, University of York, June 1989.

Sun 86
Sunview Systems Programmer's Guide, Mountain View, CA, 1986.

Sun 90
"OpenLook 1.0 Users guide", Mountain View, CA, 1990.

Wood 90
C A Wood, P F Gray, "User interface-application communication in the Chimera UIMS", Glasgow University Department of Computing Research Report CSC/90/R1, 1990.

Young 89
D A Young, "X Window Systems Programming and Applications with Motif", Prentic Hall, 1989.

Human–Computer Interaction – INTERACT '90
D. Diaper et al. (Editors)
Elsevier Science Publishers B.V. (North-Holland)

PENGUIN: A Language for Reactive Graphical User Interface Programming

Sue-Ken Yap and Michael L. Scott
Department of Computer Science, University of Rochester, Rochester, NY 14627
ken@cs.rochester.edu, scott@cs.rochester.edu

PENGUIN is a grammar-based language for programming graphical user interfaces. Code for each thread of control in a multi-threaded application is confined to its own *module*, promoting modularity and reuse of code. Networks of PENGUIN *components* (each composed of an arbitrary number of modules) can be used to construct large reactive systems with parallel execution, internal protection boundaries, and plug-compatible communication interfaces. We argue that the PENGUIN building-block approach constitutes a more appropriate framework for user interface programming than the traditional Seeheim Model. We discuss the design of PENGUIN and relate our experiences with applications.

1 Introduction

Graphical user interfaces are an essential part of current programming environments. Graphical windowing systems such as X [1] have become widely available. Unfortunately, programming tools for composing interfaces have not improved commensurately.

1.1 Event-driven programming

Windowing applications commonly use the "big loop and case statement" technique to dispatch incoming events. As a concrete example, the code for a document previewer will typically look like this:

```
display a page
loop
    get an input event
    case event of
        keystroke:
            /**/
        mouse button:
            do user command
        repaint signal:
            repaint window
    end case
end loop
```

In this program organization unrelated streams of input flow through a common dispatch point, adversely affecting modularity and the ease of revision of the interface. Suppose, for example, that the programmer decides to augment the previewer to allow the user to jump to page N. A page number is a string of digits, so digit keystrokes must be collected. The collection of keystrokes can occur within a single branch of the case statement, but then the window will be insensitive to repaint signals until the number has been entered in its entirety. Alternatively, the digits can be collected one at a time, in successive iterations of the main loop, but only at the cost of declaring global variables to retain state between digits.

Some windowing libraries use another technique: callback routines. Semantic actions need not be embedded in an explicit loop, but the program has to register callback routines with an event dispatcher at initialization time. Like the digit-at-a-time approach above, this method has the drawback of requiring routines to maintain explicit, self-contained state between events. It also complicates the handling of unexpected or exceptional events.

Similar problems arise if the programmer wishes the previewer to be sensitive to user interrupts while painting the page. There is no easy way to integrate the reading of individual document characters from the file system into the event loop or callback routines without adversely affecting the clarity of the code. System-specific interrupt handling can be used as a work-around, but will lower the portability of the previewer.

In both cases, the crucial observation is that the polling and callback methods fail to reflect the logical structure of multi-threaded interfaces. Both methods force the programmer to deal with events in isolation, despite the fact that most interesting computations comprise a series of events. Because they are designed for ordinary sequential language, both methods must explicitly mirror the potential interleaving of unrelated events.

To overcome the limitations of the polling or callback techniques, we propose a programming language that supports event-driven programming. Rather than dictating when input is expected, we suggest that programs be *reactive*. The resulting change of perspective can lead to a clearer programs.

In PENGUIN, the sequencing of input events is expressed by grammars. PENGUIN does not have input statements or input procedures. The appearance of a terminal in a grammar indicates that the program is willing to accept that terminal as input in the context of the surrounding symbols. Grammars are contained in *modules* and the composition of modules is a module that is sensitive to the input specified by union of all the grammars, taking into account the *context* (source) of the input. This decentralized module-by-module approach to input specification makes it easy to modify input syntax. Modules are also managers of private data, distinct in each instance of a module. As a result, the semantics of modules are local, decreasing the risk of inadvertent interaction between unrelated segments of code.

Previous event-driven languages include Esterel [2] and Input Tools [3, 4]. Esterel allows event specifications to be compiled into an automaton. Piecewise construction of larger programs is not supported; the automaton generated is global to the entire program. Communication is by broadcasting. Input Tools [3, 4] allows programs to be composed hierarchically, with low-level tools accepting input, processing it, and propagating information upwards to higher-level tools. There is no provision for input selection based on the source of an event, so broadcasting of events is still required. Experience with an implementation of Input Tools [5] suggests that this broadcasting is a serious source of inefficiency, particularly for large systems.

PENGUIN encourages modular construction, separates the grammatical specification of input sequencing from the bulk of the program code, and does not require broadcasting of events.

1.2 Composing applications

Another deficiency of current graphical user interfaces is the difficulty of composing graphical applications from free-standing, pre-existing pieces. Experience with pipes in the Unix operating system[1] shows that it is possible to build stream-based process communication mechanisms that are extremely easy to use. It has been suggested [6] that similar support be provided for non-linear process graphs as well, but even the linear variety has yet to be heavily used in user interface design. While most Unix programs can participate in multi-process combinations, the average graphical program is a free-standing entity, not easily connected to other programs.

We propose the PENGUIN *component* model for the composition of multi-component programs. A PENGUIN component is a set of modules linked with a parser for their grammars. A component can be free-standing or can be connected to other components in a general communication graph. Easy composition of components with compatible interfaces encourages code re-use, rapid prototyping, and the construction of flexible, general-purpose tools.

Two systems that explored facilities for the composition of graphical programs are ConMan [7] and Fabrik [8]. ConMan is a high-level visual language that allows the user to build a complex application from components on the fly. Its primary goal is the manipulation of graphical images. Its components are programs that transform or display data. Fabrik is a similar system for experimenting with visual programming, but its components are interactors or computational modules. Both systems define specialized environments.

PENGUIN provides a formal, generalized model to describe intercomponent connections. Since PENGUIN components are reactive, the composition of components can achieve more than data transformations; it can also specify the interactive behaviour of a system of interconnected objects.

The remainder of this paper describes how the design of PENGUIN achieves the goal of making user interfaces easier to build and easier to understand.

2 Language Overview

This section provides a quick overview of the PENGUIN language. PENGUIN's compilation units, *modules*, are organized around augmented context-free grammars. The design decisions taken and algorithms used by PENGUIN have already been described[9]. A PENGUIN implementation consists of a compiler that translates grammars and their associated data declarations and action routines into executable program components. Data and actions are written in a host language (currently C++) of which PENGUIN is an extension. The output of the PENGUIN compiler is a program in the host language without extensions.

The most noticeable difference between programming a user interface in PENGUIN and a conventional language is that the spurious juxtaposition of unrelated threads of execution introduced by the event loop model disappears. The programmer only needs to consider the sequencing *within* a thread of control.

2.1 Forks

The productions of a PENGUIN grammar specify valid sequences of terminals that may be received by the grammar's module. Terminals are matched by input events, following *context* matching rules, and may carry information from the outside world via *attributes*. Input events encompass more than data received by input statements in conventional languages; they also include asynchronous signals and exceptions, which are difficult to handle in a non-reactive language.

Multi-threaded execution in PENGUIN programs is achieved with *fork* productions. There are two types of fork productions: the AND fork and the OR fork. A variety of useful behaviour can be synthesized with these two variants. A fork creates one or more *subparsers*, which are disjoint, concurrent regions of parser activity. A module may be thus willing to accept terminals from multiple sources. Moreover terminals from independent sources may be accepted by a PENGUIN program in arbitrary order, without the need to accommodate their interleaving in user-written code.

```
tool &> canvas panel;
run |> work abort;
```

In the first example the AND fork (specified with a `&>` derivation symbol instead of the usual `=>`) requires that all the component windows start running in parallel and that all of them complete before the parent advances past the fork. In grammar terms, the yield of the non-terminal `tool` is some arbitrary interleaving of the yields of the non-terminals `canvas` and `panel`. In procedural terms, a subparser for `canvas` and a subparser for `panel` begin execution in parallel; when they complete, the subparser for `tool` can continue.

In the second example the OR fork (specified with `|>`) requires that only one of `work` or `abort` complete. Specifically, hitting the abort button will cancel all work in progress in the sibling window, returning the locus of control to the parent production. Completing `work` will disable the subparser for `abort`. By nesting abort productions, the programmer can allow the user to back out of multiple levels of interaction.

A PENGUIN program is thus driven from below by the arrival of events that match terminals, and from above by the creation of threads of control by fork productions. Forks are a linguistic mechanism for domesticating threads for use in user interface programs. The PENGUIN compiler handles the messy thread management which would otherwise have had to be coded by the programmer.

2.2 Context

The presence of more than one active production requires a mechanism for dispatching events. We stipulate that every input event be tagged with *context*, an attribute that uniquely identifies its source. In a typical windowing system, the source of a event would be a window, but alternative interpretations are equally valid. In a flight simulator, context attributes could be used to distinguish between mechanically similar flight controls. The PENGUIN parser contains a dispatcher that delivers incoming events to productions in which they match both in value and in context.

Here is a simple dialogue that awaits the key `k` and then creates two new sub-windows with an `&>` production. Both sub-windows must terminate before the parser proceeds. Inheritance rules are written using a notation similar to argument passing in imperative languages: `Y(@X.c1)` means that the first attribute of `Y` is copied from the `c1` attribute of `X`. In practice, default context rules eliminate much of this verbiage.

```
terminal key(context ctx) = 'k';
nonterm S(context ctx), X(context c1, context c2);
nonterm Y(context c), Z(context c);
nonterm new(|context ctx1, context ctx2);
...
S => key(@S.ctx) new X(@new.ctx1,@new.ctx2) ...;
X &> Y(@X.c1) Z(@X.c2);
```

The non-terminal `new`, whose sub-productions are not shown, causes the creation of two new windows and returns their contexts. These contexts are passed to `Y` and `Z`, so that they can operate independently, even if their token alphabets overlap.

Attribute flow rules for context, enforced by the PENGUIN compiler, ensure that at most one production will accept an incoming event. The compiler can compute in advance the locations that the parser must examine to find a match. As in regular attribute grammars, attributes other than context carry information about the symbol to which they are attached.

2.3 Modules

The unit of compilation in PENGUIN is the module. A module contains a header, declarations, private variables, and a grammar. PENGUIN does not allow the programmer to write a main program. The locus of control is retained by the PENGUIN *parser* which is the dispatcher of input events. The PENGUIN parser is the heart of an *executing* interactive program. It should not be confused with the portion of PENGUIN compiler that parses PENGUIN source. The programmer provides modules to be linked with the PENGUIN parser. The parser initially predicts a non-terminal of the topmost module. The chain of predictions eventually will require one or more terminals to be consumed.

Declarations inform the compiler of the types of attributes of symbols in the grammar. Attributes transmit information between productions. Inherited attributes pass information to descendants while synthesized attributes return information to ancestors. Attributes are attached to all symbols: terminals and non-terminals.

```
terminal lparen = '(', rparen = ')';
nonterminal S(int i|int j);
```

These declarations state that the value of the terminal `lparen` is the character code for '(' and that the nonterminal `S` carries an inherited attribute `i` and a synthesized attribute `j`

Productions may refer to non-terminals in other modules (externals). Since there may be more than one instance of an external module active, an external non-terminal is qualified with a module handle. A handle is initialized by predicting its `create` symbol (which every module must provide).

```
module canvas C;
module panel P;
...
create => C:create P:create;
tool &> C:start P:start;
```

Private data are local to each instance of a module. They provide a repository for the shared state of related events, independent of the rest of the program. The current version of the PENGUIN compiler does not check type declarations, so the data types available are those provided in the target language.

Changes to the outside world are effected via *actions*, which are symbols in productions representing executable code. The code is executed when the PENGUIN parser reaches the position of the action while recognizing its production.

```
nonterminal click(color newc);
...
click => left_button
         $( change_color(@click.newc);
            output("OK"); $);
```

In the code fragment above, an action to change the color of the button is executed after the event `left_button` has been received. As the example shows, actions may use inherited attributes, as with other items.

Ideally, actions that are triggered by events would take no noticeable time. In practice an input buffer smooths out the effect of delays in actions. As long as the input is ordered by time and buffer overrun does not occur, a PENGUIN program does not lose any input information. Communication between parallel PENGUIN *components* (discussed in the following section) provides a more general solution for programming actions that may introduce arbitrary delays.

3 Components

A set of modules linked with a PENGUIN parser is a *component*. A component may be a free-standing program or may co-operate with other components. The synergy of co-operating components makes it easy to adapt existing tools to novel applications.

PENGUIN components communicate with other components via bidirectional reliable data streams. The unit of information exchanged is the token or terminal. Each token is a complete piece of information and can be as small as a single character or as large as a picture—whatever is appropriate for the application.

Figure 1 is an example of components co-operating to implement a game-playing program. The Chess component controls the reaction of the application to user input, received via the presentation component. A second, parallel presentation component provides another display of the game in progress. Since move generation and evaluation may require substantial amounts of computation, some work is given to parallel components to preserve the interactiveness of the user interface. This is an example of a general technique that can be applied to any computation that may delay the flow of events through the grammar: do the work in a separate component and devise a protocol for sending data to, receiving results from, and querying the status of the sibling component. In response to queries the user interface might say "`Thinking`" if the move generator is still busy.

Two features of PENGUIN provide flexibility in creating networks of components. First, communication partners need not know the identity or implementation details of their peers. Second, the connection graph of components does not have to be fixed until run time, allowing alternative configurations to be created. Tokens are addressed to output streams, not to named components, and the connections between components can be established under program control. The only requirement for two components to be able to communicate is that each send only

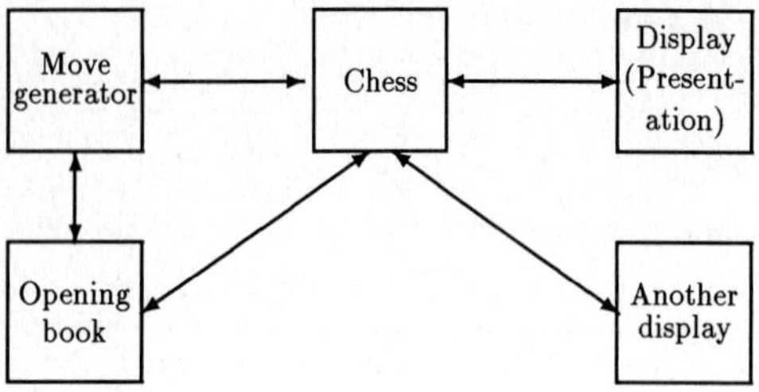

Figure 1: A multi-component Chess program.

tokens that are in the other's input alphabet. The behaviour of a component is determined by the grammar within. Alternative implementations of components can be produced to meet a functional specification. Interchangeable components are useful for selecting between different versions of components or for producing different effects. The example above, for instance, could be configured with a variety of different move generators or opening books. A logging component could also be interposed between the Chess and Display components, to record the entire session.

4 The Seeheim Model Reconsidered

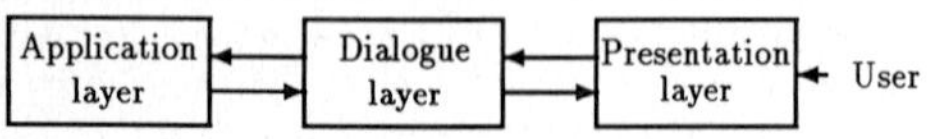

Figure 2: The Seeheim model of a UIMS.

In the original Seeheim model [10], depicted in Figure 2, a program is postulated to have three layers: application, dialogue and presentation. These layers correspond to division by semantic, syntactic and lexical functions. The Seeheim model assumes that a separation between syntax and semantics provides the most natural partition of a graphical application. The fallacy of this assumption can be seen in our game-playing example. A chess program must examine the positions of other pieces on the board to discover whether it is legal to move a king. One can imagine an implementation that allows the user, syntactically, to make an illegal move, but an interface that provides immediate feedback, indicating that the move is not allowed, is far preferable to one that accepts the illegal move, displays it, and then forces it to be rescinded after performing semantic checking. Immediate feedback requires a coupling between presentation and application not accommodated by the Seeheim model.

Separating the application from the input device through a long communication path creates long feedback loops that diminish both performance and conceptual clarity. Separating lexical checking from semantic checking works well in non-interactive programs such as compilers. It can be extended to simple devices such as buttons that have no significant semantic component and require little feedback. It does not generalize well to non-trivial interactive programs. Artificial distinctions between feedback based on the state of a logical input device and feedback based on the state of the application serve only to complicate programs. Both cases can be modeled as actions that test an internal resource. The only difference lies in the sophistication of testing.

The specification of input syntax should be separated from the specification of computation semantics, but this separation is not an appropriate basis for division into components. Syntax and semantics are too tightly bound to be placed in separate components. Components that have been segregated by lexical, syntactic or semantic functions have *logical cohesion* or, at best, *communicational cohesion*[11]. Both these types of cohesion are weaker than the *functional cohesion* exhibited by PENGUIN components.

The Seeheim model envisions a syntactic and a semantic component, both of which encompass all of the functional tasks of the application. The PENGUIN model assigns each functional task to a separate component that includes both syntax and semantics. Seen in this framework, a presentation manager is more than just the lexical front-end of the Seeheim model; it is a first-class component with internal resources and syntax (protocol). A window server such as X can be built as a PENGUIN component, and clients should be structured as components too, rather than as a completely different kind of program.

5 Experiences with PENGUIN

We have constructed a PENGUIN compiler and used it to construct reactive applications. We discuss two of these applications here.

5.1 pfig: A graphics editor

The first application is an adaptation of an existing line graphics editor called **xfig** comprising of about 15000 lines of code, of which about 2500 are concerned with the user interface. The editor interface comprises a window subdivided into a canvas area, a panel of buttons, a message window and rulers at the edges. The window hierarchy is:

```
xfig
    canvas
    panel
        buttons
    message
    rulers
```

The events that need to be handled by each window include mouse clicks, key clicks and exposure notifications. The parent window creates instances of each of the second level modules and predicts their **create** symbols. The panel module then creates buttons. The terminals generated by the windows have distinct contexts so the parser is able to dispatch all events to the correct thread.

Measurements indicate that about 700 lines of PENGUIN grammar and code expanded to 2600 lines of C++ code, which replace 2500 lines of old C code. We estimate that compiler generated C++ code is twice as bulky as good human generated C++ code, i.e. a human would have had to write about 1300 lines of C++ to replace the 2500 lines of C code. There are 102 productions in total of which 14 are **&>** productions. There are no **|>** productions, probably because exceptional conditions were already handled by the old C code. A similar editor created from scratch might profitably use **|>** productions in some places. All of the **&>** productions are used to create parallel threads of control, none of which expect to complete.

5.2 alarm: Alarm clock

Our second application is a simulated alarm clock with time and alarm displays, and buttons to set the display mode and the time of the alarm. This application demonstrates the handling of signals as events. The window hierarchy is simple:

```
wrapper
    clock
    alarm
    mode_button
    set_button
```

A run time library timer module sets up a handler for Unix alarm signals. When the operating system delivers an alarm signal, the library translates it into a PENGUIN event. Since Unix signals carry no information other than the fact that they occurred, an auxiliary queue is used to store a list of pending timer events. The library obtains the context and value of the token to create from the queue when a signal occurs.

The clock time and alarm time subwindows respond to exposure events, so they will redisplay the time when the window first appears or when it is unobscured. The clock subwindow schedules a timer event once a minute to update the digits. The alarm subwindow schedules a timer event for the time at which the clock is due to beep.

Because the alarm clock was coded from scratch, there is no old implementation to compare against. Some indication of the degree of programming help provided by the compiler can be seen from these statistics: some 650 lines of PENGUIN code generated about 2800 lines of C++ code. Another 550 lines of auxiliary routines in C++ were needed. The run time library is identical to that used by **pfig**, except for the addition of the timer module. There are some 50 productions, of which 4 are forks. Our subjective impression is that the clock would have been significantly harder to write without PENGUIN. Now that the timer code has been added to the run time library, future programs requiring timer events would be even easier to write.

5.3 Evaluation

Writing modules to react only to events that concern it and letting PENGUIN compose the modules and correctly dispatch events is pleasantly natural. The distinction between module templates and module instances is important. For example, there is only one copy of the code for a graphical button, but as many instances as there are buttons in a panel, each instance customized via attributes.

PENGUIN makes possible an interesting technique for intermodule communication we call "event forwarding." Here is an example of how this works: A panel comprises buttons. Each button may trigger a different action routine when clicked upon. Since the code template for the button is common to all buttons, it is not appropriate to put the call to the action routine in the button code. There are two traditional ways to deal with this situation. The first method is to give each button a unique index and have the code use the index to find the appropriate action. This requires a case statement or a global array somewhere. The second method is to pass a pointer to an action routine to each button (callbacks). PENGUIN has a third method: take the input event, change the context to one expected by the recipient and forward the event. In this example the buttons forward the event to the parent panel. Since the button and panel are part of the same component, the forwarding amounts to putting the modified token back on the input stream, where the parser will deliver it to a different module. As far as the panel is concerned, a click event has happened at its window, even though the presentation does not deliver any.

The alarm clock program provides another example. The button for setting the alarm time forwards button events so that they appear to come from the alarm display subwindow. The code for setting the wakeup time and the variable holding the time can be kept local to the alarm module.

It is not necessary for modules to have a parent/child relationship for forwarding to work. The pointers on the top and side rulers of **pfig** track the movement of the cursor in the canvas window. The canvas receives cursor motion events, uses them to update its display (and its internal state), and forwards them to both of the rulers, even though the canvas is a sibling of the rulers. Forwarding can also be used profitably in constructing a composite module comprising a viewport and a scrollbar. All actions on the scrollbar can be made to appear to happen in the viewport, simplifying the programming and preserving the modularity of the composite window. The PENGUIN forwarding mechanism is more powerful than the forwarding strategy of windowing systems such as X11, which can forward only to ancestor (enclosing) windows, unless extraordinary and inconvenient arrangements are made.

Finally, because all events go through the parser, it is possible in PENGUIN to isolate windowing system dependencies in the run time library. Details such as the layout of input event structures can be confined to a few routines that turn window system functions into events. Different run time libraries can interface to different window systems. The cost of porting a program to a different windowing environment will be smaller than if the program had been written for a single environment because fewer idiosyncrasies will have been introduced and because the labour of adapting the run time library can be amortized over many applications.

6 Implementation

The PENGUIN compiler was written with the help of **flex**, **bison**, and **g++**, the GNU (Free Software Foundation) C++ compiler. The PENGUIN compiler converts a module grammar into code and a set of tables.

The multithreading of forked productions can be implemented with a coroutine package or with interpretive code. In the former method, the compiler generates a conventional sequential parser (e.g. recursive descent) for each PENGUIN subparser. One subroutine is used for each production, non-terminal or start symbol. Terminals are translated to calls to a run time routine that fetches an event. Prediction points are translated to calls that peek at the next event and use it to decide which production routine to call. Fork productions are translated to calls that create new threads. A coroutine library switches between the threads of a module, giving each thread control when a event acceptable to it arrives. Some subtlety is required to re-join threads at the end of a fork production: the first OR branch or last AND branch must clean up all its siblings.

In the latter, interpretive method of parser construction, the parser runs an extension of the normal table-driven predictive parsing algorithm. It builds a branching (cactus) stack to represent parallel productions. When a production is predicted, one branch of the cactus is extended. As terminals are matched, the appropriate branch is trimmed. Forks and joins change the number of branches.

We originally planned in our implementation to use the interpretive method, but eventually switched to coroutines. Both methods are feasible but the coroutine method simplifies attribute passing. In the interpretive method, either the set of attribute types must be restricted to those known to the PENGUIN compiler, or calls to external code must be made to copy attributes. In the coroutine method, the PENGUIN compiler can generate appropriate assignment statements and let the host language compiler implement type-specific copying. The coroutine method has an additional advantage when the amount of inline code is large in comparison to the number of symbols in the grammar. The interpretive method turns every piece of inline code into a subroutine and devotes much time to linkage overhead. The coroutine method can execute inline code in line.

Prediction tables for either the interpretive or coroutine approaches are simply initialized data. They are shared between all instances of a module. Private variables are unique to every module instance. In our current host language, C++[12], private variables have a natural expression as class members. Slightly less attractive translations could be found for other languages.

7 Conclusions

Programs have traditionally been viewed as data transformers. They read their input, compute a function, write their output, and terminate. Programs that run indefinitely (operating systems for example) have been seen as exceptional cases. Programs with graphical interfaces, however, are representative of a growing class of applications with a heavy interactive component. Real-time process control is also in this class. For these applications the sequencing of acceptable input is just as important, and just as complicated, as the operations on that input.

Mainstream programming languages have no facilities for expressing this sequencing beyond the standard control flow operators. Pseudo-parallelism may be obtained by calling system dependent operations to poll for data, but the underlying procedural execution model makes the resulting code obscure and non-portable. It can be difficult to ascertain the effects of a given input sequence. This in turn makes it difficult to ensure that all valid input sequences are covered, that invalid sequences are rejected, that appropriate actions are taken in every case, and that resources are recovered when no longer in use, a particularly important consideration for long-lived programs. PENGUIN goes to the heart of the problem by providing a notation that better matches the programming tasks confronted in graphical user interfaces. This notation frees the programmer from thinking in sequential terms and instead encourages the decomposition of an interface into self-contained modules with well-defined entry points triggered by the arrival of input events. Reasoning about the effects of input sequences and the life history of resources becomes much easier.

Our experience with PENGUIN suggest that its reactive execution model, its separation of dialogue and computation, and its automatic dispatch of tokens can make complicated reactive programs easier to write, easier to read, and easier to debug and maintain. PENGUIN's component model provides a basis for building applications incrementally as a collection of co-operating components, and encourages the reuse of existing components in new combinations.

Notes

1. Unix is a trademark of AT&T Bell Laboratories.

References

[1] Robert W. Scheifler and Jim Gettys. The X window system. *ACM Transactions on Graphics*, 6(2), April 1987.

[2] G. Berry, P. Couronne, and G. A Gonthier. Synchronous programming of reactive systems: an introduction to Esterel. Technical Report 647, INRIA, March 1987.

[3] Jan van den Bos. Input tools – a new language construct for input-driven programs. In *Proceedings of the European Conference on Applied Information Technology of IFIP*, September 1979.

[4] Jan van den Bos. Abstract interaction tools: A language for user interface management systems. *ACM Transactions on Programming Languages and Systems*, 10(2):215–247, April 1988.

[5] J. Matthys. Recent experiences with input handling at PMA. In *User Interface Management Systems*. Springer-Verlag, 1985.

[6] Chris McDonald and Trevor I. Dix. Support for graphs of processes in a command interpreter. *Software Practice and Experience*, 18(10):1011–1016, October 1988.

[7] Paul E. Haeberli. ConMan: A visual programming language for interactive graphics. In *SIGGRAPH '88 Conference Proceedings*, pages 103–111, August 1988.

[8] Dan Ingalls, Scott Wallace, Yu-Ying Chow, Frank Ludolph, and Ken Doyle. Fabrik: A visual programming environment. In *OOPSLA '88 Conference Proceedings*, pages 176–190, September 1988.

[9] Michael L. Scott and Sue-Ken Yap. A grammar-based approach to the automatic generation of user-interface dialogues. In *CHI '88 Conference Proceedings*, pages 73–78, May 1988.

[10] Günther E. Pfaff, editor. *User Interface Management Systems*. Springer-Verlag, 1985.

[11] Edward Yourdon and Larry L. Constantine. *Structured Design: Fundamentals of a Discipline of Computer Program and Systems Design*. Prentice-Hall, 1979.

[12] Bjarne Stroustrup. *The C++ Programming Language*. Addison-Wesley, 1986.

Human–Computer Interaction – INTERACT '90
D. Diaper et al. (Editors)
Elsevier Science Publishers B.V. (North-Holland)

PETRI NET OBJECTS FOR THE DESIGN, VALIDATION AND PROTOTYPING OF USER-DRIVEN INTERFACES.

Rémi Bastide * Philippe Palanque **

ABSTRACT
Petri Net Objects (P.N.O.) are a high-level, object-structured dialect of Petri nets, primarily devised for the design of parallel systems. We show how this formalism can be used for the specification and design of event-driven interfaces, through the use of a real-life example. We then discuss the potential for dialogue validation, integration in UIMS and prototyping offered by this model.

KEYWORDS : User interface design, High level Petri Nets, prototyping, validation, Object oriented software design.

1. INTRODUCTION.

Nowadays, the user interface designer undertaking a development in a window-oriented environment finds himself less unprovided than only a few years ago. He has at his disposal a whole array of tools that alleviate to a great extend the non trivial task to build a user-friendly interface out of the rather low level services provided by graphical toolboxes. These tools, variously called Interface Generators or User Interface Management Systems and featuring interactive editing of the interface components generally rely on an "event driven" or "callback" style of programming [1], [2]. Interfaces produced with these systems usually exhibit a distinctive style of user/application dialogue where control flow is most of time event driven (or *external*) and application driven (internal or *modal*) only when some imperative action or confirmation is needed. It is now generally admitted that external control enables friendlier interfaces [3], where the *decision scope* of the user is broader [4].

This increased flexibility, however, causes some problems to the application programmer : event driven programming, as opposed to more conventionnal styles, does not exhibit a global and sequential control flow for the application. Even if the application is implemented in a single (sequential) computer process, the user can hold several seemingly parallel dialogues with different parts of the program, where subtle synchronisation and resource sharing problems may take place. The programmer, faced with this unforeseen complexity, generally has few conceptual tools to help him conceive and validate a global design for his application. Formalisms like finite state automata, Augmented Transition Networks or grammar and production systems are not particularly well suited to this kind of design, because they tend to model the user as a parsable sequential file, which does not fit well with the "pseudo-parallel" behavior expected in such systems [5] .

Similar problems are encountered in another area of computer science : real-time software designers have been confronted for a long time with the complexity of modelling parallel systems. Indeed, it might seem an interesting idea to undertake an event-driven interface design using concepts usually put forward in real time systems. An interface may well be thought of as a reactive system, as usual interface components such as buttons, gauges and sliders can be viewed as the sensors and actuators found out in real time systems descriptions.

* TECHLOG
Bâtiment Aurélien II
2, Rue Boudeville
31100 Toulouse France
Tél. 61.44.46.44

**L.I.S.
Université Toulouse I
1 place Anatole France
31042 Toulouse cedex France

Another aspect could incite us to bring closer the two approaches : it is the interest shown on both sides towards the object-oriented approach, which is the cornerstone of many current UIMS and which gives rise a lot or work and research in the real-time community [6], [7].

These are the points that led us to investigate the interest of using Petri Net Objects (PNO), a model whose main purpose is to describe parallel or real-time systems, in the field of user interface design. Petri nets have already been used for the description of computer-aided tasks [8] and for prototyping of interactive application [9], but not yet in the field of event driven interfaces.

spontaneous activity, not triggered by the call of its operations but processed on its own behalf.

Like in conventionnal object-oriented models, an object is described by the data structure it maintains (its attributes) and the operations it offers to its environment (its methods). The model adds another dimension to this description by adding the specification of a *behavior* for the object : this behavior is intended to describe the spontaneous activity of the object, the effect of its internal state on the availability of the operations it offers, and conversely the effect of operations on the internal state of the object.

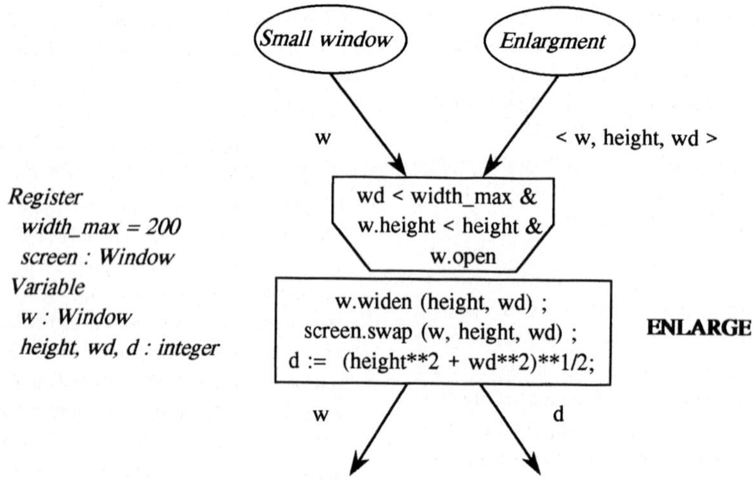

A transition featuring a pre-condition.

Figure 1

2. PNO MODEL OVERVIEW.

The description of PNO formalism will be rather informal, leaving out of scope several features of the model introduced in order to increase its modelling power in the field of real-time and parallel systems design, where timing and synchronisation constraints are somewhat tougher. A complete description of the formalism may be found in [8].

A system described by means of PNO will be modeled as a set of objects that cooperate to handle the global tasks of the system. An object in this model *is not* a sequential entity such as an ADA task or a computer process. On the contrary, we consider, like in HOOD [6], that the operations offered by an object are activated by control flows, and that an object may take place in several different control flows at the same time. An object is also not a passive entity, but often will have its own

This behavior, called the Object Control Structure (OBCS) is described by a Petri Net (PN). The Petri Net model used to describe the OBCS is of course a high level PN model, where tokens flowing in the net, instead of zero-dimensional entities found in conventional PN, will be constant or objects whose class can also feature an OBCS of its own.

Arcs in the OBCS will be labeled by typed variables that act as the formal parameters for the transitions. A transition will be made of a *precondition* (a boolean expression of the input variables of the transition) and an *action*. If variables are of simple types (integer, strings, boolean ...) their value will be used. If they are of Class type, methods described in this class will be called in the precondition or action (Figure 1).

The semantics of the cooperation between objects (through operation calls) is also expressed through the use of PN formalism. Synchronous and non synchronous communication is available, but this is beyond the scope of this paper. This formalism is oriented towards an implementation in a compiled object-oriented language such as Eiffel [9], C++ [10] or Objective C [11], in the very same way that HOOD is oriented towards an implementation in ADA. In the rest of this paper, object-oriented descriptions will be given in "quasi Eiffel" syntax.

To design an interface using this formalism, we will consider an interface as an object whose methods can be interactively triggered by the user, through interactions with usual dialogue components. The sequencing an synchronisations constraints for these methods will then be expressed in the OBCS.

3. ILLUSTRATIVE EXAMPLE.

The example chosen to demonstrate the use of this model is a fairly common one: we wish to design an editor for tuples in a relational database table. This editor will allow adding new tuples, deleting tuples from the database, selecting tuples from those already stored and changing their values. Of course, our goal is to provide a fully user-driven style of dialogue, as opposed to menu-driven interactions usually found in most of applications.

The overall look of the interface is shown on Figure 2. A scrollable list shows the tuples in the database, presenting them by a distinctive attribute such as their primary key. Items in this list are selectable by clicking on them with the mouse. The attributes of a selected object are editable through the use of standard interface components (radio buttons, check boxes, sliders, ...). Database operations (creation, deletion, ...) are launchable by clicking on command buttons.

More often than not, the application programmer will get something like the paragraph just above, along with a sketch of the dialogue window, by way of specifications for the interface he has to build. Clearly, this is not enough: nothing is said about what will make the interface a pleasure or a pain to use, i.e. the structure of the dialogue between the user and the system. What is the meaning of command *delete*, if the object has been edited ? Is the *Quit* command always available ? Are the dialogue items always active ? Such questions are left open, and finally answered according to the implementor's taste and experience. We will design this dialogue as a PNO class, in order to provide a concise, yet formal and complete specification for the control structure of the application.

As stated in section II, the interface will be thought of as an object whose methods can be interactively triggered by user actions. The method of class *Tuple_editor* are easily found out (one might think of proceeding "à la Grady Booch" and underline the verbs found in the informal specifications of the dialogue). Our class will therefore offer operations *Add, Delete, Select, Edit* (change the attribute values of the object being edited), *Replace* (to record the changes) and *Quit* to end the application. It is also a good user-interface practice to add operation *Reset*, which will allow the user to undo his changes.

An instance of class *Tuple_editor* is also a window in its own right, and therefore should be made a descendant of class *Window* in order to inherit methods such as *Move, Resize, ... Tuple_editor* will also be made a generic or

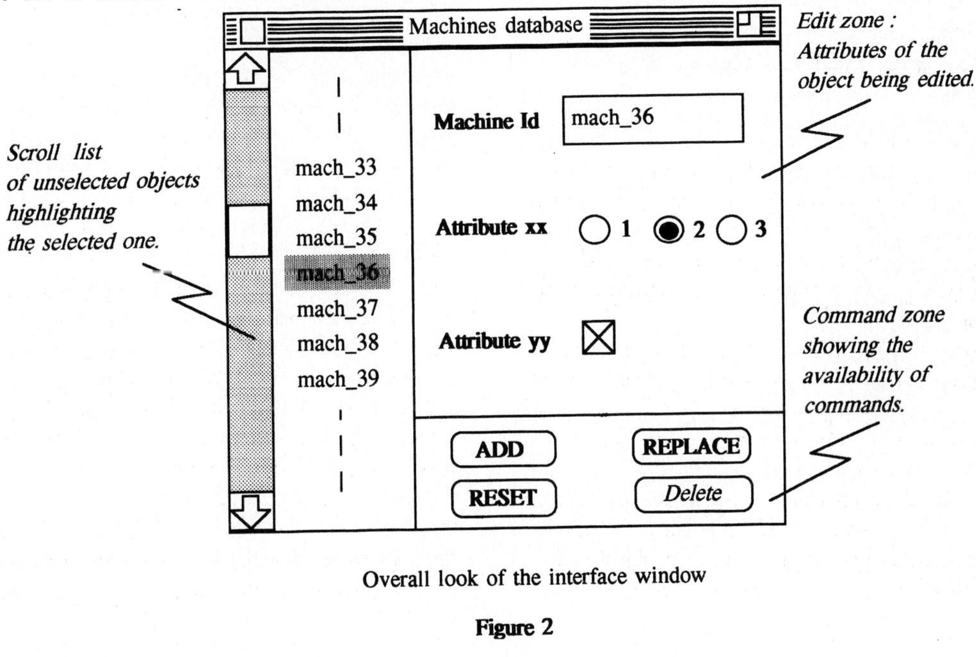

Overall look of the interface window

Figure 2

Parametrized class : we will then be able to derivate a new class for each kind of tuple we wish to edit.

The declarations for class *Tuple_editor* and its OBCS are shown in Figures 3 and 4 respectively. In order for our specification to be complete, we must provide the OBCS with an *initial marking*, defining which places will be marked at the creation of an instance and the values they will hold. In our example, place *default* should be marked with an object of class *Editable* bearing default values (presumably provided by operation *create* for class *Editable*). So, at the initialisation of the interface, the *unselected* list is empty and only operations *add* and *edit* are legal. Finally we must explicit the binding between operations offered by the class an the dialog items that will trigger these operations, which is straightforward : operation *close* is triggered by the close box of the window, *select* is triggered by any of the unselected objects in the scroll list, *edit* is triggered by any of the dialog items in the edit zone and *add, reset, replace* and *delete* are triggered by the buttons with the same name.

```
class Tuple_editor[Editable] export
      add, delete, replace, select, edit, reset, quit
inherit Window
feature
      display(Editable) is ... end;
      add is ... end;
      delete is ... end;
      ...
obcs
      o,x,old : Editable;
```

Declarations for Class Tuple_editor
Figure 3

Note how each public operation of class *Tuple_editor* is associated with transitions in the OBCS : a transition bears the name of the method it is bound to and is pictured with an incoming broken arrow to underline its distinctive role in the OBCS. Most often there is only one transition corresponding to the method (as for add, reset, replace and select). In this case the operation is legal only if the corresponding transition if *fireable*. Operation *delete* is bound to two transitions in the OBCS : the meaning of this is that the same user action will give rise to different interpretations depending on the inner state of the dialog : in our example deletion will cause another object in the unselected list to become selected if one is available, and otherwise provide an object with default values. Of course, we would like the behavior of our dialogue to be deterministic : so if the same operation is bound to several transitions in the OBCS, we will have to check that these transitions are in *mutual exclusion* : that is, any reachable marking of the net will allow at most one of those transitions to be fired.

Operation *edit* deserves special attention : first it is bound to several transitions, but it also can be triggered by any of the dialog items in the Edit zone : this highlights the fact that there is neither bijective relation between triggers and methods, nor between methods an transitions in the OBCS. The general relations between those design components are summarized in an entity-relationship fashion on Figure 5. The reader could verify that whichever the state of the dialogue, one and only one *edit* transition is fireable, meaning that the user can always interact with items in the edit zone.

In the OBCS of class *Tuple_editor* all transitions are bound to an operation of the class. This is not enforced by the model, however : an unbound transition in an OBCS will be able to occur - if it is enabled - without any need for user intervention, thus modelling a *systematic operation*, carried out by the system as soon as its preconditions are fullfilled.

The aim of private operation *display* is to map individual attributes of the object being edited to dialogue items in the edit zone. This clearly require some knowledge of the object being edited, and that is why we have made *Tuple_editor* a parametrized class.

It should be noted that operations required to virtual class *Editable* are quite different from those offered by class *Tuple_editor*: an instance of *Editable* has no method *display* or *edit* but is expected to answer calls to *is_correct* (that might check integrity constraints in the database), in addition to the usual *create* and *clone* methods. An interesting side-effect of this is that our design can be tested before the full functionnality of the application is implemented, by providing a "fake" class with minimal *create, clone,* and *is_correct* operations. This design achieves a good separation between interface and application by ensuring that the information exchanged between the application and the UIMS are application concepts [14] : an interface object manipulates application objects only through the operations offered by their class, thus allowing good semantical partitionning.

It should also be remenbered that only user-driven interaction has to be stated in the OBCS. When part of the dialog is application-driven and fully sequential, it can be ommited altogether : for example, operation *is_correct* could pop up a modal dialogue informing the user on why a creation attempt has failed and wait for him to click on a button before continuing processing.

4. DESIGN VALIDATION .

As we have seen above, Petri Nets are a powerful tool for modeling interactions between the various actions that can occur, especially if some amount of concurrency is to be highlighted. Common situations, such as resource sharing, synchronisation and parallel flow of control are expressed in a natural and convenient way, allowing easy communication of the design. Moreover, an important feature brought by the use of PN is the ability to statically check properties of the design through the use of analysis techniques, allowing the designer to prove the correctness of his specifications. A huge amount of literature has been devoted the analysis of PN, and several results are of interest to the interface designer: [15], [16].

4.1 Liveness (deadlock freedom).

Deadlocks are easy to avoid in a conventional, application driven style of dialogue. However, in a user-driven dialogue, where the flow of control cannot be predicted because the user carries on concurrent dialogue flows with several parts of the application, the designer should have a way to ensure that is specification is deadlock-free, i.e that wichever the inner state of the application, any application command will have a way to become available again, through a given sequence of commands. In our design, this problem is directly connected to the *liveness* problem in the PN theory : for a given method to be accessible, at least one of the transistions it relates to should be live in the OBCS, whichever the current marking.

4.2 Boundedness.

A place in a Petri Net is k-bounded if there exists an integer *k* such that the number of tokens in this place cannot exceed *k*. For example, given the initial marking stated in III, place *selected* is 1-bounded, thus establishing the desirable property that only one object can be selected at a time. Conversely, place *unselected* is not bounded, which is adequate since it models all the tuples in the table. This shows how bounds-checking can help establishing that the elements of design have the right semantical properties. Incidentally, the fact that the net is globally unbounded shows that it cannot be reduced to a finite state automaton.

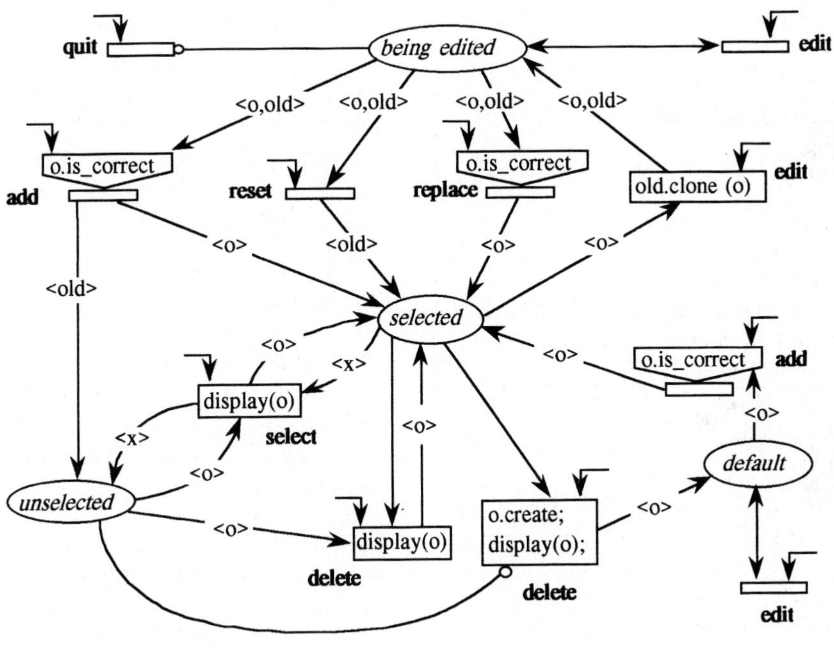

OBCS of Class Tuple_editor

Figure 4

4.3 Re-initialization.

Given an initial marking, a net is *reinitializable* if there is a finite sequence of transition firings that can bring it back to its initial state. In our design, this means for the user the ability to reproduce it's initial working environment, which might be desirable in most cases. In the example, deletion of the last tuple will reproduce the initial marking, i.e. a token in the *default* place.

4.4 Coverability.

We have stated in section III that if the same operation for a class relates to several transitions in its OBCS, those transitions should be checked for mutual exclusion. This relates to *coverability* problems in the PN theory. We must check that no reachable marking enables more than one transition relating to the same method. In our example, place *being edited* and place *selected* should not be marked at the same time, because two *edit* transitions would then be enabled. Coverability analysis could prove this requirement.

5. PROTOTYPING.

The design shown in Figure 4 features several arbitrary decisions that are worth examination : for example, command *quit* is disabled when a tuple is *being edited.* Is this the best option to choose ? Would'nt it be better to leave the command allowed and give the user a warning message ? Ultimately, the end-user should be the one to answer such questions. Many current UIMS focus on the easy definition of the external "look and feel" of the interface, and leave out of scope the definition of dialogue structure, because they provide no tool to specify reasonably complex control flow for the application. When using such systems for a prototyping purpose, there is a strong likelihood that the debate between the designer and the user will focus mainly on "cosmetic" matters such as the size or placement of dialogue items, precisely because the UIMS makes it easy to change those parameters "on the fly".
Older prototyping systems, using a finite state automaton description for a hierarchy of screens and menus were better off in this case, because the user could have a clear vision of the dynamics of the future application, and answer the "where can I go from here ?" question.
PNO formalism could fruitfully be introduced in an UIMS, by allowing the designer to relate his Petri Net design to the user interface components manipulated by an interface editor. This would result in a fully operational prototype for the application, allowing the user to interact

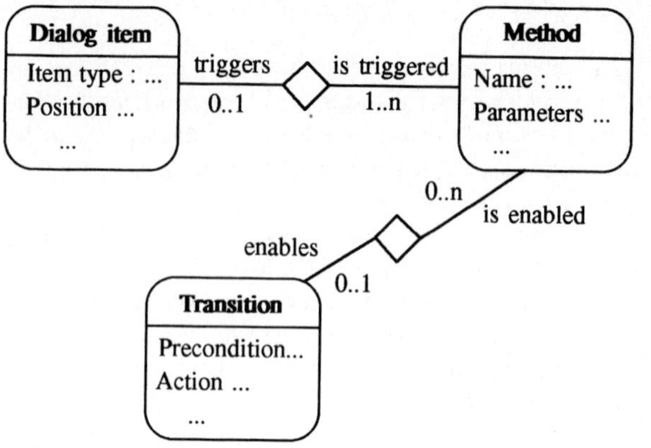

Relationships between interface components

Figure 5

and proceed through the various states of the dialogue. What is needed for this is a generic Petri Net Interpretor (sometimes called a token game player) which is not a difficult thing to build, and could act as the "run-time kernel" for the UIM environment. A PNO design can therefore be thought of as "executable specifications" for an interface.

6. CONCLUSION.

The aim of this paper is to promote the use of Petri Nets (and especially of PNO) as a valuable and efficient formalism for user interface specification and design. Several existing tools (some of which are public domain [17]) can already help the designer by providing interactive edition of PN, model analysis and simulation [18]. However, to be an efficient tool for user interface prototyping, support for the PNO formalism should be tightly integrated into an existing UIMS, providing the kind of environment needed to accomodate the frequent changes and experimentations needed in the prototyping process.

7. ACKNOWLEDGEMENTS.

The authors would like to thank Patrick ESQUIROL for being the first to use PNO for user interface specifications in real life conditions. The example used in section III is straight from his specification set for project ORIGAN, a job-shop short term scheduler whose interface has been developped on top of the X-Window system using the Open Dialog UIMS [19]

8. BIBLIOGRAPHY

[1] KARSENTY S.
Graffiti : Un outil graphique pour la construction d'interface homme-machine adaptables.
These de 3° cycle Université de Paris-Sud.

[2] HULLOT J.M.
SOS interfaces : un générateur d'interfaces homme machine.
Acte des jounées AFCET-Informatique sur les langages orientés objet.
BIGRE+GLOBULE N° 48

[3] COUTAZ J.
The Construction of User Interfaces and the Object Paradigm
ECOOP'87 special issue of BIGRE n° 54 Paris, 87.

[4] M.F. BARTHET.
Logiciels interactifs et ergonomie.
Dunod informatique 1988.

[5] MYERS B.A.
Creating user Interfaces by demonstration..
Academic Press, inc.

[6] HEITZ M.
HOOD, une méthode de conception hiérarchisée orientée objet pour le développement de gros logiciels techniques et temps réel; Bigre+Globule 57, dec. 87

[7] BOOCH G.
Software Engineering with Ada,
Benjamin/Cummings Publishing, California, 87

[8] BARTHET M.F. SIBERTIN-BLANC C.
La modélisation d'applications interactives adaptées aux utilisateurs par des réseaux de Petri à structures de données.
Actes du 3° colloque-exposition de génie logiciel, Versailles, Mai 1986.

[9] SIBERTIN-BLANC C.
Prototyping interactive applications using Petri Nets.
Le Genie logiciel et ses applications EC2, TOULOUSE 1988

[10] BASTIDE R. - SIBERTIN-BLANC C.
Conception par objets de systèmes parallèles.
Le Genie logiciel et ses applications EC2, Toulouse89

[11] MEYER B.
Object-Oriented software construction; Prentice hall, 1988

[12] STROUSTRUP B.
The C++ Programming Language ; Addison-Wesley , Mass., 86

[13] COX B. J.
Object-Oriented programming : An evolutionary approach; Addison-Wesley , Mass., 1986.

[14] COUTAZ J. Interface Homme-Ordinateur : Conception et Réalisation.
Thèse d'état Université Joseph Fourier Grenoble FRANCE. 1988.

[15] BRAMS G.W..
Réseaux de Petri : théorie et pratique.
Masson 1983 Paris.

[16] PETERSON J.L.
Petri net theory and the modeling of systems.
Prentice Hall.

[17] FELDBRUGGE F. JENSEN K.
Petri Net Tool Overview 1986
Petri Nets : Applications and relationships to other models of concurrency ;
B. Brauer, W. Reisig, G. Rosenberg editor,,Springer.

[18] TECHLOG.
SEDRIC : presentation générale
Techlog 1989

[19] APOLLO 1988
Open dialog reference manual

Human–Computer Interaction - INTERACT '90
D. Diaper et al. (Editors)
Elsevier Science Publishers B.V. (North-Holland)

An Object-Oriented UIMS for Rapid Prototyping

Yen-Ping Shan

Department of Computer Science, University of North Carolina, Chapel Hill, NC 27599-3175, U.S.A.

User interface management systems (UIMSs) that support rapid prototyping often suffer from the limited range of interfaces that they can produce and the lack of support for the connection between the produced interface and its underlying application. This paper discusses a Mode Development Environment (MoDE) that addresses these problems.

1 Introduction

Creating a good user interface for a system is a difficult task. User interface software is often large, complex, and difficult to debug and modify. It often represents a significant fraction of the code, frequently ranging from 40 to 60 percent. Good interfaces that are easy to use are also interfaces that are complex and hard to create. There are few guidelines or strategies at the design stage that will insure that the resulting user interface will be easy to learn, easy to use, and user-friendly. Instead, user interface developers rely on testing prototypes with actual end users and iteratively modifying the design. Many user interface management systems (UIMSs) have been developed to facilitate rapid prototyping [NeX88, Sme87, LIBY89, Car89]. Although they have helped in many aspects of the prototyping process, most of them suffer from lack of generality and lack of support for connecting the interface with the application.

Many UIMSs are limited in the look and feel of the interfaces they can generate. It is very hard to generate user interfaces not in the style provided. The major reason is that they have a *fixed* library of interface components. The possible interfaces are limited to those that can be composed from components in the fixed library. For a production system, this might be desirable since it maintains consistency among the interfaces. For a prototyping system where new ideas are to be tested, lack of generality becomes a serious deficiency.

Also, few of the UIMSs for prototyping provide adequate support for connecting the user interface to the underlying application. In a good interface, the semantics of the application often strongly affect the design of the user interface. Consequently, the prototype must be connected to the application or to a model of the application if it is to be tested fully. Most UIMSs that generate a set of procedures or provide a callback mechanism require programming by the interface developer to connect the interface to the application. This programming task often becomes the bottleneck in the prototyping process.

This paper presents a Mode Development Environment (MoDE) that addresses the above problems.

2 MoDE

MoDE is a general user interface management system that supports rapid creation of a wide variety of user interfaces. It is implemented on top of Smalltalk 80 [GR83] and an event-driven mechanism [Sha89]. Its dynamically expandable interaction technique library allows the interface developer to easily introduce new objects into the library. MoDE also supports creation and management of the connection between the user interface and the application through direct manipulation.

An interface developer uses MoDE's library of interaction techniques to construct new interaction techniques. Each interaction technique built using MoDE may be promoted to the library for reuse at any time. The MoDE library stores the interaction techniques in the form of live objects (with values in the instance variables retained). Each library object represents a "copy," as opposed to the class, of an interaction technique. As a consequence, when promoting an interaction technique, only a live copy of the technique needs to be created and registered; there is no need to recompile the library. Furthermore, once an interaction technique is promoted into the library, it can be reused immediately by making copies of it. The above properties allow the library to be dynamically expanded. Interactive techniques stored in the library can also be written to files. These files can be read by other interface developers' libraries to share the interaction techniques.

Each interface generated by MoDE is composed of a number of basic building blocks called *modes*. A mode is distinguished by an area on the screen that interacts differently than its surrounding areas. A user interface might be composed of a group of hierarchically structured modes. A mode in such a structured interface could contain other modes as submodes. Any given mode, however, would be a submode of only one mode – its "supermode." The set of modes in a structured interface forms a hierarchy.

To illustrate, the dialogue box shown in Figure 1 can be thought of as a mode with two submodes: a "yes" submode and a "no" submode. The yes and no buttons highlight themselves when the left mouse button is pressed within them, and they dehighlight themselves when the cursor moves away or the left mouse button is released. Their behavior is different from that of their supermode which does not respond to a left mouse button press. Notice that the text in the dialogue box is not a mode. It affects the appearance of the dialogue box, but it does not form an area that provides a different interpretation of the user's input.

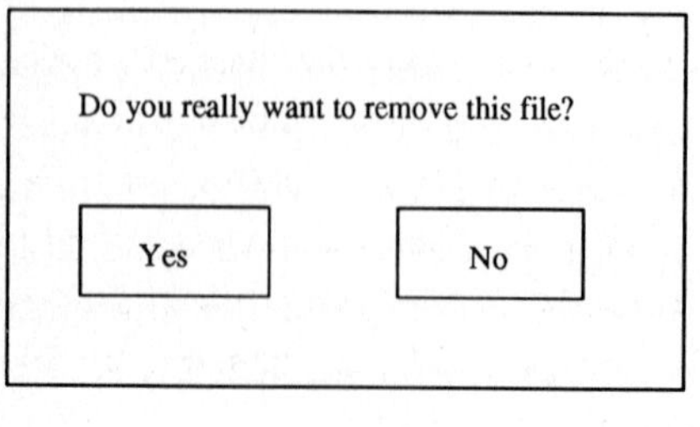

Figure 1

Each mode has a "semantic object" that supplies its semantics. The term "supply" is used instead of "generate" because in MoDE, the actual semantics are "generated" by the application but they are "supplied" to the interface by a separate "semantic object" being described here. Semantic objects can also connect to each other. They reside in a layer maintained by MoDE. Objects in the layer have knowledge of both the user interface and the application. They insulate both sides from the effects of changes. MoDE supports the creation and manipulation of semantic objects through direct manipulation. This three-level model of interface modes, semantic objects, and application is illustrated in the next section.

It is the existence of the semantic objects that allows MoDE to provide a rich support for the connection between the user interface and the application. Since all connections are made through the semantic objects, supporting routines can be built into the abstract superclass of the semantic objects. These routines keep track of the creation, deletion, and modification of the connections. They provide MoDE with sufficient information to perform searches, consistency checks, and other maintenance operations. Semantic objects also help in presenting the connections to the interface developer. Without them, the links between interface objects would need to be drawn directly from one to another (such as the link between the "yes" submode and the dialogue box in Figure 1). A display incorporating many such links would be difficult to understand.

3 MoDE in Use

Through a concrete example, this section illustrates how MoDE can be used to create a prototype of a simple binary desk calculator with one display window and three push buttons–"0," "1," and "C" (the clear button).

With MoDE, interfaces are created by dragging objects (modes) out of the interactive technique library (the right-hand window in Figure 2) and pasting them together. In Figure 2, the user has created a "Vanilla Mode" as the background of the calculator and is editing its appearance.

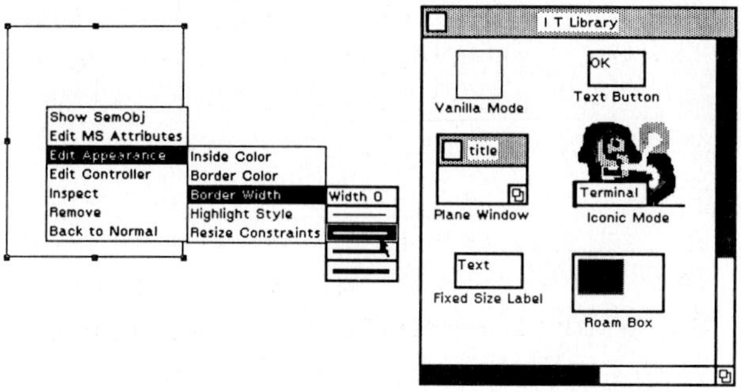

Figure 2

Next, the user creates the three buttons and the display window for the desk calculator and pastes them onto the background. This process is similar to drawing a picture with a drawing tool. The result is shown in Figure 3.

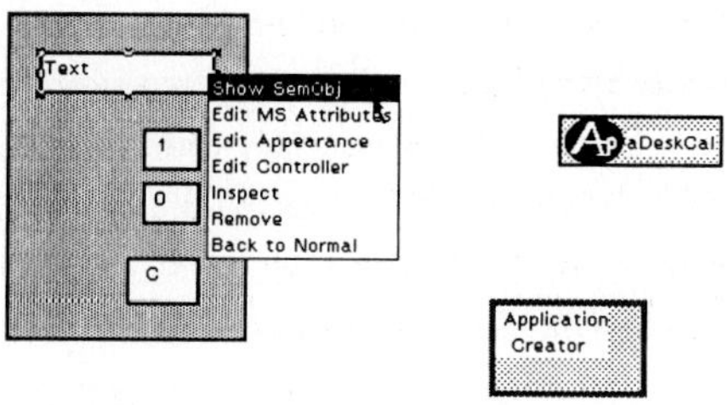

Figure 3

The "Application Creator" shown in the lower right corner of Figure 3 is used to create the representative of the computing component of the desk calculator. Because the computing component is not a visible user interface object, a visual representative is necessary for it to be displayed and manipulated directly. Here, the user decides to create the computing component from scratch. A new class named "DeskCal" is defined and an instance of the class is created. The representative of this instance (with the text "Ap-aDeskCal") is shown. Remember, the semantic objects are the points of connection. To establish the connection between the user interface and the computing component, the semantic objects must be present. In Figure 3 the user is requesting the system to show the representative of the semantic object of the display window.

Figure 4 shows the semantic objects (represented by diamond shaped icons containing an "S") for the display window and the "1" button. The user has created a link from the semantic object of the "1" button to the computing component, and would like to create another link from the computing component to the semantic object of the display window. His plan is for the semantic object of the "1" button to send a message to the computing component whenever the button is pushed. The computing component, in response, updates its states and requests the display window to display the digit "1" by sending a message to its semantic object. Since the *DeskCal* class is a new class, it does not have an instance variable to store the connection. The system infers that a new instance variable is needed and requests permission to create one, as shown in Figure 4. Once the permission is granted, the user will be prompted for the name of the new instance variable and the system will automatically change the class definition of the *DeskCal* to insert this new instance variable and update all the existing instances of the class.

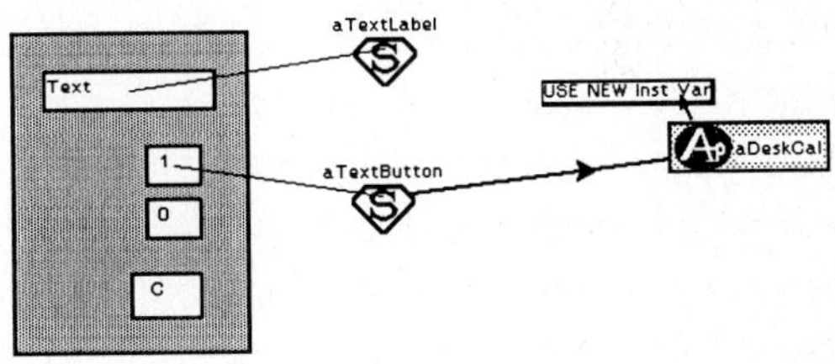

Figure 4

Next, the user selects the "Inspect" option in the menu associated with the semantic object to inspect the "1" button (Figure 5). The inspector, shown in Figure 6, indicates that the default action message for the button is "buttonPushed:" The colon at the end indicates that there is one argument for this message. By default it is the text string of the button.

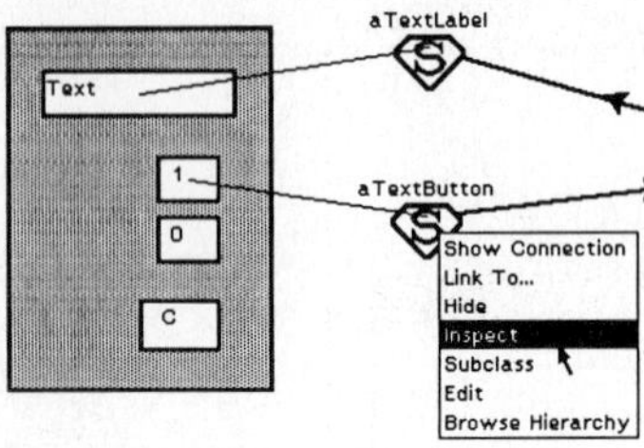

Figure 5

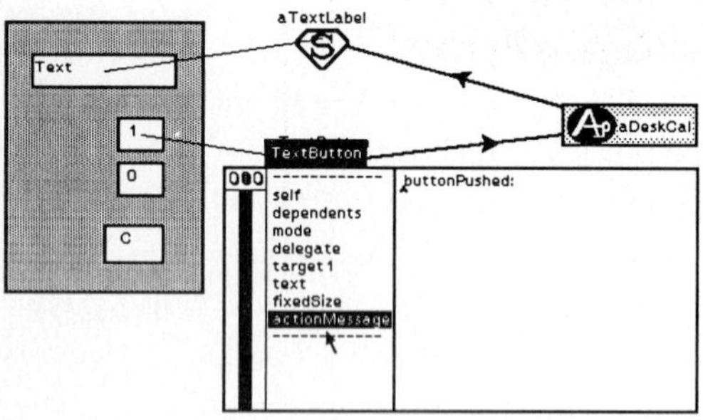

Figure 6

Since the computing component is created from scratch and does not understand the "buttonPushed:" message, the user selects the "Add Message" option in the menu associated with the link. The system will open a code editor for the user to define the "buttonPushed:" method in the *DeskCal* class.

In the process of defining the method, the user needs to know what message can be sent to the display window to display the result of a computation. The system can help by displaying the messages understood by the display window. In Figure 7, the list of understood messages is shown and the user finds that the "displayText:" method is what he needs.

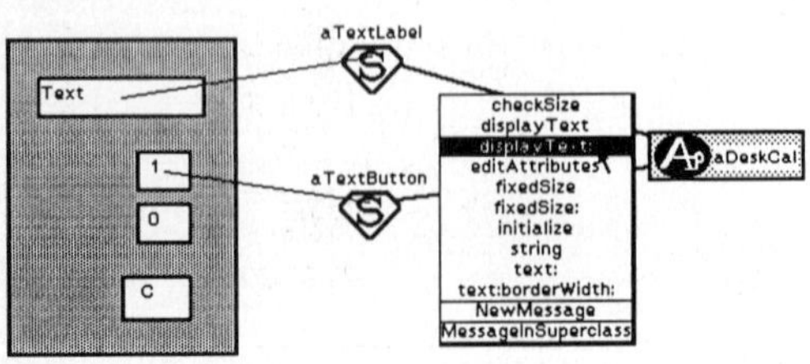

Figure 7

The other two buttons can be connected in the same manner. Figure 8 shows the fully connected desk calculator. Since all interfaces created with MoDE are immediately testable, there is no need to switch to a test state. Further, the user can test the partially implemented prototype at any point in its development. In Figure 8, for example, the button "1" was pushed and the display window of the calculator shows the correct result.

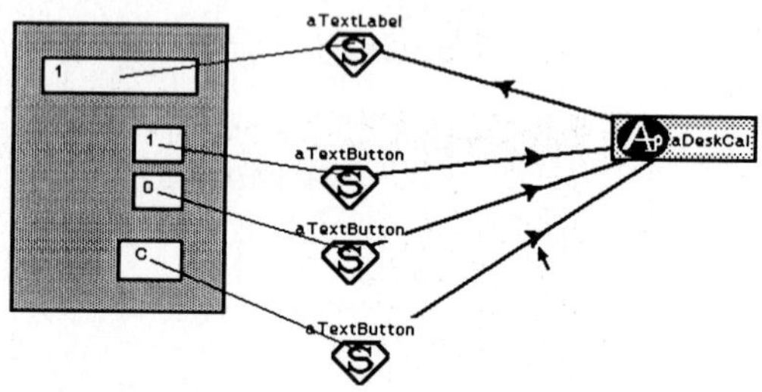

Figure 8

There are two approachs to handling the clear button. The first one is to use the default message ("buttonPushed:") and have the computing component interpret the argument "C" as a special command. An alternative is to use a different message selector (for example "clear") and define the corresponding method in the *DeskCal* class. Both approachs are valid. MoDE allows the user to choose whichever he prefers.

. After the user finishes the prototyping, he hides all the connections and promotes the calculator into the interaction technique library by dragging the desk calculator into the library. The library automatically prepares an icon for the calculator, as shown in Figure 9.

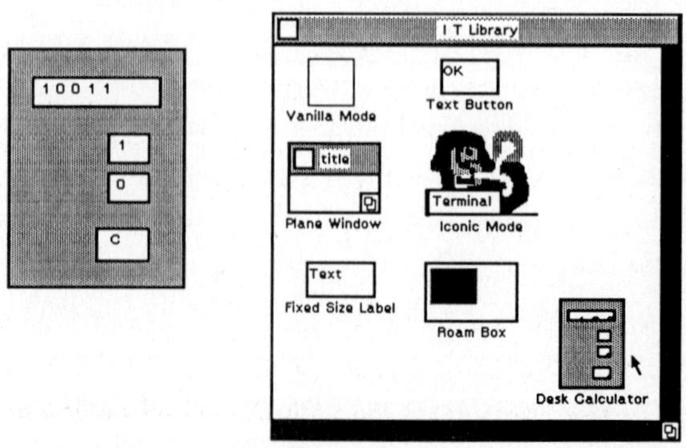

Figure 9

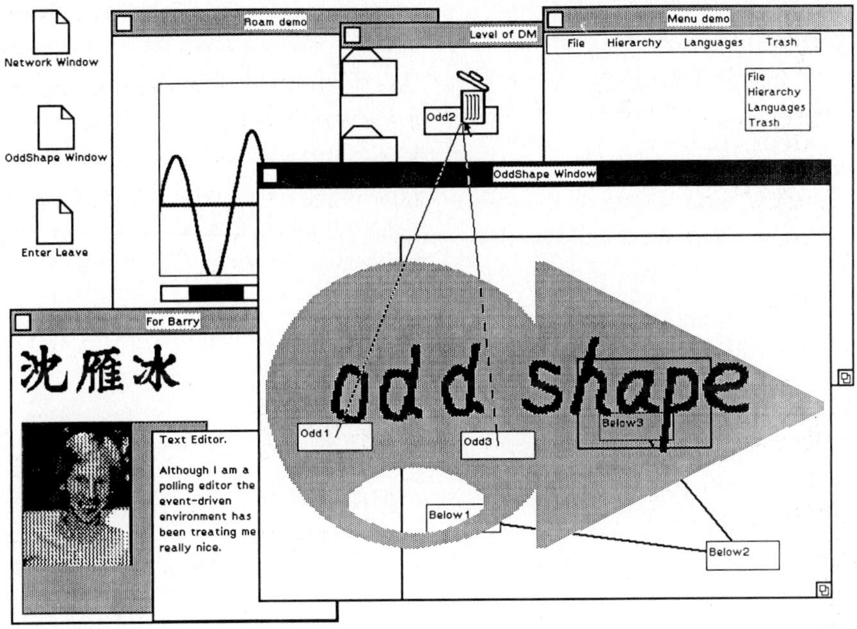

Figure 10

4 Experience with MoDE

Sample Interfaces

MoDE has been used to create many direct-manipulation user interfaces. Figure 10 shows a few sample interfaces created with it. The scroll bar in the top left window (Roam demo) scrolls the picture continuously. The top right window (Menu demo) has three types of menus: title-bar menu, tear-off menu, and pop-up menu (not displayed). Menu items can be text, foreign characters, bitmaps, and animated pictures. The lower left window (titled "For Barry") demonstrates the system's capability to incorporate scanned images and text editors. The largest window (titled "OddShape Window") contains two subwindows; both allow the user to create networks of hypertext nodes. The oddly shaped subwindow has three nodes in it. The user is dragging one of the nodes over the trash icon in another window (titled "Level of DM"). The trash icon opens to provide semantic feedback. Rubber-band lines are drawn from "Odd1" node and "Odd3" node to the node being dragged to show the connection. Notice that the oddly shaped subwindow has a hole in it through which the user can work with objects (for example, the "Below1" node) underneath the window. MoDE also supports semi-transparent windows as shown in the right half of the oddly shaped subwindow.

Self-Creation

To demonstrate the generality of MoDE, the user interface of MoDE was created using itself. Consequently, MoDE can be used to edit itself. For example, in Figure 11, the user is using MoDE to examine the connection between the "ShrinkBox" and the "Window" of the interaction technique library. The user has also made some changes to MoDE. The two scroll bars of the interaction technique library were removed, and a "Roam Box" (a two-dimensional scrolling device) has been attached.

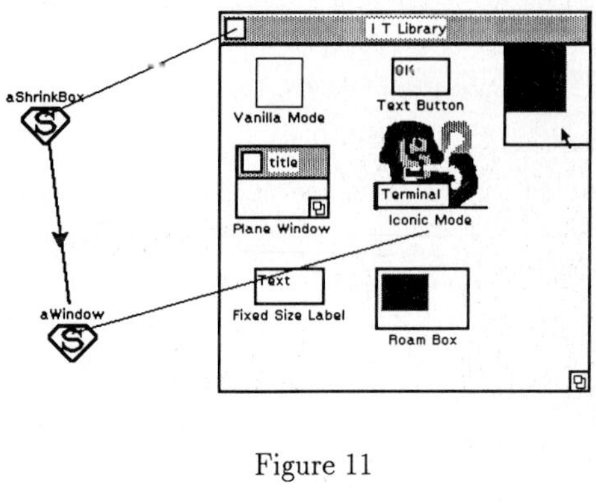

Figure 11

Since it is easy for users to customize the user interface of MoDE, the interface images shown in this document represent only a small sample of those developed by the author.

Rapid Prototyping

In an informal experiment to study the effectiveness of MoDE, two groups of subjects were asked to create the same interface. One group used MoDE exclusively; the other group used whatever tools they liked except MoDE. The group using MoDE were able to finish the assignment both faster and with fewer unimplemented features than the other group. Time data collected from this informal experiment suggest that MoDE reduces the time required to develop a prototype interface by nearly an order of magnitude.

5 Conclusion

MoDE provides an effective environment for prototyping user interfaces. The capability to easily incorporate new objects into the library results in a general system with which a wide variety of interfaces can be created. Experience with MoDE shows that its support for connection between the user interface and the application substantially facilitates the prototyping process.

To support studies of user behaviors, an experimental tracking system has been incorporated into MoDE to collect transcripts of users' interaction with prototype interfaces. The transcripts can be used to recreate the users' sessions and to support computerized analysis. MoDE is also being used to prototype interfaces for a hypertext software engineering system.

6 Acknowledgement

A number of organizations and people have contributed to the work reported here. The author is grateful to the National Science Foundation (Grant # IRI-85-19517) and the Army Research Institute (Contract #MDA903-86-C-0345) for their support of this research. This work has been done as part of the author's dissertation project under the supervision of Professor John B. Smith. Barry Elledge provided valuable comments and suggestions for this paper. The Textlab Research Group within the Department of Computer Science at the University of North Carolina at Chapel Hill has provided a provocative and supportive intellectual environment for this work.

References

[Car89] L. Cardelli. Building user interface with direct manipulation. *SIGCHI'89: Human Factors in Computing Systems*, pages 152–166, May 1989.

[GR83] A. Goldberg and D. Robson. *Smalltalk-80: the Language and Its Implementation.* Addison-Wesley, 1983.

[LIBY89] T. G. Lewis, Fred Handloser III, Sharada Bose, and Sherry Yang. Prototypes from standard user inferface management system. *Communications of the Assoication of Computing Machinery*, 22(5):51–60, may 1989.

[NeX88] NeXT, Inc., Palo Alto, Calif. *NeXT System Reference Manual*, 1988.

[Sha89] Yen-Ping Shan. An event-driven model-view-controller framework for smalltalk. In *OOPSLA'89: Object Oriented Programming, Systems and Applications*, pages 347–352, October 1989.

[Sme87] SmethersBarnes, P.O. Box 639, Portland, Ore. 97207. *SmethersBarnes Prototyper User's Manual*, 1987.

Human–Computer Interaction – INTERACT '90
D. Diaper et al. (Editors)
Elsevier Science Publishers B.V. (North-Holland)

Do-It-Yourself Iconic Displays:

Reconfigurable Iconic Representations of Application Objects§

by Philip D. Gray†, Kevin W. Waite† and Stephen W. Draper‡

†Department of Computing Science
‡Department of Psychology
University of Glasgow, Glasgow, United Kingdom, G12 8QQ

Abstract
It is often a major programming task to associate user interface objects with the application objects they are to represent. This discourages the exploration of alternative representations. In this paper we describe the architecture and interface of *Iconographer*, a system which enables iconic representations of (sets of) application objects to be specified in a highly interactive manner. At its heart is a direct manipulation "switchboard" by which attributes of application objects may be mapped on to icon attributes with a resultant change in the display.

1. Introduction

Iconographer (n.)
One who illustrates a subject by
drawings or figures.
(Derived from the Oxford English Dictionary)

Modern visual interfaces are powerful at least in part because the pictorial elements, or icons, visible to the user carry information about the (invisible) objects of interest. This information is carried by virtue of the fact that the icons represent application entities and, potentially, some of the properties of the icons represent properties of the application entities. If the users know which properties of the icons carry information and the rules which govern the representation relations, they can acquire knowledge about the underlying application objects simply by looking at the display. The seminal work in this area was the Pygmalion system [1] where icons were used as constructs in a programming language. More recently, the ideas behind Smalltalk [2] and the Xerox Star computer [3] have lead to iconic interfaces to personal computers becoming de rigueur. A survey of these and other applications is given by Lodding [4].

However it is beginning to seem as if the Xerox Star approach, especially as popularised by the Apple Macintosh[1], has not only established but frozen the idea of what an iconic interface should be like. In fact a few minutes' imagination shows how that design has only scratched the surface of what might be done with today's mouse and bit-mapped screen technology. However imagination is not the only consideration, and unfortunately for the interface designer there are no reliable rules by which the best pictorial representation for an arbitrary universe of application objects can be generated a priori.

In general it is necessary to explore alternative representations in order to discover empirically which of several alternatives is best able to provide accessible information to a user about the attributes of, relationships among, and operations on, a set of application objects. While paper mock-ups provide useful information about representation design choices, there are a number of aspects of a pictorial representation which cannot be discovered by this method. Without a computer-based prototype, it is difficult to examine, for example, the effect of display-dependent features such as resolution, colour, update time and animation.

Currently, building such prototypes is a difficult and time-consuming affair. This is due to a number of factors, of which the most important appear to be:

- the lack of software tools which enable designers to specify in a natural way the universe of application entities, the domain of pictorial entities and the relations between them, preferably without requiring programming expertise,
- the costs of recompiling and linking the reconfigured specification, and

---

§ This research has been funded by SERC grant number GR/F 67129.

- the constraints placed on the exploration of alternatives by pre-defined "tool-kits" of pictorial elements.

In the Innovative Iconic Interfaces project, we have built a prototype system which overcomes these problems, *Iconographer*, and which itself supports the rapid prototyping of iconic representations of application entities. For the purposes of this paper we define an "icon" to be a small area of the final picture which is the whole and only representation of a single application object (i.e. this definition is consistent with everyday usage in existing systems). In the remainder of this paper we consider the rationale for the Iconographer design and describe how its architecture and user interface meet the requirements arising from this rationale.

2. Degrees of Freedom in Specifying Iconic Representations

Iconic interfaces, as representational systems, carry information about the universe of entities which they represent by virtue of a selective sensitivity of the icons to (changes in) the state of the represented entities [6]. That is, the state of the icons must reflect the state of the application objects. Formally, for each application attribute represented, there must exist a function which maps from the domain of values which that attribute may take onto the set of values which the associated iconic attribute may take. Given a definition of representation in such terms, it is possible to produce a system which will automatically generate icons from a given description of the application domain [7]. However, this leaves open the question of exactly which aspects of the representation relations(s) to select for designer access via design tools — the "degrees of freedom" of specification — and how best to present in such tools the specification tasks and the elements on which they operate.

At the heart of our system (shown schematically in figure 1) is a tool, called the *Switchboard*, which enables the designer to specify graphically the particular attributes of application objects to represent iconically and to determine the nature of the function which maps values from the application domain onto the iconic domain. Together, these specifications determine the nature and amount of information which is carried by individual icons. For example, consider the case of designing an iconic representation of files. Via the switchboard, the designer may choose to represent some file attributes (e.g., filename by an icon's textual label and file size by the icon's colour), while excluding other attributes (e.g., file type, creation date, date of last access) from representation. Additionally, the function between, say, file size and colour can be modified in the switchboard by setting the range of sizes which are represented by a given colour and by determining the actual colour to employ as the representation for a given range of sizes.

On the application side of the switchboard, we provide two additional degrees of freedom of specification. Just as a designer may choose not to provide an iconic representation of some application attribute via the switchboard, the designer may also limit the set of application entities which will have an iconic representation. This is accomplished by a tool, called the *Object Filter*, enabling a function to be defined over the original application universe, which filters out objects which possess certain designer-specified attribute values.

The definition of the application universe is, strictly speaking, not part of the task of specifying a representation. However, a minimum condition of a toolkit such as ours is that it be able to deal with a variety of different application universes and that these be capable of being "plugged into" the representation system without requiring changes to the implementation of the rest of the system. In the Iconographer, a designer may select one of several pre-existing *Object Adaptors*, which provide a connection to a given application universe and which define the attributes of the objects in that universe.

The chosen object adaptor plus filter settings determine the information which arrives at the switchboard. A designer's degree of choice of informational content for icons, however, is also influenced by the class of icons which are available

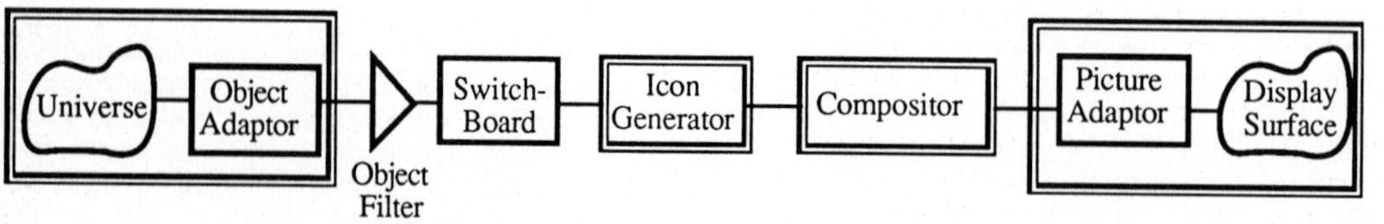

Figure 1: Main dataflow is from left-to-right. Control messages and parameters are passed in both directions. Modules selected from a set of alternatives are shown with outlined borders.

for carrying information, defined by the pictorial attributes which they possess, and the way in which they are presented at the display (e.g., the scaling of the coordinate system for two-dimensional icons, the existence of background information such as labelled axes, and the specification of the interaction among animated icons). The Iconographer separates these two aspects, icon class and method of presentation, treating them as distinct, albeit connected, degrees of freedom of specification. Each icon class is defined by an *Icon Generator* and each method of presentation by a *Compositor*. Subject to compatibility constraints, the designer selects one of each to specify the carriers of application information and the environment in which that information will be presented.

A sixth, and final, degree of freedom of specification is provided on the icon side of the switchboard and corresponds to the choice of object adaptor on the application side. A designer may "plug" into the Iconographer a *Picture Adaptor* which provides the pictorial semantics of iconic attributes in terms of the capabilities of a particular display device.

It is important to note that it is by virtue of the *relation* between object attributes and iconic attributes, that icons represent, or carry information about, application objects. The way the iconic attributes are presented pictorially is not essential to the representation relation [8], although the particular display technique may be critical in influencing the success of the user in acquiring the information so carried. For example, it is the existence and definition of the function at the switchboard which maps ranges of file size onto icon colour which determines that the icon carries information about the file's size. The particular colour used to represent each range of sizes has no bearing on the informational content of the icon. It follows that a designer of an iconic interface is engaged in two separate representation specifications:

- the relation between application attributes and abstractions of iconic attributes, e.g. colour, and

- the relation between these abstractions and their visible representation on a display, e.g. mapping the abstract value 'red' on to a particular colour table entry.

The degrees of freedom which we provide designers in the Iconographer does not make this distinction clear. Thus, some degrees of freedom are incidental to these two specification tasks (e.g., selection of an object adaptor) and other degrees of freedom conflate the tasks (e.g., in addition to defining the attributes of instances of an icon class, the icon generator also "fixes" some presentational aspects of icon attributes, while other aspects are handled by the compositor and the picture adaptor). It is still an open question whether our approach is superior to one which offers specialised tools for the two representational specifications, a question which will only be answered by future testing of the system with real designers.

3. Iconographer Architecture

This section describes the architecture of the Iconographer prototype which is shown in figure 1. In this figure, the flow of data between the modules is left to right.

3.1. Universe and Adaptor

The collection of external application objects to be considered for display, the *Universe*, is isolated from the Iconographer by means of a customised *Object Adaptor* that converts raw object values into the standard object format used by the rest of the Iconographer. To view a different universe requires only that an appropriate adaptor be provided and selected. At the time of writing, adaptors have been written for the UNIX[2] file store, the Smalltalk-80[3] class hierarchy, and a monitor of a local-area network.

3.2. Object Filter

Since a universe may be populated by a large number of objects (e.g. the thousands of files in a UNIX file system), an *Object Filter* restricts the objects currently in view (e.g. those in a single directory). The user programs the filter by drawing a directed graph of filter nodes using a graphical editor. Having built a filter, the user can store it in a file for use in a later session if desired.

Objects from the universe "flow" through this filter out to the rest of the Iconographer. Each node of the filter can be set to let through objects with certain attribute values, while blocking all others. For example, if the universe is a UNIX file store, a node may restrict passage to files below a certain size, or having particular access permissions. By default, the filter lets through all objects in a single directory.

The filter network may be of arbitrary size and use various combinations of series and parallel paths. Nodes placed in series are used to combine restrictions, while nodes in parallel provide alternative paths. The arcs connecting the filter nodes are labelled with a count of the numbering of objects flowing along them. This is useful in determining the efficacy of each node. Figure 2 shows a typical filter network for selecting certain types of file. The upper path allows through files that are greater than ten kilobytes in size and whose name does *not* contain the string 'test'. (The negation of the criterion is shown by a diagonal line through the value.) The lower path allows through all files that are directories. The output of the filter is the union of the output from these two paths.

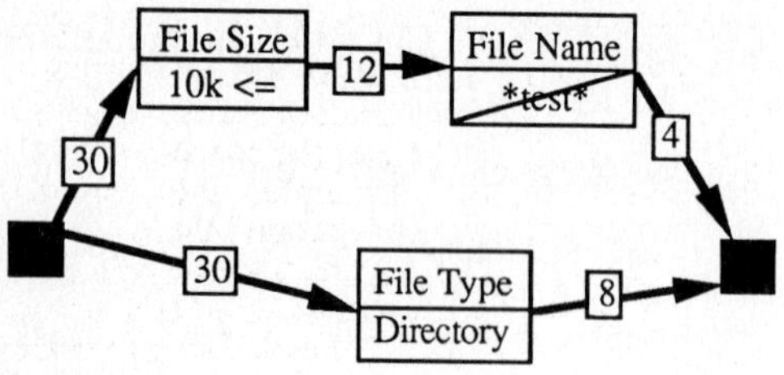

Figure 2: An Example Network in the Object Filter

When creating a new filter node the user is presented with a menu of the available object attributes from which one may be selected to form the basis of the filtering action. A node for the selected attribute is then inserted into the filter. A specialised editor is then opened on this node allowing the user to state which values are to be allowed through the node. For example, the editor for a textual attribute such as a file's name allows a regular expression to be entered as the filtering criterion. This node would only let objects pass if their filename matched this regular expression.

The filter editor has accelerators that make the creation of simple filters fast and easy. Since such filters are common, this facility provides considerable savings. The accelerators include automatic insertion of nodes into the graph where a new node is placed in series with the last node to be inserted with the appropriate "re-wiring" of the filter. The user may disable these accelerators and manually configure the filter.

3.3. Switchboard

On emerging from the filter, objects arrive at the *Switchboard* which handles their association with iconic objects. There is a one-to-one correspondence between objects and icons. The switchboard allows the user to associate object attributes with iconic attributes using one-to-many mappings. A direct manipulation graphical editor is used to specify these mappings. An example of the switchboard editor's display is shown in figure 3.

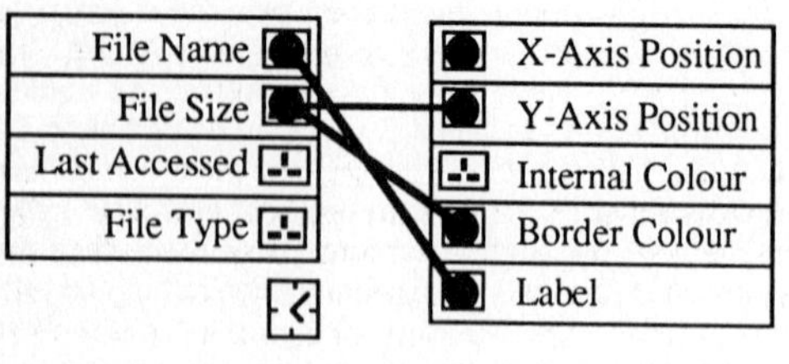

Figure 3: Example Switchboard Setting

On the left-hand side of the switchboard are the object attributes, in this example, of files. The right-hand side shows the currently available icon attributes as determined by the currently selected icon generator and compositor (as discussed in the section 3.4).

To prevent the designer from making nonsensical connections (e.g. file name on to icon colour), the switchboard constrains the attributes to be "type" compatible. For example, file name and icon label are compatible as they are both textual attributes. Type coercion is used to allow, say, the numeric attribute of file size to be mapped on to a textual attribute, such as the label. Semantic feedback is used to tell the user which connections are legal.

The small plug icons in figure 3 are intended to reinforce the metaphor of plugging new connections into the switchboard. The clock-face icon represents a metronome provided by the Iconographer that behaves as a input attribute. The periodicity of the metronome may be set by the user. When the metronome is connected to a display axis attribute (e.g. X-Axis Position), a dynamic plot of how object attribute values vary over time is generated.

Whenever the user adds a new connection, the switchboard creates a default mapping from object attribute values to icon attribute values. For example, consider the file size attribute being mapped on to icon internal colours obtained from a palette of eight different colours. In this case the switchboard asks the adaptor for the lower and upper bounds of the file size attribute for objects in the universe. It then partitions this range (with a generous margin at either end) into eight equal intervals and maps each interval on to a unique colour from the palette. The user can then edit this mapping, to change the interval sizes or the individual colour assignments, for example.

3.4. Icon Generator

The icons representing application objects are created by an *Icon Generator* which implements a class of icons sharing the same attributes. The Iconographer allows the user to dynamically select a generator from a menu of alternatives. Examples of icon classes that are provided by the Iconographer are shown in figure 4.

Each generator provides a set of icon attributes that appear on the right-hand side of the switchboard. (These may be supplemented by attributes from the compositor, described in section 3.5.) Figure 4(a) shows an icon whose attributes include label, internal image, and border colour; figure (b) shows a "squiral" whose attributes include rotation angle, number of turns, and tightness of turns; the icon in figure (c) has attributes such as mouth and nose shapes, hair style and colour, and eye direction.

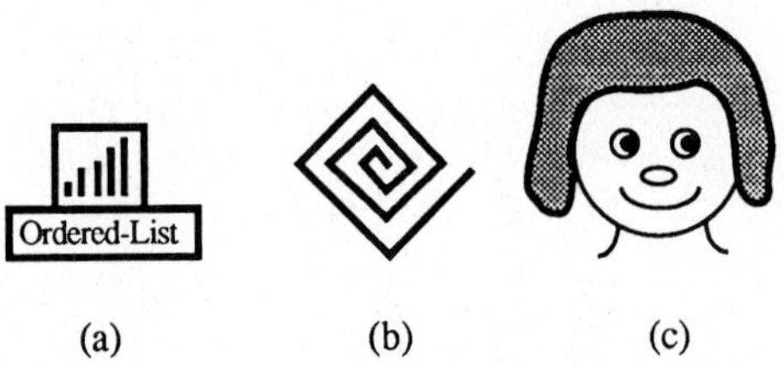

Figure 4: Example Icons

If an iconic attribute has not been connected to an object attribute in the switchboard then the default value specified by that particular iconic attribute will be used. For example, if the border colour attribute for the icon shown in figure 4(a) has not been connected then a default of black is used.

3.5. Compositor

The rest of the Iconographer regards icons as being independent entities that have no knowledge of their environment. In particular, icons are ignorant of the existence of other icons and are unaware of their eventual position on the display screen. These aspects are handled by a *Compositor* which is responsible for the presentation of the set of icons as a whole, especially their spatial arrangement. This separation of responsibility allows different compositors to be used with a given set of icons. Just as the user may choose from a menu of alternative icon generators, so a compositor may be dynamically selected from a menu. By this means, the user can rapidly switch between alternative iconic representations of the universe.

As mentioned in section 3.4, the compositor *may* supplement the set of attributes provided by the icon generator that appears on the right-hand side of the switchboard. Typically, a compositor will provide attributes that allow users to map object attributes on to spatial dimensions. However, the compositor may elect to handle the layout of icons on the display itself. A simple example of this is where icons are arranged in a rectangular grid without regard to any object attribute. In order to arrange the icons the compositor needs to know details of the display environment (e.g. the width and height of the display surface). It obtains this information from the attached picture adaptor (discussed in section 3.6).

A number of demonstration compositors have been built to explore the advantages of separating the mechanics of displaying a single icon from the arrangement of the overall set of icons. The implemented compositors include the rectangular grid mentioned above, and a Cartesian space where the user can map object attributes on to Cartesian space.

The displays produced by the above compositors are static, i.e. icons do not move after they have been placed. An experimental compositor, based on the rectangular grid, introduces the concept of dynamic displays. In this example, the compositor continuously moves icons around the screen. The icons are made to follow vectors whose directions are random but whose magnitude is determined by an iconic attribute called its *speed*. The movement of icons along these vectors is shown as an animation handled by a separate process under the control of the compositor.

Animation is not limited to movement under the control of a compositor. The icons themselves may be given dynamic attributes: what we have termed *animated icons*. For example, the head icon shown in figure 4(c) allows the eyes and mouth to move at a rate determined by an object attribute value. Although this example is amusing rather than informative, the general ability to map object attributes on to dynamic iconic representations is both powerful and novel.

3.6. Picture Adaptor

After the icon set has been arranged by the compositor, they are passed to the *Picture Adaptor* for rendering. The picture adaptor isolates the representation-independent icons obtained from the compositor from the device-dependent details of displaying those icons on the display surface.

The picture adaptor produces its display by asking each icon to display itself at the position determined by the compositor. The ability to display itself is regarded as an inherent property of any icon used by the Iconographer.

Unlike other approaches, e.g. [1], this final display stage is not hard-wired into the system but is also selectable by the user, albeit not dynamically. Currently, three picture adaptors have been built to demonstrate the potential of this approach. The first produces output on a high-resolution, bit-map display that can be panned in two dimensions, based on Smalltalk graphics. The second is a PostScript[4] engine that may be used to produce hard-copy output on a laser printer or window systems that recognise PostScript. The third adaptor produces output for an alpha-numeric terminal such as a vt100.

The three picture adaptors described above are clearly very different in their nature and capabilities. The first is best for highly dynamic displays while the second, because it uses continuous functions not bitmaps, allows a rich variety of icons with attributes limited only by the expressiveness of the PostScript display language. The third option is obviously restricted to textual output and very crude graphics. However, it does show that the Iconographer's concept of icon can encompass textual output as well as the graphical images normally associated with icons. Compositors have been written that use the textual picture adaptor and icons to produce directory listings similar to the UNIX *ls* command.

Given the different capabilities of the various picture adaptors described above, it is clear that icons cannot be displayed with the same fidelity on all display surfaces. For example, an icon that uses fine distinctions in line thickness or colour will not be rendered satisfactorily on a vt100 alpha-numeric display. However, the Iconographer does not constrain which icons may be displayed on which type of surface leaving such considerations to the user.

4. Conclusions and Future Work

Iconographer is a prototype implemented in Smalltalk, intended not only to be a test-bed for iconic interface designers, but also to explore ideas about how iconic interfaces might be designed. Currently, the system only deals with a limited range of icon classes and application universes (both growing in number); more importantly, we intend to extend the system to handle:

- explicit, specifiable iconic representation of relationships (rather than only attributes) among application objects,
- derived attributes of application objects and icons, defined by the user in terms of the primitive object attributes,
- user input.

Acknowledgements

The authors would like to thank their colleagues in the Graphics and HCI group at Glasgow University for providing a stimulating environment for this research. In particular, Catherine Wood, Tunde Cockshott, Alistair Kilgour and Stephen Todd have all helped hone our ideas and early implementations.

References

[1] Smith, D.C. *PYGMALION: A Computer Program to Model and Stimulate Creative Thought*, Birkhäuser Verlag, Boston, 1977.

[2] Ingalls, D. "Design Principles behind Smalltalk", *Byte*, August 1981.

[3] Smith, D.C., Irby, C., Kimball, R., Verplank, W., and Herslem, E. "Designing the Star User Interface", in: Degano, P. and Sandewall, E. (eds.), *Integrated Interactive Computing Systems*, (North-Holland, Amsterdam, 1983), pp. 297–313.

[4] Kenneth Lodding. "Iconic Interfacing", *IEEE Computer Graphics and Applications* **3**(2), March/April 1983, pp. 11–20.

[5] MacKinlay, J. "Automating the Design of Graphical Presentations of Relational Information", *ACM Transactions on Graphics*, **5**(2), April 1982, pp. 110–141.

[6] Dretske, F. *Knowledge and the Flow of Information*, Basil Blackwell, 1981.

[7] Fairchild, K., Meredith, G. and Wexelblat, A. "A Formal Structure for Automatic Icons", *Interacting with Computers* **1**(2), 1989, pp. 131–140.

[8] Dretske, F. *Explaining Behavior*. MIT Press, 1988.

---

[1] Macintosh is a trademark of Apple Computers Inc.
[2] UNIX is a trademark of AT&T Bell Laboratories.
[3] Smalltalk-80 is a trademark of ParcPlace Systems.
[4] PostScript is a trademark of Adobe Systems.

Human–Computer Interaction – INTERACT '90
D. Diaper et al. (Editors)
Elsevier Science Publishers B.V. (North-Holland)

Localisation of Application Knowledge in Incremental Development of User Interfaces

Philip D. Gray†, Catherine A. Wood† and Alistair C. Kilgour‡

DRUID Project,

†Department of Computing Science,
University of Glasgow,
Glasgow G12 8QQ.
email : pdg@ uk.ac.glasgow.cs
email : cathy@uk.ac.glasgow.cs

‡Department of Computer Science,
Heriot-Watt University,
79 Grassmarket,
Edinburgh EH1 2HJ.
ack@uk.ac.hw.cs

ABSTRACT

Localisation of application knowledge in user interface management systems may usefully be categorised with respect to two orthogonal dimensions: the horizontal dimension (the separation of application dependencies from dialogue control) and the vertical dimension (separation into task-related substructures).

We discuss the relation of these issues to user interface development in the context of the Chimera User Interface Management System, which supports both dimensions of modularisation by a dynamically reconfigurable linkage component encapsulating local application knowledge.

INTRODUCTION

We may compare User Interface Management Systems (UIMSs) with respect to a horizontal dimension along which UIMSs are ordered in terms of the number, and characteristics, of the actual components which mediate information flow between user and application. As Cockton [1] has argued, separation of dialogue control from application functionality requires the existence of an actual component of the UIMS, the *linkage*, which handles communication between the user interface and application.

UIMSs may be compared along this horizontal dimension of separation with respect to whether:

- there exists a distinct run-time component which handles communication between the dialogue control and the application;
- such a component, if present, is specifiable independently of dialogue control and application;
- the component is reconfigurable at run-time.

Additionally, one may identify a vertical dimension along which UIMSs may be compared with respect to the degree of modularisation of their linkage. Task structures, and the dialogue control components which reflect them, often exhibit a hierarchical or graph-like organisation. The application knowledge encapsulated in a linkage may be organised similarly, providing a number of advantages, including:

- from the point of view of design, the structure of tasks in the conceptual description of the interface will be reflected in the semantics of the application, as represented by the linkage's description of the application functionality, and
- from the point of view of software engineering, the modularisation of linkage brings attendant benefits such as information hiding and complexity control.

The Chimera User Interface Management System, built as part of Project Druid at the University of Glasgow, has a user interface-application linkage which exhibits a high degree of localisation of knowledge in both dimensions. In the remainder of this paper, we describe the this component, its relationship with dialogue control and application, and how knowledge localisation is achieved.

DIALOGUE CONTROL IN THE CHIMERA UIMS

Before looking in more detail at user interface-application communication in Chimera, it is necessary to examine briefly the dialogue control component, with which the application will communicate, as well as the overall system within which it resides. A fuller description of the system may be found in [2].

Chimera is a user interface management system intended to provide rapid prototyping via run-time reconfigurabiltity [3]. It consists of a specification language (Chisl) and an interpreter (Chip). Interfaces constructed in Chisl consist of three linked parts:

- a presentation system defined in terms of interactive objects,
- a dialogue control component defined as an acyclic directed graph of dialogue units, and
- a user interface-application linkage which consists of a set of linkage units.

Of these, the presentation system is of no direct relevance to the present discussion, and the linkage component will be described in greater detail in later sections of this paper. The dialogue control component is discussed below.

The dialogue control component is composed from dialogue units (DUs) which form the nodes of the graph structure and define the flow of control of the interface. The DUs consist of:

- definitions of presentation details such as windows, textpanes and fonts;
- declarations and definitions of interactive objects;
- declarations of local and global variables;
- options;
- entry exit and clean-up actions.

The first two categories above are actually part of the specification of the presentation system, which is itself modularised via the dialogue units, but implemented as a separately executing process. Interactive objects are presentation entities which have a visible representation and, in most cases, internal state and behaviour which can be changed as the result of user, dialogue control or application actions. Typical interactive objects include buttons, editable textfields and PostScript-defined images.

The heart of a DU is its options, which consist of condition-action pairs, and which determine the flow of control. Conditions are tests over expressions referring to dialogue unit variables and the state of interactive objects. When an option condition is evaluated as true, the option's set of actions is executed. These actions include:

- effecting changes to interactive objects,
- assigning values to dialogue unit variables,
- activating application processes,
- activating other dialogue units (subDUs).

Communication with application processes does not occur directly as a dialogue unit action, but takes place via a separate component, the linkage component, described below.

When a dialogue unit is activated via an option action, its set of options is added to the currently active options. Its parent's options are also still active unless explicitly disabled, thus allowing selection "up" the DU activation path.

THE HORIZONTAL DIMENSION

In the Chimera architecture, application functionality resides in one or more Unix processes external to the user interface, which is itself a separate process. Communication with an application process is initiated by the dialogue control component. There is a pre-defined Chisl action which, given the name of an executable file,

- launches the associated process,
- assigns a Chisl identifier with the link (called the link identifier),
- establishes the pipes to and from the application process,
- creates and activates a component to handle user interface-application communication; this component is called a linkage unit (LU).

Once the application process has been launched and the linkage established, all communication between dialogue control and the application is mediated by the linkage. Subsequent Chisl actions may merge further LUs with the linkage, or replace it with a new one. Figure 1 illustrates the arrangement for one application process. In principle, a Chisl interface may communicate with any number of processes simultaneously, each with its own communication channels and linkage.

Like DUs, LUs contain declarations of local and global variables, as well as options. However, unlike DUs, LU option conditions may include tests over the contents of the input pipe from the application and a predefined LU action is available to place data on the output pipe. LUs may not include declarations of interactive objects.

Linkage and dialogue control communicate via special linkage variables, which constitute the only shared data between the two components. These variables may be used, changed, or tested in the conditions of options in either component. Linkage variables are somewhat like active values, a communication and control mechanism used in some other UIMSs [4], in that changing the value of a variable in one component may cause associated actions to be executed in the other component.

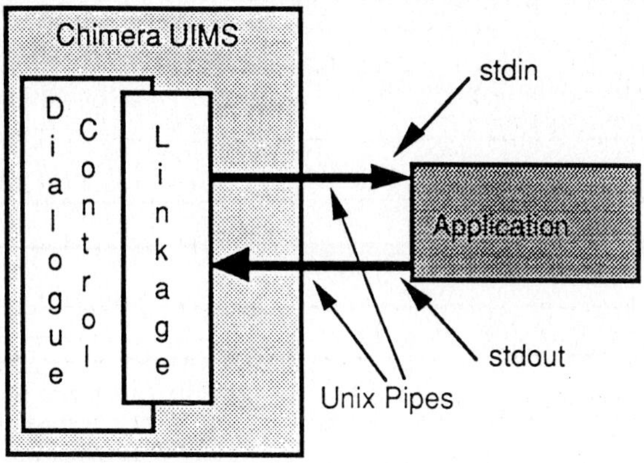

Figure 1 : The Dialogue — Application Communication

The options of both active DUs and active LUs are liable for "firing". That is, input from the application is treated no differently from input from the user, allowing interleaving of user-generated and application generated actions. In practice, DU conditions are given priority over LU conditions to enable user actions to be serviced with a minimum of delay.

We believe this approach to horizontal application knowledge localisation provides a number of advantages, the most important of which are listed below.

i. The linkage variables provide an adequate model of the application from the point of view of the dialogue control component. The particularity of the application's actual communication protocol — lexical and syntactic — are isolated from control, allowing changes to the protocol without requiring changes to control. Of course, changes to the application semantics may well demand changes to the control component.

ii. The fact that LUs have state allows a further decoupling of application from control. For example, arguments to an application operation may be collected (in any order), stored and sent when all the arguments have been received and validated.

iii. LUs are dynamic; that is, they can change their own state. This allows an LU to communicate with an application without causing any change to dialogue control state, for example when dealing with application messages of no relevance to the rest of the interface.

iv. The similarity of LU and DU structure simplifies the specification of an interface in that a designer does not need to learn two entirely separate subsets of the specification language; a single computational model and, largely, a single syntax are applicable to both components.

THE VERTICAL DIMENSION

As mentioned above, when a link to an application process is created by a DU, the associated LU is "attached" to the DU which created it. The LU's lifetime is thereafter coextensive with that of its parent DU; when the DU is de-activated, so is the LU.

Once a linkage is created, subDUs of the DU which created the linkage may add linkage units to that linkage. Typically each subDU will add a corresponding LU which deals with the application specific aspects of the task supported by the subDU. This vertical localisation of application knowledge provides a powerful method of defining communication protocol incrementally. Each DU is thus responsible for adding to the protocol the content relevant to the "task" which the DU represents.

This structure is similar to the approach of Coutaz's PAC model [5] in which each object in a PAC hierarchy may possess its own linkage to the application. The advantage of our architecture is that the overall linkage exists as a single (albeit compound) entity, thus allowing a designer to specify in terms of a single application model. Furthermore, global application actions can be handled at any level without having to pass information explicitly from one level to its predecessors. Figure 2 shows the combination of horizontal and vertical dimensions of modularity in the Chimera architecture.

AN EXAMPLE

In order to illustrate the dynamics of UI—Application communication, and the way horizontal

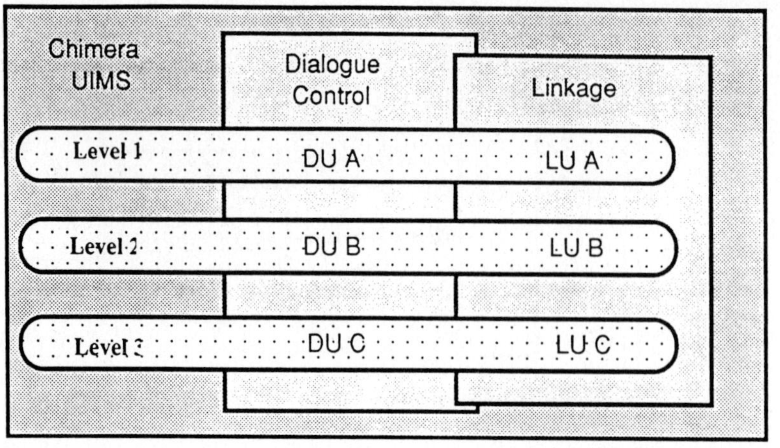

Figure 2 : The Horizontal and Vertical Modularisation of Application Knowledge

and vertical separation are implemented, we present a simple example of an interaction in Chisl.

Consider the task of saving some pre-specified data to a new file. We shall assume, for the purposes of this example, that the application can interpret the command *'Save as : <filename>'*. If the filename refers to an existing file, the application will respond with *'File exits: <filename> Overwrite (y/n)?'*. If *'y'* is received by the application, the file will be overwritten with the specified data, otherwise the operation is cancelled. To save to another filename, the entire operation must begin again. Apart from the concrete syntax, this is not unlike the Macintosh's *'save as...'* command.

Figure 3 shows the communication between the four components necessary to complete the task using a Chisl-specified interface. The presentation column describes the actions carried out by the user in terms of visible interaction objects, the dialogue column shows the dialogue unit options executed as a result of user actions and/or changes to DU or LU state (not all options are shown, only those which are in fact executed), the linkage column indicates the LU options executed as a result of changes to link variables and/or application actions, and finally, the application column describes the actions carried out by the application as a consequence of data received from the linkage.

We assume that our example interaction begins part-way through a larger interactive session. The user has already specified the data to be saved and is offered the choice of button interactive objects (referred to as *buttons* below) labelled *Save, Save As* and *Delete*. At the start of this task, the user selects the *Save As* button. The selection is tested in the dialogue control component via an option with the condition *{saveAs}*. On firing, the option executes the Chisl action *doSaveAs[]*, which represents the activation of a new DU called *doSaveAs*, which will handle the required subtask.

On activation, the DU carries out its entry actions (not shown here), which result in the display of an editable textfield interactive objects (referred to as *textfields* below), called entry, with the prompt *'Filename:'*; plus two new button, called *doIt* and *cancel*, with their usual meanings and with representations *Do save* and *Cancel*, respectively. The user enters the desired filename, 'roo', in entry and then selects the button *doIt*.. This selection is caught by the condition *{doIt}* which results in the execution of its associated actions, viz., causing the contents of the textfield to be assigned to the link variable *filename* and the link toggle (i.e., a flag which is automatically cleared after being tested) *doSave* to be set.

The linkage, as represented by the linkage unit associated with, activated by the DU *doSaveAs*, has an option whose condition tests the state of the toggle *saveAs* and if true, builds a command with the user-supplied filename and passes it to the application. In our example, we assume that the file exists, which fact is reported by the application. The string *'File exists: roo'* is then matched against the LU condition *{"File exists: %s"}*. The '%s' filters out the file name and assigns it to temporary variable, *$1*, which is in turn assigned to the link variable *existingFile*. Another toggle, *fileExists*, is then set.

The control component catches the change of state of toggle *fileExists* and in turn generates a message indicating to the user the existence of the file. The *doIt* button is replaced by a button called *overwrite* (with representation *Overwrite*) to indicate the change in semantics of a file save action. Also, the entry

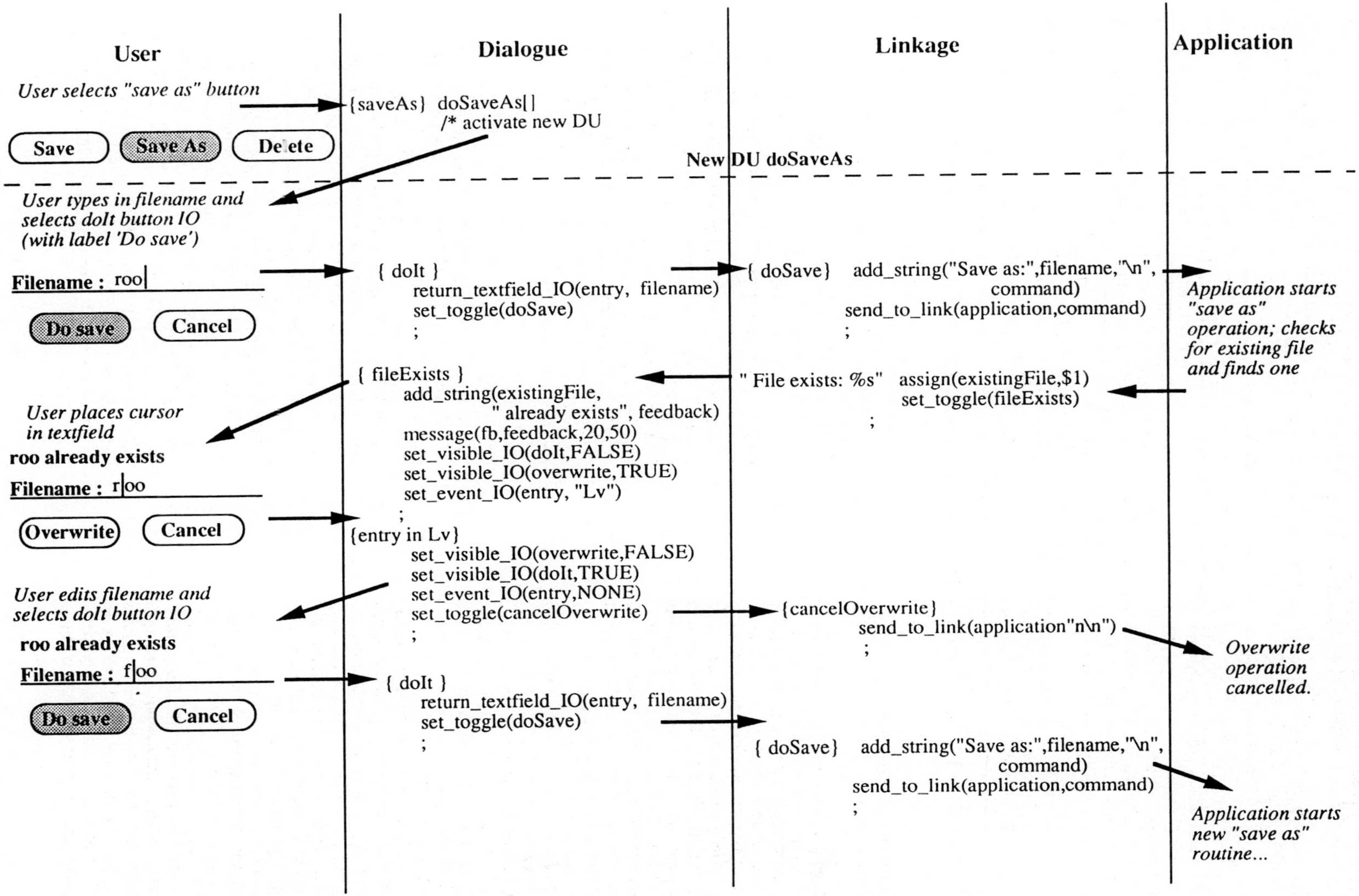

Figure 3 An Example Interaction

textfield is set up to respond to a mouse click, indicating that the user wishes to edit the filename.

If the user wished to overwrite, they would select the *overwrite* button (the options corresponding to this choice are not given in the diagram). However, we shall assume the user edits 'roo' to 'foo'. The user must click the mouse in the textfield in order to carry out the edit action; that click is caught by the altered textfield (see previous paragraph) causing the button *overwrite* to be removed and the *doIt* button to be redisplayed. This also has the side effect of cancelling the overwrite operation by sending 'n\n' to the application.

The textfield has been edited and the overwrite operation cancelled. In order to execute the save operation with the new filename, 'foo', the user would select the *doIt* button , thereby reinitiating the save as sequence started by firing the *{doIt}* condition.

In the example, communication between dialogue control and linkage was entirely by means of the following link variables.

Representing application operations:

doSave indicates that 'save as' operation is to be performed;
doOverwrite indicates that the existing file is to be overwritten;
cancelOverwrite indicate that an overwrite has been rejected.

Representing application entities:

filename holds the user specified filename
existingFile holds the name of an existing file, if any.

Representing application state:

fileExists indicates that the filename specified already exists.

Together, these link variables form the application model. The actual textual commands and application feedback which the application process understands and can generate are isolated in the linkage component and could be changed without affecting either the dialogue component or the communication between dialogue and linkage. Furthermore, note the application operation to cancel an overwrite has now been embedded in the task of selecting the textfield for editing.

Although this example describes the horizontal dimension in some detail, it does not show the vertical modularity explicitly. However, each of the other options available in the parent DU (i.e. *save* and *delete*) would have their own LUs to handle communication for those tasks.

CONCLUSIONS

In its present form, the Chimera linkage component provides an explicitly specifiable, dynamically reconfigurable and active UIMS component which modularises application functionality . We believe it provides considerable flexibility for design and that the separability it provides between dialogue specification and application linkage specification is an indispensable aid to the designer in conceptualising and prototyping the different aspects of an interface which must be combined to form an effective system.

Currently Chimera only supports string and toggle variables. More complex data structures will be necessary in order to handle sophisticated application models.

ACKNOWLEDGEMENTS

We would also like to thank Kieran Clenaghan, David England and Kevin Waite for their helpful comments on an earlier version of this paper. The initial realisation of the need for a Chimera linkage is the natural consequence of working near Gilbert Cockton.

This work in this paper is supported by the UK Science and Engineering Research Council under grant GR/D 80124. Their assistance is gratefully acknowledged.

REFERENCES

[1] **COCKTON, Gilbert;** A New Model for Separable Interactive Systems, *Proceedings of Interact'87,* Bullinger and Shackel (Eds), 1987, pp 1033 — 1038.

[2] **WOOD, Catherine A.; GRAY, Philip D.;** User Interface — Application Communication in the Chimera UIMS, Glasgow University, Department of Computing Science Research Report CSC/90/R1. 1990.

[3] **GRAY, Philip D., KILGOUR, Alistair C., WOOD, Catherine A.;** Dynamic Reconfigurability for Fast Prototyping of User Interfaces,*Software Engineering Journal,* November 1988, pp 257—262.

[4] **MYERS, Brad A. and BUXTON, William;** Creating Highly Interactive and Graphical User Interfaces by Demonstration, ACM SIGGRAPH, Vol 20, No.4, pp 249—258, 1986.

[5] **COUTAZ, Joelle;** PAC, an Object Oriented Model for Dialog Design, *Proceedings of Interact'87,* Bullinger and Shackel (Eds), 1987, pp 431 — 436.

Human–Computer Interaction – INTERACT '90
D. Diaper et al. (Editors)
Elsevier Science Publishers B.V. (North-Holland)

A UIMS FOR KNOWLEDGE BASED INTERFACE TEMPLATE GENERATION AND INTERACTION

Christian Märtin*

Fachhochschule Augsburg, FB Allgemeinwissenschaften und Informatik, Baumgartnerstr. 16
D-8900 Augsburg

A knowledge based UIMS that exploits the semi-structured nature of office objects and tasks to generate flexible, user-adapated dialogue is presented. To produce interface templates for a broad range of interactive applications, the conceptual structure of the application data and abstract dialogue objects serve as the elements of a frame-like representation of the user interface. This description is refined by a dialogue manager that evaluates rules for presentation and user preferences. A refined interface frame, which is still independent of underlying I/O-tools, is mapped to the most suitable classes of the toolkit in the preferred environment (e.g. Andrew or OSF/Motif) by a generation component. The dialogue design process is illustrated for a multimedia editor application.

1 Introduction

During the last years major advances in user interface management systems and object-oriented information systems have led to powerful and usable development environments and solutions for the office domain. The *CT-UIMS* approach (*C*onceptual *T*emplate *UIMS*) is primarily aimed at supporting applications like intelligent editors, electronic mail, and document retrieval systems. Those systems rely heavily on efficient and highly interactive user interfaces and provide an internal data or object representation that can directly be exploited for knowledge based automatic user interface construction. With the current implementation of the system productivity of application programmers and end-users can be considerably improved. At the same time a high degree of design flexibility can be realized.

Discussion of general models for interactive software systems, [see Balzert (1987), Lantz, Tanner (1987)], experience with prototypical knowledge based architectures [Märtin, Waldhör (1988)], and consequences from the dynamic evolution of prototypical and commercially available user interface tools [Myers (1989)] resulted in four major design goals for CT-UIMS:

1) Providing maximum separation of application semantics and dialogue functionality.

2) Allowing for easy integration of existing and future standard user interface toolkits into the UIMS by decoupling the high-level aspects of dialogue generation from the mapping to toolkit primitives.

3) Decomposition of applications with substantial functional contributions from low-level interaction (e.g. editors) into an abstract requirements-definition part and executable class-instances.

4) Flexible and adaptable general or user-/task-specific embedding of frame-based dialogue knowledge.

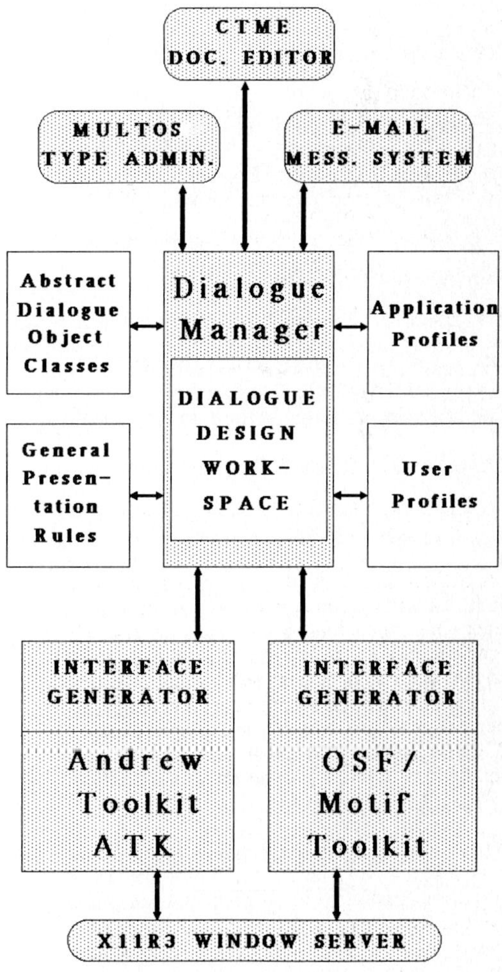

Figure 1. Architecture of CT-UIMS

*Formerly at Olivetti D.O.R. / TA Research Lab, Nürnberg, where this work was funded by the Commission of the European Communities as part of ESPRIT-Project 28 "MULTOS".

The global architecture of CT-UIMS, which is now a part of the *MULTOS* system (*Multi* Media *Office* *Server*), see e.g. [Constantopoulos, Yeorgaroudakis (1986)], is shown in figure 1. The central component of the UIMS, the dialogue manager, is responsible for controlling the user interface design process by evaluating several dialogue knowledge bases according to a given strategy. The construction process uses a central dialogue design workspace for the gradual refinement of abstract user interface objects in a way directed by the results of the knowledge base consultation. The knowledge bases of the dialogue manager contain frame-like representations of the dialogue objects, dialogue profiles for different applications as well as general, user-, and application-dependent presentation rules.

An abstract programming interface, and facilities for general user guidance and inter-application communication are also provided by the UIMS.

Different user interface toolkits can optionally be integrated into CT-UIMS without affecting the higher levels of the dialogue. Each toolkit is coupled to the UIMS by a special interface generator. The generator activates the relevant toolkit classes for presentation and mediates user inputs between the active toolkit and the dialogue manager.

Automatic user interface generation by a high-level UIMS is also discussed in [Singh, Green (1989)]. Another recent approach to knowledge based dialogue design is presented in [Wiecha, Bennett (1989)].

2 Building Applications with CT-UIMS

The requirements for generating advanced user-system dialogues with CT-UIMS and the different steps of the automatic design process will be discussed in detail for one of the MULTOS applications, a conceptual structure editor, that was implemented under CT-UIMS.

2.1 Abstract User Interface Representation

For building application user interfaces with CT-UIMS similarities between the data representation of the applications and their potential user interface structures have to be located. An abstract representation of the data objects used within applications for interaction with the user is essential, in order to allow to clearly separate the application semantics from the user interface functionality. There exist several UIMS approaches that use a declarative approach to generate direct manipulation interfaces [e.g. Olsen (1989)]. Such UIMSs use the definitions of scalar-, vector-, array-, and record-variables of application programs for building adequate user interfaces. In addition to exploiting such standard data types in CT-UIMS the definitions of conceptual document structures serve as abstract frame representations of the user interface, especially for multimedia document processing applications. During the design process such frames are refined by the dialogue manager and translated to interactive screen representations of either instances of conceptual document types or raw templates, which simplify the creation of new documents for the user.

Templates are also the principal user interface structures of the Object Lens System [Lai, Malone (1988)], where the concept of semi-structured objects is emphasized for a broad range of interactive applications. The user interface frames used by CT-UIMS, which were inspired by the more formalized MULTOS-CSD [Barbic, Rabitti (1985)], can be seen as suitable representations for such semi-structured objects. In other terms, the same data representation scheme which serves for user interface generation in CT-UIMS, could be employed for describing office tasks, procedures, evaluation rules, etc. (N.B. Ultimately, the dialogue manager - provided with the necessary knowledge and functionality - could be used to coordinate a unified, intelligent, and multi-threaded dialogue among all users, applications, and resources of the system, including databases).

2.2 Design of a Conceptual Structure Editor

Advanced information systems distinguish between a logical, a layout, and a conceptual view on the structure of a document. The conceptual view, as it was defined in the MULTOS document model [Eirund, Kreplin (1988)], describes the semantics of a document as a tree, the already mentioned *CSD* (*Conceptual Structure Definition*). A CSD identifies and names all of the essential semantic components of a document, with their associated contents and content attributes. Components may be basic, complex or refinable objects, they may be optional or mandatory, unique or iterative. The components or nodes of a CSD specify a type.

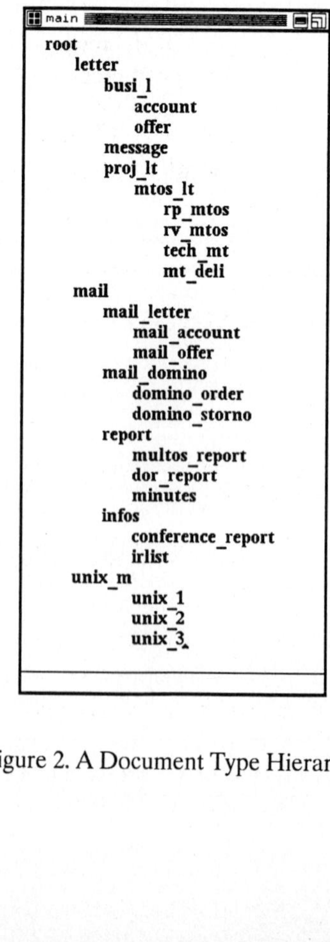

Figure 2. A Document Type Hierarchy

An example type hierarchy was defined as the basis for classifying any business document as an instance of a given type. Figures 2 and 3 illustrate the conceptual typing approach of the MULTOS system. The conceptual types serve as efficient structures for data base access, query formulation, content based retrieval, and filtering mechanisms for electronic mail distribution. In structured editors, conceptual types can be used to generate templates for the preparation of business documents with an a priori CSD for later retrieval purposes. *CTME* (*C*SD-*Tem*plate *E*ditor) was designed with this main goal in mind.

By conceiving CTME as a CT-UIMS application [Oemig (1989), Märtin, Oemig (1989)], a user-centered editor with a maximum degree of independence of the underlying toolkit and window server could be realized, which is easily portable between different target environments.

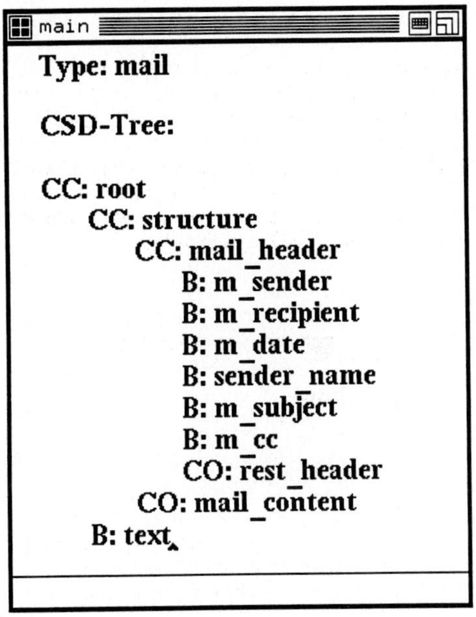

Figure 3. Textual Tree Representation of the CSD-Type Mail

In CTME, the MULTOS type hierarchy and the CSD-formalism fulfill four purposes:

- visualization of existing documents and their CSDs for structured editing,
- generation of raw templates of a specific CSD-type to facilitate the preparation of a priori CSD-structured document instances,
- automatic construction of abstract user interface frames for any new CSD,
- type refinement and interactive creation of new CSD-types.

2.3 The Dialogue Manager

Automatic dialogue design may be seen as a cooperative process based on contributions from several design knowledge bases which are evaluated and coordinated by the dialogue manager. A *design workspace* (similar to a simplified blackboard) is used for modelling the different stages of the dialogue design process, holding the dynamic user interface frames for any CT-UIMS application in their various states of completion. In contrast to the blackboard approach (Engelmore, Morgan 1988), where knowledge sources may actively access the objects located in the workspace, in CT-UIMS the dialogue manager alone controls the sequence of action by maintaining the priorities of the different knowledge bases, interpreting the abstract user interface frames, evaluating dialogue rules, and finally modifying the objects in the workspace. The dialogue control strategy, which tries to solve occurring design conflicts by allowing to restore intermediate design states, whenever necessary, is - like the rest of the dialogue manager - implemented in C, for efficiency reasons. The dialogue design process and the contents of the design knowledge bases will now be discussed for the CTME editor.

The *dialogue object classes* knowledge base contains an abstract frame-like description of standard dialogue resources like windows, menus, forms, text editor objects, images, bitmaps, graphics editor objects, animations, etc. In general, the user interface of each application is constructed as a spatial and temporal combination of different dialogue standard object instances.

For the CTME-application text-editor objects and menues are essentially important as dialogue objects. The descriptions of a simple text-editor object and a selection-list object are contained in the knowledge base and have the following structure:

```
((dialogue_object_class     text_editor_object)
 (identification            <id_number>)
 (data_object               <text>)
 (display_object            <input_output_window>
 (interactive_functions     ( <insert> <delete> ...
                              <search> <replace> ))
```

```
((dialogue_object_class     selection_list)
 (identification            <id_number>)
 (data_object               <array_of_string>)
 (display_object            <input_output_window>
 (interactive_functions     ( <select_item> ))
```

The standard set of currently more than fourty abstract dialogue object classes is easily extensible. Their interactive functions are specified in C source code notation and reside in the same KB. For the application programmer these standard dialogue objects form the building blocks for the design of the user interface of any specific application.

As the application programmer knows the data structure of the application, it is an easy task for her/him, to configure the abstract frames for the templates of the desired user interface by combining the appropriate dialogue objects from the knowledge base. Only a very limited vocabulary of keywords is needed for slot definition. If some aspects of the application data or functionality cannot be covered by existing dialogue objects, extensions to existing classes or new classes and their interactive functions have to be specified within the dialogue object classes knowledge base. Such modifications of the class specifications have to be mirrored in the toolkit primitives chosen for the actual screen representation of the user interface.

The abstract user interface frames for the templates of a document or a type, i.e. the interface between applications and CT-UIMS, are organized in *application profiles*. These profiles provide the semantic structure of the user interface that will be generated by the UIMS. They also hold the user interface frames for initialization and subtask-selection. The frames contained in the profiles are reusable by any other applications with similar user interface requirements.

As an example, interface frames for CTME's main window and for the MULTOS-type mail are given. Note, that for any new document type with no UI-frame entry in the application profile, CTME will automatically generate a default frame by parsing the type's CSD-description, before the document's user interface is created.

```
(user_interface_frame
 (application_class    document_preparation)
 (ui_frame_id          CTME_1)
 (ui_frame_class       application_frame)
 ((node_identifier     application__logo
  (dobj_type           NIL))
 (node                 application_logo__content
  (dobj_type           animation)))
 ((node_identifier     task_selection
  (dobj_type           NIL))
 (node                 task_selection_content
  (dobj_type           selection_list)
  (dobj_instance       ("Administration"
                        "Template Generator"
                        "Document Editor"
                        "Type Refinement"))))
```

Contrary to the CSD representation of the document type mail, only basic nodes have to be considered in the user interface frame of this type:

```
(user_interface_frame
 (application_class    document_preparation)
 (ui_frame_id          CTME_12)
 (ui_frame_class       conceptual_document_template)
 (presentation_mode    NIL)
 (document_type        mail)
 ((node_identifier     m_sender
  (dobj_type           no_scroll_text_output_object))
 (node                 m_sender_content
  (dobj_type           no_scroll_text_editor_object)))
                       /* semantic relation between a CSD-
                         node and its contents */
 ((node_identifier     m_recipient
  (dobj_type           no_scroll_text_output_object))
 (node                 m_recipient_content
  (dobj_type           no_scroll_text_editor_object)))
 ((node_identifier     m_date
  (dobj_type           no_scroll_text_output_object))
 (node                 m_date_content
  (dobj_type           date_object)))
 ((node_identifier     sender_name
  (dobj_type           no_scroll_text_output_object))
 (node                 sender_name_content
  (dobj_type           no_scroll_text_editor_object)))
 ((node_identifier     m_subject
  (dobj_type           no_scroll_text_output_object))
 (node                 m_subject_content
  (dobj_type           no_scroll_text_editor_object)))
 ((node_identifier     m_cc
  (dobj_type           no_scroll_text_output_object))
 (node                 m_cc_content
  (dobj_type           no_scroll_text_editor_object)))
 ((node_identifier     text
  (dobj_type           no_scroll_text_output_object))
 (node                 text_content
  (dobj_type           scroll_multimedia_editor_object))))
```

The semantic information of the user interface frames is refined and completed with presentation, style, and layout information by the dialogue manager during the design process. Thus, one and the same abstract user interface frame can result in a wide spectrum of refined frames depending on the characteristics of the application environment and the current user.

In the first refinement phase a knowledge base with *presentation and style rules* is exploited by the dialogue manager. The presentation rules and their associated functions are responsible for the general aspects of the layout design and the styles of the node contents.Some typical presentation rules are the following:

```
((if presentation_mode == NIL)
      (presentation_mode = window_mode))

((if (number(node) - 1) <= 5
 and presentation_mode == window_mode)
      (node_orientation = horizontal))

((if (number(node) - 1) >= 6
 and (number(node) mod 3) == 0))
      (nodes_per_row = 3))

(node_justify = TRUE)
```

```
((if node_identifier == product) (font = "Dutch" "bold"))

((if document_type != NIL)
        (((node_identifier     help_info_area
          (dobj_type           NIL))
         (node                 help_info_content
          (dobj_type           scroll_help_object)
          (dobj_instance       NIL)
          (dobj_position       right))))
        /* a new slot is created for a CSD-type user
           interface frame within the CTME application */
```

Rules are interpreted by the dialogue manager and are always applied to the current interface frame, which resides in the dialogue design workspace. This process triggers the creation of the *extended user interface frame,* which contains all the details of the user interface, necessary for the toolkit-dependent interface generator.

In the second design phase, the dialogue manager checks whether the current *user profile* contains any design rules that would modify some layout or style aspects of the user interface. These rules may cover both application-independent or application-specific user preferences. In CTME, these rules can influence the structure and the content styles of the extended user interface frame for each CSD type of some importance to a specific user.

The rules have the same structure as the general presentation rules. They can handle aspects such as the sequence of nodes, alias names of nodes, horizontal or vertical layout ordering, multimedia and other aspects.

Some typical user profile rules are listed below:

```
((if document_type == mail)
        (node_orientation = horizontal))

((if document_type == offer)
        ((nodes_per_row = 4)
         (header_image = TRUE)
         ((if node == sender_content)
                (dobj_type = no_scroll_raster_image))
         ((if node == date_content)
                (date_format = "(ddmmyy_/)")))

((if document_type == mail)
        ((if (node_identifier != text) and
            (node_identifier != help_info_area))
        (font = "Swiss" "italic"))

((if document_type == offer)
        ((if node_identifier == locality)
                ((alias = "Locality")
                 (font = "bold"))))

((if document_type == mail)
        ((help_exist = TRUE)
        ((if node == help_info_content)
                (dobj_instance = "help/chris/standard"))))
```

For an application like CTME the user profile entries that handle the nodes of a specific type can be grouped to a single rule in order to maintain consistency and increase design efficiency. Conditions of rules covering more than one type, can also be linked by *or*-operators.

After the user-profile evaluation the extended user interface frame for the CSD type *mail* has the following structure:

```
(user_interface_frame
 (application_class    document_preparation)
 (ui_frame_id          CTME_12)
 (ui_frame_class       conceptual_document_template)
 (presentation_mode    window_mode)
 (document_type        mail)
 (node_orientation     horizontal)
 (node_justify         TRUE)
 (help_exist           TRUE)
 (nodes_per_row        1)
 ((node_identifier     help_info_area
  (dobj_type           NIL))
 (node                 help_info_content
  (dobj_type           scroll_help_object)
  (dobj_instance       "help/chris/standard")
  (dobj_position       right)))
 ((node_identifier     m_sender
  (position            3)
  (dobj_type           no_scroll_text_output_object)
  (font                "Swiss" "italic"))
 (node                 m_sender_content
  (dobj_type           no_scroll_raster_image)
  (dobj_instance       "pictures/old_man")))
 ((node_identifier     m_recipient
  (position            4)
  (dobj_type           no_scroll_text_output_object)
  (font                "Swiss" "italic"))
 (node                 m_recipient_content
  (dobj_type           no_scroll_text_editor_object)
  (font                "Dutch")))
 ((node_identifier     m_date
  (position            1)
  (dobj_type           no_scroll_text_output_object)
  (font                "Swiss" "italic"))
 (node                 m_date_content
  (date_format         "(day), (ddmmyy_/)"
  (dobj_type           date_object)
  (font                "Dutch")))
  . . .
  . . .
  . . .
 ((node_identifier     text
  (position            bottom)
  (dobj_type           NIL))
 (node                 text_content
  (dobj_type           scroll_multimedia_editor_object)
  (font                "Dutch" "Size 14")
  (text_style          "indented" "right justified"))))
```

2.4 Interface Layout Generation

An extended user interface frame serves as the input for the interface generation component that creates a toolkit-specific interactive user interface layout with the resources of the selected toolkit. The generation component interprets the extended user interface frames and replaces abstract dialogue objects with the instances of the appropriate classes in the CT-UIMS resource set, which were built from toolkit primitives. A table that maintains the mappings from all abstract dialogue object classes to the best fitting toolkit classes is part of the generation component.

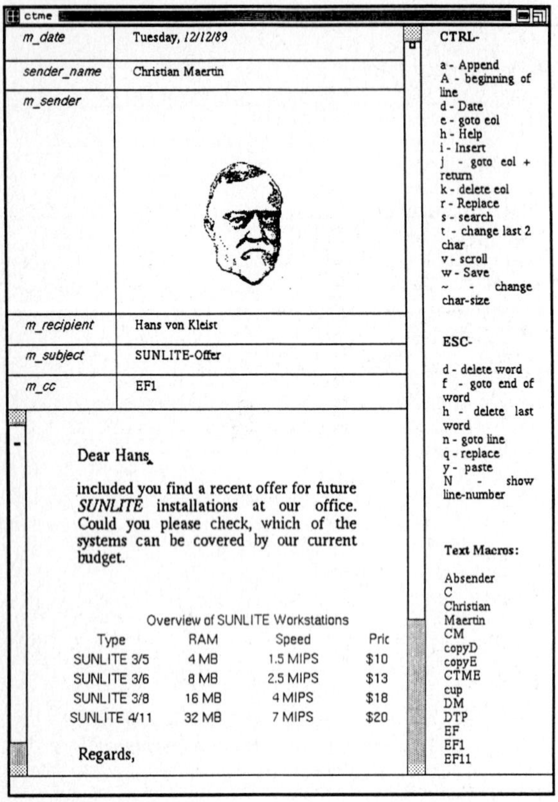

Figure 4. CTME Mail Layout for User A

Special attention is paid to programmer contributed interactive functions for data manipulation that need to be embedded into the menus of the application user interface. In an editor application like CTME, low-level functionality, which is generally seen as a logical part of the toolkit or I/O-level, forms a major part of the application functionality. Comfortable macro functions and flexible search and replace commands, that were not part of the CT-UIMS resource set, therefore had to be defined in the abstract dialogue object classes. The functions are coded in C - independent of the toolkit - as parts of the application. The generation component downloads these functions to the toolkit level before runtime, in order to maximize system performance.

By interpreting the extended user interface frame, the generation component creates an interactive document editor layout. Figure 4 shows the interface for the type mail, after a document was created. Different profile entries lead to alternative template layouts (see fig. 5).

Each node of the user interface frame is translated into a toolkit class instance. Depending on the specification of the abstract dialogue objects, the nodes differ in their functional behaviour. In the mail example, node identifiers were mapped to read-only windows, whereas the node contents where mapped to several text-editor windows, a raster image window, a multimedia-editor window for the document body, and a help window.

Each window type offers a different set of functions, which are available for the end-user to interactively prepare electronic documents.

To create balanced user interface layouts, the size of the screen representation of the extended user interface frame, which is internally computed by the generator, must be within the limits of the available screen space (especially, if a tiled window manager is used) or the default size of the new window. If some of the template nodes cannot be placed within the window area to be displayed, the generation component informs the user, via the dialogue manager, that an adequate screen representation of the template is not possible. If the user wishes, the dialogue manager selects the less space-consuming default interface frame from the root user profile, adds to it the properties of the node contents of the rejected frame and again passes it to the generator.

Document Type: mail

m_sender:

m_recipient: ***Hans von Kleist***
m_date: ***12.12.1989***
sender_name: ***Christian Maertin***
m_subject: ***SUNLITE-Offer***
m_cc: ***EF1***
text:

Figure 5. Text_mode Template Layout for User B

Note, that for any document layout produced by the generator, several additional functions for macro operations and editing are available that are not part of the standard toolkit classes. The help area on the right of the document layout contains the personal help, information, and macro environment of a specific user. Interactively, this information can be modified, extended, and stored in the user profile for later use and thus be tailored by the user, according to her/his personal needs and preferences. Standard entries for type-specific help and information areas are available as parts of the application profiles. Part of a template with vertical node orientation is shown in figure 6.

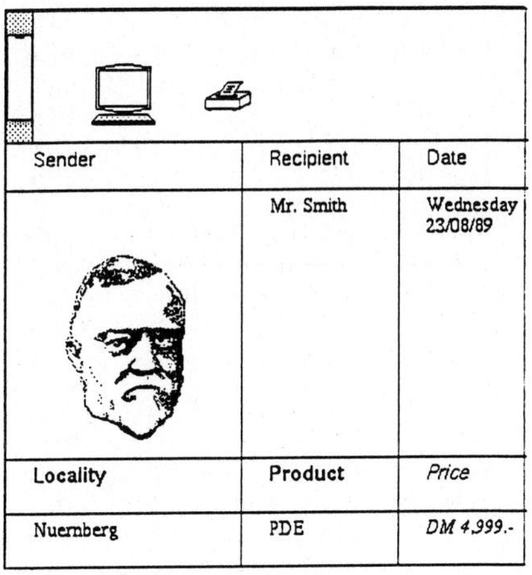

Figure 6. Vertical Node Layout for Type Offer

Documents (user interfaces and contents) can interactively be refined and modified by the user, stored for later use, or mailed. The user has the option to enable *adaptation mode*, when documents are stored after an editor session. In this case, the dialogue manager will become active again and may alter part of the right-hand sides of the type-specific rules in the user profile to the values that were selected in the current document's user interface. A mail user, who receives a CTME document may either visualize the document with the layout generated by the remote CT-UIMS, or create a version of the document with layout and style features adapted to her/his personal environment by invoking the local CT-UIMS dialogue manager. If the receiving user prefers a different toolkit, the document can even be mapped to that toolkit by invoking the relevant interface generator. For this purpose all abstract dialogue objects have to be consistently represented as classes of both toolkits.

3 Implementation and Future Work

For the current CT-UIMS implementation, which has been running for several months on top of X11R3 on SUN workstations, an interface generator for the Andrew toolkit ATK [ATK (1988)] was developed first. ATK was chosen, because of the multimedia functionality inherent to its standard toolkit classes. The next step will be the implementation of an OSF/Motif [OSF (1989)] interface generator that will allow the easy migration of the complete UIMS and its applications to a broader range of UNIX machines. Future work will be concentrated on the evolution of the current architecture and will result in the design of several new components of the UIMS, such as:

- A CT-UIMS generated rule editor with support for consistency maintenance in dialogue profiles.

- An internationalization component that provides multilinguality by replacing the names of nodes and identifiers of UI frames with the correct expressions in the goal language.

- An interface generator for a voice toolkit which will allow simple mixed visual/voice dialogues.

Acknowledgements

The author's special thanks go to Martina Oemig, who contributed many ideas and solutions to the design of the general architecture and implemented most of the prototypical CT-UIMS code as part of her diploma thesis work at TA Research.

References

ATK (1988). The Andrew System. Programmer's Guide to the Andrew Toolkit. IBM, CMU-ITC.
Balzert, H. (1987). A Blackboard Architecture for the Realization of Software-Ergonomic Demands. In Proceedings of INTERACT '87 (Eds. H.-J. Bullinger and B. Shackel), North-Holland, Amsterdam, 1041-1046.
Barbic, F., Rabitti, F. (1985). The Type Concept in Office Document Retrieval. In Proceedings 11th. Conf on Very Large Data Bases, Stockholm, 1985.
Constantopoulos, P., Yeorgaroudakis, Y. et al. (1986). Office Document Retrieval in MULTOS. Proceedings of 3rd ESPRIT Technical Week, North-Holland.
Engelmore, R., Morgan, T. (Eds.). (1988). Blackboard Systems. Addison-Wesley.
Eirund, H., Kreplin, K. (1988). Knowledge Based Document Classification Supporting Integrated Document Handling. In Proceedings of COIS '88, ACM, Palo Alto.
Lai, K-Y., Malone, T. W., Yu, K-C. (1988). Object Lens: A "Spreadsheet" for Cooperative Work. ACM Transactions on Office Information Systems, 6, 4 (Oct.), 332-353.
Lantz, K. A., Tanner, P.P. et al. (1987). Reference Models, Window Systems and Concurrency. Computer Graphics, 21, 2 (Apr.), 87-97.
Märtin, Ch., Oemig, M. (1989). CTME-CSD-Template Editor. Functional Specification. ESPRIT Project 28 (MULTOS), TA-89-02.
Märtin, Ch., Waldhör, K. (1988). BASAR - A Blackboard Based Software Architecture. In Proceedings of ECAI '88 (Ed. Y. Kodratoff), Pitman, London, 1988, 2-4.
Myers, B.A. (1989), User Interface Tools: Introduction and Survey, IEEE Software 6, 1 (Jan.).
Oemig, M. (1989). Wissensbasiertes Dialogmanagement für interaktive, mutlimediale Bürosysteme, Diploma Thesis, University of Dortmund.
Olsen, D.R. (1989). A Programming Language Basis for User Interface Management. In Proceedings of CHI '89, ACM, 171-176.
OSF (1989). OSF Motif Toolkit. External Specification. Open Software Foundation.
Singh, G., Green, M. (1989). A High-Level User Interface Management System. In Proceedings of CHI '89, ACM, 133-138.
Wiecha, Ch., Bennett, W. et al. (1989). Generating Highly Interactive User Interfaces. In Proceedings of CHI '89, ACM, 277-282.

Human–Computer Interaction – INTERACT '90
D. Diaper et al. (Editors)
Elsevier Science Publishers B.V. (North-Holland)

Incorporating Metaphor in Automated Interface Design

Brad Blumenthal †

Department of Computer Sciences
University of Texas at Austin
brad@cs.utexas.edu

Abstract

Metaphoric interface design is a useful technique for making computer applications easier to learn and use. The MAID system uses a knowledge-based description of computer applications and real-world entities to automatically produce interface designs with metaphoric characteristics. MAID employs two strategies for producing metaphoric human interfaces: one imports characteristics such as appearance, relative size, *etc.* into the application, the other imports new objects suggested by the metaphor. MAID has been implemented, and some results of its design runs are presented.

1 Motivation for automating metaphoric design

Although there is still active debate concerning the definition and role of metaphor in language and communication, the concept of a human interface metaphor can be characterized fairly precisely. In short, a human interface metaphor involves importing features from the real world into a computer application to determine the presentation and behavior of the objects and operations that the computer application makes available to the user. The real-world features that are imported range from simple attributes like appearance, relative size and location, visual and aural effects of an operation, *etc.* to more complex relations like the spatial location of a direct manipulation operation gesture with respect to the object being operated on, the collection of objects and operations which are made available at a given time, the capabilities of the application that are emphasized, *etc.*

Such interface metaphors are desirable because they allow the user of the application to bring experience and expectations from the real world to bear when attempting to perform a task involving the computer. This is especially important when the application is designed for a population of users who are solely interested in accomplishing domain-specific tasks and who know little, and care less, about the underlying machinations of the computer. By providing an appropriate interface metaphor, an application can allow the user to approach the task in a familiar manner.

To incorporate appropriate metaphors into human interface designs, the MAID[1] system represents a computer application, a number of real-world objects, and a set of metaphoric mappings between these real-world objects and the computer application. It uses these representations to produce a set of interface designs that incorporate characteristics from each of these real-world objects. By facilitating the development of a number of metaphoric interfaces, the MAID system encourages empirical comparisons of various interfaces to determine which is the most appropriate for a given user population.

In addition, the MAID system provides a testbed for experimentation with representations of metaphoric relations between computer applications and real-world objects. A context-sensitive, polymorphic representation of metaphor is used successfully in the MAID system to determine whether a real-world characteristic is appropriate for a given interface.

2 MAID overview

The MAID system architecture consists of several parts. A knowledge base contains frame-based descriptions of computer applications, real-world objects, and the metaphoric similarities between them. This knowledge is hand-coded, but the effort of encoding this knowledge is amortized over several uses. In particular, multiple interfaces can be designed for a single application, and each real-world object may be the source of a metaphoric interface for multiple applications.

In addition, the MAID system architecture contains a set of interface design heuristics and a mechanism for applying these heuristics to the goal of designing an interface for a particular application. These heuristics can produce an interface that may or may not incorporate metaphoric characteristics from some real-world object. The mechanism for applying these heuristics orders the unaddressed interface design goals, selects one to be addressed, and applies an appropriate heuristic to address the selected goal. The resulting design is specified in terms of stored graphics and interface techniques that can be implemented on specific hardware.

3 Strategies

In order to discuss how MAID incorporates real-world characteristics into an interface design, it is necessary to discuss how the system does interface design in general. This section will give an overview of the MAID architecture, discuss the techniques used to automate the interface design task,

†Support for this research was provided by the National Science Foundation under grant IRI-8620052, Apple Computer Corporations, and by the Army Research Office under grant ARO-DAAG29-84-K-0060

and then describe how real-world metaphors are incorporated.

The fundamental part of the MAID system architecture is an agenda-based, heuristic design system that takes a specification of a computer application and produces a human interface design. This rule-based design component is similar in many respects to a number of recent automated interface design systems [AMSS88, WBBG89, BBG+89, BF89]. There are two facets to performing the task of automated interface design: decomposition and instantiation. MAID decomposes the goal for designing an interface into goals for designing interfaces to the application's intermediate states, and the objects and operations that are made available in those states. MAID instantiates interfaces to individual objects and operations by selecting interface entities from a library of available interface techniques such as menus, mouse sensitive regions, graphics primitives, command line input, *etc.*

3.1 Interface design strategies

There are a number of sets of design heuristics currently available for guiding interface designers and programmers in producing usable interfaces [Cor85, Cor87, Car88, SM86, Cor89]. While helpful for improving the quality of interfaces, a common characteristic of these sets of heuristics is that they tend to be incomplete. This incompleteness may well be a fundamental characteristic of the domain of interface design, but it limits the autonomy of a rule-based system for automating such designs.

In particular, there are at least two ways in which this incompleteness manifests itself. First, rules for specifying æsthetic decisions, such as the location and size of the various interface entities are arbitrary at best, or missing altogether. Where such rules are supplied, they enforce a particular layout style which may not be appropriate for all applications.

Second, besides being incomplete, many sets of guidelines are either too specific or too vague for automating interface design. Most guidelines tend to concentrate on describing particular interface techniques available under a particular system architecture without much discussion of the appropriate uses of each technique. When general rules are given, they are sparse, and generally leave a great deal to interpretation. Rules such as "Assign more screen area (or primary optical areas) to objects that are more important" assume that the designer knows in advance what the important parts of the application are.

The MAID system addresses this incompleteness (missing or underspecified design rules) in two ways. When there is no real-world object specified as a source for an interface metaphor, MAID selects an appropriate interface technique for presenting an object or operation to the user, but leaves æsthetic decisions such as the size and location of a graphic or a menu to the designer. When there is an appropriate real-world object supplied as the source of an interface metaphor, MAID uses its description of that real-world object to determine appearances, locations, and other characteristics of the interface entities.

3.2 Metaphoric strategies

Within the context of rule-based design by systematic decomposition and appropriate instantiation, the MAID system pursues two strategies which combine to produce a metaphoric interface design. The simpler strategy is to take real-world characteristics, such as appearance, relative location, and relative size, and use them to specify the on-screen appearance, location, and size of the graphics, mouse-sensitive regions, text, command lines, *etc.*, which present the functionality of the application. For example, the appearance of a real-world object that corresponds to some application data structure is represented in a machine readable form and scaled to fit the portion of the screen allocated for the display of that data structure. Related objects are then scaled to the appropriate relative size and placed in the appropriate relative location.

In addition to importing attributes like appearance and size, the MAID system uses a second strategy that imports new objects from the real world to the application. This strategy is used when there is some part of the real-world object that is not initially mapped to any entity in the computer application. In this case, MAID imports the real-world entity into the interface and attempts to give it appropriate functionality in the application.

Operationally, when MAID finds a real-world entity that is not known to correspond to any part of the computer application, it checks the knowledge base to see if there is some entity in the computer application that should correspond to this real-world entity. If such an entity is provided, this strategy instantiates the appropriate entity, adds it to the application description, and constructs an interface to it using the characteristics of the real-world object that suggested it. Otherwise, MAID instantiates a generic, empty data structure that serves as a functionless place holder for the attribute of the real-world entity.

4 Example

To make these strategies more concrete, consider an example involving a simple data manager application and a description of a Rolodex card file as the source of the interface metaphor. The data manager application maintains a list of records, each of which has a name field, an address field, and a phone number field. It allows the user to add and delete records and browse through the records one at a time, either forwards or backwards. Working from the top level of the application down, the application has two states, the `DisplayRecord` state and the `AddRecord` state (see figure 1). The `DisplayRecord` state has a `CurrentRecord`[2] with its three fields, and operations to delete the currently displayed record, move forward or backward one record, quit the application, or go to the `AddRecord` state. The `AddRecord` state has a record template with its three fields and the operations for specifying the contents of the fields, adding the record to the list of records, or canceling the addition and going back to the `DisplayRecord` state.

Real-world entities are described in a similar fashion (see figure 2). A Rolodex has an ordered set of cards, each of which has a distinctive appearance and a canonical region where a name, address, and phone number are typically

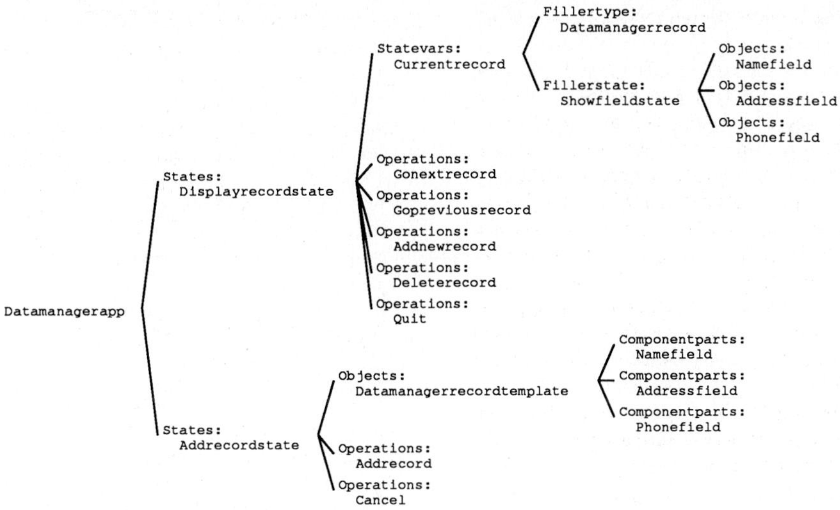

Figure 1: Part of the application description in the knowledge base.

written. A user can add or remove cards from the Rolodex and can browse through the cards by flipping them forward or backward. A Rolodex can be in one of two states: "open" or "closed." When it is open, the Rolodex presents a top card, a bottom card, a spindle, and a frame and allows the user to perform the actions mentioned above.

In the MAID knowledge base, the top card of the Rolodex is metaphorically mapped to the currently viewed record of the application. As noted in the overview, these mappings are given by the designer as part of the specification of the metaphor. MAID uses its simpler metaphoric strategy to give the currently viewed record the appearance of a Rolodex card and to place the name, address, and phone fields of the application in appropriate locations within the Rolodex card graphic. The more complex strategy is used to instantiate data structures corresponding to the spindle, frame, and bottom card, and specify appropriate graphics to enhance the metaphor.

A human interface to the data manager application which utilizes a Rolodex metaphor would thus present the currently viewed record with the appearance of the top card of a Rolodex. It would also show graphics with the appearance of the bottom card, the spindle, and the frame of the Rolodex. The operations for moving forward or backward one record are specified by MAID as direct manipulation operations on the graphics presenting the appearances of the top and bottom cards.

5 Representation of metaphoric mappings

In the MAID system, a metaphoric relation between a computer entity and a real-world entity is referred to as a metaphoric mapping ("mmap" for short). Continuing the example from the previous section: the interface designer might specify that the `CurrentRecord` in the computer applica-

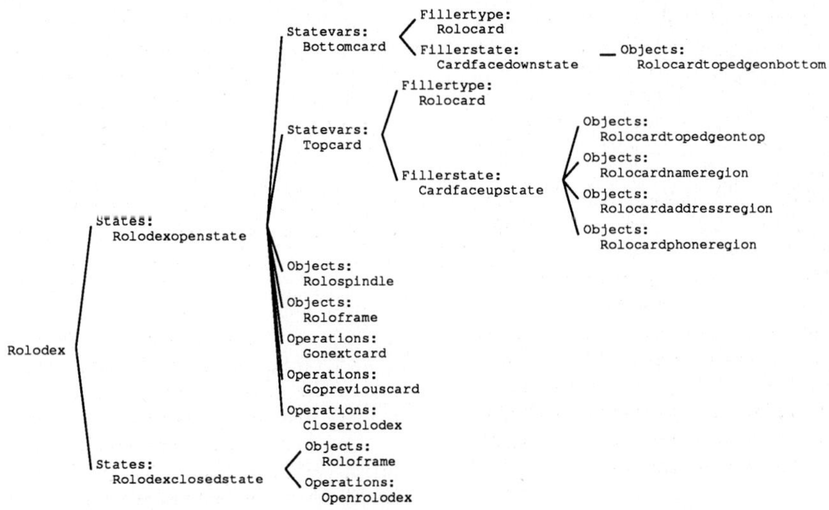

Figure 2: Part of the Rolodex description in the knowledge base.

tion is metaphorically mapped to the top card of the Rolodex; the `DisplayRecord` state is mapped to the open state; the name field is mapped to the region of the Rolodex card where a name is typically written; *etc.*

The way MAID represents metaphoric mappings is an important issue in how it produces metaphoric interfaces. There are two ways that a metaphor can be represented: it can either be implicit in a set of relations between the source and the target of the metaphor, or it can be a reified entity which can be discussed or cognitively manipulated on its own.

In order to specify the desired mappings, the interface designer would create a set of frames, each pointing to a source entity in the real-world object description, a target entity in the computer application description, and a context in which the metaphoric mapping is appropriate. In this way, the metaphor is explicitly reified as a set of frames representing the various possible mappings that might exist between the source and the target. The frames are ordered into a sub- and super- mapping hierarchy; for instance, the frame mapping the `CurrentRecord` to the top card is a submapping of the frame mapping the `DisplayRecord` state of the application to the open Rolodex (see figure 3). Similarly, the frame mapping the name field to the area on the Rolodex card where a name is typically written is a submapping of the frame mapping the `CurrentRecord` to the "top card".

The fundamental difference between the two views of a metaphor as they are represented in the MAID system is that the explicit, reified view is static while the metaphor implicit in the set of relations is dynamic. Since a number of metaphors may refer to a single entity (*i.e.,* a number of frames may have the same entity as their target or source entity), the metaphoric relations that hold at any given time must be sensitive to the context in which the metaphor is applied. This distinction is reflected in the implementation by defining an accessor for the "mmap" slot of an entity that is a function of both the metaphoric mapping frames pointing to that entity as well as the context in which the slot is accessed.

This dynamic context sensitivity is demonstrated in its most basic form by the simple presence or absence of a "current metaphor." If no metaphor is being attended to, then the value of the mmap slot is `nil`. If there is some metaphor in force, then that metaphor and all of its submappings are considered when the mmap slot is accessed. If one of these mapping frames points to the entity being queried, then the accessor for that entity's mmap slot transparently traverses the links that lead through the mapping frame to the source of the metaphor and returns the source entity as a value.

To take a more complicated example, the value of the mmap slot must be sensitive to context which is more transient than the presence or absence of a current metaphor. During interface design, this context is provided by the design goal being addressed at the time that the mmap slot is accessed. For the purposes of appearance and size, the record that comes immediately before the currently displayed record can be mapped to the bottom card of the Rolodex. However, for the purpose of presenting the fields of that previous record there is no mapping since the knowledge base description of a face down Rolodex card does not indicate that such a card displays any information.

6 Interface design

To see how MAID uses metaphor in designing human interfaces, it is necessary to first look at how the system produces an interface design with no metaphoric characteristics by using the bare application description and generic interface techniques. The bare application description is the minimum set of objects and operations that the application must make available to the user. In the case of the data manager application, this description includes the `DisplayRecord` state, the `AddRecord` state, the `CurrentRecord` and its fields, the record template and its fields, and the various operations that the application makes available.

6.1 Generic interface design

The design component of the MAID system can take this simple application description as input and use some basic interface design heuristics to produce a reasonable user interface design. The design component first decomposes the goal of designing an interface to the application into goals for designing interfaces to the various states, objects and operations that are included in the simple description. In the case of the data manager application, the knowledge base describes two modes, the `DisplayRecord` state for browsing and the `AddRecord` state for adding a new record. The goals for designing interfaces to these states are subsequently decomposed by the design rules into goals for designing interfaces for their component objects and operations.

After decomposition, the leaf objects and operations are

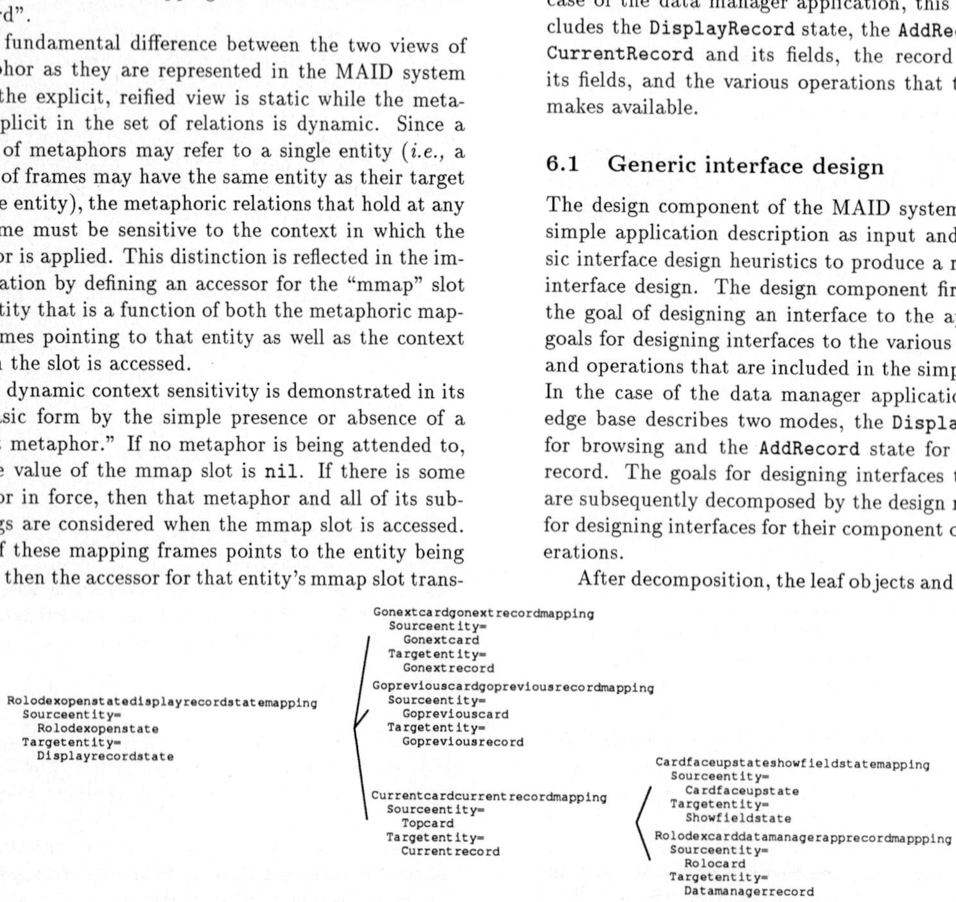

Figure 3: Part of the representation of the Rolodex – **DataManager** metaphoric mapping.

presented by generic interface techniques taken from whatever architecture was made available to the design component. For instance, if bit-mapped graphics, a mouse, and a menu system are available, the interface to the DisplayRecord state would consist of generic graphics (*i.e.*, rectangles) representing the CurrentRecord and its three fields, and a menu presenting the available operations (see figure 4). The size and location of each of these interface components would be specified by the designer. If the available architecture only provided a set of command line interface techniques, then the interface to the DisplayRecord state would consist of a prompt, keyboard input for each of the commands, and simple screen output for displaying records.

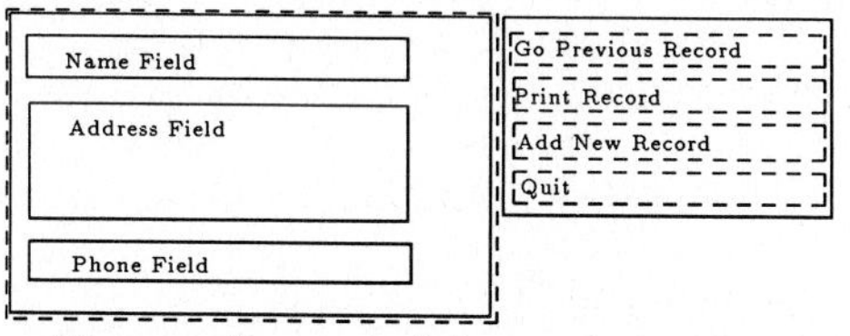

Figure 4: One part of the generic interface.

6.2 Metaphoric interface design

The design process for metaphoric interfaces is fundamentally similar to the process for generic interfaces; it follows the same decomposition and instantiation methodology. However, at certain points in the process the MAID design component checks for appropriate metaphoric mappings and imports characteristics from the real-world object whenever possible.

6.2.1 Importing characteristics

A simple example of this use of metaphoric mappings is in the selection, sizing and placement of the graphic representing the CurrentRecord when the Rolodex–DataManager metaphor is being attended to. Since the designer has specified that, in the context of appearance and data presentation, the CurrentRecord is metaphorically mapped to the top card in the Rolodex, MAID selects a graphic for representing the CurrentRecord that looks like the characteristic appearance of a face-up Rolodex card. Further, the location and size of the top Rolodex card with respect to the open Rolodex are recorded in the hand-coded knowledge base representation of the Rolodex. Because the designer has specified that the DisplayRecord state is metaphorically mapped to the open state of the Rolodex, MAID infers that it is appropriate to import the size and location of the top card into the application to determine the size and location of the graphic representing the top card. Thus, in addition to producing a more recognizable interface to the CurrentRecord, the inclusion of metaphoric mappings by the designer has increased the autonomy of the design system in selecting appropriate locations and graphics for the interface.

Similarly, the location of each of the record fields is determined by MAID from the locations given by the knowledge enterer for the canonical regions where a name, address, and phone number are written on a Rolodex card. Once again, MAID checks the appropriateness of this assumption by comparing the two contexts (top card and CurrentRecord) to determine that they are metaphorically mapped.

Appearances of real-world objects are represented in the MAID architecture as a hierarchy of graphical objects in a normalized coordinate space [Fv82]. For instance, the appearance of a Rolodex is represented as a graphical object made up of the appearances of the top card, bottom card, frame, and spindle, along with an appropriate location and scaling factor for each. The appearance of the top card (that is, the appearance of a face-up Rolodex card) is represented as an irregular polygon in a normalized coordinate space. Thus, locations and sizes are only represented with respect to a particular context. If there is no appropriate context when using a real-world appearance in a computer application, the designer is asked for an appropriate location and size. In either case, the graphics are then scaled to fit the provided space, and locations are adjusted relative to size.

6.2.2 Importing new objects

A more complicated example of incorporating characteristics of a real-world object into the interface design occurs at the level of decomposing the DisplayRecord state. Since this state is metaphorically mapped to the Rolodex open state, the design component of MAID checks to see if there are any objects in the real-world description of the Rolodex state that do not have a corresponding object in the application description. If there are some, the system attempts to import those objects into the application.

An example of this is the bottom card in the Rolodex open state. The system notices that this object is not mapped to any known object in the application description, so it looks for a corresponding object in the application. If it finds the record just before the CurrentRecord, it creates a new object of the data manager record data-type and adds it to the list of objects belonging to the DisplayRecord state. Since the bottom card of a Rolodex does not display any information, this new object does not display its fields. However, since the bottom card is the location where the go-to-the-previous-card operation is invoked in the Rolodex (*i.e.*, the user usually flips the card back by the bottom edge), the graphic is used as a location for a direct manipulation interface to the GoPreviousRecord operation.

If there is no appropriate object in the computer application that can be metaphorically mapped to a real-world object, MAID creates an empty data structure which does nothing but look like the real-world object. Examples of this include the Rolodex frame and Rolodex spindle.

Thus, by attending to the metaphoric mappings between the data manager application and the Rolodex, the MAID system has designed a more recognizable interface (see figure 5) to the application and has left fewer design decisions to be specified by the designer.

7 Results

So far, the MAID system has been used to design five interfaces to the data manager application. These interfaces include the generic interface and metaphoric interfaces corresponding to a Rolodex, an address book, an index card file, and a note pad. The generic interface specifies 9 entities and requests the designer to specify the appearance of 3 of those entities and the locations of all 9.

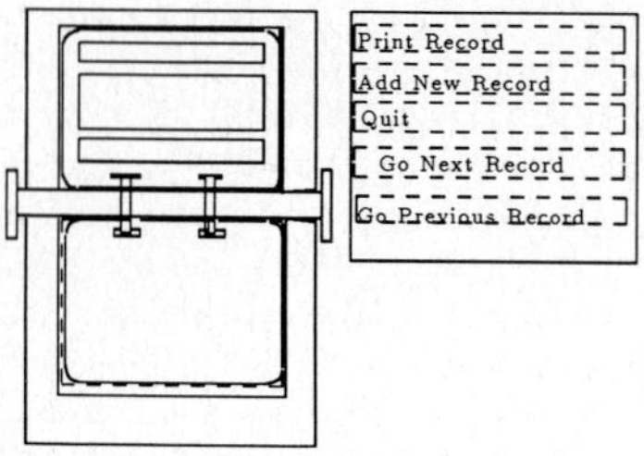

Figure 5: Part of the Rolodex metaphoric interface.

By contrast, the design incorporating the Rolodex metaphor specifies 12 entities, the appearances to all 12 entities, and the locations of 11 of the entities. Thus the addition of the Rolodex metaphor has increased the autonomy of MAID substantially. For the real world objects represented to date, the various interface metaphors import between 2 and 16 new entities into the application interface. They further specify all of the appearances in two of the cases (Rolodex and index card file), and all but one in the other two. The metaphoric mappings specify all but one of the required locations in each design.

In addition, each of the interface metaphors imports some entity that can be appropriately used as the location for the `GoPreviousRecord` command. As a result, this command is implemented as a direct manipulation command in each of the four metaphoric interfaces.

8 Conclusions

Although there are a number of design systems for producing human interfaces to computer applications with varying degrees of autonomy, none of them have explicitly incorporated metaphor into the design process. The notion of a human interface metaphor is well-defined enough to allow this incorporation to be done automatically, given an appropriate representation of real-world objects and an appropriate strategy for importing characteristics from such real-world objects.

Real-world objects which are appropriate for interface metaphors can be represented in much the same way as computer applications themselves. Essentially, this involves delineating the user-discernible objects and operations available to the user and how they are made available. Establishing designer-specified mappings between the components of the computer application and those of the real-world object provides an adequate representation for importing characteristics from the real world to the user interface.

A successful strategy for incorporating such characteristics requires that such mappings be checked for appropriateness in the context of particular design decisions. If a mapping is appropriate, then characteristics like appearance and relative size and location can be incorporated into the interface. Further, new entities may be introduced which enhance the illusion created by the metaphor (as in the case of the Rolodex frame and spindle), or actually add to the functionality of the interface (as in the direct manipulation interface to the `GoPreviousRecord` command). This representation and strategy have been instantiated in the MAID system and have been shown to substantially increase the autonomy of an automated interface design system.

[1] MAID stands for Metaphoric Application Interface Designer.

[2] Actually this "record" is a meta-variable which can be filled, at runtime, with any instance of a data manager record. Such constructs are called "state variables" in the MAID system and are represented as entities with information about the type of thing that might fill them. This note is to clarify figures generated from the knowledge base. For the purposes of the textual examples however, such entities can be thought of as simple data objects.

References

[AMSS88] Yigel Arens, Lawrence Miller, Stuart C. Shapiro, and Norman K. Sondheimer. Automatic construction of user-interface displays. In *Proceedings of the Seventh National Conference on Artificial Intelligence*, pages 808–813, USC/ISI, 1988.

[BBG+89] William E. Bennett, Stephen J. Boies, John D. Gould, Sharon L. Greene, and Charles F. Wiecha. Transformations on a dialog tree: Rule-based mapping of content to style. In *Proceedings of the ACM SIGGRAPH Symposium on User Interface Software and Technology*, pages 67–75, 1989.

[BF89] Clifford M. Beshers and Steven K. Feiner. Scope: Automated generation of graphical interfaces. In *Proceedings of the ACM SIGGRAPH Symposium on User Ineterface Software and Technology*, pages 76–81, 1989.

[Car88] Robert Carr. Developing for the user. *Dr. Dobb's Journal of Software Tools*, (139), May 1988.

[Cor85] Apple Computer Corporation. *Inside Macintosh*. Addison-Wesley Publishing Company, 1985.

[Cor87] Apple Computer Corporation. *Human Interface Guidelines: The Apple Desktop Interface*. Addison-Wesley Publishing Company, 1987.

[Cor89] Apple Computer Corporation. *Hypercard Interface Guidelines*. Addison-Wesley Publishing Company, 1989.

[Fv82] James Foley and Andrew van Dam. *Fundamentals of Interactive Computer Graphics*. Addison-Wesley Publishing Company, 1982.

[SM86] Sidney L. Smith and Jane N. Mosier. Guidelines for designing user interface software. Technical Report ESD-TR-86-278, Mitre Corporation, Bedford, MA, 1986.

[WBBG89] Charles Wiecha, William Bennet, Stephen Boies, and John Gould. Generating highly interactive user interfaces. In *Proceedings of CHI '89*, pages 277–282, Austin, TX, 1989. ACM SIGCHI.

SECTION IV: INTERACTIVE TECHNOLOGIES AND TECHNIQUES

SIV.1 Input

The role of visual and kinesthetic feedback in the prevention of mode errors
A.J. Sellen, G.P. Kurtenbach, and W.A.S. Buxton 667

Windows on tablets as a means of achieving virtual input devices
E. Brown, W.A.S. Buxton, and K. Murtagh 675

Building adaptive interfaces with neural networks: The glove-talk pilot study
S.S. Fels and G.E. Hinton 683

FINGER: A language for gesture recognition
G. Weber 689

A virtual stereographic pointer for a real three dimensional video world
P. Milgram, D. Drascic, and J. Grodski 695

Force-to-motion functions for pointing
J.D. Rutledge and T. Selker 710

Keyboard layout for occasional users
N. Marmaras and K. Lyritzis 707

Human–Computer Interaction – INTERACT '90
D. Diaper et al. (Editors)
Elsevier Science Publishers B.V. (North-Holland)

THE ROLE OF VISUAL AND KINESTHETIC FEEDBACK IN THE PREVENTION OF MODE ERRORS

Abigail J. SELLEN†, Gordon P. KURTENBACH, and William A. S. BUXTON

Computer Systems Research Institute, University of Toronto, Toronto, Ontario, Canada, M5S 1A1*

The use of visual and kinesthetic feedback in preventing *mode errors* was investigated. Mode errors were defined in the context of text editing as attempting to issue navigation commands while in insert mode, or attempting to insert text while in command mode. Twelve novices and twelve expert users of the Unix-based text editor *vi* performed a simple text editing task in conjunction with a distractor task in four different conditions. These conditions consisted of comparing the use of keyboard versus foot pedal for changing mode, crossed with the presence or absence of visual feedback to indicate mode. Both visual and kinesthetic feedback were effective in reducing mode errors, although for experts visual feedback was redundant given that they were using a foot pedal. Other measures of system usability indicate the superiority of the use of a foot pedal over visual feedback in delivering system state information for this type of task.

1. INTRODUCTION

Mode errors as originally defined by Norman (1981) occur when a situation is misclassified resulting in actions which are appropriate for the analysis of the situation but inappropriate for the true situation. Mode errors in text editing are very common. Users attempt to issue commands when the system is actually in "text insert mode" or attempt to enter text while actually in "command mode". While mode errors frequently occur with computers, examples from diary studies of action slips (Norman, 1981; Reason and Mycielska, 1982; and Sellen, 1990) reveal mode errors occur in many other aspects of everyday experience. Examples such as trying to fast forward the tape in the VCR when in "record mode", or turning the key in the ignition when the car engine is already running could both be called mode errors.

In the context of computers, any given action can have very different effects depending on the state of the system. Fortunately the consequences of most mode errors are only minor inconveniences, and in well designed systems, are usually reversible. However, such errors in poorly designed interfaces or in highly complex systems such as aircraft and nuclear power plants can result in far more serious outcomes. In such situations, the importance of preventing such errors, or at least absorbing their effects, is critical.

Errors are not the only metric with which to measure users' problems with mode identification, however. In some cases, the user may diagnose the correct mode, but only after experiencing confusion or uncertainty. In such cases, the appropriate measure is in terms of the cognitive effort or decision time required to deduce the system state. Increased cognitive effort may in turn be reflected in users' opinions of the usability of the system.

Why not just do away with modes? This was the opinion voiced strongly by Tesler (1981). But almost everything we do involves modes in one way or another, including working with so-called "modeless" computer systems such as the Apple Macintosh. Whenever dialog boxes appear, or whenever the cursor changes from an arrow to an "I-beam" depending on its location on the screen, one is in a mode. What is actually meant by a "modeless" system in this context is design in which contextual information is provided to minimize mode errors, and where modes can easily be entered and exited. Further, while the number of elemental actions available to interact with systems remains relatively constant, the number of functions within an application is growing. One has only to look at applications such as Hypercard to see how modes are used to support rich functionality.

It is not clear that we can ever hope to completely eliminate the problems associated with modes, but it certainly seems possible to reduce them. One obvious solution seems to be to give users more salient feedback[1] on system state. Apart from the practical importance for system designers, this raises some interesting theoretical questions: What kind of feedback is most salient to the user? Through what perceptual modality is the feedback best delivered? At what point does feedback become obtrusive? One objective of our research is to shed some light these issues.

There is little directly relevant literature. The exception is Monk (1986) who investigated the use of auditory feedback in preventing mode errors. In this study, Monk demonstrated that mode errors could be reduced by a third by using a key-contingent sound change depending on the mode of the system. Monk argued that sound is a good choice for system feedback in that users do not constantly look at the display while working.

† Also at the Institute for Cognitive Science, University of California, San Diego, La Jolla, CA. 92093

* This research was supported by the Natural Sciences and Engineering Research Council of Canada, Digital Equipment Corporation, and Xerox PARC.

A variation on the Monk experiment could have been to present the feedback in the form of a sustained tone whose timbre (sound quality) depended on the current mode. In contrast to the action-contingent sound used in the actual experiment, subjects in this instance could determine the current mode before initiating a possibly erroneous action. This kind of feedback might be called "action-independent".

These examples illustrate that feedback can be characterized along several dimensions, including:

• Modality of delivery (visual, auditory, kinesthetic)
Through what sensory modality is the information delivered?

• Action-contingent versus action-independent delivery
Does the feedback depend on an action being executed?

• Transient versus sustained delivery
How long does the feedback last?

• Demanding versus avoidable feedback
Can the user choose not to monitor the feedback?

These are not all necessarily orthogonal. For example, feedback using the visual channel is generally avoidable: one can easily choose not to monitor visual information. Kinesthetic and audio feedback however, are more inherently demanding and inescapable.

Choosing the best way of delivering system state information clearly must be dependent on the task. All else being equal though, it seems reasonable that the more salient the feedback, the more effective it will be in preventing mode errors. Presumably feedback which is sustained is more salient than transient feedback (with the qualification that sustained feedback may become habituated to over time). Feedback which is demanding is presumably more salient than feedback which is avoidable.

This experiment compares the effectiveness of two kinds of sustained, action-independent feedback in the context of a simple text editing task. Visual feedback was delivered by changing the colour of the screen, while kinesthetic feedback was delivered through the use of a foot pedal to change modes. The prediction was that since kinesthetic feedback is inherently more demanding than visual feedback, it would be a more effective way of preventing mode errors.

2. METHOD

2.1 Subjects

Twelve expert and twelve novice subjects were recruited from the University of Toronto and paid for their participation. An *expert* subject had extensive experience in using *vi*, a Unix-based text editing system. A *novice* subject was one who had never used *vi*, but had experience in using a computer mouse. Eleven of the experts and seven of the novices were touch typists.

2.2 Tasks

The primary task consisted of navigating through and inserting text into a pre-existing document on a Sun workstation. Subjects were instructed to insert the string "errorerror"[2] following any word in the document that was printed all in capital letters. They were instructed to complete this task as quickly as possible, only correcting typing errors if they detected them within a word before leaving insert mode. Each block of text contained approximately 190 words and a total of 75 capitalized words.

A simulated *vi* text editor was created in which only a small subset of the commands were available. In order to navigate, the keys h, j, k, and l moved the cursor left, up, down, and right, respectively. In addition, the space bar was available to move the cursor right. For keyboard conditions, in order to insert text, subjects were instructed to position the cursor over the point at which the word was to be inserted, and to press the 'i' key. Once in "insert mode", the text could then be entered. After typing the text to be inserted, the escape key returned the user to "navigation mode". For foot pedal conditions, inserting text was accomplished by positioning the cursor over the insertion point, depressing the foot pedal, and keeping the pedal depressed while typing the text. Releasing the foot pedal returned the subject to navigation mode.

In addition to the primary task, subjects were also required to perform a concurrent distractor task on a Macintosh computer positioned adjacent to the Sun workstation. Thirty seconds after the editing task was begun, after some random interval of time, beeps from the Macintosh signalled the presentation of a digit between 1 and 6 on its screen. Below the digit, 6 buttons numbered 1 to 6 appeared in a random order. The subjects' task was to use the Macintosh mouse to click on the button corresponding to the presented digit. Subjects were instructed to service this distractor task as quickly as possible. In order to encourage them to do so, the beeping would increase in frequency as time passed. The intervals between digit presentation were distributed according to a uniform distribution with an average interval between digits of 4.5 seconds and a range of 3 to 6 seconds.

2.3 Design and Procedure

Each subject performed in each of the four conditions depicted in Figure 1. *Insertion method* refers to the method by which insert mode was entered and exited. Keyboard insertion means using the 'i' and 'escape' keys, while foot pedal insertion means holding down the foot pedal to insert text. In the *visual feedback* conditions, while in insert mode, the screen changed from white to pink. The order of the conditions for each subject was counterbalanced according to a digram-balanced Latin square.

All subjects were given a practice run on the editing task using the keyboard insertion method immediately prior to performing the first keyboard condition, as well as a different practice run using the foot pedal insertion method immedi-

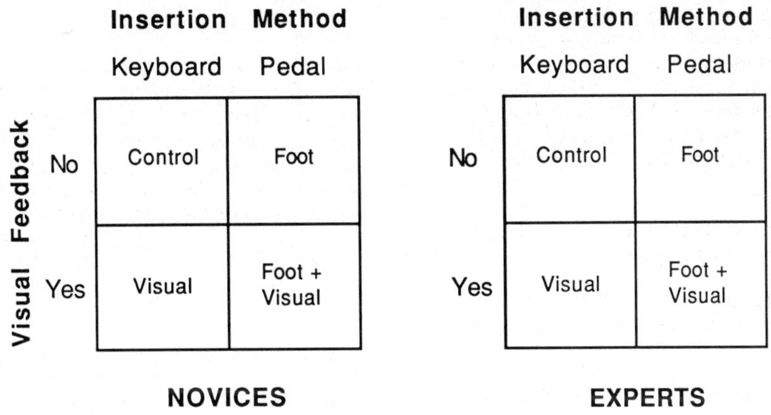

Figure 1. *Schematic diagram of the experimental design. Insertion method refers to the method of switching to insert mode, while visual feedback refers to the presence or absence of a pink screen colour while in insert mode.*

ately preceding the first foot pedal condition. Each practice run consisted of 28 insertions into a pre-existing block of text.

At the end of the experiment, subjects were asked to rank order the conditions in terms of preference and to provide comments on the comparative usability of each "system" for text editing. The entire experiment lasted approximately an hour for expert subjects and an hour and a half for novices including a five to ten minute break halfway through.

3. RESULTS

3.1 Mode Errors

Mode errors were operationally defined in the context of the task as follows, where <NAV> indicates switching to navigation mode and <INS> indicates switching to insert mode, by whichever method:

A *navigation mode error* was defined as trying to navigate while in insert mode. Operationally, this meant the appearance of h, j, k, l, or spacebar characters while in insert mode and included any unexpected characters which could be construed as aiming errors around those keys, depending on the context. The presence of the "i" command when already in insert mode was also counted as a navigation mode error.

e.g. <INS>errorerrorllk<NAV>...

An *insertion mode error* was defined as trying to insert while in navigation mode. This meant the appearance of any portion of the string "errorerror" while in navigation mode and also included anything which might be an aiming error around those keys. In addition, the appearance of the "escape" character when already in navigation mode was also counted as an insertion mode error since it indicates, at the very least, uncertainty about the state of the system if not the belief that the system is in insert mode.

e.g. llljjjjjlerr<INS>errorerror...

In addition to mode errors, a class of errors we called *synchronization errors* occurred in the foot pedal conditions. A synchronization error looked very similar to a mode error in that a navigation command would sometimes precede the release of the foot pedal, or the letter "e" would sometimes precede depression of the pedal. It was clear, though, that these errors were different from mode errors in that the time between the erroneous keystroke and the response of the pedal was very short (less than 200 msec). Thus these errors arose because of problems in synchronizing the action of the pedal with the keystrokes. Errors with times less than 200 msec. were therefore classified as synchronization errors. If there was any doubt about whether an error was a synchronization error or a mode error, it was classified as a mode error.

The mean number of mode errors of both kinds for novices and experts is shown in Figure 2. Experts made more errors than did novices ($F(1, 11) = 6.23$, $p < .030$). For both the novices and the experts, the pedal method of insertion resulted in significantly fewer mode errors than the keyboard ($F(1, 11) = 16.72$, $p < .002$). In addition, there were significantly fewer mode errors in conditions with visual feedback than those without for both novices and experts ($F(1, 11) = 6.65$, $p < .026$).

Finally, there was a significant interaction present between insertion method and visual feedback ($F(1, 11) = 6.77$, $p < .025$). In order to understand the source of this better, separate analyses were run on the expert and novice groups. The result was a significant insertion method by visual feedback interaction for experts ($F(1, 11) = 9.34$, $p < .011$) but not for novices. This indicates that for experts, while visual feedback was effective in reducing mode errors when the method of insertion was the keyboard, visual feedback was redundant in the case of the foot pedal.

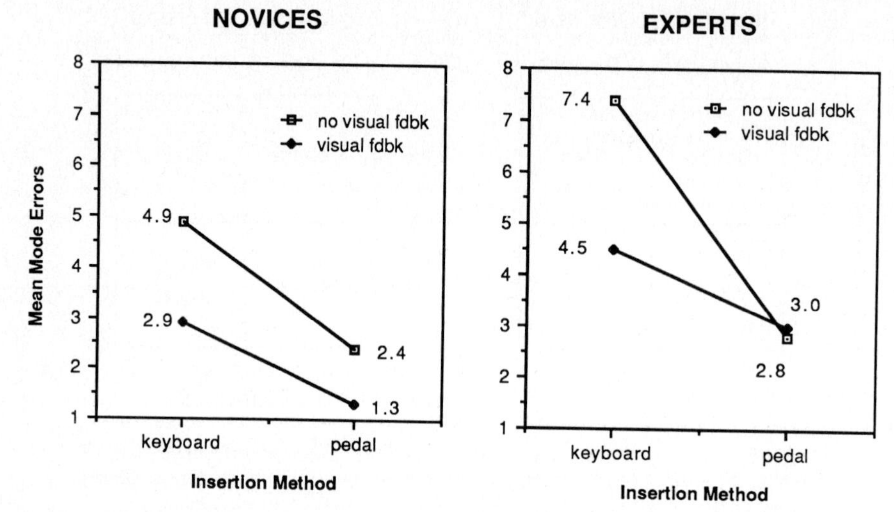

Figure 2. *Mean number of mode errors for novices and experts plotted as a function of method of insertion (keyboard versus foot pedal) and visual feedback (present versus absent).*

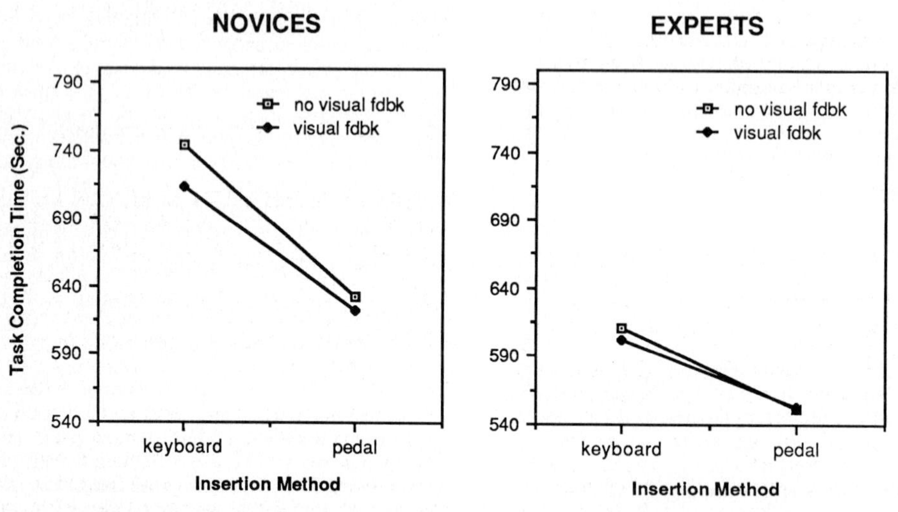

Figure 3. *Mean task completion times for novices and experts plotted as a function of method of insertion (keyboard versus foot pedal) and visual feedback (present versus absent).*

3.2 Task Completion Time

The total time to complete the task in each condition is shown in Figure 3. Experts were significantly faster than novices ($F(1, 11) = 7.35$, $p < .020$). The only other significant result was a main effect of insertion method, with the foot pedal being faster than the keyboard ($F(1, 11) = 18.42$, $p < .001$).

3.3 Effects of Switching Between Tasks

Resume time was defined as the amount of time required to make the first keystroke in the editing task after servicing the distractor task. This was taken to be a measure of confusion about the mode in the editing task. The means are shown in Figure 4.

The pedal resulted in a significantly faster mean resume time than the keyboard ($F(1, 11) = 9.41$, $p < .011$). There were no significant effects of visual feedback, no differences between novices and experts, and no interactions found.

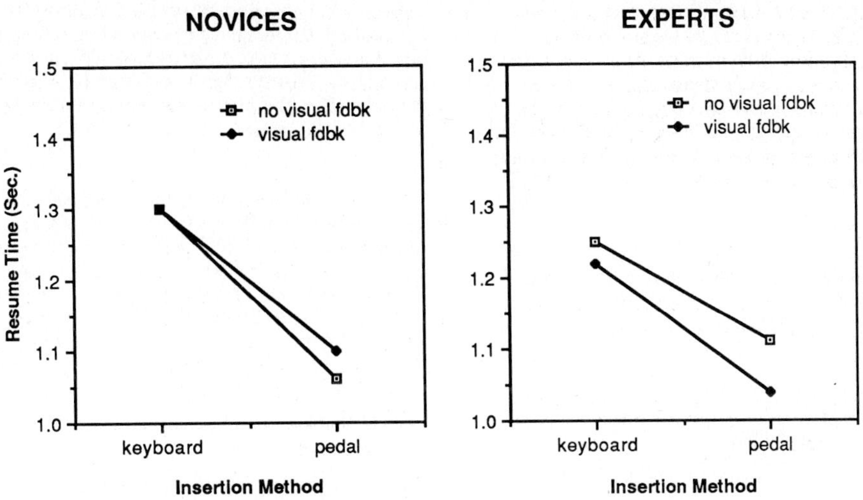

Figure 4. *Mean resume time for novices and experts plotted as a function of method of insertion (keyboard versus foot pedal) and visual feedback (present versus absent).*

Service time for the distractor task was also examined. This was defined as the time between the occurrence of an audio interruption by the distractor task and the mouse click cancelling the number on the Macintosh screen. There were no significant differences found between conditions or between novices and experts.

3.4 Ranking Data

At the end of the experiment subjects were asked to imagine that each condition represented a system that they might use to do text editing on a daily basis and to rank order each of the four "systems" according to their preference. It was clear that subjects fell into three main categories: those who preferred the foot pedal, those who preferred the keyboard, and those who preferred the "systems" with visual feedback, regardless of insertion method. Operationally, they were classified as pedal-oriented, keyboard-oriented, or visual-oriented according to which conditions they chose as their first and second preferences versus their third and fourth choices.

One expert and one novice failed to complete the ranking task properly and could not be classified. Of the remaining eleven experts, five were keyboard-oriented, five were pedal-oriented, and one was visual-oriented. Of the eleven novices, eight preferred the foot pedal systems, two preferred the visual feedback systems, and one was unclassifiable. This last subject preferred either visual feedback, or the foot pedal, but not both.

4. DISCUSSION

This experiment has shown the effectiveness of both visual and kinesthetic feedback in preventing the occurrence of mode errors regardless of whether or not the subjects were experienced users of a system with no explicit mode indicator. Thus, even though many of the expert subjects commented that they were used to keeping track of the mode "in their head", feedback significantly reduced their mode errors nonetheless.

4.1 Kinesthetic versus Visual Feedback

Not all kinds of feedback are equal, however. The results make a particularly strong case for feedback delivered via the foot pedal as opposed to a visual mode indicator. Both visual and pedal feedback reduced mode errors. In the case of experts, though, visual feedback was redundant when pedal feedback was present. This is somewhat surprising given that all but one of the experts were touch typists and frequently monitored the screen. Conversely the beneficial effect of visual feedback for the novices was also surprising given that five of the twelve were not touch typists and constantly monitored the keyboard. One might therefore expect that visual cues would be less effective for this group. What may explain these results is that we frequently observed novices making deliberate visual checks to ascertain the mode when returning from the distractor task. It could be that experts were more likely to be looking at the screen but not necessarily for the purpose of making a visual check on the mode.

Resume time is perhaps a more sensitive measure than mode errors with which to compare kinesthetic to visual feedback. It seems reasonable to assume that the amount of time required to resume the editing task in part reflected decision time during which subjects were attempting to diagnose the state of the system. Such cognitive processes are effortful and increase the mental workload of the task, especially since they are likely to involve short term memory. Any differences in resume time among conditions must reflect a difference in cognitive operations since there are no differences in the physical actions required to switch tasks.

Use of a foot pedal led to a significantly faster resume time than the keyboard while the presence of visual feedback made no difference. Further, these results are independent of level of skill, since novices and experts both benefitted from the foot pedal and not from visual feedback. On the basis of this result, we claim that pedal feedback reduces the cognitive load of the system, at least with respect to confusion about system mode. Visual feedback does not achieve this effect.

Why might the foot pedal be a better way of reducing the cognitive load imposed by confusion about modes? There are at least three possible explanations:

1. Subjects were simply not monitoring the visual feedback. That is, subjects could simply forget to monitor the screen and therefore fail to benefit from visual cues. Visual feedback is *avoidable* and therefore is not as effective.

2. Information delivered through the visual channel is simply not as *salient* as information delivered kinesthetically. This may be the case even though the visual cues in this study involved changing the entire screen area pink. If this is true, this has important implications for systems which rely on more subtle visual cues such as changing the shape of the cursor or the colour of the menu bar.

3. Visual feedback *competes* with the visual nature of the editing task. In other words, a user who is text editing has as his or her main goal the task of searching the screen or monitoring the outcome of their keystrokes. The colour of the screen may therefore compete for attentional resources required for this visual task. Thus it may be that using a different "channel" for indicating mode is more effective since it does not compete with task-specific resources.

These issues cannot be directly addressed in the context of this experiment, but they are good candidates for further research.

4.2 Other Issues of Usability

What about other aspects of the usability of the different systems? One clear difference was the faster speed with which the task was completed for foot pedal versus keyboard conditions. This was true not only for novices but also for experts (most of whom had many years of experience with *vi*). The fact that keyboard insertion caused more mode errors and therefore may have incurred more cost in terms of error recovery time, probably contributed to this difference.

A more fundamental difference between keyboard and pedal was that assigning the mode changing task to the foot pedal meant that this could be accomplished without interfering with the other tasks of navigating and typing. Both subjects who could and could not touch type commented that having to alternate between "i" and "escape" and the navigation keys meant having to constantly re-position the fingers on the keyboard. Many of them felt that this led to more errors in typing. Many of them also said that using "i" and "escape" meant they had to spend more time searching the keyboard, which made the task more effortful.Whatever the contributing factors, subjects (both novices and experts) commented that they liked the increased speed with which they could edit using the foot pedal.

There were different problems associated with the foot pedal. Most notably, from time to time there were synchronization errors where subjects would either depress or release the pedal a fraction of a second too early or too late. These were fairly infrequent though, averaging less than one error per subject during the entire experiment. In addition, some subjects commented that they thought that eventually their foot would become tired. The ergonomics of the design of a foot pedal would therefore have to be an important consideration.

Finally, we had expected that there would be some differences in service time and in "chunking" behaviour across conditions. Chunking behaviour refers to the tendency to finish one sub-task before attending to another (see Buxton, 1986). In this case, chunking was defined as the tendency to delay servicing the distractor task until completion of a sub-task within the editing task. For example, subjects had a strong tendency to complete navigation to the next word, or to complete typing of the inserted word before attending to the distractor. They did this even though they were instructed to service the distractor task as quickly as possible. We predicted that with improved feedback subjects might feel secure enough to interrupt their primary task (text editing) mid-stream, in order to service the distractor. This was not the case, however, and perhaps speaks to the strength of the tendency to chunk in all conditions.

4.3 Experts versus Novices

There was some question as to whether the experts in this study were truly "experts" since subjects could use only a restricted set of commands in the editing task. Differences between experts and novices suggest that they were in fact drawn from distinct populations.

First, experts completed the task much faster than novices in *all* conditions. Note that this was the case even though they were as naive as novices with regard to the foot pedal. This suggests that experts had no trouble integrating the new device with their previously established skills in *vi*.

Second, experts exhibited a different pattern of behaviour with regard to mode errors. Not only did experts make more mode errors over all, but they also did not benefit from visual feedback in combination with the foot pedal. This might be explained by the fact that for experts, there is less overhead involved in correcting errors. Users of *vi* make errors all the time, and are highly skilled at recovering from them. The cost of an error for an expert is thus considerably lower than the cost of an error for a novice and may explain why experts made more mode errors overall. This increased cautiousness on the part of novices may also account for why they benefitted from visual feedback given that they were already receiving feedback from the foot pedal.

Increased cautiousness on the part of novices might cause them to exploit every available cue in an effort to avoid errors.

5. CONCLUSION

The research reported brings us to three main conclusions:

- That with appropriate design, a common class of error can be significantly reduced for both novices and experts.
- That the modality (sensory channel) used for feedback is an important design consideration.
- That designing to reduce errors can also lead to other improvements in system usability including faster performance times and lower cognitive load.

As the complexity and functionality of systems grow, we must learn to anticipate the errors users will make and to design interfaces to minimize their occurrence. In order to cope with this growing responsibility, we feel strongly that interface design will be served well by looking beyond the traditional "mouse-keyboard-display" configuration and investigating other channels and modalities of interaction. We believe that the work of Monk (1986) and the research reported in this paper support this view, and hope that it will stimulate additional research and activity in this direction.

ACKNOWLEDGEMENTS

The members of the Input Research Group at the University of Toronto provided the forum for the design and execution of this project. We especially thank Scott MacKenzie for his comments and assistance. In addition, we are grateful to our colleagues at the University of Toronto: Daniel Read and Ian Spence of the Department of Psychology for their advice in statistical matters, and Alison Lee and George Drettakis of the Dynamic Graphics Project for implementation advice. We also gratefully acknowledge the financial support of the Natural Sciences and Engineering Research Council of Canada, Digital Equipment Corporation, and Xerox PARC.

NOTES

[1]We define "feedback" in this context as information about system state received through any of the human sensory modalities.

[2]The string 'errorerror' was chosen so that mode errors consisting of attempts to insert these characters in navigation mode could be clearly distinguished from navigation commands or aiming errors around the navigation keys, and similarly for errors in attempting to navigate in insertion mode.

REFERENCES

Buxton, W. (1986). Chunking and phrasing and the design of human-computer dialogues. In H. J. Kugler (Ed.) *Information Processing '86*, Proceedings of the IFIP 10th World Computer Congress, Amsterdam: North Holland Publishers, pp. 475-480.

Monk, A. (1986). Mode errors: A user-centred analysis and some preventative measures using keying-contingent sound. *International Journal of Man-Machine Studies, 24*, pp. 313-327.

Norman, D. A. (1981). Categorization of action slips. *Psychology Review, 88 (1)*, pp. 1-15.

Reason, J., and Mycielska, K. (1982). *Absent-Minded? The Psychology of Mental Lapses and Everyday Errors.* Englewood Cliffs, N. J.: Prentice-Hall, Inc.

Sellen, A. J. (1990). *Human Error Detection Mechanisms.* Doctoral dissertation in progress. University of California, San Diego, La Jolla, CA.

Tesler, L. (1981). The Smalltalk environment. *Byte*, August, pp. 90-147.

Human–Computer Interaction – INTERACT '90
D. Diaper et al. (Editors)
Elsevier Science Publishers B.V. (North-Holland)

WINDOWS ON TABLETS AS A MEANS OF ACHIEVING VIRTUAL INPUT DEVICES*

Ed BROWN, William A.S. BUXTON and Kevin MURTAGH

Computer Systems Research Institute, University of Toronto, Toronto, Ontario, Canada M5S 1A4

Users of computer systems are often constrained by the limited number of physical devices at their disposal. For displays, window systems have proven an effective way of addressing this problem. As commonly used, a window system partitions a single physical display into a number of different virtual displays. It is our objective to demonstrate that the model is also useful when applied to input.

We show how the surface of a single input device, a tablet, can be partitioned into a number of virtual input devices. The demonstration makes a number of important points. First, it demonstrates that such usage can improve the power and flexibility of the user interfaces that we can implement with a given set of resources. Second, it demonstrates a property of tablets that distinguishes them from other input devices, such as mice. Third, it shows how the technique can be particularly effective when implemented using a touch sensitive tablet. And finally, it describes the implementation of a prototype an "input window manager" that greatly facilitates our ability to develop user interfaces using the technique.

The research described has significant implications on direct manipulation interfaces, rapid prototyping, tailorability, and user interface management systems.

1. INTRODUCTION

A significant trend in user interface design is away from the discrete, serial nature of what we might call a *digital* approach, towards the continuous, spatial properties of an *analogue* approach.

Direct Manipulation systems are a good example of this trend. With such systems, controls and functions (such as scroll bars, buttons, switches and potentiometers) are represented as graphical objects which can be thought of as *virtual devices*. A number of these are illustrated in Fig. 1.

The impression is that of a number of distinct devices, each with its own specialized function, and occupying its own dedicated space. While powerful, the impression is an illusion, since virtually all interactions with these devices is *via* only one or two *physical* devices: the keyboard and the mouse.

The strength of the illusion, however, speaks well for its effectiveness. Nevertheless, this paper is rooted in a belief that direct manipulation systems can be improved by expanding the design space to better afford turning this illusion into reality. Distinct controls for specific functions, provide the potential to improve the *directness* of the user's access (such as through decreased homing time and exploiting motor memory). Input functions are moved from the display to the work surface, thereby freeing up valuable screen real-estate. Because they are dedicated, physical controls can be specialized to a particular function, thereby providing the possibility to improve the quality of the *manipulation* .

While one may agree with the general concepts being expressed, things generally break down when we try to put these ideas into practice. Given the number of different functions and virtual devices that are found in typical direct manipulation systems, having a separate physical controller for each would generally be unmanageable. Our desks (which are already crowded) would begin to look like an aircraft cockpit or a percussionist's studio. Clearly, the designer must be selective in what functions are assigned to dedicated controllers. But even then, the practical management of the resources remains a problem.

The contribution of the current research is to describe a way in which this approach to designing the control structures can be supported. To avoid the explosion of input transducers, we introduce the notion of virtual input devices that are *spatially distinct*. We do so by partitioning the surface of one physical device into a number of separate regions, each of which emulates the function of a separate controller. This is analogous on the input side to *windows* on displays.

We highlight the properties that are required of the input technology to support such windows, and discuss why certain types of *touch tablets* are particularly suited for this type of interaction.

Finally, we discuss the functionality that would be required by a *user interface management system* to support the approach. We do so by describing the implementation of a working prototype system.

* The research reported has been sponsored by the Natural Sciences and Engineering Research Council of Canada and Xerox PARC.

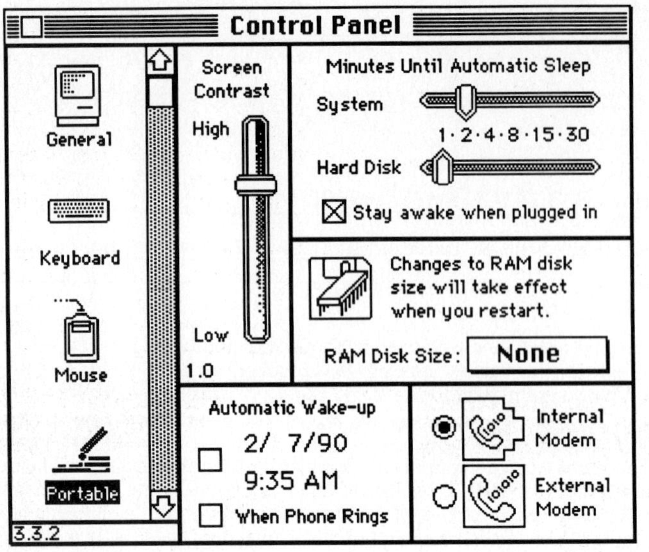

Figure 1: *Virtual Devices in the Macintosh Control Panel*

The figure shows graphical objects such as potentiometers, radio buttons and icons. Each functions as a distinct device. Interaction, however, is via one of two physical devices: the mouse or keyboard.

2. RELATIONSHIP TO PREVIOUS PRACTICE

The idea of virtual devices is not new. One of the most innovative approaches was the virtual keyboard developed by Ken Knowlton (1975, 1977a,b) at Bell Laboratories. Knowlton developed a system using half-silvered mirrors to permit the functionality of keyboards to be dynamically reconfigured. Partitioning a tablet surface into regions is also not new. Tablet mounted menus, as seen in many CAD systems, are one example of existing practice.

Our contribution:

- makes this model explicit
- develops it beyond current common practice
- develops some of the design issues (such as input transducers)
- demonstrates its utility
- and presents a prototype User Interface Management (UIMS) utility to support its use.

3. RELEVANT PROPERTIES OF INPUT TRANSDUCERS

The technique of "input windows" involves a mapping of different functions to distinct physical locations in the control space. This mapping can only be supported by input transducers that possess the following two properties:

- *Position Sensitive:* They must give absolute coordinates defining position, rather than a measure of motion (as with mice).
- *Fixed Planar Coordinate System:* Position must be measured in terms of a two dimensional Cartesian space.

Hence digitizing tablets will work, but mice, trackballs, and joysticks will not. Within the class of devices which meet these two criteria (including light pens, graphics tablets, touch screens), touch technologies (and especially touch tablets) have noteworthy potential.

Control systems that employ multiple input devices generally have two important properties:

- *Eyes-Free Operation:* Sufficient kinesthetic feedback is provided to permit the operation of the control, leaving the eyes free to perform some other task, such as monitoring a display.
- *Simultaneous Access:* More than one device can be operated at a time, as in driving a car (steering wheel and gear lever) or operating an audio mixing console (where multiple faders might be accessed simultaneously).

In many design situations, these properties are useful, if not essential. In mixing a colour in a paint program, one might assign a potentiometer to each of hue, saturation and value. In performing the task, it is reasonable to expect that the artist generally is better served by focusing visual attention on the colour produced rather than the potentiometers controlling its components values. Driving a car would be impossible if operating the steering wheel required visual attention.

Simultaneous access is also important in many situations. Within the domain of human-computer interaction, for example, Buxton and Myers (1986) demonstrate benefits in tasks similar to those demanded in text editing and CAD.

4. THE AFFORDANCES OF TOUCH TABLETS

Touch tablets are interesting in that they can be designed and employed in such a way as to afford eyes-free operation and simultaneous access. As well, they can meet our constraints of providing absolute position information in a planar coordinate system. In this, they are rare among input transducers.

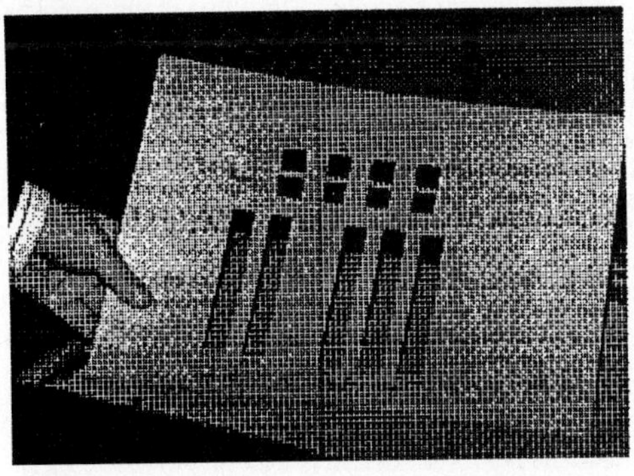

Figure 2: *Using a template with a touch tablet*

A cut-out template is being placed over a touch tablet. Each cut-out represents a different virtual device on a prototype operating console. The user can operate each device "eyes-free" since boundaries of the virtual devices can be felt (due to the raised edges of the template). If the tablet can sense more than one point of contact at a time, multiple virtual devices can be operated at once. (From Buxton, Hill, & Rowley, 1985).

The primary attribute of touch technologies that affords eyes-free operation is their having no intermediate hand-held transducer (such as a stylus or puck). Sensing is with the finger. Consequently, physical templates can be placed over a touch tablet (as illustrated in Fig. 2) and provide the same type of kinesthetic feedback that one obtains from the frets on a guitar or the cracks between the keys of a piano. This was demonstrated in Buxton, Hill and Rowley (1985). Because of the ability to memorize the position of virtual devices and sense their boundaries, usage is very different than that where a stylus is used, or where the virtual devices are delimited on the tablet surface graphically, and cannot be felt.

An interesting result from our studies, however, is the degree to which eyes-free control can be exercised on a touch tablet which is partitioned into a number of virtual devices, but which has no graphical or physical templates on the tablet surface.

Using a 3"x3" touch sensitive touch tablet (shown in Fig. 3), our informal experience suggests that with very little training users can easily discriminate regions to a resolution of up to 1/3 of the tablet surface's vertical or horizontal dimensions. Thus, one can implement three virtual linear potentiometers by dividing the surface into three uniform sized rows or columns, or, for example, one can implement nine virtual push-button switches by partitioning the tablet surface into a 3x3 matrix.

If the surface is divided into smaller regions, such as a 4x4 grid, the result will be significantly more errors, and longer learning time. In such cases, using the virtual devices will require visual attention. The desired eyes-free operability is lost.

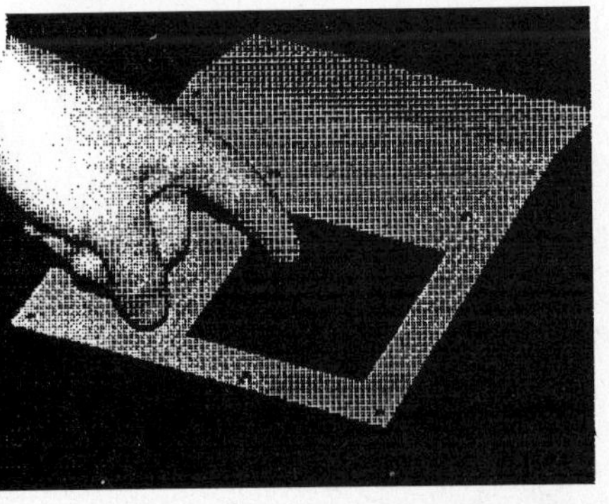

Figure 3: *A 3"x3" Touch Tablet*

A touch tablet of this size has the important property that it is on the same spatial scale as the hand. Therefore, control and access over its surface falls within the bounds of the relatively highly developed fine motor skills of the fingers, even if the palm is resting in a fixed (home?) position. (From Buxton, Hill & Rowley, 1985).

These limits are illustrated in Fig. 4. For example, we see that nine buttons for playing tick-tack-toe can work rather well, while a sixteen button numerical button keypad does not. Similarly, three virtual linear faders to control Hue, Saturation and Value work, while four such potentiometers do not.

Our belief is that the performance that we are observing is due to the size of the tablet as it relates to the size of the hand, and the degree of fine motor skills developed in the hand by virtue of everyday living. Being sensitive to these limits is very important as we shall see later when we discuss "dynamic windows." Because of this importance, these limits of motor control warrant more formal study.[1]

Finally, there is the issue of parallel access. Touch technologies have the potential to support multiple virtual devices simultaneously. Again, this is largely by virtue of their not demanding any hand-held intermediate transducer. If, for example, I am holding a stylus in my hand, the affordances of the device bias my expectations towards wanting to draw only one line at a time. In contrast, if I were using finger paints, I would have no such restrictive expectations.

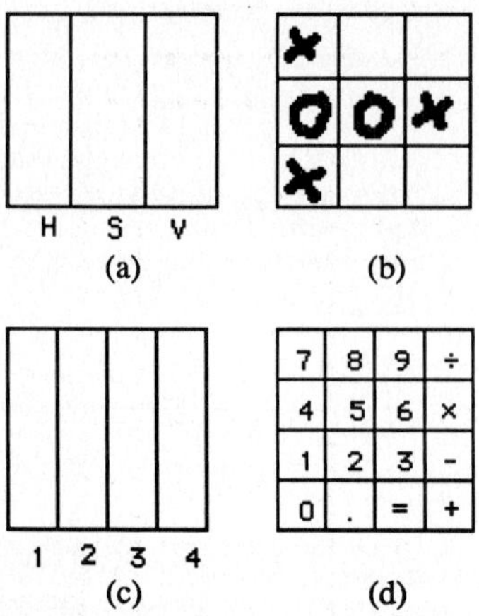

Figure 4: *Grids on Touch Tablets*

Four mappings of virtual devices are made onto a touch tablet. In (a) and (c), the regions represent linear potentiometers. The surface is partitioned into 3 and 4 regions, respectively. In (b) and (d) the surface is partitioned into a matrix of push buttons (3x3 and 4x4, respectively). Using a 3"x3" touch tablet without templates, our informal experience is that users can resolve virtual devices relatively easily, eyes-free, when the tablet is divided into up to 3 regions in either or both dimensions. This is the situation illustrated in (a) and (b). However, resolving virtual devices where the surface is more finely divided, as in (c) and (d), presents considerably more load. Eyes-free operation requires far more training, and errors are more frequent. The limits on this discrimination warrant more formal study.

A similar effect is at play in interacting with virtual devices implemented on touch tablets. Consider the template shown in Fig. 2. Nothing biases the user against operating more than one of the virtual linear potentiometers at a time. In fact, experience in the everyday world of such potentiometers would lead one to expect this to be allowed. Consequently, if it is not allowed, the designer must pay particular attention to avoiding probable errors that would result from this false expectation.

Being able to activate more than one virtual device at a time opens up a new possibilities in control and prototyping. The mock up of instrument control consoles is just one example. The biggest obstacle restricting the exploitation of this potential is the lack of a touch tablet that is capable of sensing multiple points. However, Lee, Buxton and Smith (1985) have demonstrated a working prototype of such a transducer, and it is hoped that the applications described in this current paper will help stimulate more activity in this direction.

In summary, we have seen that position sensitive planar devices readily support spatially distinct virtual input devices. Further, we have seen that touch technologies, and touch tablets in particular, have affordances which are particularly well suited to this type of interaction. Finally, it has been shown that a touch tablet capable of sensing more than one point of contact at a time would enable the simultaneous operation of multiple virtual devices.

5. VIRTUAL INPUT TRANSDUCERS

In current "menu on the tablet" practice, there is typically just one device driver which returns a single stream of coordinates. The application must decode the data according to the current partitioning of the tablet. This is all *ad hoc*, as are the means of specifying the boundaries of the various partitions. There are few tools, and little flexibility.

In our approach, the data from each virtual device is transmitted to the application as if it were coming from an independent physical device with its own driver. If the region is a button device, its driver transmits state changes. If it is a 1-D relative valuator, it transmits one dimension of relative data in stream mode. All of this is accomplished by placing a "window manager" between the device driver for the sensing transducer and the application.[2] Hence, applications can be constructed independent of how the virtual devices are implemented, thereby maintaining all of the desired properties of device independence. Furthermore, this is accomplished with a uniform set of tools that allows one to define the various regions and the operational behaviour of each region.

6. WHAT ABOUT DYNAMIC WINDOWS?

Window managers for displays can support the *dynamic* creation, manipulation, and destruction of windows. Is it reasonable to consider comparable functionality for input windows?

Our research (Buxton, Hill & Rowley, 1985) has demonstrated that under certain circumstances, the mapping of virtual devices onto the tablet surface can be dynamically altered. For example, in a paint system, the tablet may be a 2D pointing device in one context, and in another (such as when mixing colours) may have three linear potentiometers mapped onto it.

Changing the mapping of virtual devices onto the tablet surface restricts or precludes the use of physical templates. However, this is not always a problem. If visual (but not tactile) feedback is required, then a touch sensitive flat panel display can provide graphical feedback as to the current mapping. This is standard practice in many touch screen "soft machine" systems.

As has already been discussed, under certain circumstances, some touch tablets can be used effectively without physical or graphical templates. This can be illustrated using a paint mixing example. Since there are three components to colour, three linear potentiometers are used. As in Fig. 4(b), the potentiometers are vertically oriented so that there is no confusion: up is increase, down is decrease. The potentiometers are, left-to-right, Hue, Saturation, and Value (H, S & V in the figure). This ordering is consistent with the conventional order in speech, consequently there is little or no confusion for the user.

The example illustrates three conditions for using virtual devices without templates:

Property Sensed		Number of Dimensions: 1		2				3	
Position		Rotary Pot	Sliding Pot	Tablet & Puck	Tablet & Stylus	Light Pen	Floating Joystick	3D Joystick	M
		+	+O	Touch Tablet +O		Touch Screen		+O	T
Motion		Continuous Rotary Pot	Treadmill	Mouse			Trackball	3D Trackball	M
		+	Ferinstat +O	+O			X/Y Pad	+O	T
Pressure		Torque Sensor +	+	+			Isometric Joystick	+	T

Figure 5. *Taxonomy of Hand-Controlled Continuous Input Devices.*

Cells represent input transducers with particular properties. Primary rows (solid lines) categorize property sensed (position, motion or pressure). Primary columns categorize number of dimensions transduced. Secondary rows (dashed lines) differentiate devices using a hand-held intermediate transducer (such as a puck or stylus) from those that respond directly to touch - the mediated (M) and touch (T) rows, respectively. Secondary columns group devices roughly by muscle groups employed, or the type of motor control used to operate the device. Cells marked with a "+" can be easily be emulated using virtual devices on a multi-touch tablet. Cells marked with a "O" indicate devices that have been emulated using a conventional digitizing tablet. After Buxton (1983).

• a low number of devices;

• careful layout;

• strong compatibility between the virtual devices and the application.

Our objective is not to encourage or legitimize the arbitrary use of menus on tablet surfaces. As many CAD systems illustrate, this often leads to bad user interface design. What we hope we have done is identify a technique which, when used in the appropriate context, will result in an improved user interface.

7. UIMS's AND VIRTUAL DEVICES

User Interface Management Systems, or UIMS's, are sets of tools designed to support iterative development of user interfaces through all phases of development (Tanner & Buxton, 1983; Buxton, Lamb, Sherman & Smith, 1983). Ideally, this includes specification, design, implementation, testing, evaluation and redesign. Typically, UIMS's provide tools for the layout of graphic interfaces, control low level details of input and output, and (more rarely) provide monitoring facilities to aid in evaluation of the interfaces developed.

We have developed an *input window manager* (IWM). The tool consists of a "meta device" that provides for quick specification of the layout and behavior of the virtual devices. The specified configuration functions independent of the application. Users employ a *gesture-based trainer* to "show" the system the location and type of virtual device being specified. Hence, for example, adding a new template involves little more than tracing its outline on the control surface, defining the virtual device types and ranges, and attaching them to application parameters. Since the implementation of new devices can be achieved as quickly as they can be laid out on the tablet, this tool provides a new dimension of *system tailorability*.

In order to support iterative development, the tool should allow the user to suspend the application program, change the input configuration (by invoking a special process to control the virtual devices), and then proceed with the application program using the altered input configuration.

8. THE REPERTOIRE OF SUPPORTED VIRTUAL DEVICES

The impact of the physical device used on the quality of interaction has been discussed by Buxton (1983). The objective, therefore, is to make available as broad a repertoire of "virtual" devices as possible from a limited number of physical transducers. We based our initial

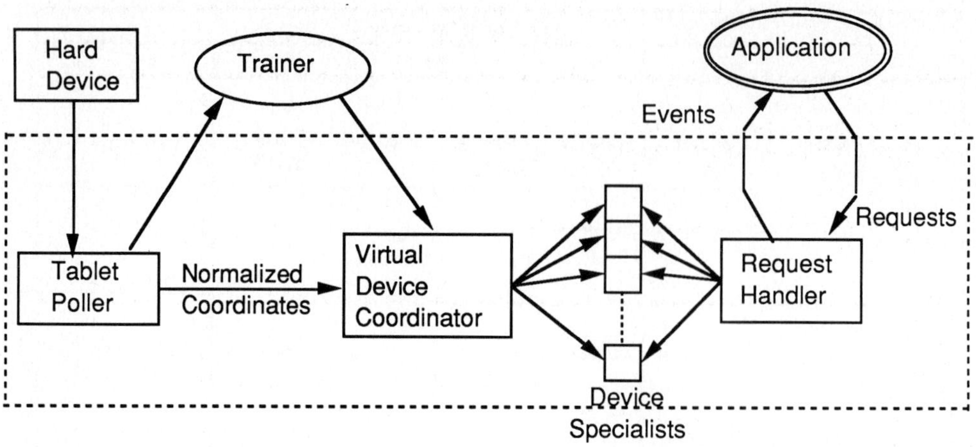

Figure 6. *Architecture of a Prototype Input Window Manager*

prototype on a conventional graphics tablet, and have designed to include future support for both single and multiple touch-sensitive tablets. The repertoire of virtual devices supported by our prototype is indicated in Fig 5.

9. A PROTOTYPE INPUT WINDOW MANAGER

The architecture of the IWM that we have implemented is depicted in Figure 6. The user interacts with the IWM at two separate points indicated by ovals in the diagram. The *Trainer* program, provides for configuring the input control structure. The *application* exists outside of the IWM, and the workings of the IWM are incidental to it (other than the interface to the request handler).

The *tablet poller* monitors the activity on the physical device, filters redundant information, and normalizes the data points before passing them on. The normalized format allows use of a range of physical devices simply by changing the tablet poller for the specific device.

The *virtual device coordinator* is active if the current activity is not a trainer session. It uses the incoming tablet data and the configuration provided by a trainer session to identify the virtual device to which the incoming data belongs. It passes the appropriate information on to the *device specialist* (device driver) for that virtual device. The device specialist determines the effect of the input and signals the *request handler* appropriately.

The virtual devices are accessed by the application program through two communication routines. One routine allows the activation and deactivation of various types of event signals. The other routine accesses the *event-queue*, returning the specifics of the last event to be signaled. A number of requests are available to the activation routine, including discrete status checks on a device, turning the device "on" or "off" for continuous event signaling, and a utility shutdown request.

The request handler module interprets and acts on requests from the application program, altering or extracting information of the device specialists as needed. It posts appropriate events to the event queue.

Finally, the architecture is such that much of the underlying software can reside in a dedicated processor, thereby freeing up resources on the machine running the main application. This includes the part of the tablet poller, the internal representation of the current mapping of the virtual devices onto the tablet, and the virtual device coordinator.

10. CONCLUSION

This paper has discussed one way of making direct manipulation interfaces more direct and manipulation more effective. The general approach has been to extend the number of discrete and continuous controllers which can be tied to different functions. This is accomplished through spatially distinct virtual devices, and an input window management system. In the process, a number of properties of input devices have been discussed, and a prototype system presented. The results have important implications on the usability and tailorability of systems, and the architecture of UIMS's.

The work described has been exploratory. Nevertheless, we feel that the results are sufficiently compelling to suggest that more formal investigations of the issues discussed are warranted. We hope that the current work will help serve as a catalyst to such research.

ACKNOWLEDGEMENTS

The work described in this paper has been supported by the Natural Science and Engineering Research Council of Canada and Xerox PARC. This support is gratefully acknowledged. We would also like to acknowledge the contribution of Ralph Hill, Peter Rowley and Abigail Sellen. Finally, we would like to thank Tom Milligan for his help in proof-reading the final manuscript.

NOTES

[1] It must be emphasized that the limits discussed here were obtained through informal study. We intend only to suggest that there is something interesting and useful here, rather than to imply that these are experimentally derived data.

[2] We thank Alain Fournier for first suggesting the analogy with window managers.

REFERENCES

Anson, E. (1982). The Device Model of Interaction. *Computer Graphics,* (16,3), 107-114.

Buxton, W. (1983). Lexical and Pragmatic Considerations of Input Structures. *Computer Graphics*, (17,1), 31-37

Buxton W., Hill R., & Rowley P. (1985). Issues and Techniques in Touch-Sensitive Tablet Input. *Computer Graphics*, 19(3), 215 - 224.

Buxton, W., Lamb, M., Sherman, D., & Smith, K.C. (1982). Towards a Comprehensive User Interface Management System. *Computer Graphics,* (16,3), 99-106.

Buxton, W. & Myers, B. (1986). A Study in Two-Handed Input. *Proceedings of CHI'86 Conference on Human Factors in Computing Systems*, 321-326.

Evans, K. Tanner, P., & Wein, M. (1981). Tablet-based Valuators that Provide One, Two, or Three Degrees of Freedom. *Computer Graphics* (15,3), 91-97.

Kasik, D. (1982). A User Interface Management System. *Computer Graphics,* (16,3), 99-106.

Knowlton, K. (1975). Virtual Pushbuttons as a Means of Person- Machine Interaction. *Proc. IEEE Conf. on Computer Graphics, Pattern Matching, and Data Structure*., 350-351.

Knowlton, K. (1977a). Computer Displays Optically Superimposed on Input Devices. *The Bell System Technical Journal* (56,3), 367-383.

Knowlton, K. (1977b). *Prototype for a Flexible Telephone Operator's Console Using Computer Graphics*. 16mm film, Bell Labs, Murray Hill, NJ.

Lee S., Buxton, W., & Smith, K.C. (1985). A Multi-Touch Three Dimensional Touch Tablet. *Proceedings of CHI'85 Conference on Human Factors in Computing Systems*, 21 - 25.

Myers, B. (1984a), Strategies for Creating an Easy to Use Window Manager with Icons. *Proceedings of Graphics Interface '84,* Ottawa, May, 1984, 227 - 233.

Myers, B. (1984b), The User Interface for Sapphire. *IEEE Computer Graphics and Applications,* 4 (12), 13 - 23.

Pike, R. (1983). Graphics in Overlapping Bitmap Layers. *Computer Graphics,* 17 (3), 331 - 356.

Tanner, P.P. & Buxton, W. (1985). Some Issues in Future User Interface Management System (UIMS) Development. In Pfaff, G. (Ed.), User Interface Management Systems, Berlin: Springer Verlag, 67 - 79.

Human–Computer Interaction – INTERACT '90
D. Diaper et al. (Editors)
Elsevier Science Publishers B.V. (North-Holland)

Building Adaptive Interfaces with Neural Networks: The Glove-Talk Pilot Study*

S. Sidney Fels and Geoffrey E. Hinton

Department of Computer Science, University of Toronto,
10 Kings College Road, Toronto, Canada, M5S 1A4

A multilayer neural network can learn complicated mappings from inputs to outputs. After learning a mapping from a set of training examples, the network can generalize to new cases. Although the learning can be slow, the network runs extremely rapidly once it has learned so it can be used for real-time applications. To illustrate the potential of this technology for adaptive interfaces, we used a VPL DataGlove connected to a DECtalk speech synthesizer via five neural networks to implement a hand gesture to speech system. Using minor variations of the standard back-propagation learning procedure, the complex mapping of hand movements to speech is learned using data obtained from a single "speaker" in a simple training phase. With a 203 gesture-to-word vocabulary, the wrong word is produced less than 1% of the time, and no word is produced about 7% of the time. Adaptive control of the speaking rate and word stress is also available. The training times and final performance speed are improved by using small, separate networks for each naturally defined subtask. The system demonstrates that neural networks can be used to develop the complex mappings required in a high bandwidth interface that adapts to the individual user.

Introduction

Neural networks are composed of simple, neuron-like processing elements which are richly interconnected. A common type of network contains some input units, one or more intermediate layers of "hidden" units, and a layer of output units. The number of layers, the number of units per layer, and the pattern of connections between layers is typically chosen by hand, but the way in which the network maps vectors of activity over its input units into vectors of activity over its output units is determined by the weights on the connections and these are typically learned from a set of training examples that specify the desired ouput vector for each input vector. Once the network has learned, it can generalize to new cases. Adaptive neural networks are being successfully applied to important real-world problems such as speech recognition (Lippmann 1989), hand drawn character recognition (LeCun, 1989) and adaptive system control (Nguyen and Widrow, 1989).

Adaptive interfaces are a natural and important class of applications for neural networks. When a person must provide high bandwidth control of a complex physical device, a compatible mapping between the person's movements and the behaviour of the device becomes crucial. With many devices the mapping is fixed and if a poor mapping is used, the device is difficult to use. Using adaptive neural networks, it may now be possible to build device interfaces where the mapping adapts automatically, tailoring control of the device to each individual who uses it. Such adaptive interfaces would simplify the process of designing the compatible mapping and allow the mapping to adapt to different users. The key features of neural networks in the context of adaptive interfaces are the following.

- Neural networks can learn to approximate any input/output function.
- Neural networks learn input/output functions from examples provided by the user who demonstrates the input that should lead to a specified output. This "extensional" programming requires no computer expertise.
- Adapting the interface to the peculiarities of a new user is simple and quick. The new user has only to create example data to retrain the network.
- Once trained, the networks run very quickly, even on a serial machine. Also, neural networks are inherently suitable for parallel computation.

Overview of the Glove-Talk system

To demonstrate the usefulness of neural networks for adaptive interfaces, we chose the task of mapping hand

*This research was supported by the Canadian National Science and Engineering Research Council and the Ontario Information Technology Research Centre. The DECtalk speech synthesizer was provided by Terry Sejnowski and the Xerion neural network simulator we used was written by Tony Plate.

gestures to speech (Kramer and Leifer, 1988). The hand gesture data is sensed by a VPL DataGlove (VPL, 1988) that has two sensors for each finger. The sensors are fibre optic transducers which measure the finger flex angles. There is also a "polhemus" sensor attached to the back of the glove which measures the x, y, z, roll, pitch, and yaw of the hand relative to a fixed source. All 16 parameters are measured every $1/60^{th}$ second. The speech synthesiser is a DECtalk model DTC01 from Digital Equipment Corporation. This synthesizer can perform text-to-speech synthesis and there is also user control of speaking rate and word stress. DECtalk has a large selection of user controllable speech parameters in addition to phoneme-to-speech capabilities.

The granularity of speech can be used to define a spectrum of possible methods for mapping from hand gestures to speech. At the finest granularity, rapid finger movements could play the role of movements of the speech articulators. This gives the user an unlimited vocabulary and analog control over the quality of the speech, but the finger movements must be extremely fast and they must be recognized with very little delay to produce speech in real-time. In the middle of the spectrum, a brief movement or hand configuration could represent a diphone or syllable. At the other end of the spectrum, a complete hand gesture could be mapped to a whole word without mapping temporal constituents of the gesture to temporal constituents of the word. This gives a fixed vocabulary which, like chinese ideographs, makes it very arduous for the user to master a large vocabulary. However, for a small vocabulary the user can learn the task quite quickly. For this pilot study we chose to map complete hand gestures to whole words.

Once trained, the Glove-Talk system works as follows: the user forms a hand-shape which represents a root word. Then s/he makes a movement forward and back in one of six directions. The direction chosen determines the word ending, and the duration and magnitude of the gesture determine the speech rate and stress. The precise time at which the word is spoken is more complex. The user imagines that the end of the forward movement is like a button press that causes the word to be produced immediately, much like a conductor producing music. To avoid delays in producing the word, the shape of the hand is actually "read" near the beginning of the deceleration phase of the forward movement. This moment is called the "strobe-time" and is detected by a hand_trajectory→strobe_time network ("strobe network") that continually monitors the directionless speed and acceleration of the whole hand using preprocessed information from the polhemus device. A block diagram of the Glove-Talk system is in figure 1.

When the strobe network detects an appropriate strobe-time, it sends a signal back to the preprocessor. The preprocessor then sends the appropriate buffered data to each of four neural networks to do the hand gesture to word mapping. The hand_shape→root_word network determines the correct root word based on the static hand shape and orientation at the strobe-time.

root word	hand shape
come	
go	
I	
you	
short	

Table 1: Examples of Glove-Talk Language

The hand_direction→word_ending network determines, from the direction of hand movement, which of the six possible endings (plural, -ed, -ly, -er, -ing, and normal) the user intended. The hand_speed→word_rate and hand_displacement→word_stress networks determine the speaking rate and whether the word is stressed or not, based on the speed and magnitude of the hand movement respectively. Once the mapping is completed, the appropriate commands (i.e. the word and the necessary rate and stress) are sent to the speech synthesizer which then speaks the word.

The current Glove-Talk vocabulary consists of 66 root words, each with up to six different endings. The total size of the vocabulary is 203 words. Five examples of the initial mapping of hand shapes (and orientations) to words are shown in table 1. Many of the hand shapes are derived from American Sign Language (ASL) letters (Wilbur 1979). Orientation differences in the hand shapes are usually reserved for semantically opposite words; for example, the hand shapes for "come" and "go" have the same finger angles but are 180° of roll apart (i.e. "come" is made with the palm up and "go" is made with the palm down). The various endings of the words are formed by different directions of the hand movement. The mapping is given in table 2.

Note that for some root words the endings do **not** correspond to the ones shown above. For example, the "-s" ending of the root word "I" is "me". When any of the 6 endings do not exist for a root word, the normal ending is used. The 66 root words and six endings were extracted from the 850 word vocabulary of Basic English (Ogden, 1968).

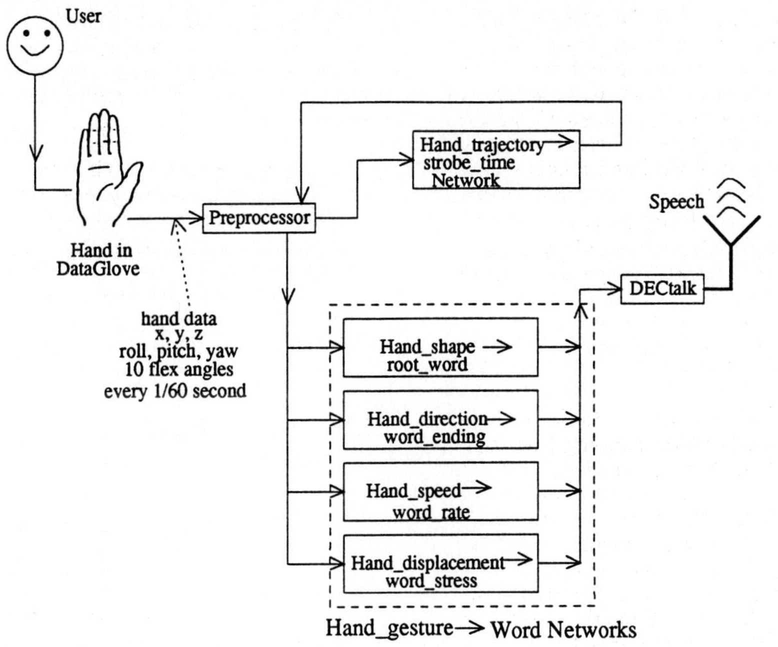

Figure 1: Glove-Talk System

	Ending	Direction
1	normal	down
2	-s	up
3	-ed	away from user
4	-ing	away from user
5	-er	to user's right
6	-ly	to user's left

Table 2: Direction of Movement to Ending Mapping

The following sections briefly describe the two most interesting neural networks. Full details of the complete system, the training data, and the performance can be found in (Fels, 1990).

Learning in a multilayer neural network

A typical multilayer neural network consists of layers of simple, neuron-like processing elements called "units" that interact via weighted connections. Each unit has a "state" or "activity level" that is determined by the input received from units in the layer below. The total input, x_j, received by unit j is defined to be

$$x_j = \sum_i y_i w_{ji} - b_j \qquad (1)$$

where y_i is the state of the ith unit (which is in a lower layer), w_{ji} is the weight on the connection from the ith to the jth unit and b_j is the bias of the jth unit. Biases can be viewed as the weights on extra input lines whose activity level is always 1, so they can be learned in just the same way as the other weights. The lowest layer contains the input units and an external input vector is supplied to the network by clamping the states of these units. The state of any other unit in the network is determined by its activation function. One example is a monotonic non-linear function of its total input (sigmoid unit):

$$y_j = \frac{1}{1 + e^{-x_j}}. \qquad (2)$$

Other activation functions can also be used. For example, the activity levels of the output units of the hand_shape→root_word or hand_direction → word_ending networks represent probability distributions across mutually exclusive alternatives. To ensure that these activity levels sum to 1, the output value, y_i, of each output unit, i, is derived from the total input received by that unit, x_i, using the following non-local non-linearity:

$$y_i = \frac{e^{x_i}}{\sum_j e^{x_j}} \qquad (3)$$

Both input and output units can be used to represent

discrete values or real values. The flexibility of the input and output representations and the ability of the hidden layers to construct new, intermediate representations allows these networks to be used to approximate many different types of functions. All the network's long-term knowledge about the function it has learned to compute is encoded by the magnitudes of the weights on the connections. The weights are adjusted by automatic learning procedures. Using suitable multi-layered networks, along with appropriate learning procedures, any input/output function can be approximated (Funahashi, 1989).

The standard method of training multilayer networks requires labeled examples each of which consists of a vector of input values paired with the desired output vector. The network trains by propagating the input vector forward through the network and comparing its actual output vector with the desired output vector. The weights are then adjusted to minimize an error function which depends on the difference between the actual and the desired output vectors. The simplest technique for adjusting the weights is to change them in the direction of the gradient of the error function with respect to the weights. This gradient can be efficiently calculated using a method called *backpropagation* (Rumelhart, Hinton, and Williams, 1986).

Many different error functions can be used. The commonest is the the sum-squared error which is simply the sum of the squared difference between actual and desired output activities. We use this error function for three of our networks, but for the hand_shape→root_word and hand_direction→ word_ending networks we use a different error-function that is appropriate to the special behaviour of the output units in these two networks (see Eq 3). The error function is simply $-\log y_i$, where y_i is the activation of the correct output unit. The backpropagation procedure for deriving error-derivatives can easily be modified to use this new error function and the more complex behaviour of the output units (Yair and Gersho, 1989).

The Hand Shape to Root Word Network

The 16 input units of the hand_shape→root_word network represent the 2 flex angles of each finger (linearly scaled to lie between 0 and 1) and the sines and cosines of the roll, pitch, and yaw of the whole hand. The input units are fully connected to 80 hidden units which, in turn, are fully connected to 66 output units. The network is trained to activate the appropriate output unit more than the others. It requires 509 sweeps through the entire set of 8912 training examples to achieve an error rate of 0.58% on the training data. The weights are updated every 66 examples (one per root word) using a learning rate of 0.01 and a momentum of 0.5 (Rumelhart *et. al.*, 1986). On test examples we only accept output values above 0.6 as identified root words, and the network gives 0.96% incorrect identifications and 2.25% misses. The details of how the training data were collected and the effects of changing the architecture of the network or the input and output encodings are described by (Fels, 1990).

Once the strobe network is working it is simple to create training and test data for the hand_shape→root_word network and the other networks. Targets (combinations of the word root, ending, rate, and stress) are presented to the user and s/he simply makes the appropriate gesture. Since the computer already knows the desired ouputs of all the networks, it is easy to create the training set.

The Hand Trajectory to Strobe Time Network

The network which we had most difficulty in designing and training was the hand_trajectory→strobe_time network which must decide when the user intends to utter a word. This network segments the continuous stream of data from the DataGlove and, as is common in pattern recognition tasks, the segmentation turns out to be much harder than it appears.

The input data to the hand_trajectory→strobe_time network is a window of 10 time steps of the Δx, Δy, Δz, and the directionless speed and acceleration of the user's hand. These values are obtained by pre-processing the raw output of the polhemus. The $\Delta x, \Delta z$, and Δz values are the difference between the current position and the previous position. The speed of the hand is calculated by $\sqrt{\Delta x^2 + \Delta y^2 + \Delta z^2}$. The acceleration is the current speed minus the previous speed. The directionless speed and acceleration are the primary source of information for detecting the beginning of the deceleration phase of the forward movement, but the Δx, Δy and Δz values are needed to allow the network to discriminate translational movements of the whole hand from translational movements of the polhemus caused by hand rotations.

The window size of 10 time steps (133 msec) is a compromise between ensuring that the network has enough information to detect a strobe-time and keeping the strobe network small. Notice that the strobe network must perform a forward propagation *every* time step to keep up with the DataGlove. The 50 input units of the strobe network are fully connected to 10 hidden units which are all connected to a single sigmoid output unit which represents a binary decision about whether the most recent time is the right time to strobe (i.e. read) the hand shape. The input units act as a 10 time step shift register with 5 data values per time step.

The network was trained on 638 hand movement examples covering 30,356 time steps. The training minimized the sum-squared difference between the actual and desired output values. We hand-labeled appropriate strobe-times in the training data and required the network to give an output of 1 at these times and an output of 0 at other times. This makes life difficult for the network since our choice of strobe-time may differ by one time step from the network's natural choice, given the other training cases it has to accommodate. Retrospectively, it would have been better to use an error function that allowed the network some temporal latitude in detecting the strobe-times. Watrous (1988) describes one method of allowing temporal latitude when recognizing phonemes.

The performance of the strobe network is critical. If the network is too sensitive, extraneous words are produced and if it is too insensitive, many intended utterances will have to be retried. If the strobe-time is detected at the wrong time, the hand shape and direction of movement may be wrong. Also, the labeled training data for the other networks cannot be created until the strobe network is working. So it is very important to have a reliable, accurate strobe signal.

To illustrate what the strobe network recognizes, consider the typical time domain waveform of the speed of a user's hand movement in figure 2. In the first 5 time steps, the hand accelerates and reaches its maximum speed. Then the user begins to slow their hand down, to change direction, and bring it back to rest. It takes 4 time steps to come to a brief stop and reverse direction.

The strobe network is trained to recognize the initial acceleration and speed increase followed by the deceleration and speed decrease. After detecting a strobe-time, the strobe network is not run for the next five time steps. This refractory period eliminates double detections and frees the processor for simulating the other networks.

The hand-labeling of the training data for the strobe network is time-consuming. The training set was created in 21 sessions, where most sessions involved making 25 hand movements. The user made exactly the decided upon number of hand movements in each session, so the correct number of strobe-times was known. Various hand shapes, hand movement directions, durations and displacements were made to capture the variability in hand movements from different word contexts.

There were 30356 input/output pairs in total and 638 of them were labeled as positive examples of strobe-times with the remainder being negative. The data was labeled by a human observer viewing the data graphically and marking the time of the first drop in speed of the user's hand after its initial acceleration. After the data had been labeled, it was possible to check the labeling accuracy by checking that the number of positive labels in each session was the same as the number of hand movements made. To save effort, data was labeled in a bootstrap manner. First, a small number of examples (approximately 60) were labeled by hand. These were used initially to train the network. The remaining unlabeled training data were then forward propagated through the network. In most cases, some activity then occurred around the locations that would have been labeled by hand. Thus, the initial, poorly trained network was used to focus the search for likely areas in the unlabeled training data where a strobe-time might occur.

The strobe network required 1325 sweeps through the entire training set with the weights being updated after each entire sweep. The learning rate was 0.001 and a momentum was 0.9. With the threshold set to 0.5, the total number of misses was 32 out of 638 and the total number of false alarms was 29 out of 29718. Even though the number of training examples was very large, the time required to train the network on one processor of a Silicon Graphics 4D/240S was only a few hours due to the small network size. The hand_trajectory→strobe_time network has a 95% (190/200) hit rate on the test data set.

Achieving real-time responses

The Glove-Talk system consists of three Unix processes. One handles the DataGlove communication and preprocessing, another runs the hand_trajectory→strobe_time network and the last runs the hand_gesture→word networks. The processes communicate using Unix sockets, allowing each process to run on separate machines. This approach does not lend itself well to real-time operation. When all the processes are running on a Silicon Graphics 4D/240S, the processing usually takes about 10 msec, but there are occasional delays of much longer duration. Using shared memory for the interprocess communication and synchronization will probably alleviate this problem and give excellent real time response, limited mainly by the 33 msec delay in getting outputs from the DataGlove.

To ensure a delay of only 20 msec in the four neural networks that identify the root word, the ending, the speech rate, and the stress, requires about 0.8 million floating point operations per second because the four networks contain 8,036 weights each of which requires a multiply and an add. The continually running strobe network is much less demanding because it is small. The delays in the DataGlove, neural network, and speech synthesizer can be effectively eliminated by reading the hand-shape before the end of the forward movement of the hand.

Concluding Remarks

Fairly rapid, intelligible speech is possible with the current Glove-Talk system. About 1% of the words spoken are incorrect, and about 7% of attempts result in no word being spoken due to failure to detect the gesture or failure to confidently identify the root word.

Obvious improvements include user control of pitch and loudness, continued "online" training while the system is in use, and a method for explicitly spelling out words that are not in the fixed vocabulary. One major improvement would be to increase the number of root words to the entire 850 words of Basic English. This

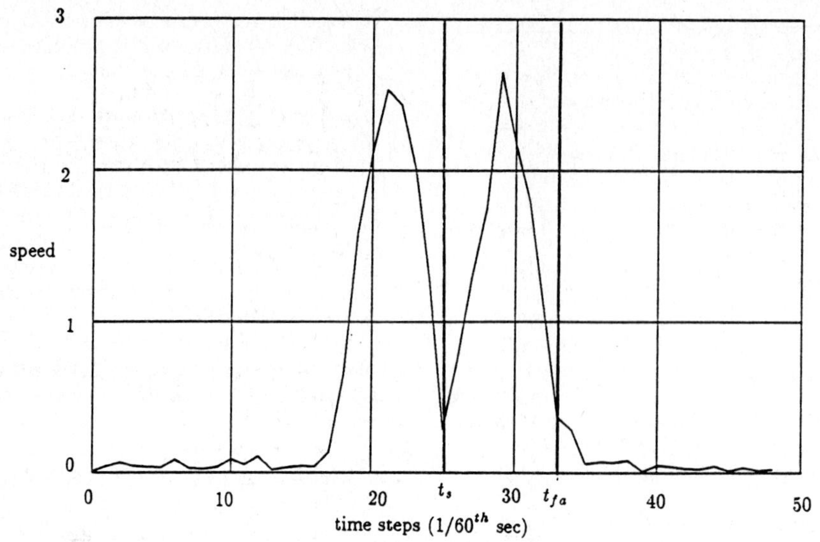

Figure 2: Speed of Hand versus Time During Hand Movement

may require substantial restructuring of the system, since static hand-shapes and orientations may not be sufficiently reproducible to allow 850 discriminable alternatives. It may therefore be necessary to use hand position or its temporal derivatives to distinguish between root words, or to encode root words by time-varying hand shapes. A sequence of two static hand-shapes would only require 30 discriminable alternatives to specify 900 root words, and a neural network should be good at adapting to co-articulation effects between the two consecutive hand-shapes.

If it proves necessary to abandon the use of static hand shapes altogether, we will investigate a finer-grained mapping in which finger movements play the role of the normal speech articulators. Such a mapping would be hard to learn, but would allow an unlimited vocabulary and much greater control of the speech.

Finally, it would be illuminating to investigate the performance that can be achieved at this kind of real-time task using other approaches such as standard pattern recognition techniques or expert systems.

References

Fels, S.S., *Building Adaptive Interfaces Using Neural Networks: The Glove-Talk Pilot Study*, Technical Report CRG-TR-90-1, University of Toronto, Toronto, Canada, 1990.

Funahashi, K., "On the Approximate Realization of Continuous Mappings by NeuralNetworks", *Neural Networks*, Vol. 2, 183-192, 1989.

Kramer, J., and Leifer, L., "The 'Talking Glove': A Speaking Aid For Nonvocal Deaf and Deaf-Blind Individuals", in *Proceedings of RESNA 12th Annual Conference*, 471–472, Louisiana, USA, 1989.

LeCun, Y., Boser, B., Denker, J.S., Henderson, D., Howard, R., Hubbard, W., and Jackel, L.D., "Backpropagation applied to handwritten zip code recognition", *Neural Computation*, in press.

Lippmann, R.P., "Review of Neural Networks for Speech Recognition", *Neural Computation*, 1:1-38, 1989.

Nguyen, D., and Widrow, B., "The Truck Backer-Upper: An example of Self Learning in Neural Networks", *Proceedings of International Joint Conference on Neural Networks*, 2:357–363, Washington D.C., USA, 1989.

Ogden, C.K., *Basic English: International Second Language*, prepared by Graham, E.C., Harcourt, Brace & World Inc., NY, USA, 1968.

Rumelhart, D.E., Hinton, G.E., and Williams, R.J., "Learning internal representations by back-propagating errors", *Nature*, 323:533-536, 1986.

VPL Research Inc, *DataGlove Model 2 Operating Manual*, CA, USA, 1989.

Watrous, R. L., Ladendorf, B., Kuhn, G., "Complete gradient optimization of a recurrent network applied to /b/, /d/, /g/ discrimination", *Acoustical Society of America*, 87(2), 1990, to appear.

Wilbur, R.B., *American Sign Language and Sign Systems*, University Park Press, BA, USA, 1979.

Yair, E., Gersho, A., "The Boltzmann Perceptron Network: A multilayered feed-forward network equivalent to the Boltzmann Machine", *Advances in Neural Information Processing Systems 1*, ed. Touretzky, D.S., Morgan Kaufmann Publishers, CA, USA, 1:116-123, 1989.

Human–Computer Interaction – INTERACT '90
D. Diaper et al. (Editors)
Elsevier Science Publishers B.V. (North-Holland)
IFIP, 1990

FINGER - A Language for Gesture Recognition

Gerhard WEBER

Institut für Informatik, Universität Stuttgart
Azenbergstr. 12, D-7000 Stuttgart , F.R. Germany

We report on the development of a new kind of interaction for blind users. The interaction centers around our large, touch-sensitive tactile pin-matrix device. The fingers of the blind user are used for reading and simultaneously for specifying input in the form of gestures.

We developed and implemented the language FINGER on a SUN workstation in C for describing gestures. Human-computer interaction based on finger-movements is thus formalized with FINGER. This formalization allows describing gestures in a textual notation, thereby providing a solid basis for their design. Furthermore, FINGER enables gestures to be adapted to the individual user by transformations of their textual representations.

1. Introduction

Gestures are part of human nonverbal communication. Even the blind use gestures in conjunction with verbal communication (see Blass (1974)). While recent research (for an overview see Buxton (1989)) concentrates on gestures which result in immediate feedback displayed on a screen, we treat gestures as a kind of pointing which needs no visual feedback. This opens up a new input channel for the blind who cannot use conventional pointing devices.

2. Pointing devices for Blind users

Modern interaction methods are not usable by blind users simply through some additional hardware since such techniques are based on visual feedback on a raster display that follows a mouse movements. Although the use of a mouse is inappropiate for a blind user, it has been shown by Hill and Grieb (1988) that active movements of a single hand clearly improves a blind user's understanding of the spatial layout of a screen.

Hill and Grieb's system "Touch 'n Talk" therefore uses a graphics tablet. Moving the stylus on the tablet results in speech output that varies according to the speed and the direction of the movement. Touch 'n Talk also realized engraved guidelines in the tablett's surface in order to allow movements that act as input commands. By moving the stylus along these lines, one can, for example, select text units or start a command for searching.

Recognition of movements of a single pointing device has been realized as a modality in a graphical user interface by Wolf et al. (1987). The "paperlike interface" consists of a transparent graphics tablet placed over an LCD-screen. Gesture recognition is done mostly for handwritten symbols on the basis of feature analysis for changes in speed and direction of the stylus. Other gesture recognition systems can be based on connectionism. However, any one of the recognized gestures is associated with one semantic action. It is our understanding that in addition, gestures are far more capable of carrying additional semantic information that could be best termed parameters of gestures (see Weber (1987)) and that gestures can be formed by parallel movements of the hands.

While speech in general isn't able to explain an icon or the layout of a window system, another accoustic approach to display spatial information is based on nonspeech audio as described by Gaver (1989). Sounds like that of knocking on a wooden material carry a meaning and are easily understood. Pointing to an icon therefore results, according to Gaver, in a single wooden sound to help to identify the icon. Non-speech audio can also be parameterized (e.g. "dark", "bright") and thus to carry additional information together with its conventionalized meaning. Gaver suggests encoding the length of a file as a parameter of a sound, namely its pitch. However, it is not clear which interaction techniques are necessary to overcome the lack of overview of a blind user if presented with non-speech audio.

In the Stuttgart research group "Applied Computer Science for the Blind", we use a large tactile display which consists of more than 7000 individually moveable pins. Unlike all other types of commercially available tactile displays known to us (e.g. Optacon described by Bliss (1970), Braille Window manufactured by EHG (1986)), the pin-matrix device allows the user to move both hands actively on the display.

The pin-matrix device is capable of displaying text in braille as well as graphics together (see Schweikhardt (1984)). While it doesn't achieve the resolution of a LCD-screen, it is possible with this prototype to study the basic interaction techniques that are necessary in order to substitute the visual channel in a WYSIWYG-style UIMS. Although a subsitution of this output channel is necessary for blind users, one could say that these interaction techniques open up an additional channel that is based on feeling for every user.

The pin-matrix device has been extended by a sensor system that allows monitoring the movements of two fingers simultaneously. The sensor system is based on magnetic induction, as the driving force for every single pin is based on electromagnetism. Both sensors are to be worn on each forefinger. Reading on the display isn't hampered by the sensors but can be constantly monitored. The resulting data are fed into a SUN 3/60 where they are interpreted (see Fig.1).

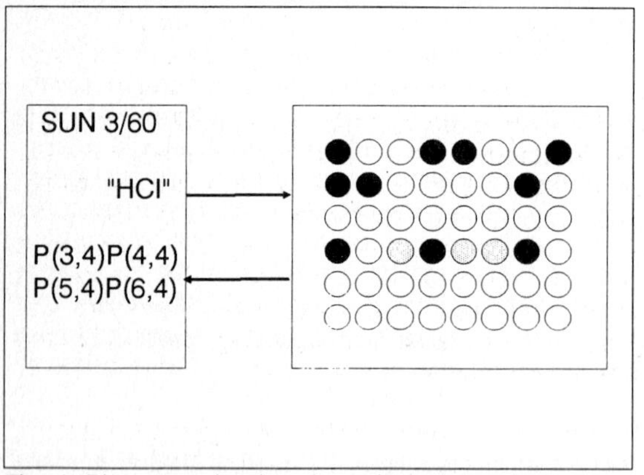

Fig. 1: Pins are raised and monitored

It is the interpretation of these data by the I/O-system, the user interface or the application program that is at the heart of a particular interaction method's design (see also Weber (1989a)). Direct manipulation, for example, requires the interpretation of pointing according to the sensitiveness of the UIMS's objects. This type of interaction for direct manipulation is further referred as direct interaction. In addition to the UIMS the application program has to monitor the movements if the interaction implies changes of the internal objects. Justification of a line along a grid in a drawing program is an example. This type of interaction is to be called active interaction.

Gestures can hardly be called representatives of active interaction, since to fulfill the movement no feedback by the computer is required. Gestures are also not used, for example, to directly drag an icon into the trashcan, so we will call gestures a kind of indirect interaction. In a dialogue system, this requires the interpretation of a gesture in a modular way, with at least a defined initial movement. Such a module acts like a filter that produces commands for the application program, similar to a menu or a command line interface. Gestures are in this respect another input modality of a multi-modal user interface.

2. Syntax of the language FINGER

With FINGER we want to present a language that formally describes the parallel movements of more than one pointing device (the fingers), specifies the resultant operation and allows calculating the actual values of the gesture's parameters. The implementation of FINGER consists of a compiler for the language and a recognition algorithm that acts according to the statements in a "gesture program".

Definition: We define a gesture in human-computer interaction as any bodily movement carrying a conventionalized meaning. Variations in the physical properties of a gesture can modify its meaning. We assume a certain standard of prototypical gesture-form as the carrier of the basic meaning. The degree of its variation in relation to the standard modifies the gesture's basic meaning.

From a language design point of view, we want FINGER to be

- declarative,
- modular ,
- recursive and
- abstract with respect to variations of a gesture.

The grammar in Fig. 2 gives a rough overview of important syntactic elements of FINGER (for a complete description of the grammar see Weber (1989b), Appendix B). The starting symbol is description. Terminal symbols are underlined. Assignments and conditional expressions are defined as in usual declarative expressions. For an example of a description for gestures see Fig. 3.

```
(1) description ← initpattern { commandpattern | basic }+
(2) initpattern  ← { clause }* commandpatterns:
                 {cmdpatt_name} + end
(3) commandpattern ←commandpattern
                 cmdpatt_name: { clause }*
                 commandclause end
(4) clause ← segment variable_name |
(4.1)        basic variable_name type basic_name |
(4.2)        comparison |
(4.3)        assignment |
(4.3)        imported_function |
(4.4)        conditional expression |
(4.5)        alternative clause
(5) basic ← basic basic_name: { clause }+ end
(6) comparison ← variable comp_operator variable
                 { with number }
(7) variable ← variable_name {. variable_name }*
             {{start | stop | len } {.X | .Y}}
```

Fig. 2: A simplified grammar of FINGER

A single gesture is described mainly by two parts: the initial pattern (hereinafter called initpattern) and the command pattern (1). Each pattern consists of a number of clauses that all together (resp. those that are encountered according to the flow of control) have to match the actual movement of a finger. The list of clauses in a command pattern is followed by a clause that defines the action that is the result of the gesture's recognition (3).

There exists only one initpattern in a description of gestures that is common to all command patterns (2). Its purpose is to specifiy the starting point of a movement that leads into one of several gestural movements. All according to (2) specified command patterns have to be checked in parallel.

A command pattern is dynamically to be correlated to the actual movement of the pointing device. The processing proceeds as soon as new data are coming from the finger's movement. The clauses therefore have to describe, in a readable way, the varieties of movements that form a gesture.

The terminal elements of clauses are segments (4). Segments are extracted from the actual movement of a finger. Geometrically seen a segment can be a straight line or an arc. For purposes of reference, every segment is named in FINGER. To allow a bundeling of segments in a generic manner, basic gestures are definable. A basic gesture is "called" by its name (4.1 and 5) within a command pattern or recursively within a basic gesture.

To include more than one alternative in a command pattern, the keyword alternative announces such a choice (4.5). The order of declaration of the alternatives does not imply in which way they are examined, but every alternative is checked in parallel. The exclusion of different command patterns and alternatives is realized by a type of clause for comparisons (4.2). If the comparison does not hold true, the corresponding alternative resp. command pattern is not further examined.

The set of usual relational operators (=, <, >, etc.) is applied to points or single coordinates. In extension of the test on equality the relation "?=" has a third operand that allows for a comparison within a range (6). (The following examples will show for purposes of implementation all numeric values referring to coordinates multiplied by 100).

By allowing any self-defined function that is written in C to be linked with a gesture description, FINGER can be extended for application specific purposes (4.3). There is already a printf function implemented for producing output after a gesture's recognition.

The function printf uses as its parameters the variables that were introduced while the gesture was reognized. Specifically, segments and basics are named. By appending these names and seperating by a dot, a specific unit of the movement as well as the starting point and the end point of a segment can be named and referred to in a clause (7). (In addition to variable names we use also a preprocessor that expands predeclared names into (mostly numeric) constants).

3. Example

Fig. 3 describes an example of a partial description for a kind of angles. Since exploration of a large canvas is a central problem for blind users and the method of using scroll bars doesn't work very easily due to the lack of overview, an angle formed with a finger can express in which direction the user wants to scoll. In addition, we want to calculate, as a parameter of the gesture, the distance of the scolling motion from the steepness of the angle .

The description starts with the initpattern. We want the user to tip at the upper left corner. That is, we are waiting for a segment produced by the left hand when touching the display (line 4) and we are waiting until the display is released (line 5). In line 6 the position of the segment at the upper left corner is verified. The initpattern declares the possible command patterns that can follow. An angle is either going upwards or downwards. In addition we could make command patterns for an angle to the left or to the right.

The basic gesture for an angle consists of two legs that are symmetrical to each other formed without lifting the finger in between. The basic in line 9 requires

```
01  #define lhand 1
02  #define rhand 2
03  initpattern:
04          segment(lhand) S
05          startsegment(sensor_up, lhand)
06          ((0,0) ?= S.START with 1000)
07          commandpatterns: up, down
08  end
09  basic angle:
10          segment(rhand) LEG1
11          segment(rhand) LEG1
12          startsegment(sensor_up, wait, rhand)
13  end
14  commandpattern up:
15          basic ANG type angle
16          ANG.LEG1.START < ANG.LEG1.STOP
17          command: printf("go backward by %d",
18          10*(ANG.LEG1.STOP.Y-ANG.LEG1.START.Y)/
19          (ANG.LEG1.STOP.X-ANG.LEG1.START.X))
20  end
21  commandpattern down:
22          basic ANG type angle
23          ANG.LEG1.START > ANG.LEG1.STOP
24          command: printf("go forward by %d",
25          10*(ANG.LEG1.STOP.Y-ANG.LEG1.START.Y)/
26          (ANG.LEG1.STOP.X-ANG.LEG1.START.X))
27  end
```

Fig. 3: Declarations for angles

two (named) segments to be produced and is waiting until the finger is released.

Since both commandpatterns are very similiar we concentrate now on command pattern down. In line 22, the basic angle is called. We name this element of the movement ANG. To seperate this command pattern from others, a test on the y-coordinate ensures that the first leg (ANG.LEG1) goes downwards. The command pattern results in a printf-function that calculates the steepness of the first leg and prints the message "goes forward by" plus the rounded value of the steepness.

4. Gesture recognition

We have implemented a compiler on the basis of lex and yacc for descriptions of gestures that transforms the clauses into state transitions.

The process of recognizing the gesture from our previous example is illustrated in Fig. 4. As mentioned earlier, the segments are recognized by a segment recognition algorithm that calculates the starting- and the endpoint of movements as well as the length of the segment. The data in Fig. 4 corresponds to a downward angle. Therefore the gesture recognition finds that the conditions for the basic ANG are fullfilled. Only the command pattern down can be processed further on after calling the basic of type angle, since the test on the cordinates holds in command pattern up not true.

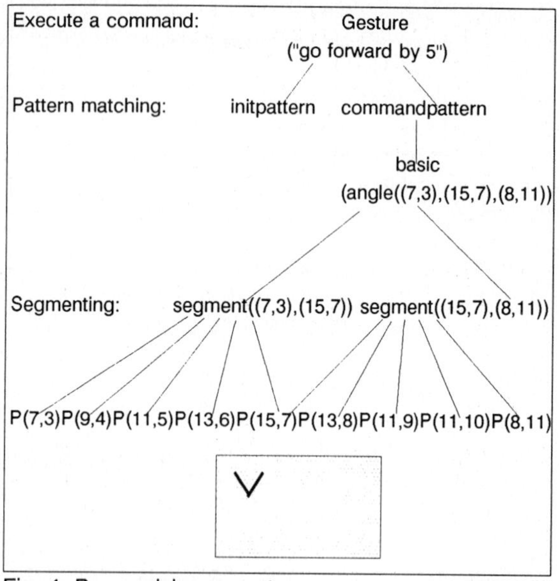

Fig. 4: Recognizing a gesture

The gesture recognition algorithm can be compared to an Augmented Transition Network (ATN) (see Woods (1970)). Fig. 5 shows the translation of our example in section 3 into an ATN. The starting state is the initpattern. All clauses of the initpattern make up the subnet that has to be processed on the transition to the command patterns. The clauses of the command pattern (terminated by the clause after the keyword command:) have to be processed in a subnet on the transition to the initpattern. The comparison of the gesture recognition algorithm with an ATN makes clear that basic gestures are similar subnets to that of a command pattern. Additionally, by naming this subnet we can call a basic gesture recursively.

At the time of the state transitions, we have to take care of the bindings from variable names that we introduce to the data for the segments since there can be backtracking necessary in our breadth-first search of possible clauses. Along with the state transitions, we build therefore a dynamically linked list of variable names. The names of the variables are not resolved into simple addresses since calculations on the values of variable names can only be done by determining from the linked list the appropiate instance of a variable. For details of the heap management of states see Wetzel (1988).

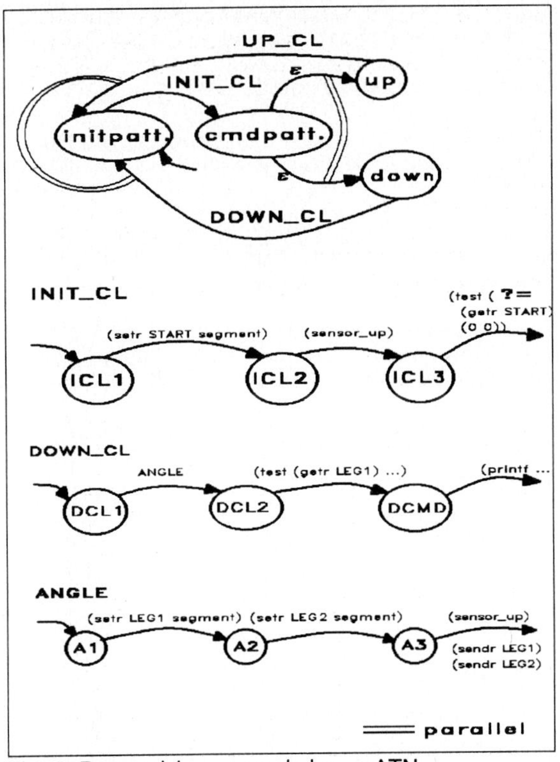

Fig. 5: Recognizing an angle by an ATN

5. Extending the example

We have found that the practical use of our example in section 3 is limited since the segment recognition algorithm introduces a new segment whenever there is a change in direction of the movement. By redefining the basic gesture for an angle, FINGER can cope with varieties in the legs of an angle without interfering with the description of the command patterns.

Fig. 6 gives a recursive definition of what a leg is as well as a new definition of an angle that omits intermediate points, if some additional segments were found. By introducing a recursive control structure, we can postpone the decision whether a new segment is part of the current leg or already part of the new leg to the clause that actually tests it. It is not clear to the author if a truely non-tail recursion is appropiate to any human gesture.

6. Conclusion

Parameterized gestures open-up an additional input channel in man-computer-communication. A gesture is a kind of interaction that does not rely on immediate feedback to the user. The language FINGER allows, in a modular way, describing gestures and defining a resultant operation that links the gesture recognition algorithm with an application program. The implementation of the gesture recognition algorithm uses state transitions that are checked in parallel. Even if the terminal elements of FINGER are now segments from two 2D pointing devices the syntax can easily be extended to deal with more pointing devices that even work in 3D-space.

```
basic angle:
        segment(rhand) LEG1
        (steep := 10*(LEG1.STOP.Y-LEG1.START.Y)/
                (LEG1.STOP.X-LEG1.START.X))
        basic FINDLEG type LEG
end
basic LEG:
        segment(rhand) TEMP
        (newsteep := 10*(TEMP.STOP.Y-TEMP.START.Y)/
                (TEMP.STOP.X-TEMP.START.X))
        alternative /* not equal within range */
                (steep ?!= newsteep with 2)
                LEG2:=TEMP
        alternative /* equal within range */
                (steep ?= newsteep with 2)
                basic FINDLEG type LEG
        alternative
                startsegment(sensor_up, wait, rhand)
end
```

Fig. 6: Improving the description for an angle

7. Acknowledgements

I wish to thank Prof. Dr. R. Gunzenhäuser and Dr. W. Schweikhardt who made this project possible.

Th. Knopik and Dr. Th. Strothotte contributed to this article through a critical review of the first draft. I wish to thank them as well as P.Wetzel and G.Wahl for the ground work with the pin-matrix device.

8. References

Blass, T.; Freedman, N.; Steingart, I. (1974). Body movement and verbal encoding in the congenitally blind. Perceptual and Motor Skills, 39, 279-293.

Bliss, J.C.; Katcher, M.H.; Rogers, C.H.; Shepard, R.P. (1970). Optical-to-tactile image conversion for the blind. IEEE Transactions on Man-Machine-Systems, 11, 58-64

Buxton, W. (1989). The pragmatics of haptic input. Conference on Human Factors in Computing Systems (CHI Tutorial 16). ACM, 8.1.

Hill, D.R.; Grieb, Chr. (1988). Substitution for a Restricted Visual Channel in Multimodal Computer-Human Dialogue. IEEE Transactions on Systems, Man, and Cybernetics. 18(2), 285-403.

Gaver, W.W. (1989). The Sonic Finder: An interface that uses auditory icons. Human Computer Interaction, 4, 67-94.

Schweikhardt, W. (1984). Representing Videotex-pages to the Blind. In Proceedings of Third Annual Workshop on Computers and the Handicapped, IEEE, 23-29.

Weber, G. (1987). Gestures as a means for the blind to interact with a computer. In Human-Computer-Interaction INTERACT '87 (Eds. H.-J. Bullinger and B. Shackel). Elsevier Science Publishers: North Holland, 593-595.

Weber, G. (1989a). Reading and pointing - modes of interaction for blind users. In Information Processing '89 (Ed. G.X. Ritter). Elsevier Science Publishers: North Holland, 535-540.

Weber, G. (1989b). Interaktive Dialogtechniken für blinde Rechnerbenutzer. Dissertation. Universität Stuttgart.

Wetzel, P. (1988). Recognizing gestures in a dialogue system (in German)., Diplomarbeit, Institut für Informatik, Universität Stuttgart.

Wolf, C.G.; Morrel-Samuels, P. (1987). The use of hand-drawn gestures for text editing. International Journal of Man-Machine Studies, 27, 91-102.

Woods, W.A. (1970). Transition network grammars for natural language analysis. Communications of the ACM, 13(10), 591-606.

Human–Computer Interaction – INTERACT '90
D. Diaper et al. (Editors)
Elsevier Science Publishers B.V. (North-Holland)

A Virtual Stereographic Pointer for a Real Three Dimensional Video World

Paul Milgram* **& David Drascic**
Dept. of Industrial Engineering, University of Toronto,
Toronto, Ontario, Canada M5S 1A4

Julius Grodski¶
Defence and Civil Institute of Environmental Medicine (DCIEM)
P.O. Box 2000, Downsview, Ontario, Canada M3M 3B9

A brief overview is given of a new display concept, involving superimposition of computer stereographic images onto a real world stereoscopic video display. The aim of the current system is to supply the user with a computer generated "virtual probe", for exploring, making measurements, and enhancing images within a real three dimensional video world. Development of the system is discussed, together with its capabilities and a number of practical considerations for its use. Although originally developed as an enhancement for telerobotic control only, use of the technology is predicted for a wide variety of novel multimedia applications.

1. INTRODUCTION

This paper offers a brief overview of a new display "hypermedium". The system which we are presenting involves the merging of two important technologies, *stereoscopic video* and *stereoscopic computer graphics*. Each of these display technologies has been widely recognised as beneficial in different domains: the former most frequently for operators of remotely controlled manipulators and vehicles, remote surveillance systems, etc., and the latter for users of CAD and medical imaging workstations, microbiologists, crystallographers, etc. The two technologies have, however, seldom been combined into one integral display system, whereby the synergistic benefits of both can be put to significant practical use.

What we are presenting in this paper is a computer generated "virtual probe", for exploring, making measurements, and enhancing images within a real three dimensional video world. Utilising the concept of *"virtual reality"*, we have created a low cost, personal computer based display system, whose aim is to provide an observer with both a high quality stereoscopic video image of a particular world, as well as a tool for interactively probing that world and enhancing its visualisation, using superimposed computer stereographic images. In using the term "virtual reality", we mean that, by taking special care to account for the physical parameters of our video display system, our computer generated virtual images appear to be *really physically present* within the video world being viewed and to move about, *in three dimensions*, as would real physical objects in that world.

In the following we give a brief description of the development of the system, an overview of its architecture, and a summary of some of the practical insights which we have gathered thus far. Our discussion of system capabilities and of future applications should be of special interest to the human-computer interaction community, as we touch there on some uses of the technology which we believe to be novel and potentially very useful for a variety of practical multimedia applications.

2. BACKGROUND AND SYSTEM OBJECTIVES

The principle underlying both stereovideo (SV) and computer stereographic (SG) technologies is *stereopsis*, the perception of three dimensionality due to the differences in an observer's retinal images which occur when viewing a scene *binocularly*. Both SV and SG technologies operate by channelling left and right eye views of a scene or object separately to a viewer's left and right eye respectively. If suitably presented, the two images will be fused into a single image in the observer's brain and will be perceived as being three dimensional. A short review of properties of both SV and SG display systems has been included in Milgram et al. (1989). A thorough treatment of the theory of stereoscopy can be found in Lipton (1982). Two recommended general reviews of stereoscopic display technology are those of Lipton (1982) and of Lane (1982).

Development of the system presented in this paper derived from our research into user issues related to closed circuit stereoscopic video (CCSV) technology (Drascic et al, 1989) and from our research on computer graphic depth cues (Sollenberger & Milgram, 1989). Especially in the former domain, it was clear that, although users of CCSV systems benefit from a greatly enhanced ability to discriminate *relative* distances and depths, they are still somewhat limited in their ability to make *absolute* judgements of distance and depth. That is, whereas it might be easy for an observer to determine that object A is farther away from the cameras than object B, for example, it is generally more difficult to estimate *how far away* the two objects are from the cameras or from each other. The ability to make such estimates can be of importance for tasks involving remote surveillance, assembly, telerobotic path planning, obstacle avoidance, etc.

In order for an operator to determine absolute world coordinates of relevant objects in a real three dimensional world, therefore, essentially three options are available:

- the human observer can estimate object coordinates directly;
- use can be made of (stereoscopic) machine vision technology to make accurate measurements of object location, using feature detection, triangulation, etc.;

* milgram@gpu.utcs.utoronto.ca
 drascic@ecf.utoronto.ca
¶ jul@zorac.dciem.dnd.ca

- use can be made of our knowledge of the geometrical and optical characteristics of the CCSV system to superimpose a computer generated pointing device, calibrated in real world units, and then rely on the human's *relative* depth acuity for pointer positioning.

To evaluate the first approach, one must understand the difference between relative and absolute distance judgement using stereo displays. The disparity between the two perspective views provided by a conventional dual camera CCSV system allows one directly to perceive differences in distances between points in the longitudinal (z) direction relative to the cameras (i.e. into the screen), without having to rely on *monoscopic* depth cues (Lipton, 1982; Milgram et al, 1989). In general, the larger the separation in viewpoints, the greater one's discriminative acuity in the z direction. However, there is no easy way for the observer to estimate *accurately* how far away any particular object is -- in metres, millimetres, or whatever absolute units are suitable to the domain-- unless some well known anchor, or comparison point, is available, to turn the task into a *relative* judgement task. Alternatively, if an object being viewed is already well known to the observer, its absolute distance from the cameras can often be estimated fairly accurately on the basis of its apparent size; however, this type of cue can clearly not be used for unfamiliar or unknown objects.

The second option listed is not only technically more complex, and thus expensive, but is still in need of a means for the human to communicate to the computing elements which points or objects in the visual scene are of interest. The third approach was therefore chosen because it was judged the most feasible option given current technology. Clearly, some combination of the second and third approaches, to make efficient use (according to traditional human factors principles) of both human and machine strengths, is an important future option.

3. SYSTEM CAPABILITIES

An illustration of the capabilities of the present system is given in Figure 1. The reader is requested to imagine that this scene has been generated with a (dual camera) stereoscopic video system and is being viewed stereoscopically, as described under System Hardware. The tree, the bench, the dustbin, the rock and the box represent "live" objects, as seen on a television monitor. The triangular, or filled "V" shaped, virtual pointer is generated by the graphics computer and appears to the observer as "floating" among the real objects in the video world. The observer is able to move this pointer about with ease, in real-time, using a three degree-of-freedom input device.

The objective behind this capability, as outlined above, is to allow the observer to obtain accurate estimates of the spatial coordinates of designated points relative to the remote camera system. Under normal circumstances, with a conventional *monoscopic* video system, the observer would perceive the tree in Figure 1 as being behind the bench (due to the (monoscopic) occlusion cue) and the dustbin also as being further away than the bench (geometric perspective cue). The box is evidently located near the centre of the bench. With our *stereoscopic* video system, the observer would have a much clearer impression of these same cues; that is, s/he would more easily perceive how far away, in a *relative* sense, the various objects are from each other. If required to estimate the locations of the objects and distances from each other in *absolute* units, however, the observer would still have some difficulty, due to the paucity of reference standards.

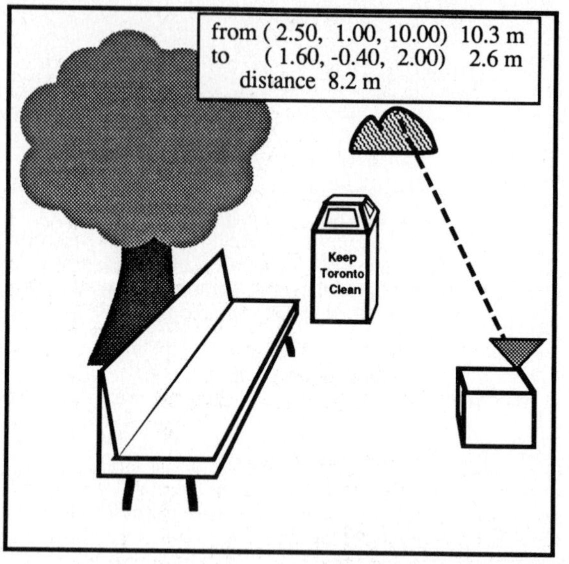

Figure 1 Simulated video scene with superimposed graphic cursor, illustrating "tape measure" option.

The software which has been written to generate the pointer is calibrated in absolute real-world units. In other words, the graphic image is not simply overlaid on the monitor and moved about in relative screen units. Rather, the positions on the screen of the pointer images are computed as a function of the SV hardware parameters. Consequently, the virtual pointer will always appear to be at the same location in the real-world scene as it would if it were actually present in that scene. It will also have the appropriate dimensions as if it were at that location in the scene. Furthermore, the computations to generate these images are carried out in real-time. As shown in Figure 1, the real-world pointer (x,y,z) coordinates can be displayed as a (real-time) readout on the screen as well.

The particular form of the pointer shown in the rendition of Figure 1 is not the only shape which is possible. Clearly, the number of choices is unlimited. We have experimented thus far also with an open V-shaped pointer, an inverted arrow, and a set of cross-hairs.

A particularly important option of the system is illustrated in Figure 1 by the dashed line running from the centre of the rock to the far right hand corner of the box on the ground. We refer to this as the *"tape-measure"* option. In this case, the point on the rock would have been specified by the operator using the pointer. After clicking the pointer at that position with the controller switch, the observer can then "drag" a (virtual) line along a three dimensional trajectory through the video picture to the second point, on the box. In addition to both sets of (x,y,z) coordinates, the readout on the screen, in this case, will also give the absolute distance between the two points.

Another capability, which will be especially useful in telerobotics, involves fixing the starting point of a superimposed line at a specified location. In that case, as the pointer is moved about, the dashed line which follows it appears as a sort of "virtual trajectory", indicating clearly the path which would be followed if a teleoperated vehicle or manipulator, for example, were to move in a straight line in that direction. This could be carried out in steps, if required, to help an operator plan the path of a manœuvre prior to its actual execution, such as might be the case for controlling a remotely operated vehicle in the presence of large time delays. Avoidance of obstacles is another case for which such a capability would obviously be of potential advantage.

A further application along these lines would involve use of a superimposed path to indicate to the operator the predicted trajectory of any projectile which might be launched from the remote system. This could have significant safety implications, especially if data were available on the estimated "spread" characteristics of the projectile. This information could then be displayed to the operator as a predicted three dimensional "cone of danger" emanating from the telerobot's weaponry.

4. SYSTEM HARDWARE

A block diagram summary of the system developed is shown in Figure 2. The operating principle behind both the stereoscopic video system and the stereoscopic computer graphic system is *alternating-field*, or *time-multiplexed,* stereoscopy, which currently is the most economical and easily implemented method of presenting three dimensional, full colour stereoscopic images, using standard display hardware (Lane, 1982). This class of stereo-pair displays involves rapidly alternating left- and right-eye viewpoint images on a video or computer monitor. The observer views the screen through an electronically-driven shuttering device, which alternately blocks and unblocks the view of the display from each eye, in synchrony with the alternating display images. The result is that the left eye is blocked whenever the right eye image is displayed and unblocked whenever the left eye image is presented, and vice versa.

The principle underlying the implementation of alternating-field stereoscopic displays is illustrated in Figure 3. Note that, although the image sources in the figure are labelled, for video applications, as Left Camera and Right Camera, these could equivalently be considered as respective left and right image buffers for computer graphic applications. For interlaced raster scan displays, which are used in most video and a few computer display systems, the method involves alternating odd (O) and even (E) *fields* (i.e. half-*frames*), using standard video scanning rates. The resulting signal shown exiting from the Alternating Field Combining Circuit is a conventional video signal, identical in form to the two entering (LO, LE, LO, etc. and RO, RE, RO, etc.), with the distinction that the fields making up the combined signal are alternating between left and right image sources (LO, RE, LO, etc.). When using vector scan or non-interlaced displays, which are characteristic of many high quality graphic workstations, the alternating field method involves alternating *complete* left (L) and right (R) display image *frames*. For the system reported here, interlaced NTSC raster scanning was used for both the video and computer graphics portions.

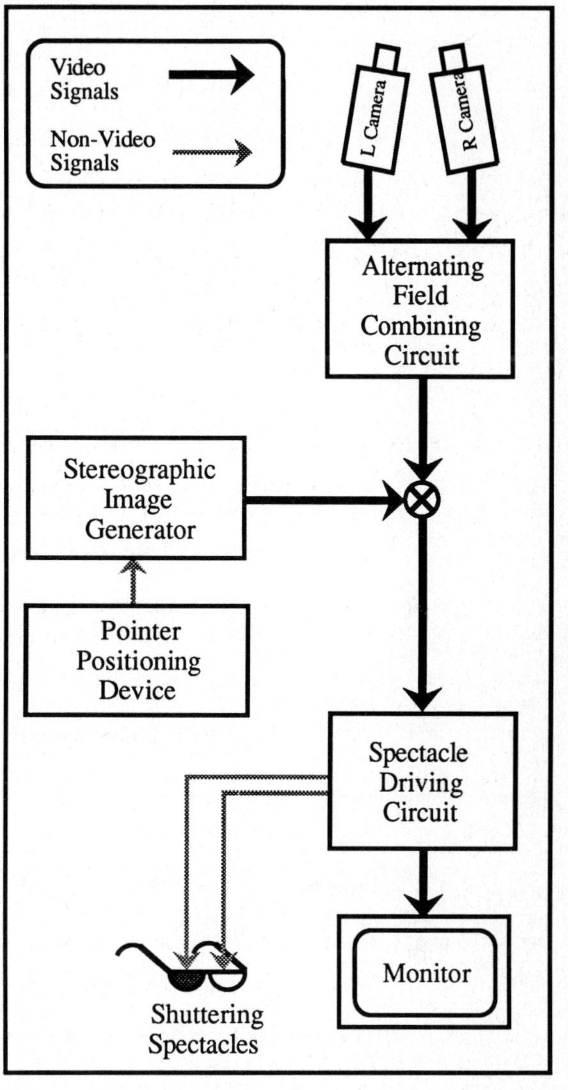

Figure 2 Block diagram of SV+SG display system.

In both Figure 2 and 3, the viewing device is illustrated symbolically as a pair of shuttering spectacles. A review of various choices of shuttering spectacle technologies is given in (Milgram & van der Horst, 1986). In our system we have used both *light-scattering* liquid crystal spectacles, whose properties are discussed in detail in (Milgram, 1987), as well as a number of *light polarising* liquid crystal spectacles. We have found that light scattering spectacles have the largest degree of light transmission of all devices reviewed (approximately 95% in the open state). This factor can be of potentially critical importance for poor quality video conditions or low ambient camera lighting levels, which are characteristic of many telerobotic operations in the field. Under standard laboratory lighting conditions, both methods have so far been found to be quite satisfactory.

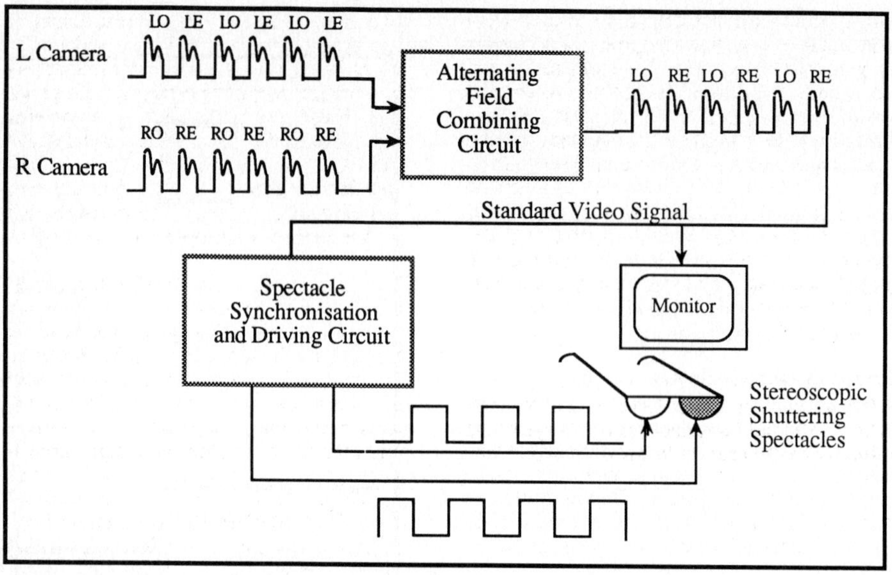

Figure 3 Schematic illustration of alternating-field stereoscopic display system.

The stereoscopic *video* (SV) component of the system in Figure 2 is shown as being driven by the dual camera plus Alternating Field Combining Circuit subsystem. The *stereographic* (SG) component comprises the Stereographic Image Generator plus Pointer Positioning Device subsystem. The combining of the two (SV+SG) occurs within a video keying device, represented here by the summation module in the centre of the block diagram. Clearly, both subsystems must share a common monitor.

In our system, we have used two Hitachi VKC150 colour CCD cameras (rated at 340 lines of resolution) as the basis of the video system, and an Amiga 2500 microcomputer as the basis of the computer display system. The monitor for both subsystems is the Amiga's Commodore 1084 colour monitor, which is capable of displaying either RGB or NTSC video. An Amiga 2300 genlock unit, capable of mixing Amiga generated graphic images with the NTSC video signal from the cameras, is the key component which allows the two subsystems to operate together. A MicroSpeed FastTrap 3D Model 8735 Trackball is used as the interactive pointer positioning device. All software was written in Manx "C".

5. ALTERNATIVE HARDWARE OPTIONS

Before expanding on practical considerations, it is worthwhile to review alternative hardware options for the SV+SG system.

Perhaps most relevant is to consider whether it is indeed necessary to use the Amiga computer as the central platform. At the time our development programme started, there were essentially no reasonable alternatives offered by other computer systems to enable construction of a relatively low-cost SV+SG system. (Our original system comprised an Amiga 500 with a Mimetics AmiGen genlock unit.) Although great strides in multimedia technology have been made since then, as reviewed by Robinson (1990) in a recent survey of Commodore, Apple, IBM/Intel and Sony / Philips systems, it still appears that none of the others offer the flexibility of the Amiga at comparable prices.

Alternative options are certainly available with higher end computer graphic workstations and peripherals. Among the advantages achievable there are:

- non-interlaced displays, which will eliminate the halving of the vertical resolution that is a necessary consequence of using alternating-field stereoscopy with interlaced display hardware;
- higher resolution graphics;
- higher speed graphic update rates;
- flicker-free displays, using increased equivalent scan rates.

Elaborating on the latter point, one of the unavoidable consequences of our alternating field technique is the presence of a noticeable flicker. This is due to the fact that (in North America) each eye is being stimulated with light at a frequency of 30 Hz (1/60 s blocked, 1/60 s unblocked)[1], a rate which, under normal circumstances, is below the human's critical fusion frequency (CFF) for flickering light stimulation. As noted, however, "frequency doubled" field-sequential systems have been introduced into the commercial market in recent years, based on either interlaced or non-interlaced methods (e.g. Lipton & Meyer, 1984). At present, due to the cost of specialised electronics, such systems are substantially more expensive than the standard NTSC or PAL interlaced methods which, as stated above, make use of "off-the-shelf" video equipment. A less expensive remedy for the problem is simply to reduce the effective intensity of the display monitor.

It is obvious that flicker and resolution reduction problems can be eliminated completely by using separate display monitors for each eye. This is essentially what is done with many head-mounted display (HMD) systems (e.g. Fisher et al., 1988; Foley, 1987). Clearly, the incremental costs of such systems, in terms of display hardware, head tracking, eye tracking, etc., will be significant.

We have not dwelt here upon the particular video cameras used, since essentially any reasonable quality commercial cameras should be satisfactory. The only necessary constraint is that it must be possible to *genlock* them to a common synchronisation source. Solid state (CCD), high resolution, colour, auto-iris, lightness, compactness and ruggedness are, of course, all properties worth having.

Finally, we have not yet investigated the full range of feasible three degree of freedom pointer positioning devices. The FastTrap device, which comprises a two degree of freedom trackball, a one degree of freedom thumbwheel and three buttons, although quite rudimentary, has proven to be reliable and adequate in the meantime.

We maintain in conclusion that, on the basis of cost, flexibility, and effectiveness, our prototype dual Hitachi camera, Amiga-based, alternating field interlaced SV+SG system is quite likely optimally configured in terms of today's technology.

6. PRACTICAL CONSIDERATIONS

The practical considerations involved in setting up a system such as that described here must not be taken lightly. Although it is fairly straightforward to set up an operating stereovideo (SV) system which will add some impression of depth to the scene being displayed, it is also fairly easy to neglect those design factors which make the difference between a "good" SV system and an "unsatisfactory" one. The same holds true for computer stereographics (SG) technology, although the design factors are somewhat different. To some extent both SV and SG technologies on their own are rather forgiving, because the human binocular visual perceptual system is very robust in correcting "errors" which can result from asymmetries or inconsistencies that have been allowed to creep into the system[2]. This robustness is somewhat diminished, however, when the two technologies are combined.

Other than *horizontal parallax*, which provides the depth information for stereopsis, all other asymmetries are undesirable. The fundamental design criterion, therefore, is straightforward: to endeavour to make the two images *as similar as possible*. According to Lipton (1982, Ch. 6) the following important asymmetries should be eliminated in stereovideo:

- Illumination Asymmetries: These are caused by differences in illumination, iris settings, and electronic gains between the two cameras.
- Aberration Asymmetries: These are caused by differences in optics, focus and CCD chip characteristics between the two cameras.
- Geometrical Asymmetries: These are caused by differences in focal length and linearity between the two cameras, or by cameras that are not co-planar or do not converge symmetrically, resulting in misalignment of corresponding image points.
- Chromatic Asymmetries: These are caused by differences in colour transformations between the two cameras.

Of the above, we have found that eliminating *geometrical asymmetries* is the most serious problem, especially when stereographics (SG) are introduced. This was actually quite an interesting finding, since we had already noted that the human visual system is able to compensate for rather large misalignments, such as vertical disparities or differential tilting of the images, with stereovideo alone. However, if it should happen that the cameras, and thus the video images, are misaligned, but the left and right graphic images are *not* misaligned, the brain can have some trouble dealing with this difference in disparities, particularly in situations where the SG image is located in the vicinity of a real-world image. In other words, the robustness found with the SV system alone appears to weaken when *both* video misalignments and graphic "nonmisalignments" are present!

The final practical consideration that we deal with here is the problem of *calibrating* the virtual pointer in real world units. As outlined above, our system has been developed such that any graphic image drawn on the screen is scaled according to its equivalent location in real video space, which provides us with a continuous direct readout of (x,y,z) coordinates. This means that, if a particular object is drawn graphically and then moved to the same equivalent location in (x,y,z) space as the corresponding real world object, the two should coincide exactly on the screen. Because space limitations preclude any description here of details of the calculations we use, we restrict ourselves only to listing the physical parameters which enter into those calculations:

- camera separation,
- camera convergence angle,
- alignment of camera optics,
- focal lengths of the lenses,
- positions of the centroids of the lenses,
- mapping betwen video CCD chips and computer display.

Suffice it to say that accurate determination of each of these factors can be quite difficult.

An interesting phenomenon is encountered whenever the *virtual* pointer is caused to pass *through* an object or surface in the real video world. Originally, it was not clear what would happen when this situation would be encountered. What we found was that whenever the pointer is in *front* of another surface, the observer is able to shift attention easily back and forth from one to the other. However, when the pointer goes *behind* that surface, this creates a contradiction between the binocular disparity cue and the apparent monoscopic occlusion cue, resulting in a breakdown of the pointer into a double image; that is, the eyes no longer fuse the left and right images. This phenomenon can be looked upon as a positive feature of the system, which provides an additional cue about the position of the pointer relative to other objects. In other words, if the pointer can no longer be fused as it approaches another object, it must therefore have gone behind that object.

7. CONCLUSION

As stated earlier, we have limited our research thus far to the domain of telerobotics. It is nevertheless quite obvious that an exciting range of other applications await. As a tool for probing and making measurements in any SV world, the current simple SG pointer is quite sufficient. We expect that SV+SG technology in its present form will also prove a useful tool in such areas as cooperative and group work, telescience, microsurgery, cellular physiology, multimedia navigation, etc. At present we are carrying out a series of initial psychophysical experiments to determine the accuracy with which one is actually able to position the SG pointer relative to real world objects in three dimensional space.

In order to extend the SV+SG technology to a broader range of applications, it will be necessary to generate SG images of objects which are more complex than the simple pointer which we now have. That capability, which is also currently under development in our laboratory, will allow us to superimpose three dimensional *wireframe* SG images onto a real SV scene. That will allow us to expand into such applications as stereovideo image enhancement for telerobotics, (landscape) architecture, anthropometric simulation and workplace evaluation.

In conclusion, we emphasise that SV+SG technology should not be looked upon solely as an attractive enhancement of existing video and computer graphic display systems, but as a means of fundamentally extending the way in which we currently use those two media. We predict that, as the SV+SG hypermedium is further developed, significant new opportunities will open up for desktop interaction with remote video worlds, teleoperation and control, and simulation of virtual reality.

ACKNOWLEDGEMENT

The work described here was carried out under contract W7711-7-7009/01-SE with Supply and Services Canada for the Defence and Civil Institute of Environmental Medicine, Downsview, Ontario, Canada.

FOOTNOTES

[1] Note that with other interlaced video standards, most notably PAL, the corresponding switching frequency is 25 frames/s or 50 fields (half-frames)/s.

[2] An extreme example of this is that a number of earlier experimental investigations into the efficacy of stereoscopic video displays are suspected to have been carried out with the left and right eye camera views *reversed*, without the subjects ever having realised this!

REFERENCES

Drascic, D., Milgram, P. & Grodski, J. (1989). Learning effects in telemanipulation with monoscopic vs stereoscopic remote viewing. Proceedings of 1989 International Conf. on Systems, Man, & Cybernetics, Boston, MA.

Fisher, S.S., Wenzel, E.M., Coler, C. & McGreevy, M.W. (1988). Virtual interface environment workstations. Proceedings of 32nd Annual Meeting of Human Factors Society, 91-95.

Foley, J.D. (1987). Interfaces for advanced computing. Scientific American, Oct. 1987, 127-135.

Lane, B. (1982). Stereoscopic displays. Proc. SPIE, Vol. 367, 20-32.

Lipton, L. (1982). Foundations of the Stereoscopic Cinema: A Study in Depth. van Nostrand Reinhold: NY.

Lipton, L. & Meyer, L. (1984). A flicker-free field-sequential stereoscopic video system. SMPTE Journal, 93(11), 1047-1051.

Milgram, P., Drascic, D. & Grodski, J. (1989). Stereoscopic video + superimposed computer stereographics: Applications in teleoperation. In Proceedings 2nd Canadian Workshop on Military Robotic Applications (Eds. Grodski, J. & Farooq, M.F.). Kingston, Ontario, Canada Aug. 1989.

Milgram, P. (1987). A spectacle-mounted liquid-crystal tachistoscope. Behavior Research Methods, Instruments, & Computers, 19(5), 449-456.

Milgram, P. & van der Horst, R. (1986). Alternating-field stereoscopic displays using light scattering liquid crystal spectacles. Displays: Technology & Applications, 7(2), 67-72.

Robinson, P. (1990). The four multimedia gospels. Byte, Feb. 1990, 203-212.

Sollenberger, R.L. & Milgram, P. (1989). Stereoscopic computer graphics for neurosurgery. In Designing and Using Human-Computer Interfaces and Knowledge Based Systems. (Eds. G. Salvendy & M.J. Smith). Elsevier Science Publishers: Amserdam. pp. 294-301.

Human–Computer Interaction – INTERACT '90
D. Diaper et al. (Editors)
Elsevier Science Publishers B.V. (North-Holland)

Force-to-Motion Functions for Pointing

Joseph D. Rutledge Ted Selker
IBM T.J.Watson Research Center, Yorktown N.Y. 10598
SELKER@ibm.com

A pointing device which can be operated from typing position avoids time loss and distraction. We have built and investigated force-sensitive devices for this purpose. The critical link is the force-to-motion mapping. We have found principles which enable a force joystick to match the function and approach the performance of a mouse in pure pointing tasks, and to best it in mixed tasks, such as editing. Examples take into account task, user strategy and perceptual-motor limitations.

1. INTRODUCTION

Various workers over the past two decades have investigated and compared a variety of analogue devices for use in computer interface pointing tasks [1, 4]. The usual conclusion has been that the mouse has the advantage over alternatives, and the current commercial fashion seems to agree.

We have been intrigued with the 1.5 [2] or so seconds required to make an excursion from the keyboard to the mouse and return; in applications which intermix pointing and typing, this can be significant. Also, the mouse has other inherent disadvantages, especially in environments which provide restricted space or where dangling wires or loose bits of equipment are a hazard.

Our thesis is that it is possible to point efficiently without moving the hands from the normal touch typing home position. This requires locating the pointing device either in the immediate vicinity of the J or F keys (the index finger being rather clearly the finger of choice), or below the space bar, convenient to the thumbs. We first investigated the use of the J or F keys themselves, to serve for both pointing and typing. This requires that the user tell the computer which use is intended. A number of mode switch possibilities are available, but after preliminary experiments we concluded that the cognitive load of making the switch was serious, and shifted attention to a miniature joy-stick, located between the G and H keys in "no-hands land" where it does not interfere with normal typing. This POINTING STICK is the subject of the studies reported here.

The constraints of space in the keyboard eliminate the kind of position-to-position mapping used for the mouse - hence an isometric or force joystick. We could map force applied to the joystick to the velocity of the cursor, to its position, or perhaps to some combination. We report here on the first choice, the conventional rate joystick. The function relating force to velocity is critical to the performance of the Pointing Stick, and leads to the principle results reported here.

The force joystick has a long history of investigation and use [2]. It has been found that pointing times could be expected to be perhaps 20% slower than for a mouse performing the same tasks. Another concern is the "feel" - the subjective impression of exact control of the cursor, and that its movements are the "natural" response to actions.

Many people find pointing with the position of a mouse natural. Can pointing with a rate joystick also feel natural? The rate joystick appears to have an immediate disadvantage here, since the most natural response to a hand motion (for many people) is a movement of proportional magnitude, independent of duration. An analogous discordance will be recalled by anyone who has taken the controls of a light aircraft for the first time - the aircraft responds to a control offset with a rate of change, not with a direct change. As in that case, we find that users very quickly become accustomed to the rate mode of response, and find it natural.

The less tangible aspect of "feel" is the positive control; here the force to motion function is critical. Good "feel" seems to correlate, up to a point, with the more easily measured speed of pointing tasks, especially with small targets.

This paper reports the result of an investigation of a class of force-to-motion functions (***transfer functions***) and their effect on the speed of several experimental pointing tasks for our in-keyboard pointing device, the Pointing Stick.

2. TRANSFER FUNCTIONS

Our exploration of the space of transfer functions began with three families of mathematically simple mappings of force to cursor velocity - linear, parabolic, and a sigmoid parabolic, obtained by reflecting the initial part of the parabola in the point 1/2,1/2 $[(v = f), (v = f^2)$, and $(v = 2 \times f^2, 0 \leq f \leq 1/2;$ $v = 2 \times (1/2 - (1 - f)^2, 1/2 \leq f \leq 1; v = 1, f > 1)]$. Force f and velocity v have scale factors (coefficients), making each of these a 2-parameter family of functions. From experience with these functions, we arrived at the following conjectures:

1. A 'solid' feel, that a point can be held, requires a 'dead band' near zero force, in which the cursor does not move, even if the finger is not perfectly steady.

2. Pointing at small targets requires accurate control of low speed motion - one pixel at a time must be possible. This needs to be done without excess strain in fine motor control, hence the slope of the function at low speed should be low.

3. For long-distance cursor movements, high speed is required. However, we found that when eye-tracking became inaccurate, overall speed was reduced. A high-speed dash off the screen, or to somewhere distant from the target, is counter-productive. In less extreme form, one has the impression of playing golf - a long-distance, partially controlled 'drive', followed by "now where is it - oh, there", then perhaps another, shorter shot, recovery, and finally a low-speed 'putt'. This suggests that a limitation of maximum speed to the eye-tracking limit will be desirable.

4. As a final touch, users like to feel that they can make the cursor dash across the screen almost instantly, and there may be occasions when one wants to reach the opposite edge and start again from there. To accommodate this, we add a steep rise near the top of the force scale. This probably adds little if anything to speed of performance, but it does no damage, and seems to increase acceptance.

Of the simple functions, the sigmoid parabolic seems the most promising, according to the conjectures. This was borne out in informal experiments. However, its behavior near zero was less than 'solid'. The addition of a 'dead slow' plateau suggested itself, following a true dead band. This gives no motion at all for very low force, followed by a region of predictably slow motion somewhat independent of force, then followed by a rapid but smooth acceleration. Similarly, in the upper range, we would like to be able to easily 'cruise' just below the eye-hand-tracking limit, without danger of exceeding it. An upper plateau provides this, reached smoothly from the acceleration regime (Figure 1).

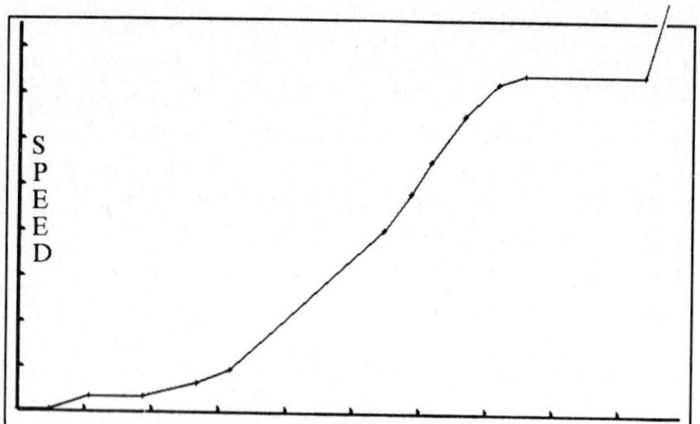

Figure 1. Transfer Function 2Plateau

The ordinate of this graph is force, the abscissa is cursor velocity, in percent of the corresponding scale factors. The velocity scale factor (multiplier of v in the above formulas) is 1500 pixels/second, or on our screen, 66 cm/second. The force scale factor (multiplier of f) was fixed for these experiments at a comfortable value of 225 grams; all sensitivity adjustments were done with the velocity scale.

3. APPARATUS

The Pointing Stick, as used in these experiments, is a steel rod of 2 mm diameter and 2 cm length, mounted on an acrylic base. A section near the base has orthogonal flats to which miniature semiconductor strain gages are bonded (Figure 2).

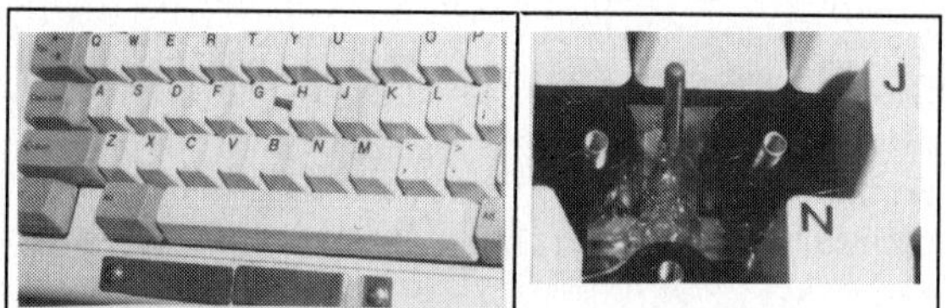
Figure 2. Pointing Stick

The base is glued on the sub-key surface of an IBM PS/2 keyboard, so that the stick protrudes approximately 4 mm above the surface of the keys in their rest position, between the G and H keycaps, which are relieved at their bases to allow space for it. The top is rounded to provide a comfortable fingertip grip. To provide mouse button signals, two microswitches and operating buttons are mounted nearly flush just below the space bar, convenient to the thumbs.

The keyboard was placed about 6 cm from the edge of the desk, allowing subjects to use it as a rest for the heel of the hand. The keyboard retains its normal function as the keyboard of a PS/2 Model 80 computer, which presented and recorded the experiments.

The strain gage outputs of the Pointing Stick are conditioned by an IBM PC/Portable computer, equipped with a LabMaster A/D, D/A, and clock board. The computer makes resistance measurements on the pointing stick gages at 10 millisecond intervals, and emits a set of four pulse trains simulating standard Hawley Mouse signals, for speeds from 2 to about 10,000 pixels/second. Either these signals or signals from a standard mouse feed the PS/2 via an interface box (supplied by Microsoft during 1988-89) converting to serial PS/2 format. The experimental display is an IBM Type 8514 PS/2 color display, displaying 640 pixels horizontal and 350 vertical. Parameters are specified and results given in a coordinate system with 0,0 at screen center and $-1000 \leq X \leq 1000$, $-750 \leq Y \leq 750$, or approximately 0.14 mm per unit. Software in the PC/Portable allows full generality in generating, modifying, and applying transfer functions. The mouse is a Microsoft InPort(tm) Mouse purchased during 1989.

4. EXPERIMENTAL PROCEDURE

Two related experimental procedures were used. In both, Subject is seated before the computer display and keyboard in normal typing position, hands on the keys. Either the Pointing Stick or the mouse may be used; if the mouse, it is located adjacent to the keyboard on the preferred side, on a foam pad at about the level of the top of the keyboard. After signing in and entering experimental parameters, Subject initiates a trial by pressing a key ("t"). At the end of the trial, a score is presented, and the experimenter may choose to commence another trial, present an average score for the most recent group of trials, change experimental parameters, or terminate the experiment. The content of the 'trial' depends on the particular experiment.

1. Target Shooting. Subject selects targets presented as circles of random size and position on the screen. The situation being abstracted here is that of a user engaged in a typing task interspersed with single pointing actions; a pointing action begins and ends with the hands in typing home position. The 'trial' consists of 10 repetitions of the following: a blank screen is presented, with the mouse cursor (arrow) somewhere on it. Subject presses the J key (F if left-handed). The arrow appears at screen center, and a target outline appears at a random position on the screen. Subject moves to the pointing device, brings the arrow to point within the target, and presses a 'mouse-button' (on the mouse if a mouse is in use, the button below the space bar if the Pointing Stick). A hit (splash) or miss (beep) is signaled by the computer.

For a hit, the target and splash symbol remain on the screen until Subject returns to the keyboard and presses the J or F key again; for a miss, the screen blanks, ready for the next shot. For each shot, six items are recorded: target position (X,Y), target size, and three times: the time from initial keypress to first pointer movement, to 'hit', and to keyboard return. Misses are generally excluded from the data in analysis. Subject identification, experimental parameters, transfer function in use, date and time, and any other relevant conditions are also recorded in the same file.

The targets are circles of diameter randomly chosen from a uniform distribution between limits specified as an experimental parameter (usually 20 and 100 screen units, corresponding to the range from one character to a representative icon). Targets which extend beyond the screen edges, or are within one diameter of the center, are excluded.

2. Maze Running. A field of targets is presented which requires a sequence of pointings of varying directions and distances. Immediately upon the initiation of a trial, the screen is blanked and a field of numerals is presented, with the arrow in screen center. The object is to select the numerals in numerical order. Initially "1" is highlighted; as soon as it is selected by pressing the appropriate 'mouse' button with the arrow within the highlight, the highlight moves on to "2", and so on. For two-digit numerals, only the first digit is highlighted. Misses (inappropriate button presses) are disrewarded with a brief low-pitched sound, and counted. Each numeral must be successfully selected before the subject can proceed. An *event* begins with one successful selection (or the beginning of the trial) and ends with the next. The duration of each event is recorded. When the last numeral has been selected, the trial ends and the total elapsed time and number of errors are reported.

The same maze is used for a series of runs, so that in place of the random pointings of the other experiment, the maze presents a fixed sequence of pointings which is quickly learned. The targets are of fixed size, and, most important for mouse - Pointing Stick comparisons, the keyboard is not involved at all - this is a pure pointing task.

5. SUBJECTS

Subjects were 6 men ages 22-30 employed as co-op students at the T.J. Watson Research Center. All were experienced and proficient mouse users, but, aside from video game experience, naive to the Pointing Stick or any similar device. Subjects performed the experiments in random order, until scores had settled (no significant difference between first and last 10 trials of a series of at least 40 trials (10 shots or 16 maze events per trial). Subjects reached different levels of proficiency, and comparisons are first within subject; those considered significant are consistent across subjects.

6. ANALYSIS

We can compare performance in our experiments in several ways. The simplest is to average measurements over enough trials for the target distance and size to average out. To see the effect of size or distance we can take a measurement as a function of the parameter in question, averaging out the other. Another option, used by previous authors [1] is to use the Fitts Difficulty Index, $DI = \log_2(D/S + .5)$, to collapse distance and size into a single parameter. We can then fit a line to the resulting point set, either before or after averaging points with similar *DI*, to obtain a two-parameter characterization and visualization of the data set, with a correlation coefficient to characterize the adequacy of the fit. This gave nice results, with correlation coefficient in the neighborhood of .98 for our larger data sets with averaging over intervals of 0.25 in *DI*.

For the maze experiment, total times are directly comparable between trials, and can be used as a sensitive measure of performance. To preserve the momentum of a sequence of pointing tasks, errors were tolerated in the maze experiment. In the target shooting experiment, to make all events directly comparable, we followed earlier workers [1] in dropping pointings in which errors occurred. One might question the effect of the different treatment of errors in the two experiments. When events in which errors occurred are eliminated from the maze data, the effect on the overall results is to increase the speed by perhaps 5%, without any qualitative change. Subjects were in part motivated by the scores which they saw at the end of each trial. In the maze the penalty for an error was loss of time, but more time might be lost in waiting to be sure of a hit before pressing the button. In the target experiment, errors did not directly affect the score, and it might be advantageous to deliberately miss a difficult target; we saw no suggestion that this occurred. The error rate was considerably higher in the maze experiment.

7. RESULTS

The velocity scale must be in a reasonable range - a control with a low top speed, or one which jumps uncontrollably at the slightest touch, is clearly unsatisfactory. The exact setting is less obvious. We repeatedly found that our intuition led to excessive sensitivity. The more interesting questions concern the shape of the transfer function, once the scaling is optimized.

In preliminary experiments we selected the following transfer functions for more careful characterization:

- Three linear functions with velocity scale factors respectively 1.5, .75 and .375. These are LIN1a, LIN1b and LIN1c.
- Two parabolic functions with velocity scale factors 1 and 2, called PAR1 and PAR2.
- Our current favorite shown above, 2Plateau. Its velocity scale factor of 1.5 puts the upper plateau of 2Plateau at 1120 pixels or about 50 cm per second.

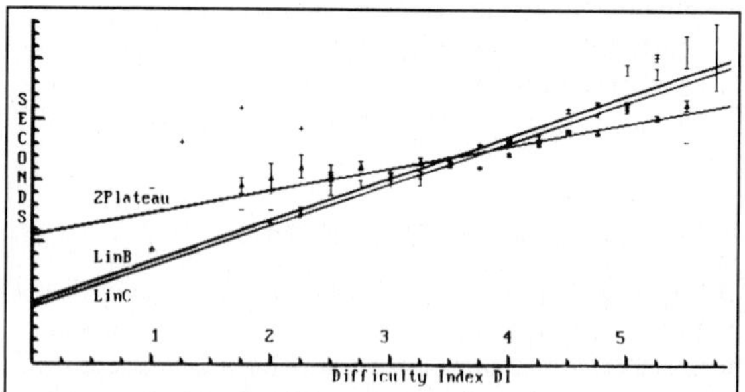

Figure 3. Comparison of 2Plateau with Linear Transfer Functions

Figure 3 is a plot of time against *DI* for 'target shooting' with 2Plateau, LIN1b, and LIN1c. The linear functions are faster at low difficulty (mainly distance - the range of target sizes in this experiment was 20 to 50 units). The simple numerical average times from keyboard to hit, for example, were 1.61, 1.71, and 1.65 seconds (average distances 645 ± 1, sizes 35.5 ± 0.5 for all three runs). Excluding points representing targets of size < 35 left the time against *DI* regression lines for 2Plateau and LIN1c essentially unchanged, but reduced the slope of the LIN1b line from .33 to .23. It appears that despite the small range of target sizes, the effect of size is significant.

The 'maze running' experiment gave a clearer distinction. Average run times and standard deviations in a sequence of runs, for one subject, were:

function	average time	S.D.	trials	slope t/*DI*
2Plateau	23.9	2.3	20	.30
LIN1b	27.9	2.4	30	.34
LIN1c	29.5	2.9	20	.51
LIN1a	27.8	2.4	30	.31
2Plateau	23.6	1.7	40	.30

LIN1a and LIN1b are not distinguished, but LIN1c differs from them at about 1 sigma, and all from 2Plateau at 2 sigma.

PAR1 and PAR2 gave performance similar to 2Plateau. Subjects reported objectionable fatigue using PAR1 and PAR2. The lower sensitivity could be compensated, but at the cost of physical effort - see discussion below. More sensitive parabolic functions were rejected in early screening as inadequately controllable for fine pointing.

Comparisons with sigmoid parabolic functions gave similar results - no significant differences in speed in either experiment, but noticeable differences in 'feel' and in fatigue effects.

8. POINTING STICK VERSUS MOUSE

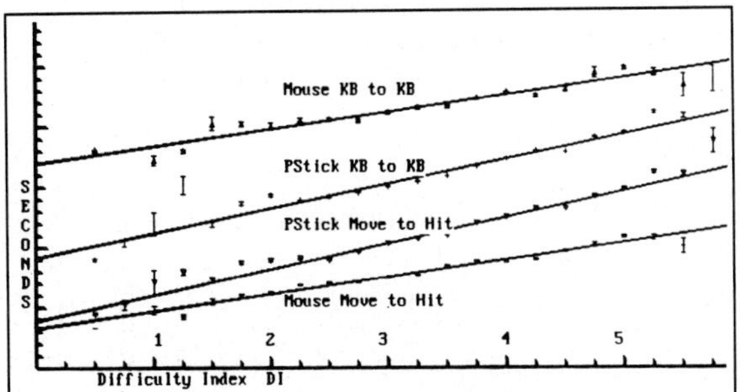

Figure 4. Mouse vs. Pointing Stick

Figure 4 shows the general result. The lower line fits the pointing time for the mouse, in the 'target shooting' experiment, taken from first movement (after 'homing') to selection of the target (hit). The upper line is the same run of the experiment, but timed from keyboard to keyboard (homing times included). The middle pair of lines gives the same information for the pointing stick. The averaged measurements for these runs are as follows:

	mouse	SD	Point	SD
Keyboard to first move	.64	.11	.39	.08
First move to hit	.76	.19	1.18	.35
Hit to keyboard	.72	.12	.09	.13
Keyboard to keyboard	2.12	.26	1.66	.39

Note that the time to reach the Pointing Stick is higher than expected, nearly 2/3 that for the mouse, despite the much shorter distance. The return time for the mouse is much longer than for the Pointing Stick.

The 'maze running' experiment, as a (nearly) pure pointing task, gives results very similar to the central part of the above experiment. The respective time against *DI* regression lines lie close to those for 'first move to hit' for both the mouse and the Pointing Stick. For most (but not all) subjects there was a significant delay between the hit on target n and the first move toward target n + 1, of the order of 0.1 second for the mouse and approaching twice this for the Pointing Stick. Best average times observed for the traversal of a sixteen point maze, starting at screen center, were 15.7 seconds, S.D. 1.8, 60 consecutive runs, for the mouse, and 20.0 seconds, S.D. 1.3, 120 consecutive runs, for the Pointing Stick.

9. DISCUSSION

In comparisons of mouse with Pointing Stick, it must be kept in mind that the subjects were highly experienced mouse users, but novices with the Pointing Stick. Therefore the comparisons can be used only as upper bounds on the differences to be expected in practice. Even so, for an isolated pointing action the Pointing Stick still has an advantage.

We have no firm explanation of the time from keyboard to first movement with the Pointing Stick, or of the difference in hit-to-first-move times in the maze between mouse and Pointing Stick. It is tempting to speculate that about 0.2 seconds is occupied in mental preparation for the move, that this is overlapped with the reaching action in the case of the mouse, and that the relative unfamiliarity of the Pointing Stick accounts for the longer time observed in the maze. The subject who exhibited very short hit-to-move times in the maze was using the LIN1 transfer functions, with slow cursor movement, and was observed to be 'shooting on the fly', never apparently stopping at a target; this strategy was not otherwise observed.

The relatively long return-to-keyboard time for the mouse is consistent with the fact that a key is a smaller target than the mouse.

The comparison of Pointing Stick transfer functions shows a wide range of subject adaptability in using strategies appropriate to the case in hand. For high sensitivity functions they automatically used intermittent contact with the stick, for low sensitivity they maintained contact and (in one case) adopted 'shoot-on-the-fly'. There may in fact be individual differences in optimum transfer function, although we have not observed this. In addition to the observed speed differences between linear and non-linear functions, differences of 'feel' and fatigue were observed, supporting our conjectures that at least two stable speeds, with an appropriate ratio between them, are desirable. The lower plateau of 2Plateau, at 1.5 cm/second, is appropriate for character-sized targets, but a bit fast for pixel targets, which would be needed for a drawing application. While subjects could perform at speed with PAR1 and PAR2, the force required for long fast movements was too much to sustain for more than a few minutes of operation, while more sensitive functions made fine pointing too difficult.

We observed time/*DI* regression line slopes in the range of 0.12 (for the mouse) to .20±.03 for the Pointing Stick with optimal transfer function, and considerably higher with other functions. These contrast with apparently corresponding slopes of about 0.10 found previously [1, 3]. The latter effect is expected, for functions with low maximum speed - time increases linearly with distance, not logarithmically. For other functions, the explanation is presumably deeper, and requires further investigation.

10. CONCLUSIONS

We have been exploring alternative analogue pointing devices for computer interfaces. Laptop computers have no space for a mouse, and space is a problem in many office and other settings as well. The distraction and time of reaching for and returning from a mouse concerns us. We first considered adding sensors to a key under the index finger in a normal keyboard; signaling the use of the key for pointing or typing was distracting. We have placed joysticks in several keyboards and find the Pointing Stick between the G and H keys very useable. In experimenting with analogue pointing devices we have found the Pointing Stick can best the mouse in many situations.

For intermixed pointing and keyboard tasks the Pointing Stick is faster than the mouse. When three or more consecutive pointings occur the mouse can be up to 25% faster than the Pointing Stick. We note also that our Pointing Stick users' pointing speed continues to improve.

Our experience has been that users consistently over estimate their ability to control a fast pointing device. Reducing the rate of change for low speeds as in the parabolic, sigmoid parabolic and 2Plateau (Figure 1) functions increases subjects' speed for selecting small objects. The presence of two plateaus, with the proper ratio between them, makes precise control possible at relatively high sensitivity, greatly improving comfort and reducing fatigue. Adding the high speed tail of 2Plateau made users more comfortable with the Pointing Stick. Before this was added, two users literally bent the Pointing Stick (probably pressing over 5 pounds with their index fingers).

11. FUTURE DIRECTIONS

Following [5, 6] we have informally modeled pointing as a feedback control process, attempting to maintain what we think of as critical damping, which we find to yield the highest speed. A more critical treatment of this area should yield improvements in ease of use and in speed.

Other classes of force-to-motion functions are possible, in particular some degree of force-to-position mapping. Pure force-to-position mapping seems infeasible, but some mixed strategy, perhaps force-to-position locally with force-to-velocity at greater distances, should be worth investigating.

We informally measured how fast a subject could run our maze with his eyes; this was about 12 seconds or 3 seconds faster than the fastest pointing measured. Could this 25% speed difference be bridged? Could an eye tracking cursor positioner or "applications smart" transfer functions improve pointing speed?

BIBLIOGRAPHY

1. S. K. Card, W. K. English, and B. J. Burr. Evaluation of Mouse, Rate-Controlled Isometric Joystick, Step Keys, and Test Keys for Text Selection on a CRT. *Ergonomics*, 21(8):601-613, 1978..

2. Stuart K. Card, Thomas P. Moran, and Allen Newell. *Psychology of Human Computer Interaction.* Lawrence Erlbaum Associates, 1983.

3. P. M. Fitts. The Information Capacity of the Human Motor System In Controlling The Amplitude of Movement.. *Journal of Experimental Psychology*, 47:381-391, 1954..

4. P. M. Fitts and J. R. Peterson. Information Capacity of Discrete Motor Responses. *Journal of Experimental Psychology*, 67(2):103-112, 1964..

5. T. O. Kvalseth. Information Capacity of Two-Dimensional Human Motor Responses. *Ergonomics*, 24(7):573-575, 1981..

6. D. E. Meyer, S. Kornblum, R. A. Abrams, C. E. Wright, and J. E. K. Smith. Optimality in Human Motor-Performance - Ideal Control of Rapid Aimed Movements. *Psychological Review*, 95(3):340-370, 1988..

Human–Computer Interaction – INTERACT '90
D. Diaper et al. (Editors)
Elsevier Science Publishers B.V. (North-Holland)

KEYBOARD LAYOUT FOR OCCASIONAL USERS

Nicolas MARMARAS and Kostas LYRITZIS

Technical University of Crete, Greece

The present study is a first attempt to solve the problem of keyboard layout for occasional users of computer-based systems. Sixty subjects, all customers of a department store, divided in four groups, have been asked to type a short phrase on specially tailored keyboards. The keyboard arrangements tested were the alphabetical-diagonal, the alphabetical-horizontal, the standard greek keyboard which is similar to the QWERTY layout, and a new alternative greek keyboard designed for typists. The obtained results showed that the alphatetical-diagonal arrangement achieved better typing speed rates, and that the differences between typing rates achieved with the other three layouts are practically insignificant.

1. INTRODUCTION

The increasing spread of computer-based systems offering public services, e.g. electronic phone book, commercial machines, airline reservation systems, library information systems etc, poses the problem of keyboard layout for occasional users. Which character set arrangement is more appropriate for these keyboards addressed to a general public, whose typing, from time to time, is rather a limited amount of characters (e.g. single letters, numbers, words, or small sentences)? Is the standard QWERTY keyboard, whose arrangement has been dictated by technological constraints of the early designed typewriter, insure an acceptable rate of typing speed and errors? Or, a keyboard with character set alphabetically arranged, could achieve better performance, given the logical ordering of the keys?

Manufacturers of such systems seem not to have faced the problem in a systematic way. Therefore, the public meets systems with keyboards using the standard QWERTY arrangement, systems using the alphabetical arrangement where letters A through Z are arranged from left to right starting at upper left of the keyboard (horizontal), or systems using the diagonal arrangement, which is also alphabetical but with letters arranged from top to bottom and then from left to right starting at upper left of the keyboard.

Ergonomic literature provides a rather limited number of studies comparing experimentaly alphabetically arranged keyboards and QWERTY.

Bodenseher (1970), produced a special-purpose keyboard with the letters keys arranged in alphabetical order, numerals like a desk calculator, and functions keys grouped in patterns for identification, according to function and frequency of use. Bodenseher concluded that this keyboard showed a reduction in error rate about 25% when compared with the typewriter keyboard. He also supported that it reduced learning time, and allowed experienced users to enter statements about twice as fast as on the standard QWERTY keyboard. However, as Noyes (1983) notes, it is not clear whether these advantages arise from the alphabetical layout or the arrangement of the numeral and special function keys.

Hirsch (1970) tested a group of non-typists on QWERTY and another group on an alphabetic-horizontal keyboard. The 40 subjects of the experiment were selected among 55 volunteers self styled as non-typists, on the basis of a 10 min pre-test on the standard keyboard. After 7 hours of practice, the QWERTY group improved their typing speed from 1.47 to 1.99 keystrokes per second. The alphabetical group, however, did not even reach their pre-experiment QWERTY typing rates.

A third experiment comparing the QWERTY keyboard with an alphabetical-horizontal arrangement was carried by Michaels (1971). He used 30 subjects divided into three groups, according to the level of typing skill they professed during a pre-test, consisting of typing on a QWERTY keyboard. Subjects were pair-matched across the two keyboards, and keyed for two sessions of about 1 1/2 hour daily with a 30 min break. Results showed that both high- and medium-skill groups were significantly faster on QWERTY, while low-skill group showed no significant difference in typing speed on the two keyboards.

Norman & Fisher (1982), tested 12 subjects on four different keyboards: QWERTY, two alphabetic keyboards (horizontal and diagonal) and a random keyboard with letters assigned to keys randomly. Subjects were given again a 10 min pre-test on the QWERTY keyboard. They were then tested for 10 min on each of the other three keyboards in counterbalanced order, with a 5 min rest between tests. Results showed that the first three keyboards were all significantly faster than the random arrangement, and that speed achieved on the QWERTY keyboard was 67% greater than the speed reached with the alphabetic keyboards.

As far as the explanation of the results observed in the last three experiments are concerned, the following assumptions are formulated:
- simple visual search is less time consuming than it is to mentaly figure out the position of the letter in the alphabet and then translate this into a keyboard location (Norman & Fisher, 1982)
- many of the more commonly used letters are centrally located in QWERTY arrangement, and therefore in the case of visual search strategy the area of search is reduced (Hirsch, 1981)
- the QWERTY keyboards are so common that most people have had at least some experience with one (Hirsch 1981, Norman & Fisher, 1982).

However, a number of objections could rise as to whether the above experiments are appropriate for testing keyboards addressed to occasional users.

a. Subjects in these experiments had to type an entire text. Consequently, they are put in the position of a novice or future typist, and not in the position of an occasional keyboard user, who would type from time to time a rather limited amount of characters.

b. It is reasonalbe to assume that the pre-tests on QWERTY keyboard lasting more than 10 min, biased the typing performance on alphabetic keyboards, specially during the early stages of the main test. The knowledge of the QWERTY arrangement undoubtly interferred with the use of alphabetical ones.

c. The sample of subjects consisting of undergraduate students and university staff, cannot be considered as representing well enough the users of computer-based systems offering public services.

These objections, as well as the contradictory results of existing studies, led us to the experiment presented in this paper. It constitutes as a first attempt to test different keyboard arrangements for occasional users, in field experiments, simulating as close as possible real-life situation. Subjects were customers of a big department store, and they had to type a small standard phrase.

2. EXPERIMENTAL EVALUATION

2.1. Keyboards to be evaluated

Considering the physical structure of the standard three-row keyboard as given, four different key arrangements were chosen for experimental comparison: alphabetical-horizontal, alphabetical-diagonal, the standard greek keyboard and a new alternative arrangement (fig. 1).

The two alphabetical arrangements were chosen based on the assumption that the logical key ordering would facilitate the visual search to find a specific key on the board. These arrangements are almost similar to the alphabetic keyboards tested by Norman & Fisher (1982). There are only two differences. First, the 25 letters of the greek alphabet are used in the place of the latin ones. Second, there is an effort to simulate an inverted "v" shape to the columns of the keys. This shape, as Kroemer (1972) supports, makes physical approach of hands to the keyboard easier and more confortable.

The standard greek keyboard, can be considered as a direct descendant of the QWERTY. Simple observation clearly indicates the similarity of the two key arrangements: 14 letters common in greek and latin alphabet, are found in the same position on both keyboards; 7 more greek letters spelled similarly with latin ones, share the same keys (e.g. Π-P, Φ-F, etc). There are only five greek letters which are totaly different from the latin ones, and these are arranged rather randomly to the remaining keys. The similarity of the two

Figure 1. The four key arrangements tested

a. The alphabetic-horizontal keyboard

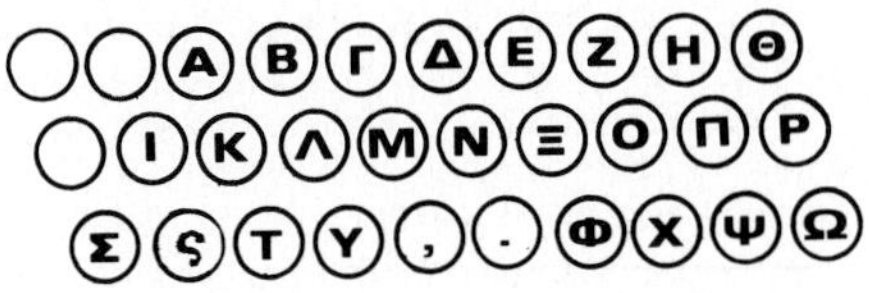

b. The alphabetic-diagonal keyboard

c. The standard greek keyboard

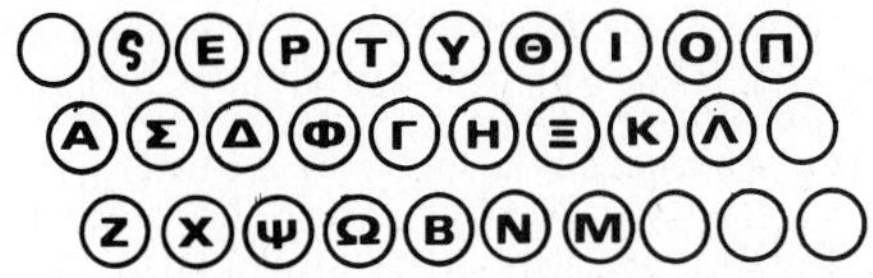

d. The alternative keyboard for typists

key arrangements makes valid the comparison of results from previous studies on QWERTY, with the results of the present study.

The fourth keyboard to be tested, is the output of an unpublished study (Marmaras, Lyritzis, 1990). The scope of this study was to design a keyboard arrangement for greek typists, based on ergonomic principles and statistical analysis of greek texts.

Technically speaking, the four keyboards were tailored through appropriate software and flexible covers, on a conventional portable personal computer. Three keyboard-drivers programs, which had the ability to change the function of every keyboard character when activated by a combination of special function keys, were developed (two for the alphabetical arrangements and one for the new alternative greek keyboard). The keyboard driver program for the standard greek keyboard, already existed on the computer used. The four covers, made from flexible nylon and small labels with letters marked on them were interchangable. Only the letters, punctuation marks and space-bar keys were visible by the user, the rest being covered for simplicity reasons (fig. 2).

2.2. The Experiment

Procedure. The personal computer described above, was installed near the entrance of a big department store of Chania (Crete). Customers were requested, on voluntary basis, to participate at an experiment of our Polytechnic University, typing a short phrase on a keyboard. The scope of the experiment as well as brief instractions were presented to the customers who accepted to participate. Subjects were told to type the short phrase shown to them, in any way they preferred (using one or both of their hands, one, two or all of their fingers). They were also told to ignore any typing error and to continue typing. The use of space-bar was explained only on request. Customers with considerable typing experience were excluded from the experiment.

The phrase. The phrase that subjects had to type was: "ΣΗΜΕΡΑ ΕΙΝΑΙ ΤΕΤΑΡΤΗ ΕΝΝΙΑ ΑΥΓΟΥΣΤΟΥ" (Today is Wednesday nine of August). It was written in upper-case letters, on a blank page and placed on the left of the keyboard. This phrase fullfills the following requirements: It is short, simple, without special terms, easy in orthograph, and it does not comprise special symbols, numeric characters, punctuation marks. We can assume therefore, that the experiment simulates quite well the task occasional users have to execute on terminals of

Figure 2. The cover used

computed-based public systems. Furthermore, the results of the test are expected not to be biased towards special user characteristics such as ability of memorisation, education level, specific knowledge and experience, nor by the use of function keys or special character keys.
Sample and measurements. In total of 60 customers participated to the experiment, during a two days period. Each keyboard layout was tested therefore by 15 subjects. Typing time of each subject was measured using an electronic chronometer, and the typed phrase was saved in the computer's memory.

Personal characterictics of each subject was also recorded. These personal characteristics were: sex, age, education level and familiarization with the type writer or computers. Table 1 presents the distribution of our sample regarding the personal characteristics and the keyboard arrangement on which they were tested.

2.3. Results and Discussion

The mean number of typing time, the sample variance (σ^2_n), and the unbiased estimator of population variance (σ^2_{n-1}) for the four tested keyboard arrangements, are presented in Table 2.
The results show a superiority of alphabetical-diagonal arrangement over the others. The mean typing time required with this keyboard is 39% less than the time required with the standard greek keyboard, 43.5% less than the time required with the new alternative greek keyboard, and 44.5% less than the time required with the alphabetic-horizontal keyboard. Furthermore, the variance of typing time with this keyboard is smaller than the variances of the other keyboards.

The three remaining keyboard layouts did not show significant differences in speed rate. Standard greek keyboard required only 3% and 4% less typing time than the new alternative greek keyboard and the alphabetic-horizontal respectively.

An analysis of variance on the collected time-data of the four keyboard arrangements, was also performed. The ANOVA control variable F=1,6491 was smaller than F(3.56) in either significance level [F(3.56)=2.78 for P=0.05 and 4.2 for P=0.01]. Thus, although typing rate on the alphabetic-diagonal keyboard is shown better, considering mean times and variances, performance differences on the four tested keyboards can not be considered as statistically significant (with a 99% possibility). Perhaps further increase of sample may be necessary for the above mentioned statistical significance criteria.

Table 1: Personal characteristics of the sample

Population "Profile"	Standard Greek kyboard	Proposed key arrangement for touch typing	Horizontal Alphabetic key arrangement	Diagonal Alphabetic key arrangement	Total Results
▪ Sex:					
Male	6	11	9	9	35 (58.3%)
Female	9	4	6	6	25 (41.7%)
▪ Age:					
≤ 20	7	5	4	4	20 (33.3%)
≤ 50	8	10	10	11	39 (65.0%)
> 50	-	-	1	-	1 (1.7%)
▪ Education level:					
Elementary	2	-	1	-	3 (5.0%)
High school	9	7	9	9	34 (56.7%)
University	4	8	5	6	23 (38.3%)
▪ Typing dexterity:					
None	8	14	11	7	40 (66.7%)
Little	7	1	4	8	20 (33.3%)

Table 2: Statistical Results of the experiment

	Standard Greek kyboard	Proposed key arrangement for touch typing	Horizontal Alphabetic key arrangement	Diagonal Alphabetic key arrangement
Mean typing time (min)	1.1034	1.1394	1.1478	0.7938
Sample Variance ($\sigma^2{}_n$)	1.7820	2.7752	2.2774	1.5703
Unbiased estimator of population variance ($\sigma^2{}_{n-1}$)	1.8443	2.8728	2.3575	1.6254

As far as typing errors are concerned, the analysis of the typed phrases showed no considerable errors. The only typing error observed, was the absence of space between words in some cases. We can conclude therefore that the four keyboard arrangements tested, did not show any significant difference in causing typing errors.

The major issue emerged from the above analysis is that, although not statistically significant, the typing performance with the alphabetical-diagonal arrangement can be considered higher than the performance with the remaining three keyboard layouts. This could be explained by the fact that the alphabetic-diagonal keyboard combines a logical structure and a high correlation between this logic (i.e. the position of a letter in the alphabet) and the location of the keys. Letters positioned at the beginning of the alphabet are located in the left area of the keyboard, letters at the middle of the alphabet are located in the middle keys, and letters at the end of the alphabet are located in the right area of the keyboard.

On the contrary, this is not the case for the alphabetical-horizontal arrangement. We can assume therefore, that occasional users, when typing on the alhabetic-horizontal keyboard, the standard greek keyboard, or the new alternative one, proceed to a visual search which is not driven by the alphabetical ordering of the letters.

Comparing the results of the present study with those of previous studies on different keyboard layouts, we have the following remarks to annotate. Although the standard greek keyboard which is similar to QWERTY, seems to achieve better performance than the alphabetic-horizontal one, the difference is not so significant as it is shown in Hirsch's (1970), Michaels' (1972) and Norman & Fisher's (1982) tests. It is reasonable to support that this is due to the experimental conditions of those studies (see introduction).

As far as the alphabetical-diagonal arrangement is concerned, the results of Norman & Fisher's study are partially corresponding to the results of the present study, and partially in contradiction. The alphabetical-diagonal arrangement in that study had also shown a superiority over the horizontal one, but was inferior compared to the QWERTY keyboard. Again, differences in the experimental conditions could explain the above.

Three more remarks have to be done regarding the assumptions formulated by Hirsch (1981) and Norman & Fisher (1982), in order to explain the advantage of QWERTY arrangement shown in their experiments. As it can be seen in Table 1, only 20 out of the 60 subjects of our experiments had some previous experience with the standard greek keyboard. If we add to them the 4 customers which were excluded from the experiment as typists, we reach a percentage of 38% department store customers having experience on a keyboard. This is a percentage which does not confirms Hirsch's assumption that most people have had at least some experience with the QWERTY arrangement.

The second remark concerns Norman & Fisher's assumption that simple visual search requires less mental activity and thus it is less time consuming than it is to mentaly figure-out the position of the letter in the alphabet and then translate this into a keyboard location. The results of the present study show

that it is not always true that a strategy which comprises more mental actions will be more time consuming than another, comprising less actions.
Finally, Hirsch's assumption according to which the QWERTY arrangement may be better because of the central location of the more commonly used letters seems not to be confirmed. Actually, the typing performance with the new alternative greek keyboard, which had as a main design criteria the central location of the more frequently used letters, is worse than the performance of the standard greek keyboard.

3. SUMMARY AND CONCLUSION

The study presented in this paper, is a first attempt to solve the problem of keyboard layout for occasional users of computer-based systems offering public services. Four groups of 15 subjects, all customers of a department store, have been asked to type a short phrase on four different specially tailored keyboards. The keyboard arrangements tested were the alphabetical-diagonal, the alphabetical-horizontal, the standard greek keyboard which is similar to the QWERTY, and a new alternative greek keyboard designed for typists.
The results showed that the alphabetical-diagonal arrangement achieved better typing speed rates, and that the differences between typing rates achieved with the other three layouts are practically insignificant.

However, in order to propose the alphabetical-diagonal arrangement as the best keyboard for occasional users, further investigation is required in terms of increasing the number of subjects, differentiating the field of study (e.g. banks, libraries etc), and by also using alternative short phrases to be typed.
Finally, the present study proves that the redesign of the keyboard layout cannot be considered as fruitless effort, like Potosnak (1988) and Noyes (1983) maintain. On the contrary, recent changes in the population of keyboard users, due to the growing use of computer-bases systems, requires in looking afresh at this problem.

REFERENCES

Bodenseher, H., (1970), A console keyboard for improved man-machine interaction, Institute of Electrical Engineers Conference, Man-Computer Interaction Conference Publication No 68, pp. 196-200.

Hirsch, R.S., (1970), Effects of standard versus alphabetic keyboard formats on typing performance, Journal of Applied Psychology, 54, pp. 484-490.

Hirsch, R.S., (1981), Procedure of human factors center at San Jose, IBM systems Journal, 20, pp. 123-171.

Kroemer, K.H.E., (1972), Human engineering the keyboard, Human Factors, 14, pp. 51-63.

Marmaras, N. & Lyritzis, K., (1990), An alternative greek keyboard, in print.

Michaels, S.E., (1971), QWERTY versus alphabetic keyboards as a function of typing skill, Human Factors, 13, pp. 419-426.

Norman, D.A. & Fisher, D., (1982), Why alphabetic keyboards are not easy to use: keyboard layout doesn't much matter, Human Factors, 24(5), pp. 509-519.

Noyes, J., (1983), The QWERTY keyboard: a review, International Journal of Man-Machine Studies, 18, pp. 265-281.

Potosnak, K.M., (1988), Keys and keyboards, in: M.Helander (ed.), Handbook of Human-Computer Interaction, Elsevier Science Publishers B.V. (North-Holland), pp. 475-494.

SECTION IV: INTERACTIVE TECHNOLOGIES AND TECHNIQUES

SIV.2 Output

The simulation of a large image terminal using Heath Robinson techniques
J.R. Harris, M.B. Harris, and D.Th. Henskes 715

Evaluation of flat panel display properties on a high fidelity display simulator
G. Spenkelink, H. Van Spijker, and T.N. White 721

Colour model integration and visualisation
P.A. Rhodes, M.R. Luo, and S.A.R. Scrivener 725

On the visibility of character features on a VDU
D. Bosman and T.N. White 729

Auditory icons in large-scale collaborative environments
W.W. Gaver and R.B. Smith 735

Interactive scientific visualization: An assessment of a virtual reality system
P.J. Mercurio and T.D. Erickson 741

A browser for dynamic multimedia documents
S. Anupindi 747

Human–Computer Interaction – INTERACT '90
D. Diaper et al. (Editors)
Elsevier Science Publishers B.V. (North-Holland)

The simulation of a large image terminal using Heath Robinson[1] techniques

J.R. Harris, M.B. Harris and D.Th. Henskes†

Department of Computer Science, Heriot-Watt University, 79 Grassmarket, Edinburgh
†SEL-Research Center; PO Box 1760; 7530, Pforzheim, West Germany

A non-existent large image terminal with screen diagonal of one metre was simulated using various software and hardware techniques. Groups of non-computer scientists were used to evaluate its potential. This information is being used as vital input to the hardware design definition phase for a new generation of interactive terminals. The users were lecturers and students from a university languages department, and the information content was based on their normal classes. The software was developed on an Apple Macintosh IIX and the hardware was prepared from various items, including mirrors and string. We show that it is possible to have limited realistic interaction; to get a close proximity to the predicted visual effect; and to use real users in appropriate realistic scenarios.

1. Introduction

In a statement at the end of the ALVEY Programme in 1988, the government criticised the HCI community for gaining a reputation of giving post hoc advice and suggested that the future of HCI depends upon the results that its practitioners provide today in the market place, not the promises for tomorrow. Reviews of the field have shown that there appears to be lack of communication between HCI researchers and computer system designers. The computing world is highly applied and is judged on its current performance; it is on this basis that HCI improved interface designs will succeed or fail, - Morgan (1989). This is a strong reminder that the needs and attitudes of real end users, i.e. the 'human' element in HCI should be included in the design stages.

In describing the successful design and implementation of the 1984 Olympics information system, Gould (1987) demonstrated the importance of early user feedback even at the cardboard and string level. We wondered what would happen if we put a collection of subjective data on an early mock-up into a controlled experiment.

This paper describes pre-production investigations of hardware development which form the early stages of a Development Life Cycle - Rouse (1984). That is to say, the research has been conducted with a view to achieving specific findings prior to a real product being developed for the market place. At such an early stage in the design process it is only possible to have an exploratory assessment based on subjective data as objective performance tests cannot be carried out, because functional equipment is not yet in existence.

The initial terms of reference were to decide upon the kind of screen and pointing mechanism that would be appropriate for a proposed 'large image terminal' (LIT) - see Esprit (1989). The investigations have encompassed design of mock-ups, choice of experimental subjects and scenario, assessment and use of existing software packages and the development of novel software. Furthermore, we endeavoured to avoid compromise by following good computer science and psychological paradigms through co-operative work shared between psychologists, computer scientists, domain experts and technicians, rather than employing a single 'HCI expert'. This has been suggested by Long (1986).

Although early research in human-computer interaction was done largely by introspection and intuition, this approach suffered from lack of validity, generality, and precision - Shneiderman (1987). It appears that work with real users at the design stage is still not the norm despite the proliferation of various 'guide-lines' - e.g.Smith and Mosier (1984). Part of the problem could be that guide-lines are so comprehensive that they are contradictory and confusing to follow. 'Knowing the user' is good advice but may be hard advice to follow when many people working within HCI are used to interacting with computers and may be, by definition, the kinds of people who find recruiting real people a difficult task. Perseverance is necessary to see this through, as using real people is more complex and far more time consuming and frustrating than other abstract methods, see Harris (1987). We decided that the empirical approach offered by an experimental evaluation with real users would offer more reliable and valid information than either observational or expert evaluation methods - Long & Whitefield (1986).

2. Background information

2.1. Target product

The first issues to be resolved concerning the LIT were: what is large, and what is a terminal? These two factors were decided by pressure from external forces: the ESPRIT programme was prepared to support development of a terminal with a large, flat, back-projected screen in order to exploit the state-of-the-art active matrix liquid crystal display (AMLCD) technology. The extrapolation of progress indicated that it would be possible to manufacture, in sufficient quantities, AMLCDs of a resolution suitable for 640 by 480 3-colour elements (pixels). A one-metre diagonal projection screen was chosen from assessment of the optical design of the system. The fact that it is a 'terminal' is to allow sufficient flexibility for its use in a range of applications. However, we assume a rather vague definition of terminal; in fact, we intend to have a system which would be better classed a networked micro-computer with video interfacing. The combination of both a 'large' and 'interactive' screen in a terminal is innovative in its potential use.

2.2. Screen parameters

The resolution and size of the screen were fixed because of the technology being employed; this introduced some further complications: because the AMLCD is made up of individually controllable elements, each one representing a pixel, and because it is being used as a 'light valve', it is impossible to avoid having a visible grid, or 'flyscreen', as part of the projected picture. This is caused by the fine opaque connecting wires built into the LCD cell as an addressing matrix for the thin film transistors used to control the pixels and the black matrix used as a light shield. The wires and screen together were designed to be approximately one-fifth of a pixel wide. In addition, in order to achieve ambient light viewability, the projection system has to have either: a high intensity light source - leading to rapid deterioration of the AMLCD, or: a screen which increases the brightness by means of some optical arrangement. This latter option is available as a lenticular screen, which incorporates a Fresnel lens and linear lenticular array so concentrating the brightness of display into a horizontal field of view. After some early tests with photographically produced simulations of pictures plus flyscreen, we noted that there was a pronounced and undesirable effect with the lenticular screen. This is known as a moiré pattern which is caused by the interaction of the flyscreen and cylindrical lenses of the lenticular screen (this looks like a water-mark or a large thumb print interfering with the picture).

2.3. Interaction device

The choice of methods of interaction was more flexible because the nature of material presented on screen, together with the acceptability and/or need to approach the larger screen, would depend on its use. The initial target markets are retailing and training/education areas, so the simplest methods for non-expert users were considered to be either touch or a remote pointing device, which would offer close proximity or distancing from the screen. For the remote pointing device, one such possible device is Intermetall's new generation infra-red remote-control tool, which has the look and feel of a light pointer and functions like a mouse, Electronics (1989).

3.1. Choice of experimental design

The type of screen to be used: whether 'plain' with a very bright light source, leading to rapid deterioration of our AMLCD; or 'lenticular' with the possible adverse interaction between flyscreen and vertical lenses. As both screens presented different problems the decisions would be made by determining the trade-offs between them.

Interaction mechanism: bearing in mind the screen and predicted resolution, how close can people stand - and therefore could they reach to touch - and/or can a form of pointing offer any useful alternative or supplement to the interaction. We chose to compare touch and light pen as interaction devices as both methods were easy to perform (thus reducing anxiety) and the remote pointer would afford distancing opportunities.

Subjects: Domain experts were consulted in both education and retailing and compared with regard to availability and commitment. Investigations into retailing scenarios revealed that these needed to be highly specific depending on such factors as location, product, customer socio-economic group, etc. We questioned the relevance of generalisation from such findings and rejected the retailing environment. The educational environment offered superior experimental control, could include domain experts and be carried out in a truly realistic setting, thus increasing validity. Although it would have been easier to use the Computer Science Department, their familiarity and acceptance of technology was not typical of the user population and we chose instead to use a group with more neutral attitudes towards computers. The Languages department within the university offered such an ideal experimental group.

3.2. Scenarios

It is hoped that eventually large image terminals would yield an interactive computing environment with multimedia facilities. Users would either obtain information for themselves or else display information to others. The teaching environment is therefore an appropriate one as the simulated LIT could be used to display information to a group of students who would be highly motivated to read that presented information. At the same time this information needs to be accessed by someone within that group, be it lecturer or student. Experimental scenarios comprised normal timetabled teaching sessions using the LIT 'as if' it were a real functioning LIT. Thus, the simulation of the new generation LIT was enacted using a Heath Robinson contraption, complete with technician inside it, executing screen changes in response to an appropriate command addressed to the screen.

3.3. Questionnaire

As operational software was not available, we rejected studying speed of performance, rate of errors on the simulation. Also subjectivity of users, rather than perception criteria, would determine take-up in the market place, (education or retailing). Therefore, the questionnaire form was chosen to provide material for the data base - although video filming of the experimental scenarios was included for reference purposes, safety back-up and for possible timings if it seemed worthwhile.

Post-session questionnaires were given manually to lecturers and students to elicit subjective opinions concerning preferred interaction methods and acceptability of screen used, together with background information on computer usage, attitudes towards technology, personal data including visual status, seating distances and angles for viewing, and various open ended questions for further opinions and suggestions regarding LIT use.

A short additional questionnaire (CUSI, 1988) was given to the lecturers before their test sessions to determine pre-test attitudes (affect & competence) to computers. This was to be used for comparison with attitudes following use of LIT and as an attitude control indicator should extreme attitudes be found in the post-session questionnaire.

4. Slides

Screens images, i.e. simulations of different screens of the LIT forming part of the lecture material, were designed using an Apple IIX (see Discussion) and consisted of graphical and textual information. Material presented on each slide was agreed between lecturer and researcher and was mostly presented in an attractive format to include as much of the screen area as possible with an acceptable mixture of textual information and graphical images - even if only colour boxes or highlighting. To achieve authentic screen images, slides were designed to expected LIT screen resolution of 1 line per five pixels resulting from an actual mesh pattern of one fifth of a pixel wide for each pixel. The flyscreen effect (see 7.4), i.e. lines in both vertical and horizontal planes, was incorporated into each slide. This effect is a result of the functional design of the interactive screen.

5. Method

5.1. Subjects

Eight university lecturers, six male and two female, from the Languages Department at Heriot-Watt University agreed to take part in the simulation exercise, plus undergraduate students (total 101) who attended their classes. Lecturer ages ranged from 39 to 49 and student ages ranged from 17 to 29. All had normal or corrected-to-normal vision.

5.2. Experimenter

The same person gave instructions, distributed questionnaires and videoed sessions throughout. Similarly, the same trained technician operated the projection equipment in all sessions from behind the screening.

5.3. Design

Two types of screen (lenticular or plain) and two interaction methods (touch screen or pointer) were compared in a between subjects design. Each subject participated in one session only. Additional data was obtained from some lecturers who were required to deliver identical lectures to two different groups of students. The eight lecturers were allocated to one screen type and either touch or pointer method of interaction, with screens and interaction methods being counterbalanced across conditions, i.e. two lecturers in each condition.

5.4. Apparatus/Materials

Two screens, measuring one metre diagonally, as specified by Thorn EMI, were compared :- plain screen ('Standard Marata') and a lenticular screen (P307 'Electrosonic' - high gain, rear-projection screen). A Hama light pen was used to simulate the hand-held interactive device. 100 colour slides, approximately 12 slides per lecturer giving graphical/textual images and devised to fit a predetermined lecture session, were developed directly from Studio/8 and Persuasion software on the Apple Mackintosh IIX via a Solitaire electronic recorder at Express Computer Graphics Ltd of Edinburgh.

Equipment needed for the simulation included 2 Kodak Carousel projectors model SAV2000 with magazines, 35 mm lens, Imatronic Manual Dissolver Unit, screen : 1 metre focal length, and control panel, one half-silvered mirror (measuring approximately 20 x 30 cms) with supports, string and clamps, all mounted on a Unicol stand, plus sufficient screening to conceal the foregoing equipment and'Velcro' to secure screens to front panel.

All experimental sessions were videoed using a Philips Camcorder mounted on a tripod. Pre-session - CUSI (1988) and post-session - Harris, Harris & Henskes, (1989) Questionnaires.

5.5. Procedure

Lecturers only completed a Computer User Satisfactory Inventory (CUSI) prior to the simulation session for comparison with the post-simulation questionnaire to determine whether or not general attitudes towards computers and competence levels were maintained after using LIT.

Simulations took place during normal timetabled teaching sessions to ensure authenticity and motivation of students and to elicit specific information concerning possible future educational use. All experimental simulation sessions were carried out in the same room with the same illumination, namely daylight and overhead fluorescent lighting.

The LIT was positioned at the front of the class before subjects entered the room. The LIT was used as if it were an interactive visual teaching aid during these lectures, i.e. a real LIT, except that lecturers knew it wasn't real. Slides were back-projected onto the screen so that the general appearance of the LIT resembled a large VDU. The same slide appeared on the screen at the beginning of all sessions so that subjects could, if they wished, select a seat according to their own inclinations, relative to the LIT.

During the lecture, when lecturers wished to develop some information on the LIT, they accessed 'stored' information by either touching a specific spot on the screen or else selecting this pre-determined selection area by pointing to it with the light pen, according to their allocated condition.

This action was recognised by the technician concealed behind the screening and resulted in her back projecting the image of the next slide in the sequence onto the screen. This dovetailing was achieved with the use of the dissolver unit. Due to the necessity for sequentially stored slides, prior collaboration with lecturers was essential to fit their lecture with a pre-planned scenario. Lecturers received a short practice session before the actual simulation session.

Lecturers were aware, therefore, of the nature of the simulation, whereas students were naive as to its extent, although were informed that their responses to screen and interaction method were valued as part of an ESPRIT evaluation study.

At the end of each 40 minute session, questionnaires taking about 10 minutes to complete, were administered and were filled in immediately by lecturers and students. Subjective ratings of screen and interactive device of LIT were obtained on the following: user computer experience, user technical competence and experience, attitude towards screen and interaction device, attitude towards LIT in general, embarrassment levels and open ended questions to allow for expression of both positive and negative feedback. Question format was mostly Likert-type, together with some bipolar adjectival ones, plus open ended questions to provide space for further suggestions, frustration and so on. Mean scores of ratings were used to compare both screens and interaction method.

Each session was video-ed for later analysis where required. Short informal semi-structured interviews were given to the lecturers a week or so after testing to elicit further suggestions concerning the experiment and possible future development.

6. Results

Two-way ANOVA (unrelated) were used to analyse the data variables for the effects of screen (plain or lenticular) and interaction device (touch or remote light pen). A full account of the results will be published elsewhere when analyses are complete, but we include a selection of the initial findings below:

6.1 Pre-session tests

Lecturers CUSI scores revealed no significant extremes of attitude towards or competence with computers.

6.2 Post session tests

No between-group differences were found for student attentiveness nor comparisons with other lectures so it can be assumed that the lectures were of the usual standard and therefore the sessions were valid. Main effects of screen were found to be highly significant ($p=0.004$) for brightness where the lenticular screen was rated brighter than the plain. But, blurring was significantly worse for lenticular screen ratings ($p=0.005$). General reactions to using the screen, rated using bipolar adjectives, yielded more positive responses in those using the plain screen ($p=0.031$). Ratings of difficulty seeing the images were significantly higher for the plain screen ($p=0.05$). Levels of embarrassment when actively using one of the interactive devices revealed no significant effect of interaction method, but this became highly significant in the passive condition, i.e. observing others interacting ($p=0.001$). Using the remote pointer was perceived as being more embarrassing than touching.

Results from other variables were more complex as interaction effects were found. For instance, quality of image was found to be the same across groups, but there were significant interaction effects ($p=0.011$); subjects rated the 'quality of image' superior when screen and interaction device were in the combinations: 'plain/remote' and 'lenticular/touch'.

7. Discussion

7.1 Interpretation of results

Interaction Device: One of the main effects of interaction device was the increased passive embarrassment expressed when the remote pointer was used. It was our expectation that remote pointing would be just as easy as touching the screen. Nevertheless, subjective ratings of perceived difficulties in interacting with the screen were significantly worse for pointing than touching. One could partly interpret this as being influenced by imperfections in the simulation, but we still have to take into account that the introduction of a more technical device introduces more difficulties than were anticipated.

Screens: Although the lenticular screen was found to be significantly brighter than the plain one, it was also reported to be significantly more blurred. The plain screen on the other hand received more favourable ratings on the 'general reactions' scale.

7.2. Choice of domain

The domain chosen for the scenarios was teaching language students as this group represented typical users being non-computer experts. This potentially allowed us a great deal of scope in choosing the material for the slides, but in reality this was restricted in a number of ways: the requirement of adding a flyscreen effect; the target resolution; the appreciation of possible range of effects by the lecturers - who were accustomed to overhead transparencies and word processors; the time scale imposed for producing the material. This latter restriction was compounded by the fact that we were using actual time-tabled classes for the experiments, which were therefore committed to planned teaching topics; if we missed the window for using the material, it would be totally useless until the following year.

7.3. Choice of software

The time scale forced the use of easy-to-use available packages; after some investigation in both Germany and Britain, the most favoured method of producing slides was using software graphics packages on the Macintosh and then to output via an electronic film recorder. We fortuitously found a bureaux service in Edinburgh (Express Computer Graphics Ltd) which gave a rapid turn around from software to slide - this was always less than two days, and in most case was closer to two hours. The pictures were produced with a pixel-based graphics package (Studio/8) and a presentation package (Persuasion) to the iterative design of the lecturers, and then doctored by PicMan - Harris (1989) to give the effect of the AMLCD.

We considered an alternative strategy for generating the graphics and the flyscreen effect utilising the user interface prototyping tool-kit developed at SEL, see Henskes (1987). This was rejected because the film recorder required Macintosh software to drive it, and we would have needed to convert from Sun picture files to Macintosh files. This extra effort would have been wasted as the resulting files, if we had been able to produce them, would have taken many hours to process by the Macintosh-Solitaire software.

7.4. Flyscreen effect

Adding a flyscreen was an interesting problem. The first trial was achieved photographically in Germany, where a grid of lines 10 microns wide and with a spacing of 50 microns was printed on emulsion. After experimenting with the contrast, we achieved the effect of dark shadows which we wanted. A section of this emulsion was sandwiched next to a normal 35 mm slide and projected on to a screen to produce the effect of the AMLCD. When we tried this using back-projection on to a sample lenticular screen (obtained from a television), we first noticed the moiré effect. Thus, we decided that it was essential to include this effect in all our material.

The flyscreen for the early stage mock-ups had used a second sheet of photographic emulsion, but the eventual effect was produced using software, so allowing total control of the picture production and the whole process to be achieved within a very short time-scale. In order to ameliorate the conversion process between aspect ratios, the PicMan program was used first to convert from 640 x 480 to 3200 x 2800, and then to add margins to make up to 4096 x 2371. The grid was included in the picture at 1 in 5 pixels at the slide resolution so giving 1/5th screen pixel wide images. This had one last minute teething problem when the samples came back from the film recorder: the flyscreen had all-but disappeared, and the moiré effect was very weak when projected onto a lenticular screen. This was rectified by specifying a wider grid line (two-fifths of a pixel wide), which, from observation, gave similar results to the photographic prototype flyscreen, which we assume will be the likely eventual effect.

7.5 Brightness

Brightness of screen used for the simulation was measured at approximately 80 cd/m^2 for the plain screen and 120 cd/m^2 for the lenticular screen. This dropped to 10 cd/m^2 and 40 cd/m^2 respectively when looking from an angle of approximately 45°.

7.6 Possible limitations of study

Unequal sizes of groups due to fixed lecture timetable - due to not all subjects turning up on the day. Some subjects regarded LIT purely as visual aid rather than computer controlled interactive device and therefore made comparisons with this in mind. However this only affected open ended questions and not readability of screen or judgement of interactive device per se.

Noise generation gave weird perceptual effects in some sensitive subjects. Although immediate feedback noise for subjects at the moment of screen change may have been an additional improvement, noise not associated with screen change was noted as an irritant factor by some respondents and therefore needs to be addressed in the final product as this may have a strong influence on use in a teaching situation and even fan noise levels such as those used in computer hard disks may prove too disruptive for some people.

Stimulus material on slides was not strictly uniform; however, the requirement was the ability to perceive material of all types, so, although this criticism is valid, in practice it did not matter as authenticity in a natural setting was maintained with adequate screen coverage of material.

8. Conclusions

The natural conclusion would be to specify a touch screen method of interaction because of its simplicity and ready acceptance. However, the remote pointer is a desirable method of interaction for some users or in some scenarios. Attention must be given to the pointing mechanism, either in its ease of use or, alternatively, in the way in which people learn to use it. The interaction device needs closer attention at the next iteration, which will be closer in functionality to the real device.

From a side-by-side comparison of the two screens, it is obvious that the technical properties of the lenticular screen are far superior to the plain one. The plain screen is unacceptable because of its inherent uneven light distribution created from back-projection. Yet, the results have shown a preference for the uncontaminated (plain) screen. Therefore, we must pay close attention to controlling the ill-effects that are produced by the combination of flyscreen and lenticular screen.

Like Gould (1987) we found using data from real users very important at this very early stage, before any committments had been made to either screen type or interaction device, and it has focussed the area of future research in eliminating the screen defects. As the evaluation was carried out at such an early stage of the design process, the results yielded somewhat weak data but has still been highly valuable in indicating the direction for further study.

We followed the ideas proposed by Gould (1987). Putting this approach into a controlled experiment forced us, from the start, to prepare a complete, realistic mock-up. This revealed the moiré effect on the lenticular screen which we would not have seen, had we conducted our experiments on a piece-meal basis, until a much later stage - with costly consequences. Further, the 'weak' data of an *early* iteration are at least as important for guiding the design process as data obtained through objective performance testing at later stages when the required functionality is available in the prototype.

Footnote

[1]Heath Robinson - 'A mechanical device of absurdly complicated design and having a simple function. Named after William Heath Robinson (1872-1944) English cartoonist who drew such contrivances.' *Collins English Dictionary, 2nd ed.*

Acknowledgements

Our special thanks to all in the Languages department at Heriot Watt University who took part and for their generous time commitment . Susan Donachie of the Computer Science Dept deserves special recognition for working the LIT. Research for this paper was partially supported by Esprit Contract No 2455.

References

CUSI, v3.4 Manual, (1988) Computer User Satisfaction Inventory, Kirakowski, J., & Corbett, M., Dept of Applied Psych. Univ.Col. Cork.

Electronics, April, 1989 p39-40

Esprit Contract No 2455 (1989) *Large Image Terminals.*

Gould, J. (1987) How to Design Usable Systems, Invited lecture : HCI-*INTERACT'87* (eds Bullinger & Shackel) Elsevier Science Publishers, North Holland.

Harris, J.R. (1989) PicMan documentation and user manual written in MPW C, (Internal Report, Heriot Watt Univ.).

Harris, J.R. and Parker, D.W. (1987), Evaluation of Rapid Prototyping Methodology in a Human Interface, *INTERACT'87* (eds Bullinger & Shackel) Elsevier Science Publishers, North Holland, 1059-1063

Henskes, D.T. and Tolmie, J.C. (1987) Rapid Prototyping of Man-Machine Interfaces for Telecommunications Equipment Using Interactive Animated Computer Graphics, *INTERACT'87* (eds Bullinger & Shackel) Elsevier Science Publishers, North Holland, 1053-1058

Long, J.B. & Whitefield, A. (1986) Evaluating Interactive Systems, Tutorial presented at *HCI '86* Sept.1986, York

Long, J.B. (1986) Invited lecture: *People & Computers: Designing for Usability,* Proceedings of 2nd Conf. of Brit.Computer Soc., HCI Specialist Group, eds Harrison & Monk., CUP

Morgan, Konrad (1989) "Individual Differences in User Performance on Command Line and Direct Manipulation Computer Interfaces" Univ.of Edinburgh, Unpublished Phd Thesis.

Rouse, W.B. (1984), Design and evaluation of computer-based decision support systems, In Salvendy, A (ed) *Human-Computer Interaction,* Elsevier Science Publ., B.V.Amsterdam 229-246

Shneiderman, B. (1987) *Designing the User Interface: Strategies for Effective Human-Computer Interaction,* Addison-Wesley Publ.Co.

Smith, S.L., Mosier, J.N. (1984), *Design Guidelines for User-System interface software,* Technical Report ESD-TR-84-190. U.S.A.F. Electronic Systems Divn., Hanscom Air Force Base, Mass.(NTIS No.AD A154 907)

Human–Computer Interaction – INTERACT '90
D. Diaper et al. (Editors)
Elsevier Science Publishers B.V. (North-Holland)

EVALUATION OF FLAT PANEL DISPLAY PROPERTIES ON A HIGH FIDELITY DISPLAY SIMULATOR

Gerd SPENKELINK, Henk VAN SPIJKER, Ted WHITE

Ergonomics Group, University of Twente, P.O. Box 217, 7500 AE Enschede, the Netherlands

A dynamic high fidelity simulator of Flat Panel Displays (FPD's) was built in the Esprit project "Modelling and simulation of modern display technologies under office work conditions".

Research methods using both experimental and subjective techniques have been developed and used for the purpose of simulator validation and the evaluation of FPD properties with respect to task performance and display acceptability for users.

The research methods can provide a valuable contribution to a better understanding of display quality and the results may be used in the design of FPD's and display fonts as well as in the development of ergonomic standards and guidelines for these new display technologies. The methods are also suitable for research outside this specific application field.

1. INTRODUCTION

Today there is a great deal of interest in Flat Panel Displays (FPD's) and much effort is put in further development of FPD technologies. In order to deal with the human factor in the development and design of FPD's there is a great need for tools to investigate the ergonomic aspects. It is also important to translate ergonomic knowledge into a system of guidelines and standards ie. design rules.

Ultimately, it is the compatibility of a display's visual properties with the properties of the human visual system and with the human information processing characteristics that determines the quality of a display. Relevant display properties pertain to the spatial, the temporal and the luminance domain. Although we would like to speak of display quality in terms of the hardware of a display, when using alphanumerics there are intricate relations between hardware properties and the font that is displayed. A further complication is that most display properties interact in producing the visual image as it is perceived by the user.

The importance of ergonomic knowledge in display development and design was recognized in the ESPRIT project 'modelling and simulation of modern display technologies under office work conditions' (DISSIM). As Placencia Porrero et al. [1] stated it: "the aim ... is to identify user requirements for flat panel display developments." In this project a display simulator was developed and built for dynamic simulations of FPD's, notably Liquid Crystal Displays (LCD's) and Electro-Luminescence Displays (ELD's). A detailed description of the simulator is provided by [1]. The most prominent feature of the display simulator is its capability to simulate spatial, luminance and temporal parameters, including their interactions, in real time over a wide range. Further simulations can be set up on two levels: either by specifying engineering parameters (layer materials, electrical constants etc.) or by specifying visual characteristics (luminance, colours, point spread functions etc.). In the first case a model translator off-line calculates the visual image characteristics that result from the entered combination of parameters. In the second case all parameters can be changed interactively. This interactive facility was used in the present research.

The ergonomic work in the DISSIM project has concentrated on three issues: the development of research tools, a validation of the simulator and the investigation of display characteristics in relation to task performance and subjective quality estimations. The research tools fall in two categories: experimental methods & procedures and subjective techniques. The quality of the simulations was investigated in a validation study involving three types of displays. The results indicate that in general the simulations are reliable, but that some specific problems remain.

Finally, performance and quality rating aspects of several display technologies and characteristics were investigated. The first results are encouraging. The continuation of the research aims at modelling subjective display quality and at the development and validation of ergonomic standards and guidelines for FPD technologies. Further the tools can be applied for the evaluation of specific FPD design solutions.

2. DEVELOPMENT OF RESEARCH METHODS

The way the simulations have been embedded in the simulator is shown in figure 1.

To create a high degree of flexibility the task and the experimental procedure have been completely separated. What cannot be seen in figure 1 is that in addition the stimulus material (the displayed information) is independent of both the task and the experimental procedure.

Setting up simulations of LCD's and ELD's by specification of visual characteristics requires that these specifications are available. For this purpose three FPD's were acquired: a reflective LCD (standard display of the HP-Vectra CS), a backlit LCD (standard display of the Zenith Z-180) and a Planar ELD, interfaced to the HP-Vectra lap-top. The data needed for setting up simulations could not be obtained from available product specifications.

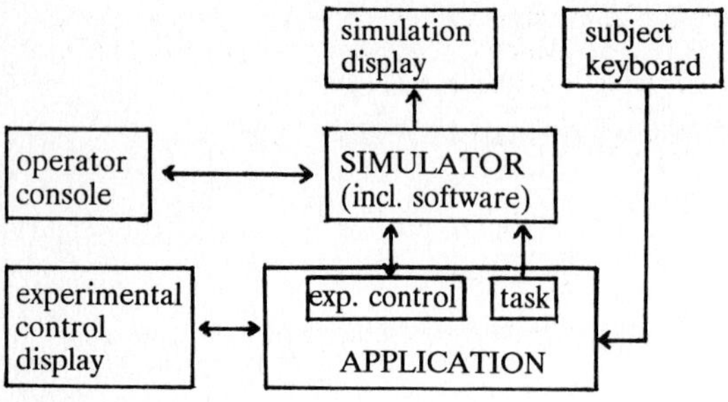

Figure 1. Schematic view of the configuration of the display simulator.

Therefore the relevant parameter values were obtained by direct or indirect measurement. Local spatial parameter values (display element sizes and separations) were obtained by indirect measurements. They were taken from projected colour slides of the displays and cross checked by calculating approximate sizes from resolution information and display area size measurements. The necessary font parameters were also obtained from the colour slides.

In setting up the simulations it appeared that it was necessary to make small corrections in the colours. The cause lies in the fact that displayed colours interact with each other and the human visual system, especially at the higher spatial frequencies. The corrections were based on subjectively matching the colours of the simulated displays with their actual counterparts. The correction process was facilitated by a specially designed colour manipulation interface, allowing direct manipulation of colours in equal luminance planes of a (quasi-)continuous colour triangle displayed on the simulation display.

The parameters in the spatial domain, as obtained from the actual FPD's had to be mapped onto the simulation display with its own spatial properties. In order to achieve eg. rectangular simulated display elements, a number of (roughly speaking round) CRT pixels had to be used. It is evident that in order to maintain relative sizes in the simulations the ultimate size of the simulated display elements and their gaps had to be determined by the smallest feature to be simulated, which was in all cases the gap between actual FPD display elements.

In order to design experimental fonts a font editor was built in which the font matrix and spatial parameters thereof can be changed interactively, immediately displaying the result of such changes. With the help of these tools simulations can be set up in a straightforward manner.

A number of experimental tasks and procedures have been developed. The experiments were designed specially for the simulator in the sense that they fit its capabilities, but are also applicable in other settings. The instruments can be used both for performance data collection (in experiments) and as a reference for the subjective technique.

There is good evidence that human observers are well able to judge displays (see eg. [2]). Therefore an instrument has been developed for the subjective evaluation of (simulated) displays. The remainder of this section is devoted to a description of the experiments and subjective techniques as they were used in the DISSIM project.

In the numerical verification task subjects are presented with a series of screens made up of three columns that in turn consist of six five-digit number strings. For each of these number strings the presence (or absence) of a specific target number has to be verified. The time needed to complete each screen and the number of errors made in verification are recorded.

In the target search task series of screens are presented that consist of Dutch text, quasi text (Dutch words in random order) or nonsense text (characters in random order, but with character frequency and word length distribution conform normal Dutch). Again the time needed to complete each screen and the number of errors made are recorded.

In the paired comparison task two simulated displays are presented simultaneously (one left, one right) on the simulator display. The half images may vary on simulation characteristics in the luminance and the spatial domain and in the lay out and contents of the presented information. This set-up can thus be applied for investigating display technology effects, font design effects or a mixture of both. In this set-up preferences can be obtained with respect to a large number of different simulated images. The method is suited for a number of psychophysical measurement techniques. Information to which the subject has to react can be presented on a separate terminal that is connected to the simulator, eg. rating scales can be administered on this terminal, so that the experimental procedure is fully automated and self paced.

A special piece of interactive software has been designed to allow subjects to change the value of parameters that are simulated in a matching task. In this task subjects try to create an accurate as possible simulation of an actual display acting as the standard. In another set-up it can be used as an optimization task in which subjects try to improve a simulation with respect to predefined features (such as colour or brightness). This user interface is designed for ergonomic research, but can be applied for other purposes as well.

In order to gather subjective responses to simulated displays a rating scale was constructed and implemented under MS-DOS. Starting from the notion that display quality is determined by a number of different visual features (ie. is of a multi dimensional nature), this Display Evaluation Scale (DES) was constructed to incorporate the relevant visual aspects of displays in the three domains. The full scale consists of 12 items, but subsets may be used for special occasions.

In the construction phase the scale was administered in connection with some of the above mentioned experimental procedures. Multi Dimensional Scaling (MDS) techniques, reliability calculations and significance tests were used to analyze ratings.

Besides the DES a rating scale was selected for the measurement of experienced work load, especially in combination with enduring tasks. For this purpose we used a Dutch translation of the Task Load indeX (TLX), a six item scale that was developed at NASA-Ames [3]. This well tested and validated [4,5] scale was chosen for reasons of economy and efficiency (fast and straightforward procedure which may be administered retrospectively) and because the TLX accounts for the multi-dimensionality of workload.

The TLX consists of 21 point subscales. In order to maintain a high degree of consistency for the raters, the DES was also developed as 21 point scales. Both scales were implemented under MS-DOS to be administered on a PC. Responses are generated by positioning a mark on a horizontal line by using the cursor keys. The initial position of the mark is exactly in the middle of the line and corresponds to a neutral answer. Only end descriptors are provided and the scales are presented as lines which are not subdivided. This creates a rather strong impression of a response continuum, even though only 21 cursor positions are possible on these lines.

3. APPLICATION OF DEVELOPED METHODS

The research methods and procedures mentioned in the previous section have been used in two studies validating the simulated images and are presently used in investigations of effects of display characteristics.

The validation was carried out in two experiments (a number verification task and a target search task) in which performance and subjective data for the three actual FPD's mentioned in section 2 and for their simulated counterparts were compared and tested against each other. The subjective data were also compared to descriptions of image properties of the actual and simulated displays.

The results indicated that performance measures were not as sensitive to variations in display properties and to differences between simulation and reality as were the subjective measures. This was probably partly a result of the relatively short experimental task durations so that no visual fatigue effects could show up. Secondly the subjective data converge with implications that followed from the descriptions of image properties. Thirdly the indicated differences between the simulated displays were somewhat smaller than those between their actual counterparts. This effect is illustrated in figure 2 that also serves as an example of how the subjective data are analyzed by scaling techniques.

This figure shows the two-dimensional MDS solution for displays which was based on the DES ratings of 16 subjects. A six item form of the DES was used. The following aspects were rated: brightness, fore-/background colour, sharpness, contrast, response speed, font. The ratings were obtained in the numerical verification task. The stress and RSQ values for this solution indicate a close fit between data and geometrical representation. With the help of regression analysis of the DES ratings over the MDS solution we were able to identify the two (orthogonal) dimensions as a font dimension and a combined contrast/brightness dimension respectively. As was noted earlier, a font (size and shape) is independent from display characteristics such as contrast and brightness. The present results indicate that subjects are well able to discriminate between these characteristics. The figure shows that the perceived qualitative differences between the simulated displays are smaller than those between the actual displays: the actual displays are drawn farther apart in space. Further it can be seen that the relative positions of the simulated displays correspond to the relative positions of the actual displays, indicating that although the ratings for the simulated displays are less extreme, the relations between the display technologies are maintained in both dimensions.

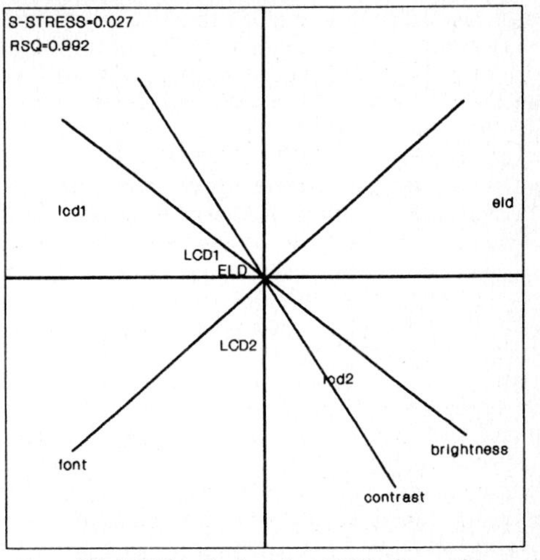

Figure 2. 2D MDS solution for DES data with n=16. The displays are plotted. Lowercase entries indicate actual displays, uppercase entries their simulated versions. 'lcd1'= reflective LCD; 'lcd2'=backlit LCD; 'eld'= ELD. Significant regressions of DES data (6 item form) are shown as lines with the DES item name at the end corresponding with a positive rating.

Summarizing over the various experiments that have been carried out it can be stated that for the implemented experimental tasks it is necessary to use a fairly large number of subjects (at least 16) to produce statistically sizeable effects. It can be expected that lengthening tasks to invoke visual fatigue will further increase the discriminative power of the tasks. The ratings offer interpretable and highly discriminating results. The first results from studies into effects of display parameters tentatively indicate that luminance (brightness and contrast) and the integrity and size of the alphanumerics (which is eg. strongly affected by gaps between display elements) are two strong determinants of the perceived quality of a display.

4. DISCUSSION

The dynamic simulator built in the DISSIM project is a unique instrument. It can dynamically produce high quality simulations of Flat Panel Displays which can be manipulated with respect to all relevant parameters in the spatial, the luminance and the temporal domain. Together with the development of flexible experimentation tools for ergonomic experiments there is now a very powerful research instrument.

A number of experimental tasks and procedures were defined, implemented and applied in validation studies. They are presently used in systematic studies in effects of visual properties of displays. The recognition of the importance of subjective aspects of display perception is reflected in the development of a rating scale for the evaluation of displays. The application of the tools has concentrated on flat panel displays, but they are equally valid for research on other display technologies.

If at an early stage in display development the ranges of values for the engineering parameters are known, the display simulator can generate images corresponding to the specified display configuration. These images can easily be subjected to an evaluation with the available tools. There are little opportunities to increase the ergonomic quality after designing or manufacturing a display. Therefore ergonomic knowledge has to be an input to Research & Development in the field of display technology. This implies that such knowledge has to be specified in terms that can be handled in the development of displays and display technologies. On the other hand guidelines must be accessible to the buyer and user of a display as a means for evaluating alternatives. Existing guidelines fall short for these purposes. They are generally drawn up for cathode ray tubes, while other technologies such as the Liquid Crystal bring about their own specific features and with that specific problems. Further, many standards conflict with each other, sometimes on important issues. This may reflect the use of different, conflicting research outcomes or different application areas aimed for. Thus there is a need for coherent ergonomic input to R&D. The notion of transparency can be applied here: a quality display is designed for compatibility with human perception, including subjective reactions, and with the way in which humans naturally cope with the tasks carried out. Therefore there is all reason to continue the work that was started in DISSIM.

In the next years the research methods and instruments are further shaped. They will be used to gain a fundamental insight in visual factors that are involved in display quality. This is achieved by developing a general weighted model of display quality. Further, for each characteristic that more or less contributes to display quality the operational relation between parameter value and a benchmark (selected visual performance aspects) can be stated and related to characteristics of human visual information processing. This means that displays, either actual or virtual (in terms of engineering parameters or in the form of a description of visual properties) can be evaluated and a contribution can made to the definition of ergonomic standards and guidelines for displays.

REFERENCES

[1] Placencia Porrero, I., Levis, J.P., Duprez, J., Bosman D., Spenkelink, G., Modelling and simulation of the visual characteristics of flat panel display technologies under office work conditions, Esprit '89 Conference Proceedings, Brussels, 27-30 november 1989, pp 915-933.

[2] Beaton, R.J., Perrin, N.A., Weiman, N., Multi-dimensional Scaling of Flat-Panel Image Quality. Baltimore: SID '89, 1989.

[3] NASA Task Load Index (TLX), Version 1.0. Moffett Field, CA: NASA Ames Research Centre, 1986.

[4] Casali, J., Wierwille, W.W., A comparison of rating scale, secondary task, physiological, and primary task workload estimation techniques in a simulated flight task emphasizing communications load, Human Factors, 1983, 25, 6, 623-641.

[5] Nataupsky, M., Abbott, T.S., Comparison of workload measures on computer generated primary flight displays, Proceedings of the Human Factors Society, 31st meeting, New York, October 19-23 1987, Vol.I, 548-552.

Human–Computer Interaction – INTERACT '90
D. Diaper et al. (Editors)
Elsevier Science Publishers B.V. (North-Holland)

COLOUR MODEL INTEGRATION AND VISUALISATION

Peter A. Rhodes, M. Ronnier Luo and Stephen A.R. Scrivener

LUTCHI Research Centre, Department of Computer Studies, Loughborough University of Technology, UK

Colour is an increasingly important element of human-computer interfaces and yet is difficult to control for a variety of reasons. In this paper, the most frequently used colour models are described and discussed. It is argued that no single model is going to be suitable for all applications. A system is proposed comprising a set of colour models that are integrated via mappings to and from the international standard colorimetric CIE XYZ System. The paper describes the models implemented to date in a system that allows interactive colour specification and communication.

1. INTRODUCTION

The increasing availability and affordability of high quality colour displays means that the use of colour is becoming more and more prevalent in today's computer systems. Consequently, the range of applications where colour selection and manipulation is a natural part of the user's task is large. In addition, colour is proving to be useful, or desirable, in many applications where colour was not available in the past (e.g. management information and office systems). The best colour monitors are capable of displaying more than 16 million colours. With so many colours to choose from, locating a specific colour becomes difficult. The key to the control of colour in any computer-based system is the method of colour specification. At present, many of colour models used to specify colours are not psychologically meaningful and are difficult to use. The solution to this problem of colour specification is to employ proper perceptual colour models at the user interface to the system.

Another area of difficulty commonly experienced is that of colour fidelity. A colour displayed on one computer monitor will generally not look the same on another monitor nor when it is printed on a hard-copy device. Where judgements have to be made on the basis of colour appearance, colour fidelity can be seen to be critical. For example, the value of a colour coding scheme can be lost if, in a map containing altitude information, two altitude ranges appear similar when presented on a particular device; this can then lead to ambiguity and misinterpretation which could be costly or even dangerous in certain situations. In order to successfully use applications involving colour, some precise means of both specifying and communicating colour information between different ranges of computer equipment is required.

This paper desribes work carried out as part of the Alvey Research Project MMI/146 entitled "Predictive Perceptual Colour Models" [1] and which is being further extended in the IED project "Colour Management in the Design of Advanced IT Systems". As a result of this work, a prototype system has been developed that allows the user to interactively visualise and manipulate various colour models by "flying through" in real-time any of the models' parameters.

2. COLOUR MODELS

The colour model is a means by which any colour may be specified according to a point within a three dimensional space. Colour models are used as a convenient way of selecting and communicating colour. A key requirement for communicating colour between different hardware is that the colours should appear similar on each device. This involves what is known as *device independency*. In order to achieve a degree of device independency, some form of device characterisation and calibration is required [2, 3, 4]. This must take into account the physical characteristics of the device (the way its primaries combine) and its gamut limitations (which colours *can* be reproduced). Additionally, the viewing conditions under which the colours are to be observed must be carefully defined and controlled - e.g. sample size and stray ambient light does affect colour appearance. Colour models may be categorised in many ways, but for our purposes, we will consider the following three classes, giving some commonly used examples of each.

2.1 Device-Dependent Colour Spaces

Device-dependent colour spaces are the most primitive means by which colour may be presented to the user. Generally, the same colours within such spaces appear different when presented on different media or using different devices.

RGB
This is the simplest model for representing colour on a CRT monitor because it relates directly to the intensities of the red, green and blue phosphors which emit the light that we then perceive as being a single colour. The same set of RGB coordinates do not produce the same colour on different monitors (i.e. this is a device-dependent colour space) due to differences in the physical characteristics of each monitor's phosphors. While this model is easy to implement on most computer systems, it is by no means easy to use: much experience is required to locate colours.

CMY
The printing industry typically uses cyan, magenta and yellow (and often black) inks as its primary colours which are combined to produce the desired colour. Device-dependency manifests itself due to differences in the inks used and variations in the printing process itself. Unlike RGB, the CMY primaries do not combine additively making their combinations difficult to predict. Both the CMY and RGB colour spaces are perceptually non-uniform; that is, human perception of lightness (or darkness), colourfulness or hue do not vary linearly with the amount of light (RGB) or ink (CMY) that is applied.

HLS
The HLS colour space was developed by Tektronix [5]. Its three attributes of hue, lightness and saturation are based on the perceptual characteristics of colour. Hue is arranged in rainbow order, with complementary hues (red and cyan, blue and yellow, green and magenta) opposite each other. The model parameters are psychologically meaningful and so this makes its use more intuitive. Its two main disadvantages are, however, that it is again device-dependent and that it is perceptually non-uniform.

2.2 Colour Order Systems

Colour order systems are based on physical samples, conventionally presented as coloured chips in the form of a book. Such a system is a rational method of sequencing and specifying colours using a certain number of representative material samples.

Munsell Colour System
The Munsell Colour System [6] is widely used in the fabric design and graphic art industries where colorimetry is less important. It is based on the *Munsell Book of Colour* [7] which contains many coloured chips. Each of these are ordered according to Munsell Hue, Munsell Value (lightness) and Munsell Chroma (colourfulness). Munsell Hue is described in terms of a combination of two of its five primary colours which are red, yellow, green, blue and purple. This can lead to problems with notation; for example, is 2.5PB closer to purple or to blue? Even with all the colours displayed for the user in Munsell Hue order, use of this hue naming system can seem confusing to the inexperienced. The system was intended to be viewed under just one special light source (known as *illuminant C*) corresponding to average daylight conditions and with a fixed background. Although each of its three attributes are intended to be perceptually uniform, it does exhibit some non-uniformity in certain areas.

Natural Colour System
The Swedish Natural Colour System (NCS) [8] is a colour-appearance model based on six elementary colours: red, yellow, green, blue, black and white. For each of these, there is an elementary attribute (redness, yellowness, greenness, blueness, whiteness and blackness) which defines on a 0 to 100 scale the degree of resemblance of a given colour to each of the elementary colours. The hue of an arbitrary colour is described by the ratio of the two neighbouring elementary hues. The system does not permit a colour to resemble both red and green or yellow and blue simultaneously; this is known as an opponent-hue system. The term chromaticness, being a colour's degree of resemblance to a completely chromatic hue, is also used by the system. This may be contrasted with the Munsell system which uses chroma to represent the degree of *difference* between the colour and a neutral colour of the same Munsell Value. Since NCS is a colour-appearance model, it may not be used to quantify differences in hue as it is not perceptually uniform in its hue scale.

2.3 Colorimetric Models

Rather than using physical samples (which can change colour with age due to contamination or fading), it is possible to specify a colour model numerically using a standardised colour measurement technique.

CIE XYZ System
This was originated in 1931 by the Commission Internationale de l'Eclairage (CIE) and has since been refined [9]. It is based on a series of experiments involving several observers who were asked to match a test colour (viewed under tightly controlled conditions) to a mixture of red, green and blue reference lights whose intensities could be varied. By combining these three primary colours, a colour of known visible wavelength can be matched. The three intensities required to match a particular colour are known as the *tristimulus values* and define three colour matching functions across the entire visible spectrum. With the CIE system, it is possible to describe numerically any colour in terms of its XYZ coordinates such that any two colours with the same tristimulus values appear the same when viewed under the same conditions (i.e. using the same media and with the same background colours and lighting conditions). The XYZ coordinates indicate the amount of reference red, green and blue lights that are needed to match a colour. This numerical quantification is known as *colorimetry*. Using colorimetry means that we can achieve a good visual match between colours presented on different monitor screens (again, provided that the viewing conditions are alike) but does not guarantee that colours produced using dissimilar media (e.g. textiles or paint samples) will appear alike. However, the main drawback of the CIE XYZ system is that it is perceptually non-uniform; equal colour differences are not represented as equally long lines in its colour space [10, 11].

CIE $L^*u^*v^*$ and CIE $L^*a^*b^*$ Uniform Colour Spaces
These two uniform colour spaces, recommended by the CIE in 1976, both share a common dimension (L^*) describing lightness. Both are based on the CIE XYZ system. Effort was made in both cases to achieve a uniform colour space. CIE $L^*u^*v^*$ [9] is a linear projective transformation of CIE XYZ. This allows it to be used in the colour television or colour photography industries because this makes it easier to use for predicting colours obtained by the additive mixture of lights. CIE $L^*a^*b^*$ [9] is actually a non-linear transformation of CIE XYZ space and is widely used in the surface colour industry (e.g. paints, textiles, plastic). Because both models are approximately uniform, this makes them suitable for quantifying colour difference, typically in quality control applications. Both spaces can be

tranformed from cartesian coordinates to polar space with chroma (similar to colourfulness) and hue angle attributes. This representation makes them easier to use since these attributes are more psychologically meaningful, i.e. they correspond closely to the metrics used by our minds when judging colour [12].

Hunt-ACAM

Hunt-ACAM [13] is a product of the Hunt 89 model [14] and the Alvey Colour Appearance Model (ACAM). It was derived as part of the Alvey project mentioned previously. By modelling the human visual process, Hunt-ACAM is able to predict colour appearance under various viewing conditions. The model provides several perceptual attributes: hue, lightness, brightness, coloufulness, saturation and chroma. Not only does it take into account the light source used and the lighting level, it also considers the effect on colour appearance of a surrounding neutral colour. Most importantly, different media are considered within the model, e.g. the differences between screen and surface colours. The model's performance has been verified using LUTCHI colour appearance data [13] (consisting of about 43,000 estimations of lightness, coloufulness and hue) obtained during the Alvey project and was found to be the best model of its kind currently available in terms of its fit to the data.

3. COLOUR MODEL VISUALISATION SOFTWARE

The above models, and many others, are in use at this time. Some industries working with colour have a strong preference for one particular model and are highly reluctant to change to another. Indeed, some models are more suited than others to certain environments, e.g. persons in the printing industry often must deal directly with the ink primary colours that are used to produce the final print. This would suggest that a system is needed that integrates the commonly used colour models. By using a computer, there are the added advantages of speed and increased control. The speed of modern systems means that it is possible to develop interactive software that allows the user to control various model parameters and see the results instantly. Although the model being shown may be based on a limited set of physical samples (e.g. Munsell), it is possible by means of interpolation to show many more colours on the computer display than can be seen using those samples. Also, physical samples deteriorate with time and hence have a limited useful life.

Such a system has been implemented as part of the Alvey project. It integrates the RGB, CMY, HLS, CIE $L^*u^*v^*$ and $L^*a^*b^*$, Munsell and ACAM models into a single interactive system. Using a "WIMP" interface, the user is able to select one model and manipulate any of its various parameters. Each model is presented on the screen as a view comprised of a series of coloured patches arranged according to that particular model's spatial definition. The views are labelled according to the dimensions shown in order that colours may be located or described numerically. Once the view of the colour model has been selected, the user can then vary just one of the model's dimensions under mouse control. This gives the ability to "fly through" the colour space of the model and gives an instant feedback of how colours change within that dimension. This is useful in learning to use new colour models and in using more familiar ones with greater efficiency.

Figure 1 illustrates the communication that exists between the various colour models comprising the system that has been developed. It also makes the distinction between device dependent and device independent models. As can be seen, the CIE XYZ system forms the central hub of the device independent models and all models must eventually produce RGB information as this is required to drive the colour monitor. Algorithms have been devised which allow reverse mappings between the models (i.e. allowing communication in the reverse direction to that shown). This permits communication between the models themselves allowing a user of one model to communicate colour information with a user of another. Using this system allows users from different environments to speak the same colour language.

4. CONCLUSION

A prototype of a colour management toolkit has been developed allowing the user to manipulate and select colour using various standard colour models. Such a system has several beneficial qualities to offer the user. Firstly, the design of its user interface provides a quick and convenient means for visualising the various colour models and selecting colours from them. Because of its speed and ease of use, it is useful for users who are inexperienced in using one or more of the models; interactive manipulation of the colour models speeds the learning process. The system is useful to a wide range of users from different backgrounds whose colour requirements are dissimilar but nevertheless need to communicate colour information. Finally, the system can be used by colour researchers to visually assess the uniformity of colour spaces and for general colour experimentation.

The system will be further extended as part of the IED project during which the user interface will be improved to increase efficiency in selecting colours. Hunt-ACAM will be further developed to include a much wider range of media, e.g. transparencies and textiles. Consequently, the software needs to be extended in order to cope with multiple-media by displaying the predicted colour appearance of samples as they would be seen when reproduced on different hardcopy devices. More standard colour systems will have to be considered (e.g. NCS, DIN and OSA) because each has its own characteristics which may be useful specifically to certain professions. Future systems will allow electronic colour communication between different industries using the CIE XYZ as intermediary. This will allow designs to be conveyed between distant sites whilst maintaining a high level of colour fidelity.

ACKNOWLEDGEMENTS

The research described here was conducted under Alvey project MMI/146 as part of the Alvey UK program. The authors would like to thank Professor R.W.G. Hunt (independent consultant) and L.W. MacDonald (project manager, Crosfield Electronics) for their guidance in this work.

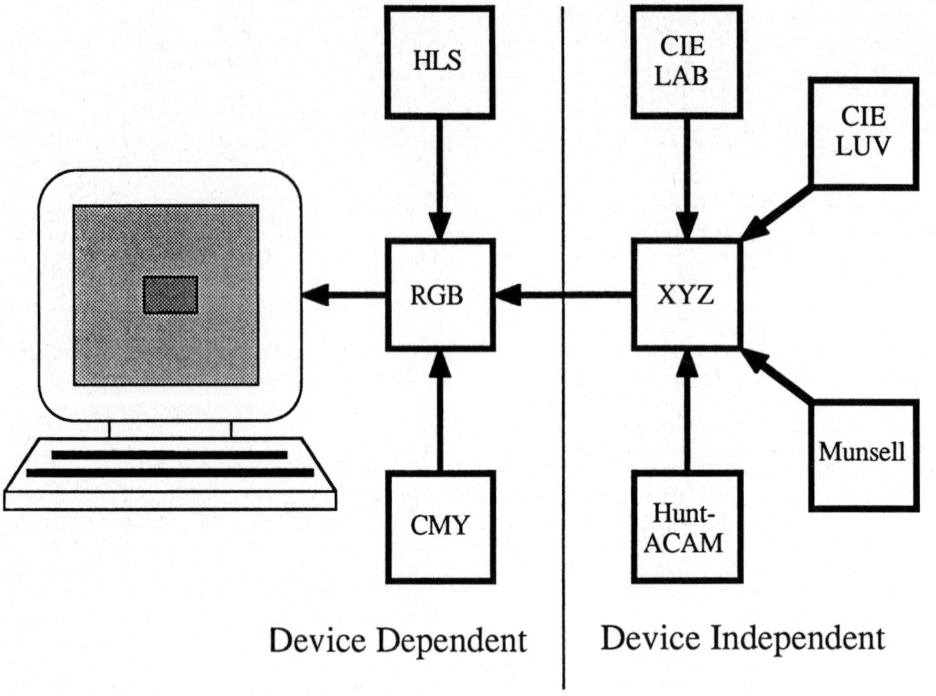

Figure 1: Communication of Colour Information between each of the models

REFERENCES

[1] MacDonald, L.W., Luo, M.R., Scrivener S.A.R., Images on a Video Display Monitor. RPS Conference, September 1989, Cambridge.

[2] Cowan W.B., An Inexpensive Scheme for Calibration of a Colour Monitor in terms of CIE Standard Coordinates. Computer Graphics, vol.17, 1983, pp315-321.

[3] Stone, M.C., Cowan, W.B., Beatty J.C., Colour Gamut Mapping and the Printing of Digital Colour Images. ACM Transactions on Graphics, 1988, pp249-292.

[4] Post, D.L.,Calhoun C.S., An Evaluation of Methods for Producing Desired Colors on CRT Monitors. Color Research and Application, vol.14, 1989, pp172-186.

[5] Foley, J.D., van Dam A., Fundamentals of Interactive Computer Graphics, Addison-Wesley, 1982, pp617-619.

[6] Newhall, S.M.,Nickerson, D., Judd D.B., Final Report of the O.S.A. Subcommittee on the Spacing of the Munsell Colors. Journal of the Optical Society of America, 1943, pp385-418.

[7] Munsell A.H., A Colour Notation Munsell Colour Co., 1946.

[8] Hård, A.,Sivik L., NCS - Natural Color System: A Swedish Standard for Color Notation. Color Research and Application, vol.6 , 1981, pp129-138.

[9] Colorimetry (Second Edition). CIE Publication No.15.2, 1986.

[10] MacAdam D.L., Specification of Small Chromaticity Differences. Journal of the Optical Society of America, vol.33, 1943, pp.18-26.

[11] Luo, M.R., Rigg B., Chromaticity-Discrimination Ellipses for Surface Colours. Color Research and Application, vol.11, 1986, pp25-42.

[12] Hunt R.W.G., The Specification of Colour Appearance I. Concepts and Terms Color Research and Application, vol.2, 1977, pp55-68.

[13] Luo, M.R. Clarke, A.A. Rhodes, P., Schappo, A., Scrivener, S.A.R., Tait. C.J., Deriving Hunt-Alvey Colour Appearance Model. LUTCHI Research Centre, Loughborough University of Technology.

[14] Hunt, R.W.G. Procedures for Using a Revised Colour Appearance Model. RPS conference, September 1989, Cambridge.

Human–Computer Interaction – INTERACT '90
D. Diaper et al. (Editors)
Elsevier Science Publishers B.V. (North-Holland)

ON THE VISIBILITY OF CHARACTER FEATURES ON A VDU

D. BOSMAN†, T.N. WHITE‡

† Faculty of Electrical Engineering
‡ Faculty of Philosophy and Social Sciences
University of Twente,
Enschede, The Netherlands

The legibility of characters depends on several factors, in the first place on the visibility of specific character features. Small character features may be difficult to perceive, even under supra-threshold conditions. Visibility of features is here taken as the probability that the corresponding amounts of light energy produce signals which can be interpreted by the brain. Therefore brightness, not luminance, determines perception. Early visual processing is modelled as a mapping of the character spatial luminance distribution into local brightness variations, measured in equal intervals. This is the basis for calculating visibility probability estimates of features of the presented characters and symbols. Influence on visibility is discussed of several common describing factors, such as average brightness, line separation, stroke width, active area and blur.

1. INTRODUCTION

From the days of the crude 5×7 matrix which only provides room to define one bilevel alphanumeric set (albeit with some legibility problems), progress allows the implementation of more sophisticated fonts approaching the quality of print. Faithfulness of reproduction now becomes the issue; inherent quantification of the shapes still remains visible. Technical specs are not sufficient to assess perceived quality; nor the ergonomic considerations applied in the design phase of the display, although these are helpful in avoiding the most common pitfalls. To verify choices of the design parameters and to obtain data on (gray level) driving signals, completed prototypes are subjected to ergonomic measurements. These are costly, their extent and number must be kept as small as possible. It would be advantageous if, at the beginning of the design, the visual appearance of the display can be modelled and subjected to a quality rating by a 'standard observer', also available in software. Such models gradually become available, for instance (Bosman, 1989; van der Meulen & Placencia Porrero, 1988). This paper reflects a first effort and its results of their application to font parameters; synergetic use of available scientific research data in the areas of physics, physiology, psychology and modelling mathematics. The legibility of characters depends on several factors, many of which are interdependent. To assess their effects the possibility of ordering must be considered, but first and foremost the relevant character details must be 'sufficiently' **visible**. These details are very local, not global features of the brightness image distribution. In this paper, the analysis is restricted to some commonly used factors which can be linked to 'visibility' of character features, in terms of probabilities to exceed the brightness threshold. To calculate 'iso-brightness' contours of characters from their luminance distributions perceived in a fixation period, a model of early visual process ing (Bakker & Bosman, 1988) is used. This maps the luminance distribution into a brightness pattern and can include comparators to detect the iso-brightness contours.

Human operator response is characterised by 'uncertainty', inability to positive identification. This is partly due to cognitive effects, partly due to ambiguous stimulation in the brightness domain. In terms of the model, the detector can be implemented with two thresholds, which results in three regions of 'yes', 'uncertain' and 'no' probabilities. 'Uncertain' responses can add information about feature visibilty: confused characters appear to have membership to features in common. Of course, (cognitive) redundancies also inherent in its members, affect the weight of visibility uncertainties associated with some features. For instance, in upper case many characters have a vertical stroke at the left side. With poor vertical performance of the display, a perceived symbol '≡' cannot be mistaken for O or Z because of strong mismatch with the sets of internal references; E and B are more likely.

Good legibility requires in the character feature space, sufficient, preferably uniform, distance distribution and the perception of specific features which force separation in spite of commonalities. It est: a lower bound on the probability to exceed the threshold of seeing "important" local features of the font in question. To study

legibility, it is imperative to understand the factors determining visibility.
In table I the factors, in some way associated with visibility, are marked. In terms of the model: features with good visibility produce sufficient changes in brightness to be detected with "high" probability (e.g.>95 %).

This is true for both the "written" features of a character and for the "empty" or "non-written" spaces in between. Difficult are the detection probabilities in the range of 50 % to 95 %; it depends on cognitive factors, e.g. the distance distribution of prime features in the feature space, whether character confusions are likely to occur. In this paper, therefore, only a single threshold is considered; 'yes' and 'no' probabilities, without inference to confusion.

Table I: LEGIBILITY FACTORS

- Symbol height	√
- Stroke width/delsize to symbol height ratio	√
- Spatial del distribution (font)	√
- Symbol width to height ratio	
- Symbol spacing	
- Size of the alphabet, redundancy in syllabes	
- Line spacing	
- Lay-out	
- Luminance contrast	√
- Colour contrast	√
- Quantisation	√
- Active area and brightness ripple	√
- Line jumping due to interlace (twinkle)	
- Reflections	
- Blur	√
- Flicker	
- Noise	√
- Shading	√
- Task dependent factors	

2. VISIBILITY

In a matrix display the smallest feature size is determined by the display elements (dels). The original images represented on the display are assumed continuous; i.e. the dimensions of dots and lines are determined by e.g. a printing technology which still are superior to the most advanced display by a factor of better than 2. There the dominant limiting factor in visibility is the eye. Ergonomic models of its performance can be applied in order to be able to predict the visiblity aspects in font qualities. Initially threshold data of perception of discs and lines have been gathered (Blackwell, 1946; Westheimer & Campbell, 1962), only the last two decades suprathreshold performance, as is the case in "normal" reading, is investigated (Georgeson & Sullivan, 1975; Campbell & Howell & Johnstone, 1978; Cannon, 1979) These data, obtained on systematic and simple shapes, are indicative only and cannot serve to predict the visibility of complex character features. Moreover, within the symbol both positive and negative contrast are present; they occur very locally. Analysis must focus on the ticked factors in Table I; in this paper is considered the discriminability of local features and their relations with character height, strokewidth, contrast, active area and blur.

3 VISIBILITY OF LOCAL FEATURES

Traditionally fonts and the quality of their representation are characterised by the factors listed in Table I. These are global measures which cannot give insight into possible confusions caused by feature distortions due to low visibility, or by missing and extra dels.
In order to model the influences of e.g. symbol height, strokewidth, modulation and blur, the local brightness distributions of the 2-D signals sent to the brain by the optic nerve can be examined; assuming that early visual processing in the eye (optical transmission properties and neural action in the retina) is mostly responsible for the quality of the image from which the brain must infer cognitive responses.
The engineering model of early visual processing providing the required brightness distributions, was available from project OS 612/1593. It is a nonlinear 2-D achrome image processor consisting

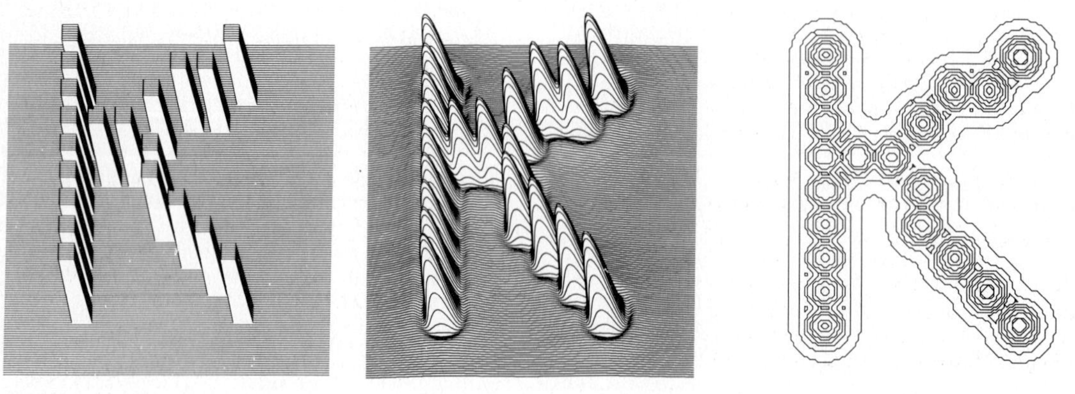

a) b) c)
Fig. 1) Symbol processing by an engineering model of vision
a) Luminance profile; b) brightness profile; c) Iso-brightness contours.

of a) an optical part including lens aberration, pupil diffraction and scatter, and b) a detector part which maps and enhances the illumination distribution at the retina into an interval scale of brightness, taking account of both photon noise and neural noise. The next step will be the translation of brightness into probability of seeing.

In figure 1 an example is depicted of:

a) luminance distribution of a character 2.5 mm high, driven at a foreground of 200 cd/m^2 and a background of 10 cd/m^2, with resolution of 3.6 dels/mm and 45 % active area;
b) the same character after being processed by the model, when viewed at a distance of 47 cm. The foreground and background now are 450 and 300 brightness unity intervals respectively.
c) iso-brightness contours obtained from b), which depict perceived shapes of the features, at several probabilities of seeing them.

With the output b) of this model it is possible to determine both average brightness contrast and local contrast modulations over the character area (achrome). The data so obtained differ per symbol; e.g. for the del distributions of e, l, m, and z. Therefore, in tests of visibility the stimuli must not have cognitive redundancy; thus be composed of numerals and unfamiliar yet pronounceable words.

3.1 Average brightness resulting from local modulation within the symbol

At the display resolution of 3.6 dels/mm it is seen that in the perceived image (figure 1b) the response to the oblique bars of the K consists of wholly separated PSFs, i.e. ≈100 % modulated; while responses to adjoining dels in horizontal and vertical directions slightly merge, with smaller modulation and thus, presumably, should give a stronger impression. These results were obtained using in the model circular symmetric point spread functions (PSFs) for the neural processing. Experimental evidence suggests that the eye-brain system adjusts its receptive fields (PSFs of locally pooled receptors and associated neurons) to elongate and align with the line direction, the model data probably are pessimistic but, in our opinion, still provide useable estimates. By the same argument, the brightness ripple (or modulation) in line pieces must be determined along the line (cross section through the peaks), instead of using volume ratios.

The eye/brain system also adjusts itself to the background brightness B_b, shifting the apparent brightness interval scale to become a ratio scale with its zero to match the background brightness. Thus, in the example of figure 1, the range over which the average level must be determined becomes: 450-300= 150. Then the peak brightness B_p equals 150, the trough of the modulation B_t depends on the amount of merging of the eye PSF. At modulations of ≈ 100 % the cross sections along the line resemble normal distributions, yielding an average brightness B_{av}

$$B_{av} = 0.6B_p + 0.4B_t \qquad (3.1a)$$

For undeep modulations the ripple tends toward symmetry and

$$B_{av} = 0.5B_p + 0.5B_t \qquad (3.1b)$$

resulting in the following table II, made for

B_p=150:

modulation index (%)	B_{av} (units)
100	90
30	115
0	150

Because the brightness unit equals 1 JND (Just Noticeable Difference) and one needs at least 7 JND (Galves & Brun, 1976) comfortable resolving power (here called critical visibility), in this example the luminance contrast is more than sufficient. A possible model for the visibility factor associated with average brightness :

$$v_{av} = 2\,\{0.5 - \operatorname{erf} B_{av} / 5\} \qquad (3.2)$$

graphically depicted in figure 2.

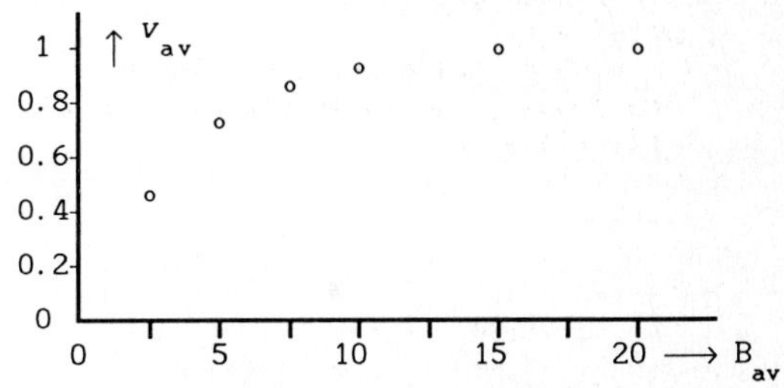

Fig. 2) Visibility factor against average foreground brightness, according to (3.2). For B_{av} = 7: v_{av} = 0.84.

3.2 Effects of stroke width and character height

If a stroke is very thin, the visibility of the stroke is low. Conversely, if character height and font in combination with the stroke width leaves little room for intrasymbol spaces, the PSFs merge reducing local contrasts of these spaces and thus their visibility. Consequently one may expect that visibility of character features, as function of the stroke width, peaks at a certain width interval.

The vision model calculates the brightness distribution across the character matrix, to which expression (3.2) can be applied, thus transforming its result into the symbol feature visibility matrix. The distribution over this matrix depends strongly on the character in question; there is a large variance within the total alpha numerical alphabet. This, then, must also be the case with 'legibility'.

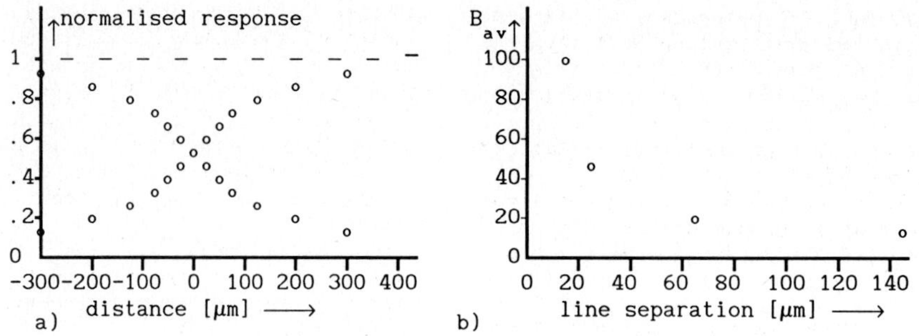

500 mm viewing distance
Fig. 3a Overlapping eye responses for 2 just touching lines
Fig. 3b Effect of separation of radiant lines on critical visibility

Insight into the modelling process is obtained by realising that the eye PSF is approximately Gaussian; the cross section of the line results from convolving the uniform stroke luminance distribution with the PSF. For thick strokes the line edge becomes S shaped, approximated by an error function. When (in negative contrast) two edges overlap as shown in figure 3a, the visibility of the dip requires that $B_{av} > 7$.

Some light emitting displays, e.g. light emitting diodes, can provide very thin lines at high brightness. That the visibility of very small gaps in LED arrays is high, is understood from figure 3b, which is derived from figure 3a for the threshold separation at $B_{th} = 7$.

Consequently, from the visibility angle, character height can be quite small. At high luminance and contrast, the young healthy eye should see every feature of familiar fonts in radiant thin strokes at character heights down to 0.7 mm at the viewing distance of 47 cm (5 arcminutes). But strong recognition requirements have drastic effect as evidenced by Osga (1984); the character must not be smaller than about 12 arcminutes and even larger for thicker strokes.
The desire to ascertain visibility of very small features relates to the reason why people tend to operate emissive displays at higher luminances.

For positive contrast, the same arguments lead to different conclusions. The brightness of the screen background and surround can be matched which is less fatiguing; at higher background luminances the eye PSF is more slender allowing sharper vision under favourable contrast/size conditions. But strong merging of the PSFs takes place for very thin strokes. Because at constant stroke width-to-symbol height ratio, the stroke width shrinks proportionally to character height and viewing distance, the contrast of the whole symbol suffers, not only certain features such as with negative contrast.
Assuming ample background brightness $B_{av} = 25$ and applying the data of figure 2, the effect is depicted in figure 4, consistent with (Reger & Snyder & Farley, 1989) for 9x12 matrix blocks or better. At very small angular character height, i.e. small del size, the smallest intra-symbol spaces (in 'a' and 'e') with area < 2' also decrease in contrast, causing sharper cutoff of the legibility. The same happens when stroke width increases at constant character height, implying that the curve of figure 4 mirrors at thicker stroke widths.

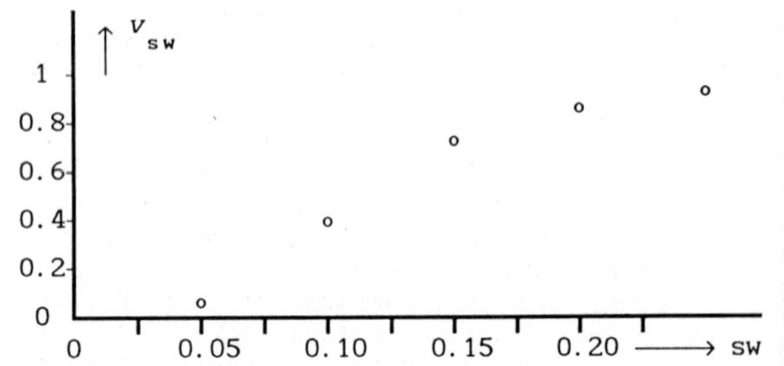

Fig. 4 Visibility v_{sw} versus stroke width sw in [mm]. Viewing distance 470 mm.

4. EFFECT OF BLUR

Natural blurring causes additional adjecent gray levels, through smearing due to point spreading in e.g. the optical transmission outside the eye; at the face of a CRT or in display cover layers and antiglare filters. Only in badly designed CRT based displays (Barten, 1984) considerable blur can be experienced, therefore analysis is restricted to effects of little blurring by whatever cause.
Hamerly & Dvorak (1981) pointed out that edge gradient softening by 0.4 arcminute in normal print causes the experience of bolder line segments. Blur is most obvious in sharp turns of line directions and narrows intra-symbol spacing, where it should be avoided.

In low to medium resolution quantised displays blur can actually improve the perception. The apparent thickening effect is used to advantage to modulate perceived stroke width as required in high quality fonts. (Ginsburg, 1977; Naiman & Farrell, 1989). For fixed circular symmetric blur PSFs (image independent), the turning point in resolution can be expected at about 2 arcminutes

per del (3.6 dels/mm at 47 cm viewing distance). At higher resolutions and high font quality requirements, simple fixed blurring operations are not satisfactory. Correlations between gray levels of display elements in characters are image-dependent and must be individually defined in each symbol matrix.
Such intended 'blur' operations, being nonlinear, can be determined with the aid of the calculated spatial brightness distribution, or determined in interactive experiments.

5. EFFECT OF ACTIVE AREA OF THE DISPLAY ELEMENT; LOCAL BRIGHTNESS MODULATION

Remain the questions of discomfort caused by the presence of the quantisation and the associated brightness ripple (modulation) of the character. This is a combined effect of visibility and of cognitive factors which are inseparable and therefore must be considered together. Much experimental effort (Shurtleff, 1974; Uphaus & Pastor, 1982; van Ness, 1986; Watson, 1989) was devoted to assessment of the quality of quantised fonts; earlier publications lack generality as they reflect the state of the art in the display technology of their epoch. Spatial resolution measured in solid angle is often not explicitly varied; usually one character height is specified in the experiment. The results have in common that for (familiar) fonts the legibility as function of quantisation shows an exponential trend from coarse to fine, a result that is intuitively acceptable.
The ANSI standard for Human Factors Engineering of Visual Display Terminal Workstations states that the minimum permissable active area or fill factor in flat panel displays be 30 %, preferred is 75 % . From the foregoing it is obvious that resulting brightness modulation greatly varies with del size. This recommendation thus is not sufficient; some function of both the number of elements in the character matrix and the active area per del should be considered. The resulting brightness modulation then depends on the adaptation state of the eye. One may specify a fixed 'standard' eye PSF or use the brightness model to calculate the resulting modulation. Based on the presumptions of the model, under good viewing conditions the modulation seems secondary as it hardly affects visibility; only deep modulations have effect but this should be verified.
Active del area convolves with the eye point spread function, producing a modified PSF with effective area about equal to the sum of both. E.g. in figure 1b), with del pitch of 2 arc-minutes and eye PSF with effective area of 1.5 minutes solid angle, the 45 % active del area results in a PSF with effective area of 3.3 arc-minutes solid angle. In the brightness pattern of adjacent dels of a line in a main direction of the display, the modulation contrast is clearly visible. With 75 % active del area the resulting effective area becomes 4.5 minutes, larger than the pitch squared. For that reason modulation contrast is only visible in oblique lines.

When more dels are addressed as in complicated shapes of characters, modulation may become objectionable, although it is not yet known how to quantify this effect. To calculate the modulation index, it is necessary to use the 2-D vision model. By the same means it is possible to design reduction of image-dependent unwanted modulation, using gray level blurring techniques discussed in section 4.
A reasonable model to estimate the modulation contrast in the brightness pattern of adjacent dels of a line in a main direction of the display is the expression

$$m = \exp - \frac{\pi\sigma^2}{(1-P)(p+\sigma)^2} \times \frac{P(p+\sigma)^2 + \pi\sigma^2}{(p+\sigma)^2 + \pi\sigma^2} \qquad (5.1)$$

with m the modulation index $m = (B_p - B_t)/(B_p + B_t)$;
P the active area in % of the display element, p the pitch of the display elements, σ the s.d. of the eye PSF. A plot of m as function of p/σ with parameter P is depicted in figure 5.

6. EVALUATION

With the exclusion of complicated effects like recognition and confusion, masking, fatigue, spatial frequency adaptation and temporal phenomena, the vision model explains some of the

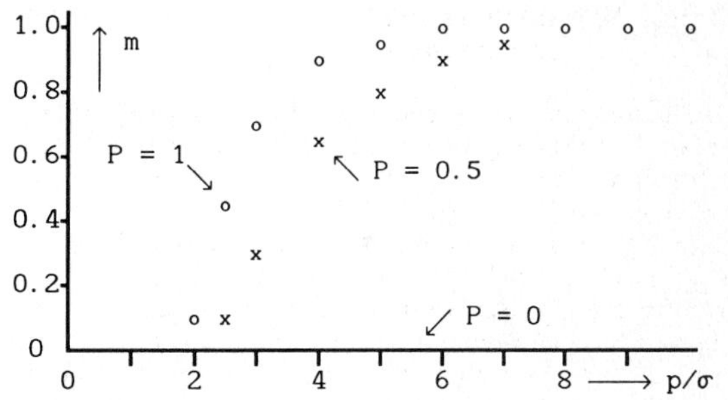

Fig.5 Effect of pitch, active area and eye PSF on brightness modulation

ergonomic facts in display viewing in terms of early visual processing. Brightness is the determining variable instead of the physical quantity luminance. Local exceedances of a minimum brightness threshold is far more important than many scientists and manufacturers are currently aware of. Moreover, the aspect of positive versus negative contrast is not a matter of preference. Many characters have a complex set of both, which may either enhance or disrupt seeing. Also the point spread function of a del and blur are important. The effect of each of these factors is reasonably understood.
To study the interrelation of these factors is relatively new. On the basis of a display simulator we are now able to investigate these factors by systematic variation in a real time setting. A discussion of Spenkelink, van Spijker and White, elsewhere in these proceedings, gives

an impression of what already has been done in this field.
Furthermore it may also provide an objective method for the evaluation of confusion effects caused by erroneously addressed and faulty display elements and for comparison of (the quality of) displays of different design; thus being a tool in the hands of the display designer which reduces design time and cost.

With the display simulator we are able to vary in software the factors mentioned above and, using the model predictions of the brightness distribution, investigate their effect on visibility and legibility. The objectively measurable human task performance and subjective ratings about perceived task performance are related to the outcomes of the vision model by applying advanced statistics such as Multi Dimensional Scaling. The research as such is focussed to provide data for improving the rapid prototyping of new displays. The display simulator affords to simulate character information, using different character sets and fonts, on different flat panel technologies in configurations yet to be designed. It is our strong conviction that this research vehicle will greatly assist in evaluating effects of modern display technology in visibility and legibility under office work conditions.

7. REFERENCES

1 Bakker W.H. & Bosman D. (1988). Engineering how we see a display. Digest International Symposium of the Society for Information Display, **XIX**, pp 439-444, ISSN 0097 966X

2 Barten P.G.J. (1984) Spotsize and current distribution of CRTs. Proceedings of the Society for Information Display, **25**, no 3, pp 155-159.

3 Blackwell H.R. (1946). Contrast thresholds of the human eye. Journal of the Optical Society of America, **36**, no 11, pp 624-643.

4 Bosman D. (1989). An engineering view on the visual system-technology interface. Display Engineering, ed. D. Bosman. pp 60-74. North Holland, Amsterdam. ISBN 0 444 87319 8

5 Campbell F.W. & Howell E.R. & Johnstone J.R. (1978). A comparison of threshold and supra-threshold appearance of gratings with components in the low and high spatial frequency range. J. Physiol., **284**, pp 193-201.

6 Cannon Jr. M.W. (1979). Contrast sensation: a linear function of contrast. Vision Research, **19**, pp 1045-1052.

7 Galves J.P. & Brun J. (1976). Colour and brightness requirements for cockpit displays: proposal to evaluate their characteristics. Conference proceedings CP-167, pp 6/1-6/8. Advisory Group for Aerospace Research and Development, Paris. ISBN 92 835 1438 6

8 Ginsburg, A.P. (1977). Visual information processing based on spatial filters contained by biological data. PhD Dissertation, Cambridge University, England.

9 Hamerly, J.R. & Dvorak, C.A. (1981) Detection and discrimination of blur in edges and lines". Journal of the Optical Society of America, 71, no.4, pp 448-452.

10 van der Meulen A. E. & Placencia Porrero, I. (1988). Requirements, specifications, and architecture for a real time display simulator. Digest International Symposium of the Society for Information Display, **XIX**, pp 454-457. ISSN 0097 966X

11 Naiman, A. & Farrell, J. (1989). Modelling the display and perception of grayscale characters. Digest International Symposium of the Society for Information Display, **XIX**, pp 424-427. ISSN 0097 966X

12 van Ness, F.L. (1986). A new teletext character set with enhanced legibility. Proceedings of the Society for Information Display, **27**, no 3, pp 239-242.

13 Osga, G.A. (1984). Legibility study of a tactical graphics language for high resolution monochrome display. Digest International Symposium of the Society for Information Display, **XV**, pp 287-290. ISSN 0097 966X

14 Reger J.J. & Snyder H.L. & Farley W.F. (1989). Legibility of emissive and non- emissive flat-panel displays under fluorescent and daylight illumination. Digest International Symposium of the Society for Information Display, **XX**, pp 364-367. ISSN 0097 966X

15 Shurtleff, D.A. (1974). Legibility Research. Proceedings of the Society for Information Display, **15**, no 2, pp 41-51.

16 Uphaus, J.A. & Pastor, J.R. (1982). Investigating the correlation between reading errors and degraded numerics. Proceedings of the National Aerospace and Electronics Conference, 2, pp 734-738.

17 Watson, A. B. (1989). Modelling character legibility. Digest International Symposium of the Society for Information Display, **XX**, pp 360-363. ISSN 0097 966X

18 Westheimer G. & Campbell F.W. (1962). Light distribution in the image formed by the living human eye. Journal of the Optical Society of America, **52**, no 9, pp 1040-1045.

19 Spenkelink, G. & van Spijker, H. & White, T.N. Evaluation of flat panel display properties on a high fidelity simulator. This volume.

Human–Computer Interaction – INTERACT '90
D. Diaper et al. (Editors)
Elsevier Science Publishers B.V. (North-Holland)

AUDITORY ICONS IN LARGE-SCALE COLLABORATIVE ENVIRONMENTS

William W. Gaver
Rank Xerox EuroPARC
61 Regent Street
Cambridge, UK

Randall B. Smith
Xerox Palo Alto Research Center
3333 Coyote Hill Road
Palo Alto, CA, USA

We discuss the potential for auditory icons to address several common problems in large-scale, multiprocessing, and collaborative systems. These problems include those of confirming user-initiated actions, providing information about ongoing processes or system states, providing adequate navigational information, and signalling the existence and activity of other users who may be working in a part of the system that is not visible. We provide several examples of useful auditory icons drawn from a large, shared, multitasking environment called SharedARK, and discuss their implications for other systems.

1. INTRODUCTION

Auditory icons are everyday sounds meant to convey useful information to computer users by analogy with the sounds produced by everyday events (Gaver, 1986, 1989). The strategy of using everyday sounds is based on the observation that, in general, we listen to the world, not just to sounds. That is, when hearing a sound while walking down a street we are, hopefully, more likely to be aware that it is made by a large car accelerating in our direction than to notice to its pitch, loudness and timbre. Pitch, loudness, and timbre are perceptual attributes of the sound itself; their experience is one of *musical listening*. Size, force, and bearing are perceptual attributes of a sound's source; their experience is one of *everyday listening* (Gaver, 1988).

In this paper, we suggest ways that auditory icons can be used to enhance the usability of systems which employ multiprocessing and modes, extended or layered displays, and collaborative workspaces. Our suggestions are illustrated by examples drawn from our work in adding auditory icons to a large, shared virtual environment called SharedARK (Smith, 1988). SharedARK is a collaborative version of the Alternative Reality Kit (ARK; Smith, 1987). The system serves as a virtual physics laboratory for distance education, allowing one or a number of users to interact simultaneously with objects in an environment that extends far beyond the view offered by their screens. Users manipulate the mouse to control hands that may pick up, carry or even throw objects in the world. This interface has been shown to be relatively easy for novices to learn and use (Smith, et. al., 1989), but several problems remain. These problems include those of confirming user-initiated actions, providing information about ongoing processes or system states, providing adequate navigational information, and signalling the existence and activity of other users who may be working in a part of the system that is not visible. Of course, these problems are not unique to this system, but shared by most (if not all) systems that rely on direct manipulation, multiprocessing, extended or layered views, and/or collaboration.

We believe that auditory icons can address many of these problems. In SharedARK, for example, we have added auditory cues that are meant to help users interact with the system and each other. The auditory icons we use in the SharedARK interface are, for the most part, recorded environmental sounds. We avoid using synthesized or musical instrument tones in accordance with the philosophy that things in the virtual world of the computer should sound like things in the everyday world to which we are accustomed. However, several "sound effects" are also used to indicate events that have no counterparts in the real world (though even these were developed by modifying naturally-occurring sounds).

In what follows, we describe three groups of auditory icons, based on their functions for a single user. First are those that provide confirmatory feedback to users which is largely redundant with visual displays. Second are those that provide information about ongoing processes and system states. Third, we discuss the use of auditory icons to aid navigation in complex systems. Finally, we address how these sounds might aid collaboration by providing users information about the existence, location and actions of others. For each group, we provide several examples drawn from SharedARK, and discuss their implications for other systems.

2. CONFIRMATORY SOUNDS

In our everyday lives, we often rely on auditory feedback as confirmation of our actions. As I type this, for instance, I rely as much on the sounds of the keys as I do on watching the letters appear (and sometimes more). Yet computer interfaces rely almost entirely on visual cues to provide confirmation that user actions have been accepted. This presents problems in many direct-manipulation systems. For instance, a common mistake in such interfaces occurs when objects are dragged to some target. Often one either misses hitting the target, or accidently hits the wrong one. The results of such errors are usually annoying, and sometimes catastrophic. Visual highlighting, perhaps the most common visual cue added to indicate target acquisition, is not entirely effective in helping users avoid these problems.

Auditory icons can be used to provide the kind of auditory confirmations that we rely on in the everyday world. A simple strategy for designing such sounds is to use simple everyday sounds (like taps, clicks and scrapes) to supplement or replace visual highlighting. For instance, in SharedARK, many of the actions users may perform are accompanied by the sorts of sounds such actions might make in the everyday world.

An example of an interaction which involves many confirmatory sounds is shown in Figure 1. In this example, the user creates a Xerox button, and uses it to copy a ball for teleportation to a user in another part of the system (so, for instance, the other user can use it to experiment with gravity). In SharedARK, commands are embodied as labeled buttons (like the Xerox button showed in Figure 1, which copies other objects). Commands are issued by placing buttons on the relevant object and then activating the button.

In A, the user selects the Xerox button on a menu; the choice is confirmed by a clicking sound like that of a key being pressed. In B, the Xerox button makes a popping sound (which depends on what size it is) as it appears from nowhere. The user then carries the Xerox button to the ball and drops it on (C). The wooden clanking sound reflects a successful button attachment to the object. When the user activates the Xerox button (D), it makes a sound like a machine going through one cycle of activity to indicate that it is processing a command. Another popping sound accompanies the appearance of the new ball. In E, the user sets a teleporter on the ball, and again a clank indicates a successful attachment. When the teleporter is activated, the ball is instantly moved to a linked teleporter, and a science-fiction-like zapping sound indicates that the move is successful. This sound is an example of a sound effect, a non-arbitrary extension of everyday sounds to those meant to provide information about wholly synthetic events (see Gaver, 1989).

The auditory icons used to represent events in these examples are almost completely redundant with visual feedback already present in the system. Menu selection is usally indicated by the appearance of a new object. Appearance itself is of course visually indicated, as is contact between a button

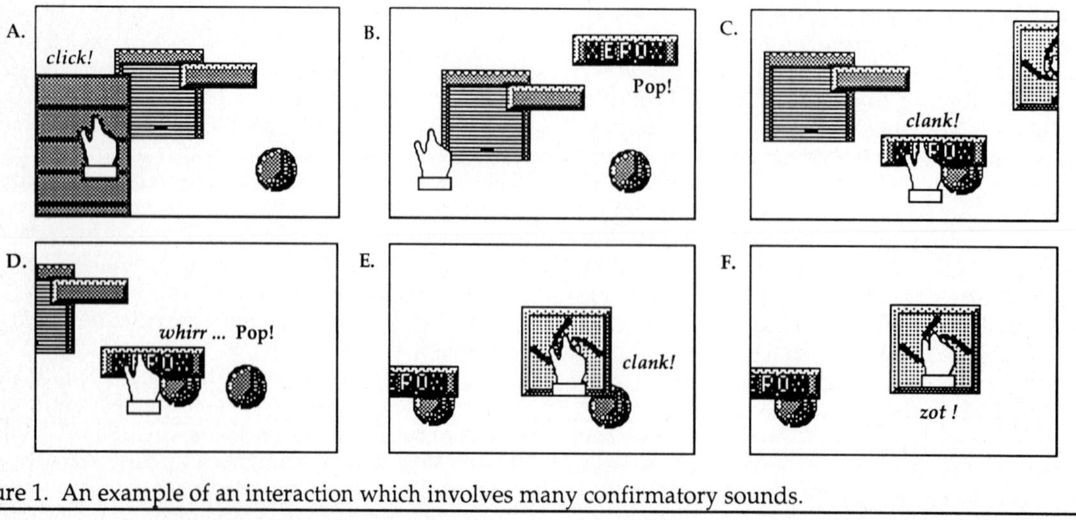

Figure 1. An example of an interaction which involves many confirmatory sounds.

and an object. Yet these sounds seem to provide feedback about actions in a way that is immediate, intuitive, and engrossing.

3. PROCESS AND STATE INFORMATION

Just as we listen to the world to tell the moment when our actions have successfully been performed, so we listen to ongoing events and processes to find out about their state. Experienced drivers seldom look at their tachometers in judging when to change gears, but instead listen to their engines. Hang-glider pilots often listen to the rush of wind around their heads to judge their speed, as watching the ground can be seriously misleading. Finally, computer users listen to the sounds their disk-drives, modems, and printers make to know what their machines are doing.

There are several reasons that sound is a particularly effective medium for displaying process and state information from computer systems. Sounds can serve to remind users about continuous states or ongoing processing without depending on windows that are likely to be occluded or to use unnecessary space. In addition, hearing auditory feedback about some change in the system does not rely on visual attention to that change. This property is important for any system, and crucial for those like SharedARK, in which events are not necessarily visible on the screen. Finally, changes in processes or state are usually most important to users, and sounds tend to be most noticeable when they change. Thus continuous sounds can be designed that fade into the perceptual background when they are unchanging, but which are quickly noticed when they change (Buxton, 1989).

A number of examples of sounds that provide information about ongoing processing and states may be found in SharedARK. Figure 2 shows several instances of processes that produce continuous sounds. In A, the user is turning on the law of motion, which is a simulated "law of nature" controlling whether objects move (a mode of the system). When this law is on, it makes a quiet, low pitched humming noise reminiscent of an electrical appliance. This sort of sound tends to fade into the perceptual background after a short time, so that it does not annoy or distract users. However, it can be heard if one wants to ascertain its status, and when motion is turned off the change to silence is immediately noticeable.

When the law of motion is turned on, two balls begin bouncing around a nearby room (B). With each collision comes a tapping sound that depends on the object's size. In C, the user has moved to a raincloud in a different area of the system and turned it on. As the raindrops fall, they make a dripping sound. The drips' repetition rate depends on the density of the rain and how fast it is falling.

Sounds that reflect the state of the system (such as the activation of a law of nature) and the activity of ongoing processes are quite helpful when the associated visual indicators are not visible or when the screen is crowded. Without the sound, one must look at the law of motion object to determine whether it is on, or throw an object to see if it moves. Such tests, simple as they might be, are often inconvenient and time-consuming, and in fact sometimes misleading. Hearing the state of the system and its processing is often more efficient than relying on graphical displays or tests of its performance.

Most systems to not include bouncing balls or falling rain, but they often do make use of multiple continuous processes and changing system states or modes. In such systems, sounds can be used as they are in this example to remind users of the state of their system and the activation of processes. Simple sounds have been shown to be effective in reminding users of the state of their system and avoiding mode errors (Monk, 1986). Similarly, other relatively continuous auditory icons can be used to represent the activity of ongoing processes such as background printing, copying, and formatting. There is great potential for using these sort of

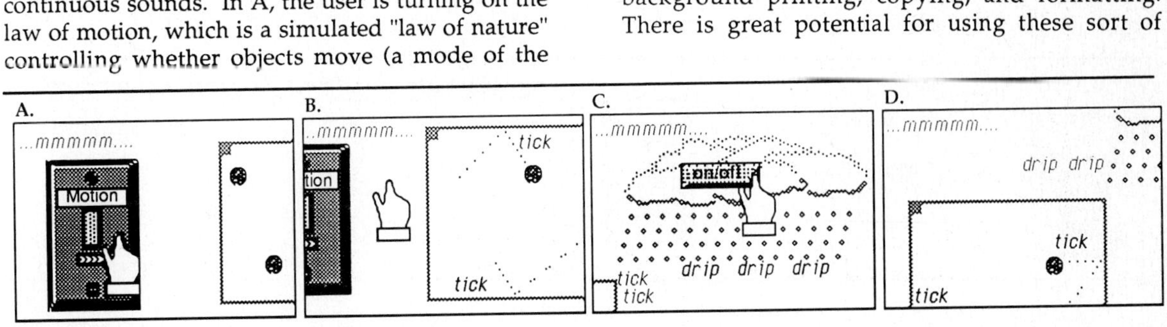

Figure 2. States and processes in SharedARK make sounds; their relative volumes depend on their distance.

auditory cues in any system which involves multitasking.

4. SOUNDS IN VERY LARGE ENVIRONMENTS

As the user moves to the raincloud in Figure 2, the balls continue to bounce around the room, but the sounds they make are quieter because the user has moved away from them. The dripping sounds, on the other hand, are relatively loud, indicating the user's proximity to them.

In general, the amplitudes of all sounds in SharedARK are changed and they are low-pass filtered to indicate the distance of their virtual sources from the user (low-pass filtering provides the attenuation of high frequency energy typical of distant sounds). In D, for instance, as the user moves back towards the bouncing balls the sounds they make become louder, while those made by the rain drops become softer. The humming noise made by law of motion remains constant, because it is a property of the entire system and is not associated with a particular location.

Auditory icons which depend on the distance between their sources and the user's virtual location have the potential to help users navigate. Such sounds produce auditory neighbourhoods, so that one can move away from one sound source and towards another without seeing either. Visually-disabled people commonly make use of continuously present sounds in their environment such as those of ventilator ducts or traffic crossings for orientation (Jenkins, 1985); we believe sounds can play a similar role in computer systems.

We have created objects we call *soundholders*, to explore the utility of such auditory landmarks. Soundholders continuously emit sounds whose volume decreases as the user moves away from them. The sounds they produce are randomly varied, with users having control over their average frequency and amplitude, as well as the frequency and amplitude ranges and the average repetition rate. By choosing different sounds and setting these parameters, a wide range of auditory environments can be created. As soundholders are associated with working areas, they make easier the task of moving around a space larger than can be seen at any given time. This seems true not only for systems with extended displays like SharedARK, but for layered systems as well.

Figure 3 shows how soundholders may be used as auditory landmarks. In A, the user has put a soundholder near one area of the system and started its sound (in this case, a series of bird calls). In B, the user has associated a different soundholder with another working space. This soundholder makes sounds like a burbling stream. As the user moves over the otherwise unmarked plane between the two regions, the rise and fall of their associated sounds provides information about the relative distance to each part of the system.

In any interface that uses sound, annoyance is an important issue. We have found that environmental sounds such as bird chirps, waves, and crickets seem to work well as continuously present auditory landmarks. They have the disadvantage that they are not meaningfully related to the areas with which they are associated; nonetheless, listening to a virtual aviary, for instance, seems much more pleasant than hearing a room full of machinery or typing. It is interesting to note in this context that there is a semantic component to sounds that make acoustically-based predictions of annoyance somewhat unreliable (Swift, et al., 1989). For instance, though birdsong is a highly abrupt and complex sound (and thus might be expected to be aversive) it is much less annoying than other more continuous sounds such as passing traffic.

Just as using auditory cues about the state of the system and processes frees users from relying solely on visual input, so do auditory landmarks enable users to navigate with reference to parts of the

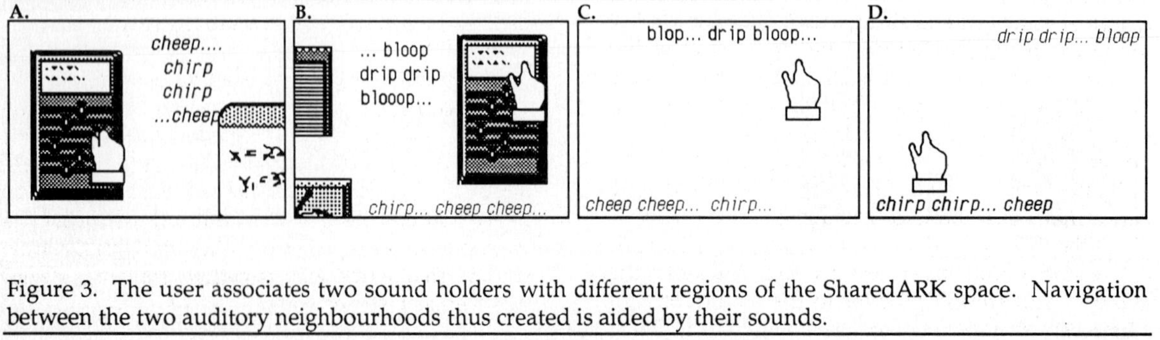

Figure 3. The user associates two sound holders with different regions of the SharedARK space. Navigation between the two auditory neighbourhoods thus created is aided by their sounds.

system they might not be able to see. Providing information about the distance between the user and important landmarks could be a useful tool in creating interfaces for the visually disabled. But as Buxton (1989) points out, we are all visually disabled to some degree when working with computers, especially those in which not all items of interest are necessarily visible. Auditory landmarks are useful for interfaces such as SharedARK, in which objects may be offscreen. Similarly, they have the potential to aid navigation in layered systems in which parts of the interface may be occluded or simply not shown. For instance, many CAD systems rely on invisible layers to simplify displays. Associating auditory landmarks with key layers to indicate proximity could help users find their way in such systems. Similarly, sounds could be used to indicate the nature and importance of linked areas in hypertext systems, helping users find paths in complex mazes of information.

5. LISTENING TO OTHER USERS

The functions outlined above are all relevant to individual users of large-scale multiprocessing environments. These auditory icons may play an equally important role in shared systems, in which more than one user may be working in the environment at a given time. For instance, all the auditory icons we incorporated into the SharedARK system are heard by all users of the system. The sounds thus perform the dual role of providing feedback to an acting user as well as new information to others. The addition of sound seems to add to the feeling of presence of other users, and to aid in coordinating activities. This is particularly true when users are working in spatially separated areas of the system.

Sounds that provide confirmatory feedback to one user might well be the only indication to another that certain actions are being performed. In the situation described in Figure 1, for instance, the sounds made in the process of copying and teleporting the ball – the pops, clanks, and whirring noises – assure the waiting user that his or her request is being carried out, and the sound of the teleporter tells him or her that the ball has arrived. Similarly, the sounds made by continuous processes and states are helpful in knowing what others are doing and the expected results of various actions ("Oh, you turned on the law of motion – I guess I'd better make sure none of my things are moving."). Finally, auditory landmarks are useful in helping to locate and guide other users ("Are you near the aviary? You should go over to the stream to find that button.").

Sound opens up a new dimension of meaningful reference points in this system which can help collaborative users overcome the limitations of the visual display. We have observed users collaborating on a spatially-distributed task in this system, both with and without sound. In general, it seems that users working with sound are much more likely to comment on each other's actions even when working in separate parts of the system That is, users working without sounds must ask one another about activities they cannot see, while those with auditory feedback can comment directly on the things they hear. In general, auditory icons can help users collaborate effectively even when they do not share the same view, as for instance when working on different portions of a document using a group editing tool.

6. CONCLUSIONS

The use of varied sounds in computer interfaces is new, but we feel it has much potential for increasing the usability of complex systems. With multiprocessing, the limitations of screen-size for representing objects and events becomes more apparent. Such limitations are inherent to complex interfaces that rely on spatial encoding. Strategies to overcome them such as layering and extending the virtual world outside the screen are potentially quite powerful, but many objects may be invisible at a given time. The same is true for many collaborative systems, in which users may work together on different aspects of a task. As more items are placed outside of view in such systems, being able to hear the status of the system could become more important.

There are a number of issues to address in designing effective auditory icons. The first involves the sort of mapping used between sounds and the information they are to convey. We believe that using environmental sounds chosen to have some semantic relation to their referents is often the best method for maintaining identifiability. It is difficult to relate synthesized or musical sounds to events in the interface in any but an arbitrary way.

A second problem is in designing sounds that will not be confused. Choosing sounds with different temporal patterns is the most effective way to create a set of discriminable sounds (Patterson, 1989). But the more sounds that are played at once, the more likely that any particular sound will be difficult to distinguish. Care must be taken to design a set of sounds that work well together, forming a well-balanced acoustic ecology.

Finally, sounds in the interface can be annoying. What seems cute and clever at first may grow tiresome after a few exposures. Sounds should be concise and unobtrusive, and should reflect a number of data dimensions at once to avoid repetition (for instance, varying sounds to reflect the size of associated objects is informative and adds variety). In general, the aim should be to use sounds that fit in with the environment in which the system will be used. In addition, users should have control over the sounds they hear, at least to the extent of being able to turn off individual sounds.

Although these issues can be difficult to resolve, auditory icons have much potential in providing feedback from complex systems. The addition of sound to SharedARK helps to demonstrate the wide range of functions that auditory icons can perform. By designing sounds that accompany user actions in the system, salient confirmatory feedback is provided to users in a way that seems more noticeable than visual cues. Sounds which reflect the status of the system and ongoing processes can be useful in allowing users to know about events without having to be in the same area of the system. Using amplitude and filtering to reflect the distance of virtual sound sources can aid navigation, and in combination with auditory landmarks helps to divide the otherwise homogeneous surface of the virtual world into distinct neighbourhoods. Finally, using these sounds in a collaborative context adds new information about other users and their activities, and provides new points of reference to all users.

ACKNOWLEDGEMENTS

We thank Allan Maclean and Judy Olson for their comments on this paper.

REFERENCES

Buxton, W. (1989). Introduction to this special issue on nonspeech audio. *Human-Computer Interaction*. 4 (1).

Gaver, W. W. (1986). Auditory icons: Using sound in computer interfaces. *Human-Computer Interaction*. 2, 167 - 177.

Gaver, W. W. (1988). Everyday listening and auditory icons. Doctoral Dissertation, University of California, San Diego.

Gaver, W. W. (1989). The SonicFinder: An interface that uses auditory icons. *Human-Computer Interaction*. 4 (1).

Jenkins, James J. (1985). Acoustic information for objects, places, and events. in Warren, W. H., & Shaw, R. E., *Persistence and change: Proceedings of the first international conference on event perception*. Hillsdale, NJ: Lawrence Erlbaum Associates.

Monk, A. F. (1986). Mode errors: A user-centered analysis and some preventative measures using keying-contingent sound. *International Journal of Man-Machine Studies*. 24, 313 - 327.

Patterson, R. D. (1989). Guidelines of the design of auditory warning sounds. *Proceedings of the Institute of Acoustics 1989 Spring Conference*. *11* (5), 17 - 24.

Smith, R. B. (1989). A prototype futuristic technology for distance education. *Proceedings of the NATO Advanced Workshop on New Directions in Educational Technology*. Nov. 10 - 13, 1988, Cranfield, U.K..

Smith, R. B. (1988). The Alternate Reality Kit: an example of the tension between literalism and magic. *Proceedings of CHI + GI 1987*. April 5 - 9, Toronto, 61 - 67.

Smith, R. B., O'Shea, T., O'Malley, C., Scanlon, E., & Taylor, J., (1989). Preliminary experiments with a distributed, multi-media, problem solving environment. *Proceedings of the European Conference on Computer Supported Cooperative Work*.

Swift, C. G., Flindell, I. H., & Rice, C. G. (1989). Annoyance and impulsivity judgments of environmental noises. *Proceedings of the Institute of Acoustics 1989 Spring Conference*. *11* (5), 551 - 555.

Human–Computer Interaction – INTERACT '90
D. Diaper et al. (Editors)
Elsevier Science Publishers B.V. (North-Holland)

INTERACTIVE SCIENTIFIC VISUALIZATION: AN ASSESSMENT OF A VIRTUAL REALITY SYSTEM

Philip J. MERCURIO

Advanced Scientific Visualization Laboratory, San Diego Supercomputer Center
Box 85608, San Diego, California 92138-5608 USA

Thomas D. ERICKSON

Human Interface Group/ATG, Apple Computer, Inc.
20525 Mariani Avenue, MS 76-3H, Cupertino, California 95014 USA

A virtual reality system, consisting of a head-mounted stereoscopic display and a computer-interfaced glove, was assessed by examining interaction with a 3-D model of the human brain. Interactions were recorded on videotape. Non-trivial user interface issues were identified, ranging from constraints imposed by the nature of the wearable interface hardware, to the choice of gestures for controlling the interaction, to problems with a metaphor used in the interface. Some possible solutions are discussed. Sound solutions to these problems, coupled with increases in the computational power of the underlying hardware, are needed for virtual reality to realize its immense potential for scientific visualization.

1. INTRODUCTION

Scientific visualization is a domain of computer science whose goal is to promote visual conceptualization in the process of scientific investigation. As a National Science Foundation report on Visualization in Scientific Computing states: "The ability of scientists to visualize complex computations and simulations is absolutely essential to insure the integrity of analyses, to provoke insights and to communicate those insights with others" (McCormick, et al. (1987)).

Interactivity is fundamental to scientific visualization. The scientific method is by nature an interactive and iterative process, and thus requires interactive graphics environments which interfere as little as possible with the scientist's explorations. Researchers from diverse fields—including fluid dynamics (Helman and Hesselink (1989)), medical research (Fuchs, et al. (1989)), and the earth sciences (Hibbard and Santek (1989))—have remarked upon the importance of the ability to interact with their data.

Traditional means of interacting with data, particularly with 3-D data models, leave much to be desired. A common approach to interacting with a 3-D model employs a knob box, an array of (typically 8) continuously-rotatable knobs assigned to parameters of the rendering transformation (typically X, Y, and Z translation and rotation, and scaling). Knob boxes are a cumbersome and non-intuitive means of interaction. Many researchers have investigated alternative means via both software and hardware innovations, with varying degrees of success. Software approaches have included rotation techniques not subject to the pitfalls of X, Y, Z rotation (Shoemake (1985)), techniques for specifying arbitrary origins of rotation (Bier (1986)), and investigations into the use of 2-D input devices for specifying 3-D rotation (Chen (1988)). Hardware approaches have included custom controllers with knobs mounted on orthogonal axes (Mosher, et al. (1986)) and numerous unique interaction devices, such as those created by Fred Brooks' laboratory at UNC Chapel Hill (Brooks (1988)). However, even the most successful of these methods requires going into a special mode to rotate objects, or lacks sufficient correlation to interaction with real-world objects.

Our goal in this investigation was to explore virtual reality as a user interface for scientific visualization. Virtual reality is a computer-generated illusion of a data space in which the user has a virtual presence. The user wears a headset containing a binocular video display; the headset also contains a position sensing device, so that as the head moves, the display is appropriately updated, creating the illusion that the wearer is looking around in a static visual environment. The user also wears a computer-interfaced glove which allows hand position and configuration to be incorporated in the interaction with the virtual world. The use of the glove allows the user to directly manipulate objects in the display using natural gestures. It was because of this potential for direct interaction via natural gestures that we felt that virtual reality offered immense potential as a scientific visualization environment.

Our approach was to bring up a scientific data set under a commercial virtual reality system so that we could evaluate it. Although we had already received demonstrations of virtual reality systems, the data sets were created by the vendors, and consisted of relatively simple displays (typically virtual rooms in which a user could move and interact). We felt a more telling evaluation would be to use an existing data set, a 3-D contour model of a human brain.

2. BACKGROUND

2.1. The Virtual Reality Platform

We were fortunate to obtain the cooperation of VPL Research, a leading vendor of virtual reality systems. VPL provided us with access to an experimental version of a single user virtual reality system—it was experimental in that it was currently under development, and also in that the rendering workstations used were of lower power than in the final, commercial system. They also gave us information about file formats and system limitations so that the data set could be appropriately transformed before our visit.

The computer hardware for the virtual reality system consists of a Macintosh II, which processes the positional data received from the head-mounted display and the computer interfaced glove, and two Silicon Graphics Personal Irises, which render the 3-dimensional image of the data set. The interface hardware consists of a binocular video display—the EyePhone , and a computer interfaced glove—the DataGlove.

The "EyePhone" consists of 2 color LCD screens fitted into a rubber mask worn on the face like a scuba mask. Lenses installed in front of the LCD screens magnify the images and help the wearer merge the images into one binocular view. The EyePhone's rubber face mask blocks all ambient light, so all that the user sees are the images presented on the EyePhone display. The field of view is 100 degrees horizontally, with 60 degrees of overlap, and 60 degrees vertically. The resolution of the EyePhone's LCD displays is 360 x 240 pixels. Considering the proximity of the LCD's to the eyes, each pixel subtends a rather large portion of the view, and the resulting resolution is relatively low.

The EyePhone weighs 4.25 lbs, with the weight of the display being counter-balanced by weights positioned behind the head. On the straps joining the display to the weights is a mount for a Polhemus 6-D tracking device. The position in 3-space and 3 degree-of-freedom orientation of the tracker are detected by a nearby rigidly-mounted receiver and transmitted to the computer managing the virtual reality. The EyePhone is connected to its interface box by a long cable.

The DataGlove is a glove fitted with fiber optic sensors to measure the amount of bend in the joints of the fingers, and its position is tracked via a separate Polhemus tracker. Like the EyePhone, it is connected to its interface box via a long cable.

2.2. The Virtual Reality Interface

In the virtual reality environment that we studied, there are two distinct ways of moving the model being viewed. One is moving about under your own locomotion. That is, if the model is floating in front of you, you can walk toward it and through it. If you are above it, you can bend over or sit down. From a stationary position, you can move your head to alter the direction of viewing. The other means of movement is gesture-controlled "flying." By pointing with your forefinger extended and the rest of your fingers curled in you fly forward, in the direction you are looking (not the direction you are pointing). Pointing with two fingers causes you to fly backwards.

The virtual reality system provides feedback on the position and configuration of the user's hand, as sensed by the DataGlove. When the gloved hand is within the user's field of vision (or what would be the user's field of vision if the user could actually see), the display shows an image of a hand in the position and configuration sensed by the DataGlove.

A third means of movement is also possible, but was not available in the version of the system which we examined. If you reach out with your hand and the image of your hand in the virtual reality intersects an object, you can make a fist and grab the object, and move it by moving your hand.

2.3. The Data

The brain data was originally acquired by embedding a human brain in paraffin. Successive thin layers were shaven off of the block of paraffin and the top of the block was photographed onto movie film in a process called "cinemorphology". The resulting film frames were then hand-digitized into a computer to produce 3-dimensional stacks of 2-D contours. The contours for different neuroanatomical structures were digitized separately and can thus be displayed independently or in selected groups. The resulting brain database consists of about 75,000 vectors, or, when converted to polygonal surface data, 150,000 polygons (Livingston and Wilson (1976)).

2.4. Data Preparation

The display limitations of the graphics hardware in the system described above is approximately 1200 polygons (at the rates necessary to achieve satisfactory interaction). To cull the brain database down to a manageable size, the contour data for each section of each brain structure was first replaced by the orthogonal rectangle bounding that section, reducing the number of vectors representing that section to four. This produced a 3-D stack of aligned 2-D rectangles which were then converted to a polygonal mesh consisting of four 3-D rectangles for each section.

Even this crude, boxy representation of the data did not make it possible to view the entire set of brain structures simultaneously. The final data set brought into the virtual reality consisted of the brainstem, cerebellum, thalamus, red nucleus, and the top inch (approximately) of the cerebral cortex, with Broca's and Wernicke's language areas of the left hemisphere represented as separate objects. This data set consisted of approximately 1000 polygons.

2.5. Evaluation Method

The virtual reality system was qualitatively evaluated by two users: a scientific visualization specialist who was familiar with the data set, and a user interface specialist who had had only slight exposure to the data set. Each evaluator used the system for about twenty minutes, with the interactions being recorded on videotape.

3. DISCUSSION

In this section we begin by giving a capsule description of the experience of interacting with the virtual reality environment. We then survey the problems we found — some of which arise from current (although not inherent) hardware limitations, and some which arise from the design of the interface.

3.1. The Interactive Experience

When the headset was put on and the system started up, the user could see a large brain (scaled up by an order of magnitude) floating in space . Although the resolution of the display was poor, the stereopsis and interactivity offered by the virtual reality environment enhanced the reality of the brain image to the extent that we quickly lost awareness of the low resolution. We were, however, continually aware of the boxiness of the image, which resulted from the transformation of the data set from 150,000 polygons to the roughly 1,000 that the rendering engines could handle in real time.

Movement in the virtual reality via real-world locomotion and head motion worked quite well. The correspondence between real-world movement and movement in the virtual world was so accurate that there was no need for a conscious translation of intent to the user interface action necessary to achieve that intent. It was very natural to walk towards the brain image, have it get bigger, and then be inside it. There was virtually no learning necessary to interact with the data set in this way. The only difficulty with this type of movement was that, in spite of the greatly simplified data set, there was still a bit of jerkiness when the image moved in sync with the user's head movements.

Flying was more problematic. First, due to a miscalculation, the speed of movement was set too high. Since this version of the virtual reality system didn't give the user interactive control over speed, flying to a particular spot was very much a hit or miss proposition. Usually, several forward and backward passes were required to get close to the target. Since the brain image was only about ten feet in diameter, flying inside it was not necessary; however, since the brain contours were opaque, this made flying much more difficult, since the target could not be seen until it was present. While flying was the most difficult part of the interaction, it still took only about two minutes to get the basics down.

3.2. Hardware and System Limitations

First of all, there are a number of pragmatic factors that spring from the fact that the user is wearing the interface hardware. The user wears the EyePhone upon his or her head. Although it is reasonably comfortable despite its weight of 4.25 lbs., the user is aware that tilting the head too far to one side could cause the unit to slip off. Because the EyePhone blocks all ambient light, and because the virtual reality display does not give any feedback about the external environment, the user must remain aware of a number of physical constraints. The cables connecting the EyePhone and DataGlove to their interfaces boxes are long, and can become tangled or twisted around the wearer. The user must also be aware of the location of the stationary Polhemus receiving units and must not walk too far from them or too close to them. Walls may also pose a problem. In this instance observers were present who were able to warn us about physical obstacles and constraints so that we were able to operate with little attention to these factors. However, for virtual reality to be a truly practical form of interaction, it will have to be usable without supervision. For example, the virtual reality environment could also reflect salient features of the surrounding physical environment.

Another limitation was the inability of the rendering hardware to handle more than about 1200 polygons without serious degradation in performance. Because of this, the brain data set had to be greatly simplified. The original data beautifully represents the folds and contours of the brain structures. All of this detail was lost in exchange for the ability to display more of the brain structures. The structures that were chosen were those which best survived the translation to boxy solids. It should be noted that this limitation is due only to the capabilities of the available graphics hardware; with sufficiently powerful real-time rendering machines, much more detailed data can be displayed.

One of the major interaction problems evident in the videotape is with the speed of movement through the data set. If the user flew, the user flew very, very fast. This particular problem was due to the fact that the software that was in development at the time we used it, and that the speed of movement through the data was linked to the scaling of the data.

Another hardware limitation is the slow update rate and unsteadiness due to the temporal and spatial resolution of the Polhemus tracking devices. This problem is not inherent in the virtual reality environment itself, and will be alleviated by advances in tracking hardware.

3.3. User Interface Problems

While the virtual reality system makes use of gestures to fly through the virtual environment, the gestures used were problematic. One problem was that the gesture used to fly (pointing with one finger to fly forward) is a relatively natural one. Both of us flew inadvertently a number of times, either because we were trying to point at something as we spoke about it, or because other habitual gestures (e.g. finger on the chin; stroking the mustache) would sometimes map onto the "fly" gesture. A second problem is that, although the gesture is a natural one, it has no meaningful connection with the command it invokes. Such semiotic gestures are difficult to learn and remember, although this is not a problem in a system with only a few gesture commands. A better example of the use of gesture is placing a 'hand' inside an 'object', and closing the hand to 'grab' it. Examples of some possible solutions are given below.

The problem with the speed of flying has already been discussed. A related problem is that you fly in the direction in which you are looking, rather than in the direction you're pointing. Flying in the direction you're looking prevents users from scanning the image as they move. That is, users should be able to look around while flying. For example, with a very detailed brain image, users might want to move slowly along the fissure between the temporal and frontal lobes, watching for the speech area. But that would be off to the side, perpendicular to the direction of movement; since the resolution is not very high, and the angle of view not that wide, it may be difficult to see it with peripheral vision.

A third problem is inherent in the verb "fly," which VPL uses to describe the mode of moving through the data without the user moving in real space. As Lakoff and Johnson (1980) have noted, a single word can evoke a whole series of expectations and beliefs, a metaphoric system. Unfortunately, flying is a poor metaphoric system for movement through a virtual reality environment. There are two reasons.

First, while "flying" is a sexy concept, the fact is that it doesn't feel like you are flying toward the object when you point at it. Rather, it feels as though the object is coming towards you. Presumably this is because there is natural kinesthetic feedback associated with movement, but no such feedback in the virtual reality. While it can be argued that users can suspend their disbelief and ignore their kinesthetic feedback, the fact is that in a very short time they'll want to be paying attention to such feedback as they walk around and through the object, or grab it to reposition it. An interface which requires users to rely heavily on kinesthetic feedback one moment, and ignore it the next, seems problematic.

The second problem with flying as a metaphor stems from the role of metaphor in an interface: the purpose of an interface metaphor is to allow users to apply some of their real-world experience to areas of the new domain with which they might otherwise have difficulty (Erickson, 1990). In this context, the problem with the flying metaphor is that we don't know how to fly in the real world. As a result, there are no intuitiive gestures for flying and it is not clear what should control the direction of flight.

3.4. A Possible Solution

It is important to emphasize that the user interface problems—as with the hardware limitations—are not inherent in the virtual reality approach. As evidence of this, we offer one possible solution to a number of the above problems.

Many of the problems noted above may be solved by choosing a different metaphor for moving through the data set. Instead of a metaphor in which the user is depicted as moving, a metaphor in which the user stayed stationary and the data set moved would be more suitable. For example, a user could push and pull the object rather than flying through it. A "push-pulling" metaphor avoids both problems of the flying metaphor: there is no contradictory kinesthetic feedback, since it is the world that is moving; and users know how to push and pull things in the real world.

Unlike flying, push-pulling also suggests some intuitive gestures for doing it: palm open, fingers together, pushing in the direction you want the object (or space) to move; clenched fist, moving in the direction you want to pull the object or data space. As with real pushing and pulling, the action should only continue as long as the hand is moving. The use of such mimetic gestures, combined with a push-pulling metaphor, also eliminates any ambiguity about what should determine the direction of movement: clearly the push-pull should act in the direction of the gesture, not in the direction of view.

Another indication that the push-pulling metaphor is a good one is that it is extensible. For example, momentum could be introduced, so that if you grab something and open your hand before stopping (i.e. throwing), the object would coast by until you grabbed it again. This would also solve the speed problem, by providing an intuitive means for the user to control speed--if you want to go fast, you throw fast. Another possibility that comes to mind is that if a system were configured with two data gloves, two-handed pushing and pulling could translate into shrinking and stretching, thus providing a way to scale the image.

Finally, the natural gestures suggested by the push-pulling metaphor make much more use of the unique features of the DataGlove. In the virtual reality system we used (since grabbing wasn't working), there seemed to be little reason to use the glove--a little box with two buttons for fly forward and backward would have worked as well.

The solution presented here is not ideal. It glosses over a number of problems. For example, suppose the data set consists of a number of separate objects: if a user grabs an object and pulls, does it move the object relative to the other objects, or does it move the entire set of objects relative to the user. The answer isn't obvious. The point here is not to offer a final solution, but to demonstrate that virtual reality environments have non-trivial interface problems which must be, and can be, addressed.

4. CONCLUSION

To read popular descriptions of virtual reality systems, one would think that there are no interface issues. Virtual reality is just like real reality, except better: a wave of the hand, a simple, natural gesture, and whatever the user had in mind happens. Such is not the case. As we have seen, there are non-trivial interface problems associated with virtual reality environments: wearable interface devices may encumber the user; inadvertent gestures may cause unintended actions; gestures may be non-intuitive; metaphors may be inappropriate. While we have suggested some solutions for these problems, the solutions are intended to indicate the nature of the design task, rather than to be the final word.

Displaying the brain data in the virtual reality was both disappointing and exciting. It was disappointing because the transformations to the data left the final image so coarse that it was little more than a curiosity. It is difficult to imagine doing useful scientific research with the data in this form. But while the hardware platforms underlying virtual reality environments are not yet sufficiently powerful to support scientific visualization of the sort of data set we have explored, they are powerful enough to offer an interactive testbed for research on the interface issues.

Nonetheless, the experience was exciting because there is clearly immense potential for displaying data in this manner. We were able to figure out how to navigate through the data with about fifteen seconds of instruction, and a few minutes of trial and error (which was necessary to learn how to cope with the time lag and circumvent some of the problems described above). Even with its problems, virtual reality was by far the easiest and most useful way in which we've been able to interact with this data. And, most importantly, none of the problems was inherent in either the system or the interaction techniques. With careful redesign of some aspects of the user interface, and with increases in the capabilities of the hardware, virtual reality systems will open new vistas in scientific visualization.

ACKNOWLEDGEMENTS

We would like to acknowledge the cooperation of VPL Research, who provided us information, technical support, and access to a version of one of their virtual reality systems which was still under development. VPL Research may be contacted at 656 Bair Island Road, Suite 304, Redwood City, California 94036.

REFERENCES

Bier, E. A. (1987). Skitters and Jacks: Interactive 3D Positioning Tools. In Proceedings of the 1986 Workshop on Interactive 3D Graphics (Chapel Hill, NC, October 23-24, 1986), 183-196. ACM: New York.

Brooks, F. P. (1988). Grasping Reality Through Illusion--Interactive Graphics Serving Science. In Proceedings of CHI '88, 1-11 (Washington, May 15-19). ACM: New York.

Chen, M., Mountford, S. J., and Sellen, A. (1988). A Study in Interactive 3-D Rotation Using 2-D Control Devices. Computer Graphics, 22, #4, 121-129.

Erickson, T. D. (1990). Working with Interface Metaphors. The Art of Human-Computer Interface Design. (Ed. B. Laurel). Addison-Wesley: in press.

Fuchs, H., Levoy, M. and Pizer, S. M. (1989). Interactive Visualization of 3D Medical Data. Computer, 22, #8, 46-52.

Helman, J. and Hesselink, L. (1989). Representation and Display of Vector Field Topology in Fluid Flow Data Sets. Computer, 22, #8, 27-38.

Hibbard, W. and Santek, D. (1989). Visualizing Large Data Sets in the Earth Sciences. Computer, 22, #8, 53-59.

Lakoff, G. and Johnson, M. (1980). Metaphors We Live By. The University of Chicago Press: Chicago and London.

Livingston, R. B. & Wilson, K. R. (1976) The Human Brain: A Dynamic View of its Structures and Organization. Film, 28 minutes. Presented by Roche Laboratories ; made by Wexler Films. Distributor: Wexler Film Productions.

McCormick, B. H., DeFanti, T. A. and Brown, M. D. (1987). Visualization in Scientific Computing. Computer Graphics, 21, # 6.

Mosher, C. E. Jr., Sherouse, G. W., Mills, P. H., Novins, K. L., Pizer, S. M., Rosenman, J. G., and Chaney, E. L. (1987). The Virtual Simulator. In Proceedings of the 1986 Workshop on Interactive 3D Graphics (Chapel Hill, NC, October 23-24, 1986), 37-42. ACM: New York.

Shoemake, K (1985). Animating Rotation with Quaternion Curves. Computer Graphics 19, #3, 245-254.

Human–Computer Interaction – INTERACT '90
D. Diaper et al. (Editors)
Elsevier Science Publishers B.V. (North-Holland)

A Browser for Dynamic Multimedia Documents

Suresh Anupindi

Computer Laboratory, University of Cambridge, Cambridge, CB2 3QG. UK.

A model for audio dominated multimedia documents is presented. Such documents are active and dynamic because of their audio content. However, revision of information is difficult because of the dynamic nature. We present static and dynamic scanning techniques which allow reviewing and describe a browser which employs these techniques. We also describe a method for customizing the presentation of dynamic documents using trails.

1 Introduction

Text, figures and pictures are generally used to present information in traditional documents. There are a number of situations like teaching, instruction, presentation, etc. where the use of an audio medium is effective. Present generation workstations are used to compose and read traditional documents. In addition to raster displays, the new generation of multimedia workstations will have audio input/output facilities and can support documents containing audio information.

Audio is an active and dynamic medium, whereas text and figures are static and passive. It is dynamic in the sense that the information is presented in time and active in the sense that the presentation is automatic without any user intervention. Because of the differences in the characteristics of the various media, a multimedia document will have variable behaviour depending on the media used for representing the information. If one wants to have a uniform behaviour throughout the document then a particular behaviour needs to be enforced on all the media. For instance, a document can be made either static or dynamic by making all the objects in the document either static or dynamic. The decision as to whether the document should have static or dynamic behaviour depends on the dominant medium. A document with the majority of information in text form will have static characteristics while a document with the majority of information in audio form will exhibit dynamic behaviour. Our interest is in considering audio dominated documents. Such documents are active and dynamic because of their audio content and existing document models are not suitable for them. In this paper we shall present a model for such dynamic documents.

Audio has some drawbacks over other media. The rate at which the information is presented is prespecified and cannot be customized by the reader, nor can the information be held continuously before the reader as with for visual media. The later drawback makes the reviewing of information difficult unless the audio information is repeatedly replayed. Audio dominated documents will inherit the same problems. Hence, a browser is required which allows the reader to review selected parts of a dynamic document. We describe one such browser for audio dominated documents in this paper.

2 Dynamic Documents

We shall first examine why traditional document models are not suitable for dynamic documents before developing a model for later. In traditional documents, logically arranged information is laid out spatially onto a sequence of pages. Where a page projects a two dimensional spatial view. Since dynamic documents are three dimensional with a two dimensional visual component and a temporal third dimension, the page model is not suitable for them.

There are two representations one can project for dynamic documents. In the first view, the dynamic document is assumed to be spatially organized on a sequential tape. Here, for every temporal movement there is a corresponding spatial movement. For example, if the user wants to review the document from a previous point in the presentation then he has to rewind the tape correspondingly. In the second case, a dynamic document is seen as a sequence of events happening in time. Here, one has to move backwards or forwards in time to review the presentation. The interface to browsers with the first representation will be familiar to the user, because of the analogy with video recorders. However, it is an indirect view, since time is a more natural unit for dynamic documents than space. We provide a temporal view to dynamic documents.

In a dynamic document with logical structure, the boundaries of logical units needs to be explicitly shown during the presentation using either visual or auditory cues, for them to be useful for browsing. If dynamic documents were to have complex logical structures then the additional information in the form of cues will be considerable and it may start to interfere with the main message [Hartman (1961)]. Hence a minimal logical structure needs to be provided for dynamic documents. Such a logical structure is also in keeping with the assumption that dynamic documents will be of a short duration only. One reason for this assumption is that the audio component is effective only if the information presented is simple.

2.1 Structure of Dynamic Documents

A dynamic document is considered as a sequence of *scenes* with a scene being the logical division of the information. A scene can also be viewed as a chunk of information whose presentation starts at a specific point in the overall presentation of the document and continues for some duration. Physically, dynamic documents are treated as a sequence of *snap shots* with a snap shot representing the information that is presented in an instant. The main drawback with dynamic documents is that the viewer cannot get an overview of the document unless the entire presentation is viewed. This drawback can be decreased by providing a static view of the dynamic document. To be able to provide such a view, a textual heading is attached to each scene and some of the snap shots within the scene are marked and annotated with textual strings. These headings and markers are used for providing a static view such as in the table of contents.

Different dynamic documents can be grouped together into *clusters*. A cluster has a title and a sequence of links to its component dynamic documents or to other clusters. This is useful for organizing the information at a gross level. For example, all the documents explaining different aspects of a topic or all the related topics can be grouped into a cluster. Clusters are not dynamic in themselves. The user has to select the appropriate document in the cluster and start its presentation.

2.2 Browsing within Dynamic Documents

In the traditional documents, browsing is done either by following the structure of a document or by content searching. As in traditional documents, the logical and physical structure of dynamic documents can be used for browsing. But content searching is not possible here due to the presence of large amounts of information in audio form. It can be done only if there is some sort of speech recognition. However, the search of the scene headings and textual annotations enables the user to access parts of dynamic documents, based upon content, with out performing speech recognition. Content searching will be really useful when the document is large. Since the dynamic documents are assumed to be of short duration only, browsing by structure is quite sufficient.

There are two ways one can scan a dynamic document, either statically or dynamically. In a static scanning, points in the presentation of dynamic documents are selected before the actual presentation and the viewer can start replaying the document from the selected points. In dynamic scanning, the selection of the required points in a document are done while it is being replayed.

The division of documents into logical units called *scenes* and the presence of text descriptors as annotations to markers helps the reader in static scanning. There are two techniques one can employ for dynamic scanning [Maxemchuk (1980)]. The first is to provide a facility to jump forwards or backwards during the presentation and the second is to provide a facility to change the rate of presentation. We have designed and implemented a browser that allows both the static and dynamic browsing of dynamic documents and is described in the next section. We also provided a facility for leaving trails while viewing the presentation and a means to use them for reviewing documents.

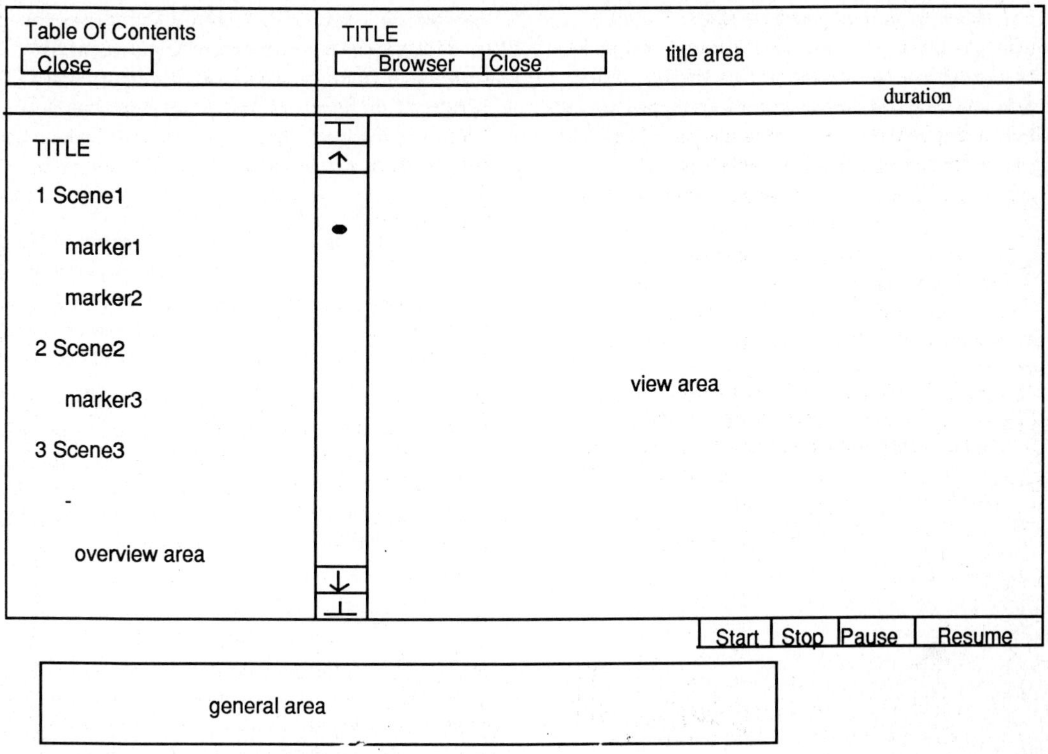

Figure 1: The screen layout of the browser

3 The Browser

Whenever a dynamic document is opened for reading, a browser is presented to the user with the current document as its context. The browser is used for both the sequential and random scanning of the document. The screen area of the browser is divided into title, view, overview and general areas. Figure 1 shows the browser with its screen layout. The title area displays the information such as title of the document and its duration. During the presentation of dynamic documents, audio information is replayed through an audio output device such as a speaker and visual information is displayed in the visual area allocated for that purpose. The overview area is for displaying the table of contents of the selected document. A scroll bar and a control panel is attached to the viewing area of the browser. The scroll bar allows the viewer to dynamically scan the document and the control panel is used for controlling the presentation of the document. The general area is for displaying the temporary information and it's use will be explained in the section on *trails*.

3.1 Presentation of Dynamic Documents

The presentation of dynamic documents is controlled by using the control panel attached to the viewing area. The control panel contains commands to *start*, *stop*, *pause* and *resume* the presentation. When the *stop* command is used to halt the presentation, restarting it, starts the presentation from the beginning. If one wants to temporarily halt the presentation and resume it from the same point then it can be done using the *pause* and *resume* commands.

During the presentation of a dynamic document, some additional information needs to be given to the user. This additional information may be in the form of audio or visual cues to show the beginning and end of scenes or to show the current position of the presentation in the overall document etc. We have used visual cues such as highlighting, to show the scene boundaries. For example, during the presentation of a scene, its heading which is being displayed in the overview area is highlighted.

We have used the scroll bar to show the relative position of the presentation point in the overall document. The vertical length of the scroll bar indicates the total duration of the document. A dot, which indicates the current position of the presentation, is displayed in the scroll bar and moves along the bar with a rate equal to that of the presentation. The offset from the top of the bar to the dot indicates the presentation already covered and the distance from the dot to the bottom of the bar indicates the duration of the presentation yet to come.

3.2 Static Scanning

Normally the presentation starts from the beginning of a document and continues sequentially from there. For quick scanning one should be able to select any point in the document and start the presentation from that point. This is done here using the table of contents displayed in the overview area. This table shows scenes and marked points which the viewer can select with a mouse interface. The next time the presentation is started, it will begin from the selected point. Since all the points in the presentation are not marked (i.e. not present in the table of contents), it is not possible to statically select any arbitrary point in the document. This is not going to be a big problem because of the availability of facilities for dynamic scanning.

3.3 Dynamic Scanning

In the dynamic scanning, the current position of a presentation can be moved forwards or backwards depending on the requirement. The amount of movement required is variable and depends on the situation. Hence, a flexible way of specifying this is required and we have used the scroll bar for this purpose. The viewer specifies this by pointing at a position in the scroll bar and the distance between the top of the bar and the point specifies the amount of movement required. This movement normally be some percent of the total duration. For instance, in our case, pointing at the bottom of the scroll bar indicates 10 percent of the total duration. Movements of less than 10 percent can be achieved by pointing further up the scroll bar.

Along with the scroll bar we also provided commands for making some operations easier. The *up* and *down* arrow commands move the presentation point backwards and forward respectively by a prespecified amount. This movement is roughly in the order of 8 percent. In dynamic scanning, backward movement needs to be slightly longer than forward movement. This is because one has to view some of the presentation before deciding to move again. The *top* and *bottom* commands in the scroll bar are used for reaching the start and end of the presentation respectively. In dynamic documents, moving the presentation point to the end is equivalent to stopping the presentation. Hence, we move the presentation to slightly before the end.

Another dynamic scanning technique is to increase the presentation rate of the information. This can be achieved by compressing the silences present in the audio information. In [Maxemchuk (1980)], it was reported that a rate increase of 20 percent can be achieved by making all silent interval that are longer than a second to 1/8 th of a second. But the prototype system we have implemented thus far does not provide this facility because of the lack of hardware support to detect silences. We recognize the importance of this facility for dynamic scanning and are considering its provision in the future.

3.4 Trails

Trails are a facility where the viewer marks points while viewing the presentation and later uses them for reviewing. These are only temporary markers and when the document is closed these markers disappear. These temporary markers are displayed in the general area and the viewer can select any of them and start the presentation from there. In a way, one can use trails for customizing the presentation. However, we have not provided a facility to leave permanent trails.

4 Implementation

In audio dominated documents, information presentation through other media is to be synchronized with the presentation of audio. Hence, a document data structure should represent this information along with the data. We have represented this in the form of a script and separated it from the main data structure. The script specifies serial and parallel actions that are to be carried out on the information. Unlike traditional documents where the only action that can be carried out is to display the information on the screen, variety of actions can be specified here. For instance one can display an image and then gradually increase its size.

The prototype system for creating and browsing through dynamic multimedia documents is implemented on the experimental *Firefly* workstation. *Firefly* is a multi processor workstation with bitmap displays, a mouse interface and a voice I/O facility [Thacker (1988)]. Using the ***Firefly*** one can record and replay telephone quality (64 kHz) speech and can store it on ordinary file servers available on the network. We organized and manipulated the speech in the prototype similarly to that of *Island* [Calnan (1988)] and *Etherphone* [Terry (1987)]. Here, operations on speech are not carried out by manipulating actual speech but by manipulating the pointers to the speech.

The creation of dynamic documents is a two step process, creating the information and the creation of scripts. Our approach is to provide separate editors for the creation of each information type and an editor for creating the script. The current prototype system consists of editors for speech and frame types. Frame is a two dimensional visual space with text and images laid in it. The system is implemented in such a way that the addition of new information types is easy. Which is useful for using the system in different application environments.

We have used an orchestration technique for reproducing the presentation from the document data structure. The presentation of different information types is carried out by separate servers and a central process controls and synchronizes the presentation by giving appropriate commands at appropriate times. When the viewer uses the browser for viewing the presentation, the browser contacts the central process, which in turn starts the presentation by sending commands to the servers. Similarly, moving the presentation point results an individual movement in all the information types involved.

5 Summary

In this paper we have presented a model for audio dominated documents. We identified the need for a powerful browser for dynamic documents and have described one such browser. This browser allows the viewer to scan the document both statically and dynamically.

Acknowledgments I would like to thank the Nehru Trust for Cambridge University for funding my studies and Prof. Roger Needham for his guidance during this project. Roger Calnan's constant encouragement during this work is appreciated. I also would like to thank Bhaskar Harita and Raphel Yahalom for their help during the writing of this paper.

References

[Calnan (1988)] Calnan, R. (1988) *The Integration of Voice within a Digital Network.* Ph.D. thesis, Computer Laboratory, Cambridge University.

[Hartman (1961)] Hartman, F. R. (1961) Single and Multiple Channel Communication: A Review Of Research and a Proposed Model. *AV Communication Review,9*,235–262.

[Maxemchuk (1980)] Maxemchuk, N. F. and Wilder, H. A. (1980) Experiments in Merging Text and Stored Speech. In *Conference Record. National Telecommunications Conference*, Houston, Texas.

[Terry (1987)] Terry, D. B. and Swinehart D. C. (1987) Managing Stored Voice in the Etherphone System. *ACM Operating Systems Review,4*, 48–61.

[Thacker (1988)] Thacker, C. P, Stewart L. C. and Satterthwaite Jr, E. H. (1988) Firefly: A Multiprocessor Workstation. *IEEE Transactions on Computers,8*,909–920.

SECTION IV: INTERACTIVE TECHNOLOGIES AND TECHNIQUES

SIV.3 Speech and Natural Language

An investigation into the use of error recovery dialogues in a user interface management system for speech recognition
M. Zajicek and J. Hewitt 755

Feedback requirements for automatic speech recognition in control room systems
C. Baber, R.B. Stammers, and R.G. Taylor 761

Spoken language interaction in a spreadsheet task
A.I. Rudnicky, M. Sakamoto, and J.H. Polifroni 767

Case study of development of a user interface for a voice activated dialing service
D. Lawrence and R. Stuart 773

A voice recognition interface for a telecommunications basic business group attendant console
I. Sola and D. Shepard 779

Observations on using speech input for window navigation
C. Schmandt, D. Hindus, M.S. Ackerman, and S. Manandhar 787

The design and implementation of a context sensitive natural language interface to management information
A. Burton and A.P. Steward 795

Recent approaches to natural language generation
L. Fedder 801

Human–Computer Interaction – INTERACT '90
D. Diaper et al. (Editors)
Elsevier Science Publishers B.V. (North-Holland)

AN INVESTIGATION INTO THE USE OF ERROR RECOVERY DIALOGUES IN A USER INTERFACE MANAGEMENT SYSTEM FOR SPEECH RECOGNITION

Mary ZAJICEK & Jill HEWITT*

Department of Computing and Mathematical Sciences, Oxford Polytechnic, Gipsy Lane, Headington, Oxford OX3 0BP. Tel: 0865 741111 Fax: 0865 819666

*School of Information Sciences, Hatfield Polytechnic, College Lane, Hatfield, Herts. AL10 9AB. Tel: 0707 279327 e-mail comqjah@hatfield.uk.ac

Experiments were carried out to assess new users' attitudes to different versions of a speech input word processing system providing different error recovery strategies. Whilst they preferred a simple error message to none at all, a more complex recovery dialogue lead to decreased satisfaction with the system. This paper describes the experiments carried out and explores possible reasons for the results.

1. INTRODUCTION

The purpose of our investigation was to assess the effects of different error recovery strategies on first time users of a speech input word processing system. The system has been developed as part of our ongoing work into speech interfaces in a project entitled the "Intelligent Speech Driven Interface Project" (ISDIP)#. The investigation forms a part of a continuous programme to improve the usability of the system following an iterative design approach.

Earlier investigations (Hewitt & Furner 1988) had highlighted the importance of error recovery in a system where the recognition rate was not 100%, and a study of user satisfaction with the system (Zajicek 1989) lead us to believe that a more informative error recovery dialogue would be well received.

Our results were not what we were expecting, and have lead us to reconsider the interface design and the form of error recovery we might offer. In particular we propose that a more close adherance to human-to-human conversational strategies should be investigated.

2. THE EVALUATION

Our experiments were designed to ascertain "Whether first-time users prefer an informative error recovery dialogue to a minimal one or none at all". The 20 participants were selected from the staff in the Computer Science department at Hatfield Polytechnic, all of them had keyboard skills, but none had used a speech recognition system before. The task they were asked to complete was to input and save to disk a short letter, using speech alone; following this they completed an attitude questionnaire and made any comments about the system. Diagnostics were recorded automatically for each session, giving us recognition rates and the types of error that occurred.

2.1 The Recognition System

The voice recognition system used was a VOTAN VPC 2000 isolated word recogniser with limited vocabularies (of up to 64 words). It was therefore necessary for the users to train all the words they would need to create edit and save the letter; these were contained in two vocabularies, the main one containing the words and editing functions and the other devoted to file handling commands. Movement between the vocabularies was to be made explicitly using a "switch" command.

2.2 An Experimental Session

Subjects were assessed individually and were not allowed to view sessions preceding their own so that the system would be new to each one of them. They were given a short demonstration of the training process followed by a part of the letter being dictated and then saved to disk. The training program was started for them and they trained each word just once before embarking on two separate attempts to create the letter.

They were told to watch the screen for possible error messages whilst inputting the letter - no error tone was used for this experiment. They had access to a limited number of editing functions and an UNDO command and were asked to try to ensure that the letter was correct, but to abandon attempts to correct a word if after 3 tries they could not get it right.

Prompts from the experimenter were given to enable them to save the file they had created and quit from the word processor.

2.3 The Word Processing System

The word processor used has been specially created for voice input, it has a limited range of editing functions

Funded by NAB under the NAB3 initiative in Artificial Intelligence.

which are sufficient for simple text creation tasks. The screen design includes special fields related to the voice recognition system, an outline is given in Figure 1. The labelled regions are used as follows:

A. The name of the file being edited
B. Reserved for the messages "Speak Louder Please" or "Speak Quieter Please"
C. The name of the vocabulary currently in use by the Recogniser
D. The main area for error messages.
E. Reserved for sub-dialogues between user and the interface management system and for auxiliary error messages.
F. A scrolling text area.

Pop-up windows appear in the text area for the file menu and the edit menu. The participants did not use the edit menu but were provided with a limited set of editing commands in the form of cursor movement, delete (previous character) and undo (last action).

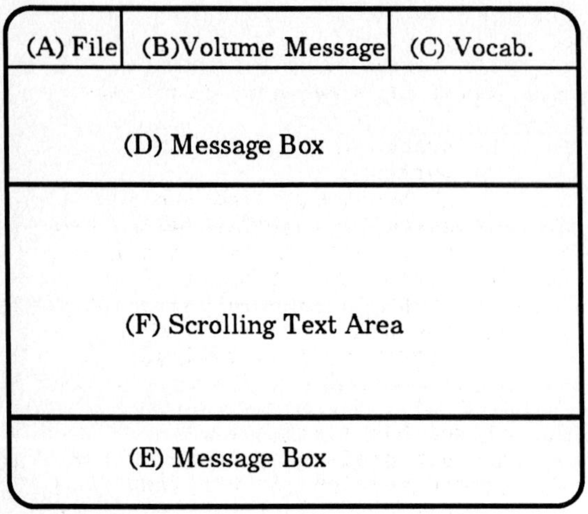

Figure 1

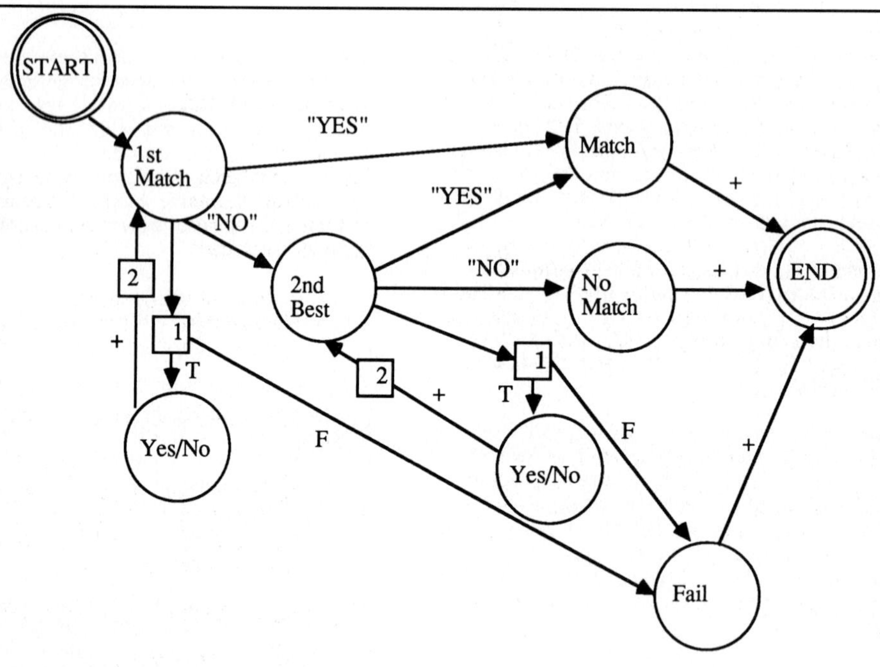

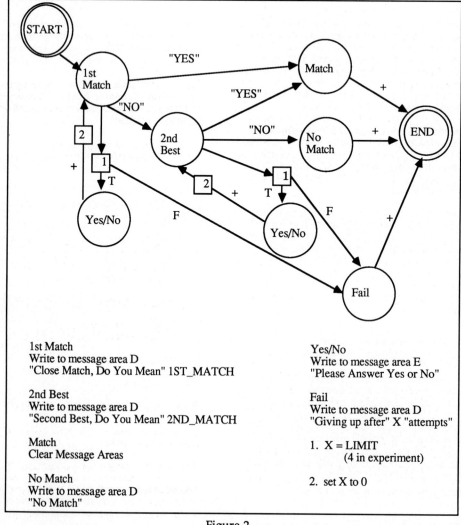

1st Match
Write to message area D
"Close Match, Do You Mean" 1ST_MATCH

2nd Best
Write to message area D
"Second Best, Do You Mean" 2ND_MATCH

Match
Clear Message Areas

No Match
Write to message area D
"No Match"

Yes/No
Write to message area E
"Please Answer Yes or No"

Fail
Write to message area D
"Giving up after" X "attempts"

1. X = LIMIT
(4 in experiment)

2. set X to 0

Figure 2

2.4 Recovery from Recognition Errors

Three strategies were used in the evaluation:

i. No error recovery:- the system will always find a match for an utterance even if it is not a good one. In this case, users will get the wrong word coming up on the screen. If they notice it immediately they can use the 'undo' command to remove it, otherwise they have to delete it character by character. It is possible that users may not be able to get the correct word if it has been badly trained and is too 'close' to another.

ii. Minimal information:- if the system does not find a good match for an utterance it will print the message "Don't recognise that word" in the error message area (D) and wait for the user to say something else. Wrong words will appear less frequently on the screen, but, depending on the setting of the recognition threshold, users may get stuck on a particular word which was perhaps poorly trained.

iii. Close Match dialogue:- in the case of an uncertain recognition, the system will offer a recovery dialogue as shown by the USE (Wasserman et al.1985) state transition diagram in Figure 2. If the first word offered is not the one they want they are offered a second choice. If that too is incorrect they will have to say the word again. The recovery dialogue uses both the message areas on the screen, the lower one being reserved for the message "Please answer Yes or No" if one of these words was not detected in answer to a question.

The system does in fact have a fourth recovery strategy - the "failsafe" which was not used for this experiment. It offers a selection of all possible words and highlights each in turn, asking the user to whistle when the required one is reached. This is essential when it is being used for 'real' work, particularly if the user is handicapped and cannot resort to using the keyboard.

Subjects were divided into two groups, the first each used two versions of the system, one with no error recovery beyond the undo command (strategy 1) and one with the minimal information (strategy 2). The second group used the version supporting strategy 3 for both tasks, but they were not told that there was no difference between the versions and were asked the same questions as the first group.

2.5 The Questionnaire

On completion of the task, subjects were asked to consider 8 statements related to the system and to score them on a scale of -3 to +3 depending on their level of agreement. These are reproduced in Figure 3. They were also asked which version of the system they preferred, if any, and whether they had a strong or marginal preference for it (question 9). They were given the opportunity to make any other comments regarding the system, including any suggestions for improvements they might have.

```
Rate the following statements (1-8)
on a scale of -3 (fully disagree) to
+3(fully agree) depending on
your level of agreement with them:

1.  The system is easy to use
2.  The system is tiring
3.  I feel happy with the system
4.  The system is complicated to use
5.  I feel in control of the system
6.  The system is confusing
7.  The system allows easy correction
     of mistakes
8.  The system is frustrating

9.  If you had a preference,
    did you prefer the first or the
    second version and was your
    preferred version much better or
    slightly better than the other one
```

Figure 3.

2.6 The Diagnostics

Whilst the subjects were using the recognition system a diagnostics program running in the background was collecting information. The statistics collected for all three strategies included:

- Number of words spoken
- Number rejected by the recognition unit
- Number of undo commands given by the subject

In addition, for the third strategy, the following were collected:

- Number of accepted 1st matches
- Number of accepted 2nd matches
- Number of rejected 2nd matches
- Number of yes/no errors

Two recognition rates were calculated automatically :-

- The basic recognition rate: words recognised/words spoken

-Rate plus Undo's
(words recognised + undo commands)/ words spoken

We felt it was necessary to also calculate an adjusted rate:-

(words recognised + undo commands + errors in finished letter) / words spoken

This was not a very exact measurement, but allowed some account to be taken of mistakes that the subject could not correct or had not noticed when creating the letter.

These diagnostics are summarised in Figure 4.

Strategy:	1	2	3
Avg. no. utterances	95	76	89
Basic Recog. Rate	100	87	93
Rec. Rate incl. undo	93	83	89
Adjusted Rate	90	82	88
Undo Commands	7	3	3
Yes/No errors	-	-	5

Figure 4.

3. RESULTS OF EXPERIMENTS

User scores on questions 1-8 of the questionnaire were totalled, providing a numeric measure of their satisfaction with the system generally. Since dialogue structure was the only variable component, changes in measure were taken to reflect different scores for dialogue structures. Diagnostic files were analysed for changes in recognition rate, the number of yes/no errors, and the number of undo commands. The letters created by subjects were examined for errors.

The results were analysed to find the answers to two questions:

3.1 Are users happier with a description of no match rather than wrong machine action?

The primary indicator was the result of question 9, which asked subjects to indicate their preference. It was found that eight out of nine preferred the description of no match. This preference was shown to be unrelated to recognition rate which in some cases was slightly better for the 'wrong machine action' version. The number of undo commands was predictably higher for this version. The number of errors in the finished letters were similar.

3.2 The hypothesis that "Users find no difference between more explanatory dialogue with the offer of a second best match and basic dialogue which either offers a no match message or wrong machine action"

The results of questionnaire answers were grouped as follows:

Group 1 - those who experienced no error recovery (wrong machine action) or minimal error recovery dialogue in the form of the error message "I don't recognise that word" (strategies 1 and 2 as described in section 2.4).

Group 2 - those who experienced error messages describing first and second best choices (strategy 3 described in section 2.4)

The score for each subject on questions 1-8 was computed, taking into account the sign change for negative questions. The scores were then subjected to a one-tailed Mann-Whitney U Test of the null hypothesis above. It was found that this hypothesis could be rejected at .02% level and a significant shift in favour of basic dialogue was detected. The results indicated that users preferred the basic dialogue with either a 'no match' message or wrong machine action.

4. DISCUSSION

The aim of experimentation was to analyse users' response to different dialogue structures, and to establish usability guidelines for speech driven dialogue design. The results have clearly shown users' preference for different dialogue structures and indicated the importance of fundamental dialogue design issues. They have also provided insight into the user's relationship, and perception of, a speech driven system, in particular the problems that are encountered when the user subconsciously expects natural human dialogue structures rather than restricted, conventional computer interaction dialogue.

4.1 Levels of sub-dialogue activity

Previous work (Zajicek 1990) had shown that users were, in principle, in favour of a high level of explanatory sub-dialogue. They expressed the opinion that it contributed to feelings of being in control of the system and gave them confidence in achieving error recovery. They made the assumption that the more explanation there was the more information they had to work with in handling the speech driven word processor, i.e. 'Knowledge is power!'

Researchers however, were aware of problems associated with information overload (Nusbaum 1986) and the need for simple dialogue on a multi-functional screen (Dye and Cruickshank 1988). Although the concept of more information more power may be sound, the increased activity involved in reading sub-dialogue messages contributed to cognitive overload, and detracted from the fluency of operation of the word processor.

The aim of experimentation was to observe subjects using the word processor and gain a rating for different forms of feedback dialogue, enabling a comparison between a users' expectations and the actual experience.

4.2 Comparison between the strategies of no error recovery and a description of no match.

The answer to question 9 of the questionnaire showed that users are happier with a description of no match rather than wrong machine action. This indicated that the dialogue displayed in the top sub-dialogue area, if in the brief form of a description of no match, was considered to be more effective than no dialogue at all. This was consistent with previous users' positive view of the value of increased sub-dialogues.

The result was also consistent with rules of human conversation in that if a word is misheard, the listener will give the equivalent of a no match message such as "Pardon" or "Can you repeat that please" rather than act on an unlikely guess. The strength of the description of no match was that it was succinct and required no further action.

4.3 User Preference for a basic dialogue or no error recovery over a more explanatory one

This result shows that although a 'no match' message was preferred to wrong machine action, users were less well satisfied with a system giving more explanatory error messages. This result was not consistent with previous experiments where users had expressed a preference for increased explanation, the experience was then in some way different from the expectation.

It is well known that help facilities which enable a user to 'get started' with a system soon become irritating when the user becomes competent, however in these experiments all users were inexperienced and persisted in overlooking useful information.

Observations showed that subjects frequently misused the yes/no answer system provided for selecting first and second best matches. They failed to answer yes or no even when prompted and often continued to scan the upper dialogue area for clues to their apparent deadlock. This is substantiated by the large number of yes/no errors in their diagnostic files (a yes/no error occurs when the system is expecting one of those words and the user says something else). It must be noted that even the most experienced researchers sometimes forgot to consult the lower sub-dialogue area for information when error situations arose. The yes/no dialogue had been flagged as a problem in previous prototypes and these experiments have helped to clarify aspects of the problem.

4.4 Mapping Dialogue to the User's Conceptual Model

Although a yes/no response is an effective method for clarifying the user's intention in keyboard interfaces where typing 'y' or 'n' is quicker than re-typing a command, subjects' behaviour has shown its use to be at variance with their conceptual model of a speech driven interface.

The user's conceptual model of a speech driven interface appears to be more closely related to human conversation than conventional keyboard dialogue, although other researchers (Newell, 84) maintain that people use unnatural speech when addressing machines. The usual conversational response to a misheard word is to repeat it. The preferred basic dialogue mode offered the no match message and the chance to repeat the utterance of the word. Although it is less sophisticated it provides a close match to human conversational strategies.

However if we pursue the analogy with human conversation, there are situations when if a word is misheard the listener will say 'did you say ....' and the speaker will naturally say yes or no rather than repeat the misheard word. This dialogue strategy is usually employed after several repetitions have been tried.

4.5 Dealing with information overload

As described above, feedback dialogue is presented in several areas above and below the main text of the word processor. It was hoped that users would become familiar with the function of individual sub-dialogue areas, automatically scanning them when particular information was needed. The results of experimentation have shown that the sub-dialogue area below the word processor text was not easily recognised by the user as performing a yes/no dialogue role.

Reasons for the apparent neglect of the lower sub-dialogue area have not yet been established, but two explanations are offered. Firstly that the position of the lower sub-dialogue area does not correspond to the user's conceptual model of the interface and their expectation that all information will be displayed *above* the word processing text; secondly, that the sub-dialogue itself is not comfortable for the user.

It is possible that a sub-dialogue utilising speech output would be more acceptable, satisfying the user's expectations of a more natural conversational mode. If the dialogue (whether spoken or screen output) was invoked only after several attempts to recognise a word it would conform more closely to a human to human conversational strategy.

5. CONCLUSIONS

The experiments have provided insight into natural assumptions made by users of a speech driven interface. Recognition rates are good enough to instill feelings of confidence in word recognition leading users to assume that dialogue structure emulates human conversation. They overlooked confirmation messages in sub-dialogue areas and in fact behaved as though they assumed 100% recognition.

The two particular dialogue strategies offered for assessment in these trials differed in that the basic dialogue strategy emulated natural conversation when a word is misheard. The more explanatory dialogue strategy, while conforming to normal computer interaction confirmatory rules, did not conform to the model of natural conversation. It was found to introduce confusion, and was less popular with subjects.

These results indicate that there exists a point at which expectation and conceptual models of a speech driven interface cease to be those of standard computer interaction, and take on the characteristics of natural conversation. The point may be determined by the level of confidence in the recognition of utterances. The ISDIP system appears to have reached this point indicating that consideration should be given to a dialogue modelled more closely on natural conversation.

Further trials will need to be completed to investigate the usefulness of speech output in a dialogue and the degree to which a 'natural' conversation can be emulated. It is important also to assess more experienced users, particularly those who *have* to use the system in order to complete a task (i.e. disabled users), since their perceptions of the usefulness of the various strategies may be different from those of new users described in this paper.

6. REFERENCES

Dye, R. and Cruickshank. (1988) A System for Composing and editing text using natural spoken language. Proc. Speech '88, Institute of Acoustics.

Hewitt J.A. & Furner S.(1988) Text Processing by Speech: Dialogue Design and Usability Issues in the provision of a System for Disabled Users, in People & Computers IV, Jones D.M. & Winder R. (eds.)

Newell, A.F. (1984) Speech - The Natural Modality for Man-Machine Interaction. Proc. Interact '84.

Nusbaum, H.C. (1986) Human Factors Considerations in the Design Large Vocabulary Speech Recognition Devices in Proc. Speech Tech 1986.

Wasserman A.I., Pircher P.A. Shewmake D.T. and Kersten M.L. (1987) Developing Interactive Information Systems with the User Software Engineering Methodology in Readings in Human Computer Interaction, Baecker R.M., and Buxton W.A.S. .

Zajicek, M. (1990) Evaluation of a Speech Driven Interface, Proc. IEE UK IT 1990.

Human–Computer Interaction – INTERACT '90
D. Diaper et al. (Editors)
Elsevier Science Publishers B.V. (North-Holland)

FEEDBACK REQUIREMENTS FOR AUTOMATIC SPEECH RECOGNITION IN CONTROL ROOM SYSTEMS

C. BABER, R.B. STAMMERS, and R.G. TAYLOR

Applied Psychology Division.
Aston University,
Aston Triangle,
Birmingham.
B4 7ET

Previous research into feedback requirements for users of ASR has tended to concentrate on verbal feedback: presented via text or via synthetic speech. In control room systems, auditory feedback is not viable for ASR, and textual feedback is potentially problematic. To counter these problems, feedback could be presented using symbols on exisiting displays. In this study, textual and symbolic feedback are compared for an error detection task, one of the prime uses of feedback for ASR. It was found that although performance using symbolic feedback did improve over time, it was significantly lower than that for textual feedback. Further, the type of symbol used also effected performance.Therefore, for error detection at least, textual feedback is preferable to symbolic feedback. However, the role of symbolic feedback in more direct task control is yet to be explored.

1.INTRODUCTION

Automatic Speech Recognition (ASR) is gradually gaining acceptance as a means of controlling computer systems. Several successful applications have been reported from industry and telecommunications. However, ASR is unlikely to be 100% efficient. This means that errors are inevitable. Because of this, the user needs to be informed of the performance of the device being used. Therefore, feedback is a topic of major importance to ASR research.

1.1. Uses of Feedback in ASR

Schurick et al (1985) distinguish between primary feedback, in which a spoken command causes a desired action by the system, and secondary feedback, in which the user is informed of the words recognised by the device. We extend these definitions to consider what the user requires the feedback for. Initially, feedback will indicate that something has been recgonised by the device. This information is provided by primary feedback. However, feedback can also be used for the detection of errors. This will require the user to perform a verbal decision task. The aim of this study is to examine whether such a task is best supported by textual or symbolic feedback.

1.2. Types of Feedback Secondary feedback could be provided using synthetic speech. But there are a number of problems associated with auditory feedback (Martin and Welch, 1980). Furthermore, in control rooms, the auditory channel is generally reserved for alarm information. Therefore, visual feedback will be preferable for such appications.

Screen space is at a premium in control rooms. Much of the screen is required to display plant diagrams and data. Textual feedback will require space that may be more usefully employed for the display of other information. It will also require the operator to rely on two areas of screen space for feedback. Symbolic feedback could be incorporated in the plant diagram. This would reduce the amount of screen space required and the amount of information given to the operator. It has been convincingly argued that user performance will be most effective when the user deals with as few sources of information as possible (Carroll, 1984).

Symbolic feedback could provide a very useful means of primary feedback. Intuitively, this ought to make the monitoring of the plant easier. The feedback from the diagram will allow a direct interaction between operator and plant. Diagrams are the most efficient format for presenting data concerning decisions about the structure of a system (Gerstendörfer and Rohr, 1984). The use of symbolic feedback could support such findings. When using ASR, feedback should also be secondary. This will support decisions concerning the correctness of the recognised words, either in terms of verbal decisions (error detection), or semantic decisions for wider issues of system performance. This study questions whether symbolic feedback will provide the same level of performance as textual feedback, in terms of error detection.

1.3. Text and Symbol Recognition

There has been limited research comparing text with symbols as a means of feedback to users of computer systems. We are not aware of any studies addressing the issue of symbolic feedback for ASR. Previous studies comparing symbolic and textual feedback, in other contexts, provide conflicting results.

Alphanumeric displays have been shown to yield faster search and identification times than symbolic symbols (Christ and Corso, 1983). Dewer et al (1976) showed that verbal road signs produced faster recognition times than graphical ones. In contrast graphical road signs have been shown to be recognised faster than verbal signs (Dewer et al 1965).

It is clear that a major component of recognising different types of sign is the familiarity of the sign for the subject. Christ and Corso (1983) argue that their results stem form the fact that subjects are more familiar with words and numbers, that with abstract geometric shapes. However, they also demonstrate that after nine months of practice, subjects could identify and search through all sets of symbols with equal speed. If text and symbols of comparable familiarity were compared, then unequivocal results could be obtained. Richardson Simon et al (1988) showed subjects colour patches, shapes, and the corresponding words. It was found that decisions were made the fastest for colours and shapes. Thus, information presented in pictorial formats ought to be processed faster than that presented in words.

The conflicting results from these studies also reflect the different uses to which feedback is put. For example, Dewer et al (1976) asked subjects to name the signs as soon as they recognised them. He measured the time between presenting the sign, and the subjects response. In naming textual signs, subjects only need to read the word. But for symbols, subjects need to recognise the symbol, recall its name, and speak the name In other words, some form of translation is required between symbolic presentation and naming. Therefore, one would expect people to name a word faster than a symbol. Further, subjects can classify an object faster than they can classify a word (Potter and Faulconer, 1975). Some interesting research into the processing of faces has a bearing on this point. Young et al (1986) found that subjects could classify faces of famous people as being actors, politicians etc. faster than they could name them, and that they could speak the name faster than they could classify it. It has also been shown that objects and words can be used to prime recognition of each other (Guenther et al 1980). This suggests that the recognition and naming processes overlap.

1.4. Text and Symbol Processing

Seidenberg and McClelland (1989) propose a distributed model of word recognition and naming. In this model, naming is the result of a process which constructs an articulatory motor program from the phonological code for the word. Decisions of word meaning, on the other hand, are computed for phonological and semantic information. Warren and Morton (1982) also argue that words can access both a semantic representation and pronunciation mechanism simultaneously. But the pronunciation mechanism gives a faster output. Objects must access the semantic representation before a name can be assigned to be pronounced. Therefore, assigning an object to a particular class will take less time than recalling its name.

We draw a parallel between user correction of errors in ASR use and naming words and objects. A word is spoken, feedback appears and the user must decide if it is correct. If the feedback is textual, then the verbal decision process is akin to naming. If the displayed word matches the spoken word then the feedback is correct. If feedback is symbolic, then users have to recall the symbols name, and compare it with the word they spoke. Thus, decision requires a translation between the recognition of a symbol and the recall of its name. For this reason we expect textual feedback to yield faster decision times that symbolic feedback.

1.5.Symbols

A second hypothesis relates to the familiarity of symbols. In control room systems,

symbols will be arbitrarily assigned meanings, ie, they do not necessarily bear a natural correspondence to their meaning. This means that whenever symbols are used, some learning of their meaning will occur for the user.
Graphical symbols can be defined in terms of their depictive qualities or in terms of assigned meanings. The latter are commonly called symbols and the former pictograms (Barnard and Marcel, 1984). Mead and Modley (1968) distinguish between image related symbols (termed pictograms here), and concept related symbols, such as a right turn arrow. Concept related symbols rely on a strong analogy between symbol and assigned meaning. This suggests that three types of graphical symbol can be used in displays.
Graphical symbols can represent pictograms: objects in defined states, e.g. an open switch. They can be concept related, e.g. in terms of spatial indications. And they can be abstract symbols, such as command words. The latter category is often the most difficult to design. Graphical symbols cannot easily represent verbs, e.g. open . It is possible to show the action off a particular verb, but not its intention.
The classification of pictograms, spatial symbols,and command symbols can be assumed to be in decreasing order of concreteness. Command symbols are the least concrete because they have an arbitrary pairing of meaning and symbol, whilst the other two types use cultural stereotypes to inform the pairings. This level of concreteness can be expected to affect decision times, with the least concrete symbols taking longer to recognise. It is also expected that some learning could occur. This will be less marked for the textual feedback, as it assumed that the words will be familiar to the subjects.

2. METHOD

2.1.Outline of study

This study will compare subjects reaction time to different types of visual feedback when they use ASR. Reaction times can be used to provide an index of the speed with which subjects can understand information in a given stimulus (Keele, 1973).
Subjects speak a word, and feedback is given; either textual or a type of symbol. Subjects decide as quickly as possible whether the display matches the word they said. Reaction times are used to compare performance across the different types of feedback.

2.2.Subjects

Fourteen students were paid £2.00 for participation in a study which lasted approximately half an hour. They were told that they were helping to assess the style of feedback to be used for ASR. Subjects were told that the device was speaker independent, so that it would recognise their speech without the need to enrol it. Subjects were assigned to two groups. Group 1 were tested using textual feedback. Group 2 were tested using symbolic feedback.

2.3. Equipment The experiment was run on an Archimedes p.c. Rather than using an ASR device, we relied on a simulation. This permitted errors to be introduced at defined points in the interaction. The simulation required the experimenter to hit the return key as soon as the subject spoke a word. A second response key was provided for the subject. The time between depressing the return key and the response key was recorded on the computer.The vocabulary used consisted of twenty two words comonly found in control room systems (each with an associated symbol).
The words were divided into three categories. Spatial words: up, down, left, right, above, below. Commad words: stop, go, increase, decrease, open, close, move, check. Objects:, boiler, furnace, valve, temperature, pipe, condenser, switch, telephone.

2.4.Procedure

Group 1 were given a list of the twenty two words used in the study, and asked to read them aloud. They were asked to say if any of the words were unfamiliar. This constituted the learning phase for subjects in group 1. After this, they completed the recognition test. The experimenter prompted subjects verbally, i.e. "Please say the word 'condenser'", and subjects repeated the word. This was assumed to minic the process of word recall in using ASR. When the subject said the word, the experimenter pressed a key to call up a word. The words were programmed to appear in a set order, so the experimenter only had to hit the reurn key. When the word appeared, the subject had to decide whether this was the word she had said, and press a 'yes' or a 'no' key. At each trial the list of

words was presented twice, thus giving forty four items per trial. This procedure was repeated five times. At each trial the order in which the subject was prompted to say the words was varied. This allowed some errors to be introduced into the feedback. The rate of error was 25%, which was assumed to mimic poor industrial use.
Group 2 were shown a table containing all the symbols used in the study. Each word had an associated symbol. The experimenter described each of the symbols to the subject. The subject then carried out the learning phase of the study. They were prompted with a word on the screen, which appeared below a box containing the symbols. They had to move a cursor onto the correct symbol for that word. This was carried out until all the symbols were correctly identified. The recognition terst was similar to that for group 1, except that instead of words for feedback, group 2 received symbols. Reaction times were measured for the two conditions, and compared in terms of type of item (object, spatial, command) using a three way ANOVA.

3.RESULTS

A comparison of the overall mean reaction times for the two groups shows a significant difference (p<0.01) between textual and symbolic feedback. This difference is constant across trials. There are no significant differences between items for textual presentation. Graph 1 shows that there are differences between type of item under symbolic presentation. These differences are significant (p<0.0001). However, these differences need to be examined in terms of results per trial. In trial 1, there is a significant difference (p<0.01) between all item types. In trial 2, this difference is only between objects and spatial items, and objects and commands. There are no significant differences between items in the other trials.
The times to make decisions for correct and incorrect feedback were also recorded. It does not seem viable to compare the changes in reaction time across trials for such decisions as a different script was used for each trial. This means that the difference in results over time could be explained by subjects improvement in performance or by the variations in script.

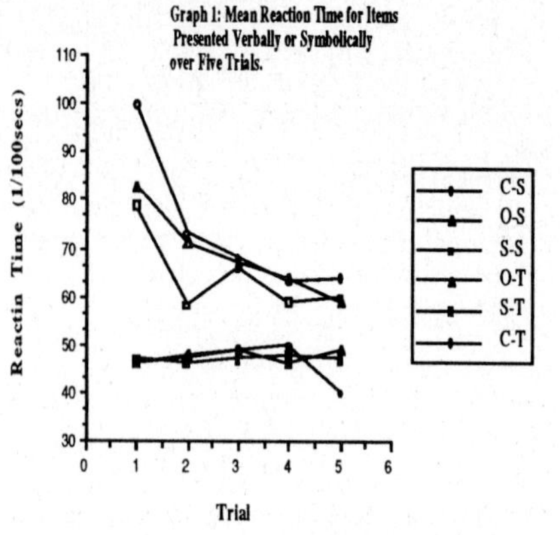

[In the key, the letters t and s indicate whether feedback was textual or symbolic. c,s,and o indicate whether the symbols were spatial, object, or command.]

Overall the differences between textual and symbolic feedback can be broken down into reaction times for 'yes' and 'no' decisions. The time taken to respond to correct textual feedback was, on average, 405 ms and the time taken to respond to incorrect textual feedback was, on average, 540 ms. This gives a difference of 45 ms between 'yes' and 'no' decisions.The time taken to respond to correct symbolic feedback was, on average, 672 ms and the time taken to respond to incorrect symbolic feedback was, on average, 707 ms. This gives a difference of 35 ms.

4.DISCUSSION

4.1.Overall Results

Comparison of the mean times for the two groups shows that textual feedback produces consistently a faster reaction time than symbolic feedback, across all trials.

4.2.Effects of Practice

There was no learning effect for textual feedback; performance was constant across all item types and across all trials. There was a definite learning effect for symbolic feedback, in the first two trials. This can be explained by several factors. Loftus and Bell (1975) show that speed of picture recognition increases with the amount of visual detail encoded.

This would relate to an increase in recognition as subjects saw the pictures more often. Also, speed of recognition increases as subjects verbalise more information of picture details. At a simple level, assigning a name to the pictures could contribute to such information. Finally, subjects would be learning the pairing of symbol with name more efficiently over time.

4.3. Types of Symbol

In the first trial, the significant differeneces in performance lay between all item types for symbolic feedback. The spatial symbols were recognised fastest, with objects next and then command words. This supports the notion of levels of concreteness proposed in the Introduction. Results in the second trial also reflect this pattern, although performance between spatial items and commands has reached nonsignificance. Over the remaining trials, there is no difference between items. This suggests that although a relationship may exist between the concreteness of a symbol and ease of recognition, this effect can be reduced through practice.

4.4.Correct vs. Incorrect Feedback

Subjects in both groups reported that once they had spoken a word, they imagined the appropriate feedback, either word or symbol. If the feedback on the screen matched this, they pressed the 'yes' button. It is difficult to propose why it should take longer to press the 'no' button if the feedback did not match the word or symbol they had imagined. It is suggested that negation involves the construction of the positive state first, and then the negation of this statement. If this is the case, then the forming of an anticipated image for the decision task in this experiment can be analogous to forming a positive statement. Negation will be expected to take longer. It is well established that decisions for negative information take longer than for positive information (Ratcliff, 1985).

4.5.Processing Codes

The results could also be explained by saying that verbal feedback is a more natural pairing with speech than symbolic feedback (Wickens, 1984).
Both speaking and reading require the same processing code (Baddeley, 1986). Therefore, tasks requiring the same code ought to provide faster performance times than ones which require translation between codes. However, the effect of translation will depend as much on the task as on the codes used. The studies comparing naming and classifying words and objects support this assertion.

4.6.Conclusions

We have suggested that error detection in ASR will require similar processing to naming tasks, because both are verbal decision tasks. Therefore, error detection, at least, requires textual feedback.Textual feedback gave consistent performance across all trials, and no differences between type of item.
Symbolic feedback showed differences on both of these measures.
In control room systems, screen displays are most often used for monitoring plant activity. This requires decisions about the status and functioning of objects. Such decisions could be classed as semantic. It has been argued that symbolic feedback is more effective than textual feedback for semantic decisions. Also, if feedback was provided near the relevant object, the operator would not need to concentrate on two areas of the screen at the same time. The use of symbolic feedback for direct task control will be investigated in a further study.

5.REFERENCES

Baddeley, A.D.(1986) **Working Memory** Oxford: Clarendon Press

Barnard, P. and Marcel, T. (1984) Representation and Understanding in the Use of Symbols and Pictograms. In: Easterby, R. and Zwaga, H.(eds.) **Information Design** Chichester: Wiley

Carroll, J.M. (1984) Minimalist Design for Active Users. In: **Interact '84** 1st. IFIP Conference on Human Computer Interaction. Amsterdam: Elsevier

Christ, R.E. and Corso, G.M. (1983) The Effects of Extended Practice on the Evaluation of Visual Display Codes. **Human Factors 25** (1) pp.71-84

Dewer, R.E., Nicolay, R.C., and Stearns, C.R. (1965) Comparative Accuracy of Recognising American and International Road Signs. **Journal of Applied Psychology 49** pp.322-325

Dewer, R.E., Ells, J.G., and Mundy, G. (1976) Reaction Time as an Index of Traffic Sign Perception. **Human Factors 18** (4) pp.381-392

Gerstendörfer, R.K. and Rohr, G. (1987) Which Task Representation on What Type of

Interface. In: Bullinger, H.J. and Shackel,B.(eds.) **Interact '87** Amsterdam: Elsevier

Guenther, R.K., Klatzky, R.L. and Putnam, W. (1980) Commonalities and Differences in Semantic Decisions about Pictures and Words. **Journal of Verbal Learning and Verbal Behaviour 19** pp.54-74

Keele, S.W.(1973) **Attention and Human Performance** Englewood Cliffs, N.J.: Prentice Hall Inc.

Loftus, G.R. and Bell, S.M. (1975) Two Types of Information in Picture Memory. **Journal of Experimental Psychology: Human Learning and Memory 1** pp.103-115

Martin, T.B. and Welch, J.R. (1980) Practical Speech Recognisers and Some Performance Effectiveness Parameters. In: Lea, W.A. (ed.) **Trends in Speech Recognition** Englewood Cliffs, N.J.: Prentice Hall Inc.

Mead, M. and Modley, R. (1968) Communications Among All People, Everywhere. **Natural History 77**(7) pp.56-63

Potter, M.C. and Faulconer, B.A.(1975) Time to Understand Pictures and Words. **Nature 253** pp.437-438

Ratcliff,R. (1985) Theoretical Interpretations of the Speed and Accuracy of Positive and Negative Responses **Psychological Review 92** pp.212-225

Richardson Simon, J. Peterson, K.D., and Wang, J.H. (1988) Same- Different Reaction Times to Stimuli Presented Simultaneously to Separate Cerebral Hemispheres. **Ergonomics 31** (12) pp.1837-1846

Schurick, J.M., Williges, B.H. and Maynard, J.F. (1985) User Feedback Requirements with ASR. **Ergonomics 28** (11) pp.1534-1555

Seidenberg, M.S. and McClelland, J.L. (1989) A Distributed, Developmental Model of Word Recognition and Naming. **Psychological Review 96** (4) pp.523-568

Warren, C. and Morton, J. (1982) The Effects of Priming on Picture Recognition. **British Journal of Psychology 73** pp.117-130

Wickens, C.D. (1984) **Engineering Psychology and Human Performance** Columbus, Ohio: Charles E. Merrill Pub. Co.

Young, A.W.,McWeeny, K.H., Ellis, A.W., and Hay, D.C. (1986) Naming and Categorising Faces and Written Names. **Quarterly Journal of Experimental Psychology 38a** pp.297-318

Human–Computer Interaction – INTERACT '90
D. Diaper et al. (Editors)
Elsevier Science Publishers B.V. (North-Holland)

Spoken language interaction in a spreadsheet task

Alexander I. Rudnicky, Michelle Sakamoto, and Joseph H. Polifroni

School of Computer Science, Carnegie Mellon University, Pittsburgh, Pennsylvania 15213 USA

To study the spoken language interface in the context of a complex problem-solving task, we had a group of users perform a spreadsheet task, alternating voice and keyboard input. A total of 40 tasks were performed by each participant, the first thirty in a group (over several days), the remaining ones a month later. The voice spreadsheet program used in this study was extensively instrumented to provide detailed information about the components of the interaction. These data, as well as analysis of the participants's utterances and recognizer output, provide a fairly detailed picture of spoken language interaction.

1 Introduction

Recent advances in speech recognition technology [2] have made it possible to build "spoken language" systems that create the opportunity for interacting naturally with computers. Spoken language systems combine a number of desirable properties. Recognition of *continuous speech* allows users to use a natural speech style. *Speaker independence* allows casual users to easily use the system and eliminates training and its associated problems (such as drift). *Large vocabularies* make it possible to create habitable languages for complex applications. Finally, a *natural language* processing capability allows the user to express him or herself using normal locutions.

While the recognition technology base that makes spoken language systems possible is rapidly maturing, there is no corresponding understanding of how such systems should be designed or what capabilities users will expect to have available. For example, it seems intuitively apparent that speech will be suited for some functions (e.g., data entry) but unsuited for others (e.g., drawing). We would also expect that users will be willing to tolerate some level of recognition error, but do not know what this is or how it would be affected by the nature of the task being performed or by the error recovery facilities provided by the system.

Meaningful exploration of such issues is difficult without some baseline understanding of how humans interact with a spoken language system. To provide such a baseline, we implemented a spoken language system using currently available technology and used it to study humans performing a series of simple tasks. We chose to work with a spreadsheet program since the spreadsheet supports a wide range of activities, from simple data entry to complex problem solving. It is also a widely used program, with a large experienced user population to draw on. We chose to examine performance over an extended series of tasks because we believe that regular use will be characteristic of spoken language applications.

2 The voice spreadsheet system

2.1 General

The voice spreadsheet (henceforth "VSC") consists of the UNIX-based spreadsheet program SC interfaced to a recognizer embodying the SPHINX technology described in [2]. Figure 1 shows the structure of the system used in this study. Additional description of VSC is available elsewhere [3].

An interaction cycle goes through the following stages: the recognizer is enabled and becomes "live" until an utterance is

Figure 1: System block diagram

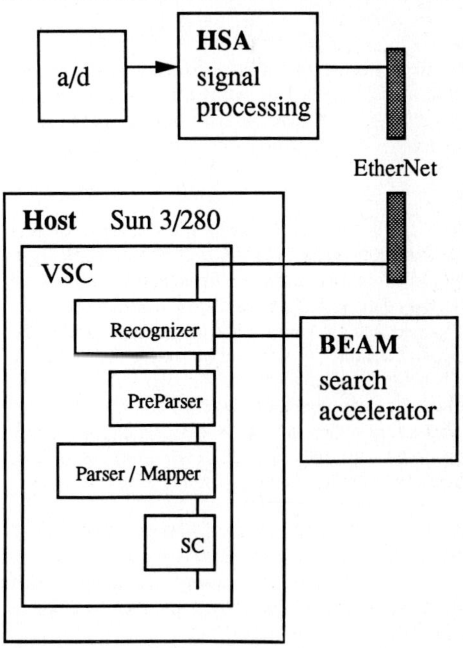

detected. While the system is processing this utterance, all other input is ignored until recognition has been carried out. Once ready, the resulting word string is passed to a **preparser** module, whose role is to check for syntactic legality and to translate task non-specific components, such as the numbers. The SC-specific **parser/mapper** converts the utterance into an actual SC command and enters it into the SC processing queue. Errors in parsing (i.e., grammatically illegal strings) are rejected and the user is asked to supply a new utterance. To aid the user in distinguishing the two cases, a synthesized 100 msec tone is emitted after each parse attempt, an ''acccpt'' tone (a quasi-pure 250 Hz tone) indicates success, a ''reject'' tone (frequency of 100 Hz) indicates parser failure. SC performs the specified action, then returns to listening to the user. For purposes of this study, the system was instrumented to provide detailed information about the interactive session.

2.2 The spreadsheet language

We conducted a ''wizard'' experiment, described more fully in [6], to determine an appropriate language for a spoken language spreadsheet. On the basis of the protocols collected in that experiment, we defined a language that allows users to express the actions necessary to carry out the tasks we set in a fairly natural manner.

The spreadsheet language has a vocabulary of 271 words, with a task-set perplexity of about 52, using a word-pair grammar[1]. The spreadsheet vocabulary includes all lexical items necessary for controlling the SC program, including many that were of no use in the current study (for example, commands for modifying the display format and trigonometric functions). On the other hand, the vocabulary included task-specific words (such as SALARY and MORTGAGE) that allow the users to refer to particular cell locations within the worksheet used for the present tasks.

2.3 Method

Since we were interested in not only how a casual user approaches a spoken language system, but also how his or her skill in using the system develops over time, we constructed a set of 40 spreadsheet tasks. All participants did each of these tasks.

2.3.1 Task description

The general task chosen for this study was the entry of personal financial data from written descriptions of various items in a fictitious person's monthly finances. An attempt was made to make each version of the task comparable in the amount of information it contained and in the number of complex arithmetic operations required. On the average, each task required entering 38 pieces of financial information, an average of 6 of these entries required arithmetic operations such as addition and multiplication. Movement within the worksheet, although generally following a top to bottom order, skipped around, forcing the user to make arbitrary movements, including off-screen movements.

Users were presented with preformatted worksheets containing appropriate headings for each of the items they would have to enter. In addition, each relevant cell location was given a label that would allow the user to access it using symbolic movement instructions (see [6]).

The information to be entered was presented on separate sheets of paper, one entry to a sheet, contained in a binder positioned to the side of the workstation. This was done to insure that all users dealt with the information in a sequential manner and would follow a predetermined movement sequence within the worksheet. To aid the user, the bottom of each sheet gave the category heading for the information to be entered and, if existing, a symbolic label for the cell into which the information was to be entered.

2.3.2 Procedure and Design

All participants performed 40 tasks. The first 30 tasks were completed in a block, over several days. The last ten were completed after an interval of about one month. The purpose of the latter was to determine the extent to which users remembered their initial extended experience with the voice spreadsheet and to what degree this retest would reflect the performance gains realized over the course of the original block of sessions.

All sessions were limited to about one hour, to minimize fatigue effects. Most people took five sessions to complete the first 30 tasks, finishing about six per session.

At the beginning of each session, each participant was given a standard-format typing test to determine their facility with the keyboard. The typing test revealed two types of participants, touch typists (3 people) with a mean typing rate of 63 words per minute (wpm) and ''hunt and peck'' typists (5 people), with a mean typing rate of 31 wpm[2]. Task modality (whether speech or typing) alternated over the course of the experiment, each successive task being carried out in a different modality. To control for order and task-version effects the initial modality and the sequence of tasks (first-to-last *vs* last-to-first) was varied to produce all possible combinations (four). Two people were assigned to each combination.

Since we were interested in studying a spoken language system in an environment that realistically reflects the settings in which such a system might eventually be used, we made no special attempt to locate the experiment in a benign environment or to control the existing one. The workstation was located in an open laboratory and was not surrounded by any special enclosure. Apart from being the location of the experiment, the laboratory served as permanent workspace for four people and might be occupied by several others at any given point in time. A second workstation was located within 2 m of the one used for the experiment. The setting was witness to such events as door slams, normal-voice conversations, and telephone ringing. We feel that these features allow us to validly characterize what to expect in office-like environments.

The participants were informally solicited from the university community through personal contact and bulletin board announcements. There were 3 women and 5 men, ranging in age from 18 to 26 (mean of 22). With the exception of one person who was of English/Korean origin, all participants were native speakers of English. All had previous experience with spreadsheets, an average of 2.3 years (range 0.75 to 5), though currently usage ranged from daily to ''several times a year''. None of the participants reported any previous experience with speech recognition systems (one had seen a SPHINX demonstration).

3 Results

The data collected in this study consisted of detailed timings of the various stages of interaction as well as the actual speech uttered over the course of system interaction.

When a spoken language system is exposed to speech generated in a natural setting a variety of acoustic events appear that contribute to performance degradation. Spontaneous speech events can be placed into one of three categories: ***lexical***, ***extra-lexical***, and ***non-lexical***, depending on whether the item is part of the system lexicon, a recognizable word that is not part of the lexicon, or some other event, such as a breath noise. These categories, as well as the procedure for their transcription, are described in greater detail in [5]. Table 1 lists the most common non-lexical events encountered in our corpus. The number of events is given, as well as their incidence in terms of words in the corpus. Given the nature of the task, it is not surprising to find that a large number of paper rustles intrudes into the speech stream. These events were transcribed for 893 of the 12507 utterances used for this analysis (7.14% of the utterances). Figure 2 show the proportion of transcribed utterances that contain extraneous material (such as coughs and environmental sounds). This function was generated by calculating grammaticality with both non-lexical and extra-lexical tokens included in the transcription. As is apparent, the incidence of extraneous events steadily decreases over sessions. Users apparently realize the harmful effects of such events and work to eliminate them (conversely, the user does not appear to have absolute control over such events, otherwise the decrease would have been much steeper). The top line in the graphs shows utterance error rate, the percent of utterances that are incorrectly recognizer and therefore lead to an unintended action; it includes errors due to both the presence of unanticipated events and to more conventional failures of recognition. The similarity in the shape of the two functions suggests that speech recognition accuracy is fairly constant across sessions, major variations being accounted for by changes in ambience (as tracked by the lower curve).

Existing statistical modeling techniques can be used to deal with the most common events (such as paper rustles) in a satisfactory manner [7]). However, more general techniques will need to be developed to account for low-frequency or otherwise unexpected events. A spoken language system should be capable of accurately identifying novel events and disposing of them in appropriate ways.

3.1 The time it takes to do things

Of particular interest in the evaluation of a speech interface is the potential advantages that speech offers over alternate input modalities, in particular the keyboard. On the simplest terms, a demonstration that a given modality provides a time advantage is a strong *a priori* argument that this modality is more desirable than another.

To understand whether and how speech input presents an advantage, we examined the times, both aggregate and specific, that it took users to perform the task we gave them.

3.1.1 Aggregate task times

The total time it takes to perform a task is a good indication of how effectively it can be carried out in a particular fashion. Figure 3 shows the mean total time it took users to perform the spreadsheet tasks. As can be seen, keyboard entry is faster. The

Figure 2: Utterance and grammatical error rates

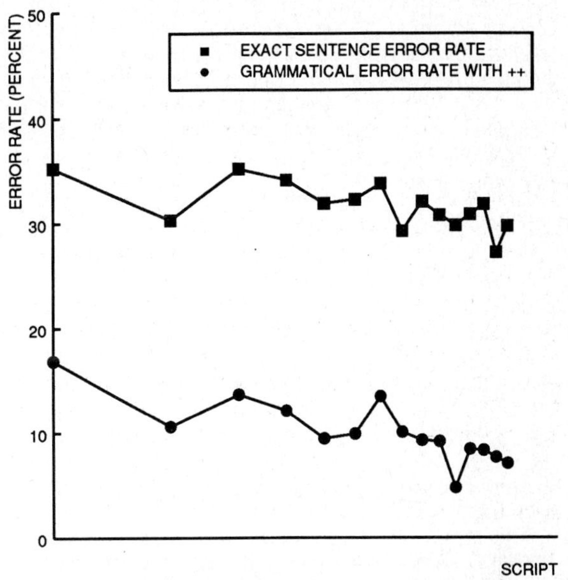

comparable speech time, while improving initially, seems to asymptote to a level above that of keyboard input. Since the tasks being performed are essentially (and over individuals, exactly) the same, we must infer that the lack of improvement is due in some fashion to the nature of the speech interface. After a month away from the system, users show a 21% slow-down for voice input. The slow-down for keyboard input is greater, 40%, possibly because task optimizations discovered in the keyboard condition were more easily forgotten.

Figure 3: Total task time, over sessions

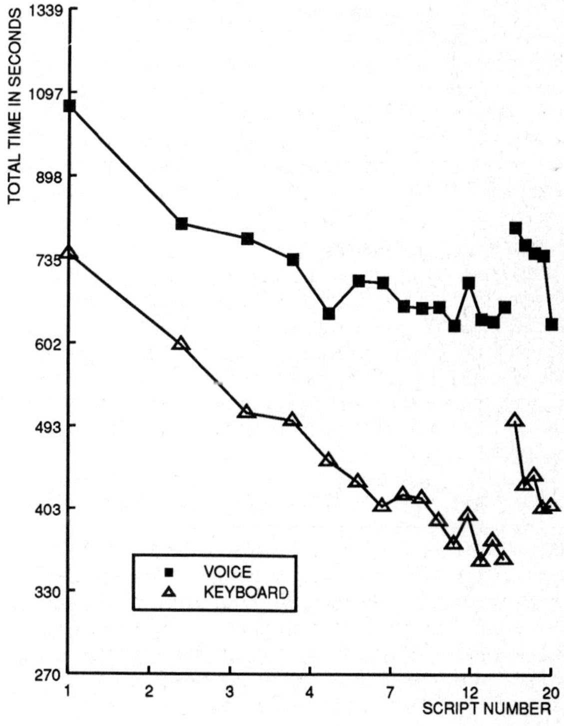

The reasons for this become clearer if we examine in greater detail where the time goes. The present implementation incurs substantial amounts of system overhead that at least in principle could be eliminated through suitable modifications. Currently, sizable delays are introduced by the need to initialize the recognizer (about 200ms), to log experimental data (about 600ms), and by the two times real-time performance of the recognizer. What would happen if we eliminate the overhead due to our current implementation?

If we replot the data by subtracting these times, but retain the time taken to prepare for and speak an utterance, we find that the difference between speech and keyboard is reduced, though not eliminated (see Figure 4, only the first 15 sessions are shown). This result underlines the importance of designing tightly-coupled spoken language systems for which the excess time necessary for entering information by speech has been reduced to a value comparable to that found for keyboard input. In a personal workstation environment this would essentially have to be nil, and we believe this represents a *minimum* requirement for successful speech-based applications that support goal-directed behavior.

There is an additional penalty imposed on speech in the current system—recognition error. In terms of the task, the only valid inputs are those for which the utterance is correctly recognized. If an input is incorrect, it has to be repeated. We can get an idea of how fast the task could actually be performed if we discount the total task time by the error rate. That is, if a task is presently carried out in 10 min, but does so with a 25% utterance error, then the task could actually have been carried in 7.5 min, had we been using a system capable of providing 100% utterance recognition. Figure 4 compares total task time corrected by this procedure. If we do this, we find that the amount of time taken to carry out the task by voice is actually faster than by keyboard.

The above calculations are, of course, an exercise in arithmetic, and cannot take the place of an actual demonstration. We are currently working towards the goal of creating a true real-time implementation of our system. Note that system performance could also be improved by reconfiguring the system for speaker-dependent operation. Doing so would halve the existing error rate (as training experiments with one of the talkers in this study have shown).

3.1.2 Time for individual actions

The tasks we have chosen are very simple in nature and can be decomposed into a small number of action classes (see [6]). Our detailed logging procedure allows us to examine the times taken to perform different classes of actions in the spreadsheet task. In the following analysis, we will concentrate on the three classes that allow the user to perform the two major actions necessary for task completion, movement to a cell location and entry of numeric data.

Movement actions. Examination of the movement data shows that users adopt very different strategies for moving about the spreadsheet, depending on whether they are using keyboard input or speech input. As Figure 5 shows, when in keyboard mode users rely heavily on relative motion (the "arrow" keys on their keyboard). In contrast, users use symbolic and absolute movements in about the same proportion when in speech mode. A detailed discussion of the reasons for this shift are beyond the scope of this paper. Briefly stated, the strategy shift can be traced to the presence of a system response delay in the voice condition. Delays affect the perceived relative cost of the two movement actions, making absolute and symbolic movements

Figure 4: Session times, adjusted for non real-time and error

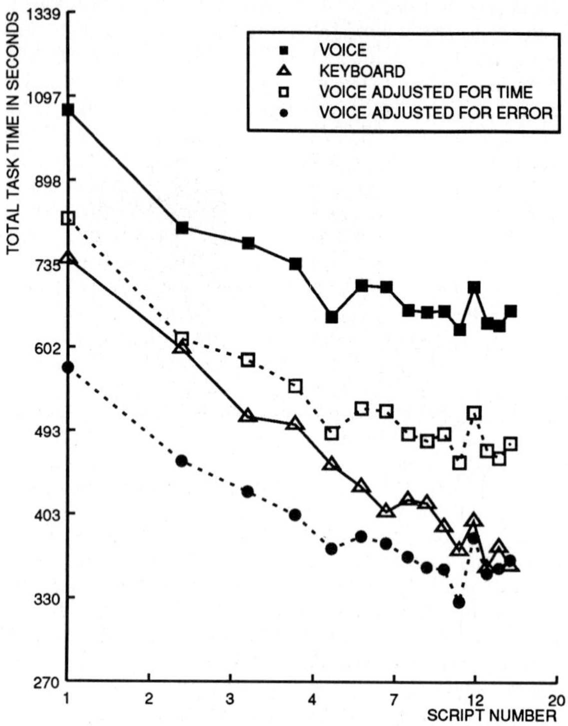

more attractive. A more thorough presentation, with additional experimental data, can be found in [4].

Figure 6 shows the total time taken by movement instructions within each modality. Surprisingly, voice movement commands take less overall time than movement commands in keyboard mode, at least initially. As the user refines his or her task skills, total keyboard movement time overtakes the voice time. For example, users learn the absolute locations of cells and begin to use row-column coordinates for movement. Voice time initially also improves, but eventually appears to asymptote, very likely because of a floor imposed by the combination of system response delay and recognition accuracy. These data appear to support, at the very least, the assertion that total movement time is comparable for the two modalities and that spreadsheet movement can be carried out with comparable efficiency by voice and by keyboard. Of course, contemporary workstations make available alternate options for movement. The hand-operated mouse is one example, which might prove to be more efficient for some classes of movement. A controlled comparison of speech and mouse movement would be of great interest, but lies beyond the scope of the current study.

Number Entry. The input time data for number entry (or more properly numeric expression entry, since the task could require the entry of arithmetic expressions) clearly show that speech is superior in terms of time. It took a median of 1906 ms to enter a number or expression by voice and 3301 ms to enter it by keyboard. These durations did not change over the course of the study.

Figure 5: Number of Movement actions, by class

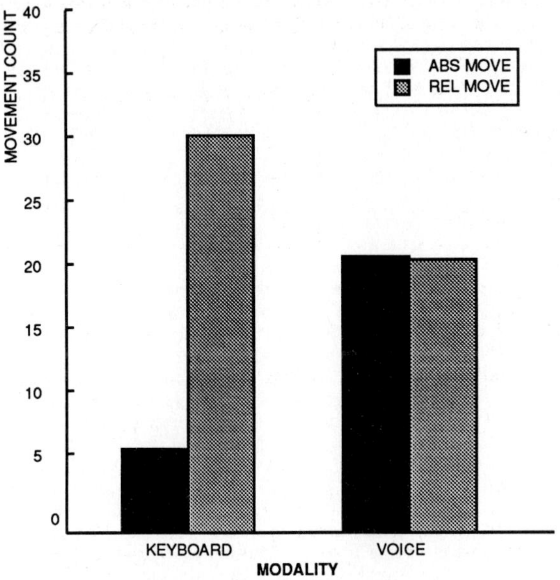

Figure 6: Total time for movement actions over sessions

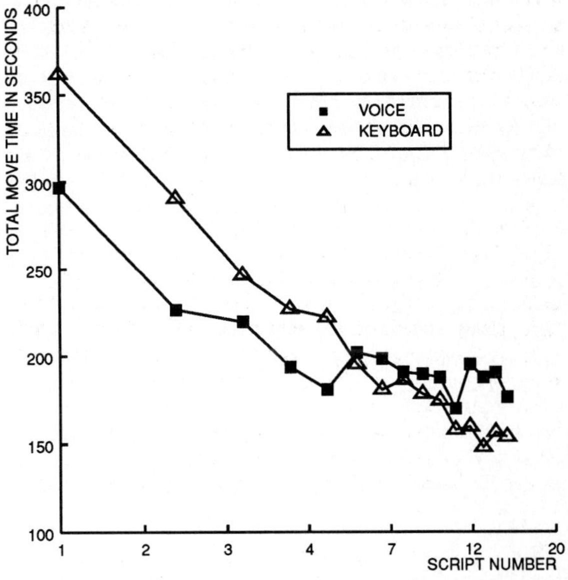

The advantage for speech entry is due to a number of factors. First, it may be faster to say a number than to type it (a digit-string entry experiment [1] shows that the break-even point occurs between 3 and 5 digits). Second, when working from paper notes (a more likely situation for this task in real life), users do not need to shift their attention from paper to keyboard to screen when speaking a number. They would have to do so if they were typing, particularly if they are hunt-and-peck typists. Data supporting this interpretation can be found in [1].

Of course, we should not lose sight of the fact that the current implementation produces longer total task times for speech than for keyboard and that this system cannot show an overall advantage for speech input. Nevertheless, it clearly demonstrates that component operations can be at least as fast and in some cases faster than keyboard input. These characteristics will only be present in the full system when system response and recognition accuracy exceed a critical threshold.

4 Discussion

The results obtained in this study provide a valuable insight into the potential advantages of spoken languages systems and allow us to identify those aspects of system design whose improvement is critical to usability of such systems.

4.1 User performance

Our analysis shows that the component actions in the spreadsheet task can be carried out as fast, and in some cases faster, by voice as by keyboard. Note, however, that time advantages can appear not only by virtue of shorter input duration, but also by virtue of the fact that a given modality allows users to spend more time attending to the problem-solving aspects of the task. The more time spent problem-solving (relative to input), the higher the quality of the completed task. At the same time, it should be realized that inputs that are more complex than the present ones may require more sophisticated spontaneous speech processing, otherwise the user will be forced to devote substantial preparation time to the formulation of inputs, at which point the speed and cognitive load advantages of speech could disappear.

4.2 System characteristics

Although we found that total task time was greater for speech input than for keyboard, this was not due to any intrinsic deficit for voice input. In fact, if we examine the component actions performed by the user, we find that they could be completed faster by voice than by typing. The failure of the speech mode to achieve greater throughput can be attributed to two shortcomings of our spoken language system.

A *time penalty* is imposed by the current implementation, which processes speech at about 2 times real-time and incorporates a substantial overhead. The penalty is reflected not only in longer task times, but also in changes in user strategies. Fortunately, real-time performance can be achieved with a suitable implementation and sufficient hardware resources. We are currently reimplementing the system on a multi-processor computer and expect to achieve sub-real-time performance in the near future.

While speed is a tractable problem, *low accuracy* is less so. We can expect to improve utterance recognition on the order of 10% if we properly model extraneous events, but even if we do so, recognition performance may still be at a level that significantly interferes with task performance. Judging from Figure 4, it may be sufficient to provide a moderate improvement in recognition accuracy, which together with real-time recognition would allow a spoken language system to perform at a level equivalent to a keyboard system. At that point, it may be possible to give speech a further advantage through the use of appropriate confirmation style and the provision of suitable error repair facilities, features that improve the usability of the system.

5 Conclusion

This paper has described the design of a spoken language system based on a speaker-independent continuous speech recognition system. To provide a realistic evaluation of its capabilities, we evaluated it with a complex task performed under natural ''office'' conditions, comparing it to an equivalent task carried out by keyboard. We found that spoken language input, compared to keyboard was degraded due to two characteristics of the system, a high error rate and non real-time response. The high error rate was attributable to the lack of provision for ambient event modeling and to the choice of speaker independence. Both sources of error, however, were shown to be controllable. Second, we found that non real-time system response had a significant impact on performance, not only in terms of preventing the natural input speed of speech from being realized, but also by forcing changes in the users' choice of task strategy.

Solutions to these problems are necessary before the potential of speaker-independent continuous speech interfaces will be practical for complex applications such as the spreadsheet.

References

1. Hauptmann, A.H. and Rudnicky, A.I. A comparison speech versus typed input. In *Proceedings of the June DARPA Speech and Natural Language Workshop* , Morgan Kaufmann, San Mateo, 1990, pp. in press.

2. Lee, K.-F. *Automatic Speech Recognition: The Development of the SPHINX System.* Kluwer Academic Publishers, Boston, 1989.

3. Rudnicky, A.I. The design of voice-driven interfaces. In *Proceedings of the February DARPA Speech and Natural Language Workshop* , Morgan Kaufmann, San Mateo, 1989, pp. 120-124.

4. Rudnicky, A.I. System response delay and user strategy selection in a spreadsheet task. CHI'90 invited poster, April 1990.

5. Rudnicky, A.I. and Sakamoto, M.H. Transcription conventions for spoken language research. Tech. Rept. CMU-CS-89-194, Carnegie Mellon University School of Computer Science, October, 1989.

6. Rudnicky, A.I., Polifroni, J.H., Thayer, E.H., and Brennan, R.A. "Interactive problem solving with speech". *Journal of the Acoustical Society of America 84* (1988), S213(A).

7. Ward, W.H. Modelling non-verbal sounds for speech recognition. In *Proceedings of the October DARPA Workshop on Speech and Natural Language*, Morgan Kaufmann, San Mateo, 1989, pp. 47-50.

Notes

A number of people have contributed to the work described in this paper. We would like to thank Robert Brennan who did the initial implementation of the voice spreadsheet program and Takima Hoy who produced the bulk of the transcriptions used in our performance analyses. The research described in this paper was sponsored by the Defense Advanced Research Projects Agency (DOD), ARPA Order No. 5167, monitored by SPAWAR under contract N00039-85-C-0163. The views and conclusions contained in this document are those of the authors and should not be interpreted as representing the official policies, either expressed or implied, of the Defense Advanced Research Projects Agency or the US Government.

[1]Perplexity is roughly the average number of words that can follow a given word in a legal phrase. Speech recognition systems will normally exhibit a higher error rate when grammar perplexity is high. Fifty-two is a moderately high perplexity. Task-set perplexity was calculated over transcripts of actual sessions taken from the study. It is the *mean* of the perplexities for individual utterances comprising the sessions. Agrammatical utterances were excluded from this calculation. Since agrammatical utterances typically result in misrecognition and the user therefore has to repeat the input in question, the set of grammatical utterances fairly represents the perplexity of the task if carried out ''correctly''. A word-pair grammar provides fairly weak constraint on recognition, specifying the allowable transitions between pairs of words. It does not indicate their relative likelihood, as would a bigram grammar. In addition, no sentence-level constraints are enforced, as would be the case for a finite-state grammar.

[2]In terms of characters per second, the touch-typists produced characters at a rate of one per 190 msec, while the others typed at a rate of 386 msec per character.

Table 1: Frequency and incidence of non-lexical spontaneous speech tokens.

1.332	585	++RUSTLE+
0.469	206	++BREATH+
0.098	43	++MUMBLE+
0.041	18	++SNIFF+
0.029	13	++BACKGROUND-NOISE+
0.025	11	++MOUTH-NOISE+
0.022	10	++COUGH+
0.013	6	++YAWN+
0.011	5	++GIGGLE+
0.009	4	++PHONE-RING+
0.009	4	++NOISE+
0.009	4	++DOOR-SLAM+
0.009	4	++CLEARING-THROAT+
0.009	4	++BACKGROUND-VOICES+
0.005	2	++SNEEZE+
0.002	1	++SIGH+
0.002	1	++PING+
0.002	1	++BACKGROUND-LAUGH+

Note: A total of 43901 speech tokens were transcribed. The first column gives the percentage of all items labeled as indicated. The second column gives the actual number of items for the given non-lexical token.

Human–Computer Interaction – INTERACT '90
D. Diaper et al. (Editors)
Elsevier Science Publishers B.V. (North-Holland)

Case Study of Development of a User Interface for a Voice Activated Dialing Service

Deborah Lawrence, Rory Stuart
NYNEX Science and Technology
500 Westchester Ave./White Plains NY 10604

ABSTRACT

A user interface for a Voice Activated Dialing service was designed and evaluated. The service will use speaker dependent recognition technology based in the telephone network to allow users to place a call by saying a name into a regular touch tone or rotary telephone. The interface was designed iteratively in three design-evaluation cycles, each with 20 subjects selected to represent the population of adult telephone users. Evaluations examined user errors, task completion, names used, recognition performance, responses to Likert-like questionnaires rating the interface, and responses to open-ended questions. A comparison was made of design variations (alternative menus, access methods, and voice- vs. tone-prompts), and of usability of the interface with different types of telephones. Subjects had little difficulty understanding and following the prompted procedures for adding, erasing, reviewing and voice-dialing names. Few errors were common across subjects. However there were several types of user difficulty in interacting with the recognizer, and the human factors of human-recognizer interaction is discussed.

INTRODUCTION

As the performance of speech recognition technology improves (and as its cost decreases), the design of speech interfaces to control telephony services is becoming an area of practical interest. Speech is often named as a desirable mode for human-machine interaction because it is direct and immediate (e.g. Martin, 1989). However, there has been limited experience with automated speech recognition in applications with broad user bases, such as telephone interfaces for the general public. Members of the Intelligent Interfaces Group of the Artificial Intelligence Laboratory at NYNEX Science and Technology were asked to design a user interface for a Voice Activated Dialing service which would allow telephone users to place a call by saying a name into a telephone. Design and evaluation of this interface was an opportunity to observe the interaction of novice users with a speaker-dependent recognizer and to learn about both their behavior and recognizer performance under these conditions. This case study will document the iterative design and evaluation of the interface and discuss human factors considerations in the development of speech recognition-based systems.

Though dialing a telephone number is a well-known and well-accepted human-machine interaction, it has the disadvantage of requiring the user to remember or look up an arbitrary telephone number. Voice dialing could increase the ease and transparency of placing a call by eliminating use of a telephone number to place a call.

The Voice Activated Dialing service (VAD) will use speaker-dependent recognition based in the telephone network. Users will be able to voice-dial calls from regular touch tone or rotary telephones. Entering names and phone numbers will require both voice and keypress (or dialed pulse) responses by the user, and the implemented VAD system will have the ability to convert dialed pulses to touch tones.

Interface development goals were to provide an interface which telephone customers could learn and use easily and with minimal advance information. Emphasis was on first time use, since it was felt that the product should require minimal learning time, and frustrations encountered in first time use were expected to be an impediment to further use. The interface was designed iteratively in three design-evaluation cycles. An initial design, which included alternate versions of portions of the interface, was prototyped on a Compaq 286 with a Dialogic board and a Dragon speech recognizer[1]. (A different recognizer may be used in the actual implementation.) Subjects were recruited to use the prototyped service, and modifications in the prototypes were made on the basis of those results.

Each evaluation cycle tested the current version of the entire interface. In addition, the first evaluation compared two alternate main menus and two alternate versions of the prompt used to indicate that VAD was available. One was a voice prompt ("Please begin"), and one was a tone (200 msec dialtone, 200 msec silence, 200 msec dialtone). The second iteration compared two alternate modes of access, "Off-hook", where VAD becomes available whenever the phone goes off-hook and "Voluntary", where the user dials a code to access the service. Rotary functionality was simulated, and subjects used the system from touch tone, rotary or both types of telephones, depending on the equipment they used at home. The third iteration included comparison of two alternate versions of the key assignments and tested a module not included in earlier versions, which was a method for erasing directory names by selection (versus recognition). Subjects who had a home phone with the keypad in the handset used the system with that type of telephone.

1. (Dragon Systems, 90 Bridge Street/ Newton MA 02158)

To use the VAD service, the user accesses the service as described above. At the top level prompt, the user can either voice dial a call (by saying a previously entered name) or access the directory by pressing a key. Within the directory, the user would choose from an auditory menu to either add, erase, or review names. These procedures are prompt-guided. Adding a name involves saying the name, repeating it once or more, as required by the recognizer for building a template, and finally keying in (or dialing) the phone number.

METHOD

Subjects

There were three rounds of evaluation (VAD-1, -2, and -3) with 20 subjects per round. Subjects selected to roughly represent the population of adult telephone users were recruited and paid to participate in individual sessions at NYNEX Science and Technology. Each study included about half men and half women, an approximately even distribution of ages from 20 to late sixties, and a range of occupations. In addition, VAD-2 included four teenagers. In VAD-1 and -3, all subjects had touch tone service at home, and the third study included seven who had a phone with the keypad in the handset. In VAD-2, ten had touch tone service, and ten had rotary. Of those in VAD-2 with touch tone, five had at least one rotary phone in use.

Overview of procedure

Sessions were between one and two hours in length, and usually about an hour. An experimenter met with the subject in an office-like room and gave subjects a brief verbal description of the service and a sheet with the minimal instructions required to use the service. Instructions covered:

1. Accessing the service
2. Accessing the directory
3. Tips about names and pronunciation.
4. Changing directory entries when numbers change

Subjects were asked to create a voice-dial directory of names and numbers, make voice-dialed calls, erase names, browse the directory, change directory entries to accomodate changes in phone numbers. In VAD-1 they were also asked to make two entries for the same person (e.g. home and office). Instructions to subjects did not name the tasks with the same terms used in the interface. Instead, subjects were required to link real world goals to the interface. For example, subjects were asked to "Check and see what names are in there". In VAD-1, subjects were given a set of names to use. In VAD-2 and -3, they generated their own names.

In VAD-1, the experimenter remained in the room, and the sequence of tasks was controlled to insure that all subjects used all parts of the interface. In the two subsequent evaluations, the experimenter gave the subject a written list of tasks and left the room. The subject was allowed to control the task sequence.

Alternate versions of the main menu and alternate access modes were each tested as within-subject variables. Half of the subjects received one version first, and half received the other first. Between versions, the experimenter returned to the room, asked about reactions to the first version, and explained that the subject would now try a somewhat different version. The alternate initial prompts, alternate key assignments, and telephone type were between-subject variables. After the subject completed the tasks, the experimenter asked questions about the subject's reactions, and subjects filled out an objective questionnaire evaluating the interface, which was adapted from Chin, Diehl, and Norman, (1988).

Sessions were videotaped. Evaluations examined user errors, task completion, names used, recognizer performance, questionnaire responses, and responses to open-ended questions.

RESULTS

Overview

In all three iterations, *user* errors, defined as a less than optimal path for performing a function, were low, and failures to perform a function were infrequent (Tables 1 and 2). Subjects did have problems interacting with the recognizer. Some did not understand its limitations, and others reacted to it in ways more appropriate to human-human communication (e.g. by exaggerating pronunciation in response to an utterance not being recognized).

User Errors

Users were able to follow the logical procedures and to apply them to real world goals. Because of bugs in the prototype it sometimes behaved erratically, and user errors often occurred on those occasions (especially in VAD-3). Only one of the total 60 subjects was unable to enter names into the directory or voice dial calls. This subject (VAD-3) correctly began the procedure to add a name but became confused and quit afer the recognizer repeatedly failed to register that anything had been spoken.

Table 1. Mean and Median User Error Rates as Percent of Total Attempts to Perform Functions

	Overall		Second Half	
	Median	Mean	Median	Mean
	%		%	
VAD-1	4.0	4.2	N/A	N/A
VAD-2	4.2	10.2	0	9.9
VAD-3	3.7	10.4	0	3.7

Note: Tasks varied in VAD-1,-2, and -3, so comparison of overall error rates between versions is not meaningful. User errors are defined as use of a less than optimal path in attempting to perform a function.

Table 2. Task Completion: Number of Ss Successfully Completing a Task at Least Once

	Add Names	Voice Dial	Erase Names	Review Directory	N
VAD-1	20	20	20	19	20
VAD-2	20	20	19	20	20
VAD-3	19	19	18	19	20

Procedural Errors. The most common procedural error was attempting to add a name at the top level prompt, where the user can either say a name to be voice-dialed or dial 3 to enter the directory (and then add, erase, or review names). In order to make the voice-dialing procedure as fast and transparent as possible, we wanted to use a very brief prompt at this level. In VAD-1, 15 subjects heard a voice prompt ("Please begin"), and nearly half (7/15) of this group attempted to add a name by saying the name at that point, without accessing the add function. All other subjects (VAD-1, -2, -3) heard two short tones instead of "Please begin". With this group, the error was less frequent but was still made by 26% (12/45) at least once. However only 11% (5/45) ever repeated the error. In VAD-2 and -3, an extended prompt was added which made these top level choices explicit when a name spoken at the top-level prompt was not recognized after three attempts: "The name you are calling was not recognized. To add, review or erase a name, dial 3. Or, to try calling again repeat the name now". Those who heard this prompt recovered quickly from the error.

The only other common procedural error, made by 10% (4/40) of subjects in VAD-2 and -3 using the Voluntary access mode, was attempting to voice dial a name by saying the name over dial tone without accessing VAD.

Access mode. For Off-hook vs. Voluntary access, error rates overall were equivalent, and preferences were mixed. The real test of the two modes will come from field testing, which should determine how often unintended inputs are accepted by the recognizer as attempts to voice-dial.

Rotary vs.Touch Tone. Rotary functionality was simulated (Wizard-of-Oz style) in VAD-2 for subjects who used rotary or both rotary and touch tone at home. Use of the interface on a rotary phone by rotary users presented no special usability problems, nor were any special difficulties experienced by subjects who used rotary after a touch tone session.

Rotary users had comparable (though slightly higher overall) error rates to those of touch tone users. A single subject (S #25) who contributed 35.3% of the total errors in VAD-2 was a rotary user; excluding that subject, the rotary users had more similar performance to the touch tone users: mean procedural error rate for rotary was 8.75%, vs.mean procedural error rate for touch tone of 8.54%. Though we suspect that there may be some differences between rotary and touch tone users, voice-dialing was comparably usable by both groups.

Keypad-in-handset. Subjects who used a keypad-in-handset phone at home used that type for the second half of the session in VAD-3. Use of the service from this type of phone did not cause higher error rates or special problems: the mean procedural error rate by the subjects using keypad-in-handset phones was 1.6%, vs. 5.3% for the subjects using standard touch tone phones in the second half of VAD-3.

Recognizer concept errors and voice directory maintenance. About a third of the subjects in VAD-2 and -3 made at least one error which involved failing to maintain an orderly directory. Twelve percent added names they had already added, and 25% attempted to place calls to names which had not been added. We distinguished these directory maintenance errors, which involved whether a function (such as add) was performed appropriately, from procedural errors, which involved how a procedure was performed or attempted. The reasons for directory maintenance errors were not clear in each case. Often they occurred after the subject had made one or more unsuccessful attempts to build a template for a name; the subject seemed to be either unobservant or forgetful about whether the name had been successfully added. However, in some cases, subjects seemed to have erroneous models of how automated recognition operates. For example, some thought that a name added twice and erased once would be gone because "that name" had been erased. These subjects behaved as though they thought the system had some higher order representation of the "content" of the voice templates as opposed to a record of acoustics only. Subjects sometimes did not remember the exact version of a name they had used (e.g. "Gran H" vs. "Grandma H") and some of this group expressed surprise that the system would not recognize the two forms as equivalent. Subjects did not always distinguish computer abilities (e.g. treating a class of variants as equivalent) from recognizer abilities.

Written instructions were given for the procedure required when a phone number for a name in the directory changes. It is necessary to first erase the name and then readd it with the new number. All who attempted this task (37 subjects) were able to follow the procedure. In this case at least, explicit instructions about directory maintenance worked well even when the user's mental model was faulty.

Names used

In VAD-1, subjects used names specified in the directions. In VAD-2 and VAD-3, users generated their own names, and instructions avoided indicating what type of names were expected. The only instructions on names were that names should not be too similar to each other, and that names of more than one syllable work best.

Type of names. A total of 260 names were generated in VAD-2, and 236 in VAD-3, or a mean of 12 per subject. Overall, 81.2% were person names, and 63.9% were first names only. Names of business were 6.0%, names of services ("weather","fire department") were 4.2%, and descriptive names ("Frank's parents", "Home phone number") were 4.4%. Seven subjects (18%) entered names for emergency services, such as "Police" or "Fire department". Since speech changes under stress, (Cooper, 1987) voice-dialing may not be suitable for dialing emergency numbers, and instructions should contain this caution.

Name length. 70.3% of all names were single words. Though instructions cautioned that names of more than one syllable work best, 25.8% of the names used were one syllable.

Recognizer performance

Recognizer performance in VAD-1, -2, and -3 is summarized in Table 3. Rates varied across iterations. Part of the variability was due to changes in the settings which determine the stringency with which the Dragon compares the tokens used to create a template. In VAD-1 and -3, the most stringent settings were used; in VAD-2, settings were at a middle level. Problems in the prototype software also contributed to the variability in recognizer performance and to the relatively poor recognizer performance overall. Recognition rates were equivalent for males and females.

User tolerance for having to repeat names varied greatly. Some subjects were undisturbed at having to repeat names a number of times, and some were annoyed. A few were intolerant of even the single repetition minimally required by the recognizer for creating a template. Subjects sometimes seemed insulted when asked to repeat, as though they felt their utterance had been "rejected".

Table 3. Mean Recognizer Success Rates

% Success			
Adding a name*	VAD-1	VAD-2	VAD-3
With one attempt	75.2	86.5	64.7
With two attempts	9.2	6.7	14.7
With three or more attempts	10.4	3.7	13.6
Failure	5.2	3.6	6.9
Calling			
With one token	77.7	70.7	68.6
With 2 tokens	12.0	13.9	12.5
With three or more tokens	6.7	5.5	6.0
Failure/ misrecognition	3.5	10.1	13.0

*An attempt to add required two tokens.

Considerably better recognition performance was observed in earlier NYNEX testing of the same recognizer under more controlled conditions. Part of the difference may have been due to prototype problems, but at least part was due to differences in conditions. The more controlled testing was conducted over telephone lines (as the user interface evaluations were), but speakers were recorded in an anechoic room; their position relative to the microphone was held constant; all speakers recorded the same set of words; and speakers recorded only: they were not interacting with a recognizer.

Response to Questionnaires and Open-Ended Questions

Subjects' responses on questionnaires evaluating the interface were moderately positive. The mean and median ratings (on a scale of 0 [very negative] to 9 [very positive]) were positive on all items. The mean for all subjects on all questions was 6.8 (median 7.5). The mean response to all items for individual subjects varied greatly; they ranged from 3.4 to 8.5. Subjects in VAD-2 and -3 who gave the lowest ratings (mean response < 5) had both higher procedural error rates (26.0% vs. 6.4%) and worse recognizer performance (59.6% vs. 71.9% success at calling in 1 token, 9.6% vs. 4.0% misrecognitions) than other subjects.

Thirty-six subjects (60%) said they would want VAD, fifteen (25%) said they would not, and 5 (8%) were not sure [4 gave no response]. Usability of the user interface procedures was not cited as a reason for not wanting VAD. The reasons cited were: "no need for it" (4/15), "too unreliable" (4/15), "too slow" (2/15). "maybe at office, but not at home" (2/15); no reasons were given by three subjects.

CONCLUSIONS

(1) Although a proliferation of new tone prompts could be very confusing to telephone users, our results show that tone prompts can be less ambiguous than voice prompts, since words necessarily have multiple interpretations. We think this is a timely area for research. (2) Some user expectations and communication habits are incompatible with the way recognizers work, and more user knowledge and/or experience may be necessary for smooth human-recognizer interaction. (3) These studies demonstrate that speech recognition technology should be evaluated within the application, since many factors affect recognizer performance.

Tones vs. voice prompts. Results from the first iteration found that the one significant procedural problem was the design for representing the two choices at the top level of the interface, calling vs. accessing the directory (for adding, erasing, or reviewing). To maximize the speed and transparency of calling, we wanted a minimal prompt at this top level. The final design used a tone prompt here since an abbreviated voice prompt ("Please begin") was often interpreted differently at different times by the same user. We found that users were more likely to treat the tone prompt as having a unique meaning. The pros and cons of tone vs. voice prompts may become a more significant issue as the number of new telephone services grows. Though a tone can be mystifying to an uninformed user, words or phrases in isolation can be ineffective because they are ambiguous.

Human-recognizer interaction. Though there were few problems following the procedures per se, many subjects had problems interacting with the recognizer. Joost, James, and Moody (1986) have observed that people may have unrealistic expectations when speaking to speech recognizers. They may "expect to converse with the computer as if it were another human being" (p. 45) and become frustrated when their expectations are not met. In the VAD studies, we encountered two levels of mismatch between habits of human-human communication and interaction with the recognizer. Some individuals did not understand the limits of the recognizer (e.g., that it would not recognize two forms of the same name as equivalent). Other users who understood the basic idea sometimes "reverted" to old human-human communication habits in frustration when an utterance was not recognized. For instance they would enunciate slowly and loudly as a habitual way of "being clearer"and as an expression of annoyance. These exaggerated pronunciations may in fact hinder recognition. The first type of mismatch could be reduced by greater user awareness of how recognizers work. We think user documentation for VAD should explain the consequences of certain actions -- for example that adding the "same name" a second time does not replace the earlier entry. Our users were able to follow explicit procedure for changing a phone number. But the second type of mismatch may be harder to eliminate because it involves intrusion of well- established habits and natural expression of emotion. It would be interesting to determine whether explicit instructions would help users to avoid uttering exaggerated pronunciations which are unlikely to be recognized.

Recognizer performance. Doddington and Schalk (1981) pointed out the need for the empirical evaluation of a recognizer's performance in a given context since there are too many combinations of parameters possible to make a comprehensive prediction of performance. Our experience corroborates this view. Recognizer performance in testing of the VAD interface was significantly worse than performance in recognizer evaluations which had better acoustic conditions and used prerecorded voice inputs, without direct human-recognizer interaction. Because problems with the prototype may have contributed to the low recognition rates we observed and because real world conditions are not replicable in the lab, a field test will be required to determine the actual recognizer performance.

REFERENCES

Chin, J.P., Diehl, V.A., & Norman K.L. (1988). Development of an Instrument Measuring User Satisfaction of the Human-Computer Interface. *CHI'88 Conference Proceedings*, ACM 213-218.

Cooper, M.B. (1987). Human Factors Aspects of Voice Input/Output. *Speech Technology*, March/April, 82-86

Doddington, G. R. & Schalk, T. B. (1981). Speech Recognition: Turning Theory Into Practice. *IEEE Spectrum 18* (9), 26-32.

Joost, M. G., James, F.G., & Moody, T. (1986). Ergonomics Research in Speech I/O. *Speech Technology, 3* (2) 42-47.

Martin, G. L. (1989). The Utility of Speech Input in User-Computer Interfaces. *International Jourtnal of Man-Machine Studies. 30,* 355-375.

Human–Computer Interaction – INTERACT '90
D. Diaper et al. (Editors)
Elsevier Science Publishers B.V. (North-Holland)

A VOICE RECOGNITION INTERFACE FOR A TELECOMMUNICATIONS BASIC BUSINESS GROUP ATTENDANT CONSOLE

Authors: Ismail Sola, Don Shepard

HMI and Database Group, Second Design Engineering, Switching Systems Division, NEC America, Inc., 1525 Walnut Hill Lane, Irving, Texas 75038. USA.

The Human Machine Interface (HMI) Group at NEC America has designed a voice recognition interface for the Basic Business group (BBG) Attendant Console. The personal computer (PC) based console provides call processing services to telephone operating company Business Group customers. Voice recognized commands have been implemented to facilitate more effective and efficient call processing. An experimental analysis is presented which shows the effectiveness of the voice interface in this product.

1. INTRODUCTION

The BBG Attendant Console (ATND) product has been designed to operate with the NEC NEAX61E Digital Switching System. This system is the equipment used by telephone operating companies for processing telephone calls on the public telephone network. Telephone lines to business and residential subscribers are subtended from the switch. At present the switch is deployed worldwide by telecommunications service providers in over fifty countries.

The Console's primary function is to allow an attendant to receive phone calls and transfer those calls to extensions within the business environment. To maximize the efficiency of processing phone calls and control the business phone environment, many other features are provided on the console.

The ATND has been marketed since October 1988 and was originally designed without the voice interface. All call processing functions were activated by inputting commands using the console keyboard.

Within a large business environment, the attendant typically receives phone calls sequentially for long periods of time. Improvements in call processing time and the ATND user ergonomics were the prime objectives in introducing a voice recognition interface. The keyboard interface is still available and supplements the voice interface.

Following the integration of the voice recognition hardware and software, an experimental analysis was performed to determine the effectiveness of the interface in meeting the objectives. The experiment used untrained subjects to evaluate call processing efficiency and human factors of the voice interface compared to the keyboard interface.

This paper describes the ATND with the keyboard and the voice interface. The experiment and it's results are then presented.

2. THE PRODUCT

2.1 The ATND with a Keyboard Interface

The ATND is a PC based product. A special adapter card, the NEC TA1001, which slots into the PC bus provides connection to the NEAX61E Digital Switch via an Integrated Services Digital Network (ISDN) Basic Rate interface.

The color monitor is used to display information about incoming or outgoing calls. The screen layout with an incoming call extended to a BBG phone station is shown in Figure 1.

The Six loops on the console can be viewed as independent telephone sets. Call processing may occur on any loop. Loop processing has the following general characteristics:

- A loop can be in an IDLE, ACTIVE or HELD state.
- Calls may be held on a loop. Call processing can then continue on any available idle loop.
- Call type information is displayed in the loop indicator window.

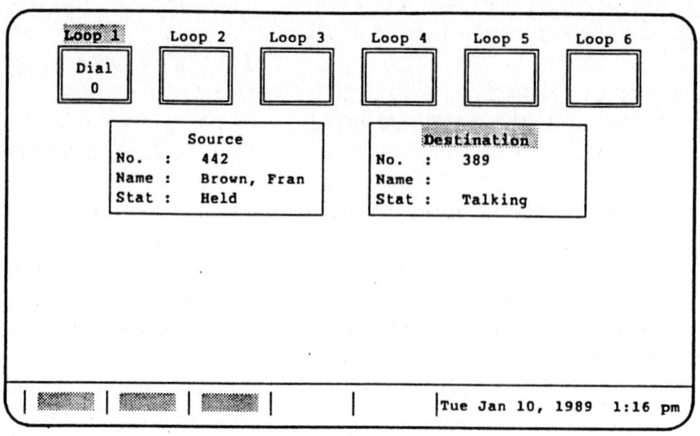

Figure 1: NEC Attendant Console Screen Layout with Two Parties

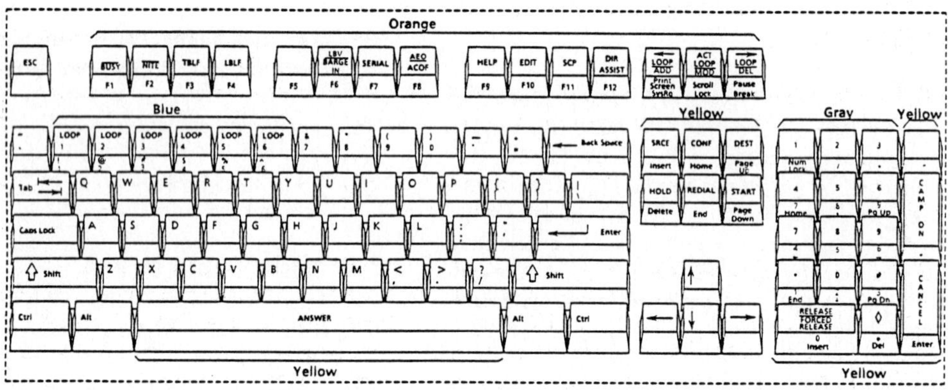

Figure 2: NEC Attendant Console Keyboard Layout

An incoming call is presented in the form of a flashing Loop Window, ring tone, and the appearance of a Party Information Window (PIW). This PIW is termed as the source (Figure 1). The source party number and name, if available, are displayed within the PIW. The state of the party is also displayed and can be INCOMING (ringing), TALKING, or HELD.

The attendant transfers calls by dialing the appropriate number. This action will cause a second PIW to appear on the display, termed the destination (Figure 1). This party's state can be RINGING, TALKING, BUSY, CAMPED-ON, HELD, or IDLE.

The layout of the ATND keyboard is shown in Figure 2. Customized keycaps with ATND functional labels are used on the keyboard interface. In the majority of ATND call processing, the following keys are used:

- DIAL (0 - 9): These are depressed to dial digits for outgoing calls.

- ANSWER: This key is depressed to answer an incoming call.

- RELEASE: This key is depressed to release calls on a loop.

- CANCEL: This key is depressed to release a destination party, but not the source party.

- CAMP-ON: This key is depressed when the destination party is BUSY. This case is described in detail in the following text.

- REDIAL: This key is depressed to redial the last dialed party.

The most frequent attendant function is to answer incoming calls and transfer them to the required destination parties. This is accomplished by the following scenarios:

1. An incoming call is presented on the screen by means of a flashing loop indicator and a source PIW.

2. The attendant answers the call by depressing the ANSWER key.

3. The attendant converses with the source party and is informed of the desired destination party.

4. The attendant 'extends' the call by dialing the destination party number using the DIAL keys.

5. *EITHER:* If the destination PIW goes to the RINGING state, the RELEASE key is depressed. This results in call transfer, removal of PIWs from the display, and transition of the loop indicator to the IDLE state. The scenario then returns to step 1. The attendant also hears ringback tone simultaneously with the PIW RINGING display.

6. *OR:* If the destination PIW goes to the BUSY state, the CANCEL key is depressed to release the destination party. The attendant hears busy tone simultaneously with the PIW BUSY display.

7. The source party is reconnected and the attendant asks if the party will hold until the destination party is free. If the source agrees to wait, then the REDIAL key is depressed.

8. If the destination PIW again goes to the BUSY state, the CAMP-ON key is depressed. The loop will then be in the HELD state. The source party hears ringback tone, informing that the destination is being alerted.

9. When the destination is free and answers the call, the loop automatically transitions into the IDLE state. This indicates to the attendant the call was successfully transferred. The scenario now returns to step 1.

2.2 The Voice Recognition Interface

The voice recognition system was selected according to the following specifications:

- A speaker independent system was required, due to multiple ATND users.

- A vocabulary of six commands is required for call processing functions.

- Recognition of discrete commands, in explicit states of a phone call, is required. Recognition of continuous speech is not necessary.

- ATND product marketing required that the voice system cost less than $2000.

- The voice product must be designed for integration with a PC and provide the necessary tools for software and hardware integration with the existing ATND.

- The development cost should be limited to three man-months.

The selected product is a commercially available speaker independent system with memory resident vocabulary limited to 160 words. Unique vocabulary generation and training is allowed with the manufacturers supplied development system. Independent voice recognition of 99% is achieved with a system trained by fifty users, three training passes per user. This feature allows recognition which compensates for stress, illness, or other phonetic altering circumstances.

Figure 5 shows the software structure of the ATND integrated with the voice recognition product.

2.3 ATND Voice Recognition Interface

Providing an easy transition from the keyboard to a voice interface, for experienced users, required the use of existing keyboard definitions for the voice command language set. The Call Processing scenarios described in section 2.1 show the keyboard actions necessary for the attendant to accomplish tasks. These keyboard actions directly translate to the required voice commands:

ANSWER, RELEASE, CAMP-ON, CANCEL, REDIAL, 0 - 9 (DIAL keys).

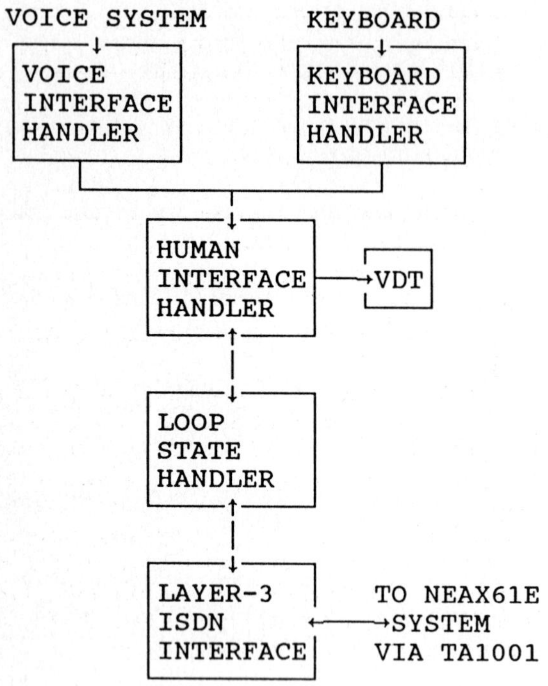

Figure 3: ATND Software Structure

In most ATND user environments, the number of digits dialed are three or more. Investigations with the chosen voice product showed that, for experienced keypad users, use of spoken digit commands was approximately 300% slower then using the keyboard dial keypad (for three digits). Since one of the design goals was to decrease call processing time, it was decided to use the keyboard rather than the voice interface for dialing digits.

In this voice recognition application the attendant has two vocal functions:

- Conversing with callers.
- Issuing voice commands to process calls.

This presents two possible problems:

- Inadvertent recognition of commands during continuous speech with callers.
- Voice commands might be heard by the caller.

To alleviate the first problem, voice recognition parameters were adjusted such that only discrete words could be recognized. Periods of silence must be present at the beginning and end of command keywords. The most effective settings for these end-point parameters were determined to yield a compromise between speed of voice command issuance and rejection of voice commands in continuous speech.

The second problem occurs when a talking path exists between the attendant and another party. This situation is step 7 in the scenario explained in section 2.1: the REDIAL function has to be performed while the attendant is speaking to the source party. The solution to this problem was to assign a natural conversational phrase as a command. When this situation occurs, the attendant says the key-phrase 'PLEASE HOLD'. This puts the source party on hold, thereby removing the caller from the voice path. The attendant can then continue issuing voice commands.

3. EXPERIMENTAL EVALUATION

The experiment was conducted in a lab simulated environment. The actual ATND product was used in conjunction with PC resident software simulating incoming BBG call traffic.

The evaluation was broken into three phases. The first phase consisted of selection of test subjects. The second phase established an effective command language set. The third phase consisted of testing and evaluation of command interfaces. Objective data was collected by automatically logging attendant inputs. Subjective data was collected in the form of questionnaires concurrent with, and immediately following the objective tests.

3.1 Selection of Test Subjects

The goal in selecting effective test subjects was to find users that had no previous ATND experience. This was important in order to evaluate learning time, retention, and comparative call processing times between interface types. Twelve subjects were chosen that met the requirements, four females and eight males.

3.2 Command Language Generation

The command definitions are multi-syllable words, and difficult to enunciate repeatedly. An independent survey of possible commands was performed. All test subjects were sent a list containing descriptions of ATND call processing scenarios. The subject was asked to provide the most effective command, based on the following guidelines (Barnard(1988)):

- Commands should be spontaneous, natural.
- Synonyms are allowed, provide several if applicable.
- Names should directly relate to the definition rather than semantically unrelated commands or pseudowords.
- Names should be mono-syllable if possible, and frequently used commands should be easy to enunciate.

The responses were reviewed and the most common mono-syllable commands were selected as synonyms to the related keyboard defined commands (Table 1).

COMMAND	SYNONYM
ANSWER	TALK
RELEASE	DROP
CANCEL	BACK
REDIAL	DIAL
CAMP-ON	CAMP

(Note: *PLEASE HOLD* is a conversation key-phrase command, no synonym can be used.)

TABLE 1: Command Synonyms

3.3 ATND Command Interface Testing

The third phase was to train the subject on ATND use, and perform interactive tests. These tests were broken into three stages. The first stage tested the subject as a first time novice user on one of the three interface types: keyboard, mono-syllable voice, or multi-syllable voice. Objective test data was collected to provide call processing time, help requests, and errors made during the test. This information was evaluated to compare the three interface types for novice users unfamiliar with the other interface types.

The second and third test stages tested the subjects using the remaining interface types. Subjective data was collected by the completion of questionnaires. This information was evaluated to compare human factors of the three interface types.

The subjects were divided into three groups. Each group was tested in the first stage using a different interface type. Table 2 shows the order which these groups performed the test stages.

STAGE	GROUP1	GROUP2	GROUP3
1st	MONO	MULTI	KEYBD
2nd	MULTI	MONO	MONO*
3rd	KEYBD	KEYBD	MULTI*

(*: the GROUP3, stage 2&3 interface types were alternated)

Table 2: Group Test Stage Order

The tests represented a maximum traffic call processing environment, in that as soon as a call loop was released from the ATND, another call was presented on the display. The test scenario is the same as described as the most common ATND function in section 2.1. The first test stage was run for fifteen minutes, in which an average of 75 calls were processed from ANSWER to RELEASE. The second and third stages were run for five minutes, in which an average of 21 calls were processed.

3.3.1 Objective Tests

Objective testing was done in the first test stage only. Each group was trained on the interface type to be used in the first stage. Call processing data was automatically logged. Help requests and error count was monitored by the test administrator. This data provided the following information:

- Average call processing time:

-Voice Mono-syllable:	11.4 sec/call
-Voice Multi-syllable:	13.5 sec/call
-Keyboard:	12.0 sec/call

- Average errors made in processing:

-Voice Mono-syllable:	1.0 per test stage
-Voice Multi-syllable:	1.5 per test stage
-Keyboard:	4.2 per test stage

- Average times help was requested:

-Voice Mono-syllable:	1.5 per test stage
-Voice Multi-syllable:	2.0 per test stage
-Keyboard:	2.1 per test stage

The average call processing (CP) time showed an advantage of 5% for the mono-syllable voice interface as compared to the keyboard interface. There was a 15.5% reduction in multi-syllable CP time, compared to the mono-syllable interface. This was attributed to difficulty in repetitive multi-syllable enunciation and command length.

There was no significant difference in learning time between the voice and keyboard interface types. Yet a clear difference in average errors and help requested indicated the voice training retention was better, and/or the voice command set was easier to remember than keyboard command key locations.

3.3.2 Subjective Tests

Subjective testing consisted of questionnaires after each test stage. There were two types of evaluation questionnaire. The first asked questions, requiring scaled answers, to evaluate human factors of the first stage command interface. The results are summarized in Table 3. The data in this table is the average scaled score for the human factor under consideration. The scale was of this form:

NONE: 1 2 3 4 5 6 7 8 9 10 : VERY MUCH

FACTOR	KBD	MONO	MULTI
NATURALNESS	5	7	6
CONFIDENCE	6	7	7
IRRITATION	4	1	1

TABLE 3: First Test Stage Independent Interface Ratings

The other questionnaire type was given after the second and third test stages. It asked human factor comparison questions between the mono-syllable and multi-syllable voice interfaces (Table 4), and between the keyboard and voice interfaces (Table 5). The data in these tables shows the number of test subjects who preferred the particular command interface for the human factor under consideration. Table 5 combines both voice interface types. This is because the keyboard versus voice comparison questions were asked after both voice interface type test stages were completed.

Confidence factor data in Table 3 shows that when the voice and keyboard interfaces were used independently, confidence ratings were approximately the same. Yet in Table 5 the Confidence factor *comparison* favored the keyboard. This was primarily due to the familiarity of the test subjects with keyboard usage. They are confident of the fact that when a key is depressed, action will result. The voice interface is a new experience, and confidence will come with it's use.

The voice interface was advantageous in all other categories. An important enhancement with the voice interface is the ability of the user to focus on the call processing task rather than keyboard command key locations. The ease of remembering the voice command language allows this.

FACTOR	MONO	MULTI	N/P
NATURAL	7	3	2
EASE OF USE	9	1	2
TIRING	0	4	8
CONFIDENCE	7	0	5

(Note: *N/P* indicates no preference)
TABLE 4: Later Stage Mono versus Multi-syllable Interface Comparison

FACTOR	KYBD	VOICE	N/P
NATURAL	3	9	0
EASE OF USE	3	9	0
TIRING	7	1	4
CONFIDENCE	6	3	3
TASK FOCUS	3	9	0
OVERALL	0	8	4

(Note: *N/P* indicates no preference)
TABLE 5: Later Stage Keyboard versus Voice Interface Comparison

4. CONCLUSIONS

The simulator test environment showed that the mono-syllable voice interface, combined with the use of the keyboard dial keypad, decreased call processing time, processing errors, and learning time of the product. Careful selection of the voice command language is an important factor in the success of a voice recognition application which requires repetitive use of voice commands. Mono-syllable, easy to enunciate words are more successful.

The results of the tests indicate that the voice interface has a strong potential of providing improved product ergonomics for real field users. As a result, the product will be introduced at selected trial sites for further evaluation.

The international markets of this product require that a multi-language vocabulary be developed and tested. Customizing the user command interface to each country and language will improve product human factors with relatively small development costs. The voice recognition technology allows the convenient, inexpensive provision of multi-language command sets.

Although present voice recognition technology has limitations (Levinson(1990)), this application shows that products with relatively simple voice requirements can be ergonomically enhanced by the use of a voice command interface.

For the future, when appropriate voice recognition technology is available, elimination of the keyboard interface will be attempted. This will allow attendants to perform other tasks. This product could also be used by handicapped attendants.

5. REFERENCES

Barnard, P.J.(1988). Command Names. In Handbook of Human-Computer Interaction (Ed. M. Helander). Elsevier Science Publishers: The Netherlands. 239-253.

Blohm, W. and Prussog, A.(1989). Multiservice Telecommunications Terminals: Performance and Design Concepts for the User Interface. In Proceedings of the Third International Conference on Human-Computer Interaction. Elsevier Science Publishers: The Netherlands. 579-586.

Card, S.K. and Moran, T.P. and Newell A.(1983). The Psychology of Human-Computer Interaction. Lawrence Erlbaum Assoc: Hillsdale, New Jersey.

Helander, M.(1988). Systems Design for Automated Speech Recognition. In Handbook of Human-Computer Interaction (Ed. M. Helander). Elsevier Science Publishers: North Holland. 301-319.

Levinson, S.E. and Roe, D.B.(1990). A Perspective on Speech Recognition. IEEE Communications Magazine. January 1990. 28-34.

Ogden, W.C.(1988). Using Natural Language Interfaces. In Handbook of Human-Computer Interaction (Ed. M. Helander). Elsevier Science Publishers: North Holland. 281-299.

Human–Computer Interaction – INTERACT '90
D. Diaper et al. (Editors)
Elsevier Science Publishers B.V. (North-Holland)

Observations on Using Speech Input for Window Navigation

Chris Schmandt, Debby Hindus, Mark S. Ackerman and Sanjay Manandhar

Media Laboratory, M.I.T.
Cambridge, MA 02139 USA
email:geek@media-lab.media.mit.edu

We discuss the suitability of speech recognition for navigating within a window system and we describe *Xspeak*, an implementation of voice control for the X Window System. We made this interface available to a number of student programmers, and compared the use of speech and a pointer for window navigation through empirical and observational means. Our experience indicates that speech was attractive for some users, and we comment on their activities and recognition accuracy. These observations reveal pitfalls and advantages of using speech input in windows systems.

Introduction

Considering the high expectations of speech input technology, there have been few convincing studies of its utility in an office environment. This paper describes an evaluation of speech recognition in a computer window system, where speech may provide an auxiliary channel to support window navigation tasks. In this study, speech was seen as assuming some of the functions currently assigned to the mouse, rather than as a keyboard substitute. We expected that allowing users to keep their visual and manual attention on the keyboard and the screen could provide an improved interface.

To do this, we built *Xspeak*, a speech interface to the X Window System. Xspeak allows words to be associated with each window; a window rises to the front of the screen and the cursor moves into it when the window's name is spoken. Thus a number of windows can be managed without removing hands from the keyboard or eyes from the screen.

We evaluated this interface empirically to determine the tradeoffs between voice and mouse navigation. However, we were not looking to compare the relative merits of voice input versus mouse input. Voice is an additional input medium that may augment the mouse in some respects and supplant it in others; some pointer operations, such as moving a window, would be difficult with voice alone.

We also wished to observe the acceptance and utility of this voice interface. A group of student programmers used Xspeak for several months. We were interested in whether these subjects would choose voice and under what circumstances, and how the addition of voice input would change their window system use.

In the next section we discuss issues in speech recognition as a user interface. The section following addresses navigation in window systems and the role voice might play. Following these, we describe our methodology and results.

Speech Recognition

Although speech recognition has received much positive publicity, the actual devices available today leave much to be desired, particularly in terms of recognition accuracy. Many variables affect error rates, including vocabulary size and composition, user's attitudes and speaking style, ambient noise, and microphone type and placement [Nusbaum, 1986, Biermann, 1985]. In short, it is difficult to get recognition to work well outside of controlled laboratory conditions. Because of these difficulties, the most successful applications for recognition to date have been in hands-and-eyes-busy situations [Visick, 1984], e.g., baggage sorting [Nye, 1982] or inspections of printed circuit boards [Harper, 1985], where the user is visually connected to the instrument. These are cases where the added benefit of hands-free input may outweigh other device-related problems.

The role of speech recognition in the office has yet to be established. There is little conclusive evidence that recognition is superior to the keyboard for data entry, much less for free-form typing and editing. For an excellent survey of the literature, we refer the reader to Martin [Martin, 1989]. Voice input may be more valuable when used in *conjunction* with other input devices (such as keyboard and mouse) for situations in

*This work was funded by the MIT X Consortium and Sun Microsystems.

which different tasks may be multiplexed across the different input modalities. To the extent that the tasks are separable, a performance improvement may be expected by splitting the input [Wickens, 1981].

Such considerations led Martin to design an experiment using speech recognition as an alternate input channel in a CAD system employing both keyboard and mouse. Her subjects were indeed more productive with the addition of voice, which she attributed in part to the speed of speech recognition versus typing longer command names, and in part to the ability of users to split attention across channels; that is, to remain visually focused on the screen while using speech. This second finding was particularly interesting in terms of expected utility of speech as an interface to a potentially visually complex window system. This paper was pivotal in motivating us to build our speech interface.

Window Navigation and Voice

Window systems allow the screen to be divided into smaller regions of input and output. Windows are used to organize work spatially, and, to a lesser extent, to perform tasks in parallel. For example, a user may have one window in a semi-permanent location on the screen running a text editor, and another window for the debugger.

There has been surprisingly little study of how people use windows, in terms of number, degree of overlap, distribution of tasks, or reasons for preference of a particular window system interface. Gaylin [Gaylin, 1986] discusses frequency of use of some window operations. A key study by Bly [Bly, 1986] compared tiled and overlapped windows in a task involving searching for information between windows. When the text to be searched was not all visible (in a tiled situation), she found that overlapping windows were more effective, with an interesting bimodality. For the most experienced users, overlapping windows were faster. For some less experienced users, overlapping windows were significantly slower. She attributed this to the added navigational tasks of manipulating the various windows. Overlapping windows were preferred among her users despite this added load.

This suggested to us that in a complex window environment, especially with users who like to create a large number of windows, an interface designed to improve navigation might be beneficial, providing faster access to various windows. Further, to the extent that navigation might be differentiated as a separate task from the activities occurring within each window, multi-modal input might lessen the user's cognitive load. This might allow successful use of a larger number of windows dedicated to specific tasks.

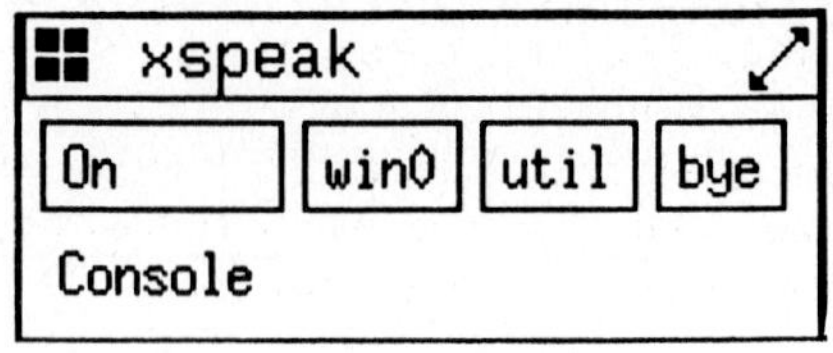

Figure 1: Xspeak control panel

Our application, Xspeak, allows access to windows by voice in the X Window System. Speaking a window's name causes it to pop up to the foreground and moves the mouse pointer to the middle of the window, at which point the window receives keyboard input focus. Thus users may move between windows and rearrange them without removing their hands from the keyboard.

Xspeak includes a graphical control panel (see Figure 1) which provides additional feedback on recognition results and can invoke utility functions to test, calibrate, and retrain the recognizer. (See [Schmandt, 1990] for a more detailed description of Xspeak operations.)

Xspeak runs on Sun workstations (it should run on any X server) using a Texas Instruments speech card in a PC-based audio server. We mounted a super-cardioid microphone (Sennheiser ME-80) on a stand next to the workstation screen, pointing out and at the user.

A consequence of not using noise canceling microphones is the tendency to pick up background noise as speech, that is, *insertion* errors. Recognizers are in general poor at discriminating whether a particular word is within their universe of names, being optimized to determine *which* known word was spoken. Since the consequence of insertion errors is window reconfiguration, which can be especially annoying if keyboard noise caused the error (suddenly user input goes to the wrong window), we set a high rejection threshold on the recognizer.

Evaluation Methodology

Having built this speech interface, we wanted to find out how it would be used, how it would affect users' overall workstation usage, and what problems existed with the interface that we needed to address. Since there are few other examples of speech interfaces to desktop windowing environments, we initially wanted to collect observations of this new interface in use. At this early stage of discovery, observation was more suited to our task of hypothesis generation.

Much of the work done on speech interfaces has simulated the recognition hardware [Gould, 1978]. This is due in part to the considerable practical problems of making speech recognition technology work reliably in relatively uncontrolled environments. However, we felt that it was important to observe usage over a longer period of time than is possible with simulations. In particular, how would having speech affect other post-acclimatization interactions? We preferred that our users be doing real work, since the artificiality of assigned tasks could confound our attempts to understand the ramifications of speech.

Furthermore, we felt that the reactions, both emotional and functional, to the long-term use of imperfect speech technology would be an important part of what was to be learned. This aspect of speech interfaces is often disregarded in studies.

Therefore, we enrolled four full-time student programmers from the speech group as our pilot users. They were experienced enough with window systems to have learned how to take advantage of windows and improved navigation. Although they had little, if any, exposure to speech recognition, they were certainly interested in its use; this made it likely they would try it enough to allow us to study their interactions.

Following an entry interview, our users were trained on how to use the system and given assistance in their selection of vocabulary names and initial configuration files. After this, they were observed for as much as two months.

We tracked Xspeak usage via extensive automatic logging, videotaping, and frequent short interviews. Logging recorded each word recognized and its recognition score, all Xspeak utility activities (such as retraining words and naming new windows), and all top level X window events.

Our users were all developing X Window System applications. Their basic screen layouts varied, but typically included a large editing window, a local terminal window for compiling the edited programs, a remote terminal window to receive mail and news, a local console window, Xspeak's window, and accessories such as a clock. The editing, terminal, and console windows were all text-based.

Empirical Analysis

We present empirical data on the tradeoffs between the mouse and voice below. Observations on the extended use of the system follow.

Timing

Input technologies are often compared on the basis of speed because of the belief that users will pick the most efficient interface. Therefore, we decided to join the fray, and we looked at the time required to complete a window transition using Xspeak versus the mouse. Table 1 shows the results. Speech was slightly slower than mousing for time to transition to another window. There was less variability in the spoken commands than in the mouse movements, perhaps due to differing window geometries and distances between windows.

		Times (secs)		
		Mouse	Xspeak	
User A	Mean	2.1	2.6	df=13, t=1.73
	Stddev	.6	.4	n.s. at .05
User B	Mean	2.0	2.5	df=14, t=1.66
	Stddev	.4	.9	n.s. at .05

Table 1: Timings

Table 1 shows the times, from videotape analysis, for each medium for two users. Times were measured from the start of the action (the user's hand moving off keys for the mouse and the start of speech for voice) to the first keystroke in the destination window (after the mousing motion). We excluded rejection errors (when a spoken name results in no action), transitions where the user clearly reads or thinks before typing, and all mouse transitions involving a button press.

Given the slowness of speech and the delays in recognition, we were not surprised that the mouse is faster. The difference is small enough that speech should be considered a viable input device.

However, these were optimal situations, and one might expect different behaviors in suboptimal situations. For Xspeak transitions, the user might experience rejection errors and have to repeat the window name. For mouse transitions, a user might need to move or lower several windows in order to find the desired window, or go through a sequence of mouse actions (such as handling a menu) to expose a buried window.

We were curious about how these more complex mouse motions would compare to speech times. In more realistic mouse interactions, times were as long or longer than speech. For user A, clicking on the title bar of a partially obscured window to raise it required a mean time of 2.8 seconds (s.d. = .3). Moreover, using a menu to expose a completely obscured window required a mean time of 4.2 seconds (s.d. = .6), a time substantially greater than speech. For user B, a double-click to raise a window required 2.5 seconds (s.d. = 1.0), a time that was comparable to speech.

Window Transitions

Window transitions, switching the pointer from one window to another, were the predominate navigational activity, and they occurred more often than we had anticipated.

	Session length (mins)	Xspeak chances	Xspeak use %	Mouse use hand on mouse %
User A	40	44	84	14
User B	40	73	63	22
User C	40	38	89	0
User D	20	22	100	–
Expert E	40	51	98	2
Expert F	45	49	96	2

Table 2: Xspeak Use within a Session

Users used Xspeak to navigate between windows about once per minute, based on our analysis of representative sessions on videotape. Within sessions, however, transitions were not evenly distributed; there were often flurries of window activity.

How often were window transitions made using Xspeak instead of the mouse when the window was named? As Table 2 shows, the percentages varied from 63% to 100%. (An Xspeak chance, in the table, is a window transition where the user could have used either Xspeak or the mouse. Window transitions to test Xspeak were not included.) When the user's hand was already on the mouse, the rate was substantially lower. These data were derived from videotapes of a single session with each user, and all window transitions in those sessions were included.

Recognition errors

Table 3 shows the *recognition* errors (when a spoken name results in no action) for six sessions analyzed in detail. Only recognizer errors are reported; user errors (e.g., speaking the wrong name) are not included.

Rejection errors varied considerably, from 16% to 58% of attempts. As mentioned, Xspeak was tuned to give rejection errors over insertion or substitution errors, and the consequences of an error were not very high. Table 3 presents the rejection data.

Because the rejection rates were higher than expected (an average of 35% with a standard deviation of 16%),

	Session length (mins)	Words spoken to recognizer	Rejection error rate (%)
User A	40	50	16
User B	40	70	47
User C	40	46	26
User D	20	28	43
Expert E	40	80	58
Expert F	45	62	23

Table 3: Rejection Error Rates

we wondered whether the nature of the window navigation task was causing additional errors. So we conducted an additional study, involving three of the original six subjects, to obtain "pure" recognition rates. We asked the subjects to speak each window name, one after the other, for six cycles, at the beginning, middle and end of a half-hour of working session. In these results the navigation task did not have a statistically significant effect on recognition accuracy.

The high error rate may surprise most readers; there is a common perception that speech recognition (especially small vocabulary, speaker dependent, isolated word recognition) is a solved problem. Although experienced users with proper microphones and a quiet environment can achieve high accuracy, recognizers are not well behaved in natural settings. For example, Biermann [Biermann, 1985] reported error rates of 2% to 25% and Martin [Martin, 1989] reported rejection errors of 4% to 27%. With a head mounted noise canceling microphone (which both these studies used), these levels of errors are not unusual and simply reflect the variability of human speech without some practice. Our results are not inconsistent with these, given that we were using less robust microphones. (We must caution that comparing recognition results is risky without knowing the number and content of the words in the recognizer's vocabulary [Nusbaum, 1986].)

In our study, we chose not to use the head-mounted microphones traditionally used for speech recognition. Our informal evaluation of Xspeak with a head-mounted microphone gave recognition scores of over 90%. However, headsets are not, we feel, suited to everyday office use; they're uncomfortable over time, tend to slip, and interfere with common activities such as drinking coffee or answering the telephone. Although an even more directional microphone than the one we used might decrease background noise from fans and telephones, it would also be more sensitive to the speaker's exact position, and would also cause substantial rejection errors.

Users' reactions to their rejection rates varied considerably. As will be discussed below, users adopted a number of retraining and coping strategies.

Observational Analysis

Our users were a varied lot. Table 4 summarizes their working style and prior experience.

	Work Style	X Windows prior use
User A	typing with brief pauses	moderate
User B	typing with brief pauses	moderate
User C	typing with lengthy pauses	minimal
User D	typing with brief pauses	extensive
Expert E	constant typing	extensive
Expert F	constant typing	extensive

Table 4: Window System Use

Three of the four subjects programmed steadily; the other programmed for a while after a significant amount of thinking time. All of them had developed some navigation methods before using Xspeak; those with the longest exposure to windowing systems had developed the most extensive range of window behavior. For example, Subject D used the mouse extensively, e.g. for iconifying windows and for moving around inside his text editor.

In addition, we observed two of the coauthors, who are expert users. They both had substantial experience with windowing systems and used windows extensively for performing tasks in parallel.

Acceptance of Xspeak differed widely among our users, for a variety of reasons, as shown in Table 5. Subject A used Xspeak in the majority of his sessions for two months, and regularly asked other users to move if they were on an Xspeak workstations. He reported preferring Xspeak because it allowed him to have larger windows with more overlap. Indeed, his screen was typically much more cluttered at the end of the study than at the beginning.

Subject B liked fast machines, and Xspeak did not run on the fastest machines in the lab. After initial enthusiasm for Xspeak, he lost interest because of his poor recognition rates and began to use the faster machines exclusively. He also noted that if he already had his hand on the mouse, he preferred to continue using the mouse for window actions.

Subject C's navigation activity was minimal because of his low input rates. Moreover, he was fixed in his use of the mouse; he just did not find Xspeak to be sufficiently interesting to justify its use. Subject D used Xspeak for several weeks but thereafter his research work required hardware that conflicted with Xspeak, so we have limited data for him.

Expert E said using Xspeak allowed him larger windows with more overlap. When using Xspeak, Expert F allowed more window overlap, and typically used one to two additional windows than when limited to the mouse. Expert F, with his relatively high recognition, also believed that he had higher throughput with Xspeak, and therefore favored using it.

In summary, two users, including one author, preferred Xspeak to other input methods. Two users rejected Xspeak as being insufficiently interesting to outweigh their preferred system usage. One user found Xspeak interesting, but left the study for other equipment. The other user, an author, found Xspeak interesting, but his low recognition rates hampered his use.

Coping Behaviors

Poor recognition accuracy, in our opinion, was the greatest impediment to acceptance of Xspeak. The users who stuck with it had some of the higher overall recognition rates and developed successful strategies to overcome errors, as shown in Table 6.

Users retrained single window names (or the entire vocabulary), and calibrated audio levels in mixed amounts. Our most active user, A, had a strategy of retraining a single word when his recognition was low. He rarely trained the entire vocabulary (4 times, a

	Use of Xspeak	Recognition	Subjective Evaluation of Xspeak	Navigation Preference
User A	extensive	very good	enthusiastic	Xspeak preferred
User B	moderate	poor	not as useful as a faster workstation	fastest method
User C	minimal	moderate	not interesting	mouse motions
User D	minimal	poor	has potential	iconification
Expert E	moderate	very poor	positive although frustrating	all methods
Expert F	extensive	moderate	positive	Xspeak preferred

Table 5: User Experiences with Xspeak

to verify recognizer active:
calibrate the microphone
speak each window name in turn
to verify recognizer discrimination:
speak some nonsense words
speak some other window names
to improve overall recognition:
retrain the whole vocabulary
verify that recognizer was responding
improve single name recognition:
retrain a window name
rename a window

Table 6: Coping Strategies

minimum amount), but he often retrained a single word (109 single words in 79 sessions). On the other hand, two users with low recognition rates, B and E, showed the highest percentages of retraining the entire vocabulary and calibrating the recognizer.

All users, except one of the authors, had problems guessing which names would be most suitable for success with this particular recognizer. We expected our users to find suitable names for themselves with a minimum of training; this may have been unrealistic.

Although we began the experiment believing that navigation was a separate user task, our users did not distinguish between using the mouse for navigation among applications and using it for direct manipulation interactions within an application. As a consequence, Xspeak seemed incomplete to them.

Adaptive behaviors

We also observed users displaying behaviors that used speech in novel and creative ways. These behaviors would be present at any recognition rate.

We observed users speaking window names while in physical positions from which they could not operate a keyboard or mouse (such as answering the telephone). Even when sitting directly in front of the computer, users took advantage of the "hands-off" nature of speech input (see Table 7). Interestingly, both experts began to use Xspeak to "warp" the mouse. That is, they used Xspeak to move to the desired application and then used hand motions to fine-tune the mouse position.

physical freedom from keyboard
hands in lap, scratching head
hands in motion to or from keyboard
hand on mouse
physical freedom from workstation
yawning, stretching
drinking coffee
using the telephone
looking in manuals
flexible window names
sounds with emotional content
words unrelated to window function
words representative of a window shape
words from a foreign language

Table 7: Adaptations to Voice Input

Conclusions

The reader is cautioned against generalizing from our results. This set of case histories is very small. Furthermore, Xspeak was a prototype system under development during the evaluation, and simply did not work well during some periods.

Having said that, we believe we have observed several important behaviors on the part of our users, and some interesting characteristics. First, the individual differences we observed were substantial. For our most satisfied student user, speech input worked very well and gave him opportunities for creativity. This user has a strong preference now for speech input. For our least satisfied student user, speech held no attraction even though his recognition scores were quite good. For the other two students the results were mixed.

Our experiences suggest that users' preferences for an auxiliary speech interface may vary a great deal and, for some users, be unrelated to their success with speech recognition. Designers and evaluators of speech input systems should anticipate a wide range of user responses, depending upon the users' experience level, ability to achieve consistent recognition, their current strategies for managing windows, and the nature of their work.

Second, speech recognition is clearly still difficult to use, and expertise is required in setting up the recognition device, choosing a vocabulary, and training users. We decided against head-mounted microphones, and therefore we needed to have Xspeak's design minimize the impact of rejection errors. We observed several of our users developing interesting and successful coping strategies for times when the recognizer was not working well. Nonetheless, recognition rates are important and were the most consistently cited complaint about Xspeak. In a second version of Xspeak, we will address this by subsetting the user's vocabulary for recognition purposes.

Third, we observed that having Xspeak allowed users a greater range of physical motions and positions, since they were not so tied to the keyboard and mouse. Fourth, we saw some evidence for increased number and degree of overlap of windows while using voice. Longer term studies will be required to substantiate this point, however.

Finally, a speech interface to a window system needs to support direct manipulation interactions. As mentioned, our users did not distinguish between the use of the mouse within an application and among applications. We intend to add this capability in our second version as well, so that spoken words can invoke, for example, mouse button presses.

Acknowledgments

We would like to thank Gale Martin, for her insightful early discussion on evaluation methodologies; Wendy Mackay, for her invaluable help with our use of video as an evaluation tool and ongoing review of the work; Barbara Frederickson, whose comments on an early version of this paper were of great assistance; and Ralph Swick, for key advice on some obscure aspects of X.

References

[Biermann, 1985] A. W. Biermann, R. D. Rodman, D. C. Rubin, and F. F. Heidlage. Natural language with discrete speech as a mode for human-to-machine communication. *Communications of the ACM*, 28(6):628–636, 1985.

[Bly, 1986] S. A. Bly and J. K. Rosenberg. A comparison of tiled and overlapping windows. In *Human Factors in Computer Systems - CHI'86 Conference Proceedings*, pages 101–106, New York, 1986.

[Gaylin, 1986] K. B. Gaylin. How are windows used? Some notes on creating an empirically-based windowing benchmark task. In *Human Factors in Computer Systems - CHI'86 Conference Proceedings*, pages 96–101, New York, 1986.

[Gould, 1978] J.D. Gould. How experts dictate. *Journal of Experimental Psychology: Human Perception and Performance*, 4(4):648–661, 1978.

[Harper, 1985] R. Steve Harper. Voice data entry applications at Texas Instruments. In *Proceedings of the 1985 Conference*, pages 217–221. American Voice I/O Society, 1985.

[Martin, 1989] Gale L. Martin. The utility of speech input in user-computer interfaces. *International Journal of Man-Machine Studies*, 30:355–375, 1989.

[Nusbaum, 1986] Howard C. Nusbaum, Christopher N. Davis, David B. Pisoni, and Ella Davis. Testing the performance of isolated utterance speech recognition devices. In *Proceedings of the 1986 Conference*, pages 393–408. American Voice I/O Society, 1986.

[Nye, 1982] J. M. Nye. Human factors analysis of speech recognition systems. *Speech Technology*, 1:36–39, 1982.

[Schmandt, 1990] Chris Schmandt, Mark S. Ackerman, and Debby Hindus. Augmenting a window manager with speech input. *IEEE Computer*, August 1990.

[Visick, 1984] D. Visick, P. Johnson, and J. Long. The use of simple speech recognizers in industrial applications. In *Proceedings of INTERACT '84, First IFIP Conference on Human-Computer Interaction*, London, 1984.

[Wickens, 1981] C. D. Wickens, S. J. Mountford, and W. Schreiner. Multiple resources, task-hemispheric integrity, and individual differences in time-sharing. *Human Factors*, 23:211–230, 1981.

Human–Computer Interaction – INTERACT '90
D. Diaper et al. (Editors)
Elsevier Science Publishers B.V. (North-Holland)

THE DESIGN AND IMPLEMENTATION OF A CONTEXT SENSITIVE NATURAL LANGUAGE INTERFACE TO MANAGEMENT INFORMATION

Alan Burton and Anthony P. Steward.

School of Computer Studies & Mathematics
Sunderland Polytechnic

Natural Language Interfaces (NLIs) make database (DB) query easier for infrequent computer users. Interfaces to management information are particularly problematical because of the unpredictability of queries. This paper describes ATMI a context sensitive NLI to a working Oracle DB in a managerial environment. We discuss why context free grammars cannot provide an adequate model of the range of English which needs to be covered. A knowledge based approach which enables pronouns and other ambiguous terms to be resolved intelligently is described. Our current system demonstrates the feasibility of this approach.

1. INTRODUCTION

Arguments exist both for and against Natural Language (NL) as a means of querying computer DBs. It is argued that for knowledgeable and frequent computer users, a concise command language is preferred (Shneiderman (1987)). Experimental evidence shows that experienced users of a structured query language do not perform any better when using NL (Small & Weldon (1983), Jarke (1985)).

Menu driven interfaces provide information about actions and objects in the DB domain, this guides unfamiliar users through a range of pre-determined options. However users with extensive domain knowledge require less guidance, they are frustrated by repeated menu interactions and become 'lost' inside extended menu hierarchies (Shneiderman (1987)).

In a managerial environment a wide range of unpredictable queries occur, these cannot easily be covered by menus. In addition we must cater for intermittent users who have not learned the syntactic details of a structured query language. However managers are familiar with the DB domains that interest them. Under these circumstances we believe that NL is the ideal interaction technique: a view supported by Shneiderman (1987).

The ATMI project (Access To Management Information), aims to develop techniques for NL DB query, and to implement a working system interfacing to ORACLE. Input is not translated into an intermediate query language, instead it is used to construct a Prolog query, exactly as if addressing a Prolog DB. Further software provides a link between Prolog and ORACLE. As much of the implementation as possible is DB independent.

It is impossible to provide *full* NL capabilities. We therefore support the view of Diaper (1988) that what is needed is a sublanguage of English, reduced in lexical and syntactic complexity, but nevertheless providing the flexibility expected of NL interaction.

NL is fraught with ambiguity. This paper describes a distinct knowledge based approach to the resolution of ambiguous terms, applying context to select from the possibilities allowed by the lexicon, grammar and other interface components.

2. THE DATABASES

ATMI has been developed in Prolog on a Vax 6210 computer under the VMS operating system. The DB highlighted in this paper holds instrument and borrower details in a Stores Inventory system. 'Stores' is a relational ORACLE DB comprising 11 tables or entities in all. Figure 1 shows a simplified Entity-Relationship diagram for Stores.

3. CONTEXT FREE GRAMMARS

In Context Free Grammars (CFGs) the words of a language are identified by terminal symbols. Phrases are identified by non-terminal symbols and each rule specifies the possible form of a non-terminal. The analysis of a sentence by a CFG yields a parse tree showing the constituent phrases of the sentence. A CFG for the sentence "The dog ate the bone." would be as follows:

```
sentence --> np,vp.
vp --> verb,np.
np --> determiner,noun.
verb --> [ate].
noun --> [dog].
noun --> [bone].
```

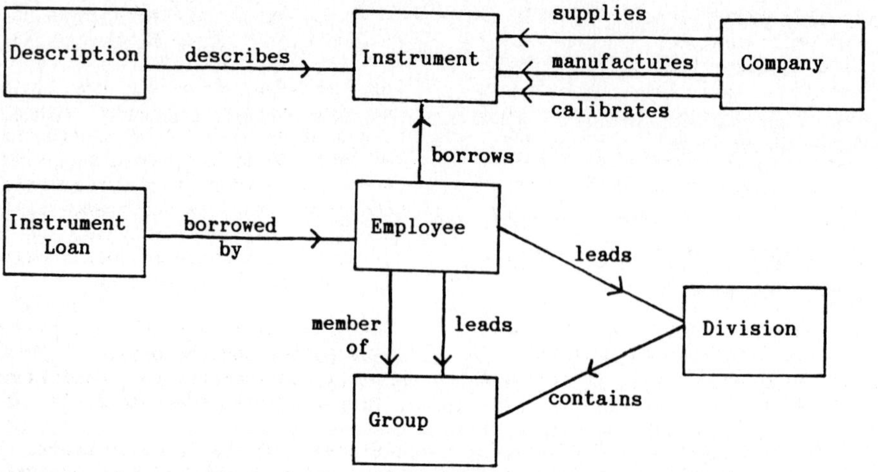

Figure 1 - A simplified Entity-Relationship diagram for 'Stores'.

```
determiner --> [the].
```

Definite Clause Grammars (DCGs) are an extension of CFGs. By augmenting a CFG with arguments the parser can then assign values to these arguments corresponding to the nodes and leaves of the tree. This provides a means of actually building a structure corresponding to the parse tree during the process of parsing. The structure can be represented as:

```
sentence(np(det(the),
            noun(dog)),
         vp(verb(ate),
            np(det(the),
               noun(bone)))).
```

and can be read as: the sentence consists of an initial noun phrase (np) followed by a verb phrase (vp). The noun phrase is made up of the determiner (det) *the* and the noun *dog*. The verb phrase is composed of the verb *ate* and a noun phrase consisting of the determiner *the* followed by the noun *bone*.

Space does not allow for a more detailed explanation of CFGs and DCGs in this paper. The reader is therefore referred to Pereira & Warren (1980) who describe the formalisms more fully, and show in detail how such grammars and their parsers can be implemented in Prolog.

4. THE INADEQUACIES OF CONTEXT FREE GRAMMARS

CFGs can sometimes be used to derive two different parse trees which have the same sequence of leaf nodes (Allen (1987)). Though there are rules for determining preferred interpretations: such as the rules of Minimal Attachment and Right Association (Allen (1987)). In the context of the DB query, it is not easy to decide which rules to use. Semantic/pragmatic knowledge is required to resolve syntactic ambiguity.

Winograd (1983) suggests that phenomena such as agreement need to be handled by adding constraints that cannot be conveniently expressed in the formalism of CFGs. Thus it is difficult to provide precise forms for such constraints as "the subject and verb of sentence must agree in person and number".

Chomsky (1957) explains that restrictions must be placed on the choice of a verb in terms of subject and object in order to permit such sentences as "John admires sincerity." while excluding the inverse "Sincerity admires John." At a strictly syntactic level both sentences are equally valid, the latter however is meaningless.

Finally, ambiguities arising from anaphora (such as an occurrence of the pronoun "he"), or from the use of WH-words in the role of interrogative pronouns (such as "who" or "what"), cannot be resolved purely on the basis of syntactic information obtained during parsing. Therefore context sensitive issues must be addressed either in the grammar, or elsewhere in the NL processor, if ambiguous terms are to be properly resolved, and if invalid interpretations are to be excluded.

5. CONTEXT SENSITIVE GRAMMARS

The arguments of non-terminal symbols in a DCG can be used not only to build structures but also to carry context sensitive information. Thus for example it is possible to implement rules for the agreement in number required between nouns and verbs. A grammar incorporating such rules would permit sentences like (1) and (2) while excluding (3) and (4).

(1) The dog eats the bone.
(2) The dogs eat the bone.
(3) The dog eat the bone.
(4) The dogs eats the bone.

A grammar containing such rules can provide a very detailed syntactic analysis. The resulting parse tree forms a stronger foundation for the resolution of ambiguity than that provided by a CFG. However it will be shown in the next section of this paper that such a rigorously constrained grammar is unsuited to the types of NL input expected in a managerial environment.

6. A GRAMMAR FOR MANAGERIAL DATABASE QUERY

In a managerial environment we are able to make certain assumptions about our target user group, and about the likely forms of input to an NLI. These assumptions do not necessarily apply in other environments.

We may suppose that managers will ask questions that make sense: since managers have an overall familiarity with the DB domains that interest them, and a good idea of the likely response to a given query, they will not ask questions that fall beyond the scope of the DB.

Most managers are infrequent computer users, and few are trained typists. We have observed that they tend to abbreviate their input by the omission of redundant words or word endings. These observations are supported by the findings of Eastman & McClean (1981) who analysed 700 DB queries collected from educated subjects, they reported that 32.8% of the queries were grammatically ill-formed.

A grammar for DB query must therefore be sufficiently unconstrained to allow deviations from strictly grammatical English, yet sufficiently constrained to enable the resolution of ambiguity by reference to syntactic structure.

Gazdar (1983) has suggested that the surface structure parse obtained from a CFG is sufficient to provide the basis for semantic interpretation. This appears to be the case, provided that processes for the resolution of ambiguous terms are supported by a detailed knowledge based domain model, and that free interaction is allowed between the grammar and the other interface components.

7. A KNOWLEDGE BASED DOMAIN MODEL

Three types of knowledge need to be included in the domain model: structural knowledge; semantic knowledge; and pragmatic knowledge. Syntactic knowledge resides in the grammar and is independent of any specific DB.

Structural knowledge provides a description of the tables in the DB. For example the table EMPLOYEE with four attributes can be represented in Prolog by the structure

```
employee(emp_name,initials,payroll_no,gp_code).
```

in which each of the four arguments corresponds to a given attribute in the ORACLE table.

Joins between tables are modelled by specifying the two tables concerned along with their common attributes. These attributes need not be referred to by the same name. Where a useful verb can be identified, it is included in the model so that its occurrence in a query can guide, though not constrain, the selection of attributes on which to join a pair of tables. For example, the structures

```
join_tables(company,co_code,instrument,
   supplier_code,supply).
join_tables(company,co_code,instrument,
   manufacturer_code,manufacture).
```

indicate that in the presence of the verb *supply*, tables COMPANY and INSTRUMENT should be joined on attributes co_code and supplier_code. In the presence of the verb *manufacture* the tables should be joined on co_code and manufacturer_code. This enables the system to respond correctly to two distinct queries such as "Who supplies widgets" and "Who makes widgets". Further data provides information useful during query optimisation.

Semantic knowledge provides possible interpretations for ambiguous terms. For example the WH-word "who" might refer to a company or to an employee. The domain model specifies the allowed interpretations as a series of prolog structures like those shown below. In the interest of efficiency the most likely interpretation for a given word is placed first. Thus if "who" usually refers to a company, and only infrequently to an employee, then ordering ensures that the Prolog processor selects the most likely interpretation first.

```
interpret(who,company).
interpret(who,employee).  etc.
```

Knowledge vital to the resolution of anaphora is modelled on the different types of noun occurring in the domain. Thus it is possible, for example, to specify the types of DB objects which might reasonably be referred to as *he*, or *it*, or *one* . This part of the model is based on the simple *isa* hierarchy shown in Figure 2 and represented in Prolog as:

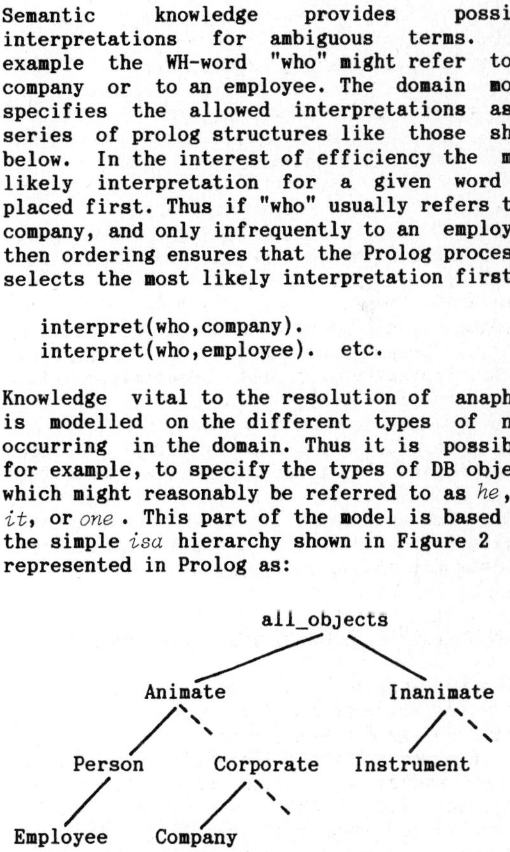

Figure 2 - An 'isa' hierarchy for 'Stores'

```
isa(employee,person).
isa(person,animate).   etc.
```

Data held in the domain independent core lexicon relates given anaphoric words to specific nodes in the hierarchy. If a given node is specified for a word then that word can be said to potentially refer to any one of the leaves arising from that node. For example, the lexicon identifies the word *he* with all nouns of type *person*, and the domain model relates all objects of type *person* with DB objects of type *employee*. Thus the antecedent of *he* must be an *employee* or one of the other leaves arising from the *person* node.

Pragmatic knowledge specifies the allowed relationships which exist in the DB. These relationships are derived in the first instance from the entity-relationship diagram, and are usually identified by the main verb in a NL query. Structures such as

```
supply(company,instrument).
manufacture(company,instrument).
borrow(employee,instrument).
lead(employee,division).
```

specify that *companies supply instruments, companies manufacture instruments, employees borrow instruments, employees lead divisions,* and so on. In this way a query such as "Which employee has borrowed a video recorder" is permitted since the lexicon determines that a video recorder is a valid instance of an instrument, and the domain model confirms that *employees borrow instruments*. In like manner the query "which employee supplies video recorders" is rejected as being pragmatically ill-formed on the grounds that there is no rule of the form supply(employee,instrument).

The domain model provides a means of filtering out ill-formed queries before any call to the DB is implemented. Apart from the obvious advantage in terms of efficiency, this filtering process provides access to knowledge which can be used in recovering from dialogue failures resulting from pragmatic errors. This is in contrast to most existing DB query systems which are cannot respond intelligently to ill-formed queries. Tools to support model building have not been implemented.

8. RESOLVING AMBIGUOUS TERMS

In the previous section of this paper we showed how a domain model can be used to check the pragmatic well-formedness of queries. In this section we describe how pragmatic knowledge can be used to direct resolution of ambiguity.

We have identified four important sources of ambiguity: syntactic ambiguity; anaphoric references; ambiguous WH-words; ambiguous nouns. Our method of resolution is essentially as follows: one possible interpretation is selected by reference to the domain model and a dialogue-history module. If according to pragmatic knowledge this leads to an ill-formed query, then the interpretation is rejected and Prolog backtracks in search of an alternative. If the resulting query is well-formed then it is passed forward and the DB is accessed. Knowledge in the model is ordered by the system designer so that the most likely interpretations are tried first. If no valid interpretation exists then the knowledge in the model is exploited to elicit further information from the user, or to guide him in rephrasing the query.

The most obvious danger in this approach is that Prolog might backtrack pathologically in an endless search for a valid interpretation. However the domain model specifies only a very limited set of interpretations for any given ambiguous term, so that the only real restriction which needs to be imposed concerns how far back to look in the previous dialogue for the candidate antecedents of pronouns. Recent work suggests that in about 95% of cases, the knowledge required to resolve an anaphoric reference occurs within the previous two items of dialogue (Diaper (1986)).

Each component of the NL interpreter has free access to the domain model and its lexicon. Free interaction via backtracking then enables a sequence of naive algorithms to work together to give satisfactory interpretations.

Figure 3 shows a block diagram of the ATMI NLI. The short horizontal line "--" indicates the point at which backtracking is constrained. Straight arrows indicate a flow of information, and the curved arcs indicate where backtracking can be particularly active. Boxes represent the different components of the interface, nesting indicates how given processes are called from within others.

9. EXAMPLES

The following short dialogue illustrates in detail how the domain model supports the NL processor in selecting interpretations for ambiguous terms. The dialogue is summarised in Figure 4. The initial query is the sentence typed by the user. After the query has been processed the resulting interpretation is displayed. This interpretation is used to construct a Prolog query which is not seen by the user. Finally the prolog query is passed to the Prolog/ORACLE link.

A first pass through the lexical analyser reveals that the word *borrowed* in "Who has borrowed the video recorders" is potentially ambiguous. The analyser is unable to determine whether *borrowed* is the past tense of the verb *borrow*, or part of a compound noun (e.g. *date_borrowed)*. It makes no attempt to resolve

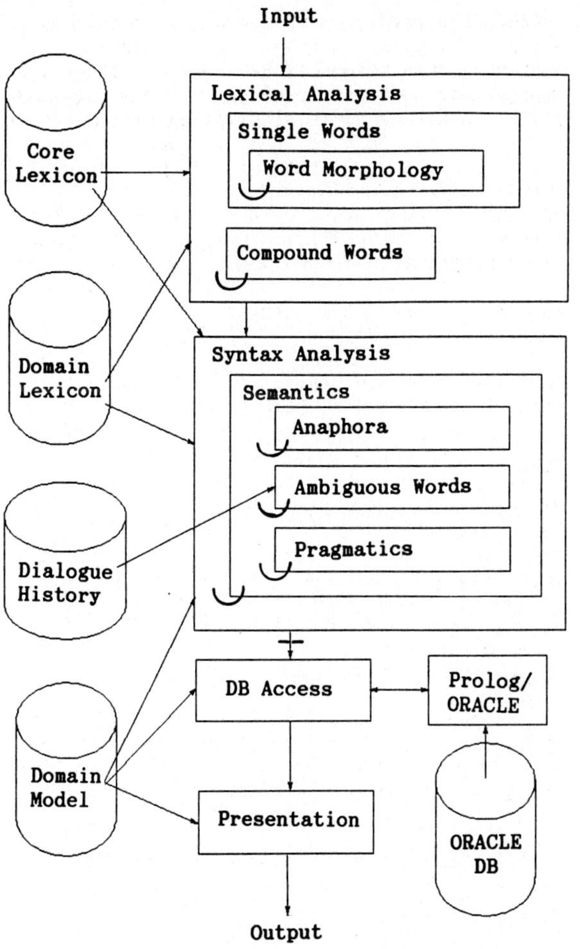

Figure 3 - Block diagram of the ATMI NLI.

this issue but passes the sentence on to the next process. There is no spell-checker, unknown single word forms the focus of a sub-dialogue in which the system attempts to elicit an alternative that it recognises.

A second pass through the lexical analyser invokes a pattern matching algorithm. This scans the sentence for compound structures, such as *video_recorder*, which are taken to be single lexical items. At this stage *borrowed* is found to be a single word occurring in isolation, morphological analysis labels it as the past tense of the verb *borrow*. Any incorrect interpretations are repaired when later syntactic failure causes backtracking into the lexical analyser. Unknown items again form the focus of a sub-dialogue with the user.

An initial pass through the syntactic analyser produces a surface structure parse which acts as the locus for semantic interpretation:

```
Query 1: Who has borrowed the video recorders.
Interpretation: Which employee has borrow  the
                Video Recorder.
Response:
   2 Items Found.
    EMPLOYEE                   INSTRUMENT
   ---------------------------------------------
    HUDSON                    Video Recorder
    CHRISTIAN                 Video Recorder

Query 2: Who makes them.
Interpretation: Which company manufacture Video
                Recorder.
Response:
   2 Items Found.
    COMPANY                    INSTRUMENT
   ---------------------------------------------
    PANASONIC                 Video Recorder
    SONY                      Video Recorder
```

Figure 4 - Two queries to ATMI.

```
sent(whq(ambig_wh(who),
     vp(vgp(aux_verb(has),verb(borrow)),
     np2(np(det(the),
            np(noun('Video Recorder'))))))))
```

who is labelled as an ambiguous WH-word. The reader will note that the occurrence of *who* in the role of a relative pronoun would not be ambiguous, neither would its occurrence in a sentence of the form "Who is the X of Y".

At no stage is the query translated into a logical form; quantifiers like *some, all, each,* and so on being interpreted by default as *all*. As far as the ATMI system is concerned, the importance of syntactic analysis lies in the resolution of ambiguity.

The semantic analyser consults the domain model and concludes that *who* means *which company*, however pragmatic knowledge invalidates this on the grounds that there is no rule saying anything about companies borrowing instruments. The second attempt interprets *who* as *which employee*, the resulting query is found to be pragmatically well-formed and so the final interpretation is obtained: "Which employee has borrow the video recorder", these confirmation messages are not reformed into full NL.

Structural knowledge provides a means of matching nouns in the query to tables and attributes in the DB. The verb *borrow* directs attention to the tables EMPLOYEE and INSTRUMENT (see Figure 1), and enables a join to be implemented. A second join links DESCRIPTION and INSTRUMENT. The following Prolog query is invoked by the Prolog/ORACLE link:

```
query(X,'Video Recorder'):-
    description('Video Recorder',Y),
    instrument(Y,_,_,_,_,_,_,Z,_,_),
    employee(_,_,X,Z).
```

Argument 2 in the predicate 'description' and argument 1 in 'instrument' are bound to the same variable name, thus activating the required join. The same applies to argument 9 in 'instrument' and argument 4 in 'employee'. Argument 1 in 'query' represents the attribute employee_name which also occurs as argument 3 in 'employee'. The second argument in 'query' is instantiated to 'Video Recorder' as is argument 1 of 'description'. The remaining arguments are instantiated at random, they play no important role in the Prolog query and are represented by the Anonymous variable '_'. The system retrieves two items of data indicating that the video recorders are currently borrowed by Hudson and Christian.

Query 2 is processed in much the same way except that the pronoun *them* is an additional source of ambiguity. Pronoun resolution uses a naive algorithm based on the principle of last occurrence (Charniak (1973)). The algorithm initially matches *them* with the employees listed in response to Query 1, however this is invalidated by pragmatic knowledge and the system backtracks to obtain *video_recorder* as antecedent. Two items of data are retrieved showing which companies make video recorders.

10. CONCLUSIONS

Most managers are infrequent computer users who have not acquired expertise in computer command languages. They are familiar with the DB domains that interest them. The ad-hoc and unpredictable nature of queries in a managerial environment indicates the unsuitability of menu driven interfaces. These factors suggest that only NL can provide the flexibility required for DB query.

Context Free Grammars are not powerful enough to interpret the range of English needed for DB query. However the introduction of context sensitive rules would constrain the grammar too tightly, resulting in an interface that is intolerant of abbreviations and minor deviations from strictly correct grammar.

The surface structure parse obtained from a CFG seems to be sufficient to provide a locus for semantic and pragmatic interpretation, provided that it is supported by extensive domain knowledge and a detailed lexicon.

Knowledge in the domain model provides a means of filtering out ill-formed queries before DBs are accessed. It also provides information useful for recovering from a dialogue failure.

Each component of the NL interpreter has free access to the domain model and its lexicon. Free interaction via backtracking then enables a sequence of naive algorithms to work together to give satisfactory interpretations.

ACKNOWLEDGEMENTS

This paper arises from work financially supported by British Gas Engineering Research Station and the National Advisory Board.

REFERENCES

Allen, J. (1987). Natural Language Understanding. Benjamin Cummings.

Charniak, E. (1973). Context and the Reference Problem. In: Rustin, R., (ed.) Natural Language Processing. Algorithmics Press, New York, pp311-331.

Chomsky, N. (1957). Syntactic Structures. Mouton, The Hague.

Diaper, D. (1986). Identifying the Knowledge Requirements of an Expert System's Natural Language Processing Interface. In: Harrison, M.D. & Monk, A.F. (eds.), People and Computers: Designing for Usability. Cambridge University Press.

Diaper, D. (1988). Natural Language Communication with Computers: Theory, Needs and Practice. In: Proceedings of the Conference on KBS in Government. pp19-44.

Eastman, C.M. & McClean, D.S. (1981). On the Need for Parsing Ill-Formed Input. In: American Journal of Computational Linguistics, 7, p257.

Gazdar, G. (1983). NLIs, CFLs and CF-PSGs. In: K. Sparck Jones & Y. Wilks (eds.). Automatic Natural Language Parsing. Ellis-Horwood.

Jarke, M., et al. (1985). A Field Evaluation of Natural Language for Data Retrieval. IEEE Transactions on Software Engineering, SE-11,1. January. pp97-113.

Pereira, F.C.N. & Warren, D.H.D. (1980). Definite Clause Grammars For Language Analysis - A Survey Of The Formalism And A Comparison With Augmented Transition Networks. Artificial Intelligence, Vol.13, pp231-278.

Shneiderman, B. (1987). Designing The User Interface: Strategies For Effective Human-Computer Interaction. Addison-Wesley.

Small, D. & Weldon, L. (1983). An Experimental Study of Natural and Structured Query Languages. Human Factors, 25. pp253-263.

Winograd, T. (1983). Language As A Cognitive Process, Volume 1: Syntax. Addison - Wesley.

Human–Computer Interaction – INTERACT '90
D. Diaper et al. (Editors)
Elsevier Science Publishers B.V. (North-Holland)

Recent Approaches to Natural Language Generation

Lee Fedder,

University of Cambridge, Computer Laboratory, Pembroke Street,
Cambridge CB2 3QG, England.

1 Abstract

An HCI system can produce speech or text output if it is coupled with a language generation component. Such a module should be capable of producing reliable text that uses the resources of the language to produce the best description of the data in the current context. Past language generators have been criticised on several counts, and developments are underway to improve the situation. This paper examines the criticisms, and their implications for HCI systems. We look at the new approaches, and present our own solutions.

2 Introduction

An HCI system will include an application program, perhaps an expert advisor or a database system, and perhaps a natural language interface. When the application has some data to be communicated to the user, it will issue a "message" to the language generation component, which produces a linguistic realisation of the message. The application usually has no linguistic knowledge, and so the message carries just the semantic content of the output, and perhaps some information about the functional status of the various parts of the semantics. The idea of such a message is familiar from computational models of language generation (for example Appelt [2]), as well as psychological ones (see Levelt [4]). The semantic content might for consist of a clause of logic (as in Shieber [13]), or perhaps some sort of frame based data structure (see Danlos [3]). Functional data might, for example, identify parts of the data structure as being the current topic or focus (see McKeown [9]). We have adopted this model for the current report and in our work, but the division between application and language generator may not always be so clear cut (see McDonald [7] for an alternative breakdown of the processes involved).

The generator itself usually consists of a lexicon and a grammar component. The lexicon holds descriptions of the words in the system, whilst the grammar component contains knowledge about how to combine words into sentences. Generation then consists of a combination of the processes of lexical selection and grammatical construction, although the nature and order of these processes varies (see for example Appelt [1], McKeown [9], Tait [15], McDonald [7], and many more).

There are two classes of criticisms which have been made of these generators. One might be described as "overgeneration". The linguistic data in the system is not sufficient to prevent certain errors at the surface level. The other criticism relates to inflexibility. Amongst the many ways language may possess for describing a concept, one is usually "hard wired" in.

3 Criticism of Generation systems

Marcus (Marcus [5]) says of typical generation systems that they:-

> "... operate by incrementally specifying fragments of linguistic structure in a top-down fashion, typically inserting specific lexical items only when the frontier of the structure is encountered."

And again :-

> "Current systems by and large fail to represent lexical meaning, and back away from most issues of lexical choice."

Take the following input data (simplified) to Simmons' generator (see Simmons [14]) :-

TOKEN SAW
DATIVE TOKEN JOHN
OBJECT TOKEN BOTTLE

The tokens "SAW","JOHN" and "BOTTLE" represent the concepts they name. The grammatical data is encoded in an ATN which is traversed, incrementally describing the input data until individual words are reached. The concept tokens map directly to specific words.

The input data above would probably be realised as :-

John saw the bottle.

A language reflects the views of its culture in the way it divides up the world conceptually. There is no compelling reason why the concepts represented in an application should match directly the language concepts. Further, more than one language concept may be capable of describing a given application concept. The language may possess a whole range of ways of describing the same event, depending on the viewpoint of the speaker or on other aspects of the context in which the expression occurs. This leads to the need for "conceptualisation" in language generation. That is, the mapping of application concepts to language ones.

What tends to happen, as in the Simmons system, is that these linguistic decisions are smuggled into the message. Concepts from the application are "hard wired" to linguistic ones. There is no real choice between different words, or ways of describing the event.

This direct mapping also ignores the interaction between words at a linguistic level, which can lead to errors in the surface structure. Usually, the domain is limited and the lexicon is small, and the vocabulary can be constrained to avoid these pitfalls. The words which are hard wired to the semantics symbols can be selected to be feasible in the particular domain and range of contexts.

The following are simple examples of what can go wrong. They demonstrate that a whole range of linguistic data is needed for each word :-

1a. ?A bar owner was assassinated by gunmen.

1b. ?John rumoured that Jane was pregnant.

1c. ?He had a strong motorbike.

The verb "assassinate" requires a famous person in object position, and in 1a this requirement is not met. 1b shows the verb"rumour" in a construction which is acceptable for other verbs of the same type, but which is unacceptable for "rumour". 1c uses a modifier which doesn't suit the noun.

A further example of missing linguistic data comes from Danlos (Danlos [3]). She investigated linguistic constraints placed on clauses by relationships between events. In particular, the relationship of direct causality was examined. Danlos suggested that a whole stratum of data, relating to clause linearisation, and thematic form, had been overlooked.

For example, if we want to express the relation of direct causality between the events "shoot" and "kill" we can use the following constructions :-

2a. John shot Mary. He killed her.

2b. Mary was killed by John. He shot her.

However, the following expressions sound awkward :-

3a. ?John shot Mary who was killed by him.

3b. ?John killed Mary who was shot.

(see Danlos [3], p90)

A system like Simmons' would be capable of producing these unfelicitous constructions. Some data about the combination of these forms at the linguistic level, is missing from the language model.

So, we might say that generation systems are prone to over-generate if not properly controlled. On the other hand, due to the direct mapping technique mentioned earlier, most generation systems can't take advantage of the diverse ways a language possesses for describing an event. A given symbol need not be described using the same language concept in all situations.

Most events involving some sort of transfer, for instance, can be described in English from two perspectives, that of the sender, and that of the receiver. So, a selling event could be described using the ideas "buy", "sell", "give" (as in "John gave $20 for the picture"), and so on. Linking each application concept directly to a word makes these possibilities difficult to realise. A similar effect can be seen with the phrases "I planned to go ...." and "I would have gone ..." (originally formulated by Sergei Nirenburg at a recent workshop). These can be seen as alternative realisations of a single conceptual unit. This would pose problems for conventially organised generators.

A related problem, implicit in the direct mapping approach, is that concepts in the application may not be represented directly in language. If we allow more flexible concept mapping, this will become apparent. A simple example of this is pronominalisation in English. When generating pronouns, there is a choice which depends on knowing the gender of the referent. If the application is not interested in the gender of its entities, this data won't be recorded. Adding a language component, however, demands that this data come from somewhere. The language Kilivila displays a further charming example. Demonstratives, numerals, and adjectives carry affixes that relate to the class of the object they modify. Classes are determined by properties of objects such as whether they are wooden and long, or round and stony (see Levelt [4]). Generation systems for Kilivilan would only be able to talk about these classes of objects, whereas the application may use a different set of classes.

4 Why haven't these problems been encountered with language analysis?

Language analysis has been studied in depth, but on the whole, the problems described above have not been encountered. Though language analysis and generation are closely related, there are some problems special to generation, mainly related to choice. Analysis systems, in general, are designed to derive the semantic content of a text. It is not necessary to worry about how the user arrived at a particular conceptualisation of an event, or a particular lexical structure. A useful amount of semantic information can still be extracted. The information about the differences between possible realisations is not included in the language model. However, for generation, choices must be made. There may be no "neutral" way of expressing some domain data using language, so the correct choice must be made. Current models of language are far from complete, and the parts of the model required for analysis and generation are not the same, although there may be a big overlap.

5 What are the consequences for HCI systems?

Ideally, we would like a generalised generation module that we can use as the back end to HCI systems. This would take some input from the application, and produce appropriate text. However, we have seen that current systems only work in limited domains. For each new application, much of the data must be re-coded, the systems are inflexible in their use of language, and there is the risk of errors in surface structure due to a lack of linguistic data.

To make the generator more flexible, there should be a more complex mapping between domain and language concepts. To make generation more reliable, more linguistic data needs to be included. This will hopefully give a more modular generation system in which the description of the language is less tied to particular domains, and so more portable.

However, this increase in linguistic sophistication will lead to an increase in choice between words, surface structures, and so on. Some form of data will need to be forthcoming to enable choice between these possibilities. Thus for pronominalisation in English, gender data is needed, and for choosing between "take" and "bring", some form of perspective data is necessary. This data will either have to be supplied by the application, or be derivable from elsewhere, from a knowledge base within the generator for example.

6 Recent Approaches

Recent generation research has aimed at addressing the issues outlined above. There seem to be three main approaches, each aimed at a different problem. One is to boost the amount of language knowledge in the message before entering the generator, thus aiding the domain to concept mapping and allowing more accurate linguistic descriptions. The second is to give the generator its own knowledge base, and the third is to base the semantic structures of the application on those dictated by the language, that is, to make the application "think" in language based concepts.

The first approach is taken by McDonald and Meeter (McDonald [7]), and recognises the fact that application concepts don't necessarily match linguistic ones. Parts of the message are associated with "templates" which fill in any linguistic data which might be lacking in the original. For instance the symbol "53RD-MECHANISED-DIVISION" has no number or gender. This data is simply not necessary in the application. The template for this symbol adds these features to the data structure, with the appropriate values, before passing the new message to the generator. Reference to the symbol can then be pronominalised correctly

The second approach might be seen as a more general version of the first. Linguistically required knowledge is not added to the input data, but is included in the generator as a knowledge base, making it more general, and more flexible. Generation is then based on lexical selection, which consists of some sort of match between the data in the message, and the knowledge base (see for example Pustejovsy and Nirenburg [12], Nirenburg [11], Mattieusen [6], and Miezitis [10]). The knowledge made available during lexical selection allows more accurate and appropriate choices to be made.

The third approach, is also being developed by McDonald (McDonald [In press]). This addresses the issue of flexible mapping from domain to language concepts. The emphasis in this work is to explain the change in perspective in semantically equivalent phrases like :-

4a. I can stay until 4.

4b. I must leave by 4.

This example illustrates well the deficiencies of "hard wiring". The two realisations must at some point be derived from the same domain concept.

McDonald proposes that both the above examples would be generated from the central domain concept "transition-at-4pm". This concept would then be mapped to a set of lexical objects, in this case consisting of the pair "stay until" and "leave by". This set is called a "lexical cluster". A discrimination net chooses between the possibilities in the cluster depending on the current perspective.

McDonald suggests the perspective is so closely related to the workings of the application, in this case an appointments manager, that the program data structures must reflect it themselves. The description of the temporal properties of the phrases requires a certain representation of events. The application then adopts this same representation. McDonald suggests applications must take the language into account in this way, if we are to have coherent descriptions of the data.

7 Ongoing research

To address the problems of text reliability and flexibility, we have also adopted an approach based on lexical choice. As we have seen, the concepts that a language uses in its description of the world are culturally based rather than being defined by some canonical system. So, unless an application is to be coerced into using language based concepts (as McDonald suggests), there needs to be some way of mapping application concepts to linguistic ones. This mapping may unavoidably introduce some perspective or point of view.

Our work is aimed at representing this mapping process explicitly, and at making it flexible enough to break away from the "hard wiring" approach seen earlier. This should produce a more comprehensive account of what data is needed for conceptualisation.

The basic approach is to take the data structure presented as the message, and massage it into a language dependent form before realising the surface structure. This involves choice of the particular language concept to be used for the description. Modifiers may need to be used if no language concept is quite sufficient.

In addition, a discourse model is maintained, recording the entities and events already introduced into the conversation, and the domain to language mapping must take this into account as well.

The domain being investigated is that of home banking. Natural language may be used to respond to a customer enquiry, or a to produce descriptions of the course of the bank's transactions, as may be recorded in a log. A person, describing what goes on in a bank, might like to use terms such as "pay in", "draw out", "deposit", "cash cheques" and so on. These are particular types of event which English has the facility for describing. The bank log may not record events using predicates such as "cash", "deposit" and so on, and there is no reason why it should. These are concepts which describe events in a particular way, depending on the identities of speaker and hearer, and on the context. The log should record the data in a manner independent of these considerations, and it is up the speaker to know the conditions under which each of the linguistic concepts is appropriate. As an example, imagine there is a transfer event which may occur as part of the records. This event can be used to record the transfer of money from customer to bank, and vica versa, or the transfer of funds between banks. It is recorded as an event with three roles:-

1. Object
2. From
3. To

An example might be the following:-

TRANSFER($200,John, Bank)

So, how might this event be described? Remember, in many previous generation systems, the predicate head "TRANSFER" would be used to retrieve the verb "to transfer".

- John paid in $200.
- John brought in $200.
- The bank received $200 from John.
- John took in $200.
- John deposited $200.

The concepts of "pay","bring","take", and "receive", can all be used to describe the predicate in the context of a banking system. However, use of any one of them introduces some perspective. The generation system needs to know which one is the most appropriate.

There are two stages in the process of lexical choice First, the domain concept is mapped onto a language concept. The mapping defines how domain parameters map into the lexical semantics. Second, specific lexical entries, which are linked to the language concepts, may be retrieved. As we saw above, many concepts may be capable of describing an event. So, from any given domain event, many candidate words may be retrieved. The map and lexicon encode parameters describing the conditions under which each concept or word is most appropriate. These conditions may be lexically based, such as collocations, or contextually based, such as point of view, or style restrictions. We may also need to consider such things as the unavailability of parameters. If the filler of the"from" role were unknown, we might want to consider a realisation where that role was not involved.

For instance :-

CONCEPT MAPPING

∃e TRANSFER(object,from,to,e) ⇒
∃e (AND (DEPOSIT from object e)
(IN e to))
Conditions: [to=an account,focus=from]

This example shows the domain based concept "TRANSFER", mapping to the language based concept of "DEPOSIT". The "DEPOSIT" concept leads to the selection of the verbs "deposit" and "put". Other mappings will lead to other verb selections. Appraisal of the conditions for each leads to the selection of a single verb.

8 Conclusions

For reasons of flexibility, portability, and accuracy, generation components of HCI systems need to include more sophisticated mappings between domain and language concepts, and more lexical knowledge. This could have consequences for applications programs, since the data supplied in the message may need to take the requirements of the generator into account.

9 Acknowledgements

The author is supported by the Science and Engineering Research Council, and by Logica UK. Thanks are due to the many colleagues who have provided support and encouragement, especially Dr. S. G. Pulman, Julia Galliers, Richard Crouch, Ann Copestake, Nick Youd and Derek Bridge.

References

[1] Appelt, D. 1985. Planning English Sentences. Cambridge University Press.

[2] Appelt, D. 1987. Bidirectional Grammars and the design of Natural Language Generation systems. Position papers - TINLAP 3, New York State University.

[3] Danlos, L. 1987. The linguistic basis of text generation. Cambridge University Press.

[4] Levelt, W. 1989. Speaking. MIT press.

[5] Marcus, M. 1987. Position papers - TINLAP 3, New York State University.

[6] Mattieusen, C. 1988. Lexico/Grammatical choice in text generation. Abstract presented to the Catalina workshop on generation.

[7] McDonald, D. and Meeter, M. 1988. From Water to Wine. Proceedings of the ACL conference.

[8] McDonald, D, In press. On the place of words in the generation process. In Natural Language Generation in Artificial Intelligence and Computational Linguistics, by C. Paris, W. Swartout, and W. Mann (Eds.) Kluwer, Dordrecht.

[9] McKeown, K. 1985. Text generation. Cambridge University Press.

[10] Miezitis, M. A. 1988. Generating lexical options by matching in a knowledge base. Tech. report CSRI-217. University of Toronto.

[11] Nirenburg, S. 1988. Lexical selection in a Blackboard Based generation system. Abstract presented to the Catalina workshop on generation.

[12] Pustejovsky, J. and Nirenburg, S. 1987. Lexical selection in the process of language generation. Proceedings ACL conference.

[13] Shieber, S. 1988. A uniform architecture for parsing and generation. Proceedings of Coling conference.

[14] Simmons. 1972. Networks. Communications of the ACM, Vol 15.

[15] Tait, J. 1985. An English Generator For Case Representations. Proceedings of ACL conference.

SECTION V: APPLICATIONS AND CASE STUDIES

SV.1 Knowledge-Based Systems

User centered explanations in knowledge based systems
K. Waldhör and H. Anschütz 809

Intelligent user interface for a conventional program
J. Junger, G. Bouma, and Ph. Letanoux 815

Knowledge acquisition and hypertext in manufacturing
S.M. Hajsadr, A.P. Steward, and V. Carroll 821

Knowledge based user interfaces for scientific programs
H.J. Van Zuylen and H. Gerritsen 827

Human–Computer Interaction – INTERACT '90
D. Diaper et al. (Editors)
Elsevier Science Publishers B.V. (North-Holland)

USER CENTERED EXPLANATIONS IN KNOWLEDGE BASED SYSTEMS

Klemens Waldhör Hans Anschütz

OLIVETTI Research, c/o TA TRIUMPH-ADLER AG, Fürther Str. 212, D-8500 Nürnberg 1

One advantage of expert systems is the ability to explain its reasoning process. Many commercial systems support explaining only at rule trace level. Knowledge engineers understand such explanations; the everyday user who is not expert in that area is confused. Our approach allows the definition of user centered explanations and justifications by knowledge engineers. These explanations and justifications of conclusions are adapted to the way the user solves problems by cutting off irrelevant details and presenting only main steps in the reasoning process. A sophisticated user interface allows the user to ask questions about the system behaviour in various ways.

1. Motivation

Explanation is a great theme in knowledge based systems. Each book about knowledge based systems describes explanations as one of the major advances of such systems. Some interesting results and implementations have been achieved in this area (e.g. Swartout, 1981; Clancey, 1981, 1983). But looking at the commercial available tools one must conclude that the explanation capabilities of such systems are very poor (if existing) and do not reflect the state of the art in this area (in contrast to the knowledge representation schemes used !).

One aim of our research (and of our implemenation) was to fill this gap between theory and research implementations and a commercially available tool (in our case the knowledge representation LUIGI of TA). The other aim was to show that explanations are not only of use for a special user group but can be adapted in various forms to different user groups and as an important fact can be understood by these different user groups.

2. User groups

When discussing explanations it is important to distinguish the different user groups a knowledge based system is aimed. In our paper we will distinguish between four groups:

1) The *knowledge engineer*: He creates and maintains the knowledge base.
2) The *expert*: He knows about the domain and in many cases his expert knowledge is the basis of the system; he uses the knowledge based system as a software tool.
3) The *student*: He uses the knowledge base to learn from it; his aim is to become an expert.
4) The *naive user*: He has no knowledge about the domain and wants to get some useful information from the system (e.g consultation).

It is evident that it is possible to construct other user group taxonomies but we think that this taxonomy is structured sufficiently for our purposes.

What are the differences between these user groups with regard to explanations ?

Three different areas can be identified:

The first difference is the *knowledge of the domain*. While the expert has a lot of knowledge the student and the naive user may have a very limited knowledge of the domain. The knowledge engineer will have in many cases the same status as a student. Two general areas of application domains must be distinguished:

- *common domains* (e.g. journey consultation) - in such a domain commonsense knowledge is available und useful for understanding the terms and results of the reasoning process.

- *special domains* (e.g. share consultation; medical consultations) - such a domain requires very special knowledge and uses a specialized terminology which needs a lot of time to become acquainted with it.

The difference between these two domains becomes important as far as explaining is concerned.

If the system gives some support how to plan a journey and any user asks for explanations the system can assume that the terms of these domain are generally known (e.g. the system needs not explain in detail for any user group "what is a journey"). The system may assume some general background knowledge of the domain which needs no explanation.

If the system gives advice, e.g. in the domain of buying shares, the naive user may not be aware about the terms used in this domain. As a result he needs another explanation as the knowledge engineer or expert. The contrast to the student may be that the student gets a deeper explanation about the mechanism how the share market works than the naive user, who is not so much interested in such details.

The second difference comes from the *knowledge about the knowledge representation scheme* used.

The knowledge engineer knows the knowledge representation and its syntax and semantics. From that he has no problems to interprete entities and reasoning processes which are very closely related to the chosen knowledge representation (e.g. he understands a frame like structure, a rule trace). This cannot be be assumed by the other groups. They are not interested in the knowledge representation syntax and semantics but in the goal they can achieve with it.

This leads us to the third difference - *the user expectations*. The knowledge engineer will use the explanation component to test and maintain the knowledge base, while the other groups use it as a tool. The knowledge engineer wants to know if his implementation works correctly, e.g. if the conclusions drawn are the conclusions he expects. So from his point of view explaining also means support in debugging the knowledge base. The expert may use it as a tool to get some work done which he cannot do because of lackage of time or because the most actual data are automatically entered into the system by some device. He needs the explanations as a kind of control too, e.g. if the reasoning is correct. Through the fact that the other two user groups have a very limited knowledge of the domain they must rely on the reasoning and the knowledge in the system. The explanations thus clarify on which assumptions and conclusions the reasoning process is based on. These groups must trust that the reasoning process is correct.

When keeping this facts in mind it is obvious that an explanation system has to offer the opportunity to support different user groups. Looking at knowledge based systems which exist today one comes to the conclusion that such a support does not exist. One aim of our explanation system LUX was therefore to enable such user specific explanations.

3. Task of an explanation component in knowledge based systems

Generally two areas for explanations can be found in knowledge based systems - explanations concerning the domain model and explanations for the problem solving model. The domain model contains the descriptive knowledge of the domain, e.g the objects and their taxonomy, their relations, types of possible values and so on. The problem solving model contains knowledge how the domain model is used for a specific task; its knowledge is stated in terms of rules, strategies and meta rules (problem solvers).

The task of explanation components is to support the user in understanding the results of conclusions taken by knowledge based systems as well as to provide the user with information about objects (classes, components, instances, affairs, ...) in the domain. Two kinds of explanations can therefore be distinguished: explaining domain knowledge and explaining problem solving knowledge.

Both domain and problem solving knowledge can be generated with the following methods: using canned text (sometimes with "blanks" within the text to fit in the actual context) for both static and dynamic knowledge; paraphrasing knowledge for objects and rules; displaying the fired rules and their instances (see MYCIN, Shortliffe 1976; Schulman & Hayes-Roth 1987); display of the strategies of the rule selection (NEOMYCIN: Clancey & Letsinger 1981; Clancey 1983; XPLAIN: Swartout 1981; Kassel 1987, Neches 1984; Chandrasekaran et al. 1988 and 1989; Cleal & Heaton 1988); condensing the inference trace (Wick et. al, 1988; Waldhör, 1990); using deep knowledge as a means for better explanations (Chandrasekaran et al. 1988; Kassel 1987); adapting the explanation to the user within a user model (Wahlster 1983; Wick et. al, 1989) and taking into account the users goals and plans (Van Beck, 1987). For explaining domain knowledge see Belaid & Herin-Aime,1988 or Waldhör, 1990.

Another important point is the preparation of the explanation for the user. This requires a user model, an advanced text generation component and the possibilty to display graphics, tables ... The explanations have to be improved to be understandable for the end user; this requires in many cases the application of linguistic knowledge and the translation into natural language (NUGGET: Rösner 1986; Jablonski et al. 1988); using instantiable texts (KOKON, a knowledge based system for configuring real estate constracts, Strasser & Gerl, 1988); using ATNs (Miller & Rennels, 1988; Waldhör, 1990) or a "journalistic approach" (Wick & Slage, 1988) based on the experience of how journalists explain questions.

4. The explanation system LUX

The explanation system LUX supports user specific multilingual explanations. It generates explanations for two areas: the domain model and the problem solving model.

4.1. User specific explanations

As a first step the knowledge engineer defines the possible user groups (e.g. expert, naive user ...). The knowledge engineer may define as many user groups as he likes, esp. he is not constrained to the user groups of the taxonomy we have presented. For each user group different explanations can be defined, both for the domain and the problem solving knowledge. When using the UIMS of LUX, a user group can be chosen and only the explanations relevant for this user group are displayed.

4.2. Text generation and multilingual explanations

Most of the texts which are generated within LUX are defined using ATNs (augmented transistion networks: Woods, 1970; Miller & Rennels, 1988; Waldhör & Anschütz, 1989). The ATN-approach, which is used as a powerful programming language for LUX text generation, enables the knowledge engineer to specify texts in a comfortable way. He can refer to the concepts which are available in the domain model and adapt explanations for the domain model in the way he likes.

The current implementation allows the knowledge engineer to create language specific versions of explanations and store them in a file. When the user starts LUX he can change to his native language and will get the explanations in the selected language. He also can change the language during a LUX session. This will be supported by special lexica which allow the translation of terms into different languages.

4.3. Explanation for the domain model

Explanations in the domain model are supported in two ways:

First LUX is able to create default explanations for all entities within the domain model. Depending on the application domain and the user groups these explanations may be appropriate for the user. One must keep in mind that when creating default explanations LUX can only create explanations which reflect the semantics of the LUIGI knowledge representation scheme. The default explanations are aimed at the knowledge engineer and in some cases at the expert, but are not of much help for the other two user groups. It assumes that the user knows that the knowledge representation is based on a special frame concept.

For the two other user groups it is necessary to create specific domain model explanations. The knowledge engineer may define ATNs for all entities of the domain and these specific ATNs will be used instead of the ATNs of the default explanations. LUX allows to specify for which entities defaults may be created or not; thus entities which are of no relevance for a special user group can be hidden. LUX controls the access to the entities in such a way that entities which should not be visible for the user are not accessible.

For all entities in the domain model question types were chosen to give the user access to the whole information concerning his user group:

1) *WHAT* describes the specified entity in terms of existing examples, its position in the taxonomy.
2) *EXAMPLES OF* describes all instantiated entities (instances of affairs and objects).
3) *STRUCTURE OF* describes the structure of entities in terms of their components, possible values of the components.
4) *ALL ABOUT* combines WHAT, EXAMPLES and STRUCTURE.
5) *COMMON* describes what two entities of the domain have in common (e.g. the common components of two objects, common values ...).
6) *DIFFERENCE* describes the differences between two entities (e.g. different components, different values ...).

If some questions are not intended for a user group they can be omitted.

In addition to the specified explanations a lexicon facility is provided. Within this lexicon the KE may specify entities and information which is not represented within the domain model in more details. This is a facility which is clearly aimed for user groups like student and naive user.

4.4. Explanations for the problem solving model

LUX supports two kinds of explanations within the problem solving domain:
- task explanations
- explanations within rules (conclusion explanations)

Tasks organize either rules or other task (subtasks). This enables the knowledge engineer to structure the knowledge base in an appropriate way (Beetz & Barth, 1988).

4.4.1. Task explanations:

Within a task three different explanations can be provided:
- a general information of the content of the problem solver
- a description of the situation when the task was activated (precondition of the problem solver)
- a description of the goal of a task (goal of a problem solver)

If no user specific explanation for a task is available, LUX may create an explanation for the three explanation possibilities using special defaults. Like in the domain model explanations are represented as ATNs. Each activation of a task creates an entry in the task explanation net which is used to construct explanations. Each of the three explanations is represented as a component of the corresponding task. Defaults are mainly intended for the first two user groups while the special explanations are intended for students and naive users.

Task explanations are activated by the following questions:

(1) *OVERVIEW* displays the subtasks or conclusions within a task. It describes in a short way how the reasoning process took place in a task.
(2) *SUBTASK OF* describes within which task a task was activated. With these two questions the user may navigate through the whole task explanation net.
(3) *TASK DESCRIPTION* informs the user about the general aims and the task of a problem solver.
(4) *SITUATION* describes the activation condition of the task.
(5) *GOAL* explains the situation which has to be achieved or was achieved when the task terminates.

4.4.2. Conclusion explanations:

Within rules a special function call (named *explain*) creates an explanation conclusion node and stores it in an explanation conclusion net. Two types of nodes are distinguished in this net: conclusion nodes and basic assumptions. Conclusion nodes are justified by other conclusions or basic assumptions, while basic assumptions are not justified within the system.

The knowledge engineer has to specify at which point of the reasoning process he wants explanations for the actions of rules to be created. For each explanation he may specify an ATN which describes the conclusion and the justification of the conclusion (which is a subset of the precondition of the rule). The KE need not define an explanation for each rule when he thinks that it is not necessary (condensing the reasoning process). But he also can specify a more fine grained explanation process by entering more explanations within a rule (this may be useful, if the inference process should be explained in more detail as is available through the precondition of the explanation or if the rule itself represent condensed problem solving knowledge). For each conclusion explanation the user type to which it fits can be stated.

The following questions are available for conclusions:

(1) *HOW* was a conclusion reached. As a result the justifications of a conclusion are displayed).
(2) *WHY* describes what could be inferred from a conclusion (the consequences of a conclusion).
(3) *WHERE OF* states the ultimate assumptions where a conclusion is based on. These assumptions are generated as explanations without justifications.
(4) *SUBTASK OF* describes the task within which the conclusion was performed.
(5) *SITUATION* describes the activation condition of the task within which the conclusion was reached.
(6) *GOAL* describes the terminating situation of the corresponding task of the conclusion.
(7) *RULE DESCRIPTION* returns a general information about the background of a rule.

Additionally problemsolving knowledge may also be described and justified within the lexicon.

Through the combination of questions for tasks and conclusions the user can navigate between the task and conclusion explanation nets.

In addition to the textual display of the problem solving process the user can display the reasoning process also as a graph both for tasks and for conclusions to get a global overview.

5. The User Interface

Special care was taken to implement an easy to use user interface. The user interface supports the questioning process of the user in two ways:

(1) The user may enter a query with the keyboard. The disadvantage of this methods comes from the limitations of the parser which translates the query of the user into an internal format. Keyboard is therefore used mainly for questions concerning the domain model because questions concerning the problem solving model are not easy to interprete. Currently we are working on a translation procedure which allows the user to communicate with the problem solving model in a convenient way, too.

(2) Using the mouse and menus. We think that using menus is the appropriate way to generate queries in our case. This method has some advantages:
a) the user cannot ask incorrect questions. When asking a question (by clicking on a the appropriate question type in the question menu) the possible parameters are displayed. In such a way the user cannot mix e.g. a question concerning conclusions with a paramter from the domain model.
b) Typing is unnecessary. Misspelling is not possible.
c) The question types give the user an overview of the capabilities of the system. Each question type is also explained in a detailed way in a special help facility (syntax, semantics of the question type).
d) Using menus gives the user a first feeling of the content of the knowledge base and he may get a feeling of the concepts or conclusions which are interesting for him.
e) Persons who are accomodated to the editors of the knowledge representation get a similar interface which enables the transfer of knowledge from the editors to our interface (button usage, window activation ...).

Picture 1 presents the user interface for a SYMBOLICS. A similar interface exists on a SUN workstation.

Additionally each user has the possibilty to adapt the user interface in the way he likes (e.g. by specifying how menu entries should be sorted, content of menu entries, length of texts and so on). The interface parameters are stored in a file and are used the next time the same user starts a specific application.

It is obvious that such an interface may not be useful in every case. If an application needs a specific interface a set of interface functions have been implemented which allows the application programmer to integrate the functionality of LUX.

6. Conclusions

The described concepts been implemented for the knowledge representation system LUIGI and shown to be useful in different applications. Using this approach in an investment counselling system the reasoning process of the system could be presented in a much cleaner and understandable way to the end user as in the case of a rule trace. The same is true for the entities of the domain which could be described in a very concise way - even to people with no experience in this area.

We are now considering extending the system in some directions: a) to make some adaptations towards a tutoring system; b) extending the question types (e.g. the WHY NOT question) and c) special support for non monotonic reasoning (e.g. explaining consequences of drawing back some assumptions).

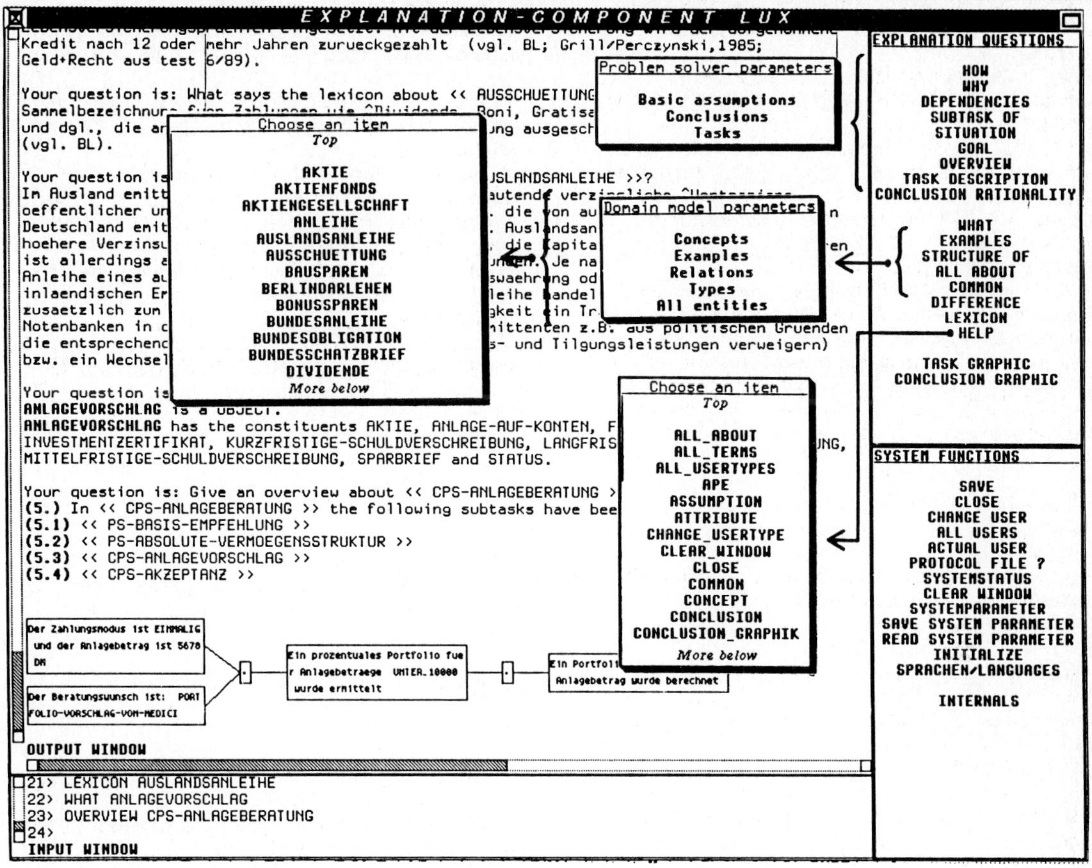

Picture 1: User interface of LUX

7 . Literature

Beetz, M (1987). Specifying Meta-level Architectures for Rule-Based Systems. Proc. GWAI 87, Springer, New York, 149-159.

Belaid, F., Herin-Aime, D. (1988). Explanations for an object-oriented knowledge base. Proc. of the 4th International Expert Systems Conference, London.

Chandrasekaran, B., Tanner, M.C., Josephson, J.R. (1988). Explanation: The Role of Control Strategies and deep models. In: Hendler, J.A. (ed.) Expert systems: The User Interface, Ablex, Norwood, pp. 219-247.

Chandrasekaran, B., Tanner, M.C., Josephson, J.R. (1989). Explaining Control Strategies in Problem Solving. IEEE Expert, Spring 1989.

Clancey, W., Letsinger, R. (1981). Neomycin: Reconfiguring a Rule-Based Expert System for Application to Teaching. Proc. of the 7th IJCAI, 829-835

Clancey, W. (1983). The Advantages of Abstract Control Knowledge in Expert System Design. Proc. of the Third National Conference on Artificial Intelligence (AAAI).

Cleal, D.M., Heaton, N.D. (1988). Knowledge-Based Systems: Implications for human-computer Interaction. Ellis Horwood, Chichester.

Jablonski, K., Rau, A., Ritzke, J. (1988). NUGGET: A DCG-based Text Generation System, WISBER-report B27, Nixdorf Computer AG, Paderborn.

Kassel, G. (1987). The use of deep knowledge to improve the explanation capabilities of Rule-Based Expert systems. In: Balzert, H., Heyer, G., Lutze, R., Expertensysteme 1987, Teubner.

Miller, P.L., Rennels, G.D. (1988). Prose Generation from Expert Systems. AI Magazine, Fall 1988, 37-44.

Neches, R., Swartout, W.R., Moore, J. (1984). Enhanced Maintenance and Explanation of Expert Systems through Explicit Models of their Development. in: Workshop an Principles of Knowledge Based Systems, 173-183, IEEE.

Roesner, H. (1986). Generation of Explanations in Knowledge Representation. LVD-Forum 4-1, 3-19.

Schulman, R., Hayes-Roth, B. (1987). ExAct: A Module for Explaining Actions, Report No. KSL 87-8, Computer Science Department, Standford University.

Shortliffe, E.H. (1976). Computer Based Medical Consultations: MYCIN. New York: American Elsevier.
Strasser, A., Gerl, G. (1988). The Explanation Component of KOKON-III. FB-TUM-88-30, München.
Swartout, W.R. (1981). Explaining and Justifying Expert Consulting Programs. Proc. of the 7th IJCAI, 815-823.
Van Beek, P. (1987). A Model For Generating Better Explanations. ACL '87. Proceedings of ACL '87, Stanford, California.
Waldhör, K. (1990). Die Erklärungskomponente LUX des Wissensrepräsentationssystems LUIGI; to be published in: Stoyan, H. (1990). Proc. of the Workshop: Explanation as Man Machine Communications, Springer, New York.
Waldhör, K., Anschütz, A. (1989). Definition of an ATN-Grammar for the Explanation Component in LUIGI, SPEC-01-89-03, TA Triumph Adler, Nürnberg.
Wahlster, W. (1983). Explanation Components as Dialogue Tools. Office Management: Sonderheft, 45-48.
Wick, M.R., Paris, C.L., Swartout, W.B., Thompson, W.B.: (Eds.) (1988). Proceedings of the 1988 AAAI Workshop on explanation. American Association for Artificial Intelligence, Menlo Park, California.
Wick, M.R., Slage, J.R. (1989). An explanation Facility for Today's Expert Systems, IEEE Expert, Spring 1989.
Woods, W.A. (1970). Transition Network Grammars for Natural Language Analysis, CACM 13, 591-606.

Human–Computer Interaction – INTERACT '90
D. Diaper et al. (Editors)
Elsevier Science Publishers B.V. (North-Holland)

INTELLIGENT USER INTERFACE FOR A CONVENTIONAL PROGRAM

J. Junger, G. Bouma, Ph. Letanoux
Research Institute for Knowledge Systems
Maastricht, The Netherlands

ABSTRACT

In this paper we describe an intelligent user interface to CHEMSIM, a mathematical simulation program. The interface is added to the already existing and completed program as a separate front-end. In this paper three aspects of the interface will be described: the task model represented as a hierachical tree, the use of the tree for knowledge-representation and the graphical component. The choice of an object-oriented approach enables including in the class definitions both task aspects and domain knowledge aspects, and this way integrating the two. This approach simplifies the architecture as well. In addition, the same hirarchical tree representation is used also for the graphical component consisting of windows, menus and icons. The dynamic icons, governed by rules give the user direct feedback on his/her actions and help.

1. INTRODUCTION

The importance of user friendly interfaces is in recent years widely recognized, and the user interface of systems is a topic which gets increasing attention already at the stage of preparing the design. This development, however, is fairly recent. Therefore, there still are many in themselves very good systems (databases, systems for industrial-control, simulators) with rather user unfriendly interfaces, needing a good interface. Redesigning and reimplementing these systems is often too expensive. Hence for practical reasons the only possibility is adding the intelligent interface to the existing conventional system. This goes against the claim that in order to have a good user interface, it should be part of the initial design and of the whole development process of the system. This paper describes a user interface added to a completed system, which still has all the functionality of an interface that is integrated in the system from the design stage.

The user interface described here is to a simulation program, whose original interface is extremely user unfriendly. [1] The interface which we added to it differs from one which would be integrated in the system from the very beginning in that it is a separate front-end, not a module in the system, but a small system in itself; this adds extra requirements such as a separate knowledge-base. In addition the output of the interface is a batch file which forms the input for the application program (i.e. the main system). Hence, there is no interaction with other modules, such as for example in an interface with a blackboard architecture.

After a general description of the application program and of our user interface, follows a detailed description of one aspect of the interface which is of more general interest: the use of the task model for constructing the knowledge-base of the interface, and its use in the object oriented implementation.

2. GENERAL DESCRIPTION

This section is a short general description of the user interface: its functionality, components, architecture and implementation environment. Due to space limit only the task model, the knowledge-base and the use of classes and objects will be described properly; all the other components of the interface are described only very shortly.

2.1. Functionality

CHEMSIM (as mentioned in the footnote, a fictive name but based on the real interface) simulates the production processes in a chemical plant. The simulation program itself is a mathematical program written in Fortran. For running it the user has to supply a set of input parameters, which are processed by the mathematical program. The output of the user interface is a batch file with calculations that can be used for monitoring the chemical plant, for planing a new pant, for testing safety, for controll or for optimalization of the processes.

Hancock and Chignell (1989) classify intelligent user interfaces into two groups: those acting as an intermediary, and those acting as a machine reasoning system. The CHEMSIM interface is based on the intermediary approach. Its main function is supporting the user in providing a correct list of input parameters for the simulator. This general functionality demand is further specified into the following points:

1. Support: providing the user with help in specifying the input parameters, and with explanation on each parameter and the relations between them.
2. Flexibility: allowing the user as much freedom as possible in the order of executing the individual tasks of specifying each input parameter.
3. Feedback: a very elementary feature of a user-friendly interface is giving feedback to the user on his/her actions. In our case the feedback is twofold, realized by means of icons. One icon indicates whether specifying a parameter is obligatory, optional or forbidden (in some cases choosing parameter X entails that parameter Y should not be specified); another icon indicates whether a parameter's value has been specified or not, and if yes the source of the value: system default, specified by the user or loaded from a previous run.
4. User adaptiveness: the interface has two modes: for power (experienced) users and for casual users. The literature gives 5 criteria for judging the costs and benefits of a user model. For details on them the reader is referred to Kass and Finin (1988) and Gillis (1989). Considering their guidelines, we concluded that only two of them apply to CHEMSIM. Within our limits of time and resources it was preferable to concentrate on aspects like graphic representation, direct manipulation, flexibility and a good help facility, and use only a coarse user model (power vs. casual users). Furthermore, the client expressed clear preference to a graphic, if possible direct manipulation system rather than one which is adaptive to individual users.

2.2. Components and architecture

The interface consists of three modules: a presentation engine (PE) which is responsible for the graphical appearance (windows, menus, icons etc.), a knowledge base (KB) including all the knowledge specific to the simulation program and a controller which handles the interaction between the knowledge base and the presentation engine.

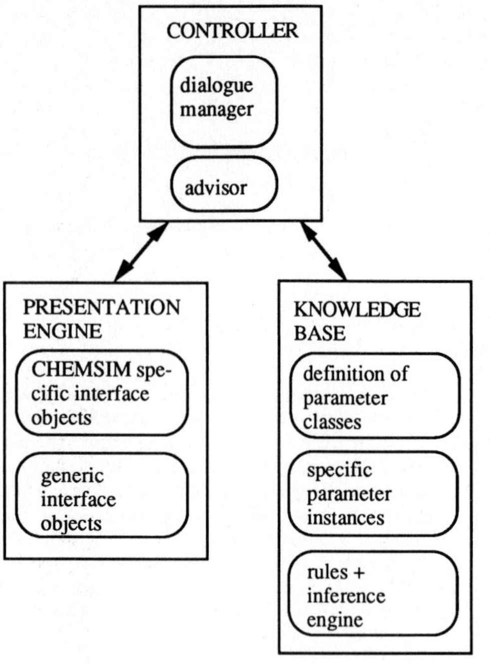

figure 1: the components

Both the presentation engine and the controller are generic; the application specific knowledge is all concentrated in the knowledge base. This way there is a separation of the generic reusable components (PE and Controller) and the application specific component (the KB).

The KB contains the hierarchical tree of all the parameters as they are organized in the task model. That is, the tasks, sub-tasks and input parameters are directly translated into the nodes and the leaves of the hierarchical tree of the KB. The KB also contains rules and a forward chaining inference engine. The inference engine can be of course more complex too, but for our application a simple forward chaining one is enough, as the only reasoning is for correlations between input parameters.

3. THE TASK ANALYSIS AND THE TASK MODEL

The typical design and implementation process of a user interface starts with the task analysis (Chignell and Hancock, 1988).

A task is defined as a meaningful unit of work performance, consisting of a set of related actions which typically has a discernible beginning and end so that it can be fully accomplished before accomplishing another task. There are various approaches for making a task analysis for a user interface. Philips, Bashinsky, Ammerman and Fligg (1988) present several methods for task analysis which are a straightforward way of describing a whole cycle of activities. However, they do not include also the knowledge required from the user for performing them. A different type of task analyses are those based on a psychological model of the user. Kieras (1987) and Polson (1987) analyse the types of knowledge a user has with regard to a task: 'knowledge how it works', 'knowledge how to do it' and 'knowledge of job situations'. An 'in between' approach, trying to encompass both the knowledge of the user and the activities, is GOMS (Card, Moran and Newell, 1983) and Command Language Grammar (Moran, 1981).

We chose for the task analysis a method which reflects both the activities that take place during a session and the knowledge about the organization of the input parameters. That is, both 'knowledge how to do it' and 'knowledge how it works', though the latter has been as yet implemented only with regard to the tasks, not to the simulation program itself. The resulting task model is an object oriented model, used also for the knowledge representation. The tasks are organized into a hierarchical tree. The tree reflects both the domain of the simulator and the activities of the user. The domain of the simulation program is reflected in that the tree structure reflects directly the internal organization of the input parameters. For example:

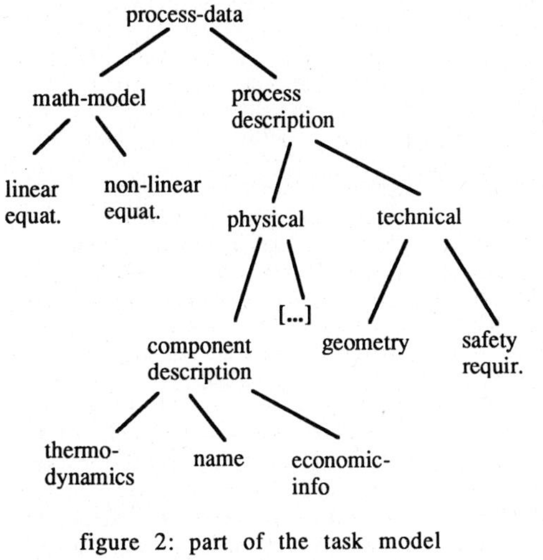

figure 2: part of the task model

There are two types of tasks: a simple task, following the definition given above, based on it being one discernible action, and a 'complex task' . A complex task is represented by a node and a simple one by a leaf. Thus "specify process data" is a complex task. Accomplishing it consists of the subtasks: "specify mathematical model" and "specify process description". These sub-tasks too are complex, consisting of several tasks. "Specify mathematical model" consists of tasks (=leaves) for specifying the particular linear or non-linear equation to be used by CHEMSIM. The other sub-task, specifying the process description, consists of the complex sub-tasks "specify physical description" and "specify technical description" of the components. By the same principle, "specify technical description" consists of the simple tasks "specify geometry" and "specify safety requirements", and "specify component description" consists of the simple tasks "specify theromdynamic data", "specify name of component" and "specify economic information on the component".
Such a task model integrates the conceptual model of the simulator's domain with the tasks which the user has to fulfil. Namely: the main task is specifying all the necessary input parameters. The relations between them are represented by the hierarchical tree above. The basic simple tasks refer to one parameter. The complex tasks can be seen as referring to a complex input parameter, since the nodes are meaningful not only when seen as complex tasks, but also within a conceptual model of the domain. The node "component description" stands for a group of input parameters which are all related within the domain of the simulation program, as they together provide the description of the chemical components.
Although from the example it may look ad hoc, in fact the principle is general and applicable to any domain/task model which can be represented as a hierarchical tree. (There might be problems in translating a domain network to a task model- we have not looked into that).

The task model also directly reflects some of the domain expertise in the simulator, namely when and which parameters are necessary to provide a good input file. This is implemented by the "completed" mechanism. A complex task is "completed" if all its sub-tasks are completed. That is, a node is completed when the values of all the parameters which are its leaves have been specified by the user. Thus when the highest task, "make input file for CHEMSIM" is completed, this means also that all the necessary input parameters are provided. Or, for example, the complex task "specify process description" is partially completed if the sub-task "specify technical details" is completed, and fully completed if also the sub-task "specify physical details" is completed. These subtasks are completed when the leaves (parameters) have the correct values as specified by the rules. The rules expressing when a task is completed or not are in fact "domain rules" of the simulator. They are part of the knowledge-base and will be discussed in the next section. These rules also have a visual aspect, the feedback to the user in the form of icons, discussed in section five.

4. OBJECT ORIENTED KNOWLEDGE REPRESENTATION

The knowledge-base of the interface consists of a hierarchical tree of the input parameters and of rules stating how they should be specified: limits on the acceptable value, correlations between parameters, statements about when certain parameters should or should not be specified by the user and unit types that have to be consistent. For the representation of the input parameters an object oriented approach was chosen. A similar approach is used in Pierret-Golbreich (1988), with the difference that the object oriented knowledge representation in CHEMSIM is not based only on the conceptual model of the domain, but on a model integrating the task model with a domain model, as shown in figure 2 above.

4.1. Classes and instances

The use of object oriented programming (Smalltalk) for simulation environments is described for example in Baudel, Cantegrit and Toulotte (1988) and Stephanopolous, Johnston, Kriticos, Lakshmanan, Mavrovouniotis and Siletti (1987). Our implementation is in two different environments: the graphic aspects are in the C-based X-windows, and the knowledge base is in CLOS (object oriented Lisp, see Keene, 1988). Here the inheritance mechanism of CLOS and the use of accessors will be explained only very shortly.
The whole knowledge is represented in a hierarchical tree. The conceptual entities are represented as objects in the tree: nodes and leaves. The objects are organized in classes, and each class has attributes and facets. These specific characteristics of object oriented programming will not be dealt with here, as they are described in detail in numerous articles.
The leaves of the tree, which are the input parameters specified by the user are arranged into classes. The whole tree is represented as follows:

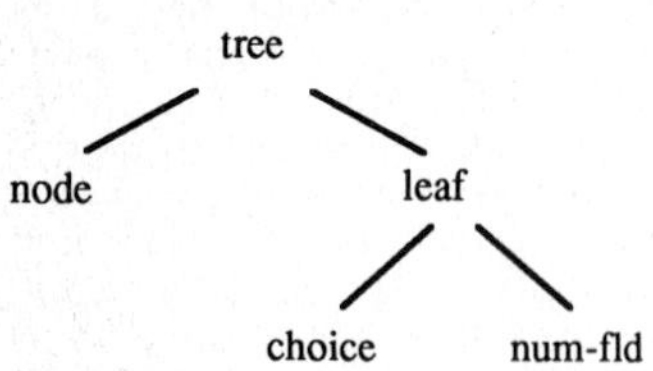

figure 3: the hierarchical tree underlying the knowledge-representation

This tree overlaps the task-model shown in figure 2 above: the root-node "tree" is the meta task of creating the batch file which is the output of the interface and the input to CHEMSIM. A node is a complex task, and a leaf is a simple task. Leaves can be of two types: choice and numerical (num-fld). The choice type tasks involve choosing an option from a menu, and the numerical type tasks involve specifying a numerical value for a task.
The definitions of the classes are:

```
(defclass tree (gr-tree)
     ((father :initarg :father :accessor t-father)
      (symb-name :initform nil accessor t-sname)
      (status :initform :opt :accessor t-status)
      (rules :initform nil :accessor t-rules))
     (:documentation "Tree"))
```

The class has a type, namely gr-tree ("gr" standing for "graphic"), hence its instance is graphic. A class has slots, which have an initial value indicated by the keyword :initform; in the class "tree" it is "nil". The initial value can be changed by means of acessors. The class 'tree' has slots for father, symbol-name and status, which can be accessed with the t-father, t-sname and t-status respectively. The "symb-name" slot specifies the name used to refer to this class and its instances in methods and rules. Interesting here is the "status" slot, which can have the values "optional", "obligatory" and "forbidden". These define whether an input parameter may be, should be or must not be specified. The value can be changed by means of the "t-status" accessor, which is activated by means of rules. The slot "rules" is for the methods, which mostly describe correlations between input parameters and change their "status". Nodes are defined as follows:

```
(defclass node (tree gr-node)
     ((children :initform nil :accessor t-child)
      (completed :initform nil :accessor t-compl))
      (:documentation "Complex parameter"))
```

A node inherits from "tree" the slots for "status", "symb-name" , "rules"and "father". It also has a slot for children and a slot indicating whether it is "completed" or not. In principle a node is completed if all the parameters (simple of complex) under it are specified. But there are also cases when a node can be considered as completed, even if not all its children are specified. These cases are treated by rules.
Since a node is defined to be of type "tree gr-node", a node inherits all the slots and methods of "tree" and the graphical methods. The graphical aspect is treated in section 5. The nodes can be plain or of type "choice"; the former have individual parameters as children and the latter "items". Items are the options on a choice menu, which is the graphic realization of some nodes. For example, the node "mathematical model" can be of choice type, with "linear equation" and "non-linear equation" as items. The node "process description" has two children: "physical" and "technical descr", whose children are leaves. Leaves, which stand for simple input parameters, are defined to be of one of the types: numerical (when the user's input is a numerical value), or text (when the user's input is a string, eg. for the name of a component). The node "component description" has two leaves of "text" type, for the name of the component and economic information on it, and one numerical leaf for "thermodynamics".
The class definition for leaves is:

```
(defclass leaf (tree gr-leaf)
    ((source :initform nil :accessor t-source)
     (value :initform nil :accessor t-value)
     (default :initform nil :accessor t-default))
     (:documentation "Simple parameters"))
```

A leaf inherits the slots of the tree class, and has slots for the source of its value (either from the user or as default value in the simulator). Note that leaves do not inherit from nodes. The reason is that nodes are complex parameters which are treated differently than leaves, which are simple parameters.

The definition for numerical parameters is:

```
(defclass num-fld (leaf gr-num-fld)
    ((fld-min :initform nil :accessor t-min)
     (fld-max :initform nil :accessor t-max))
      (:documentation "Numerical parameter"))
```

Thus num-fld inherits from "tree" (via the class "leaf") the slots "father", "status", "symb-name" and "rules" and from the class "leaf" the slots "source", "value" and "default". All these slots are valid also for text-type leaves. Numerical parameters can also have a limit for the acceptable minimum and maximum values, hence the slots "fld-min" and "fld-max". The individual input parameters are instances of leaves. The rules regulate how the tasks on the leaf-level should be accomplished.

4.2. The rules

The relations between the leaves and the nodes, as well as between the leaves internally are expressed by rules. The rules correlate the input parameters (leaves) to each other by making use of the t-value slot-accessor to regulate the status of the parameter.
Thus many of the rules are of the type

if: t-status of parameter A is obligatory
then: set t-status of parameter B to obligatory

or

if: t-source of parameter C is :user
then: set t-status of parameter D to forbidden.

The first rule correlates two parameters which must be specified together; the second rule specifies a relation of "exclusiveness" between two parameters, so that if the user specifies one of them (expressed by the source being the user), than the other parameter must not be specified. Another relation is "at least one", that is out of two or three input parameters specifying one only is obligatory and the rest are optional. The precise relations between the parameters are an important part of the domain expertise. Such as for example under which circumstances the choice of "linear equations" in the mathematical model is desirable, or if "lienar equations" has been chosen, which "technical description" parameters are obligatory and which are optional or forbidden. These correlations are in fact the rules which at the same time both specify the relations between the input parameters and also guide the user in specifying them.

In practice this mechanism works as follows: the individual input parameters are instantiated to "obligatory" or "optional". Their "status" can be changed by rules as the ones illustrated above. Then methods are executed which look at the "status" of the parameter, and decide when a leaf and a node should be considered as completed.

5. THE GRAPHIC COMPONENT

The graphical component of the interface is implemented in X-windows, making use of the same object-oriented model as the knowledge base. The graphical component gives information to the user both on the individual parameters and on the relations between them.
The graphic mechanism for the individual parameters gives information on each individual parameter. As we saw the graphic part is included in the class definition for the tree, the nodes and the leaves, by defining them to be of type "gr-tree", "gr-node" etc. The graphic definitions define how the component in question appears on the screen. In the separate graphic component (the Presentation Engine) there is a graphic tree, similar to the knowledge representation tree.

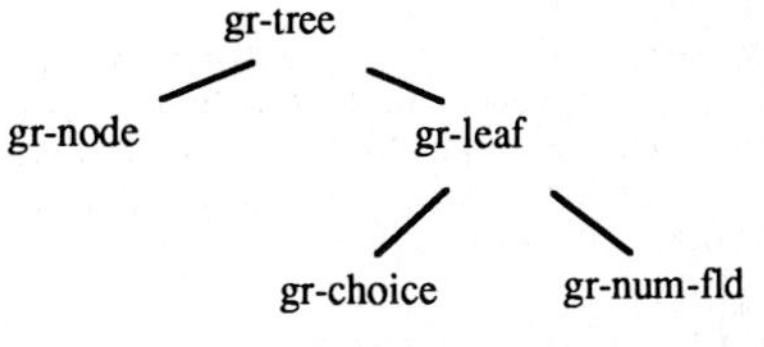

figure 4: the tree representation of the graphic component

There is, however, no complete mapping between this tree and the knowledge representation tree in order to avoid double inheritance, by which for example a leaf would inherit graphic features from tree both via the "tree" class of which it is a child (remeber that "tree" is defined of the type "gr-tree") and directly from "gr-tree" of which it is also a child. Such a double inheritance would cause problems within our present CLOS environment. This is, however, a technical problem which we hope to solve in the final product by using another CLOS environment.
The graphical aspect plays also an important role in the feedback to the user, and contains the rules on how to specify the input parameters.
As mentioned in section 2.1 and 4.2 the user gets information on the "status" and the "source" of each input parameter, both expressed by means of icons in small buttons next to the parameters. Thus there is an icon for expressing the "status" of a parameter: "obligatory", "optional" and "forbidden", and an icon for the "source": "user" and "default". The graphic mechanism provides the user also with support on accomplishing the tasks. For complex tasks there is an icon indicating whether it is

completed or not, i.e. whether all its sub-tasks are completed or not. This icon can indicate "completed", "partially completed" or "not specified at all". For the individual parameters (simple tasks) the icon expresses only "completed" or "not completed". Similarily, if one parameter in a pair of two which are exclusive is specified by the user, the other cannot be selected.

6. CONCLUSIONS

This paper illustrated two points: the first one that adding a user friendly interface to a completed program is possible. Such an interface, which is not integrated in the program is in fact a knowledge-based system on its own. It reproduces the domain knowledge of the application program. Although this means a certain redundancy, it is a practical solution in that it enables leaving the application program unchanged. The second point was illustrating how the task analysis and task model of the interface can be used for the knowledge representation and for the implementation of the graphic aspects. This is possible due to using an object-oriented approach, where the task units, (i.e individual simple tasks), the conceptual units of the domain and the graphical objects could be made to overlap.

This paper described only several aspects of the interface to CHEMSIM. Some other aspects were not described here. These are the help and the support, the consistency checks performed by the rules, the flexibility in performing the tasks and the internal check on the correctness of the user's specifications. Some of these features are still in a phase of completion. Thus for example we hope to further exploit the object-oriented approach in a more complete model of the simulation program's internal structure and use it for generating an intelligent explanation. Such an explanation would be able to tell the user not only how to use CHEMSIM but also why certain actions are possible and others not, that is give a real insight into how the program works. We believe that such an explanation facility is an indispensable feature of a really user friendly interface.

FOOTNOTES

[1]The application program CHEMSIM described here is fictive. The real application program is kept confidential on request of the client. Except for the content of the examples, however, the interface described here is exactly as the real one.

REFERENCES

Baudel, B. , Cantegrit, E. and Toulotte, J.M. (1988). Smalltalk and Simulation of Batch Processes. In

Card, S.T., Moran, T.P. and Newell, A. (1983). The psychology of Human Computer Interaction.

Chignell M. H. and Hancock, P.A. (1988). In M. Helander (ed.) 969-995

Hancock, P.A. and Chignell M.H. (1989). Intelligent Interfaces: Theory, Research and Design, North-

M. Helander (ed.) Handbook of Human Computer Interaction, North-Holland: Amsterdam

Caroll, J.M. (ed.) (1987). Interfacing Thought: Cognitive Aspects of Human-Computer Interaction,

Gillis, S. (1989). User Models: The Long and Short of

Kass, R. and Finin, T. (1988). Modeling the user in natural language systems. In Computational

Keene, S.E. (1988). Object Oriented Programming in Common Lisp. Addison-Wesley Publishing

Kulikowski, C.A., Huber, R.M. and Ferrate G.A. (eds.) (1988). Artificial Intelligence, Expert Systems and Languages in Modelling and

Moran., T.P. (1981). The Command Language Grammar: A Representation for the User Interface of Interactive Computer Systems. In Int. J. Man-

Stephanopolous, G., J. Johnston, T. Kriticos, R. Lakshmanan, M. Mavrovouniotis and C. Siletti (1987). Design-Kit: An Object Oriented

Philips, M.D., Bashinski, H.L., Ammerman, H.L. and Fligg C.M. (1988). A task analytic approach to

Pierret-Golbreich, C. (1988). Object-centered Knowledge Representation for Modelling in

Polson, P.G. (1987) A Quantitative Theory of Human-Computer Interaction. In Caroll (ed)

Human–Computer Interaction – INTERACT '90
D. Diaper et al. (Editors)
Elsevier Science Publishers B.V. (North-Holland)

KNOWLEDGE ACQUISITION AND HYPERTEXT IN MANUFACTURING

S. M. Hajsadr (School of Computer Studies and Mathematics,
A. P. Steward (Sunderland Polytechnic

V. Carroll (Fasson Cramlington Ltd.

Abstract

The particular nature of manufacturing knowledge is proposed and the demands that this nature places on a company are outlined. To respond to this situation many companies have instituted problem solving teams that gather, organise and consolidate worthwhile knowledge. To assist this process in a particular company we have designed two software tools; one is based on an expert system shell and the other on hypertext. These tools are available to machine operators in the company to browse or to contribute to the knowledge. The forms of these tools are described and the advantages of hypertext as being closer to production knowledge is discussed. We finally suggest that the benefits of the rule-based approach can be embedded in hypertext.

1. Introduction

Our experience of building an expert system in a manufacturing domain (Fasson Cramlington Limited) leads us to make the following observations about production know-how.

If we define Total Production Knowledge (TPK) as the complete, existing production and problem solving expertise in a manufacturing domain, then the following statements we believe are true;

* Only a minority of operators are aware of most of the TPK

* The majority of operators know only some of the TPK

Although the final responsibility for quality and production is placed on the production personnel and the product department as a whole, nevertheless some valid production related knowledge exists within other departments such as engineering and process engineering.

Thus we believe that

* Not all TPK resides with operators or even the production department as a whole

The competitiveness in quality and productivity demanded of today's manufacturers means that they have to keep abreast of advances in their sector and continually improve their performance. Thus,

* The TPK needs to be continually updated, improved and enlarged.

Production operators in such a domain accumulate knowledge of certain skills and problem solving actions during their years of experience. The depth and scope of this knowledge varies from one individual to another and is therefore not standard. Thus,

* The TPK is inconsistent

The TPK can be partially consistent. At Fasson the consistent part of the TPK includes standard procedures which are clearly defined steps to deal with well understood problems. However, the TPK also includes problem solving, defined as the actions which may be taken by operators in the belief that they will reduce delays in production. Two types of problem need to be addressed in a manufacturing environment, those that can be dealt with by the operator on the line and those that require a modification of the manufacturing system itself. Both of these types are usually found to be multi-disciplinary in nature and lend themselves to "team" problem solving. These two problem situations are often difficult to distinguish, not well understood, are beyond the control of operators and occur in such situations as machine or material failure. Problem solving knowledge of this scope comprises the inconsistent part of the TPK.

One of the main causes of inconsistency in the TPK is the existence of different criteria for deciding what is the best solution. To some operators the best solution is that which solves the problem quickest while others believe that the best solution is the simplest one.

To sum up we have a TPK which is not possessed by any one person is continually changing and which has included inconsistencies with the potential to harm production. The next section addresses these problems and describes the objectives of acquiring, standardising and optimising production behaviour.

2. The Objectives of a Knowledge Related System

The application of a knowledge-related system was considered at Fasson in order to achieve the following prime objectives;

1. Reduction of set-up-time and hence scrap rates

2. Reduction of problem-solving time and hence scrap rates

Meeting these objectives can be assisted by improving the quality and productivity in a collaborative manner through cyclic stages of standardisation and optimisation of operators production behaviour (Fukuda, 1983). A knowledge-based system can assist through the establishment of a communication channel between the Problem-Solving Teams (PST's) and production personnel.

3. Methods Adopted and Implementation Tools

In order to fulfil the objectives described in the previous section for such a domain, features of which were explained earlier, we suggested a computerised knowledge elicitation/delivery system.

The proposed knowledge-related system should work like a bulletin board, where multiple experts can offer information on how to solve different problems on the production line or carry out a task. On such a bulletin board, one problem can therefore receive many inputs by different production personnel. This variety of ideas are then to be optimized by a problem solving team where the best solutions are decided on and hence delivered to the operators, as standard procedures via the same media.

To build such a channel we employed Xi-plus an ES shell and Hyper Card, a hypermedia development tool.

3.1 Expert System Version

Our first choice as a development tool was an expert system shell. In order to build a communication channel using this software we decided to acquire a general model of production behaviour on which more detailed knowledge could be placed. This model, by which we represented production knowledge, was built during a period of knowledge engineering when various techniques were employed (Hajsadr and Steward 1990).

Figure 1 shows this model to be in the form of a tree diagram, two main branches of which are "problem solving" and "standard procedures" (see Introduction).

The standard procedure side of the model was designed to contain knowledge with 100% certainty so that when the system is prompted with a query, on how a particular task has to be done, it offers a number of very certain steps in a sequence, namely it acts very much like a check list. The exact settings of production parameters such as oven temperature and line speed for a particular product, or the correct steps and the correct order to take these steps to say shut down the production line are examples of the type of information found on this side of the system. The steps taken to deal with a problem, when confirmed by a problem solving team can also be repositioned on the standard procedures side of the system.

The result of our knowledge acquisition on one of the production lines at Fasson was a "problem solving" tree which contained almost all possible problems on that line.

To give the system built upon this design some dynamism, a mechanism was devised using Xi-plus commands whereby the contributor could add new branches to the tree without having to manually add lines of code to the knowledge base.

At the bottom of the "problem solving" tree, attached to a problem name (figure 1), there is the possibility of viewing someone's idea about the solution to that

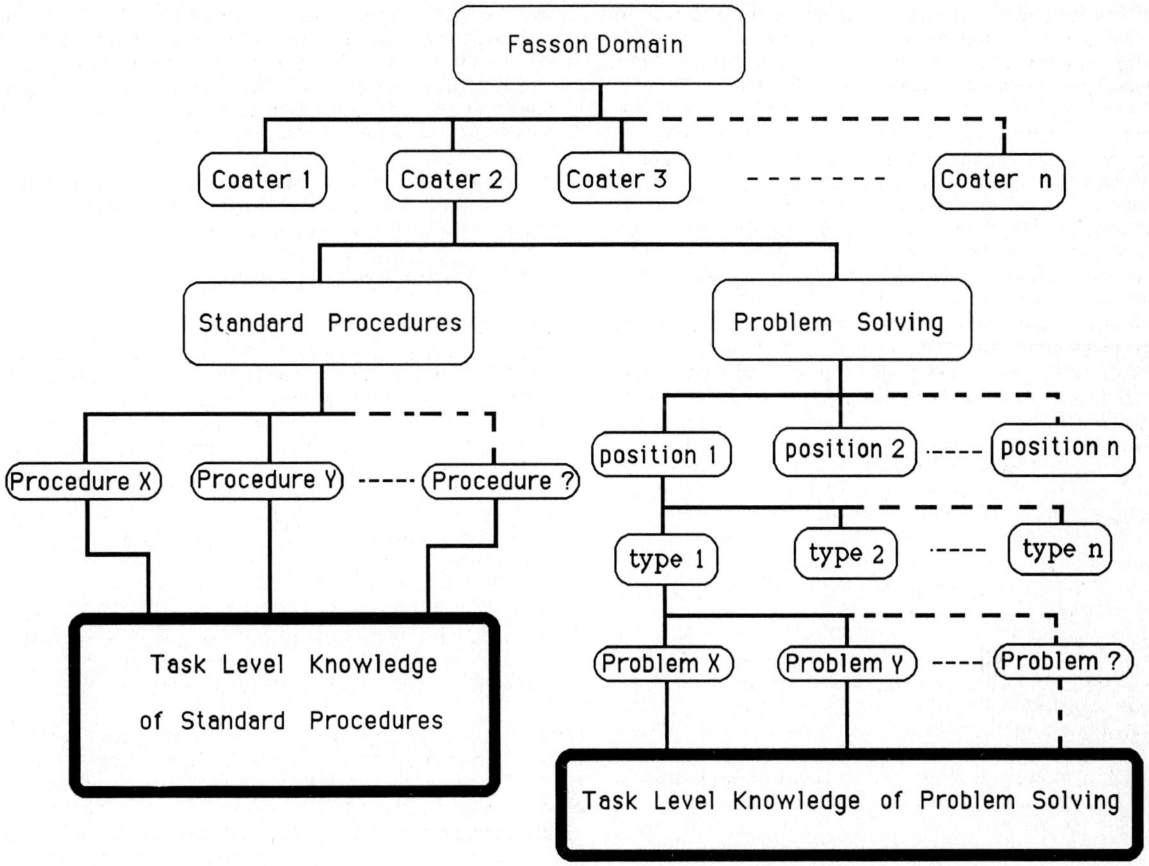

Figure 1 A Tree Model of Total Production Knowledge

problem or enter ideas if none has already been entered. Therefore using these slots, information could either be conveyed to the users or elicited from them.

Figure 2 shows two sample screens of a computerised knowledge elicitation session. They depict the first and the fifth "Cause and Action" (solution alternatives) which the user "d.patton" has offered for the problem identified by the "Index Card".

Although using the simple model shown in Figure 1 enabled us to build a rule-based system which offered some flexibility in the content and size of its knowledge-base, however using an ES shell demands coding knowledge in the form of causal rules. The more complex model which could offer the type of flexibility that we expected of a knowledge elicitation/delivery medium may not be

```
Index Card
Name : d . Patton            Certainty factor :

Problem specifications :
   Section      :- Adhesive Section <Meyer Bar>
   Problem Type :- Build up
   Problem Name :- Adhesive Buildup
Cause & Action 1
Contributor d . Patton      Probability factor 95

Cause  : Edge wipers are set for wrong gum width
Action : You have to re-set edge wipers' spacing.
```

```
Index Card
Name : d . Patton            Certainty factor :

Problem specifications :
  Section      :- Adhesive Section <Meyer Bar>
  Problem Type :- Build up
  Problem Name :- Adhesive Buildup
Cause & Action 1
 Cause & Action 2
  Cause & Action 3
   Cause & Action 4
    Cause & Action 5
    Contributor d . Patton      Probability factor 60

    Cause  : Air leak somewhere on bladder tube
    Action : If air leak spotted then switch off air
    supply (short term) and when convenient call
    fitter.
```

Figure 2 Sample Screens of Computerised Elicitation

representable in a rule form. The expected flexibilities were that, the view of almost all production personnel about a particular production matter could be stored and retrieved through this medium.

These views include, ideas, reasons, comments, votes of confidence, namely all relevant material on which the problem solving team could base their discussions. These views could also include decisions made by problem solving teams, reasons, clear steps to follow, namely material by which the production personnel are informed of the PST's decisions and adjust their production behaviours.

3.2 Hypertext Version

A hypertext system is essentially a Database Management System that allows the connection of screens of information using associative links (Begeman and Conklin, 1988a). In others words it can be a form which represents a network of contributions. As a delivery medium the choice of what a node should contain in this semantic net is decided by the developer who has to make sure all nodes contain logical units of information and nodes are placed in their logical positions on the network according to their context.

The flexibility expected of our knowledge-based system for production knowledge is achieved using Hypercard, a hypertext-type developing tool. (Kitza, 1989). Since you need no domain rules to develop a hypertext system you need no knowledge even that of a model for the domain to initiate the system, and therefore no pre-development knowledge elicitation is necessary. However, we needed a design for the system. This design is shown in Figure 3.

The textual information can be divided into 3 levels referred to as stacks. At the top level, the issue stack contains pages of topics and production matters giving an indication of the related materials in the lower stacks. The issue stack can be automatically enlarged giving this stack a single dimension of flexibility. Figure 4a shows a sample screen of this stack. The link between an issue and the relative stack of ideas is established automatically as soon as a new issue is entered. Through these links the user is guided to the relative stack of ideas. Figure 4b also shows a sample screen from this stack. At each card in the ideas stack there is a possibility of using a cross-level link to see the related votes and comments on a particular idea or a inter-level link to see other ideas on the same issue.

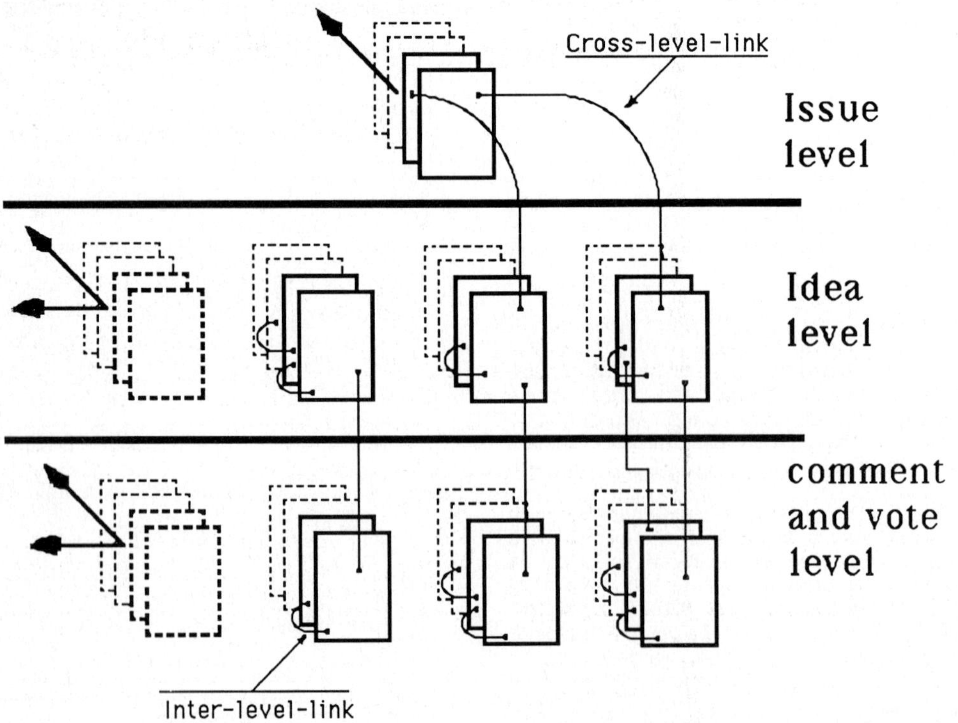

Figure 3 Hypertext Design for TPK

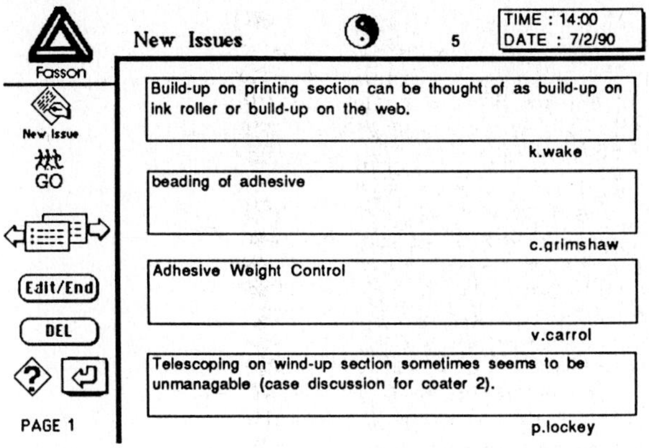

Figure 4a

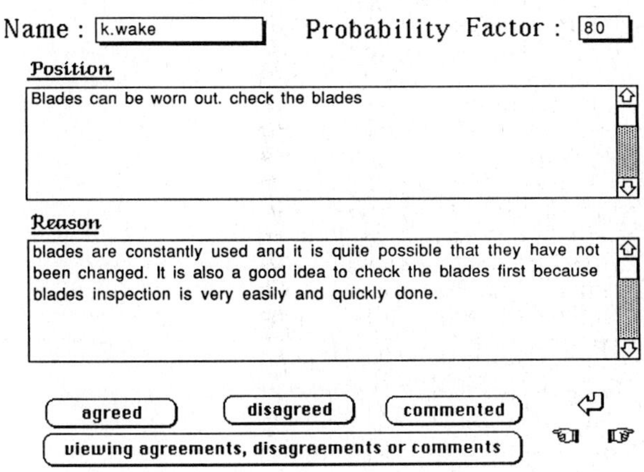

Figure 4b

Figures 4a and 4b
Sample Screens of Issues and Ideas

This stack has two dimensions of flexibility, indicated by the bold arrows in the figure. Either new ideas can be added to the stacks or new stacks on the same level, creation of each will automatically create the necessary links. The bottom level, the vote and comment stack has the same characteristics and dimension of flexibility as that of the ideas stack.

This hypertext form is now being tested as a knowledge elicitation tool for production personnel. Its contents are made available to problem-solving teams whose job is to identify and resolve the inconsistencies which the system uncovers. We intend to develop similar software, based on the same three levels, to deliver production knowledge when this becomes available as a result of the deliberations of problem-solving teams. The work of these teams is particularly valuable in addressing these problems which require input from a range of expertise for their solution; as we have described in the Introduction. Software which reflects the working methods of the PST's is clearly important here, our first model described above is based on the triangular structure of I.B.I.S. (Issue Based Information System, Conklin and Begeman, 1988b). The three elements that form this structure being issue, position and argument.

This looser structure of hypertext contrasts with the more rigid system we have built in the expert system shell. However, we believe that both have their role in representing the TPK and more generally that the benefits of both approaches can be brought together (Rada and Barlow, 1988).

4. Conclusions

We have described the special nature of manufacturing knowledge as we have found it in one particular company. The features that it exhibits are that it is multi-disciplinary, dynamic and inconsistent. To respond to these features requires problem solving teams that provide the breadth of expertise necessary to solve many problems and the opportunity to reduce the inconsistencies. To perform the knowledge elicitation task for these teams we have provided two software tools; an expert system shell and a hypertext structure. The shell was found to be restricting in that knowledge had to be entered as a consistent set of rules which was not appropriate for all contributions. A more suitable tool which can accommodate the inconsistencies of production knowledge is a hypertext version and we have outlined its current simple form. However, in adopting this approach we feel that the benefits of a rule-based approach can be retained within hypertext, particularly when standard procedures achieve general agreement in the company.

Acknowledgements

We thank Fasson Cramlington Limited for permission to publish this paper and its employees for their assistance.

References

Conklin, J. and Begeman, M. L. (a) "The Right Tool for the Right Job", BYTE, October 1988.

Conklin, J. and Begeman, M. L. (b) "gIBIS : A Hypertext Tool for Exploratory Policy Discussion". Proc. Conf. on Computer Supported Cooperative Work, Portland, Oregon, September 1988.

Fukuda, R. "Managerial` Engineering, Techniques for Improving Quality and Productivity in the Workplace", Productivity Press, 1983.

Hajsadr, M. and Steward, A. P. "An Approach to Knowledge Elicitation of Manufacturing Skills and Production Behaviour in an Industrial Environment", to be presented at UKIT 90 Southampton, March 1990.

Kitza, W. "Inside Hypercard II". Addison-Wesley Publishing Co., 1989.

Rada, R. and Barlow, J. "Expert Systems and Hypertext". The Knowledge Engineering Review, 3, No. 4, pp285-301, 1988.

Human–Computer Interaction – INTERACT '90
D. Diaper et al. (Editors)
Elsevier Science Publishers B.V. (North-Holland)

KNOWLEDGE BASED USER INTERFACES FOR SCIENTIFIC PROGRAMS.

Henk J. van Zuylen, Herman Gerritsen
Delft Hydraulics, POB 177, 2600 MH Delft, The Netherlands

SUMMARY

In a pilot study, a knowledge based support system has been developed for a scientific computer program. Some interesting phenomena have been observed during this process. The need for a non-linear development process could be shown. The development of a knowledge based support system for this complicated application program resulted in a specification of a system that could be considered as a user interface. The approach to use knowledge elicitation to get a user interface design showed to have some useful possibilities.

1. INTRODUCTION.

1.1 Knowledge based support of computer programs

Some computer programs are difficult to use. In a feasibility study, a knowledge based support system has been developed for the program GETIJSYS for the analysis of a tidal time series. The system started as a knowledge based system, but the support system that was implemented, finally got the character of an extended user interface. The specific features of knowledge based system, such as a separate knowledge base, an inference mechanism and explanation facilities, played only a minor role.
Although the development method used is intended for knowledge based systems, the method appears to be very well suited for the development of the extended user interface for this case.

An interesting result of the knowledge elicitation phase was, that the expert responsible for the computer program became more conscious of the decision process of the program user and found alternative ways to reduce the skill and knowledge necessary to use the program. These solutions were outside the scope of user interfaces and knowledge based systems.
This resulted in a different way of working with the program. In the end the support system had to be adapted to the modified task. Other knowledge had to be applied in the system and the knowledge used originally, appeared to be obsolete.

1.2 Numerical programs.

Numerical calculations have been one of the first applications of computers. Since the early days of digital computers many programs have been written to calculate the solution of numerical problems. Many of these problems are related to physics.
The long tradition in computational physics has resulted in a vast amount of computer programs, often designed by mathematicians and physicists, and meant to be used by mathematicians and physicists.
At present many of those programs have proved their value and have become a valuable production means of researchers and consultants.

The spread of the use of these programs, however, has not always been accompanied by an adaption of the functionality of the programs. While the original programs were intended for specialists who knew much about the domain for which the programs have been developed, the physical and mathematical theory underlying the program and the technical solutions used in the programs, nowadays the users have less knowledge about these subjects and like to use the programs as tools to support the real task: the solution of a physical problem. The main part of their task is now often the preparation of the input and the use of the program, which prevents them from concentrating on the real problem.
Most programs in the described category have a large utility but a low usability: the user needs to know much about technical details of the program, which have little to do with the underlying physical problem.

1.3 GETIJSYS.

At Delft Hydraulics many programs are developed to study the physical properties of water flows. One of them is the program GETIJSYS, which builds a mathematical model of the tide. It uses a time series of measured water levels, to calibrate a mathematical model. The preparation of input data, the use of the program and the interpretation of the output required much knowledge of the user. In order to improve the possibilities to have the programs used by a larger group of experts, an attempt has been made to support the use of the program with a knowledge based system.

The development of the supporting knowledge based system for GETIJSYS has started with knowledge elicitation according to the KADS method (Wielinga et al. 1988). A model for the inference structure for the GETIJSYS program has been made by Jonathan Killin, who reports this in the book of Hickman et al. (1989). After the development of a conceptual model and the description of a task model, a prototype has been implemented. During the project it became more and more clear, that the main task in the development of the knowledge based system became focused on the development of a good user interface.

2. THE USE OF GETIJSYS.

The program GETIJSYS tries to fit a formula of a form like

$$H(t) = A_0 + \Sigma_j A_j \sin(\Omega_j t + \Phi_j) \qquad (1)$$

where H(t) is the calculated water level as a function of the time t the sum over j is a sum over frequencies Ω_j occurring in the tidal waves. The variables A_0, A_j and Φ_j have to be estimated from observed values of H(t).

The possible values for the frequency come from astrophysical theory. More than 200 hundred possible tidal frequencies of tidal components have been determined. Tidal analysis with GETIJSYS is the determination of the minimum set of tidal frequencies with which the tidal wave part of the series can be described (formula 1). This is called the mathematial model for the series at that specific location. The next step is the estimation of the values of A_0, A_j and Φ_j, e.g. via least squares analysis. So the user first has to make a selection of components which can be possibly used in the mathematical model. For the frequencies in the resulting model, the parameters A and Φ are estimated by the program. The result of this estimation and the deviation of the calculated water level from the observations give further information to the user, with which he may improve the model.

To do so, the user needed to have knowledge about a variety of subjects. For instance:

- the mathematics of parameter fitting,
- the theory of geometrical series,
- the numerical techniques used in the program,
- the format and sequence of the input data,
- Fourier analysis,
- the quality of the measured input data,
- the possible frequencies,
- physics of tidal flow,
- geography.

It is not our purpose to give an exhaustive treatment of this knowledge in this paper, but to focus of the concept of the support system which contains a part of this knowledge.

3. THE USER TASK.

The main features of the user task are given in figure 1.

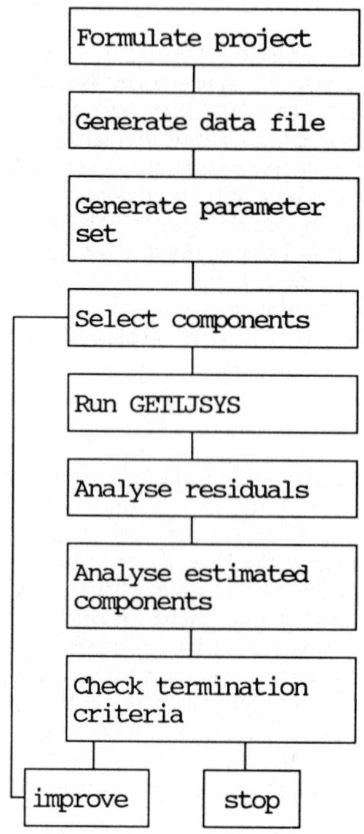

figure 1
User task for GETIJSYS.

The user starts with a project definition. Given a set of observed data (time series of water levels at regular time intervals) he has to quality control the data, remove invalid data, trace unlikely data, verify the possible local circumstances (storm, heavy rain fall). From this analysis of the data set he determines some parameters which describe the data quality.
His next action is to prepare the first analysis. This implies the choice of the first set of components in the tidal model (formula 1). There are some constraints to this choice. Frequencies which are too high or too low should not be used in the formula, since no reliable estimation of the corresponding parameters can be given. Also, components with frequencies which are close together can not be resolved independently, and can therefore not be used simultaneously in the tidal model (formula 1). If two components are too close together, they should be combined or one of them should be eliminated from the model.

After a first analysis with GETIJSYS, the resulting model is used for an estimation of the tidal part and the calculation of the residual, i.e. the difference between the estimated and the observed water level. A further analysis of this residual is used to get an indication which components should be added to the tidal model. This is done by making a transformation of the residual to a frequency spectrum (Fourier analysis). Peaks in this spectrum which correspond to the frequency of a component indicate that this component should be included in the next estimate of the tidal model.

The model is further refined by the elimination of components which appear to have a contribution to the tidal model (formula 1) which is too unreliable. These components follow from the output of GETIJSYS. The amplitudes A_j are estimated by the program, together with a measure of the accuracy, i.e. the range within which the amplitude with some certainty will be. If the range is large compared to the value of the amplitude, the estimation is unreliable. The user has to consider the elimination of such components from the model.

4. THE KNOWLEDGE BASE.

The rules for the selection of new components and the elimination of chosen components are rather simple and could be formulated in a very small knowledge base. A part of the knowledge identified concerns the decision whether the model is sufficiently well determined or whether more iterations are needed. This knowledge is related to the objective of the model. A model which has to be used to estimate the tide near a harbour for submarines or for the design of offshore platforms should be more accurate than a model used to estimate the tide for use in a sailing contest.
The structure of the knowledge, as described by Killin is given in fig. 2.
The boxes represent knowledge of some kind. The ellipses mean transformations of the knowledge to derive other knowledge. The ellipses are called the knowledge sources. Examples of such transformations are abstraction (removing details from the knowledge), specification (adding details), comparison (pattern matching), selection, etc.

There is some similarity between the inference structure and the task structure. This is not completely accidental: each activity of the task requires knowledge and the knowledge needed for a subsequent activity can be derived partially from the knowledge of the previous activity. However, it can not be concluded, that in general the task structure and the inference structure are similar or even identical.

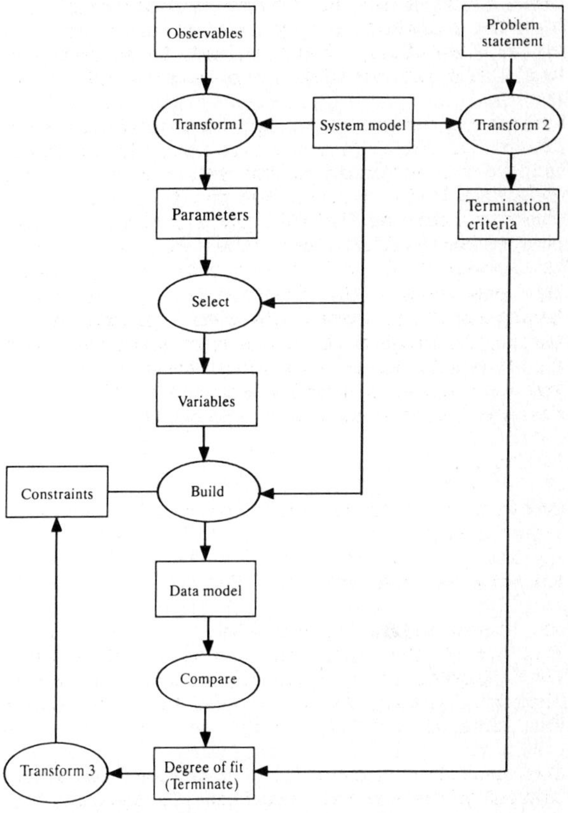

fig. 2 The inference structure of the knowledge involved in the use of GETIJSYS.

5. THE IMPLEMENTATION OF THE SUPPORT SYSTEM.

Expert systems without a good user interface are useless, how ingenious they may be (Hendler 1988). A knowledge based system in which the user has to enter data, which he has already entered earlier for a different purpose or which are calculated by another program, is unacceptable. In the case of GETIJSYS the need for interfaces was clear: the support system should have access to the input and output of GETIJSYS, apart from access to its own knowledge base.

The support system for GETIJSYS has been implemented as an extended user interface, including an input processor and output analyser. There was no need for a complicated inference mechanism to derive conclusions from a rule and fact base. The problem to be solved was more to give the support system access to the facts (i.e. the program input and output) and to present the user with the right amount of information necessary to take the right decisions. E.g. the support system should have access to the output file, analyze the data, extract evidence for conclusions and present the user with the evidence in such a way, that he can interpret the information easily and draw his conclusions. The residual had to be presented graphically instead of numerically, with the possible components to be included as a choice indicated on the graph so, that the user task to choose new components is much reduced by the fact that the support system prepares all necessary information needed for the choice and presents it in a comprehensive way. The presentation of the information got most attention in the implementation, the application of knowledge could be included largely implicitly in the functionality of the user interface.

The same applied to the analysis of the estimates in the output. Instead of presenting the whole output of GETIJSYS to the user, the support system analyses the output, interprets it, applies the rules as formulated and presents to the user only the information necessary to take a decision.

The preparation of the input could also be supported by a system which can be considered as a fairly conventional user interface with a small application coupled to it, i.e. to check the validity and consistency of the parameters, calculate appropriate defaults and give advise how to proceed.

The implementation of the knowledge could largely be done in a procedural form and as a context sensitive help system. As a result the knowledge elicitation has been an efficient technique to obtain a good functional specification of a new user interface and new requirements for GETIJSYS itself.

6. CONCLUSIONS ABOUT KNOWLEDGE ELICITATION.

In order to obtain the knowledge and determine the structure, several interviews were held, mostly on practical cases, in order to find out what knowledge the expert uses when he makes a calculation with GETIJSYS. The task structure (fig. 1) was not surprising and also the structure of the knowledge (fig. 2) did not reveal much new information: the expert was aware that the program was used in this way and that the knowledge elicitated by the knowledge engineer, was required in order to use the program correctly. In fact, the objective of the knowledge engineer was mainly to discover how the expert built a model of the physical phenomenon. In retrospect, the information was especially valuable for the knowledge engineer, who wanted to structure the knowledge involved in this process. On the other hand, the expert became conscious of possibilities for improvement in the use of the program, by the process of explaining it to someone who was a layman in the domain of his expertise.

The interviews were therefore very valuable to make the expert aware of the user problems which were due partly to a primitive user interface, partly to the functionality of the program and partly inherent to the domain of the analysis of tidal time series.

While the support system was implemented, the GETIJSYS program itself was also modified to improve its usability.

A conclusion from this experience is that knowledge elicitation is very useful to become aware of certain problems in the use of a program and to find solutions. The knowledge gained can be used in the support system as well as in the functionality of the program itself. If it is implemented in a support system, it is not necessary that the implementation is done with techniques for knowledge based systems. Much knowledge needed for the use of a program can be applied in the structuring of the user interface, the presentation of input and output data or the calculation of defaults for the input data.

7. IMPACT OF THE SUPPORT SYSTEM.

By the fact that the support system made certain activities more simple, the use of the program changed. Originally the user tried to keep the number of iterations small by starting with a first estimate which was "as good as possible". With the iteration, decision and preparation process much better supported, the importance of the first estimate decreased. This had an impact again on the requirements for the user interface.

The original choice of the components for the tidal model was based on the geographical situation and on tidal theory. Some components are always important in the tidal wave model, independent on the location on earth. Other components are only important in some places and those components are difficult to choose in advance. More difficult to estimate is the influence of the distance to the coast and the question whether the measurements have been done in open sea or in a harbour or upstream a river.

Known tidal representation models for reference locations in the same area (often harbours) are looked up in tables and the main components can be used in an initial tidal model, but often the local situation is different from the reference location. The expert adds more components, which can be considered as combinations of the primary components. The selection of those components is based on his experience. The same applies to the choice of the location where he draws the choice of the main components from.

Since iterations are now easier to make, the choice of the initial tidal model is less important. In most cases a reasonable guess is sufficient, which means that only the main components of locations in the environment are taken into account. The selection of additional components, i.e the improvement of the tidal model, is done after the first run.

Originally the components which could be selected were seen in a geographical context. The structure is given in fig. 3.

Details of the meaning of this structure are not relevant for this paper and can be found in Gerritsen (1989).

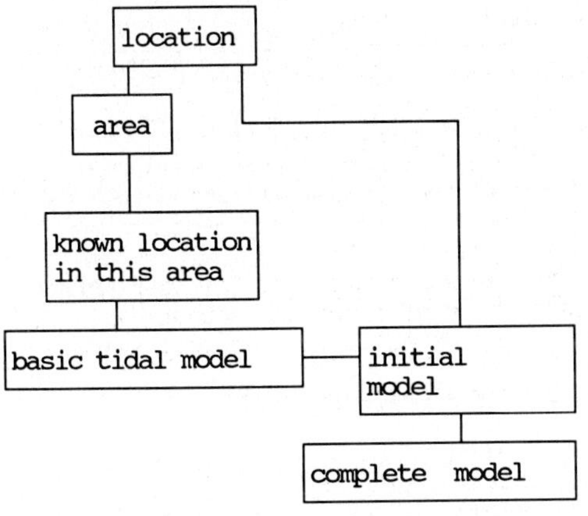

fig. 3 Logical structure of the initial component set

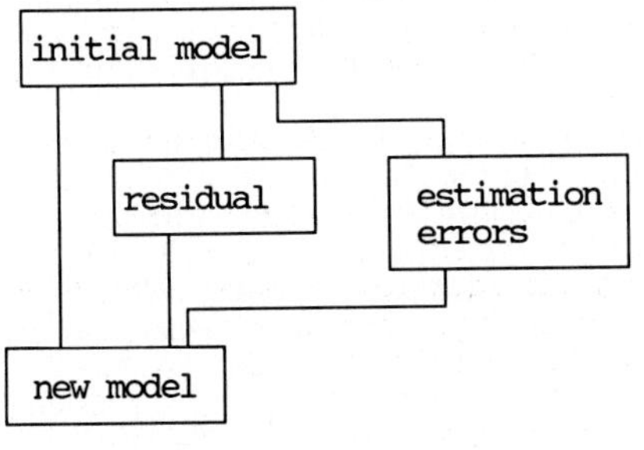

fig. 4 Logical structure of the model after the introduction of the support system.

The initial model or component set is copied right away from the basic model in a location in the neighbourhood, after which a first run an be made. From the analysis of the residual new components can be selected.

In the new situation the initial model is less important. The emphasis is now on the detection of new components from the analysis of the residual and the elimination of unreliable components.

As a result, the presentation of the components to the user had to be changed. The first entry in the selection should be the location on earth. Depending on the location and the duration of the series, there are a few initial models to choose from. Further components are selected after the analysis with GETIJSYS. This structure is different from the original structure, which was based on a more analytic approach based on detailed knowledge of the local situation.

The conclusion of this experience is, that a linear development of the support system, starting with an analysis, followed by a specification, a design and the implementation, is not sufficient. Feedback from all phases is necessary and, as will be shown in the next section, is essential for all systems which will create a new situation. An iterative approach can not be replaced by a very elaborated task, knowledge or requirements study. The behaviour of the users and their intentions change by the fact that a new situation arises after the creation of the system, which makes certain functions obsolete, other inappropriate and requires new functionality.

8. THE STRUCTURE OF THE DEVELOPMENT PROCESS.

The development of a system which is an adequate tool for a task, starts with the analysis and the determination of the requirements. The system developer gathers information from the user (either the real end user of the system but often a representative of the end user, who is responsible for the system to be built). The system has to be used for a task to be done by a user in his work environment. The assumption which is normally made implicitly, is that the requirements of the new system are independent of this system, that the users are independent of the system developer, that the environment is independent of the users. In reality all these components are interacting and form a coherent system.

The requirements for the new system have their meaning in the context of the users, their task and their environment and the developer. The formulated requirements are not passive: they have their influence on the users. Due to the analysis of the needs and the situation of the users, they make the users aware of their problems and possible solutions. This changes their situation and needs.

When the developer asks his questions, he is a part of the user system (the word user system will be used for the system consisting of the user, his tasks, tools and environment): he is not only gathering information from the user, he influences the user by his questions, his ideas and as soon as a prototype is available, also by the new computer system (Winograd 1986).

What happens in this interaction is unpredictable. Even the most profound analysis of the user requirements can not reveal what the user will really need when he can use the new system, unless the user has no freedom to change. The same applies to the environment and the task: they may change in an unpredictable way when the new system is introduced. The unpredictability of the behaviour of the user system can be understood, when one realises that the whole system is in fact a chaotic system (Prigogine 1984) with interactions between all components. Even when the interaction is completely known, the way the system evolves is practically unpredictable.

Prototyping and iterative development are a way to live with the unpredictability of the requirements. By providing the user with prototypes during the definition of the system, the user will integrate the new system in his world, extend his mental model of the reality and discover new possibilities and problems. A prototype is an excellent way to transfer ideas to the (future) users and to stimulate them to use their creativity and express their needs in terms of a new medium: the functionality of the prototype system.

However, prototyping in itself is no general cure for the problem to capture requirements. If the first prototype is far from the system that is really needed, it may confuse the user, invoke requirements which are not very relevant and may hide other requirements. In fact the prototype offers some kind of language to reason about the new system and to express the requirements. If this language does not have the right elements and structure, it is unsuited to be a proper vehicle to carry the development process. Therefore a first exhaustive requirements analysis is also needed when prototyping is applied. Only if the first prototype already incorporates the essential features of the system, the iterations can converge to a system which solves the real problem and satisfies the needs of the users.

ACKNOWLEDGEMENTS.

The authors wish to thank Jonathan Killin for his work on the knowledge elicitation and for his permission to use his results and also the many people who contributed to the implementation of the first prototype.

REFERENCES

Gerritsen, H. (1989). GETIJSYS, Analysis and Prediction of Tides. Delft Hydraulics report Z385.

Hendler, J.A. (1988). Expert Systems: The User Interface. Ablex Publishing Corp. Norwood N.J.

Hickman, F.R., J.L.Killin, L.Land, T.Mulhall, D.Porter and R.M.Taylor (1989). Analysis for Knowledge-based Systems, a pratical guide to the KADS methodology. Ellis Horwood Ltd Chichester.

Prigogine, I., I.Stengers (1984). Order out of Chaos. Bantam Books Toronto.

Wielinga, B.J., B.Bredeweg, J.A.Breuker (1988). Knowledge Acquisition for Expert Systems. ACAI-88.

Winograd, T., F.Flores (1986). Understanding Computers and Cognition. Ablex Publishing Corp. Norwood N.J.

SECTION V: APPLICATIONS AND CASE STUDIES

SV.2 Computer Supported Co-operative Work

Concurrent editing: the group's interface
J.S. Olson, G.M. Olson, L.A. Mack, and P. Wellner 835

Characteristics of well-designed electronic communications systems
P.A. Holleran and R.W. Haller 841

Process modelling and CSCW: An application of IPSE technology to medical office work
J. Maresh and D. Wastell 849

Tools that support human–human communication in the automated office
I.D. Benest and D. Dukić 853

Human–Computer Interaction - INTERACT '90
D. Diaper et al. (Editors)
Elsevier Science Publishers B.V. (North-Holland)

CONCURRENT EDITING: THE GROUP'S INTERFACE

Judith S. Olson
Gary M. Olson
The University of Michigan
Ann Arbor, MI USA

Lisbeth A. Mack
Andersen Consulting,
Chicago, IL USA

Pierre Wellner
Rank Xerox EuroPARC,
Cambridge, UK

We review aspects of systems built for group work that allow real-time, concurrent editing of a single work object. Existing systems vary in both what group functions they offer users (e.g., whether simultaneous editing is possible or it must proceed one by one) and how these functions appear in the user interface (e.g. what signals are given to the user that the window is public or private). Design alternatives suggested by existing systems are analyzed in terms of their value for various phases of group work and their support for individuals' needs in coordinating their work.

1. INTRODUCTION

One important class of software function that is emerging in the area of computer supported cooperative work (CSCW) is what one might call a **group editor**, which allows the members of a group to have synchronous access to a single information object. Members can see all changes to the object, and may be able to edit it. Concurrent access is over a network. The editors can be used to assist interactions that are either face-to-face or remote. This contrasts with systems that give the members of a group asynchronous access to a single object, such as document authoring tools that coordinate comments and changes from a number of readers. It also contrasts with a system consisting of one machine whose display is projected onto a publicly viewable screen, run by a scribe or facilitator.

A number of systems have been built to explore this group editing function. There are two broad classes of such systems. In one class, the group editing function allows true concurrent access by all participants. Examples include MCC's GROVE (Ellis, Gibbs, & Rein, 1988) and Michigan's ShrEdit (CSMIL, 1989). In a second class of systems, a single-user editor is "groupified" through one of several mechanisms. Timbuktu on the Macintosh (Farallon, 1987) and shared windowing systems on Unix machines (Gust, 1988; Lantz, 1988; Lauwers & Lantz, 1990) achieve this by creating shared access to a single machine's application. In the Capture Lab (Mantei, 1988; Elwart-Keys, Halonen, Horton, Kass, & Scott, 1990), a similar function was achieved by means of a series of individual machines networked with a group machine that one member of the group controls at a time. Systems of the second type allow one person to edit at any given moment, though rapid shifts of control may be possible.

In either class, potentially any kind of object could be presented to the group for editing: text, outlines, images, spreadsheets, drawings, hypertext systems, etc. There are likely to be object-specific issues about how to implement a group editor, affecting both the functions and the interface But in this paper we focus on the issues that cut across the specifics of the information objects.

We could evaluate these functions by the sets that are possible given a certain system architecture. For example, choosing the Timbuktu or shared windowing scheme can limit the kind of access one could have to the work object. But in this paper we come at these issues the other way around. We focus on the functions themselves, the conditions under which they might be useful, and the interface issues in providing such functions to users. This should guide the choice of features as new architectural possibilities emerge.

2. CHARACTERISTICS OF GROUP EDITORS

Our analysis of the group functions and interfaces for group editors was motivated by an in-depth review of ten existing systems. But our goal here is not to evaluate or comment on these systems. Rather, we aim to highlight general issues pertaining to the interfaces, illustrating our discussion with examples from specific systems. We first review some general features that such systems can provide, then discuss a series of design issues that arise as implementation of these features is considered. Since none of the systems we review implements all of these features, the overall set of features can be thought of as an attempt to define the design space of interface characteristics for group editors.

2.1 Single object.

One of the criterial features of a group editor is that it makes available to the group a single work object that is the focus of whatever their collaborations are about. There must be a common referent on which each participant can work, either in reading its contents or making changes to it via the edit functions provided.

This singleness is often achieved through a range of complex architectures which use various mechanisms to maintain an illusion of a single work object. One way to implement group editors is to have replicated copies of the work object, and to maintain the illusion of singleness through rapid, coordinated updates to the copies of each of the participants (cf. Lauwers & Lantz, 1990). But even an architecture with a single object could have trouble keeping up the impression of a common object if there are transmission delays.

2.2 Single or multiple entry points.

Some group editors allow users to edit the object simultaneously. These systems include ShrEdit, Shared ARK (Smith, O'Shea, O'Malley, Scanlon, & Taylor, 1989), Cognoter (Stefik, Foster, Bobrow, Kahn, Lanning, & Suchman, 1987; Foster & Stefik, 1986), and Grove. Other group editors provide serial access to the workspace, as if the keyboards and mice were connected octopus style to one machine. Timbuktu, rIBIS (Rein, 1989), and the shared screen in Capture Lab have this style. Other group editors share not a whole screen but a window: shared windows, Rapport (Ahuja, Ensor, Horn, & Lucco, 1988), and MMConf (Crowley & Forsdick, 1989).

2.3 Support for turn taking.

Single entry systems allow only one person at a time to enter commands or material. Some systems (e.g., Timbuktu) take inputs on a first come first served priority. Others (Capture Lab and Rapport) require each person to indicate by pressing a button that they want "the floor". Rapport further requires the floor to be relinquished by someone before another can take it. This explicit control keeps people from producing jumbles of actions from overlapping keystrokes or simultaneous mouse movements. The other freer systems avoid jumbles by social control, asking and giving permission verbally. The Capture Lab has explored various system-based turn-taking schemes (Mantei, 1988), and Lauwers & Lantz (1990) discussed a variety of schemes for shared window systems.

2.4 Mix of public and private work.

All group editors have at the core a mode of access that is fully public and shareable. But many group editors have explored a variety of different mechanisms for mixing public and private work. Total privacy is achieved when some aspect of the work is available only to one person. MCC's Grove system also allows intermediate forms of permission for subgroups.

The principal kinds of private material are:

1) *Private views,* such that an individual can scroll to view any part of the object on their own. Grove additionally allows sections of its outline format to be opened and closed by individuals separately. This kind of privacy differs from those below in that the object is not changed or transformed in any way, just looked at from a different vantage.

2) *Private transformed views*, which are qualitatively different formats for displaying the information object. For instance, an outline could be viewed as a standard textual outline, a hierarchical tree, or bullet charts by different individuals. We know of no actual systems that have implemented this.

3) *Private workspaces* which are totally unconnected with the shared workspace, such as a separate window or, in the case of the Capture Lab, a separate machine with a shared clipboard. In these it is possible to copy material between the two. Many group editors provide this for free, in that they are embedded in multiprocessing or multitasking environments that give the user other windows than the one that houses the group editor.

4) *Private objects attached* to the shared object. Grove allows users to link private objects such as notes or initial ideas for possible inclusion directly into the public object. Later, this private material can be made public by changing its permissions.

3. DESIGN ISSUES RAISED BY GROUP FEATURES

The availability of the various group features described in the previous section raises a number of design issues.

In general, the designers of group editors envisioned users having additional communication channels available, such as face-to-face interactions, voice connections through telephone, or audio/visual connections via television. One very general design question is the extent to which features required to support the group use of such editors should be provided as an aspect of the editor itself, versus being left to social control among the participants via one of these other channels.

3.1 Individual identities of group members.

Who are the participants in a group editing session? If the editor is being used in a face-to-face session, this information can be provided in part from natural visual or verbal channels. But even then, it is often useful to know who is currently logged into the session. This information is provided in a variety of ways in existing systems: names or icons always visible on the screen, names in menus or dialog boxes.

3.2 Identity and location of current editing operations.

For systems with single editing points, such as Timbuktu or shared window systems, one can tell that editing is going on but has only extra-system information about who is doing it. In systems like Grove or Shredit that allow concurrent editing, the editing locations of individuals are not even shown, let alone the identity of the person at that location. Shared ARK identifies who is making a change because each cursor (a hand) has the owner's name on the cuff. It also allows users to "zoom out" to see the whole object and where each participant is.

3.3 Updating and synchronization.

With multiple insertion points and parallel editing, there can be both a chance for delays and divergence between views, and a lot of potentially disruptive change occurring in an individual's view of the work object. Some systems update after each small change (e.g., letter by letter), while others like Cognoter update only at the completion of a whole unit entry, such as the end of a word title or a text paragraph.

3.4 Conflict resolution.

Systems differ in the manner in which conflicts are eliminated, minimized, or resolved. All systems require some degree of social control, especially since they are weak on showing who is doing what. Thus, each person would be given a sense as to where the others are working, whether it be in a distant but related or unrelated part, or nearby.

Other systems offer no such view, but rather lock out a user from an area that another is working in. Cognoter, for example, will gray out an item that someone else is currently working on. Both Grove and ShrEdit minimize the lockout, by resolving conflicts centrally (e.g., first come first served). ShrEdit has locking of the insertion point. This means another user cannot backspace or sweep/select over another's insertion point. To minimize unnecessary conflicts, users who are not editing can "park" their insertion point so they stay out of the way of others. Unfortunately, in both Grove and ShrEdit, the user has no visual signal as to where someone is working before they try to do something, and are beeped only after they have tried something that is disallowed. Though in both those systems the results of edits and entries are visible after they are made, there is no warning of where someone is *about* to do something.

3.5 View convergence.

Systems allowing any degree of private control over views of the shared object make it very likely that individuals will diverge. The troubles caused by such divergence can in part be forestalled by following a more or less strict WYSIWIS principle -- what you see is what I see (Stefik, Bobrow, Foster, Lanning, & Tatar, 1987). Xerox PARC's C-noter (Tatar, 1989) resorted to strict WYSIWIS after negative, confusing experience with the relaxed WYSIWIS of its predecessor, Cognoter.

3.6 Telepointers.

Even when individuals' views are totally aligned, it can be useful to have some means of directing the attention of group members to some particular location within the display. In a system like Timbuktu, the single visible cursor serves as a pointer to aid conversation. rIBIS has a telepointer that can be controlled by one individual at a time. It has to be explicitly returned to a neutral spot before another person can take control of it, making the pass-off very explicit and controlled. A variety of telepointer ideas have been considered within shared windowing systems (Lauwers & Lantz, 1990).

4. HOW DOES ONE DECIDE UPON FEATURES?

Assessing the value of these features is important to design, since each impacts the architecture, the performance, and, of course, cost. The benefits to group work must be compared to the costs in terms of implementation, performance, and training. For example, it may be hard to coordinate simultaneous inputs while keeping system response time down. The question naturally arises, "Do you *really* need immediate update of all group members' inputs?" Only with an argument about the **value** to the participants can these tradeoff questions be answered.

Following the principles of user centered design, we believe that systems should be designed to fit users' work, needs and capabilities (Norman & Draper, 1986; Olson & Olson, 1990). We have found it helpful to evaluate design alternatives in relation to the major activities in collaborative problem solving and in consideration of what capabilities they have to process the personal and group generated information.

4.1 Individual and group information processing.

We know that people who participate in groups come with a cognitive architecture that has some very well known characteristics. Perception is excellent, short-term memory is severely limited, recall from long-term memory is flexible and rich but slow and inaccurate, and learning is powerful but similarly very slow.

In group situations, however, other aspects of individuals' architecture loom large. Group work differs fundamentally from individual work in the **pacing** of the interaction, both in the order in which each participates and the simultaneity of their contributions. There is also the critical role of **communication** that helps them acquire a shared understanding. One must capture others' attention, present ideas in an appropriate representations, and present at a pace that fosters learning. In our observations, we have seen major pitfalls in group work when individuals cannot learn quickly enough, when their attention wanders as the pace moves too slowly, and when members have constructed mental representations and external notes that differ in disastrous ways. Thus, individuals engaged in group work are driven not only by their own thinking processes but by the demands of interacting with others. Ideas often come from the members of a group in an unstructured associative stream. The pacing of group work, especially the communication activities, often conflicts with the pacing of individual cognition.

4.2 Group work as shared problem solving.

We see group work as consisting of various amounts of time spent in 1) stating the goal, 2) ideating potential solutions, 2) structuring the sets of ideas, 4) evaluating the ideas, 5) selecting an idea, and 6) carrying out the solution or detailing further the issue just decided upon. Different kinds of groups and different kinds of tasks require more time on some of these activities than on others.

Each of these activities requires different levels of focused communication versus information gathering that could be performed simultaneously. Stating and understanding the goal requires the group to focus until everyone has a shared view. In ideating, however, we might want individuals to generate their own ideas rapidly.

4.3 Analysis of features of group editors from this view.

Some of the alternative features of group editors can be evaluated on the basis of this analysis of people's tasks and their capabilities. For those activities that require a common focus of attention such as stating the goal or selecting a solution, a **common public view** would help, and focused discussion follows the group members **one-at-a-time**. Deliberate baton passing control serves well to support focused discussion.

For those stages, such as brainstorming and evaluating, that benefit from quick associations from the group members, a system that allows **simultaneous work,** either on the **public screen or in private work areas**, would be of value. Simultaneous entry can be distracting if not used with conscious control over the timing of the display. Although the public addition of an idea or thought might be advantageous to the individual who just thought of it (capturing it before it is forgotten), having this entry be publicly viewed is potentially disruptive. A private annotation might be better.

Although uncontrolled simultaneous entry is potentially disruptive to focused work, it could serve as the basis for a new way to work. Brainstorming itself is known to trigger ideas, but in the group setting people wait for a turn to report their ideas. The number of ideas generated in a group is usually below the sum of the ideas generated individually. Perhaps simultaneous entry could support *silent* brainstorming, where people could both freely associate and enter ideas without waiting for the social slot in which to say them. Or it could allow breakout sessions without people having to change locations, where people work on different parts of the object and then report to each other their changes, allowing coordination of ideas without delay.

Furthermore, having private workspaces can support another new kind of group work. Structuring is difficult work, in our experience, and normally the group adjourns to have time to think. What we really need in this phase is the absence of distraction. Having individual work areas available in this setting would allow an "in-room" breakout session.

What is needed *after* that period of quiet work, however, is a new feature that seems not to exist explicitly in any of these group editing systems. This would be the ability to take the individuals' thoughts from this breakout session and share them simultaneously side-by-side. It helps others to see various individuals' inputs simultaneously, so that patterns can be detected and new integrations seen. Furthermore, a new shared space is needed in which key ideas from each individual input can then be gathered and edited to form a cohesive whole. This requires the public display and editing of each individual's previously private work, and a smooth transition between kinds of permission.

In sum, focused activities are supported by public views and an explicit passing of editing control. Simultaneous activities are supported by concurrent access and public or private views, followed by more focused activity in sharing ideas with other group members. Simultaneous private entry captures fleeting individual thoughts; focused shared views support the pacing and communication of group work.

5. EXTENDING THE GUIDELINES ON USABILITY TO INCLUDE GROUP EDITORS.

Whatever the functionality of a group editor, the interface may be the key to success or failure. There exist a host of guidelines that bear on the design of interfaces that support individual users. Many of these have straightforward extensions to interfaces to groups (e.g., consistency), but there are some special considerations about how some of the guidelines can be extended to include the special characteristics of group work.

5.1 Representation Fits the way the User Thinks.

Flexibility in representations is much more important in group work, since the members often have very different backgrounds and skills. It may be necessary to display the information object in different ways, either privately or publicly. For example, a project manager needs to see a schedule of the work and assess impacts of late components, whereas the managers of subtasks within the project need to see the local resource allocation to the task at hand. Although these are working on the same aggregate information, they are decidedly different views.

5.2 Visual Display.

The visual display can serve as reminders of special group features. For example, Timbuktu will show an eye in the upper corner when someone has read only access to the work on the host machine, and a hand when they can take control. On other systems that have public and private windows, there is a need for signals indicating which are which. When one is privately working on the group object that looks very similar to the public display, this signal is acutely important.

Visual signals can also indicate the presence of others' work. In Cognoter, for example, an item is grayed when it is locked out because someone is working on it. Ellis (Ellis, Gibbs, & Rein, 1988) described an indicator for another's work progressing without showing the potentially disruptive changes keystroke by keystroke. Clouds could indicate that work is progressing, with the cloud getting bigger as the hidden work extends. Then, under user control, a "cloudburst" could display the contents of the work. This is a nice solution to the potentially disruptive aspect of simultaneous access.

5.3 Command structure.

Command structures should be consistent and similar to the way the user forms the task goal in his head. Group editors conform in general to this prescription except in the way in which the group session is started and stopped, or in how individuals enter and leave during a session. In order to support the easy flow of group work, this aspect of the task will have to have the same kind of care as the core group editing aspects.

5.4 Error Recovery.

Being able to undo the last action is as much a value in a group as it is in individual work. Complications arise, however, in implementing an "undo" in a group setting. If there is single access point, it is natural to undo the latest action. However, if two individuals' actions occur close in succession, the author of the action to be undone may not enter the undo command until another group member's action had taken place--a situation likely to create enormous confusions.

In systems that have multiple simultaneous input, the situation is much more complex. Many architectures can undo the last action in time, but it may not be, like above, the action desired. Moreover, "undo my last action" may not even make sense if others' intervening actions have altered the very object on which that action operated.

6. CONCLUSIONS.

We have proposed in this review a way of assessing the benefits against which to weigh the costs of a variety of features that support the group editing of a common work object. One has to assess the kinds of group work that go on in their setting (e.g., design, policy, presentation meetings), and unfold for these the necessity of single versus simultaneous access, and for public and private views.

The list of extended usability principles should assist in evaluating or designing aspects of the user interface for these group editors. There are important considerations beyond those of individual applications, because of the interleaving of various people's inputs and of the additional burden the group places on the limited capabilities of the individual.

In all of the above, we have used the review of a currently set of prototype and product software to introduce the notion that the way to evaluate any new system is to consider the needs and capabilities of the group. Although this involves time and thought, it is likely to save enormous costs in designing features that either won't support the end user's real needs or are too costly for their final benefit.

ACKNOWLEDGEMENTS

Our work on collaboration technology is supported by the National Science Foundation (Grant No. IRI-8902930), by Andersen Consulting, by Steelcase, Inc., and by Apple Computer. This paper was written during sabbatical leaves by the first two authors in Cambridge, England, and we are grateful to our hosts, Rank Xerox EuroPARC and the Applied Psychology Unit, for providing supportive environments.

REFERENCES

Ahuja, S. R., Ensor, J. R., Horn, D. N., and Lucco, S E. The Rapport multimedia conferencing system: A software overview. *Proceedings of the Second IEEE Conference on Computer Workstations.* IEEE, March (1988) 52-58.

Cognitive Science and Machine Intelligence Laboratory, ShrEdit, A Multi-user Shared Text Editor: Users Manual. The University of Michigan.(1989)

Crowley, T., and Forsdick, H. MMConf: The Diamond multimedia conferencing system. *Proceedings Groupware Technology Workshop.* IFIP Working Group 8.4, (1989).

Ellis, C. A., Gibbs, S. J.and Rein, G. L Design and use of a group editor. MCC Technical Report Number STP-263-88. (1988)

Ellis, C. A., Gibbs, S. J.and Rein, G. L. Groupware: The Research and Development Issues. Tech Report STP 414-88. Austin, TX: Microelectronics and Computer Technology Corporation.(1988)

Elwart-Keys, M., Halonen, D., Horton, M., Kass, R. Scott, P. User interface requirements for face to face groupware. *Proceedings of CHI'90 Human Factors in Computing Systems*, (1990).

Farallon Computing, Timbuktu: the next best thing to being there. (1987).

Foster, G., and Stefik, J. Cognoter: Theory and practice of a Colab-orative tool. *Proceedings of the Conference on Computer-Supported Cooperative Work* (1986).

Gust, P. SharedX: X in a distributed group work environment. Presentation at the 2nd annual X conference, MIT, (January 1988).

Lantz, K. A. An experiment in integrated multimedia conferencing. in I. Greif (Ed.) *Computer Supported Cooperative Work: A Book of Readings.* (Morgan Kaufman Publ.,San Mateo, CA, 1988) pp. 533-552.

Lauwers, J. C., and Lantz, K. Collaboration awareness in support of collaboration transparency: Requirements for the next generation of shared window systems. *Proceedings of CHI'90 Human Factors in Computing Systems,* (1990).

Mantei, M. Capturing the Capture Lab concepts: A case study in the design of computer supported meeting environments. *Proceedings of the 1988 Conference on Computer Supported Cooperative Work,* (1988), 257-270.

Norman, D. A. and Draper, S. W. *User Centered System Design.* Lawrence Erlbaum Associates, Publ., Hillsdale, NJ, (1986)

Olson, G., and Olson, J. User-centered design of collaboration technology. *Organizational Computing,* (1990, in press).

Rein, G. Personal communication, (1989).

Smith, R. B., O'Shea, T., O'Malley, C., Scanlon, E., and Taylor, J. Preliminary experiments with a distributed, multi-media problem solving environment. *Proceedings of European Conference on Computer Supported Cooperative Work,* (1989).

Stefik, M., Foster, G., Bobrow, D. G., Kahn, K., Lanning, S., and Suchman, L. Beyond the chalkboard: Computer support for collaboration and problem solving in meetings. *Communications of the ACM,* (1987) 30(1), 32-47.

Stefik, M., Bobrow, D. G., Foster, G., Lanning, S., and Tatar, D. WYSIWIS Revised: Early experiences with multi-user interfaces. *ACM Transactions on Office Information Systems* (1987) 5(2), 147-167.

Tatar, D. Personal communication on the C-noter. (December, 1989)

Human–Computer Interaction - INTERACT '90
D. Diaper et al. (Editors)
Elsevier Science Publishers B.V. (North-Holland)

Characteristics of Well-Designed Electronic Communications Systems

Patrick A. Holleran

Apple Computer, Inc.
20525 Mariani Ave., MS 35-G
Cupertino, CA 95066
e-mail: holleran@apple.com

Richard W. Haller

Computing Center
University of Oregon
Eugene, Oregon 97403
e-mail: rhaller@oregon.uoregon.edu

Software designed to facilitate communication among people has tremendous potential to improve the quality and consequences of human cooperative effort. The success of integrated electronic communications systems depends on both the usability and functionality of the software. The present paper briefly discusses both general principles of software design and those specifically relevant to communications systems. It offers recommendations for the design of communications systems which will optimize the accessibility, usability and utility of this software.

Increased connectivity between computers, particularly via networks and other high speed information channels, enhances the opportunity for software which facilitates collaborative effort via communication. Products in an emerging category of computer programs, *social software*, provide services which make previous styles of communication more efficient and enable completely new methods of information exchange and cooperative enterprise. Products of this type include project management systems (Sathi, Morton, & Roth, 1986), group problem solving software (Stefik, Foster, Bobrow, Kahn, Lanning, & Suchman, 1987), multi-user graphic & design software (Lakin, 1987), "mark-up"or "collaborative editing" systems (Leland, Fish, & Kraut, 1988), multi-person electronic calendars (Greif & Sarin, 1987), and multi-user hypermedia systems (Yoder, Akscyn, & McCracken, 1989).

Perhaps the most heavily used network-based communications programs are interpersonal message systems. These include electronic mail, which is usually based on the model of person-person communications, and conferencing, which integrates person-group and group-group communications capabilities (Meeks, 1985). Both types of software may provide asynchronous and synchronous or "real-time" communications. Additionally, computer networks now may facilitate teleconferencing (Egido, 1988), voice mail (Aucella & Ehrlich, 1986), and facsimile transmission (FAX). Typically, these types of capabilities are contained in separate software systems, although integration of electronic communications capabilities is likely in the the future.

As in other areas, success of electronic communications packages depends not only on the functionality which they provide but the way in which people can use and interact with them. Even accessible, full-featured communications packages may not be heavily used (Hiltz, 1988). A mix of useful capabilities and a well designed human interface will enhance the probability that communications systems are used to their fullest potential. The present paper suggests some specific features of electronic communications systems which will maximize their functionality and usability.

General Design Principles

The design of electronic communications systems should be based on principles derived from knowledge of human capabilities and characteristics gained from research in cognitive science (Card, Moran, & Newell, 1983; Hammond, Gardiner, Christie, & Marshall, 1987). For example, usable software should be consistent with human memory capacity and capabilities. Since recognition memory is typically superior to recall (Luh, 1922), interfaces which provide recall cues or allow users to choose from lists of commands or options reduce the load on "short term" or "working" memory, which is fairly small (Miller, 1956). Recall of information presented graphically may be superior to that presented in words or sentences (Shephard, 1967), and in certain situations users may more easily process graphical, rather than verbal, information (Pellegrino, Rosinski, Chiesi, & Siegel, 1977), so interfaces which take advantage of graphical capabilities may provide powerful advantages. Consistency within and among applications will enhance the transfer of skills (Polson, 1988) and reduce the effects of proactive inhibition (Underwood, 1957). Similarly, avoidance of modality, in which identical or similar actions on the part of the user have different effects depending on the "mode" or "state" of the program, reduces memory demands.

While humans have powerful abilities to process information, there are well documented limitations to these abilities that have implications for human-computer interface design. Programs should present information so that the user can quickly select what is important by grouping related items, utilizing consistent display formats (Pakin, Sherwin, & Wray, 1982), avoiding distraction through the display of irrelevant or unimportant items, and using organizational and emphasis cues such as color (Christ, 1975; Durett and Trezona, 1982; deWeert, 1988). Complex data structures, commands, or relationships can be made understandable though the use of concrete "objects" such as icons or other graphic representations (Rogers, 1986) and by "direct manipulation" of the objects themselves (Schneiderman, 1987). Since humans may efficiently process multiple streams of information, especially when presented across multiple sensory modalities (Wickens, Mountford, & Schreiner, 1981), software which makes use of visual, auditory, and other output capabilities (Lamb & Buckley, 1984, cited in

Marshall, Christie, & Gardiner, 1987; Eberts, 1987) has the potential to increase the user's attentional bandwidth.

Typically, humans learn not by passively accepting information but by exploring their environment (Carroll & Rosson, 1987). Software should be designed to allow people to learn about capabilities of products by trying out their features. Programs should be written to reduce the risk of experimentation by eliminating the possibility a user can inadvertently destroy data and by providing reversibility (e.g. an "undo" function) for most actions. Furthermore, as they explore, people attempt to make sense of the environment by associating new information with existing knowledge structures. Software which facilitates incorporation of new information about how a system operates into existing cognitive structures enhances the probability that the user's mental model of the system will be an accurate reflection of how the system actually works. One important way of using the user's experiences and knowledge is by utilizing metaphors which relate software operations to the operation of systems in the "real world" (Carroll & Thomas, 1982; Carroll & Mack, 1985; van der Veer & Feldt, 1988).

Finally, it is also essential to realize that significant differences exist among potential users of any program. These exist in areas such as memory capacity, cognitive processing abilities, cognitive style, physical capabilities, age, experience, cultural background, and motivation. Software must be written to accommodate different sorts of people and should not demand that users adapt to the idiosyncrasies of programs or programmers. Programs must be designed so that the user can customize them to fit their own characteristics and the properties of the task and the environment.

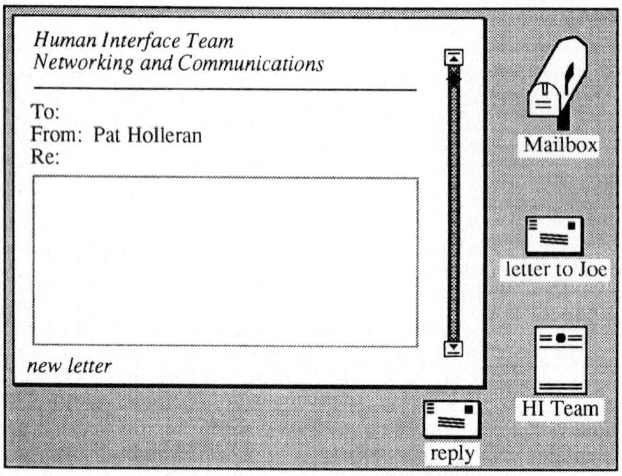

Figure 1. Mail Application Interface

Special Considerations for Communications Software

While electronic communications systems share these principles with other software, there are special considerations with communications packages or other types of social software. In addition to the usual *computer—human* interface, communication packages involve a *human-human* interface as well. In addition to the general relevancy of findings derived from research in cognitive psychology, attention to knowledge derived from work in social psychology is also important (Kiesler, Siegel, & McGuire, 1984). Creation of an "organizational interface" so that computer systems fit naturally into formalized group structures (Malone, 1987) may also be required for software which will be used collaboratively.

Computer-mediated communications differ from face-to-face communications in a variety of ways. Normal social cues such as facial expressions, gestures, bodily posture, and voice level and intonation present in typical interpersonal interactions are absent in computer-mediated communications. Normal face-to-face conversation is interactive even when only one individual is speaking, as additional social cues serve as a "back-channel" of communication (Hampton, 1987) which play a significant role in altering and modulating the communication of each participant. Absence of these cues in electronic systems contributes to increased potential for misunderstanding and miscommunication and may alter the content of messages altogether. Computer-mediated communication among groups of people may also result in the reduction of status and position cues for participants, enhanced equity of social feedback, and deindividuation of participants. Finally, there are at present fewer widely shared norms governing this type of communication (Kiesler, Siegel, & McGuire, 1984), and those which do exist have "tended to evolve haphazardly" (Thorngate, 1985, p. 191). This may magnify the effects of other differences on electronic communication.

Preliminary investigations into computer-mediated communications have yielded some data about the effects of communicating via computer. It is popularly believed that computer-mediated communication is characterized by high levels of emotions such as sarcasm, anger, or irony (Eckerson, 1989), and some evidence has accumulated that increased levels of antagonism and hostility are characteristic of electronic interactions (Sproull & Kiesler, 1986), although such evidence is preliminary and equivocal at this point.

Other effects include include disturbances in organizational structure (Winograd, 1988) and prescribed channels of communication flow (Crowston, Malone, & Lin, 1988), reduction in operation of normative influences, lessening of the influence of group leaders and other dominant individuals, and a decline in off-task interaction (Weeks & Chapanis, 1976, cited in Kiesler, et al., 1984). Eveland and Bikson (1988) have also found significant enhancements on involvement in group work, a higher degree of contact, and less communication isolation for a workgroup supported by electronic communications compared with one working on the same task without electronic support.

Finally, Mackay (1989) has found substantial differences among people in the use of electronic communications tools and in reactions to electronic communications tools in general. These differences are surprisingly large even among people in similar positions working on the same project. It must be expected that the effects of electronic communications will differ considerably from individual to individual and organization to organization, and communications interfaces must be designed flexibly to accommodate, and even take advantage of, these differences.

Characteristics of Communications Systems

Clearly, electronic mail systems must be designed with the information presented above in mind. Powerful features will only be utilized if they are accessible, convenient, and easy to use. Those principles which appear to increase usability must be applied to a variety of powerful and innovative communications capabilities. A number of these capabilities are presented below. Some similar general recommendations are presented by Scragg (1985), Borden (1985), and Beckwith (1987).

It is essential that communication packages be understandable to potential users. The use of real-world metaphors, as discussed above, can provide important assistance in this area, and mail packages ought to be designed to capitalize on the very obvious metaphors which present themselves in this area. Electronic mail systems resemble postal services, and they involve letters, mail boxes, post offices (servers), delivery receipts, etc. Mail systems also involve addresses, enclosures, and many other features which have analogs in real-world, non-electronic message systems. A well written mail system must take advantage of these natural metaphors both visually and conceptually. For example, messages themselves are like letters, and the metaphor of a piece of paper can be used to great advantage in assisting users in preparing their messages. Or letters can be "deposited" in icons which represent mail- or outboxes using direct manipulation techniques, analogous to placing real envelopes in mailboxes in the office environment. An illustration of such a system is presented in Figure 1, representing a computer screen on a system with integrated electronic mail. In this system, the mail box icon represents the mail system, and a list of incoming mail can be viewed by "opening" this mailbox, perhaps by clicking on the door. Mail can be transmitted by "dragging" icons representing mail or files onto the mailbox and providing an appropriate address. Also displayed on the screen are icons representing letters and stationery and an open letter being composed. Use of the metaphor in this way makes it quite easy for a new user of the system to accomplish basic mail tasks, or for a sophisticated user to accomplish these same tasks quickly and with a minimum of trouble

Date 11/26/89
Topic RE: Test
From RHALLER@oregon.uoregon.edu
To Patrick Holleran

Mail*Link™ RE: Test
Received: by gateway.qm.apple.com; 26 Nov 89 15:16:17
Received: from apple.com by goofy.apple.com (5.51/25-eef)
id AA17203; Thu, 23 Nov 89 10:03:21 PST
for Patrick_Holleran.NC_PROJ_LEAD@gateway.qm.apple.com
Received: from oregon.uoregon.edu by apple.com (5.59/25-eef)
id AA18724; Thu, 23 Nov 89 10:03:15 PST
for Patrick_Holleran.NC_PROJ_LEAD@gateway.qm.apple.com
Message-Id: <8911231803.AA18724@apple.com>
Date: Thu, 23 Nov 89 10:03 PST
From: Rich Haller <RHALLER@oregon.uoregon.edu>
Subject: RE: Test
To: Patrick_Holleran.NC_PROJ_LEAD@gateway.qm.apple.com
X-Vms-To: IN%"Patrick_Holleran.NC_PROJ_LEAD@gateway.qm.apple.com"

It arrived 22-NOV-1989 16:33:23.01.

Above all, communications systems must allow people to send information to one another in ways which are at the least as good as and preferably better than traditional media. Communication in non-electronic forms involves a variety of different types of information, and a significant percentage of correspondence contains graphic images or information (Hansen, 1980). Electronic communication should provide equivalent or superior capabilities. Thus, support for various text characteristics such as font or typeface, text styles (bold, italic, etc.), and font size is essential. One advantage of such a capability is the potential mitigation of the effects of absent interpersonal cues (Swart, 1985), as such styles may be used to add emphasis, highlight information, and convey attitudes or emotion. It should also be possible to send graphic images or integrate them into a message because of the communicative power such images may provide. Permitting the user to save such images for consistent reuse—as "stationery"—may also contribute to the reduction of the effects of missing cues and enhance communication of personal and affective characteristics of messages. However, it is also important that communications software provide capabilities for processing or filtering graphic images, text characteristics, or device-dependent information so that individuals who do not have hardware which supports these capabilities may still receive a "version" of the message. Providing the sender with a "preview" capability which will indicate at least in a general way how the message will appear to the recipient in a particular computing environment is also an essential feature to avoid miscommunication. Finally, since preparation of messages represents a substantial percentage of interaction with mail packages (Akin & Rao, 1985), incorporation of powerful and easy-to-use text and graphics editors, or permitting users to incorporate their own favorite editors seamlessly into the package, will significantly enhance usability of the system.

Communication packages should permit inclusion of a variety of types of special information about messages themselves (*meta-message* information) into the message without special effort by the sender. This includes a **clear** display of the identity of the sender and when the message was sent, whether copies of the message have been sent to other individuals, and who has seen the message. More detailed routing information, including forwarding nodes, etc., should be available to the receiver but should not be imposed (as do many mail systems which force the user to wade through half a screen or more of extraneous routing information to read a message). Figure 2 illustrates how the imposition of unwanted routing and addressing information can overwhelm actual message content in a simple electronic communication. It is also important that the sender should be offered the option of incorporating previous messages into a reply in a simple, perhaps automatic, way if a more powerful method of establishing context is not provided. This provides contextual cues about the information in a message, which can have major effects on the receiver's interpretation of the message itself.

Additionally, an ordinary message sent via inter-office, campus, or U.S. mail may include any number of other items in the envelope. In fact, anything which will fit physically into the envelope can be included. Similarly, electronic mail should permit files of various types, including binary and other format specific information, to be "attached" to the electronic message or sent alone. The existence of an attachment should be quite obvious to the receiver, since the message to which it is attached may be unwittingly deleted before the file is retrieved. Ideally, the user should be able to easily inspect the contents of the attachment without losing contact with the note which accompanies it, again for the contextual value that represents.

Another feature which will prove useful is voice communication. It is often considerably quicker for the sender to dictate a voice message than to type a written one, so many users will wish to use this form of message composition, and an integrated communications system should support this capability. Among other considerations, it must be clear to the recipient when a voice-based message has been included. However, human memory for information contained in voice messages may be limited (Gardiner, 1987), and it is somewhat difficult to extract the important information from them even while they are still accessible. This problem is exacerbated by the fact that people may not recognize that leaving or including voice messages is not exactly like having a interactive conversation.

While initial research indicates that people may follow auditory instructions in a mail system almost as well as written ones (Potosnak & van Nes, 1984), insufficient research has yet been done on information extraction from auditory versus written communication in an electronic mail application. Similarly, digital representations of voice messages are storage-intensive. For these reasons, voice mail capabilities should be offered as supplementary to and not a replacement for basic electronic mail features. For example, voice annotation of written messages can be a very useful feature.

Notification of the arrival of new messages is very important. The user should be notified of the arrival of new mail in a way which is conspicuous (Scragg, 1985) but not intrusive. It should be possible to continue ongoing activities without any interruption, and so there should be no **required** action on the user's part to "turn off" notification. Since an individual may not be present when the message arrives the notification should "leave a trace" which can be seen after returning. Ideally, users will be notified in a similar way about the arrival of other material—FAX images, transmitted files, etc., although it is useful to permit the user to customize this feature so the method of notification will be most appropriate and effective in the user's particular environment.

Handling of new mail should also be easy. It should be possible to read through unread messages with a single keystroke or click of a mouse or other input device. Since a high percentage of mail messages are replies to other messages (Wilbur, Rubin, & Lee, 1986), initiation of a reply should require only a single command or action; this action should provide all addressing and routing information needed by mail systems and any necessary routers or gateways. Similarly, forwarding a message should be done in the same way as replying to one, and should be no more difficult. The user should be able to optionally specify a time when the message should be transmitted, permitting use of the system for reminding individuals, including the sender, of timely information and events.

Selecting a local or frequently used address should be quite easy, but specification of a more complex address, when possible, should also be possible. Among other features, this should allow creation and use of an address book or list of common receivers, and choosing of a receiver from the list, preferably with a keystroke or mouseclick. The capability to associate "synonyms" or "aliases" with long or complex addresses is also desirable. Allowing the user to save return addresses from messages which have been received into an address book will eliminate the need to type many complex addresses, or understand details of routing or addressing.

Reliability of mail delivery is essential. Users typically assume once they have sent a message that it will be received, and misunderstandings may arise from unreliable communication. On a personal computer or workstation, which people may turn off at the end of the day or when they are out of the office, having mail acceptance, delivery, and transmission handled by a server elsewhere on a network is desirable. This also permits coherent management of the system by a network administrator or postmaster which should enhance the system reliability and reduce management effort by individual users. If problems develop which might result in the loss of messages or other information, the mail system must provide users with this information.

Connectivity capabilities of a mail system are extremely important. The utility of any communications medium is partially dependent on the number of accessible individuals or systems. A mail package which allows users to communicate only with people in the same geographical area with the same kind of computer and mail system is of limited use. Secondly, to the extent that a particular communications system lacks connectivity, people will be forced to use other electronic packages and media. This increases the amount of information a person must learn, enhances the potential for inconsistency in user interfaces of separate packages, and limits the effectiveness of the mail package as both a communication and information retrieval tool. Modern mail systems should provide connectivity tools which permit communication with the "rest of the world" (where hardware connections are in place). Typically, this means a communications architecture built on international standards, such as SMTP or the emerging ISO/OSI electronic message protocol, X.400 (Lisker, 1988), or alternately by providing gateways between proprietary systems and these protocols.

However, a well-designed interface should shield the user **entirely** from the complexities of routing which are presently inherent in interconnected systems; it should be as simple for the user to address a message to a person across the ocean as it is to send something across the room. As Wilson (1985) has suggested, "...the networks are of no interest to the user except in terms of reliability and cost" (p. 322), and so addressing which requires substantial knowledge of routing is not in the best interest of usability. Clearly, creation of an interface which provides this shield is difficult; it is nevertheless worth the designer's effort from the point of view of the enhancement of the usability of mail systems in general. Adoption of international mail standards for addressing and directory services (x.500) will make this task much easier. Until this is a reality, however, there are several ways the designer can make the task of addressing messages easier for the user. Intelligent local routing, in which the addresses of individuals on local network can be "looked up" or accessed by the mail system in the course of mail delivery or address specification, are useful. Easily accessible name servers with addresses of many individuals provide valuable assistance in the specification of addresses. It should not be necessary for the mail user to search for these servers; the mail system should provide that service itself. Similarly, it should not be necessary for a user or administrator to provide all of the entries in the server. Addressing information can be gathered and retained from messages which are routed through the network on which the server resides. Finally, in situations in which the specification of a complex address which includes routing or other arcane information is inescapable, preparation of **addressing templates** which provide the user with a framework for specifying information will provide the same advantages as does form-based input in other areas (Jeffries & Rosenberg, 1987).

An additional major concern of users of electronic communications systems is security and confidence that the flow of information can be adequately restricted when necessary. This type of confidence is essential to the utility of a communications system, as people will not communicate openly with unclear expectations about information dissemination. Security and privacy features may take a variety of forms. Data encryption capabilities are important, as with many mail systems it is possible to "listen in" to network transmission, or to inspect message archives stored on a public disk. Password-protected access to mail "accounts" is desirable to prevent others from using one's own personal "mailbox".

There are additional features which may prevent unintended distribution of information. It is important that, as the user prepares to initiate transmission of a message, receivers are displayed clearly. Having separate screens or windows which display **only** the message or **only** the receivers enhances the possibility that information may be sent to the wrong people by accident. As "undo" capabilities limit the amount of damage a person may do in exploring a system's capabilities, so the mail equivalent of undo, "unsend", is a valuable and necessary feature of a mail system. It also should be possible to send a message with a "no forward" flag to indicate that it should not be forwarded to others after it has been received by the intended recipient. Such a feature would at least discourage (although probably not prevent) unwanted forwarding of private messages. In addition, users should be able to specify that they receive automatic notification when a message they originated has been forwarded so that they can keep track of the dissemination of information they originated.

While early electronic communications systems remained close to a basic metaphor—"mail" or simple one-to-one message delivery capabilities—it is likely that future systems will integrate this capability with the ability to communicate among and share information with groups of individuals, as conferencing systems do (Hiltz & Turoff, 1985). In fact, in situations in which group communications are well supported, as in the COM conferencing system, 92% of messages are addressed to conferences (groups of individuals) as opposed to single persons (Palme, 1984). So well-designed systems should provide a number of features which can facilitate communications among collections of individuals. These systems should provide the ability to use "routing" or "group distribution" lists which provide a single identity for a number of individuals. It should be easy for users to create such lists, to access existing distribution lists of general interest to other network users, and to combine these in ways they choose. Systems should provide users with the ability to become members of groups themselves, as with conferencing systems such as COM or SuperCom, EIES, Participate, and CoSy (Meeks, 1985; Palme, 1988), where group communication is the focus rather than an afterthought. A system designed in this way provides more flexibility in the evolution, maintenance, and dissemination of information about groups of addresses, routing of messages, expiration dates of communications, etc.

Among the most important implications of electronic message systems is the degree of control over transmitted information conferred on senders and receivers. Typically, mail systems grant large amounts of control over the routing of information to the sender who may determine the contents of messages, who receives them, when they are transmitted, etc. The receiver usually has little control. This provides a substantial risk of "information overload" (Hiltz & Turoff, 1985) where the individual can be overwhelmed by the amount of transmitted information, and as a result the usefulness of the delivery system is seriously compromised. One example of this problem is the proliferation of "electronic junk" (Denning, 1982), or unsolicited, unwanted information which has afflicted electronic mail system users for some time. But it is not just unwanted information which creates the problem, as electronic communication provides potential also for receiving a great deal of valuable information. What is needed is a way to deal with this information in a manageable way both as it comes in and after it has been received.

Some fairly simple features provide assistance in managing this information. Providing users with the ability to specify a level of importance or priority for each message and receivers with the capability to be alerted distinctly (with, for example, different, user-specifiable sounds or screen displays) about messages of different priority levels can help. Another useful feature for handling information is for mail systems to provide users with the ability to create and use forms in which specific data or "redundant" information (Winograd, 1988) is located in particular "fields" or consistent locations on the screen (Malone, Grant, Turbak, Brobst, & Cohen, 1987). This allows the receiver to immediately recognize the type of message and to quickly locate information of importance on the form. Use of such forms to produce "semistructured messages" has been shown to be both natural and extremely useful (Malone, Grant, Lai, Rao, & Rosenblitt, 1987). Also, providing conferencing or "group discussion" capabilities also furnishes users with another tool to avoid information overload by allowing them to choose groups of past and future messages they know they'll want to review (Hiltz & Turoff, 1985) and to avoid those which hold little interest.

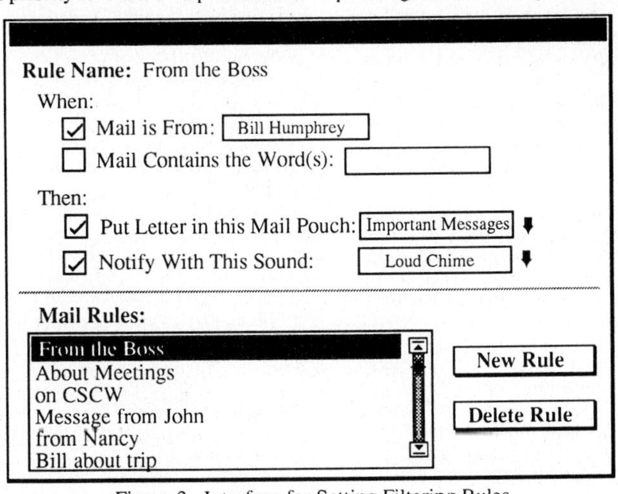

Figure 3. Interface for Setting Filtering Rules

However, systems which allow more sophisticated forms of filtering of incoming messages are essential for the avoidance of information overload. It should be possible for the user to specify characteristics of messages, such as the sender, subject, time of arrival, and occurrences of strings in messages, and make a determination about what the mail system should do with those messages. For example, messages of a certain type might be placed in a particular "unread mail" folder, or messages of another type might cause the user to be immediately alerted when they arrive, and placed at the top of an "important unread messages" list. Other messages might be rejected entirely, or deleted as they arrive. Work on various types of rule-based filtering mechanisms have been done by Malone, et al. (1987), and Pollock (1989).

The power of filtering functions is limited, however, by the interface. Unless it is easy to specify these "rules" they will not be used and their power will be irrelevant. Figure 3 provides an example of a very simple tool which could be used to specify rules for filtering incoming messages in a hypothetical mail system, but which would nevertheless provide substantial functionality. This tool allows users to create new filtering "rules" or to select old ones from a list to edit. Incoming messages from particular individuals or containing particular strings of characters may be routed to separate unread mail receptacles, and the user may choose to be alerted by different auditory signals based on these conditions. Mackay, Malone, Crowston, Rao, Rosenblitt, and Card (1989) provide a similar but somewhat more powerful example of a similar tool used with their "Information Lens" system as well as evidence that users who are not programmers use and derive substantial value from it. Advanced systems which make intelligent inferences on the importance of received mail and where it should be stored based on rules or information apparent to an expert system (Chang & Leung, 1987) or past actions by or "profiles" of the user (Boyle & Clarke, 1985) could also contribute significantly to the usability of filtering systems.

It is also essential that information be accessible **after** it has been been acquired. There are a variety of essential functions a mail system should provide to facilitate access to stored messages. First, the system should create and maintain a complete log of mail activity. This log should contain records of messages sent and received, message type, destinations, time stamps, and confirmation of receipt and attention. Copies of messages sent and received should be retained by the system for later access by the user unless specifically deleted (although this should be configurable so that both the user and the system administrator can make determinations about the amount of information which can be retained). Related messages (ones which are replies or comments on other messages) ought to be saved with pointers to one another so that the communication "chain" can be reconstructed if desired. This provides information about the context of communications which will not in many cases be otherwise available to the user.

Additionally, it should be possible to organize information in a logical and accessible way, such as hierarchically. It should be as simple to save a message into a specific folder, directory, mail pouch, or other location as it is to delete the message or read the next one. Once stored, it should be possible to access saved messages with all the power of database-style searching capabilities. A user ought to be able to select all messages from Dr. Smith sent after July 10 on the topic of multidimensional scaling, for example. It should be possible to build various kinds of lists of messages and sort them or extract subsets in various ways. Summary information about messages, such as the number from a specific individual or on a particular topic during a particular period of time, should also be accessible. Ability to retrieve and access information is critical, and mail systems designed to provide users with high levels of access will prove particularly valuable.

Summary

Computer and network-mediated communications are already a reality. Electronic mail and related software is heavily used already in business and academic environments, and many operations are dependent on them. Mackay (1989), in a study of the use of electronic mail in research settings, finds users receiving 30-75 messages per day and sending up to 30 themselves. The authors of the present paper, long-time heavy users of electronic communications systems, may deal with several dozen messages in a typical work day.

However, the degree to which these system truly enhance communications and human cooperative effort depends largely on the design of the software which mediates them. And, unfortunately, despite the fact that many commercial communications packages exist, only a few incorporate more than a few of the features recommended in this paper. The true promise of this technology has not yet been realized. Electronic communication systems which provide much of the functionality outlined here, and which are based on sound interface design principles derived from knowledge of human cognitive capabilities and characteristics, offer the strongest possibility that the full promise of this technology will be fulfilled.

References

Akin. O., & Rao, D. (1985). Efficient computer-user interface in electronic mail systems. *International Journal of Man-Machine Studies, 22*, 589-612.

Aucella, A.F., & Ehrlich, S.F. (1986). Voice messaging enhancing the user interface design based on field performance. *Human Factors In Computing Systems: CHI'86 Conference Proceedings.*

Beckwith, D. (1987). Group problem-solving via computer conferencing: The realizable potential. *Canadian Journal of Educational Communications, 16*, 89-106.

Borden, B. (1985). Mail in the electronic age. *UNIX Review*, July, 40-89.

Boyle, C. D. B., & Clarke, M. R. B. (1985). An intelligent mail filter. In P. Johnson & S. Cook (Eds.), *People and computers: Designing the interface.* Cambridge: Cambridge Univ. Press.

Card, S. K., Moran, T.P., & Newell, A. (1983). *The psychology of human-computer interaction.* Hillsdale, N.J.: Lawrence Erlbaum Associates.

Carroll, J.M., & Mack, R.L. (1985). Metaphor, computing systems, and active learning. *International Journal of Man-Machine Studies, 22*, 39-58.

Carroll, J.M., & Rosson, M.B. (1987). The paradox of the active user. In J.M. Carroll (Ed.), *Interfacing thought: Cognitive aspects of human computer interaction.* Hillsdale, N.J.: Lawrence Erlbaum Assc

Carroll, J. M., & Thomas, J. C. (1982). Metaphor and the cognitive representation of computing system. *IEEE Transactions On Systems, Man, And Cybernetics, 12*, 107-116.

Chang, S.-K., & Leung, L. (1987). A knowledge-based message management system. *ACM Transactions on Office Information Systems, 5(3)*, 213-236.

Christ, R.E. (1975). Review and analysis of color coding research for visual display. *Human Factors, 17*, 542-570.

Crowston, K., Malone, T.W., & Lin, F. (1988). Cognitive science and organizational design: A case study of computer conferencing. *Human Computer Interaction, 3(1)*, 59-85.

de Weert, C. M. M. (1988). *The use of color in visual displays.* In G. C. van der Veer & G. Mulder (Eds.), Human-computer interaction: Psychonomic aspects. Berlin: Springer-Verlag.

Denning, P. (1982). Electronic junk. *Communications of the ACM. 23(3).* 163-165.

Durrett, J., & Trezona, J. (1982). How to use color displays effectively: A look at the elements of color vision and their implications for programmers. *Byte, April*, 50-53.

Eberts, R. (1987). Human computer interaction. In Hancock, P. A. (Ed.), *Human Factors Psychology*, Amsterdam: Elsevier Science Publishers, 249-304.

Eckerson, W. (1989). Techniques for improving etiquetter in E-mail. *Network World, May 8*, 19-20.

Gardiner, M. (1987). Episodic and semantic memory. In Gardiner, M. M., & Christie, B., (Eds.), *Applying cognitive psychology to user-interface design.* Chichester: John Wiley & Sons.

Greif, I., & Sarin, S. (1987). Data sharing in group work. *ACM Transactions on Office Information Systems, 5*, 187-211.

Hammond, N. (1987). Principles from the psychology of language. In Gardiner, M. M., & Christie, B., (Eds.), *Applying cognitive psychology to user-interface design.* Chichester: John Wiley & Sons.

Hammond, N., Gardiner, M. M., Christie, B., & Marshall, C. (1987). The role of cognitive psychology in user-interface design. In Gardiner, M. M., & Christie, B., (Eds.), *Applying cognitive psychology to user-interface design.* Chichester: John Wiley & Sons.

Hansen, P. (1980). Perspectives of mass communications and telecommunications. In Bjørn-Anderson (Ed.), *The human side of information processing.* Amsterdam: North-Holland.

Hiltz, S. R., & Turoff, M. (1985). Structuring computer-mediated communications systems to avoid information overload. *Communications of the ACM. 28(7).* 680-689.

Hiltz, S. R. (1988). Productivity enhancement from computer-mediated communication: A systems contingency approach. *Communications of the ACM, 31*, 1438-1454.

Jeffries, R., & Rosenberg, J. (1987). Comparing a form-based and a language-based user interface for instructing a mail program. *Proceedings Of Human Factors In Computing Systems And Graphic Interface*, 261-266.

Kiesler, S., Siegel, J., & McGuire, T. (1984). Social psychological aspects of computer-mediated communication. *American Psychologist, 39*, 1123-1134.

Lakin, F. (1987). A performing medium for working group graphics.

Lamb, M., & Buckley, V. (1984). New techniques for gesture-based dialogue. In B. Shackel (Ed.), *Interact '84: First IFIP Conference on Human Computer Interaction.* Amsterdam: IFIP, North-Holland.

Leland, M. D. P., Fish, R. S., & Kraut, R. E. (1988). Collaborative document production using Quilt. *Proceedings Of The Conference On Computer-Supported Cooperative Work, Sept 26-28, 1988, Portland, Oregon*, 206-215.

Lisker, P. (1988). Around the world in eighty seconds. *Connect, 2*, 52-54.

Luh, C.W. (1922). The conditions of retention. *Psychological Monographs, 31*, No. 142.

Mackay, W. E. (1989). Diversity in the use of electronic mail: A preliminary inquiry. *ACM Transactions on Office Information Systems, 6(4)*, 380-397.

Mackay, W. E., Malone, T. W., Crowston, K., Rao, R., Rosenblitt, D., & Card, S. K. (1989). How do experienced Information Llens users use rules? *Human Factors In Computing Systems: CHI'89 Conference Proceedings*, 211-216.

Malone, T. W., Grant, K. R., Lai, K.-Y., Rao, R., & Rosenblitt, D. (1987). Semistructured messages are surprisingly useful for computer-supported coordination. *ACM Transactions on Office Information Systems*, 5(2), 115-131.

Malone, T. W., Grant, K. R., Turbak, F., Brobst, S. A., &

Cohen, M. D. (1987). Intelligent information sharing systems. *Communications of the ACM, 30*, 390-400.

Marshall, C., Christie, B., & Gardiner, M. M. (1987). Assessment of trends in the technology and techniques of human-computer interaction. In Gardiner, M. M., & Christie, B., (Eds.), *Applying cognitive psychology to user-interface design.* Chichester: John Wiley & Sons.

Marshall, C., Nelson, C., & Gardiner, M. M. (1987). Design guidelines. In Gardiner, M. M., & Christie, B., (Eds.), *Applying cognitive psychology to user-interface design.* Chichester: John Wiley & Sons.

Meeks, B.N. (1985). An overview of conferencing systems. *Byte, 10(13)*, 169-184.

Miller, G.A. (1956). The magical number seven, plus or minus two: Some limits on our capability for processing information. *Psychological Review, 63*, 81-97.

Muter, P., & Mayson, C. (1986). The role of graphics in item selection from menu. *Behaviour and Information Technology*, 5, 89-95.

Pakin, S.E., Sherwin E., & Wray, P. (1982). Designing screens for people to use easily. *Data Management, 20(7)*, 36-41.

Palme, J. (1984). Computer conferencing is more than electronic mail. Unpublished manuscript, Stockholm University Computing Centre--QZ.

Palme, J. (1988). SuperCOM—a distributed computer conference system. QZ University Computing Centre, Stockholm, Sweden.

Pellegrino, J. W., Rosinski, R. R., Chiesi, H. L., & Siegel, A. (1977). Picture-word differences in decision latency: An analysis of single and dual memory models. *Memory And Cognition, 5*, 383-396.

Pollock, S. (1989). A rule-based message filtering system. *ACM Transactions on Office Information Systems, 6*, 232-254.

Polson, P.G. (1988). The consequences of consistent and inconsistent user interfaces. In R. Guindon, (Ed.), *Cognitive science and its applications for human-computer interaction.* Hillsdale, N.J.: Lawrence Erlbaum & Associates.

Potosnak, K. M., & Van Nes, F. L. (1984). Effects of replacing text with speech output in an electronic mail application. *IPO Annual Progress Report, 19*, 123-129.

Rogers, Y. (1986). Pictorial representation of abstract concepts relating to human-computer interaction. *SIG-CHI Bulletin, 18(2)*, 43-44.

Sathi, A., Morton, T. E., & Roth, S. F. (1986). Callisto: An intelligent project management system. *AI Magazine*, Winter, 34-52.

Schneiderman, B. (1987). *Designing the user interface: Strategies for effective human-computer interaction.* Reading, MA: Addison-Wesley

Scragg, G. W. (1985). Some thoughts on paper notes and electronic messages. *SIG-CHI Bulletin, 16(3)*, 41-44.

Shepard, R.N. (1967). Recognition memory for words, sentences and pictures. *Journal of Verbal Learning and Verbal Behavior, 6*, 156-163.

Sproull, L., & Kiesler, S. (1986) Reducing social context cues: Electronic mail in organizational communication. *Management Science, 32*, 1492-1512.

Stefik, M., Foster, G., Bobrow, D. G., Kahn, K., Lanning, S., & Suchman, L. (1987). Beyond the chalkboard: Computer support for collaboration and problem solving in meetings. *Communications of the ACM, 30*, 32-47.

Swart, E. R. (1985). Electronic conferencing: A new mode of communication. In *Proceedings Of The Workshop On Computer Conferencing And Electronic Mail, University Of Guelph, Guelph, Canada, Jan. 22-23.*

Thorngate, W. (1985). Social psychology and the design of computer conferencing systems. *Computer Conferencing And Electronic Messaging Conference Proceedings, University Of Guelph, Ontario, Canada*, 188-193.

Underwood, B. J. (1957). Interference and forgetting. *Psychological Review, 64*, 49-60.

van der Veer, G. C., & Felt, M. A. M. (1988). Development of mental models of an office system: A field study on an introductory course. In G. C. van der Veer & G. Mulder (Eds.), *Human-computer interaction : Psychonomic aspects.* Berlin: Springer-Verlag.

Wickens, C. D., Mountford, S. J., & Schreiner, W. (1981). Multiple resources, task hemispheric integrity, and individual differences in time-sharing. *Human Factors, 25*, 227-248.

Wilbur, S., Rubin, T., & Lee, S. (1986). A study of group interaction over a computer-based message system. In M. D. Harrison & A. L. Monk (Eds.), *People and computers: Designing for usability.* Cambridge: Cambridge University Press.

Wilson, P. A. (1985). Mailbox advances and MMI needs In P. Johnson & S. Cook (Eds.), *People And Computers: Designing The Interface.* Cambridge: Cambridge University Press.

Winograd, T. (1988). A language/action perspective on the design of cooperative work. *Human Computer Interaction, 3(1)*, 3-30.

Yoder, E., Akscyn, R., & McCracken, D. (1989). Collaboration in KMS: A shared hypermedia system. *Human Factors in Computing Systems: CHI'89 Conference Proceedings*, 37-42.

Human–Computer Interaction – INTERACT '90
D. Diaper et al. (Editors)
Elsevier Science Publishers B.V. (North-Holland)

PROCESS MODELLING AND CSCW: AN APPLICATION OF IPSE TECHNOLOGY TO MEDICAL OFFICE WORK

Janet MARESH and David WASTELL

Department of Computer Science, University of Manchester, Oxford Road, Manchester, M13 9PL, U.K.

An Integrated Process Support Environment (IPSE) refers to a work environment (typically software development) in which the cooperative activities of men and machines are coordinated by a computer system according to a formally defined schema. In this paper we demonstrate the use of the process modelling language PML (developed in the Alvey-supported IPSE 2.5 project) to represent the cooperative structure of work underlying the administration of hospital outpatients activity. The semantics of PML and the methodology of process modelling are discussed and consideration is given to the implications of IPSE technology for the design of office systems.

1. INTRODUCTION

The field of Computer-Supported Cooperative work (CSCW) has emerged over the last five years or so as an area of research distinctively concerned with the social dynamics of work and the design of computer systems to support group work. The recent compilation edited by Irene Grief (1988) provides an excellent overview of the rich variety of studies that are grouped under the CSCW rubric. Such work runs the gamut from well-established applications of computer support in group decision-making and structured communication (e.g. computer conferencing, the Delphi process etc. see Linstone and Turoff, 1975) to empirical studies of the impact of CMC (computer mediated communication) upon group dynamics (decision shifts etc., see Kiesler et al, 1988).

This paper deals with forms of CSCW that have been specifically developed with software production in mind and considers their more general application to white-collar work. Kedzierski (1988) presents one view of the organisational problems that are endemic to the systems development process, highlighting the importance of effective group communication to the success of software development. She describes a support environment (CHI) to enhance communication amongst designers. We describe an alternative form of group support, namely the Integrated Process Support Environment or IPSE (Warboys, 1989), which has been developed by the software engineering community, by and large independently of the CSCW field. Although specifically developed to deal with the much discussed problems facing that industry, i.e. poor quality systems, low productivity etc., IPSE technology has obvious application beyond these boundaries.

This paper looks at the technology and in particular the modelling techniques developed in the Alvey funded IPSE 2.5 project involving ICL, Plessey, British Gas and the University of Manchester, amongst others. We describe the PML formalism (Process Modelling Language) that has been developed to model the cooperative structure of group work, and illustrate the application of IPSE technology to non-software environments by constructing a process model of the administrative procedures involved in scheduling and following up hospital outpatients appointments.

The fieldwork described arose out of a project known as the Clinical Information Systems Project (CISP) which was set up in 1988 to devise a general specification for an information system for a clinical department (Wastell et al, 1987). The resulting work was based in the Cardiology department of the Manchester Royal Infirmary and the focus of the investigation was the medical office. Medical office work embraces a range of activities: liaison, coordination, communication and record keeping, all of which serve the purpose of 'enabling' the clinical work of the medical and paramedical staff (Kings's Fund, 1985). Our initial analysis followed the traditional design practices of documenting data flows, processes and data models. It became clear, however, that the conventional information modelling techniques were limited in their perspective on office work. In particular, they seemed inadequate to express the richness of office work as cooperative social activity. What was needed was a broader view of office work and of the ways and means by which computer support could increase the effectiveness of the service provided by clinical departments. IPSE 2.5 appeared to provide such a richer perspective.

2. PROCESS MODELLING AND IPSE 2.5

Warboys (1988) defines a 'process support environment' (PSE) as a work environment in which a computer system supports work by actively coordinating the work of a number of cooperating actors, making sure that resources and tools are available at the right place and the right time and automating the more straightforward and laborious procedures. A PSE must, of course, have comprehensive knowledge of the process it supports. Process modelling refers to the task of developing a formal representation of the tasks and division of labour in a particular setting.

A central part of the IPSE 2.5 project has thus been the development of a Process Modelling Language (PML) which allows process models to be expressed. PML models are articulated in terms of three main concepts: roles, activities and interactions. Broadly speaking, PML breaks cooperative work down into *actions* (which may be carried out either by people or by computer systems embedded in the support environment), *roles* (holding a role confers upon some agent, the entitlement and obligation to perform certain tasks, rights to the necessary resources and defines the relationships of the role to other roles) and *interactions* which express the mutual dependencies between activities that embody the formal cooperative structure of the work process. Figure 1 shows the main diagrammatic conventions used in this document and expands on the formal nature of roles and actions.

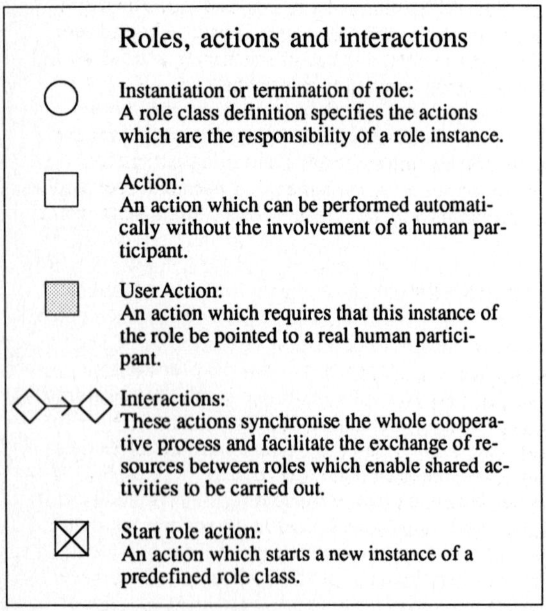

Roles, actions and interactions
Instantiation or termination of role:
A role class definition specifies the actions which are the responsibility of a role instance.
Action:
An action which can be performed automatically without the involvement of a human participant.
UserAction:
An action which requires that this instance of the role be pointed to a real human participant.
Interactions:
These actions synchronise the whole cooperative process and facilitate the exchange of resources between roles which enable shared activities to be carried out.
Start role action:
An action which starts a new instance of a predefined role class.

Figure 1

PML has a distinctive object-oriented flavour and the definitive implementation of PML was indeed written in SMALLTALK (Goldberg, 1984). The principal constructs are all conceptualised as objects (roles, actions, resources etc.). An important distinction is made between the generic definition of an object (e.g. a role-class, action-class, resource-class etc.) and particular instantiations of that class (role-instances, action-instances etc.). To help construct and display PML models, which are actually written in a SMALLTALK-like script, a diagramming tool called the Role Activity Diagram (RAD) has been adopted.. These diagrams are inadequate to express the full complexity embodied in a PML model, but are useful to give some idea of the modelling concepts.

3. THE CASE STUDY

To illustrate PML, a set of RAD diagrams is discussed which have been developed to express a logical view of the cooperative structure of work supporting the organisation of outpatients clinics in a typical hospital setting. Typically this process begins with a referral letter from a general practitioner (GP) which is then assessed for urgency and an appointment made to see a doctor at an outpatients clinic. The process proceeds after the visit through a number of possible stages (e.g. laboratory investigations) culminating in a letter from the consultant to the GP reporting his expert assessment. In real life, a large number of people are involved in this process: patients, secretaries, clerks, records staff, porters, doctors, nurses etc. Frequently the process fails in various ways, e.g. notes cannot be traced, patients wait interminably, communication with GPs takes much longer than it ought.

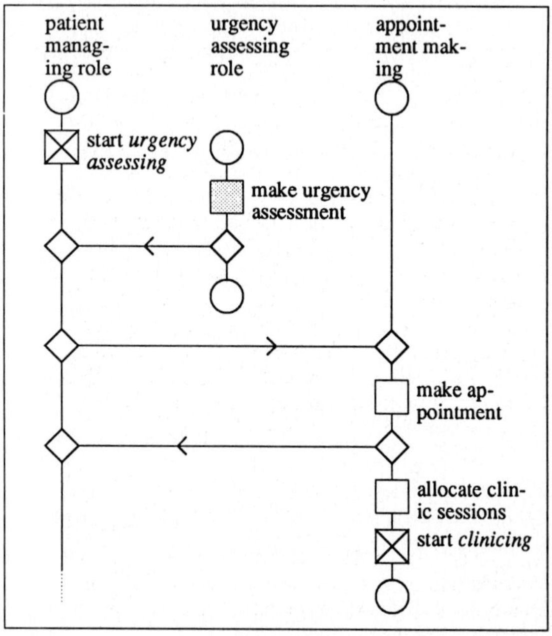

Figure 2

Figure 2 shows an RAD diagram of the early stages involved in dealing with a referral letter from a GP. Three roles are shown. In particular, we have chosen to define an overarching *patient managing* role which takes overall responsibility for coordinating the progress of a single outpatient episode. A fresh instance of this role is assumed to be associated with the receipt of the GP letter. During its instantiation certain necessary resources (the referral details for the patient) become bound to the role instance. We have chosen to split off the activity associated with assessing the urgency of the case with a second role, *urgency assessing*, which is triggered by *patient managing*. Again the necessary resources are bound on instantiation, but an interaction must occur with *patient managing* to transfer the results of the assessment.

A central distinction in PML is made between Actions (which are carried out automatically by the PSE) and UserActions (figure 1) which require a human agent. The dynamic assignment of UserActions to agents is mediated by the role concept; at any time a role-instance 'points at' a particular user who is responsible for carrying out the UserActions (if any) associated with the role. Such assignments may be varied with great flexibility allowing considerable latitude in the division of labour. As new tools become available, more and more of the process can be transferred to the PSE (i.e. UserActions become internal Actions) relieving the user of the more repetitive and routine aspects of their work. By such means, PML allows the man-machine boundary to be drawn and redrawn with considerable flexibility without radical change to the structure of the model.

UserActions, as we have said, require a human agent. Because urgency assessment is a UserAction, the *urgency assessing* role will refer to a real user currently associated with this role instance. This real participant might be the consultant to whom the patient is referred or it might be a junior doctor or even a secretary to whom the task has been delegated, via the appropriate role reassignment. Because an instance of the *appointment making* role already exists (we have decided in developing our model, that such a role should be continuously present, i.e. not linked to a particular patient), *patient managing* does not have to start this role but interacts with it , transferring the information necessary to make an appointment. The reader will note that all the activities of this role are Actions, i.e. they will be run off automatically. Of course, it would make no fundamental difference to the model if they were changed to UserActions with real participants being provided with appropriate tools to perform the tasks.

Coordination in PML is expressed in terms of a system of start conditions and other predicates. Actions and UserActions, for instance, are triggered when the start conditions defined in their generic classes are fulfilled. For interactions to take place, start conditions in both interacting roles need to be realised. Similarly roles are terminated when the terminating conditions in the state

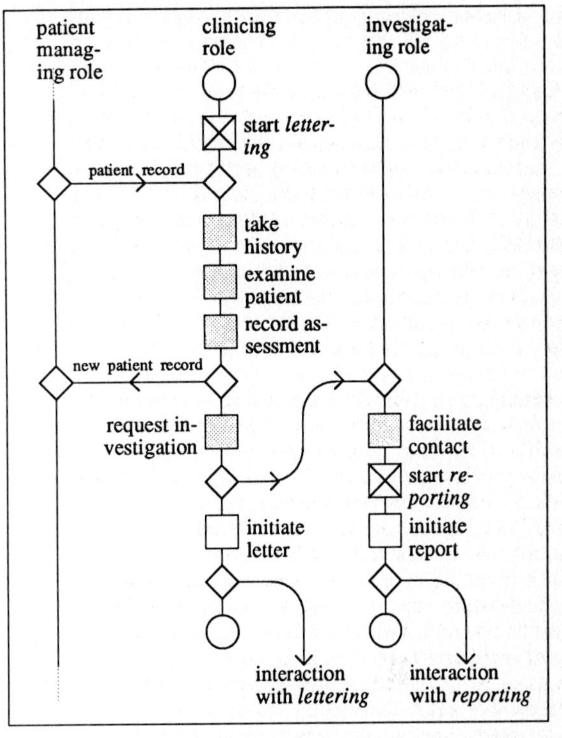

Figure 3

of the role apply. The *clinicing* role in figure 3, for instance, is instantiated for a single doctor in an outpatient clinic with the list of patients he should see in the clinic in question. The role is terminated when all the patients in the clinic list have been seen (a condition of the resources). At any point during the lifetime of the role, an action or interaction will be activated if its start conditions are right. So, for instance, the *examine patient* UserAction will execute if the *take history* UserAction for the same patient has been executed and the 'get patient record' interaction has taken place etc..

4. DISCUSSION

The importance of IPSE 2.5 is that PML models are not simply descriptive but can be 'brought to life' given a suitable computer system (e.g. a network of SUN workstations), to provide an actual working environment for a community of users. Such a working PSE is supported by a Process Control Engine (PCE). The PCE is a computer system which can 'execute' a process model expressed in PML to provide what Warboy's has described an 'active work environment', i.e. an environment in which the process model actively structures the user's work, providing, for instance, an overview of outstanding work, 'enforcing' the correct observance of procedures, making sure that users always have the correct tools and resources available, that jobs are not begun prematurely or overlooked etc. In short, the IPSE assists users to organise their affairs and ensures that processes involving several actors are properly coordinated.

We can gain some impression of what this means by considering the user's view of the IPSE. The scene we have in mind is the medical office of the future, a working IPSE based on a network of SUN workstations. After logging on first thing in the morning, the secretary, for instance, will be confronted by her *role agenda* which provides a list (in the form of a set of icons) of those role-instances pointing at her which are associated with outstanding UserActions. Thus in figure 2, the secretary would be informed that there were outstanding GP referrals to be assessed by the appearance of the *urgency assessing* icon in her 'role agenda' window . Other work would be reflected in the presence of other role icons and the secretary would choose which task she felt to be the most appropriate (i.e. the IPSE does not remove her usual discretion). On selecting a particular role, she would then be presented with an *action agenda*, which (again in iconic form) would specify the full list of outstanding UserActions for the selected role, i.e. those UserActions whose start conditions are currently satisfied. On selecting a particular UserAction, the appropriate tools (e.g. word processor) and resources (e.g. an embryonic standard letter, including basic patient data) would be automatically provided.

Although originally conceived of as a means of introducing project discipline into software development environments, it is apparent that the benefits of IPSE technology extend well beyond this application. IPSE 2.5 provides both a modelling technique for representing cooperative activity and a means of creating working CSCW systems which are characterised by a high degree of flexibility. In many office environments, considerable inefficiencies arise because administrative procedures are not properly understood or carried out. This is particularly true in some settings such as health care where procedures are complex and staff are often inexperienced and overworked. By incorporating knowledge of organisational processes, the IPSE supports and controls the process of cooperative work and thus augments the effectiveness of group working. In our hospital example, for instance, many benefits may be anticipated: patients will be seen on time and with full documentation; doctors will be able to assess patients accurately; investigations will be carried out and reported promptly; vital data will not be lost; communication with GPs will occur without needless and possibly significant delay.

ACKNOWLEDGEMENTS

We would like to express our gratitude to Central Manchester Health Authority who have provided the financial support for Janet Maresh's post.

REFERENCES

Kedzierski, B.I. (1988). Communication and management support in system development environments. In *Computer Supported Cooperative Work* (Ed Grief). Morgan Kauffman: California.

Kiesler, S. *et al* (1988). Social Psychological Aspects of Computer-Mediated Communication. In *Computer Supported Cooperative Work* (Ed Grief). Morgan Kauffman: California.

King's Fund (1985). *Enabling clinical work.*

Goldberg, A. (1984). *Smalltalk-80 The Interactive Programming Environment.* Addison-Wesley: London.

Greif, I. (1988). *Computer Supported Cooperative Work.* Morgan Kaufmann: California.

Linstone, H.A. and Price, C.R.(1975). *The Delphi Method.* Addison-Wesley: London.

Warboys, B. and Veasey, P. (1989). Twenty years with support environments. *ICL Technical Journal.*

Wastell, D.G. *et al* (1987). Computing in clinical departments: implications for the design of hospital information systems, *Health Policy*, 8 , 347-354.

Human–Computer Interaction – INTERACT '90
D. Diaper et al. (Editors)
Elsevier Science Publishers B.V. (North-Holland)

TOOLS THAT SUPPORT HUMAN-HUMAN COMMUNICATION IN THE AUTOMATED OFFICE

I D BENEST and D DUKIĆ

Department of Computer Science, University of York, York, England, YO1 5DD

This paper reports on the progress made so far on the development of a new office automation environment. Such an environment must support the technical access to the very large quantities of information available in an office. It must also provide instinctive mechanisms that offer both casual and formal access to that information. It attempts to widen the keyhole effect that is present in other office information systems, and also imposes a surreptitiously managed work environment. This contribution describes a set of tools (for example electronic mail and computer conferencing) developed to support human-human cooperative work in this automated office.

1. INTRODUCTION TO THE ENVIRONMENT

The desk-top metaphor developed at Xerox (Smith et al. (1982)) and made famous by Apple (Birss (1984)) has become synonymous with a style of interface where objects in the real office are reflected in some of the graphical symbols displayed on the screen.

The application of windows, to represent the electronic form of sheets of paper that can be overlaid one on top of the other, helps to reinforce the impression of a desk on a screen. The impression is weakened when the user needs to navigate via a menu button or scroll bar and his progress through the document is one of moving over a continuous roll. Some systems have attempted to improve this situation by adopting hypertext mechanisms that provide a web (Yankelovich et al. (1985)) of paths through the material. Unfortunately such environments cause users to feel lost (Conklin (1987)); quite the opposite to the comfortable 'know-where-you-are' environment exhibited by real documents that dominate a real office. Since the visual display is so much smaller than the real desk top (Henderson and Card (1986)), it is necessary for users to fiddle with their graphics environments by moving, resizing, deleting, closing and opening windows, quite effectively resulting in a chaotic 'desk-top' (Benest and Dukić (1989)).

The desk-top metaphor is only a thin covering on top of a computer system. The authors believe that a higher-level metaphor is needed to cushion the user from the underlying computer system, in order to provide a more natural interface to the paper-less office of the future. The system is being designed to offer a task-level infrastructure that is capable of surreptitiously managing the work environment not only at the graphics level, but also at the task level.

2. HIGH-LEVEL INTERFACE OBJECTS

Two high-level user-interface objects: the Book Emulator and the Rôle Controller, are being developed to provide the interaction mechanisms for the user to access information. These have been described elsewhere (Benest (1990b), Benest & Dukić (1989)) and have been applied in other areas (Benest (1990a)). Figure 1 shows the general arrangement.

2.1. Rôle Controller

The Rôle Controller provides a means of accessing software tools, each of which supports a user task, and together serve a user rôle (Newman (1980), Woo et al. (1985)). So for example, a self-manager rôle controller would provide access to self-management tools such as a diary, telephone directory, project planner, etc. There is no restriction as to the level of functionality each tool may assume. However it is expected that within a rôle there is commonality in purpose, and that when the user has finished using a tool, a quite definite task-closure (Miller (1968)) is experienced by the user.

There are two presentation formats that are set by the rôle's governing files: a stylised shelf of books, and a set of large square buttons that may uniquely and visually identify the functionality invoked by the button. Each format may either be dynamic (in which case the books/buttons may be moved left or right within their containing window) or be static (in which case they cannot be moved). For the dynamic Rôle Controller, two buttons on the mouse enable the user to browse along the bookshelf in either direction. A momentary press causes some movement, continued pressure on the key causes quite rapid movement. The third key is for selecting a tool, catalogue or volume of information from the dynamic Rôle Controller. At any time, more than one tool may be invoked from a rôle. Currently, up to two levels of Rôle Controller can be present in a system; the number of levels and the precise structure of the information being dependent on the amount of information and the number of categories required by the specific office. At the top level, selection invokes up to four Rôle Controllers that can be present on the screen simultaneously.

2.2. Book Emulator

The Book Emulator is a constrained hypermedia system (Benest (1990b)) and presents information in the form of an open book. Two mouse keys enable the user to turn forward or back a page, the turn being animated across the screen to give implicit feedback that the page has been turned and to indicate the direction of travel. Holding down the mouse keys causes the pages to be flicked and as the reader

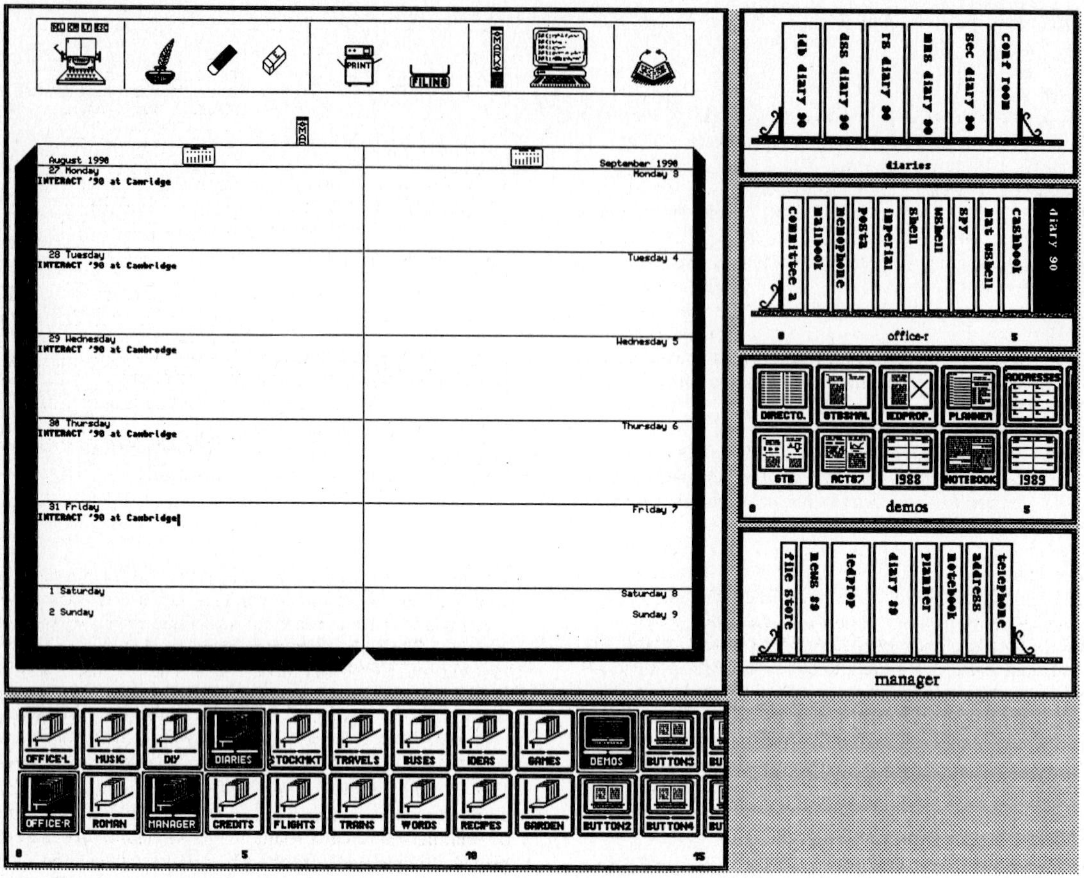

Figure 1: General arrangement of environment illustrating two levels of Rôle Controller, four formats for the Rôle Controller, and the Book Emulator containing a diary.

progresses through the book, the black bands down the side and along the bottom of the book, simulating the user's position within the material, grow and shrink to reflect the user's changing location. This mechanism provides for true browsing and helps to reduce the 'tunnel-vision' effect notable of other more computer-oriented navigation mechanisms. It supports the casual approach to finding information that is either deliberately sought by the user, or eye-catchingly provoked. Where appropriate the Book Emulator quite accurately mimics the structure of real documents, but can also provide networked links to arbitrary pages within the book and to other books. The information contained in the book may be static, as with a real book, or dynamic (animation) (Benest (1990a)).

The keyboard may be used to provide typewritten annotation; the emphasis here is on annotation rather than editing, though of course characters and whole lines may be deleted. Normally these annotations are private to the owner, subject of course to the file protection mechanisms available on the computer system, but they may also be shared. In such cases, the owner must specify which users can have access to his annotations. This specification includes whether they have observer status, or full annotation status. If a book is shared and the concurrent users have write permission and they exercise that right, only one is able to do so at any one time. The annotation facility is then locked on a first come first served basis, and all other users who have access to the information are notified as to who is updating. The lock is removed when the new annotation has been written to disk and all other viewers, who have the book on display, are then automatically updated with the new annotation a few seconds later.

The Book Emulator is the centre of attention around which are the Rôle Controllers. At all times, the user is spatially conscious of his location within the information. Although more than one Book Emulator may be 'out' at any one time, they are placed directly on top of each other. When the user wants to use a tool that is covered, he selects again at the Rôle Controller and the book at the front gradually disappears (de-materialises) from the screen and the required book is then materialised into view and is ready for instant use. Thus the graphics environment is controlled by the user through the Rôle Controllers, removing the requirement for the user to manipulate the window manager independently of the task.

3. HUMAN-HUMAN COMMUNICATION TOOLS

3.1. Shared Diaries

The diary presented through the Book Emulator, is just like a conventional paper diary, with one page-per-week for fifty-three weeks. The previous year, current year and next year calendars are provided at the front of the book where they would normally be located in a real diary. Notes in the diary are made using the typing annotation facility. Each working day may have up to eight lines of text. This diary clearly offers a different user-interface on to information compared with previous systems (Gifford (1980)). The Book Emulator enables the user truly to browse through his appointments instead of laboriously stepping through. The system does not exhibit the user interference mechanisms such as those identified in the study by (Kincaid et al. (1985)).

Not everyone is in favour of having their diaries open to inspection by colleagues. Nevertheless there are situations where it is desirable for others to have access to these annotations. For example, the secretary/manager relation (Kincaid et al. (1985)), the sales manager/sales team relation, and a central room booking facility. There are systems (Gifford (1980), Kincaid et al. (1985), Sarin and Greif (1985)) that offer views on to other people's diaries and though technically powerful, demand that a conventional database query be the means of specification. Such systems are difficult to browse. An alternative approach to sharing diaries is offered here by using a shelf of diaries where, for example, each diary is owned by a member of the sales team. Similarly, every member of a department might have access to a central diary for booking a room.

3.2. On-Line Support For Meetings

The Meeting support tool is a book of pages that are designed specifically for those meetings that do not require the benefits of face-to-face interaction. Members join the meeting at times that are convenient for them. The front page (Figure 2) is filled in by the Chairman. In principle, any number of observers may also be 'present' at the meeting.

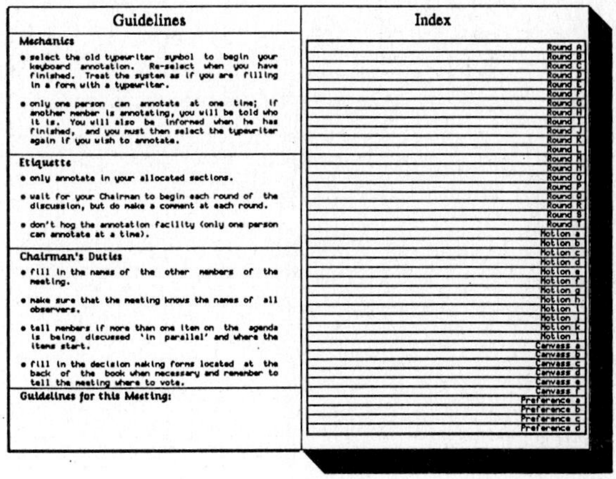

Figure 3

On the next two pages (Figure 3) there are general guidelines as to how members should conduct themselves during the meeting and there is room for additional rules for the specific meeting. The right hand page of Figure 3 shows an index that may be annotated; this index also provides a means for direct access to each round of the discussion (Figure 4) and to the voting (Figure 5) and preference forms (Figures 6 and 7) located at the back of the book. Each round (two pages) is divided up into eight numbered sections (Figure 4), one for each member of the meeting. Each person has to restrict his comments to his section (ten lines of typing). The comments of each person at each round of the discussion are inherently provided in parallel, and the Chairman continues the discussion on to the next round, repeating this until a consensus is reached; a simple set of concluding statements should suffice for the record. If no consensus is reached, the voting forms (Figures 5, 6 and 7) are available for use, and all votes are visible to the meeting.

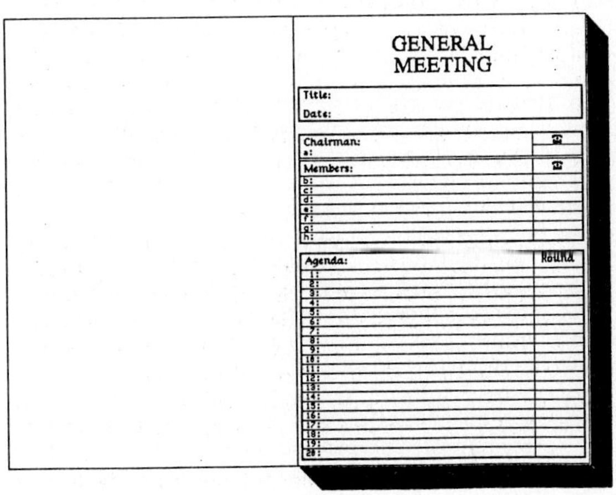

Figure 2

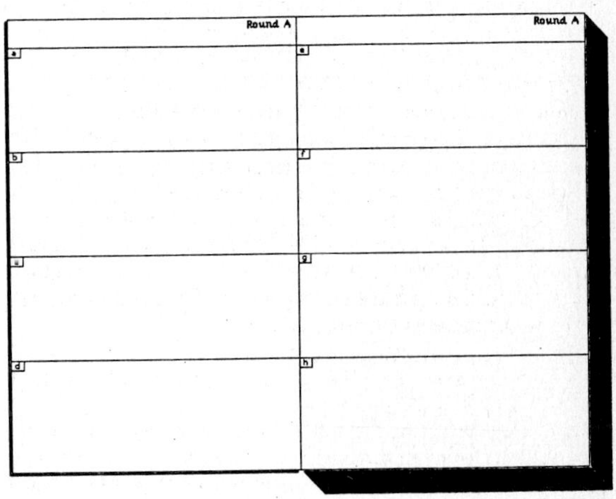

Figure 4

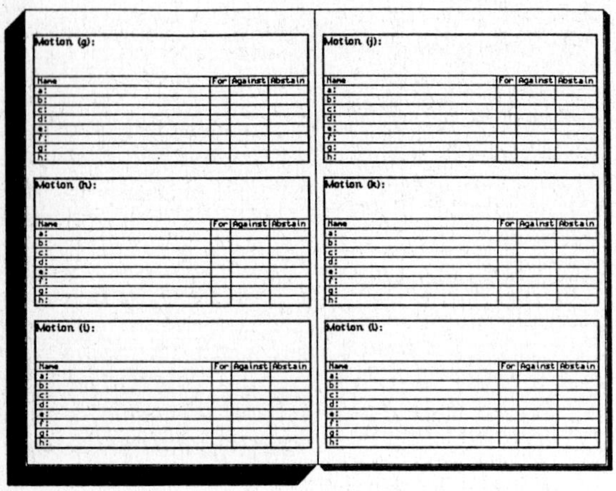

Figure 5

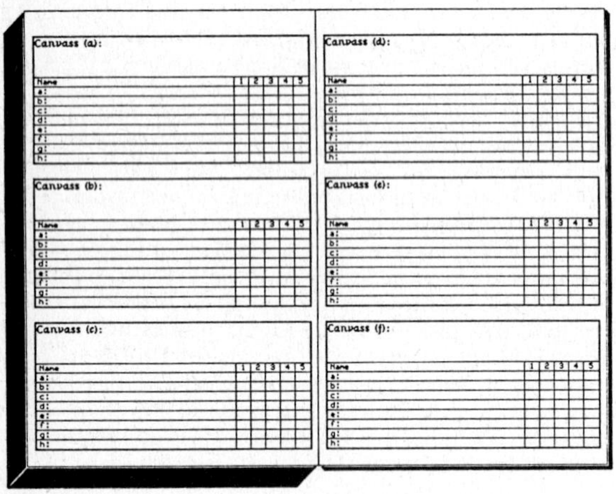

Figure 6

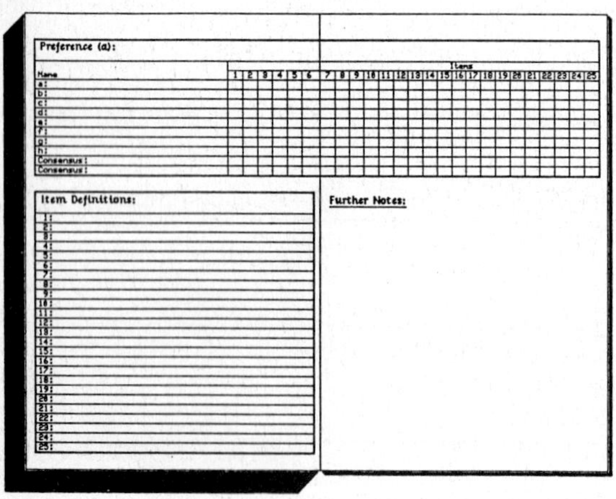

Figure 7

The parallel nature of the medium means that each item on the agenda can be started at the same time; the Chairman would decide on which page the item should begin and this he would annotate either in the index, or in the agenda, or in both. The medium, together with light meeting control from the Chairman, should ensure that the discussion 'sticks to the point' (Maude et al. (1984)). If members wished to consult documents relevant to a discussion point, then they have access through their Rôle Controllers to specific volumes (eg. the papers for the meeting) all through the same style of interface. If a member is away for a week and the meeting progresses during that time, then when he returns he can make his response at the correct position within the discussion, ensuring that 'old' issues are not muddled with the latest. When a meeting is judged to have finished, the whole book can be filed as the minutes of the meeting without further minutes being written.

This tool supports an orderly structured electronic conference in which people do not have to be at the same place at the same time. In comparison with older systems (Palme (1984), Pankoke-Babatz (1984)), it offers an improved ability to browse through earlier discussion, and to see the arguments in a more parallel fashion than that exhibited in the older 'serial' systems. However, it must be said that the ten line restriction would severly hamper the activities of on-line writing of technical papers (Maude et al. (1984), Wilson (1984)); and alternative support for such activity within the environment is being given consideration. The system can be used for 'real-time' conferences in the sense that all members can be present on the computer system at the same time. However, it is estimated from work reported in (Richer (1980)), that about ten minutes can be expected for a user to compose a ten line contribution. During that time there is no immediate updating of participants' screens as the annotations are being made, but the system does ensure that each person making his comment is not interrupted. All others present on the computer at the same time are informed as to who is annotating. The technical difficulties (Sarin and Greif (1985)) in which more than one person might attempt to update the current state of the meeting at the same time, does not arise. Finally, it is only necessary to change the layout of pages (less than a day's effort) in order to change the supporting structure for a meeting and perhaps to allow for a different number of members.

3.3. Meeting Scheduler

This sharing of information can also be exploited to schedule face-to-face meetings using tables in which columns represent hours in the day or days in a fortnight and the rows are filled in by the organiser of the meeting with the names of the people required to attend (Figure 8). Then each individual can fill in the times/dates when he is/is not available for the meeting. An advantage is that all attendees can see the organisational difficulties and, where possible, modify their response to accommodate the schedule. It is felt that this is an improvement over those data base oriented systems (Sarin and Greif (1985)) that provide access to individual's diaries, because those systems rely on the diary being up-to-date and correct; they do not take account of the fact that the diary is only a person's memory support tool with many unnoted considerations locked in his head. Only he knows whether he can attend a meeting at a specific time. The work in (Kincaid et al's (1985)) identifies a less than enthusiastic approach to such automated scheduling systems, a surprising result when manufacturers place great emphasis on this

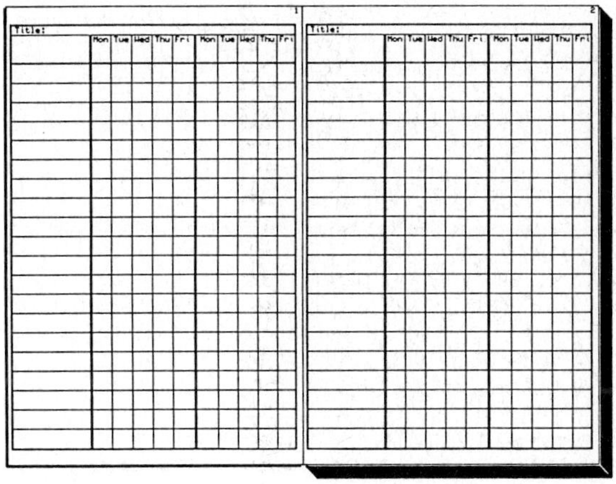

Figure 8

facility in their products. The meeting scheduler can be made in a number of guises depending on the level of secrecy that pervades the organisation. For example, an open organisation would ensure that all members of a Department, via a common meeting scheduling book (Figure 9), could know which meetings were being arranged in their department even though not all people attended or needed to attend every single meeting that took place. Such a system could provide an interesting impact on the social fabric of the organisation!

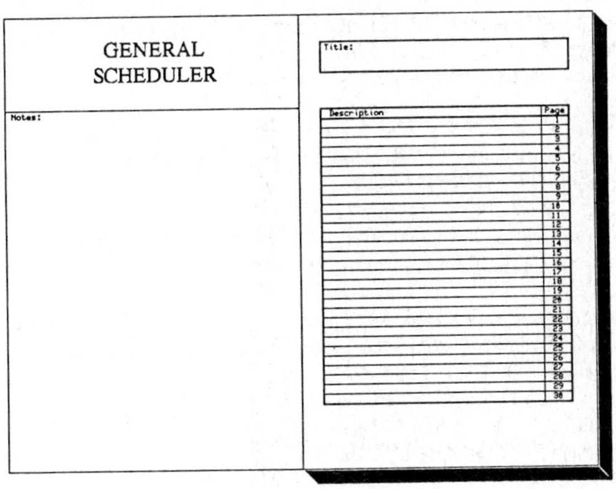

Figure 9

3.4. Whiteboard

A further use for the sharing facilities of the Book Emulator, inspired by the more extensive and elaborate work in (Donahue and Widom (1986)) is that of providing the electronic equivalent to a Group's or Department's central whiteboard. A blank book that enabled people to write dated news information could be simply implemented, but unlike a real whiteboard, it would not have to be wiped clean so often and indeed could be used to provide an informal record of the Group's activity.

3.5. Electronic Memoranda

Electronic mail (Innocent et al. (1987)) is a common facility in a computer system and their benefits have long been recognised (Uhlig (1977)). Usually they provide a window on to a continuous roll of mail that the user can scroll around. The necessary functionality is now well-known, but the user-interface does not readily support the human handling of mail in a manner that encourages efficiency and formality. Figure 10 illustrates the presentation of memoranda within the new environment. This system encourages users specifically to schedule time (or times) in the day when mail will be handled, rather than deal with items as they arrive. It accesses the normal mail file on the computer system, and uses the ordinary mail command to send mail. Thus it is a new user-interface to a well established electronic mail system and is fully integrated into the developing environment.

The items of mail are presented in book form, with the oldest item at the front and the newest (which can be located directly with a book-mark) at the back. At the front there exists a Contents section (Figure 11) that serves both to indicate the amount of mail that requires attention, and to provide a gateway to specific items. Selecting on an item in the Contents pages causes the mail book to be turned directly to that item. A book-mark is automatically placed in the Contents section for direct return. The system enables the user to browse through all his mail reminding him of what is still outstanding. He can bin an item (Figure 12), reply to an item or file an item. The mail is not deleted, filed, or the reply sent, until the book is closed. This allows the user to retrieve or correct an item.

Messages received cannot be changed by the receiver. Thus the volatility (Shapiro and Anderson (1985)) inherent in other mail systems is not present with the typed annotation facility. Furthermore, the user can write a reply without filling in the 'Reply' line, enabling him to dwell on his response for an extended period of time. Such a facility might well reduce the incidence of flamming (Shapiro and Anderson (1985)). The reply always follows the original message so that it is presented in the correct historical order. This makes reviewing the progress of a discussion, that has passed many times between sender and receiver, a straightforward linear read.

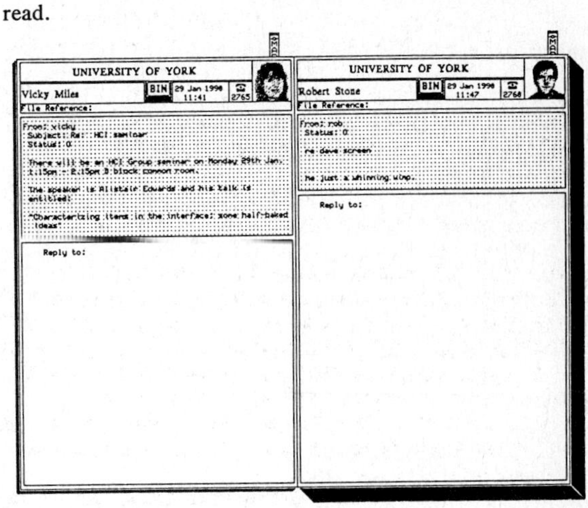

Figure 10

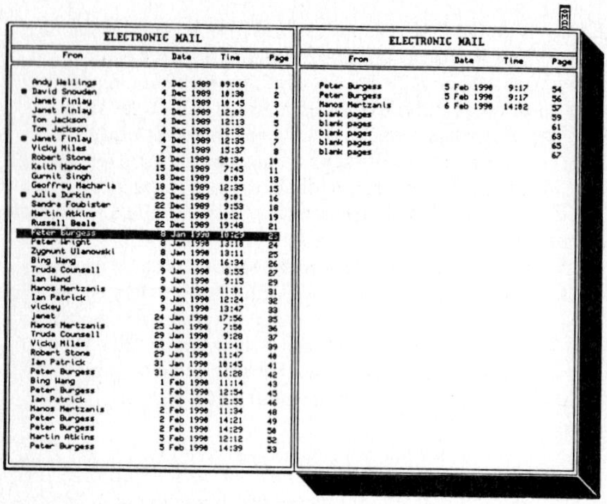

Figure 11

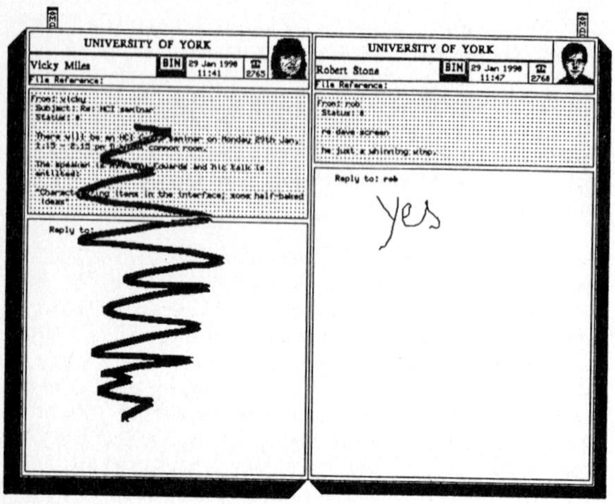

Figure 12

Mail may include free hand annotation (Figure 12) as allowed for by the Book Emulator. The picture of the sender, the name of his organisation, and his telephone number are currently derived from system files, though it is planned to enable pictures to be received from the sender.

Separate books for creating new memoranda and telephone messages (Figure 13) are available to the user, illustrating the principle of using standard forms to provide "additional cues to the level of formality intended (Shapiro and Anderson (1985)). Though such forms are restricted in length, the authors have been guided by (Shapiro and Anderson (1985)) who commented: "the message that makes its point and fits on one screen does its job best, and you will be well regarded".

ACKNOWLEDGEMENTS

This work has been supported by UK SERC grant number GR/F 37535/IED4/1/1220.

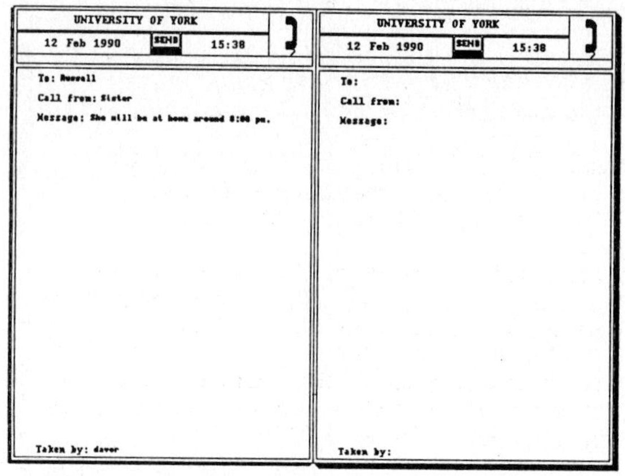

Figure 13

REFERENCES

Benest, I.D. (1990a). Computer-Assisted Learning Using Dynamic Electronic Books. In Computer Assisted Learning (Ed. M. Kibby). Pergamon Press, 195-203.

Benest, I.D. (1990b). A Hypertext System with Controlled Hype. In Hypertext: Theory into Practice II (Eds. C. Green and R. McAleese). Intellect, (to be published).

Benest, I.D. and Dukić, D. (1989). "High-Level User-Interface Objects", In Designing and Using Human-Computer Interfaces and Knowledge Based Systems (Eds. G. Salvendy and M.J. Smith). Elsevier, 597-604.

Birss, E.W. (1984). The Integrated Software and User Interface of Apple's Lisa. National Computer Conference, 53, AFIPS Press, 319-328.

Conklin, E.J. (1987). Hypertext: An Introduction and Survey. IEEE Computer, 20(9), 17-41.

Donahue J. and Widom J. (1986). Whiteboards: A Graphical Database Tool. ACM Transactions on Office Information Systems, 4(1), 24-41.

Gifford, D.K. (1980). Violet, An Experimental Decentralized System. In Integrated Office Systems - Burotics, (Ed. N. Naffah). IFIP, North-Holland, 27-41.

Henderson, D.A. and Card, S.K. (1986). Rooms: The Use of Multiple Virtual Workplaces to Reduce Space Contention in a Window-Based Graphical User Interface. ACM Transactions on Graphics, 5(3), 211-243.

Innocent, P.R. et al. (1987). Experiments With the User Interface for Unix Mail. Proceedings of European Unix Systems User Group Conference.

Kincaid, C.M. et al. (1985). Electronic Calendars in the Office: An Assessment of User Needs and Current Technology. ACM Transactions on Office Information Systems, 3(1), 89-102.

Maude, T.I. et al. (1984). An Experiment in Group Working on Mailbox Systems. IFIP Conference on Human-Computer Interaction, Vol.1. Elsevier, 396-400.

Miller, R.B. (1968). Response Time in Man-Computer Conversational Transactions. Fall Joint Computer Conference, 33(1). AFIPS Press, Virginia, USA, 267-277.

Newman, W. (1980). Office Models and Office Systems Design. In Integrated Office Systems - Burotics, (Ed. N. Naffah). IFIP, North-Holland, 3-10.

Palme, J. (1984). COM/PortaCOM Conference System. Design Goals and Principles. IFIP Conference on Human-Computer Interaction, Vol.1. Elsevier, 271-272.

Pankoke-Babatz, U. (1984), The Computer Conferencing System KOMEX. IFIP Conference on Human-Computer Interaction, Vol.1. Elsevier, 269-270.

Richer, I. (1980). Voice, Data and the Computerized PABX. In Integrated Office Systems - Burotics, IFIP, North-Holland, 55-69.

Sarin, S. and Greif, I. (1985). Computer-Based Real-Time Conferencing Systems. IEEE Computer, 18(10)., 33-45.

Shapiro, N.Z. and Anderson, R.H. (1985). Toward an Ethics and Etiquette for Electronic Mail. Rand Report R-3283-NSF/RC.

Smith, D.C. et al. (1982). The Star User Interface: An Overview. National Computer Conference, 51. AFIPS Press, 515-528.

Uhlig, R.P. (1977). Human Factors in Computer Messaging Systems. Datamation, 121-126.

Wilson, P. (1984). Structures for Group Working in Mailbox Systems. IFIP Conference on Human-Computer Interaction, Vol.1. Elsevier, 388-395.

Woo, C. et al. (1985). Document Management Systems. In Office Automation Concepts and Tools, (Ed. D.C. Tsichritzis). Springer-Verlag, 21-40.

Yankelovich, N. et al. (1985). Reading and Writing the Electronic Book. IEEE Computer, 18(10)., 15-30.

SECTION V: APPLICATIONS AND CASE STUDIES

SV.3 Applications

Smartwriter: A tool-based wordprocessor for adult literacy students
D. Ellis, J. Horton, and P. Black 863

The interface to a hypertext journal
A. Simpson 869

A fisheye presentation strategy: Aircraft maintenance data
D.A. Mitta 875

Supporting exploratory learning
A. Howes and S.J. Payne 881

Application of cognitive modeling and knowledge measurement in diagnosis and training of complex skills
Y.M. Yufik 887

Human–Computer Interaction – INTERACT '90
D. Diaper et al. (Editors)
Elsevier Science Publishers B.V. (North-Holland)

SMARTWRITER: A TOOL-BASED WORDPROCESSOR FOR ADULT LITERACY STUDENTS

David Ellis, Jane Horton and Philip Black

System Applied Technology Limited, Sheaf House, Sheaf Street, Sheffield, S1 2BA

This paper describes the design and development of a computer-based Literacy Tutor centred on a mouse-driven wordprocessor. The appropriateness of the design for literacy students is emphasised; the design objectives being simplicity and consistency rather than the implementation of a large collection of 'interesting' features. A novel tool-based approach has been adopted for the wordprocessor and associated learning modules. The suitability of using an object-oriented design methodology for this research project is clearly demonstrated. The subsequent development of the system for profoundly deaf students further exposes the advantages of this approach. Both systems have been evaluated in the field.

INTRODUCTION

The initial eighteen month research and development project funded by the Learning Technology Unit of the Training Agency began in December 1987. The aim was to develop a flexible, easy to use wordprocessor specifically for adult literacy students which would include a dictionary, thesaurus, spelling checker and computer-based learning materials. The scope of this Literacy Tutor was subsequently extended to include the development of a fast grammar checker. Full details of this project are given in a report by Horton [1]. The initial target hardware was the Acorn Archimedes microcomputer.

The research phase of the project involved assessing the precise needs of literacy students and their tutors. Tutors clearly understood the potential that word processing could offer literacy students but suitable software packages were not available. Whereas literate users of word processors have only to contend with the functionality of the system (not always an insignificant task on its own) literacy students also lack basic understanding of the medium itself. Since the aim of using a computer in the first place is to break down barriers to learning and increase the students' self-confidence the word processor had to be simple and straightforward to use.

In addition, the target population were adults, and simple word processors designed for Primary Education, Folio (Tediman Software) and Pendown (Logotron), were as equally unsuitable as the countless general purpose word processors then available. At their worst, general purpose word processors are a collection of features roughly assembled into incoherent packages. Eventually mastered they are capable of a multitude of ingenious functions such as multiple phrase buffers and complex indent and tab functions. Good design principles such as transparency, simplicity and consistency are often sacrificed for the sake of including more and more features.

During the research phase of this project the important features to include within the system were elicited which avoided *unnecessary* complexity.

The final version of the Literacy Tutor is referred to as Smartwriter.

OVERALL SYSTEM DESIGN

Smartwriter contains many of the writing aids available on microcomputer systems such as a spelling checker, thesaurus and dictionary. The grammar checker, implemented using a form of GPSG (Generalised Phrase Structure Grammar) proposed by Gazdar et al [2], and the computer-based learning materials designed specifically for this project also operate from within the wordprocessor interface. The learning materials focus on literacy skills such as form filling and writing CVs.

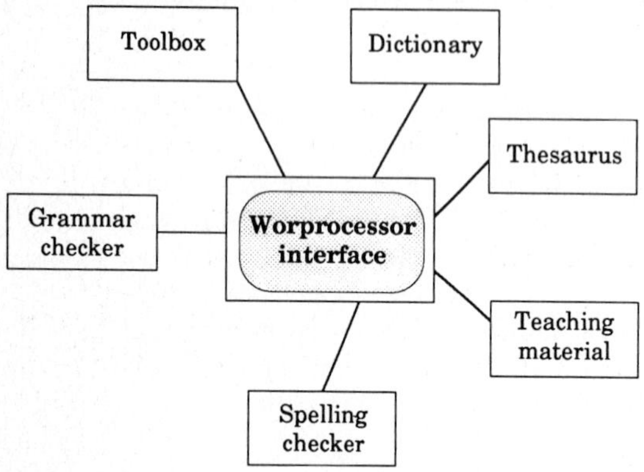

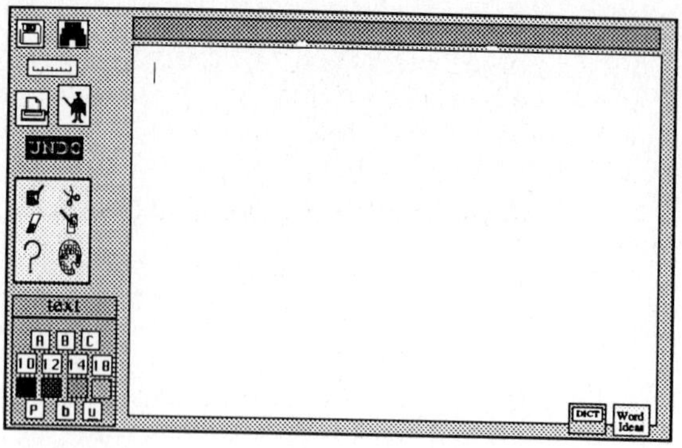

Having the wordprocessor central to the whole system provides two major benefits. Firstly, students only need to learn how to operate one interface and are never 'transported' to any other screen. This alleviates the common problems associated with navigating through a system (eg getting lost!). Secondly, all tools (eg spelling checker, dictionary, undo and copy) are constantly available to the student even within the learning modules themselves. This puts the user in control of the system by allowing them the flexibility of having instant access to a universal set of tools. The consistency of the system is thus maintained.

Smartwriter has utilised a mouse-driven windowing interface with pop up windows, buttons and other icons in common with many graphical interfaces such as the Macintosh, Motif and NextStep. It avoids the use of pull down or pop up menus by having all functions immediately accessible in the form of tool icons or buttons. Where an application contains a limited number of commands and functions this seems an obvious solution.

The design of the interface has naturally been influenced by other graphical interfaces such as the Macintosh, but as Jones [3] points out, learning to use the MacWrite wordprocessor is not at all straightforward and leaves naive users with an incorrect mental model of the system. The interface needed improving to make the system simpler and more overt to the target group. This was achieved by clearly identifying the needs of the user with respect to creating, editing and printing written documents. A number of design ideas are outlined below.

All windows (except the wordprocessor itself) are moveable to allow the user to leave tools such as the dictionary permanently on screen in a convenient position, but are *not* scaleable since this would add unnecessary complexity to the interface and increase the time spent on window management. The text windows do not have the ubiquitous scroll bars for the same reason. Documents produced by literacy students rarely exceed two pages in length and an easier method of scrolling text windows was investigated. The eventual solution was to turn the pointer into a 'hand' whilst pressing the second mouse button (the Acorn Archimedes has a three button mouse) and allow the user to push the text up and down. This function is universal and used for instance in the dictionary to scroll through definitions. This method is also encountered as an option on some Apple Macintosh graphics programs for moving the graphics page inside the window.

It was essential that the literacy students were able to enter and format text on screen and produce an exact copy via a graphics printer. Initial research showed that students became frustrated if the printout did not match the screen display. A truely What You See Is What You Get (WYSIWYG) wordprocessor was therefore essential. The students needed to be able to enjoy their writing, so three different fonts, in four sizes and colours with three styles (plain, bold and underline) were made available. Text was limited to these options, not because it was difficult to increase the number of fonts or sizes, but because the mechanism for selecting text attributes would have been much more complex.

THE TOOLBOX

The basic toolbox contains five tool icons for editing text: erase, cut, copy, paste and paint (to change text attributes). The Macintosh interface avoids plunging the user into obscure modes such as 'copy mode' by requiring the user to select an area (by highlighting) *before* selecting the operation. This is opposite to the naive user's model of the real life process of, say, rubbing out words on paper. Smartwriter adopts this more familiar approach by allowing the user to 'pick up' a tool (the pointer changes to the tool icon when the user clicks on that tool) and drag it over the chosen area of text to perform the operation. The complex cut and paste operation is outlined below to illustrate this use of editing tools.

A. The cat sat on the fluffy mat.

Pick up 'cut' tool, click and drag over text, release mouse button.

B. The cat sat on the mat.

Fluffy is deleted and tool immediately changes to the 'paste pot'. Place tool (if required) to insert text and click mouse.

C. The fluffy cat sat on the mat.

Fluffy is inserted and the 'paste pot' is still available for inserting text at another point.

Tools can be returned to the toolbox at any time by, clicking within the toolbox area. The UNDO button will undo the last operation but *not reundo it*, since this often leads to conceptual problems. Changing text attributes (font, size, colour, style) can be difficult to comprehend and usually involves changing one attribute at a time. This is handled by the 'paint brush' tool. The user clicks on this tool and a painter's palette appears. The user can 'dip' their brush into any of the fonts, sizes, colours or styles (selecting all four if required) and 'paint' the area of text by highlighting and releasing the mouse. Only those attributes that have been set in the palette will be changed. This method more accurately models the user's real life experience.

The final tool in the toolbox provides a simple level of help. The student can pick up the '?' tool and click on any object on the screen. A short help pop up is displayed whilst the button is pressed. For instance clicking the '?' tool on the eraser in the toolbox will pop up the message 'Use this to rub out text' and clicking on the title bar of any moveable window will pop up 'You can move the box by dragging this bar'. This simple level of help has been provided to give the literacy student an extra degree of independence in using the system which is a key element in developing their confidence.

OBJECT-ORIENTED DESIGN

Most WIMP interfaces are not designed or implemented using an object-oriented methodology, one exception being NextStep, the interface for the NeXT workstation. In order to achieve the flexibility and consistency that underlies the design of Smartwriter it was necessary for the internal program design to mirror the external interface design. The model presented to the user is hence very similar to the model of the real system. There is thus no need to disguise the basic program model, and the simplicity of the object-oriented program design can be made transparent to the user. One could say that good building materials are more likely to produce a good house. Good interfaces can, of course, be achieved using other program design methodologies but it is much more difficult.

In Smartwriter everything that appears on the screen from a button to a whole text document is defined as an object. The system operates on the basis of message passing between these objects.

Objects have a good degree of autonomy and since they are allowed to act independently the user is free to manipulate them in any context. Hence the delete tool (the 'eraser') can be used at any time to rub out any piece of editable text. The flexibility of the system is thus increased without any significant programming overhead.

There are many advantages in using an object-oriented design methodology apart from aiding interface design. An excellent justification for using these techniques is given by Meyer [4]. These include amendability, reusability and reliability.

In the case of Smartwriter the decision to build the system using an object-oriented methodology has been particularly fruitful. It has facilitated the development of a complex piece of software in a very modular fashion; designing and implementing new tools and facilities as and when they were required and knowing that they would easily fit within the system. Smartwriter has proved to be particularly reliable despite many modifications. The relatively short timescale for this development and the ability to cope with the evolving nature of the design, which is particularly inherent in such research projects, have demonstrated the suitability of an object-oriented approach.

With the aid of further funding from the Training Agency, Smartwriter has since been adapted for use by deaf students. This group, especially pre-lingually deaf student, have similar literacy needs to the original target group but also require additional support in the form of graphical representation of words in the dictionary to aid comprehension using BSL (British Sign Language) and pictures where appropriate.

Modifying Smartwriter to meet these new requirements has been relatively painless from the software engineering point of view due to the coherence and inherent adaptability of the original object-oriented design. The objects within the system were designed to make programming using these objects very easy by completely hiding the fast (and hence complex) low level graphics and windowing routines. Programmers new to this project have been able to extend the system without becoming involved in complex coding.

THE USERS' VIEW

Evaluation of Smartwriter took place at eight trial sites which included Open Learning Centres, Colleges of Education and Community Colleges in the UK. Initial trials were held to evaluate the usability of the interface whilst the system was still under development and resulted in modifications to the interface. Further trials were used to evaluate the complete system by asking tutors to explain to the literacy students how to use the system, to set them tasks, provide assistance when necessary and monitor their progress.

Most students found the mouse quite useable but a small number simply found it difficult to control. Overall, students were motivated by the degree of control a mouse allowed them and after only one session were able to manipulate the mouse well enough. The toolbox (containing cut, copy, paste etc) was well received although some students had difficulty manipulating the mouse to highlight precisely the text they wanted to change. Students enjoyed being able to change the size, colour and style of their text. One student thought that it was 'glamorous' and many agreed that it was quick and easy to use. The following report from a literacy student summarises general remarks about the system.

"Having used Smartwriter for a few hours I was soon deep into the text and having lots of fun, unlike some word processors where you have to sit down with a manual for a few days and learn a lot of complicated commands to do the simplest task.

I like the icons a lot, it made using Smartwriter very easy for some one like me who has never used a word processor before. Being able to insert text, change the style, and change the size at the click of the mouse was very clever.

I also liked the thesaurus, and though it was a good idea to include it in the word processor I thought the colour options were irrelevant unless you have access to a colour printer, although it was pretty to look at, the memory could have been used to include a larger dictionary.

Not having the world's greatest education I also found the spell checker a real help, it gave me more confidence to actually sit down and type a letter knowing that at the click of the mouse help was there if I needed it.

It's nice to be able to mangle the English language and know that you can put it right without having to consult a load of experts first. Once I had the letter looking something like I wanted it, I found it a simple task to print out my finished document.

My opinion, for what it is worth, is yes I really liked using Smartwriter, it was fun, easy to use, and it also taught me how to spell a few words I had problems with."

The version of Smartwriter developed for deaf students was trialled with twenty four profoundly deaf students and five students with partial hearing. The following report is from the tutor responsible for the trials (himself profoundly deaf) at the Two-Can Resource Unit, Derby.

"All the students except one found that there were no major difficulties in using the system for the first time as they had a one hour session to work on and at the end of the session, almost all of them mastered the skills with some help from the observer, with some of them needing extra time to control the mouse. They were pleased with the basic tools, but one had problems with the palette (text) because of his eyesight problems. This could be expanded a bit, so that the student can work on it on his own. Some weaker students needed guidance from the tutor to help them gain confidence to work, before working on their own. But there should not be a main problem after a few hours, except for the grammar checker, spelling checker, dictionary words and word ideas."

At the end of the trial period all students except one particularly weak student felt that they understood the use of the toolbox. As far as being able to use the tools practically, seventeen (out of twenty nine) were fully confident to use the tools on their own, eleven had almost mastered them and required a little help from the observer and one did not attempt to use them. Eleven students consistently needed help with the UNDO function. Again, controlling the mouse was the major reason for not being able to use the tools.

The trials population were young adults with moderate or severe learning difficulties. The Smartwriter interface proved to be highly usable by most students who quickly gained a sufficiently good mental model of the system to be able to use the word processor unaided after a short time.

CONCLUSIONS

The research project demonstrated that good design principles of consistency and simplicity have produced a highly useable word processor interface for adult literacy students to learn. This paper has emphasised the necessity to clearly identify the needs and abilities of the target group in order to produce an interface design that is appropriate to the user.

The text editing tools have been designed so that their functionality closely models the real life process. The tools have been well received by users. Trials of the interface have been well received by users. Trials of the interface have highlighted the problems that some users have in manipulating a mouse. Although there are many advantages in adopting a WIMP interface this potential barrier to controlling the interface should be borne in mind especially for users with special needs.

Using an object-oriented design methodology has great benefits for the interface designer since the underlying program design can mirror the external interface design. The user's model of the interface is therefore consistent with the computer model. The object-oriented methodology has facilitated the evolution of the interface over the life time of this project and has allowed the system, to be easily amended and extended for use by a different target group.

REFERENCES

[1] Horton, J., Computer Based Learning and Application Software in Adult Literacy

(Learning Technology Unit, the Training Agency, Sheffield, 1989).
[2] Gazdar, G., Klein, E., Pullum, G.K., and Sag, I.A., Generalised Phrase Structure Grammar (Blackwell, 1985).
[3] Jones, S., A Mouse's Tale, HCI Newsletter, No. 14 (December 1989) BCS HCI Specialist Group.
[4] Meyer, B., Object-Oriented Software Construction (Prentice Hall, 1988).

Human–Computer Interaction – INTERACT '90
D. Diaper et al. (Editors)
Elsevier Science Publishers B.V. (North-Holland)

THE INTERFACE TO A HYPERTEXT JOURNAL

ANNETTE SIMPSON

HUSAT Research Institute, The Elms, Elms Grove, Loughborough, Leics, LE11 1RG. UK.

This paper reports some of the findings of a study comparing two interfaces to a hypertext database of academic journal articles. The design of the interface to the individual articles was derived from the results of previous studies by the author. The aim of the present investigation was to determine whether those features found to assist readers in navigating through, and extracting information from, individual journal articles were of benefit when applied to the interface to a database of such articles. The influence of interface type on readers' ability to locate the information required to answer two essay-type questions was examined. Performance, both in terms of the amount of information located and the efficiency with which it was located, was significantly better when using an interface containing these features as compared to an interface whose features were derived from the paper medium.

1. Introduction

1.1 The Academic Journal

There are well-established conventions regarding the structure of both academic journals and the articles within them. Typically, a journal comprises a number of volumes (usually one per year), each of which comprises several issues, which contain the individual articles. This format has been largely dictated by developments in the paper-making and print industries, and it imposes certain restrictions. For example, limitations concerning the size and weight of volumes, and, as a consequence, the number and length of the articles within them.

For a long time paper has been the only viable presentation medium for journals. However, recent advances in computer-based technology make it possible to present journals electronically, and the considerable advantages of the electronic storage and retrieval of information have also been demonstrated. The use of the electronic medium removes restrictions such as those mentioned previously and, furthermore, permits the exploration of alternative structures.

Nevertheless, there are a number of reasons for preserving the structure of the paper journal at the individual article level. First, it follows the structure of the research process itself. Second, studies described by McKnight, Dillon and Richardson (1989) have demonstrated that readers possess a model of a journal article which permits them to judge whereabouts in the article certain information may be located. Furthermore, it has been shown that people rarely read journal articles in a sequential manner (e.g., Dillon, Richardson and McKnight, 1988), but adopt various strategies according to their reason for accessing the article. Consequently, a structure capable of supporting a wide variety of tasks is required. An additional argument against merely reproducing the linear presentation style of paper articles in the electronic medium (e.g., Benest, Morgan and Smithurst, 1987) is that people may dislike reading from screen, and will therefore always prefer the paper version. However, if electronic documents permit the reader to do things they would find useful, but which are difficult or impossible when using paper documents (e.g., nonsequential access to its constituent parts), the electronic version may be considered preferable. It is therefore proposed that the existing components of the journal article should be preserved in a hypertext environment, but that the linear form of presentation used in the paper medium may not be the optimum.

1.2. Navigation in hypertext

Some writers speak of the possible navigation problems associated with hypertext. As Monk, Walsh and Dix (1988) point out, in paper documents, "the underlying object manipulated by the user has a serial or sequential structure" (p.422), and, even if the reader does not choose to access the information in this order, its sequence remains the stable. However, the increased flexibility of access permitted in the hypertext environment means that the reader may not be able to conceptualize an overview of a document's structure. It has been shown that readers are often confused about where they are within a hypertext document and unsure if they have seen all of the information, or whether they will be able to find something they read earlier (Nielsen and Lyngbaek, 1989).

Canter, Rivers and Storrs (1985) draw an analogy between database navigation and navigation through the physical environment, proposing that in both situations people construct mental maps of objects and the relationships between them. At both the article and database level, knowing where one is, where one has been and where else there is to go "clearly represent navigational matters" (Canter, Powell, Wishart and Roderick, 1986).

A series of studies by the present author (see Simpson, 1989) attempted to determine what the interface to a

presentation order of the two questions was counterbalanced.

2.2 Subjects

The 32 subjects used in the study were final year and postgraduate students from the Department of Human Sciences at Loughborough University. They were each paid £5 for participating in the experiment. All had some experience of using a Macintosh computer.

2.3 Materials

The database was presented using SuperCard™, and displayed on a Macintosh II computer. It contained 18 articles taken from the human factors journal 'Behaviour and Information Technology'. All of the articles referred to at least one other article in the database, some of them to several other articles. The construction of the individual articles was the same for both interface types.

On selecting an article from the database, subjects were shown a 'title page', containing the author/s' names(s) and address(es) and the title of the article. This card also showed a list of the other articles in the database either referred to by the selected article, or referring to it. The articles in the list were selectable, so that readers could go directly to them without having to go back to the database level.

The structure of an article was shown by a series of tree diagrams, each of which displayed one level of the hierarchy, with arrows indicating the links to other levels (see figure 1). Readers were able to move up and down the hierarchy, and the sections of text were selectable. Reverse video was used to show readers which sections of the text they had visited, and the 'footprint' was a small marker cross by the title of a section.

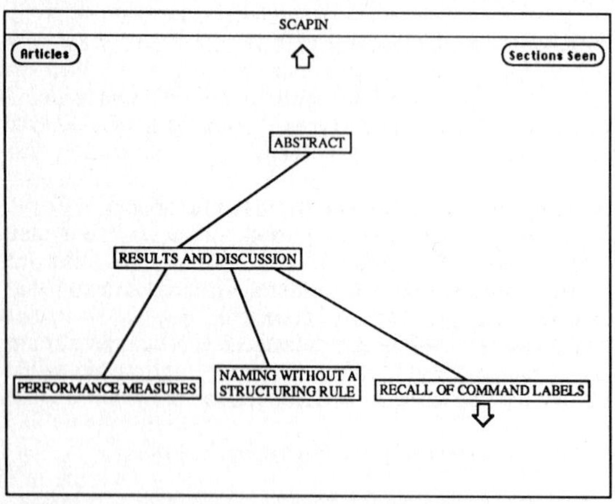

Figure 1. Tree diagram of the article's structure.

It was possible to access both the contents of the database and the hierarchical representation of the structure of the current article from all text cards. If a reference to another article in the database was made by an author, then a small arrow was placed in the text after the reference, and clicking the mouse on this arrow took readers to the 'title page' of that article. Thus there were three possible methods of moving between articles: at the database level, from the 'refers to/referred to by' on the title page of an article, and via the arrows embedded in the text.

The two interfaces to the database were as follows. For the first (map), the articles in the database were displayed graphically, with directional lines indicating the cross-references, thus producing a network type of display (see figure 2). Articles were selected by clicking the mouse in the appropriate box. When an article had been accessed, its author and title were displayed in reverse video, thus providing readers with a record of the articles they had visited. An ordered list of the articles visited was obtainable by clicking on a button at the top of the screen. A small marker cross, or 'footprint' showed readers which article they had just come from. For the second interface (list), subjects were shown a chronological list of the 18 articles (see figure 3). Clicking the mouse on an author's name moved readers to that particular article.

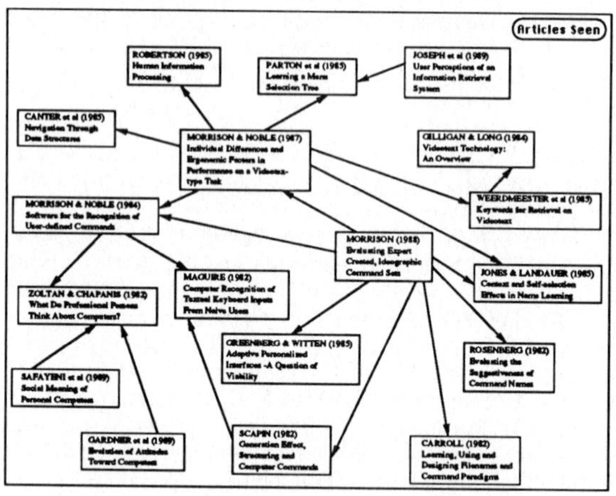

Figure 2. Map type interface to the database.

Information relevant to each of the two questions was contained in a different set of seven articles. The questions differed in the number of these articles which referenced one or more of the other seven, i.e., which were linked within the database. For question one (linked), all of the articles were linked to at least one other article, but for question two (unlinked), none of the articles referenced any other article in the database.

A questionnaire given to subjects after they had completed the question-answering task required them to indicate their computer experience and prior knowledge of the topics addressed by each of the questions.

2.4 Procedure

After a short practice session in which to familiarize them with the system, subjects were given a printed instruction

hypertext document should look like, and what features it should provide, in order to help readers overcome such problems. The main findings of these studies are discussed briefly below.

1.3 Previous Studies

A textual representation of a document's structure was found to assist readers in locating information from within a document, and in forming a map of its structure, but a graphical representation was of even greater benefit. The importance of spatial location is widely discussed in the literature, it being an 'incidental' cue, processed automatically (Hasher and Zacks, 1979). A number of writers (e.g., Rothkopf, 1971; Haas and Hayes, 1985) have investigated incidental memory for the location of text, both in the paper and electronic media. The results of these studies indicate that incidental memory for such an attribute is significantly more accurate than by chance.

The finding that performance in an information retrieval task was better when readers used a graphical, as compared to a textual, representation of a document's structure supports the hypothesis that people form mental maps of documents they read (e.g., Waller, 1985). The graphical representation more closely matched the reader's own internal model of the document's structure.

Providing a 'footprint' on a representation of the document's structure, indicating which section of text the reader had just come from, was found to be helpful. The importance of knowledge of present location is emphasized by Canter (1984), "Any future navigation is probably built upon knowledge of present location" (p.247). The footprint helped readers to answer the question 'Where am I?' in relation to the document as a whole.

Showing readers which parts of a document they had already seen was also beneficial, eliciting superior performance in an information relocation task and assisting in the formation of a mental map of the document's structure. Providing a record of the sections of text visited helped to answer questions such as 'Where was I when I saw...?', 'Have I seen everything?' and 'Where else is there to go?'.

Thompson (1971) describes a hierarchically structured document retrieval system which displayed a list of the selections made by the user during a session. The provision of information concerning the order of access may be of particular benefit in view of Canter's (1984) proposition, that "knowledge of earlier location will then be linked to knowledge of present location by the person's understanding of how he traveled between" (p.248). The results of a study by the present author support this proposition; navigation efficiency was considerably improved by the addition of an ordered list of the sections of text visited. As the document was presented in hypertext, it would appear that temporal sequence was the important factor, rather than any sequence suggested by the structure of the document.

To summarize, the results of the studies described above indicated that the interface to a hypertext document should
(i) display the structure of the document graphically,
(ii) provide the reader with a record of the sections of text visited, (iii) indicate the order in which these were accessed, and (iv) have a 'footprint' showing the reader which section of text they have just come from.

1.4 The present study

These features were applied to the interface to both the individual articles in the database used in the study reported in this paper, and to one version of the interface to the database itself.

The second version of the interface to the database was a chronological list of the articles it contained, with no additional features. The study therefore contrasted performance using an interface from the paper medium with one taking advantage of the facilities offered by the electronic medium.

The hierarchical structures of the individual articles were shown as tree diagrams, each section comprising a node. Engel, Andriessen and Schmitz (1983) speak of the difficulties arising when the structure of an information system is too large and/or complex to display on a single screen. The authors propose that there are three possible solutions to showing the user where they are and what is available: (i) 'zooming in', (ii) panning across the structure, and (iii) a hierarchical series of screens. In the present study, the structure of an individual article could not all be displayed on a single screen, and the latter of these three strategies was adopted.

The task used in the study was considered to be particularly important. It was felt that subjects should be required to use the database to perform a task for which they would normally use academic journals. In view of the fact that the subjects were students, the task selected involved the location of information relevant to answering two questions of the type commonly set for class or examination essay. The students were drawn from a population familiar with the area covered by the journal from which the articles were taken.

Marchionini and Shneiderman (1988) consider that a document and a database have some similarity in that they both provide information and cues for the selection of further information. It was therefore hypothesized that those features found to be of benefit for individual articles would also be of utility at the database level, readers being able to locate relevant information more efficiently when using an interface containing such features.

2. Method

2.1 Design

The design was a 2 x 2 mixed ANOVA. Factor one (Interface type) was between subjects, and factor two (Question type) was a within subjects variable. The

sheet. These instructions stated that information relevant to each question would be found in more than one article, and subjects were asked to write down each piece of information located, together with the author of the article from which it came. When subjects had read the instructions they were given a piece of paper containing their first question. They were told that there was no time limit for the task, and asked to indicate to the experimenter when they were ready for the second question.

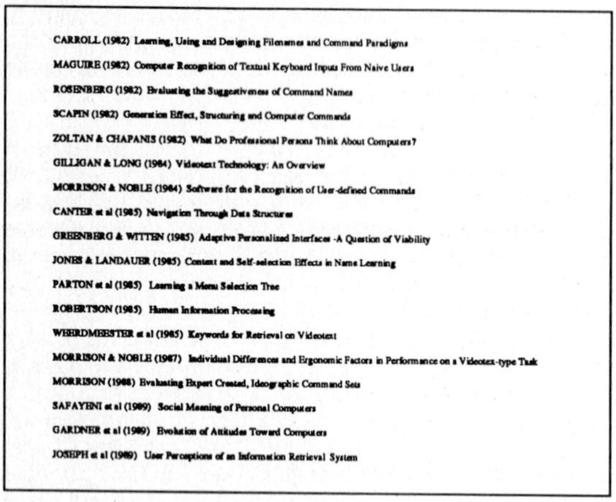

CARROLL (1982) Learning, Using and Designing Filenames and Command Paradigms
MAGUIRE (1982) Computer Recognition of Textual Keyboard Inputs From Naive Users
ROSENBERG (1982) Evaluating the Suggestiveness of Command Names
SCAPIN (1982) Generation Effect, Structuring and Computer Commands
ZOLTAN & CHAPANIS (1982) What Do Professional Persons Think About Computers?
GILLIGAN & LONG (1984) Videotext Technology: An Overview
MORRISON & NOBLE (1984) Software for the Recognition of User-defined Commands
CANTER et al (1985) Navigation Through Data Structures
GREENBERG & WITTEN (1985) Adaptive Personalized Interfaces -A Question of Viability
JONES & LANDAUER (1985) Context and Self-selection Effects in Name Learning
PARTON et al (1985) Learning a Menu Selection Tree
ROBERTSON (1985) Human Information Processing
WHERDMEESTER et al (1985) Keywords for Retrieval on Videotext
MORRISON & NOBLE (1987) Individual Differences and Ergonomic Factors in Performance on a Videotex-type Task
MORRISON (1988) Evaluating Expert Created, Ideographic Command Sets
SAFAYENI et al (1989) Social Meaning of Personal Computers
GARDNER et al (1989) Evolution of Attitudes Toward Computers
JOSEPH et al (1989) User Perceptions of an Information Retrieval System

Figure 3. List type interface to the database.

After the second question had been completed, the questionnaire was administered. Finally, subjects were shown a screen dump of the alternative version of the interface to that they had used, and asked to state their preference. General comments on the database were also noted.

The software recorded the articles and cards visited by readers during the question-answering task.

3. Results

3.1 Question scores

The questions were scored as follows. The points pertaining to each question were extracted from the relevant articles, there being 21 points for to the linked question and 17 for the unlinked question. The number of points recorded by each subject for each question was calculated as a percentage of the maximum possible number of points for that question. A 2 x 2 ANOVA (Interface type x Question type) on the resulting data indicated there to be both a main effect of interface type ($F_{[1,30]} = 43.90$, $p < 0.0001$) and a significant interaction between the interface and question variables ($F_{[1,30]} = 12.25$, $p < 0.01$). Further analysis indicated that the difference between four of the five significantly different pairs of means could be accounted for by the effect of interface type ($T_{0.01} = 9.86$). The mean question scores for the four conditions were as follows:

Map/Linked = 45.24%; Map/Unlinked = 36.76%; List/Linked = 15.78%; List/Unlinked = 21.69%.

3.2 Number of moves between articles

The number of moves between articles made by subjects while locating information was calculated. A 2 x 2 ANOVA revealed a main effect of interface type on this measure ($F_{[1,30]} = 4.85$, $p < 0.05$). Significantly fewer moves were made by readers using the map (mean = 7.88) than by those using the list (mean = 10.10).

3.3 Number of different articles visited

A 2 x 2 ANOVA indicated that neither interface type or question type, nor the interaction between these two variables, had a significant influence on the number of different articles visited during the question-answering task ($F_{[1,30]} = 6.65$, $p > 0.05$).

3.4 Number of different relevant articles visited

A 2 x 2 ANOVA revealed a main effect of interface type ($F_{[1,30]} = 4.29$, $p < 0.05$) and a significant interaction between this and the question variable ($F_{[1,30]} = 4.31$, $p < 0.05$). Further analysis indicated that for the linked question, significantly more relevant articles were visited by subjects using the map (mean = 5.50) than by those using the list (mean = 3.94) ($T_{0.01} = 1.52$), and for the map interface, significantly more relevant articles were opened for the linked question (mean = 5.50) than for the unlinked question (mean = 4.25).

3.5 Number of different irrelevant articles visited

A 2 x 2 ANOVA indicated there to be a main effect of interface type on this measure ($F_{[1,30]} = 6.57$, $p < 0.05$). Fewer irrelevant articles were visited by subjects using the map type interface (mean = 1.94) than by those using the list (mean = 3.04).

3.6 Correlations

The number of relevant articles visited by subjects was positively correlated with the scores obtained for the question-answering task (r = 0.60).

For the map interface, there was a positive correlation between the number of times the ordered list of articles seen was accessed and the number of relevant articles visited (r = 0.69), and a negative correlation between the former measure and the number of irrelevant articles visited (r = -0.68). Question scores were also positively correlated with the number of times the ordered list of articles visited was accessed (r = 0.66).

4. Discussion

The study reported in this paper examined the hypothesis that the interface to a hypertext database would have a significant influence on readers' ability to locate information relevant to two essay-type questions. It was proposed that performance would be superior using an interface whose features were found to be of benefit to readers of individual hypertext articles. This hypothesis was supported, with significantly higher scores being obtained by subjects using such an interface than by subjects using a straightforward list of the articles in the database. The effect of interface type on the number of relevant points located was particularly strong ($p < 0.0001$), with the mean percentages of the total number of points available being 41% in the map condition and 18.70 in the list condition. Furthermore, the significant interaction between interface type and question type could mainly be accounted for by the effect of the former variable.

The scores obtained by subjects in the question-answering task were not correlated with subjects' prior knowledge of the two question topics. This finding would suggest that differences in the amount of relevant information located from within the database may be attributed to characteristics of the interface and task requirements.

Although subjects using the map interface made fewer moves between articles than those using the list interface, interface type had no significant influence on the number of different articles visited during the question-answering task. Taken together, these findings indicate that subjects in the list condition revisited more articles than those in the map condition. The most obvious explanation for this is that both a record and an ordered list of articles visited were available to subjects using the map type interface, but neither were available to those using the list.

The analysis of the number of different relevant articles visited indicated that, while answering the linked question, subjects using the map type interface visited significantly more relevant articles than those using the list type interface. In addition, for subjects using the map interface, more relevant articles were visited for the linked question than for the unlinked question. It be therefore be concluded that subjects using the graphical interface found the illustration of the way in which the articles referred to each other to be of benefit. This proposition is supported by the comments made by subjects, a number remarking that once they had found one relevant article, they used the map to see which other articles were linked on the display, and therefore likely to be relevant. Although similar information was available on the 'title page' of each article (for both interface types), it was not found to be as easy to assimilate – hence the performance difference for the two interface types.

The finding that, in the map condition, more different relevant articles were visited for the linked question than for the unlinked question may also indicate that it was the depiction of the links between the articles which was the important feature, rather than the record of the articles that had been visited. The results of an earlier study (Simpson, 1989) support this hypothesis. In this investigation, performance in an information location task was compared using textual and graphical representations of a document's structure. A record of the text sections visited was provided in both conditions, and performance by subjects using the graphical representation was found to be superior to that by subjects using the textual one. Billingsley (1982) concluded that "exposure to a pictorial representation of the structure of a menu system helps subjects to develop a workable mental model of the way data elements interrelate" (p.106). The findings of both the earlier study and that reported in the present paper are in agreement with this proposition.

Two criticisms of the present study are (i) that there were only a limited number of articles available to readers, and (ii) the database only contained articles from one journal. When there are a larger number of articles in the database, it will obviously not be possible to show the entire contents on a single screen. What may be the most appropriate solution to this problem is one of the issued to be addressed in future research.

The results of a previous study suggested that temporal sequence was an important cue at the article level, and this was also found to be so at the database level. Subjects who accessed the ordered list of 'articles seen' the greatest number of times scored higher in the information location task, visited more relevant articles and fewer irrelevant ones. Again, comments by subjects support this conclusion. The questions comprised several distinct parts, and a number of subjects made remarks such as "I remembered that I had seen something relevant to the second part when I started the question, and I could see from the list which article I had looked at first".

It was found that the number of relevant articles visited was positively correlated with the scores obtained for the question-answering task. This indicates that once subjects had decided an article was relevant, they were able both to decide which sections were likely to contain relevant information and to locate this information. This supports the proposition by McKnight, Dillon and Richardson (1989), that readers have a mental model of the structure of an article, which is used to judge where particular information may be located.

Finally, it would appear that subjective measures obtained from readers are in agreement with the objective ones reported here. When subjects were shown a screen dump of the alternative interface to the database, 87.00% of those in the map condition and 81.25% of those in the list condition said they preferred the map type of interface, discussing the benefits of the various features and facilities it provided.

The data reported in this paper comprises a small part of that obtained from the study. Other findings, such as the influence of question type (linked vs. unlinked), methods of moving between articles, and more general navigation features, together with a fuller discussion of subjects' comments, will be reported elsewhere.

5. Conclusion

In conclusion, the results of the present investigation indicated that those features found to be of benefit for an interface to a hypertext document are also useful for an interface to a database of such articles.

Although the aim of the study was not to compare paper and electronic media, the majority of subjects said that an electronic journal of this kind was far preferable to the existing paper journal system, e.g., "Why hasn't this been done before? I'd use it all the time if I had one – marvellous!".

According to Elm and Woods (1985) "Getting lost in a display network means that the user not have a clear conception of the relationships within the system, does not know his present location in the system relative to the display structure, and finds it difficult to decide where to look next within the system" (p.927). There is evidence that those users of the database described in the present study did not 'get lost', but were able to use the database in order to perform a realistic task.

All of those who used the database responded very favourably, a number of them asking if they could come back and use it again. Comments such as "It's all here, what more could you want?" were not uncommon, and the majority of users were of the opinion that such a database would be far preferable to the present, paper-based, journal system.

Acknowledgments

This research was conducted while the author held a CASE studentship, jointly funded by the Social and Economic Research Council and the British Library Research and Development Department. The author would also like to thank Taylor and Francis for permission to use the articles from 'Behaviour and Information Technology' for research purposes.

References

Benest, I.D., Morgan, G. and Smithurst, M.D. (1987). A humanized interface to an electronic library. In *Human-Computer Interaction–INTERACT '87*. (Eds. H.-J. Bullinger and B. Shackel). Elsevier Science Publishers: North-Holland, 905-910.

Billingsley, P.A. (1982). Navigation through hierarchical menu structures: Does it help to have a map?. *Proceedings of the Human Factors Society 26th Annual Meeting,* 103-107.

Canter, D. (1984). Wayfinding and signposting: Penance or prosthesis? In *Information Design.* (Eds. R. Easterby and H. Zuraga). J. Wiley and Sons: Chichester, 245-264.

Canter, D. Rivers, R. and Storrs, G. (1985). Characterizing user navigation through complex data structures. *Behaviour and Information Technology,* 4(2), 93-102.

Canter, D., Powell, J., Wishart, J. and Roderick, C. (1986). User navigation in complex database systems. *Behaviour and Information Technology,* 5(3), 249-257.

Dillon, A., Richardson, J. and McKnight, C. (1988). Towards the development of a full text, searchable database: implications from a study of journal usage. *British Journal of Academic Librarianship,* 3(1), 37-48.

Elm, W.C. and Woods, D.D. (1985). Getting lost: A case study in interface design. *Proceedings of the Human Factors Society 29th Annual Meeting,* 927-931.

Engel, F.L., Andriessen, J.J. and Schmitz, H.J.R. (1983). What, where and whence: means for improving electronic data access. *International Journal of Man-Machine Studies,* 18, 145-160.

Haas, C. and Hayes, J.R. (1985). *Effects of text display variables on reading tasks: Computer screen vs. hard copy.* Communications Design Centre Technical Report No.3. Pittsburgh: Carnegie-Mellon University.

Hasher, L. and Zacks, T.T. (1979). Automatic and Effortful Processes in Memory. *Journal of Experimental Psychology: General,* 108(3), 356-388.

Marchionini, G. and Shneiderman, B. (1988). Finding facts vs. browsing knowledge in hypertext systems. *IEEE Computer*, January 1988, 70-80.

McKnight, J. and Dillon, A. C., Richardson, (1989). Journal articles as learning resource: what can hypertext offer? Paper presented at the NATO Advanced Workshop "Designing Hypertext/Hypermedia for Learning, Rottenburg, July 1989.

Monk, A.F., Walsh, P. and Dix, A.J. (1988). A comparison of hypertext, scrolling and unfolding as mechanisms for program browsing. In *People and Computers IV.* (Eds. D.M. Jones and R. Winder). Cambridge University Press: Cambridge, 421-435.

Nielsen, J. and Lyngbaek, U. (1989). Two field studies of hypermedia usability. Proceedings of Hypertext 2 Conference, York, June 1989.

Rothkopf, E.Z. (1971). Incidental memory for the location of information in text. *Journal of Verbal Learning and Verbal Behaviour,* 10, 608-613.

Simpson, A. (1989). Navigation in hypertext: Design issues. Paper presented at the 13th International Online Information Meeting, London, December 1989.

Thompson, D.A. (1971). Interface design for an interactive information retrieval system: A literature review and a research system description. *Journal of the American Society for Information Science,* December 1971, 36-373.

Waller. R.H.W. (1985). Skimming, scanning and browsing: problems of studying from electronic text. IEE Computing and Control Division Colloquium on *'Paper versus screen: The Human Factors Issues'*. Digest No.1985/80.

Human–Computer Interaction – INTERACT '90
D. Diaper et al. (Editors)
Elsevier Science Publishers B.V. (North-Holland)

A FISHEYE PRESENTATION STRATEGY: AIRCRAFT MAINTENANCE DATA

Deborah A. Mitta

Department of Industrial Engineering, Texas A&M University, College Station, TX 77843

A computer interface that presents information in a usable format will typically improve the quality of human-computer interaction (HCI). One presentation technique recently developed as a means of enhancing the quality of HCI is known as the fisheye lens viewing strategy. This paper will discuss an application of the fisheye lens viewing strategy to the presentation of aircraft maintenance data. The research results presented in this paper will demonstrate that the fisheye strategy, through its ability to prioritize interface information, can be used as a mechanism for filtering details of maintenance data.

1. INTRODUCTION

Devising an effective information presentation strategy for computer-based system information is an essential interface design task. Computer interfaces that facilitate users' abilities to access and interpret information will typically enhance the quality of human-computer interaction. A user often experiences difficulties in accessing and interpreting information because his knowledge of both the underlying information structure and the relationships between information currently observed and other information elements in the structure is limited. An effective presentation strategy must also address, if not alleviate, those situations in which the amount of information to be presented exceeds the amount of space provided by the display medium. Traditional solutions for solving the navigation and information quantity problems described above incorporate hierarchical menu facilities, windowing techniques, and scroll/zoom features.

One technique recently developed as a means of enhancing the quality of human-computer interaction is known as the fisheye lens viewing strategy [1]. This technique presents information related to points of interest (focus points) in great detail; less relevant information is presented as an abstraction. In this manner the user is provided detailed information concerning a specific item of interest; however, the global aspects of the entire information data structure are not eliminated from the user's view. The motivation for incorporating fisheye presentations in a computer interface is to provide users with a balance between local detail and global context.

This paper discusses the application of the fisheye lens viewing strategy to the presentation of aircraft maintenance data, where the presentation medium is a computer interface. The focus of this paper is on computer-based maintenance aids, of which online reference manuals and troubleshooting and diagnostic tools are of particular interest [2]. The following scenarios depict the types of conditions for which information presentation strategies potentially influence the quality of human-maintenance aid interaction.

Scenario 1: In order to complete a set of diagnostic procedures, a maintenance technician is required to navigate through a number of screen displays.

Scenario 2: Diagnostic information is presented on a visual display for which the amount of information displayed per viewing screen is restricted.

Scenario 3: An experienced maintenance technician is provided with information that is unnecessarily detailed.

Human-computer interaction researchers suggest that fisheye views might facilitate navigation within informational data bases (Scenario 1), enable information abbreviation (Scenario 2), and capture the correct balance of detail and context required to satisfy both the novice and experienced maintenance technicians (Scenario 3). Furnas [1] implemented the fisheye concept as a presentation strategy for online text and as a navigation tool for a hierarchically structured data base. Also implemented was an interactive fisheye calendar that provided hourly information for a given day; limited details of weekly and monthly schedules were also available. More recently, a fisheye approach was used to present topographic information [3], [4]. Computer-based images of a subway map were presented via a fisheye environment, and users were required to determine optimal routes between sets of subway stations.

2. FISHEYE LENS VIEWING STRATEGY

In order for information to be presented from a fisheye perspective, the underlying structure of the associated informational data base must be represented in network form. In such a network, nodes define information elements within the data base, and arcs identify relationships between data base elements. Furnas' [1] implementation is directed to hierarchical tree graphs, that is, acyclic, hierarchies of nodes originating with a top level root node and branching to nodes at lower hierarchical levels.

Each network node (information element) is assigned a metric known as its degree of interest (DOI). The DOI indicates a presentation *value* or *priority* for the information contained at the node. Applying the fisheye concept to the presentation of interface information requires implementation of a DOI function. This function assigns a DOI to each node, where the DOI value is the degree of interest a user has in viewing a particular information element for a given scenario.

A node's degree of interest is expressed as a difference of two parameters: importance and distance. For a network consisting of the set of nodes $\mathbf{N} = \{x_1, x_2, \ldots, x_{n-1}, x_n\}$, where x_n is a point of interest, referred to as a focus point, the degree of interest for any node in **N** is determined by the following function:

$$DOI_{fisheye}(x_i | .= x_n) = API(x_i) - D(x_i, x_n), \quad (1)$$

where

$DOI_{fisheye}(x_i | .= x_n)$ = degree of interest for node x_i given a focus point x_n

$API(x_i)$ = importance rating assigned to node x_i

$D(x_i,x_n)$ = path distance between node x_i and focus point x_n.

The importance rating $API(x_i)$, as defined by Furnas, is actually the distance of node x_i from the root node and is assigned a negative value; therefore, nodes closer to the root node are assigned greater importance than nodes a greater distance from the root.

From Equation (1) it is evident that the degree of interest associated with a given node increases with its importance rating and decreases with its distance from the current information focus point. Additionally, if the importance rating strategy described by Furnas is employed, degrees of interest are negative. The convention is such that an arithmetically larger degree of interest implies a greater presentation value for information contained at a particular node. Information having a high presentation value is more useful to successful human-computer interaction than is information having a lower presentation value.

2.1. Establishing DOI Threshold Levels

Through the setting of DOI thresholds, Furnas [1] demonstrates that fisheye views with varying degrees of information content can be provided. For a given threshold level, t, the set of network nodes satisfying the condition $DOI_{fisheye}(x_i | .= x_n) \geq t$ has the greatest presentation value. When the threshold level, t, is decreased, a greater amount of information is displayed. Nodes having the highest degrees of interest are placed in a *zero-order* fisheye view. The zero-order view contains the minimum amount of information necessary to present detail associated with a focus point and maintain global context. As the order of a view is increased (threshold is decreased), more information is presented.

3. MAINTENANCE DATA AND FISHEYE VIEWS

The United States Air Force Human Resources Laboratory is currently developing an integrated computer-based information system to aid in tasks associated with aircraft maintenance [5], [6], [7]. This system is known as the Integrated Maintenance Information System (IMIS). IMIS will consolidate existing information systems and data bases used in aircraft maintenance into a comprehensive information data bank. It will provide maintenance technicians with a direct link to various maintenance information systems and data bases: supply data, historical data bases, and automated technical orders. IMIS will provide diagnostic and troubleshooting recommendations, test procedures, and graphics-based information (e.g. locator diagrams, schematics); it will also enable technicians to obtain fault data from built-in tests.

The primary intent of this research is to demonstrate how the fisheye strategy, through its ability to prioritize information, can be used as a mechanism for filtering details of aircraft maintenance data [8]. In addition, the results presented in this paper extend the original research concept. The first extension allows the fisheye technique to be applied to any type of information network, not only hierarchical tree graph structures; the second extension illustrates that fisheye views resulting from selections of multiple focus points are possible. In these views, detail surrounding each focus point is presented, and the global context associated with each point is maintained.

3.1. Structuring of Information: General Networks

Furnas [1] applies the fisheye presentation strategy to information having a hierarchical tree graph structure. In a hierarchical tree network, arcs connect nodes that are at most one level apart such that the link between any two nodes specifies a *family* relationship, that is, a *parent-child* relationship. This type of relationship is also referred to as a *system* relationship in which *system-*

subsystem pairs are identified. When information has a general network structure, additional types of relationships between nodes are specified. Additional family or system relationships can be defined, for example, sibling (system-system) or grandparent (supersystem-subsystem) links; however, system relationships, or links between functional units of a system, are not the only identifiable relationships. *Physical* relationships typically shown to maintenance technicians through graphics-based information (mechanical parts diagrams or circuit schematics) can also be introduced. For example, a network arc may establish that Part P1 *snaps_into* Socket S1 or Output Pin 1 on Gate G1 *is_connected_to* Input Pin 2 on Gate G2.

3.2. Multiple Focus Points

Furnas [1] describes scenarios in which selection of multiple focus points is of potential interest. In such instances, it is perhaps desirable for detail associated with two or more focus points to be emphasized, while global context associated with each point is maintained. This type of interaction scenario is appropriate from a maintenance perspective. Suppose a technician is performing an electronics troubleshooting task and suspects that two integrated circuit chips, IC_1 and IC_2, are likely to be responsible for a particular fault; IC_1 and IC_2 would be the focus points. Fisheye views based on these focus points would provide detailed information concerning the physical connections and functional relationships in close proximity to each chip. Additionally, these views would provide global context information, describing the physical/functional relationships existing between IC_1 and IC_2 and the electronics system of which they are components.

To develop fisheye views that are based on multiple focus point selection, Equation (1) is slightly modified. A change of notation is adopted to distinguish between the development presented here and Furnas' original development. For a network containing the set of nodes $N' = \{y_1, y_2, \ldots, y_{n-1}, y_n\}$, a *presentation value* for any node in this set is determined according to the following function:

$$V_k = I_k - \sum_j D_{k,j}, \qquad (2)$$

where

V_k = presentation value of node y_k
I_k = importance rating of node y_k
$D_{k,j}$ = minimum path distance between node y_k and focus point y_j.

The function of Equation (2) incorporates the importance and distance parameters originally identified by Furnas [1]. V_k, while analogous to the original degree of interest metric, is dependent upon the sum of path distances between node y_k and each focus point, as well as the importance rating assigned to y_k. It should be noted that for informational data bases in which no underlying hierarchical structure is apparent, that is, a root node does not exist, importance must be defined in terms other than path distance from a root node.

4. PROTOTYPE SYSTEM

To demonstrate how the fisheye concept might be applied to aircraft maintenance data, a prototype system was developed. Recall that the primary motivation for implementing the fisheye presentation strategy was to provide a mechanism for filtering maintenance data (Scenario 3). Conceptually, a fisheye environment would enable a technician to obtain additional detail available in higher order fisheye views only after he initiates a specific request for that type of information. Example fisheye views were developed in HyperCard® [9]. The information content presented in each nth-order view was specified according to values for V_k determined from Equation (2). It should be noted that the HyperCard® environment will not serve as the final presentation medium; however, it was a convenient software tool for initially demonstrating the concept of information filtering.

Several types of maintenance data were selected for fisheye presentations. These data were selected from two types of graphics-based information: circuit schematics and mechanical parts diagrams. Both types of data typically appear in repair manuals and technical orders used by Air Force technicians. Figure 1 is an example a mechanical parts diagram as it might appear in a technical order (TO); it is an exploded view of a mechanical assembly called a clearing solenoid. Underlying the network representation of the parts data appearing in Figure 1 is a hierarchical structure; therefore, because this network has an identifiable root node, I_k was defined as the minimum path distance between node y_k and the given root node.

Suppose during a routine maintenance task, a technician is required to disassemble the clearing solenoid assembly. If screws 1 and 9 (Figure 1) are selected as focus points, Figures 2 and 3 illustrate how the fisheye algorithm was used to eliminate levels of detail from the original TO graphics. The MORE and LESS buttons allow access to higher and lower order views, respectively. When the clearing solenoid assembly is represented in network form, nodes specify its components, and arcs establish the physical and functional relationships existing between these components. Two examples of the functional relationships established from Figure 1 are provided below:

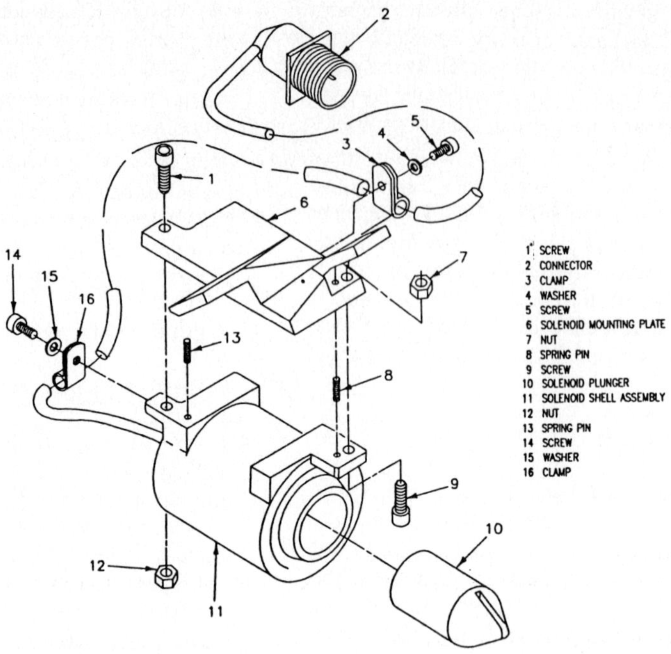

Figure 1. Clearing Solenoid Assembly.

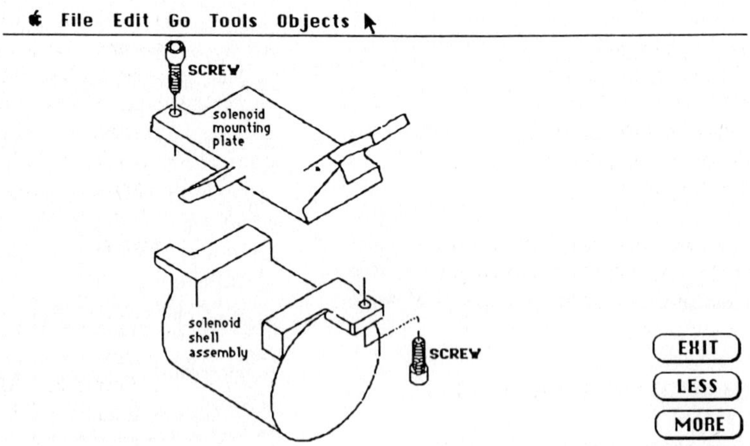

Figure 2. Clearing Solenoid Assembly: Zero-Order Fisheye View.

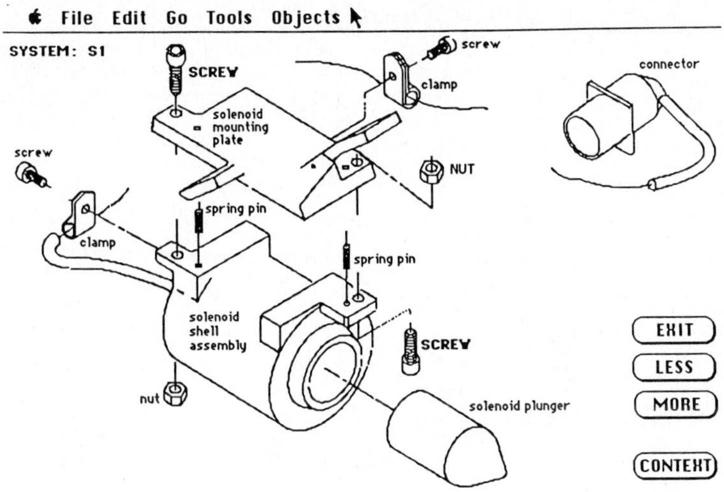

Figure 3. Clearing Solenoid Assembly: Third-Order Fisheye View.

(1) solenoid mounting plate ***is_part_of*** clearing solenoid assembly
(2) screw 9 ***is_linking_device_of*** solenoid mounting plate.

Physical relationships establish physical orientations of components of the clearing solenoid assembly: *attachment*, *adjacency*, or *insertion*. The physical orientations of several components can be described as follows:

(1) connector ***is_attached_to*** solenoid shell assembly
(2) solenoid shell ***is_adjacent_to*** solenoid mounting plate
(3) solenoid plunger ***inserts_into*** solenoid shell.

The CONTEXT feature provides global context for the clearing solenoid assembly, allowing a user to view the clearing solenoid assembly with respect to a larger system of mechanical assemblies (Figure 4).

5. FUTURE RESEARCH AND CONCLUSIONS

The results of this research represent an initial attempt to implement the fisheye viewing strategy to the presentation of aircraft maintenance information. The intent of the research was to demonstrate how this particular presentation approach might be applied to a subset of maintenance data and used to filter information; graphics-based data were considered. It is apparent from the fisheye examples offered in this paper that further research on the design of a user interface is required. As presented in this paper, the existing interface allows users to (1) access higher and lower order fisheye views (more and less information, respectively), (2) obtain additional global context, and (3) exit the environment.

It is suggested that several interface design issues require further examination. One issue is the selection of focus points. At this stage in the research, an emphasis has been placed on using values of V_k to specify the information content of each nth-order view for a given set of focus points. It is assumed that the selection of focus points has already occurred. Thus, future research efforts are to examine *how* information should be selected, in addition to *what* information should be presented. Design of an interface feature facilitating the process of focus point selection is suggested. Additionally, this feature should enable users to select new focus points from within any nth-order fisheye view.

As with any research pertaining to human-computer interaction, the motivation in examining fisheye views is to enhance the quality of interaction and thus improve human performance. Furnas [1], Hollands [3], and Hollands et al. [4] document human performance improvements with a fisheye presentation approach. At this point it appears that further experimentation is required to obtain an understanding of the full benefits researchers and designers might expect from this particular information presentation technique.

This research has demonstrated the results of using the fisheye presentation strategy as a mechanism for filtering aircraft maintenance information. Two extensions to the

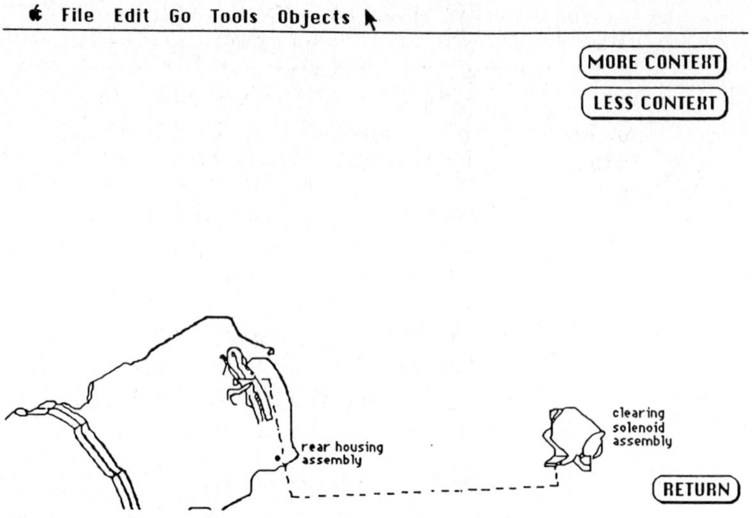

Figure 4. Global Context: First-Order Fisheye View.

original concept have been presented. Information represented by a general network type structure can be represented through fisheye views. Fisheye views resulting from multiple focus point selection are considered. An approach for specifying the information content of these views is presented, where the information content of any nth-order view is specified according to the presentation value metric, V_k.

ACKNOWLEDGMENTS

This research was sponsored by the Air Force Office of Scientific Research/AFSC, United States Air Force, under Contract F49620-88-C-0053.

REFERENCES

[1] Furnas, G. W., "Generalized Fisheye Views." *PROCEEDINGS CHI'86 HUMAN FACTORS IN COMPUTING SYSTEMS*, ACM Special Interest Group on Computer and Human Interaction, 16-23 (1986).

[2] Gunning, D., "The Fisheye View of Knowledge: A Heuristic for Selecting Relevant Information." Working Paper, Wright-Patterson Air Force Base, OH: Air Force Human Resources Laboratory (1987).

[3] Hollands, J. G., *Presenting a Network Graphically: A Comparison of Performance Using Fisheye View and Scrolling*, Master's thesis, The University of Guelph, Ontario, Canada (1988).

[4] Hollands, J. G., Matthews, M. L., McCann, C. A. and Carey, T., "Presenting a Graphical Network: A Comparison of Performance Using Fisheye and Scrolling Views." *PROCEEDINGS OF THE THIRD INTERNATIONAL CONFERENCE ON HUMAN-COMPUTER INTERACTION: DESIGNING AND USING HUMAN-COMPUTER INTERFACES AND KNOWLEDGE BASED SYSTEMS*, 313-320 (1989).

[5] Chenzoff, A. P., Evans, D. C., Joyce, R. P., and Roth, J. T., *Man-Machine Interface Concepts for an Advanced Integrated Maintenance Information System*, Technical Paper AFHRL-TP-86-30, Wright-Patterson Air Force Base, OH: Air Force Human Resources Laboratory (September, 1986).

[6] Link, W. R., Von Holle, J. C., and Mason, D., *Integrated Maintenance Information System (IMIS): A Maintenance Information Delivery Concept*, Technical Paper AFHRL-TP-86-30, Wright-Patterson Air Force Base, OH: Air Force Human Resources Laboratory (November 1987).

[7] Thomas, D. L., and Clay, J. D., *Computer-Based Maintenance Aids for Technicians: Project Final Report*, Technical Report AFHRL-TR-87-44, Wright-Patterson Air Force Base, OH: Air Force Human Resources Laboratory (August 1988).

[8] Mitta, D. A., *Fisheye Representation of Information: IMIS User Interface*, Technical Report Air Force Office of Scientific Research/AFSC, Contract F49620-88-C-0053, 1989 USAF-UES Summer Faculty Research Program (September 1989).

[9] *HyperCard® User's Guide*, Apple Computer, Inc. (1988).

Human–Computer Interaction – INTERACT '90
D. Diaper et al. (Editors)
Elsevier Science Publishers B.V. (North-Holland)

SUPPORTING EXPLORATORY LEARNING

Andrew HOWES & Stephen J. PAYNE

Departments of Computing and Psychology
University of Lancaster, Lancaster, LA1 4YD, UK

Andrew Howes now at, MRC Applied Psychology Unit, 15 Chaucer Rd. Cambridge, CB2 2EF, UK. andrewh@mrc-apu.cam.ac.uk

Stephen J. Payne now at, IBM Thomas J. Watson Research Center, Box 704, Yorktown Heights, NY 10598, USA. payne@ibm.com

This paper introduces the notion of a Learning Support Environment (LSE), which is a collection of tools designed to support exploratory learning of computer applications. An implementation of an LSE for a particular interactive device is motivated in terms of an analysis of the cognitive problems faced by the exploratory learner. The implementation includes four support tools; a Task-action Trace, a Metaphor Micro-world, an Animation Machine and a Buddy Learner.

1. INTRODUCTION

1.1. Supporting exploration

Learners spend a lot of time exploring, whether out of choice or out of necessity. For some users, no documentation is available, for others, it is too much trouble to read. For some, there is an urgent need to accomplish particular practical tasks, for others, exploration is fun. Whatever the reasons, learning by exploring is an everyday reality for many. Fortunately, there is evidence that exploratory learning may, if properly supported, be an effective means of acquiring practical computing skills (Carroll, 1990). However, as most readers will testify, unsupported exploration can quickly lead to frustration.

How can we insure that exploratory learning is properly supported? Our approach is pragmatic and problem based. We do not pretend that exploratory learning is a unitary phenomenon that can be supported within a single instructional paradigm. Instead, we analyse a variety of problems faced by exploratory learners, and use each problem to motivate the design of an interface tool. Because we expect different learners to face different problems at different times, each tool, although its prime objective is instructional, is under the learner's control. Indeed much of our work has been to make the tools as responsive and interactive as possible.

Our way of working, then, has been to analyse users' problems, and develop tools, ad hoc, that help to overcome them. But we would note the close relationship between this pragmatic approach and psychological theory. As the descriptions below illustrate, we have found models of the user to be helpful both for the expression of problems and the framing of design solutions.

In the following sections we describe four separate tools that have been implemented to support exploratory learning of a device called RATES.

1.2. The target device

RATES is a device used by British Telecommunications engineers to test telephone lines. The device allows the user to access and test a line via designated test points, without having to travel to the exchanges in which they are located. An example of a commonly used test is to apply a tone at one test point and measure the received value at another.

The RATES system provides the user with a menu interface and screen display of two of the accessed test points. This display is dynamically incremented with information about the tests and measurements that the user has performed during the current session. The menu is displayed horizontally, and an option is selected by hitting the corresponding function key (f1 .. f8). Selecting an option results in a new menu, or a prompt to type in a value, and perhaps a change in the state of the device/telephone-network.

Whilst the LSE being reported here is implemented for RATES, for clarity in the face of detailed remarks about the interface, we draw some of the examples from the more familiar Apple Macintosh system.

2. TASK-ACTION TRACE

2.1 The problem: "How did I do what?"

Even when exploration successfully achieves some device transformation, the user may not be aware exactly what has happened, and may not remember the sequence of actions that led to the effect. In exploring RATES, it is not unusual for learners, after a long sequence of menu traversals, to successfully attach an oscillator to a line, only to fail to recognize the significance of their achievement, and fail to remember the sequence of actions that would enable it to be repeated.

Furthermore, to learn most effectively, learners need to parse their interaction with the device into minimal meaningful task units. The RATES learner would ideally separate the preparatory phase of isolating a telephone line from the actual specification and placement of an oscillator, for only at this finer grain is generalization across methods possible.

To use a more familiar example, someone engaged in learning the copy/paste operation on the Macintosh would ideally want to acquire three component tasks, one to select an object, one to copy it to the system buffer and one to paste the contents of the buffer onto the workspace. Such a "deconstructed" account (Payne, 1987) of this operation provides the user with sufficiently flexible methods to do things such as multiple pastes or changing the operation without having to repeat the object selection.

Learners have two sources of evidence for parsing their behaviour into task units; feedback from the device and expectations derived from their knowledge of the states of the "external" world that can be manipulated with the device. So in our example we can see that the device feedback provides some help for the user to infer that selection is a meaningful task (the selected object is highlighted and remains highlighted across the copy operation), but provides no help at all for the user to infer a buffer, and hence to separate the copy and paste tasks. In this case expectations derived from the "external" world are equally unhelpful, a buffer is not a readilly available concept in the domain of text editing. The result is that, in the terms of Payne (1987), the user will initially acquire an operational account of copy/paste, that is copy/paste will form one task unit with each operation only having a meaning by virtue of its place within this method.

So an LSE should contain a tool that helps users recognise the appropriate task units in their behaviour and to recall the actions that realised these units.

2.2 The tool

A Task-action Trace is a tool which displays a history of the users' actions and, whenever a task is completed, "collapses" the sequence of actions into a description of the task. Figure 1 shows a Task-action Trace display during RATES use. In our implementation tasks and actions appear in separate panes, and collapsed tasks may be expanded to reveal their component actions by a click of the mouse over the task description.

```
Tasks                 Actions

Circuit accessed
Select test point 10
>>>
                      press test&measure
                      press equipment
                      type "oscillator on"
```

Figure 1: Example Task-action Trace display.

The design of the collapsing trace draws on a Task-action grammar analysis of the RATES interface language (Payne and Green, 1986). The level of the task description is critical. If the collapse/expand mechanisms are to communicate useful "how-to-do-it" knowledge, then verbal descriptions of tasks in the trace need to be at the level at which the mapping from tasks to actions is best encoded. Our approach was therefore to produce a task-action grammar for RATES, exposing the "simple-task" level at which patterns in the action sequences could be exposed.

3. METAPHOR MICRO-WORLD

3.1 The problem: the device-domain dependency paradox

Most device learners start with a good understanding of the domain in which the device operates. For example the novice wordprocessor user invariably understands the concepts of text and text-editing. However this is not always the case. For example, with RATES the novice user is often not only unfamiliar with the device but also with the concepts of telephone line testing. As computer technology becomes more prevalent and a new generation of novice users emerges it will become increasingly true that novices are not just learning about the device and its concepts but also about the nature of the domain in which the device operates.

To appreciate the learning problem this introduces it is necessary to understand the knowledge that device users need to acquire. Device users must understand the device's representation of the task domain (Payne, 1987; Payne, Squibb and Howes, in press), but how can this relational knowledge be acquired incrementally? To simply teach the domain before the device would be to discard one of the richest potential learning aids - the device itself. We might dub this the "device-domain dependency paradox". It is easier to learn the domain if it can be actively explored but to explore the domain the learner must do so through the medium of the device. On the other hand, the device cannot be learned in isolation, as its vital properties are determined by the way it interacts with the domain.

3.2 The tool

One possible way around this problem is to provide the learner with a Metaphor Micro-world (MMW). This is a device which is structurally isomorphic to the target device but which operates in a domain which is already familiar to the novice. The use of metaphor is ubiquitous in education. The MMW simply embodies this teaching technique in a computer program.

For RATES the MMW is constructed around the metaphor of a railway line using the mappings in Figure 2.

RATES	RAILWAY
telephone line	-> track
oscillator	-> train
meter	-> timer
test-point	-> station
received level	-> time

Figure 2: Metaphor mapping for RATES MMW.

So where a typical task in RATES would involve sending a signal from an oscillator on a particular test-point along a telephone line to a meter on another test-point, the corresponding task with the Railway MMW would involve sending a train from a station along a track to a timer on another station.

The hope is that when the learner comes to use the original device she will, with the help of the analogical mapping between the devices, be able to transfer task-action mapping knowledge and screen interpretation knowledge from the MMW.

A simple illustration of the transfer of task-action mapping knowledge is in the organisation of the RATES menu. RATES menu functions are grouped into semantic categories. The metaphor is sufficiently consistent that this semantic hierarchy transfers from Railway MMW to the target domain as easily as the basic domain objects transfer. Similarly the structure of the mapping between screen objects and domain objects is the same for both the MMW and RATES. There is also the possibility that the learner will transfer strategic knowledge of how to solve the overall task. For example, due to the infrequency of faults, efficient line testing in RATES involves testing the whole line and ascertaining that there is a fault at least somwhere on the line before testing each individual section. Given similar fault frequencies on the Railway MMW this strategic knowledge can be acquired using the MMW and carried across to the target domain.

4. ANIMATION MACHINE

4.1 The problem: teaching display-based methods

Allowing novices to actively explore a system creates at least two problems which stem directly from a lack of direct tuition. One is in actually getting started - exploring a system is fun once you're underway but completely novice users can suffer a paralysis when first sat in front of the machine. The other, termed the assimilation paradox (Carroll, 1987) is that users tend to get stuck in a rut - they learn the minimal system functionality to get by and are unwilling to seek, or simply fail to come across more advanced device features.

One proposed response to this problem is the Did-you-know system (Owen, 1986), which is a simple database of hints, available on-line for the user to browse. But the textual nature of such hints may limit their effectiveness in menu-driven systems like RATES, where skill is heavily dependent on the extraction of information ad hoc from the display (Howes and Payne, in press; Payne, in press), making accurate verbal description lengthy, and ill-matched to the targetted competence.

4.2 The tool

So we require an LSE tool to help the novice get started and to overcome the assimilation paradox, that does not depend on detailed textual descriptions. The tool that we are going to report is inspired by arcade machines. Whilst not in use these machines play an animation of their game. Watching this animation is often an essential precursor to playing the game, the animation provides the potential warrior, pilot or racing car driver with essential information on strategies to avoid being blown-up, straffed or shunted. In experimental simulations, using the MacDraw package, we have shown that such animated demonstrations do indeed confer large learning advantages to novices (Payne, Chesworth and Hill, 1990).

The standard form of arcade machine provides the user with no control over which aspect of the animation is played. A useful animation for a complex device such as RATES is almost invaraibly going to be rather long. Our LSE tool therefore uses a video-machine control metaphor to allow users to randomly select a segment of the animation to be played. The animation is indexed by task descriptions identical to those used by the Task-action Trace tool. The animation-machine also has fast-forward and pause buttons.

The animation-machine supports the acquisition of task-action mapping knowledge by providing the user with examples of device use. Further, these examples are presented in a way which maintains the dynamic context of the device. That is it's not just the users commands that are presented in the example but all of the feedback from the device. This may be particularly important, given the display-based nature of skill with interactive devices (see Howes and Payne, in press; Payne, in press).

5. BUDDY-LEARNER

5.1 The problem: Generalizing from imperfect "demonstrations"

The central task for the exploratory learner is to generalize methods from the raw data of the actions performed on the device and the device's responses to those actions. The exploratory learner is provided only with examples generated by her own interaction. Many of these examples are suboptimal and none of them carry any explicit explanation. It therefore seems appropriate that an LSE should provide some support for generalization.

The first step in generalizing from an interaction trace is to partition the interactions into meaningful task units. As we have seen, the Task-action Trace tool (reported in section 2) provides support for this. In addition novice user needs to make detailed analysis of the interactions within a task unit. Such an analysis will determine which actions contribute to which aspects of the task achieved. This understanding will facilitate generalization by providing the necessary structural information to construct an analogy from goals with known methods to a new goal.

There are many reasons why analysis is difficult. Amongst them are the following,

* exploratory learners often make unnecessary actions on their way to completing a task. Hence although learners can assume, superstitiously (Lewis, 1988), that repeating the exact same sequence of actions will reachieve the task, they cannot assume that all actions contributed to the outcome of the task. It is necessary to decide which actions were unnecessary in order to make appropriate generalizations.

* tasks may have default outcomes, that is outcomes that do not have individually identifiable causes in the actions of the method. For example the creation of a box in Macdraw - the outcome not only includes the box but also the enlargement handles.

* methods often contain hidden events. Not all system events have immediate consequences for the display of the device, for example a "save file" operation.

* methods often consume their parameters, that is a parameter has no immediately identifiable counterpart in the outcome. For example arithmetic operations produce a result which is only related to the parameters through the semantics of the particular operation.

5.2 The tool

Keeping within the spirit of LSE, active learner/interactive tool, we adopt the notion of a Buddy Learner. A Buddy Learner is a program that attempts to learn from a student's interaction with a device. As it does so it reports its acquired knowledge to the novice. A Buddy Learner has a number of motivational advantages, stemming from the increased activity of the student (Chan & Baskin, 1988).

It is important that the Buddy Learner acquires knowledge in a psychologically plausible way so as to maintain its credibility with the human learner. To this end we have been developing a semantic theory of analysis during exploratory learning (Howes & Payne, 1990). This theory is embodied in a program called Explor. Explor uses a combination of lexical semantics and causal heuristics to constrain the assignment of roles to actions.

The causal heuristics are borrowed from EXPL (Lewis, 1988), a model of causal attribution in the domain of simple procedures in Human Computer Interaction. EXPL's causal heuristics are the identity heuristic, the loose-ends heuristic and the previous-action heuristic. The identity heuristic (Lewis, 1986) is characterized as, "if something appears in a user action, and in a later system response, the user action is probably a cause of the system response." The loose-ends heuristic assumes that all user actions contribute to the goal, hence if there is a system response which contributes to the goal, and there is a prior user action which hasn't yet been related to the goal, then hypothesize that the user action caused the system response. The previous-action heuristic says that if an event follows an action immediately it is plausible that the action caused the event.

Explor emphasises the role of semantic knowledge in analysis. It uses Procedural Semantics (Miller & Johnson-Laird 1976, Johnson-Laird 1983) to represent the meaning of lexical items in terms of their effect on a mental model of the world, by encoding a routine that changes the state of the model. The mental model is a structural model of a single state of affairs. Explor is given definitions of device-relevant verbs that capture their meaning in everyday usage. When Explor comes across one of these verbs in an exploratory trace, it creates an analogical mapping between the procedural semantics of the verb and the trace. For example, if Explor finds the verb 'multiply' in a trace, then the word's procedural semantics tell it to look for two numerical parameters in the trace, and to expect a system response which contains the result of the arithmetic computation on these parameters.

Explor is implemented in lisp. It uses its knowledge of lexical semantics to constrain the mapping of user actions to system responses. The model provides an account of how users learn from behaviour which contains erroneous and unnecessary actions, hidden events default outcomes and paramater consumptions.

The use of Explor as the mechanism underlying a Buddy Learner raises several issues. Amongst them are, should Explor's semantics be biased toward the correct system semantics? Will learners expect too much of Explor? We are yet to implement Explor as a Buddy Learner: when we do we hope to gain answers to these questions.

6. DISCUSSION

We have illustrated four component tools of an LSE. The Task-action Trace provides support for users partitioning their actions into task units. The Metaphor Micro-world helps the user who is unfamiliar with a domain to learn about the structure of the device. The Animation Machine eases the assimilation paradox and the Buddy Learner helps users acquire appropriately general methods by analysing their behaviour.

The Task-action Trace and Buddy Learner both draw on psychological theory for their design. The Task-action Trace uses a task-action grammar analysis of the interface to give the appropriate level of abstraction for the task units and the Buddy Learner relies on a theory of analysis-based learning to construct accounts of the interaction. The Metaphor Micro-world and the Animation Machine are less directly theory-based, but we have nevertheless found theory helpful to articulate the learning problems which they address. The notion of an LSE provides a framework within which psychological theory can genuinely be a mother of invention.

ACKNOWLEDGEMENTS

This work was supported by Alvey/SERC grant GR/D 60355, a collaborative project between Lancaster University and British Telecommunications plc.

REFERENCES

Carroll, J.M. & Rosson, M.B. (1987). Paradox of the Active User. In (Ed. J.M. Carroll) *Interfacing Thought.* MIT Press.

Carroll, J.M. (1990). *The Nurnberg Funnel: Minimalist Training for Practical Computer Skills.* Cambridge, MA: MIT Press.

Chan, T.W. & Baskin, A.B. (1988). Studying with the prince. The computer as a learning companion. *Proceedings ITS88*, Montreal. p194-200.

Howes, A. & Payne, S.J. (1990). Semantic Analysis during Exploratory Learning. *Proceedings CHI 90.* New York: ACM.

Howes, A. & Payne, S.J. (in press). Display-based Competence: Towards user models of menu-based systems. *International Journal of Man-machine Studies*, in press.

Johnson-Laird, P.N. (1983). *Mental Models.* Cambridge University Press.

Lewis, C.H. (1986). A model of mental model construction. *Proc. CHI'86*, New York: ACM Press.

Lewis, C.H. (1988). Why and how to learn why: Analysis-based generalization of procedures. *Cognitive Science*, 12, 211-256.

Miller, G.A. & Johnson-Laird, P.N. (1976). *Language and perception.* Cambridge University Press.

Owen, D. (1986). Answers first, then questions. In D.A. Norman and S.W. Draper (Eds.) *User-Centered System Design.* Hillsdale, NJ: Erlbaum.

Payne, S.J. (1987). Complex Problem Spaces: Modelling the knowledge needed to use interactive devices. In H. Bullinger and B.Shackel (Eds.) *Human-computer Interaction - INTERACT'87.* Amsterdam: Elsevier.

Payne, S.J. (in press) Display-based action at the user interface. *International Journal of Man-Machine Studies*, in press.

Payne, S.J. & Green, T.R.G. (1986) Task-action grammar: a model of the mental representation of task languages. *Human-Computer Interaction, 2*, 93-133.

Payne, S.J., Squibb, H. & Howes, A. (in press) The nature of device models; the yoked state space and some experiments with text editors. *Human-Computer Interaction*, in press.

Payne, S.J., Chesworth, L. and Hill, E. (1990) Animated demonstrations for exploratory learners. IBM T.J. Watson Research Center: RC 15714.

Human–Computer Interaction – INTERACT '90
D. Diaper et al. (Editors)
Elsevier Science Publishers B.V. (North-Holland)

APPLICATION OF COGNITIVE MODELING AND KNOWLEDGE MEASUREMENT IN DIAGNOSIS AND TRAINING OF COMPLEX SKILLS

Yan M. Yufik, Ph.D.

Institute of Medical Cybernetics, Inc. Philadelphia, USA

We discuss an innovative approach to the design of intelligent training systems (ITS), integrating methods of Artificial Intelligence, Cognitive Modeling and Hypermedia. New ITS will facilitate personalized training in complex technical domains, and will support a. acquisition of expert domain models, b. simulation of expert strategies of models manipulation, c. analysis and visualization of models structure, and d. quantitative comparison of students and expert models. The advantage of the proposed approach is the underlying semiformal format of domain knowledge representation which is both cognitively compatible and computer executable. The paper starts by defining the problem of knowledge measurement and transfer in complex interactive tasks, and then discusses ITS architecture and training methods.

1. The problem of expert knowledge transfer.

To operate competently in complex technical domains, for example, to control a power plant or modern weapon, one needs intimate informal knowledge of these domains. Such knowledge enables experts to recognize significant domain relations and respond in a manner consistent with the task demands. The problem of delivering such knowledge through traditional instructional media and computer assisted training proved to be overwhelming for generations of training designers. The major reasons, we believe, are as follows.

Proficiency in complex tasks is most naturally acquired through direct interaction with the domain and, preferably, through apprenticeship. Experts do not usually concern themselves with the designing and administering of formal training. Instead, they manage to communicate, both explicitly and implicitly, their models of the domain and their strategy of models manipulation. The machinery of human mind is such that knowledge and skills acquired in this manner are readily assimilated and retained, while the results of formal instruction tend to evaporate easily. Unless instruction in complex interactive tasks is augmented by other methods facilitating transfer of expert models, interactive skills learned in training will remain fragile and will break down under pressure. Presently, there is no technology efficiently addressing the problem of expert knowledge transfer in complex interactive tasks. In the space of this paper we will outline research directed towards filling this gap. The intewntion is to develop generic tools allowing training designers to capture expert domain models and then engage trainees in their exploration. The diagnosis of skills and performance feedback can be provided based on the assessment of relative proximity of experts' and trainees' models. In our view, computer-based training systems endowed with such capabilities will create training opportunities unavailable otherwise.

The remainder of this paper is organized in four sections. First, we contrast the model-based training strategy to conventional methods adopted in computer-assisted training. Second, we suggest a format to represent domain models and consider ways to measure expert/trainee differences. Third, we discuss our approach to cognitive modeling. Fourth, we introduce the overall architecture of the demonstration system KnowledgePlex (TM), and give example of training possibilites the system offers.

2. Taxonomy of training systems.

For the purpose of this discussion, we will distinguish three major classes of training devices: conventional systems, knowledge-based systems, and simulators. Conventional and knowledge-based systems administer training, while simulators provide environment to explore.

Conventional systems differ by their organization and the form of user interaction this organization affords. Linear organization implies a predetermined sequence of training steps from which the system does not deviate regardless of network organization. Networks anticipate user input at the nodes, and apply it to decide among alternative directions offered by the links emanating from the nodes. Goal-driven network systems choose directions based on some computational criteria defined on the network paths and apply the criteria, for example, to traverse certain target nodes or to minimize the cumulative cost of steps in the path.

In conventional systems the knowledge of the domain, trainee and training strategy is implicit in the system organization. By contrast, knowledge-based systems contain explicit representation of the domain model and knowledge needed for training delivery. The power and flexibility of knowledge-based systems stem from the compartmentalized and explicit representaion of relevant knowledge. However, here also lies the possibility for excessive demands imposed on system developers and users. Namely, developers often encounter situations of "diminishing return," when exponential growth in system complexity and cost produces only modest linear improvements in training quality. Users might find the expression of knowledge in the system incompatible with their model of the domain and reasoning patterns. The motivation behind this research is to employ representation that is both cognitively compatible and computer processible. It is also important to mitigate computational bottlenecks resulting from viewing training quality as contingent upon the system capability to monitor the trainee and account for all the eventualities in the learning process. Instead, less forceful approaches, emphasizing modeling and exploration rather than supervision might prove beneficial in the complex skills training. An approach allowing acquisition and exploration of expert domain models is discussed next.

3. Cognitive models and their dynamics in training.

Cognitive model is a knowledge structure encoding a set of knowledge primitives in a particular relationship [1]. More precisely, a cognitive model Q is a brain-executable representation of the domain specifying a set of objects (knowledge primitives) M, their attributes P, and relationships R defined on $M \wedge P$.

$$Q = \langle M, P, R \rangle.$$

In a computer-executable representation objects can be expressed as descriptions, diagrams, or procedures, and are defined as elements m M, with relations to other elements expressed as functions of object attributes. In general, model Q can be defined as a semantic graph where nodes are associated with the elements $m \in M$, and links represent relationships $r \subset R$.

Execution of model Q involves two operations: graph composition and graph traversal. In other words, memory contains an archive of representational elements. When responding to a task, elements are retrieved and assembled into a graph so that the resulting structure is isomorphous to the perceived relationships among the task components [2]. Subjectively, successful compositions are experienced as task understanding. Resolving the task involves various forms of graph traversal.

For example, consider the problem of controlling a large scale technical system. The operator needs knowledge of control functions associated with individual instruments, and knowledge of interrelations among control actions and system responses. Understanding the task requires composing a subgraph sufficient to account for the system condition, followed by mapping task characteristics onto the subgraph [3]. Successful mapping allows one to comprehend the task and identify a group of relevant functions. Control plan is produced by tracing links in the graph leading from the current state to the task objective. Of course, this example can be generalized to represent problem solving as path finding in any problem space defined by the vocabulary of objects, interobject relations, procedure for tracing relations, and termination criteria [4].

Training causes modification of cognitive models through chunking [5] and simplification. Chunking involves gradual "consolidation" of structural groups into pieces manipulated as indivisible gestalts. Such groups are stored and retrieved simultaneously, based on their relations with other chunks. Simplification involves various forms of graph contraction. Contraction eliminates redundant elements by deleting unused links and merging nodes. Chunking and simplification serve to reduce the complexity of cognitive models, which leads to effortless, competent performance. Thus, highly organized and optimally simplified models distinguish experts from novices.

There are two other important characteristics of the cognitive models dynamics. First, in the course of training rules emerge capturing some global regularities in the domain. Such rules govern models processing without necessarily reaching the level of conscious awareness, and can be expressed as graph grammars. Second, development of models through chunking and simplification increases adaptation to a certain class of tasks. When exposed to different tasks, models need to be transformed. The transformational theory of learning [6] predicts partial destruction of models and temporary loss of performance efficiency. Also, some marginal destruction of individual chunks can be expected before the evolving models finally stabilize. A more detailed discussion of the dynamics of models development can be found elsewhere [7].

To summarize, this section offered a definition of cognitive models in terms of graphs and computations on graphs. Although speculative, the definition provides a consistent framework in which fundamental concepts of learning theory, such as chunking and structural transformation, can be expressed. We also suggested four distinct types of cognitive operations involved in models processing: formation and archiving of discrete knowledge units, composition of these units into knowledge structures, modification of knowledge structures in the course of training, and manipulation of structures in response to problem situations. There is certain experimental and theoretical evidence in support of these distinctions. The neuropsychological theory of decision making [8] distinguishes two major stages in a decision act: afferent synthesis, when current sensory input is synthesized with prestored information, and anticipatory excitation, when the synthesized information structure is acted upon based on the extrapolation of previous experience. These stages are similar to knowledge structures composition and manipulation correspondingly. The concept of discrete knowledge units is resonant with the Headed Records model of memory [9], proposing memory structure made up of individual unconnected records, with records having no restriction on the amount or format of information they contain. The graph-based representation has been extensively researched by the Conceptual Graphs theory [10] of human information processing, where operations of composition and manipulation received concrete computational substantiation.

The graph-based representation is inherently computer processible, provides powerful language for expressing domain knowledge, and promotes various forms of knowledge measurement. The next section discusses how this representation can be employed to develop training environment compatible with human cognitive operations. Some methods of knowledge measurement will be also introduced.

4. KnowledgePlex (TM) - knowledge acquisition and training shell.

The purpose of KnowledgePlex (TM) is a) to represent knowledge units at the level of granularity adopted by domain experts, b) to represent expert structural grammars capturing regularities in the domain, c) to simulate expert strategies in manipulating cognitive models, d) to help trainee to visualize and explore expert models, and e) to compare expert and trainee performance.

To accomplish this purpose, KnowledgePlex employs knowledge processing architecture different from the architecture of conventional knowledge-based systems. The architecture contains three functional components: a Knowledge Base, or Archive to store knowledge units, a Composition Engine to associate knowledge units into labeled graphs (plexes), a Computation Engine to manipulate graphs, and a Navigation Engine to analyze and display graphs and their components.

Knowledge units in the Knowledge Base are defined by their informational content, which can be represented as text, drawings, programs, or audio and video sequences. From a structural standpoint, a unit is a node in a plex. In other words, units are nodes in a composed labeled graph, with relations among the units represented as labeled links. In composing graphs, compatibility of units is defined in terms of functions on the labels. More precisely, a plex P is defined as P:P = Q (m1, m2, ..., mk), where mi is a knowledge unit, and Q is a composition square matrix in which the element qij is the list of interconnections between mi and mj. A grammar on the plex is a four-tuple G = < S, A, B, R>, where S is the initial unit, A is the set of terminal units in the plex, B is the set of the auxiliary (non-terminal) components, and is a set of productions defined on the alphabet A V B.

It is easy to see that knowledge units are, in a sense, a generalization of the frame concept. Namely, a frame is identified by its slot structure and informational links to other frames. By contrast, plex-based representation is insensitive to the internal organization of knowledge units, but emphasizes instead the structure in which the units are embedded. In the result, the representation allows new forms of execution and analysis, concentrated on the structure's topological properties. The basic form of execution is composition, i.e., association of units in one-, two-, and, ultimately, multidimensional models. Composition rules (graph grammars) determine compatibility relations among classes of units, thus reflecting global organizational properties of the domain the model represents. This makes the plex-based representation suitable for capturing and expressing holistic cognitive patterns of domain experts.

When the number of links incident to and from the node exceeds two, a plex can be viewed as a hypergraph where each hyperpath represents an admissible alternative relation among the domain entities, for example, relations among the parts of a complex object. The meaning of the hypergraph formalism is particularly apparent when knowledge units represent steps in a procedure. Then a hyperpath represents an admissible sequence of steps, and the plex represents the entire set of admissible alternative procedures. For example, mission decomposition scenarios compiled to analyze operational procedures in complex systems, such as an aircraft, can be naturally expressed in terms of the hypergraph formalism. To acquire expert pilot generic knowledge of the ways in which missions can unfold, a grammar should be abstracted sufficient to generate plausible mission scenarios.

Before discussing functions performed by the Composition Engine we will consider an important generalization of the plex concept. Namely, we will allow weights to be assigned to the plex nodes to represent subjective preferences associated with alternative plex components. Consider, for example, operation planning in controlling a large scale industrial system such as a nuclear power plant. Operators are often confronted with multi-objective control problems when they have to consider simultaneously several criteria of the operational situation. In the plant, a number of variables are critical for the overall operational status and have to be maintained within certain safety limits at all times. As far as cognitive models of plant operators are concerned, not much is known. It is established, however, that operators' decision process is inherently based on assessing the set of goals combined with explicit or explicit utility judgment determining the order of priority on the set. The essence of plant control expertise is the capability to translate situational data into specific goals and to prioritize these goals appropriately. Therefore, to represent operators' knowledge structures, the knowledge acquisition procedure should employ representational format allowing operators to communicate their sense of relative operational priorities.

Analysis of a broad variety of models simulating performance in diverse technical domains [11] pointed at three major classes of composition strategies distinguished by the nature of constraints imposed on the resulting structure. Constraints of the first class are expressed in terms of compatibility relations among knowledge units and take the form of functions defined on the symbolic labels and, more generally, graph grammars. Constraints of the second class are expressed in terms of some computable characteristics of the resulting structure and take the form of functions defined on the weights associated with the graph elements. Finally, constraints of the third class are expressed in the form of input/output relationships defined on the structure and take the form of functions associated with individual units. The latter class of composition problems is the most general. For example, let units represent functions associated with individual instruments on a control panel and established on the input and output variables. Composition of such functions defines then the overall input-output characteristics of the device. Constraints can limit compatibility of functions within operational procedures, define the required outcome, and establish preference order on the outcome components. The Composition Engine is designed to assemble connected graphs in compliance with the constraints of various classes.

The Computation Engine is designed to perform two types of operations on graphs: simplification, and measurement of informational complexity. Both types involve various forms of graph partitioning. Simplification is accomplished by eliminating redundant links, and by partitioning graphs into strongly connected components (chunks) followed by replacing chunks by hypernodes. To determine chunks, weights are assigned to links based on the degree of their involvement in graph manipulation. For example, when the graph represents a model of control procedures, weights are assigned to links based on the relative frequency of links traversal. Heavy links indicate cohesive, highly correlated components of the model that tend to be manipulated as wholes. The concept of graph partitioning into strongly connected groups as a mechanism of model simplification in the course of training was introduced in [12]. It is encouraging that grouping strategy was independently proposed for neural network models as a way to reduce complexity and speed up learning [13].

Assessment of informational complexity is one of the forms of knowledge measurement on cognitive models. Informational complexity is computed as entropy of partitioned graphs. It can be shown that the upper bound of model complexity corresponds to unpartitioned graphs. Training causes models to evolve towards some optimal partitioning scheme corresponding to the lower bound of complexity. For models of technical systems, a reasonable correspondence was found between graph parameters contributing into informational complexity and experimentally identified factors of psychological complexity of interactive tasks [14].

Another form of knowledge measurement involves comparing models acquired from the expert and trainee. Comparison is done by computing the distance between the graphs. Two methods are employed, one involving entropy measurement, and another computing the distance as subjective "cost" of transforming one graph into another. In more detail these and other forms of knowledge measurement are discussed elsewhere.

Finally, the Navigation Engine is designed to analyze graphs and identify their topological components, such as paths, and properties, such as connectivity. For example, the following graph characteristics can be computed by the Engine: connectivity relations between the given components, paths between the given nodes traversing or circumventing an intermediate node, nodes assessible and reverse accessible from the node. The primary purpose of the Engine is to simulate manipulation processes on models and support their visualization by displaying graph components and results of components manipulation.

In summary, the architecture of KnowledgePlex follows the trend of fusing features of a knowledge-based system with Hypertext [15]. A unique advantage of KnowledgePlex resides in the capability to compose and analyze knowledge structures. The composition process is organized to accommodate major classes of global structural constraints. This, combined with computational tools for navigating structures, comparing them, and measuring their informational properties creates a very supportive environment for knowledge acquisition and transfer. Some of the procedures available or scheduled for delivery on KnowledgePlex-0.1 are illustrated in the next section. The 0.1 version is being developed in C language for IBM 286.

5. Acquisition and transfer of expert models.

5.1. Expert domain taxonomy.

The acquisition process starts by eliciting the vocabulary of knowledge units. Units are registered on cards in the form of textual descriptions and drawings. A standard set of drawing tools is provided with the system. No special requirements are observed in cards formatting.

Domain taxonomy is reflected in the distribution of cards within Archive, i.e., a hierarchical data base where cards are grouped according to the expert classification of knowledge units. Standard facilities are provided for card sorting, copying, etc. Components of the hierarchy, i.e., leaves and branches, can be moved, swapped or deleted. Often experts were found reluctant to name some of the subgroups. The system resolves this naming problems by color coding and clustering of cards images.

In acquiring the domain taxonomy, a special consideration should be given to verifying its completeness and stability. In short, completeness and stability can be assumed when admissible and meaningful compositions of units can be generated as permutations and distributions within the Archive. However, this issue merits a separate discussion outside of this paper.

5.2. Acquisition of domain relations.

KnowledgePlex offers facilities to create a relational data base containing structural tokens. A token is created by generating a node with incident links, followed by assigning labels to the links. User can scroll the data base, search for tokens with a given combination of labels, and sort tokens into sets. A special facility is provided to associate tokens with cards in the Archive. In this way, labeled links become attached to the previously formed cards. Separate formation of cards and relational tokens emphasizes two distinct perspectives on the knowledge structure, and adds flexibility to the acquisition process.

5.3. Composition and visualization of plexes.

To be considered for composition, tokens have to be accessed and marked by the user. Groups of tokens specified through their associations with cards, can be marked simultaneously, by identifying the class of cards. Composition is accomplished in two modes: manual and automatic. A general composition rule dictates that only links carrying identical labels can be connected. In the manual mode, the user composes plexes by retrieving tokens from the data base and positioning them on the screen. In the automatic mode, the user supplies a list of tokens to serve as starting and target nodes in the graph, and composition is conducted by the system. Two types of constraints can be defined: required and suggested. The former have to be observed for the resulting structure to be legal. The latter can be violated at the expense of some fine. When the cumulative fine exceeds a certain threshold, the structure is rejected. Compatibility constraints are expressed as requirements and prohibitions: required sequences of classes, required adjacency of nodes, required inclusion of a node in a sequence, and prohibited sequences of classes, prohibited adjacency, and prohibited inclusion.

When weights are associated with the nodes, the user can request that the cumulative weight of any path does not exceed a threshold value. Otherwise, the structure is considered inadmissible.

For simulation purposes, functions can be selected from a library of functions and associated with the nodes. Input-output values can then be computed along any path, and constraints can expressed in terms of output bounds for a given range of input values.

Plex structures can be scrolled both vertically and horizontally. For each node, the associated card can be displayed. Within a viewing window, several cards can be displayed simultaneously. Completed plexes can be placed in the archive and manipulated as tokens.

5.4. Analysis of plexes.

As indicated earlier, the system can compute some topological components and relations in plexes. In particular, the system computes paths connecting any pair of nodes, paths traversing any node, sets of nodes accessible and reverse-accessible from any node. The system can also sort nodes by rank, and find superfluous components, i.e., nodes with links not connected to other nodes.

5.5. Training modes.

Consider a task of controlling a technical system. Cards contain images and descriptions of control devices. Links of the associated tokens are labeled by pre- and post conditions of device manipulations. The acquisition process has produced an expert's model of control procedures stored in the Archive, and a list of expert rules and constraints registered in the Composition Engine.

The trainee starts by creating his/her own Archive and token data base, or by reviewing plexes generated by the expert. Active training consists largely in exposing the trainee to a representative sample of control tasks and comparing trainee's solutions to the expert ways of approaching these tasks. Training scenarios are as follows.

When presented with a task, the trainee scrolls through the data base and selects tokens for composition. This defines a set of control functions the trainee considers relevant to the task. Selected tokens are associated with the corresponding cards and composed manualy into a plex. Next the trainee will attempt answers to a list of questions:
for given starting and target conditions, identify all possible control sequences;
identify collateral sequences providing some of the controls are not operational;
for given conditions, identify relative weights of target nodes;
for a given distribution of weights, identify preferable procedures;
for a given control action, identify all the control elements affected by the action;
for a given control action, identify all possible immediate predecessors;
for a given sequence of actions with vacancies, identify all possible actions to complete the sequence;
for a given control action, identify all possible immediate consequences (e.g., what controls are enabled or disabled by the action), etc.

Answers are produced by direct manipulation, i.e. by positioning and connecting tokens. Future version of KnowledgePlex will support active cards containing generic images of devices capable of interacting with the user. Expert answers are simulated computationally by identifying paths, accessible and reverse accessible sets, and other components in the expert's plex. The diffrences between answers provide a basis for diagnostic feedback.

A series of sample tasks is concluded by the request to sort tokens in the data base into subsets representing control "blocks," i.e., cohesive groups of control elements.

Feedback to the trainee includes measures of complexity and relative distance between the trainee's and expert's models. The content and utility of this important measures are beyond the scope of this paper. Also, representation of temporal relations in the domain and assessment of indicators knowledge structures stability were omitted because of the space limitations. These issues will be addressed elsewhere.

To conclude, the paper reported the state-of-affairs in a research project investigating a new representational format and strategy for complex interactive skills acquisition and transfer. The project intends to formulate a new measurement and knowledge processing methodology derived from recent results in cognitive modeling and information theory. Some of the intermediate deliverables of this project have been successfully demonstrated in the medical domain [16].

REFERENCES

[1] Anderson, J.R., The Architecture of Cognition (Harvard University Press, 1983).
[2] Vekker, L. Cognitive Processes, Part II. (Leningrad University Press, 1982). In Russian.
[3] Yufik, Y.M. & Sheridan, T.B., Large Scale Systems (1986), 10, 133-146.
[4] Ohlsson, S. & Langley, P. Psychological Evaluation of Path Hypothesis in Cognitive Diagnosis, in: Mandl, H. & Lesgold, A. (eds.) Learning Issues for Intelligent Tutoring Systems. Springer-Verlag (1988).
[5] Laird, J.E., Rosenbloom, P.S., Newell, A. Towards Chunking as General Learning Mechanism. Carnegie-Mellon University (1985).
[6] Venda, V.F. Hybrid Intelligence Systems, in print.
[7] Venda, V.F. & Yufik, Y.M. Functional and Psychological Complexity of Mental Activity, in print.
[8] Anochin, P., Problems of Decision Making in Psychology and Physiology, Problems of Psychology, 1974. In Russian.
[9] Morton, J., Hammersley, R. H., Bekkerian, D.A., Cognition (1985) 20, 1-23.
[10] Sowa, J.F., Conceptual Structures (Addison-Wesley, 1984).
[11] Yufik, Y.M., Graph-Algebraic Approach to Heuristic Configuration Design (FMC Artificial Intelligence Center, 1987).
[12] Yufik, Y.M. & Hartzell, E.J., Design for Trainability: Assessment of Cognitive Complexity in Man-Machine Systems, in: Salvendy, G. & Smith, M.J. (eds.) Designing and Using Human-Computer Interfaces and Knowledge Based Systems (Elsevier, Amsterdam, 1989).
[13] Zipser, D. A Subgrouping Strategy That Reduces Complexity and Speeds Up Learning in Recurrent Networks (University of California, San Diego, 1989).
[14] Venda, V.F. Engineering Psychology (Moscow, 1983). In Russian.
[15] Carando, P., IEEE Expert (1989) 4, 65-78.
[16] Yufik, Y.M. & Zheleznyak, J., Proc. XII International Congress on Cybernetics (Namur, Belgium, 1989).

SECTION V: APPLICATIONS AND CASE STUDIES

SV.4 Software Development

Software Reusability: Delivering productivity gains or short cuts
A. Sutcliffe and N. Maiden 895

A project-orientated view of CSCW
N.R. Seel, G.N. Gilbert, and M.E. Morris 903

Satisfying the need to know: Interpersonal information access
R.E. Kraut and L.A. Streeter 909

Conversationbuilder: An open architecture for collaborative work
S.M. Kaplan 917

Human–Computer Interaction - INTERACT '90
D. Diaper et al. (Editors)
Elsevier Science Publishers B.V. (North-Holland)

SOFTWARE REUSABILITY: DELIVERING PRODUCTIVITY GAINS OR SHORT CUTS

Alistair Sutcliffe and Neil Maiden

Department of Business Systems Analysis,
City University,
Northampton Square,
London EC1V 0HB, U.K.

It has been claimed that software reuse can produce considerable productivity gains in system development. Although much software engineering research has been undertaken to deliver reusability in CASE tools there is little knowledge about how system developers actual reuse specifications. This paper reports practical research into reuse scenarios based on providing analogous specifications for systems analysts. The results are encouraging for reuse but caution that reuse may also create mistakes in specifications by erroneous transfer of knowledge.

1. INTRODUCTION

Software reuse has been proposed as a panacea for many software engineering problems, (Rich, Waters and Reubenstein 1987); however, in practice even expert programmers required considerable time and mental effort to modify unfamiliar programs (Pennington 1987), whilst novices often fail to achieve any successful modifications (Holt at al. 1987). Little is known about how software engineers actually reuse software modules and specifications, hence the design of CASE tools embedding reusability has little sound theoretical or empirical basis.

The role of analogy in problem solving has been the subject of considerable research (e.g. Hall 1989). Providing software developers with analogous conceptual models for new problems has been suggested as one way of reusing of software specifications held in large repositories.

Cognitive analyses of software development have yet to produce a clear model of the process, although the some studies (Vitalari and Dickson 1983, Guindon and Curtis 1988) do suggest some cognitive determinants of good performance for system developers. However, the cognitive implications of software reusability have received no attention. The objective of this study was to investigate how software engineers may reuse specifications.

The use of abstraction in the construction of conceptual models, represented as data flow diagrams or entity life histories, to describe application domains at a high level is widely advocated by software engineers. Furthermore the use of abstract templates and generic objects has been proposed as a method of delivering reusability (Rich, Waters and Reubenstein 1987). However, software engineering authors rarely evaluate the usability of their products consequently little evidence exists on how abstract and generic concepts may help systems development. In light of this we investigated the reuse of specifications presented in concrete and abstract forms, as concrete presentation of analogy is often advocated in HCI whereas abstraction is valued for problem understanding in software engineering.

2. METHOD

The 30 (23 male, 7 female) subjects were full-time MSc students in Business Systems Analysis and Design. They had knowledge of several structured analysis and Jackson (JSD) techniques. All but 6 of the subjects had previous systems development experience. The subjects, whose age ranged from 21 to 36 years, volunteered their services, for which they received practice and supplementary tuition on JSD techniques.

A video camera recorded all written work, and verbal protocols were tape recorded. Subjects were asked to develop a JSD process structure diagram for a scheduling function allocating videos to hotels. The problem built upon domain knowledge already acquired by subjects from a case study.

A between subjects, two conditions experiment was conducted with:
a Control group, where subjects were given the problem narrative alone,
an Abstract Analogy Group (Group AA), where subjects were provided with the problem narrative and an abstract JSD template of a general scheduling problem,
a Concrete Analogy Group (Group CA), where subjects were given the problem narrative and a JSD specification of a real analogous production planning application.
Each group of 10 subjects was balanced with respect to subjects' experience.

Retrospective protocols and a written questionnaire captured problem-solving and reuse strategies.

The hypothesis was that both supplementary analogical specifications would promote reuse and improve specification completeness and accuracy. Measurable dependent variables included solution completeness and errors. For full details of experimental materials and procedure see Sutcliffe and Maiden (1990).

In concurrent protocols, Groups CA and AA subjects were requested to verbalise: (i) similarities between the reusable specification and the problem, and; (ii) how these similarities were used to solve the problem. Subsequent retrospective analysis probed subject's general problem-solving strategies and their understanding of the analogy and the target problem. The main concept was the functional requirement to allocate a resource within certain constraints. This was manifest as scheduling a resource, (or video copies in the target domain) within certain constraints (e.g. time and hotel preference in the target domain).

Subjects' solutions were scored for completeness and validity. Completeness was measured against a solution provided by an experienced JSD analyst. Subjects solutions were scored for the correct number of actions in the diagram and for use of JSD design constructs (e.g. Backtracking). The validity of solutions was measured by the quantity and severity of errors. Errors were counted and ranked on a 1-8 scale according to their severity, by examining the extent to which the specification was incorrect in terms of domain knowledge and JSD syntax. Solutions were independently cross-marked by two experts, who agreed on scoring in 91% of all cases for completeness scores.

3. RESULTS

Completeness scores for subjects are shown in Table 1. Solution completeness scores indicate that the subjects who were given reusable specifications produced more complete solutions than the control group. This effect was significant for the abstract analogy (AA group) (T test, using the approximating Z distribution for non-normal populations; $Z = 2.23$, $p = 0.05$); however, although the CA group showed better scores than the control group, this difference was non significant. Control subjects made more errors than both experimental groups although these differences were also non-significant (see Table 1).

Table 1 - Average completeness (as % of ideal solution and Error scores for solutions developed by subject group

	Control Group	Abstract (Group-AA)	Concrete (Group-CA)
%age completeness	24.4	41.1	32.8
Average error score	11.8	10	10.1

Recognition of the analogy was evaluated by asking subjects whether they recognised three key analogical associations: the functional requirement of allocation/scheduling, the concept of resources, and the requirements needing the resources. All the AA subjects recognised at least one key association, 8 out of 10 CA subjects also recognised one association but none of the subjects recognised all three.

Three mappings which involved JSD method knowledge as well as domain knowledge were analysed in more detail. Subjects were asked whether they recognised and used three features and their solutions were checked for inclusion of the same. The three features of the Allocation function were: integrity of the top-level sequence, an iteration of hotel-to-video allocations, and a backtracking selection for each allocation. Most of the control subjects failed to recognise these features (5 out of 30 features recognised) whereas the experimental subjects performed better, with Group-AA having a higher overall score (23/30) than Group-CA (16/30). This suggests that the transfer of structural knowledge about the target problem was effective, particularly with the abstract analogy prompt.

Subjects' attitude, recorded by the post-test questionnaire, underlined the effectiveness of the abstract analogy. Group-AA subjects rated the abstract analogy to be more helpful in developing a solution than did CA subjects for the concrete analogy.

The reasons for failure to use the analogical prompt appear to be a matter of motivation and comprehension of the analogical prompt. Five group CA subjects failed to use the analogical material. Two of these 5 subjects retrospectively reported that they rejected the analogous specification since it contained too much information to be absorbed in the time allowed, whilst another 2 totally ignored the analogical prompt. The other Group-CA subject was unable to reuse the scheduling function, even though the analogy was recognised. Two Group-AA subjects also failed to reuse the abstract analogous prompt because they misunderstood the functionality in the analogous prompt, although they did recognise the potential analogy with target problem domain. This indicates that the concrete analogy may be more difficult to assimilate than the abstract version.

Analytic strategies which caused errors were identified in retrospective protocols, backed up by analysis of subject's solutions. Three strategies were apparent:

(i) Creation of unnecessary components in the target specification, apparently caused by the motivation of mapping all components across from the analogous prompt (4 AA and 2 CA subjects),
(ii) Making false analogies, apparently caused by trying to link all structures in the prompt with a structure in the target domain (1 CA subject),
(iii) Choice of the structure to map from the prompt was based on its general familiarity (2 CA subjects).

Some subjects used more than one weak strategy. It was noticeable that weak heuristics were also used to attempt to solve other aspects of the analogy problem.

3.1 Effect of Experience

No significant interaction was found between experience and solution completeness or errors with a two-way analysis of variance. Inexperienced subjects made proportionally less syntax errors (1 error in 3 made was syntactic, whilst other subjects made 1 syntactic error in 2), which appears to contradict their lack of experience. This result may be caused by a copying strategy from the analogical prompt, which could also explain their higher rate of domain errors.

3.2 Analysis of the Use of Analogy

The quality of reuse of the prompt made by the subjects was rated in four bands according the completeness scores and reuse strategies reported by the subjects. In all cases the strength of assertions made retrospectively about analogical transfer agreed with the quality of subjects' solutions. Five Group-CA subjects and 8 Group-AA subjects, who had completeness scores of >= 7/18 components, verbalised a clear model of the analogy and its association to the problem domain in retrospective protocols. Five subjects did not effectively transfer any information from the analogical prompt. Poor usage was shown by 2 CA subjects who misunderstood the analogical prompt, made false inferences about component details and mapped to an inappropriate JSD process structure. Two AA subjects partially used the analogy and employed some of the prompt's components in their solutions. Results are given in Table 2.

Good and partial reuse subjects were grouped as Successful Reusers while others were classified as Unsuccessful Reusers - see Table 3a. Although the completeness scores, predictably, were better for successful subjects, this effect was not present for errors. This suggests that although reuse may promote a more complete solution, accuracy of the result may not be improved. There was no significant difference in scores of successful subjects between the CA and AA groups- see Table 3b.

The type of errors made by transferring knowledge from the reusable specification was

Quality of applicatn.	Number of Group-AA subjects	Number of Group-CA subjects
Good	6	5
Partial	2	0
Poor	0	2
None	2	3

Table 2 - Application of analogous knowledge by Group-AA and -CA subjects

	No. of subjects	Average % Completeness Scores	Average Error Scores
Successful Subjects	13	49.2	9.23
Unsuccessful Subjects	7	14.3	11.57

Table 3a - Average completeness and error scores for successful and unsuccessful subjects

	No. of subjects	Average % Completeness Scores	Average Error Scores
Group-AA	8	47.2	11.125
Group-CA	5	52.2	6.2

Table 3b - Average completeness and error scores of successful subjects in AA and CA Groups

investigated by looking at constraint checking, an important part of the scheduling function. All 5 successful Group-CA subjects modelled individual constraint checks correctly used components in the analogical prompt. However for the 8 successful Group-AA subjects: 4 subjects modeled the constraints in non-specific terms, (e.g., 'Check Constraints' component, or '1st', '2nd', 3rd', etc Constraints'), 2 subjects only modeled two of the 4 individual constraints, 1 subject specified incorrect constraints, and only 1 subject correctly modeled the constraints as required.

The better performance of the CA subjects may be caused by the extra mental effort they had to make to understand the concrete analogy. The number and naming of the check constraints components by the AA subjects were closely related to the reusable specifications from which they were derived, suggesting they may have been copying the material rather than reasoning about it.

Specification copying in the sense of direct transfer and lexical tailoring of specification components, without reasoning, accounted for many errors. Errors in eleven of the 13 successful subjects' solutions, combined with their retrospective reports, suggested a general failure to understand the analogical prompt. One subject included the sort component within the allocation iteration while the remaining 10 subjects had errors related to the backtracking concept, from duplication of conditions and posits, and use of conditional rather than backtrack symbols in the posit\admit components. Retrospective questioning also revealed that no subject understood the reusable specification to their satisfaction, although this did not inhibit reuse. For example, 9 subjects transferred the backtracking concept, although post-test questioning revealed only 3 of these subjects understood it.

Among the successful subjects, only 6 developed solutions that supplemented the material derivable from the analogy. One Group-CA and 3 Group-AA subjects added minor components or structural features, while two Group-AA subjects expanded the abstract solution, and retrospectively claimed that the abstract constraint checking component was insufficient. It was more common for subjects to omit components from the reusable specification; e.g. all but one subject omitted backtracking quits from their solutions. Retrospective probing suggested that such omissions may have been caused by failure to understand the role of the components in the analogous prompt.

3.3 Subjects' behaviour

Analysis of the video tapes suggested successful reuse required considerable effort, since the successful subjects spent 90% of the protocol session time attending to the reusable specification. There was a significant correlation between time spent analyzing the reusable specification and subject completeness scores (Spearman Rank Order Coefficient $r = +0.657$, $p = 0.05$). Most subjects took some time to recognise similarities between the two systems and understanding of the analogy appeared to be incremental.

Failure to understand the analogy led to mappings based on surface similarities between the problem and the reusable specification. Subjects were unable to construct mappings where no surface similarities existed (e.g. Booking to Task entities). An analysis of false mappings made by both groups emphasised dependence on surface similarities.

4. DISCUSSION

Reuse of software poses two problems: first, retrieval of code modules or specifications which are appropriate for the new application, and secondly comprehension of the problem and reusable components by system developers so that the software is reused correctly. The findings reported in this paper bear particularly on the second problem.

Reuse of specifications appears to improve the completeness of solutions produced by system analysts, and reusable material presented in an abstract form appears to enhance performance more than presentation of concrete analogies. This may be because abstract analogies are more easily recognised. Abstract concepts in software engineering are thought to reflect expert performance and require considerable learning (Gilmore and Green 1988), so a stronger effect may have been expected from the concrete analogy, especially for less experienced subjects. Although both types of reusable specifications improved completeness, they produced similar error rates hence abstraction does not appear to help creation of more accurate specifications. A possible explanation is that the skill level of our subjects was insufficient for them to be familiar with abstraction, even though no significant interaction between experience and the abstract/concrete condition was found.

Although recognition was effective, understanding of the analogies was not. Even successful reusers made mistakes many of which could be attributed to lack of detailed reasoning about the specification. Subjects appeared to exhibit a mental laziness which was manifest in copying rather than reasoning while reusing specification components. This was particularly noticeable with the copying of the JSD backtracking construct without understanding it. While this effect may be ascribed as a lack of motivation among the subjects, this was not our impression as most expressed keen interest in the experiment and its outcome. A more probable explanation is that reuse offers developers a mentally easy cognitive strategy for problem solving.

Understanding a problem domain requires construction of a mental model, based on analysis and knowledge of similar domains held in memory (e.g. Gentner and Stevens 1983, Pennington 1987). However, as Sheil suggested (cited in Sein 1988), novice analysts are unlikely to have many domain analogies to draw on when constructing new mental models. Furthermore, novice analysts tend to follow weak problem solving strategies and have difficulty in initial scoping of problem spaces (Sutcliffe and Maiden 1989). It is therefore not surprising that when presented with an analogical prompt they take it as a potential ready-made solution.

A frequent mistake made by the relatively inexperienced systems analysts in this study was to focus on surface, lexical properties of the analogical prompt. This concords with the tendency of novices to incorrectly categorise problems by surface similarities found by Chi et al. (1982). The subjects' poor understanding of the analogy was probably caused by a lack of reasoning which is consistent with Novick's

(1988) observation that subjects invoke cognitively-easy strategies when exploiting analogies.

We suggest that specification reuse in a CASE environment is unlikely to succeed without tutorial support. The situation is analogous to learning to use new applications. Here strategies which encourage learning by experience and partial exposure to the full functionally (i.e. less than the whole problem domain) have been found to be effective (Carroll et al. 1988). The key to correct reuse of specifications may be partial exposure, coupled with a didactic dialogue to encourage understanding. Studies of errors during learning (Lewis and Anderson 1985) suggest an iterative approach promotes more effective problem understanding. A possible strategy for reusability may be to help structuring the problem space, by providing analogous specifications and promoting iterative learning with techniques for gradual exposure of analogical links between knowledge structures in the two domains.

Formation of mental models in software engineering requires building on the analyst's knowledge of the target domain, and appropriate abstract concepts are thought to be important in promoting problem understanding (Guindon and Curtis 1988). This study supports the potential of abstract templates for requirements analysis. Specification reuse appears to assist in structuring the problem space and defining the problem scope. Specifications of analogous applications could reduce the analyst's mental load during model formation by provision of ready-made mental schema for the problem domain. Mental models in software engineering are often used to simulate scenarios in order to evaluate candidate designs (Adelson and Soloway 1985, Guindon and Curtis 1988). In this case analogy could help development of alternative scenarios.

ACKNOWLEDGEMENTS

We wish to thank the students on the Msc in Business Systems Analysis and Design who participated in this study. N. Maiden is supported by SERC post-graduate studentship number 88803006.

REFERENCES

Adelson B. and Soloway E., [1985], "The Role of Domain Experience in Software Design", *IEEE Trans. on Software Engineering* SE-11, No 11, November 1985, 1351 - 1360.

Carroll J.M., Smith-Kerker P.A., Ford J.R. and Mazur-Rimetz S.A., [1988], The Minimal Manual, *Human Computer Interaction*, 3, 123-133.

Chi M.T.H., Glaser R. & Rees E., [1982], "Expertise in Problem Solving", in *Advances in the Psychology of Human Intelligence*, ed. R. Sternberg, Lawrence Erlbaum Associates, 7 - 75.

Gentner D., and Stevens A.L., [1983], *Mental Models*, Lawrence Erlbaum Associates.

Gilmore D.J. and Green T.R.G., [1988], "Programming plans and programming experience", *The Quarterly Journal of Experimental Psychology*, 40A, 423-442.

Guindon R. & Curtis B., [1988], Control of Cognitive Processes During Software Design: What Tools are Needed ?", Proceedings of CHI '88, ed. E. Soloway, D. Frye and S.B. Sheppard, 263 - 269.

Hall R.P., [1989], "Computational Approaches to Analogical Reasoning: A Comparative Analysis", *Artificial Intelligence*, 39, 39 - 120.

Holt R.W., Boehm-Davis D.A. and Shultz A.C., [1987], "Mental Representations of Programs for Student and Professional Programmers", in *Empirical Studies of Programmers: Second Workshop*, ed. G.M. Olson, S. Sheppard & E. Soloway, Ablex, 33 - 46.

Lewis M.W. and Anderson J.R., [1985], "Discrimination of Operator Schemata in Problem Solvers", *Journal of Experimental Psychology: Learning, Memory and Cognition*, 8, No 5, 484 - 494.

Novick L.R., [1988], "Analogical transfer, problem similarity and expertise" *Journal of Experimental Psychology: Learning, Memory and Cognition*, 14, No 3, 510 - 520.

Pennington N., [1987], "Stimulus Structures and Mental Representations in Expert Comprehension of Computer Programs", *Cognitive Psychology*, 19, 295 - 341.

Rich C., Waters R.C. & Reubenstein H.B., [1987], "Towards a Requirements Apprentice", MIT Artificial Intelligence Laboratory internal paper, August 1987.

Sein M.W., [1988], "Conceptual Models in Training Novice Users of Computer Systems: Effectiveness of Abstract Vs Analogical Models and Influence of Individual Differences", Ph. D. Thesis, School of Business, Indiana University, January 1988.

Sutcliffe A.G. & Maiden N.A.M., [1989], "Analysing the Analyst (Cognitive Models in Software Engineering)", submitted for publication.

Sutcliffe A.G. & Maiden N.A.M., [1990], "Specification Reusability: Why Tutorial Support is Necessary", Proceedings of SE-90 Conference, Brighton UK, July 1990.

Vitalari N.P. and Dickson G.W., [1983], "Problem Solving for Effective Systems Analysis: An Experimental Exploration", *Comm. of the ACM*, 26(11), November 1983, 948 - 956.

Human–Computer Interaction – INTERACT '90
D. Diaper et al. (Editors)
Elsevier Science Publishers B.V. (North-Holland)

A PROJECT-ORIENTATED VIEW OF CSCW[1]

N. R. Seel*, G. N. Gilbert**, M. E. Morris*

* STC Technology Ltd, London Road, Harlow, Essex CM17 9NA.
** Social and Computer Sciences Research Group, University of Surrey, Guildford GU2 5XH

Project Support Environments (PSEs), a type of computer supported cooperative work (CSCW) system, are examined in terms of the management forms which their designs appear to assume. Data-oriented PSEs can be seen as aiming to support management by direct authority. Process-oriented PSEs are aligned to the exercise of technical authority. However, much of the work of the 'professional communities' found in organisations is conducted, not under either of these two more traditional forms of management, but under a pluralist form, in which professionals are given a degree of responsible autonomy. Neither data- nor process-oriented PSEs are well suited to this management form.

The characteristics of a PSE designed to support professional communities are outlined. Such a PSE, a 'Professional Community Support' system, needs to provide resources for negotiated cooperation in order to support what is argued to be the key activity of professionals – issue handling. These resources must be designed to support explicitly both globally and locally managed interactions, with it being possible to embed either within the other.

1. INTRODUCTION

This paper examines the interplay between certain kinds of social processes which occur within organisations and the nature of the computer systems which are intended to support them. We focus in particular on *projects* and their computer support systems which we call 'Project Support Environments' (PSEs).

It is not easy to define what is meant by the word project. The difficulty is compounded by variation in the definition of what constitutes a project amongst the organisational actors involved in its creation and prosecution. Rather than attempting a considered taxonomy, we will talk of a space of *project models*. Only a few such models will be discussed in what follows.

A computer system supporting a certain type of project model necessarily objectifies certain project-significant entity types and relationships within its architecture. As a result, the insertion of such a PSE into the social context of a real project often causes problems. A better understanding of these problems might be offered by either of two directions of analysis: (i) start from a sociological analysis of a project model and deduce a PSE system architecture; or (ii) start from a given type of PSE and induce a notional project model presupposed by its architecture. The former direction of analysis is impeded by the fact that the designers of most existing PSEs have not spelled out in detail the sociological model of projects to which they were working. Much attention has been lavished on detailed requirements analysis and specification of the *functionality* of such PSEs, but this does not amount to the same thing.

We therefore intend in this paper to follow the second direction, to 'reverse-engineer' project models from some existing 'state of the art' PSEs, and through assessment and criticism of these models, to develop a more adequate model of many of the projects which commonly occur in organisations. This will in turn lead to some proposals for a novel project support environment which integrates some of the advanced systems currently being developed under the general rubric of CSCW.

2. CURRENT PSEs

The Alvey Software Engineering Strategy identified three generations of 'Integrated Project Support Environments' (IPSEs) (Talbot and Witty 1983). The first generation was considered to be currently available environments, such as those provided by UNIX tools, where integration was *ad hoc*; the second generation was to be based around the idea of a database of project artifacts, with a collection of project specific tools interworking over the database; the third generation was speculatively supposed to be based upon AI techniques.

For the purposes of this paper, we will call the second generation IPSEs *data-oriented PSEs*. In Alvey, the second generations IPSEs were represented by projects such as ASPECT and ECLIPSE (discussed in McDermid 1985), loosely characterised by an architecture of a central project database, together with a number of compatible tools (editors, compilers, configuration managers). The artifacts maintained by the system (such as requirements documents, specifications, executable code, test data, configuration information, evaluation reports, documentation, etc.) would be checked out of the database, transformed (by a project actor using appropriate IPSE tools) and the results entered into the database under configuration control. The Alvey Programme did not attempt to develop any third generation IPSEs, but did commission a project to examine support for *process* in projects: IPSE2.5[2] (Snowdon 1989).

The requirement for support for process arises from the following observation: data-oriented PSEs say almost nothing about the properties of project actor-types (rôles), the interaction between rôles, the assignment of particular actors to rôles, the structure and temporal sequencing of rôle activities etc. Thus significant project uniformities are not represented by the data-oriented PSE and are consequently unsupported. A process-oriented PSE augments the data-oriented PSE with explicit support for these and other aspects of project process by providing a process model.

The process model may be conceptualised in terms of participating rôles, which have access to certain resources, which can undertake certain kinds of transformational operations, and which can conduct interactions with other rôles[3]. The benefits of having an executable process model are considerable. During process model execution, the process-oriented PSE can maintain a global project context, ensuring the routing of deliverables; manage resources and agendas for individual actors; provide overall visibility within the project for participants; and support various management techniques such as 'management by exception'.

3. PSEs AND MANAGEMENT STYLE

The reason why effort has been devoted to the design and development of PSEs is that the carrying out of projects involves complex problems of coordination and control of organisational tasks, often ones whose success is critical for the organisation. Coordination is required to prevent the wasteful and haphazard use of physical and human resources, and control is needed to ensure that all the components of the work, including the coordination itself, are achieved satisfactorily. Often control and coordination tasks are allocated to the same rôle, the 'project manager', but in some forms of management, they may be separated.

PSEs can be seen as attempts to transfer some of the managerial work which is required to achieve coordination and control onto a software system. Their design can be examined to extract the types of management relationship which they are primarily intended to support.

Because PSEs never offer support for all possible control and coordination functions, particular PSEs are best suited for particular forms of management. Below we suggest three 'ideal type' characterisations of management style which are useful for examining PSEs. It is not suggested that any actual work situation will fit into one of the categories precisely; rather, that the categories represent extreme forms which can be found combined in various ways in real organisations.

Perhaps the simplest form of control is the direct exercise of authority by one manager over a set of subordinates who have little say about the nature of their work. This simple model of *direct authority* requires the manager to see, know and decide everything, and the subordinates to accept passively the manager's commands. The manager has not only to determine the tasks of each subordinate, but also to handle the coordination requirements.

This form of control tends to break down for tasks of any but the most straightforward kind because of the demands made on the manager, who alone is responsible for the detection and correction of problems arising from poor planning and exogenous change. In at least some contexts, the effectiveness of control suffers from subordinates' resistance to what can be perceived as a highly coercive form of management. Coordination is also a problem if the number of subordinates is not small, because of the potential complexity of the interactions between subordinates' tasks, all of which the manager has to monitor and understand.

A partial solution to the coordination problem can be seen as the aim of the data-oriented PSEs reviewed above. These PSEs assume that the supervisory structure, the division of labour and the criteria for acceptance of work have all been laid down and can be enforced by the project manager or other authority figure: thus control remains with the manager. The integration of project data and data-transformation tools in the data-oriented PSE may provide significant support, however, for coordination. Nevertheless, the disadvantages of this first style of management, especially the difficulties of control, remain.

A second management form, based on a model of *technical authority*, divides up the work into pre-ordained tasks, and assigns each subordinate to one or more of these tasks. The subordinate's job is to complete the task within the specified time in the specified manner. The manager's job becomes largely one of coordination, control having been transferred to the task specification. Taken to its extreme form, with minute division of tasks, this is akin to Taylorism (Taylor 1915; see Littler 1982) and suffers from some of the same problems.

First, the ability to construct viable plans and specifications of the work requires great skill, experience and knowledge which may not be available or may be expensive to provide. Second, there is difficulty in responding to exogenous changes, which may have unpredictable effects on the specification. Third, this form of management also tends to encourage resistance from subordinates. Subordinates can find themselves allocated to tasks without consultation, and often with only vague notions of how their work fits into the wider whole. This may lead to opposition, with specifications being interpreted by the subordinates in ways which differ from that intended in order to wrest some autonomy for themselves.

The process-oriented PSE model can be aligned to this form of management in a fairly straightforward way. The control aspect of management may be largely delegated to the process model, which determines what is to be done, by whom and how. The process-oriented PSE, in executing the process model, supports the coordination of activities. The function of management, in principle, reduces to the handling of anomalies, which remain unencoded in the model[4].

Creating such a process model requires the identification of the actor relationships constitutive of carrying out the project. These are then reified into algorithmic code. For projects of significant size and complexity, this is a non-trivial task, itself resembling a software development project. Furthermore, the resulting process-modelling code may be intelligible only to specialists, and safely modifying the process model in mid-project poses difficult, and currently under-explored problems. These points are not perhaps of decisive importance where projects are highly routinised and stable, hence where there is a possibility of getting the process right, and then using it on many subsequent occasions. If the code correctly captures the actual processes which are appropriate to the project, and which are consensually supported by project participants, such support may be useful. For projects which are not of this type however, the 'frozen' social interactions supported by the PSE may be, or may rapidly become, inappropriate. The system may then be experienced as coercive, unhelpful and perhaps unusable.

A third form of management, recognising the difficulties of the second form, aims to recruit subordinates to assist in the management of the project by giving them a degree of 'responsible autonomy' (Friedman 1977). This helps to ensure that the subordinates identify with the aims of the project and that they react constructively to contingencies. A part of the manager's authority is given away to the subordinates, in exchange for their cooperation in advancing the aims of the project. In particular, partial responsibility for coordination is devolved to individuals, yielding a 'flatter' organisational structure in which decisions are frequently made by negotiation rather than by managerial *fiat*[5].

There is a price to be paid, however, for this more apparently consensual form of management. Conflicts, which in other management forms are suppressed by the coercive effect of either the authority of the manager in person or by the reified authority of the project's plans and specifications, become visible and the source of potential discord and delay. Lacking an authoritative central direction, the aims of the project may fail to cohere, or may be diverted from the original intentions. Lacking a central focus, the web of interactions between subordinates may become too complex and too expensive to sustain. The communication costs are compounded if meta-issues (not just what to do and how to do it, but also, for example, how success is to be measured) are open for negotiation.

Few PSEs have been designed in a way which would make them useful for supporting this third form of management, which we shall label *pluralist* (Fox 1974). This is surprising as much of the work of the 'professional communities' found in many organisations is at least nominally organised in this style. In the rest of this paper, we will examine more carefully the characteristics of 'project work' as carried out by professional communities organised according to the pluralist form of management. Flowing from this analysis, we will make some proposals as to the form of suitable project support environments.

4. WHAT DO PROFESSIONALS DO? THE CASE OF ISSUE HANDLING

In an organisational model comprising a collection of professional communities organised according to the pluralist form of management, the collective execution of agreed-upon activities to accomplish agreed-upon goals is just one moment of a much more complex negotiated process. This includes monitoring the environment, setting up new work groups, negotiating and advancing problem solutions, maintaining knowledge, deciding on the next activity, and so on. Not all of these activities can be related to a specific project. We will call this constellation of technical and managerial activities *issue-handling*.

Issue handling is the key activity for many professionals. Issues are often worked on in a negotiated manner, with each professional bringing a different viewpoint. For example, different professionals may address the financial and the technical aspects of an issue. Issue-handling itself can be analysed into sub-activities, with the proviso that rigid sequencing is not implied[6]. Some of the sub-activities are themselves decomposable in a fashion similar to the overall 'issue-handling' analysis.

4.1 AN ISSUE-HANDLING LIFE CYCLE

- Event detection and problem acceptance. A trigger event may occur within an organisation, or it may occur in the external environment. If an event is missed it can mean an opportunity lost or a threat not recognised, with subsequent deleterious consequences for the organisation.
- Identification of and interaction with appropriate colleagues to establish the scope of the problem, who 'owns' it and where it will be handled. To do this effectively a professional needs access to organisational models.
- Task-analysis, plan formation, and resource acquisition. Many issues have certain features in common and can be considered to form a class, all members of which can be handled in a similar fashion. Part of the planning activity may involve searching corporate archives for previous exemplars on which to base current activities. The extent of the search will be dependent on the ease with which such information is available and the difficulty of adapting the process to the current situation.
- Workgroup formation i.e. the allocation of resources to the issue for a specific period of time. The members of the workgroup may be drawn from within just one community within an organisation. However, many issues require workgroups drawn from many communities including, increasingly, those located in other organisations. The composition of the workgroup is likely to vary over time as different aspects of the issue are addressed.
- The workgroup undertakes synchronous activities (meetings), and individually coordinated asynchronous activities (deliverable production and exchange) in order to develop the issue. A variety of proposals may be produced, evaluated and modified until eventually an acceptable 'solution' is produced.
- Agreement to the solution is negotiated with the problem owners.
- The solution is implemented and its effects monitored. The implementation and monitoring of the solution may raise further issues, both for the original workgroup, for other parts of the organisation and for organisations in the external environment.
- The issue-handling process, history, deliverables, etc. are further processed and archived.

If we take the issue-handling life cycle above to be a species of project model, we can see that it is much more sophisticated than the process models induced from existing PSEs. The context for the project is an organisational community with many professional sub-communities, where problem negotiation, organisational localisation, resource acquisition and process development are as important as the 'straightforward' execution of pre-defined processes.

5. PROFESSIONAL COMMUNITY SUPPORT SYSTEMS

We will call a PSE capable of supporting technical and managerial professionals organised in communities according to the pluralist management model, a *Professional Community Support system.*

What would such a system be like? This question is not academic, since the recent technologies of relatively low-cost, high-powered distributed workstations permits an organisation to equip its professionals with significant interconnected computing power. Many demonstrator systems exist which offer technical support for issue-handling, by providing, for example:

- shared-screen conferencing, often with additional audio/video facilities, providing the simulation of co-presence of people and artifacts;
- structured messaging systems, providing communication and coordination resources for communities;
- hypermedia systems which potentially provide a means of storing and accessing structured, shareable, multi-media information and navigating over the resulting 'information-bases'.

While all these technologies will be required for an effective Professional Community Support system, current commercial efforts to integrate them coherently into a networked multi-media workstation configuration are unlikely in themselves to yield a usable Professional Community Support system. An autonomous level of design of the end-user computing environment is required, which responds to the requirements of the pluralist management form. One important aspect of interaction under this form of management is its diversity: open-ended conversations, structured work in an organisationally-agreed context and considerations of process seamlessly coexist. As we shall now explain, the key to providing a coherent support system for these apparently diverse interactional styles is the distinction between *local* and *global* management systems.

5.1 A Professional Community Support system for negotiated cooperation

An influential trend in current CSCW research assimilates cooperation between people to a *conversational* paradigm. A similar idea has begun to take root in software engineering (Finkelstein and Fuks 1990). Systems such as Coordinator (Winograd 1987, Winograd and Flores 1986) maintain explicit conversational models (such as 'Conversations for Action') which enforce a turn-taking protocol on users. The Coordinator model fails, however, to distinguish between what Bowers and Churcher (1989) term local and global management systems.

A feature of everyday conversation is that it is *locally managed* (Sacks, Schegloff and Jefferson 1974): speakers take turns, and there are an arbitrarily large number of possible rejoinders which, in various contexts, count as appropriate conversational continuations. As Bowers and Churcher (ibid) observe in relation to Coordinator-like systems, "the localism and situatedness of conversation is somewhat missed by network models of conversation, where only certain options are represented at particular junctures as an extended, non locally-managed representation unfolds".

At the other extreme, Bowers and Churcher continue, there are "'speech-exchange systems', in which all (from first to last) turns are pre-allocated. At any given turn, you will know who will be speaking (and usually for that matter, what they'll be saying). By contrast to Sacks et al's local management notion, we can say that such communication activities are subject to global management systems". Such systems are found typically in institutional rituals.

Although the notion of local management has most often been applied to conversation and systems explicitly modelled on conversation (e.g. Frohlich and Luff, 1989), it was initially developed for understanding social *action* generally and may usefully be applied to many social events in organisations, including projects and office procedures. Often these combine local and global structuring. For example, the large scale structure of a process may be organisationally pre-agreed, even standardised, as a globally-managed framework, while the fine-grained interactions in the interstices of the framework are not pre-agreed, and constitute locally-managed interactions.

A global management system, by virtue of its pre-allocation of turn structure and content, may be represented independently of its enactment by actors: think of it as a script (as for a play). A locally-managed system, by contrast, cannot be scripted, because the 'fan-out' of possible continuations from any juncture in the interaction is too contextual, representing the 'situatedness' of the interaction.

We can now put these observations to work in the case of CSCW systems. The global/local distinction finds its reflection in the asynchronous/synchronous distinction in CSCW (although the use of temporal terminology does not properly express, nor wholly coincide with, the conversation-analytic distinction). Because a *globally managed system* can be scripted, it is possible to develop a script notation - such as a process-modelling language - and to build a CSCW system as the language interpreter.

A *locally-managed system*, however, cannot be successfully scripted. Hence existing CSCW systems have concentrated on permitting synchronous conversations to be achieved by non co-located participants (using audio/video links) and in achieving co-presence with computer environments (as in CoLab (Stefik et al 1988) and shared-window conferencing systems (Sarin and Greif 1988)).

Within the issue-handling model, professionals participate in both locally managed and globally managed interactions, and either style of interaction may be embedded within the other. This contrasts with the process-oriented PSE model, in which PSE-mediated cooperation occurs only under the auspices of an already-running (global-management) process model[7].

The embedding of globally managed systems within a wider framework of activity suggests that the process models which describe them should be *first class citizens* of the professional's computing environment. It should be possible to store process models, view them, transform them and run them.

The transition from global to local management can sometimes be a scripted event (for example, a project meeting, locally-managed, can be scheduled in a process model for the first Thursday of the month). Hence the process-modelling language is required to provide primitives to invoke a computer support environment for locally-managed interactions. This support environment for locally-managed interactions must also be directly available to the user at the workstation. Since process models are first-class citizens, they may be freely discussed, modified, simulated and perhaps even run in the context of a computer-mediated locally-managed interaction.

Between the extremes of globally-managed process support on the one hand, and locally-managed 'conversational' computer conferencing on the other, lie several intermediate interactional styles, also worthy of promotion to first-class citizenship. We consider briefly store-and-forward messaging and computer-mediated meetings.

At first sight, computer-based messaging systems appear to be the analogue of face-to-face conversations – because of the time delays, a kind of 'slowed-down discourse'. Bowers and Churcher (1989) argue that there are in fact significant differences (which they term "Asynchronies"), but suggest that a local management regime still obtains. Accepting this, there are clearly some conversations which by virtue of their embedding context, are stereotyped/scripted, and it makes sense to permit such constraints to be computer-supported where they exist. This points to the need to integrate the messaging system with the process modelling system[8].

Meetings appear to be examples *par excellence* of local management. Participating in, and chairing meetings are clearly arts, not reducible (in the foreseeable future) to any algorithmic process model. Nevertheless, meetings are generally structured by topics (the agenda), are organised to solve problems, and often produce results which are intended to be constraints on future actions. A meeting support subsystem can be envisaged which permits computer supported contexts to be anchored to agenda items, provides computer support for problem-solving (*cf* gIBIS, Conklin and Begeman 1988), and accommodates 'active minutes', incorporating a variety of multi-media objects, including process models agreed at the meeting.

6. CONCLUSIONS

In this paper we have examined three kinds of support environments for cooperative work in a project context. We contrasted data-oriented and process-oriented project support environments, arguing that they supported aspects of rather traditional forms of management.

We then examined a 'pluralist' form of management characterised by the delegation by management of significant autonomy to 'professional' subordinates, in the context of an organisational structure of professional communities. By exploring what such professionals do, and how they do it – under the rubric of 'issue-handling' – we identified the requirements for a more adequate support environment, which we termed a Professional Community Support system.

We then attempted to characterise a Professional Community Support system as being one which supports a heterogeneous collection of interactional processes in an organisational/community context, structured by the global/local management system distinction.

In particular we do not propose that the top-level environment of the user is necessarily embedded within (dominated by) any particular institutional process model: instead, process models, peer-to-peer discussion links, computer-based meeting environments, configurable structured messaging facilities (*cf* Malone et al 1987, Lai et al 1988), and a plethora of computer-supported multi-media artifacts, could all be resources available within the user's structured personal environment at the workstation.

ACKNOWLEDGEMENTS

The work of the two authors at STL was funded by the MultiWorks project (ESPRIT 2105). They particularly acknowledge the contribution of colleagues in the Professional Community Support team at STL, and at Triumph-Adler in Nuremberg, in thinking about Professional Community Support environments.

FOOTNOTES

1 CSCW – Computer Supported Co-operative Working

2 The '2.5' indicates an interpolation for *process* in the generational sequence.

3 The distinction between a process model, and an instance of a process-model in execution, (the latter being a project), permits a dynamic binding to be made between rôles and the actors which activate them. Hence some rôles might be executed by a person on one occasion, and by a machine-agent on another.

4 It is important to realise that there is very little *practical* experience with any real PSE's which, in some some sense, can be assimilated to the idealised model discussed here. The introduction of such systems over the next few years promises to constitute some fascinating and instructive social experiments.

5 Note that the ideology of 'professionalism' can be seen as an attempt to come to terms with the bounded autonomy accorded to skilled subordinates in this model.

6 Indeed, professionals are subject to interruptions from a wide variety of sources (*cf* Mintzberg 1973).

7 It could be argued that a central problem with process-oriented PSE's is the failure to make the global-local distinction, coupled with a view that *all* significant interactions can be subsumed under the global management apparatus of process-modelling.

8 The COSMOS system (Bowers and Churcher 1989) provides a user oriented 'Structure Definition Language' (SDL) for end-user definition of process models. SDL has illocutionary force operators which could be used in principle to tailor stereotyped conversation models.

REFERENCES

J. Bowers and J. Churcher (1989). 'Local and global structuring of computer mediated communication: developing linguistic perspectives on CSCW in Cosmos'. in *Office: Technology and People* Vol 4 No. 3 pp. 197-227. Elsevier Science Publishers.

J. Conklin, M. L. Begeman (1988) 'gIBIS: A Hypertext Tool for Exploratory Policy Discussion'. *ACM Transactions on Office Information Systems.* Vol 6, No. 4.

A. Finkelstein and H. Fuks (1990) 'Conversation Analysis and Specification' in P.Luff, D. Frohlich and G.N. Gilbert. *Computers and Conversation.* Academic Press, forthcoming.

D. Frohlich and P. Luff (1989) 'Conversational Resources for Situated Action' *Proceedings of CHI '89*, Austin, Texas.

A.Fox (1974). *Beyond Contract: Work, Power and Trust Relations.* Allen and Unwin.

A. Friedman (1977) *Industry and Labour.* London, Macmillan.

I. Greif (ed.) (1988) *Computer-Supported Cooperative Work: A Book of Readings.* Morgan Kaufmann.

C.R. Littler (1982). *The Development of the Labour Process in Capitalist Societies.* Heinemann.

K-Y Lai, T. W. Malone, K-C Yu (1988) 'Object Lens: A "Spreadsheet" for Cooperative Work'. *ACM Transactions on Office Information Systems.* Vol 6 No 4.

T. W. Malone et al. (1987). 'Semistructured Messages are Surprisingly Useful for Computer-Supported Coordination'. *ACM Transactions on Office Information Systems* Vol. 5 No. 2.

J. McDermid (ed.) (1985). *Integrated Project Support Environments.* Peter Peregrinus Ltd.

H. Mintzberg (1973), *The Nature of Managerial Work.* Prentice-Hall.

R. A. Snowdon (1989) 'An Introduction to the IPSE2.5 Project'. *ICL Technical Journal* Vol 6, No 3.

M. Stefik, G. Foster, D. Bobrow, K. Kahn, S. Lanning, L. Suchman (1988), 'Beyond the Chalkboard: Computer Support for Collaboration and Problem Solving in Meetings'. In Greif, 1988.

S. Sarin, I. Greif (1988). 'Computer-Based Real-Time Conferencing Systems'. In Greif, 1988.

H. Sacks, E. Schegloff, G. Jefferson (1974). 'A simplest systematics for the organisation of turntaking in conversation'. *Language* Vol. 50, pp. 696-735.

F. W. Taylor (1915), *The Principles of Scientific Management* Harper and Brothers.

D. Talbot, R. W. Witty (1983). Alvey Programme Software Engineering Strategy.

T. Winograd (1987). 'A Language/Action Perspective on the Design of Cooperative Work'. *Human-Computer Interaction* Vol. 3 pp. 3-30.

T. Winograd and F. Flores (1986) *Understanding Computers and Cognition.* Addison-Wesley 1986.

Human–Computer Interaction – INTERACT '90
D. Diaper et al. (Editors)
Elsevier Science Publishers B.V. (North-Holland)

SATISFYING THE NEED TO KNOW: INTERPERSONAL INFORMATION ACCESS

Robert E. Kraut and Lynn A. Streeter
Bellcore
445 South Street
Morristown, NJ 07960-1910
USA

ABSTRACT

We examine the ability of traditional and computer-based communication technologies to spread organizational and task knowledge in large scale software development environments. It is our contention that the principal problems in software development are social and organizational, rather than cognitive. We review: (1) factors that make improving software development formidable, and (2) technological aids and project management methods that have been tried as possible "solutions," (3) a survey we are conducting on coordination techniques in large projects and conclude by (4) discussing candidate information/communication technologies to support coordination.

1. COORDINATION IN SOFTWARE DEVELOPMENT

The coordination of activity while developing large software systems represents both an important practical problem and an interesting site to test theories of organizational communication more generally. When studying software development, most psychologists have focused on individual programmers and the problems that result from creating, understanding, and debugging relatively small programs. For example, virtually all the the 48 research articles reprinted in Curtis's (1985) *Human Factors in Software Development* take this approach. We believe that this approach is fundamentally flawed and cannot address some very real problems with large software systems. Rather we believe that these fundamental problems are social and organizational, not cognitive, and that results from studying small problems do not generalize to large ones.

In a field study of software design, Curtis, Krasner and Iscoe (1988) identified three major problems areas that occurred in virtually all large projects studied:

1. thin spread of knowledge of the application
2. changing and conflicting requirements
3. communication bottlenecks and breakdowns

These problems remain as central today as they were in the 1970s, despite massive attempts to deal with the "software crisis." In this paper we deal with coordination of tasks and activities in large software projects, which are difficult because of the three problems highlighted by Curtis et al. We picked coordination since it is central to the software development process, is harder to "get right" in software than in simple manufacturing, and gets harder at a nonlinear rate as the project grows in size.

We briefly review those factors that make improving software development formidable and then the literature on software engineering -- the technological aids and project managements methods that have been offered up as "solutions" to date. Next, we review a survey we have conducted of coordination techniques in large projects and conclude by discussing possible information/communication technologies to support coordination.

1.1. Scale

A fundamental characteristic of many software systems in the real world is that they are very large and far beyond the ability of any individual to create or to understand in detail. The software to run ground control for the Apollo spacecraft in the 1970s contained about 23 million lines of code (Fox, 1982). The software to allocate lines in a telephone network contains over 10 million lines of code. The source code that comes with a standard release of the Unix operating system has several million lines of code. It is useful to give a concrete sense of the magnitude of these software efforts. A million lines of code without comments occupies a stack of paper over 5 feet tall. A typical programmer can write 6,000 lines of new or changed production-quality code per year (Martin, personal communication); at this level of productivity, over 160 programmer years are needed to produce a million lines of code.

But of course, the creation of large software systems requires more than programmers to write code. Crucial actors in the software development process include analysts to determine what the software needs to do, software architects to shape the basic structure of the programs and their communication with other programs, databases, and users, software testers to insure the code meets requirements, support staff to create tools and maintain hardware, documenters to write users' manuals, an administrative infrastructure to prioritize requests for features and for resources, and sales and clients support personnel to handle feedback from users. Given this cast of players, software productivity is closer to 2,000 lines of code per staff year. Thus, in the final accounting to produce a software system with one million lines of code requires 500 staff-years of effort.

1.2. Uncertainty

A central feature of software development is uncertainty. The specification of what the software is supposed to do invariably changes over time (Brooks, 1987; Fox, 1982; Curtis, et al., 1988). In part change in software specification comes about because the external world that the software was designed to support also changes. Moreover, it is often only by using software that purchasers and users understand its capabilities and limitations. Especially as they use software in circumstances for which it wasn't explicitly designed, the users demand new capabilities that had not been envisioned at the software's creation. It is primarily for this reason that in the human-interface domain a method of rapid prototyping and iterative design is preferred to one of user interface specification. Designers don't know how users will react until the users have tried the system.

Software also changes because specifications for it are invariably incomplete. Incompleteness partially results from the limited domain knowledge that Curtis et al. (1988) identified and by the division of labor used in large software projects. Typically, analysts with knowledge of the domain to which the software applies write specifications describing what the software should do in that domain. It is inevitable that some of the analyst's tacit knowledge, relevant to the software under construction, will not be reflected in the specifications. Thus, one of the major coordination problems in software development is that at many points the information that software architects and programmers need to make decisions is not available to them through documents, although others involved in the project have the knowledge necessary for these decisions.

1.3. Interdependence

The large size and inevitable uncertainty in software work would be less of a problem if software didn't require a strong degree of integration of its components. Software is composed of thousands of modules or components that must mesh with each other perfectly for the software system as a whole to operate correctly. As Fox (1982) notes, with large size and this degree of interdependence, it is impossible to exhaustively test any large software system.

2. SOFTWARE ENGINEERING SOLUTIONS

Software professionals are obviously aware of the problems in large-scale software development and have attempted over the past twenty years to develop procedures and tools as a remedy. (See Yourdon, 1979 and 1982 for a representative sampling of these software engineering innovations). Although productivity figures on software are notoriously unreliable and difficult to interpret, the data suggest that despite massive investment in new computers, workstations, languages, and software engineering techniques, the productivity gains -- measured as lines of code per staff year -- have been a modest three to five percent a year for the past 20 years.

At the risk of oversimplification, one can say that most proffered solutions to the software crisis have taken one of three approaches: (1) technical aids for the individual developer, (2) procedures to formalize communication among program pieces and among development personnel, and (3) techniques to encapsulate the behavior of individual programmers and thus reduce needs for coordination. We will briefly outline previous contributions to making software development a humanly doable occupation. We conclude by identifying a potentially fertile middle ground that has been neglected by prior software engineering techniques: tools for facilitating informal information exchange.

2.1. Powertools for Programmers

Probably the greatest effort has been spent developing new tools in the form of languages and operating systems for individual programmers. That these tools should be aimed at improving individual rather than group productivity should come as no surprise. The vast majority of languages and operating systems have begun as academic or research projects, where the inventors were keen to improve their individual productivity and environments. It has been rare that any of these inventors has had even modest familiarity with programming in production environments. As a result, these tools necessarily miss the mark in dealing with the hard problems in software development.

Of the technical solutions to software development, high-level languages have had the most effect on overall productivity. For example, it is said that the effect due to high level languages is a 5 times increase in productivity (Brooks, 1987). Thus, modern day C programmers would be five times more productive than their assembly language (BC) counterparts. However, other commentators are much less enthusiastic. Boehm (1987) claims that the software productivity increase since 1981 from all factors, including languages, is only 7% per year. Martin's (a Bellcore VP in charge of software development) analysis of the data is that there has been about a 3% increase per year due to programming languages alone. With compounding, this amounts to a 19% increase over the six years from 1981 to 1987. Whatever the exact rate of increase, there is reason to believe that this trend will continue at a modest though significant rate.

The second biggest contributor to productivity gains has been new operating systems, such as UNIX and LISP environments. For instance, UNIX radically changed the way programmers did business. The introduction of (1) pipes coupled with (2) a high level command language (the Shell) to manipulate processes, as well as (3) the simple notion of device (everything communicates as if it were a terminal) meant that many people could write programs without having to understand much about the internals of the software they called. The operating system was designed to support and encourage the modularity that is so fundamental to good software development.

2.2. Formalization of Communication

A major emphasis in software engineering is an attempt to formalize knowledge and communication that occurs within the software development at various levels: requirements, programming, and project management. To the extent that these attempts are successful, they reduce the cost of coordination, by allowing coordination procedures to be routinized and even automated.

Requirements specificiation languages. Brooks (1987), Curtis et al.(1988), and Fox (1982) all note that problems in accurately and completely describing stable software requirements and communicating them to members of a software project are among the most difficult in software development. Everyone agrees that English is simply too expressive and too ambiguous for specifying and interpreting software requirements. Given that the cost of fixing errors goes up logarithmically with the software development phase in which the error was detected (Williams, 1984), it is critical to discover problems in the requirements phase. To this end various data flow modeling languages have been developed (e.g., PSL/PSA, Teichroew & Hershey, 1977) in which the inputs and outputs from a module are shown explicitly. On the other hand, requirements specification languages, such as PAISLEY (process-oriented, applicative, interpretable specification language; Zave & Yeh, 1981) go far beyond characterizing inputs and outputs, forcing users to "write" requirements in a special-purpose language, that does not admit the looseness and ambiguity of English.

However, a new language introduces problems of its own. Firstly, languages like PAISLEY have not benefited from eons of evolution. Thus, users of such languages find that they often do not have the necessary scope of coverage for their particular application, let alone for systems that are not as yet in the minds of any conceivers. Add to this the sizable cost and time involved in teaching people to write and read these new languages, and it becomes difficult for us not to draw the Esperanto analogy. However, in these languages' defense, anecdotal evidence suggests that the exercise of using a formal representation system to express requirements uncovers flaws that would not have been obtained through the normal course of requirements writing and analysis.

Formalization of project management. Over the past twenty years, the term software development has changed from meaning "coding" to encompass the entire process from conceptualization to maintenance. Each phase of the development cycle from system requirements, to preliminary design, to detailed design, to coding, to testing, to operation and maintenance has well-defined products and milestones. Thus, it is specified in advance what will be delivered at each stage and how the deliverables can be tested or scrutinized to insure that they do what they were advertised to do. Not only code, but all official project documents are under change control. Naming conventions must be adhered to project-wide. No source code can be delivered without "makefiles" or some automatic ways to show dependencies and to produce executables. Code cannot be written without design reviews; code can't be tested before code walk-throughs; errors/bugs/changes cannot be made without issuing a modification request; no piece of code can go to system test without a prior integration and unit test.

Thus, a major the effort in software development has been to formalize the process in order to track and monitor it. As general manager of IBMs Federal Systems Center reviewing the Houston Manned Space Center, Fox (1982) reports being "appalled" by the "sheer bureaucracy" of a formal development system, until he visited other sites where the process was less formal and the projects were "out of control". While formal software methodologies are necessary, they place an extra burden on development in terms of increased staff, increased interfaces, and increased project information. Fox (1982) estimates that in large software projects, 50% of the cost is involved in planning, checking, scheduling, management, and control.

2.3. Making Programming in the Large Seem Small

A theme running through many software engineering techniques is to make programming in the large behave like programming in the small. If the programmer has a well-defined interface, they can program their modules independently with minimal interaction. Similarly, rapid prototypes make the programming team smaller. Layered architectures subdivide the work into modular pieces. So, many techniques currently employed are attempts to minimize the number of interfaces and consequently reduce the amount of communication that would result otherwise.

Quality of personnel is the single most influential factor for success in software development (Boehm, 1987). A concomitant of this is that virtually all successful software projects have a chief designer or guru. The existence of skilled designers means that at least one person in a project has sufficient knowledge of both the application domain and possible software architectures to integrate the two. Problems arise when the design is distributed in more than one head or worse (and probably more typical) is not in anybody's head. According to Curtis et al (1988), skilled designers often assume responsibility for communicating their technical vision to other project members and for coordinating the work of the project.

3. INFORMAL COMMUNICATION AND COORDINATION

.Both past experience and organizational theory suggest that these prior efforts in software engineering cannot by themselves solve the software crisis. Powertools for individual programmers simply do not address the coordination problem. No matter how successfully layered architectures and structured programming methodologies are in reducing the number of interfaces between modules, at some point pieces of a software project have to fit together, and the information sharing and coordination dilemmas that were avoided at one level surface at another.

Although previous organizational research has not looked at software development per se, much of it has investigated communication patterns within research and development organizations. The major findings are easy to summarize. First, informal, interpersonal communication is the primary way that information flows in research and development organizations. For example, Allen (1977) showed that fully half of the information that engineers use comes from personal contacts, rather than from any written source. Second, in the world of research and development as in many other domains, the ease of acquiring information is at least as important as the quality of the information in determining the sources that are used. Thus, for example, Allen (1977) demonstrated that physical proximity is a major determinant of whom engineers talk to about work related matters. Communication declines exponentially with distance, so that engineers are half as likely to talk to a colleague two offices away as they are to talk to one next door. This relationship asymptotes at 30 meters, so that one has the same, low likelihood of communication with a colleague 30 meters away and one a kilometer away. When engineers get information from written sources, they do so only when the information is in their personal files. Third, getting information and achieving coordination through informal, interpersonal communication is valuable both for individuals and for their organizations.

The implication of this research for the software development process is clear. Given the uncertainty and change associated with large software development projects and the sparse and uneven distribution of domain knowledge, software development needs some degree of informal, interpersonal communication to achieve effective coordination.

4. A STUDY ON COORDINATION IN SOFTWARE

Given this state of affairs, we are studying the variety of coordination techniques used in software development projects and the conditions under which they are successful or unsuccessful. We hope this project will lead to both theoretical and practical outcomes. The theoretical goal is a better understanding of the interplay between uncertainty, interdependence, and scale in organizational coordination. The practical goal is to identify or develop coordination tools and techniques that are responsive to the unique tensions between uncertainty, interdependence, and scale in software development.

The research consists of a survey of the intergroup coordination practices in one large software development company. The survey focuses on three factors: 1) coordination practices used, 2) structural characteristics of projects and groups that might interact with the practicality and utility of various coordination techniques, and 3) the success of the projects and groups on several dimensions.

4.1. The Research Site

Our research site was a large software development division of a research and development company. Approximately 3,000 managers, analysts, software engineers, programmers, testers, and documentation specialists are employed by the divisions. Collectively, they work on the development of a wide range of projects for the telecommunications industry using a wide range of techniques in the development process. In terms of scale, they range from small-group projects with development on PCs to large mainframe systems, with 14 million lines of code already developed and 150 people on staff at one time. In terms of uncertainty, the projects range from those in the specification stage with active negotiations with clients and with other development organizations to more maintenance-oriented projects, where new releases are designed to fix bugs and add small numbers of features.

While all projects use both formal and informal communication to coordinate activity, the balance differs across projects. For example, in some projects requirement specification documents are written by members of a different vice presidential area than those who design software architecture. Information about needed software capabilities is done through these formal specification documents. In other projects the responsibility for assessing software capabilities and for designing software architecture reside within the same 30-person department and communication is through informal, interpersonal contacts supplemented by sketchy requirements documents. Similarly, some departments make extensive use of electronic mail and bulletin boards to distribute project knowledge, while others do not use these facilities.

4.2. Sample and Measures

Our sample consists of 500 individuals in 150 different supervisory groups involved in some aspect of software development, representing approximately 60 different software systems. Depending on the question being asked and other data available, analysis are based on the 150 groups or the 60 software projects.

Data come from three sources. 1) A paper and pencil survey collected from the group supervisor and up to four members of the group; 2) software metrics routinely collected as part of project management, such as staffing levels, lines of code per staff-month, errors found in code inspection, and numbers of requests of modifications outstanding; and 3) evaluations by senior managers and clients about the quality of the software development process within each project and about the quality of the deployed software itself.

The survey of project members attempted to measure the following aspects of software development within a project: *Structural characteristics of groups and projects* (project and group size, project age, project uncertainty, need for integration with other groups); *Formal coordination techniques used* (e.g., data dictionaries, formal requirements documents, formal project scheduling techniques, modification request tracking, and formal reviews of design, code, or test plans); *Informal coordination techniques used* (e.g., informal group meetings, co-location of requirements and design staff, and project bulletin boards); and *Success of coordination techniques* (respondents' assessments of how well their projects are going and integrating with the work of other organizations).

We are currently analyzing data and will have complete results to report at the conference. Some of the gross findings, however, are already clear. First, in software development, as in R&D more generally, the primary source for information is informal communication with colleagues, supervisors, and others who are close at hand. Second, both informal communication and formal management programs (e.g., Schedule Tracking and Modification Requestion Tracking) are crucial devices for coordination within large software projects. Third, different stages in the software development cycle have different communication and coordination needs. In particular, personnel who work in the planning stages of the cycle (i.e., requirements specifiers and software architects) need substantial communication with people in different companies and organization who are physically remote from them. On the other hand, most of coordination among those involved in the coding stages of software development is among people in the same 30-person department. Fourth, the more involved people are in planning, the less useful formal project management techniques are to their ability to coordinate their work. Fifth, it follows from these previous findings, that planners are especially ill-served by current coordination techniques.

5. TECHNOLOGY TO SUPPORT INFORMAL COMMUNICATION

Even though much information currently follows through software projects by informal communication, practical considerations suggest that in large software projects, informal communication as mediated by direct personal contact cannot be the major mechanism for coordination. Simply put, in large projects the transaction costs of pairwise, informal communication are too high. The amount of communication needed increases too rapidly with the numbers of individuals and groups whose activities and products must be coordinated. Moreover, physical proximity, which is the major device used to support informal communication, doesn't meet the needs of planners, who must have their informal communication across organization and site.

Yet it may be possible to use information technology to support informal communication more efficiently. In particular, discretionary databases and computer-based communication systems may allow informal, interpersonal communication across a much larger community than can be supported by physical proximity and other conventional mechanisms.

However, if information technologies for informal communication are to be valuable, two major problems must be solved. First, is the difficulty of insuring that the relevant information that some project members know is made explicit and available for others to use. When information can be thought of as a common good, it will tend to be undersupplied. This is because it is in most people's best interest to partake of the pool of information, but not to contribute to it. Second, once the information becomes explicit and publically available, it must then be retrievable by those project members who need it without overwhelming them. Given the vast quantities of information that are potentially relevant to personnel in a software project, it is easily imaginable that any individual will be unaware of or unable to find that portion of it that is relevant to a task at hand, but will be bombarded with information he or she considers irrelevant. Below we outline some partial technological solutions to the inefficiencies of informal communication in large projects, and in doing so discuss difficulties of information supply and information access that they raise.

5.1. Electronic Mail

One existing technology that has notable success at supporting and extending information communication and information gathering is electronic mail. The reasons for its deserved success are numerous. First, the effects of physical distance are minimized. Those variables that control whether or not one can effectively communicate electronically with another person are the connectivity of the network, its reliability and average speed. Thus electronic mail effectively expands ones informal "working group" from the few people next door. In addition to a larger working group, electronic mail makes available a larger amount of information and potential contacts than can be supported by more traditional organizational mechanisms. Yet most studies of electronic mail, including our own, suggest that it is mainly used for communication among those who frequently see each other face-to-face. Second, the transaction cost associated with each mail encounter is low. The cost of attending a face-to-face meeting, walking down the hall to have a conversation, or reading a document is much higher than sending a typical electronic mail message. Third, since the medium is asynchronous, message initiation and response are determined much more by the user than by the demands of the medium. Thus, it even becomes possible to coordinate work efforts on different continents.

5.2. Find me an Expert Service

As we have seen, in software projects satisfying information requirements is more often accomplished by talking to the right (or even the wrong) person rather than by reading relevant documents. Yet identifying the right person is hard, particularly in large organizations. The problem is compounded when the information need is ill-formed or when a query is not expressed in appropriate, technical vocabulary. Often this the case when the question-asker is not an expert in the field.

We created a system that helps identify relevant experts, by comparing an information query with the documents that domain experts in a project have written. This system returns a list of experts, ranked in order of the maximally relevant documents they have written recently (Streeter & Lochbaum, 1988, Lochbaum & Streeter, 1989). This system works because: (1) the experts do not need to contribute new information to the public pool to describe themselves accurately. The documents they write are part of their normal work effort--technical memos and project plans, (2) because of this, there is extensive coverage of the company, (3) the user need not read these documents, (4) the matching algorithm used to pair requests with experts does not require that the expert and the person with the query use the same exact terminology.

5.3 Does Anybody Know...?

A more general form of the find an expert service is a broadcast service in which the question-asker broadcasts a question via electronic mail to all or a "relevant" subset of users. Any person who has an answer reports back. The messages that are returned from these information queries can be archived to benefit others who might have similar questions. Although this would clearly be a useful and efficient way to get information, implicit in its design are some thorny technical and social problems. First, why should one person answer a random person's question ("does anybody care?"). Without a reward system, responding just takes away valuable time from work. If the rewards were nontrivial, broadcast questions would get many answers. However, many of the answers might be of low quality or irrelevant. So, there would have to be some mechanism whereby the recipient of an answer judges usefulness. This explicit evaluation again represents a contribution to the common pool of knowledge and doesn't directly benefit the evaluator. At first glance it is not easy to see how to implement successfully a payoff scheme.

5.4. Alerting Services

One of the advantages of informal communication for information exchange is that other people sometimes tell you more than you thought you wanted to know. Often in conversation other people reveal information that they infer you would want to know, even though you did not know it was available, and therefore did not ask for it. The proffered information may be direct project information, for example, changed plans or specifications, or it may be pointers to sources of information, for example, the name of someone who is relevant to ones own work.

Information systems could monitor relevant project information and send an alert to relevant parties when that information changed. (See Fish, Kraut, Leland, and Cohen, 1988 for a description of alerting features for small-scale projects.) For example, a suitable alerting system might be one way to deal with the perpetually changing requirements in large software systems. Change control software that monitors requirements documents, for example, could send off messages to the relevant development organizations when the requirements documents were altered. While practical problems of privacy violations and information overload may result from such monitoring, it provides one method for keeping up with changing personnel and responsibilities in a large software project.

6. CONCLUSIONS

Whereas past efforts in software engineering have concentrated on formalizing communication and providing better individual tools, we have argued that software development needs informal, interpersonal communication to effectively coordinate work. Technological support for information communication and access resides in the construction and maintenance of discretionary databases and computer-based communication systems.

ACKNOWLEDGEMENTS

Jolene Galegher and Michael Muller were invaluable colleagues in the initial planning stages of the project described here.

REFERENCES

[1] Allen, T. (1977). *Managing the Flow of Technology*. Cambridge, MA: MIT Press.

[2] Boehm, B. W. (1987). Improving software productivity. *IEEE Computer, 20,* (9), 43-57.

[3] Brooks, F. P. (1987, April). No silver bullet: Essence and accidents of software engineering. *IEEE Computer, 20,* 10-18.

[4] Curtis, B. (1985). *Human Factors in Software Development*. Washington, DC: IEEE Computer Society.

[5] Curtis, B., Krasner, H. & Iscoe, N. (1988). A field study of the software design process for large systems. *Communications of the ACM, 31,* 11, 1268-1287.

[6] Fish, R. S., Kraut, R. E., Leland, M. D. P. & Cohen, M. (1988). Quilt: A Collaborative Tool for Cooperative Writing Proceedings Conference on Office Information Systems pp. 30-37, March, 1988, Association for Computing Machinery

[7] Fox, J. M. (1982). *Software and its Development.* Englewood Cliffs, NJ: Prentice-Hall.

[8] Lochbaum, K. E. & Streeter, L. A. (1989). Comparing and Combining the Effectiveness of Latent Semantic Indexing and the Ordinary Vector Space Model for Information Retrieval. *Information Processing and Management, 25,* 665-676.

[9] Martin, Robert (1989). Personal communication.

[10] Streeter, L. A. & Lochbaum, K. E. (1988). An expert/expert-locating system based on automatic representation of semantic structure. *Proceedings of the Fourth Conference on Artificial Intelligence Applications,* March 14-19, IEEE, 345-350.

[11] Teichroew D. and Hershey, E. A. III (1977). PSL/PSA: A cmputer-aided technique for structured documentation and analysis of information systems. *IEEE Transactions on Software Engineering,* 41-43.

[12] Weinberg, G. M. (1971). *The Psychology of Computer Programming*. New York: Van Nostrand Reinhold Co.

[13] Williams. R. D. (1984). Management of software development. In *Handbook of Software Engineering,* C. R. Vick and C. V. Ramamoorthy (Eds.) New York: Van Nostrand Reinhold Co., 456-468.

[14] Yourdon, Edward (1979). *Classics in Software Engineering*. New York, NY: Yourdon Press.

[15] Yourdon, Edward (1982). *Writings of the Revolution*. New York, NY: Yourdon Press.

[16] Zave, P. and Yeh, R. T. (1981). Executable requirements for embedded systems. *Proceedings of the 5th International Conference on Software Engineering,* San Diego, CA, March, pp. 295-304.

Human–Computer Interaction – INTERACT '90
D. Diaper et al. (Editors)
Elsevier Science Publishers B.V. (North-Holland)

CONVERSATIONBUILDER: AN OPEN ARCHITECTURE FOR COLLABORATIVE WORK*

Simon M. KAPLAN

Department of Computer Science
University of Illinois at Urbana-Champaign
1304 W. Springfield Avenue, Urbana, Illinois 61801, USA

Software process support tools of necessity be highly tailorable to mesh with the culture of, and tools used by, groups of programmers. They must also support the activities of groups in a natural and integrated manner. The ConversationBuilder is an 'open' tool in which provides support for cooperative, goal-directed group activities such as the software process.

1. INTRODUCTION

Software development is a process with the following characteristics [10, 11, 12]:

It is *collaborative*: The process is carried out by many people, who play different roles in the process, (e.g. clients, analysts, programmers, managers, lawyers, accountants, etc) and who can be divided into subgroups in many different ways.

It is *multi-faceted*: There are many things to be done, and each of the players in the process sees a different subset of these. This in turn influences that players view of the process as a whole.

It is *context-sensitive*: The context in which the process is carried out — time, funding, quality of the players in the process, knowledge of clients, etc — all have an impact on the process itself.

It is *creative*: The process is not simply a matter of mechanically selecting templates and connecting them together, it requires creative insights on the part of the players. For example, an insight could be quite radical, leading to a new design technique or approach to a problem; or it could be the more prosaic but still insightful ability to 'put oneself in the shoes of' another player (e.g. a client) and comprehend his point of view, thereby affecting one's own, or take any one of a number of different forms.

It is (partially) *mechanizable*: Significant portions of the process are amenable to mechanization (e.g configuration management, version control, some kinds of tracking, etc), and most parts of the process benefit from support tools of various kinds.

It is *historical*: To understand how to maintain some piece of code, for example, it is often useful to understand why it is like it is, as opposed to merely what it does. Thus it is useful to have complete design histories that track the evolution of a system, as opposed to simply maintaining a database of code fragments.

The next generation of interactive support environments will have to come to terms with the real nature of the software process; tools based on models which support a single approach or which claim to provide a 'silver bullet' need to be superceded by tools based on models which recognize the open, collaborative nature of the process. To coin a phrase, we call such systems COS (collaborative open system) tools.

In order to build COS tools one needs a 'meta-model' of collaborative activity within which specific models of collaborative activity can be constructed. We hypothesize that the Language/Action perspective of Winograd and Flores [18] provides such a meta-model and that we can use this as the basis for developing a framework for COS tools. The ConversationBuilder (CB) is the framework we are constructing to test this hypothesis.

The Language/Action perspective takes the view, based on the hermeneutics of Heidegger [7] and Gadamer [6], that human intellectual activity should be viewed as *conversational*. The speech act theory developed by Searle [17] and Austin [1] provides the 'bridge' between abstract hermeneutic philosophy and realizing systems on a computer. The idea of speech acts is used as the basis for the concepts of 'protocol' and 'utterance' which allow CB to be an open, collaborative system.

*This research supported in part by the National Science Foundation under grant CCR-8809479 and by AT&T through the Illinois Software Engineeering Project.

This paper outlines the Language/Action perspective of Winograd and Flores, introduces our model of process specification and discusses how open systems may be realized within this model.

2. HERMENEUTICS

Winograd and Flores' Language/Action perspective is based in hermeneutic philosophy [6, 7, 18]. Hermeneutics gives us a view of how knowledge is accrued and transmitted. Space does not permit more than a thumbnail sketch of the arguments; see [10] for more information.

The scope of ones knowledge at any time is termed one's *horizon* (the term is due to Gadamer). Language has no literal meaning, but instead is always interpreted relative to the horizon of the listener/reader. Similarly, when one wishes to articulate some information to another, there is no literal way in which to do this; one has to try express it in terms which explain it within ones horizon. The implications of this are that passing information is always a cultural event in that the horizons of speaker/writer and listener/reader must overlap in order for the transmission of information to make sense. Ones horizon is intensely personal and depends on ones entire history.

Shared horizons provide the potential for the transfer of information, but do not guarantee it. The actual flow takes place through language: I express an idea and because our horizons overlap you understand it. Of course, that which you understand is seldom exactly what I meant. Sometimes the conversation is brought to a halt because of a lack of communication. Such a point is called a *breakdown*; breakdowns and their resolutions are the critical points for information transfer.

The dual of breakdown is the concept of *thrownness.* Thrownness can be thought of as a response at an unconscious level. A related concept is *blindness* — the inability to recognize the applicability of some course of action in a given situation, either through ignorance or because one is trained not to see it.

It is important to note that breakdowns are very personal and, like horizons, are dependent on the past history of the person experiencing the breakdown. For example, to the experienced software developer once the decisions is made to use a set data type, the choices of possible implementations are well known and present no problems. For the novice, though, the choices may not be at all obvious and some time may need to be spent reading literature to find out about possible implementation strategies and their relative ad- and disad- vantages. When one is a novice in some field, many breakdowns occur. It is through repeated experience that situations become familiar and thrown.

The major relevence of hermeneutics to our work is the argument that *actions occur through language.* Language is the medium through which both the need for action and the results of actions are expressed. The sets of utterances which drive actions form conversations around the actions. For example, one may tell a programmer to modify some code. This is a request for action. The conversation may revolve around why the modification is needed, exactly what should be done, etc. The resolution of the conversation will be some action, which may be the implementation of the modification, the realization that the suggested modification is not needed or incorrect, or any one of a number of other alternatives.

3. RELATIONSHIP TO PROCESS

What does hermeneutics have to say about process, in particular the software process. We can draw two major conclusions:

There is no one model of a process. Except for purely clerical processes, such as automated system builds, it is not possible to build a model of a process that all participants in the process will share. This is because: (a) Not all participants have the same motivations and interests (and backgrounds) in the process. The interests of a client are not those of the programmers implementing the system, which are not those of the project managers, and so on. The interests of the participants are colored by their needs and background, and could not therefore be expected to be the same. This means that for different groups different breakdown points will exist; and (b) The horizons even of those participants who share common goals (such as the programmers) will not be the same, because they in general have different backgrounds and will therefore break down differently.

Because every participant has a different background, it is not reasonable to expect commonality of breakdown. Since a process model must anticipate breakdowns, this means that every participant will need a different model.

There is still hope. As groups work together, their horizons naturally tend to meld together and overlap; we usually refer to this by terms such as "corporate culture" or "project folklore". Rather than denigrating this, we should see it as an advantage; people with overlapping horizons will tend to work in the same way, so there is at once the hope of sharing parts of process models and the challenge of modeling and coping with diversity.

4. PROTOCOLS, UTTERANCES AND GAPS

The hermeneutic perspective gives a theoretical foundation for process modeling, but does not indicate how we might expect to realize process models on the computer. There is, however, a closely related area which does give such an insight, namely *speech act theory* (SAT) [17]. Hemeneutics claims that knowledge accrual and action occur through language and conversations, and speech act theory gives a basis for modeling conversations. SAT forms the basis (see [10, 11] for the *conversation modeling language* (CML) in which we specify our processes.

In SAT, a conversational structure is always focused towards some goal. The utterances in the conversation move in a 'dance' towards that goal. Thus one can think of a conversation in a SAT structure as a state machine, in which the utterances change state until one of the goals terminating the conversation is reached. This is precisely the model we want for CML. A particular conversation is implemented as a *protocol* on which a set of utterances are defined. For convenience and flexibility, protocols should be small; the concept of digression allows protocols to be composed to make larger conversational structures. This composition forms the basis of our view of process modeling.

When talking about CML we use the following vocabulary:

Protocol The 'template' which models some conversational structure. A protocol is analogous to a class in a multiple-inheritance object-oriented language such as CLOS [13] (which is used as the implementation language for the current version of CB).

Utterance A 'move' in a protocol. An utterance is analogous to a method in an object-oriented language. Utterances are made either by users (through menu selection, keyboard entry, dialog boxes, etc) or can be made by tools, allowing a symbiosis between human and automated support tools via utterances.

CSD A 'conversation state descriptor', this holds information shared by all participants in the conversation. Analogous to an instance of a class, i.e. a CSD is conceptually created by instantiation of a protocol. The state information is used by utterances to determine if they are applicable in certain contexts, identify the participants in the conversation, and store any other shared information that may be useful.

Gap State information in a conversation local to a particular user. This information, also, can be consulted when determining the applicability of an utterance.

Node Persistent storage arranged in a hypertext structure [3]. There is an inheritance hierarchy of node types. Nodes are used to store the "trails" created by conversations. For example, bug reports, design documents, code versions, etc.

User Each user in CB is represented by a user object which holds information specific to that user.

User Interface The way that information is displayed to, and received from, the users. Detailed discussion of the user interface is beyond the scope of this paper.

Conversation A conversation is the "execution" of a protocol. This involves instantiating a protocol to make a CSD, which then accepts utterances. The conversation is complete when the CSD reaches a state in which it no longer accepts utterances, or when it is 'garbage' in the usual Lisp sense of the word, i.e. no user can access the CSD directly or indirectly.

A process is modeled in CML as a set of protocols. Each protocol defines some part of the total process, and the utterances for each protocol determine the space of actions a user can take within the protocol. The set of available utterances consists of the utterances local to the protocol together with any utterances inherited by the protocol. Multiple inheritance is very important in CML as it provides a way to build libraries of protocols and then mix-and-match them when implementing or tailoring processes.

A CSD is shared among the participants in a process, and records information global to all participants. Some of this information is required in all CSDs, for example the list of participants. Others are specific to the semantics of the protocol being implemented. For example, a protocol may allow the posting of positions and arguments, as in the IBIS protocol[4]. We could imagine extending this protocol with a "lock" utterance: A user of management class could foreclose the discussion, after which no further comment may be posted. The CSD for the protocol would record the value of the lock, and all utterances would have to check the lock as part of the process of checking their applicability.

Each time an utterance is made, a space of potential actions is opened for the participants in the conversation. This space is termed a *gap* (the term is due to Terry Winograd). Considering again the IBIS example, posting an issue (a kind of node in the IBIS structure to which other users can respond with supporting or opposing positions and arguments) creates a space in which all users can post a response. The protocol designer has to decide how to represent this space to the user. Two possible solutions are (a) do nothing, the user must find the issue by browsing, and (b) notify the user by creating a gap. A gap is unique to a user and holds context-specific state information (such as the conversation in which the gap was created, and the particular issue in the conversation record).

When a gap is received by a user object (each user is represented by a user object), the user object has control over how that information is presented to the user. One solution is to maintain a set of 'job jars' of gap information. The user can then work by selecting a gap from a jar and performing one of the possible actions relative to that gap and the CSD to which it is related. In our example, choose to post a reply to an issue, ignore it, or save the gap for possible later action. The gap concept allows the user to participate in multiple conversations simultaneously by switching among gaps, giving a high degree of flexibility so that the tool does not restrict the users work habits too greatly.

Each job jar can have its own filtering and display hooks. Thus one jar may list gaps as possible tasks directly, another may filter these and just give the user summary information, a third may have a complex interface that schedules tasks for the user in some way, and so forth. The user can define any scheduling and/or filtering strategy that he likes (of course some could be more complex to implement than others).

Conversations produce data. In the IBIS protocol, this data is issues, positions and arguments. In a maintenance protocol, the data could be bug reports and code versions. This data is stored in the nodes of the CB system. Nodes are arranged in a hypertext-like fashion, i.e. they are linked together, and a standard protocol for browsing hypertext structures is provided which all other protocols can inherit. Nodes are instances of classes in the node hierarchy. Thus, arbitrary hypertext objects can be defined and linked together. In the IBIS protocol, for example, nodes and links are typed to indicate issue, position or argument, whether they support or refute, etc. A gap is always created relative to the CSD controlling the conversation, and usually relative to a node as well. In our IBIS example of posting an issue, a node is created recording the issue which is then pointed to by the gap created for each user informing him about the issue. Then if a user decides to post a response, the CSD controlling the conversation as a whole can use this information to determine where the conversation is "restarting from" for that user.

The semantics of protocols are defined through their utterances. Each utterance must be able to do the following:

- Check its own applicability. An utterance is always made relative to a CSD and a gap. These must contain enough state information to allow an utterance to determine if it is applicable.
- Modify the state of the CSD.
- Create new nodes and/or modify interconnections among existing nodes.
- Create new gaps for the appropriate participants in the conversation.
- Send messages to the user interface requesting it to display relevent information.
- Invoke digressions (this will be discussed below).
- Any other appropriate actions.

Since utterances are currently programmed in CLOS this can be done, but writing protocols and utterances can sometimes get a little tricky. A higher-level notation is under development to ease some of this burden.

In order to keep protocols managable and flexible they must be small. This means that a protocol should define one 'level' of a task and then use other protocols to define the other levels. The ability to invoke a protocol from within a protocol is termed a *digression*. We illustrate the usefulness of digression with an example.

Consider the action of creating and tracking a bug report. Such a document has a 'life' and history of its own, and accrues information such as fix dates, who fixed the bug, etc. When a user generates a bug report, he does so from within the framework defined by some protocol and represented by a CSD. A digression (another CSD) is created whose role is to track the bug report. The report has a protocol that goes along with it, indicating what one can do with bug reports.

A bug report could have several fields: 'From' and 'to' fields indicate who is reporting the bug and who is receiving it, a 'module' field indicates where the bug occurred, an 'information' field gives information about the problem. If the system runs on multiple machines there could also be systems fields indicating machine type, operating system, etc. This report requires a fair amount of data be generated, and the user may not want to (or be able to) fill the report in top-down. He may want to fill in the information field first, while the details are fresh in his mind; he may want to rerun the program to get more information while he is in the middle of filling out the report, and so on. To have a state variable in the protocol which indicates 'a bug report is being filled out, dont do anything else', or worse 'the only legal action is to fill in the module data on the report' straitjackets the user in the worst way. A far better solution is to use a 'form-filling' protocol to get the form created. Such a protocol would be set up such that on instantiation a set of gaps get created for the user wanting to fill the form, one for each field on the report. This is in turn a digression from the bug reporting protocol. As the fields get filled in the gaps go away, until at last the 'file report' utterance becomes applicable. The user would be able to fill in the fields as he likes, or go off and do other tasks (the gaps would wait in an appropriate job jar), as desired. This approach provides a maximal amount of flexibility to the user. When the report is complete it is mailed to the appropriate users by the protocol of the CSD created for the bug report. How does this protocol know when the form is filled? It must generate a gap that waits on the termination of the form-filling protocol.

The protocol in which the bug report digression was initiated could in turn, if appropriate, leave a gap waiting on the resolution of the bug report, or simply ignore the spawned sub-conversation which will then proceed independently. Thus digressions allow: (a) *Modularity*: one can write protocols fairly independently and then compose them to model processes; (b) *Flexibility*: Lots of small flexible protocols allow the user to move around his various tasks in such a way that the system intrudes and impedes him as little as possible; and (c) *Tailorability*: Which protocols to instantiate as digressions can be as state information in a CSD; thus different groups can use different protocols for digression. This is extremely important in large organizations. It means that management can lay down broad organizational guidelines which can be supported by fairly high-level protocols, but groups can have independence within by tailoring through digression.

5. CB IS A COLLABORATIVE OPEN SYSTEM

We have claimed that CB is a collaborative, open system. One way in which we meet this goal is through gaps. These are the basic unit of collaboration. When one user performs an action, those that need to find out about it are informed by having gaps placed on their user objects. The recipients can then respond as they see fit. In our bug report example, when a programmer receives a bug report the space of actions implied by the gap include viewing the report, commiting to fix the problem, refiling it in another jar or handing it off to another programmer or another group. If the process, though its set of protocols, requires the originator be notified of these or other actions, gaps are then imposed back on this user, who in turn will have certain actions possible: delete the message, complain to a manager, initiate some subconversation with the person who takes on the responsibility to fix the problem, etc.

One way in which the goal of openness is met is through digression. A protocol controlling some task is "closed" in the sense that the set of possible actions is predetermined by the protocols utterances. This is good in that this information can be used to help guide the user, but bad in that the user is trapped in that model. By careful composition of protocols through digression, a sense of flexibility can be maintained. Suppose in the bug report protocol the postcondition is established that 'any bug report must eventually lead to one of a set of possible outcomes'. Then any digression protocol can be employed to manage the bug report providing that the results are constrained to be one of the possible outcomes. This allows for a mix of flexibility and management.

Another way in which we meet the goal of openness is through the concepts of *automated conversations* and *enveloping*. An automated utterance is one which, when invoked, does not require any user interaction. This provides a way to model tasks that can be automated without user assistance. For example a make protocol can be set up to obtain initial parameters from the user and then run through the compilation and linking process automatically. The big advantage over regular make is that if there is a failure the user can be brought back into the loop. On the other hand, there are certainly times when one wants to (or must) use tools other than CB. Such tools are integrated into the system using enveloping techniques. This means that a protocol is created which externally looks like any CB protocol but whose utterances are internally defined to invoke an external tool, taking care of issues such as data representation mappings. This technique is well understood at this time, and a standard way to enable tools to link with other existing tools in a coherent way [9]. The effect is to treat the automated tools in the system as if they were other users.

6. CB CAPTURES PROCESS

The Language/Action model provides a new way of viewing the concept of process as linguistic interaction among the players in the process (since automated tools can be considered to be 'users' in the system as well, querying a tool and getting data is no different conceptually from querying any other user; this is just another kind of linguistic interaction).

The CML provides a powerful and flexible way of modeling these linguistic interactions. The concepts of breakdown and thrownness tell us that we can expect people with common horizons to share ways of doing things, but break down in different ways. The entire nature of the software process is such that there are groups whose members have similar backgrounds and interests, but the needs and viewpoints of the different groups may clash. Thus single models of process are insufficient; a way had to be found to provide models of parts of the process that can be composed flexibly and deal flexibly with breakdown.

The idea of many small protocols is designed to deal with this. 'Umbrella' process models can be imposed by protocols, with details left to digressions into other protocols. This allows users to share high-level common goals and structure, while allowing flexibility in the way the goals are met (different subgroups can use different digression protocols). Another role of digression is to provide a mechanism for dealing with breakdown, in that the user can digress to resolve the breakdown. For example, when doing a code walk-through, if a programmer does not understand something the ability to digress into an IBIS-style protocol to discuss the problem with others in the group allows breakdown resolution within the scope of CB.

Dealing with clashing viewpoints is also supported through support for breakdown. A classic example of the clash in viewpoint arises in the requirements analysis process; the analyst has one idea of the needs of the client, the client another which, because he is thrown in his work, are hard to articulate. The analyst has a mechanism to extract information from the user: Find out what data, how much volume, who gets the data, what do they do with it, when, what information must be generated, to whom must it be sent, etc. A protocol that tries to extract this information can be defined which at every step allows for backtracking, digression to discussion protocols of the IBIS kind to resolve misunderstandings, uses lots of gaps so the analyst can follow the clients usually jumbled attempts to provide information, etc. When the process is complete all the gaps must be filled in — they do play an important prescriptive role in helping the analyst to make sure he hasnt forgotten anything — and the information thus obtained is structured 'correctly' (ie the way the analyst's organization needs it), but it may have been obtained in an arbitrary order.

7. RELATED WORK

The project most closely related to CB is Conklin's gIBIS system [4]. This system, like CB, assumes a conversational model of process; the major difference is that in gIBIS the model is fixed, whereas in CB extensive user tailoring is permitted. Conklins work has had a profound influence on the CB project, and one of the first simulations undertaken in CB was to model the IBIS approach.

Software Process Modeling [15] has become increasingly popular as a way of controlling software development. In the classic use of the term one views software development as a 'program' whose 'execution' leads to the development of the code. The problems with this solution are that the assumption that the space of the process can be *a priori* constrained into a 'program' is (as we have argued above) unreasonable, that there is no provision for breakdown or recovery from breakdown, and that "Expressions like 'code wrong: change_code' or 'create_design' in the body of a Process Program do nothing to clarify the *process.* They are either trivial, a stilted form of a natural language, or their meaning [for the Process Program] is undefined and their expression merely creates the *illusion* of progress." [14].

On the other hand, it is easy to misinterpret the Language/Action approach as saying that no models are possible, and that anarchy is the correct solution. The path taken by CB in realizing the Language/Action approach is to try blend process and flexibility: Protocols define processes, and can, if desired, be just as rigid as a process program. It is more useful, however, to build protocols that provide flexibility and breakdown recovery through digression. Indeed, this is the way in which we can make create_design become meaningful: it becomes the root of a digression from one protocol to another which provides specialized support for design.

Another area of related work is research into software development methodologies, such as Parnas' rational design process [16], Jackson's structured design [8], Boehm's waterfall model [2], structured programming [5] and stepwise program refinement [19]. All of these approaches provide the information necessary to write protocols, i.e. protocols should not be written in a vaccuum, but rather to support effective program development structure. We do not see CB as superceding existing methodologies but rather as complementing them, placing them in their proper role in a more general environment.

REFERENCES

[1] J. L. Austin. *How to Do Things with Words.* Harvard University Press, Cambridge, MA, 1962.

[2] Barry Boehm. *Software Engineering Economics.* Prentice-Hall, Englewood Cliffs NJ, 1981.

[3] Jeff Conklin. Hypertext: an introduction and survey. *IEEE Computer*, 20(9), September 1987.

[4] Jeff Conklin and Michael Begeman. GIBIS: a hypertext tool for exploratory policy discussion. *ACM Transaction on Office Information Systems*, October 1988.

[5] O-J. Dahl, E. W. Dijkstra, and C. A. R. Hoare. *Structured Programming.* Academic Press, New York, 1972.

[6] Hans-Georg Gadamer. *Truth and Method.* Seabury Press, New York, 1975.

[7] Martin Heidegger. *Being and Time.* Harper and Row, New York, 1962.

[8] M. Jackson. *Structured System Development.* Prentice-Hall International, 1983.

[9] Gail E. Kaiser, Peter H. Feiler, and Steven S. Popovich. Intelligent assistance for software development and maintenance. *IEEE Software*, 40–49, May 1988.

[10] Simon M. Kaplan. Coed: a conversation-oriented tool for coordinating design work. In *Proceedings IFIP Conference on Human Factors in Information Systems*, Elsevier, Scharding, Austria, June 1990.

[11] Simon M. Kaplan and Alan M. Carroll. Understanding software process. In *Proceedings 1990 SAE Conference*, Peoria, Illinois, April 1990.

[12] Simon M. Kaplan and Medhi T. Harandi. Adding design expertise to coed. In *Proceedings International Conference on CASE*, London, UK, August 1989.

[13] Sonya Keene. *Object Oriented Programming in Common Lisp: A Programmers Guide to CLOS.* Addison-Wesley, 1989.

[14] M. M. Lehman. Process models, process programs, programming support. In *Ninth International Conference on Software Engineering*, pages 14–16, IEEE Computer Society, IEEE Computer Society Press, Washington D.C., April 1987.

[15] Leon Osterweil. Software processes are software too. In *Ninth International Conference on Software Engineering*, pages 2–13, IEEE Computer Society, IEEE Computer Society Press, Washington D.C., April 1987.

[16] David Parnas and Paul Clements. A rational design process: how and why to fake it. In *Proceedings TAPSOFT 85, LNCS 186*, pages 80–100, Springer-Verlag, 1985.

[17] John Searle. *Speech Acts.* Cambridge University Press, Cambridge, 1969.

[18] Terry Winograd and Fernando Flores. *Understanding Computers and Cognition.* Addison-Wesley, Reading, Mass., 1987.

[19] N. Wirth. Program development by stepwise refinement. *Comm. ACM*, 14(4):221–227, April 1971.

SECTION V: APPLICATIONS AND CASE STUDIES

SV.5 Programming

Learning to program in another language
J. Scholtz and S. Wiedenbeck 925

ϒπADAPTερ: Individualizing hypertext
H.-D. Böcker, H. Hohl, and T. Schwab 931

Minimalist planning tools in an instructional system for smalltalk programming
M.K. Singley and J.M. Carroll 937

Why program comprehension is (or is not) affected by surface features
B.T. Mynatt 945

The generalized unification parser: Modelling the parsing of notations
T.R.G. Green and A. Borning 951

Program comprehension beyond the line
S.P. Robertson, E.F. Davis, K. Okabe, and D. Fitz-Randolf 959

Expert programmers re-establish intentions when debugging another programmer's program
R. Waddington and R. Henry 965

Difficulties in designing with an object-oriented language: An empirical study
F. Détienne 971

The spreadsheet interface: A basis for end user programming
B.A. Nardi and J.R. Miller 977

Action representation for home automation
S. Sebillotte 985

Browsing through program execution
H.-D. Böcker and J. Herczeg 991

Compressing and comparing metric execution spaces
J. Domingue 997

Human–Computer Interaction – INTERACT '90
D. Diaper et al. (Editors)
Elsevier Science Publishers B.V. (North-Holland)

Learning to Program in Another Language

Jean Scholtz

Computer Science Department, Portland State University, Portland, OR 97207.

Susan Wiedenbeck

Computer Science and Engineering Department, University of Nebraska, Lincoln, NE 68588.

Our objective in this study was to examine how programmers go about learning new programming languages and to identify which areas of program development presented difficulties. Verbalizations from think aloud protocols were classified as one of five kinds of knowledge: syntax, semantics, strategic planning, tactical planning, and implementation planning. Implementation planning occupied over 50 percent of subjects' efforts, irrespective of language and level of expertise. Difficulties in a dissimilar language were due to subjects' failure to construct appropriate tactical plans. In a similar language difficulties centered on subjects' inability to locate appropriate constructs.

1. Introduction: Motivation and Background

We are studying how people who already know how to program go about learning a new programming language. The impetus for our work on this problem is twofold. First we are interested in the problem of transfer of skills, per se; and second we are interested in aiding programmers who are faced with the task of learning a new language.

Most educational programs are built on the premise that skills acquired for one purpose can be used as a basis to acquire skills for another purpose. Skills transfer has been classified as near transfer or far transfer (Salomon & Perkins, [6]). Near transfer is transfer between two areas that are closely related. Far transfer is transfer from one skill to another far afield from it. In the domain of computing, near transfer has been studied extensively in text editing and word processing systems. Much promising work has been based on a common elements theory of transfer, (Polson, Muncher & Englebeck, [5]; Polson & Kieras, [4]; Polson, Bovair, & Kieras, [3]; Singley & Anderson, [7]). Systems are described by using a set of production rules. Transfer between systems is assumed to occur whenever two systems possess common productions.

Studies of transfer of skills in programming have concentrated on far transfer, that is, transfer of logical problem solving skills to such distant domains as algebra, geometry, logic, and planning tasks. Studies to date have found little evidence of transfer of programming skills to other domains (Olson, Catrambone, & Soloway, [2]; Kurland, Pea, Clement & Mawby, [1]; Solomon & Perkins, [6]).

A more favorable area in which to observe transfer of programming knowledge is transfer from one programming language to another. The fact that the transfer is in the same domain means that programmers will easily recognize the applicability of their previous knowledge. However, the transfer task is still much more complicated than in text editing because programming is a complex problem solving activity. It is unlikely that the programmer transferring to a new language will be able simply to take production rules from previous languages and fire them in the new language.

Practical reasons also exist for studying the problem of learning new programming languages. Learning a new language, often without any formal instruction, is a task which regularly arises among both students and working programmers. This learning task is often a frustrating and time consuming experience. We are interested in building tools to aid the programmer in learning new languages. This work was aimed in part at discovering what kinds of help the programmer needs.

In the study reported below we carried out a protocol analysis of programmers at two levels of expertise, intermediate and expert, writing their first program in a new language. Some programmers were observed working in a language similar to ones they already knew and others in a language quite different from ones they already knew. Our objective was to characterize the kinds of knowledge programmers were able to bring to bear from their past experience in learning a new language and to determine in what areas they needed help. Since we wanted to get a broad idea of how programmers learn a new language, we decided to look at their activities in terms of the categories of programming knowledge they used, without breaking their behavior down to the microlevel where it can be described by a set of productions.

2. Framework for the Study of Learning a New Language

In writing a program, whether in a familiar or a new language, programmers use three basic kinds of programming knowledge: 1) syntactic knowledge, 2) semantic knowledge, and 3) planning knowledge. These different kinds of knowledge are explained below and some quotations from our protocols are given as illustrations of how such knowledge (or a need for such knowledge) is expressed by programmers in the process of writing a program in a new language.

Syntax is the formal set of rules which defines whether a program is correctly expressed in a language. A program will not run if the syntax is even slightly wrong, so programmers must and do attend to it. (Example: "I'm trying to figure out what the proper syntax for decrementing a variable is.") The semantics of a programming language describes how constructs in a language actually behave when the program is executed. A failure to understand semantics may result in errors at run time or unexpected program results. (Example: "So I assume that the READ function reads in one line exactly. A fair assumption perhaps.") Planning a program is the process of structuring a solution to the problem. Planning is an ambiguous term because several distinct kinds of planning occur in programming. Soloway, Bonar, Ehrlich and Greenspan [8] broke planning down into strategic, tactical, and implementation planning. Strategic planning is high-level, language independent planning which represents a global strategy for solving a problem. (Example: "So we need some kind of control loop . . . Just read in a line at the top of the control structure, reverse the line, fill out, well, break it up if necessary, fill out any lines that need to be, and then translate. Translation could be done when reversing the line.") Tactical planning is also language independent but is somewhat lower level, expressing a local strategy or algorithm for solving part of a problem. (Example: "Find the intersection between that character and the whole upper case character set and, if that returns the original character you gave them, then you know it's an upper case.") Implementation planning, on the other hand, is language dependent and deals with how to actually achieve the strategic and tactical plans using the constructs of a particular programming language. (Example: "FOR -- does that exist? If not, I'll be in trouble.")

We believe that what programmers must learn in transferring to a new programming language is structured around the five kinds of knowledge outlined above: syntax, semantics, strategic planning, tactical planning, and implementation planning. Therefore, we used these categories to classify subjects' verbalizations as they solved a problem in a new language. We expected that language independent knowledge would transfer smoothly to a new language and that this would be reflected in our protocols in relatively little effort being expended on strategic and tactical planning. On the other hand, we expected the language dependent syntax, semantics, and implementation planning to occupy a great deal of the programmer's attention. Here, however, our expectations were modified somewhat by the target language. In any new language implementation planning presents a strong challenge, because it is there that the programmer must find the proper constructs to express language independent plans in the unknown language. However, it seems likely that one would see less attention devoted to implementation planning in a language similar to a subject's known languages than in a language very different from the known languages, because of the greater overlap of constructs in similar languages. Likewise, because of their greater overlap, syntax and semantics seemed likely to present fewer difficulties in a near language than in a far language.

3. Methodology

For our protocol analysis, we selected six intermediate subjects and six expert subjects who were all familiar with Pascal. Our intermediate subjects were graduate students in computer science who all had extensive student programming experience. Many of them had also worked part-time as programmers. Our expert subjects had worked between two and twelve years as professional programmers with their average work experience being six years. The experts also had university training in computer science. A short interview was conducted with subjects prior to their protocol session. Subjects were asked what programming languages they knew and to estimate how many programs they had written in each. The following discussion is based on only the languages in which subjects had written ten or more programs. Experts knew between 4 and 9 languages with an average of 5.7. Intermediates knew between 2 and 6 languages with an average of 4.5. There was a large difference in the number of programs written between the two groups. Intermediates, with one exception, had not written over 50 programs in any one language. Experts, on the other hand, had written over 100 programs in at least one language. The majority of the languages that subjects were familiar with were procedural languages. Two of the experts were familiar with APL. One of those experts was, in addition, familiar with LISP and SNOBOL, although his SNOBOL experience was not recent.

Half of the subjects at each level were asked to write a program in Ada, a language whose constructs are similar to Pascal. The other half were asked to write the same program in Icon, a language dissimilar to Pascal. Subjects were asked to think aloud as they went about solving the problem. They were allowed to refer to a language text and to write and run any test programs that they wished. Their actions, verbalizations and computer input were videotaped. Subjects worked until one of three events occurred: 1) the problem was completed, 2) the allocated time of two hours was up, or 3) they felt they were at a complete impasse. The videotapes of these sessions served as the basis for analysis.

The problem that the subjects were asked to solve is shown in Figure 1. From their past experience most of our subjects were familiar with algorithms to solve all parts of the problem. A good Pascal-like solution to the problem is based on a character at a time approach. That is, each character in a line of text is converted from one case to another and a loop is used to print them out in reverse, filling out and breaking up the line as necessary. It was feasible to solve the problem in Icon by using this same Pascal-like approach. However, Icon is a string processing language modeled in part after SNOBOL4. By correctly utilizing Icon's string handling features subjects could produce a much more elegant and compact solution based on functions applied to entire lines of text at a time. In Ada the Pascal-like one-character-at-a-time implementation is an efficient and appropriate way to solve the problem. However, one must still find the proper Ada constructs to use in the implementation.

The RJE problem
You are asked to simulate a (simplified) version of a remote job entry facility which modifies and transmits data between two computers. Your program will do three things to each line of text read in:
1)Reverse the order of the characters.
2)Translate the upper case characters to lower case and vice versa.
3)If a line is less than 60 characters long, fill it with *'s and write out a line of length 60. If a line is greater than 60, write it out as separate lines of exactly 60, filling the last line with *'s if necessary.

Figure 1: The RJE Problem

4. Completion of the Problem

Of the six subjects working in Ada, none was able to solve the entire problem, although all of them had solutions to several of the individual parts. Of the subjects working in Icon, two of the intermediates and one of the experts completed the program. Again, those who failed to complete the whole program completed several of the parts.

For the subjects working in Ada the two common difficulties in completing the program were using the correct I/O package in order to determine an end of file condition and discovering the Ada equivalents to the Pascal ORD and CHR functions (needed for the upper and lower case conversion). The Icon subjects failed to complete the program for several reasons. One expert simply ran out of time, having spent a great deal of time looking at constructs which the subject (correctly) speculated, "weren't useful in the solution, but looked interesting." The other expert could not find the function needed to solve the case conversion part of the problem and spent over an hour trying to implement a solution with various inappropriate constructs. The Icon intermediate had trouble understanding the differences between procedures and functions and, therefore, used many Icon built-in functions incorrectly. Understanding the semantics of several Icon constructs was also a problem for this subject.

5. Analysis of the Protocols

The transcripts of the twelve think aloud protocols were first broken into episodes where an episode was defined as behavior distinct from other surrounding behaviors. Two specific criteria were used to determine where a new episode started. First, a new episode began when there was a shift to a different physical activity, such as finishing reading the book and beginning to write code. Second, a new episode was signified by a shift in focus, for example, the programmer might abandon a search for a definite loop construct and look for an indefinite loop instead. The episodes were then classified independently by each of the authors, using the fivefold classification of programming knowledge explained previously. Some episodes were not classified. The think aloud protocols included a substantial amount of time (an average of 30 percent of each subjects' total time) devoted to essentially non-problem solving activities. Included in this time were activities such as clarifying the meaning of the problem with the experimenter, typing in program code at the terminal, waiting for the program to translate or compile, entering test data, and waiting for the program to execute and error messages to be produced. During many of these episodes the subjects were not verbalizing and, even if they were, the content was usually unrelated to the problem they were solving.

The twelve protocols analyzed constituted 1569 episodes. The level of agreement in classification of the two judges was 93 percent. For individual subjects the lowest percentage of agreement was 83 percent for one Ada expert. All other subjects had percentages of agreement above 90 percent, with the highest being 98 percent.

6. Results

Figure 2 contains the results of the analysis showing the percentage of classified episodes and the percentage of actual clock time that these episodes occupied in each area of program development. Over 50 percent of the episodes occurred in the area of implementation planning, while about 28 percent of the episodes concerned syntax. Semantics and tactical planning were the subject of 12 percent and 8 percent of the episodes respectively, while strategic planning occupied less than 1 percent of the subjects' episodes. The actual clock times of the episodes were also examined in order to see if the percentage of time spent in each of the five areas matched closely the percentage of episodes. A fairly close correspondence was found. The only major divergence was in the syntax category, where the percentage of time was about 7 percent less than the percentage of episodes.

% of	Syntax	Semantics	Impl. Planning	Tactical Planning	Strategic Planning
episodes	27.8	11.8	52.2	7.7	0.7
time	21	13.8	55.5	9.3	0.6

Figure 2: percentage of episodes and time in each area of program development

In accord with our expectations, the language independent strategic and tactical planning occupied a relatively small portion of the attention of subjects working in a new language. The problem which our subjects solved was similar to ones they had solved before in Pascal, so some high-level plans for it were known to them. We seldom observed a subject completely at a loss either for an overall strategy or for an algorithm for a specific part of the program. However, while subjects were always able to suggest some language independent plan, they were not always able to implement the plan in the new language, for reasons discussed below.

Of the three language dependent areas of program development, implementation planning was far more difficult than syntax or semantics, as the very high percentage of implementation planning episodes suggests. Subjects did have many questions about the syntax and semantics of the new languages. The reason why syntax and semantics were, nevertheless, easier seems to be that subjects had well defined ways of resolving their uncertainty. If they were unsure of the correct syntax for a statement in the new language, they were able either to consult the documentation for the correct usage or run the program and let the language translator tell them if the statement was incorrect. We frequently observed subjects making assumptions about syntax based on their knowledge of Pascal and other languages and only checking the documentation if an error was flagged when they ran the program. The relative ease of resolving syntactic questions is suggested by the fact that syntactic episodes made up 28 percent of the subjects' episodes but occupied only 21 percent of their time. Likewise for semantics, we observed the subjects efficiently answering their own questions by reference to the documentation or by writing and running small test programs. Any constructs which they were unsure of after consulting the documentation or running tests, they simply avoided.

Implementation planning caused much more serious problems for our subjects. Implementation planning consisted of realizing the high-level strategic and tactical plans using the constructs available in the new languages. Subjects had difficulties with implementation planning because: 1) a construct with which they were familiar from their past experience of other languages had a different name in the new language or 2) constructs that they wanted to use did not exist in the new language. Both of these situations were hard to resolve from the documentation, since programming books and manuals are not set up to lead the user from a language independent goal to the constructs which can be used to achieve it. With a slow, thorough reading of the documentation, subjects could generally find the construct that they wanted if it was a simple matter of a different name in the new language. However, we observed several subjects who were very unsystematic in searching the documentation and failed to find desired constructs which existed in an unexpected form.

If the constructs which the subject envisioned using did not exist, the outcome was even more uncertain. Some subjects searched for a desired construct exhaustively but without success. They had trouble deciding when to give up the search because they could never be certain that they had not overlooked or misunderstood something in the documentation. In the end, they usually discarded their language independent tactical plan and tried to develop a new one which would be easier to implement given the constructs of the new language. Thus, we saw a strong interplay between tactical and implementation planning. While tactical plans are formally language independent, they are strongly influenced by what is convenient to implement in a subject's known languages. Thus, our subjects often started with a tactical plan which was inappropriate for the new language they were using and were forced to revise it substantially because of implementation difficulties. This revision process often led to a more nearly ideal solution in the new language but at the price of a great deal of time and effort.

Figure 3 shows the percentages of episodes and time in each of the five areas by language. The results show some differences between Ada subjects and Icon subjects, but the differences are relatively modest overall. We had expected all of the language dependent areas of program development, syntax, semantics, and implementation planning to present fewer difficulties in the similar language, Ada, than in the dissimilar language, Icon. This expectation was not supported in the case of syntax, where Ada subjects spent 25 percent of their time but Icon subjects only 17 percent. Although Icon is basically a string processing language with features quite distinct from Pascal's, paradoxically its syntax is actually simpler and more Pascal-like than is Ada's. Subjects were more often able to make (correct) assumptions about Icon syntax based on their knowledge of Pascal. The Icon subjects' higher percentage of semantic episodes confirms that more semantic questions or problems arise in transferring to a dissimilar language. However, the percentage of time spent on semantics in Ada and Icon was almost identical. Constructs in Ada behave in a way very similar to the corresponding constructs in Pascal, while constructs in Icon are quite different and often have no corresponding equivalence in Pascal at all. However, close study was needed by both groups in order to verify this.

Language	percent	Language concept				
		syntax	semantics	impl planning	tactical planning	strategic planning
Ada	episodes	29.9	9.8	54.2	5.4	0.6
	time	25.2	13.7	53.5	8.7	0.5
Icon	episodes	25.7	13.7	50.1	9.9	0.7
	time	17.2	13.9	57.7	10.0	0.8

Figure 3: Percentage of episodes and time in each area of program development by language

Although the percentage of implementation planning episodes is higher for Ada than Icon, the percentage of actual time tends to support our expectation that the dissimilar language would present greater implementation challenges. Nevertheless, Ada subjects also spent a high percentage of their time dealing with implementation planning. Ada subjects encountered difficulties because constructs which were parallel to the Pascal constructs which they wanted had different names in Ada. As a result, they spent a great deal of effort on implementation as they repeatedly searched the documentation for the constructs that they needed. Icon subjects most often began with a Pascal-influenced tactical plan, unsuited to Icon, then discovered from the documentation that the features available in Icon were very different from what they had anticipated, based on their past experience. This led them to revise their tactical plan (reflected in a higher percentage of tactical planning episodes) rather than making repeated attempts to implement their original plan. Thus, the difficulties of Icon subjects were reflected in a greater iteration between tactical and implementation planning as higher levels plans were adjusted to fit the capabilities of the new language.

The breakdown of percentage of episodes and time by level of expertise showed few large differences between levels and hence is omitted. Experts spent a smaller percentage of time on syntax and tactical planning than intermediates but a larger percentage of time on semantics and implementation planning. Experts were more capable of handling questions about and syntax and more adept at formulating suitable tactical plans. As experts solved a greater portion of the problem and utilized more language constructs, they spent more time dealing with semantic and implementation planning issues. These results were in accordance with the experts' greater experience with programming languages.

7. Baseline Comparison

Think aloud protocols were also collected from three intermediate subjects who were asked to solve the RJE problem using Pascal. Although all three intermediates working in Pascal produced a runnable solution, they needed an average of 77 minutes to do so (compared to Ada and Icon where most of the subjects spent the full two hours allowed). The lesser but still substantial time required by the Pascal subjects confirms our assumption that the problem required significant effort even in a known language. The Pascal protocols were broken down into episodes and the episodes were classified as syntax, semantics, strategic, tactical, or implementation planning. The results were compared to the results of the Ada and Icon subjects to see how programmers differ when working in a known and an unknown language. Figure 4 presents the average percentage of classified time spent by the Pascal subjects in each area of program development. By comparison with the Ada and Icon subjects, much less time was spent in the areas of syntax and semantics, as would be expected with programmers writing code in a language they already know. With little time spent on syntax and semantics, the resulting percentage of time spent on planning activities is bound to be high. Implementation planning still occupied a majority of the subjects' time, and the figure was only a little lower for Pascal than for Ada and Icon. But working in a known language subjects spent a larger percentage of time on tactical planning and also a slightly larger percentage of time on strategic planning.

syntax	semantics	implementation planning	tactical planning	strategic planning
11.8	2.3	52.7	30.5	3.3

Figure 4: Percentage of time spent in program development areas by Pascal subjects.

Although most of the Pascal programmers' time was spent in implementation, observation of the protocols showed that their implementation efforts were straightforward, unlike the iterative approaches we observed in the Ada and Icon protocols. The protocols also showed that the Pascal subjects verbalized at a higher level of planning than did Ada and Icon subjects, usually at the tactical level. As these subjects knew implementation methods for their tactical algorithms, they were able to concentrate more on developing better tactical plans for their programs. Indeed, examination of the Pascal subjects' code showed that not only were their tactical plans appropriate and correctly implemented for the language, but they also uniformly exhibited good programming methods and style. Attention to the higher level strategic and tactical issues of modularity and parameter passing were observed in the Pascal subjects' protocols, while we saw virtually no attention to them in the Ada and Icon protocols. For Ada and Icon the subjects' problem was at the basic level of finding tactical plans which could be successfully implemented to solve each subproblem. They never reached the level of refinement where they had time to worry about program structure and data flow techniques, but were overloaded with simply developing algorithms that would work in the new language.

8. Summary and Conclusions

The results indicate that, regardless of language, the two areas that consume much of the attention of programmers learning a new language are syntax and implementation planning. Since the syntax must be completely correct for a program to run, it is axiomatic that programmers will spend a good deal of effort on it. However, our observations from the protocols showed that the many syntactic questions which subjects had were answered quickly and efficiently. Implementation planning, on the other hand, was truly a hard task. Subjects many times failed to implement their initial language independent tactical plan. Sometimes, especially in the dissimilar language, Icon, they failed because their initial tactical plan was impossible or extremely difficult to implement with the constructs available in the new language. This led to one or more iterations of tactical planning followed by more implementation planning until the programmer developed an appropriate tactical plan which could be implemented using the facilities of the language. Other times, more often with the similar language, Ada, subjects simply failed to discover the correspondence between the construct which they would have used in their preferred language and the symmetrical construct in the new language. Sometimes this failure to discover a corresponding construct occurred for reasons as simple as different naming conventions.

Overall, the differences between Ada and Icon were quite modest. This similarity between languages is somewhat surprising. We observed that, though implementation planning was the biggest area of difficulty in both languages, the reasons were different, i.e., in Ada the failure to locate constructs corresponding to known constructs in Pascal and in Icon the need to develop higher-level tactical plans suited to the unique capabilities of the language.

For the understanding of transfer between programming languages this work indicates that implementation of language independent plans is a major area where transfer fails to occur. In more disparate languages this failure of transfer ultimately leads back to plan revisions at the tactical level. Thus, tactical planning, while language independent in a formal sense, tends to be closely tied to what has proven convenient for a programmer to implement in known languages. The close link between these two types of planning needs to be recognized. Our analysis of Pascal subjects showed that programs exhibiting good programming structure and methods were produced when subjects were able to spend a larger percentage of time on tactical planning activities. For the development of an automated system to help in the process of learning a new language, the results show that tools which aid in evaluating the appropriateness of tactical plans and finding the constructs to implement those plans are the most critical needs. Other areas of program development, such as syntax and semantics, seems to be handled fairly efficiently using conventional documentation.

9. References

1. Kurland, D., Pea, R., Clement, C. and Mawby, R. (1986). A study of the development of programming ability and thinking skills in high school students. *Journal of Educational Computing Research*, Vol. 2 (4), 429-458.
2. Olson, G., Catrambone, R., and Soloway, E. (1987). Programming and algebra word problems: A failure to transfer. In *Empirical Studies of Programmers: Second Workshop* (G.M. Olson, S. Sheppard, & E. Soloway, Eds.), Norwood, NJ: Ablex, 1-13.
3. Polson, P., Bovair, S. and Kieras, D. (1987). Transfer between text editors. In *Chi + GI 1987 Conference Proceedings: Human Factors in Computing Systems and Graphics Interface* (J.M. Carroll & P.P. Tanner, Eds.), 27-32.
4. Polson, P. and Kieras, D. (1985). A quantitative model of the learning and performance of text editing knowledge. In *Chi'85 Conference Proceedings: Human Factors in Computing Systems* (L. Borman & B. Curtis, Eds.),207-212.
5. Polson, P., Muncher, E., & Englebeck, G. (1986). A Test of a Common Elements Theory of Transfer. In *CHI '86 Conference Proceedings: Human Factors in Computing Systems* (M. Mantei & P. Orbeton, Eds.), 78-83.
6. Solomon, G. and Perkins, D. (1987). Transfer of cognitive skills from programming: When and how? *Journal of Educational Computer Research*, 3(2), 149-169.
7. Singley, M.K. and Anderson, J. R. (1988). A keystroke analysis of learning and transfer in text editing. *Human-Computer Interaction*, 3(3), 223-274.
8. Soloway, E., Ehrlich, K., Bonar, J., and Greenspan, J. (1984). What do novices know about programming? In *Directions in Human-Computer Interaction* (A. Badre & B. Shneiderman, Eds.). Norwood, NJ: Ablex, 27-54.

Human–Computer Interaction – INTERACT '90
D. Diaper et al. (Editors)
Elsevier Science Publishers B.V. (North-Holland)

ΥπADAPTερ – Individualizing Hypertext

Heinz-Dieter Böcker, Hubertus Hohl, and Thomas Schwab

Institut für Informatik, Universität Stuttgart, Herdweg 51, D-7000 Stuttgart 1

ΥπADAPTερ is an adaptive Hypertext system that offers individualized access to and presentations of tutorial information. Depending on the user's current knowledge state which is represented in a dynamic user model, it identifies and suggests nodes of the network of tutorial topics which may serve as starting points for a succeeding browsing session. Within this browser, the presentation of tutorial information is determined by the data contained in the user model. During the browsing session, the sequence of knowledge units explored by the user is analyzed to infer the user's current knowledge state and maintain the user model.

1 Introduction

The good old days of having one or two specialized applications running on a small computer are gone. Today's systems tend to be "integrated" with lots of tools "sitting around", waiting to be used, offering solutions to almost any conceivable problem, whatsoever. This trend can be observed in several areas of computer usage. It is obvious in the domain of programming languages and programming environments. Languages like COMMONLISP offer hundreds or thousands of built-in functions, variables, etc., thousands of chunks of knowledge to be learned and, eventually, mastered by the programmer.

On the other hand, it has been empirically shown that programmers effectively use only a small percentage of the available functionality [Fischer et al. 85]. The growing functionality and complexity of modern programming environments results in huge systems that tend to be unusable because of their size.

There are at least two complementary answers to these problems. First, we will have to recognize that the problem may be a different one than we thought it is. We will have to recognize that today's most advanced programming environments are sufficiently complex that nobody masters them completely *and nobody will, ever*. We will have to concede that the very goal of being a master fails. The best we can hope for is being a knowledgeable person in certain subdomains.

Second, it automatically follows that if there is no way to become a master there should be no need to be an apprentice. Thus, we will have to think of ways to make feeling like being an apprentice obsolete. As a long term goal, we suggest to build systems that act as intelligent assistants when needed [Teitelman 79, Böcker 88]. They provide just the right kind and amount of information that is needed by the user to solve the problem at hand. To do this, the envisioned assistants will need some means to sense the direction that the user is working. They will also need to model and remember the experience an individual user has with a particular system; since no two users are alike they will have to be able to adapt to their users' view of the world.

By having given up the guild's paradigm of master and apprentice another long standing dichotomy broke down: the clear cut distinction between learning and working. Both, instead, become tightly intertwined; in the future, information gathering on demand and learning on demand will become standard practice. Due to the lack of appropriate terminology we cast general procedures and principles in terms of learning terminology. What we are really interested in are system components that are supportive in general human problem-domain communication [Fischer, Lemke 88]. In this article describing ΥπADAPTερ we choose programming as prototypical problem-domain.

2 The ΥπADAPTερ system

ΥπADAPTερ is one answer to some of the questions posed. ΥπADAPTερ (pronounced: Hypadapter) was designed to individually support learning and working activities in the domain of the programming language COMMONLISP [Steele Jr. 84]. ΥπADAPTερ is an adaptable as well as adaptive source for help; it generates individualized presentations of tutorial information and allows the user to lay out and maintain his or her private Hypertext like paths through the information jungle. Typical users of the system are programmers with different knowledge states concerning COMMONLISP. ΥπADAPTερ is implemented as a Hypertext system [Conklin 87] augmented by a user modelling facility

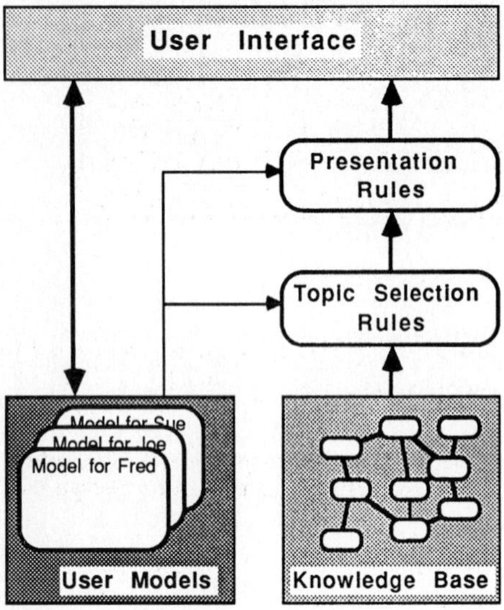

Figure 1: Architecture of $\Upsilon\pi$ADAPT$\epsilon\rho$

[Rich 83, Schwab 89]. Figure 1 displays the architecture of $\Upsilon\pi$ADAPT$\epsilon\rho$.

The available topics, that describe the application domain, are represented as knowledge units in a richly structured *knowledge base*. A topic selection component identifies and suggests topics according to the user's knowledge state represented in a dynamic *user model*. The selection process is controlled by *topic selection rules*. Topics are visualized on a direct manipulation user interface that supports Hypertext design principles. The presentation of topics is determined by *presentation rules* that are controlled by the contents of the user model. The user model of $\Upsilon\pi$ADAPT$\epsilon\rho$ is dynamic: to model the learning progress of the user the model is automatically updated during the navigation process.

2.1 The knowledge base

The knowledge base describes a subset of programming knowledge relevant for COMMONLISP programming. It is structured as a network of heterogeneous information nodes that represent tutorial topics. Topics are separated into the following *spaces*, each containing interrelated nodes that are linked to nodes of other spaces as well:

meta-topics — describe the conceptual structure of the knowledge base itself. There is one meta-topic for every space that among other things provides links to all its space-topics. Thus, meta-topics may serve as starting points for searching or navigating in the knowledge base.

programming concepts — form the abstract framework of any programming language. Aside from links to other spaces, concept topics are embedded in a heterarchy that represents conceptual generalizations and specializations. The layers of this heterarchy refine from general concepts at the top (e.g. *function*, *recursion*) to COMMONLISP-specific concepts (e.g. *list*, *macro*).

functions — collect knowledge about the individual COMMONLISP functions (including special forms and macros).

goals — specify normative categories for a LISP programmer, e.g. stylistic characteristics or efficiency issues.

optimization rules — describe transformation rules that can be used to optimize program code according to guidelines specified in the goals.

errors — collect information about typical programming errors, e.g. errors that may be detected by program code analysis.

The properties of a topic are completely defined by a set of *attributes*. Every topic includes the following general attributes as well as attributes that are specific to a single space: topic-name, level of difficulty, preconditions, links to related- and sister-topics, a link to its meta-topic, description, examples, notes, summary and page references to CLtL [Steele Jr. 84].

The attributes *description*, *examples*, and *notes* come in different flavours to select among depending on the user's overall knowledge state. The values of these attributes are implemented as formatted texts containing markup that defines a declarative markup language [Symbolics 88]. Besides textual information, graphics and bitmapped images these texts may include *active elements*. When presented to the user, they can be activated by pointing with the mouse to trigger arbitrary actions.

2.2 The User Model

$\Upsilon\pi$ADAPT$\epsilon\rho$ builds up and exploits *dynamic, individual user models* [Rich 83] that represent the information about each individual user. Each model contains a set of attribute-value pairs that characterize the user. These characteristics range from personal data, experience with particular computer systems to the user's current knowledge state of tutorial topics and preferences concerning the presentation of tutorial information.

To infer additional facts about the user $\Upsilon\pi$ADAPT$\epsilon\rho$ uses *stereotypes* [Schwab 89]. A stereotype defines a collection of attribute-value pairs that often occur together.

Knowledge level of topic depending on stereotype and difficulty					
	difficulty level of topic				
stereotype	mundane	simple	advanced	complex	esoteric
novice	FAMILIAR	UNFAMILIAR	UNKNOWN	UNKNOWN	UNKNOWN
beginner	KNOWN	FAMILIAR	UNFAMILIAR	UNKNOWN	UNKNOWN
intermediate	KNOWN	KNOWN	FAMILIAR	UNFAMILIAR	UNKNOWN
expert	KNOWN	KNOWN	KNOWN	FAMILIAR	UNFAMILIAR

Figure 2: Stereotypes in ΥπADAPTϵρ.

If some of these properties apply to a user he or she is supposed to possess the other stereotype characteristics as well, unless the system is able to infer otherwise.

The possible stereotypes in ΥπADAPTϵρ are *novice*, *beginner*, *intermediate* or *expert*. They model the learning progress of users by differentiating relative to their current knowledge state. Every stereotype masters topics up to a fixed level of difficulty (cf. Figure 2). Based on the information already represented in the user model each user is assigned to exactly one of these stereotypes by classification rules.

Whilst the knowledge base is relatively stable, the user models behave *dynamic*. The known facts about each user may change during the dialogue and the user may learn new things while working with the system. This causes model adjustments — e.g. stereotype reclassifications — that immediately affect the presentation of tutorial information.

ΥπADAPTϵρ exploits the user model for topic selection and presentation. The *topic selection rules* that select the appropriate topics for a specific user are controlled by the information represented in the user model. The goal is to prevent users from being confronted with topics that are not up to their qualification and to support the incremental expansion of the user's knowledge space. The system does this by applying topic selection rules to the topic-oriented model of the user's current knowledge state according to the following criteria:

- Avoid known topics.
- Avoid topics with unknown preconditions.
- Prefer topics that are needed immediately.
- Prefer topics that are related to topics already known.
- Match topic's level of difficulty with the user's qualification, e.g. prefer easy and avoid complex topics for beginners.

Topics are presented individually by focusing on those attributes and links that most closely match the user's needs and interests as determined by the data contained in the user model. To this end, *presentation rules* are formulated according to the following strategy:

- The presentation of attributes like *description* should correspond to the user's overall classification.
- The user's preferences for certain attributes have to be considered.
- Different levels of detail have to be supplied.
- Additional information has to be presented according to the user's learner type.

2.3 The User Interface

The Model Inspector

To avoid acceptance problems the user model must be made transparent to the user. This is realized by a *model inspector*, which gives a user insight into stored model values and discloses a user's current stereotype classification.

The model inspector allows further customization of the learning environment by providing a questionnaire to specify or adjust model values that cannot be inferred implicitely. This includes user characteristics like personal data, general information about computers, information about LISP usage, and individual preferences concerning the visualization and presentation of topics (e.g. the preferred explanation style, the information's level of detail, and overall interest).

The Topic Browser

ΥπADAPTϵρ provides a direct manipulation, window-based user interface that mainly supports selection-oriented interaction techniques. Operations on objects are invoked by single point-and-click actions using the mouse.

Navigation by browsing is the primary means for retrieving information from the knowledge base. The user explores the universe of connected topics by following links

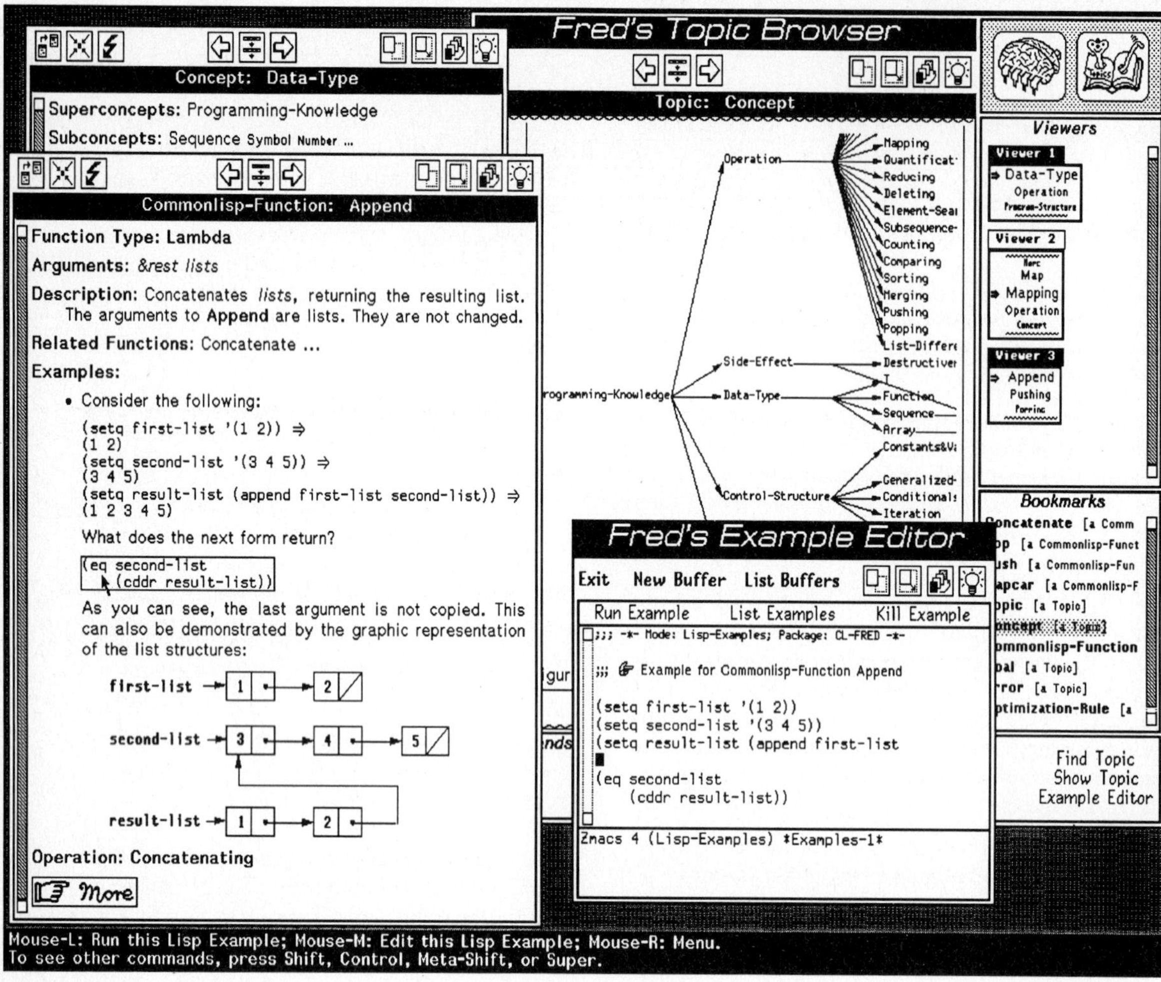

Figure 3: Fred's Topic Browser.

from topic to topic. Thus the dialogue is fully controlled by the user, who determines the order of topics to be acquired by selecting from the set of system-suggested topics.

Viewers — realized on screen as multiple, overlapping windows of arbitrary size — are used to present topics from the underlying knowledge base. Every viewer maintains and provides access to its own chronological history of visualized topics.

Representing topic histories is one means to prevent users from getting lost while travelling through the large and complex network of information nodes. Introducing alternative access facilities on topics is another means to cope with disorientation and to control browsing and searching:

Knowledge maps — provide two-dimensional, graphical views of parts of the underlying knowledge base structure by showing topics and their local context. They are used to visualize and browse through the generalization hierarchy in the space of concepts. Figure 4 shows the subconcepts of **data-type**. This graph was activated by selecting the subconcepts area of Viewer 1 contained in Figure 3.

Bookmarks — provide a way to keep track of important points in a user's browsing session. By defining bookmarks users build a personal trail of interesting topics that can later be accessed directly.

Name-based access — complements navigation by allowing users to directly access topics known by name (including a facility to complement partially specified names). This avoids inefficient search

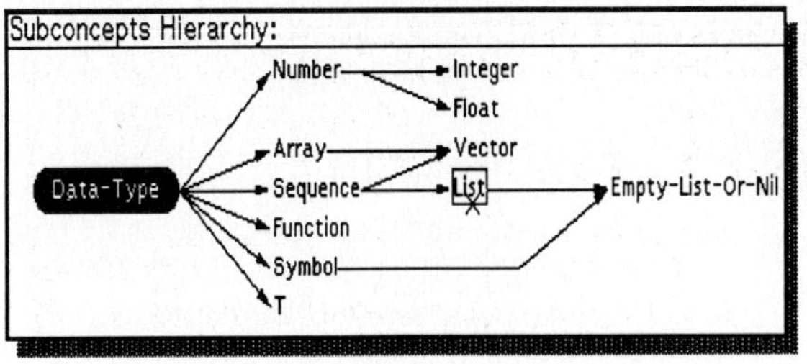

Figure 4: Subconcept hierarchy of `data-type`.

> processes that are caused by following paths imposed by the structure of the knowledge base.

As an example, Figure 3 shows the user interface for a user named Fred. The Topic Browser contains an integrated viewer, a graphic menu listing all other viewers, a menu of bookmarks and a command interface that among other things allows direct access to topics. In Viewer 3 (on the left side of the screen), the topic `append` is visualized by presenting a subset of its attributes, depending on the presentation rules that operate on Fred's user model. This model characterizes Fred as a beginner. Thus description and examples are tailored for beginners.

Going beyond conventional Hypertext systems like the Document Examiner [Walker 88] — a system by SYMBOLICS that provides online access to the user documentation of their lispmachines — ϒπADAPTερ is *adaptive*. While navigating through the knowledge base, the user model is automatically maintained: each inspection of a topic by the user leads to a slight increment of the corresponding knowledge state in the user model. Thereby, the system models the transition of a user from a novice to an expert.

The user interface always reflects an individual view of the underlying knowledge base. However, the presentation of topics — controlled by the topic selection rules and the presentation rules — that filters tutorial information by highlighting relevant and eliding inappropriate aspects doesn't restrict the user to a fix learning path. The user may at any time zoom into information elided in the initial presentation of a topic.

Integration in LISP

ϒπADAPTερ supports example-based programming by supplying topics with attributes that contain examples, especially LISP-code. Examples play an important role in the process of learning and programming (cf. [Rissland 84]). Beginners often reuse code from books and manuals as a "recipe" for standard tasks and as a base for generalizations. More advanced programmers tend to use the structure inherent in examples as templates for own problem solving. Moreover examples may serve as a reminder for syntactic forms.

The LISP-code contained in example-attributes is active: by clicking the mouse on active examples, the corresponding code can be evaluated or copied into an Example-Editor for further experimentation (see Figure 3). Thus, active examples support a motivating "learning by doing" mode that encourages users to get hands-on experience with stated problems.

3 Implementational Aspects

ϒπADAPTερ is composed of several subsystems that are based on the COMMONLISP [Steele Jr. 84] platform of a SYMBOLICS lispmachine. The knowledge base is represented by classes and instances of OBJTALK [Girgensohn, Rathke 88], a powerful, object-oriented extension of COMMONLISP. The user modelling component is implemented with the general user modelling toolkit MODUS described in [Schwab 89]. The user interface makes heavy use of the user interface toolkit and the SAGE text formatter provided by SYMBOLICS' GENERA programming environment.

4 Discussion

The ϒπADAPTερ system is a first step toward a new class of systems, adaptive Hypertext systems that simultaneously support learning as well as working activities. By using a highly structured knowledge base about the COMMONLISP domain as a reference point the system builds up a detailed model of the user's knowledge state which it utilizes to provide individualized assistance. The internal structure of the knowledge base is much more complex, manifold and variable than usual Hypertext databases. In addition to the proper topics, there exists an explicit representation that reflects the conceptual level of the knowledge base.

Future developments of the system will have to address the following issues:

- The startup user models are rather primitive; we will have to develop more realistic ones by integrating diagnostic components that analyze users' already existing programs to arrive at differential initial user models.
- Currently, the system models progress only; to build more realistic user models a theory of forgetting will have be developed and put to use.

- The underlying knowledge base was built up "by hand". We will have to further develop and adapt authoring and editing tools that are common in standard Hypertext systems to cope with the issue of semi-automatic knowledge acquisition.
- Authoring and editing tools would also become helpful if we were to port the system to domains different from COMMONLISP. To do this, we would also provide new rules and stereotype definitions for the user modelling component. The user interface and the basic user modelling framework could be ported unchanged.
- The way the stereotype mechanism is used by ΥπADAPTερ leaves some room for improvement. Currently, ΥπADAPTερ defines mutually exclusive stereotypes which to some extent contradicts the very idea of stereotypes. It would be more appropriate to augment or even replace the current stereotypes that relate to the users' global experience by content-based stereotypes. It seems reasonable, for example, to dissect the space of COMMONLISP functions into certain subdomains (e.g., numerical, list processing) and to associate stereotypes accordingly.

Acknowledgements

Numerous people have contributed to ΥπADAPTερ over the last three years. We wish to thank Susanne Reicherter for building an initial version of the user modelling component. We are also grateful to Matthias Ressel who worked on the COMMONLISP knowledge base and implemented the topic selection and presentation rule mechanism. Special thanks go to Rul Gunzenhäuser for his continuous support.

References

[Böcker 88] H. D. Böcker. OPTIMIST: Ein System zur Beurteilung und Verbesserung von Lisp-Code. In R. Gunzenhäuser und H. D. Böcker (Hrsg.), *Prototypen benutzergerechter Computersysteme*, Kapitel 9. Verlag Walter de Gruyter & Co., Berlin - New York, 1988.

[Conklin 87] J. Conklin. Hypertext: An Introduction and Survey. *Computer*, 20(9):17–41, September 1987.

[Fischer et al. 85] G. Fischer, A. Lemke und T. Schwab. Knowledge-based Help Systems. In L. Borman und B. Curtis (Eds.), *CHI-85, Human Factors in Computing Systems Conference Proceedings*, pp. 161–167, New York, April 1985. ACM SIGCHI/HFS.

[Fischer, Lemke 88] G. Fischer und A. Lemke. Construction Kits and Design Environments: Steps Toward Human Problem-Domain Communication. *Human-Computer Interaction*, 3(2), 1988.

[Girgensohn, Rathke 88] A. Girgensohn und C. Rathke. ObjTalk - Version 16.0. INFORM Manual, Institut für Informatik, Universität Stuttgart, August 1988.

[Rich 83] E. Rich. Users are individuals: individualizing user models. *International Journal of Man-Machine Studies*, 18:199–214, 1983.

[Rissland 84] E. L. Rissland. Explaining and Arguing with Examples. In AAAI (Ed.), *Proceedings of the National Conference on Artificial Intelligence. August 1984, University of Texas at Austin*, Los Altos, 1984. American Association for Artificial Intelligence, W. Kaufmann, Inc.

[Schwab 89] T. Schwab. Methoden zur Dialog- und Benutzermodellierung in adaptiven Computersystemen. Dissertation, Fakultät Informatik der Universität Stuttgart, October 1989.

[Steele Jr. 84] G. L. Steele Jr. *Common LISP: The Language*. Digital Press, Digital Equipment Corporation, 1984.

[Symbolics 88] Symbolics, Inc., Cambridge, MA. *Concordia*, Symbolics Reference Manual #999065 edition, July 1988.

[Teitelman 79] W. Teitelman. A Display Oriented Programmers Assistant. *Int. J. Man-Mach. Stud.*, 11(2):157–187, 1979.

[Walker 88] J. Walker. Supporting Document Development with Concordia. *Computer*, 21(1):48–59, January 1988.

Human–Computer Interaction – INTERACT '90
D. Diaper et al. (Editors)
Elsevier Science Publishers B.V. (North-Holland)

MINIMALIST PLANNING TOOLS IN AN INSTRUCTIONAL SYSTEM FOR SMALLTALK PROGRAMMING

Mark K. Singley
John M. Carroll

User Interface Institute
IBM T.J. Watson Research Center
P.O. Box 704
Yorktown Heights, NY 10598

We describe the design of an instructional system for Smalltalk that attempts to reify students' goals and plans through the application of *minimalist planning dialogues*. Minimalist planning dialogues are sparse in that the planning knowledge is not stated explicitly but rather is imbedded into the structure of a planning "tool." They are situated in that the planning tools are fully integrated into the physical problem space and in essence provide an elaborated view of that space. We contrast our system with other current attempts at reifying students' goals and plans and sketch out problems and prospects for future work.

1.0 INTRODUCTION

Evidence is mounting that the representation of the student's task embodied by an instructional system plays a major role in determining student performance (Singley, in press, Anderson et al., 1985). This suggests that perhaps more effort should be spent on the system's conceptualization and structuring of the task (providing the system with *proactive* intelligence) and less on the system's diagnosis and response to student errors (*reactive* intelligence). This view stresses the role of an instructional system as a tool rather than a remediator and brings into greater prominence the role of interface design in intelligent tutoring systems work. The specific challenge faced by interface designers in this area is to find ways of representing abstract cognitive structures such as students' goals and plans as concrete visual or textual objects that can be made the focus of student action and discourse.

2.0 COMMUNICATING PLANNING STRUCTURES

Our claim is that a great deal of instructional leverage comes from an accurate and complete task analysis of the domain and the successful communication of that analysis to the student. This is especially true for the more strategic aspects of a skill. The strategic, meta-level knowledge is what drives problem solving, yet its explication is typically absent from traditional pedagogy. The successful tutor captures this knowledge and uses it in some way to structure and support student problem solving. To do this well is a feat of cognitive engineering that is currently not systematically understood.

One example of the successful communication of planning structures to students is in the Related Rates Tutor (Singley, in press). The Related Rates Tutor helps first-year calculus students solve related-rates word problems. In an initial experiment with a prototype version of the system, it was discovered through analyses of verbal protocol data that students were attempting to execute a fairly standard means-ends strategy to solve systems of equations, but were having trouble formulating and maintaining the requisite subgoals. To remedy this problem, an enhancement to the interface of the tutor was designed which allowed students to post and display the subgoals required by the means-ends strategy. As students progressed through problems, individual subgoals were boxed and shaded to indicate which were active and which had been satisfied, respectively. An experiment testing the effects of this type of planning discourse showed that student problem solving performance improved in terms of both speed and quality of moves while the goal blackboard was present. Furthermore, many of the positive effects persisted after the goal blackboard was taken away, suggesting that the blackboard was not only a performance aid but also a learning catalyst.

This work supports the view that planning structures should be made the subject of tutorial discourse. However, the usefulness of this principle may be limited by the fact that it may be difficult to find a transparent representation for goals and plans in some domains. The problem is that the planning space is typically positioned at a level of abstraction far above what Newell and Simon (1972) call the physical problem space, the space where actual operations are carried out. It may be that the goal manipulation worked in the Related Rates Tutor simply because the usual distinction between the planning space and the physicial problem space was for the most part degenerate: the goals themselves were very similar to the kinds of objects that students were manipulating in the physical problem space. This meant that students were not burdened with learning a new and abstract vocabulary for conversing about goal structures in this domain. However, in other domains, such as programming (which is our current interest), the planning structures are more abstract and may have little meaning to the novice.

Wanting to support the planning process in their systems, some researchers have adopted the view that the planning structures they have discovered and codified can be communicated more or less directly to the student with beneficial effects. So, for example, a system that teaches legal reasoning asks students to create a semantic network to represent the meaning of legal text (Feifer et al., 1988), or a system that teaches Pascal programming asks students to first code the algorithm in terms of planning icons which are themselves a fully-executable programming language (Bonar, 1988). To date, these systems have not been evaluated empirically, so it is not clear what pedagogical effect these abstract representations might have, but it is our suspicion that in these domains this brute force approach to conveying abstract knowledge probably overwhelms the student with additional complexity. It is quite likely that learning to use these formalisms is at least if not more difficult than mastering the domain itself. To be successful, we must take a more indirect and artful approach. We would like to apply the *minimalist* instructional philosophy (Carroll, in press) to the design of planning dialogues.

3.0 MINIMALIST PLANNING DIALOGUES

A minimalist planning dialogue has two main features: it is *sparse* and it is *situated.* It is sparse because the planning knowledge is not stated explicitly but rather is imbedded into the structure of a planning "tool." In using the tool, the student is invited to draw his or her own inferences about the nature of planning in the domain and is pointed in the direction of the right conclusions. Sparseness has at least three advantages over the brute force approach: (1) The student actively constructs his or her own representations of the planning knowledge. An active learner is both more motivated (Carroll and Mack, 1985) and more retentive (Black et al., 1989) than the passive learner. (2) Since the planning knowledge is only implicit in the tool, the student is spared the pain of learning an abstract planning language which in all likelihood would make no contact with existing student knowledge and thus would be poorly integrated. (3) If the tool is reasonably transparent, a student can operate in the physical problem space with no explicit awareness of the planning space and can shift attention to it when cognitive resources are available. Studies of novice problem solvers (e.g. Kotovsky et al. (1985), Sweller (1986)) suggest that procedures in the physical problem space must be automated before the learner can profit from instruction on planning.

A minimalist planning dialogue is situated because the planning tool is in fact used to operate in the physical problem space and is fully integrated with that space. It does not sit alone on a separate level. The planning tool in a sense simply presents an elaborated view of the physical problem space which suggests constraints on operator selection. (In this sense, the interface technique of menu dimming is a weak yet clear example of a minimalist planning tool.) The situated nature of minimalist planning is both a strength and a weakness. It is a strength because it acknowledges that people learn best in context and that planning knowledge must be richly and inextricably linked to execution knowledge. It is a weakness in that students may acquire representations of planning knowledge that are too closely tied to the planning tools themselves and may be unable to do the task without the tool. (If the tool can be supplied as a permanent part of the student's environment, this may not be a problem.)

One example of a minimalist planning tool is the equation table used in the Algebra Word Problem Tutor (Singley and Anderson, in preparation). Figure 1 shows the table as it appears to students after solving the following word problem: *Eighteen pennies and nickels have a total value of 38 cents. How many pennies are there?* Singley and Anderson's task analysis of algebra word problem

	pennies	nickels	coins
number	x	18 - x	18
value of coin	.01	.05	
total value	.01x	.05(18-x)	.38

Figure 1. The equation table in the Algebra Word Problem Tutor.

solving claims that solving a problem involves the generation and combination of primitive equations in such a way that the answer variable is expressed in terms of known quantities. Thus, solving a word problem is largely a matter of search: Many primitive equations can be generated, and these can be combined in many ways, but only one set of equations and several sets of combinations yields the answer. The equation table supports both phases of this search process: First, each row and column in the table represents a separate primitive equation that is potentially relevant, and the presence of the table cues these equations for the student. Thus, the generation of equations is supported. Second, the two-dimensional structure of the table reveals the systematicity of the primitive equations, most importantly which equations share variables and therefore can be combined. Thus, the combination of equations is supported. In fact, the presence of the table turns the entire search process into a straighforward fill-in-the-blanks procedure, a procedure that Singley and Anderson call the diagram strategy: *Wherever there is a row or column that has a single value missing, generate the equation for that row or column and use the two known values to generate the missing value. Iterate until a row or column is filled in entirely by other rows or columns. Generate the equation for that row and solve for the goal variable.* It is important to note that the table doesn't communicate the diagram strategy directly; it simply provides a representation that suggests and facilitates the strategy. Empirical tests of the equation table have shown that students master particular classes of algebra word problems more quickly with the table than without it. However, student performance degrades somewhat when the tables are taken away. As mentioned previously, this pattern of results typifies situated learning.

One possible remedy to this overdependence on the tool is to make the tool itself the subject of instruction. We saw this in the Related Rates Tutor, where students were taught to create the goal structures for themselves from the beginning and had no degradation of performance once the goal structures were taken away. To duplicate this result, Singley and Anderson redesigned the Word Problem Tutor so that students would be required to construct the tables for themselves, and indeed this mitigated the problem somewhat. In both of these cases, students achieved independence from the tool by learning to reconstruct it for themselves. Another domain where this technique might be especially attractive is programming, where presumably any type of planning aid could be written in the target language.

4.0 PLANNING TOOLS FOR SMALLTALK

Presently, we are designing an instructional system for Smalltalk (written in Smalltalk) which we hope will exemplify the principles of minimalism. In our current vision, the system is composed of four integrated components, each of which is potentially useful inside and outside of a tutoring context:

Video Guru. Rather than present planning information textually, we will present it using the more situated medium of video. A *video guru* will be available online to provide visual demonstrations of coding along with auditory commentary explicating underlying intentions and goal dependencies. There is a principled reason for using video in this way. It does not overload the visual channel with an unholy mixture of planning information and code, which is typically done in programming tutors. By dividing the message cleanly and distributing it across both channels, we are replicating the kind of "show and tell" instruction that occurs naturally in everyday apprenticeship situations. The video library of example plans and procedures can be accessed not only by the tutor but also by the student, thus facilitating its use outside of the tutor.

Goal Poster. As an extension of the calculus goal posting work, we will provide a goal blackboard to maintain the student's current goal tree. Again, both the tutor and student can write to the goal blackboard. The tutor writes to it in two ways. First, the Video Guru can leave a textual goal trace of the auditory commentary. Second, as students write code, browse the class hierarchy, or engage the debugger, a plan parser automatically updates the contents of the blackboard to reflect the tutor's current interpretation of the student's actions. The interpretation may be that the student is doing something wrong, i.e. that the student is pursuing a buggy plan. This would be communicated graphically to the student, perhaps with the use of color. Although textual, the presentation of individual goals would be telegraphic: several words at most. Hierarchical relationships would be presented using indentation, as they are in the Smalltalk Class Hierarchy Browser (CHB)(Goldberg, 1984). At any point, the student can expand one of telegraphic nodes in the goal blackboard for further explanation.

Commentator. The Commentator is designed to facilitate code comprehension and reuse, which is a large part of Smalltalk programming. As students search the Smalltalk method library with the method editor, they can select any syntactically-meaningful chunk of code with the mouse and get a context-sensitive explanation of the code they have selected in a separate window. (Context sensitivity is implemented naturally using the Smalltalk inheritance hierarchy.) Also, as students write code in the tutor, it is automatically annotated with the tutor's comments. (The student will be encouraged to abridge or elaborate any of these comments to make them more meaningful.) For example, if code is copied from another method, the tutor will record the name of the source. Thus, after leaving the tutoring environment, in addition to the system code, the student's own exercises have meaningful annotations that can be accessed by the Commentator. This presumably will facilitate reuse.

Adaptive Index. Many newcomers to Smalltalk are experienced programmers who know what they want to do but simply cannot find the right method in the voluminous class hierarchy. The Adapative Index is a search tool that provides a bridge between familiar procedural functionality (e.g. accessing records, appending strings) and Smalltalk functionality. After entering a keyword query in terms of their favorite programming language (in fact, we plan to support LISP and C) or perhaps generic computing functionality, students get pointers to appropriate methods in the class hierarchy. In the context of the tutor, students can enter queries composed of problem-specific terms for additional searching power. The Commentator will access the Adaptive Index to generate cross-references to more familiar languages in its explanations of Smalltalk code. The design of the index will be informed by detailed empirical studies of how procedural programmers represent functionality and how they search the Smalltalk hierarchy.

5.0 SMALLTALK INSTRUCTIONAL SCENARIO

We will now illustrate the integration and coordination of these tools in a Smalltalk instructional scenario.

Student's Goal: Add functionality to a window so that all alphabetic input is transformed to upper case. (This goal is purposely stated to reveal very little about the solution, i.e. it does not say "Create a subclass of TextEditor."

Smalltalk solution: Create a new subclass of TextEditor called UpperCaseEditor, intercept the alphabetic input that normally is passed to the TextEditor method processInputKey:, and transform it to upper case before inserting it into the model for the pane.

The student's activity in this scenario is broken down into the two major phases that typify Smalltalk programming: (1) Finding the right classes and methods to specialize in the Smalltalk class hierarchy, and (2) designing and implementing the modifications. In a sense, the process of programming in Smalltalk for the novice is not unlike the process of enhancing a large unfamiliar program in a more conventional procedural language like C.

5.1 Finding the functionality

First, the student has to find out how character input from the keyboard is processed and displayed in Smalltalk windows. The student may know nothing about TextEditor, the Smalltalk class that normally handles this function. Once the proper functionality is found, the student can make the appropriate decision about specialization.

The student engages the Smalltalk tutor by a selection from the System Menu. Once in the tutor, a variety of projects can be selected from the window menu (tutor mode), or the student can use the tutor as an enriched CHB (tool mode). The student clicks on the title bar to display the menu and selects the project *uppercase window*. This starts up the Video Guru which presents orienting commentary about the problem and how to attack it, i.e. the Guru presents the top-level goal structure outlined above.

As the Video Guru overviews the problem, the goals that are described appear in the Goal Poster: find functionality and specialize functionality. The student can expand these nodes using the pane menu for the Goal Poster. For example, find functionality expands into various methods for navigating the class hierarchy in search of the appropriate class, and specialize functionality expands into subclassing the appropriate class, followed by copying and modifying the appropriate method. The student can request further rationale and procedural detail for any node in the goal structure: selecting a nonterminal subgoal like "find functionality" would produce a problem-specific rationale for searching the class hierarchy (i.e., to find how character input is processed and displayed); selecting a terminal subgoal would explain in explicit terms how to carry out a primitive action to satisfy the goal. The windows for these node expansions contain selectable icons which provide more focussed Video Guru help.

To proceed, the student must discover that the TextEditor class handles keyboard input. One strategy for discovery is to browse the class hierarchy for possibilities. The tutor simplifies this search by presenting only a subset view of the class hierarchy to the student, using the Bittitalk Browser tool (Rosson et al., 1990). The student can also use the Adaptive Index tool, typing any number of keywords into a prompter to obtain a new view of the class hierarchy in which classes indexed under the searched terms are displayed in bold font. For example, the student can type "input, text, uppercase." All the dispatcher classes will match "input," some of the pane and dispatcher classes will match "text" (for example, TextPane and TextEditor) and the Character class will match "uppercase." Although there are still multiple classes to consider, the search space is substantially reduced.

The student eventually selects the TextPane class, and the Commentator explains that panes work with dispatchers to manage window interactions. This relationship can be explored in more detail by selecting the defaultDispatcherClass method, which specifies TextEditor as the dispatcher for TextPane.

Having understood the relationship between TextPane and TextEditor, the student must continue the search to identify the specific method that needs to be specialized. This part of the search is again supported by the Commentator. When a method is selected in the class hierarchy browser, a description of its function appears in the Commentator pane. Likely candidates in this case are the various "process input" methods in the TextEditor class. After a fair amount of browsing, the student finds that the method processInput handles the input first and determines its type (e.g. mouse event, function key, character). It invokes processInputKey: if the input is a alphabetic. This latter method then is the one that needs to be specialized.

5.2 Specializing the functionality

Typically in Smalltalk, one creates new functionality by first subclassing the appropriate class and then adding new methods that augment or supercede the existing methods of the parent. This preserves the integrity of the original hierarchy and allows for inheritance of existing methods that require no modification.

In this case the student wants to subclass TextEditor and create a specialized version of the method processInputKey:. Once the method is copied from TextEditor to UpperCaseEditor, the student can add the code to transform the input. The student begins by selecting the class TextEditor in the CHB and then selecting the *add subclass* option from the CHB menu. In response to each student action, the Goal Poster reconfigures itself, expanding nodes as the student takes on new subgoals and shading and contracting nodes as goals are satisfied. Here is a portion of the underlying goal tree that guides student action during this episode:

specialize: TextEditor
  preserve: TextEditor
    subclass: TextEditor
      selectTextEditor in CHB
      select *add subclass* from menu
      name new subclass
    copyMethod: processInputKey:
      store source
        choose method in CHB
        select full contents
        copy selection
      create new method from copy
        select new subclass in CHB
        select *new method* from Selectors menu
        select template
        paste buffer
  code: uppercase transformation

As mentioned previously, at any point students can choose to expand a goal node to get help text or, where warranted, a video narrative. One subgoal particularly amenable to video instruction is the copyMethod: subgoal shown above. The procedure for copying methods is much more difficult to describe textually than it is to demonstrate visually with an audio commentary.

Errors are always possible. When an error is diagnosed, the Goal Poster displays an error subgoal in the goal structure. For example, the student might have decided that the processLastInput: method in the Displatcher class has the functionality that is to be specialized. Consequently, the student might try to subclass the Displatcher class instead of the TextEditor class. The tutor would block this action, displaying a red error subgoal in the Goal Poster and an explanation in a pop-up window: "The Dispatcher class does not contain the functionality you need to specialize." The student's next correct action deletes the error subgoal and the pop-up window. If the student's error is closer to the target performance, more specific feedback is provided. For example, the student might have decided that

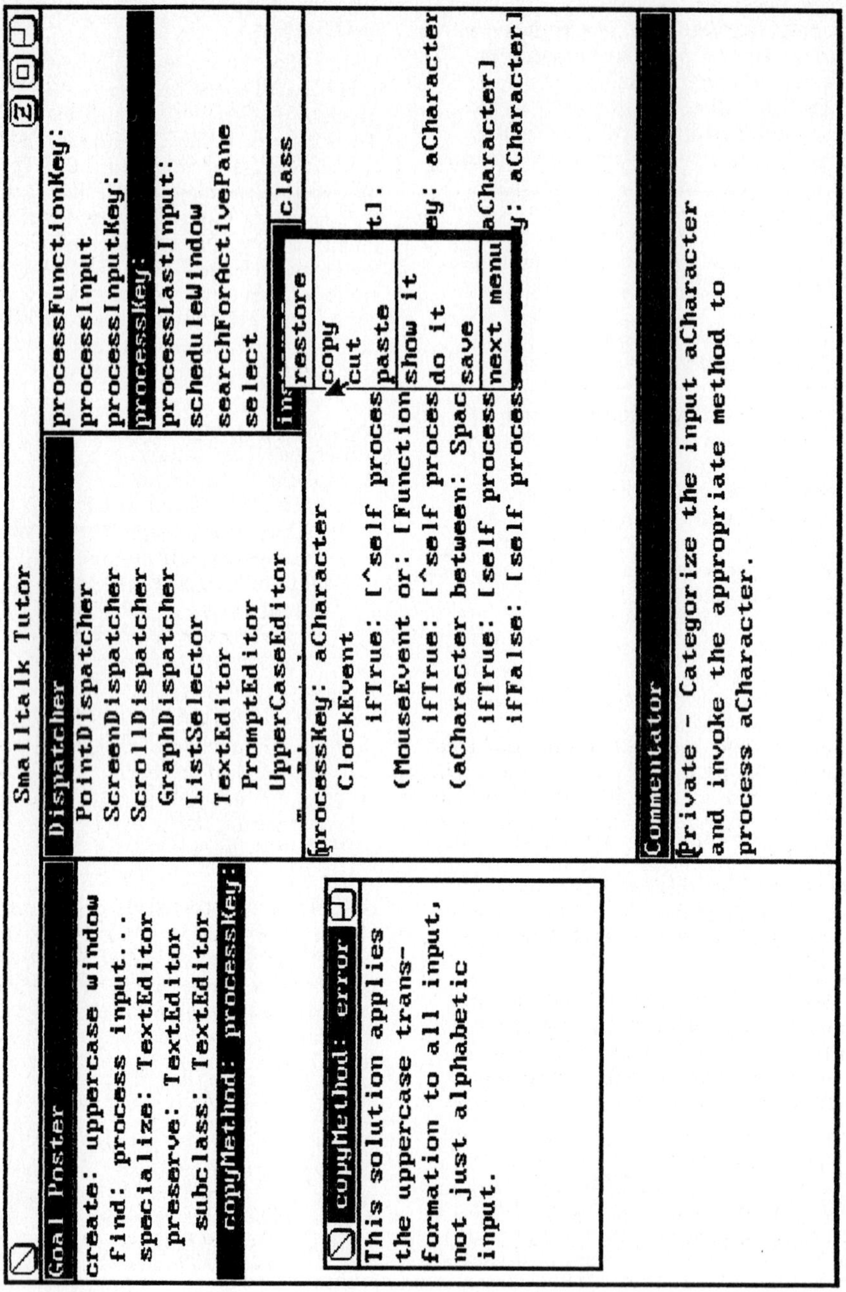

Figure 2. The Smalltalk Tutor responding to a student error.

processKey: was the method to specialize. In this case the tutor could provide a specific critique of the error: "This solution applies the uppercase transformation to all input, not just alphabetic input." See Figure 2 for a view of the system's interface as it responds to this error.

Our hypothetical student is now ready to write new code for processInputKey:. Here's the method as it was copied from TextEditor:

```
processInputKey: aCharacter

pane isGapSelection
   ifFalse: [pane hideSelection].
newSelection :=
   pane replaceWithChar: aCharacter.
modified := true.
pane
   selectAfter: newSelection corner;
   makeSelectionVisible
```

The student needs to add the following two lines of code to the beginning of the method:

```
|aChar|
aChar := aCharacter asUpperCase.
```

In addition, the student must substitute the local variable aChar for the parameter aCharacter as the argument to the method replaceWithChar:. To write this code correctly, the student has to know two non-obvious features of Smalltalk:

- Parameters cannot be assigned new values. This necessitates the declaration of a local variable and the reassignment of the parameter to that local variable.
- Methods are sent to objects and not *vice versa*. A common slip for procedural programmers is to reverse the ordering of method and object in a message so as to more closely approximate a standard function call.

Should the student make either of these or similar mistakes, the tutor will display an error goal in the Goal Poster and a message in a pop-up window. Specific mention of the differences between Smalltalk and procedural languages will be made.

As students write correct code, annotations are automatically supplied and permanently stored by the tutor in the Commentator. (These annotations can be edited by the student to render them more meaningful.) This means that students come away from their collaboration with the tutor with well-documented code that can be searched by the Adaptive Index. Thus, the code that they write becomes well-integrated into the environment which enhances its lasting pedagogical impact and encourages its reuse.

6.0 SUMMARY

Our proposed Smalltalk instructional system is a set of integrated tools that can function effectively inside or outside of a tutoring context. The system supports real-world situated learning by easing the transition between a tutored and an untutored environment. The planning tools are minimal in that they provide sparse explanations under the control of the student, and in most cases allow students to operate in the physical problem space without manipulating planning representations directly.

REFERENCES

Anderson, J. R., Boyle, C. F., & Yost, G. (1985). The geometry tutor. *Proceedings of the Ninth International Joint Conference on Artificial Intelligence.* Los Altos, CA: Morgan Kaufmann.

Black, J. B., Bechtold, S., Mitrani, M., & Carroll, J. M. (1989). On line tutorials: What kind of inference leads to the most effective learning. *Proceedings of the CHI '89 Conference on Human Factors in Computing Systems.* Boston, MA: Association for Computing Machinery.

Bonar, J. (1988). Intelligent tutoring with intermediate representations. *Proceedings of ITS '88 Intelligent Tutoring Systems Conference.* Montreal: Association for Computing Machinery.

Carroll, J. M. (in press). *The Nurnberg funnel: Designing minimalist instruction for practical computer skill.* Cambridge, MA: MIT Press.

Carroll, J. M., & Mack, R. L. (1985). Metaphor, computing systems, and active learning. *International Journal of Man-Machine Studies*, 39-57.

Feifer, R., Dyer, M., & Baker, E. (1988). Learning procedural and declarative knowledge. *Proceedings of ITS '88 Intelligent Tutoring Systems Conference.* Montreal: Association for Computing Machinery.

Goldberg, A. (1984). *Smalltalk-80: The Interactive Programming Environment.* Reading, MA: Addison-Wesley.

Kotovsky, K., Hayes, J. R., & Simon, H. A. (1985). Why are some problems hard? Evidence from tower of Hanoi. *Cognitive Psychology,* 248-294.

Newell, A., & Simon, H. A. (1972). *Human problem solving*. Englewood Cliffs, NJ: Prentice-Hall.

Rosson, M. B., Carroll, J. M., & Bellamy, R. K. (1990). Smalltalk scaffolding: A case study of minimalist instruction. *Proceedings of the CHI '90 Conference on Human Factors in Computing Systems.* Seattle, WA: Association for Computing Machinery.

Singley, M. K. (in press). The reification of goal structures in a calculus tutor: Effects on problem solving performance. *Interactive Learning Environments,* 44-66.

Singley, M. K., & Anderson, J. R. (in preparation). *Promoting abstract representations in algebra word problem solving*. Pittsburgh, PA: Department of Psychology, Carnegie-Mellon University.

Sweller, J. (1986). *Cognitive load during problem solving: Effects on learning*. Sydney: University of New South Wales.

Human–Computer Interaction - INTERACT '90
D. Diaper et al. (Editors)
Elsevier Science Publishers B.V. (North-Holland)

WHY PROGRAM COMPREHENSION IS (OR IS NOT) AFFECTED BY SURFACE FEATURES

Barbee T. Mynatt

Computer Science Department
Bowling Green State University
Bowling Green, OH 43403 USA

The literature contains a variety of conflicting reports on the effect of various surface features such as variable naming style, indenting and commenting on program comprehension. In some cases these features appear to aid comprehension as intended, and in other cases they do not. Studies done at Bowling Green State University, reported here, have likewise shown conflicting outcomes. Pennington's (1987) model of programmer comprehension based on text structure knowledge is used to reconcile many of the results. According to her model different levels of knowledge, ranging from operational to functional, are extracted during comprehension. It was hypothesized that poor variable names would affect a programmer's comprehension of function, but would not affect the other sorts of knowledge. An experiment comparing comprehension of programs using either meaningful or nonsense variable names found the predicted result. The implications of the results vis-a-vis the true effects of surface features are discussed.

INTRODUCTION

It has been approximately 20 years since the systematic study of the psychology of programming began (see Sheil, 1981, for a review of early work in the area). Studies have ranged over topics including programming notation, programming practices, and programming tasks such as debugging and design. From the earliest stages, it has been apparent that program comprehension is a central issue to these topics. Program notation and programming practices should influence program understanding. Programming tasks such as debugging and modification require program comprehension. Shneiderman and Mayer's (1979) syntactic/semantic model of programmer behavior, for example, recognizes the central role of program comprehension in many programming tasks.

One facet of programming that raised immediate interest was the relationship of programming practices such as commenting, indenting and variable naming to the comprehension of programs. An understanding of how these factors affect comprehension could be important in two domains. First, the results could be used by software engineers as empirical bases for programming guidelines. Currently, most style guidelines are based on convention and intuition (e.g., Kernighan and Plauger, 1974). If researchers could show the actual value of following certain practices, organizations might be more likely to adopt strict guidelines and programmers might be more willing to forego a personal style and adopt the new guidelines. Second, the research could provide insights into the cognitive processes used by programmers in comprehending code, and, eventually, into how code is written and maintained. For example, evidence that language-structure-based indenting aids comprehension (compared to no indenting or random indenting) would suggest that the hierarchy implied by the indenting corresponds in some way to the mental representation build by a programmer through comprehension.

As research reports began to appear, however, it became clear that factors related to programming practice were not as powerful as might be expected. While some significant results turned up, many experiments failed to show the expected effects. That this state of affairs was unexpected and frustrating is illustrated by the following quotes:

"Although the evidence for the utility of comments is equivocal, it is unclear what other pattern of results could have been expected. Clearly, at some level comments *have* to be useful." (Sheil, 1981, p. 111)

"...the body of research they surveyed fails to provide clear experimental confirmation for what every programmer knows: a program's appearance dramatically effects its comprehensibility and usability." (Baecker and Marcus, 1986, p. 51)

"... we cannot yet prove with hard empirical evidence that these methods of display make programs more readable, comprehensible and maintainable. We can only submit that the figures in this paper...provide compelling visual evidence of the appropriateness and efficacy of the proposed techniques." (Baecker and Marcus, 1986, p. 57)

As suggested by these quotes, it seems obvious and intuitive to at least some people that programming practices are important determinants of comprehension. And if experimental data will not show it, then common sense and "compelling visual evidence" will.

PRIOR RESEARCH

Before exploring possible causes of these conflicting findings, let us look more closely at some examples of research that have been done on the effects of programming practices on comprehension.

A few published studies have attempted to explore the effects of variable naming styles on program comprehension. An early study by Weissman (1974) explored six different factors related to program understanding. Five of the ten experiments reported by Weissman examined variable naming. He used three styles of naming: long mnemonic, short mnemonic and meaningless. Different versions of the same program were created using the three variable-name styles and different groups of second-year student subjects carried out hand executions. Although the results of the five studies were conflicting and significant results were not always found, Weissman concluded that both the short and long mnemonic names were better than the meaningless names, and the long mnemonics were slightly better than the short ones. However, in subjective ratings, the subjects with the long mnemonic names rated themselves higher in performance than the other groups.

In an experiment reported by Shneiderman (1980), the use of short mnemonic variable names and meaningless names was compared for novice FORTRAN programmers using a comprehension quiz. The mnemonic names produced significantly higher quiz scores than the meaningless names. A second similar study used intermediate-level students and a debugging task. No significant effects were found due to the use of mnemonic variable names. Likewise, Sheppard, Curtis, Milliman & Love (1979) found no evidence that mnemonic names aided professional programmers in memorizing FORTRAN programs.

An experiment done at Bowling Green State University by Michael Rudd looked at the effects of different sorts of variable names on program comprehension by beginning programmers. Alternate versions of a short Pascal program to find the minimum, maximum and sum of a series of input values were created. In one version the variable names were meaningful in terms of the purpose of the program. In a second version meaningless single-letter names were used. In a third version, nonsense words such as Dog and Cat were used as variable names; and in the fourth version misleading names (e.g., Min for the maximum value) were used. The subjects were told to study the program until they felt they understood the program, then answer a set of comprehension questions without referring back to the program. There was a significant effect of variable name type. The misleading names (mean correct = 7.41 out of 12) and the meaningful names (mean = 7.50) both produced higher comprehension scores than the meaningless (mean = 5.45) and the nonsense names (mean = 5.50). While the effect of the meaningful names was expected, the high comprehension associated with the misleading names was unexpected. One explanation for this unexpected finding is that although the misleading names were connected to the "wrong" variables, they nonetheless tipped the reader off as to the function of the program. The reader was able to infer the purpose of the program and then sort out the names.

A second study done at Bowling Green (BGSU Study 2) examined the effect of different sorts of variable names on program understanding using a debugging task instead of a comprehension quiz. The types of variable names used were meaningful, meaningless (single letters) and misleading (related to a different problem domain). In this study, second-semester computer science majors were asked to spend up to 25 minutes searching a 116-line Pascal program for "3 to 6 errors". In fact, 5 errors of various sorts were seeded in the program. The subjects also rated how confident they were that they had found all of the errors in the program, and how well they understood the program. The subjects examining the program with meaningful names found a mean of 3.31 errors, while the meaningless variable names produced a mean of 2.87 and the misleading, 2.13. These means were significantly different using ANOVA, $F(2,41) = 7.41$, $p < .01$). There were no overall differences on the subjective ratings concerning confidence of finding all errors or program understanding.

Another group of experimenters at Bowling Green (BGSU Study 3) argued that procedures and parameters might represent more semantically important components of a program than simple, local variables and thus might be more affected by the "goodness" of their names. To test this idea, they created three forms of a Pascal program consisting of two procedures, one function and a main program. One version used meaningful parameter and procedure names, a second used ambiguous names and a third used meaningless names (one or two characters). Three groups of junior-level students (a total of 33 subjects) were given up to 20 minutes to study the program and answer multiple-choice questions on a comprehension quiz. Dependent measures were scores on the quiz and time to complete the task. No significant effects were found.

Finally, an experiment at Bowling Green (BGSU Study 4) also looked at variable naming, but combined variable naming and the presence or absence of comments. The comments included both module headers and line comments. Two levels of variable naming were used: meaningful and meaningless, thus creating four experimental conditions. It was expected that the group with the meaningful variable names and comments would exhibit the best performance. A 52-line Pascal program consisting of three procedures and a main program formed the basis of the materials.

The subjects were 31 students in a senior-level data base course. The subjects were given a maximum of 30 minutes to study the program and answer a set of program comprehension questions. They concluded by rating how difficult it was to understand the program. Dependent variables included a score for the comprehension questions, time to complete the task, and a difficulty rating. No main effects or interactions were significant for any of the dependent variables.

Results from other studies of commenting have produced mixed results. Shneiderman (1977) found that high-level comments were of significant help in a FORTRAN program modification task compared to low-level (line) comments. On the other hand, Sheppard, Curtis, Milliman & Love (1979) found that neither high level nor low level comments had any significant effects on either total time or accuracy in a modification task.

A number of studies have looked at the effects of source code indenting on program comprehension or tasks requiring program comprehension (e.g., debugging or reconstruction). Some of these studies found a significant effect (Norcio, 1981; Miara, Musselman, Navarro & Shneiderman, 1983; and others cited in Miara, et al.), while others did not (Weissman, 1974; Love, 1977).

One approach to synthesizing these disparate result might be to isolate methodological differences and/or subject variables. However, the weakness of the effects and the counterintuitive nature of some of these findings calls out for a more basic explanation. What is it about the underlying cognitive processes involved in comprehension that makes the effect of surface features such as variable naming and indenting so elusive? Pennington (1987, 1988) proposes that programmers have various kinds of information available after studying program text and that these different types of knowledge have different mental representations. She suggests that programmers' comprehension typically is based on text structure knowledge, and is achieved "bottom up". Comprehension is built up from a recognition of operations, through control flow and understanding of local purpose. More specifically, Pennington identified five levels of knowledge, including:

- operation: actions the program performs at the level of source code
- control flow: execution sequence of the program
- dataflow: the series of transformations data objects undergo
- state: connections between execution of an action and the state of all aspects of the program that are necessarily true at that point in time
- function: relations concerning the main goals and subgoals of the program.

Major functions and goal information are available only after lower-level relations have been acquired.

To test these ideas, Pennington had expert programmers read eight 15-line program segments for a short period of time. They then answered a series of true-false questions on the segments, followed by free-recall of the segment. The study-test sequence was repeated three times in a row for each of the eight program segments. A recognition test followed each block of three trials. The true-false questions probed all of the five levels of knowledge. She found that subjects made the most errors on questions concerning state and function, and fewer on those related to the lower-levels of knowledge. She concluded that these findings, combined with those from the other dependent variables, support the idea that comprehension of the lower-levels of knowledge precedes understanding of program functions.

Assuming that comprehension proceeds as Pennington suggests, one can ask the question "What would be the effect of good versus bad variable names on program comprehension?" By definition, good variable names relate to the functions performed by the program. Therefore, good variable names should enhance understanding of program function, while bad variable names should hinder such understanding. However, understanding of operations, control flow, data flow and state information can all be achieved independently of understanding of function. Therefore, bad variable names should not inhibit comprehension of these levels of knowledge. An experiment directly testing this reasoning is presented below.

METHOD

Subjects: Subjects were 43 computer science majors currently enrolled in two sections of the author's advanced programming course. The course is the second programming course the students are required to take and uses Pascal. The experiment was administered at the beginning of the fourth week of the term. The students were assured of anonymity, and were given a few points towards their total course points for participating.

Materials: Two 21-line Pascal programs, each consisting of a main program and one procedure, were created. One program (program Alpha) reads in a sentence typed in capital letters and ending with a period, counts the occurrence of each letter of the alphabet, and displays the occurrences. The second program (program Beta) reads in three different integers, sorts them by finding the minimum, maximum and middle values, and displays the sorted order. The *writeln* statements which display the final results were altered so that they contained no explicit verbal clues as to the purpose of the program. Two versions of each program were created. One version used variable names meaningful to the function of the program (e.g., Nextchar and Occurrence for program Alpha; Min and Max for program Beta). (See Table 1.) The second version substituted single, distinctive random letters for every variable name and a three-letter word for the procedure name. All programs were indented to reflect the structure of the code, and none contained comments.

TABLE 1

The Meaningful Variable Name Version of Program Alpha

```
program Alpha (input, output);
type Counters = array ['A'..'Z'] of integer;
var Occurrence: Counters; Letter: 'A'..'Z';

procedure CountChars (var Occurrence: Counters);
var Nextchar: char;
begin
   writeln ('Enter a sentence using all capital letters.
      End with a period.');
   read (Nextchar);
   while Nextchar <> '.' do
      begin
         if ('A' <=Nextchar) and (Nextchar <='Z')
         then Occurrence[Nextchar] :=
            Occurrence[Nextchar] + 1;
         read (Nextchar)
      end;
   readln; writeln
end;

begin
   for Letter := 'A' to 'Z' do Occurrence[Letter] := 0;
   CountChars (Occurrence);
   for Letter := 'A' to 'Z' do writeln ( Letter,
      Occurrence[Letter])
end.
```

TABLE 2

Sample Questions for the Meaningful Version of Program Alpha

TYPE	QUESTION
Operation	Is the value of Nextchar compared to 'Z'?
Control Flow	Is each cell of the array Occurrence displayed before the procedure CountChars is called?
State	When the procedure CountChars is exited, will Nextchar have the value '.' ?
Functional	Is the frequency of each letter in the input sentence counted?

A pool of 30 true-false questions concerning each program was created. The questions were constructed to probe four of the five categories of program information proposed by Pennington (1987). The middle category, data flow, was not tested to reduce the overall number of questions asked, and because the predicted effect is for only one of the five possible types of questions (functional). Nine questions related to Operations, 6 to Control Flow, 6 to State and 9 to Function. (See Table 2 for sample questions.) The 30 questions were randomly divided into three sets (Sets A, B and C), with the restriction that each set contain 3 Operations, 2 Control Flow, 2 State and 3 Function category questions. The questions were altered to reflect the appropriate variable names for the program they accompanied. Each set of 10 questions was randomized and printed on a separate page.

Booklets were constructed which contained materials for two replications of a mini-session. Each mini-session consisted of three copies of the program alternating with one of each of the three sets of appropriate questions. All possible orders of the three sets were used as equally as possible. For example, some booklets contained the order ABC, others BCA, etc. Each booklet contained one mini-session which dealt with a meaningful variable program, and another mini-session dealing with the meaningless variable names. Booklets containing all four possible combinations of program (Alpha or Beta) and variable naming (meaningful or meaningless) were created.

Procedure: Subjects were instructed to read the programs until a signal to turn the page was given. At that time, they were to turn the page and answer the 10 true-false questions. They were instructed to guess if necessary, and to be sure to answer all ten questions. At the signal, they were to turn the page and study the program again. They were told the study/question cycle would be repeated a total of six times and that they should never turn back to a previous page. Following Pennington's procedure, the subjects were given 1.5 minutes to study the program. Two minutes was allotted to answer the true-false questions. Thus, the entire task required 21 minutes.

RESULTS

Each subject's responses were scored for percent correct by question type by program (Alpha or Beta). While the responses were being scored, it was discovered that one of the Alpha program questions (a state-type question) and 2 of the Beta program questions (one operational and one functional) were somewhat ambiguous. These items were excluded from further consideration.

A MANOVA was used to test for overall differences among the question types. This test was significant $F(7,42) = 6.46$, $p < .01$). Individual ANOVAs were then used to look for specific effects. Overall, program Beta produced significantly higher scores (mean percent correct= .798) than program Alpha (mean = .711), $F(1,42) = 20.08$, $p < .001$, indicating that program Beta was somewhat easier to understand than program Alpha. Overall, there was no difference between each subject's first program scores (regardless of whether the subject had Alpha or Beta first) and her/his second program scores. This indicates there was no overall practice effect due to working through two mini-sessions. There was a significant main effect of trials, $F(2,84) = 7.30$, $p < .002$. The overall mean percent correct on trials 1, 2 and 3 was .698, .734 and .782, respectively. This indicates that subjects were understanding more about each program as trials progressed within each mini-session.

Of greatest interest, however, is the scores on the different types of questions as a function of variable-naming style. Figure 1 shows the mean percent correct for each of the four question types for the programs with meaningful variable names and for the programs using nonsense names. As predicted, variable naming style had a significant effect only on functional questions, $F(1,42) = 8.81$, $p < .005$. (The other three comparisons were all nonsignificant.) This suggests that poor variable names slow down or disrupt the acquisition of program function knowledge, but *do not* disrupt acquisition of lower-level knowledge.

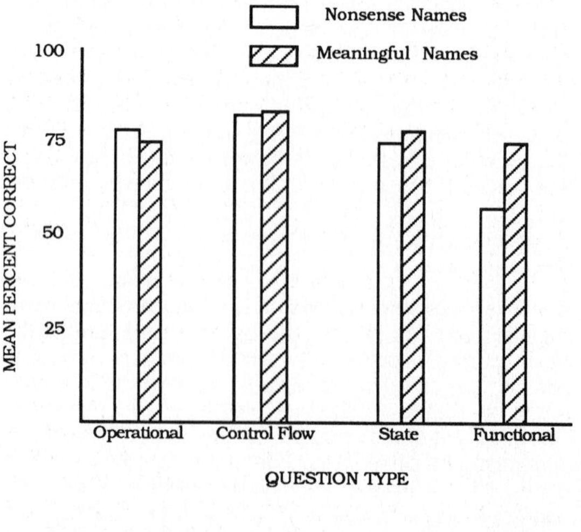

FIGURE 1 : Mean percent correct answers on four different types of program comprehension questions as a function of variable naming style used in the program.

There was one way in which the present results did not replicate Pennington's 1987 study. She found that performance was worse on state and functional questions than on operations and control flow questions. In the present study the mean percent correct for the four types of questions for the meaningful variable name programs are all approximately equal. Analyses and examination of the data did not indicate that the relative performance was different across trials or by program. The cause of this discrepancy is unclear, although it might be related to the fact that Pennington used experts, while the current study used novices.

DISCUSSION

The results show, perhaps surprisingly, that variable naming style affects the comprehension of only one of at least four different sorts of knowledge programmers glean from reading programs. Poor variable names produced decreased comprehension of program function, but did not affect the programmers' understanding of operational, control flow or state information.

The present findings offer problems for a model of program comprehension based on plans (e.g., Soloway & Ehrlich, 1984). This model says that comprehension proceeds by the recognition of patterns that implement known programming plans. Plans represent functional units. These plans are activated by partial pattern matching, and additional details are either sought or assumed. Plans have been used to explain why and how experts chunk programs during free recall. Plan knowledge is used to encode the functions of the program to be recalled. Details of the program need not be encoded, because the programmer need only expand the recalled plan to reconstruct details. Using a plan-based comprehension model, poor variable names should disrupt the recognition of plans, and thus the build up of chunks in memory.

Let us consider whether the present results and Pennington's model of program comprehension can help explain the results of existing experiments. Clearly, the findings vis-a-vis variable-naming have been inconclusive. Some studies find an effect, while others do not. One explanation, assuming Pennington is correct, is that some studies used dependent measures that tested comprehension of the programs' functions, while others tested comprehension at lower levels, and still others tested a mixture of levels. If a study tested solely or primarily functional knowledge, then Pennington's theory would predict an effect of variable naming. If a study tested a mixture of levels of comprehension, the failure of variable names to effect comprehension of the lower-level knowledge would obscure the effect of the good names on comprehension of function.

Some support for these notions comes from the study by Sheppard, et al. (1979), which found no evidence that mnemonic variable names aided professional programmers in memorizing FORTRAN programs of approximately 50 lines. Normally, one would expect that mnemonic names would help experts form chunks, thus enabling them to more rapidly and completely memorize the programs, as outlined above. This presupposes, however, that chunks are only based on program functions. Pennington's theory suggests that their are other sorts of knowledge and other sorts of mental representations that comprise the comprehension process. The fact that the task asked for line-by-line memorization may have actually caused the increased use of these other sorts of knowledge representations, obscuring the effects of variable naming. Another study (Schmidt, 1983) compared recall of meaningful-structured code, structured-but-meaningless code, and randomly arranged lines of code. The randomly arranged lines were most poorly recalled, while there was no difference in recall of the two types of structured code. Pennington might say that the structured but "meaningless" code in fact had many understandable (meaningful) components, and lacked only functional meaning.

This model of comprehension also suggests why the study of the effects of style differences on debugging (BGSU Study 2) showed an effect of style. A programmer arguably requires an understanding of a program's functions to effectively debug. Poor variable names may reduce such comprehension.

In summary, recent models of program comprehension which suggest that comprehension is based on text structure knowledge offer an insight into why variations in surface features do not always have a profound effect on comprehension. As these models become more fully articulated, they should afford guidance for programming practice as well as explanations of program comprehension.

ACKNOWLEDGEMENTS

Although they are too numerous to list, I would like to acknowledge the contributions of the students who designed and carried out the research reported in the introduction. Special thanks to Keith Instone and Kathy Falgout for their aid in data analysis. Thanks also to my colleague Laura Marie Leventhal for her many-faceted assistance.

REFERENCES

Baecker, R. & Marcus, A. (1986) Design principles for the enhanced presentation of computer program source test. *Proceedings of Human Factors in Computer Systems*, ACM: Washington, D.C., 51-58.

Kernighan, B. W. & Plauger, P. J. (1978) *The Elements of Programming Style*. New York: McGraw-Hill.

Love, T. (1977) An experimental investigation of the effect of program structure on program understanding. *Proceedings of the ACM Conference on Language Design for Reliable Software*, ACM: Washington, D.C., 105-113.

Miara, R. J., Musselman, J. A., Navarro, J. A. & Shneiderman, B. (1983) Program indentation and comprehensibility. *Communications of the ACM*, 26(11), 861-867.

Norcio, A. F. (1981) Indentation, documentation and programmer comprehension. *Proceedings of Human Factors in Computer Systems*, ACM: Washington, D.C., 118-120.

Pennington, N. (1987) Stimulus structures and mental representations in expert comprehension of computer programs. *Cognitive Psychology*, 19, 295-341.

Pennington, N. (1988) Comprehension Strategies in Programming. In G. Olson, S. Sheppard & E. Soloway (Eds.) *Empirical Studies of Programmers: Second Workshop*. Norwood, N.J.: Ablex Publishing, 114-131.

Schmidt, A. L. (1983) *Comprehension of computer programs by expert and novice programmers*. Unpublished doctoral dissertation, Southern Illinois University, Carbondale, IL.

Sheil, B. A. (1981) The psychological study of programming. *ACM Computing Surveys*, 13(1), 101-120.

Sheppard, S., Curtis, B., Milliman, P. & Love, T. (1979) Modern coding practices and programmer performance, *IEEE Computer*, 12, 41-49.

Shneiderman, B. (1980) *Software Psychology*, Cambridge, MA: Winthrop Publishers.

Shneiderman, B. & Mayer, R. (1979) Syntactic/semantic interactions in programmer behavior: A model and experimental results. *International Journal of Computer Information Science*, 7, 219-239.

Soloway, E. & Ehrlich, K. (1984) Empirical studies of programming knowledge. *IEEE Transactions on Software Engineering*, SE-10, 595-609.

Weissman, L. M. (1974) Psychological complexity of computer programs: An experimental methodology. *ACM SIGPLAN Notices*, 6(June), 25-36.

Human–Computer Interaction – INTERACT '90
D. Diaper et al. (Editors)
Elsevier Science Publishers B.V. (North-Holland)

The Generalized Unification Parser: Modelling the parsing of notations

T R G Green and Andrea Borning

MRC Applied Psychology Unit, 15 Chaucer Road, Cambridge, UK

Experienced readers of notations pick out structures such as 'plans' or 'clichés'. It has been claimed that these are easier to perceive in some notations than others, making some notations more 'role-expressive'. We present a computational model of parsing, derived from a natural language parsing model, which has been applied to programming clichés and is capable of using typographical features as parsing aids. Preliminary results suggest that languages where cliché-structures are marked by lexical key-words (e.g. the Pascal family) are easier to parse than languages where cliché-structures are not marked by surface cues (e.g. Prolog), and more significantly, that the difference will increase rapidly with the complexity of the program. Experiments are in progress to test this prediction, which implies that support tools for illuminating program structure may be needed.

Introduction

An experienced programmer quickly perceives 'beacons' which give clues as to the function of a program (e.g. exchanges of values suggest a sort algorithm), and part of the process of program comprehension appears to be driven by such beacons (Wiedenbeck, 1986). The comparison with expert perception of chess configurations has often been made. We assume that this is true for other notational systems. This paper takes steps towards a theory of structural obviousness in notations. What is required is a theory of obviousness not just at the level of syntax, but at the level of 'programming plans' (also called schemas or clichés, depending on the type of notation and on the author's predilection).

Gilmore and Green (1988) claimed that notations differ in the degree to which they reveal or obscure the functional role of components. This dimension was called by them 'role-expressiveness' and has been made part of Green's framework of 'cognitive dimensions of notations' (Green, 1989). For a notation to be highly role-expressiveness it needs more than structural obviousness (the programmer needs not only to discover the structures but also to discover what functions they serve), but clearly, locating the structures is a first step.

If we are to understand this aspect of cognition, and ultimately to make use of it in designing effective notations and support environments, we need to model it and to test our predictions. We propose a model of parsing (Generalized Unification Parsing, or GUP) which possesses the following properties:

it derives from a cognitive model of natural language parsing, and therefore has 'coherence validity' – it does not propose special mental arrangements solely for the purposes of HCI;
it can handle the syntax of programming languages;
it can operate at the cliché (plan) level;
it can operate on visually presented material, accounting for the help given by typographic cues such as indenting;
and it makes intuitively plausible predictions which can be empirically tested.

Relationships between parsing and comprehension

We shall distinguish between *parsing* and *comprehension.* Although the model we propose is able to search for typical clichés, it is not a theory of comprehension. Our model is strictly limited to putting together surface components of the text and looking for patterns which can be assembled into possible clichés. Pennington (1987a) showed that program comprehension involves creating a model of the effects of the program in terms of the domain in which the program operates. Our model does none of that; nor does our model do any genuine data-flow analysis to be sure that what it perceives as clichés really are such. The model describes the programmer's perception of what *look like* programming units. When appearances are misleading, it will be fooled – just as a programmer would also be fooled at first.

Now, it is no longer fashionable to propose staged theories of human language perception – that is, theories in which the listener/reader first parses for syntax, then comprehends the meaning. It is widely accepted by psycholinguists that language perception involves many interleaved processes. We share that view. But it is noticeable that the working computational models that psycholinguists use are almost without exception models of sentence parsing, rather than of comprehension (e.g. Frazier and Fodor, 1978; Marcus, 1980; Kempen and Vosse, 1989). It has proved convenient to maintain a separation between these research areas, for the time being, and we shall continue this tradition.

Why use a natural language parser?

The differences between programming language and natural language (NL) are often very considerable. Programming languages have a smaller vocabulary and a smaller range of syntactic constructions. The parse tree of a entire program could easily be huge, far larger than normal sentence structures, but of course programmers do not necessarily attempt to parse the whole thing as one utterance; instead they work on selected parts. In contrast, human NL sentence parsing works with units that are well-bounded and quite small. Parsing a program may be more like discourse processing than sentence parsing, in that discourse processing implies pieces together related utterances which are complete in themselves. Yet another difference is that programming languages make heavy use of constructions where the same identifier is mentioned twice (e.g. X := X + 1), or other devices for the same purpose. NL rarely mentions the same material more than once per sentence except by using anaphora.

One might well ask, therefore, why we have chosen the quixotic-seeming course of trying to stuff a highly artificial notation down the throat of a natural language parser. An immediate reason for doing so is simply that research on the perception and imposition of structure has been done mainly on NL. True, many linguists, psycholinguists, and even neuropsychologists consider NL to be special, and would raise eyebrows at this extension, pointing for instance to research on the various types of dyslexia (Shallice, 1988). However, we believe that there are likely to be strong similarities between the way one part of the human cognitive architecture functions and the way another part functions; so the properties that cause the distinctive phenomena of NL parsing (such as 'minimal attachment') are likely to cause parallel phenomena in processing artificial languages, and indeed the principles of NL parsing seem to work well in their new domain. To say that is not to dispute the possible specialness of NL.

Unification Parsing

We shall use as our starting point a model of NL parsing developed by Kempen and Vosse (1989). This parser uses unification grammar (Kay, 1985) as its underlying formalism, according to which the entries in our mental lexicon are marked with features to indicate their syntactic roles. Examples of features as used by Kempen and Vosse are case, e.g nominative; person, e.g. 3rd; category, e.g. verb, noun phrase, etc. There are also functional roles, such as subject. Each lexical entry (roughly, each sense of a word) has its own matrix of features, and each feature has a set of permitted values, e.g. gender = (masculine, feminine). To build a sentence, related entries must *unify* across all their shared features. Features unify by set intersection. Thus gender = (masculine, feminine) unifies with gender = (masculine, neuter) to yield gender = (masculine). If the intersection is null, unification fails. Kempen and Vosse's model applies unification to *segments,* which comprise two nodes (root and foot) and an arc. Parsing proceeds by unifying the root of one segment with the foot of another, thereby growing parse tress. Figures 1 and 2 illustrate two segments, with their feature matrices, and their concatenation into a structure.

So much for the underlying formalism. Now, how does the parsing process operate? They propose that as words are read, the corresponding lexical entries are located. Each entry specifies one or more segments; a verb like 'give', for example, will specify three segments, to describe the two associated noun phrases (for subject and object) and the prepositional phrase (for the recipient). These segments are placed in what they call the 'unification space' (or, more colloquially, a 'mental test-tube'). The sentence

(1) I gave Jane tea.

will generate segments corresponding to each of the four words. Each segment is given an initial activation level, which spontaneously decays during the parsing process.

As the segments arrive in the 'unification space', they are randomly brought together in a search for pieces that can be unified. (This operation is assumed to happen in parallel, although their computational realisation uses a sequential simulation.) The probability of attempting to unify any two nodes depends on their activation levels, and on a parameter S which is used to bias the parser towards unifications that preserve word order. This bias is not so much as to prevent other occurrences, and so sentence (1) could give rise to structures in which the verb 'gave' had unified its subject segment with 'I', 'Jane', or 'tea' (as in 'Tea gives Jane hiccups'). But the segment for 'I' will not unify at any other position, so the if other structures are attempted they will come to a standstill.

When two nodes unify they form a single node with an activation which is less than the sum of its constituents, so that as larger structures form activation is reduced. (This is in addition to spontaneous decay with time.)

Random unification is one component of Kempen and Vosse's theory. The other component is disintegration. Their model incorporates 'simulated annealing', by which they mean that every now and again structures are disintegrated at random. The probability that a structure will disintegrate depends on its activation value. When a tree disintegrates, its broken segment is removed from the unification space. This process they compare to the events

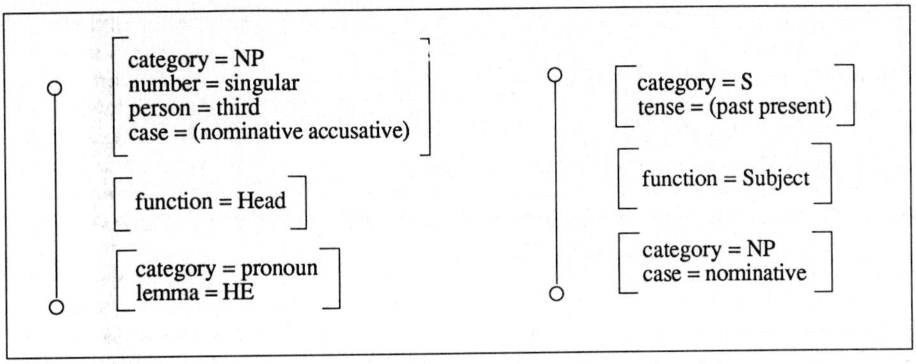

FIGURE 1. Two segments plus feature matrices (from Kempen and Vosse, 1989).

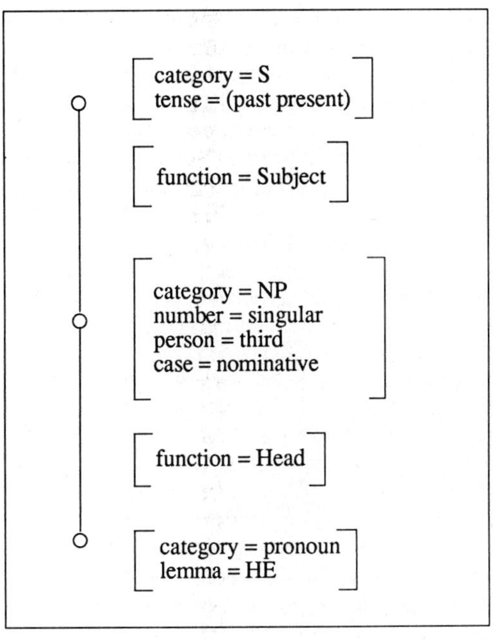

FIGURE 2. Concatenation of the segments of Figure 1 (from Kempen and Vosse, 1989).

occurring during annealing of metals, and they compare the total activation level in the unification space to the temperature of the metal: as activation falls, the structures settle down. Returning to sentence (1), parses that assign 'Jane' or 'tea' to the subject position stand a good chance of being disintegrated, allowing the system another chance. The correct parse also stands a chance of disintegration, but since it has not been blocked, the tree will be more likely to have grown larger, causing the activation level to decrease and thus improving its chances of survival. In general, better parses, ones that include more material, will settle down faster.

Finally, from all this activity they compute a metric of parsing difficulty, the percentage of correct parses obtained during a set of 100 runs. They show that their model successfully displays many of the well-known phenomena of human sentence processing; for instance, it parsed sentence (2) successfully 77 attempts, but sentence (3), which violates the 'minimal attachment' principle, was only parsed successfully 8 times.

(2) The horse raced past the barn yesterday.

(3) The horse raced past the barn fell.

(–i.e. "The horse *that was* raced past the barn fell.")

Kempen and Vosse's model offers several useful possibilities for modelling the comprehension of program texts. It can readily be adapted to modelling reading rather than listening. In reading, the reader has considerable control over the order of arrival of words, and that is particularly true of reading large documents like program texts. Certain other models of human sentence perception (such as Frazier and Fodor's 'sausage machine' model) make little sense when applied to unpaced reading. It can also used to model the focussing of attention when reading a large document, by the simple mechanism of raising the activation values of attended material.

What would a program parse look like?

Figure 3 shows a simple Basic program, performing a computation familiar in studies of novice programmers. Pennington (1987) showed that an understanding of text structure is important in comprehension of procedural languages, using Fortran and Cobol versions, but it has also been argued repeatedly by Soloway and his co-workers (e.g. Soloway and Ehrlich, 1984) that the plan-based abstraction shown in Figure 4 is a component of program comprehension. Evidence for the psychological reality of plan structures in procedural languages, in certain circumstances, has been reported by Détienne (1986), Gilmore and Green (1988), and Davies (1988). We therefore want this second abstraction to be extracted from the parsing process, as well as the first.

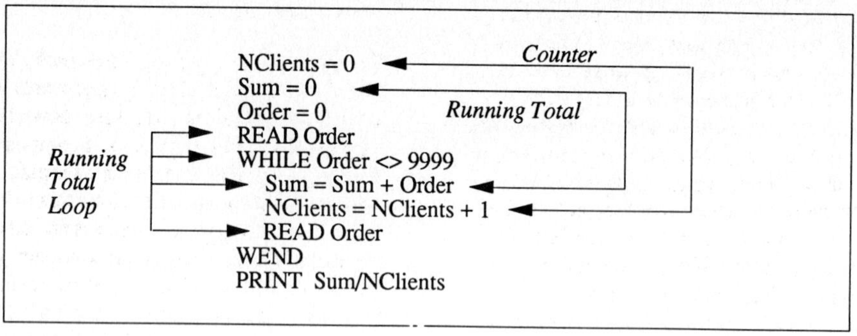

FIGURE 3: A short Basic program to compute the average value of customers' orders (no guard on division by zero), showing 'plan' structures.

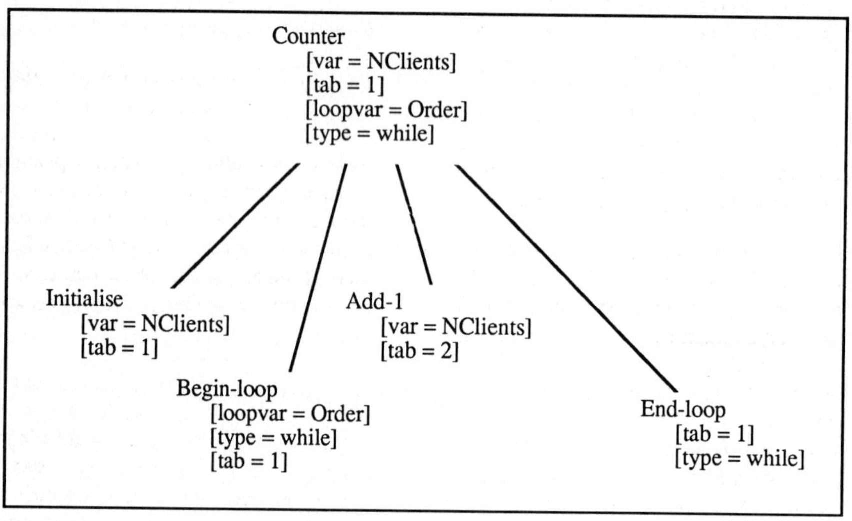

FIGURE 4: Overview of the structure representing a Counter plan. Further details lie below the nodes shown.

Although our model is only doing pattern-matching, it can easily perceive a probable instance of say a Counter plan (Figure 3). These plans have an initialisation component (something is set to zero) and an add-1 component (the same something is incremented by 1). The add-1 component must occur inside a loop, and the initialisation must occur before the loop. (We say a 'probable' instance because the pattern could be misleading, if side-effects get in the way; conversely, it is also possible to create a program that will have the same effect without meeting the pattern. This is as it should be. Our model is only supposed to make first guesses.)

Generalized Unification Parsing

We have extended the Kempen and Vosse model in a number of ways to make it able to parse program text, naming the resulting process 'Generalized Unification' since it preserves the general approach but has increased power. We have programmed a version of the model and an elementary grammar of procedural-language clichés. Work is ongoing to extend this grammar and to develop an equivalent grammar of Prolog clichés.

The approach works well for procedural clichés; patterns

strongly indicating Counter plans, for instance, are easily picked out (see Figure 4). They start with an *initialisation statement,* in which some identifier is set to an *exceptional value,* typically 0. (Italics denote terms used in our grammar of procedural-language clichés.) They continue with a *start-of-loop* and then with an *add-1* statement in which an identifier is set to itself plus 1. We ensure that the initialisation statement and the add-1 statement refer (probably) to the same variable by passing the identifier as a feature, which must, of course, unify. Finally, there will be an *end-of-loop*. This completes the Counter pattern. Of course extraneous material may intervene between the various components; the parser will ignore it.

We now consider the main extensions in turn.

Display-based features

There is ample evidence that the readability of programs can be enhanced by judicious use of typographic cues (Baecker and Marcus, 1983) and by colour-coded perceptual cues or by well-judged indentation cues(Gilmore and Green, 1988; Davies, 1989; van Laar, 1989). All programmers will also be acquainted with the opposite case, where the typographical cues are misleading and we misread the program in consequence! Languages with unobtrusive semicolons, like C and Pascal, are the worst offenders in this respect: a semicolon creeps in after a DO and gets overlooked.

To model this, we allow the values of features to be set by *inspection of the display*. Thus a statement "X := X + 1" will be assigned a feature for its indentation level, or for its colour coding, or for its typographical weight – aspects that are perceptually salient and do not need reasoning. The parser can then base its unification on these features as well. Moreover, we allow unification to be a probabilistic process. When nodes are brought together to consider unification, they are not certain to be unified even if their features match perfectly. Instead, we declare that the more features they have in common, the more likely they are to match. We regard these display-based features as the most important extension of the model.

Modelling 'beacons'

In our model the 'beacon' constructions, which are highly indicative of program structure, have been assigned *permanently* raised activation values in the lexicon. This will have the effect of making the model 'search' for beacons first, since they will be unified early.

More generally, we suppose that the experienced programmer or notation user knows what constructions are likely to be the most efficient ones to parse first, and that activation levels are raised for these strongly diagnostic constructions.

Beyond the sentence

Kempen and Vosse's model uses each syntactic segment no more than once per parse, as is conventional in NL parsing. However, to obtain the structure shown above, it is necessary to use the loop segment as a component of both the Running Total plan and the Counter plan. Therefore we have extended the model to allow this to happen by adding a feature called 'persistent' to certain constructions, including loops, so that once built they remain part of the Unification Space. If the loop structure is then made part of another structure, such as Running Total, a copy of the loop structure is kept available. The mental process we want to simulate, of course, is one where certain constructions are allowed to have more than one parent.

The same would be necessary if the model were used as a discourse-level parser of NL sentences, since one sentence can probably be a component of several discourse structures.

Extending the 'feature'

To make these extensions work, we have found it necessary to assume that the lexical entries contain parsing directives, which we have expressed as special features. One of these we have already noted, the 'persistence' feature. Another example is a matching directive for indentation: in the Running Total loop, the initialisation statement is expected to occur at a lower indentation level than the increment statement, so the features must be unified not by looking for identity but by looking for a greater-than relation.

Essentially, these directives can be viewed as small packets of code. As such they significantly extend the power of the parser. If unrestricted, they would allow the parser to become a universal Turing machine, exactly as ATN parsers were (since they allowed arbitrary code on any arc). By expressing them as features we have limited them to a finite set, and although a more principled form of restriction would be desirable, at least the current set clearly do not generate anything like the power of a universal Turing machine.

Interestingly, however, these directives do give the parser a more active style than the purely data-driven model of Kempen and Vosse. It appears now to occupy a promising position, somewhere between the unlimited power of a production system and the too-limited power of a conventional NL parser.

Comparative predictions

Parsing difficulty in this model will increase sharply when there are many nodes in the Unification Space that could easily be wrongly unified. This condition will occur when the programming language contains few lexical cues.

Parsing difficulty will also increase when there are few display-based features to aid parsing.

We are now in the process of extending the range and detail of our grammar of procedural-language clichés and developing a corresponding grammar for Prolog clichés. A Prolog version of the example is shown in Figure 5. It is immediately clear (even without knowing Prolog) that there are fewer distinctive constructions to help the parser, and that there are no conventions of indentation. Thus, we would expect the model to find the Prolog version harder to parse.

```
average( L, A ) :-
    sumAndCount( L, Sum, N ),  A is Sum/N.

sumAndCount( [ ], 0, 0 ).
sumAndCount( [ A|B ], S, N ) :-
    sumAndCount( B, S1, N1 ),
    S is S1 + A, N is N1 + 1.
```

FIGURE 5: The Prolog version of the program in Figure 3 has fewer lexical clues to its cliché structure.

But there is a much stronger prediction, and that concerns the composition of plan structures. Figures 6 and 7 show an extended version of the same program in which a filter plan has been introduced. The addition makes virtually no difference to the complexity of parsing the procedural version, because the keywords *if* and *then* act as signals. In the Prolog version, the lack of any distinctive features makes the number of available wrong unifications go up dramatically. We expect the model to perform very poorly on this input.

The prediction, therefore, is not just that Prolog will be harder to parse than the procedural version, but that the difference between them will increase very quickly as the program complexity increases. Certainly folklore has it that comprehending Prolog programs can be extremely difficult. Experiments are currently in progress to test these predictions, using Prolog and Modula-2.

Looking at the comparative figures, it may seem unsurprising that the Prolog version should be harder to parse. Nevertheless, we regard this as a significant prediction. Prolog has had a poor track record as a teaching language. Much attention has gone on looking for reasons, and most of the reasons proposed have been to do with the nature of the underlying model and the difficulty of determining the execution path from the program text. In consequence, extremely impressive animations of Prolog execution have

```
NClients = 0
NActive = 0
Sum = 0
READ Order
WHILE Order <> 9999
   Sum = Sum + Order
   IF Order > 0 THEN NActive = NActive + 1
   NClients = NClients + 1
   READ Order
WEND
PRINT Sum/NActive, Sum/NClients
```

FIGURE 6: The program of Figure 3 modified to compute the average of the active clients. The new plans (Running Total and Filter) are easily spotted.

```
average2( L, A1, A2 ) :-
   sumAndCount2( L, Sum, NClients, Nactive ),
   A1 is Sum/Nactive, A2 is Sum/NClients.

sumAndCount2(  [ ], 0, 0, 0 ).
sumAndCount2(  [ 0|B], S, Nt, Na ) :-
    sumAndCount2( B, S, Nt1, Na ), Nt is Nt1 + 1.
sumAndCount2(  [ A|B], S, Nt, Na ) :-
    A>0,
    sumAndCount2( B, S1, Nt1, Na1 ),
    S is S1 + A, Nt is Nt1 + 1 , Na is Na1 + 1.
```

FIGURE 7: Prolog version of Figure 6. Note the extensive changes from Figure 5. The cliché structure is even less evident.

been developed (Brayshaw and Eisenstadt, in press). However, we do not know of previous suggestions that the difficulty of parsing Prolog correctly may have contributed to the difficulty experienced by novices. A corollary of our work would be that a Prolog parser which picked out and labelled familiar clichés could significantly assist the learner (and could also assist the experienced programmer in reading a large program), just as Van Laar's 'Colour Coding Support Tool' assisted comprehension of Pascal (Van Laar, 1989). This would be a Prolog version of the 'Programmer's Torch' project (Green and Cornah, 1984) which was designed to illuminate cliché structures in Basic programs, but which unfortunately was never brought to a testable form.

Conclusions

The Generalized Unification Parser has extended an existing NL parsing model to handle programming clichés. By doing so, we have shown that the model has potential for handling elementary forms of discourse analysis and can be made responsive to aspects of typographical layout that have not previously been taken into account. It has led us to make a powerful and testable prediction about the relative difficulty of two programming languages as a function of complexity of program, and it has suggested that a previously unconsidered source of beginners' difficulty with Prolog could be difficulty in parsing.

Norman (1986) proposed a now well-known analysis of 'stages of user activity', and it has many times been remarked subsequently that HCI research has had far more to offer on the side of action planning and execution than on the side of perceiving and interpreting. The GUP is a contribution towards filling that gap. Specifically, it takes us closer to understanding what makes some notations 'role-expressive'.

Acknowledgements We have relentlessly picked our colleagues' brains, and wish to thank in particular George Houghton, Chuck Clifton, and William Marslen-Wilson for helpful conversations, advice, and information.

References

Baecker, R. and Marcus, A. (1983) On enhancing the interface to the source code of computer programs. *Proc. CHI '83 Conf on Human Factors in Computing Systems.* New York: ACM.

Brayshaw, M. and Eisenstadt, M. (1989) A practical tracer for Prolog. Technical Report no 42, Human Cognition Research Laboratory, Open University, Milton Keynes, U.K. To appear in *International Journal of Man-Machine Studies.*

Clifton, C. E. (1990) The use of lexical information in sentence comprehension. Paper presented at Eighth European Workshop on Cognitive Neuropsychology, Bressanone, Italy.

Davies, S. P. (1989) Skill levels and strategic differences in plan comprehension and implementation in programming. In A. Sutcliffe and L. Macaulay (Eds.) *People and Computers V.* Cambridge University Press.

Détienne, F. (1986) Program understanding and knowledge organization: the influence of acquired schemata. *Proc, 3rd European Conference on Cognitive Ergonomics,* Paris. Rocquencourt, France: INRIA.

Frazier, L. and Fodor, J. D. (1978) The sausage machine: a new two-stage parsing model. *Cognition,* **6**, 291-325.

Gilmore, D. J. and Green, T. R. G. (1988) Programming plans and programming expertise. Quarterly J. Exp. Psychol. 40A, 423-442.

Green, T. R. G. (1989) Cognitive dimensions of notations. In A. Sutcliffe and L. Macaulay (Eds.) *People and Computers V.* Cambridge University Press.

Green, T. R. G. and Cornah, A. (1984) The Programmer's Torch. In B. Shackel vEd.) *Interact '84 - Conf. on Computer-Human Factors.* Elsevier.

Kay, M. (1985) Parsing in functional unification grammar. In D.R. Dowty, L. Karttunen and A.M. Zwicky (Eds.), *Natural Language Parsing: Psychological, computational, and theoretical perspectives.* Cambridge University Press.

Kempen, G. and Vosse, T. (1989) Incremental syntactic tree formation in human sentence processing: an interactive architecture based on activation decay and simulated annealing. *Cahiers de la Fondation Archives Jean Piaget.*

Marcus. M. P. (1980) *A Theory of Syntactic Recognition for Natural Language.* MIT Press.

Norman, D. A. (1986) Cognitive engineering. In D.A. Norman and S.W. Draper (Eds.) *User-Centered System Design.* Erlbaum.

Pennington, N. (1987a) Comprehension strategies in programming. In G. M. Olson, S. Sheppard, and E. Soloway (Eds.), *Empirical Studies of Programmers: Second Workshop.* Ablex.

Pennington, N. (1987b) Stimulus structures and mental representations in expert comprehension of computer programs. *Cognitive Psychology,* **19**,295-341.

Shallice, T. (1988) *From Neuropsychology to Mental Structure.* Cambridge University Press.

Soloway, E. and Ehrlich, K. (1984) Empirical studies of programming knowledge. *IEEE Trans. on Software Engineering,* **SE-10**, 595-609.

Van Laar, D. (1989) Evaluating a colour coding support tool. In A. Sutcliffe and L. Macaulay (Eds.) *People and Computers V.* Cambridge University Press.

Wiedenbeck, S. (1986) Processes in computer program comprehension. In E. Soloway and E. Iyengar (Eds.) *Empirical Studies of Programming.* Ablex.

Human–Computer Interaction – INTERACT '90
D. Diaper et al. (Editors)
Elsevier Science Publishers B.V. (North-Holland)

Program Comprehension Beyond the Line

Scott P. Robertson, Erle F. Davis,
Kyoko Okabe, and Douglas Fitz-Randolf

Psychology Department
Rutgers University
Busch Campus
New Brunswick, NJ 08903

Comprehension of computer program code has often been compared with text comprehension. We argue, though, that the requirements of code comprehension make it more of a problem-solving task that happens to use text-like material. We present data on search patterns and reading times in code comprehension that support this view. Specifically, we found that programmers examine code in repeated cycles that cover functionally relevant units. We suggest some problem-solving goals that guide search through code and show that line scanning times vary with hypothesized problem-solving activities. In a direct comparison of programmers reading isolated lines versus lines in the context of program comprehension we show that a simple model of microstructure parsing predicts reading times better for isolated lines than for lines in the context of a program.

1. Introduction

Understanding how programmers comprehend computer program code is a challenge both to the cognitive science community and to researchers interested specifically in computer-human interaction. Several researchers have used an analogy to reading comprehension when characterizing code comprehension. For example, Mayer (1987) successfully predicted the reading times of BASIC statements using a model of microstructure parsing which has similarities to parsing models from the text comprehension literature (Kintsch, 1974). Dyck & Auernheimer (1989) extended Mayer's model to Pascal.

Other researchers have been concerned with the knowledge structures used by programmers during code comprehension (Ehrlich & Soloway, 1984; Pennington, 1987; Rist, 1989; Robertson & Yu, in press). Task knowledge and plan knowledge have emerged as the most important information structures used by programmers, although theories of the content and application rules of this knowledge remain under-developed.

We have undertaken to examine code comprehension as a problem-solving process rather than a reading process. By this we mean a process of strategic search through code which results in the construction of a representation of the code's funtional properties. In this view, syntactic parsing and even the application of knowledge structures are parts of a larger process in which search strategies and comprehension goals play an important role and change the processing that occurs when particular lines are studied.

In the study reported here we allowed subjects to search through a program in an attempt to understand it. We collected data on their search patterns and line-by-line reading times. Also we collected verbal protocol data from another group of subjects who examined the same code. Our goal was to show that the behavior of programmers studying code is better understood when strategic goals related to problem solving and search are considered. We hoped to show a reduction in the effectiveness of simple models of line-by-line comprehension when programmers were actually studying a long program.

2. Method

2.1. Subjects

Fifteen graduate students in computer science at Rutgers University were recruited by advertisement. Each was paid for participation. The subjects were assigned to one of three groups which determined how the code was presented to them and whether or not they were to provide verbal protocols.

2.2. Materials

A 136-line Pascal program that formats text was used as the stimulus material. The program consists of 9 procedures (4-28 lines) and a 29-line main section. The program was presented one line at a time on a video display terminal. By pressing the up-arrow and down-arrow keys subjects could view previous and subsequent

The work described here is sponsored by the Office of Naval Research under contract number N00014-86-K0876 from the Perceptual Sciences Program. Jurgen Koenemann and Chiung Chen Yu also contributed significantly to the project.

lines. Subjects in two of the conditions could jump to the beginning of procedures by pressing "home" (for a previous procedure) or "end" (for the next procedure). Subjects who provided verbal protocols were tape recorded as they inspected the code.

2.3. Design and Procedure

Subjects in one group viewed the lines of the program in scrambled order. Reading times for these subjects were considered to be "pure reading," reflecting only the cognitive processes required to parse and store the information in each line. A second group of subjects viewed the lines of the program in the coherent order in which it was originally written and were expected to be able to describe how it worked. Reading times and search patterns for these subjects should reflect comprehension processes beyond simple line-by-line reading. A third group of subjects viewed the lines of the program in coherent order but were instructed to talk about what they were doing as they inspected the code. Only their verbal comments and search patterns were analysed.

3. Results and Discussion of Non-Protocol Data

In this section the data from subjects who did not talk during code inspection is discussed. Reading times from these subjects reflect cognitive processes associated with reasoning about the code. We hope to demonstrate here the varied nature of cognitive processes during code comprehension.

3.1. Descriptive Information

Subjects who saw the coherent program averaged 5.6 looks at each line with a range of 2.4 to 13.6 looks/line. These subjects spent an average of 50m,16s studying the program lines (range=26m-64m,43s) while the subjects who read through the scrambled lines spent an average of only 6m,20s (range=3m,43s-10m,12s) looking at the lines.

3.2. Search Was Not Linear

Virtually every subject who viewed the coherent program made several short retrogressions through code segments. In order to summarize this phenomenon we categorized each action that the subjects performed as either a forward move (from one line to the next after another forward move), backward move (from one line to the previous line after another backward move), or switch in direction. Switches in direction were either forward-backward (a return to a previous line after a forward move), or backward-forward (a return to a subsequent line after a backward move).

Overall, about 11% of the activity of subjects involved switches in direction, 16.6% of the the search activity involved going backwards through the code, and the remaining 72.4% was forward movement. The proportions of each type of activity did not change over time suggesting that the same strategies were being used throughout the experiment.

3.3. Study involved local episodes

In order to characterize the search patterns we segmented each subject's protocol into "episodes." An episode consisted of a forward pass through a section of code, a forward-backward switch, a backward pass through the code, a backward-forward switch, and a second forward pass. Each subjects' data contained a number of episodes defined in this manner, with the mean number being 18.2 (sd=6.1). This number did not vary over quartiles, with the mean number of episodes/quartile being 4, 3.6, 5.2, and 5.4 respectively. Over one-third of subjects' activities were categorized as being within episodes.

Subjects read more quickly within episodes (mean=287ms/syllable) than they did between episodes (mean=385ms/syllable), $F(1,4)=7.96$, $p<.05$. The difference in reading times lends credence to the episode/non-episode distinction and may be due to the highly goal-directed nature of processing within episodes. Between-episode processes are likely to include more discovery processing whereas subjects are searching for particular information within episodes.

Table 1. Mean reading times (ms/syllable) across move categories.

Movement Type	Between Episodes	Within Episodes
Forward	408	———
Backward	141	146
Forward-Backward	1581	1027
Backward-Forward	569	410
First forward pass	———	387
Second forward pass	———	225
Episode begin	———	348
Episode end	———	411

The hypothesized information processing steps for each type of activity within an episode led to predictions about the time spent in each activity. We predicted that switching times would be high relative to other times because they involved decision making, and that the forward-backward switching time would be the longest since this involves hypothesis generation and planning for the episode whereas the backward-forward switching time involves only a match to the target line. We also predicted that it would take longer to read and parse a line than to check if it is a target line by some partial matching process, hence the forward moves should take longer than the backward moves.

Table 1 presents the mean time/syllable observed across all of the move types. Here we distinguished between moves occuring between episodes and within episodes. Analysis of variance showed the time differences among types of moves to be reliable, $F(3,12)=22.12$, $p<.001$ for the data between episodes and $F(6,24)=12.90$, $p<.001$ for the data within episodes. As predicted, the forward-backward switch time was longest, which we interpret as reflecting the time to make a decision to re-examine a code segment or find some information. Backward times were extremely short and, in fact, one could question whether 141-146ms/syllable is enough time to actually read the code. One possibility is that subjects' were not reading but performing a partial matching process on the lines as they searched backwards toward a target line. The backward-forward switch, though longer than other forward moves, was much shorter than the forward-backward switch. Processing at this point may involve verification of information and is not as involved as decision-making for the forward-backward switch. The second forward pass through an episode was faster than the first, possibly because processing is minimal at this stage.

3.4. Certain Lines Trigger Switch Operators

Further evidence that the episode analysis captures meaningful problem-solving activity comes from the non-randomness of types of program statements at the switching locations that define episode boundaries. We examined the "switching pairs" and categorized them according to the links that the two program statments had. For example, if a subject switched direction in a statement containing the variable "rightmost," searched backwards and then switched direction again on an earlier line also containing that variable, then the switching pairs were said to be linked by common variable names.

Twenty-three percent of the switching pairs were linked such that the first switch occured on a statement within a very local construct (like a conditional or iteration) and the second switch occured on the first line of that construct (like an "if" or "while" statement). This may be evidence that subjects are reasoning about local plan units. Twenty-one percent of the switches were between a statement within a procedure and the first line of that procedure. One interpretation of this is that subjects' are building a chunk in memory to represent the procedure itself and they are double-checking the name to store with this representation. Eighteen percent were linked by common variable names. An interpretation of this result is that subjects are building a representation of data flow (Pennington, 1987). Twelve percent were between seemingly unrelated statements within a procedure and ten percent were within a functional group within a procedure. All of the above switches, 84% of the total, were within procedure boundaries and only 6% ever crossed procedure boundaries, demonstrating the local quality of search in this task. These categories accounted for 90% of the observed switch pairs, leaving only 10% uncategorized.

3.5. Prediction of Reading Times

Regression models of reading time have been very successful in predicting text comprehension (Haberlandt & Graesser, 1985) and parsing of code microstructure (Mayer, 1987). We predicted that a simple model of microstructure parsing would be a good predictor of the reading time for scrambled lines but a poor predictor of reading time for the lines in coherent order. Our simple equation for the microstructure model is

Reading Time =
#operators
\+ #variables
\+ #commands
\+ #delimiters.

This model contains components that are completely determined by code statements in isolation and that correspond well to other models of microstructure representation.

When predicting the reading times for the scrambled lines the microstructure equation resulted in a mean multiple $R^2=.54$ (across subjects). The R^2 values were large and significant for every subject. When predicting the reading times for the lines in coherent order the microstructure equation resulted in a mean multiple $R^2=.231$. The multiple R^2 values for these subjects, though significant, were all much smaller.

Table 2. Frequenceies of comments in each move category.

	Movement Type			
	Forward	Backward	Forward-Backward	Backward-Forward
Expected Frequency	114.7	45.5	10.9	10.9
Observed Frequency	102.0	13.0	23.0	44.0

This result supports two conclusions. First, the significant proportions of variance accounted for supports the view that a microstructure analysis of the code is carried out both when subjects read scrambled lines and lines in the coherent program order. Second, however, the microstructure analysis plays a small role in explaining the observed reading times of subjects who are actually studying the code. We claim that this difference in prediction strength is the result of the application of problem-solving rules and strategic knowledge to the task of code comprehension.

This view is supported further by the observation that the proportion of variance accounted for by the microstructure equation varies considerably across movement types. The mean multiple R^2 values were .17 and .22 for forward and backward movement categories respectively between episodes, and .34, .22, and .27 for the first and second forward passes and the backward pass repectively within episodes.

4. Results and Discussion of Protocol Data

In this section some of the data from subjects who provided verbal protocols is discussed. These programmers were asked to stop whenever they wished as they looked through the code and explain what they had just done or learned. They were also encouraged to describe what they planned to do next or hoped to discover in the future.

4.1. Comparison of Movement Types

The movements of subjects in this group were also categorized into forward, backward, forward-backward, and backward-forward types. Switches in direction accounted for 12.6% of the subjects' activites, backward movements accounted for 24.8% of the activities, and the remaining 62.6% of the activities were forward movement through the code. A comparison with the same percentages for the non-protocol subjects (section 3.2) suggests that the behavior of subjects who were talking was similar to the behavior of subjects who did not talk.

4.2. Distibution of Comments Across Movement Types

The five programmers in this study provided 182 comments about their activities. By assuming that the comments should be evenly distributed across the movement types by chance, it was possible to determine the expected frequencies of comments in each of the movement categories based on the proportion of movements in each category. Table 2 shows the expected frequencies and the observed frequencies of comments that occured in each movement category. There were many more comments than expected (by chance) that occured in conjunction with switches in direction x^2=138.3, p<.001. Together with the observation that line reading times tended to be very high at these positions we conclude that considerable problem-solving activity is associated with switches in direction in the search sequences.

4.3. Comment Types and Movement Categories

The programmers' verbal comments were categorized into six groups: Analyse, Assume, Question, Answer, Function, and Strategy. An *analyse* comment was one in which the programmer offered an explanation of a code segment. An *assume* comment was one in which the programmer offered a prediction about what was coming up. A *question* was a query about the code. An *answer* was a statement that could be clearly linked to an earlier question. A *function* comment was a statement about what the code did functionally. A *strategy* comment was a statement about what the programmer planned to do next, usually where they wanted to go in the program or what kind of information they wanted.

Table 3 shows the proportion of comments of each type within each movement category. The two most frequent comment types in each movement category are shown in boldface. Note that the functionality of the code was the topic of most of the programmers' comments. This was true for each type of movement except backward movements. Apparently subjects did not discover as much about code functionality when they were moving backwards. Inspection of the backward movement category shows that *questions* and *strategy* were the primary concerns when programmers regressed through the code. *Strategy* comments were also prevalent when programmers switched from the forward to the backward direction.

Table 3. Proportions of comment types within each move category.

Comment Category	Movement Type: Forward	Backward	Forward-Backward	Backward-Forward
Analyse	.078	.053	0	.074
Assume	**.219**	.158	.167	**.220**
Question	.078	**.263**	.125	.118
Answer	.094	.105	.083	.118
Function	**.422**	.158	**.250**	**.368**
Strategy	.109	**.263**	**.375**	.103
	1.0	1.0	1.0	1.0

The unequal distribution of comment types across movement categories shows that programmers had qualitatively different things in mind as they moved around in the code. We are working now on a model of programmers' goals and comprehension strategies that would account for the differences in reading times and comment types that co-occur with changes in reading direction.

5. Conclusions

In this study we demonstrated that code comprehension is not simple line-by-line reading comprehension. Instead code comprehension involves complex search strategies that persist throughout the study session. We showed that subjects structure their search activities in episodes that involve re-examination of local code segments. These episodes range over functionally meaningful units of the code typically within procedures, and these units tend to be small. Different reading times and different comment types during parts of an episode demonstrate that different operators are applied depending on the currently active problem-solving goal. Finally, we showed that models of code microstructure analysis are good for simple reading of isolated code statements, but poor as overall predictors of study time in the context of real programs and real comprehension goals.

6. References

Dyck, J., & Auernheimer, B. (1989). *Comprehension of Pascal statements by novice and expert programmers*. Poster presented at CHI-89.

Haberlandt, K., & Graesser, A. (1985). Component processes in text comprehension and some of their interactions. *Journal of Experimental Psychology: General, 114*, 357-374.

Kintsch, W. (1974). *The representation of meaning in memory*. Hillsdale, NJ: Erlbaum.

Mayer, R.E. (1987). Cognitive aspects of learning and using a programming language. In J.M. Carroll (Ed.), *Interfacing thought: Cognitive aspects of human-computer interaction*. Cambridge, MA: MIT Press.

Pennington, N. (1987). Stimulus structures and mental representations in expert comprehension of computer programs. *Cognitive Psychology, 19*, 295-341.

Rist, R. (1989). Schema creation in programming. *Cognitive Science, 13*, 389-414.

Robertson, S.P., & Yu, C.C. (in press). Common cognitive representations of program code across tasks and languages. *International Journal of Man-Machine Studies*.

Ehrlich, K., & Soloway, E. (1984). An empirical investigation of tacit plan knowledge in programming. In J.C. Thomas & M.L. Schneider (Eds.), *Human factors in computer systems*, Norwood, NJ: Ablex.

Human–Computer Interaction – INTERACT '90
D. Diaper et al. (Editors)
Elsevier Science Publishers B.V. (North-Holland)

Expert Programmers Re-establish Intentions When Debugging Another Programmer's Program

Ray Waddington

Dept. of Computing and Information Science, University of Guelph, Guelph, Ontario, Canada N1G 2W1, ray@snowhite.cis.uoguelph.ca

and

Roger Henry

Dept. of Computer Science, University of Nottingham, University Park, Nottingham NG7 2RD, UK, rbh@uk.ac.nott.cs

When discussing software debugging, some authors have discussed the experience of debugging another programmer's program as being somehow different from that of debugging one's own program. Software psychologists attempt to understand the nature of debugging expertise, but have ignored the potentially fruitful method of looking empirically at the differences between debugging in the two situations.

We discuss a model of debugging expertise which addresses the relationship of program authorship to debugging strategy. This model predicts that when debugging another programmer's program, experts will use a strategy of re-establishing the original author's intentions in order to debug it.

We report an experiment, conducted with expert programmers, which supports this prediction. We also discuss the implications of this result for the design of debugging aids to support expert programmers when they are debugging another programmer's program.

1. Introduction

Novice programmers generally spend their time debugging their own programs. In contrast expert programmers spend their time debugging other programmers' programs as well as their own, since they are more likely to be involved in software maintenance. Although it has been suggested that program authorship (i.e., whether a programmer originally wrote the program s/he is working on as opposed to working on one written by a different programmer) plays a significant role in the debugging process (e.g., Gould, 1975), software psychologists have not investigated its effect empirically.

Our contention in this paper is that a closer examination of programmers within the context of the tasks they perform is the most likely approach that will lead to more cognitively appropriate designs for software tools and environments. This is an example of user-centred design (see papers in Norman and Draper, 1986), in which the users are programmers and the software is used to help produce other software.

We have previously investigated empirically the effect of program authorship on the debugging performance of novice programmers (Waddington and Henry, 1989). In this paper we report further empirical work on the effect of program authorship on the debugging strategy adopted by expert programmers.

2. A Model of The Relationship between Program Authorship and Expert Debugging Strategy

In this section we propose a model of expert debugging performance which takes into account the factor of program authorship.

Wertz (1982) draws attention to the distinction between what he calls conceptual and teleological bugs. Conceptual bugs manifest themselves as a discrepancy between actual program behaviour and required program behaviour (as might be stated in a program specification document, for example). In contrast, teleological bugs are a discrepancy between actual program behaviour and program behaviour as intended by the original author independently of the required behaviour. Consider the following example. Suppose a program is written to issue credit card statements and invoices to a credit company's customers. Suppose, further, that a requirement of this program is that it issue statements regardless of the balance of the customer's account, but that it issue invoices only in those cases where the balance of the account is in debit to the customer. Suppose, finally, that there is a bug in this program such that it issues invoices regardless of the balance of the account. This bug is a conceptual bug when considered from the perspective of the program being debugged by a programmer who did not write it, since the symptom is a descrepancy between how the program actually behaves and how it is required to behave. However, from the perspective of the same program being debugged by the programmer who wrote it, it may be either a conceptual or a teleological bug. If the original author was aware of the requirement not to issue invoices in cases of credited or blank accounts, and s/he also intended the original program not to issue invoices in these cases, then the bug is a teleological one. In contrast, if, for whatever reason, the original author overlooked this requirement, and s/he also intended the original program to issue invoices in these cases, then the bug is a conceptual one.

When a programmer is required to debug another programmer's program s/he is, initially at least, unaware of the behaviour of that program, as it was intended by the original author. Hence at this stage, all the bugs in the code are conceptual bugs (in the sense of Wertz, 1982). However, s/he will usually have access to some statement of the required behaviour of the program.

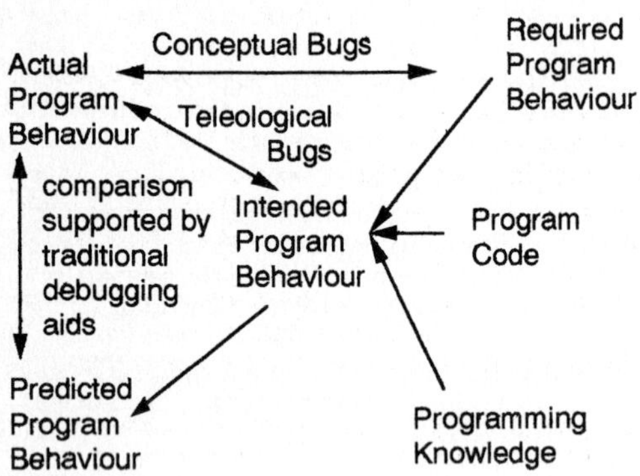

Figure 1. The relationship between teleological and conceptual bugs and their possible effect on expert debugging strategies.

Figure one represents the proposed model of expert debugging strategy diagrammatically. Most debugging aids implicitly assume a debugging process in which the software development environment reveals the actual behaviour of the program being debugged; the person performing the debugging is assumed to compare this behaviour with some prediction s/he makes about how a correct program should behave (Adrion, Branstad and Cherniavsky, 1982). We refer to these as traditional debugging aids to distinguish them from more advanced debugging aids such as PHENARETE (Wertz, 1982). The model attempts to address the issues of where these predictions might originate and why they might be useful to expert programmers as debugging strategies.

The model assumes that, ultimately, the predictions originate from some knowledge of the intended behaviour of the program. However, as explained above, it is reasonable to assume that in the case where one is debugging another programmer's program one is initially unaware of what the intended behaviour of the program is. The model predicts that an expert programmer will re-establish those intentions for her/himself. The model proposes that the expert will be able to do this as a result of her/his knowledge of required behaviour, the actual program code, and programming knowledge[1]. The model says nothing about the details of what programming knowledge might be, or how it might be represented in long term memory. This is a topic for further research in the field of software psychology. However, it is generally agreed that experts have a richer programming knowledge than do novices.

The experiment reported in the following section investigates the hypothesis that in order to debug a program written by a different programmer, expert programmers will attempt to re-establish what the behaviour of the program is according to its original author's intentions.

3. Empirical Investigation of The Effect of Program Authorship on Experts' Debugging Strategies

3.1 Introduction

The experiment reported in this section is taken from research in the area of the psychology of concurrent programming (Waddington, 1989). The subjects used had received special trainning before this experiment took place. This training had been in the use of one of two concurrent micro-languages. Micro-languages are small scale versions of real programming languages, and are designed to be identical in every respect except for those features under investigation. This methodology has been used previously by Sime, Green and Guest (1973) to evaluate the design of conditional constructs, Gannon (1977) to evaluate the effect of strong typing and by Soloway, Bonar and Ehrlich (1983) to evaluate the design of looping constructs. These experiments used this methodology to evaluate the design of constructs to express interprocess communication in concurrent programming languages (Waddington and Henry, in preparation). The two constructs under evaluation were the semaphore (Dijkstra, 1968) and rendezvous (Hoare, 1978) constructs.

3.2 Design

Eleven expert, male programmers volunteered to take part in the experiment. They were all professional computer programmers, who were employed by a company specialising in the provision of telecommunications hardware and software. Their projects involved extensive use of concurrent programming techniques. They had been assigned randomly to one of the two micro-language conditions.

The subjects varied considerably with respect to their programming experience. Here we present a summary of the group profile; full details are given in Waddington (1989). Their ages ranged from 23 to 39 years, with a mean age of 28.2 years. Their programming experience, in terms of number of years of programming, ranged from 1 to 17 years, with a mean of 5.8 years. It might be suggested that some of these subjects were more likely to be intermediate than expert programmers. However, even those with less experience in terms of number of years had a comprehensive programming background in terms of diversity of languages and projects. It was therefore felt appropriate to consider them to be experts.

The subjects were required to test and debug a program written in the micro-language they had already learned. Bugs had been artificially placed into this program. The program implemented a concurrent version of the 'quicksort' algorithm (Hoare, 1962). The program listings may be found in Waddington (1989). Subjects were required to debug by hand/mental simulation. This was so that the experimental design made no assumptions about what information about actual program behaviour they would require to perform successfully.

It may be that experts explicitly use the strategy of re-establishing intended program behaviour in order to debug another programmer's program. On the other hand it may be that experts re-establish intended program behaviour once a bug has been detected, as a consequence of having debugged the program. To distinguish between these two possibilities the experiment was designed as follows. Four bugs were devised to be used to form the 'buggy' versions of the program. Each subject received a version of the program with only two of these bugs in it. The decision as to which two bugs each subject received was made randomly for each subject. Associated with each of the four bugs devised, were two English-language assertions that purportedly described the behaviour of the program that the subject had received. Thus there were eight assertions in total.

The truth of these assertions was determined by the rules listed below. It may be helpful to consider these rules in the context of an example: One of the bugs placed in the program involved changing a procedure, *SwapElements*, so that the variables *firstPos* and *secondPos* were swapped instead of the variables *list [firstPos]* and *list [secondPos]*. This meant that no swapping occured of the actual numbers stored in the array of elements read in. The two assertions associated with this bug were:

1) A call to execute SwapElements (3, 5) in the process running Sort on the array 3 1 7 6 4 2 0 5 will result in the array becoming 3 1 7 6 4 2 0 5.

2) A call to execute SwapElements (3, 5) in the process running Sort on the array 3 1 7 6 4 2 0 5 will result in the array becoming 3 1 4 6 7 2 0 5.

Notice that assertion 2 is true of intended program behaviour, but assertion 1 is false of intended program behaviour. Thus, rule 1:

1) One of the assertions was always true of intended program behaviour, the other was always false of intended program behaviour.

Notice that the truth of both assertions about intended program behaviour holds independently of whether the particular bug with which it is associated is present in the program. Thus rule 2:

2) The truth of each assertion with respect to intended program behaviour is independent of whether the subject received its associated bug.

Notice that whereas assertion 2 is always true of intended program behaviour, it is false of actual program behaviour if the bug with which it is associated is present in the program; but it is true of actual program behaviour if the bug with which it is associated is not present in the program. Thus, rule 3:

3) The assertion that was true of intended program behaviour was false of actual program behaviour if the subject had received its associated bug; but it was true of actual program behaviour if the subject had not received its associated bug.

Notice that whereas assertion 1 is always false of intended program behaviour, it is true of actual program behaviour if the bug with which it is associated is present in the program; but it is false of actual program behaviour if the bug with which it is associated is not present in the program. Thus, rule 4:

4) The assertion that was false of intended behaviour was true of actual program behaviour if the subject had received its associated bug; but it was false of actual program behaviour if the subject had not received its associated bug.

The rationale behind this design is as follows. Subjects may adjudge the truth of each assertion from their memory of the behaviour of the (original) program after they have worked with it. However, their memory of actual program behaviour may be different from their memory of intended program behaviour. Thus, when asked to adjudge whether an assertion is true of actual program behaviour (an actuality judgement) subjects may be able to make this decision from memory faster or slower than a similar judgement about whether an assertion is true of intended program behaviour (an intentionality judgement).

If experts re-establish intended program behaviour as a consequence of having debugged, one would predict that they would make intentionality judgements faster for those assertions associated with bugs they received (and diagnosed and fixed successfully) than for those bugs they did not. One would also predict that intentionality judgements associated with those bugs not received (or received but not diagnosed or fixed successfully) would be made slower than actuality judgements for those bugs not received (or received but not diagnosed or fixed successfully). This is because they would not have considered the behaviour proposed by the assertion from the point of view of whether the original author intended it that way but would be likely to have considered it from the point of view of whether the program actually behaved that way. If, on the other hand, experts re-establish intended program behaviour in order to debug, one would predict no differences between the times to make judgements of either type about assertions associated with bugs they received (and diagnosed and fixed successfully) and those bugs they did not. One would also predict no interaction between whether a bug was received (and diagnosed and fixed successfully) and judgement type. This is because they would be as likely to have considered the behaviour proposed by the assertion from the point of view of whether the original author intended it as they would be to have considered it from the point of view of whether the program actually behaved that way.

Thus the experiment was designed to test the hypothesis that in order to debug a program written by a different programmer an expert programmer will attempt to re-establish what the behaviour of the program was according to the original author's intentions. Each subject was required to judge each of the eight assertions. The independent variables of judgement type (actuality versus intentionality) and bug presence were manipulated. The experimental hypothesis was tested by mixed analysis of variance on subjects' reaction times to make each judgement.

3.3 Procedure

Each subject attended one experimental session lasting a maximum of one hour. The experimental sessions were administered by purpose-built software running on an Apple Macintosh[2] XL computer, which also recorded the reaction time data.

The subjects were given a description of the program and its requirements, but were not told what algorithm was implemented. They were told that the program may or may not be a correct implementation of the requirements, but that it had been written by an expert programmer who had been attempting to write a correct implementation.

For the first phase of the experiment (the debugging phase) the subjects were given instructions, a program description, code listings appropriate to their experimental condition and a pen and rough paper to perform any hand simulation they desired. When they had read the instructions the experimental software was set running. A window was presented on the screen containing two buttons (in the usual Macintosh interface style; see Rose, Hacker, Anders, Withey, Metzler, Chernicoff, Espinosa, Averill, Davis and Howard, 1985). These were labelled 'Bug Found' and 'Program Correct'. When a subject had found a bug he was to press in the 'Bug Found' button. Then the software replaced the first window with a second one. This window was the screen of a display editor, into which subjects were to type a description of the bug they had found and their proposed fix. Then the screen returned to that which contained the two buttons. When the subject considered he had found and diagnosed all the bugs in the program he was required to press in the 'Program Correct' button. Subjects were allowed a maximum of forty minutes in this phase of the experiment.

Then the second phase of the experiment (the judgement phase) began. The experimenter removed the program listings and any rough work from the subject and gave him the second phase instructions to read and set the experimental software running. Here two windows were presented on the computer screen. In the first window appeared the text of an assertion. In the second window appeared two buttons labelled either 'actual' and 'not actual' or 'intended' and 'not intended', depending on the type of judgement being made. The order of presentation of the assertions and judgement types was randomised independently for each subject by the software. The subject made his judgement by pressing in the appropriate button. Visual feedback was achieved in the usual Macintosh interface style.

3.4 Results

Table 1 below shows the mean percentage of correct answers in each condition[3].

Table 2 shows the mean reaction time in each condition. Only correct answers are included in this table[3]. Also, the data have only been included in the bug received condition if the bug was present, and diagnosed and fixed successfully.

Condition	Correct Answers (%)	
Bug Presence	Judgement Type	
Bug	*Intentionality*	65.8
Received	*Actuality*	46.2
Bug	*Intentionality*	52.9
Omitted	*Actuality*	52.9
Mean		54.5

Table 1. Percentage of correct answers by bug presence and judgement type (N = 11).

Condition	Mean Reaction Time (seconds)	
Bug Presence	Judgement Type	
Bug	*Intentionality*	31.2
Received	*Actuality*	42.7
Bug	*Intentionality*	35.9
Omitted	*Actuality*	30.3
Mean		35.0

Table 2. Mean reaction time per response by bug presence and judgement type (N = 11).

The data could not be analysed as originally intended, due to missing cells in the condition semaphores, bug received, actuality judgement. Therefore, the data from the rendezvous condition were analysed separately using analysis of variance. This analysis revealed no significant main effect of bug presence ($F_{1,4} = 0.004$), or judgement type ($F_{1,4} = 0.498$) nor a significant interaction between bug presence and judgement type ($F_{1,4} = 1.008$).

In order to analyse the data together, they were collapsed first across the judgement type variable and second across the bug presence variable. In the first case analysis of variance revealed no significant main effect of language construct ($F_{1,9} = 0.962$), nor of bug presence ($F_{1,9} = 0.094$) nor a significant interaction between language construct and bug presence($F_{1,9} = 0.039$). In the second case analysis of variance revealed no significant main effect of language construct ($F_{1,9} =$ 1.172), or of judgement type ($F_{1,9} = 0.079$) nor a significant interaction between language construct and judgement type ($F_{1,9} = 1.867$).

3.5 Discussion

Although it was only possible to carry out a full statistical analysis for those subjects who had been instructed in the rendezvous micro-language, the results of this analysis, and the data shown in Table 2, indicate that subjects did not make actuality judgements any faster than they made intentionality judgements. These results also indicate that there was no interaction between bug presence and judgement type.

The data support the overall conclusion that expert programmers acquire as much information about intended program behaviour as they do about actual program behaviour when debugging a program they did not write. Additionally, it seems that, since this result is unaffected by the presence of a bug in the program, expert programmers adopt this strategy in order to debug rather than as a consequence of having debugged.

This conclusion supports the model of the effect of program authorship on expert debugging strategy proposed in Figure 1. However, this model provides a very gross description of that effect. This experiment has not considered the extent to which the factors of Required Program Behaviour, Program Code and Programming Knowledge contribute to the process of acquiring information about Intended Program Behaviour. Also, it may be the case that other factors are involved when experts adopt this debugging strategy.

Further research on this topic might consider not only the issues of whether other factors play a role in the information acquisition process, and to what extent different factors mediate that process, but also how the different kinds of available information might best be represented. For example, there are many ways of expressing (specifying) the required behaviour of a program. Likewise, programmers will differ in the way they write program code in the hope of expressing their intentions to other programmers (for example, their use of naming conventions, high-level comments etc.). Finally, it is unlikely that any two programmers will have precisely the same programming knowledge. It will be necessary to understand both the structure and content of expert programming knowledge in order to assess its likely effect on the debugging strategy described here.

4. Implications for The Design of Debugging Aids

In this section we discuss the implications of these results for the design of debugging aids for expert programmers.

Traditional debugging aids are used to support programmers debugging their own programs as well as other programmers' programs. In either case, the person debugging the program must make predictions about intended program behaviour which may be compared with actual program behaviour, as this is revealed by the software development environment (see Section 2). In the case of debugging aother programmer's program, traditional debugging aids are unsupportive of the debugging strategy in which the expert seeks to establish information about the original author's intended program behaviour.

The *Proust* system (Johnson and Soloway, 1985) was designed to analyse a program in a way that allows intended program behaviour to be revealed to a novice programmer debugging her/his own program. The philosophy behind this approach is that novices are not fully aware of their own intentions when they write programs (Johnson, 1986). However, the intentions are not really re-established by Proust in the way that an expert programmer might re-establish them; rather *Proust* relies on knowledge of the specific goals of the programming assignment as provided by humans externally to the actual program code. The results obtained in this experiment suggest that a similar approach to that adopted in *Proust* might be appropriate to inform the design of debugging aids to support expert programmers when debugging other programmers' programs.

As Ward (1986, p.1) indicates, there is no getting away from the fact that programming involves debugging: "To write programs that work, you must know how to debug. It's that simple. In fact, if you produce working programs, you will spend at least half of your time debugging". Hanson and Rosinski (1985) have observed that of all the different types of tool that might be available in a software development environment, expert programmers consider debugging aids to have the greatest effect on productivity. Further investigation of the cognitive processes involved in the adoption of the expert's strategy of re-establishing intentions might allow the designers of future debugging aids to produce effective design solutions.

Acknowledgements

This research was undertaken whilst the first author was a graduate student in the Department of Psychology at Nottingham University, UK. It was supported by ESRC grant # H00428425013.

Endnotes

[1] In Waddington and Henry (1989) we discuss why novice programmers ought not to be able to re-establish another programmer's intentions.

[2] Macintosh is a trademark of McIntosh Laboratory, Inc. Apple is a trademark of Apple Computer, Inc.

[3] The data shown here have been collapsed across the conditions of type of micro-language. This was because there was neither a significant main effect of micro-language type nor a significant interaction between micro-language type and either bug presence or judgement type.

References

Adrion, W. R., Branstad, M. A. and Cherniavsky, J. C. (1982). Validation, Verification, and Testing of Computer Software. *ACM Computing Surveys*, 14, 2, 159-192.

Dijkstra, E. W. (1968). Co-operating Sequential Processes. In *Programming Languages* (Ed. F. Genuys). London: Academic Press.

Gannon, J. D. (1977). An Experimental Evaluation of Data Type Conventions. *Communications of the ACM*, 20, 8, 584-595.

Gould, J. D. (1975). Some Psychological Evidence on How People Debug Computer Programs. *International Journal of Man-Machine Studies*, 7, 2, 151-182.

Hanson, S. J and Rosinski, R. R. (1985). Programmer Perceptions of Productivity and Programming Tools. *Communications of the ACM*, 28, 2, 180-189.

Hoare, C. A. R. (1962). Quicksort. *Computer Journal*, 5, 10-15.

Hoare, C. A. R. (1978). Communicating Sequential Processes. *Communications of the ACM*, 21, 8, 666-677.

Johnson, W. L. (1986). *Intention-Based Diagnosis of Novice Programming Errors*. Pitman, Los Altos, Calif.

Norman, D. A., and Draper, S. W. (Eds.) (1986) *User Centered System Design: New Perspectives on Human-Computer Interaction*. Hillsdale, N. J.: Lawrence Erlbaum Associates.

Rose, C., Hacker, B., Anders, R., Withey, K., Metzler, M., Chernicoff, S., Espinosa, C., Averill, A., Davis, B. and Howard, B. (1985). *Inside Macintosh Volumes I, II, and III*. Reading, Mass.: Addison-Wesley.

Sime, M. E., Green, T. R. G. and Guest, D. J. (1973). Psychological Evaluation of Two Conditional Constructions Used in Computer Languages. *International Journal of Man-Machine Studies*, 5, 1, 105-113.

Soloway, E., Bonar, J. and Ehrlich, K. (1983). Cognitive Strategy and Looping Constructs: An Empirical Study. *Communications of the ACM*, 26, 11, 853-860.

Waddington, R. (1989). *User-Centred Design of Software Development Environments: An Example from Program Debugging*. Unpublished Ph. D. Thesis, Department of Psychology, University of Nottingham, University Park, Nottingham NG7 2RD, U.K., March, 1989.

Waddington, R. and Henry, R. (1989). The Effect of Program Authorship on Novice Debugging Performance. In *Proceedings of the 3rd International Conference on HCI* (Eds. G. Salvendy & M. J. Smith. Boston, Mass. September 18-22, 1989.

Waddington, R. and Henry, R., (in preparation). A Micro-Language Approach to The Psychology of Concurrent Programming. *Manuscript in preparation.*

Ward, R. (1986) *Debugging C*. Indianapolis, ID.: Que Corporation.

Wertz, H. (1982). Stereotyped Program Debugging: An Aid for Novice Programmers. *International Journal of Man-Machine Studies*, 16, 4, 379-392.

Human–Computer Interaction – INTERACT '90
D. Diaper et al. (Editors)
Elsevier Science Publishers B.V. (North-Holland)

DIFFICULTIES IN DESIGNING WITH AN OBJECT-ORIENTED LANGUAGE: AN EMPIRICAL STUDY*

Françoise Détienne

Institut National de Recherche en Informatique et en Automatique (National Institute for Research on Computer Science and Automation), Ergonomic Psychology Project, Rocquencourt B.P.105
78135 Le Chesnay Cedex, France
email: detienne@psycho.inria.fr

An experiment has been conducted to study the activity of program design developed by programmers experienced in classical procedural languages as they use an object-oriented programming (OOP) language. This paper focuses on the analysis of the difficulties programmers experienced in designing with OOP language. An important difficulty is to articulate the declarative and the procedural characteristics of the solution. This study highlights the importance of a representation of the procedure so as to construct the static relations between objects.This result does not support the hypothesis on naturalness of design with an OOP language made by advocates of OOP. This experiment also show that previous knowledge of programming languages may produce negative effects in the acquisition of a new language.

1. THEORETICAL FRAMEWORK AND GOALS

An experiment has been conducted to study the design activity developed by programmers experienced in classical procedural languages as they use an object-oriented language. We assume that experienced programmers possess in memory numerous schemas which are abstract knowledge structures they have constructed through practice in their domain of expertise. These schemas represent classes of problems or/and classes of solutions. Evidence supporting this hypothesis has been found in various studies [1, 2, 3].

It has been shown that experienced programmers possess schemas dependent on the task domain and schemas dependent on the programming domain. These schemas are evoked and used whenever programmers perform programming tasks. It is likely that they are more or less dependent on programming languages (specifically the type of language such as declarative, procedural, object-oriented) and on methodologies of design.

The activity of program design has been analyzed as a mapping between representations of entities in, at least, two domains: the task domain in which the designer construct a representation of the problem and the programming domain in which a solution is developed. The cognitive mechanisms involved in design are: problem understanding mechanisms, mechanisms for decomposing the problem into a solution and coding mechanisms. These cognitive processes are assumed to be driven by schematic knowledge. For example, inferences based on schemas in the task domain and, possibly, in the programming domain, allow to construct a coherent representation of the problem. The search for a solution is driven by schemas about the problem and about design solutions.

The originality of this study is double.

First, there is, as far as we know, no empirical study on object-oriented programming. Most psychological studies on software design [4, 5] were conducted with programmers using procedural languages or, more recently, declarative languages.

There is an important difference between the object-oriented paradigm and the procedural paradigm. With a procedural paradigm, data and functions are separated. On the contrary, with an object-oriented paradigm they are integrated. Objects are program entities which integrate a structure defined by a type as well as functionalities. Objects are instances of classes.

An empirical study of programming with an object-oriented language seems particularly interesting to evaluate the claim made on the easiness to program or the "naturalness" of design with this kind of languages.

Second, this study allows to analyze the learning mechanisms of experts. Most psychological studies on learning programming were focused on knowledge acquisition by novices. Inasmuch as experienced programmers tend to have, more and more, new languages at their disposal, the learning of new programming languages by experts seems an important psychological question to address.

In our experiment, we collected data on the activity of program design with an object-oriented data base system, the "O2 System" [6, 7] which is being developed by the GIP ALTAIR.

* This research was supported by the GIP ALTAIR. Altaïr is a consortium funded by IN2 (a Siemens Subsidiary), INRIA (Institut National de Recherche en Informatique et Automatique) and LRI (Laboratoire de Recherche en Informatique, Université Paris XI).

2. HYPOTHESES

Advocates of object-oriented programming make a strong hypothesis about the naturalness of design with an OOP language [8, 9]. According to this hypothesis the mapping between a representation of the problem composed of problem entities and a representation of a solution composed of computational entities is assumed to be more straightforward with an OOP paradigm than with a procedural paradigm. Concerning problem understanding, it is assumed that the identification of objects (or classes as objects are classes' instances) would be easy inasmuch as objects form natural representations of problem entities. According to Meyer, the world can be naturally structured in terms of objects, thus, it seems particularly relevant to organize a model of design around a software representation of these objects.

With an OOP language, decomposing the problem into a solution consists in identifying the relations between objects and the associations between the structures and the functionalities of objects. It is assumed that decomposing a problem into objects and actions to operate on these objects is natural. This activity is assumed to be driven by knowledge in the task domain such as schemas representing problems characteristics and by general knowledge in the programming domain. On the contrary, with a procedural paradigm this activity would be driven by design knowledge representing classes of solution in the programming domain.

However, this hypothesis seems to be very optimistic for novices and for experts in programming. There is no psychological evidence supporting the assumption that objects form natural entities of problem representation. On the contrary, studies [10] highlight the procedural nature of knowledge transferred from the task domain in learning by novices. Furthermore, from studies on program design by experts, it appears that schemas in the programming domain play an important role in the design process and that representations of the procedure in terms of functions performed as well as in terms of control flow are constructed by programmers for performing programming tasks [11, 12]. These studies highlight the importance of a procedural representation in programming activities. Some results suggest that constructing a syntactic representation of the procedure (in terms of control flow) may precede the construction of a more abstract representation in terms of functions and objects involved in the solution.

With OOP languages, constructing a representation of the declarative aspects of the solution is required for structuring the solution. So programmers are encouraged to develop these aspects before developing the procedure. This may cause difficulties because declarative and procedural aspects are very dependent and the preferred strategy of experts may consist in developing the procedural aspects first.

This study does not aim to compare the object-oriented paradigm and the procedural paradigm. However, it collects data on the difficulties encountered by programmers with an OOP language so as to evaluate how easy (or how difficult) the design activity with this kind of language is for programmers experienced with more "classical" procedural languages.

This will be evaluated relatively to different kinds of design problems. We assume that problems may be more or less easy (or difficult) to design with an OOP paradigm. An OO representation could be more natural for certain kinds of problems. We chose to give subjects two different problems. One problem is "declarative"; it has been shown by Hoc, in a previous study [13], that the data structure guides the program development. The other problem is "procedural"; the structure of the procedure has been shown to guide the program development. In the paradigm of object-oriented programming, identifying objects and their characteristics is important in the design process and in a declarative problem, these aspects should be more obvious to analyze. So an object-oriented language could make the design activity, at least in a learning phase, easier for a declarative problem than for a procedural problem.

Another question this study addresses is how subjects which are experienced in programming learn new concepts in their domain of expertise. We expect experienced programmers to use the schemas they have constructed in the programming and the task domains so as to construct new solutions more adapted to the new language which is, in our study, an object-oriented language. However it is likely that having programming schemas at their disposal may have positive effects as well as negative effects. Trying to apply programming schemas already constructed may produce negative effects whenever these knowledge structures are not modified so as to take into account the rules of the new programming device. In this case the programmers should develop non adequate solutions.

3. METHODOLOGY

3.1. The O2 System

The O2 system is an object-oriented data base system. A "classical" language is used mainly to write the methods. In the version of the system used for our experiment, this is the CO2 language, which is a slightly modified version of C. An object-oriented layer, the O2 language, is added to the "classical" language. Subjects have been chosen so as to be familiar with the C language.

The object-oriented programming paradigm is based on the concepts of class, inheritance, message passing, late-binding. A class is defined as a structure (a type) and methods. A method is a function attached to a class that describes one part of the behavior of the objects which are instances of this class.

There are various possible relations between classes. The "is-a" relation defines a specialization between a class and its superclass. The "is-part-of" relation defines an imbrication between classes. A class inherits the properties of its superclasses. This inheritance property apply on structural properties of classes and on functional properties of classes, i.e., a class inherits the structure of its superclass and the methods associated to it.

A subclass can redefine methods; thus a method can have the same name and be associated to different classes with different code. When the program is executed, one of these methods will be called according to the class of the object on which this method is applied: this is the principle of late-binding. A method call is termed passing a message. The syntax for message passing is: [Receiver NameOfTheMethod (parameters)]. The receiver must be an object of the class to which the method is attached, or to a subclass. At the execution, a method is called according to the receiver's class.

A program is composed of two parts

-a *declarative part* in which are defined computational entities and the relations between entities. This part is called the "model of classes" (or "schema" in the terminology of O2 system designers) and is written in O2. It consists of:
*the type specification, i.e., the names of classes, the types and names of attributes, the relations between classes
*the method specification, i.e., the signatures of methods which are names and parameters of methods

-a *procedural part* which consists of the bodies of methods. This is written in CO2.

The following excerpt illustrates the declarative part of a program:

```
add class Book
   type tuple (title:string,
               year: integer)
   method title: string
   method show
...
add class Proceedings inherits Book
   type tuple (place: string)
   method show
...
add class Journal inherits Book
   type tuple (vol: integer)
   method show
...
```

The following excerpt illustrates the procedural part of the same program as above:

```
body title: string in class Book
{return (self->title);}
...
body show in class Book
{printf("title=%s, year=%d", self->title, self-
>year);}
....
```

In this example, the classes Proceedings and Journal are subclasses of the class Book. Thus they inherit its structure. This means that the type of the class Proceedings is a tuple with three fields: title, year and place. The subclasses also inherit the functionalities of their superclass. This means that the methods "title" and "show" are inherited by the class Proceedings. In this example, the method "show" is redefined in the two subclasses. Whenever this method is called, the method associated to the class of the receiver is run. This may be the method associated to the class Proceedings or the method associated to the class Journal.

3.2. Subjects

Eight professional programmers participated in this experiment. All had several years of programming practice with classical procedural languages such as C, Cobol, Basic. Four of them were "beginners" in object-oriented programming (OOP). They had no practice with this programming paradigm. The four others, "experienced" in OOP, had several weeks of practice with the object-oriented language under study.

3.3. Material

The material consisted of two problems of management:
-a financial management problem which was a slightly modified version of a problem classified in a previous experiment [13] as a declarative problem
-a library management problem which was a slightly modified version of a problem classified as a procedural problem

The task domain was familiar to the subjects.

3.4. Procedure

Each subject had the two problems to program with the O2 system. The order of problems presentation was counter-balanced. The programmers not experienced in object-oriented programming had one day for programming each problem whereas the programmers "experienced" in object-oriented programming had half a day (which has been proved to be sufficient to develop the program at least as much as what beginners did). Previously to the phase of program design, the four subjects "beginners in OOP" received a one-day theoretical formation. Subjects were asked to verbalize while designing their programs. They were allowed to ask questions to several experts in object-oriented programming whenever they had problems they were not able to overcome.

All subjects had at their disposal a manual for the system, a theoretical paper on object-oriented programming and an example-program i.e., a program written in CO2 and O2, solving a problem different from the experimental ones. After the programming phase, subjects had to answer questions on the difficulties they had experienced during the experiment.

We collected the subjects' verbalizations, successive versions of programs under development, notes written during the realization of the task, questions asked to the experts, the order in which the different traces of the activity were made, i.e., the order for writing notes and coding programs with the verbalization recorded simultaneously.

The final versions of programs have been given for evaluation to experts in object-oriented programming. They were asked to detect and report errors as well as "inelegances" in design and style. They had to rank them by order of seriousness, to classify them and to make explicit their criteria of classification.

4. RESULTS

Programmers developed fairly rapidly programs with the new programming language. The use of their previous knowledge in programming had a positive effect in the acquisition of the new concepts of the object-oriented language. However, it is not possible to measure how easy it was to learn this new language compared to other languages.

Although designing with an object-oriented language seemed easy in some aspects, we will focus, in this paper, on the analysis of the difficulties encountered by programmers in performing their task. First, the activity of design followed by the programmers is characterized. We analyze the mechanism of mapping between problem entities and computational entities. This allows to evaluate the hypothesis on naturalness of design with an OOP language. Second we will analyze the effect of the problem's type. Then we analyze some reasons of programming difficulties which are mostly negative effects of transferred knowledge. Although we observed programmers simulating partial solutions developed at various levels of abstraction, the description and the role of simulation in design will not be developed in this paper.

4.1. Characteristics of design activity

A plan subjects try to follow when designing their program is to define the model of classes before defining the processes which are expressed by methods. Thus they try to define the most declarative aspects of the program composed of classes and relations between classes before defining the most procedural aspects. Remark that this is driven by constraints of order in the version of the O2 system under study: in a method body, it is not possible to use a class or an object which has not been completely specified before. The plan programmers try to follow is hierarchical. They try to develop first the most abstract aspects of the solution before writing the code of methods which is a refinement of some functional aspects defined in the declarative part.

In a first phase of design, the programmer thus try to map problem entities to computational entities, which are classes with their type, their functionalities and the relation between them. We observed that the subjects had difficulties in doing that. They had difficulties to construct all aspects of the model of classes before developing the procedural part of the program.

The way programmers develop the declarative part of the solution, which can be described as following a hierarchy of abstraction, is not strictly from abstract levels toward more detailed levels. We observed that the solution development is done either in a top-down way or in a bottom-up way. In the process of class creation, we observed that classes were defined by programmers either in a top-down direction (from super-classes to sub-classes) or in a bottom-up direction. Novices in OOP had many difficulties to construct classes, to use the "is-a" and "is-part-of" relationships between classes, and to associate methods to classes. Programmers tried to anticipate the different classes and methods they will need in the detailed coding of methods, i.e., the procedural aspects of the program. However, we observed they were not able to anticipate all these aspects.

They were not able to construct the computational entities only from the schematic knowledge they have on the problem and from general knowledge in the programming domain. They needed to construct a representation of the procedural aspects in the program so as to construct the declarative representation. This is shown in the numerous modifications made to the model of classes while writing the methods. When the subjects judge the model of classes to be sufficient they started the coding of methods. We observed the programmers made many modifications in the declarative part defined previously while writing the procedural part . These modifications are of two types: refinement of entities defined previously and change of entities defined previously at abstract levels.

When they refine the functions by writing the code of methods, programmers are able to refine some characteristics of the structure of objects already defined at higher levels of abstraction: addition of attributes in a class, addition of parameters in a method signature. However they also make changes and additions concerning choices of the solution previously defined at abstract levels: addition of classes, addition of methods, modification of association between methods and classes (move a method from one class to another).

This result exhibits the difficulties subjects have to articulate declarative characteristics of a solution with more procedural characteristics of a solution. In doing the mapping between problem entities and computational entities, they do need knowledge on the procedure they will develop in the procedural part so as to develop the static aspects of the solution, i.e. the structures and the functionnalities of classes. These knowledge on the procedural aspects of the solution is dependent on the programming domain.

However, the programmers experienced in OOP may anticipate some aspects of the procedural part while writing the declarative part. On the contrary, the beginners in OOP made incorrect anticipations. They use their schematic knowledge constructed in programming with others languages or with non OOP methods so as to anticipate some aspects of the solution. By transferring knowledge they construct parts of the solution which are either modified later on or not modified and cause errors or inelegances. This will be developed in the section 4.3 on knowledge transfer in design.

Our results do not support the hypothesis on naturalness of design with object-oriented language formulated by the advocates of OOP. This study highlight the importance of a procedural representation of the solution so as to construct the declarative structure of the solution. This suggests that constructing a representation of some procedural aspects of a solution may precede the construction of a representation of more declarative aspects.

4.2. Effect of problem type

From our data, the declarative problem does not appear to be more adequate for an object-oriented paradigm than the procedural problem. Although the declarative problem is preferred by novices, the analysis of the design activity shows that both kinds of problems are difficult to solve with an object-oriented paradigm.

The difficulty to program was judged different according to the type of problem solved. Beginners in OOP tended to judge the procedural problem more difficult than the declarative one: three over four beginners in OOP found designing the procedural problem more difficult than designing the declarative problem, the fourth one finding them equivalent. Two subjects "experienced" in OOP also found the procedural problem harder to program whereas the two others found the declarative problem harder to program.

The same kinds of reasons were given to compare the two problems by the beginners in OOP and the programmers experienced in OOP. It is noteworthy that the declarative problem was judged more difficult for the structuration and composition of classes and for the association between functionalities and classes; this is precisely what is assumed to be easy with this kind of language by the advocates of OOP. From the data on the design activity, it appears that programmers, specifically the beginners in OOP, experienced many difficulties for both kinds of problems. In a further analysis of our data we will evaluate whether or not some kinds of difficulties are problem specific.

4.3. Knowledge transfer in design

We observed that programmers use transfer of knowledge in designing their solution, i.e., they evoke solutions or parts of solution, more or less abstract, that they try to reuse. These solutions come from internal source, i.e., the memory of the programmers, as well as from external sources, i.e., other programs (the example-program or programs written previously by the subject him/herself) or parts of the program being written.

Transfer of knowledge may have a positive effect as well as a negative effect. It has positive effects inasmuch as it allows subjects to use already constructed knowledge structures in their solutions without having to reconstruct them which would be more expensive. A transfer produces a structure which can be adapted to a new device. It has negative effects whenever the knowledge structure is used without being correctly adapted. In this case, transfer mechanisms cause errors.

Many errors and "inelegances" have been detected by the evaluators in the final versions of the programs. From the analysis of the protocols collected on the design activity, we have been able to analyze how some of them are produced. It appears that the transfer of various kinds of knowledge has negative effects which explain many errors and "inelegances" in design. Subjects, beginners as well as experienced in OOP, transfer schematic structures they have constructed through their practice of programming. Whereas these transfers are useful in the learning process, the programmers, in some cases, just apply the old structure without taking into account the new constraints and functionalities of the new device.

In this section we present examples of these negative effects of the transfer mechanism. We differentiate different cases according to the kind of schematic knowledge which have been transferred.

4.3.1. Schematic knowledge dependent on the task domain

Programmers possess schemas dependent on the task domain they evoke as soon as they have information on the problem they have to solve. From these schemas they can infer data structures and functions to perform for solving a certain kind of problems. For example, they know that, for data base management, which is the kind of problems they had to solve, there must be some kind of set of records in the program and some functions are to be performed: creation, modification, deletion.

According to the hypothesis on the naturalness of OOP, schematic knowledge dependent on the task domain is assumed to help programmers so as to develop solutions adequate for OOP. Our data suggest that it is not the way it happens.

We observed that beginners in OOP experienced difficulties in structuring their solution. From the problem statements and from their schematic knowledge in the task domain, they inferred functions and objects to use in their solution. However, they found difficult to relate one to each other, so as to construct the model of classes, and often tried several solutions. The model of classes seems not to be transparent in the problem statements.

Furthermore, it appeared that very soon in the design process, the programmers, mostly the beginners in OOP, inferred elements of solution which do not conform to OOP principles. Although the representation they worked on was a very abstract one and still very close to the problem statements, they added elements of schematic knowledge relative to a methodology of design (different from OOP), or relative to a solution in classical procedural language. We develop below several examples of these mechanisms.

4.3.2. Schematic knowledge dependent on a methodology of design

Very early in their design activity, we observed that beginners in OOP may evoke and use schematic knowledge dependent on a methodology of design which do not conform to OOP principles. For example, a subject evoked elements of a solution constructed with a relational approach of data base management. According to this methodology, different objects have a number which is used as a cue to link together objects and to help the search in the data base. Evoking this schematic knowledge, the subject added an attribute of type "number" to each class he had constructed previously. Then he constructed a kind of "flat" structure of classes, without using the "is-part-of" relationship to link together classes. According to the evaluators, the final solution, which was a development of this abstract solution did not conform to principles of OOP.

4.3.3. Schematic knowledge dependent on classical procedural languages

Very early in their design activity, we observed that beginners, as well as experienced programmers in OOP, evoked schematic knowledge dependent on classical procedural languages. For example, a beginner added a parameter "type of object" in a class which allowed him to do different processing (method calls) according to the value taken by this parameter in a structure "case of" or "Ifs". This is typically a solution constructed for classical procedural language. In doing so, he does not take into account the functionalities of OOP. By the late-binding and inheritance properties, he could let the system decide during the execution which kind of object is under process so as to call the adequate method without using a "type" parameter and a structure of selection.

4.3.4. Schematic knowledge dependent on the OOP language

In their learning process, subjects construct new structures which are dependent on the OOP language and they try to transfer these structures in order to apply them in different situations. This is a learning process which sometimes causes errors by overgeneralization of the use of a structure. For example, when they had several methods which performed the same functionality in different classes, they tried to use the inheritance properties. This is possible when the signature of the method is the same for the method associated to the superclass as for the methods associated to the subclasses. However, many errors were produced as they generalized this structure without taking care of the signature of methods.

5. DISCUSSION

It appears from our study that designing a program with an object-oriented language is not so easy and so natural as the advocates of OOP say. The hypothesis on naturalness of design with an OOP language is not confirmed by our data. Our observations show that decomposing a problem into a solution is not easy, specifically for identifying classes and articulating objects and functions and, more generally, declarative aspects and procedural aspects. Whatever the type of the problem is, programmers experience many difficulties in understanding and using the new concepts and constructs of the OOP language.

The analysis of the mapping between problem entities and computational entities show that it is not so straightforward as the advocates of OOP assume. Although knowledge in the task domain helps in structuring the solution in terms of objects, it is not enough. Beginners need to develop the procedural aspects of the program so as to refine and evaluate their schema of classes. As they try to anticipate these procedural aspects, they use knowledge in programming they have constructed previously with procedural languages and, more generally, with other programming devices. This transfer of knowledge has been shown to cause errors and inelegances whenever these knowledge structures are not adapted to the rules of functioning of the new programming device.

In the learning process of a new language by experts, we have stressed the importance of transfer and reuse of solutions. We have seen that previous knowledge of programming languages may produce negative effects in the acquisition of a new language. Beginners as well as experienced programmers in object-oriented programming tend to not fully use the functionalities of the new programming paradigm. They sometime use inappropriately the syntax of the new language so as to translate an old solution.This result highlights the need for training the subjects with examples which take into consideration their previous knowledge and, in particular, the transfers they may do. Experts in programming learn a new programming language by the evocation and the adaptation of old schemas. However, our data suggest that, in many cases, the schemas were not adapted. From questions programmers asked and from errors or inelegances made in programs, it appeared that beginners in OOP did not have a good representation of data flow and control flow in programs written in the object-oriented language. This suggests that data flow and control flow representations may be important in the mechanisms involved so as to adapt old schemas and construct new schemas.

This research has been conducted while the O2 system is still under development. The designers of this system are interested in our observations on programmers' difficulties so as to take them into account for the further development of the language, for the training of the system's users and for the development of a methodology of design and the documentation.

REFERENCES

[1] Détienne, F. Program Understanding and Knowledge Organization: the Influence of Acquired Schemas, in: Falzon, P. (ed.), Cognitive Ergonomics: Understanding, Learning and Designing Human-Computer Interaction (Academic Press, London, 1990).

[2] Détienne, F. and Soloway, E., An Empirically-Derived Control Structure for the Process of Program Understanding. Research report 886, INRIA, Rocquencourt, (1988).

[3] Soloway, E. and Ehrlich, K., Empirical Studies of Programming Knowledge, IEEE Transactions on Software Engineering, SE-10 (5), (1984) pp. 595-609.

[4] Adelson, B. and Soloway, E., A Model of Software Design. Research report 342, Yale University, New Haven (1984).

[5] Visser, W., Strategies in Programming Programmable Controllers: A Field Study on a Professional Programmers. in: Olson, G., Sheppard, S. and Soloway, E. (eds.), Empirical Studies of Programmers: second workshop. (Ablex Publishing Corporation: NJ, 1987) pp. 217-230.

[6] O.Deux et al., The Story of O2. Technical report 37-89, GIP Altaïr, Rocquencourt (1989).

[7] Lecluse, C. and Richard, P., The O2 Database Programming Language. Proceedings of International Conference on Very Large Data Bases (Amsterdam, 26 Août 1989).

[8] Meyer, B., Object-Oriented Software Construction (Prentice Hall, International Series in Computer Science, 1988).

[9] Rosson, M. B. and Alpert, S. R., The Cognitive Consequences of Object-Oriented Design. Research report, RC 14191, IBM, N.Y (1988).

[10] Hoc, J-M., Analysis of Beginner's Problem Solving Strategies in Programming, in: Green, T.R.G., Payne, S.J. and Van der Veer G. (eds.), The Psychology of Computer Use. (Academic Press, London, 1989) pp.143-158.

[11] Détienne, F., Expert Programming Knowledge: The Schema-Based Approach, in: Hoc, J-M., Green, T.R.G., Samurçay, R. and Gilmore, D. (eds), (Academic Press, People and Computer Series, to appear).

[12] Pennington, N., Stimulus Structures and Mental Representations in Expert Comprehension of Computer Programs. Cognitive Psychology, 19, (1987), pp. 295-341.

[13] Hoc, J-M., Une méthode de classification préalable des problèmes d'un domaine pour l'analyse des stratégies de résolution: la programmation informatique chez des professionnels. Le Travail Humain, 46 (3), (1983), pp. 205-217.

Human–Computer Interaction – INTERACT '90
D. Diaper et al. (Editors)
Elsevier Science Publishers B.V. (North-Holland)

The Spreadsheet Interface: A Basis for End User Programming

Bonnie A. Nardi
James R. Miller

Hewlett-Packard Laboratories, Human-Computer Interaction Department, 1501 Page Mill Road, Palo Alto, CA 94304 U.S.A.

This paper describes the properties of the spreadsheet interface and the ways in which spreadsheets support users with little or no formal training in programming. We analyze the spreadsheet formula language through which users express mathematical relations and the tabular grid which permits users to view, structure and display data. Based on our analysis of the formula language and the tabular grid, we argue that user programming environments should be characterized by (1) a limited set of carefully chosen, high-level, task-specific operations that are sufficient for building applications within a restricted domain, and (2) a strong visual format for structuring and presenting data.

Introduction

A key question in human-computer interaction research is: How can we design software so that non-programmers can build their own applications? One way to study this question is to analyze existing user programming environments such as spreadsheets, HyperCard, the Metaphor Capsule, New Wave, fourth generation database management systems, style sheets in word processing programs, and statistical packages such as SPSS and SAS. We can learn much from their successes and failures. Unlike most research systems, these commercially available programs have large user populations, enabling us to study the programs as they are actually used in offices and homes.

Our work focuses on spreadsheet software. Spreadsheets have proven enormously popular with personal computer users, and their benefits have been enumerated by Kay (1984), Hutchins, Hollan and Norman (1986), and Lewis and Olson (1987). These investigators have noted that spreadsheets provide a concrete, visible representation of data values, immediate feedback to the user, and powerful features such as applying formulas to blocks of cells.

These characteristics of spreadsheets are important. However, the single biggest advantage of spreadsheets is not cognitive but motivational: after only a few hours of work, spreadsheet users are rewarded by simple but functioning programs that model their problems of interest. Many users lack formal programming education, and perhaps more importantly, they lack an intrinsic interest in computers. The key to understanding non-programmers' interaction with computers is to recognize that non-programmers are not simply underskilled programmers who need assistance learning the complexities of programming. Rather, *they are not programmers at all.* They are business professionals or scientists or other kinds of domain specialists whose jobs involve computational tasks. It is not enough to say that these users need systems that are "easy to use." User programming systems should allow users to solve simple problems within their domain of interest in a few hours.

Methodology

To understand user programming, we believe it is necessary to find out how people actually use software in the everyday contexts of homes and offices. We have chosen to study a small number of people in some depth to learn how they construct, debug, and use spreadsheets. We are interested in the kinds of problems for which people use spreadsheets and how they themselves structure the problem solving process – topics that by their very nature cannot be studied under the controlled conditions of the laboratory.

For the study, we interviewed and tape recorded conversations with spreadsheet users in their offices and homes, and collected examples of their spreadsheets.[1] Study participants were found through an informal process of referral. We told prospective participants that we are interested in software for non-programmers and that we want to talk to people actively using spreadsheets. The interviews were conversational in style, intended to capture the users' experiences in their own words. A fixed set of open-ended questions was asked of each user, though the questions were asked as they arose naturally in the context of the conversation. Part of the interview session was devoted to viewing users' spreadsheets on-line and discussing their uses and construction. Material in this paper is based on about 335 pages of transcribed interview material from a total of eleven users. User names given in this paper are fictitious.

Why do spreadsheets work so well?

The usefulness of spreadsheets derives from two properties of their design:

- Computational techniques that match users' tasks and that shield users from the low-level details of traditional programming, and
- A table-oriented interface that serves as a model for users' applications.

The power of spreadsheets comes from the combination of these properties – either separately would be inadequate to solve the spreadsheet user's two basic problems: *computation* and *presentation*. Our intent in this paper is to understand the reasons for the success of spreadsheets, and to look for general principles that might be applied to other user programming environments.

Computation: The spreadsheet formula language[2]

The spreadsheet formula language allows users to compute values in their models by expressing relations among cell values.[3] To use the formula language, the user must master only two concepts: cells as variables, and functions as relations between variables. With relatively little study, the user acquires the means to solve the basic computational problems of any modeling task: creating entities that represent the variables in the problem, and expressing relations among the entities.

As users become more proficient at using spreadsheets, they learn more advanced programming concepts such as relative and absolute cell references, iteration, and conditionals. Knowing these more advanced concepts is immensely useful, but we want to emphasize that they are not necessary for beginning users building simple spreadsheets. Spreadsheets allow users to perform useful work with a small investment of time, and then to go on to more advanced levels of understanding as they are ready. In our research we found that users may add new programming concepts to their repertoire very slowly.

For example, Jennifer, a user in our study, has been using spreadsheets for about five years. She has an accounting position of considerable responsibility in a high technology firm. Jennifer knows how to write nested conditionals, to link individual spreadsheets, and to create simple macros. She has not, however, learned how to iterate operations over a cell range (a group of contiguous cells), though she is aware of this capability, and plans to learn how to do it. Despite what would be a fatal gap in her knowledge in a traditional programming language, Jennifer is a successful spreadsheet user. Moreover, she is continuing to expand her knowledge about spreadsheets, at her own pace.

The spreadsheet formula language is characterized by:

- High-level, task-specific functions.
- Very simple control constructs.

This combination of attributes in the spreadsheet formula language strikes a fine balance between expressivity and simplicity. Users have sufficient means to model their problems, but at a very attractive price in terms of learning and development time.

High-level, task-specific functions

The formula language offers a small number of arithmetic, financial, statistical, and logical functions. Most spreadsheets also offer simple database functions, date and time functions, and error trapping functions. In our study we found that most users normally use fewer than ten functions in their formulas. Users employ those functions pertinent to their domain (e.g., financial analysis) and do not have need for other functions.

Spreadsheet users are productive with a small number of functions because the functions are high-level, task-specific operations that do not have to be built up from lower level primitives. For example, a common spreadsheet operation is to sum the values of a range of cells within a column. The user writes a simple formula that specifies the sum operation and the cells that contain the values to be summed. The cell range is specified compactly by its first and last cell; e.g., SUM(C1:C8) sums cells 1 – 8 in Column C. In a traditional programming language, computing this sum would require at least writing a loop iterating through elements of an array, and creating variable names for the loop counter and summation variable. Spreadsheet functions obviate the need to create variable names (cells are named by their position in the grid), and to create intermediate variables to hold results – non-task-related actions that many users find confusing and tiresome (Lewis and Olson, 1987).

Control constructs

Lewis and Olson (1987) stated that a strength of spreadsheets is the "absence of control model." They noted that flow of control is a difficult programming concept. However, it is not the case that control mechanisms are absent in spreadsheets – they are just conceptually simple. Formulas can be written as if-then-else statements. A conditional in a spreadsheet formula is easy to understand because it does not transfer control from one part of the spreadsheet to another; its effects are local to the individual cell. Iteration is also quite simple; users can select a range of cells over which to iterate an operation. These conditional and iterative capabilities were routinely used by those in our study and added a great deal of functionality to their spreadsheets.

Users' own formulas contain an implicit flow of control as any arbitrary cell can be related to any other. When a value in one cell changes it may trigger a series of changes in dependent cells. This is the very basis of the spreadsheet's functionality, and it is quite powerful. Users can begin by building quite simple cell relations, and move on to more elaborate models as their knowledge expands.

User Programming Languages

Several lines of research on user programming proceed from the assumption that graphical techniques such as as program visualization, visual programming (Myers, 1986), and program induction (Maulsby and Witten, 1989)[4] will provide significant leverage to non-programmers. Since the spreadsheet formula language is textual, we question whether graphics *per se* is really the key to user programming languages. A limited language of high-level functions is more important than the particular form the language takes. In our study we asked users to discuss the disadvantages of spreadsheets. Not one user mentioned difficulties with the formula language (though users had other specific complaints about spreadsheets). Syntax is often suggested as a problem area in textual languages, but in our study users reported that syntax errors were few once they were familiar with a spreadsheet. Users noted that in any case, most such errors are immediately caught by the spreadsheet itself which will not permit poorly formed formulas. Proper syntax checking appears to be sufficient to enable users to cope with syntax errors. Textual languages are compact, efficient, and can be developed in less time than graphical languages. These are significant advantages which should be considered in the development of user programming languages.

Another line of user programming research suggests that users can program by modifying existing example programs (Lewis and Olson, 1987; Neal, 1989). These researchers believe that the complexity and difficulty of general purpose programming can be reduced by giving non-programmers a "head-start" with existing code which they then modify for their particular applications.[5] Even assuming that the daunting problem of information access were to be solved such that users could easily locate apposite examples, we think that general purpose programming languages, no matter how well supported, are not appropriate for the large population of users who lack intrinsic interest in computers, and have very specific jobs to accomplish. These users should be supported at their level of interest, which is to perform specific computational tasks, not to become computer programmers.

What about programming by modifying domain-specific examples? This solution still does not solve the problem of having to depend on the existence of appropriate example code. True user programming systems allow users to build a meaningful application without reliance on obtaining code from other more sophisticated users. No programmer wants to lack the skills with which to create a program from scratch, since that is so often necessary. If it is impossible to begin a program without an existing program, the user is denied real control over the computational environment. It is not clear whether users who modify existing example programs ever really come to understand the programs they modify. Without a firm grasp of the language in which the examples are written, the ability to modify a program to suit one's needs would seem very limited.

There is a need to draw a distinction between programming by modifying example programs and the reuse of software modules. Reusable software modules are clearly desirable. In the spreadsheet world there is software reuse in the form of templates used by groups of users (Nardi and Miller, 1989). However users are not dependent on templates, and they routinely create their own applications using the spreadsheet formula language. We asked users what they liked about spreadsheets, and several users reported that they can be "creative" with spreadsheets, that it is "easy" to build their own models. One user captured a general feeling about spreadsheets in noting that he thinks of the spreadsheet as a "blank canvas" – a medium in which to directly express his own thoughts; just the opposite of an artifact created by someone else that must be re-worked before it is of any use.

The large variety of applications modeled with spreadsheets (Lewis and Olson, 1987) does indeed suggest a blank canvas. Spreadsheet applications include mathematical modeling (Arganbright, 1986), simple databases, managing small businesses, forecasting trends (Janowski, 1987), analyzing scientific and engineering data, and of course the financial applications for which they were first intended. Users have programmed these diverse and sometimes sophisticated applications (see Arganbright, 1986) without the aid of example programs.

Presentation: The tabular grid

The second major element of the spreadsheet interface is a strong visual format for organizing and presenting data – the tabular grid into which users put data values, labels and annotations. The table helps users solve three crucial problems: viewing, structuring and displaying data.

Viewing data

Virtually every user in our study reported that an advantage of spreadsheets is the ability to view large quantities of data on one screen. Applications modeled with spreadsheets are data-rich, and users in our study had a strong preference for being able to view and access as much data as possible without scrolling the screen. How do spreadsheets manage large amounts of data such that users feel that it is well-presented and comprehensible?

Spreadsheets have done well at data display by borrowing a commonly used display format – that of the table. Cameron (1989) pointed out that tables have been in use for 5000 years. Inventory tables, multiplication tables and tables of reciprocal values have been found by archaeologists excavating Middle Eastern cultures. Ptolemy, Copernicus, Kepler, Euler, and Gauss used tables. Modern times brought us VisiCalc, the first personal computer spreadsheet. VisiCalc was modeled directly on the tabular grid of accountants' columnar paper which contains numbered rows and columns. It is interesting that today's spreadsheets, while much enhanced in functionality, have not changed the basic VisiCalc format in the smallest detail. A tabular grid in which rows are labeled with numbers and columns are labeled with letters characterizes all commercially available spreadsheets.

Tables are so familiar and common in our everyday lives that we are unlikely to pause to appreciate their clever design – they are extraordinarily simple and viewable. It is quite easy, even in a large table, to ascertain the categories represented in the vertical and horizontal dimensions, to scan for individual data values, and to get a sense of the range of values and other characteristics such as a rough average. The perceptual reasons for tables' exceptional capability to effectively display data are not well understood, but Cleveland's notion of "clustering" – the ability to hold a collection of objects in short-term memory and carry out further visual and mental processing (personal communication, 1989) – seems relevant. The arrangement of data items in rows and columns appears to permit efficient clustering, as users can remember the values in a row or column and then perform other cognitive tasks that involve the values.

The familiarity of tables further enhances the ease with which we use them; our schooling explicitly trains us in table use from reading calendars to learning matrix algebra, and everyday experience provides ample opportunity to both create and view tables.

Tables provide good information access as users can locate data in a simple geometric space. In a large spreadsheet though the data are not continually visible (a desideratum of proponents of direct manipulation) as the entire spreadsheet will not fit on one screen, the geometric organization of the grid permits users to find their data quickly.

For example, Jennifer was discussing a spreadsheet that contained about 300 rows and we asked her how she "gets around" in this large spreadsheet. Notice that in the following exchange she thinks we want to know the mechanics of navigating with mouse and keyboard. She adds the comment about the geometric layout of her spreadsheet as a clarification, though we have not talked about layout at any time in her interviews:

Interviewer: Now when you're actually using a spreadsheet this big, how do you get around to the places you want to be?

Jennifer: I use the mouse on the gray bar. It lets you leap down a page. It's kind of like page-up and page-down. But I can page-right and -left more easily than you can with the keyboard.

Interviewer: OK, so that's not really an issue. Even though you do have a lot of data it's pretty easy to find it.

Jennifer: UmmHmm. I'm so familiar with the spreadsheet too, that I know that if I'm here [points to a place on the spreadsheet] in Municipal Bonds, that I know I'm in the middle of the document, and I know that Preferred Stocks is above that, and I know that Collaterized Mortgage Obligations are below that, so depending on what the next transaction is, I know whether to go up or down.

Today's spreadsheets also allow users to assign names to cell ranges. In our study, some users assigned range names in large spreadsheets and then located the range by typing in the name, rather than scrolling to it. Spreadsheets thus offer both logical and spatial clues to data location that enable users to quickly find data even in very large spreadsheets.[6]

Structuring data

A spreadsheet table is much more than an effective data display – it is a problem solving medium. We tend to think of data presentation as largely a matter of setting forth information for the user to view and browse. But the means by which data are presented strongly affect the problem solving process. The table inhabits problem solving cognition in two ways.

First, the very structure of the table is the means by which users come to organize their models. Data are arranged into rows, columns, and cells. The spreadsheet provides a structure into which a model is cast. *Users do not have to invent a structure* – it is given to them. The initial phase of a modeling problem is reduced to simply recognizing a format into which a problem is framed, rather than being faced with the necessity of inventing a format from scratch.

Second, in the very process of laying out data in a spreadsheet, the user is viewing and studying the data which are immediately reflected back from the table. This contrasts sharply with traditional programming where the parameters and variables of a model are implicit in the procedures that manipulate them, and have no explicit visual representation.[7]

The structured visual format for data presentation provided by the spreadsheet table plays an active role in helping users to *structure* and then *critique* their models. We now look in more detail at how users structure and critique spreadsheet models.

The most striking thing about spreadsheets is how they help users to think through problems. *The tabular format provides a simple but powerful framework onto which users map their problems.* The importance of this structure became evident as users described how they use spreadsheets to model problems *even when their initial ideas about the problem solution are extremely ill-defined.* We were struck by the fact that many users reported that when they begin a spreadsheet they have only a general goal in mind (e.g., "maximize profits over the next three quarters" or "decide how much house we can afford"), and very little idea of how to achieve the goal. When beginning work on a new spreadsheet, users often do not even know what the parameters of a problem are. They only find out about all the relevant aspects of a problem in the process of actually trying to solve it.

For example, Jeremy, one of the participants in our study, described how he learned to use spreadsheets. A job assignment required developing business plans for joint ventures with foreign companies. Large, complex spreadsheet models were part of the plans. Although programmers were available to help, Jeremy discovered that not only was it easier to be in control of spreadsheet development himself, but that he could use the spreadsheet to work through the problem, in particular to identify the variables of interest and to make sure that the model was complete.

Jeremy described this process:

Jeremy: We had to have rather large complex spreadsheets [for the business plans] where you had lots of variables. And I found it easier to develop that myself than to go to somebody and say here's what I want, here's what I want, here's what I want. And that's what really got me going on [spreadsheets]...

Interviewer: Why was it easier for you to do this yourself than to specify it for a programmer?

Jeremy: ...I think it was quicker and easier because I felt that I was learning as I went, as I was developing the spreadsheets, I was *learning* about all the variables that I needed to think about. It was [as] much a prop for myself as [a way of] ...getting the outcome ... And there were a lot of false *endings*, I should say, not false starts. I'd get to the end and think, "I'm done," and I'd look at it and I'd say, "No, I'm not, because I've forgotten about one thing or the other."

How do spreadsheets help users give shape to fuzzy ideas?

The spreadsheet provides an overall organizing framework of rows, columns and cells within which users organize the parameters, variables, formulas and subparts of their models.

Rows and columns are used to represent the main parameters of a problem. Users know that related things go in rows and columns, and all spreadsheet applications take advantage of the simple but powerful semantics provided by the row/column convention.

Each cell represents and displays one variable. A cell value may be a constant, or may be a calculated value derived from a formula. In the case of calculated values, the spreadsheet associates a visual object, the cell itself, with a small program, the formula. Program code is thus distributed over a visual grid, providing a system of compact, comprehensible, easily located program modules. The spreadsheet itself automatically updates dependent values as independent values change; therefore the user's the task is to write a series of small formulas, each associated with a distinct visual object, rather than the more difficult task of specifying the full control loop of a program as a set of procedures.

Tables provide a simple mechanism for segmenting models into smaller subparts: leaving empty cells between segments. A spreadsheet can be modularized, at least visually, for the purpose of showing its subparts. In our study, we found that users segment spreadsheets by such criteria as years, months, geographic regions, companies, and departments.

Spreadsheets relieve users of the necessity of inventing

their own modeling frameworks – a demanding task which would force them to build a problem solving infrastructure before getting to work on their actual goals. The spreadsheet table, by virtue of a structured visual format for presenting data, provides the hooks upon which a user hangs a model. The advantages of this structure are amplified by the fact that as the user builds the model, it emerges in a highly visible way. The model is not buried in a text file of many lines of computer code, it is not littered with obscure variable names, but instead consists of an orderly set of parameter names and variable values laid out in a simple two-dimensional space. Users can see exactly what their parameters and variables are as they add them to the model.

The visibility of the emerging model is very important in the problem solving process. In our study we found that users critique their models by visually inspecting them. As Jeremy noted, he evaluated the completeness of his model by *looking at it*: "I'd look at it and I'd say, 'No, I'm not [done], because I've forgotten about one thing or the other.'" Other users also described the process of visually inspecting their models as they were building them. For example, one user stated: "I may not even ... know the final form, look and feel of the spreadsheet that I want. I'll just start getting the data in, and then I'll start ... playing with moving rows and columns around and doing things until *I see*, until I get what I want" (our emphasis). The act of viewing data in a spreadsheet table is thus not merely a means by which to find a data value, or check out the bottom line; it is a key aspect of the active process of model construction.

To summarize, the way data are presented – that is, what the user *sees* – shapes the problem solving process. As a user begins developing a spreadsheet, the tabular grid provides an overarching structure into which the parameters and variables of a model are cast. As the spreadsheet begins to take shape, the user views the emerging model and evaluates its accuracy and completeness. Within the framework of the rows and columns the user can restructure the model by re-arranging rows and columns and by adding new parameters as they become known. A spreadsheet model is grounded in the distinct tabular format of rows and columns, and is constructed in successive approximations as the user critiques the emerging model.

Displaying data

Users welcome structure in modeling the parameters and variables of their problems, but seek flexibility in creating their own displays. In office environments many spreadsheets are viewed and used by a group of co-workers, and users in our study emphasized the importance of creating effective presentations – often paper copies or slides of their spreadsheets.

The spreadsheet table has some useful flexibility. All spreadsheets allow users to vary column width, and modern spreadsheets allow users to vary individual column widths and row heights. Spreadsheets allow users to split the screen so that non-contiguous portions of a spreadsheet may be viewed on the screen (or printed out) at once. Spreadsheet cells are flexible building blocks; they are used not only to hold variables, but also to display labels and annotations, and to segment large spreadsheets into subparts by means of empty cells, as noted. All users in our study used some or all of these capabilities. All users in our study who had spreadsheet products that give users control over color, fonts, shading and outlining used these techniques to highlight important data. In short, spreadsheets give users a reasonably good user interface toolkit.

Summary

Of course, spreadsheets are not without their problems, many of which derive from the same properties that give them their strength. The ability to build spreadsheets through assigning small pieces of code to specific cells means that it is difficult to get a global sense of the structure of the spreadsheet, which requires tracing the dependencies among the cells. Many users in our study described awkward pencil and paper procedures for tracing cell dependencies in debugging spreadsheets. For the same reason, spreadsheets are not particularly modular: since the code that implements a particular piece of a spreadsheet is distributed over a potentially large and unpredictable set of cells, it is difficult to reuse a piece of one spreadsheet in another new spreadsheet.

Nevertheless, the strengths of spreadsheets are profound. Spreadsheets suggest that two key characteristics for user programming environments are:

1. A limited set of carefully chosen, high-level, task-specific operations that are sufficient for building applications within a restricted domain, and

2. A strong visual format for structuring and presenting data.

The ability to create applications with only a few functions is an important benefit of spreadsheets. Users have specific tasks to accomplish within their domain of interest. They want functionality that matches those tasks at a high level such that they do not have to either learn or use lower level primitives. Task-specific functions allow users to develop quick facility with a program and to build a real application, however simple, in a short time. The motivational barrier is thus breached as users achieve rapid success. As users continue to use a program they are not constantly faced with the job of stringing together lower level functions as they work, but can concentrate on the actual problem solving itself.

Spreadsheets succeed because they combine an expressive high level programming language with a powerful visual format to organize and display data. The user is actively engaged with the spreadsheet table as a problem solving device throughout the process of model building. The tabular structure of rows, columns and cells provides a modeling framework. The visibility of the emerging model allows the user to monitor and evaluate its accuracy and completeness.

The spreadsheet experience suggests that general programming languages are not the answer for non-programmers. Users who lack intrinsic interest in computers and who have specific tasks to get done are more likely to respond to a software system that provides high-level functionality in their area of expertise than to tolerate the slow detour of a general programming language. Insofar as techniques such as program visualization, visual programming, programming by example modification and program induction support general programming, they are unlikely, in our view, to succeed at helping non-programmers gain increased computational power. A more fruitful line of endeavor is to identify ways to support the development of high-level, task-specific languages and appropriate visual formats for new user programming environments.

Notes

1. The interviews were conducted by the first author. We use the plural "we" here for expository ease.

2. We refer to "the formula language" because most spreadsheet programs have nearly identical languages which differ only in small syntactic details.

3. Spreadsheets also have macro languages, but they are used by many fewer users and do not constitute the basic interface to spreadsheet functionality that we are concerned with here.

4. Programs are "induced" by generalizing from concrete examples created by the user via graphical direct manipulation techniques.

5. Example modification is not the same as the use of didactic examples which have an important role in learning and enhancing skill in programming (and many other areas of endeavor). Didactic examples are especially helpful in learning language syntax as part of a larger program of study in which the fundamental concepts of a programming language are learned.

6. In our study the largest spreadsheets had about a thousand rows.

7. The spreadsheet provides immediate feedback. When the user changes data values, other values related through formulas are immediately updated. This compression of the test-evaluate-debug cycle is an important feature of spreadsheets, but one that has been discussed by other investigators (Hutchins et al., 1986; Lewis and Olson, 1987) so we do not expand on it here.

Acknowledgments: We are grateful for comments from Lucy Berlin, Martin Griss, Jeff Johnson, Nancy Kendzierski, Jasmina Pavlin and Craig Zarmer.

References

Arganbright, D. (1986). Mathematical modeling with spreadsheets. *Abacus* 3:4:18-31.

Cameron, J. (1989). A cognitive model for tabular editing. OSU-CISRC Research Report, June, 1989. Ohio State University.

Cleveland, W. (1989). Personal communication.

Hutchins, E., Hollan, J. and Norman, D. (1986). Direct manipulation interfaces. In *User Centered System Design* (Eds. D. Norman and S. Draper). Erlbaum Publishers: Hillsdale, NJ.

Janowski, R. (1987). Spreadsheets: An initial investigation. Internal Technical Report, Hewlett-Packard Laboratories, Bristol, England.

Kay, A. (1984). Computer software. *Scientific American* 5:3:53-59.

Lewis, C. and Olson, G. (1987). Can principles of cognition lower the barriers to programming? In *Empirical Studies of Programmers: Second Workshop* (Eds. G. Olson, S. Sheppard and E. Soloway). Ablex Publishing Corporation: Norwood, NJ.

Maulsby, D. and Witten, I. (1989). Inducing programs in a direct-manipulation environment. In *Proceedings of CHI'89, Conference on Human Factors in Computing Systems.* April 30 - May 4, 1989. Austin, Texas.

Myers, B. (1986). Visual programming, programming by example, and program visualization: A taxonomy. In *Proceedings of CHI'86 Conference on Human Factors in Computing Systems.* April 13 - 17, Boston.

Nardi, B. and Miller, J. (1989). Twinkling lights and nested loops: Distributed problem solving and spreadsheet development. Hewlett-Packard Laboratories, Palo Alto, STL-Report 89-30.

Neal, L. (1989). A system for example-based programming. In *Proceedings of CHI'89, Conference on Human Factors in Computing Systems.* April 30 - May 4, 1989. Austin, Texas.

Human–Computer Interaction – INTERACT '90
D. Diaper et al. (Editors)
Elsevier Science Publishers B.V. (North-Holland)

ACTION REPRESENTATION FOR HOME AUTOMATION

Suzanne SEBILLOTTE*

Projet de Psychologie Ergonomique, Institut National de Recherche en Informatique et Automatique. Rocquencourt BP 105. 78153. Le Chesnay-Cedex. France.

A study on the representation of the actions in the context of programming various home devices (oven, TV, heating etc.) is reported. Previous studies have shown that: 1) in a work situation, subjects' representations of their task are based on hierarchical levels of abstraction, 2) in the context of programming home devices subjects referred to general concepts of activities (e.g."tuning").Two experiments, inspired by those of Galambos (1986) were conducted in order to specify more fully these general concepts. Results showed that these concepts were deeply rooted in subjects' representations, independently of the devices. Implications of these results for home interface design are described, concerning especially command naming.

1. INTRODUCTION

In a work situation, previous studies [1] have shown that subjects' representation of their tasks are based on hierarchical levels of abstraction. In other contexts i.e. situations of programming various home devices (oven, TV, heating etc.) subjects referred to general concepts of activities (e.g. "tuning") [2]. These general concepts seem to form the basis of device use representations in various domains of everyday life. Having the knowledge of these concepts is useful for user interface design.

Many research studies related to understanding and memory for text [3, 4, 5, 6, 7, 8] have shown that the scripts when they are activated, organize the understanding of situations based on events. More recently, Galambos [9, 10] examined the relationships among action components of scripted activities as well as those between the actions and the general concepts (script headers). For the author, the *activity* refers to a self-contained series of actions performed to attain a goal in a particular situation (synonymous with *script*) and the *action* refers to the component actions of the activity. Through a series of experiments he studied the main features of representations of actions of an activity or scripts of everyday life, especially the centrality and the distinctiveness of actions.Usually an activity involves carrying out several actions (or sub-goals). Galambos showed that the central actions which are often the main goals or sub-goals, serve to organize groups of actions within activities. This implies a hierarchical representation, where less central actions (steps in a plan) are subordinated to the more central goal actions. This goal structure is close to those discussed by other authors [11, 12, 13]. The activity name would be the highest node in the hierarchy of goals since that is the goal which organizes the sub-goals (or the actions).

In a study [2] with the pratical objective of elaborating a user interface for a home automation system, subjects were interviewed, in order to record elements which made it possible to definite a limited system for designing a model and the first command languages. The subjects were interviewed about the programming and the use of their home devices and we noted that to describe the use of these devices, some subjects referred to the general activity, which is not specific to a particular device, for example : putting on, tuning, choosing etc.
In order to specify more fully these general concepts of activity, two experiments were conducted, inspired by Galambos [10] : In the first experiment, subjects were asked to provide *action clusters,* the second experiment required a "*membership decision task.*".

2. EXPERIMENT 1 : ACTION CLUSTERS

The aim of this experiment is to identify and suggest some classes of activity or classification of actions from a large corpus of expressions used by subjects in discourse concerning devices.

2.1. Method and material

We were inspired by one of Galambos' experiments [10] : action clusters.Ten subjects were asked to sort together a set of 94 cards as they wanted (i.e. according to criteria they had previously chosen). On each card, an expression about an activity or an action was written (for example : "switch on a piece of equipment" or " press the button *program* ").

The set of written expressions had been built up from the interview protocols. It included all the expressions of actions used by subjects to describe commands (in the sense of interaction with a machine) and found in the interview protocols. These interviews concerned the use of devices by users and how they imagined simultaneously programming several devices with a fictive system [2].
The subjects of the experiment were permitted to make as many clusters as they wished as long as they ended up with fewer than 10 and more 4 clusters. In addition, they were asked to choose 3 cards which they judged the most representative of each cluster.The task was individual and the subjects were not timed.

---

* The study was conducted under a contract with the Centre Commun d'Etudes de Telediffusion et Telecommunications (CCETT). Rennes France.

2.2. Results

Above all the main results concern the criteria of classification and the actions which represent the classes [14].

* *Remark : The expressions are translated from french and correspond to the subjects' verbalizations. As certain of the original french expressions have two meanings, we have given the english translation for these two meanings . For example the french "régler" means both "tune" and "set".*

2.2.1. Action clusters or the criteria of classification

At first, only two main criteria were chosen by the subjects : cluster around the tasks and cluster around the devices.

Cluster around tasks

These clusters were also named by some subjects "around kind of actions" or "around intention and action". The average number of clusters is 7.2.

The same classes noted previously were found again : preparation or prerequisites of use, putting on, choosing or selection and tuning. In addition to these clusters, the subjects put together the expressions :
- which specify that a function or a key is activated,
- all those which concern programming,
- and the various expressions judged too general or unclassifiable.

The classification by type of task or action concurs with the results obtained by Byrne [15] which suggest that the mental representation in a everyday task (mental cookery) is economical and hierarchically structured into "subroutines".
The additional clusters "activating a function key" and "programming" may be explained because some interviews here concerned programming several devices. This is to be emphasized because it must be taken into account for future interactive systems allowing the programming of several devices.

Clusters arround devices

The average number of clusters is 6.2.
The first choice is a classification by device, but the subjects met difficulties because the number of authorized classes was limited and because certain expressions were ambiguous (the actions did not concern a particular object such as "put on" or, on the contrary,concerned several devices such as "video cassette recorder (VCR) and tape-recorder").
Then the subjects solved the problem by clustering certain devices (e.g. the decoder with the video-tape) and above all by making a cluster including commands which are valid for all the devices. The cluster is named by the subjects "common cluster" or "undefined cluster". One subject did not create this category, but she spread these commands over device clusters in order to be able to work all the devices.

It is interesting to note that out of 5 subjects who chose this classification, 3 specified subclusterings : into each class they clustered the cards around the actions. This corresponds to the previous classification i.e. cluster around tasks.

The main device clusters are "common cluster", "cooking" and "audiovisual aids" (VCR, television, and music). The cluster "heating" and "washing machine" are less systematic and that can be explained because there were few cards related to these devices and subjects hesitated to make particular clusters so they put them into the "common cluster" or they decided that they were unclassifiable.

The results confirm what we had observed elsewhere : there are two ways of going about programming several devices, but we cannot say that one is more used than the other. It is possible either to follow the programming progress and only single out the devices when it is necessary or to program each device separately . The fact that neither way dominated implies for interface design that both strategies have been provided with a system destined for widespread use.

Another comment concerns the kind of task or activity intended by the subjects when they use particular tools (here devices which are in a home): to put on and stop a process, to program, to tune, to control etc. We may well find them again in other contexts. This mental representation of the "machine" aspect in a man-machine system seems to be deeply rooted in subjects' representations since even the subjects,who chose device clusters, made subclusters within each cluster according to the tasks. It is important to take this into account either for defining menus or for the first screens of commands in order that the subjects can find the class of actions which they wish to carry out.

2.2.2. Representative actions of classes

In the experiment, the subjects were asked to choose 3 cards which were the most representative of each class (or cluster). We analysed each classification separately : clusters around tasks and clusters around devices, because often the same cards were chosen for both classifications. In this paper we are particularly interested in actions which were judged representative of a class by the subjects and also other classes with the same type of classification.

Representative actions of clusters around tasks

Among the 25 different actions (from 105 chosen actions as a whole) to represent the classes by task, 9 were judged representative of different classes :

- 3 concerned programming and related either to programming in general, or the part of the programming which concerned the timing or the recording. We can consider that there is not a divergence but only a varying degree of precision : recording/enter the program, programming the duration, programming the days, hours, and minutes.
- 3 indicated an action on a specific key or button and concerned particularly the "record/enter" key. This key or button is also found as a characteristic of the programming : press the "record/enter" button.
- finally the 3 other actions are spread over the tuning, the selection and the programming : "hear and tune", "program the channel, the frequency or the radio", and "set (cf tune) at 19°C".

It seems that these classes remain badly defined unlike the classes related to prerequisites or putting on/off, so we must continue our investigations into the features of actions concerning the programming, recording/entering, selection, tuning/setting etc. in order to define more precisely what these activities represent for future system users.

Representative actions of clusters around devices

Among 64 different actions (from 89 chosen action as a whole) to represent the device classes, 18 were judged representative of different classes.

- 9 related to the "audiovisual aids". In this cluster, subjects sorted out together 2 or 3 devices. This explains that a same action can represent 2 classes e.g. "channel 4 with decoder" or "channel 4 with VCR". As previously for the programming, the classification did not really diverge. The differences concern only varying degrees of precision (i.e. subclusters).
- 7 conflicted the "comon cluster" with another device cluster.
- 2 concerned the temperature which was clustered indifferently around "cooking" or around "thermostat".

That shows the reality of the "common cluster" which has to be considered and defined in relation to the specificities of the devices. Also in a class including for example all the audiovisual aids, it is necessary to clearly define the subclasses which have to be specified and verified.
A significant difference must also be noted between the chosen actions concerning both types of classification. The representative actions of clusters around tasks are more often the same than those of clusters around devices. In the first case 25 different actions were found out of 105 chosen actions whereas in the second case 69 different actions out of 89.
The classes seem less well defined in the latter case and support the fact that there were more actions judged representative of different classes.

2.3. Discussion

The experiment showed that there were two ways of going about programming several devices. But the representation of the use of a machine as a set of subgoals to carry out independently of the type of a device used is essential (as the subjects who spontaneously have a repressentation of an individual device also possess the other underlying type of representation).

If the actions chosen by subjects to support their classification make it possible to say that certain classes are well defined, they emphasize the ambiguity of other classes. The classes which have no problem are those related to :
- the preparation or the prerequisites necessary to attain fixed objectives (e.g. to place an objet somewhere),
- the activating or stopping of a process or putting it on/off,
- and the activating of a function (except the function "recording/enter").

On the other hand, it appears that actions could be representative of different acivities according to the subjects : tuning/setting, selection, programming and recording/entering. We noted also that one subject specified that he made a difference between "choosing an element" and "tuning" or "programming" although he had sorted out the cards in the same class.

Concerning this problem, we will mainly retain among the most significant actions :
- *press or push "recording/enter"* and *enter the programming*. The actions represent indifferently either the clusters "activating a function" or "programming" in general.
- *program the channel, the radio, the frequency and set (cf tune) at 19°C*. The actions apply just as well to the activities : "tuning/setting", "selection" or "programming".

Why are there these ambiguities? A possible explanation can be found in Galambos [10] who claimed that the features of action components of activities differ particularly as concerns the centrality and distinctiveness. Because the subjects were asked to choose representative expressions for each cluster, they might have understood the sense of the word "representative" differently. So, *push "recording/enter"* may be a distinctive action for the "activating a function" activity and a central action for the "programming" activity. In the same way *set (cf tune) at 19°C* may be a central action for the "tuning/setting" activity and a distinctive action for the "selection" or "programming" activities.

In order to verify and define these clusters and specify certain activity concepts and their action components, we conducted a second experiment.

3. EXPERIMENT 2 : ACTIVITIES AND ACTIONS

The main research studies in psychology concerning the tasks of classification are related to categorizations of objects [16,17]. More recently researchers have extended their interest to categorizations of scripts of routine activities [3,4,18]. The scripts are divided into scenes. Focusing on the scenes of environment, Twersky and Hemenway [19] obtained similar results to those of Rosch [3,4] i.e. a hierarchical organization and a preferred intermediate level of abstraction or "basic level". At this basic level they noted particular knowledge which they called "knowledge about the parts". The names of parts refer to perceptive entities or functional roles [20].

Referring to previous works which had shown that the basic concepts are specific and distinctive and the superordinate concepts are distinctive but not specific, Murphy and Wisniewski [21,22] studied the mental representation of these concepts at both levels (basic and superordinate). The results of their experiments suggest the qualificative differences between the use of basic and superordinate categories and the representation of their corresponding concepts.
That also appears in our experiment 1 for the cluster"programming". Both levels were found : the superordinate concept is "programming" in general and the basic concepts are "programming the time", "entering the data" and "recording/enter". Experiment 1 showed also that certain classes could be ambiguous.With a view towards tools or system design for human users, it is very important to clearly identify the parts and their functional roles. It is often recommended [23] to distinguish particularly the separate parts and the similar parts.

In order to specify the results of experiment 1, where specific actions (basic level) may represent various activities (superordinate level) we proposed a *"member decision task"* experiment to other subjects. The experiment is inspired by one carried out by Galambos [10] : subjects are asked to decide whether an action is involved or not in performing a given activity.

3.1. Method and material.

From the expressions of action chosen as representative of a given class in the previous experiment, we selected a set according to various degrees of typicality [12]. For each of the 6 activities or classes (preparation, putting on/off, activating a function, tuning/setting, selection and programming),we selected :

- 2 actions representing unambiguously the activity,
- 2 actions chosen for the activity by at least 2 subjects,
- 2 actions representative of another activity (never chosen for the activity)
- and for the problematic classes, the actions which were also chosen to represent other classes.

37 actions were selected in all and 10 subjects took part in the experiment.

Subjects were presented individually with statements, where an action was associated with an activity of the type : "When...(action), I ...(activity).", for example : "When I enter the start or end time, I program".
Each statement was written on a card.
The subjects were asked to reply quickly whether they agreed or not with the statement. The experimenter noted if the subject hesitated or not.

3.2. Results

We attempted in particular to make a clearer distinction between the activities of "tuning/setting", "selection" and "programming" and to specify the action "recording/enter".

Activities of "tuning/setting", "selection" and "programming"

* *"Tuning/setting"*

The activity "tuning/setting" seems precise in the subjects' representations. For 4 of the 6 statements presented, all the subjects replied without hesitation.
This activity can be defined according to a subject of the first experiment, as being:"feeling, seeing, hearing and modifying or making data evolve ".
The data here represent then a continuous variable, as the subjects didn't hesitate over statements such as "play with the amplifier", "vary the temperature" or "set (cf tune) at 19°C". . On the other hand, there were hesitations concerning the TV channel ("modify or program the TV channel").

* *Selection*

Unlike "tuning/setting", "selecting" concerned rather the choice of discontinuous variables. There was no hesitation in choosing a washing program, entering a time or indicating a TV channel . On the other hand, subjects hesitated with "set at 19°C" and one subject insisted saying "no, I don't select". These results support the definitions of this class, given previously by subjects such as "make a choice or decide an object or element or specify data."

* *Programming*

The programming is linked in the subjects' representations by the idea of time : there are no or few hesitations when an hour or duration are specified and by the idea of "enter the operations in memory". The hesitations concerned the actions "set at 19°C" and "program the channel", which, as we have seen, were linked with the activities of "tuning/setting" and "selection".

The action "record /enter"

We particularly selected 2 actions "press on record/enter" and "record/enter the programme or the programming". These actions were judged representative of either the programming or the activating of a function.

In the experiment, "press on record/enter" was no problem. The 10 subjects didn't hesitate, for them it is activating a function and not programming (one subject emphasized this point). On the other hand, "record/enter the programme" caused hesitations concerning the programming.

If we make a comparison with the actions "press on the memory key" and "memorize the operations", which seem unambiguous for the subjects, one concerning activating a function and the other programming, an explanation is possible. In "memorize the operations" several variables, including the time, are in subjects' representations, whereas "record/enter the programme" may be understood as referring to the TV and thus like a selection (of a channel) in the same way as "programming the channel".

3.3. Discussion

To conclude, we recommend for future applications not to use the word "choice " which is not precise enough but rather to use the words "tuning/setting" for the continuous variables (temperature, sound, light..) and "selection" for discontinuous variables (elements, data having a previously defined value, number etc.). Finally we must use the word "programming" only when there is an idea of time and avoid using it when the word "selection" is better suited, for example "selecting the channel" rather than "programming the channel".

The word "record/enter" in our practical application (home interactive automation model) must be kept to specify an objective to be attained : recording a movie or TV broadcast. In all cases, expressions of the type "record/enter the program" must be excluded.

4. GENERAL DISCUSSION

The study related has its limits. The general and practical objective was to bring together elements for the design of a home automation model, with the methodological constraint of studying the mental representations of future users.These mental representations are based on what the subjects know and use in everyday life. In fact the study has an exploratory character, so criticisms may be formulated :

- some expressions designating actions, extracted from interviews, are sometimes imprecise or could have several possible interpretations outside the context of interview ;
- the experimental groups were made up of few subjects without any particular selection criteria, so the individual variable couldn't be controlled and might have had effects ;
- in experiment 2, actions which were not chosen by many subjects as representative of classes, in order to vary the degree of typicality, was not of great interest and might lead the subjects to hesitate.

So, it would be preferable to constitute a more rigorous corpus of subjects' expressions (expressions with a clearer meaning), to present more items in experiment 2 and finally to extend the experiment to a great number of subjects.
Nevertheless, this research confirms the observations made during interviews, i.e. faced with several devices subjects' representations of their use are planned according to either a logical order or by device. This result supports those given by Byrne : when subjects were asked "what ingredients would you need to cook a certain dish?" they "mentally cooked" and the ingredients were reported in the order of use in cooking, the longer pauses segmented the task into logical phases. The phases are mostly components of many dishes.Two knowledge structures exist certainly in memory, but in a given situation one or the other can be preferred. So it is important to propose both approaches for the design of new tools, for example for the use of devices.

On other hand, experiment 1 showed that subjects classed an action according to the similarity of member of the class [8] and not according to attributes . The part naming (or classes) referred also to functional roles.
Finally, we have shown that the limits of certain activities were badly defined in the subjects' representations. Experiment 2 clarified a little but systematic and precise studies must be carried out.

We mentioned that the practical objective of the research was the elaboration of the first interfaces of a limited home automation system. The results were useful for the realisation of the model [2] :
- at first, subjects may plan their devices separately or together, as they wish ;
- the expression "programming" is maintained but with a wide sense i.e. the programming concerning both the time and the selection of an element : device, part of device (oven, grill, roasting spit) or discontinuous variables.
- the word "tuning/setting" concerned only the continuous variables ;
- and the word "record/enter" is kept, only in the sense of recording i.e. to designate the function of recording with a tape-recorder or a VCR.

Through this hierarchical approach to the concepts of actions and activities, concerning the use of devices, we want to emphasize the interest of studying the mental representations of users. Studies of this type would permit the designing of interfaces, name commands or propose user manuals which the future users would understand easily and without ambiguity. This study is an example ; specifiying and naming clusters could be a way forward for future research in various contexts.

REFERENCES

[1] Sebillotte,S., Hierarchical Planning as Method for Task Analysis. Behavior and Information Technology. 7,3. (1988) pp.275-293.

[2] Sebillotte,S., Agli-Garcia,G., Bisseret, A., Laborne, M.P., Scapin, D.L. Ergonomie Cognitive des Interfaces-Utilisateurs de Systèmes Domotiques. Report INRIA. (1990).

[3] Schank,R.C., Abelson,R..Scripts, Plans, Goals and Un-derstanding. (Hillsdale. NewJersey. L.Erlbaum Associates, 1977).

[4] Black, J.B., Bower, G.H.. Episodes as Chunks in Narrative Memory. Journal of Verbal Learning and Verbal Behavior, 18. (1979) pp. 309-318.

[5] Bower, G.H., Black, J.B., Turner, T.J.. Script in Memory for Text. Cognitive Psychology, 11. (1979) pp.177-220.

[6] Anderson, J.R..Cognitive Psychology and Its Implica-tions. (W.H. Freeman and Company. San Francisco, 1980).

[7] Anderson,J.R.. The Architecture of Cognition.(Harvard University Press, London, 1983).

[8] Abelson, R.P.. Psychological status of the script con-cept. American Psychologist, 36. (1981) pp. 715-729.

[9] Galambos, J.A., Rips L.J..Memory for Routines. Journal of Learning and Verbal Behavior, 21. (1981) pp. 206-281.

[10] Galambos, J.A.. Knowledge Structures for Common Activities.in : Galambos, J.A., Abelson, R.P., Black, J.B. (eds), Knowledge Structures (Hillsdale, New Jersey. L.Erlbaum Associates, 1986). pp. 21-47.

[11] Graesser, A.C.. How to Catch a Fisch : The Memory and Representation of Common Procedures. Discourse Processes, 1. (1978), pp. 72-89.

[12] Graesser, A.C.,Robertson, S.P., Anderson, P.A.. Incorporating Inferences in Narratives Representations : A study of How and Why. Cognitive Psychology, 13. (1981) pp. 1-26.

[13] Lichenstein, E.H., Brewer,W.F.. Memory for Goal Directed Events. Cognitive Psychology, 12. (1980) pp. 412-445.

[14] Sebillotte, S.. Les actions et les concepts generaux d'activités dans l'utilisation d'appareils domestiques. Research report INRIA. (1990) in print.

[15] Byrne, R.. Mental Cookery : An Illustration of Retrieval from Plans.Quarterly Journal of Experimental Psychology, 33A. (1981) pp. 31-37.

[16] Rosh,E., Mervis, C.B., Gray, W., Johnson,D., Boyes-Braem, P.. Basic Objects In Natural Categories. Cognitive Psychology,8. (1976) pp. 382-439.

[17] Mervis, C.B., Rosch, E.. Categorization of Natural Objects. Annual Reviews of Psychology,32. (1981) pp. 89-115.

[18] Abelson, R.P. Psychological status of script concept. American Psychologist,36. (1981) pp. 715-729.

[19] Tversky, B., Hemenway, K. Categories of Environmental Scenes. Cognitive Psychology,15. (1983). pp. 121-149.

[20] Tversky, B., Hemenway, K.. Objects, Parts and Categories. Journal of Experimental Psychology General, 113,2. (1984) pp. 169-189.

[21] Murphy, G.L., Wisniewski,E.J.. Categorizing Objects in Isolation and in Scenes : What a Superordinate is Good For. Journal of Experimental Psychology : Learning, Memory and Cognition,15,4. (1989) pp. 572-586.

[22] Wisniewski, E.J., Murphy, G.L.. Superordinate and Basic Category Names in Discourse : A Textual Analysis. Discourse Proceses, 12. (1989) pp. 245-261.

[23] Norman, D.A.. Steps toward a Cognitive Engeneering : Design Rules Based on Analyses of Human Errors. in Proc. of Conf. on Human Factors in Computer Systems. (1982). Ed : Gaithsburg, M.D..

Human–Computer Interaction - INTERACT '90
D. Diaper et al. (Editors)
Elsevier Science Publishers B.V. (North-Holland)

Browsing Through Program Execution

Heinz-Dieter Böcker and Jürgen Herczeg

Institut für Informatik, Universität Stuttgart, Herdweg 51, D-7000 Stuttgart 1

The system TRACK is a trace component for animation and debugging of SMALLTALK-80 programs. Unlike traditional tracers it is designed as a construction kit utilizing interaction techniques based on graphical visualization and direct manipulation. A trace is specified by manipulating graphical objects in a trace window. Different trace windows may provide insight into different parts of a program. This paper describes how TRACK interacts with the standard programming tools of SMALLTALK-80 (class browsers, inspectors, debuggers, etc.) and how tracing and browsing techniques are combined to visualize the execution of a program.

1 Introduction

Today, constructing or analysing complex systems, as for example electronic devices, is only possible with the help of various tools and instruments, e.g. when troubleshooting an electronic device an engineer uses different measuring instruments, like oscilloscopes or frequency spectrum analysers, which are sophisticated electronics systems themselves. These kinds of measuring instruments are most useful when they are connected to the system while it is in operation. They give the engineer insight into internal processes of the system which are normally invisible and may possibly reveal malfunctions of the device that cannot be derived from external symptoms of a system fault. So, these instruments give the engineer a feel of how a system works or why it does not work.

The problems of implementing and analysing computer programs are not so much different from the problems described above. Nevertheless, existing tools that help implementing, testing, and debugging a program are usually not as handy and easy to use for a programmer as, for example, electronic measuring instruments for an engineer. The problem is not that a programmer does not know which internals of the program would be of interest for him. It is much more the problem of how the programmer specifies what he wants to see and how the internal processes of a program are presented to him, i.e. a problem of communication. The task is complicated by the fact that the programmer has to communicate with the program and the "measuring instruments" via the same devices – a computer screen, a keyboard, and possibly a mouse. So, how should the "software oscilloscope" (cf. [Böcker et al. 89a]) be hooked up with the program, how should it look like – how should it work?

2 Programming tools for object oriented programming

Object oriented programming languages need powerful programming tools more desperately than other, ordinary programming languages. Typical application programs deal with hundreds or thousands of only loosely connected objects and even more different messages to be sent between them when the program runs.

According to the nature of programs two types of tools can be identified:

- Tools to analyse *data* structures, which may be used to inspect static program structures. Class and instance browsers are typical examples of tools of this kind.
- Tools to analyse *control* structures. Again, they may be used to inspect static program structures, as for example method browsers, or they may be invoked to inspect the execution state of an interrupted program part, e.g. the invocation hierarchy of a method stopped at a break point. On the other hand, there are tools to inspect the dynamic behaviour of a program while it is running, e.g. tracing components recording the execution of specified program parts.

The SMALLTALK-80 programming environment [Goldberg 84] provides different kinds of tools to analyse the static program structure, such as class, instance, and method browsers, as well as a debugger and stepper, which may invoke each other. All of these tools provide and rely on a homogeneous textual user interface. Tools to analyse the dynamic program behaviour are not included in standard SMALLTALK-80. Also, none of the tools provided makes use of the graphical capabilities that are an integral part of the SMALLTALK-80 system. Although several program animation and visual programming systems have used Smalltalk as implementation language [Brown 88, Smith 77] with a few exceptions (e.g. [Kleyn, Gingrich 88]) there is hardly any general, graphical tool to support the visualization of dynamic aspects of standard SMALLTALK-80 programs.

Since in object oriented programming control and data structure are tightly interwoven we need tools that visualize both data structures (classes and instances) and control structures (messages and methods) while the program is running. For example, the method invoked by a message depends on the class (and its position in the class hierarchy) of the instance receiving the message, which is determined at runtime. To make both types of information inspectable in one browsing and tracing tool, a combination of textual and graphical interaction and visualization techniques is required. The usability of this tool, as that of any other programming tool, critically depends on a tight integration with the rest of the environment, i.e. how much it is based on the knowledge represented in the system (system kernel and application) and how smoothly it interacts with the other programming tools included.

The TRACK system provides a trace component for SMALLTALK-80 which textually and graphically visualizes both the static world of objects as well as the dynamic world of messages sent between these objects. TRACK may not only be used for debugging means but for *program visualization* and *algorithm animation* in general. In the following we will discuss how TRACK is used as a browsing and tracing tool and how it interacts with the standard programming tools of SMALLTALK-80, the browsers, inspectors, and debuggers.

3 TRACK

The system TRACK (trace construction kit) was originally built as a trace component for SMALLTALK-80

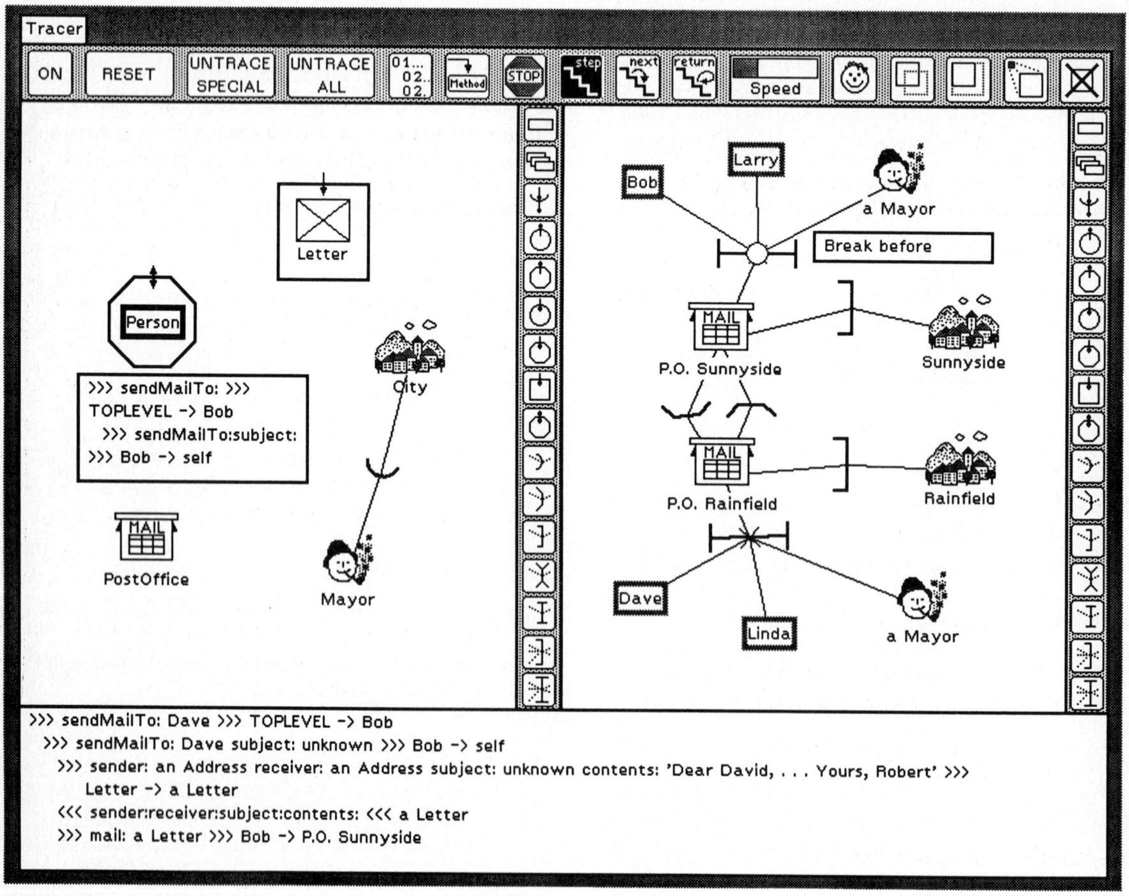

Figure 1: A graphical tracer of TRACK tracing a small application program dealing with the inhabitants of two cities corresponding with each other by sending mail

programs, which traces the messages sent and methods invoked in a running program. It is based on the internal toolkit TRICK, which provides building blocks to implement arbitrary tracers for SMALLTALK-80. In contrast to traditional text oriented tracers, well known from procedural and functional languages, the tracers of TRACK employ a direct manipulation graphical user interface for both the specification and visualization phase of the tracing task [Böcker, Herczeg 90]. In TRACK, the tracing task is strongly supported by browsing activities, commonly used in object oriented programming.

3.1 TRACK as a construction kit

In its overall design philosophy TRACK follows the idea of *construction kits*, which has become popular in connection with artificial laboratory and gaming environments [Böcker et al. 89b, Budge 83] and has recently been applied to programming environments [Ingalls et al. 88]. Following the construction kit paradigm (cf. [Fischer, Lemke 88]) complex systems may be easily constructed by selecting, connecting, and modifying elementary building blocks provided by the system. The building blocks within TRACK are:

- Representations of internal objects of the application program to be traced (classes and instances).
- Obstacles that may be set up between or around the classes and instances. They represent the trace specifications, i.e. what is to be traced.
- Textual trace windows that hold the textual trace produced at the obstacles.
- Graphical visualizations for traced messages.

Figure 1 shows a TRACK tracer for a small application program. It consists of

- two graphical trace windows, in which the building blocks are connected, one for icons representing all the instances of a specific class (the "class window") and one for icons representing specific instances (the "instances window"),
- a global textual trace window collecting all textual trace output generated by any of the obstacles,
- graphical menus for global operations and for selecting the building blocks, e.g. the different obstacles.

With TRACK, the trace for a program resembles a "jumping course" where "hurdles" and "fences" are built up around and between objects forcing the interchanged messages to follow the course and, thus, make them visible, interruptable, inspectable, etc.

3.2 Browsing with TRACK

The specification of a trace for object oriented programs is based on the selection of *methods*, determined by their classes, selectors, and arguments, or *messages*, determined by their senders, receivers, selectors, arguments, and maybe their results. This basically corresponds to the task of inspecting the network of instances connected with each other by slot–value relations and organized in class hierarchies defining methods. To inspect these networks and hierarchies, typically, browsing techniques are used that let the programmer navigate through the complex static structures of an application program. Tools fulfilling this task are class, instance, and method browsers.

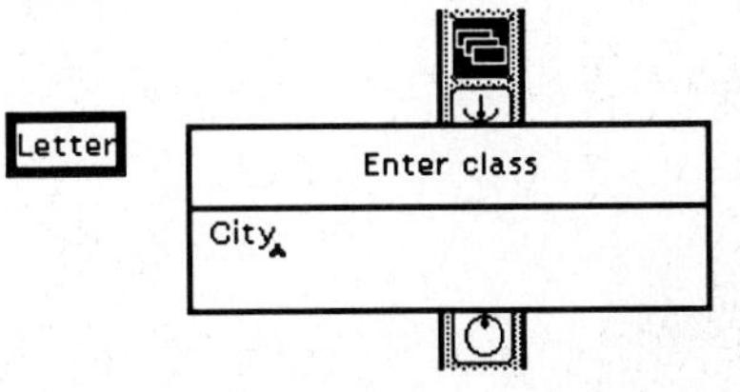

Figure 2: Inserting the class `City` in the class window

To select and inspect the classes, instances, and methods that are to be included in a trace specification, TRACK mainly utilizes browsing techniques and, thereby, makes use of standard programming tools of SMALLTALK-80, the `System Browser` and the `Inspector`. Objects to be inserted in a graphical trace window may be specified by global variables or Smalltalk expressions yielding access to objects, e.g. classes may be referenced by their unique name. In figure 2, for example, the class `City` is inserted in the class window. Alternatively, objects may be inserted via objects already included in the tracer, which is more useful in most cases. For a class, the corresponding metaclass and all or individual superclasses, subclasses, and instances may be added; for an instance, just the corresponding class may be added. In figure 3 all instances of class `City` are inserted. Instead of the default textual representations objects may be visualized by individual bitmaps and textual descriptions (see figure 1). By default, instances obtain the graphical representations of their corresponding classes (cf. figure 3).

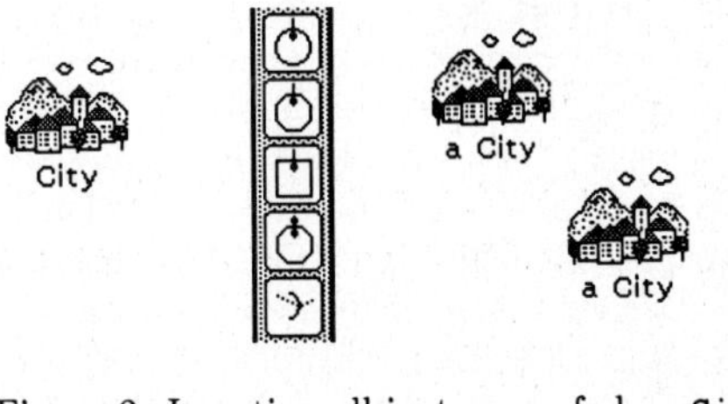

Figure 3: Inserting all instances of class `City`

Classes and instances contained in a graphical tracer may be inspected by standard browsers and inspectors, respectively (cf. figure 4). Conversely, from a browser classes may be added to the tracer, and from an inspector those instances may be added which are accessible as slot values of the inspected instance. Methods (or messages) affected by an obstacle depend on the type of the obstacle and may be restricted with respect to the classes they stem from or by selecting specific method (or message) selectors from a menu or form (see figure 6). Thus, specifying a trace with TRACK means browsing through the object world of the application and picking up the objects and methods of particular interest to include them in the specification.

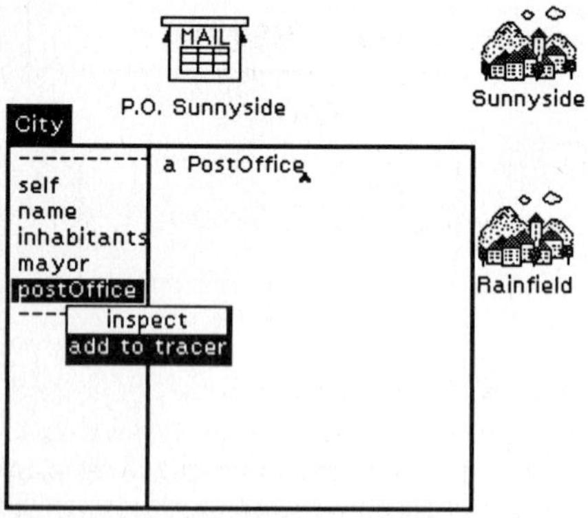

Figure 4: Inspecting the city named `Rainfield` and adding its post office to the tracer

3.3 Tracing with TRACK

A trace is specified by inserting objects, setting up obstacles, and by selecting the messages and methods to be affected by the obstacles. The selection of objects, messages, and methods is performed by browsing as described above. The obstacles are selected from a set of predefined types (cf. figure 1). Their semantics differ in the number of objects they are connected to (none, one, two, more than two), the amount of messages being traced (one, some, all), and the direction in which messages may pass the obstacle (unidirectional, bidirectional). The semantics of an obstacle is represented by its shape. There are "closed fences" surrounding a single object, "hurdles" between two or more objects, and hurdles connecting no objects. Their form is rectangular as for obstacles tracing all messages, or round for obstacles tracing just one specific message. Arbitrary messages may be selected for obstacles with the shape of an octagon. The latter type is most useful, it can, for example, be used to separately trace methods of certain categories, e.g. those that modify an object, and those that read certain slots.

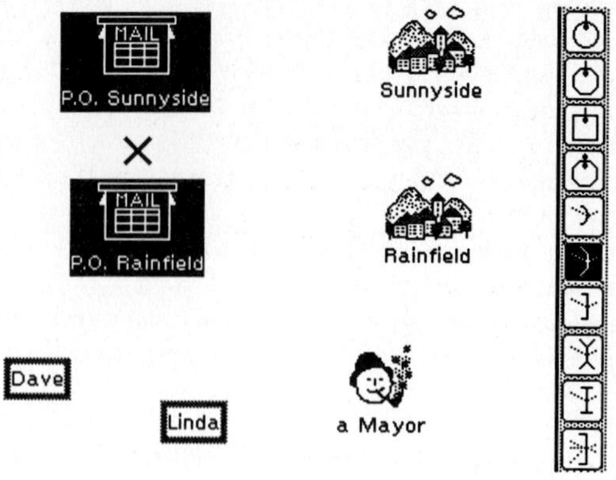

Figure 5: Positioning a hurdle

To set up an obstacle its type is selected from the graphical menu for the appropriate trace window. The position and thereby the affected objects are determined by moving the mouse within the trace window. For each position of the mouse pointer the objects that would currently be affected are highlighted (see figure 5). The final position of the obstacle is confirmed by a mouse click. Directions of unidirectional hurdles are chosen by moving the mouse in either direction starting from the position of the obstacle. To complete a trace specification classes and method selectors are selected from context sensitive, dynamic menus and forms, i.e. for a hurdle connecting two instances only those selectors are presented which correspond to messages possibly sent between the instances (cf. figure 6). By clicking onto the obstacle with the mouse a movable and resizable trace text window opens for textual trace output referring to messages traced by the obstacle.

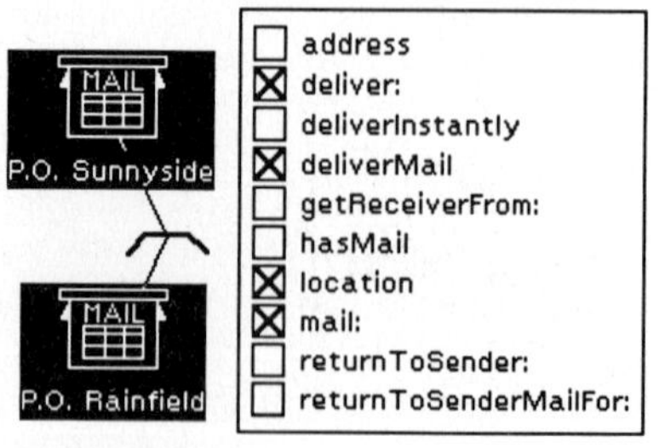

Figure 6: Choosing the selectors of traced messages sent from one post office to the other

When the application is executed the messages to be traced are visualized (1) textually by notifications in the global trace text window and the local trace text window corresponding to the obstacle by which the message is being traced and (2) graphically by a little ball moving over the obstacle from its sender to the receiver (see figure 7). A slider in the top menu of the trace window may be used to adjust the speed of the animation.

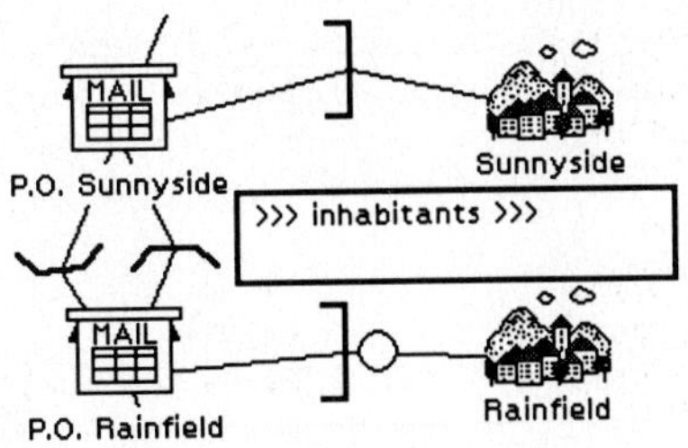

Figure 7: A traced message is sent from a post office to the corresponding city

For each obstacle break points may be set that interrupt program execution before and/or after a message has been sent. *Before* break points are encountered when the message visualized as a white ball crosses the obstacle. In figure 1, for example, a break point has been encountered by a message sent from the person named `Bob` to the post office. *After* break points are reached after the corresponding method has been evaluated in the receiver and its result is returned, in which case the message is visualized as a grey ball in the obstacle (cf. figure 8). When the break point is encountered the animation of the program freezes. The interrupted message may be inspected either by invoking an `Inspector` for the sender, receiver, one of the arguments, or possibly the result. Also, a `Debugger` may be invoked to show the method invocation hierarchy and the code and execution states of the invoked methods (see figure 9). At this point, the user may again browse through the application, add new objects to the tracer, and add or modify obstacles. Program execution continues when the user clicks onto the visualized message.

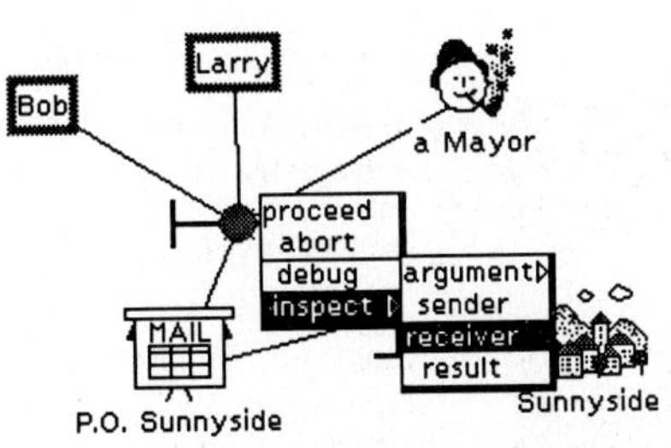

Figure 8: Inspecting a message at an *after* break point

Program execution may also be interrupted in real time by pressing the `STOP` button in the top menu, in which case the message currently crossing an obstacle will be halted. Alternatively, the user may choose to execute the trace in a *stepping mode*. In each step, one traced message is sent. Normal execution and stepping mode may be switched to, any time.

For experienced programmers TRACK offers facilities to interactively define additional filters and actions for the messages traced by an obstacle. *Trace filters* are constraints either restricting the objects the message refers to, e.g. the arguments of the message, or referring to the current system state, e.g. the value of global variables. *Trace actions* may be either additional textual output, e.g. specific slot values of the message sender or receiver, or arbitrary actions, i.e. messages to be sent as a side effect of a traced message, e.g. to notify and update other programming tools.

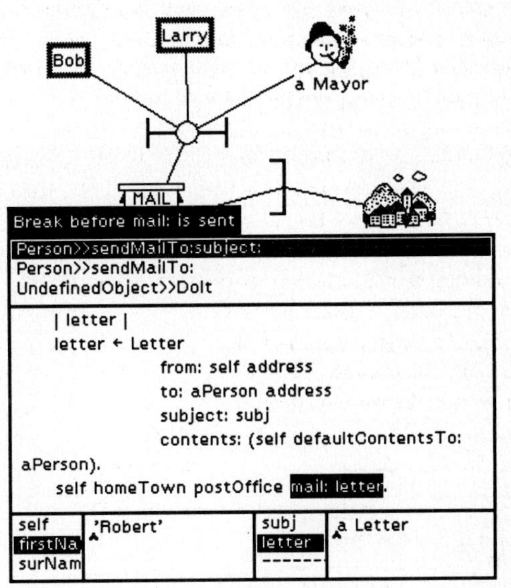

Figure 9: Invoking a `Debugger` for an interrupted message

3.4 Execution browsing

The reason for tracing a program all too often is debugging. The very concept of debugging implies the idea of not knowing, what's really going on. In a real program lots of things are happening, and in debugging it is critical to be sensitive to the right thing at the right moment in order to identify the malfunctioning parts. Very often, the programmer has only a vague idea about what's wrong. The possibility to set up traces incrementally within TRACK by zooming in and out of computational contexts, together with the fact, that the state of a trace specification is always visible allows the programmer to browse through the execution path of a program and thereby gradually bring a bug into focus.

Unlike tracing tools in traditional languages, in TRACK it is quite natural to set up multiple trace specification, i.e., to have multiple tracers some of which may be active while others are deactivated. Multiple tracers may be employed to monitor different parts of a program, methods belonging to certain categories, or to look at a program at different abstraction levels. Figure 10, for example, displays two graphical tracers being used to analyse the *Model–View–Controller* concept in different parts of the SMALLTALK-80 window system.

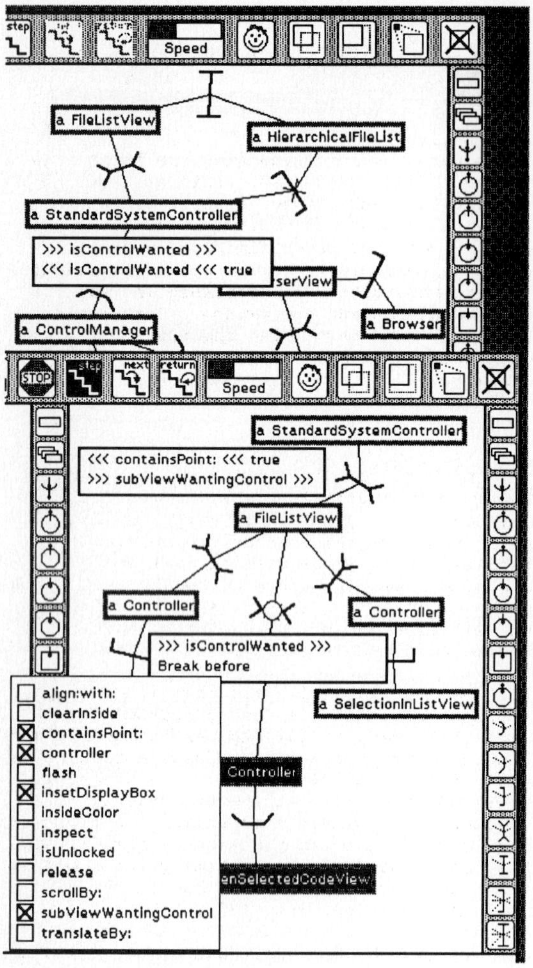

Figure 10: Multiple tracers

4 Conclusion

TRACK is a tool tightly integrated into the SMALLTALK-80 programming environment. Its usability heavily depends on the efficient use of already available tools. There are several pathways leading from other tools into TRACK, and vice versa.

There are still some things to be done. Occasionally, some program behaviour visualized by TRACK escapes the attention of the programmer. It would be a great advantage to have a replay, or alternatively, an undo–redo mechanism, to browse in time. Also, much could possibly be gained, if TRACK would include (or have access to) graphical inspectors for data structures, that would run in parallel to simultaneously show the effect of program execution on selected data structures.

References

[Böcker et al. 89a] H. - D. Böcker, G. Fischer and H. Nieper-Lemke. The Role of Visual Representation in Understanding Software. In D. Partridge (Ed.), *Artificial Intelligence and Software Engeneering.* Ablex Publishing Corporation, Norwood, NJ, 1989.

[Böcker et al. 89b] H. - D. Böcker, J. Herczeg and M. Herczeg. ELAB — An Electronics Laboratory. In *Proceedings of the Fourth Conference on Artificial Intelligence and Education*, pp. 15–24, Amsterdam, Springfield VA, Tokyo, May 1989. IOS.

[Böcker, Herczeg 90] H. - D. Böcker and J. Herczeg. TRACK — A Trace Construction Kit. To appear in *CHI-90, Human Factors in Computing Systems Conference Proceedings*, ACM SIGCHI/HFS, 1990.

[Brown 88] M. H. Brown. Exploring Algorithms. *Computer*, 21(5):14–36, May 1988.

[Budge 83] B. Budge. *Pinball Construction Set (Computer Program).* Electronic Arts, San Mateo, Ca., 1983.

[Fischer, Lemke 88] G. Fischer and A. Lemke. Construction Kits and Design Environments: Steps Toward Human Problem-Domain Communication. *Human-Computer Interaction*, 3(2), 1988.

[Goldberg 84] A. Goldberg (Ed.). *SMALLTALK-80, The Interactive Programming Environment.* Addison-Wesley, Reading, Ma., 1984.

[Ingalls et al. 88] D. Ingalls, S. Wallace, Y. Y. Chow, F. Ludolph und K. Doyle. Fabrik — A Visual Programming Environment. In N. Meyrowitz (Ed.), *OOPSLA '88 Proceedings*, pp. 176–190, New York, September 1988. ACM Sigplan.

[Kleyn, Gingrich 88] M. F. Kleyn and P. C. Gingrich. GraphTrace – Understanding Object-Oriented Systems Using Concurrently Animated Views. In N. Meyrowitz (Ed.), *OOPSLA '88 Proceedings*, pp. 191–205. Schlumberger-Doll Research, November 1988.

[Smith 77] D. Smith. *Pygmalion, A Computer Program to Model and Stimulate Creative Thought.* Birkhäuser Verlag, Basel, 1977.

Human–Computer Interaction – INTERACT '90
D. Diaper et al. (Editors)
Elsevier Science Publishers B.V. (North-Holland)

COMPRESSING AND COMPARING METRIC EXECUTION SPACES*

John DOMINGUE

Human Cognition Research Laboratory, the Open University, Milton Keynes, MK7 6AA, U.K.
Telephone: +44 908 655014 Email: jb_domingue@uk.ac.open.acs.vax

To help programmers evaluate the efficiency of their code during debugging, we are developing the Transparent Rule Interpreter Monitoring System (TRIMS). This provides the user with a visual representation of both behavioural and performance aspects of rule-based programs. Up to now, visualization within TRIMS has been applied only to the qualitative behaviour of a program. This paper describes the recent incorporation of metric information into the system, enabling the programmer to visualize the time various parts of the program take to run. The use of metric information is described in relation to two facilities currently available in TRIMS: *compression* and *comparison*. Compression enables the programmer to hide away parts of the execution, permitting the visualization of arbitrarily large execution spaces. The comparison of similar execution spaces can answer such questions as, 'Why does my program run so slowly with this particular working memory set?'

1. INTRODUCTION

1.1. Background

The work described in this paper has been carried out within the KEATS-II project [1, 2]. The aim of KEATS-II is to provide software and methodological support for building very large knowledge-based systems. One problem encountered in the construction of such systems is that of maintenance. We addressed this problem by constructing a visualization system called the Transparent Rule Interpreter (TRI) [3, 4], which enables programmers to graphically display the behaviour of large rule-based programs. A second problem often found when building large knowledge-based sytems is efficiency. To address this we are constructing a new system: the Transparent Rule Interpreter Monitoring System (TRIMS) [5] which will display both behavioural and performance information. In this paper we concentrate on two aspects of TRIMS: *compression* and *comparison*. Compression refers to the collapsing of segments of the execution history. By comparison we mean the ability to systematically compare two different execution histories.

1.2. The Aim of TRIMS

In this paper the 'behaviour' of a program refers to the primitive operations carried out during its execution. For forward chaining inference systems this would include operations such as a rule matching against working memory or a rule firing. The term 'program performance' refers to how long each operation took to execute.

* This research was funded by British Telecom p.l.c.

Once the behaviour of a program has been finalised, the programmer begins the task of performance analysis. This involves 'fine-tuning' the program in order to determine the most efficient representation. Here the programmer needs to pinpoint two factors which reduce efficiency: (i) slow segments of code, and (ii) portions of the execution that do not contribute to the solution.

In this paper it is claimed that in order to pinpoint these factors, the programmer needs to access both behavioural *and* performance related aspects of the program. We believe that rather than being two distinct attributes of program execution, behaviour and performance are intricately entwined. For example, a trace of program behaviour can highlight inefficiency, while an excessively large timing for a portion of a program can be due to a bug in the program's behaviour (see [5]).

Because both the behaviour and the performance of a program can be useful in detecting behaviour bugs and improving efficiency, a programmer should be able to see the two aspects of program execution in an integrated, coherent fashion. Thus one of our goals is to enable the programmer to investigate any segment of code that is suspected of behavioural or performance bugs using a single debugging tool. We are therefore extending the existing facilities available in TRIMS to incorporate metric information. The existing facilities are:

Navigation aids
In order to manage large execution spaces the user needs an abstract or coarse-grained view. This is described in section 3.1.

Selective synchronised fine-grained views
From the coarse-grained view TRIMS allows very detailed slices of the execution history to be selected. Each fine-grained view is synchronised with the coarse-grained view. When the coarse-grained view is

replayed (see below) all the displayed fine-grained views are automatically updated.

Replay
TRIMS enables the user, via the coarse-grained view, to move to any point in the execution space. A video-recorder style replay panel allows the execution to be replayed from a selected point, either forwards or backwards.

Compression
The user can group rules into a single set. Each set can then be displayed as a single rule.

Comparison
The comparison facility enables the user to highlight small differences between similar execution spaces.

Extensions to the first three facilities are described elsewhere [5]. Here we present extensions to the last two facilities: compression and comparison.

2. RELATED WORK

Several previous attempts have been made to display performance information in a graphical form. For example, clocks, dials, bar charts, and graphs are frequently used for portraying metric information on a number of workstations, e.g. Apollos™, Macintoshes™, SUNs™ and Symbolics™. In the theorem proving literature this type of assistance has been provided in the Gauge system [6]. Gauge is a logic programming environment designed specifically for observing and subsequently analysing the performance of programs. Gorlick and Kesselmann introduce the notion of performance experiments which the user designs with the system's help, and which the system subsequently analyses graphically. A major theme in their research is the discovery of ways to place probes within the code at a cheap cost to the computation of the program as a whole. The information gained by such means can be used for the purpose of performance monitoring.

There is also evidence supporting the use of visualization techniques for the improvement of program performance. For example, the use of BALSA [7, 8, 9], a visualization system for animating algorithms, has directly resulted in the improvement and enhancement of several algorithms, notably Knuth's Dynamic Huffman tree [10], and Shell-sort [11]. The Joshua Metering System [12] provides metric information for a rete-based rule system using three different sets of canonical steps. These sets show different aspects of the program performance, such as working memory assertions and looking for a rule to fire for a given working memory assertion. The information is displayed on a predicate basis and so does not map onto the execution of the program.

In contrast TRIMS presents metric information in a form which maps directly onto the behaviour of the program.

3. BEHAVIOURAL VISUALIZATIONS IN TRIMS

In this section we describe the behavioural aspects of the TRIMS dislay (see [3] and [4] for a more detailed description).

3.1. TRIMS' Coarse-Grained View

A simple example of TRIMS' coarse-grained view, called a *rule graph*, is shown in Figure 1. Here we can see the execution of the rules rule-a, rule-b and rule-c over nine cycles. The + means that a rule fired; a triangle means that a rule fired and backward chaining occurred; a box means that a rule entered the conflict resolution set but did not fire. It can be seen that TRIMS' coarse-grained view is cycle-based, mapping onto an OPS5-style match/fire cycle execution model [13].

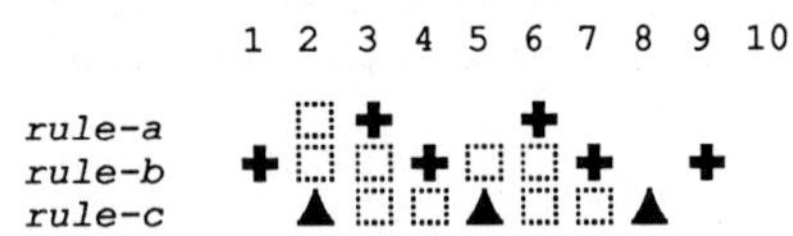

Figure 1

3.2. Compression in TRIMS

A rule graph can be compressed either along the vertical rule axis (rule compression) or along the horizontal temporal axis (temporal compression).

3.2.1. Rule Compression

The programmer can group a number of rules into a single row. For example, the rules rule-a and rule-c in Figure 1 may be compressed. This would result in the new compressed rule graph shown in Figure 2. Here, the rules rule-a and rule-c have been compressed into the single row a-c. The compressed row can be expanded again by mousing on the row name.

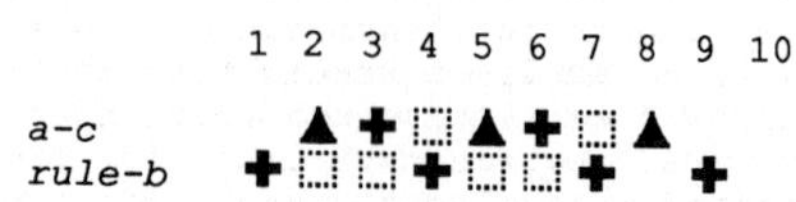

Figure 2

In selecting a symbol for a compressed row we use the following symbol hierarchy: ▲, ✚, ☐, <space>. Thus, if a triangle occurs in one of the rows we draw a triangle in the compressed row; if there is no triangle and a cross occurs in one of the rows, we draw a cross, and so on. The symbol hierarchy means that each symbol within a compressed row represents the most specialised event•occurring within the group of rules at a particular cycle. This rule compression facility allows the user to display the execution of very large rule bases.

3.2.2. Temporal Compression

Execution graphs can be temporally compressed in one of two ways. The user can specify that certain cycles be compressed or that certain cliches be compressed. Notice in Figure 1 the recurrent pattern of the symbols ✚, ✚, ▲ in a diagonal line. This pattern corresponds to the rules rule-a, rule-b and rule-c firing and is called a *cliche*. TRIMS allows the user to ring this cliche and to display each occurrence of the cliche as a single cycle.

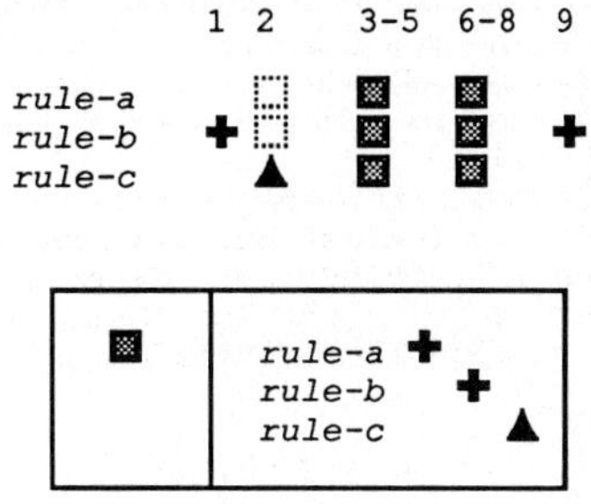

Figure 3

Figure 3 presents a temporally compressed version of the rule graph in Figure 1. Here, each occurrence of the cliche has been replaced by another icon. The compressed cycle can be expanded again by mousing on either the cycle number or the icon.

As well as facilitating the display of large execution spaces, cliche compression enables the programmer to quickly locate 'friendly' or 'hostile' segments of the execution history. For example, it may be that rule-c firing outside this cliche is treated as a bug.

3.3. Comparison in TRIMS

One of the novel features in TRIMS is the ability to compare execution spaces. The comparison is carried out on a node-by-node basis. Thirteen different symbols are used to represent the differences between any two nodes. If both the nodes are the same a space is drawn, otherwise a combination of both symbols is used. These combinations are shown in Figure 4. Notice that triangles and crosses are treated in the same manner when combined with other symbols.

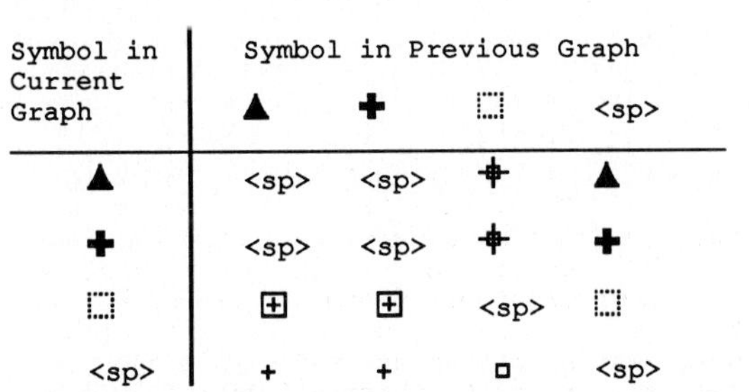

Symbol in Current Graph
Symbol in Previous Graph
<sp>

Figure 4

Comparison enables the user to quickly find out where two executions differ. This facility would be used when a run of the interpreter gave an unexpected answer after one or more 'successful' runs.

An example of the comparison of two rule graphs is shown in Figure 5. If no symbol appears in the first graph, the symbol from the second graph is used. In Figure 5, rule-a has a blank in cycle 2 in graph one, whereas there is a box for rule-a in cycle 2 graph two, so a box has been drawn in the comparison graph. If a symbol is present in the first graph and no symbol is present in the second, the symbol from the first graph is used but it is shrunk to give the impression of being further away. An example of this is shown by the node for rule-b at cycle 4. If the same node in both graphs contained non-identical symbols, a combination is used. The node for rule-a cycle 3 contains a cross in graph one and a box in graph two. The comparison graph displays this as a large box and a small cross.

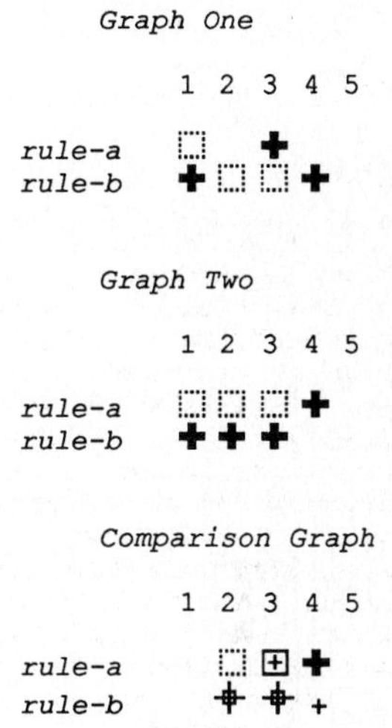

Figure 5

4. ADDING METRIC INFORMATION TO TRIMS

In section 3 we discussed how TRIMS presents the qualitative behaviour of execution spaces. However, in order to assess the efficiency of a program it is important to have a quantitative measure of how fast the program runs. For the purpose of metering, a program can be viewed as a series of operations or steps. The performance of a program can be monitored in terms of these steps either by a weighted count of the steps that have been executed, or by measuring how long it takes for all these steps to execute. The advantage of counting the steps is that the metric information maps directly onto the program behaviour and can therefore be easily interpreted by the programmer. The disadvantage of counting is that one step may take different amounts of time to execute on different occasions. Weighted counting of steps can therefore be inaccurate.

Timing information, on the other hand, is an accurate measure of how long it takes a number of rules to execute. The disadvantage of using timing is that the information does not map directly onto the qualitative behaviour of the program and is therefore not easily interpreted. Ideally, both measures of performance are required so that a programmer can know how long a step takes to execute, and therefore whether or not a large number of steps will be a performance problem. TRIMS presents both counting and timing information in conjunction with the behavioural information described in section 3.

4.1. Adding Metric Information to Rule Graphs

Figure 6 shows a coarse-grained metric view in TRIMS, each node showing its 'price' compared to the most 'expensive' node in the graph. This representation incorporates both behavioural and metric information. The behaviour symbols are now shown in the top right-hand corner of each node. Metric information is displayed here as an intensity square, although it is possible to have it displayed as a pressure bar or numeral if the user prefers. The intensity of the colour of a square represents either the percentage of the total execution time or the percentage of the time taken by the most expensive node. Thus a darker node symbolises a more expensive execution.

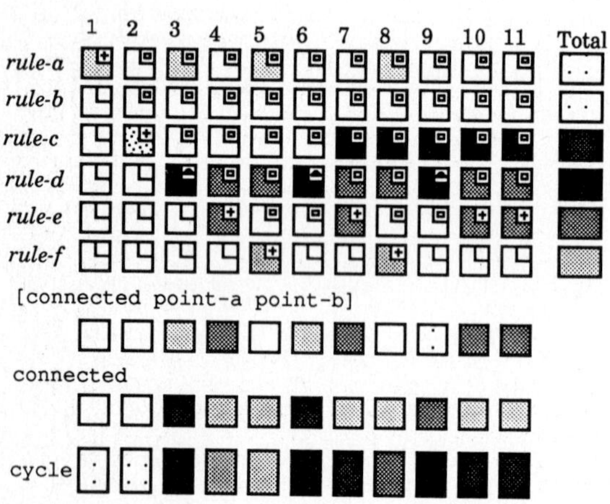

Figure 6

The rightmost column in Figure 6 shows the total amount of time taken by one rule. We can see that rule-d is the most expensive, rule-c was slightly less so and rules rule-a and rule-b were relatively cheap. It can be seen that for each of the more expensive nodes in rule-c, the rule entered the conflict set without firing. The bottom row in the graph shows the relative performance of each cycle. The most expensive cycle is cycle 9. Mousing on the triangle in the node for rule-d at cycle 6 would produce the fine-grained behavioural view shown in Figure 7.

The top window in Figure 7 shows the definition of the rule rule-d; the bottom window shows all the instantiations for the rule present at cycle 6. The first instantiation in the lower window is in italics as it fired in cycle 6. From the fine-grained view it can be seen that rule-d uses the predicate 'connected'. Since this node is expensive, the user might choose to access information about the behaviour of this individual predicate throughout the whole execution by selecting a menu option.

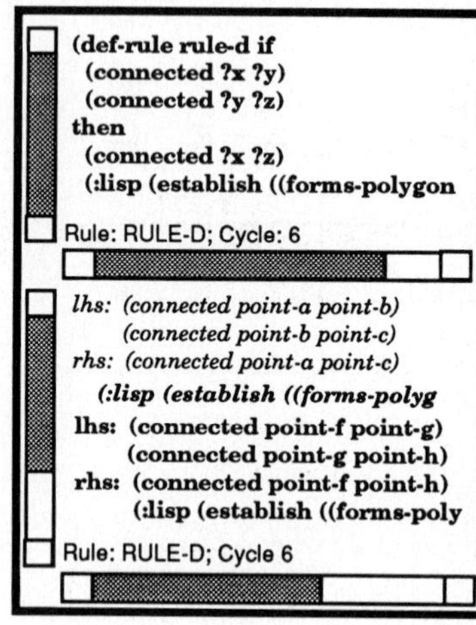

Figure 7

The second from bottom row in Figure 6 contains metric information for this predicate. This row shows the percentage of each cycle's execution time taken by the predicate 'connected'. From this row we can see that 'connected' seems to be the 'guilty' predicate on each of the cycles when rule-d fired. A first guess, from the fine-grained view shown in Figure 7, may be that the working memory pattern [connected point-a point-b] is responsible. The row above shows metric information selected for this pattern. Each node in the row represents the percentage of time taken by the working memory pattern, compared to all the other working memory patterns for the same predicate, in a particular cycle. We can see here that although [connected node-a node-b] did take a large percentage of the execution time on certain cycles these were not the cycles when the 'connected' predicate was expensive, nor when rule-d fired. From this we can conclude that although the predicate 'connected' is at least partly 'guilty' for the performance problems, the working memory pattern [connected node-a node-b] is 'innocent'. Notice that we used both behavioural and metric information in our search for the performance problem.

4.2. Compression in Metric Rule Graphs

Because metric and behavioural information is displayed in a single node, it is possible to carry out compression of metric graphs in the same way as in the strictly behavioural rule graphs (see section 3.2).

4.2.1. Rule Compression

We use the same symbol hierarchy and simply add up the metric information for each of the nodes in a column. Compressing the rows in Figure 6 would lead to the graph shown in Figure 8. Notice that, in this example, the most expensive node is now the node for the group in cycles 7, 10 and 11. This facility would allow the programmer to compress sets of rules that were known to not be contributing to the performance problem, such as initialisation rules that simply asserted constant working patterns.

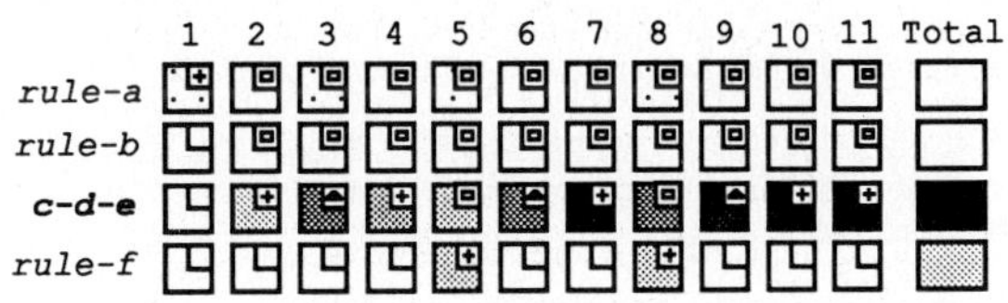

Figure 8

4.2.2. Temporal Compression

Figure 9 shows Figure 6 compressed temporally around the cliche ▲, ✚, ✚. Notice how, in this example, the most expensive cycle has changed from cycle 9 to the compressed cycles 6-8. TRIMS allows the user to include metric information in the cliche specification. In addition to selecting particular nodes it is posssible to specify a cost range for each node. This is done by setting the lower and upper limits using the icon shown in Figure 10. The left box determines the lower limit; the right box the upper limit.

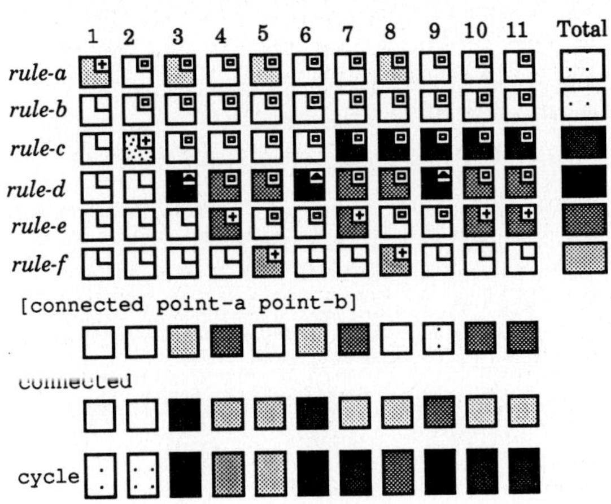

Figure 9

Figure 10

Figure 11 shows how a metric cliche would look. The left hand side of each node represents the lower limit, the right hand side the upper limit. Thus the cliche in Figure 11 specifies the following:

the three rules rule-d, rule-e and rule-f have fired in order

when rule-d fired it was at least half as expensive as the most expensive node in the graph;

rule-e was between 15% and 50% as expensive as the most expensive node; and

rule-f was no more than half as expensive as the most expensive node.

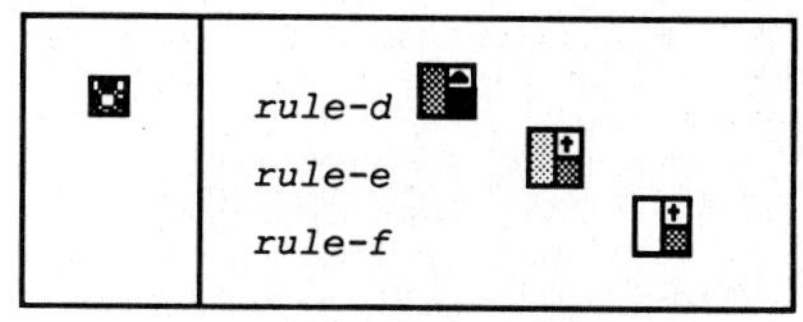

Figure 11

Metric cliches will enable programmers to highlight expensive segments of the execution history. For example, a programmer could highlight all nodes taking more than 10% of the total execution time. The interface is flexible enough, however, to answer more complex questions such as, 'Did any node taking at least 75% as much of the execution time as the most expensive node not fire?', and 'Are there any rules which fired at least three times in succession without taking more than 5% of the overall execution time?'

4.3. Adding Metric Information to Comparison Graphs

Figure 12 shows a comparison of two graphs in TRIMS. In the first graph the node for rule-b in cycle 2 was the most expensive and rule-a was relatively cheap in all four cycles. In the second graph, where both rules fired the same number of times as in the first graph, rule-a was the most expensive. The comparison graph combines the behavioural symbols in the same way as described in section 3.3.

The intensity of each node is calculated from the difference in metric steps between the two compared nodes. If there is no difference then the node is coloured in a 50% grey tone. If the node in the first graph was more expensive a lighter tone is used, and vice-versa: if the node in the second graph was more expensive a darker tone is used. So the nodes for rule-a and rule-b in cycle 2 were equally expensive in both graphs. From this we can deduce that although rule-b was relatively cheaper in the second graph when it fired, it was actually taking the same amount of absolute execution space. This means that rule-a was more expensive when it fired in the second graph than either rule-a or rule-b firing in the first graph. This is confirmed by rule-a being darker in the comparison graph for cycles 3 and 4 when it fired.

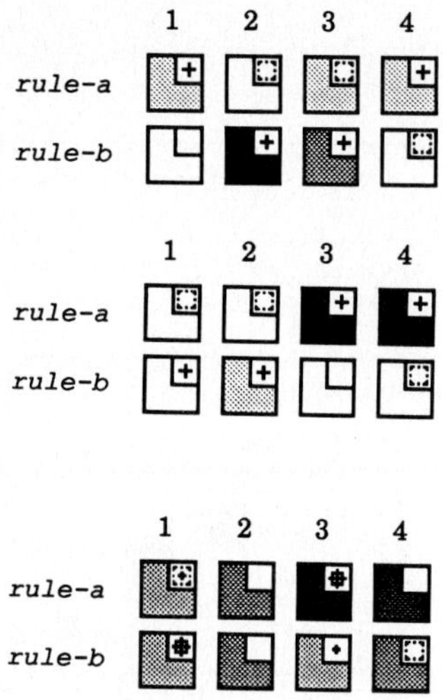

Figure 12

5. SUMMARY

In this paper we have claimed that in order to analyse the efficiency of a program, programmers need access to both behavioural and performance aspects of their programs. Rather than being two distinct attributes, we see performance and behaviour as two complementary parts of the total execution story. The overall goal in our visualization program (see [15]) is to present the execution of a program in a readily interpretable form, whilst allowing the programmer to quickly access detailed information at various levels of description.

Within TRIMS our overall goal is to provide programmers with metric information without losing any of the benefits of visualization. Ideally both behavioural and performance aspects of a program should be presented at a level of description most suited to the programmer. A first step to this goal is the user definable compression mechanism we have described. We are currently investigating techniques which would allow users to define metric abstractions in a less constrained fashion.

Programming is an incremental process; programmers often build new systems on top of old large systems. Large programs will often work successfully for a time and then suddenly crash. The intelligent comparison of relatively similar execution spaces could save enormous time and effort in debugging. The work we have presented here is but a first step towards this goal and we are currently looking at 'smarter' matching algorithms.

ACKNOWLEDGEMENTS

The ideas in this paper arose from discussions with Mike Brayshaw, Marc Eisenstadt, Enrico Motta, Tim Rajan and other members of the Knowledge Engineering Group. Mike Brayshaw, Marc Eisenstadt and Enrico Motta provided extensive comments on earlier drafts.

REFERENCES

[1] Motta, E., Eisenstadt, M., Pitman, K. and West, M. KEATS: Support for Knowledge Acquisition in the Knowledge Engineer's Assistant (KEATS), Expert Systems, 5(1), pp.6-28, 1988.

[2] Motta, E., Rajan, T. and Eisenstadt, M. Knowledge Acquisition as a Process of Model Refinement, International Journal of Man-Machine Studies, in print.

[3] Domingue, J. TRI: The Transparent Rule Interpreter. In Shadbolt, N. (Ed.) 'Research and Development in Expert Systems VII', Cambridge University Press, 1988.

[4] Domingue, J. and Eisenstadt, M. A New Metaphor for the Graphical Explanation of Forward Chaining Rule Execution, Proceedings of the International Joint Conference on Artificial Intelligence (IJCAI-89), Detroit, 1989.

[5] Brayshaw, M., Domingue, J. and Rajan, T. An Integrated Approach to Monitoring the Behaviour and Performance of Inference Systems'. In Sutcliffe, A. and Macaulay, L. (Eds.) 'People and Computers V', Cambridge University Press, 1989.

[6] Gorlick, M. & Kesselman, C. Gauge: A Workbench for the Performance Analysis of Logic Programs. In Kowalski, R. A. and Bowen, K. A. (Eds.), 'Logic Programming: Volume 1', MIT Press, 1988.

[7] Brown, M. H., and Sedgewick, R. Progress Report: Brown University Instructional Computing Laboratory, Technical Report CS-83-28, Department of Computer Science, Brown University, Providence, RI, 1983.

[8] Brown, M. H., and Sedgewick, R. Techniques for Algorithm Animation, IEEE Software, 2(1), pp.28-39, 1985.

[9] Brown, M. H. 'Algorithm Animation', MIT Press, 1987.

[10] Vitter, J. L. Design and Analysis of Dynamic Huffman Coding, Proceedings of the 26th Annual Symposium on Computer Science, 1985.

[11] Incerpi, J. M. A Study of the Worst-Case Behavior of Shell-sort, Unpublished Ph.D. Thesis, Department of Computer Science, Brown University, Providence, RI, 1986.

[12] Symbolics Inc. Joshua Reference Manual, Cambridge, MA, 1988.

[13] Forgy, C. L. OPS5 User's Manual, 1981.

[14] Forgy, C. L. Rete: A Fast Algorithm for the Many Pattern/ Many Object Pattern Matching Problem, Artificial Intelligence, 19, pp.17-37, 1982.

[15] Eisenstadt, M. and Brayshaw, M. The Transparent Prolog Machine (TPM): an Execution Model and Graphical Debugger for Logic Programming, Journal of Logic Programming, 5(4), pp.1-66, 1988.

DOCTORAL PROGRAMME

A psychology of programming for design
R.K.E. Bellamy 1005

Cognitive style and intelligent help
L. Coventry 1007

Support for understanding and participation in a distributed problem solving system
C.M. Duursma 1009

The role of analogy in training computer users
J. Elcock 1011

Linguistic models in the design of cooperative help systems
C. Elliot 1013

An environment to support the use of program examples while learning to program in LISP
K.W. Getao 1015

Modelling cognitive aspects of complex control tasks
S. Grant 1017

Using temporal logic to prototype interactive systems
C.W. Johnson 1019

A development environment for the design of multimodal, colourgraphic human–computer interfaces
M. Langen and G. Rau 1021

Advanced user interfaces for distributed group communication
L. Navarro 1025

Logic descriptions in rapid prototyping of applications
L. Oestreicher 1029

Graphical treatment of natural language in HCI
R.A. Singer 1031

Run time interface specification, using direct manipulation
R. Tibbitt-Eggleton 1033

Learning a word processing task: About documentation, help and task complexity
A. Van Laethem 1035

Human–Computer Interaction – INTERACT '90
D. Diaper et al. (Editors)
Elsevier Science Publishers B.V. (North-Holland)

A Psychology of Programming for Design

Rachel K. E. Bellamy

IBM T.J. Watson Research Center, P.O. Box 704, Yorktown Heights, NY 10598, USA; and MRC Applied Psychology Unit, 15 Chaucer Rd, Cambridge CB2 2EF, UK.

1.0 INTRODUCTION

Software artifacts don't appear in the world as *faits accomplis*, but evolve through a cyclical process of use and redesign. Software version numbers epitomize this process; a particular piece of software is built to support a task, but then the very existence of the software changes the task it was designed to support introducing further requirements for redesign. This characterization of design has been used to develop an approach to designing more useful and usable software artifacts (Carroll, 1990).

The approach assumes that artifacts embody theories of usability. Articulating and reflecting on the validity of the psychological theory embodied by an artifact can drive its redesign. Carroll and Kellogg (1989) suggest claims analysis as a representation for capturing the theory embodied by an artifact. In the initial formulation a claims analysis describes the psychological consequences of individual features of the interface. These claims are organized by Norman's (1986) theory of action and general interface techniques. Assessing the truth of the claims embodied by an artifact drives its redesign.

This paper outlines an ongoing research project which develops and tests this approach through redesigns to Smalltalk/V.

2.0 A CLAIMS ANALYSIS OF SMALLTALK/V

Positing a structured representation for design does not necessarily mean it can be used. A methodology for producing claims analyses is needed. I have explored scenarios-of-use as a method for developing a claims analysis of Smalltalk/V.

Scenarios-of-use were collected by observing expert Smalltalk programmers, and analyzed to show how the Smalltalk system either supported or detracted from the programming task. In particular, I focused on aspects of the interface that seemed frustrating, led to errors, or, compared to other programming environments, made the task particularly facile. To date the analysis of Smalltalk/V consists of over 40 claims, articulated as trade-offs, and organized by scenario-of-use. Organizing claims by scenario seems to more accurately reflect the concerns of, and types of questions asked by designers than a Norman-style task analysis. Trade-offs also reflect the nature of design, in that design decisions tend to depend on whether the positive psychological consequences of an interface feature outweigh the negative ones.

One of the claims in the analysis, for the scenario 'move a class from one branch of the hierarchy to another' is: *blocking reorganizations of the class hierarchy pre-empts the need to respecify inheritance relationships, but imposes a top-downs order on code development because inheritance relations must be specified before object behavior.* This claim reflects the fact that in Smalltalk/V there is no direct support for moving a class from one location in the hierarchy to another. This is a kind of error blocking technique, pre-empting code inconsistences that would arise if the moved class were making use of inheritance from its original super class, and thereby finessing the need to support the explicit correction of such inconsistencies. However, constraining reorganization of the class hierarchy in this way imposes a top-down methodology where the inheritance relationships of objects are designed before considering their behavior. Actual programming practice resists strictly top-down regimens and so imposing a top-down ordering causes usability problems.

Re-evaluation of psychological trade-offs supports redesign. For instance, in the example above, perhaps it is more important to support a flexible code development order than to provide error blocking? Many redesign options are possible (for example, providing operations for moving classes), but it is important to understand how the complete set of claims embodied by the system change with redesign. The analysis would never of course generate designs, but it could place specific and articulate constraints on the design process.

3.0 REDESIGN BY DESIGN

Limitations of cognitive processing mean that not all the relevant information can be considered in design (Guindon *et al.*; 1987). Bellamy and Carroll (1990) investigate what information gets left out during design and show how claims analysis can help.

Programmers who had personalized their Smalltalk/V system were asked to describe their redesigns, motivations for the redesign, and typical scenarios-of-use before and after redesign. Using these scenarios and the claims analysis of Smalltalk/V outlined above, claims analyses showing the psychological theory embodied by the generic system and that embodied by the redesigned system were developed. Comparison of the designers' motivations for the redesign with the claims analyses shows that: the designers tended to focus on particular aspects of the design problem; they often only thought about the problems with the generic Smalltalk/V, and only advantages of their redesign; they were not always aware of the particular interface features causing a usability problem; and finally, they did not take into account all of the tasks supported by the generic system, or those supported by their redesign.

One of the designers discussed how in the generic system both the class description, which shows the instance variables, and method code appear in the same pane of the class hierarchy browser. Thus to see both, a programmer must either use a second class hierarchy browser, which means lots of window management, or the same class hierarchy browser which causes memory and navigation problems. The designer responded to these problems by emulating a Smalltalk-80 facility that on request displays a class' instance variables in a pop-up window. Thus both instance variables and code can be seen at the same time without requiring management of multiple class hierarchy browsers.

Conducting the claims analysis of this redesign revealed that the pop-up window only partially solves the problem. The pop-up appears over the method text, so the programmer is still unable to see both method text and the instance variables. The claims analysis also suggests that the design facilitates not only the task of finding the class' instance variables, but also code comprehension. Not realizing that the redesign supports this additional task has not affected this particular redesign, but unless articulated, future redesigns could remove this support for code comprehension.

This study suggests that claims analysis of an artifact can support redesign. The use of scenarios to organize claims articulated as trade-offs seems to resonate with how designers think about redesign. When given the claims analysis of their redesigns, the designers in this study were able to produce more usable redesigns of the generic system.

4.0 A CLAIMS MOTIVATED DESIGN

The claims analysis of Smalltalk/V suggests some major usability problems, e.g. a lack of support for evaluation of code at the application level. Currently I am redesigning the Smalltalk/V browser to alleviate this and other problems. I am using projected scenarios-of-use (Carroll and Rosson, 1990) to describe the functionality of the redesign.

One of the reasons evaluation of applications is difficult in the existing system is that application code is distributed throughout the hierarchy. The following scenario describes the task of finding methods and classes representing a subset of application functionality in the redesigned Smalltalk browser. *You want to borrow some functionality from a database application you have been using. The code for this application is distributed throughout the class hierarchy and so is difficult to find. So using the currently open class hierarchy browser, you select 'application view' from the top pane menu. A pane containing a list of applications currently supported by the system pops-up. Selecting 'recipe database' from the list results in all the classes and methods composing this application becoming highlighted in the class hierarchy browser. You can now browse the reduced set of classes and methods to understand how the database application was coded.* Claims analyses of projected scenarios-of-use will be used to explore design possibilities prior to implementation.

I am also articulating the claims embodied by existing designs to enable design by emulation. For example, Helgon (Fischer and Nieper-Lemke, 1989) and TaskMapper (Carroll *et al.*; 1987) both support information retrieval by query reformulation but make different claims. In TaskMapper, when an item is created it is automatically added to the database with the attributes: creator, time of creation, task context and size. In Helgon, on the other hand, all items must be added to the database explicitly. Obviously there are advantages and disadvantages to both approaches: e.g. automatically adding items to the database reduces the amount of work the user needs to do, but could make them less memorable than if explicit steps have to be taken to add the item.

5.0 CONCLUSIONS

These studies have shown that psychological claims analyses can support the design process. However, some issues still need to be addressed. Firstly, a more rigorous methodology for claims analysis must be developed. Here I suggest scenario analysis as the basis for such a methodology. Secondly, existing examples of analyses need to be combined into a coherent theory expressing the relationship between interface features and psychological consequences.

6.0 REFERENCES

Bellamy, R.K.E. and Carroll, J.M. (1990) *Redesign by Design.* IBM Internal Report.

Carroll, J.M. (1990) Infinite Detail and Emulation in an Ontologically Minimized HCI. *Proceedings of CHI'90*, Conference on Human Factors in Computing, Seattle.

Carroll, J.M., Herder, R.E. and Sawtelle, D.S. (1987) TaskMapper. In H.J. Bullinger and B. Shackel (Eds.), *Human-Computer Interaction: Proceedings of Interact'87.*

Carroll, J.M. and Kellogg, W.A. (1989) Artifacts as Theory Nexus: Hermeneutics Meets Theory-Based Design. In K. Bice and C. Lewis (Eds.), *Proceedings of CHI'89*, Conference on Human Factors in Computing Systems, Austin.

Carroll, J.M. and Rosson, M.B. (1990) Human-Computer Interaction Scenarios as a Design Representation. In B.D. Shriver (Ed), *Proceedings of the 23rd Annual International Conference on Systems Sciences*, Hawaii.

Fischer, G. and Nieper-Lemke, H. (1989) HELGON: Extending the Retrieval by Reformulation Paradigm. In K. Bice and C. Lewis (Eds.), *Proceedings of CHI'89*, Conference on Human Factors in Computing Systems.

Guindon, R., Krasner, H. and Curtis, B. (1987) Breakdowns and Processes during the Early Aquisition of Software Design by Professionals. In G. Olson, S. Sheppard, and E. Soloway (Eds.), *Empirical Studies of Programmers: Second Workshop*, Ablex, NJ.

Norman, D.A. (1986) Cognitive Engineering. In D.A. Norman and S. Draper (Eds.), *User Centered System Design: New Perspectives on Human-Computer Interaction.* Lawrence Erlbaum Associates, NJ.

Human–Computer Interaction – INTERACT '90
D. Diaper et al. (Editors)
Elsevier Science Publishers B.V. (North-Holland)

COGNITIVE STYLE AND INTELLIGENT HELP

Lynne Coventry

Department of Computing Science, University of Stirling, Stirling.

1. AIMS OF THE PROJECT

This project is concerned with establishing the importance of a particular psychological user characteristic, cognitive style, to the human computer interaction process. To this end, the approaches of different users to learning and using an operating system are investigated. The intention is to develop and compare two levels of help system which will accommodate different cognitive styles. The first level will be a simple, user-driven menu system and the second will provide adaptive help.

This approach will investigate the following questions:

- What is the nature of cognitive style on learning and using UNIX? This includes the types of errors made, approaches to novel situations and the number of commands known.
- How can such differences be compensated for by the system? What facilities are required to cope with the different approaches?
- Is it necessary to prime the system with the characteristics of the user before the user proceeds, or can sufficient information be obtained from the interaction itself to enable the system to adapt in a timely and appropriate manner?

2. COGNITIVE STYLE

Previous studies have highlighted the existence of differences in the cognitive style adopted by individuals [1, 2, 3, 4]. Two identified styles are field-dependence and field-independence. These styles affect the way a person structures and processes information. This may have an affect on the way a person learns and uses a computer system. Little interest has been paid to these style differences because they emphasise an equal but different approach, where any differences observed are qualitative rather than quantitative and therefore may not result in a significant difference in overall performance.

3. THE EFFECTS OF COGNITIVE STYLE

When learning a system, users build models of the system, what it can do and what they must do with the system to complete their task [5]. In studies which have looked at unassisted exploration of large systems, vast individual differences have been found in the way people manage their time, the parts of the system they explore and the methods they employ [1]. These differences may result from a difference in cognitive style. It is hypothesised that field-independent people explore more of the system in a shorter space of time, they form a model of the system and actively structure the information they find. They then generalise that information to other situations. Field-dependent people are more likely to investigate less of the system, will not form models or generalise, but will learn each command individually, using a rote learning approach [1, 2].

4. COGNITIVE STYLE AND UNIX

With systems such as UNIX, neither approach will result in maximal learning. The field-independent people may make errors as there are many inconsistencies in the UNIX command set which makes generalisation inappropriate.The field-dependent people may never learn a vast amount of the system because the system is so big and the information is lacking in structure and difficult to acquire.

UNIX was chosen as an area to explore for the following reasons:

- It is a large and complicated system of which different people learn different parts in different orders.
- People will never know the whole system. As their objectives change, they may learn different parts of the system and therefore the opportunity for learning is always present.
- Most people only learn a very small subset of the available commands and there are many commands available which could make the interaction more efficient [6, 7, 8].

5. ACCOMMODATING COGNITIVE STYLE

Differences in the way people learn a system may be best accommodated by an adaptive system. The definition of an adaptive system adopted for the purpose of this proposal was put forward by E.A. Edmonds [9] and is "a system which changes automatically in response to its experience with users". Such systems must adapt their behaviour to changes in the abilities, needs and objectives of the users. This requires a model of the user on which to base adaptation. UNIX, despite providing profile files which can be configured by trained users, shell programming which allows users to build up commands and aliases which allow users to rename commands, is not adaptive because it cannot change in response to user behaviour.

6. INCORPORATING USER CHARACTERISTICS

Cognitive style is often cited as a characteristic of the user which should be incorporated into a model of the user. The purpose of such a model is to provide the system with the information required for the system to 'adapt' to individual users. The most common type of user model is based on stereotypes[10]. This sort of model classifies the user as a certain type and as a result infers certain characteristics to that user. This approach has been shown to have several limitations [3, 11]. The approach proposed for this project is to use only the information which is available from the interaction itself. The model will be based on actual user behaviour.

7. PROJECT OUTLINE

This project has four stages.

1. An observational prestudy of UNIX users. User session logs were collected over a period of time to establish the order in which people built up their command repertoire, difficulties and errors observed in normal use of the system and the size of command set established.
2. From the prestudy, a number of tasks were outlined for the user to perform in a controlled experiment. These tasks ranged from ones which were used often to ones which had not been used by any user during the prestudy. Subjects were asked to attempt each task. The subjects could either make use of the standard help system or a human expert. A test was then carried out to establish the subjects' cognitive style and data was analysed for group differences.
3. As a result of observations made in the experimental study, a number of design criteria for a help system were established. Different types of help were required to facilitate the different groups. A prototype static and adaptive system is now being built. The static system is menu-driven while the adaptive system incorporates an embedded user model, which collects information from the interaction on the behaviour of the user. The information provided by this model will be used as a basis for adaptation. The features incorporated will include, protective interrupts, verification of command execution and synonym capabilities.
4. The experiment of phase two will be repeated to establish whether or not either of the new systems aid the interaction and users' reactions to the systems.

REFERENCES

[1] C.J.H. Fowler, L.A. Macauley, and J.F. Fowler. The relationship between cognitive style and dialogue style. In P. Johnson and S. Cook, editors, *People and Computers : Designing the Interface*, Cambridge University Press, 1985.

[2] C.J.H. Fowler and D. Murray. Gender and cognitive style differences at the human-computer interface. In *Interact '87*, pages 709–714, 1987.

[3] L.E. Tyler. *Individual Differences.* Meredith Corporation, USA, 1974.

[4] H.A. Witkin and D.R. Goodenough. *Cognitive Styles : Essence and Origin.* International University Press, 1981.

[5] A.D. Saja. The cognitive model : an approach to designing the human-computer interface. *SIGCHI Bulletin*, 16(3):36–40, 1985.

[6] A.G. Sutcliffe and A.C. Old. Do users know they have user models? some experiences in the practise of user modelling. In *Interact '87*, pages 35–41, 1987.

[7] M.P. Anderson, J.E. McDonald, and R.W. Schvaneveldt. Empirical user modelling : command usage analysis for deriving models of users. In *Proceedings Of The Human Factors Society 31st Annual Meeting*, pages 41–45, 1987.

[8] M.C. Desmarais and M. Pavel. User knowledge evaluation: an experiment with unix. In *Interact '87*, pages 151–156, 1987.

[9] E.A. Edmonds. Adaptive man-computer interfaces. In MJ Coombs and JL Alty, editors, *Computing Skills and the User Interface*, Academic Press, London, 1981.

[10] E. Rich. Users are individuals : individualizing user models. *International Journal of Man-Machine Studies*, 18:199–214, 1983.

[11] G.N. Gilbert. User models : can they be good enough? In *Proceedings of the Alvey Special Interest Group on Intelligent Interfaces*, pages 25–29, 1986.

Human–Computer Interaction – INTERACT '90
D. Diaper et al. (Editors)
Elsevier Science Publishers B.V. (North-Holland)

Support for Understanding and Participation in a Distributed Problem Solving System

An overview of a PhD research programme

C.M Duursma,

JRC Ispra, CITE, Knowledge Base Systems Lab,
TP 440, I-21020 Ispra, Italy.

1. Background

The author has received a M.S degree In computer science specialisation Artificial Intelligence from the University of Amsterdam in 1986. After having worked for a three year period in the research and the development of a help system shell for office automation systems (Eurohelp ESPRIT P180 (Breuker et al. 89)) he has started a PhD study in December 1989 at the Communities Joint Research Centre (JRC) in Ispra where there is an on-going research activity in the area of Distributed A.I. (cooperating intelligent agents architectures). The aim of this current phase of research is to investigate the applicability of help system techniques used in the office systems area, to support users in participation with distributed problem solving systems solving high level tasks. This research is related to Esprit II project p2256 called ARCHON, an Architecture for Cooperative Heterogeneous On-line systems.

2. Thesis

The goal of this research is to investigate how human participation in Cooperative Distributed Problem Solving (CDPS) systems can be understood and supported. The approach is to design a model that makes cooperation acts explicit, and to develop an assistant agent that uses this model to support the user for participation in a problem solving environment.

The ideal mental model for understanding non distributed problem solvers has always been the reasoning of a human expert (Wenger 87, Clancey 86, Brown et al. 82); explaining what she is thinking while solving a problem. In distributed problem solvers this kind of models can still be applied at some level of abstraction by hiding the distributed nature. However, another natural metaphor is to take the view of an expert upon the group of his cooperating colleague experts as a mental model. In this approach the group solving process is made explicit; the distributed expertise, the reliability of the individual experts, their capacities and dependencies are explained. This knowledge is necessary to support the user towards a new role with the problem solver, participation.

Efficient participation in the this environment requires the understanding of the group problem solving behaviour. The goal is to design a conceptual structure that links the models of the individual agents and makes their cooperation explicit. This model will be the base for the users assistant. This assistant is constantly following the problem solving behaviour and models the behaviour of the agents. The user will be able ask her assistant to provide an explanation of high level decisions, of strategy and of justifications of the problem solving behaviour at the cooperation level. Moreover the assistant should assist the user in analyzing internal decisions, strategies and justification of the problem solving agents.

3. Methods

This research will be be phased as follows. First current approaches for understanding single agent problem solvers will be investigated. The focus will be on the explanation of strategies, decisions and justifications of such systems at appropriate levels of abstraction ((Chandrasekaran et al. 89), (Clancey 86), (Swartout 83)). Then the aspects of CDPS systems will be investigated ((Smith & 81), (Bond & 88)). I will focus on the systems that allow and need high level participation of the user . A model for explanation of cooperation will be designed for a suitable subset of these systems. Finally the user's assistant agent will be constructed to maintain this model and present it to the user. The research will be concentrated on the *content* of the explanation. Other aspects of explanation, like the adaptation to the user's knowledge and presentation issues will not be dealt with intensively.

4. Findings to date

In this first phase of this research I concentrated on explanation aspects for single agent problem solving systems, and on dimensions of cooperative problem solving systems relevant for the users understanding.

For the generation of the explanation's content for single agent problem solving systems the following aspects are considered important. In (Chandrasekaran et al. 89) three types of explanation are identified that refine the 'causal story' (Clancey 86) and provide more insight in the different 'why' questions provided by various problem solvers. They identify explaining decisions, providing justification and explaining strategy. Furthermore, levels of abstraction are a basic requirement for models that support explanation (Clancey 86) and also different viewpoint may be required (Swartout 83). The assistant agent should explain these decisions and provide justification to convince the user that the CDPS has found a correct answer to the problem, and it should provide an explanation of strategy to support the understanding of the problem solver itself (for debugging and maintenance).

Three aspects of CDPS systems appeared to be particularly important in this context; organisational structure, high level cooperation strategy and granularity. If the organisational structure does not reflect any human approach to problem solving explanation of cooperation is difficult. This is the case of ill-defined inter-node relationships which result in loose organisational structures and loosely modelled and poorly understood problem solving behaviour. In this case the explanation of strategy and decisions cannot be created at the architectural level; an intermediate model need to be created of the cooperation process.

Two major strategies for problem solving of agents exist; either agents solve tasks or agents make hypotheses. .In general task sharing works in a top down fashion. Nodes decompose tasks and make the sub-tasks available to other nodes. Decomposition is continued until nodes can solve the tasks. Result sharing works in a bottom up way. Nodes create hypothesis about data and make the hypotheses available to other nodes. Nodes use these hypotheses to create new hypotheses or to establish facts. Composition continues till all hypotheses have either been approved or rejected (Smith & 81). The cooperation that results from these two strategies can be entirely different. Problem solvers that use a 'divide and conquer' strategy, in which top level tasks are decomposed into smaller tasks, show a problem solving behaviour that lies closest to human approaches to problem solving.

The grain size of the problem decomposition at the level of the single agent and the related complexity of the individual agent define the system granularity. A system can be characterized as fine grained when the top level problem has been finely decomposed at the level of the individual agent (Sridharan 86). If agents are of low complexity, and therefore allocated low level tasks, a lot of cooperation is necessary to solve complex tasks. Explaining the behaviour of the simple agents is less complex, but in this case the understanding of the systems behaviour depends a great deal on the understanding of this cooperation. However, the user's participation in and focusing of problem solving is a difficult task in such a fine grained system. This is due to:
- The great disparity in terms of knowledge, skills and tasks which can be handled between the user and the individual agents.
- The high distribution of control and the inherent concurrency of these systems.

The only realistic opportunities for user participation in fine grain systems is by setting up the top level goal and checking the final solution. For the latter task a justification of the solution will be required.

User participation is easiest in CDPS systems that have a natural mapping to real world situations. Preliminary results of this work show that CDPS systems built out of coarse grained agents using the task sharing strategy have the most direct mapping in this respect. The architectural level of these systems represents a structure that reflects human approaches in cooperation. For CDPS systems that apply the result sharing strategy and are built out of fine grained elements user participation will be much less natural, requiring extensive support based on intermediate models.

Key References

(Bond & 88) Bond, A. H. and Gasser, L., (1988), "Readings in Distributed Artificial Intelligence", Morgan-Kaufmann.

(Breuker et al 89) J. Breuker , C. Duursma , R. Winkels, M. Smith, "Knowledge Representation in Eurohelp: Modelling Operation and Understanding of Computer Applications for Help Systems", Proceedings of Esprit'89, pp 258- 270, Kluwer Academic Publ. Brussels, November 1989.

(Brown et al. 82) J. S Brown, R. R Burton, J de Kleer, "Pedagogical, natural language and knowledge engineering techniques in SOPHIE I, II and III. in Intelligent Tutoring Systems, Sleeman and Brown eds. Cambridge, MA: Academic Press, 1982, pp227-279

(Sridharan 86) N.S Sridharan "1986 Workshop on Distributed AI- workshop report", AI Magazine, vol. 8, no 3, pp 75-85, Fall 1987.

(Chandrasekaran et al. 89) B. Chandrasekaran, M. C. Tanner, J. R. Josephson, "Explaining Control Strategies in Problem Solving" in IEEE Expert, Spring 1989.

(Clancey 86) W. C. Clancey, "Qualitative student models" in The First Annual Review of Computer Science, 1986.

(Smith & 81) R G. Smith, R Davis; "Frameworks for cooperation in Distributed Problem Solving", IEEE Transactions on Systems, Man and Cybernetics, pp 61-70, January 1981.

(Swartout 83) W. R. Swartout "XPLAIN: a System for Creating and Explaining Expert Consulting Programs" in Artificial Intelligence 21 1983 pp 285-325.

(Wenger 87) E. Wenger, "Artificial Intelligence and tutoring systems - Computational and cognitive Approaches to the Communication of Knowledge" Morgan Kaufmann Los Altos, CA

Student's name and address:
Cuno M. Duursma
JRC , CITE, KBS Laboratory,
TP 440, I 21020, Ispra, Italy
cDuursma%jrc@mcsun.uucp
Phone: +39 332 789 111 int. 5628

Supervisors:
Joost Breuker
Social Science Informatics Dept
Herengracht 196
NL-1016 BS Amsterdam
breuker%swivax@mcsun.uucp

Nichos Avouris
JRC , CITE, KBS Laboratory,
TP 440, I 21020, Ispra, Italy
nAvouris%jrc@mcsun.uucp

Human–Computer Interaction – INTERACT '90
D. Diaper et al. (Editors)
Elsevier Science Publishers B.V. (North-Holland)
IFIP, 1990

THE ROLE OF ANALOGY IN TRAINING COMPUTER USERS

Jonathan Elcock

Psychology Department, Polytechnic South West, Drake Circus, Plymouth, England, PL4 8AA.

This paper summarises work on training by analogies. Four studies are discussed. The conclusions drawn from these studies is that while analogies have an effect in training that effect is not simply beneficial. Theoretical issues arising from these studies are then discussed.

INTRODUCTION

This paper describes a programme of work on the effects of analogies in the domain of training people to use computer operating systems, but it is hoped that the work will be applicable to the more general issue of using analogies in training for a range of computer applications. While there is a body of literature on analogy it comes from varied sources. Ranging from the training of general thinking skills to applications in system management. In the last decade there has been an upsurge of interest in how people understand information from other domains by the use of analogy. The impetus for this increased awareness has come from Gentner's (1981) work on a structure mapping theory of analogies and Gick and Holyoak's (1983) work on a pragmatic theory of analogical problem solving. The underlying idea of these theories is the belief that using an analogy may lead to the formation of a knowledge structure around which the new information may be organised.

However in the HCI literature the use of analogies for training is generally mistrusted. This may be because the work on analogies that has shown there is not a beneficial effect. The work on which recommendations were based may not apply to HCI and this research thesis in part aims to clarify these issues. At the end of the research programme it is hoped, to clarify the theoretical issues arising from applying the current theories in use to more complex systems.

METHODS OF RESEARCH AND RESULTS

The first experiment involved a training paradigm for MS-DOS. Two conditions, procedural training which included minimal explanation of what the system did and analogy training which explained the system in terms of the 'integrated office' analogy. Subjects were screened so that they did not have a knowledge of MS-DOS. Subjects were given one of the two training manuals followed by a test consisting of multiple choice and short answer questions. In addition the subjects received scales designed to test the acceptability of the training material. The experiment showed that the analogy training material had some positive benefits, however when subjects got the answers incorrect they were mislead by distractors in the multiple choice questions that were analogy consistent. These subjects were also better able to accurately rate the success of the training material than subjects in the other group.

The next study involved three conditions, procedural training, the 'integrated office' analogy and conceptual training material designed to give the same level of information as the analogy condition but in terms of what the system actually does. The procedure was similar to the experiment described above, but a prior expertise score was taken. The test questionnaire included more multiple choice questions. Subjects in the analogy condition and the conceptual condition, as expected. However there was little difference in the average scores of the conceptual and analogy groups. Unexpectedly the analogy group had a much wider range of scores than the conceptual group and the variance of these groups was significantly different. Two main explanations can be put forward for why this large variability in results was found. Firstly that there is a general analogical ability that is subject to individual differences. Secondly, that there is a variation in people's understanding of the analogies, which would lead to a difference in performance as different knowledge structures would be transferred. Again the analogy trained subjects and only these subjects could accurately rate their individual success.

The next experiment was designed to look at whether or not there is a general analogical ability. Two other measures of analogical ability were used. It was hypothesised that if there was a general analogical ability then this would be reflected by the subjects scores across the range of measures. A correlational design was utilised in order to test this hypothesis. The experimental results allow for the suggestion that there is no such general ability, as very low correlations were found between the three measures.

Another experiment currently being run is designed to look at the issue of using an integrated analogy, that may not necessarily explain each component of the system fully, or using component analogies that should give a better explanation of an area of a system but which make no attempt to link with each other. This study includes measures of the knowledge that people have about the analogy domain in an attempt to verify the alternative explanation about why there is a large variance in test scores of those trained with analogies.

IMPLICATIONS OF RESEARCH

The research has a number of possible implications for HCI. First of all it is an attempt to apply psychology theories to HCI in a systematic way. The theories on which analogy research is based in psychology tend to deal with the creative use of analogies or analogies in problem solving. In order to apply these theories to a more complex situation, such as HCI, it is necessary to restructure them. For example while the pragmatic reasoning schema put forward by Gick and Holyoak (1983) provides a good explanation for problem solving where there are limited parameters to the problem it is difficult to apply this to a computer system. Gentner's generative analogy hypothesis gives a good explanation of the general principles involved in the formation of knowledge structures from analogies but fails to give a detailed explanation of how this transfer of knowledge structures takes place. It was therefore necessary to re-examine these theories for an application to HCI. As well as the empirical findings derived from the studies outlined above it is also possible to describe in theoretical terms how analogies lead to the formation of knowledge structures. For a knowledge structure about a new domain to be generated using an analogy it is important that the person being trained is exposed to the new ideas and terminology as well as the terms from the analogy, which they should already be familiar with. This approach is different to that used in teaching device models to people or using a metaphor. With both of these techniques inexperienced computer users who are unlikely to know any other terminology, may be constrained by the metaphorical vehicle chosen. With an analogy they are able to apply the syntactic, or pragmatic benefits of the analogy domain but should also be able to then build upon this knowledge structure as their understanding of the system deepens.

The other benefit of analogies that has been identified in these studies, the increase in the individuals metacognitive awareness of the state of their knowledge also has implications for HCI. The effect of underestimating knowledge about a computer system is that people tend to use the more time-consuming, but familiar, operations that they are comfortable with. Over-estimating knowledge of a computer application can lead to frustration at best when something goes wrong, at worst it can lead to losing valuable data or crashing the system. Neither outcome is desirable for the user. This effect, although it is valuable in increasing the confidence of the inexperienced user is expected to become less marked for more experienced users.

Finally the research will allow for the definition of the terms mental model and schema to be re-evaluated. These terms, especially in the case of mental model, are used without adequate explanation by many authors. In order to use the term in any meaningful way it is necessary to systematically encode users' knowledge about a domain. Rather than rely solely on performance based tasks and inferring a knowledge structure from them.

REFERENCES

Gentner D. (1981) Structure-mapping: A theoretical framework for analogy. Cognitive Science 7, 155-170.

Gick M.L. and Holyoak K.J. (1983) Schema induction and analogical transfer. Cognitive Psychology 12, 1-38.

Human–Computer Interaction – INTERACT '90
D. Diaper et al. (Editors)
Elsevier Science Publishers B.V. (North-Holland)

LINGUISTIC MODELS IN THE DESIGN OF COOPERATIVE HELP SYSTEMS

Charles Elliot

Department of Computer Studies, Sheffield City Polytechnic, Pond Street, Sheffield, S1 1WB

1. SCOPE

The starting point for the project is the premise that there is a limit to the extent to which usability can be designed into a 'passive' interface, no matter how ingenious the graphical representation of functionality or the 'analogy' with some known scenario. In order for an interface component to take dialogue or other initiatives, it must be, to some degree, intelligent. Some recent attempts at this have focussed on the notion of adaptivity but the conceptual conflicts between adaptivity and interface consistency, coupled with a dearth of knowledge about what aspects of a system are appropriate for adaptation, underlie the mostly disappointing results of such research [2].

An alternative is to have the interface actively help the user to adapt to the system. Some precedents can be found in [1], [3], [4], [7], [8], [11] and [14]. An ideal help system would take a form analogous to an expert user observing the interaction and interceding only when an error has been or is about to be made. This contrasts with conventional help systems which the user has to 'call up', requiring the user already to know that a problem exists and the nature of that problem.

2. SOLUTIONS

In order to provide helpful information at any point during the interaction, such a component would need to be capable of 'following' the interaction, assessing the consequences of user actions and of making intelligent inferences concerning the intentions of the user from user behaviour. One of the main aims of the project is to discover to what extent this is possible in a direct-manipulation or WIMPS environment and also to discern how such factors as the kind of application, dialogue design and so on, affect this aim. The project does not address directly the problem of the form that such help information should take, although it is acknowledged that this is equally important.

3. METHODS

The first stage of the project is concerned with the identification of an appropriate description of the interaction. Just what 'appropriate' means in this context is discussed below. It is also an aim of the project to determine the extent to which a linguistically orientated characterisation of WIMPS interaction is possible. Linguistics provides a rich source of description and classification for communicational phenomena and seems particularly apposite in the WIMPS context. There are good reasons for this; WIMPS is, perhaps surprisingly, semantically much richer than the command language interface, thus making the natural language analogy appealing. It is also far less complex than full natural language interaction and does not suffer the same limitations of seriality.

It should be stressed, however, that the linguistic analogy is pursued not for its own sake but because it is held that interface design which reflects 'natural' communicative processes will be easier to learn and use than one which does not. In addition, it is felt that the interaction can be better characterised, and therefore understood, in these terms. It is also worth noting that the analysis of an existing interface mimics the linguists' task of taking 'surface form' and attempting to characterise the 'deep structure' of a language.

4. RESULTS

Of course, interaction models which use a natural language analogy already exist; Moran's 'Command Language Grammar' [10] is a case in point, and such analyses formed the basis for part of this investigation. There is not sufficient space here for a full critique of all the models reviewed. However, some brief remarks may serve to give the 'flavour' of what is being proposed.

Interaction (or task) models can be divided, for our purposes, into two groups; those with a semantic component and those without. The latter group includes GOMS, Reisner's Task Action Language and Keiras and Poulson's two-pronged, GOMS-like model [13]. These are of little value to the present endeavour (although it is not a criticism of them in themselves) in that, being essentially syntactic, they do not provide access to what user actions 'mean', this being vital to current concerns.

Models which deal with interaction semantics include TAG [5], TAKD [13], and Tauber's ETAG [12]. Although these models address the semantics of tasks, they do so mostly in a manner designed to highlight the underlying similarities between tasks in order to facilitate consistent interface design. While this is laudable, the task/action lists or dictionaries that these analyses produce do not represent dependence relationships (eg: exclusivity) that may exist at various levels between tasks. Again, this is vital to present concerns.

Having identified some of the features of the required model and found some of those features lacking in models reviewed, the model outlined below was developed on the basis of a case study involving a Macintosh database application. The model has many similarities with CLG but there are important differences. Firstly CLG's semantic level contains descriptions of procedures and methods for completing tasks described in the task level. The semantic level of the model proposed here is constituted by a description of the conceptual objects involved in the task in terms of their attributes, value ranges and relations between these various features.

Procedures for higher-level tasks are stated in terms of the structure of the task level hierarchy. Lower level tasks can be described in terms of the setting of values to attributes of objects and the methods required to achieve this are usually quite straightforward. Thus procedures and methods are largely implicit. If necessary, explicit procedures and methods may be generated by tracing a task from the conceptual level through to a description of the actions appropriate for the kinds of symbols involved. The consequence of this is that there are not the mapping difficulties of CLG [9]. The task level description is entirely in semantic level terms except at the very lowest level, where it impinges on the communication level. For example, the task hierarchy for a database file-creation goal has as a sub-task that of field-definition. This latter is achieved by choices of values for attributes of a field, actions which have direct correlates in terms of symbolic manipulations.

Secondly, the communication level of CLG is inappropriate to the WIMPS style interface and is replaced by a component describing the 'lexical' or 'symbolic' constituents of the interface and a 'syntactic' description conveying the relationships between the symbolic objects. For a particular dialogue, the relationships between the various symbolic objects effectively defines the syntax for that dialogue. These relationships stem from the semantic description and should, if the software design is valid, accurately reflect the semantic level. Command-key and palette options for entering commands can be thought of as sources of synonymous productions when compared with the menu (etc) style. Certain symbolic features of the interface are seen as relating to dialogue control as opposed to dialogue content and there are strong relations between symbolic form and semantic feature. For example, dialogue control features most easily fit the 'button' form.

5. THE LINGUISTIC ANALOGY

With regard to natural language, we can talk (loosely) of lexicon (words), syntax (how the words can be combined into sentences), semantics (what the sentences mean) and pragmatics (how the 'meanings' are used). In the WIMPS environment we can distinguish a similar classification. The interface provides certain symbols (lexicon) which may be used in restricted combinations (syntax). These uses have 'significance' for the objects to which the symbols relate (or refer) (semantics) and, typically, there are discernible, rational principles (pragmatics) governing sequences of 'significant' uses.

Unlike natural language, an interface will normally prohibit the production of items not in the lexicon, non-grammatical 'utterances' or nonsensical, grammatical utterances. These will either be 'unsayable' or they will be rejected on production. However, just as it is possible to say perfectly meaningful things in English which are, under the circumstances, 'unfelicitous', typically, an interface will not restrict all 'less than cogent' sequences of behaviour.

An utterance has logical, semantic or rational implications, giving rise to expectations on the part of the 'interlocutor'. If these expectations are not satisfied ('flouting' occurs) the utterance/action is unfelicitous or has to be interpreted non-literally (there is a conflation and simplification of Speech Act and Conversational Implicature theories here but there is not the space to enlarge). Whereas in the linguistic case expectations arise from cooperative maxims [6], in the human-computer interaction, they are generated by principles and maxims of cogent usage. And whereas in natural language, the flouting of these maxims may serve the purpose of conveying non-literal meanings and metalinguistic devices, such as sarcasm or irony, there is no place for the deliberate 'flouting' of these maxims in human-computer interaction.

Case study analysis reveals that the semantic level description does give rise to what might be called 'pragmatic principles'. That is to say that when the 'meaning' of certain action sequences is considered, certain 'felicity conditions' present themselves in relation to the felicitous use of the application. For example, some of the relations between field attributes are conceptual dependencies and this means that, while it is possible to define a dependent attribute in advance of its super-attribute, it is usually inadvisable, since the latter setting may 'undo' the former. While the two actions 'make sense' in isolation, the combination is 'unfelicitous'. It is rather like saying to a baker "Have you anything with currants in it, perhaps a plain wholemeal loaf?".

The existence of such phenomena allows us to define general pragmatic rules which may apply to many aspects of an application and its interface and which can be used to monitor users' performance and provide context-sensitive help. It is also worth pointing out that the process of analysing an application in this way is liable to show up sharply any inconsistencies in the design of the interface. This is a not unwelcome byproduct of the investigation and may have important ramifications for design methodologies.

The implications for the planning level have yet to be assessed and the model is to be regimented and extended to all aspects of the WIMPS environment. Some prototype formalisation of part of the dBASE dialogue syntax, semantics and pragmatics have been successfully implemented in Prolog.

6. IMPLICATIONS

While the motivation for the project is the provision of intelligent help, the model outlined above has corollaries for design, evaluation and theory. The stated aim of CLG is to separate out the conceptual model of a system from its command language and to show the relationship between them in order to allow the structure of the command language to reflect the conceptual structure of the task. This appears possible with great clarity in the proposed model and may be applied to design or evaluation.

It is hoped that a linguistically orientated approach can be shown to be not only viable but useful in the design of non-natural-language and non-command-language systems. In the long term, a design methodology, or the basis for one, may be a result of developing the ideas outlined above.

REFERENCES

[1] Carroll, J.M & Aaronson, A.P. (1988) 'Learning by Doing with Simulated Intelligent Help' in *Communications of the ACM* Sept 1988, v. 31, No. 9, pp. 1065-79.

[2] Cooper, P. & Totterdell, P. (1986) 'Design and Evaluation of the AID Adaptive Front-End to Telecom Gold' in *People and Computers: Designing for Usability.*, Harrison, M.D & Monk, (eds) C.U.P, Cambridge, pp. 281-95.

[3] Davenport, C. & Weir, G. (1986) 'Plan Recognition for Intelligent Advice and Monitoring.' in *People and Computers: Designing for Usability.*, Harrison, M.D & Monk, (eds) C.U.P, Cambridge, pp. 297-315.

[4] Erlandson, J. & Holm, J. (1987) 'Intelligent Help Systems' in *Information and Software Technology*, vol. 29, No. 3, Apr., pp. 115-21.

[5] Green, T.R.G., Schiele, F. & Payne, S.J. 'Formalisable Models of User Knowledge in Human-Computer Interaction' in *Working with Computers: Theory versus Outcome*, Van der Veer, C.G., Green, T.R.G., Hoc, J., Murray, D.M. (eds) Academic Press, San Diego, Calif., pp. 3-45.

[6] Grice, H.P. (1975) 'Logic and Conversation' in Cole, P., Morgan, J. L. (eds), *Studies in Syntax*, vol. 3, New York Ac. Press.

[7] Hecking, M. (1987) 'How to Use Plan Recognition to Improve the Abilities of the Intelligent Help System *Sinix Consultant*' in *Interact '87* Elsevier Publishers, N. Holland, pp. 657 - 62.

[8] Jerrams-Smith, J. (1985) 'Susi - A Smart User-System Interface' in *People and Computers: Designing the Interface.*, Johnson, P. & Cook, S. (eds), C.U.P., Cambridge, pp. 211-20.

[9] Johnson, P. (1985) 'Towards a Task Model of Messaging: An Example of the Application of TAKD to User Interface Design.' in *People and Computers: Designing the Interface.*, Johnson, P. & Cook, S. (eds), C.U.P., Cambridge, pp. 47-62.

[10] Moran, T.P. (1981), 'The Command Language Grammar: A Representation for the User Interface of Interactive Computer Systems' in *Int. J. Man-Machine Studies*, 15, pp. 3-50.

[11] Sandberg, J., Breuker, J. & Winkels, R. (1988) 'Research on Help Systems: Empirical Study and Model Construction' in *Proceedings of the European Conference on A.I.*, Munich, pp. 106-11.

[12] Tauber, M.J. (1988) 'On Mental Models and the User Interface' in *Working with Computers: Theory versus Outcome*, Van der Veer, C.G., Green, T.R.G., Hoc, J., Murray, D.M. (eds) Academic Press, San Diego, Calif., pp. 89-119.

[13] Wilson, M.D., Barnard, P.J., Green, T.R.G., Maclean, A. (1988) 'Knowledge-Based Task Analysis for Human-Computer Systems' in *Working with Computers: Theory versus Outcome*, Van der Veer, C.G., Green, T.R.G., Hoc, J., Murray, D.M. (eds) Academic Press, San Diego, Calif., pp. 47-87.

[14] Woodroffe, M.R. (1988) 'Plan Recognition and Intelligent Tutoring Systems' in *Artificial Intelligence and Human Learning*, Self, J. (ed), Chapman and Hall, London, pp. 213-25.

Human–Computer Interaction – INTERACT '90
D. Diaper et al. (Editors)
Elsevier Science Publishers B.V. (North-Holland)
IFIP, 1990

An Environment to Support the Use of Program Examples While Learning to Program in LISP

Katherine Wanjiru Getao

Department of Computing, Lancaster University, Lancaster, U.K.

1. Introduction

This extended abstract describes a computer system to support learning to program in LISP using examples. We aim to investigate how examples could make it easier to learn to program in LISP by providing the learner with an environment that:

* facilitates progressive learning of subsets of LISP;
* dynamically selects and presents examples to aid concept learning.

From the educational (Tennyson [1]) and machine-learning (Michalski [2]) literature the process of learning from examples can be categorised into two dominant schools:

* Induction - the system uses a collection of general purpose heuristics to learn concepts by comparing a set of examples with a set of counter-examples and abstracting a set of definitive attributes and rules.
* Analysis - the system deductively generates an explanation of the concept membership of an exemplar using a collection of domain-specific facts and rules. In machine learning, this is known as explanation-based generalization and is similar to 'worked-examples' described in the educational literature.

Learning occurs in an environment where events generate example data which in turn provides the conditions for events to take place. Our hypothesis is that learning depends on the environment as well as the state of the learner. The learner's strategy is affected by the amount and quality of the example data presented for concept learning (Wiedenbeck [3], Berwick [4]).

A learning environment with examples, instructional text and a language interpreter is complex. It is important to maintain coherence by ordering the presentation of concepts and examples so that the student is only required to infer a few productions in order to understand the latest example.

2. LISP environments and textbooks

LISP environments provide powerful tools for interactive program development including syntax-sensitive editors, pre-processors with diagnostics, optimising programs and interactive support - such as trace facilities. LISP textbooks provide: a list of contents, subject index, exercises, summaries, bibliography, glossary, and in some cases software, which may include an interpreter debugger, on-line manual, tutorial and example programs. The goal of a programming text affects the ordering of the content and consequently the context of a particular example. Some textbooks provide an index of examples, but this often consists of a list of their names, and is unlikely to the discovery of relationships between examples by the novice.

In this system design a hypertext organisation has been selected for storing the instructions, definitions, explanations and examples needed to provide learner support in the LISP environment, because it provides flexible access to text and examples from a variety of contexts.

3. An Environment Design for LISP Learners

The main aims of the design are to provide:

* a LISP environment;
* an instructional hypertext;
* tools to support the acquisition of models helpful to programming;
* **intelligent access to a rich set of examples;**
* **coherent management of these facilities.**

Figure 1 illustrates the environment design. It consists of two independent

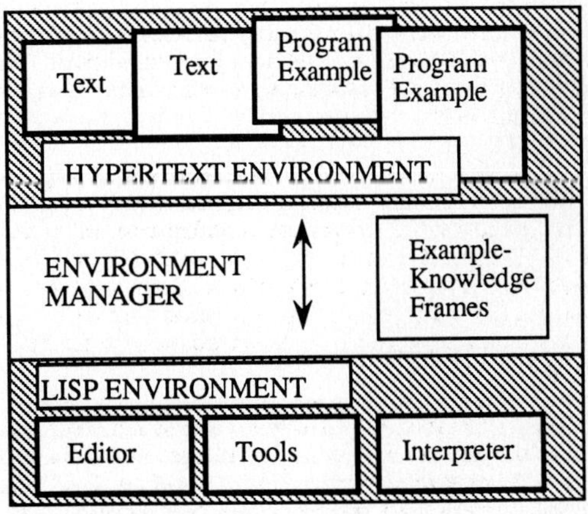

Fig 1 LISP Environment Design

environments: a hypertext of textual nodes (HE) and a LISP environment (LE). An Environment Manager (EM) interfaces between the two. HE contains the instructional text and can be read: sequentially, by following explicit links, hierarchically, by using the list of contents, or browsed. LE has a LISP interpreter, debugger and editor and supports some modelling tools. EM maintains coherence by introducing its own LISP evaluator into the LE to interpret a defined subset of LISP. EM can select an appropriate example at any time during the interaction using static frames corresponding to nodes in HE and dynamic frames created as the student works with the modelling tools. Fig 1 shows the design of the LISP learning environment.

4. System Interaction Example

An example exercise could be to write a LISP function MEETQ which takes a list L as an argument and returns T if the atom Q occurs at the top-level of L, and returns NIL otherwise.

MEETQ can be implemented using condition-action pairs. There are several different ways of implementing this control structure in LISP. In this scenario, the student would analyse the MEETQ specification,for example, by using a tool to make its structure explicit, and then attempt to write the MEETQ function.

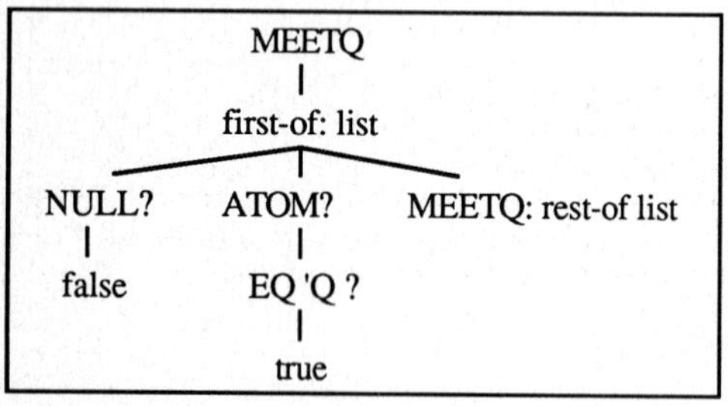

Fig 2 Example structure Diagram for MEETQ

EM uses the structure diagram and the student-created function to select examples for presentation. Depending on the system/learner interaction the system could either select a typical implementation, such as:

```
(defun colours (wave-l)          ;
prototypical cond
   (cond        (((> wave-l  .8)  (< wave-l
1.0))  'RED)
         ((> wave-l .5) 'YELLOW)
         ((> wave-l .2) 'BLUE)
         (t 'NEUTRAL)))
```

or an example that implements the same control structure in a different way to help the student to generalize his concept, for example using 'if' statements:

```
(defun  c-member (record)
   (if   (not  (member  record  c-members))
(checkout record) t )

(defun checkout (record)
   (if (eq (car record)  '(the rich)) (add-
member record c-members) f)
...
```

5. Conclusions and Future Work

An Analysis of LISP textbooks literature review has led to the hypothesis that learners can make powerful use of examples. We aim to discover if the use of available computer technology can enhance learning from examples by augmenting a LISP environment with a system which will intelligently select examples to support user interaction.

The research method to be used is user study with subject protocol and system history analysis.

The system is to be implemented using the LispWorks system in an X-Windows environment. We envisage that the initial system will consist of approximately 50 textual nodes and 100 examples. The tools and manager will be implemented in LISP.

Experimental work will consist of a pilot study with computer science students who are familiar with at least one other programming language but are LISP novices. One group will use the system with all the facilities apart from the environment manager. The second group will use the complete system including the manager. The aim is to study the differences in strategies employed by the two different groups, and their mastery of a defined set of LISP concepts.

6. References

[1] Tennyson R.D., Park O-C.; (1980); The Teaching of Concepts: A Review of Instructional Design Research Literature; REVIEW OF EDUCATIONAL RESEARCH **50(1)**; 55 - 70.

[2] Michalski R.S.; (1986); Understanding the Nature of Learning: Issues and Research Directions; in: [5];3 - 25.

[3] Wiedenbeck S.; (1989); Learning Iteration and Recursion from Examples; INT. J. MAN-MACHINE STUDIES **30**; 1 - 22.

[4] Berwick R.C.; (1986); Learning from Positive-Only Examples: The Subset Principle and Three Case Studies; in [5].

[5] Michalski R.S., Carbonell J.G.; Mitchell T.M., (eds.); MACHINE LEARNING AN ARTIFICIAL INTELLIGENCE APPROACH; **2**; Morgan Kaufmann; Los Altos.

Human–Computer Interaction – INTERACT '90
D. Diaper et al. (Editors)
Elsevier Science Publishers B.V. (North-Holland)

Modelling Cognitive Aspects of Complex Control Tasks

Simon Grant

University of Strathclyde, Scottish Human-Computer Interaction Centre
36 North Hanover St., Glasgow, Scotland G1 2AD

1 Introduction

As technology becomes more sophisticated, the consequences of its use or abuse have become more significant. The problems associated with the situation of fewer and fewer people controlling more and more technically complex and powerful systems, have led to several widely-known and reported disasters, commonly attributed to human error.

There is a wide range of complex, non-adversarial tasks, including process control, traffic control and the control of complex vehicles, for which we might attempt to improve the interaction between human and complex system by introducing computer-based decision aids. However, for such aids to be accepted and effective, they need to be in harmony with practical human representations of the task.

Machine learning studies invite a particularly focussed concept of representation, and this thesis seeks to make use of the clarity of that concept, in conjunction with more established methods, to help progress towards 'cognitive' task analysis [1], and the construction of detailed rule-based mental models of task performance.

Such models could be used to design interfaces suited to particular individuals or groups of individuals; and they could be used in safety and risk assessment, by giving clearer insight into the mental structures and functions underlying human error. A sequence of models of trainee task performance would enable more feedback from training than is currently possible. Further study could then lead to improvements in training methods. In the longer term, if further research reveals general principles governing the structure of human representations, this would inform the design of interfaces to novel systems where no useful prior analogy exists.

2 Studies defining the main scope

2.1 Machine learning of dynamic control

Dynamic control problems have often been solved using control engineering methods, which rely on detailed quantitative or mathematical analysis of the system to be controlled. These solutions can be brittle, and they typically lack any close relationship with human ways of doing similar tasks.

In contrast, as early as the 1960s there were attempts to apply machine learning to dynamic systems, such as the "pole and cart" system, in which a pole is balanced on a cart, the cart being constrained to move in one dimension. Qualitative, rule-based strategies for balancing the pole have been devised, but there is no unique solution. This variety of possible solutions links pole-balancing with the control of more obviously complex systems.

Success in learning pole-balancing depends crucially on representing the task in an adequate way, in terms of the dimensions used to describe situations, and the way in which those dimensions are divided into areas of the problem space. For the pole and cart, just four obvious quantities span the system's state space (x, $\dot{x}$, θ, and $\dot{\theta}$). For more complex systems, however, the choice of dimensions of the state space may not be so clear-cut, and may involve qualitative variables. Furthermore, where the variables are quantitative, in order to establish qualitative control rules for a system, some "landmarks" must be fixed, to divide up the state space into a finite number of regions (hence the term "boxes"). Even in the pole and cart studies, the method for establishing the landmarks appears to be more intuitive than systematic.

Chambers and Michie [2] proposed a method for machine learning of control rules for the pole and cart system based on human performance, but without full results. Nor has there been any widely known follow-up of their proposals to date. One could plausibly account for this lack by noting that they did not address the issue of discovering representations which match human performance of such a task.

2.2 Focusing of the scope

For the purposes of this study, complexity of a task was taken to be associated with a practical ability to perform the task in a large number of different ways, which may differ in wholesale strategy as well as in tactical detail.

In the literature, there are many calls for a better understanding of human cognition in complex control tasks, and much speculation about the form and content of human mental models in general (e.g., [3, 4, 5]), but there is very little evidence to support the attribution of a particular detailed mental model to a particular person engaged in a particular task—especially for tasks which are complex on the above definition. Since a good representation would enable the creation of a rule-based model (with the help of machine learning techniques), investigation of human representations could be an important first step to detailing human models of a task. Equally, knowing the human representation of a task could help greatly in defining the content (but not the form) of an appropriate interface.

The focus of this work then became the study of human models of a non-manual task of moderate complexity, using the concept of representation, and some of the methods, from machine learning.

3 Methods of the main study

3.1 Identification of a suitable task

A dynamic control task of suitable nature and complexity was sought using the following criteria.

Independence from physiological limits. This ruled out the large majority of current computer games.

Complexity of the task. This had to be high enough to provoke variant strategies, but low enough to allow achievement and stabilisation of skilled performance within an experimentally reasonable time. This ruled out both simple games and full-scale engineering or training simulators.

Adaptability of the interface to allow the construction of variations to match supposed mental models. This again ruled out, e.g., nautical or aviation simulators.

Obtainability. Enough knowledge had to be available to implement the chosen task in a suitably realistic way.

A naval mine-hunting task fitted the criteria and suited the commercial sponsor of the research (YARD Ltd.).

3.2 Implementing this task

The system consists of a moderately realistic simulation of a ship, and less realistic (but plausible) simulations of a remotely operated underwater vehicle, and the cable attaching the two. A scoring system defines a task with conflicting constraints. The base interface is low-level, in the sense that the sensors are directly related to observable quantities, and the effectors related directly to elements of the simulation.

3.3 User-controlled experiments

The simulation game proved interesting enough to attract some unpaid volunteers. The object was to encourage the development of skill, then to ascertain the principal features of the strategies, or models, employed, by taking protocols, noting suggestions, and using machine learning.

3.4 Elaboration of interfaces

At least two higher-level interfaces are being developed, with substantial differences, following the analysis of protocols and logged data. The interfaces should be each fitted to one person or group of people, in an attempt to match particular human models of task performance.

3.5 Controlled experiments

Using subjects from the first stage. The original subjects will try out the different higher-level interfaces, varying the order in which they are presented.

With new subjects. The same procedure will be preceded by training, to encourage a particular model of task performance. The training will be explicit for some, and for others implicit in starting with a higher-level interface.

3.6 Application of rule induction

The researcher's model of a subject's representation of the task can be tested, by specifying the way in which the situations and actions are represented, and then applying a rule-induction algorithm to see how efficient and concise are the rules that emerge. This enables representations to be compared in an objective way.

4 Conclusions to be drawn

Subjects have needed a few hours to develop competence at the task, and even experienced players continue to err. It is clear that there are at least some differences in task strategy. Also, there are obviously some common-sense action concepts (e.g., turning) that are not implemented straightforwardly in the simulation.

The hypothesis that a particular representation is close to that of a particular person would be supported by a number of observations: firstly, if that person performs better with, and prefers, an interface implementing that representation, while other people favour other interface representations; secondly, if rule induction using that representation produces clearer and more concise rules; thirdly, if those rules are able to govern a performance like that of the person; and lastly, if the language used by the person fits the concepts of the representation.

5 Implications

If the suggested approach, as expected, gives some measure of the closeness of correspondence between a representation and that of a particular person, that would enable the search for better and better representations of that person's task performance. Allied with rule induction, this would allow the creation of closer approximations to what we could imagine as the 'actual' mental model of that person (though this is continually liable to change).

In any event, this study is also likely to shed light on methodological problems in determining mental representations and models possessed by users and operators performing complex tasks.

References

[1] Grant, A. S., and Mayes, J. T. (1990). Cognitive task analysis? In *Human-Computer Interaction and Complex Systems*, G. R. S. Weir and J. L. Alty, Eds., Academic Press, London. Forthcoming.

[2] Chambers, R. A., and Michie, D. (1969). Man-machine co-operation on a learning task. In *Computer Graphics: Techniques and Applications*, R. Parslow, R. Prowse, and R. E. Graan, Eds., Plenum Publishing, London, pp. 179–186.

[3] Gentner, D., and Stevens, A. L., Eds. (1983). *Mental Models.* Erlbaum, Hillsdale, NJ.

[4] Goodstein, L. P., Andersen, H. B., and Olsen, S. E., Eds. (1988). *Tasks, Errors and Mental Models.* Taylor & Francis, London.

[5] Rasmussen, J. (1986). *Information Processing and Human-Machine Interaction: An Approach to Cognitive Engineering.* North-Holland, New York.

Human–Computer Interaction – INTERACT '90
D. Diaper et al. (Editors)
Elsevier Science Publishers B.V. (North-Holland)

Using Temporal Logic To Prototype Interactive Systems

C.W. Johnson*
Human Computer Interaction Group, Dept. of Computer Science,
Univ. of York, Heslington, York, United Kingdom, YO1 5DD.

Keywords: *Formal Methods, Prototyping, Rendering, Temporal Logic.*

1 Introduction

Formal methods provide a means of reasoning about implementation independent descriptions of interactive systems. They are, however, often terse, mathematical and inaccessible to the user who is typically not a software engineer. Prototypes provide a far better impression of the 'look and feel' of what it would be like to interact with a system. This paper describes how the author's research has extended executable subsets of first order logic to model dynamic interfaces. Prelog, a tool for Presenting and REndering LOGic specifications of interactive systems, has been implemented. It provides a means of both reasoning about and implementing prototypes by combining the dynamic descriptive powers of a higher order logic with a declarative graphics system.

2 Prototyping Using Temporal Logic

Prolog provides a means of implementing specifications written in first order logic. Many interfaces benefit from graphical images, in order to support prototyping. Prolog must be extended, therefore, to include tractable representations of graphical objects which can be reasoned about. Bitmaps would not be appropriate. Tools which use Prolog to prototype interactive systems must also address the problem of incorporating interaction devices, such as mice and tracker balls, into a logic programming language. There are technical problems which make a specification more difficult to reason about. For instance, predicates such as *write* rely upon side-effects irrelevant to the logic of the specification.

Prelog, a tool which links the screen management system Presenter [5] with the executable temporal logic of Tokio [1] is designed to resolve some of these problems. It extends Pereira's [4] structured graphics in order to handle input from a variety of interaction devices. It achieves this by representing physical devices, such as mice and keyboards, by the events they generate. Events are associated with the virtual devices that a user interacts with. For example a mouse or cursor keys might be used to generate a selection event for a menu [3].

Temporal logic provides a means of describing the dynamic properties of interactive systems and provides a convenient means of maintaining a graphical database. For instance, a temporal property of a VCR might be that a tape is requested and correctly inserted *before* it is played:

$$\begin{array}{l} vidplay1(V,T):- \\ \quad \bigcirc(tapein(V,T), \bigcirc(select(V,play))), \\ \quad display(V,\ 'Insert\ \ Tape'). \end{array}$$

A VCR V plays a tape T if in the present interval $Insert\ Tape$ is displayed by V and in the next interval a tape T is in V and in the next again interval *play* is selected for V. The introduction of the $\bigcirc$ (read as 'next') operator has provided the designer with a notion of sequence which was lacking in previous clauses. The designer cannot assume, however, that the user will press the play button immediate after entering the tape, the previous requirement could be refined as follows:

$$\begin{array}{l} vidplay2(V,T):- \\ \quad display(V,\ 'Insert\ \ Tape'), \\ \quad \bigcirc(tapein(V,T), \diamond(select(V,play))). \end{array}$$

A VCR V plays a tape T if in the present interval $Insert\ Tape$ is displayed by V and in the next interval a tape T is in V and eventually *play* is selected for V. Temporal logic provides the $\diamond$ (read as 'eventually') operator to express such properties.

As mentioned, temporal logic also provides a convenient means of maintaining a graphical database. For instance, it might be specified that:

$$\begin{array}{l} broken(V):- \\ \quad \bigcirc image(V, vidoff, viderror). \end{array}$$

A VCR V is broken if in the next interval the iconic image of a *vidoff* V is *viderror*.

$$\begin{array}{l} working(V):- \\ \quad \bigcirc image(V, vidon, vidwork). \end{array}$$

A VCR V is working if in the next interval the iconic image of *vidon* V is *vidwork*. Restricting the temporal domain of axioms allows the designer to map changes in the state of the system to changes in the display [2]. Clauses like those given above are executable. In order to support prototyping, however, there needs to be some means of incorporating the graphical components of an interface into a design without compromising the behavioural specification.

*Thanks are due to Prof. M.D. Harrison who supervised this work. This research was supported by a CASE studentship funded by British Telecom and by SERC grant number 88503497.

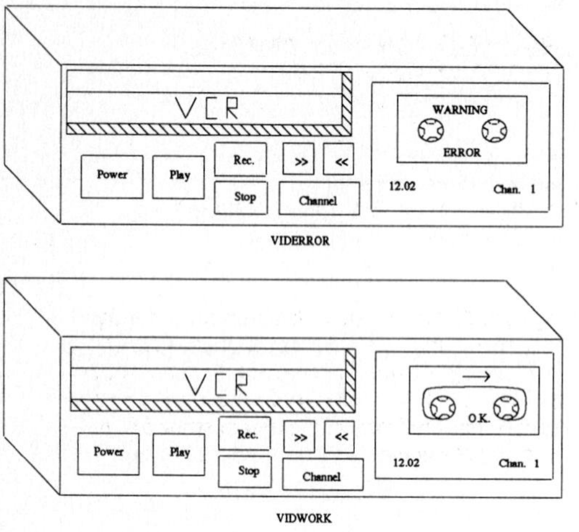

Figure 1: Two VCRs displaying possible icons for *vidwork* and *viderror*.

3 Rendering Using Temporal Logic

Rendering adds the detail necessary to rapidly transform specifications into prototypes, which possess much of the 'look and feel' of the final system. There must be some means of incorporating the pragmatics of interaction without compromising the behavioural specification. Using temporal logic to render interactive systems allows the designer to synchronise competing behavioural and interface requirements. For example, a requirement strictly related to the interface of a VCR might be that all commands from the user are displayed:

$$\begin{aligned}&getcomm1(C,V) :- \\ &\quad \bigcirc(image(V,C,I), display(V,I)).\end{aligned}$$

A command C is received by a VCR V if in the next interval the image, I, of that command for V is displayed by V. A behavioural requirement might be that the system stops playing as soon as the end of tape is reached and that this is displayed:

$$\begin{aligned}&endtape(T,V) :- \\ &\quad \bigcirc(stopplay(V), \\ &\quad image(V, finishtape, I), \\ &\quad display(V,I)).\end{aligned}$$

The end of a tape T is reached by a VCR V if in the next interval V stops playing and the image, I, of a finished tape is displayed by V. Given the limited display resources of most VCRs it may not be possible to fulfill both of the above. In order to render these specifications executable the designer must synchronise competing requirements, one of the *display* events must be delayed:

$$\begin{aligned}&getcomm2(C,V) :- \\ &\quad image(V,C,I), \Diamond(display(V,I)).\end{aligned}$$

A command C is received by a VCR, V, if the image, I, of that command is eventually displayed by V. Alternatively the *display* of *finishtape* could be delayed, however, this might have serious consequences for future interaction, a user might attempt to play beyond the end of a tape.

4 Conclusion

Temporal logic provides the designer with a powerful tool for rendering specifications into executable prototypes. It is well suited to the design and implementation of dynamic systems and can be used to resolve the synchronisation problems which often arise in complex systems. Implementations of the formalism have been extended and a tool for producing tractable, and hence economically justifiable, prototypes has been developed. Further work will address presentation problems for process control systems. Many of these problems are temporal, for example, rapid change in the environment can stretch the resources of both system and operator. The structured, tractable representation of dynamic systems, advocated in this paper, should make this task significantly easier.

References

[1] M. Fujita, M. Ishisone, H. Nakamura, H. Tanaka, and T. Moto-Aka. Using the temporal logic programming language TOKIO for algorithm description and automatic cmos gate array synthesis. In E. Wada, editor, *Logic Programming '85*, pages 246–255. Springer-Verlag, Berlin, FDR, 1986.

[2] C.W. Johnson. Temporal logic applied to interactive systems. Technical Report 89/7, Open University, Milton Keynes, England, May 1989.

[3] C.W. Johnson and M.D. Harrison. Prelog - a system for presenting and rendering logic specifications of interactive systems. Technical report, (Accepted for EUROGRAPHICS'90) Department of Computer Science, University of York, England, 1989.

[4] F. C. N. Pereira. Can drawing be liberated from the Von Neumann style ? In M. Van Caneghan and D. H. D. Warren, editors, *Logic Programming And It's Application*, pages 175 – 187. Ablex Publishing, Norwood, New Jersey, 1986.

[5] R. Took. Text representation and manipulation in a mouse driven interface. In M.D. Harrison and A.F. Monk, editors, *People And Computers : Designing For Usability*, pages 386–401. Cambridge University Press, Cambridge, England, 1986.

Human–Computer Interaction - INTERACT '90
D. Diaper et al. (Editors)
Elsevier Science Publishers B.V. (North-Holland)

A DEVELOPMENT ENVIRONMENT FOR THE DESIGN OF MULTIMODAL, COLOURGRAPHIC HUMAN-COMPUTER INTERFACES

M. Langen, G. Rau

Helmholtz-Institute for Biomedical Engineering, Aachen University of Technology, FR Germany.

The following object-oriented concept improves the design procedure of complex human-computer interfaces by a suitable development environment. This environment supports the process of evolutionary prototyping, i.e. prototypes are iteratively modified until a satisfying version is achieved. In addition to conventional approaches, this development environment integrates software tools for multimodal interaction and interactive colour manipulation. The application of this environment is demonstrated in the design of the human-computer interface of an anesthesia expert assist system.

1. INTRODUCTION

Today's technology provides many devices for human-computer interaction, e.g., high resolution colour graphics, touch input, and voice in- and output. This offers a wide range of facilities for structuring and coding information, such as iconic representation, use of colour and shape, or multimodal interaction technique (mouse-, touch- and speech-input and speech-output within one application).

However, suitable methods are required to apply these techniques efficiently to a complex human-computer interface. Often, in spite of a comprehensive task analysis, it is difficult or impossible to determine how information presentation and interaction could provide optimal support for the user. Therefore, the design of complex human-computer systems usually is an iterative process, which must be supported by appropriate prototyping methods and software engineering tools [10].

2. DESIGN OF AN OBJECT-ORIENTED USER INTERFACE MANAGEMENT SYSTEM

If conventional software development methods are used for prototyping, the implemented code deteriorates with the increase of prototype versions [6]. In addition, often in-depth programming skills are required, if the program must be extended or modified. In order to reduce this effort the idea of reusable "Software IC's" is applied [1]. A "Software IC" is an object consisting of a data structure and related methods. The internal structure of the "IC" is hidden, so that a program developer only has to take into account the description of the IC's "behaviour", which depends on its implemented methods. The mechanism of data encapsulation avoids the deterioration of code during the prototyping process - the predefined data and algorithms provide consistency in the use of these objects.

In the following described approach reusable software objects are organized in such a way that they form a user interface management system (UIMS). This UIMS has been developed considering several requirements:
- hierarchical structure of user interfaces
- direct manipulation and user guidance
- multimodal interaction
- portability and network capability

It is known from cognitive psychology that a goal is accomplished by a step to step approach each of which is representing a subgoal. We use a complementary approach in the interface design by structuring the user interface in a composition of subtask-interfaces. This concept of hierarchically structured interfaces is reflected in the object's hierarchy. The class of "Interactor" branches into two subclasses (Fig. 1): interaction "Elements" such as virtual keys and value sliders on one hand and "Constructors" on the other hand. "Constructors" enable the implementation of hierarchically structured interfaces by binding together elements or other (lower level) "Constructors". An interaction "Element" can be considered as elementary "interface cell". E.g. "Slider" contains the typical presentation and interaction capabilities of a virtual slider.

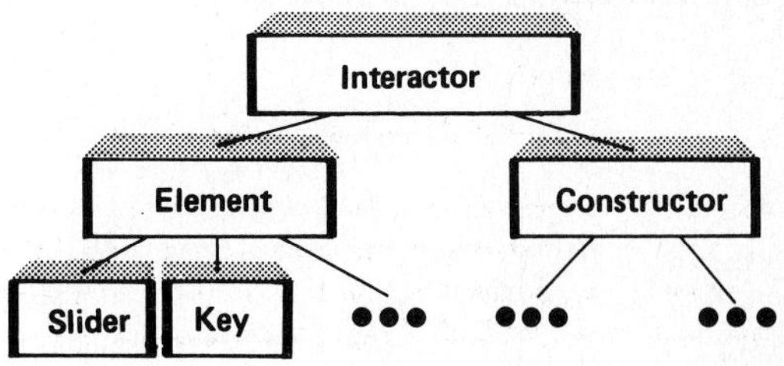

Fig. 1: "Interactor" class hierarchy

The described multimodal UIMS has been structured under the influence of the well known "Seeheim-Model" [2]. However, this model has been revised, since a strict separation of presentation- and dialog-level is unsuitable for direct-manipulation interfaces [5]. As a solution a low-level dialog handling is integrated in the objects while a complex dialog is handled application dependant. A low level dialogue is already prepared for multimodal user input and corresponding reactions. User input is handled according to the event-model, since this offers the choice from several input actions at the same time. Servers for touch-, speech-, keyboard- and mouse-input work in parallel and feed one event-queue, which is processed by an object named "Event-Controller" (Fig. 2).

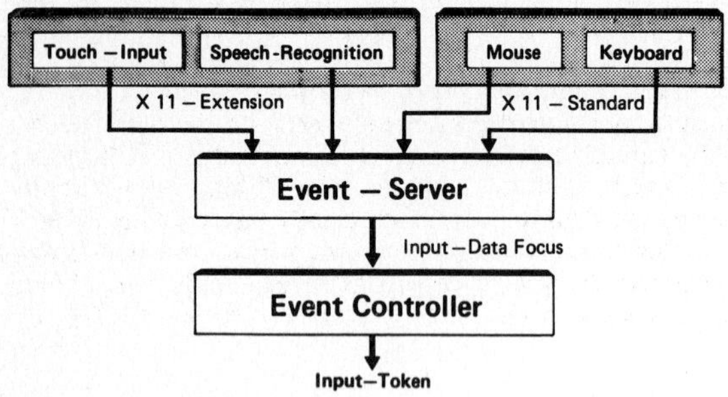

Fig. 2: Multimodal input-handling.

The "Event-Controller" addresses an input-message directly to the receiver object -for example to a virtual key-, if this key was activated by touch input or a voice command.

The use of UIMS-objects considerably reduces the amount of program statements for an application program. Since each program statement itself expresses its effect on the interface, this object-oriented source code is easy to understand. The level of programming is higher than for example in C or Pascal and more related to the task of designing a user interface.

3. SOFTWARE TOOLS OF THE DEVELOPMENT ENVIRONMENT

During the prototypical development of user interfaces several design problems have to be solved. These concern the graphical structure of an interface, colour design and the integration of multimodal interaction facilities. Therefore, a user interface development environment (Fig. 3) was developed to support the interface designer by several tools, which are related to the aspects mentioned above.

A graphical editor for interactive screen layout has been built to provide rapid generation and modification of interaction objects and their geometrical arrangement on the display. Since the screen format is a relevant factor to user acceptance and performance, this software tool supports modification of an application's layout early in the design process. This tool replaces a tedious try-compile-retry-recompile procedure of editing coordinate values in the program source text by the use of direct manipulation procedures and automatic code generation. An additional integrated component of the editor provides the evaluation of geometrical layouts using a modification of the approach from Tullis [9].

A colour editor (CEDI) for interactive colour manipulation was developed to support the designer in colour selection. The use of colour provides an effective way to code the state of interaction objects for user guidance (active, standby) or the state of monitored system components (normal, alarm). But available principles give only qualitative advices for the use of colour. On a screen layout the effect of simultaneous contrast must be taken into account [11]. Therefore, colour selection is an iterative process which should start with suitable default values and enable easy modification.

CEDI provides the use of three colour spaces: the well known RGB colour space, the more intuitive HSV (Hue, Saturation, Value) colour space and the perceptually uniform CIELAB colour space. Each colour space has certain advantages, dependent on the context of a colour selection problem, e.g. a gradual transition between two colours can only be calculated in CIELAB. Direct manipulation by mouse-input is used to adjust a colour within one of the three colour spaces. CEDI is connected to a colour data base; colour values can be read or stored by means of a specified colour term (e.g. "cyan", "active"). For a fine tuning of colours CEDI can be used on a second display which is linked with an application by means of a network. This enables interactive modification during a heuristic evaluation.

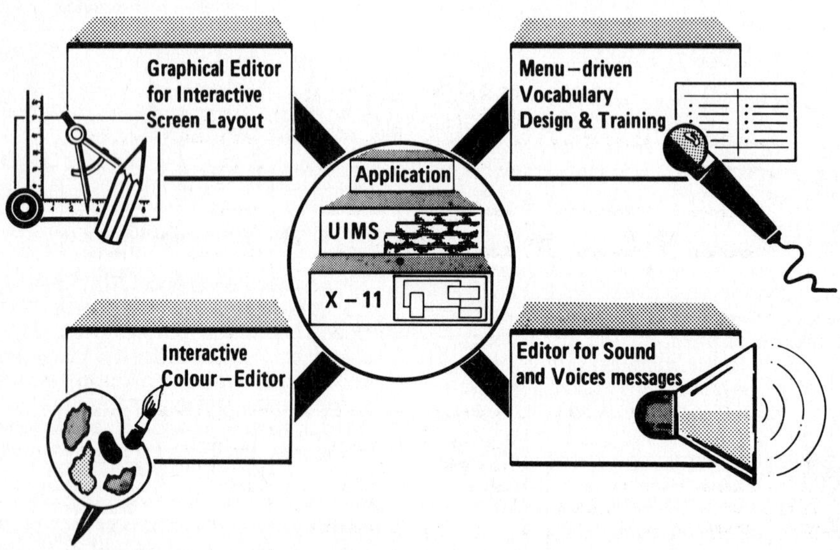

Fig. 3: User interface development environment.

A speech recognition device needs a software tool for design and training of a vocabulary. Such a tool was developed to facilitate the use of speech input in human-computer interaction. During vocabulary design it provides an analysis of the vocabulary to detect similar words. In the phase of word training it gives hints for pronunciation. After training a test procedure can estimate the recognition rate and compute a confusion matrix before a vocabulary is applied for speech recognition in a real environment.

The UIMS not only provides graphical presentation but also acoustic output by "Speaker"-objects. Acoustic messages can be either digitized speech or synthesized sounds. A special tool in form of a dictionary was built to generate, modify and archive these messages. "Speaker" objects from the UIMS access this dictionary at run time.

As shown, this concept of an integrated user interface development environment contains tools concerning many important aspects of human-computer interface design. In contrast to other approaches evaluation is facilitated in several ways during the prototyping process. Therefore, iterative prototyping becomes more comfortable and both the number of prototyping cycles and the time for each cycle should decrease. A satisfying prototype can even be used as the final product, because the negative side-effect of deteriorating code is eliminated by object-oriented programming.

4. HUMAN-COMPUTER INTERFACE DESIGN OF A KNOWLEDGE-BASED SYSTEM

The described prototyping process is being applied in the field of medicine. An expert assist system AES-2 [8] is being developed as an additional component of an anesthesia information system (AIS) for monitoring and automatic documentation [3]. AES-2 is based on a state variable model, i.e. the patient's state is described by the evaluation of so-called state variables such as "myocardial contractility" or "vascular tone". The values of these variables are the result of complex reasoning processes combining the values of vital parameters (bloodpressures, heart frequency, etc.) with additional data such as recent drug administrations. State variables can reach a state of "normal", "below normal" or "above normal" thereby considering a gradual transition between these states. If a state variable leaves a range of "normal" this is indicated to the physician. This "intelligent alarm" function is superior to any conventional alarm which only considers the value of a single signal without considering any context. Therapy recommendations depend on the actual evaluation of state variables and on the effect of recently administered drugs.

For the design of the human-computer interface of AES-2 a model of the anesthesiologist's cognitive behaviour in monitoring and controlling the patient's state was designed (Fig. 4). This model was adapted from Rasmussen's model for a plant operator's task [7]. The basic idea of the display structure of AES-2 is to map different phases of this model into different windows ("Frame" objects of the UIMS-class "Constructor") on the screen. This way each phase of the cognitive model is supported by properly coded information in a related "Frame".

These "Frames" contain (Fig.5):

(A) the evaluation of five state variables coded by coulored bar graphs and their actual trend
(B) monitoring data (bloodpressures, etc.)
(C) patient's history data
(D) therapy recommendations
(E) schedule of administered drugs
(F) information to remember routine tasks
(G) control panel to select a physiologic subsystem (at present only the cardio-vascular system is implemented).

Interaction is performed by touching virtual keys (e.g. icon-keys) or sliders directly on the screen. The user himself can open or close additional "Frames", as it is required in order to access data of the patient's history (Fig. 5). Thus, the user can adapt the amount of displayed information to his actual task, thereby reducing the workload on his visual system.

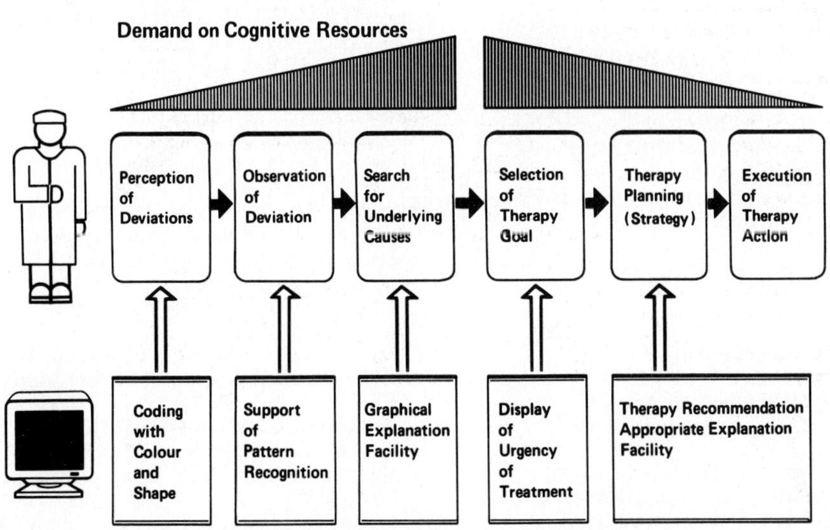

Fig. 4: Proposed model of the anesthesiologist's task. From [4].

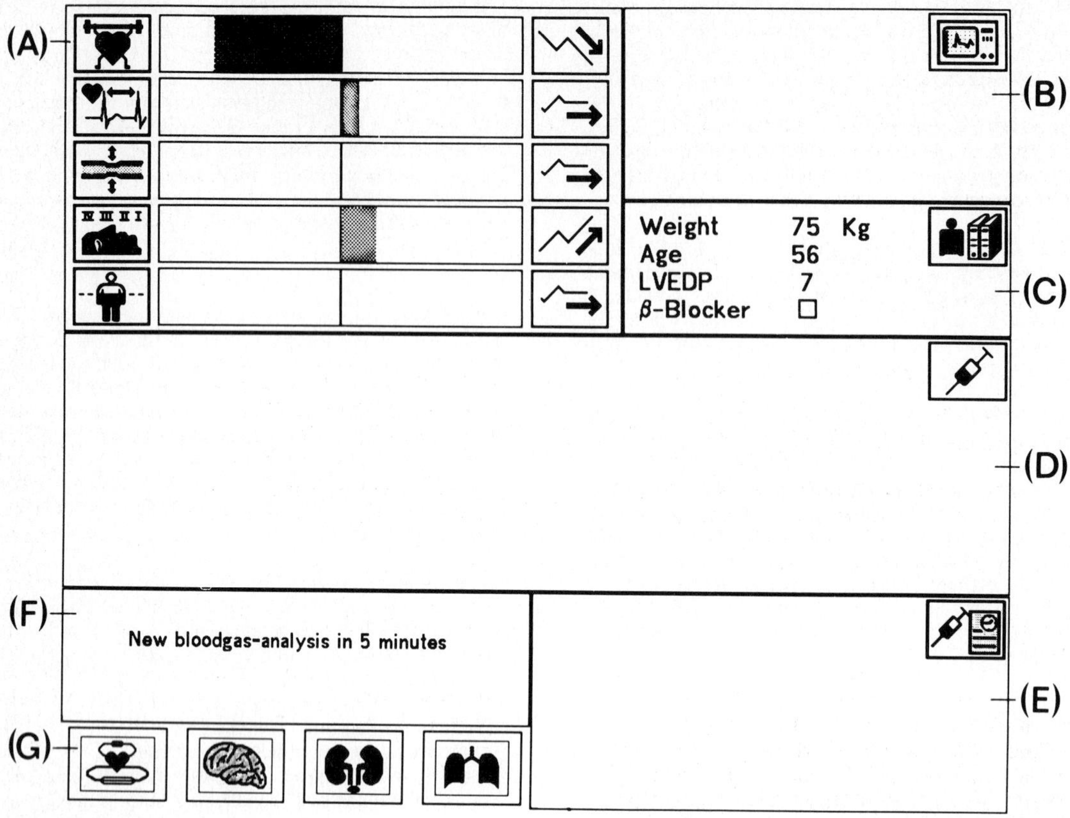

Fig. 5: Screen layout of AES-2

5. CONCLUSION

The described interface development environment has been utilized in several applications, i.e. the development of the AES-2 user interface is only one example. An application for the intensive care unit using auditive input and output - not used in AES-2- is currently tested.
These projects have shown that the predefined objects of the UIMS are an effective support for easy implementation and modification. The tools of the development environment provide visual information coding, e.g. icons for the state variables, colour coded alarms, that support the idea of "catching the situation at a glance". In summery, the described interface development environment enhances the effciency and quality of the system designer's work in the development of interactive, multimodal interfaces.

REFERENCES

[1] Cox, B., Object-oriented Programming - An Evolutionary Approach. Addison Wesley 1986.
[2] Green, M., The University of Alberta User Interface Management System. ACM Siggraph Vol. 19, No. 3, pp. 205-213, 1985.
[3] Klocke, H.; Trispel, S.; Rau, G.; Hatzky, U.; Daub, D., An Anesthesia Information System for Monitoring and Record Keeping During Surgical Anesthesia. Journal of Clinical Monitoring, Vol 2, No 4, October 1986: 246-261, 1986.
[4] Langen, M.; Thull, B.; Schecke, T.; Rau, G.; Kalff, G.: Prototyping Methods and Tools for the Human-Computer Interface Design of a Knowledge-Based System. In: G. Salvendy and M. Smith (eds.), Designing and Using Human-Computer Interfaces and Knowledge Based Systems, Elsevier Science Publishers, 861-868, Amsterdam 1989.
[5] Lowgren, J., History, State and Future of User Interface Management Systems SIGCHI Bulletin, Vol. 20, No. 1, July 1988, pp. 32-44.
[6] Pressman, R., Software Engineering - A Practitioner's Approach. Mc Graw Hill, 1988.
[7] Rasmussen, J.: Models of mental strategies in process plant diagnosis, in: J. Rasmussen , W. Rouse (eds.), Human detection and diagnosis of system failures, New York, Plenum, 241-258, 1981.
[8] Schecke, Th.; Langen, M.; Rau, G.;Käsmacher, H.; Kalff, G., Knowledge-Based Decision Support for Monitoring in Anesthesia: Problems, Design and User Interaction. In: Rienhoff, O.; Piccolo, U. (eds.), Expert Systems and Decision Support in Medicine. Springer, pp. 256-263, 1988.
[9] Tullis, T., The formatting of alphanumeric displays: a review and analysis. Human Factors, 25(6), pp 657-682, 1983.
[10] Williges, R.C.; Williges, B.H.; Elkerton, J., Software Interface Design. In: Salvendy, G. (Ed.), Handbook of Human Factors. John Wiley & Sons, pp. 1416-1449, 1987.
[11] Wyszecki, G., Color Appearance, in: K. Boff (Ed.), Handbook of Perception and Human Performance. John Wiley & Sons, Chp. 9, 1986.

Human–Computer Interaction – INTERACT '90
D. Diaper et al. (Editors)
Elsevier Science Publishers B.V. (North-Holland)

Advanced User Interfaces for Distributed Group Communication

Leandro Navarro

Universitat Politècnica de Catalunya (UPC)
Dep. d'Arquitectura de Computadors
P.O. Box 30.002, E-08080 Barcelona, Spain

The aim of this work is to define an architecture framework of User Interfaces (UI) for Group Communication (GC) activities. After a brief presentation of the background and objectives of this work we will discuss several topics in the scenario of human to group interaction processes.

The resulting UI model is based on the integration of several technologies and components: object orientation, multimedia, intelligent agents, UI languages.

1. INTRODUCTION

The first Message Handling System appeared in the early seventies. The specification in 1984 of X.400 and MOTIS standards has enabled the diffusion of e-mail not only in experimental environments but also in offices. However, experiences in offices made clear that pure exchange of messages was not sufficient. Specific support for Group Communication (GC) is required in addition.

AMIGO *(see Pankoke [3] and Smith [4])* is the name of an initiative of the COST-11ter Action Programme of the CEC. One result is the AMIGO Model of Distributed Group Activities, which is used in the work for ISO Group Communication standardization. The AMIGO Model can describe group activities such as news distribution, bulletin boards, computer conferencing, decision taking, project planning, scheduling, coordinated work, etc.

In parallel with AMIGO, the UPC has developed the User Interface of a distributed X.400 based mail system *(CEC's ESPRIT 718 CACTUS)*. Design and feedback from users and reviewers has arisen several unexpected design requirements.

This paper will present topics and elements to be considered in the design of an architecture framework of User Interfaces for Distributed Systems supporting Activities based in the AMIGO Model.

The objective of this work is to define a UI architecture to support complex cooperation patterns in distributed groups.

2. COMMUNICATION TECHNOLOGY

Group Communication and inter-personal electronic mail are two situations with common functionality. For this reason we should look for an integrated solution, a communication platform flexible and powerful enough to *support* and *enhance* both user-to-user and group communication.

2.1 Group Communication

Existing GC applications such as computer conferencing (EuroKom) and USENET News have already proved the vast potential of group communication services, but they suffer from some limitations:

- *Activities are presented as a continuous stream of information*. High level information management functions are essential to avoid the "information overload".

- *The UI presents nude and crude messages.* Messages are meaningful inserted in context, a conversation.

- *There is no support for reuse of data.* The user must reformat, and sometimes retype, data coming and going to the net.

- *Lack of dialogue structuring* makes complex GC activities difficult to support/understand (electronic newspapers).

- *They do not employ OSI standards* for communication. They are restricted to islands of users, they prevent people to freely communicate. OSI standards can provide an space for open group communication.

This work has been partly supported by the Spanish Government (CICYT 262).
Electronic mail address: `leandro@ac.upc.es`

2.2 Interpersonal communication

Electronic mail is a good tool for human communication. Nowadays, email is the primary source of information and it is used to manage daily work. The number of users is increasing, so the number of messages is increasing. People is expecting more functionality from the mail system because they rely on it more and more for daily activities.

The use of email is diverse. Depending on their use, different management strategies are necessary:

- *information management:* archive messages,
- *time management:* prioritize messages,
- *task management:* delegate tasks.

In addition, feelings of control are diverse among users, relating to the number and structure of messages.

Email systems must provide flexible and high level primitives that capture the important dimensions of use and provide adaptability for a wide range of users [2].

3. INTERACTION

There are two main communication streams in the human to group interaction: *man to machine* interaction and *man through machine* group interaction.

3.1 Man through machine interaction

The user has not only an application interface, but also a complex context that reflects the fact that he is interacting with a group of users. The difference with single user environments is in the *group context*.

Multi-user issues: a great amount of work has been dedicated to existing group interaction patterns: bulletin boards, electronic meetings, computer conferencing, electronic whiteboards, but the design of multi-user systems and interfaces should take into account new interaction patterns appearing as result of human interaction with new tools.

Geographical issues: delay, time, distance have strong influence on the interaction process. Email is based on an store and forward protocol whereas face-to-face communication is based on high speed data networks. Email is asynchronous and face-to-face is synchronous. The delay is the main difference.

Technological issues: underlying technologies have influence on the hardware/software architecture of systems. It is important to study the impact of advanced means for the collection, processing, storing, transport and presentation of information, and the impact of advanced telecommunications networks: broadband (ATM), multimedia electronic mail X.400 and distributed directory X.500.

3.2 Man to Machine interaction

User *diversity* is the most obvious outcome *(see Medina [1])*. Deviation from models are extreme. The UI should be adjustable enough to help to bridge differences in knowledge, experience, use, etc.

Diversity can be found on users, media, support, languages: the wide range of cultures within Europe provides a good field to test diversity.

4. UI DESIGN ISSUES

The design should be oriented to the integration of known techniques into an overall solution for group communication/coordination. There is nothing new under the sun, we only have to put it together.

4.1 Model of the UI

The UI architecture has three parts, the *Man-Machine Interface* (MMI), the *User Command Manager* (UCM) and the *Operations Sequencer and Translator* (OST).

The MMI is in charge of interacting with the human user. It translates user actions on input devices to messages (commands) that the UCM can understand. On the other side, it presents messages coming from the UCM in the particular style for each user and each output device.

The UCM is a block independent of device and interaction style. It supports the dialogue with the MMI (the user) and OST (the system). It can support several concurrent interaction channels (human user and agents: scripts written in UCM language). On user inputs, it checks correctness and completeness of commands coming from the MMI. The UCM can complete commands using information stored in an internal database, the *Profile*.

Model of the UI

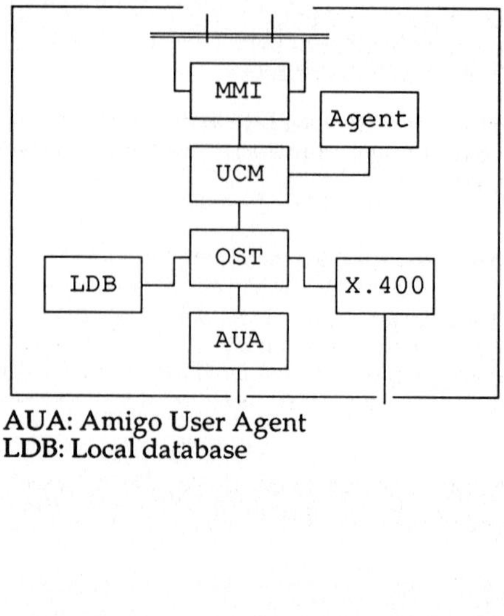

AUA: Amigo User Agent
LDB: Local database

The OST is in charge of interacting with other UI independent subblocks. It can support distributed multi-client/server systems. It is independent of the human interaction procedure and gives to the MMI and UCM independence of the underlying structure. In our case, it will interact with the AMIGO User Agent and X.400, X.500 User Agents.

Let us look to some desired characteristics for the User Interface:

4.2 The object oriented paradigm

Object oriented (OO) design provides several advantages in a complex distributed environment. The AMIGO Activity model can be seen as OO.

- OO models are very appropriate tools for clearly describing and presenting data and their relationships for complex objects such as multimedia documents and AMIGO Group Activities.

Amigo Model

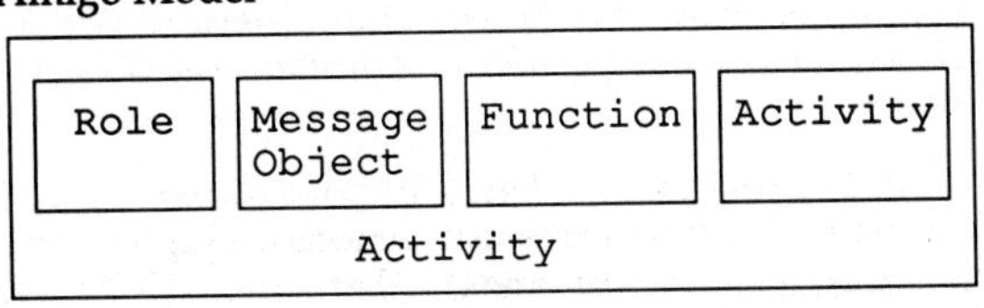

- simplified UI: objects clearly identified, common methods *(messages)* to different objects.

- Object Collection management methods [5]. Used for: store, organize, search, retrieve, share and archive objects.

- Object specialization: Objects in different contexts have different interfaces (hierarchical objects). Objects can present different interfaces to human and agent interaction.

4.3 Multimedia documents

Documents will be mostly created, live and die within computer systems, on display devices (reusable objects) instead of paper. The limitations of paper do not have to appear.

Operations with Multimedia Objects are: selecting, extracting, transfer, merging, creating, formatting, etc.

4.4 Very High Level manipulation language

This language can help to separate two dissimilar processes: *communication* and *interaction*. It can help to adapt the UI to the evolution and diversity of users and to reduce user overload by automating tasks.

The Language can be used to automate low-level, easy, repetitive tasks: semi-autonomous processes (agents). It must be easy to program, (programmer friendly) because the programmer will be the user. Object oriented languages like HyperTalk, based on Smalltalk, are suitable for this task.

4.5 Agents

Agents are software robots that act as user assistants. They can manipulate the information using an alternative view of the system (equivalent to the user's view)

The information is represented in such a way that both people and agents can process it intelligently. Messages have several structured fields that are easy to examine for agents.

Agents are convenient for easy and repetitive tasks as forwarding, moving to folders, showing, annotating, prioritizing, deleting, suggesting intelligent answers, etc.

4.6 Other characteristics

Customization: the UI should support user customization for:

- Dialogue: modify scripts (automate, ask for parameters). This information is stored in the UCM Profile.

- Objects: user view (define screen filters, redesign the presentation style). Diversity should be supported and estimulated. Views are the result of the specification on how objects should be presented to the user. This information is stored in the MMI Profile.

The communication process is a structured dialogue, with frequent references to other sources of information. Representation (views) for communication entities: activities, conversations, users involved, etc. should be provided.

Integration: it should be possible to share parts of a document across different applications without losing information. It is important for multimedia, and it should be transparent to the user.

5. References

[1] Medina M., *CACTUS UI Functional Specification*, Internal report (1986).

[2] Mackay, W.E., *Diversity in the Use of Electronic Mail*, ACM TOIS, (October 1988).

[3] Pankoke-Babatz U., *Computer Based Group Communication* (Ellis Horwood, 1989).

[4] Smith H., *Distributed Group Communication* (Ellis Horwood, 1989).

[5] Fuller, I.J., *An Overview of the HP NewWave Environment*, HP Journal, (August 1989).

Human–Computer Interaction – INTERACT '90
D. Diaper et al. (Editors)
Elsevier Science Publishers B.V. (North-Holland)

Logic descriptions in rapid prototyping of applications

Lars OESTREICHER

Computing Science Department, Uppsala University, P.O.Box 520, S-751 20 Uppsala, Sweden*

This paper presents a description method for design of new systems, using formal descriptions combined with rapid prototyping. The basic formalism is First Order Predicate Logic in the shape of Horn Clauses. The descriptions are used as conceptual models of the functionality, formed with main input from task analysis of the user's expected work tasks with the system. The possibility to immediately execute the description as an executable specification of the new system also brings this research result into the area of rapid prototyping of new designs.

Introduction

The users' understanding of what is happening in the system they are using is a major problem in Human Computer Interaction. This is often due to a bad agreement between task and function in the system. Therefore, it is necessary to study the way a system is being designed in order to find better ways to support the user in his/her work. User participation in the design process and rapid prototyping has been suggested as a solution. However, it has also been shown that users of a system have difficulties defining what they want from their systems [1]. Various techniques are used in the attempts made to deduce the needs of the users when the systems are designed but in many cases it is still very difficult for the user and the designer to agree on the meaning of concepts used in the system.

Task analysis

It is necessary to start from the users' tasks to find a definition of concepts that users and designers can agree upon. We have to define the task to be performed, and use this definition in the design of the system so that the functions better conform to the user's conception of the tasks and thereby becomes easier to learn, use and understand.

Task analysis methods currently used are not sufficient in order to define the tasks to be performed using a computer as a tool. Hjalmarsson et al. [1] have made an attempt is made to conceptualise tasks with the users' work situation as primary point of departure. The descriptions are on a level of detail that should be sufficient for the definition of the functionality of systems. However, the description is also designed to use only concepts that a user can understand without extensive knowledge of computers. When a task analysis has been performed the next step is to model the result into a description of a suitable system for this work situation. In such an approach rapid development of prototype systems is necessary for the evaluation of the functionality. The process of transferring the results of a task analysis into a model is the subject of this paper.

* The project has been sponsored by grants from COST11-ter and the Swedish Research Programme: People, Computers, Work.

Descriptive Formalisms

Previous methods used to describe systems from this more user-oriented perspective have to a large extent been based on grammar formalisms, like BNF-inspired grammars, e.g. TAG by Payne and Green [2], and ETAG by Tauber [3] (see also van der Veer et al. [4]). The grammatical approaches have formal properties, suggesting that they may be used to analyse the application, e.g., for consistency, but they are often poor tools for studying the behaviour of the application. Some of the attempts use more process oriented methods, e.g., automata theory, and Petri-nets, to put the issue of executability in focus. On the other hand, here we have problems of readability and complexity, especially when larger and more complex systems are modelled. Even small changes in structure, functionality and the set of concepts could cause widespread changes in the model. These methods offer little or no manipulative power to the descriptions, causing problems, e.g., to judge the similarity between different descriptions.

A description of a mail system

We have developed a way of describing systems with the previously described attempts as sources of inspiration, combining the analytical properties of the grammar-based approaches with the executability of logic programming. Logic formalisms are by definition grammatical, with a semantic counterpart, but through the use of logic programming methods we also achieve an execution based view of the descriptions. The possibilities to use the description to a great extent depend on the chosen representation. We use Horn clause logic, and the notation of the programming language Prolog [5] for the representation. This means that it is possible to use existing methods for logic manipulation of the descriptions and the Prolog environment for interpretation of the description. Although ordinary first order predicate calculus (FOPC) is good for logic manipulation at present it cannot be executed in machines. For the purpose of logic manipulation the Horn Clause formalism can be said to be restricted. However, it performs well under computational circumstances. The manipulative properties of Horn Clauses are sufficient *for our purposes*, and additionally, through the use of logic programming techniques, we get the power of easy interpretation of the description.

Prolog combines analytical properties of logical reasoning with functional properties of programming. This has as an immediate consequence that we can restructure the functionality description of the application using the formal properties of Prolog, and at the same time test the functionality. The description is based on primitive building blocks that have been chosen to use the conceptually smallest parts involved in the task. The analysis developed in this paper attempts to map a conceptual description of a system, in these user-oriented terms, onto the functionality of the system. This is done by successive applications of rules of logic reasoning to the initial description. The result is a functional specification on the computational level which can be studied further for functionality, e.g., by interpretation, see below.

We use a small example to illustrate this. The user's task is to preserve the text of the current message in a file. The name of this file is given as argument. Additionally, the next letter is displayed on the screen afterwards. This is a conceptual model of the task, written as a Horn Clause Formula (the notation used in the examples that follow is a simplified version of the original descriptions):

```
command(save_text,File):-
  move_Text_to_file_and_show_next_message(File).
```

After a first restructuring step we get the following definition by "explaining" the meaning of the operation through a partition into smaller conceptual units. The predicate "attribute(current,Message)" is used to locate the message currently operated on.

```
move_Text_to_file_and_show_next_message(File):-
  move_Text_of_message_to_file(File),
  get_next_message,
  show_message.
```

The restructuring can be seen as successive unfolding of each of the terms in the body, repeated until a definition in terms of primitives is reached. In this example we have reached the primitives after the next step. The three clauses below represent the step across the border between task knowledge and knowledge of the procedures needed for the task.

```
move_Text_of_message_to_file(File):-
  attribute(current,Message),
  decompose(Message, [Header,Text]),
  copy(Text,File).

get_next_nessage:-
  attribute(current,Message),
  set_attribute(current,next(Message)),
  set_attribute(not_current,Message).

show_message:-
  attribute(current,Message),
  display(Message).
```

These three clauses could be said to constitute the interface between the conceptual functionality and the machine specific procedures. They also have a specific use in that they give indications of how to administer metacommunication. Each conceptual definition on this level indicates the need for knowledge on the interaction, i.e., a need for the user to know that something has happened.

By backsubstitution of terms and variables in the clauses we arrive at a functional specification of the command, and consequently also of the task above. We propose that it can be used as such by the programmer in the design of new systems.

```
commandsave_text,User):-
  attribute(current,Message),
  decompose(Message, [Header,Text]),
  copy(Text,File),
  set(current,next(Message)),
  set(not_current,Message),
  display(next(Message)).
```

It is also possible to use the model for simulation, and study the behaviour of the new design. Execution adds possibilities to study the description, and in this respect this method is different from most modelling methods used. It closely combines grammatical analysis with interpretation of the model. This idea has been proposed previously by Davis [6] to determine program correctness. The work in this paper maintains the advantage of Prolog, over grammar based attempts, not only for the description of program designs, but also for conceptual modelling of computer applications and systems.

Initially the work situation of a computer user has been studied, and from this a corresponding conceptual model of the most basic functions in a mail system has been built. This description has been analysed, using the restructuring possibilities of the logic formalism as illustrated above. The restructuring resulted in a functional specification of a simple mail system. This description has been compared to a corresponding analysis of an existing mail system, Unix (bin)mail. The comparison shows that Unix mail has some functionality which is difficult to understand for a user. Furthermore, it can be shown that the full functionality of Unix mail is included in the functionality of the new, simpler mail system.

This method cannot only be used for analysing existing applications, but through interpretation also facilitates user participation in system design. Different descriptions can be suggested to or by users, i.e., we can let an interpreter execute the description showing the results of different actions on a database. Thus we give the designers and users a better understanding of the functionality of the resulting system before it is developed. In the practical work forming the basis of the thesis the description has also been put to a first, simple test to see if it is executable. The description of the existing old system has been interpreted by a simple Prolog environment. The results of giving the same commands to the interpreted model and the real application showed good correspondence between the systems. Steps will be taken to extend this possibility to use the description, which hopefully will result in a tool that will make it possible to enhance the communication between, e.g., designers and prospective users during the design of new systems.

Key References

[1] Hjalmarsson A., Oestreicher L. & Waern Y., 1989, Human Factors in Mail System Design. In: Behaviour and Information Technology . vol 8, No. 6 pp. 461-474

[2] Payne S.J. & Green T.R.G. 1986, Task-action grammars: A model of the mental representation of task languages. Human-Computer Interaction, 2, pp. 93-133.

[3] Tauber M.J., 1986, Top down design of human computer interfaces. In: Chang S.-K., Ichikawa T. & Ligomenides P.A. (eds.) Visual Languages. New York: Plenum Press.

[4] van der Veer G.C., Groenendijk C., Guest S., Haselager W.C.G., Hjalmarsson A., Innocent P., Oestreicher L., Tauber M.J., Vos U., & Waern Y. 1988, An Interdisciplinary Approach to Cognitive Based User-interface design: Theory, Methodologies, Methods, and Tools. 2nd Progress Report to COST11-ter, Amsterdam.

[5] Clocksin W.F. & Mellish C.S. 1981. Programming in Prolog, Springer-Verlag, Heidelberg

[6] Davis R.E., 1982, Runnable Specification as a Design Tool, In: Logic Programming, Clark, K. & Tärnlund S.-Å. (eds.), Academic Press, London, pp. 141-149.

Human–Computer Interaction – INTERACT '90
D. Diaper et al. (Editors)
Elsevier Science Publishers B.V. (North-Holland)

Graphical Treatment of Natural Language in HCI

Ronald A. Singer

Institute of Educational Technology,
The Open University, Walton Hall, Milton Keynes. MK7 6AA. United Kingdom.
Tel. (0908) 652397

This paper discusses on-going research which indicates that graphical interfaces can offer users a more effective means of communicating their intentions to the system than is possible with NL. The relationships between user thoughts and graphical objects, must if they are to be natural and effective, reflect the structure of human discourse. This requires an interface which can understand the relation of subsequent thoughts to preceding ones. Circuit I (Singer, 1989), an object-oriented prototype has clearly demonstrated that the notion of embedding discourse phenomena (anaphora and ellipsis) as handled by SOPHIE (Brown, Burton, et al,1982) within a graphics environment is a viable alternative to that of NL given the current unresolved problems. A small scale evaluation of the prototype has been carried out, and preliminary findings have been very encouraging.

1. RESEARCH QUESTIONS

Given that implementing NL understanding is hard and enjoys limited success, the main question this research seeks to address is "What is the dialogue capability of SOPHIE in a modern context?", i.e. in a graphical context. To answer such a question will involve rationally reconstructing SOPHIE's dialogue in an effort to establish (a) if the NL dialogue between SOPHIE and users can be modelled graphically within an interface, and (b) given that the goals of (a) can be achieved, to see if it is possible to embed some human discourse capabilities within the graphical interface.

2. BACKGROUND TO CURRENT RESEARCH

In an effort to decide if the NL dialogue between SOPHIE and user could be modelled graphically within an interface, three decisions were made; firstly, that SOPHIE's dialogue be categorised into three groups, category 1 (easy), category 2 (moderately hard), and category 3 (very hard). Secondly, that a simple electronic circuit should be constructed which has sufficient components to allow all of category 1 utterances to be modelled. Thirdly, that discourse phenomena such as anaphora and ellipsis, which are considered to be fundamental building blocks of NL utterances, and present within category 1 should be modelled graphically if possible.

Before embarking on this research it was decided to see how, if at all, current graphical packages handled user-machine dialogue. The macintosh user-interface offered a graphical approach to handling user-machine dialogue and so it was decided to review some macintosh applications (e.g. MacDraw, MacPaint, SuperPaint, Word 3.0, and Writenow) in the light of their ability to represent certain discourse phenomena. The results of this review were encouraging since it established that all packages, in varying degrees, supported discourse phenomena.

Encouraged by these findings an object oriented prototype Circuit I (Singer, 1989), was developed based on the three criteria given above which took category 1 SOPHIE dialogue and attempted to model it graphically. Circuit I demonstrated that it is possible to express simple dialogue graphically. Within the context of the sample dialogue, Circuit I handles anaphoric references and ellipsis well. This implies the possibility that more complicated SOPHIE dialogue may be modelled in this way, although not perhaps with the same ease.

3. CURRENT RESEARCH

Based on the research findings so far, work on Circuit II has commenced which seeks to expand the complexity of the Circuit I from the perspective of (a) computational complexity, and (b) providing a larger and more complex repertoire of graphical sentences using SOPHIE dialogue categories 2 and 3

Given that more complex graphical sentences can be constructed which can be understood by users using categories 2 and 3, future work will seek to embed discourse capabilities within the interface, such as the notion of conversational coherency (Reichman, 1978).

4. FINDINGS TODATE

A preliminary evaluation of Circuit I has shown that experienced electronic users enjoyed using the graphical interface despite its limitations, and felt that they could express themselves more easily than would be possible with a NL system.

In a NL interface a user's underlying intentions can be interpreted by the system by parsing the input sentence, breaking it down into its constituent parts and executing its underlying meaning using some computational model of performance in the task domain. The correct interpretation of a NL sentence may be hard because of surface features which are present, for example anaphora, ellipsis or deictic expressions.

Circuit I's graphical interface attempts to provide a short hand way of allowing users to express their underlying intentions to the system. That is, given that a user can express their underlying intentions in NL, we believe that an abbreviated form of graphical interaction may be used which is not only more intuitive to use, avoiding the issue of how to phrase a question which can be understood by the system, but which also circumvents many of the surface features mentioned above.

Whether or not users actually form mental equivalents of NL statements which in some sense can be said to be analogous to the actions they would perform if using a NL interface is the subject of on-going experiments. Preliminary results seem to indicate this is in fact so, but only under certain circumstances. For example, when users performed simple tasks in e.g. Word 3.0 and Circuit I they were automatic. However, when asked to do more complex tasks in Circuit I or use a package they were unfamiliar with, results seem to indicate that users had to engage in a conscious reasoning process. Users questions resulting from these processes were presented to the computer as 'mouse clicking' actions. This seems to imply that user actions which are equivalent to anaphora, ellipsis, deictic expressions, or indeed to other equivalent NL functions must be analyzed with respect to the extent to which they are learned (or overlearned) and automatic and with respect to the explicit reasoning, planning or problem-solving the user must do before executing the action.

NL and graphical interfaces seem to support *some* of the same cognitive processes which to some extent help form our intentions and control our subsequent actions, whether they be the 'pointing to' and the 'clicking on' of screen objects with a mouse or the typing in of a NL sentence. If the interface has the ability to react to users actions in a way that relates meaningfully to their conscious reasoning processes as they occur at the cognitive level, then the Human-Computer graphical interaction which is taking place becomes more natural, where users actions echo their thoughts more closely than can be the case in graphical interfaces designed without consideration for the space of possible dialogue structures. These are some of the issues that this research seeks to address.

REFERENCES

Brown, J.S., Burton, R.R. and DeKleer. (1982) Pedagogical, natural language and knowledge engineering techniques in SOPHIE I, II and III. Chapter 11 in Sleeman Brown, Intelligent Tutoring Systems.

Reichman, R. (1978) Conversational Coherency. Cognitive Science 2, 283-327 (1978).

Singer, R.A. November, 1989. Graphical Treatment of Anaphora & Ellipsis. Open University CITE Report No: 94

Human–Computer Interaction – INTERACT '90
D. Diaper et al. (Editors)
Elsevier Science Publishers B.V. (North-Holland)

RUN TIME INTERFACE SPECIFICATION, USING DIRECT MANIPULATION

Robert Tibbitt-Eggleton

Research Assistant, Department of Computing, Staffordshire Polytechnic, Blackheath Lane, Stafford. ST18 0AD

A brief overview is given of a prototype User Interface Management System (UIMS) that is being produced as part of a research degree. One of the main features of this UIMS is the ability to create/alter the interface to an application as the application runs.

1. Introduction and background

The arguments for effective user interfaces and their inherent complexities and lengthy development time, have provided the inspirations for User Interface Management Systems (UIMS). UIMS have two main functions (1) To help develop interfaces in isolation from the application without programming ability or knowledge. (2) To manage the interfaces produced at run time (if necessary).

The advantages of generating an interface via a UIMS are numerous and well documented, see [Myers 89]. A few of the more important advantages are (1) Development time is decreased. (2) A single application may have many interfaces. (3) The designer needn't have programming experience. (4) The interfaces produced by a good UIMS are very reliable. For a comparison of features provided by currently available UIMS see [Prime 89].

2. Area of research

The direction of research being reported here is the result of apparent deficiencies identified within current UIMS. Specifically the initial aims of this research are to prototype:

1. A more dynamic method of interface specification. This is to alleviate the wasted time and loss of concentration caused by a sequence of: edit interface description, write description to file, quit editor, compile and link, run application, check results, edit description ...

2. Techniques for specifying and handling inter-related interaction primitives. These are to facilitate such things as synchronising different Interaction Primitives (IP's) being used to generate identical events.

3. Techniques for specifying large and complex event structures. This is a very important element often missing or underdeveloped in most UIMS. The idea is that a number of IP's can be linked together so that a "higher level" event may be formed and passed onto the application. To achieve this, facility must be given for storing a current value within an IP and flags for identifying whether the high level event should be raised when a given IP is activated.

4. Methods that will allow users to modify the interface. This includes making the specification technique simple enough for users to use but also, and perhaps more importantly, succinct enough and fun enough to make users want to learn how to make the alterations.

5. Methods of communication between interface and application that will tolerate alterations being made without having to alter/compile both interface and application. For example, providing facility for an application to swap the functions that are to receive events from a particular IP or set of IP's at runtime (and thus avoid redundancy in the interface specification).

6. Interaction Primitives which can generate a range of types - thereby providing greater inter-changeability and flexibility.

It is generally acknowledged that the design of most applications and interfaces are iterative processes. In the same vane, the research being carried out is being progressed by building and evaluating prototypes.

3. Work carried out

3.1 An initial prototype

An initial prototype UIMS was implemented, as a research tool, which catered for specification of soft buttons only. The functionality of this UIMS was basic including creation, deletion, movement and initialisation of buttons plus saving and restoring an interface.

As a result of the implementation, four

distinct sections of a UIMS were identified, which simplified the development process. The sections were:

1. Specification of individual interaction primitives.

2. Specification of simple relationships between IP's, eg positioning.

3. Storage and retrieval of an interface.

4. Runtime control of interface and linkage to application.

For simplicity, a tabular method was used to store the interface definition thus obviating the compilation phase necessary for storing the interface in executable format. To control the interface at run time many of the functions used for creating the interface had to be re-used, eg locating IP being pointed at. To facilitate this the interface generation program was linked to the process for run time control. As a result of this the application was able to alter its own interface at run time.

As a simple tool the UIMS worked well. Interfaces could be generated quickly and with an element of fun. To facilitate the construction of more complex interfaces than soft buttons alone could provide, all user generated events which were not button related were passed onto the application as a separate event class. This allowed the application to use any other input interactor, provided they were coded in the application.

3.2 A second prototype

A second prototype has almost been completed which is intended to provide a fully working UIMS. Its design is based upon the aims of the research given earlier and the results of the first prototype. The UIMS is formed in two parts. (1) The interface editor, that facilitates specification by direct manipulation and form filling. (2) The interface control unit which controls the running of all active interfaces.

To facilitate run time editing of an interface, the interface editor must be accessible from the application. Linking the application to the editor would increase its size by many fold To avoid this the UIMS has been implemented as a separate process to the application. This has the added benefit of allowing the UIMS to control many interfaces (including the interface to the interface editor). Communication between UIMS and application is achieved using the unix pipe facilities. Communication is controlled for the application by a small set of functions linked to the application at compile time. These functions accept messages from the UIMS in the form <channel no> <data>. The channel number is used as an index to an array for determining the relevant application function to be called at run time. The application may change the function associated with a channel at any time. This allows the design of the interface to be made in isolation from the application and for different functions to use the same IP's.

The interface is defined semantically in terms of its functions and parameters. This frees the interface designer from time being wasted in correcting syntax errors and from having to learn a possibly complex grammar. When defining the IP's to be used to present parameters to a function, the interface editor forms links between the IP's containing information on ordering. This allows a user to enter the parameters in any order, freeing the interface from a fixed prompt and reply style.

4. Summary and Conclusions

A new UIMS is being developed that seeks to correct some of the faults identified in current systems and make UIMS more accessible to non-programmers.

One of the major contributions to be made towards interface specification is the use of direct manipulation in a run time environment; ie as the application runs.

Current work is progressing by building and evaluating prototypes. When a version is ready that is sufficiently complete, a full evaluation is to be made using students to produce interfaces to various applications.

This research suggests that the concept of runtime interface specification, using direct manipulation is feasible. The advantages of being able to alter the interface at runtime cannot be ignored by future UIMS. In particular this feature would be most useful at the design stage of prototyping an interface.

References:

[Myers 89] Brad Myers, "User-Interface Tools: Introduction and Survey" IEEE Software, January 1989.

[Prime 89] Martin Prime, "User Interface Management Systems - A Current Product Review". Rutherford Appleton Laboratory report "RAL-88-028", version 3.0.

Human–Computer Interaction – INTERACT '90
D. Diaper et al. (Editors)
Elsevier Science Publishers B.V. (North-Holland)
IFIP, 1990

LEARNING A WORD PROCESSING TASK: ABOUT DOCUMENTATION, HELP AND TASK COMPLEXITY.

Anne VAN LAETHEM

Unité de Psychologie du Travail et des Organisations
Faculté de Psychologie et des Sciences de l'Education
Université Catholique de Louvain
voie du Roman Pays, 20
1348 - LOUVAIN-LA-NEUVE - BELGIQUE

This work is about learning to use a personal computer for a task of medium complexity.

1. THE PROBLEM

Users of hardware and software tools have to learn how to use them. Yet very little is known about this learning process in the context of specific tasks and/or equipments (Waern, 1989). This makes it especially difficult to design an adequate documentation. Actually, most designers provide maximal documentation just because they don't know what information is relevant and what information is not. The consequence of this is that the end user has to make the selection himself, but the end user usually lacks a clear conception of the system. What the user would need is a mental model of the system. This model could be provided by the designer or elaborated by the user himself on the basis of previous and subjectively similar experiences. In both cases more or less serious misconceptions can occur.

2. WHAT THE EXPERT IS NOT...

Although precise and specific criteria to prepare documentation are not available, most designers rely on a few commonly accepted presuppositions about what expertise is and design the documentation accordingly.

Draper (1985) has made a critical examination of some of these ideas:

"Experts know more than novices (definition)
Experts know things that novices do not (logically entailed)
Experts know everything that novices know
A system can be optimized for experts or novices but not both
A system should have two modes -a novice mode and an expert mode-
Novices need more help than experts
Novices will use the help facilities more"

Most of the time documentation is divided into a "novice" part and an "expert" part.

3. GENERAL RESEARCH OBJECTIVES

The first question is the nature of expertise in complex tasks like word processing. Again very few studies have been devoted to this question. Draper (1985) deals with UNIX expertise. His results directly contradict the common presuppositions mentioned above. It can even be said that in a sense, according to Draper, there is no such thing as an UNIX expert.

Draper has a multidimensional conception of expertise, related to the task and the user experience. This experience has several components which include knowledge:

"- of using this system for this task
- of this task independent of any computer system
- of this computer system (independent of this task)
- general knowledge of other similar systems

plus
- knowledge how to acquire information on this system."

Draper concludes that what experts actually have learned is how to use the documentation: a complex task in itself, but a different one. This contrasts with an intuitively appealing view according to which experts would possess a readily generalizable and transferable knowledge of the system. In our sense such a knowledge probably does exist and is embodied in a model of the system but, nevertheless, Draper's results indicate that, in many cases, the subject faces tasks or subtasks for which the mental model provides little or no relevant information. This may be the reason why experts and novices seem to behave similarly in his experiments.

On the other hand it should be noted that UNIX is a complex system and probably cannot be fully mastered by any single user. We wondered wether Draper's conclusions were valid for complex but more reasonably sized systems implemented, for instance on personal computers.

4. EMPIRICAL WORK

A first experiment has been run to compare 15 novices and 15 experts and to replicate Draper (1985) using a word processing task on a personal computer. Several dependent variables were used to describe the experts' and the novices' behaviour. We hypothesized that in a new task, experts would react as novices.

A second experiment, again using 15 novices and 15 experts studied the subjects' capability to access documented information. We hypothesized that experts would access that information faster and succeed more frequently in finding the elements of information they need.

A third experiment compared two different formats for presenting useful information to novices. One format was especially designed to force the subject to actively create links between topics. This should contribute to improve the mental model and result in better retention and better performance in a transfer task.

5. CONCLUSION

The results of these experiments allow to briefly conclude what follows:

a. when the expert is faced to a new task, his mental model of the system doesn't lead him to better performances than novices;

b. consulting documentation constitutes a particular task in itself, which need a particular learning, and in which experts perform better and faster than novices;

c. when novices have the opportunity to actively elaborate a mental model of the system, which comprises links between its elements, they perform better and with lesser errors than when they learn with a traditional manual. These results happen not only for recall tasks but also for transfer tasks.

It seems thus necessary to conceive learning aids which are easy to understand and to use, and which conduct the user to actively elaborate an integrated mental model of the system.

REFERENCES

(1) Adelson, B. When novices surpass experts: the difficulty of a task may increase with expertise, Journal of Experimental Psychology: learning, memory and cognition, 1984, 10/3, 483-495.

(2) Chechile, R.A., Eggleston, R.G., Fleischman, R.N. & Sasseville, A.M. Modeling the cognitive content of displays, Human Factors, 1989, 31/1, 31-43.

(3) Colley, A.M. & Beech, J.R., Eds. Acquisition and performance of cognitive skills, John Wiley & sons, Chichester, 1989.

(4) Draper, S.W. The nature of expertise in UNIX, in: Shackel, B. (ed.), Human-computer interaction - INTERACT'84, Elsevier Science Publishers B.V., North-Holland, 1985, pp. 465-471.

(5) Hartley, J.T. & Hartley, A.A. Acquisition and application of expertise at computer text editing by younger and older adults, In: Gruneberg, M.M., Morris, P.E. & Sykes, R.N. (eds.) Practical aspects of memory: current research and issues - vol. 2. John Wiley & sons, Chichester, 1988, pp. 149-154.

(6) Hollands, J.G. & Merikle, P.M. Menu organization and user expertise in information search tasks, Human Factors, 1987, 29/5, pp. 577-586.

(7) Kay, D.S. & Black, J.B. Changes in knowledge representations of computer systems with experience, In: Proceedings of the Human Factors Society 28th Annual Meeting, Santa Monica, 1984, pp. 963-967.

(8) Ortega, K.A. Problem-solving: expert/novice differences, Human Factors Society Bulletin, 32/3, march 1989, pp. 1-4.

(9) Perruchet, P. (ed.) Les automatismes cognitifs, Mardaga, Liège, 1988.

(10) Schriver, K.A. Designing computer documentation: a review of the relevant litterature, CDC Technical Report N°31, Carnegie-Mellon University, Pittsburgh, 1986.

(11) Waern, Y. Cognitive aspects of computer supported tasks, John Wiley & sons, Chichester, 1989.

(12) Weiss, E.H. How to write a usable user manual, ISI Press, Philadelphia, 1984.

(13) Wilson, M., Barnard, P. & Maclean, A. Learning to use a computer system: its assessment via multiple behavioural methods, Hursley Human Factors Laboratory, Human Factors Report N°135, 1987.

PANEL SESSIONS

HCI seen from the perspective of software developers
Moderator: J.L. Bennett
Panelists: P. Conklin, K. Guevara, W. Mackay, and T. Sancha 1039

User participation in HCI research: Effects on processes and results
Panel Organiser: Y. Waern
Panelists: L. Bannon, T. Timpka, and W. Schneider 1043

Interactively supporting the software process
S.M. Kaplan, A. Finkelstein, G. Kaiser, K. Ryan, and W. Schafer 1047

Task analysis: The oft missing step in the development of computer–human interfaces; its desirable nature, value, and role
Organiser/Moderator: R.I. Anderson
Panelists: J.M. Carroll, J. Grudin, J.F. McGrew, and D.L. Scapin 1051

New approaches to theory in HCI: How should we judge their acceptability?
Organiser: A. Monk
Panelists: J.M. Carroll, M. Harrison, J. Long, and R. Young 1055

Multi-agent interaction
Organiser: N. Seel
Panelists: J. Galliers, G. Kiss, and S. Scrivener 1059

Multi-dimensional interfaces for software design
Organiser: T. Dudley
Panelists: R. Baecker, M. Eisenstadt, E. Glinert, and M.B. Rosson 1063

Usability engineering on a budget
Moderator: J. Nielsen
Panelists: S.M. Dray, J.D. Foley, P. Walsh, and P. Wright 1067

Human–Computer Interaction – INTERACT '90
D. Diaper et al. (Editors)
Elsevier Science Publishers B.V. (North-Holland)

HCI Seen from the Perspective of Software Developers (Panel)

Moderator: John L. Bennett, IBM Research, Almaden
650 Harry Road, K08/282
San Jose, CA 95120, USA
408-927-1856, bennett@ibm.com

Panelists: Peter Conklin, Digital Equipment Corp.
Hudson, MA , USA

Karmen Guevara, Consultant
London, UK

Wendy Mackay, Digital Equipment Corp. and MIT
Cambridge, MA, USA

Tom Sancha, Senior Designer
Cambridge, UK

INTRODUCTION

John Bennett

John Bennett is a Research Staff Member in the User Interface Institute, T. J. Watson Research Center, residing at the IBM Almaden Research Center. He has worked on information retrieval systems, decision support systems, user interface design for office systems, and architecture for user interfaces. His publication "Tools for Building Advanced User Interfaces", IBM Systems Journal, No. 3/4, 1986, addressed developments in technical support on both the user and the computer sides of user-computer interface design. He is co-author (with Whiteside and Holtzblatt) of "Usability Engineering: Our Experience and Evolution", in Handbook of Human-Computer Interaction; M. Helender, editor. In 1989 he received an Outstanding Innovation Award from the IBM Research Division for developing a novel and effective approach to the engineering of system usability.

He has been active in professional societies and has given tutorials at CHI'87, CHI'88 and CHI'89 and in IBM on topics related to integration of measurable, testable usability objectives into the system development cycle. At the INTERACT '84 Conference, (London) he organized four theme sessions on "Behavioral Issues in the System Development Cycle" to highlight what it is like to do human factors work in software development projects. He is currently on the Editorial Board for the journal Behaviour and Information Technology.

He received a BS in Engineering Science from Stanford in 1959 and an MS in Electrical Engineering from MIT in 1961. At IBM Research he has been manager of Geographic Data Systems and of Interactive Problem-Solving Systems.

During recent years usability (in the form of effective access to computer-based function) has become an important issue in development -- in addition to the familiar issues of function, cost, and schedule. By usability we refer to shaping the function as presented so that:

- it is truly useful,
- the learning time is acceptable to the intended users,
- the performance of the users is supported, and
- the users choose to continue use of the function.

The panelists have been especially invited to INTERACT to bring to the audience business and development experiences that could be of value to those who normally participate. A number of the conference delegates will be seeking to have various aspects of human factors expertise be ***used*** effectively in development projects, and this panel will provide an opportunity for them to hear and question development experts. These outstanding European and U.S. panelists are qualified to explore experiences of people in the "real world of development".

We anticipate addressing several issues, and the following are offered as examples:

- How do we establish the commercial value of usability as a quality at the planning stage so that development resources necessary to achieve a truly useful system are allocated from the start?
- How important is it to establish a valid basis (empirical rather than "by declaration") for determining during development whether we are on track toward a product that is useful and usable from a user viewpoint?
  What counts as evidence sufficient to warrant continued allocation of development resources?

- How do we demonstrate the needed success convincingly to those who market products and to the ultimate users or purchasers? That is, if we allocate resources, how do we make sure that the result is recognized?
- What information and what techniques would be particularly valuable in the business of bringing usability into the development process?

The actual issues we cover will, of course, be developed among the members of the panel in the course of the discussion.

The panelists can speak from the experience of leading (or being part of) teams that have delivered software found valuable by intended users in terms of function and in terms of productive user access to that function. This provides a background of proven success.

Issues of meeting schedules and of managing development costs are also handled credibly as part of such an engineering project. Thus, the panel will address "What counts as success in such development projects, how do we know when we have achieved it, and how could the skills represented at INTERACT '90 be used most effectively in these enterprises?" Our focus is on illumination rather than controversy, and we see this panel as an opportunity for delegates to ask questions leading to their effective action.

PANELISTS' STATEMENTS

Peter Conklin

Peter Conklin is Software Director of the Advanced Systems group of Digital Equipment Corporation. In his 20 years of managing software and hardware development projects, he has addressed architecture, product management, and product marketing concerns. He has participated in the design of keyboards, command languages, compilers, data management systems, hardware systems, distributed subsystems, network interfaces, VAX and VMS operating systems, and various desktop systems. This work has included consultation with research groups on the architecture and design of user interfaces. He fostered close collaboration between usability engineers and developers, and this has resulted in a number of breakthrough results. The formal reports have formed an important historical record and educational base for future work within Digital.

He received an AB in Mathematics from Harvard University in 1963. In his 25 years in the computer business he has balanced theoretical principles, compatible evolution, and industry standards. This has made him well qualified to address the discussion of resource allocation in the design and development of HCI systems.

For twenty years, experts in human factors have been called upon to advise project teams in the usability of their products. And throughout this time, the efforts of the human factors experts have been recognized as improving the ergonomics, user interface, and documentation of these products. However, it is an unfortunate fact that many of what are apparently reasonable and useful recommendations end up being rejected. Why is this, and what might these expert consultants do about it?

When a project is planned and a budget is established, a need for attention to human factors qualities is frequently identified, and this leads to budget allocation for consulting services. However, the project is likely to be well underway before the consultant is actively engaged. Or, in other cases, the details of the user interface and ergonomics are not known until late in the project. So the expert, sometimes a group of human factors specialists, is asked to "do what you need to do to review the product and make recommendations to fix any problems". The expert or the team undertakes the activity, performs experiments, and produces a thorough report. By then, however, the project is approaching final qualification and the changes are often too large to undertake in this version. In addition, the product is under severe schedule and cost pressures. Finally, the project team determines that, while the human factors report looks reasonable, none of the recommendations can be traced back to the market and product requirements documents.

During the panel, I will represent the project leader's perspective and suggest ways that consultants can remedy the situation outlined above. This may lead to increased achievement of the results that are now potentially possible in the work with the project team.

Karmen Guevara

Karmen Guevara has been a consultant for the past 10 years on topics of design and use of interactive office systems for government and industry clients in the UK, including British TeleCom, DEC, ICL, and Wang. In addition, she has taught courses on "Design of User Interfaces" and workshops for management in industry on "How to Develop User Requirements for the Design of Office Systems". She has recently completed her Ph.D at Loughborough University, UK, where her thesis addressed attention to user needs in the design process. In 1982-4 she worked with major manufacturers in the "Office Automation Pilot Program" sponsored by the Department of Trade and Industry. From 1987 to 1989 she was on the research staff at EuroPARC. She is Chair of the Human Sciences Special Editorial Board for the journal "Interacting With Computers". She has specialized in matching the development of office systems to users' requirements so that peoples' needs for usable function are met.

Those of us in the human factors community know that the usability of interactive systems is closely linked to how well users' requirements are mapped onto the system at every stage of design and development. This means that the designers, particularly in the early stages of the design cycle, must find a way to gain a robust understanding of the requirements of the potential system users. This goes beyond acceptable learning times, functionality, and system response time to include an understanding of typical tasks in users' application domains.

I participated as a consultant in one office system project in which the designers sought from the outset to provide innovative text and mail functions that would meet the needs of demanding professionals. The project members were conscientious about gaining an in-depth understanding of user requirements because this particular team had a previous personal experience of trying to design from requirements documents that they had not taken the time to understand in depth. In that prior case they had the experience of being stuck because they did not have an adequate picture of the potential users. This time they studied, represented for themselves, and argued over an existing document until they formed a picture that they felt was clear to them. Users were considered by types and each type was assigned a set of functional and personal characteristics. Designers referred to these user types throughout the process, checking design decisions against each user type. They reconciled engineering compromises with their understanding of user requirements, and they documented working assumptions and implications.

From their conviction of the value that would result, the design team went beyond the requirements document and their interpretation of it to study videos of users working in the application domain. This combined with their categorization of the user types helped designers envision the potential user community to a depth that would not have been possible if they had only given superficial attention to a conventional requirements document. Their extended work gave them a more personal and realistic concrete picture of who they were designing for as they made tradeoff decisions during system development.

This result became possible because the consultant was able to ask the kind of questions about requirements that led to an early team understanding of the need for, and impact of not having, a keen insight. We will address in the panel ways that others might bring about a similar level of insight sufficient to prevent user considerations from diminishing during development.

Wendy Mackay

Wendy Mackay has worked for Digital Equipment Corporation for over ten years. In 1979 and 1980 she wrote Digital's first two (and still top-selling) educational software products. She then became manager of Digital's Computer-Based Course Development Group, which produced the industry's first integrated educational software for personal computers, the first industrial interactive videodisc product (IVIS), and the Producer authoring language. In 1983, she established and managed Research and Development for Digital's Educational Services, which developed hypermedia learning environments, multi-media object-oriented databases, and software to support iterative design and software prototyping.

In 1986, Wendy became Digital's liaison to MIT's Project Athena, where she continues to work on multi-media software and intelligent filtering of electronic messages. She developed EVA, the Experimental Video Annotator, to provide researchers with a tool to analyze multi-media research data. She led the development of Pygmalion, a multi-media message system, with collaborators from the MIT Media Lab, the Sloan School of Management, and MIT's Project Athena. She also managed the development of Argus, a general purpose electronic message annotator and filter, based on empirical studies she conducted at Xerox PARC and MIT. The latter was recently released to the Open Software Foundation and is widely available.

Wendy received her Bachelor's degree in Experimental Psychology from the University of California at San Diego, and her Master's degree in Experimental Psychology from Northeastern University. She was a Visiting Scientist at MIT's Laboratory for Computer Science and is currently on a fellowship from Digital to complete her Ph.D. in Management of Technological Innovation at MIT. Wendy is Co-Chair of the Association of Computing Machinery Special Interest Group on Computer-Human Interaction (SIGCHI), author of over 20 papers, and an editor for ACM/TOIS.

Academia and industry have different time lines, value systems and rewards. Therefore, it is not surprising that the human interface issues and techniques discussed in the academic world do not always translate easily into the production of actual products. I have conducted experimental and field research in human-computer interaction as well as managed the production and successful delivery of over 35 software products, under tight deadlines and budgets. I found that iterative design processes developed for research can be successfully modified for industry, improving usability while reducing costs and improving efficiency.

Unfortunately, these techniques require fundamental changes in the way product goals are understood, the way success is measured, and in the software development process chosen to meet those goals. In the traditional development cycle, programmers are isolated from users and measured on their ability to implement the functional specification within time and budget constraints. They are rarely measured on whether users in the field find the functionality in the resulting product appropriate or useful. Worse, software engineering goals (program speed, functionality, architectural elegance) are orthogonal to usability goals (ease of use, efficiency in accomplishing tasks, generating a sense of satisfaction in the users) making it difficult for programmers and HCI practitioners to even communicate in view of the differences in value scales and perspectives. A non-technical Psychology graduate student hired by an engineering group to "fix the user interface" is likely to be overwhelmed by the power of circumstances.

I will briefly discuss how people with different levels of influence within the company can incorporate usability goals into products:

HCI practitioner: Adjusting from graduate school to industry, communicating with programmers and users.
Project leader: Modifying the process, managing perceptions of success.
Manager: Changing the goals of the project to fit marketplace needs, broadening the measures of success, creating and sustaining a process that will support delivery of the needed results.

Tom Sancha

Tom Sancha co-founded Cambridge Interactive Systems (CIS) in 1977, where he designed MEDUSA, a well-known CAD/CAM system for mechanical engineering. He was Chief Executive Officer and Director of CIS, President and Director of CIS, Inc. (Cambridge, Massachusetts, USA). When CIS was sold to ComputerVision he became Chairman, and he retired in late 1985.

Previously at CAD Centre he was chief designer of GINO-F, a precursor to the GKS standard, PDMS, the first CAD system for complex plant design, and the ASEA Parametric Design System. He was a founding member of the ACM Graphics Committee and represented the UK on international graphics standards committees.

He graduated from Cambridge with a degree in mathematics in 1969, began programming at IBM, London, and worked with C. Strachey in his Programming Research Unit at Oxford. He has been a director of several CAD companies including, currently, Synoptics Ltd, Cambridge, UK. As a leading participant and invited speaker at several IFIP and NATO workshops, his published papers include "Methodology of Interaction", "Methodology in Computer Graphics" and "Fundamental Algorithms for Computer Graphics".

As a senior designer of several CAD/CAM systems, and as an executive in companies offering software for professional users, he brings to the panel a special understanding of the requirements of software for highly trained and skilled technical people.

Most system developers start by hacking into data structures and algorithms and leave the user interface until the 'real work' is completed. Some then call in HCI 'experts' to smooth their gargoyles. Such systems are usually tedious to use and rarely successful.

HCI issues must be considered from the outset. HCI experts can represent users' performance requirements (golf buggies for casual use, or racing cars for professional drivers) and functional requirements (number of passengers, type of cargo). These influence how the user will form a model of the system, appropriate learning curves, level of productivity, functional complexity, etc., and they must be understood first. But without a development team and management recognition of the early need for this information and the potential value, the experts are called in too late.

Engineers drafting for 8 hours a day will invest time in learning a system to maximize performance; authors using drawing programs for occasional illustrative diagrams need ease of use, not high throughput performance. Similarly, pupils who will do a variety of word processing tasks during their years as students are willing to spend time learning to use a general purpose tool; students can not afford to waste time learning to drive a special-purpose program teaching a single topic.

When users' needs have been understood, a system under development can be modelled so that the designers can understand issues important to these potential users. Then, even harder, designers must anticipate the mental perceptions of users and how the eventual users will think of the system (the "users' model") as they learn to use it. This model shapes how users interact with the system and how they predict the consequences of their actions. The system must conform to these expectations for effective ease of use.

User psychology is not well enough understood to design systems analytically. HCI experts can only give generalized guidance and can not fully predict user behavior reliably. Therefore, most successful systems are developed iteratively, through a partnership of users, designers, programmers, and HCI experts evaluating a series of prototypes.

We will discuss a variety of opportunities for effective partnerships between HCI experts and software technology experts.

Human–Computer Interaction – INTERACT '90
D. Diaper et al. (Editors)
Elsevier Science Publishers B.V. (North-Holland)

USER PARTICIPATION IN HCI RESEARCH - EFFECTS ON PROCESSES AND RESULTS

Panel organizer: Yvonne Waern
Department of Psychology
University of Stockholm
S-106 91 Stockholm
E-mail: Yvonne.Waern@Psyk_Inst.QZ.SE
Telephone: +46 -8163894
Fax: +46 -8159342

Panelists:
Liam Bannon
Department of Information Processing Science
University of Oulu
Finland
bannon@tolsun.oulu.fi

Toomas Timpka
Department of Computer Science
University of Linköping, S-581 83 Linköping.
Phone: +46 -13 2810 00

Werner Schneider,
Center for Human-Computer Studies,
Uppsala University, Stureg. 9, S-752 23 Uppsala.
Phone: +46 -18187866

Yvonne Waern as above

1. Introduction

Several people in Sweden have for quite a while been engaged in studies related to work environment research. In order to promote an interaction between these researchers and people engaged in computer system design research and development a new programme was recently started, called MDA; in English: People, Computers, and Work.

One of the important subgoals of this programme is to promote user participation in both technological development and research. Since we know we are not alone in this endeavour, we have invited an experienced researcher in this field to enrich our experience and ideas. Even though the goal is common to the panelists, means to reach the goal and experience from work towards the goal differ.

2. Issues

The following issues will be discussed:
1. The view of users in HCI research and development.
2. What role do laboratory studies and studies of noncomputerized work play in software development?
3. What about informal, "artistic" software development versus a more formal, "scientific" one?
4. What effects do you see on the research process and the results?

3. Panelists and their contributions

Liam Bannon is currently Visiting Professor at the Dept. of Information Processing Science, University of Oulu, Finland. Trained in cognitive psychology and computer science, he has been involved in the HCI field for a number of years. His focus of interest has been on widening the perspectives adopted within the field. This has lead him to an interest in the context of use of computer systems and to a greater emphasis on user involvement in the design process.

Position

1. I believe that there needs to be a better understanding among HCI researchers, and many system designers too, about the users of computer systems and the settings in which they work. Part of the problem resides in an implicit view of ordinary people which, if surfaced, would seem to treat people as, at worst, idiots who must be shielded from the machine, or at best, as simply sets of elementary processes or factors that can be studied in isolation in the laboratory.

2. Although psychology, particularly as represented by the field of human factors (HF), or ergonomics, has had a long tradition of contributing to computer systems design and implementation it has often neglected vitally important issues such as the underlying values of the people involved and their motivation in the work setting.

3. Understanding people as actors in situations, with a set of skills and shared practices based on work experience with others, requires us to seek new ways of understanding the relationship between people, technology, work requirements and organizational constraints in work settings. Studying such a multi-facetted and multi-layered issue requires us to go beyond more traditional controlled laboratory studies that are the hallmark of experimental human-computer interaction (HCI) studies.

4. In this panel I recount some experiences and point out some problems. I suggest some alternative perspectives and directions for more fruitful research on, or rather with, people in work settings that may assist in the design of more usable and useful computer systems.

3.2. *Yvonne Waern* , Ph.D., is Associate Professor at the Department of Psychology, Stockholm University and at the Department of Manufacturing Systems, Royal Institute of Technology. She is the head of a research group, working mainly with cognitive aspects of Human-Computer interaction. Several projects of this group involve collaborations with computer scientists and manufacturing engineers.

Position:

1. Users are specialists in their own field but may still have similar requirements on computer systems. We have found the same strengths and weaknesses regarding users´ participation in HCI design both in CAD and office automation systems. In general system designers focus the task level of systems and neglect the semantic, syntactical and lexical levels, which later will cause the users problems while working with the systems.

2. Studies of noncomputerized work give you very little help in the design of computerized work.

3. Informal system design may be successful, but in order to expand our knowledge and to speed up software design, we also have to work towards formal specification tools to get from the task analysis to the implementation.

4. Although users are experts in their own tasks, they cannot predict what may happen when a computer tool is introduced. The cooperation between users, software designers and HCI researchers requires a careful consideration of both the users´ situation and the designers´ opportunities in terms of computer hardware and software as well as design tools.

3.3. *Toomas Timpka,* MD., PhD., is Assistant Professor at the Department of Computer and Information Science, Linköping University. He is also practicing physician at the Department of Community Medicine, Linköping University Hospital. Currently he leads an interdisciplinary research project into the design, implementation and use of hypermedia information systems in primary health care.

Position:

1. Computer use during patient- practitioner consultations in health care represents a situation where the one- user-one-machine model is not appropriate.

2. We have studied non-computer supported consultations to understand what really is going on during a consultation in health care and found that the organisational context is essential. A patient talks to, for instance, secretaries and nurses before seeing a physician during a health care event. These practitioners face different dilemmas during their "subconsultations", and use of computers in one subconsultation may solve the problem at hand but create a dilemma at next level.

3. It is impossible to describe and understand the interaction between patient and practitioner in entirely formal, scientific terms. Hence, use of theories and abstract specification languages from the different disciplines are postponed as long as possible in the systems development. Direct interaction (i.e., discussing, showing, and doing) between group members from different backgrounds is instead used in the group work.

4. The basic issue is that the consultation should control the computer system and not vice versa. Available methods for study and development of human-computer interaction in organisations are weak on interpersonal relations. The group process perspective on the development puts the focus on interdisciplinarity, the collaboration between people from very different backgrounds regarding theoretical education and practical experience, which might be the key to usable computers systems in the work environment.

3.4. *Werner Schneider,* Ph.D. in physics, is director of the common computer center of the Universities of Uppsala and the University Hospital (UDAC) and professor in the field of human computer studies at Uppsala University. He was named a Doctor h.c. in medicine by the University of Uppsala in 1978 and by the Medical Academy of Dresden in 1987. Since 1963 he has specialized in research work concerning the possibilities and limitations of formal representation of human knowledge and know-how, the domains of special interest being theory formation in clinical psychology and man-computer interaction.

Position:

1. From analyses of a wide range of computer applications (management information systems, electronic mail and conference systems, office automation, national and international drug information systems, computer base workstations and information systems for hospital laboratories, wards, intensive care units, dental practices etc) we have learned the following:
- An appropriate specification and design of any computer support is work context specific, i.e. there is no "portable" HCI.
- Most of the existing user problems have their origin in the fact that an analysis of the entire human use and handling of information at the work places affected was not done prior to the design and implementation of the applications. It could be shown that the human workers perform, without being awareof it, a lot of information processing and handling processes in an 'autopilot´- controlled automated mode. Obviously, this non-awareness must result in a faulty basis for specifying and designing a computer support.

2. Our research has clearly revealed that the availability of methods and tools for the analysis of the entire human use and handling of information in a specific work context is crucial. A part of our research has therefore been

devoted to the development and evaluation of such methods and tools.

3. Our research has shown that the use of informal, innovative, ´artistic´ software development is crucial.

4. Although user participation is a necessary condition for success it is not a sufficient one. An interdisciplinary research team and the collaboration of ´artistic´ graphic designers increase the probability of success.

Human–Computer Interaction – INTERACT '90
D. Diaper et al. (Editors)
Elsevier Science Publishers B.V. (North-Holland)

PANEL: INTERACTIVELY SUPPORTING THE SOFTWARE PROCESS

Simon M. KAPLAN (University of Illinois)
Anthony FINKELSTEIN (Imperial College)
Gail KAISER (Columbia University)
Kevin RYAN (Trinity College)
Wilhelm SCHAFER (STZ Dortmund)

How should we support the software process? Clearly, 'silver bullet' solutions are not going to solve the problem: what are needed are interactive systems which are designed from the perspective of a solid understanding of the nature of the process and which address the fundamental issues of how people work and how computers can reasonably be expected to support this. In keeping with the stated desire of the conference organizers that panels be be forward-looking and contentious, the panelists have been chosen to represent a range of opinions across the spectrum of how such automated support can be provided and what forms it should take.

The next generation of tools supporting the software process should reasonably be expected to, *inter alia*: Support group work; Support the mechanizable aspects of the process directly through integration of families of intelligent tools; Support the nonmechanizable aspects of the process by capturing design information (tracing the evolution of systems), supporting common representation logics for requirements, providing browsers of design histories, etc; Integrate the tools together to provide a unified system, and be open in the sense that the user can mix-and-match tools and methodologies to suit. The panelists represent a spectrum of opinion concerning the feasibility of such systems, what philosophies to use in implementing them, and where we stand in our goals of providing such high levels of support.

POSITION STATEMENT: ANTHONY FINKELSTEIN. I am interested in conducting work in the area of "fine-grain" software process modelling. By fine-grain software process modelling I mean the analysis and description of the detailed structure and organisation of development activities. In general this structure and organisation is ignored by those who are concerned with modelling software development at the level of tool invocation and interworking. I believe that many important gross features of software development such as verification, validation and cooperation arise from the complex interplay of fine-grain activities. These features of software development are not simply embedded in a matrix of routine "house-keeping" tasks. Rather they are emergent properties that derive from the underlying fine-grain organisation. In particular I am interested in modelling the processes that underlie requirements elicitation and the validation of formal specifications so as to envisage novel tool and environment support.

Much current work in the area of software process modelling ignores the relation between the software process and the product representation. It also ignores the heuristics and expertise built up and used by software developers. These areas which are dealt with in "software development methods" deserve more attention. I am interested in: unifying models of software process and models of software structure through methods; supporting the use of multiple product representation schemes within methods; providing a systematic basis for constructing and presenting methods. Configuration and version management - particularly of "upstream" software development objects - is a challenging area. I am interested in how software process modelling and configuration management can be brought together. In particular I am interested in modelling strategies for coordinating group work which are important, I believe, for both areas.

Anthony Finkelstein is Lecturer at Imperial College, Department of Computing, an engineer and a graduate of the London School of Economics and the Royal College of Art. His research is in the area of software engineering with a particular focus on requirements specification and methods. Particular areas of research include theory and practice of constructing formal models of dialogue and conversation as a framework for tool support for requirements elicitation.

POSITION STATEMENT: GAIL KAISER. We have been working for several years on rule-based modeling of the software process and have defined a general architecture for rule-based development environments (RBDEs) that assist the user in carrying out the software development process. In our architecture, each rule defines an activity, including the software artifacts to be manipulated by the activity, the condition that must be satisfied to initiate the activity, the tools or other facilities that are employed in carrying out the activity, and the effects of completing the activity with respect to the status of the software project. The user is assisted by forward and backward chaining on the rules, to automate certain activities, ensure consistency in the project database, and/or monitor user actions to determine conformance to the designated process and detect divergence from this process.

We have implemented several prototype RBDEs, and the most recent, Marvel 2.5, is available for licensing to educational institutions and industrial sponsors; an example environment for programming in C on Unix and over 350 pages of documentation are provided as part of the distribution. Marvel 2.5 is a single-user system that supports automation of the software process and integration of external tools. The Marvel administrator tailors the Marvel 2.5 kernel by providing an object-oriented data model defining the objectbase and a rule-based process model specifying the behavior of the environment. The Marvelizer tool aids the Marvel administrator in immigrating the existing artifacts of an ongoing software project into a Marvel objectbase, in order to gain the important human-computer interaction benefits of Marvel's assistance in the software development process.

Gail E. Kaiser is Associate Professor of Computer Science at Columbia University, and has received the NSF Presidential Young Investigator and Digital Equipment Corporation Incentives for Excellence awards in 1986. Professor Kaiser has published over fifty papers in a wide range of software areas and received her PhD and MS from Carnegie Mellon University and her ScB from the Massachusetts Institute of Technology.

POSITION STATEMENT: KEVIN RYAN. Research has shown that the most expensive errors are made in the earliest stages of the lifecycle, yet it is these phases and activities that received the least research attention up until very recently. This might be because of the natural tendency of research to proceed from the bottom up, but it might also be because we have concentrated on the easy tasks first. Given the ever increasing size of the applications backlog and the need to achieve previously unheard of levels of quality it is time to address the problem of providing effective, interactive support for the task of requirements capture.

One promising approach, until AI has solved the natural language problem, is to build up domain-specific models which can constrain and, to some extent, guide the person performing requirements analysis and definition. Such models would be rich enough to express a significant fraction of novel applications and would include sufficient semantic knowledge to allow more than simple syntactic checks. Over time the model would be expanded and extended to cover related domains so that its guidance facility would be similarly improved.

Prerequisites for this approach to succeed are: suitable knowledge representation formalisms, the ability to define tractable domains and a set of specification/design methods that cover most of the lifecycle. At the present time none of these is demonstrably present, but it is reasonable to expect all three to emerge in the near future.

Kevin Ryan is Senior Lecturer in Computer Science at Trinity College, Dublin. He received the BA (Maths, Economics) and BAI (Engineering) degrees from Trinity College in 1971 and PhD (Computer Science) fromTrinity in 1978. Research interests are in Software Engineering, especiatlly AI applications. From July 1st, 1990 he will be Professor of Information Technology in the University of Limerick.

POSITION STATEMENT: WILHELM SCHAFER. The indeterminate nature of the software process suggests that a rule-based approach finally yielding a 'expert system' for software process modelling looks like a promising avenue. Our first experiments and a prototype we have built show that the suitability of rule-based systems is based on their flexibility (an explicit representation of a process is easily and incrementally extensible by new rules) and the possibility to describe complex situations and dependencies in a comprehensive manner (by exploiting the declarative notion of rules).

However, conventional rule-based systems lack important features which are inevitably necessary for process modelling. Usually, rule sets become rather large and appropriate mechanisms controlling side effects via proper interface definitions (like in conventional procedural languages) are missing. Furthermore, the notion of persistency has to be provided as well. All intermediate states (even on a fine-grained level!) have to be stored such that a running process can be stopped and resumed at any time. Such persistent storage should not cause any inefficiency during run-time. An underlying object management system which also allows storage and manipulation of the complex structured software objects (documents) is therefore an absolute must. This goes much beyond what is usually provided by an expert system. Finally rule-based systems lack an explicit notion of expressing concurrency.

Based on those observations, the way ahead in developing process modelling languages is to take an approach which is often called multi-paradigm. Such languages should merge features like the declarative notion of rules with the structure capabilities of modules with well defined interfaces and the concept of tasks or coroutines for expressing concurrency.

Wilhelm Schaefer is leading a group of researchers at the STZ (Software Technology Center), a spin-off research establishment of the University of Dortmund. Dr. Schaefer is the leading technical authority on process modelling in the multi-nation (6) multi-partner (15) effort ESF (Eureka Software Factory). This project is building a process centered environment for supporting large scale software development over distributed sites.

POSITION STATEMENT: SIMON KAPLAN. The software process is inherently conversational and collaborative in nature. Software process models, and tools based on these models, that do not recognize these fundamental facets of the process can never be expected to provide the kinds of rich, interactive, autopoetic support that we believe support tools *should* provide.

Because of the conversational nature of the software process, it is impossible to specify *a priori* exactly the process by which a piece of software evolves, because the very process depends on the participants. Any support tool must therefore be extremely flexible, and mold itself to the culture of its user groups, not the other way around.

This is not to say that there is no role for the technology or approaches used in single-user support tools. Rule-based technology, for example, is extremely useful when the problem domain is well defined and meshes with the culture of the group using the tool, or at the downstream ends of the process (because there is generally better agreement about what is needed at that point).

We are currently building a conversation-based software process tool, the ConversationBuilder. The goal of this project is to allow the generation of group-based process support tools which can be tailored to the group culture and integrate existing methodologies and tools to support a groups software process model. ConversationBuilder is an example of a new generation of software environments which we term collaborative open systems.

Simon M. Kaplan has been assistant professor of Computer Science at the University of Illinois since 1985. His research interests focus on the development of programming languages and environments. Currently he is involved in two major projects: The ConversationBuilder, which is a collaborative open systems prototype, and the Δ project, which is investigating visual languages for concurrent systems. Kaplan's research is supported by AT&T and the National Science Foundation.

Human–Computer Interaction - INTERACT '90
D. Diaper et al. (Editors)
Elsevier Science Publishers B.V. (North-Holland)

Task Analysis: The Oft Missing Step in the Development of Computer-Human Interfaces; Its Desirable Nature, Value, and Role

Organizer/Moderator
Richard I. Anderson, Pacific Bell
2600 Camino Ramon, Room 2E850, San Ramon, CA 94583 (ria@PacBell.COM; 415-823- 3715)

Panelists

John M. Carroll, IBM Watson Research Center
P.O.Box 704, Yorktown Heights, NY, 10598 USA
(carroll@ibm.com; 914-784-7733)

Jonathan Grudin, Aarhus University (on leave from MCC)
Computer Science Dept., Ny Munkegade, Bygn. 540, 8000 Aarhus C Denmark (jgrudin@daimi.dk; 45 86-127188)

John F. McGrew, Pacific Bell
2600 Camino Ramon, Room 2E750, San Ramon, CA, 94583 USA(jfmcgrew@PacBell.com; 415-867-7204)

Dominique L. Scapin, I.N.R.I.A
Domaine de Voluceau, 78153, Le Chesnay Cedex, France
(scap@archie.inria.fr; 1 39-63-55-07)

Introduction

Although basing initial system design on an understanding of users and their tasks has been advocated for years, confusion reigns as to what it means. Some claim that the needed clarity resides in traditional approaches to task analysis (for an overview of these, see Drury et al., 1987), but not only are these approaches infrequently used (see, for example, Rossen et al., 1988), several question their adequacy and usability (e.g., Phillips et al., 1988). Meanwhile, designers and human factors specialists fumble with the concept.

Why is task analysis so confusing and often not done or not done well? Is it because of inadequate tools or techniques? Is it because task analysis is infrequently taught? Is it because task analysis receives no mention in some highly visible lists of ingredients of successful user interface development (e.g., Shneiderman, 1988)? Is it because the global nature and scope of user interfaces have been shifting since the early days of computers (see Grudin, 1990), impacting the appropriate meaning of task analysis and producing a multiplicity of appropriate meanings?

This distinguished panel takes aim at the confusion surrounding task analysis and offers ideas about what task analysis needs to be.

John Carroll

"Task analysis" refers to schemes for hierarchical decomposition of what people do. The premise is that understanding the parts and their structural relationships can be instrumental in designing performable and learnable tasks, artifacts to facilitate these tasks, prerequisite instruction, etc. The twin limitations of task analysis are that it can be too hard for designers to use and not useful enough to justify its difficulty. One account of this is that schemes for task analysis often seek to characterize tasks outside of any context of doing or learning. Good examples are functional specification documents or so-called object-action analysis, enumerations and clusterings of system objects with respect to the actions that can apply to them. Such analyses seek to be complete from a formal point of view, but do not represent tasks as they are coherent to users, and simply omit momentous aspects like potential error tangles. Accordingly, such analyses can fail to justify the cost of bothering to construct them.

An option is to seek highly contextualized, user-centered representations of tasks. Detailed scenario descriptions of how users accomplish representative tasks are an example: they are concrete for both users and designers, and support envisioning the system under development; they necessarily and coherently foreground aspects of tasks that matter to users; moverover, they are required for the design of user testing instruments and task-oriented instruction and documentation. Task analysis must face the issue of its own usability and value in design: user interaction scenarios are a pragmatically viable option.

Jonathan Grudin

Perhaps no one would categorically reject "task analysis" in system design. However, controversy does break out when one suggests a detailed definition for "task." Tasks may be defined at almost any level of granularity. Some writers claim an overriding importance of "situated cognition" and a very global focus on the workplace or claim that users must be educated to participate as equal partners in the analyses --

which others see as an ill-afforded luxury, fiddling vaguely when fire-fighting at lower levels would be more productive. Alternatively, many task analyses focus exclusively on "atomic" steps taken by "operator-users" in carrying out system-defined actions -- open to the charge that such efforts are often counterproductive, losing the forest in the trees.

One consideration in positioning oneself is to examine the consequences of omitting task analyses of different sorts. I have found that optimizing even low-level interface design features may require a surprisingly high-level task analysis -- the optimal placement of function keys, patterns of menu defaults, positioning of pop-up menus may vary according to the work patterns of system users or the availability of system features. Of course, an adequate (rather than optimal) design may sometimes be the goal. However, this does not justify abandoning task analysis. Identifying and "getting acquainted with" users may be difficult, but their voice needs to be heard in development environments. Engineering is a process of compromising, making tradeoffs. The human-computer interface is one consideration among many. It will inevitably be compromised. For that reason, the users' representatives in the development process must begin the negotiation with the strongest hand possible, and that can only come from knowledge about what the users need.

John McGrew

The purpose of task analysis is the transfer of information or knowledge from one group to another for such purposes as requirements definition, information analysis, and user interface design. Presently there is a lack of formal methods, or agreement on procedures, for extracting and analyzing information from users. Present methods: 1) are descriptive, such as text outlines or data flow diagrams; 2) are resource intensive, they are done by hand, and require extensive interviewing and iteration; 3) imply a relationship among task elements that does not usually exist (when task descriptions are output as text, a list is implied as the basic structure among the task elements; in reality, this is seldom the case); 4) do not provide any analytical tools for guidance in eliciting information, verifying the information obtained, or deciding on design trade-offs; and 5) do not output information in a form that is useful to designers or programmers.

A system using graphs and matrices has proven useful for task analysis. The graphs and matrices are a good representation of the information in a task analysis, are able to provide insights about a task not available through other means, and provide tools and techniques for analysis and transfer of information. This method has three purposes: 1) gathering and verifying information from the user; 2) processing the information using analytical methods; and 3) applying the analytical results to design.

Dominique Scapin

Some amount of human factors reasoning can be envisioned when the interface designers look at available literature, particularly recommendations. Unfortunately, what is directly available leads them to often consider mainly low level interface aspects, from a human factors point of view. When major questions arise about the more abstract aspects of interface design, most handbooks just mention the need for taking the users and the tasks into consideration. Designers do not have the available means to integrate these aspects. In addition, task analyses are often time consuming because there are no software supporting tools; task analyses are not always systematic, and their outcome may be dependent on the analyst. This situation should stimulate the human factors profession to investigate these aspects.

Two research items seem to be worth looking at: the definition of software tools (ideally "intelligent") for task analysis; the formalization of the human factors expertise in the matching of task requirements to interface characteristics. Concerning the first research item, a first attempt has been made to define a task description model. This model aims to represent procedural knowledge processing by structured objects and to generalize the concept of procedural attachment to high level tasks which can call a structured concatenation of sub-tasks. The model is based on generic objects tasks which allow the hierarchical decomposition of a task with some logical and synchronization relationships. A prototype tool implementing this model has been developed, but it needs further validation, added features concerning its usability, and some design-related features, the definition of which is expected to result from the study of interface design activities and the expertise involved.

Final Comments

How does task analysis fit in and compare with other design/development activities? What exactly is its goal?

Recently-presented conceptual/procedural frameworks for or which encompass task analysis provide inadequate answers to these key questions. Typical waterfall- like models of system lifecycles (e.g., Mantei & Teorey, 1988) or of user interface design methodologies (e.g., Mountford, 1989) that incorporate human factors engineering position task analysis relative to other development stages* but reveal little of its nature or scope. Perlman's (1989) model of an "asynchronous" system development process is far more revealing but is rather specific to the development of a particular product. Open systems analysis (Harker & Eason, 1985) and usability engineering's understanding "experience of use" (Bennett et al., 1988) appear to more effectively address issues involving organizational functions and user participation, respectively, but their descriptions are vague.

With the advisability of understanding user tasks prior to system design receiving increased attention (e.g., Norman, 1989) and acceptance in the computer-human interaction community, and with ISO/WD 9241-14 (1990) stating that the standard is not to be used unless "the designer has done a proper task analysis," the confusion surrounding task analysis must be targeted for destruction. Good conceptual/procedural frameworks would help. Watch for their (re)emergence in the '90s; look also for significant change in that which typifies task analysis.

----

*Some task analysis techniques cannot be applied prior to initial system design (Keane & Johnson, 1987; Scapin & Pierret-Golbreich, in press). A good framework that positions task analysis techniques of different purposes would also be helpful.

About the Participants

Richard Anderson provides human factors engineering services at Pacific Bell. His undergraduate studies were at Iowa State University; his masters and doctoral work was done at the University of Illinois at Urbana-Champaign. He has been active with software development, research, consulting, and teaching for 18 years. [Anderson, R. I. (April 1990). Task analysis - Its nature, value, and desirable role in the development of computer-human interfaces. Special interest group session at CHI '90, Seattle, Washington.]

John Carroll is Manager of User Interface Theory and Design at the IBM Watson Research Center in Yorktown Heights, New York. His research is in the analysis of learning, problem-solving, and language capacities that underlie human endeavor and experience. His most recent books are "What's In A Name" (W.H. Freeman, 1985), "Interfacing Thought" (Bradford/MIT Press, 1987), and "The Nurnberg Funnel" (MIT Press, 1990). [Carroll, J. M. & Rosson, M. B. (January 1990). Human-computer interaction scenarios as a design representation. Proceedings of the 23rd Hawaii international conference on system science, vol. II (Software Track). Kona, HA.]

Jonathan Grudin is a Visiting Associate Professor at the Computer Science Department of Aarhus University, Denmark, on leave from the Human Interface Laboratory of the Microelectronics and Computer Technology Corporation (MCC). He spent several years working in product development organizations as a programmer and software engineer, and his MCC research focuses on user interface development practices in large development companies. [Grudin, J. (1989). The case against user interface consistency. Communications of the ACM, 32, 1164-1173.]

John McGrew specializes in human factors, knowledge acquisition for expert systems, and cognitive modeling at Pacific Bell. He worked previously at the Jet Propulsion Laboratory and The Army Research Institute. He taught psychology at the University of Tulsa and at the College of Wooster. His BA and MA are from California State University, Fresno, and Ph. D. - the University of Georgia. [McGrew, J. F. (1990). The use of graphs and matrices in task analysis. To appear in J. Karat (Ed.), Taking design seriously: Techniques useful in HCI design.]

Dominique Scapin is a Research Director at I.N.R.I.A., Rocquencourt, France, where he is heading a project dedicated to research activities in software psychology. He has been involved in research, teaching, and consulting for the last 12 years in France or the US. He holds a Doctorate in Applied Psychology and various credits in computer science and human factors. His current research focuses on the specification of software environments for the design of interfaces. [Pierret-Golbreich, C., Delouis, I., & Scapin, D. L. (August 1989). Object- oriented tool for extracting and representing tasks (Report No. 1063). Le Chesnay, France: Inst. Nat. Recherche Inf. Autom.]

References

Bennett, J., Butler, K., & Whiteside, J. (1988). Usability engineering. CHI '88 tutorial notes. ACM.

Drury, C. G., Paramore, B., Van Cott, H. P., Grey, S. M., & Corlett, E. N. (1987). Task analysis. In Gavriel Salvendy (Ed.), Handbook of human factors. New York: John Wiley & Sons.

Grudin, J. (1990). The computer reaches out: The historical continuity of interface design. In J.

Chew & J. Whiteside (Eds.), Empowering people: CHI '90 conference proceedings.

Harker, S. & Eason, K. (1985). Task analysis and the definition of user needs. In G. Mancini, G. Johannsen, & L. Martensson (Eds.), Analysis, design and evaluation of man-machine systems. Oxford: Pergamon Press.

ISO TC159/SC4/WG5 (January 1990). Ergonomic requirements for office work with visual display terminals (VDTs): Part 14: Menu dialogues. (Working Draft Version 4.2).

Keane, M. & Johnson, P. (1987). Preliminary analysis for design. In D. Diaper & R. Winder (Eds.), People and computers III. Cambridge: Cambridge University Press.

Mantei, M. M. & Teorey, T. J. (1988). Cost/benefit analysis for incorporating human factors in the software lifecycle. Communications of the ACM, 31, 428- 439.

Mountford, S. J. (December 1989). A case study in designing navigable multi- media data. User interface strategies '90: A live, interactive satellite broadcast. University of Maryland Instructional Television.

Norman, D. A. (May, 1989). Whither CHI in the 1990s? Plenary panel during CHI '89, Austin, Texas.

Perlman, G. (1989). Asynchronous design/evaluation methods for hypertext technology development. Hypertext '89 Proceedings. New York: ACM.

Phillips, M. D., Bashinski, H. S., Ammerman, H. L., & Fligg, Jr., C. M. (1988). A task analytic approach to dialogue design. In M. Helander (Ed.), Handbook of Human-Computer Interaction. Amsterdam: North-Holland, 835-857.

Rossen, M. B., Maass, S., & Kellogg, W. A. (1988). The designer as user: Building requirements for design tools from design practice. Communications of the ACM, 31, 1288-1298.

Scapin, D. L. & Pierret-Golbreich, C. (in press) Towards a method for task description: MAD. Working with display units. Amsterdam: Elsevier.

Shneiderman, B. (October 1988). New user interface ideas and hypertext. User interface strategies '88: A two-day satellite TV course. University of Maryland Instructional Television & NTU.

Human–Computer Interaction – INTERACT '90
D. Diaper et al. (Editors)
Elsevier Science Publishers B.V. (North-Holland)

NEW APPROACHES TO THEORY IN HCI: HOW SHOULD WE JUDGE THEIR ACCEPTABILITY?

Organiser: Andrew MONK
Department of Psychology, University of York, York, YO1 5DD, U.K., AM1@uk.ac.york

1. PANEL

John Carroll

User Interface Institute, IBM T. J. Watson Research Center, Yorktown Heights, NY, 10598, U.S.A.; carroll@com.ibm.almaden

John Carroll is Manager of User Interface Theory and Design at the IBM Watson Research Center in Yorktown Heights, New York. His research is in the analysis of learning, problem-solving, and language capacities that underlie human endeavour and experience, especially human interaction with computers. His most recent books are "What's In A Name?" (Freeman, 1985), "Interfacing Thought" (MIT, 1987), and "The Nurnberg Funnel" (MIT, 1990).

Michael Harrison

Department of Computer Science, York University, York, YO1 5DD, U.K.; mdh@uk.ac.york.minster

Michael Harrison spent about ten years in industry. He moved to York in 1983 and is now Professor of Human Computer Interaction. He manages several research projects concerned with the use of mathematical models to design, implement and evaluate interactive systems. These methods have been applied to real systems including interactive conferencing and a system to support the formal description of concurrent systems using diagrams. He has recently completed an edited book (with Harold Thimbleby) "Formal Methods in Human Computer Interaction" published by Cambridge University Press.

John Long

Ergonomics Unit, University College London, 26 Bedford Way, London, WC1H OAP, U.K.; ucjtsjl@uk.ac.ucl.euclid

John Long has first degrees in modern languages and psychology and a Ph.D. in psychology. He has worked for Shell International in Africa and the far east and spent some time at the UK Medical Research Council's Applied Psychology unit at Cambridge as a senior scientist. He is now Professor of Cognitive Ergonomics and director of the Ergonomics Unit, University College London. His current interests are in the human factors of HCI including: performance setting, systems design and performance evaluation.

Richard Young

MRC Applied Psychology Unit, 15 Chaucer Road, Cambridge, CB2 2EF, U.K.; rmy@uk.ac.cam.mrc-apu

Richard Young studied Engineering and Artificial Intelligence (AI) before gaining his PhD in Psychology from Carnegie-Mellon University in 1973. Since 1978 he has been on the scientific staff of the UK Medical Research Council's Applied Psychology Unit in Cambridge. His research interests lie in human-computer interaction and the use of AI for the computer simulation of thinking, problem solving and cognitive skills.

2. THEME

Recent years have seen a variety of new approaches to theory in HCI. The question to be addressed in this panel is how an account or explanation of some issue in HCI should be judged within each of these approaches i.e., what are the criteria by which we discriminate a good account from a bad one.

Three approaches will be examined. The first, most notably developed by Richard Young and his colleagues at the Applied Psychology Unit in Cambridge, has been to apply models and architectures developed in Cognitive Science to HCI. Cognitive architectures describe the basic building blocks of human cognition. Richard will show how this knowledge of human information processing can guide the design process and then go on to discuss the question of how the use of a particular architecture should be validated.

The second approach to be considered has largely been pioneered by Michael Harrison and his group at York. This uses mathematical notations to describe interactive computer systems at a relatively high level of abstraction. The models they generate make explicit the link between user and system behaviour. Principles of good design can be specified within these abstractions. Michael will give some examples of this approach and then discuss how the principles should be justified.

The third approach to be considered is equally radical. This is the framework developed by John Carroll and his group at IBM, Yorktown Heights, which takes as its basis a study of artifacts i.e., the systems built. John will illustrate how this approach can inform practice and theory in HCI and how the validity of a claims analysis is demonstrated.

Each of the above approaches is different enough to be considered as a separate discipline of research. Their proponents will discuss the internal criteria for discriminating a good account or explanation from a bad one within each of these disciplines. There remains the question of whether these accounts can support design practice. The paper by John Long will discuss the more general criteria concerned with the transformation of a largely descriptive account to prescriptive advice for designers.

3. POSITION PAPERS

3.1 Evaluating cognitive simulation models in HCI - Richard M. Young

One of the hard problems facing all theorists in HCI is that of how to convey the theory to the designer in a form that is accessible and practical to use. An important current line of theorising proposes the use of cognitive simulation models, i.e. computer-based models which simulate the cognitive processes performed by a user, thereby serving to make predictions about users' behaviour with a proposed design and to draw the designer's attention to any problems of usability.

Along with other approaches, one of the difficult challenges this kind of modelling faces is that of being genuinely predictive, i.e. able to say things about the user's behaviour ahead of time, before there has been the chance to perform empirical studies, e.g. with an early prototype of the proposed design. (When this is done, the model exerts great leverage by bringing considerations of usability to bear at a very early stage of design.) Unlike the other approaches (and despite its critics), cognitive modelling is providing growing evidence of its ability to provide this kind of prediction (see for example [1, 2]).

In assessing a simulation model, it is conventional to distinguish between scientific criteria and practical criteria, although many of us challenge this because we believe that responding to the issues of application is one of the most effective ways to advance the science. Within HCI, the modelling work respects the usual scientific concerns of accuracy and generality, although some of the work reverses the priorities usual in Experimental Psychology and emphasises scope, where necessary at the expense of accuracy [3,4]. Other criteria directly responsive to the HCI context are:

(a) Applicability: Are the models applicable to the users, interface, and task? Do they make contact with the relevant phenomena? [3,4]

(b) Usability: Are the models practical for the designers who are their intended users?

(c) Perhaps most importantly of all, do the models provide the designer with "tools for thought"? Do they give the designer a new way to conceptualise the design space, with an enhanced control over usability?

[1] John, B.E., Extensions of GOMS analyses to expert performance requiring perception of dynamic visual and auditory information, in: Proceedings of CHI'90, (ACM, 1990).

[2] Olson, J.R. & Olson, G.M. The growth of cognitive modeling in human computer interaction since GOMS. Human Computer Interaction, in press.

[3] Young, R.M. & Barnard, P.J. The use of scenarios in human-computer interaction research: Turbocharging the tortoise of cumulative science, in: J.M.Carroll & P.Tanner (Eds) Human Factors in Computing Systems and Graphics Interface (CHI & GI 87), (ACM, 1987).

[4] Young, R.M., Barnard, P.J., Simon, A.J. & Whittington, J.E. (1989) How would your favourite user model cope with these scenarios? ACM SIGCHI Bulletin, 20 (4) (April), 51-55.

3.2 Modelling interactive behaviour from a system perspective - Michael D. Harrison

The main motivation for the development of formal specification techniques in software engineering is the *correctness problem*: the problem of producing a provably reliable system from a specification that satisfies a set of requirements. We argue that it is possible to use these techniques to analyse particular aspects of the system such as *security, performance* or *interactivity.*

The York group is concerned with *interactive* properties of such systems. We have developed a number of models [1,2] of interactive behaviour that have a role in the process of engineering computer software systems:

requirements ⇒interaction model ⇒specification ⇒ implementation

They also help the designer to appreciate how the user will perceive the system. These models of interactive behaviour may encapsulate claims about how the system will be used [3]. We develop *state* and *display templates* to feature information with claimed relevance to the user's performance of a task.

By considering collections of display and state templates, and the mappings between them, we may consider a number of models of how the system is perceived by the user. Each model may be described in terms of components of the state and display that are extracted by the state and display templates respectively. The user envisages a mapping between them that is constrained by structural properties such as cycles, predictability and state display conformance [1].

Norman argues [4] that interaction from the user's perspective is an iterative process of system input formulation and system output evaluation. It is clear that these formulations and evaluations are themselves products of complex cognitive processes, probably drawing on various sorts of prior knowledge. Using the methods described above we can postulate the components of the system and display that are interpreted by users during this process. State templates extract those parts of the system state that are relevant to the user's goals. They are what change as a consequence of goal directed action and they serve to provide users with information about system state that is relevant to the evaluation of goals. The user extracts this information from the display.

These modelling methods lay the basis for experiment. The data derived from such experiment may be used to improve the usability of the system design.

[1] Dix, A.J., Harrison, M.D., Runciman, C. & Thimbleby, H.W. Interaction models and the principled design of interactive systems, in: Nichols, H. & Simpson, D.H. European software engineering conference, (Springer lecture notes, 1987).

[2] Harrison, M.D. & Dix A.J. A state model of direct manipulation, in: Harrison, M.D. & Thimbleby, H.W. Formal models in human computer interaction, (Cambridge University Press, 1990).

[3] Harrison, M.D., Roast, C.R. & Wright, P.C. Complimentary methods for the iterative design of interactive systems, in: Salvendy, G. & Smith, M.J., Designing and using human-computer interfaces and knowledge based systems (Elsevier Scientific, 1989).

[4] Norman, D.A. Cognitive engineering, in: Norman, D.A. & Draper, S. User centered system design (Erlbaum, 1986).

3.3. Toward an emulation-based design theory - John M. Carroll

The User Interface Theory and Design group at the IBM T.J. Watson Research Center is developing an emulation-based design theory for human-computer interaction. This work starts from an examination of technological evolution in interface and application design (and elsewhere) to identify the kinds of abstractions and processes that have proven useful. It then attempts to develop these by designing methodologies and other tools and by undertaking "model farm" development projects.

Most technological evolution occurs through emulation or direct synthesis of new artifacts and techniques, as opposed to the popular myths of the heroic inventor -- James Watt and the tea kettle -- or of design-by-deduction from a science base. Our approach is to acknowledge, coordinate with, and leverage off the manifestly successful structure of technological evolution. We urge that objects of obvious practical importance in the everyday commerce of HCI design and development be taken seriously as potential scientific objects.

In HCI, the important objects are user tasks and designed artifacts. In the practice of the field, these objects play important and effective scientific roles. User task scenarios are simple and appropriate design representations, increasingly used to supplement or even replace traditional techniques for functional decomposition. They are also critical components of task-oriented instruction and other user support and of usability evaluation instruments.

Designed artifacts (hardware, systems, applications, interfaces) are also important scientific objects in HCI. They implicitly embody myriad psychological claims (what would have to be true of users if the artifact is usable). Designers can clearly make use of this embodied psychology: new HCI systems often emulate momentous prior art or directly synthesize aspects of several important precursors. The significant issues in HCI research are typically pursued and resolved through successive design and redesign of this sort. In this sense, HCI artifacts are the effective codifications of theory in the field as practiced.

We are developing methods and tools to make HCI tasks and artifacts even more generally and reliably useful in research and practice. For example, the psychological import of an artifact can be more explicitly understood by interpretive analysis and empirical evaluation. This in turn can both enrich the science base of the field, via task and artifact abstractions, and can more ballistically guide the subsequent design of user interaction scenarios for future HCI artifacts.

Much of our work adopts a "model farm" approach: we are using our own developing methodologies and tools to design and to understand in an integrated research activity. For the most part, these projects are enhancements to our local Smalltalk environment (an intelligent tutor, a set of tools to support design by reuse, a tool for developing task-oriented views of the class hierarchy). Our goal is to make it more feasible to take the important objects of HCI practice seriously and thereby to empower designers.

3.4 The effectiveness of knowledge supporting HCI practice (or how to judge the acceptability of new approaches to theory in HCI) - John Long

This position paper proposes that any new approach to theory in HCI is acceptable if: (i) it advances knowledge to support practices which solve the general design problem of HCI; and (ii) the support is effective.

The discipline of HCI has been characterised as: 'the use of knowledge to support practices seeking solutions to the general problem of HCI' [1]. The general problem of HCI is to design human interactions with computers for desired performance. (Performance expresses:(i) the quality of the work carried out ('product quality') and (ii) the costs incurred therein, both by the user and the computer ('production costs') [2]). Any new approach to theory in HCI is acceptable if it advances knowledge to support practices for the development of interactive worksystems having a desired performance.

Three alternative conceptions of the discipline of HCI, each with its own knowledge and practices, have been identified [1]: HCI as a craft, as an applied science and as an engineering discipline. HCI as a craft discipline has practices of implementation then evaluation supported by heuristic craft knowledge. HCI as an applied science discipline has practices of specification and implementation supported by (some transformation of) descriptive scientific knowledge. HCI as an engineering discipline has practices of specification then implementation supported by prescriptive engineering knowledge. New approaches to theory in HCI are acceptable if they meet the requirements of their own conception. However, conceptions vary in effectiveness. Craft heuristics cost little to establish, but offer little guarantee in solving the general design problem of HCI. Engineering principles cost much to establish but offer a guarantee in solving the general design problem of HCI. Any new approach to theory in HCI may be characterised within one of these three conceptions. Thus, any new approach to theory in HCI may be effective within the limits of its own conception but still be less effective than an alternative approach having a different conception.

Taken together, the three approaches to theory in HCI presented in the other position papers may be understood to espouse an applied science conception of HCI as a discipline. Each presupposes scientific knowledge (and/or some transformation therefore) to support system development processes (Young - cognitive science (cognitive modelling); Harrison - computer science (formal specification techniques); and Carroll - psychology (emulation-based design theory). The acceptability of these three approaches to theory in HCI, thus, depends on: (i) the status of their scientific knowledge; and (ii) the status of any transformation or modification to render the descriptive knowledge prescriptive. (Since the general problem of science is the explanation and prediction of phenomena (and not the design of artefacts), its knowledge is descriptive and cannot be prescriptive (either in substance or method). Some transformation is thus required (for example, into design guidelines, or into a method) before it can be used prescriptively to support the design of interactive worksystems).

For the three approaches to theory in HCI to be acceptable, both their descriptive and their prescriptive knowledges must be: (i) conceptualised (coherently and completely), (ii) expressed explicitly (in an appropriate form or notation); (iii) operationalised (with respect to their domains of application); (iv) tested (for their capability to support desired performance); (v) validated; and (vii) generalised (with respect to worksystems having desired performance). Such knowledge would offer a solution to the general design problem of HCI and be effective in supporting HCI practice (and so be acceptable).

In summary, any approach to theory in HCI is acceptable if: (i) its knowledge supports practices for the development of interactive worksystems having a desired performance in terms of product quality and production costs; and (ii) its prescriptive (and descriptive) knowledge(s) are: conceptualised; expressed explicitly; operationalised; tested; validated; and generalised. These criteria can be applied to the different approaches to theory in HCI presented in the other panel session papers (and to other approaches, for example, [2][3]).*

Acknowledgement - helpful comments from John Dowell.

[1] Long, J. & Dowell, J. Conceptions of the discipline of HCI: craft, applied science and engineering, in: Sutcliffe, A. & Macaulay, L. People and Computers V (Cambridge University Press, 1989).

[2] Dowell, J. & Long, J. (1989) Towards a conception for an engineering discipline of human factors. Ergonomics, 32(II), 1513-1535.

[3] Whiteside, J., Bennett, J. & Holtzblatt, K. Usability engineering: our experience and evolution, in: Helander, M. Handbook of human-computer interaction (North Holland Press, 1987).

* Note that it would be possible for a new approach to theory in HCI to claim that although: (i) its knowledge(s) lacked the required status; and/or (ii) its knowledge(s) failed to address interactive worksystems having a desired performance, it nevertheless supports system development practices with some success and that the level of success is acceptable. The claim, however, would not constitute a solution to the general design problem of HCI, and so the knowledge offered by the new approach could not be considered (ideally) effective.

Human–Computer Interaction – INTERACT '90
D. Diaper et al. (Editors)
Elsevier Science Publishers B.V. (North-Holland)

MULTI-AGENT INTERACTION (PANEL)

Organiser: Nigel Seel, STC Technology Ltd

Panelists: Julia Galliers, Cambridge University
George Kiss, Open University
Stephen Scrivener, Loughborough University

INTRODUCTION

There is increasing interest in augmenting human-computer interfaces by including agents: computer systems able to accomplish delegated tasks on behalf of the user. Such agents will need to be knowledgeable both about accomplishing tasks, and about the beliefs and goals of users and each other.

Designing effective agents is hard work. The basic problems of knowledge-representation and automated reasoning are compounded by the requirement to model the cognitive states of other agents, and of human users. In addition, usability requires facilities for high-level dialogue between agents and users, perhaps using speech and natural language, and then feeding the results of such dialogues back into belief and goal revisions.

Given the difficulties of tackling these problems separately, it is not surprising that creating an integrated solution of any sophistication has scarcely been attempted. But progress continues to be made, and perhaps there is utility in constructing less sophisticated agents, as an interim measure.

The panel will consider what tasks are suitable for agent-solutions based upon foreseeable technology, and how agents can represent and modify beliefs and goals. Consideration will also be given to architectural questions of agent-design.

Having a collection of computer-based assistants at the user's disposal has long been a dream of hci-designers. We hope that this panel session will clarify how near we are to this goal, and how much more remains to be done.

THE PANELISTS

Julia Rose Galliers received her M.Sc in Cognition, Computing and Psychology in 1985 at Warwick University, on the topic of 'an intelligent communication aid for the non-vocal'. She then went on to study computational models of dialogue at the Human Cognition Research Laboratory at the Open University, where she completed her Ph.D in 1988. She is currently a SERC Postdoctoral Research Fellow at the Computer Laboratory at Cambridge University.

George Kiss is a senior lecturer in AI at the Open University. His research interests are in the theory and design of agent systems and their applications. He has studied engineering and psychology and has worked for the Medical Research Council and at the Universities of Birmingham, London and Warwick. He leads an Alvey project on High-Level (inter-agent) Dialogue in MMI.

Stephen A. R. Scrivener studied Fine Art at Leicester Polytechnic and the Slade School of Fine Art, London and has a Ph.D in Computing. Since 1979 he has been actively involved in interactive computing with a special interest in systems that support designers and communication through pictures. He is currently a lecturer in the Computer Studies Department at Loughborough University of Technology.

JULIA GALLIERS: DESIGNING MECHANICAL AGENTS CAPABLE OF INTERACTING WITH EACH OTHER AND HUMAN COMPUTER USERS.

My interest is in the nature of cooperative interaction. We need to understand this in order to design mechanical agents appropriately for cooperative problem solving (Human-Computer Interaction or Distributed Artificial Intelligence). In human social interaction, conflict and its resolution is believed by social scientists to be a positive factor in cooperation. In AI, it is at best something to be coped with. AI also has a view of dialogue as information passing - like water into an empty bucket. And if there is something already there that conflicts with what is being put in, then either it is ignored, or it is always replaced by the incoming "truth". Alternatively, belief states can be viewed as never empty, but also never fully informed in a multi-agent context.

Conflict considered as positive in this context offers the joint resolution of differences between belief states of dialogue participants, autonomously and to mutual satisfaction as contributory to cooperation. Autonomously means that the hearer and speaker share control over the effects of the speaker's actions. There are no automatic assumptions of persistence of current belief, or truth and greater wisdom of the speaker. Dialogue is then a series of negotiated belief revisions. My current research is attempting to establish and model principles of autonomous belief revision, which must therefore be taken into account in utterance planning for cooperative problem solving.

GEORGE KISS: WHY DO AGENTS NEED TO BE COMPLEX DISTRIBUTED SYSTEMS?

A minimal set of significant concepts with which to characterise interesting agents comprises knowledge, goals and actions. Knowledge deals with the relationship between the state of the world and the state of the agent; goals describe the direction of state changes; and actions produce those state changes. Normally we expect that the complexity of the agent's internal state space structure matches the complexity of that of its environment.

Interaction between multiple agents needs to be analysed with respect to all three concepts. Interesting new problems arise with respect to all three, compared to the situation when a single agent is embedded in a "non-agent" environment. The reason for this is that interesting agents have complex state spaces. Participants of multiple-agent systems therefore need complex internal state-space structures in order to be well matched to their environment.

In terms of knowledge, this leads to concern with a range of possible knowledge states within a multi-agent system. Some points on this range can be described, with respect to a single fact, as follows:

(1) implicit, distributed knowledge: obtainable only by pooling the individual knowledge of several agents about the fact;
(2) explicit, localised, individual knowledge of the fact by at least one agent;
(3) everyone knows: explicit knowledge of the fact by all agents;
(4) one agent knowing that another agent knows the fact;
(5) everyone knowing that everyone knows the fact;
(6) common knowledge: everyone knows that everyone knows that everyone knows ... the fact.

Similar considerations apply to the concepts of goal and action. The interesting challenge for the design of artificial agents is to determine what kind of agent architecture can sustain such complex state spaces. I argue that only distributed systems are capable of this.

STEPHEN SCRIVENER: HUMAN-COMPUTER CO-OPERATION

Human co-operation between humans can be viewed as a method of pooling individual skills and information to solve problems that would be difficult or impossible for an individual to tackle. Such pooling of resources can be beneficial when the emphasis is on achieving a correct or good early answer.

The idea of co-operation between of this kind is implicit in early writings on human-computer interaction, particularly Computer-Aided Design (CAD), where the human-computer dyad was seen as providing potential for exploring many more solutions than would otherwise be possible. In fact, this vision has not yet been realised, and CAD systems tend to be used for the refinement, analysis and testing of solutions generated by the designer before interaction begins. Computer involvement in the intellectual activity of design is minimal.

For human-computer co-operation it is necessary to view the machine as an active agent rather than as a provider of information on request. For a machine to exhibit co-operative behaviour it must 'know' what goal it shares with its human partner. In other words the machine must be capable of goal oriented working. Secondly the machine must have the competence to work towards goals autonomously. Hence the machine must embody task domain knowledge. Thirdly the machine must have access to information generated by its human partner and be able to communicate; in order to question, answer, and offer or seek advice and suggestions. It is suggested here that the mechanisms of Goal Orientated Working, the Partner Model, and the Agreed Definition Knowledge Base implemented in the Alvey HCC project offers a prototype architecture for co-operative machines.

Human–Computer Interaction – INTERACT '90
D. Diaper et al. (Editors)
Elsevier Science Publishers B.V. (North-Holland)

Multi-dimensional Interfaces for Software Design

Organizer: Tim Dudley
Bell-Northern Research
PO Box 3511, Sta. C
Ottawa, Ontario, Canada K1Y 4H7
dudley@bnr.ca

Panelists: Ronald Baecker, CSRI, University of Toronto, Canada
Marc Eisenstadt, HCRL, The Open University, Milton-Keynes, UK
Ephraim Glinert, Rensselaer Polytechnic Institute, Troy, New York, USA
Mary Beth Rosson, IBM's T.J.Watson Research Center, Yorktown Heights, New York, USA

The Panelists

Tim Dudley has twenty-four years of experience in the field of computer graphics in the areas of CAD/CAM, application and language design, design and implementation of user interfaces, and customer support of commercially available products. He holds degrees in Computer Science and in Mathematics from Montana State University, and has worked at Lockheed Missiles and Space Company, Xerox Corporation, and Cognos Inc. He undertook early extensive work with intelligent graphics terminals and device-independent graphics systems, and has produced several papers dealing with software engineering, graphics system design, device independence, user interfaces, and visual programming. He recently re-joined Bell-Northern Research, where his current research is in graphical, direct manipulation, visual programming interfaces.

Ronald Baecker received a B.Sc., M.Sc., and Ph.D from MIT. He is Professor of Computer Science, Electrical Engineering, and Management at the University of Toronto, and co-Director of the Dynamic Graphics Project of the Computer Systems Research Institute at the University. He has been a Summer Staff Member at the Xerox Palo Alto Research Center, and a Senior Visiting Scholar in the Human Interface Group of Apple Computer. He is co-author, with William Buxton, of the book *Readings in Human-Computer Interaction: A Multidisciplinary Approach*, and co-author, with Aaron Marcus, of the book *Human Factors and Typography for More Readable Programs.*

Marc Eisenstadt received a B.A. from Washington University, where he studied Biology and Psychology, and a Ph.D from the University of California at San Diego. Following post-doctoral research at the Department of Artificial Intelligence at the University of Edinburgh, he joined the Open University, where he designed the SOLO "semantic network" language for teaching AI to Open University undergraduates. This was followed by research on human-computer interaction and automatic program debugging systems, which were to become the mainstay of research within the OU's Human Cognition Research Laboratory (HCRL). He has collaborated on several books, and has published over 40 articles on HCI and artificial intelligence.

Ephraim Glinert is with the Department of Computer Science at Rensselaer Polytechnic Institute. His research interests include multiparadigm and graphical programming environments, non-textual human-computer interfaces, computers and the physically handicapped, and CAD environments for VLSI design. He holds the Ph.D from the University of Washington, where he was an IBM graduate fellow. Together with his graduate students, he has designed and implemented numerous visual environments. He has lectured widely on his research, including an intensive graduate-level course at the National Chiao Tung University, Taiwan, has authored several tutorials and articles on visual programming environments, and is

Vice Chair of the ACM Special Interest Group for Computers and the Physically Handicapped.

Mary Beth Rosson is project leader of the Software Psychology project in the User Interface Institute at IBM's T.J. Watson Research Center in Yorktown Heights, New York. Her current research centers on the cognitive processes underlying the design and implementation of software, especially the consequences of the object-oriented programming paradigm for these activities. She is on the Human Sciences editorial board of Interacting with Computers, and is a member of ACM SIGCHI, the Human Factors Society, and the Society for Computers in Psychology. She has a B.A in Psychology from Trinity University, and a Ph.D in Experimental Psychology from the University of Texas.

Theme Description:

An enormous body of useful interactive graphical techniques has been developed for use in the areas of hardware design, molecular and solid modeling, and most notably in scientific visualization. These techniques include highly interactive interfaces, 3-D representations of data, animation, use of video, and the full range of techniques used in the area of artificial reality (including head-mounted displays, data gloves, etc). Some of these techniques are slowly beginning to spill over into the area of research into software design. On that front, "visual programming" and "program visualization" are relatively recent terms (the IEEE Workshops on Visual Languages has been held only seven times), and the techniques to which they refer are being largely ignored by people working at the design and implementation of large, complex, commercially available software systems. With rare exception, we seem to be using these advanced techniques primarily to teach people to produce , and/or to understand, code that is written in third- and fourth-generation languages. Practically none of them are finding their way into the software industry. The few examples of commercially available systems that utilize these techniques, while somewhat interesting, are generally not suitable for use with real design work for large, complex systems.

The purpose of this panel is to determine the level of application of these advanced visualization and interaction techniques as they apply to software design, to assess the feasibility of some of these techniques, and to propose potentially fruitful research topics in this area.

Panelists' Positions:

Research Issues in Program Visualization

Ronald Baecker
Dynamic Graphics Project
Computer Systems Research Institute and
Department of Computer Science
University of Toronto
Toronto, Ontario, Canada

Program visualization is the use of graphics (including typography, graphic design, animation, cinematography, and interactive computer graphics) to enhance the crafts of program design, construction, and presentation and thereby to facilitate the development, understanding, and effective use of computer programs by people [1], [3]. Whereas the complementary discipline, *visual programming*, attempts to develop new visual paradigms for expressing programs, program visualization concentrates on creating new systems, methods, and forms of imagery for displaying programs that have typically been written in conventional programming languages.

My presentation will focus on a number of research issues important to achieving progress in program visualization in the 90's:

• Users should not have to modify program source in order to specify visualizations, but should have *unobtrusive* methods of *control*. One system in which this has been done successfully is described in [2].

• The use of multiple sensory modalities, especially colour and sound, can enrich our powers of perception with respect to displays of complex software systems. I shall discuss some principles that can guide such usage.

• One area in which multiple modalities are essential is in the increasingly important area of the visualization of concurrent algorithms. I shall sketch an approach to this problem [4].

• Finally, I shall speculate on the role of three-dimensional representations in program visualization.

References

[1] Baecker, R.M. (1981). *Sorting out Sorting*. 30 minute colour sound film, Dynamic Graphics Project, Computer Systems Research Institute, University of Toronto. (Excerpted and "reprinted" in *SIGGRAPH Video Review* 7, 1983.) (Distributed by Morgan Kaufmann, Publishers.)

[2] Baecker, R.M. and Buchanan, J. (1990). A Programmer's Interface: A Visually Enhanced and Animated Programming Environment. *Proceedings of the Twenty-third Annual Hawaii International Conference on System Sciences*, pp 531-540.

[3] Baecker, R.M. and Marcus, A. (1990) *Human Factors and Typography for More Readable Programs*, ACM Press, Addison-Wesley Publishing Company, 346 pp.

[4] Price, B.A. (in progress). Automatic Visualization and Animation of Large Concurrent Programs. M.Sc. Thesis, Department of Computer Science, University of Toronto.

Visual Programming and Program Visualisation for Knowledge Engineers

Marc Eisenstadt
Human Cognition Research Laboratory
The Open University
Milton-Keynes, U.K.

AI software has for many years made extensive use of graphical software tools. However, knowledge engineers have not had access to visual programming tools which assist them during the critical early phases of knowledge acquisition. Moreover, during later phases of knowledge base debugging, knowledge engineers have had to work with program tracing tools (whether graphical or textual) which are inherently incapable of scaling up o the monitoring demands imposed by large knowledge bases. To address these deficiencies, and to satisfy the needs of knowledge engineers throughout the software design, development, and debugging cycle, we have developed several novel visual programming and programming visualisation technologies. Foremost amongst these are (i) a "direct graph manipulation" semantic network sketchpad, and (ii) "dependency viewers" which allow the knowledge engineer to examine and manipulate temporal and logical dependencies. Direct graph manipulation allows the knowledge engineer to sketch out objects and relations (including control flow), from which code can be generated. Dependency viewers allow the knowledge engineer to observe an "instant replay" of rule execution, focussing either on temporal dependencies (what each rule did on each execution cycle) or logical dependencies (how a proof is supported by subordinate proofs). These techniques are incorporated in a homogeneous fashion in KEATS, the Knowledge Engineer's Assistant.

The talk emphasizes why visual programming and program visualisation offer "just another representation" but *not* a panacea. The presentation also makes a novel distinction among four different ways of manipulating the "navigational space" produced by large programs and knowledge bases: (a) by resolution, i.e. coarse vs fine; (b) by scale, i.e.close-up vs. far away; (c) by compression, i.e. the use of a single compact display region or symbol to indicate additional territory" at the same granularity and scale; (d) by abstraction, i.e. a movement away from the raw Prolog code and towards a representation closer to the programmer's own plans and intentions.

Visual Programming: Challenges and Directions for the 90's

Ephraim Glinert
Computer Science Department
Rensselaer Polytechnic Institute
Troy, New York, USA

The past decade has witnessed the accumulation of an impressive body of evidence [1] that visual and iconic environments often prove highly beneficial, both to computer users and to programmers. Indeed, with the exception of a few diehards (cf.[2, pg.1403]), it is now universally accepted that graphics can and should play a significant role in human-computer communication. Nevertheless, visual programming is a relatively new area whose tantalizing potential remains as yet unfulfilled because of a number of unresolved fundamental issues:

1. *The need to develop a "hard science" foundation*, including good notations for both visual languages and interfaces, and formal models that lead to provable counter-intuitive results.

2. *The need to affirmatively answer the skepticism* as to whether the approach can scale up to effectively handle more than "toy" programs, preferably in the general case but at least for specific domains/paradigms.

3. *The need to compile a proven "graphical vocabulary"* and uniform representations for all aspects of programming (code, data types and structures, etc.)

4. *The need to define and validate useful metrics* for assessing the relative merits (a) of alternative environments, and (b) of programs composed in a given environment.

Additionally, we believe there are at least three areas in which future success for the visual approach is assured:

1. *Parallel and distributed computation.*
2. *Large scale software engineering.*
3. *Visual environments for the visually handicapped.*

We believe that programming environments will, in the not too distant future, be vastly different from those in common use today, and that visual programming definitely will have a place in this future — although the extent of its role will depend upon our success in finding answers to the open problems enumerated above.

References

[1] Glinert, E.P. (editor) *Tutorial:Visual Programming Environments (in two volumes).* IEEE Computing Society Press, Washington, DC, 1990, to appear.

[2] Dijkstra, E.W. On the Cruelty of Really Teaching Computer Science. *CACM*, 32(12):1398-1404, December, 1989.

Multidimensional Interfaces: Position Paper

Mary Beth Rosson
IBM T.J. Watson Research Center
Yorktown Heights, New York, USA

In our design of tools to support the learning and using of Smalltalk, we have found the provision of multiple complementary representations of Smalltalk applications to be effective in aiding program understanding. Using the View Matcher for learning [1], new users of Smalltalk analyze a paradigmatic interactive application via several synchronized views: the external interface to the application itself, a message execution stack being evaluated, and commentary describing relationships among application objects. In some situations, the message stack is animated as messages are processed - although this animation mode was originally designed for novices, to serve as an "advance organizer" for understanding the message execution stack, we have seen that this dynamic representation of the program can produce insights into Smalltalk message passing even for more accomplished users.

Our more recent work focuses on a View Matcher for code re-use. As in the learning situation, we provide multiple views onto example interactive applications. However, because users' goals are different in this situation (i.e., users are hoping to understand how to re-use something, not how it works), the synchronized representations convey different information. In particular, the representations orient users to the design structure and communication protocol supporting the application's *usage* of the target object.

References

[1] Carroll, J.M., Singer, J.A., Bellamy, R.K.E., and Alpert, S.R. (1990). A View Matcher for learning Smalltalk. In *Proceedings of CHI'90*, New York, ACM.

Human–Computer Interaction – INTERACT '90
D. Diaper et al. (Editors)
Elsevier Science Publishers B.V. (North-Holland)

Usability Engineering on a Budget

Moderator:
Jakob Nielsen, Technical University of Denmark
Panelists:
Susan M. Dray, IDS Financial Services, USA
James D. Foley, George Washington University and Computer Graphics Consultants, USA
Paul Walsh, STC Technology, Ltd., U.K.
Peter Wright, University of York, U.K.

This panel will discuss how to get the "most bang for the buck" in usability engineering. What should one do when the budget is restricted and it is impossible to do everything by the book? How can one introduce usability methods in companies that currently have no systematic usability efforts?

The Panelists

Susan M. Dray is director of People/Technology Services at IDS Financial Services where she has been since 1988. Before then she was at Honeywell and she received her Ph.D. in psychology from UCLA in 1980. Address: Susan M. Dray, IDS Financial Services, IDS Tower 10, Minneapolis, MN 55440, USA.

James D. Foley is professor of computer science and chair of the Department of Electrical Engineering and Computer Science at the George Washington University. He is coauthor of *Fundamentals of Interactive Computer Graphics*. Address: James D. Foley, Department of Electrical Engineering and Computer Science, George Washington University, Washington, DC 20052, USA. Email: `foley@seas.gwu.edu`

Jakob Nielsen is assistant professor of user interface design at the Technical University of Denmark. His research interests include usability engineering and hypertext. Nielsen's latest book is *Hypertext and Hypermedia* (Academic Press 1990). Address: Jakob Nielsen, Technical University of Denmark, Department of Computer Science, DK-2800 Lyngby Copenhagen, Denmark. Email: `datJN@NEUVM1.bitnet`

Paul Walsh graduated in Psychology from U.C. Galway, Ireland in 1981. He worked as a Research Assistant at the City of London Polytechnic for three years, and also registered for and was awarded a Ph.D. in Cognitive Psychology on the topic of metaphor comprehension. In 1987 he joined the Ergonomics Unit, University College London, where he managed a project aimed at integrating Human Factors with JSD. He joined STC Technology Ltd in 1989. Since then, he has worked on such areas as HCI for Knowledge-Based Systems, Office Automation Systems, and Usability Evaluation. Address: Paul Walsh, STC Technology Ltd. London Road, Harlow, Essex CM17 9NA, UK. Email: `paw@stl.stc.co.uk`

Peter Wright is a research fellow with Dr. A. Monk and Prof. M.D. Harrison at York. His research interests are evaluation techniques, formal methods and user modelling. Address: Peter C. Wright, Department of Psychology, University of York, York Y01 5DD, U.K. Email: `PCW1@york.ac.uk`

Making Usability Engineering Work and Pay

Paul Walsh

The information technology (IT) industry, at least in Europe, is in the midst of a difficult phase. In the UK, for example, factors such as high interest rates seems to have depressed the demand for IT investment. More than ever, usability engineering has to be seen to be cost-effective. Our traditional focus on promoting system learnability, usability and likability (to name but three factors) may not be as important to those who make strategic decisions about IT investment as we would like to think.

However, the prospects for usability engineering are not completely negative. Over the past three to four years, HCI has become better integrated with the system development process in general. Although still a craft rather than an engineering discipline [Long 1989], HCI has come a long way with respect to industrial applicability.

It goes without saying that the usability engineering approach can be made more secure by maximising its importance to the computer industry. There are three main issues in ensuring this, which are **(1)** making alliances with other groups, e.g. marketing, business analysis, rather than engage in "HCI hegemony;" **(2)** stressing the cost-effectiveness of usability engineering, by keeping simple accounts of usability engineering costs and product (or other) benefits; and **(3)** learning to use business requirements as a basis for usability engineering, such that evaluations of prototypes can satisfy the constraint of meeting business as well as end-user requirements.

The Portable Usability Lab

Susan M. Dray

I will discuss *in vitro* and *in vivo* evaluations where both our traditional fixed lab at IDS and our portable lab facilities are used to do usability evaluations of diverse systems, processes, and services.

In addition, I will discuss ways we have included designers as observers and trained them in traditional (and some unorthodox) human factors tools and techniques in order to conduct the evaluations themselves.

Discount Usability Engineering

Jakob Nielsen

Several studies have shown abysmally low usage of systematic usability methods in development projects. For example, Milsted et al. [1989] found that only 6% of Danish companies with software development projects used the thinking aloud method and that nobody used *any* other other empirical or formal evaluation methods. Gould and Lewis [1983] found that American developers used on the average only 1.3 out of four extremely simple methods.

"Discount usability engineering" [Nielsen 1989; 1990] aims at alleviating this problem by using very cheap methods that people can start using without too much preparation or investment, since we know that many practitioners are intimidated by the perceived complexity of usability methods [Bellotti 1988]. One might then hope that more careful usability methods could be used on later projects, but it is essential to help companies get started with usability as quickly as possible. In my experience, the hurdle of getting started keeps many companies from using any usability methods at all.

Specifically, I advocate the use of prototyping, heuristic evaluation [Nielsen and Molich 1990] and simplified thinking aloud studies.

Even novice experimenters can use the thinking aloud methods successfully. I have found that computer science students with a minimum amount of training (corresponding to a one-day course) can find about 75% of the usability problems in an interface by running only 4–5 subjects. Furthermore, well-run experiments give better results than poorly-run experiments, so I would conjecture that more experienced experimenters should be able to make do with only 3 subjects for a simplified thinking aloud experiment.

Studies at the Technical University of Denmark have shown that HyperCard can be learned in an average of two working days and since the software itself is free, the total cost of starting to use HyperCard for prototyping will be $640, using the perhaps somewhat low hourly rate estimate from Mantei and Teorey [1988]. This is in contrast to their cost estimate of a minimum of $16,080 for starting to use a more traditional prototyping system (where they do not even try to include estimate of the cost of the learning time). Again we see how the discount approach drastically reduces the start-up cost associated with usability engineering.

Achieving Cost-Effective Evaluation by Training Designers

Peter Wright

The approach to evaluation advocated by Gould and Lewis [1985] requires the building of prototypes and the careful 'measurement' of the way users behave with them. The main obstacle to the widespread adoption of this approach is the potential time and expense incurred by user testing. It takes time and effort for designers to brief human factors specialists about a design. The specialists then have to test users, analyse results and report back to the designers. The pressures of commercial development often make this communication process impracticable. Savings would be made if designers could be trained to evaluate their own designs directly. This would also bring the designer and user closer together [Gould and Lewis 1985].

This solution is workable only if the evaluation methods used can be understood by designers with no human factors training. At York we have carried out studies in which trainee designers evaluated an interface by using an interactive think aloud method called **Co-operative Evaluation.** The instruction received by the designers took the form of a how-to-do-it manual [Wright and Monk 1989].

In the first study, the trainees evaluated a bibliographic database. The problems detected by each team were compared with the problems detected by the authors in a separate evaluation [Wright and Monk 1989]. The trainees detected over 70% of the problems detected by the authors.

In a second study, paper-based prototypes of an electronic form interface were evaluated, once by the designers of the systems and once by some other trainee designers. The designers of the systems also made predictions about expected problems. Significantly more problems were detected by the designers of the systems, but the problems they found did not match their predictions.

We conclude that it is possible to train designers to carry out their own user testing. This is not only a cost-effective solution to the evaluation bottleneck but also may yield a better standard of evaluation.

Managing Usability

James D. Foley

Foley will discuss the management of usability work. The problem of convincing corporate management that usability is worth the investment will also be addressed.

References

Bellotti, V. (1988): "Implications of current design practice for the use of HCI techniques," in Jones, D.M. and Winder, R. (eds): *People and Computers IV*, Cambridge University Press, Cambridge, U.K., 13–34.

Gould, J.D. and Lewis, C. (1983): "Designing for usability—key principles and what designers think," *Proc. ACM CHI'83* (Boston, MA, 12–15 December), 50–53.

Gould, J.D., and Lewis, C. (1985): "Designing for usability: Key principles and what designers think," *Communications of the ACM* **28**, pp. 300–311

Long, J.B. (1989): "Cognitive ergonomics and human computer interaction: An Introduction," In Long, J.B. and Whitefield, A. (eds): *Cognitive Ergonomics and Human Computer Interaction*, Cambridge University Press, Cambridge, U.K.

Mantei, M.M. and Teorey, T.J. (1988): "Cost/benefit analysis for incorporating human factors in the software lifecycle," *Communications of the ACM* **31**, 428–439.

Milsted, U., Varnild, A., and Jørgensen, A.H. (1989): "Hvordan sikres kvaliteten af brugergrænsefladen i systemudviklingen" ("Assuring the quality of user interfaces in system development," in Danish). *Proc. NordDATA'89 Joint Scandinavian Computer Conference* (Copenhagen, Denmark, 19–22 June), 479–484.

Nielsen, J. (1989): "Usability engineering at a discount," in Salvendy, G. and Smith, M.J. (eds.): *Designing and Using Human-Computer Interfaces and Knowledge Based Systems,* Elsevier Science Publishers, Amsterdam, pp. 394–401.

Nielsen, J. (1990): "Big paybacks from 'discount' usability engineering," *IEEE Software* **7**, 3 (May).

Nielsen, J. and Molich, R. (1990): "Heuristic evaluation of user interfaces," *Proc. ACM CHI'90* (Seattle, WA, 1–5 April).

Wright, P.C. and Monk, A.F. (1989): "Evaluation for design," In Sutcliffe, A. and Macaulay, L. (eds.): *People and Computers V,* Cambridge University Press, Cambridge, U.K., pp. 345–358.

AUTHOR INDEX

Abowd, G.D., 143
Acar, B.S., 345
Ackerman, M.S., 787
Ader, M., 535
Anderson, R.I., 1051
Ankrah, A., 73
Anschütz, H., 809
Anupindi, S., 747
Atwood, M.E., 29

Baber, C., 761
Baecker, R., 1063
Bannon, L., 1043
Barnard, P.J., 61, 457
Bastide, R., 625
Bellamy, R.K.E., 199, 1005
Bellotti, V.M.E., 207, 213
Benest, I.D., 853
Bennett, J., 365, 1039
Benyon, D., 573
Bevan, N., 357, 435
Black, P., 863
Blumenthal, B., 659
Böcker, H.-D., 931, 991
Boonzaier, D.A., 499
Booth, P.A., 47
Borning, A., 951
Bosman, D., 729
Bouma, G., 815
Bradford, J.H., 43
Brigham, F., 357
Brockett, M., 505
Brodbeck, F.C., 35
Brooke, J., 357
Broos, D., 169
Brouwer-Janse, M., 253
Brown, E., 675
Burton, A., 795
Buxton, W.A.S., 449, 667, 675

Campion, J., 505
Carey, T.T., 43, 101, 581
Carroll, J.M., 199, 937, 1051, 1055
Carroll, V., 821
Case, K., 345
Catterall, B.J., 377
Charles, S., 493
Chen, J., 415
Cockton, G., xix
Colgan, L., 253
Conklin, P., 1039
Coventry, L., 1007
Cowan, W.B., 555
Crellin, J., 329, 389
Curtis, B., xxxv

Damodaran, L., 289
Darses, F., 135
Davis, E.F., 959
De Souza, F., 435
Denley, I., 407
Détienne, F., 971
Diaper, D., 277
Dillon, A., 587
Dix, A., 15
Domingue, J., 997
Donau, K., 169
Draper, S.W., 473, 639
Drascic, D., 695
Dray, S.M., 1067
Dudley, T., 1063
Duff, S.C., 61
Dukić, D., 853
Duursma, C.M., 1009
Dzida, W., 239

Eason, K.D., 295
Edmonds, E., 601
Edmondson, W., 441
Eisenstadt, M., 1063
Elcock, J., 1011
Elliot, C., 1013
Ellis, D., 863
England, D., 613
Erickson, T.D., 741

Fedder, L., 801
Fels, S.S., 683
Finkelstein, A., 1047
Finlay, J., 149
Fitz-Randolf, D., 959
Fokke, M.J., 169
Foley, J.D., 1067
Freitag, R., 239
Frese, M., 35
Frohlich, D.M., 73

Galliers, J., 1059
Gaver, W.W., 735
Geddes, N.D., 283
Gerritsen, H., 827
Getao, K.W., 1015
Gilbert, G.N., 73, 903
Glinert, E., 1063
Goble, C.A., 247
Grant, S., 1017
Gray, P.D., 473, 639, 645
Gray, W.D., 29
Green, A.J.K., 457
Green, T.R.G., 79, 463, 951
Grodski, J., 695

Grudin, J., 219, 1051
Guevara, K., 1039

Hagiwara, N., 601
Hajsadr, S.M., 821
Haller, R.W., 841
Haring, G., 469
Harker, S.D.P., 295, 357
Harris, J.R., 715
Harris, M.B., 715
Harrison, M., 149, 1055
Hendry, D.G., 101
Henry, R., 965
Henry, S.C., 337
Henskes, D.Th., 715
Herczeg, J., 593, 991
Hewitt, J., 265, 755
Hindus, D., 787
Hinton, G.E., 683
Hobson, J., 265
Hofer, E., 303
Hoffmann, C., 239
Hohl, H., 931
Holleran, P.A., 841
Hoppe, H.U., 567
Horan, B., 247
Horn, T., 329
Horton, J., 863
Howes, A., 115, 881
Howkins, T.J., 247
Hunt, W.T., 581

Ip, W.K., 289

Jennings, F., 573
Jeremaes, P., 155
Jerke, K.-H., 593
John, B.E., 29
Johnson, C.W., 1019
Johnson, H., 259
Johnson, P., 259, 383
Jones, M.R., 21
Jørgensen, A.H., 561
Junger, J., 815

Kaiser, G., 1047
Kaplan, S.M., 917, 1047
Karat, C.-M., 351
Karat, J., 365
Kay, S., 247
Keller, L.S., 3
Kellogg, W.A., 193
Kilgour, A.C., 645
Kinoshita, K., 513
Kiss, G., 1059
Klein, E., 485
Kobayashi, M., 513
Kornbrot, D., 401
Kraut, R.E., 909
Kurisaki, M., 529
Kurtenbach, G.P., 667

Lagneau, O., 607
Langen, M., 1021
Lavigne, V., 607
Lawrence, D., 29, 773
Lee, A., 121
Lee, J., 479
Lesch, A., 593
Letanoux, Ph., 815
Lewis, J.R., 337
Lim, K.Y., 225
Lloyd, E.J., 55
Lochovsky, F.H., 121
Long, J.B., 225, 407, 1055
Lopez-Suarez, A., 581
Löwgren, J., 395
Lu, G., 535
Luo, M.R., 725
Lyritzis, K., 707

Mack, L.A., 835
Mack, R.L., 337
Mackay, W., 1039
MacLean, A., 207
Macleod, M., 401, 429
Maguire, M.C., 289
Maiden, N., 895
Manandhar, S., 787
Manhartsberger, M., 469
Maresh, J., 849
Marmaras, N., 707
Märtin, C., 651
Martin, D., 505
Matsushita, Y., 513
McGrew, J.F., 1051
McKnight, C., 587
Mercurio, P.J., 741
Milgram, P., 695
Miller, J.R., 977
Mills, Z., 423
Minor, E., 607
Misue, K., 521
Mitta, D.A., 875
Miyazawa, M., 513
Monk, A., 1055
Morris, M.E., 903
Murray, D., 573
Murray, W.D., 43
Murtagh, K., 675
Mynatt, B.T., 945

Nardi, B.A., 977
Navarro, L., 1025
Neal, L., 93
Nicolosi, E., 383
Nielsen, J., 315, 1067
Nordqvist, T., 395
Nowlan, W.A., 247

Oestreicher, L., 1029
Okabe, K., 959
Olphert, C.W., 289, 295

Olson, G.M., 835
Olson, J.S., 835
Orring, R., 323

Palanque, P., 625
Payne, S.J., 185, 881
Penz, F., 469
Petre, M., 463
Pineda, L.A., 485
Polifroni, J.H., 767
Powrie, S.E., 233
Preece, J., 3, 329
Prime, M., 423
Prümper, J., 35

Rate, M., 505
Rau, G., 1021
Rector, A.L., 247
Reisner, P., 175
Rhodes, P.A., 725
Richardson, J., 587
Rivers, R., 87
Robertson, S.P., 959
Rosson, M.B., 1063
Rößler, H., 593
Roudaud, B., 607
Rudnicky, A.I., 767
Ruggiero, F., 303
Rutledge, J.D., 701
Ryan, K., 1047

Sakamoto, M., 767
Sancha, T., 1039
Sapsford-Francis, J., 265
Sauer, A., 561
Scapin, D.L., 1051
Schafer, W., 1047
Schiele, F., 567
Schmandt, C., 787
Schneider, W., 1043
Scholtz, J., 925
Schwab, T., 593, 931
Scott, M.L., 619
Scrivener, S.A.R., 493, 725, 1059
Sebillotte, S., 985
Seel, N.R., 903, 1059
Selker, T., 701
Sellen, A.J., 667
Sewell, D.R., 283
Shalit, A., 499
Shan, Y.-P., 633
Sharratt, B., 271
Shepard, D., 779
Siemieniuch, C.E., 233
Silcock, N., 225
Simpson, A., 869
Singer, R.A., 1031
Singley, M.K., 937
Smith, R.B., 735
Sneath, E.L., 247
Sola, I., 779
Spall, R., 129
Spenkelink, G., 721
Stammers, R.B., 761
Stark, H.A., 67
Steele, R., 129
Steward, A.P., 795, 821
Stewart, T., xxix
Streeter, L.A., 909
Stuart, R., 29, 773
Sugiyama, K., 521
Sutcliffe, A., 895
Szabo, P., 593

Tauber, M.J., 163
Taylor, B., 371
Taylor, R.G., 761
TeWinkel, S.T., 101
Tibbitt-Eggleton, R., 1033
Tillson, P., 429
Timpka, T., 1043
Tscheligi, M., 469

Vainio-Larsson, A., 323
Valder, W., 239
Van Der Veer, G.C., 9, 169
Van Laethem, A., 1035
Van Spijker, H., 721
Van Zuylen, H.J., 827
Vanneste, C., 535

Waddington, R., 965
Waern, Y., 1043
Waite, K.W., 473, 639
Waldhör, K., 809
Walsh, P., 1067
Wastell, D., 107, 849
Weber, G., 689
Wein, M., 555
Wellner, P., 835
White, T.N., 9, 721, 729
Whittington, J., 115
Wiedenbeck, S., 925
Wilson, A., 247
Windsor, P., 309
Wood, C.A., 645
Wright, P., 1067

Yang, Y., 543, 549
Yap, F., 169
Yap, S.-K., 619
Yokoyama, T., 513
Youmans, D., 357
Young, R., 115, 207, 1055
Yufik, Y.M., 887

Zajicek, M., 755
Zapf, D., 35
Zeevat, H., 479

SUBJECT INDEX

Page numbers refer to the first page of the indexed paper.

Accuracy, 423
Adaptive systems, 683, 1007
Agent Partitioning Theory, 175
AI, 887
Air traffic control, 309
Aircraft, 875
Alphabetical keyboards, 707
Analogies, 1011
Analysis, 47, 155, 169, 225, 371, 377, 401
Animation, 991
Apple Macintosh, 21, 115
Applications, 1029
APT, 175
Artificial intelligence, 887
ATND Attendant Console, 779
Attitudes, 21, 755
Audio, 747
Auditory icons, 735
Automotive industry, 233
Behaviour, 107, 115, 121, 129, 149, 441, 561, 567, 959
Benchmarks, 337
Bibliographic databases, 149
Blackboard systems, 407
Blind people, 689
Blur, 729
Broadband communications, 233
Browsing, 101, 513, 587, 593, 747, 931, 991
CAD systems, 135, 345, 383, 463, 485
Casual users, 707, 795
Characters, 729
Charts, 289
Classification, 47
Coding, 505, 959, 997
Cognitive factors, xxxv, 79, 283, 457, 881, 1017
Cognitive maps, 587
Cognitive models, 55, 87, 887
Cognitive processes, 135, 271
Cognitive skills, 887
Cognitive strategies, 499, 505
Cognitive style, 1007
Collaboration, 303, 521, 529, 735, 917
Colour, 561, 725, 1021
Command dialogues, 121, 555
Command naming, 985
Communication systems, 265, 303, 499, 841, 909
Complexity, 35, 87, 93, 271, 951, 1035
Comprehension, 87, 101, 473, 945, 951, 959, 1009
Computer aided design systems, 135, 345, 383, 463, 485
Computer artifacts, 193
Computer assisted instruction, 499, 931, 937, 1007
Computer assisted learning, 863, 881, 887
Computer learning, 1017
Concurrent tasks, 535, 835
Consistency, 175, 271 337
Constraint, 135
Control, 1017
Control centres, 761
Conversation behaviour, 185
CONVERSATIONBUILDER, 917
Cooperation, 107, 155, 849, 909, 917, 1009, 1013
Coordination, 909
Cost benefit analysis, 351
Customisation, 561, 1025
Data, 155, 277, 473, 977
Data processing, 15, 155, 277, 323, 329, 389, 415, 875
Databases, 149, 493, 795, 869
Deaf people, 863
Debugging, 607, 965, 991, 997
Decision support systems, 247
Design, 79, 93, 143, 169, 175, 193, 199, 219, 225, 239, 247, 289, 295, 323, 345, 365, 383, 389, 429, 435, 499, 543, 549, 573, 607, 625, 651, 659, 773, 795, 841, 863, 887, 971, 1005, 1013, 1017, 1021, 1029
Design processes, xxxv, 135, 207, 213, 225, 283, 303, 315, 365, 371, 715
Design tools, 259, 289, 295, 371, 377, 383, 395, 613
Designers, 135, 199, 259, 371, 377, 383, 389, 435, 463
Deutsches Institut fur Normung, xxix
Development, 607, 1021
Diagrams, 521
Dialling, 773
Dialogue generators, 645, 651
Dialogue managers, 309, 535, 607, 651
Dialogues, 155, 415, 479, 937
Diaries, 853
DIN, xxix
Direct manipulation, 73, 423, 449, 601, 633, 675, 991, 1033
Disabled people, 499
Discretion, 35
Displays, 505, 639, 695, 721, 725
Doctors, 247
Document formats, 903
Document organisation, 581, 747
Documentation, 1035
Dynamic documents, 747
Dynamic systems, 87
Editing, 521, 543, 549, 555, 651, 667, 835
Education, 9
Electronic books, 513
Electronic communications, 841

Electronic conferencing, 853
Electronic documents, 587
Electronic journals, 869
Electronic mail, 529, 555, 841, 853, 909, 1025
End users, 535, 977
Engineering, 253
Error recovery, 755
Errors, 35, 43, 47, 175, 435, 667, 773
Europe, xxix
Evaluation, 337, 389, 395, 407, 415, 505, 715, 721, 773, 779, 787, 997
Evaluation methods, 323, 329
Examples, 1015
Experienced users, 561, 667, 965, 1035
Expert systems, 155, 247, 395, 529, 651, 795, 809, 821, 827, 1021
Expertise, 115, 129, 529
Experts, 561, 667, 965, 1035
Explanations, 809
Feedback, 93, 219, 667, 735, 761
FINGER, 689
Fisheye views, 875
Flat panel displays, 721
Fonts, 721
Formal queries, 593
Functionality, 377, 841
Games, 87, 93
German National Standards Organisation, xxix
Gestures, 683, 689, 741
Goals, 283
Goals Operators Methods and Selection Rules, 29, 213, 283, 365
GOMS, 29, 213, 283, 365
Graphical dialogues, 469, 479
Graphical programming, 499, 601, 619
Graphics, 449, 463, 473, 485, 493, 521, 815, 991, 1021, 1031
Graphics tools, 613
Greek, 707
Group communication, xxxv, 1025
Guidelines, 435, 543, 721, 835
Handicapped people, 499
Hearing impaired people, 863
Help, 93, 169, 1007, 1035
Help systems, 389, 529, 581, 1013
Heuristic evaluation, 315
Home users, 985
Hospitals, 849
Human behaviour, 107, 115, 121, 129, 149, 441, 561, 567, 959
Human computer interfaces, xxix, 129, 169, 219, 239, 309, 315, 323, 329, 357, 383, 389, 395, 415, 469, 499, 521, 535, 549, 555, 601, 613, 619, 625, 645, 659, 683, 725, 741, 773, 779, 795, 815, 827, 869, 875, 977, 1017, 1021, 1025, 1031, 1033
Human factors, 225, 407, 435
Human human interaction, 853
Human memory, 67, 271
Human performance, 107, 707
Hydraulics, 827
Hypercard, 315, 383, 429, 499
Hypermedia, 303, 401, 593, 887
Hypertext, 67, 101, 521, 581, 587, 613, 821, 869, 931
ICONOGRAPHER, 639
Icons, 457, 469, 473, 639, 815
Implementation, 795
Inconsistency, 175, 337
Information, 485, 735, 795, 853, 909
Information processing, 15, 521
Information technology, 289, 295
Input, 449
Input devices, 675
Instructions, 61
Intelligent interfaces, 129
Intelligent tutoring systems, 863, 887, 931, 937
Interactive systems, 143, 1019
Interface layouts, 651, 659
Interfaces, xxix, 129, 169, 219, 239, 309, 315, 323, 329, 357, 383, 389, 395, 415, 469, 499, 521, 535, 549, 555, 601, 613, 619, 625, 645, 659, 683, 725, 741, 773, 779, 795, 815, 827, 869, 875, 977, 1017, 1021, 1025, 1031, 1033
Integrated Project Support Environments, 407, 849, 903
International Standards Organisation, xxix, 357
Interviews, 277
IPSE, 407, 849, 903
ISO, xxix, 357
Job design, 107, 289
Joysticks, 701
Keyboard layouts, 707
Keying, 767
Kinaesthetic feedback, 667
Knowledge, 115, 931
Knowledge acquisition, 395, 821, 887
Knowledge based systems, 155, 247, 395, 529, 651, 795, 809, 821, 827, 1021
Knowledge elicitation, 329, 389, 827
Knowledge representation, 815
Languages, 163
Learnability, 169
Learning, 55, 61, 129, 345, 401, 499, 863, 881, 925, 1007, 1015, 1035
Legibility, 729
Life cycle design methods, 303
Linguistics, 1013
LISP, 931, 1015
Logic, 1019, 1029
Macintosh, 21, 115
Maintenance, 875
Management, 903
Management information systems, 795
Manufacturing, 821
Manufacturing companies, xxix
Mathematics, 815, 827
Medical systems, 247, 849
Meetings, 853
Memoranda, 853
Memory, 67, 271

Mental workload, 107
Menu selection, 423, 441
Menus, 423, 429, 435, 441, 815
Mice, 701
Microcomputers, 21, 115, 1035
MoDE, 633
Moded editing, 667
Modelling, 87, 143, 149, 185, 213, 225, 247, 265, 271, 345, 407, 449, 505, 725, 849, 887, 951, 1013, 1017
Monitoring, 401, 415, 997
Multimedia, 233, 593, 651, 695, 747, 1025
Naive users, 529, 561, 667, 1035
Names, 945
Natural language, 479, 529, 801, 951, 1031
Natural language interfaces, 795
Navigating, 101, 401, 581, 587, 735, 787, 869, 881
Netherlands, 9
Neural networks, 683
Notations, 185, 271, 441, 463, 951
Novices, 441, 463, 529, 561, 667, 1035
Object oriented programming, 971, 991
Object oriented systems, 309, 469, 535, 625, 633, 815, 863, 1021, 1025, 1031
Occasional users, 707, 795
Office automation, 535, 853
Office systems, 265, 337, 535, 651, 849
Online searching, 493, 869
Online tutoring, 863, 931
Operating systems, 1011
Organisation, 35
Organisation structures, 219
Organisational issues, xxxv, 21, 295, 909
Organisations, 219
Paging, 555
Paper, 315
Parsing, 951, 959
Pattern recognition, 149
PENGUIN, 619
Performance, 107, 407, 707
Personal computers, 21, 115, 1035
Personal computing, 115
Petri nets, 625
Physiology, 107
Planning, 283, 371, 377, 407, 937
Pointing, 689, 695, 701, 787
Prior knowledge, 61
Privacy, 15
Problem solving, 61, 155, 767, 809, 821, 959
Problem solving systems, 1009
Product development, 219
Professionals, 3, 9, 247, 903
Programmers, 239, 529, 561, 917, 945, 959, 965, 971
Programming, 601, 619, 925, 951, 977, 997, 1005, 1015
Programming of devices, 985
Programming languages, 925
Programming tools, 991
Programs, 945, 959
Project control systems, 903
Protocols, 567, 917
Prototyping, 253, 309, 383, 607, 625, 1019, 1021
Prototyping tools, 303
Psychology, 107, 193, 555, 587, 965, 1005
Queries, 493, 593
Qwerty keyboards, 707
RAPID, 659
Rapid prototyping, 389, 613, 633, 645, 675, 1029
RATES, 881
Reading, 101, 513, 689, 869, 959
Redesign, 199, 225, 435, 1005
Representations, 169, 639, 997
Resistance to change, 79
Reuse, 895
Reviews, 587
Rule based systems, 573, 821, 997
SCENARIOO, 607
Screen brightness, 729
Screen size, 715
Scripting, 555
Searching, 493, 869, 959
Seeheim model, 601, 619
Semantics, 485
Simulation, 303, 715, 721, 815
SMALLTALK, 199, 937, 991, 1005
SMARTWRITER, 863
Social impact, 35
Social issues, 21, 909
Software, 219, 351, 945, 959
Software design, xxxv, 259
Software development, 239, 909, 917
Software engineering, 265, 895
Software tools, 389, 909, 1021
Specification, 371, 377, 1033
Speech input, 755, 761, 767, 773, 779, 787
Speech output, 801
Speech synthesis, 683
Speed, 423
Spreadsheets, 401, 767, 977
Standardisation, xxix, 79, 357
Standards, xxix, 435, 505, 721
Stereoscopy, 695, 741
Strategies, 101, 207
Stress, 107
Students, 401, 937
Symbols, 485, 761
System adaptability, 561
System adaptation, 567, 573
System design, 93, 259, 289
System development, 895
Systems, 79
Systems analysis, 295
Tables, 977
Tablets, 675
Tactical systems, 505
TAKD, 277
Task action grammars, 163, 169, 175
Task allocation, 289

Task analysis, 61, 259, 265, 277, 283, 383, 441, 535, 567, 815, 827, 1017, 1029
Task Analysis for Knowledge Description, 277
Task characteristics, 505
Task complexity, 271
Task consistency, 271
Task descriptions, 271
Task design, 239
Tasks, 35, 107, 169, 199, 271, 371, 377, 567, 835, 1035
Teaching, 3, 863
Team work, xxxv, 303, 365, 835
Telecommunications, 779
Teleconferencing, 853
Telephone workstations, 29
Testing, 351, 607
Text, 463, 761, 801
Text editing, 667
Three dimensional images, 695, 741
Touch input, 675, 689
Tracing, 991
TRACK, 991
Training, 3, 55, 887, 1011
Trees, 185, 513, 815
TRIMS, 997
Typewriting, 701, 707
Typing, 701, 707
UIMS, 129, 309, 395, 473, 601, 607, 613, 625, 633, 645, 651, 675, 755, 1021, 1033
Understanding, 87, 101, 473, 945, 951, 959, 1009
Undo commands, 543, 549, 755
UNIX, 43, 169, 239, 529, 1007, 1035
Usability, 73, 169, 193, 199, 213, 259, 315, 323, 329, 351, 357, 371, 429, 549, 667, 735, 773, 835, 841, 1013
Usability metrics, 351
Usage, 21, 115, 129, 185
User analysis tools, 383
User attitudes, 21, 755
User characteristics, 55, 371, 1007
User experience, 561
User identification, 219
User interface generators, 129, 309, 395, 473, 601, 607, 613, 625, 633, 645, 651, 675, 755, 1021, 1033
User interface management systems, 129, 309, 395, 473, 601, 607, 613, 625, 633, 645, 651, 675, 755, 1021, 1033
User interfaces, xxix, 129, 169, 219, 239, 309, 315, 323, 329, 357, 383, 389, 395, 415, 469, 499, 521, 535, 549, 555, 601, 613, 619, 625, 645, 659, 683, 725, 741, 773, 779, 795, 815, 827, 869, 875, 977, 1017, 1021, 1025, 1031, 1033
User involvement, 219, 253
User knowledge, 573
User learning, 809
User modelling, 55, 115, 129, 573
User models, 253, 573, 931
User participation, 1009
User performance, 337
User requirements, 233, 259, 289, 371, 377, 389, 555
User support, 543, 809, 881, 903, 977
Users, 35, 115, 121, 149, 371, 377, 389, 535, 561, 567, 977, 1011
Validation, 625, 721
VDUs, 729
Video, 695
Videotex, 315
Virtual devices, 675
Virtual reality systems, 741
Visibility, 729
Visual feedback, 667
Visual perception, 741
Visual searches, 457
Visually impaired people, 689
Voice input, 755, 761, 767, 773, 779, 787
Voice output, 801
Voice synthesis, 683
Windowing systems, 67, 309, 337, 555, 675, 787, 815, 991
Word processing, 555, 755, 863, 1035
Xspeak, 787